THE APOCRYPHA AND PSEUDEPIGRAPHA

OF THE

OLD TESTAMENT

IN ENGLISH

WITH INTRODUCTIONS AND CRITICAL AND EXPLANATORY NOTES
TO THE SEVERAL BOOKS

EDITED IN CONJUNCTION WITH MANY SCHOLARS BY

R. H. CHARLES, D.Litt., D.D.
FELLOW OF MERTON COLLEGE, OXFORD
FELLOW OF THE BRITISH ACADEMY

VOLUME I

APOCRYPHA

OXFORD
AT THE CLARENDON PRESS
1913

OXFORD UNIVERSITY PRESS
LONDON EDINBURGH GLASGOW NEW YORK
TORONTO MELBOURNE BOMBAY
HUMPHREY MILFORD M.A.
PUBLISHER TO THE UNIVERSITY

PRINTED IN ENGLAND.

PREFACE

For students both of the Old and New Testaments the value of the non-Canonical Jewish literature from 200 B.C. to A.D. 100 is practically recognized on every side alike by Jewish and Christian scholars. But hitherto no attempt has been made to issue an edition of this literature as a whole in English.[1] Indeed, such an undertaking would have been all but impossible at an earlier date, seeing that critical editions of some of the Apocrypha and Pseudepigrapha have not been published till within the last few years.

The method observed in this work.

In all the contributions one and the same method has been observed. Each contribution consists of an introduction, an English translation from the best critical text—in a few cases the Revised Version has been adopted and emendations suggested in the notes—and of a critical and exegetical commentary.[2] As regards the introductions, the subjects dealt with in them have, so far as possible, been treated in the same order to facilitate the use of the work. Though a large discretion has naturally been given to the various editors, the following order has more or less been observed as a guide or been actually carried out.

§ 1. Short account of the book, embodying its leading features and the editor's chief conclusions.
§ 2. Title of the book.
§ 3. The MSS.
§ 4. The Ancient Versions.
§ 5. Date of (*a*) the original text, (*b*) of the Ancient Versions.
§ 6. Integrity or composite nature of the text.
§ 7. Authorship.
§ 8. Influence of the book on later literature—(*a*) Jewish; (*b*) Christian.
§ 9. Theology of the book.
§ 10. Bibliography—
  (*a*) Chief editions of the text (and of the Ancient Versions).
  (*b*) Chief critical inquiries.
  (*c*) Chief editions of the book.

[1] Kautzsch published an edition in German in 1900, but on a smaller scale than the present work and embracing fewer books of this literature (vol. i. 1–507; vol. ii. 1–540).

[2] In the case of Sirach and Tobit the editors have been allowed much beyond the normal number of pages for their critical apparatus, which they have used to good purpose.

PREFACE

The extent of the present work.

The first volume contains what is generally known as the Apocrypha Proper, which constitutes the excess of the Vulgate over the Hebrew Old Testament, which excess was in turn borrowed from the LXX. But this volume differs from the Apocrypha Proper at once in the way of excess and in the way of defect. 3 Maccabees has been added after 2 Maccabees, since it is contained in many MSS. of the LXX, and 4 Ezra has been transferred to Volume ii since it is essentially a Pseudepigraph.

Volume ii contains all the remaining extant non-Canonical Jewish books written between 200 B.C. and A.D. 100 with possibly one or two exceptions. The greater part of these books have hitherto been accessible only in expensive editions—such as Jubilees, 1 Enoch, Testaments of the XII Patriarchs, 2 Baruch, 4 Ezra, Psalms of Solomon, Pirkē Aboth, the Story of Aḥiḳar, &c. As regards the last two, it is not necessary to make any apology for their introduction into the present work, although they do not properly fall within the true limits above defined, but they were used, at all events partially, by Jewish readers within this period, nor can they be rightly designated Pseudepigraphs. The Fragments of a Zadokite Work are of an historical character, and are valuable in throwing light on a lost chapter of Jewish religious history. They contain likewise apocalyptic material of an interesting nature.

The General Editor, in conclusion, wishes to express his thanks to the Delegates of the Press for undertaking this work, and to the Officers of the Press, whose help and counsel were always ready to meet each difficulty as it arose. The Editor is also under deep obligations to the many scholars who, notwithstanding the pressure of other duties, have yet given themselves so unsparingly to the tasks they had undertaken, that in every instance most valuable service has been rendered to the student and the scholar, while in not a few instances their contributions form actual monographs within the limits assigned. His thanks are due to Messrs. A. and C. Black, the publishers of his editions of Jubilees, Martyrdom of Isaiah, Testament of the XII Patriarchs, Assumption of Moses, 2 Baruch, for permission to reprint the translation and make use of the introduction and notes contained in those editions. Finally, he would acknowledge his indebtedness to the Rev. A. Ll. Davies, who has acted throughout as his secretary and also made the General Index.

R. H. CHARLES.

24 BARDWELL ROAD, OXFORD.
March, 1913.

CONTENTS OF VOLUME I

CONTRIBUTORS TO VOLUME I

BALL, C. J., M.A., D.Litt., Queen's College, University Lecturer in Assyriology, Oxford: *The Epistle of Jeremy.*

BENNETT, W. H., Litt.D., D.D., Professor of Old Testament Exegesis, Hackney College, London: *The Prayer of Azariah and the Song of the Three Children.*

BOX, G. H., M.A., formerly Scholar of St. John's College, Oxford; Lecturer in Rabbinical Hebrew, King's College, London; Rector of Sutton, Beds.: *Sirach* (along with Dr. Oesterley).

COOK, S. A., M.A., Ex-Fellow and Lecturer in the Comparative Study of Religions, and Lecturer in Hebrew and Aramaic, Gonville and Caius College, Cambridge: 1 *Esdras.*

COWLEY, A. E., M.A., D.Litt., Fellow of Magdalen College, Oxford: *Judith.*

DAVIES, T. WITTON, B.A., Ph.D., Professor of Semitic Languages, University College, Bangor: *Bel and the Dragon.*

EMMET, CYRIL W., M.A., formerly Scholar of Corpus Christi College, Oxford; Rector of West Hendred: 3 *Maccabees.*

GREGG, J. A. F., D.D., Archbishop King's Professor in Divinity, Trinity College, Dublin: *The Additions to Esther.*

HOLMES, SAMUEL, M.A., Lecturer in Theology, Jesus College, Oxford: *The Wisdom of Solomon.*

KAY, D. M., B.D., Professor of Oriental Languages, St. Andrews: *Susanna.*

MOFFATT, JAMES, D.D., Yates Professor of New Testament Greek and Exegesis, Mansfield College, Oxford: 2 *Maccabees.*

OESTERLEY, W. O. E., D.D. (Cambridge): 1 *Maccabees*, *Sirach* (jointly with G. H. Box).

RYLE, RIGHT REV. BISHOP HERBERT E., D.D., Dean of Westminster; formerly Hulsean Professor of Divinity, Cambridge, and Bishop of Exeter and Winchester: *The Prayer of Manasses.*

SIMPSON, D. C., M.A., Lecturer in Theology and Hebrew, St. Edmund Hall, and Reader in Hebrew and Old Testament in Manchester College, Oxford: *Tobit.*

WHITEHOUSE, O. C., M.A., D.D., Theological Tutor, Cheshunt College, Cambridge: 1 *Baruch.*

INTRODUCTION TO VOLUME I[1]

§ 1. *The origin of the term apocryphal.*

How the term 'Apocryphal Books' (*ἀπόκρυφα βιβλία*) arose has not yet been determined. It did not, as Zahn (*Gesch. des Neutestamentlichen Kanons* I. i. 123 sq.), Schurer, Porter, N. Schmidt, and others maintain, originate in the Late Hebrew phrase ספרים גנוזים, 'hidden books.'[2] But Talmudic literature knows nothing of such a class. The Hebrew word *ganaz* (גנז) does not mean 'to hide', but 'to store away' things in themselves precious. Indeed, so far is it from being a technical term in reference to non-Canonical writings, that it is most frequently used in reference to the Canonical Scriptures themselves. When writings were wholly without the pale of the Sacred books—such as those of the heretics or Samaritans—they were usually designated *ḥiṣonim*, i.e. 'outside' (Sanh. x. 1 ספרים חצונים and ספרי המינים). To this class the Apocrypha were never relegated, save Sirach, according to a statement found only in Sanh. x. 1 in the Palestinian Talmud, where it is stated that 'whoso reads the outside books would have no part in the life to come'. But it is clear that there is some error either in the text or the interpretation; for Sirach is very frequently cited by the Rabbis (see the *Original Hebrew of a Portion of Ecclesiasticus*, Cowley and Neubauer, pp. xix–xxx), and two passages of it (Sir. vii. 10 in Erubin 65^{a} and xiii. 16 in Baba Qama 92^{b}) are cited as belonging to the Hagiographa. The facts show that Sirach was read—read at all events for private edification though not in the synagogues.

§ 2. *Extent of the Jewish apocryphal writings.*

We are not here of course concerned with all Jewish apocryphal writings, but with those which were written between 200 B.C. and A.D. 120. The most notable of these in the past centuries were those which we may define as the Apocrypha Proper, i.e.

1 Esdras	Epistle of Jeremy	
2 Esdras	Additions to Daniel—	The Prayer of Azariah and the Song of the Three Children
Tobit	" "	Susanna
Judith	" "	Bel and the Dragon
Additions to Esther	Prayer of Manasses	
Wisdom of Solomon	1 Maccabees	
Ecclesiasticus or Sirach	2 Maccabees	
1 Baruch		

If we compare the collection of the Sacred books as they are found in the Hebrew Old Testament, the LXX, and the Vulgate, we shall find that the Apocrypha Proper constitutes the excess of the Vulgate over the Hebrew Old Testament, and that this excess is borrowed from the LXX. But the official Vulgate (1592) does not include 1 and 2 Esdras (i.e. 4 Ezra in this edition) and the Prayer of Manasses among the Canonical Scriptures, but prints them as an appendix after the New Testament. The Roman Church excludes them from the Canon.[3] Only 1 Esdras is

[1] This Introduction is not intended to be a General Introduction to the Apocrypha, but only to bring forward a few important points in connexion with the Apocrypha.

[2] This error appears to have arisen from Aboth R. N., I. i, where it is said, 'Formerly because Proverbs, the Song of Solomon and Ecclesiastes, contained only proverbs, and did not belong to the Hagiographa, they were stored away (גנוזים) until the men of the Great Synagogue explained them.' Here many scholars have rendered the Hebrew word wrongly as 'hidden'.

[3] The rest of the Apocrypha Proper was declared to be Canonical by the Council of Trent (1546), which pronounced an anathema on the man who did not accept *libros ipsos integros cum omnibus suis partibus, prout in Ecclesia Catholica legi consueverunt et in veteri vulgata Latina editione habentur, pro sacris et canonicis.*

found in the LXX. That 2 Esdras (i.e. 4 Ezra) was not incorporated can only have been due to an accident. Further, it is to be observed that, whereas 3 and 4 Maccabees and Psalm 151 are found in most manuscripts of the LXX, they are absent from the Vulgate and the Apocrypha Proper.

Thus the difference between the Protestant Canon and that of Rome represents the difference between the Canon of the Palestinian and the Alexandrian Jews. This difference is not due, as it was thought at one time, to the difference in the language of the originals—a view which appears as early as the controversy of Africanus with Origen; for, as we are now aware, the bulk of the Apocrypha was originally written in Hebrew.

But besides the Apocrypha Proper there was a vast body of literature in circulation in Judaism to which is now generally attached the term 'Pseudepigrapha', i.e. books written between 300 B.C. and A.D. 120 under the names of ancient worthies in Israel. Since these will be briefly dealt with in the Introduction to vol. ii we shall not discuss them here.

To the Apocrypha Proper in this volume we have added 3 Maccabees—a quasi-historical work—which is found in very many manuscripts of the LXX. It might have been advisable to have included also Pseudo-Philo's *Liber Antiquitatum Biblicarum*, which was written originally in Hebrew and possibly soon after A.D. 70. But this work has not yet been critically edited. Of lost apocrypha we might mention the *History of Johannes Hyrcanus*, mentioned in 1 Macc. xvi. 23, 24, *Jannes and Mambres* (i.e. Jambres), *Book of Joseph and Asenath*.

§ 3. *Various meanings of the term 'apocryphal'.*

(1) In its earliest use this term (ἀπόκρυφος) was applied in a laudatory signification to writings which were withheld from public knowledge because they were vehicles of mysterious or esoteric wisdom which was too sacred or profound to be disclosed to any save the initiated. In this sense it is found in a magical book of Moses, which has been edited by Dieterich (*Abraxas* 169) and may be as old as the first century A.D. This book is entitled 'A sacred secret Book of Moses' (Μωυσέως ἱερὰ βίβλος ἀπόκρυφος).

But we have still earlier indications of the existence and nature of the Apocrypha in this sense. The Book of Daniel is represented as withheld from public knowledge until the time came for its publication: xii. 4, 'But thou, O Daniel, shut up the words and seal the book, even unto the time of the end.' The writer of 1 Enoch speaks of his revelations as designed not for his own, i. 2, cviii. 1, but for the elect of later generations: xciii. 10

And at its close shall be elected
The elect righteous of the eternal plant of righteousness,
To receive sevenfold instruction concerning all His creation.

Similarly, the writer of the Assumption of Moses enjoins that his book is to be preserved for a later period, i. 16–17. That with large bodies of the Jews this esoteric literature was as highly or more highly treasured than the Canonical Scriptures is clear from the claims made by the Rabbis on behalf of their oral, which was originally in essence an esoteric, tradition, since it was not to be committed to writing. Though they insisted on the exclusive canonicity of the twenty-four books, they claimed to be the possessors of an oral tradition that not only overshadowed but frequently displaced the written Law. In 4 Ezra xiv. 44 sq. we have a categorical statement as to the superior worth of this esoteric literature: 'So in forty days were written ninety-four books. And it came to pass when the forty days were fulfilled, that the Most High spake unto me saying: The twenty-four books[1] that thou hast written publish, that *the worthy and the unworthy may read* (*them*): But the seventy last thou shalt keep to deliver to the wise among thy people.

[1] The twenty-four books are, of course, the Old Testament: the seventy are the apocryphal, but especially the apocalyptic books.

For in them is the spring of understanding,
The fountain of wisdom,
And the stream of knowledge.'

In a like laudatory sense Gregory of Nyssa reckons the New Testament Apocalypse as ἐν ἀποκρύφοις (*Oratio in suam ordinationem*, III. 549: Ed. Migne).

(2) But the word was applied to writings that were withheld from public circulation, not on the ground of their transcendent worth, but because their value was confessedly secondary or questionable. Thus Origen differentiates writings that were read in public worship from apocryphal works (*Comm. in Matt.* x. 18, xiii. 57). This use became current, and prepared the way for the third and unfavourable sense of the word.

(3) The word came to be applied to what was false, spurious, or heretical. This meaning appears also in Origen, *Prolog. in Cant. Cantic.*: Lommatzsch, xiv. 325).

§ 4. *The attitude of the Christian Church to the Apocrypha.*

The degree of estimation in which the apocryphal books have been held in the Church has varied with age and place.

(1) The Greek Fathers such as Origen and Clement, who used the Greek Bible, which included these books, frequently cite them as 'scripture', 'Divine scripture', 'inspired', or the like. Later Greek Fathers[1] rejected in various ways this conception of the Canon, but it was accepted and maintained in the West by St. Augustine. Where the Greek differed from the Hebrew Augustine held that the difference was due to Divine inspiration, and that this difference was to be regarded as a sign that in the passage in question an allegorical—not a literal—interpretation was to be looked for. Since he habitually used a Latin Bible, which embraced the Apocrypha, he appealed to the authority of these books as of the rest of the Scriptures. The Council of Hippo (A.D. 393)[2] and that of Carthage (A.D. 397), at both of which Augustine was present respectively as a presbyter and a bishop, drew up a list of Canonical writings, which, though formed by Latin-speaking bishops, was the chief authority on which the Council of Trent based its own decision. In fact the list authoritatively issued by the Council of Hippo and that of Trent agree in nearly every respect, save that the Tridentine divines appear to have misunderstood the meaning of 1 and 2 Esdras in the list of the African Council. That in this list 1 Esdras meant the apocryphal book which Augustine acknowledged as Scripture (*De Civ. Dei*, xviii. 36) and 2 Esdras meant the Canonical Ezra and Nehemiah there is no reason for doubt; but the Tridentine divines, taking 1 Esdras as = the Canonical Ezra and 2 Esdras as = the Canonical Nehemiah,[3] through a misunderstanding declared 1 Esdras (i.e. the apocryphal Esdras) apocryphal.

(2) On the other hand, teachers connected with Palestine and familiar with the Hebrew Canon, like Africanus and Jerome, declared all books outside the Hebrew Canon as apocryphal.

(3) Alongside these two opposing views arose a third which held that, though these books were not to be put in the same rank as those in the Hebrew collection, they nevertheless had their value for moral uses, and should be read in the Church services. Hence they were called 'ecclesiastical'—a designation that is found first in Rufinus (ob. A.D. 410). Notwithstanding many variations in the attitude of different authorities and councils these three opinions maintained their ground down to the Reformation.

At the Reformation the above ecclesiastical usages were transformed into articles of belief, which may be regarded as characteristic of the Churches by which they were adopted. As we have already remarked, the Council of Trent adopted the Canon of the Council of Hippo and of Augustine, declaring: 'If any one receive not, as sacred and canonical, the said books entire with

[1] In the next century Athanasius, in an Easter letter (A. D. 365), states that the books of the Old Testament were twenty-two in number according to the letters of the Hebrew alphabet. Other books not included in the Canon, such as Wisdom, Sirach, Esther, Tobit, Judith, might be used for the instruction of catechumens. It is noteworthy here that the Maccabees are omitted, and Esther is treated as an apocryph.

[2] Zahn, *Gesch. des N. T.lichen Kanons*, II. i. 246–253.

[3] Council of Trent, April 8, 1546. 'Testamenti veteris . . . Esdrae primus et secundus, qui dicitur Nehemias.'

all their parts, as they have been used to be read in the Catholic Church, and as they are contained in the old Latin Vulgate . . . let him be anathema.'[1] All the Apocrypha except 1 Esdras, 4 Ezra, and the Prayer of Manasses belonging to the Apocrypha Proper were declared Canonical.

On the other hand, the Protestant Churches have universally declared their adhesion to the Hebrew Canon of the Old Testament. Yet amongst these a milder and a severer view prevailed. While in some Confessions, i. e. the Westminster, it is decreed that they are not 'to be any otherwise approved or made use of than other human writings', a more favourable view is expressed regarding them in many other quarters; e.g. in the preface prefixed to them in the Genevan Bible: 'As books proceeding from godly men (they) were received to be read for the advancement and furtherance of the knowledge of history and for the instruction of godly manners: which books declare that at all times God had an especial care of His Church, and left them not utterly destitute of teachers and means to confirm them in the hope of the promised Messiah'; and in the Sixth Article of the Church of England: 'the other books the Church doth read for example of life and instruction of manners.'

In addition to the spiritual and moral service rendered by these books, the modern student recognizes that without them it is absolutely impossible to explain the course of religious development between 200 B.C. and A.D. 100. In this respect the Apocrypha is to be regarded as embracing the Pseudepigrapha as well. If the Canonical and Apocryphal Books are compared in reference to the question of inspiration, no unbiased scholar could have any hesitation in declaring that the inspiration of such a book as Wisdom or the Testaments of the XII Patriarchs is incomparably higher than that of Esther.

§ 5. *Editions—partial or complete—of the Apocrypha.*

Fritzsche und Grimm, *Kurzgef. exeget. Handbuch zu den Apokryphen des A. T.*, 1851–60. Fritzsche, Lief. I, 3 *Esra, Zusätze zu Esther und Daniel, Gebet Manasses, Baruch, Brief Jer.;* II. *Tobit und Judith;* V. *Sirach.* Grimm, Lief. III, 1 *Makk.;* IV. 2–4 *Makk.;* VI. *Wisdom.*

E. C. Bissell, *The Apocrypha of the Old Testament, with historical Introductions and Notes Critical and Explanatory*, New York, 1880. This work contains the Apocrypha Proper (though 2 Esdras (i. e. 4 Ezra) is added in an Appendix); also 3 Macc. and a summary of 4 Macc. In a second Appendix a short account is given of some of the Pseudepigrapha.

Wace, *Apocrypha* (in the 'Speaker's Commentary'), 2 vols., London, 1888. This edition is furnished with a good introduction by Salmon. The various books are edited by different English scholars.

O. Zöckler, *Die Apokr. des A. T. nebst einem Anhang über die Pseudepigraphenliteratur*, 1891.

Ball, *The Ecclesiastical or Deutero-Canonical Books of the Old Testament, commonly called the Apocrypha* (1892).

Kautzsch, *Die Apokryphen und Pseudepigraphen des Alten Testaments*, 2 vols., Tübingen, 1900. This is the best work that has hitherto appeared on this literature as a whole. But many parts of it are already antiquated.

§ 6. *General literature dealing directly or indirectly with the period of this literature.*[2]

Weber, *System der altsynagogalen palästinischen Theologie* (1880). The last edition of this work was published under the title *Lehre des Talmuds*, 1897.

Bacher, *Die Aggada der Tannaiten*, 2 vols., 1884–90.

Stade, *Geschichte des Volkes Israel*, vol. ii, Das Ende des jüdischen Staatswesens (by O. Holtzmann). 1888.

Drummond, *Philo Judaeus*, 2 vols., 1888.

Bois, *Essai sur les origines de la philosophie judéo-Alexandrine*, 1890.

Toy, *Judaism and Christianity*, 1890.

[1] This decree of the Council of Trent was ratified by fifty-three prelates, 'among whom (Westcott, *Bible in the Church*, 257) there was not one German, not one scholar distinguished by historical learning, not one who was fitted by special study for the examination of a subject in which the truth could only be determined by the voice of antiquity.'

[2] This list includes only a few of the works interesting to the student of this literature.

Smith, G. A., *Historical Geography of the Holy Land*, 1894, 1901[7].
Mahaffy, *The Empire of the Ptolemies*, 1895.
Bertholet, *Die Stellung der Israeliten und der Juden zu den Fremden*, 1896.
Schechter, *Studies in Judaism*, 1896.
Cheyne, *Jewish Religious Life after the Exile*, 1898.
Streane, *The Age of the Maccabees*, 1898.
Kent, *A History of the Jewish People*, Part III, 1899.
Wellhausen, *Israelitische und jüdische Geschichte*[5], 1901.
Schürer, *Geschichte des jüdischen Volkes*[3], 1898–1901.
Bevan, *The House of Seleucus*, 2 vols., 1902.
Volz, *Jüdische Eschatologie von Daniel bis Aqiba*, 1903.
Bousset, *Die Religion des Judentums im neutestamentlichen Zeitalter*, 1903, 1906[2].
Baldensperger, *Die Messianisch-Apokalyptische Hoffnungen des Judenthums*, 1903.
Porter, *The Messages of the Apocalyptical Writers*, 1905.
Friedländer, *Die religiösen Bewegungen innerhalb des Judenthums im Zeitalter Jesu*, 1905.
Marti, *Geschichte der israelitischen Religion*[5], 1907. See Sections V and VI.
Oesterley and Box, *The Religion and Worship of the Synagogue*, 1907.
Kent, *The Sermons, Epistles, and Apocalypses of Israel's Prophets from the Beginning of the Assyrian Period to the End of the Maccabean Struggle*, 1910.
H. Pentin, *International Journal of Apocrypha*.

ADDENDA ET CORRIGENDA TO VOLUME I

P. 60 (1 Macc.), l. 28 from bottom, *delete comma after* 'although'

P. 99, l. 29 from bottom, *read* 'v. 25' *for* '*v.* 25'

P. 118, l. 20 from bottom, *read* 'Sion' *for* 'Zion'

P. 123, l. 3 from top, *read* 'enemies'' *for* 'enemies'

P. 174. The evidence referred to in § 3 will be published in the *J. T. S.*, July, 1913, under the title: 'Original Text of Tobit'.

P. 197 (Tobit), l. 26 from top, *read* 'eternal' *for* 'external'

P. 534. To the literature *add* 'Goodrick, *The Book of Wisdom*, 1913'—a very valuable commentary.

P. 559 (Wisdom). In xv. 5 *for* 'leadeth fools into lust' (*which gives the sense well*) *render more literally* 'for fools leadeth into lust'.

P. 579 (1 Baruch), l. 25 from bottom, *read* '130 A. D.' *for* '130 B. C.'

SYMBOLS AND ABBREVIATIONS EMPLOYED IN INTRODUCTIONS, TEXT AND NOTES

See special lists as under :—

1 Esdras	vol. I. 19, 20.
Tobit	„ I. 201.
Sirach	vol. I. 315.
Prayer of Manasses	„ I. 620.
1 Enoch	„ II. 187.
Test. XII Patr.	vol. II. 295.
2 Baruch	„ II. 475.
4 Ezra	„ II. 560.

See also under Versions and MSS. in the different books.

A^1 &c.	See 2 Bar. § 7
A.J.Th.	*American Journal of Theology*
Aboth	Pirkē Aboth
Ab. R. Nathan	= Aboth Rabbi Nathan
ἀπ. λεγ. or εἰρ.	ἅπαξ λεγόμενον or εἰρημένον
Apoc. Abrah.	Apocalypse of Abraham
Apoc. of Baruch	= 2 Baruch
Apoc. Zeph.	Apocalypse of Zephaniah
Aq.	Aquila
Ar.	Arabic
Aram. Frag.	Aramaic Fragment. See Test. *App.* II
Arm.	Armenian
Asc. Is.	Ascension of Isaiah
Ass. Mos.	Assumption of Moses
Aug.	Augustine
B^1 &c.	See 2 Bar. § 7
B.D.	*Bible Dictionary*
B.S.	Deissmann, *Biblical Studies*
1 Bar.	Apocryphal Book of Baruch
2 Bar.	Syriac Apocalypse of Baruch
3 Bar.	Greek Apocalypse of Baruch
Ber. Rabb.	Bereshith rabba
Berach. or Berakh.	= Berachoth
Beresh.	Bereshith
C.I.G.	*Corpus Inscriptionum Graecarum*
C.O.T.	*Cuneiform Inscriptions and the Old Testament.* See K.A.T.
Cat. Niceph.	Catalogue of Nicephorus
Chag.	Chagigah (Talmud)
Chron. Pasch.	= *Chronicon Paschale*
Clem. Alex.	Clement of Alexandria
Clem. Recog.	*Pseudo-Clementine Recognitions*
Cod.	Codex
D.B.	*Dictionary of the Bible*
Dan.	Daniel
Diod. Sic.	Diodorus Siculus
Diog. Laert.	Diogenes Laertius
E.A.	See 4 Ezra, § 7, and ii. 560
E.B. or Bi.	*Encyclopaedia Biblica*
Edd.	Editions
1 En.	1 Enoch or Ethiopian Enoch
2 En.	2 Enoch or Slavonic Enoch
Encyc. Brit.	*Encyclopaedia Britannica*
Ep. Barn.	Epistle of Barnabas
Ep. Jer.	Epistle of Jeremy
Epiph.	Epiphanius
Eth.	Ethiopic
Eus.	Eusebius
Ev. Nicod.	*Evangelium Nicodemi*
4 Ez.	Fourth Book of Ezra
Fayum P.	Fayum Papyri
Fr. or Frag.	Fragment
𝕲	Greek Version
G. d. Jud.	*Geschichte des Judenthums*
G.J.V.	Schürer's *Geschichte des jüdischen Volkes*
G.V.I.	*Geschichte des Volkes Israel*
Gen. rabb.	Genesis rabba
Gk.	Greek
Gk. Frag.	Greek Fragment. See Test. *App.* II
Gr.	Grimm
Gr. of O.T.	*Greek Grammar of Old Testament Greek* (Thackeray)
H.D.B.	Hastings' *Dictionary of the Bible*
H.J.P.	*History of the Jewish People*
Heb. Gr.	Hebrew Grammar
Herm.	Hermas, *Pastor*
Hes.	Hesiod
Hiph.	Hiphil
Hom.	Homer
Il.	Iliad
Int. Crit. Comm.	= *International Critical Commentary*
Intr.	Introduction
J.E.	*Jewish Encyclopaedia*
J.Q.R.	*Jewish Quarterly Review*
J.R.A.S.	*Journal of the Royal Asiatic Society*
J.T.S.	*Journal of Theological Studies*
Jalkut Schim.	= Jalkut Shimeoni
Jashar	Book of Jashar
Jer. Joma &c.	= Joma in Jerusalem Talmud
Jerus. Targ.	Jerusalem Targum
Jos. *Ant.* &c.	Josephus, *Antiquities*, &c.
Jub.	Book of Jubilees
Jüd. Theol.^{2}	*Jüdische Theologie*^{2} (Weber)
K.	Kautzsch
K.A.T.	Schrader, *Die Keilinschriften und das Alte Testament*
Kit.	Kittel
L.A.E.	Deissmann, *Light from the Ancient East*
L.d.T.	Weber, *Die Lehren des Talmuds*
L. & S.	Liddell and Scott
LXX.	Septuagint Version
Lact.	Lactantius
Lib. V.T.	*Libri Veteris Testamenti*
Luc.	Lucian
Lucr.	Lucretius
MS.	Manuscript
MT.	Massoretic Text
1 Macc. &c.	First, &c., Book of Maccabees
Macrob.	Macrobius
Mart. Is.	Martyrdom of Isaiah
Mass.	Massoretic
Megill.	Megilla
Menach.	Menachoth (Talmud)
Mg.	Margin
Midr.	Midrash
N.H.W.	*Neuhebräisches Wörterbuch*
N.T.	New Testament
O.T.	Old Testament
Onk.	Onkelos, Targum of
Onom. Sacr.	*Onomasticon Sacrum*
Or. Sibyll.	Sibylline Oracles
Orph. Frag.	Orphic Fragment
P.E.F.	Palestine Exploration Fund
P.P.	Petrie Papyri
P.R. Eliezer	Pirke Rabbi Eliezer
P.R.E.	*Real-Encyclopädie für protest. Theologie und Kirche*
P.S.B.A.	*Proceedings of the Society of Biblical Archaeology*
Pesikt.	Pesikta
Ps. Clem. Recog.	= Pseudo-Clementine Recognitions
Ps. Jon.	Targum Pseudo-Jonathan
Ps. of Sol.	Psalms of Solomon
R.	Rabbi
R.E.	*Real-Encyklopädie*
R.E.J.	*Revue des Études juives*
Rel. des Jud.	*Religion des Judenthums*
Sam.	Samaritan
Sam. Chron.	Samaritan Chronology
Sanh.	Sanhedrin
Schürer, E.T.	Schürer's *History of the Jewish People*, English Translation
Sept.	Septuagint
Shabb.	Shabbath
Sir.	Sirach
Slav. Bar.	See vol. ii. 131
Slav. Vit.	Slavonic *Vita Adae et Evae*. See Books of Adam and Eve
Soph.	Sophocles
Stob.	Stobaeus
Symm.	Symmachus
Syncell.	Syncellus
Syr.	Syriac
Syr. H.	Hexaplaric Syriac
Syr. W.	Syriac Version in Walton's Polyglot
Sok.	Sokolov's Text of 2 Enoch
T.A. &c.	See under 'Testaments' in list of symbols prefixed to Index.
T.b.	Babylonian Talmud
Targ. Jer.	Jerusalem Targum
Targ. Jon.	Targum Pseudo-Jonathan
Th. *Gram.*	Thackeray, *Grammar of Old Testament Greek*
Theod.	Theodotion
Theoph.	Theophilus
Tebt. P.	Tebtuneh Papyrus
Tert.	Tertullian
Test.	Testament
Test. Sim.	See vol. ii. 153
Test. XII Patr.	= Testaments of the Twelve Patriarchs
Tisch.	Tischendorf
Tob.	Tobit
V.L. or Vet. Lat.	= Versio Vetus Latina, Old Latin Version
Vit. Ad.	Vita Adae
Vulg.	Vulgate
W.P.	Walton's Polyglot
Wellh.	Wellhausen
Wisd.	Book of Wisdom
Z.A.T.W.	*Zeitschrift für die A. T. Wissenschaft*
Z.D.M.G.	*Zeitschrift der Deutschen Morgenländischen Gesellschaft*
Z.N.T.W.	*Zeitschrift für die N. T. Wissenschaft*
Z.W.T. or Z.f.W.T.	= *Zeitschrift für wiss. Theologie*

[ ]	indicate an intrusion into the original text
† †	indicate that the word or passage so enclosed is corrupt
( )	or italics indicate that the word or words so enclosed or printed are supplied for the sake of clearness.
+	indicates that the authority or authorities quoted insert the word or words following this mark.
>	indicates that the authority or authorities quoted omit the word or words following this mark.
⟨ ⟩	indicate a restoration in the text.
Thick type	indicates an emendation in the text.

I ESDRAS

INTRODUCTION

§ 1. Preliminary Account of the Book.

THE first book of the Apocrypha stands in a class by itself in that it is, with the exception of one portion, a somewhat free Greek version of the biblical history from Josiah's Passover (2 Chron. xxxv.) to the Reading of the Law by Ezra (Neh. viii.). It differs, however, in several important particulars both from the corresponding canonical passages and from the more literal Greek translation of them (also preserved in the Septuagint), and an adequate treatment of its text and contents belongs properly to the commentaries and handbooks on Chronicles, Ezra, and Nehemiah. Consequently, in order to keep the Introduction and Notes within limits, it has seemed desirable to print the Revised Version of the 'apocryphal' and 'canonical' passages side by side, and to restrict all remarks to those points which appeared to be essential for the study of the relation between the texts and their significance for the period which they cover. Further reference to the commentaries and other works dealing with the period in question is therefore recommended.

The contents of 1 Esdras comprise:—

E i.[1] = 2 Chron. xxxv. 1–xxxvi. 21. Josiah's passover and death; the last kings of Judah to the fall of Jerusalem, 586 B.C.

ii. 1–15. = E i. The decree of Cyrus permitting the rebuilding of the Temple and the return of Sheshbazzar with the temple-vessels and a band of exiles, 538–537.

ii. 16–30. = E iv. 7–24. The Samaritan opposition to the rebuilding in the reign of Artaxerxes, 465–425.

iii. 1–v. 6. wanting in E. The successful oration of Zerubbabel, one of the bodyguard of *Darius*, in the second year of his reign (D. I, Hystaspes, 521–486), and the king's decree permitting a return of exiles to rebuild the city and Temple; brief statement of the journey.

v. 7–73. = E ii. 1–iv. 5, 24 (*v.* 6 is wanting). List of Zerubbabel's band, the rebuilding of the Temple hindered by the Samaritans from the time of *Cyrus* to the second year of Darius (520).

vi.–vii. = E v.–vi. The successful rebuilding of the Temple through the intervention of Darius in 520, and its completion in 516.

viii. 1–ix. 36 = E vii.–x. The decree of Artaxerxes in his seventh year (458), the return of Ezra and a body of exiles, the separation of the people from the foreign wives.

ix. 37–55 = N vii. 73–viii. 13 *a*. The reading of the law by Ezra, placed in N *l. c.* after the return of Nehemiah in the king's twentieth year (444).

The outstanding features are:—

(1) The presence of the Artaxerxes record before the reign of Darius, whether after the return of Sheshbazzar (*E* ii. 16–30) or after the commencement of the rebuilding by Zerubbabel (E iv. 7–24), both of which are placed in the time of Cyrus.

(2) The inclusion of *E* iii. 1–v. 6, the story famous for the Praise of Truth and the well-known dictum 'magna est veritas et praevalet', and the decree of Darius (which excludes any prior return).

(3) The confusion caused by the presence of this section (*E* iii. 1–v. 6) in the history of the exiles who returned in the time of Cyrus (*E* ii. 1–15 = E 1) and at once commenced the work of rebuilding (*E* v. 7–73 = E ii.–iv.).

(4) The omission in *E* of N i.–vii. 72, with the result that the continuation of the story of Ezra (N viii.) is placed in immediate connexion with E vii.–x., whereas the canonical books leave a gap of twelve years between E vii.–x. and N i. seqq.

(5) Numerous readings in *E* of greater or less value, which are often important for the textual criticism of the MT, and sometimes affect the literary and historical problems of the sources.

E ceases abruptly; cf. the close of 2 Chron., 'and let him go up' (=E i. 3), also Mark xvi. 8. The R.V. rendering of ix. 55 implies that this is intentional (so Ewald, Bissell, Lupton, Bayer, and others). Hence it is often supposed that *E* is a self-contained work, written and compiled for some

[1] For the abbreviations *E*, E, N, &c., see below, p. 19 seq.

specific purpose, e.g. to influence Gentiles in favour of the Jews, or (Lupton) to prepare the way for the building of the temple of Onias at Alexandria, or simply, perhaps, to bring together narratives relating to the Temple; cf. the conclusion of $\mathfrak{L}^{c}$ 'explicit Esdrae liber primus de templi restitutione'. But the feature may also be explained on the view that the book, which begins somewhat abruptly, is merely a fragment of a larger work (Michaelis, Eichhorn, Trendelenburg, Rödiger, Treuenfels, Howorth, Torrey, and others). This raises several interesting questions; in particular, ix. 38–55 belong in N viii. to the concluding chapters of Ezra's history, and it is very noteworthy that Josephus finishes his account of Ezra before his introduction of Nehemiah—what was the original sequel of *E*? Moreover, not only was *E* used by this orthodox Jewish historian, the book was important enough to find a place in the Greek Bible, it was known to early Christian writers, and is referred to in terms which indicate that its canonicity and value were not doubtful (see § 2).

Now, the criticism of the O.T. has advanced sufficiently to prove that the biblical records E–N bristle with the most intricate and serious difficulties, the extent of which is manifest in the widely-differing conclusions that prevail. As can be seen from other sources (see § 4, iv. *c*), the history of the Persian period is plunged in obscurity, upon which some light has only recently been shed by contemporary records (Babylonian inscriptions, Jewish-Aramaic papyri from Upper Egypt). It can no longer be assumed that the MT necessarily represents a more trustworthy record of the age, and that *E* is necessarily arbitrary and methodless. Both share fundamental imperfections. *E*, therefore, in any case deserves impartial consideration, and its problems involve those of E–N. These problems, owing to the absence of decisive and independent evidence, can be handled only provisionally; but enough is clear to permit the conclusion that *E* represents a text in some respects older than the *present* MT, to which, however, some attempt seems to have been made to conform it (cf. Ewald, 138 n. 6; Howorth, *PSBA*, xxiii. 306 seq.). From a comparison of both with Jos. and other sources (notably Daniel) it would further appear that *E* represents one of the efforts to give an account of a period, the true course of which was confused and forgotten, if not intentionally obscured; different attempts were made to remove difficulties and inconsistencies, and the desire to give greater prominence to the priestly Ezra than to the secular governor Nehemiah is probably responsible for the arrangement of the extant texts.

E–N and *E* (with Jos.) exhibit diverging views of the history. But *E*, even in its present incomplete form, overlaps with Chronicles–Ezra–Nehemiah, and since it provides a distinctly paraphrastic and free rendering of the MT, it seems probable that when it was superseded by the more literal Greek translation—of Theodotion (cf. the two Greek texts of Daniel)—this confused and self-contradictory book (or fragment) was preserved mainly on account of the excellent story of Zerubbabel (cf. Howorth, *PSBA*, xxiv. 167). To the Jews, both Zerubbabel and Nehemiah pale before the growing majesty of Ezra; to the early Christians, the Praise of Truth was a familiar passage, and Augustine (*de Civ. Dei*, xviii. 36) saw in it a prophecy of Christ.[1] Dating, apparently, about the first century B.C., *E*'s view of history was familiar to Josephus and his readers, to the Hellenist Jews, and to the Christians. The form in E–N, with the omission of the story of Zerubbabel (and the chronological confusions which attend it), represents that of the Rabbinical schools, and subsequently (through Jerome) of the Christian Church. Through these vicissitudes *E* fell into unmerited neglect, and by this omission (apparently intentional) there was removed a story which could not fail to interest the Christians—for it is surely significant that although the two genealogies of Jesus are hopelessly inconsistent, the two lines of ancestry of 'David's greater Son' converge in the person of Zerubbabel.

§ 2. Title and Standing.

The book is known as (1) Esdras A or 1 Esdras, so $\mathfrak{G}^{BA}$, $\mathfrak{L}$, $\mathfrak{S}$, and English Bibles since the Geneva edition of 1560 (where the name 'Ezra' is reserved for the canonical book); or (2) as Esdras B or 2 Esdras, so $\mathfrak{G}^{L}$ (where 1 Es. = Ezra and Nehemiah); or (3) as 3 Esdras, so Latin Bibles since Jerome, the 'Great Bible' of 1539, and also the Anglican Article VI in the Prayer-book. The name 3 *Paraleipomenōn* (i.e. Chronicles) is found in a Florentine Greek MS., cf. the title *Sermones Dierum* (the Heb. title of Chron.) *Esdrae* in Hilary's list (H. B. Swete, *Introd. to O.T. in Greek*, 210). It is also styled *Tertius Neemiae* by Franciscus Robles, 1532 (Lupton, 4). A convenient name for the book is the 'Greek Ezra', to distinguish it from the other and literal translation of the canonical books.[2]

[1] A late Midrash (Jellinek, ii. 54–7) makes Zerubbabel the centre of 'a short apocalypse on the certainty of the ultimate appearance of the Messiah son of David, on his precursor the Messiah son of Joseph, and on their friends and foes' (Ew. 128).

[2] On the title ὁ ἱερεύς in $\mathfrak{G}^{A}$ (to distinguish *E* from 2 or 4 Esdras of the Apocrypha?), see Nestle, 29.

It is a significant fact that, as emphasized by Whiston in 1722, the Jewish historian Josephus uses *E* for his account of King Josiah, follows its order of events, and is influenced by its language, although for the other books he employs the LXX. Equally significant is the appearance of *E* with the canonical E–N in the best Greek MSS., either before ($\mathfrak{G}^{BA}$, and presumably ℵ) or after ($\mathfrak{G}^{L}$) these. It is quoted by several early Greek and Latin Fathers,[1] and Augustine and Origen cite iv. 41 and 59 respectively from 'Esdras' without indicating that another than the canonical book is meant. Moreover, a Greek synopsis (Lag. 84) and a Syriac Catena (see on *E* ix. 55) treat *E* as 1 Esdras, and give the title 2 Esdras to N[2]. But Jerome meanwhile had condemned the two apocryphal books of Esdras with their 'dreams' (*Praef. Esd. et Neh.*), and his ruling was confirmed in due course by the Church. *E* is wanting in the early MSS. of the Vulgate, and it was rejected by the Council of Florence (1442). It is found in the Latin bibles of 1474, 1480, &c., but is regarded as apocryphal by De Lyra (1498), Karlstadt (1520), and Stephanus (1528). It is wanting in the Complutensian Polyglot (1514–17), and Luther ignored it—though not perhaps primarily (Bayer, 6 seq.)—for its triviality. There was even a belief that it did not exist in Greek (Torrey, 13 n. 1). The Council of Trent rejected it in 1546, but it is printed in an appendix in small type in the Tridentine edition of the Vulgate. Although it appears as 1 Esdras in the 1587 edition of the Septuagint (Rome), it was omitted three years later from the Sixtine Vulgate (Rome, 1590). In spite of the occasional attention paid to it by a few scholars, *E* has since too often been overlooked and neglected, and has only recently come into deserved prominence through the persistence of Sir Henry H. Howorth from 1893 onwards (see further Torrey, 13 seqq.).

E, on closer inspection, proves to be no free or less careful treatment of the Greek translation of the canonical books, as had been held by Keil, Zöckler, Bissell, König (*Einleitung*, § 97), and formerly Schürer (contrast his *Gesch. Volk. Isr.*, 3rd ed., iii. 328). There is an overwhelming body of opinion that it is translated from a Semitic (Hebrew and Aramaic) original. There are, it is true, various readings, identical or apparently connected with the literal Greek translation, but they do not outweigh the many considerable and characteristic differences of rendering, the variations in the transliteration or translation of proper names, and the numerous readings in *E* which can be explained only from the MT (see especially Bayer, 156 seqq.). That *E* is an independent version older than the $\mathfrak{G}$ of the canonical books was suggested by Grotius (1644, see *PSBA*, xxv. 139), Whiston (1722), Pohlmann (1859), Ewald (1864), Lagarde (1874), and others, and has since been more cogently shown by Howorth and Torrey. It is pointed out that the $\mathfrak{G}$ of E–N presents features characteristic of Theodotion's translation (viz. transliteration of gentilics, and of difficult or uncertain words) and parallel to his translation of Daniel. The $\mathfrak{G}$ of *E*, on the other hand, as Gwynn also noticed, finds parallels in the 'Septuagint' text of Daniel, especially the first six chapters. Moreover, the $\mathfrak{S}$ of *E* claims to be made from the Septuagint, and it is very probable that *E* took the place of the $\mathfrak{G}$ of E–N in Origen's Hexapla. Volz, however, has properly drawn attention to the varying quality of the different sections of *E*, a feature which 'excludes the supposition that the Greek version can have been produced *aus einem Guss*'. In general, all the evidence tends to show that *E* held a more authoritative position than has been usually conceded to it (in consequence of Jerome), but that its unevenness as a translation and the complexity of its contents make its true origin and structure a more intricate problem.[3]

§ 3. Text Versions, Date, etc.

(*a*) *Character of Translation.* *E*, on account of its peculiar relationship to the O.T., cannot be studied textually apart from the versions based directly upon the MT (see more fully, Torrey 62–114). While the $\mathfrak{G}$ of E–N is un-Greek, literal and mechanical, *E* is the very reverse of servile, and its language both elegant and idiomatic. The vocabulary is extensive, containing several words that occur nowhere else in 'Septuagint' Greek, or only in other books of the Apocrypha, notably 2 Macc. (see Moulton's list, *ZATW*, xix. 232 seqq.). Semitic idioms are usually happily replaced by natural Grecisms. There is often a free treatment of the article, pronouns, and conjunctions; hypotaxis for the parataxis of MT; active verbs for passive. Condensation, paraphrase, and re-arrangement are frequent, and the translator has generally made the best of the original text, gliding over or concealing the difficulties. Sometimes he has misunderstood the original; but the rendering is carefully worded and thus presents an apparently plausible result (see e.g. i. 10–12, 38, 51). He

[1] e.g. Tertullian, Clement of Alexandria, Athanasius; see Pohlmann, 263 seqq., and the tables in André, 22 seqq.

[2] Augustine, also, in a list of canonical books (*de doctr. Christ.* ii. 8) enumerates two books of Ezra 'of which our 1 Esd. was certainly one' (Volz). See, on the other hand, Bayer, 4.

[3] See Howorth, *PSBA*, xxiii. 156 seqq., xxiv. 164 seqq., xxix. 31 seqq., xxxiii. 26 seqq.; Torrey, ib. xxv. 139 seqq., and his *Ezra Studies*, Chap. I; J. Gwynn, *Dict. Christ. Biog.*, 'Theodotion', and *Extracts from the Syro-Hex. Version of the LXX* (London, 1909), xx. seqq.

manifests his intelligence when the skilful paronomasia ἄνεσιν καὶ ἄφεσιν (iv. 62), suggestive of a Greek *composer*, goes back none the less to a Semitic original (cf. Susanna, 54 seqq.), and the use of the name Sisinnes (vi. 3) in place of the MT Tattenai is typical of his care. *E*, it is clear, was made to be read, it is a version rather than a translation, and its value for the criticism of the MT must not blind us to its imperfections (on which see Bayer, 11 seqq.). Consequently, a mean must be sought between a promiscuous and haphazard use of *E* and a whole-hearted though indiscriminate reliance upon its readings and paraphrases. The attempt must invariably be made to distinguish between the underlying text and the features which (as in the Septuagint elsewhere) are due to the translator alone, and the difficulty of this task in certain crucial cases is vital for the disentanglement of the problems of *E*.[1]

(*b*) *E and the MT.* It is abundantly plain that *E* is not derived from the 𝔊 (Theodotion) of the Canonical Books. Where there is agreement, the evidence points to accident or absence of intention, and is not strong enough to prove dependence (see the most recent study by Bayer, 156–61). In certain cases where they agree against the MT they sometimes are due to an easy misunderstanding, and sometimes point to a preferable reading; now and then the more literal version alone preserves an older text. It is highly significant that *E* is occasionally conflate, and presents simple doublets (e.g. ii. 25, vi. 29, ix. 8, 46), or more elaborate combinations made with some little care (e.g. v. 50, 58, 72 seq., vi. 5, 10, &c. [see Marq. 44–7]). This revision appears to have been made from the MT, and *E* vi. 25 actually presents the incorrect 'new' (חדת) of the MT by the side of the correct 'one' (חד). Revision has also been made for the purpose of removing difficulties (so, probably v. 73*b*, in view of the date in vi. 1), or of making identifications (Zerubbabel, vi. 18, 27, 29). These adjustments, which are not found in Theodotion, seem to have been made first in the Greek version, and thus might appear to confirm the view that *E* is based upon an earlier Greek version (Ewald). The question of the underlying original, however, would still remain, and it is very important to notice that not only does *E* often presuppose a better text than the MT, but that some of the readings raise questions of literary structure and historical criticism. Consequently, *E* is not directly based either upon Theodotion's literal translation or the extant MT; the marks of revision point rather to an attempt to adjust to the MT an earlier version which differed from it in some material respects, large (nos. 1, 2, 4, on p. 1 above) and small (e.g. v. 39 seq., 47, vi. 28, vii. 1, ix. 38, 49).[2]

(*c*) *MSS. and Versions.* The GREEK MSS. fall into two main classes, (1) Lucianic (MSS. 19, 108), and (2) B, A, &c. The former stand in a class by themselves, reveal many signs of correction and improvement in order to agree with the MT, and can be used only with great caution (see Torrey, 106 seqq.). The latter comprise two main subdivisions, B and A. B is distinctly the inferior, but shows fewer traces of correction. For a full grouping of all the MSS., see the elaborate discussion by Moulton, *ZATW*, xix. 211 seqq. ℵ, it may be added, lacks *E*, but its subscription Εσδρας β (N xiii. 31) presupposes an 'Esdras A.'

Two old LATIN translations were printed by Sabatier (*Bibl. Sacr. Lat.* iii. 1041 seqq.), with a collation of MS. Sangermanensis—$\mathfrak{L}^{C}$ (Cod. Colbertinus; no. 3703), and a later which in a revised form was used as the Vulgate. A summary from a Lucca MS. was edited by Lagarde, *Sept. Stud.* ii. 16 seqq. (𝔏 Lag.). These differ from, and, on the whole, are purer than $\mathfrak{G}^{L}$.

The SYRIAC Peshitta is without Chron., Ezra, and Neh. *E* 𝔖 is the Syro-Hexapla of Paul of Tella, printed in Walton's Polyglot and by Lagarde (*Lib. Vet. Test. Apocr. Syr.*, 1861). It is explicitly said to be from the Septuagint, and the same is stated at the head of a collection of excerpts in the old Syriac Catena, British Museum, Add. 12168 (see on ix. 55). The variants of the latter and its selections from N are printed by Torrey, 5 seqq., and these selections, with a retranslation into Greek, collation, and complete introductory discussion by Gwynn (see p. 3 n. 3). 𝔖 has many points of contact with $\mathfrak{G}^{L}$, especially in i. 1–9, but on the whole a relationship with $\mathfrak{G}^{B}$ is more distinct.

The ETHIOPIC translation (ed. Dillmann, *Vet. Test. Aeth.*, Vol. V) represents the text of $\mathfrak{G}^{B}$, 𝔖, &c., in contrast to $\mathfrak{G}^{A}$, and, according to Torrey (101), 'is a valuable witness to the Hexaplar text. It must have been made with unusual care from a comparatively trustworthy codex.'

The Arabic translation awaits study (*PSBA*, xxiv. 169); the Armenian is valueless (Volz, § 2).

(*d*) *Josephus.* The Jewish historian (first cent. A.D.), with his continuous history of the monarchy and post-exilic age, stands nearest (of extant compilations) to the chronicler in point of antiquity. He is a valuable exponent of the attempt to weave heterogeneous material into a readable and more or less consistent whole, and his greatest claim to attention lies in the evidence he

[1] On the general features of *E's* version, see further Moulton, 226; Thackeray, 760*a*; Torrey, 83 seq.

[2] For the textual value of *E* see, in addition to the commentaries on E–N, the discussions by Riessler (*Biblische Zeitschrift*, v. 146 seqq.) and Bayer.

furnishes for a comparative study of the traditions encircling the names and events of the period from Josiah to the Samaritan schism. Jos. is the earliest witness to *E*; the relationship is unmistakable as regards material and even language (Eichhorn, *Einleit. Apokr.* [1795], 347 seqq.; Treuenfels, *Der Orient* [1850–1]; H. Bloch, *Quellen d. Fl. Jos.* [1879], 69 seqq.). There are several points of agreement with 𝔊[A] as against 𝔊[B] (Thackeray, 762 *b*), and also with 𝔊[L]; Torrey (103) assigns the text an intermediate position. Unfortunately, Jos. is often extremely paraphrastic, and is therefore no safe guide for restoring the original of *E*. None the less, it is noteworthy that he is without the faults of *E* i. 29, 34 seq., he presupposes a text more complete and older than that in vi. 18, viii. 55, he uses a slightly different version of iii. (see Büchler, 64, 100), and, while obviously harmonizing in some places, elsewhere presents singular divergences or additions which do not appear to be arbitrary. In particular, his treatment of the stories of E and N is highly suggestive (see appendix to note on ix. 55). Besides utilizing the canonical sources (Jer., Dan., Est.), he has had access (as in Est.) to other Jewish traditions (see on vii. 15), and possessed some acquaintance with external history (see p. 11, and on i. 25). But although Jos. is not a direct witness to *E*'s text—and G. Hölscher has suggested that he made use of Alexander Polyhistor (*Quellen d. Jos.* [1904], 36, 43 seqq., 51)—he testifies to the authority of *E*'s history, and it is unnecessary to assume (Swete, Thackeray, Bayer, 140) that he used it simply because it was written in good Greek.

(*e*) *Date and place.* While Jos. is evidence for the earlier existence of *E*, it is not certain that it then had precisely its present form. As a translation the linguistic features suggest that it belongs to the time of the old Greek translation of Daniel, and was perhaps due to the same translator (Torrey, 84 seq.). The date of the original is bound up with that of Chron.-Ez.-Neh., and must be some time after 333 B.C. The Persian period was past, and its history had become obscure, the identity of Darius and Apame (iv. 29) was forgotten, and the points of contact with Dan. and Est. (not necessarily in their present form), would suggest the late Greek age. The problem also involves the question whether iii. 1–v. 6 is a secondary insertion or part of the original compilation, and this naturally affects the discussion of the home of the book (see pp. 29, 32). Although the section seems to some scholars to point to the influence of Alexandrian thought and philosophy (Lupton, André, Thackeray, Volz), to others it is Palestinian (Zunz), or not necessarily Alexandrian (Torrey). The identification of Apame speaks for Egypt or Antioch; the knowledge of the topography of Jerusalem (v. 47, ix. 38) is not that of the compiler or translator but of his source, and therefore cannot be claimed to support a Palestinian home. Egypt is suggested by the free irony in iii., iv., the unveiled women (iv. 18), the references to navigation (iv. 15, 23), and piracy (*v.* 27), and elsewhere by the use of Coelesyria (see ii. 17). Thackeray (762 *a*) compares the 'friends' of the king (viii. 26; E 𝔊 *σύμβουλοι*) with the 'first friends' who were third in scale of the courtiers at Alexandria, and with *ἂν φαίνηται σοι* (ii. 21, not in E) the phrase *ἐὰν φαίνηται* in Aristeas and frequently in Egyptian papyri. In so far as these data point to Egypt one may recall the interest in history-writing among the Hellenists Demetrios, Eupolemos, Artapanos, Alexander Polyhistor and others.

(*f*) *English versions.* It may be added that the old Geneva Bible, according to Lupton (6), is 'in some respects closer to the Greek than that of 1611'. Various improvements to the A.V. are suggested by Ball in the *Variorum Apocrypha*, and even the R.V. is not such an advance as might have been anticipated. Note, for example, the archaic 'Artaxerxes his letters' (ii. 30), 'cousin' (iii. 7), 'Jewry' (v. 7), and the gliding over of the obscurities of an imperfect 𝔊 in viii. 8, and especially in the concluding words, ix. 55.

§ 4. Problems of Literary and Historical Criticism.

I. *The Period.*

The problems of *E* and its relation to E–N involve that more complete and continuous series Chronicles-Ezra-Nehemiah which is united by sequence of contents and the recurrence throughout of similar features of language, interest, standpoint, and compilation. The 'chronicler's history'[1] of the post-exilic period deals with the fall of Jerusalem (586 B.C.), the return from exile under Zerubbabel and Jeshua, the reorganization of the Jewish people, the restoration of the Temple and

[1] By 'chronicler' is meant the hand which, by writing, compiling, or revising, brought the three consecutive books into practically their present form. Owing to the complexity of the compilation the term may not be an adequate one, but there seems no reason to doubt that there has been a single editorial process *at some stage in the literary growth* (the objections of Jampel, i. 108, 112, 115 seqq., and Davies, 16 are unnecessary). In any case, historical criticism cannot start from the untrustworthiness of Chronicles, and minimize the extent of the 'chronicler' in E–N (Davies, 16 seq.), or exaggerate it (Torrey, 145 seqq., on the E-story), or assume that all other records are necessarily relatively superior (so apparently Meyer, *Entstehung*). See below, pp. 17–19.

the furtherance of religious conditions, the separation from the Samaritans and other non-Israelite neighbours, and the inauguration of a church under the Mosaic Law. It is the period during which a considerable portion of the O.T., after passing through the hands of Judaean writers and editors, was reaching its present form, and the sole consecutive canonical source for this period, the chronicler's work, cannot be dated before the Greek age (333 B.C.). This source ignores all events between 586 and the decree of Cyrus, and omits other details which also refer to the period (see e.g. 2 Kings xxv. 22–30, Jer. xl.–xliv., lii. 28–34, Daniel, Esther). This feature, like the failure to record the history of (north) Israel after the fall of Samaria, cannot be wholly unintentional. Interest is concentrated upon exiles and reformers from Babylon, and upon their labours in rebuilding the Temple and in purifying religious and social conditions in the face of opposition within and without. A new and reformed Jewish community with its new Temple is linked historically with the old Judah of the Monarchy and the Temple of Solomon. The climax is reached partly in the great Covenant inaugurated by Ezra (N x.), after the Introduction of the Law (444 B.C.), and partly in the Samaritan schism initiated by Nehemiah (N xiii.). But such are the gaps and the one-sided standpoints that the records cannot be said to give us objective history. We have, rather, specific representations of certain events of vast importance for post-exilic Judaism, and, just as the account of the settlement of the old Israelite tribes in the land of their ancestors is found to contain conflicting traditions and the gravest difficulties, so also here, the compilation as a whole is dominated by certain larger views which tend to obscure the contradictions and intricacies that arise in any critical study of the data. In both cases the method of criticism is similar, and unfortunately the evidence is frequently insufficient for any confident recovery of the actual events during that period which is of such profound importance for the study of the O.T.[1]

II. *The Age of Cyrus and Darius.*

(*a*) *Paucity of trustworthy evidence.* It is evident that the fall of Jerusalem could not have had the catastrophic effects that the traditional view assumes. We cannot picture Judah between 586 and 537 as half-empty.[2] Neither the number of deported Judaeans nor that of those who returned points to any depopulation, and even the events under Gedaliah's governorship and the account of the flight of the survivors into Egypt indicate that the disasters ending in 586, when taken by themselves, had no ruinous consequences for the land. Subsequent history is ignored in Chron., but it is known that Jehoiachin in later years received some favour, and that Tyre had once more a king. The thread is resumed in E i.–vi. (*E* ii.–vii.), in the reigns of Cyrus and Darius, but the narratives contain serious difficulties and conflicting representations (§ 6, *a*) which are increased by the independent prophecies of Haggai and Zech. i.–viii. (see on *E* ii. 1 seqq.). Not until we reach the time of Artaxerxes are the sources more extensive, and the light they throw upon preceding years renders the value of E i.–vi. extremely doubtful. That is to say, between 586 and 458 (E's return), or rather 444 (N's first visit to Jerusalem), there is a lengthy period of the greatest significance for the internal history leading up to Judaism and Samaritanism, and the only continuous source is both scanty and untrustworthy (see Marq., 67, Torrey, 156, and, partly, Meyer, 74).

(*b*) *The evidence of the prophets.* The prophecies of Haggai and Zechariah, dated in the second year of Darius, 520, mention neither any previous important return nor any earlier attempt to rebuild the Temple. Zerubbabel now resumes dynastic history (Hag. ii. 23, contrast Jehoiachin, Jer. xxii. 24), and the high-priest Jeshua (grandson of Seraiah, 2 Kings xxv. 18–21), whose return in Dan. ix. 24–26 dates an epoch, is now officially installed. Yahweh had been angry seventy years (Zech. i. 12, cf. Jer. xxix. 10 seq., Dan. ix. 2); but is aroused and returns to Jerusalem (i. 16, ii. 10–13; contrast his departure in Ezek. x. 18 seq., xi. 23). He is jealous for Zion and full of wrath against her enemies; they shall be punished and his people shall enjoy increased happiness (i. 15, ii. 9). City and temple shall be rebuilt and the land re-inhabited (i. 16 seq., ii. 4, cf. vii. 7). The dispersed shall be rescued and again dwell in Jerusalem. The community in Babylon is bidden to escape to Zion (ii. 7, cf. Jer. li. 45). Babylon is threatened (vi. 1-8), and a passage which suggests that small bands of exiles might occasionally return heralds the forthcoming building of the temple (vi. 9–15). Haggai declares that the Temple is waste (i. 4, 9, *ḥārēb*, cf. the term in N ii. 3, 17) and he stirs the people to the work of rebuilding. The appeal is to the 'remnant' (i. 12, 14, ii. 2, cf. Zech. viii. 6), that is, not the

[1] Modern criticism is influenced by the radical conclusions of W. H. Kosters and the forcible defence by E. Meyer (*Entstehung*) whose own position, however, is in many respects opposed to the purely traditional; see S. R. Driver, *Lit.* 552 (and on the introductory literary questions, ib. 544 seqq.). A striking advance has recently been made by Torrey (*Ezra Studies*), to whose work the present writer gratefully records his indebtedness, and since reasons are given in these pages for adopting certain radical conclusions of Kosters, Torrey, and others, it may be well to refer readers to the writings (see § 8) of Davies, Driver, Holzhey, Jampel, Nikel, Ryle, and G. A. Smith, for the arguments adduced in support of a generally consistent traditional position.

[2] See Wellhausen, *GGN*, 1895, p. 185 seq.; Kosters, *Th. T.* xxix. 560; G. A. Smith, *Jerusalem*, ii. 268; Torrey, 290 seq., 297 seqq.; Kennett, *Journ. Theol. Stud.*, 1905, pp. 172 seqq.

40,000 of E ii., but those who had escaped deportation (cf. Zeph. ii. 7, 9, Jer. xlii. 2, 15, &c., see Jahn, p. xxxviii.). Zerubbabel is the one to rebuild and complete the undertaking (Zech. iv. 8–10, vi. 12 seqq.). The people fetch wood and the work is begun on the twenty-fourth of the sixth month (Hag. i. 14 seq.); as yet one stone had not been set upon another (ii. 15). The foundations are laid on the twenty-fourth of the ninth month (ii. 10–19), and two years later, in 518, Zech. viii. 9 seqq. look back upon the happier period which had thus been inaugurated. But the exilic fasts were still being celebrated (vii. 3–5), the return of the dispersed was still an event to be anticipated. From these data it is reasonable to infer—with an influential number of scholars—that 'no considerable band of exiles can have returned—none that was able materially to influence the Jewish community' (Cheyne, *Ency. Bib.*, 1481 n. 4).

(*c*) *Objections.* Various counter-arguments, influenced by the chronicler's history in E–N, have been brought forward (see p. 6 n. 1). Those based upon a representation of events which has perplexed a generation of scholars naturally tend to beg the question. For example, it is urged that the prophets address returned exiles and it was unnecessary to describe the people as such; that they do not say that the builders were not returned exiles; that only E i.–iii. explain the events of 520–516 and subsequent history; that the Temple could not have been built by the native 'heathen' Judaeans; that the main stream of Jewish life had been diverted to Babylon and only the presence of a Babylonian 'leaven' explains the prophecies of Hag. and Zech. While some scholars recognize and seek to explain the silence of the prophets touching a return and rebuilding before 520, others contend that there are indeed references to these events. Some, observing the profound difference between the promises of the 'Deutero-Isaiah' (xl.–lv.) and the history in E iii. seq., are of opinion that, since 'the reality was a bitter disenchantment,' the disillusionment so great, the prophets naturally do not refer to the events. But others argue that unless these promises had been essentially fulfilled there would have been so fatal a falsification of popular expectation that the oracles of Is. xl. seqq. would scarcely have survived. It is obvious that the preservation of prophecies is hardly conditioned by their fulfilment, however partial, and the difference between the anticipations and the reality was surely sufficient, on the most conservative view, to throw Is. xl. seqq. into oblivion. Haggai, it is objected, ignores a future return and may well have ignored previous events—but his contemporary Zech. excludes a previous return, testifies to the continuation of the exile, and looks forward to a return. The *argumentum e silentio* is undoubtedly valid. Zech. (i. 2–6), in appealing to the people to repent, alludes to past experience, but does not refer to the return —which would have been the most immediate proof of the might of Yahweh. Was there a wish to put courage into the poor hearts of the returned exiles? There was one practical illustration of divine grace, but there is no allusion to it. In fact, the urgent supplication to Yahweh (i. 12) is unintelligible had a new era dawned as in E i.–iii.; one may note Daniel's prayer for divine intervention (Dan. ix., cf. also N i.) and the prayers of E after his return (E ix. 8, N ix. 30 seq.). In point of fact, Zech. sees the punishment and misery of the past (vii.), and the 'decalogue of promises' belong to the future (viii.). Did the prophets intentionally refrain from mentioning the material help the exiles had received in the time of Cyrus, in order to emphasize the necessity of relying upon spiritual help? The very passage which has been quoted in support of this view refers to the small beginnings recently inaugurated by Zerubbabel (iv. 6, 9 seq.), and ignores E i.–iv.

There is no explanation of the gap between 537 and 520; there is no hint of any hindrance, cessation, or of any more or less continuous rebuilding (see § 6 *a*): the people are negligent and remiss, and according to Haggai the distress caused by the failure of the rains was a punishment for not rebuilding the Temple (i., cf. 2 Sam. xxi. 1–10, Zech. xiv. 17). It hardly required a Babylonian exile to teach this. Haggai certainly refers to an altar (ii. 14, 'there'), but this does not prove the accuracy of E iii. 3 or its context. A holy place is not necessarily deserted when the sanctuary is ruined, and Jer. xli. 5 already presupposes an altar; to contend that the existence of this altar throughout the exile ought to have been mentioned in the O.T. is unreasonable. Indeed, the references to priests and sacrifices (Hag. ii. 10–14, cf. Zech. vii. 3 seqq.) go further and suggest that the cult of Yahweh was independent even of the existence of a Temple (cf. Sellin, *Stud.* 53 seq.; Torrey, 305). There is, moreover, no good reason for believing that native Judaeans would be 'heathenish', and that if they had rebuilt the Temple they would have been treated otherwise by the reformers E and N. If Jer. and Ezek. bear witness to low religious conditions, Hag., Mal., and Is. lvi.–lxvi. indicate no great improvement after the return; and the degenerate community which all scholars recognize in the latter sources and which needed the reforms of E and N include—on the traditional view—the Babylonian 'leaven.' Yet the Judaeans and Samaritans felt themselves to be heirs of Israel and the latter could claim to worship Yahweh (2 Kings xvii. 32 seq., 41, Jer. xli. 5, Ezek. xxxiii. 24, E iv. 2). The fall of Jerusalem and the Exile do not exclude the presence—even among 'the poorest of the land'—of men who might follow in the footsteps of the Rechabites (Jer. xxxv.), or of such seers as Amos, Hosea, Micah or Jeremiah; and considering the piety of the Jews in distant Elephantine (Sachau-papyri), there is clearly no necessity to deny the possibility of the continuous worship of Yahweh during the exile, or to demand after 538 the presence of a 'leaven' which nevertheless did not preclude the abuses confronting E, N, Mal., and the writers in Is. lvi. seqq. It is obviously impossible to start with presuppositions of what was orthodox Yahwism and what was heathenism whether in Elephantine or in Palestine (before or after 536). If, too, Meyer's argument (177) is valid, that the Levitical family of Henadad (E iii. 9, wanting in E ii.) was indigenous, indigenous also was the family of Iddo to which Zech. belonged (see *E* vi. 1); and this scholar's recognition of the prominence in and around Jerusalem of Calebite and other families who had never tasted exile (see § 5 *c*) is extremely important for any estimate of the internal conditions. The evidence of Hag. and Zech. outweighs other evidence which might appear to be contrary; hence one can hardly assume that the deliverance of Jeshua (Zech. iii. 2) necessarily refers to his return seventeen years previously, or that the *name* Zerubbabel suggests that other Jews with him were necesssarily 'begotten in Babylon'. Nor can decisive objections be based upon references in E vii.–x., N i. seqq. to an earlier return. That men (? exiles) should come and assist in the rebuilding of the Temple is a promise for the future in Zech. vi. 15. The references in E ix. 4, x. 6 seq. present their own peculiar difficulties on any view, and in all probability the story of E should come after N i.–vi. (see III. *a*). N i. 2 seq. are inconclusive: they may be used to support a theory (Kosters, 45, Berth., 47, Torrey, 301 n. 27, Davies, 161), although Ryle (149), who maintains an independent, though strictly conservative position, refers the passage to the people who had escaped the exile—the passage, in any case, must be considered in the light of evidence for some disaster between the age of Zerubbabel and the return of N (see further, § 5 *f*). It is to be remembered, also, that the belief in a great return under Cyrus (or Darius) might influence the description of subsequent events even as the complete Mosaic legislation appears at first sight to be confirmed by the form which the revised and redacted history has taken in the books that follow the Pentateuch.

(*d*) *Summary.* The account of a large return to rebuild the Temple, whether in the time of Cyrus or Darius, must be tested by the independent Hag. and Zech. Great weight is often laid upon the circumstantial list in E ii., and its genuineness has been upheld, particularly by Meyer (73, 98 seqq., 191 seqq.; note the criticisms of Kosters, *Th. T.* xxxi. 530–41); see below, p. 35. He, however, rejects in the main the rest of the Cyrus-history (49, 73, 99, 191, 193; Driver, *Lit.*, 552), although the decree of Cyrus is in itself entirely plausible (Nikel, 31–7; Torrey, 144 n. 12), and the list is closely bound up with the whole series E i.–vi. His position appears inconsistent from any traditional standpoint (see Nikel, 42 seq., Davies, 14, 80 seq.), as well as from one more consistently critical, although his recognition that the list (which contains names recurring throughout E–N) is fundamental for the criticism of the post-exilic history is thoroughly sound. But the list stands or falls with its context, and when it is admitted that the success of the opposition in E iv. proves that the return has been exaggerated (see Sellin, *Stud.* 1; O. C. Whitehouse, *Isaiah*, ii. 228; G. A. Smith, *Jerus.* ii. 298 seq.), or that the list has been re-edited (Holzhey, 15; Davies, 51), it is necessary to determine what details in E i.–vi. may be regarded as even essentially accurate. The tolerance and kindness of Amil-Marduk (to Jehoiachin), Nabunaid (who sent back Merbaal to be king of Tyre), Cyrus, Cambyses, and Darius[1] certainly allow the probability of the return of bands of exiles, even as the Sachau-papyri show how Cambyses might favour *native* Jewish communities. But E i.–vi. are so closely interconnected as a piece of history that if we accept—as we must—the testimony of Hag. and Zech., it is difficult, if not impossible, to reconstruct from E the course of events. On the one hand, we gain new presuppositions regarding the internal conditions of the age. On the other, there is remarkable confusion in the traditions of Cyrus and Darius in E and *E*, E ii. is repeated in the history of the time of Artaxerxes, and a narrative of this later period is actually inserted in E i.–vi.; these combine with other features to extend the problems of E i.–vi. to those connected with the work of E and N.

III. *The Work of Ezra and Nehemiah.*

(*a*) *Ezra.* In the story of E there is considerable intricacy in the description of the separation from the heathen on the part of the 'children of the captivity' (i. e. E's small band of exiles, or the congregation presumably formed in 536–516), and the inauguration of the new community, consisting of these and the elect of the 'seed of Israel'. The whole story is closely interconnected, and much difficulty is caused by N i.–vii. which sever E vii.–x. from N viii. seqq. by twelve years. There is, moreover, a very strong presumption that the Reading of the Law was originally described shortly after E's arrival (cf. *E* ix.), and not (as in N viii.) after this lengthy interval, during which we hear nothing of him. Finally, on independent grounds there seems to be no place for E before the *first* visit, at all events, of N. It is indeed allowed that 'it is impossible to decide upon the evidence at our disposal' (G. A. Smith, *Expositor*, July, 1906, p. 16), or that this later position of E is only a possibility (Wellhausen); but it seems very doubtful whether the story is trustworthy (H. P. Smith, Torrey, Jahn), and, even if it be historical, many agree that it cannot be placed before N i.–vi. (Berth., Buhl, Cheyne, Guthe, Hoonacker [esp. *Rev. Bibl.*, x. 15 seqq.], Kennett, Kent, Kosters, Marq., Sellin, Wildeboer). See further the notes on *E* viii–x.

(*b*) *Nehemiah.* N was governor from the 20th year of Artaxerxes (Jos. xi. 5 7, 25th of Xerxes) to the 32nd (N v. 14), i. e. 444–432, and we hear of a return to the king and a second visit (xiii. 4–6). But N xiii. is joined to xii. so closely as to imply that only on the occasion of the *later* visit were the walls dedicated, although the ceremony is ostensibly the immediate sequel of their completion, two months after his *first* visit (vi.).[2] This must be due to defective compilation (cf. Nikel, 196 n. 1),

[1] For the external evidence see Berth., 26 seq.; Jampel, i. 502 seqq., ii. 11 seqq.

[2] Rawlinson and Klostermann (so Davies, 267), Howorth (*PSBA*, xxv. 18 seq.), G. A. Smith (*op. cit.* 10–12), R. H. Kennett (*Camb. Bibl. Essays*, 120); the dates N vi. 15, vii. 73, ix. 1 were evidently meant—by the compiler—to be consecutive. That the walls were actually completed in 52 days may be 'hardly credible' (Ew. 157 n. 5); Jos. (§ 179) allows 2 years and 4 months (hardly an invention, Ew.), and dates the completion in the ninth month (cf. 2 Macc. i. 18) of the 28th year of *Xerxes*.

which will also explain the description of N's social reforms (v.) amid the intrigues during the hurried rebuilding of the walls, where N looks back upon the period of his governorship (v. 14). In fact, his strong position as reformer in v. seems more in harmony with that in xiii. than with the picture of suspicion and hostility represented in iv., vi., and this serious difficulty touching the course of N's work (vii. 2 may hint at his departure) hampers every attempt to trace the history of his period. Consequently N, even with the elimination of the E-story, cannot be in its original form, as is clear also from the literary features of xi. and xii. (see also Torrey, 225 seq., 248 seq.).

(*c*) *The List N vii.* N's proposal to summon the people in order to augment Jerusalem (vii. 4 seqq.) is severed by part of the E-story (N viii.–x.) from the list of inhabitants (xi.), other lists (xii. 1–26), the dedication of the walls and arrangements for the Temple officials (xii. 27–47), &c. His story is no longer autobiographical (contrast, however, xiii. 4–31) and fresh sources are to be recognized. Since the list found by him (vii. 5) is that of the return of Zerubbabel (E ii.), it is often assumed that the sequel in xi. must also refer to this earlier period (Ewald, Smend, Stade, Meyer, &c.). But xi. differs so widely from vii. 6 seqq. that both cannot be authentic (Meyer, 189). It is more probable, however, that xi. belongs to the story of N and follows upon vii. 4, 'though the narrative is hardly continued *uno tenore*' (Driver, 551). Yet, on any theory, the presence of N vii. 6–73 is inexplicable, since it is difficult to see why even a compiler should quote an *ancient* list which excluded the more recent return of E (E viii. 1–14; cf. Holzhey, 37). If 'a genealogical register was necessary' (Davies), this would have been out-of-date, and although lapse of time and later adjustment might explain—on this view—the various differences between E ii. and N vii., there are far more significant differences in N x. 1–27, a list which is referred to N's time. Now, its conclusion (N vii. 73 *b*) is the proper introduction to the Reading of the Law (viii.), which is in a more natural position between E viii. and ix., and Torrey (256 seqq., cf. Kent, 369) points out that N vii. 70–3 *a*, also, are more in harmony after the account of E's return. Indeed, vii. 66–9 (the enumeration) and 61–5 (the expulsion of the impure in Zerubbabel's time, see on *E* v. 38) would be useless for N's purpose, and in fact H. P. Smith would place the entire list (from vii. 5) after E viii. 36 (393 n. 1; see, however, Torrey 259 n. 9). Accordingly, through compilation and revision the account of N's work, with its own chronological embarrassments, has been broken by a portion of the story of E, the first part of which is now found before N i., while the list in vii. (*vv.* 5 *a*, 73 suggest a gathering of the people) records details which are not in keeping with the context, whereas in E ii. it is in a consistent context, albeit an unhistorical one. While the Reading of the Law (vii. 73 *b*–viii.) abruptly introduces E, the preceding material is partly (at least) connected with E's return in E vii. seq., and partly belongs to the (unhistorical) account of Zerubbabel's return. A considerable portion of the E-story is sundered from N viii. seqq., but the description of the separation from the heathen is confused and closely interrelated, and the list of those who had married strange women (see on *E* ix. 21–36) includes families who are not mentioned in E's band (E viii. 1–14), but appear in the list of E ii., which in ∥ N vii. is connected with the return of E! Finally, this great list, though used for the time of Cyrus (or Darius, *E* v.) and treated in N vii. as a document of that period, reveals traces of the age of N himself, and of having been adjusted to the earlier context (see on *E* v. 24 seq., 40, 44 seq., 46 seq.). Hence it would seem that E ii. N vii. originally belonged to an account of a return in some record of the history of the times of N, E, and Artaxerxes. On its repetition, see p. 19 (§ 6).

(*d*) *The Ezra-story.* The well-supported view that E came to Jerusalem after N i.–vi. implies some rearrangement of the material; and the suitability of N vii. (some portion) and viii. between E vii. seq. and ix. suggests, not that the *latter* part of the E-story has been removed from E x. and placed after N vi., but that the whole once stood after that chapter. The complexity of the list vii. (which overlaps with E viii.) still remains, and it is at this point in the book that the critical problems become most intricate. But it must be noticed that the E-story is certainly composite and not in its original form, and some of the confusion may have arisen when it was divided and part of it placed before N i.[1] If, moreover, the E-story stood after N vi. it may be observed that there is a certain relationship between the stories of E and N: the reference to the son of Eliashib, E x. 6, cf. N xiii. 4, 28; the suitability of N xiii. 1–2, between E x. 9 and 10 (W. R. Smith; Berth., 89); the coincidence in the day of arrival of each (see *E* viii. 6); the twelve-years' gap in the history of each, and the parallel features in their measures on behalf of temple, priests and people. E, however, is mentioned only incidentally in the story of N (xii. 36, doubtful, see the comm.), and it is impossible that the two laboured together. On the other hand, the Tirshatha is prominent at the Reading of the Law (N viii. 9) and the signing of the Covenant (x. 1), and also in the list, vii. (*v.* 65, the degradation of the priests; *v.* 70, gifts to the treasury); he is identified with N (see on *E* ix. 49), and N is

[1] For the interrelation between the now sundered portions see p. 47, and cf. JE in Ex. xxxiii. seqq. and Num. x. 29–36, xi.; and also the contents of 2 Sam. v.–viii., xxi.–xxiv.

equally prominent in his own story (especially v., xiii.). N was not the only governor in post-exilic Jerusalem (N v. 15, Mal. i. 8), but it is noteworthy that the E-story, especially in the narrative-portions, shows no interest in either the governor or the high-priest; the story seems to be written from an independent standpoint, and is focussed upon the austere figure of E alone. The story represents a period of divine favour and royal clemency after the sufferings of Israel (Dan. ix., N i. presuppose an earlier situation); it obviously comes after the disappearance of Zerubbabel, but it cannot be placed before the introduction of N. There are independent arguments for the tradition of a return under N and religious reorganization (see § 5 *b*, *d*), and this appears to be supplemented by the account of E. The latter describes the return of E and a representative community to a temple, but one sorely in need of replenishing (E vii. 15–27, viii. 36); to an ecclesiastical body (note E viii. 17), but a negligent one (N x. 32 seqq.); to a community that worshipped Yahweh, but had fallen from the ideal. It can hardly be called an Autobiography (Meyer, 205) or a Memoir, and there is no evidence to prove it to be a mere invention or fiction. Rather is it based upon facts which link the energy of N with the subsequent appearance of an established orthodox Jewish Church. It may be regarded as an ideal description of the inauguration of Judaism, and the introduction of the 'Book of the Law of Moses' (the Pentateuch is probably meant) is a later parallel to the story of the (re-)discovery of the 'Book of the Law' (Deuteronomy) in the reign of Josiah; cf. also the chronicler's accounts of Asa, Jehoshaphat and Hezekiah (2 Chron. xiv. 4, xv. 3, 10–13, xvii. 7, 9, xxix. 10). It does not seem to have been written by the *compiler* of the series Chron.-E–N; it appears rather as a tradition of independent origin, written around the age of N, combined with the story of N and ultimately with the great post-exilic history of Jerusalem and the Temple.

IV. *Interrelation of Data.*

(*a*) *Intricacy of parallels.* The intricacy of the list E ii. N vii. for the history of Cyrus, Darius (*E*) and Artaxerxes does not stand alone. The close connexion in the narratives relating to Cyrus and Darius appears in E iii. 7 compared with *E* iv. 48, in iii. 1 with *E* v. 6, and in E iii. 2 with *E* v. 4–6. The Temple, according to Hag. and Zech., was not commenced before the time of Darius, in contrast to E iii.; but the laments in E iii. 12 in the time of Cyrus curiously recall Hag. ii. 3 seqq. The social and religious reorganization implied in E ii. 59, 62, vi. 21 finds a parallel in the reforms of E, and while E ii. 70, iii. 1, introduce the erection of the altar, the text in *E* v. 46 seq. presupposes a later period, and in fact these verses in N vii. 73, viii. 1, form the prelude to the Reading of the Law. The latter event is the sequel to the record of a return (N vii.) which in *E* ix. is that of E himself. E iii. is unhistorical, and has probably been influenced by material relating to the time of N; thus Meyer (73, 99) points to N viii. 17 seq., and Jahn compares iii. 10–13 with N xii. 40–3. The account of the opposition in E iv. is untrustworthy, and there is a marked resemblance between the details and N iv., vi., enhanced by the insertion in E iv. 7–24 of a record of the time of Artaxerxes. This record attests a return of some importance, which, however, has yet to be identified, and while the decrees of Cyrus and Darius agree (cf. also Artaxerxes and E) in presenting several very similar features (Torrey, 125 seqq., 158; Bayer, 117 seqq.), the historical basis for any decree on the lines they take cannot be found in their reigns. For parallels in the stories of E and N see above, p. 9 (*d*). Such is the interrelation of the contents that it is hardly surprising that later sources should not infrequently combine Zerubbabel and Ezra (Lag. 18; Torrey, 49 n. 17) and that both should be united with Jeshua in a return in the time of Darius (Lag. 84). Even N xii. 47 looks back and mentions together Zerubbabel and N (see Berth.); and if Hashabiah and Sherebiah in N xii. 24 may be identified with the names in E viii. 18 seq., Joiakim (son of Jeshua) and E appear to be correlated much in the same way that N xii. 12–26 seem to confuse the times of Joiakim, N and E (see also the view of Kosters, 91 seq.).

(*b*) *Some modern views.* The endeavour to recover the historical facts has led to very divergent conclusions among modern scholars. One favourite view has retained Ahasuerus and Artaxerxes in E iv., between Cyrus and Darius, by the simple device of changing the names or of assuming an alternative nomenclature. Equally popular has been the theory that Artaxerxes and Darius are to be identified with the second bearer of each name, and, indeed, this may have been the view of the compiler or writer (see Torrey, 38 seq., 178 seq.). Although this leaves an astonishing gap between Cyrus and Darius II, the belief that the Artaxerxes of the stories of N and E was the later king (404–359 B.C.) has found very weighty support (de Saulcy, Maspero, Hoonacker, and Howorth [partly], Marq., H. P. Smith [382], &c., see further Berth., 30; and *PSBA*, xxiii. 319 seqq.). It has also been proposed to identify the Cyrus of the narratives with Darius and Darius with Art. I, and so close is the interconnexion of events that N viii.–x. has been placed in the time of Zerubbabel, and the whole of E–N (extending from 537 to 432) has been compressed within a few years (see H. Winckler, *Helmholt's World's Hist.* iii. 216 seq., and the summaries in Jampel, ii. 1 seq.). Others hold that Zer. first returned in the time of Darius, and that E iii. 8 seqq. properly belongs to that later period. Moreover, the historical and prophetical writings are necessarily co-ordinated, and thus Hag. and Zech. have appeared to some to be of or about the time of Cyrus, although if Darius be D. II they are brought down to (about) 423–404 (see Howorth, *PSBA*, xxiii. 324). So, also, the prophecies in Is. xl.–lxvi., are subdivided and connected with the history of the times of Cyrus and Artaxerxes, although, under the influence of another theory of the history, the chapters are once more treated as virtually a whole, either relatively early (*c.* 537–520; Sellin, *Stud.* 160; Rothstein) or relatively late (H. P. Smith, 371 n. 1, 379 n. 3; Torrey, 288 n. 8, 314; Kennett). In contrast to these efforts to overcome the difficulties are the views of those scholars who do not admit the intricacies but continue to maintain the essential trustworthiness of E–N, the unhistorical character of Chron. itself being, nevertheless, almost unanimously realized. In so far as this is based upon the manner in which the narratives appear to be mutually confirmatory—cf. the conservative attitude to the criticism of the Pentateuch—and superficially, at least, consistent, it is necessary to observe that the chronicler's history is singularly simple compared with the forms taken in *E*, or in Jos., or in the traditions that prevailed elsewhere in ancient times.

(*c*) *Some ancient views.* Jos., who is well-informed on the last Babylonian kings, asserts that the kingdom fell to Cyrus the Persian and Darius the Mede; the two were kinsmen and the latter, whose father was Astyages, had another name among the Greeks (x. **11**, 2, 4). Cyrus, son of Cambyses, was the father of the better-known Cambyses; his mother, according to tradition, was the sister of Cyaxares and daughter of Astyages. Astyages, the last Median king, was the son of Cyaxares and was defeated by Cyrus. But this name is also given by Alexander Polyhistor and others to Cyaxares (*c.* 624–584), the founder of the Median empire, who took part with Nabopolassar in the attack upon Assyria.[1] When the father of Darius is called Ahasuerus (Dan. ix. 1; cf. the synopsis, Lag. 15, where he is born of Vashti), and the latter and Nebuchadrezzar capture Nineveh (Tobit xiv. 15), the names Ahasuerus and Cyaxares have evidently been confused (Rawlinson). The Ahasuerus of Esther was certainly placed soon after the deportation of Jehoiachin by Nebuchadrezzar (so ii. 5 seq.), but in Judith iv. 1–6 the last-mentioned reigns over the Medes at a time when the Jews had recently returned from captivity and the high-priest was one Joiakim. The historical foundation for Esther's king can only be Xerxes, although Jos., LXX, and early writers identify him with Artaxerxes. Jos., moreover, states that he was also called Cyrus—in Dan. v. 31, vi. 28, Darius the Mede becomes king after the fall of Babylonia and is followed by Cyrus—and gives the name Xerxes to the Artaxerxes of the stories of E and N. The difficulty of distinguishing the names would obviously be increased by the fact that Darius I was actually followed by Xerxes (485–465), and D. II (423–404) by Art. II (404–359), and that D. II had a son Cyrus, famous for the unsuccessful expedition against his elder brother Art. II. Not to pursue the confusing details further, it is enough to notice that the later historians had behind them a series of events of vital importance. During a relatively brief period the power of Assyria was broken up, Scythians and Medes entered into W. Asiatic politics, a new Babylonian empire was restored only to fall before the Persian régime under Cyrus; a little more than a century later another Cyrus created a turmoil in W. Asia (400), and finally the Greeks, who had been gradually coming into closer touch with the Oriental world, established a new age under Alexander the Great. How soon history became enwrapped in legend is obvious from Herodotus and Xenophon (fifth century B.C.) and from Ctesias, who is even said to have drawn upon Persian records. Jos., for his part, endeavoured to reduce the confusion into some order; the Seder Olam (ch. xxx) ingeniously identifies all the Persian kings: Cyrus, Darius, Ahasuerus and Artaxerxes—Dan. xi. 2 knows only of four—and the whole of the Persian age from the restoration of the Temple to the time of Alexander the Greek was even compressed into a few decades. The appearance of simplicity in the chronicler's history of the period is misleading; see further § 6 *e*.

§ 5. DATA FOR RECONSTRUCTION.

The foregoing survey of the intricacies of E–N, the prevailing confusion in regard to the period, and the efforts made by ancient and modern writers to present the historical facts, will perhaps be convincing proof that the difficulties in E–N are genuine. They concern both E–N and *E*, and any attempt to discuss the origin and structure of *E* must form some preliminary conception of the underlying history. For this the story of N seems most fruitful.

(*a*) *The Samaritans.* N's age was one of intermarriage and close intercourse between the Jews, Samaritans, and other neighbours (vi. 18, xiii. 3, 4, 23, 24, 28). The elliptical repulse of the Samaritans in N ii. 20 implies that they, as in E iv. 2 seq., had some claim 'to a share in the fortunes of Jerusalem' (Ryle, 171), and that they 'would have had no quarrel with the Jews if they had been permitted to unite with the latter in their undertakings and privileges' (Davies, 177). These details, the character of the intermarriages, the efforts to compromise with N (vi. 2–4), the close relationship presupposed by the subsequent bitterness after the schism, the fact that Samaritanism was virtually a sister-sect of Judaism—these preclude the present position of E's return and marriage-reforms and make it extremely doubtful whether there had as yet been any serious Samaritan hostility. They also suggest that the records of E–N have been written and revised under the influence of a bitter anti-Samaritan feeling, the date of which can hardly be placed before N xiii. Indeed, it is not improbable that the Samaritan schism should be placed (with Jos. xi. 7 seq.) at the close of the Persian period (see further Marq., 57 seq.; Jahn, 173 seqq.; Torrey, 321 seqq., 331 seq.).

(*b*) *Place of Ez. iv.* 7–23. This undated record of the reign of Artaxerxes, in spite of some

[1] See *Ency. Brit.*, 11th ed., on these names.

internal difficulties (see criticisms in Berth., 18 seq., Nikel, 182), probably illustrates the story of N when 'Tobiah sent letters to put me in fear' (vi. 19).[1] It points to some new reconstruction of the city by returned exiles—evidently after an earlier disaster—and requires the assumption that the story of N is focussed upon the governor alone and that N and his military escort (ii. 9, cf. *E* v. 2, contrast ib. viii. 51 seq.) brought back a band of exiles (so Jos.); see below (*d*). Against this the objection has been brought that N, in spite of the royal command (E iv. 21 seq.), continued to build and actually did complete the walls. On the other hand, the walls were already practically finished (vi. 1, vii. 1, see Ryle, 219), and some time would necessarily elapse before letters could reach Artaxerxes and his reply come to hand (cf. the situation in E v. 5). The king does not order the walls to be destroyed or weakened; N naturally had other building operations to attend to in addition to the walls, and these may well have been stopped 'by force and power' (E iv. 23). The letter to Artaxerxes urges that the rebuilding of Jerusalem would be detrimental to the security of the province (iv. 13, 19 seq.), and disloyalty was the strongest charge brought against the governor (N ii. 19, vi. 6–7). In fact, N vii. 2 seq. may suggest that the perturbed governor left his brother in charge of the city while he visited the king—his leave had been limited (ii. 6)—and although the sequence of events is admittedly obscure there is a distinct gap between his position in N i.–iv., vi. and that as represented in xiii. (cf. v.). The formal steps of the Samaritans in E iv. 7 seqq. (similarly the satrap in E v. seq.) stand in contrast to the confusing account of the hostility in N iv., vi. against one who had come armed with royal authority, and undue weight must not be laid upon the present form of the N-story (see above [*a*]). All in all, the evidence does not exclude the helpful conjecture that E iv. 7–23 illustrate the troubles of N at that stage where the continuation of the book (after vi. 19) is almost inextricably complex.

(*c*) *The semi-Edomite population.* In the list of those who helped to rebuild the wall (N iii.) it is noteworthy (1) that very few of the names can be at all plausibly identified with the families who apparently returned with either Zerubbabel or Ezra (Kosters, 47), and (2) that some of the names have Calebite affinities.[2] The list is evidence for the poverty of the Babylonian section of population and for the prominence of the Judaeans, who include both the natives and those Calebite and allied groups who moved up from the south of Judah some time after 586. The presence of the latter is only to be expected, and the fact, pointed out by Meyer himself in 1896, is obviously fundamental for the criticism of the book of Ezra (see Kosters, *Th. T.* xxxi. 536).[3] In this Calebite or semi-Edomite Judah—and to call these groups 'half heathen' (with Nikel, 56, 64) is to beg the question—we may find a starting-point for our conception of the district from the time of their immigration northwards to the date of the far-reaching reorganization associated with the names of N and E. Further, the list of the inhabitants of Jerusalem in N xi. recurs, though with variations, in 1 Chron. ix., where it represents the compiler's conception of the post-exilic population after the captivity. According to his perspective of history, there was an old Israel which included a Judah of Calebite and Jerahmeelite origin (1 Chron. ii. and iv.) and some later stage which corresponds closely with N xi. N xi., however, differs widely from the lists in E ii. and viii. and ignores the return of Zerubbabel and Ezra. Its disagreement is hardly a proof that these lists are authentic; what is significant is the agreement between the Judaean clans Perez, Shelah and the semi-Edomite Zerah in N xi. and the mixed genealogies in 1 Chron. ii. and iv. The chronicler, it will be observed, knows of no earlier Judah; his evidence in ii., iv. is (in his view) pre-Davidic, and it agrees with this that his lists of the Levitical orders of David's time illustrate the close bond uniting these ecclesiastical bodies with people of south Palestinian and Edomite affinity.[4]

(*d*) *A decree and a return.* The introduction to the Jerusalem list reads like the sequel to the account of some return (N xi. 3, 1 Chron. ix. 2; cf. E ii. 70, N vii. 73, and see Ewald, 159 n. 2). The list itself, after dealing with priests, Levites, &c., proceeds to refer to those who dwelt in the country, and it is noteworthy that N xi. 23 seq. have in view the fulfilment of some royal decree touching the singers (cf. *E* iv. 54 seq., E vii. 24). The singers, also, are subsequently collected from the Netophathite and other villages which they had built at some unspecified period (xii. 28 seq.; cf. the Levites in 1 Chron. ix. 16), and the explicit references to the rest of Israel and their cities (xi. 20, 25), before the assembling at the dedication of the walls (xii. 27), recall the situation before

[1] H. P. Smith, 348; Kent, 358; see also the remarks of Sellin, *Ser.*, 53 seqq., *Stud.* 16–35. With Tobiah, cf. the Aram. form Tabeel, E iv. 7 (Hoonacker, *Rev. Bibl.* x. 183 n. 6; Sellin, *Stud.* 33).

[2] See for (2) Meyer, *Ent.*, 114–19, 147, 167, 177 seq., 181, 183, and his *Israeliten*, 352 n. 5, 399, 402, 409, 429 n. 5, 430. See also on *E* v. 26.

[3] Cf. also H. Guthe, *E. Bi.* 2249; T. K. Cheyne, ib. 3385; H. P. Smith, *Hist.* 354 n. 1; R. Kittel, *Chron.* 14, 16; Jahn, 99; Kennett, *Essays*, 117, 123; Torrey, 328, n. 53; E. L. Curtis and A. A. Madsen, *Chron.* 89, 98, 104.

[4] See also E. Meyer and B. Luther, *Israel.*, 442 seqq., for evidence connecting Judah and the Edomites; in their opinion, however, the data, found in literature relating to pre-monarchical times, refer to pre-Davidic conditions.

the exiles were assembled in Jerusalem after their return and settlement in the Zerubbabel-story (E ii. 70, iii. 1). Thus, the difficult and much revised narratives of N's work, between vi. and xiii., are connected with the list of the return in vii., with the return of E (see p. 9 *c*), and with some return associated with the figure of N himself. G. A. Smith observes that the reforms of N 'are best explained through his reinforcement by just so large a number of Babylonian Jews under just such a leader as E' (*Expos.*, July, 1906, p. 7 seq.). On the other hand, there is insufficient historical evidence for the presence of E and his band, and the above details strongly suggest that there was an account of some other return in connexion with the activity of N, although it is still impossible to reconstruct the course of N's work (see § 4, III. *b*).

(*e*) *The Temple.* The history after the rise of the Davidic Zerubbabel is a blank which can be filled only by conjecture (see e.g. Ewald; Sellin, *Ser.*; Nikel, 142–6, and others). The situation in Jerusalem at the return of N cannot be explained by the disasters at the fall of Jerusalem about 140 years previously. The city was in great affliction and reproach, and N's grief, confession, and prayer recall E's behaviour at the tidings of the heathen marriages. The ruins of Jerusalem were extensive (N i. 3, ii. 3, 8, 13, iii., cf. Ecclus. xlix. 13), and it is disputed whether the *bīrāh* (ii. 8) refers to the fortress on the north side of the Temple (G. A. Smith, *Jerus.*, ii. 347 seq., 461), or the Temple itself (cf. 1 Chron. xxix. 1 and see Jahn, pp. iv, 93). According to 2 Macc. i. 18, N built both the Temple and the Altar, and Jos. (independently) asserts that he received permission to build the walls of the city and to finish the Temple. An old Latin synopsis (Lag. 18 seq.) states that E restored the foundations of Zerubbabel's temple, and an old Greek summary of 'Second Esdras' refers to N as a builder of the Temple (Lag. 84, l. 27: αὐτὸς ἠξίωσε περὶ τῆς οἰκοδομῆς τοῦ ἱεροῦ). These can scarcely all be based upon the references to the Temple in the Artaxerxes-record in *E* ii. 18, 20. It is at least noteworthy that, both in *E* and E, compilers have placed this episode in the history of the Temple, and the different readings in E iv. 12, 14, might be due to the alternative position of the story (see below, § 6 (*c*)) after the account of the opposition in the time of Cyrus.[1] Moreover, the mention of the '*decree of* Cyrus, and Darius, and *Artaxerxes king of Persia*' (E vi. 14, see *E* vii. 4) is unintelligible—for even a gloss or interpolation must express some plausible belief—unless there was a tradition associating Artaxerxes with the building of the Temple. Again, in view of the parallels between E iv. and N ii. iv., vi., in the account of the Samaritan opposition, it is surely significant that the abrupt allusion in N ii. 20 to the repudiation of the Samaritans can only be explained in the light of E iv. 3, where the building of the Temple is concerned.[2] Finally, the E-story represents a period of favour during which the Temple had been restored or repaired through God's mercy and the clemency of Persia (E ix. 8 seq.). This brief 'moment' (*v.* 8) cannot date back from the decree of Cyrus and the work of Zerubbabel, rather must one read the whole situation—the strengthening of a neglectful community, the furthering of a poor temple—as a supplement to the disorganization and confusion in the story of N's measures. Hence, it may be concluded that there is sufficient evidence for some tradition of a rebuilding of the Temple and of a return in the time of N.

(*f*) *The recent disaster.* The disaster which explains N's grief, anxiety, and energetic labours may probably be ascribed in part at least to Edom. Friendly or neutral relations between Judah (and its semi-Edomite population, see *c*) and the 'brother' Edom appear to have continued at a relatively late period, until for some reason Edom is denounced for its unbrotherly conduct.[3] The origin of the enmity is generally connected with the fall of Jerusalem in 586. But it cannot be found in the time of Jehoiakim (the conjecture 'Edom' for 'Aram' in 2 Kings xxiv. 2 is against Jer. xxxv. 11), or of Zedekiah (when Edom was among the allies of Judah; Jer. xxvii., Ezek. xvii. 11 seqq.); the Chaldeans alone destroyed the Temple, and Jews had even taken refuge in Edom and elsewhere (Jer. xl. 11). The very explicit statement that the Edomites burned the Temple 'when Judaea was made desolate by the Chaldeans', and occupied Judaean territory (*E* iv. 45, 50), points to the reality of a tradition which, however, has been connected with the events of 586. The various allusions to Edom (Obad., Ezek. xxv. 12, xxxv. 10, 12, xxxvi. 5, Lam. iv., Ps. cxxxvii. 7), though possibly referring to different periods, cannot be based upon the history of the Chaldean invasion. The very circumstantial references to Edomite aggression (*E* iv. 50, Ezek. xxxv. 10, xxxvi. 3, 5) have led to the view that the Jewish exiles recovered their land through Persian aid.[4] This, however, finds no support in the history of either Cyrus or Darius. But may it not be later (Nikel, 57 n. 1), before

[1] See also Sellin, *Ser.* 56 n. 1, 58; *Stud.* 18 seq.; Grünhut, *Einleitung* (cited by Jampel, i. 105).

[2] Parallel traditions elsewhere explain each other, cf. Ex. xvii. 6 with Num. xx. 8; Ex. xvii. 10 with Num. xiv. 40, 44; Ex. xxxiii. with Num. xi.

[3] Mal. i. 2–5; see Kennett, *Essays*, 117.

[4] See the discussions of Ewald, 80 seqq., 88; Herzfeld, *Gesch.* (1847) i. 475 seq.; Smend, 22, 24; Stade, *Gesch.* ii. 112; F. Buhl, *Gesch. d. Edomiter* (1893), 77.

the prophecy of Mal. i. 2–5, and between the times of Zerubbabel and N?[1] If so, it is tempting to associate the relatively simple and unadorned decree attributed to Darius in *E* iv. 48–56 (which points to a return to rebuild the Temple after a period of Edomite hostility) with the situation that underlies the narratives of N, cf. *d* above.

(*g*) *Summary*. The internal difficulties of E–N are exceedingly complex owing to the numerous untrustworthy features, the remarkable and suspicious parallels, and the intricacies of rearrangement, adjustment, and revision. The sources throw little (if any) light on the period before the return of N, and traditions originally associated with him or his age appear to underlie the rest.[2] His story forms the starting-point for the problems of E–N, but it has too many serious difficulties for any confident theory of the order of events. Yet it seems clear that in N's time there had not as yet been any previous Samaritan hostility of any extent, any separation from the 'heathen', any important return of exiles. It is not improbable that in the time of Zerubbabel there was a monarchy of some size (cf. Sellin, *Ser.*, 89), and it is interesting to notice that the Samaritan opposition in the time of Artaxerxes is aimed especially at the apparent political pretensions of N (ii. 19, vi. 6–8, cf. E iv. 13). The population in and around Jerusalem consisted partly of the old indigenous stock and partly of the southern groups of Edomite affinity who moved northwards after 586. This semi-Edomite people had suffered from a disaster, due, in some measure, to the 'brother' Edomites who had burned the Temple and occupied Jewish territory, and to repair the lamentable conditions was the object of N's return. The southern groups in question are only to be expected after 1 Chron. ii. and iv., and the history in Chron. seems to reveal some traces of their perspective: their presence in the Levitical bodies, the stories of the reconstruction of Temple and cult, and the traditions of invasions of hostile southern peoples. On independent grounds it is probable that other traces of the presence and prominence of these groups may be observed elsewhere, and we may notice that the O. T. *preserves* the tradition of the high reputation of the eponymous Caleb, the 'servant of Yahweh', and that late traditions even ascribe a southern origin to some of the prophets.[3]

In the chronicler's compilation the rise of the new Jewish Church and the opposition of the Samaritans are dated at the commencement of the Persian age, and in the light of this the later history was meant to be read, even as other writers presuppose the patriarchal ancestors of pre-Mosaic days or the elaborate Levitical ritual associated with Moses and Aaron. Although this view shapes the compilation, the study of the age of Artaxerxes throws a different light upon its value. There are persistent and independent traditions of some return in his reign, and of some reconstruction of the people. Subsequent to the situation represented in N iii. (see *c* above) a new community was formed, and since it would be composed of elements of exilic (Babylonian) and non-exilic ancestry, some of the names of the latter class (found e.g. in N iii.) might naturally recur in (the later) lists referring to earlier periods (for such names, see Nikel, 154 seqq.). From 1 Chron. ii. and iv., and from the place of Caleb and Jerahmeel among the 'sons' of Perez—Gen. xxxviii seems to record his superiority over the rival and semi-Edomite Zerah—it is obvious that there has been a genealogical readjustment of the groups of southern origin. Moreover, elsewhere, the specific traditions of such groups as these have been revised or mutilated, and it is probable that all these features may be connected with the intricate development of the priestly and Levitical figures, suggestive of rival representations and compromise.[4]

E–N is written from the standpoint of a reorganized community which admitted no relationship with the semi-Edomite or native Judaean groups. The Babylonian exiles piqued themselves on their superiority to the Judaeans, who none the less could boast of their father Abraham—the hero of the Calebite city of Hebron (Ezek. xxxiii. 24). To the exiles from Babylon and thence (E ii.) to the old Judah which fell in 586, the community persistently attributed its origin. The Jews of the post-exilic theocracy laid most weight upon an ancestry from the deportation by Nebuchadrezzar, even as the old Israel ignored the large indigenous and mixed element in Palestine, and descent was claimed from the immigrant tribes from Egypt and thence from the pre-Mosaic sons of Israel. Different disasters were focussed upon 586, and traditions of return and rebuilding were concentrated upon the return of Zerubbabel. Consequently, by thus passing over the native groups, whether akin or not to the hated Edomites, the mixed origin of the Jews was rendered less conspicuous. The significance of this has been well pointed out by Torrey (155, 236 seq., 321 seqq., and,

[1] Some later Edomite invasion has been inferred by J. Ley, *II. Jesaia* (1893), 150; T. K. Cheyne, *Introd. Is.*, 210 seq.; *E Bi.* col. 2701; H. Winckler, *Keilinschr. u. d. A. T.* 295; R. H. Kennett, *Journ. Theol. Stud.*, 1906, p. 487. Note also the earlier views of Kuenen and Sellin (*Ser.*, 82) that Is. lxiii. 18, lxiv. 10 seq., point to another destruction of the Temple after 516.

[2] Note the tradition in 2 Macc. ii. 13 that N collected writings and 'letters of kings about sacred gifts'.

[3] Habakkuk and Zephaniah of Simeon, Obadiah an Edomite proselyte, Nahum of Elkosh.

[4] See further *Ency. Brit.*, 11th ed., artt. 'Genesis' (xi. 584 seq.); 'Jews' (xv. 387, 389–91); 'Levites' (xvi. 513 seq.); 'Palestine' (xx. 615 seq.), and art. 'Edomites' in Hastings' *Dict. of Rel. and Ethics*.

especially, 328 n. 53). Both Jews and Samaritans were of mingled ancestry, but the latter could at all events claim to have been associated with the land longer than the former. The question of kinship between the two divisions was, as we see from Jos. (ix. **14** 3, xi. **8** 6, xii. **5** 5), always a debatable one, and the knowledge of past history would only increase the bitter enmity at the rise of the rival cult on Mt. Gerizim. But the chronicler's compilation very carefully conceals the course of events and upholds for Judah alone the sole right to be the legitimate descendant of the ancient confederation of Israel.[1]

§ 6. Structure of the Sources.

It may often be possible to point out conflicting data, to indicate traditions which seem to be older or more original, and to arrive at positive or negative conclusions regarding the underlying facts; but the endeavour to trace the literary growth of complex sources which are certainly the result of intricate reshaping and revision is a delicate problem of literary criticism and distinct from the historical criticism of the period they describe.

(*a*) *The Sheshbazzar-Cyrus Tradition.* The story of Zerubbabel and the first return of the Jews in the time of Darius (*E* iii. 1–v. 6) is the pivot upon which the problems turn. Our starting-point is the Aramaic section E v. seq., where Darius confirms and extends a decree of Cyrus, who had ordered the rebuilding of the Temple and had sent back the vessels with Sheshbazzar (v. 13–15). This tradition is supported by E i., which refers also to Mithredath the treasurer who apparently was once mentioned in E v. (see on *E* vi. 18). But E i. is written in a different style and in Hebrew; it gives a highly-coloured form of the decree (note the parallels with the story of E, Marq. 56, Torrey, 157 seq.), and tends to minimize the importance of Cyrus by emphasizing the direct influence of Yahweh (contrast the initiative of Darius in *E* iv., E vi. 8–11; see also on *E* vii. 1). Consequently, E v. seq., which have various marks of incompleteness (see on *E* vi. 7 seq., 23), presuppose an account of Cyrus and the return of Sheshbazzar (probably also in Aramaic), some part of which at least has been replaced by E i. Further, Sheshbazzar returned to build the Temple, but instead of any account of his work, Jeshua and Zerubbabel are abruptly introduced in the great list, E ii. 2. These two erect the altar (iii. 2), and (mentioned in the inverse order) commence the rebuilding (iii. 8–10), repulse the 'adversaries' (iv. 2 seq.), and subsequently, in the time of Darius, are encouraged by the prophets to begin operations (v. 2, note the repetition of the ancestry). Zer., as in *E* iii. 1–v. 6, is the leading figure, whereas the Shesh. tradition in v. seq. refers to the 'elders' (E v. 5, 9, vi. 8, 14; in vi. 7 𝔊[B] omits the unnamed governor, see Berth., 19). From the point of view of historical criticism Shesh. and Zer. are two distinct individuals, but it seems obvious that the compiler of E i.–vi. regarded them as the same, although it was left for ancient and modern harmonists to make the identification. And in fact it is implied and made in *E* vi. 18, 27, 29, after the introduction of Zer. in iii. seq., but naturally not in *E* ii. 1–15 (=E i.); yet in E, strangely enough, it is nowhere made, although the return of Shesh. in E i. 11 evidently corresponds to the appearance of Zer. in ii. 2 (‖ *E* v. 8 immediately after the Zer. story). Hence Jos. is obliged to harmonize (xi. **1** § 14, **3** § 32). Moreover, it is noteworthy that the Aramaic sources (v. 3–vi. 12) do not clearly indicate that the Jewish builders were exiles (contrast E iv. 12), and that there is no explicit reference in E v. 15 to any return of exiles under Sheshbazzar; on the other hand, the conflate text of *E* vi. 5, 8 clearly alludes to the Jews as being of the Captivity (cf. vii. 6, 10), and *E* ii. 15 shows more distinctly than E i. 11 that exiles returned with Shesh. That there is a gap after this verse has often been suspected. Accordingly, there are two important features: (1) the Shesh. tradition has been mutilated and otherwise adjusted in order to give the greater prominence to Zer. and *his* return, and (2) while it is not certain that Shesh. was originally the leader of a band of exiles, the text in *E* partly identifies him with the more illustrious Zer., and partly seems to treat his return as that of the 'captivity' also. Finally, the Shesh. tradition is that of a continuous building of the Temple since the time of Cyrus (E v. 16). This may be supported by E iv. 4, 5, which refer to unceasing troubles and intrigues, and by *v.* 6, where the accusation in the reign of Ahasuerus means, in this context, that the Temple was still under construction. On the other hand, the presence of the Artaxerxes-episode would imply that the work was definitely brought to a stop (see iv. 21–24), and with this agrees the statement in v. 2 that Zer. and Jeshua, encouraged by the prophets, 'rose up . . . and *began* to build the house of God'. Since the presence of these conflicting views can hardly be original, the Artaxerxes-episode and the cessation of the building may probably be regarded as foreign to the Shesh. tradition. Hence, although E does not present *E*'s remarkable confusion of the sequence of events in the reigns of Cyrus and Darius—a confusion which Jos. has

[1] In so far as the foregoing paragraphs bear upon the prophetical writings, it must be remembered that the dates of the latter depend upon our knowledge of the historical conditions in the light of which they are to be explained.

done his best to remedy—it contains, on closer inspection, a very singular combination of conflicting traditions of the Temple, and of Shesh. and Zer.

(*b*) *The Zerubbabel-Darius tradition.* Since Jewish tradition has it that Darius was the son of Ahasuerus the Mede (Dan. ix. 1), and the Ahasuerus in Esth. was called Artaxerxes (although, historically, Xerxes must be meant), and since the sequence Art.-Darius is true of Art. I-Dar. II (or even of Art. III-Dar. III), compilers might be justified in placing the story of the opposition before a tradition of Darius, whether in *E* ii. 16 seqq., iii., or E iv. 7–24, v. But it is not easy to decide which of the two is the earlier position. The cessation of the building of the Temple would be intelligible before *E* iv., which really describes a new era in the history, and would equally agree with the commencement of work mentioned in E v. 2. In either case it leads up to Zerubbabel. But whereas in *E* it forms a necessary link between Cyrus and Darius, in E it breaks the connexion (iv. 5, v. 1) and conflicts with the Shesh. tradition. The assumption that *E* gives the older position of the episode may be suggested by the fact that its text presents some features distinctly sounder than that in E iv. (note, however, the textual relation of Chron. to Sam.-Kings). On the other hand, in *E* v. 66 seqq. (E iv. 1 seqq.) the compiler has made use of iv. 1–5, 24, and it is possible that he found iv. (6 ?) 7–24 before him, but naturally omitted the passage he had already used. In any case, iv. 1–5 is obviously most closely connected with the preceding chapters, and since these presuppose certain material found only in *E* iii. 1–v. 6, E's account of Sheshbazzar and Zerubbabel in the time of Cyrus thus presupposes data in *E* of the time of Darius! The simplest explanation of these intricacies is that the MT has suffered by excision (see Torrey, 27 seq.), and it remains to determine whether the material in question originally belonged to the Darius period (as in *E*) or to that of Cyrus (as in E). Torrey alone has discussed this problem, and he has presented a complete, clever, and attractive hypothesis. He treats the Darius-Zer. story in *E* iii. 1–iv. 42 as an interpolation in the history of *Cyrus*, rejects or emends all that is impossible in such a context, and regards *E* ii. 16 seqq. as a transposition from E iv. made by the interpolator (see p. 32). But this leaves the complexity of E i.–vi. untouched. It treats as redactional certain passages that have by no means that appearance (viz. *E* iv. 43–7*a*, 57–61), and if E iv. 7–24 was deliberately borrowed, it is strange that no effort was made to form a reasonable link between ii. 15 and 16, as Jos. has done. The compiler used *E* ii. 16 seqq. to link Cyrus and Darius, but this theory assumes that for no apparent reason whatsoever a story of Darius has been introduced into the Cyrus-history and combined with it by (redactional ?) material, which is partly of considerable independent value, and partly introduces a *new* tradition of Cyrus (iv. 44, 57) in conflict with all other evidence. The story, moreover, would hardly have been used in Jewish history unless it was associated with Zerubbabel, Darius, and the return of the Jews; hence its presence, general character, independence, and the confusion arising from the attempt to unite it with *other* traditions plead for the view (also held by Howorth and Bayer) that it is original.

(*c*) *Result of combination.* On this alternative theory, then, *E* preserves a Zer.-Darius nucleus corresponding to a Shesh.-Cyrus nucleus in E, and it seems probable that the intricacies in *E* and E have arisen from the endeavour to combine and compromise. *E* iii. 1–v. 6 commence like an independent story, presupposes no prelude, and quite excludes any current story of Cyrus. iv. 44, 57, it is true, refer to his inability to fulfil a vow, but this has neither any foundation in history nor support in extant tradition, and appears to be an early effort to connect the section with Cyrus. Thenceforth we apparently have the building-up of narratives. The Artaxerxes episode was taken from a source relating to the time of N (§ 5*b*), and the sequel of the story, the list v. 7 seqq., also has a Nehemian background. The connexion between v. 1–6 and 7 seqq. is not close (note repetition 4, 7*a*, the preliminary *vv.* 5 and 7), and it is possible that iii. 1–v. 6 once had another sequel, or that there has been later adjustment. In any case, the references to Cyrus (iv. 44, 57), the treatment of the Shesh. tradition, and the fact that *E* ii. 1–15 are not in their original form, unite to show that there has been much revision, the stages in which cannot be traced. The list itself, partly connected with E's return in N vii., has been applied to the return of Zer., and then treated (in N) by the compiler of E–N as a quotation from the earlier period. It presents a materially older text, and its immediate continuation in *E* v. 47 seqq. (E iii.) is also based upon N viii. 1, and describes events in which one may recognize the influence of other passages in N (Meyer, 73, 99; Marq., 58 seq.; Volz, § 9). But the material is adjusted to Zerubbabel and Cyrus, with the result that while *E* v. 8 (the introduction of Zer.) is explained by the preceding story, and v. 47 (the date) by v. 6; v. 55 has in view iv. 48 (Darius), but its context is of the time of Cyrus (note the harmonizing efforts of Jos., xi. 4 1, 3 seq.).

Haggai and Zech., in the second year of Darius, know of no return or earlier rebuilding. So far this agrees with the Zer. story, which, however, while excluding any earlier rebuilding, describes the first return of the Jews. The Shesh. story throws back the commencement of the temple, but in E does not clearly point to any return (contrast *E*). In so far as Darius is concerned, these stories are mutually contradictory, and neither is supported by the prophets, and in so far as the fortunes of the temple are concerned, it is possible that a compromise was found in the belief that the work was brought to a stop and that the building was *re*-commenced in the time of Darius. This explains the motive of the Artaxerxes episode, and if the references to the Temple in *E* ii. 18, 20 are reliable, their absence in E iv. 12, 14 may be due to its new position. Further, if E v. 1 once had (as in *E* vi. 1) the precise date, this would be in order after iv. 5 (see Berth., 19), but might naturally be omitted after the insertion of iv. (6) 7–24; and since also the retention of the date in *E* vi. 1 would be unnecessary after v. 73 (=E iv. 24), the present unintelligible wording of the latter verse may be due to intentional alteration and not to corruption of the text. Thus, *E* partly presents material in an older text and form than E, partly shows signs of revision (apparently in the Greek), either to harmonize details or to conform with the MT, and partly is influenced by the form of E, whose imperfections it shares. The root of the problem lies in the two nuclei: Zerubbabel-Darius, Sheshbazzar-Cyrus-Darius, and in the endeavour to co-ordinate them; but in addition to the complexity touching Cyrus and Darius, it is obvious that the present form of the narratives cannot be viewed apart from the literary treatment of the events of the time of Artaxerxes.

(*d*) *The Ezra-story.* The narratives involved are an account of N's work, partly autobiographical, but now in a much revised and intricate form, which is divided by the E-story, also not from one hand, and itself split into two. These have suffered various changes and adjustments in the course of being combined with each other and with the great history of the 'chronicler'. On both literary and historical grounds we may postulate a stage when the whole of the E-story was found after the first appearance of N (p. 9 *d*). To suppose that N viii.–x. also once stood before N i. (Torrey, 265 seq.) only increases the difficulties. E appears relatively late in tradition, but continues to grow in reputation. He is absent from both Ben Sira xlix. 12 seq. and 2 Macc. i. seq., and here N is particularly prominent; but N's prominence, though in agreement with all the evidence, has not been made so obvious in the E-story (see § 4. III. *d*). Moreover, the effort has apparently been made to give greater significance to E by placing the most important part of his mission—the Reading of the Law (and the sequel, the Covenant)—in the account of the completion of the walls of Jerusalem, and also by introducing the rest of the story before N's arrival. *E* has gone further, and in ix. 37 seqq. has read part of N viii. after E x. Now, although *E* presents in some cases a better text, it is noteworthy that in reproducing N viii. and the introductory vii. 73*b*, the compiler has also unnecessarily removed *v.* 73*a*, which can hardly stand after *E* ix. 36 = E x. 44 (cf. Volz, 1492). This deliberate transference perhaps explains the text in *vv.* 38, 49, and suggests that *E*'s recension is here based upon the MT, with the E-story divided as at present. Consequently, both *E* and E–N share that complicated treatment of the purification of Israel which seems to have arisen when the story of E was rearranged. It is uncertain how *E*, if more complete, would have continued. There is indeed some evidence, perhaps not of great value, for an account of E's passover, suggesting that some portion of the story has been lost (see on ix. 55). However, if the whole of the *present* story had been placed before N i., both N i.–vi., xi.–xiii. and E vii.–x., N viii.–x. (or in any rearranged form) would still be in a confused, and certainly not original shape. The one source which actually effects this transposition is Jos., who finishes the life of E before dealing with N. His treatment is brief and paraphrastic, but it seems to be extremely significant that he does not point to the existence of the story of N in either the form or the sequence which it now has. To reconstruct the continuation of *E* is to make the overlapping with N more conspicuous; this is clear from the synopses cited below on p. 58, and it is interesting to notice that an old Syriac catena, which follows *E*, endeavours to readjust to N—it passes from *E* ix. 1–10 to 46*b*–47 (= N viii. 6) and thence to N i. 1–4, and places the Reading of the Law (N viii.) in the context it now has in the MT. *E*, it is evident, does not enable us to go behind the MT, but, together with Jos., it tends to show that the MT is the late outcome of a very intricate literary development.

(*e*) *The Compilation.* At the stage when the stories of E and N were shaped in their present form, and when the traditions of the time of Artaxerxes had been used directly or indirectly for the age of Cyrus and Darius, we reach the complete historical work Chron.-E-N., and the structure of E–N really involves close attention to that of Chron. itself. Here it must suffice to observe that both Chron. and E–N furnish evidence representing different stages in the vicissitudes of the priests and Levites (see on *E* viii. 28), and it is noteworthy that there are several traces of textual variation and confusion where these are concerned (see, e.g., i. 5 seqq., 10, 15, v. 56, vii. 9, viii. 42, ix. 43 seqq.). It is also significant of the relative lateness of E–N that the age at which the Levites serve agrees with *secondary* passages in Chron. (see on v. 58), and that an apparent anti-Aaronite bias has found its way into both (see on vii. 10–12). Perhaps the most important feature in the compilation is the presence of gaps (e.g. before E v. 1, N i.), the more striking when we observe that the chronicler has ignored pertinent material in Kings, Jer., Daniel, and Esther. The book of Daniel was familiar in the Greek age and later (cf. 1 Macc. ii. 59 seq., and, for the Targums, *Prot. Realency.*, iii. 107 seq.), and was used by Jos. The story in *E* iii. seq. has literary points of contact with both Dan. and Est. (Marq. 66, 68, 72; Torrey, 47 seq.; Bayer, 110 seqq.), and the former of these records traditions of the Temple-vessels (see on ii. 10).[1] The sacrilegious use of the holy objects by Belshazzar was followed by the fall of Babylon to the Medes and Persians, and forthwith *Darius the Mede*, son of Ahasuerus, became king (v. 31, ix. 1). He was led to proclaim the God of Daniel (vi. 25–7), and to the first year of his reign is ascribed the prayer of Daniel (ix.). Here, the seventy years of desolation foretold by Jeremiah are complete, and Daniel prays on behalf of the Jews in Jerusalem and afar off, and on behalf of the ruined sanctuary. The tradition—irrespective of its present setting—is so far in harmony with *E* iii. seq., the story of Zerubbabel in the second year of Darius (cf. Büchler, 7 seq.), where, as in Daniel's prayer, an earlier return is excluded. It is difficult not to believe that these traditions are related, and it is noteworthy that while the references to Cyrus in the story of Zerubbabel appear to be due to later revision, Cyrus, according to Dan. vi. 28, x. 1, reigned after Darius. Thus, not only is it more intelligible that the Cyrus tradition is relatively the later, and probably grew out of the Darius tradition, than the reverse, but a tradition evidently once prevailed which placed Darius before Cyrus.

But it was also known that Cyrus preceded Darius, and in Bel and the Dragon he follows after Astyages (see above, p. 11) and—like Darius in Dan. vi.—becomes convinced of Daniel's God. This correct sequence is that represented by Jos. and the 'chronicler', with one important difference, that while the former does his best to combine all the varying traditions of Cyrus and Darius, the *present* MT ignores Dan. and *E* iii. 1–v. 6 and the complications these would introduce into the history. Accuracy of sequence does not necessarily prove greater antiquity of source. It depends upon accuracy of information, and if Jos. (xi. 2) knows that Cambyses and not Artaxerxes (*E* ii. 16 seqq.) reigned before Darius, he is confused in his treatment of Xerxes and Artaxerxes, and while the chronicler wrongly retains these two between Cyrus and Darius, he has, however, avoided the incorrect sequence of the latter two in Daniel. The traditions of this period (§ 4 IV. *c*.) combine in an inextricable manner trustworthy and untrustworthy data with the result that mere mechanical rearrangement of material or correction of names is inadequate for the recovery of the historical facts. Whether or no there was a continuous chronicle of the Kings of Media and Persia (Est. x. 2), if a compiler of Jewish history followed the tradition which also appears in Dan., Darius the Mede reigned before Cyrus, and Darius, after *E* iii. seq., was the first to permit the Jews to return. On the other hand, Cyrus was really the first king, and it is easy to understand the endeavours to adjust the traditions. It may not be possible to trace all the steps in the process, nevertheless, *E*'s recension is a valuable witness to the efforts made to effect a compromise, and it is significant that while all the evidence points to the relative lateness of the Cyrus tradition in the form it now has in *E* ii. 1–15 or E i., the immediate prelude in *E* i. represents a text materially older in some respects (though more corrupt in others) than the corresponding 2 Chron. xxxv. seq.

(*f*) *Conclusion*. In the nature of the case, any explanation of the structure of *E* and E–N must be a provisional one. At all events, Bayer's view (93 seq., 102, 139), that *E* is a secondary and deliberate self-contained compilation dealing with the Temple, is inadequate, in that it accounts for only a small proportion of the textual features. Howorth, whose merit it has been to force the attention of biblical students to the importance of *E*, undoubtedly goes too far in championing the textual and historical value of *E*. As regards its text, used by Jahn with a certain lack of discrimination and by Bayer somewhat unduly underestimated, Torrey and Volz support an intermediate position, pointing out the general relative superiority of MT. Torrey justly observes, also, that as a history *E* is not in its original form, and he has proposed a hypothesis of its relationship with E–N which he works out with much skill and thoroughness (18 seqq., 30 seqq., 255 seqq.). He starts from the chronicler's history in almost its present form (dated *c*. third cent. B.C.), and assumes two important changes: (1) the transference of N vii. 70–x. 39 from their 'original' position between E viii. and ix. to the place where they now stand, and (2) the interpolation of the story *E* iii. 1–iv. 42, in the history of *Cyrus*, with redactional expansion, alteration, &c., and with the transposition of the Artaxerxes episode from E iv. 6–24 to *E* ii. 16–30. Subsequently, two rival forms arose: one (A) with the retransposition of N vii. 73–x. 40, this time between E x. and N i.; the other (B) with the excision of the Story of the Three Youths (*E* iii. seq.) together with a part of the 'original' history. The latter is represented by the MT; the former, after being translated into Greek, survives only in the fragmentary *E*, which is defined as 'simply a piece taken without change out of the middle of a faithful Greek translation of the chronicler's History of Israel in the form which was generally recognized as authentic in the last century B.C.' (18). This hypothesis is complicated (see Bayer's criticisms,143 seq.), though not unduly so. On the other hand, there are objections to the view that

[1] It is disputed whether *E* iii. seq. is later than these (Bayer, 128 seq.), or earlier (Torrey); in any case the canonical books, whatever their date, may well incorporate or be based upon older traditions.

the Story of the Three Youths is an interpolation in the alleged original Cyrus-history, viz. in E i., *E* iv. 47–56, iv. 62–v. 6, E ii. seqq. (see p. 16), and to the assumption that the place of the E-story before N i. is the earlier (see p. 17). Further, although *E* is obviously imperfect, to restore a complete work in which it should correspond to E in the chronicler's series necessitates the belief that Jos., the only early source which places the E-story before N, is witness to the MT form of the stories of both E and N, and this cannot be said to be certain (see p. 57 seq.). The latter part of *E* presupposes the present structure of E vii.–x., N . . . vii. 73–viii. 13 . . ., whereas the first half presents older traits in i., ii. 16 seqq. (the position of the Artaxerxes episode), iii. 1–v. 6 (the Zerubbabel story), v. 7–70 (the background of the list, E ii.), and v. 71 (the immediate sequel, the prelude to the work of the returned exiles). Finally, the criticism of *E* inevitably raises the problem of the entire series Chron.-E–N, which at one stage was a literary whole, and consequently we cannot take the chronicler's history as a fixed starting-point. As a matter of fact, apart from the literary questions arising out of Chronicles alone, it seems that the books were regarded by the Rabbis with some suspicion (Curtis and Madsen, *Chron.* 2), and now stand after E–N 'as if it were an afterthought to admit them to equal authority' (W. R. Smith, *Old Test. Jew. Church*, 182). It is not improbable that this severance involved some subsequent alteration and revision (cf. Marq., 29). Moreover, the recurrence of 1 Chron. ix., N xi., in a single work hardly looks like an original feature; like the more remarkable repetition of the list E ii., N vii. (see Jampel, i. 306; Howorth, *PSBA*, xxvi. 26; Holzhey, 37 n. 2) the feature seems to point to the combination of sources which were primarily distinct.

All the data suggest that *E* and E–N represent concurrent forms which have influenced each other in the earlier stages of their growth. They are rivals, and neither can be said to be wholly older or more historical than the other. The endeavour was made to correct *E* to agree with the MT—and 𝔊^{L} is a conspicuous example of the extent to which the revisers could go—and the presence of such efforts and in particular the doublets (see § 3 *b*) are of essential importance in indicating that *E*'s text does not precisely represent a Heb.-Aram. work, and that when all allowance is made for correction and revision of the Greek, problems of the underlying original text still remain. But it was impossible to make any very satisfactory adjustment, *E* diverged too seriously from the MT, which had cut the chronological knot by the excision of the story of Zerubbabel, and we may suppose that this facilitated the desire for the more literal translation of Theodotion (p. 3 seq.).

§ 7. Value.

Although our O.T. has lost the story of Zerubbabel and the Praise of Truth, there is no doubt that there is something 'unbiblical' in the orations. In the course of the growth of the O.T., compilers and revisers have not unfrequently obscured or omitted that to which they took exception, and some light is thus often thrown upon other phases of contemporary Palestinian or Jewish thought. While the orations themselves remind us of the old 'Wisdom' literature (Proverbs, Ben Sira, Wisdom), their combination with narrative will recall the interesting story of Ahikar. *E* remains 'apocryphal' in so far as it was deliberately rejected by Jewish and Christian schools. It had indeed found a place in the Bible of the Greek-speaking Jews, and was familiar to Jews and Christians, either indirectly through Jos., or directly as a separate work. To the Christians the prominence of Zerubbabel must have been of no little interest (see § 1, end). But the value of *E* does not lie merely in this story. The book (or fragment) furnishes useful evidence for the criticism of the text and contents of the canonical passages, and illustrates methods of compilation and revision, swing of traditions, and play of motives. It clearly indicates the importance of the comparison of related traditions as apart from the ultimate question of the underlying facts, and shows, in conjunction with Jos., how a relatively straightforward account of history as in E–N may be the last stage in the effort to cut the knots formed by imperfect compilation. In its final form, the MT, the result of 'Rabbinical redaction' (Marq., 29), is ascribed by Howorth to the School of Jamnia in the time of Rabbi Akiba (*PSBA*, xxvi. 25), and although it is difficult to find decisive arguments in favour of this conjecture—or against it—it is not impossible that the chronicler's history, as it now reads, may be dated about the beginning of the Christian era. It is significant that it is wanting in the Syriac Peshitta. Such a view, it should be observed, no more expresses an opinion on the dates of the component sources or sections than it would were the work in question a composite and much edited portion of Mishnah or Midrash.

§ 8. Select Bibliography and Abbreviations.

A, ℵ, B = Codices of the Greek version.
André, L. E. T. = *Les Apocryphes de l'A. T.* (1903).
Ball, C. J. = *The Variorum Apocrypha* (1896).

I ESDRAS

Bayer, E. = 'Das dritte Buch Esdras und sein Verhältnis zu den Büchern Esra-Nehemia', in *Biblische Studien*, ed. Bardenhewer, vol. xvi. (1911).

Bertholet, A. = *Die Bücher Esra und Nehemia* (1902).

Büchler, A. = 'Das apokryphische Esrabuch', *MGWJ*, xli. (1897), 1–16, 49–66, 97–103.

Charles, R. H. = 'Third Book of Ezra', *Ency. Brit.* 11th ed., vol. x. 104–6.

Cheyne, T. K. = *Introduction to the Book of Isaiah* (1895). *Jewish Religious Life after the Exile* (1898). See also *sub* Kosters.

Davies, T. W. = 'Ezra, Nehemiah, and Esther', *The Century Bible* (1909).

Driver, S. R. = *Introd. to the Lit. of the O.T.* (1909).

E = Ezra (the book or man).

E = 1 Esdras.

E Bi. = *Encyclopaedia Biblica* (1899–1903).

Ew. = Ewald, H., *History of Israel*, 2nd ed. (1880). vol. v.

Fr. = Fritzsche, O. F., Comment. on 1 Esdras in *Kurzgef. exeget. Handbuch* (1851).

$\mathfrak{G}$ = Greek version.

$\mathfrak{G}$ Chron., $\mathfrak{G}$E, &c. (or Chron. $\mathfrak{G}$, E$\mathfrak{G}$, &c.) = Greek version of Chronicles, Ezra, &c.

$\mathfrak{G}^{BA\aleph L}$ = Codices of the Greek.

Geissler, J. = *Die litterarischen Beziehungen der Esramemoiren* (1899).

Guthe, H. = *1 Esdras*, in Kautzsch, *Die Apok. u. Pseudepig. d. A. T.* (1898). See also *SBOT.*

Holzhey, C. = *Bücher Ezra u. Nehemia* (1902).

Hoonacker, A. van = *Néhémie et Esdras* (1890). *Zerubabel et le second Temple* (1892). *Nouvelles Études sur la Restauration juive* (1896). Articles in *Revue Biblique*, 1901, January, April.

Howorth, Sir Henry H. = *Academy*, 1893, January–July (*passim*), *Transactions of Oriental Congress, London*, ii. 69–85 (1893). *Proceedings of Soc. of Bibl. Archaeology*, 1901–10 (*passim*).

Jahn, C. = *Die Bücher Esra (A u. B) u. Nehemja* (1909).

Jampel, S. = 'Die Wiederherstellung Israels unter den Achämeniden', *MGWJ*, xlvi. and xlvii. (1902–3); here cited as i. and ii.

Jos. = Josephus, ed. Niese.

Kennett, R. H. = 'Hist. of the Jew. Church from Nebuchadnezzar to Alexander', *Cambridge Biblical Essays* (ed. Swete, 1909), 91–135. *Journal of Theological Studies*, 1905, January, 161–86; 1906, July, 481–500.

Kent, C. F. = *Israel's Historical and Biographical Narratives* (1905).

Kosters, W. H. = *Die Wiederherstellung Israels in der persischen Periode* (Germ. ed., by Basedow, 1895).

„ *Th. T.* = Articles in the *Theologisch Tijdschrift*, xxix. (1895), 549 seqq.; xxx. (1896), 489 seqq., 580 seqq.; xxxi. (1897), 518 seqq.

„ *E Bi.* = Articles 'Cyrus', 'Ezra', 'Ezra-Nehemiah', 'Nehemiah' (with additions by T. K. Cheyne), in *E Bi.*

L = Lucian's recension of the Greek version.

$\mathfrak{L}$, $\mathfrak{L}^{C}\mathfrak{L}$ Lag. = Latin Versions, see above, § 3 *c*.

Lag. = Lagarde, P. de, *Septuaginta-Studien*, ii. (1892).

Lupton, J. H. = 1 Esdras in *The Apocrypha*, ed. H. Wace (1888).

Marq. = J. Marquart, *Fundamente israel. u. jüd. Geschichte*, pp. 28–68 (1896).

Meyer, E. = *Die Entstehung des Judentums* (1896).

„ *Isr.* = *Die Israeliten u. ihre Nachbarstämme* (1906), by E. Meyer and B. Luther.

MGWJ = *Monatsschrift f. Gesch. u. Wissenschaft des Judentums.*

Moulton = 'Über die Überlieferung u. d. textkritischen Wert d. III. Esr.' in *ZATW*, xix. 209–58 (1899); xx. 1–35 (1900).

MT = Massoretic Text.

N = Nehemiah (the book or man).

Nestle, E. = *Marginalien u. Materialien* (1893), 23 seqq.

Nikel, J. = 'Die Wiederherstellung des jüd. Gemeinwesens nach den bab. Exil', in *Biblische Studien*, ed. Bardenhewer, vol. v (1900).

Pohlmann = 'Über das Ansehen des apokryphen Buches Esra', *Tübinger Theolog. Quartalschrift*, 1859.

PSBA = *Proceedings of the Society of Biblical Archaeology.*

Ryle, H. E. = 'Ezra and Nehemiah' in the Cambridge Bible (1901).

$\mathfrak{S}$ = Syriac version.

Sachau, E. = 'Drei aram. Papyrusurkunden aus Elephantine' (*Abhandl. königl.-preuss. Akad. Berlin*, 1907).

SBOT = *The Sacred Books of the O.T.*, ed. P. Haupt: 'Ezra and Nehemiah', by H. Guthe (and, pp. 56–71, L. W. Batten).

Schrader, E. = 'Die Dauer des zweiten Tempelbaues', *Theolog. Stud. und Kritiken*, 1867, pp. 460 seqq.

Sellin, E., *Ser.* = *Serubbabel* (1898).

„ *Stud.* = *Studien zur Entstehungsgeschichte d. jüd. Gemeinde*, vol. ii. (1901).

Smend, R. = *Die Listen der Bücher Esra u. Nehemia* (1881).

Smith, G. A. = In *The Expositor*, 1906, June–August.

Smith, H. P. = *O.T. History* (1903).

Th. T. = *Theologisch Tijdschrift.*

Thackeray, H. St. J. = Art. 'Esdras', Hastings' *Dict. Bible*, i. 758–63.

Theis, J. = *Gesch. u. literarkrit. Fragen in E i–vi* (1910).

Torrey, C. C. = *Ezra Studies* (Chicago, 1910).

„ *Comp.* = 'Composition and Historical Value of Ezra-Nehemiah', *Beiheft zur ZATW*, 1896.

Trendelenburg = 'Apokr. Ezra', Eichhorn, *Allgem. Bibl. d. bibl. Litt.* (1787), 178–232.

Treuenfels = Articles in *Der Orient* (ed. J. Fürst), 1850–1.

Volz, P. = 'The Greek Ezra', *E Bi.* vol. iv, cols. 1488–94.

Wellhausen, J. = 'Die Rückkehr der Juden aus dem bab. Exil', in *Nachrichten d. Göttinger Gelehrten Gesellschaft*, 1895, pp. 166 seqq. Review of E. Meyer, *Entstehung u.s.w.*, in the *Gött. Gel. Anzeigen*, 1897, pp. 89 seqq.

ZATW = *Zeitschrift für Alttest. Wissenschaft.*

I ESDRAS.

ESDRAS

1 1 AND Josias held the passover in Jerusalem
unto his Lord, and offered the passover the four-
2 teenth day of the first month; having set the
priests according to their daily courses, being
arrayed in their vestments, in the temple of the
3 Lord. And he spake unto the Levites, the
temple-servants of Israel, that they should hallow
themselves unto the Lord, to set the holy ark of
the Lord in the house that king Solomon the son
4 of David had built: *and said*, Ye shall no more
have need to bear it upon your shoulders: now
therefore serve the Lord your God, and minister
unto his people Israel, and prepare you after your
5 fathers' houses and kindreds, according to the
writing of David king of Israel, and according to
the magnificence of Solomon his son:

and stand-
ing in the holy place according to the several
divisions of the families of you the Levites, who
minister in the presence of your brethren the
6 children of Israel, offer the passover in order, and
make ready the sacrifices for your brethren, and
keep the passover according to the commandment
7 of the Lord, which was given unto Moses. And
unto the people which were present Josias gave
thirty thousand lambs and kids, *and* three thousand calves: these things were given of the king's
substance,

according as he promised, to the peo-
8 ple, and to the priests and Levites. And Helkias,
and Zacharias, and Esyelus, the rulers of the
temple, gave to the priests for the passover two
thousand *and* six hundred sheep, *and* three hundred calves.

9 And Jeconias, and Samaias, and
Nathanael his brother, and Sabias, and Ochielus,
and Joram, captains over thousands, gave to the
Levites for the passover five thousand sheep, *and*
seven hundred calves.

10 And when these things

2 CHRON.
35

AND Josiah kept a passover unto the Lord in 1
Jerusalem: and they killed the passover on the
fourteenth *day* of the first month. And he set 2
the priests in their charges, and encouraged them
to the service of the house of the Lord.

And 3
he said unto the Levites that taught all Israel,
which were holy unto the Lord, Put the holy ark
in the house which Solomon the son of David
king of Israel did build; there shall no more be
a burden upon your shoulders: now serve the
Lord your God, and his people Israel.

And 4
prepare yourselves after your fathers' houses by
your courses, according to the writing of David
king of Israel, and according to the writing of
Solomon his son. And stand in the holy place 5
according to the divisions of the fathers' houses
of your brethren the children of the people, and
let there be for each a portion of a fathers' house
of the Levites. And kill the passover, and sanc- 6
tify yourselves, and prepare for your brethren,
to do according to the word of the Lord by
the hand of Moses. And Josiah gave to the 7
children of the people, of the flock, lambs and
kids, all of them for the passover offerings, unto
all that were present, to the number of thirty
thousand, and three thousand bullocks: these
were of the king's substance. And his princes 8
gave for a freewill offering unto the people, to
the priests, and to the Levites. Hilkiah and
Zechariah and Jehiel, the rulers of the house of
God, gave unto the priests for the passover offerings two thousand and six hundred *small cattle*,
and three hundred oxen. Conaniah also, and 9
Shemaiah and Nethanel, his brethren, and Hashabiah and Jeiel and Jozabad, the chiefs of the
Levites, gave unto the Levites for the passover
offerings five thousand *small cattle*, and five
hundred oxen. So the service was prepared, 10

Josiah's passover and death, the last kings of Judah, and the exile. Ch. i. = 2 Chron. xxxv. seq. (cf. 2 Kings xxiii. 21–xxv. 30 and the relevant portions of Jeremiah), cf. Jos. *Ant.* x. 4 5–xi. 7 (who uses the canonical books, including Daniel, *E*, and unknown sources). On the text and contents, see the Comm. on Chronicles, also, for the versions, Moulton, *ZATW*, xix. 234 seqq. The whole chapter when compared with MT and 𝔊 of Chron. and Kings furnishes an instructive illustration of the methods and merits of the translator.

2. **arrayed** (ἐστολισμένους), cf. v. 59, vii. 9. Perhaps an Aramaizing mistranslation (Nestle, 24).

3. **temple-servants,** mg. *the Nethinim*, a misreading of MT הַמְּבִינִים. Note the indirect narration in *E* and Chron. 𝔊.

5. **magnificence** (μεγαλειότητα), $\mathfrak{G}^{L}$ (cf. 𝔖) and Chron. $\mathfrak{G}^{BA}$ διὰ χειρός, perhaps interpreted 'by the might'. Charles conj. עַל יְדֵי for MT במכתב (a repetition of כתב), misread in *E* as בגדל (private communication).

The paraphrastic 5–7 represent a rather different MT.

8. **Esyelus** ($\mathfrak{G}^{L}$ 'Joel'), mg. *Jehiel* (after MT); perhaps Haziel is intended (Fr., Guthe; cf. 1 Chron. xxiii. 9).

were done, the priests and Levites, having the unleavened bread, stood in comely order according
to the kindreds,

11 and according to the several
divisions by fathers' houses, before the people, to
offer to the Lord, as it is written in the book of
12 Moses: and thus *did they* in the morning. And
they roasted the passover with fire, as appertaineth: and the sacrifices they sod in the brasen
13 vessels and caldrons with a good savour, and set
them before all the people: and afterward they
prepared for themselves, and for the priests their
14 brethren, the sons of Aaron. For the priests
offered the fat until night: and the Levites prepared for themselves, and for the priests their
15 brethren, the sons of Aaron. The holy singers
also, the sons of Asaph, were in their order,
according to the appointment of David, *to wit*,
Asaph, Zacharias, and Eddinus, who was of the
16 king's retinue. Moreover the porters were at
every gate; none had need to depart from his
daily course: for their brethren the Levites pre-
17 pared for them. Thus were the things that belonged to the sacrifices of the Lord accomplished
18 in that day, in holding the passover, and offering
sacrifices upon the altar of the Lord, according
19 to the commandment of king Josias. So the
children of Israel which were present at that time
held the passover, and the feast of unleavened
20 bread seven days. And such a passover was not
held in Israel since the time of the prophet
21 Samuel. Yea, all the kings of Israel held not
such a passover as Josias, and the priests, and the
Levites, and the Jews, held with all Israel that
were present in their dwelling place at Jerusalem.
22 In the eighteenth year of the reign of Josias was
23 this passover held. And the works of Josias were
upright before his Lord with a heart full of godli-
24 ness. Moreover the things that came to pass in
his days have been written in times past, concerning those that sinned, and did wickedly against
the Lord above every people and kingdom, and
how they grieved him exceedingly, so that the
words of the Lord were confirmed against Israel.

and the priests stood in their place, and the
Levites by their courses, according to the king's
commandment. And they killed the passover, 11
and the priests sprinkled *the blood, which they
received* of their hand, and the Levites flayed
them. And they removed the burnt offerings, 12
that they might give them according to the
divisions of the fathers' houses of the children of
the people, to offer unto the Lord, as it is written
in the book of Moses. And so did they with the
oxen. And they roasted the passover with fire 13
according to the ordinance: and the holy offerings sod they in pots, and in caldrons, and in
pans, and carried them quickly to all the children
of the people. And afterward they prepared for 14
themselves, and for the priests; because the
priests the sons of Aaron *were busied* in offering
the burnt offerings and the fat until night: therefore the Levites prepared for themselves, and for
the priests the sons of Aaron. And the singers 15
the sons of Asaph were in their place, according
to the commandment of David, and Asaph, and
Heman, and Jeduthun the king's seer; and the
porters were at every gate: they needed not to
depart from their service, for their brethren the
Levites prepared for them.
So all the service 16
of the Lord was prepared the same day, to keep
the passover, and to offer burnt offerings upon
the altar of the Lord, according to the commandment of king Josiah. And the children of Israel 17
that were present kept the passover at that time,
and the feast of unleavened bread seven days.
And there was no passover like to that kept in 18
Israel from the days of Samuel the prophet;
neither did any of the kings of Israel keep such
a passover as Josiah kept, and the priests, and
the Levites, and all Judah and Israel that were
present, and the inhabitants of Jerusalem. In 19
the eighteenth year of the reign of Josiah was
this passover kept.

10–12. A good example of misunderstanding and adjustment. **Unleavened bread** = *commandment* (מַצּוֹת, for מִצְוֹת), **morning** (cf. v. 50) = *oxen* (בָּקָר, 𝔊 in *E* and Chron., for בֹּקֶר); **good savour** = *pans* (εὐωδίας for εὐοδίας [cf. A.V. mg.], 𝔊 in Chron. εὐωδώθη; a misunderstanding of the root צלח in וּבַצֵּלָחוֹת; for parallels, see Ecclus. xliii. 26, *Ascens. Isaiah*, vi. 17, and *Journ. Royal Asiatic Soc.*, 1901, p. 169). For 𝔊[L]'s text, see Torrey, 107.

15. 'To wit', implying that these choir-masters were at Josiah's passover (cf. Chron. 𝔊) is of course erroneous.

Zacharias, may be supported by 1 Chron. xv. 18, xvi. 5, where he ranks next to Asaph; see Benzinger, *Chron.* 74.

was, mg. *were* (𝔊[B]). 𝔊[L] 𝔏[c] + the prophets (so 𝔊 in Chron.); some MSS. of MT read 'seers', cf. 1 Chron. xxv. 1.

23 seq. An addition partly with reference to 1 Kings xiii. 2, 32, 2 Kings xxiii. 14 seqq. (see also 𝔊's addition in Chron.). See further Nestle, 27; Torrey, 88 seq.; Bayer, 95 seq.

24. Better: 'and the things pertaining to him had been written in times past, on account of those . . . and grieved him . . . and the words . . .' (after Ball).

exceedingly (𝔊[A] ἐν αἰσθήσει [cf. 𝔖], 𝔊[L] ἔτι), mg. *sensibly*; cf. Judith xvi. 17.

confirmed (ἀνέστησαν), a Hebraism, cf. Jer. xliv. 29.

25 Now after all these acts of Josias it came to
pass, that Pharaoh the king of Egypt came to
raise war at Carchemish upon Euphrates: and
26 Josias went out against him. But the king of
Egypt sent to him, saying, What have I to do
27 with thee, O king of Judæa? I am not sent
out from the Lord God against thee; for my
war is upon Euphrates: and now the Lord is
with me, yea, the Lord is with me hasting me
forward: depart from me, and be not against
28 the Lord. Howbeit Josias did not turn back
unto his chariot, but undertook to fight with
him, not regarding the words of the prophet
29 Jeremy *spoken* by the mouth of the Lord: but
joined battle with him in the plain of Megiddo,
and the princes came down against king Josias.
30 Then said the king unto his servants, Carry me
away out of the battle; for I am very weak. And
immediately his servants carried him away out
31 of the host. Then gat he up upon his second
chariot; and being brought back to Jerusalem
he died, and was buried in the sepulchre of his
32 fathers. And in all Jewry they mourned for
Josias; and Jeremy the prophet lamented for
Josias, and the chief men with the women made
lamentation for him, unto this day: and this was
given out for an ordinance to be done continually
33 in all the nation of Israel. These things are
written in the book of the histories of the kings
of Judæa, and every one of the acts that Josias
did, and his glory, and his understanding in the
law of the Lord, and the things that he had done
before, and the things now *recited*, are reported
in the book of the kings of Israel and Judah.
34 And the people took Joachaz the son of
Josias, and made him king instead of Josias his
father, when he was twenty and three years old.
35 And he reigned in Judah and in Jerusalem three
months: and then the king of Egypt deposed
36 him from reigning in Jerusalem. And he set a
tax upon the people of a hundred talents of
37 silver and one talent of gold. The king of Egypt
also made king Joakim his brother king of Judæa
38 and Jerusalem. And Joakim bound the nobles:
but Zarakes his brother he apprehended, and
brought him up out of Egypt.

After all this, when Josiah had prepared the 20
temple, Neco king of Egypt went up to fight
against Carchemish by Euphrates: and Josiah
went out against him. But he sent ambassadors 21
to him, saying, What have I to do with thee,
thou king of Judah? *I come* not against thee
this day, but against the house wherewith I have
war; and God hath commanded me to make
haste: forbear thee from *meddling with* God,
who is with me, that he destroy thee not.
Never- 22
theless Josiah would not turn his face from him,
but disguised himself, that he might fight with
him, and hearkened not unto the words of Neco,
from the mouth of God, and came to fight in the
valley of Megiddo. And the archers shot at 23
king Josiah; and the king said to his servants,
Have me away; for I am sore wounded. So 24
his servants took him out of the chariot, and put
him in the second chariot that he had, and brought
him to Jerusalem; and he died, and was buried
in the sepulchres of his fathers. And all Judah
and Jerusalem mourned for Josiah. And Jere- 25
miah lamented for Josiah: and all the singing
men and singing women spake of Josiah in their
lamentations, unto this day; and they made them
an ordinance in Israel: and, behold, they are
written in the lamentations.

Now the rest of the 26
acts of Josiah, and his good deeds, according to
that which is written in the law of the Lord, and 27
his acts, first and last, behold, they are written
in the book of the kings of Israel and Judah.
Then the people of the land took Jehoahaz 2 CHRON.
the son of Josiah, and made him king in 36 1
his father's stead in Jerusalem. Joahaz was 2
twenty and three years old when he began to
reign; and he reigned three months in Jerusalem.
And the king of Egypt deposed him at Jeru- 3
salem, and amerced the land in an hundred talents
of silver and a talent of gold. And the king of 4
Egypt made Eliakim his brother king over Judah
and Jerusalem, and changed his name to Jehoiakim. And Neco took Joahaz his brother, and
carried him to Egypt.

25. Jos. x. **5** 1 explains the march of Neco as an attack upon the Medes and Babylonians who had overthrown Assyria. On the Median empire see *Introd.*, pp. 11 *c*, 17 *e*.

26. **king of Egypt,** based on a misunderstanding of 'messengers' (מלאכים).

27. **upon Euphrates,** similarly Jos.

28. **unto his chariot,** mg. *his chariot from him* ($\mathfrak{G}^{L}$).
undertook (so Jos., and 𝔊 in Chron.), see Torrey, 221; Charles conj. יְחַשֵּׁב (private communication).
prophet. Neco (so Jos.) misread (נביא for נכו) and plausibly expanded by the addition of the prophet's name.

29. **princes came down**; another misreading (וירדו השרים for וירו הירים with which 𝔊 Chron. and Jos. agree).

30. **host,** better 'line of battle'; apparently reading מערכה for מרכבה.

32. **chief men**; reading שָׂרִים for שָׁרִים.
The dirge, according to Jos., was still extant.

33. With the paraphrase cf. *v.* 42.

34. **Joachaz** (i. e. Jehoahaz), but mg. *Jeconias* (i. e. Jeconiah=Jehoiachin, *v.* 43), so $\mathfrak{G}^{B}$ 𝔏 and Matt. i. 11. Jos. x. **5** 2 follows 𝔊 of Chron. with which cf. 2 Kings xxiii. 31–35. All the texts show some confusion here; see the comm.

35. **Judah,** mg. *Israel* ($\mathfrak{G}^{B}$ 𝔏); $\mathfrak{G}^{L}$, Jos. . . and MT (with 𝔊) omit.

38. Hopeless confusion arising from misreadings of the MT.

39 Five and twenty years old was Joakim when
he began to reign in Judæa and Jerusalem; and
he did that which was evil in the sight of the
40 Lord. And against him Nabuchodonosor the
king of Babylon came up, and bound him with
a chain of brass, and carried him unto Babylon.
41 Nabuchodonosor also took of the holy vessels of
the Lord, and carried them away, and set them
up in his own temple at Babylon.
42 But those
things that are reported of him, and of his
uncleanness and impiety, are written in the
chronicles of the kings.

43 And Joakim his son reigned in his stead: for
when he was made king he was eighteen years
44 old; and he reigned three months and ten days
in Jerusalem; and did that which was evil before
the Lord.
45 So after a year Nabuchodonosor sent and
caused him to be brought unto Babylon with
46 the holy vessels of the Lord; and made Sedekias
king of Judæa and Jerusalem,
when he was one
and twenty years old; and he reigned eleven
47 years: and he also did that which was evil in
the sight of the Lord, and cared not for the
words that were spoken by Jeremy the prophet
48 from the mouth of the Lord. And after that
king Nabuchodonosor had made him to swear
by the name of the Lord, he forswore himself,
and rebelled; and hardening his neck, and his
heart, he transgressed the laws of the Lord, the
49 God of Israel. Moreover the governors of the
people and of the priests did many things
wickedly, and passed all the pollutions of all
nations, and defiled the temple of the Lord,
50 which was sanctified in Jerusalem. And the
God of their fathers sent by his messenger to
call them back, because he had compassion on
them and on his dwelling place.
51 But they
mocked his messengers; and in the day when
the Lord spake *unto them*, they scoffed at his
prophets:
52 so far forth, that he, being wroth with
his people for their great ungodliness, commanded to bring up the kings of the Chaldeans
53 against them; who slew their young men with
the sword, round about their holy temple, and

Jehoiakim was twenty and five years old when 5
he began to reign; and he reigned eleven years
in Jerusalem: and he did that which was evil in
the sight of the Lord his God. Against him came 6
up Nebuchadnezzar king of Babylon, and bound
him in fetters, to carry him to Babylon.
Nebuchad- 7
nezzar also carried of the vessels of the house of
the Lord to Babylon, and put them in his temple
at Babylon. Now the rest of the acts of Jehoi- 8
akim, and his abominations which he did, and
that which was found in him, behold, they are
written in the book of the kings of Israel and
Judah: and Jehoiachin his son reigned in his
stead.
Jehoiachin was eight years old when he began 9
to reign; and he reigned three months and ten
days in Jerusalem: and he did that which was
evil in the sight of the Lord.
And at the return 10
of the year king Nebuchadnezzar sent, and brought
him to Babylon, with the goodly vessels of the
house of the Lord, and made Zedekiah his brother king over Judah and Jerusalem.
Zedekiah was twenty and one years old when 11
he began to reign; and he reigned eleven years in
Jerusalem: and he did that which was evil in the 12
sight of the Lord his God; he humbled not himself before Jeremiah the prophet *speaking* from
the mouth of the Lord. And he also rebelled 13
against king Nebuchadnezzar, who had made
him swear by God: but he stiffened his neck,
and hardened his heart from turning unto the
Lord, the Lord God of Israel.
Moreover all the 14
chiefs of the priests, and the people, trespassed
very greatly after all the abominations of the
heathen; and they polluted the house of the
Lord which he had hallowed in Jerusalem. And 15
the Lord, the God of their fathers, sent to them
by his messengers, rising up early and sending;
because he had compassion on his people, and on
his dwelling place: but they mocked the messen- 16
gers of God, and despised his words, and scoffed
at his prophets, until the wrath of the Lord arose
against his people, till there was no remedy.
Therefore he brought upon them the king of the 17
Chaldeans, who slew their young men with the
sword in the house of their sanctuary, and had
no compassion upon young man or maiden, old
man or ancient: he gave them all into his hand.

39 seqq. For Joakim's history *E* does not use the fuller 𝔊 of Chron. Jos. incorporates material from Jer. and elaborates the traditions; cf. Dan. i. 1 seq. On the text see further Torrey, 89.

43. **Joakim**, an error for Jehoiachin.

eighteen, mg. *eight* ($𝔊^B$ $𝔏^c$ 𝔖).

49. **and passed all**, mg. *even above all* ($𝔊^L$).

50. **messenger**; read the plural, as in *v.* 51. The Jeremian 'rising up early and sending' (השכם ושלוח, cf. Jer. xxix. 19, &c.) is wanting.

51. **in the day**, a misreading, בְּיוֹם for בוזים ('despised').

spared neither young man nor maid, old man
nor child; but he delivered all into their hands.
54 And they took all the holy vessels of the Lord,
both great and small, with the vessels of the
ark of the Lord, and the king's treasures, and
55 carried them away unto Babylon. And they
burnt the house of the Lord, and brake down
the walls of Jerusalem, and burnt the towers
56 thereof with fire: and as for her glorious things,
they never ceased till they had brought them all
to nought: and the people that were not slain
57 with the sword he carried unto Babylon: and
they were servants unto him and to his children,
till the Persians reigned, to fulfil the word of the
58 Lord by the mouth of Jeremy: Until the land
hath enjoyed her sabbaths, the whole time of her
desolation shall she keep sabbath, to fulfil threescore and ten years.

And all the vessels of the house of God, great 18
and small, and the treasures of the house of the
Lord, and the treasures of the king, and of his
princes; all these he brought to Babylon. And 19
they burnt the house of God, and brake down the
wall of Jerusalem, and burnt all the palaces thereof
with fire, and destroyed all the goodly vessels
thereof.

And them that had escaped from the 20
sword carried he away to Babylon; and they
were servants to him and his sons until the reign
of the kingdom of Persia: to fulfil the word of 21
the Lord by the mouth of Jeremiah, until the
land had enjoyed her sabbaths: *for* as long as
she lay desolate she kept sabbath, to fulfil threescore and ten years.

2 1 In the first year of Cyrus king of the Persians,
that the word of the Lord by the mouth of
2 Jeremy might be accomplished, the Lord stirred
up the spirit of Cyrus king of the Persians, and
he made proclamation through all his kingdom,
3 and also by writing, saying, Thus saith Cyrus
king of the Persians; The Lord of Israel, the
Most High Lord, hath made me king of the

EZRA 1

Now in the first year of Cyrus king of Persia, 1
that the word of the Lord by the mouth of Jeremiah might be accomplished, the Lord stirred up
the spirit of Cyrus king of Persia, that he made
a proclamation throughout all his kingdom, and
put it also in writing, saying, Thus saith Cyrus 2
king of Persia, All the kingdoms of the earth
hath the Lord, the God of heaven, given me;

53. **child**, MT יָשִׁישׁ (? 'aged', cf. Ar. *wathwāth*, 'weak, impotent').

54. **the vessels**, mg. *the arks of the Lord* (𝔊^BL, 𝔖); based upon a confusion of אוצר ('treasure') and ארון.

56. *Lit.* 'and they made an end of spoiling . . .' (συνετέλεσαν . . . ἀχρεῶσαι); MT כל כלי ('all the goodly . . .') treated as כל ('made an end of') כלו.

that were not slain: τοὺς ἐπιλοίπους ἀπήγαγεν μετὰ (𝔊^A ἀπὸ, cf. 𝔏^C) ῥομφαίας 'the people that were left he led away with the sword'.

58. The passage (see Jer. xxv. 12, xxix. 10; Lev. xxvi. 34 seq.) is treated as a quotation (cf. comm. on E ix. 11 seq.); on the statements, see Torrey, 286 n. 2.

The decree of Cyrus and the return under Sheshbazzar, ii. 1–15=2 Chron. xxxvi. 22 seq., E i.; cf. Jos. *Ant.* xi. 1. (*a*) The compiler passes over the years of exile, ignores the tradition of the Median empire represented in Daniel, and proceeds to the first year of Cyrus the Persian, the divinely-appointed agent inspired to fulfil the prophecy of Jeremiah (see Jer. xxiv. 6, xxv. 12 seq., xxix. 10–19, xxxiii. 10–13). His decree (to be contrasted with vi. 24 seqq.) has a marked Jewish tinge, as is recognized even by those who accept it as mainly genuine (Ewald, 49; Sellin, *Stud.* 154; Holzhey, 14), and should be compared with those of Darius (*E* iv.) and Artaxerxes (viii. 8 seqq.), and with the royal decrees in the 'canonical' and 'apocryphal' Esther; see Torrey, 144 n. 12, 158. The place of Cyrus in Jewish tradition (see Is. xli. 25, xliv. 28, xlv. 1–13) has been idealized; the story of Bel and the Dragon reveals another view of his character. He was not a monotheist, nor did he fulfil all the expectations of the prophecies. On the other hand, the parallels between his 'cylinder Inscription' and Is. xliv. 28–xlv. 4 (see Kittel, *ZATW*, xviii. 149 seqq.) could suggest that the biblical writers had been directly influenced by the inscription of this patron of the Babylonian gods. Tradition is embellished further in Jos., who refers to a prophecy of Jeremiah heralding the rebuilding of the Temple (x. 7 3, xi. 1 1–2; cf. on v. 61), and attributes the enthusiasm of Cyrus to his perusal of the prophecies of Isaiah (cf. similarly Alexander the Great and Daniel, xi. 8, 5, § 337).

(*b*) The section E i.–vi. is mainly from the chronicler (Driver, *Lit.* 545 seq.), and while Chron. itself can be controlled by the parallel portions of Samuel and Kings, the criticism of this section rests upon internal data and the independent testimony of Haggai and Zech. i.–viii. From a study of these prophecies it is urged that the rebuilding of the Temple at Jerusalem was first begun in the reign of Darius, and not Cyrus (as in E iii.), that the builders were the 'remnant' of Judah, no considerable body of exiles having as yet returned (as in E i. seq., *E* iv.–v. 6), that no serious Samaritan hostility had as yet arisen, and that no separation from the heathen of the land had as yet led to the inauguration of a Jewish 'congregation' or 'church'. See, in the first instance, Schrader, 460–504, and for fuller details *Introd.* § 4 (II).

On the text of ii. 1–15 see the comment., Moulton, *ZATW*, xix. 243 seqq., and Torrey, 120 seqq.

II. 3. **Most High**, MT 'God of Heaven', so also in vi. 31, viii. 19, 21. Definite conclusions can with difficulty be drawn from the numerous and often noteworthy variations in the form of the Divine name; for a summary of the data see Moulton, *ZATW*, xix. 226 seqq. The title 'Most High' (ὕψιστος = עֶלְיוֹן) recurs frequently in Daniel (14 times), Psalms (21), Ecclus. (48), and in Jubilees; more rarely in the Pentateuch (6); see the details in R. H. Charles, *Jubilees*, pp. lxvi, 213, who observes that it was most used in the second cent. B.C. On the Greek title see E. Schürer, *Theolog. Lit.-zeit.*, 1897, nos. 9 and (with a review of F. Cumont's *Hypsistos*) 19; J. Skinner, *Genesis*, 270 seq.

4 whole world, and commanded me to build him
5 a house at Jerusalem that is in Judæa. If therefore there be any of you that are of his people,
let the Lord, even his Lord, be with him, and
let him go up to Jerusalem that is in Judæa, and
build the house of the Lord of Israel: he is the
6 Lord that dwelleth in Jerusalem. Of such therefore as dwell in divers places, let them that are
7 in his own place help each one with gold, and
with silver, with gifts, with horses also and cattle,
beside the other things which have been added
by vow for the temple of the Lord which is in
Jerusalem.
8 Then the chief of the families of Judah and of
the tribe of Benjamin stood up; the priests also,
and the Levites, and all they whose spirit the
Lord had stirred to go up, to build the house for
the Lord which is in Jerusalem.
9 And they that
dwelt round about them helped them in all things
with silver and gold, with horses and cattle, and
with very many gifts that were vowed of a great
number whose minds were stirred up *thereto*.
10 King Cyrus also brought forth the holy vessels
of the Lord, which Nabuchodonosor had carried
away from Jerusalem, and had set up in his temple
11 of idols. Now when Cyrus king of the Persians
had brought them forth, he delivered them to
12 Mithradates his treasurer, and by him they were
delivered to Sanabassar the governor of Judæa.
13 And this was the number of them: A thousand
golden cups, a thousand cups of silver, censers of
silver twenty nine, vials of gold thirty, and of
silver two thousand four hundred and ten, and
14 other vessels a thousand. So all the vessels of
gold and of silver were brought up, even five

and he hath charged me to build him an house
in Jerusalem, which is in Judah. Whosoever 3
there is among you of all his people, his God
be with him, and let him go up to Jerusalem,
which is in Judah, and build the house of the
Lord, the God of Israel, (he is God,) which is in
Jerusalem. And whosoever is left, in any place 4
where he sojourneth, let the men of his place help
him with silver, and with gold, and with goods,
and with beasts, beside the freewill offering for
the house of God which is in Jerusalem.

Then 5
rose up the heads of fathers' *houses* of Judah and
Benjamin, and the priests, and the Levites, even
all whose spirit God had stirred to go up to build
the house of the Lord which is in Jerusalem.
And all they that were round about them 6
strengthened their hands with vessels of silver,
with gold, with goods, and with beasts, and with
precious things, beside all that was willingly
offered.
Also Cyrus the king brought forth the 7
vessels of the house of the Lord, which Nebuchadnezzar had brought forth out of Jerusalem,
and had put them in the house of his gods; even 8
those did Cyrus king of Persia bring forth by the
hand of Mithredath the treasurer, and numbered
them unto Sheshbazzar, the prince of Judah.
And this is the number of them: thirty chargers 9
of gold, a thousand chargers of silver, nine and
twenty knives; thirty bowls of gold, silver bowls 10
of a second sort four hundred and ten, and other
vessels a thousand. All the vessels of gold and 11
of silver were five thousand and four hundred.

5. **people.** 𝔊^{L} + 'who desireth to go up'; cf. *v.* 8, viii. 10 seq.
let the Lord, mg. *let his Lord be, &c.* (𝔊^{B}), cf. Chron. *Yahweh his God.*
the Lord that dwelleth, cf. E R.V. mg.: *he is the God which* . . . (with omission of the brackets).

7. **horses**, reading רֶכֶשׁ for רְכוּשׁ (cf. *v.* 9); perhaps wrongly, see Torrey, 121.
added by vow (or 'in accordance with vow'), cf. *v.* 9, viii. 13, and see *ZATW*, xix. 231.

9. **in all things**, בכל, for MT בכלי.
of a great number, reading לָרֹב (i.e. 'with precious things *in abundance*') in place of the incorrect לְבַד ('beside').

10. **holy vessels.** For the rendering cf. i. 45, vi. 18, 26; Dan. i. 2 (MS. 87) and Moulton, *ZATW*, xix. 228 seq.
There is an obvious effort to link the new Temple with that of Solomon (cf. similarly the Register of the exiles in v. 1–46), but the details are intricate. *Some* of the Temple-vessels were removed in the reign of Jehoiakim (2 Chron. xxxvi. 7, Dan. i. 2; wanting in 2 Kings). Later, in the time of Jehoiachin *all* were cut up or carried away (2 Kings xxiv. 13 seq., a doubtful passage, see the comm.). In Zedekiah's time, nevertheless, many evidently were left (Jer. xxvii. 16 seqq., xxviii. 3), and a prophecy of their removal also promises their restoration, although this latter feature is absent from 𝔊's text (xxvii. 16–22). Finally, at the fall of Jerusalem they were broken up and removed (2 Kings xxv. 13–17, Jer. lii. 17 seqq.). (The evidence in Judith iv. 1–3 for a return of exiles and vessels in the time of Nebuchadrezzar and the high-priest Joakim can hardly be discussed.) The sacrilegious use of the vessels by Belshazzar was avenged by the division of the Babylonian empire among the Medes and Persians, and Darius became king (Dan. v.). The tradition of their restoration in the reign of Cyrus clearly conflicts with *E* iv. 44, 57, where Darius effects what Cyrus had been unable to accomplish, and this belief can hardly have been current among those who knew of their return as described in E i. Moreover, the prophets Hag. and Zech. (time of Darius) do not imply that the vessels had been restored; E received rich supplies (*E* viii. 17), and returned with gifts something over £2,500,000 in value (Meyer, 69 seq.). But in the story of N the Temple appears to be neglected and poor, and Is. lx. 5–7 look forward to wealthy gifts. Another aspect is presented when it is supposed that the Temple-furniture had been concealed (see 2 Macc. ii. 4–8; *Apoc. Baruch*, ed. Charles, vi. 7 seqq., lxxx. 2, and p. 168).

12. **Sanabassar** (𝔊^{A}), mg. *Samanassar* (𝔊^{B} in *v.* 14, but 'Sanamassar' here). On the numerous variant forms see Guthe (*SBOT*) and Torrey, 136 seq. See below, vi. 18.

13 seq. On the variations in this passage see Torrey, 123 seq., 138 seq.

15 thousand four hundred threescore and nine, and
were carried back by Sanabassar, together with
them of the captivity, from Babylon to Jerusalem.

16 But in the time of Artaxerxes king of the Persians Belemus, and Mithradates, and Tabellius, and Rathumus, and Beeltethmus, and Samellius the scribe, with the others that were in commission with them, dwelling in Samaria and other places, wrote unto him against them that
dwelt in Judæa and Jerusalem the letter follow-
17 ing: To king Artaxerxes our Lord, Thy servants, Rathumus the storywriter, and Samellius the scribe, and the rest of their council, and the judges that are in Cœlesyria and Phœnicia.

18 Be it now known to our lord the king, that the Jews that are come up from you to us, being come unto

All these did Sheshbazzar bring up, when they of the captivity were brought up from Babylon unto Jerusalem.

Ezra 4

And in the reign of Ahasuerus, in the begin- 6
ning of his reign, wrote they an accusation against the inhabitants of Judah and Jerusalem.
And in the days of Artaxerxes wrote Bishlam, 7
Mithredath, Tabeel, and the rest of his companions, unto Artaxerxes king of Persia; and the writing of the letter was written in the Syrian *character*,
and set forth in the Syrian *tongue*. Rehum the 8
chancellor and Shimshai the scribe wrote a letter against Jerusalem to Artaxerxes the king in this
sort: then *wrote* Rehum the chancellor, and Shim- 9
shai the scribe, and the rest of their companions; the Dinaites, and the Apharsathchites, the Tarpelites, the Apharsites, the Archevites, the Babylonians, the Shushanchites, the Dehaites, the
Elamites, and the rest of the nations whom the 10
great and noble Osnappar brought over, and set in the city of Samaria, and in the rest *of the*
country beyond the river, and so forth. This is 11
the copy of the letter that they sent unto Artaxerxes the king; Thy servants the men beyond
the river, and so forth. Be it known unto the 12
king, that the Jews which came up from thee are come to us unto Jerusalem; they are building

15. Neither MT nor the explicit *E* supports the conjecture (Meyer, 193; cf. Holzhey, 15 seq., Davies, 47) that Sheshbazzar returned to prepare the way for Zerubbabel.

The opposition in the reign of Artaxerxes, ii. 16–30 = E iv. 7–24 (Aramaic), cf. Jos. *Ant.* xi. 2 1–2.

(*a*) This passage cannot, in either E or *E*, come between the reigns of Cyrus and Darius. There is an obvious gap after *v.* 15, and Jos., who ingeniously changes Artaxerxes into Cambyses, avoids it by an introduction (§ 19 seq., to be compared with § 88 = *E* v. 72 seq.), and ends with the statement of a delay of nine years (including 6 of Cambyses, 2 of Darius). The passage has hardly 'strayed' to its place in E (Davies, 84); it is not indispensable in E, whereas in *E* it is a necessary link between the return of Sheshbazzar and the tradition in iii. seq. Various attempts have been made to show that it is in its true position before the accession of Darius, whether by identifying the latter with D. II, or, like Josephus, by treating Artaxerxes as a mistake for Cambyses (cf. Sellin, Winckler, Torrey, and see references by Howorth in *PSBA*, xxiii. 313, 319, and Jampel, i. 103 seqq., ii. 97 seq.). These only cut the knot. Allowance must be made for a compilation based on a particular though erroneous theory of the Median and Persian kings (see Torrey, 38, 286, 302), but the real difficulty is the occurrence of this document relating to the time of Artaxerxes immediately after the reign of Cyrus. On its place, see further below, p. 56, and *Introd.* § 5 (*b*).

(*b*) The text in *E* is certainly from an Aramaic original. Note the translation of בעל טעם 'story-writer' (mg. 'recorder') in 17, 25, but the transliteration in 16 and (with a doublet) 25; the different renderings in E𝔊 (e.g. *ἐν εἰρήνῃ* for MT Bishlam, *E* Belemus, *v.* 16); and such variant renderings as 'cities' (*v.* 22 for 'provinces'), 'passage' (*v.* 24 and Jos. § 25; הלך for MT חלק 'portion'). *E*, although free and paraphrastic, preserves (as noticed by Volz, 1490) some better readings: 'our lord, the king' (*vv.* 17 seq., 21, cf. vi. 8; in agreement with Aramaic diplomatic usage), 'be it now known' (*v.* 18, see Torrey, 146, 186; 𝔏c prefixes 'peace'); 'books' (*v.* 21), 'the Jews' (*v.* 23). Sometimes, however, decision is difficult; so in *vv.* 25 seq., 28, the references to the Temple in *vv.* 18, 20, and especially the introduction compared with E iv. 6–11. In the MT 7 and 8 imply *two* letters, but the relationship is not clear; both 8 *b* and 10 *b* (ending 'and now' as in *v.* 11) point to the immediate commencement of a letter. The (Hebrew) reference to Ahasuerus (Xerxes) in *v.* 6 (cf. the story of Esther) is wanting in *E*, although *v.* 16 (end) seems to represent MT 6 *b*, and *v.* 17 covers MT *vv.* 8 (end), 9 (omitting the names after 'Dinaites', *E* 'judges'), and 10 (the reference to 'beyond the river'). Thus *E v.* 18 begins the letter and corresponds to MT 12 (cf. 11 *b* with 10 *b*). The intricacies may be due partly to the compiler's effort to quote a source and also to use it in his narrative (cf. on *E* vi. below), partly also to the revision of *E* after E and the reverse. It is noteworthy that E (where i.–iv. 6 is in Hebrew) takes care to state that the document was in Aramaic and needed translating (*vv.* 7 and 18 R.V. mg.); this is ignored in *E*, as also is the debatable מְפָרַשׁ in *E* ix. 48. See further the comment. and Torrey, 172 seq., 178 seqq., Bayer, 33 seq.

17. **Cœlesyria and Phœnicia.** The geographical term in MT ('Transflumen', 'Transpotamia') represents the Persian province west of the Euphrates, and to this the earlier use of the term Coelesyria (before the first cent. B.C.) corresponds. *E*'s rendering (contrast E𝔊's literal *πέραν τοῦ ποταμοῦ*) may point to an Egyptian locale where the geography of Palestine and Syria was unfamiliar (Torrey, 83). Jos. names Syria and Phoenicia, and adds Ammon and Moab; cf. perhaps Tobiah the Ammonite and Sanballat (if a native of Horonaim).

Jerusalem, do build that rebellious and wicked
city, and do repair the marketplaces and the
walls of it, and do lay the foundation of a temple.
19 Now if this city be builded and the walls *thereof*
be finished, they will not only refuse to give
tribute, but will even stand up against kings.

20 And forasmuch as the things pertaining to the
temple are now in hand, we think it meet not to
21 neglect such a matter, but to speak unto our lord
the king, to the intent that, if it be thy pleasure,
search may be made in the books of thy fathers:
22 and thou shalt find in the chronicles what is
written concerning these things, and shalt understand that that city was rebellious, troubling both
23 kings and cities: and that the Jews were rebellious, and raised always wars therein of old time;
for the which cause even this city was laid waste.
24 Wherefore now we do declare unto thee, O lord
the king, that if this city be builded again, and
the walls thereof set up anew, thou shalt from
henceforth have no passage into Cœlesyria and
25 Phœnicia. Then the king wrote back again to
Rathumus the storywriter, and Beeltethmus, and
Samellius the scribe, and to the rest that were in
commission, and dwelt in Samaria and Syria and
26 Phœnicia, after this manner: I have read the
epistle which ye have sent unto me:

therefore
I commanded to make search, and it hath been
found that that city of old time hath made in-
27 surrection against kings; and the men were given
to rebellion and war therein: and that mighty
kings and fierce were in Jerusalem, who reigned
and exacted tribute in Cœlesyria and Phœnicia.
28 Now therefore I have commanded to hinder
those men from building the city,

and heed to
be taken that there be nothing done contrary to
29 this *order*; and that those wicked doings pro-
30 ceed no further to the annoyance of kings. Then
king Artaxerxes his letters being read, Rathumus, and Samellius the scribe, and the rest that
were in commission with them, removing in haste
unto Jerusalem with horsemen and a multitude
of people in battle array, began to hinder the
builders; and the building of the temple in Jeru-

the rebellious and the bad city, and have finished
the walls, and repaired the foundations.

Be it 13
known now unto the king, that, if this city be
builded, and the walls finished, they will not pay
tribute, custom, or toll, and in the end it will
endamage the kings. Now because we eat the 14
salt of the palace, and it is not meet for us to see
the king's dishonour, therefore have we sent and
certified the king; that search may be made in 15
the book of the records of thy fathers: so shalt
thou find in the book of the records, and know
that this city is a rebellious city, and hurtful unto
kings and provinces, and that they have moved
sedition within the same of old time: for which
cause was this city laid waste.

We certify the 16
king that, if this city be builded, and the walls
finished, by this means thou shalt have no portion
beyond the river.
Then sent the king an answer 17
unto Rehum the chancellor, and to Shimshai the
scribe, and to the rest of their companions that
dwell in Samaria, and in the rest *of the country*
beyond the river, Peace, and so forth. The letter 18
which ye sent unto us hath been plainly read
before me. And I decreed, and search hath been 19
made, and it is found that this city of old time
hath made insurrection against kings, and that
rebellion and sedition have been made therein.
There have been mighty kings also over Jeru- 20
salem, which have ruled over all *the country*
beyond the river; and tribute, custom, and toll,
was paid unto them. Make ye now a decree to 21
cause these men to cease, and that this city be
not builded, until a decree shall be made by me.
And take heed that ye be not slack herein: why 22
should damage grow to the hurt of the kings?

Then when the copy of king Artaxerxes' letter 23
was read before Rehum, and Shimshai the scribe,
and their companions, they went in haste to
Jerusalem unto the Jews, and made them to cease
by force and power.

Then ceased the work of

18. **lay the foundation . . .**, *καὶ ναὸν ὑποβάλλονται* (BA; *ὑπερβάλλοντα θεμελιοῦσιν*, L).

20. **temple . . . in hand** (*ἐνεργεῖται τὰ κατὰ τὸν ναόν*), lit. 'are being urged on'. MT *Now because . . . palace* ($\mathfrak{G}^{BA}$ om.) may mean that the writers are in the king's service, or have entered into a covenant with him, or (reading 'our salt is the . . .'; Nestle, Strack) receive the dues of the palace or temple (cf. E vii. 22, 1 Macc. x. 29, xi. 35). *E* apparently rests upon some confusion of מלח ('salt'), with מלאכת ('work of'), מלת ('the matter of'), or perhaps מלא ('be full, complete'). In any case the reference to the Temple here and in *v.* 18 is noteworthy; either it may be part of a deliberate aim to introduce allusions to the Temple (see Bayer, 87 seqq., 94 seq., 102), or there was a tradition of the building of the Temple in the time of Artaxerxes. The latter finds independent support (see *Introd.* § 5 *e*), and the text in MT may be explained by the fact that, while in *E* and E Sheshbazzar had returned to rebuild the Temple, in E only is there an account of the commencement of the work and the delay. See also *Introd.* 15 seq.

23. Rather 'rebellious and still continuing sieges therein from of old' (Ball).

30. **horsemen**, &c.; MT *force* (*lit.* 'arm') *and power* (lit. 'strength' or 'army'). Cf. the situation in N iv. 2, 8.

salem ceased until the second year of the reign of Darius king of the Persians.

the house of God which is at Jerusalem; and it ceased unto the second year of the reign of Darius king of Persia.

3 1 Now king Darius made a great feast unto all his subjects, and unto all that were born in his house,
2 and unto all the princes of Media and of Persia, and to all the satraps and captains and governors
3 that were under him, from India unto Ethiopia, in the hundred twenty and seven provinces. And
when they had eaten and drunken, and being satisfied were gone home, then Darius the king went
into his bedchamber, and slept, and awaked out of his sleep.
4 Then the three young men of the body-guard, that kept the king's person, spake one to another:
5 Let every one of us say one thing which shall be strongest: and he whose sentence shall seem wiser
than the others, unto him shall Darius the king give great gifts, and great honours in token of

The Story of the Three Pages and the Decree of Darius, iii. 1–v. 6, wanting in E; see Jos. xi. 3 2–6.

(*a*) This section, famous for the Praise of Truth and for the familiar though often misquoted saying in iv. 41, is the centre of the problems of *E*. The story, well-known to early Christian Fathers and Synoptists, appears to be a piece of popular literature (cf. Susanna, Bel and the Dragon), not originally connected with Zerubbabel (see iv. 13, v. 5). Although ascribed to the early part of the reign of Darius (iv. 43, v. 6), it was evidently not written for the present context, which, indeed, it throws into great chronological confusion (see iv. 44, 57; v. 2, 55, 71, 73). In fact, the name Apame (iv. 29) suggests the time of Darius III (Codomannus), and the original scene, not laid in Babylon (iv. 57, 61), though ostensibly in Susa, was probably Egypt (so most scholars) or Antioch in Syria (Marq. 66). The orations are not distinctively biblical. That on drink stands in contrast, e.g. to Prov. xxiii. 29–35, Ecclus. xxxi. 25–30; and iv. 20 and 39 do not necessarily indicate any acquaintance with Gen. ii. 24 and Deut. x. 17 respectively. Allusions to Samson (so Lupton) are not obvious in iv. 17, 24, 26. The religious colouring is weak, but has been deepened by translators (see iv. 35 seq., 41, 59). Even the fine Praise of Truth seems to be an early addition: it is loosely appended to the paean of women, which, again, is out of touch with O.T. thought. Yet, even though the story be somewhat removed from biblical ideas, it may still be Jewish. The Praise of Truth, for example, may be a specimen of Palestinian wisdom (Zunz), and although Volz (1493) thinks it shows contact with Alexandrian religious philosophy, Torrey (46 seq.) fails to find anything 'hellenistic' or suggestive of the influence of Greek literature or philosophy.

(*b*) Ewald has suggested a connexion with the Sibylline books (iii. 293 seq.), where allusion is made to Persian kings inspired by *dreams* to further the restoration of the Temple. This is as little convincing or helpful as the alleged parallel between the questions debated by the Three Pages and the propositions put to the Jewish elders in the Letter of Aristeas. On the other hand, the opening of the story is clearly reminiscent of Est. i. 1–3; iii. 9 seems to be connected with Dan. vi. 2 (Torrey, 48), and several other interesting points of contact with Esther and Daniel have been noticed by Bayer (110 seqq.). Lagarde (*Mittheil.* iv. 358) conjectured that the story once followed after Dan. vi. 1. It is not improbable that the compiler identified Darius with the Mede in Dan. v. 31 (Hitzig, Reuss), and Büchler (51) further points out that Daniel's prayer in the first year of Darius (ix.) knows of no earlier return of exiles and may be associated with *E*'s story of Zerubbabel, which is placed in the king's second year. The story contains data which ignore and exclude *E* ii. 1–15 (note that Cyrus follows Darius in the book of Daniel). The land is waste and is partly occupied by Edomites who had burned the Temple. Neither exiles nor Temple-vessels had as yet returned, and now for the first time the favour of Persia had been gained and permission was given to return. For some reason Cyrus had been unable to fulfil his vow, and that of Darius is virtually a duplicate. It is, as Ewald (129) trenchantly observes, 'as if these kings had been in the habit of thinking of the God of Israel and the fate of his people at every critical moment of their lives, and the history of the whole world had strictly hinged in consequence upon the changes of its lot'. Ewald, however, accepts the decree of Cyrus, and this leaves no room for that of Darius, which is as credible, in itself, as that of the other Persian kings. See below, p. 32.

(*c*) It is very generally agreed that, with the exception of v. 1–6, the section was probably or certainly composed in Greek. But signs of a Hebrew original have been noticed by Schrader, Renan, Ball, and especially Jahn, who offers a Hebrew retranslation (177–88). Torrey (20–25, 37–61) argues for a Hebrew or Aramaic original, on the grounds of internal linguistic features, antecedent probability (viz. the close connexion between v. 1–6 and the end of iv.), and the characteristic interest in the ecclesiastical bodies (iv. 51–56). He notices several 'Aramaisms' (e.g. use of τότε, Aram. אדין; ἤρξατο, שׁרי), and concludes that the Story of the Three Pages was in Aramaic, and metrical (p. 47); *vv.* 43–46 were also in Aramaic, but the sequel in Hebrew (pp. 29 seq., 58). Bayer (123 seqq.) agrees, but urges that the whole of iii. and iv. was in Aramaic. See further Torrey's retranslation and notes (50 seqq.), and below on iv. 42 seqq. Jos. reproduces the section, with a necessary introduction to account for the presence of Zerubbabel; he seems to have used a slightly different version (Büchler, 57 seqq., 100; see on iii. 3). An abbreviated version is given in the Latin summary published by Lagarde (*Sept. Stud.* ii. 16 seqq.; here cited as Lag.), and in Josippon (see Büchler, 59 seqq., 62 seq., 100 seq.). For other witnesses see on iv. 36, 41, 59.

III. 3. **slept, and awaked**: ἐκοιμήθη καὶ ἔξυπνος ἐγένετο, 'lay down and was sleepless', cf. ἔξυπνος in mod. Greek 'wide-awake' (J. C. Lawson, *Mod. Gr. Folklore*, p. 31). According to Jos. § 35, cf. § 57, the king was restless (cf. Est. vi. 1), and was the first to suggest the orations and to promise and specify rewards. This conflicts with *v.* 8 seq., but seems to be hinted at in iv. 42 (πλείω τῶν γεγραμμένων). On the other hand, *E* does not allow that the suggestion came from the king, who is asleep (*vv.* 8 seq., 13). Jahn proposes to read ἔνυπνος (p. 177); Torrey (24, 50) conjectures that the original Aramaic text read: '(*v.* 3) . . . Darius . . . slept. (*v.* 4) Then stood on the watch (or "bestirred themselves" מתערין הוו) three young guardsmen (who protected the person of the king: a gloss), and they said . . . .'

5. **thing** (λόγον), i.e. sentence, as in *v.* 16.

strongest (ὑπερισχύσει), i.e. shall prevail.

sentence (ῥῆμα), i.e. argument.

honours, &c., ἐπινίκια μεγάλα, (*v.* 6) καὶ πορφύραν περιβαλέσθαι; Jos. § 35 νικητήριον πορφύραν ἐνδύσασθαι. Cf. Dan. v. 7.

6 victory: as, to be clothed in purple, to drink in gold, and to sleep upon gold, and a chariot with
7 bridles of gold, and a headtire of fine linen, and a chain about his neck: and he shall sit next to
8 Darius because of his wisdom, and shall be called Darius his cousin. And then they wrote every
9 one his sentence, and set to their seals, and laid *the writing* under king Darius his pillow, and said,
When the king is risen, some shall give him the writing; and of whose side the king and the three
princes of Persia shall judge that his sentence is the wisest, to him shall the victory be given, as it is
10, 11, 12 written. The first wrote, Wine is the strongest. The second wrote, The king is strongest. The
third wrote, Women are strongest: but above all things Truth beareth away the victory.
13 Now when the king was risen up, they took the writing, and gave it unto him, and so he read it:
14 and sending forth he called all the princes of Persia and of Media, and the satraps, and the captains,
15 and the governors, and the chief officers; and sat him down in the royal seat of judgement; and the
16 writing was read before them. And he said, Call the young men, and they shall explain their own
17 sentences. So they were called, and came in. And they said unto them, Declare unto us your
mind concerning the things ye have written.
18 Then began the first, who had spoken of the strength of wine, and said thus, O sirs, how exceeding
19 strong is wine! it causeth all men to err that drink it: it maketh the mind of the king and of the
fatherless child to be all one; of the bondman and of the freeman, of the poor man and of the rich:
20 it turneth also every thought into jollity and mirth, so that a man remembereth neither sorrow nor
21 debt: and it maketh every heart rich, so that a man remembereth neither king nor satrap; and it
22 maketh to speak all things by talents: and when they are in their cups, they forget their love both
23 to friends and brethren, and a little after draw their swords: but when they awake from their wine,
24 they remember not what they have done. O sirs, is not wine the strongest, seeing that it enforceth
to do thus? And when he had so spoken, he held his peace.
4 1, 2 Then the second, that had spoken of the strength of the king, began to say, O sirs, do not men
3 excel in strength, that bear rule over the sea and land, and all things in them? But yet is the king
stronger: and he is their lord, and hath dominion over them; and in whatsoever he commandeth
4 them they obey him. If he bid them make war the one against the other, they do it: and if he
5 send them out against the enemies, they go, and overcome mountains, walls, and towers. They
slay and are slain, and transgress not the king's commandment: if they get the victory, they bring
6 all to the king, as well the spoil, as all things else. Likewise for those that are no soldiers, and
have not to do with wars, but use husbandry, when they have reaped again that which they had sown,
7 they bring it to the king, and compel one another to pay tribute unto the king. And he is but one
8 man: if he command to kill, they kill; if he command to spare, they spare; if he command to
smite, they smite; if he command to make desolate, they make desolate; if he command to build,
9, 10 they build; if he command to cut down, they cut down; if he command to plant, they plant. So
all his people and his armies obey him: furthermore he lieth down, he eateth and drinketh, and

9. **some** (i. e. they) **shall give**, *δώσουσιν*. 𝔏 *dabimus*.
three princes, cf. Est. i. 14 (𝔊, but MT 7, as in *E* viii. 11).
as it is written, Jahn restores *according to his writing*.

12. **above all things** . . . (*ὑπὲρ δὲ πάντα* . . .), i. e. 'Truth is victor over all' (Torrey, p. 24, cf. נצח על). 'The third appears to have a double thesis to maintain, thus interfering with the symmetry' (Lupton).

13. 𝔊^{L} 'writings', and similarly in *v.* 15.

14. 𝔊^{L} om. *satraps*. Cf. Dan. iii. 2 for this list.

15. **sat**; 𝔏 𝔖 *they sat*.
seat of judgement (*χρηματιστηρίῳ*), council-chamber (cf. A.V. mg.).

16. **he**, 𝔊^{L} 𝔖 *they*.

17. **they said**, 𝔏 he said, 𝔊^{L} 𝔏^{c} and the king said.

18. 𝔏 *quam* (+facile 𝔏^{c}; cito Lag.) *praeualet* (𝔏^{c} vincit) *vinum omnibus hominibus* (𝔏^{c} omnes homines) *qui bibunt illud.*

21. **speak . . . by talents**, 𝔊^{L} + *καὶ πάντα διὰ γραμμάτων ποιεῖ ὅταν δὲ πίνωσι.*

23. **awake**, 𝔊^{B} *ἐγερθῶσιν*, 𝔊^{A} *γενηθῶσιν*, 𝔊^{L} *γένωνται*, 𝔏^{c} *et cum digesserit vinum et surrexerint* (Lag. cum a vino fuerint . . .).

24. 𝔊^{L} how is not wine . . ., cf. iv. 12, 32.

IV. 2. **that bear** . . ., rather 'in bearing rule . . .'

3. **their lord**, 𝔊^{A} lord of all, cf. A.V.; 𝔏 rex autem super omnia praecellit, 𝔏^{c} . . . super fortis est.
and hath . . . them, 𝔊^{L} om.
obey, 𝔊^{B}𝔖 *ἐνακούουσιν*, 𝔊^{L} *αὐτὸς, ἀκούουσι τοῦ ἑνός*, 𝔊^{A} *ποιήσουσιν* (cf. L Lag. faciunt); 𝔏^{c} om. 'and in . . . him'.

5. **as well the spoil** . . . 𝔊 *καὶ* (A + *ὅσα*) *ἐὰν προνομεύσωσιν καὶ τὰ ἄλλα πάντα* (i. e. 'and if they raid—and all else' [in like manner]), 𝔏 they bring to the king whatsoever they spoil. Torrey (52) conjectures a confusion of Aram. אחד 'take' and אחר 'other'.

7. **but one man**, mg. *one and alone*; 𝔊 *καὶ αὐτὸς εἰ* (𝔊^{BabAL} *εἷς*) *μόνος ἐστίν*, cf. Josh. xxii. 20, Judith i. 11 (so Torrey, 52, who would join the words to *v.* 6).

8. 𝔊 om. *if* in *v.* 8 seq. 𝔊^{A} om. *εἶπεν ἐρημῶσαι ἐρημοῦσιν*. Cf. generally Dan. v. 19.

11 taketh his rest: and these keep watch round about him, neither may any one depart, and do his own
12 business, neither disobey they him *in anything*. O sirs, how should not the king be strongest, seeing
that in such sort he is obeyed? And he held his peace.
13 Then the third, who had spoken of women, and of truth, (this was Zorobabel) began to speak.
14 O sirs, is not the king great, and men are many, and wine is strong? who is it then that ruleth them,
15 or hath the lordship over them? are they not women? Women have borne the king and all the
16 people that bear rule by sea and land. Even of them came they: and they nourished them up that
17 planted the vineyards, from whence the wine cometh. These also make garments for men; these
18 bring glory unto men; and without women cannot men be. Yea, and if men have gathered together
gold and silver and every other goodly thing, and see a woman which is comely in favour and beauty,
19 they let all those things go, and gape after her, and even with open mouth fix their eyes fast on her;
20 and have all more desire unto her than unto gold or silver, or any goodly thing whatsoever. A man
21 leaveth his own father that brought him up, and his own country, and cleaveth unto his wife. And
22 with his wife he endeth his days, and remembereth neither father, nor mother, nor country. By this
also ye must know that women have dominion over you: do ye not labour and toil, and give and
23 bring all to women? Yea, a man taketh his sword, and goeth forth to make outroads, and to rob
24 and to steal, and to sail upon the sea and upon rivers; and looketh upon a lion, and walketh in the
25 darkness; and when he hath stolen, spoiled, and robbed, he bringeth it to his love. Wherefore a man
26 loveth his wife better than father or mother. Yea, many there be that have run out of their wits for
27 women, and become bondmen for their sakes. Many also have perished, have stumbled, and sinned,
28 for women. And now do ye not believe me? is not the king great in his power? do not all regions
29 fear to touch him? Yet did I see him and Apame the king's concubine, the daughter of the illus-
30 trious Bartacus, sitting at the right hand of the king, and taking the crown from the king's head,
31 and setting it upon her own head; yea, she struck the king with her left hand: and therewithal the
king gaped and gazed upon her with open mouth: if she laughed upon him, he laughed also: but
if she took any displeasure at him, he was fain to flatter, that she might be reconciled to him again.
32 O sirs, how can it be but women should be strong, seeing they do thus?
33 Then the king and the nobles looked one upon another: so he began to speak concerning truth.
34 O sirs, are not women strong? great is the earth, high is the heaven, swift is the sun in his course,
for he compasseth the heavens round about, and fetcheth his course again to his own place in one
35 day. Is he not great that maketh these things? therefore great is truth, and stronger than all

13. *οὗτός ἐστιν Ζορ.*, $\mathfrak{G}^{L}$ $\mathfrak{L}^{c}$ $\mathfrak{S}$ + the son of Salathiel, Lag. + of the house of David, of the tribe of Judah, cf. v. 5. The identity of the unknown third youth (note *v.* 58), thus parenthetically introduced, is stated also by $\mathfrak{G}^{L}$ in *v.* 61, by $\mathfrak{L}^{c}$ in 33, 43, 58, and by Jos. regularly after iv. 40.

14. **is not . . .** $\mathfrak{G}^{L}$ by omitting the negative, makes the statement, and joining the verse on to *v.* 15, reads 'have not women borne the king? and all the people . . . land were even of them'.

men are many, or are mighty, see Torrey, 24, 53.

From *v.* 14 seq. Büchler (61 seq.) conjectures that the first and second orations have been transposed; cf. August. *de Civ. Dei*, xviii. 36 'quum reges unus dixisset, alter vinum, tertius mulieres,' &c.

17. **garments . . . glory**, probably a doublet (Torrey).

18. **and see . . .**, $\mathfrak{G}^{A}$ do they not love (cf. A.V.).

comely . . . beauty *καλὴν . . . τῷ κάλλει*, an evident sign of translation (Torrey, 53).

21. **endeth his days,** $\mathfrak{G}$ *ἀφίησι τὴν ψυχήν*; or 'loseth his life' (Ball, who cfs. Gen. xxxv. 18 $\mathfrak{G}$); otherwise '. . . for the sake of (ב misunderstood) his wife' (Jahn, 178), or 'abandoneth himself' (Torrey, 53, cf. $\mathfrak{S}$). Jos. § 52 *καὶ τὰς ψυχὰς ἀφιέναι μετ' αὐτῶν* (*ἀξιοῦμεν καί*, see Niese) *καρτεροῦμεν*.

22. **ye must know . . . over you,** $\mathfrak{G}^{L}$ 'we . . . us'.

23. **make outroads,** $\mathfrak{G}^{BL}$ *ἐξοδεύειν* (cf. 1 Macc. xv. 41), $\mathfrak{G}^{A}$ *εἰς ἐξοδίαν*, $\mathfrak{L}^{c}$ 'to waylay', $\mathfrak{S}$ 'to travel'.

and to steal, $\mathfrak{G}^{L}$ om.

24. **looketh upon** (i.e. faces or confronts), $\mathfrak{G}$ *θεωρεῖ*, $\mathfrak{L}$ *contemnit*, Lag. *vidit*; Treuenfels conj. *θηρεύει*, 'hunts'.

25. **Wherefore,** *lit.* 'and', similarly in *vv.* 35 ('therefore'), 49 ('moreover').

27. **stumbled,** $\mathfrak{G}^{BA}$ *ἐσφάλησαν*, $\mathfrak{G}^{L}$ *ἐσφάγησαν* (cf. $\mathfrak{L}$), $\mathfrak{S}$ 'erred'.

28. **do ye not,** $\mathfrak{G}^{L}$ 'if ye'.

29. **I see him and,** Torrey, 339 conj. *I myself* (*αὐτός*) *saw* . . .

the illustrious Bartacus. $\mathfrak{G}$ Βαρτακου (BA; Βαζακου, L; *ῥαβεζακου*, Jos.; Bezacis, Bezzachi, Lat.; r-b-'-'r-t-k $\mathfrak{S}$) *τοῦ θαυμαστοῦ* (*θεμασίου* Jos., ? a proper name, cf. *Θαμάσιος*, Herod. vii. 194). The reference may be to no historical person (Bayer, 116), or to Apame daughter of the satrap Artabazos III, or of the Bactrian satrap Spitamenes; the former was given to Ptolemy Lagos, the latter to Seleucus Nicator. Thus the story may relate to Egypt or to Antioch, and date from the time of Darius III, Codomannus (*c.* 300 B.C.). See further, Marq. 65 seq.; Torrey, 40 seqq., 54, 102; Josippon (Büchler, 66 n. 2) would make Apame the daughter of Axios (?) the Macedonian.

30. **struck,** $\mathfrak{G}$ *ἐράπιζεν*, 'was slapping'.

31. **therewithal,** $\mathfrak{G}$ *καὶ πρὸς τούτοις*, 'and moreover' (Lupton, cf. *v.* 10), or, 'and in spite of this' (Torrey, 25, 54).

33. **one upon another,** $\mathfrak{G}^{B}$ *εἷς* [*ἕτερος πρός*, A] *τὸν ἕτερον*; $\mathfrak{G}^{L}$ *ἕτ. τῷ ἑτέρῳ* (see Torrey, 54 *g*).

35. **maketh,** rather 'doeth'; the reference is transferred from the Sun to the Deity (see esp. Jos.).

therefore, *καί*, rather 'but'.

36 things. All the earth calleth upon truth, and the heaven blesseth her: all works shake and tremble,
37 but with her is no unrighteous thing. Wine is unrighteous, the king is unrighteous, women are
unrighteous, all the children of men are unrighteous, and unrighteous are all such their works; and
38 there is no truth in them; in their unrighteousness also they shall perish. But truth abideth, and
39 is strong for ever; she liveth and conquereth for evermore. With her there is no accepting of
persons or rewards; but she doeth the things that are just, *and refraineth* from all unrighteous and
40 wicked things; and all men do well like of her works. Neither in her judgement is any unrighteousness; and she is the strength, and the kingdom, and the power, and the majesty, of all ages. Blessed
41 be the God of truth. And with that he held his tongue. And all the people then shouted, and said,
Great is truth, and strong above all things.
42 Then said the king unto him, Ask what thou wilt more than is appointed in writing, and we will
give it thee, inasmuch as thou art found wisest; and thou shalt sit next me, and shalt be called my

36. **calleth upon**, A.V. mg. *praiseth the truth*, Lag. *invocat*; Athanasius, *Or. II. c. Arian.* ii. xx, quotes the passage ('all . . . tremble'), and argues that if all the earth 'praiseth' (ὑμνεῖ) the Demiurge and Truth, the former is the Logos.

works, ἔργα, perhaps originally 'created things' (Torrey), Lag. *quae mouentur trement.*

with her (so Jos.), but *him* (mg.) is a well attested reading and refers to the Deity as in *v.* 35 (see Torrey, 55).

37. **and there is**, Torrey (25) conj. 'if (εἰ) there is . . .'

38–40. See Cyprian, *Ep.* lxxiv., August. *de Civit. Dei*, xviii. ch. 36.

38. **for evermore**, εἰς τὸν αἰῶνα τοῦ αἰῶνος, a Semitism.

39. **rewards**, 𝔊^{B} διαφορά (cf. 𝔏 𝔖), 𝔊^{AL} διαφθορά; Torrey, 56 *a*, compares 2 Chron. xix. 7.

and refraineth, similarly 𝔊^{L} 𝔏^{C} 𝔏 Lag.; the text implies a misunderstanding of the comparative particle: 'things that are just *rather than* all . . .' (Fr., Ball, Torrey, 25, 56).

do well like, εὐδοκοῦσι, cf. Matt. iii. 17.

40. **she**, αὕτη; 𝔊^{L} αὐτῆς 'hers'; read perhaps αὐτῇ 'to her' (cf. Lag. *ipsi*). With the doxology cf. 1 Chron. xxix. 11, Dan. ii. 37, Matt. vi. 13.

Blessed . . ., or, since Truth is praised, restore 'blessed of God be Truth' (Torrey, 56).

41. 𝔊 Μεγάλη ἡ ἀλήθεια καὶ ὑπερισχύει; 𝔏 *magna est veritas et praevalet* (𝔏^{C} + *omnibus*). There is no good authority for the erroneous *praevalebit*. Jos. ignores the saying. Cyprian (*Ep.* lxxiv. 9) quotes it as *veritas manet et invalescet.* August. (*de Civ. Dei*, xviii. 36) refers to this passage as a prophecy of Christ. See further, for citations, Pohlmann, 263 seq.

The appendix on Truth (*vv.* 33–41) does not seem to be part of the original story; one may perhaps compare the various embellishments in the story of Ahikar. André (192) points out parallels in the praise of Wisdom and refers to Wisd. iii. 9, where Truth has a deeper mystical signification as though synonymous with the God of Truth.

The decree of Darius and the return of Zerubbabel, iv. 42–v. 6. (*a*) The vow of Darius practically duplicates that of Cyrus, and both kings are curiously associated with the capture of Babylon in Jos. x. II 4. That Cyrus was unable to fulfil his vow need not imply, as Büchler supposes, the existence of some specific tradition; it may be merely an attempt to justify this story of Darius, see *Introd.* p. 16. In any case the return of exiles under Zerubbabel in the reign of Darius (v. 6) is complicated by the references in v. 7 seqq. (E ii. seq.) to that of Cyrus. Since ii. 1–15 seems to be incomplete, it has been urged that the gap between E i. and ii. may be filled, partly at least, by *E* v. 1–6, reading *Cyrus* for *Darius* in *v.* 2 and adjusting or omitting *v.* 6 (see Ewald, 86; the comm. of Bertheau and Ryssel; Sellin, *Stud.*, 112 seq.; Davies, 49 seq.). Against this see Schrader, 482 n. *b*. It is otherwise held that v. 1–6 refer to a return, perhaps under Joakim (see v. 5), in the reign of Darius (De Saulcy and Kaulen [so Nikel, 52, 126]; Schrader; Reuss; Ryle, 15; André, 137–40). But it has been shown by Schrader (*loc. cit.*) and Torrey that this passage cannot be severed from the close of iv, and that both are of Semitic origin. The relationship between E i. and *E* iv. v. 1–6, 7 seqq. (E ii.) thus becomes more difficult, and Torrey (followed by Kent) would treat the Story of the Three Youths as an (Aramaic) interpolation in the (Hebrew) history of the time of Cyrus. Hence iv. 43–7, 57–61, and v. 6 *a* are regarded as redactional, linking the interpolated Darius story with the main narrative. The latter thus comprises E i. (*E* ii. 1–15), *E* iv. 47 *a*, 48 *a* ('and *Cyrus* the king wrote . . .'), 48 *b*–56, 62 seq., v. 1 seqq. (with *Cyrus* in *v.* 2, and in *v.* 6 reading only 'in the second year of the reign of Cyrus, king of Persia, in the month . . .'); see Torrey, *Journ. Bibl. Lit.*, xvi (1897), 168 seq., *Ezra Stud.*, 26, 32 seq., 58, 133; Kent, 340 seq. This would represent an earlier stage than the MT, but still furnishes a narrative, which both scholars regard as unhistorical, and which has been expanded by transferring E iv. 7 seqq. from its incorrect position before the reign of Darius to one equally incorrect in *E* ii. 16 seqq.

(*b*) Although the effort has been made to link together traditions of Cyrus and Darius, the interpolation-hypothesis brings fresh difficulties. The Story of the Three Pages (iii. 1–iv. 41), whatever its true origin and form, can only have been used because of its sequel. True, it could only have been inserted here, but a compiler was under no obligation to insert it, and the exhibition of rhetorical skill evidently served his purpose. The royal favour once obtained is turned to good account (cf. Est. v.), and unless the story had been already connected with Jewish history it is difficult to explain its presence. Only the fact that it deals with Darius and not Cyrus explains its survival, and the confusion arising from the effort to combine it with the history of the exiles is evidence of deliberate method. On these grounds, then, we have a bona-fide tradition—not necessarily a valuable one—of a return in the reign of Darius. Hence it is that ii. 16 seqq. seek to explain the delay between the time of Cyrus (who belongs to the past, ii. 30, iii. 1, iv. 44, 57) and that of Darius, and that Darius is represented partly as initiating (iv. 43, 47–56) and partly as endorsing (iv. 44, 57, see vi. 34) the return of the Jews. The whole is the result of a compromise. iv. 43–6 (Aramaic, Torrey, 29 n. 13) and 57–61 (Hebrew, *id.* 59) bear no resemblance to redactional patches (against Torrey, 57 seqq.). They actually being new details (the valuable *v.* 45), and *vv.* 44, 57, by ignoring the return of the vessels in ii. 10–15, link conflicting traditions, but do not link an otherwise unnecessary interpolation with the tradition which runs through E i.–iii. Besides, it is not clear that the gap between E i. and ii. is filled by Torrey's restoration (see Bayer, 134) or that the attempt to fill it is (in view of the development of the Cyrus-tradition) at all necessary. It may be concluded,

43 cousin. Then said he unto the king, Remember thy vow, which thou didst vow to build Jerusalem,
44 in the day when thou camest to thy kingdom, and to send away all the vessels that were taken out
of Jerusalem, which Cyrus set apart, when he vowed to destroy Babylon, and vowed to send them
45 again thither. Thou didst also vow to build up the temple, which the Edomites burned when Judæa
46 was made desolate by the Chaldeans. And now, O lord the king, this is that which I require, and
which I desire of thee, and this is the princely liberality that shall proceed from thee: I pray therefore that thou make good the vow, the performance whereof thou hast vowed to the King of heaven
with thine own mouth.

47 Then Darius the king stood up, and kissed him, and wrote letters for him unto all the treasurers
and governors and captains and satraps, that they should safely bring on their way both him, and
48 all those that should go up with him to build Jerusalem. He wrote letters also unto all the
governors that were in Cœlesyria and Phœnicia, and unto them in Libanus, that they should bring
49 cedar wood from Libanus unto Jerusalem, and that they should build the city with him. Moreover
he wrote for all the Jews that should go out of his realm up into Jewry, concerning their freedom,
50 that no officer, no governor, no satrap, nor treasurer, should forcibly enter into their doors; and that
all the country which they occupied should be free to them without tribute; and that the Edomites
51 should give over the villages of the Jews which then they held: and that there should be yearly
52 given twenty talents to the building of the temple, until the time that it were built; and other ten
talents yearly, for burnt offerings to be presented upon the altar every day, as they had a command-
53 ment to offer seventeen: and that all they that should come from Babylonia to build the city should
54 have their freedom, as well they as their posterity, and all the priests that came. He wrote also *to*
55 *give them* their charges, and the priests' vestments wherein they minister; and for the Levites he
wrote that their charges should be given them until the day that the house were finished, and
56, 57 Jerusalem builded up. And he commanded to give to all that kept the city lands and wages. He
sent away also all the vessels from Babylon, that Cyrus had set apart; and all that Cyrus had given
in commandment, the same charged he also to be done, and sent unto Jerusalem.

58 Now when this young man was gone forth, he lifted up his face to heaven toward Jerusalem, and
59 praised the King of heaven, and said, From thee cometh victory, from thee cometh wisdom, and
60 thine is the glory, and I am thy servant. Blessed art thou, who hast given me wisdom: and to thee
61 I give thanks, O Lord of our fathers. And so he took the letters, and went out, and came unto
62 Babylon, and told it all his brethren. And they praised the God of their fathers, because he had

therefore, that *E* iii. 1–v. 6 furnish a distinctive tradition of some return in the reign of Darius in accordance with his decree in *vv.* 48–56. See further on vi. seq.

On the text of iv. 42 seqq., see especially Torrey, 125 seqq.

43. **Remember**, 𝔊^{L} + O king.

44. **he vowed . . . Babylon**, 𝔖 om.; Gaab (see Fr.) and Torrey conj. 'when he began' (ἤρξατο); 𝔏 *cum excideret* (*desolavit*) *B*. Jos. § 58 omits all reference to Cyrus—'the vessels which Neb., having pillaged, carried to B.'

45. **Edomites**, cf. viii. 69. 𝔊^{B} Ἰουδαῖοι; 𝔏 Lag. '. . Chaldei cum desolata esset Iudea.' Fr. cites MS. 44: . . . ἐνεπύρισε Ναβ. See *Introd.* § 5 *f.*

46. **O lord the king**, cf. Dan. iv. 24.

and this is the . . .; 'and since such munificence is thine' (Torrey, 29 n. 13).

the vow . . . vowed, lit. 'the vow which thou didst vow.'

47. **letters**, lit. 'the letters', viz. which he desired. The reference is naturally to Darius and Zerubbabel; but on the theory that the story is an interpolation, Cyrus writes for Sheshbazzar (Torrey, Kent).

48. The grant of wood; see v. 55.

49. **enter . . . doors**. According to Jos. § 61 the royal taxes are remitted, cf. E vii. 24.

50. **Edomites** (𝔊^{B} Chaldeans). Jos. adds the Samaritans and people of Coelesyria.

51. **twenty talents**, 𝔊^{L} 𝔖 + 'of silver'. Jos. reads 'fifty', but omits the numbers in *v.* 52.

temple, τὸ ἱερόν, probably בית האלהים; for היכל *E* usually has ναός.

52. **and other . . . yearly**, 𝔊 𝔏 𝔖 at end of verse, perhaps rightly.

seventeen should probably be omitted (Lupton, 69; Torrey, 127).

53. The reference to freedom seems out of place, see Büchler, 98 seq., who joins the last words ('and for all the priests . . .') to *v.* 54.

54. **to give them**, cf. 𝔊^{L} δοθῆναι.

charges, χορηγία. In *v.* 55, Jos. § 62 has 'for the Levites, the musical instruments (τὰ ὄργανα) wherewith they praise God'. With the interest in the Levites, cf. E vii. 24, and especially N xi. 23.

56. **kept** (φρουροῦσι) **the city**; Jos. + 'and the temple'; on his paraphrase of the verse, see Büchler, 99 n. 3.

58. **toward Jerusalem**, cf. Dan. vi. 10, Tob. iii. 11 seq. With the prayer cf. E vii. 27, Dan. ii. 19, 20, 23.

59. 𝔊^{L} 'counsel (βουλή) and wisdom and victory, and thine is the glory'; so 𝔏^{c}, transposing 'wisdom' and 'victory'. Origen, *Hom. ix. in Iosuam*, quotes from 'Esdras': 'a te Domine est victoria et ego servus tuus, benedictus es Deus veritatis' (cf. *v.* 40).

60. **give thanks**, rather 'praise'.

62. **God of their fathers**, cf. E vii. 27, viii. 28, x. 11.

63 given them freedom and liberty to go up, and to build Jerusalem, and the temple which is called by
his name: and they feasted with instruments of music and gladness seven days.
5 1 After this were the chiefs of fathers' houses chosen to go up according to their tribes, with their
2 wives and sons and daughters, with their menservants and maidservants, and their cattle. And
Darius sent with them a thousand horsemen, till they had brought them back to Jerusalem safely,
3 and with musical instruments, tabrets and flutes. And all their brethren played, and he made them
go up together with them.
4 And these are the names of the men which went up, according to their families amongst their
5 tribes, after their several divisions. The priests, the sons of Phinees, the sons of Aaron: Jesus the
son of Josedek, the son of Saraias, and Joakim the son of Zorobabel, the son of Salathiel, of the
6 house of David, of the lineage of Phares, of the tribe of Judah; who spake wise sentences before
Darius the king of Persia in the second year of his reign, in the month Nisan, which is the first
month. EZRA
7 And these are they of Jewry that came up | Now these are the children of the province, **2** 1

63. **which is called . . .** 𝔊 οὗ ὠνομάσθη τὸ ὄνομα αὐτοῦ ἐπ' αὐτῷ; a Hebraism, cf. 2 Chron. vi. 33, vii. 14, *E* vi. 33.
feasted, Jos. § 66 τὴν ἀνάκτησιν καὶ παλιγγενεσίαν τῆς πατρίδος ἑορτάζοντες.

V. 2. **brought . . . back,** 𝔊^{BA} ἀποκαταστῆσαι, 𝔊^{L} ἀποκατασκηνῶσαι.
safely, mg. *with peace*, a literal rendering in the Greek of the Hebrew term. For the escort, cf. E viii. 22, N ii. 9.
3. **And all . . .**, 𝔊 MSS. nos. 55, 58 omit 'and'; the brethren were naturally the musicians, cf. *v.* 42 below.
he made . . ., 𝔊^{L} 'they'. Restore perhaps (after Torrey, 130) 'played and were sending them (on their way) as they went up'. Cf. Jos., and possibly (so Lupton) Tertullian, *De Cor. Milit.* ix. 'facilius cum tympanis et tibiis et psalteriis revertens de captivitate Babyloniae quam cum coronis', &c.
4. Cf. viii. 28; the *tribal* arrangement also recalls E's twelve lay-families.
5. Read 'of the priests' (Torrey, 131), cf. E viii. 2, where also priests are mentioned first (cf. E iii. 2, but contrast iv. 3, v. 2).
Phinees (Phinehas), the son (𝔊^{L} 𝔖) + of Eleazar the son of Aaron (𝔊^{L}).
and Joakim the son of Z. 𝔊^{L} ὁ καὶ Z., thus identifying, cf. Zer. and Sheshbazzar in vi. 18. This genealogy conflicts with that of Zerubbabel in 1 Chron. iii. 19 seqq., and Joakim the priest was the son of Jeshua (N xii. 10, 26). Some (e.g. Fr., Reuss) accept Joakim as the original hero of the story in iii. seq. and as the leader of a return in the reign of Darius. Büchler (56) would read 'and Zer. the son of Shealtiel the son of Joakim' (i.e. the king), corresponding to Jeshua the grandson of the priest Seraiah. Similarly Bayer (121 seq.) who also reads 'Jeshua the son . . . of Seraiah, the son of Phinehas, the son of Aaron the priest'. Torrey (131) suggests 'and there rose up with him Zer.' (ויקם בו, cf. ii. 8). This is attractive but seems rather abrupt. The analogy of E viii. 2 would suggest the presence of priestly and Davidic representatives. Such is the confusion, however, in the history of the return that 'Joakim the son of' may conceivably be an insertion on the view that Zer. (identified with Sheshbazzar) had already led a return in the time of Cyrus. On the intricacies see *Introd.* p. 15 seq.
6. **which is . . .**, rather 'on the first of the month' (Fr.; Jahn; Torrey, 27, 61). The date is properly not that when Zer. gained the king's ear (cf. N ii. 1, also the first month), but of the departure (see *E* viii. 6), and, although it conflicts with *v.* 57, the mention of the year is presupposed by the reference in *v.* 47. Note the care to give dates in E vii. 7 seq., viii. 31, &c.

The Register of the Return. v. 7–46 = E ii, N vii. 6–73; Jos. xi. 3 10 merely gives a brief summary. This list is the foundation-stone of the canonical post-exilic history, its authenticity a matter of keen dispute among those who have investigated this period, its essential trustworthiness accepted even by those who reject almost all that remains for the time of Cyrus (*E* i.–iv. 5). Its problems involve the entire structure of E–N. It is the list of those who returned 'every man to his own city' (*E v.* 8), thus connecting in the most realistic manner the large community (the *ḳāhāl*) which returned to the land of their ancestors with the pre-exilic population. It is no less closely connected with subsequent events in E–N; note the families in Ezra's band several decades later (see on *E* viii. 28–40), the enumeration in *E* ix. 21 seqq., the signatories of the covenant (N x.), and the various lists in N xii. As a whole the list may be likened to the register of the children of Israel before the Exodus (Gen. xlvi. 8–27) and after the settlement (Num. xxvi. 1–51, 1 Chron. ii.–viii.).

As a Register of the Return it ignores both the many Jews who had never left Palestine or who may have fled (perhaps temporarily) into Egypt, and the South Judaean families who had moved northwards into the neighbourhood of Jerusalem (1 Chron. ii.). Confining itself to the deportation by Nebuchadrezzar it ignores other returns (on the assumption that Zech. vi. 9 seq. do not represent an isolated occurrence). It implies the possibility of a very easy settlement by the exiles among the people of the land (contrast the tradition in *E* iv. 50); and the manifest improbability that the families could return after many years each to its old abode cannot be explained away (with Meyer, 151, and others) in view of the explicit statements in *v.* 46 seq. Moreover, the list includes the common people (see 2 Kings xxiv. 14–16), numbers Zerubbabel alone among the Davidic descendants, and apparently excludes guilds of artisans (2 Kings, *l.c.*). Although the numbers (*v.* 41) have been skilfully defended, considerable perplexity is caused by the place-names enumerated (see Elhorst, *Th. T.* xxix, 97 seq.; Kosters ib. xxx, 499 seq., xxxi, 531; Nikel, 57 seq.). Whether the list enumerates families carried off at the exile or applies to the new settlers—and those who accept the list are divided on this very important question—it is very difficult to account for the absence of some places (Nikel, 54 seq.) and the presence of others (Meyer, 105 seqq., 190). Moreover, the list implies a careful retention of the various local origins and divisions of the ecclesiastical and lay families during the years of exile, although once in Palestine there are, as is to be expected, continual changes and developments (Kosters, *E Bi.* col. 1483, § 8). No doubt some of the personal names are old, but it is improbable that such family-names as Jeshua, Pahath-moab, Elam, Bigvai (better Bagoi *E v.* 14), and Aspadath (*E* Aspharasus *v.* 8) are of pre-exilic date. It also assumes the existence

from the captivity, where they dwelt as strangers,
whom Nabuchodonosor the king of Babylon had
carried away unto Babylon.

8 And they returned
unto Jerusalem, and to the other parts of Jewry,
every man to his own city, who came with Zorobabel, with Jesus, Nehemias, *and* Zaraias, Resaias,
Eneneus, Mardocheus, Beelsarus, Aspharasus,
9 Reelias, Roimus, *and* Baana, their leaders. The
number of them of the nation, and their leaders:
the sons of Phoros, two thousand a hundred
seventy and two: the sons of Saphat, four
10 hundred seventy and two: the sons of Ares,
11 seven hundred fifty and six: the sons of Phaath
Moab, of the sons of Jesus and Joab, two thousand eight hundred and twelve:
12 the sons of
Elam, a thousand two hundred fifty and four:
the sons of Zathui, nine hundred forty and five:
13 the sons of Chorbe, seven hundred and five: the
sons of Bani, six hundred forty and eight: the
sons of Bebai, six hundred twenty and three:

that went up out of the captivity of those which
had been carried away, whom Nebuchadnezzar
the king of Babylon had carried away unto
Babylon, and that returned unto Jerusalem and
Judah, every one unto his city; which came with 2
Zerubbabel, Jeshua, Nehemiah, Seraiah, Reelaiah,
Mordecai, Bilshan, Mispar, Bigvai, Rehum, Baanah. The number of the men of the people of
Israel:
the children of Parosh, two thousand 3
an hundred seventy and two.

The children of 4
Shephatiah, three hundred seventy and two.
The children of Arah, seven hundred seventy 5
and five. The children of Pahath-moab, of the 6
children of Jeshua *and* Joab, two thousand eight
hundred and twelve. The children of Elam, a 7
thousand two hundred fifty and four. The chil- 8
dren of Zattu, nine hundred forty and five. The 9
children of Zaccai, seven hundred and threescore.
The children of Bani, six hundred forty and two. 10
The children of Bebai, six hundred twenty and 11

of trustworthy genealogies (*v.* 37 seqq.) which apparently were not preserved at Babylon, but were cherished by the natives of Judah. Such lists as are incorporated in Chron. (especially 1 Chron. xxiv., which has several points of resemblance with the E–N lists) are on critical grounds practically valueless for the pre-exilic age, and it is necessary, therefore, to suppose that—if the great list is genuine—the older genealogical records have disappeared (see Meyer, 140, 160 seqq.). On the other hand, one important list which vitally conflicts with this is preserved in Neh. iii., and, as Ed. Meyer was the first to observe, testifies to the prominence of an indigenous population, secular and ecclesiastical, wherein the presence of the South Judaean groups may be recognized. But that list testifies also to the weakness of any body of Babylonian exiles; see *Introd.* § 5 (*c*).

While this list forms the backbone of the biblical post-exilic history and is in a context where the events are closely interconnected (viz. the generous decree, the great return, the steps to reorganize religious conditions), the evidence of Haggai and Zechariah (520 B.C.) renders the whole context untrustworthy (so even Meyer, pp. 49, 73, 98 seq., 191). These prophets ignore the presence of this great community (see *Introd.* § 4. II.), and the successful opposition as described in *E* v. 66 seqq. 'shows how small a number had really returned' (G. A. Smith, *Jerusalem*, ii, 298 seq.). Certain considerations might support the genuineness of the list and its context (see Davies, 14, 80; Torrey, 144), but the weight of evidence, and the recognition that the list has been subsequently 'edited' (Holzhey, 15; Davies, 51), or may comprise the result of several returns between 538 and 520 or 516 (Sellin, *Ser.* 7, *Stud.* 42, 108 seq., 115, 158), indicate that whatever return or returns took place the list and the context describe events in such a way that the historical facts cannot be recovered by any internal criticism of the narratives.

The list appears in the account of Nehemiah (*c.* 444) where it is treated as that of 'the children of the province', and should incorporate those native families who had separated from the heathen (*E* vii. 6. 13); see *Introd.* p. 9. On internal grounds N vii. (not necessarily in its present form) appears to be its earlier form, and it is noteworthy that *E* and to a greater extent E show traces of some adjustment of the list to the history before the building of the Temple (see below). On the minutiae of the list, see Smend (who notes frequent agreement with N, so also Bayer, 38); Moulton, *ZATW*, xix, 246 seq.; Meyer, 141 seqq., and Bayer, 42 seqq., and, besides the comm., the several articles in *E Bi.* The readings in the R.V. mg., with the identifications of the more difficult names, have been omitted in the notes here and in the other lists, viii. 29 seqq., ix. 19 seqq., &c.

7. **captivity** . . . , 𝔊 τῆς αἰχμαλωσίας τῆς παροικίας (𝔊[L] ἀποικεσίας).

8. The leaders are twelve in number (cf. the tribes, and see on *v.* 4) through the insertion of Eneneus (= Nahamani N vii. 7). N𝔊 reads 'who came with Zer. and Jeshua and Neh.: Azariah . . . Mispereth, Ezra, Bigvai . . . Baanah, Masphar'; cf. the old view that the return of Zer. was contemporary with that of N or E (see *Introd.* p. 10 *a*). Among the important variants are *E Zaraias* (E *Seraiah*, N *Azariah*); *Resaias* (E *Reelaiah*, N *Raamiah*, see *E Bi.*, 3997); *Beelsarus* (EN *Bilshan*, see *E Bi.*, 574); *Aspharasus* (? Pers. Aspadata; Marq. 35); *Reelias* (i.e. Reelaiah, EN *Bigvai*); *Roimus* (E *Rehum*, N *Nehum* = 𝔊[L] in E). Jos. xi. 3 § 73 seq. mentions besides Zer. and Jeshua two names of prominent donors (see *v.* 44 seq.), Mordecai (see on vii. 15) and Sherebiah.

9–23. The lay-families. *E* 15 seq. add *Kilan* (? Keilah), *Azetas* (? Azekah), *Azaru* or *Azuru* (cf. Asara *v.* 31, or Azzur N x. 17), *Annis* or *Annias* (cf. Hananiah, or Hodiah N x. 18). For *Arom* cf. *Harim*, E 32 (wanting in *E*, unless *Chorbe v.* 12 represents it and not *Zaccai*; see N x. 14) or *Hashum* (E 19 before *Gibbar* [see below]; N x. 18 before *Bezai* [*E* Bassai]). On these additions see also Bayer, 43 seqq., 75. For the compound *Arsiphurith*, cf. *Jorah* E 18 = *Hariph* N vii. 24 (𝔊[ℵ] + 'the children of Asen'), x. 19. *Baiterus* (note the number) takes the place of *Gibbar* (E) or *Gibeon* (N); cf perhaps Bether, Josh. xv. 19 𝔊 and see Guthe, *SBOT*. With the *Chadiasai*, cf. perhaps Hadashah, Josh. xv. 37, or Adasa, 1 Macc. vii. 40; and with the *Ammidioi*, perhaps Modin, 1 Macc. ii. 1, or Migdal-Gad, or Middin (Ball); Bayer (45 seq.) discovers the names Hashum and Hodijah. In *v.* 21 Ai is wanting, and if *Niphish* represents *Magbish* (E only, cf. Magpiash N x. 20), the men of Nebo, the other Elam (cf. E 31) and Harim (see E 39, *E* 25) are absent. *Calamolalus* (𝔊[B] -calus) and *Onus* represent *Lod*, *Hadid* and *Ano*.

the sons of Astad, a thousand three hundred
14 twenty and two: the sons of Adonikam, six
hundred sixty and seven: the sons of Bagoi, two
thousand sixty and six:
the sons of Adinu, four
15 hundred fifty and four: the sons of Ater, of
Ezekias, ninety and two: the sons of Kilan and
Azetas, threescore and seven: the sons of Azaru,
16 four hundred thirty and two: the sons of Annis,
a hundred and one: the sons of Arom: the sons
of Bassai, three hundred twenty and three: the
17 sons of Arsiphurith, a hundred and twelve: the
sons of Baiterus, three thousand and five: the
sons of Bethlomon, a hundred twenty and three:
18 they of Netophas, fifty and five: they of Ana-
thoth, a hundred fifty and eight: they of Bethas-
19 moth, forty and two: they of Kariathiarius,
twenty and five: they of Caphira and Beroth,
20 seven hundred forty and three: the Chadiasiai
and Ammidioi, four hundred twenty and two:
they of Kirama and Gabbe, six hundred twenty
21 and one: they of Macalon, a hundred twenty
and two: they of Betolion, fifty and two: the
sons of Niphis, a hundred fifty and six:

22 the sons
of Calamolalus and Onus, seven hundred twenty
23 and five: the sons of Jerechu, three hundred
24 forty and five: the sons of Sanaas, three thousand three hundred and thirty. The priests:
the sons of Jeddu, the son of Jesus, among the
sons of Sanasib, nine hundred seventy and two:
the sons of Emmeruth, a thousand fifty and two:
25 the sons of Phassurus, a thousand two hundred
forty and seven: the sons of Charme, a thousand
and seventeen.
26 The Levites: the sons of Jesus,
and Kadmiel, and Bannas, and Sudias, seventy
27 and four. The holy singers: the sons of Asaph,
28 a hundred twenty and eight. The porters: the
sons of Salum, the sons of Atar, the sons of
Tolman, the sons of Dacubi, the sons of Ateta,
the sons of Sabi, in all a hundred thirty and nine.

29 The temple-servants: the sons of Esau, the sons
of Asipha, the sons of Tabaoth, the sons of
Keras, the sons of Sua, the sons of Phaleas, the

three. The children of Azgad, a thousand two 12
hundred twenty and two. The children of 13
Adonikam, six hundred sixty and six. The 14
children of Bigvai, two thousand fifty and six.
The children of Adin, four hundred fifty and 15
four. The children of Ater, of Hezekiah, ninety 16
and eight.

The children of Bezai, three hundred 17
twenty and three. The children of Jorah, an 18
hundred and twelve. The children of Hashum, 19
two hundred twenty and three. The children of 20
Gibbar, ninety and five. The children of Beth- 21
lehem, an hundred twenty and three. The men 22
of Netophah, fifty and six. The men of Ana- 23
thoth, an hundred twenty and eight. The chil- 24
dren of Azmaveth, forty and two. The children 25
of Kiriath-arim, Chephirah, and Beeroth, seven
hundred and forty and three. The children of 26
Ramah and Geba, six hundred twenty and one.
The men of Michmas, an hundred twenty and 27
two. The men of Beth-el and Ai, two hundred 28
twenty and three. The children of Nebo, fifty 29
and two. The children of Magbish, an hundred 30
fifty and six. The children of the other Elam, 31
a thousand two hundred fifty and four. The 32
children of Harim, three hundred and twenty.
The children of Lod, Hadid, and Ono, seven 33
hundred twenty and five. The children of 34
Jericho, three hundred forty and five. The 35
children of Senaah, three thousand and six
hundred and thirty. The priests: the children 36
of Jedaiah, of the house of Jeshua, nine hundred
seventy and three.
The children of Immer, a 37
thousand fifty and two. The children of Pashhur, 38
a thousand two hundred forty and seven. The 39
children of Harim, a thousand and seventeen.
The Levites: the children of Jeshua and Kad- 40
miel, of the children of Hodaviah, seventy and
four. The singers: the children of Asaph, an 41
hundred twenty and eight. The children of the 42
porters: the children of Shallum, the children of
Ater, the children of Talmon, the children of
Akkub, the children of Hatita, the children
of Shobai, in all an hundred thirty and nine.
The Nethinim: the children of Ziha, the children 43
of Hasupha, the children of Tabbaoth; the chil- 44
dren of Keros, the children of Siaha, the children

24 seq. The priests. The family of Jedaiah is ascribed to Sanasib (𝔏[c] Enassibe) i.e. Eliashib, grandson of Jeshua and grandfather of Jaddua (N xii. 10–12); Meyer, 169; Batten, *SBOT*, 59. The omission of Eliashib in EN is more explicable (in view of the foreign alliance in N xiii. 4, 28) than its presence in *E*. The reference to Jeshua may be due to insertion. Apart from this, it is noteworthy that there is little variation in the versions, perhaps an indication of the lateness of the list of the priests (*SBOT loc. cit.*).

26. The Levites. As regards the small number, it may be noticed that certain Levitical families, at all events, appear not to have been deported, so Henadad (see *v.* 58), and also the Korahites (Meyer, *Israel.*, 352 n. 5), see Meyer, *Ent.* 167, 177, Nikel, 86 (from another standpoint), and *Introd.* § 5 (*c*).

29 seqq. The Nethinim. *E* (but not 𝔊[L], which is as usual corrected after the MT) adds *Uta* (? cf. *Uthai*, E viii. 14), *Ketab* (or Ketam, cf. N vii. 48 𝔊[NA], and see Torrey, 89 seq., Bayer, 52), *Chaseba* (? cf. Chezib, Cozbi), *Asara* (see *Azaru*, *v.* 15, and cf. Hasrah, 2 Chron. xxxiv. 22), *Pharakim* (see *E Bi.*, 3686) and *Cutha* (? cf. the Cuthaeans, or, with Bayer, Sotai, E 55).

30 sons of Labana, the sons of Aggaba, the sons of
Acud, the sons of Uta, the sons of Ketab, the
sons of Accaba, the sons of Subai, the sons of
Anan, the sons of Cathua, the sons of Geddur,
31 the sons of Jairus, the sons of Daisan, the sons of
Noeba, the sons of Chaseba, the sons of Gazera,
the sons of Ozias, the sons of Phinoe, the sons of
Asara, the sons of Basthai, the sons of Asana,
the sons of Maani, the sons of Naphisi,
the sons
of Acub, the sons of Achipha, the sons of Asur,
32 the sons of Pharakim, the sons of Basaloth, the
sons of Meedda, the sons of Cutha, the sons of
Charea, the sons of Barchus, the sons of Serar,
the sons of Thomei, the sons of Nasi, the sons of
Atipha.
The sons of the servants of Solomon:
33 the sons of Assaphioth, the sons of Pharida,
the
sons of Jeeli, the sons of Lozon, the sons of
34 Isdael, the sons of Saphuthi, the sons of Agia,
the sons of Phacareth, the sons of Sabie, the sons
of Sarothie, the sons of Masias, the sons of Gas,
the sons of Addus, the sons of Subas, the sons of
Apherra, the sons of Barodis, the sons of Saphat,
35 the sons of Allon. All the temple-servants, and
the sons of the servants of Solomon, were three
36 hundred seventy and two. These came up from
Thermeleth, and Thelersas, Charaathalan lead-
37 ing them, and Allar; and they could not shew
their families, nor their stock, how they were of
Israel: the sons of Dalan the son of Ban, the
sons of Nekodan, six hundred fifty and two.
38 And of the priests, they that usurped the office
of the priesthood and were not found: the sons
of Obdia, the sons of Akkos, the sons of Jaddus,
who married Augia one of the daughters of
39 Zorzelleus, and was called after his name. And
when the description of the kindred of these men
was sought in the register, and was not found,
they were removed from executing the office of
40 the priesthood: for unto them said Nehemias
and Attharias, that they should not be partakers

of Padon; the children of Lebanah, the children 45
of Hagabah, the children of Akkub; the children 46
of Hagab, the children of Shamlai, the children
of Hanan; the children of Giddel, the children of 47
Gahar, the children of Reaiah; the children of 48
Rezin, the children of Nekoda, the children of
Gazzam; the children of Uzza, the children of 49
Paseah, the children of Besai; the children of 50
Asnah, the children of Meunim, the children of
Nephisim; the children of Bakbuk, the children 51
of Hakupha, the children of Harhur; the chil- 52
dren of Bazluth, the children of Mehida, the
children of Harsha;
the children of Barkos, the 53
children of Sisera, the children of Temah; the 54
children of Neziah, the children of Hatipha.
The children of Solomon's servants: the children 55
of Sotai, the children of Hassophereth, the children of Peruda; the children of Jaalah, the 56
children of Darkon, the children of Giddel; the 57
children of Shephatiah, the children of Hattil,
the children of Pochereth-hazzebaim, the children of Ami.

All the Nethinim, and the chil- 58
dren of Solomon's servants, were three hundred
ninety and two. And these were they which 59
went up from Tel-melah, Tel-harsha, Cherub,
Addan, *and* Immer: but they could not shew
their fathers' houses, and their seed, whether
they were of Israel: the children of Delaiah, the 60
children of Tobiah, the children of Nekoda, six
hundred fifty and two. And of the children of 61
the priests: the children of Habaiah, the children
of Hakkoz, the children of Barzillai, which took
a wife of the daughters of Barzillai the Gileadite,
and was called after their name. These sought 62
their register *among* those that were reckoned
by genealogy, but they were not found: therefore were they deemed polluted and put from
the priesthood. And the Tirshatha said unto 63
them, that they should not eat of the most holy

33 seq. Servants of Solomon. *E* (but not $\mathfrak{G}^{L}$) omits *Sotai*, severs (with 𝔊 of E–N) *Pochereth-hazzebaim*, and between the latter and *Ami* (E; N *Amon*, *E* Allon) inserts eight names, on which see *E Bi.*

36. See the comm. *Leading* is apparently based upon a doublet of *Tel-harsha* (חרשא), as though connected with ראש (רשא) 'head, leader'; but see *v.* 8 end.

37. **Dalan,** $\mathfrak{G}^{B}$ *ασαν*, MT Delaiah. *Ban*, marg. *Baenan* ($\mathfrak{G}^{B}$), but MT Tobiah (? cf. N vi. 17 seq., xiii. 4), though with the addition of *βουα*, E$\mathfrak{G}^{B}$, N$\mathfrak{G}^{A}$. *Nekoda*(*n*), cf. *v.* 31 (*E* Noeba).

38. **And of the priests** (similarly N 63), they that claimed . . . (*οἱ ἐμποιούμενοι* [$\mathfrak{G}^{L}$ *μεταποι.*] *ἱερωσύνης*). *Obdia*, $\mathfrak{G}^{B}$ Obbeia, N Hobaiah. The family of Hakkoz, according to the traditional view, had been legitimate (1 Chron. xxiv. 10), was now deposed, but was subsequently reinstated and held a prominent place (N iii. 4, 21, E viii. 33). If this list is of the time of Zerubbabel we must explain the retention of the name in N vii. 63 and its omission in N x., xii. (cf. Kosters, *Th. T.*, xxxi, 539). The passage has not the value set upon it (notably by Meyer, 170, who compares the Calebite Ḳoṣ, 1 Chron. iv. 8; see also Jampel i, 313), but only shows that at some period the legitimacy of the family was evidently doubtful.

the sons of Jaddus, apparently Jaddua; note the variant text in E.

40. **Attharias,** i.e. the Tirshatha (cf. ix. 49). The verb (*εἶπεν*) is in the singular and $\mathfrak{G}^{L}$ (see A.V. mg.) identifies the two. 𝔖 reads only *Nehemiah*, and MT only the *Tirshatha* (cf. the variants in *E* ix. 49). Even if the identification be due to a gloss (Fr., cf. Bayer, 53) it must serve a purpose (as in iv. 13, vi. 18), and it is only intelligible if the list belonged originally to the history of N's age (see W. R. Smith, *Ency. Brit.*, 9th ed., art. 'Haggai', xi, 370; Harvey, *Expos.*, 1893, vii. p. 440; Howorth, *PSBA*, xxiii, 309 seq.). The mitigated form of the decision in the MT is probably

of the holy things, till there arose up a high
41 priest wearing Urim and Thummim. So all
they of Israel, from twelve years old *and upward,* beside menservants and womenservants,
were *in number* forty and two thousand three
42 hundred and sixty. Their menservants and
handmaids were seven thousand three hundred
thirty and seven: the minstrels and singers, two
hundred forty and five:
43 four hundred thirty and
five camels, seven thousand thirty and six horses,
two hundred forty and five mules, five thousand
five hundred twenty and five beasts of burden.
44 And certain of the chief men of their families,
when they came to the temple of God that is in
Jerusalem, vowed to set up the house again in
45 its own place according to their ability, and to
give into the holy treasury of the works a thousand pounds of gold, five thousand of silver, and
a hundred priestly vestments.
46 And the priests
and the Levites and they that were of the people
dwelt in Jerusalem and the country; the holy
singers also and the porters and all Israel in their
villages.
47 But when the seventh month was at hand,
and when the children of Israel were every man
in his own place, they came all together with
one consent into the broad place before the first
48 porch which is toward the east. Then stood up
Jesus the son of Josedek, and his brethren the
priests, and Zorobabel the son of Salathiel, and
his brethren, and made ready the altar of the
49 God of Israel, to offer burnt sacrifices upon it,
according as it is expressly commanded in the

things, till there stood up a priest with Urim
and with Thummim. The whole congregation 64
together was forty and two thousand three
hundred and threescore,

beside their menservants 65
and their maidservants, of whom there were seven
thousand three hundred thirty and seven: and
they had two hundred singing men and singing
women. Their horses were seven hundred thirty 66
and six; their mules, two hundred forty and
five; their camels, four hundred thirty and five; 67
their asses, six thousand seven hundred and
twenty. And some of the heads of fathers' 68
houses, when they came to the house of the
Lord which is in Jerusalem, offered willingly for
the house of God to set it up in its place: they 69
gave after their ability into the treasury of the
work threescore and one thousand darics of gold,
and five thousand pound of silver, and one hundred priests' garments. So the priests, and the 70
Levites, and some of the people, and the singers,
and the porters, and the Nethinim, dwelt in their
cities, and all Israel in their cities.

And when the seventh month was come, and 3 1
the children of Israel were in the cities, the
people gathered themselves together as one
man to Jerusalem.
Then stood up Jeshua the 2
son of Jozadak, and his brethren the priests,
and Zerubbabel the son of Shealtiel, and his
brethren, and builded the altar of the God of
Israel, to offer burnt offerings thereon, as it is
written in the law of Moses the man of God.

less original (Guthe, Bertholet, Jahn); instead of being removed, the priests are forbidden to share in the most holy things, which were restricted to the Aaronites.

41. For the age-limit (also in Jos.) cf. Luke ii. 42.

42. For the minstrels cf. *v.* 2 seq., and see Meyer, 192.

43. The horses and mules are wanting in good MSS. of N.

44 seq. *E* and E omit N vii. 70, which refers vaguely to the donations of the heads 'to the work' and mentions the gifts of the Tirshatha (i.e. Nehemiah, so $\mathfrak{G}^{B}$), and also ib. 72, the gifts of the rest of the people, although the priestly garments are recorded. The emphasis upon the proposed building of the temple, natural in *E*E, is wanting in N, although the record there professes to be taken from the history of the time of Zerubbabel (N vii. 5). For the view that *E*E represent a less original form of the passage, see Meyer, 195; Wellh., *GGN*, 1895, p. 176; Nikel, 75 n. 1; Sellin, *Stud.*, 110; Guthe, *SBOT*. For the general situation, cf. 1 Chron. xxix. 6 seqq.

46. On the data of MT and the versions, see the comm. The mention of Jerusalem here and ix. 37 presupposes the completion of the rebuilding of the city; the omission in MT may be due to the context: in E, the city has not yet been restored, in N it is still poorly inhabited and barely ready. Elsewhere, in 1 Chron. ix. 2, N xi, 3. 20 there is a distinction between Jerusalem and the outside villages. In N xi. some of the ecclesiastical body dwell in the city (*v.* 21), but others live in the villages (N xii. 28 seq., cf. 1 Chron. ix. 16), and in N xiii. 10 Levites and singers have deserted and returned to their abodes. In 1 Chron. xiii. 2, 2 Chron. xxiii. 2, they are summoned, especially when new conditions are inaugurated, or when (xxix. 4) the temple-service is resumed (cf. the dedication of the walls, N xii. 27 seq.), or when fresh arrangements are made for them (2 Chron. xxxi. 19).

The Rebuilding of the Altar and the Foundation of the Temple. v. 47–65 = E iii., cf. Jos. xi. 4 1–2. The description of the resumption of the Levitical service (cf. 1 Chron. xxiii. 31, 2 Chron. ii. 4, viii. 12 seq.) begins with the congregating of the exiles (now 'the children of Israel') in the seventh month. This is the first year of the return (cf. *v.* 56 [Cyrus] and the preliminary date *v.* 6 [Darius]). In ‖ N vii. 73 *b*, viii. 1, it is the first year of N's return (after the completion of the walls, vi. 15), and it introduces the Reading of the Law, which in ‖ *E* ix. 37 *b*, 38 seqq. is the sequel to the purging of the community (cf. probably *E* v. 36–40 and the allusions in vii. 6, 13). The scene of the assembly in *v.* 47 (cf. 2 Chron. xxix. 4, a story of the restoration of the Temple after some disaster, *v.* 9) presupposes the existence of the Temple, as in ix. 6 (E x. 9), 38 (N viii. 1), and, therefore, a later context in the history (cf. the later background of the preceding list). The MT has consequently altered the wording (see Bertholet, Guthe).

50 book of Moses the man of God. And certain
were gathered unto them out of the other nations
of the land, and they erected the altar upon its
own place, because all the nations of the land
were at enmity with them, and oppressed them;
and they offered sacrifices according to the time,
and burnt offerings to the Lord both morning
51 and evening. Also they held the feast of tabernacles, as it is commanded in the law, and *offered*
sacrifices daily, as was meet:
and after that, the
52 continual oblations, and the sacrifices of the
sabbaths, and of the new moons, and of all the
consecrated feasts.
53 And all they that had made
any vow to God began to offer sacrifices to God
from the new moon of the seventh month,
although the temple of God was not yet built.
54 And they gave money unto the masons and
55 carpenters; and meat and drink, and cars unto
them of Sidon and Tyre, that they should bring
cedar trees from Libanus, *and* convey them in
floats to the haven of Joppa, according to the
commandment which was written for them by
56 Cyrus king of the Persians. And in the second
year after his coming to the temple of God at
Jerusalem, in the second month, began Zorobabel
the son of Salathiel, and Jesus the son of Josedek,
and their brethren, and the priests the Levites,
and all they that were come unto Jerusalem out
57 of the captivity: and they laid the foundation of
the temple of God on the new moon of the second
month, in the second year after they were come
58 to Jewry and Jerusalem. And they appointed
the Levites from twenty years old over the works

And they set the altar upon its base; for fear 3
was upon them because of the people of the
countries: and they offered burnt offerings
thereon unto the Lord, even burnt offerings
morning and evening.
And they kept the feast 4
of tabernacles, as it is written, and *offered* the
daily burnt offerings by number, according to
the ordinance, as the duty of every day required;
and afterward the continual burnt offering, and 5
the offerings of the new moons, and of all the set
feasts of the Lord that were consecrated, and of
every one that willingly offered a freewill offering
unto the Lord. From the first day of the seventh 6
month began they to offer burnt offerings unto
the Lord: but the foundation of the temple of
the Lord was not yet laid.
They gave money 7
also unto the masons, and to the carpenters; and
meat, and drink, and oil, unto them of Zidon,
and to them of Tyre, to bring cedar trees from
Lebanon to the sea, unto Joppa, according to
the grant that they had of Cyrus king of Persia.
Now in the second year of their coming unto 8
the house of God at Jerusalem, in the second
month, began Zerubbabel the son of Shealtiel,
and Jeshua the son of Jozadak, and the rest of
their brethren the priests and the Levites, and
all they that were come out of the captivity unto
Jerusalem;
and appointed the Levites, from
twenty years old and upward, to have the over-

50. **upon its own place**; cf. E R.V. mg. *in its place.*
And certain . . . and **because all . . .** are doublets ($\mathfrak{L}$ om. the latter), MT has only *for fear . . . countries* (בְּאֵימָה represented in *E* by בָּאִים; E$\mathfrak{G}^{B}$ om. the clause). *E*'s reading finds parallels in 1 Macc. v. 1–2, and possibly N iv. 12 (MT *v.* 6), where the enemy come up against the builders (see comm.).
oppressed (*κατίσχυσαν*), may point to וַיִּתְחַזְּקוּ 'and they strengthened themselves' (see Berth.), or וַיְחַזְּקוּ 'and they [the foreigners] strengthened them' (Ewald, 101 n. 4; Bayer 25 compares v. 66).
to the Lord and **according to the time** ($\mathfrak{L}$ om.) are based on doublets in $\mathfrak{G}$ (*κύριος, καιρός*); for the sacrifices, cf. 1 Chron. xvi. 40. Jos. § 76 reads simply *ταῦτα δὲ ποιοῦντες οὐκ ἦσαν ἐν ἡδονῇ τοῖς προσχωρίοις ἔθνεσιν πάντων αὐτοῖς ἀπεχθανομένων.*
52. **sabbaths**; appropriate, see Num. xxviii. 9 seq.; 2 Chron. ii. 4, viii. 13.
53. **seventh month,** mg. *first* ($\mathfrak{G}^{B}$).
although . . ., Jos. § 78: 'they also began the building of the temple.' MT *laid*; for the use of יסד, see E iii. 10, 2 Chron. iii. 3, xxiv. 27 (R.V. mg.).
55. Cf. 2 Chron. ii. 8–10, 15 seq.
cars (MT and $\mathfrak{G}$ *oil*), *χάρα* ($\mathfrak{G}^{B}$? שמחה for שמן), *καρρα* (A) *καρυα* (L), *καρπούς* (58), *καρδα*, &c., &c. $\mathfrak{G}^{B}$ explains Jos. § 78 *τοῖς τε Σιδωνίοις ἡδὺ καὶ κοῦφον ἦν*, &c., and $\mathfrak{L}$ *cum gaudio et dederunt carra* (cf. A.V.). The grant in question is referred to only in the decree of *Darius* (iv. 48, cf. N ii. 8, Artaxerxes). Jos. here and in *v.* 71 characteristically combines Cyrus and Darius on the lines of iv. 57 (D. commands what had been commanded by C.). But, apart from other questions, was Cyrus in a position to make this grant (Ryle, 43)?
56. A new paragraph, note the order Zer. and Jeshua (contrast *v.* 48), and the parentage (see v. 68 and vi. 2).
second year, $\mathfrak{G}^{L}$ (which is often corrected after MT) and $\mathfrak{L}^{C}$ add 'of Darius' (but E$\mathfrak{G}^{L}$ *τῆς ἐλεύσεως αὐτῶν εἰς τὸν οἶκον . . .*) in agreement with Haggai and Zechariah; see *Introd.* p. 16 (foot). For the *second month* cf. 1 Kings vi. 1.
the priests the Levites, $\mathfrak{G}^{L}$ inserts *and* with MT, cf. *v.* 63.
58. For the age-limit of the Levites, cf. the secondary passages 1 Chron. xxiii. 24, 27; 2 Chron. xxxi. 17–19. The reference to the oversight of the works presupposes the statement in *v.* 57 which is wanting in MT. E *v.* 9 is very confused and the names of the Levites are severed; *E* has doublets, and Jos. § 79 points to the reading 'Kadmiel the brother of Judah (= Hodaviah, E ii. 40) the son of Amminadab'; see Bayer, 64 seq. Meyer observes that the Levites of Henadad (wanting in the preceding register) apparently were not of exilic origin; see on *v.* 26.

of the Lord. Then stood up Jesus, and his sons
and brethren, and Kadmiel his brother, and the
sons of Jesus, Emadabun, and the sons of Joda
the son of Iliadun, and their sons and brethren,
all the Levites, with one accord setters forward
of the business, labouring to advance the works
in the house of God. So the builders builded
59 the temple of the Lord. And the priests stood
arrayed in their vestments with musical instruments and trumpets, and the Levites the sons
60 of Asaph with their cymbals, singing songs of
thanksgiving, and praising the Lord, after the
61 order of David king of Israel. And they sang
aloud, praising the Lord in songs of thanksgiving, because his goodness and his glory are
62 for ever in all Israel. And all the people
sounded trumpets, and shouted with a loud
voice, singing songs of thanksgiving unto the
Lord for the rearing up of the house of the
63 Lord. Also of the priests the Levites, and of
the heads of their families, the ancients who
had seen the former house came to the building
of this with lamentation and great weeping.
64 But many with trumpets and joy *shouted* with
65 loud voice, insomuch that the people heard not
the trumpets for the weeping of the people: for
the multitude sounded marvellously, so that it
was heard afar off.

66 Wherefore when the enemies of the tribe of
Judah and Benjamin heard it, they came to
know what that noise of trumpets should mean.
67 And they perceived that they that were of the
captivity did build the temple unto the Lord,
68 the God of Israel. So they went to Zorobabel
and Jesus, and to the chief men of the families,
and said unto them, We will build together
69 with you. For we likewise, as ye, do obey
your Lord, and do sacrifice unto him from the

sight of the work of the house of the Lord. Then 9
stood Jeshua with his sons and his brethren,
Kadmiel and his sons, the sons of Judah, together, to have the oversight of the workmen in
the house of God: the sons of Henadad, with
their sons and their brethren the Levites.

And 10
when the builders laid the foundation of the
temple of the Lord, they set the priests in their
apparel with trumpets, and the Levites the sons
of Asaph with cymbals, to praise the Lord, after
the order of David king of Israel.

And they 11
sang one to another in praising and giving thanks
unto the Lord, *saying*, For he is good, for his
mercy *endureth* for ever toward Israel. And all
the people shouted with a great shout, when they
praised the Lord, because the foundation of the
house of the Lord was laid.

But many of the 12
priests and Levites and heads of fathers' *houses*,
the old men that had seen the first house, when
the foundation of this house was laid before their
eyes, wept with a loud voice; and many shouted
aloud for joy: so that the people could not dis- 13
cern the noise of the shout of joy from the noise
of the weeping of the people: for the people
shouted with a loud shout, and the noise was
heard afar off.

Now when the adversaries of Judah and 4 1
Benjamin heard that the children of the captivity builded a temple unto the Lord, the God
of Israel;

then they drew near to Zerubbabel, 2
and to the heads of fathers' *houses*, and said
unto them, Let us build with you: for we seek
your God, as ye do; and we do sacrifice unto
him since the days of Esar-haddon king of

59. **stood**, so 𝔊 and some MSS. of the MT.

61. For the refrain see 2 Chron. v. 13, and especially Jer. xxxiii. 10 seq., a prophecy of the repopulating of the desert land (cf. *v.* 7 seq.), which is followed by the promise of the ideal king (*vv.* 14–18).

62. **sounded, shouted**, apparently doublets of ויריעו; cf. *v.* 64 seq.

63. **came** (i. e. באים), but MT *many* (רבים) is wanting.

the former house . . ., E R.V. mg. *the first house standing on its foundation, when this house was before their eyes*; cf. Hagg. ii. 3 (Darius). For the mingling of joy and sorrow cf. *E* ix. 50–4, and for the last words of *v.* 65, cf. Neh. xii. 43.

The Samaritan opposition. v. 66–73 = E iv. 1–5, 24; cf. Jos. xi. 4 3–4, §§ 84–8. The result of the opposition indicates that there could have been no large return of exiles fortified with the decree of a generous king. Jos. (xi. 2 1), and many modern scholars attempt to explain the success of the opponents, but the Sachau-papyri from Elephantine prove that, whatever may have been the case with Cyrus, Cambyses was ready to assist the Jews. Moreover, Haggai and Zechariah do not refer to any persisting opposition of the kind here implied, and, according to the former, when the Temple was ultimately taken in hand in the reign of Darius, not external history, but the desire to remove the distress caused by the failure of the rains was the main factor. The term 'enemies' (*v.* 66) is applied prospectively (Reuss), and, as Ewald (103 n. 4) remarks, 'this severe designation only belongs to the later period in which the mutual hostility of the neighbours on either side had quite broken out.' In fact the situation in 66 seqq. has many untrustworthy features (so even Meyer, 119 seqq., 124 seqq.; Cornill, *Introd.* 252), and the proposal of Rothstein (15, 20) to ascribe 47–55 and 56–73 *a* to the reigns of Cyrus and Darius respectively, though insufficient in itself, illustrates the difficulties. Indeed, all the indications point to an initial absence of Samaritan hostility (see Davies, 81), and there are some striking resemblances between the details here and in N ii., iv., vi., the relation between *v.* 68 seq. and N ii. 20 being especially interesting. See *Introd.* § 5 *a*, *b*, *e* (end).

days of Asbasareth the king of the Assyrians,
70 who brought us hither. Then Zorobabel and
Jesus and the chief men of the families of Israel
said unto them, It is not for you to build the
71 house unto the Lord our God. We ourselves
alone will build unto the Lord of Israel, according as Cyrus the king of the Persians hath
72 commanded us. But the heathen of the land
lying heavy upon the inhabitants of Judæa, and
holding them strait, hindered their building;
73 and by their secret plots, and popular persuasions
and commotions, they hindered the finishing of
the building all the time that king Cyrus lived:

so they were hindered from building for the
space of two years, until the reign of Darius.

6 1 Now in the second year of the reign of Darius,
Aggæus and Zacharias the son of Addo, the

Assyria, which brought us up hither.
But Zerub- 3
babel, and Jeshua, and the rest of the heads of
fathers' *houses* of Israel, said unto them, Ye have
nothing to do with us to build an house unto our
God; but we ourselves together will build unto
the Lord, the God of Israel, as king Cyrus the
king of Persia hath commanded us. Then the 4
people of the land weakened the hands of
the people of Judah, and troubled them in
building, and hired counsellors against them, 5
to frustrate their purpose, all the days of Cyrus
king of Persia, even until the reign of Darius
king of Persia.
Then ceased the work of the 24
house of God which is at Jerusalem; and it
ceased unto the second year of the reign of
Darius king of Persia.
Now the prophets, Haggai the prophet, and 5 1
Zechariah the son of Iddo, prophesied unto the

69. **Asbasareth** (𝔊^A), mg. *Asbacaphath* (B and partly 𝔖), but L αχορδαν; see Torrey, 169 n. Jos. has Shalmaneser (cf. E iv. 10 𝔊^L and Tobit i.); he ascribes the origin of the Samaritans to Cutha and Media (§ 85, cf. § 19), and, in his version of *v.* 71 (where Cyrus and Darius are associated), allows them and other peoples to come to Jerusalem for worship (similarly xviii. **2** 2).

70. **for you**, mg. *for us and you* (𝔊^A, 𝔖).

71. **alone**; E *together*, which would be more appropriate in E iv. 2. For the spirit of the reply, cf. Neh. ii. 20 and see 2 Chron. xiii. 5–12, xxv. 7, and 2 Kings xvii. 7–41, xviii. 12.

72 seq. **lying heavy**, ἐπικοιμώμενα (BA), ἐπικοινωνοῦντα (L), *gentes autem terrae quae commixtae erant* (𝔏), 'that were set over them' (𝔖). Fr. conj. ἐπικείμενα.

holding them strait (πολιορκοῦντες), mg. *besieging them.*

by their secret plots, &c., mg. *leading the people astray in counsel and raising commotions*: καὶ βουλὰς (ἐπιβουλάς, A) καὶ δημαγωγοῦντες (-ας, B^ab; δημαγωγίας, AL) καὶ συστάσεις (ἐπιστάσεις, L) ποιούμενοι. See further, Moulton, *ZATW*, xx. 1 seq. The language (E v. 4 seq.) implies that the Jews were slandered at the Persian court (Ryle, Bertholet); the whole situation is illustrated by Neh. ii. 19 seq., iv., vi.

73. **for the space of two years**; the MT is correctly reproduced in *E* ii. 30; see *Introd.* p. 17 *c.* Jos. (§ 89), who has filled in the gap between *E* ii. 15 and 16 (§ 19) and consistently placed *E* v. in the reign of Darius (who carries out the wish of Cyrus), refers to the new opposition (as in the days of Cyrus and Cambyses), ignores the actual cessation and the fresh 'beginning' (*E* vi. 2), and passes on to the visit of Tattenai.

The rebuilding and completion of the Temple in the reign of Darius. vi.–vii. = E v.–vi., cf. Jos. xi. **4** 1–8, whose treatment of the material is highly instructive. (*a*) In MT the narrative, apart from E vi. 19–22, is, like E iv. 8–24, in Aramaic, and the dialect, though in close agreement with Eg.-Aram.-papyri of the fifth cent., is certainly later; see Bevan, *Daniel*, 34; T. Nöldeke, *Ency. Brit.* xxiv. 624; A. Kamphausen, ib. 1010 n. 1; Driver, *Lit.* 504, 515; Torrey, 161 seqq. The excerpts show some traces of Jewish colouring and of compilation and adjustment (see *E* vi. 8, 18, 23, 26, 33), and the whole concludes with an account, in the chronicler's style, of the dedication of the Temple. To what extent reshaping and revision have been effected is of course uncertain (see Torrey, 142 seqq.). *E* is especially noteworthy for its doublets (vi. 5, 10, 12, 15, 28, see further Marq. 44 seq.), perplexing paraphrases (e.g. vi. 19 seq., 26 seqq.), and for a few interesting material variations (see vi. 4, 18, 26 seq., 32, vii. 1 seq., 5 seq., 9).

(*b*) The narrative represents a zealous satrap anxious to ascertain whether the Jews had really received permission from Cyrus to rebuild the temple. His procedure is quite formal (cf. E iv. 8 seqq., contrast N. iv., vi.), and Darius, having found the 'memorandum' of Cyrus, not only confirms that king's permission, but goes further in his benevolence. Such a representation agrees with the traditional friendliness of Darius (see also vi. 26), but utterly conflicts with his own decree already given in *E* iv. The wording does not suggest that the Jews, whether before or after the intervention of Darius, were rewarded for any act of loyalty, e.g. abstinence from the intrigues at his succession. Nor does it point to any serious Samaritan hostility (see Kosters, *Th. T.* xxxi. 545 seq.; Meyer, 124; Sellin, *Ser.* 88). In thus agreeing with Hag. and Zech. it also does not state that the Jewish builders were exiles from Babylon (Kosters, 26; contrast the explicit E iv. 12; see on *E* vi. 5, 18). Both sources agree, moreover, in dating the founding of the Temple in the second year of Darius (see on vi. 1 seq.), and this narrative, implying that the building was in course of erection, might be taken to refer to a slightly later date.

(*c*) It throws another light upon the decree of Cyrus (vi. 17–20, 24–26, see ii. 1 seqq.). It confirms the return of the vessels (contrast iv. 44, 57), but gives prominence to Sheshbazzar (cf. E i.) and not to Zerubbabel (E iii., see on *E* vi. 18 seq.). These two are identified by harmonists (see 18, 27, 29), but to the latter alone do the independent prophecies ascribe the commencement and completion of the Temple (see *Introd.* § 4, II). In addition to this, while vi. 1 seq. relate the 'beginning' by Zer. and Jeshua, the context combines the representation of *continuous* operations since the return of Sheshbazzar (E v. 16) with a complete cessation (iv. 24) which is attributed to the decree of a Persian king. See further *Introd.* § 6. On the text, see also Torrey, 189 seqq., 201 seqq.

1 seq. The opening verses agree with Hag. in the date of the beginning of the building, yet not 'before a stone was laid upon a stone' (Hag. ii. 15), but after a complete cessation (E iv. 24); contrast, however, *v.* 20 below.

Addo, mg. *Eddin* (𝔊^B). A *priest* Zechariah son of Iddo is mentioned in the time of Joiakim the son of Jeshua

prophets, prophesied unto the Jews in Jewry
and Jerusalem; in the name of the Lord, the
2 God of Israel, *prophesied they* unto them. Then
stood up Zorobabel the son of Salathiel, and
Jesus the son of Josedek, and began to build
the house of the Lord at Jerusalem, the prophets
of the Lord being with them, *and* helping them.
3 At the same time came unto them Sisinnes the
governor of Syria and Phœnicia, with Sathrabuzanes and his companions, and said unto them,
4 By whose appointment do ye build this house
and this roof, and perform all the other things?
and who are the builders that perform these
things?
5 Nevertheless the elders of the Jews
obtained favour, because the Lord had visited
6 the captivity; and they were not hindered from
building, until such time as communication was
made unto Darius concerning them, and his
answer signified.
7 The copy of the letter which Sisinnes, governor
of Syria and Phœnicia, and Sathrabuzanes, with
their companions, the rulers in Syria and Phœnicia,
wrote and sent unto Darius;
8 To king Darius,
greeting: Let all things be known unto our lord
the king, that being come into the country of
Judæa, and entered into the city of Jerusalem,
we found in the city of Jerusalem the elders of
9 the Jews that were of the captivity building a
house unto the Lord, great *and* new, of hewn
10 and costly stones, with timber laid in the walls.
And those works are done with great speed, and
the work goeth on prosperously in their hands,
and with all glory and diligence is it accom-

Jews that were in Judah and Jerusalem; in the
name of the God of Israel *prophesied they* unto
them. Then rose up Zerubbabel the son of 2
Shealtiel, and Jeshua the son of Jozadak, and
began to build the house of God which is at
Jerusalem; and with them were the prophets of
God, helping them.
At the same time came to 3
them Tattenai, the governor beyond the river,
and Shethar-bozenai, and their companions, and
said thus unto them, Who gave you a decree to
build this house, and to finish this wall?
Then 4
spake we unto them after this manner, What are
the names of the men that make this building?
But the eye of their God was upon the elders of 5
the Jews, and they did not make them cease, till
the matter should come to Darius, and then
answer should be returned by letter concerning it.

The copy of the letter that Tattenai, the 6
governor beyond the river, and Shethar-bozenai,
and his companions the Apharsachites, which
were beyond the river, sent unto Darius the
king: they sent a letter unto him, wherein was 7
written thus; Unto Darius the king, all peace.
Be it known unto the king, that we went into 8
the province of Judah,
to the house of the great
God, which is builded with great stones, and
timber is laid in the walls, and this work goeth
on with diligence and prospereth in their hands.

(N. xii. 16); but the family of Iddo, though among the priests in N. xii. 4, is not named in the great list (E ii., &c.). Did the four families in E ii. 36–9 suddenly expand into the twenty-two in Neh. xii. 1–7 or the twenty-four in 1 Chron. xxiv., or were the latter incorporated into four great classes? On the traditional view some explanation is necessary.

unto them (ἐπ' αὐτούς), E, R.V. mg. *which was upon them*, cf. Jer. xv. 16.

3. On the identification of the names (Uštani, a prefect of Transpotamia temp. Darius, or Taddanu a Bab. name; and Mithrabuzanes, or perhaps Satibarzanes), see the comment. and Torrey, 172. *E*'s Sisinnes, though probably incorrect, is a thoroughly authentic name and typical of the cleverness of the translator.

his (E *their*) **companions.** On the variation in the possessive pronoun, see Guthe, *SBOT*.

4. **roof,** E wall, אֻשַּׁרְנָא (𝔊 χορηγία, 'charges' in *E* iv. 54 seq.). The readings represent (so Torrey, 175 seq.) אגרא (*iggarā* 'roof', *agrā* 'pay'), cf. אגורא 'shrine, temple', in the Aram. papyri from Egypt (Sayce and Cowley, E 14 J 6, Sachau I, 6, &c.). אשרנא, also in Sachau I, 11, denotes some part of a temple, whether fore-court (Sach.), colonnade (Torrey), or the temple as a whole (see Haupt, Delitzsch, *SBOT*, 34, 63, Nikel 130 n. 2, Jampel i. 494). Jos. (§ 89) finds a reference to the porticoes (στοαί, see on vii. 9) and the walls of the city. Was אגרא altered in MT because of its heathen associations? Cf. its use in the Targums of a heathen altar, and the Bab. *ekur*; cf. also the distinction observed in MT between כֹּהֵן and כֹּמֶר.

and who. E 'then spake we' (𝔊 𝔖 'then spake they'), an actual quotation from the report, cf. ib. 9 seq.

5. **the captivity** (cf. E𝔊), and see *vv.* 8, 27 seq.; based upon a doublet שָׂבֵי 'elders [of]' and שְׁבִי 'captivity'.

7. 𝔊 'The copy of the letter which he (𝔊[L] 'they') wrote unto D. and sent: Sis., the governor, &c., to king Darius greeting' (cf. 𝔏).

7 seq. **Let all things . . .** 𝔏[c] combines this with the reading of E.

our lord the king, rightly, cf. 21 seq., ii. 17 seq.

The reference to the arrival at Jerusalem and the discovery is quite appropriate (Marq., 46 seq.); MT has apparently condensed.

9. **new,** apparently based upon *v.* 25, where it represents MT חדת an error for חד 'one'; the doublet combines both corrigendum and correctum (see Berth. xvi. seq., 24).

11 plished. Then asked we these elders, saying,
By whose commandment build ye this house,
12 and lay the foundations of these works? Therefore, to the intent that we might give knowledge
unto thee by writing who were the chief doers,
we questioned them, and we required of them
13 the names in writing of their principal men. So
they gave us this answer, We are the servants of
14 the Lord which made heaven and earth. And
as for this house, it was builded many years ago
by a king of Israel great and strong, and was
15 finished. But when our fathers sinned against
the Lord of Israel which is in heaven, and provoked him unto wrath, he gave them over into
the hands of Nabuchodonosor king of Babylon,
16 king of the Chaldeans; and they pulled down
the house, and burned it, and carried away the
17 people captives unto Babylon. But in the first
year that Cyrus reigned over the country of
Babylon, king Cyrus wrote to build up this
18 house. And the holy vessels of gold and of
silver, that Nabuchodonosor had carried away
out of the house at Jerusalem, and had set up in
his own temple, those Cyrus the king brought
forth again out of the temple in Babylonia, and
they were delivered to Zorobabel and to Sanabassarus the governor,
19 with commandment that
he should carry away all these vessels, and put
them in the temple at Jerusalem; and that the
temple of the Lord should be built in its place.
20 Then Sanabassarus, being come hither, laid the
foundations of the house of the Lord which is in
Jerusalem; and from that time to this being still
a-building, it is not yet fully ended.
21 Now there-
fore, if it seem good, O king, let search be made
among the royal archives of our lord the king
22 that are in Babylon: and if it be found that the
building of the house of the Lord which is in
Jerusalem hath been done with the consent of
king Cyrus, and it seem good unto our lord the
king, let him signify unto us thereof.
23 Then commanded king Darius to seek among
the archives that were laid up at Babylon:
and

Then asked we those elders, and said unto them 9
thus, Who gave you a decree to build this house,
and to finish this wall? We asked them their 10
names also, to certify thee, that we might write
the names of the men that were at the head of
them.
And thus they returned us answer, say- 11
ing, We are the servants of the God of heaven
and earth, and build the house that was builded
these many years ago, which a great king of
Israel builded and finished.
But after that our 12
fathers had provoked the God of heaven unto
wrath, he gave them into the hand of Nebuchadnezzar king of Babylon, the Chaldean, who
destroyed this house, and carried the people away
into Babylon.
But in the first year of Cyrus 13
king of Babylon, Cyrus the king made a decree to
build this house of God.
And the gold and 14
silver vessels also of the house of God, which
Nebuchadnezzar took out of the temple that
was in Jerusalem, and brought them into the
temple of Babylon, those did Cyrus the king
take out of the temple of Babylon, and they
were delivered unto one whose name was Sheshbazzar, whom he had made governor; and he 15
said unto him, Take these vessels, go, put them
in the temple that is in Jerusalem, and let the
house of God be builded in its place.
Then 16
came the same Sheshbazzar, and laid the foundations of the house of God which is in Jerusalem:
and since that time even until now hath it been
in building, and yet it is not completed. Now 17
therefore, if it seem good to the king, let there be
search made in the king's treasure house, which
is there at Babylon, whether it be so, that
a decree was made of Cyrus the king to build
this house of God at Jerusalem, and let the king
send his pleasure to us concerning this matter.

Ezra 6

Then Darius the king made a decree, and 1
search was made in the house of the archives,
where the treasures were laid up in Babylon.
And there was found at Achmetha, in the palace 2

13. **the Lord which made** (τοῦ κτίσαντος), cf. 2 Chron. ii. 12 (ἐποίησεν) and the quotation in Eupolemos (ἔκτισεν), second cent. B.C. (Swete, *Introd.* 370; Torrey, 82); also Jer. x. 11 and the late Gen. xiv. 19 R.V. mg.

15. **Lord . . . heaven.** A conflate reading.

Note that even the Aram. source presents the later and inaccurate form of the name Nebuchadrezzar.

18. **his own temple**, cf. ii. 10.

and to Sanabassarus (mg. *Sabanassarus*). Some MSS. omit *and*; this and the sequel ('that *he* should carry') indicate that the attempt has been made to identify Sheshbazzar (E i.) with the more prominent Zerubbabel (Nikel, 42 n. 1, 45). Note the introduction of the latter in *vv.* 27, 29.

E 'whom he had made' . . ., but $\mathfrak{G}^{BA}$ 'to the treasurer . . . who was over the treasury'. This must refer not to Shesh., but to Mithredath (E i. 8) whom Jos. combines with Zer. here (§ 92, cf. ib. xi. 3 §§ 11, 14), although in his version of *E* 20, 26, he mentions only Shesh. The allusion to the treasury may be supported by E v. 17, vi. 1. That the texts are not in their original form is obvious.

19. **all these vessels**, mg. *the same* ($\mathfrak{G}^{A}$).

21. **of our lord** (Κυρίου), $\mathfrak{G}^{L}$ $\mathfrak{S}$, curiously 'of Cyrus' (so A.V.).

so at Ecbatana the palace, which is in the
country of Media, there was found a roll where-
24 in these things were recorded. In the first
year of the reign of Cyrus king Cyrus commanded to build up the house of the Lord
which is in Jerusalem, where they do sacrifice
25 with continual fire: whose height shall be sixty
cubits, and the breadth sixty cubits,
with three
rows of hewn stones, and one row of new wood
of that country; and the expenses thereof to
26 be given out of the house of king Cyrus: and
that the holy vessels of the house of the Lord,
both of gold and silver, that Nabuchodonosor
took out of the house at Jerusalem, and carried
away to Babylon, should be restored to the
house at Jerusalem, and be set in the place
where they were before.
27 And also he com-
manded that Sisinnes the governor of Syria
and Phœnicia, and Sathrabuzanes, and their
companions, and those which were appointed
rulers in Syria and Phœnicia, should be careful
not to meddle with the place, but suffer Zorobabel, the servant of the Lord, and governor of
Judæa, and the elders of the Jews, to build that
28 house of the Lord in its place. And I also do
command to have it built up whole again; and
that they look diligently to help those that be
of the captivity of Judæa, till the house of the
29 Lord be finished: and that out of the tribute of
Cœlesyria and Phœnicia a portion be carefully
given these men for the sacrifices of the Lord,
that is, to Zorobabel the governor, for bullocks,
30 and rams, and lambs; and also corn, salt, wine,
and oil, and that continually every year without
further question, according as the priests that
be in Jerusalem shall signify to be daily spent:

that is in the province of Media, a roll, and
therein was thus written for a record.
In the 3
first year of Cyrus the king, Cyrus the king
made a decree; Concerning the house of God at
Jerusalem, let the house be builded, the place
where they offer sacrifices, and let the foundations thereof be strongly laid; the height thereof
threescore cubits, and the breadth thereof threescore cubits; with three rows of great stones, 4
and a row of new timber: and let the expenses
be given out of the king's house:
and also let 5
the gold and silver vessels of the house of God,
which Nebuchadnezzar took forth out of the
temple which is at Jerusalem, and brought unto
Babylon, be restored, and brought again unto the
temple which is at Jerusalem, every one to its
place, and thou shalt put them in the house of
God. Now therefore, Tattenai, governor beyond 6
the river, Shethar-bozenai, and your companions
the Apharsachites, which are beyond the river,
be ye far from thence:
let the work of this house 7
of God alone; let the governor of the Jews and
the elders of the Jews build this house of God in
its place. Moreover I make a decree what ye 8
shall do to these elders of the Jews for the building of this house of God:
that of the king's
goods, even of the tribute beyond the river,
expenses be given with all diligence unto these
men, that they be not hindered. And that 9
which they have need of, both young bullocks,
and rams, and lambs, for burnt offerings to the
God of heaven, wheat, salt, wine, and oil,
according to the word of the priests which are

23. **roll** (𝔊[A], Jos.), mg. *place* (𝔊[BL] 𝔏 𝔖), a confusion of τόμος and τόπος. The 'memorandum' (דכרון) recalls the זכרן (Sach. Pap. III) relating to the rebuilding of the Jewish sanctuary at Elephantine. The fact that the roll was sought for at Babylon but found at Ecbatana points to some condensation in the narrative.

24. **continual fire.** A slight change of the MT supported by most scholars.

25. Jos. (§ 99) applies these measurements to the altar, although in xi. 1 3 (see below on *v.* 26) he rightly refers them to the Temple.

one row of new wood (similarly Jos.) **of that country,** 'one' and 'new' are doublets, (see *v.* 9), and 'country' seems to be some confusion of the Heb. ארץ (land) and אֶרֶז (cedar), so Jahn; or of the Aram. ארע (land) and אע (wood), so Marq. For the details see 1 Kings vi. 36, vii. 12.

26. Note the changes of person and number in MT (E 6 has *their* companions). The compiler turns the decree of Cyrus into a command to Shesh. (*and thou shalt place*), and then passes on to the commands of Darius (see Meyer, 47); a clear case of compilation. *E*, however, takes E 6 to belong to the old decree, and Jos. actually attributes the whole (to the end of *v.* 33) to Cyrus, which Darius (as in *v.* 34) simply endorses. Hence, in his history of Cyrus, Jos. (xi. 1 3) gives a lengthy decree on these lines in the form of a letter to Tattenai and Shethar-bozenai, an interesting and instructive example of history-making.

27. **the servant of the Lord.** Jos. (§ 101) 'the servants of God (cf. *v.* 13), the Jews and their leaders'. Here and in *v.* 29 Zer. appears to be due to later insertion (Jos. omits); perhaps the translator misunderstood עבידת ('work') in the MT, where 𝔊[B] om. 'the governor (𝔊[AL] governors, or leaders) of the Jews and'. In E v. 5, 9, vi. 8, 14 only the 'elders of the Jews' are mentioned; see Guthe, *SBOT.*

28. **till . . . finished,** a natural limitation, cf. iv. 51, and the stipulation in N ii. 6; with MT cf. the free hand given to Ezra (E vii.).

29. **of the Lord . . . ,** cf. 𝔖; 𝔊 τῷ κυρίῳ (𝔊[L] + τοῦ, cf. Dan. vi. 26, Bel and Dragon, 41) Ζορ. ἐπάρχῳ (𝔊[L] om.).

30. **question,** a misunderstanding (as in E𝔊) of שלו, as though from שאל.

31 that drink offerings may be made to the Most
High God for the king and for his children, and
that they may pray for their lives.
32 And that
commandment be given that whosoever shall
transgress, yea, or neglect anything *herein*
written, out of his own *house* shall a tree be
taken, and he thereon be hanged, and all his
33 goods seized for the king. The Lord therefore,
whose name is there called upon, utterly destroy
every king and nation, that shall stretch out his
hand to hinder or endamage that house of the
34 Lord in Jerusalem. I Darius the king have
ordained that according unto these things it be
done with diligence.
7 1 Then Sisinnes the governor of Cœlesyria and
Phœnicia, and Sathrabuzanes, with their companions, following the commandments of king
2 Darius, did very carefully oversee the holy works,
assisting the elders of the Jews and rulers of the
3 temple. And so the holy works prospered, while
Aggæus and Zacharias the prophets prophesied.

4 And they finished these things by the commandment of the Lord, the God of Israel, and with the
consent of Cyrus, Darius, and Artaxerxes, kings
5 of the Persians. *And thus* was the house finished
by the three and twentieth day of the month
6 Adar, in the sixth year of king Darius. And the
children of Israel, the priests, and the Levites,
and the other that were of the captivity, that were
added *unto them*, did according to the things
7 *written* in the book of Moses. And to the dedication of the temple of the Lord they offered a
hundred bullocks, two hundred rams, four hun-

at Jerusalem, let it be given them day by
day without fail: that they may offer sacri- 10
fices of sweet savour unto the God of heaven,
and pray for the life of the king, and of his sons.
Also I have made a decree, that whosoever 11
shall alter this word, let a beam be pulled
out from his house, and let him be lifted up
and fastened thereon; and let his house be
made a dunghill for this:
and the God that 12
hath caused his name to dwell there overthrow
all kings and peoples, that shall put forth their
hand to alter *the same*, to destroy this house of
God which is at Jerusalem. I Darius have
made a decree; let it be done with all diligence.
Then Tattenai, the governor beyond the river, 13
Shethar-bozenai, and their companions, because
that Darius the king had sent, did accordingly
with all diligence.
And the elders of the Jews 14
builded and prospered, through the prophesying
of Haggai the prophet and Zechariah the son of
Iddo. And they builded and finished it, according to the commandment of the God of Israel,
and according to the decree of Cyrus, and Darius,
and Artaxerxes king of Persia. And this house 15
was finished on the third day of the month Adar,
which was in the sixth year of the reign of
Darius the king.

And the children of Israel, the 16
priests and the Levites, and the rest of the children of the captivity, kept the dedication of this
house of God with joy.
And they offered 17
at the dedication of this house of God an
hundred bullocks, two hundred rams, four hun-

31. For the praying cf. Baruch i. 10 seq., 1 Macc. vii. 33, Sach. Pap. I, 25 seq. $\mathfrak{G}^{L}$ reads *θυσίαι κ. σπονδαί* and adds *ἐνδελεχῶς* at end of verse.

32. **written**, mg. *afore spoken or written* ($\mathfrak{G}^{A}$).

goods seized, similarly Jos.; cf. Dan. ii. 5, iii. 29, 𝔊. This interpretation of MT נולו (נולי) 'dunghill' is supported by Jahn (55) and by Torrey (85, who compares Ar. *nāla* 'take, obtain'). Bayer, 30, emends.

33. **therefore**, MT *for this*, end of *v*. 11.

whose name . . ., the Jewish colouring in this verse (cf. Deut. xii. 11, xiv. 23) is commonly admitted (Meyer, 51, Holzhey, 25, &c.).

VII. 1 seq. The more active intervention of the strangers (*ἐπεστάτουν . . . ἐπιμελέστερον*), though in harmony with viii. 67 (E viii. 36), is less emphatic in MT '. . . their companions did according to the decree which . . . sent', cf. above, 27 seq., with E vi. 7.

2. **rulers of the temple** (*ἱεροστάταις*; Jos. 'princes of the Sanhedrin'), cf. i. 8 (2 Chron. xxxv. 8), and the addition in E𝔊 'and the Levites'.

4. **consent** (A.V. mg. *the decree, γνώμη*) . . . **Artaxerxes** (Jos. omits Art., $\mathfrak{G}^{L}$ transposes with Darius), **kings** ($\mathfrak{G}^{BL}$ and MT *king*) . . . The name can hardly be explained even as a careless interpolation; the reading *king* suggests that only one name was originally written; see *Introd.* § 5 (*e*).

$\mathfrak{G}^{A}$, 𝔖, 𝔏 add 'until (by) the sixth year of Darius king of the Persians'.

5. **the house**, mg. *the holy house* ($\mathfrak{G}^{A}$).

Jos. confirms the 23rd day (adopted by Bertholet, Torrey, 195, but treated by Bayer, 83, as a misreading, עשרים for עד יום), but reads the *ninth* year of Darius; in *C. Apion.* i. 21 he states that the foundations of the Temple were laid in the second year of Cyrus and it was finished again in the *second* year of Darius.

6. **that were added**, explained by *v*. 13, although this act of separation is not recorded, contrast N ix. 2, xiii. 3 (see below, p. 47).

book of Moses, cf. v. 49, and especially N. viii. 1, x. 29, xiii. 1.

8 dred lambs; *and* twelve he-goats for the sin of all
Israel, according to the number of the twelve
9 princes of the tribes of Israel. The priests also
and the Levites stood arrayed in their vestments,
according to their kindreds, for the services of the
Lord, the God of Israel, according to the book of
Moses: and the porters at every gate.
10 And the children of Israel that came out of
the captivity held the passover the fourteenth
day of the first month, when the priests and the
11 Levites were sanctified together, and all they that
were of the captivity; for they were sanctified.
12 For the Levites were all sanctified together, and
they offered the passover for all them of the captivity, and for their brethren the priests, and for
13 themselves. And the children of Israel that came
out of the captivity did eat, even all they that
had separated themselves from the abominations
of the heathen of the land, and sought the Lord.

14 And they kept the feast of unleavened bread
15 seven days, making merry before the Lord, for
that he had turned the counsel of the king of
Assyria toward them, to strengthen their hands
in the works of the Lord, the God of Israel.

8 1 And after these things, when Artaxerxes the
king of the Persians reigned, came Esdras the

dred lambs; and for a sin offering for all Israel,
twelve he-goats, according to the number of the
tribes of Israel. And they set the priests in 18
their divisions, and the Levites in their courses,
for the service of God, which is at Jerusalem; as
it is written in the book of Moses.

And the children of the captivity kept the 19
passover upon the fourteenth *day* of the first
month. For the priests and the Levites had 20
purified themselves together; all of them were
pure: and they killed the passover for all the
children of the captivity, and for their brethren
the priests, and for themselves.

And the chil- 21
dren of Israel, which were come again out of the
captivity, and all such as had separated themselves unto them from the filthiness of the
heathen of the land, to seek the Lord, the God
of Israel, did eat, and kept the feast of unleavened 22
bread seven days with joy: for the Lord had
made them joyful, and had turned the heart of
the king of Assyria unto them, to strengthen
their hands in the work of the house of God, the
God of Israel.

Now after these things, in the reign of Artax- 7 1
erxes king of Persia, Ezra the son of Seraiah, the

8. **princes**, mg. *twelve tribes of Israel* (𝔊ᴸ).

9. Cf. v. 59. For the *porters* (also in Jos.), cf. i. 16, and 2 Chron. viii. 14, xxiii. 18 seq.; Jos. adds that the Jews also built the cloisters (στοάς) of the inner temple. See vi. 4 above.

10. From this verse onwards the MT, with the exception of E vii. 12-26, is in Hebrew. With this account of the celebration of the Passover, cf. 2 Chron. xxx. (after the purification of the Temple by Hezekiah), xxxv. = *E* 1 (after Josiah's reforms); see also p. 58.

of Israel, lit. 'of Israel, of those that were of the captivity.'

when the priests, several MSS. *because.*

11 seq. mg. *and they that were of the captivity were not all sanctified together: but the Levites were all sanctified together. And, &c.*; cf. 𝔊ᴸ 𝔏 𝔖, but not Jos. For the textual variants see *ZATW*, xx. 12 seq. Since the Levites perform the slaughtering there may be an anti-Aaronite bias, as also in 2 Chron. xxix. 34 (cf. perhaps xxx. 3, 15 17); see Kittel, *Chron.* 160.

13. **even**, wanting in 𝔊.

15. Jos. (§§ 111–13) after summing up with an account of the constitution, &c., appends (§§ 114–19) a new story of Samaritan enmity and of the intervention of Darius. The Jews send Zerubbabel and four nobles, including Ananias and Mordecai (see for the latter, v. 8 above) to complain that the Samaritans did not carry out the royal commands and were hostile. Darius accordingly writes to the eparchs and council (βουλή, cf. ii. 17), viz. to Taganas and Sambas (or Sambabas), the eparchs, and to Sadrakes and Bouēdōn (var. Bouēlōn, &c.), 'the rest of their fellow servants' (σύνδουλοι, cf. 𝔊 E v. seq. for 'companions'). On the conjectural origin of these corrupt names, see Marq. 52, 54 (Tag. from Tattenai, Sad. and Bou. from Shethar-bozenai).

The Work of Ezra. (*a*) The narratives are severed in the MT, which places E vii.–x. (*E* viii. 1–ix. 36) in the seventh year of Artaxerxes (458 B.C.), and N viii. seqq. (*E* ix. 37–55 + . . .) in the twentieth. They are of composite origin: note the introductory impersonal E vii. 1–10 (see Driver, *Lit.*, 548 seq.), the change from 'I' (vii. 27–ix.) to the impersonal form in viii. 35 seq., the use of 'I' (ix.), 'he' (x.), and 'we' (N ix. 38, x. 30). In spite of parallels (Torrey, 244 seq.), these changes seem to prove diversity of source. Various signs of revision and condensation are to be noticed in vii. (see *E* viii. 8–24), x. (Meyer, 96 n. 1), and elsewhere.

(*b*) Although N viii. seqq. interrupt the history of Neh., and both E and N are engaged in reorganizing religious conditions, the story of N ignores the work of E, and the story of E mentions N only somewhat incidentally (N viii. 9, x. 1). The two groups of narratives have different backgrounds. The E-story shows no trace of the desolation and misery which N sought to remedy. E is intent upon the Temple and the law, and comes to an apparently peaceful city, whereas N appears as a reformer of elementary civic, social, and religious conditions at a time when E was presumably in Jerusalem. The secular pioneer builds up and reconstructs; the priestly scribe gives, as it were, a finishing stroke in the way of important, though less initial, reforms. While N laments the ruin and distress, E recognizes the manifestation of God's favour, which the people had ill requited by their heathenish marriages. The former encounters suspicion, hostility, and treachery; the latter, armed with most remarkable powers, finds a people anxious to hear and obey the law, eager to remove the stain of the marriages, and ready to carry out measures which N, with characteristic impulsiveness, seems merely to initiate in N xiii. The whole situation in the E-story forbids

son of Azaraias, the son of Zechrias, the son of
2 Helkias, the son of Salem, the son of Sadduk,
the son of Ahitob,
the son of Amarias, the son
of Ozias, the son of Memeroth, the son of
Zaraias, the son of Savias, the son of Boccas,
the son of Abisue, the son of Phinees, the son
of Eleazar, the son of Aaron the chief priest.
3 This Esdras went up from Babylon, as being
a ready scribe in the law of Moses, that was
4 given by the God of Israel. And the king did
him honour: for he found grace in his sight in
all his requests.
5 There went up with him also
certain of the children of Israel, and of the priests,
and Levites, and holy singers, and porters, and
6 temple-servants, unto Jerusalem, in the seventh
year of the reign of Artaxerxes, in the fifth
month, this was the king's seventh year;
for they
went from Babylon on the new moon of the first
month, and came to Jerusalem, according to the
prosperous journey which the Lord gave them
7 for his sake. For Esdras had very great skill, so
that he omitted nothing of the law and commandments of the Lord, *but* taught all Israel the ordinances and judgements.

son of Azariah,
the son of Hilkiah, the son of 2
Shallum, the son of Zadok, the son of Ahitub,
the son of Amariah, the son of Azariah, the son 3
of Meraioth, the son of Zerahiah, the son of Uzzi, 4
the son of Bukki, the son of Abishua, the son of 5
Phinehas, the son of Eleazar, the son of Aaron
the chief priest:
this Ezra went up from Baby- 6
lon; and he was a ready scribe in the law of
Moses, which the Lord, the God of Israel, had
given: and the king granted him all his request,
according to the hand of the Lord his God upon
him. And there went up some of the children 7
of Israel, and of the priests, and the Levites, and
the singers, and the porters, and the Nethinim,
unto Jerusalem, in the seventh year of Artaxerxes the king. And he came to Jerusalem in 8
the fifth month, which was in the seventh year
of the king. For upon the first *day* of the first 9
month began he to go up from Babylon, and on
the first *day* of the fifth month came he to Jerusalem, according to the good hand of his God
upon him. For Ezra had set his heart to seek 10
the law of the Lord, and to do it, and to teach
in Israel statutes and judgements.

the identification of E's return with that in E iv. 12 (*E* ii. 18). The rebuilding mentioned in the latter is excluded in the E-story and ignored in N i.–vi., where there is neither any reference to an earlier attempt to rebuild nor any hint of such a return as that in E vii.–x.

(*c*) E vii.–x. are severed from E i.–vi. by nearly sixty years. A large body of exiles, 'children of the captivity' (iv. 1), had rejected the families of doubtful blood (ii. 59–63), and had been reinforced by those who had separated from the heathen (vi. 21). Jewish exclusivism had apparently been established. Now, however, E returns with a representative band (vii. 7), 'children of the captivity' (viii. 35), and, after an interval (the vague ix. 1), hears of the deplorable extent of intermarriage among the people of Israel, the 'holy seed' (ix. 2), 'the captivity' (ix. 4). The sin is admitted, and it is proposed to make a solemn covenant (x. 3). 'The children of the captivity' are summoned from their settlements under the penalty of excommunication from 'the congregation of the captivity' (x. 6–8). The area affected proves to be extremely restricted (x. 9). The congregation agrees to the separation (*vv.* 10–12). There is, however, an inquiry lasting three months, and as a veritable anti-climax we have an extremely small list of offenders (see on *E* ix. 21–36). Forthwith (so *E*), or apparently some twelve years later (so N viii.), E reads the law to the people, and 'all the congregation, those who had returned from captivity' (N viii. 17, cf. E vi. 21), celebrate the feast of Tabernacles. After a solemn confession of sin, the erring 'seed of Israel' separate from the heathen (ix. 1 seq.), and this epoch-making event, which (see E x. 1–12) might be expected after the prayer in E ix. 6 seqq., is followed by a second prayer on behalf of the backsliding people. Finally, there is a covenant (N ix. 38) signed by the congregation and all that separated themselves from the people of the land (x. 28). Whether we follow the tradition or any modern hypothesis, these data are extremely complicated (see Kosters, 67, 96 seqq., *Th. T.*, xxix, 554 seqq.). They point to a close literary connexion in the E-story, which makes it improbable that E vii.–x. should be severed, as in MT, from N viii. seqq. They reveal a serious literary intricacy which must be due to revision and reshaping, and they do not show at all clearly that the 'children of the captivity' who returned (E viii. 35) found a people constituted as E ii. 59–63, vi. 21, would imply. It is possible that the E-story (of independent origin, see *Introd.* p. 9 *d.*) has confused the accounts of the purification of the exiles who returned with E and the separation of the native Judaeans from the heathen, the two events which are kept more distinct in E i.–vi.

The return of Ezra, viii. 1–67 = E vii., viii., cf. Jos. xi. **5** 1–2 (who replaces Artaxerxes by Xerxes). In addition to the comm., see Torrey, 196 seqq., 205 seqq., 265 seqq.

2. **Azaraias** and **Zechrias** ($\mathfrak{G}^B$; 'Εζερίου A, 'Αζαραίου L) = Seraiah and Azariah. The former was contemporary with the fall of Jerusalem (1 Chron. vi. 14 seq.), but the genealogy would make him identical with the Seraiah in Neh. xi. 11 (|| 1 Chron. ix. 11, Azariah), priest at the renovation of the city.

$\mathfrak{G}^B$ omits the names Memeroth—Savias (Uzzi).

5. **temple-servants**, mg. *the Nethinim*, cf. i. 3, and for the sequence of the classes cf. the arrangement in v. 9 seqq.

6. The date of arrival (E 8) probably coincides with that of Nehemiah (departure in the first month, ii. 1; arrival at the beginning of the fifth, interval of three days, ii. 11; and, after fifty-two days, the completion of the walls on the 25th of the sixth month, vi. 15).

seventh year ($\mathfrak{G}^B$ 'second', cf. v. 6, vi. 1), the absence of a date in *v.* 1 is noticeable. On the chronological and other details in the verse see the comm.

for his sake, $\mathfrak{G}^B$ ἐπ' αὐτῷ, $\mathfrak{G}^A$ om., $\mathfrak{G}^L$ (*v.* 7) ἐπ' αὐτὸν γὰρ ὁ Ἔζδρας ἦν, ὃς . . .

7. **but taught**, so $\mathfrak{G}^A$ διδάξαι. For the variants see Moulton, *ZATW*, xx. 14.

8 Now the commission, which was written from
Artaxerxes the king, came to Esdras the priest
and reader of the law of the Lord, whereof
this that followeth is a copy;
9 King Artaxerxes
unto Esdras the priest and reader of the law of
10 the Lord, greeting: Having determined to deal
graciously, I have given order, that such of the
nation of the Jews, and of the priests and Levites, and of those within our realm, as are
willing and desirous, should go with thee unto
11 Jerusalem. As many therefore as have a mind
thereunto, let them depart with thee, as it hath
seemed good both to me and my seven friends
12 the counsellors; that they may look unto the
affairs of Judæa and Jerusalem, agreeably to that
13 which is in the law of the Lord, and carry the
gifts unto the Lord of Israel to Jerusalem, which
I and my friends have vowed;
and that all the
gold and silver that can be found in the country
14 of Babylonia for the Lord in Jerusalem, with that
also which is given of the people for the temple
of the Lord their God that is at Jerusalem, be
collected: even the gold and silver for bullocks,
rams, and lambs, and things thereunto apper-
15 taining; to the end that they may offer sacrifices
unto the Lord upon the altar of the Lord their
God, which is in Jerusalem.
16 And whatsoever
thou and thy brethren are minded to do with gold
and silver, that perform, according to the will of
17 thy God. And the holy vessels of the Lord,
which are given thee for the use of the temple of
thy God, which is in Jerusalem:
18 and whatsoever
thing else thou shalt remember for the use of the
temple of thy God, thou shalt give it out of the
19 king's treasury. And I king Artaxerxes have
also commanded the keepers of the treasures in
Syria and Phœnicia, that whatsoever Esdras the
priest and reader of the law of the Most High
God shall send for, they should give it him with
20 all diligence, to the sum of a hundred talents
of silver, likewise also of wheat even to a hundred measures, and a hundred firkins of wine,
and salt in abundance.

Now this is the copy of the letter that the king 11
Artaxerxes gave unto Ezra the priest, the scribe,
even the scribe of the words of the commandments of the Lord, and of his statutes to Israel.
Artaxerxes, king of kings, unto Ezra the priest, 12
the scribe of the law of the God of heaven, perfect and so forth. I make a decree, that all they 13
of the people of Israel, and their priests and the
Levites, in my realm, which are minded of their
own free will to go to Jerusalem, go with thee.

Forasmuch as thou art sent of the king and his 14
seven counsellors, to inquire concerning Judah
and Jerusalem, according to the law of thy God
which is in thine hand;
and to carry the silver 15
and gold, which the king and his counsellors
have freely offered unto the God of Israel, whose
habitation is in Jerusalem, and all the silver and 16
gold that thou shalt find in all the province of
Babylon, with the freewill offering of the people,
and of the priests, offering willingly for the house
of their God which is in Jerusalem;
therefore 17
thou shalt with all diligence buy with this money
bullocks, rams, lambs, with their meal offerings
and their drink offerings, and shalt offer them
upon the altar of the house of your God which
is in Jerusalem. And whatsoever shall seem 18
good to thee and to thy brethren to do with the
rest of the silver and the gold, that do ye after
the will of your God. And the vessels that are 19
given thee for the service of the house of thy
God, deliver thou before the God of Jerusalem.
And whatsoever more shall be needful for the 20
house of thy God, which thou shalt have occasion
to bestow, bestow it out of the king's treasure
house. And I, even I Artaxerxes the king, do 21
make a decree to all the treasurers which are
beyond the river, that whatsoever Ezra the priest,
the scribe of the law of the God of heaven, shall
require of you, it be done with all diligence,
unto 22
an hundred talents of silver, and to an hundred
measures of wheat, and to an hundred baths of
wine, and to an hundred baths of oil, and salt

8–24. Jos. xi. **5** 1, §§ 123–30 reproduces this remarkable decree more carefully than he does the rest of the Ezra story. The document, which is in Aramaic, should be compared with the decrees of Cyrus and Darius (see Torrey, 158): its value rests upon the Ezra-story as a whole and is variously estimated (see Berth., 34 seq., Nikel, 167 seqq.). According to Jewish tradition, of course, the book of Esther, with the story of the favour of Xerxes, would precede the present situation. *v.* 8 𝔊 has no conclusion and there are signs of unevenness especially in 9 seq. and 22.

9 seq. Read, perhaps E 12 seq., 'perfect peace, and now I make . . .' (cf. E v. 7).

10. Some words are probably missing at the beginning (Lupton).

and of those, mg. *being within* 𝔊[AL] 𝔏 𝔖.

17. Jos. prefixes ἀναθήσεις, 𝔏[c] 'pones', cf. MT *deliver* (rather 'hand over wholly'). The MT *God of Jerusalem* (𝔊[BA] 'before God [𝔊[L] 'the God of Israel'] in J.') is very strange.

18. **remember** (ὅσα ἂν ὑποπίπτῃ σοι), rather, 'shall occur to, or befall thee', MT 'thou shalt have to give'.

19. **send for** (E *shall require*), a misreading (שלח for שאל; so Ball, Moulton), or merely a paraphrase.

20. **salt** (𝔏 and some MSS. of 𝔊), mg. *other things* (𝔊[A] 𝔏; B om.); 𝔏[c] 'sal sine mensura et caetera sine men.'; 𝔊[L] 𝔖 'and other things according to the law of God' (see *v.* 21).

21 Let all things be per-
formed after the law of God diligently unto the
Most High God, that wrath come not upon the
kingdom of the king and his sons.
22 I command
you also, that no tax, nor any other imposition,
be laid on any of the priests, or Levites, or
holy singers, or porters, or temple-servants, or
any that have employment in this temple, and
that no man have authority to impose anything
23 upon them. And thou, Esdras, according to the
wisdom of God ordain judges and justices, that
they may judge in all Syria and Phœnicia all
those that know the law of thy God; and those
that know it not thou shalt teach.
24 And whoso-
ever shall transgress the law of thy God, and of
the king, shall be punished diligently, whether
it be by death, or other punishment, by penalty
of money, or by imprisonment.

25 Then said Esdras the scribe, Blessed be the
only Lord, the God of my fathers, who hath
put these things into the heart of the king, to
26 glorify his house that is in Jerusalem: and hath
honoured me in the sight of the king, and his
counsellors, and all his friends and nobles.
27 Therefore was I encouraged by the help of the
Lord my God, and gathered together out of
Israel men to go up with me.
28 And these are the
chief according to their families and the several
divisions thereof, that went up with me from
29 Babylon in the reign of king Artaxerxes: of
the sons of Phinees, Gerson: of the sons of
Ithamar, Gamael: of the sons of David, Attus
30 the son of Sechenias: of the sons of Phoros,
Zacharias; and with him were counted a hun-
31 dred and fifty men: of the sons of Phaath
Moab, Eliaonias the son of Zaraias, and with
32 him two hundred men: of the sons of Zathoes,
Sechenias the son of Jezelus, and with him three
hundred men: of the sons of Adin, Obeth the
son of Jonathan, and with him two hundred
33 and fifty men: of the sons of Elam, Jesias son
of Gotholias, and with him seventy men:

without prescribing how much. Whatsoever is 23
commanded by the God of heaven, let it be done
exactly for the house of the God of heaven; for
why should there be wrath against the realm of
the king and his sons? Also we certify you, 24
that touching any of the priests and Levites,
the singers, porters, Nethinim, or servants of this
house of God, it shall not be lawful to impose
tribute, custom, or toll, upon them.

And thou, 25
Ezra, after the wisdom of thy God that is in
thine hand, appoint magistrates and judges,
which may judge all the people that are beyond
the river, all such as know the laws of thy God;
and teach ye him that knoweth them not. And 26
whosoever will not do the law of thy God, and
the law of the king, let judgement be executed
upon him with all diligence, whether it be unto
death, or to banishment, or to confiscation of
goods, or to imprisonment.
Blessed be the Lord, the God of our fathers, 27
which hath put such a thing as this in the king's
heart, to beautify the house of the Lord which
is in Jerusalem; and hath extended mercy unto 28
me before the king, and his counsellors, and
before all the king's mighty princes. And I was
strengthened according to the hand of the Lord
my God upon me, and I gathered together out
of Israel chief men to go up with me.
Now these are the heads of their fathers' 8 1
houses, and this is the genealogy of them that
went up with me from Babylon, in the reign of
Artaxerxes the king. Of the sons of Phinehas, 2
Gershom: of the sons of Ithamar, Daniel: of
the sons of David, Hattush. Of the sons of 3
Shecaniah; of the sons of Parosh, Zechariah:
and with him were reckoned by genealogy of
the males an hundred and fifty. Of the sons 4
of Pahath-moab, Eliehoenai the son of Zerahiah;
and with him two hundred males. Of the sons 5
of Shecaniah, the son of Jahaziel; and with him
three hundred males. And of the sons of Adin, 6
Ebed the son of Jonathan; and with him fifty
males. And of the sons of Elam, Jeshaiah the 7
son of Athaliah; and with him seventy males.

22. The decree is now addressed to the Persian officials in Palestine, cf. the direct address E vi. 6 seq., and the abstract in *E* iv. 49 seqq.

that have employment, πραγματικοῖς τοῦ ἱεροῦ; 𝔏 𝔖 'scribes of the temple' (as though γραμματικοῖς).

24. **punishment,** 𝔊^{BA} τιμωρία, L, ἀτιμία, 𝔏 cruciatu, 𝔏^{C} tormentis, E *banishment*, prop. 'uprooting', 𝔊 παιδεία.

imprisonment, mg. *captivity*, 𝔊^{BA} ἀπαγωγή, L δεσμεῦσαι, 𝔏 abductione, 𝔏^{C} exilio. Jos. + ἔρρωσο, cf. 𝔏 Lag. *bene valeas*.

25. **Then . . . scribe,** 𝔊^{BL} om., 𝔏^{C} om. *the scribe*.

Blessed . . ., or 'blessed alone be the Lord' (Ball).

28–40. Ezra's band. With the priestly families (*v.* 29), cf. Eleazar and Ithamar, 1 Chron. xxiv. 2 seqq., where the priesthood is not restricted to the Zadokites but as a compromise a share is given to the subordinate family of Ithamar. For the priestly and Davidic families, cf. *E* v. 5. With the preferable reading: Hattush of the sons of Shechaniah (*v.* 29), cf. 1 Chron. iii. 22. The names of the *twelve* (see v. 4) lay families recur in the great register *E* v.; Pahath-moab and Joab (*vv.* 31, 35) are, however, severed (contrast v. 11). The sons of Zattu (*v.* 32) are wrongly omitted in E (but see 𝔊^{A} ib.). *Zaraias* represents Zerahiah in *v.* 31, but Zebadiah in *v.* 34; *Jezelus* (*v.* 35) = Jehiel, cf. on i. 8. The family of Bani (*v.* 36) is wanting in E (but see 𝔊^{A} ib.). *Istalcurus* (*v.* 40) = Zabbud or Zaccur; see *E Bi.*, art. Zabud (2); Bayer 56 would restore עותי בן יזכור. For other details see the comm.

34 of the
sons of Saphatias, Zaraias son of Michael, and
35 with him threescore and ten men: of the sons
of Joab, Abadias son of Jezelus, and with him
36 two hundred and twelve men: of the sons of
Banias, Salimoth son of Josaphias, and with him
37 a hundred and threescore men: of the sons of
Babi, Zacharias son of Bebai, and with him
38 twenty and eight men: of the sons of Astath,
Joannes son of Akatan, and with him a hun-
39 dred and ten men: of the sons of Adonikam,
the last, and these are the names of them, Eliphalat, Jeuel, and Samaias, and with them
40 seventy men: of the sons of Bago, Uthi the son
of Istalcurus, and with him seventy men.

41 And I gathered them together to the river
called Theras; and there we pitched our tents
42 three days, and I surveyed them. But when
I had found there none of the priests and
43 Levites, then sent I unto Eleazar, and Iduel,
44 and Maasmas, and Elnathan, and Samaias, and
Joribus, Nathan, Ennatan, Zacharias, and Mo-
sollamus, principal men and men of understand-
45 ing. And I bade them that they should go unto
Loddeus the captain, who was in the place of
46 the treasury: and commanded them that they
should speak unto Loddeus, and to his brethren,
and to the treasurers in that place, to send us
such men as might execute the priests' office in
47 the house of our Lord. And by the mighty
hand of our Lord they brought unto us men of
understanding of the sons of Mooli the son of
Levi, the son of Israel, Asebebias, and his sons,
and his brethren, who were eighteen,
48 and
Asebias, and Annuus, and Osaias his brother, of
the sons of Chanuneus, and their sons were
49 twenty men; and of the temple-servants whom
David and the principal men had appointed for
the service of the Levites, two hundred and
twenty temple-servants, the catalogue of all their
50 names was shewed. And there I vowed a fast
for the young men before our Lord, to desire of
him a prosperous journey both for us and for
our children and cattle that were with us:
51 for
I was ashamed to ask of the king footmen, and
horsemen, and conduct for safeguard against
52 our adversaries. For we had said unto the
king, that the power of our Lord would be with

And of the sons of Shephatiah, Zebadiah the 8
son of Michael; and with him fourscore males.
Of the sons of Joab, Obadiah the son of Jehiel; 9
and with him two hundred and eighteen males.
And of the sons of Shelomith, the son of Josi- 10
phiah; and with him an hundred and threescore
males. And of the sons of Bebai, Zechariah the 11
son of Bebai; and with him twenty and eight
males. And of the sons of Azgad, Johanan the 12
son of Hakkatan; and with him an hundred and
ten males. And of the sons of Adonikam, *that* 13
were the last; and these are their names, Eliphelet, Jeuel, and Shemaiah, and with them threescore males. And of the sons of Bigvai, Uthai 14
and Zabbud; and with them seventy males.

And I gathered them together to the river 15
that runneth to Ahava; and there we encamped
three days: and I viewed the people, and the
priests, and found there none of the sons of Levi.
Then sent I for Eliezer, for Ariel, for Shemaiah, 16
and for Elnathan, and for Jarib, and for Elnathan,
and for Nathan, and for Zechariah, and for Meshullam, chief men; also for Joiarib, and for Elnathan, which were teachers. And I sent them 17
forth unto Iddo the chief at the place Casiphia;
and I told them what they should say unto Iddo,
and his brethren the Nethinim, at the place
Casiphia, that they should bring unto us ministers for the house of our God.
And according 18
to the good hand of our God upon us they
brought us a man of discretion, of the sons of
Mahli, the son of Levi, the son of Israel; and
Sherebiah, with his sons and his brethren, eighteen; and Hashabiah, and with him Jeshaiah of 19
the sons of Merari, his brethren and their sons,
twenty;
and of the Nethinim, whom David and 20
the princes had given for the service of the
Levites, two hundred and twenty Nethinim: all
of them were expressed by name.
Then I pro- 21
claimed a fast there, at the river Ahava, that we
might humble ourselves before our God, to seek
of him a straight way, for us, and for our little
ones, and for all our substance. For I was 22
ashamed to ask of the king a band of soldiers
and horsemen to help us against the enemy in
the way: because we had spoken unto the king,
saying, The hand of our God is upon all them

41. **called**, perhaps a better reading (Ew. 137 n. 4).
Theras ($\mathfrak{G}^{B}$ om.), see *vv.* 50, 61. Jos. § 134 'beyond (? πέραν for Θεράς, Lupton) the Euphrates'.

42. In E only the Levites are absent, see *v.* 29 and note the textual difficulties in 42 seqq. (see Berth.), and elsewhere where the priests and Levites are concerned.

43 seq. **sent I unto**. Omit *unto*; the accusatival ל (see esp. 2 Chron. xvii. 7) was misunderstood.

45. **place of the treasury**, E *Casiphia*, but cf. $\mathfrak{G}$ ib. Cf. also *v.* 46, where, too, the Nethinim are ignored.

47. **men**, mg. *a man* ($\mathfrak{G}^{BL}$).

48. **Annuus** = MT *itto* 'with him' (to be read *eth*, a mark of the accusative).
Chanuneus (E *Merari*) might suggest Chenani(ah), Neh. ix. 4, 1 Chron. xv. 22, &c.

50. **for the young men**, an obscure statement, perhaps a misreading of E's *river* (נער for נהר), *Ahava* being omitted (Ball).

them that seek him, to support them in all ways.
53 And again we besought our Lord as touching
these things, and found him favourable *unto us.*
54 Then I separated twelve men of the chiefs of the
priests, Eserebias, and Assamias, and ten men of
their brethren with them:
55 and I weighed them
the silver, and the gold, and the holy vessels of
the house of our Lord, which the king, and his
counsellors, and the nobles, and all Israel, had
56 given. And when I had weighed it, I delivered
unto them six hundred and fifty talents of silver,
and silver vessels of a hundred talents, and a hun-
57 dred talents of gold, and twenty golden vessels,
and twelve vessels of brass, even of fine brass,
58 glittering like gold. And I said unto them, Both
ye are holy unto the Lord, and the vessels are
holy, and the gold and the silver are a vow unto
59 the Lord, the Lord of our fathers. Watch ye,
and keep them till ye deliver them to the chiefs
of the priests and Levites, and to the principal
men of the families of Israel, in Jerusalem, in
the chambers of the house of our Lord.
60 So the
priests and the Levites, who received the silver
and the gold and the vessels which were in
Jerusalem, brought them into the temple of the
Lord.
61 And from the river Theras we departed the
twelfth day of the first month, until we came to
Jerusalem, by the mighty hand of our Lord
which was upon us: and the Lord delivered us
from *assault by* the way, from every enemy, and
62 *so* we came to Jerusalem. And when we had
been there three days, the silver and gold was
weighed and delivered in the house of our Lord
on the fourth day unto Marmoth the priest
63 the son of Urias. And with him was Eleazar
the son of Phinees, and with them were Josabdus
the son of Jesus and Moeth the son of Sabannus,
the Levites: all *was delivered them* by number
and weight.
64 And all the weight of them was
written up the same hour.
65 Moreover they that
were come out of the captivity offered sacrifices
unto the Lord, the God of Israel, even twelve
bullocks for all Israel, fourscore and sixteen rams,
66 threescore and twelve lambs, goats for a peace
offering, twelve; all of them a sacrifice to the

that seek him, for good; but his power and his
wrath is against all them that forsake him. So 23
we fasted and besought our God for this: and
he was intreated of us. Then I separated twelve 24
of the chiefs of the priests, even Sherebiah,
Hashabiah, and ten of their brethren with them,
and weighed unto them the silver, and the gold, 25
and the vessels, even the offering for the house
of our God, which the king, and his counsellors,
and his princes, and all Israel there present, had
offered: I even weighed into their hand six 26
hundred and fifty talents of silver, and silver
vessels an hundred talents; of gold an hundred
talents; and twenty bowls of gold, of a thousand 27
darics; and two vessels of fine bright brass,
precious as gold. And I said unto them, Ye are 28
holy unto the Lord, and the vessels are holy;
and the silver and the gold are a freewill offering
unto the Lord, the God of your fathers. Watch 29
ye, and keep them, until ye weigh them before
the chiefs of the priests and the Levites, and the
princes of the fathers' *houses* of Israel, at Jerusalem, in the chambers of the house of the Lord.
So the priests and the Levites received the 30
weight of the silver and the gold, and the vessels,
to bring them to Jerusalem unto the house of our
God.

Then we departed from the river of Ahava on 31
the twelfth *day* of the first month, to go unto
Jerusalem: and the hand of our God was upon
us, and he delivered us from the hand of the
enemy and the lier in wait by the way. And 32
we came to Jerusalem, and abode there three
days.

And on the fourth day was the silver and 33
the gold and the vessels weighed in the house of
our God into the hand of Meremoth the son of
Uriah the priest; and with him was Eleazar the
son of Phinehas; and with them was Jozabad
the son of Jeshua, and Noadiah the son of Binnui, the Levites; the whole by number and by 34
weight: and all the weight was written at that
time. The children of the captivity, which were 35
come out of exile, offered burnt offerings unto
the God of Israel, twelve bullocks for all Israel,
ninety and six rams, seventy and seven lambs,
twelve he-goats for a sin offering: all this was
a burnt offering unto the Lord.

54. **Eserebias** (= Sherebiah), 𝔊[BA] prefix 'and'; there are thus twelve Levites (cf. *v.* 47 seq., N xii. 24) and twelve priests (**cf.** *v.* 60). E includes the two men and their brethren among the twelve priests.

55. **all Israel,** Jos. 'who remained at Babylon' (cf. *v.* 13 seq.), some qualification is necessary.

57. **twelve,** 𝔊[B] 'ten'.

58. **holy,** cf. Is. lii. 11.

and the vessels . . . , mg. *and the vessels and the silver and the gold, &c.* (𝔊[B]).

60. **which [were] in Jerusalem,** the words belong to the end of the verse.

61. **every enemy,** reading ואויב for ואורב. 𝔊[B] confuses the first and the third person (for the latter see 65–7) and omits 'our' in *v.* 62. See on *vv.* 68 seqq.

66. **peace offering,** or thank-offering, cf. the Geneva Bible 'for salvation'. For E cf. vii. 7 seq. (E vi. 17).

67 Lord. And they delivered the king's commandments unto the king's stewards, and to the
governors of Cœlesyria and Phœnicia; and they
honoured the people and the temple of the Lord.

68 Now when these things were done, the prin-
69 cipal men came unto me, and said, The nation
of Israel, and the princes, and the priests and
the Levites, have not put away *from them* the
strange people of the land, nor the uncleannesses of the Gentiles, *to wit*, of the Canaanites,
Hittites, Pherezites, Jebusites, and the Moabites,
70 Egyptians, and Edomites. For both they and
their sons have married with their daughters,
and the holy seed is mixed with the strange
people of the land; and from the beginning of
this matter the rulers and the nobles have been
71 partakers of this iniquity. And as soon as I had
heard these things, I rent my clothes, and my
holy garment, and plucked the hair from off my
head and beard, and sat me down sad and full of
72 heaviness. So all they that were moved at the
word of the Lord, the God of Israel, assembled
unto me, whilst I mourned for the iniquity: but
I sat still full of heaviness until the evening sacri-
73 fice. Then rising up from the fast with my clothes
and my holy garment rent, and bowing my knees,
and stretching forth my hands unto the Lord,

74 I said, O Lord, I am ashamed and confounded
75 before thy face; for our sins are multiplied above
our heads, and our errors have reached up unto
heaven,
76 ever since the time of our fathers; and we
77 are in great sin, even unto this day. And for our
sins and our fathers' we with our brethren and
our kings and our priests were given up unto the
kings of the earth, to the sword, and to captivity,
and for a prey with shame, unto this day.
78 And
now in some measure hath mercy been shewed
unto us from thee, O Lord, that there should be
left us a root and a name in the place of thy
79 sanctuary; and to discover unto us a light in the
house of the Lord our God, *and* to give us food in
80 the time of our servitude. Yea, when we were in
bondage, we were not forsaken of our Lord; but
he made us gracious before the kings of Persia, so
81 that they gave us food, and glorified the temple

And they 36
delivered the king's commissions unto the king's
satraps, and to the governors beyond the river:
and they furthered the people and the house of
God.

Now when these things were done, the princes 9 1
drew near unto me, saying, The people of Israel,
and the priests and the Levites, have not separated themselves from the peoples of the lands,
doing according to their abominations, even of
the Canaanites, the Hittites, the Perizzites, the
Jebusites, the Ammonites, the Moabites, the
Egyptians, and the Amorites. For they have 2
taken of their daughters for themselves and for
their sons; so that the holy seed have mingled
themselves with the peoples of the lands: yea,
the hand of the princes and rulers hath been
chief in this trespass. And when I heard this 3
thing, I rent my garment and my mantle, and
plucked off the hair of my head and of my beard,
and sat down astonied.
Then were assembled 4
unto me every one that trembled at the
words of the God of Israel, because of the trespass of them of the captivity; and I sat
astonied until the evening oblation. And at the 5
evening oblation I arose up from my humiliation,
even with my garment and my mantle rent;
and I fell upon my knees, and spread out my
hands unto the Lord my God; and I said, O my 6
God, I am ashamed and blush to lift up my face
to thee, my God: for our iniquities are increased
over our head, and our guiltiness is grown up
unto the heavens. Since the days of our fathers 7
we have been exceeding guilty unto this day;
and for our iniquities have we, our kings, and
our priests, been delivered into the hand of the
kings of the lands, to the sword, to captivity,
and to spoiling, and to confusion of face, as it is
this day. And now for a little moment grace 8
hath been shewed from the Lord our God, to
leave us a remnant to escape, and to give us
a nail in his holy place, that our God may
lighten our eyes, and give us a little reviving in
our bondage.
For we are bondmen; yet our 9
God hath not forsaken us in our bondage, but
hath extended mercy unto us in the sight of the
kings of Persia, to give us a reviving, to set up

67. **honoured**, ἐδόξασαν (so E𝔊), cf. viii. 25, 81, and Is. lx. 13; a weak and inappropriate rendering (Ew. 138 n. 6).
The mixed marriages, *vv*. 68–90 = E ix., cf. Jos. xi. 5 3. See below on ix. 37 seqq. 𝔊L gives the narrative in the third person.

69. **the uncleannesses** . . ., mg. *nor their uncleannesses* (to wit) *of the Gentiles, &c.* (𝔊B).
Edomites, see iv. 45, 50.

72. **So all they**, 𝔊A + 'that were zealous and all they'.

73. **fast**, cf. E R.V. mg. *fasting*.

75. **multiplied above** . . ., 𝔊L 𝔏 𝔖 'multiplied more than the hairs of our head', cf. Ps. xl. 12.

77. **we with our brethren** (אנחנו 'we' read as אחינו).

78. **root** (cf. *v*. 88), perhaps influenced by 2 Kings xix. 30 seq. (Bayer, 15).

79. **food**, E *reviving* (מִחְיָה, cf. Judg. vi. 4).

of our Lord, and raised up the desolate Sion, to
give us a sure abiding in Jewry and Jerusalem.
82 And now, O Lord, what shall we say, having these
things? for we have transgressed thy commandments, which thou gavest by the hand of thy
83 servants the prophets, saying, That the land,
which ye enter into to possess as an heritage, is a
land polluted with the pollutions of the strangers
of the land, and they have filled it with their uncleanness.
84 Therefore now shall ye not join your
daughters unto their sons, neither shall ye take
85 their daughters unto your sons. Neither shall
ye seek to have peace with them for ever, that
ye may be strong, and eat the good things of
the land, and that ye may leave it for an in-
86 heritance unto your children for evermore. And
all that is befallen is done unto us for our wicked
works and great sins: for thou, O Lord, didst
87 make our sins light, and didst give unto us such
a root: *but* we have turned back again to transgress thy law, in mingling ourselves with the
88 uncleanness of the heathen of the land. Thou
wast not angry with us to destroy us, till thou
hadst left us neither root, seed, nor name.
89 O Lord of Israel, thou art true: for we are left a
90 root this day. Behold, now are we before thee
in our iniquities, for we cannot stand any longer
before thee by reason of these things.

91 And as Esdras in his prayer made his confession, weeping, and lying flat upon the ground
before the temple, there gathered unto him
from Jerusalem a very great throng of men and
women and children: for there was great weep-
92 ing among the multitude. Then Jechonias the
son of Jeelus, one of the sons of Israel, called out,
and said, O Esdras, we have sinned against the
Lord God, we have married strange women of
the heathen of the land, and now is all Israel aloft.
93 Let us make an oath unto the Lord herein, that
we will put away all our wives, which *we have*
94 *taken* of the strangers, with their children, like as
seemeth good unto thee, and to as many as do obey
the law of the Lord.
95 Arise, and put in execution:
for to thee doth this matter appertain, and we

the house of our God, and to repair the ruins
thereof, and to give us a wall in Judah and in
Jerusalem. And now, O our God, what shall 10
we say after this? for we have forsaken thy
commandments, which thou hast commanded by 11
thy servants the prophets, saying, The land,
unto which ye go to possess it, is an unclean
land through the uncleanness of the peoples of
the lands, through their abominations, which
have filled it from one end to another with their
filthiness. Now therefore give not your daugh- 12
ters unto their sons, neither take their daughters
unto your sons, nor seek their peace or their
prosperity for ever: that ye may be strong, and
eat the good of the land, and leave it for an
inheritance to your children for ever.
And after 13
all that is come upon us for our evil deeds, and
for our great guilt, seeing that thou our God
hast punished us less than our iniquities deserve,
and hast given us such a remnant, shall we again 14
break thy commandments, and join in affinity
with the peoples that do these abominations?
wouldest not thou be angry with us till thou
hadst consumed us, so that there should be no
remnant, nor any to escape? O Lord, the God 15
of Israel, thou art righteous; for we are left
a remnant that is escaped, as it is this day:
behold, we are before thee in our guiltiness; for
none can stand before thee because of this.
Now while Ezra prayed, and made confession, **10** 1
weeping and casting himself down before the
house of God, there was gathered together unto
him out of Israel a very great congregation of
men and women and children: for the people
wept very sore. And Shecaniah the son of 2
Jehiel, one of the sons of Elam, answered and
said unto Ezra, We have trespassed against our
God, and have married strange women of the
peoples of the land: yet now there is hope for
Israel concerning this thing. Now therefore let 3
us make a covenant with our God to put away
all the wives, and such as are born of them,
according to the counsel of my lord, and of those
that tremble at the commandment of our God;
and let it be done according to the law. Arise; 4
for the matter belongeth unto thee, and we are

81. **Sion.** G. A. Smith (*Jerusalem*, i. 150 seq.) observes that the term is not found in Ezek., Chron. (except the quotations 1 Chron. xi. 5, 2 Chron. v. 2), E and N.

82. **having . . . transgressed**, presumably based upon misreadings אחזי for אחרי, עברנו for עזבנו (see Ball).

86. **make . . . light**, cf. E𝔊.

88. **Thou wast not**, mg. *wast thou not*, &c., see E.

The marriage-reforms, viii. 91–ix. 36 = E, x., cf. Jos. xi. **5** 4.

92. **Israel** (Jos. 'Jerusalem'), E *Elam*, cf. E x. 26.

aloft, mg. *exalted* (with a reference to Deut. xxviii. 13, לְמַעְלָה). This points to the reading מַעַל 'trespass' (E ix. 2, 4, x. 6) for מקוה 'hope' ($𝔊^L$ 𝔖 here) and is preferred by Jahn. 𝔏 et nunc es super omnem Israel ($𝔏^c$ et nunc de populo I.). Bayer (16) conj. ἐπάνω corruption of ὑπομονή (E𝔊).

'Concerning this thing' in E is read by $𝔊^{BA}$ 𝔏 at the beginning of *E* 93.

94. $𝔊^L$ 𝔖 'and as many as obeyed . . . having arisen, said unto Ezra, Arise . . .' (reading קמו החרדים).

95. **put into execution**, כַּלֵּה has probably dropped out from the MT (Guthe, *SBOT*).

96 will be with thee to do valiantly. So Esdras
arose, and took an oath of the chief of the priests
and Levites of all Israel to do after these things;
and *so* they sware.

9 1 Then Esdras rising from the court of the
temple went to the chamber of Jonas the son of
2 Eliasib, and lodged there, and did eat no bread
nor drink water, mourning for the great iniquities
of the multitude.

3 And there was made proclama-
tion in all Jewry and Jerusalem to all them that
were of the captivity, that they should be gathered
4 together at Jerusalem: and that whosoever met
not there within two or three days, according as
the elders that bare rule appointed, their cattle
should be seized to the use of the temple, and
himself cast out from the multitude of them that
were of the captivity.

5 And in three days were all they of the tribe
of Judah and Benjamin gathered together at
Jerusalem: this was the ninth month, on the
6 twentieth day of the month. And all the multitude sat together trembling in the broad place
before the temple because of the present foul
7 weather. So Esdras arose up, and said unto
them, Ye have transgressed the law and married
strange wives, *thereby* to increase the sins of
8 Israel. And now make confession and give
glory unto the Lord, the God of our fathers,
9 and do his will, and separate yourselves from
the heathen of the land, and from the strange
10 women. Then cried the whole multitude, and
said with a loud voice, Like as thou hast spoken,
11 so will we do. But forasmuch as the multitude
is great, and it is foul weather, so that we cannot
stand without, and this is not a work of one day
or two, seeing our sin in these things is spread
12 far: therefore let the rulers of the multitude
13 stay, and let all them of our habitations that
have strange wives come at the time appointed,
and with them the rulers and judges of every
place, till we turn away the wrath of the Lord
from us for this matter.

14 *Then* Jonathan the son
of Azael and Ezekias the son of Thocanus accordingly took the matter upon them: and Mosol-
lamus and Levis and Sabbateus were assessors

with thee: be of good courage, and do it. Then 5
arose Ezra, and made the chiefs of the priests,
the Levites, and all Israel, to swear that they
would do according to this word. So they
sware. Then Ezra rose up from before the 6
house of God, and went into the chamber of
Jehohanan the son of Eliashib: and *when* he
came thither, he did eat no bread, nor drink
water: for he mourned because of the trespass
of them of the captivity. And they made pro- 7
clamation throughout Judah and Jerusalem unto
all the children of the captivity, that they should
gather themselves together unto Jerusalem; and 8
that whosoever came not within three days,
according to the counsel of the princes and the
elders, all his substance should be forfeited, and
himself separated from the congregation of the
captivity.

Then all the men of Judah and Ben- 9
jamin gathered themselves together unto Jerusalem within the three days; it was the ninth
month, on the twentieth *day* of the month: and
all the people sat in the broad place before the
house of God, trembling because of this matter,
and for the great rain. And Ezra the priest 10
stood up, and said unto them, Ye have trespassed, and have married strange women, to
increase the guilt of Israel. Now therefore make 11
confession unto the Lord, the God of your
fathers, and do his pleasure: and separate yourselves from the peoples of the land, and from the
strange women. Then all the congregation 12
answered and said with a loud voice, As thou hast
said concerning us, so must we do. But the 13
people are many, and it is a time of much rain,
and we are not able to stand without, neither is
this a work of one day or two: for we have
greatly transgressed in this matter. Let now 14
our princes be appointed for all the congregation,
and let all them that are in our cities which have
married strange women come at appointed times,
and with them the elders of every city, and the
judges thereof, until the fierce wrath of our God
be turned from us, until this matter be despatched. Only Jonathan the son of Asahel and 15
Jahzeiah the son of Tikvah stood up against this
matter: and Meshullam and Shabbethai the
Levite helped them.

96. **the chief** (rather **chiefs**, as in viii. 49) . . . **and Levites**, for *and* see Guthe, *SBOT*.

IX. 2. **lodged there**, rightly reading וילן for וילך.

6. **in the broad place**. According to Jos. § 149 there was a meeting of the elders in the upper room (but Niese ὑπαίθρῳ) of the temple.

8. 𝔊[BA] 'Give confession (𝔊[L] + and) glory'; a doublet of תּוֹדָה (Fr., &c.).

11. **forasmuch as**, wanting in 𝔊.

13. **for this matter**, cf. E R.V. mg. *as touching this matter*.

14. **took the matter** (ἐπεδέξαντο, cf. with Fr. 1 Macc. i. 42); cf. E R.V. mg. *were appointed over this (matter)*. On the conflicting interpretations of this passage see the comm.

Ezekias, mg. *Ezias* (𝔊[BL] 𝔖).

Levis . . ., E 𝔊[L] 'the Levites'.

assessors, 𝔊 συνεβράβευσαν, 𝔏 cooperati (𝔏[c] consenserunt).

15 to them. And they that were of the captivity
did according to all these things.
16 And Esdras the priest chose unto him principal
men of their families, all by name: and on the
new moon of the tenth month they were shut in
17 together to examine the matter. So their cause
that held strange wives was brought to an end
by the new moon of the first month.
18 And of the
priests that were come together, and had strange
19 wives, there were found; of the sons of Jesus
the son of Josedek, and his brethren; Mathelas,
20 and Eleazar, and Joribus, and Joadanus. And
they gave their hands to put away their wives,
and *to offer* rams to make reconcilement for
21 their error. And of the sons of Emmer; Ananias,
and Zabdeus, and Manes, and Sameus, and
Hiereel, and Azarias.
22 And of the sons of Phaisur;
Elionas, Massias, Ismael, and Nathanael, and
23 Ocidelus, and Saloas. And of the Levites;
Jozabdus, and Semeis, and Colius, who was called
Calitas, and Patheus, and Judas, and Jonas.
24 Of
25 the holy singers; Eliasibus, Bacchurus. Of the
26 porters; Sallumus, and Tolbanes. Of Israel, of
the sons of Phoros; Hiermas, and Ieddias, and
Melchias, and Maelus, and Eleazar, and Asibias,
27 and Banneas. Of the sons of Ela; Matthanias,
Zacharias, and Jezrielus, and Oabdius, and Hieremoth,
28 moth, and Aedias. And of the sons of Zamoth;
Eliadas, Eliasimus, Othonias, Jarimoth, and
29 Sabathus, and Zardeus. Of the sons of Bebai;
Joannes, and Ananias, and Jozabdus, and Ematheis.
30 theis. Of the sons of Mani; Olamus, Mamuchus,
Jedeus, Jasubus, and Jasaelus, and Hieremoth.
31 And of the sons of Addi; Naathus, and Moossias,
Laccunus, and Naidus, and Matthanias, and Sesthel,
32 thel, Balnuus, and Manasseas. And of the sons
of Annas; Elionas, and Aseas, and Melchias, and
33 Sabbeus, and Simon Chosameus. And of the
sons of Asom; Maltanneus, and Mattathias, and
Sabanneus, Eliphalat, and Manasses, and Semei.
34 And of the sons of Baani; Jeremias, Momdis,
Ismaerus, Juel, Mamdai, and Pedias, and Anos,
Carabasion, and Enasibus, and Mamnitanemus,
Eliasis, Bannus, Eliali, Someis, Selemias, Nathanias:
and of the sons of Ezora; Sesis, Ezril,
35 Azaelus, Samatus, Zambri, Josephus. And of
the sons of Nooma; Mazitias, Zabadeas, Edos,
Juel, Banaias.

And the children of the 16
captivity did so. And Ezra the priest, *with*
certain heads of fathers' *houses*, after their fathers'
houses, and all of them by their names, were
separated; and they sat down in the first day of
the tenth month to examine the matter. And 17
they made an end with all the men that had
married strange women by the first day of the
first month. And among the sons of the priests 18
there were found that had married strange
women: *namely*, of the sons of Jeshua, the son
of Jozadak, and his brethren, Maaseiah, and
Eliezer, and Jarib, and Gedaliah. And they 19
gave their hand that they would put away their
wives; and being guilty, *they offered* a ram of
the flock for their guilt. And of the sons of 20
Immer; Hanani and Zebadiah. And of the 21
sons of Harim; Maaseiah, and Elijah, and Shemaiah,
and Jehiel, and Uzziah. And of the sons 22
of Pashhur; Elioenai, Maaseiah, Ishmael, Nethanel,
Jozabad, and Elasah. And of the 23
Levites; Jozabad, and Shimei, and Kelaiah (the
same is Kelita), Pethahiah, Judah, and Eliezer.
And of the singers; Eliashib: and of the porters; 24
Shallum, and Telem, and Uri.
And of Israel: 25
of the sons of Parosh; Ramiah, and Izziah, and
Malchijah, and Mijamin, and Eleazar, and Malchijah,
and Benaiah. And of the sons of Elam; 26
Mattaniah, Zechariah, and Jehiel, and Abdi, and
Jeremoth, and Elijah. And of the sons of 27
Zattu; Elioenai, Eliashib, Mattaniah, and Jeremoth,
and Zabad, and Aziza. And of the sons 28
of Bebai; Jehohanan, Hananiah, Zabbai, Athlai.
And of the sons of Bani; Meshullam, Malluch, 29
and Adaiah, Jashub, and Sheal, Jeremoth.
And 30
of the sons of Pahath-moab; Adna, and Chelal,
Benaiah, Maaseiah, Mattaniah, Bezalel, and Binnui,
and Manasseh. And *of* the sons of Harim; 31
Eliezer, Isshijah, Malchijah, Shemaiah, Shimeon;
Benjamin, Malluch, Shemariah. Of the sons of 32, 33
Hashum; Mattenai, Mattattah, Zabad, Eliphelet,
Jeremai, Manasseh, Shimei. Of the sons of 34
Bani; Maadai, Amram, and Uel; Benaiah, 35
Bedeiah, Cheluhi; Vaniah, Meremoth, Eliashib; 36
Mattaniah, Mattenai, and Jaasu; and Bani, and 37, 38
Binnui, Shimei; and Shelemiah, and Nathan, and 39
Adaiah; Machnadebai, Shashai, Sharai; Azarel, 40, 41
and Shelemiah, Shemariah; Shallum, Amariah, 42
Joseph. Of the sons of Nebo; Jeiel, Mattithiah, 43

16. **chose**; read accordingly in E 'separated for himself' (Eichhorn, Bayer, &c.), or better (Torrey) 'they separated'.
to examine . . ., MT לְדַרְיוֹשׁ; the singular Heb. word has a no less singular resemblance to 'Darius' (דָּרְיָוֶשׁ).
20. Read in E 19 'and for their guilt offering . . .' (וַאֲשָׁמָם for וַאֲשֵׁמִים 'and being guilty').

21–36. In view of the tenour of the whole narrative viii. 68–ix. 20 this list of 113 (E, 111 𝔊) offenders is an anticlimax. On the one hand, the separation of the people of Israel generally, though anticipated at this juncture (see viii. 91–ix. 17), is not recorded until N ix. 2, after the reading of the law. On the other hand, the list cannot refer only to 'the congregation that had come out of captivity' with E (N viii. 17, combined with the purified Israel in x. 28), since the families of Harim, Hashum and Nebo did not return with E, but many years earlier under Zerubbabel.

On the variants see the comm. and *E Bi.* There are omissions in *vv.* 21, 25, much confusion in *vv.* 31 seqq., and Zaccur should be added after Eliashib in E 24 (cf. $𝔊^L$).

36 All these had taken strange wives,
and they put them away with their children.

37 And
the priests and Levites, and they that were of
Israel, dwelt in Jerusalem, and in the country, on
the new moon of the seventh month, and the
children of Israel in their habitations.
38 And the whole multitude were gathered together with one accord into the broad place before
39 the porch of the temple toward the east: and
they said unto Esdras the priest and reader,
Bring the law of Moses, that was given of the
40 Lord, the God of Israel. So Esdras the chief priest
brought the law unto the whole multitude both
of men and women, and to all the priests, to hear
the law on the new moon of the seventh month.
41 And he read in the broad place before the porch
of the temple from morning unto midday, before
both men and women; and all the multitude gave
heed unto the law.

42 And Esdras the priest and
reader of the law stood up upon the pulpit of
43 wood, which was made *for that purpose*. And
there stood up by him Mattathias, Sammus, Ananias, Azarias, Urias, Ezekias, Baalsamus, upon
44 the right hand: and upon his left hand, Phaldeus,
Misael, Melchias, Lothasubus, Nabarias, Zacha-

Zabad, Zebina, Iddo, and Joel, Benaiah. All 44
these had taken strange wives: and some of
them had wives by whom they had children.
So the priests, and the Levites, and the Neh. 7
porters, and the singers, and some of the people, 73
and the Nethinim, and all Israel, dwelt in their
cities. And when the seventh month was come,
the children of Israel were in their cities.
And all the people gathered themselves together Neh. 8 1
as one man into the broad place that was before the
water gate; and they spake unto Ezra the scribe
to bring the book of the law of Moses, which the
Lord had commanded to Israel.
And Ezra the
priest brought the law before the congregation, 2
both men and women, and all that could hear
with understanding, upon the first day of the
seventh month. And he read therein before the 3
broad place that was before the water gate from
early morning until midday, in the presence of
the men and the women, and of those that could
understand; and the ears of all the people were
attentive unto the book of the law. And Ezra 4
the scribe stood upon a pulpit of wood, which
they had made for the purpose; and beside him
stood Mattithiah, and Shema, and Anaiah, and
Uriah, and Hilkiah, and Maaseiah, on his right
hand; and on his left hand, Pedaiah, and Mishael, and Malchijah, and Hashum, and Hash-

36. The MT cannot be translated (R.V. mg. has 'some of the wives had borne children') and E's reading is eminently more intelligible.

The division between the books E and N which occurs at this point is a relatively late feature in the MT. The scribes counted them as one book. This is important in considering questions of the transposition and rearrangement of the contents.

The Reading of the Law, ix. 37–55 = Neh. vii. 73–viii. 13 *a*, cf. Jos. xi. 5 5. The view is strongly urged (Hoonacker, Ryle, Meyer, Bertholet, Nikel, Jampel, Driver, &c.) that E iv. 7 seqq. (*E* ii. 16 seqq.), which cannot refer to the return of Ezra, fills partially at least the gap between the books E and N. This would imply a new catastrophe, a new and important return, and a somewhat extensive work of rebuilding in the time of Artaxerxes, after E x. and before N i. On the other hand, the formal proceedings of the adversaries in E iv. 7 seqq. and the words of the king do not suggest that the opponents would be likely to exceed instructions which, in themselves, are not necessarily sufficient to explain the ruined Jerusalem which so deeply moved Nehemiah. Further, it cannot be assumed that the disgrace of 113 offenders in the matter of the mixed marriages aroused the hostility that is represented in N i.–vi. The people themselves had recognized their sin (*E* viii. 68 seqq.), they feel themselves to be the 'holy seed', and the proposed covenant and the willingness of the people to act 'according to the law' (*v.* 94, E x. 3), would make the entire tenour of the narrative unintelligible unless the writer was describing the successful issue (despite the obscure opposition in E x. 15) of steps initiated, not by Ezra, but by the community (Meyer, 228, 240, 241 n. 2, Torrey, 278). Moreover, the close literary connexion between E ix. seq. and N viii. seqq. forbids the severance of these portions (see above, p. 47 *c*). The sequence of events in *E* ix. is adopted by many (Michaelis, Fr., Berth., &c.), but can hardly be original, since there is still a lacuna between the reforms and the Reading of the Law, and ix. 37, though the natural introduction to the latter, is not in place after *vv.* 1–36 (note the awkward dates *vv.* 17, 37). *v.* 37[a] more properly concludes the account of *some* return, as in v. 46, where *vv.* 47 seqq. describe another religious event, also dated in the seventh month. Finally, it is a very natural supposition that the law brought by Ezra was being made known during the four months' interval between viii. 67 and 68 (E viii. and ix.); see A. P. Stanley, *Jew. Church*, iii. 118; Lupton, 60. Hence it is highly probable, following Torrey (*Comp.* 29 seqq., *Essays*, 253 seqq., 260 seq.), H. P. Smith (*Hist.* 393), and Kent (ii. 369 seqq.), that the introduction of the law to the notice of the people came at the beginning of Ezra's work (after E viii.), and thus explains the people's recognition of their sins. Such an arrangement is found in the Greek summaries of Esdras Book I (= *E*) and Esdras Book II (= N) in Lag. *Sept. Stud.*, ii, 84 (see below, p. 58).

38. For the locality cf. v. 47, ix. 6. Perhaps the compiler who placed this narrative before N i.–viii. believed that the water-gate was in ruins (see N iii. 26); cf. the adjustment in E iii. 1.

39. 𝔊[A] 'the chief priest', *vv.* 40, 49 (contrast N).

40. **the priests**, a misreading of כהן for מבין (see E viii. 16, 1 Chron. xxv. 8), or merely a paraphrase; in any case in an unsuitable position.

41. **all the multitude** . . ., mg. *they gave all heed* (𝔊[B]).

43 seq. *E* adds Azariah after Anaiah, reads Hezekiah for Hilkiah, and perhaps rightly omits Meshullam. For other variants see *E Bi.* and comm.

45 rias. Then took Esdras the book of the law
before the multitude, and sat honourably in the
first place before all.
46 And when he opened the
law, they stood all straight up. So Esdras blessed
the Lord God Most High, the God of hosts,
47 Almighty. And all the people answered, Amen;
and lifting up their hands they fell to the ground,
48 and worshipped the Lord. Also Jesus, Annus,
Sarabias, Iadinus, Jacubus, Sabateus, Auteas,
Maiannas, and Calitas, Azarias, and Jozabdus,
and Ananias, Phalias, the Levites, taught the law
of the Lord,
and read to the multitude the law of
the Lord, making them withal to understand it.
49 Then said Attharates unto Esdras the chief priest
and reader, and to the Levites that taught the
50 multitude, even to all, This day is holy unto the
Lord; (now they all wept when they heard the
law:)
51 go then, and eat the fat, and drink the
sweet, and send portions to them that have
52 nothing; for the day is holy unto the Lord:
and be not sorrowful; for the Lord will bring
you to honour.
53 So the Levites published all
things to the people, saying, This day is holy;
54 be not sorrowful. Then went they their way,
every one to eat and drink, and make merry,
and to give portions to them that had nothing,
55 and to make great cheer; because they understood the words wherein they were instructed,
and for the which they had been assembled.

baddanah, Zechariah, *and* Meshullam. And 5
Ezra opened the book in the sight of all the
people; (for he was above all the people;) and
when he opened it, all the people stood up: and 6
Ezra blessed the Lord, the great God. And all
the people answered, Amen, Amen, with the lifting up of their hands: and they bowed their
heads, and worshipped the Lord with their faces
to the ground. Also Jeshua, and Bani, and 7
Sherebiah, Jamin, Akkub, Shabbethai, Hodiah,
Maaseiah, Kelita, Azariah, Jozabad, Hanan,
Pelaiah, and the Levites, caused the people to
understand the law: and the people *stood* in
their place. And they read in the book, in the 8
law of God, distinctly; and they gave the sense,
so that they understood the reading. And 9
Nehemiah, which was the Tirshatha, and Ezra
the priest the scribe, and the Levites that taught
the people, said unto all the people, This day is
holy unto the Lord your God; mourn not, nor
weep. For all the people wept, when they heard
the words of the law. Then he said unto them, 10
Go your way, eat the fat, and drink the sweet,
and send portions unto him for whom nothing
is prepared: for this day is holy unto our Lord:
neither be ye grieved; for the joy of the Lord
is your strength. So the Levites stilled all the 11
people, saying, Hold your peace, for the day is
holy; neither be ye grieved. And all the 12
people went their way to eat, and to drink, and
to send portions, and to make great mirth,
because they had understood the words that
were declared unto them.
And on the second day were gathered to- 13
gether . . .

46. 𝔊 𝔏 (but not 𝔊[L]) transliterate the familiar יהוה צבאות, and add the paraphrase Παντοκράτωρ, *omnipotentem* (wanting in 𝔏[c]). On the use of this paraphrase, see H. St. J. Thackeray, *Gram. of O.T. in Greek*, 9, and for the distribution of the term 'Lord of Hosts', see M. Löhr, *Buch Amos* (*Beiheft* to *ZATW*, 1901), 38 seqq.

47. **Amen,** 𝔊[B] 𝔖 + Amen, cf. N.

48. The teachers are Levites, cf. 2 Chron. xvii. 8 seq., and contrast N *and*. On the forms in *E* see *E Bi.*; *Annus* is apparently a corruption of Banaias.

and read . . . Lord, 𝔊[A] 𝔏 om.

The texts are confused, see N𝔊.

49. In N, some read 'and N and E', omitting 'which was the Tirshatha' (Smend, Stade, Wellh., Nikel, &c., cf. 𝔊[BNA] 𝔖); others omit 'N which was' (Fr., Schlatter, Guthe, Torrey, &c.); and yet others read simply 'and E', omitting all reference to N (Meyer, 200 n. 3; Howorth, *PSBA*, xxv. 15 seq.; Berth., Jahn, Davies). The difficulty caused by the presence of N or of an unnamed Tirshatha makes it still more difficult to remove it by simple excision. The identification of N and the Tirshatha, even if a gloss, expresses a plausible view (cf. N x. 1), and its omission in *E* may be due to the presence of the passage before N i. seqq. (cf. Meyer, 200 n. 3). N and especially *E* may seem to give the Tirshatha undue prominence, but this may be supported by v. 40, N vii. 70 (his gifts), and the position of the governor Bagohi in the Sachau papyri.

52. **honour,** חדות, 'joy', misread הדרת (Ball).

53. **published,** ἐκέλευον, an error for κωλύω, or מחשים ('stilled') read as מחוים.

55. **understood,** mg. *were inspired by*; ἐνεφυσιώθησαν (cf. John xx. 22); cf. *v.* 48 ἐμφυσιοῦντες ἅμα τὴν ἀνάγνωσιν.

and for the which . . . This conceals the abruptness of 𝔊: καὶ ἐπισυνήχθησαν. N𝔊 reads καὶ ἐν τῇ ἡμέρᾳ τῇ δευτέρᾳ συνηχ., but *E*, which handles the MT more freely (cf. the dates in viii. 62, ix. 37), probably placed the date after the verb. Bayer's explanation (90 seq.) seems too artificial. 𝔊[L] cites the whole of N 13. 𝔏 reads: et coadunati (congregati) sunt omnes (universi) in Ier. iocundari (celebrare laetitiam) secundum dispositionem (testamentum) Domini dei Israel; 𝔏[c] + explicit Esdrae liber primus de templi restitutione. Jos., whose treatment of the story of E is free and summary, proceeds to refer to the feast of tabernacles (N viii. 16 seqq.), the return of the people to their homes, the death of the aged E, and his burial in Jerusalem contemporary with the death of the high-priest Joiakim and the succession of Eliashib (cf. N xii. 10). He then gives a summary of the labours of N, either an extremely arbitrary version or else based upon another recension (xi. 5 6–8). N, hearing of the desolation and captivity, returns with a band of exiles in the 25th year of Xerxes (cf. N i.–ii. 9). He appeals to the people (cf. ii. 17 seq.) and the work of rebuilding is distributed (cf. iii.). Ammon, Moab, Samaria, and Coelesyria are hostile, but the walls (evidently begun in the 5th month, cf. vi. 15) are completed in 2 years 4 months, in the 9th month of the 28th year of Xerxes (N v. is ignored). The walls are dedicated (cf. xii. 27 seqq.) and there is a feast of eight days. The surrounding peoples are enraged at the completion of the building (cf. vi. 16). The population of the city is augmented (cf. vii. 4, xi.), and arrangements are made for the priests and Levites (cf. xii. 44, xiii. 10–13). N dies an old man, and the walls of the city are his eternal monument (cf. Ben Sira, xlix. 13). Next follows the story of Esther (xi. **6**), and the Samaritan schism (cf. N xiii.) is placed at the close of the Persian age (xi. **7**, **8**). Thus Jos. does not testify to the present fragmentary condition of *E*; he treats the life of E independently of and before that of N, and his points of agreement with the MT make his divergences the more significant.

A Syriac Catena (Brit. Mus. Add. 12168), representing a text of the seventh cent., illustrates the relationship between *E* and the MT in an interesting manner. It uses 1 and 2 Chron., '1 Ezra' (i.e. *E*), '2 Ezra' (i.e. N) and Daniel; *E* is said to be 'according to the tradition of the Seventy (i.e. the Septuagint).' It passes from 2 Chron. xxxv. 20–25 to *E* ii. 1–15, 16, 24–30, iv. 35 *b*–36, 38–40, 49–57, v. 47–73, vi. 1–2, vii. 6–15, viii. 1–26, 68–72, 91–6, ix. 1–10, 46 *b*–47. Then follow N i. 1–4 *a*, ii. 1–8, iv. 1–3, 10–16, vi. 15–16, vii. 73 *b*–viii. 18, ix. 1–3 (the references are to the R.V.). This removal of the Reading of the Law appears to be a compromise between *E* (note the retention of ix. 46 *b*–47) and the MT of N. But there is some evidence that *E* may have had another sequel, and that it or a following book may have treated the life of E and of N on other lines (cf. H. Bloch, *Quellen d. Fl. Jos.*, 1879, p. 79 seq.). Thus according to Justin Mart. (*Dial. Tryph.* lxxii) an account of the passover celebrated by E was among the passages cancelled by the Jews. The passage quoted recurs in Lactantius (*Inst.* iv. 18): 'Apud Esdram ita scriptum est: Et dixit Esdras ad populum: Hoc pascha Salvator noster est, et refugium nostrum, cogitate et ascendat (Just. *καὶ ἐὰν διανοηθῆτε καὶ ἀναβῇ*) in cor uestrum, quoniam habemus humiliare eum in signo (Just. *ὅτι μέλλομεν αὐτὸν ταπεινοῦν ἐν σημείῳ*), et post haec sperabimus (but Epit. xlviii. -*avimus*) in eum, ne deseratur (J. *ἐρημωθῇ*) hic locus in aeternum tempus (J. *ἅπαντα χρόνον*), dicit Dominus Deus virtutum (*λέγει ὁ θεὸς τῶν δυνάμεων* [= יהוה צבאות]). Si non credideritis ei neque exaudieritis annuntiationem eius, eritis derisio (*ἐπίχαρμα*) in gentibus.'

The quotation may be compared generally with the spirit of E's prayers (E ix., N ix.). It can hardly be based upon E viii. 35, which recalls the sacrifices at the dedication of the Temple by Zerubbabel (vi. 17) mentioned before the celebration of the passover by the 'children of the captivity' (vi. 19 seqq.). Elsewhere the chronicler deals at length with the passover celebrated by Hezekiah and Josiah (2 Chron. xxx., xxxv.), in each case after a restoration or reform of the Temple, and 2 Chron. xxx. 6–9 illustrate the importance attached to the celebration. It is very noteworthy, also, that the Latin Lucca Synopsis (Lag. 18 seq.), after using *E* iii. seq., combines the return of Zerubbabel with that of E (using *E* viii.) and asserts that the passover was celebrated on reaching Jerusalem. Moreover, a Greek synopsis of 1 Esdras and 2 Esdras (= N) testifies to E's passover. According to 1 *E*, Jeshua, E and Zer. were the three youths of *E* iii. seq., and the statement of the return is followed immediately by the notice that the builders were Zer., Jeshua and N; E brings the law, reads it, casts out the foreign wives and the people observe the passover and a fast. As for 2 *E*: *ἐν τούτῳ τῷ βιβλίῳ τὰ αὐτὰ μὲν τῷ πρώτῳ λέγει* Ἕ. *περὶ τῆς ἐπανόδου χωρὶς τῶν προβληθέντων.* But it is chiefly concerned with 'N. the eunuch' and his building of the Temple. E reads the law and celebrates the passover, and in the seventh month there is a fast and the Feast of Tabernacles. E then notices the foreign marriages (Ashdodite women are mentioned, see N xiii. 23) and persuades the people to promise to observe the law and expel the women. They swear to keep the law and after being cleansed rejoice and depart each to his own home (Lag. *Sept. Stud.* ii. 84). It seems clear from the foregoing evidence that the form of the narrative whether in the present EN or in *E* was not the only one extant. See further, *Introd.*, p. 17.

THE FIRST BOOK OF MACCABEES

INTRODUCTION

§ 1. Title.

THE Greek title Μακκαβαίων[1] α′ takes its origin from the surname applied, in the first instance, to Judas (cp. 1 Macc. ii. 4. 66; 2 Macc. viii. 5. 16; x. 1. 16, &c.), but later on to all the members of the family and their followers. The title is transliterated by Origen (Eusebius, *Hist. Eccl.* vi. 25. 2) Σαρβὴθ Σαβαναιέλ (= ספר בית חשמנאי 'the book of the house of the Hasmonæans', see further, Dalman, *Aramäische Grammatik*, p. 7 [2nd ed.]); but this title is Aramaic, and is not likely to have stood at the head of a book written in Hebrew (see § 6); it was, therefore, probably, the title of an Aramaic translation of the original Hebrew. What the actual title of the book in its original form was, is not known.

§ 2. Contents.

The book is a sober and, on the whole, trustworthy account of the Jewish struggle for religious liberty and political independence during the years 175–135 B.C., i.e. from the accession of Antiochus Epiphanes to the death of Simon the Maccabee. The narrative is, with few exceptions, written in chronological order, and is concerned almost wholly with military events. The main part of the book deals with the exploits of Judas Maccabaeus, who is regarded as the central figure in the whole struggle. The divisions of the book are clearly marked, and are as follows:

- i. 1–9. A brief introduction in which reference is made to the conquests of Alexander the Great, and the division of his kingdom.
- 10–64. The original cause of the Maccabaean struggle.
- ii. 1–70. The beginning of the struggle, under the leadership of Mattathias.
- iii. 1–ix. 22. The account of the events during the leadership of Judas. The purification of the Temple and re-dedication of the altar. The acquisition of religious liberty.
- ix. 23–xii. 53. The leadership of Jonathan; the establishment of the Hasmonaean high-priesthood.
- xiii. 1–xvi. 24. The leadership of Simon; political independence secured. A brief reference to the rule of John Hyrcanus.

§ 3. The Author.

There are no direct indications in the book as to who the author was, nor is anything to be gathered elsewhere regarding him; but some points concerning him may be inferred from certain *data* in his book. It is clear that he was a rigid adherent of orthodox Judaism, and his patriotism is everywhere evident. That he was a native of Palestine is equally clear, for he manifests an intimate, and even minute knowledge, both of the geography and topography of the land. There are grounds for believing that he belonged to the circle of the Sadducees; although a loyal upholder of the Law, his zeal is not characterized by any approach to Pharisaic fanaticism; his sympathy for the Jewish high-priesthood is frequently manifested; his tolerant attitude towards the profaning of the Sabbath (ii. 41; ix. 43 ff.) is very different from that which would have been adopted by a Pharisee; there is not the slightest hint of a belief in the life after death, see ii. 52 ff. where a reference to this would have been eminently appropriate, had it been believed in. These reasons go far in justifying the opinion that the author was a Sadducee.

[1] The name is derived, most probably, from the Hebrew מַקָּבָה 'hammer' (cp. Judges iv. 21); another derivation is suggested by S. J. Curtiss (*The name Machabee*, Leipzig, 1876), namely מַכְבִּי 'quencher' (cp. Isa. xliii. 17), i.e. he who exterminated the enemies of his people. Earlier commentators explained the name as consisting of the initial letters of the words מי כמכה באלם יהוה ('who is like unto thee among the gods, Yahweh', Exod. xv. 11); but there is no reason to suppose that a cryptic title of this kind would have been adopted by those whose special boast was loyalty to their God and His Law.

§ 4. Date of the Book.

The passages which throw light on the date of the composition of the book are:

(*a*) In reference to the sepulchre which Simon the Maccabee built for his parents and his four brothers at Modin, the writer says in xiii. 30: 'This is the sepulchre which he made at Modin, and it is there unto this day.' The sepulchre in question was an elaborate one, as is clear from the description given (xiii. 27–29); it consisted of seven pyramids with 'great pillars' around them; when, therefore, it is spoken of as being in existence 'unto this day', it must have been standing for some considerable time when the author wrote this book. The building of this sepulchre is described as having taken place immediately after the death of Jonathan (xiii. 25), i. e. in 143 B. C., and Simon was murdered in 135 B. C. When the writer, therefore, speaks of the sepulchre standing 'unto this day', we must allow at the least the lapse of about thirty years, probably more, from the time the year 143 B. C. to the time when the writer made this statement. That would make the earliest possible date of the book about 110 B. C.

(*b*) But in xvi. 23, 24 we have the following: 'And the rest of the acts of John, and of his wars . . . behold, they are written in the chronicles of his high-priesthood, from the time that he was made high-priest after his father'; the formula here used is very frequent in the O.T., but it is invariably employed in reference to a ruler whose reign has been concluded. These chronicles, that is to say, took up the narrative at which our author ceased his account; therefore he was writing at a period subsequent to the time at which the chronicles of John's high-priesthood had been compiled. Now John (Hyrcanus) died in 105 B. C., so that even if the records of his doings were being kept from year to year during his rule, they were not finished until the year 105 B. C., and therefore the writer of 1 Macc. did not begin his work until, at the earliest, after this year. On the other hand, the book cannot have been written after the year 63 B. C., for it was in the autumn of this year that Pompey took Jerusalem, and desecrated the Temple by entering into the Holy of Holies (cp. Josephus, *Antiq.* XIV. iv. 2–4; *Bell. Iud.* I. vii. 3–6); it is inconceivable that the book would have contained no reference to this, had it been written after this calamity had taken place. Cf. the references to the faithfulness of the Romans as allies (viii. 1. 12, xii. 1, xiv. 40). Roughly speaking, therefore, the book must have been finished some time between the years 100–70 B. C., nearer the former than the latter date. But this does not mean to say that the writer did not *begin* his work at an earlier period; for, although, the author made use of certain documents (see below), which implies, of course, that he was writing some time subsequent to the events recorded, there are passages which certainly give the impression that he wrote as a contemporary of those who took the leading part in those events; such a passage, e. g. as xiv. 4–15, in which the details of Simon's reign are described, reads like the account of an eye-witness; it was a period of peace ('And the land had rest all the days of Simon'), and therefore conducive to literary work. There seems to be nothing that can be urged against the belief that the writer began his work during the reign of Simon; the looking-up of records, and the compiling of a book which is, upon the face of it, a very careful piece of work, must have taken some time to complete. The conclusion, therefore, is that the gathering of materials began as early as the time of Simon (142–135 B. C.), but that the completed work must be dated some time later. We cannot be far wrong in assigning the work in its final form to somewhere during the last quarter of the second century B. C.

§ 5. Literary and Religious Characteristics.

Although a translation (see § 6) the literary style of the book is admirable; the narrative is written in a simple, straightforward manner, with an entire absence of anything artificial; the reader's interest is engaged throughout, both on account of the easy flow in the style of writing, as well as on account of the graphic way in which the details are presented. The author writes as a historian, whose duty it is to record the facts without colouring them with personal observations; he is impartial, but this does not prevent him from sometimes bursting out into a poetical strain. While, as might be expected, there are frequent reminiscences of the language of the Old Testament, the author in no wise imitates this, his writing being marked throughout by his own individual style. On the other hand, there are not infrequent exaggerations, especially in point of numbers; and considerable freedom is observable in the way in which discourses are put into the mouths of important persons; but in these things the author only shows himself to be the child of his age; his substantial accuracy and trustworthiness are not affected thereby.

From the religious standpoint the book is likewise marked by special characteristics; these are to be explained partly by the writer's sober and matter-of-fact way of looking at things, and partly by the somewhat altered religious outlook of the age as compared with earlier times. The most striking characteristics here are (i) that the direct divine intervention in the nation's affairs is not nearly so prominently expressed as in the books of the Old Testament; and (ii) that God is not mentioned by name in the whole book. The writer is very far from being wanting in religious belief and feeling; his conviction of the existence of an all-seeing Providence who helps those who are worthy comes out strongly in such passages as ii. 61, iii. 18 ff., iv. 10 ff., ix. 46, xii. 15; but he evidently has an almost equally strong belief in the truth expressed in the modern proverb, that 'God helps those who help themselves'. This very sensible religious attitude, which is as far removed from scepticism as it is from fatalism, fully corresponds to the writer's sober impartiality as a historian. But his attitude was, doubtless, also due to the influence of certain tendencies which were beginning to assert themselves. These centred round the Jewish doctrine of God. Just as there was a disinclination, on account of its transcendent holiness, to utter the name of God, and instead, to substitute paraphrases for it, so there arose also a disinclination to ascribe action among men directly to God, because of His inexpressible majesty. One result of this was the further tendency to emphasize and extend the scope of human free-will. These tendencies were only beginning to exert their influence, but they largely explain the religious characteristics of the book.

§ 6. Original Language.

In his *Prologus Galeatus* Jerome distinctly states that Hebrew was the language in which the book was written: 'Machabaeorum primum librum hebraicum repperi' (cp. also the title given by Origen, see § 1 above). The question arises, nevertheless, as to whether Hebrew proper or Palestinian Aramaic is meant; two considerations, however, make it almost certain that it was Hebrew. In the first place, the writer clearly takes as his pattern the ancient inspired Scriptures (cp. Grimm, p. xvii), so that the obvious presumption is that he would have written in the holy tongue. And, secondly, there are many indications in the book itself that it was translated from Hebrew rather than from Aramaic, many of these will be found in the commentary; in some cases, mistakes in translation are most easily and naturally accounted for on the supposition that they were translated from Hebrew, e.g. i. 28 καὶ ἐσείσθη ἡ γῆ ἐπὶ τοὺς κατοικοῦντας αὐτήν: this presupposes an original על which was translated 'against' instead of 'because of'; it can mean either of these, according to the context; other examples are found in ix. 24, xiv. 28, see notes in commentary. There are, furthermore, many examples of Hebrew idiomatic phrases translated literally into Greek. There can, therefore, be no reasonable doubt that the book was originally written in Hebrew. But it seems clear that this original Hebrew text was little used, and disappeared altogether at a very early period; the reasons which lead to this supposition are firstly that not even does Josephus show any signs of having used it, and secondly, as Torrey (*E. B.* 2866) points out: 'There is no evidence of correction from the Hebrew, either in the Greek, or in any other of the versions . . . on the contrary, our Greek version is plainly seen to be the result of a single translation from a Hebrew manuscript which was not free from faults.'

§ 7. The Sources of the Book.

One of the chief sources of information utilized by the writer of 1 Macc. seems to have been the accounts given to him by eye-witnesses of many of the events recorded; one is led to this conviction by considering the wonderfully graphic descriptions of certain episodes (cp., e. g., iv. 1–24, vi. 28–54, vii. 26–50, ix. 1–22, 32–53, x. 59–66, &c.), the sober presentation of the facts, and the frequent mention of details obviously given for no other reason than that they actually occurred. That the writer had also written sources to draw from is to be presumed from such passages as ix. 22: 'And the rest of the acts of Judas, and his wars, and the valiant deeds which he did, and his greatness, they are not written,' the implication being that in part these acts had been written (cp. xi. 37, xiv. 18, 27, 48, 49), and xvi. 23, 24: 'And the rest of the acts of John . . . behold, they are written in the chronicles of his high-priesthood. . . .'

Besides these sources, there are a certain number of documents which have been incorporated in the book; the genuineness, or otherwise, of these requires some more detailed consideration. They fall into three groups; but for reasons which will become apparent the documents belonging to each group respectively cannot in every case be kept separate.

i. *Letters of Jewish origin.*

(*a*) The letter from the Jews in Gilead asking Judas to send them help because they were being attacked by the Gentiles (v. 10–13). This purports to contain the very words which were written; but it is probably merely a summary of what the author of the book had derived from some well-informed source; that it represents, however, in brief, the contents of some written document, and was not simply a verbal message, may be assumed, as it stands in contrast to what is said to have been a verbal message in v. 15.

(*b*) The letter from Jonathan to the Spartans (xii. 6–18). Concerning this it must be said that the artificial way in which it has been pressed into the text is sufficient to arouse suspicion. In xii. 1 we are told of an embassy being sent to Rome; the narrative is broken by *v.* 2 which refers to a letter which was sent to the Spartans, and 'to other places'; in *v.* 3, which comes naturally after *v.* 1, the thread of the narrative is taken up again. Then in *v.* 5, where one might reasonably have expected further details about the embassy to Rome, it goes on to say: 'And this is the copy of the letter which Jonathan wrote to the *Spartans*.' The copy of this letter then follows; but the main subject with which the chapter began, obviously a more important one, is left without further mention. On considering the letter itself, it must strike one that it is not easy to understand what the purpose of it was. In *v.* 10 the purpose is stated to be the renewing of brotherhood and friendship; but in the same breath, as it were, it is said that the Jews needed none of these things, 'having for our encouragement the holy books which are in our hands.' Then, again, in *v.* 13, after reference has been made to the afflictions which the Jews had endured, the letter continues (*vv.* 14, 15): 'We were not mindful, therefore, to be troublesome unto you . . . for we have the help which is from heaven to help us. . . .' Thus, in the same letter, brotherhood and friendship are desired, on the one hand, while on the other it is said that this is not required. The object of the letter is, therefore, not apparent; nor can it be said that it reads like a genuine document. That a relationship of some kind existed between the Jews and the Spartans need not be doubted; the letter probably reflects the fact of this relationship, which the writer of this book, or more probably a later editor, desired to place on record, while not wishing to make it appear that his people had any need to depend upon foreign help in struggling with their enemies (see further the notes on this passage in the commentary). In connexion with this letter the following one must be considered.

(*c*) The letter from Areios, king of the Spartans, to Onias the high-priest (xii. 20–23). This owes its presence here to the fact that in the letter just dealt with Jonathan cites the existence of former friendship between the Jews and the Spartans as a reason for renewing the same (xii. 7–9); it is added as an appendix to Jonathan's letter. The original of this document must have been written about 150 to 200 years earlier than that in which it is incorporated (see the notes on the passage in the commentary). It is only of indirect importance in the present connexion as it does not bear on the history of the Maccabaean struggle. But the fact of a letter written so long before this period being quoted here shows with what care such documents were preserved, and thus tends to inspire confidence in the general historicity of our book, since it is clear that the writer (or, as in this case, probably a later editor) had recourse to the national archives for information; for even if, as some commentators rightly believe, this letter was added by a later editor, it is equally true that he depended on ancient documents for his additions.

(*d*) In xiv. 27–47 we have a source of an entirely different character. This passage contains a panegyric on Simon, together with a *résumé* of his prosperous reign. It is stated to have been engraved on tables of brass, and to have been set up in a conspicuous place within the precincts of the sanctuary; copies of it are also said to have been deposited in the treasury (cp. *vv.* 27, 48, 49). On comparing the details of Simon's reign given in this section with those in chaps. xi–xiii, however, it will be found that there are several chronological discrepancies. The course of the history, as given in the book itself, is acknowledged on all hands to be, on the whole, of a thoroughly trustworthy character; but if the passage in question be really the copy of an official document, as it purports to be, the accuracy of other portions of the book is, to some extent, impugned. It is difficult to suppose that one and the same author would write the historical account of Simon's reign in chaps. xi–xiii, and then in the very next chapter give a *résumé* of what had preceded differing from it in a number of particulars. The suggested explanation of the difficulty is as follows: The original writer of the book gave in chaps. xi–xiii a substantially correct account of the period of history in question, but was inaccurate in the sequence of events; a later editor added a copy of the document under consideration, to which the original author of the book, for some reason or other, did not have access; or perhaps he gathered his materials from different eye-witnesses of the events recorded, and therefore saw no purpose in utilizing this document. The later editor was not concerned with the discrepancies between the written history and the copy of the document which he added, because he saw that, in the main, they were in agreement. If this solution be the correct one it will follow that for the historical period in question we have two independent accounts as far as the main history is concerned.

ii. *Letters from the suzerain power (Syrian kings) to Jewish leaders.*

(*a*) The letter from Alexander Balas[1] to Jonathan (x. 18–20). There can scarcely be two opinions regarding this document; it is not a copy of the letter, but merely its purport which our author has woven into his narrative, much after the same manner in which he incorporates the general sense of the various speeches he records. It is far too short and abrupt to be the actual letter of one who was seeking the help and alliance of the Jewish leader, and for whose friendship this aspirant to the Syrian throne was bidding. The author of our book, moreover, adds some words of his own in the middle of the letter, a thing he is scarcely likely to have done had he been quoting the actual words of the letter itself. On the other hand, there is not the slightest reason to doubt that a genuine document has been made use of here.

(*b*) The letter from Demetrius I to the nation of the Jews (x. 25–45). This was written for the purpose of out-bidding Alexander Balas in promises of favour, remitting of taxes, and conferring of privileges, &c., on the Jews in return for their support in his struggle to retain his throne. While it must be admitted that the letter is based upon an original document—all the probabilities go to support this—there are two reasons for questioning the accuracy of the details. The promises and concessions made to the Jews are of such an exaggerated character that, had they really been made, they would have defeated their object by arousing suspicions among the Jews regarding the writer's sincerity; this, indeed, was actually the case (see *v.* 46), but the reason of Jonathan's incredulity is not the character of the promises, but the fact that Demetrius had before done 'great evil in Israel', and 'had afflicted them very sore'; that does not tally with the contents of the letter as given. If one compares the sober contents of another letter from Demetrius on the same subject, not actually quoted, but incorporated in the narrative (x. 3–6), the document under consideration must strike one as untrustworthy as regards details. Then, in the second place, a number of the things actually promised in the letter correspond so exactly with the highest aspirations of the Jews at this time, that they suggest rather the expression of Jewish ideals than actual promises; such are, the promise that Jerusalem is to be 'holy and free' (*v.* 31), a thing which would have been impossible for the Syrian king to grant if he was to have any real hold upon this part of his kingdom, a Syrian garrison in Jerusalem being essential to his overlordship; the promise to permit the full observance of all the ancient feasts and holy-days, together with 'immunity and release'[2] for all Jews during these periods, as well as during three days before and after each (*vv.* 34, 35); this would have meant an end to the hellenization of Jewry which the Syrian kings had always regarded as indispensable if the Jews were to be their genuine subjects; the promise that the Jews were to have their own laws (*v.* 37), a thing which would have meant an *imperium in imperio*, a dangerous state of affairs from the Syrian point of view; and finally, the promise to remit a large amount of taxation, and to give princely gifts to the sanctuary (*vv.* 39 ff.); this would have meant considerable loss to the royal coffers at a time when there was the highest need of increasing monetary supplies. For these reasons, the letter we are considering must be regarded as ungenuine so far as most of its details are concerned.

(*c*) The letter from Demetrius II to Jonathan, enclosing one to Lasthenes (xi. 30–37). Most of what has been said regarding (*b*) applies to this document as well. It represents an original letter, the contents of which were utilized by the author of 1 Macc., and elaborated in accordance with his ideas of things.

(*d*) The letter from Antiochus VI to Jonathan (xi. 57). This is clearly a succinct summing-up of the contents of the original letter; its extreme shortness and the absence of salutation show that, although written in the first person, it does not profess to do more than to give the general sense of the original.

(*e*) The letter from Demetrius II to Simon (xiii. 36–40). This letter, in which the Syrian king acknowledges receipt of certain presents from the Jewish high-priest, and confirms earlier privileges, is stamped with the mark of genuineness; it reads like an original, and is doubtless a copy of this.

(*f*) The letter from Antiochus VII to Simon (xv. 2–9). To some extent what was said in reference to (*b*) and (*c*) applies also to this letter; it is probably not a verbatim copy of the original, but represents in part the contents of this; on the other hand, there are elements in it which are the expression of ardent desires rather than the actual facts of the case.

iii. *Letters from the rulers of foreign kingdoms.*

(*a*) The document containing the treaty of alliance between the Romans and the Jews (viii. 23–32). In *vv.* 24 ff. it is stated, as one of the articles of the treaty, that if the Romans are attacked, the Jews

[1] He was, of course, not yet king when he wrote this letter.
[2] See, on this, the notes in the commentary.

must not render the enemy any help, whether of 'food, arms, money, or ships' (*v.* 26); this mention of ships is held by several commentators to be a proof that this document belongs to a later date than the time of Judas, when the Jews were not in possession of any ships, and that therefore the whole section is a later interpolation. But it is quite possible that the foresight of the Romans sufficiently explains this mention of ships; they might, indeed, very naturally have assumed the possession of ships by the Jews, as they must have been aware of the long stretch of coast-land which belonged to Palestine. It was, as a matter of fact, not long after the time of Judas that the Jews acquired a harbour: 'And amid all his glory he (i. e. Simon) took Joppa for a haven, and made it an entrance for the isles of the sea' (xiv. 5), cp. also xiii. 29. There seems no sufficient reason to doubt that the author of 1 Macc. made use here of the actual document in question, though it may be that he gives only its general contents, and not a verbatim copy.

(*b*) *The letter from the Spartans to Simon* (xiv. 20–22). We are confronted here with the same difficulty which occurs in the letter from Jonathan to the Spartans (xii. 6–18, see i. (*b*) above). The section opens (*v.* 16) with the words: 'And it was heard at Rome that Jonathan was dead, and even unto Sparta, and they were exceedingly sorry;' it then goes on to say that the Romans wrote to Simon (who had succeeded his brother) on tables of brass to renew 'the friendship and the confederacy' (*v.* 18); but then, instead of giving a copy of this letter, as might reasonably have been expected, it goes on to say: 'And this is a copy of the letter which the Spartans sent.' In this letter it is stated that the two Jewish ambassadors who were the bearers of it were Numenius, the son of Antiochus, and Antipater, the son of Jason. But then the narrative (in *v.* 24) goes on: 'After this Simon sent Numenius to Rome with a great shield of gold of a thousand pound weight, in order to confirm the confederacy with them.' On the previous occasion on which mention is made of a *rapprochement* between the Jews and the Romans on the one hand, and the Spartans on the other, the same two ambassadors were sent, first to the Romans and then to the Spartans, on the same journey (see xii. 16, 17); on the present occasion it is to be presumed, for the text implies it, that this was also done; but if so, how is one to account for the fact that in the letter to the Spartans these ambassadors are said to be the bearers of it, while immediately after (*v.* 24) it is said that Numenius started on his journey? Then there is this further difficulty; is it likely, as stated in the text, that on the death of Jonathan the Romans would have taken the initiative in renewing the treaty with the Jews? This seems to be directly contradicted by *v.* 24. It seems probable that *vv.* 17–23 are an interpolation added later; this would also explain the otherwise unaccountable words 'and even unto Sparta' in *v.* 16, which was presumably put in because of the interpolation; the text of this verse, as it stands, cannot fail to strike one as suspicious: *καὶ ἠκούσθη ἐν Ῥώμῃ ὅτι ἀπέθανεν Ἰωναθάν, καὶ ἕως Σπάρτης, καὶ ἐλυπήθησαν σφόδρα.* The contents of the letter read like an official document; the probability seems to be that use has been made of some genuine record which, as already remarked, was interpolated at a later period.

(*c*) The letter from Lucius, the Roman consul, to Ptolemy Euergetes II, king of Egypt (xv. 16–21). This is the copy of a circular letter written in the name of 'Lucius the consul', and brought back by Numenius. In it the friendship between the Romans and the Jews is proclaimed; copies of it are sent not only to the kings of Egypt and Syria, but also to a number of small separate States which enjoyed complete independence. Now Josephus (*Antiq.* XIV. viii. 5) mentions a letter from the Roman Senate, written in the name of the praetor Lucius Valerius in reply to a message brought by a Jewish embassy; as in the case just referred to, Numenius, the son of Antiochus, is one of the ambassadors,[1] and he brings a gift of a golden shield; the contents of the letter are similar, and it is, likewise, sent to a number of independent petty States. But, according to Josephus, this happened in the ninth year of Hyrcanus II, who reigned 63–40 B.C. Now if, as is maintained by some (especially by Willrich, in his *Juden und Griechen vor der makkabäischen Erhebung*, pp. 70 ff.), Josephus is right here, the passage in question is an interpolation, and must have been added shortly before the beginning of the Christian era. Mommsen (*Hermes* ix. 284 ff., cp. Kautzsch, *Die Apokryphen und Pseudepigraphen des alten Testamentes*, i. p. 30) has proved that Josephus is recording genuine history in saying that the praetor Lucius Valerius sent a letter to the Jews, with the contents as given, during the reign of Hyrcanus II. But this does not constitute an insuperable difficulty, for one of the consuls in 139 B.C. was named Lucius Calpurnius Piso, and the 'Consul Lucius' spoken of in the text (xv. 16) could quite well refer to him. What is more difficult is the fact of the great similarity in the contents between the letter as given in 1 Macc., and that given in Josephus; Mommsen maintains that they are not identical, which would mitigate the difficulty; but the mention of Numenius, the son of Antiochus, in both documents is more serious; the explanation

[1] Two other ambassadors, Alexander the son of Jason, and Alexander the son of Dositheus, accompany him, according to this account.

given by Torrey (*E.B.* 2865) that Josephus 'omitted the portion of 1 Macc. containing the mention of Numenius and the golden shield, but took occasion to introduce this important name, and the most interesting details, at the next opportunity', is not very illuminating. Probably Willrich is right in regarding the passage as a later interpolation, added because it seemed appropriate in a place where Simon's treaty with Rome was mentioned (*op. cit.* p. 72); this conclusion was arrived at independently by the present writer, on the following grounds:—Numenius is mentioned in 1 Macc. in connexion with an embassy to Rome in xii. 16, in the letter of *Jonathan* to the Spartans, which, as we have already seen reasons to believe, is a later interpolation; he is also referred to incidentally in a similar connexion in the time of *Simon* xiv. 24, cp. xv. 15. But a Numenius, in all respects identical, so far as description and name are concerned, is mentioned by Josephus as taking part in an embassy to the Romans, and having presented a shield of gold of a thousand pounds' weight, in the reign of *Hyrcanus II*; it seems, on the face of it, highly improbable that both references can be correct; either the episode of the shield in connexion with Numenius took place in the reign of *Simon*, or in that of *Hyrcanus II.* The account given by Josephus, and the letter as quoted by him (*Antiq.* XIV. viii. 5), appear to be undoubtedly genuine; it follows that 1 Macc. xv. 15–24 is due to an interpolator; there are also independent reasons for regarding this passage as an interpolation, since it breaks the narrative in a very obvious and awkward manner. The interpolator, knowing that negotiations had actually taken place between Simon and the Romans, has transferred an incident describing a Jewish embassy to Rome, which belongs to a later period, to the time of Simon. Josephus, in his edition of 1 Macc., did not read the section xv. 15–24 as we have it (see *Antiq.* XIII. vii. 3); he does, however, follow 1 Macc. xii. 16 ff. (see *Antiq.* XIII. v. 8) in associating Numenius, the son of Antiochus, and Antipater, the son of Jason, with an embassy sent to Rome in the reign of *Jonathan*; but we have already seen that the whole of this letter in 1 Macc. is a later interpolation; it follows, therefore, that Josephus had this interpolation in his copy of 1 Macc., though the Lucius letter (xv. 16–24) seems to have been absent from the text he used.

§ 8. The Greek Manuscripts.

The most important of these are the three uncials *Cod. Sinaiticus* (א), *Cod. Alexandrinus* (A), *Cod. Venetus* (V), the latter belonging to the eighth or ninth century. *Cod. Vaticanus* (B) does not contain the books of the Maccabees. The text represented in א V is, on the whole, better than that represented in A; but all three are undoubtedly the offspring of a single Greek MS. Whether, however, it can be said that *all* our texts, as well as the Versions, come from one Greek MS. (Torrey, in *E.B.* 2867) is not so certain; for there are isolated readings (small in number, it is true) in some of the cursives which presuppose a better text in the passages in question than that represented in the three uncials; in some cases these readings are supported by one or other of the Versions. Of the cursives which have been used, 52, 106, 107 follow, now א A against V, now א V against A; in a somewhat less degree this is also true of 56, 62, as well as of 55; but this latter has retained some readings, peculiar to itself, which are superior to those in any other MS., uncial or cursive (see e. g. iii. 47, 48, 49, iv. 61, v. 22, 67, vii. 7, 38), and it is possible that these represent echoes of a MS. or MSS. other than the single Greek MS. which is the parent of the three uncials; at the same time the fact is not lost sight of that in other cases the variations in 55 are merely explanatory additions, and in this, as well as in its agreement at times with $\mathfrak{S}^{luc}$ (see below), betrays a Lucianic colouring. Another group is formed by 19, 64, 93;[1] these are Lucianic in character, but 64 less so than the other two; with these three $א^{c.a}$ sometimes agrees against all other Greek MSS.; very frequently 19, 93 and $\mathfrak{S}^{luc}$ (see below) go together against all other authorities; this occurs in about fifty cases. The cursive 71 offers a curious phenomenon on account of its large number of omissions; these are usually skilfully manipulated; they have been recorded in the *apparatus criticus* because it quite looks as if in some instances a better reading were afforded by the omission. That in spite of these omissions 71 here and there shows signs of Lucianic colouring is an interesting fact. So far as the cursives are concerned, with the exception of 19, 64, 93, and 71, only those readings are recorded in the *apparatus criticus* which seemed to be of importance.

The collations used for the above are, for the uncials, Swete's *The Old Testament in Greek*, vol. iii., and for the cursives the *apparatus criticus* of Holmes and Parsons.

§ 9. The Syriac and Latin Versions.

(*a*) The Syriac text exists in two forms; one is represented in *Cod. Ambrosianus* (sixth century);[2] this follows in the main the text of the Greek uncials ($\mathfrak{S}^{g}$ in the *app. crit.*), and is preserved up to

[1] = Luc in the *apparatus criticus*.
[2] Edited by Ceriani (Milan, 1876).

xiv. 25ᵃ, from there onwards it = 𝔖luc; the other is the text found in the Peshitta,[1] which is, however, Lucianic in character, and has, as we have seen, great affinity with the Lucianic group of cursives 19, 64, 93.[2] See the very useful notes on the two Syriac recensions by G. Schmidt, 'Die beiden syrischen Uebersetzungen des I. Makkabäerbuchs,' in *ZATW*, 1897, pp. 1 ff., 233 ff.

(*b*) The Latin Version is also preserved in two recensions; both are pre-hieronymian; one is that found in the Vulgate (𝔏1), the other is that contained in *Cod. Sangermanensis*;[3] (𝔏2) the latter is only preserved up to the beginning of chap. xiv.

Both the Syriac and Latin Versions are translations from the Greek.

LITERATURE.

Grimm, in *Kurzgefasstes Exeg. Handbuch* . . . (1853 . . .).
Bissell, in Lange-Schaff's *Commentary* . . . (1880).
Fairweather and Black, *The First Book of Maccabees*, in the Cambridge Bible for Schools (1897).
Kautzsch, in *Die Apokryphen und Pseud. des A. T.* (1900).
Knabenbauer, in *Cursus Scripturae Sacrae* (1907).
For the older literature see Grimm, and Schürer *HJP*. II. iii. pp. 9 ff. (E. T. 1890).
Other works which have been of use are referred to in the body of the work.

[1] Edited by P. de Lagarde, *Libri vet. test. apocryphi Syriace* . . . (Leipzig, 1861).
[2] It is represented by 𝔖luc in the *app. crit.*; the sign 𝔖 denotes the consensus of these two recensions.
[3] Edited by Sabatier, *Bibl. Sacr. Latinae versiones antiquae*, ii. pp. 1017 ff.

THE FIRST BOOK OF MACCABEES

INTRODUCTION. I. 1–9.

I. 1–4. *The Victory of Alexander the Great over the Persians, and the founding of his empire.*

1 1 And it came to pass after Alexander, the son of Philip the Macedonian[a], who came from the land
of Chittim, had smitten Darius, king of the Persians and Medes[b], that he reigned in his stead[c].
2, 3 And he waged many wars, and won strongholds[d], [e]and slew kings[f], and pressed forward to the ends
of the earth, and took spoils from many peoples[e]. But when the land was silenced[g] before him, [h i]he
4 became exalted[h], and his heart was lifted up[i]. Then he gathered together [k]a very mighty army[k],
and ruled over lands and peoples and principalities[l]; and they became tributary unto him.

I. 5–9. *The sickness and death of Alexander; the division of his empire.*

5, 6 And after these things he took to his[m] bed, and perceived that he was about to die. Then he
called his chief ministers, men who had been brought up with him from his youth, and divided his
7 kingdom among them while he was yet alive. And Alexander had reigned twelve years when he
8, 9 died. And his ministers ruled, each in his particular domain. And after he was dead they all

I. [a] + who first reigned in Greece 𝔏^1 [b] *the repetition of the verb* (και επαταξεν) *is not required*; > 𝔏^1 [c] προτερον (προτερος 𝔖^{luc} Luc) επι την Ελλαδα *is probably a gloss*; > 𝔏^1 [d] + many 𝔏^2 + all 𝔏^1 [e–e] > 𝔖^{luc} [f] + of the earth ℵ V 𝔏^1 [g] was silent and quiet 𝔖^{luc} [h–h] > 𝔖^{luc} [i–i] > ℵ [k–k] a strong and numerous host 𝔖^{luc} [l] princes ℵ [m] αυτου ℵ A 𝔏^2

I. 1. **And it came to pass.** The Hebrew original of the book is indicated at the outset, καὶ ἐγένετο being the usual Septuagint rendering of ויהי.

Alexander the 'Great', 356–323 B.C., the third Macedonian king of this name.

Chittim. i.e. the people of the islands and coastlands of Greece, cp. Jer. ii. 10 אִיֵּי כִתִּיִּים. In Gen. x. 4 the *Chittim* are called 'sons of Javan' (Greece). They took their name originally, according to Phoenician inscriptions, from *Kiti* (the Greek *Kition*), the chief city on the island of Cyprus, now called Larnaca. The original colonists were Phoenicians, later on many Greeks settled down there, hence the term 'sons of Javan' applied to these *Chittim*.

Darius. The third of the name, known as Codomannus.

he reigned in his stead. Cp. Dan. viii. 21, where Alexander is spoken of as מלך יון, and xi. 2, where his kingdom is spoken of as מלכות יון.

2. **kings.** Not to be taken in a literal sense, generals, governors, and the like, are meant.

3. **the ends of the earth.** A constant O.T. expression: עד אפס הארץ.

his heart was lifted up. Cp. Dan. xi. 12. ורם לבבו.

4. **principalities.** The reading of ℵ (τυράννων for τυραννιῶν) is perhaps preferable; *satrapies* (or *satrap*), the Persian province is presumably meant, though in Esther ix. 3 a difference is made between the ruler of a province and a 'tyrannos' (οἱ ἄρχοντες τῶν σατραπειῶν καὶ οἱ τύραννοι).

they became tributary unto him. In Judges i. 28 (= Sept. i. 30) this phrase occurs, but the Heb. ויהיו למס = 'they were subject to task-work', cp. Gen. xlix. 15.

6. **chief ministers.** παῖς is used in 1 Sam. xix. 1 of the chief officers of Saul (עבדיו).

brought up with him. τοὺς συνεκτρόφους αὐτοῦ, cp. Acts xiii. 1 Μαναήν τε Ἡρῴδου τοῦ τετράρχου σύντροφος.

divided his kingdom . . . Grimm, *in loc.*, gives numerous references to ancient authors in which this is referred to, but shows that the statement is unhistorical; he says that the story was probably circulated by the partisans of the various Hellenic kings in order to make their assumption of kingship appear legitimate in the eyes of the people.

while he was yet alive. When one remembers how young Alexander was at his death, the improbability of the whole tradition is obvious. 'Greater likelihood attaches to the statement of Justin (xii. 15), Diodorus Siculus (xviii. 2), and Curtius (x. 5. 7), that when no longer able to speak, the dying Macedonian took off his signet-ring and handed it to Perdiccas, the captain of his body-guard, in token of his desire that he should reign after him' (Fairweather and Black, *in loc.*; this is also referred to by Grimm); but as an hereditary monarchy existed in Macedonia (cp. *v.* 9), this statement must also be regarded as unhistorical.

7. **he died.** He was taken ill with fever in the night of May 31, 323 B.C., and died eleven days after.

8. **And his ministers . . .** This is a continuation of the unhistorical statement just referred to.

9. **they all assumed . . .** This is inexact, as only five of Alexander's generals assumed the title of king, and that not till 306 B.C., seventeen years after his death.

assumed the diadem, and their sons after them [did likewise; and this continued for] many years. And these wrought much evil on the earth.

THE CAUSE OF THE MACCABAEAN REVOLT. I. 10–64.

I. 10–15. *Antiochus Epiphanes and the Hellenistic party in Judaea.*

10 And a sinful shoot came forth from them, Antiochus Epiphanes, the son of Antiochus the king,
who had been a hostage in Rome, and had become king in the one hundred and thirty-seventh
11 year of the Greek kingdom. In those days [n]there came forth out of Israel lawless men[n], and persuaded many, saying: 'Let us go and make a covenant with the nations that are round about us;
12 for since[o] we separated ourselves from them many evils have come upon us.' And the saying
13 appeared good in their eyes; and as certain of the people were eager (to carry this out), they went
14 to the king, and he[p] gave them authority to introduce the customs of the Gentiles. And they built
15 a gymnasium[q] in Jerusalem according to the manner of the Gentiles. They also submitted themselves to uncircumcision[r], and repudiated the holy covenant; yea, they joined themselves to the
Gentiles, and sold themselves[s] to do evil.

I. 16–19. *Antiochus subdues Egypt.*

16 And when, in the opinion of Antiochus, the kingdom was (sufficiently) established, he
determined to exercise dominion also over the land of Egypt, in order that he might rule over two
17 kingdoms. So he pushed forward into Egypt with an immense force; with chariots, and elephants

n–n ℵ 𝔏[1]   [o] + the day Luc 𝔏[2]   [p] the king Luc 𝔖 𝔏[2]   [q] stadium 𝔖   [r] *lit.* they drew forward the prepuce 𝔖[luc]   [s] were tempted ℵ[c.a] 19 𝔖[luc]

---

the diadem. Cp. viii. 14, xi. 54; Josephus, *Antiq.* XII. x. 1; a blue and white band which was worn around the Persian royal hat as a badge of royalty; to be distinguished from the crown worn on state occasions. The Heb. equivalent is צָנִיף and מִצְנֶפֶת. It was also worn by the Parthian kings, and by the Byzantine emperors.

wrought much evil. Heb. הִרְבּוּ לַעֲשׂוֹת הָרַע; cp. Ecclus. xlviii. 16 (Sept.; the Heb. is different).

10. **a sinful shoot.** Cp. Ecclus. xl. 15; in Dan. xi. 21 he is called a 'contemptible person'.

Antiochus Epiphanes. The fourth of the name; he seized the Syrian throne in 175 B.C., on the murder of his elder brother Seleucus IV; he died in 164 B.C. (cp. 1 Macc. vi. 1–16, 2 Macc. i. 10–17). The title 'Epiphanes' (the 'Illustrious') which he assumed on coming to the throne, was in mockery changed to 'Epimanes' (the 'Madman') on account of the outrageous acts of which he was guilty. On his coins are found the epithets Θεός and Νικηφόρος; the former title is applied to him by the Samaritans in their letter to him asking him to permit their temple to be called 'The Temple of Hellenius' (Josephus, *Antiq.* XII. v. 5).

the son of Antiochus. i.e. the 'Great'; the third of the name, who reigned 223–187 B.C.

who had been a hostage in Rome. The reference is to Antiochus Epiphanes, who was sent as a hostage to Rome after the defeat of his father at the battle of Magnesia (190 B.C.); he remained in Rome for twelve years.

in the . . . of the Greek kingdom. The reference is to the Seleucid era, which began on October 1, 312 B.C., on the accession of Seleucus I (cp. Josephus, *Antiq.* XIII. vi. 7); the author of this book reckons according to the months of the Jewish calendar, according to which the year begins on the first of Nisan (April), so that his dates are all six months earlier than those of the Seleucid era.

11. **In those days.** An indefinite reference to date occurring very often in the O.T. as well as the N.T.; Heb. בימים ההם.

there came forth . . . Cp. Deut. xiii. 13 (14 in Sept.); the reference is to Jason, cp. *v.* 13 and 2 Macc. iv. 7–10.

make a covenant. The regular Heb. phrase, כרת ברית. The object of this was, according to Josephus (*Antiq.* XII. v. 1, *Bell. Iud.* I. v. 1), solely the acquisition of temporal advantage.

since we separated ourselves . . . The reference here cannot be to any particular time, for the observance of the Mosaic Law was the cause of this separation; it had always been intended to be the means of keeping Israelites free from the contamination of the Gentiles.

many evils have come upon us. Lit. 'have found us', thoroughly Hebraic, cp. e.g. Deut. xxxi. 21. תמצאן . . . רעות רבות:.

12. **appeared good.** Cp. the Hebr. phrase, 'to do what is pleasing in the eyes of'; עשה הטוב בעיני which is of frequent occurrence in the O.T.

13. **and he gave them authority.** Cp. 2 Macc. iv. 9.

14. **And they built a gymnasium.** Cp. Josephus (*Antiq.* XII. v. 1), 2 Macc. iv. 9, 12.

15. **They also submitted . . .** See the rendering of the Syriac in the critical note; cp. 1 Cor. vii. 18. Those who submitted to this operation were called *Meshukim* (from a root meaning 'to draw back'), according to the Roman name, *Recutiti* (Grimm, *in loc.*).

repudiated the holy covenant. Since circumcision was the covenant-mark (Gen. xvii. 11), its obliteration was *ipso facto* the repudiation of the covenant.

sold themselves to do evil. Hebraism, cp. 1 Kings xxi. 20: הִתְמַכֶּרְךָ לַעֲשׂוֹת הָרַע.

16. **the kingdom . . . established.** Hebraism, cp. 1 Kings ii. 12: וַתִּכֹּן מַלְכֻתוֹ.

two kingdoms. i.e. Syria and Egypt.

17. **with an immense force.** Lit. 'a heavy force'; Hebrew usage, cp. בְּעַם כָּבֵד; cp. Dan. xi. 22–24.

18 and horsemen[t], together with a great fleet[u]. And he waged war against Ptolemy, the king of
Egypt. And Ptolemy turned back[x] from before him, and fled; [y]and there fell many wounded[y z].
19 And they[a] captured the fortified cities in Egypt[b]; and he took the spoils from the land[c] of Egypt.

I. 20–28. *The Desecration of the Temple; slaughter of the Jews.*

20 And Antiochus, after he had smitten Egypt, returned in the one hundred and fifty-third year,
21 and went up against Israel and[d] Jerusalem with a great army. And in (his) arrogance he entered
into the sanctuary, and took the golden altar, [e]and the candlestick for the light[e], and all its acces-
22 sories, and the table of the shewbread, and the cups, and the bowls, and the golden censers[f], and the
veil, and the crowns, and the golden adornment on the façade of the Temple, and he scaled it all off.
23 Moreover, he took the silver, and the gold, and the choice vessels; he also took the hidden treasures
24 which he found. And having taken everything, he returned[g] to his own land[h].

25 'And there was great mourning in Israel[i] in every place;
26 And[k] the rulers and elders groaned;
Virgins and young men languished,
And the beauty of the women faded away;
27 Every bridegroom took up (his) lament,
She that sat in the bridal-chamber mourned[l].
28 And the land was moved for her inhabitants,
And all [m]the house of[m] Jacob was clothed with shame.'

I. 29–40. *Jerusalem occupied by Apollonius; massacre of the people; desecration of the Sanctuary.*

29 After the lapse of two years the king[n] sent a chief collector of tribute to the cities of Judah; and
30 he came to Jerusalem with a great host. And he spoke unto them peaceful words in subtilty, so
that they had confidence in him; but he fell upon the city suddenly, and smote it with a grievous
31 stroke, and destroyed much people in Israel. And he took [o]the spoils of the city[o], and burned it
32 with fire, and pulled down the houses thereof and the walls thereof[p] round about. And they led
33 captive the women and the children, and [q]took possession of[q] the cattle. And they fortified the
city of David with a great and strong wall with strong towers, so that it was made into a citadel for
34 them. And they placed there a sinful nation, lawless men; and they strengthened themselves
35 therein. And they stored up (there) arms and provisions, and collecting together the spoils of
36 Jerusalem, they laid them up there. And it became a sore menace, for it was a place to lie in wait
in against the sanctuary, and an evil adversary to Israel continually.

[t] > 64 [u] with great pomp 𝔖 [x] ℵ; ενετραπη A ℵ[c.a] V (= 𝔏[1]) [y–y] > 𝔖[g] [z] fled ℵ were slain 𝔖[luc] [a] he 𝔖[g] 𝔏[1] [b] the land of Egypt A V 93 [c] > land ℵ V [d] + went up against 𝔖[luc] 𝔏[2] 𝔏[1] [e–e] > V [f] the instruments of the sacrifices and offerings 𝔖[luc] [g] carried (*them*) V [h] + And he (A they) made a great slaughter and he (A they) spake with great arrogancy; *all authorities* (*exc* 𝔖[g]); + and he made a great slaughter 𝔖[g], *omitting the rest. The words have probably got out of place, and should come after v.* 21. [i] Jerusalem 64 [k] Therefore 𝔖 [l] ℵ; εγενετο εν πενθει A V επενθησε Luc [m–m] > 93 [n] Antiochus the king Luc [o–o] much spoil 𝔖 [p] of Jerusalem 𝔖 [q–q] > ℵ; + for themselves ℵ[c.a] Luc 𝔖[luc]

---

18. **Ptolemy.** The sixth of the name, Philometor, 181–146 B.C.; he was only sixteen years old at this time.
there fell many wounded. The Hebrew equivalent וַיִּפְּלוּ חֲלָלִים רַבִּים would imply that they were wounded to death (cp. R.V.), but in Greek the word has not this intensive force.
20. **went up against . . . Jerusalem.** Cp. 2 Macc. v. 11 ff.
21. **the golden altar.** Cp. Exod. xxx. 1–6.
the candlestick. Cp. Exod. xxv. 31–9.
22. **the table of the shewbread.** Cp. Exod. xxv. 23–30; cp. Josephus, *Antiq.* III. vi. 6.
23. **the hidden treasures.** Cp. 2 Macc. iii. 10–12; Josephus, *Bell. Iud.* II. ix. 4.
25–8. This lament was probably originally in poetical form, and is largely made up from the language of the O.T. poetical books. Cp. for some verses cast in a somewhat similar mode 2 (4) Esdras x. 22.
25. **great mourning.** Cp. Job xxx. 31.
26. **the elders.** Cp. Lam. i. 19, ii. 10.
faded away. Cp. Sept. of Ps. cviii. 24, ἠλλοιώθη (cix. 24 in Hebr.).
virgins and young men . . . Cp. Lam. i. 4, 18, ii. 10, 20.
27. **took up (his) lament.** Cp. Sept. of Lam. v. 13 κλαυθμὸν ἀνέλαβον (the Heb. reads differently).
28. **clothed with shame.** Cp. Job. viii. 22; Ps. xxxv. 26, cxxxii. 18.
29. **a chief collector of tribute.** i.e. Apollonius, according to 2 Macc. v. 24.
After the lapse of two years. Lit. 'After two years of days'; Heb. מִקֵּץ שְׁנָתַיִם יָמִים, cp. Gen. xli. 1.
30. **he spoke peaceful words.** A Hebrew idiom: וַיֹּאמֶר דִּבְרֵי שָׁלוֹם. Cp. Deut. ii. 26.
he fell upon . . . suddenly. Cp. 2 Macc. v. 24 ff.
33. **into a citadel.** εἰς ἄκραν, i.e. Acra.

37 And they shed innocent blood on every side of the sanctuary,
And they defiled the sanctuary[r].
38 And because of them the inhabitants of Jerusalem fled,
And she became a dwelling for strangers,
Being herself estranged to her offspring,
And her children forsook her.
39 Her sanctuary became desolate as a wilderness,
[s]Her feasts were turned into mourning[s],
Her sabbaths [t]into shame[u],
Her honour[t x] into contempt.
40 According as her glory[y] (had been) [z]so was (now) her dishonour increased[z],
And her high estate was turned to mourning[a].

I. 41–53. *Edict of Antiochus, forbidding Jewish Worship.*

41, 42 And the king[b] wrote unto his whole kingdom, that all should be one people, and that every one
should give up his [religious] usages. And all [c]the nations[c] acquiesced[d] in accordance with the com-
43 mand of the king. And many in Israel took delight in [e]his (form of) worship[e], and they began
44 sacrificing to idols, and profaned the sabbath[f]. Furthermore, the king sent letters[g] by the hand of
messengers to Jerusalem and to the cities of Judah (to the effect that) they should practise customs
45 [h]foreign[i] to (the traditions of) the land[h], and that they should cease the (sacrificing of) whole burnt
offerings, and sacrifices, and drink offerings in the sanctuary, and that they should profane the sabbaths
46, 47 and feasts, and pollute the sanctuary and [k]those who had been sanctified[k]; that they should (moreover) build high places, and sacred groves, and [l]shrines for idols[l], and that they should sacrifice
48 swine and (other) unclean[m] animals; and that they should leave their sons uncircumcized, and make
49 themselves abominable by means of (practising) everything that was unclean and profane, so that
50 they might forget the Law, and change all the (traditional) ordinances. And whosoever should not
51 act according to the word of the king, should die. In this manner did he write unto the whole[n] of
his kingdom; and he appointed overseers[o] over all the people; and he commanded the cities of Judah
52 to sacrifice, every one of them. And many of the people joined themselves unto them, all[p] those
53 [namely] who had forsaken the Law; these did evil[q] in the land, and caused Israel to hide in all
manner of hiding-places.

I. 54–64. *Idolatry forced upon the people of Judah; destruction of copies of the Scriptures; massacre of Israelites.*

54 And on the fifteenth[r] day[s] of Chislev in the one hundred and forty-fifth[t] year they set up upon the
altar an 'abomination of desolation', and in the cities of Judah on every side they established high-

[r] + of the Lord V [s–s] > 𝔖g [t–t] > ℵ *but added by* ℵc.a [u] humiliation 19 [x] *plur. in* 𝔖g 𝔏1 [y] her children ℵ* [z–z] the land was filled with shame ℵ [a] humiliation 64 𝔖luc [b] + Antiochus 𝔏 [c–c] > 𝔖g [d] 𝔏2 [e–e] the worship of the king 𝔖g [f] sanctuary Aa sabbath A* [g] > 64 93 [h–h] of the Gentiles in the land 𝔏 [i] > 93 [k–k] the holy things 𝔖 𝔏2 [l–l] idols A Va 𝔖 𝔏 [m] all ℵ* (unclean ℵc.a) [n] > A V 𝔖 𝔏 [o] + over all his kingdom and 𝔖g [p] all 𝔖g 𝔏1 [q] much evil 64 93 [r] twenty-fifth 𝔖g [s] + in the month Luc [t] forty-fifth A

37–40. Another lament in poetical form originally, the language of which is again largely borrowed from that of the O.T. poetical books.

37. **they shed innocent blood.** Cp. Ps. lxxix. 3.

they defiled the sanctuary. Cp. Ps. lxxix. 1.

38. **a dwelling for strangers.** Cp. Ps. liv. 3; Lam. v. 2.

Being herself estranged. Cp. Lam. i. 1.

her children forsook her. Cp. Lam. i. 5.

39. **Her feasts . . .** Cp. Amos viii. 10.

Her sabbaths into shame. Cp. Lam. ii. 6.

40. **And her high estate . . .** Cp. Lam. ii. 9, 10.

41. **one people.** i. e. as regards religious practice.

44. **letters.** *βιβλία*, Heb. סְפָרִים.

47. **swine and unclean animals.** i.e. animals holy to heathen gods and goddesses; the pig and the hare were holy to Astarte, and as holy animals occupied an important place in the religions of Greece and Asia Minor.

51. **appointed overseers.** Cp. 2 Macc. v. 22.

54. **the fifteenth day of Chislev.** We should read here with 𝔖g 'the twenty-fifth day', see *v.* 59. Chislev is the ninth month of the Hebrew calendar (= December approximately).

the one hundred and forty-fifth year. i.e. 168 B.C.

an abomination of desolation. Cp. Dan. xi. 31, xii. 11; i.e. the abomination which brought about profanation (= desolation); it was a small heathen altar which was set up on the altar of burnt-offering, see *v.* 59.

55, 56 places; and [u]they offered sacrifice[u] at the doors of the houses and in the streets. And the books of
57 the Law which they found they [x]rent in pieces, and[x] burned them in the fire. And with whomsoever
was found a book of the covenant, and if he was (found) consenting unto the Law, such an one was,
58 according to the king's sentence[y], condemned to death. Thus did they in their might to the Israelites
59 who were found[z] month by month in their[a] cities. And on the twenty-fifth day of the month they
60 sacrificed upon the altar which was upon the altar of burnt-offering. And, according to the decree[b],
61 they put to death the women who had circumcised their children, hanging their babes round their
(mothers') necks, and they put to death their (entire) families[c], together with those who had circum-
62 cised them. Nevertheless many in Israel stood firm[d] and determined in their hearts[e] that they would
63 not eat unclean things, and chose rather to die so that they might not be defiled with meats, thereby
64 profaning the holy covenant[f]; and they did die. And exceeding great wrath came upon Israel.

Mattathias. II. 1–70.

II. 1–5. *The Genealogy of the Maccabees.*

2 1 In those days rose up Mattathias, the son of John, the son of Simeon, a priest of the sons of
2 Joarib, from Jerusalem; and he dwelt at Modin. And he had five sons: John, who was surnamed
3, 4, 5 Gaddis; Simon, who was called Thassis; Judas, who was called Maccabaeus; Eleazar, who was
called Auaran; and Jonathan, who was called Aphphus.

II. 6–14. *A Dirge over the desecration of the Holy City.*

6, 7 And he saw the blasphemous things that were done in Judah and in Jerusalem, and said, 'Woe is
me, why was I born to behold the ruin of my people and the ruin[a] of the holy city, and to sit still
there while it was being given into the hand of enemies, and the sanctuary[b] into the hand of
strangers?'

8 [c]Her house[d] is become like (that of) a man dishonoured[e][c];
9 [f]Her glorious vessels are carried away captive;
Her infants have been slain in her streets,
Her young men with the sword of the enemy.
10 What nation hath the kingdom not taken possession of,
(Of what nation) hath it not seized the spoils?
11 Her adornment hath all been taken away,
[g]Instead of a free woman she is become a slave[g].
12 And, behold, our holy things, and our beauty, and our glory have been laid waste,
13 And the heathen have profaned them! To what purpose should we continue to live?
14 And Mattathias and his sons rent their garments, and covered themselves with sackcloth, and
mourned greatly.

[u–u] they burned incense and offered sacrifice 𝔏^{1} they burned incense 𝔏^{2} [x–x] > 𝔖 [y] edict 𝔏^{2} [z] + and they led them away by force 𝔖^{g} [a] V; the ℵ A &c. [b] the command of the king 𝔖 the command of king Antiochus 𝔏^{2} [c] houses ℵ V their entire houses 𝔏 (𝔖^{g} = A) + and plundered ℵ$^{c.a}$ 𝔖^{luc} [d] were hanged A 19 [e] > 19 𝔖^{luc} [f] the holy Law of God 𝔏^{2}

II. [a] > 19 93 𝔖^{luc} 𝔏^{2} [b] her sanctified ones 𝔖^{g} + were delivered 𝔖^{g} [c–c] T.R. 𝔏^{2}; Her temple was like an illustrious man ℵ A V 𝔖^{luc} 𝔏. They did clothe her temple with glory as a man (*is clothed*) 𝔖^{g} [d] people 93 [e] 19 𝔏^{1} [f] + And now Luc [g–g] Her freedom is become bondage 𝔖^{luc}

---

55. **at the doors of the houses.** The reference is to sacrifices offered to the 'deities of the street', i. e. images of Greek gods which stood in the porches of houses.

56. **the books of the Law.** i. e. rolls of the Pentateuch.

58. **to the Israelites who were found.** A literal translation of the Hebrew לישראל הנמצאים.

63. **and chose rather to die.** Cp. 2 Macc. vi, vii.

II. 1. **In those days . . .** Cp. Josephus, *Antiq.* XII. vi. 1.

the son of Simeon. Josephus adds τοῦ Ἀσαμωναίου, from whom the adjectival form of the family name, Asmonaean or Hasmonaean, was derived; the name does not occur in the books of the Maccabees, though Josephus often uses it, and it is found in the Mishnah (*Middoth* i. 6), and frequently in the Gemara (e. g. *Shabbath* 21 *b*, *Baba Kama* 82 *b*), where the name Hasmonaeans is always used for Maccabaeans.

the sons of Joarib. Cp. 1 Chron. xxiv. 7 ff.

Modin. Cp. v. 70, xiii. 25. The present El-Medije, east of Lydda.

4. **Maccabaeus.** See Introduction.

7. **The holy city.** עיר הקדש Isa. xlviii. 3; cp. 2 Macc. i. 12, iii. 1, ix. 14.

8–12. Another dirge in poetical form.

14. **rent their garments . . .** The usual signs of mourning in the East, see further Nowack, *Hebräische Archäologie* I. 192 ff.

II. 15–28. *The commencement of the Maccabaean Revolt.*

15 And the king's officers who were enforcing the apostasy came to the city of Modin [h]to make them
16 sacrifice[h]. And many from Israel went unto them ; but Mattathias and his sons[i] gathered themselves
17 together. Then the king's officers answered and spake unto Mattathias, saying: 'A ruler art thou,
18 and illustrious and great in this city, and upheld by sons and brothers. Do thou, therefore, come
first, and carry out the king's command, as all the nations have done, and all the people[k] of Judah,
and they that have remained in Jerusalem; then shalt thou[l] and [m]thy house[m] be (numbered among)
the friends of the king, and thou and thy sons shall be honoured with silver and gold, and with many
19 gifts.' Thereupon Mattathias answered and said with a loud voice: 'If all the nations that are
within the king's dominions obey him by forsaking, [n]every one of them[n], the worship of their fathers,
20 and have chosen for themselves to follow his commands, yet will I and my sons and my brethren
21 walk in the covenant of our fathers. Heaven forbid that we should forsake the Law and the ordi-
22 nances; (but) the law[o] of the king we will not obey by departing from our worship either to the
23 right hand or to the left.' And as he[p] ceased speaking [q]these words[q], a Jew came forward in the
24 sight of all to sacrifice[r] upon the altar in Modin in accordance with the king's command. And
when Mattathias saw it, [s]his zeal was kindled[s], and his heart quivered (with wrath); and his indig-
25 nation burst forth for judgement, so that he ran and slew him on the altar; and [t]at the same time[t]
26 he [also] killed the king's officer who had come to enforce the sacrificing, pulled down the altar, and
[thus] showed forth his zeal for the Law, just as Phinehas had done in the case of Zimri the son of
27 Salom. And Mattathias cried out with a loud voice in the city, saying, 'Let everyone that is
28 zealous for the Law and that would maintain the covenant come forth after me!' And he and his
sons fled unto the mountains, and left all that they possessed in the city.

II. 29–38. *A strict observance of the Sabbath results in the massacre of a thousand Jewish people.*

29 At that time many who were seeking righteousness and judgement went down to the wilderness to
30 abide there, they and their sons, and their wives, and their cattle; for misfortunes [u]fell hardly[u] upon
31 them. And it was reported to the king's officers and to the troops that were in Jerusalem, the city
of David, that men who had set at nought the king's command[x] had gone down into hiding-places
32 in the wilderness. And many ran after them, and having overtaken them, [y]they encamped against

[h–h] to sacrifice 64 𝕷²; + and burn incense and forsake the Law of God 𝕷¹ [i] they that were with him 64 93
[k] rulers ℵ V [l] + and thy sons V 64 [m–m] and thy sons ℵ^c.a 𝕾 𝕷 [n–n] > 𝕾^luc [o] the word ℵ V Luc
[p] Mattathias 64 93 [q–q] > ℵ (*hab* ℵ^c.b) [r] to burn incense A 𝕾^g [s–s] 𝕾^g *places this after* quivered [t–t] > 𝕷
[u–u] + and were multiplied ℵ* ℵ^c.a were multiplied V [x] counsel ℵ [y–y] > 𝕾^luc 𝕷¹

18. **the friends of the king.** There were, according to Polybius (xxxi. 3. 7), two orders of royal favourites under the Graeco-Syrian kings, viz. those of the 'Companions' and the 'Friends'; these occupied the position of a military aristocracy. Cp. x. 65, xi. 27; 2 Macc. viii. 9.

19. **the king's dominions.** ἐν οἴκῳ τῆς βασιλείας τοῦ βασιλέως, cp. Amos vii. 13 οἶκος βασιλείας, בית ממלכה, in reference to Bethel.

have chosen for themselves. Cp. 2 Chron. xxix. 11 (Sept.).

21. **Heaven forbid.** ἵλεως = חלילה, cp. 2 Sam. xx. 20.

22. **either to the right hand or to the left.** Cp. 2 Sam. xiv. 19.

24. **his heart.** Lit. 'his kidneys', the seat of the emotions and affections, cp. Ps. lxxiii. 21 וכליותי אשתונן, 'for my kidneys were in a ferment.'

for judgement. Heb. כמשפט; what, according to the statute, he was bound to do.

and slew him. Cp. Deut. xiii. 9; 2 Chron. xxx. 16.

26. **as Phineas had done . . .** Cp. Num. xxv. 7, 8.

27. **Let everyone . . . come forth after me.** Grimm quotes (from Livy xxii. 53) the cry of the Roman patriots in time of danger: *Qui rempublicam salvam volunt me sequantur.*

28. **fled unto the mountains.** This would enable him, with a comparatively small number of followers, to defy almost any force that might be brought against him, an attacking party being always at a great disadvantage in mountain warfare.

29. **righteousness and judgement.** Cp. Ps. lxxxix. 14, xcvii. 2; righteousness (צדקה) = ethical right-doing; judgement (משפט) = sense of justice; the technical terms are 'to do (עשה) righteousness', and 'to keep (שמר) judgement', cp. Isa. lvi. 1; the terms are generally used in the reverse order, and rightly so as the more logical; the inward sense of justice has as its result outward acts of righteousness; this is also borne out by the verbs used, 'to keep,' 'to do.'

the wilderness. i.e. the wilderness of Judaea, west of the Dead Sea; it was called Jeshimon, cp. 1 Sam. xxiii. 19, 24, xxvi. 13, meaning 'desolation'.

30. **their cattle.** In the wilderness of Tekoa, which lay to the north of the district just mentioned, there was sufficient vegetation to support cattle, cp. Amos i. 1, vii. 14.

31. **hiding-places in the wilderness.** Cp. 1 Sam. xxiv. 3; Isa. xlii. 22.

33 them, and[y] set the battle in array against them on the Sabbath day. And they said unto them:
'[z]Let it suffice now[z]; come forth, and do according to the command of the king, and ye shall live.'
34 And they answered, 'We will not come forth, nor will we do according to the command of the king,
35, 36 and thereby profane the Sabbath day. Thereupon they immediately attacked them. But they
37 answered them not, nor did they cast a stone at them, nor even block up their hiding-places, saying,
'Let us all die in our innocency; Heaven and earth bear us witness that ye destroy us wrongfully'[a].
38 And they attacked them on the Sabbath; and they died, they and their wives, and their children,
and their cattle, about a thousand souls.

II. 39–48. *Mattathias, supported by the Chasidim, continues the war with success.*

39, 40 And when Mattathias and his friends knew[b] it they mourned greatly for them. And one said to
another, 'If we all do as our brethren have done, and do not fight against the Gentiles for our lives
41 and our ordinances, they will soon destroy us from off the earth.' And they took counsel on that
day, saying, 'Whosoever attacketh us on the Sabbath day, let us fight against him, that we may not in
42 any case all die, as our brethren died in their hiding-places.' Then were there gathered unto them
[c]a company of the Chasidim[c], mighty men of Israel who willingly offered themselves for the Law,

z–z Do ye resist still even now? 𝔏 a uncharitably 𝔖g b heard 𝔖luc c–c the whole company of Jews ℵ V

---

32. **on the Sabbath day.** From the words in *v.* 33 it is evident that the enemy had no desire of taking a mean advantage by fighting on a day on which they knew the Jews would make no resistance.

34. **and thereby profane the Sabbath day.** The profanation of the Sabbath would, according to the preceding words, consist in coming forth and doing according to the command of the king; i.e. the command of the king was that they should come forth and submit themselves. This the Jews would not have done at any time, but to do so on the Sabbath would have been an aggravation of the offence, since, apart from the act of renegades which submission would, under the circumstances, have implied, the coming forth with their belongings would, in itself, have constituted a breaking of the Sabbath.

36. **nor did they cast a stone.** i.e. there was not even the semblance of resistance.

37. **in our innocency.** ἐν τῇ ἁπλότητι ἡμῶν, i.e. 'in our integrity' (תם); cp. Ps. xxvi. 1, 11, xxv. 21, xli. 13.

wrongfully. Cp. xv. 33 where R.V. renders ἀκρίτως 'wrongfully'; this is a better rendering than 'without trial' as R.V. translates here, for the revolt having been entered upon by the events recorded in *vv.* 15–28, the idea of a trial is out of the question. Cp. Ps. lxix. 4, 'They that would cut me off, being mine enemies wrongfully, are mighty.'

38. **they attacked them.** This hardly bears out the statement of Josephus: 'they burned them as they were in the caves without resistance, and without so much as stopping up the entrances of the caves' (*Antiq.* XII. vi. 2).

and they died . . . about a thousand souls. Josephus adds: 'But many of those that escaped joined themselves to Mattathias, and appointed him to be their ruler, who taught them to fight, even on the Sabbath day' (*ibid.*), cp. *vv.* 40, 41.

39. **they mourned greatly for them.** ἕως σφόδρα = עד־מאד; ἐπ' αὐτούς, the verb אבל ('to mourn') is usually followed by על ('upon' or 'over').

40. **and one said to another.** καὶ εἶπεν ἀνὴρ πρὸς τὸν πλησίον αὐτοῦ is another Hebraism: ויאמר איש אל־רעהו.

41. **and they took counsel . . .** Cp. ix. 44 ff., xi. 34, 43 ff.; the counsel ('Whosoever attacks . . .') taken was a modification of the Law; but, as a matter of fact, the Written Law did not forbid necessary labour on the Sabbath. What we have here is an ordinance of the Oral Law, framed by the rigid legalists as the interpretation of the Written Law. The mention of the *Chasidim* in the next verse is significant, as they were responsible, in large measure, for the strict interpretation of the Written Law. The passage shows that the party of the *Chasidim* was already in existence, and was not created by the persecution under Antiochus; see next note.

42. **a company of the Chasidim.** The Ἀσιδαῖοι (= חסידים) are here referred to as though well known, a fact which further substantiates what was said in the preceding note. The *Chasidim* ('pious') were those, frequently referred to in some of the later Psalms (e.g. xii. 2, xxx. 4, xxxi. 23, xxxvii. 28, cxlix. 1–9), who remained true to the traditions and customs of their fathers when, in the third century B.C. and onwards, the Jews of the Dispersion, and also of Palestine, were becoming lax in their observance of orthodox Judaism owing to the rise of the Hellenistic spirit. They were animated by a hatred of everything and everyone that savoured of Hellenism, for, according to them, this implied unfaithfulness to the God of Israel. Although in existence beforehand, it was only during the Maccabaean struggle that they commenced to play an important rôle in the political life of the nation. In 1, 2 Macc. they are referred to three times; the data regarding their characteristics seem, at first sight, to be conflicting. In 1 Macc. ii. 43, 44 they are described as warlike; in vii. 12–14 they appear as the peaceful party, while in 2 Macc. xiv. 6 they are said to 'keep up war, and are seditious, not suffering the kingdom to find tranquillity'. It is probable that these descriptions both witness to the true facts of the case; the natural inclination of these strict observers of the Law would obviously be in the direction of peace; but as soon as they realized that the cherished object of their existence was imperilled, it behoved them to be up and doing. This is borne out by what we read in the Psalms concerning them, for at one time they are spoken of as peaceful worshippers (xxx. 4), and as the lovers of the Lord (xxxi. 23, xxxvii. 28); while at another time they are represented as warriors zealous for the honour of God, and fighting His enemies (cxlix. 6–9). It is not without significance that after the Maccabaean struggle, when the victory for orthodox Judaism had been won, nothing further is heard of the *Chasidim*. They seem to have gradually developed into the Pharisaic party, which was characterized by the same zeal for the Law (cp. Moritz Friedländer, *Geschichte der Jüdischen Apologetik*, pp. 316 ff., 464 ff.).

mighty men of Israel. Cp. 1 Chron. vii. 2, 7 (Sept.).

43 every one of them. And all they that fled from the evils were added unto them, and reinforced
44 them. And they mustered a host, and smote sinners in their anger, and lawless men in their wrath;
45 and the rest fled to the Gentiles to save themselves. And Mattathias and his friends[d] went round
46 about[e], and pulled down altars[f], and they circumcised by force the children that were uncircumcised,
47 as many as they[g] found [h]within the borders[h] of Israel. And they pursued after the sons of pride,
48 and the[i] work prospered in their hand. And they rescued[k] the Law out of the hand of the
Gentiles, and [l]out of the hand[l] of the[m] kings, neither suffered they the sinner to triumph.

II. 49–70. *The last words of Mattathias; his death.*

49 And the days drew near that Mattathias should die, and he said unto his sons: 'Now have pride
50 and rebuke[n] gotten strength and a season of destruction and wrath of indignation. And now (my)
51 children, be zealous for the Law, and give your lives for the covenant of your[o] fathers[q]. [p]And call
to mind the deeds of the[r] fathers[s p] which they did in[t] their generations[q]; [u]that ye may receive[u]
52 great glory and an everlasting name. Was not Abraham found faithful in temptation, and it was
53 reckoned unto him for[x] righteousness? Joseph, in the time of his distress, kept the commandment,
54 and became lord of Egypt. Phinehas, our father, for that he was zealous exceedingly, obtained the
55 covenant[y] of an everlasting[z] priesthood. Joshua, for fulfilling the word[a], became a judge in Israel.
56, 57 Caleb, for bearing witness in[b] the congregation, obtained [c]land (as) an heritage[c]. David, for being
58 merciful, inherited[d] the throne of[d] a [e]kingdom for ever and ever[e]. Elijah, for that he was exceeding
59 zealous for the Law, was taken up into heaven[f]. Hananiah, Azariah (and) Mishael, believing (in
60 God)[g], were saved from the flame. Daniel, for his innocency, was delivered from the mouth of the
61 lions[h]. And thus consider ye [i]from generation to generation[i];—all who hope in Him shall want for
62 nothing. And[k] be not afraid of the words of a sinful man, for his glory [shall be][l] dung and worms[m].
63 To-day he shall be lifted up, and to-morrow[n] he shall in no wise be found, because he is returned
64 unto his dust, and his thought is perished. [o]And ye[o], (my) children, be strong and show yourselves
65 men [p]on behalf of the[q] Law[p]; for therein shall ye obtain glory. And behold Simeon your[r] brother,
66 I know that he is a man of counsel[s]; give ear unto him alway[t]; he shall be a father unto you. And

[d] sons A; they that were with him 𝔖[g] [e] commanded ℵ [f] their altars A V [g] he A V [h–h] among the sons ℵ [i] their 19 [k] took 𝔖[g] [l–l] > 64 [m] their ℵ[c.a] 64 93 [n] famine 𝔖[g] [o] our A [p–p] > 𝔖[luc] [q–q] > 71 [r] our A [s] first ones 𝔖[g] [t] > A [u–u] and ye shall receive 𝔏[2] [x] > A [y] the lot of a covenant ℵ [z] holy A > 71 [a] words Luc. + of the Lord 𝔏[1] [b] > A [c–c] the heritage ℵ 𝔏[1] a heritage of land V a land of heritage 𝔖[luc] [d–d] > 71 [e–e] an everlasting kingdom A 71 [f] verses 59–63 are omitted by 71 [g] 𝔏[1] [h] lion ℵ 64 [i–i] according to generation A [k] > 𝔖[luc] [l] Luc [m] a worm 19 𝔖[luc] 𝔏[1] [n] > A [o–o] > ℵ (*hab* ℵ[c.a]) [p–p] > 71 [q] your A [r] our 93 [s] good counsel 𝔏[2] counsel and intelligence 𝔖 [t] > 𝔏[1]

44. **sinners . . . lawless men.** i.e. the renegade Israelites.

46. **the children . . . Israel.** An eloquent witness to the way in which the Hellenistic spirit had influenced the Jews. The same applies to the mention of altars (i.e. idol-altars), for these verses evidently refer to Jews, cp. the words of Josephus: '. . . and overthrew their idol-altars, and slew those that broke the laws, even all that he could bring under his power, for many of them were dispersed among the nations round about them for fear of him (i.e. Mattathias).'

47. **sons of pride.** Hebraism, cp. 'sons of tumult' (בני שאון) Jer. xlviii. 45; the reference is to the Syrians; cp. i. 21.

48. **neither suffered they the sinner to triumph.** οὐκ ἔδωκαν κέρας τῷ ἁμαρτωλῷ, Hebraism; cp. Ps. lxxv. 5, 'Lift not up your horn on high'; a frequent O.T. figure for strength.

49. **And the days drew near . . .** A frequent O.T. phrase, cp. Gen. xlvii. 29; 1 Kings ii. 1.

50 ff. With this enumeration of the deeds of the fathers, cp. Ecclus. xliv–xlix.

51. **an everlasting name.** On the ideas connected with this cp. the writer's *Life, Death, and Immortality; Studies in the Psalms*, Lecture III.

52. **. . . in temptation.** Cp. Gen. xxii. 1.
reckoned unto . . . Cp. Gen. xv. 6.

53. **kept the commandment.** Cp. Gen. xxxix. 9.

54. **was zealous exceedingly.** Cp. Num. xxv. 7, 13.

55. **a judge.** שֹׁפֵט in the sense of 'ruler', cp. Mic. iv. 14.

56. **for bearing witness . . .** Cp. Num. xiii. 31, xiv. 24; Joshua xiv. 14.

57. **the throne of a kingdom.** Cp. 2 Sam. vii. 16.

58. **exceeding zealous . . .** Cp. 1 Kings xviii. 40, xix. 10.
was taken up . . . Cp. 2 Kings ii. 11.

59. **Hananiah . . .** Cp. Dan. i. 6 ff.
believing. Cp. Dan. iii. 17.

60. **. . . of the lions.** Cp. Dan. vi. 22.

61. **shall want for nothing.** Cp. Ps. xxxiv. 10.

63. **To-day . . .** Cp. Ps. cxlvi. 3, 4; Ecclus. x. 10.

64. **Be strong . . .** Cp. Joshua x. 25; 1 Sam. iv; 1 Kings ii. 2.

Judas Maccabaeus, he[u] hath been strong and mighty[v] [w]from his youth[w]; he shall be your captain and
67 shall fight[x] the battle[y] of the people[z]. And ye, take you unto you all those who observe the Law,
68 and avenge the wrong of your people. [a]Render a recompense to the Gentiles, and take heed to the
commandments of the Law.'
69, 70 And he blessed them, and was gathered unto his[b] fathers. [c]And he[d] died in the one hundred and
forty-sixth[e] year[f c]; [g]and his sons buried him[g] [h]in the sepulchres[i] of his fathers[h] at Modin; [k]and
all Israel made great lamentation for him[k].

JUDAS MACCABAEUS. III. 1—IX. 22.

III. 1–9. *A Song of praise in honour of Judas Maccabaeus.*

3 1, 2 And his son Judas, [l]who was called[l] Maccabaeus, rose up in his stead.
And all his brethren helped him,
And all they that clave unto[m] his father,
And they fought with gladness the battle of Israel.

3 And he[n] extended the glory [o]of his people[o],
And put on a breastplate as a giant,
And girt on his weapons of war.

[p]He set battles in array,
He protected [q]the army with the sword[q p].
4 And he was like a lion in his[r] deeds:

And as a lion's whelp roaring for prey,
5 He pursued the lawless, seeking them out,
And burnt up those that troubled [s]his people[s].

6 And the lawless lost heart for fear of him,
And all the workers of lawlessness were sore troubled;
[t]And deliverance prospered in his hand.[t]

7 And he angered many[u] kings,
And made Jacob[x] glad with his acts.
And his memorial is blessed for ever.

8 And he went about among the cities of Judah,
And destroyed the ungodly[y] thereout[z],
And turned away wrath from Israel.

9 And he was renowned unto the utmost part of the earth,
And gathered together [a]those who were perishing[a].

III. 10–26. *Victories of Judas Maccabaeus over Apollonius and Seron.*

10 [b]And Apollonius gathered[b] the Gentiles[c] together, and[d] a great host from Samaria, to fight
11 against Israel. And Judas perceived it, and went forth to meet him, and smote him, and slew him;

[u] > ℵ Luc [v]in might A [w–w] > 71 [x]ye shall fight A [y]battles Luc [z]for the people 71 𝔏[1] 𝔖 [a] > *this v.* 71 [b]their ℵ* (his ℵ[c.a]) [c–c] > 71 [d]Mattathias Luc [e]forty-eighth ℵ 𝔖[luc] [f] + of the kingdom Luc [g–g]he was buried ℵ 71 𝔏[1] [h–h] > 71 [i]sepulchre Luc [k–k] > 71

III. [l–l] > 𝔖[luc] [m]followed 64 [n]Judas Luc 𝔏[2] [o–o]by his word V [p–p]So that they fell in the battle; and he raised up shields against the fortresses 𝔖[g] [q–q]with his sword in battle V [r] > ℵ [s–s] > A [t–t] > 93 [u] > 93 𝔖[g] [x]Israel Luc [y]kings 64 [z]thereon A [a–a]Apollonius (*as subject*) V[a] [b–b] > V[a] [c] > 19 [d] > 𝔖[g]

68. **Render a recompense.** Cp. Ps. cxxxvi. 11 (Sept.).
69. **and was gathered . . .** A regular O.T. phrase, cp. e.g. Gen. xxv. 8; Deut. xxxii. 50, cp. also Acts xiii. 36.
70. **in the one hundred and forty-sixth year.** i.e. 167–166 B.C.

III. 1. **Judas.** Hebr. יהודה.
who was called Maccabaeus. Cp. ii. 4, 66, v. 24; 2 Macc. ii. 19, viii. 1.
3–9. In his panegyric on Judas Maccabaeus the author adopts a poetical form.
3. **giant.** *γίγας* is not a good rendering of גבור, which means 'hero'; for the Sept. usage see, e.g., Gen. x. 9, Isa. iii. 2.
weapons of war. *τὰ σκεύη τὰ πολεμικά* = כלי מלחמה, cp. 1 Sam. viii. 12.
4. **like a lion.** Cp. 2 Macc. xi. 11.
5. **burnt up.** Better 'exterminated', according to the sense of בער in 2 Sam. iv. 11; unless it is meant literally cp. *vv.* 5, 44, 2 Macc. viii. 33; this was regarded as the most degrading death, cp. Lev. xx. 14, xxi. 9; Deut. xxi. 23; Joshua vii. 25; Amos ii. 1.
7. **his memorial . . .** Cp. Prov. x. 7.
10. **Apollonius.** Cp. i. 29 and 2 Macc. v. 24; Josephus, *Antiq.* XII. v. 5, vii. 1.

12 and many fell wounded to death, and the rest fled. And they[e] took their spoils[f]; and Judas took
the sword of Apollonius, and therewith fought he all (his) days.
13 And Seron, the commander of the host of Syria, heard that Judas had gathered [g]a gathering and[g]
14 a congregation of faithful men with him, [h]and[i] of such as went out to war[h]; and he said: 'I will make
a name for myself, and get me glory in the kingdom; and I will fight against Judas[k] and them that
15 are with him, that[l] set at nought the word of the king.' [m]And he went up again[m]; and there went up
16 with him a mighty army of the ungodly to help him, to take vengeance on the children of Israel.
And he[n] came near to the ascent of Bethhoron; and Judas[o] went forth to meet him[p] with a small
17 company. But [q]when they[r] saw the army coming to meet them[q s], they said unto Judas: 'What?[t] shall
we be able, being a small company, to fight against so great [u]and strong[u] a multitude? And we, for
18 our part, are faint, having tasted no food this day.' And Judas said: 'It is an easy thing for many
to be shut up in the hands of a few, and there is no difference [v]in the sight of[v] Heaven[w] to save by
19 many or by few; for victory in battle standeth not in the multitude of an host, but strength is from
20 Heaven[x]. They come unto us in[y] fulness of insolence and lawlessness, [z]to destroy us and our wives
21, 22 and our children, for[a] to spoil us[z]; but we fight for our lives and our laws. And He Himself[b] will
23 discomfit them before our face; but as for you, be ye not afraid of them.' Now when he[c] had left
off speaking, he[d] leapt suddenly upon them, and Seron and his army were discomfited [e]before him[e].
24 And they pursued them[f] at the descent of Bethhoron unto the plain; and there fell of them about
eight hundred men; and the rest fled into [g]the land of[g] the Philistines.
25 Then began the fear of Judas [h]and of his brethren[h], and the dread (of them) fell upon the nations[i]
26 round about them. And his name came near even unto the king; and [k]every nation[k] told of
the battles[l] of Judas.

III. 27–37. *Lysias is commissioned to continue the war against the Jews during the absence of Antiochus in Persia.*

27 But when Antiochus the king[m] heard these words he was full of indignation; and he sent and
28 gathered together all the forces [n]of his kingdom[n], [o]an exceeding strong army[o]. And he opened his
treasury and gave his forces pay for a[p] year, and commanded them to be ready[q] for every need[r].
29 And he saw that the money failed from his treasures, and that the tributes of the country were
small, because of the dissension and harm which he had brought upon the land (in seeking) to take
30 away the laws which had been (in vogue) from the earliest times; and he feared (therefore) that he
would not have (enough), as (he had had) at other times, for the charges and the gifts which he gave

[e]he 19 [f]arms (*lit.* vessels) A [g–g]> 𝔖luc [h–h]> 𝔖 [i]> Luc [k]+ the son ℵ [l]and those that A [m–m]*Reading* και προσεθετο του αναβηναι (ויוסף לעלות); and he prepared himself 𝔏[1] > 𝔏[2] [n]they V Luc [o]he 𝔖g [p]them V 64 [q–q]> 71 [r]+ that were with him Luc [s]him A V[a] (them V) [t]How 71 [u–u]> A [v–v]𝔏[1]; 𝔊 *lit.* before [w]the God of Heaven ℵ V him that dwelleth in Heaven 𝔖g [x]the Heavenly One 19 64 [y]> A [z–z]> 𝔖g [a]and 71 𝔖luc 𝔏 [b]the Lord Luc 𝔖luc [c]Judas Luc [d]they 𝔖g [e–e]> 93 [f]him ℵ [g–g]> V [h–h]> 19 [i]all the nations 𝔏[1] [k–k]the nations ℵ 64 93 [l]acts 93 𝔖 [m]> 𝔖luc [n–n]> 71 [o–o]> ℵ* (*hab* ℵ c.a) [p]the A [q]+ for a year A [r]all things 𝔏[2]

15. **and he went up again.** See critical note.

16. **the ascent of Bethhoron.** About five hours' journey north-west of Jerusalem. 'From a military point of view Bethhoron was an important outpost, and to an invading force from the maritime plain the key to Jerusalem; cp. Joshua x. 16–26' (Fairweather and Black, *in loc.*).

18. **to save by many or by few.** Cp. 1 Sam. xiv. 6.

22. **He Himself.** Thus avoiding the mention of the name of God; this is characteristic of later usage; cp. ii. 61.

23. **were discomfited.** συντρίβειν has a stronger meaning, 'were utterly crushed'.

28. **pay for a year.** This suggests that his forces could not always be relied upon. The extravagance of Antiochus Epiphanes (cp. *v.* 30) and the way in which he squandered money on public displays, games, and the like, must have often made it difficult to find the wherewithal to pay his soldiers, in consequence of which discontent would have manifested itself. The Jews had a great advantage here, since, in fighting, they were actuated solely by patriotic motives. According to Josephus (*Bell. Iud.* I. ii. 5) the Jews never employed mercenary troops until the time of Hyrcanus I (135–107 B.C.).

to be ready for every need. The meaning is, presumably, that they were not necessarily to be employed against the Jews only, but that they were to be prepared to go anywhere; this provision was necessary, for with his Egyptian campaigns Antiochus was always in need of soldiers. In 2 Macc. v. 5–11, e.g., we are told that he was hurriedly called back from an Egyptian campaign in order to quell an outbreak in Judaea under Jason.

30. **the gifts which . . . with a liberal hand.** Cp. the words of Polybius (xxvi. 1): 'Rational people were at a loss what to think about him. Some regarded him as a simple and homely man, others looked upon him as crazed. . . . To some he gave bone dice, to others dates, to others gold. But if perchance he should meet anyone whom he had never seen before, he would give him unexpected presents' (quoted by Fairweather and Black, *in loc.*). Grimm mentions that in one of his Egyptian campaigns Antiochus gave a piece of gold to every Greek in Naukratis (Polybius, xxviii. 17. 11); cp. also Dan. xi. 24, 'In time of security shall he come even upon the fattest places of the

31 aforetime with a liberal hand,—[s]and he was more lavish than the kings that were before him[s]. He
was (therefore) exceedingly perplexed in his mind; so he[t] determined to go to Persia, and to take
32 tributes of the countries[u], and (thus) to gather much money. And he left[v] Lysias, an honourable
man, and [w]one of the seed royal[w], (to be) over the affairs of the king from the river Euphrates unto
33, 34 the borders of Egypt, and to bring up his son Antiochus until he should return. And he delivered unto
him the half of the forces, and the elephants, and gave him charge over all the things that he would
35 have done and concerning them[x] [y]that dwell in Judaea and Jerusalem, (namely) that he should send
a host [z]against them[z] to root out[a][y] and destroy the strength[b] of Israel and[c] the remnant of Jerusalem,
36 and [d]to take away[d] their[e] memorial from the place; and that he should make strangers to dwell in
37 all their borders, and that he should [f]divide their land by lot[f]. And the king took the half that
remained of the forces, and removed from Antioch, [g]from his[h] royal city[g], [i](in) the one hundred and
forty-seventh year[i]; and he passed over the river Euphrates, and went through the upper countries.

[s-s] > A [t]they A Antiochus Luc [u]country 𝔖[luc] [v]sent ℵ* (left ℵ[c.a]) [w-w]by race (belonging) to the king 𝔖[luc] . . . the kingdom 𝔖[g] . . . the country 𝔏 [x]all them A [y-y] > 93 [z-z] > 𝔖[g] [a]to drive out AV 64 93 [b]name 𝔖[g] [c] + to take away Luc [d-d] > Luc [e]its A [f-f]take possession of their land A take possession of their land and divide it by lot 𝔏 [g-g] > 𝔏[1] [h]the 𝔖[g] [i-i] > 71

---

province; and he shall do that which his fathers have not done, nor his fathers' fathers; he shall scatter among them prey, and spoil, and substance.'

31. **Persia, and to take . . . countries.** i. e. the countries east of the Euphrates under the rule of the Seleucidae; cp. vi. 56, where the reference is to Media and Persia.

to gather much money. 'The temples of the Asiatics had hitherto been for the most part respected by their European conquerors, and large stores of the precious metals were accumulated in them. Epiphanes saw in these hoards the means of relieving his own necessities, and determined to seize and confiscate them. Besides plundering the temple of Jehovah at Jerusalem (see i. 21–23), he made a journey into the south-eastern portion of his empire, about 165 B. C., for the express purpose of conducting in person the collection of the sacred treasures. It was while he was engaged in this unpopular work that a spirit of disaffection showed itself; the East took arms no less than the West; and in Persia, or upon its borders, the avaricious monarch was forced to retire before the opposition which his ill-judged measures had provoked, and to allow one of the doomed temples to escape him' (cp. vi. 1–4), Rawlinson, *The Seventh Great Oriental Monarchy*, p. 5.

32. **Lysias.** For the part played by this general during the Maccabaean struggle, see, besides this passage, iv. 1 ff., 28 ff., vi. 5 ff., 28 ff., 51 ff.; he was put to death at the accession of Demetrius I, in 162 B. C. (vii. 1–4); see also 2 Macc. x. 11 ff., xi–xii. 1, xiii. 1–xiv. 2; the two accounts are not always in agreement.

one of the seed royal. [מ]זרע המלוכה as in 1 Kings i. 46; Jer. xli. 1; Dan. i. 3, or זרע הממלכה as in 2 Kings xi. 1; 2 Chron. xxii. 10.

the affairs of the king. For the phrase cp. 2 Macc. viii. 8, x. 11, xi. 1.

33. **his son Antiochus.** The future Antiochus V, surnamed Eupator (cp. vi. 17), 'on account of the virtues of his father,' according to Appian (quoted by G. A. Smith in *EB* 187); he was murdered, after two years' reign, together with Lysias (see vii. 1–4; 2 Macc. xiv. 2).

34. **elephants.** The Persians were the first to use elephants in warfare, as far as is known; they are first mentioned in this connexion as having been used in the army of Darius at the battle of Arbela, in 331 B. C. They are referred to several times in this book; vi. 34 ff., where they are described as being furnished with towers of wood, and as being driven by an Indian (cp. 2 Macc. xiv. 12); see also viii. 6, xi. 56; 2 Macc. xi. 4, xiii. 15.

35. **to root out.** *τοῦ ἐκτρῖψαι*; Cod. A has the milder word *τοῦ ἐκρῖψαι*, 'to drive out.'

the strength. The Syriac Version reads 'the name', which in the Old Testament is not infrequently used as equivalent to 'seed', Num. xxvii. 4; Deut. xxv. 6; Ruth iv. 5, 10; 1 Sam. xxiv. 22; Isa. xiv. 22, &c.

36. **strangers.** *υἱοὺς ἀλλοτρίους* is a Hebraism, בְּנֵי נֵכָר.

divide their land by lot. i. e. apportion it to others, cp. Ps. lxxviii. 55; this is the reading of ℵ *κατακληροδοτῆσαι*.

37. **Antioch.** Not, of course, the Pisidian Antioch, though this, too, was founded by the Seleucid kings about 300 B. C.; but the Syrian Antioch, built (300 B. C.) by Seleucus Nicator on the left bank of the Orontes. It was situated just where the Libanus range joins the Taurus range. 'Holm has summed up in a striking sentence the historical position of Antioch under the Seleucid kings. Although close to the sea (*ἀνάπλους αὐθημερόν*, Strabo, p. 751), it was yet no seaport; on the borders of the desert, it was yet something more than a centre for the caravan trade between the East and the West. The city reflected the character of the kingdom of which it was the capital, a kingdom which itself also was neither a genuine naval nor a genuine land power. Antioch was a Greek city, just as the Seleucid kingdom was an attempt to impose upon the Orient the political ideas and forms of Hellas. Yet, in the capital, as in the kingdom at large, there was no true Hellenism; the commingling of Oriental and Western elements resulted in the perpetuation of the worst features of both races, and the moral worthlessness of the Syrian found in the brilliance and artistic temperament of the Greek merely the means of concealing the crudities of his own life. The characteristic failing of the Greek also was exhibited on a great scale. A third element, and that the one most important for biblical history, was provided by the Jews. The colony was in fact coeval with the city, for it dated from the time of Seleucus Nicator, who gave the Jews the same privileges as he gave the Greeks (Josephus, *Antiq.* XII. iii. 1). For this connexion with the Syrian kings see 1 Macc. xi. 42 ff.' (*EB* 185.)

the one hundred and forty-seventh year. 166–165 B. C.

the upper countries. Cp. vi. 1, 2 Macc. ix. 25. Grimm quotes Polybius (v. 40. 5) and Arrian (iii. 6. 12) as referring in similar terms to Persia and Media.

III. 38–60. *Lysias dispatches an army into the land of Judah under Ptolemy, Nicanor, and Gorgias. Judas Maccabaeus prepares for the coming struggle.*

38 And Lysias chose [k]Ptolemy the son of[k] Dorymenes, and Nicanor, and Gorgias, mighty men of the
39 king's friends; and with them he sent forty[l] thousand footmen, and seven thousand horse, to go into
40 the land of Judah, and to destroy it, according to the king's command. And they[m] removed with
41 all their host, and came and pitched near Emmaus in the plain country. And the merchants of the
country heard tell of them, and took silver and gold exceeding much, together with fetters[n], and
came into the camp, to take the children of Israel as slaves. And there were added unto them
troops from Syria and from the land of the Philistines[o].
42 And Judas and his brethren saw that evils were multiplied, and that the forces (of the enemy)
were encamping[p] in their borders; and they[q] took knowledge of the king's[r] commands which he had
43 put forth (with a view) to bring about the destruction and annihilation of the people. So they said,
each man to his neighbour: 'Let us raise up the ruin[s] of our people, [t]and let us fight for our people[t]
44 and the Holy Place.' And the[u] congregation was gathered together, so as to be ready for battle, and
to pray and to ask for mercy and compassion.

45 And Jerusalem was uninhabited like a wilderness,
There was none of her offspring that went in [v]or went out[v].
And the Sanctuary was trodden down,
And the sons of strangers (dwelt) in the citadel,
A lodging-place for Gentiles (it became);
And joy [w]was taken away[w] from Jacob,
And the pipe and the harp ceased.

46 And they gathered themselves together, and came to Mizpeh[x], over against Jerusalem; for in
47 Mizpeh there had been aforetime a place of prayer for Israel. And they fasted that day, and put on

[k-k] > V [l] fifty V ten 𝔖 [m] + who were round about Ptolemy Luc [n] bands and fetters 𝔖; servants (παιδας for πεδας) 𝔊 (= 𝔏); 'fetters' Josephus [o] 𝔖; *lit.* strangers 𝔊 𝔏 [p] had surrounded 𝔖g [q] he 𝔖g [r] royal A [s] kingdom 𝔏² [t-t] > A V [u] all the V [v-v] > ℵ* (*hab* ℵ^c.a) V 71 𝔏¹ [w-w] was brought to an end 64 [x] Massepha 𝔊

---

38 ff. With this section cp. 2 Macc. viii. 8–22; Josephus, *Antiq.* XII. vii. 3.

Ptolemy the son of Dorymenes. Cp. 2 Macc. iv. 45, viii. 3, x. 12, in this last passage he has the surname Macron, and is described as being friendly disposed to the Jews; he committed suicide by taking poison because he was regarded as a traitor for abandoning Cyprus. This is the only mention of him in 1 Macc.

Nicanor. Cp. vii. 26–50; 2 Macc. viii. 9, xiv, xv.

Georgias. Cp. v. 56 ff.; 2 Macc. x. 14, xii. 32–7.

forty thousand. See critical note. In 2 Macc. viii. 9 the number is 20,000, no mention being made of horsemen.

to destroy it. Better 'to lay it waste'.

40. **Emmaus.** Not the Emmaus of Luke xxiv. 13, but a city in the plain into which the mountains of Judaea slope down; it is twenty-two Roman miles from Jerusalem on the road to Joppa; the modern *Amwas*. It was fortified by Bacchides, cp. ix. 50.

41. **the merchants of the country.** In earlier days the Edomites are mentioned as slave-dealers (cp. Amos i. 6, 9); in Ezek. xxvii. 13 Javan (Greeks), Tubal, and Meshech (probably peoples of Asia Minor) are said to have traded with 'the persons of men'; from the fifth century B.C. onwards Syrian slaves, among whom Jews were reckoned, were in great demand in Greece (cp. Robertson Smith, in the *Encycl. Brit.* xiii. 705). The Phoenicians played a leading rôle in the slave-market; Rawlinson (*Hist. of Phoenicia*, p. 296) says: 'The traffic in slaves was one in which the Phoenicians engaged from very early times. They were not above kidnapping men, women, and children in one country and selling them in another; besides which they seem to have frequented regularly the principal slave-marts of the time. They bought such Jews as were taken captive and sold into slavery by the neighbouring nations.' See further 2 Macc. viii. 11, 34.

fetters. See critical note.

troops from Syria . . . According to Josephus these were 'auxiliaries (σύμμαχοι) out of Syria and the country round about, as also some of the renegade Jews' (*Antiq.* XII. vii. 3), i. e. presumably volunteers who joined either from the love of fighting, or from the hope of plunder, or possibly out of sheer hatred of the Jews.

Philistines. See critical note.

43. **each man to his neighbour.** See note on ii. 40.

45. This verse was probably in poetical form in the original; it is full of O.T. thoughts and expressions.

uninhabited. Cp. Isa. v. 9, vi. 11; Jer. ix. 11, xlvi. 19.

there was none of her offspring. Cp. Jer. xxxiii. 10.

that went in or went out. Cp. Jer. xxxvii. 4; Zech. viii. 10.

the Sanctuary . . . Cp. Ps. lxxix. 1.

the sons of strangers. See note on v. 36.

A lodging-place . . . Cp. Isa. i. 8.

joy was taken away. Cp. Lam. v. 15; Isa. xxiv. 11; Hos. ix. 1.

the pipe . . . ceased. Cp. Isa. xiv. 11, xxiv. 8.

46. **aforetime a place of prayer.** Cp. 1 Sam. vii. 6–9.

48 sackcloth, and put[y] ashes upon their heads[z], and rent their clothes. And they spread out the roll
of the Law, (one of those) concerning which the Gentiles were wont to make search [a b]in order to depict
49 upon them[a] likenesses of their idols[b]. And they brought the priestly garments, and the firstfruits, and
50 the tithes; and they shaved[c] the Nazirites who had accomplished their days. And they cried aloud[d]
toward heaven, saying: 'What shall we do with these men, and whither shall we carry them away?
51 For[e] thy Holy Place is trodden down and defiled, and thy priests are in heaviness and brought low.
52 And, behold, the Gentiles are gathered together against us to destroy us; thou knowest what things
53, 54 they imagine against us. How shall we be able to stand before them unless thou help us?' And
they sounded with the trumpets[f], [g]and cried with a loud voice[g].
55 And after this Judas appointed leaders of the people, captains of thousands, and captains of
56 hundreds, [h]and captains of fifties[h], and captains of tens. And he said to them that were building
houses, and were betrothing wives, and were planting vineyards, and were fearful, that they should
57 return, each man to his own house, according to the Law[i]. And the army removed, and encamped[k]
58 on the south of Emmaus. And Judas said: 'Gird yourselves, [l]and be[l] valiant men; and be ready
on the morrow to fight against these Gentiles that are assembled together against us to destroy us,
59 and our Holy Place; for it is better for us to die [m]in battle[m] than to look upon the evils (that have
60 come) upon our nation and the Holy Place. Nevertheless, as may be the will in heaven, [n]so shall
he do[n].'

IV. 1–25. *Victory of Judas over Gorgias.*

4 1 And Gorgias took five thousand (foot-) men, and a thousand chosen horse; and the[a] army moved
2 by night so that it might fall upon the army of the Jews[b] and smite them suddenly; and (certain)[c]
3 men from the citadel were his[d] guides. And Judas heard thereof, and he removed, he and the valiant
4 men, that he might smite the king's host, which was at Emmaus, while as yet the forces were
5 dispersed from the camp. And Gorgias came into the camp of Judas by night[e], and found no man;
6 and he sought them in the mountains, for he said: 'These men flee from us.' And as soon as it was
day, Judas appeared in the plain with[f] three thousand men; howbeit, they had not armour nor
7 swords as they would have wished (to have had). And they saw the camp of the Gentiles strong
8 (and) fortified, and horsemen compassing it round about; and these were experienced in war. And
Judas[g] said to the men that were with him: 'Fear ye not their multitude, neither [h]be ye afraid of[h]
9 their onset. Remember how our fathers[i] were saved in the Red Sea, when Pharaoh pursued them
10 with a host[k]. And now, let us cry[l] unto heaven[m], [n]if he will have mercy upon us[n], [o]and[p] will

[y] > 𝔊 (*exc* 55); 𝔖[luc] 𝔏[1] *supply the verb* [z] head ℵ V Luc [a-a] > 𝔊 (*exc* 55 71) [b-b] and mourned before the Holy One concerning the Gentiles, because they forced them to imitate their ways 𝔖[luc] [c] raised up 𝔊 (*exc* 55) [d] *lit.* with a voice; with a great voice 93 [e] And 𝔊 > 𝔖[g] [f] + fortiter 𝔏[1] [g-g] > 𝔏[1] [h-h] > ℵ* (*hab* ℵ[c.a]) 𝔖[g] [i] + of Moses 𝔏[1] [k] assembled 𝔏[1] [l-l] > 93 [m-m] > 93 [n-n] so be it done 𝔏 𝔖[g]

IV. [a] his 19 93 𝔖[luc] [b] Judah 𝔖[luc] + by night 19 93 𝔖[luc] [c] the A [d] to them 𝔖[luc] 𝔏 [e] > 𝔖[luc] [f] + only 𝔏[1] [g] he 𝔖[luc] [h-h] > 71 [i] brethren 𝔏[1] [k] a great host 𝔖[luc] 𝔏 [l] we will cry ℵ [m] the Lord 71 our Lord 𝔏[1] [n-n] *Several cursives* 𝔖[g] 𝔏[1]; if he will have us ℵ A V [o-o] > 71 [p] + the Lord 𝔖[luc]

---

48. **they spread out . . .** In order that the roll of the Law might bear witness before God against the blasphemous proceeding of the Gentiles.

49. **and they brought . . .** All these acts were intended to witness against the evils which the Gentiles had wrought, and thus call down upon them the divine wrath.

54. **they sounded with the trumpets.** Cp. Num. x. 1 ff.

58. **be valiant men.** Cp. 2 Sam. ii. 7, xiii. 28 (Sept.).

be ready on the morrow. Cp. Exod. xxxiv. 2, xix. 15.

60. **so shall he do.** Another instance of the way in which the mention of the name of God is avoided in this book.

IV. With *vv.* 1–25 cp. Josephus, *Antiq.* XII. vii. 4.

1. **Gorgias . . .** The non-mention of Nicanor, the commander-in-chief (cp. 2 Macc. viii. 23, 24), does not necessarily imply that he was not the guiding spirit; the writer is giving the details of one episode in the campaign, in which Gorgias is the leading figure; he is, therefore, not concerned with the question as to under whose orders Gorgias was acting. That there was not one in chief command responsible for the general conduct of the operations, is difficult to believe. Cp. Josephus: 'But when the enemy sent Gorgias . . .'

2. **men from the citadel.** *οἱ υἱοὶ τῆς ἄκρας*, Hebraism. Josephus speaks of them as 'renegade Jews'.

3. **Emmaus.** See note on iii. 40.

5. **and he sought them in the mountains.** i. e. in the mountainous district south and east of Emmaus; Judas was thus drawing this detachment of the enemy further and further away from the main body with which he intended to deal (see *v.* 13); cp. Josephus: 'And he resolved to fall upon those enemies that were in their camp, now that their forces were divided.'

6. **three thousand men.** So, too, according to Josephus; in 2 Macc. viii. 16 the number is given as 6,000.

7. **experienced in war.** *διδακτοὶ πολέμου*, Hebraism, cp. Song of Songs iii. 8 מלמדי מלחמה.

11 remember [q]the covenant of the[r] fathers[q], and destroy this army before our[s] face to-day[o]; and (then)
12 all the Gentiles will know that there is one who redeemeth [t]and saveth[t] Israel.' And the strangers[u]
13 lifted up their eyes and saw them coming against them, and they went out of the camp to battle.
14 And they that were with Judas sounded the trumpets, [v]and joined battle[v], [w]and the Gentiles
15 were discomfited, and fled unto the plain. And all[x] the hindmost fell by the sword; and they
pursued them unto Gazera, and unto the plains of Idumaea[y] and[z] Azotus and Jamnia; and there
fell of them about three thousand men.
16, 17 And Judas and (his)[a] host returned [b]from pursuing after them[b]; and he[c] said unto the people:
18 'Be not greedy of the spoils, for (another)[d] battle is before us, and Gorgias and (his)[e] host are nigh
unto us [f]in the mountain[f]. [g]But stand ye now against our enemies[g], and fight (against) them, and
19 afterwards take the spoils with boldness.' While Judas was yet saying[h] these things, there appeared a
20 part of them peering out from the mountain; and they saw that (their host) had been put to flight,
and that (the Jews)[i] were burning the[k] camp,—for the smoke [l]that was seen[l] made manifest what had
21 been done. And when they perceived these things they were sore afraid; and perceiving also the
22, 23 army of Judas [m]in the plain[m] ready for battle, they[n] all fled into the land of the Philistines[o]. And
Judas returned to the spoil of the camp, and took much gold and silver, and blue[p], and [q]sea-purple[q],
24 and great riches. And as they returned they sang a song of thanksgiving, and blessed [rs](God[t],
looking up) to heaven[s], (and saying):

'Good (is the Lord), for his mercy endureth for ever.'[r]

25 And Israel had a great[u] deliverance that day.

IV. 26–35. *Victory of Judas over Lysias.*

26 But as many of the Gentiles[v] as had been saved came and reported to Lysias all that had happened.
27 And when he had heard all[w] he was confounded [x]and discouraged[x], both because it had not
happened unto Israel as he had wished, and because the things which the king had commanded him[y]
had not come about.
28 And in the next year he[z] gathered together sixty thousand chosen [foot-]men, and five thousand
29 horse, to make war upon them[a]. And they came into Judaea[b], and encamped at Bethsura, and Judas

[q–q] the first covenant 𝔖   [r] our, *several cursives*   [s] your 64   [t–t] > ℵ* (*hab* ℵ[c.a])   [u] the Greeks 𝔖[g]   [v–v] > 𝔖[g]   [w] with them Luc   [x] > 𝔖[g]   [y] Judæa A V 19   [z] + unto Luc   [a] 19 93 𝔖[luc]   [b–b] > 𝔏[l]   [c] Judas Luc   [d] Luc 𝔖[luc]   [e] 64 93   [f–f] > 𝔖[g]   [g–g] > 93   [h] T.R. 𝔖 𝔏; *lit.* filling up ℵ A V &c., *reading* ממלא *for* ממלל   [i] they that were with Judas Luc   [k] their Luc   [l–l] > 93   [m–m] > 𝔖[g]   [n] and they 𝔖[luc]   [o] 𝔖; *lit.* strangers 𝔊   [p] precious hyacinth stones 𝔖[luc]   [q–q] purple and sea A   [r–r] > 71   Possibly ηὐλόγουν εἰς οὐρανόν here and in *v.* 55 = וברכו לשמים (cf. 1 Chron. xxix. 20 for construction) where, therefore, οὐρανός = θεός. Hence 'they blessed Heaven; for He is good, &c.' [Gen. Editor]   [s–s] the Lord that is in the heavens 𝔖   [t] T.R.   [u] > Luc   [v] *lit.* strangers 𝔊; the Greeks 𝔖[g]   [w] > ℵ V   [x–x] > V   [y] > 19 93 𝔖[luc] 𝔏   [z] Lysias T.R.   [a] Israel Luc   [b] ℵ; B reads Ιδουμαιαν

---

12. **and the strangers lifted up their . . .** From *vv.* 3, 4. Judas evidently intended a surprise attack, but this verse shows that his intention was frustrated. On the other hand, Josephus definitely states that the enemy's defeat was due to Judas's unexpected attack; 'so he commanded the trumpeters to sound for the battle; and by thus falling upon the enemies when they did not expect it, and thereby astonishing and disturbing their minds, he slew many of those that resisted him.'

15. **Gazera.** The ancient Gezer, cp. Joshua x. 33, xii. 12, xvi. 3, &c.; see further the note on xiii. 43.

Azotus. Ashdod, cp. Joshua xi. 22; 1 Sam. v. 5; 2 Chron. xxvi. 6, &c., the modern *Asdud.*

Jamnia. Jabneel, cp. Joshua xv. 11, called Jabneh in 2 Chron. xxvi. 6.

the plains of Idumaea. This reading cannot be right, for the border of Idumaea lay at least two days' journey to the south-east of the scene of the battle, and the next day was the Sabbath, cp. 2 Macc. viii. 26, 27; in the next verses Judas and his army are described as being near the mountainous region again; had four days intervened some mention would assuredly have been made of it. Moreover, the three places 'Gazera, Azotus, and Jamnia' lie close together, and the mention of Idumaea in such a connexion is quite out of place. The reading 'plains of Judaea' is equally strange, for Judaea lay behind the pursuers where the country was mountainous. It is possible that 'Emmaus' stood here originally (cp. iii. 40 'Emmaus in the plain country'), the reference being to the plain in which Emmaus stood.

23. **blue and sea-purple.** תכלת 'violet stuff', cp. Ezek. xxiii. 6, xxvii. 7; used in reference to the Temple hangings 2 Chron. ii. 6, 13, 14; ארגמן 'purple-red cloth', generally mentioned with the former; 'sea-purple' refers to the fact that the colour was not a manufactured dye, but that it was the slimy substance from a sea-shell (*Murex trunculus*) found in great quantities on the Phoenician coast; the slime from these shells is white, but becomes gradually darker when exposed to the rays of the sun, until it assumes a deep red, or a deep blue-red colour which never fades. Immense numbers of these shells have been found on the site of an ancient dye-factory near Tyre. According to Judges viii. 26 it would appear that the Midian kings wore a purple garment when going into battle.

24. **for his mercy . . .** Cp. Ps. cxviii. 1–4, and the oft-repeated refrain in Ps. cxxxvi.

29. **Judaea.** This is what Josephus reads, as well as 2 Macc. xi. 5 (the parallel passage), see note *v.* 15.

Bethsura. 'The house of rock' (cp. Joshua xv. 58), in southern Judaea; 'Bethsuron' in 2 Macc. xi. 5.

30 met them with ten thousand men. And he saw that the army[c] was strong, and he prayed, and
said:
'Blessed art thou[d], O Saviour [e]of Israel[e], who didst bring to nought the onslaught of the giant[f] by
the hand of [g]thy servant[g] David, and didst deliver the army of the Philistines into the hands of Jonathan
31 [h]the son of Saul and of his armour-bearer[h]. Shut up[i] this army in the hands of thy people Israel,
32 that with their host and their horsemen they may be put to shame. [k]Give them fearfulness of heart,
and cause the boldness of their strength to melt away, and let them quake at[l] their destruction[k].
33 Cast them down with the sword of them that love thee, [m]and let all that know[n] thy name praise
thee with songs of thanksgiving[m].'
34 And they joined battle; and there fell of the army of Lysias about five thousand men, and[o] they
35 fell down over against them. But when Lysias[p] saw that his array had been put to flight, and the
boldness[q] that had come upon them that were with Judas, [r]and how ready they were either to live
or die nobly[r], he removed to Antioch, [s]and gathered together mercenary troops, that he might come
again into Judaea with an even greater (army)[s].

IV. 36–61. *The Purification and Re-dedication of the Temple; the fortification of the Temple-Mount and Bethsura.*

36 But Judas and his brethren said: 'Behold, our enemies are discomfited; let us go up to cleanse[t]
37 the Holy Place, and re-dedicate[u] it. And all the army was gathered together, and they[v] went unto
38 mount Sion. And they saw our[w] sanctuary laid desolate, and the altar profaned[x], and the gates[y]
burned up, [z]and shrubs growing in the courts as in a forest or upon one of the mountains, and the
39 chambers[a] (of the priests) pulled down[b z]; [c]and they rent their garments[c], and made great lamenta-
40 tion, and put ashes [d]on their heads[d]; and they fell on their faces to the ground, [e]and they [f g]blew
41 the solemn blasts[f] upon the trumpets[g], and cried unto heaven[e h]. Then[i] Judas appointed (a certain
number of) men to fight against those (that were) in the citadel, until he should have cleansed
42 the Holy Place. And he chose blameless priests, such as had delight in the Law; and they[k]
43, 44 cleansed the Holy Place, and[l] bare out the stones of defilement[m] into an unclean place. And they

[c] + of them that were opposed Luc [d] + Lord ℵ [e–e] > 71 [f] *lit.* mighty man, + Goliath 71 [g–g] > 71 [h–h] > 71 [i] + Lord 𝔏 [k–k] > 71 [l] in 19 93 𝔖luc [m–m] > 71 [n] that have seen A [o] > 𝔖g [p] he 71 [q] + and steadfastness 𝔏[1] [r–r] > 71 [s–s] *the MSS. and Versions vary here considerably; but the general sense is clear, and in accordance with the text above* [t] that we may cleanse ℵ c.a Luc [u] that we may re-dedicate ℵ c.a Luc that we may renew it 𝔖luc [v] he 93 [w] the ℵ V [x] waste 93 𝔖luc [y] doors ℵ [z–z] > 71 [a] adornments 𝔖g [b] disruta et detracta 𝔏[2] [c–c] 𝔖g *places these words after* heads [d–d] > ℵ 19 93 [e–e] et clamaverunt ad caelum in tubis signorum 𝔏[1] [f–f] > 𝔖g [g–g] blew with glorious horns 𝔖luc [h] the Lord 71 [i] and 𝔖g [k] he Luc 𝔖g [l] + they Luc 𝔖g [m] + and placed them 𝔖g + and cast them 𝔖luc

30–32. In 2 Macc. xi. 6–8 this prayer is only referred to, not quoted; but instead, mention is made of 'one on horseback in white apparel, brandishing weapons of gold', who appeared at the head of the Jewish army, and led them on to victory. This fantastic elaboration is perhaps based on the two stories of David (1 Sam. xvii. 40–54) and Jonathan (1 Sam. xiv. 1–16); in each case a champion came forth and delivered Israel.

34. **they fell down over against them.** i.e. they were struck down and fell at the feet of each individual Jewish warrior, so fierce was the onslaught of the Jews.

36. **cleanse.** טָהֵר is used of cleansing the Temple from unclean things in 2 Chron. xxix. 15, 16, 18, and from the pollution of idolatrous images in 2 Chron. xxxiv. 3, 5, 8.

re-dedicate. The ritual of cleansing and re-dedicating is detailed in the verses which follow. The Hebrew word for 'dedicate' (חנך) means lit. 'to train up a child' (Prov. xxii. 6); it is used in the sense of dedicating a house in Deut. xx. 5, of the Temple in 1 Kings viii. 63 (= 2 Chron. vii. 5).

38. **the gates burned up.** We have but scanty details of Zerubbabel's temple; mention is made of the Miphkad Gate (Neh. iii. 31) and of the Prison Gate (Neh. xii. 39); in Josephus (*Contra Ap.* i. 22, quoting Hecataeus) there is a reference to 'double gates' in the Temple, but this seems only to refer to one of the ordinary gates. These are the only gates of which mention is made in the O.T., but there must certainly have been others, as there were in the first temple.

the chambers (of the priests). τὰ παστοφόρια, cp. Ezra viii. 28, x. 6; Neh. iii. 30, x. 37 ff., xii. 44, xiii. 5 ff.; Josephus *Antiq.* XI. iv. 7, XIV. xvi. 2.

40. **solemn blasts upon the trumpets.** The reference is to the long drawn-out blasts on the ram's-horns. Cp. Num. x. 10.

41. **in the citadel.** Cp. i. 33 ff.

42. **blameless.** ἀμώμους, lit. 'without blemish', i.e. Levitical purity; used originally in reference to physical blemish, but later the idea of innocence and integrity is included, cp. Prov. i. 12, where the word (תמים) is used for soundness in health; see Deut. xviii. 13, where it occurs in the figurative sense, cp. Ps. cxxxii. 9, 16. That a physical blemish was, also in later times, an obstacle to the performing of the priestly office may be gathered from Josephus, *Antiq.* III. xii. 2: 'He ordered that the priest who had any blemish should have his portion indeed among the priests, but he forbad him to ascend the altar, or to enter into the holy house.' In the Talmud no less than 147 physical blemishes are enumerated which make a man unfit to perform ministerial duties, cp. Krauss *Talmudische Archäologie*, i, p. 250.

43. **the stones of defilement.** Cp. i. 54.

an unclean place. What is meant can be seen by a reference to Deut. xxiii. 12–14.

took counsel concerning the altar of burnt offerings, which had been profaned, what they should do with
45 it. And a good idea occurred to them[n] (namely) to pull it down, lest it should be a reproach unto
46 them, because the Gentiles had defiled it; so they pulled down the altar, and laid down the stones
in the mountain of the House, in a convenient place, until a prophet should come and decide[o] (as to
47 what should be done) concerning them. And they[p] took whole stones according to the Law, and
48 built a new[q] altar after the fashion of the former (one); [r]and they built the Holy Place, and the
49 inner parts of the house, and hallowed[s] the courts. And they made the holy[t] vessels new[r], and they
brought the candlestick, and the altar of burnt offerings and of incense, and the table, into the
50 temple. And they burned incense upon the altar, and they lighted the lamps that were upon the
51 candlestick [u]in order to give light[v] in the temple[u]. And they set loaves upon the table, and hung up
52 the veils, and finished all [w]the works[w] which they had undertaken. And they rose up early in the morning [x]on the twenty-fifth (day) of the ninth[y] month, which is the month Chislev, in the [z]one hundred
53 and[z] forty-eighth[a] year[x][b], and[c] offered sacrifice, according to the Law, [d]upon the new altar of burnt
54 offerings which they had made[d]. At[e] the corresponding time (of the month) and on the (corresponding) day on which the Gentiles had profaned it, on that day[f] was it dedicated afresh, with songs
55 [g]and harps[g] and lutes, and with cymbals. And all [h]the people[h] fell upon their faces, and worshipped[i],
56 and gave praise, (looking up) unto heaven, to him who had prospered them. And they celebrated
the dedication of the altar for eight days, and offered burnt offerings [k]with gladness[k], [l]and sacrificed
57 a sacrifice of deliverance [m]and praise[m][l]. And they decked the forefront of the temple with crowns
of gold[n] and small shields, and dedicated[o] afresh the gates and the chambers (of the priests), [p]and
58 furnished them with doors[p]. [q]And there was exceeding great gladness among the people, and the
59 reproach of the Gentiles was turned away[q]. And Judas and his brethren and the whole congregation
of Israel ordained, that the days of the dedication of the altar should be kept [r]in their seasons year
by year for eight days, from the twenty-fifth (day) of the month Chislev, with gladness and joy[r][s].
60 And [t]at that season[t] they built high walls[u] and strong[v] towers around mount Sion, lest haply the
61 Gentiles should come and tread them[w] down, [x]as they had done aforetime[x]. And he set there[y]
a force to keep it[z], and they fortified Bethsura [a]to keep it[a], that the people might have a stronghold over against Idumaea.

V. 1–8. *Victories of Judas over the Edomites, Baeanites, and Ammonites.*

5 1 And it came to pass, when the Gentiles round about heard that the altar[b] had been built[c] and the
2 sanctuary dedicated[d], [e]as aforetime[e], that they were exceeding wroth. And they determined[f] to

[n] him 𝔖[luc] [o] speak 𝔖 answer 𝔏 [p] he A V [q] > 𝔖[luc] [r–r] > 71 [s] he hallowed A V [t] > 93 [u–u] > 71 [v] to be visible Luc [w–w] > 𝔖[luc] [x–x] > 71 [y] > ℵ [z–z] > 64 [a] ninth 𝔖[g] [b] > ℵ + of the kingdom Luc [c] > 𝔖[g] [d–d] > 71 [e] And at ℵ V [f] > A [g–g] > Luc [h–h] > 71 [i] + God 71 [k–k] > 71 [l–l] and a sacrifice of deliverance 𝔏[2] [m–m] > 71 [n] > ℵ* (*hab* ℵ[c.a]) [o] he dedicated A [p–p] > 𝔖[luc] [q–q] > 71 [r–r] > 71 [s] great joy 𝔏[1] [t–t] > 71 [u] a high wall Luc [v] high ℵ* (strong ℵ[c.a]) [w] it ℵ[c.a] 93 [x–x] > 71 [y] > 71 [z] them ℵ* (it ℵ[c.a]) [a–a] > 55 𝔖

V. [b] house 𝔖[g] [c] > 71 [d] > 𝔏[2] [e–e] > 71 [f] were wroth ℵ* (determined ℵ[c.a])

---

46. **the mountain of the House.** Cp. Mich. iii. 12; Jer. xxvi. 18 (הר הבית).

a prophet should come . . . The reference is probably to Deut. xviii. 18, which is not a 'Messianic' passage, however it may have been interpreted subsequently.

47. **according to the Law.** Cp. Exod. xx. 25; Deut. xxvii. 6.

49. **the candlestick . . . the altar . . . and the table.** These had been taken away by Antiochus Epiphanes, see i. 21, 22; the three are again specifically mentioned in the two next verses.

52 ff. The inauguration of the feast of *Chanukkah*, which has been observed ever since by the Jews. The month Chislev corresponds to December. Ewald (*Geschichte des Volkes Israel* iv. 407 [3rd ed.]), followed by Wellhausen (*Israelitische und Jüdische Geschichte*, p. 210), believes that on the 25th Chislev a winter solstice feast had been celebrated long before this time, and that this was adapted and turned into the historical feast of *Chanukkah*. This feast was early known as the Feast of Lights (Φῶτα in Josephus, *Antiq*. XII. vii. 7); two methods were in vogue regarding the lighting of the lamps; the followers of Shammai lit eight lamps on the first day of the festival, and one less on each succeeding day until the end of the feast; the Hillelites lit one lamp on the first day of the feast, and added one on each succeeding day, so that on the last day eight lamps were lit. 'The Talmudic sources . . . ascribe the origin of the eight days' festival, with its custom of illuminating the houses, to the miracle said to have occurred at the dedication of the purified Temple. This was that the one small cruse of consecrated oil found unpolluted by the Hasmonean priests when they entered the Temple, it having been sealed and hidden away, lasted for eight days, until new oil could be prepared for the lamps of the holy candlestick' (*Jewish Encycl.* vi. 224 *a*). For a legend of somewhat similar character see 2 Macc. i. 18–ii. 15.

57. **crowns of gold and small shields.** Perhaps wreaths of gold, which with the small shields, were temporary ornaments, cf. 1 Kings x. 17.

60. **strong towers.** Cp. i. 31.

V. 1–8. Cf. Josephus, *Antiq.* XII. viii. 1.

destroy (those of) the race[g] of Jacob [h]that were in the midst of them[h], and they began [i]to slay and
3 to destroy among the people[i]. And Judas fought against the children of Esau in Idumaea[k] at
Akrabattine, because they annoyed Israel[l] by their attacks; and he smote them with a great
4 slaughter, [m]and humbled[n] them[m], and took spoils from them. And he remembered the malice of
the children of Baean, who were unto the people[o] a snare and a stumbling-block, lying in wait for
5 them [p]in the ways[p]. And they were shut up by him in the towers; and he encamped against[q]
them, [r]and utterly destroyed them[r], and burned[s] [t]with fire[t] [u]the towers of the place[v][u], with all that
6 were[w] therein. Then he[x] passed over to the children of Ammon, and found (there) a mighty band,
7 and much people[y], and Timotheus (who was) their leader. And he fought many battles with them,
8 [z]and they were discomfited before him, [a]and he smote them[a][z]; and he gat possession of Jazer and
the villages[b] thereof, and returned[c] again into Judaea[d].

V. 9–68. *Victories of Simon in Galilee, and of Judas in Gilead.*

9 And the Gentiles that were in Gilead gathered themselves together against the Israelites that
10 were on their borders, to destroy them; and they fled unto the stronghold of Dathema[e]. And they
sent letters unto Judas and his brethren, saying: 'The Gentiles that are round about us are gathered
11 together [f]against us[f] [g]to destroy us; and they are preparing to come and get possession of the
12 stronghold[g] whereunto we[h] have fled for refuge; and Timotheus is leading their host. Now, there-
13 fore, [i]come and deliver us from their hand, for a number of us are fallen, and all our brethren[i] that
were in the (parts) of Tubias have been put to death, and they have carried into captivity their wives
14 and their children and their[k] belongings, and have destroyed there about a thousand men.' While
the[l] letters were yet being read, behold, there came other messengers from Galilee with their
15 garments rent, bringing a report to the following effect, saying[m]: 'There be gathered together
against them (men) from Ptolemais, and Tyre [n]and Sidon[n], and all Galilee of the Gentiles, to

[g] seed Luc [h–h] > 71 [i–i] to persecute and to kill them 𝔏[1] [k] Judaea A [l] Amalek ℵ* (Israel ℵ c.a) [m–m] > 𝔏[1] [n] scattered 𝔖g [o] + of Israel 𝔖g [p–p] > 𝔖g [q] cast aside A [r–r] > 𝔏[1] [s] they burned 𝔖luc [t–t] > V [u–u] their towers 𝔏[1] [v] *lit.* thereof > 𝔖luc [w] dwelt ℵ c.a 55 [x] Judas 64 93 𝔏[1] [y] + and a mighty band ℵ V Luc [z–z] > 𝔏[1] [a–a] > 19 [b] *lit.* daughters [c] they returned ℵ Judas ret. 64 93 [d] Idumaea V 𝔖luc [e] Ramoth 𝔖g [f–f] > ℵ [g–g] and have carried us off and are occupying the stronghold 𝔏[1] [h] they ℵ* (we ℵ c.a) [i–i] > 71 [k] > 𝔖luc [l] these 55 𝔖luc [m] *The words which follow are in direct narration in* 𝔖g, *but in oblique narration in* 𝔊 𝔏 [n–n] > 𝔖luc

2. **(those of) the race of Jacob.** The reading 'seed of J.', though not well attested, is more likely to be correct, being more in accordance with O.T. usage, cp. Ps. xxii. 23, Isa. xlv. 19, Jer. xxxiii. 26, &c.

3. **the children of Esau.** Cp. Gen. xxxvi. 10, 19.

Akrabattine. Cp. מעלה עקרבים (Joshua xv. 3, Judges i. 36); a spot in the hill-country in the south-west of Palestine, which formed the boundary of Judaea, cp. Num. xxxiv. 4.

and he smote them with a great slaughter. A characteristic Hebrew phrase: ויך אתם מכה גדולה.

humbled them and . . . For the phraseology cp. Deut. xxviii. 29.

4. **the children of Baean.** This name does not occur elsewhere; Blau (quoted by Bissell, *in loc.*) says: 'The region in which the event described in 1 Macc. v. 1–6 took place is the same as that which the table by Karnack calls Bajaa, near Kapharbaruk, east from Hebron, where in the time of the Maccabees Idumaeans settled. In my opinion, בְּנֵי בַּיָּן signifies simply the inhabitants of the place Bajjan.' Grimm holds that Baean can only refer to the ancestor of a tribe, on the analogy of 'the children of Esau'.

a snare and a stumbling-block. Cp. Ps. lxviii. 23 (Sept.), = lxix. 22 (E.V.).

5. **utterly destroyed.** ἀναθεματίζω = החרים; cp. 1 Sam. xv. 8.

burned . . . the towers. Cp. Judges ix. 49.

6. **the children of Ammon.** Like the Edomites, traditional enemies of Israel, cp. Judges xi. 4, 12; 2 Sam. x. 6–14.

a mighty band. Lit. 'a mighty hand'; a Hebraism, יד חזקה, used in Num. xx. 20 of the fighting power of the Edomites.

Timotheus . . . their leader. Probably an Ammonite who had assumed a Greek name, in accordance with a frequent custom in those times.

7. **and he smote them.** Cp. note on *v.* 3.

8. **he gat possession.** προκαταλαμβάνεσθαι implies a sudden taking possession.

Jazer. A place on the east of Jordan occupied by the Amorites originally (Num. xxi. 32), later by the tribe of Gad (Num. xxxii. 25; Joshua xiii. 25; 1 Chron. vi. 81).

the villages thereof. Lit. the 'daughters thereof', a Hebraism; the 'land of Jazer' was a fertile region with villages dependent upon the city; see Num. xxxii. 1; Isa. xvi. 8; Jer. xlviii. 32.

9. **Gilead.** The reference here is to the 'land of Gilead', i.e. the mountainous district on the east of Jordan between the Yarmuk in the north, and the Arnon in the south; the river Jabbok cuts this region into two parts (cf. Num. xxxii. 29; Joshua xxii. 9; Judges x. 8, xx. 1).

Dathema. This place has not been identified. On the letter contained in *vv.* 10–13 see *Intr.* § 7. 1 (*a*).

13. **Tubias.** Cp. 2 Macc. xii. 17; 'the land of Tob' (Judges xi. 3, 5; 2 Sam. x. 6, 8), twelve miles south-east of the Sea of Galilee.

15. **Ptolemais.** The Accho or Akka of the O.T., cp. Judges i. 31; Joshua xix. 24–31. It is uncertain when this name was changed to Ptolemais; the city had already received it for some time by the end of the third century B.C.

16 consume us.' Now when Judas and[o] the people[p] heard these words, there assembled together
a great gathering to consult what they should do [q]for their brethren who were in tribulation and
17 being attacked by the enemy[r q]. And Judas said unto Simon his brother: 'Choose out men for
thyself, and go and deliver thy[s] brethren in Galilee, while I and Jonathan my brother will go into
18 Gilead.' And he left Joseph the son of Zacharias, and Azarias, as leaders of the people, with the
19 rest of the army, in Judaea, to guard it. And [t]he commanded them, saying[t]: 'Take ye the charge of
20 this people, and engage not in battle with the Gentiles until we return.' And three thousand men were
allotted unto Simon to go into Galilee, and eight thousand men[u] unto Judas (to go)[v] into Gilead.
21 And Simon went into Galilee, and engaged in many[w] battles with the Gentiles, and the Gentiles
22 were discomfited before him. And he pursued them unto the gate[x] of Ptolemais; and there fell of
23 the Gentiles[y] about three thousand men, and he took their spoils. And he[z] took [a]those (that were)[a]
in[b] Galilee and Arbatta with (their) wives and children, and brought[c] them[d] into Judaea [e]with great
gladness[e].
24 And Judas Maccabaeus[f] and [g]his brother[g] Jonathan passed over Jordan, and went three days'
25 journey in the wilderness; and they fell in with the Nabataeans, and these met them in a peaceable
26 manner, and recounted to them all things that had befallen their brethren in Gilead; and how that
many of them were shut up in Bosora, and Bosor, and Alema, Casphor, Maked, and Carnaim,—all[h]
27 these cities (being) strong and great; [i]and how that they were shut up in the rest[k] of the cities of
Gilead[i], and that on the morrow (the enemies) had planned[l] to encamp [m]against the stronghold[n m],
28 and to take (it)[o], and to destroy all those[p] (who were in it) in one day. And Judas and his army
turned suddenly [q]by the way of[q] the wilderness unto Bosora[r]; and he took[s] the city, and slew all the
males[t] [u]with the edge of the sword[u], and took all their spoils, and burned[v] it (i.e. the city)[w] with fire.
29, 30 And he[x] removed thence[y] by night, and went on[z] until (he reached) the stronghold. And when it
was morning they lifted up their eyes[a], and behold (there was) a great multitude [b]which could not
be numbered[b], bearing ladders and engines (of war), to take the stronghold[c]; and they were fighting
31 against them (that were in the stronghold). And when Judas saw that the battle had begun, and
32 that the cry of the city[d] went up to[e] heaven, with trumpets and [f]a great sound[f], he[g] said unto the
33 men of his host: 'Fight this day for your[h] brethren.' And he[i] went forth behind them in three
34 companies, and they[k] sounded with trumpets, and cried out in prayer. And the army of Timotheus
perceived that it was Maccabaeus, and they fled from before him; and he[l] smote them with a great[m]

[o] + all 55 64 𝔖g [p] his brethren 𝔖g [q–q] > 71 [r] by them ℵ V &c. by him A [s] > ℵ 93 our 55 64 [t–t] and he said unto them 71 [u] > 71 [v] *this is expressed in* 𝔖luc [w] > V [x] cities A gates 55 > 19 71 93 𝔖luc [y] + in that day 55 [z] Simon Luc [a–a] them A [b] *lit.* from [c] they brought A V [d] all as many as were with them 𝔖g [e–e] > 71 [f] > 71 [g–g] > 71 [h] > ℵ* (*hab* ℵ c.a) 71 [i–i] > 71 [k] other ℵ > 𝔖g [l] intended to attack (*lit.* to trouble) 64 [m–m] > 93 [n] *plur.* 𝔊 𝔖 𝔏; *but see next note and note* [c] *below* [o] them 19 64 + and the rest of the cities of Gilead 71 [p] > 𝔖luc [q–q] to 55 [r] + a journey (*lit.* a way) of three days 55 [s] fell upon 𝔖luc [t] + thereof 55 [u–u] > 71 [v] they burned ℵ [w] it 𝔊 𝔖 𝔏 [x] Judas 64 93 [y] > 71 [z] they went on ℵ 64 93 [a] + and saw 𝔖luc 𝔏1 [b–b] > ℵ* (*hab* ℵ c.a) [c] *plur.* 19 [d] battle 𝔏1 [e] unto (εως for εις) A 55 (= 𝔖luc) [f–f] > 71 + from the city 𝔏1 [g] Judas 55 64 93 [h] our ℵ c.b A V [i] Judas 64 93 [k] he A [l] they 𝔏1 [m] > 71

Ptolemy Lagi destroyed it in B.C. 312 when it was still called Akka; very possibly the renovated city which subsequently arose took its name from him; but as he only had possession of it for a very short time, it seems more likely that it was named after Ptolemy II, who conquered the whole of Phoenicia, and retained possession of it. For the history of the city during the Maccabaean struggle see 1 Macc. x. 1, 39, 48–66, xii. 45 ff.; Josephus, *Antiq.* XII. viii. 1, ii. 6, XIII. ii. 3, iv. 1. 6. 9, vi. 2.

all Galilee of the Gentiles. i.e. Upper Galilee with its mixed Gentile population; cp. Isa. viii. 23, ix. 1.

18. **Joseph . . . and Azarias.** See *vv.* 56–62; they are not mentioned otherwise.

23. **Arbatta.** Probably = *Arabah*, i.e. the valley of the Dead Sea (cp. Deut. i. 7; Joshua xi. 16, xii. 8, xviii. 18).

25. **the Nabataeans.** The Ishmaelite tribe of Nebaioth of the O.T. (Gen. xxv. 13), according to Josephus (*Antiq.* I. xii. 4); Petra, their capital, became a great commercial centre in later days. G. A. Smith (*Historical Geography of Palestine*, p. 547) says: 'Their inscriptions are scattered all over eastern Palestine, where they had many settlements, and in Arabia, but have even been discovered in Italy, proving the extent of their trade.'

in a peaceable manner. Cp. ix. 35.

26. **Bosora.** i.e. Bozrah in Moab (cp. Jer. xlviii. 24), not the Bozrah in Edom (Isa. lxiii. 1).

Bosor. i.e. most likely = Bezer 'in the wilderness', in the inheritance of the Reubenites (Deut. iv. 43, Joshua xx. 8, xxi. 36); mentioned also on the Moabite Stone.

Alema, Casphor, Maked. These places are not otherwise mentioned; they cannot be identified further than that they were cities of Gilead, see *v.* 36.

Carnaim. Cp. Gen. xiv. 5; Deut. i. 4; Am. vi. 13; 2 Macc. xii. 21, 26.

29. **the stronghold.** i.e. Dathema.

33. **And he went forth . . .** Cp. Judges vii. 16.

cried out in prayer. i.e. a battle-cry which was also a prayer, cp. Judges vii. 18, where the cry is: 'For the Lord and for Gideon,' which was also preceded by the blowing of trumpets. Cp. the battle-cry, 'Allah, Allah!' of the Turks (Grimm), and 'For God and St. George!' of the English.

35 slaughter; and there fell of them [n]on that day[n] about eight thousand men. And he[o] turned aside[p]
to Mizpeh and fought against it, [q]and took it[q], and slew[r] all the males thereof, and took[s] the spoils
36 thereof[t], and burned it with fire. From thence he[u] removed, and took Casphor, Maked, Bosor, and
the other cities [v]of Gilead[v].
37 Now after these things Timotheus gathered another army, and encamped over against Raphon,
38 beyond[w] the brook. And Judas sent (men) to espy the army[x]; and they reported to him, saying[y]:
'All the Gentiles [z]that are round about us[a z] are gathered together unto them[b], an exceeding[c] great
39 host; and they have hired Arabians to help them, and are [d]encamping beyond the brook[d], ready to
40 come against thee[e] to battle.' And Judas went to meet them. And Timotheus said unto the
captains of his host, when Judas [f]and his army[f] drew nigh unto the brook of water: 'If he pass over
41 unto us first, [g]we shall not be able to withstand him[h], for[g] [i]he will mightily prevail against us[i]; but
[k]if he be afraid, and[k] encamp beyond the river, we will cross over [l]unto him[l], [m]and prevail against
42 him[m n].' Now when Judas came nigh unto the brook [o]of water[o], he placed the officers[p] of the people
[q]by the brook[q], and [r]commanded them, saying[r]: [s]'Suffer no man to encamp[s], but let all[t] come to
43 the battle.' And he crossed over first against them, and all[u] his[v] people after[w] him; and all[x] the
Gentiles were discomfited before his[y] face, and cast away their[z] arms, and fled unto [a]the temple of[a]
44 Carnaim. And they[b] took the city[c], and burned the temple[d] with fire, together with all [e]that were[e]
therein. [f]And Carnaim was subdued[f]; neither could they[g] stand any longer before the face of
Judas.
45 And Judas gathered together all Israel, them that were in Gilead, [h]from the least unto the
greatest[h], and their [i]wives, and their[i] children, and their belongings, an exceeding great army, that
46 they might come into the land of Judah. And they came as far as Ephron; and this was a large
city at[k] (the entrance of) the pass, exceeding strong; it was not (possible) to turn aside [l]from it[l]
47 either to the right or the left, but (one had) to go through the midst of it. And they of the city shut
48 them out, and stopped up the gates with stones. And Judas sent [m]unto them[m] with words of peace,
saying: 'We[n] would pass through[o] thy[p] land to go into our own land; and none shall harm you,
49 we will only pass by on our feet.' But they would not open unto him[q]. And Judas [r]commanded
proclamation to be made[r] in the army, that each man should encamp in the place where he was.
50 [s]And the men of the host[t] encamped[s]; and they[u] fought against the city all that day and all that

[n–n] > 71 [o] Judas Luc [p] enclosed 𝔏[1] [q–q] > 𝔖[luc] [r] they slew 𝔖[luc] [s] they took 𝔖[luc] [t] > 𝔖[luc] [u] Judas Luc [v–v] > 𝔖[g] [w] in front of ℵ at 𝔏[1] [x] the land 𝔖[g] [y] > 71 [z–z] > 71 [a] you A [b] him ℵ 𝔏 𝔖[g] [c] > 71 [d–d] > 71 [e] us 𝔏[1] [f–f] > 71 𝔖[g] [g–g] > 71 [h] before the face of him 55 𝔖[luc] [i–i] > 𝔏[1] [k–k] > 71 [l–l] > 71 unto them 𝔖[g] [m–m] > A [n] them 𝔖[g] 𝔏[2] [o–o] > 71 [p] *lit.* scribes [q–q] > 71 [r–r] said 71 [s–s] leave no man behind 𝔏[1] [t] > 71 [u] > 71 [v] > ℵ V [w] before A [x] > ℵ 19 93 𝔖[luc] [y] their ℵ 𝔏[1] [z] all their A [a–a] > 𝔏[1] [b] + that were round about Judas Luc he 𝔖[g] 𝔏[2] [c] + of Carnaim 55 [d] the place 𝔏[1] [e–e] > ℵ V Luc [f–f] > 𝔏[1] [g] he A 93 [h–h] > 71 [i–i] > 71 [k] ℵ V (επι *instead of* η) [l–l] > 64 93 [m–m] > 𝔖[g] [n] I A 19 64 [o] into A [p] your 𝔖[luc] 𝔏[2] [q] them ℵ* (him ℵ[1]) 𝔖[luc] 𝔏 [r–r] proclaimed 71 [s–s] > 71 [t] city A [u] he ℵ

35. **Mizpeh** in Gilead; cp. Judges xi. 29.

36. **Casphor . . .** See notes on *v.* 26.

37. **Raphon.** According to Pliny (quoted by Grimm) this was one of the cities of 'Decapolis'; Josephus (*Antiq* XII. viii. 4) speaks of it as a 'city'.

the brook. χειμάρρους = נחל, 'a torrent' of water in a narrow channel; cp. Judges v. 21, &c.

39. **Arabians.** Cp. 2 Macc. xii. 10.

40. **For he will mightily prevail against us.** Grimm aptly refers to 2 Chron. xxxii. 13 (Sept.) = יָכֹל יוּכַל לָנוּ.

42. **officers.** τοὺς γραμματεῖς = שֹׁטְרִים. Cp. Deut. xx. 5 ff. (Kautzsch).

43. **and he crossed over first.** That no attempt was made by Timotheus to oppose the Jews during this crossing shows extraordinary ineptitude; bad leadership on the part of the enemy must evidently have had much to do with many of their defeats during the Maccabaean struggle.

the temple. τέμενος is the entire piece of consecrated ground in which a temple stands; regarding this temple of Carnaim cp. 2 Macc. xii. 26.

45. **from the least unto the greatest.** A characteristic O.T. expression, מקטן ועד־גדול.

46. **Ephron.** According to Kautzsch, identical with the Γεφροῦς or Γεφροῦν, mentioned by Polybius V. lxx. 12, as having been conquered by Antiochus the Great. From *vv.* 43, 52 (cp. 2 Macc. xii. 27 f.) it must have lain in the stretch of land between Ashtaroth and the Jordan, opposite Scythopolis or Beth-Shan (Grimm). The situation of the city explains why it was not possible 'to turn aside from it either to the right or the left', i.e. the land was precipitous on either side.

48. **we would pass through . . .** Cp. the similar request preferred by Moses to the king of Edom (Num. xx. 17) and to the king of the Amorites (Num. xxi. 22).

we will only pass by on our feet. Cp. the Hebrew phrase ברגלי אעברה 'let me pass through with my feet' (Num. xx. 19), the idea being that of rapidly passing through; cp. Ps. ciii. 16.

49. **each man should encamp . . .** In view of what is said in the next *v.*, that they fought 'all that day', it can only be a temporary halt that is here referred to, not an encampment proper.

51 night; and [v]the city[v] was delivered into his[w] hands; and he[x] destroyed all the males[y] with the edge
of the sword, and rased[z] the city, and took[a] the spoils thereof[b], and passed[c] through the city over
52 them that were slain. And they[d] went over Jordan into the great plain over against Bethshan.
53 [e]And Judas gathered together those that lagged behind, and encouraged the people all the way
54 through until[e] he came into the land of Judah. And they went up to mount Sion with gladness
and joy, and offered whole burnt offerings, because not so much as one of them was slain [f]until they
returned in peace[f].
55 And in the days when Judas and Jonathan[g] were in the land[h] of Gilead, and Simon [i]his brother[i]
56 in Galilee [k]before Ptolemais[k], Joseph[l] the son of Zacharias, and Azarias, leaders[m] of the armies[n] (in
57 Judaea), heard of their exploits and of the war,—[o]what things they had done[o]; and they said: 'Let
us[p] also make a name for ourselves, and [q]let us go[q] fight[r] against the Gentiles that are round about
58 us.' [s]And they gave charge unto the (men) of the host[t] that was with them[s], and went toward
59, 60 Jamnia. And Gorgias and his men came out of the city [u]to meet them[u] in battle. And Joseph and
Azarias were put to flight, [v]and were pursued[v] unto the borders of Judaea[w]; and there fell on that
61 day [x]of the people[x] of Israel about two thousand men. And there was a great overthrow [y]among
62 the people[y], because they hearkened not unto Judas [z]and his brethren, thinking to do some exploit[a z].
63 But they were not of the seed of those men, by whose hand deliverance was given unto Israel. [b]But
[c]the man[c] Judas and his brethren were glorified exceedingly in the sight of all Israel, and of all[d] the
64 Gentiles, wheresoever[e] their name was heard of[b]; [f]and[g] (men) gathered unto them, acclaiming
(them)[h f].
65 And Judas and his brethren went forth, and fought against the children of Esau in the land toward
the south; and he smote Hebron and the villages[i] thereof[k], and pulled down the strongholds[l] thereof[m],
66 and burned the towers thereof round about. [n]And he[o] removed[n] to go into the land of the Philis-
67 tines[p], and he went through Marisa[q]. In that day (certain) priests fell in battle, desiring[r] themselves[s]
68 to do exploits, in that they[t] went out to the war unadvisedly. And Judas turned aside to Azotus, to
the land of the Philistines, and pulled[u] down their altars, and burned the carved images of their gods[v],
and took the spoil of their cities, and returned into [w]the land of[w] Judah.

v–v it 71   w their V 55   x they 55 93   y + thereof Luc 55   z they rased 19 $\mathfrak{S}^{luc}$ a they took 19 $\mathfrak{S}^{luc}$ b of the city A   c they passed 19 $\mathfrak{S}^{luc}$ d he $\mathfrak{S}^{g}$ e–e > 71   f–f > 71   g + his brother 19 93 $\mathfrak{S}^{luc}$ h > A   i–i > 71   k–k > 71   l Josephus Luc   m *lit.* rulers   n army $\aleph$ V   o–o which Judas had waged (*lit.* done) Luc > $\mathfrak{S}^{luc}$ p + we 55   q–q > 71   r > V let us fight 71   s–s > 71   t > $\mathfrak{L}^{1}$ u–u and they stood before him V   v–v > $\mathfrak{L}^{1}$ w Idumaea 19 (*but wrongly spelt*) $\mathfrak{S}^{luc}$ x–x > V   y–y > 71 in Israel $\aleph^{c.a}$ among them 93   z–z > 71   a + him (*sic*) A + they also Luc   b–b > 71   c–c > $\mathfrak{S}^{luc}$ d > $\mathfrak{S}^{g}$ e and wheresoever $\mathfrak{S}^{g}$ f–f > 71   g > $\mathfrak{S}^{g}$ *making one sentence with the foregoing*   h 64 him 93   i *lit.* daughters   k > 71   l *sing.* A   m > 71   n–n And Judas removed from thence Luc   o they $\mathfrak{S}^{g}$ p *lit.* strangers   q $\mathfrak{L}^{2}$ Samaria $\mathfrak{G}$ $\mathfrak{S}$ $\mathfrak{L}^{1}$ (*see note below*)   r *reading* βουλευομενοι *with* $\aleph$*   s *reading* αυτοι *with* 55   t *reading* αυτους *with* T.R.   u *this and the following verbs in the plur.* $\mathfrak{S}^{luc}$ v + in fire $\aleph$ T.R.   w–w > A

---

50. **the city was delivered.** For the expression cp. Gen. xiv. 20; Deut. iii. 3; Judges xi. 21; the idea was that the Lord of hosts (i.e. of the Israelite hosts) brought this about; cp. 2 Macc. xii. 36.

52. **the great plain.** i.e. the plain of Esdraelon, between the Jordan and mount Gilboa; Kautzsch suggests that it was called the 'great' plain because it was here much broader than the continuation of it east of Jordan.

Bethshan. Beth-Shean; called Scythopolis in Judges i. 27 (Sept.); 2 Macc. xii. 29; Josephus, *Antiq.* XII. viii. 5, XIII. vi. 1; *Bell. Iud.* III. ix. 7; one of the cities of the Decapolis, the only one of the ten lying on the west of Jordan; the modern *Beisan.*

56. **Joseph . . . and Azarias.** Cp. *v.* 18.

58. **Jamnia.** See note on iv. 15.

59. **Gorgias.** Cp. iii. 38; 2 Macc. viii. 9, 'a captain and one that had experience in matters of war.'

61. **because they hearkened not . . .** i.e. to the command given to them by Judas in *v.* 19. Josephus (*Antiq.* XII. viii. 6) says concerning this: 'For besides the rest of Judas' sagacious counsels, one may well wonder at this concerning the misfortune that befel the forces commanded by Joseph and Azarias, which he understood would happen, if they broke any of the injunctions he had given them.'

62. **But they were not of the seed . . .** i.e. not Hasmonaeans; the writer apparently resents the idea that any not belonging to the Hasmonaeans should take part in the national deliverance; cp. note on iii. 28.

63. **the man Judas.** Cp. Exod. xi. 3, xxxii. 1; Num. xii. 3.

65. **Hebron.** The ancient Kirjath-Arba (Judges i. 10).

the villages thereof. Cp. note on *v.* 8.

the strongholds. Cod. A reads 'stronghold', i.e. the citadel.

66. **Marisa.** i.e. Mareshah in the plain of Judaea. The reading of all authorities, excepting $\mathfrak{L}^{2}$ and Josephus, *Antiq.* XII. viii. 6), viz. 'Samaria' cannot be right, for to go from Hebron to Philistia via Samaria without very special reasons is unthinkable; no reasons are given, but they certainly would have been given by the intelligent and careful author of this book if this enormous *détour* had been undertaken.

67. **In that day . . .** This episode is not mentioned by Josephus; but in 2 Macc. xii. 38–40, where, however, no mention of priests is made, these men are said to have fallen because under their garments were found 'consecrated tokens of the idols of Jamnia'.

68. **Azotus.** See note on iv. 15.

pulled down their altars . . . Cp. x. 84.

VI. 1–17. *Death of Antiochus Epiphanes, and accession of his son, Antiochus Eupator.*

6 1 And king Antiochus was journeying through the upper countries; and he heard that Elymais[a], in
2 Persia, was[b] a city [c]renowned for riches, for silver and gold[c], and that the temple which was in it
(was) rich exceedingly, and that therein (were) golden shields, and breastplates, and arms, which
Alexander, son of Philip[d], the Macedonian[e] king, who reigned first among [f]the Greeks[f], had left
3 behind there. So he came and sought to take the city, [g]and to pillage it[g]; but he was not able (to
4 do so) because the thing had become known to them of the city. And they rose up[h] against him to
battle[i]; and he fled, and removed[k] thence with great heaviness, to return to Babylon.
5 And [l]there came one bringing him tidings[l] into Persia[m] that [n]the armies, which went against
6 [o]the land of[o] Judah[n], had been put to flight; and that Lysias had gone forth at the head of a strong
army, and had been put to shame before them; [p]and that they had waxed strong by reason of
arms [q]and power, and with store of spoils[q], which they took from the [r]armies that they had cut off[r p s];
7 and that they had pulled down [t]the abomination which he had built[u] upon the altar that was in
Jerusalem[t]; and that they had compassed about the sanctuary[v] with high walls, [w]as (had been the
8 case) formerly[w], and Bethsura, [x]his city[x]. And it came to pass, when the king heard these words,
he was struck with amazement and greatly moved; and he laid him down upon (his) bed, and fell
9 sick for grief, because it had not befallen him as he had looked for. And he was there many days,
10 because great[y] grief was renewed upon him; and he[z] reckoned that he was about to die. And he
called for all his Friends, and said unto them: 'Sleep departeth from mine eyes, and (my)[a] heart
11 faileth [b]for care[b]. [c]And I said in (my) heart[c], Unto what tribulation am I come, and how great
12 a flood is it wherein I now am! For I was gracious and beloved in my power. But now I remember the evils which I did at Jerusalem, and that I took all[d] the vessels [e]of silver and gold that were
13 therein, and sent forth (armies) to destroy the[f] inhabitants[e] of Judah without a cause. I perceive
that on this account these evils are come upon me, and, behold, I perish [g]through great grief[g] in
14 a strange land.' And he[h] called for Philip, [i]one of his Friends[k i], and set him over all his kingdom,
15 and gave him (his) diadem, and his robe, and (his) signet-ring, [l]to the end that he should educate[l]

VI. [a] ενλυμαις ℵ V (εν ελυμαις 55) ελυμες A [b] had ℵ [c-c] glorious, and full of riches, possessing gold and silver 𝔏[2l] [d] > 71 [e] > 71 [f-f] them ℵ [g-g] > 𝔖[g] [h] withstood 𝔏[1] [i] > 93 [k] > 𝔏[1] [l-l] there came (men) bringing tidings to him 𝔖[luc] [m] + to Antiochus 19 93 𝔖[luc] [n-n] the encampments in the land of Judah 𝔏[1] [o-o] > ℵ [p-p] > 71 [q-q] > A [r-r] the encampments 𝔏[1] [s] smitten Luc [t-t] the execrable thing, the monstrous thing which they had built in Jerusalem 𝔏[1] [u] had been built 19 93 𝔖[luc] [v] > 71 the altar and the sanctuary 𝔖[g] [w-w] > 71 [x-x] > ℵ their city 19 93 𝔖[luc] [y] > 𝔖[luc] [z] Antiochus 64 93 [a] 19 93 𝔖[luc] [b-b] > 71 [c-c] > 71 [d] > 55 71 𝔖[luc] [e-e] > 71 [f] all the 55 [g-g] > 71 [h] Antiochus 64 93 [i-i] his friend 𝔏[2] [k] servants V [l-l] to bring them to Luc 𝔖

VI. 1. **Elymais.** See critical note. Most commentators take Elymais as the name of a province (Elam of the O.T. lying between Media and the Persian Gulf), and retain the ἐν, because a city of this name is unknown; but the preposition does not belong to the original text, and the whole context necessitates our regarding Elymais as a city, and not as a province. Josephus (*Antiq.* XII. ix. 1) speaks of 'a very rich city in Persia, called Elymais', and says that Antiochus 'went in haste to Elymais, and assaulted it, and besieged it'. Elymais is mentioned in Tobit ii. 10, where, however, it is thought of as a province; but it is possible, and even probable, that the text in this passage is based on a misunderstanding of an original Semitic form (see Dillon in the *Contemporary Review*, March, 1898, referred to in *EB* col. 1284). See next note.

2. **the temple which was in it.** Cp. 2 Macc. i. 12–17, where this episode is clearly referred to; here this temple is spoken of as that of Nanaea, one of the primeval Babylonian deities, = Innanaea, called in later times Nana, and identified with Ishtar; she is spoken of as the 'goddess of the world', and also as the 'goddess of war' (see further Jastrow, *Die Religion Babyloniens und Assyriens*, i. 76 f.). The chief centre of the cult of this goddess was the city of Erech, and continued so to the very end of the Assyrian Empire. There is, therefore, the possibility that in the name Elymais there lurks a corruption of some form of the name of Erech in the original Hebrew text.

had left behind there. i. e. as votive offerings.

5. **the armies . . . had been put to flight.** i. e. those of Seron (iii. 23), Nicanor (iv. 14), and Gorgias (iv. 22).

7. **the abomination . . .** Cp. i. 54.

10. **Sleep . . .** Cp. Gen. xxxi. 40 (Sept.). With this and the following *vv.* cp. 2 Macc. ix. 12–17; in Josephus (*Antiq.* XII. ix. 1) this speech is merely summarized.

13. **these evils are come upon me.** According to Polybius (xxxi. 11), who is, however, only repeating a tradition (ὥς ἔνιοί φασιν), 'these evils' constituted a species of madness, for he died δαιμονήσας . . . διὰ τὸ γενέσθαι τινὰς ἐπισημασίας τοῦ δαιμονίου κατὰ τὴν περὶ τὸ προειρημένον ἱερὸν παρανομίαν. The author of 1 Macc. is evidently preserving some tradition based on fact, though he assigns the cause of Antiochus' disorder to his desecration of the temple at Jerusalem, while Polybius traces it to strange apparitions seen during his attempt to rob the temple in Elymais. Cp. the argument in Josephus (*Antiq.* XII. ix. 1) who certainly does *not* take the will for the deed!

in a strange land. This is a natural addition by a Jew who wishes to represent things as bad as possible for the arch-enemy of his race, cp. for the conception Amos vii. 17. Antiochus the Great was killed while plundering the temple at Elymais.

14. **Philip.** Cp. 2 Macc. v. 22, vi. 11, viii. 8, ix. 29, see also 1 Macc. i. 6.

15. **signet-ring.** Cp. Gen. xli. 42; Esther iii. 10, viii. 2.

that he should educate . . . This duty had been assigned to Lysias (iii. 32–4); the reason for the change is

16 Antiochus his son, [m]and bring him up to be king[m]. And king[n] Antiochus died there [o]in the one
17 hundred and forty-ninth year[o]. And when Lysias knew that the king was dead, he set up
Antiochus his (i.e. the king's) son to reign[p], whom he had nourished up while yet young, and he
called his name Eupator.

VI. 18–54. *The struggle between Judas and the forces under Lysias and Eupator for the possession of Jerusalem and Bethsura.*

18 And they that were in the citadel kept enclosing Israel round about the sanctuary, and continually
19 sought their hurt, [q]and (acted as) a support to the Gentiles[q]. And Judas[r] purposed to destroy
20 them, and called all[s] the people together to besiege them. [t]And they were gathered together, and
besieged them[t] in [u]the one hundred and fiftieth year[u]; and he[v] constructed siege-towers[w] against
21 them, and engines (of war). And there came forth some [x]of them[x] that were shut up, and unto
22 them were joined certain ungodly men of Israel[y]. And they went unto the king and said: 'How
23 long wilt thou not execute judgement, and (when wilt thou) avenge our brethren? We were willing
24 to serve thy father, and to walk after his words, [a]and to follow his commandments[a]. [b][c]For this cause[c]
the children of our people [d]besieged it (i.e. the citadel)[e][b], and were alienated from us, and[f] [g]as
25 many of us as they could light on[g] they killed[h], [i]and they spoiled[k] our inheritances[i]. And not
26 against us only did they stretch out their hand, but also against all their[l] borderlands. And, behold,
they are encamped this day against the citadel in Jerusalem with the object of capturing it, and
27 they have fortified the sanctuary[m] and Bethsura. And if thou art not[n] beforehand with them quickly
they will do greater things than these, and thou wilt not[o] be able to control them.'
28 And the king was angry when he heard (this); and[p] he gathered together all his Friends, (who
29 were) the leaders of his host, and them that were over the horse[q]. And there came unto him[r] from
30 other kingdoms[s], and from [t]the isles of the sea[t], bands of mercenaries. And the number of his forces
was a hundred thousand footmen, and twenty thousand horsemen, and thirty-two elephants trained
31 for war. And they went through Idumaea, and encamped against Bethsura, and fought against (it)
many days, and made engines (of war); but [u]they (that were besieged)[u] came out and burned them
32 with fire, and fought manfully. And Judas removed from the citadel, and encamped at Beth-
33 zacharias, over against the king's camp. And the king rose early in the morning, and removed the
army in its eagerness [v]along the road to Beth-zacharias[v]; and his forces prepared themselves[w] for
34 the battle, and sounded with trumpets. And they showed the elephants the blood of grapes and
35 mulberries, that they might prepare them for the battle. And they divided the beasts among the
phalanxes[x], and they set by each elephant a thousand men armed with coats of mail, and helmets

[m-m] that he should reign Luc [n] > $\mathfrak{S}^{g}$ [o-o] > 71 [p] + in his stead A V 19 64 $\mathfrak{S}^{g}$ [q-q] > 71 $\mathfrak{S}^{g}$ [r] > $\mathfrak{S}^{g}$ [s] > 71 [t-t] > ℵ* (*hab* $ℵ^{c.a}$) A 71 [u-u] 71 [v] they 𝔏 𝔖 [w] turrets to fight (from) 𝔖 [x-x] thereof A [y] Jerusalem ℵ [z] + to the king $\mathfrak{L}^{1}$ [a-a] > 71 [b-b] > 71 [c-c] and ℵ V [d-d] A 55 [e] T.R. $\mathfrak{S}^{luc}$ [f] but A V [g-g] > ℵ* (*hab* $ℵ^{c.a}$) [h] *pass. in* 𝔊 𝔏 $\mathfrak{S}^{luc}$ *act. in* $\mathfrak{S}^{g}$ [i-i] > 71 [k] > ℵ* (*hab* $ℵ^{c.a}$) [l] thy $\mathfrak{L}^{1}$ [m] > V the fortress $\mathfrak{L}^{1}$ with high walls 55 [n] ye be not ℵ V 55 64 $\mathfrak{S}^{luc}$ [o] ye will not $\mathfrak{S}^{luc}$ [p] + he sent and 55 [q] tribute 55 chariots 𝔖 𝔏 [r] them $\mathfrak{S}^{g}$ $\mathfrak{L}^{2}$ [s] kings A V [t-t] many isles $\mathfrak{S}^{luc}$ [u-u] the children of Israel 55 [v-v] > 71 [w] + in order that they might be ready 55 [x] defiles A 71

---

not given; cp. Josephus (*Antiq.* XII. ix. 2), who adds: 'But it was Lysias that declared his death to the multitude, and appointed his son Antiochus to be king, of whom at present he had the care, and called him Eupator.' The appointment of Philip was fraught with evil consequences, see *vv.* 55–63.

16. **one hundred and forty-ninth year.** 163 B.C.

17. **while yet young.** Appian (*Syr.* xlvi) says he was: *ἐνναετὲς παιδίον*.

and he called his name. A very frequent O.T. phrase ויקרא את־שמו.

Eupator. Appian (*ibid.*) says: *προσέθηκαν ὄνομα Εὐπάτωρ οἱ Σύροι διὰ τὴν τοῦ πατρὸς ἀρετήν*.

18. **kept enclosing . . .** This is explained by Josephus (*Antiq.* XII. ix. 3): 'For the soldiers that were in that garrison rushed out suddenly, and destroyed such as were going up to the temple in order to offer their sacrifices; for this citadel adjoined to, and overlooked the temple.'

20. **the one hundred and fiftieth year.** 162 B.C.

21. **ungodly men of Israel.** Cp. i. 11.

26. **they have fortified . . .** Cp. iv. 60, 61.

30. **a hundred thousand footmen . . .** These numbers, which are also given by Josephus, are probably exaggerated; in 2 Macc. xiii. 2, the number of horsemen given is still larger, but the other forces are smaller, though there are added, 'three hundred chariots armed with scythes.'

32. **Beth-zacharias.** A place between Jerusalem and Beth-zur, an hour's walk to the south of Bethlehem; the present Beth-zacharieh.

34. **they showed the elephants . . .** Grimm refers to Aelian, *De Animal.* xiii. 8 in support of the fact that spirituous liquors were given to elephants in order to excite them. In the present case the liquor was only shown to them, for had they drunk of it they would have got out of control. Josephus omits all reference to this. In 3 Macc. v. 1, 2 there is an account of the intention to give unmixed wine to elephants, and, when thoroughly maddened, to drive them into an enclosure full of Jews, in order that the latter might be trampled upon.

36 of brass [y]on their heads[y]; and for each beast were appointed five hundred chosen horsemen. These
had previously been (with the beasts) [z]wherever a beast was[z]; [a]and whithersoever it went, [b]they
37 went together with (it)[b]; they did not leave it[a]. And towers of wood (were) upon them, strong
38 (and) covered, (one) upon each beast, girt fast [cd]upon them with[d] (special) contrivances[c]; and upon
each were †thirty-[e]two† men[e], fighting [f]from them[f], [g]and (each beast had) its Indian[g]. [h]And the
residue of the horsemen he placed on this side and that side, on either wing of the army, [i](thus)
39 striking terror (into the enemy, while) covering the phalanxes[ih]. Now when the sun shone upon the
40 shields of gold [k]and brass[k], the mountains shone therewith, and blazed like torches [l]of fire. And
a part[l] of the king's[m] army [l]was spread[l] upon the high[n] mountains, and some on the [o]low ground[o],
41 and they went on [p]safely[q] and in order[p]. And all that[r] heard the noise of their multitude, [s]and of
the marching of the multitude, and the rattling of the arms[s], did quake; for the army was exceeding[t]
42 [u]great and[u] strong. And Judas and his army drew near for battle, and there fell of the king's army
six hundred men.
43 And Eleazar Avaran saw one of the beasts armed with royal breastplates, and he was higher than
44 all the (other) beasts, so that it appeared as though the king were upon it; and he gave himself to
45 deliver his people and to acquire an everlasting name; and he ran upon it courageously into the
midst of the phalanx[v], and slew on the right hand and on the left, and they parted asunder [w]from
46 him[w] on this side and on that; and he crept under the elephant, [x]and[y] thrust him from beneath[x],
47 and slew it; and it fell to the earth upon him, and he died there. And when they[z] saw the strength
of the royal[a] (army), and the fierce onslaught[b] of the hosts, they[c] turned away from them.
48 [d]But they[d] of the king's army went up to Jerusalem to meet them, and the king encamped toward
49 Judaea, and toward mount Sion. And he made peace[e] with them of Bethsura; for[f] they[g] came out
of the city, because they had no food there[h] to be shut up therein (any longer), [i]because it was
50 a sabbath to the land[i]. And the king took Bethsura, and appointed[k] a garrison there to keep it.
51 And he encamped against the sanctuary many days, and set there siege-towers[l], and engines (of war),
52 and instruments for casting fire [m]and stones[m], and pieces to cast darts and slings. And they (who
53 were besieged) also made engines against their engines, and fought for many[n] days. But there were
no victuals in the store-chambers[o] [p]because it was the seventh year[p], and they that had fled for
54 safety [q]to Judaea[q] from the Gentiles had eaten up the residue of the store; and there were (but)
a few men left in the sanctuary, because the famine prevailed against them, and they were scattered,
each man to his own place.

VI. 55–63. *An abortive treaty of peace.*

55 And Lysias heard that Philip, whom Antiochus the king[r]—while he was yet alive—appointed to
56 nourish up his son Antiochus[s] that he might be king, had returned from Persia [t]and Media[t], and

y–y > 𝔖g   z–z > 𝔖luc *which joins the preceding sentence to this verse*   a–a > 71   b–b > 𝔏1   c–c > 71   d–d under it ℵ   > 𝔖g   e–e men of strength ℵ V   > two 19 55 64   f–f against them [*i.e. the foes*] A   g–g > 71   h–h > 71   i–i striking with weapons 𝔖g   moving together in close order in legions 𝔏2   k–k > A 55 71   l–l > ℵ* (*hab* ℵ c.a)   m > 𝔖luc   n > ℵ* (*hab* ℵ c.a)   o–o low mountains 𝔖luc   p–p cautiously 𝔏1   q with confidence 𝔖   r + inhabited the earth 𝔏2   s–s > 71   t > V   u–u > 𝔖g   v defile A 71   w–w > 64   x–x > 𝔏1   y + the sword 19 64   z Judas Luc   a *lit.* of the kingdom   b *plur.* A   c Judas Luc   d–d and some A 𝔖luc   e > A   f *lit.* and   g he; *but the sense of the passage shows that this is wrong*   h > 93 𝔖luc   i–i > 𝔏1   k smote A   l turrets to fight (from) 𝔖   m–m > V 71   n > ℵ V   o T.R. V   sanctuary ℵ A &c.   p–p > 71   q–q > 𝔖luc   r > 𝔖luc   s > 𝔖luc   t–t > 71

37. **thirty-two.** This is, of course, an impossible number; Grimm, following Michaelis, suggests in the original the reading שלש שנים ('two (or) three') which, through a copyist's error, became שלישים ושנים ('thirty-two'); Fairweather and Black offer the ingenious suggestion that 'possibly the original text may have read שָׁלִשִׁים ("picked warriors"), the term used in Exod. xiv. 7, xv. 4 of the picked men in Pharaoh's chariots, which the translator mistook for שְׁלֹשִׁים ("thirty")'; some Greek MSS. read 'thirty', and ℵ V read 'thirty men of strength'. The usual number of warriors on an elephant was three or four.

its Indian. This name came to be applied to the driver whether an Indian or not.

39. **the shields of gold . . .** This is merely a rhetorical picture.

43. **Eleazar Avaran.** Cp. ii. 5.

45. **they parted asunder from him.** i.e. they could not withstand his onslaught.

47. **they turned away from them.** An instance of the general trustworthiness of the writer, who does not conceal the fact of defeat; that he does not enlarge upon it is very excusable; cp. Josephus, *Bell. Iud.* I. i. 5. In 2 Macc. xiii. 22, 23 the Jewish defeat is represented as a victory.

49. **it was a sabbath to the land.** i.e. a Sabbatical year, cp. Exod. xxiii. 10, 11; Lev. xxv. 2–7; cp. *v.* 53.

51. **pieces.** *Lit.* 'little scorpions,' so called because part of the 'piece', or instrument, resembled the uplifted tail of a scorpion. The Hebrew word עקרבים occurs in 1 Kings xii. 11, 14; 2 Chron. x. 11, 14.

53. **they that had fled for safety . . .** i.e. those from Gilead and Galilee, see v. 23, 45.

55. **Philip.** Cp. *v.* 14.

with him the forces that went with[u] the king, and that he was seeking to take unto him the govern-
57 ment[v]. And he[w] made haste, and gave consent to depart; and he[x] said [y]to the king and[y] to the
leaders of the host and to the[z] men: '[a]We languish daily[a], and our food is scant, and the place which
58 we are besieging is strong[b], and the affairs of the kingdom lie upon us; now therefore let us give the
59 right hand to these men, and make peace [c]with them[c], [d]and with all their nation[d]; and let us settle
with them that they (be permitted) to walk after their own laws, as aforetime; for because of their
60 laws which we abolished were they angered, and did all these things.' And the saying pleased the
61 king and the leaders, and he sent unto them to make peace[e]; and they[f] accepted thereof. And the
king [g]and the leaders[g] sware unto them in accordance with these (conditions); (thereupon) they[h]
62 came forth from the stronghold, and the king entered into mount Sion. But (when) he saw the
strength of the place, he set at nought the oath [i]which he had sworn, and gave commandment[i] to
63 pull down[k] the wall round about. And he[l] removed in haste, and returned unto Antioch, and found
Philip master of the city; and he fought against him, and took the city [m]by force[m].

VII. 1–20. *Demetrius becomes king of Syria; Bacchides and Alchimus sent against the Jews.*

7 1 In the one hundred and fifty-first[a] year Demetrius the son of Seleucus came forth from Rome, and
2 went up with a few men [b]unto a city[c] by the sea[b], and reigned there. And [d]it came to pass[d], when
he had formed the purpose of entering into the house of the kingdom of his fathers, that the soldiery[e]
3 laid hands on Antiochus and Lysias, to bring them unto him. [f]And when the thing was made known
4 to him[g], he[f] said: 'Show me not their faces.' And the soldiery slew them. And Demetrius sat
5 upon the throne of his kingdom. And there came unto him all the lawless and ungodly men of
6 Israel; and Alcimus[h] led them, desiring to be (high)[i] priest. And they accused the people unto the
king, saying: 'Judas and his brethren have destroyed all thy Friends, and have scattered us from
7 our[k] land[l]. Now therefore send a man whom thou trustest, and let him go and see [m]all the havock
which he hath made of us and of the king's country[m], and [n]let him punish[n] them and all that[o] helped

[u] > A 55 𝔏[1] [v] regni negotia 𝔏[2] the affairs of the kingdom 𝔖[luc] [w] they A [x] Lysias Luc [y–y] > 𝔏[2] [z] + great 64 93 [a–a] it is all up here 𝔖[luc] [b] is firm and strongly fortified 𝔖[luc] [c–c] > ℵ [d–d] > 71 [e] + with them Luc [f] he A [g–g] > 71 [h] he A [i–i] > 71 [k] and they (he 64 71) pulled down A Luc [l] they A [m–m] > 𝔖[g] 𝔏

VII. [a] fiftieth 𝔖[g] [b–b] to abide in a city 𝔏[1] [c] *plur.* 𝔖[luc] [d–d] > 71 [e] the captains of the forces 𝔖 [f–f] and when they had been brought, Demetrius 𝔏[1] [g] > V [h] + their leader ℵ [i] 𝔖 [k] their 𝔖[g] [l] + and from our people 55 [m–m] these things 71 [n–n] 55; ℵ A V &c. he hath punished [o] those that 71

59. **to walk after their laws.** To achieve this was the one object, originally at any rate, of the Maccabaean struggle.

63. **returned unto Antioch.** See the further details given by Josephus (*Antiq.* XII. ix. 7); cp. also 2 Macc. xiii. 4–7.

VII. 1. **the one hundred and fifty-first year.** 162–161 B.C.

Demetrius the son of Seleucus. The first of the name, called also Soter, on account of his having delivered the Babylonians from the satrap Heraclides; he reigned 162–150 B.C. His father was Seleucus IV, surnamed Philopator.

came forth from Rome. i.e. he escaped from Rome, mainly through the help of Polybius the historian, where he was as a boy sent as a hostage in place of Antiochus Epiphanes, his uncle. He escaped to Tripolis, the 'city by the sea' (cp. 2 Macc. xiv. 1; Josephus, *Antiq.* XII. x. 1).

a few men. According to Polybius, five men and three boys; in 2 Macc. xiv. 1 he is said to have arrived in Tripolis 'with a mighty host and a fleet'.

and reigned there. Rather, proclaimed himself king there, cp. x. 1, xi. 54; Josephus (*Antiq.* XII. x. 1) says: 'and set the diadem on his own head.' Polybius (xxxi. 20. 4 f.) says that while Demetrius was yet in Rome his guardian Diodorus brought him the news from Syria that distrust had arisen between Lysias and the Syrians, in consequence of which there was much turmoil in the land of his fathers. It was owing to the advice of Diodorus, who assured him that he would be welcomed in Syria, that he determined to escape. The event proved that he was well advised.

2. **the house of the kingdom.** i.e. Antioch, the royal city, cp. Dan. iv. (27) 29.

the soldiery. The Syriac rendering is probably more strictly correct, 'the captains of the forces.'

3. **And when the thing was made known to him.** See critical note.

Show me not their faces. A hint that they should be put away; Josephus says they were 'immediately put to death by the command of Demetrius'.

4. **the throne of his kingdom.** He was the rightful heir.

5. **the lawless and ungodly men.** i.e. those who did not obey the Law (Torah), the Hellenizing element.

Alcimus. According to Josephus Ἰάκειμος, a graecized form of יָקִים abbreviated from אֶלְיָקִים (= Eliakim), cp. 2 Kings xviii. 18, &c., another form of the name is Jehoiakim.

desiring to be (high-) priest. According to 2 Macc. xiv. 7 he had already been high-priest, but had 'laid aside' his 'ancestral glory,' meaning the high-priesthood. Josephus (*Antiq.* XII. x. 1) speaks of him as 'high-priest', and makes no mention of his now desiring to be so; and, again, in XX. x. 1 he says: 'Antiochus (Eupator) and Lysias, the general of his army, deprived Onias, who was also called Menelaus, of the high-priesthood, and slew him at Beraea, and put Jacimus into the place of the high-priest, one that was indeed of the stock of Aaron, but not of this house' (i.e. of Onias). The words before us are, therefore, not strictly correct, and must be understood in the sense of desiring to be confirmed in the office by the new king, cp. *v.* 9.

8 them.' And the king chose Bacchides, (one) of the king's friends[p], who was ruler in the country
9 beyond the river, [q]and was a great man in the kingdom, and faithful to the king. And he sent him[q],
and the ungodly Alcimus, and made[r] sure to him the (high-) priesthood[s]; and he commanded him
to take vengeance upon the children of Israel.
10 And they[t] removed, [u]and came[u] with a great host into [v]the land of Judah[w v]; and he[x] sent
11 messengers to Judas and his brethren with words of peace, deceitfully. But they gave no[y] heed to
12 their words; for they saw that they were come[z] with a great host. And there was gathered together
13 unto Alcimus and Bacchides a company of scribes, to seek for justice. And the Chassidim were the
14 first among [a]the children of[a] Israel that sought peace of them; for they said: 'One that is a priest
15 of the seed of Aaron is come [b]with the forces, and he[c] will do us no wrong[b]. And he spake with
them words of peace, and sware unto them, saying: 'We will seek the hurt neither of you nor of your
16 friends.' And they believed him; and he laid hands on threescore men of them, and slew them in
one day, according to the [d]words which (the psalmist)[e] wrote[d]:

17 The flesh of thy saints and their blood
They poured out around Jerusalem;
And there was no man to bury them.

18 And the fear [f]and the dread[f] of them fell upon all the people, for they said: 'There is neither truth
19 nor judgement in them; for they have broken[g] the covenant and the oath which they sware.' And
Bacchides removed from Jerusalem, and encamped in Bezeth; and he sent[h] and took many[i] of the
deserters that were with[k] him, and certain of the people, and slew them, (and cast them) into the
20 great pit. And he delivered the land to Alcimus, and left with him a force to aid him; and
Bacchides went away unto the king.

VII. 21–50. *Judas takes vengeance on the deserters; his victories over Nicanor.*

21, 22 And Alcimus strove for the high-priesthood[l]. And there were gathered unto him all they that
troubled their people, and they got the mastery of the land of Judah, and did[m] great hurt in Israel.
23 And Judas saw all the mischief that Alcimus and his company had wrought among the children of
24 Israel, worse than (that of) the Gentiles; and he went out into all the coasts of Judaea[n] round about,
and took vengeance on [o]the men[p] that had deserted from him[o], and they were restrained from going
25 forth into the[q] country. But when Alcimus saw[r] that Judas and his company waxed strong, and

[p] the king's Friend V [q-q] > 71 [r] they made A V [s] high priesthood V [t] he A [u-u] > 71 [v-v] Judaea V Judah 64 93 [w] > 𝔏[1] [x] they 𝔖[luc] [y] > Luc [z] + against them Luc 𝔖[luc] [a-a] > 𝔖[g] [b-b] to us 𝔏[1] [c] they 𝔖[luc] [d-d] word which the prophet spoke 𝔖 word of Asaph the prophet 55 𝔏[1] [e] the prophet ℵ[c.a] Luc 𝔖 Asaph the prophet 55 [f-f] > 𝔖[luc] 𝔏[2] [g] + the judgement and 19 93 𝔖[luc] [h] > 𝔖[g] [i] > 𝔖[luc] [k] from Luc [l] priest-hood ℵ 55 > 93 [m] he did 𝔖[luc] [n] + and A [o-o] the children of the deserters 𝔏[1] [p] + and (on those) A [q] their 𝔖[g] [r] heard 𝔏[2]

8. **Bacchides.** Cp. Josephus (*Antiq.* XII. x. 2), who speaks of him as 'a friend of Antiochus Epiphanes, a good man (a reading which Grimm disputes), and one that had been entrusted with all Mesopotamia.'

the river. i.e. the Euphrates, cp. Isa. viii. 7; Zech. ix. 10.

13. **the Chassidim.** See note on ii. 42.

14. **one that is a priest.** ἄνθρωπος ἱερεύς, a Hebraism אִישׁ כֹּהֵן, cp. Lev. xxi. 9.

16. **which (the psalmist) wrote.** In different MSS. the subject ('the psalmist') varies; 'the prophet', 'David', 'Asaph' occur.

17. **The flesh . . .** A shortened form of Ps. lxxix. 2, 3.

thy saints. חֲסִידֶיךָ, i.e. Chassidim, cp. *v.* 13; this word was most probably the reason for which the writer quoted the passage, for the circumstances of the Psalm are not analogous to the occurrence here described.

18. **the fear and the dread of them.** Cp. Isa. viii. 13.

neither truth nor judgement. Cp. Ps. cxi. 7.

they have broken the covenant. παρέβησαν τὴν στάσιν, *lit.* 'they have transgressed the statute'; in the O.T. the usual phrase is עבר את־ברית (Joshua vii. 11, &c.), but ברית, 'covenant', is not infrequently = to חק (חקה), 'statute' (e.g. Isa. xxv. 5; Ps. l. 16).

the oath which they sware. See *v.* 15.

19. **Bezeth.** Josephus (*Antiq.* XII. x. 2, xi. 1), 'the village called Bethzetha' (= Βηθζαιθά, 'the house of the olive', cp. Judith v. 2), Hebr. בית זית; in *Bell. Iud.* V. iv. 2 Josephus speaks of Bezetha as the new quarter of Jerusalem (καινὴ πόλις). Probably the place is to be identified with this.

the deserters that were with him. i.e. that had been with him (Bacchides). Judas did likewise, see *v.* 24.

the great pit. φρέαρ, *lit.* 'well' or 'cistern' (= באר); the use of the definite article shows it was well known.

21. **strove for . . .** Cp. note on *v.* 5; the meaning is that he strove to retain the office he already possessed, cp. Josephus (*Antiq.* XII. x. 3).

24. **into all the coasts.** i.e. the whole border of, cp. Judges xxix. 19. בכל גבול ישראל.

they were restrained . . . i.e. they were besieged in their fenced cities.

25. **But when Alcimus . . .** In 2 Macc. xiv. 26 the return of Alcimus is stated to be the understanding that had been arrived at between Judas and Nicanor; the account in Josephus (*Antiq.* XII. x. 3, 4) does not agree with this.

knew that he was not[s] able to withstand them[t], he returned to the king[u], and brought evil accusations
against them[v].
26 And the king[w] sent Nicanor, [x]one of his honourable princes, a man that hated Israel and was their
27 enemy[x], and commanded him to destroy the people. And Nicanor came to Jerusalem with a great
28 host; and he sent unto Judas and his brethren deceitfully[y] with words of peace, saying: 'Let there
be no battle between me and you[z]; I[a] will come with a few men, that I may see [b]your faces[b] in
29 peace.' And he[c] [d]came to Judas[d], and they saluted one another peaceably[e]. But the enemies were
30 ready to take away Judas by violence. And the thing became known to Judas, (namely) that he
31 came unto him with deceit; and he was sore afraid of him, and would see his face no more. And
(when) Nicanor knew that his purpose was discovered, he went out to meet Judas [f]in battle[f] beside
32 Capharsalama; and there fell of those (that were) with Nicanor about five hundred[g] men, and they
fled into the city of David[h].
33 And [i]after these things[i] Nicanor went up to mount Sion; and there came some of the priests out
of the sanctuary, and some of the elders of the people, to salute him peaceably, and to show him the
34 whole burnt sacrifice that was being offered for the king; but he mocked them, and laughed at them,
35 and polluted them, and spake haughtily, and sware in a rage, saying: 'Unless Judas and his army
be now delivered into my hands, it shall be that, if I come again in safety, I will burn up this house.'
36 And he went forth with great[k] wrath. And the priests entered in, and stood before the altar and
37 the temple[l], and wept and said: 'Thou[m] didst choose this house to be called by thy name, to be a
38 house of prayer [n]and supplication[n] for thy people; take vengeance on this man and his army, and
let them [o]fall by the sword[o]; remember their blasphemies, and suffer them not to live any longer.'
39 And Nicanor went forth from Jerusalem, and encamped in Bethhoron, and there met him the host
40 of Syria. And Judas encamped in Adasa with three thousand men; and Judas prayed, and said:
41 'When they that came from the king blasphemed, thine angel went out and smote among them one
42 hundred and eighty-five thousand. Even so crush[p] this army before us to-day; and let all the rest
know that he hath spoken wickedly against thy sanctuary; and judge him[q] according to his wicked-
43 ness.' And the armies joined battle [r]on the thirteenth (day) of the month Adar[r]; and Nicanor's
44 army was discomfited, [s]and he himself was the first to fall in the battle[s]. Now when his army saw
45 that Nicanor was fallen, they cast away their arms, and fled. And they[t] pursued after them a day's
journey from Adasa until thou comest to Gazara, and they sounded an alarm after them [u]with the

[s] > A [t] him 𝔖g [u] to them 𝔏1 [v] him 93 [w] + Demetrius 64 93 [x–x] that was Israel's enemy 71 [y] > 𝔖g [z] thee 𝔖g [a] and I 19 93 𝔖luc [b–b] thy face 𝔖g [c] they 𝔖luc [d–d] Judas came to him 𝔖g [e] > 71 [f–f] > A Luc [g] thousand A V [h] Judah 71 [i–i] > 71 [k] > A [l] the steps of the altar (καταστρωμα, cp. Joel ii. 17) 𝔖luc + and called upon God 55 [m] + O Lord 55 71 𝔏1 [n–n] > 71 𝔏1 [o–o] all fall by the mouth of the sword 55 [p] he crushed A [q] them Luc 55 [r–r] > 71 [s–s] > 71 [t] + that were with Judas 64 93 [u–u] > 71

26. **Nicanor.** Cp. iii. 38; Josephus (*l. c.*) speaks of Nicanor as 'the most kind and most faithful of all his (Demetrius') friends; for he it was who fled away with him from the city of Rome'; Polybius (xxxi. 22. 4) also speaks of him as one of Demetrius' intimate friends in Rome.

28. **that I may see your faces in peace.** i. e. that I may have friendly intercourse with you; it is a Hebraism (ראות פנים); but it is also used of simply appearing before someone, e. g. Exod. x. 28, and cp. *v.* 30.

31. **he went out to meet Judas in battle.** A Hebrew phrase, cp. Num. xx. 18 פן־בחרב אצא לקראתך, 'lest with the sword I go forth to meet thee.'

Capharsalama. Called 'a village' by Josephus; possibly to be identified with the modern Salame, a village distant from Jaffa about an hour's walk (Kautzsch).

32. **and there fell . . .** According to Josephus, Nicanor 'beat Judas, and forced him to fly to that citadel which was in Jerusalem'; an obvious error since the citadel ('Akra') was in the hands of the enemy!

33. **there came . . . out of the sanctuary.** i. e. the outer court; they came from the inner court into which Nicanor, as a Gentile, was not permitted to enter.

offered for the king. Cp. Jer. xxix; Ezra vi. 10; Josephus, *Bell. Iud.* II. xvii. 2.

34. **polluted them.** Most probably by spitting on them; this was, according to the Rabbis, one way whereby Levitical purity was lost (cp. Krauss, *Talm. Arch.*, i, pp. 251, 704).

35. **unless.** *ἐὰν μή* = אם לא; the threat is conditional on his winning the victory.

37. **to be called by thy name . . .** Cp. with this verse 1 Kings viii. 38, 43.

39. **Bethhoron.** See note on iii. 16.

40. **Adasa.** An hour and a half north-east of Bethhoron; Josephus (*Antiq.* XII. x. 5) speaks of it as 'a village which was thirty furlongs distant from Bethhoron.'

41. **when they that came from the king . . .** The reference is to Sennacherib, see 2 Kings xviii. 22 ff.

one hundred . . . Cp. 2 Kings xix. 35; reference to the same event is made in Ecclus. xviii. 21.

43. **Adar.** The twelfth month of the Jewish ecclesiastical year, corresponding roughly to March; in leap-years there is what is called *Adar Sheni* (the 'Second Adar'), which is then the thirteenth month.

45. **a day's journey.** From Adasa to Gazara is about fifteen miles.

Gazara. See note on iv. 15.

46 solemn trumpets[u]. And they came forth out of all the villages of Judaea round about[v], [w]and closed
them in[w]; and these turned back on those (behind), and they all fell by the sword, and there was
47 not one of them left. And they took the spoils and the booty, and they smote off Nicanor's head,
[x]and his right hand, which he stretched out so haughtily, and brought them[x], and hanged them up[y]
48 near Jerusalem. And the people was exceeding glad, [z]and they kept that day as a day of great
49 gladness[z]. And they ordained that this day should be observed year by year (on) the thirteenth
50 (day) of Adar. And [aa]the land of[aa] Judah had rest [bb]a little while[bb].

VIII. 1–32. *Judas concludes a treaty with the Romans, after having heard of their power and rule.*

8 1 And Judas heard of the fame of the Romans, that they were valiant men, and that they were
friendly disposed towards all who attached themselves to them, and that they offered friendship[a] to
2 as many as came unto them, [b]and that they were valiant men[b]. And they told him about their
wars and exploits which they had done among the Galatians, and [c]how they had [d]conquered them[d],
3 and brought them under tribute; and (they told him also of) what things they had done in the land
4 of Spain[c], how they had acquired [e]the mines of silver and gold there[e]; [f]and how that by their
policy and persistence[g] they had conquered the whole[h] land (and the land was exceeding far [i]from
them[i]); also (they told) of the kings that had come against them from the uttermost part of the
earth, until they had discomfited them[f], and smitten them very sore; and how the rest had given
5 them tribute year by year. Furthermore, (they told) of how they had discomfited in battle [k]Philip,

v > $\mathfrak{S}^{luc}$ w–w *lit.* outflanked them > 71 x–x > $\mathfrak{L}^1$ y *lit.* stretched them out z–z > 71 in that day $\mathfrak{L}^1$ aa–aa > V bb–bb *lit.* a few days.

VIII. a + and to as many as held to them A b–b > $\mathfrak{S}^{luc}$ c–c > 71 d–d won their land $\mathfrak{L}^1$ e–e The mountains from whence silver and gold are sought out $\mathfrak{S}^g$ f–f > 71 g wisdom $\mathfrak{L}^1$ h > $\mathfrak{S}^g$ i–i > $\mathfrak{S}^g$ k–k > $\mathfrak{S}^g$

---

the solemn trumpets. *Lit.* 'the trumpets of signals', i. e. to give a signal to their friends in the villages round about, see next verse.

46. **closed them in.** ὑπερεκέρων αὐτούς, 'outflanked them', thanks to the alarm given by the signal trumpets.

47. **smote off . . .** Cp. 1 Sam. xxxi. 9; Judith xiii. 8–15.

stretched out . . . hanged them up. ἐξέτεινεν . . . ἐξέτειναν, a word-play quite after the Hebrew fashion.

49. . . . **the thirteenth (day) of Adar.** This festival was originally called 'Nicanor Day', but it was displaced (when, is not known) by the Fast of Esther, which was kept on this day in memory of Esther's fasting, mentioned in Esther ix. 31 (cp. Esther iv. 3, 16); this fast was a preparation for the feast of Purim, which occurs on the fourteenth of Adar. 'Nicanor Day' is mentioned in the Jerusalem Talmud (*Megillah*, ii. 66 *a*), where it is spoken of as a semi-festival.

50. **the land . . . had rest.** Cp. ix. 57, xiv. 4, and for the Hebrew שקטה הארץ cp. Joshua xi. 23.

a little while. *Lit.* 'a few days', i. e. about a month, cp. ix. 3.

VIII. 1–32. 'The details of this narrative have been called in question by many critics, although the fact of a treaty having been concluded between the Jews and the Romans has been generally admitted. Wellhausen, e.g., while asserting that the journey to Rome, the negotiations with the Senate, and the return to Jerusalem, could not have been accomplished in a single month, goes on to say: "This would be decisive, only I am not convinced that the usual assumption is correct. For the festival of Nicanor's day is unintelligible, if the sensation of victory had been forthwith effaced through a reverse of the worst description. It is not maintained that the statement of 1 Macc. viii. 17 (2 Macc. iv. 11) is drawn purely from the imagination" (*Isr. und Jüd. Gesch.*², p. 250, note 3). That the narrative does contain inaccuracies (*vv.* 8, 15, 16) is not to be denied. These, however, may be accounted for by the defective means of international communication in those days, and still more by the fact that the interests of the Jews were practically confined to agriculture and their ancestral religion. The writer's graphic picture is, upon the whole, "not unfaithful" (Rawlinson), and has "quite the character of that *naïveté* and candour with which intelligence of that sort is propagated in the mouth of the common people" (Grimm). In spite of what is said in *v.* 13, he is apparently blind as to the dangers attending negotiations with Rome' (Fairweather and Black, p. 157).

1. **all who attached themselves to them.** Rawlinson points out that 'the Romans had received into alliance Attalus of Pergamus, Ariarathes of Cappadocia, Ptolemy Philometor, and the Rhodians.'

2. **the Galatians.** Kautzsch thinks it improbable that the reference is to the Gauls in Asia Minor who were conquered by Manlius Vulso, 189 B.C.; he thinks, with Mommsen and others, that the Gauls of Upper Italy are meant; these were subjugated by the Romans in 190 B.C., and laid under tribute.

3. **the land of Spain.** This came under the Roman dominion in 201 B.C., though only that portion of it which had belonged to the Carthaginians; it was not until nearly two centuries later that the whole country became incorporated into the Roman Empire.

the mines of silver and gold there. Pliny (*Hist. Naturalis*, xxxiii. 4, §§ 21, 23) speaks of the gold and silver found in Spain, the former in the shape of gold-dust in the bed of the Tagus; Diodorus Siculus (v. 35, § 1) says: 'Spain has the best and most plentiful silver from mines of all the world' (cp. Rawlinson, *Hist. of Phoenicia*, pp. 313 ff.).

4. **the whole land.** τόπος is used here of the whole country as in 1 Sam. xii. 8 (Sept.); Jer. xvi. 2, 3 (Sept.); the Hebrew word (מקום) is used in the same way in these passages. The statement here is an exaggeration, see note on *v.* 3.

5. **Philip.** i.e. Philip V, King of Macedonia, 220–179 B.C.; he was finally defeated at the battle of Cynoscephalae in Thessaly (197 B.C.) by T. Quinctius Flaminius.

[l]and[k] Perseus[l], king of Chittim, and them that lifted themselves up against them, and had conquered
6 them; Antiochus also, the great[m] king of Asia, who had come against them to battle, having
a hundred and twenty elephants, with cavalry, and chariots, and an exceeding great host,—he had
7 also been discomfited by them[n], and they had taken him alive, and had appointed that both he and
such as reigned after him should give them a great tribute[o] and should give hostages, and a 'tract'
(of land), (namely) the country of India, and Media, and Lydia, and of the goodliest of their
9 countries; and how they had taken them from him, and had given them to king Eumenes. Also
10 (they told of) how they of Greece had purposed to come and destroy them, and the thing had
become known to them, and they had sent against them a captain, and had fought against them,
and many of them had fallen, [p]wounded to death[p]; and (of how) they had made captive their wives
and their children, [q]and had spoiled them and conquered their land, and had pulled down their
11 strongholds[r][q], and had brought them into bondage unto this day. And (they told of) how they had
destroyed the residue of the kingdoms [s]and of the isles[s], as many as had risen up against them[t], and
12 had made them their servants; but that with their friends and such as relied upon them they kept
amity; and (of) how they had conquered the kingdoms[u] that were nigh and those that were far off,
13 and that all who heard of their fame were afraid of them. Moreover (they told) that whomsoever
they will to succour and to make kings, become kings[v]; and that whomsoever they will, do they
14 depose; and they are exalted exceedingly; and that for all this none of them did ever put on
15 a diadem, [w]neither did they clothe themselves with purple, to be magnified[x] thereby[y].[w] (They told)
also how they had made for themselves a senate house, and how day by day three hundred [z]and

[l-l] > 19 93 [m] > 71 [n] him Luc [o] + year by year Luc [p-p] > L[1] [q-q] > 71 [r] + and spoiled them 𝔊 &c. [s-s] > 𝔏[1] the rest of the isles 𝔖[luc] [t] + and had plundered them Luc + and had plundered them and taken them captive 𝔖[luc] [u] kings ℵ V 19 93 𝔖[luc] [v] will become kings A [w-w] > 71 [x] > ℵ* (*hab* ℵ[c.a]) [y] to exalt themselves (*in the sense of assuming too much power*) 𝔖[g] [z-z] > 𝔖[g]

Perseus. The illegitimate son and successor of Philip; he was conquered by L. Aemilius Paullus at the battle of Pydna (168 B.C.), whereby the Macedonian kingdom was brought to an end.

Chittim. See note on i. 1.

and them that lifted . . . Probably the reference is to those who sent reinforcements to Perseus, viz. the Epirots, Thessalians, and Thracians (Grimm).

6. **Antiochus also . . .** i.e. Antiochus III, the Great, King of Syria 223–187 B.C., son of Seleucus Callinicus.

Asia. See note on xi. 13.

discomfited. At the battle of Magnesia, 190 B.C., by Scipio Africanus (Polybius, iii. 3. 4).

7. **taken him alive.** 'Here the author has been misled by a false report. According to the unanimous testimony of the classical writers, Antiochus succeeded in making his escape' (Fairweather and Black); Kautzsch suggests that possibly the author has mixed up Antiochus with Perseus here.

such as reigned after him. Seleucus IV, Philopator (187–176 B.C.), and Antiochus IV, Epiphanes (175–164 B.C.), with whom the tribute ceased.

a great tribute. According to Polybius, xxi. 14. 3–6, 15,000 Euboic talents, 500 of which had to be paid at the conclusion of the negotiations, 2,500 when peace was ratified, and 1,000 a year for the next twelve years (quoted by Knabenbauer, p. 152).

hostages. See note on i. 10.

a tract. διαστολή, the word is apparently used in the same sense as in Rom. iii. 22, a 'distinction', i.e. the land in question was to be distinguished in the future from the rest of his possessions by being assigned to the Romans.

8. **India.** This never belonged to Antiochus, so he could not have ceded it to Rome.

Media. According to Livy xxxvii. 56, xxxviii. 38 it was only his possessions on this side of the Taurus (i.e. on the west) that Antiochus was forced to give up. We must probably see here, as elsewhere in this section, a rhetorical exaggeration. The ingenious attempts which have been made to emend to the text, and read 'Ionia and Asia', or 'Mysia', may or may not be justified, but they have absolutely no support either from MSS. or Versions.

. . . to king Eumenes. Eumenes II, king of Pergamos (197–158 B.C.), and son of Attalus I; these territories were given to him by the Romans in recognition of the help rendered during the war with Syria, and especially at the battle of Magnesia (see further, Smith's *Dict. of Class. Biog.* s.v.).

9. **Also . . .** What this all refers to is not known. Kautzsch thinks that very probably the reference may be to the Roman victory over the forces of the Achaean Alliance (147–146 B.C., i.e. fifteen years after the death of Judas Maccabaeus); in this case the 'captain', mentioned in *v.* 10, would be L. Mummius. The war, which was short and decisive, resulted in the subjugation of the whole of Greece, which was reduced to the status of a Roman province, under the name of Achaia.

11. **the isles.** i.e. Sicily, Sardinia, and Corsica, together with the isles of the Grecian Archipelago.

12. In this and the next few verses the subjects of *vv.* 1 ff. are again reverted to.

with their friends . . . they kept amity. This is not in accordance with the facts; the statement is, no doubt, due to insufficient knowledge.

15. **and how day by day . . .** As Fairweather and Black point out, 'this is quite a mistake. The regular sittings of the Senate were confined to the Kalends, Nones, Ides, and Festivals. In case of emergency, however, it could be summoned in a moment, as its members were not allowed to leave Rome for more than a day, and only a few of them at a time. In the later days of the Republic the Senate sat on all lawful days in February to receive foreign ambassadors, but there is no evidence that the practice was as old as the time of the Maccabees. If it was, the writer's mistake is easily explained.' The reference to three hundred and twenty members of the Senate is also a mistake, it never reached more than three hundred.

twenty[z] men sat in council, consulting alway for the people, to the end that they[a] might be well
16 ordered; and how they committed their government to one man year by year, that he should be over
them, and be lord over all[b] their country; and that all are obedient to this one, and that there is
neither envy nor emulation among them.
17 And Judas chose Eupolemus, the son of John, the son of Accos, and Jason, the son of Eleazar, and
18 sent them to Rome, to make a league of amity and confederacy [c]with them[c], and that they should
take the yoke from[d] them, when they saw that the kingdom of the Greeks did keep Israel in
19 bondage. And they[e] went to Rome, [f]and the way was exceeding long[f]; and they entered into the
20 Senate house, [g]and answered[g] [h]and said[h]: 'Judas, who is also (called) Maccabaeus, and his brethren,
and the whole people of the Jews, have sent us unto you, to make a confederacy and peace with you,
21 and that we might be registered (as) your confederates and friends.' And the thing was well-pleasing
22 in their sight. And this is the copy of the writing[i] which they wrote back again on tablets of brass,
and sent to Jerusalem, [k]that it might be with them there[k] for a memorial of peace and confederacy:
23 'Good success be to the Romans, and to the nation of the Jews, by sea and by land for ever; the
24 sword also and the enemy be far from them. But if war arise for Rome[l] first, [m]or for any of their
25 confederates in all their dominion[m], the nation of the Jews shall help them as confederates as the occasion
26 shall prescribe [n]to them[n], with all their heart; and unto [o]them that make war[o] they (i.e. the Jews)
[p]shall not give[p], neither supply, food, arms, money, or ships, as it hath seemed good unto Rome; and
they (i.e. the Jews) shall observe their obligations, receiving nothing (in the way of a bribe). [q]In the
27 same manner[q], moreover, if war come first[r] upon the nation of the Jews, the Romans shall help them
28 as confederates with all their soul, as the occasion shall prescribe to them; and to them that are
confederates[s] there shall not be given corn, arms, money, [t]or ships[t], as it hath seemed good unto

[a] *the reflex pron.*, A V *suggesting that the Senate was looking after its own interests* [b] > 71 [c–c] > ℵ* (*hab* ℵ$^{c.a}$) [d] > A [e] + that were with Eupolemus Luc [f–f] > 𝔏^2 [g–g] > 𝔏^1 [h–h] > A [i] letter ℵ [k–k] > 𝔖luc [l] the Romans 𝔖luc 𝔏 [m–m] > 71 [n–n] > 𝔖luc 𝔏 [o–o] 𝔖 *in* 𝔊 *the reference seems to be to the Romans* [p–p] > ℵ* (*hab* ℵ$^{c.a}$) 93 [q–q] > 𝔖luc [r] > 𝔖g [s] that make war 55 𝔏^2 [t–t] > A

---

16. **one man.** Another instance of inadequate knowledge; there were, of course, two consuls.

neither envy . . . This also is contrary to fact; on this, however, Grimm remarks that 'it is psychologically very comprehensible that, having regard to the assistance to be looked for by an alliance with Rome, the darker side of the conditions which obtained in the Roman State, of which the writer might have been cognisant, were naturally overlooked or left unnoticed.' At any rate, it is not to be expected that the writer should have had much intimate acquaintance with the internal affairs of Rome; and even if he had, his knowledge of the deplorable conditions in his own country would unconsciously tend to make him take a bright view of all that concerned the powerful people from whom so much was hoped.

17. **Eupolemus.** 'Perhaps identical with that Eupolemus who is known to us as a Hellenistic writer' (Schürer, *The Jewish People* . . ., Div. I, vol. i, p. 231, see also Div. II, vol. iii, pp. 203 ff.); he was a Palestinian Jew who wrote about 158–157 B.C. or shortly afterwards.

the son of John. See 2 Macc. iv. 11.

Accos. More correctly Hakkoz, cp. 1 Chron. xxiv. 10; Ezra ii. 61; Neh. iii. 4, 21, vii. 63, belonging to a priestly family.

Jason the son of Eleazar. Perhaps the same Jason who is mentioned as the father of Antipater in xii. 16, xiv. 22.

18. **the yoke.** i.e. the Syrian yoke; this implies either that the victory over Nicanor, recorded in ch. vii, had not yet taken place, or else that it was, after all, not of a wholly decisive character; Schürer thinks that 'from the general drift of the First Book of Maccabees, it may be assumed that Judas had first arranged the embassy after the victory over Nicanor' (op. cit. Div. I, vol. i, p. 232 note).

22. **tablets of brass.** The usual way of preserving documents of this kind; Grimm quotes Polybius, iii. 26. 1, who says, in reference to the treaties between Rome and Carthage, that they were preserved in this way, and that they were kept in the Capitol. Josephus (*Antiq.* XII. x. 6) says regarding this treaty that the Romans 'also made a decree concerning it, and sent a copy of it into Judaea; it was also laid up in the Capitol, and engraven in brass.'

23. **Good success be to the Romans.** The equivalent, as Grimm points out, of the usual Roman formula: *Quod bonum, faustum felixque sit populo Romano* . . .

26. **unto them that make war . . . ships.** Kautzsch sees in this mention of ships, which at this time (161 B.C.) the Jews could not have supplied, one of the reasons for regarding this whole section (*vv.* 22–32) as having been added later, whether in the Hebrew original or when the translation was made; but there is much in Grimm's contention that the mention of ships shows the far-seeing character of Roman policy, especially as not long after this the Jews got possession of a harbour (cp. xiv. 5). At the same time, it is worth while noting that in Josephus' account the ships are not spoken of in reference to the Jews; in *Antiq.* XII. x. 6 the decree runs: 'It shall not be lawful for any that are subject to the Romans to make war with the nation of the Jews, nor to assist those that do so, either by sending them corn, or ships, or money'; this is the only mention of ships. It is, therefore, just possible that the form of the decree in 1 Macc. is due to a misunderstanding of the original Roman form of it.

as it hath seemed good unto Rome. This, together with the phrase in *vv.* 25, 27, 'as the occasion shall prescribe to them', made the treaty far more advantageous to the Romans than to the Jews; see also the same words in *v.* 28. It is true that in *v.* 30 there is a *proviso* that modifications might be made by either party by mutual consent, but this does not appear to be part of the actual treaty, the words of which clearly stop at the end of *v.* 28.

29 Rome[u]; and they shall observe these obligations, and that without deceit.' [x]According to these
30 words have the Romans made (a treaty) with the people of the Jews. But if hereafter the one
party [y]or[z] the other[y] shall determine to add or to diminish anything, they shall do it at their
31 pleasure, and whatsoever they shall add or take away shall be established. And as touching the
evils which king[aa] Demetrius doeth [bb]unto you[bb cc], we have written [dd]to him[ee] saying[dd]: 'Wherefore hast
32 thou made thy yoke heavy upon our friends (and)[ff] confederates the Jews? If, therefore, they plead
any more against thee, we will do them justice[gg], and fight thee by sea and by land.'

IX. 1–22. *Death of Judas Maccabaeus.*

9 1 And when Demetrius had heard that Nicanor [a]was fallen[a] with his forces [a]in battle[a], he sent
Bacchides and Alcimus again into the land of Judah [b]a second time[b], and the right wing (of his army)
2 with them. And they[c] went by way of Gilgal[d], and encamped against Mesaloth, which is in Arbela,
3 [e]and gat possession of it[e], and destroyed[f] much people. And [g]in the first month of the one
4 hundred and fifty second year[g] they encamped against Jerusalem. And they removed and went
5 unto Berea, with twenty thousand footmen and two thousand horse. And Judas was encamped at

[u] the Romans ℵ 𝔖luc 𝔏 [x] + thus Luc [y-y] + 𝔖luc [z] and A V Luc 𝔖luc 𝔏 [aa] > ℵ* (*hab* ℵ c.a) [bb-bb] > 𝔏 [cc] them ℵ (*not* ℵ c.a) A Luc 𝔖 [dd-dd] and sent unto him 𝔖luc [ee] thus 𝔖g [ff] + our Luc [gg] vengeance 55 vengeance and justice 𝔖luc

IX. [a-a] had waged battle A [b-b] > 𝔖g [c] + that were with Bacchides Luc [d] Gilead Luc 𝔖luc [e-e] > 𝔖g and occupied it 𝔏² [f] he destroyed A V [g-g] > 71

31. **we have written to him . . .** But, as Schürer truly points out, this came too late, for through the energetic action of Demetrius the overthrow of Judaea had already been completed before there was any possibility of interference on the part of the Romans (cp. ix. 1–21).

wherefore hast thou made thy yoke heavy. A Hebraism הכביד עול (cp. 2 Chron. x. 10, 14).

32. **we will do them justice.** Another Hebrew phrase עשה משפט ('to do justice', lit. 'judgement'), Deut. x. 18, &c.

IX. 1. **that Nicanor was fallen.** Cp. vii. 43, 44.

he sent . . . a second time. προσέθετο . . . ἀποστεῖλαι, 'he added to send', a Hebrew phrase ויסף לשלח.

the right wing. The Jews faced eastwards so that from their point of view the right would be the Syrian troops in the south, but the actual right wing of the Syrian army was that part of it stationed towards the north; see next note, Bacchides probably came from the north, Josephus directly states that he 'marched out of Antioch' (*Antiq.* XII. xi. 1).

2. **Gilgal . . . Mesaloth . . . Arbela.** The identification of the place which 'Gilgal' represents is extremely difficult, perhaps impossible. The best attested reading is Γάλγαλα = Gilgal; but there are at least three places of this name mentioned in the O.T.; Joshua's Gilgal, the Gilgal by Bethel, and the Gilgal by Mount Gerizim (on this see G. A. Smith in *EB* 1729 ff.). Some MSS., followed by the Lucianic Syriac, read Γαλαάδ = Gilead; and Josephus has Γαλιλαίαν = Galilee. Assuming, as is permissible, that the two last readings are to be rejected, and that 'Gilgal' is the right reading, it seems upon the whole best to identify this with the Gilgal by Mount Gerizim; 'if', says G. A. Smith (*EB* 291 f.), 'Bacchides wished to avoid the road which had proved so fatal to Nicanor, he may have taken the road from Esdraelon south through Samaria. . . . On this route Masaloth might be Meselieh or Meithalūn, respectively 5 or 8 miles south of Jenīn, each of them a natural point at which to resist an invader. A greater difficulty is presented by ἐν Ἀρβήλοις. The plural form evidently signifies a considerable district. Now, Eusebius (*OS*(2) Ἀρβηλά) notes the name as extant in his day, on Esdraelon, 9 Roman miles from Lejjūn, while the entrances from Esdraelon on Meselieh and Meithalūn are 9½ Roman miles from Lejjūn. It is therefore possible that the name Ἀρβηλά covered in earlier days the whole of this district. The suggestion is, however, far from being capable of proof. The chief points in its favour are the straight road from the north, which was regarded as a natural line of invasion, and the existence along the road of a Jiljūljeh [= Gilgal], a Meselieh, and a Meithalūn.'

3. **the first month.** If, as there is every reason to suppose (cp. i. 54, vii. 43), it is the Jewish first month that is meant, it is the month Nisan, corresponding roughly to April. This would mean that only six or seven weeks had elapsed since the defeat of Nicanor on the 13th of Adar (= March); that does not allow much time for the news of Nicanor's defeat to have reached Demetrius in Antioch, and for the latter to dispatch the reinforcements under Bacchides, especially as some time must have been taken up in encamping against Mesaloth, and getting possession of it, and destroying much people (see *v.* 2), on the way to Jerusalem. This feat is not impossible, but rather improbable, unless we suppose (with Michaelis, quoted by Grimm) that it was leap-year, in which the month Adar Sheni with its twenty-nine days came between Adar and Nisan. Otherwise the most obvious explanation is that the writer has made a mistake of about a month.

they encamped against Jerusalem. Presumably Bacchides thought Judas was in Jerusalem; otherwise it is difficult to understand why he should have encamped here. It is surprising how badly Bacchides must have been informed about the movements of his opponents; bad generalship and an inefficient intelligence department on the part of the Syrians, both of which are several times unconsciously implied by the writer of this book, must evidently have had much to do with the success of the Maccabees against overwhelming odds. In this particular case the disparity was so great that even bad generalship could not save the Jews from disaster.

4. **they removed . . . unto Berea.** They had scarcely settled themselves down before Jerusalem before they had to break up the camp again. It is not known where Berea was.

5. **Judas was encamped at Elasa.** This place is also unknown; Josephus says that 'Judas pitched his camp at a certain village whose name was Bethzetha' (*Antiq.* XII. xi. 1).

6 Elasa, and three thousand chosen men with him. And (when) they saw the multitude [h]of the
forces[h], [k]that they[i] were many[k], they feared exceedingly; and many slipped away from the army;
7 there were not left [l]of them[l] more than eight hundred men. And (when) Judas saw that his army
slipped away, [m]and that (nevertheless) the battle was imminent for him[m], he was sore troubled in
8 heart, for that he had no time to gather them together. [n]And he became desperate[n], and said to
them that were left: 'Let us arise and go up against our adversaries, if peradventure we may be able
9 to fight against them.' And they turned from him, saying: 'We shall in no wise be able [o](to withstand them)[o]; but let us rather save our lives now[p]; let us return (later on) with our brethren, and
10 fight [q]against them[q]; we are (now too) few.' Then Judas said: 'Far be it [r]from me[r] to do this
thing, to flee from them! [s]And if[t] our time is come[s], let us die manfully[u] for our brethren's sake
11 [v]and not leave a cause (of reproach) against our glory[v].' And the (Syrian) host removed from the
camp, and (the Jews) stood to encounter them; and the horse was divided into two companies, and
the slingers and the archers went before the host together with [w]all the mighty men that fought in
12 the front (of the line of battle)[w]. But Bacchides was on the right wing; and the phalanx drew near
from both sides, and they blew with their trumpets, and the men of [x]Judas' side[x] also blew [y]with
13 their trumpets[y]; and the earth shook [z]with the shout[z] of the[a] armies. And the battle was joined,
14 (and continued) from morning until evening. And (when) Judas saw that Bacchides and the main
strength of (his) army were on the right wing, [b]his followers concentrated their whole attention (upon
15 them)[b], and the right wing[c] was discomfited by them, and they pursued after them unto the mount
16 Azotus[d]. And (when) they that were on the left wing[e] saw that the right wing[e] was discomfited,
17 they turned (and followed) upon the footsteps of Judas and those that were with him. And the
18 battle waxed sore, and many[f] [g]on either side[g] fell [h]wounded to death[h]. And Judas fell, and the
19 rest fled. And Jonathan and Simon [i]took Judas their brother, and[i] buried him in the sepulchre of
20 his[k] fathers at Modin. And they bewailed him[l], and all Israel [m]made great lamentation for him
and[m] mourned[n] many days, [o]and said[o]:
21 '[p]How is the mighty one fallen, the saviour of Israel![p]'
22 And the rest of the acts of Judas, [p]and (his) wars[p], and the valiant deeds [q]which he did[q], [p]and his
greatness[p],—they are not written; for they were exceeding many.

h-h > 71 i + who were opposed (to them) Luc k-k > 71 𝔏[1] l-l > 𝔖luc m-m > 71 n-n > 71 𝔏[1] o-o to fight against them ℵ V 55 p > 𝔖g 𝔏[2] q-q > 𝔖g r-r > ℵ V s-s > 71 t > A u > 𝔏[1] v-v > 71 w-w all the men who are skilled in war 𝔏 x-x Judah ℵ V y-y > 71 z-z because of (*lit.* from) A a their A b-b 𝔖luc and there went with him all that were brave in heart 𝔊 𝔖g 𝔏 c part ℵ 19 93 d Gazara 𝔏 e part 𝔖luc f > 19 93 𝔖luc g-g of those ℵ h-h > 𝔖luc i-i > 93 k their 64 93 l + there A Judas 19 93 𝔖luc m-m > 71 n > 𝔏 o-o > 71 p-p > 71 q-q > 𝔖luc

three thousand chosen men. It is strange that so many of these 'chosen men' should have 'slipped away' at the critical moment; Josephus gives their number as only one thousand, but this is obviously a mistake, as he says that 'they all fled away, excepting eight hundred'!

8. **he became desperate.** Cp. Deut. xx. 3 (Sept.).

10. **far be it from me to do this thing.** Μή μοι γένοιτο ποιῆσαι τὸ πρᾶγμα τοῦτο, a very Hebraic phrase: חלילה לי מעשׂות זאת (cp. xiii. 5), see Gen. xliv. 7, 17; Joshua xxii. 29, xxiv. 16; 1 Kings xxi. 3.

13. **the earth shook.** Cp. 2 Sam. xxii. 8.

from morning until evening. Josephus says the battle continued 'till sun-set', but does not mention when it began; the statement in the text is probably a rhetorical exaggeration; eight hundred against twenty-two thousand, holding out all day, can scarcely be literally true, especially as no hint is given that the smaller number occupied any advantageous position; from the account in the text, as well as in Josephus, the two armies met on equal terms as far as position was concerned.

15. **the mount Azotus.** Josephus, 'a mountain called Eza' (or Aza); no such mountain is known; the text is clearly corrupt.

17. **and the battle waxed sore.** καὶ ἐβαρύνθη ὁ πόλεμος, a Hebrew phrase ותכבד המלחמה; cp. 1 Sam. xxxi. 3; 1 Chron. x. 3; Isa. xxi. 15.

19. . . . **took Judas their brother.** According to Josephus (*Antiq.* XII. xi. 2) they 'received his dead body by a treaty from the enemy'; this is more likely to be correct, for it is hardly to be expected that the Syrians would have treated the body of the Jewish rebel chief, as they regarded him, with more respect than that which the Jews accorded to the body of the Syrian general Nicanor (see vii. 47), unless there were special reasons for this. Josephus does not mention the terms of this 'treaty'.

Modin. Cp. ii. 1, xiii. 27.

20. **great lamentation.** Cp. xiii. 26.

21. **How is the mighty one fallen.** Cp. 2 Sam. i. 19, 25, 27.

the saviour of Israel. Cp. Judges iii. 9; 2 Kings xiii. 5.

22. **And the rest of the acts . . .** For the phraseology cp. xvi. 23; it occurs often in the Books of the Kings.

they are not written. This statement implies that for this part of the narrative (i.e. the 'rest of the acts') no documents were available; which, on the other hand, implies that what is recorded in our book was based on extant documents.

'With the overthrow of Judas', says Schürer (*op. cit.*, I. i, p. 233), 'it was finally and definitely proved that it

JONATHAN MACCABAEUS. IX. 23—XII. 53.

IX. 23–31. *Jonathan succeeds Judas.*

23 And it came to pass after the death of Judas that the lawless put forth their heads in all the
24 borders of Israel, and all they that wrought iniquity rose up ; in those days [r]there arose exceeding
25 great murmuring that the land made peace with them[r]. And Bacchides chose out the ungodly men,
26 and made them lords of the country. And they sought out and searched for the friends of Judas,
and brought them to Bacchides, and he took vengeance on them, [s]and treated them with mockery[s].
27 And there was great tribulation in Israel, such as was not since the time that a prophet appeared
28 unto them[t]. And all the friends of Judas were gathered together, and they said unto Jonathan :
29 'Since thy brother Judas hath died, we have no man like him to go forth[u] against our enemies and
30 Bacchides, [v]and against them of our nation that are inimical (to us)[v w]. Now therefore we have
chosen thee this day to be our ruler and leader [x]in his stead[x], [y]that thou mayest fight our battles[y].'
31 [z]And Jonathan took[a] [b]the leadership upon him at that time[b], and rose up in the stead of his brother
Judas[z].

IX. 32–73. *Jonathan's struggle with Bacchides.*

32, 33 And (when) Bacchides knew it, he sought to slay him. But (when) Jonathan, [c]and Simon his
brother, [d]and all that were with him[d c], knew it, they fled into the wilderness of Tekoah, and

r–r *See note below*   s–s > 𝔏   t Israel 𝔖g 𝔏²   u + and to enter in ℵ V 𝔖g   v–v > 𝔏¹   w 19 64   x–x > 𝔖luc
y–y for battle 𝔏¹   z–z And they chose Jonathan as leader in place of his brother Judas 𝔏¹   a chose 19 𝔖g   b–b > 71
c–c > 71   d–d > 93

---

was a vain endeavour on the part of the Jewish nationalists to measure swords with the mighty forces of Syria. Brilliant as the earlier achievements of Judas had been, he was largely indebted to the recklessness and self-confidence of his opponents. Continuous military success was not to be thought of if only the Syrian authorities seriously roused themselves to the conflict. The following age cannot show even one conspicuous victory of the kind by which Judas had won renown. What the Maccabaean party finally reached, it won through voluntary concessions of claimants to the Syrian throne contending with one another, and generally in consequence of internal dissensions in the Syrian Empire.'

23. **the lawless.** Cp. vii. 24, 25.

put forth . . . rose up. Cp. Ps. xcii. 7 (Sept. xci. 8).

24. **murmuring.** Prof. Torrey (*EB* 2859) thinks the rendering λιμός is due to a misreading of the original Hebrew which had רעם ('murmuring'), not רעב ('famine') ; this, if correct, would certainly make the next clause less difficult.

that the land made peace with them. *καὶ αὐτομόλησεν ἡ χώρα μετ' αὐτῶν.* The verb with *μετά* only occurs once in the Septuagint, 2 Sam. x. 19, where the Hebrew has וישלימו את־ישראל, ('and they made peace with Israel'). If we are to be guided by this, the passage before us must mean (if we accept 'famine' as the right reading) that owing to the famine, the land, by which here can only be meant the followers of Judas, made peace with them, i.e. the 'lawless'. This must, however, be rejected ; firstly, because 'the land' cannot be restricted in this way, and, secondly, because the sequel shows that there was no peace between the followers of Judas and the 'lawless'. Fairweather and Black take 'the land' to mean 'the country in general, as distinguished from staunch patriots' ; but the text gives no justification for this distinction ; for the writer of 1 Macc. there are only two parties in the Jewish State, the Maccabaean party and the 'lawless'. Grimm holds that the real meaning of the passage is shown by the paraphrastic rendering of the Syriac Version : 'And the land too has become corrupt with them' ; i.e. the land, through the famine, had, as it were, joined hands with the apostates in antagonism against the faithful. This is in accordance with Josephus (*Antiq.* XII. i. 1). Kautzsch concurs in this : 'The land, otherwise so fruitful, seemed to have allied itself with the lawless for the purpose of destroying the godly' ; and he renders : 'So that (in the same way) the land fell off (or "deserted") with them, i.e. the lawless.' Against this it is to be urged that the Septuagint nowhere uses the verb in question in this sense (1 Sam. xx. 30, where the participle is used in the sense of 'rebellious' is not *à propos*). If, now, we follow Torrey in regarding 'famine' as a mistake for 'murmuring' (in the sense of indignation), and interpret the verb in the sense in which it is used in 2 Sam. x. 19 (see above), its only other occurrence with *μετά*, we get : 'there arose exceeding great murmuring (i.e. on the part of the faithful) that the land made peace with them,' i.e. the enemy, as the next verse goes on to show ; indeed, the verses that follow seem thoroughly to justify this rendering, as offering further grounds for the 'murmuring'. By 'the land' is meant everyone excepting the faithful, who were now obviously in a minority ; it must also be remembered that the author of 1 Macc. writes as one of the faithful.

26. **took vengeance on them.** *ἐξεδίκα αὐτούς*, for which T.R. reads *ἐξεδίκει ἐν αὐτοῖς*, cp. Jer. v. 9, 29 (Sept.) = התנקם ב 1 Sam. xviii. 25 ; נקם ב Judges xv. 7 (Grimm).

treated them with mockery. The reference must be to their religious practices ; Josephus, however, says : 'tortured and tormented them.'

27. **since the time that a prophet appeared unto them.** That the writer implies the prophet Malachi here (so Grimm, Bissell, Fairweather and Black, Knabenbauer) is not necessarily certain ; we have in the O.T. fragments of the writings of prophets who lived later than the time of Malachi (some short time before 450 B.C.) ; if they are anonymous, 'Malachi' is pseudonymous ; the former may have exercised as great an influence as the latter, although their names have not come down to us. Josephus makes no reference to a prophet, but says : 'They had never experience of the like since their return out of Babylon.' In either case it is a rhetorical exaggeration.

33. **the wilderness of Tekoah.** The wilderness got its name from the city six miles south of Bethlehem, on the borders of the wilderness ; the name still exists, *Tekua* ; the site of the ancient city lies on the top of a hill with

34 encamped by the water [e]of the pool Asphar[e]. [f]And Bacchides got to know of this on the Sabbath
day, and he came, he and all his army, over Jordan[f].
35 And (Jonathan)[g] sent his brother, a leader of the multitude, and besought his friends, the Nabath-
36 aeans, that they might leave with them their baggage, which was much. But the children of Ambri
37 came out of Medaba, and took John, and all that he had, and went their way [h]with it[h]. [i]But after
these things[i] they brought word to Jonathan [i]and Simon[i] his brother, that the children of Ambri
were making a great marriage, and were bringing the bride from Nadabath with a great train,
38 a daughter of one of the great nobles of Canaan. And they remembered[k] John their[l] brother, and
39 went up, and hid themselves under the covert of the mountain ; [m]and they lifted up their eyes[m], and
saw, and behold, a great ado and much baggage ; and the bridegroom came forth, and his friends
and his brethren to meet them (i.e. those forming the bridal procession) with timbrels, and minstrels,
40 and [n]many[o] weapons[n]. And they rose up [p]from their ambush[p] against them, and slew them ; and
many fell wounded to death, and the rest fled into the mountain ; and they took all their spoils[q].
41 And the marriage was turned into mourning, and the voice of their[r] minstrels into lamentation.
42 And (thus) they avenged fully the blood of their brother ; and they turned back to the marsh-land[s]
of Jordan.
43 And (when) Bacchides[t] heard it[u], he came on the Sabbath day unto the banks of the Jordan
44 with a great host. And Jonathan said unto his brethren[v] : 'Let us arise now and fight [w]for our
45 lives ; for it is not (with us) to-day, as yesterday and the day before. For, behold, the battle is
before us and behind us[w] ; moreover, the water of the Jordan is on this side and on that side, and (this
46 is) marsh-[x] and wood-land, and there is no place to turn aside. Now, therefore, cry unto heaven,
47 that ye may be delivered out of the hand of your[y] enemies.' And the battle was joined, and
48 Jonathan stretched forth his hand to smite Bacchides, and he turned away back from him. And
Jonathan, and they that were with him[z], leapt into the [a]Jordan, and swam over to the other side ;

[e–e] > 𝔏[1] [f–f] B. and all his army crossed the Jordan on the Sabbath day 𝔏[1] [g] T.R. [h–h] > 𝔏[1] [i–i] > 71 [k] + the blood of ℵ 𝔖[g] 𝔏[2] And Jonathan remembered 𝔖[luc] [l] his ℵ* (their ℵ[c.a]) 93 𝔖[luc] [m–m] > 71 [n–n] much people 55 64 [o] > 71 [p–p] > 19 [q] vessels A [r] the 19 [s] mountainous-land A V 55 71 bank 𝔏[1] ford 𝔖[luc] [t] > 𝔖[luc] [u] that Jonathan had returned Luc 𝔖[luc] (*with slight variations*) [v] them that were with him ℵ V [w–w] > 71 [x] > 𝔖[luc] [y] our A [z] + behind Luc [a–a] > 𝔖[g]

---

sloping sides ; the top is of considerable extent, and is covered with ruins spread over four or five acres of ground (cp. 1 Chron. ii. 24 ; 2 Chron. xx. 20 ; Amos i. 1 ; Jer. vi. 1).

the pool Asphar. 'The Be'er Asphar is probably the modern *Bīr-Selhūb*, a considerable reservoir in the wilderness, six miles WSW. of Engedi, and near the junction of several ancient roads ; the hills around still bear the name *Ṣafrā*, an equivalent of Asphar' (G. A. Smith, *EB* 343).

34. This verse, which is a variant of *v.* 43, has got out of place ; it should be deleted.

35. **his brother.** i. e. John ; cp. *vv.* 36, 38.

the Nabathaeans. See note on *v.* 25.

36. **the children of Ambri.** The reading 'Ιαμβρεί is probably due to dittography, the ι of the preceding υἱοί having been repeated by mistake (Kautzsch). Cheyne, however, thinks that the form Jambri (or Jamri) is correct, as the name יעמרי has been found on an Aramaic inscription at *Umm er-Reṣāṣ*, about twelve miles SSE. of Medeba (*EB* 2317). The name is not otherwise met with ; but, as the text shows, they belonged to an Arab clan of this name living at or near Medeba. Josephus has οἱ 'Αμαραίοι παῖδες, i. e. Amorites ; cp. Num. xxi. 29–31, where Medeba is spoken of as a city of the Amorites.

Medaba. Mentioned on the Moabite Stone : '. . . Now Omri annexed the (land) of Medeba, and dwelt therein' (ll. 7, 8). It was situated on the high land of Moab to the south of Heshbon ; cp. Joshua xiii. 9, 16. The ruins still survive and are called Medaba (see the *Quarterly Statement* of the Pal. Expl. Fund, July 1895 and July 1901).

37. **they brought word.** Presumably some escaped.

Nadabath. Possibly = Nebo ; Clermont-Ganneau (*Journal of the American Oriental Soc.*, 1891, pp. 541 ff.) thinks it is a mistake for Rabatha = Rabbath Ammon, twenty-two miles east of Jordan, on the river Jabbok (cp. 2 Sam. xii. 26–28) ; the modern *'Amman*.

39. **his friends.** Cp. Judges xiv. 11.

42. **the marsh-land.** τὸ ἕλος ; at the present day the ford nearest the Dead Sea is called *el Helu* ; it is no doubt owing to this that the Syriac Version reads 'the ford' ! (cp. Grimm).

44. **for it is not . . .** i. e. the state of affairs is more desperate than hitherto on account of the hopeless position they are in, as described in the next verse.

45. **on this side and on that side.** i. e. they were caught in a bend of the river.

47. **and he turned . . .** The exact meaning here is not quite clear ; in view of the words : 'The battle was joined,' it is probable that the reference is not to a personal conflict between Jonathan and Bacchides, but that their names here refer to their respective parties. In this case, the meaning of *vv.* 47, 48 would be that Jonathan and his followers made such a vigorous onslaught upon the enemy that the latter gave way temporarily ; Jonathan, thereupon, seeing the indecision of the enemy, took advantage of the momentary respite, and plunged into the river, followed by his men. That he gained some advantage at the commencement of the battle seems evident from the fact that Bacchides is afraid to pursue ; he is, presumably, deterred by the courage of despair which had been evinced by his opponents. The mention of the loss of a thousand Syrians also points to a conflict which at the start, at all events, was not one-sided.

49 and they (i.e. Bacchides and his followers) did not pass over[a] Jordan against them. And there fell[b]
[c]of Bacchides' company[c] [d]that day[d] about a thousand[e] men.
50 And they[f] returned[g] to Jerusalem; and they[h] built strong cities in Judaea, (namely), the stronghold that is in Jericho, and Emmaus, and Bethhoron, and Bethel, and Timnath[i], Pharathon, and
51 Tephon, with high walls, [k]and gates and bars[k]. And they[l] set garrisons[m] in them to vex Israel.
52 And they[n] fortified [o]the city Bethsura[o], and Gazara, and the citadel; [p]and they[q] put forces in them,
53 and store of victuals[p]. And they[r] took the sons[s] of the chief men of the country for hostages, and
put[t] them in ward in the citadel at Jerusalem.
54 Now in the one hundred and fifty-third year, [u]in the second month[u], Alcimus commanded to pull
down the wall of the inner court [u]of the sanctuary[u], (in so doing) he pulled down[v] also the works of
55 the prophets. [u]And (when) he began to pull down[u], at that (very) time, Alcimus was stricken, and
his works were hindered; and his mouth was stopped, and he became palsied, [u]and he could no more
56 speak anything, (nor) give order concerning his house[u]. And Alcimus[w] died at that time with great
57 torment. And (when) Bacchides saw that Alcimus was dead, he returned to the king. And the
land of Judah had rest two years.
58 And all the lawless men took counsel, saying: 'Behold, Jonathan, and they of his part are dwelling
at peace, (and) in security; [x]let us therefore now bring[x] Bacchides, and he will lay hands on them
59, 60 all[y] in one night.' And they went and consulted with him. And he[z] removed, and came with
a great host, and sent letters privily to all his confederates that were in Judaea, that they should lay
hands on Jonathan, and (on) them that were with him; but they were[a] not able (to do so), because
61 their plan became known to them[b]. And they (that were of Jonathan's part) laid hands on [c]about
62 fifty men[c] of the country that were the ringleaders in the wickedness, and slew[d] them. And Jonathan, and Simon, and they that were with him, gat them away[e] to Bethbasi, which is in the wilder-
63 ness, and he built up [f]that which had been pulled down thereof[f], and made[g] it strong. And [h](when)
Bacchides knew it[h], he gathered together all[i] his multitude, and sent word to them that were in Judaea.
64 And he [k]went and[k] encamped against Bethbasi, and fought against it [k]many days, and made[k]
65 engines[l] (of war). And Jonathan left his brother Simon in the city, and went forth into the country;

[b] there went through A   [c–c] by the side of Bacchides A   [d–d] > 71   [e] three thousand ℵ V 55 $\mathfrak{S}^g$ [f] he ℵ V Luc 𝔏
[g] + Bacchides 64 93   [h] he $\aleph^{c.a}$ [i] + and ℵ A V   [k–k] > 71   [l] he ℵ   [m] V *only*   [n] he ℵ V   [o–o] 𝔖 𝔏;
Bethsura ℵ 64 93   the city and Bethsura A   the city near (*lit.* in) Bethsura V   [p–p] > 71   [q] he ℵ V Luc 𝔏
[r] he ℵ V 𝔏   Bacchides 64 93   [s] + of Israel 55   [t] he put ℵ V 𝔏 64 93   [u–u] > 71   [v] destroyed 𝔏   [w] > $\mathfrak{S}^g$
[x–x] V^a *only*   we will bring ℵ A V*   let us lead Luc   [y] > 19 64 $\mathfrak{L}^1$ [z] Bacchides Luc   [a] he was not A
[b] > ℵ   him $\mathfrak{S}^g$ [c–c] > ℵ   [d] he slew ℵ A $\mathfrak{L}^1$ [e] + from them ℵ   [f–f] > 71   [g] they made ℵ $\mathfrak{L}^1$ T.R.   [h–h] > $\mathfrak{L}^1$
[i] > $\mathfrak{S}^{luc}$ [k–k] > 71   [l] with engines 71

---

50. **they.** i.e. the Syrians; cp. critical note.

the stronghold that is in Jericho. Grimm refers to the two citadels by Jericho mentioned by Strabo as having been destroyed by Pompey, namely Taurus and Thrax; the reference here must be to one of these.

Emmaus. See note on iii. 40.

Bethhoron. See note on iii. 16.

Bethel. About ten miles north of Jerusalem, the modern *Beitin*, nearly 3,000 ft. above the sea-level.

Timnath. Several places of this name are mentioned in the O.T.; the one here must be either the Timnath-Serah in Mount Ephraim, where Joshua was buried (Joshua xix. 50, xxiv. 30; Judges ii. 9), or the Timna (called also Timnatha) in Danite territory about fifteen miles to the west of Jerusalem; the latter is, perhaps, the more likely.

Pharathon. The Syriac and O.L. versions, like Josephus, omit 'and'. This place is the Pirathon of the O.T. (Judges xii. 13, 15), in Ephraimite territory (but cp. xi. 34), the modern Ferata, about six or seven miles south-west of Nablous, the ancient Sichem.

Tephon. Probably a corruption of Tappuach, also in the inheritance of Ephraim (Joshua xvi. 8).

52. **Bethsura, and Gazara.** See notes on iv. 29. 15.

the citadel. Cp. i. 33, and the note on v. 53.

54. **the one hundred and fifty-third year.** i.e. 159 B.C.

the second month. Iyar in the Jewish calendar.

the wall of the inner court. The inner court was restricted to Israelites, so that the pulling down of its wall implied the obliteration of all religious difference between Israelites and Gentiles; this was to undo the work of the prophets whose aim was to keep the Israelites distinct from their idolatrous neighbours.

56. **Alcimus died.** Josephus places the death of Alcimus earlier, before the death of Judas, see *Antiq.* XII. x. 6; he says that Alcimus was 'smitten suddenly by God'.

57. **he returned to the king.** Assuming, no doubt, that the country had now been subjugated; but, as the sequel shows, the period of rest which the land had enjoyed, was utilized by the national party to good purpose.

62. **Bethbasi, which is in the wilderness.** G. A. Smith says that 'in the wilderness of Judaea, east of Tekoa, there is a *Wady el-Bassah*, which name as it stands means 'marsh', an impossible term, and therefore probably an echo of an ancient name' (*EB* 550); possibly Bethbasi is to be identified with this.

65. **and went forth into the country.** For the purpose of creating diversions, and to come to the relief of his brother at the right moment.

66 and he went with a (small) number. And he smote Odomera and his brethren, and the children of
67 Phasiron in their tents. And he[m] began to smite (them) and to go up with (his) troops. Then Simon
68 and they that were with him went out of the city and set on fire the engines (of war); and they
fought against Bacchides, and he was discomfited by them, and they afflicted him sore, [n]for his plan
69 and his attack had been in vain[n]. And they[o] were very wroth with the lawless men that gave him
counsel to come into the country, and they slew many of them. And he determined to depart into
70 his own land. And (when) Jonathan had knowledge (thereof), he sent ambassadors [p]unto him[p], to
the end that they should make peace with him, and that he should restore unto them[q] the captives.
71 And he[r] accepted (the thing), [s]and did according to his words[s], and sware unto him that he would
72 not seek his hurt all the days of his life. And he restored unto him the captives which he had taken
captive aforetime out of [t]the land of[t] Judah; and he[u] returned and departed into his own land, and
73 came[v] not any more into their borders. And the sword ceased from Israel. And Jonathan dwelt
at Michmash. And Jonathan began to judge the people[w]; and he destroyed the ungodly out of
Israel[x].

X. 1–66. *Jonathan supports Alexander Balas in his struggle with Demetrius I.*

10 1 In[a] the one hundred and sixtieth year Alexander [b]Epiphanes, the son of Antiochus[b], went up
2 and took possession of Ptolemais, and they[c] received him, and he reigned there[d]. And (when) king
Demetrius heard (thereof), he gathered together exceeding great forces, and went forth to meet him
3 in battle. And Demetrius sent letters unto Jonathan with words of peace, so as to magnify him.
4 For he said: 'Let us be beforehand to make peace with them, ere he make peace with Alexander
5 against us. For he will remember all the evils which we have done [e]unto him[e], and unto his
6 brethren and unto his nation[f].' And he gave him authority to gather together forces, and to provide
arms, and to be his confederate; and he commanded that they should deliver up to him the hostages
7 that were in the citadel. And Jonathan came to Jerusalem, and read the letters [g]in the ears of all[h]

[m] they ℵ V 64 93 [n-n] > 71 [o] he ℵ c.a V Bacchides 19 93 𝔖luc [p-p] unto them ℵ 93 > V [q] him 55 𝔏 𝔖g
[r] Bacchides Luc [s-s] > 71 [t-t] > ℵ 𝔖g [u] Bacchides 19 93 𝔖luc [v] looked Luc [w] + of Israel 19 93 𝔖luc
[x] of it 𝔖luc

X. [a] And in 𝔊 𝔏 𝔖luc [b-b] the son of Antiochus Epiphanes 𝔖luc > Antiochus 𝔏2 [c] it A 93 ℵ c.a [d] (over) them 𝔏1 [e-e] > 𝔏1 [f] race V [g-g] > 71 [h] > 𝔖g

---

with a (small) number. ἀριθμῷ, cp. Isa. x. 19 (Sept.).

66. **Odomera.** Another reading is Odoarres; presumably the name of the head of some Bedouin clan; this applies also to Phasiron.

and to go up with (his) troops. i.e. to lead his troops against the enemy; for the Hebrew phrase 'to go up' (עלה על) for the purpose of fighting cp. 1 Sam. xiv. 10; Judg. vi. 3, xv. 10, xviii. 9, &c.

70. **the captives.** i.e. those who had been taken captive aforetime (see *v.* 72).

73. **And the sword ceased . . .** 'With this laconic notice the First Book of Maccabees passes over the following five years. This can only mean that Jonathan, while the official Sanhedrim of Jerusalem was still filled by those friendly to the Greeks, established at Michmash a sort of rival government, which gradually won the position of main influence in the country, so that it was able even to drive out (ἀφανίζειν) the ungodly, that is, the Hellenizing party. The Hellenistic or Greek-favouring party had no root among the people. The great mass of the Jews had still the distinct consciousness that Hellenism, even if it should tolerate the religion of Israel, was irreconcilable with the religion of the scribes. So soon, then, as pressure from above was removed, the great majority of the people gave themselves heart and soul to the national Jewish movement. The Maccabees, therefore, had the people soon again at their back. And this is the explanation of the fact that during the struggles for the Syrian throne now beginning, the claimants contended with one another in endeavouring to secure to themselves the goodwill of the Maccabees' (Schürer, *op. cit.* i. 1, p. 239).

Michmash. Nine miles north of Jerusalem, the modern *Mukhmas*.

and he destroyed . . . This shows how the power of the national party had been consolidated.

X. 1. **In the one hundred and sixtieth year.** 153 B.C.; the last date given was 159 B.C. (see ix. 54), and in *v.* 57 we are told that the land had rest for two years; seven years have, therefore, elapsed since the time that Bacchides thought the land was subjugated (see note on ix. 57); and during this interval nothing is recorded save an abortive attempt on the part of Bacchides to subdue Jonathan (ix. 58–73).

Alexander Epiphanes. Alexander Balas was a low-born native of Smyrna who, owing to his resemblance to Antiochus Eupator, gave himself out to be the son of Antiochus Epiphanes. He was taken up by Attalus II, King of Pergamum, from whom he received the name of Alexander, and who supported his claims to the kingdom of Syria against Demetrius. Although, according to Polybius (xxxiii. 14. 6), it was well known that the claims of Alexander were without justification, he was, nevertheless, recognized by the Roman Senate, who promised to support him. His success was largely due to the fact that Demetrius was hated by his own people (see Josephus, *Antiq.* XIII. ii. 1) on account of his 'insolence and difficulty of access', and because he was 'slothful and negligent about the public affairs'.

Ptolemais. See note on v. 15, and cp. Josephus, *l. c.*

2. **went forth to meet . . .** See note on vii. 31.

3. **with words of peace.** See note on i. 30.

7. **in the ears of all the people.** Cp. Isa. xxxvi. 2 באזני העם.

8 the people, and of them that were in the citadel[g]; and they were sore afraid when they heard that
9 the king had given him[i] authority to gather together forces. And they [k]of the citadel[k] delivered up
10 the hostages unto Jonathan, and he[l] restored them to their parents. And Jonathan dwelt[m] in
11 Jerusalem, and began to build [n]and renew[n] the city. And [o]he[p] commanded them that did the work
to build[o] the walls and the mount Sion round about with square[q] stones for defence; and they[r] did
12, 13 so. And the strangers, that were in the strongholds that Bacchides had built, fled away; [s]and
14 each man left his place[s], and departed into his own land. Only in Bethsura were there left certain
of those that had forsaken the Law, [s]and the commandments; for it was a place of refuge unto
them[s].
15 And king Alexander heard all the promises which Demetrius had sent unto Jonathan; and they
told him of the battles and the valiant deeds [t]which he and his brethren had done, [u]and of the toils
16 which they had endured[tu]; and he said: 'Shall we find another such man? And now [v]let us make[v]
17 him our Friend [w]and confederate[w].' And he wrote letters, [xy]and sent (them) unto him[y], according to
18, 19 these words, saying[x]: 'King Alexander to his brother Jonathan, greeting[z]! We have heard
20 concerning thee, that thou art a mighty[a] man of valour, [b]and meet to be our Friend[b]. And now we
have appointed thee [c]this day[c] (to be) high-priest of thy nation, and (it is our will) that thou shouldest
be called the king's Friend'—and he[d] sent unto him a purple robe and a crown[e] of gold[f]—'and that
21 thou shouldest take our part, and keep friendship[g] with us.' And Jonathan put on the holy garment
[h]in the seventh month of the one hundred and sixtieth year[h], at the feast of Tabernacles, and he
gathered together forces, and provided arms in abundance.
22, 23 And (when) Demetrius heard [i]these things[i], he was grieved, and said: 'Why have we permitted
this to be done, that Alexander hath been beforehand [k]with us in establishing friendship with the
24 Jews[k], to strengthen himself? I also will write unto them words of encouragement, [l]and of honour,
25 and gifts, that they may be with me for (my) aid.' And he sent unto them according to these words[l]:
26 'King Demetrius unto the nation of the Jews, greeting! Forasmuch as ye have kept covenant with
us, and have continued in our friendship, [m]and have not joined yourselves to our enemies, we, (who)
27 have heard (hereof), rejoice. And now continue ye still[m] to keep faith with us, and we will recom-
28 pense unto you [n]good things[n] [o]in return for what ye do in our behalf[o]; and we will grant you many
29 immunities, and will give you gifts. [p]And now I (herewith) free you, and release all the Jews from
30 the tributes[p], and from the custom on salt, and from (the presenting of)[q] the crowns; and instead of

[i] them A [k-k] > $\mathfrak{L}^2$ [l] they A [m] heard A [n-n] > 71 [o-o] > 71 [p] Jonathan 64 93 [q] four-foot ℵ V 55 [r] he ℵ V $\mathfrak{L}^1$ [s-s] > 71 [t-t] > 71 [u-u] > $\mathfrak{S}^{luc}$ [v-v] we will make ℵ V 19 64 [w-w] > 71 [x-x] unto him 71 [y-y] > Luc [z] > V [a] good A [b-b] > 71 [c-c] > 71 [d] they A [e] a royal crown $\mathfrak{S}^g$ [f] + and saying ℵ[c.a] [g] *plur.* ℵ Luc [h-h] > 71 [i-i] > 71 [k-k] > V [l-l] > 71 [m-m] > 71 [n-n] > $\mathfrak{S}^g$ [o-o] > 71 [p-p] And now I release all Jews from tribute $\mathfrak{L}^2$ [q] the custom of 55

8. **they were sore afraid.** ἐφοβήθησαν φόβον μέγαν, cp. Luke ii. 9.

11. **square stones.** Cp. 1 Kings vi. 36, vii. 9; Isa. ix. 9; called in Hebrew אַבְנֵי גָזִית; not אבני מחצב ('hewn stones'), which were smaller, and not necessarily 'square'.

14. **Bethsura.** See note on iv. 29.

16. **Friend.** See note on ii. 18.

18. **King . . . greeting!** A Greek formula which often occurs in 1–2 Macc.; the Hebrew equivalent for 'greeting' would be שָׁלוֹם 'Peace'.

19. **a mighty man of valour.** A very frequent O.T. expression, גִּבּוֹר חַיִל.

20. **high-priest.** This office had been vacant for seven years, i. e. since the death of Alcimus.

a purple robe and a crown of gold. Cp. xi. 58, xix. 43; Esther viii. 15; Dan. v. 7.

21. **the holy garment.** i. e. the specific high-priestly robe (מְעִיל); the 'robe of righteousness' (Isa. lxi. 10).

the seventh month. Tishri, corresponding roughly to October.

the feast of Tabernacles. Called *Sukkoth* ('Booths'); the feast began on the 15th of Tishri, and lasted seven days (Lev. xxiii. 34); nowadays it lasts nine days, and is called 'the season of Rejoicing'; cp. Josephus, *Antiq.* VIII. iv. 1.

he gathered together forces . . . Jonathan evidently thought it wisest, in the long run, to trust to himself only.

27. **we will recompense . . .** These promises were of such an extravagant character that Jonathan would in any case have regarded them with suspicion; but he evidently knew the real state of affairs, and foresaw that the doom of Demetrius was sealed.

29. **the tributes.** This was the principal burden laid upon the people, the poll-tax; 'it was, strictly speaking, a kind of trade-tax, a percentage that varied according to the nature of the work and the means of the individual, not a personal tax, uniform and unchanging' (*EB* 4909, after Aristotle, *Oeconom.* ii. 1. 4).

the custom on salt. A very large quantity of salt is deposited upon the marshy land around the Dead Sea when the annual spring floods, which cause the sea-level to rise several feet, subside. The tax on this was called ἡ ἁλική; the very words here used, ἀπὸ . . . τῆς τιμῆς τοῦ ἁλός, have been found on an Egyptian ostrakon. See further on the whole subject of salt-taxes in Palestine under the Seleucidae, Wilcken, *Griechische Ostraka aus Aegypten* . . ., i. pp. 141 ff.

and from . . . crowns. These were originally voluntary gifts given to the sovereign, but afterwards exacted as of right. For another instance of the remission of taxes to the Jews see Josephus, *Antiq.* XII. iii. 3, where we are told of 'poll-money, and the crown tax, and other taxes' being remitted.

the third part of the seed, and instead of [r]the half of[r] the fruit of the trees, which falleth to me
to receive, I release (them) from this day and henceforth, so that I will not take (them) from the
land of Judah, and from the three governments which are added thereunto from the country of
31 Samaria and Galilee, [s]from this day forth and for all time[s]. And [t]let Jerusalem be[t] holy and
32 free, [u]together with the outlying districts, (regarding)[v] the tenths and the tolls. [w]I yield up[w]
also my authority over[u] the citadel which is at Jerusalem, and give (it) to the high-priest[x], that
33 he may appoint in it (such) men as he shall choose, to keep it. And every soul of the Jews that
hath been carried away captive from the land of Judah into any part of my kingdom, I set at
34 liberty [y]without price[y]; and let all remit the tributes of their cattle also. And all the feasts, and
the Sabbaths, and new moons, and appointed days, and three days before a feast, [z]and three days
after a feast[z], [a]let them all be days of immunity and release for all the Jews [b]that are in my king-
35 dom[a b]; and no man shall have authority to exact (anything) from any of them, or to trouble them
36 concerning any matter. And let there be enrolled among the king's forces about thirty[c] thousand men
37 of the Jews, and pay shall be given unto them, as belongeth to all[d] the king's forces. [e f]And of them
some shall be placed in the king's[e] great strongholds, and some of them shall be placed over the
affairs of the kingdom[g], which are of trust; and let those that are over them, and their rulers, be
from among themselves, and let them walk after their own laws, even as the king hath commanded
38 in the land of Judah. And the three governments that have been added to Judaea from the country
of Samaria[h] [i]let them be added to Judaea, [k]that they may be reckoned[i k] to be under one (man),
39 that they obey not any other authority than that of the high-priest[f]. As for Ptolemais, and the land
pertaining thereto, I have given (it [l]as) a gift[l] to [m]the sanctuary that is at[m] Jerusalem, for the
40 expenses [n]that befit[n] the sanctuary. And I (undertake to) give every year fifteen thousand shekels
41 of silver [o]from the king's revenues[o], [p]from the places which are (most) convenient[p]. [q r]And all the

r–r > 𝔖luc   s–s > 71   t–t J. shall be V   u–u > 𝔏1   v and I remit A V 19 𝔖   w–w > A 19 71 𝔖   x to the holy house 𝔖g   y–y > 71   z–z > 71 𝔏1   a–a *paraphrased in* 𝔖   b–b > 71   c three 𝔖luc   d > 𝔖luc   e–e > ℵ 𝔏1   f–f > 71   g of the king 𝔖luc   h + and Galilee Luc   i–i let them be reckoned with Judaea 𝔖g 𝔏1   k–k > 19 𝔖luc   l–l > 𝔖luc   m–m > 𝔖g   n–n > 𝔖luc   o–o > 71 from the king's treasury 𝔖g from the treasury 𝔏2   p–p > 𝔖luc   q–q All that is owing to me 𝔖luc   r–r > 71

30. **the seed.** Josephus (*Antiq.* XIII. ii. 3): 'the fruits (of the field),' cp. τὰ σπειρόμενα, XIV. x. 6.

half of the fruit . . . A larger proportion of this was appropriated because the produce involved less labour.

the three governments. Cp. xi. 28, 34, called 'toparchies'.

and Galilee. This is an erroneous addition; the three toparchies mentioned belonged to Samaria, cp. xi. 34; in *v.* 38 of this chapter a similar error is made in some MSS., see critical note there.

and for all time. Cp. xi. 36.

31. **let J. be holy.** What is meant is made very clear by referring to a rescript of Antiochus III, the Great, quoted by Josephus (*Antiq.* XII. iii. 4): 'It shall be lawful for no foreigner to come within the limits of the Temple round about; which thing is forbidden also to the Jews, unless to those who, according to their own custom, have purified themselves. . . . Let them only be permitted to use the sacrifices derived from their forefathers, with which they have been obliged to make acceptable atonements to God. And he that transgresseth any of these orders, let him pay to the priests three thousand drachmae of silver.

free, . . . the tenths and the tolls. The reference is to the tithes, and the tax on the revenues of the Temple, which had been exacted by the Syrian rulers; Josephus makes this clear (*Antiq.* XIII. ii. 3): 'I also release to you those ten thousand drachmae which the kings received from the Temple, because they appertain to the priests that minister in that Temple' (cp. also 2 Macc. xi. 3). The Temple dues which were thus taxed were: (1) 'the third part of a shekel for the service of the house of our God' (Neh. x. 32), which every Israelite of twenty years and upwards had to pay annually; originally it was a half-shekel (about one shilling and twopence halfpenny), for rich and poor alike (Exod. xxx. 14, 15); but on this see Schürer, *op. cit.* ii. 1. 250; (2) the votive offerings (cp. Lev. xxvii; Deut. xxiii. 22–24; see also Josephus, *Antiq.* IV. iv. 4) = נדרים; and (3) the free-will offerings (נדבות). On the whole subject of these offerings see the Mishnic tractate *Shekalim*.

33. **and let all remit.** The 'all' must refer to the king's officials, 'their cattle' to the property of Jews; what is meant is explained by Josephus (*Antiq.* XIII. ii. 3): 'I also give order that the beasts belonging to the Jews be not pressed for our service.'

34. **days of immunity . . .** i.e., as the next verse shows, on these days the Jews were to be left unmolested, whether as regards the payment of taxes or debts (cp. *v.* 43) or as regards service for the king.

36. **And let there be enrolled . . .** This would give a *status* to the Jews which they had not hitherto enjoyed; but Demetrius' main object was to increase his forces in order to withstand Alexander.

pay. ξένια = the clothing, food, and pay given to mercenary troops.

37. **and some of them shall be placed . . .** Josephus (*Antiq.* XIV. ii. 3) says: 'And some of them I will place in my garrisons, and some as guards about mine own body, and as rulers over those that are in my court;' cp. *Antiq.* XII. ii. 5.

38. **the three governments.** See note on *v.* 30.

39. **As for Ptolemais . . .** As Alexander had taken possession of this (see *v.* 1), the promise was merely a bribe to induce Jonathan to attack the rival of Demetrius.

40. **from the places . . . convenient.** i.e. those which could best afford it; the clause is omitted by the Lucianic Syriac, and Josephus makes no reference to it.

41. **all the overplus.** Fairweather and Black are probably right in understanding this to refer to the additional

overplus [q] which the officials paid not in—as (has been done) in former years [s]—they shall from
42 henceforth give towards the works of the [t] house [r]. And [u] beside this [u], the five thousand shekels of
silver, which they used to take from the **dues** of the sanctuary [v] [w] out of the income [w] year by
43 year, [x] [y] this also is released, because it appertaineth [x] to the priests that minister [y]. And whosoever
shall flee unto the temple that is in Jerusalem, and in all the precincts thereof, (because) he oweth
money to the king, or for any other reason, let (such) go free, together with all, whatsoever they possess,
44 in my kingdom. And for the building and renewing of the works of the sanctuary the expense
45 shall be given also out of the king's revenue. [z] And for the building of the walls of Jerusalem, and
the fortifying thereof round about, [a] shall the expense be given also out of the king's revenue [b] [z],
and for the building of the walls (of other cities) in Judaea [a].'
46 Now when Jonathan and the people heard these words, they gave no credence unto them [c], nor
received they (them), because they remembered the great evil that he had done in Israel [d], and that
47 he had afflicted them very sore. And (moreover) they were well pleased with Alexander, because
he was the first that spake [e] words of peace [e] unto them, and they remained confederate with him
always.
48 And king Alexander gathered together [f] great forces [f], and encamped over against Demetrius.
49 And the two kings joined battle, and the army of Alexander [g] fled, and Demetrius [h] followed after
50 him [i], and prevailed against them. And he continued the battle [k] obstinately until the sun went
down; and Demetrius fell that day.
51 And Alexander [l] sent ambassadors to Ptolemy, king of Egypt, [m] according to these words [m],
52 saying: 'Forasmuch as I am returned to my kingdom, and am set on the throne of my fathers, and
have gotten the dominion, and have overthrown Demetrius, [n] and have gotten possession of our
53 country [n]—yea, I joined battle with him, and he and his army were discomfited by us, and we [o] sat
54 upon the throne of his kingdom,—let us now establish amity [p] one with the other [p]; and give me
now [q] thy daughter to wife; and I will make affinity with thee, and will give both thee and her gifts
55 worthy of thee.' And Ptolemy the king answered, saying [r]: 'Happy is the day wherein thou didst
56 return into the land of thy fathers, and didst sit upon the throne of their kingdom. And now will
I do to thee (according to) the things which thou hast written. But meet (me) [s] at Ptolemais, that
57 we may see one another; and I will make affinity with thee [t] even as thou hast said [t].' And Ptolemy
went out of Egypt, he and Cleopatra his daughter, [u] and came unto Ptolemais, in the one hundred
58 and sixty-second year [u]; and he bestowed on him his daughter Cleopatra, and celebrated her
marriage at Ptolemais with great pomp, as the manner of kings is.
59, 60 And king [v] Alexander wrote unto Jonathan, that he should come to meet him. And he [w] went

[s] nations Luc $\mathfrak{L}^2$ [t] this Luc [u-u] > 71 [v] + as in former years A V 55 71 $\mathfrak{S}$ $\mathfrak{L}$ [w-w] > $\mathfrak{S}^{luc}$ [x-x] > $\mathfrak{S}^{g}$ [y-y] > 71 [z-z] > $\mathfrak{S}^{g}$ [a-a] > 64 [b] house 19 93 $\mathfrak{S}^{luc}$ [c] him $\mathfrak{S}^{luc}$ > 71 [d] Jerusalem 64 [e-e] > 71 [f-f] all the forces ℵ + and many 19 93 [g] Demetrius ℵ$^{c.a, c.b}$ V 19 64 [h] Alexander ℵ$^{c.a}$ V 19 64 [i] them ℵ$^{c.a}$ 19 $\mathfrak{S}^{luc}$ [k] $\mathfrak{S}^{g}$ *is wanting from here to* year *in v.* 67 [l] + in that day Luc $\mathfrak{S}^{luc}$ [m-m] > 71 [n-n] > 71 [o] I Luc [p-p] with him A with them ℵ [q] > ℵ 19 71 93 $\mathfrak{S}^{luc}$ $\mathfrak{L}$ [r] > 71 [s] *expressed in* ℵ$^{c.a}$ 19 93 [t-t] > 71 [u-u] > 71 [v] > 71 [w] Jonathan Luc

---

yearly subsidy granted for the Temple service out of State funds, and regularly paid ('as in former years') under the Persians, Ptolemies, and Seleucidae, prior to Antiochus Epiphanes.

the works of the house. i.e. the affairs of the Temple, see preceding note.

42. **the five thousand shekels of silver, which . . .** This item has already been dealt with in *v.* 31.

dues. Text reads χρειῶν = צרכי, corrupt for ערכי [Gen. Editor].

43. **shall flee unto the temple.** Jewish law granted the right of asylum only to those who had committed murder accidentally; the places of asylum were the altar in the Temple, and the six cities of refuge (cp. Exod. xxi. 14; 1 Kings i. 50, ii. 28, 29).

44. **for the building . . .** Cp. Ezra vi. 8, vii. 20.

46. **they gave no credence.** The promises were far too extravagant to inspire confidence.

47. **the first.** ἀρχηγός, i.e. he took a higher place in their estimation.

49, 50. This laconic account can only be understood by the aid of Josephus, who says (*Antiq.* XIII. ii. 4): 'And when it was come to a battle, the left wing of Demetrius put those who opposed them to flight, and pursued them a great way, and slew many of them, and spoiled their camp. But the right wing, where Demetrius happened to be, was beaten; and as for all the rest, they ran away. But Demetrius fought courageously, and slew a great many of the enemy; but as he was in pursuit of the rest, his horse carried him into a deep bog, where it was hard to get out, and there it happened, that upon his horse's falling down, he could not escape being killed; for when his enemies saw what had befallen him, they returned back, and encompassed Demetrius round, and they all threw their darts at him; but he being now on foot, fought bravely; but at length he received so many wounds that he was not able to bear up any longer, and fell.'

51. **Ptolemy.** The sixth of the name, surnamed Philometor; he reigned 180–146 B.C., first under the guardianship of his mother, Cleopatra, and jointly with his brother until 170, when he became sole king of Egypt.

52. **I am returned to my kingdom . . .** This insolent falsehood had been so sedulously propagated that many believed Alexander to be the rightful heir; presumably the author of 1 Macc. also believed this.

54. **thy daughter.** Cleopatra, the issue of the incestuous union between Ptolemy and his sister, Cleopatra.

[x]with pomp to Ptolemais[x], and met the two kings, and gave them and their Friends silver and
61 gold, and many[y] gifts; and he found favour in their sight. And there were gathered together
against him [z](certain) pestilent fellows out of Israel[z], men that were transgressors of the Law, to
62 complain against him; but the king [a]gave no heed to them. And the king[a] commanded[b], and they[c]
63 took off Jonathan's garments, and clothed him in purple; [d]even so did they do[d]. And the king[e] made
him sit with him, and said unto his princes: 'Go forth with him into the midst of the city, and make
proclamation, that no man complain against him [f]concerning any matter[f], and let no man trouble
64 him for any manner of cause.' And [g]it came to pass[g], when they that complained against him[h] saw
his glory [i]according as (the herald) made proclamation[i], and (saw) him clothed in purple[k], that they
65 all fled away. [l]And the king showed him[h] honour, and wrote[m] him among his Chief Friends, and
66 made him a captain, and governor of a province[l]. And Jonathan returned [n]to Jerusalem[n] with
peace [o]and gladness[o].

X. 67–89. *Victory of Jonathan over Apollonius, the general of Demetrius II; he is rewarded by Alexander.*

67 And in the one hundred and sixty-fifth year came Demetrius, the son of Demetrius, out of Crete
68 into the land of his fathers. And (when) king Alexander heard (thereof) he[p] was grieved exceed-
69 ingly, and returned[q] unto Antioch. And Demetrius appointed Apollonius, [r]who was[r] over
Coelesyria[s], (captain); and he gathered together a great host, and encamped in Jamnia, and sent
70 unto Jonathan the high-priest, saying: 'Thou alone liftest up thyself against us; but I am had in
derision and in reproach because of thee. [t]And why dost thou vaunt thy power against us in the
71 mountains?[t] Now therefore, if thou trustest in thy forces, come down to us in the plain, and there
72 let us try conclusions with one another, for with me is the power of the cities[u]. Ask and learn who
I am, [v]and the rest[w] (of those) that help us; and they (will) say, Your[x] foot cannot stand before
73 our face; for thy fathers have been twice put to flight in their own land. And now thou wilt not

[x–x] > 71 [y] > 𝔖luc [z–z] > 93 [a–a] > 93 [b] + them A [c] he A [d–d] > 71 𝔏[1] [e] kings ℵ [f–f] > 71
[g–g] > 71 𝔖luc [h] Jonathan Luc [i–i] > 71 [k] linen A [l–l] > 71 [m] appointed 55 [n–n] > ℵ [o–o] > 71
[p] the king ℵ [q] sent 19 [r–r] leader 55 𝔏[1] defender 𝔖g [s] Syria 𝔖luc [t–t] > 71 [u] wars 64 [v–v] > 71
[w] > 𝔖luc [x] Thy 𝔖g

60. **and he found favour in their sight.** A Hebrew expression (מָצָא חֵן בְּעֵינֵי) which frequently occurs in the O.T., e.g. Gen. xxx. 27, xlvii. 25, 29; 1 Sam. i. 18, &c.

61. **pestilent fellows.** ἄνδρες λοιμοί, cp. 1 Sam. xxx. 22 (Sept.) ἀνὴρ λοιμός; 1 Sam. xxv. 25 . . . τὸν ἄνθρωπον τὸν λοιμόν . . . (אִישׁ בְּלִיַּעַל).

62. **clothed him in purple.** 'It is still the custom of oriental kings to bestow upon State officials, vassals, governors, ambassadors, and scholars, as a mark of honour, not, it is true, purple, but a costly garment, called *Khila* . . . and especially also those whom they wish publicly and solemnly to declare innocent of some charge do they clothe in gorgeous apparel, and cause them to be led through the royal city' (Grimm); references to the accounts of travellers are given. Cf. Gen. xli. 43; Esther vi. 11.

65. **Chief Friends.** There were evidently different grades among the King's Friends, just as in an aristocracy; Jonathan had already been made a Friend of the King (see *v.* 16).

a captain, and governor of a province. 'Στρατηγός and μεριδάρχης may be taken as equivalent to military and civil governor. . . . It specially deserves notice, that, in spite of Jonathan's appointment as στρατηγός, a Syrian governor still continued to occupy the citadel of Jerusalem' (Schürer).

66. **with peace and gladness.** The rebuff which the Hellenistic Jews had received, and the honours which had been heaped upon Jonathan, occasioned him outward and inward peace.

67. **the one hundred and sixty-fifth year.** 147 B.C.

Demetrius. The second, surnamed Nicator. Josephus (*Antiq.* XIII. iv. 2) adds further that he came with a large number of mercenary troops, brought to him by Lasthenes, a Cretan, and sailed to Cilicia. He had been living in exile in Crete since the war between his father and Alexander began.

68. **returned unto Antioch.** i.e. from Ptolemais.

69. **Apollonius.** According to Polybius (xxxi. 21. 2), the foster-brother (σύντροφος) of Demetrius I. Josephus (*Antiq.* XIII. iv. 2) calls him 'Apollonius Daus', i.e. belonging to the Dahae, a great Scythian people who led a nomad life over a large tract of country east of the Caspian Sea, still called Daghestan.

Coelesyria. i.e. 'hollow (κοίλη) Syria', so called because it included, and was originally restricted to, the depression between the two Lebanons (cp. Joshua xi. 17 בִּקְעַת הַלְּבָנוֹן, 'the valley of Lebanon'); but in the Greek period it included the whole of eastern Palestine; Josephus (*Antiq.* XIV. iv. 5) says that it stretched from 'as far as the river Euphrates and Egypt'; it is in this extended sense in which the name is here used. It occurs for the first time in 1 Esdras ii. 17. In the Roman period Coelesyria was again used in the restricted sense, as it was made a separate province.

Jamnia. See note on iv. 15.

72. **for thy fathers . . .** As Apollonius is writing from Jamnia (Jabneel), i.e. from what was formerly Philistine territory, he is probably referring to Israelite defeats at the hands of the Philistines; the two most signal instances were the battle of Aphek, at which the Philistines captured the Ark (1 Sam. iv. 1–11), and the battle of Mount Gilboa,

be able to withstand the horse and such an host as this in the plain, where there is neither stone
74 [y] nor flint [y], nor (any) place [z] to flee unto [v].' Now when Jonathan heard the words of Apollonius, he
was [a] moved in his mind [a]; and he chose out ten thousand men, [b] and went forth [b] from Jerusalem;
75 and Simon his brother met him for to help him. And he encamped against Joppa; and they of the
city shut him [c] out, because Apollonius (had) a garrison [d] in Joppa [d]; and they [e] fought against it.
76 [f] And they of the city, being afraid, opened (the gates) [f], and Jonathan became master of Joppa.
77 And (when) Apollonius heard (of this), he gathered [g] an army of three thousand horse, and a great
host, and went to Azotus as though (intending) to journey on, but [h] at the same time [h] moved
78 forward [i] into the plain, because he had a multitude of horse, and relied on this. And he [k] pursued
79 after him [l] to Azotus, and the armies joined battle [m]. Now Apollonius had left a thousand horse
80 [n] behind him [n], hidden [o]; but Jonathan realized that there was an ambushment [p] behind him [p]. And
they surrounded his army, and cast (their) [q] darts at the people from morning until [r] late in the
81 afternoon [r]; but the people stood still, as Jonathan (had) commanded, while the (enemy's) horses
82 were wearying (themselves). And Simon drew forth his host, and joined battle with the phalanx—
83 for the horsemen [s] were spent—and they were discomfited by him, [t] and fled. And the horsemen [s]
were scattered in the plain [t]; and they fled to Azotus, and entered into Beth-dagon, their idol's tem-
84 ple [u], to save themselves. And Jonathan burned Azotus, and the cities round about it, and took
85 their spoils; [v] and the temple of Dagon, [w] and them that fled into it [w], he burned with fire [v]. And
they that had fallen [x] by the sword [x], with them that were burned, were about eight thousand men.
86 And from thence Jonathan removed, and encamped against Askalon, and they of the city came forth
87 to meet him with great pomp. And Jonathan, with them that were on his side, returned to Jerusalem,
88 having many spoils. And [y] it came to pass [y], when king Alexander heard these things, he honoured
89 Jonathan yet more; and he sent unto him a buckle of gold, as the use is to give to such as are of
the kindred of the kings; moreover, he gave him Ekron and all the borders thereof for a possession.

y–y > 𝔏 z + whither A a–a enraged and moved 𝔖g b–b > 𝔖luc c ℵ* V 𝔖luc 𝔏1 *make this refer to the city* d–d therein 𝔖luc e he 𝔖g f–f And they were afraid and departed from the city 𝔏1 g interposed 93 𝔖luc h–h > 𝔖luc i led forward A 55 k Jonathan T.R. 𝔖 l + for battle ℵ V m + after him 𝔊 (*exc.* Luc) 𝔖 𝔏 n–n > 71 o in a hiding-place T.R. p–p > 𝔖 q *expressed in* 19 93 r–r evening T.R. the sinking (*of the sun*) 𝔖g s–s > 71 t–t > 𝔖g u > 93 𝔖luc 𝔏1 v–v > 19 93 𝔖luc w–w and its (i.e. *the city's*) temple A > 71 x–x > 𝔏1 y–y > 71 𝔖luc 𝔏2

---

when king Saul was slain (1 Sam. xxxi. 1–7). These were by no means, however, the only occasions on which the Israelites were defeated by the Philistines, and perhaps for this reason Josephus (*Antiq.* XIII. iv. 3) says that 'these are the very men who *always* conquered thy progenitors', though this, again, is a gross exaggeration, cp. e.g. 2 Sam. v. 17–21, when David defeated them at the battle of Baal-perazim (2 Sam. viii. 1; 1 Chron. xviii. 1, &c.).

73. **neither stone nor flint.** An exaggeration, to emphasize the contrast between the mountainous country and the plain.

75. **Joppa.** The modern Jaffa, 3½ miles from Jamnia; its chief importance lay in its harbour, which was the best, though not an ideal one, on the coast of Palestine; cp. 1 Macc. xii. 33, 34, xiii. 11, xiv. 5, 34, xv. 28–30, 35; 2 Macc. xii. 3–7.

77. **Azotus.** See note on iv. 15.

but . . . moved forward. With the purpose of enticing Jonathan out.

79. **hidden.** Lit. 'in secret', Josephus, more explicitly, 'in a gully.'

80. **realized.** Lit. 'knew', presumably by means of spies.

cast (their) darts. 'Shot their arrows' (Hebr. ירה חץ, as in, e.g. 1 Sam. xx. 36).

81. **but the people stood still.** This is explained by Josephus, who says that Jonathan commanded his army 'to stand in a square battle array'; they covered themselves with their shields, against which the enemy hurled their missiles in vain.

82. **Simon drew forth his host.** Evidently having been held in reserve all this time.

83. **Beth-dagon.** Dagon was one of the chief gods of the Philistines (cp. Judges xvi. 23, 24; 1 Sam. v. 1–5), whose worship they took over when they first entered into the land; his name occurs on the Tell-el-Amarna tablets, and has also been found inscribed on the walls of the temple of Mukair in southern Babylonia. Although it cannot be proved that Dagon was a fish-god, it is probable that this was the case, though Philo Byblius speaks of him as a corn-god (deriving the name from דגן 'corn', instead of דג 'fish').

84. **the cities . . .** Josephus, more correctly, 'the villages about it.'

86. **Askalon.** One of the five chief cities of the Philistines (Joshua xiii. 3), lying on the coast between Ashdod and Gaza; the modern *Askalûn*.

88. **he honoured . . . yet more.** προσέθετο δοξάσαι, a Hebraism (יסף ל).

89. **a buckle of gold.** Cp. xi. 58, xiv. 44; the golden buckle and the purple robe (see *v.* 21) were only worn by the most distinguished men of the kingdom, or by 'the kindred of the kings'.

Ekron. The most northerly of the chief Philistine cities; it lay between Ashdod and Jamnia towards the east; the modern Akir.

XI. 1–19. *Alliance between Ptolemy VI and Demetrius II, resulting in the downfall of Alexander Balas. Demetrius becomes king of Syria.*

11 1 And[a] the king of Egypt gathered together [b]great forces[b], as the sand which is by the sea shore
(for multitude), [c]and many ships[c], and sought to make himself master of Alexander's kingdom by
2 deceit, and to add it to his own kingdom. And he went forth into Syria with[d] words of peace; and
they of the cities opened unto him (the gates), and met him, and king Alexander's command was
3 that they should meet him, because he was his father-in-law. Now when [e]Ptolemy entered into the
4 cities[e], he placed in each city[f] his forces ([g]for) a garrison[g]. And when he came near to Azotus, they
showed him the temple of Dagon (which had been) burned with fire, [h]and Azotus, (which) together
with the suburbs thereof, had been pulled down, and the bodies scattered about, and them that had
been burned, [i]whom he had burned[i] [k]in the war[k], for they had made heaps of them in his way[h].
5 And they told the king what things Jonathan had done, in order to cast blame on him; and the
6 king[l] held his peace. And Jonathan met the king[m] [n]with pomp[n] at Joppa, and they saluted one
7 another, and they slept there. [o]And Jonathan went with the king[o] as far as the river [p]that is called[p]
Eleutherus, and returned to Jerusalem.
8 But king Ptolemy made himself master of the cities upon the sea coast, unto Seleucia [q]which is by
9 the sea[q], and he devised evil devices concerning Alexander. And he sent ambassadors unto king
Demetrius, saying: 'Let us make a covenant with one another, and I will give thee (to wife) my
10 daughter whom Alexander hath, and thou shalt reign over thy father's kingdom; for I have repented
11 that I gave my daughter unto him, for he sought to slay me.' [r]But he cast blame on him (thus),
12 because he coveted his kingdom[r]. And taking his daughter (from Alexander), he gave her to
13 Demetrius, and [s]was estranged from Alexander[s], and their enmity became manifest. And Ptolemy

XI. [a] + Ptolemy 71 [b-b] an army 𝔏[2] [c-c] > 𝔏[1] [d] speaking ℵ [e-e] he entered into the cities of Ptolemais A V ℵ[c.a] [f] of them 𝔖[luc] [g-g] to guard (*it*) ℵ[c.b] V 55 [h-h] > 71 [i-i] who had been killed 𝔏[1] [k-k] with fire 𝔖[g] [l] + went forth and 55 + when he heard it 𝔖[luc] [m] him 71 [n-n] > 71 [o-o] And they went 71 [p-p] > 19 [q-q] > 𝔏[1] [r-r] and to obtain my kingdom 𝔏 [s-s] T.R.; Alexander changed his face A it became known unto Alexander ℵ

XI. 1. **the king of Egypt.** Ptolemy VI, Philometer, cp. x. 51.

as the sand . . . For this frequently used O.T. metaphor cp. Joshua xi. 4; Judges xvii. 12; 1 Sam. xiii. 5, xvii. 11, &c.

by deceit. Cp., on the other hand, Josephus (*Antiq.* XIII. iv. 1), according to whose account Ptolemy came in perfect good faith.

4. **the suburbs thereof.** Cp. xi. 61.

5. **held his peace.** So as not to commit himself either for or against Jonathan.

6. **met the king.** Cp. x. 86, where συνάντησις is used in the sense of a meeting for the purpose of submitting oneself (Kautzsch); the verb here used is συναντᾶν, cp. Gen. xlvi. 28 (Sept.) where this verb is used in the sense of meeting some one with the purpose of showing honour to him (Jacob sending Judah to Joseph).

7. **Eleutherus.** The modern *Nahr al-Kebir*, the most important river in Phoenicia; it rises in the Lebanon and reaches the sea a little north of Arka; Jonathan therefore accompanied Ptolemy for a considerable distance. Burckardt (*Travels in Syria and the Holy Land*, p. 161) says: 'It is a large torrent, dangerous at this period of the year (March) from its rapidity. The Hamah caravans have been known to remain encamped on its banks for weeks together, without being able to cross it.'

8. **Seleucia which is by the sea.** Five miles north of the spot where the Orontes flows into the sea; one of the four most important cities of northern Syria; the port of Antioch, which was sixteen miles distant; it was founded by Seleucus I Nicator (reigned 312–280 B.C.), the founder of many cities. Mentioned in connexion with the missionary journey of Paul and Barnabas, Acts xiii. 4.

9. **sent . . . unto king Demetrius.** He was presumably in Cilicia; cp. x. 67, and *v.* 14, where it is said that the people of Cilicia had revolted against Alexander.

10. **for he sought to slay me.** The occasion of this is not mentioned in our book; the author was biassed in favour of Alexander because of the friendship between him and Jonathan; but Diodorus does not refer to it either, he says that Ptolemy only turned against Alexander when he realized what a hopeless weakling he was (cp. Grimm). On the other hand, Josephus refers to the occurrence in a circumstantial manner (*Antiq.* XIII. iv. 6): 'But as Ptolemy was at Ptolemais, he was very near to a most unexpected destruction, for a treacherous design was laid for his life by Alexander, by means of Ammonius, who was his friend; and as the treachery was very plain, Ptolemy wrote to Alexander, and required of him that he should bring Ammonius to condign punishment, informing him what snares had been laid for him by Ammonius, and desiring that he might be accordingly punished for it. But when Alexander did not comply with his demands, he perceived that it was he himself who had laid the design.' It is difficult to believe that there was not some truth in Ptolemy's allegation.

11. **because he coveted . . .** This can scarcely have been the case originally, otherwise why should he have given his daughter in marriage to Alexander? A pretext for quarrelling could easily have been found if, in the first instance, Ptolemy had intended to seize the kingdom. It seems more likely that it was the proof of Alexander's enmity which was the reason of Ptolemy's determination to wrest the kingdom from him.

entered into Antioch, and put on himself the diadem of Asia; so he (now) had put two diadems
upon his head, the diadem of Egypt and that of Asia.
14 But king Alexander was in Cilicia at that season, [t]because they of those parts were in revolt[t].
15 And Alexander heard of it, and he came against him in war; and Ptolemy led forth[u] (his host)[v], and
16 met him with a strong force, and put him to flight. And Alexander fled into Arabia, [w]that he might
17 be sheltered there; but king Ptolemy was exalted[w]. And Zabdiel the Arabian took off Alexander's
18 head, and sent it to Ptolemy. And king Ptolemy died the third day (after); and they that were in
19 his strongholds were slain [x]by them that dwelt in the strongholds[x]. And Demetrius became king
in the one hundred and sixty-seventh year.

XI. 20–37. *Jonathan secures the favour of Demetrius II.*

20 In those days Jonathan gathered together [y]them of Judaea[y] to take the citadel that was in
21 Jerusalem; and he made many engines (of war) against it. And [z]certain ones that hated their[a] own
nation[z], men that transgressed the Law, went unto the king, and reported unto him[b] that Jonathan
22 was besieging the citadel. And (when) he heard it he was angered; but immediately [c]on hearing it[c]
he set forth, and came to Ptolemais, and wrote unto Jonathan that he should not besiege it[d], and that
23 he should meet him and speak with him at Ptolemais with all speed. But when Jonathan heard (this),
he commanded (that the citadel should continue) to be besieged; and he chose (certain) of the elders
24 of Israel and of the priests[e] and put himself in peril, and taking silver and gold and raiment, and
25 divers presents besides, went to Ptolemais unto the king. And he found favour in his sight. And
26 certain lawless men of them that were of the nation made complaints against him; but the king did
unto him even as his predecessors had done unto him[f], and exalted him in the sight of all his Friends[g],
27 and confirmed him in the high-priesthood, and whatsoever other honours he had before[h], and gave
28 him pre-eminence among his Chief Friends. And Jonathan requested of the king, that he would make
Judaea[i] and the three provinces of the country of Samaria[j] free from tribute; and he[k] promised him
29 [l]three hundred[l] talents. And the king consented, and wrote letters unto Jonathan concerning all these
things after this manner:
30, 31 'King Demetrius unto (his) brother Jonathan and unto the nation of the Jews, greeting; The copy
of the letter which we wrote unto Lasthenes our[m] kinsman concerning you, we have written also unto
32, 33 you, that ye may see (it). King Demetrius unto Lasthenes (his) father, greeting; We have determined

t–t > 71 u went forth 55 $\mathfrak{S}^{luc}$ v *expressed in* ℵ c.a Luc w–w > 71 x–x > $\mathfrak{L}^2$ y–y Israel $\mathfrak{S}^g$ z–z > 71 a our ℵ* b + saying Luc c–c > 71 d the citadel ℵ c.a Luc e Jews ℵ > $\mathfrak{S}^g$ f + and glorified him with great glory 55 g enemies $\mathfrak{L}^1$ h + and exalted him 19 93 $\mathfrak{S}^{luc}$ i Idumaea 64 j *Reading, with Grimm,* τῆς Σαμαρείτιδος *for* καὶ τὴν Σαμαρίτην k they A l–l thirty 55 m your ℵ* A*

13. . . . **entered into Antioch.** Cp. Diodorus (quoted by Knabenbauer), who says that Hierax and Diodotus, who had been left in charge of Antioch by Alexander, gave up his cause as hopeless, and induced the people of Antioch to offer the crown and kingdom to Ptolemy.

Asia. Not the Roman province of this name, which was formed in 133 B.C., and included Mysia, Lysia, Caria, the western part of Phrygia, together with the Dorian, Ionian, and Aeolian coast-cities, with the islands lying off the coast (Ramsay, in *HDB*, s.v.); nor the continent; but the Asia as understood after it had been reduced about 285 B.C., and when the name Asia was 'restricted to the coast-cities and the lower valleys of the Maeander, Cayster, Hermus, and Caicus' (Ramsay).

15. **and met him.** According to Strabo, Ptolemy attacked Alexander at the river Oenoparas, on the plains of Antioch (Schürer, *op. cit.* i. 1, p. 244). Josephus says that Ptolemy was accompanied by Demetrius.

17. **Zabdiel.** 'A prince among the Arabians' (Josephus). The name occurs on a Palmyrene inscription (A.D. 155) in the form Zabd-ila (Waddington, *Inscriptions grecques et latines de la Syrie* 2590; cp. G. A. Cooke, *North Semitic Inscriptions*, p. 272).

18. . . . **died the third day (after).** Josephus (*Antiq.* XIII. iv. 8) says that Ptolemy was thrown from his horse in the battle, and wounded in the head by his enemies; he was unconscious for four days, but partially recovered on the fifth, and died 'a little while after'.

they that were in his strongholds. Cp. *v.* 3.

19. **the one hundred and sixty-seventh year.** i.e. 145 B.C.

21. **men that transgressed . . .** As on several other occasions, it was the renegades of their own race who were the worst enemies of the Jewish leaders.

24. **he found favour in his sight.** For the Greek phrase cp. Sept. of Gen. vi. 8, xviii. 3, xxx. 27.

26. **as his predecessors had done . . .** Cp. x. 6, 18–20, 25 ff., 61–65.

27. **confirmed him in the high priesthood.** Cp. x. 20.

28. **the three provinces . . .** Cp. x. 30, and especially xi. 34; these provinces had been taken from Samaria; the reading καὶ τὴν Σαμαρίτην, though supported by all MSS. and Versions, cannot be right, see crit. note.

29. **after this manner.** With the Greek cp. 2 Macc. i. 24.

30. **unto (his) brother.** Cp. x. 18, 25.

31. **Lasthenes our kinsman.** Cp. Josephus (*Antiq.* XIII. iv. 3), where it is said that it was Lasthenes, the Cretan, who brought a great number of mercenary soldiers to Demetrius. 'Kinsman', like 'brother' in *v.* 30, is a title of honour; the same is the case with 'father' in the next verse; cp. *Antiq.* XII. iii. 4, where Antiochus III addresses Zeuxis, the general of his forces and his 'intimate friend', as 'father'.

to do good to the nation of the Jews, who are our friends, and observe what is just toward us, because
34 of their good will toward us. We have confirmed unto them, therefore, the districts of Judaea, and
the three governments of Aphaerema[n], and Lydda, and Ramathaim—(these) were added unto Judaea
from the country of Samaria—and all things appertaining unto them, for all such as do sacrifice in
Jerusalem, instead of the king's[o] dues which the king received of them yearly aforetime from the
35 produce of the land and the fruits of trees. And as for the other things which appertain unto us,
[p][q]from henceforth[q], of the tenths and the tolls [r]that appertain to us[r], [s]and the saltpits, and the crowns
36 that appertain to us[p], all these we will bestow upon them[s]. [t]And not one of these things shall be
37 annulled[t] from this time forth and for ever. Now therefore be careful to make a copy of these things,
and let it be given unto Jonathan, and let it be set upon the holy mount in a fitting [u]and conspicuous
place[u].'

XI. 38–53. *Jonathan assists Demetrius in opposing Tryphon.*

38 And (when) king Demetrius saw that the land was quiet before him, [v]and that no resistance was
made to him[v], he sent away all his forces, each man to his own place,—except the [w]foreign forces[w],
which he had raised from the isles of the Gentiles—and (therefore) all the forces [x]of his fathers[x]
39 were inimically disposed towards him. Now Tryphon was of those who aforetime had been of
Alexander's part, and he saw that all the forces murmured against Demetrius, and he went to
40 Imalkue[y] the Arabian, who was nourishing up Antiochus, the young child [z]of Alexander[z], [a]and
pressed sore upon him that he should deliver him unto him[a], that he might reign[b] in his father's
stead; and he[c] told him all that Demetrius had done, and the hatred wherewith his forces hated
him; and he abode there many days.
41 And Jonathan sent[d] unto king Demetrius, that he should cast out of Jerusalem them of the citadel,
42 and them that were in the strongholds; for they fought against Israel continually[e]. And Demetrius

[n] Ephraim 𝔖 > $\mathfrak{L}^1$ [o] > $\mathfrak{S}^g$ $\mathfrak{L}^1$ [p-p] > 71 [q-q] > $\mathfrak{S}^{luc}$ [r-r] > $\mathfrak{S}^{luc}$ [s-s] we remit unto them 𝔏 [t-t] > 71 [u-u] > 71 $\mathfrak{S}^{luc}$ [v-v] > 71 [w-w] > $\mathfrak{S}^{luc}$ [x-x] > 71 [y] Malchus $\mathfrak{L}^2$ $\mathfrak{S}^g$ = Josephus [z-z] > $\mathfrak{S}^g$ [a-a] > ℵ [b] make him king Luc [c] they A [d] + letters 71 [e] > $\mathfrak{L}^1$

34. **Aphaerema.** i.e. Ephraim (2 Sam. xiii. 23), or Ephron (2 Chron. xiii. 9); according to Josephus (*Bell. Iud.* IV. ix. 9) it lay not far from Bethel, '. . . he took Bethel and Ephraim, two small cities.' Cp. also John xi. 54 (see further, Robinson, *Researches in Palestine*, iii, pp. 67 ff.).

Lydda. *Lod* in Hebr., afterwards called Diospolis, the modern Ludd; between Joppa and Jerusalem; one of the toparchies of Judaea, according to Josephus (*Bell. Iud.* II. xx. 4).

Ramathaim. Cp. 1 Sam. i. 1, where it is called *Ramathaim Zophim* (but see Driver, *Notes on the Hebrew Text of the Books of Sam.*, in loc.), and located on Mount Ephraim; the usual form of the name is *ha-Ramah* ('the height'), which is, however, to be differentiated from the Ramah belonging to the tribe of Benjamin, nearer Jerusalem. It is probably to be identified with the modern *Beit Rima*, north-east of Lydda, in the neighbourhood of Thamna; this agrees with the accounts of Eusebius and Jerome (see Schürer, *op. cit.* i. 1, p. 246).

from the country of Samaria. Cp. x. 30, xi. 28.

as do sacrifice in . . . i.e. the privilege is for the orthodox Jews; the 'transgressors of the Law', as well as the Samaritans living in the three provinces, are excluded.

instead of . . . The text is clearly not in order, something having dropped out; in Josephus (*Antiq.* XIII. iv. 9) it says: 'I remit to them the three provinces . . . as also what the kings, my predecessors, received from those that offered sacrifices in Jerusalem, and what are due from the fruits of the earth, and of the trees, and whatever else belongs to us . . .'; cp. x. 29–31.

35. See notes on x. 29, 30.

all these . . . It is noteworthy that there is no mention about the siege of the citadel in Jerusalem (*vv.* 20–23); presumably the siege was raised in consideration of all these concessions; the Syrian garrison, therefore, still remained in possession.

37. **a copy.** On tables of brass, cp. viii. 22.

38. **the foreign forces . . . from . . .** From Crete and from the other islands (Josephus), i.e. of the Grecian Archipelago.

were inimically disposed. The real reason for this was their loss of pay; Josephus (*Antiq.* XIII. iv. 9) says that the kings before this used to give pay to the soldiers in time of peace, 'that they might have their goodwill, and that they might be fully prepared to undergo the difficulties of war, when any occasion should require it.' This short-sightedness of Demetrius is only to be explained by the natural slothfulness which seems to have been characteristic of him; cp. Justin. xxxvi. 1. 1, 9, referred to by Grimm.

39. **Tryphon.** 'Diodotus, who was also called Trypho, an Apamaean by birth, a commander of Alexander's forces' (Josephus).

Imalkue the Arabian. On a Palmyrene inscription (A.D. 162) the name *Maliku* (מלכו) occurs (de Vogüé, *La Syrie Centrale*, 9); on another of later date (A.D. 242) we have *Zabdila the son of Maliku, the son of Maliku*, cp. *v.* 17 (Vogüé, 15; cp. G. A. Cooke, *op. cit.*, pp. 276, 278). In Josephus the form is Malchus, so also the Syriac and one Latin Version. Schürer (*op. cit.* i. 1. 247) refers to Nöldeke, in Euting's *Nabatäische Inschriften*, p. 74, where a Palmyrene inscription is given in which the name ימלכו (= Imalku) occurs; Diodorus gives Iamblichus, which also is nothing else than ימלכו.

41. **. . . that he should cast out . . .** Nothing could better illustrate the broken power of the Seleucidae, and the way in which Jonathan was able, in consequence, to draw advantage from it.

sent unto Jonathan, saying: 'I will not only do this for thee and thy nation, but I will greatly honour
43 thee [f]and thy nation[f], if I find favourable occasion. Now therefore thou shalt do well, if thou send me
44 men who shall fight for me; for all my forces are revolted.' And Jonathan sent him[g] three thousand
valiant men unto Antioch. And they came unto the king; and the king[h] was glad at their coming.
45 And they of the city gathered themselves together [i]into the midst of the city[i], to the number of a
46 hundred and twenty thousand men; and they were minded to slay the king[j]. And the king fled
into the palace, and they [k]of the city[k] seized [l]the thoroughfares of the city[l], and began to fight.
47 And the king called the Jews to (his) aid[m], and they were gathered together unto him [n]all at once[n];
and they dispersed themselves [o]in the city[o]; and they slew that day to the number of a hundred
48, 49 thousand. And they set the city on fire, and got many spoils [p]that day[p], and saved the king. And
(when) they of the city saw that the Jews had made themselves masters of the city [q] [r]as they would[q],
50 they waxed faint in their hearts[r], and cried out to the king with[s] supplication, saying: 'Give us (thy)
51 right hand, and let the Jews cease from fighting against us and the city.' And they cast away their
arms[t], and made peace. And the Jews [u]were glorified in the sight of the king, and before all that
52 were in his kingdom[v] [u]; and they[w] returned to Jerusalem, having many spoils. And (when) king[x]
53 Demetrius was seated on his throne of his kingdom (again), and the land was quiet before him, he
lied in all that he had spoken, and estranged himself from Jonathan and recompensed (him) not
([y]according to)[z] the benefits with which he (had promised to) recompense him[y]; but he afflicted
him sore.

XI. 54–74. *Friendship between Jonathan and Antiochus VI.*

54 Now after this Tryphon returned, and with him the young child Antiochus; and he reigned, and
55 put on a diadem. And there were gathered unto him all the forces which Demetrius had sent away
56 in disgrace; and they fought against him, and he[a] fled, [b]and was[c] put to rout[b]. [d]And Tryphon
57 took the elephants[d], and became master of Antioch. And the young Antiochus wrote unto
Jonathan, saying: 'I confirm unto thee the high-priesthood, and appoint thee over the four govern-
58 ments, and to be one of the king's Friends. And he sent unto him golden vessels and furniture for
the table, and gave him leave to drink in golden vessels, and to be clothed in purple, and to have
59 a golden buckle. And his brother Simon he made governor (over the district) from the Ladder of
60 Tyre unto the borders of Egypt. And Jonathan went forth, and took his journey beyond the river,
and through the cities; and all the forces of Syria gathered themselves unto him for to be his
61 confederates. And he came to Askalon, and they of the city met him honourably. And he
departed thence to Gaza, and they of Gaza shut him out; and he lay siege unto it, [e]and burned the
62 suburbs thereof with fire[e], and spoiled them. And they of Gaza made request unto Jonathan, and
he gave them his right hand, and took the sons of their princes for hostages, and sent them away to
Jerusalem. And he passed through the country as far as Damascus.
63 And Jonathan heard[f] that Demetrius' princes were come to Kedesh, which is in Galilee, with

[f–f] > 71 [g] of them A 55 64 93 [h] > 71 [i–i] > 55 𝔏[1] [j] + Demetrius 64 93 [k–k] > 93 [l–l] (it) 93 [m] palace 𝔏[2] [n–n] > 71 55 𝔖[luc] 𝔏 [o–o] > 71 𝔖[g] [p–p] > 71 [q–q] > ℵ* (*hab* ℵ[c.a]) [r–r] > 19 [s] + much 64 [t] + and gave him their right hand 𝔖[luc] [u–u] > 71 [v] + and they were named in his kingdom ℵ 𝔏[1] [w] the Jews 71 [x] > 71 𝔏[1] [y–y] > ℵ 93 [z] *expressed in* V [a] Demetrius 64 93 [b–b] > 𝔏[1] [c] they were ℵ [d–d] > 55 [e–e] and they burned it 𝔖[g] [f] saw 𝔏[1]

43. **all my forces are revolted.** According to Josephus (*Antiq.* XIII. v. 3), the inhabitants of Antioch revolted, but all the troops which Demetrius had not dismissed (see *v.* 38) remained faithful to him; 'he took the mercenary soldiers which he had with him . . . and assaulted the Antiochians.'

45. **a hundred and . . .** This is an evident exaggeration, so too the number of the slain, *v.* 47.

48. **they set the city on fire.** Josephus adds that the houses were close together, and mostly built of wood.

49. **they waxed faint in their hearts.** For the Greek cp. Isa. vii. 4, Sept. (Grimm).

53. **afflicted him sore.** Josephus, more specifically, says that 'he threatened that he would make war upon him unless he would pay all the tribute which the Jewish nation owed to the first kings' (i. e. of Syria).

57. **the four governments.** i. e. Judaea and the three governments mentioned in *v.* 34.

58. **clothed in purple, . . . golden buckle.** See notes on x. 20, 62, 89.

59. **the Ladder of Tyre.** Cp. Josephus (*Bell. Iud.* II. x. 2), who says it is a high hill, a hundred stadia north of Ptolemais.

60. **beyond the river.** πέραν τοῦ ποταμοῦ = עבר הנהר, i. e. the territory this side of the Euphrates from the point of view of the Israelites, that side of the Euphrates from the point of view of the Babylonians (cp. 1 Kings v. 4); the reference here is, therefore, to Syria; cp. the words in this verse, 'all the forces of Syria gathered themselves unto him.'

Askalon. See note on x. 86.

61. **Gaza.** The southernmost of the five chief Philistine cities, the modern *Ghuzzeh.*

62. **Damascus.** The modern *Esh-Sham*; it lies 120 miles north-east of Jerusalem, and 200 miles south of Antioch.

63. **Kedesh.** Cp. Joshua xxi. 32; Judges iv. 6, 11; situated on the northern frontier of Palestine, among the mountains of Naphtali. Josephus speaks of it as belonging to the Tyrians (*Bell. Iud.* II. xviii. 1, IV. ii. 3); it still retains its ancient name.

64 a great host, with the object of hindering him from his purpose; and he went to meet them, but
65 Simon his brother he left in the country. And Simon encamped against [g] Bethsura, and fought
66 against it many days, and shut it [h] up; and they made request to him that he would give them his
right hand, and he gave it to them; but he put them out from thence, and took possession of the
67 city, and set a garrison over it. And Jonathan and his army encamped at the water [i] of Gennesar [i],
68 and early in the morning they got them to the plain of Hazor [k]. And, behold, an army of strangers
met him [l] in the plain, and they laid an ambush for him [m] in the mountains, but they themselves met
69 (him) [n] face to face. But they that lay in ambush [m] rose out of their places, and joined battle; and
70 all they that were of Jonathan's side fled; not one of them was left, except Mattathias the son of
71 Absalom, and Judas the son of Chalphi, captains of the forces. And Jonathan rent his clothes, and
72 put earth upon his head, and prayed. And he turned again unto them in battle, and put them to
73 rout, and they fled. And (when) they of his side who were fleeing saw it, they returned unto him,
74 and pursued (them) with him unto Kedesh to their camp; and they encamped there. And there
fell of the strangers [o] on that day [o] about three thousand men. And Jonathan returned unto
Jerusalem.

XII. 1–38. *Jonathan renews his alliance with Rome, and enters into a league with the Spartans. He defeats the followers of Demetrius.*

12 1 And Jonathan saw that the time served him, and he chose men, and sent them to Rome, to confirm
2 and renew the friendship that they had with them. [a] And to the Spartans, and to other places, he
3 sent letters after the same manner [a]. And they [b] went unto Rome, and [b] entered into the senate
house, and said: 'Jonathan the high-priest, and the nation of the Jews, have sent us, to renew for
4 them the friendship and the confederacy, as in former time [c].' And they gave them letters unto (the
governors) of every place, that they should bring them on their way to the land of Judah in peace.
5, 6 And this is the copy of the letter which Jonathan wrote to the Spartans: 'Jonathan the high-priest [d],
and the Council [e] of the nation [e], and the priests, and the rest of the people of the Jews, unto their
7 brethren the Spartans, greeting! Even before this time were letters sent unto Onias the high-priest
from Areios [f], who was reigning among you, (to the effect) that ye are our brethren, as the copy
8 (here) underwritten showeth. And Onias treated honourably [g] the man that was sent [g], and received [h]
9 the letters, wherein declaration was made of confederacy and friendship. Therefore we also—albeit

[g] in A 64 $\mathfrak{S}^{luc}$ [h] them Luc $\mathfrak{L}^1$ $\mathfrak{S}^{luc}$ [i-i] > V [k] Nazor A V 55 64 [l] them 55 $\mathfrak{S}^{g}$ [m-m] > $\mathfrak{S}^{luc}$ [n] *expressed in* 55 [o-o] > $\mathfrak{L}^1$

XII. [a-a] > 71 [b-b] > $\mathfrak{L}^1$ [c] + and they that were in Rome welcomed them 19 93 $\mathfrak{S}^{luc}$ [d] + of the nation A [e-e] > A $\mathfrak{S}^{luc}$ [f] $\mathfrak{L}^1$ = Josephus; *all other authorities read* Dareios [g-g] those who were sent $\mathfrak{L}^1$ [h] gave 71

his purpose. i. e. of helping Antiochus.

65. **Bethsura.** See note on iv. 29.

67. **the water of Gennesar.** i. e. the lake of Gennesareth; the name occurs here for the first time.

the plain of Hazor. Cp. Joshua xi. 1, xii. 19, xix. 36; Judges iv. 2; 1 Sam. xii. 9; 1 Kings ix. 15; Josephus (*Antiq.* V. v. 1) says it was near the lake Semechonitis, or Merom; it lay, therefore, right in the north of Palestine.

74. **three thousand.** Josephus says two thousand (*Antiq.* XIII. v. 8).

XII. 1. **he chose men.** i. e. Numenius and Antipater, see *v.* 16, xiv. 22.

to confirm . . . Cp. viii. 17 ff.

2. **and to other places.** It is not specified either in this book or in Josephus what these 'other places' were.

6. **the Council of the nation.** This *Gerousia* is mentioned as being already in existence in the time of Antiochus the Great (cp. Josephus, *Antiq.* XII. iii. 3); the earliest reference to it is, however, 2 Chron. xix. 8. It developed later into the Sanhedrin, a name which occurs for the first time in the reign of Hyrcanus II (cp. *Antiq.* XIV. ix. 4). The head of this Council was the high-priest, as the head also of the State; it exercised judicial and administrative functions (cp. 1 Macc. xiv. 20). The measure of its authority varied according to the amount of autonomy granted by the suzerain power; but its moral influence over the Jews, whether in the Dispersion or in Palestine, was always very considerable.

the rest of the people. ὁ λοιπὸς δῆμος; Grimm pointedly remarks that it is probably not without a purpose that the Greek translator of this book almost invariably restricts the use of the word δῆμος to documents sent to or received from a foreign nation (viii. 29, xiv. 20, 25, xv. 17); his object in doing so is to place on record the fact that the Jewish people is one that is free and independent.

7. **Onias.** The first of the name, son of Jaddus (*Antiq.* XI. viii. 7) or Jaddua (Neh. xii. 11), father of the high-priest Simon I, the Just. There is great uncertainty as to his date, some scholars putting it at about 320–300 B.C., while others contend for some fifty years later; others, again, place it between these two extremes.

Areios. The first of the name, who reigned over the Spartans 309–265 B.C. This is the correct form of the name Areus. All Greek MSS. wrongly read Dareios (see crit. note). That Areios is the right reading is evident from Josephus; the form Oniares occurs in *v.* 20; Cod ℵ reads there *ονιααρης* (= Ὀνίᾳ Ἄρης). The Old Latin Version alone has preserved the right reading.

8. **the man that was sent.** Named Demoteles, according to Josephus (*Antiq.* XIII. v. 8).

10 [i] we need none of [i] these things, having for our comfort the holy books which are in our hands—have
assayed to send that we might renew our brotherhood [k] and friendship [k] with you, to the end that we
should not become estranged from you altogether; for long time is passed since ye sent unto us.
11 [l] We therefore at all times without ceasing, both at our feasts, and on other convenient days, do
remember you in the sacrifices which we offer, and in our prayers, as it is right and meet to be
12, 13 mindful of brethren; and, moreover, we are glad for your glory [l]. But as for ourselves, many
[m] afflictions and many wars [m] have encompassed us, [n] and the kings that are round about us have
14 fought against us [n]. We were not minded, however, to be troublesome to you, or to the rest of our
15 confederates [o] and friends, in these wars; for we have the help that is from heaven [p] to help us [p], and
16 we have been delivered from our enemies, and [q] our enemies [q] have been humiliated. We chose,
therefore, Numenius the son of Antiochus, and Antipater the son of Jason, and have sent (them)
unto the Romans, to renew the friendship that we had [r] with them [r], [s] and the former [t] confederacy [s].
17 We commanded them, therefore, to go also unto you, and to salute you, and to deliver you our letters
18 concerning the renewing [u] (of friendship) and [u] of our [v] brotherhood. And now ye shall do [w] well if
19 ye give us an answer thereto.' And this is the copy of the letters [x] which they [y] sent [x] to Onias:
20, 21 'Areios [z], king of the Spartans, to Onias, the chief priest, greeting! [a] It hath been found in writing,
concerning the Spartans and the Jews, that they are brethren, and that they are [b] of the stock [b] of
22 Abraham; and now, since these things have come to our knowledge, ye shall do well to write unto us
23 of your prosperity. And we, moreover, do write on our part to you [a], that your cattle and goods
are ours, [c] and ours are yours. We do command, therefore, that they [d] make report unto you on
this wise [c].'
24 And Jonathan heard that Demetrius' princes were returned to fight against him with a greater
25 force than afore, so he removed from Jerusalem, and met them in the country of Hamath; for he
26 gave them no respite to set foot in his country. And he sent spies into their [e] camp; and they
returned, and reported unto him that in such and such a way they had planned to fall upon him by
27 night. But as soon as the sun was down, Jonathan commanded his men to watch, and to be in arms,
that all the night long they might be ready for battle; and he sent forth sentinels (and placed them)
28 round about the camp. But (when) the adversaries heard that Jonathan and his men [f] were ready
for battle, they were afraid and trembled in their heart; and they kindled fires in their camp, [g] and
29 departed [g]. But Jonathan and his men knew it not till morning; for they saw the fires burning.
30 And Jonathan [h] pursued after them, but did not overtake them; [i] for they had gone over the river
31 Eleutherus. And Jonathan turned aside (and fought) against the Arabians, who are called Gaba-
32 daeans, and smote them [i], and took their spoils. And he set out from thence, and came to Damascus, [k] and took his journey through all the country.
33 And Simon went forth [k], and took his journey as far as Askalon, and the strongholds that were

i–i we do not put our trust in 𝔖g k–k > 71 l–l > 71 m–m > V n–n > 71 o + and brethren 𝔖g
p–p > 71 𝔏1 q–q they that are before us Luc 71 r–r > 𝔖g s–s > 71 t > 𝔖luc u–u > 𝔖luc 𝔏1 v your 𝔖luc
w ye have done A x–x > 71 y he ℵ c.a 64 93 z 𝔏1 (> 𝔏2) *alone* a–a > 71 b–b > 𝔖g 𝔏2 c–c and if ye
command anything we will readily fulfil it 71 d we 𝔖g 𝔏2 e his 𝔊 (*exc.* Luc) 𝔖luc 𝔏 > 𝔖g f fathers ℵ
g–g Luc 𝔖 *only* (= Josephus) h > A i–i > 71 k–k > 𝔖g

9. **the holy books.** Cp. i. 56, 57, iii. 48.
15. **we have been delivered . . .** Cp. iii. 18 ff., iv. 30 ff., &c.
21. **concerning the Spartans and the Jews . . .** 'The fiction of a relationship between the Jews and the Spartans, which constituted the motive for the Spartans to write their letter (1 Macc. xii. 6, 7, 21, cp. 2 Macc. v. 9), was not unheard of during the era of Hellenism. Freudenthal, *Alexander Polyhistor*, p. 29, note, refers in illustration and for proof to Stephen of Byzantium under the word 'Ιουδαία . . . ὡς Κλαύδιος 'Ιούλιος ἀπὸ Οὐδαίου Σπάρτων ἑνὸς ἐκ Θήβης μετὰ Διονύσου ἐστρατευκότος. In a decree of the Pergamenes (Josephus, *Antiq.* XIV. xviii. 22) there is also mention of a relation between the Jews and the Pergamenes' (Schürer, *op. cit.* i. 1. 251). On the other hand, as S. A. Cook and W. J. Woodhouse (*EB* 4744) contend: 'There is no reason to doubt the fact of diplomatic relations with Sparta having been set on foot by Jonathan. For Sparta was too obscure at the time to have suggested itself to a forger eager to magnify his hero by inventions of the kind. Again, the incident leads to no result in the sequel; the reverse would have tended to throw doubt upon the entire episode.' The probability is that while the details can scarcely be regarded as historical, the broad fact of diplomatic relations of some kind between the Jews and the Spartans is to be accepted as true (see further, *Intr.* § 7). The Greek legend of the Spartans having been descended from the Phoenicians may not have been without influence upon the subject (see, further, Stade, *Geschichte des Volkes Israel*, ii, pp. 372 f.). Grimm's important pages (187–191) should, however, also be consulted; while not prepared to accept the copy in 1 Macc. as representing the original document, he holds that since diplomatic relationships were in existence between the two nations, documents of some kind must have been exchanged.
24. **And Jonathan heard . . .** The narrative, interrupted by *vv.* 1–23, is now taken up from xi. 74.
25. **Hamath.** On the Orontes; the modern Hamah. Cp. Num. xiii. 21; 1 Kings viii. 65.
30. **Eleutherus.** See note on xi. 7.
31. **Gabadaeans.** Probably the small tract of land, about eight miles north of Damascus, now called *Zabdini*. 𝔊, 𝔏, 𝔖 read 'Zabadaeans'.
33. **Askalon . . . Joppa.** See notes on x. 75, 86.

34 near unto it. And he turned aside to Joppa, and took possession of it, for he had heard that they
were minded to deliver the stronghold unto the men of Demetrius; and he placed a garrison there
to keep it.
35 And Jonathan returned, and called the elders of the people together; and he took counsel with
36 them to build strongholds in Judaea, and to make the walls of Jerusalem higher, and to raise a great
mound between the citadel and the city, [l] for to separate it from the city [l], [m] so that it might be
37 isolated [m], [n] that they (within it) might neither buy nor (they without) sell [n]. And they were
gathered together to build (the city) [o]; and (a part of) the wall by the brook that is on the east side
38 had fallen down, and [p] he repaired that which is called Chaphenatha [p]. And Simon also built Adida
in the plain country, and made it [q] strong, [r] and set up gates [s] and bars [r] [s].

XII. 39-53. *The capture of Jonathan through treachery.*

39 And Tryphon sought to reign over Asia and to put on himself the diadem, and to stretch forth
40 his hand against Antiochus the king [t]. And he was afraid lest haply Jonathan should not suffer
him (to do so), [u] and lest he should fight against him [u]; so he [v] sought a way [w] how [v] to take him,
41 [x] that he might destroy him [x]. And he [y] removed, and came [y] to Bethshan. [z] And Jonathan came
42 forth [z] [a] to meet him [a] with forty thousand men chosen for battle, and came to Bethshan. And
(when) Tryphon saw that he came with a great host, he was afraid to stretch forth his hand against
43 him; and he received him honourably, and commended him unto all his Friends, [b] [c] [d] and gave him
gifts [d], and commanded his Friends [b] and his forces to be obedient unto him, [e] as unto himself [c] [e].
44 And he said unto Jonathan: 'Why hast thou put all this people to trouble, seeing there is no war
45 betwixt us? And now, send them away to their homes, but choose for thyself a few men who shall
be with thee, and come thou with me to Ptolemais, and I will give it up to thee, [f] and the rest [g] of the
strongholds and the rest of the forces, and all the (king's) officers; then I will return and depart; for,
46 for this cause did I come [f].' And he trusted him and did even as he said, and [h] sent away his
47 forces, and they departed into the land of Judah. But he reserved to himself three thousand men,
48 two thousand [i] of whom [i] he left in Galilee, but one thousand went with him. But when Jonathan
had entered into Ptolemais, [k] they of Ptolemais shut the gates, and [k] took him; and all they that
49 had come with him they slew with the sword. And Tryphon sent forces and horsemen into Galilee,
50 [l] and [m] into the great plain [l], to destroy all Jonathan's men. And they perceived that he was taken
and had perished, and they that were with him; nevertheless they encouraged one another, and went
51 on their way close together, ready for war. And (when) they that were following (upon them) saw
52 that they were ready (to fight) for their lives, they turned back again. And they all came in peace
to the land of Judah, and they mourned for Jonathan and them that were with him, [n] and they were
53 sore afraid. And all [o] Israel mourned [n] with a great mourning. And all the Gentiles that were
round about them sought to destroy them utterly, for they said: 'They have not [p] a man [p] (that is)
leader and (who will) help (them); [q] now therefore let us fight against them [q], and take away their
memorial from among men.'

[l-l] > ℵ* (*hab* ℵ c.a) [m-m] > 𝔖g [n-n] > ℵ* (*hab* ℵ c.a) [o] *expressed in* ℵ cities V [p-p] he pulled down the mound which is called Chesphonitho 𝔖 [q] > A [r-r] > A [s-s] > 55 𝔖g [t] the younger 𝔖g [u-u] > 71 [v-v] was desirous 𝔏 [w] > ℵ [x-x] > 𝔖g [y-y] came stealthily V [z-z] > 𝔖g [a-a] > 64 93 [b-b] > ℵ* (*hab* ℵ c.a) V [c-c] > 71 [d-d] > 𝔖g [e-e] likewise A [f-f] > 71 [g] many A [h] + Jonathan ℵ c.a 19 93 𝔖luc [i-i] about ℵ A [k-k] > 𝔖luc [l-l] > 71 [m] > A [n-n] > 71 [o] > A 98 [p-p] > ℵ V [q-q] > 71

37. **the brook that . . .** i.e. the Kidron.

Chaphenatha. The meaning of this word is unknown; it does not occur elsewhere; Josephus does not mention it.

38. **Adida.** The Chadid of Ezra ii. 33; Neh. vii. 37, xi. 34, four miles east of Lydda; Josephus (*Antiq.* XIII. vi. 5) says it is 'upon an hill, and beneath it lie the plains of Judaea'. The modern *el-Chadite*.

the plain country. Σεφηλά = the lowland region west of the mountainous country of Judaea.

40. **Bethshan.** See note on v. 52.

41. **with forty thousand men.** The number shows how Jonathan's power and influence had increased; it was not without reason that Tryphon recognized Jonathan's power to hinder him in his designs (cp. *v.* 40). Josephus (*Antiq.* XIII. vi. 1) says that the reason why Jonathan came with such a large army was because he expected to be attacked by Tryphon.

43. **commended.** For this sense of συνίστημι cp. 2 Macc. iv. 24; Wisd. vii. 14; Rom. xvi. 1; 2 Cor. x. 18; for further references see Schleusner *s.v.*

49. **the great plain.** See note on v. 52.

50. **had perished.** But see xiii. 23, though it was natural to suppose that he had been murdered.

52. **they mourned . . .** Cp. ix. 20, xiii. 26; ἐπένθησεν . . . πένθος μέγα, a Hebraism.

53. **They have not . . .** Both the rival kings were now at enmity with the Jews; hitherto the Jewish leader had always managed to have the support of one or other of the claimants to the throne.

let us fight against them. This intention does not appear to have been carried out.

. . . take away their memorial . . . Cp. iii. 35, Ecclus. x. 17.

SIMON MACCABAEUS XIII. 1—XVI. 24.

XIII. 1–11. *Simon elected leader.*

13 1 And Simon heard that Tryphon had gathered together a numerous [a] host to come into the land of
2 Judah, and destroy it utterly. And he saw that the people were troubled [b] and (were) in great fear [b];
3 so he went up to Jerusalem, and gathered the people together, and encouraged them, and said unto
them: 'Ye yourselves know what things I, and my brethren, and my father's house, have [c] done for
4 the [d] laws and the sanctuary [d], and the battles [e] and the distresses [e] [f] which we have seen [f]; by reason
5 whereof all my brethren have perished for Israel's sake, and I alone am left. And now be it far from
me that I should spare my own life in any time of affliction; [g] for I am not better than my brethren [g].
6 Howbeit I will take vengeance for my nation, and for the sanctuary, and for our [h] wives and [h] children;
7 because all [i] the Gentiles are gathered together to destroy us [k] of very hatred [k].' And the spirit of
8 the people, [l] as soon as [l] they heard these [m] words, revived. [n] And they answered with a loud voice,
9 saying [n]: 'Thou art our leader instead of Judas and Jonathan thy brethren [o]. Fight thou [p] our war [p],
10 and all that thou shalt say unto us, that will we do.' And he [q] gathered together all the men of war,
11 and made haste to finish the walls of Jerusalem, and fortified it round about. And he sent Jonathan
the son of Absalom, and with him a great host, to Joppa; and he cast out them that were therein,
and abode there [r] [s] in it [s].

XIII. 12–24. *Simon defeats Tryphon.*

12 And Tryphon removed from Ptolemais with a mighty host to enter into the land of Judah; and
13, 14 Jonathan was with him in ward. But Simon encamped at Adida, [t] over against the plain [t]. And
(when) Tryphon knew that Simon was risen up instead of his brother Jonathan [u], and meant to join
15 battle with him, he sent ambassadors unto him, saying: 'It is for the money which Jonathan thy
brother owed unto the king's treasure, [v] by reason of the offices which he had [v], that we hold him fast.
16 And now send a hundred talents of silver, and two of his sons (as) hostages, that when he is set at
17 liberty he may not revolt from us,—and we will set him at liberty.' And Simon knew [w] that they
spake [x] unto him [x] deceitfully, but sent the money and the children, lest peradventure he should bring
18 upon himself great hatred on the part of the people [y], (in that they should be) saying: 'Because I sent
19 him not the money and the children [z] [a] he perished [b].' [c] And he sent the children [z] [c] and the hundred
20 talents; and [a] he [d] dealt falsely, and did not set Jonathan at liberty. And [e] after this [e] Tryphon came
to invade the land [f], and destroy it, and he went round about by the way (that leadeth) to Adora;

XIII. [a] great 𝔖[g]   [b–b] > 71   [c] + all ℵ V   [d–d] the holy laws 𝔏   [e–e] > ℵ* (*hab* ℵ[c]) V 71   [f–f] T.R. ℵ[c.b]
[g–g] > 71   [h–h] > 𝔖[luc]   [i] > 𝔖[g]   [k–k] > 71   [l–l] αυτου (*for* αμα του) *in reference to people*   [m] his 19 93 𝔖[luc]
[n–n] And they said 𝔏   [o] 55 𝔖[luc]; brother 𝔊 𝔏   [p–p] > 𝔏   [q] Simon 64 93   [r] > ℵ* (*hab* ℵ[c.a]) V 𝔖[g]
[s–s] > 𝔖[luc] 𝔏   [t–t] in the sight of the temple 𝔏   [u] > 71   [v–v] > 71   [w] knew not V 55   [x–x] > 71
[y] Israel 55 𝔖[luc]   + Israel Luc   [z–z] > ℵ   [a–a] > 𝔖[g]   [b] > 55 64   [c–c] > 71   [d] Tryphon Luc   [e–e] > 71 𝔏
[f] city A   + of Judah Luc

XIII. 1. **Simon.** The last survivor of the five Maccabaean brothers. He completed the work so brilliantly carried out by Jonathan, and made his people entirely independent of the Syrian kings.

3. **which we have seen.** i. e. experienced; ἰδεῖν is used in this sense like ראה, see Jer. v. 12, xiv. 13, &c.

4. **my brethren have perished.** According to the general belief Jonathan had been murdered, but he was still alive at this time, see *vv.* 12, 23.

I alone am left. Cp. the words of Elijah, 1 Kings xviii. 22.

5. **I am not better . . .** Cp. the similar words of Elijah, 1 Kings xix. 4.

7. **the spirit . . . revived.** Cp. Gen. xlv. 27 ἀνεζωπύρησε τὸ πνεῦμα Ἰακώβ.

9. **and all that . . .** Cp. Exod. xix. 8; Joshua i. 16.

10. **to finish the walls . . .** This work had been begun by Jonathan, see xii. 36, 37.

11. **Absalom.** Cp. xi. 70.

. . . to Joppa . . . Cp. xii. 33, according to which Joppa was already in possession of the Jews; Josephus (*Antiq.* XIII. vi. 4) makes the matter clear: 'And sent . . . Jonathan the son of Absalom, to Joppa, and gave him command to cast out the inhabitants out of the city, for he was afraid lest they should deliver up the city to Trypho.'

13. **Adida.** See note on xii. 38.

the plain. πεδίον here, in xii. 38 σεφηλά.

14. **to join battle with him.** For the Greek phrase cp. Deut. ii. 14 (Sept.).

15. **the king's treasure.** i. e. the royal treasury, cp. 2 Macc. iii. 13.

the offices which . . . Cp. x. 65, xi. 63.

20. **he went round about by the way.** Cp. 1 Kings iii. 9 (Sept.); κυκλοῦν ὁδόν = סַב דֶּרֶךְ (Grimm), i. e. he purposely made a *détour* by way of Adora.

Adora. Adoraim in the O.T., cp. 2 Chron. xi. 9, one of the cities fortified by Rehoboam, the modern *Dûra* (Josephus calls it Dora, *Antiq.* XIII. vii. 2), five miles south-west of Hebron.

21 and Simon and his army marched over against him to whatsoever place he went. Now they of the
citadel sent [g] unto Tryphon [g] ambassadors, hastening him to come [h] unto them through the wilderness,
22 and to send them victuals [h]. And Tryphon made ready all his horse to come; and in that night
there fell [i] a great quantity of [i] snow, and he did not (find it possible to) come because of the snow;
23 so he removed, and came into the country of Gilead. But when he came near to Bascama, he slew
24 Jonathan, and he was buried there. And Tryphon returned, and went away into his own land.

XIII. 25–30. *Jonathan's sepulchre at Modin.*

25 And Simon sent, and took the bones of Jonathan his brother, and buried him [k] at Modin, the city
26 of his fathers. And [l] all Israel [l] made great [m] lamentation over him, [n] and mourned for him many
27 days [n]. And Simon built (a monument) upon the sepulchre of his father and of his brethren, and
raised it aloft, [o] so that it could be seen [o] (from afar); (he built it) with polished stone behind and
28 before. And he set up [p] seven pyramids, [q] one over against another, for (his) father, and mother, and
29 four brethren [q]. And [r] for these [r] he made cunning devices, setting about them [s] great [t] pillars,
and upon the pillars he fashioned [u] all manner of arms [u] for a perpetual memory, and beside [u] the
30 arms [u] [v] carved ships [v], that they should be seen of all that sail on the sea. This is the sepulchre
which he made at Modin, (and it is there) unto this day.

XIII. 31–42. *Murder of Antiochus. Treaty between Simon and Demetrius II.*

31, 32 Now Tryphon dealt deceitfully with the young [w] king [x] Antiochus, and slew him, and reigned in
his stead, and put on himself the diadem of Asia, and brought great calamity upon the land.

g-g > A   h-h > 71   i-i > 𝕷   k them T.R.   l-l they 71   m > Luc   n-n > 71   o-o *lit.* to the sight
p + upon it 55 Luc   q-q > 71   r-r > 𝔖luc   s + four 𝕷   t > 55   u-u panoplies *Gk.* propitiatory
offerings 𝔖g (?)   v-v various carved things A   + he set up 𝔖luc   w great 64 93   x > 𝔖g

---

marched over against him. i.e. marched parallel with him, Simon in the mountain country and Tryphon in the plain.

21. **hastening.** For the Greek *καταστεύδειν* cp. Sept. of Exod. v. 13 ('And the taskmasters were urgent . . .').

22. **because of the snow.** It is but rarely that snow falls south of Hebron, though it is not altogether unknown even so low down south as that; see further, Nowack, *Hebr. Archäologie*, i. 49.

23. **Bascama.** This place is not mentioned elsewhere, its position is quite uncertain; see, further, Buhl, *Geographie des alten Palästina*, p. 241.

25. **Modin.** See note on ii. 1.

26. **great lamentation.** Cp. ii. 70, ix. 20.

27. **the sepulchre . . .** 'Ever since, in the fourth century B.C., Artemisia, widow of Mausolus, King of Caria, erected at Halicarnassus a stately monument to his memory—hence the word *mausoleum*—the custom of building similar sepulchred edifices had been spreading in the East' (Fairweather and Black, *op. cit.*, p. 230).

28. **seven pyramids.** Josephus (*Antiq.* XIII. vi. 6) says that these had 'been preserved to this day'; he seems to be referring to some additional source of knowledge in adding: 'And we know that it was Simon who bestowed so much zeal about the burial of Jonathan, and the building of these monuments for his relations;' cp. in *v.* 30 the words 'unto this day'. The seventh pyramid Simon presumably set up for himself.

29. **carved ships.** Josephus makes no mention of these.

30. **unto this day.** Concerning the bearing of this on the date of the book see *Intr.* § 4. Grimm quotes Eusebius, who says in his *Onomasticon*: 'Modeim . . . unde fuerunt Maccabaei, quorum hodieque ibidem sepulchra monstrantur.'

31. **and slew him, and reigned in his stead.** 'There are coins of Antiochus VI from 167 to 170 of the Seleucid era, or from 146–145 to 143–142 B.C. Coins of Trypho bear the number of the years III and IV. Josephus assigns to the reign of Antiochus VI a period of four years, and to Trypho a period of three years (*Antiq.* XIII. vii. 1, 2). This is in agreement with the statement of Porphyry, who gives to Demetrius, before his imprisonment, only a three years' reign (Eusebius, *Chron.*, ed. Schoene, i. 257, 263 ff.), from Olympiad 160. 1, which is really Olym. 159. 4, or 141–140 B.C., to Olympiad 160. 3, or 138–137 B.C. Porphyry evidently reckons the reign of Demetrius as beginning with the displacement by conquest or murder of Antiochus VI. In thorough accord with this, too, is the chronology of 1 Macc. xiii. 31–41, which unhesitatingly assigns the murder of Antiochus by Trypho to the Seleucid year 170, or 143–142 B.C. Finally, it is no serious discrepancy when, in 1 Macc. xiv. 1 the Parthian campaign of Demetrius is dated from the Seleucid year 172, or 141–140 B.C.; while Porphyry, on the other hand, assigns it to Olympiad 160. 2, or 139–138 B.C. In direct contradiction, however, with the foregoing, stands the statement made by many writers (Josephus, *Antiq.* XIII. v. 11, vii. 1; Appian, *Syr.* 67, 68; Justin. xxxvi. 1), that Antiochus was not murdered by Trypho before the time of the Parthian campaign by Demetrius, and indeed not till after Demetrius had been taken prisoner. This, however, is in opposition not only to the chronology of 1 Macc., but also to the circumstance that then there is not left a three or four years' reign for Trypho, which yet, according to Josephus and the coins, must be admitted. Then Trypho's death occurs almost contemporaneously with the seizure of Demetrius by the Parthians in 138 B.C. . . . It therefore seems to me hazardous to assume, with many modern critics, that the last-named authorities should have precedence over 1 Macc.' (Schürer, *op. cit.* i. 1, pp. 176 f.). Regarding the death of Antiochus, Grimm quotes Livy (*Epit.* 55) to the effect that 'Alexandri filius, rex Syriae, decem annos admodum habens, a Diodoto, qui Tryphon cognominabatur, tutore suo, per fraudem occisus est, corruptis medicis, qui eum calculi dolore consumi ad populum mentiti, dum secant, occiderunt.'

32. **Asia.** See note on xi. 13.

33 And Simon built the strongholds [y] of Judaea, and fenced (them) about with high towers, and great
34 walls [z], and gates, and bars; and he laid up victuals in the strongholds. And Simon chose men, and
sent to king Demetrius, to the end he should give the country an immunity, [a] because all that
35 Tryphon did was to plunder [a]. [b] And king Demetrius sent unto him according to these words, and
36 answered him, and wrote a letter unto him, after this manner [b]: 'King Demetrius unto Simon the
37 high-priest and Friend of kings [c], [d] and unto the elders and nation of the Jews [d], greeting. The golden
crown, and the palm-branch [e], which ye sent, we have received; and we are ready to conclude
38 a lasting peace with you, and to write to the officers to grant immunities unto you. [f] And whatsoever
things we (have now) confirmed unto you, they are confirmed [f]; and the strongholds which ye have
39 builded, [g] let them be [g] your own. [h] As for any oversights and faults (committed) unto this day, we
forgive (them [i]) [h]; and the crown which ye owed [k] (we remit); and if there were any other toll
40 exacted in Jerusalem, [l] let it no longer be exacted [l]. And if (there be) some of you meet to be
enrolled among those round about us, let them be enrolled; and (thus) let there be peace betwixt
41 us.' [m] In the one hundred and seventieth year (therefore) was the yoke of the heathen taken away
42 from Israel [m]. And the people of Israel [n] began to write in their instruments and contracts: [o] 'In
the first year [o] of Simon the great high-priest and captain [p] and leader of the Jews.'

XIII. 43–53. *Simon captures Gazara and the citadel of Jerusalem.*

43 In those days he [q] encamped against Gazara [r], and compassed it round about [s] with armies; and he
44 made [t] an engine of siege [t], and brought it up [s] to the city, and smote one tower, and took it [u]. And
they that were in the engine of siege leaped forth into the city; and there was a great uproar in the
45 city; and they of the city rent their clothes, and went up [v] on the wall [v] with their wives and children,
46 and cried with a loud voice, making request to Simon to give them right hands. And they said:
47 'Deal not with us according to our wickednesses, but according to thy mercy.' And Simon was
reconciled unto them, and did not fight against them; but he drove them out of the city, and cleansed
the houses wherein the idols were, and so [w] entered into it with [x] singing and giving of praise [x] [y].
48 [z] And he put all uncleanness out of it [z], and caused to dwell in it men who observed the Law; and
he made it stronger (than it was before), and he built therein a dwelling-place for himself.
49 But they of the citadel of Jerusalem were hindered from going forth, [a] [b] and from going [a] into the
country [b], [c] and from buying and selling [c]; and they hungered exceedingly, and many of them
50 perished through famine. And they cried out to Simon [d] to take right hands; which thing he
granted them [d]; but he cast them out from thence; and he cleansed the citadel from pollutions.

[y] stronghold A [z] + and towers A [a-a] > 71 [b-b] And he sent unto him a writing thus 71 [c] of the king 𝔖luc [d-d] > 71 [e] palm-branched ℵ embassy 93 *so probably* 𝔖luc שלחיותא (*'robe'*) *being a mistake for* שליחותא (*'embassy'*) [f-f] > 71 [g-g] they are 𝔏 [h-h] > 71 [i] you A [k] owe V [a] [l-l] > 71 [m-m] > 71 [n] > ℵ V 64 93 [o-o] > 71 [p] > 71 [q] Simon T.R. [r] *with Josephus, Antiq.* XIII. vi. 7; *Bell. Iud.* I. ii. 2; Gaza *all the MSS. and Versions, wrongly* [s-s] > 71 [t-t] > A a strong wooden tower 𝔖luc; *in* 𝔖g *the Gk. is transliterated* [u] the city 𝔖luc [v-v] > 19 93 𝔖luc [w] then 𝔖g 𝔏 [x-x] > 71 [y] + to God V 𝔏 [z-z] > 71 [a-a] > A 71 93 [b-b] > 𝔖g [c-c] > 71 [d-d] > 71

---

33. **And Simon built . . .** Simon was not slow to utilize the opportunity for strengthening his own position which the struggle for the Syrian throne afforded him.

34. **And Simon chose men . . .** This is not mentioned by Josephus.

36. **King Demetrius . . .** On this letter see *Intr.* § 7. ii. (*e*).

the elders. See note on xii. 6.

37. **the palm-branch.** So critical note. The reading βάϊν is to be preferred, βαϊνὴν of Cod. ℵ being most likely due to the following ἣν, cp. 2 Macc. xiv. 4, where it is said that 'a chaplet of gold and a palm' (φοίνικα) were presented to Demetrius. The reference here is most likely to a sceptre the top of which was shaped into palm-leaves. In the O.T. the palm-tree is referred to as a symbol of prosperity (cp. Ps. xcii. 12); it is with this signification that it is depicted on some Jewish coins, see De Saulcy, *Numismatique Juive*, Pl. I, fig. 6; Madden, *Coins of the Jews*, p. 71.

to grant immunities . . . Cp. x. 28–35.

39. **the crown . . .** Cp. x. 29.

41. **In the one hundred and seventieth year.** i.e. 143–142 B.C.

42. **And the people of Israel began to write . . .** On the importance of the study of numismatics in connexion with this statement see Schürer, *op. cit.* i. 1, pp. 257 ff., and his Appendix IV.

43. **Gazara.** See critical note. For the correctness of this reading see *v.* 53; xiv. 7, 34; xv. 28; xvi. 1. On Gazara see note on iv. 15. On the situation of Gazara, Eusebius, *Onom.*, ed. Lagarde, p. 244 (quoted by Schürer, *op. cit.* i. 1, p. 261), remarks: καὶ νῦν καλεῖται Γάζαρα κώμη Νικοπόλεως ἀπέχουσα σημείοις δ' ἐν βορείοις. It is the modern Tell-Jezer discovered by Clermont-Ganneau in 1873, and excavated by the *Pal. Explor. Fund* during the years 1902–9; see the 'Quarterly Statement' for these years.

an engine of siege. ἑλέπολις (see critical note); on this machine see Smith's *Dict. of Class. Antiq.*, s. v.

46. **Deal not with us . . .** Cp. Isa. i. 16 (Sept.); Jer. xxxiii. 5.

51 And he[e] entered into it[f g] on the three and twentieth day of the second[h] month, in the one hundred
and seventy-first year[g], with praise, and palm-branches, [i]and with harps and with cymbals, [k]and
with viols, and with hymns[k], and with songs[i]; because a great[l] enemy had been destroyed out of
52 Israel[m]. And he ordained that they should keep that day every year [n]with gladness[n]. [o]And the
hill of the temple that was by the citadel he made stronger (than it was before); and he dwelt there,
53 (both) he and his men[o]. And Simon saw that John his son was (grown to be) a man, and he made
him leader of all his forces; and he dwelt at Gazara.

XIV. 1–3. *Demetrius II imprisoned by Arsaces, king of Persia.*

14 1 In the one hundred and seventy-second year Demetrius the king gathered his forces together, and
2 went into Media, to get him help, that he might fight against Tryphon. And (when) Arsaces, the
king of Persia [a]and Media[a], heard that Demetrius was come into his borders, he sent one of his leaders
3 to take him alive; and he went and smote the army of Demetrius, and took him, and brought him to
Arsaces; [b]and he put him in ward[b].

XIV. 4–15. *Simon's beneficent rule; an ode in his honour.*

4 And the land[c] had rest all the days of Simon; and he sought the good of his nation; and his
5 authority [d]and his glory[d] was well-pleasing to them [d]all his days[d]. And [d]in addition to all his
(other) glory (was this that)[d] he took Joppa for a haven, and made it a place of entry for the ships[e]
of the sea.

6 And he enlarged the borders of his nation,
  [f]And ruled over the land[f]:
7 And he gathered together [g]many that had been in captivity[g],
  And he ruled over Gazara, and Bethsura, [f]and the citadel.
And he took away uncleannesses therefrom[h f],
  And there was none that could resist him.
8 And they tilled their land in peace;
  And the land gave her increase,
And the trees of the plains their fruit.
9 Old men sat in the streets[i],
[k]All spoke together of the (common) weal[k],
  And the young men put on glorious and[l] warlike apparel.

[e] they ℵ 19 93 𝔖luc [f] the citadel Luc [g–g] > 71 [h] > 19 93 𝔖luc [i–i] > 71 [k–k] > 𝔖luc [l] > 64
[m] Jerusalem V + and no enemy rose up any more to fight Luc 𝔖luc [n–n] > A [o–o] > 71

XIV. [a–a] > 71 [b–b] > ℵ (*hab* ℵ c.a) [c] + of Judah ℵ V 19 55 𝔖 𝔏 [d–d] > 71 [e] Luc 𝔖; isles *all other authorities* [f–f] > 71 [g–g] much treasure 𝔖g [h] from them 64 93 [i] assemblies ℵ (streets ℵ c.a) [k–k] > 71
[l] + not Luc 𝔖g

---

51. **the three and twentieth day . . .** The 23rd of Iyyar (= Ziv in O.T., cp. 1 Kings vi. 1) 171 = the 23rd May 142 B.C.

palm-branches. Cp. 2 Macc. x. 7; John xii. 13.

with harps . . . Cp. iv. 54.

52. **And he ordained . . .** This feast is referred to in *Megillath Ta'anith* ('The scroll of Fasting', so called because fasting is forbidden on the days enumerated), ch. ii, which enumerates thirty-five days of joy in Jewish history which were kept as feast-days; it was compiled about the beginning of the Christian era. Possibly this feast is included in the words contained in Judith viii. 6, but it has long ceased to be celebrated.

And the hill of the temple . . . On this statement, and that of Josephus (*Antiq.* XIII. vi. 7), that Simon had the hill on which the citadel stood removed, in order that the Temple might stand higher than any other building in Jerusalem, see Schürer, *op. cit.* i. 1, p. 263.

53. **John.** i. e. John Hyrcanus I.

XIV. 1. **one hundred and seventy-second year.** On the Parthian expedition see note on xiii. 31.

2. **Arsaces.** i. e. Mithridates I, king of the Parthians. The name Arsaces was assumed by all the kings of Parthia after the founder of the Empire of this name.

7. **Gazara . . .** Cp. iv. 29, xiii. 43, 49–51.

8. **they tilled . . .** Cp. Lev. xxvi. 4; Ezek. xxxiv. 27.

the land gave . . . Cp. Zech. viii. 12.

the trees . . . Cp. Deut. viii. 8; Hag. ii. 19.

9. **Old men . . .** Cp. Zech. viii. 4, 5.

10 For the cities he provided victuals,
[m] And furnished [n] them with defensive works,
Until his glorious name was proclaimed to the end of the earth.
11 He made peace in the land,
And Israel rejoiced with great joy.
12 And each sat under his vine [o] and his fig tree [o],
And there was none to make them afraid [m];
13 And no one was left in the land to fight them
[p] And the [q] kings were discomfited in those days.
14 And he strengthened all that were brought low of his people;
He sought out the Law,
And put away the lawless and wicked.
15 [r] He glorified the sanctuary [p],
And multiplied [r] the [s] vessels of the Temple.

XIV. 16–24. *Renewal of the alliance with Rome.*

16 And (when) [t] it was heard [t] in Rome that Jonathan was dead, [u] and [v] (even) unto Sparta [u], they
17 were exceeding sorry. But as soon as they heard that his brother Simon was made high-priest [u] in
18 his stead, and ruled the country, and the cities therein [u], they wrote unto him on tablets of brass, to
renew with him the friendship and the confederacy which they had established with [u] Judas and [u]
19, 20 Jonathan [u] his brethren [u]; and they were read before the congregation in Jerusalem. And this is the
copy of the letter which the Spartans sent: 'The rulers and the city [vv] of the Spartans, unto Simon the [w]
high-priest, and unto the elders, [u] and the priests, and the rest of the people of the Jews, (who are)
21 brethren [u], greeting; [u] The ambassadors that were sent unto our people made report to us of your [x]
22 glory and honour; and [u] we were glad for their coming. And we did register the things that were
spoken by them in the public records, after this manner: Numenius, son of Antiochus, and Anti-
pator, son of Jason, the Jews' ambassadors, came unto us to renew the friendship they had with us.
23 And it pleased the people to receive the men honourably, and to place the copy of their words
among the public records, to the end that the people of the Spartans might have a memorial thereof.'
24 Moreover they [y] wrote a copy of these things unto Simon the high-priest. After this Simon sent
Numenius to Rome having a great shield of gold of a thousand pound weight [z], in order to confirm
the confederacy with them.

XIV. 25–49. *The hereditary High-priesthood conferred upon Simon; a memorial tablet to Simon and the Maccabaeans is set up in the Temple.*

25 But when the people heard these things, they said: 'What thanks shall we give to Simon [a] and his
26 sons? For he, and his brethren, and his father's house have [b] made themselves strong [b], and have
chased away in fight the enemies [c] of Israel from them, [d] and established liberty for it [d].' And they
27 wrote on tablets of brass, and set them upon a pillar [e] in mount Zion. [f] And this is the copy of the
writing: 'On the eighteenth day of Elul, in the one hundred and seventy-second year—that is the

[m–m] > 71 [n] strengthened $\mathfrak{S}^{luc}$ [o–o] > ℵ [p–p] > 71 [q] their A [r–r] > ℵ [s] And the ℵ [t–t] he heard A they heard Luc 55 71 [u–u] > 71 [v] + it was heard Luc [vv] cities $\mathfrak{L}^{1}$ $\mathfrak{S}^{luc}$ [w] + great Luc 55 [x] peace and your Luc [y] we V 93 [z] > $\mathfrak{S}^{g}$ [a] + the high priest $\mathfrak{S}^{luc}$ [b–b] acted valiantly $\mathfrak{S}^{luc}$ [c] the sons 64 [d–d] and they gave the inheritance to Simon and established (him) Luc, *making 'the people' in v. 25 the subject* [e] pillars ℵ V [f–f] > 71

---

12. **each sat under . . .** Cp. 1 Kings iv. 25; Mic. iv. 4; Zech. iii. 10.
And there was none . . . Cp. Deut. xxviii. 26; Jer. vii. 33; Zech. i. 21.
14. **all that were brought low.** *πάντας τοὺς ταπεινούς*; cp. Ps. xvii. 28; Isa. xiv. 32; Amos ii. 7 (all in Sept.).
He sought out the Law. Cp. Ps. civ. 45 (Sept.).
16. **and (even) unto Sparta.** See *Intr.* § 7. iii. (*b*).
18. **the friendship and the confederacy . . .** Cp. viii. 17–30, xii. 1–4.
20. **The rulers and . . .** On this letter see *Intr.* § 7. iii. (*b*). The rulers were the *Ephors* ever since the year 192 B.C., when Nabis, the last of the 'tyrants', was murdered.
22. **Numenius.** Cp. xii. 16.
24. **After this . . .** See *Intr.* § 7. iii. (*c*).
a thousand pound weight. An obvious exaggeration, cp. xv. 18.
27. **Elul.** The sixth month in the sacred year (= September approximately); cp. Neh. vi. 15.
the one hundred and seventy-second year = 141 B.C.

28 third year of Simon [g] the [h] high-priest [g], [i] and the **prince of the people of God** [i]—in a great congregation of priests and people and princes of the nation, and of the elders of the country, [k] (the following)
29 was promulgated by us [k]; Forasmuch as oftentimes there have been wars in the country [f], Simon the
son of Mattathias, [f] the son of the children of Joarib [f], and his brethren, put themselves in jeopardy,
and withstood the enemies of their nation, that their sanctuary and the Law might be upheld; and
30 they glorified their nation with great glory. [l] And Jonathan assembled their [m] nation together [l], and
31 became high-priest to them; and he was gathered to his people. Then their enemies determined to
invade their country, [n] that they might destroy their country utterly [n], and stretch forth their hands
32 against their sanctuary. Then rose up Simon and fought for his nation; and he spent much of his own
33 substance, and armed the [o] valiant men of his nation, and gave them wages. And he fortified the cities
of Judaea, and Bethsura (that lieth) upon the borders of Judaea, where the arms of the enemies were
34 aforetime, and set there a garrison of Jews. [p] And he fortified Joppa which is by the sea, and Gazara
which is upon the borders of Azotus, wherein the enemies dwelt aforetime; and he placed Jews there [p],
35 and whatsoever things were needful for the sustenance [q] of these he put in them. And (when) the
people saw the faith [r] of Simon, and the glory which he sought to bring unto his nation, they made him
their leader [p] and high-priest, because he had done all these things, and because of the justice and the
36 faith which he kept to his nation, and because he sought by all means to exalt his people [p]. And in
his days things prospered in his hands [s], [t] so that the Gentiles were taken away out of their (the
Jews') country; and they also that were in the city of David, they that were in Jerusalem, who had
made themselves a citadel, out of which they issued, and polluted all things round about the sanc-
37 tuary, and did great hurt unto its purity (these did he expel) [t]; and he made Jews to dwell therein,
and fortified it for the safety of the country and of the city; and he made high the walls of Jeru-
38 salem. And king Demetrius confirmed him in the high-priesthood [u] in consequence of these things [u],
39, 40 and made him one of his Friends, [v] and honoured him with great honour [v]. For [w] he had heard [w]
that the Jews had been proclaimed by the Romans friends, and confederates, [v] and brethren [v], and
41 that they had met the ambassadors of Simon honourably. And [x] the Jews and the priests were well
pleased that Simon should be their leader and high-priest [v] for ever, until a faithful prophet should

[g-g] > 𝔖luc [h] + great א V Luc 55 [i-i] in Asaramel (Saramel A = שר עם אל) 𝔊 the prince of Israel 𝔖 [k-k] he made known to us א A V &c. we made known to you Luc 𝔖luc these things were made known 𝔏 (= הוֹדַע) [l-l] > א 71 [m] his V 𝔖luc 𝔏¹ [n-n] > א* (*hab* א c.a) V [o] his א [p-p] > 71 [q] nourishment and sustenance 𝔖luc [r] deeds 𝔖luc 𝔏¹ + deeds V [s] + and fortified Jerusalem 71 [t-t] > 71 [u-u] *lit.* according to these things; > 71 𝔖luc [v-v] > 71 [w-w] it had been heard A Luc 71 [x] 71; *all other authorities add* that

---

the third year . . . Cp. xiii. 42.

28. **the prince of the people of God.** Greek ἐν Σαραμέλ, see critical note, where, however, the meaning of this expression given does not account for the ἐν; Schürer thinks that this represents the remains of σεγεν (= סגן, the Hebr. for στρατηγός [τοῦ ἱεροῦ], cp. Jer. li. 23, 28, 57; Ezek. xxiii. 6, 12, 23; Ezra ix. 2; Neh. ii. 16, iv. 8, xii. 40, xiii. 11; Dan. iii. 2, 27, vi. 8; Acts iv. 1), *op. cit.* i. 1. 265; ii. 1. 258 f.; but, in this case, what has become of the σεγ? It seems more natural to follow Wernsdorf (quoted by Grimm and Kautzsch) and see in σαραμέλ the transliteration of שׂר עם אל, 'Prince of the people of God'; the translator, assuming that this was the name of a place, would then have inserted ἐν. The difficulty here is the mention of God, which is uniformly avoided in this book; it may, therefore, be that the Syriac Version has retained the original reading, 'a prince of Israel,' שׂר ישׂראל; the Hebrew script in use before the square characters were introduced might easily account for reading an m (מ) for the second s (שׂ); the translator, who was obviously puzzled, may also have taken exception, through ignorance, to the repeated שׂר.

was promulgated by us. See critical note.

29. **Joarib.** Cp. ii. 1.

33. **Bethsura.** Cp. iv. 29.

34. **he fortified Joppa.** Cp. xii. 33, 34.

Gazara . . . upon the borders of Azotus. Cp. xiii. 43–8. This is a mistake as Gazara was 17 miles distant from Ashdod; Grimm thinks the error is due to the translator.

wherein. ἐν ᾗ . . . ἐκεῖ, a Hebraism; cp. e. g. Deut. iv. 5, 14, 26, ἡ γῆ εἰς ἣν ὑμεῖς εἰσπορεύεσθε ἐκεῖ; and often.

35. **they made him . . .** But cp. xiii. 8 ff.; on the chronological discrepancies between the details given in this letter and those in xi. 16–xiv. 24 see *Intr.* § 7. iii.

40. **and brethren.** σύμμαχοι is the more usual expression, cp. v. 18, viii. 20, xv. 17; ἀδελφοί is scarcely original.

41. **leader and high-priest.** Simon has three official titles: ἀρχιερεύς, as spiritual ruler; στρατηγός, as military chief; and ἐθνάρχης, as civil governor; see xiii. 42, and *v.* 47 of this chap., cp. also xv. 1, 2.

for ever. i. e. that it should be hereditary in his family.

until a faithful prophet . . . By this is meant that 'this popular decree should remain in force until an authentic communication from God should make some other enactment. . . . The significance of this popular resolution lies not so much in the fact that it conveyed to him (Simon) any new dignity, but rather in this, that it legitimized and pronounced hereditary those dignities which he already had. In this way a new high-priestly and princely dignity was founded, that of the Asmoneans' (Schürer, *op. cit.* i. 1, p. 265).

42 arise [v]; and that he should be a captain over them [y], to set them over their works, and over the country,
43 and over the arms, and over the strongholds, [v] and that he should take charge of the sanctuary, and
that he should be obeyed by all, and that all instruments in the country should be written in his
44 name [v], and that he should be clothed in purple, and wear gold; and that it should not be lawful for
anyone among the people or among the priests to set at nought any of these things, or to gainsay
the things spoken by him, or to gather an assembly [z] in the country [z] without him, or that any (other)
45 should be clothed in purple, or wear a buckle of gold; [aa] but that whosoever should do otherwise,
46 or set at nought any of these things, should be liable to punishment [aa]. And all the people con-
47 sented to ordain [bb] for Simon that it should be done according to these words. And Simon accepted
(hereof), and consented to fill the office of high-priest, and to be captain and governor of the Jews
[aa] and of the priests, and to preside over all matters [aa].'
48 And they commanded to put this writing on tablets of brass, and to set them up within [cc] the
49 precinct of [cc] the sanctuary in a conspicuous [dd] place; and copies of this (they caused) to be placed in
the treasury, to the end that Simon and his sons might have them.

XV. 1–9. *Antiochus VII (Sidetes) seeks the throne, and solicits the help of Simon.*

15 1 And Antiochus, son of Demetrius the king, sent letters from the isles of the sea unto Simon the
2 priest [a] and governor of the Jews, and to all the nation [b]; [c] and the contents thereof were after this
manner [c]:
'King Antiochus to Simon the high-priest and governor, and to the nation of the Jews, greeting:
3 Forasmuch as pestilent fellows have made themselves masters of the kingdom of our [d] fathers, and my
purpose is to claim the kingdom, that I may restore it [c] as before,—I have, moreover, raised a mul-
4 titude of foreign soldiers, and have prepared ships of war [c], and I have determined to land in the country,
that I may punish them that have devastated our country, and them that have made many cities in the [e]
5 kingdom desolate,—I therefore (herewith) confirm [f] unto thee [f] (the release from) all the exactions which
6 the kings that were before me remitted unto thee, [c] and whatsoever gifts [g] besides they remitted unto
7 thee [c]; [h] and I give thee leave [h] [i] to coin money [k] for thy country [k] with thine own stamp [i]. And Jerusalem and the sanctuary shall be free; [c] and all the arms which thou hast prepared [c], and the strongholds
8 [c] which thou hast built, which thou hast in thy possession [c], let them remain unto thee. And everything
owing to the king, [l] and the things that shall be owing to the king, let them be remitted unto thee
9 from now and unto all time [l]. Moreover, when we shall have established [m] our kingdom, we will
glorify thee and thy nation and [n] the Temple with great glory [n], so that your glory shall be made
manifest in all the earth.'

XV. 10–14. *Antiochus VII besieges Tryphon in Dor.*

10 In the one hundred and seventy-fourth year Antiochus went forth into the land of his fathers;
11 and all the forces came together unto him, so that there were (but) few men [o] with Tryphon. And
12 king Antiochus pursued him, and in fleeing he [p] came to Dor, which is by the sea; for he perceived
13 that [q] troubles were come upon him, and that his forces had forsaken him. And Antiochus encamped
against Dor, and with him a hundred and twenty thousand men of war, and eight thousand horse.
14 And he compassed the city round about, [r] and the ships joined in the attack from the sea; and he
pressed the city sore [r] by land [s] and sea [s], and suffered no man to go out or in.

[y] + and should take charge of the sanctuary 𝔊 𝔖luc 𝔏¹; *these words have crept into the text by mistake, they occur again in the next verse* [z–z] > 𝔖luc [aa–aa] > 71 [bb] + these things 64 93 [cc–cc] > 𝔖luc [dd] safe A

XV. [a] high-priest 55 64 [b] + of the Jews 71 [c–c] > 71 [d] my 55 𝔖luc [e] my ℵ V [f–f] > 𝔖luc [g] exactions A [h–h] > A [i–i] to make laws and to put forth decrees according to thine own will 𝔖luc [k–k] > 𝔖luc [l–l] > 71 [m] obtained 𝔏¹ [n–n] our Temple 55 [o] + that were left T.R. [p] Tryphon 64 93 [q] + all Luc [r–r] > ℵ [s–s] > 𝔖luc

43. . . . **clothed in purple, and wear gold.** Cp. viii. 14, x. 20, 89, and *v.* 44 of this chap.
49. **in the treasury.** Cp. 2 Macc. iii. 6, 28, v. 18; John viii. 20.

XV. 1. **Antiochus.** Called *Sidetes* on account of his having been brought up in the city of *Side* in Pamphylia (cp. *v.* 23). According to Josephus (*Antiq.* XIII. viii. 2), he was also called the 'Pious' (Εὐσεβής), because of 'the great zeal he had concerning religion'. He was the seventh of the name; son of Demetrius I, and brother of Demetrius II.
from the isles of the sea. Schürer quotes Appian, *Syr.* c. 68, to the effect that while at Rhodes Antiochus learned of his brother's captivity (πυθόμενος ἐν Ῥόδῳ περὶ τῆς αἰχμαλωσίας).
2. **the contents thereof . . .** On this letter see *Intr.* § 7. ii. (*f*).
6. **to coin money . . .** See Schürer, *op. cit.* i. 1, pp. 257–60.
10. **In the one hundred and seventy-fourth year.** i.e. 139–138 B.C.
11. **Dor.** Cp. Joshua xi. 2, xii. 23, xvii. 11; Judges i. 27; an ancient Phoenician town on the Mediterranean coast, about nine miles north of Caesarea; the modern *Tanturā*.

XV. 15–24. *The return of the Jewish envoys from Rome.*

15 And Numenius and his company came from Rome, having letters to the kings, and to the countries, wherein were written these things:
16, 17 'Lucius, consul of the Romans, unto king Ptolemy, greeting: The Jews' ambassadors came unto
us (as) our friends and confederates, to renew the old friendship and confederacy, being sent from
18 Simon the high-priest, [t]and from the people of the Jews[t]; moreover, they brought a shield of gold
19 of a thousand[u] pound[v]. It pleased us, therefore, to write unto the kings and unto the countries,
[w]that they should not seek their hurt, nor fight against them[w], [x]and their cities, and their country[y],
20 nor be confederates with such as fight against them[x]. And it seemed good to us to accept the
21 shield from them. If, therefore, any pestilent fellows should have fled from their country unto
you, deliver them unto Simon the high-priest, that he may take vengeance on them according to
their law.'
22 And the same things wrote he to Demetrius the king, and to Attalus, and to Ariarathes[z], and to
23 Arsaces, and unto all the countries, and to Sampsames[a], and to the Spartans, and unto Delos, and
unto Myndos, and unto Sicyon, and unto Caria[b], and unto Samos, and unto Pamphylia, and unto
Lycia, and unto Halicarnassus, and unto Rhodes, and unto Phaselis, and unto Cos, and unto Side, and
24 unto Aradus, and Gortyna, and Cnidus, and Cyprus and Cyrene[c]. And a copy hereof they wrote to
Simon the high-priest.

XV. 25–41. *Antiochus VII breaks his covenant with Simon.*

25 And Antiochus the king encamped against Dor the second (day)[d], bringing his forces up to it
26 continually, and making engines (of war); and he shut up Tryphon[e] from going in or out. And
Simon sent him two thousand chosen men to fight for him, and silver and gold, and instruments (of
27 war) in abundance. But he would not receive them, [f]but set at nought everything that he had
28 previously covenanted [g]with him[g f]; [h]and he was estranged from him[h]. And he sent unto him
Athenobius, one of his Friends, to commune with him, saying; 'Ye hold possession of Joppa and
29 Gazara, and the citadel that is in Jerusalem, [f]cities of my kingdom. The borders thereof have ye
wasted, and done great hurt in the land[f], and have got the dominion of many places in my kingdom.
30 Now, therefore, deliver up the cities which ye have taken, [f]and the tributes of the places whereof ye
31 have gotten dominion outside of the borders of Judaea[f]; or else give me for them five hundred talents
of silver; and for the harm that ye have done, and the tributes of the cities, other five hundred
32 talents; otherwise we[i] will come and make war upon you.' And (when) Athenobius, the king's
Friend, came to Jerusalem, and saw the glory of Simon, and the[k] cabinet with gold and silver vessels,
33 and his great attendance, [l]he was amazed[l], and reported to him[m] the king's words. And Simon
[n]answered, and[n] said unto him: 'We have neither taken other men's land, nor have we possession
of that which appertaineth to others, but of the inheritance of our fathers; [n]howbeit, it was had in
34 possession of our enemies wrongfully for a certain time[n]. But we, having (taken) the opportunity,

t–t > 71 u five thousand A 55 v talents 55 w–w > ℵ (*hab* ℵc.a) 55 x–x > 71 y countries A 93 𝔖luc 𝔏1
z Arathes A 55 71 a Sampsaces A 𝔖luc Lampsacus 𝔏1 b Caris A c Smyrna V d *expressed only in* ℵc.a
Luc e + from all sides 𝔖luc f–f > 71 g–g > 𝔖luc h–h > 55 i they A k + golden Luc 𝔖luc
l–l > 𝔖luc m them A Simon Luc n–n > 71

---

16. **Lucius . . .** On this letter see *Intr.* § 7. ii. (*c*).
Ptolemy. The seventh of the name; Euergetes II, Physcon; he reigned jointly with his brother, Ptolemy VI, Philometor, 170–164 B.C., and alone from 164–117.
22. **Attalus.** King of Pergamum, but uncertain whether the first or second of the name (Grimm).
Ariarathes. The fifth of the name, king of Cappadocia, 162–130 B.C.
Arsaces. Mithridates I, king of Parthia; see note on xiv. 2.
23. **Sampsames.** Possibly the harbour on the Black Sea between Sinope and Trebizond, but uncertain.
Delos. This and Samos are islands in the Archipelago.
Myndos. Like Halicarnassus and Cnidus, in Caria, the country on the south-west coast of Asia Minor.
Sicyon. On the north coast of the Peloponnesus, west of Corinth.
Pamphylia. The country on the coast of Asia Minor between Lycia and Cilicia; Side is a sea-port of Pamphylia.
Rhodes. The island lying south off the coast of Caria.
Phaselis. A city on the coast of Lycia.
Cos. An island lying off the coast of Caria.
Aradus. An island close to the Phoenician coast, nearly opposite the mouth of the Eleutherus (see xi. 7).
Gortyna. A town on the island of Crete.
Cyrene. The capital of Libya, the country lying to the west of Egypt.
The disordered enumeration of all these shows that the writer's knowledge of their geographical positions was extremely meagre.

35 hold fast [o] the inheritance [o] of our fathers. Nevertheless, as touching Joppa and Gazara which thou
demandest,—(though it was) they that did great harm among the people [n] and in our land [n]—we will
36 give a hundred talents for them.' And he [p] answered him not a word, but returned in a rage to the
king, and reported unto him these words, [n] and the glory of Simon, and all things whatsoever he had
seen [n]; and the king was exceeding wroth.
37, 38 But Tryphon embarked on board a ship, and fled to Orthosia. And the king appointed Cende-
39 baeus chief captain of the sea-coast, and gave him forces of foot [q] and horse [q]; and he commanded
him to encamp before Judaea; also [r] he commanded him [r] to build up Kedron, [r] and to fortify [s] the
40 gates [t] [r], and that he should fight against the people; but the king pursued Tryphon. And Cendebaeus came to Jamnia, [r] and began to provoke the people [r], and to invade Judaea, and to take [r] the
41 people [r] captive and to slay them. And he [u] built Kedron, and set horsemen there, and forces of
foot, to the end that, [v] issuing out, they might make outroads upon the ways of Judaea [v], according
as the king had commanded him.

XVI. 1–10. *Judas and John, the sons of Simon, defeat Cendebaeus.*

16 1, 2 And John went up from Gazara, and told Simon, his father, what Cendebaeus was doing. And
Simon called his two eldest [w] sons, Judas and John, and said unto them: 'I and my brethren and my
father's house have fought the battles of Israel [x] from our youth, even unto this very day [x]; and things
3 have prospered in our hands, [x] (so that we were able) to deliver Israel oftentimes [x]. But now I am
old, and ye moreover, [x] by (God's) [y] mercy [x], are of sufficient age [z]; be ye (then) instead of me [x] and
my brother, and go forth [x] and fight for our nation; [x] and let the help that is from Heaven be with
4 you [x].' And he [aa] chose [bb] out of the country [bb] twenty thousand men of war and horsemen; and they
5 went against Cendebaeus, and rested at Modin. And rising up in the morning, they went into the
plain, and, behold, a great host came to meet them, of footmen and horsemen; and there was
6 a brook betwixt them. And he encamped over against them, [x] he and his people; and he saw that

[o-o] our inheritance and (that) A [p] Athenobius T.R. [q-q] > V 93 [r-r] > 71 [s] to build up ℵ [t] cities A
[u] Cendebaeus Luc [v-v] they might fight Judaea 71

XVI. [w] > 71 [x x] > 71 [y] *expressed in* 𝔖luc [z] > 𝔖luc [aa] John Luc [bb-bb] > V 71

---

37. **Orthosia.** A town on the Phoenician coast, north of Tripolis; the name is preserved to the present day, the ruins of the ancient town being still called *Arthûsi*.

38. **Cendebaeus.** According to Schürer (*op. cit.* i. 1, p. 270) a name derived from Κάνδυβα, a town in Lycia, cp. Sidetes, from *Side* (see *v.* 1).

39. **Kedron.** Probably identical with Gederoth (Joshua xv. 41), the present Katra, south-west of Ekron, near Modin, according to xvi. 4 ff.

40. **Jamnia.** See note on iv. 15.

XVI. 2. **his two eldest sons.** A third, Mattathias, is mentioned in *v.* 14.

things have prospered in our hands. Cp. the Hebr. phrase הוֹשִׁיעַ יָד לְ 'to gain success for'.

3. **I am old.** Cp. Joshua xxiii. 2 זקנתי.

by (God's) mercy. ἐν τῷ ἐλέει, again the avoidance of the divine name which is characteristic of this book; cp. 'the help that is from Heaven' further on in this verse.

of sufficient age. Lit. 'sufficient in years'.

go forth and fight. According to Josephus (*Antiq.* XIII. vii. 3), Simon himself took the lead: '... Taking a resolution brisker than his age could well bear, he went like a young man to act as general of his army ...'; this is also borne out by the *vv.* that follow here, in spite of 'be ye instead of me' in this verse.

4. **he chose.** Logically 'Simon' is the subject; 'John' of the Lucianic MSS. (see critical note) was presumably inserted because of the words, 'I am old ...'.

out of the country. The point of these words is not quite clear (see critical note); the Jews had not yet had any idea of employing mercenaries, so that the words cannot be supposed to imply native-born soldiers as distinct from foreigners; nor could they have been new recruits, since they were 'men of war'. The MSS. which omit the words are perhaps justified in doing so.

horsemen. This is the first time mention is made of the Maccabees using horsemen, though their use in warfare was not new to the Jews (cp. Isa. xxxi. 1, xxxvi. 9; Hos. i. 7; Neh. ii. 9, &c.); that more use had not been made of them during the Maccabaean war was due to the method of warfare on the part of the Maccabaeans; it was more advantageous for them to adopt mountain warfare.

rested. Lit. 'slept', = 'passed the night', the Hebr. לוּן.

Modin. See note on ii. 1.

5. **they went into the plain.** Cp. Job xxxix. 10 (Sept.).

a great host. δύναμις πολλή, cp. Ps. lxxvii. 12 (Sept.).

to meet them. εἰς συνάντησιν αὐτοῖς, cp. the same phrase in Gen. xiv. 17 (Sept.).

a brook. See note on v. 37.

6. **he encamped.** See notes on *vv.* 3, 4.

his people. λαός is used in the sense of an army in Joshua x. 5 (Sept.) for the Hebrew מחנה.

the people were afraid to pass over the brook, so he passed over first [x]; and (when) the men saw him
7 (doing this), they passed over after him. And he divided the people, [cc] and (set) the horsemen in the
8 midst of the footmen, for the enemies horsemen were exceedingly numerous [cc]. And they sounded
with the [dd] trumpets; and Cendebaeus and his army were put to the rout, and there fell of them [ee]
9 many wounded to death; and they that were left fled to the stronghold. At that time was Judas,
John's brother, wounded; but John pursued after them, till he came to Kedron, [ff] which [Cendebaeus] [a]
10 had built [ff]. And they fled unto the towers that are in the fields of Azotus; and he burned it with
fire; and there fell of them about a thousand [b] men. And he returned to Judaea in peace.

XVI. 11–24. *Murder of Simon and his two sons, Mattathias and Judas, by Ptolemy; John Hyrcanus escapes.*

11 And Ptolemy the son of Abubus had been appointed captain [ff] for the plain [ff] of Jericho; and he
12, 13 had much silver and gold, for he was the high [c]-priest's son-in-law. [ff] And his heart was lifted up [ff],
and he was minded to make himself master of the country; and he took counsel deceitfully against
14 Simon and his sons, to make away with them. Now Simon was visiting the cities that were in the
country, and taking care for the good ordering of them. And he went down to Jericho, he himself
and Mattathias and Judas, [d] his sons [d], [e] in the one hundred and seventy-seventh year, in the eleventh
15 month, the same is the month Sebat [e]. And the son of Abubus received them deceitfully into the
little stronghold that is called Dok, [e] which he had built [e]; and he made them a great banquet; and
16 he hid men there. And when Simon and his sons had drunk freely [f], Ptolemy and they that were
with him rose up, and took their arms, and came upon Simon [e] into the banqueting hall [e], and slew
17 him and his two sons, and certain of his servants. [e] And he committed (thus) a great act of
18 treachery [g] [e], and recompensed evil for good. And Ptolemy wrote these things, and sent to the king,
that he should send him forces to aid (him), and that he should deliver to him their [h] country and the
19 cities. And he sent others to Gazara to make away with John; [e] and unto the captains of thousands
20 he sent letters to come unto him that he might give them silver and gold and gifts [e]. And others he
21 sent to take possession of Jerusalem, [e] and of the mount of the Temple [e]. And one [i] ran [k] before to
Gazara, and told [k] John [e] that his father and brethren had perished, 'and', (said he), 'he hath sent to

[cc–cc] > 71 [dd] + holy V T.R. [ee] it A (*in reference to the army*) > 71 [ff–ff] > 71 [a] they Luc 𝔖luc [b] two thousand ℵ V 71 three thousand Luc 𝔖luc [c] > V 55 [d–d] his brother ℵ* (his sons ℵ c.a) [e–e] > 71 [f] + and were merry 𝔖luc [g] a godless act A [h] the Luc 71 [i] > A 71 93 𝔖luc [k–k] *plur.* 93 𝔖luc

---

7. **the horsemen in the midst . . .** An unusual proceeding; Grimm cites an instance of the Romans having done so. The object here was two-fold; to accustom the horsemen to their new duties, and to avoid their meeting the full force of the enemy's cavalry, which was numerically superior.

8. **they sounded with . . .** Cp. Num. x. 8; the addition of ἱεραῖς in some MSS. is probably due to the mention of the priests in Num. x. 8, from which the phrase here seems to be borrowed; *οἱ ἱερεῖς σαλπιοῦσιν ἐν ταῖς σάλπιγξιν*, cp. 1 Chron. xv. 24 (Sept.).

the stronghold. i.e. Kedron, see xv. 39–41.

10. **they fled.** i.e. those of the enemy who had not been able to get into Kedron, and who had, therefore, been forced to continue their flight.

the fields of Azotus. i.e. the open country round the city. The 'towers' (מגדל) were used both for the defence of cities and for the protection of flocks; for the former use cp. 2 Kings xvii. 19, xviii. 8.

he burned it with fire. i.e. the city of Azotus; Jonathan had done this to Azotus ten years before (see x. 84), but it is not necessary to suppose that either then, or on this occasion, the city was wholly obliterated.

about a thousand men. See critical note.

11. **Ptolemy the son of Abubus.** He was the son-in-law of Simon, see below.

the plain of Jericho. ערבות יריחו Joshua v. 10, see also Sept. of this. The plain was 'seventy furlongs long, and twenty broad; wherein it (i.e. the fountain near Jericho) affords nourishment to those most excellent gardens that are thick set with trees' (Josephus, *Bell. Iud.* IV. viii. 3).

12. **the high-priest's son-in-law.** See further Josephus (*Antiq.* XIII. vii. 4, viii. 1).

13. **his heart was lifted up.** See note on i. 3.

14. **went down to Jericho.** For the phrase cp. Luke x. 30.

the one hundred and seventy-seventh year. i.e. 135 B.C.

the month Sebat. Properly Shebat (שבט); cp. Zech. i. 7. It corresponds approximately to February; the fifth civil and eleventh ecclesiastical month in the Jewish Calendar; the month, according to Jewish tradition, in which demons prevail.

15. **Dok.** Δώκ, Josephus (*Antiq.* XIII. viii. 1; *Bell. Iud.* I. ii. 3) calls it Δαγών. 'The name is still retained in that of the fountain *'Ain ed-Duk*, north of Jericho, on the border of the mountain land, in a position very suitable as the site of a fortress' (Schürer, *op. cit.* p. 271). Grimm says that *Duk* is mentioned as a mountain fortress lying between Jericho and Bethel, and belonging to the Templars; this was still standing in the thirteenth century.

16. **had drunk freely.** ἐμεθύσθη means that Simon was intoxicated cp. the murder of king Elah by Zimri under similar circumstances (1 Kings xvi. 9, 10).

17. **act of treachery.** See critical note. Cp. 2 Macc. xv. 10.

22 slay thee also [e].' And when he[1] heard (it), he was sore amazed; and he laid hands on the men [m] that
came to destroy [n] him [m], and slew [n] them; [o] for he perceived that they were seeking to destroy him [o].
23 And the rest of the acts of John, and of his wars, and of his valiant deeds [o] which he did [o], and of
24 the building of the walls which he built, and of his (other) deeds, behold they are written in the
chronicles of his high-priesthood, from the time that he was made high-priest after his father.

[1] John Luc m–m > 93 $\mathfrak{S}^{luc}$ n–n > V o o > 71

---

23. **acts.** Lit. 'words', but the Hebr. word דבר means 'act' as well; cp. 2 Sam. xi. 18 ἀπήγγειλε τῷ βασιλεῖ Δαβὶδ πάντας τοὺς λόγους τοῦ πολέμου.

the building of the walls. i.e. the walls of Jerusalem which had been broken down by Antiochus VII Sidetes (Josephus, *Antiq.* XIII. viii. 3).

24. **in the chronicles.** ἐπὶ βιβλίου ἡμερῶν; cp. the Hebrew name of the Books of Chronicles, דברי הימים, lit. 'the acts of the days'.

Grimm mentions that 'Sixtus Senensis (*Bibliotheca sancta*, lib. i, p. 39) declares that he saw in the library of Santes Pagninus in Lyons the manuscript of a very hebraic Greek book of the Maccabees, which embraced the history of thirty-one years (according to Josephus, *Antiq.* XIII. x. 7, Hyrcanus reigned this number of years), and which began with the words, καὶ μετὰ τὸ ἀποκτανθῆναι τὸν Σίμωνα ἐγενήθη Ἰωάννης ὁ υἱὸς αὐτοῦ ἱερεὺς ἀντ' αὐτοῦ; a book which, according to this description, must either have contained the chronicles here mentioned, or have been, at any rate, one which contained their substance. Unfortunately, soon after Sixtus Senensis had given this news to the world, the library in question was destroyed by fire'. Schürer (*op. cit.* ii. 3, p. 14) says regarding this manuscript: 'Judging from the enumeration of the contents as given by Sixtus, this book simply narrates *the history of John Hyrcanus*, and precisely as in Josephus (the same facts and in the same order). With regard to this he himself observes: "*Historiae* series et narratio eadem fere est quae apud Iosephum libro Antiquitatum decimo tertio; sed *stylus, hebraicis idiotismis abundans*, longe dispar." Consequently he ventures to conjecture that it may have been a Greek translation of the history of Hyrcanus mentioned at the end of the First Book of the Maccabees. Many modern writers have concurred in this conjecture. . . . But in view of the enumeration of the contents given by Sixtus, it seems to me there can hardly be a doubt that the book was simply a reproduction of Josephus, the style being changed perhaps for a purpose.'

THE SECOND BOOK OF MACCABEES

INTRODUCTION

§ 1. CONTENTS AND CHARACTERISTICS.

2 MACCABEES is the anonymous ἐπιτομή (ii. 26, 28) or digest of an earlier Maccabaean history which had been composed by a Hellenistic Jew called Jason of Cyrene. The writer condensed Jason's five books into one. It is unnecessary to hold that his statements to this effect are simply a literary device, as though he were a Jewish Defoe who thus attempted to gain the fictitious authority of age for his own composition (so e.g. Kosters in *Theolog. Tijdschrift*, 1878, 491 f., and Kamphausen). Had this been the case, the contents would have been more of a unity than they are, and the *lacunae* would have been fewer. Besides, more than once, the style (e.g. in xiii. 22 f.) suddenly corresponds to that of an historian who is hurriedly compressing as well as popularizing some earlier source. Upon the whole the materials, the contents, and the style of the book answer fairly to the writer's account of his own method and aims (in ii. 19–32, vi. 12–17, xv. 37–9). His work is an abridgement and at the same time more than an abridgement. He must have omitted large sections of Jason's treatise and summarized even what he took over, but, instead of preserving invariably either the language or the shape of his selections, he embellished the former to suit the popular taste and enlarged the latter, for the sake of edification, with pious amplifications of the miraculous element.

The outline of the epitome is thus characterized by a unity of religious feeling, rather than by any historical sequence. The introductory documents of i. 1–ii. 18, containing two letters, are followed by a naïve preface (ii. 19–32), after which the epitome proper begins, with five successive pauses (iii. 40, vii. 42, x. 9, xiii. 26, xv. 37, perhaps after Jason). The only formal interruption is a short passage upon the doctrine of retribution as the clue to Jewish history (vi. 12–17). Judas Maccabaeus comes on the scene in v. 27, and, once his story is resumed (in viii. 1 f.), it runs on to the end, the only digression being the highly-coloured tale of Antiochus' death (ix. 1–29; x. 1–8 resumes the narrative dropped at viii. 33). The epilogue (xv. 37–9) echoes the prologue. Indeed the aim of even the prefixed letters corresponds to the general purpose of the book, which is to magnify the two festivals of the Ḥanukka and Nicanor's day,[1] as the ceremonial glories which recall the heroism of Judas Maccabaeus.[2]

2 Maccabees is not a sequel to 1 Maccabees. It is, in Luther's words,[3] *a* second book upon the Maccabaean struggle, not *the* second book. As the period of its narrative (175–161 B.C.) coincides with part of 1 Maccabees, a comparison of the two books might be expected therefore to clear up the problem of their relative value, and furnish a standard for valuating the second. To some extent this expectation is realized. But critical opinion has swayed curiously between an undue depreciation of 2 Maccabees as an historical document and an exaggerated claim on its behalf. The former tendency is represented by modern critics like Willrich and (especially) Kosters; the latter by Niese (*Kritik der beiden Makkabäerbücher*, 1900), who not only succeeds in vindicating the trustworthiness of the book at several points, but attempts to prove that it is older and more authentic than 1 Maccabees—an attempt which has failed to carry conviction (cp. e.g. the articles of Lévi in *Revue des études juives*, 1901, 222–30, Abrahams in *Jewish Quarterly Review*, 1901, 508–19, Kamphausen in *Theolog. Literaturzeitung*, 1901, 287–90, and Wellhausen in *Nachrichten der kgl. Gesellsch. d. Wiss. zu Göttingen*, 1905, pp. 117–63). The parallel narratives of the two books are as follow:—

[1] On the improbability of any connexion between the Purim festival of the book of Esther and Nicanor's day see L. B. Paton's 'Esther' (*Intern. Crit. Comm.*), pp. 78 f.

[2] Cp. Hochfeld in *ZATW*, 1902, pp. 264–84, who emphasizes, after Geiger, the Pharisaic interests and methods of the writer.

[3] 'Man wolt es denn heissen ein anders buch und nicht das ander buch Maccabeorum, alium vel alienum scilicet non secundum.'

II MACCABEES

1 Macc.	2 Macc.
Accession of Antiochus Epiphanes: i. 10.	iv. 7: accession of Antiochus Epiphanes.
	iv. 7–8: sacerdotal intrigues of Jason.
Gymnasium, &c., introduced in Jerusalem: i. 11–15.	iv. 9–17: gymnasium, &c., introduced in Jerusalem.
	iv. 18–22: fresh intrigues of Jason.
	v. 23–50: high-priesthood of Menelaus.
Expedition of Antiochus against Egypt: i. 16–19.	v. 1: expedition[1] of Antiochus against Egypt.
	v. 2–10: intrigues and death of Jason.
Antiochus plunders Jerusalem: i. 20–8.	v. 11–21: Antiochus plunders Jerusalem.
His royal commissioner completes secularization of Jerusalem: i. 29 f.	v. 22 f.: Apollonius, his deputy, completes the work.
The Maccabees leave Jerusalem: ii. 1 f.	v. 27: Judas Maccabaeus and his followers leave Jerusalem.
Hellenizing decree of Antiochus brought by messengers to Jerusalem: temple profaned and pagan customs established: i. 41–59.	vi. 1–9: Athenian commissioner of Antiochus has temple profaned and pagan customs established.
Jewish mothers and their children[2] killed: i. 60–1.	vi. 10: two Jewish mothers and their children[2] killed.
Jews massacred for keeping sabbath: i. 29–38.	vi. 11: Jews burnt for keeping sabbath.
Jews martyred for refusing to eat swine's flesh: i. 62 f.	vi. 18–31: Eleazar martyred for refusing to eat swine's flesh.
	vii. 1–42: mother and seven sons martyred for refusing to eat swine's flesh.[3]
Mattathias and his sons refuse to sacrifice: ii. 15–26.	
Mattathias organizes a revolt: ii. 27 f.	
Judas Maccabaeus succeeds Mattathias: ii. 49–70.	
Successful revolt of Judas: iii. 1–9.	viii. 1–7: successful revolt of Judas.
He defeats Apollonius and Seron: iii. 10–26.	
Lysias commissioned by Antiochus to exterminate the Jews: iii. 27 f.	
Lysias commissions Ptolemaeus, Nicanor, and Gorgias to devastate Judaea: iii. 38 f.	viii. 8 f.: Ptolemaeus, Nicanor, and Gorgias commissioned to devastate Judaea.
Slave-dealers join expedition: iii. 41.	viii. 10–11: slave-dealers join expedition.
Mustering of Jews: iii. 42–60.	viii. 12–23*a*: mustering of Jews.
Withdrawal of some: iii. 55–6.	viii. 12 f.: withdrawal of some.
Defeat of Gorgias: iv. 1–25.	
	viii. 23*b*–29: defeat of Nicanor.
	viii. 30: defeat of Timotheus and Bacchides.
Defeat of Lysias[4]: iv. 26–35.	
Entry into Jerusalem: iv. 36–7.	viii. 31 f.: entry into Jerusalem.
	ix. 1–28: miserable death of Antiochus.
Purification of temple: iv. 38–51.	x. 1–5: purification of temple.
Celebration of Ḥanukka-feast: iv. 52–61.	x. 5 f.: celebration of Ḥanukka-feast.
	x. 9–11: accession of Antiochus Eupator.
Judas subdues Idumaeans, Baeanites, Ammonites under Timotheus: v. 1–8.	x. 15 f.: Judas[5] defeats Idumaeans, Timotheus, &c.
Judas subdues pagans under Timotheus in Gilead, Galilee, &c.: v. 9–54.	
Gorgias defeats Joseph and Azarias outside Jamnia: v. 55–62.	

[1] This invasion of Egypt by Antiochus is not 'second' to the preliminary march south in iv. 21 (Bevan, *House of Seleucus*, ii. 297–8), but the second of the campaigns against Egypt (cp. Dan. xi. 25 f., which agrees better with 1 Maccabees), the first of which (170 B.C.) was really followed by the attack upon Jerusalem.

[2] The question of circumcision.

[3] The earliest martyrology—an important tradition preserved by Jason, though the presence of the king at the tortures, even if the scene is transferred from Jerusalem to Antioch, is dramatic rather than historical.

[4] The epitomist (xi. 1–12) not only transfers this to the next reign but embellishes it in order to glorify the success of Judas. On the other hand, he dates the death of Antiochus too early. Whether the one error led to the other, and, if so, which was primary, it is impossible to determine.

[5] These wars on the neighbours of the Jews may have lasted longer than 1 Maccabees implies, and it is even probable that some details which the epitomist has supplied in xii. 1 f. are to be credited, but Niese (pp. 55–60) is not justified in proceeding to set aside the fact that they began before the death of Antiochus. At his death the king had only heard (1 Macc. vi. 5–8) of the Jewish rebellion as recorded up to iv. 61, but this does not imply that the Jews had not already embroiled themselves with the surrounding tribes. The motive assigned in 1 Macc. v. 1 for the rising of these tribes is perfectly natural, and is not to be explained as a mere unhistorical echo of Neh. iv. 1.

1 Macc.	2 Macc.
Judas subdues Edomites and Philistines: v. 63–8.	
Miserable death of Antiochus: vi. 1–16.	
Accession of Antiochus Eupator: vi. 17.	
Judas attacks citadel of Jerusalem: vi. 18 f.	
	xi. 1–12: defeat of Lysias.
	xi. 13 f.: Lysias arranges terms of peace.
	xii. 1 f.: Judas punishes Joppa and Jamnia, &c., defeats pagans under Timotheus[1] in Gilead, &c.
Lysias and Eupator invade Judaea: vi. 28–54.	xiii. 1 f.: Lysias and Eupator invade Judaea.[2]
Lysias concludes a treaty of peace: vi. 55–63.	xiii. 22 f.: treaty of peace.
Accession of Demetrius I: vii. 1–4.	xiv. 1–2: accession of Demetrius I.
Alcimus installed high-priest by Bacchides: vii. 5–22.	xiv. 3 f.: Alcimus to be re-instated high-priest by Nicanor.[3]
Nicanor's mission, attempt to seize Judas by treachery, threats against temple, defeat and death: vii. 23–47.	xiv. 15–xv. 35: Nicanor's mission, friendliness to Judas, attempt to seize him, threats against temple, defeat and death.
Institution of feast: vii. 48–50.	xv. 36: institution of feast.

A broad survey of the two documents puts it beyond reasonable doubt that upon religious questions like the resurrection of the body (e. g. vii. 11, xiv. 46) and the prohibition of warfare on the sabbath (viii. 27, xv. 1 f.), 1 Maccabees is decidedly more primitive than 2 Maccabees. It is probably the latter interest, among other things, which led the anti-Hasmonean epitomist to omit all reference to Mattathias (cp. 1 Macc. ii. 39 f.; also ii. 49 with its absence of any allusion to the resurrection). Niese (pp. 45 f.) attempts to turn the force of this argument against the accuracy and impartiality of 2 Maccabees by ascribing the introduction and prominence of Mattathias in 1 Maccabees to tendency—i. e. to the desire of glorifying the later Hasmoneans through Simon his son. But the probabilities are against this theory. It is incredible that Jewish traditions went wrong in glorifying the rôle of Mattathias; 'the Rabbinic tradition (which is independent of both books of the Maccabees) recognized Mattathias as the principal figure in the struggle for religious liberty' (Abrahams, *op. cit.* 516), and this consideration corroborates the impression that it is the omission of Mattathias in the epitome, not his rôle in 1 Maccabees, which is secondary.

The chronological disorder of 2 Maccabees, as has been already noted, further tells against the hypothesis of its superiority to 1 Maccabees. The first part of the epitome closes with the feast of the purification (x. 1–8), the second with the feast of Nicanor's day (xv. 36). The former feast is apparently[4] dated after the death of Antiochus Epiphanes; but there is really no sound reason for doubting that 1 Maccabees has preserved the correct tradition in the reverse order of these events (iv. 36 f., vi. 1 f.) as well as in its description of the manner in which Antiochus died, while the entire account of Lysias' subsequent actions (in 2 Macc. xi. 1 f.) shows that the writer, or the sources on which he relied, must have confused the two defeats of Lysias. It is not possible, with Niese, to establish the historical inferiority of 1 Maccabees on the basis of these incidents.

The historicity of the Roman correspondence in xi. 34 f. is also supposed to be corroborated not only by the fact that, in keeping with contemporary usage, the cognomen is omitted (Niese, 31), but by the likelihood that the Romans would no more hesitate to negotiate with the Jews against Demetrius at this juncture than they hesitated to deal with Timarchus who was in arms against the same opponent (Diod. Sic. xxxi. 27 a; cp. Niese 63 f., 88 f., and, for a more cautious statement, Laqueur, *op. cit.*, pp. 30 f.). Still, these considerations do not amount to more than the possibility that such documents (as e. g. the letters from Antiochus III in Josephus, *Antiq.* XII. iii) were composed at an early period by some Alexandrian writer who possessed good knowledge of the situation. At most they may reflect an historical nucleus, but in their present form the epistles of xi. 16 f. are almost certainly manufactured documents, like those in i–ii.

Here, as elsewhere, Niese's arguments and researches prove that the sources (i. e. especially Jason) used by the epitomist evince a knowledge of the age which is hardly likely to have been possessed

[1] An instance of the compiler's carelessness: he had already killed Timotheus (x. 37).

[2] Even Niese (pp. 76 f.) admits that 1 Maccabees at this point is plainly superior to the self-contradictions and patriotic evasions of 2 Maccabees. It is the inferior character of xii f. which has led some critics (from Grotius onwards) to suspect that Jason is no longer used.

[3] 2 Maccabees, fusing the missions of Bacchides and Nicanor, obliterates the real course of events, but gives a not incredible account of the latter's policy and temper.

[4] Laqueur (*Kritische Untersuchungen zum zweiten Makkabäerbuch*, 1904, pp. 30 f.), arguing that the Antiochus of xi. 22 f. was originally Antiochus Epiphanes, not Antiochus V, proposes to transfer x. 1–8 and xi to their true position before viii. 30 f. But this is a *tour de force* of criticism.

by a Jewish writer after the second century B.C. There are vivid touches which are more than circumstantial, and independent notices which point upon the whole to the information of eye-witnesses and contemporaries behind some of Jason's narratives. Upon the other hand, 2 Maccabees exaggerates numbers generally (cp. e. g. xiv. 1 with 1 Macc. vii. 1) and horrors invariably, abounds in confused and contradictory notices (cp. e.g. on i. 17, ix. 18, xi. 5, xiii. 23), and is repeatedly unhistorical (see on iv. 21, ix. 2, 9, x. 11, xiii. 22, xv. 33), besides containing some references (e.g. to the vicarious suffering of the martyrs, vi. 28, and to sacrifices for the dead, xii. 43) which at any rate suggest that it is less primitive than its predecessor.[1] The result is that Niese must be pronounced more successful in establishing afresh the historicity of some details which are peculiar to 2 Maccabees, in opposition to ultra-scepticism, than in depreciating 1 Maccabees in favour of the general trustworthiness of the epitome. The epitomist, in fact, has the artistic temperament as well as the pious aim of edification; on both grounds he is naturally careless of the exact accuracy which an historian pursues, and satisfied if he can produce his effects in a picturesque manner. The relative position of the two Maccabaean books may be, therefore, summed up in Wellhausen's verdict (*Geschichte*[4], p. 246): 'Niese's criticism of the two Maccabean books has taught me a great deal, but it has not convinced me that the second book is older than the first and that it deserves preference. . . . We must not indeed look at everything through the spectacles of the first book. Nevertheless we have no alternative but to make it our basis.'

§ 2. MSS. and Versions.

Second[2] Maccabees (Μακκαβαίων B, Machabaeorum liber secundus), like 1 Maccabees, is preserved in A and V, as well as in a number of minuscules. Probably owing to the influence of Athanasius, who objected to the Maccabaean books, it was omitted from the Ethiopic version (Rahlfs, *ZATW*, 1908, pp. 63–4). The Syriac version is paraphrastic and of less value than in the case of 1 Maccabees. On the other hand, in addition to the pre-Hieronymian Old Latin or Vulgate version, there is a version reproduced in Codex Ambrosianus E 76 inf. (cp. A. Peyron's *Ciceronis orationum pro Scauro, pro Tullio et in Clodium fragmenta inedita*, 1824, pp. 73–117), and yet another in Codex Complutensis (cp. S. Berger's *Notices et Extraits de la Bibliothèque Nationale*, 1895, pp. 147–52). Four fragments (iv. 39–44, 46–v. 2, v. 3–14, x. 12–26, x. 27–xi. 1) recently published by Mercati (*Revue Biblique*, 1902, 184–211, 'Frammenti Urbinati d' un' antica versione latina del libro II de' Maccabei editi ed illustrati') seem to be connected with the Peyron-text; iii. 13–iv. 4 and iv. 10–14, which also occur in a fragmentary Breslau MS. (eighth or ninth century), are now published by W. Molsdorf in *ZATW* (1904, pp. 240–50). It is thus from the Latin versions, as representing varied types, that most help is to be gained in the determination of the text. Still, the extant Greek text has been so badly preserved at certain points, that neither the aid of the versions nor of conjecture is sufficient to yield any sure confidence that we can have a text before us which approximates to the original.

§ 3. Date.

The date of the epitome, and inferentially of Jason, cannot be fixed except within approximate limits. It has indeed been argued by Niese (see below) that, as i. 1–ii. 18 represent a composition of the author in 125–124 B.C. (i. 7, 10 a), this will date the entire epitome. But the integrity of the introductory section must be abandoned (see below); i. 10 a only dates (or professes to date) the particular letter to which it is appended; and, even on Niese's showing, the loose connexion between the introduction and ii. 19 f. would invalidate any argument from the date of the former to that of the latter. Furthermore, even supposing that 1 Macc. xvi. 23–4 formed part of the original work, these verses do not necessarily presuppose a date subsequent to the death of Hyrcanus (cp. Torrey in *Ency. Bib.* 2859 f., as against Niese on the one hand and Destinon, Wellhausen, and Abrahams on the other), so that 1 Maccabees need not be assigned to a period (after 104 B.C.) subsequent to the supposed date of the epitome (when the latter, or its source, is placed shortly after the last event which it records). The utmost that can be said, with any degree of certainty, as opposed to Niese on the one hand and to Willrich (*Judaica*, 1900, pp. 131 f.) on the other, is that the *terminus ad quem* is fixed by the use of 2 Maccabees not only in Fourth Maccabees and the Epistle to the Hebrews (especially xi. 35 f.) but in Philo (*quod omnis probus liber*, § 13), while the *terminus a quo* for its source is 161 B.C., the date of Nicanor's defeat by Judas (xv. 1–36)—although, if xv. 36 is an

[1] 'The Pharisaic author of 2 Maccabees may scatter angel appearances and surprising wonders over his romantic work. But the pious contemporaries . . . of the Maccabean brethren were content with the providential wonders of history' (Cheyne, *Origin of Psalter*, 344 f.).

[2] The first occurrence of the title is in Eus. *Praep. Euangel.* viii. 9 ἡ δευτέρα τῶν Μακκαβαίων.

allusion to the book of Esther (ix. 21), the source of the epitome can hardly have been written earlier than *c.* 130 B.C., while the epitome itself must be later than 125 B.C. Jason's work may be dated, therefore, roughly after 130 B.C.; the epitome probably falls not later than the first half of the first century B.C. The internal evidence, as compared with that of 1 Maccabees, offers remarkably few reliable clues to its distance from the period of its subject. The predilection for the supernatural in the shape of apparitions (*ἐπιφάνειαι*, ii. 21), prodigies, and visions, vouchsafed from heaven to its favourites in need, is neither unexampled in Greek historians—indeed the apparition of the two youths (iii. 6 f.) recalls the cult of the Dioscuri—nor is it necessarily any proof of late composition. Legends spring up early on such soil, especially at some distance from the scene, and popular tales of the miraculous (so far as they go back to the sources) may be contemporaneous in the main with the events which they embellish (cp. Niese, pp. 34 f.). But the matter-of-fact air which pervades 1 Maccabees, in spite of its tendencies and omissions, invests it with superiority as an historical document to 2 Maccabees, and superiority here is practically equivalent to priority.

There is no obvious reason for conjecturing (so e.g. Kosters recently) that the latter is deliberately and primarily an attack on the former, although there is perhaps as little for suspecting that the epitomist (not Jason) was not familiar with the earlier document.[1] In any case, he had a fine, if uncritical, enthusiasm for the heroes (private as well as public) and the principles of the Maccabaean rising; more specifically, as his pages prove, he was an Alexandrian Jew, a rhetorical adherent of the Pharisees, who wrote, probably during the third or fourth generation afterwards, in order to foster reverence for the temple in Jerusalem and also strictness in the observance of the Maccabaean festivals as a bond of union between the Jews of Palestine and Egypt. If the anti-Hasmonean bias of the book is emphasized, a more precise *terminus a quo* for its composition might be found *c.* 106 B.C., when the Pharisees broke with the Hasmoneans (so Hochfeld). But this is not inevitable; 2 Maccabees might have been compiled shortly before that date, under stress of the growing antagonism, as naturally as after it.

§ 4. Integrity and Composite Nature of the Text.

2 Maccabees, says Luther in his brief preface, appears to be 'zusammen geflickt aus vielen büchern'. This is evident (*a*) in i. 1–ii. 18, where some critics, like Grätz ('Das Sendschreiben der Palästiner an die ägyptisch-judäischen Gemeinden wegen der Feier der Tempelweihe', in *Monatsschrift für Geschichte und Wiss. des Judentums*, 1877, pp. 1–16, 49–72), N. Brüll ('Das Sendschreiben der Palästiner an die Alexandriner', in *Jahrbücher für jüdische Geschichte und Literatur*, 1887, pp. 30–40), and B. Niese (*op. cit.* pp. 10 f.), have contended that there is only one letter, opening properly at i. 10 after the introductory preface of i. 1–9, while others, e.g. Bruston (*Zeitschrift für die alttest. Wissenschaft*, 1890, pp. 110 f.), Willrich (*Juden und Griechen vor der makkab. Erhebung*, 1895, pp. 76 f.), and Laqueur (*op. cit.* pp. 52 f.), have detected no fewer than three (in i. 1–7 a, 7 b–10 a, 10 b–ii. 18); the majority, however, rightly distinguish only two, in i. 1–10 a and i. 10 b–ii. 18, although opinion is still seriously divided upon the precise extent, date, and trustworthiness of both (cp. generally the older pamphlets by F. Schlünkes: *Epistulae quae secundo Machabaeorum libro cap. I. vv* 1–9 *legitur explicatio*, 1844, *Difficiliorum epistulae quae II Mach. I.* 10 *ad II.* 18 *legitur locorum explicatio*, 1847, with Kosters' essay in *Theol. Tijdschrift*, 1898, 68 f., C. Torrey's article in *Zeitschrift für die alttestam. Wissenschaft*, 1900, pp. 225–42, and H. Herkenne's full monograph, in Bardenhewer's *Biblische Studien*, viii. 4, on *Die Briefe zu Beginn des Zweiten Makkabäerbuches*, 1904). It is fair to start from the likelihood that, just as in xi. 21, 33, 38, the date of the first letter is placed at the end (i. 10 a). The date in ver. 6 (i.e. 144–143 B.C.) refers to a previous communication, to which the writer (or editor) awkwardly refers in order to lend verisimilitude to his present production as one item of a correspondence between the Palestinian and Egyptian Jews. The date assigned to this later epistle is 124 B.C. Those who join i. 10 a to the following letter are involved in the double awkwardness not only of beginning the letter with the date but of placing a full stop after *ὑμῖν* in i. 7 (so Torrey), or else (cp. D. M. Sluys, *De Maccabaeorum libris I et II quaestiones*, 1904, pp. 1–79) of taking i. 2–6 as an interpolation. The second letter apparently comes from a different source; it is undated, except generally after the death of Antiochus Epiphanes, and the writers precede the receivers in the address (i. 10 b, c). But the object is the same (i. 18 a, ii. 16 f. = i. 9)—to bring out the historical and religious significance of the Maccabaean feast of the Ḥanukka. Both epistles, as they stand, are specimens of the Alexandrian epistolography which was fond of producing such documents for purpose of edification. At the same time, the language of i. 18 a (*μέλλοντες ἄγειν κτλ*) and of ii. 16 (*μέλλοντες οὖν ἄγειν κτλ*) is

[1] So e.g. Montet (*Essai sur les Origines des Partis Saducéen et Pharisien*, 1883, pp. 13 f.).

a watermark of interpolation, the intervening paragraphs being a legendary insertion based on the tradition of x. 3 and perhaps on Epist. Jerem. 4–6. The retrospective allusion to Judas in ii. 14 is incompatible with the position assigned him in i. 10 b, but it fits in with the aim of setting Judas within the great succession of Moses, Solomon, Jeremiah, and Nehemiah; he ranks with Nehemiah as a collector of the sacred scriptures, and with the others as a transmitter of the holy fire which was essential to the sacrifices of the temple.

Whether authentic or not, these letters did not belong to the Jason-source, as the position of the preface (ii. 19–32) and the discrepancy between the two accounts of the death of Antiochus (i. 12 f. and ix. 1 f.) are enough to show, but there is scarcely sufficient evidence to indicate decisively whether both came from the same pen, and if so, whether it was the pen of the epitomist or of another. As the insertion (i. 18 b–ii. 15) is in all likelihood his own work, the two letters which form the framework may have been found by him in some other source and prefixed to his abridgement proper, instead of being placed chronologically in the narrative. It is a further question whether he translated one (the second, according to Ewald's *History of the Jews*, Eng. Tr. v, pp. 467 f.; the first, according to Schlünkes) or both (so e.g. Grätz, Brüll, and Torrey) from the original Hebrew (Aramaic). Upon the whole, it seems difficult to give a satisfactory answer in the negative, with any positive evidence, to such a query, although the rest of the book was undoubtedly written in Greek ('Machabaeorum . . . secundus Graecus est; quod ex ipsa quoque φράσει probari potest', Jerome's *Prologus Galeatus*).

(*b*) This opens up the intricate problem of the sources which lay before the epitomist. Without refusing to deny that he had access to a Jason-source, we may conjecture that not only in i. 1–ii. 18 but in the body of the epitome (e.g. x. 32 f. and xii. 2 f.) he occasionally employed traditions and even documents from other quarters,[1] e.g. (i. 10) from the famous Alexandrian Jew Aristobulus (cp. Schürer's *Geschichte*, iii, pp. 512 f.). The conjecture, however, cannot be worked out with any approach to definiteness. Büchler, in his important *Die Tobiaden u. die Oniaden im II Makkabäerbuche*, &c. (1899), pp. 277 f., 396–8, and Laqueur (*op. cit.* pp. 72–87) have recently elaborated precise theories of the use made respectively of Jason and of a supposed second source, involving frequent transpositions of material. The patent variations of style may lend some colour to the hypothesis that Jason is specially employed e.g. in viii. 1 f., and that throughout the writer is often an interpolator (e.g. in iii–v, cf. Büchler, pp. 277 f.) as well as an epitomizer. But as the available data (even e.g. in iv. 5–6 and viii. 20) are purely internal, they seldom enable us to check such theories, and the possibility—amounting to a probability—that Jason's large work already contained a variety of oral traditions counterbalances any attempt to run literary analysis into a confident scheme of results. Unfortunately we possess no independent clue to the character and scope of Jason's treatise. While the second book of τὰ Μακκαβαϊκά is an abridgement, it is not on the same footing as e.g. the *periochae* of the lost books of Livy. 2 Maccabees is neither a bare synopsis nor the summary of a summary; it is a literary composition, whose materials were selected from the original work of Jason. The latter's work has not survived, however, and even his personality is in dispute. He has been precariously identified (Herzfeld: *Geschichte des Volkes Israel*, 1855, 445 f.) with the Jason of 1 Macc. viii. 17 (= the Judas[2] of 2 Macc. i. 10, ii. 14), and even more arbitrarily his Jewish nature has been denied (Sluys, *op. cit.* pp. 74 f.). The name (Ιασων Κυρηναιος) has been found in an Egyptian temple of Thothmes III (cp. Sayce in *Revue des études grecques*, 1894, p. 297), apparently dating from the third century B.C., but, while this does not necessarily tell against a Jew, the individual need not, on the other hand, be the author of the epitomist's source. His connexion with Cyrene would suggest a more accurate knowledge of Palestinian sites and affairs than the epitome reveals; its references to the latter are less reliable than in the case of the Syrian realm.

§ 5. Authorship.

While the relation of the book to 1 Maccabees resembles on the whole that of the books of Chronicles to the books of Kings, in so far as a definitely religious pragmatism controls the epitomist, the affinities of the latter are with the Pharisaic type of Jewish piety. He lays emphasis e.g. upon legal praxis, the divine providence, recompense, the temple cultus, the sabbath, angels, and the resurrection. The last-named feature is bound up with the martyr-stories (cpp. vi–vii) which have floated the book into wide popularity throughout Christianity as well as throughout Judaism. They are told with a detailed ghastliness which jars on modern taste. Probably 'the

[1] It is impossible to ascertain whether an extra-Biblical touch like viii. 19 f. was due to the author or to Jason.

[2] Attempts have often been made to identify this Judas not with Judas Maccabaeus but with some other Judas (so e.g. Ewald and Niese), or to emend the text into τῶν Ἰουδαίων or Ἰουδαίας (Syr., so e.g. Torrey), or Ἰούδας Ἀριστόβουλος Ὀνίᾳ (Sluys), but in vain (cp. Grimm 36–7, Herkenne 65).

stories had already clothed themselves for the writer in a halo of legend, and he tricks them out in that poor rhetoric, that stifled literary jargon, which was the curse of third-rate authors in the Hellenistic world; but if you can penetrate through this repellent medium, you can still touch an anguish that was once real and quivering' (E. Bevan, *Jerusalem under the High Priests*, 1904, p. 83). The anonymous author belongs to Alexandrian rather than to Palestinian Judaism, but beyond this general inference it is not possible to pass with any confidence to theories, for example, like the ingenious but unconvincing guess of Büchler (*op. cit.* pp. 396 f.), that the author or final editor was a Hellenistic Jew who reversed the polemic of the original (written by a Samaritan in Egypt) against the temple in Jerusalem.

§ 6. Influence on Later Literature.

(*a*) The use of 2 Maccabees in Philo[1] and in 4 Maccabees (see above, § 3) is clearer than the evidence for Josephus' acquaintance with it; none of the latter's relevant passages (*Antiq.* XII. v. 1 = 2 Macc. iv. 1 f., XII. v. 5 = 2 Macc. vi. 2, XII. ix. 7 = 2 Macc. xiii. 3–8, XII. x. 1 = 2 Macc. xiv. 1) makes such a conjecture necessary. More is to be said for the hypothesis that the epitome is echoed in the *Assumptio Mosis* (cp. v. 1–4 = 2 Macc. iv. 11 f., v. 8, &c.; viii. 3 f. = 2 Macc. vi. 4 f., 11, 28, &c.; ix. 1 f. = 2 Macc. vi. 18 f.; ix. 6 = 2 Macc. vi. 11, vii. 2, x. 6, &c.). The edifying narratives of the martyrs in especial led to haggadic developments in Jewish literature (cp. Zunz, *Die gottesdienstlichen Vorträge der Juden*, pp. 130 f.), and also (*b*) in early Christianity where the Maccabaean martyrs were eventually canonized[2] and accorded a yearly festival (August 1st) in the Greek and Latin churches (cp. Maas in *Monatsschrift für Geschichte u. Wiss. des Judenthums*, 1900, pp. 145–56). This tallies with the early and widespread diffusion of the book, from the period of the epistle to the Hebrews down to Clement of Alexandria, Hippolytus, Origen, Chrysostom, and Jerome. Portions of it are read in the Roman Breviary (for October).

§ 7. Theology.

The later popularity of 2 Maccabees is due as much to the support found in it by the Roman Church for dogmas like prayers for the dead (xii. 43, 45) and the intercession of the saints (xv. 11–16) as to the martyr-stories or the miraculous and legendary incidents (ἐπιφάνειαι). Otherwise,[3] the theological ideas resemble those of the Pharisaic school during the latter half of the second century B.C. The doctrine of retribution and chastening is naturally worked out with particular care (vi. 12–17). The worst punishment is to be left severely alone by God, as is the case with pagan nations; the Jews, on the contrary, are chastened and thus prevented from lapsing into the excesses of sin which draw down upon their neighbours (individuals as well as nations) the shattering penalties of God even in this life (cp. e.g. iv. 38, v. 9–10, ix. 5–6, xiii. 4 f., xv. 32 f.). The sufferings of the martyrs, again, although due to the sins of their nation, avail to expiate God's just anger (vii. 33–8) on their fellows. After death, only the righteous rise, and rise with their bodies (vii. 11, 22 f., xiv. 46) to life eternal, i.e. apparently to participation in the messianic kingdom (vii. 29, 33, 37, xiv. 15) on earth. The similarity of this conception to that of Eth. En. lxxxiii–xc, where the scene of the messianic kingdom is also on earth, suggests that 2 Maccabees, in its eschatological outlook at this point, 'belongs essentially to the second century' (R. H. Charles, *Eschatology*, 1899, p. 230). The outlook on the future, as might be expected from the nature of the subject, has nothing of the catholic hope which dominated the best of the O.T. prophets.

§ 8. Special Literature.

In addition to essays and monographs already cited: (*a*) critical editions of text in editions of LXX by Holmes and Parsons (*Vetus Testamentum Graece*, v, 1827), Fritzsche (*Libri Apocryphi Vet. Testam. Graece*, 1871), Tischendorf (*Vet. Test. Graece*, 6th ed., 1880), and H. B. Swete (*The Old Testament in Greek*, iii, 1894); (*b*) annotated editions by Grotius (*Annotationes in Vet. Testamentum*, 1644), Grimm (*Kurzgefasstes exeget. Handbuch zu den Apocryphen des AT*, 1857), Keil (Leipzig, 1857), Reuss (*La Bible*, vii, 1879), E. C. Bissell (*The Apocrypha of the O.T.*, 1880, New York, pp. 550-614), W. R. Churton (*Canon. and Uncan. Scriptures*, pp. 481 f.), Rawlinson (*Speaker's Comm.*, 1888, London), Kamphausen (Kautzsch's *Apokryphen u. Pseudepigraphen des AT*, 1901), and Knabenbauer (in *Cursus sacr. s. Comment. in Vet. Test.*, 1908); (*c*) general literature, Westcott in Smith's *Dict. of Bible* (ii. 174–8), Welte in *Wetzer und Welte's Kirchenlexicon* (viii. 418–22), André's *Les Apocryphes de l'Ancien Testament* (Florence, 1903, pp. 86–115), Schürer's *Geschichte des Jüdischen Volkes*[4] (iii, 1909, pp. 482–9), Fairweather in Hastings' *Dict. of Bible* (iii. 189–92), Torrey in *Encycl. Biblica* (2869–79), C. F. Kent in *Israel's Historical and Biographical Narratives* (pp. 38 f., 387 f.), Bertholet in Budde's *Geschichte d. althebräischen Literatur* (pp. 345–50), and F. Bechtel in *Catholic Encyclopaedia* (ix. 497–8).

[1] Cp. Lucius, *Der Essenismus* (1881), pp. 36–9.

[2] Cp. the Acts of the Christian Felicitas and her Seven Sons, a variation of the same theme. The scene of the Maccabaean martyrdom was transferred from Jerusalem to Antioch, where a basilica was erected in their honour.

[3] The book's angelology is allied to a belief in dreams (xv. 11).

THE SECOND BOOK OF MACCABEES

I. 1–10 a. *First document.*

1 1 To the brethren, the Jews in Egypt, greeting. The brethren, the Jews in Jerusalem and
2 throughout the land of Judaea, wish you perfect peace; yea, may God do good unto you, and
3 remember his covenant with Abraham and Isaac and Jacob, his faithful servants; may he give you
4 all a heart to worship him and do his pleasure with hearty courage and a willing soul; may he give
5 you an open heart for his law and for his statutes, and make peace, and hearken to your supplica-
6 tions; may he be reconciled to you, and not forsake you in time of evil. Such, then, are our
7 prayers for you in this place. In the reign of Demetrius, in the hundred threescore and ninth year,
we the Jews have already written unto you in the extreme tribulation that came upon us during
these years, from the time that Jason and his company revolted from the holy land and the kingdom,
8 setting the porch on fire and shedding innocent blood: but we besought the Lord, and were heard;
we offered sacrifice and made the meal offering, we lighted the lamps, and set forth the shewbread.
9, 10 See that ye keep the days of the feast of tabernacles in the month Chislev. Written in the hundred
fourscore and eighth year.

I. 10 b—II. 18. *Second document.*

They that are in Jerusalem and they that are in Judaea and the senate and Judas, unto
Aristobulus, king Ptolemy's teacher, who is also of the stock of the anointed priests, and unto the
11 Jews that are in Egypt, send greeting and health. Having been saved by God out of great perils,
12 we render great thanks, as befits us to thank **One who arrayeth himself** against a king. For He
13 flung away into Persia those who had arrayed themselves against the holy city. For when the leader
arrived, with a force that seemed irresistible, they were cut to pieces in the temple of Nanaea by
14 the treachery of Nanaea's priests. Antiochus, on the pretext of marrying her, came into the place,
he and his Friends who were with him, that they might take a great part of the treasures by way
15 of dowry; but when the priests of the Nanaeon had set the treasures forth, and he had passed
with a small company inside the wall of the precincts, they shut to the temple when Antiochus had
16 entered: then opening the secret door in the panelled ceiling, they threw stones and struck down
17 the leader, and hewing the company in pieces threw their heads to those who were outside. Blessed
18 for all things be our God who gave the impious doers for a prey. Whereas we are now about to
celebrate the purification of the temple in the month Chislev, on the five and twentieth day, we

I. 7. **already written**, i.e. referring to some previous communication. The alternative (see *Introd.* § 4) is to take the perfect (γεγράφαμεν) in the sense of the epistolary aorist (ἐγράψαμεν, ii. 16), and render: *we write*, as if the context dated the present letter.

extreme tribulation (ἐν τῇ θλίψει καὶ ἐν τῇ ἀκμῇ), i.e. that under Demetrius (see 1 Macc. xi. 53). The hendiadys of the exaggeration is too obvious to justify Herkenne's (pp. 42–4) conjecture of ἀλκῇ (= warlike attack) for ἀκμῇ (cp. iv. 13).

the kingdom, i.e. the theocracy; Jason's apostasy is described in iv. 13 f. The following words are a loose summary of the outrages subsequent to Jason's movement, and of the restoration under Judas (1 Macc. iv. 38, 50 f.).

9. **see that ye keep**: i.e. in Egypt, as we do in the Holy Land; or, by sending representatives to Jerusalem. The Maccabaean festival of the temple's reconsecration was called either τὰ ἐγκαίνια (cp. John x. 22) or ἡ σκηνοπηγία (John vii. 2) τοῦ Χασελεύ, being celebrated for the same time and almost on the same lines (cp. 2 Macc. x. 6–7) as the feast of tabernacles, only during Chislev (December) instead of during Tisri (October).

11. **arrayeth himself.** Reading, with Bruston and Herkenne, παρατασσομένῳ (cp. Zech. xiv. 3, LXX) for παρατασσόμενοι.

13. **in the temple of Nanaea.** i.e. the temple in Elymais of Artemis or Aphroditê (cp. Polyb. xxxi. 2; Josephus, *Ant.* XII. ix. 1, and Appian. *Syr.* 66) as identified with the Persian goddess Anaea (Anaitis), or of the Babylonian Nanâ.

14. **take . . . by way of dowry.** For this diplomatic trick see Seneca's *Orat. Suas.* 1, where Antony agrees to marry Athenê at Athens for a dowry of a thousand talents. Antiochus is said to have tried a similar device at Hierapolis in Syria.

17. **gave the impious doers for a prey.** In 187 B.C. Antiochus III lost his life in an attempt to plunder a shrine of Bel in the Elymaean hills, and Antiochus VII (Sidetes) perished, in 129 B.C., in battle against the Parthians; ἡσσώμενος ἑαυτὸν ἔκτεινεν (Appian. *Syr.* 68). The writer of the letter may have been so barren in imagination as to have embellished the death of this king (so recently Torrey and Niese) with legendary traits drawn from the fate of Antiochus Epiphanes, but it is the latter who is (erroneously) meant.

deem it our duty to inform you, that you too may keep the feast of tabernacles.—Now ⟨concerning⟩
the fire, on the occasion of Nehemiah offering sacrifices, after he had built both the temple and the
19 altar (, you must know that) when our fathers were to be led into the land of Persia, the godly priests
of that time took some of the fire of the altar, and hid it secretly in the hollow of a sort of empty
20 cistern, wherein they made it sure, so that the place was unknown to all men. Well, after many
years, when it pleased God, Nehemiah was sent on a mission by the king of Persia, and he sent in
quest of the fire the descendants of the priests who had hid it. When they announced that they had
21 found no fire, but thick liquid, he commanded them to draw out some and bring it to him: and when
the sacrifices had been duly placed (on the altar), Nehemiah commanded the priests to sprinkle the
22 liquid both on the wood and on the sacrifices. When this was done, after some time had elapsed
and the sun, formerly hidden in clouds, had shone out, there was kindled a great blaze, so that all
23 men marvelled. And the priests offered prayer, while the sacrifice was being consumed,—priests
24 and all, Jonathan leading and the rest saying it after him, as did Nehemiah. The following was the
prayer: O Lord, Lord God, the creator of all things, who art terrible and strong and righteous and
25 merciful, who alone art King and gracious, who alone suppliest every need, who alone art righteous
and almighty and eternal, thou that savest Israel out of all evil, who madest the fathers thine elect,
26 and didst sanctify them: accept this sacrifice for all thy people Israel, guard thine own Portion,
27 and consecrate it. Gather together our dispersion, set at liberty them that are in bondage among
the heathen, look upon them that are despised and abhorred, and let the heathen know that thou
28, 29 art our God. Torment them that oppress us and in arrogancy shamefully treat us. Plant thy
30, 31 people in thy holy place, even as Moses said. Then the priests sang the hymns. Now as soon as
the sacrifice was consumed, Nehemiah ordered the rest of the liquid to be poured on large stones.
32 And when this was done, a flame was kindled; but, when the light from the altar shone over against
33 it, it was extinguished. And when the matter became known, and it was told the king of the
Persians, that, in the place where the captive priests had hid the fire, there had appeared the liquid with
34 which Nehemiah and his company purified the sacrifice, then the king, after verifying the matter,
35 had the place made a sacred enclosure. And the king exchanged gifts with those in his favour.
36 Nehemiah and his company called this thing Nephthar, which is by interpretation, Cleansing; but
most people call it Nephthai.

2 1 It is also found in the records, that Jeremiah the prophet commanded them that were carried
2 away to take some of the fire, as has been already noted: and how that the prophet charged them
that were carried away, after giving them the law, that they should not forget the statutes of the
Lord, neither be led astray in their minds, when they saw images of gold and silver, and the adorn-
3 ment thereof. And with other such words exhorted he them, that the law should not depart from
4 their heart. This also was in the writing, that the prophet, being warned by God, commanded the
tabernacle and ark to accompany him, and that he went away to the mountain which Moses had

18. **the feast of tabernacles.** Several critics (from Schlünkes and Grimm to Kosters and Kamphausen) supply *τὰς ἡμέρας* before *τῆς σκηνοπηγίας*, while Herkenne adds *τά*. Something like *τοῦ ἀνευρεθέντος* or *δοθέντος* or *φανέντος* is usually supposed, also, to have dropped out after *πυρός*. But if (as the Syriac version suggests) *περί* is read for *καί*, the text may be rendered as above (so Torrey). Here the long interpolation (i. 18 b–ii. 15) begins.

built. The *v. l.* *οἰκονομήσας* (125, so Herkenne) for *οἰκοδομήσας* is an attempt to get rid of the unhistorical statement about Nehemiah, whose prestige is exaggerated in another direction in ii. 13.

20. **announced.** The meaningless *ἡμῖν* (*to us*) between *διεσάφησαν* and *μή* is rightly omitted by Rawlinson (with 64, 93, *Syr.*) as the result of dittography (*ησαν* repeated from *διεσάφησαν* and then amended into *ἡμῖν*).

26. **thine own Portion.** Deut. xxxii. 9.

29. Cp. Baruch ii. 28–35.

31. **to be poured on.** This involves the reading of *καταχεῖν* (A, vg.) for *κατέχειν* or *κατασχεῖν*, and either the addition of *ἐπί* (or *εἰς*) before *λίθους* or the construction of *καταχεῖν* with a double accusative, but there is no more satisfactory explanation of a corrupt and obscure passage.

33–5. The writer appeals to the testimony of the pagan monarch, whose respectful attitude to the phenomenon of the fire—as befitted a Persian—adds glory to this Jewish portent.

35. **exchanged gifts,** &c. Reading, with V, *ἐχαρίζετο* after *οἷς*—a naïve Oriental method of expressing pleasure at some happy occurrence (cp. Esth. ix. 19, 22; Apoc. John xi. 10).

36. **Nephthai.** An inflammable oil, like the modern naphtha, is in the writer's mind, but the etymology of the word is beyond recovery. The writer equates N. with *καθαρισμός*, and this is the point of the legend, which connects the discovery of the fiery liquid with the purification of the temple (*v.* 18). The least improbable line of explanation is that which connects the word with the Persian *naptar; naptar apanm* was a Zend epithet for the sacred elemental water (*arduisur*), which possessed purifying qualities (cp. Benfey and Stern's *Ueber die Monatsnamen einiger alter Völker*, 1836, pp. 204 f.).

II. 1. Legend had no scruple in transforming a prophet who was radically indifferent, if not hostile, to the ritual of the temple into a pious conservative (cp. further, xv. 14).

5 climbed to view the inheritance of God. On reaching it Jeremiah found a cavernous chamber, in
which he placed the tabernacle, and the ark, and the altar of incense; and he made fast the door.
6, 7 And some of his followers drew near in order to mark the road, but they could not find it. Now
when Jeremiah came to know this, he blamed them, saying, Unknown shall the spot be until God
8 gather the people again together, and mercy come; then indeed shall the Lord disclose these things,
and the glory of the Lord shall be seen, even the Cloud, as in the days of Moses it was visible, and
9 as when Solomon prayed that the Place might be consecrated with solemn splendour. It was also
10 narrated how he, in his wisdom, sacrificed at the consecration and completion of the temple; as
Moses prayed to the Lord, and fire descended from heaven to consume the sacrifice, so Solomon also
11 prayed, and the fire descended and burned up the holocaust; [and Moses said, Because the sin
12 offering had not been eaten, it was consumed in like manner with the rest;] and Solomon kept the
eight days.

13 These things were narrated also in the archives or memoirs of Nehemiah; as well as how he
founded a library and collected the books about the kings and the prophets, and the books of David,
14 and letters of kings about sacred gifts. Even so did Judas collect for us all the writings which had
15 been scattered owing to the outbreak of war. They are still with us. So, if you need them, send
some messengers to fetch them for you.

16 Seeing therefore that we are about to keep the purification, we write thus to you. You will do well,
17 then, to keep the days (of the festival). Now God, who saved all his people, and restored to all the
18 heritage, and the kingdom, and the priesthood, and the hallowing, even as he promised through the
law,—in God have we hope, that he will speedily have mercy upon us, and gather us together from
under the (wide) heaven to the holy place: for he did deliver us out of great evils, and did purify the
place.

II. 19–32. *The preface of the epitomist.*

19 Now the things concerning Judas Maccabaeus and his brothers, and the purification of the great
20 temple, and the dedication of the altar, and further the wars against Antiochus Epiphanes and
21 Eupator his son, and the heavenly apparitions vouchsafed to those that vied with one another in
manful deeds for the religion of the Jews—so that, in spite of their small numbers, they plundered
22 the whole country, and routed the barbarian hordes, and regained the temple renowned all the world
over, and freed the city, and restored the laws which were on the verge of abolition, since the Lord
23 showed favour graciously to them: (all) this, recounted by Jason in five books, we will try to compress
24 into a single volume. For, in view of the flood of statistics and the difficulties presented by the mass
25 of material to those who desire to go into the narratives of the history, we have aimed at attracting
those who are fond of reading, at smoothing the path for those who like to memorize their facts, and
26 at being of some service to our readers in general. As for ourselves, we have not found this self-
imposed task of abridging to be a light business. On the contrary, we have sweated and sat up late
27 over it—just as there is no lack of work for any one who has to superintend a banquet and look after
the interests of others. Still, to reap the gratitude of many, we will cheerfully undertake this
28 toilsome labour; leaving the historian to investigate details, we will exert ourselves to prepare
29 an epitome upon the usual lines. For as the masterbuilder of a new house has to look after
the entire edifice, while the decorator who undertakes to inlay and paint it has only to look out
30 what is suitable for embellishing the house, so, methinks, is it with us. To enter into details and
31 general discussions and elaborate researches is the business of the original historian; on the other
hand, any one who simply recasts the material must be allowed to aim at conciseness of expression
and to eschew any thoroughgoing treatment of the subject.

32 Well now, let us begin the story. We have no more to add, by way of preface; for it is truly
stupid to expatiate in introducing a history and then cut short the history itself.

10. **fire descended . . . sacrifice.** A midrashic expansion of Lev. ix. 23–4. The Solomonic legend follows the midrash of 2 Chron. vii. 1 in preference to 1 Kings viii. 62 f., and a precedent for the Maccabaean ceremonial is artificially found in the tradition of 1 Kings viii. 66 (2 Chron. vii. 8). The origin of the incoherent touch in verse 11 must have been also a midrashic paraphrase of Lev. x. 16 f.

13. **about sacred gifts,** i.e. about presents made to the temple. A specimen is preserved in Ezra vii. 12 f. The interest of 2 Maccabees in the temple comes out incidentally even in this allusion; such letters are ranked alongside of the sacred scriptures in Nehemiah's library. The next verse reflects the companion interest in the prestige of Judas Maccabaeus.

18. Cp. Exod. xix. 6; Deut. xxx. 1–10.

21. **plundered the whole country.** In the sense in which Cromwell's troops swept over England during the Civil War.

27. **superintend a banquet.** For the duties of the ἀρχιτρίκλινος (?) see Sir. xxxii. 1–2; John ii. 8–9.

28. **exert ourselves.** Reading διαπονοῦντες for ἀτονοῦντες.

III. 1–39. *The miraculous discomfiture of Seleucus and Heliodorus in their attack upon the temple at Jerusalem.*

3 1 When the holy city was inhabited in unbroken peace, and the laws were kept right strictly,
2 owing to the godliness of Onias the high-priest and his hatred of wickedness, it came to pass that
even kings themselves did honour the Place and glorify the temple with the noblest presents;
3 so much so that Seleucus the king of Asia actually defrayed, out of his own revenues, all the expenses
4 connected with the ritual of the sacrifices. But a certain Benjamite, Simon, who had been appointed
5 warden of the temple, fell out with the high-priest over the management of the city-market. Unable
to get the better of Onias, he betook himself to Apollonius of **Tarsus**, then governor of Coelesyria
6 and Phoenicia, and informed him that the treasury in Jerusalem was full of such untold sums
of money that the wealth of the funds was past counting; they did not belong, he said, to the
7 accounts of the sacrifices, and they could be got into the hands of the king. So when Apollonius
met the king, he informed him of the money which had been mentioned to him, and the king
chose his chancellor, Heliodorus, and dispatched him with orders to carry out the removal of
8 the aforesaid money. Heliodorus at once started on his journey, giving out that he intended to
visit the cities of Coelesyria and Phoenicia, though his real object was to execute the king's design.
9 On reaching Jerusalem, where he was courteously welcomed by the high-priest and the city, he
submitted the information which had been given him, and explained why he had come, inquiring
10 further if this information was really true. The high-priest pointed out to him that there were
11 deposits belonging to widows and orphans, besides monies belonging to Hyrcanus, the son of Tobias,
a man of extremely high position (by no means what that impious Simon had alleged), and that in
12 all there were four hundred talents of silver and two hundred of gold; it was utterly impossible, he
added, that injury should be inflicted on those who had put their trust in the sacredness of the Place
13 and in the majesty and inviolable sanctity of the temple, honoured over all the world. Heliodorus
had his orders from the king, however, and he replied that in any case these monies must be
confiscated for the king's treasury.
14 So, having appointed a day, he went in to superintend the investigation of the treasure. And
15 there was no small distress throughout the whole city. The priests, arrayed in their priestly robes,
flung themselves before the altar, and called to heaven on him who had appointed the law regarding
16 deposits, beseeching him to preserve these treasures safe for the depositors. And no one could look
at the mien of the high-priest without feeling a pang of heart. His countenance and changed colour
17 betrayed the anguish of his soul. For terror and a shuddering of the body had come over the
18 man, which plainly showed to the onlookers the grief that was at his heart. As for the people in
the houses, they flocked out with a rush to join in common supplication that the Place should not be
19 dishonoured. The married women, girt under their breasts with sackcloth, thronged the streets, while
the maidens who were kept in ward ran together, some to the porticoes, others to the walls, and
20 others to look out at the windows; but all, stretching forth their hands toward heaven, made their
21 solemn supplication. One could not but pity the populace all prostrate with one accord, and the
anxiety of the high-priest in his sore distress.
22 Meantime, however, as they were invoking the all-powerful Lord to keep the deposits safe and
23, 24 sure for the depositors, Heliodorus proceeded to execute his orders. But when he and his guards
had got as far as the front of the treasury, the Sovereign of spirits and of all authority prepared
a great apparition, so that all who had presumed to enter were stricken with dismay at the power
25 of God and fainted with sheer terror. For there appeared to them a horse with a terrible rider, and

III. 4. **warden of the temple.** Whether this office corresponded to that of the sĕgan (or στρατηγὸς τοῦ ἱεροῦ) or of the γαζοφύλαξ (Josephus, *Antiq.* XX. iii. 11, &c.) depends largely on the meaning assigned to τῆς κατὰ τὴν πόλιν ἀγορανομίας (the *v. l.* παρανομίας being an attempt to smooth out the difficulty). According to Büchler (*op. cit.* pp. 33 f.; cp. Bevan, *House of Seleucus*, ii. 163) Simon the Tobiad, as στρατηγός, was also ἀρχιερεύς in the sense that he exercised a certain political control of the temple affairs. This identification of Simon with the Simon of Josephus, *Antiq.* XII. iv. 10, is preferable to the alternative identification of Onias II (*Antiq.* XII. iv. 1–10) with the Onias of 2 Macc. iii (so e.g. Schlatter, Willrich, and Guthe in *Encycl. Biblica*, 3504 f.).

5. **of Tarsus.** Adopting Hort's convincing conjecture of Θαρσέα for the Θρασαίου of the MSS.

7. **Heliodorus.** Probably the Heliodorus of the Delian inscriptions (cp. Deissmann's *Bible Studies*, pp. 303–7). The payment of the annual instalment of the war indemnity to Rome was one of the causes which made the government press for money in any likely quarter. Simon's information suggested a welcome and unexpected source of revenue.

9. **and.** Inserting καὶ (V) after ἀρχιερέως.

11. **Hyrcanus.** Perhaps the Jewish Alcibiades of Josephus, *Antiq.* XII. iv. 2–11, whom Wellhausen sees behind Zech. xi. 4–17.

24. **Sovereign of spirits.** This is the same expression as Lord of spirits in 1 Enoch xxxvii. 2, &c.

presumed to enter. The implied insolence (cp. v. 15) is described in 1 Macc. i. 21. In the following account, the first horseman (ver. 25) seems to belong to a different tradition from that of the other two (26 f.). The latter do all the work. Similar traces of fusion occur in ix. 6 f., as if the author had embroidered his source with outside matter.

it was decked in magnificent trappings, and rushing fiercely forward it struck at Heliodorus with its
26 forefeet. And the rider seemed to be armed with a golden panoply. Two youths also appeared
before Heliodorus, remarkable for their strength, gloriously handsome, and splendidly arrayed, who
27 stood by him on either side, and scourged him unceasingly, inflicting on him many sore stripes. He
dropped suddenly to the ground, and thick darkness wrapped him round, but (his guards) caught him
28 up and put him into a litter, and carried him away—carried him who had just entered the aforesaid
treasury with a large retinue and all his guard, but who was now absolutely helpless—recognizing
29 clearly the sovereign might of God. And so he had been laid prostrate, deprived of speech owing to
30 God's strong hand, bereft of all hope and succour. But the Jews blessed the Lord who had done
marvellous honour to his own place; and the temple, which a little before had been full of terror and
alarm, was filled with joy and gladness, thanks to the manifestation of the all-powerful Lord.
31 Now some of Heliodorus' intimate friends at once besought Onias to call upon the Most High,
32 and so grant life to him, as he lay quite at the last gasp. The high-priest suspected that the king
might imagine the Jews had perpetrated some foul play against Heliodorus, and he offered a sacrifice
33 for the recovery of the man. But as the high-priest was offering the sacrifice of propitiation, the same
young men appeared again to Heliodorus, arrayed in the same robes; and they stood and said, Give
Onias the high-priest hearty thanks, since it is for his sake that the Lord has granted thee thy life;
34 and do thou, since thou hast been scourged from heaven, publish abroad to all men the sovereign
35 majesty of God. And when they had spoken these words, they vanished out of sight. So Heliodorus
offered sacrifice to the Lord and vowed very great vows to him who had preserved his life, and, after
36 taking a friendly farewell of Onias, he returned with his army to the king, testifying to all men the
37 deeds of the supreme God which he had witnessed with his own eyes. And when the king asked
Heliodorus what sort of person would be suitable for another mission to Jerusalem, he said, If thou
38 hast any enemy or conspirator against the state, send him thither, and thou shalt get him back well
scourged—supposing he escapes with his life; for the Place is really haunted by some power of God.
39 He who dwells in heaven above has his eye upon that Place and defends it, smiting and destroying
those who approach it for ill ends.

III. 40—IV. 22. *Intrigues of Simon and Jason over the high-priesthood.*

40 Such was the history of Heliodorus and the preservation of the treasury. But the aforesaid
4 1 Simon, who had informed about the money and betrayed his country, proceeded to slander Onias,
alleging that it was he who had maltreated Heliodorus and who had contrived the whole mischief.
2 He dared to accuse of conspiracy the very man who had proved the benefactor of the city, and the
guardian of his fellow-countrymen, and a zealot for the laws! And when the feud between them
3 went to such a pitch that one of Simon's trusted followers actually committed several murders, Onias,
4 recognizing the danger of the contention, and observing that Apollonius, **the son of Menestheus**, as
5 governor of Coelesyria and Phoenicia, was fanning Simon's malice, betook himself to the king—not
that he went about to accuse his fellow-citizens, but simply with a view to the good of all the people,
6 both public and private; for he saw that, unless the king intervened and interested himself, it was
impossible for the State to be at peace, nor would Simon abandon his insensate attempt.
7 But when Seleucus died, and Antiochus, who was called Epiphanes, succeeded to the kingdom,
8 Jason the brother of Onias supplanted his brother in the high-priesthood, promising in a petition to
9 the king three hundred and threescore talents of silver, besides eighty talents from another fund; in
addition to which he undertook to pay a hundred and fifty more, if he was commissioned to set up
10 a gymnasium and ephebeum and to register the Jerusalemites as citizens of Antioch. And when
the king had given his assent, Jason at once exercised his influence in order to bring over his fellow-
11 countrymen to Greek ways of life. Setting aside the royal ordinances of special favour to the Jews,
obtained by John the father of Eupolemus who had gone as envoy to the Romans to secure their
friendship and alliance, and seeking to overthrow the lawful modes of life, he introduced new customs
12 forbidden by the law: he deliberately established a gymnasium under the citadel itself, and made

28. **recognizing.** Reading ἐπεγνωκότες, with the majority of MSS., instead of ἐπεγνωκότα.

IV. 4. **Menestheus.** Reading Μενεσθέως, Hort's certain emendation of μαίνεσθαι ἕως or ὡς. Cp. ii. 21; Apollonius was naturally exasperated at the miscarriage of his little plot.

7, 8. **Jason . . . promising,** &c. If Josephus is correct, however, the charge of simony is undeserved; Jason succeeded to his brother's position, as Onias died leaving only an infant son (cp. *Antiq.* XII. v. 1).

9. **to register . . . as citizens of Antioch.** The coveted title of 'Antiochenes' (cp. Schürer, *Gesch. jüd. Volkes*[4], ii. 166–7), i.e. 'loyalists' (to the Seleucid dynasty and policy), carried with it certain privileges (cp. ver. 19). The cognate promise (ix. 15) to confer on the Jews the privileges of Athenian citizens is true to the Hellenistic and Athenian proclivities of Antiochus (Niese, pp. 29–30), who probably tried to atticize his Antiochene subjects.

11. See 1 Macc. viii. 17–32.

13 the noblest of the young men wear the petasus. And to such a height did the passion for Greek
fashions rise, and the influx of foreign customs, thanks to the surpassing impiety of that godless
14 Jason—no high-priest he!—that the priests were no longer interested in the services of the altar, but
despising the sanctuary, and neglecting the sacrifices, they hurried to take part in the unlawful
15 displays held in the palaestra after the quoit-throwing had been announced—thus setting at naught
16 what their fathers honoured and esteeming the glories of the Greeks above all else. Hence sore
distress befell them; the very men for whose customs they were so keen and whom they desired
17 to be like in every detail, became their foes and punished them. For it is no light matter to act
impiously against the laws of God; time will show that.
18 Now games, held every five years, were being celebrated at Tyre, in the presence of the king,
19 and the vile Jason sent sacred envoys who were citizens of Antioch to represent Jerusalem, with
three hundred drachmas of silver for the sacrifice of Heracles. The very bearers, however, judged
20 that the money ought not to be spent on a sacrifice, but devoted to some other purpose, and, thanks
to them, it went to fit out the triremes.
21 Now when Apollonius the son of Menestheus was sent to Egypt to attend the enthronement
of king Ptolemy Philometor, Antiochus, on learning that the latter was ill-disposed to him, proceeded
22 to take precautions for the security of his realm. Thus he visited Joppa, and travelled on to
Jerusalem, where he had a splendid reception from Jason and the city, and was brought in with
blazing torches and acclamation. Thereafter, he and his army marched down into Phoenicia.

IV. 23–50. *Intrigues of Menelaus.*

23 Now after a space of three years Jason sent Menelaus, the aforesaid Simon's brother, to convey the
24 money to the king and to remind him of some matters which required attention. But Menelaus got
into favour with the king, whom he extolled with an air of impressive authority, and secured the high-
25 priesthood for himself, outbidding Jason by three hundred talents of silver. On receiving the royal
mandate, he appeared in Jerusalem, possessed of no quality which entitled him to the high-priesthood,
26 but with the passions of a cruel tyrant and the rage of a wild beast. So Jason, who had supplanted
his brother, was in turn supplanted by another man, and driven as a fugitive into the country of the
27 Ammonites. Menelaus secured the position, but he failed to pay any of the money which he had
28 promised to the king, although Sostratus the governor of the citadel demanded it. As the latter
29 was responsible for collecting the revenue, the king summoned both men before him; Menelaus left
his brother Lysimachus to act as his deputy in the high-priesthood, while Sostratus left (as his
deputy) Crates, the viceroy of Cyprus.
30 At this juncture, it came to pass that the citizens of Tarsus and Mallus raised an insurrection,
31 because they were to be assigned as a present to Antiochis, the king's mistress; so the king went
off hurriedly (to Cilicia) to settle matters, leaving Andronicus, a man of high rank, to act as his
32 deputy. Then Menelaus supposed he had got a favourable opportunity, so he presented Andronicus
with some golden vessels which he had stolen from the temple;—others he had already sold to Tyre
33 and the surrounding cities. On ascertaining the truth of this, Onias sharply censured him, withdrawing
34 for safety into the sanctuary of Daphne, close to Antioch. Whereupon Menelaus took Andronicus
aside and exhorted him to kill Onias. So Andronicus went to Onias, gave him pledges by guile and
also his right hand with oaths (of friendship), and persuaded him, despite his suspicions, to come out of
35 the sanctuary. He then **killed** him at once, regardless of justice. This made not only the Jews but

12. **the petasus,** i.e. a broad-brimmed felt hat, which, as the mark of Hermes, was the badge of the *palaestra*. The otiose ὑποτάσσων of V probably arose from dittography with the following ὑπὸ πέτασον.

16. For this idea of the punishment fitting the crime see ver. 38 (= Herod. iii. 64), v. 9–10, viii. 33, ix. 6, xiii. 8, xv. 32, Wisd. xi. 16, Test. Gad v. 10.

18. The celebration of games, in imitation of the Olympic festival and the Panathenaea, was an important part of the Hellenizing policy (cp. vi. 7). For the games held by Alexander the Great at Tyre see Arrian ii. 24. 6, iii. 6. 1.

20. **thanks to them.** Reading, with V, τῶν παρακομιζόντων, instead of τῶν παρόντων.

21. **Antiochus, on learning that the latter was ill-disposed,** &c. Apollonius, the representative of Antiochus at the enthronement (πρωτοκλισία or πρωτοκλησία = the ἀνακλητήρια of Polybius xxviii. 12. 8, τὰ νομιζόμενα γίνεσθαι τοῖς βασιλεῦσιν ὅταν εἰς ἡλικίαν ἔλθωσιν) of the young Ptolemy, evidently reported to his master that a move was on foot to regain Coelesyria for Egypt. Antiochus took the initiative by concentrating his forces in Phoenicia. The writer, however, merely narrates the episode for the purpose of branding Jason's servility. In the following episode (30–8), either he or his source must be assumed to have coloured and shaped the death of Onias from the story of prince Seleucus' murder at the hands of Andronicus (so Willrich's *Juden und Griechen*, pp. 86 f., 120 f., and Wellhausen's *Geschichte*[3], pp. 243 f.), even though the murder of Onias is taken (as e.g. by Niese and Guthe) to be historical.

29. **deputy.** In the semi-technical sense of διάδοχος, the Egyptian court-title (cp. ver. 31 and xiv. 26). As Cyprus belonged to the Ptolemies, Crates can only have been viceroy of the island during the later and brief occupation by Antiochus. The phrase is therefore proleptic.

34. **pledges.** Reading πίστεις (62, so Niese) for πεισθείς, with δεξιὰς θεὶς μεθ' ὅρκων, and ἀπέκτεινεν (so Niese after vg. and $\mathfrak{S}$) for παρέκλεισεν.

36 many people of other nationalities indignant and angry over the unjust murder of the man. So
when the king returned from the regions of Cilicia, the Jews of the capital (with the support of the
37 Greeks who also detested the crime) complained to him about the illegal murder of Onias. Antiochus
was heartily sorry about it, and was moved to pity and tears for the dead man's sober and well-
38 ordered life; inflamed with passion, he at once had Andronicus stripped of his purple robe, and
led, with rent under-garments, all round the city to the very spot where he had committed the
outrage upon Onias; there he had the murderer dispatched, the Lord rendering to him the punishment he had deserved.
39 Now when many acts of sacrilege had been committed in the city by Lysimachus, with the
connivance of Menelaus, the report of these spread abroad throughout the country, till the people rose
against Lysimachus; for by this time a large number of gold vessels had been sold in all directions.
40 But when the people rose in a frenzy of rage, Lysimachus armed about three thousand men and
took the offensive with a bold charge, led by a certain Auranus, a man well up in mad folly no less than
41 in years. On realizing that Lysimachus was attacking them, however, some of the people caught
up stones, others logs of wood, and some snatched handfuls of ashes that lay near, flinging them all
42 pell-mell upon Lysimachus and his troops. In this way they wounded many, felled some to the
ground, and routed the whole band, slaying the sacrilegious robber himself beside the treasury.
43, 44 In connexion with this affair, proceedings were taken against Menelaus, and when the king
45 reached Tyre, three men sent by the senate laid their accusation before him. Menelaus felt that all
was now over with him, but he promised a large sum of money to Ptolemy the son of Dorymenes,
46 in order to get the king talked over. So Ptolemy took the king aside into a gallery, as though to
47 get some fresh air, and induced him to change his mind, the result being that he acquitted Menelaus,
who was responsible for all the trouble, and condemned to death the hapless trio, who would have
48 been discharged as innocent, even had they pled before Scythians. This unjust punishment was
49 inflicted instantly upon these spokesmen for Israel's city and folk and sacred vessels; which moved
50 some Tyrians, who hated the crime, to provide magnificent obsequies for them. Menelaus, however,
still remained in power, thanks to the covetousness of the authorities, and, waxing more and more
vicious, he proved a great plotter against his fellow-citizens.

V. 1–27. *Profanation of temple and oppression of Jews by Antiochus Epiphanes.*

5 1, 2 Now about this time Antiochus made his second inroad into Egypt. And it so befell that
throughout all the city of Jerusalem for almost forty days horsemen were seen charging in mid-air,
3 wearing robes inwrought with gold, armed with lances, and arrayed in troops: swords flashing,
squadrons of horse in array, assaults and charges repeated from one side and another, shields shaken,
spears massed together, darts hurtling to and fro, the sheen of golden trappings, and corselets of all
4 kinds. Which made all men pray that the apparition might betoken good.
5 Now a false rumour got abroad that Antiochus had died. Whereupon Jason took not less
than a thousand men, and made a sudden attack on the city; the troops stationed on the walls were
6 routed, and, as the city was now practically captured, Menelaus took refuge in the citadel, while
Jason proceeded to slaughter his fellow-citizens without mercy, reckless of the fact that to get any
advantage over kinsfolk is the worst kind of disadvantage, and imagining to himself that he was winning
7 trophies from foes and not from fellow-countrymen. He failed to secure the place of power,
however; and in the end he reaped only shame from his conspiracy, and had to pass over again as
8 a fugitive into the country of the Ammonites. As for the end of his wretched career—imprisoned
under Aretas the Arabian prince, flying from city to city, pursued by all men, hated as an apostate
from the laws, and loathed as a butcher of his country and his fellow-citizens, he was expelled into
9 Egypt. He who had driven so many into exile, died himself in exile, crossing over to the Lace-
daemonians, with the idea of finding shelter there among kinsfolk. He who had flung out many

40. **Auranus.** The variant reading 'Tyrannus' (Τυράννου, V; cp. Acts xix. 9) is more likely to have arisen from the uncommon Αὐράνου (A, 55, 74, 106) than vice versa. The latter, even when read as Αὑράνου, cannot mean 'homo in Auranitide', which would be Αὐρανίτιος or Αὐρανιτίτης. Nor is there any connexion between this assassin's name and Eleazar's title of Avaran (Αὐαράν) or the 'stabber' (?) in 1 Macc. ii. 5.

V. 8. **imprisoned.** Owing to the compressed style of this passage, which recapitulates generally the closing adventures of Jason, the conjectural reading ἐγκληθείς (= arraigned; so read many editors from Luther and Grotius to Grimm), instead of ἐγκλεισθείς (cp. Nestle's *Septuaginta-Studien*, iv, p. 22), is plausible, but the lack of connexion in the epitome here is enough to explain how Jason could be described as fleeing from city to city after being a prisoner. Probably ἔτυχεν goes with ἐγκλεισθείς (cp. iv. 32), and πέρας with κακῆς ἀναστροφῆς. The easier *v. l.* ἔλαβεν (V) enables πέρας to be taken not in an absolute construction but in close connexion with the verb.

9. **kinsfolk.** Cp. 1 Macc. xii. 21; Josephus, *Wars*, i. 26. 1. On the origin of the legend see Büchler, *op. cit.*, pp. 126 f. H. Winckler (*Altorient. Forschungen*, ii. 3. 565 f.) takes the Maccabaean references as editorial additions based on a misunderstanding of the original כתים.

a corpse to lie unburied had none to mourn for him, nor had he a funeral of any kind or place in the
11 sepulchre of his fathers. Now when tidings of what had happened reached the king, he thought
12 Judaea was in revolt. He therefore started from Egypt in a fury, stormed the city, and commanded
his soldiers to cut down without mercy any one they met, and to slay those who sheltered in their
13 houses. So there was a massacre of young and old, an extermination of boys, women, and children,
14 a slaughter of virgins and infants. In the short space of three days eighty thousand were destroyed,
15 forty thousand of them in close combat, and as many again were sold into slavery. Not content
with this, he dared to enter the most holy temple on earth, under the guidance of Menelaus, who
16 proved himself a traitor both to the laws and to his country; he laid polluted hands on the sacred
vessels, and swept off with his profane hands what other kings had dedicated to enhance the glory and
17 honour of the Place. Uplifted in spirit, Antiochus did not consider that it was on account of the sins
of those who dwelt in the city that the Sovereign Lord was provoked to anger for a little while; hence
18 His indifference to the Place. Had they not been involved in so many sins, this fellow would have
fared like Heliodorus, who was sent by king Seleucus to pry into the treasury—he would have been
19 scourged as soon as he pressed forward, and turned back from his presumption. But the Lord did not
20 choose the nation for the sake of the Place; he chose the Place for the sake of the nation. And so
the Place, after partaking in the calamities that befell the nation, shared afterwards in its prosperity;
forsaken in the wrath of the Almighty, it was restored again in full glory when the great Sovereign
became reconciled.
21 Antiochus, then, carried off from the temple eighteen hundred talents and hurried away to
Antioch, thinking in his arrogance to make the land navigable and the sea passable by foot—so
22 uplifted was he in heart. He also left governors behind him to ill-treat the Jewish people: at
Jerusalem, Philip, a Phrygian by race, whose disposition was more barbarous than that of his
23 master; at Gerizim, Andronicus; and, besides these, Menelaus, who lorded it worst of them all
24 over the citizens. And in malice against the Jews he sent the Mysian commander Apollonius with an
army of two and twenty thousand, under orders to slay all those that were of full age and to sell
25 the women and the younger men. This fellow, on reaching Jerusalem, played the rôle of a man of
peace, waiting till the holy day of the sabbath; then, finding the Jews at rest from work, he com-
26 manded his men to parade in arms, put to the sword all who came to see what was going on, and
27 rushing into the city with the armed men killed great numbers. Judas Maccabaeus, however, with
about nine others got away, and kept himself and his companions alive in the mountains, as wild
beasts do, feeding on herbs, in order that they might not be polluted like the rest.

VI. 1–31. *Enforced Hellenization of the Jews.*

6 1 Shortly after this the king sent an old Athenian to compel the Jews to depart from the laws
2 of their fathers, and to cease living by the laws of God; further, the sanctuary in Jerusalem was to
be polluted and called after Zeus Olympius, while the sanctuary at Gerizim was also to be called
3 after Zeus Xenius, in keeping with the hospitable character of the inhabitants. Now this proved a sore
4 and altogether crushing visitation of evil. For the heathen filled the temple with riot and revelling,
dallying with harlots and lying with women inside the sacred precincts, besides bringing in what
5 was forbidden, while the altar was filled with abominable sacrifices which the law prohibited. And
6 a man could neither keep the sabbath, nor celebrate the feasts of the fathers, nor so much as
7 confess himself to be a Jew. On the king's birthday every month they were taken—bitter was the
necessity—to share in the sacrifice, and when the festival of the Dionysia came round they were
8 compelled to wear ivy wreaths for the procession in honour of Dionysus. On the suggestion of
Ptolemy, an edict was also issued to the neighbouring Greek cities, ordering them to treat the Jews
9 in the same way and force them to share in the sacrifices, slaying any who refused to adopt
10 Greek ways. Thus any one could see the distressful state of affairs. Two women, for example,
were brought up for having circumcised their children; they were paraded round the city, with

23. **And in malice against the Jews.** Omitting (with V) πολίτας in ver. 23, and taking ἔχων . . . ἀπεχθῆ with what follows (so Grimm, and R.V. margin).

24. **the Mysian commander.** τὸν μυσάρχην may be either a derogatory epithet or an official title; probably it is both. The Mysians (Μυσοί, cp. Polyb. xxxi. 3. 3) formed a special division or guard in the Seleucid armies, and the unique formation Μυσάρχης means 'commander of the Mysians' (cp. Κυπριάρχης, xii. 2 = ὁ ἐπὶ τῶν Κυπρίων, for the form, though μυσιάρχης would mean 'governor of Mysia'). But the ill-repute of the Mysians (Μυσῶν ἔσχατος, a scoundrel) suggested a play on the term, as if it meant 'detestable ringleader'.

27. Cp. x. 6, Heb. xi. 37–8.

VI. 2. **Zeus Xenius.** i.e. the protector of strangers or guests.

7. **the king's birthday every month.** For the monthly celebration of a royal birthday see the evidence from Egypt, Commagene, and Pergamum, collected by Schürer in Preuschen's *Zeitschrift für die neutestamentliche Wissenschaft* (1901), pp. 48–52.

11 their babies hanging at their breasts, and then flung from the top of the wall. Some others, who
had taken refuge in the adjoining caves in order to keep the seventh day secretly, were betrayed
to Philip and all burnt together, since they scrupled to defend themselves, out of regard to the
honour of that most solemn day.
12 Now I beseech the readers of this book not to be discouraged by such calamities, but to reflect
13 that our people were being punished by way of chastening and not for their destruction. For
indeed it is a mark of great kindness when the impious are not let alone for a long time, but
14 punished at once. In the case of other nations, the Sovereign Lord in his forbearance refrains from
punishing them till they have filled up their sins to the full, but in our case he has deter-
15 mined otherwise, that his vengeance may not fall on us in after-days when our sins have reached
16 their height. Wherefore he never withdraweth his mercy from us; and though he chasteneth his
17 own people with calamity, he forsaketh them not. So much by way of a reminder to ourselves;
after these few words we must come back to our story.
18 Eleazar, one of the principal scribes, a man already well stricken in years and of a noble counten-
19 ance, was compelled to eat swine's flesh. But he, welcoming death with renown rather than life
20 with pollution, advanced of his own accord to the instrument of torture, affording an example of
how men should come forward who have the courage to put from them food which, even for the
21 natural love of life, they dare not taste. Now those in charge of that forbidden sacrificial feast took
the man aside, for the sake of old acquaintance, and privately urged him to bring some flesh of his
own providing, such as he was lawfully allowed to use, and to pretend he was really eating of the
22 sacrifice which the king had ordered, so that in this way he might escape death and be kindly treated
23 for the sake of their old friendship. But he with a high resolve, worthy of his years and of the
dignity of his **descent** and of his grey hair reached with honour and of his noble life from childhood
and, still more, of the holy laws divinely ordained, spoke his mind accordingly, telling them to
24 dispatch him to Hades at once. 'It ill becomes our years to dissemble,' said he, 'and thus lead
many younger persons to imagine that Eleazar in his ninetieth year has gone over to a heathenish
25 religion. I should lead them astray by my dissimulation, for the mere sake of enjoying this brief
26 and momentary life, and I should bring stain and foul disgrace on my own old age. Even were I for
the moment to evade the punishment of men, I should not escape the hands of the Almighty in
27 life or in death. Wherefore, by manfully parting with my life now, I will show myself worthy of my
28 old age, and leave behind me a noble example to the young of how to die willingly and nobly
29 on behalf of our reverend and holy laws. With these words he stepped forward at once to the
instrument of torture, while those who a moment before had been friendly turned against him,
30 deeming his language to be that of a sheer madman. Now, just as he was expiring under the
strokes of torture, he groaned out, The Lord, who hath holy knowledge, understandeth that,
although I might have been freed from death, I endure cruel pains in my body from scourging and
31 suffer this gladly in my soul, because I fear him.' Thus he too died, leaving his death as an
example of nobility and a memorial of virtue, not only to the young but also to the great body of
his nation.

VII. 1–42. *Martyrdom of seven brothers and their mother.*

7 1 It also came to pass that seven brothers and their mother were arrested and shamefully lashed
with whips and scourges, by the king's orders, that they might be forced to taste the abominable
2 swine's flesh. But one of them spoke up for the others and said, Why question us? What wouldst
3 thou learn from us? We are prepared to die sooner than transgress the laws of our fathers. Then
4 the king, in his exasperation, ordered pans and cauldrons to be heated, and, when they were heated
immediately, ordered the tongue of the speaker to be torn out, had him scalped and mutilated
5 before the eyes of his brothers and mother, and then had him put on the fire, all maimed and
crippled as he was, but still alive, and set to fry in the pan. And as the vapour from the pan spread

18. **of a noble countenance, was compelled.** Reading κάλλιστος τυγχάνων ἠναγκάζετο (19, 52, 62, 93, Syr.; V om. ἀναχαίνων) with Niese and Nestle (*Sept.-Studien*, iv. 20).

20. **affording an example.** For προπτύσας δέ (= but spat out the flesh first), which comes in awkwardly, read προτυπώσας (so one minuscule: Nestle, pp. 20–1) as above, which tallies with 27–8 better than πρωτεύσας (V^a). The less natural alternative is to omit δὲ (with Niese) and read τόπον (so Grotius) for τρόπον.

23. **descent.** For γήρους (A) or γήρως (V) read, with Niese, γένους. The two considerations of age and race are developed in the following clauses, where ἀναστροφῆς (R.V. margin, so A, 52, 55, 62) is preferable to ἀνατροφῆς (R.V. text).

26. Cp. Heb. x. 31, xi. 35; also *vv.* 19 and 30 with Heb. xi. 35 (ἄλλοι δὲ ἐτυμπανίσθησαν), and vii. 28 with Heb. xi. 3.

VII. 4. **scalped.** Περισκυθίσαντας refers to the practice of the Scythians, the typical savages (see above, iv. 47) and Red Indians of the ancient East, who flayed and scalped their victims (Herod. iv. 64).

6 abroad, they and their mother exhorted one another to die nobly, uttering these words: The Lord
God beholdeth this, and truly hath compassion on us, even as Moses declared in his Song which
testifieth against them to their face, saying,
And he shall have compassion on his servants.
7 And when the first had died after this manner, they brought the second to the shameful torture,
tearing off the skin of his head with the hair and asking him, Wilt thou eat, before we punish thy
8 body limb by limb? But he answered in the language of his fathers and said to them, No. So he
9 too underwent the rest of the torture, as the first had done. And when he was at the last gasp, he said,
Thou cursed miscreant! Thou dost dispatch us from this life, but the King of the world shall raise
10 us up, who have died for his laws, and revive us to life everlasting. And after him the third was made
a mocking-stock. And when he was told to put out his tongue, he did so at once, stretching forth
11 his hands courageously, with the noble words, These I had from heaven; for His name's sake
12 I count them naught; from Him I hope to get them back again. So much so that the king
himself and his company were astounded at the spirit of the youth, for he thought nothing of his
13 sufferings. And when he too was dead, they tortured the fourth in the same shameful fashion.
14 And when he was near his end, he said: 'Tis meet for those who perish at men's hands to cherish
hope divine that they shall be raised up by God again; but thou—thou shalt have no resur-
15, 16 rection to life. Next they brought the fifth and handled him shamefully. But he looked at the
king and said, Holding authority among men, thou doest what thou wilt, poor mortal; but dream
17 not that God hath forsaken our race. Go on, and thou shalt find how His sovereign power will
18 torture thee and thy seed! And after him they brought the sixth. And when he was at the point
of death he said, Deceive not thyself in vain! We are suffering this on our own account, for sins
19 against our own God. That is why these awful horrors have befallen us. But think not thou shalt
20 go unpunished for daring to fight against God! The mother, however, was a perfect wonder; she
deserves to be held in glorious memory, for, thanks to her hope in God, she bravely bore the sight
21 of seven sons dying in a single day. Full of noble spirit and nerving her weak woman's heart with
the courage of a man, she exhorted each of them in the language of their fathers, saying, How you
22 were ever conceived in my womb, I cannot tell! 'Twas not I who gave you the breath of life or
23 fashioned the elements of each! 'Twas the Creator of the world who fashioneth **men** and deviseth
the generating of all things, and he it is who in mercy will restore to you the breath of life even
24 as you now count yourselves naught for his laws' sake. Now Antiochus felt that he was being
humiliated, but, **overlooking** the taunt of her words, he made an appeal to the youngest brother,
who still survived, and even promised on oath to make him rich and happy and a Friend and
25 a trusted official of State, if he would give up his fathers' laws. As the young man paid no atten-
26 tion to him, he summoned his mother and exhorted her to counsel the lad to save himself. So,
27 after he had exhorted her at length, she agreed to persuade her son. She leant over to him and,
befooling the cruel tyrant, spoke thus in her fathers' tongue: My son, have pity on me. Nine
months I carried thee in my womb, three years I suckled thee; I **reared thee** and brought thee up
28 to this age of thy life. Child, I beseech thee, lift thine eyes to heaven and earth, look at all that is
therein, and know that God did not make them out of the things that existed. So is the race of
29 men created. Fear not this butcher, but show thyself worthy of thy brothers, and accept thy death,
30 that by God's mercy I may receive thee again together with thy brothers. Ere she had finished, the
young man cried, What are you waiting for? I will not obey the king's command, I will obey the
31 command of the law given by Moses to our fathers. But thou, who hast devised all manner of evil
32 against the Hebrews, thou shalt not escape the hands of God. We are suffering for our own sins,
33 and though our living Lord is angry for a little, in order to rebuke and chasten us, he will again be
34 reconciled to his own servants. But thou, thou impious wretch, vilest of all men, be not vainly
35 uplifted with thy proud, uncertain hopes, raising thy hand against the heavenly children; thou hast
36 not yet escaped the judgement of the Almighty God who seeth all. These our brothers, after

6. **Song which testifieth . . . face.** This sententious description of the Song (Deut. xxxii. 36) is not only out of keeping with the *mise en scène*, but far-fetched; the testimony of the Song in question was borne against faithless Israel, not against outside oppressors.

18. Some MSS. insert διό before, or γάρ after, ἄξια. Niese, reading the latter, and following V[a] (ἄξιοι) and V (γεγόναμεν), conjectures κολασμοῦ for θαυμασμοῦ (i.e. *and have deserved punishment*). But the above reading, though characteristically abrupt, yields a good sense.

23. **men.** For ἀνθρώπου γένεσιν read with Niese ἄνθρωπον (or ἀνθρώπους), the first γένεσιν being repeated *per incuriam* from the second.

24. **overlooking.** For ὑφορώμενος ('suspecting') read ὑπερορώμενος (Vg. = *exprobrantis uoce despecta*) with Kamphausen. For the promised rank of Friend (i. 14, viii. 29, 1 Macc. ii. 18, &c.) see Deissmann's *Bible-Studies*, pp. 167 f.

27. **reared thee.** Omitting (with 71, Vg, 𝔖) the anticlimax of καὶ τροφοφορήσασαν (= *and sustained thee*, lit. nursed).

enduring a brief pain, have now **drunk** of everflowing life, in terms of God's covenant, but thou shalt
37 receive by God's judgement the just penalty of thine arrogance. I, like my brothers, give up body
and soul for our fathers' laws, calling on God to show favour to our nation soon, and to make thee
38 acknowledge, in torment and plagues, that he alone is God, and to let the Almighty's wrath, justly
39 fallen on the whole of our nation, end in me and in my brothers. Then the king fell into a passion
40 and had him handled worse than the others, so exasperated was he at being mocked. Thus he also
41 died unpolluted, trusting absolutely in the Lord. Finally after her sons the mother also perished.
42 Let this suffice for the enforced sacrifices and the excesses of barbarity.

VIII. 1–36. *Revolt and early successes of Judas Maccabaeus.*

8 1 But Judas, who is also called Maccabaeus, together with his companions, went round the
villages by stealth, summoning their kinsfolk and mustering those who had adhered to Judaism, till
2 they collected as many as six thousand. And they invoked the Lord to look upon the people whom
3 all men oppressed, to have compassion on the sanctuary which the godless had profaned, and also
to pity the ruined city which was on the point of being levelled with the ground, to hearken to the
4 blood that cried to him, to remember the impious **massacre of the innocent babes** and the blasphemies
5 committed against his name, and to manifest his hatred of evil. Now as soon as Maccabaeus had
got his company together, the heathen found him irresistible, for the Lord's anger was now turned
6 into mercy. He would surprise and burn both towns and **villages**, gaining possession of strategic
7 positions and **routing** large numbers **of the enemy**. He took special advantage of the night for such
attacks. And the whole country echoed with the fame of his valour.
8 So when Philip saw that the man was gaining ground inch by inch and adding daily to his
successes, he wrote to Ptolemy, the governor of Coelesyria and Phoenicia, for support in maintaining
9 the king's cause. The latter lost no time in selecting Nicanor, the son of Patroclus, one of the foremost among the king's Friends, whom he dispatched at the head of no fewer than twenty thousand
troops of all nationalities to exterminate the entire population of Judaea; and with him there was
associated Gorgias, a military commander who had considerable experience of active service.
10 Nicanor, however, determined to sell the Jews into slavery, and so to make up the sum of two
11 thousand talents which the king owed by way of tribute to the Romans. He therefore sent at once
to the maritime towns, inviting them to purchase Jewish slaves, whom he promised to sell at the rate
of ninety a talent—little imagining the judgement that was to overtake him from the Almighty.
12 Now when Judas was informed of Nicanor's inroad, and when he told his followers about the
13 arrival of the host, those who were cowardly and sceptical about **God's judgement** ran off and decamped,
14 while others sold all their remaining possessions and withal besought the Lord to deliver **those**
15 **whom** the impious Nicanor had already **sold before the battle**; and this, if not for their own sakes,
at least for the sake of the covenants made with their fathers and for the sake of His reverend and
16 glorious name, by which they were called. But when Maccabaeus had got his men together, **six**
thousand in number, he bade them have no fear of **chains and slavery** and no dread of the vast
17 number of the heathen who had attacked them wrongfully; let them fight nobly, keeping before their
eyes the wanton and lawless outrage of the heathen upon the holy place, the shocking and despiteful
18 violence done to the city, and further the overthrow of their ancestral polity. They trust to arms
and daring deeds, he said, but we rely upon the Almighty God, who **by a nod** can lay low our
19 enemies, **aye and the whole world**. Then he rehearsed to them the aid repeatedly vouchsafed in the
days of their ancestors, as in the days of Sennacherib, when a hundred and eighty-five thousand
20 perished, and as at **the battle** fought against the Galatians **in Babylonia**, where only eight thousand

36. **drunk.** Hort's conjecture, *πεπώκασι*, for the MSS. *πεπτώκασι*, restores the original sense of the passage.

VIII. 4. **massacre of the innocent babes.** Cp. above, vi. 10, and 1 Macc. i. 61.
6. **villages.** *κώμας* ('villages') is to be read for *χώρας*.
routing . . . enemy. Cp. Heb. xi. 34.
13. **God's judgment.** i. e. on their foes (cp. ver. 11). Contrast the account of 1 Macc. iii. 56.
14. **those whom . . . sold before the battle.** i. e. not stray captives picked up by the way but the speakers themselves, whom Nicanor had sold in advance.
16. **six thousand in number.** But this was the original number of the army (ver. 1)!
slavery. For *τοὺς πολεμίους* (V) or *τοῖς πολεμίοις* read *τοῖς δεσμοῖς*, which has been altered in A into *τοῖς δεσμίοις*, as the variant (19, 62) *τοῖς πολέμοις* has been altered into *τοῖς πολεμίοις*.
18. **by a nod.** Cp. Apoc. Bar. xxi. 5, &c.
and the whole world. For the turn of expression see 1 John ii. 2.
20. **the battle . . . in Babylonia.** Nothing is known of the engagement which forms the subject of this exaggerated boast. The eight thousand, who are obviously Jews, may have been fighting either under Antiochus the Great against a body of Gallic mercenaries under Molon, the rebellious satrap of Media (221–220 B.C.), or, earlier, in the ranks of Antiochus Soter (281–261 B.C.), who is said to have won his title (Appian, *Syr.* 66) from his efforts against the Gallic raiders in Asia Minor.

men, together with four thousand Macedonians, took the field, and where, after the Macedonians were
hard pressed, the eight thousand slew the hundred and twenty thousand, owing to the aid vouchsafed
21 them from heaven, and won rich booty. With these words he inspirited them and got them ready
22 to die for the laws and for their country. He then divided his army into four, and put his brothers
at the head of the various divisions, Simon, Joseph, and Jonathan each being in command of fifteen
23 hundred men; he also made Eleazar read aloud the holy Book, and taking 'God's Help' as a watch-
24 word put himself at the head of the first division, and engaged Nicanor. And, since the Almighty
fought on their side, they slew over nine thousand of the enemy, wounded and disabled the greater
25 part of Nicanor's army, and forced them all to flee. They also secured the very money of those who
26 had arrived for the purpose of buying them. Then, after pursuing them for some distance, they were
obliged to turn back on account of time; it was the day before the sabbath, and therefore they made
27 no effort to follow them up. So, after collecting the arms of the enemy, and stripping them of their
spoils, they attended to the duties of the sabbath, loudly blessing and praising the Lord who had
28 preserved them unto this day and thus begun to show them mercy; after the sabbath, when
they had apportioned part of the spoils to their own wounded and to the widows and orphans, they
29 shared the remainder among themselves and their children. This done, they united in supplication,
beseeching the Lord of mercy to be fully reconciled to his servants.
30 In an encounter with the forces of Timotheus and Bacchides, they also killed over twenty thousand
and got possession of some extremely high strongholds, securing a large quantity of plunder which
they distributed equally with themselves not only among the wounded, the orphans, and the widows,
31 but also among the older people. Then, after collecting the arms of the enemy, they stored them all
32 carefully in the most important forts, conveying the rest of the spoils to Jerusalem. They also slew
Phylarches, who belonged to Timotheus' forces, a most impious scoundrel who had inflicted serious
33 injuries on the Jews. And while they were celebrating the victory in the city of their fathers, they
burned Callisthenes and some others, who had set fire to the sacred gates, and who had taken refuge
34 in a small house; thus did these men receive the due reward of their impiety. As for the thrice-
35 accursed Nicanor, who had brought the thousand merchants to buy the Jews for slaves, those whom
he reckoned of no account humbled him by the help of the Lord; doffing his splendid uniform, he
had to make his way alone, like a runaway slave, straight across country to Antioch, having fared
36 disastrously in his expedition and having left his army annihilated. So the man who undertook to
secure tribute for the Romans by selling the Jerusalemites into captivity, proved the means of
showing that the Jews had a Champion and that they were invulnerable since they followed the laws
which He enacted.

IX. 1–29. *The miserable death of Antiochus Epiphanes.*

9 1 Now about that time it happened that Antiochus had to beat a disorderly retreat from the region
2 of Persia. He had entered the city called Persepolis and tried to rob temples and get hold of the
city; whereupon the people flew to arms and routed him, with the result that Antiochus was put to
3 flight by the people of the country and broke up his camp in disgrace. And while he was at
4 Ecbatana, news reached him of what had happened to Nicanor and the forces of Timotheus. So, in

22. **Joseph,** here and in x. 19, is an error of the author or of a copyist for John (cp. 1 Macc. ix. 36 f.).

23. **made Eleazar read aloud.** Reading (Vg, 𝕾, 19, 62, 64, 93, so Grimm, Rawlinson, and Kamphausen) *παραγνῶναι* for *παραναγνούς* (A.V. Fritzsche, Swete). 'God's Help' is a play on the name of Eleazar.

26, 27. The real reason was not sabbatarian strictness (cp. 1 Macc. iv. 17 f.), and the spoiling of the enemy is ante-dated (cp. 1 Macc. iv. 18, 23). On the Sabbatarianism see above, vi. 11, and Jub. 7. 6–13.

27. **after collecting the arms.** Here, though not in ver. 31, *ὁπλολογήσαντες αὐτούς* might also be rendered, 'having piled their arms' (contrast 1 Macc. iv. 6).

thus begun to show them mercy. The pretty reading, *στάξαντος* ('distilled'), is less well supported than *τάξαντος* (as above, cp. ver. 5) or *τάξαντι* (62). Niese, reading the latter, with *καί* after *αὐτούς*, renders, 'to him who had preserved them and appointed this day to be the beginning of mercy for them.'

29. **to be fully reconciled.** i.e. to show the permanence of his favour by continuing to crown their efforts with success. Grimm quotes a similar phrase from Euseb. *H. E.* viii. 16. 2 (*τῆς θείας προνοίας . . . τῷ μὲν αὐτῆς καταλλαττομένης λαῷ*, of the cessation of persecution).

33. **a small house.** The point of mentioning the smallness of the house (*οἰκίδιον*, a real diminutive) is obviously to contrast the number who took refuge in it. This tells, together with the position of *ὑφῆψαν* after *Καλλισθένην*, in favour of *πεφευγότας* instead of *πεφευγότα* (as if Callisthenes was the only incendiary who hid himself in the hut or cottage), of *καί τινας ἄλλους* after *Καλλισθένην*, and of *ἐκομίσαντο* for *ἐκομίσατο*.

reward of their impiety. For the phrase cp. 2 Pet. ii. 13.

35. **fared disastrously.** Reading *ὑπεράγαν δυσημερηκώς*.

IX. 2. **Persepolis** was not in Elymais; consequently, unless 'Elymais' in 1 Macc. i. 6 is a corruption (cp. Cheyne in *Encyclopaedia Biblica*, 1284, 3660), there is a geographical contradiction between the two narratives. See i. 12 f.

tried successfully, according to Appian (*Syr.* 66).

3. **Ecbatana**, the capital of Media, was not near the route of his flight to Babylon (1 Macc. vi. 4).

a transport of rage, he determined to wreak vengeance on the Jews for the defeat which he had
suffered at the hands of those who had forced him to fly, and ordered his charioteer to drive
on without halting till the journey was ended. Verily the judgement of heaven upon him was
imminent! For thus he spoke in his arrogance: When I reach Jerusalem, I will make it a common
5 sepulchre of Jews. But the all-seeing Lord, the God of Israel, smote him with a fatal and unseen
stroke; the words were no sooner out of his mouth than he was seized with an incurable pain in
6 the bowels, and his internal organs gave him cruel torture—a right proper punishment for one who
7 had tortured the bowels of other people with many an exquisite pang. He did not cease from his
wild insolence, however, but waxed more arrogant than ever, breathing fire and fury against the Jews,
and giving orders to hurry on with the journey. And it came to pass that he dropped from his
8 chariot as it whirled along, so that the bad fall racked every limb of his body. Thus he who in his
overweening haughtiness had supposed the waves of the sea were at his bidding and imagined he
could weigh the high mountains in his scales, was now prostrate, carried along in a litter—a manifest
9 token to all men of the power of God. Worms actually swarmed from the impious creature's body;
his flesh fell off, while he was still alive in pain and anguish; and the stench of his corruption turned
10 the whole army from him with loathing. A man who shortly before had thought he could touch
11 the stars of heaven, none could now endure to carry, such was his intolerable stench. Then it was
that, broken in spirit, he began to abate his arrogance, for the most part, and to arrive at some knowledge of the truth. For, as he suffered more and more anguish under the scourge of God, unable
12 even to bear his own stench, he said: Right is it that mortal man should be subject to God, and not
13 deem himself God's equal. The vile wretch also made a vow to the Lord (who would not now
14 have pity on him), promising that he would proclaim the holy city free—the city which he was
15 hurrying to lay level with the ground and to make a common sepulchre—that he would make all
the Jews equal to citizens of Athens—the Jews whom he had determined to throw out with their
16 children to the beasts, for the birds to devour, as unworthy even to be buried—that he would
adorn with magnificent offerings the holy sanctuary which he had formerly rifled, restoring all the
sacred vessels many times over, and defraying from his own revenue the expense of the sacrifices;
17 furthermore, that he would even become a Jew and travel over the inhabited world to publish abroad
18 the might of God. But when his sufferings did not cease by any means (for God's judgement had
justly come upon him), he gave up all hope of himself and wrote the following letter, with its humble
supplication, to the Jews:
19 To his citizens, the loyal Jews, Antiochus their king and general wisheth great joy and health
20 and prosperity. If you and your children fare well and your affairs are to your mind, I give thanks
21 to God, as my hope is in heaven. As for myself, I am sick. Your esteem and goodwill I bear in
loving memory. On my way back from Persia I have fallen seriously ill, and I think it needful to
22 take into consideration the common safety of all my subjects—not that I despair of myself (for,
23 on the contrary, I have good hopes of recovery), but in view of the fact that when my father marched
24 into the upper country, he appointed his successor, in order that, in the event of anything un-

8. Cp. v. 21; Isa. xl. 12, li. 15.

9. **worms**, &c. A conventional doom for blasphemous persecutors (cp. Acts xii. 23). The narrative of Jason probably described the disease as a result of the fall from the chariot. The epitomist not only puts in the supernatural touch of ver. 5, but some of the high colouring in the edifying sequel.

11. **broken in spirit.** V's reading (ὑποτεθραυσμένος) may mean either that he grew steadily worse (Bissell) or that he was suffering severely (an instance of meiosis, so Grimm and Kamphausen); but the variant of A (τεθραυσμένος, so Fritzsche, Rawlinson, &c.) gives a better sense, and Niese's conjecture that κατὰ στιγμήν has arisen by dittography from μάστιγι (cp. 62, μάστιγμην) is very plausible. 'Ferner muss man mit 19, 62, 64, 93 lesen: καὶ εἰς ἐπίγνωσιν ἔρχεσθαι ἀληθείας· θείᾳ γὰρ μάστιγι ἐπιτεινόμενος ταῖς ἀλγηδόσι καὶ μηδὲ τῆς ὀσμῆς δυνάμενος ἀνέχεσθαι κτλ' (*Kritik*, p. 113). In ver. 12 ὑπερήφανα (A, 55, 71, 74, 106, 243) is probably (so Grimm, Bissell, Kamphausen) a gloss upon ἰσόθεα (cp. Phil. ii. 6; Aesch. *Persae*, 820, &c.).

17. **become a Jew**, &c. The narrative makes Antiochus outdo even Nebuchadrezzar (Dan. iv. 37) in the way of abject penance, or at least of promises.

18. **the following letter, with its humble supplication.** The letter does not answer to this description, and, as addressed to Judas and his party, is entirely out of keeping with the facts of the situation. Bevan (*House of Seleucus*, ii. 177, 298), like Niese (30), defends it by supposing that it was originally meant for the Hellenizing Jewish community of Jerusalem, which Antiochus affected to regard as the genuine article. He calls them χρηστοί in the sense in which the Cavaliers in seventeenth-century England were called the 'honest' party (cp. e. g. Aristoph. *Frogs* 783 ὀλίγον τὸ χρηστόν ἐστιν), and describes himself as their στρατηγός (general) by way of flattery, implying that he was proud to be *strategos* in Jerusalem no less than in Athens. Had the author, or Jason, composed the letter, he would probably have coloured and shaped it to fit the context. Its very discrepancies with the present setting tell in favour of the hypothesis that it reflects some authentic document.

21. **I am sick. Your esteem**, &c. The asyndeton is awkward, but it is more awkward to insert εἰ μή before ἀσθενῶς or ἄλλως γάρ before ὑμῶν, and translate (with Rawlinson): 'I am sick, otherwise I would have remembered, &c.' (retaining the ἄν before ἐμνημόνευον, which probably arose from the last syllable of the preceding εὔνοιαν).

23. **marched into the upper country.** Cp. 1 Macc. iii. 37.

24. **anything unexpected.** A euphemism for the king's death, like 'the coming event' (ver. 25).

expected occurring or any unwelcome news arriving, the residents at home might know whom the
25 State had been entrusted to, and so be spared any disturbance. Besides these considerations, as
I have noticed how the princes on the borders and the neighbours of my kingdom are on the alert
for any opportunity and anticipate the coming event, I have appointed my son Antiochus to be king.
I have often committed and commended him to most of you, when I hurried to the upper provinces.
26 I have also written to him what I have written below. I therefore exhort and implore you to
remember the public and private benefits you have received and to preserve, each of you, your
27 present goodwill toward me and my son. For I am convinced that with mildness and kindness he
will adhere to my policy and continue on good terms with you.
28 So this murderer and blasphemer, after terrible suffering such as he had inflicted on other people,
29 ended his life most miserably among the mountains in a foreign land. His bosom-friend Philip
brought the corpse home; and then, fearing the son of Antiochus, he betook himself to Ptolemy
Philometor in Egypt.

X. 1–8. *The temple purified and the feast of dedication instituted.*

10 1 Now Maccabaeus and his followers, under the leadership of the Lord, recaptured the temple and
2 the city, and pulled down the altars erected by the aliens in the market-place, as well as the sacred
3 inclosures. After cleansing the sanctuary, they erected another altar of sacrifice, and striking fire
out of flints they offered sacrifices after a lapse of two years, with incense, lamps, and the presentation of
4 the shew-bread. This done, they fell prostrate before the Lord with entreaties that they might never
again incur such disasters, but that, if ever they should sin, he would chasten them with forbearance,
5 instead of handing them over to blasphemous and barbarous pagans. Now it so happened that the
cleansing of the sanctuary took place on the very day on which it had been profaned by aliens, on
6 the twenty-fifth day of the same month, which is Chislev. And they celebrated it for eight days
with gladness like a feast of tabernacles, remembering how, not long before, during the feast of
7 tabernacles they had been wandering like wild beasts in the mountains and the caves. So, bearing
wands wreathed with leaves and fair boughs and palms, they offered hymns of praise to him who had
8 prospered the cleansing of his own place, and also passed a public order and decree that all the
Jewish nation should keep these ten days every year.

X. 9–38. *Further campaigns of Judas.*

9, 10 Such was the end of Antiochus, who was called Epiphanes. We will now explain what occurred
under Antiochus Eupator, the son of that godless man, summarizing the calamities of the wars.
11 When he succeeded to the throne, he appointed a certain Lysias as his chancellor and as supreme
12 governor of Coelesyria and Phoenicia. For Ptolemy, who was called Macron, had set an example
of justice to the Jews in righting wrongs done to them, and had endeavoured to deal amicably
13 with them. For this he was arraigned before Eupator by the king's Friends; on every side he heard
himself called a traitor for having abandoned the island of Cyprus which Philometor had entrusted
to him, and for having sided with Antiochus Epiphanes: so, feeling unable to maintain the prestige of
his position, he took poison in a fit of despair and made away with himself.
14 But when Gorgias became governor of this district, he maintained a force of mercenaries and kept
15 up war with the Jews at every turn. Besides that, the Idumaeans, who were in possession of important
strongholds, harassed the Jews and did their utmost to keep the feud going by welcoming the refugees
16 from Jerusalem. But Maccabaeus and his men, after solemnly imploring and beseeching God to

29. **bosom-friend.** A Hellenistic court title (cp. Fränkel in *Alterthümer von Pergamon*, viii. 1, pp. 111 f.) here as in Acts xiii. 1 and in the inscription of Delos (see above, on iii. 7) which assigns it to Heliodorus.

X. 3. **striking fire out of flints.** According to the ancient view that only fire obtained thus fresh from nature, i.e. struck from flints or otherwise (cp. i. 22 f.), could be used to rekindle altar-fires. 'Two' years is a mistake for 'three' (cp. 1 Macc. iv. 54).

6. **wandering,** &c. v. 27, Heb. xi. 37–8.

11. **a certain Lysias.** The off-hand allusion to Lysias (*τινά*) is on a par with the unhistorical conception of the regent's position (cp. 1 Macc. iii. 32, vi. 17, &c.).

12. **For** gives the reason why Lysias was made governor of Coelesyria and Phoenicia, which Ptolemy (cp. viii. 8) had hitherto ruled. The boy-king must have been a puppet in the hands of Lysias; the latter was responsible for the impeachment of Ptolemy, who was evidently suspected by the anti-Semites on much the same flimsy pretext as Desdemona ('She did deceive her father, marrying you. And . . .').

13. **the king's Friends.** This title was revived by the phalanx of political mercenaries in the eighteenth century who intrigued for George III. As though, said Junius, the mass of Englishmen were enemies of the king!

prestige. Grimm's conjecture, *εὐγενίσας*, for the textual variants (*εὐγενναίσας, εὐγεννασίας, εὐγεννασίαν*, &c.) gives an excellent sense, but the words *ὑπ' ἀθυμίας* (56), though poorly supported by MS. evidence, are too vivid and essential to be a gloss.

15. **the refugees.** i.e. Hellenistic Jews expelled by Judas.

17 fight on their side, rushed at the strongholds of the Idumaeans and, after a vigorous assault, captured
the positions, beating off those who manned the walls, slaying any whom they came across, and
18 slaughtering no fewer than twenty thousand. No less than nine thousand took refuge in two
19 extremely strong towers, which were well equipped to stand a siege; so Maccabaeus left Simon and
Joseph, together with Zacchaeus and his division, as a force adequate for the siege, and went off
20 in person to various places where he was needed. But the covetous retinue of Simon allowed themselves to be bribed by some of those inside the towers, and let some of them slip out, on payment of
21 seventy thousand drachmas. When Maccabaeus learned of what had occurred, he summoned the
leaders of the nation and accused them of selling their brethren for money, by setting their enemies
22 free to fight against them; then he slew these men for having turned traitors and instantly stormed
23 the two towers. Successful in every feat of arms which he undertook, he destroyed in the two
strongholds more than twenty thousand men.
24 Now Timotheus, who had been previously defeated by the Jews, mustered a foreign force of vast
size, and raised a large detachment of Asiatic cavalry, and arrived in Judaea as though he meant
25 to capture it by force of arms. But on his approach Maccabaeus and his men sprinkled earth upon
26 their heads and girded their loins with sackcloth, in supplication to God, and falling down upon the
step in front of the altar besought Him to show favour graciously to them, to be the enemy of their
27 enemies, and the adversary of their adversaries, as the law affirmeth. Then rising from prayer they
took up their arms and advanced some distance from the city, halting when they drew near to the
28 enemy. And when the dawn came, the two armies joined battle; one had a pledge of success and
victory, not only in their valour but in their appeal to the Lord, while the other side were impelled
29 to the struggle by their own passions. And as the fight waxed fierce, the enemy saw five resplendent
30 men from heaven on horses with golden bridles, who led on the Jews and took Maccabaeus between
them, sheltering him with their armour and preserving him scatheless; they also showered arrows
and thunderbolts on the enemy till, blinded and disordered, they were utterly bewildered and cut to
31, 32 pieces. Twenty thousand five hundred were slain, with six hundred horsemen, and Timotheus
himself took refuge in a stronghold called Gazara, which was very strongly fortified under command
33 of Chaereas. The troops of Maccabaeus laid eager siege to this fort for twenty-four days, during
34 which time the besieged, who relied on the strength of the place, blasphemed furiously and gave
35 vent to impious cries. But, as the twenty-fifth day dawned, twenty youths from the Maccabaean army,
burning with anger at all this blasphemy, stormed the wall like men, and in a wild fury of passion
36 proceeded to cut down every one they met. Meantime others had followed them up by a wheel
movement and had set fire to the towers, kindling fires and burning the blasphemers alive, while
37 some burst the gates open and admitted the rest of the band. So they captured the city, and killed
Timotheus, who had concealed himself in a cistern, and his brother Chaereas, and Apollophanes.
38 Having accomplished this feat, they sang hymns of thanksgiving, blessing the Lord who rendereth
great services to Israel and giveth them the victory.

XI. 1–38. *Defeat of Lysias, and terms of peace arranged.*

11 1 Quite soon after this, Lysias, the king's guardian and kinsman and chancellor, who was seriously
2 annoyed at what had taken place, collected about eighty thousand infantry with all his cavalry and
3 marched against the Jews, intending to make the city a residence for Greeks, to levy tribute on the
temple as on the other sacred places of the nations, and to put up the high-priesthood for sale
4 every year; for he never reckoned with the might of God, but was puffed up with his own myriads

19. **Zacchaeus** (cp. viii. 22) is otherwise unknown, unless his name is explained from 1 Macc. v. 56. Thus Grotius conjectured that the original reading here was *καὶ τὸν τοῦ Ζακχαίου*.

21. **selling their brethren for money.** i. e. betraying the wider interests of the nation for the sake of pecuniary advantage to themselves.

24. **Asiatic cavalry.** The Iranian cavalry were a famous item in the Seleucid armies; but if *ἵππους* here is equivalent to *horses*, probably Media is intended specially.

25. **sprinkled earth upon their heads.** See xiv. 15 and 1 Macc. xi. 71.

26. **as the law affirmeth.** Cp. Exod. xxiii. 22.

28. **came.** Literally 'succeeded the night' (*διαδεχομένης* as in Wisd. vii. 30).

30. **led on the Jews**, &c. Reading *Ἰουδαίων, οἳ καὶ κτλ.* (instead of *Ἰουδαίων οἱ δύο καὶ κτλ.*). *Δύο* is the gloss of a scribe who wished to emphasize that Judas was escorted by two of the angels, one on each side (so Grimm).

32. **Gazara.** Gezer was really captured by Simon (1 Macc. xiii. 43 f.), but, in this extract, the credit of the exploit is assigned to the troops of Judas, the only Maccabee in whom the book is interested, and the story is retold in order to bring out the religious fanaticism of the Jewish army (cp. Kosters in *Theolog. Tijdschrift*, 1878, pp. 519 f.). This strong post, on a ridge of the Shephelah, was 'virtually the key of Judaea at a time when Judaea's foes came down the coast from the north' (G. A. Smith, *Hist. Geogr. of Holy Land*, pp. 215 f.). But, if the story is taken as an independent narrative, Gazara must be identified with Jazer (1 Macc. v. 8) in Gilead.

5 of infantry and thousands of cavalry and eighty elephants. On entering Judaea, he came up to
6 Bethsuron, a strong fort about five leagues from Jerusalem, and pressed it hard. Now when Maccabaeus
and his men learned that he was besieging the strongholds, they and all the people wailed and wept,
7 beseeching the Lord to send a good angel to save Israel. Maccabaeus himself was the first to take
up arms, and he urged the others to join him at the hazard of their lives, in order to succour their
8 brethren. So they sallied forth, all together, right willingly. And ere ever they had left Jerusalem,
9 a rider appeared at their head, in white apparel, brandishing weapons of gold; and they joined in
blessing God the merciful and were still more encouraged; ready now to break through not only
10 men but ferocious beasts and walls of iron, they advanced in array with their heavenly ally—for the
11 Lord had mercy on them. And leaping like lions upon the foe, they slew eleven thousand of
12 their infantry, and sixteen hundred of their cavalry, and forced all the rest to flee. The majority
only escaped with wounds and the loss of their arms, while Lysias himself had to save his life by
13 a disgraceful flight. Now Lysias was no fool. Thinking over the defeat he had sustained, and
14 recognizing that the Hebrews were invincible, thanks to the mighty God who was their ally, he sent
to persuade them to agree to a fair and comprehensive settlement, undertaking that he would even
15 induce the king to become their friend. Maccabaeus agreed to all the terms proposed by Lysias,
thereby showing a sagacious regard for the interests of the people, since the king did grant all the
16 written demands which Maccabaeus made to Lysias on behalf of the Jews. Now the letter addressed
by Lysias to the Jews was to this effect:
17 Lysias to the people of the Jews, greeting. Your envoys, John and Absalom, have presented the
18 appended petition and asked for a decision upon its contents. I have therefore informed the king
19 of whatever had to be laid before him, and he has agreed to all that could be granted. If you will
20 maintain your goodwill toward the State, I will endeavour in future to promote your interests, and,
as for this particular business, I have instructed your representatives and my own to confer with
21 you. Fare ye well. Written in the hundred and forty-eighth year, on the four and twentieth day
of the month Dioscurus.
22 The king's letter ran as follows:
23 King Antiochus to his brother Lysias, greeting. Now that our father hath passed over to the
gods, it is our pleasure that the subjects of the realm should live undisturbed and attend to their own
24 concerns. As for our Jewish subjects, we understand that they object to our father's project of
bringing them over to Hellenism, preferring their own ways of life and asking permission to follow
25 their own customs. It is our will therefore that this nation also shall not be disturbed, and we have
decided to give them back their temple and to permit them to live after the manner of their
26 ancestors. Thou wilt do well therefore to send messengers to them and give them the right hand
of fellowship, that they may know our purpose and be of good heart and cheerfully settle down to
their own business.
27 The king's letter to the nation was as follows:
28 King Antiochus to the senate of the Jews and to the rest of the Jews, greeting. If you fare well,
29 it is as we wish; we too are in good health. Menelaus has informed us of your desire to return
30 home and attend to your own affairs. Those Jews then who return home up to the thirtieth day of
31 Xanthicus shall have our friendship, with full permission to use their own food and to observe their
32 own laws as of yore; none of them shall be molested in any way for any unwitting offence. More-
33 over, I have sent Menelaus to reassure you. Fare ye well. Written in the hundred and forty-eighth
year, on the fifteenth day of Xanthicus.

XI. 5. **Bethsuron** (Βεθσούρων, gen. after συνεγγίσας as in 1 Macc. xi. 4, xiii. 3, &c.) in 1 Macc. iv. 29 is the strategic fort of Beth-zur, commanding the highroad from Jerusalem to Hebron. The *v. l.* σχοίνους (σχοῖνος = thirty stadii) for σταδίους is probably an attempt to correct the error of placing B. so near to Jerusalem, unless the writer (or his source) confused the place with another of the same name in the vicinity of the capital, e. g. Bèt Sâhûr (Grimm), or Kefr-et-Tûr (on the Mount of Olives, cp. Schick in *Palest. Explor. Fund Quarterly*, 1895, p. 37). The σχοίνους-reckoning, which brings up its distance to 150 stadii, would almost harmonize with the statement of Eusebius that Beth-zur lay 160 stadii from Jerusalem, but this reckoning never occurs elsewhere in 2 Maccabees (cp. xii. 9, &c.).

6. **a good angel.** Cp. xv. 23; Tobit v. 21. He came in white apparel, the conventional guise of angels.

14. **induce the king.** Text corrupt. Translation omits ἀναγκάζειν.

16. **to this effect.** For an analogous expression see Acts xxiii. 25.

people. πλῆθος here, as in 1 Macc. viii. 20, &c., is used in its official and political sense of δῆμος (see below, ver. 34).

17. **Absalom.** Possibly the same as the Absalom of 1 Macc. xiii. 11.

21. **the month Dioscurus.** The Διοσκορινθίου of A, &c. (cp. the Διοσκορίδου of V in ver. 28) is either a corruption of Δυστροῦ (read by some MSS. in Tobit ii. 12; Addit. Esth. xiii. 6, as an equivalent for Adar), or some intercalary month between Dystrus and Xanthicus (cp. below, vers. 33 and 38), or, most probably, an error for Διοσκυροῦ (i. e. the third month of the Cretan calendar). When Διὸς Κορινθίου is read, the first month of the Macedonian calendar is perhaps meant (Δῖος = Marcheshvan, the Μαρσουάνης of Josephus, *Antiq.* I. iii. 3, &c.), and the name betrays the king's love of introducing Hellenic novelties into the very calendar of the East.

29. **to return home.** Literally 'to go down' (i. e. from Jerusalem to the country-districts).

34 The Romans also sent them a letter to this effect:
Quintus Memmius and Titus Manlius, ambassadors of the Romans, to the nation of the Jews,
35 greeting. With reference to what Lysias, the king's kinsman, has granted you, we hereby give our
36 consent. As for the points which he decided were to be referred to the king, send some one at once
37 to advise on them, that we may act in your interests. We are off to Antioch; make haste, then, to
38 send some of your number, that we may know what your mind is. Fare ye well. Written in the
hundred and forty-eighth year, on the fifteenth day of Xanthicus.

XII. 1–45. *Fresh campaigns of Judas.*

12 1 After these agreements had been concluded, Lysias went away to the king, while the Jews
2 devoted themselves to husbandry. But some of the local governors, Timotheus and Apollonius,
the son of Gennaeus, with Hieronymus and Demophon, and also Nicanor, the governor of Cyprus,
3 would not let them alone or leave them at peace. Some inhabitants of Joppa also perpetrated the
following crime: they invited the Jewish residents to embark, with their wives and children, in boats
which they provided, as if they meant no harm at all but were simply acting according to the public
4 regulations of the town. The Jews agreed to go, since they wished to be peaceable and had no
suspicions; but, when they were out at sea, the men of Joppa drowned no fewer than two hundred
5 of them. Now when Judas heard of this brutal cruelty to his fellow-countrymen, he summoned his
6 men, called on God the righteous Judge, and attacked the murderers of his brethren, setting fire to
7 the haven by night, burning the boats, and putting to the sword those who had fled thither. Then,
as the town was shut against him, he retired, intending to come back and extirpate the entire
8 community of Joppa. And on learning that the inhabitants of Jamnia meant to carry out the same
9 kind of plot against the local Jews, he attacked them also by night, and set fire to the haven and
the fleet, so that the glare of the light was seen at Jerusalem, two hundred and forty furlongs distant.
10 Now when they had drawn off nine furlongs from thence, on their march against Timotheus, they
11 were attacked by no fewer than five thousand Arabs, with five hundred horsemen, and a stiff fight
was waged in which, by God's help, Judas and his men won the victory. The vanquished nomads
besought Judas to be their friend, promising to give him cattle and to be of service in other ways,
12 and Judas, with the idea that they would really be of use in a number of ways, agreed to keep
peace with them; whereupon, after pledging friendship, they departed to their tents.
13 He also fell upon a town which was strongly fortified with earthworks and walls, and inhabited
14 by a mixed population; its name was Caspin. The inhabitants, relying on the strength of their
walls and their ample provisions, scoffed insolently at Judas and his men, and, more than that,
15 blasphemed and uttered cries of impiety; but Judas and his men, invoking the great Sovereign of
the world, who without rams and instruments of war had laid Jericho low in the days of Joshua,
16 made a furious attack on the walls, and, capturing the town by the will of God, they massacred an
unspeakable number, so much so that the adjoining lake, which was two furlongs broad, looked as
though it were filled with the deluge of blood.
17 Drawing off seven hundred and fifty furlongs from thence, they made their way to Charax, to the
18 Jews who are styled Tubieni. Timotheus they did not find in that locality; he had gone off without
19 achieving any success, and left behind him in a certain post an extremely strong garrison. But
Dositheus and Sosipater, captains of Maccabaeus, sallied out and destroyed the troops left by
20 Timotheus in the stronghold, over ten thousand men. Whereupon Maccabaeus, arranging his men
in divisions, set a **leader** over **each** division, and hurried after Timotheus, who had with him

34. **Titus Manlius.** In 163 B.C., two years later than the date of this letter, a certain Manius Sergius was one of the envoys to Antiochus Epiphanes (Polybius, xxxi. 9. 6), and in 164 B.C. T. Manlius Torquatus went on a mission to Egypt (Livy, xliii. 11), but there is no record of any Roman envoys to Syria bearing the names of Q. Memmius and T. Manius (or Manlius). Niese (72 f.), in his desire to identify one of them, emends the reading of V (Μανιος Ερνιος) into Μάνιος Σέργιος, and takes Τίτος as the corruption of a name ending in -tius. But this is too heavy a price to pay for vindicating the historicity of the passage. For πρεσβύτης (*senex*) = πρεσβευτής (*legatus*) see 1 Macc. xiv. 22, xv. 17, Philemon 9.

XII. 6. **thither.** i.e. to the coast, where refugees from the interior were trying to escape by sea.
13. **earthworks.** For γεφυροῦν (om. V, Syr., &c.) read γεφύραις (55, Vg. = *firmam pontibus*) with Grimm and Kamphausen, in sense of 'embankments' or 'earthworks'. In 1 Macc. v. 26–36 Judas, during his raid into Gilead, captures Casphor among other towns, and subsequently (46 f.) storms Ephron, an 'extremely strong' town. When 'Gephyrun' is retained here, it may be identified with this Ephron, as the 'Gephyrus' of Polyb. v. 70. 12, or with Heshbon, which had a large reservoir adjacent (ver. 16). Otherwise the town's name, Caspin (or Caspis), must be connected with Casphor, i.e. the modern el-Muzeirit, 'the great station on the Hajj road' (so G. A. Smith, *Encycl. Biblica*, i. 707–8, who pronounces Furrer's identification of Casphon with Chisfin as 'philologically improbable').
20. **over each division.** Reading τούς, Grimm's conjecture for the MSS. αὐτούς.

21 a hundred and twenty thousand infantry and two thousand five hundred cavalry. Now as soon as
Timotheus heard of the onset of Judas, he sent forward the women and children and also the
baggage into a place called Carnaim, which was hard to besiege and difficult of access owing to its
22 narrow approaches on all sides. But when the first division of Judas appeared in sight, panic seized
the enemy, who were terrified by the manifestation of Him who beholdeth all things; they took
to flight in all directions, so that many got hurt by their own men and wounded by the points of
23 one another's swords, while Judas kept up a hot pursuit, putting the wicked wretches to the sword,
24 and destroying as many as thirty thousand men. Timotheus himself fell into the hands of Dositheus
and Sosipater, whom he adjured with plenty of specious guile to spare him and let him go, on the
ground that he had the parents of many and the brothers of some in his power, and that (if he were
25 not released) it would be the worse for them. So, to save their brethren, they let him go, after he
26 had solemnly pledged himself with many an oath to restore them unhurt. Then Judas attacked
27 Carnaim and the temple of Atergatis, massacring twenty-five thousand persons, and after this rout
and slaughter he made war against Ephron, a strong city, where Lysias had a residence and where
the inhabitants came from all nationalities. Stalwart young men drawn up in front of the
28 walls offered a resolute defence, and the place held ample stores of military engines and darts, but
the Jews invoked the Sovereign who crusheth forcibly the strength of his enemies, and got the city
29 into their hands, destroying as many as twenty-five thousand of the inhabitants. Setting out from
thence they marched in haste against Scythopolis, which is six hundred furlongs from Jerusalem,
30 but since the local Jews testified to the goodwill shown them by the Scythopolitans and to their
31 humane conduct during periods of misfortune, they simply thanked them and enjoined them to
continue well-disposed to their race in future. Then they marched up to Jerusalem, as the feast
of weeks was close at hand.
32, 33 After the feast called Pentecost they hurried against Gorgias, the governor of **Jamnia**, who came
34 out to meet them with three thousand foot soldiers and four hundred cavalry. And when they
35 joined battle, it came to pass that a few of the Jews fell. But a man Dositheus, belonging to the
Tubieni, who was a powerful horseman, caught hold of Gorgias and, gripping his mantle, dragged
him off by main force, meaning to capture the accursed wretch alive. A Thracian horseman bore
36 down on him, however, and disabled his arm, so that Gorgias managed to escape to Marisa. And
as Esdris and his men were now exhausted by the long fight, Judas called upon the Lord to
37 show he was their ally and leader in the fight; then, raising the war-cry and songs of praise in the
language of the fathers, he made an unexpected rush against the troops of Gorgias and routed them.
38 And Judas took his army to the town of Adullam, where, as the seventh day was coming on, they
39 purified themselves according to custom and kept the sabbath. Next day, when the troops of Judas
went—as it was high time they did—to pick up the corpses of the slain, in order to bring them
40 home to lie with their kinsfolk in their fathers' sepulchres, they discovered under the shirts of every
one of the dead men amulets of the idols of Jamnia—a practice forbidden the Jews by law. All saw
41 at once that this was why they had perished, and, blessing the (dealings) of the Lord, the just Judge
42 who revealeth what is secret, all betook themselves to supplication, beseeching that the sin committed might be wholly blotted out; and the noble-hearted Judas exhorted the people to keep themselves from sin, after what they had seen with their own eyes as the result of sin committed by those

21. **Carnaim.** The Carnaim of I Macc. v. 26, 43, where Derkĕto, the fish-goddess (cp. W. R. Smith's *Religion of Semites*², pp. 171 f.; Cheyne in *Encycl. Biblica*, i. 379), was worshipped as Atargatis (see below, ver. 26).

26. **Then,** &c. Resuming the narrative of ver. 23, after the interlude of vv. 24–25.

29. **Scythopolis,** the Bethshan of I Macc. v. 52, is so named in Judith iii. 10 and Polybius v. 70. 4 (cp. Rix, *Tent and Testament*, pp. 152 f.). Though a Hellenistic town under the Syrian power, it was not bitterly anti-Semitic at this period.

32. **Jamnia.** The change (Grotius) of Ἰδουμαίας into Ἰαμνείας brings the narrative more into line with ver. 40, I Macc. v. 58–9, and Josephus, *Ant.* XII. viii. 6 (where Gorgias is called Ἰαμνείας στρατηγός).

35. **Dositheus.** Evidently a different man from the Dositheus of vv. 19 and 24. For τοῦ Βακήνορος read (with 19, 62, 64, 93; so Niese) τῶν Τουβιηνῶν (Τωβιηνῶν). Dositheus belonged to the Tubieni Jews of ver. 17.

36. **Esdris.** The Γοργίαν of A 44, 64, &c., is more probably a correction of Ἐσδρίν, due to the feeling that Esdris (for the name cp. I Chron. xxvii. 26) has not hitherto been mentioned, than of Ἔσδραν (i. e. priests called after Ezra, Ewald). The epitomist, with characteristic carelessness, has forgotten to transcribe from Jason any previous allusion to this Jewish captain; hence the abruptness of his introduction. The earlier part of the engagement seems to have been costly and doubtful (for the reason assigned in ver. 40), but Judas as usual, with divine aid, proves successful in the end.

38. **the town of Adullam.** Not far from Marisa (the Mareshah of I Macc. v. 66); cp. Micah i. 15; 2 Chron. xi. 7; Neh. xi. 30.

purified themselves. i. e. from the stains of recent contact with pagans as well as of bloodshed.

40. **a practice forbidden.** Deut. vii. 26, &c. These ἱερώματα were small portable idols, worn as amulets (see W. Robertson Smith, *Religion of Semites*², pp. 208–9, and L. Blau, *Das altjüd. Zauberwesen*, pp. 86–7).

43 who had fallen. He then collected from them, man by man, the sum of two thousand drachmas of
silver, which he forwarded to Jerusalem for a sin-offering. In this he acted quite rightly and
44 properly, bearing in mind the resurrection—for if he had not expected the fallen to rise again, it
45 would have been superfluous and silly to pray for the dead—and having regard to the splendour of
the gracious reward which is reserved for those who have fallen asleep in godliness—a holy and
pious consideration! Hence he made propitiation for the dead, that they might be released from
their sin.

XIII. 1–26. *Lysias and Eupator forced to make terms with Jews.*

13 1 In the hundred and forty-ninth year tidings were brought to Judas and his men that Antiochus
2 Eupator was marching with large troops against Judaea, accompanied by Lysias his guardian and
chancellor, each commanding a Greek force consisting of a hundred and ten thousand foot-soldiers,
five thousand three hundred cavalry, twenty-two elephants, and three hundred chariots armed with
3 scythes. Menelaus also attached himself to them and, making loud pretences of patriotism, abetted
Antiochus—not that he cared for the safety of the fatherland, but because he thought he would
4 be appointed to office. But the King of kings stirred the anger of Antiochus against the
scoundrel, and, learning from Lysias that he was responsible for all the troubles, he ordered him to
5 be taken to Beroea and put to death there in the local fashion. For at Beroea there is a tower, fifty
cubits high, filled with (hot) ashes, and a revolving contrivance which drops the victim sheer into the
6 ashes. To this they **bring** any one who is guilty of sacrilege or other heinous crimes, and they all
7 **push** him on, to meet his doom. By such a fate it befell that Menelaus, the law-breaker, died,
8 not even getting a grave in earth. And this was perfectly just. Many a sin had he committed
against the altar, whose fire and ashes were holy; by ashes, then, he got his death.
9 Now the king was coming in hot indignation to inflict on the Jews the very sorest of the sufferings
10 that had befallen them in his father's time. But when Judas heard this, he bade the people call day
and night on the Lord, that he would succour them, now if ever, as they were on the point of losing
11 the Law, their country, and the holy temple, and that he would not allow the people, after their brief
12 and recent revival, to fall into the hands of profane pagans. Now when they had all done so with one
accord, and implored the merciful Lord for three days without ceasing, weeping and fasting and
13 lying prostrate, Judas addressed them and ordered them to get ready. After consulting privately
with the elders, he determined that, before the king could throw his army into Judaea and master
14 the city, they would march out and decide the issue by the help of God. So, committing the
outcome of it to the Creator of the world, and charging his men to fight stoutly, even to death, for
15 laws, temple, city, country, and polity, he pitched his camp near Modin, and, giving his troops the
watchword of VICTORY IS GOD'S, he and a picked body of his bravest young men made an onset
by night upon the royal tent and slew as many as two thousand men within the camp; they also
16 **stabbed** the chief elephant and his mahout, and finally, after filling the camp with panic and
17 confusion, got away triumphantly, just as the day began to dawn. This was due to the help of
God's protection.
18, 19 After this taste of the Jews' prowess the king used stratagem in attacking their positions. Thus
he moved upon Beth-sura, a strong fortress of the Jews, was routed, dashed at it (again), was worsted.
20, 21 Judas got the necessaries of life conveyed to those inside. But Rhodocus, a Jewish soldier, betrayed
the secrets of the Jews to the enemy; search was made for him, he was arrested and imprisoned.
22 Again the king made overtures to the residents in Beth-sura, pledged his right hand, took theirs,

43. **man by man.** κατ' ἀνδρολογεῖον (Swete) or κατ' ἀνδραλογίαν (V, 74, Fritzsche) is a corruption of κατ' ἄνδρα λογίαν (44, 71, cp. Deissmann's *Bible-Studies*, pp. 219–20) or λογείαν. The following κατασκευάσματα is to be omitted (with 52, 55, 74, 106, 243) as a gloss. The sacrifice for the dead is recounted in such a way as to suggest that the writer anticipated, not unnaturally, objections to it on the score of novelty. It is, from the religious standpoint, one of the remarkable contributions made by this book to our knowledge of contemporary Judaism.

XIII. 2. **elephants.** The elephants and their mahouts (ver. 15) were imported by the Seleucid monarchs from India. The 'futile device' of the scythed chariot (ἅρμα δρεπανηφόρον, *currus falceatus*) was used as late as the battle of Magnesia (cp. Livy xxxvii. 40–1), 'but it may be questioned whether after the experience of that day they were used again' (Bevan, *House of Seleucus*, ii. 290).

5. Nothing otherwise is known of this local custom at Beroea (the modern Aleppo), 'but suffocation in a pit full of ashes was a recognized Persian punishment, and one frequently inflicted upon offenders of a high class' (Rawlinson). See Ovid's *Ibis*, 317–18.

6. **they bring.** Reading ἄραντες (Niese) for the unintelligible ἄπαντες of the MSS., and προωθοῦσιν below ('push on') for the προσωθοῦσιν of the MSS. With 7–8 cp. iv. 26, ix. 5–6, Wisd. xvi. 1.

15. **stabbed.** Reading συνεκέντησε (cp. xii. 23), Grimm's ingenious correction of the meaningless συνέθηκεν of the MSS.

17. **just as . . . dawn. This.** Omitting (with V) the δέ after ὑποφαινούσης and adding (with V, so Niese) δέ after τοῦτο. Judas still believed in night-attacks (viii. 7).

21. Rhodocus apparently was more leniently treated than the earlier traitors (x. 22).

22. **pledged his right hand, took theirs,** &c. See xii. 12. The writer, or the source which he is hurriedly recapitu-

23 departed, attacked the forces of Judas, was defeated, heard that Philip who had been left as
chancellor in Antioch had become desperate, was confounded by the news, proposed peace to the
Jews, submitted with an oath to all their equitable conditions, came to terms with them and offered
24 sacrifice, honoured the sanctuary and the sacred Place, behaved humanely, took gracious farewell
25 of Maccabaeus, left Hegemonides in command from Ptolemais to **Gerar**, went to Ptolemais. The
men of Ptolemais felt sore over the treaty; they were excessively indignant with the Jews and
26 wanted to annul the articles of the agreement. Lysias advanced to the bêma, defended it as well
as possible, convinced them, pacified and won them over, departed to Antioch. Such was the course
of the king's inroad and retreat.

XIV. 1–46. *Intrigues and threats of Nicanor.*

14 1 Now after the space of three years Judas and his men learned that Demetrius the son of Seleucus
2 had sailed into the haven of Tripolis with a powerful army and fleet, and had seized the country,
3 after making away with Antiochus and Lysias his guardian. And Alcimus, a former high-priest,
who had voluntarily polluted himself in days when there was no trafficking (with the Gentiles), and
who therefore judged he was no longer safe and that he was now debarred entirely from the holy
4 altar, came to king Demetrius in the hundred and fifty-first year with the present of a golden crown
and palm, and, in addition to these customary gifts, some of the olive-branches from the temple.
5 The first day he said nothing. But when he did get a chance of furthering his infatuated enterprise,
on being summoned to confer with Demetrius and being asked about the temper and aims of the
6 Jews, he replied: It is the Jews called Hasidaeans, led by Judas Maccabaeus, who are keeping up the
7 feud and stirring sedition; they will not let the kingdom settle down in peace. Wherefore, deprived of
8 my ancestral glory—I mean, the high-priesthood—I have now come hither, primarily from a sincere
concern for the king's interests, and secondly from anxiety on behalf of my own fellow-citizens; for
9 the recklessness of the aforesaid party has involved our nation in no small misfortune. Acquaint
thyself, O king, with the details of this business, and take measures on behalf of our country and our
10 sorely tried nation, according to the gracious kindness which thou showest to all. For as long as
11 Judas is alive, it is impossible for the State to be at peace. When he said this, the rest of the king's
Friends, who cherished ill will against Judas, hastened to inflame Demetrius still further against him,
12 and, after instantly summoning Nicanor, formerly master of the elephants, and appointing him
13 governor of Judaea, he dispatched him with written instructions to make away with Judas and to
14 scatter his troops and to set up Alcimus as high-priest of the great temple. Now all the heathen
throughout Judaea, whom Judas had driven to flight, flocked to join Nicanor, anticipating that the
15 misfortunes and calamities of the Jews would mean gain to them. But when the Jews heard of
Nicanor's inroad and the onset of the heathen, they sprinkled earth upon their heads and solemnly
invoked Him who had established his own people to all eternity and who ever upholds those who
16 are his Portion with visible aid. Then, by order of their leader, they at once started out and joined
17 battle with them at a village called Lessau. Now Simon, the brother of Judas, had already
encountered Nicanor and, thrown suddenly into consternation by the foe, had sustained a temporary
18 check. Nevertheless, Nicanor shrank from deciding the issue at the sword's point, as he had
heard of the manliness and the courage shown by the troops of Judas in fighting for their country.
19 He therefore sent Posidonius and Theodotus and Mattathias to give and receive pledges of friend-
20 ship. After full consideration, when the proposals were laid by the general before the troops, and
21 it appeared they were all of one mind, the compact was agreed to, and a day was fixed for the two

lating, glosses over the fact that the fortress was starved into surrender (1 Macc. vi. 49–50), and that Judas was routed (cp. Josephus, *Ant.* XII. ix. 5).

23. Cp. v. 22, ix. 29, where a different tradition emerges. It was really Lysias, not the king, who was upset by the news of Philip's move (cp. 1 Macc. vi. 55 f.).

24. **Hegemonides.** If *ἡγεμονίδην* is equivalent to *ἡγεμόνα*, the story is guilty of another historical error in making Lysias appoint Judas as governor. But the word is more probably a proper name, formed on the analogy of Ἡγεμόνιος, especially as *στρατηγόν* would otherwise be superfluous.

Gerar. For Γερρηνῶν (V), = 'the inhabitants of Gerrha', read Γεραρηνῶν (Γεραρήρων 55) = Gerar, SE. of Gaza (so Ewald), or Garar (Syr.), i. e. Gezer (Gazara) near Lydda (1 Macc. xv. 28, 35). The phrase means 'from Ptolemais on the north to G. on the south'. Gerrha (Gerra), between Rhinocura and Pelusium, belonged at this time to Egypt. Hence, unless the writer is held guilty of a serious error, the other reading is preferable.

XIV. 3. **voluntarily polluted himself**, &c. The Hellenistic proclivities of Alcimus were aggravated, to the writer's mind, by their gratuitousness; he had not been forced to adopt Syro-Greek customs, and he had not the excuse of any syncretistic current during his high-priesthood (cp. ver. 38).

14. **whom Judas had driven to flight.** A solecism (*πεφυγαδευκότες τὸν* Ἰούδαν) apparently based on the analogous uses of *φεύγειν τινά* = 'to fly from one' (e. g. Herod. v. 62).

16. **Lessau.** The *v. l.* Δεεσαού is connected by Ewald with the Adasa of 1 Macc. vii. 40, 45; otherwise neither Lessau nor Dessau can be identified.

17. **a temporary check.** Reading *βραχέως* (V) instead of *βραδέως* (A, 19, 44, 62, &c.).

22 leaders to meet by themselves. A litter was carried forward from each army; chairs of state were
placed; Judas stationed armed men ready in suitable positions, lest the enemy should spring any
23 treacherous attack; they carried through the conference duly. Nicanor stayed a while in Jerusalem
24 and did nothing amiss; he even disbanded the hordes who had flocked to join his standard;
25 he kept Judas always beside him; he had become heartily attached to the man, urged him to
marry and beget children. He did marry, settled down, and enjoyed life.
26 But when Alcimus saw their mutual goodwill, he got hold of the treaty which had been concluded
and went to Demetrius, alleging that Nicanor was ill affected toward the State, since he had
27 appointed that conspirator Judas to be his successor. At this the king fell into a passion
and, exasperated by the calumnies of the scoundrel, wrote to Nicanor that he was displeased
at the compact, and ordered him to send Maccabaeus instantly as a prisoner to Antioch.
28 Nicanor was confounded by this news and sadly vexed at the thought of annulling the terms
29 arranged, as the man had done no wrong. However, as the king could not be gainsaid, he bided
30 his time to carry out the business by a stratagem. But Maccabaeus noticed that Nicanor was
treating him with less friendliness and behaving more rudely than was his wont; so, reckoning this
harshness was of a sinister character, he gathered a considerable number of his men and hid from
31 Nicanor. The latter, conscious that he had been pluckily outwitted by Judas, went to the great and
holy temple, while the priests were offering the usual sacrifices, and commanded them to deliver up
32, 33 the man. And when they swore they did not know where the man was whom he sought, he
stretched forth his right hand toward the sanctuary, and swore this oath: Unless you hand over
Judas as my prisoner, I will raze this shrine of God to the ground, and break down the altar, and
34 erect on this spot a temple of Dionysus for all to see. With these words he went away. But the
priests stretched forth their hands to heaven, invoking Him who ever fighteth for our nation, thus:
35 O Lord, who hast no need of aught, as it hath pleased thee to have among us a sanctuary where thou
36 dwellest, so now, O holy Lord, from whom is all hallowing, keep free from defilement for evermore
this house so lately cleansed, and shut every impious mouth.
37 Now information was laid before Nicanor against a Jerusalemite elder called Razis, a patriot who
was very highly esteemed, and addressed as Father of the Jews on account of his benevolence. For
38 in bygone days, when there was no trafficking (with the Gentiles), he had been accused of Judaism,
39 and had most resolutely risked body and life for Judaism. So Nicanor, with the intention of
40 showing his hostility to the Jews, sent over five hundred soldiers to arrest him. For he meant to
41 strike a blow at the Jews by this arrest. But when the troops were on the point of capturing the
tower, forcing the outer door of the courtyard and calling for fire to set light to the doors, he fell
42 upon his sword, seeing he was surrounded on every side; he preferred to die a noble death rather
43 than fall into the scoundrels' hands and suffer outrages unworthy of his noble character. Owing to
the hurry of the struggle, however, he missed his stroke, and, as a crowd of men was now pouring
through the door, he pluckily ran up to the wall and threw himself bravely down among the crowds.
44, 45 They drew back at once, so that he fell between them on the open street. Still alive, however, he
got up in a fury of anger and ran, with blood pouring from him, sore wounded as he was, right
46 through the crowds; then, standing on a steep rock, his blood now drained from him, he tore out
his bowels, taking both his hands to them, and flung them at the crowds. So he died, calling on
Him who is lord of life and spirit to restore them to him again.

XV. 1–36. *Attack, defeat, and death of Nicanor.*

15 1 Now, learning that Judas and his men were in the region of Samaria, Nicanor determined to
2 attack them without any risk upon the day of rest. And when the Jews who were forced to accompany him said, Destroy them not so savagely and barbarously, but show honour to the day which
3 He who beholdeth all things hath hallowed in his holiness, the thrice-accursed wretch asked them
4 if there was a Sovereign in heaven who had ordered the observance of the sabbath day. And when
they declared, There is the living Lord, himself a Sovereign in heaven, who bade us observe the
5 seventh day, he replied, I too am a sovereign on earth, and my orders are to take arms and execute
the king's business. Nevertheless he did not succeed in executing his shocking purpose.
6 Now Nicanor, in the height of his overweening pride, had determined to erect a public trophy of
7 victory over Judas and his men; but Maccabaeus still ceased not to trust with absolute confidence

24. **the hordes**, i.e. the supporters mentioned in ver. 14.
36. **and shut every impious mouth.** So 19, 62, *φράξον δὲ πᾶν στόμα ἄνομον* (*φράξεις . . . ἄδικον*, 64, 93 *a*), and S.
42. A higher motive for suicide than in the case of Ptolemy Macron (x. 13).

XV. 5. **he did not succeed**, &c. The writer gives no account of what transpired. The purpose of the excerpt is simply to exalt, in ultra-Pharisaic and unhistorical fashion (cp. 1 Macc. ii. 41), the rigid sabbatarianism of the Maccabaean army.

8 that he would obtain help from the Lord, and exhorted his company not to dread the onset of the
heathen, but to keep in mind all the help they had formerly received from heaven and to expect at
9 the present hour the victory which would be theirs from the Almighty; and comforting them out
of the law and the prophets, as well as recalling the struggles they had endured, he made them
10 more eager (for the fray). Then, after rousing their spirits, he issued his orders, and at the same time
11 pointed out the heathen's perfidy and breach of their oaths. He armed each man, not so much with
confidence in shields and spears as with the heartening which comes from apt words, and also
12 cheered them all by recounting a reliable dream, a **sort of vision**. This was what he had seen: Onias,
the former high priest, a good and great man, of stately bearing yet gracious in manner, well-spoken
and trained from childhood in all points of virtue—Onias with outstretched hands invoking blessings
13 on the whole body of the Jews; then another man in the same attitude, conspicuous by his grey
14 hairs and splendour, and invested with marvellous, majestic dignity. This, Onias explained to him,
is the lover of the brethren, who prayeth fervently for the people and the holy city, Jeremiah the
15 prophet of God. And Jeremiah held out his right hand to present Judas with a golden sword, and
16 as he gave it he addressed him thus: Take this holy sword as a gift from God, and with it thou
shalt crush the foe.
17 So, encouraged by these truly heroic words of Judas, which had the power of rousing young souls
to valour and stirring them to manliness, they determined not to pitch camp but manfully to set
upon the foe and, by engaging them right valiantly hand to hand, to decide the issue, since the city
18 and the sanctuary and the temple were in danger. For their anxiety about wives and children, as
well as about brethren and kinsfolk, weighed less with them than their supreme and chief anxiety
19 about the consecrated sanctuary. Whereas those left behind in the city were uneasy about the
20 encounter in the open country, and suffered no slight anguish. All were now waiting for the critical
moment, the enemy had now **united their forces** and drawn up their line of battle, the elephants
21 were arranged for easy action, and the cavalry stationed on the wings, when Maccabaeus, surveying
the hordes in front of him, with their varied weapons and fierce elephants, held up his hands to
heaven and called upon the Lord, the worker of wonders, for he knew that victory is not decided
22 by weapons but won by the Lord for such as He judgeth to deserve it. And his prayer was in these
terms: Thou, Sovereign Lord, didst send thine angel in the days of Hezekiah king of Judaea, and
23 he slew as many as a hundred and eighty-five thousand of Sennacherib's host; so now, O heavenly
24 Sovereign, send a good angel before us to scare and terrify the foe; by the great strength of thine
25 arm may those who have blasphemously assailed thy holy sanctuary be utterly dismayed. And as
26 he ended with these words, Nicanor and his men advanced with trumpets and paeans. But Judas
27 and his men joined battle with the enemy, calling upon God and praying; and so fighting with their
hands, while they prayed to God with their hearts, they slew no fewer than thirty-five thousand men,
28 mightily cheered by the manifest help of God. The battle over, they were returning with joy, when
29 they recognized Nicanor lying dead in full armour; a shout of excitement arose, they blessed the
30 Sovereign Lord in the language of their fathers, and he who was ever in body and soul the protagonist
of his fellow-citizens, he who retained through life his youthful patriotism, ordered Nicanor's head
31 and arm to be cut off and carried to Jerusalem. When he arrived there, and had called his country-
32 men together and set the priests before the altar, he sent for the garrison of the citadel, showed them
the vile Nicanor's head and the impious creature's hand which he had stretched out vauntingly
33 against the holy house of the Almighty; then, cutting out the impious Nicanor's tongue, he said he
would throw it piecemeal to the birds and hang up the rewards of his insensate folly opposite the
34 sanctuary. And they all lifted to heaven their cry of blessing to the Lord who had manifested
35 himself, saying, Blessed be He who hath preserved his own Place undefiled. And he hung Nicanor's
36 head from the citadel, a clear and conspicuous token to all of the Lord's help. And all decided, by
public decree, never to let this day pass uncelebrated, but to celebrate the thirteenth day of the
twelfth month—called Adar in Syriac—the day before the day of Mordecai.

11. **a sort of vision.** Reading *ὕπαρ τι* for *ὑπέρ τι*. This intercessory function of the saints is denied in Slav. En. liii. 1.

20. **united their forces.** Reading *συμμιξάντων* (V) for *προσμιξάντων* (A).

21. **and fierce elephants.** Omitting, with V, *ἐπὶ μέρος εὔκαιρον*.

24. **sanctuary.** Reading *ναόν* (V) for *λαόν* (A). Cp. xiv. 33.

33. **the rewards of his insensate folly.** i.e. the mutilated head and hand (cp. 1 Macc. vii. 47), which were the miserable recompense of his insensate attack on the Jews. The citadel was not in the hands of the Jews at this period, however, but held by a Syrian garrison.

34. **to heaven . . . to the Lord.** Cp. 1 Macc. iv. 24, 55.

35. Cp. 1 Sam. xxxi. 10, Judith xiv. 1. For 'head' (as a rendering of *προτομήν*) R. V. prefers 'head and shoulder' (cp. ver. 30).

XV. 37–39. *Epilogue of the epitomist.*

37 Such was the history of Nicanor; and as the city was held from that period by the Hebrews,
38 I will make this the end of my story. If it has been well told, if it has been skilfully arranged, such
39 was my desire; but if it is poor and indifferent, that was all I could manage. For just as it is bad
to drink wine alone or again to drink water alone, whereas wine mixed with water proves at once
wholesome and delightful, so the skill with which a book is composed is a delight to the taste
of readers.
And here shall be the end.

37. **the city was held from that period.** A pious exaggeration; the citadel was not captured by the Jews till 142–141 B.C., and Antiochus Sidetes recaptured the city in 133 B.C.

39. This verse carries on the thought of the first part of the preceding verse; it has nothing to do with the second part. The writer expresses himself obscurely, although the obscurity may be due to some corruption of the text, but it is clear that he is not comparing graphic and prosaic passages in his narrative to wine and water, as if defending the blend of the two. He did his best, he pleads, to be pointed. For good style, blended with sound matter, adds to the reader's profit and pleasure; facts alone, and style alone, are alike inferior to this combination of history and literature.

THE THIRD BOOK OF MACCABEES

INTRODUCTION

§ 1. Contents and Main Conclusions.

The scene of *3 Maccabees* is placed in the reign of Ptolemy IV (Philopator) at the time of the battle of Raphia (217 B.C.). It narrates an attempt made by the king to enter the Temple at Jerusalem, and his miraculous repulse. In consequence he determines to wreak his vengeance on the Jews of Alexandria, and of Egypt as a whole, first by interfering with their religion, and altering their political status, and afterwards by letting loose drunken elephants to trample them to death in the Hippodrome of Alexandria. After his purpose has been several times providentially delayed, it is finally foiled by a vision of angels which turns the elephants upon the persecutors. The king repents and becomes the patron of the Jews, who return in safety and rejoicing to their homes. The story as it stands is full of impossibilities and bombastic exaggerations, but each one of the incidents taken singly may well rest on some basis of fact, though they certainly did not all take place in the same reign. The general accuracy of the technical and official language of the book is confirmed by a comparison with Ptolemaic Papyri, and the book as a whole has striking points of contact with *2 Maccabees* and the *Letter of Aristeas*. It would seem to have been written in Alexandria at about the same time as these books, not far from 100 B.C., a date which is confirmed by indications drawn from Papyri. The writer apparently used the lost memoirs of the reign of Philopator, written by Ptolemy Megalopolitanus shortly after his death. He seems to have combined a narrative of Philopator's attempt to enter the Temple with a later story, preserved in another form by Josephus, of a persecution of Egyptian Jews by Physcon.

§ 2. Title.

Maccabees is really a misnomer, unless with Fritzsche we consider the book to be part of a prolegomena to a complete history of the Maccabees. Πτολεμαικά (see below, § 9) would be more accurate. Syncellus (I. 516) cites the *Letter of Aristeas* as πτολεμαικά. It is probable that the present title is not original. It may easily have arisen from its collocation with the other books of Maccabees in the MSS.

§ 3. MSS. and Versions.

The book is found in A and V (= Holmes and Parsons 23), and in many cursives; see Fritzsche, *Libr. Apocr. Graece*, p. xx, and Swete, *Intr. to the O.T. in Greek*, pp. 148 ff.; 19, 62, 64, 93 agree continually and give a Lucianic Text. It is not in the Vulgate, but is found in the Syriac Peshitta, the text of which represents a free and expanded rendering, sometimes agreeing with the Lucianic Text. There is also an Armenian version, which is probably to be dated A.D. 400–600, in the golden age of Armenian literature. It is a loose, but very literary, translation in the style of the fifth-century historian, Faustus of Byzant, and is found in most MSS. of the Armenian Bible.[1]

The text is generally well preserved and presents as a whole no serious problems. The variations of reading seldom affect the sense, and usually arise from the desire to substitute for the forced phraseology of the writer a simpler and more familiar expression. Even in cases where the MSS. seem to be corrupt, the general meaning is clear, and the confusion always appears to be due to the difficulties raised by the verbose and obscure style of the book. Emendation is very uncertain, as the ordinary canons of language and grammar can hardly be applied. There are interesting examples of probable conflation, e.g. in ii. 6, 24, v. 43.

[1] For these facts, and for the readings from the Armenian version in the critical notes, I am indebted to the ready help of Mr. F. C. Conybeare.

§ 4. Date and Origin.

The date must be determined by internal considerations. There is no early attestation to the existence of the book (see below, § 9), but it cannot have been written after the destruction of the temple. It clearly belongs to the Jewish apologetic literature which sprang into being in the second century B.C. and continued to be popular for some time. It has points of contact with *Esther* and *Judith* on the one hand, though unlike them it has no hero, and with *Sirach*, *Wisdom*, and *4 Maccabees* on the other. But the connexion is specially close with *2 Maccabees* and the *Letter of Aristeas*.

(*a*) *Relation to 2 Maccabees.* (α) Many of the leading ideas and incidents are the same :— The repulse of Heliodorus (2 Macc. iii. 22–31), and the punishment of Antiochus (ix. 4 ff., cf. 3 Macc. ii. 21–4); miraculous visions (iii. 25, x. 29, xi. 8; cf. 3 Macc. vi. 18); stress on the sanctity of the temple and prayers for its defence (iii. 15–22, viii. 2–4, xiv. 34–6; cf. 3 Macc. i. 11 ff., ii. 1 ff.); attacks on religion (vi. 9, &c.; cf. 3 Macc. ii. 27 ff., iii. 21); attempts to enforce an alien citizenship (iv. 9; cf. 3 Macc. ib.); stress laid on memorial feasts (x. 6, xv. 36; cf. 3 Macc. vi. 30–6. An aged and pious Eleazar appears in both books (vi. 18; cf. 3 Macc. vi. 1); official letters are included (ix. 18 ff., xi. 16 ff.; cf. 3 Macc. iii. 12 ff., vii. 1 ff.); the picture of the general horror in iii. 15 ff. is like that in 3 Macc. i. 16 ff., iv. 3–8.

(β) There is a strong resemblance in style and language. Both books present the same type of literary, or pseudo-classical, Greek. Crasis of the definite article, and various classical syntactical forms, are common to the two books and found nowhere else in the LXX[1]; both show the same fondness for connecting sentences with δέ. The following words found in both occur nowhere else in the LXX :—

[2] *διακομίζω* i. 2; iv. 5, ix. 29 in passive.
δοριάλωτος i. 5; v. 11.
ἀντίπαλοι i. 5; xiv. 17.
εὐταξία i. 10; iv. 37.
παραναγιγνώσκω i. 12; viii. 23.
φρυάσσομαι ii. 2; vii. 34 [cf. Acts iv. 25].
κραδαίνω ii. 21; xi. 8.
ἀντιλήμψεως τεύξασθαι ii. 33; xv. 7 [the same peculiar form of the Aorist; see Thackeray, *o. c.*, p. 287].
ἀλιτήριοι iii. 16; xii. 23, xiii. 4, xiv. 42.
ὑψαυχενῶν iii. 19; xv. 6.
ὑφορώμενος iii. 23; vii. 24.
πρὸ τῶν ὀφθαλμῶν λαμβάνειν iv. 4; viii. 17.
ὁμοεθνής iv. 12, vii. 14; iv. 2.
μιᾶς ὑπὸ καιρὸν ἡμέρας iv. 14; vii. 20.
ἐλεφαντάρχης v. 4, &c.; xiv. 12.
μεγαλομερῶς vi. 33 [adj. v. 8]; iv. 22, 49.
προσημαίνω v. 13, 47; iv. 23.
ἀθέμιτος v. 20; vi. 5, vii. 1, x. 34.
ὁ ἐπιφανὴς Κύριος v. 35; xv. 34.
ἀλογιστία v. 42; xiv. 8.
ἰσόπεδος v. 43; viii. 3, ix. 14.
ἄτρωτος v. 47; viii. 36, x. 30 [in classical sense = unwounded].
καταστέλλω vi. 1; iv. 31.
τερατοποιός [of God] vi. 32; xv. 21.
οἰωνόβρωτος vi. 34; ix. 15.

The following words are found in both books, and are rare otherwise :—

κατάκλειστος i. 18; iii. 19 [in both cases with *παρθένοι*]; Wisd. xviii. 4.
ἀγερωχία, -ος i. 25, ii. 3; ix. 7; Wisd. ii. 9.
ἀπροσδεής [of God] ii. 9; xiv. 35; 1 Macc. xii. 9 [not of God].
ἐπόπτης [of God] ii. 21; iii. 39, vii. 35; Ad. Esth. v. 1.
ἀνίκητος iv. 21; xi. 13; 4 Macc. *ter*.
ἀπεχθής, -ως iii. 4, v. 3; v. 23; Wisd. xix. 15.
ἀπήμαντος vi. 6; xii. 25; Wisd. vii. 22.
ἀδιαλείπτως vi. 33; iii. 26, &c.; 1 Macc. xii. 11.
ξενίζων [as adj.] vii. 3; ix. 6; Esther iii. 13.
εὐσταθεῖν vii. 4; xii. 2, xiv. 25; Jer. xxx. 9.
ἄδεια vii. 12; xi. 30; Wisd. xii. 11.
καθιδρεύειν vii. 20; iv. 12; Ep. Jer. 17.
προειρημένος five times in 3 Macc.; six times in 2 Macc.; 1 Esdras vi. 32 [A].

The similarity of phrase in the following cases is noticeable :—

χειρονομία i. 5; *ἐν χειρῶν νομαῖς* v. 14.
κισσόφυλλον ii. 29; *κισσοί* vi. 7 and reference to Dionysiac worship.
χείριστος μόρος iii. 1; *οἴκτιστος μόρος* ix. 28.
ἀποτυμπανίζω iii. 27; *τύμπανον* vi. 19, 28.
πασῆς δυνάμεως δυναστεύων v. 7 [cf. *δυνάστης* v. 51]; *πασῆς ἐξουσίας δυνάστης* iii. 24 [all of God].
βασιλεὺς τῶν βασιλευόντων v. 35; *β. βασιλέων* xiii. 4 [both of God].
'Scythian' cruelty vii. 5; iv. 47.

Add also the idea of the *ἐπιφάνεια* of God, and the use of *τόπος* for the temple, which are frequent in both books.

Though these resemblances are sufficiently striking, there are differences which prevent our ascribing the books to the same author. The style of 2 Maccabees is much better than that of 3 Maccabees; it is less involved and exaggerated, and more akin to the style of Polybius. Nor

[1] See Thackeray, *Gr. O.T. in Greek*, pp. 138, 248, 279.
[2] In each verse the reference to 3 Macc. is given first.

is it easy to establish a direct literary dependence on either side.[1] The impression left is that both books belong to the same school of thought, and probably to the same period.

(*b*) *Relation to the Letter of Aristeas.* (*a*) There is a general similarity in the idea and purpose of the books. Both aim at glorifying the Jew in his own eyes and in the eyes of the Greek world; stress is laid on the importance of his position, and his fidelity to the Ptolemies (*Aristeas*, 36, &c.).[2] A Ptolemy is the central figure in each book, and he is represented as acknowledging the protection of the God of the Jews (16, 19, 37; cf. 3 Macc. iii. 21, v. 31, vi. 24 ff., vii. 6 ff.). Much is made of the inviolability and beauty of the temple (83 ff.) and the overwhelming awe inspired by it (99); the latter would seem to be a simpler expression of the physical terror and helplessness which in 3 Macc. ii. 21 overtakes Philopator; cf. also the punishments of those who profaned the secrecy of the text of the law (313 ff.). Other points of contact are the discussion of Jewish separateness in food and life (128 ff.; cf. 3 Macc. iii. 3 ff.), the place played in each story by the repeated royal feasts (187 &c., 3 Macc. iv. 16, v, vi), the inclusion of official letters, and the position of the typical priest Eleazar (22, 29, 33, 41; cf. 3 Macc. iii. 12, vii. 1; 33, 41, &c.; vi. 1).

(β) *Style and language.* The most striking resemblances are found in the official letters, or decrees:—[3]

χαίρειν καὶ ἐρρῶσθαι iii. 12, vii. 1; 35; cf. 41.
προστετάχαμεν iii. 25, vii. 8; 24.
μηνύειν τὸν βουλόμενον ἐφ' ᾧ . . . iii. 28; τὸν βουλόμενον προσαγγέλλειν περὶ τῶν ἀπειθησάντων ἐφ' ᾧ . . . 25 [reward follows in each case].

Cf. also iii. 25 with 25 [διειλήφαμεν γάρ, &c.]; and ὑπομαστιαίων in iii. 27 with ἐπιμαστιδίων in 27.
ὁ τῆς ἐπιστολῆς τύπος οὕτως ἐγέγραπτο iii. 30; ἐπιστολὴ τὸν τύπον ἔχουσα τοῦτον 34.
καθ' ὀντινοῦν τρόπον vii. 7; 24.

Remarkable words or phrases common to both books include the following:—[4]

†ἐντυχία [technically of a petition] vi. 40: 1.
†ἀπόλυσις vi. 37, 40; 16.
ὁ πάντων ἐπόπτης θεός ii. 21; 16.
ὁλοσχερής v. 31; 27 [-ῶς].
†ἀλόγως vi. 25; 24, 107.
θεωρία v. 24; 31.
καταχωρίζω [technically] ii. 29; 36.
παραναγιγνώσκω i. 12; 42.
ἀδιάλειπτος, -ως vi. 33; 86, 92, 294.
†ἕως [dawn] v. 46; 88.
†ἰδιότης vii. 17; 97.
παρὰ πόδας ὁρῶντες, or ἔχοντες iv. 8, v. 8; 135.
δυναστεύων [of God] v. 7; 168, 195.
†ἄπταιστος vi. 39; 187.
τραπῆναι εἰς [πρὸς] εὐφροσύνην v. 36; 202, 294.
ἀπροσδεής ii. 9; 211.
ἀλόγιστος v. 42, vi. 12; 213.
εὐστάθεια iii. 26, vi. 28; 217, 261.
†κατευφημεῖν vii. 13; 217.
†ἀνέφικτος ii. 15; 223, 283.
†μεγαλομερής v. 8; 226, 319.
ἐπιφάνεια [of God] v. 8; 264.
ἐνέργεια [of God] iv. 21, v. 12; 266.
†ἄληκτος iv. 2 [V]; 269.
ἐπιείκεια καὶ φιλανθρωπία [in technical sense, of king] iii. 15; 290.

As with *2 Maccabees*, the connexion seems to be of school and date. The similarity in the use of technical and official language is specially remarkable; as we shall see in the next paragraph, this language was that actually in use in documents of the Ptolemaic period.

(*c*) *Relation to Papyri.* The evidence of the papyri confirms the general accuracy of the official and technical language of the book, and suggests that it belongs to the Ptolemaic period, not the Roman.

Applying Thackeray's test[5] of οὐθείς (μηθείς) as against οὐδείς (μηδείς), we find the θ form in i. 13 (A), ii. 28 (V), vii. 8 (A), as against six times where the MSS. agree with the spelling with δ. The fluctuation is much the same as in Wisdom (see Introd. to Wisdom *in loc.* in this volume), and both books are probably to be referred to the 'period of transition' 132 B.C. to 100 B.C., or rather later.

Again, the formula χαίρειν καὶ ἐρρῶσθαι κτλ. (iii. 12, vii. 1), which it will be remembered is found in the *Letter of Aristeas*, seems 'to point to a date at the end of the second or the beginning of the first century B.C.'[6] Earlier papyri usually have a conditional sentence; papyri of the end

[1] It is usually assumed without any serious attempt at proof that the writer of *3 Maccabees* used *2 Maccabees*. Willrich argues, on the other hand, that the reverse is true (*Iudaica*, pp. 163 ff.).

[2] The references are to Wendland's paragraphs, as printed in Mr. Thackeray's edition in Swete's *Intr. to the O.T. in Greek*². The English translation with critical and exegetical notes will be found in vol. ii of this work.

[3] Thackeray has already called attention to some of these in Swete, *o. c.*, p. 502, n. 3. As before, the reference to 3 Macc. is in each case given first.

[4] Those marked with † do not occur elsewhere in the LXX.

[5] *Grammar O.T. in Greek*, pp. 58 ff.

[6] For the facts and references in this paragraph I am indebted to information kindly placed at my disposal by Mr. Thackeray in a private letter.

of the first century B.C. and onwards have πλεῖστα χαίρειν. Cf. especially *P. Grenf.* ii. 36 (95 B.C.) and *P. Lips.* 104 (*c.* 96 B.C.), where the resemblance to *3 Maccabees* is peculiarly close.

λαογραφία (ii. 28),[1] which had been supposed to point to the Roman period, has been proved to be entirely in place in the Ptolemaic age; and again the dating by Egyptian months alone (vi. 38), in which Willrich[2] finds a sign of late date, occurs much earlier, the equalizing of the Egyptian and Macedonian months having taken place in the reign of Euergetes II (Physcon).[3]

In *Tebt. P.* 5 (an official document of the beginning of the same reign) we find οἱ ἐπὶ τῶν προσόδων (cf. 3 Macc. vi. 30); οἱ τεταγμένοι ἐπὶ πραγμάτων [χρειῶν] (cf. vii. 1, v. 14); καθ' ὀντινοῦν τρόπον (cf. vii. 7 and *Letter of Aristeas*, 24). In *Louvre P.* 63 (an official letter of Philometor's reign) occur the words τιθηνεῖσθαι (cf. iii. 15), σκεπάζειν (cf. iii. 27), εὐχρηστία (cf. ii. 33), ἀσχολία (cf. v. 34), the first two words being used in the same technical sense. καταχωρίζω (= enroll, ii. 29; *Aristeas* 36) occurs in the Canopus and Rosetta inscriptions, and frequently in Papyri; the same inscriptions speak of records on a στήλη (ii. 27, vii. 20), and afford evidence of the popularity of commemorative feasts (vi. 36, vii. 19). μηνύειν τὸν βουλόμενον (iii. 28),[4] παρουσία[5] (iii. 17, of a royal visit), φιλανθρωπία (of royal clemency, iii. 15–18), ἐντυγχάνω (= petition, vi. 37–40), are all familiar in Papyri. γραφικοὶ κάλαμοι (a hitherto unparalleled phrase, iv. 20) occurs in *Grenfell P.*, ii. 38 (first century B.C.); οἰκετικός (ii. 28) in *B.M.P.* cccci (*c.* 116 B.C.); κακοτεχνεῖν (vii. 9) in *P. Eleph.* I (311 B.C.); θεωρία (v. 24) in *P. Tebt.* 33 (112 B.C.); σκυλμός (iii. 25 metaphorically) in *P. Tebt.* 41 (119 B.C.).

(*d*) We have therefore converging lines of evidence. There are good reasons for connecting *2 Maccabees* with Alexandria;[6] Jason is probably to be placed between 130 and 100 B.C., and *2 Maccabees* not much later. The *Letter of Aristeas* is certainly Alexandrian and of the same period.[7] Indications derived from the papyri (the nature of the official language, the greetings in the letters, and the use of the forms οὐθείς and μηθείς) suggest a date somewhere about 100 B.C. As we regard the connexion between *3 Maccabees* and the other books as one of school and thought, and not of direct literary indebtedness, it may possibly have been written shortly before them. Its superior limit is fixed by the apparent quotation in 6[6] from *The Song of the Three Children* (LXX), which probably dates from the last quarter of the second century B.C.

Mahaffy[8] points out that polemical tracts for and against the Jews came into vogue during the reign of Physcon (146–117 B.C.), and they certainly continued to be the fashion. Our book clearly belongs to this class of literature. It was apparently written primarily for Jews to encourage and confirm their faith in themselves and their destiny,[9] but it was certainly meant to be read by the outside world as well. It is an apology, representing the Jew as the Ptolemies' most loyal supporter, just as later apologists represented the Christian as the Emperors' best citizen. There is also, not far below the surface, the further suggestion that it is not prudent to interfere too far with him or his religion. The book is further a tract on the orthodox side, supporting the strict view of the Ḥasidim, as against the laxer Hellenizing section,[10] which must have been even stronger in Egypt than in Palestine. There is, however, little evidence that this polemic was specially directed against a Samaritan element, or even very definitely against the Onias temple.

(*e*) The chief alternative date is that suggested by Ewald.[11] He connects the book with the attempt of Caligula to place his image in the temple, and with the persecutions of the Alexandrian Jews which took place in his reign. Philo tells the story in the *adv. Flaccum*, and the *Legatio ad Caium*.[12] Certain points are found in his story and in *3 Maccabees* as well, e.g. the injustice of the persecution, the loyalty of the Jews, the punishment of the persecutor. But these are commonplaces. We miss the characteristic features of the Caligula story, the attempt to force the Emperor's image into the temple and the synagogues of Alexandria, the attacks on the synagogues, and Caligula's claim to divine honours;[13] since the Ptolemies were θεοί, this feature could have been easily transferred. Further, in Philo the hostility comes first from the populace, the outbreaks in Alexandria *precede* the events in Jerusalem, and the Jews in fact suffer severely. Those who accept this date are therefore forced to hold with Grimm that the author was afraid to work out his parallel too closely. But the tone of *3 Maccabees* is not that of a period of oppression and martyrdom; it belongs rather to a time when the nation is prosperous, and its position has been triumphantly vindicated.

[1] See note on ii. 28.
[2] *Judaica*, p. 166.
[3] Mahaffy, *The Ptolemaic Dynasty*, p. 205.
[4] Deissmann, *Bible Studies*, p. 343.
[5] Deissmann, *Light from the Ancient East*, pp. 372 ff.
[6] *E. B.*, art. *2 Maccabees*.
[7] Wendland and Thackeray, 100–80 B.C.
[8] *Emp. Ptol.*, p. 390.
[9] It may also have been intended to be read publicly on the occasion of the festivals commemorating the deliverances (vi. 36, vii. 19).
[10] Cf. ii. 31, vii. 10.
[11] *Hist. Isr.* v, pp. 468 ff.
[12] See also Josephus, *Ant.* XVIII. viii.
[13] See Schürer, *G. J. V.* (1909), ii, iii, pp. 493 ff.

And tempting though Ewald's suggestion appears at first sight, it cannot outweigh the positive indications of an earlier date which we have gained from other sources.

Attempts have also been made to find the occasion for the writing of the book in Pompey's attack on the Temple in 64 B.C., or in the incidents narrated of Herod (Josephus, *Ant.* XVII. vi. 5) or Pilate (ib. XVIII. iii. 1). But the resemblances in these cases are still slighter, and could only be seriously considered if there were independent grounds for ascribing the book to the Roman period.

§ 5. Historical Basis.

(*a*) *Relation to Polybius.* Generally speaking the account of the battle of Raphia, and the picture of Philopator's character, agree with Polybius v. But there are important differences in detail, for which there is no obvious reason; see notes on ch. i. Now there was a certain Ptolemy of Megalopolis (a fellow-townsman of Polybius), who is mentioned by him as governor of Cyprus (xviii. 55. 6, &c.), and who wrote an anecdotic account of the reign of Philopator, giving a very unfavourable picture of the king.[1] Scala[2] shows that he was one of the sources used by Polybius, particularly in the story of Agathocles (xv. 25–33);[3] the comment which he appends to that story (xv. 34. 1) probably refers to Ptolemy's history. 'I am quite aware of the miraculous occurrences and embellishments which the chroniclers of this event have added to their narrative with a view of producing a striking effect upon their hearers, making more of their comments on the story than of the story itself and the main incidents. Some ascribe it entirely to Fortune, and take the opportunity of expatiating on her fickleness, and the difficulty of being on one's guard against her. Others dwell on the unexpectedness of the event and try to assign its causes and probabilities.'[4] Mahaffy,[5] apparently independently, also arrives at the conclusion that this Ptolemy is the authority for the Agathocles section, and is 'probably the source which has blackened the name of Philopator'. Now on the other hand it has been recognized that the author of *3 Maccabees* apparently used some good authority, other than Polybius, for his account of Raphia and the character of Philopator.[6] Can we not then identify this unknown source with the lost history of Ptolemy Megalopolitanus? The characteristics which Polybius ascribes to him, love of 'miraculous occurrences and embellishments', and the fondness for tracing out causes, are exactly those of *3 Maccabees*, and would make him a congenial pattern for the author of the latter book. It is noticeable that in one of his extant fragments[7] he speaks of Philopator's boon companions, of whom we hear so much in *3 Maccabees*. There are again many features in the Agathocles section which remind us of the Jewish story, e.g. the stress laid on the popularity of Arsinoe (cf. 3 Macc. i. 4 ff.), the picture of the confusion in the streets of Alexandria, the debaucheries, the cruelties, the unexpected escape of Moeragenes.[8] These are sufficient to show that the sort of story told in *3 Maccabees* is just that which was narrated by Ptolemy in his anecdotes. I would suggest then that the narrative of the opening verses of *3 Maccabees* may be derived directly from him, and that amongst the stories which he told of Philopator were some which a pious Jew could adapt for the glorification of his own nation.

(*b*) *Relation to Josephus.* In *c.* Ap. ii. 5 there is a story which is certainly in some way connected with that of *3 Maccabees*. After the death of Philometor the Alexandrian Jews supported Cleopatra against his brother Physcon (Ptolemy IX, 146–117 B.C.). The latter in revenge exposed the Jews and their families to drunken elephants, which, however, turned on Physcon's followers and slew many of them. A phantom also appeared to the king, preventing him from further attempts to injure them. But the parallel does not stop here. Earlier in the chapter Josephus mentions a visit of Ptolemy Euergetes I to Jerusalem to offer thankofferings after a victory; stress is laid on the services of Onias and *Dositheus*, Jewish generals; and reference is made to the intercession of Ithaca, or Irene, Physcon's concubine, on behalf of the Jews, as well as to a memorial feast kept by the Alexandrian Jews on the day of their deliverance. It is at once obvious that Josephus' version is far more probable than the exaggerated and sensational narrative of *3 Maccabees*.[9] The mention of the festival in both suggests that some historical incident lies

[1] See Müller, *Frag. Hist. Graec.* iii, p. 66.

[2] *Studien des Polybius*, pp. 58–60, 263–7.

[3] Also in the character of Philopator, xiv. 11, 12; Cleino, his cup-bearer, mentioned there, is also mentioned in one of the extant fragments of Ptolemy.

[4] Shuckburgh's translation.

[5] *Empire of the Ptolemies*, p. 272, n. 1; *Ptolemaic Dynasty*, pp. 143 ff.

[6] e.g. by Mahaffy (*Emp. Pt.*, p. 267); Willrich (*Klio*, vii, p. 293); Büchler (*Tobiaden und Oniaden*, p. 174).

[7] *apud* Athen. vi, p. 246 C.

[8] There is no striking resemblance in the language, which is that of Polybius himself; but ἀμετάθετος and παραδειγματίζειν, which occur in 3 Macc. v. 1, 12, iv. 11, and nowhere else in LXX, are found in this section (32. 7, 32. 5); also cf. 31. 5 (χωρήσαντες εἰς τὴν ἐξ ἀρχῆς διάθεσιν) with ii. 28, 29.

[9] Josephus clearly did not know, or at any rate care to use, *3 Maccabees*.

behind the legends, and there is indeed no *a priori* reason for doubting this. But is Josephus right in placing it in Physcon's reign? The evidence of the papyri tends to show that the Jews as a whole were well treated by this king, and this fact has led Mahaffy and others to reject Josephus' setting of the incident.[1] But the evidence is somewhat scanty and refers to the latter part of the reign. Josephus places the persecution at the very beginning, and implies, as does the author of *3 Maccabees* even more clearly, that the persecutor afterwards became a protector of the Jews. In neither story is there any question of a long continued oppression, but only of a single abortive attempt at vengeance. Further, in the troubles which broke out on the death of Philometor, it is in every way probable that his widow Cleopatra and her infant son were supported by Onias and the loyal Jews of Leontopolis;[2] it is equally probable that in the reprisals with which Physcon signalized his success[3] he may have attempted to punish the Jews. Such a view agrees with the impression left by *3 Maccabees* that the main attack was made on Fayûm Jews brought to Alexandria for the purpose.[4] Again, the fact that in Justin 38. 8 we may have 'traces of an edict [of Physcon] by which Egyptians and Syrians (Jews) were granted the privileges of Alexandrian citizenship'[5] harmonizes exactly with 3 Macc. ii. 30, iii. 21.

On the other hand the Jerusalem incident is probably rightly placed by the writer of *3 Maccabees* in the reign of Philopator. In his triumphal progress after Raphia the king would not be likely to leave out the Jewish capital.[6] With his love of architecture and interest in religion he would certainly wish to enter the Temple. The Jews would no less certainly have tried to prevent him, and his superstitious fears may well have been worked on in some such manner as to give rise to the highly coloured narrative of our book.[7] It is even possible that the story may have been taken in substance from the memoirs of Ptolemy Megalopolitanus.

The hypothesis that two independent stories have been united in *3 Maccabees* is confirmed by an examination of the book itself. The connexion between the Jerusalem episode and the subsequent persecution in Egypt is very artificial. No doubt it is difficult to set bounds to the ἀλογιστία of a despot, but it is not very probable that Philopator should have wished to destroy the innocent and loyal Jews of Egypt merely on account of an insult offered by their fellow-countrymen in Jerusalem, and the narrative itself in its references to taxation and local religious differences affords a far more reasonable explanation of the origin of the persecution.

It would seem, then, that the writer of *3 Maccabees* has combined the Physcon and Philopator stories, transferring the former to the earlier reign. There was an obvious advantage in doing so, since in the original narrative as preserved by Josephus the position of the Jews was a little ambiguous. It is true they had been loyal to Cleopatra, but they had unfortunately sided with the defeated party, and from the point of view of the conqueror they could be regarded as rebels. No such objection attached to the representation in *3 Maccabees*. The writer has also, by the way, worked in a reference to another story glorifying the Jew. Dositheus is mentioned in the Physcon story side by side with Onias as a Jewish general who did good service to the Ptolemies. In the *Hibeh P.* 90 and elsewhere a Dositheus *son of Drimylus* is found as an Alexander priest of 222 B.C. The writer in i. 3 apparently identifies the two, and turns the *son of Drimylus* into a renegade Jew. At the same time he makes him play the rôle of a Mordecai and save the king's life.[8] It is possible that the reference to Arsinoe in i. 1, 4 may be explained on similar lines. She plays no further part in the story and her introduction seems quite pointless. But the writer may have intended that she should play the rôle which Ithaca plays in Josephus, and intercede for the Jews; for some reason he dropped this feature, but omitted to expunge the earlier references to her. On the other hand the episode may have been taken directly from Ptolemy Megalopolitanus, in whose narrative she seems to have figured prominently. In that case she is simply part of the historical setting of the picture, and her introduction was never intended to have any further significance.

It is at any rate clear that the aim of the writer was to combine in a single picture as many

[1] *Ptolemaic Dynasty*, pp. 192 ff.; Willrich, *Juden und Griechen*, pp. 151 ff.

[2] Mahaffy, ib., p. 183.

[3] e.g. the massacre of Cyrenaeans, Diod. xxxiii. 13.

[4] v. inf. § 6, and cf. Abrahams, *J. Q. R.* ix, pp. 39 ff.

[5] Mahaffy, ib., p. 190.

[6] Ib. p. 134.

[7] *The Letter of Aristeas* 99 speaks of the ἔκπληξις and θαυμασμὸς ἀδιήγητος inspired by the Temple; Stanley compares the story of Ibrahim Pacha struck down on attempting to enter the shrine of Isaac (*Hist. J. Ch.* iii, p. 219, n. 1).

[8] See Willrich, *Klio*, vii (1907), p. 293 f. The same writer in *Iudaica*, p. 19 f., and *Hermes*, xxxix. 244 ff., calls attention to the undoubtedly curious coincidence that in Ad. Esth. xii. 1 Tharra the Eunuch slain by Mordecai is called, in Lagarde's *a* text, Thedeutos or Theudetos, while Josephus (*Ant.* XI. vi. 4) calls him Theodosites, or in *Ant.* XI. vi. 10 Theodestes; cf. the Theodotus of 3 Macc. i. 2. Again in Ad. Esth. xi. 1 *Dositheus* a priest and Levite is named as the bearer of the book to Egypt. But his elaborate attempt to reduce all these narratives to versions of a single legend can hardly be followed; it involves a theory of Esther which 'has found no favour thus far among critics' (Paton, *Esther* [in *Int. Crit. Com.*], p. 77).

features as possible, all tending to the glorification of the faithful Jew. We thus have brought together in a single canvas the frustrated attempt to enter the Temple, the saving of the king's life by a Jew, the attacks on religion and attempts to hellenize, affecting both the Jews in Alexandria and in Egypt as a whole, the testimonies to their great influence and unswerving loyalty, the marvels of divine intervention, and the vengeance on renegades. The result is not very convincing artistically or historically. But on the other hand each feature, taken by itself and stripped of its sensational colouring, is entirely credible and probably has some foundation in fact. Our knowledge of the history of the Jews in Egypt under the Ptolemies is too fragmentary to justify us in denying the possibility of sporadic outbreaks of anti-Semitism in the second and third centuries B.C. As we have seen, the papyri confirm in various ways the general accuracy of the writer, and we shall probably be justified in giving his work a somewhat higher historical value than has usually been assigned to it.

On one point all are agreed. The character of Philopator is in full accordance with the picture which history had come to form of him. 'Noctes in stupris, dies in conviviis consumit.'[1] Whether the picture is quite a fair one is another question. It may be due to the bias of Ptolemy Megalopolitanus, and inscriptions suggest that there was something to be said on his side.[2] At any rate they prove an interest in architecture and religion, and a ready liberality to cities and temples, which agree with the statements of *3 Maccabees*.

§ 6. Integrity of the Book.

It is sometimes held that the book is only a fragment of a larger work (Ewald, Fritzsche), or that at any rate the opening has been lost (Grimm). The arguments for this view are found in the abruptness of the introduction,[3] the reference to the plot of Theodotus in i. 2 as though it were well known, and to the 'before-mentioned companions' in ii. 25, who have not in fact been introduced previously. But if we accept the hypothesis of the writer's dependence on Ptolemy Megalopolitanus, it will be more reasonable to suppose that these are slips, due to a careless reproduction of the source. In i. 2 we have 'a *certain* Theodotus', as though from the writer's standpoint he was being mentioned for the first time, while the following words imply a previous reference to his treachery. The source is evidently only imperfectly adapted; the *τις* shows that Theodotus cannot have been already named in a lost opening of the book itself.

Büchler,[4] on the other hand, argues that *3 Maccabees*, as it stands, has been drastically edited, and contains copious interpolations which have introduced confusion into the story. He points out that in the concluding chapters the Alexandrian Jews are hardly mentioned; they deal solely with the return of country Jews to Moeris and the Arsinoite nome. He suggests that the original narrative dealt with a persecution of Fayûm Jews, who had refused to join in a birthday feast to Dionysus on some occasion when Philopator attempted to establish his cult at Bakchis and Dionysias on the banks of Moeris. The references to renegades point to a Samaritan element which was ready to fall in with a lax syncretism. In accordance with this theory he makes very considerable excisions in the book. There are no grounds for doing this, and it is more probable that the writer himself combined various stories and is responsible for the resultant confusion. At the same time Büchler's hypothesis as to the reasons which led to the persecution of the Fayûm Jews is probable enough, and may well indicate one of the historical elements in the story.

§ 7. Style.

The book is a product of Alexandrian literature, exemplifying in its extremest form the pseudo-Classicalism of the Atticists. It would, however, be misleading to speak of it as written in the most *literary* style, since its artificiality and extravagance make it hardly worthy of the name of literature. Particularly when the writer attempts in descriptions to introduce purple passages, he succeeds only in being obscure and bombastic: e.g. i. 16 ff., iv, v. 6 ff. His sentences are full of repetitions and awkwardly constructed, and for all their attempt at rhetoric are marked by an excessive use of the weak introductory particle δέ; e.g. of the first 11 verses, 10 begin with it. The vocabulary is varied; Swete[5] gives a selection of 32 words not found elsewhere in the LXX, but in fact the list can be extended to over 100; its character may be judged from the fact that it includes 20 adjectives compounded with *α* privative; many again are poetical, such as *πανόδυρτος*, or *πολύδακρυς*. There are also about 14 words not found elsewhere in Greek literature, verbs such as *ψυχουλκεῖν*, *προσυστέλλειν*, and compound adjectives of the type of *βυθοτρεφής*, *μισοὔβρις*, *μυροβρεχής*, *ποντόβροχος*, *φοβεροειδής*, *πυρόπνους*.

Among the Classical forms, unique or unusual in the LXX, which mark the writer as an Atticist,

[1] Justinus xxx. 1. 8; his nickname was Τρύφων.

[2] Mahaffy, *Emp. Ptol.*, pp. 270 ff.

[3] Xenophon's *Oecon.* and Josephus' *Life* also begin with a δέ clause, but apparently in neither case were they meant to be regarded as independent works.

[4] *Tobiaden und Oniaden*, pp. 172 ff.

[5] *Intr. O.T. in Greek*, p. 312.

are the following[1]:—τέλεον, τελέως, δεσμά, ἴστε, διηρπάσθην, καθειστάντες, ᾤκτειρα, and the use of crasis with the definite article (τοὐνάντιον, τἀληθές).

At the same time the writer shows the influence of the κοινή in such forms as τεύξασθαι, κατεσχέθη, ἠνέωξα, εἰάσθησαν, θεέ, τετάρτη (for τέτρας). In iv. 19 there is an interesting example of a superfluous ἐν with dative after χρᾶσθαι.[2]

§ 8. THEOLOGY.

The book represents the most orthodox type of old-fashioned Judaism, with its devotion to the temple, the law, and the peculiar position of the chosen people. The business of God is to act as their champion; there is no trace of universalism, or even any desire for proselytes; Philopator is forced to respect God, but he does not worship Him, as does Nebuchadnezzar, nor is there any of the syncretism which we find in the *Letter of Aristeas*. At the same time, side by side with the tone of somewhat arrogant self-satisfaction and narrow materialism, there is a real piety and an absolute faith in the power of prayer. There are no references to the Messianic hope, or apocalyptic ideas, or the future life. An angel vision terrifies Ptolemy and his followers, but it is not seen by the Jews; there is no sign of the desire to interpose intermediaries between God and man, nor is He described by periphrases; e.g. His πρόνοια is mentioned, but in no way personified (iv. 21, v. 30). He is addressed directly, and the variety and number of the attributes ascribed to Him is remarkable. The heaping up of such attributes in prayer was a feature of Hellenistic Judaism[3] (ii. 2 ff., 21, v. 7, vi. 2–9, 18, 28; cf. 2 Macc. i. 24, Pr. Man. 1–4). Among the titles of God not found elsewhere in the LXX are the following:—μόναρχος (ii. 2), προπάτωρ (ii. 21), μεγαλοκράτωρ (vi. 2), μισύβρις (vi. 9), ἔντιμος (vi. 13), μεγαλόδοξος (vi. 18), as well as several phrases of the type of πάσης δυνάμεως δυναστεύων.[4] Unusual titles are πάντων ἐπόπτης (ii. 21), ἅγιε ἐν ἁγίοις (ii. 2, 21), ὁ ἐπιφανὴς Κύριος (v. 35), τερατοποιός (vi. 32), ῥύστης Ἰσραήλ (vii. 23).

From the theological standpoint, therefore, the book seems to belong to the strict and conservative school of the Ḥasidim, devoted to the law, and finding its inspiration in the lessons of the national history (ii. 2–20, vi. 1–15). It expresses a bitter opposition to the attempts at hellenizing, which so nearly overwhelmed Judaism in the second century B. C., and shows no sympathy with the developments of thought and doctrine, which at that time were growing up within the Jewish Church. Though it belongs to Alexandria, it shows no trace of the influence of the typical Alexandrian ideas.[5] The keenest heresy-hunter could have found no fault with its uncompromising orthodoxy.

§ 9. USE OF THE BOOK.

The references to *3 Maccabees* are very few, and entirely confined to Christian writers. They include *Apost. Canons* 85, the *Stichometry* of Nicephorus, *Synopsis Athanasii*, Eus. *Chron.* ii. 122. The Stichometry of Codex Claromontanus implies a knowledge of the book, by mentioning the fourth book of Maccabees. In the *Synopsis Athanasii* we find Μακκαβαικὰ βιβλία δ' Πτολεμαικά, where Credner's emendation of καί for δ' is usually followed; Zahn's πολεμικά has found little support. Theodoret of Antioch summarizes the book and treats it as historical (*ad* Dan. xi), and Swete[6] calls attention to an interesting combination of Isa. lvii. 15 with 3 Macc. ii. 2 in the *Liturgy of St. Clement*. It will be seen that the attestation is entirely Eastern; the book was not accepted in the Western Church and does not appear in the Vulgate.

§ 10. BIBLIOGRAPHY.

(*a*) *Text*—Holmes and Parsons, vol. v; Fritzsche, *Libri Apocryphi Graece*; Tischendorf and Nestle, *Septuagint*; Swete, *O.T. in Greek*, vol. iii (collates A and V). The Syriac is printed in Walton's *Polyglot*, vol. iv (with Latin trans.), and in Lagarde's *Apocr. Syriace*.

(*b*) *Editions*—Grimm in *Kurz. Ex. Handb.* (far the fullest); Kautzsch in *Die Apokr. u. Pseudepigr. des A.T.*; Churton, *The Uncanonical and Apocryphal Scriptures*; Bissell in *Lange-Schaff Commentary*.

(*c*) *Critical inquiries*—Articles in the Bible Dictionaries, &c.; Ewald, *Hist. Isr.* v. 468 ff.; Schürer, *G.J.V.* (1909), ii, iii, pp. 493 ff. [Eng. trans. ii, iii, pp. 216–19]; André, *Les Apocr. de l'A. T.*, pp. 115–32 (full with many references); Swete, *Intr. O.T. in Greek*, pp. 278 ff.; Abrahams, *J.Q.R*, ix, pp. 39 ff. (discusses historicity of the story); Mahaffy, *Empire of the Ptolemies*, pp. 267 ff.; *Ptolemaic Dynasty* (vol. iv of Petrie's *Hist. Egypt*), chs. v, viii; Willrich, *Juden u. Griechen*, pp. 145 ff.; *Iudaica*, pp. 163 ff.; *Klio*, vii, p. 293 f.; *Hermes*, xxxix (1904), pp. 244–58; Büchler, *Tobiaden und Oniaden*, pp. 172 ff. (a very full and suggestive study).

The translation which follows is based to some extent upon Churton's, but is practically a new one. The attempt has been made to give an idea of the characteristics of the Greek by preserving the complexity of the sentences, and the use of out-of-the-way words. A smoother and more literary rendering would have given a wrong impression of the book.

In the notes *Gr.* and *K.* refer to the editions of Grimm and Kautzsch.

[1] These examples are collected from Thackeray, *Gr. O.T. in Greek*; the references will be readily found in the index to that book.

[2] Cf. Moulton, *Grammar of N.T. Greek*, pp. 75, 104.

[3] Deissmann, *Bible Studies*, pp. 297 ff.

[4] v. 7, 28, 51, vi. 2, vii. 9; cf. 2 Macc. iii. 34; Esther viii. 13; Wisd. xiv. 3.

[5] The attempts made to find characteristic features of Philonian thought are very unconvincing.

[6] *Intr. O.T. in Greek*, p. 472.

THE THIRD BOOK OF MACCABEES

1 1 Now when Philopator had learned from those who had returned of the capture by Antiochus of the
places which had been held by him, he issued orders to all his forces, foot and horse, and taking with
him his sister Arsinoe, marched to the district over against Raphia, where the army of Antiochus
2 was encamped. But a certain Theodotus, determining to carry out his plot, took with him the
bravest of the soldiers of Ptolemy who had been previously assigned to him, and went by night to
3 the tent of Ptolemy, intending to kill him single-handed, and thereby put an end to the war. But
Dositheus, called the son of Drimylus, who was by birth a Jew, but had subsequently abandoned
the observance of the law, and renounced his ancestral faith, had conveyed Ptolemy away, and put
some obscure person to sleep in the tent; and so it happened that on this man fell the vengeance
4 intended for the other. And when a fierce battle had begun, and things were favouring Antiochus,
Arsinoe went frequently up and down the ranks, and her hair dishevelled, exhorted them with
lamentation and tears to fight manfully for themselves, their children, and their wives, promising to
5 give them if they conquered two minae of gold each. And thus it came about that their adversaries
6 were destroyed in the encounter, and that many were also taken captive. So Ptolemy, having
7 crushed the attack, determined to visit the neighbouring cities, and encourage them. And having
8 done this, and given gifts to their shrines, he inspired his subjects with confidence. And when the
Jews had sent to him some of the senate and elders to greet him, and bring him gifts, and con-
gratulate him on what had happened, he became the more eager to visit them as quickly as possible.
9 And when he had come to Jerusalem he sacrificed to the Most High God and offered thankofferings,
acting in some measure according to what was suitable to the place. And entering into the *holy*
10 place, and being struck by the care *displayed*, and the beauty, and admiring also the good order of
11 the temple, it came into his mind to purpose to enter into the sanctuary. And when they said that
this was not allowed, since not even members of their own nation could enter, or all the priests, but
12 only the high-priest who was chief of all, and he once a year, he was by no means convinced. And
when the law had been read out to him, not even then did he desist from his claim that he himself
13 should enter, saying, Even if they are deprived of this honour, I must not be so. And he asked
14 why, when he entered into every shrine, none of those present hindered him? And some one

I. 9. μεγιστω] πιστω A   των εξης τι] ων εξεστι 64: περιττον τι, or εξοχον τι Arm

---

I. 1. The opening describes the relations between Ptolemy IV, Philopator (222–204 B.C.), and Antiochus III, the Great (224–187 B.C.), immediately before the battle of Raphia, which took place in the spring of 217; Antiochus had captured Seleukeia, and occupied Syria and Palestine. See Pol. v. 40 ff.; 82 ff.; Mahaffy, *Empire of the Ptolemies*, ch. vii. The story of Raphia is in substantial agreement with the account of Polybius, but there are certain divergences; (*a*) in Polybius the two armies reach Raphia at about the same time; (*b*) Arsinoe encourages the army in concert with Philopator *before* the battle; Antiochus is at first victorious on the right wing, but at the crisis it is the king himself who changes the fortune of the day; (*c*) Polybius refers to the ready submission of Coele-Syria and to Ptolemy's visits to its cities, but he lays stress on their gifts and homage to him, not on his to them, as in 3 Macc. i. 6, 7. On the significance of these differences see Intr. § 5 *a*; see also § 6 for the abruptness of the opening, and § 5 *b* for character of Philopator. Raphia is referred to in Dn. xi. 11, 12.

his sister Arsinoe. This is correct at the date of Raphia; subsequently, according to Egyptian custom, she became Ptolemy's wife; Livy (xxxvii. 4) calls her Cleopatra; Justinus (xxx. 1. 7) Eurydice. On the significance of her mention here see Intr. § 5 *b*.

2. This Theodotus was a deserter from Ptolemy, who had been of great service to Antiochus (Pol. v. 40, 46, 61). His attempt is narrated ib. 81; there he takes two men with him, Dositheus is not mentioned, Ptolemy is saved because he did not sleep in his official tent, and Theodotus wounds two men and kills Andreas the king's physician (? = the ἄσημός τις of v^3). See further Intr. § 5 *b*.

ὅπλων Πτολεμαικῶν τὰ κράτιστα. The translation given above is that of most Edd., and κράτιστα makes it probable. But the reference may be to arms and equipment which were Πτολεμαικά, and therefore not noticed (n. b. ὡς μόνος κτεῖναι). Polybius remarks that the varieties of dress in the two armies prevented discovery.

3. **Dositheus**, see Intr. § 5 *b*.

4. The promise seems impossibly extravagant, but it must be remembered that Egyptian queens had large private property, and Abrahams suggests that the promise was only made to the Greek mercenaries.

5. According to Polybius, Antiochus lost nearly 10,000 infantry, 300 cavalry, and 4,000 prisoners; Ptolemy 1,500 infantry and 700 cavalry.

9. τόπος the temple, as regularly in 2, 3 Macc. and elsewhere.

13. πᾶν τέμενος. Gr. and K. (with hesitation) understand this of the Jewish temple, as though it were πᾶν τὸ τέμενος; why had he been allowed to enter at all, if he might not penetrate into the inmost shrine? But the argument is weak even for a despot, and the translation given above is more pointed.

15 answered thoughtlessly that he did wrong to make this boast. But since this is so, he said, why
16 should I not enter in any case, whether they wish it or not? Then the priests in all their robes fell
down, and besought the Most High God to aid them in that which had come upon them, and to
turn the violence of him who was making this wicked attack, filling the temple with lamentation
17 and tears; and those who were left in the city hurried forth in confusion, concluding that something
18 strange was happening. The virgins who had been shut up in their chambers rushed forth with
their mothers, and covering their hair with dust and ashes, filled the streets with groanings and
19 lamentations. And those who had been lately married, leaving the chambers prepared for *wedded*
20 intercourse and forgetting their proper modesty, ran about in confusion through the city. And as
for the new-born children, the mothers and nurses who had charge of them left them here and there,
in the houses or in the streets without care, and came in crowds to the temple which is high above all.
21 And manifold were the supplications of those gathered here because of the impious enterprise of the
22 king. And with them the bolder from among the citizens would not endure his carrying the matter
23 to an extremity, or his determination to complete his project; but calling *on one another* to rush
to arms, and to die bravely for the law of their fathers, they made great confusion in the place,
and being with difficulty turned from their purpose by the elders and the priests, they joined in
24, 25 supplication with them. And the multitude continued meanwhile praying as before. But the
elders who were with the king tried in many ways to turn his haughty mind from the purpose he
26 had conceived. But being emboldened and now setting them all aside, he was even beginning to
27 approach, thinking that he would complete the *design* aforesaid. Therefore those who were with
him seeing this, joined with our own people in beseeching him who has all power to defend them in
28 their present need, and not to disregard the lawless and insolent deed. So incessant and vehement
29 was the united cry of the multitude that an indescribable uproar arose. For it might have been
thought that not only the people, but even the walls and the whole pavement were crying out, since
all preferred death to the profanation of the *holy* place.

2 1 Then the High-Priest Simon bowing his knees before the holy place, and spreading out his hands
2 in calm reverence, prayed after this manner: Lord, Lord, king of the heavens, and sovereign of all
creation, holy among the holy ones, only ruler, almighty, give ear to us who are grievously troubled
3 by one wicked and profane, made wanton in insolence and might. For thou who hast created all
things, and governest the whole world, art a righteous ruler, and judgest those who do aught in
4 violence and arrogance. Thou didst destroy those who aforetime did iniquity, among whom were
5 giants trusting in their strength and boldness, bringing upon them a boundless flood of water. Thou
didst burn up with fire and brimstone the men of Sodom, workers of arrogance, who had become
known of all for their crimes, and didst make them an example to those who should come after.
6 Thou didst try with manifold and grievous punishments the insolent Pharaoh when he enslaved thy
7 holy people Israel, and didst make known thy mighty power. And when he pursued with chariots
and a multitude of peoples thou didst overwhelm him in the depth of the sea, but those who trusted
8 in thee, the ruler of all creation, thou didst bring safely through. And they seeing the works of thy
9 hands did praise thee, the almighty. Thou, O King, when thou didst create the boundless and

15. *παντως*] *παντων* A; *παντες* V 16. *πασαις ταις εσθησεσιν*] A V 44, 55, 74; *ταις αγιαις εσθ. al*; *πασαις ταις αγιαις εσθ.* Arm 18. *σποδω και*] *απεδωκαν* A V 44, 55, 71, 74; > Arm *γοου τε* V 44, 55, 74 Arm; *που γε* A; *γοων τε al.* 19. *τους προς απαντησιν διατεταγμενους παστους*] *τους προς απαν νυν διατεταγμενους* (A *-ην*) A V 55; *απαντας* 44, 74, with further variations in cursives; 'were sitting veiled (*or* curtained off) and prepared' Arm. The parallel in iv. 6 confirms *παστούς*, and *διατεταγμένην* in A suggests that *ἀπάντησιν* is the original reading. 23. *ιερεων*] Luc text, Syr; *γεραιων* A Arm *al*; *γερεων* V 28. *συναγομενης*] *-ων* Syr Arm and Edd

II. 1. A V 55, 71 > whole verse; *και ειπον ομοθυμαδον* 44, 74; 'they began to pray and said' Arm 6. *δοκιμασας τιμωριαις εγνωρισας το μεγα σου κρατος*] V; + (after *εγνωρισας*) *την σην δυναμιν εφ αις εγνωρισας* A Arm and most cursives with variations; a conflate reading *δοκιμασας*] *εδ.* A; *δαμασας* Luc text 9. *ηγιασας . . . σοι*] + (before *σοι*) *εις σον ονομα* A Arm; *εις ονομα σου* (> *σοι*) V

---

15. Text and grammar are in some confusion, but the general meaning is clear.

18, 19. The same remark applies; cf. 2 Macc. iii. 19 for the general picture. *προσαρτίως* is not found elsewhere; L. and S. 'lately'; Edd. 'completely'.

ἐσταλμέναι. There is no parallel for the meaning 'married', which is required by the verse. Gr. and K. suggest 'secluded', others *vestem* (sc. *nuptialem*) *indutae*. Arm. translates 'who had just then only been newly introduced', which is probably right.

II. 1. Simon II, son of Onias II (219–199 B.C.). Perhaps referred to in Sir. l. 1, but it is doubtful whether Simon the Just is to be identified with Simon I or II.

2. This heaping up of the attributes of God is characteristic of Hellenistic Judaism; see Intr. § 8. *ἅγιε ἐν ἁγίοις* (ii. 21); cf. Isa. lvii. 14; see Intr. § 9 for the liturgical use of the phrase. *μόναρχος* occurs in Eus. and later writers as a title of God.

4. For **giants** cf. Judith xvi. 7; Sir. xvi. 7; Wisd. xiv. 6; Enoch vii. 2, ix. 9, xv. 8; Jubilees v. 7. See also 2 Pet. ii. 5–6, where we have *angels*, the flood, and Sodom.

measureless earth, didst choose this city and sanctify this place [for thy name] for thyself, who hast
need of nothing, and didst glorify it by a splendid manifestation, establishing it to the glory of thy
10 great and honourable name. And loving the house of Israel, thou didst promise that if there should
be a falling away, and distress should overtake us, and we should come to this place and make our
11, 12 supplication, thou wouldst hear our prayer. And indeed thou art faithful and true. And seeing
that oftentimes when our fathers were afflicted thou didst succour them in their humiliation, and
13 didst deliver them from great evils, behold now, O holy king, for our many great sins we are
14 grievously troubled and put into subjection to our foes, and faint in *our* weakness. In our low
estate this insolent and profane man seeketh to do violence to the holy place which is consecrated
15 upon earth to the name of thy glory. For man cannot reach thy dwelling place, the heaven of
16 heavens. But since thy good pleasure was in thy glory amongst thy people Israel, thou didst
17 hallow this place. Punish us not by the uncleanness of these men, neither chastise us by their
profane doings, lest the transgressors boast in their wrath or exult in the insolence of their tongue,
18 saying, We have trodden down the house of the sanctuary as the houses of the abominations are
19 trodden down. Blot out our sins and scatter abroad our offences and manifest thy mercy at this
20 hour. Let thy compassion speedily overtake us, and put praises in the mouth of the fallen and
broken in heart, granting us peace.
21 Then the God who beholds all, the Father of all holy among the holy ones, hearing the supplication *spoken* according to the law, scourged him who was greatly uplifted in violence and inso-
22 lence, shaking him to and fro as a reed by the wind, so that lying on the ground powerless and
23 paralysed in body he could not so much as speak, being smitten by a righteous judgement. Whereupon his friends and body-guard, seeing that the chastisement which had overtaken him was swift,
and fearing lest he should even die, speedily drew him out, being overwhelmed by an exceeding great
24 fear. But having after some time recovered himself, he by no means came to repentance though he
had been thus punished, but departed with bitter threats.
25 So, arriving in Egypt, and going on further in his wickedness, through his boon companions and
26 associates, who have been already mentioned, utter strangers to all justice, he was not content with
his countless excesses, but even reached such a pitch of insolence that he raised evil reports in those
parts, and many of his friends watching carefully the royal purpose, themselves also followed his
27 will. He purposed publicly to inflict a disgrace upon the Jewish nation, and erected a pillar on the
28 tower in the palace with the inscription, That none who did not sacrifice should be allowed to enter
their temples; and that all Jews should be degraded to the rank of natives and the condition of
29 serfs, and that those who spoke against it should be taken by force and put to death; and that
those who were registered should even be branded on their bodies with an ivy-leaf, the emblem of

24. *απειλας δε πικρας θεμενος*] V Luc text; *μετα απειλης δε πικρας al*; *μετα απειλης δε πικρας θεμενος* A (a clearly conflate reading)

---

10. 1 Kings viii. 33.
18. **abominations** is of course a slip from the standpoint of the supposed heathen speaker.
21. πάντων ἐπόπτης, cf. 2 Macc. vii. 35, ix. 5; Ad. Esth. xv. 2; *Letter of Aristeas*, 16; see Deissmann, *Light from the Ancient East*, p. 429.

ἔνθεσμος expressing the law; cf. v. 10.

For the incident cf. the repulse of Heliodorus in 2 Macc. iii. 22–30, where the resemblance in language is great, and the punishment of Antiochus ib. ix. 4 ff.

25. **already mentioned**; either a slip from a careless use of a source (see Intr. § 6), or a reference to the supposed lost beginning of the book.
26. **evil reports**—whether against himself, or the Jews, is not clear.
28. i.e. the Jews might only enjoy their own worship if they also conformed to the official cult; cf. Josephus, *Ant.* XII. iii. 2; *c. Ap.* ii. 6. No other example of the word λαογραφία was known till the discovery of the Papyri. Grenfell and Hunt (*Tebt. P.* [1902] pp. 445–8) discuss this passage with reference to Wilcken's view that the word implies the 'poll-tax' of the Roman period, and is therefore an anachronism in a decree ascribed to Philopator, and in fact proves that the book dates from the Roman period. They show that the word does occur in Ptolemaic papyri, but not in its fully developed technical sense; it means not a tax, but 'a taxing list of persons, most, or all, of whom were native Egyptians'. λαός is the technical term for Egyptians as contrasted with Greeks (ib. p. 552). This exactly fits the context here.

διάθεσις is freq. in Polybius = condition; cf. esp. xv. 31. 5 χωρήσαντες εἰς τὴν ἐξ ἀρχῆς δ. For the idea cf. Philo, *Leg. ad Cai.* 17.

29. Ewald finds here an allusion to the vine as 'the symbol and arms of Jerusalem'; i.e. it is maliciously suggested that the Jews have been worshippers of Dionysus all along. This, however, is rather far-fetched. There is good evidence that Bacchus was the family god of the Ptolemies (*vide* Satyrus *ap. Theophr. ad Autolyc.* ii, p. 94). Philopator apparently allowed himself to be branded (Γάλλος, ὁ Φιλοπάτωρ Πτολεμαῖος διὰ τὸ φύλλα κισσοῦ κατεστίχθαι ὡς οἱ Γάλλοι, *Steph. Thes. s. v.*); cf. also Büchler, *Tob. u. On.* pp. 197 ff., for traces of the cult in Egypt during this period. In 2 Macc. vi. 1 Antiochus introduces the worship of Bacchus into Jerusalem.

For **branded** cf. Philo, *De Mon.* i. 8 (Jews who allowed themselves to be branded), and Isa. xliv. 5 (a probable reference to branding the name of J″ on the hand).

30 Dionysus, and be reduced to their former limited status. But that he might not appear an enemy
to all, he added: But if any of them prefer to join those who are initiated into the mysteries, they
shall have equal rights with the citizens of Alexandria.
31 Some †obviously hating the price paid for the religion of *their* city† readily gave themselves up,
32 expecting to gain great glory from their association with the king. But the greater part stood firm
with a noble courage, and departed not from their religion; and paying money as a ransom for
33 their lives fearlessly attempted to save themselves from the registration. And they remained of
good hope that they should find help, and abhorred those who parted from them, accounting them
as enemies of their nation, and excluding them from social intercourse and the rendering of any
service.
3 1 The impious *king* perceiving this was so greatly enraged that he was not only wroth with those
who dwelt at Alexandria, but was even more bitterly hostile to those in the country, and ordered
that they should all be speedily gathered together, and put an end to by the most cruel death.
2 While this was being arranged a malicious report was noised abroad against the *Jewish* nation on
the part of men who agreed together to do them hurt, an occasion being afforded for representing
3 that they hindered them from the observance of the laws. But the Jews continued to maintain
4 their goodwill towards the kings and their unswerving fidelity. Yet worshipping God, and living
according to his law, they held themselves apart in the matter of food; and for this reason they
5 were disliked by some; but adorning their conversation by the good practice of righteousness they
6 were established in the good report of all. But of this good practice, which was the common talk
7 of all men with regard to the nation, the foreigners took no account; but they talked continually of
the difference *they made* with regard to worship and food, alleging that they were friendly neither
to the king nor his army, but ill-disposed, and bitterly hostile to his interests; thus they cast no
8 small opprobrium upon them. But the Greeks in the city having been in no way injured by them,
9 seeing the unexpected disturbance about them, and the unlooked-for concourse, were not able to
help them—for they lived under a tyranny—but tried to comfort them and were indignant, expecting that this affair would take a change for the better; for so great a community could not be thus
10 allowed to perish when it had committed no fault. And already some of their neighbours and
friends and business associates, taking aside some of *the Jews* secretly, gave pledges of their protection and earnest endeavours for their assistance.
11 So *the king*, puffed up by his present prosperity, and regarding not the power of the most high
God, but supposing that he himself would always hold firmly to the same purpose, wrote this letter

31. επιπολαιως] V^a Arm; επιπολειως A; επι πολεως V* *al* τα (τας A^1) της πολεως ευσεβειας επιβαθρα A; τας . . . επιβαθρας V *al*, with numerous variations of ευσεβους, επιβαθροις, and alterations of order   στυγουντες] -αι A; στοιχουντες Arm Luc text (with variations of spelling)

III. 4. επι τω κατα τας τροφας] V 62, 64; επι τω καταστροφας A; επι τινων και καταστροφας *al*   ενιοις] -οι A

29. καταχωρίζω is technical = 'enrol' or 'enter'; cf. papyri, *Letter of Aristeas*, 36, Canopus and Rosetta inscriptions. The latter also speak of records set up on a stelé (v. 27).

30. The question of Alexandrian citizenship and its different grades is complicated; cf. Mahaffy, *Ptol. Dyn.*, p. 58. According to the repeated statements of Josephus (*Ant.* XII. i; XIX. v. 2, &c.) the Jews already possessed a full citizenship. But there is no doubt that whatever such privileges they had at this period they enjoyed as individuals and not as a nation, and very little is known of citizenship outside Alexandria. There was therefore room for such a grant as this; and there are in fact independent traces of it in Physcon's reign (Intr. § 5 *b*). Abrahams suggests that Alexandrian citizenship was offered to the Fayûm Jews in order to simplify organization or taxation. Cf. 2 Macc. iv. 9 for attempt to impose Antiochene citizenship on the Jerusalem Jews, and Josephus (*Ant.* XII. iii. 2) for close connexion of citizenship with religion.

31. The first part of the verse is very obscure. K., 'who on account of the citizenship in a city hated the approaches to the city of piety'. Gr. takes ἐπὶ πόλεως, 'some who were over a district, or community, in Alexandria,' and the last part is translated by some 'hated the advances of the religion of the city'. I suggest with hesitation the translation given above, which keeps the best attested reading. ἐπιπόλαιος in Aristotle frequently means 'evident' or 'obvious'. ἐπίβαθρον means 'a fare', or more generally 'price paid'; cf. Plut. 2. 727 *f*, where the stork by its destruction of snakes pays ἐπίβαθρόν τι γῆς.

The reference would be to the heavy demands made by the Jewish law, or more specifically to the Temple tax, and it is possible, as Büchler suggests, that the renegades may be Samaritans; at any rate they are the lax, Hellenizing section of the Egyptian Jews (cf. Kennett, *Schweich Lectures* [1909], Lect. III). The Arm. gives a similar sense: 'Many of them, shallow-witted people [taking ἐπιπολαίως as meaning "superficially"] who aforetime indeed were irresolute in the ancient law.'

If 'city of piety' be the right translation, it confirms Prof. Burkitt's emendation of חסד for חרס in Isa. xix. 18, though there the reference is not to Jerusalem.

III. 4. On the unpopularity caused by Jewish peculiarities see an exhaustive study by Dobschütz, *Amer. J. Theol.* 1904, pp. 728 ff.; cf. the defence in *Letter of Aristeas*, 128 ff. For the hostility of the populace see Philo's account of the violence of the Alexandrian mob in the outbreak under Caligula.

8. The **Greeks** are the better-class Macedonian element. There is evidence that their position too was attacked by Physcon (Mahaffy, *Emp. Ptol.*, p. 388).

12 against them. King Ptolemy Philopator to his generals and soldiers in Egypt and every place
13, 14 greeting and prosperity. I myself and our affairs prosper. Our expedition into Asia, of which you
yourselves are aware, having been brought to an expected conclusion by the help of the Gods
15 granted us deliberately, we thought, not by force of arms, but by kindness and much benevolence
to foster the peoples of Coele-Syria and Phoenicia, bestowing benefits upon them with all readiness.
16 And having granted large revenues to the temples in the cities, we came to Jerusalem as well, going
up thither to show honour to the temple of the accursed people who never cease from their folly.
17 Seemingly they welcomed our presence, but their welcome was insincere; for when we were eager
18 to enter their shrine and to honour it with magnificent and beautiful offerings, carried away by their
ancient pride they prevented us from going in, being left unhurt by our power on account of the
19 benevolence we have to all. But they show plainly their ill-will towards us, and standing alone
among nations in their stiff-necked resistance to kings and their own benefactors, they refuse to take
20 anything in a proper spirit. We accommodated ourselves to their folly, and returning victoriously
21 to Egypt, and treating all nations with kindness, have acted as was right. And under these circumstances, making known to all our ready forgiveness of their fellow-countrymen, on account of
their alliance, and the numerous matters which have been freely entrusted to them from of old, we
have ventured to make a change, and have made up our mind to hold them worthy even of Alex-
22 andrian citizenship, and to give them a share in our religious rites from time to time. But they
taking this in the opposite spirit and rejecting the good *offer* with their inborn ill-feeling, and
23 continually inclining to evil, not only refused the invaluable citizenship, but also show their contempt silently and by words for the few among them who behave properly towards us, in every case
secretly expecting that through their infamous behaviour we should speedily alter our
24 policy. Therefore having good proof for our persuasion that they are evilly disposed towards us
in every way, and taking precautions lest when some sudden tumult is raised against us hereafter
25 we should have these impious people behind our backs as traitors and barbarous foes, we give order
that, as soon as this epistle reaches you, you shall at once send to us with harsh and violent treatment those who dwell among you with women and children, binding them fast in every way with
26 iron chains, to meet a terrible and ignominious death, as befits traitors. For we believe that when
they have been punished together, our estate will be established for the future in the surest and
27 best condition. And whoever shall harbour any Jew, old man or child or very suckling, shall with
28 all his house be tortured to death with the most horrible torments. Information may be given by
any one; *the informer* to receive the estate of the guilty party, with two thousand drachmae from
29 the royal treasury, and to be honoured with freedom. And every place where a Jew shall be
detected at all in concealment shall be made a waste and burnt with fire, and shall become entirely
30 useless to any mortal creature for all time. Thus ran the letter.

4 1 In every place where this decree reached, a feast at the public charges was made for the heathen
with exultation and joy, the hatred which had long before become inveterate in their hearts being now
2 freely displayed. But among the Jews there was unceasing grief and a lamentable crying with
tears, their heart being all aflame with their groanings, as they bewailed the unlooked-for destruction
3 which had been suddenly decreed against them. What district or city or what habitable place at

14. + (after *συμμαχια*) *και ημετερα δε ρωμη* inferior cursives 21. *και μετοχους . . . καταστησαι*] > V 62, 64 Arm 25. *εννεμομενους*] *ενσημαινομενους* Luc text, Syr; *εμμαινομενους* Arm (*ut videtur*) 28. *της ελευθεριας στεφανωθησεται*] A V 55, 74; + (after *ελ.*) *τευξεται και al*; 'honoured with a crown of freedom' Arm

IV. 2. *αληκτον*] V 44, 55, 74 (cf. *Letter of Aristeas*, 269); *αλεκτον* A; *ανηκεστον al* 3. *οικητος*] *οικτιστος* A V; unparalleled = 'habitable', in 2 Macc. ix. 28 = pitiable

---

13. On the papyri evidence for the technical terms in this letter see Intr. § 4 *c*; on the parallels with similar official documents in the *Letter of Aristeas* see § 4 *b*.

21. For the confidence reposed in Jews see vi. 25, vii. 7; *Aristeas*, 36, and the Josephus passages quoted on ii. 30. The Elephantine Papyri show that as early as the fifth century B.C. Jewish garrisons had been established by the Persians at Elephantine and Assuan to guard the southern frontier of Egypt.

τῶν ἀεὶ ἱερέων, Edd. tr. 'eternal religious rites'. Mahaffy emends to *ἱερειῶν*, which he translates by 'priesthood' = *ἱερωσυνῶν* (*Emp. Ptol.*, p. 268, n. 2). But with this reading, the translation of the text seems better, giving *ἀεί* its idiomatic classical meaning; for the meaning of *ἱερειῶν* cf. 2 Kings x. 20.

28. The shorter reading, omitting *τεύξεται καί*, is to be preferred. Deissmann (*B. S.*, p. 341) emends further to *ἐλευθερίᾳ* (cf. the reading of the Arm.), the *ς* being due to the following *στεφανωθήσεται*. He gives examples from Polyb. xii. 9. 5 and the papyri of the use of *στεφανοῦν* in the metaphorical sense of 'reward'. Freedom is opposed to the practical slavery with which the Jews were threatened; cf. *ἐλεύθεροι* in vii. 20. But it is not probable that the Jews themselves should be expected to be the only informers. Accepting his emendation, it would be better to see a reference to native-born Egyptians, who were practically serfs, and more likely to be specially hostile to the Jews (cf. *Aristeas*, 36), in contrast to the Greeks who favoured them (iii. 8). But much is to be said for the emendation *τοῖς ἐλευθερίοις* ('at the Eleutheria'); *ἐλευθερεύς* and *ἐλεύθερος* were names of Dionysus, and the Eleutheria sometimes meant a festival of Dionysus (v. *Steph. Thes. s. v.*). Though there is no evidence of the Eleutheria in Egypt under the Ptolemies, there is abundant evidence of the cult of Dionysus at this period.

4 all or what streets were not filled with wailing and lamentation for them? For in such manner with
harshness and pitiless heart were they sent away with one accord by the generals in the cities, that
at the sight of their unusual sufferings even some of their enemies, with common pity before their
5 eyes, remembering the uncertain issue of life, wept at their hapless departure. For there was carried
away a multitude of old men, covered with their wealth of grey hairs, forcing to a swift journey
their feet bent and sluggish from old age under the violence of their rough driving which knew no
6 shame. And the young women who had but lately entered the marriage chamber for the society of
wedded life, with lamentations instead of joy, and with their perfumed locks covered with dust, were
carried away unveiled, and with one accord sang a dirge in place of the wedding hymn, scarred by
7 the cruel treatment of the heathen; and as prisoners *exposed to* public *gaze* they were dragged
8 along with violence until they were embarked on board. And their consorts, with ropes on their
necks instead of garlands, in the flower of their youthful age, spent the remainder of the days of their
marriage feast in dirges instead of mirth and youthful ease, seeing the grave already yawning at their
9 feet. And they were brought on board driven like wild beasts under the constraint of iron bonds;
some were fastened by the neck to the benches of the ships; others had their feet secured in the
10 strongest fetters; and further they were shut off from the light by the thick planks above, that in
entire darkness they might be treated as traitors throughout the whole voyage.
11 When they had been brought to the place called Schedia, and the voyage was completed as
determined by the king, he ordered them to be imprisoned in the hippodrome that was before the
city, a place of immense circuit and very suitable for making them a gazing stock to all who entered
the city, and to those of the inhabitants (?) who went into the country to sojourn, so that they might
12 neither communicate with his army, or in any way claim protection of the walls. But after this had
been done, hearing that their fellow-countrymen in the city often went out in secret and bewailed the
13 shameful fate of their brethren, he was enraged and ordered that they should be treated in exactly
14 the same way as the others, receiving in no respect a lesser punishment. And *he commanded* that
the whole race should be registered by name, not for the wearisome service of labour which was briefly
described before, but that they should be tortured with the torments to which he had sentenced
15 them, and finally be made an end of in the space of a single day. The registration therefore was
carried on with bitter haste and zealous diligence from sunrise to sunset, coming to an end after
forty days but still uncompleted.
16 But the king was greatly and continually filled with joy, ordering feasts in the temples of his
idols, with a heart far astray from the truth and profane lips, praising dumb *idols* which could not speak
17 to them or help, and uttering words which were not fitting against the most high God. But after
the aforesaid space of time the scribes reported to the king that they were no longer able to continue
18 the registration of the Jews on account of their incalculable number; although the greater number
of them were still in the country, some still remaining in their homes and others on the journey, it
19 was impossible for all the generals in Egypt. And after he had threatened them fiercely as having
20 been bribed to contrive their escape, he was at length clearly convinced on this point, when they told
him and proved that even the paper manufactory and the pens which they used for writing had
21 already given out. But this was the working of the invincible providence of him who was aiding the
Jews from heaven.

5. γεραιων πληθος πολια πεπυκασμενων] V *al*, with variations; γερων πληρης πολιας πεπυκασμενων A 10. το φεγγος αποκλειομενοι] > A V Luc text, Arm; but the phrase is necessary to the grammar and sense, and is hardly a glossator's 11. τοις εκ τουτων] This can hardly mean 'those of the inhabitants'. For τουτων read ταυτης: 'those who set out from it to the country' (R. H. C.) περιβολων] V *al*; -ω A; -ου Luc text 16. εις δε τον μεγιστον θεον] > τον μεγιστον θεον A 55, 64, 93; > whole concluding clause V 18. κατα τον πορον] Luc text; κατα τον τοπον A; κατα τροπον V; κατα τοπον *al*; Kautzsch suggests a lacuna at the end of the verse, 'to gather them all together'

IV. 5. The verse is obscure and probably corrupt, but the general sense is clear.

6. Cf. i. 18 ff.

11. Schedia was three miles from Alexandria (Strabo xvii, p. 800); probably a landing-place nearer the city is here intended. The Hippodrome was before the east gate of the city (ib. p. 795).

καταξιῶσαι περιβόλων. Edd. supply αὐτούς as object, 'honour them with the protection of walls'. But this is very awkward grammatically, since it is the subject of the previous clause. For meaning of καταξιοῦν as given in the translation adopted cf. 2 Macc. xiii. 12.

14. See ii. 28 (condition of serfs).

16. Cf. Dn. iv. 4.

20. χαρτηρία is not found elsewhere; cf. Pliny, *N. H.* xviii. 10 *Chartariae officinae*. For γραφικοὶ κάλαμοι cf. Grenfell, *P.* ii. 38. Philo, *c. Fl.* 6, gives the number of Jews in Egypt as a million, but it is impossible to defend the bombastic exaggerations of this chapter. There are also some inconsistencies; *vv.* 12 ff. seem to imply that the Jews in Alexandria had not yet been interfered with, and according to *v.* 18 many of the country Jews are still at large; contrast ii. 27 ff., iv. 1 ff.

5 1 Then he called Hermon who was in charge of the elephants, and filled with bitter anger and
2 wrath, and altogether inflexible, ordered him for the next day to drug all the elephants—in number
five hundred—with copious handfuls of frankincense, and abundance of unmixed wine, and then when
they were maddened by the plentiful supply of drink to bring them in to compass the fate of the Jews.
3 And giving this order he turned to his feasting, having gathered together those of his friends and
4 army who were most hostile to the Jews, while [Hermon] the ruler of the elephants attended to the
5 injunction with all care. And the servants who were in charge of the Jews went out in the evening
and bound the hands of the hapless wretches, taking all other precautions to keep them safe through the
6 night, imagining that the nation would at one blow meet its final destruction. But the Jews who
seemed to the heathen to be destitute of all protection, on account of the constraint and bonds
7 which encompassed them on every side, with crying that would not be silenced, all called with tears
8 on the almighty Lord and ruler of all power, their merciful God and father, beseeching him to
frustrate the wicked design against them and to deliver them by a glorious manifestation from the
9 fate yawning ready before them. So their prayer ascended fervently to heaven; but Hermon,
10 having given the pitiless elephants drink till they were filled with the plenteous supply of wine and
sated with frankincense, came early in the morning to the palace to report to the king about this.
11 But the good creature, bestowed night and day from the beginning of time by him who gives the
12 portion of sleep to all, *even* to whomsoever he will, *this* he sent upon the king; and he was over-
borne by a sweet and heavy *slumber* by the operation of the Lord, thus being greatly foiled in his
13 lawless purpose, and utterly disappointed in his unchangeable design. But the Jews having escaped
the appointed hour praised their holy God, and again besought him who is ready to forgive to
14 manifest the might of his all-powerful hand before the proud eyes of the heathen. But when the
middle of the tenth hour had nearly come he who was in charge of the invitations, seeing the guests
15 assembled, went to the king and shook him. And having woken him up with difficulty, he pointed out
16 that the hour for the banquet was already passing, reminding him of the circumstances. And the
king considering these, betook himself to his cups and ordered those who had come for the banquet
17 to take their places over against him. And when this had been done he called on them to give themselves up to revelry, and counting themselves highly honoured to reckon as a joy the feast, late as it
18 was. And when the entertainment had gone on for some time, the king called Hermon and asked with
19 fierce threats why the Jews had been allowed to survive that day. But when he pointed out that he
20 had completely carried out the order overnight, and his friends confirmed him, the king with a rage
more fierce than Phalaris, said that *the Jews* might thank his sleep for the *respite* of the day; but,
he added, make ready the elephants in the same manner without further delay for the following day
21 to destroy utterly the accursed Jews. When the king had spoken, all who were present readily
22 assented with joy with one accord, and each one departed to his own house. But they did not
spend the night season in sleep, so much as in devising all manner of cruel insults for those whom
they thought to be in such wretched plight.
23 So as soon as the cock had crowed in the morning, Hermon harnessed the beasts and began to
24 put them in motion in the great colonnade. And the multitudes in the city assembled for the
25 piteous spectacle, eagerly looking for the break of day. But the Jews drawing their last breath for
but a brief moment more, with tearful supplications and strains of woe, raising their hands to heaven,
26 besought the most high God again to help them speedily. The rays of the sun were not yet scattered
abroad, and the king was receiving his friends, when Hermon came to his side and invited him to go
27 forth, explaining that the desire of the king was ready to be fulfilled. When the king understood
him, he was astonished at the unusual *summons* to go forth, having been overwhelmed with complete
28 ignorance, and asked †what was the matter on account of which this had been so zealously completed†.
But this was the operation of God the ruler of all, who had put in his mind forgetfulness of his former
29 devices. But Hermon and all his friends pointed to the beasts and the army; It is prepared, O king,

V. 4. Ερμων] τω Ερμωνι Luc text, Syr, reading *ἀραρότως* as a proper name, *αροραωτ*. But H. is the *ἐλεφαντάρχης*; the position suggests the name is a gloss; Arm > 12. *κατεσχεθη*] A V *al*; *κατασχεθεις υπνω απο εσπερας εως εννατης* Luc text, Syr 17. *το παρωρον της συμποσιας . . . εις ευφροσυνης* (-*ην* V) *καταθεσθαι μερος*] V Luc text, Arm; *το παρον . . . εις ευφροσυνην* A *al* 27. *τι το πραγμα εφ ου τουτο αυτω μετα σπουδης τετελεσται*] *οτι το διασαφουμενον ετι αυτω ει μετα σπουδης τετελεσται* A 19, 93 (A > *ει*); *οτι το διμαφουν . . . τετελεσθαι* V; apparently a primitive corruption, though the general sense is clear

---

V. 2. Philadelphus had 300 elephants; Philopator had 73 at Raphia.
5. The mention of the binding has been supposed to be inconsistent with iii. 25, iv. 9; but it is to be presumed that once the Jews were safe in the hippodrome, their fetters were taken off.
14. i. e. 3.30 p.m., the Babylonian reckoning being in use in Egypt.
20. **Phalaris**—the tyrant of Agrigentum in the sixth century B. C., whose cruelty had become proverbial (Polyb. xii. 25); cf. *inf. v.* 42.

30 according to thine eager purpose. But he was filled with fierce anger at the words, because by the
providence of God he had entirely lost his wits on this matter, and looking on him said threaten-
31 ingly, If thy parents or offspring were here, I would have furnished them as this rich banquet for the
fierce beasts in place of the Jews against whom I have no charge and who have shown in a pre-
32 eminent degree a full and unshaken loyalty to my ancestors. And indeed, if it were not for the
33 affection *kindled* by our life together and thy service, thou shouldst have died instead of these. So
34 Hermon met with an unexpected and dangerous threat, and his eyes and countenance fell. And
the king's friends, slinking away sullenly one by one, sent away the assembled crowds, each to his
35 own business. And the Jews hearing the words of the king, praised the Lord God who had
manifested *his glory*, the king of kings, having obtained this help also from him.
36 But the king, having arranged the banquet once more in the same way, ordered them to turn to
37 their pleasures. And calling Hermon he said threateningly, How often, thou wretched creature,
38 must I give thee orders about these very things? Even now make ready the elephants for the
39 morrow to destroy the Jews. But his kinsmen who sat at table with him wondered at his shifting
40 purpose, and remonstrated, How long, O King, dost thou make trial of us as though we were fools,
now for the third time giving orders for their destruction, and once more when the matter is in
41 hand changing and cancelling thy decree? Wherefore the city is in a tumult through its expectation, and being crowded with throngs of people has now been several times in danger of being put
42 to plunder. On this the king, a Phalaris in all things, was filled with madness, and, reckoning
nothing of the changes of mind which had been wrought in him for the protection of the Jews,
swore strongly a fruitless oath that he would without delay send to the grave the Jews mangled by
43 the knees and feet of the beasts, and would march against Judaea and quickly level it to the ground
with fire and sword, †and burning to the earth their temple which we might not enter would quickly
44 make it empty for all time of those who sacrificed therein†. Then his friends and kinsmen went
away joyfully with good confidence, and ordered the army to the most convenient places of the city
45 to keep guard. And the ruler of the elephants, having driven the beasts into a state almost, one
might say, of madness by fragrant draughts of wine mingled with frankincense, and having fitted
46 them in a fearful guise with implements, at dawn, the city being now filled with countless multitudes
thronging towards the hippodrome, entered the palace and urged on the king to the business that
47 lay before him. And he, his impious heart filled with fierce anger, started forth with all his force
with the beasts, determined with an unfeeling heart and his own eyes to gaze on the grievous and
48 piteous destruction of the afore-mentioned *Jews*. And when they saw the dust raised by the
elephants going out at the gate, and the armed force accompanying them, and the movement of the
49 crowd, and heard the far-sounding tumult, thinking that the last crisis of their life had come and the
end of their miserable suspense, they betook themselves to lamentation and groans, and kissed one
another, embracing their relatives and falling on their necks, parents and children, mothers and
50 daughters; and others with new-born babes at their breast drawing their last milk. But none the
less, reflecting on their former deliverances sent from heaven, with one accord they threw them-
51 selves on their faces, and took the babes from their breasts, and cried out with an exceeding loud
voice, beseeching the ruler of all power by a manifestation to show pity upon them now that they
were come to the gates of death.
6 1 But a certain Eleazar, a man of note among the priests of the country, whose years had already

29. At the end of this verse 64 has a long addition (14 lines in *Holmes and Parsons*), according to which the king is inclined to spare the Jews; his friends, including Hermon (who is mentioned as though for the first time), remind him of his decree, and the dangerous character of the Jews 30. μετα απειλης] + εις τον Ερμωνα και δυσμενεσι λογοις λοιδορησας Luc text 31. εσκευασα αν] 62; εσκευασαν A V 40. ως αλογους] V *al*; > 19, 93; > αλογους A; 'in thy mind' Arm 42. Φαλαρις] σφαλερος Arm (a tempting variant, but cf. v. 20) 43. πυρι πρηνεα εν ταχει και των συντελουντων εκει θυσιας ερημον τον απαντα χρονον καταστησειν] πυρι πρην A V; > και A V *al*; > ερημον A V Arm *al*; + εις (before τον) A V *al*; Arm paraphrases freely. The verse is in confusion, and we seem to have a conflate reading (n. b. repetition of πυρί, στήσεσθαι—καταστήσειν, διὰ τάχους—ἐν τάχει). Swete emends πρην to πρησαντα, but the verse remains unintelligible with the omission of καί and ἔρημον in the Uncials. Perhaps πυρι πρην conceals some adj. governing τῶν συντελούντων. Or a tempting emendation would be πυραν, which a scribe might have altered to πυρην, hesitating as to the form, πυραν πυρην giving rise to πυρι πρην: 'make [the temple] the funeral pyre of those who sacrifice there.' The objection is that it becomes necessary to omit τὸν ἅπαντα χρόνον.

VI. 1. ιερεων] Ιουδαιων A, evidently objecting to the presence of Jewish priests in Alexandria

---

31. The first part of the verse is an iambic, apparently an unidentified quotation from a poet.
39. **kinsmen**—the συγγενής was the regular term for the higher officials at the Ptolemaic court.
43. **we**—from the king's point of view, as though the clause was in *oratio recta*.
45. i. e. scythes, knives, &c. were attached to the elephants.

VI. 1. Eleazar is the typical old man of piety and faith; cf. 2 Macc. vi. 18; 4 Macc. vi. 5, vii. 1, and *Letter of Aristeas*, 41, &c.

priests: vii. 13 shows that this reading is right. They are the priests of the temple at Leontopolis and the fact

reached old age, and who was adorned with every virtue of life, made the elders who were round
2 him cease from calling on the holy God, and prayed thus: King of great power, most high, almighty
3 God, who governest all creation with loving-kindness, look upon the seed of Abraham, the children
of Jacob thy sanctified one, the people of thy sanctified inheritance, who are unjustly perishing,
4 strangers in a strange land. O Father, thou didst destroy Pharaoh, the former ruler of this Egypt,
with his multitude of chariots, when he was lifted high in his lawless insolence and a tongue
speaking great things, drowning him together with his proud host, and didst cause the light of thy
5 mercy to shine upon the race of Israel. Thou, when Sennacherib, the cruel king of the Assyrians,
was puffed up by his countless hosts, after he had taken the whole earth captive by his sword, and
was lifted up against thy holy city speaking grievous words of boasting and insolence, thou, Lord,
6 didst break him in pieces, making manifest thy power to many nations. Thou, when the three
friends in Babylonia freely gave their life to the flames that they should not serve vain things, didst
make as dew the fiery furnace, and deliver them unharmed even to the hair of their head, turning the
7 flame upon all their adversaries. Thou, when Daniel was cast through the slanders of envy to the
8 lions beneath the ground as food for wild beasts, didst bring him up to the light unhurt. And when
Jonah was languishing unpitied in the belly of the sea-born monster, thou didst restore him,
9 O Father, uninjured to all his household. And now thou hater of insolence, rich in mercy, protector
of all, quickly manifest thyself to the saints of Israel's line, in their insolent oppression by the
10 abominable and lawless heathen. And if our life has been ensnared in impious deeds during our
sojourning, save us from the hand of the enemy, and destroy us, O Lord, by whatever fate thou
11 choosest. Let not the men whose thoughts are vanity bless their vain *gods* for the destruction of
12 thy beloved, saying, Neither has their God delivered them. Thou who hast all might and all
power, the Eternal, look now upon us; pity us who by the mad insolence of lawless men are
13 being sent to death as traitors; and let the heathen to-day fear thy invincible might, thou glorious
14 one, who hast mighty works for the salvation of the race of Israel. The whole multitude of babes
15 with their parents beseecheth thee with tears. Let it be shown to all heathen that thou art with us,
O Lord, and hast not turned thy face away from us; but as thou hast said, Not even when they
were in the land of their enemies have I forgotten them, even so bring it to pass, O Lord.
16 And when Eleazar was even now ending his prayer, the king with the beasts and the whole
17 insolent array of his army came to the hippodrome. And the Jews beholding it raised a great cry
to heaven, so that now the surrounding valleys re-echoed it, and caused in all the hosts an incon-
18 trollable trembling. Then the greatly glorious, almighty, and true God, making manifest his holy face,
opened the gates of heaven, from which two glorious angels of terrible aspect descended, visible to
19 all but the Jews, and withstood them and filled the army of the adversaries with confusion and
20 terror, and bound them with immovable fetters. And a great horror seized on the body of the
21 king as well, and his fierce insolence was forgotten. And the beasts turned round against the
armed hosts that followed them and began to tread them under foot and destroy them.
22 And the king's wrath was turned to pity and tears on account of that which he had devised
23 before. For hearing the outcry and seeing them all prostrate to meet their death, he wept and
24 angrily threatened his friends, saying, Ye usurp the kingly power, surpassing even tyrants in your
cruelty; and me myself, who am your benefactor, ye plot to deprive of my dominion and my life,
25 devising secretly things that are unprofitable to the kingdom. Who hath driven each one from his
home the men who have faithfully held the fortresses of our country, and gathered them here without

8. αφειδως] -ων 55; αφιδων A; αφελων V; επιδων Luc text 9. σκεπαστα] δικαστα A αγιοις] απο V 17. πτοην] A, Luc text (ποιην 62); οιμωγην *al*; > V 55

---

that the writer recognizes them shows that the bias against the Onias temple, which Willrich and others have found in the book, is not very marked.

6. Cf. Dn. iii. 50 (LXX) *ἐποίησεν τὸ μέσον τῆς καμίνου ὡσεὶ πνεῦμα δρόσου διασυρίζον*; and iii. 94 (Heb. iii. 27) for 'hair of the head'.

8. The restoration of Jonah to his home is not mentioned in the O.T., but is easily inferred.

15. Lev. xxvi. 44.

18. **greatly glorious.** Cf. 1 Enoch xiv. 20; T. Lev. iii. 4, where God is called 'the Great Glory'. For the relation to the narrative of Josephus see Intr. § 5 *b*. For the terror inspired by visions cf. 2 Macc. iii. 24 ff., x. 29; Wisd. xvii. 3, 15, xviii. 17, the repulse of Heliodorus in the first passage being the nearest parallel. Similar ideas meet us in Greek history, e.g. the apparitions at Marathon and Salamis. The peculiar feature here is that the vision is not seen by the Jews themselves. The suggestion that they were already sufficiently terrified is not very convincing. Possibly the current Jewish version of the story ascribed the fright of the elephants to some other cause. But it is noticeable that there are no other references to angels in the book, even in the reference to Sennacherib in vi. 5; the writer did not belong to the school which delighted in them, and he makes as little of their appearance as he can.

25. For the services of the Jews cf. passages quoted on iii. 21.

26 reason? Who hath thus lawlessly overwhelmed with indignities those who from the beginning have
been in all things conspicuous beyond all nations in their goodwill towards us, and have ofttimes
27 encountered the worst dangers man *can undergo*? Loose, yea loose, their unjust bonds; send
28 them to their homes in peace, asking pardon for what has been already done. Set free the sons of
the almighty living God of Heaven, who from the days of our ancestors until now hath granted an
29 unimpaired stability and glory to our estate. Thus he spake; and they, having been set free in
a moment, praised the holy God their saviour, having but now escaped death.
30 Then the king returning to the city called the officer who was over the revenues, and ordered him
to supply to the Jews for a space of seven days wines and all else necessary for a feast, decreeing
that they should keep a festival of deliverance with all manner of rejoicing in the very place in
31 which they had thought to meet their fate. Then those who before were reviled and nigh to the
grave, or rather had already one foot therein, instead of a bitter and most lamentable death, held
a banquet to celebrate their deliverance, and full of joy they portioned between their companies the
32 place which had been prepared for their destruction and grave. And ceasing the piteous strain of
dirges, they took up the song of their fathers, praising God the saviour of Israel and doer of wonders;
and laying aside all wailing and lamentation they formed dances in token of joy for their safe
33 deliverance. And likewise the king too convening a great banquet in celebration of this, unceasingly
34 gave thanks in exalted terms to heaven for their unexpected deliverance. And those who before
supposed that they (the Jews) were doomed to destruction and to be food for birds, and had joyfully
carried out the registration, groaned at finding themselves covered with confusion and their fiery blast
35 of insolence quenched ingloriously. And the Jews, as we have already said, formed the dance which
36 we have before described, and spent their time in feasting with joyful thanksgiving and psalms. And
establishing a public ordinance about this, to be observed for all their sojourning from generation to
generation, they appointed the days mentioned to be kept as a festival, not for the sake of drinking
37 or gluttony, but in memory of the salvation granted them by God. And they petitioned the king,
desiring to depart to their home.
38 Now they were registering them from the twenty-fifth day of Pachon to the fourth of Epiphi,
for forty days; and they were appointing their destruction from the fifth of Epiphis to the seventh,
39 three days. And on these did the ruler of all with great glory manifest his mercy and deliver them
40 one and all unhurt. And they feasted, provided with all things by the king, till the fourteenth day
on which they also made petition for their return.
41 And the king granting their request wrote for them the following letter to the generals in the
cities, generously declaring his purpose.
7 1 King Ptolomaeus Philopator to the generals in Egypt and to all set over his affairs greeting and
2 prosperity. We ourselves and our children prosper, the great God directing our estate as we will.
3 Certain of our friends with evil heart by frequently urging the matter upon us persuaded us to gather
together in a body the Jews in the kingdom, and to inflict upon them extraordinary punishments as
4 traitors, urging that our state would never be firmly established, on account of the enmity which
5 they have to all nations, until this was done. And they, bringing them bound with harsh treatment
as slaves, or rather traitors, without any inquiry or examination, attempted to put them to death,
6 girding themselves with a cruelty fiercer than Scythian customs. But we severely threatened them
for this, and of the clemency which we have to all men scarcely granted them their lives; and
knowing that the God of heaven surely protects the Jews, fighting on their side continually as a

26. επιδεδειγμενους] A V 55, 93; επιδεδεγμενους *al* 31. δυσαιακτου] δυσατακτου A V (? a *vox nihili*); δυσαχθους Luc text; > Arm 33. αυτων] A 55, 93 Arm; αυτω *al*; > V

VII. 2. πραγματα] προσταγματα A

---

31. **companies** (κλισίας): cf. Luke ix. 14.

36. Cf. Jos. *c. Ap.* ii. 6. The institution of festivals is a common feature at this period; cf. Esth. ix. 15; 1 Macc. iv. 56, vii. 59, xiii. 50; 2 Macc. x. 6, xv. 36; Judith xvi. 25 (Vulg.). The Canopus stone shows that they were equally popular outside Jewish circles.

37. ἐντυγχάνω, technical of a petition to a king, &c. (cf. ἐντυχία, v. 40); see Intr. § 4 *c*.

38. **Pachon**, April 26–May 25; **Epiphi** (in Papyri, Epeiph), June 25–July 24. The names are Egyptian. The Macedonian and Egyptian calendars were combined towards the end of the second century B.C. Accordingly the dropping of the older double dating by months of both systems does not prove that this book belongs to the Roman period.

VII. 1. On the official language of the letter see ii. 12.

For ὁ ἐπὶ τῶν πραγμάτων (cf. 2 Macc. iii. 7) see Deissmann, *B.S.*, p. 306. In inscriptions it is technical, as here, 'first minister', but in Polybius and Josephus it stands for the viceroy of an absent king.

2. Philopator had no legitimate son till 208 B.C.

For this and the following verses cf. *Letter of Aristeas*, 37, and vi. 25–8 *sup.*

5. Cf. 2 Macc. iv. 47 for Scythian cruelty.

7 father for his children, and taking into account the goodwill as of a friend which they have shown
unswervingly to us and our ancestors, we have rightly absolved them from all blame on whatsoever
8 account. And we have ordered them each to return to his own home, and that no one in any place
9 should injure them at all or reproach them for their unreasonable sufferings. For know well that
if we devise any evil against them, or harm them in any way, we shall have not man but the ruler
of all power, the most high God as an adversary to avenge what is done, *and that* in every way and
at all time without being able to escape him. Fare ye well.
10 *The Jews* receiving this epistle did not at once make haste to prepare for their departure,
but desired further of the king that those of the Jewish race who had of their own will transgressed against the holy God [and the law of God] should receive at their hand fitting punishment,
11 urging that those who for their belly's sake had transgressed against the divine commands would
12 never be well disposed to the king's commands either. And he acknowledging the truth of what
they said and praising them, gave them full indemnity to destroy in every place in his dominions those who had transgressed against the law of God, *and this* with all freedom without any
13 further authority or inquiry from the king. Then having received his words with applause, as was
14 fitting, their priests and the whole multitude with shouts of hallelujah departed in joy. So as they
went on their way they slew whomsoever they met of their countrymen who had been defiled, and
15 put them to death with ignominy. And on that day they slew over three hundred men, and they
16 kept it as a joyful festival, having destroyed the impious. But they themselves who had held fast
to God even unto death, and had entered into the full enjoyment of their safe delivery, departed
from the city crowned with all manner of fragrant flowers and with cries of joy, in praises and
melodious hymns giving thanks to the God of their fathers, the eternal saviour of Israel.
17 And when they had reached Ptolemais, called on account of the peculiarity of the place, The
18 rose-bearing, the fleet according to their general wish waited for them seven days, and they held
there a banquet to celebrate their deliverance, the king having generously provided for them all
19 things for their journey until each one had come to his own home. Having reached the end of
their voyage in peace with befitting thanksgivings, there too in like manner they determined to
20 observe these days as well as a festival during the time of their sojourning; and having inscribed
them as holy on a pillar, and having dedicated a place of prayer on the spot where they had
held their festival, they departed unharmed, free, and full of joy, being brought safely on their
journey by land and sea and river according to the king's command, each to his own country,
21 having even greater authority than before in the eyes of their enemies with glory and respect,
22 and being despoiled by no one at all of their goods. And they all recovered the whole of their
property according to the registration, so that those who held any of it returned it with great fear,
the great God having perfectly wrought great things for their salvation.
23 Blessed be the deliverer of Israel for ever and ever. Amen.

10. *και του θεου τον νομον*] > *και* A V; *και τον του θεου νομον* Luc text. The omission of *καί* and the variation in order shows that the words are a gloss 16. *σωτηριας απολαυσιν*] *σωτηριαν απολυσιν* A *αιωνιω*] V *al*; *αγιω* A 44, 74 20. *προσευχην*] 19, 93; *-η* 62; *-ης* A V *al* (due to the attraction of *τόπον*) 20, 21. *εις την ιδιαν και πλειστην η εμπροσθεν*] > *ιδιαν . . . η* A; > *η* V; V is clearly right, the homoioteleuton in *εις την* and *πλειστην* explaining A's omission + *Μακκαβαιων γ'* A V

17. **Ptolemais**—not the famous city in Upper Egypt, but 'Ptolemais at the harbour', on the widening of the canal, 12 miles SW. of Cairo. See Grenfell and Hunt, *Fayum P.*, pp. 12 ff. The epithet *ῥοδόφορος* is not found elsewhere.

20. **sea** has been criticized as a gross error, but Abrahams refers it to Lake Moeris, a view which Wilbrich questions (*Hermes*, xxxix, p. 244). We may compare the use of *θάλασσα* for the Lake of Galilee. But the choice of the word is probably due to the writer's love of rhetoric. On any view of the book it comes from Alexandria, and shows considerable local knowledge. It is therefore beside the point to attempt to convict the writer of a childish geographical error.

In *Tebt. P.* 86 (second century B.C.) we find a Jewish *προσευχή* at Arsinoe.

22. Nothing was said of any confiscation of property connected with the registration, unless the reference is to cases where informers had received a reward (iii. 28). More probably we have here a reminiscence of some occasion on which there was some general attempt at confiscation; the feature of the book is its combination of a variety of attacks on the Jews (Intr. § 6 *b*).

THE BOOK OF TOBIT

INTRODUCTION

§ 1. Short Account of the Book.

THIS book, composed, possibly in Aramaic, in the last quarter of the third century B.C., probably emanated from orthodox circles in Egypt. It therefore throws considerable light upon the religious and ethical conditions of the Diaspora in that country some 150 years after the date of the recently discovered Aramaic papyri.

The evidences of its popularity, almost from the moment of its composition until the eighteenth or nineteenth century of our era, in themselves constitute a long and interesting history. Its influence is apparent alike in Jewish writings, in the New Testament, in the early Church and in mediaeval art. Carefully revised by A.D. 150 in Jewish circles into the form most common to-day, but almost immediately translated into Aramaic from the first Greek version and later, and more than once, into Hebrew, and yet again revised in Greek in Christian circles, it remained on the one hand a favourite Jewish work, and on the other hand, translated into various languages, it followed the spread of the Christian religion to Edessa in the East, to Rome and Africa in the West, and Ethiopia in the South.

Its religious and moral outlook, with a delightful mixture of real piety and Oriental superstition, is still refreshing to the modern reader. The author's chief merit, however, lies not so much in the originality of his conceptions as in his artistic genius and inimitable art in combining, and working up, strong priestly and prophetic tendencies, distinct pagan and Jewish sources, various written and oral information, definite religious and moral precepts, into a work of singular aesthetic beauty and remarkably liberal sympathies. 'Is it history?' wrote Luther. 'Then is it a holy history. Is it fiction? Then is it a truly beautiful, wholesome, and profitable fiction, the performance of a gifted poet.'

§ 2. Title.

The original Greek title was Βίβλος λόγων Τωβειθ which was only modified in R^V in the spelling of the last word—Τωβίτ Cod. Vat.—είτ Cod. Al.[1] The title is not extant in R^C. For the other versions see *critical synopsis*.

§ 3. Greek MSS. and Papyrus.

These fall into three groups, representative, along with the versions mentioned in § 4, of three distinct recensions. Their interrelation constitutes a problem of such extreme intricacy and length as to preclude little more than a bare statement of the main conclusion to which the present writer has come. A full statement of his reasons and further details, with a *résumé* of the modern treatment of the problem, he is therefore compelled to publish elsewhere.[2]

[1] Müller supposes that father and son were originally the same individual, whom some editor, later than the author, artificially separated into two when he re-wrote the work in its present form, since in the later portion of the book Sarah appears as a parallel figure to Tobias, but in the earlier portion remnants still remain, e.g. iii. 16, 17, of her original connexion with Tobit. This hypothesis is connected with Müller's theory that the author of Tobit was not a Jew, and that *Tobit* was a foreign name of which *Tobiah* was a welcome variation. But no relics of undigested paganism remain in the work. The forms Τωβείθ (R^S) and Τωβείτ (chiefly R^V, R^C) are Semitic names in Greek dress. Γεννησαρέθ and Ναζαρέθ with their by-forms Γεννησαρέτ and Ναζαρέτ are quite analogous.

[2] The evidence, however, derived from the literary and linguistic characteristics of the respective recensions, is overwhelming. That from the *contents* of the book is equally strong, since it demonstrates that the redaction we shall call R^V is a modification of R^S inasmuch as it reflects (1) the general presuppositions and ideas, (2) the historical conditions, and (3) the religious characteristics and theological developments of an age long subsequent to that in which R^S was written.

INTRODUCTION

i. Codex Sinaiticus (ℵ). This MS. presents the longest and clearest text, with only two lacunae of great importance[1] and eight slight and practically unimportant ones,[2] a comparatively trustworthy orthography of proper names,[3] only one or two additions to the original text,[4] and only a few—mostly natural—cases of internal textual corruption.[5] All the evidence, as will be seen, points to the comparative originality of the recension of Tobit contained in ℵ, which stands in a few cases alone, but is supported especially by the Old Latin, very frequently by the Aramaic, often by the Münster Hebrew, and—by no means rarely—by the recension of the Greek which we shall term R^C. Some of those scholars, who regard ℵ as only secondary, have described it as *the B text*, or simply B, a nomenclature which, apart from prejudging the problem, at least introduces considerable confusion since B is universally recognized as the symbol for Codex Vaticanus, which, according to these scholars, along with Cod. Alex., represents *the* A *text*.[6] In the following pages, therefore, we have avoided this begging of the question and much confusion by referring to the text of ℵ and its auxiliaries not as *the* A *text* (as we believe it to be) but as R^S, i. e. *the Sinaitic recension, the nearest approach which can be made to the original text whether the latter first appeared in Greek or in a Semitic language*. It is this text which has been translated and commented upon in the following pages.[7] The corrector denoted by $ℵ^{ca}$ began to emend the first scribe's text of ℵ, but seems to have recognized that it was essentially divergent from the later one better known in his time and abandoned the task.

ii. Codex Vaticanus (B) and Codex Alexandrinus (A) give the second type of text. It is accepted in some quarters as more original than ℵ. In the following pages it is referred to as R^V, i. e. the recension best preserved in Cod. Vat. A number of minuscules[8] belong to this class, but their practical unimportance, except in one or two isolated cases,[9] is admitted by all scholars. The differences between Codd. A and B are comparatively few,[10] and the Syriac, when it follows R^V, follows it practically unerringly and continuously, as do some other versions mentioned below.[11] On the other hand, the differences between R^V as a whole and R^S in its original form are extraordinarily numerous and important in spite of the number of points in which they agree. When R^S faithfully records an incident in detail, R^V summarizes; when R^S retains the poetic and aesthetic beauty of the original, R^V ruthlessly substitutes a brief prosaic narrative. That the text of R^V was finally settled in the reign of Antoninus Pius, not in Christian but in Jewish circles of the Diaspora in touch with the official heads of the Jewish Church in Palestine, is more than sufficiently proved by its general presuppositions and ideas, historical background, and its religious and theological developments in comparison with R^S. R^V, moreover, in spite of its own internal solidity, presents a much corrupted text with the proper names badly written, its grammar that of the vernacular and its style

[1] viz. iv. 6^b–19^a; xiii. 6^b–10^a. They are peculiar to this MS., not derived from its archetype, not destructive of its reputation for general reliability, and easily explicable; see notes *ad loc.*

[2] viz. i. 2, 4, 5; ii. 2, 8; ix. 5; xi. 12, 13; xiii. 11, chiefly single words, at times only the copula and a conjunction.

[3] See notes to i. 1, 2, 15; v. 6; vi. 13; xi. 18; xiv. 10, 15.

[4] xi. 15, due simply to dittography; xii. 9 (merely a gloss).

[5] ii. 1 (case ending), 12; iv. 19^b (owing to the omission in verses 6^b–19^a); v. 6 (already mentioned in previous note); vi. 13 (12); viii. 3, 15; xi. 1 (?), 4; xiii. 16; exclusive of xiv. 4 where the textual corruption ℵ shares with all extant MSS. and versions is outweighed by its unique preservation of the original *Nahum*.

[6] Müller's 𝔏 for R^S and 𝔎 for R^V avoid this difficulty, but lay too much stress on the comparative length of the two recensions to the exclusion of more important and characteristic differences.

[7] The text of ℵ is printed by Swete below that of B in vol. ii of *The Old Testament in Greek* with the variations of A noted at the bottom of each page, an arrangement which, in addition to the premium it allows B, has led, as Nestle, *Septuagintastudien*, iii, 1899, has shown, to some slight confusion in the critical apparatus. This text has, however, been used for the present translation. Swete's verse-numbering of ℵ has also been adopted, that of the Revised English Version appearing in brackets wherever it differs from Swete's. In Fritzsche's *Kurzgefasstes exegetisches Handbuch zu den Apokryphen*, 1853, the readings of the Alexandrine and Sinaitic are at times interchanged! In *La Sainte Bible Polyglotte, Ancien Testament*, vol. iii, 1902, edited by F. Vigouroux, B appears on the extreme left, next to it ℵ, on the right-hand page the Vulgate and a French translation. This work is therefore more convenient to consult, but is not ideal, since its critical apparatus notices only a *minimum* of variants of ℵ, B, A, P^2 (= Holmes 243), P^3 (a hitherto uncollated MS. identical, it is claimed, with Holmes 106), and makes no comparative collation of any of the other MSS. and versions. As long ago as 1870 Fr. H. Reusch published an emended text of ℵ with a carefully constructed synopsis of the various readings of the Old Latin MSS. in his *Libellus Tobit e codice Sinaitico editus et recensitus*—a work, to which the present writer is much indebted, though it presents no synopsis at all of the various recensions of R^V and R^C nor even of the more important translations other than the Old Latin.

[8] Their variations are noted by Fritzsche in most cases, but only a few instances, e. g. in ch. vi, appear in our critical synopsis.

[9] e. g. xiv. 15; cf. note *ad loc.*

[10] Cod. A is not, however, quite unimportant since it frequently inclines to R^S, thus showing the antiquity of this latter redaction and its refusal to be ousted entirely by R^V. For the relation of these two MSS. to each other, see Schulte, *Biblische Zeitschr.*, 1908, pp. 262–5.

[11] The solidity of R^V is naturally no guarantee of its antiquity.

abrupt. A minute analysis of these and many other indications of its inferiority as compared with R^S can be seen in the critical apparatus (or, as it might be better described, synopsis) of the differences in the case of each verse and often each word which is printed below the translation of R^S in the following pages.[1]

iii. Between vi. 7 (8) and xiii. 8 THE MINUSCULES 44 (CITTAVIENSIS) 106 (FERRARIENSIS) and 107 (FERRARIENSIS, written *c.* 1337, agreeing almost entirely with 106), furnish a fragment of a third type of text.[2] Before vi. 7 (8) and after xiii. 8 these cursives follow R^V, but it has now been demonstrated by the discovery of the OXYRHYNCHUS PAPYRUS No. 1076 [3] that R^C commenced at any rate as early as ch. ii.[4] R^C presents a few characteristics avowedly late, and it is noteworthy that we have no contemporary evidence for the use of a single reading peculiar to it prior to 2 Clem. *ad Cor.* xvi. 16, which presupposes the recension of R^C in Tob. xii. 8. Dr. Rendel Harris [5] has argued that, since this admittedly finer version—at least from the Christian standpoint—of R^C in xii. 8 was known to the author of 2 Clem., it is consequently the original text, though differing from both R^S and R^V. But, if any argument as to the date or originality of the verse can be based on 2 Clem., it is surely that its use in 2 Clem. is evidence for its existence not at an early time but at a period later than R^S, even if it was more or less contemporary with R^V. Moreover, at Alexandria R^V was still in use in the time of Clement of Alexandria, and it is not till the sixth century [6] that the Oxyrhynchus papyrus witnesses definitely to the existence of R^C in Egypt. On the other hand, individual readings in R^C, not now extant in ℵ or BA, may conceivably go back to a considerably earlier date, if not to the original writing, if they are supported by a version which is either itself admittedly ancient or known to contain a text which—on independent grounds—follows R^S in the great majority of cases. Accordingly in ii. 8 it has been possible to restore the original reading of R^S from R^C as preserved in the papyrus, owing to its agreement with the invaluable Old Latin MSS. *α* and *β* which so constantly, if not invariably, attest ℵ's general trustworthiness. R^C in fact is a *mediating* redaction, representing a compromise between R^S and R^V. A sentence is preserved in part as it appears in the former, and in part recast in the mould of the latter. It would appear that R^V was in general vogue at the time when R^C arose, but, while the brevity and other characteristics of R^V appealed to its readers, the extent and character of its deviations from R^S precluded its complete popularity everywhere. R^C is therefore an attempt to combine the improvements of R^V with the ancient and well-established R^S.

§ 4. NON-GREEK VERSIONS.

These are indispensable for a critical investigation of the text (*a*) as showing the form in which the book was read in various quarters of the world in several different languages; (*b*) as being by no means insignificant aids to the recovery of the true text of the various chief recensions (R^S, R^V, R^C) to which they belong; (*c*) as conceivably containing among their unique readings a few potentially original ones. Consequently the older versions appear in the critical synopsis below the new translation of R^S in the following pages. The less ancient and less literal, with the exception of Fagius' Hebrew, have not been taken into account there owing to the lack of space in the present volume and their comparative unimportance. A few of their more important readings are enumerated by Marshall, *HDB*, art. 'Tobit.'

A. Aramaic.

The Aramaic version of our book demands our careful attention. This is the case not simply because, as a result of the pronouncements of Neubauer and Bickell,[7] it has been popularly regarded

[1] A less exact idea of the relations of R^S and R^V may be obtained by comparing this translation of R^S with that of the Revised English Version, which, presenting R^V, follows chiefly the readings of Cod. Alex. against Cod. Vat. when the former is supported by the majority of the minuscules. See also C. J. Ball, *Variorum Apocrypha*, 1892.

[2] Printed in full by Fritzsche with a collation of the majority of the variants of 44, 106, 107, to which the present writer is chiefly indebted. Vigouroux claims that his P^3 ('supplément grec 609'), hitherto uncollated, is identical with 106. He prints it in full where its variants from R^S and R^V are very numerous. He holds that this revision was made at the commencement of the fourth century by Hesychius.

[3] See A. S. Hunt, *Oxyrhynchus Papyri*, viii, 1911. No. 1076 (9·5 × 13·9 cm.) is the lower part of a vellum leaf, the text being written in two columns, and one side of the leaf has shrivelled so that the letters were considerably larger originally.

[4] See ii. 2–4, 5, 8, note *ad loc.* That this fragment belongs to R^C has been proved beyond dispute by Dr. Hunt, *op. cit.*, pp. 6–9; see further notes to ii. 2–8 on pp. 205 f. below.

[5] *A. J. Th.*, iii, 1899, pp. 547–9.

[6] This is the date assigned to 1076 by Dr. Hunt in view of its carefully formed, large round uncials, the similarity to other papyri of the same date, and the brown colour ink commonly found in the Byzantine period.

[7] *Zeitschr. f. kathol. Theol.* ii, pp. 216 ff., 764 ff.

as one of the most genuine representatives of the original form of the book, and is still supposed by some scholars to be the 'Chaldee' text used by Jerome,[1] but also on account of the problem of the Aramaic dialect in which it appears, and finally on account of the subsidiary evidence it supplies in favour of the antiquity and originality of R^S. It was first published by Neubauer in 1875, being the fifth part of a MS.[2] in the Bodleian Library, and is headed והוא כתוב במדרש רבה דרבה. This Midrash Rabbah of Rabbah is identified by Neubauer with the *B'reshith Rabbah major* of Martini, which in turn is identified by Zunz,[3] but not by Neubauer, with the *Bereshith Rabbah* of R. Moses had-Darshan.

The linguistic characteristics of this version were first subjected by Nöldeke to a scientific criticism and treatment in the appendix to his epoch-making essay, to which we shall have reason constantly to refer. His investigations at once showed how optimistic was the supposition of Neubauer and Bickell[4] that it usually represents the oldest and most genuine form of the original work even when it differs from R^S and R^V. Nöldeke, on the contrary, came to the conclusion that its dialect was Palestinian, and intermediate between the so-called Babylonian Targums and the more modern Palestinian dialect of the Palestinian Talmud, Midrashim, and Targums, and that consequently this extant form of the Aramaic goes back only to *c.* A. D. 300.

Nöldeke himself, in framing this hypothesis, recognized many of its difficulties, and endeavoured to explain them by the supposition that the text has suffered considerably from errors, mutilations, and grammatical and syntactical alterations of 'ignorant and careless' copyists who had no knowledge whatsoever of the influence of grammatical rules, dialectic variations, or the earlier and later forms of the language other than their own vernacular.

May not many of these characteristics that Nöldeke regards as secondary and scribal corruptions be as primary as those he regards as the most original? Are they not too numerous to allow of the supposition that they are less characteristic than those of the earlier dialects which also survive? Dalman, in fact, is probably correct in his supposition that *the linguistic peculiarities in our MS.* did not appear earlier than the seventh century in circles which were influenced by both Talmuds and by the more ancient Targums.

THE SOURCE OF *Ar.* The extant Aramaic text goes back to an earlier Aramaic version,[5] but the question still remains as to whether—through that earlier Aramaic text—it is to be regarded as a translation and redaction from a Semitic or a Greek original. In Neubauer's judgement 'the pure Semitic idiom of the Chaldee text does not admit for a moment the possibility of its being a translation from a non-Semitic text.[6] Dalman writes: '*Possibly* a source in the style of the Targum of Onkelos might have been utilized and might have been the text known by Jerome, but it is also probable that the Aramaic text is a translation from the Latin.'[7] Nöldeke, on the other hand, rightly argues that the language of *Ar.* certainly does not prevent the recognition, in parts of it, of even a fairly literal, though never a slavish, rendering of the Greek B (=R^S).' Thus, in spite of Bickell's explanations,[8] the forms ראגיש (רגאש, רגאיש, ריגש) רגש presuppose the translation from the Greek Ῥαγοῖς or Ῥαγαῖς, whereas a Semitic original would have resulted in the appearance of רג or רגא.[9] Similarly אגבתנים is a transcription of Ἐκβατάνοις,[10] whereas a Semitic original would have known the Hebrew form אחמתא. For תיגרין see note to vi. 2 (1). טובי represents the dative Τωβεί. אשר i. 2 in M = Ἀσσήρ (= Ἀσσώρ?), whereas a Semitic original would have preserved the correct חצור, just as עשאל = Ἀσιήλ, which in LXX regularly represents יחציאל. Supposed misreadings in *Ar.* of a Semitic original and the absence of the dog in *Ar.* and M[11] are equally futile (see notes to vi. 3, 16) as evidence of the translation of *Ar.* and M from a non-Greek original. The forms and partial omissions of Aḥiḳar in *Ar.* and M are also emphatically in favour of a Greek original.

TYPE OF *Ar.'s* TEXT. In Neubauer's judgement *Ar.* 'agrees for the greater part with the Sinaitic text, and consequently with the Itala. However, the Chaldee text has sentences which are to be found sometimes in one, sometimes in another.' Nöldeke, as mentioned above, believes that the original Aramaic was a translation from a Greek MS. of R^S. *Ar.* is, therefore, a not unimportant witness to R^S as the most original text extant, while to some small extent it illustrates among Aramaic-speaking peoples a gradual evolution of the text on lines somewhat

[1] See p. 178.
[2] This MS., containing a collection of smaller and larger Midrashim, is written in Greek-Rabbinical characters and dates from the fifteenth century.
[3] *Die Gottesdienstlichen Vorträge der Juden*, 1832, pp. 287 ff.
[4] *Zeitschr. f. kathol. Theol.* ii, pp. 216 ff., 764 ff.
[5] See *Münster Hebrew* below.
[6] The same view is taken by Bickell, *Zeitschr. f. kathol. Theol.* ii, pp. 764 ff.
[7] *op. cit.*, p. 37. [8] *op. cit.*, p. 219. [9] See Nöld., *op. cit.*, p. 56, footnotes 1, 2.
[10] For g = k cf. אגדיקום = ἔκδικος.
[11] See pp. 184, 195 below.

parallel to those which culminated in the publication of R^{V}. On the other hand, the fact that it was translated from a Greek MS. is far from supporting the theory that the book was originally written in Hebrew or Aramaic (see § 6). The use of the third person throughout is paralleled in the Vulgate.

B. Latin Versions.

I. OLD LATIN VERSIONS[1] AND QUOTATIONS.

The old Latin MSS. with which we are chiefly concerned[2] are: 1. Codex Regius, No. 3564, in Paris (= α); 2. Codex, No. 4, in the Library of G. Germain (= β); 3. Codex Sangermanensis, No. 15 (= γ); 4. Codex Vaticanus, No. 7 (=δ), which once belonged to Christina of Sweden. The four were collated and edited by P. Sabatier.[3] Joseph Blanchini[4] produced a more exact edition of δ than Sabatier's, while Neubauer included in his *Book of Tobit* a carefully corrected text of Sabatier's edition of αβγ.

αβ are probably to be traced back to a common ancestor, from which Sabatier thought they were transcribed in the ninth century, while γ, in most of its deviations from αβ, represents a later and slight redaction of one of their ancestors, and texts in which it agrees with αβ therefore go back to a still earlier period and one much closer to the time of translation from R^{S}. δ, on the other hand, was transcribed about the tenth century,[5] and up to vi. 12 (11)[6] contains either an independent and somewhat free translation of R^{S}, or, in view of its close approximation to R^{C} in vi. 7(6)–11(10), a fair example of the existence of R^{C} in the Western Church.

Most of the Latin patristic quotations[7] agree more or less closely with αβγ. While the fragments of Tobit which appear in the Mozarabic Breviary[8] also mostly follow αβγ or δ, S. Augustine's *Speculum*[9] presupposes a third Latin text differing both from αβγ and δ.

The Old Latin with its three types of text is thus one of the most important versions. One type, αβγ, is almost as constant a representative of R^{S} as is ℵ, and through Reusch's careful handling and analysis the Old Latin versions and patristic quotations have become a primary authority for the original text. In the critical synopsis beneath the accompanying translation, therefore, the readings of the various MSS. are given where they are of moment instead of the less detailed 𝔏 denoting the Old Latin as a whole. In a few cases the original reading, lost in ℵ, can thus be restored; see notes to i. 4, ii. 2, 12, iv. 6^{b}–19^{a}, v. 6, viii. 3, ix. 5, xiii. 6^{b}–10^{a}, 16.

2. VULGATE.[10]

This is S. Jerome's translation. His own explanation of its origin he gives in his Preface[11] to the book. Neubauer has argued that his *Ar.* 'in a more complete form was the original from which the translation of the Vulgate was made'. This supposition is not supported by the evidence derived from a comparison of the two texts.

Nöldeke's strictures upon S. Jerome's accuracy and possibly upon his truthfulness are therefore more or less justifiable. Somewhat but not essentially different is Schulte's hypothesis[12] that the saint (i) actually used 'a Chaldee', i. e. an Aramaic text, presumably the parent of *Ar.*, but (ii) with constant reference to 𝔏 and (iii) with considerable freedom in the insertion of his own sentiments.

C. Hebrew Versions.

I. THE MÜNSTER HEBREW.[13]

Neubauer's *Book of Tobit* contains a collation of Münster's text with (1) No. 1251 of the

[1] = 𝔏 in following pages.
[2] For further MSS. see Berger, *Notices et Extraits des Manuscrits de la Bibliothèque Nationale et autres Bibliothèques*, xxxiv. 2, 1893, p. 142.
[3] *Bibliorum sacrorum Latinae versiones antiquae*, Paris, 1751.
[4] *Vindiciae Canonicarum Scripturarum*, Rome, 1740.
[5] Blanchini, *op. cit.*, p. ciii.
[6] From this point it has the text of 𝔙.
[7] The more lengthy quotations are enumerated by Reusch, and are noticed frequently in our critical apparatus.
[8] See Migne, *P. L.* lxxxvi. 151.
[9] *Spicilegium*, ix, edited by Angelus Maius.
[10] = 𝔙 in the following pages. Cf. Berger, *Histoire de la Vulgate pendant les premiers siècles du moyen âge*, 1893.
[11] Quoted in full by Neubauer, *op. cit.*, p. ii.
[12] *Die aramäische Bearbeitung des Büchleins Tobias verglichen mit dem Vulgatatext* (*Theol. Quartalschr.*, 1908, pp. 182–204).
[13] = M in the following pages.

Hebrew MSS. in the National Library in Paris [1]; (2) the Persian translation of M,[2] made in the Pehlewi idiom, written in Hebrew characters, No. 130 of the Hebrew MSS. in the National Library, dating from A. D. 1400 [3]; (3) No. 194 of De Rossi's Catalogue,[4] which agrees closely with (2).[5]

Purpose of M. The circle in which M flourished was Jewish and orthodox, with its thoughts directed to the Torah and its hopes centred on the rise of still another generation of 'children busied with the Torah,' for whose edification the translation of its Hebrew may have been made. Its reverence for the Deity is expressed by its use of the periphrasis 'the Holy One blessed be he'; its angelological development is exemplified by the application of the title השר הממנה על־הרפאות to Raphael. For the omission of Noah and the dog and the stress on the later procedure in marriage contracts see p. 184, *infra*. Ginsburg surmises that M dates from the fifth century A. D. Nöldeke points out that the language is not the לשון חכמים, but an imitation of the Biblical language, not, however, entirely uninfluenced by the former,[6] though considerably more ancient than F.

M's Source. It was at one time natural to regard M as a redaction based on a translation of R^S, and usually of that form of R^S extant in the Old Latin rather than that in א. The grounds for this supposition are best stated by H. Sengelmann, *Das Buch Tobit*, 1857, pp. 61–3. Its usefulness as a quite subsidiary, but not as an independent, witness to the comparative originality of R^S was even then of some small moment. But the evidence thus collected for the closeness of M's agreement with R^S became of more vital importance for the solution of the interrelation of R^S and R^V after the discovery of *Ar.* *Ar.* and M are closely and essentially connected (*a*) in phraseology and vocabulary,[7] (*b*) in the sequence and displacements,[8] (*c*) in contents [9] and point of view.[10] They are a unity as distinct from R^V and a clearly deliberate redaction of R^S.[11] But M, having been subjected to changes as a result of the special circumstances and point of view outlined above,[12] is a less perfect representative of this redaction than *Ar.* But while *Ar.* is therefore not derived from M, the latter is evidently not derived from the extant form of the Aramaic. This is shown by a comparison of M and *Ar.*, e.g. in i. 16 (where *Ar.* omits דעמי), 18 (where M retains part of the blasphemy charge omitted by *Ar.*), iii. 3, 5 (where *Ar.* but not M has small omissions), as well as by the abbreviations at the beginning of the book, the avoidance of Raphael's ascension, and the use of the third person throughout the book. We must, therefore, conclude with Nöldeke that *Ar.* and M go back to a common Aramaic ancestor, which was a translation from R^S (cf. p. 177, *supra*). Thus, in spite of its comparatively modern date and secondary character, M's agreement in many important points with R^S adds considerable weight to the great mass of evidence in favour of the antiquity and originality of R^S.

2. FAGIUS' HEBREW.[13]

This is a translation based chiefly on R^V, and is usually regarded as dating from the twelfth century. This late date naturally robs the version of much of the critical value it would otherwise possess, and it has not therefore been necessary to tabulate the minutiae of its readings in full detail. Still it is not without considerable importance. It is an excellent illustration of the type of text in use in Western Europe [14] amongst the Jews of that period. From the literary point of view F is of

[1] Neubauer uses the sign P, while additions peculiar to it are enclosed in square brackets [ ]. These signs have been retained in the following pages.

[2] = Pr. in Neub. and the following pages.

[3] Some of the errors of this translation are due to the translators' ignorance and literalness, see Neub. p. xiii, footnote 2; others form an interesting parallel to F's treatment of proper names, e. g.

מדי = עראק, בבל = בגדאד, אררט = קוסטנטנייה, אשור = מוצל.

[4] = Π in Neub. and following pages.

[5] Neub.'s brackets ( ) are retained, signifying passages appearing in M and Π but not in P.

[6] Note the presence of a few נתפעל forms; אותו once as a demonstrative; לירש and לידע; טרם ש and קודם ש beside טרם and בטרם.

[7] e. g. בדרך בכל־הארץ = באורח כל־ארעא, iii. 8.

[8] e. g. iv. 13–16, &c.

[9] e. g. the two *bonds* for the two *bags* in v. 3, &c.

[10] e. g. 'king of the demons' as a title of Asmodaeus, &c.

[11] Theories of mistranslation or mis-reading of a common original as explanations of the deviations of *Ar.* and M from R^S are as inadequate as they are in the case of the differences of R^S and R^V. See note to vi. 16 and pp. 181 f.

[12] Nöldeke further emphasizes the paraphrase of xi. 2 end in M as compared with *Ar.*'s literal translation of R^S, the abridgement in i. 16 f. (see note *ad loc.*), x. 1–7, the expansion in i. 19, the reconstruction of the prayer in viii. 5.

[13] = F in following pages.

[14] This is probably the reason for his interpretation of the reference to Elymais which he understands as Germany, ii. 10. In vi. 2 (1) he is usually supposed to refer to Laodicea but the reference may be to some otherwise

interest as showing a still further development than appears in R^V, and even *Ar.* and M, to introduce biblical phraseology and texts, e. g. iii. 5 f.; iv. 13, and *passim*. It belongs to a strict legal circle which sought for precision in matters of the cultus, e. g. i. 4, current commercial terms, e. g. iii. 17; vii. 10 (9): v. 14 (13), and liturgical formulae, e. g. iii. 16 and *passim*. Special importance was attached to the hope for the rebuilding of the Temple, i. 8. Moreover, in contrast with R^S, R^V, and R^C it insists on the importance of the Halachah as well as the Torah, vii. 12 (13), and consequently describes the marriage rite in the terms of contemporary usage, vii. 13. An element of speculative philosophy, if not of Kabbalistic lore, appears in its insistence upon the Divine foreknowledge of the marriage of Tobias and Sarah on the sixth day of creation, vi. 17 (16). Stress is laid upon the Fatherhood of the transcendent God, who himself hearkens to mortals' prayers, iii. 16. It reflects the point of view of a period in which Noah's reputation had recovered from the stigma which attached to it in the time of the common ancestor of *Ar.* and M (see p. 184). Unlike the original author, he believes in a judgement beyond the grave, a judgement of Gehenna, iv. 11, and speaks of 'the eternal home', iii. 8. The fragmentary character of ch. xiv is probably due to accidents of transmission.

3. THE LONDON HEBREW.

This text was found by Gaster in the British Museum. It is *Add.* 11639. It is of little critical value, but is interesting as showing the culmination of the tendency, observable in germ in R^V and active in F, to approximate to biblical phraseology. The problem of the close interrelation of this version and the Vulgate is probably to be settled in favour of the priority of the latter and the indebtedness of the former to it in some way which is not at present clear.[1] See further, Gaster, *PSBA*, vol. xviii, pp. 208 ff., 259 ff.; vol. xx, pp. 27 ff.

4. THE GASTER HEBREW.

This version was taken by Gaster from a Midrash on the Pentateuch. The tendency to *abbreviate* the original story reaches its culmination in this version. Its affinities are closest with *Ar.* See Gaster, *PSBA*, vol. xix, pp. 33 f.

D. Two Syriac Versions.

1. The first, commencing at i. 1, and extending to vii. 11, is a close translation of R^V. Nestle supposes that this text was once complete, and that all the extant MSS. are descended from one of early date which had been accidentally mutilated.[2] This version, moreover, represents, as Nöldeke thinks, the work of Paul of Tella, and therefore dates from the beginning of the seventh century.

2. The second has ousted the first and taken its place from vii. 11[3] to the end of the book. It belongs almost entirely to R^C, though at times it shows even greater reverence for R^S than usually characterizes R^C.

E. Ethiopic Version.

This is based on R^V. Abbreviations and errors in translation are numerous.

§ 5. Original Language.

A. The only *external evidence* is supplied by Origen[4] and Jerome,[5] and, on the whole, leaves the question quite open.

B. *A priori considerations*. From the Yeb papyri it can be seen that while the proper names of their period were mostly Hebrew, the colony employed Aramaic for literary purposes. Thus *c.* 200 B.C. it is far more likely that a popular work such as Tobit would be written in Aramaic

unknown locality near his own home. The change of Media to Midian, i. 14, is due on the other hand to his extreme subservience to Biblical language and scenery.

[1] Hence Gaster was too optimistic in his belief in its close relationship to Jerome's 'Chaldee'.

[2] For details see Nöldeke, *op. cit.*, p. 46, footnote 1.

[3] That the text after vii. 11 is a remnant of a version entirely distinct from that before this verse is apparent not only from the transference of allegiance from R^V to R^C at this point, but from differing orthography in ii. 10, xiv. 10 (Aḥiḳar), vii. 2, 13 (14) (Edna), iv. 1, 20, ix. 2 (Raga). One MS., moreover, in the British Museum, which extends only to v. 14 (13), contains the earlier text, while another in the same collection like the three MSS. at Paris and the one at Oxford (Payne-Smith, *Cat. Col.* 18) contains i. 1–vii. 11, and from that point gives the other Syrian text. It is noteworthy that the Syriac glosses mentioned by Masius in his *Syrorum Peculium* agree with this Syriac version and do not extend beyond ch. vii.

[4] Origen remarks in *Ep. ad Afric.* ch. xiii, with reference to Tobit: περὶ οὗ ἡμᾶς ἔχρην ἐγνωκέναι ὅτι Ἑβραῖοι τῷ Τωβίᾳ οὐ χρῶνται οὐδὲ τῇ Ἰουδήθ. οὐδὲ γὰρ ἔχουσιν αὐτὰ καὶ ἐν ἀποκρύφοις ἑβραϊστί, ὡς ἀπ' αὐτῶν μαθόντες ἐγνώκαμεν.

[5] See p. 178, *supra*.

rather than Hebrew, especially if written in Egypt. In Palestine, it must be remembered, Hebrew remained the sacred language, as is shown by Daniel and many Maccabean Psalms, and also the official language of the nation, as can be seen on the coins. Greek, on the other hand, was making headway about this time, particularly in Egypt. Moreover, in the century in which our book was written, the Pentateuch was probably translated into Greek, and in the next century still more of the Scriptures, including Ben-Sirach, also appeared in Greek at Alexandria.

C. The *internal evidence* should be dealt with in four departments:

1. Evidence favouring a *Greek* original—

(*a*) Greek sentences and verbal combinations such as *could not* result at least from literal translation appear in i. 6 ff.. iii. 8, iv. 6, vii. 7, xii. 7. Their importance for the problem is emphasized by Nöldeke and André. On the other hand, it is conceivable that the Greek idiom is due either to a translator's conscious attempt to render the original into good Greek or to later correction.

(*b*) It is at least evident that the forms of the proper names in i. 1 f. are the proper and usual Greek equivalents of Hebrew names, not the unfortunate results of misreadings of a Semitic script. See notes *ad loc.*

(*c*) Nöldeke points out (*op. cit.*, p. 60) that there is a considerable difference between the Greek style of our book and that of the translations of Judith and 1 Maccabees. Nöldeke, however, bases his arguments on R^V instead of the original R^S, to which this objection does not apply to the same extent.

2. Evidence *slightly* in favour of a *Semitic* original, but not necessarily so if a Greek original is presupposed; some few at least of these words and phrases belong as much to the κοινή as to the vocabulary of a Greek-speaking Jew. If on the other hand there is independent evidence pointing to a Semitic original, most of them, not being characteristic of the κοινή, will be explicable as literal translations of that Semitic original, and will thus afford subsidiary proof of its existence.

(*a*) The etymological value of names such as Raphael,[1] Azariah,[2] Ananiah,[3] though known sufficiently to be appreciated both by a Greek-writing Jewish author and by his Greek-reading Jewish public, would be the more appropriate if the book was written in a Semitic language.

(*b*) The list Müller gives,[4] though not complete, is sufficiently illustrative of the vocabulary, style, and phraseology which should be included under this section. It is, however, especially in this sphere, that the minor changes of R^V are important. R^V tends to remove them, thus reflecting a consciousness of their non-Greek character.

3. Evidence pointing more or less *definitely* to a *Semitic* original—

(*a*) A few constructions remain which, unlike the preceding, seem to demand for their explanation not simply a Jew who wrote in Greek as their author, but one who thought and wrote in Hebrew or Aramaic.[5]

(*b*) The hypothesis of independent translation from a Hebrew or Aramaic original in the various recensions and translations is frequently resorted to, not only to explain the divergences of R^S, R^V, and R^C, and even of each of the versions (e.g. 𝔖, *Ar.*, M, F), but also to prove the existence of a Hebrew or Aramaic original.[6] Various scholars have thrown out suggestions,[7] but Dr. Marshall[8] presents it in its most attractive and logical form. Even if, however, no other solution of the divergences of R^S and R^V existed, it must be confessed that Dr. Marshall's hypothesis would have

1 'God heals.' 2 'Jahveh helps.' 3 'Jahveh has compassion.'

4 *op. cit.*, pp. 28 ff.

5 e.g. (i) In iv. 18 the Greek presupposes בוז על or בסר על. (ii) v. 19 (18), see note *ad loc.* (iii) Cases such as καὶ θάψω, ii. 4; καὶ εὐφρᾶναι, xiii. 10; καὶ ἀπέθανεν (cf. Judges ii. 21), i. 8. (iv) v. 19 (18) and xiii. 3, see notes *ad loc.* and Müller, *op. cit.*, p. 32 f. (v) εἰς τὸν αἰῶνα καὶ ἔτι in xiii. 18 seems to presuppose immediate translation of לעולם ועד, cf. LXX Exod. xv. 18, Theod. in Dan. xii. 3, Aq. Theod. Sym. Ps. xxi. 5. Similarly ἐν αὐτῷ τῷ καιρῷ, iii. 14, 16, might be a literal translation. (vi) ἡμέραι τοῦ γάμου ἃς ὤμοσεν ποιῆσαι τῇ θυγατρὶ αὐτοῦ, x. 7, might possibly point to a Hebrew or Aramaic original if ποιῆσαι should be taken in the sense of 'spend'. But see Barton, *Eccles.* (*Inter. Crit. Comm.*), p. xxiii and note to Eccles. vi. 12. (vii) προσηλύτοις τοῖς προσκειμένοις in i. 8 may be a doublet translation of גֵּר or the participle of גור. πρόσκειμαι = גור in Lev. xvii. 8. On the LXX's equivalents to this Hebrew root see W. C. Allen, *Expositor*, vol. xx, 1894, p. 264 ff.

6 So precarious and unscientific has this method proved in the past in the exegetical (see notes to ii. 10, iv. 17, xiv. 4) and other spheres (see notes to v. 3, vi. 3, viii. 3, xii. 6), that it would be beside the point even to allude to it here were it not so intimately bound up with the problem of the original language of the book and consequently to some extent with those of the place and date of composition (see § 6, 7) and the sources of the various non-Greek versions (see above).

7 Cf. Fuller, *op. cit.*, *Excursus I*, pp. 164–8.

8 *HDB*, vol. iii, *sub* 'Tobit', where he employs the results of his investigations as an argument for an Aramaic original.

to be pronounced untenable for reasons of which the following are only the more important and are only stated here in outline form:—(i) At the outset it is clear that, to use Dr. Plummer's words with reference to Dr. Marshall's attempt to explain certain divergences in the Synoptic Gospels by a similar hypothesis of independent translation from the Aramaic,[1] 'these possibilities seem to be too isolated and sporadic to be of great value in accounting for differences'.[2] (ii) It is almost inconceivable—both on the analogy of other books and from the evidence we possess of the derivation of *Ar.* and M from R^S, and of 𝔖 and F, &c., in part from R^V and in part from R^C—that each and every secondary translator or redactor in turn had recourse—and that, too, independently of all the others—to this hypothetical Aramaic original, safely preserved and handed down apparently for the sole purpose that they might independently consult it! (iii) Before such a hypothesis could be accepted as a working basis for further research, the independent evidence for the composition of the book in Aramaic would have to be much stronger and certain than it is at present. (iv) Most of the instances Marshall adduces are far more easily and rightly explicable in other ways,[3] while in some cases the reasoning is purely subjective[4] and in others self-evidently weak and erroneous in its premises.[5] (v) If attempts such as Marshall's and Resch's more laborious studies[6] are rightly passed over, along with the oral hypothesis of Gieseler and Dr. A. Wright, by New Testament scholars as being inadequate and useless contributions to the solution of the Synoptic Problem, hypotheses such as this of Marshall's and Bickell's[7] must also fail in the case of Tobit, and for the same fundamental reason. In the case of R^S and R^V especially, and also in that of non-Greek versions of Tobit, as in the Synoptic Gospels, *the problem to be solved is not simply that of the causes for the existence of numerous and important* **divergences**, *but along with, and in spite of, these divergences the reason for the far more numerous and unobtrusive sections, verses, and words,* **exactly alike** *in themselves and in their order in the various recensions, and particularly in the Greek of* R^S *and* R^V. Thus the hypothesis of independent translation is neither adequate nor needed for the solution of the problem of the interrelation of R^S, R^V, and R^C. At the most the *mere possibility* can be admitted that in a few cases R^S (cf. p. 181, footnote 5) and 𝔙 (see e.g. xi. 18, note) contain an instance or two of translations suggestive of their Semitic origin, if indeed the latter can first be shown to have existed, while other versions (see e.g. vi. 16, note) may contain a few readings due ultimately, but not directly, to a recollection—i.e. in an oral, not written manner—of a different or corrupt form of the text in existence in Semitic circles. But this is not evidence that the *original* tongue was Semitic. (vi) Finally it will suffice here to observe that granted the Greek text preserved in R^S was translated—as it must have been if it is indeed a translation—very soon after the original Semitic work was composed, corruptions in the Hebrew would at that time naturally be *very few*. And only a very few even of these select cases can bear the test of an unbiased examination.[8] Even in some passages of real difficulty the true explanation often lies elsewhere,[9] and the possibility of intentional corruption must be taken into account.[10]

4. Evidence pointing to an Aramaic rather than a Hebrew original, e.g. the forms Ἀθήρ and Ἀθουρειάς in xiv. 4, 15. Even these Aramaisms, pronounced as they are, do not, however, settle the question.[11] The possibility will always remain that these two words are an early scribal error,[12] or are even due to the Aramaic environment in which the earlier Greek writers among the Jews found themselves.

It must be admitted that the evidence in favour of a Semitic original is not strong enough to put the matter beyond controversy.

[1] *Expositor*, April and Nov., 1891. His arguments were refuted by W. C. Allen in the *Expositor*, vol. xvii, 1893, pp. 386–400, 454–70, the prefatory note on the linguistic issue by Professor Driver on pp. 386 f. being specially pertinent in connexion with Tobit as well as with the Synoptists.

[2] Plummer, *S. Luke* (*Inter. Crit. Comm.*), p. 154, footnote 1, cf. pp. 102, 186, 222.

[3] e.g. see notes to i. 15, 18.

[4] e.g. רחמותא in i. 13 might equally well be said to be an internal corruption of דמותא, itself a translation of μορφήν!

[5] e.g. iv. 3, see note *ad loc.*

[6] *Agrapha* in *Texte und Untersuch.*, v, Heft 4, 1889, and *Aussercanon. Paralleltexte*, x, Heft 1 and 3, 1893–5.

[7] According to this scholar R^S was a revision made from the original translation with the assistance of the Hebrew original. Nöldeke's reply (*op. cit.*, p. 50) to Bickell applies with even more force to Marshall.

[8] Cf. notes to i. 2, 15, 18; ii. 3, 10; iii. 7; iv. 3; v. 3, 19 (18); vi. 3 (2); xii. 6, &c.

[9] e.g. iv. 17, vi. 16 (15), viii. 3, see notes *ad loc.*

[10] See note to xiv. 4.

[11] See Ed. Meyer, *Der Papyrusfund von Elephantine*, 1912, p. 108.

[12] Compare the copyists' variations of the Aramaic quotations in the Greek MSS. of the New Testament, e.g. Mark v. 41, xv. 34.

§ 6. Date of Composition.

That *Tobit* is not an autobiography [1] written in the seventh century B. C., is evident from the writer's historical inaccuracies, e. g. i. 15, chronological blunders, e. g. i. 4 as compared with i. 15–22 and xiv. 1, and knowledge of events long subsequent to 722 B. C., e. g. xiv. 4 f., 15. He differentiates between the return from the Babylonian exile, which has therefore taken place already, and the promise of a further return and the dawn of a still more glorious era, xiv. 5. He betrays a religious as well as literary dependence on the latest portions of the Pentateuch.[2] Similarly a date at the very earliest a little subsequent to the rise and establishment of Judaism is necessitated by his religious and moral teaching (see § 10). The same *terminus a quo* is favoured by the author's general outlook, developed style, and artistic composition, the product of an age accustomed to the chronicling of singular experiences, xii. 20, as well as to the somewhat formal drawing up of marriage contracts, vii. 13 (14). Financial and commercial relations had superseded purely agricultural and pastoral pursuits, and the writer and his contemporaries had grown more or less accustomed to the foreign domination.

The *terminus ad quem* is more debatable, but the book is certainly pre-Maccabean. While the author has some knowledge, derived from the historical books of O.T., of historical events prior to, and including, the Return, and reflects the general religious point of view of the period subsequent to Ezra, he reveals no knowledge of the stirring historical crises of the later Greek domination and the Hasmonean period, and lacks the intense hatred of the heathen they inspired. Not only does he not accept, but in most cases he shows no knowledge of those explicit dogmas of Judaism which first came into prominence at or after the time of Antiochus Epiphanes, such as advanced apocalyptic expectations, formulated doctrines of a personified and hypostatized Wisdom, stereotyped descriptions of the Messianic age, explicit belief in a resurrection and immortality. He knows practically nothing of the problem Job was the first to raise, the Hellenizing apostasy, the Essenes' self-abnegation, or the long fight of Pharisaic progressiveness against Sadducean conservatism.[3] The comparatively early date of the book, as it appears in the earliest form known to us, R^S, is perhaps most clearly demonstrated by comparison with R^V, which dates from the second century of the Christian era (see § 3).

There are, too, certain other features which also point more or less definitely to this pre-Maccabean period, though some are much less significant than is usually allowed. To this latter class belongs xiv. 4–6, once a mainstay alike of the more conservative critics [4] in their defence of the book's pre-Herodian date, and also of extremists, like Hitzig,[5] to whom it presents equally circumstantial evidence of composition after the destruction of Herod's Temple in 70 A. D. But while the words καὶ οὐχ ὡς τὸν πρῶτον must certainly have been written before that event, they are quite as likely in the mouth of a pious contemporary of Christ, scandalized by the paganizing tendencies of Herod's Temple architecture and the spiritual unreality of its services, as in the mouth of faint-hearted worshippers in Zerubbabel's Temple (cf. Hag. ii. 3)! It is equally unfortunate that Tobit's scrupulous care for the burial of the dead has been exalted to a position of primary importance for the settlement of the date, e. g. by Graetz, who consequently assigns the book to the reign of Hadrian; by Kohut, who dates it *c.* A. D. 226; and by W. R. Smith and Riggs, who, comparing 2 Macc. v. 10, refer it to the Maccabean revolt. This trait is ultimately due, so far as the author, not later redactors, is concerned, not to contemporary political troubles, but, in the case of Tobit's own action in chs. i, ii, chiefly to his literary dependence on *The Grateful Dead*,[6] and, in the case of advice to the same effect, to the influence of Aḥiḳar [7] and especially to the book of Genesis and its traditional exegesis [8]. Again the stress which, it is usually alleged, is laid by the author on the agnatic or consanguineous marriages led Graetz [9] to suppose that he endeavoured to inculcate the *laity's* observances of the (late) Talmudic regulation [10] which was originally intended to regulate only *Priests'* marriages.

[1] The historicity of the book is still defended by F. Vigouroux (*Les Livres Saints et la critique rationaliste*, fifth edition, 1901, p. 551 ff.). On the other hand, as Cosquin (*Revue Biblique*, vol. viii, 1899, p. 82) points out, several Roman Catholics—Jahn, Dereser, Movers, and Antoine Scholtz—have held that the book is not a history but either an allegory or homiletic treatise. Moreover, the Council of Trent in affirming its canonicity made no pronouncement as to its historicity.

[2] See p. 192, footnote 6.

[3] The hypothesis that the book was written by a Sadducee might account for such silence, but is inadmissible in view of the nascent angelology and the childlike belief in Providence it inculcates—both, in their full growth, leading dogmas of the Pharisees' creed and the butt of the Sadducees' cold logic.

[4] e. g. Fuller, W. R. Smith, Riggs, André.

[5] *ZWT*, 1860, pp. 250 ff.

[6] § 8. ii.

[7] § 8. iii.

[8] See § 8. iv, and I. Abrahams, *JQR*, 1893, vol. i, p. 348.

[9] *Monatsschrift f. Gesch. d. Judentums*, 1879, pp. 509–13.

[10] *Kiddushin*, 76ª.

The author himself appeals to the Pentateuch (vi. 13; vii. 12)! Kohut's explanation [1] that it is due to Zoroastrian influence, is open to the same objection, as well as being contradicted, as Gutberlet [2] first pointed out, by Kohut's own theory, that the book is a protest against Zoroastrianism. To Rosenmann [3] belongs the distinction of having first partially unravelled this problem of the agnatic marriages, while Müller has advanced a stage nearer the true solution. The former scholar has demonstrated that the Talmud nowhere insists on its actual observance by any generation except that of the wilderness wanderings, that even before the destruction of the Temple, A. D. 70, an annual festival on the 15th of Ab had been instituted in celebration of the abolition of the custom, that it had never been recognized by the Pharisaic party, and that 'therefore in practice agnatic marriage was no longer known to the first pre-Christian century'.[4] Thus also Rosenthal's theory that *Tobit* emanated from the School of Rabbi Akiba is bereft of the support it claims from this quarter. In Rosenmann's judgement the author wrote in order 'to break a lance on behalf of agnatic marriage which was already in a moribund condition'. If, however, the author's main interest, as seems to be the case [5], was in Jewish as opposed to international marriage, and his references to agnatic unions were only subsidiary to that and primarily the result of his close dependence on his chief sources, he must have lived in an earlier period, the pre-Maccabean, when agnatic marriages were still to some extent in vogue even in the Diaspora, where the most pressing danger of the day was that of international marriage.

With equal clearness Rosenmann [6] has disproved the inferences which have been drawn from vii. 11–13 (14) in favour of a late date.[7] The ceremony described in these verses differs only from those of the O.T. in its mention of 'an instrument of cohabitation'. Graetz, followed by Rosenthal, understands this συγγραφή as the Greek equivalent to the technical כתובה which appears in *Ar.* and M, and which, he supposes, was first coined in the reign of Queen Salome by Simon ben Shetah But the כתובה was in existence before that time, for Simon did not invent it; he only modified the details of its working. To identify, however, this כתובה with the συγγραφή of the present passage is to remove from the narrative all mention of betrothal or marriage-rite. Moreover, the usual Greek equivalent of כתובה was φερνή or ἀντιφέρνη which also represent מהר in LXX of Ex. 22. 15 f., the passage from which the Talmudic rite of the כתובה and its amount are derived.[8] The term συγγραφή, on the contrary, is the usual equivalent of שטר של אירוסין or שטר של נישואין. Tob. vii. 11–13 (14) therefore casts an interesting side-light on the early forms of the procedure before it had assumed the stereotyped character of the Talmudic age. Here the father prepares and signs the συγγραφή; in the fully developed Talmudic ceremony it should be done by the bridegroom.[9] Here the marriage is consummated the same night; in Talmudic times a virgin could not be married until twelve months, and a widow till one month, after this solemn betrothal.[10]

Finally the references to the *dog* (vi. 2 (1), xi. 5),[11] the number (seven) of Sarah's husbands, vi. 14 (13), vii. 1, and the statement that Noah, like Abraham, Isaac, and Jacob, was a prophet and a 'father' of the nation who contracted an agnatic marriage, contribute additional evidence of the comparatively early origin of the book. In the Talmudic period it was prescribed that no one should keep a dog unless it was led by a chain;[12] no woman might marry again whom death had already bereft of *three* husbands in succession;[13] and admiration for Noah, displayed e.g. in Jub., ch. xxv (where the very features of his life appear to which *Tobit* alludes)[14] gave way to the view that Noah was saved not by his own good works—which did not exist—but by the grace of God.[15] So well known and widely accepted, in later times, were these specifically Rabbinical points of view, that in *Ar.* and M, the common Aramaic ancestor of which dates from this period, the dog was not mentioned; in the Addition to the Midrash Tanḥuma,[16] as in the ספר שעשועים,[17] Sarah's seven husbands were reduced to three; and in M no reference at all was made to Noah.[18]

Is it possible to define the date more closely? Ewald [19] favoured 350 B. C., but a number of

[1] Geiger's *Zeitschrift*, vol. x, p. 61 f.
[2] *Das Buch Tobias*, Münster, 1877, p. 47.
[3] *Studien zum Buche Tobit*, Berlin, 1894, pp. 1–7.
[4] Rosenmann, *op. cit.*, p. 7.
[5] See p. 196.
[6] *op. cit.*, pp. 15–19.
[7] Even if R^V were the more original text, its καὶ εὐλόγησεν αὐτούς (vii. 12) is based on Gen. xxiv. 60, and does not therefore necessarily presuppose the Talmudic formula of the ברכת חתנים (*Kethubhoth* 8[a]), as Rosenthal, *op. cit.*, p. 132, note 1, urges in his attempt to prove the late origin of the book.
[8] *Kethubhoth* 10.
[9] See *Qiddushim* 9[a].
[10] *Kethubhoth* 57.
[11] See § 9.
[12] *Baba Kama* 83[a], cf. 69[b].
[13] *Yebhamoth* 64[b], *Niddah* 64[a].
[14] Cf. also Sir. xliv. 17 for an appreciation of Noah's righteousness.
[15] *Sanhedrin* 108[a], *Midrash Rabba* to Genesis, § 29.
[16] Neub., *op. cit.*, p. 36.
[17] In יין לבנון, Paris, 1866, p. 18.
[18] The author's explanation of the term Pentecost (ii. 1, see note *ad loc.*) and other details all point to a comparatively early date, but are quite subsidiary to the more important points already mentioned.
[19] *History of Israel*, vol. v, p. 209 ff.

considerations, more or less cogent, point to a date much closer to 170 B.C. The period subsequent to Alexander the Great seems to be demanded by the use of the Greek drachma, v. 15 (14), the Greek name of the month, ii. 12, the wide extent of the Diaspora which the author presupposes, and by the fact that Rages, iv. 1, &c., probably the Ragha of the Avesta,[1] was comparatively unknown before it was rebuilt by Seleucus Nicator, 321–281 B.C.[2] The second tithe, i. 7 (still less the third of R^V, i. 8), was still unknown to the Chronicler (*c.* 300 B.C.), though it appears in Jubilees and in the LXX of Deut. If the author wrote in Egypt, his enthusiastic description of Tobit's marriage to the beautiful Jewess, his relative Sarah, is probably an attempt to substitute a more edifying story for the scandal, still fresh in his own and his readers' minds, of that apostate descendant of another Tobias, Joseph the notorious tax-collector.[3] This did not take place before 230 B.C.[4] Further, the author's affinities—in thought and point of view—with Sirach certainly lead one to suppose that they belonged to the same tendency and type of thought within the pre-Maccabean period. Unfortunately they are far from being sufficiently close, immediate or numerous as to warrant the assumption that either writer was dependent on the other.[5]

To sum up, *Tobit* was written at the very earliest, *c.* 350 B.C.; at the latest, *c.* 170 B.C., probably much nearer the latter than the former date.[6]

§ 7. Place of Composition and Purpose.

The nameless author of *Tobit* was not a Palestinian Jew.[7] The characters of his book, as well as the geographical setting, belong to the Diaspora; his readers are in exile (xiii. 3), and he counts himself among them (xiii. 6), while distance lends enchantment to Jerusalem, the goal of all his hopes (i. 4–9, xiii. 7–18). Moreover, his staunch adhesion to Judaism is accompanied by a belief in demons and magic, side by side with a breadth of culture and a liberal outlook on life unequalled by any Palestinian writer whose work has survived. The widespread use of the Greek Verss., the scarcity and comparative lateness of the oriental Verss., and the almost complete ignorance of the book in the Syrian Church, do not favour theories such as Ewald's of the Far East, Kohut's of Persia, or Vetter's of Assyria or Babylonia, or Professor J. H. Moulton's of Media. The internal evidence is in fact antagonistic to any such hypothesis. Such surmises are, at the outset, negatived by the author's ignorance of Eastern geography and his acceptance of the ordinary standards of Greek and Roman geographies. That the Tigris flowed between Nineveh and Media was an idea common among the Greeks; that Ecbatana was situated in a plain was a constant Western fallacy, and is repeated in Diod. ii. 13. 6 in a passage dependent on Ctesias.[8]

The hypothesis that Egypt was the place of composition alone serves to explain all the phenomena, and, at the same time, raises no additional difficulties, and encounters no legitimate objections on the part of the upholders of the Palestinian or Eastern origin of the work. This happy solution of the problem was first stated by Nöldeke, and has been accepted by Löhr, W. R. Smith, André, and others. It has lately received additional support from the discovery of the actual sources upon which the author depended for the plot, outline, literary allusions, and the non-Jewish stratum of his religious and speculative materials. Only Egyptian Jews could need an antidote to the *Tractate of Khons*. No trace can be found in Palestinian literature of any acquaintance with the *Fable of the Grateful Dead*. Only in Egypt, so far as is known, did either Jews or pagans read Aḥiḳar's fortunes at the Assyrian court *in exactly the chronological order* in which they

[1] *Vendidad*, i. 16; *Yasna*, xix. 18; cf. Marquardt, *Eransahr*, pp. 122 ff.

[2] Strabo, 524 C.

[3] Josephus, *Antiq.* xii. 4. 6. Joseph had sought a *liaison* with a dancing-girl of the Egyptian Court and had only been saved from it by the crafty action of his brother Solymius, who substituted his own daughter. Possibly a covert reference to him is to be found in v. 14, 'Semelias the great.'

[4] The date cannot be fixed definitely and many of the details are fictitious and self-contradictory, see Bevan, *The House of Seleucus*, vol. ii, p. 168, note 1; Schürer, *GJV*, fourth edition, i. 183, 195 f.; ii. 99 f. To his credit, Joseph, too drunk at first to notice the deception, afterwards became attached to his niece, and a son, Hyrcanus, was born of the agnatic marriage.

[5] § 8, iv.

[6] Since the foregoing was written, Professor J. H. Moulton has very kindly pointed out to me that the comparatively early date for which I have argued is supported by the fact that, while the book reflects many of the most significant points of ancient Magianism, *it betrays no knowledge of the newer Zoroastrianism*, much less of the still later fusion of those two mighty currents of Persian thought. The importance of this significant argument, for which I am entirely indebted to him, is self-evident in the light of the new and fuller information about Zoroastrianism contained in his *Hibbert Lectures* (see § 8, v, below).

[7] Müller, in spite of his theory that between the present Jewish work of Tobit and the ultimate sources stands a pagan Tobit, holds the view that the Jewish author or redactor lived in Palestine. How the Jewish writer living in *Palestine* could obtain the pagan original or, if it was well known in Palestine, dared to adapt it, retain the *pagan* title, and yet publish it as a genuine autobiography of a seventh-century *saint*, Müller does not explain.

[8] Even R^V still insists that Rages was near Ecbatana.

appear in *Tobit*.[1] The author's environment in Egypt fostered Magian presuppositions[2] and allusions which would be incredible in an author writing in an eastern land such as Persia or Media, where Semitic and Iranian elements first met in deadly antagonism,[3] and highly improbable in Palestine. It was in Egypt, too, that the Jews especially indulged in demonological speculations and practices.[4] Moreover, while the fish, vi. 2 (1)–9 (8), primarily mythological and probably inspired by the details of *The Grateful Dead*, symbolizes[5] the pagan empire endeavouring to seize what portions it could of the pious Diaspora, the fact, on the other hand, that its inner organs are subsequently employed for medicinal and magical purposes suggests that the author, perhaps unconsciously, identified it with the crocodile of the Nile, on the banks of which he lived. 'This conjecture is raised almost to certainty when we read in Ḳazwini i. 132 that the smell of the smoke of a crocodile's liver cures epilepsy, and that its dung and gall cure leucoma, which was the cause of Tobit's blindness.[6] Very similar statements as to the medicinal virtues of the crocodile occur in Greek and Latin writers.' Again, the binding of Asmodeus in Upper Egypt, though mythological in its origin (viii. 3, cf. *note ad loc.*), expresses the author's conviction that Egypt, where he was compelled to live in exile, was the veritable dumping-ground of wickedness and sin, exactly as Zechariah regarded Babylon, the land of exile he knew best, whence some of his hearers had just returned and where exiles still lived, as the goal of the flying Ephah, wherein Wickedness was imprisoned, Zech. v. 5–11. Consequently our author excludes all unnecessary references to the specifically Egyptian life around him.[7] His heroes are made to live out their lives in that distant part of the Diaspora, where Aḥiḳar, like Nehemiah, had held important positions at court. The rustic simplicity and idyllic life of the patriarchs[8] fill in the details of the pictures. This, too, is the motive for the author's careful substitution of Elymais in ii. 10 for Egypt, which appears in Aḥiḳar as the country whither the sage journeyed to demonstrate his wisdom; he felt that Aḥiḳar was too good and noble a Jew ever to have been domiciled in Egypt or compelled to participate in the deliberations of the Egyptian court.[9]

The writer does not, however, forget the practical needs of his readers. The present book, as already pointed out, was a reply to the tractate of the priests of Khons, and was designed to dissuade his co-religionists from apostasy, and convert if possible any pagan who might read it. It is still more pointed in its warning against marriages with non-Jews, and incidentally condemns imitation of the immorality and apostasy of Joseph, the son of another Tobias, an allusion not without point in Egypt, where the scandal had occurred. While the major portion of the Jews in Egypt were probably never deeply influenced by Greek Philosophy, and many of them remained unaffected by the rising tide of Hellenism,[10] the writer, aware of these nascent dangers, makes the pertinent and emphatic statement of iv. 19.

Lastly, our hypothesis illustrates and gives point to the author's position with regard to sacrificial and legalistic religion. The fortunes and religious life of the Jewish exiles in Egypt were

1 Cf. p. 191. 2 Cf. p. 193 f.

3 The hypothesis of Media as the writer's home is, however, most unlikely on other and independent grounds. It involves the following highly improbable suppositions: (i) that our author was a descendant of such of the ten tribes as were deported to Media in 722 B.C. (see 2 Kings xvii. 6); (ii) that the tribe or family to which our author belonged not only preserved the purer religion of Jahveh, but also by some inexplicable means advanced from that comparatively undeveloped faith to the fuller and richer Judaism of the early post-exilic period (see § 10), *along the lines laid down by Jeremiah, Ezekiel, and Deutero-Isaiah*, and even knew almost immediately and accepted unreservedly the *newly-introduced Law Code of Ezra* as well as *the presupposition of Jerusalem's unique sanctity*, of which his forefathers had naturally known nothing: (iii) that the book, when written, by some equally inexplicable means not only found its way to Jerusalem in the pre-Christian period, but was received with applause by the confessedly narrow-minded religious leaders of the post-exilic community!

4 See Deissmann, *Light from the Ancient East*, second edition, 1911, pp. 306 ff.

5 This symbolism need not have been based on that of the whale (= the Babylonian Empire) in Jonah, but may, like Jonah, have originated through an allegorical treatment of Jer. li. 34–6.

6 W. R. Smith, art. 'Tobit', in *Ency. Brit.*[9].

7 Maspero and Spiegelberg (see Budde, *Das Hohelied*, p. xvi f.) have shown the application of the term *sister* to a wife (Tobit v. 21 (20); vii. 15 (16); viii. 4, 7) was common in the old Egyptian songs. Our author, however, had no need to avoid the term on account of its Egyptian associations as it was also genuinely Hebrew: see Gen. xx. 12; Song of Songs iv. 9, 10, 12.

8 See p. 192, footnote 7.

9 Or possibly in the version of Aḥiḳar in use among his co-religionists in Egypt this motive had already eliminated the reference to Egypt. It is, therefore, probably more than a mere coincidence that, as Sachau (*op. cit.*, p. xxii) points out, in the Aramaic papyri, which retail the history of Aḥiḳar, 'there is no trace of the Egyptian episode'. But see Ed. Meyer, *Der Papyrusfund von Elephantine*, 1912, pp. 110 f.

10 Müller (*op. cit.*, pp. 23 f.), however, seems to deny even the possibility of a single Jew resident in Egypt being unaffected by Hellenism in the pre-Maccabean period, the sole but 'decisive' argument, in his judgement, against *Tobit's* composition in Egypt! And yet he himself (p. 20) sees in iv. 19 so clear and definite a refutation 'of the well-known pre-Maccabean efforts in the direction of Hellenism and culture' as to be able to use, and quite rightly, this as an argument in favour of a pre-Maccabean date for the book!

till lately almost unknown to us. But from the papyri we now know, for instance, that, even before the Exile, Jews had migrated to Egypt, become mercenaries in the Egyptian army, and formed a colony as a permanent garrison at Yeb, where they built a temple to Jahveh; that this temple survived the destruction of the Egyptian ones by Cambyses, but towards the close of the fifth century B.C. was destroyed at the instigation of the priests of Chnum, the ram-headed god of the island; and that an appeal was made to Bagoas, the governor of Judaea. It is not clear, however, whether the temple was rebuilt or not. But two important inferences in connexion with the religious evolution of the Jews in Egypt at the time of this catastrophe seem to Sachau to be justified.[1] On the one hand, neither Monotheism nor the Law had there undergone the full development which had resulted from Ezra's establishment of Judaism and the Law some few years before at Jerusalem. On the other hand, even before the catastrophe, reforms in the interests of Judaism, as established at Jerusalem by the priestly school, may have been initiated at Yeb by a party powerful enough at any rate to enforce the principle, if not the details, of the High-priesthood and the imposition of a tax of two shekels of silver in imitation of Ezra and Nehemiah's innovation.[2] If it had been possible for his book to have been written so early, and if he had modelled his work on some tractate of Chnum instead of Khons, our author might well have been one of these pioneers of progressive, and therefore living, though legal, religion in Egypt.[3] But teaching such as our author's with regard to the duty of Egyptian Jews to the Law and the temple must have been needed still more in later days in that part of the Diaspora. A need of that kind must necessarily have produced efforts like the present one to inculcate such principles.[4] This explains the purity of his moral outlook, the true spirituality of his religion, and the depth and reality of his adhesion to the Law. His struggle in Egypt for religious expansion and broad-minded progressiveness, hand in hand with its practical application for the actual lives of his co-religionists, antedated a somewhat different fight in Palestine by only a few years. Because our author's was less sharp than the latter, it left him without much of the rich theology the Ḥasidim's plight evoked. But, because its objective was primarily the establishment of a progressive Judaism and only secondarily the preservation of religion against pagan encroachments and was still less in opposition to a Hellenizing liberalism, it left him fortunately without the Ḥasidim's narrow bigotry.

§ 8. Sources.

Popular religious and magical speculations, current mythology and demonology, ethical and moral maxims of his day, traditional folklore and romantic legend, all contributed their quota to the education of the author. They widened his outlook on life without vitiating the spirituality of his religion or the reality of his adhesion to Judaism. They endowed him with the culture necessary to a writer whose appeal was probably directed to the educated pagan as well as the enlightened Jew of the Diaspora in its early days. They did this without loosening his grip on his own countrymen's practical difficulties of everyday life, and without stultifying the real usefulness of his literary work with the veneer of a superficial philosophy.[5] But to the following four sources—partly literary, partly oral—he was especially indebted in writing the present work.

i. *The Tractate of Khons.*

A copy of this tractate, designed for the propagation[6] of the cult of the Egyptian God Khons of Thebes, has been preserved on the Bentres Stele, which dates from about 500 B.C. In a town called *Bchtn* (= Ecbatana?) there lived a princess possessed by a demon. 'Khons, the beautifully resting one', the God of Thebes, despatched 'Khons, the executor of plans', to her assistance; the demon was expelled and the princess was healed. It is probable that, conscious of the baneful tendency of this and similar propaganda of Egyptian paganism to encourage apostasy

[1] The line of argument pursued above is, of course, quite independent of Sayce's deductions ('The Jews and their Temple in Elephantine') in the *Expositor*, Nov., 1911.

[2] A long tax list containing more than a hundred names survives, while the personal names in the papyri belong on the whole to the type in vogue at Jerusalem in the later period.

[3] His high ideals for reunion with Jerusalem were in turn destined to receive a set-back, when in the time of Antiochus V Eupator (164–162 B.C.), Onias IV went to Egypt and established the temple at Leontopolis 'in the province of Heliopolis' (Josephus, *Ant.* xii. 9. 7; xiii. 3. 2, and 10. 4; xx. 10; *Bell. Iud.* i. 1. 1; vii. 10. 3).

[4] This would naturally commend the book to the notice of the authorities at Jerusalem. Moreover, the fact that the book is also an abridgement of the main features of Aḥiḳar's history and maxims would win for it an enthusiastic, unanimous, and early reception in Palestine. Thus its wide acceptance there and elsewhere cannot be adduced as an objection to the hypothesis of its composition in Egypt.

[5] See p. 186.

[6] Naville, *The Old Egyptian Faith*, 1909, p. 257, terms it 'a puff advertisement for the God Khons'. On Khons, or Chunsu, see further, Wiedemann, art. 'Religion of Egypt', in *HDB*, Extra vol., p. 185.

among his fellow exiles in Egypt, our author conceived the idea of writing a rival tractate to illustrate Jahveh's sole sovereignty over supernatural as well as human beings, and His ability to protect and assist in dangers, sickness, and exile all who fulfilled his moral and ceremonial requirements. H. Schneider [1] has endeavoured to prove that *Tobit* is a *direct* 'remodelling' of this tractate. The author seems at least dependent upon it for one place-name and for the ideas of demon-possession, supernatural assistance sent from afar to relieve the maiden of high position, the father's unwillingness to allow the instruments of his daughter's deliverance to depart from his roof, his loading them with riches, if not also for the mention of Egypt in connexion with the expulsion of the demon. Such borrowing from a pagan source, with a view to disprove a pagan god's pretensions by ascribing his attributes and work to Jahveh, is more than paralleled among the Jews in Babylon, e.g. by P's use of the Babylonian Tablets of Creation in praise of Marduk in order to work up their contents into a dogmatic statement of Monotheism, of Jahveh's creation of the world, and of the duty of Sabbath observance in Gen. i–ii. 4[a]. But our author's work is more complex than the *Tractate of Khons* in the weaving and working out of its plot, and richer in details, while he abandoned many of the detailed characteristics [2] of the Egyptian story in favour of other sources equally well known to pagan and Jew, but less subversive of the Jewish Faith.

ii. *The fable of the Grateful Dead.*

It was more probably this cycle of stories—either written or oral—which provided the author with the major portion of the general outline of his story, infused the romantic interest, and furnished several of the most exciting crises in the plot—a fact denied by only a very few scholars.[3] The corpse of a debtor, the outline of the fable runs, was rescued from his murderers and buried at great personal self-sacrifice by a traveller or itinerant merchant, whom the dead man's spirit, appearing in human form, afterwards delivered from mortal peril, bestowing on him a bride and rescuing him from death by drowning; the supernatural being only revealed his own identity at the end of the series of adventures to the surprise alike of the merchant and of the reader. Such legends might well be as widespread in antiquity as at the present day and would be speedily assimilated and conformed by the Jews to their own peculiar religious and aesthetic tendencies: finally only an artistic mind such as our author's would be required to transform one or more of these fables into the Apocryphal story of Tobit. Simrock in his collection of seventeen variants of the fable,[4] was the first to point out their importance in relation to *Tobit*. Mostly indigenous in their present form to Germany, they have parallels in Holland, France, and Italy. Andersen's *Reisercamarad* witnesses to the existence in Denmark of a recension closely akin to No. 10 in Simrock, while Cicero, *De Divinatione*, i. 27, proves that the kernel of the fable was already in existence in his day. Further parallels are given by Benfey in *Pantschatantra* and Pfeiffer's *Germania* xii. Considerably closer parallels to *Tobit* appear in the Armenian [5] and Russian [6] forms of the fable.

Though the parallels are numerous, there are a number of significant differences both in outline and detail. The pertinent question is therefore raised by Schurer [7] as to whether, quite apart from the uncertainty as to the antiquity of the fable, these differences are so vital as to make the hypothesis of our author's dependence on the fable improbable.

In the first place, however, it is likely that the primitive story from which all the modern forms of it are *ex hypothesi* derived, underwent considerable changes in outline as well as in detail between the date of our author's use of it and the moment when these modern variants branched off from the main stock. Fortunately Simrock's seventeen versions, though they all assumed their present literary form in one country and at the same time, themselves provide an excellent example of this peculiar adaptability of the fable to transformations and modifications.[8]

Secondly, not a few of the important traits peculiar to *Tobit* and contradictory of all the extant forms of the fable, are explicable as deliberate modifications by the author of *Tobit* in conscious deference to his own aesthetic tendencies, his Jewish prejudices, his readers' edification, or his desire at the moment to utilize some other source or copy some other pattern.[9]

[1] *Kultur und Denken der Babylonier und Juden*, Leipzig, 1910, pp. 638 f.

[2] See Naville's description, *op. cit.*, pp. 249–58.

[3] e.g. Preiss, *ZWT*, 1885, pp. 24–51 (in reply to Linschmann); Geiger, *Katholik*, 1904, vol. i, pp. 367–77 (in reply to Plath), but accepted e.g. by Sepp., *Kirchliche Reformentwürfe*, 1870, pp. 27–45, and *Altbayerischer Sagenschatz*, 1876, pp. 678–89; Linschmann, *ZAT*, 1882, pp. 359–62; Cosquin, *Revue Biblique*, 1899, pp. 513–20; Plath, *Th. Stud. und Krit.*, 1901, pp. 402–14 (especially valuable); Joh. Müller, *Beihefte zur ZATW*, xiii, 1908, pp. 2–10.

[4] Published under the title *Der gute Gerhard und die dankbaren Toten*, Bonn, 1856.

[5] Printed in Haxthausen's *Transkaukasia*, 1856, i, pp. 333 f., reprinted in Pfeiffer's *Germania*. iii, 1858, pp. 202 f., by Köhler.

[6] Schiefner, *Orient und Occident*, ii, 1864, pp. 174 f.

[7] *GJV*[4], 1909, iii, p. 241.

[8] See Plath, *op. cit.*, pp. 404–6.

[9] The various differences are minutely traced to these causes by Plath, *op. cit.*, pp. 408–14.

iii. *The story and wisdom of Aḥiḳar.*[1]

A. *Antiquity of Aḥiḳar.*—G. Hoffmann[2] was the first scholar to point out the striking resemblances between this work and our book. To-day its value as a primary source of a portion at least of Tobit, as well as the multiplicity of problems it raises on its own account and in relation to the Jewish colony at Yeb, is generally recognized. Still read in the *Arabian Nights* and *Aesop's Fables*, it was widespread in the ancient world. Quite apart from the numerous versions which survive, it has left an indelible impression on the literature and thought of the past. It was well known to the Greeks and Romans, and it has been argued that this is proved apart from its appearance in *Aesop's Fables*, by numerous parallels in the fragments of Menander,[3] S. Clement of Alexandria's reference[4] to its alleged use by Democritus,[5] as well as by the statement of Diogenes Laertius (v. 30) that Theophrastes (371–264 B.C.) composed a work entitled Ἀκίχαρος, and the allusion of Strabo[6] to Ἀχαΐκαρος. The use of Aḥiḳar is unmistakable in the Qoran.[7] The Talmud[8] is not entirely free from its influence, and some Christian writers knew it at second hand.[9] At the beginning of the Christian era Aḥiḳar was still somewhat popular in Palestine: this much is clear from the New Testament.[10] It is consequently by no means surprising that certain of the latter parts of the Old Testament itself are to some extent dependent upon Aḥiḳar. Dr. Rendel Harris points out the parallels in thought and language between Aḥiḳar, e.g. in Ps. cxli. 4, 5, 10 (in both the Massoretic text and the LXX), in Dan. ii. 2, 11; iv. 10; v. 7, 16. In the case of Sirach, with which Tobit is intimately connected in sentiments and date (see iv. below), the dependence on Aḥiḳar is beyond dispute.[11] Thus before the beginning of the second century B.C.—how much earlier we cannot tell—Aḥiḳar must have been reverenced in Palestine, and even regarded there as sacred if not actually inspired, and its vogue had declined considerably before New Testament times on account of its partial incorporation in Tobit. In Egypt, however, we have contemporary evidence from the Elephantine papyri[12] that between the fifth and sixth centuries B.C. the Jewish community there read, in Aramaic, some portions at least both of the history (see p. 186, foot-note 9) and of the parables and fables. Consequently Hoffmann's supposition that an author later than Tobit wrote the legend to explain the references to Aḥiḳar in Tobit, and Mr. E. H. Dillon's that

[1] For the Greek, Armenian, Syriac, and Arabic texts, and an English translation of these, and of Jagić's German rendering of the Slavonic, with an Introduction (including an examination of the relation of *Tobit* to *Aḥiḳar*), see (in addition to vol. ii of this work) *The Story of Aḥiḳar*, Cambridge, 1898, by F. C. Conybeare, J. Rendel Harris, and Agnes Smith Lewis. More recent works are: *Alter und Herkunft des Achikar-Romans und sein Verhältnis zu Aesop*, by Rudolph Smend, being the second part of *Beihefte zur ZATW*, xiii, 1908; and *Histoire et Sagesse d'Aḥikar l'Assyrien*, 1909, by F. Nau, containing a full history of the criticism of Aḥiḳar, an up-to-date bibliography (especially with regard to works on the Syriac, Ethiopic, Slavonic, Roumanian, and Greek versions), with indispensable concordances of the relative order of the sayings and proverbs in the various versions; Benfey, in *Ausland*, 1859, pp. 457 ff., 511 ff., demonstrated the existence of the legend among the Hindus. For further articles and works see below.

[2] *Abhandlungen für Kunde des Morgenlands*, vol. viii, 1880, p. 182 f.

[3] Nau, *op. cit.*, pp. 41–6.

[4] *Stromata*, i. 15, in *Migne*, p. 772; see H. Diels, *Fragmente der Vorsokratiker*, p. 439.

[5] Rendel Harris, in vol. ii *Story of Aḥiḳar*, Introd. § 3 *a*; Nau, *op. cit.*, pp. 35–41. Sachau, however, confesses himself unable to find any connexion between the proverbs of Aḥiḳar and those of Democritus, whether Democritus or a pseudo-Democritus, and attaches but little importance to the evidence quoted above.

[6] XVI. ii. 39. The pertinence of this allusion remains unaffected whether παρὰ δὲ τοῖς Βοσπορηνοῖς is understood with Reinach (*Revue des Études juives*, xxxviii, 1899, pp. 1–13) as pointing to Borsippa in Babylonia, or with Halévy (*Revue Sémitique*, 1900, p. 44) to Bostra in Syria.

[7] Especially in the 31st Sura entitled *Lokman*, Rendel Harris, *op. cit.*, lxxii f. Nau, *op. cit.*, pp. 68–70.

[8] Nau, *op. cit.*, pp. 66 f.; cf. L. Ginzburg, art. 'Aḥiḳar', in *Jewish Ency.*, vol. i, p. 289.

[9] e.g. S. Clement of Alexandria (referred to above). For Origen see Rendel Harris in *The Story of Aḥiḳar*, Cambridge, 1898, p. xliv.

[10] While Vetter, Ginzburg, and Nau, in opposition to Dr. Harris and Halévy, may possibly seek unduly to minimize Aḥiḳar's influence upon the New Testament, the extent of the latter's immediate dependence upon the former is certainly exaggerated if passages such as Matt. iii. 10 (Luke iii. 9); Luke vii. 39; 1 Cor. i. 27, v. 11; 2 Tim. iv. 17 be included. It may be presumptuous to inquire whether it was the History of Aḥiḳar or Tobit's reference to Aḥiḳar which was present to the mind of our Lord when he uttered the parable of the Wicked Servant recorded in Q (especially Matt. xxiv. 48–51; Luke xii. 14, 15), and whether the Wisdom of Aḥiḳar is the background of the parable of the Barren Fig-tree (Luke xiii. 6–9). The details, or at least the literary presentation, of the death of Judas may have been influenced quite as much by the book of Tobit as by the Story of Aḥiḳar. The latter certainly moulded the thought of 2 Pet. ii. 22. But, in view of the extent of the evidence—afforded especially by the papyri and Sirach—of the popularity of Aḥiḳar in early post-exilic days as compared with the paucity of definite evidence for its use the nearer the Christian era is approached, it may not be too bold to assume that Aḥiḳar's vogue had at least taken second place to Tobit before New Testament times (see p. 198 f.). This is not without importance in connexion with the questions of the date of the book, the integrity of the text, and the priority of R^S.

[11] Sir. iv. 7, 26, 32, 34; v. 17; vi. 7, 14, 24; vii. 25; viii. 1, 8; ix. 8 f., 14; xix. 26 f.; xxii. 26 f.; xxvii. 17, 28; xxx. 17; xli. 16, 27; xlii. 1, all demand careful examination in this connexion.

[12] See Eduard Sachau, *Aramäische Papyrus und Ostraka aus Elephantine*, 1911, Tafel, 40–50, and Arthur Ungnad, *Aramäische Papyrus aus Elephantine*, 1911, pp. 62–82.

Aḥiḳar, though earlier than Tobit, was only composed in the third century B. C., are *finally*[1] disproved. The interpolatory hypotheses (see § 9) are seen to be almost as unjustified as Ginzburg's scepticism as to the identity of the Aḥiḳar of Tobit with the Aḥiḳar of this legend or Plath's doubts (*op. cit.*, p. 391) as to whether our author had written or only oral acquaintance with Aḥiḳar.

The further problems of Aḥiḳar's exact date and place of composition concern us in so far as it is of interest to discover whether or not this source of Tobit was written in some non-Semitic language and by an author of non-Jewish nationality and religion.[2] The fact that the Assyrian kings are alluded to by name but in a somewhat impersonal and general manner, as well as the absence of all indications that the Assyrian empire was still in existence, points to a date of composition subsequent to 608 B. C. The proper names, on the other hand—even to some extent those in the latest forms of Aḥiḳar—preserve their genuine Assyrian form to a greater extent than the same and similar words have done within the Old Testament Canon. The author is acquainted with official titles (e. g. רביא, כותא), which might have been no longer understood if the Assyrian empire had long since passed away, while the Persian names, even in the later strata, are very few. Still it is probable that even if the name Aḥiḳar is a very ancient Babylonian one,[3] an author writing under Cyrus would borrow the name of a person famous for wisdom in the ancient days of Babylon. These considerations lead Sachau to suppose that it cannot have been composed earlier than the last decades of the Babylonian empire, and finally he decides that 'in its present form the book of Aḥiḳar may have been composed somewhere between 550–450 B. C.'.[4] Its author would therefore be a contemporary of Deutero-Isaiah and Jonah. Though Halévy and Dr. Rendel Harris have endeavoured to show that on internal grounds the hypothesis of a Babylonian and pagan original cannot be maintained, in Bousset's judgement 'there can scarcely be any doubt as to the legend being heathen in origin'.[5] Sachau finds nothing specifically *Hebrew* in the book of Aḥiḳar and surmises 'that such a work, possibly resting on a more ancient Babylonian pattern, might perhaps have arisen in the circle of the priests of Nebo', a cult which 'was one of the most extensive in those days' (*op. cit.*, p. xxiii). Reinach, too, urged that the original author was a pagan, and the work, which was polytheistic[6] with a mythological *motif*,[7] was translated and expurgated theologically and ethically by the Jews before our author's use of it. Nor is it quite improbable that a polytheistic work of this kind composed in Babylon would so quickly find its way to Egypt and having so quickly lost its polytheistic tendency, become a sacred book of the Jews at Yeb. Thus the papyri may fail both to favour and to disprove the hypothesis of a Jewish not a pagan author. The fact that they are written in Aramaic equally fails to solve the problem of the rival claims of Hebrew and Aramaic to be the language of the original work.

B. *Alleged divergence in detail.*—The Aramaic papyri of Aḥiḳar, in addition to the undeniably complete proof they afford of the use of Aḥiḳar among the Jews prior to the composition of Tobit, are equally useful in removing at least one of the alleged differences between the references to Aḥiḳar in Tobit and the history of Aḥiḳar as it was formerly known to us only from

[1] The weakness of Hoffmann's position was pointed out by G. Bickell in the *Athenaeum*, ii, 1890, p. 170. The priority of the composition of Aḥiḳar to that of Tobit has also been maintained by Bruno Meissner (so far only as the end of the history is concerned) in *Zeitschr. d. Morgenl. Gesellschaft*, xlviii, 1894, pp. 171–97; by M. Lidzbarski (in reply to certain statements by Meissner) in the same magazine, pp. 671–5; by E. J. Dillon in the *Contemporary Review*, March, 1898, pp. 362–86; by E. Cosquin, *Revue Biblique*, viii, 1899, p. 30 ff.; Th. Reinach, *Revue des Études juives*, xxxviii, 1899, pp. 1–13; J. Halévy, *Revue Sémitique*, 1900, p. 23; by M. Plath in the *Theologische Studien und Kritiken*, Gotha, 1901, pp. 377–414, as well as by Rendel Harris, *op. cit.*, and in 'The Double Text of Tobit' in the *American Journal of Theology*, ii, pp. 541–54.

[2] Nau (*op. cit.*, p. 35) stands practically alone in his belief in the genuineness and authenticity of *Aḥiḳar*, though he admits that the story has undergone several redactions.

[3] Ungnad and Ed. Meyer (*Der Papyrusfund von Elephantine*, 1912, p. 109) regard it as an Assyrio-Babylonian name *Aḫû jaḳar*, 'the brother is dear', probably to be vocalized אֲחִיקָר in ancient Aramaic. In Sachau's estimation, too, the name Aḥiḳar is Babylonian and belongs to a much more ancient period of Babylonian history than that of the later Babylonian or Persian empire (*op. cit.*, p. xxiii). If it was pronounced Aḥîḳâr, it would be interpreted in Syriac ܐܚ ܐܝܩܪ, 'brother of honour' (*op. cit.*, p. 148). It 'belongs to the numerous western Semitic names which the Amorites of the First Dynasty of Babylon brought to Babylonia, and at this time is quite frequent', Ed. Meyer, *Der Papyrusfund von Elephantine*, 1912, p. 119.

[4] *op. cit.*, p. xxii; cf. Ed. Meyer, *op. cit.*, p. 107.

[5] *Die Religion des Judentums*, second edition, 1906, p. 565. Cf. the same writer in *Beiträge zur Achikarlegende* in *ZATW*, 1905, pp. 180–93.

[6] e. g. in the Armenian version Aḥiḳar's prayer is addressed to the gods Belšim, Šimil, and Samin. The various adaptations, versions, and MSS. naturally differ very considerably in details, and even in more important features of the legend. For example, the MS. B of the Syriac gives two invocations, one to the idols and one to the true God, whereas L and C record only the latter, and the Armenian version, with its usual retention of the earlier form of the legend, only the former.

[7] Aḥiḳar in the Armenian employs magic and astrology and has sixty wives and sixty palaces, corresponding to the sixty solar houses and the sixty degrees of the primitive division of the celestial phenomena.

the MSS. of the various versions. In the latter Aḥiḳar lives in the reign of Sennaḥerib, who is represented as the son and successor of Esarhaddon, whereas in Tobit the inverse and correct order appears and the accuracy of R^S is incidentally vindicated. Schürer[1] has already pointed out that in the papyri[2] we read 'the history of Aḥiḳar under Sennaḥerib and Esarhaddon in this correct sequence, not the reverse as in our MSS.' of Aḥiḳar. The papyri, moreover, present in general an earlier form of the text than even those versions and redactions of Aḥiḳar in which the hero is an idolater and only worships the true God when the idols fail to hear him. Still the presentation of Aḥiḳar in our book as a Jew and a nephew of Tobit, may be due to our author's desire to enhance the fame of Tobit by making so famous a man his relative (Smend, p. 63). The same motive probably dictated the description of Aḥiḳar as a friend and benefactor of Tobit, though in his own legend Aḥiḳar appears simply as a shrewd man. In Aḥiḳar the hero is delivered from prison because he is righteous; in Tobit because he has done alms (Tobit xiv. 10). Doubtless, even if Dr. Rendel Harris's arguments[3] with regard to the Syriac in this connexion do not entirely commend themselves to all scholars, the transition from the idea of righteousness to that of almsgiving was easy if not unconscious in view of the widespread expression of the two ideas by one Hebrew word (צדקה) at the time when Tobit was written.[4] For the true explanation of the transformation of Aḥiḳar's journey to Egypt into one to Elymais (Tobit ii. 10) see p. 186 and note *ad loc.*

C. *Extent of dependence.*—(1) He borrowed directly from the history of Aḥiḳar in i. 21 f.; ii. 10; xi. 18; xiv. 10. 15.[5] The principal textual divergences and corruptions in the tradition of the proper names are referred to elsewhere (see notes *ad loc*). Nau (*op. cit.* p. 11) gives the following table of consanguinity as that presupposed by these references.

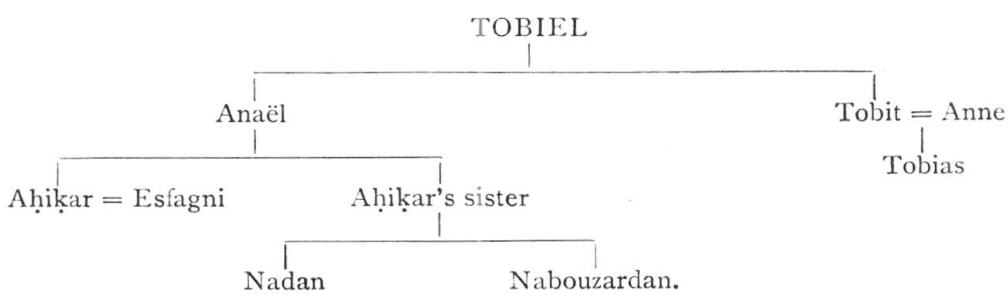

In iv. 10 'suffereth not to come into darkness' is a pertinent reference to Aḥiḳar's unhappy plight in prison and Nadan's ultimate fate mentioned more clearly in xiv. 10; it is still more generalized in Sir. xxix. 12. Especially noteworthy is the *juxtaposition* of the terms *Assyria* and *Nineveh* in the earliest recension of Tobit in xiv. 4 as well as in xiv. 15, proving conclusively the immediate dependence of Tobit upon the legend of Aḥiḳar where this curious double description of the empire is used.[6] It would appear that the legend lay before him in a written form.

(2) The legend of Aḥiḳar seems to have supplied our author with several literary and structural models. With the title i. 1. cf. the Syriac C 'I write the proverbs, to wit, the story of Aḥiḳar' and the Armenian 'the maxims and wisdom of Khikar'. As far as iii. 6[7] our author followed the example set him by Aḥiḳar of representing the hero as recounting his own history. Tobit, too, like Aḥiḳar, gives a brief summary of his previous fortunes (i. 3 ff.). Moreover, in addressing two series of exhortations to his son (iv. 3 ff., xiv. 3 ff.) and two prayers to God (iii. 2 ff., xiii) he is surely imitating the legend of Aḥiḳar, which, though the details are different, is constructed according to this plan.

(3) Our author has assimilated a not inconsiderable amount of Aḥiḳar's parenetic sections. The prologue (Tobit iv. 5) and the epilogue (iv. 19) to the 'teaching' of Tobit find their prototype in the prologue in the Syriac to Aḥiḳar's teaching: 'My son, listen to my speech, follow my opinion, and keep my words in remembrance', and in the Arabic, 'O my son, hear my speech and follow my advice and remember what I say', and in the epilogue to the same in the Armenian, 'Son, receive into thy mind my precepts, and forget them not'. As iv. 12 finds a place within *this*

[1] *GJV*, fourth edition, 1909, vol. iii, p. 253.
[2] e.g. Papyrus 49, Tafel 40, lines 3–5, 15; Papyrus 50, line 11, in Sachau, *op. cit.*
[3] Camb. ed., pp. xlviii–l, lxxxii–lxxxvi. Cf. Nau, *op. cit.*, p. 59, footnote 2.
[4] See Rendel Harris, *op. cit.*, xlix f.; *A.J.Th.*, p. 548; cf. the various readings in Matt. vi. 1, and the modern *charity* as opposed to the original meaning of *caritas*.
[5] e.g. in Syriac text on pp. 58, 67 (*bis*), 69 (*bis*), &c., of the Camb. ed.
[6] e.g. in Syriac text on pp. 58, 67 (*bis*), 69 (*bis*), &c., of the Camb. ed.
[7] Where he was compelled to abandon the direct narration, see p. 195.

'teaching', so the *same* thought appears in the *same* discourse of Aḥiḳar.[1] With iv. 15 cf. *App.* ii. 198; with iv. 18 cf. Camb. ed., p. 61, No. 12 (iii. 16 in Nau). In the case of several other verses in ch. iv a less verbal dependence on Aḥiḳar can be established as the latter appears, for instance, on pp. 60–6 of the Cambridge Aḥiḳar. With 14b, 16, 18 cf. Nos. 9, 11, 12, 43, 73; with 15 cf. Nos. 20, 39, 60. Moreover, *unless immediate dependence on Aḥiḳar is presupposed, a few obscure passages cannot be elucidated.* Of this iv. 17 (see note *ad loc.*) is an excellent example. Its meaning and phrasing are clear when read in conjunction with Aḥiḳar's, 'My son, pour out thy wine on the graves of the righteous, and drink it not with evil men'.[2] Again, in iv. 14b the precept to be πεπαιδευμένος[3] finds its original context in Sachau's Aramaic Papyrus 53 (Tafel 44) line 2. ברא זי יתאלף ויתסר[4] ויתשים ארחא ברגלו[הי] = 'the son who is trained and disciplined and at whose feet . . . is laid'. The importance Tobit attaches to the burial of the dead (e.g. i. 20, ii. 3–9, iv. 3, 5, xiv. 12) also finds a prototype in Aḥiḳar.[5] Finally, as Aḥiḳar orders his last discourses to Nadan to be written down, so Raphael bids Tobit write the record of his acts and maxims (xii. 20).

iv. *The Old Testament and Apocrypha.*

The author, as a devout Jew, was naturally well versed in the sacred writings of his own people and religion. They served as a source of the truest inspiration—historical, literary, and religious—and as a standard of orthodoxy by which he might test and repudiate all that was *essentially* alien to Judaism as he wrote this tractate, which, as shown above, was parallel but in opposition to that propagated by the priests of the god Khons, not uninfluenced by echoes of Zoroastrianism and dependent upon the pagan fable of *The Grateful Dead* and upon *Aḥiḳar*, which at the best was not *specifically* Jewish or deeply religious.

His style, phraseology, religious conceptions, and moral advice are fundamentally influenced by the Pentateuchal narratives and legislation in all their various strata.[6] The literary affinities with Genesis are of more than passing interest, for they illustrate the peculiar indebtedness of the author to that book. It was the source from which he derived not only his idea of writing a new patriarchal history, but also the materials with which he paints with consummate art the more important scenes.[7] Above all, the author was most deeply influenced by the fact that in Genesis 'there are more references to the duty of burial of the dead than in any other Scriptural book'.[8] Gen. xlvii. 49 is decisive, where Rashi, following the *Midrash Rabba*, annotates 'the kindness that a man shows the dead is *kindness of truth* for the doer has no hope of (receiving) a reward (from the corpse)'. Accordingly, the somewhat frequent references to the burial of the dead are properly and fully explained not only by the influence exerted upon the author by *The Grateful Dead* and the parallels in Aḥiḳar, but also by his close dependence upon Genesis, resulting in his belief that he could thus best inculcate disinterested charity such as Providence only can reward.

For his knowledge of the periods and scenery which he chose as the background of his story and his *vaticinium post eventum* he was dependent upon the historical books of the O.T.

[1] Camb. ed., p. 60, No. 6; in Nau's translation, iii. 9.

[2] Cf. Camb. ed., p. 61, No. 10; in Nau, iii. 13. The Arabic texts agree with the Syriac's retention of 'on the graves of the righteous', which is omitted by the Armenian.

[3] By Lévi wrongly supposed to prove dependence on Sirach; see p. 193, footnote 3, *infra*.

[4] Possibly to be punctuated יִתְּסַר (Sachau) or יִתַּסַּר, instead of the more regular יִתְיַסַּר, for which it may be a scribal error or a passive with assimilated ת. Ungnad compares the Arabic *ittaṣala* for *iwtaṣala*, and the Assyrian *ittašab* for *iwtašab*. But in any case it is יסר in Hebrew.

[5] e.g. Camb. ed., pp. 69, 71; chs. ix. 6, xiv, in Nau.

[6] viz. (*a*) *JE* in i. 22 (Gen. xli. 40, 42); iii. 6 (Num. xi. 15); iii. 10 (Gen. xlii. 38; xliv. 31); v. 17 (16) (Gen. xxiv. 7); vi. 2 (1) (*Tigris*, Gen. ii. 14); vii. 4 (Gen. xliii. 27 f.); vii. 11, 12 (11, 12, 13) (Gen. xxiv. 33, 59; and v. 60 is more closely imitated in R^V in which a point of contact with Gen. xxix. 27 is also introduced in xii. 1 (xi. 19); viii. 6 (Gen. ii. 7, 18, 22); xi. 9 (Gen. xlvi. 29 f.); (Gen. xxix. 27); xiii. 12 (Gen. xii. 3, xxvii. 29); xiii. 12 (Num. xxiv. 9). (*b*) The Code of the Covenant in i. 6 (Exod. xxii. 29); and J.'s counterpart in ii. 1 (Exod. xxxiv. 22); while an approximation to the code itself (Exod. xx. 12) was introduced by R^V in iv. 3. (*c*) D.'s legislative kernel in i. 6–8 (Deut. xii. 6, xviii. 4, xvi. 16, xiv. 25–9); ii. 13 (Deut. xxii. 1); iv. 7 (Deut. xv. 7, 8); the parenetic prefixes in iv. 5 (Deut. viii. 11); xiv. 8 (9) (Deut. iv. 40); the hortatory additions in iii. 4 (Deut. xxviii. 37); xiii. 5 (Deut. xxx. 3); and the song of Moses in xiii. 2 (Deut. xxxii. 39). (*d*) H. in i. 3 (Lev. xxv. 35); iv. 14 (Lev. xix. 13). (*e*) P. in i. 7 (Num. xviii. 21); i. 9 (Num. xxxvi. 6, 7); i. 21 (Gen. viii. 4): ii. 9 (Num. xix. 11); v. 18 (17) (Num. xxvii. 17); vi. 13 (12) (Num. xxvii. 8, xxxvi. 8, xv. 30 f.); vii. 12 (13) (Num. xxxvi. 6); viii. 21 (Num. xxvii. 8); xii. 10 (Num. xvi. 38).

[7] e.g. Tobit calls Tobias to hear, as it seemed to him, his last injunctions in ch. iv, and his grandchildren in ch. xiv, just as Jacob had done (Gen. xlix); Raphael performs the part angels played in the lives of the Patriarchs, and like them returns to heaven when his work is accomplished. Again, the story of Joseph and his Egyptian wife encouraged a romantic treatment, lending colour and interest to the inculcation of purely Jewish marriage, and even, by way of antithesis, suggesting agnatic ones, such as non-canonical writings attributed to the earlier patriarchs; the journey culminating in the discovery of a wife for Tobias has its counterpart in the journey of Eliezer to find in Rebecca a wife for Isaac, as R^V recognized and therefore made the author's reference more explicit in vii. 1.

[8] I. Abrahams, *JQR*, 1898, vol. i, p. 348.

It would be, however, an injustice to our author if we were to suppose that, while he knew the historical books well in the uncritical manner of his age and knew the minutiae of the legal system, he did not study the non-legalistic and prophetic writings in existence in his time.[1]

With some of the latest books of the O.T. not yet in existence, e. g. Daniel, many Maccabean Psalms, late portions of Proverbs, and other books or sections only composed after his time, he was necessarily unacquainted.

The question of Tobit's dependence upon Sirach cannot be dismissed so summarily. If literary dependence upon the Greek of Sirach were properly and thoroughly substantiated, it might seriously complicate or facilitate the solution of the problem of the date of Tobit's composition. In Fuller's judgement 'the general impression will probably be that Tobit is more precise and definite than Ecclesiasticus; and this would indicate that of the two Ecclesiasticus is the older book', but he does not deduce from this that Tobit exhibits any literary dependence upon any form of the text of Sirach. Israël Lévi,[2] however, has endeavoured to produce evidence from the text not only of our author's similarity of expression, but also of his use and misunderstanding of the text of Sirach. Granted Lévi were correct—and well-authenticated misreadings of the text would be a strong confirmation—it would be possible to fix exactly the date of Tobit. The evidence in favour of the pre-Maccabean date would not be weakened, for his arguments are based on supposed misreadings, not of the Greek translation of Sirach (*c.* 132 B.C.), but of the *Hebrew* original (*c.* 190–180 B.C.); Tobit must, then, have been written between 190–170 B.C. Lévi, however, brings forward only two passages in confirmation of this theory of textual dependence and misunderstanding, and in neither case can his reasoning be pronounced sound or his conclusions be accepted.[3] Moreover, if the parallels appear 'more precise and definite' (Fuller) in Tobit than in Sirach, it is just because in the former they present themselves in more of the original freshness of their ultimate sources.

v. *Magian Influences.*

It cannot any longer be alleged either that the author was influenced by the Zoroastrian religious system, or that he necessarily borrowed, as has been argued by W. R. Smith[4] and Prof. J. H. Moulton, from *written* Iranian sources, and lived in Media to do so, as Prof. J. H. Moulton formerly[5] suggested.[6]

For a complete refutation of the supposition of his indebtedness to Zoroaster we are indebted to Professor J. H. Moulton's recent researches.[7] *It was non-Zoroastrian Magianism which influenced the author of Tobit.* There are numerous parallels between Tobit and 'the most important factors in Magianism as distinguished from the other strata in complete Avestan Parsaism'. Professor Moulton, for instance, points out the parallels in the use made of the fish's heart, the stress laid on burial, the consanguineous marriages, the unnecessary appearance of the dog, and the demon Asmodeus, whose name finds its exact counterpart in the later Avestan *Aēšma daēva.* On the other hand, the absence of any eschatology in Tobit would be inexplicable if the author had been acquainted with the system of Zarathushtra, who 'enlarged and enhanced' the eschatology of 'the earliest Iranian stratum', writes Professor Moulton, 'till it became the very centre of the Religion'. Again, the *seven angels* of Tobit xii. 15 need not point back to the Amesha Spenta, since the latter in Zoroaster's own system were *six.* The later substitution of *seven* was probably under Semitic influence; and of the two alternative additions, that of the Deity is expressly excluded by the text of Tobit *l.c.*, while that of Sraosha has no claim to antiquity.

[1] He quotes Amos viii. 10 in ii. 5. His text may be reminiscent of Amos v. 15 and Jonah iii. 9 in xiii. 6^b; of Mic. iv. 2, Zech. viii. 22 in xiii. 11^a; of Mic. ii. 3 in xiv. 4 (see note *ad loc.*); of Isa. ii. 18 (cf. Mic. v. 13) in xiv. 6; of the Trito-Isaiah in i. 16 (cf. Isa. lviii. 7), in xiii. 11 (cf. Isa. lx. 6–10), 14 (Isa. lxvi. 10), 16 (Isa. liv. 11). He appeals to Nahum for the verification of his *vaticinium post eventum* in xiv. 4 (cf. Nahum iii. 7 for its fulfilment in xiv. 15). He utilizes Hag. ii. 3 in xiv. 5. He bases his description of the glorious future on prophetic passages such as Jer. xxxi. 1–14; l. 4, 5.

[2] *Revue des Études juives*, vol. xliv, No. 88, April–June, 1902.

[3] In the case of Tobit iv. 3 and Sir. iii. 12, it is noteworthy that (1) עזב twice, but עצב never, in LXX is thus translated; (2) ὑπερίδης would not naturally represent either in this connexion; (3) R^v, which Lévi follows, is certainly inferior to R^s here. In the case of Sir. xxxi. 19, (1) according to Strack נבון not נכון is correct, (2) πεπαιδευμένος in Tobit iv. 14 is a reminiscence of Aḥiḳar (cf. p. 192 *supra*).

[4] *Encyc. Brit.*^{9}, art. 'Tobit'.

[5] 'The Iranian Background of Tobit', published in the *Expos. Times*, vol. xi, pp. 257–60.

[6] Cf. *supra*, p. 186, footnote 3.

[7] *Hibbert Lectures* (New Series), 1912, delivered in Manchester College, Oxford, and in the University of London. His Excursus, *Magianism and the Book of Tobit*, attached to Lecture II, containing an interesting conjectural restoration of a supposed Magian archetype of our book, entirely supersedes his earlier essay in the *Expos. Times.* I am indebted to Professor Moulton for allowing me to read and make several quotations from this Excursus before its publication.

It was in Egypt, and practically in Egypt alone,[1] that an author such as ours could have made the use he has of those 'most important factors in Magianism'. The recent discoveries of papyri in Egypt [2] have thrown new light upon the conditions of the Jews there. The Jews in Egypt would look with the less suspicion upon Persian ideas and customs inasmuch as the Persian empire, under Cambyses, had spared their temple on the island of Elephantine. Many of the worshippers at that shrine had once been mercenaries in the employ of the Egyptian military authorities. In the course of time Persian officers had been appointed over them, Persian soldiers quartered in Syene, and, towards the end of the fifth century B.C., a Persian, by name Vidarna, had been in command of the entire garrison of the southern border. The descendants of these Jewish soldiers became military colonists, farmers, and ordinary burghers. But their environment for long remained partly Persian, for business was transacted with Persian weights and measures, and dates were reckoned according to the reigns of the various Persian kings. Thus we have a glimpse into the life of the Jew in Egypt, for the general conditions were probably much the same throughout the country. In some such environment the author of Tobit lived.[3] Possibly he knew but little of Magianism as a system of thought—in this book he is certainly not waging a polemic against it [4] or against Zoroastrianism—but was fairly well acquainted with the popular stories and legends Persians—soldiers and others—had introduced into the circles in which he moved. In our story, for instance, prefaced as it is by a reference to the careful burial of the dead, which is further inculcated in the body of the narrative, the surprising references [5] to the dog as the companion of the wayfarers (vi. 2 (1), xi. 5) may well be due to a confused recollection of fables originally of Magian tendency,[6] which emphasized, like the *Vendidad*, the importance of properly building 'the tower of silence' for the dead, and recorded Parsi funerals in which 'a dog (with certain spots) is brought in to look at the corpse and so exorcise the *Nasu*'. But the dog is no longer a companion of Tobit and a participant in the funeral rites; he simply accompanies the travellers. Similarly, the consanguineous marriages only form a subsidiary part of his argument and the particular form and motive of their introduction, as already shown, are determined by other considerations. So too the name Asmodeus comes ultimately from Media but the *meaning* of the name cannot be pressed.

§ 9. Integrity.

The integrity, unity and originality of the book as a whole have not remained unchallenged. As early as A.D. 1800 Ilgen endeavoured to prove that while i. 1–iii. 6 was written by Tobit himself (*c.* 689 B.C.) in Assyria, iii. 7–xii. 22 were not composed till *c.* 280 B.C. in Palestine, and xiii was only inserted *c.* 10 B.C. But the book is characterized throughout by a unity of purpose well conceived in its plan and natural and simple in its development, the work in short of a single author of more than average taste and ability. In spite, however, of Plath's unanswerable demonstration—with one possible exception—of the integrity of the book, the allusions to Aḥiḳar as well as the didactic sections (especially iv, xii), the superficial contradictions, the use of the first person in i. 1–iii. 6 and the supposed irrelevancy of portions of xiv have been utilized, in the most radical manner by Erbt, to prove that *Tobit* in its present form is the result of a lengthy process of accretion, elaboration and chance conglomeration, and that a number of interpolations must first be removed and certain further redactional features (inserted, according to Erbt, as late as the second century A.D.) must be discarded before it is possible to make a conjectural reconstruction of the original story such as he himself attempts. Others, less radical than Erbt, find difficulties in only one or two of the following problems.

Allusions to Aḥiḳar's history. Are these original? The discovery at Elephantine of *Aḥiḳar* papyri earlier than 400 B.C. has removed the *a priori* objection that *Aḥiḳar* is later than *Tobit*. On the contrary, if our author wrote in *Egypt* where *Aḥiḳar* was so popular, even supposing it was not elsewhere quite so well known a legend as R. Harris, Cosquin and others suppose, he might even

[1] See above, p. 186, footnote 3.

[2] See especially Eduard Sachau, *op. cit.*, pp. xiii–xxvii.

[3] With Professor J. H. Moulton's permission I quote the following extract from one of his letters to me on the subject: 'My earlier suggestion that the Jewish adaptation of a Median folk-story was actually made in Media by a Jew living there is not in the least necessary to my theory. Provided that a Jew in Egypt or elsewhere was able to get hold of this story, in oral or written form, all that I postulate is fully met. Indeed, your theory that Persian soldiers of Cambyses may have brought the story into Egypt suits admirably my argument that Zoroaster's Reform did not enter into the religion of the Achaemenian Kings before Darius, and it was a good deal later that it reached the people.'

[4] As Kohut, dating the work in the third century A.D., has argued.

[5] See p. 195 for their genuineness.

[6] Erbt (*EB*, col. 5128), however, traces the dog not to Zoroastrian influence, but to 'one of the variations of the tales of the spirit' of *The Grateful Dead* which occasionally appears in animal form. Rosenmann refers it to the influence of Greek customs and literature, e.g. the Homeric poems (*Odys.* xvii. 29 ff., where the dog plays a similar rôle), which he thinks were not unknown to the Jews.

be *expected* to introduce some references to the fortunes of that hero and sage, especially in view of the non-Jewish background and models of his work and of the great use he has made of Aḥiḳar's wisdom. But i. 21 f.; ii. 10; xi. 18; xiv. 10, are all rejected by Erbt, Riggs, Müller, Smend, Toy. xiv. 10, however, is certainly essential to the climax of the author's argument since it serves as a celebrated example of his dictum that divine justice always triumphs. That much is admitted by Reinach, who, unlike Ilgen, regards all the other allusions as spurious and supposes that the story of Aḥiḳar was originally a Babylonian solar myth of essentially polytheistic colouring. Moreover, Müller and Smend, who like Ilgen, and in opposition to Reinach, find most difficulty in xiv. 10, admit that all the passages, though interpolations, were *very* early accretions to the text, in fact pre-Christian. It is only the earliest versions and recensions which preserve the tradition, the later ones tending more and more to misunderstand, confuse or omit the names. Thus R^{S} is clearest (as Erbt acknowledges more than once); R^{V} has partly lost the point of the references, conjectured Haman and preserved a somewhat corrupt text; *Ar* M. omitted it altogether; 𝔖 has suffered textual corruption; F has conjectured *Aaron*. 𝔙, avowedly useless for textual criticism, so far supports the interpolatory theory (except in xi. 20 [1]) that Erbt yields to the temptation to gain support for his hypothesis by entering a special plea on behalf of Jerome's superiority to the uncials in this particular!

The Didactic Sections. Erbt and Riggs, consistently with their rejection of the allusions to the *history* of Aḥiḳar, endeavour to set aside also the allusions to the *wisdom* of Aḥiḳar, particularly iv. 6 b–19 a. Toy holds that both iv and xii are the insertions of the late editor. But א's omission of iv. 6 b–19 a, to which Erbt appeals, does not support the interpolatory hypothesis (see note *ad loc.*). Moreover, the parenetic contents of these verses, to which Erbt demurs as unsuitable to and disturbing the context, are justified by the situation—Tobit believes himself to be dying and desires to communicate to his son the wisdom he himself has acquired that it may help Tobias on his journey to Media and throughout his life. Verses 12 and 13 have special reference to the immediate problems of that journey, and are therefore carefully marked off from the rest by a freer rhythm.

The Dog. That the references to this animal as the companion of the wayfarers were made by the author, not by an interpolator, is attested not simply by their presence in R^{S}, but also from their vicissitudes in the various recensions and versions. vi. 2 (1) is possibly the allusion to which suspicion might most easily attach itself, for R^{V} omitted it. He did so, however, simply because the sentence seemed tautologous. He introduces it without prejudice in v. 17 (16) and xi. 4. In the latter case an original $\overline{\kappa\upsilon}$ (= κύων) preserved in 𝔏's version of R^{S} has accidentally become $\overline{\kappa\varsigma}$ (= Κύριος) in א, whereas Semitic prejudice and Jewish legalism reasserted itself in *Ar.* followed by M, though in F the ancient tradition returned. That R^{V} copied from R^{S} and not R^{S} from R^{V} is shown conclusively in xi. 4, where the former retained the *συνῆλθεν*, though he omitted its complement *αὐτοῖς*. R^{C} removed the clause back to 11^{a} (?), made the dog run *before* the party (cf. *et quasi nuntius adveniens* 𝔙), and reintroduced him, v. 9, where *blandimento suae caudae gaudebat* was added in 𝔙. Were Löhr [2] right in regarding *τοῦ υἱοῦ αὐτῆς* of א as a corrupt anticipatory dittography from v. 5 and in reading *αὐτῶν* for *αὐτοῦ καί*, R^{S} would still be prior to R^{V}. But even if R^{V} were the earlier, the dog could only be the work of the author, not an interpolator.

Internal Contradictions and Signs of Non-unity. (1) In the Introduction (i. 3–iii. 17) and Conclusion certain difficulties of this nature have led to the denial of the originality or genuineness of these sections either as a whole or in part. The change, however, from the narration in the first person in i. 1–iii. 6 to that in the third in the subsequent chapters is not inexplicable. It was necessitated by the summary of Sarah's previous history (iii. 7–15) and the author's desire to paint in his own inimitable manner the contrast between the reader on the one hand, who has been initiated into the intentions of the merciful Providence (iii. 16 f.), and the heroes of the story on the other hand, who can only 'walk by faith'. The author has lessened the harshness of the transition by the insertion of Tobit's preparatory prayer (iii. 1–6). Moreover, Plath quite pertinently [3] points to similar alternations of third and first persons in the Aramaic *Aḥiḳar* and the Acts of the Apostles. Again, if i. 6 seems to contradict i. 14 it is only because 'the individual interest is stronger than the interest in the harmony of the parts' (Plath), while the contradictions between i. 20 and ii. 1 f. are merely superficial. Nor is there any internal contradiction in either R^{S} or R^{V} as to the duration of Tobit's blindness.[4] Finally, the style of xiv is in no way different from that of the preceding chapters, and its thought and contents (including *v.* 10) are sufficiently akin to the rest of the book to allow of its originality, unless indeed *a priori* presuppositions of the way in which the book should end are allowed undue weight. From the fact that two proper names of an Aramaic form (xiv. 10)

[1] Dr. Marshall regards this as an interpolation.
[2] *ZATW*, xx, p. 258.
[3] In spite of Erbt's strictures, *EB*, col. 5117.
[4] The two years of ii. 10 appearing in R^{S} not in R^{V}, and the eight years of xiv. 2 in R^{V} not R^{S}.

point to an *Aramaic* original, it cannot be logically argued, as is done in the *Ency. Brit.*^{11}, that the chapter is *later* than the rest of the book! True, *Ar.* and M betray no knowledge of it, but that is due to intentional and conscious omission in their common ancestor, the purpose of which is as clear as their dogmatic modifications of ch. xiii.

(2) In the central portion of the book. The inconsistency of vi. 17 (16) and v. 13 (12) is due to Raphael's increasing anxiety for the consummation of the marriage in reaction from Tobit's disinclination to espouse Sarah. Müller, who supposes that the exorcism of the demon by prayer (viii. 4–8) is a later feature of the story than that by magic, has examined the alleged contradictions involved in the various references to the fatal results of Sarah's previous espousals. If Raguel had acted illegally in giving his daughter successively to seven men on whom he had no right to bestow her, Raguel himself should have paid the penalty, vi. 13 (12), whereas Raguel himself survived, but the seven were slain in satisfaction not of Jahveh's just wrath but of a demon's lust. Raguel anticipated that the same fate awaited Tobias, though he was confessedly the preordained husband for Sarah. Raphael, like Tobias, foresaw danger only to Tobias, not to Raguel, since if the latter alone had been expected to suffer, Sarah and Tobias would have escaped and inherited Raguel's fortune at once. These inconsistencies after all are only superficial and result from the author's attempt—on the whole admirably carried out—to utilize demon-possession, like other ideas he had derived from his sources, in order to inculcate the importance of obeying the law and preserving the purity of Jewish marriages. It is in this connexion, however, that Müller[1] discusses another problem which has a more serious bearing upon the purpose and date of the book (see pp. 183 f.) as well as upon its integrity. In iii. 17 Sarah states that her father has no near relative whose offspring she is bound to marry, but in vii. 2–9 her parents have not forgotten Tobit's existence. Tobit has no premonition of the happy duty of marrying his relative Sarah in store for Tobias, contenting himself with the general statement of iv. 12, whereas in vi. 10 (9)–18 (17) Raphael is aware not only of the relationship but of Sarah's legal obligations to marry Tobias, and the latter shows no surprise, if he is not in fact already as well aware of it as Raphael, and only shrinks from the dangers it involves to his own person. There is the further difficulty that, in spite of vi. 13 (12), vii. 12 (13), Holy Writ nowhere commands 'agnatic' marriages, i. e. marriages within the particular family or tribe of the contracting parties as opposed to inter-tribal unions. The case is not covered by Num. xxvii. 1–11, xxxvi, which at the best was only theoretical and dealt only with the case of heiresses owning *landed* property in *Palestine*. Even Tobit's reference to the patriarch's action (iv. 12) rests not upon Genesis but on traditions in vogue in the earlier post-exilic period such as *Jubilees* has preserved. Müller therefore supposes—and it is an exceedingly happy supposition—that the *author sought to inculcate not tribal as opposed to inter-tribal, but Jewish as opposed to Jewish-pagan marriages.* Sarah's seven former husbands were slain because they were *pagans*, but Tobias had a right superior to that of any other possible suitor at the moment, because he was the only Jew in the neighbourhood. Thus ἀδελφός in this book properly means a brother Jew, ἀδελφή = a term of endearment for the only legal wife a Jew may have, i. e. a Jewess,[2] vii. 15 (16), viii. 4, γένος = kindred, not in the narrower sense of tribal relationship but with the wider connotation of the Jewish nation, e. g. in i. 17, τινὰ τῶν ἐκ τοῦ ἔθνους μου can only be intended as a synonym for, not as an antithesis to, τοῖς ἐκ τοῦ γένους μου in v. 16. The example of the patriarchs is quoted in iv. 12 not to inculcate their marriage with near relatives as such, but to exemplify by the fact that their wives were near relatives how careful to avoid marriage with non-Jewesses were these patriarchs, the 'fathers of old time' (iv. 12) of the whole Hebrew race. Attractive as Müller's theory is, and though successfully explaining the apparent contradictions of the story, it is not entirely supported by any version or recension. Müller falls back on an eclectic text, the result of the rejection of all readings of R^S, R^V, and R^C which militate against his theory. This procedure presupposes that each and all of these revisions embodies an attempt (only partially successful in each case) to transform a story, originally inculcating only Jewish marriages, into one advocating agnatic marriages. But could all these revisions possibly have shared this purpose in common? Certainly they could have done if—an impossible condition—they could *all* be proved to have been made *before* the irksome duty of agnatic marriage was annulled in the first century B. C. Whereas those revisions which were made *after* that date—i. e. at least two of them (irrespective of the rival merits of R^S and R^V)—if they made any alterations at all, would tend to obscure and remove the agnatic *motif*; Müller (p. 7, note 4) admits that R^C actually did so in vi. 16 in deference to R^S. Hence the agnatic interest must have figured to some extent in the original story, probably, however, only in the half-hearted way in which it appears in R^S. The author's advice might be summed up: At all costs marry Jewesses of the purest possible descent, like the patriarchs; marry your own sisters or cousins, if no other Jewesses are available.

[1] *op. cit.*, pp. 3–9.

[2] Cf. p. 186, footnote 7.

§ 10. Religious and Moral Teaching.

The theological, religious, and moral outlook of our author is far from unimportant. Unfortunately the comparatively lengthy treatment which the other problems of the book have claimed allows only of a very brief *résumé*.

A. The author's—as opposed to the later redactors'—*religious presuppositions* are those of the popular mind tinged with the point of view of the newest developments of the official and orthodox leaders of the post-exilic period, in its earlier rather than its later phases. This is amply justified by the following considerations:—

(1) *Doctrine of God.* The full Monotheism of the post-exilic period is presupposed.[1] The descriptions of Jahveh's qualities are manifold.[2] Since He is a transcendental Deity, He hears men's prayers through angelic mediation. The tendency to distinguish between Jahveh, the invisible and ineffable, and His personified self-manifestation and revelation also appears, but only in the two expressions, 'the Glory', iii. 16, xii. 12, 15, and 'the Name', iii. 11, viii. 5, xi. 14, xii. 6, xiii. 18.

(2) *Angelology.*[3]—The angelology of the author as compared with that of Jubilees, 1 Enoch and R^V, is at a somewhat embryonic stage of its evolution. As compared, on the other hand, with that of the Old Testament as a whole, it seems to stand well within the threshold of the subsequent period. It is especially noticeable that Raphael here represents in germ the ideas which afterwards crystallized in the fully developed doctrine of Michael, with whose functions Raphael's should therefore be carefully compared.[4]

Chapter xii is without parallel in the extant literature of Judaism. The whole story illustrates the free, untutored, and vigorous type of speculation existent a little before the rise of Pharisaic regulations of the dogma. This belief in the angel's intervention, moreover, always remained essentially characteristic of the people's religion as opposed to that of the learned and cultured.[5] With iii. 16 f., xii. 12, 15 (14), cf. Jub. xxx. 20, Testaments of Dan vi, of Asher vi, of Levi v.

(3) *Eschatology.* The author shows no advance upon the pre-exilic period in his conceptions of death and its consequences. The grave is external in its annihilating effects, iii. 6, 10, cf. iv. 10, xii. 9. In relation to the nation, however, he stands possibly almost on a threshold of the Apocalyptic tendency. He has worked out for himself a crude and simple, but yet unmistakable, philosophy of the future. Jerusalem at the end of a given period will be rebuilt and the Temple sumptuously restored, the scattered tribes reunited, and—to his credit—the heathen will worship the God of Israel, xiii. 7–18 a, xiv. 4–6. See further, Charles, *Eschatology*, 1899, pp. 165 f.

B. It is in the *practical sphere* that our author's religious and moral outlook find their fullest expression. His hero is a rare instance of an almost perfect combination and realization, in actual life, of the priestly and prophetic ideals.

(1) *The cultus*,[6] as practised at Jerusalem, the precepts of the *law* (tithes, marriage,[7] purity, &c.) and *Jerusalem* itself, are primary factors in the author's life, i. 3–13; ii. 1–9, and their future perfection is painted in glowing colours, xiii. 7–18 a, xiv. 4–7.

(2) The 'Three Pillars of Judaism', *prayer*, *almsgiving*, and *fasting* are inculcated. Fasting (ii. 4) has not reached the culmination of its development.[8] Almsgiving, however, as in Sirach,[9] ranks high among the non-sacrificial duties of Judaism, i. 3, 16, ii. 14, iv. 7 ff., 16, xii. 9 f., xiv. 9, is the *sine qua non* of a long and prosperous life, a virtue, to be practised by the richest, i. 16 f., ii. 10, and the poorest, ii. 14, and occupies a prominent position in the 'teaching' both of Tobit, iv. 3–19, and of Raphael, xii. 8. 'Righteousness' is thus already tending to take the lower level and become synonymous to some extent with almsgiving,[10] but devotion to the cultus and legalism do not result in this book in hypocrisy or externalism, since the whole is pervaded with a mysticism which finds its highest expression in heart-felt prayer as the immediate means of communion with God.[11]

This is evident not simply from the number and length of the prayers which are quoted, but from the care which has been devoted to their position, structural arrangement, and contents.[12]

[1] See iv. 14; xiii. 1, 2, 5, 6, 11; xiv. 6.

[2] See vii. 17 (18); viii. 5; xiii. 4, 7, 11, 15.

[3] The demonology and magical elements are relics of the author's sources and Jewish-Egyptian environment and do not belong to the circle of his own constructive ideas, and are therefore not dealt with here.

[4] See Wilhelm Lueken, *Michael*, 1898.

[5] Cf. W. Bousset, *Die Religion des Judentums*, second edition, p. 379.

[6] See Bousset, *op. cit.*, p. 123.

[7] Cf. pp. 183 f., 196, *supra*.

[8] Note the addition in x. 7 in R^V.

[9] Cf. Sirach iv. 10 (Heb.); vii. 10, 32; xvi. 14 (Heb.); xvii. 22, &c.

[10] Cf. p. 191, *supra*.

[11] For the important place of prayer and its function in this connexion in Judaism, see *Communion with God*, 1911, pp. 106–13, by Dr. Darwell Stone and the present writer.

[12] Cf. Plath, *op. cit.*, pp. 382, 390, 401.

Tobit's (iii. 16 f.) and Sarah's (iii. 10–15) prayers, uttered with face turned to Jerusalem, and the immediate answer to them in iii. 16, 17, are the climax to the Introduction (i. 3–iii. 17). Both are probably typical of the form in which prayers were cast in the writer's day. Each contains an invocation,[1] followed by an act of adoration (iii. 2, 11), and the specific supplication with a lengthy retrospective explanation. Both are of almost equal length, in spite of Sarah's preliminary history (iii. 7–15) being otherwise much briefer than Tobit's (i. 3–iii. 6). Sarah's is the more concrete and individualistic, Tobit's the wider in its outlook and the more intercessory. The same structural arrangement characterizes viii. 5–7, 16 f. and the frequent thanksgivings. The liturgical *Amen* appears in viii. 8.[2] Finally, Raphael sets prayer in its rightful position in xii. 8 and asserts its efficacy in xii. 12, which is followed by the exile's prayer of exhortation and consolation, xiii. 1–6. In none of them, however, is there a single petition for the conversion of the non-Jewish world.

(3) *Morality* and *ethics* are inculcated in all departments of life, e. g. piety towards parents, the duty of Jewish marriage, the purity of wedlock,[3] and in matters of everyday life,[4] from a standpoint as high as, if not higher than, Aḥiḳar's. It was such moralizing precepts as these, rather than theological dogmas, which did most to regulate and direct contemporary life—both Jewish and pagan.

(4) A special plea seems to be entered in relation to contemporary *conduct towards the dead.* Though from a literary point of view our author is dependent upon Aḥiḳar directly for iv. 17, yet it is quite clear that he is inculcating an actual religious practice. In fact, at the time our author lived, it would appear to have been a subject of considerable dispute as to whether such offerings were right and proper and a matter of duty (cf. Sir. vii. 33; Job iv. 17) or whether they were definitely to be excluded by Judaism[5] and its adherents (Sir. xxx. 18, 19; Ep. Jer. 31, 32; Wisdom xiv. 15, xix. 3; Sibyl. Or. viii. 382–4). At the time when Jubilees xxii. 17 was written they were apparently regarded as characteristic of the Gentiles. See, further, Charles, *op. cit.* pp. 23–31.

§ 11. Influence of the Book on Later Literature.

A. *Jewish.* There is considerable evidence to show that Tobit was held in high repute alike by early and by later Judaism. (*a*) There are possibly traces of its use in Daniel, in the later Psalms, in the book of Jubilees (*v.* note iv. 16, 18, 21 f.; x. 4–6), the Test. of Job, &c.[6] (*b*) While the references to it in New Testament (*v. infra*) exemplify its use by the Jews of our Lord's day, R^V is the best evidence of its extraordinary popularity between *c.* 200 B.C. and *c.* A.D. 150. (*c*) In M an example survives of its use among pious orthodox Jews. (*d*) The fact that the latter found a place in the *Midrash Rabba de Rabbah* together with the passage contained in the addition to the *Midrash Tanchuma*,[7] illustrates best of all how thoroughly our story permeated the thought of later Judaism. (*e*) Finally in F as also in Gaster's Hebrew, if not also in the London Hebrew, we have an unmistakable example of Jewish interest in the book in the Middle Ages.

B. *Christian.*[8] Interest in the question of the presence in the New Testament of allusions to Tobit and of passages tinged whether directly or indirectly with a recollection of Tobit's history or maxims, has been damped in the past by the credence which the theories of Graetz, Kohut and others once unfortunately gained. More lately the field has been occupied by the attempts of students of Aḥiḳar to find traces of the use of that legend in the New Testament, instead of admitting that the probabilities may point to the latter's comparative supersession by Tobit, into which, as already stated, its most permanent features had by now[9] been merged.

Christianity appealed, at least at the outset, to the very classes to whom Tobit would be especially dear with its simple but sympathetic narrative of the fortunes of Jews of previous days who had lived under the yoke of a foreign domination—classes, too, who would give an equally enthusiastic welcome to the most crudely painted Apocalyptic. The fact that our book, though never in the Jewish Canon, survived the shock of this religious revolution and found a still more honourable position in the Bible of the new community than it had ever done under the old Covenant,

[1] 'Lord' in Tobit's own, 'Lord my God' in Sarah's.
[2] Cf. Judith xiii. 20.
[3] See p. 196, *supra*.
[4] Cf. Budde, *op. cit.*, p. 406; André, *op. cit.*, p. 178; Bousset, *op. cit.*, p. 490.
[5] See Deut. xxvi. 14; Jer. xvi. 7; Isa. viii. 19, xix. 3.
[6] See 'Tobit' in *HDB*, vol. iv, p. 789.
[7] Printed and translated by Neub., *op. cit.* See Nöldeke, *op. cit.*, p. 63.
[8] Cf. J. Moffat, *Introd. to the Lit. of N.T.*, 1911, pp. 34 f.
[9] It should be remembered that this holds good even if the parallels to Aḥiḳar be regarded as interpolations, since, for example, Müller and Smend frankly admit Aḥiḳar's presence in the text of Tobit prior to the Christian era. See pp. 194 f.

speaks volumes for its intrinsic charm and adaptability for the spiritual requirements of the new religion.

(i) *In the New Testament.* It has already been hinted (p. 189, footnote 10) that, instead of Aḥiḳar directly, it might be right to see a reference to Aḥiḳar only as mediated through Tobit in the Parables of the Wicked Servant and the Barren Fig-tree. Thus Tobit would stand in the same relation to these parables as Isa. v. 1–7 to the parable of the Wicked Husbandmen. Again, to insist that Aḥiḳar itself, not Aḥiḳar as abridged in Tobit, influenced the diction of the Biblical as well as the non-Biblical stories of Judas' death is to come very near denying even the general historicity of the kernel of the story in order to find its kernel in Aḥiḳar. In the case of our Lord's words, which were uttered in Aramaic, verbal, as distinct from literary, coincidence with the Greek must be expected generally only in so far as the evangelists have modelled their Greek on that of the LXX. The following parallels, however, even if only accidental, are noteworthy: xi. 9[1] and Luke xv. 20; xii. 8 and Matt. vi. 1–18; a materialistic interpretation of iv. 9 condemned in Matt. vi. 20 f.; iv. 15 and Matt. vii. 12, Luke vi. 31;[2] iv. 7 and Luke xi. 41;[3] iv. 16 and Matt. xxv. 35 f. But do the remarkable parallels to the commission and Ascension of Raphael which are collected in the note to xii. 16–22 fall into the same category? Do their completeness and detail suggest that our book exercised a direct and important formative, if not creative, influence upon the expression of the truths of the Transfiguration, Resurrection, and Ascension of our Lord? Or are we to suppose both only represent the popular vocabulary in which such events were wont to be related? True, angels ascended in the Old Testament; the *Ascension of Isaiah* and *Assumption of Moses* must once have related something similar, but nowhere is there so exact a coincidence of religious presupposition, literary expression and dramatic climax as in Tobit xii. 16–22.

S. Paul is possibly conscious of his indebtedness to Tobit, 'which must certainly have been a part of his library'.[4] With iv. 12 a cf. 1 Thess. iv. 3; xii. 10 cf. Rom. vi. 23; iv. 8 cf. 1 Cor. xvi 2 and 2 Cor. viii. 12; iv. 7, 16 cf. 2 Cor. ix 7 a[5]. R. Harris[6] has already pointed out the use S. Paul made of Tobit iv. 10 in Gal. vi. 10.

In the third group of Pauline Epistles, Eph. v. 18, though expressed in the language of Prov. xxiii. 31 in LXX, recalls the advice of Tobit iv. 15 b.

Still more important are the alleged parallels between Tobit and the Pastoral Epistles. The uncommon phrase βασιλεὺς τῶν αἰώνων occurs in Tobit xiii. 6 and 1 Tim. i. 17, in both cases in an ascription of praise. With iv. 9 cf. 1 Tim. vi. 19; Tobit iv. 21 cf. 1 Tim. vi. 6. The form of address 'my child Timothy' reminds us of Tobit's recurring formula. Is it possible to go further? What abuses or heresies was the writer of the Pastorals combating? Are we quite sure that there is no alternative to the rival claims of Rabbinism and Gnosticism? Granted undue reverence for tractates of mythological, demonological and useless—non-religious, though moral—proverbial tendencies, such as we meet with in Tobit; granted, too, possibly the presence to some small extent of the numerous speculations and vicious by-products of a debased Apocalyptic—is it not probable that the writer of the Pastorals had ample justification for the remarks upon which the theories of Gnostic or Rabbinic polemics are based?

It only remains to mention two other points of contact between Tobit and the New Testament. The ethical and moral point of view and forms of literary self-expression in vogue among the circles which produced the early chapters of Acts were similar in some respects to Tobit's—on the positive and good side of the latter. With Tobit 1. 3 cf. Acts ix. 36 b; Tobit ii. 1 cf. Acts ii. 1 (Pentecost); Tobit iii. 16 with Acts ix. 18; xi. 12, 13 (13); and Tobit xii. 12 with Acts x. 4. Lastly—apart from the parallelism of demonological technicality in Tobit viii. 3 and Rev. xx. 2 independently borrowed from current formulae—Rev. xxi. 10–21 is as much dependent on Tobit xiii. 16 and Rev. xix. 1–7 on Tobit xiii. 18 as upon other Old Testament and Apocryphal literary models of this type.

(ii) *In post-Apostolic Christian Writers* Tobit is quite unmistakably placed on as high a pedestal as the other books of the Apocrypha not known at the time to have been written in Hebrew, and most often it was even venerated as highly as any other Scriptures—a fact well illustrated by Clem. Alex's. quotation[7] of iv. 16 as ἡ γραφή. For numerous other Patristic quotations, decisions of Church Councils, and use and influence in the Anglican Church, see Fuller *op. cit.* Marshall, *op. cit.*, and cf. p. 178, *supra*, footnote 7.

[1] A closer parallel at any rate, in thought and language, than Gen. xlvi. 29.

[2] The scriptural antiquity of which is vouched for by οὗτος γάρ ἐστιν ὁ νόμος καὶ οἱ προφῆται. Hillel, like Tobit, expressed himself only negatively, see Taylor, *Pirqe Aboth*, 37.

[3] τὰ ἐνόντα has been rendered more or less in conformity with Tobit by *quae sunt* (b d g), *ex his quae habetis* (f), *quod superest* (Vulg.), *ea quae penes vos sunt* (Beza), *quantum potestis* (Grotius); cf. Luther's *von dem, das da ist.* See Plummer, *S. Luke, Int. Crit. Comment., ad loc.*

[4] *A.J. Th.*, p. 546.

[5] Just as 7 b is a quotation from Prov. xxii. 8, LXX.

[6] *op. cit.*, p. 545.

[7] *Strom.* ii. 23, § 139.

§ 12. Bibliography.

(*a*) Chief Editions of the Ancient Versions.

Greek MSS. and Papyrus.

Reusch, *Libellus Tobit e codice Sinaitico editus et recensitus*, 1870.
Fritzsche, *Die Bücher Tobiä und Judith erklärt* (*Exeget. Handbuch zu den Apokryphen*, ii), Leipzig, 1853.
Tischendorf, *Vetus Testamentum Graece iuxta LXX interpretes*, 2 vols., 1850.
Swete, *The Old Testament in Greek according to the Septuagint*, vol. ii, 1891.
Vigouroux, *La Sainte Bible Polyglotte, Ancien Testament*, vol. iii, 1902.
Hunt, *Oxyrhynchus Papyri*, viii, 1911, No. 1076.

Aramaic Version.

Neubauer, *The Book of Tobit, a Chaldee Text*, &c., Oxford, 1878.

Old Latin Versions.

Sabatier, *Bibliorum sacrorum Latinae versiones antiquae*, Paris, 1751.
Blanchini, *Vindiciae Canonicarum Scripturarum*, Rome, 1740.
Neubauer, *The Book of Tobit, a Chaldee Text*, &c., Oxford, 1878.

Hebrew Versions.

1. The Münster Hebrew (first printed in Constantinople, 1516).
   Sebastian Münster, 1542.
   Neubauer, *op. cit., supra.*
2. Fagius' Hebrew.
   Fagius, 1542.
   Walton's Polyglot.
3. The London Hebrew.
   Gaster, *PSBA*, vol. xviii, pp. 208 ff., 259 ff., vol. xx, pp. 27 ff.
4. The Gaster Hebrew.
   Gaster, *PSBA*, vol. xix, pp. 33 f.

Syriac Versions.

Walton's Polyglot.
Lagarde, *Libri apocryph. Syriace.*
Ceriani, *Le edizioni e i manoscritti delle versioni siriache del Vecchio Testamento*, 1870, p. 22; and Rahlfs in Lagarde, *Bibliotheca Syriaca*, 1892, pp. 32 b–32 i.

Ethiopic Version.

Dillmann, *Biblia Veteris Testamenti aethiopica*, v, 1894.

(*b*) Chief Critical Inquiries.

Ilgen, *Die Geschichte Tobi's nach drey verschiedenen Originalen*, &c., Jena, 1800.
Steinschneider, *Catalogus librorum Hebraeorum in Bibliotheca Bodleiana*, 1852–60.
Fritzsche, *Die Bücher Tobiä und Judith erklärt* (*Exeget. Handbuch zu den Apokryphen*, ii), Leipzig, 1853.
Reusch, *Das Buch Tobias übersetzt und erklärt*, Freiburg, 1857.
Sengelmann, *Das Buch Tobit erklärt*, Hamburg, 1857. *Journal of Sacred Literature and Biblical Record*, iv, 1857.
Hitzig, *Zeitschr. für wissenschaftl. Theol.*, 1860.
Hilgenfeld, *Zeitschr. für wissenschaftl. Theol.*, 1862.
Reusch, *Libellus Tobit e codice Sinaitico editus et recensitus*, Bonnae, 1870.
Kohut, *Etwas über die Moral und die Abfassungszeit d. B. Tobias* in Geiger's *Jüdische Zeitschr. f. Wissenschaft u. Leben*, x, 1872; also separate.
Gutberlet, *Das Buch Tobias übersetzt und erklärt*, Münster, 1877.
Neubauer, *op. cit., supra.*
Bickell, *Zeitschr. f. kathol. Theol.*, 1878.
E. Schürer, *Theol. Literaturzeit.*, 1878.
Nöldeke, *Monatsberichte der Berliner Akademie*, 1879.
Grätz, *Monatsschr. f. Gesch. und Wissensch. des Judenth.*, 1879.
Grimm, *Zeitschr. für wissenschaftl. Theol.*, 1881.
Linschmann, *Zeitschr. f. wissenschaftl. Theol.*, 1882.
Preiss, *Zeitschr. für wissenschaftl. Theol.*, 1885.
Rosenthal, *Vier apokryphische Bücher aus der Zeit und Schule R. Akiba's*, 1885.
Hilgenfeld, *Zeitschr. für wissenschaftl. Theol.*, 1886.
Fuller, in Wace's *Apocrypha*, London, 1888.
W. R. Smith, art. 'Tobit' in *Ency. Brit.*, ninth edition, 1888.
Scholz, *Commentar zum Buche Tobias*, 1889.
Nestle, *Marginalien und Materialien*, 1893.
Dalman, *Grammatik des jüdisch-palästinischen Aramäisch*, 1894.
Rosenmann, *Studien zum Buche Tobit*, 1894.
Dillmann, *Biblia Veteris Testamenti aethiopica*, v, 1894.
Gaster, *Two unknown Hebrew versions of the Tobit Legend* (*Proceedings of the Society of Bibl. Archaeol.*, vol. xviii, 1896; xix, 1897).
I. Abrahams, *Jewish Quarterly Review*, 1898, p. 348.
Kohler, *Kleinere Schriften zur Märchenforschung*, 1898.
Nestle, *Septuagintastudien*, iii, Maulbronn, Progr., 1899; iv, 1903.
Rendel Harris, *American Journal of Theology*, iii, 1899, pp. 541–54; also *The Story of Aḥiḳar*, Cambridge, 1898 (by F. C. Conybeare, J. Rendel Harris, and Agnes Smith Lewis).

Cosquin, *Revue biblique*, 1899, pp. 513–20.
Löhr, *Zeitschr. für die alttest. Wissensch.*, xx, 1900.
Simonsen, *Tobit-Aphorismen* (*Gedenkbuch zur Erinnerung an David Kaufmann* herausg. von Brann und Rosenthal, 1900).
Plath, *Theol. Stud. und Krit.*, 1901.
Marshall, art. 'Tobit', Hastings' *Dictionary of the Bible*, vol. iv, 1902, pp. 788 ff.
Lévi, *Revue des Études juives*, xliv, 1902, pp. 288–91.
Erbt, art. 'Tobit' in *Encyclopaedia Biblica*, iv, 1903.
André, *Les Apocryphes de l'A. T.*, 1903.
Sieger, *Das Buch Tobias und das Märchen vom dankbaren Toten* (*Katholik*, 1904).
Vetter, *Theol. Quartalschrift*, 1904.
Nestle, *Zeitschr. für die alttest. Wissensch.*, xxv, 1905.
Müller, *Beiträge zur Erklärung und Kritik des Buches Tobit*, Göttingen, Diss., 1907; also in *Beihefte zur Zeitschr. f. d. alttest. Wissensch.*, xiii, 1908.
Schulte, *Theol. Quartalschr.*, 1908, and *Biblische Zeitschr.*, 1908.
Müller and Smend, *Beihefte zur Zeitschr. f. die alttest. Wissensch.*, xiii, 1908.
Schürer, *GJV^4*, vol. iii, 1909.
Ed. Sachau, *Aramäische Papyrus und Ostraka aus Elephantine*, 1911 (small edition by A. Ungnad, 1911).
Ed. Meyer, *Der Papyrusfund von Elephantine*, 1912.
J. H. Moulton, *Zoroastrianism*, *Hibbert Lectures*, 1912 (in the press), especially Lecture II and the excursus on *Magianism and the Book of Tobit*.

(*c*) Chief Editions of the Book.

Fuller in Wace's *Apocrypha*, vol. i, 1898.
C. J. Ball, *Variorum Apocrypha*, 1892.
Löhr, *Das Buch Tobit* in Kautzsch's *Übersetzung der Apokryphen und Pseudepigraphen*, 1900.

§ 13. Chief Abbreviations.

R^S	= Sinaitic and most original form of text	See § 3.
R^V	= Recension best preserved in Cod. Vat.	See § 3.
R^C	= Third recension	See § 3.
Ox	= Oxyrhynchus Papyrus, No. 1076	See § 4.
Ar.	= Extant Aramaic text	See § 4.
M	= Münster Hebrew	See § 4.
[M], II, Pr.	varieties of Münster Hebrew (see p. 179, footnotes 1, 2, 4, 5)	See § 4.
𝔏	= Old Latin, of which α β γ δ are MSS.	See § 4.
𝔖	= Syriac Versions	See § 4.
F	= Fagius' Hebrew	See § 4.
𝔙	= Vulgate	See § 4.

κ., &c. = καί, &c.
ἀδελ., &c. = ἀδελφός, &c.
κ.$^{1\circ}$, κ.$^{2\circ}$, κ.$^{3\circ}$, &c. = first, second, third occurrence of καί, &c., in a verse.

TOBIT

PREFACE, i. 1, 2.

1 1 The book of the words of Tobit, the son of Tobiel, the son of Hananiel, the son of Aduel, the son of Gabael, the son of Raphael, the son of Raguel, of the seed of Asiel, of the tribe of Naphtali;
2 who in the days of Shalmaneser king of the Assyrians was carried away captive out of Thisbe, which is on the right hand of Kedesh Naphtali in upper Galilee above Asser, behind the <road> leading west, on the left of Phogor.

INTRODUCTION, i. 3–iii. 17.

A. Tobit's Earlier History, i. 3–iii. 6.

i. Tobit's Previous Fortunes, i. 3–22.

3 I Tobit walked in the ways of truth and in acts of righteousness all the days of my life, and I did many almsdeeds to my brethren and my nation, who went with me in the captive band into
4 the land of the Assyrians, to Nineveh. And when I was in mine own country, in the land of Israel, and when I was young, all the tribe of Naphtali my father fell away from the house of David my father and from Jerusalem, the city which <was chosen> out of all the tribes of Israel for all the tribes of Israel to sacrifice *there*, and wherein the temple of the habitation of God was hallowed and

I. 1. B. λογ.] עובדא הוה *Ar* זה ספר M F Τωβειθ] -ειτ B ιτ A Thobis *αβ* Tobis *γδ* ܛܘܒܝܬ 𝔖 טובי *Ar* טוביה F *pr.* בחד חסידא ושמיה *Ar* Τωβιηλ] ܛܘܒܝܐܝܠ 𝔖 > F Ανανιηλ] > *Ar* Αδουηλ] Ναυη A ܕܐܕܘܐܝܠ 𝔖 > 𝔏 *Ar* (אריאל) M Γαβαηλ] Γαμ. A > *Ar* גבריאל F τ. Ραφαηλ] > BA 𝔖 𝔏 *Ar* M F τ. Ραγουηλ] > BA 𝔖 𝔏 *Ar* M F εκ τ. σπ. Ασιηλ] filii Asihel (+f. Gadalel, f. Arabei) > *Ar* בן עשאל בן נתניאל M φυλ.] *pr.* τ. BA 2. ος] *pr.* (אשר הגלה משומרון עם הגולה אשר הגלתה בימי הושע בן אלה) M ταις] > BA *post* Θισβης F Ενεμεσσαρου] ܫܠܡܢܐܣܪ 𝔖 𝔏 *Ar* M F τ. Ασσυριων] Ασσ. BA ܕܐܬܘܪܝܐ 𝔖 דאתור *Ar* אשור M F εκ Θισβης] εκ Θιβης A ܡܢ ܬܚܒ 𝔖 Bihel civitate [?] והוא היה מתושבי *Ar* והוה יתיב בתשבי קרתא עיר M מתושבי F η ε. εκ δεξ.] > *Ar* M F Κυδιως] -ιων A ܩܕܫ 𝔖 Edisse civitatis 𝔏 > *Ar* M F εν τη . . . Φογωρ] > *Ar* F ανω Γαλειλ.] Γαλιλ. B?A in superioribus G *αβ*𝔙 in superiore G *γ* super G . . . am *δ* דבגלילא *Ar* M עם כל יושב הגליל F υπερανω] υπερ|ανω B* υπερα|νω B[b] υπερ (*sed vide annot.*) א[2] contra 𝔏 > M Ασσηρ] Ασηρ BA ܕܐܫܝܪ 𝔖 Naasson 𝔏 > M οπ. δυσ. ηλι.] > BA 𝔖 post viam quae ducit in occidentem *αβγ*𝔙 quae est ad occidentem solem *δ* על גבול ימה M εξ αριστ. Φογ.] > BA 𝔖 M Φογ.] Raphain 𝔏 3. Εγω Τ.] ויאמר ט' זכרה לי אלהי לטובה על ש M *tert. pers. ubique Ar* αληθ.] תמים M εποp.] + לפניך M εν δικαιοσυναις] -νη B -νης A 𝔖 *αβγ* > *δ* *Ar* צדקות רבות M τ. ζω.] > *Ar* εποι.] שעשיתי M μου3°] > B πορευθ.] προπορ. B συνπορευομ. A דהוו *Ar* > M μετ' εμ.] > M εν τ. αιχμ.] > BA 𝔖 την] > BA των] > BA 4. εν τ. χ. μου] > *Ar* M γη] *pr.* τη BA κ.2° . . . νεος] νεωτερου μου οντος BA 𝔖 inter omnes iunior 𝔏 טליא *Ar* F בהיותי נער *Ar* η] > BA Νεφ.] *pr.* του BA τ. πατ. μου] > *Ar* M απεστησαν] -εστη BA מרדו *Ar* M > F απο τ. οικ.] במלכותא *Ar* Δ. τ. πατ. μ. κ. απο] > BA D. et ab *αβγδ* דדויד *Ar* M F Ιερουσαλημ] Ιεροσολυμων BA ומנעו גרמיהון למיסק לירו' *Ar* M πολ. . . . αιωνος] > *Ar* πολεως της] τ. εκλεγεισης BA 𝔖 + civitate quae est electa 𝔏 + אשר בחר יי MF *pr.* הקדש F εκ] απο BA φυλων] *pr.* των BA εις τ. θυσ. . . . κ. ηγ. . . . κ. ωκ. . . . εις πασ. τ. γεν. τ. αιωνος] ubi altare constitutum est . . . quod sanctificatum est in saecula. Tunc, cum . . . aedificatum esset . . . ut sacrificaret in ipso omnis progenies in aeternum et 𝔏 ושם מזבח יי המקודש לכל שבטי יש' והיכל יי בנוי בתוכה להעלות

I. 1. Ῥαγουήλ = רעואל as Φογώρ (*v.* 2) = פעור (*cf.* Γόμορρα = עמרה, and other transliterations of hard ע).

2. Ἐνεμεσ. Ball conjectures that של' was misread ענ', but even if this was the ultimate cause of the form, Ἐνεμεσ. was well known as a recognized Greek equivalent of של' since all the Vss, translating from the Greek, were able to substitute Shal. for it; therefore the mistake of ענ' for של', if that be the correct explanation, had probably taken place before Tobit was written. Κυδιώς probably = Kadesh. Cod. 248 and the Complut. have κυριῶς, hence A.V. 'which is properly called N.' In the crit. appar. Swete has been followed. Nestle (*Septuag.* iii, p. 23), however, urges that Swete is wrong in his reference to the last three letters of ὑπεράνω; it was the ανω before Γαλ. which a secondary hand cancelled by placing dots above it. Ἀσσήρ = Hazor. After ὀπίσω insert ὁδοῦ in א with *αβγ* (conjectured by Reusch, accepted by Müller), cf. אחרי דרך מבוא השמש, Deut. xi. 30.

4. Restore in א τ. ἐκλεγ. (omitted through haplography of εκ) after πόλεως (which R[v] in turn omitted) and in *v.* 5 insert καί before ἐπί.

5 built for all ages. All my brethren and the house of Nephtalim my father, they sacrificed to the
6 calf, which Jeroboam the king of Israel made, in Dan <and> on all the mountains of Galilee. And
I alone used often to journey to Jerusalem at the feasts, as it hath been ordained in all Israel by an
everlasting decree. I used to go to Jerusalem with the firstfruits and the firstlings and the tenths of
7 the cattle and the first shearings of the sheep, and give them to the priests, the sons of Aaron, for
(7) the altar, and the tenth of the corn and the wine and oil and pomegranates and the rest of the fruits
to the sons of Levi, who ministered at Jerusalem. And the second tenth I tithed in money for
8 the six years, and went and spent it each year at Jerusalem: and gave it unto the orphans
and the widows and the proselytes who attached themselves to the children of Israel; I brought it
and gave it unto them in the third year, and we did eat it according to the decree which was decreed
concerning it in the book of Moses and according to the commands which Deborah, the mother of
9 Hananiel our father commanded, because my father left me an orphan when he died. And when
I became a man, I took a wife of the seed of our own family, and of her I begat a son and called his
10 name Tobias. After the carrying away captive to Assyria when I was carried away captive, I came
to Nineveh, and all my brethren and those that were of my kindred did eat of the bread of the

עולות ושלמים ליי של׳ פעמ׳ ובשנה M (*cf.* F) πασ. φυλαις] πασ. τ. -λας BA omn. nationibus γ (o. tribubus αβδ) Ισρ.3°] > BA 𝔖 κ. ηγ.] > 𝔖 (*corrupt.*) του θ.] τ. υψιστου BA 𝔖 𝔏 ῳκ.] οικ. A αυτῃ] > BA Hierusalem 𝔏 5. παν. οι αδελ. μου (ου ℵ* μ *superscr.* ℵ a(vid))] κ. (> 𝔖) πασ. αι φυλ. (+ [illegible] 𝔖) συναποστασ. BA 𝔖 (*cf.* F) > *Ar* κ.1° . . . πατ. μ.] *post* δαμαλ. ℵ c a mg BA 𝔖 (*cf.* F) > *Ar* מטה נפתלי M omnisque (et γ) domus *&c.* αβγδ Νεφ.] *pr.* του A εθυσιαζ.] εθυον ℵ c a mg BA + זבחים ועולות M ויעבדו F εκεινοι τ. μοσχῳ] τη Βααλ τη δαμαλει ℵ c a mg BA 𝔖 vitulo aureo 𝔏 לעגליא *Ar* לעגלי הזהב M את הבעלים ואת העגלים F ον εποι. . . . Γαλειλ.] > BA 𝔖 F Ιεροβ.] + בן נבט M. εν Δαν] *post* εθυσιαζον 𝔏 *pr.* בבית אל *Ar* M επι . . . Γαλ.] > *Ar* M et omnibus altissimis montibus G. αβ cum omnibus superioribus partibus G. γ et in excelso omnium gentium. G. δ 6. καγω] κ. εγω A והוא (*et ubique*) *Ar* μονωτατ.] μονος BA 𝔖 > M + עובד יהוה F πολλακις] πλεονακ. BA aliquoties αβγ aliquotiens δ > *Ar* M F εις Ιεροσολυμα1° ℵ B ab A] εν -οις B* vid εν1° ℵ B ab A] > B* vid εν2°] > BA εν π. Ισρ.] > *Ar* M על יש׳ M παντι] + τ. BA προστ. αι.] בספר אוריתא דמשה *Ar* בתורת יי M (+) F τ. πρωτογεν. κ.] > BA αβγ *Spec.* 59 MF אפרשותא *Ar* τ. δεκ.] > δ κτηνων] γενηματ. BA 𝔖 armentorum (-ti γ argenti *Spec.*) et pecorum (-odum γ) αβγ *Spec.* pecorum δ > *Ar* M F πρωτοκουρας] τ. προκουριας B (*post* τας *seq* ρας *in* B: π B? *mg sinistr*) τ. πρωτοκυριας A > δ *Ar* ובכורות M τ. προβατων] > BA δ *Ar* M F εχων] והוא מוביל *Ar* απετρεχ. εις Ιερ.] > BA 𝔏 M לתמן *Ar* *aliter* F 7. κ. εδιδ.] > M αυτα] αυτας B *ante* εχων 𝔏 > M τ. υι. A. . . . Ιερουσ.1°] וללויאי לכל חד וחד מאי דחזי ליה *Ar* Ααρων] Αρ. A πρ. τ. θυσ.] + παντ. των γενημ. ℵ c a mg B ab A + των γεν. B* 𝔖 ad aram δ > αβγ *Spec.* M F κ.2° τ. δεκατην] τ. δεκατην εδιδουν BA 𝔖 et quod moris erat de tritico αβγ et decimam frumenti δ et secundum morem legis de trit. *Spec.* > M + ראשון F τ. οιν. . . . ακροδ.] > BA 𝔖 F τ. οιν. κ. τ. σιτ.] τ. σιτ. κ. τ. οιν. ℵ c a de tritico vino αβγ ελαιων ℵ*] -ου ℵ c a αβγ *Spec.* κ. ροων] + κ. τ. συκων ℵ c a mgg M et (de) ficu malorum granatorum αβγδ *Spec.* ακροδρ. ℵ c a] κροδρ. ℵ* τ. θεραπουσιν] τ. -ευου. BA [illegible] 𝔖 et servientibus Domino, qui praesto erant 𝔏 (*cf.* M) *plen.* F εν1°] εις B > A δεκ. τ. δευτ. *usque ad* νομ. Μωσ. (v. 8)] ומעשרא תניינא ומעשרא עניא הוה אכיל ויהיב ככל מה דכתו׳ בספרא דמשה *Ar* ומ׳ שני ומ׳ שלישי לגר ליתום ולאלמנה (והלכתי בכל שנה ושנה עם כל אלה לירו׳) כמצות יי M δεκ. τ. δευτ.] δευτ. δεκ. BA απεδεκ. αργυριω] απεπρατιζομην BA 𝔖 commutans in pecunia (*vide Reusch*) αβ τ. εξ ετων] > BA 𝔖 F Ιερουσαλημ2°] Ιεροσολυμοις BA (+ αβ) in loco sancto αβγ *Spec.* > δ 8. εδιδ. αυτα . . . εισεφερ. κ. εδιδ. αυτοις εν τ. τριτ. ετ.] τ. τριτην εδιδ. BA 𝔖 (*cf.* M *supra*) F tertii ad decimationem ferebam . . . et dabam illis in tertio anno αβ decimationem dabam . . . in Israel γ tertia autem decima dab. . . . et dabam *&c.* δ ita ut Tertii anni decemationem darem . . . in Isr. *Spec.* τ. ορφαν. . . . υιοις Ισρ.] οις (B b vid τοις B*) καθηκει BA 𝔖 proselytis et orph. et viduis (et v. > δ) αβγδ *Spec.* לבדק הבית F τοις προσκ. τ. υι. Ισρ.] faciens omnia quae pracepta sunt (+ a Domino *Spec.*) in Isr. αβγ *Spec.* adpositis in Isr. δ τ. υιοις] *pr.* εδιδουν ℵ c a vid κ. ησθ. . . . Μωσῃ κ.] > BA 𝔖 F ησθ.] manducabam 𝔏 κατα τ. εντολ. ας] καθως BA 𝔖 > *Ar* F ας ενετ. . . . απεθαν.] והדין ט׳ אשתאר · · · ורבת · · · והיא אדרכתיה באורחא קשיטא *Ar* Δεββ.] Δεμβ. A Αν. τ. πατ. ημ.] τ. πατ. μου BA 𝔖 M F patris mei Thobihel matri meae et patri meo αβ Danihel δ > γ οτι] διοτι BA ορφανον . . . απεθ.] -νος κατελειφθην υπο τ. πατρος μου (+ ומאמי M F) BA 𝔖 M 9. εγεθην ℵ*] εγενηθ. ℵ c a εγενομην BA γυν.] *pr.* Ανναν BA 𝔖 δ uxorem nomine Annam αβ (A. > γ) εκ τ. σπ. . . . ημων] מזרעיתה *Ar* M + ושמה חנה *Ar* M εγγεν. εξ αυτ.] וילידת ליה *Ar* M F υιον . . . ονομα αυτ.] > BA 10. μετα . . . ηχμαλωτισθην] κ. οτε ηχ . . . σθην (-ημεν B F + מארין נפ׳ M) BA 𝔖 γ *Ar* M F et postquam in captivitatem deveni ad Assyrios αβ

5. τῇ βάαλ (R v) is an imitation of LXX, e.g. 4 Kings xxiii. 5 (cf. the papyrus fragment of the Ascension of Isaiah, ii. 12), not an andrygonous deity (Baudissen, Herzog's *R.E.* sub *Baal*, *Astarte*) or a corruption of Bethel (Graetz, Neub.); בבית אל in *Ar*, however, is a mistake, reproduced in M, for בבעל.

6. The non-classical word γένημα, common in LXX, is found in papyri, Mayser, *Gramm. d. griech. Pap. aus d. Ptol.-zeit*, p. 214. Deissm. *B.S.*, pp. 109 ff. ἐν Ἱερ. (Cod. Vat.) after a verb of motion belongs to the distinctly vernacular style of the R v text, cf. v. 5, vi. 6, ix. 2, while the form Ἱεροσόλυμα (R v ἱερὸς Σόλυμοι ?) is Hellenistic.

7–9. See Müller, *op. cit.*, pp. 37–48, for minute textual criticism of 𝔏.

11, 12 Gentiles. But I kept myself from eating of the bread of the Gentiles; and, when I remembered my
13 God with all my soul, the Most High gave me grace and favour in the sight of Shalmaneser and
14 I used to buy for him all things for his use, and go into Media and buy for him thence, until he
died. And I left purses in trust with Gabael the brother of Gabri in the land of Media, ten talents
of silver.
15 And when Shalmaneser was dead and Sennacherib his son reigned in his stead, the roads of
16 Media were unsafe, and I could no more go into Media. In the days of Shalmaneser I did
17 many almsdeeds to my brethren who were of my kindred: I used to give my bread to the hungry,
(17) and garments to the naked: and if I saw any of my nation dead, and cast forth behind the wall of
18 Nineveh, I buried him. And whomsoever Sennacherib slew, when he had come fleeing from Judaea
in the days of the judgement which the King of heaven wrought upon him for the blasphemies
wherewith he had blasphemed, I buried. For in his wrath he slew many of the children of Israel,
and I stole away their bodies and buried them. And Sennacherib sought them and found them not.

(*cum* δ *cf.* א) αιχμαλ. א*] + με א ca N.] + קרתא רבתא *Ar* M εποր.] > BA 𝔖 *a* β F morarer δ *Ar* M κ.2°] > BA 𝔖 μου2°] > B ησθ.] *pr.* הוו מסאבין נפשיהון *Ar* 11. והוא לא אכל דהוה דחיל מן אלהא *Ar* ואנכי לא נגאלתי בפתבגם מפני יראת יי M (*cf.* F) εκ τ. αρτ. τ. εθν.] > BA 𝔖 de escis (v. 10 panibus) illorum 𝔏 12. ורחים יתיה בכל לביה *Ar* (*cf.* F) κ. οτε] καθοτι BA et quoniam 𝔏 μου1°] > BA 𝔖 𝔏 + בכל לבי M F 13. κ1°.] > (*v. supra* κ. οτε) 𝔏 μοι] > BA ο υψιστ.] אלהא *Ar* M יהוה אל׳ F χαρ. κ. μορφ.] חנא וחסדא *Ar* M (*cf.* F) Εν.] (*vide* v. 2) + regem Assyriorum *a* β δ *Ar* M + regem γ *Ps.-Aug.* F ηγορ. . . . χρησιν] ημην αυτου αγοραστης BA 𝔖 ומני יתיה על כל מה דהוה ליה *Ar* M τα προς τ. χρησιν] quaecumque volebat in usu suo 𝔏 14. κ. εποր. . . . εκει.] > *Ar* M κ. εποր.] εποր. B iens 𝔏 Μηδιαν] -δειαν B ab *pr.* τ. BA *pr.* regionem 𝔏 *pr.* בכל מלכותו וגם F κ. ηγορ. αυτ. εκειθ.] > BA 𝔖 𝔏 F εως αυτ. αποθαν.] > BA 𝔖 F παρεθ.] *pr.* ובההיא זימנא *Ar* Γαβηλῳ א*] -αηλω א ca BA Gabelo 𝔏 גבאל *Ar* גביאל M עביאל F βαλλαντια] > BA 𝔖 *a* β γ *Ar* M F τ. αδ.] fratri meo *a* β M fratri δ > γ τῳ2°] > BA M filio *a* β γ F et δ Γαβρει] -ρια BA Gabahel *a* β Gabeli γ Gabin δ קברי *Ar* + קריביה *Ar* > M גבריאל F τῃ χωρᾳ] Ραγοις BA 𝔏 ܒܪܓܐ 𝔖 Μηδιας] -δειας B ab regionis Medorum *a* β civitate M γ in terra M. δ + בקורי רגש *Ar* ובמדינת רגאש M 15. Ενεμασσαρ] -μεσσαρ B -μεσσαρος A ܐܢܡܤܪ: 𝔖 *Ar* M + מלכא דאתור *Ar* M המלך F κ.2°] > BA 𝔖 𝔏 Σενναχηρειμ] Αχηρειλ B Αχηρεια B b *vid* ܣܢܚܪܝܒ 𝔖 סנחריב *Ar* M κ.3°] + ובהלין יומיא סגיאו אנגרייתא *Ar* οδοι . . . απεστ.] דפסקו עברי אורחא מטול ביהלתא *Ar* והיה רע וקשה ודרכיו מקולקלים F της M.] αυτου BA terrae Medorum 𝔏 απεστησαν] ηκαταστατ. B κατεστ. A ܠܐ ܡܬܩܢܢ 𝔖 constantes erant *a* β incon. er. γ recesserant δ (+ (*cf.* *Ar*) ויסגרו מפני המלחמות אשר היו בארץ) M κ. ουκετι . . . Μηδ.] ולא נסב בכספיה מידא דגב׳ *Ar* (*cf.* M *post* Μηδ.) κ. ουκετι ηδ.] et nemo poterat . . . postea 𝔏 *pr.* ומפחדו F πορευ.] לשוב F εις τ. M.] illuc *post* pot. 𝔏 16. εν] *pr.* κ. א ca BA 𝔖 𝔏 εν . . . Εν] (ואחריכן) M Ενιμεσσαρου] -σαρ BA ܐܢܡܤܪ: 𝔖 F סנחריב *Ar* εποιησα] -οιουν (ουν sup ras 4 litt A a) BA τ. αδ. μου τ. εκ τ. γεν. μου] τ. αδ. μου BA 𝔖 omnibus de natione mea 𝔏 לחשיכיא *Ar* (*cf.* (*plen.*) M) לכל אחי F τ. αρτ. . . . γυμν.] > M πειν.] + ויתמין *Ar* 17. ιματ.] *pr.* τ. A + μου A > M κ.2°] + והיה גמיל חסדא סני *Ar* τ. εκ τ. εθν. μ.] > *Ar* εθν.] γεν. BA 𝔖 τεθν.] חללי *ante* εκ τ. εθ. M (*cf.* F) κ.3°] > *Ar* M ερριμ.] ρεριμ. B εριμ. A οπισω τ. τειχ. Νιν.] באורחא דיהודאי *Ar* οπισω] επι A מחוץ M Νιν.] *pr.* εις A εθαπ.] *pr.* לא שקטתי ולא נתתי עד אשר M 18. *multa verba apud M addita e Script. et aliis locis. simil.* F ει τ. απεκτ.] > *Ar* Σενναχηρειμ1°] Αχηρειλ B ܣܢܚܪܝܒ 𝔖 + ο βασιλευς א ca (*vid*) BA 𝔖 𝔏 סנחריב *Ar* M + מלך אשור M απηλθ.] ηλθ. BA 𝔖 φευγων] בביהות אפין *Ar* M + מיהודה אלנ׳ M εν ημ. . . . εβλασφ.] > BA 𝔖 אזל לניג׳ בתקוף רגז על עשר שיבטיא דבארעא דאתור וקטל מנהון סגי והות ניבלתהון רמיין באורחה ולית קביר *Ar* (+ *simil.* M) εν ημ. . . . κρισ.] propter defensionem 𝔏 εξ αυτ.] de illo 𝔏 ο βασ.] Dominus 𝔏 εθαψ. . . . Ισρ.] כד חמא טובי כדין סגי באיש עליה *Ar* εθαψ.] + αυτους κλεπτων BA 𝔖 𝔏 M εκ τ. υι. . . . κ. εθαπτ.] > BA 𝔖 κ.2°] ego 𝔏 *pr.* וקם בליליא *Ar* εκλ.] involvebam 𝔏 εζητ. . . . ευρ. αυτ.] -ηθη υπο τ. βασ. τα σωμ. κ. ουχ ευρεθη BA 𝔖 זימנא חדא תבע סנחריב פגרי

14. ἠγόραζον (without the πάντα . . . χρῆσιν of *v.* 13) may refer to journeys to Media for the purchase of *slaves*, the sense in which ἀγοράζειν is used in the will of Attalus III, Dittenberger, *Orient. Graeci Inscript. Select.* No. 338, cf. 1 Cor. vi. 20, vii. 23.

15. 'Αχηρεὶλ (Vat.) is the result of haplography ΕΒΑΣΙΛΕΥΣΕΝ[ΣΕΝ]ΑΧΗΡΕΙΜ. The phonetic interchange of β and μ is frequent; consequently Marshall's hypothesis, that ב was misread מ in a supposed Aramaic original, is needless: see Introd., p. 182. ἠκαταστάτησαν (Vat.) exemplifies the tendency of new verbs to take an external augment.

16. In *Ar* Levi reads חשיכיא but חשיכיא is correct as ס appears elsewhere, e.g. vii. 16; xvi. 5, 9, 13; דעמי has dropped out after it, and a similar omission occurs in *v.* 18, where M shows that the common parent of *Ar* and M originally followed the tradition of R[s] fairly closely.

17. In ῥεριμ. (Vat.) initial ρ is reduplicated contrary to the Attic rule.

18. 𝔏's *involvebam* is due to the influence of xii. 13, or the presence of περιστέλλειν in his MS. of R[s], not to independent translation of גנבת misread ענבת, a corruption ingeniously but quite unnecessarily invented by Marshall.

19 And a certain one of those of Nineveh went and informed the king concerning me, that it was I who
buried them, and that I was hid. And when I perceived that the king knew concerning me and
20 that I was sought for to be put to death, I was afraid and ran away. And all that I possessed was
seized, and there was nothing left unto me which was not taken to the royal treasury save my wife
21 Anna and my son Tobias. And there passed not forty days before two of his sons slew him. And
they fled into the mountains of Ararat, and Esarhaddon his son reigned after him. And he
appointed over all the accounts of his kingdom **Aḥiḳar**, my brother Anael's son, and he had authority
22 over all his affairs. Then **Aḥiḳar** made request for me, and I came down to Nineveh. For **Aḥiḳar**
was chief cupbearer, and keeper of the signet, and steward, and overseer of the accounts in the days
of Sennacherib king of Assyria, and Esarhaddon appointed him a second time. And he was my
brother's son and of my kindred.

ii. The starting-point of the present story, ii. 1–14.

2 1 And when **Esarhaddon** was king I came home again, and my wife Anna was restored unto me,
and my son Tobias. And at our feast of the Pentecost, which is the holy Feast of the Weeks, there

19. κ. επορευθη] +וכדין עבד זימנין סגיאין *Ar* αυτα] > 𝔏 Σ.2°] rex 𝔏 קטיליא ולא אשכח יתהון *Ar* τις] > BA εκ της Ν.] εν Ν. B Νινευιτων A 𝔖 εις τις] אנשי *Ar* εμορ. . . . εμου] renuntiatum est illi 𝔏 -θεις δε BA 𝔖 ואזלו *Ar* υπεδειξεν] -ξε B אכל קורציה *Ar* +*multa verba* M εγω] > BA θαπτω] εθαπτον A κ. εκρ.] > α β γ δ *Luc.* *Ar* F κ. οτε επεγνων] επιγνους δε BA 𝔖 οτε . . . αποθ.] quaerebat me occidere 𝔏 פקיד מלכא למקטליה כד שמע טובי *Ar* (*cf.* F) εγνω . . . οτι3°] > BA 𝔖 του] > BA εφοβηθην κ. απεδρασα] φοβηθεις ανεχωρησα BA 𝔖 ego autem fugi 𝔏 קם וערק *Ar* ברחתי מפניו M (*cf.* F) 20. ופקיד מלכא למישלל ית ביתיה *Ar* (*cf.* +*multa verba* M) *simil.* F ηρπαγη] δι- BA direpta est 𝔏 οσα υπηρχεν μοι] τ. υπαρχοντα μου BA 𝔖 substantia mea 𝔏 ο ουκ . . . βασιλικ.] > BA 𝔖 𝔏 Τωβια] -βειτ B -βιου A 21. ου διηλθ. ημ. + εως ου] contigit dum laterem post dies α β contigit (+ut γ) post dies γ *Luc.* latui diebus δ ואיטמר מקמיה ··· יומין עד *Ar* F *plen. et aliter* M τεσσερακοντα] ν' א ca mg πεντηκ. BA 𝔖 quadraginta quinque α β γ δ *Ar* > M תשעה עשר F απεκτ.] +בחרבא *Ar* οι δυο υι.] *pr.* אדרמלך ושראצר *Ar* M F εφυγον א c a] -γεν א* τ. ορη] montem 𝔏 לארע *Ar* M F Αραρατ] -αθ B 𝔏 קרדו *Ar* Σαχερδονος] -δαν A ܣܪܚܐܕܘܢ 𝔖 Archedonossar α β γ δ *Luc.* אסרחדון *Ar* M F υιος] *pr.* ο BA μετ' αυτον] αντ' αυτου BA 𝔏 *Ar* M F > 𝔖 εταξ.] +מלכא אסרחדון *Ar* Αχειχαρον] -ειαχαρον א c a -ιαχαρον BA ܐܚܝܩܪ 𝔖 Achicarum α β γ δ אקיקר *Ar* M אהרון F Αναηλ] חמאל *Ar* חננאל M F τ. του αδελ. μ. υιον] υι. (*pr.* τ. A) τ. αδ. μ. BA M אחי F εκλογιστιαν] -ειαν B curam α β γ δ כל דליה *Ar* M (*cf.* F) αυτος ειχ. τ. εξουσ.] > BA 𝔖 *aliter* F τ. διοικ.] ארעא דאתור *Ar* M 22. 𝔏 *vide apud Reusch* τοτε] κ. BA 𝔖 *Ar* ηξιωσ.] *pr.* ומליל אקיקר מלין טבין על טובי למלכא *Ar* (*cf.* M) Αχειχαρος1° 2°] Αχιαχαρος BA ܐܚܝܩܪ 𝔖 Achirarus α β γ δ אהרון F εμου] +erat enim consobrinus meus α β מיניה *Ar* κατηλθ.] ηλθ. BA 𝔖 ואתביניה *Ar* (*cf.* M) F την] > BA Αχειχ2°. . . δευτ.] > α β *Ar* M γαρ] δε BA 𝔖 αρχιοινοχοος] οιν. B 𝔖 F οινοδοχος A διοικητης] על המם F επι Σεν. βασιλεως (א* -εα א c a) Ασσυρ.] > BA 𝔖 F Σαχερδονος] *pr.* ο א c a BA -δονοσος A ܣܪܚܐܕܘܢ 𝔖 Acedonassar δ > F εκ δευτερας] *pr.* υιος BA ܕܝܠܗ ܗܘ ܠܕܘܬܪܝܢ 𝔖 iterum δ > F ην] η א* > F δε] enim 𝔏 *Ar* εξαδ.] רחימיה *Ar* M > F κ. εκ τ. συγ. μ.] > BA 𝔖 𝔏 F

II. 1. κ.1°] οτε δε (δ. > A) BA 𝔖 > 𝔏 M επι Σ. Βασ.] > BA 𝔖 > 𝔏 M וגדר המלך באנונה ההיא *Ar* אם' F κατηλθ.] > 𝔏 *Ar* M F εις τ. . . . μου3°] *post* Νιν. 1 22 𝔏 > *Ar* κ. απεδ.] אהדרו *Ar* M ונתן F η γυν.

19. ἀπέδρασα, a form occurring elsewhere in LXX only in א Judith xi. 3.

20. βασιλικόν, cf. Dan. ii. 5 (LXX ἀναλημφθήσεται ὑμῶν τὰ ὑπάρχοντα εἰς τὸ βασ.), 1 Esdras i. 7.

21. Rv has 'graecized' the name of Esarhaddon; for א by its ἐπὶ Σαρχεδόνος βασ. ii. 1, shows that Rs had Σαχερδών (cf. Cod. Al. Σαχερδάν). For Aḥiḳar cf. note to xi. 18.

22. *a second time* (cf. Mark xiv. 72): so Ball, Rendel Harris, the fem. being employed on the analogy of שֵׁנִית. Rv, however, preferred 'son by a second wife', unless it is right to accent and punctuate ὁ Σαχερδονὸς υἱός, ἐκ δευτ. = Sacherdonus' son appointed him a second time. Dr. Charles conjectures that υἱός is a dittograph of the last three letters of Σαχερ.

II. 1. In א the gen. was written for τῇ ἑορτῇ under the influence of the following genitive unless τῇ ἡμέρᾳ is to be understood. πεντ. (*sc.* ἡμέρα cf. 2 Macc. xii. 32; 1 Cor. xvi. 8; Jos. *Ant.* iii. 10. 6; cf. Philo, *De Septenar.* 21) = חג חמשים יום, a somewhat new and unusual name for the 'feast of weeks' at the time when our author wrote; hence he defined it as ἥ . . . ἑβδ. which is an integral part of Rs (not lacking in א as Hatch and Red. *Concord.*, p. 361, sub. ἑβδομάς, incorrectly state), and Rv undoubtedly witnesses to subsequent misunderstanding of his purpose.

With *vv.* 2–4, 5 (first letter) and 8 cf. *Ox. papyr.* No. 1076. Presenting the recension of Rc, it shows the usual deference of that recension for the ancient tradition of Rs against the less antique Rv in several respects, e.g. *v.* 2 βάδιζε (-ζον Rv) πτωχ. (against ἐνδ. of Rv though the latter's order is followed); *v.* 3 κ. ἐπορ. T., ἀναστρέψ. (= ἐπιστρέψ. Rs) against ἐλθών of Rv, ἰδού2° (> Rv), ἔθνους (γεν. Rv); in *v.* 4 ἦρα (ἀναιροῦμαι Rs) against ἀνειλόμην (Rv), ἐκ τ. πλατ. (> Rv), ἐν τῶν against τι of Rv, μέχρι and infin. against ἕως οὗ and indic. in Rv, retention of the clause 'in order to bury him'; see above for *Ox.*'s coincidence with Rv, and Introd., p. 176, for the emendation in *v.* 8.

2 was a good dinner prepared me; and I laid me down to dine. And the table was set for me, and
abundant victuals were set for me, and I said unto Tobias my son, Go, my boy, and what poor man
soever thou shalt find of our brethren of the Ninevite captives, who is mindful <of God> with his
whole heart, bring him and he shall eat together with me; and lo, I tarry for thee, my boy, until
3 thou come. And Tobias went to seek some poor man of our brethren and returned and said,
Father. And I said to him, Here am I, my child. And he answered and said, Father, behold, one
of our nation hath been murdered and cast out in the marketplace, and he hath but now been
4 strangled. And I sprang up and left my dinner before I had tasted it, and took him up from the
5 street and put him in one of the chambers until the sun was set, to bury him. Therefore I returned
6 and washed myself, and ate food with mourning, and remembered the word of the prophet which
Amos spake against Bethel, saying,

> Your feasts shall be turned into mourning,
> And all your ways into lamentation.

7, 8 And I wept. And when the sun was set, I went and digged a grave and buried him. And my

μ. A.] A. η γυν. μ. BA   υι. μου] + כי צוה המלך אשור וג׳ M   κ.4°] > BA 𝔏   τ. πεντ.] > *Ar* F   ובשנה ההיא M   τ. εορτης] -ρτη (*pr.* τ. A) BA   ημων] > BA 𝔖 *Ar*   η . . . εβδ.] דשבועיא *Ar* M F   εβδομ.] *pr.* επτα BA 𝔖   a septem annis *a β*   ex (a *γ* de *Aug.*) septimanis *γ Luc. Aug.*   septimanarum *δ* (*vide Reusch*)   εγεν.] הכינותי M F   μοι αρ. καλ.] αρ. καλ. μοι BA   κ.5°] > B ܘ 𝔖   ανεπεσα] ανεπαυσαμην A   αριστησαι] φαγειν (*a sup ras* A[a]) BA 𝔖   2. a [πλειο]να usque ad [επιστ.] ουν v. 5 *cf. Ox*   κ.1°. . . τραπεζα > BA 𝔖 *Ar* M F   παρ. μοι 2°] εθεασαμην BA 𝔖 *a β γ Luc.*   > *δ Ar* M F   οψαρια πλειονα] οψα πολλα BA 𝔖   > *δ Ar* M F   πλειονα] [πολ]λα *Ox*   τ. T.] > BA 𝔖 *Ox*   παιδ.1°] > BA *Ox* 𝔏 *Ar* M   βαδιζε] -σον BA   ον] *pr.* αγαγε BA *Ox* 𝔖 𝔏   αν] εαν BA *Ox*   ευρης] υρης *Ox*   πτωχ. τ. αδ. ημ.] τ. αδ. ημ. ενδεη B 𝔖 (*cf. Ar* M)   τ. αδ. ημ. A F   εκ τ. αδ. ημ. πτωχων *Ox*   εκ N. . . . μεχρι του *non exst. Ox*   εκ N. αιχμ.] > BA *Ar* M F   ος μεμν.] > A F   + τ. κυριου BA 𝔖   Deum *a β γ Cypr. Luc.*   dom. suum *δ*   דחליא דאלהא *Ar*   > M   εν ολ. καρδ. αυτ.] > BA 𝔖 *Ar* M   αγαγε . . . εμου κ.] > (*v. supra*) BA (*cf. Ox*) 𝔖   κ. φαγ.] ut manducet 𝔏   κοιν. μετ᾿ εμου] panem nobiscum et prandium hoc *γ*   pariter nobiscum prandium hoc *a β*   עמנא *Ar* M F   ιδε א*] ιδου א[c a] BA 𝔖   > *Ar* M   אל תאחר F   προσμενω] μενω BA   *pr.* וכל היושבים עמי M   παιδ.2°. . . ελθειν] > BA 𝔖 F   παιδ.] > *Ar* M F   σε ελθ.] [παραγενε]σθαι σε *Ox*   3. επορευ. . . . κ.2°] > BA 𝔖   ואזל *Ar*   ζητ. . . . ημ.1°] > *Ox*   πτωχ.] + captivum 𝔏   τ. αδελ.] > M   επιστρεψας] ελθων BA 𝔖   αναστρεψας *Ox*   > *Ar* + מר נפש M   λεγ. . . . εθνους ημων] ואשכח *Ar*   λεγ. . . . αποκριθ.] > BA *Ox* 𝔖 M   λεγει] dixit mihi 𝔏   αυτῳ] > 𝔏   αποκρ. ειπεν] ait 𝔏   πατερ] μοι *Ox* 𝔏   ιδου2°] > BA 𝔖 M   εκ] των απο *Ox*   εθνους] γεν. BA 𝔖   ex fratribus nostris *a β δ* (*γ Luc.* = א) M   מבני ישראל F   πεφ. *usque ad* γευσ. μ. αυτ. (v. 4) *non exst. Ox*   πεφ. κ. ερρ. εν τ. αγ. κ. αυτ. ν. εστρ.] εστραγγαλωμενος (-λημενος B[ab] A > M) ερρ. εν τ. αγ. BA 𝔖 *a β γ δ* + גברא חד קטיל רמא באורחא וחוי לאבוהי *Ar*   נפל בשדה F   4. κ.1°] καγω BA 𝔖   וכד שמע *Ar* M F   αναπηδ.] *post* με BA   > *Ar* F   נבהלתי ויצר לי מאד M   αφηκα τ. αριστ. + κ.2°] > BA 𝔖   כן קם מן פתורא *Ar*   πρ. η γευσ. με] *ante* αναπηδ. BA (*cf.* F)   ולא אכל *Ar*   > M   η] > A   αυτου > BA   αναιρουμαι] ανειλομην BA 𝔏   ηρα *Ox*   *pr.* ואזל *Ar* M   εκ τ. πλατ.] > BA 𝔖   + דקרתא *Ar*   κ.3°] > BA *Ox* 𝔖 𝔏   εν τ. οικιδιων] τι οικημα BA   εν τ. οικηματων *Ox*   ܒܒܝܬܐ 𝔖   in domum apud me 𝔏 (*cf.* F)   בחד ביתא *Ar*   ברשותי M   εθηκα] > BA *Ox* 𝔖 𝔏   μεχρι τ. τ. ηλιον δυειν] εως ου εδυ ο ηλ. BA   μεχρι δυειν τ. ηλιον *Ox*   κ. θαψω αυτ.] > BA 𝔖 F   κ. θαπτω αυτ. *Ox*   ut illum sepelirem 𝔏   5. επιστρ. ουν] κ. επιστρ. BA 𝔖 𝔏 M   κ. (*reliqua non exst.*) *Ox* + לביתה *Ar* M   > F   ελουσ.] > *Ar* M   + ידיי F   αρτον] + μου BA 𝔖 𝔏   μετα πενθ.] εν λυπη BA 𝔖   *pr.* באילוא *Ar*   *pr.* בדמעה M   + ואנחה F   6. εμνησ. . . . λεγων] דאיתקיים בנא *Ar*   τ. ρηματος τ. προφητου] τ. προφητειας (-ιας A) BA 𝔖 F   sermonum prophetae 𝔏   הדבר M   οσα . . . λεγων] καθως ειπεν BA 𝔖   עמוס הנביא F   οσα] quod 𝔏   A.] *post* προφ. BA 𝔖 𝔏   επι Βαιθηλ] in Bethleem 𝔏   στραφησ.] והפכתי *Ar* M   > F   υμ. αι εορτ.] αι εορτ. υμ. BA   omnes dies festi vestri 𝔏   > F   κ. πασ. . . . θρην.] > *Ar* F   וג׳ M   οδοι] ευφροσυναι BA 𝔖   cantica *a β Luc.* (viae *γ* semitae *δ*)   θρηνος] -ον BA   7. εκλ.] + בכיה רבא לחדא *Ar* M   κ. οτε . . . ηλ.] בערב F   ορυξ.] > *Ar* M   8. *simil* F   οι] *pr.* omnes 𝔏   πλησ.] קריבוהי *Ar*   וקרובי ומשפחתי M   μ.] > BA   κατεγ.] επεγ. BA   deridebant me 𝔏   *cum* ου φοβ. . . . ιδου *cf. Ox*   ου

2. R[s] had τοῦ θ. which *a β γ* have preserved; א omitted (or they have fallen out after αὐτοῦ) and R[v] varied to κυρίου.

3. On the surface the ἀναστρέψας of *Ox.* and the ἀποκριθείς of א might seem to suggest independent translation of a Heb. or an Aramaic word. This, however, apart from the general difficulties (see Introd., p. 182) of the independent translation hypothesis, is precluded by the fact that ἀναστρέψ. of *Ox.* corresponds to ἐλθών of R[v] (= ἐπιστρέψ. not ἀποκριθ. of R[s]), λέγει . . . ἀποκριθ. being omitted in conformity with R[v] and only κ. ἐπορ. T. retained in R[c]'s usual compromising tendency in the first clause of the verse.

4. κ. θάψω (-τω *Ox.* = R[c]) > R[v], an instance of the resolution of an infin. into a finite verb in Hebraistic style and of its rejection or modification in a subsequent recension.

6. R[s] (cf. *γ δ* in addition to א's αἱ ὁδοί read by Swete but διοδοί by Reusch) had 'ways' (used metaphorically like דרך and well paraphrased by R[v]). The emendation ᾠδαί which was made as long ago as *a β* (and accepted even by Reusch) is preferred by the partisans of R[v] (e.g. Nöldeke, Löhr) as giving colour to the fiction that R[s] is merely a secondary revision undertaken in the interests of Biblical style and Semitic idiom.

neighbours mocked, saying, Is he no longer afraid?—for already I had been sought after to be put
to death for this matter—And yet he fled away <and lost all his possessions> and lo, again, he
9 burieth the dead! And the same night I washed myself and came into my courtyard and lay down
10 to sleep by the wall of the courtyard, and my face was uncovered because of the heat. And I knew
not that there were sparrows in the wall above me; and their dung settled warm into mine eyes and
brought up white films; and I used to go to the physicians to be healed; and the more they
anointed me with their medicaments, the more mine eyes were blinded by the films, until they were
totally blinded. And I was impotent in mine eyes four years. And all my brethren did grieve for
me, and **Aḥikar** nourished me two years until he went to Elymais.
11, 12 And at that time my wife Anna used to work for hire in the tasks of women, and would send
the tasks back to their owners: and they would pay her the wages. And on the seventh of Dystrus,
she cut off the web, and sent it home to the owners and they gave her all her wages, and gave her
13 **in addition to the wages** a kid of the goats. And when she came into my house, the kid began to
cry, and I called her and said, Whence is this kid? is it stolen? Render it to its owners; for we
14 have no right to eat anything that is stolen. And she said unto me, It hath indeed been given me

φοβ. ουκετι] ουκετι φοβ. BA εκινδυνευσεν *Ox* quomodo non &c. 𝔏 φοβ.] + hic homo 𝔏 + מן נפשה *Ar* M ηδη γαρ επεζητηθην] -θη א[a b?] 𝔏 > BA *Ox* 𝔖 *Ar* M τ. φον. . . . απεδ.] > *Ar* M του¹] > BA *Ox* φον.] αποθανειν *Ox* περι τ. πραγ. τουτ.] > *Ox* απεδ.] αποδ. A + κ. απωλεσεν παντα τα υπαρχοντα αυτου *Ox* + et perdidit substantiam suam *αβ* κ. παλιν ιδου] κ. ιδου BA *Ox* iterum 𝔏 παλ. ιδ.] > *Ar* M θαπτ.] sepelire coepit 𝔏 νεκρ.] + ego autem intentus in mandatis Dei non timebam quid loqueretur homo *Spec.* 30 9. αυτ. τ. νυκτι ελουσ.] εν αυτ. τ. νυκτι ανελυσα (ανελυσ. *sup ras* B[ab]) θαψας BA 𝔖 iterum lavi ea hora postquam sepelivi *αβ* illum sepelivi *γ* sepelivi δ אחרי קברי את המת M ελουσ.] לא טבל מן מיתא *Ar* עשיתי טבילה M κ.2° . . . αυλ. μ.] > BA 𝔖 *Ar* *plen. et aliter* M αυλ.] domum 𝔏 εκοιμ.] + μεμιαμμενος BA 𝔖 τ. τοιχ. της αυλ.] parietem 𝔏 על ערסיה סטר כותלא *Ar* אצל הקיר M αυλης] + μου BA ανακεκαλυμμεν.] ακαλυπτ. BA δια τ. καυμα] > BA 𝔖 *Ar* M 10. στρουθια] דרור F επανω μ.] > BA εισιν] εστ. BA residebant 𝔏 (*cf. Ar*) κ.2°] + τ. οφθαλμων μ. ανεωγοτ. BA 𝔖 (*cf.* F) εκαθ.] > 𝔏 εκαθ. τ. αφοδ. αυτ.] αφωδευσαν τ. στρουθια BA F εκαθ.] insiderunt *γ* residerunt δ > BA θερμ.] *ante* εις BA > *Ar* M κ.3°] > A επηγαγ.] εγενηθη B *Ar* M (*cf.* F) λευκ.] + εἰς τ. οφθαλμους (-οις B[edit]) μ. B 𝔖 *Ar* M (*cf.* δ F) επορευομην] -θην BA + caecus 𝔏 *pr.* cotidie δ *pr.* כל צפר וצפר *Ar* *pr.* בבקר M τους] > BA θεραπευθ. . . . ετη τεσσερα] κ. ουκ ωφελησαν με BA 𝔖 (*cf.* F) לאסאה עייני ולא איתסי אלא אסגי חיורא וג׳ *Ar* לרפאת אותי ולא יכלו M κ. παντ. . . περι εμ.] > BA 𝔖 F οι αδελφ.] + et amici mei 𝔏 *Ar* M περι εμ.] על עודות עיני M κ.8° Αχειαχαρος] Αχιαχαρος δε BA ܐܚܝܩܪ 𝔖 Achicarus autem 𝔏 אקיקר *Ar* M + קרובי M ואחי אהרון F ετη δυο] > BA 𝔖 *Ar* M προ τ. αυτον βαδισαι] εως ου επορευθην BA 𝔖 F priusquam iret 𝔏 > *Ar* M τ. Ελυμ.] τ. Ελλυμ. BA Limaidam 𝔏 > *Ar* M באלמנייא F 11. κ.] > 𝔏 εν τ. χρον. εκειν.] > BA 𝔖 ליומין סגיאין *Ar* הנה F A. η γυνη μ.] ∽ BA ηριθευετο] ܦܠܚܐ 𝔖 deserviebat *αβ* mercede serviebat *γ* operabatur δ εργοις τ.] > BA 𝔖 עבידתא *Ar* γυναικιοις] -ειοις B ܦܠܚܐ ܕܢܫܐ 𝔖 mulierum *αβγ* muliebribus (= mulieribus) δ + lanam faciens et telam ex mercedibus suis pascebat me *αβ* l. f. et conducens telas texendas et ex &c. δ לנשייא חורנייתא *Ar* לנשים M F 12. απεστ. . . . παντα κ.] > *Ar* (*cf.* F) ואורגת יריעות לאחרים M mittebant et adducebant (duc. *γ*) illam ad texendum et dabant ei mercedem suam *αβγ* quae accipiebat et texebat et cum detexuisset (detexisset?) remittebat domino rerum et ille mercedem dabat ei δ αυτων . . . κυριοις2°] > BA 𝔖 εξετεμε τ. ιστον] consummavit texturam 𝔏 εδωκ. αυτ.] απεδωκ. αυτ. κ. αυτοι BA 𝔖 παντα] > BA 𝔖 κ.6° εδωκαν αυτῃ] προσδοντες κ. BA et insuper dederunt ei *αβγ*δ *pr.* ויהי היום M εφ' εστιᾳ] > BA δ pro detexto *αβ* telaticum *γ* + ad manducandum *αβ*δ בגין אגרה *Ar* M F εξ αιγων] > BA 𝔖 *Ar* M 13. κ.1° . . . κραζ.] והוה שמע גדיא זעיק בביתא *Ar* (+ F *cf.* M) κ. οτε] οτε δε BA εισηλθ.] ηλθ. BA והביאתו F ο εριφ.] > BA 𝔖 F κραζειν] κραυαζ. A εκαλ. αυτ. κ. ειπα] ειπα (-πον A) αυτῃ BA 𝔖 M F vocavi ad me uxorem et dixi illi 𝔏 ושאל יתה *Ar* τουτο] > BA 𝔖 + qui balat 𝔏 μηποτε . . . κλεψιμ.] השמרי בנפשך שלא יהיה גנוב M μηποτε] μη BA κυριοις] למריה *Ar* αυτου] > BA εξουσ. εχομεν ημεις] θεμιτον εστιν BA 𝔖 𝔏 ουδεν] > BA 𝔖 F κλεψιμ.2°] supra mercedem 𝔏 14. κ. λεγ. μ. αυτῃ] η δε ειπεν BA 𝔖 et respondit mihi et dixit 𝔏 (*cf. Ar*) F δοσει . . . μισθῳ] ליתוי מן גניבתא ברם באגר עובד

10. Müller finds in *θερμόν* of R[s], which he regards as the original Greek, an improbable epithet for *ἀφόδευμα* and conjectures that חורי (= dirt) has been mistranslated. *ἀνεωγότων* R[v] perf. act. in *late* passive sense. Dillon's conjecture (*Contemp. Rev.* 1898, p. 367) that 'Ελλυμ. (Cod. Vat., but elsewhere 'Ελυμ.) is a misunderstood transliteration of a Hebrew word = 'hiding-place' derived from עלם is favoured by Dr. Harris, *Story of Aḥiḳar*, p. lii, n. 1, but see Introd., p. 186.

12. *ἐφ' ἑστίᾳ* (Swete). Reusch conjectures *ἐπὶ τοῦ ἐσθίειν* (cf. δ) or *ἐπὶ τῷ μισθῷ* (telaticum *γ* = mercedem pro tela = *ἵστιον*? *v.* 11). *αβ* presuppose the existence of both these conjectures. Dr. Charles suggests that of an original ΕCΤΙΑΤΟΡΙΑΙ (=*for a meal*) the last five letters were lost before *ἔριφον* and the remaining six became ΕCΤΙΑΙ. For *ἱστός* see Deissm. *B.S.*, p. 135.

14. The presence of *ποῦ εἰσίν* in R[s] shows that *δικαιοσύναι* here keeps its old sense. At times however (as here in R[v]) it appears in R[s], e.g. xii. 9, beside *ἐλεημ.* as an early gloss or doublet translation and should be omitted.

over and above the wages. And I did not believe her, and I bade her render it to the owners; and I was abashed at her because of this. Then she answered and said unto me, And where are thine alms-deeds? Where is thy righteous course of life? Behold, this thy case is known.

iii. **Tobit's Prefatory Prayer,** iii. 1–6.

3 1, 2 And I was much grieved in my soul and groaned and wept. And I began to pray with groanings: O
Lord, thou art righteous, and all thy works are righteous, and all thy ways are mercy and truth: thou
3 judgest the world. And now, O Lord, remember thou me, and look upon me; and take not vengeance
4 on me for my sins, both for mine ignorances and my fathers'. They sinned against thee and disobeyed
thy commandments, and thou gavest us for spoil and captivity, and death, and for a proverb and
5 a by-word and a reproach among all the nations among whom thou didst disperse us. And now
thy many judgments are true in exacting from me the penalty of my sins, because we did not keep
6 thy commandments and walked not truly before thee. And now deal with me according to thy
pleasure, and command my spirit to be taken from me, that I may be released from off the earth
and become earth: for it is more profitable for me to die than to live, because I have heard false
reproaches, and there is much sorrow in me. Lord, command that I be released from this distress,
let me go to the everlasting place, and turn not thy face, O Lord, away from me. For it is more
profitable for me to die, than to see much distress in my life, and not to hear reproaches.

B. Sarah's Previous History, *vv.* 7–15.

7 On this day it happened unto Sarah the daughter of Raguel who was in Ecbatana of Media,

ידאי קבילתיה *Ar* > F δοσει] δωρον BA $ *pr.* לא כן הדבר כי M αυτη] למילתא *Ar* > F κ. ελεγ. . . . αποδουν.] sed magis dicebam illi Furtivis est redde illum 𝔏 > *Ar* וצעקתי עליה וג' M αποδουναι] -διδοναι BA + αυτο BA $ προσηρυθ.] -ηρυθ. BA ܡܬܟܬܫܐ $ contendebam et erubescebam 𝔏 ונצא עמיה *Ar* והיינו מתקוטטים יחד M > F χαριν τουτ.] > BA $ F על גדיא *Ar* M ειτα] η δε BA $ ענת חנה אנתתיה *Ar* > F λεγει] ειπεν κ.5° BA ܦܘܡܐ $ > F > B Ae κ. που . . . δικ. σου] ubi sunt iustitiae tuae *a β Cypr. Aug.* (*bis*) ubi sunt eleemosynae tuae δ ubi sunt el. tuae quas faciebas γ *aliter* F που εισιν2°] κ. BA ιδε (א*) ταυτ. μετα σ. γνωστ. εστ.] ιδου (א c a) γν. παντα μ. σ. BA $ ecce quae pateris omnibus nota sunt 𝔏 (*cf.* F) וקלנך אתגלי לכולא *Ar* M *pr.* שלא יועילו לך בעת צרתך M

III. 1. κ.1°] + כד שמע *Ar* (*cf.* F) περιλ. γεν.] λυπηθεις BA ܘܟܕ ܐܬܟܪܝܬ $ contristatus 𝔏 מעי המו F τ. ψυχ.] > BA $ *Ar* M עלי F κ. στεν. εκλ.] εκλ. BA $ *Ar* F ingemui lacrymans 𝔏 ונחלתי על שברי *Ar* ηρξ. προσευχεσθαι] προσευξαμην BA $ M *pr.* introivi (intravi γ δ) in atrium meum (aulam meam δ) et *a β γ δ* > F μετ. στεν.] μετ' οδυνης BA $ + animae meae 𝔏 *Ar* לפני יי M במר נפש F 2. δικ.] *pr.* λεγων BA $ (*cf. Ar* M F) Κυριε] אלהא רבא *Ar* יי M + וישר משפטך M F παν. τ. εργ.] > F δικαια] > BA $ F magna 𝔏 (*cf. Ar* M) ελ. κ. αλ.] misericordiae et verit. plenae 𝔏 -συνη] -ναι BA $ συ] σοι A *pr.* κ. κρισιν αληθινην κ. δικαιαν BA $ F *pr.* et iudicium verum *a β γ* (δ = א) τον] *pr.* εις BA $ 𝔏 *pr.* לכל באי F αιωνα] כל ארעא *Ar* הארץ M + ואתה צדיק · · · · · ואני הרשעתי M 3. *simil. sed plen.* M F κ.1°. . . επιβλ. κ.] > *Ar* κ. νυν σ. Κυρ.] > BA $ επιβλ.] + επ' εμε BA $ respice in me 𝔏 κ.3°] > BA 𝔏 με] > B εκδικησ.] εκδικ. B תזכר F ταις αμ.] de pecc. 𝔏 κ. εν τ. αγν. μ.] > *Ar* וכעווני M εν] > BA $ *Ar* de 𝔏 ημαρτ.] *pr.* α. B *pr.* οι א c a A $ *a β* *pr.* si quid γ quia δ ואנא ואבהתאי חבנא *Ar* (*cf.* δ F) εναντ.] ενωπ. BA 𝔏 *Ar* F 4. *simil. sed plen.* (*verba e Script.*) M κ. παρ.] παρ. γαρ BA $ 𝔏 παρηκουσα א*] -σαν א c a BA $ *a β γ* contempsimus δ (*cf. Ar*) κ.2°] > B δ αρπαγ.] διαρπαγ. B *post* αιχμ. *Ar* > M αιχμ.] > M θαν.] > *Ar* M F εις2°] > BA κ. λαλ. κ.] > BA $ *Ar* ονειδισμον] -μου BA $ *ante* παρα B *Ar* > F εν1°] > BA εθν.] + הארץ F ημ. διεσκορπισας] εσκορπισμεθα BA $ אתגליתא יתנא *Ar* 5. *simil.* M *plen.* F νυν] + Domine 𝔏 אלהא *Ar* σου αι κρ.] αι κρ. σ. BA *pr.* רחמך *Ar* υπαρχ.] εισιν BA αληθ.] + αι οδοι σου א c a + ܟܐܢܐ $ *pr.* et 𝔏 ποιησ. . . ενωπ. σ.] לא תגמול עמי בחובאי *Ar* ποι. εξ εμ.] εξ εμ. ποι. BA quae de me exigas 𝔏 μου] + κ. τ. πατερων (πρων א c a) μου א c a BA $ *a β γ* (> δ) κ. ουκ] ου γαρ BA $ non 𝔏 αληθινως] εν -θεια BA $ 6. *aliter et plen.* F κ. νυν . . . εμου] ברם כחסדך וקביל נפשי מן ידאי סניא עביד עמי *Ar* σου1°] *pr.* ενωπιον A + הישר M κ.2°] > BA $ επιταξ. . . . γη] *Ar* (*cf.* M F) εξ εμ.] > BA $ 𝔏 απ. . . . γης] > BA $ *Ar* M שתאספני אל אבותי בית מועד לכל חי F κ. γενωμαι γη] > 𝔏 διο] διοτι BA αποθαν.] חסדך F μαλλον] > B κ.4°] > B οτι ονειδ. *usque ad v. fin.*] במסכנות רבתא ובחיסודא אלין ולא אשמע קלנא עוד *Ar* ולא אשמע חרפתי עוד M λυπ.] + εστιν BA μετ' εμ.] εν εμ. BA $ Κυρ.1°] > BA $ απολυθω] -θηναι με BA απο2°] > BA ταυτ.] > BA $ απολ. με] ηδη BA $ et da mihi refrigerium 𝔏 τοπ. τ. αιων.] αι. τοπ. BA κ.5°] > BA $ Κυρ.2°] > BA $ 𝔏 διο2°. . . ονειδ.] > BA $ βλεπειν] vivere et pati 𝔏 7. *brev.* F ημ. ταυτ.] αυτ. ημ. BA $ 𝔏 συνεβ.] > *Ar* Σ.] *post* Ραγ. BA τη2°] > A του] > BA Εκβ.] > F τ. Μ.] *pr.* מדינתא בארעא *Ar*

III. 7. Israël Lévi (*Revue des Études juives*, vol. xliv, April–June, 1902, pp. 289 ff.) points out the disproportion

8 that she also heard reproaches by one of her father's maidservants; because that she had been given
to seven husbands, and Asmodaeus the evil demon had slain them, before they had been with her as it
is appointed for women. And the maidservant said unto her, It is thou that slayest thy husbands;
behold thou hast already been given to seven husbands, and thou hast not been named of one of
9 them. Wherefore dost thou scourge us on account of thy husbands because they have died? Go thy
10 ways with them and let us see neither son nor daughter *of thine* for ever. In that day she was grieved
in her soul and wept; and she went up into her father's upper room, and desired to hang herself; and
again she considered and said, *Nay*, lest they reproach my father; and shall say unto him, Thou
hadst one beloved daughter, and she hath hanged herself because of her calamities! and I shall bring
down my father's old age with sorrow to Hades. It is fitter for me not to hang myself, but to
11 supplicate the Lord that I may die and no longer hear reproaches during my life. At the self-same
time she stretched forth her hands towards the window and prayed, and said, Blessed art thou,
12 O merciful God, and blessed is thy name for ever: and let all thy works bless thee for ever. And
13 now unto thee my face and mine eyes I lift up: command that I be released from the earth, and
14 that I no more hear reproaches. Thou knowest, Master, that I am pure from all uncleanness with
15 man, and that I never polluted my name, nor the name of my father either, in the land of my

(*cf.* M) *pr.* בארץ F αυτ.] ταυτ BA ipsa 𝕷 ακουσ. ονειδισμ.] -δισθηναι BA 𝕾 שמעת חיסודא רבתא *Ar* שפחותיה F משפחות אביו M υπο . . . εαυτης] > *Ar* הרעו F (*sed* v. F v. 8) מחרפים אותה ומלעיגים בה M ואומרים לה לא יש ראוי לקרא לך שרה אלא צרה + M υπο] απο A 𝕷 μιας τ.] > BA 𝕾 του2°] > B εαυτ.] αυτ. BA 8. *plen.* F εκδεδ.] δεδ. BA επτα] + ולא על עלה איניש באורח כל ארעא *Ar* (*cf.* M) Ασμοδεος] -δαυς B -δαιος A ܐܣܡܘܕܐܘܣ 𝕾 אשמדאי *Ar* F אשמדי M δαιμ. τ. πον.] πον. δ. BA מלכא דשידי *Ar* M απεκτεννεν] -κτεινεν BA πριν . . . αυτ.] ea hora qua ad illam introiebant ad concumbendum *αβ* qua hora introibant ad illam *γ* M antequam fierent cum illa in coniugio *δ* καθ. . . . ταις] ως εν BA 𝕾 sicut solitum est mulier *αβ* sicut traduntur mulieres *δ* > *γ* באורח כל ארעה *Ar* בדרך כל הארץ M > F ειπεν] -αν B 𝕾 η παιδ.] > BA 𝕾 + sua 𝕷 Συ ει η] Ου συνιεις BA 𝕾 למה את M αποκτεννουσα] -πνιγουσα BA 𝕾 F suffocas *αβγ* suffocasti *δ* τ. ανδρ. σ.] σ. τ. ανδρ. BA ιδου ηδη] ηδη BA מטול ד *Ar* > M απεκδεδ. επτα ανδρ.] επτα εσχες BA 𝕾 > M κ.3°. . . ωνομασθης א B$^{a?b}$] κ.3°. . . ωνασθης BA 𝕾 et nullo eorum fruita es *αβγ* frunita es *δ* > M F וחד מנהון לא עאל עלך דאנת מקלה יתהון *Ar* 9. τι ημας . . . ανδρ. σ.] ותלקי אותנו על הדבר הרע הזה M (*cf.* F) περι τ. ανδρ. σ.] > BA *pr.* aut 𝕷 οτι απεθ. . . . αυτων] וטוב יהיה לאבותיך שתמותי תחתם M (*cf.* F) οτι] ει BA 𝕾 F qui L απεθανον] -ναν BA -νε̄ B$^{a?}$ תמותי F κ.] > BA 𝕾 ιδοιμεν] יראו M υιον א*] *pr.* σου BA 𝕾 + σου א^{ca} *pr.* ex te *ante* videamus 𝕷 μηδε] η BA 𝕾 10. εν τ. ημερ. εκειν.] ταυτα ακουσασα BA 𝕾 (*cf. Ar* (*cf.* M) F) eadem hora *αβ* in illa hora *γ* in illa die *δ* ελυπ.] חרה M εν τ. ψυχ.] σφοδρα BA 𝕾 *Ar* M עד למות F κ. εκλαυσ.] > BA 𝕾 ותצר לה F κ.2° αναβασ. . . . ηθελ.] ωστε BA 𝕾 ובקש F ηθελ. . . . ελογ.] ותזעק לפני יי בקול מר M ηθελ. . . . κακων] *mult. aliter et plen.* M. *hab. supplicationem* παλ. ελογ. κ. λεγ.] ειπεν BA 𝕾 cogitavit 𝕷 Μη . . . κακων] Μια μεν ειμι τ. πατρι μου εαν ποιησω τουτο ονειδος αυτῳ εσται (εστιν A) BA 𝕾 *supplicationem et dissim. verba habet* M אם אעשה הדבר הזה F αυτῳ] > 𝕷 απο τ. κακ.] > 𝕷 καταξω] *post* αυτου BA 𝕾 ולאחתא *Ar* τ. πατρος μ.] αυτου BA 𝕾 + אמי F λυπης] οδυν. BA + animi 𝕷 αδου א^{ca} BA] αδους א* χρησ. . . . ζωῃ μ.] > BA 𝕾 M F + neque ego neque pater meus *αβγ* + pater meus *δ* χρησ. μοι] *pr.* כן לית *Ar* αλλα] ברם טב לי *Ar* Κυρ.] אלהא *Ar* οπως αποθ.] > *Ar* 11. > M εν αυτ. τ. καιρ.] κ. BA 𝕾 אז F διαπ. τ. χειρ.] > BA 𝕾 הלכה ונפלה τ. θυριδα] τῃ -δι BA 𝕾 קדם אלהא *Ar* εδεηθη] *ante* προς BA 𝕾 בצלו *Ar* + וכדין אמרת *Ar* θεε ελ.] κυριε ο θεος μου BA 𝕾 Domine Deus misericordiarum 𝕷 יי אלהים רחמנא וחננא *Ar* יהוה אלהינו F σου1°] + τ. αγιον κ. εντιμον BA 𝕾 𝕷 קדשך דמפרש בכל עלמיא *Ar* שמו הגדול הגבור והנורא F κ.3°] > BA 𝕾 𝕷 *Ar* ευλογησατωσαν] -γησαισαν BA σου] ידך *Ar* εις τ. αι.] לעלם ולעלמי עלמין *Ar* *post* הנורא F + ולך משבחים כל בשר F 12. > M νυν] + κυριε BA 𝕾 *Ar* + יהוה אלהינו F επι σε] εις σε *post* μου2° BA 𝕾 προσ.] > F τ. προσωπ. μ. τ. οφθ. μ.] ∽ BA μου1°] + levo *αβ Ar* + verto *γ* ανεβλεψα] δεδωκα BA 𝕾 dirigo *αβγ* respiciunt *δ* תליין *Ar* *aliter* F 13. *plen. et aliter* M F ειπον] ܠܡܐܡܪ 𝕾 απολυθηναι] -λυσαι BA ܕܐܫܬܪܐ 𝕾 דאתיב *Ar* ותאבדני F απο τ. γης] לעפרי *Ar* מן העולם F ακουειν] -σαι BA ονειδισμους] -μον BA 𝕾 14. *plen.* F δεσποτα] Κυρ. BA *Ar* > F ακαθαρσιας] αμαρτ. BA ανδρος] *pr.* και B (*sed non* B^{ab} A) 𝕾 15. ουχι] ουκ BA μου τ. ον.] τ. ον. μου BA corpus

---

between the cause—*servant's* gibes—and the result—desire for death; the strangeness of 9^{b} in the mouth of servants (but rightly used by parents, x. 11, R^{s}, 12, R^{v}), Sarah's anxiety for her *father's* sake; the *figurative* use elsewhere in Tobit of μαστιγόω (e.g. xi. 15, xiii. 2, 5, 9). He ingeniously conjectures that **her mother** (אִמָּהּ) not **a maid** (אָמָה) taunted her, that πατρὸς αὐτῆς was a gloss inserted afterwards, and ἡμᾶς (*v.* 9) = the parents. Even if Levi were right, R^{s} (a *single* maid) would be nearer to the intention of the author than R^{v}.

8. ἀπόκτενν. (+ vi. 14 f. א, xiv. 11 א), Th. *Gram.*, p. 225. ὠνάσθ. (R^{v}), Th. *Gram.*, p. 200.

captivity. I am the only daughter of my father, and he hath no other child to be his heir, nor has he kinsman near him, nor has he relation, that I should keep myself for a wife unto him. Seven husbands of mine are dead already; and why should it be mine to live on? And if it pleaseth thee not to slay me—O Lord, now hear my reproach.

C. The Union of Sarah's and Tobit's Destinies, *vv.* 16, 17.

16, 17 At the self-same time the prayer of both was heard before the glory of God. And Raphael was sent to heal them both: *in the case of* Tobit to remove the white films from his eyes, that he might see the light of God with his eyes; and *in the case of* Sarah the daughter of Raguel, to give her for a wife to Tobias the son of Tobit, and to unbind Asmodaeus the evil demon from her; because it belonged to Tobias that he should inherit her rather than all those which wished to take her. At that time did Tobit return from the courtyard into his house, and Sarah the daughter of Raguel herself also came down from the upper chamber.

THE JOURNEY OF TOBIAS, iv–xiii.

A. Its Cause and the Preparations, iv. 1–v. 17a.

i. **The Cause**, *vv.* 1, 2.

4 1 In that day Tobit remembered the money which he had left in trust with Gabael in Rages of
2 Media, and he said in his heart, Behold, I have asked for death. Why do I not call my son Tobias and shew unto him concerning this money before I die?

meum *α β* > *γ* κ.2°] > BA ουδε] + dehonestavi *α β* πατρος μ.] אבותי F αιχμ. μ.] גלותינו F της] > A ετερον] > BA 𝕾 *Ar* M F τεκνον] παιδιον BA filium vel filiam 𝕷 בר *Ar* M יורש F ινα] ο BA 𝕾 qui 𝕷 κληρονομηση] -σει BA αυτου] אחסנתיה *Ar* M αδελφ.] > *Ar* M αυτῳ2°] > BA 𝕾 𝕷 *Ar* M εγγ. ουτε συγγ.] vel proximus aut propinquus 𝕷 ουτε] ουδ. BA συγγ. αυτ. υπαρχει] -χων αυτ. υιος (ι *sup ras* Aa) BA 𝕾 קריב *Ar* M בן לאחיו F αυτῳ3° υπαρχει] *post* αδελφος 𝕷 *aliter* F συντηρ. εμ.] custodiat me 𝕷 *Ar* שיורשני M ואסברה F εμαυτην ℵ ca BA] αυτην ℵ* > M αυτῳ γυναικα] αυτ. γυ. *sup ras* ℵ1 αυτῳ γυναι *sup ras* Aa (*seq ras* 2 litt.) > M *aliter* F γυν.] > *Ar* ηδη] והרי *Ar* M επτα] *pr.* viri 𝕷 (*plen.* F) κ.4°] > BA εστιν ετι] > BA 𝕾 adhuc 𝕷 מה יתרון M > F ζην] חיי *Ar* לחיות M + בעולם M > F σοι δοκ.] ∽ BA Κυρ.] > BA *Ar ante* αποκτ. 𝕷 νυν] επιταξον BA 𝕷 > 𝕷 *Ar* εισακουσ. ονειδ. μ.] επιβλεψαι (*pr.* impera et δ) επ' εμε (ε. ε. > *γ Ar*) κ. ελεησαι με κ. μηκετι ακουσαι με ονειδ. BA 𝕾 *α β γ δ Ar* M *plen.* F 16. Εν αυτ. τ. καιρ.] κ. BA 𝕾 ביומא ההוא *Ar* ובאותה שעה F εισηκουσθη] -σεν κ̅ς̅ A exauditae sunt 𝕷 עלת *Ar* F η] > B της A προσευχη ℵ Ba] -χης B* A preces 𝕷 τ. δοξ. τ. θεου] τ. δ. τ. μεγαλου Ραφαηλ BA ܩܕܡ ܐܠܗܐ 𝕾 *pr.* summi 𝕷 כורסי יקרא דאלהא רבא *Ar* כסא הכבוד (כסא ולפני השכינה + כבוד יי + *verba pauca* M *et* Π) M אבינו בשמים F 17. απεστ.] ושלח *Ar* M וצוה (*pr. verba pauc.*) F Ρ.] *ante* κ. BA (*v.* 16) *pr.* מלאכא *Ar* M + השר הממנה על הרפואות M Τωβειθ1° απολ. τ. λ. απο τ. οφθ. αυτου] του Τ. λεπισαι (λιπεισαι A* *ras* λι A? ܠܡܣܚܦܘ 𝕾) κ. τ. λ. BA 𝕾 id est T. curare a maculis oculorum *α β* sanare a mac. oc. *γ* desquama maris (= desquamare) δ לרפאתו מחלי עיניו M (*cf.* F) ινα . . . θεου] > BA 𝕾 *Ar* M F et reddere ei (ei > *γ*) aspectum luminis *α β γ* lumen coeli δ Σαρρᾳ ℵ*] -ραν ℵ1 BA 𝕾 𝕷 τῃ ℵ*] την ℵ ca BA 𝕾 𝕷 Ραγ.] *pr.* του ℵ ca BA αυτην] > BA 𝕷 Τωβειθ] *pr.* του A λυσαι] δησ. BA 𝕾 colligare *α β γ* alligare δ לאעדאה *Ar* M ולגעור ולהבריחו F Ασμοδεον] -δαυν B -δαιον A 𝕷 ܠܐܣܡܘܕܐܘܣ 𝕾 (*cf.* 38) אשמדאי *Ar* F אשמדי M δαιμ. τ. πον.] π. δ. BA מלכא דשידי *Ar* M > F διοτι . . . αυτην3°] > *Ar* M כי לט' משפט הגאולה F απ' αυτ.] > BA 𝕾 επιβ. κλ. αυτην2°] destinata erat haereditas eius 𝕷 παρα . . . αυτην3°] > BA 𝕾 εν εκ. τ. καιρ.] וכד שיצי ט' ית צלותיה *Ar* M (*cf.* F) εκεινῳ] αυτ. BA 𝕾 επεστρ. Τ. απο τ. αυλης] επιστρεψας Τ. εισηλθεν BA 𝕾 תב *Ar* M ונכנס F κ. αυτ.] > BA 𝕾 *post* κατεβη 𝕷 υπ.] + αυτης BA 𝕾 + כד שיציאת לצלאה *Ar* (*cf.* M F)

IV. 1. του] *pr.* περι BA 𝕾 αργυριου] *inter* ρ2° *et* ι *parva ras in* B vid ο] ου BA Γαβαηλῳ] -ηλ BA 𝕷 ܠܘܬ ܓܒܐܝܠ 𝕾 גבאל *Ar* גביאל M עביאל F εν Ραγοις] ܒܪܓܝܣ 𝕾 בקורי ריגש *Ar* במדינת רגאש M > F Μηδιας] -ειας B ab 2. τ. καρδ. αυτ.] εαυτῳ B αυτῳ A ܒܗ 𝕾 בדעתו F ιδου] > BA 𝕾 ουχι] ουχ BA *pr.* ܘܗܫܐ 𝕾 > *Ar* M למה אינני F Τ.] > A κ.2°] ινα αυτῳ BA 𝕾 υποδειξω] ואצונו F αυτῳ . . .

12. ἀναβλ. causative as in Is. xl. 26 (= נשׂא).

17. λῦσαι (Rs) and δῆσαι (Rv) were both technical terms in contemporary magic, Deissm. *L.A.E.* 306–10. It is noteworthy that in Dan. iv. 12 these two words both correspond to the Aramaic שׁרא; cf. 1 Enoch viii. 3.

IV. 3. F's *immediately* may be due to his intimate acquaintance with some recension based on an Aramaic text in which בהדרא had been corrupted into בהדדה, but this particle is very characteristic of F's style (*e.g.* iv. 3 *et passim*) and but little weight therefore can be attached to its appearance here.

ii. The 'Teaching' of Tobit, *vv.* 3–21.

3 And he called Tobias his son and he came unto him and he said unto him, Bury me well, and
honour thy mother; and forsake her not all the days of her life, and do that which is pleasing before
4 her, and grieve not her spirit in any matter. Remember her, child, that she hath experienced many
5 dangers for thee in her womb; and when she is dead, bury her by me in one grave. My child, be
mindful of the Lord all thy days, and let not thy will be set to sin and to transgress his commandments: do acts of righteousness all the days of thy life, and walk not in the ways of unrighteousness.
6 <For if thou doest the truth, success shall be in thy works, and *so it shall be* unto all that do
7 righteousness. Give alms of thy substance: turn not away thy face from any poor man, and the
8 face of God shall not be turned away from thee. As thy substance is, give alms of it according to
thine abundance: if thou have much, according to the abundance thereof, give alms; if thou have
9 little bestow it, and be not afraid to give alms according to that little: for thou layest up a good
10 treasure for thyself against the day of necessity: because alms delivereth from death, and suffereth

τουτου] > BA 𝔖 + quam commendavi 𝔏 ליה עסקא דכספא *Ar* (*cf.* M F) 3. κ.1°] מיד F εκαλεσεν] καλεσας BA 𝔖 T. τ. υιον αυτ.] αυτον BA 𝔖 filium suum 𝔏 F κ. ηλθ. πρ. αυτ.] > BA 𝔏 𝔖 *Ar* M F κ.] > BA 𝔖 αυτῳ] > BA 𝔖 + Fili: et (et > γ) ille respondit: Quid est pater et Thobis dixit (et dixi γ) α β θαψ.] *pr.* Παιδιον εαν αποθανω BA α β γ δ 𝔖 *Ar* M F καλως] > BA 𝔖 diligenter 𝔏 מיד F τιμα] μη υπεριδῃς BA 𝔖 (*cf.* F) κ. μη εγκ.] τιμα BA 𝔖 αυτης] σου BA 𝔖 F κ. ποι . . . πραγμ.] > 𝔖 ενωπ. αυτ.] αυτῃ BA illi . . . in conspectu eius 𝔏 λυπησ.] תסרב *Ar* תמרה M τ. πνευ. αυτ.] αυτην BA על מימר פומהא *Ar* את פיה M + ואל תמרר את חייה M > F εν π. πραγ.] > BA *Ar* M F 4. αυτης1° 2°] > BA α β γ δ *Spec.* κινδ. πολ.] ∽ BA quanta pericula 𝔏 > *Ar* כמה צרות M *pr.* הרבה הטרחות נטרחה עליך F εωρακ.] εορ. B passa sit 𝔏 אתעיקת *Ar* עברו עליה M εν τ. κοιλ. αυτ.] > *Ar* *pr.* בהיותך M F κ.] > BA 𝔖 εν ενι ταφ.] *pr.* בכבוד M 5. *paene simil.* M κ.1°] > BA π. τ. ημερ.] *cum praeced. coniung.* A*vid* σου] > BA του Κυρ.] + τ. θεου ημων BA 𝔖 *Ar* Deum 𝔏 בוראך M יהוה אלהיך F κ.2°. . . αδικιας] *plen.* F κ.2°] > B αμαρτειν κ.] > B -τανειν κ. B*ab mg* A δικαιοσυνας] -ην BA α β δ *Cypr. Luc.* *pr.* κ. A 𝔖 > γ ποιει] -ειν A 𝔖 > γ ταις οδ.] in viam α β γ δ (in vias *Spec.* 24) עם גבר חטוף *Ar* 6. > M οι ποιουντες] ποιουντος σου BA α β γ δ *Luc. Cypr.* 𝔖 αληθειαν] -ιαν B* א A *pr.* την BA ex (in β) veritate α β γ *Luc. Cypr.* veritatem δ ευοδωθησ.] ευοδιαι εσονται BA 𝔖 erit respectus α β γ *Cypr.* -tio *Luc.* bene tibi erit δ תצליח F εν τ. εργοις αυτων] εν τ. ε. σου BA α β γ 𝔖 + omnibus (+ in (ex *Cypr.*) substantia *e versu seq.* δ *Cypr.*) δ operibus tuis *Luc.* operum tuorum *Cypr.* בכל דלך *Ar* את דרכיך ואז תשכיל F κ. π. τ. ποιουσιν δικ.] *cum* v. 19 *coniung.* א (Swete) + טוביהון *Ar* > F δικαιοσ.] *pr.* την BA > F 7–19a. > א [7 *usque ad* 19a B:—] 7. *simil.* M σοι] σου A κ. μη φθ. . . . ελεημοσυνην] > 71 106 𝔖 α β γ δ *Spec.* 24 *Ar* M σε] > A κ.2°] > A ου μη . . . θεου] אלהא לא יכסה שכינתיה *Ar* לא יעלים ממך אל׳ F προσ-ωπον] *cf.* עיניך M F πτωχ.] *cf.* מענִיי ישראל M + ואביון F του θεου] > 𝔖 8. *simil.* M ברי עד דאית יוכלא בידך למעבד צדקתא עביד ואם מתרחק מינך עותרה עביד צדקתא *Ar* υπαρχ.] ܐܝܟ ܕܒܟ ܐܝܬ ܩܢܝܢܐ 𝔖 + fili 𝔏 εξ αυτων ελεημ.] + εαν πολυ σοι υπαρχῃ κατα το πολυ εξ αυτων ποιησον ελεημοσυνην 249 α β γ (> δ *et reliqua verba huius versus* > δ) *Cypr. Aug.* (*cf.* F?) κατα το ολιγ.] + communica et α β γ *Cypr. Spec.* 24 *Aug.* ποιειν] cum (quia β) facies (facis γ *Cypr.*) α β γ *Cypr.* (*cf. Spec.* 24) φοβου ποιειν] ου ποι *sup ras* B*ab* 9. *simil. et plen.* M ותקנה נכסין ואם תעביד צדקתא דרופתק טב תקנה ביום ריתחא *Ar* γαρ] > α β γ δ *Cypr. Caes.* 10. ελεημοσυνη] -ην (ν *ras* A?) A* היא *Ar* צדקה M και ουκ . . . σκοτος] וכל המתעסק בצ׳ יחזה

5. Cf. Test. Job xlv, 'Behold I die; only forget not the Lord.'

6b–19a, full of reminiscences of Aḥiḳar (see Introd. pp. 191 f.), certainly stood in R^s. Apart from the fact that their presence in 𝔏 cannot be attributed to later insertion from R^v or R^c, a comparison of *v.* 5 with *v.* 19c shows that some ethical instruction of the type found in 𝔏 and R^v intervened in R^s between these two verses. The omission therefore is simply confined to א and is explicable on the supposition either of the loss of a page in a MS. or that the eye and mind of a scribe passed from the objective fact expressed in ποιοῦσιν δικ. *v.* 6 to the cause and subjective motive for such action stated in δώσει . . . βουλ. ἀγαθ. The gap has been filled in above from R^v except in a few cases (v. *infra*) in which that recension has evidently and seriously departed from the more ancient R^s.

7. The words *and when . . . grudging* seem to be an interpolation in R^v from *v.* 16. The combination of 71, 106, α β, *Spec.* 24, 𝔖, *Ar*, M is emphatically against their originality in R^s.

8. The parallelism demands the text of R^s preserved in 𝔏 and the Patristic quots.:—ὡς σοὶ ὑπ. παιδίον οὕτως ποίει ἐὰν πλῆθός σοι ὑπάρχῃ κατὰ τὸ πλῆθος ποίησον ἐξ αὐτῶν ἐλεημ.· ἐὰν ὀλίγ. σοι ὑπάρχῃ, κατὰ τὸ ὀλίγ. μεταδός (*Communico* = μεταδίδωμι in Wisd. vii. 13, cf. Test. Issachar vii. 5; Test. of Zeb. vi. 4. 7).

9. Possibly γάρ should be omitted and the verse construed closely (cf. 𝔏. *Cypr. Caes.*) with the preceding:—μὴ φοβοῦ· ὅτι ἐν τῷ ποιεῖν σε ἐλεημ. θέμα ἀγαθ. θησ. *Ar*'s רופתק should be read *either* הופתק = ὑποθήκη (Neaub.) or הפתק = ἀποθήκη (Nöld.).

10. Cf. Prov. xi. 4 (generalized in Sir. xxix. 12) with its counterpart in Syriac Aḥiḳar (R. Harris, *Story of Aḥiḳar*, pp. xlvii f.).

11 not to come into darkness. Alms is a good offering in the sight of the Most High for all that give
12 it. Beware, my child, of all whoredom, and take first a wife of the seed of thy fathers, take not
a strange wife, which is not of thy father's tribe; for we are the sons of the prophets. Noah,
Abraham, Isaac, Jacob, our fathers of old time, remember, my child, that they all took wives of
13 their kinsmen, and were blessed in their children, and their seed shall inherit the land. And now,
my child, love thy brethren, and scorn not in thy heart thy brethren and the sons and the daughters
of thy people so as not to take one of them; for in scornfulness is destruction and much trouble,
14 and in idleness is decay and great want, for idleness is the mother of famine. Let not the wages of
any man, which shall work for thee, tarry with thee, but render it unto him out of hand: and if thou
serve God, recompense shall be made unto thee. Take heed to thyself, my child, in all thy works,
15 and be discreet in all thy behaviour. And what thou thyself hatest, do to no man. Drink not wine
16 unto drunkenness, and let not drunkenness go with thee on thy way. Give of thy bread to the
hungry, and of thy garments to them that are naked: of all thine abundance give alms; and let not
17 thine eye be grudging when thou givest alms. Pour out thy bread and thy wine on the tomb of the

11. *Corrupt. et e Script. multa addita Ar* εασει] -εις A ומגנת בעושיה ומצלת מדינה של גיהנם F פני אלהים ככתוב וגו' M ומתנה גדלה וטובה משלמים לפני הקדוש ברוך הוא לעושי M ועוסקים עמו מן השמים (+ הם M) πασι B] -σιν A δωρον] ܩܘܪܒܢܐ 𝕾 γαρ] > A צדקה F 12. προσεχ.] + מכל עצת חטאין *Ar* מכל טמאה M γυν. πρωτον λαβε] accipe primum uxorem δ ux. primo acc. γ ux. proximam acc. αβ ux. acc. *Cypr.* וסב לך אתתא מזרעיתך *Ar* (*cf.* M) וקח אשה ממשפחתי ומבית אבי F μη] *pr.* κ. A 𝕷 F εσμεν] + qui in veritate prophetaverunt priores αβ et secundum veritatem ambulamus δ > F Νωε] + prophetavit prior αβ + propheta fuit prior γ quia prophetavit primus δ > M *pr.* מטול דנביאי קדמאי *Ar* (*cf.* F) Αβρ.] *pr.* και 𝕷 *Ar* F Ισ.] *pr.* και A 𝕷 Ιακ.] *pr.* και A 𝕷 *Ar* M F αυτοι] ουτ. A 𝕷 των αδελφ.] genere patrum αβ semine fratrum γ sem. patrum δ ממשפחותם M ευλογηθ.] ηυλογισθ. A *pr.* לא אבו להתחתן בבני נכר M σπερμ. αυτ.] semen filiorum 𝕷 זרעייהו *Ar* > M κληρονομ.] אחסינו *Ar* > M 13–16. *similiter* (?) *sed ord. confus. Ar* M νυν] tu αβγ (nunc δ) *Arm* propter quod et tu *Spec.* 13 *et* 34 τους αδελφ. σου] לריעך כמוך F απο τ. αδελφ. κ. τ. υιων κ. θυγατ.] filiabus filiorum αβγ filiis et filiabus δ 𝕾 *Ar* filiabus filiarum *Spec.* 13 *et* 34 אחיך ובני עמיך F του λα. σου] > *Ar* λαβειν σεαυτῳ εξ αυτων γυν.] ut non accipias unam ex illis αβγ accipe unam ex illis δ (*cf. Spec.* 13 *et* 34) > *Ar* εν τ. υπερηφ. . . . πολ.] כי לפני בזדונא שנושיא אית *Ar* שבר גאון וג' F κ. εν τῃ . . . μεγαλη] > δ *Ar* τῃ αχρεοτ.] ܠܐ ܡܣܟܢܘܬܐ 𝕾 חרפה F η γαρ . . . λιμου] > αβγ iugalitas est mater inopiae δ luxuria mater est famis *Ambr. multo plura sed confusa et corrupta exhibet Spec.* > *Ar* απωλια B] -εια B[ab] A 14. '*In nonnullis diversus fuisse videtur textus Sin. ab' Vat.* (*vide* αβγδ *Ambr Spec.*) *apud Reusch sim.* M αλλα . . . παραυτικα] > *Ar* מן היום אשר תסתכם עמו M (*cf.* F) εαν . . . σοι] ופעולתך ישלם לך האל' M *aliter* F εαν 2°] *pr.* κ. A προσεχε . . . σου 2°] > M εν πασ. αναστρ. σ.] in omnibus sermonibus tuis αβ (> γ) in univers. serm. tuis *Spec.* 91 in omn. cogitationibus tuis δ בכל-דרכיך F 15. και ο μισ. μηδενι ποι.] ο μισεις αλλῳ συ ποιησεις *Clem. Strom.* ο μισ. αλλῳ μη ποι. *Chrys.* ο συ μισ. αλλῳ μη ποι. *Did. de Trin.* et quod oderis alio (alii γ) ne feceris αβγ *cf. Const. Apost.* 3. 15. 7. 2 *Aug. Serm. Bened. Reg. Ether. c. Elep. Fastid. de v. Chr. Greg. Mor. Paulin. Ep. Valer. Cemel. hom.* (*apud Reusch*) ודסנאני לך לחורני לא תעביד (*post v.* 13) *Ar* ואשר תש' לנפשך לא תעשה לאחרים (*post v.* 13) M לא תקים ולא תטור F οινον . . . οδῳ σ.] > *Ar* ומנע את עצמך משכרון ולא יאנה לך כל און M εις μεθ.] in ebrietate 𝕷 μεθη] οινος 44. 106 nequitia (*pr.* ulla αβ) αβγ שכור F τῃ οδ.] omni vita γ (δ *haec tantum habet*: ab ebrietate abstine) omni via αβ 16. διδου] διαδιδ. A πεινωντι] -ωσι 58, 74, 76, 249 αβδ (-ντι γ *Spec.* 24) *Ambr. de Tob.* τοις γυμν.] τοις *sup ras* B[ab] nudos lege αβ nudum veste γ da nudis δ lege nudis *Spec.* 24 παν . . . ελεημ.] > *Ar* M περισσευσῃ] -ευη A (בכל עניניך F) μη . . . οφθαλ.] ולא יקשה בעינך *Ar* M ולא ידע לבבך F σε] > A 17. εκχεον] funde αβ frange (+ funde) γ *Aug. Serm.* distribue δ effunde *Auct. imperf. in Mth. hom.* 26 אשוד *Ar* שפוך M constitue 𝔙 שלח F τ. αρτ.] *pr.* vinum tuum et

---

11. δῶρον = offering (cf. 𝕾), Lev. i. 2, Mark vii. 11. F's paraphrase is good.
12. See Test. Job xlv, Jub. iv. 33. See Introd., pp. 183 f., 186, and espec. 196.
13. Restore R[s] from 𝕷:—τοῦ μὴ λαβεῖν μίαν ἐξ αὐτῶν. On ἀχρεότης (R[v]) see Th. *Gram.*, p. 82.
16. Restore in R[s] τοὺς γυμνοὺς and *pr* περίβαλε (Is. lviii. 7) on basis of 𝕷.

17. The impossibility of *literally* 'pouring out bread' (R[v]) and the alleged paganism of the funeral rite here inculcated have led to numerous emendations and suggestions as to how a hypothetical Hebrew or Aramaic original could have been misread. Graetz (cf. δ) suggested שלח לחמך בקרב הצדקים; Hilgenfeld conjectured לבר הצדיקים misread as לקבר הצ'; Hitzig רחמיך misread לחמך; others שׁפע misread שׁפך. The difficulty, even if R[v] were the true text, is not sufficiently great to warrant these hypotheses. But the zeugma in R[s] (recovered from 𝕷 *Ar* M) is quite defensible and its claim to be the original text is now beyond controversy through the discovery of the Syriac and Arabic texts of Aḥiḳar (see Introd. p. 192, footnote 2, and Cambr. Aḥiḳar, pp. xlvii f.). It is, however, quite conceivable that 𝔙's *constitue* may be a mistranslation of an Aramaic imper. סך. For the custom of offering such sacrifices see Introd. p. 198.

18 just, and give not to sinners. Ask counsel of every man that is wise, and despise not any counsel
19 that is profitable. And bless the Lord thy God at all times, and ask of him that thy ways may be
made straight, and that all thy paths and counsels may prosper: for every nation hath not >good
counsel; <but> the Lord will give to them <all good things>; and whom he will the Lord
humbleth unto the nethermost Hades. And now, child, remember these commandments, and let them
20 not be blotted out of thy heart. And now, child, I shew thee that I left ten talents of silver in
21 trust with Gabael the brother of Gabri at Rages of Media. And fear not, my child, because we
have become poor: thou hast much wealth, if thou fear God and avoid every kind of sin and do
the things which are good in the sight of the Lord thy God.

iii. **The Preparations,** v. 1–17.

1 Then answered Tobias and said unto Tobit his father, All things, whatsoever thou hast com-
2 manded me, I will do, father. But how shall I be able to fetch it from him, seeing he knoweth
me not nor do I know him? What token shall I give him that he may recognize me and trust me
3 and give me the money? And the roads to Media I know not to journey there. Then answered
Tobit and said unto Tobias his son, His note of hand he gave me and a note of hand I gave him and
I parted it in two and we took to each of us *a part*, and I put it with the money, and now lo, it is
twenty years since I left this money in trust. And now, child, seek thee a trusty man which shall

α β +funde vin. t. γ *Aug. Serm.* +vin. t. δ vin. t. *Auct.* *pr.* ברי +וחמרך *Ar* +ויינך M επ. τ. ταφ.] super sepulcra α β γ 𝔖 cum iustis δ δικ.] +לעולם F και μη . . . αμαρτ.] > *Ar* M אל תתן עצת עקשות לרש׳ F δως] +illud 𝔏 18. ושמע למלכא טבא בכל עדן *Ar* (*cf. plen.* M) ζητησ.] אל תנח F καταφρονησης] μεταφρον. A επι . . . χρησ.] quoniam omne consilium utile est 𝔏 19ª. *plen. et multa e Script. addit.* F και1° . . . και2°] > *Ar* M και1°] > 𝔏 Κυρ. τ. θ.] Deo 𝔏 לבוראך F παρ' αυτ.] אלהך *Ar* οπως . . . ευοδωθωσιν] והוא יכשר אורחותך *Ar* (*cf.* M) διοτι . . . αγαθα] ארום לית לאינש מלך טב אלהין אלהא *Ar* כי אין ביד אדם שום עצה אלא ביד הב״ה (לבד) M παν εθν.] caeterae nationes α β γ omnes gentes δ βουλην] +bonam (-um δ) α β γ δ αλλ' αυτος . . . αγαθα] > α β γ Dominus dat nobis omnibus δ 19ᵇ *usque ad* 13: 6ª א:— δωσει Κυριος] αλλα αυτος ο Κυρ. διδωσιν BA 𝔖 (*Ar* M *v. supra*) βουλ. αγ.] παντα τ. αγαθα BA 𝔖 (*v. Ar* M *supra*) ον αν] ο εαν B ον εαν A quem ergo α β γ quemcunque δ Κυρ.] > BA 𝔖 ipse α β Deus γ (Dom. δ) > *Ar* M ταπεινοι] *pr.* allevat et quem voluerit ipse α β γ *pr.* exaltat et quemc. vult δ *pr.* מרים וכל רצבי *Ar* (*cf.* M F) εως ᾳδ. κατ.] καθως βουλονται (-εται A 𝔖) BA 𝔖 usque ad inferos γ (deorsum α β sub terram δ) α β γ δ > *Ar* M και νυν . . . σου] > 𝔖 ברי טר אמרי פומי ופקודי ולא ילכון מעינך *Ar* (*cf.* M) τ. εντολας ταυτ.] τ. -λων μου BA 𝔏 +ובכל נפשך . . . . וחזק M 20. παιδ.] > BA 𝔖 υποδεικνυω] επιδεικ. B οτι] τα BA 𝔖 > *Ar* M αργυρ.] *pr.* του BA *pr.* עסק *Ar* (*cf.* M) παρεθ.] *pr.* α BA 𝔖 *Ar* M Γαβαηλῳ] Γαμ. A Gabelo 𝔏 ܓܒܐܝܠ 𝔖 גבאל *Ar* גביאל M עביאל F Γαβρει] -ρεια B -ια A Gabahel α β Gabrin δ Gabeli γ > 𝔖 *Ar* אחרי קרובי M גבריאל F Αργοις] Ραγοις BA 𝔏 ܪܓܝܣ 𝔖 בקורי ריגש *Ar* במדית רגאש M +ארום לא ידעית יום מותי *Ar* M > F 21. και μη . . . επτωχ.] > *Ar* M και] > 𝔖 παιδ.] -διον *absciss. est in* A αγαθ.1°] > BA θεον] κ̄ν̄. A φυγης] αποστ. BA recesseris 𝔏 תיטר גרמך *Ar* ποιησ. . . . θ. σου] ובצנעה תהך עמיה *Ar* > M τ. αγαθ.] τ. αρεστον BA 𝔖 bene 𝔏 הישר F ενωπ. . . . σου] > 𝔏 Κ. τ. θεου σου] αυτου BA 𝔖 F +ולא תחסר כלום F

V. 1. τοτε] κ. BA M F ܗܝܕܝܢ 𝔖 > *Ar* Τ. τ. πατ. αυτ.] αυτῳ BA 𝔖 לאבוהי *Ar* M > F ποι. πατ.] πατ. ποι. *ante* παντα BA 𝔖 אעביד *Ar* 2. πως δε] αλλα π. BA 𝔖 *Ar* Quomodo autem 𝔏 *pr.* ועתה אבי תן לי עצה M αυτο] το αργυριον BA 𝔖 *Ar* M F hanc pecuniam α β γ pec. δ παρ' αυτ.] > BA מיד גבאל *Ar* M מן האיש F αυτος . . . εγω] > BA 𝔖 τι σημ. . . . εκει] > BA 𝔖 F *pr.* vel 𝔏 δῳ] אומר M κ. επιγνῳ με] > *Ar* M κ. πιστευ. μ.] > M το] hanc 𝔏 τ. εις Μ.] regionis illius 𝔏 τ. πορ.] > 𝔏 דיובילני (*ante* εις Μ.) *Ar* שילכו בהם M εκει] > 𝔏 *Ar* M 3. τοτε . . . ειπεν] > F τοτε . . . τουτο εγω] κ. εδωκ. αυτῳ το χειρογρ. BA 𝔖 τ. υιῳ αυτ.] ברי דין לך סימנא *Ar* M +אשר תאמר לו M > F χειρογρ. εδωκα αυτῳ . . . μετα τ. αργυρ.] et meum similiter accepit et divisit in duas partes unum accepi ego et alium posui cum ipsa pecunia α β γ et cyrographum meum accepit in quo posui pecuniam apud illum et alterum habeo δ טועניה יהב לי וטועני יהבית ליה (M קבל מידי) כמה דשויתי בספא ופקדתיניה (M > ופ׳) בידיה *Ar* M מיד הוציא כתב ידו ונתן לו ואמר הראה לו זה כתב ויתן לך הכסף F κ. νυν . . . τουτο εγω] ש׳ ע׳ דין יומא עד יומא ההוא ומן יומא *Ar* היום עשרים שנה M > F νυν παιδ.] ειπεν BA 𝔖 ומהר בני F πιστον] > BA 𝔖 F πορευσ. μ. σου] συμπ. σοι

19. Trans. presupposes Reusch's restoration of R^s. κατωτάτω (R^s), Th. *Gram.*, p. 183.

V. 3. R^v, in abridging, has altered the story considerably, and *Ar* and M substitute *bag* for *bond*, possibly through a confused recollection of a debased form of the Heb. original, e.g. Perles proposed either חרט (= *a writing* Isa. viii. 1, and *a bag*, 2 Ki. v. 23), or the Talmudic דיסקא.

go with thee, and we will give him wages, until thou return: and fetch thou this money from him.
4 And Tobias went out to seek a man who would go with him into Media and knew the way well;
(5) and he went out and found Raphael, the angel, standing before him. And he knew not that he was
5 an angel of God, and said unto him, Whence art thou, young man? And he said unto him, Of the
children of Israel thy brethren; and I am come hither to work. And he said unto him, Knowest
6 thou the way to go to Media? And he said unto him, Yea, I have often been there, and I know it
well and I know all the ways; many times did I go unto Media and lodged with Gabael our kinsman,
who dwelleth in **Rages** of Media; and it is two regular days' journey from Ecbatana to **Rages**;
7 for it lieth in the hill country, but Ecbatana in the middle of the plain. And he said unto him, Wait
for me, young man, until I go in and shew my father; for I need that thou go with me and I will
8, 9 give thee thy hire. And he said unto him, Behold, I will wait, only tarry not. And Tobias went
in and shewed Tobit his father and said unto him, Behold, I have found a man of our brethren
the children of Israel. And he said unto him, Call me the man, that I may know what is his family
and of what tribe he is, and whether he be a trusty man to go with thee, child.
10 (9) And Tobias went forth, and called him and said unto him, Young man, my father calleth thee.
And he came in to him, and Tobit saluted him first. And he said unto him, Much cheer to thee!
And Tobit answered and said unto him, What cheer have I any more, who am a man impotent in

BA eat tecum 𝔏 δωσομεν] -σω BA 𝔖 εως οτ. ελθ. κ. λαβε] εως ζω κ. λ. BA 𝔖 *Ar* M (בטרם אמות M) et dum adhuc vivo recipe *αβγ* vade fili dum vivo accipe *δ* ואולי תשובו בעודני חי מיד לקח בידו כספים F παρ' αυτ.] πορευθεις BA 𝔖 זל (*ante* εως) *Ar* M > F τουτο] > BA 𝔏 𝔖 *Ar* M F + וי׳ אלהי יש׳ וג׳ M 4. εξηλθ. δ.] κ. επορευθη BA et exiit 𝔏 + לשוק F Τωβιας] > BA 𝔖 ος πορ. . . . εξηλθ.] > BA 𝔖 דיהך עמיה *Ar* M πορ. μετ. αυτ.] eum duceret 𝔏 Μηδ.] *pr.* regionem 𝔏 > F ος] *pr.* et 𝔏 οδ.] + regionis illius 𝔏 > F κ. εξηλθ.] > 𝔏 F κ. ευρεν . . . εστιν] ומלאך ר׳ נדמה בדמות אדם ועמד בשוק ראה אותו ט׳ F Ρ.] *pr.* τον A 23, 64, 243, 248 τ. αγγελον] ος ην -λος BA 𝔖 + יו׳ M εστηκ.] > BA 𝔖 απεν. αυτ.] > BA 𝔏 𝔖 *Ar* εγνω] ηδει BA + ט׳ M οτι . . . εστιν] > BA 𝔖 + (צבאות) M 5. κ. ειπ. αυτ.] שאליה *Ar* ויאמר המלאך אל ט׳ M Ποθεν . . . ειπεν αυτ.3°] > BA 𝔖 F *reliq. v.* 5 *et* 6ª *aliter* F νεαν.] > *Ar* κ. ειπ. αυτῳ2°] אתיביה *Ar* ויען טוביה ויאמר M τ. αδελφ.] *pr.* חד *Ar* [מבני ישראל אנכי] M κ. εληλ.] veni 𝔏 > *Ar* M ωδε εργατ.] > *Ar* M ειπ. αυτ.3°] + Thobias 𝔏 *Ar* M επιστ. τ. οδ. πορ.] ει δυναμαι πορ. μετα σου BA 𝔖 nosti viam quae ducit 𝔏 אדני התדע ללכת עמי M εις Μηδ.] εν Ραγοις τ. Μηδ. BA 𝔖 in regionem Mediam 𝔏 + κ. ει εμπειρος ει τ. τοπων BA 𝔖 6. αυτῳ] + ο αγγ. BA 𝔖 *Ar* M Ναι . . . εκει] πορευσομαι μετα σ. BA 𝔖 multa ego (cog- *γ*) novi *αβγ* multa sunt quae scio *δ* > *Ar* εμπ. κ. επιστ. τας οδ. πασ.] της οδ. εμπ. BA teneo vias omn. *αβγ* vias omnes novi *δ* ידענא אורחיה *Ar* M (+ כלם M) πλεονακ. . . . Μηδ.] > BA 𝔖 *Ar* M aliquoties ivi in illam reg. 𝔏 ηυλιζ.] ηυλισθην *post* ημων BA במדי הוינא אושפיזא *Ar* M Γαβ. τῳ αδ.] Γαβαηλ τον αδ. BA 𝔖 עביאל F τ. οικουντι . . . πεδιῳ] > BA 𝔖 F εν Εκβ. τ. Μ.] in Rages civitate Medorum *αβγδ* ברגיש מדינת המדי M באגבתנים *Ar* κ. απεχει . . . τ. πεδιῳ] et est iter bidui ex Bathanis usque Rages civitatem Phagur quae posita est in monte et est Bathanu in medio campo *αβ* et est b. iter a Batanis usq. ad R., quae pos. est in m. et haec in m. c. *γ* et continet Ecbathnis dierum duo stadiorum R. pos. est in montem Ecbathana in m. c. *δ* עד ראגיש והיא בנויה בטורא ואגבתנים במישרא *Ar cf.* M (*v. Neub.*) εις Γαρρας . . . Εκβατανα] > א* *vid* (*hab.* א1 *mg*) 7. κ.1°] > *Ar* αυτ.] + Τωβιας BA 𝔏 𝔖 *Ar* M μενον με] υπομεινον με BA sustine 𝔏 הרף M νεαν.] > BA 𝔏 𝔖 ציבחר *Ar* מעט בחסדך M אדוני מעט F μεχρ. οτ. εισελθ.] κ. BA 𝔖 *Ar* υποδειξω] ερω BA 𝔖 hoc ipsum . . . nunciem 𝔏 + את הדבר M μου] > B *Ar* χρειαν . . . μισθ. σ.] > BA 𝔖 F דרגיג · · · · אגר אורחה *Ar* M 8. ειπ.] + Raph. ang. 𝔏 ιδου . . . προσκ.] πορευου BA 𝔖 + te 𝔏 *pr.* לך מהר כי M אל תאחר F ιδου] > *Ar* μον. μη χρ.] עד דתיתי *Ar* μονον] κ. BA M > 𝔖 F *pr.* עד שתשוב אלי M 9. Τωβειας . . . κ.2°] > BA 𝔖 *Ar* αυτῳ] τῳ πατρι BA 𝔖 *Ar* F ιδου] > *Ar* M F ανθρ.] > BA *γ* 𝔖 + טוב M בחור אחד F ευρον] -ηκα BA 𝔖 > *γ* τ. αδ. ημ.] > BA 𝔖 F ex (de *δ*) frat. nostr. *αβδ* > *γ* τ. υι. Ισρ.] ος συνπορευσεται (-μπ. B ᵇ A) μοι BA *αβδ* (> *γ*) 𝔖 *Ar* M מנוסה במקום ההוא F κ.3°] ο δε BA 𝔖 > F αυτ.] > BA 𝔏 𝔖 + Τωβ. *Ar* M אביו F καλεσ.] φωνησον BA roga 𝔏 *pr.* זל *Ar* μοι] προς με BA > *Ar* F τ. ανθρ.] αυτον BA 𝔖 *Ar* M F οπως] ινα BA 𝔖 τι . . . κ.] > BA 𝔏 𝔖 *Ar* M εκ] > BA 𝔖 φυλης] מקום M F εστιν2°] > B 𝔖 (*hab.* A 23, 64, 243, 248, 249) ινα πορ. μ. σου] του πορευθηναι μ. σ. BA 𝔖 *Ar* M F cui tu committaris 𝔏 παιδ.] > BA 𝔏 𝔖 *Ar* F εξηλθ. Τωβ. κ.] > BA 𝔖 F κ. ειπ. . . . σε] > BA 𝔖 *Ar* M F Νεαν.] + intra 𝔏 πατηρ] + meus 𝔏 10. προς αυτ.] רפאל לט׳ *Ar* M εχαιρ. . . . πρωτ.] ησπασαντο αλληλους BA 𝔖 F > *Ar* M κ. ειπ. αυτ. Χαιρ. . . . γινωσκω] > BA 𝔖 F ειπ.] *pr.* ille 𝔏 αυτ.] > 𝔏 *Ar* χαιρ. . . . γενοιτο] gaudium tibi semper sit (frater *αβ*) *αβγ* pax super te *δ* + איש האלהים M τι . . . χαιρειν] ut quid mihi gaudium *αβγ* quis dixit

6. The tradition of R[s] seems to have been handed down in slight confusion, but the mistakes are easily rectified. In א Ῥάγοις should be read with 𝔏 for Ἐκβατάνοις. Reusch emends καὶ Ῥάγαι for εἰς Γάρρας but εἰς Ῥάγας is simpler, and it is possibly an explanatory gloss. In *δ* Ecbatana has been dittographed, *stadiorum* written for *statutorum*; in *αβ quae* before *posita* is possibly a remnant of *Rages quae*.

the eyes, and I behold not the light of heaven, but lie in darkness like the dead which no more see
the light; while I live I am among the dead; the voice of men I hear, and themselves I behold not.
And he said unto him, Be of good cheer! it is nigh with God to heal thee; be of good cheer! And
Tobit said unto him, My son Tobias wisheth to go unto Media; canst thou go with him and direct
him? And I will give thee thy hire, brother. And he said unto him, I shall be able to go with
him, and I know all the ways, and often have I gone to Media and passed through all its plains
11 (10) and mountains, and all its ways I know. And he said unto him, Brother, of what family art thou,
12 (11) and out of what tribe? Shew me, brother. And he said, What need hast thou of a tribe? And he
13 (12) said unto him, I would know truly of what *tribe* thou art, brother, and what thy name. And he said
14 (13) unto him, I am Azarias, the son of Ananias the great, of thy kinsmen. And he said unto him, Welcome
and safety, brother; and be not bitter towards me, brother, because I wished to know the truth and
thy family. And thou chancest to be a kinsman, and thou art of a noble and good lineage: I knew
Ananias and Nathan, the two sons of Semelias the great, and they used to go with me to Jerusalem
and worship with me there and they went not astray. Thy brethren are good men; thou art of
15 (14) a good stock, and I bid thee welcome. And he said unto him, I give thee a drachma a day as

mihi pax δ ואית שלם עלי למה אירע לי כל דא *Ar* M κ. εγω . . . οφθαλ.] > *Ar* κ. ου . . . ουρ.] > M κειμαι] יושב עור M οι νεκρ. οι μηκ. θε. τ. φ.] > 𝕷 *Ar* M ζων εγω εν νεκρ.] mortuus inter vivos *αβγ* > δ *Ar* M φωνην . . . βλεπ.] > M ανθρωπων] מלין *Ar* αυτους ℵ*] αυτος ℵ^{c a} ipsos 𝕷 וגברא *Ar* αυτῳ 3°] + Raph. ang. 𝕷 רפ׳ *Ar* המלאך M Θαρσ. 1°] > δ *Ar* M εγγυς . . . ιασ. σε] יכיל אל׳ לאסאה עינך ארום גבר חסידא את *Ar* (יאמר יי) מי שעור אותך ממאור עיניך הוא ירפאך כי צדיק אתה ויען טובי ויאמר כן M θαρσ. 2°] > *αβγ* *Ar* M ε. Μηδ.] in regionem Mediam 𝕷 κ. αγαγ. αυτ.] > *Ar* M κ. δωσ.] dabo 𝕷 וניתן *Ar* αδελ.] > *Ar* ειπ. 5°] + Raph. ang. 𝕷 המלאך M αυτῳ 6°] > 𝕷 M Δυνησ. . . . μετ' αυτ.] יכילנא גברא שליחא אנא *Ar* כן אוכל M επιστ.] > *Ar* M κ.] quoniam 𝕷 Μηδ.] *pr.* regionem 𝕷 κ. πολλακ. . . . διηλθ. παντα] > *Ar* M παντα, πασ.] > *Ar* τ. ορη] תחומיא *Ar* כל הגבולים M πασ. τ. οδους] > M 11. ειπ.] + Tobis 𝕷 *Ar* M αυτῳ] > 𝕷 *Ar* M Αδελ.] > *Ar* M ποι. πατριας ει κ. εκ π. φ.;] εκ π. φ. κ. εκ π. πατριδος συ ει BA𝕾F מאיזה מקום אתה ומאיזה שבט אתה ומאי זה *Ar* מאדין שבטא את ושום קרתא דאת דייר בה עיר M αδελ.] > BA𝕷𝕾 *Ar* F 12. ειπ.] + αυτῳ BA𝕾 + Thobis 𝕷 רפ׳ *Ar* המל׳ M Τι χρ. εχ. φυλ.;] φυλην κ. πατριαν συ ζητεις η μισθιον ος συμπορευσεται μετα του (τ *sup ras* B^{ab}) υιου σ. BA δ *Salv. Ep.* 9 𝕾 (*cf.* F) עוד תבקש ויש לך שכיר שילך עם בנך כרצונך *Ar* אם לית אנא כשר בעינך זיל ובליש גברא חורנא דיהך עם ברך M εχ. φυλ.] scire genus meum vel tribum meam mercenarium desideras genus et tribum meam cur quaeris (desid. aut tribum et patriam meam γ) sed si valde exigis *αβγ* κ. ειπ. αυτ. Βουλ. . . . σου] > *αβγ* (*hab.* δ) *Salv. Ep.* 9 αυτ.] + Τωβ. BA𝕾M γνων.] επιγν. BA *pr.* לא תכעום עלי ד *Ar* τα κατ' αλ.] > BA𝕾 MF τινος ει] το γενος σου BA𝕾F + זרעיתא *Ar* > M αδελ.] *post* βουλομαι BA τι] > BA𝕾F ומאי זו M σου] > BAF + משפחה אתה M 13. κ. . . . αυτ.] > *αβγ* κ.] ος δε B ο δε 64, 71, 74, 76, 243, 248, 249 αυτ.] > BA𝕾 + המל׳ M Εγω] > A + sum 𝕷 Αναιαν] *pr.* ממשפחת F τ. μεγαλου] *pr.* de domo Sellemmiae δ *pr.* מביתא דשלמיה *Ar* *pr.* מבית שלומית M *pr.* בן עזריה F τ. αδελφ. σ.] > F 14. αυτ.] + Thobis 𝕷 ט׳ *Ar* M κ. σωζ.] > BA𝕾 πικραν.] οργισ. BA𝕾 *Ar* F irascaris 𝕷 αδελ.] > BA𝕷𝕾F τ. αληθ. εβουλ. γνωναι κ. τ. πατριαν] εζητησα τ. φυλ. σ. κ. τ. πατριαν σ. (σ. > B^{ab} A 23, 55, 58, 64, 71, 74, 76, 106, 108) επιγν. BA𝕾 vere (-um γ) scire de genere tuo *αβγ* scire veritatem generis tui δ מבקש לדעת דבר אבות ממשפחתך M τ. αληθ.] > *Ar* F κ. σ. τυγχ.] והא *Ar* M עתה ידעתי F ων] μου BA𝕾 ex fratr. meis 𝕷 > *Ar* M κ. εκ γεν. καλ. κ. αγ.] εκ τ. καλ. κ. α. γ. BA𝕾 מזרעיתא טבא *Ar* ει συ] > BA𝕷𝕾 εγινωσκον] επεγιν. γαρ εγω B εγιγν. γ. ε. A Nosti *αβγ* Uno vero foderas δ אתה ידעת M Ναθαν] Ιαθ. BA Athanian γ Nathanian δ (Nathan *αβ*) ܢܬܢ 𝕾 יותם F δυο] > BAγF υιους] > γ Σεμελιου] Σεμεου B -ειου A Semeiae *αβ* Sellemmiel δ (> γ) ܫܡܥܝܐ 𝕾 דשלמיה *Ar* שלומית M שלמון F τ. μεγαλ.] novi magni viri δ (magni viri *αβ*) > γ κ. α. συνεπ. μ.] ως επορευομεθα κοινως BA𝕾 *pr.* et dixit ille angelus γ κ. προσεκυν.] -κυνειν BA𝕾 *pr.* כד יתיבנא בארעא ישראל *Ar* M > F μετ' εμ. εκει] αναφεροντες τ. πρωτοτοκα κ. τ. δεκατας τ. γενηματων BA𝕾F επλαν.] + εν τῃ πλανῃ B𝕾 τ. πλανῃ 64, 248, 249 την πλανην A 23, 55, 71, 74, 76, 236 + באנונא דטעו *Ar* + אחרי אלהי נכר הארץ כאשר תעו M לא עזבו · · · · · ולא טעו אחרי ההבל אשר טעו F οι αδ. σου] τ. αδελφων ημ. BA𝕾 hi omn. fratr. nostri *αβ* > γδ אחינו MF ανθρωπ. αγαθ.] > BAγδ𝕾 optimi sunt *αβ* > *Ar* M בני ישראל F αγαθ.] καλ. B μεγαλ. A 55, 58, 64, 71, 74, 76, 236, 243, 248, 249 > M *pr.* מזרע קדושים F συ] αδελφε BA𝕾 > MF κ. χαιρ. ελθ.] > BA𝕾MF salvus eas et salvus venias *αβ* salvus sis γ cum pace venias δ 15^{a} *post* 15^{b} M κ. ειπ. αυτ.] αλλ' (-λα A) ειπον μοι BA אם תרצה F Εγω . . . μισθ.] τινα σοι εσομαι μισθ. διδοναι BA διδωμι] dabo 𝕷 τ. ημεραν δραχ.] δρ. της ημερας (*in* της *parvam ras prae se fert* B) BA ܙܘܙܐ ܒܝܘܡܐ 𝕾 didragmam diurnam 𝕷 טרפעיקא כל יומא *Ar* זוז בבל יום M בבל יום בקע משקלו F τ. δεοντα] ומיכלך *Ar* M > F ομοιως] ως κ.

---

15. The periphrastic future ἔσομαι διδόναι is characteristic of R^{v}'s strong vernacular style.

16 (15) wages, and those things that be necessary for thee, as unto my son; and go thou with my son, and
I will add something to thy wages. And he said unto him, I will go with him, and fear thou not;
17 (16) we shall go safe and return safe unto thee, because the way is secure. And he said unto him,
Blessing befall thee, brother! And he called his son, and said unto him, Child, prepare what is
needful for the journey and go forth with thy kinsman. And God which is in heaven preserve you
there and restore you to me in safety and his angel accompany you with deliverance, child.

B. The Departure, v. 17^b–vi. 1.

And he went forth to go upon his journey; and he kissed his father and mother, and Tobit
18 (17) said unto him, Farewell. And his mother wept, and said unto Tobit, Why is it that thou hast sent
19 (18) away my child? Is he not the staff of our hand, and doth he not go in and out before us? Let
20 (19) not money be added to money: but let it be a ransom for our child. As the Lord hath given
21 (20) us to live, so doth it suffice us. And he said unto her, Trouble not; our child shall go in peace, and
in peace come unto us and thine eyes shall see *him* in the day when he shall come unto thee in peace.
22 (21) Trouble not: fear not for them, sister; for a good angel shall go with him, and his journey shall be
6 1 (22) prospered, and he shall return in peace. And she was silent from her weeping.

16. κ.1°] עד אשר תלכו F ובשלום תבואו בעזרת האל + M > BA 𝕾 *Ar* κ. πορ. . . . μου] > F BA 𝕾 τ. μισθῳ] επι τ. μισθον BA 𝕾 adiiciam 𝕷 επιπροσθ.] ετι προσθ. BA ואם ישיבכם הק"בה בשלום עוד + M (*cf.* F) ad merc. tuam 𝕷 + εαν υγιαινοντες (τε *sup. ras.* A ^a?) επιστρεψητε BA + כראוי F κ. ειπ. . . . ασφαλ.] > BA 𝕾 αυτῳ] אמר לו כדבריך כן אעשה F ענא רפ׳ לא תחדל דאנא אחך עם ברך וניתב בשלום *Ar* (*cf.* M) + Raph. ang. 𝕷 המל׳ M κ. μη] ne 𝕷 προς σε] > M 17. ειπ.1°] > BA *pr.* Thobis 𝕷 𝕾 > *Ar* F αυτ.1°] > BA 𝕷 *Ar* F Ευλογια σοι γεν.] ευδοκησαν (*pr.* κ. A) ουτως BA 𝕾 bene iter age frater et contingat tibi α β bene iter agere contingat tibi γ > δ *Ar* M F bene ambulatis 𝖁 κ. εκαλ.] > BA 𝕾 + ט׳ *Ar* M τ. υι. αυτ.] > BA 𝕾 *pr.* Thobiam 𝕷 *Ar* F αυτῳ] προς Τωβιαν BA Παιδ.] > BA 𝕷 𝕾 *Ar* M ετοιμ. τα] Ετοιμος γινου BA 𝕾 praepara te 𝕷 *Ar* πρ. τ. οδ.] + κ. ευοδωθειητε BA > 𝕷 𝕾 *Ar* לאלתר F κ.4°] + ητοιμασεν ο υι. αυτ. τα προς τ. οδον BA et praeparavit (-erunt ea quae in itinere haberent δ) se ad viam Thobias (*post* σωτηριας) α β γ δ (*cf.* F) εξελθε] Πορευου *pr.* κ. ειπ. αυτῳ ο πατ. αυτου BA ובא לצאת לדרכו F αδελφου σου] ανθρωπ. BA 𝕾 והתחיל אביו מברכו כך F κ. ο θ. ο εν τ. ουρ.] ο δε εν τ. ουρ. οικων (κατοικ- A 58, 243, 248, 249) θ. BA 𝕾 Deus autem q. in caelo est 𝕷 אלהא דשמיא *Ar* אל שדי M יי אלהי השמים השכן בשמי מרים F διασ. υμ. εκ.] ευοδωσει τ. οδον υμων BA 𝕾 F perducat vos ibi cum pace 𝕷 *Ar* M κ. αποκ. υμ. πρ. εμ. υγ.] > BA 𝕾 κ. ο αγγ. . . . μετα σωτ.] וישלח מלאכיה עמכון ויצליח אורחכון *Ar* M F συνοδ.] συνπορευθητω (συμ- B ^b A) BA comitetur 𝕷 μ. σωτ.] > BA 𝕾 παιδ.] > BA 𝕷 𝕾 *Ar* M εξηλθεν πορ. τ. οδον αυτου] -θαν (-ον A 44, 58, 64, 71) αμφοτεροι απελθειν BA 𝕾 F exiit ut iret α β γ egressi sunt ut proficiscerentur δ *Ar* M κ.9°] + ο κυων τ. παιδαριου μετ᾽ αυτων BA 𝕾 F εφιλ. τ. πατ. αυτ. κ. τ. μητ.] > BA 𝕾 F κ. ειπ. αυτ. T.] > BA 𝕾 F + pat. suus 𝕷 ואמרו ליה *Ar* M Πορ.] > BA 𝕾 F + fili 𝕷 F υγ.] > BA 𝕾 F + venias 𝕷 18. κ. εκλ.] εκλ. δε BA + Αννα B ותחל אמו לבכות M Τωβ.] patri eius 𝕷 אל בעלה M F οτι απεστειλ.] εξαπ. BA 𝕾 F לא דחילתא למשלח *Ar* M μου] ημων BA 𝕷 𝕾 > *Ar* M F ουχι αυτος] η ουχι η BA ܠܐ ܗܘ 𝕾 ארום *Ar* ραβδ. τ. χειρ. ημων] בר יחידאי הוא לנא *Ar* בן זקונים הוא (לנו) M κ. αυτος . . . εκπορευεται] εν τ. εισ—εσθαι αυτον κ. εκ—εσθαι BA 𝕾 ενωπ. ημ.] > F 19. Nunquam esset pecunia illa sed purgamento sit (filio meo γ) α β γ ܟܣܦܐ ܠܟܣܦܐ ܠܐ ܢܬܬܘܣܦ ܐܠܐ ܦܘܪܩܢܐ ܢܗܘܐ ܕܒܪܢ 𝕾 19, 20. בלא כספא פרנסנא אלהא *Ar* ובלא אותו כסף יחיינו אלהינו M *plen. et aliter* F 20. > M ως א*] + γαρ א ^ca BA 𝕾 ικ. ημ.] + υπαρχει BA 𝕾 sufficiebat nobis 𝕷 21. αυτῃ] + T. BA 𝕷 𝕾 *Ar* M εχε] + αδελφη BA 𝕾 πορ. . . . υγιαιν.2°] > BA 𝕾 + 21^c *et* 22^a *Ar* *plen. et aliter* F προς ημ.] > BA 𝕾 *Ar* οψοντ.] + αυτον BA 𝕷 𝕾 *Ar* εν τ. ημ. η αν ελθ.] > BA 𝕾 F דיתוב *Ar* > M πρ. σε υγ. μη λογ. εχ.] > BA 𝕷 𝕾 M F בשלום *Ar* μη φοβ.] > BA 𝕾 F π. αυτων] > BA δ 𝕾 F de illo α β γ *Ar* M αδελ.] *supr.* BA *post* εχε > F 22. αγγ. . . . οδ. αυτου] ישלח מלאכו עמו ויצליח דרכו M (*v. supra v.* 21 *Ar*) συνελευσεται] συνπορευσεται B συμπ. B^b συνπορευεται A 23, 249 𝕾 𝕷 ευοδ.] bene disponet 𝕷

VI. 1. εσιγ.] επαυσατο BA 𝕾 cessavit 𝕷 ומנעי *Ar* F ותוסף M κλαιουσα] מלמבכי *Ar* F לבכות עוד M

16^b. Cf. *quoniam in via recta est*, Jub. xxvii. 17.
18. ἔκλαυσεν. Cf. *flevit*, Jub. xxvii. 13.
19. φθάσαι. lit. *come*, φθάνω having almost entirely lost its anticipatory force in the LXX (Th. *Gram.*, p. 289); Müller can only understand the phrase as a translation from a Semitic original.

A ransom for: this translation can be justified by a comparison with Ignatius, *Ep. to Ephes.* viii. 1, while xviii. 1 of the same epistle suggests the alternative 'offscouring for our child'.

21 f. R^s more closely than R^v resembles the words 'et dixit Isaac ad Rebeccam, Soror, noli flere Iacob filium meum, quoniam in pace ibit et in pace rediet . . . dirigentur omnes viae eius . . . quousque revertatur ad nos in pace et videbimus eum cum pace. Noli ergo timere de illo, soror mea' in Jub. xxvii. 14-17.

C. The Events of the Journey, vi. 2–ix. 6.

i. **Tobias' Adventure with the Fish, vi. 2–9.**

2 (vi. 1) And the young man went forth, and the angel with him, and the dog went forth with him and
journeyed with them; and they journeyed both of them together. And once night came upon
3 (2) them, and they lodged by the river Tigris, and the young man went down to wash his feet in the river
Tigris. And a great fish leaped up out of the water, and would have swallowed the foot of the young
4 (3) man. And he cried out. And the angel said unto the young man, Grasp and take hold of the fish.
5 (4) And the young man caught hold of the fish, and hauled it up on to the land. And the angel said
unto him, Open the fish, and take out its gall and the heart and liver and put them by thee, and cast
6 (5) away the inwards; for its gall and heart and liver are for an useful medicament. And the young
man opened the fish and collected the gall and the heart and the liver, and he roasted part of the
7 (6) fish and did eat, and left part thereof salted. And they journeyed both of them together until they
drew nigh to Media. And then the young man asked the angel and said unto him, Brother Azarias,
8 (7) what is the medicament in the heart and the liver of the fish and in the gall? And he said unto him,
As regards the heart and the liver of the fish, make thou a smoke before a man or a woman who hath

2. κ. εξ. . . . αυτων] > BA 𝔖 F עמיה (*pr.* המלאך M) ורפאל (+לדרכו M) אזל טליא *Ar* M παιδ.] + illorum 𝔏 εξ. μετ' αυτου κ.] > 𝔏 επορ. μετ' αυτων] secutus est eos 𝔏 κ. επορ. αμφ.] οι δε πορευομενοι τ. οδον BA 𝔖 F > *Ar* M עד הערב (*cum hac sententia*) F κ. ετ. αυτ. νυξ μια] ηλθον εσπερας BA 𝔖 *Ar* M et comprehendit illos proxima nox 𝔏 κ. ηυλισθ. επ. του Τιγρ. ποτ.] επ. τον Τιγριν ποταμον (בעיר לדיקיאה F) κ. ηυλιζοντο εκει BA 𝔖 *Ar* M F 3. κ. κατεβη τ. παιδιον] τ. δε παιδαριον κατ. BA 𝔖 et descendit Thobias 𝔏 M ורחט ט' *Ar* והלך הנ' ונכנס F περινιψ.] περικλυσ. BA לקרר גופו F τ. ποδ.] > BA 𝔖 ε. τ. Τιγριν ποτ.] > BA 𝔖 in flumine 𝔏 לנהרא (*ante* περινιψ.) *Ar* M F αναπηδησας] -επηδησεν (*seq. ras.* 2 *circ. litt. in* B) BA נפק *Ar* M F *pr.* ובשלו *Ar* M μεγας] > BA 𝔖 *Ar* M εκ τ. υδ.] απο τ. ποταμου κ. BA 𝔖 *Ar* F εβουλ. . . . παιδ.] circumplexus est pedes eius pene puerum devoraverat (-ravit γ) α β γ ut puerum devoraret δ εβουλετο] -ηθη BA > *Ar* M καταπειν] -πιειν B^ab A τ. ποδ. του παιδ.] τ. παιδαριον BA 𝔖 F לחמא דטליא *Ar* M κ. εκρ. ℵ*] κ. απο τ. φοβου εκρ. ℵ^ca > BA 𝔖 et exclamavit puer α β γ δ + Domine, piscis invadit me (*cf.* 𝔙) δ + טליא *Ar* והיה המלאך רץ והיה צווח לנער אל תירא אלא F 4. κ. ο . . . ειπ.] > F κ. ο] ο δε BA 𝔖 רפ' *Ar* τ. παιδ. ειπ.] ειπ. αυτω BA 𝔖 *Ar* M κ. εγκρατ. γεν.] > BA 𝔖 ולא תשבקיניה *Ar* M כאיש חיל F τ. παιδ. του ιχθ.] τον ιχθ. τ. παιδ. BA 𝔖 + מיד F ανηνεγκ.] ανεβαλ. BA 𝔖 eduxit 𝔏 > M αυτ. . . . γην] > M מן־הנהר F 5. ο αγγ.] רפ' *Ar* + רפ' F Αναςχ.] Ανατεμε BA בזע נונא במציע *Ar* M εξελε] λαβων BA 𝔖 tolle 𝔏 χολ. . . . καρδ. . . . ηπ.] καρδ. . . . ηπ. . . . χολ. BA 𝔖 F ליביה *Ar* הלב ואת המרה M αυτου] > BA F κ. αποθες αυτα μετα σαυτου] θες ασφαλως BA 𝔖 F > *Ar* κ. τ. εγκ. εκβ.] > BA 𝔖 *Ar* M F *post* utilia 𝔏 ε. φαρμ. χρησ. . . . αυτ.] > BA 𝔖 *Ar* F necessaria haec ad medicamenta utilia 𝔏 כי טובים הם לרפאות M 6. *post* v. 9 *Ar* αναςχ. τ. παιδ. . . . ηπαρ.] εποιησεν τ. παιδ. ως ειπ. αυτω ο αγγ. BA 𝔖 F עבד בן ט' ונסב ליבא ומררתא דנונא *Ar* ויעש בן הנער M κ. ωπτ. του ιχθ. κ.] τ. δε ιχθυν οπτησαντες BA 𝔖 et partem piscis assaverunt et α β et partem pis. adsumptos γ piscem vero assavit δ assavit carnes eius 𝔙 ואת הדג תקנו F εφαγεν] -ον BA 𝔖 tulerunt in via α β sustulerunt in victu γ manducaverunt δ secum tulerunt 𝔙 κ. αφηκεν εξ αυτ. ηλισμ.] > BA 𝔖 caetera autem (> γ) salierunt α β reliquum autem eius in via reliquit δ caetera salierunt quae sufficerunt eis quosque etc. 𝔙 ומותרא שבק באורחה *Ar* והנותר הניח M > F επορ.] ωδευον BA 𝔖 ואזלו עד מדי *Ar* *pr.* ועמדו F αμφ.] > 𝔏 *Ar* M F κοιν.] > BA 𝔏 𝔖 *Ar* M εως . . . ηγγισ.] > *Ar* M εις M.] εν Εκβατανοις BA 𝔖 in regionem Mediorum 𝔏 > *Ar* אינקבמנים F 7. *A versu* 7 *in codicibus* 44, 106, 107 *incipit graec. textus R^c* > *Ar* τοτε] > BA 𝔏 𝔖 ηρωτ. τ. παιδ. τον αγγ. κ. ειπ. αυτω] ειπ. τ. παιδ. (ט' M) τω αγγ. BA 𝔖 M τι τ. φαρμ. εν] τι εστιν BA 𝔖 F quod remedium est 𝔏 מה רפואה תעשה M τ. καρδ. . . . τ. ηπ. του ιχθ. . . . τ. χολ.] το ηπαρ κ. η καρδ. κ. η χολ. του ιχθ. BA 𝔖 F hoc fel cor et iecur piscis 𝔏 מלב הדג והמרה M vv. 8, 9 *pr.* v. 6 *Ar* 8 *aliter* F ειπ.] *pr.* ang. 𝔏 > *Ar* αυτ.] > 𝔏 *Ar* η καρδ.] τ. -ιαν ℵ^ca הוא טב *Ar* κ. τ. ηπ.] > *Ar* M τ. ιχθ.] αυτου ιχθ. ℵ* > BA 𝔏 𝔖 *Ar* M καπν.] -σαι ℵ^ca ταυτα δε -σαι (τ. εδει -σαι A) *post* πονηρ.

VI. 2. Even *Ar* and M employ the Greek word *Tigris* to denote the river known in O.T. as חדקל and in most North Semitic lands as דקלת (so Syriac) or דגלת (Jewish Aramaic and Mandaic).

3. *Ar* would directly support the originality of R^s if his 'ate the bread of the young man' was written with a knowledge or indistinct recollection—Bickell believed *Ar* was a direct translation—of a Hebrew text in which ויאב ללחם had been changed into ויאכל לחם after the loss of רגל. Nöld.'s objections (p. 59) to the use of אבה would apply only to classical Hebrew (but even so, see Job xxxix. 9, Is. i. 9). ἔκραξεν (Th. *Gram.*, p. 234) of R^s is supported by F (which attributes the cry to Raphael) as well as *Ar* M.

8. ἀπάντημα = פגע only in 3 (1) Kings v. 4 (18), ואין פגע רע אין שטן, and in Eccles. ix. 11, and appears in Sym. Ec. ii. 14, and Hos. xiii. 14. It is not a medical term. R^v has evidently rewritten this verse with due regard to the technicalities

an attack of a demon or an evil spirit; and every attack will flee from him, and they shall nevermore
9 (8) find an abode with him. And as for the gall—anoint a man's eyes, upon which white films have
come up, <or> blow into them on the white films, and they become well.

ii. Tobias at Raguel's Home and his Marriage with Sarah, vi. 10–viii. 20.

Raphael's plans for Tobias' marriage, vi. 10–18.

10 (9) 11 (10) And when he had entered into Media and was already drawing nigh to Ecbatana, Raphael
saith unto the young man, Brother Tobias. And he said unto him, Here am I. And he said unto him,
In the house of Raguel we must lodge this night, the man being thy kinsman; and he hath a daughter
12 (11) whose name is Sarah. And he hath no son nor daughter but Sarah alone, and thou art nearer kin
to her than any man to inherit her, and what things are her father's it is right for thee to inherit;
(12) and the maid is wise and steadfast and exceeding honourable, and her father is an honourable man.
13 And he said, It is right for thee to take her; and hear me, brother, and I will speak this night unto
her father concerning the maid, that we may take her to be thy bride. And when we return from
Rages we will celebrate her marriage. And I know that Raguel can in no wise keep her back
from thee or marry her to another—to incur liability to death according to the decree of the book
of Moses—and because he knoweth that the inheritance appertaineth to thee to take his daughter
before any man. And now, hear me, brother, and let us speak concerning the maid this night and
we will betroth her to thee; and, when we return from Rages, we will take her and let us lead her

BA 𝕾 fumigatur 𝕷 לא קטרא מיניה *Ar* יועיל להקטיר ממנו M η γυν.] > *Ar* M η] et 𝕷 ῳ] > BA 𝕾 απαντ.] > BA 𝕾 *Ar* M (*cf.* לנוזקים F) δαι. η πν. πον.] εαν τινα οχλῃ δ–ιον η πν–α π.–ρον BA (*cf.* 𝕾) רוח רעה או רוח השדים M φευξ. . . . αιωνα] ου μηκετι (ουκετι ου μη A) οχληθῃ BA 𝕾 ταυτα θυμιασεις εμπροσθεν αυτου κ. φευξεται απ' αυτου 44, 106 ויערקון מיניה *Ar* M μειν. μετ' αυτ.] apparebit 𝕷 (*cf.* 6, 18) 9. κ. η] η δε BA ενχρ.] εγχρ. B^{a?b} 44, 106 facit ad unguendos 𝕷 למימשח מיניה *Ar* תועיל למשח M אם ימשח F ανθρ. οφθ. ου λ. αν. επ. αυτ.] -ον ος εχει λ. (λ–μα A) εν τοις οφθ. BA 𝕾 οφθαλμους εν οις αν λευκωμα (-ατα 106) 44, 106 עינין דאית בהון חיורא *Ar* M בעיני כל בעלי שבלול בע' F εμφ. . . . λευκ.] > BA 𝕾 *Ar* M η εμφ. εις αυτους 44, 106 *pr.* vel 𝕷 κ. υγ.] κ. ιαθησεται BA 𝕾 M -ουσιν 44, 106 *Ar* F ut ad sanitatem perveniat α β γ 10. κ. οτε] Ως δε BA F κ. 44, 106, 107 > *Ar* M εισηλθ. . . . ηδη] > BA 44, 106, 107 𝕾 M F εισηλθεν] -ον α β γ *Ar* Μηδ.] *pr.* regionem 𝕷 κ. ηδη] > 𝕷 *Ar* M ηγγιζ.] προσηγγισαν BA 𝕾 α β γ F παραγινονται 44, 106, 107 ואתו *Ar* M εις Εκβατανων] τ. Ραγη BA εις Εκβατανα 44, 106, 107 civitati Bathanis α β civ. Exbathanis γ ܠܐܚܡܬܢ 𝕾 לאג־בתנים M לעיר ריגו F 11. λεγει] ειπ. BA F κ. ειπ. 44, 106, 107 𝕷 𝕾 *Ar* M Ρ.] ο αγγελ. BA 𝕾 44, 106, 107 F Raph. ang. α β γ τ. παιδ.] > 44, 106, 107 α β γ *Ar* M Τ.] > BA 𝕾 44, 106, 107 α β F לט' *Ar* M αδελ.] > 44, 106, 107 α β F κ. ειπ.1° . . . αυτῳ2°] > BA 44, 106, 107 α β 𝕾 *Ar* M F αυτῳ Ιδου εγω] quid est γ Εν τοις Ρ.] παρα Ραγουηλῳ (-ηλ A) *post* αυλισθησ. BA 𝕾 τ. νυκ. ταυτ.] Σημερον (*post* αδελφε) BA 44, 106, 107 > *Ar* M F δει ημ.] > BA 𝕾 *Ar* M *ante* σημερον 44, 106, 107 אם תיצה F αυλισθη.] -σομεθα (*post* σημερον) BA 𝕾 M F תיתי *Ar* ο ανθρωπ.] αυτος BA 𝕾 *Ar* M F συγγεν. σ.] גבר סב *Ar* M + ממשפחת בית אביך F εστ. αυτ.] > 44, 106, 107 θυγ.] + μονογενης A 𝕾 + speciosam 𝕷 + μια υπαρχει αυτῳ κ. αυτ. καλ. τ. ειδει 44, 106, 107 M F שפירתא לחדא *Ar* η ον. Σ.] > 44, 106, 107 η ονομα] -ατι BA 12. κ.1°] > BA sed 𝕷 υι. . . . μον.] λαλησω περι αυτης του δοθηναι (דיתנינה *Ar* M) σοι αυτην εις γυναικα BA *Ar* M (*cf.* F) > 𝕾 κ.2°] οτι BA 𝕾 συ] σοι A 𝕾 εγγ. . . . δικ. κληρ.] επιβαλλει η κληρονομια αυτης κ. συ μονος ει εκ του γενους αυτης BA 𝕾 το δικαιωμα αυτης εστι κληρονομησαι πατερα αυτης κ. σοι δικαιωμα λαβειν αυτην σοι εγγιζει παρα παντας 44, 106, 107 > *Ar* M κληρον. αυτην . . . κορασιον] ut possideas (+ eam et α β) haereditatem illius et omnem substantiam patris eius; accipe illam uxorem; etenim (est autem γ) puella haec α β γ (*cf.* F) > *Ar* M τ. κορ.] αυτη 44, 106, 107 *Ar* M φρον. κ. ανδρ. κ. καλ. λιαν] καλ. κ. φρον. εστιν BA 𝕾 ανδρεια κ. φρονιμη (+ κ. καλ. 106, 107) 44, 106, 107 sapiens, fortis et bona valde et constabilita 𝕷 והיא יחידה לאביהא (*post* νυμφην v. 13) *Ar* טובת שכל M ואתה יחיד ואת יחידה F κ. ο π. αυτ. καλ.] > BA 𝕾 F καλ.] αγαπᾳ αυτην 44, 106, 107 M diligit illam 𝕷 והוא רחים לה טובא והיא אתתא טבתא ודחלת שמיא *ante* κ. οταν επιστρεψ. v. 13 *Ar* M F 13. κ.1° . . . αυτην1°] > BA 44, 106, 107 𝕾 *Ar* M F (et α β) quaecunque possedit (-sidet γ) illi tradet (dabit ei γ); tibi ergo destinata est haereditas patris eius et te oportet accipere illam α β γ ακουσ.] *pr.* νυν BA 44, 106, 107 𝕷 𝕾 M F > *Ar* αδελ.] > BA 44, 106, 107 𝕾 *Ar* M בקולי F λαλησω] loquere α β γ M נדבר F τ. πατ.] + αυτης BA 𝕾 F > 44, 106, 107 α β γ M לית *Ar* π. τ. κορ. . . . νυμφ.] > BA 𝕾 F דיתנינה לך לאנתו *Ar* בעבורה M π. τ. κορ.] π. αυτης 44, 106, 107 α β γ

---

of the magico-medical profession (cf. Nestle, *Septuag.* iii, p. 27), an interesting parallel to St. Luke's treatment of St. Mark (cf. Hobart, *The Medical Language of St. Luke*). Moreover, ὀχλεῖν (R^v) and its compounds are characteristically medical and Lucan (see Luke vi. 18; Acts v. 16, xv. 19). For a less speedy ophthalmic cure in papyri see Deissm. *L.A.E.*, p. 132.

13. R^s had *Rages* in 13^a, as in 13^b, not *Raguel*, and ὀφειλήσειν not -σιν (א) or -σει (R^v), leaving it indeterminate whether the subject is Raguel (α β) or the suitors (γ); see Introd., p. 196.

14 (13) back with us to thy home. Then Tobias answered and said unto Raphael, Brother Azarias,
I have heard that already the maid hath been given to seven men, and they have died in their
bridal-chambers; even in the night when they went in unto her they died. And I have heard them
15 (14) say that a demon slayeth them. And now for my part I fear—for her he harmeth not, but the
man who would come in unto her, him he slayeth, *and* I am my father's only child—lest I should
die and bring my father's and my mother's life to the grave with sorrow because of me: and they
16 (15) have no other son to bury them. And he saith unto him, Dost thou not remember the commands
of thy father, that he commanded thee to take a wife of thy father's house? And now hear me,
17 (16) brother; and make thou no reckoning of this demon, but take her. For I know that this night she

τ. νυκ. τ.] *σημερον* (*post αυτην*) 44, 106, 107 *ινα*] *κ.* 44, 106, 107 et *αβγ* *λημψ. σ. αυτ. νυμφ.*] *αρμωσωμεθα* (*-ομεθα* 106) *σ. αυτ.* 44, 106, 107 *επιστ.*] *υποστ.* BA *επαναστ.* 44, 106, 107 *Ραγουηλ*] *Ραγων* BA 44, 106, 107 *αβγ* 𝕾 *Ar* M F *ποιησ.*] *-ωμεν* B 44, 106, 107 *αυτης*] > BA 𝕾 *Ar* M שמחתך F *κ.*5°] *διοτι* BA 𝕾 > 44, 106, 107 *Ar* M F *επιστ.*] *οιδα* 44, 106, 107 > F *οτ. Ραγ.*] *Ραγ. οτ.* BA 𝕾 כי האיש M *ου μη*] *ου* 44, 106, 107 *δυνηθῃ Ρ. κωλ. . . . εγγ.*] *δῳ αυτην* BA 𝕾 *δυναται αντειπειν σοι οτι συ αρχεις αυτης παρα παν. τ. εθνη οτι γινωσκεις εαν* (*οτι -κει οτι* 106) *δωσῃ αυτην* 44, 106, 107 negabit illam tibi novit enim quia (certus sum autem quoniam *γ*) si dederit illam *αβγ* יסרב פומך ויתן יתה לך *Ar* נשבע ימרה את פיך ולא יתן אתה M שלא יתנה וג' F *ετερ.*] *pr. ανδρι* BA 44, 106, 107 *αβγ* [illegible] 𝕾 M F > *Ar* *οφειλησιν*] *-λεσει* B *-λησει* A 44, 107 *-λει σοι* 106 periet *αβ* perient *γ* [illegible] 𝕾 > *Ar* M F *κ. τ. κρ. τ. βιβλ. Μω.*] *κ. τ. νομον Μωυση η* (*ante οφειλ.*) BA 𝕾 M > *Ar* *pr.* ותשאנה (P) M *κ. δια τ. γινωσκειν*] > BA 44, 106, 107 𝕾 *Ar* M F *οτι σοι κληρονομια καθ. λαβ. την θυγ. αυτ. παρα παντα ανθρ.*] *οτι την κληρ. σοι κ. λ. η π. ανθρ.* BA 𝕾 > 44, 106, 107 *Ar* M tibi maxime (m. t. *γ*) aptam esse haereditatem (+accepta filia *γ*) illius *αβγ* (*aliter* F) *την θυγ.* ℵ[1 c.a]] *αυτην θυγ.* ℵ* *κ. νυν . . . οικον σου*] > BA 𝕾 F *κ. νυν . . . Ραγων*] > 44, 106, 107 *Ar* M *τ. νυκ. ταυτ.*] > 𝕷 *λημψ. αυτ.*] *κ. λαβοντες απ.* 44, 106, 107 > 𝕷 *Ar* M *ημων*] *εαυτ.* 44, 106, 107 *εις τ. οικ. σου*] *προς τ. πατερα σ.* 44, 106, 107 *Ar* M 14. *τοτε*] *κ.* 44, 106, 107 > F *αποκριθ.*] > BA 44, 106, 107 𝕾 *Ar* M *Τ. ειπ.*] *ειπ. τ. παιδαριον* BA 𝕾 F *ειπ. Τ.* 44, 106, 107 *Ρ.*] *αγγελῳ* BA 44, 106, 107 𝕾 M Raph. ang. 𝕷 *Αζαρια*] > 44, 106, 107 *Ar* M *αδελ.*] > *Ar* *ηκουσα*1°] *ακηκοα εγω* BA *ante αδ.* 44, 106, 107 +על הנערה F *οτ. επ. ηδη εδ. αν.*] *τ. κορασιον δεδοσθαι επ. αν.* BA 𝕾 *οτ. εδ.* (+iam 𝕷 M) *αν. επ.* 44, 106, 107 𝕷 *Ar* M F *εδοθ.* ℵ[c a]] *εδθ.* ℵ* *κ. απ. εν τ. νυμφωσι αυτ.*] *κ. παντας εν τ. -ωνι απολωλοτας* BA > 𝕾 *Ar* M F *τ. νυκτα . . . αποκτ. αυτ.*] > BA *τ. νυκτα οποτε*] *νυκτος* 44, 106, 107 nocte ea hora qua 𝕷 [illegible] 𝕾 עד לא *Ar* M בלילה הראשון F *εισεπ. προς αυτ.*] [illegible] 𝕾 > F *κ. απεθν.*] > 44, 106, 107 *αβγ* *κ. ηκ.*] *κ. εγω ηκ.* 106 > 𝕾 F *λεγοντ. αυτ.*] > 44, 106, 107 𝕾 *Ar* M F quosdam dicentes *αβγ* *δαιμ.*] דאשמדאי מלכא דשידי *Ar* M > 𝕾 F *αποκτεννει*] *-ειvει* 44, 106, 107 > 𝕾 F 15. *φοβουμαι . . . πατρι μου*] *εγω μονος ειμι τ. πατρι κ. φοβ.* BA 𝕾 F *φοβ. εγω απο του πνευμ. τ. ακαθαρτου* (hoc daemonium *αβγ*) *οτι φιλει αυτην κ. ταυτην* (*αυτ.* 106) *ουκ αδικ. αλ. ος εαν* (*αν* 106) *θελ. εγ. αποκτενει αυτον* (+unicus sum patri meo *αβγ*) 44, 106, 107 *αβγ* אנא דחיל מן שידא *Ar* ירא אני מאד M *αποθανω*] *pr. εισελθων* BA 𝕾 *pr. ποτε* (*τε* 44) *ουν κ. εγω* 44, 106, 107 *pr.* forte *αβγ* יקטלינני *Ar* פן יהרגני אשמדי M *κ. καταξω*] *pr. καθως κ. οι προτ. οτι* (*διοτι* A) *δαιμ. φιλει αυτην ο ουκ αδικει ουδενα πλην των προσαγ. αυτην κ. νυν εγω φοβουμαι* BA 𝕾 (*cf.* F) *τ. ζωην*] *τ. γηρας* 44, 106, 107 *Ar* M F *επ' εμε*] > 44, 106, 107 *αβγ* *Ar* M F *κ. υιος*] *pr. οτι μονογενης ειμι* 44, 106, 107 *ετερος*] +*η θυγατηρ* 44, 106, 107 *Ar* M *ινα θαψῃ αυτ.*] *ος -ει αυτ.* BA 𝕾 *pr. οταν αποθανωσι* 44, 106, 107 *Ar* M qui sepeliat illos et possideat haereditatem illorum *αβ* qui sit eis haeres *γ* 16. *κ. λεγ.*] *ειπεν δε* BA 𝕾 (*cf.* F) *κ. ειπ.* 44, 106, 107 𝕷 M אמר *Ar* *αυτῳ*] +*ο αγγ.* BA 𝕾 F *ο αγγ.* 44, 106, 107 Raph. ang. 𝕷 ר' *Ar* *ου μ.*] memor esto 𝕷 M *pr.* ירא את יי וזכר אותו M *τ. εντ.*] *τ. λογων* BA 𝕾 (*cf.* F) *pr. πασ.* 44, 106, 107 *τ. πατ. . . . ενετ. σοι*] *ων ενετ. σοι ο πατ. σου* (*ο πη̄ρ σου sup. ras. et in mg.* A[a]) BA 𝕾 F *τ. π. σου* 44, 106, 107 *λαβ. γυν.*] *υπερ του λαβειν σε γυναικα* BA 𝕾 *υπερ του λογου τουτου το λαβει̃ σε γυναι sup. ras. et mg.* A[a]? > 44, 106, 107 *εκ τ. οικ. τ. πατ. σ.*] *ε. τ. γενους σ.* BA 𝕾 > 44, 106, 107 de domo patris tui *αβγ* de genere patris tui *Auct. de voc. gent.* מזרעיתא דא' *Ar* (*cf.* M F) *ακουσον . . . γυνη*] *μη φοβηθης οτι εγω οιδα οτι δοθησεται σοι κ. μη λογον εχε περι του εν αυτῃ πνευμ.* 44, 106, 107 קביל מני ולא תדחל מן שידא (+כי M) ידענא דתסבינה לילא הדין לאינתו *Ar* M *κ. μη λογ. . . . γιν. εγω*] *διοτι σοι εσται εις γυν. κ. του δαιμ. μηδενα λογ. εχε* BA 𝕾 *κ. λαβε*] postula illam *αβγ* (*cf. Auct. de Voc. Gent.*) *γυνη*] *αυτη* (> A) *εις -αικα* B 𝕾 17. *κ. οταν*] *κ. εαν* BA 𝕾 *οταν δε λαβῃς αυτην* 44, 106, 107 *εις τ. νυμ.*] *τον ν. sup. ras.* B[ab] *pr. προς αυτην* 44, 106, 107 +עמה M *λαβε . . . θυμιαμ.*] *λημψῃ τεφραν θυμ. κ. επιθησεις απο της καρδ. κ. του ηπ. του ιχθ.* BA 𝕾 *επιθησ. την καρδ. του ιχθ. κ. τ. ηπ. επι τ. θερμην τ. θυμ.* 44, 106, 107 סיב ליבא דנונא *Ar* M *επι τ. τ. τ. θυμ.*] super carbones

16. 𝕷's *postula* may possibly have arisen through the translator's (or a reviser's) knowledge of a Heb. MS. in which ל had been dittographed (שאל לה for שא לה) just as *Ar* (which M follows) in *v.* 17, though actually translated from the Greek, might have been influenced by a Hebrew text in which תחת לבונה had been corrupted into ת' לבושה, but *direct* translation from such a text is precluded by the phrasing of viii. 2 in *Ar* as well as by the fact that he chiefly used R[s] (Nöld. *op. cit.*, p. 50, n. 1). More probably *Ar*'s 'under her garments' is an independent version of a baser process of exorcism (cf. a similar story in *The Arabian Nights*). F's affinities with *Ar* and M, especially in viii. 2, are noteworthy.

shall be given to thee to wife. And when thou comest into the bride-chamber, take of the liver of
18 (17) the fish with the heart and place them upon the ashes of the incense and the smell shall go forth,
and the devil shall smell it, and flee away, and never appear any more to her. And when thou art about to be with her, rise up both of you first and pray and supplicate the Lord of heaven that mercy and deliverance may be extended to you. And fear not, for she was set apart for thee before the world was; and thou shalt save her, and she shall go with thee. And I suppose that thou shalt have children of her and they shall be as brothers unto thee. Take no reckoning. And when Tobias heard the words of Raphael, and that she was his sister of the seed of his father's house, he loved her exceedingly, and his heart clave unto her.

Arrival and welcome at Raguel's, vii. 1–9[a].

7 1 R[s] And when he came into Ecbatana, he saith unto him, Brother Azarias, lead me straight to Raguel our brother. And he led him to the house of Raguel, and they found him sitting by the door of the court; and they saluted him first, and he said unto them, Much cheer to you, brethren, and ye are well come in safety. And he brought them into his house.

And they came to Ecbatana, and arrived at the house of Raguel. But Sarah met them; and she saluted them, and they her; and she brought them into the house. R[v]

2, 3 And he said unto Edna his wife, How like is this young man to Tobias my kinsman! And Edna
asked them and said unto them, Whence are ye, brethren? And they said unto her, We are of the
4 sons of Naphtali, which are captives in Nineveh. And she said unto them, Know ye Tobit our

a β Auct. de Voc. Gent. super carbonesi gnis ardentis *γ* עליה אש *Ar* κ. η οσμη πορευ.] κ. καπνισεις BA 𝔖 > 44, 106, 107 ואקטר מיניה תחות לבושה *Ar* M עד שיעשן F 18. κ. οσφρ. . . . μετ' αυτ.] > 44, 106, 107 ουκετι . . . αυτην1°] ουκ επανελευσεται (*post* επανε *ras. aliq.* B1? a? b) BA 𝔖 *Ar* M F τ. παν. αιωνα] (εις A) τ. αι. του αι. BA κ. οταν] οτ. δε BA μελλης . . . μετ' αυτ.] προσπορευη (-ση A) αυτη BA 𝔖 וכד תצבי למיעל לותה *Ar* M וכשתרצה לדבר עמה F εξεγερθητε] εγ. BA ποιεις αυτην εγερθηναι 44, 106, 107 + מן ערסא *Ar* M πρωτ.] > BA 𝔖 *Ar* M F αμφ. κ. προσ. κ. δεηθ. τ. κυρ. τ. ουρ.] α. κ. βοησατε προς τ. ελεημονα θ. BA 𝔖 (*cf. Ar* M F) προσ. εκατεροι κ. δεηθ. τ. κυρ. 44, 106, 107 ambo et deprecamini dominum caeli 𝔏 *pr.* ואמרו כן F αμφ.] > *Ar* M ιν. ελ. γεν. κ. σωτ. εφ' υμ.] κ. σωσει υμ. (ημ. A) κ. ελεησει BA 𝔖 κ. δοθησεται αυτη ιασις κ. ελεον 44, 106, 107 (*cf. Ar* M) ut detur vobis misericordia et sanitas κ. μη φοβ. . . . σωσεις κ.] > 44, 106, 107 *pr.* ובכן תיעיל ··· בנין *Ar* M κ.8°] > BA 𝔏 [illegible] 𝔖 σ. γαρ] οτι σοι BA εστ. μεμ.] αυτη ητοιμασμενη ην BA 𝔖 (𝔏 *cf.* 6, 12) προ του א1] προ ου א* απο του BA 44, 106, 107 𝔖 מיומא דעל' *Ar* (*cf.* M) משׁשת ימי בראשית F σωσεις] + מן שידא *Ar* M > F μετ. σ. πορ.] πορ. μετ. σ. BA εισελευση προς αυτην (*pr.* F) 44, 106, 107 > *Ar* M υπολαμβ. οτι] > 44, 106, 107 *Ar* M F εσονται σοι1°] σ. εσται BA γεννησεις 44, 106, 107 > *Ar* παιδια] τεκνον 44, 106, 107 > *Ar* M κ. εσονται2° . . . λ. εχε] > BA *Ar* M ο τι σοι εστι τ. δικαιωμα λαβειν αυτην απο τ. αιωνος (*v. supra*) 44, 106, 107 בשמחה F κ. οτε ηκ. . . . εκολλ. εις αυτ.] > 44, 106, 107 M οτε] ως BA τ. λογ. P.] ταυτα BA 𝔖 *Ar* F + angeli 𝔏 κ. οτι . . . πατ. αυτ.] > BA 𝔖 *Ar* F κ.] *ante* εκ τ. σπερμ. 𝔏 λιαν ηγαπ.] εφιλ. BA 𝔖 > 𝔏 F עלת רח' דש' בלביה *Ar* αυτην] *in* η *ras. aliq.* B? > 𝔏 κ. η καρδ. αυτ. εκολλ. εις αυτ.] κ. η ψυχ. αυτ. εκολλ. αυτη (κεκολλητο A) σφοδρα BA 𝔖 (*cf.* F) haesit cordi eius 𝔏 > *Ar* + קודם שיראנא F

VII. 1. κ. οτε . . . P.2°] ועלו בבית רע' באגבתנים *Ar* M וכיון שנכנסו בעיר F οτε] > BA εισηλθεν] ηλθ. B ηλθον A 44, 106, 107 𝔖 *a β γ* Εκβ.] civitatem Ec. 𝔏 λεγει . . . ημων] > BA 44, 106, 107 𝔖 αυτῳ] Th. angelo 𝔏 αδελ. ημ.] > 𝔏 απηγ. αυτον] παρεγενετο B παρ-οντο A 44, 106, 107 𝔏 τ. οικον] τ. -ιαν BA > 44, 106, 107 𝔏 P.] > 𝔏 κ. ευρ. αυτ. καθ. παρα τ. θυρ. τ. αυλ.] Σ. δε υπηντησεν αυτῳ (-οις A F) BA 𝔖 F εν. αυτ. καθ. π. τ. αυλειαν θυραν 44, 106, 107 et inven. ill. sed. in atrio (> *γ*) circa ostium domus suae (d. s. > *γ*) *a β γ* ואשכחו יתיה סטר תרע ביתיה *Ar* M εχαιρετισαν] -εν BA ησπασατο 44, 106, 107. *pr.* [illegible] 𝔖 αυτον] -τους A 44, 106, 107 > F πρωτοι] κ. αυτος αυτους B κ. -τοι -την A [illegible] 𝔖 > 44, 106, 107 *Ar* וישב להם שלום M הוא והיא F κ. ειπ. . . . υγιαιν.] > BA 𝔖 κ. ειπ. εν ειρην. αδελ. εισελθ. εις τ. οικ. τ. αδελ. υμων 44, 106, 107 א' ל' עולו בשלום לביתא *Ar* ואמר לו המלאך זאת הנערה F αυτοις] > 𝔏 καλ. ηλθ. υγ.] intrate salvi et sani 𝔏 ηγαγεν αυτους εις τ. οικον αυτ.] εισηγ. ε. τ. -ιαν BA 𝔖 εγενετο οτε εισηλθοσαν 44, 106, 107 ועלו לביתא *Ar* אז נכנסו בבית רע' אביה F 2. κ.] + Ραγ. 44, 106, 107 𝔖 *Ar* M F Εδ.] Annae (*et ubique*) 𝔏 [illegible] 𝔖 ουτος] > BA Τωβειᾳ] -ειτ B 44, 106, 107 τῳ -ιτ A αδελ.] ανεψιῳ BA 𝔖 consobrini *a β* -no *γ* Εδ.] Ραγ. BA 𝔖 F Anna 𝔏 κ. ειπ. αυτ.] > BA 44, 106, 107 𝔖 *Ar* M F dicens 𝔏 Ποθ. εσ. αδελ.; κ.] > 44, 106, 107 αδελ.] > *Ar* F ειπαν] -εν A > 44, 106, 107 αυτη] -τῳ BA F > 44, 106, 107 εκ τ. υι. . . . εν N.] 44, 106, 107 ex f. N. sumus ex captivis N. 𝔏 מן שביתא דבניג' משיבטא דנפ' *Ar* M מגלות נפ' אשר בניג' F ημ.] > BA εν] εκ B *pr.* των A 4. κ.] tunc 𝔖 > *Ar* γινωσκετε] -εται A ημ.] μου 106 𝔖 κ.

kinsman? And they said unto her, We know him. And she said unto them, Is he in good health?
5, 6 And they said unto her, He is in good health and alive. And Tobias said, He is my father. And
7 Raguel sprang up, and kissed him, and wept; and he spake and said unto him, Blessing be unto thee,
lad, who art the son of a noble and good father. Oh, dire calamity, that a man, righteous and
almsdoing, should have become blind! And he fell on the neck of Tobias his kinsman and wept,
8, 9 and Edna his wife bewept him, and Sarah their daughter also wept. And he killed a ram of the
flock and received them gladly.

The negotiations and the marriage, vv. 9^{b}–14.

And when they had bathed, and washed their hands and laid them down to dine, Tobias said unto
10 (9) Raphael, Brother Azarias, speak unto Raguel that he give me Sarah my sister. And Raguel heard
(10) the word and said unto the young man, Eat and drink, and make merry this night: for there is no
man unto whom it appertaineth to take Sarah my daughter except thee, brother; and likewise, further,
I have not power to give her to another man than thee, because thou art my nearest kin. Yea,
11 verily, I will shew thee the truth, lad. I have given her to seven men of our brethren and all died

ειπαν αυτη] > B *οι δε ειπᾱ* A 𝔖 M *κ. ειπον αυτ.* 44 + *τ. εκ τ. υι.* N. *κ. ειπε ναι κ. απεκριναντο* 44, 106, 107 *γινωσκ.*] > B *γιγν.* A *ημ. αυτ.*] > BA 44, 106, 107 𝔖 𝔏 F דישלם ליה *Ar* *κ. ειπ.*] > BA *Ar* *-αν* 106 *αυτοις*] > B 44, 106, 107 𝔏 *Ar* לו F *υγιαιν.*] > B *Ar* fortis est 𝔏 5. *κ.*1° . . . *κ. ζ.*] > 44, 106, 107 𝔖 *Ar* *κ.*1°] *οι δε* BA 𝔏 *αυτη*] > BA 𝔏 M F *υγ. κ. ζ.*] *κ. ζ. κ. υγ.* BA שלום M F *κ. ειπ. . . . εστ.*] והנה ט' בנו זה F *ο*] > BA 44, 106, 107 *pr.* טובי אחיכם M *εστ.*] + de quo quaeris *α β* d. q. interrogas *γ* 6. *ανεπ.*] *επηδ.* 44, 106, 107 רהט לקדמותיה *Ar* M *pr.* מיד F *κατεφ.*] *pr.* נפיק *Ar* M F *κ. εκλαυσεν*] *κ. -ε* BA > 𝔖 lacrymans 𝔏 ובכו *Ar* (*cf.* M) *ελαλ. κ.*] *ευλογ.* (*ηυ-* A) *αυτ. κ.* BA 𝔖 F > 44, 106, 107 *α β γ* אמר ר' *Ar* M *αυτῳ*] > 44, 106, 107 *α β γ Ar* M F *ευλογια σοι γενοιτο*] > BA 𝔖 *ευ. σ. -ηται* 44 בריך ט' *Ar* *παιδ.*] > BA 44, 106, 107 *Ar* + ליי M F *ο του*] *υιε ανδρος* 44, 106, 107 *pr.* כי M *πατρ.*] *ανθρωπ.* BA > 44, 106, 107 𝔖 *ω ταλ. . . . ελεημ.*] ורפיונא דידא חוא לנשי חיסדא על דאתעוור גבר עביד זכ' ומצו' סגיאן *Ar* > M *ω ταλ.*] > BA 𝔖 F *μεγαλ.* 44, 106, 107 O infelicitas 𝔏 *κακων*] *κ. ακουσας* BA 𝔖 (*cf.* F) *ετυφλ.*] *T. απωλεσεν τ. οφθαλμ. εαυτ.* (*ε.* > A) BA 𝔖 (*cf.* F) *επηρ.* 44, 106, 107 *ανηρ δικ.*] > BA 𝔖 F *κ.*] > BA 44, 106, 107 𝔖 F *ποι. ελεημ.*] > BA 𝔖 F *π. δικαιοσ.* 44, 106, 107 *επιπεσ. . . . αδελ. αυτ.*] *ελυπηθη κ.* BA 𝔖 *περιελαβ. αυτον* (*T. τ. υιον τ. αδελ. αυτ.* 106 𝔏) *κ.* 44, 106, 107 𝔏 *Ar* > M F *εκλαυσ.*] + *επι τ. τραχ. αυτ.* 44, 106, 107 𝔏 *Ar* > M F 8. *κ.*] + *εφιλησεν αυτον* 44, 106, 107 ויוסיפו M התחילו F *αυτου*] P. 44, 106, 107 *εκλαυσ. αυτ.*] > BA 44, 106, 107 *α β γ* M בכו עליו *Ar* לבכות עמו ר' M F *αυτων*] *-της* BA 44, 106, 107 (*cf.* F) *εκλαυσεν*] *-αν* BA (*-εν* B$^{a\,b}$) 𝔏 > 44, 106, 107 𝔖 *Ar* M F *κ. αυτη*] > BA 44, 106, 107 𝔏 *Ar* M F 9. *κ.*1°] *pr. κ. υπεδεξαντο* (*-ατο* 106 𝔖 *εδ-αντο* 44, 107) *αυτ. προθ.* BA 44, 106, 107 F *εθυσεν*] *-αν* BA 44, 106, 107 𝔏 *pr.* רע' *Ar* *εκ προβ.*] *προβ.* BA 106 𝔖 > 44, 107 𝔏 *Ar* M F + ובשלו F *υπεδεξατο αυτ. προθ.*] *παρεθηκαν* (ܣܡܘ 𝔖) *οψα πλειονα* BA 𝔖 ואתקינו להון שירו *Ar* M *κ. οτε . . . δειπν.*] > BA 𝔖 ואכלו ושתו עד לא אכלו *Ar* (*cf.* M) *plen.* F *κ. οτε*] *κ.* 44, 107 *κ. ενιψ.*] > 44, 106, 107 *α β γ* *κ.*5°] > 𝔏 *ανεπεσαν*] *-σον* 44 *δειπνησαι*] *εις τ. δειπνον* 44, 106, 107 *ειπ.*] + *δε* BA$^{a\,?}$ 𝔖 *κ. ειπ.* 44, 106, 107 𝔏 + T. ad ang. 𝔏 P.] המלאך M F Aζ. *αδελ.*] > *Ar* *ειπον . . . αδελ. μου*] *λαλησον υπερ ων ελεγες εν τ. πορεια* (*-ια* A) *κ. τελεσθητω* (*-στητω* A) *τ. πραγμα* BA 𝔖 (*cf.* F) *λαλ.* (+ *δη* 106) *προς* P. *περι της θυγ. αυτ. κ. δωσει μοι αυτ. εις γυν.* 44, 106, 107 *Ar* M 10. *ηκ.* P.] *μετεδωκεν* BA 𝔖 (*cf.* *Ar* F) > 44, 106, 107 *τ. λογ.*] + *τῳ* P. BA 𝔖 *Ar* F > 44, 106, 107 *κ.*2°] > 44, 106, 107 *Ar* *τ. παιδι*] P. *προς* T. (*-ιαν* B^{b} A) BA 𝔖 *Ar* illi 𝔏 *φαγ. . . . ταυτ.*] > *Ar* M *κ.*3°] > B *τ. νυκτα ταυτ.*] > BA 𝔖 F *τ. νυκτι ταυτ.* 44, 106, 107 *ου γαρ . . . ῳ*] *σοι γαρ* BA 𝔖 *επισταμαι γ. οτι αλλῳ ου* 106, 107 *κ. ελαλ. ταυτα* Aζ. *προς* P. 44 > *Ar* M F *καθηκει . . . πλην σου*] *καθ. παιδιον μ. λαβ.* BA 𝔖 *καθ. λαβ. τ. θ. μ. ει μη σοι* 106, 107 > 44 *Ar* M F *αδελ.*] > BA 44, 106, 107 𝔖 𝔏 *Ar* M F *ωσαυτ. . . . εγγ. μου*] > BA 44, 106, 107 𝔖 טב דאתן יתה לך מדאתן וג' *Ar* M כי לך טוביה בני משפט הגאולה F *εγγισ. μου*] + et tibi Sarra *α β γ* *κ. μαλα τ. αλ. σοι υποδ. παιδ.*] *πλην υποδ.* (+ *σοι* A *Ar*) *τ. αλ.* BA 𝔖 *Ar* F *κ. ερω τ. αλ. προς σε τεκνον* 106, 107 𝔏 M > 44 11. > 44. *εδωκ.*] *pr. ηδη* 106, 107 *Ar* *pr.* דע כי כבר M *αυτην*] *τ. παιδιον μ.* (*παιδαριον* A* *παιδειον* (*e sup. ras.*) A$^{a\,?}$) BA 𝔖 F *ζ'*] *επτα* BA 106, 107 *τ. αδελ. ημ.*] > BA 106, 107 𝔖 *Ar* M *παντες . . . προς αυτ.*] *οποτε εαν* (*αν* A) *εισεπ. πρ. αυτ. απεθνησκον* (*-κοσαν* B^{a}A) *υπο* (+ *την* A) *νυκτα* BA 𝔖 *απεθ.* 106, 107 וכלהון מיתו עד לא עלו לותה *Ar* M (*cf.* F) *τ. νυκτ.*] > 𝔏 *κ. νυν . . . πιε*] *αλλα το νυν εχων* (*-ον* B$^{a\,b}$A) *ηδεως* BA *κ. Κυρ. . . υμιν*] > BA 106, 107 *αβγ Ar* ܘܗܫܐ ܐܟܘܠ ܘܐܫܬܝ ܘܐܬܒܣܡ 𝔖 והנה הדבר M ובבקר כטוב בעיניך עשה F *κ. ειπ.*] ܘܐܡܪ 𝔖 *ου μη . . . πιω*] *ου γενομαι* (*-σομαι* A) *ουδεν ωδε* BA *ου μη φ. ουδ' συ μη π.* 106, 107 לא אכול *Ar* F *εως αν*] *ε. ου* 106, 107 *εως διαστ.*

VII. 11. The precise and legalistic emendation of R^{v} seems to mean 'until ye make covenant with me and have your covenant ratified by me', Th. *Gram.*, p. 254, n. 1, *θνησκοσαν* (B^{a}A), Th. *Gram.*, p. 214. With this verse commences the second 𝔖 recension, with affinities to R^{s} and R^{c} instead of R^{v}.

in the night when they came in unto her. And now, child, eat and drink, and the Lord will deal
mercifully with you. And Tobias said, I will taste nothing here nor will I drink until thou settle
(12) mine affairs. And Raguel said to him, I do so; she is given to thee according to the decree of the
book of Moses, and from heaven it hath been decreed that she is given to thee; take thy sister.
From henceforth thou art her brother, and she is thy sister; she hath been given to thee, from to-day
even for ever. And the Lord of heaven give success to you, child, this night, even to do mercy and
12 (13) peace towards you. And Raguel called his daughter Sarah, and she came to him and he took
her by the hand, and gave her to him, and said, Take her according to the law and according to
the decree which is written in the book of Moses to give her unto thee to wife. Have her and
13 (14) lead her away to thy father in peace; and the God of heaven prosper you with peace. And he
called her mother, and told her to bring a book, and he wrote an instrument of co-habitation, even
14 (15) that he gave her to him to wife according to the decree of the law of Moses. Then they began to
eat and to drink.

Sarah's recovery and the consummation of the marriage, vii. 15–viii. 9[a].

15 (16) And Raguel called Edna, his wife, and said unto her, Sister, prepare the other chamber, and
16 (17) bring her in thither. And she went and spread the bed in the chamber as he bade her and
17 (18) brought her thither; and she wept for her and wiped away her tears, and said unto her, Be

προς εμε] στησητε κ. σταθητε προς με BA ܕܬܩܝܡ ܥܡܝ 𝔖 mecum rem confirmes 𝔏 (*cf.* F) דתיתנינה לי *Ar* M εἰπε] απεκριθη 44 αυτῳ] > BA 44, 106, 107 *Ar* M οτι Ποιω . . . σοι] κομιζου αυτην απο τ. νυν BA (*cf. Ar* M) τι δυναμαι ποιησαι κ. αυτη εστι δεδομ. υπο τ. νομου κατα αγχιστειαν ιδου αυτη σοι δεδοται 106, 107 ιδου διδωμι ταυτ. γυναικα 44 ܗܟܢܐ ܥܒܕ ܐܢܐ ܠܟ ܕܝܗܒܐ ܗܝ ܡܢ ܢܡܘܣܐ ܠܟ ܗܝ ܐܢܬܬܐ 𝔖 facio: tibi S. destinata est *etc.* γ ne dubites fili facio quod vis et his dictis adiecit dicens Thobi tibi *etc.* αβ הנה הנערה לפניך תהיה לך לאשה F κ. τ. κρισιν τ. β. Μ.] כתורה וכהלכה F τ. βιβλ. Μ.] > BA τ. νομου εις γυν. 44, 106, 107 (*cf.* ܗܘܐ ܠܟ ܠܗ ܐܢܬܬܐ ܐܝܟ ܕܝܢܐ ܕܢܡܘܣܐ ܕܡܘܫܐ 𝔖) אוריתא דמ׳ *Ar* M + וישראל M κ. εκ . . . εις τ. αιωνα] > 44, 106, 107 𝔖 M κ. εκ . . . τ. νυν] > BA *Ar* M συ] + δε B (*hanc sent. ante* וכען יהיבה *hab. Ar* M) αδελφη] > BA σου] + εστιν BA κ. ο κυρ. τ. ουρ.] ο δε ελεημ. θ. BA ⸢τ. ουρ. κυρ. 44 ܘܐܠܗܐ 𝔖 יי אלהא דשמיא *Ar* M אל־שדי F ευοδ.] > F υμας] -ιν BA[a] 44 ημιν A* 106, 107 παιδ.] > BA 44, 106, 107 𝔖 *Ar* M F τ. νυκτα ταυτ.] τ. καλλιστα BA τ. νυκτι τ. 44 > F κ. ποι. . . . ειρην.] > BA 44 ܘܢܥܒܕ ܥܡܟܘܢ ܛܝܒܘܬܐ 𝔖 (*cf. Ar* M F) υμας 2°] ημ. 106, 107 12. > 44, 106, 107 𝔖 εκαλ.] ודבר *Ar* Ρ.] > BA κ. ηλθεν προς αυτον] > BA *Ar* M F λαβομενος] -βων BA > *Ar* M παρεδ.] > F αυτῳ] Τ. (*pr.* τῳ A) γυναικα BA *Ar* M > F κ. ειπ. . . . ειρην.] ויברכם M Κομισαι] ιδου BA ראה בני הרי זאת מקודשת לך F κ. κατα . . . βιβλῳ] > BA כהלכת אוריתא דמ׳ *Ar* כדת יהודה וישראל F δουναι . . . γυναικα] > BA *Ar* F εχε] κομιζου αυτην BA > *Ar* F απαγαγε] απαγε BA ולך F υγιαινων . . . ειρηνην] κ. ευλογησεν (ηυλ. A) αυτους BA *pr.* fili 𝔏 > *Ar* F 13. > 𝔖 ומיד קרא עדים וקדש אותה בפניהם וכתבו וחתמו שטר כתובתה ומיד ברכו שבע ברכות F (*cf. Ar* M *infra*) εκαλ.] ויאמר M τ. μητερα αυτης] Ε. (ܥܕܢܐ 𝔖) τ. γυναικα αυτου BA *Ar* M matrem et puellam 𝔏 ειπ.] > BA *Ar* M ενεγκειν] λαβων BA -γκαι 107 κ. ηνεγκε 44 βιβλιον] chartam αβγ גיירא *Ar* גליון M κ.3° . . . συνοικ.] > M κ.3°] > BA ut αβγ *Ar* συγγραφην] συγγ. B[ab] 44, 106, 107 conscriptionem αβγ כתובתא *Ar* βιβλιου συνοικησεως] > BA συνοικιουσαν 44, 106, 107 coniugii αβγ לברתיה *Ar* κ. ως διδ. . . . νομ.] ויכתב עליו את הכתובה ויחתם אותה בעדים M (*cf.* F *supra*) ועבדת כן וכתבו כתובתא וחתמו יתה סהדיו *Ar* κ. ως διδωσιν] κ. εσφραγισαντο BA ως διδοται κ. εδωκαν (εδοσαν 44) 44, 106, 107 quemadmodum tradidit αβγ αυτην . . . κρισιν του] > BA α. α. γ. κ. τ. συγκρισιν 106 Μ. νομου] > BA βιβλιου Μ. κ. ηνεγκαν η μητ. αυτ. κ. εγραψε κ. εσφραγισαντο (κ. εσ. > 44) 44, 106, 107 αβγ 14. απ' εκεινου] κ. BA *Ar* M F κ. τοτε 44, 106, 107 𝔖 ex illa hora αβγ ηρξ. . . . πειν] εφαγον κ. επιον 44, 106, 107 𝔖 *Ar* M + וישמחו M ηρξαντο] -ατο B[ab] φαγειν] εσθιειν BA κ. πειν] > BA 15. εκαλ. . . . γυν. αυτ. κ.] > 44, 106, 107 𝔖 *Ar* M Ρ.] > A αυτῃ] Ρ. Ε. (Ε. > 44) τῃ γυν. αυτ. 44, 106, 107 𝔖 *Ar* M Αδελ.] > 𝔏 *Ar* M τ. ταμι. τ. ετ.] τ. ε. ταμι. (-ει. B[a]) BA τ. ταμιειον 44, 106, 107 אידרון בית משכבא *Ar* החדר M חדר הפנימי F εισαγαγε] εισαγε B αυτην] puellam 𝔏 F > *Ar* אותם M εκει] > BA 44 ܠܩܝܛܘܢܐ 𝔖 *Ar* 16. βαδισασα . . . αυτῃ] εποιησεν ως ειπ. BA 𝔖 επ. ουτως Ε. 106, 107 *Ar* abiit in cubiculum (secretum γ) et stravit sicut *etc.* αβγ > 44 M F ηγαγεν] εισ- B 44, 106, 107 𝔖 𝔏 εισηγαγον A > *Ar* M αυτην] filiam suam 𝔏 F > *Ar* M εκει] εις τ. κοιτωνα 44, 106, 107 + ܠܩܝܛܘܢܐ 𝔖 > *Ar* εκλαυ.] *pr.* περιελαβεν αυτ. (𝔖) η μητ. αυτ. κ. (> 𝔖) 44, 106, 107 𝔖 (*cf. Ar* M) והתחילה הנערה לבכות F περι αυτ.] > BA 44, 106, 107 *Ar* ܥܠܝܗ ܘܒܟܬ 𝔖 עמה M במרת נפשה F κ. απεμ. τ. δ.] > 44, 106, 107 𝔖 *Ar* M וקבל הקדוש ברוך הוא דמעתה F κ. απεμαξ.] κ. απεδεξ. BA τ. δακρυα] + της θυγ. αυτης BA αυτῃ] > 44, 106, 107 *Ar* 17. Θαρ.] > *Ar* M *pr. verba e Script.* F

13. συγγραφήν. Cf. the Isis Inscription from Ios. ἐγὼ συγγραφὰς γαμικὰ[ς] εὗρα (i. 33 in reproduction in Deissm. *L.A.E.*, p. 136).

16. Some of the changes made by the later redactors and versions are pleasing, e.g. R[v]'s alterations (incorporated as usual in F) to make the daughter weep and the mother catch her tears, and F's 'the Holy One, Blessed be He, received her tears', but R[c] lacks the poetic imagination.

of good comfort, daughter: the Lord of heaven give thee joy for thy sorrow: be of good
8 1 comfort, daughter. And she went forth. And when they had finished eating and drinking,
they desired to sleep, and they led the young man away and brought him into the chamber.
2 And Tobias remembered the words of Raphael, and took the liver of the fish and the heart
3 out of the bag which he had, and put them on the ashes of the incense. And the smell of the
fish baffled the demon, and he ran away into the upper parts of Egypt; and Raphael went and
4 fettered him there and bound him straightway. And they went forth and shut the door of the
chamber. And Tobias rose up from the bed, and said unto her, Sister, arise; let us pray and make
5 supplication to our Lord that he may work mercy and deliverance for us. And she arose, and they
began to pray and make supplication that deliverance might be wrought for them, and he began to
say, Blessed art thou, God of our fathers, and blessed is thy name for ever and ever; let the
6 heavens bless thee, and all thy creation to all the ages. Thou madest Adam, and madest Eve his

θυγ.] τεκν. BA κυρ.] θ. 44, 106, 107 *Ar* ουρ.] + κ. τ. γης BA 𝔖 *pr.* אלהי F + εν τ. νυκτι ταυτ. 44, 106, 107 𝔖 *Ar* M δῳη σ.] δῳ σ. A *pr.* ελεος επιδῳ (-ωσῃ 106) επι σε (+ δωσει σοι 106) 44, 106, 107 𝔖 *Ar* M F χαραν] χαριν BA *Ar* M ששון ושמחה F της] > 44 σου] + ταυτ. BA (*cf.* F) + τ. εμπροσθεν 44, 106, 107 𝔖 *Ar* (*cf.* M) θαρ. θυγ.] > 𝔏 *Ar* κ. εξηλθ.] > BA 44, 106, 107 𝔖 *Ar* M + inde 𝔏

VIII. 1. κ. οτε] οτε δε BA κ. εγενετο οταν (-ε 44) 44, 106, 107 והוה כד *Ar* M συνετ.] > 𝔖 עמדו F το φαγ. κ. π. ℵ*] του φ. ℵ^{c a} δειπνουντες BA ευφρανθηναι (+ κ. 106) 44, 106, 107 ܟܕ ܫܡܠܝܘ ܠܡܐܟܠ 𝔖 coenam 𝔏 לאתקנא אידרונא וערסא *Ar* M מן חשולחן F ηθελ. . . . νεαν. κ.] > BA 44, 106, 107 𝔖 *Ar* F εισηγ. . . . ταμ.] ועלו לתמן ט' וש' אנתתיה *Ar* (*cf.* M) αυτ.] T. B 44, 106, 107 𝔖 F εις] προς BA F ταμειον] αυτην BA (*cf.* F) τ. κοιτωνα 44, 106, 107 ܠܓܢܘܢܐ 𝔖 2. κ.1°] ο δε πορευομ. BA וקודם שיכנם F εμνησθη . . . P.] צוה והביאו לו מחתה עם הגחלים F εμνησθη] -ημονευσε 44, 106, 107 T.] > BA 44, 107 P.] + ang. 𝔏 κ. ελαβ.] > F τ. ηπ. τ. ιχθ. κ. τ. καρδ.] τ. καρδ. τ. ιχθ. κ. τ. ηπ. (+ המרה F) *post* επεθηκ. BA (*cf.* F) τ. καρδ. τ. ιχθ. 44, 106, 107 *Ar* M εκ τ. βαλ. ου ειχ.] > BA 44, 106, 107 𝔖 *Ar* M F κ. επεθ.] > 44, 106, 107 επι τ. τεφρ. του θυμι.] τ. τεφρ. των θυμι. *post* ελαβ. BA > 44, 106, 107 ܥܠ ܓܘܡܪܐ ܕܢܘܪܐ ܘܣܡܐ ܐܢܘܢ ܥܠ ܓܘܡܪܐ 𝔖 super carbones vivos (ignis γ) αβγ (*cf.* F) על מחתה *Ar* M (*cf.* F) 3. κ. η οσμη τ. ιχθυος εκωλ.] κ. (> A) εκαπνισεν οτε δε ωσφρανθη τ. δαιμ. τ. οσμης BA > 44, 106, 107 וקטר תחות גלימת שרה ואשמדאי קביל ריחא *Ar* M ונכנם והעשין את נערה ואת עצמו וגם כל הבית וכשהריח אש' וג' F εκωλ.] ܐܦܪܥ 𝔖 prohibuit αβγ κ. απεδραμ.] εφυγ. BA κ. εξεβαλε 44, 106, 107 *pr.* [ויצא ממנה] M τ. δαιμ.] > (*v. supra*) BA 𝔏 *Ar* M F τ. ακαθαρτον πνευμα (+ κ. απεστη 106) 44, 106, 107 *ante* κ.2° 𝔏 ανω εις τα μερη] εις (*pr.* εως A) τα ανωτατα BA εις τα ανω μερη 44, 106, 107 ܠܥܠܝܬܐ ܕܡܨܪܝܢ 𝔖 in superiores partes αβγ בסייפי ארעה *Ar* (*cf.* M F) βαδ. . . . παραχ.] > F βαδ.] > BA 44, 106, 107 𝔖 *Ar* abiit . . . et 𝔏 P.] ο αγγελος *post* αυτ. BA + ang. 𝔏 M συνεποδ.] εδησ. BA 44, 106, 107 𝔖 αυτον] -το BA 44, 106, 107 εκει] > BA *post* εποδ. *Ar* κ. εποδησ. παραχρ.] > BA 44, 106, 107 𝔖 M et reversus est continuo αβγ ואסריה *Ar* 4. κ. εξηλθ. . . . κλιν. κ.] > 44, 106, 107 𝔖 κ.1°. . . ταμ.] ως δε συνεκλεισθησαν αμφοτεροι BA ואז יצאו משם האנשים וסגרו הבית F εξηλθ.] ויצא M + מן אידרונא *Ar* M τ. ταμ.] בדיל תרויהון *Ar* M κ. ηγερθ.] ανεστ. BA απ. τ. κλιν.] > F ειπ. αυτῃ Αδελ. αναστηθι] κ. ειπ. ανα. αδ. κ. BA κ. T. ειπ. προς Σ. αδ. αναστα κ. 44, 106, 107 ܐܡܪ ܛܘܒܝܐ ܠܣܪܐ ܩܘܡܝ ܚܬܝ 𝔖 dixit S. surge soror 𝔏 *Ar* M προσευξωμ.] ξ *sup. ras.* B^{ab} -ομ. 106 κ. δεηθ.] > BA *Ar* M τ. κυριου ημ. οπως ποι. εφ. ημ. ελεος κ. σωτ.] ινα (*pr.* Deum 𝔏) ημ. ελεησῃ ο. κυρ. (> 𝔏) BA 𝔏 (*cf.* F) τ. προσωπου κυρ. οπως π. εφ. ημ. ελ. κ. σωτ. εν τ. νυκτι ταυτ. 44, 106, 107 ܩܕܡ ܡܪܝܐ ܕܢܥܒܕ ܥܡܢ ܚܢܢܐ ܘܦܘܪܩܢܐ ܒܠܠܝܐ ܗܢܐ 𝔖 קדם א' דיפקיד עלנא חיסדיה וטיבותיה (המקום M) *Ar* (*cf.* M) 5. ανεστ. . . . σωτ. κ.] > BA 44, 106, 107 𝔖 *Ar* M מיד עמדו יחד בתפלה F ανεστη] surrexerunt 𝔏 δεηθ.] + Dom. 𝔏 ηρξατο λεγ.] ηρξ. T. λεγ. BA ειπ. T. 44, 106, 107 ܘܨܠܝܘ ܩܕܡ ܡܪܝܐ ܘܐܡܪ ܛܘܒܝܐ 𝔖 dixerunt 𝔏 וצלי ט' קדם א' ואמר *Ar* (*cf.* M) התחיל ט' מברך F ευλογ. . . . αιωνας 2°] *aliter* M ει] κυριος 44, 106, 107 + ܡܪܝܐ 𝔖 𝔏 *Ar* F τ. πατ. ημ.] דישראל *Ar* (*cf.* F) σου1°] + τ. αγιον κ. ενδοξ. BA (*cf.* F) παν. τ. αιωνας τ. γεν.] τ. αιωνας BA ܠܥܠܡܝܢ 𝔖 *Ar* τ. γενεας τ. αιωνων 44, 106, 107 in omnia saec. saeculorum αβγ *Aug.* ευλογ. . . . κτ. σου] > 𝔖 *aliter* F π. η κτισις] π. αι -εις BA εις π. τ. αιωνας] > BA 44, 106, 107 αβγ *Aug. Ar* 6. τον Αδαμ] A. BA τ. ανθρωπ. 106 ܠܐܕܡ ܘܝܗܒܬ 𝔖 + הראשון F εποι.] εδωκας BA 44, 106, 107 αβγ *Ar* M F βοηθ. στηρ. Ευ. τ. γ. αυτ.] β. Ευ. στ. τ. γ. αυτ. BA β. Ευ. τ. γ. 44, 106, 107 *Ar* M ܠܚܘܐ ܡܥܕܪܢܝܬܐ 𝔖 adiutorium Evam αβγ *Aug. Spec.* 56 חוה אשתו F κ. εξ . . . βοηθον 2°] > M αμφοτ.] τουτ. BA 𝔏 *Ar* > γ *Aug. aliter* F εγεν.] multiplicasti αβ > γ *Aug.* *aliter* F τ. σπ. τ. ανθρ.] τ. ανθρ. σπ. BA τ. γενος τ. ανθρ. 44, 106, 107 > γ *Aug.* כל בני

VIII. 3. In R^s εἰς τὰ ἄνω μ. (cf. αβγ) was written, which was retained in R^c and paraphrased in R^v. In ℵ (which Swete, *Expos. Tim.*, vol. xi, p. 39, appears to treat as the sole authority in this verse for R^s !) the ἄνω has been accidentally inserted before εἰς τά. The reference to Egypt is pertinent historically (see Introd. p. 186) and mythologically (Jeremias, *A.T.L.A.O.*, pp. 180, 432), and Kohut's emendation מצנדרן for מצרים is pointless, but see J. H. Moulton, *Hibbert Lectures*, excursus to lecture ii. 𝔏's *reversus est* may possibly have crept into the text from the mg. where it had been placed by a reader who had before him an Aramaic text in which חזר had taken the place of חבר.

wife for a helper *and* a stay for him: of them both came the seed of men: and thou didst say, It is
7 not good that the man should be alone; let us make him a helper like unto him. And now
I take not this my sister for lust, but in truth: command that I and she may find mercy and grow
8, 9 old together. And they said together, Amen. And they slept the night.

The parents' joy and the ensuing feast, vv. 9^b–21.

10 And Raguel arose and called his servants with him and they went and digged a grave, for he
11 said, Lest he perish, and we become a derision and a reproach. And when they had finished
12 digging the grave Raguel came into the house, and called his wife, and said, Send one of the maidservants and let her go in and see if he be alive: and if he is dead that we may bury him, that no
13 man know it. And they sent the maidservant and lighted the lamp and opened the door, and she
14 went in and found them sleeping and slumbering together. And the maidservant came forth, and

אינשא *Ar* > γ *Aug.* *aliter* F κ. συ . . . βοηθ.2°] > 44, 107 α β γ *Aug.* κ. συ] συ BA οτι] > BA 106 τ. ανθρ.] ܐ̈ܢܫܐ 𝔖 *Ar* ποιησωμ.] ܐܥܒܕ 𝔖 *Ar* F 7. νυν] + Κυριε BA 𝔖 + Κυριε συ γινωσκ. οτι 44, 106, 107 α β γ *Aug.* (*in* 4 *loc.*) *Ar* M ουχι] ου BA δια πορνιαν] δ. -ειαν BA 44, 106, 107 luxuriae causa 𝔏 τ. αδελ. μ. ταυτ.] uxorem sororem meam α β αλλ' επ' αληθ.] αλλα ε. α. A αλλα κατα (τα 44) δικαιωμα (-ατα 44) τ. νομου σου (σ > 106 𝔖) 44, 106, 107 𝔖 sed ipsa veritate 𝔏 כהלכת אוריתא *Ar* בישר לבב כדת משה וישראל M לקיים דברך האמת F επιτ. . . . κοιν.] *plen.* F επιτ. ελεησ. με κ. αυτην] ε. ελ. μ. BA επι τω ελεηθηναι ημας κυριε (+ εμε τε κ. αυτην 106, 107) 44, 106, 107 ܕܬܪܚܡ ܥܠܝ ܘܥܠܝܗ̇ ܡܪܝܐ 𝔖 ut (> γ) misereris nostri Domine α β γ *Aug.* חוס עלנא והב לנא חסדך *Ar* (*cf.* M) κ. συνκαταγηρασαι κοινως] κ. αυτη (ταυτ. A) συνκαταγηρασαι (συγ. B^ab συνκαταγηρασομε (αγηρα *sup. ras.* A^a) A) BA κ. συγκαταργησαι (= συ καταρασαι?) τῳ ακαθαρτ. δαιμ. κ. δος ημιν κυριε τεκνα κ. ευλογιαν 106, 107 et (ut γ) consenescamus pariter sani cum pace α β γ ולאתחברא אך חדא *Ar* M + (+ ועוסקים תורתך M) ܟܚܕ̈ܐ ܘܢܣܝܒ ܟܠܢ ܕܒܫܝܢܐ 𝔖 α β *Ar* M 8. ειπαν μεθ' εαυτων] -εν μετ' αυτου BA -αν κοινως 44, 106, 107 ܘܐܡܪܘ ܐܡܝܢ 𝔖 (*cf.* F) dixerunt 𝔏 ואתיבת ש' ואמרת *Ar* M 9. εκοιμ.] + αμφοτεροι BA (*cf.* F) ועל לוותה *Ar* M et receperunt se α β γ τ. νυκτα] εν τη ν. εκειν. 44, 106, 107 𝔖 F *post* ταφον α β γ αναστ. P. εκαλ. τους οικετ. μ. εαυ. κ.] αναστ. P. BA F ειπ. (*pr.* ויקם + לילה M) P. τοις οικ. αυτ. 44, 106, 107 𝔖 M והות בפילגות ליליא קם ר' ואמר לעבדוהי *Ar* ῳχοντο κ. ωρυξαν ταφ.] επορευθη κ. -εν τ. BA (*cf.* F) ορυξατε τ. νυκτι ταυτ. (+ ܒܗ̇ ܒܠܠܝܐ 𝔖) 44, 106, 107 𝔖 + per noctem 𝔏 לחפרא קברא בליליא *Ar* M 10. ειπ. γαρ] λεγων BA > 44, 106, 107 ואמר להון *Ar* Μη ποτε] μη κ. ουτος (αυτ. A) BA ινα εαν 44, 106, 107 אם *Ar* αποθανῃ] η τεθνηκως (+ טליא *Ar*) θαψω (נקבריניה *Ar*) αυτον νυκτος κ. μηδεις γνῳ (*cf.* *v.* 12) 44, 106, 107 𝔖 *Ar* *simil.* (*pr.* אל קבורת) F κ. γεν. καταγ. κ. ονειδ.] > BA ινα μη γενωμαι (יהא לנא *Ar*) εις ονειδισμον κ. καταγελωτα 44, 106, 107 *Ar* (*cf.* F) ܘܠܐ ܢܗܘܐ ܠܟܠ ܡܘܝܩܐ 𝔖 et omnibus fiam derisio et opprob. 𝔏 11. οτε . . . οικον] > *Ar* M οτε . . . ταφον] > BA F εγενετο (> 44) οταν εξηλθοσαν οι οικετ. (+ ܘܟܕ ܫܠܡܘ ܡܢ ܕܚܦܪܘ 𝔖) 44, 106, 107 𝔖 οτε] > 𝔏 ηλθ. P.] > 44, 106, 107 𝔖 τ. οικον] τ. -ιαν εαυτου BA F > 44, 106, 107 𝔖 εκαλ. την γυν. αυτ. κ.] > BA 44 F εκ. P. (P. > *Ar*) Εδ. (Εδ. > 𝔖) τ. γ. αυ. 106, 107 𝔖 *Ar* M 12. ειπ.] + E. (P. 44) τη γ. αυτ. BA F + αυτῃ 106, 107 𝔖 *Ar* M Αποστ.] + δη 44, 106, 107 κ. εισελθ.] > BA 𝔖 F εις τ. κοιτωνα κ. 44, 106, 107 𝔏 *Ar* M + דבוצינא בידה *Ar* ιδετω] ειδετωσαν (ιδ. B^b) BA ζῃ] + εν ειρηνῃ 44, 106, 107 > F κ. ει . . . γνῳ] ει δε μη (an mortuus est 𝔏) ινα θαψ. αυτ. (+ טדם אור הבקר M) κ. μηδ. γνῳ (-ωτω A) BA 𝔏 *Ar* M שמא נפטר גם הוא ואקברהו F > 44, 106, 107 𝔖 13. απεστ. . . . λυχν. κ.] εισηλθ. η παιδισκη BA F απεστ. Εδνα τ. παιδ. κ. 106, 107 𝔖 *Ar* M απηλθ. η παιδ. κ. 44 + לאדרונא *Ar* M misit unam ex ancillis et α β γ ηνοιξαν] ανοιξασα BA ανεωξε 44, 106, 107 𝔖 α β γ > *Ar* M F θυρ.] + του κοιτ. 106, 107 𝔖 > *Ar* M F εισηλθ. κ.] > BA *Ar* M F ο λυχνος εν τη χειρι αυτης κ. 44, 106, 107 𝔖 κ. ευρ. αυτους καθευδ. κ. υπν. κοιν.] κ. ευρ. τ. δυω καθευδ. BA 𝔖 κ. ιδου αυτοι καθευδ. κοιν. 44, 106, 107 et invenit illos pariter dorm. 𝔏 (+ יחד בשלום M) וחזת והא שכבין תרויהון *Ar* M ומצאתם יושבים F 14. εξελθουσα] εξηλθε (+ Εδ. 44) κ. 44, 106, 107 𝔖 *Ar* M η παιδ.] > BA 44, 106, 107 𝔖 𝔏 *Ar* M F υπεδ. αυτ.] ואמרת להון בריכו מרי עלמא *Ar* ואמר להם F υπεδειξ.] απηγγειλ. BA 44, 106, 107 αυτοις] Εδ. τ. ανδρι αυτης 106, 107 𝔖 > 44 + (ותאמר להם) M

---

9. In the original story (R^s), along with his servants (who are omitted in R^v, accidentally or for brevity's sake, as Müller admits), Raguel digs the grave and returns from doing so before he addresses his wife (*v.* 11). R^c, however, denies Raguel's presence at the digging and his share in the manual labour, as it is inconceivable 'that a rich man should himself do such work' (Nöld., *op. cit.*, p. 48, who with singular inaccuracy attributes this alteration and motive to R^s!).

12. εἰδέτωσαν. B* A, misplaced augment, Th. *Gram.*, p. 209.

13. The three chief recensions, particularly R^c, have not retained their individuality in this verse, but both the later ones seem as usual to have been based on R^s either in the form it assumes in ℵ or in that of 𝔏.

15 told them that he was alive and that there was naught amiss. And he blessed the God of heaven
and said,
16 Blessed art thou, O God, with all pure blessing; let them bless thee for ever. And blessed
art thou, because thou hast made me glad: and it hath not befallen as I supposed, but thou hast
17 dealt with us according to thy great mercy. And blessed art thou, because thou hast had mercy on
two that are the only begotten children of their parents: shew them mercy and deliverance, O
Lord; and fulfil thou their life with gladness and mercy.
18, 19 Then he bade his servants fill the grave before the morning came. And he bade his wife
make many loaves. And he went to the herd, and fetched two oxen and four rams, and bade
20 prepare them; and they began to make ready. And he called Tobias and said unto him, For
fourteen days thou shalt not stir hence, but shalt stay here eating and drinking at my house, and
21 shalt gladden my daughter's sore afflicted soul. And all that is mine take thereof the half, and go
in safety to thy father; and the other half, when I and my wife die, is yours. Be of good cheer,
child! I am thy father, and Edna is thy mother; and thine now are we and thy sister's; from
henceforth we are for ever. Be of good cheer, child!

οτι . . . εστ.] *ο. ζ.* BA *Ar* > 44, 106, 107 𝔖 illum vivere et nihil mali passum 𝔏 חי הוא M (*cf.* F) 15. *κ.*1° . . . *ειπαν*] ואמר רעואל *Ar* *ευλογησαν*] *-εν* (*ηυ-* A) P. (P. > γ) BA αβγF *τον*] *pr.* יי M F *τ. ουρ.*] > BA 44, 106, 107 𝔖 F הגדול M *κ. ειπ.*] *λεγων* BA 𝔏 > *Ar* + ר' M *θεε*] *συ ο θεος* BA *κυριε ο θεος* (*θ.* > 𝔖) *τ. ουρ κ. τ. γης* 44, 106, 107 𝔖 *Ar* + את מחי ומסי *Ar* (*cf.* M *v.* 16) יי אלהי אבותינו M כל בשר F *εν π. ευλ. καθαρᾳ*] *ε. π. ευ.* B *ε. π. ευ. καθ. κ. αγια* B^ab mg A α β *ε. π. ευ. αγιε κ. καθαρε κ. αμιαντε* 106, 107 *αγιε καθαρε κ. αμιαντε* 44 omni benedictione sancte et munde γ וברכתך קדישא ודכיא *Ar* > 𝔖 M *aliter* F *ευλογειτωσαν σε*] *-ησατ.* 106, 107 > 44 𝔖 *pr. κ. ευλογ. σε οι αγιοι σου κ. πασ. αι κτισ. σου παντ.* (*pr. κ.* A) *οι αγγ. σου κ. οι εκλεκτ. σου* (*κ. οι ε. σ.* > *Ar*) BA (*cf. Ar* F) + omnes sancti tui γ et benedicant tibi omnes electi tui et omnis creatura tua benedicat tibi α β > M *εις παντας τ. αιων.*] *εις τ. αι.* B *Ar* *παντες οι αιωνες σου* (> 44) *ο τυπτων κ. ιωμενος ευλογ. σε παντ. οι αγγ. σου ευλογ. σε* (*ε. σ.* 44 *κ.*) *παντ. οι εκλεκτ. σου* 44, 106, 107 > 𝔖 M in omnia saecula saeculorum α β in saeculum s—li γ 16. ܕܐܢܬ ܗܘ ܡܫܒܚ ܘܐܢܬ ܗܘ ܡܒܪܟ 𝔖 (*cf.* M) *aliter* M *simil.* F *κ.*1°] > BA 44, 106, 107 𝔏 *ει*] שום יקרך *Ar* *ευφρ.*] *ηυ.* (*ευ.* B^a) B* b A *με*] *ημας* 44, 106, 107 *Ar* *εγενετο*] + *μοι* BA 𝔏 + *ημιν* 44, 106, 107 > *Ar* *υπενοουν*] *-ουμεν* 44, 106, 107 *Ar* *αλλα . . . ημων*] בסגיאות טיבותך *ante κ. ουκ Ar* *πολυ*] > 44, 106, 107 17. *simil.* F *κ.*1°] > BA 44, 106, 107 𝔖 𝔏 *Ar* *ευλ. ει*] > 𝔖 M + *κυριε* 44, 106, 107 + אלהא *Ar* *ελεησ.*] עצית הפלא הזה M *δυο*] תרויהון *Ar* שני אלה M *μονογ.*] + *κ. τ. γονεις αυτων* 106, 107 𝔖 > *Ar* M *ποιησ. . . . ελεου*] הב להון שלמא וחסדא וחדוה בחייהון לעלם *Ar* *aliter* M *ελεος κ.*] > 𝔖 *κ. σωτ. κ.*] > BA *συντελ.*] ܒܚܕܘܬܐ ܠܐܢܫܝܢ ܘܚܢܢܐ 𝔖 *μετ' ευφ. κ. ελεου.*] *εν υγειᾳ* (*-ιειᾳ* B^ab *-ιᾳ* A) *μετα ευφ. κ. ελεους* BA *μετα ελεους κ. ευφ.* 44, 106, 107 𝔏 > 𝔖 18. *τοτε ειπ. τοις οικ. αυτου*] (*pr.* ומיד F) *εκελευσεν δε τ. οικ.* BA F *κ. ηλθοσαν οι οικ. κ. ειπ. αυτοις* 44, 106, 107 𝔖 *Ar* + ר' M *χωσαι*] ܕܢܛܡܘܢ 𝔖 ומלאו F *ταφ.*] + quam fecerunt 𝔏 + עפר F *προ τ. ορθρον γεν.*] > BA F *π. τ. ημερ.* (ܨܦܪܐ 𝔖) γ 44, 106, 107 𝔖 עד לא ירגיש בנא בר נש *Ar* (+ 𝔖 M) 19. *κ. εποιησεν αυτοις γαμον ημεραν δεκα τεσσ.* BA (*cf.* F) *τ. γυν.*] E. (> 44 𝔖) *τ. γ. αυτου post ειπεν* 44, 106, 107 𝔖 > M *ποιησ.*] *ετοιμασον* 44, 106, 107 𝔖 + *pauc. verb.* M *τ. βουκ.*] *τας* (*τους* 44) *βοας* 44, 106, 107 *βαδισ.*] *εδραμ. αυτου* (*αυ.* > 44 𝔖) *κ.* 44, 106, 107 𝔖 M abiit ipse 𝔏 ורהוטי *Ar* *ηγαγεν*] וסיבי מתמן *Ar* *δυο*] > 44, 106, 107 *Ar* M *τεσσ.*] > 44 *Ar* + ܕܟܪܐ 𝔖 M *ειπ. συντελ.*] *εταξ.* (+ ܠܡܥܒܕ ܡܫܬܘܬܐ 𝔖) *ετοιμαζ.* 44, 106, 107 𝔖 𝔏 *Ar* ופקיד למעבד אריסטוון טב *Ar* *κ. ηρξ. παρασκ.*] > 44, 106, 107 𝔖 𝔏 M ועבדת כן *Ar* 20. *εκαλ. T. κ.*] > BA 𝔖 *Ar* M + *ωμοσεν αυτῳ κ.* 44, 106, 107 𝔏 ור' נשבע F *αυτῳ*] *-τοις* A + P. *πριν η συντελεσθηναι τ. ημερας τ. γαμου ενορκως* BA > 44, 106, 107 𝔏 ܒܡܘܡܬܐ 𝔖 *Ar* M *δεκα τεσ. ημερων*] *εαν μη πληρωθωσιν αι δ. τεσ. ημ. τ. γαμου post αυτον* BA (*cf.* F) *εως ημερων δεκατεσ.* 44, 106, 107 *post οικον σ.* 44, 106, 107 ܥܕܡܐ ܕܢܫܠܡܘܢ ܝܘܡܬܐ ܕܡܫܬܘܬܐ *post μη κιν.* 𝔖 *ου μη κιν. εντευθ.*] *μη εξελθειν αυτον* BA *ου μη εξελθης εκ τ. οικου σ.* 44, 106, 107 *Ar* M ܠܐ ܬܦܘܩ 𝔖 ולא אניחך וג' F *αλλ' . . . κατωδ.*] > BA F *αλλ' . . . εμοι*] > 44, 106, 107 𝔖 *Ar* M *κ. ευφρανεις*] *ινα -ῃς* 44, 106, 107 𝔖 *τ. ψυχ.*] > *Ar* M *κατωδυνωμενην*] *-οδ.* 44 *-ωδυνομ.* 106 multis adflictam doloribus 𝔏 21. *οσα μοι . . . το ημισυ κ.*] *τοτε λαβοντα τ. ημ. τ. υπαρχοντων αυτου* BA *τ. ημ. των υπαρχ. μοι λαβε παραχρημα* 44, 106, 107 𝔖 *Ar* (*cf.* F) *pr.* ואחרי מלאת הימים F *υπαγε υγιαιν.*] *πορευεσθαι μετα υγειας* (*-ιας* B*A *-ιειας* B^ab) BA *υπ. εν ειρηνῃ* 44, 106, 107 > 𝔖 *Ar* vade salvus et sanus cum pace 𝔏 ותלך בשמחה M ולך F *πρ. τ. πατ.*] > 𝔖 *Ar* *σου*] > BA 𝔖 *Ar* *τ. αλλο ημ.*] *τ. λοιπα* BA F *τ. ημ.* 44 תיסב כולא *Ar* M *οταν*] *εως* 44, 106, 107 *εγω τε*] > BA *εγω* 44, 106, 107 *υμετ. . . . παιδ.*2°] > BA M נתונים המה לך F *υμετ.*] *σου* 44 > *Ar* *θαρσ.*1°] > 𝔖 *Ar* *παιδ.*1°] *τεκν.* 44, 106, 107 > 𝔖 את תהא לי לבר יקיר *Ar* *σου ο*] > 44, 106, 107 Eδ.] + אנתתי *Ar* *η*] > 44, 106, 107 *κ. παρα σ. . . . παιδ.*2°] > 44, 106, 107 𝔖 עד עלם *Ar* *θαρσ. παιδ.*2°] > 𝔏

15. R^s wrote *εὐλόγησεν . . . κ. εἶπεν* which should be read in ℵ. See Introd., p. 174, footnote 2, for the importance of liturgical and theological additions in R^v and R^c.

ii. **Raphael's journey to Gabael,** ix. 1–6.

9 1, 2 Then Tobias called Raphael, and said unto him, Brother Azarias, take along with thee four
servants, and two camels, and go to Rages and get thee to Gabael, and give him the bond ; receive the
4 money and bring him with thee to the wedding feast. For thou knowest that my father will count
3 the days, and if I tarry one day, I shall sorely grieve him ; and thou seest what Raguel hath sworn,
5 and I cannot break his oath. And Raphael went on his way with the four servants and the two
camels to Rages of Media and they lodged with Gabael, and Raphael gave him his bond ; and (he)
made known to him concerning Tobias, Tobit's son, that he had taken a wife and that he invited
him to the wedding-feast. And he arose and counted out to him the bags with their seals and placed
6 them together < on the camels >. And they rose up early in the morning together and came to
the wedding-feast. And they came into the house of Raguel, and found Tobias lying at meat.
And he sprang up and greeted him. And he wept and blessed him and said unto him, Honest and

IX. 1. τοτε] κ. BA P.] *pr.* τον BA 44, 106, 107 + ang. 𝕷 F 2. παραλαβε] λαβε BA 44, 106, 107 μετα σ.] εντευθεν 44, 106, 107 𝕾 + hinc 𝕷 *Ar* M τεσσαρ. οικετ.] παιδα BA > 44, 106, 107 κ.1°] > 44, 106, 107 καμ. δυο] δυο καμ. BA 44, 106, 107 εις Ραγας] εν Ραγοις τ. Μηδειας (-ιας A) BA ܒܪܓܝ 𝕾 in civitatem Rages 𝕷 > F κ. ηκε] > 44, 106, 107 𝕾 𝕷 *Ar* M F παρα] προς 44, 106, 107 Γαβ.] + בעל הפקדון F δος] > BA αυτῳ] > BA αυτοις 44, 106, 107 τ. χειρ.] > BA ܟܬܒܐ ܗܘ 𝕾 + suum 𝕷 מרצופיה *Ar* אמתחתו M κομισαι] + μοι BA λαβε 44, 106, 107 יתן *Ar* M F *pr.* κ. א1 (> א*) 𝕾 44, 106, 107 *Ar* M F παραλαβε αυτ.] αυτ. αγε μοι (μ. > A) BA αγαγε αυτον (-το 44) 44, 106, 107 וזמין *Ar* M F μετα σ.] > BA 𝕷 *Ar* M τους γαμ.] τον γ. BA 4. *pr.* v. 3 BA *Ar* συ . . . εσται] κ. BA *Ar* γαρ] > 44 αριθμων ο πατ.] ο π. μ. αριθμει BA ο π. μ. αριθμων 44, 106, 107 𝕷 *Ar* ܠܐ ܟܠ ܒܡܢܝܢܐ 𝕾 + ואמי M τ. ημερ.] > 44, 106, 107 χρονισω] ܐܘܚܪ 𝕾 F יעבר עדנא *Ar* M ημερ. μιαν] μεγα (γ *sup. ras.* Aa) BA μιαν ημερ. 44, 106, 107 una plus die 𝕷 > F λυπησω αυτ.] οδυνηθησεται BA ܗܘܐ ܒܝܫ ܠܗ 𝕾 F contristabo animam eius 𝕷 (*cf. Ar* M) λιαν] > 44, 106, 107 𝕾 𝕷 *Ar* 3. κ. θεωρ. τι] διοτι BA κ. 44, 106, 107 ܚܙܐ 𝕾 Sed vides quomodo 𝕷 מטול דאנא לא יכילנא למיזל לתמן בדיל *Ar* M > F ωμοσεν P.] ομωμοχεν (-κεν Ba b) P. BA 44, 106, 107 + μη εξελθειν με (+ מן ביתיה עד ארבסר יומיו *Ar* M F) BA *Ar* M F + μειναι με (μοι 44) δεκατεσσαρες (ܐܪܒܥܣܪ 𝕾) ημερας (δ. η. 44) παρ' αυτῳ 44, 106, 107 𝕾 κ. ου. . . . ορκ. αυτ.] > BA 106 *Ar* M δυναμαι] -ησομαι 44, 107 possumus 𝕷 παραβηναι] αθετησαι 44, 107 spernere 𝕷 5. επορευθη] ויקם M P.] + ang. 𝕷 κ. οι τ. . . . οικ. κ. αι δ. καμ.] > BA F κ. οι οικ. αυτου 44, 106, 107 *pr.* ויקח M εις P. τ. M.] > BA εις P. 44, 106, 107 M ܠܪܓܝ ܕܡܕܝ 𝕾 in civ. M. 𝕷 לקורי ראשיג *Ar* > F ηυλισθησαν] -θη BA 𝕷 *pr.* ηλθον προς Γ. κ. 44, 106, 107 𝕾 F > M + בלילה ההוא F παρα Γ.] εκει 44, 106, 107 ܠܘܬܗ 𝕾 αυτῳ 1°] + Ραφ. 44, 106, 107 𝕾 𝕷 *pr.* ובבקר F τ. χειρ.] ܫܛܪܐ ܕܝܠܗ 𝕾 αυτου] > BA 44, 106, 107 𝕾 κ. υπεδ. αυτω] > BA F ܘܐܘܕܥܗ ܥܠ 𝕾 π. T. υι. T.] > BA π. τ. υι. Τωβια 44, 106, 107 > 𝕾 F οτι ελαβ.] > BA F + ܕ 𝕾 γυν.] > BA + τ. θυγ. P. 44, 106, 107 𝕾 𝕷 ש' ב' ר' *Ar* M κ.7°] > BA οτι καλ.] > BA εστιν εκει καλων (κ. > 44) 44, 106, 107 ܘܐܙܡܢܗ ܗܘ ܕܢܐܬܐ ܠܗ 𝕾 *pr.* ט' *Ar* + ר' M > F εις τ. γαμον] > BA 44 + ט' M > F κ. αναστας] ος δε BA κ. ανεστη T. 44, 106, 107 כד שמע גבאל כן *Ar* > M F παρηριθμ.] προηνεγκεν BA F εξηνεγκε 44, 106, 107 > *Ar* M αυτῳ 3°] > BA 44, 106, 107 *Ar* M συν τ. σφραγισιν] εν τ. σφ. BA κ. εδειξε τας σφ. 44, 106, 107 𝕾 + suis 𝕷 > *Ar* M בחותמו של ט' F συνεθηκαν αυτα] εδωκεν αυτω BA ηριθμησε τ. αργυριον κ. επεθηκεν επι τας καμ. 44, 106, 107 𝕾 + supra camelos αβγ טען כספא על גמליא *Ar* M ולקח ר' הכסף ואת עביאל F 6. ωρθρισαν] ωρθρευσαν B > 44 *Ar* M vigilaverunt 𝕷 κοιν. κ.] > 44 *Ar* M F εισηλθον 1°] ηλθοσαν B*b 44, 106, 107 αβγ ηλθον BaA ואתא M εις τ. γαμον] > 44 + ܘܩܕܡܘ 𝕾 κ. εισηλθ. . . . εκλαυσ. κ.] > F κ. εισηλθ.2°] > BA 44, 106, 107 𝕾 αβγ *Ar* M εις τα P.] > BA 𝕾 αβγ *Ar* M προς P. 44, 106, 107 κ. ευρ. T. ανακειμ.] > BA et invenit Gabelus Th. discumb. (accumb. γ) αβγ κ. ανεπ.] > BA 44, 106, 107 *Ar* M κ. ησπ.] > BA 44, 106, 107 𝕾 αυτον 1°] > 44, 106, 107 ܘܢܫܩܗ 𝕾 αβ *Ar* M κ. εκλ.] > 44, 106, 107 𝕾 + Gabelus αβ + מסגיאות חדואתא *Ar* M κ. ευλογ.] > 44, 106, 107 𝕾 γ αυτον] Τωβειας τ. γυναικα αυτου BA (*cf.* F) > 44, 106, 107 𝕾 γ Deum αβ κ. ειπ. . . . ομοιον αυτῳ] > BA F κ. ειπ.] + T. 44, 106, 107 𝕾 dicens 𝕷 αυτῳ] > 44, 106, 107 𝕷 *Ar* M Καλε . . . ελεημοπ.] ευλογητ. ο κυρ. ος εδωκε σοι ειρην. (+ bone et optime vir αβ) οτι υιος ει (ευλ. . . . ει > γ) ανδρος καλ. κ. (κ. κ. > 44 𝕾) αγαθ. κ. ελεημοσυνας ποιουντος 44, 106, 107 (+ et benedictus tu fili αβ) 𝕾 αβγ ברוך יי אלהי ישראל *Ar* אלהא דשמיא יברך גבר טב וקשיט עבד צדק' ובריך אל' ט' קריבי אשר התבירך בשמחה עם האשה M δωῃ . . . γυν. σ.] ευλογημενος ει κ. ευλογ. (ευ. > 44) ο πατ. σου κ. ευλογ. (ευ. > 44 𝕾) η γυν. σου κ. ο πατ. κ. η μητ. (κ. η. μ. > 106) αυτης 44, 106, 107 𝕾 דיהב לך ולאבוך ולאמך אתתא טבתא הדא

IX. 3. ὀμώμοχεν (R^v), Th. *Gram.*, p. 205.

5. συνέθηκαν αὐτά is possible alone, but probably ἐπὶ τ. καμήλους should be restored from αβγ *Ar* and M. On the other hand αβγ *Ar* M inadvertently wrote κ. εἰσῆλθον only once in the next verse and then omitted εἰς τὰ 'P. R^c clings at any rate to the mention of Raguel though its compromise has suffered in 44 and is lost in 𝕾. R^v so radically abridged the verse that the second half was unintelligible to the copyists, but restore κ. εὐλ. 'P. τὸν T. κ. τὴν γυν. αὐτοῦ in R^v.

good *lad*, son of a man honest and good, just and merciful! The Lord give thee the blessing of heaven, and unto thy wife and thy father and thy wife's mother! Blessed be God that I have seen Tobias my cousin like him.

D. THE HOME-COMING, x. 1–xi. 17.

i. **Tobias' sorrowing parents,** x. 1–7ª.

10 1 Now day by day Tobit kept counting how many days he would spend in going and how many
2 return in. And when the days were expired, and his son was not come, he said, Is he perchance
3 detained there? or is Gabael perchance dead, and there is no man to give him the money? And
4 he began to grieve. And Anna his wife saith, My child hath perished, and is no longer among the
5 living; and she began to weep and bewail her son, and said, Woe is me, *my* child, that I let thee
6 go, the light of mine eyes. And Tobit kept saying unto her, Hold thy peace, trouble not, sister, he is in
good health; doubtless some distracting business hath befallen them there; and the man who went
7 with him is trusty and one of our brethren; grieve not for him, sister, soon he will be here. And

Ar והוא ברחמיו יתן לך ממנה בנים זכרים ועוסקים בתורת יי M δωη σοι κυρ. ευλογ. ουρ.] det tibi benedictionem (ben. det tibi γ) Dom. coeli α β γ κ. τ. πατ. . . . γυν. σου] > γ ευλογ. . . . ομ. αυτ.] > 44, 106, 107 𝕾 *Ar* M οτι ειδ. . . . ομοιον αυτῳ] quoniam video Thobi consobrini mei similem α β et benedicat Deus Thobi consobrinum meum γ

X. 1. *brev.* M εκαστ. . . . επιστρ.] κ. T. ο πατ. αυτ. ελογισατο (-ζετο A) εκαστ. ημερ. BA (*cf.* F) κ. T. ηριθμει (-ησε 44) τ. ημ. αφ' ης εξηλθε T. ο υιος αυτ. 44, 106, 107 𝕾 δε] et 𝕷 *Ar* ημερ.] + בריה *Ar* πορευσ.] יכיל למיזל לקבל כספא *Ar* εν ποσ.2°] > 𝕷 επιστ.] + filius eius 𝕷 οτε συνετελ.] ως επληρωθ. BA επλεονασαν 44, 106, 107 ημεραι] + τ. πορειας (-ιας A) BA F + חושבניה *Ar* ο υι. αυτ.] > BA 44, 106, 107 *pr.* 'ט *Ar* κ. . . . ου παρην] ουκ ηρχετο (-οντο A F) BA κ. ελυπηθη Τωβιας (T. > 44) 106, 107 (+ F) ܟܪܝܐ ܠܗ ܠܛܘܒܝܐ 𝕾 2. *brev.* M ειπ.] + T. A *pr.* κ. 44, 106, 107 𝕾 + בנפשיה *Ar* (*cf.* F) Μη1° . . . η] > 44, 106, 107 𝕾 κατεσχεθη] κατησχυνται BA דלמא עכבוניה *Ar* קראהו אסון F εκει] > BA בדרך F απεθ.] τεθνηκε 44, 106, 107 ο] > BA 44, 106, 107 ουδεις] ου 44, 106, 107 *Ar* ܘܐܢܫ ܠܐ 𝕾 et nemo 𝕷 αυτ. διδ.] διδ. αυτ. BA διδ. τ. υιῳ μου 44, 106, 107 𝕾 יהבו ליה *Ar* (*cf.* F) 3. κ. ηρξ. λυπ.] κ. ελυπειτο λιαν BA > 44, 106, 107 𝕾 ושרי לאתענאה *Ar* (*cf.* M) *ante v.* 2 F 4. *brev.* M κ. A. η γ. αυτ. λεγ.] ειπ. δε αυτῳ η γυνη (+ αυτου A) BA F κ. ειπ. A. 44, 106, 107 𝕾 + ליה *Ar* τ. παιδ. μ.] τ. π. BA ο υι. μ. 44, 106, 107 𝕾 κ. ουκ. . . . ζ.] (+ *Ar*) διοτι κεχρονικεν BA *Ar* κ. ουκετι ζη 44, 106, 107 𝕾 quare tardat (-tur γ) α β γ > F ηρξ. . . . υι. αυτ.] ηρξ. θρηνειν αυτον BA εθρηνει περι αυτ. 44, 106, 107 𝕾 κ. ειπ.] εθρηνει λεγουσα 44 5. > M Ουαι μοι] ου μελει μοι (μ *sup. ras.* Aª) BA οιμοι 44, 106, 107 𝕾 οτι] προς τι 44, 106, 107 𝕾 πορευθ.] > BA 𝕾 απελθειν απ' εμου 44, 106, 107 𝕾 + לארע רחיקתא *Ar* *aliter* F τ. φ. τ. οφθ. μ.] *ante* τεκν. 44, 106, 107 𝕾 + למה שבקתיה למיזל *Ar* + בני ט' F 6. *brev.* M F T. ελεγεν αυτῃ] T. λεγει αυτη BA παρεκαλει αυτην T. κ. ειπ. (κ. ε. 44 λεγων) 44, 106, 107 𝕾 σιγ. . . . υγ.] θαρσει αδελ. παρεσται ο υιος ημ. υγιαινων 44, 106, 107 𝕾 αδελ.] > BA *Ar* κ. μαλα . . . ηδη παρεστ.] > BA κ. μαλα] > 44, 106 107 𝕾 sed forsitan 𝕷 ברם *Ar* περισπασμ.] ܒܥܘܦܢܐ 𝕾 mora 𝕷 מורע *Ar* αυτ. εγ. εκει] detinet illos 𝕷 αυτοις . . . ο ανθρ.] τις αυτων (-τῳ 44 𝕾) γεγονε μη λυπου οτι κ. (κ. > 𝕾) 44, 106, 107 𝕾 αυτοις] ליה κ. εις] εκ 44, 107 et ex 𝕷 > 106 *Ar* τ. αδελ. ημ.] > 106 *Ar* μη λυπ. . . . παρεστ.] μη θῃς επι την καρδ. σ. κακον 106, 107 𝕾 > 44 περι αυτ. αδελ.] ארום *Ar* 7. κ. ειπ. . . . παιδ. μ.] ותמאן להתנחם M (*pr.* F) αυτῳ] Αννα 44, 106, 107 𝕾 > 𝕷 + חנה *Ar* Σιγ. . . . πλανα] > 44, 106, 107 𝕾 Σιγ. απ' εμ. κ.] σιγ. BA *Ar* F tace molestus es mihi α β molestus es mihi esse noli γ μη με πλ.] μη πλ. με BA (+ F) ולא תנחמינני *Ar* F απωλ.] > *Ar* παιδ.] τεκν. 44, 106, 107 על ברי *Ar* εκπηδ. περιεβλ. τ. οδ.] επορευετο καθ' ημερ. εις τ. οδ. BA F εκπηδ. επι τ. οδου περιεβλ. 44, 106, 107 ܚܘܪܐ ܘܢܦܩܐ ܠܫܒܝܠܐ ܘܐܙܠܐ ܗܘܬ ܒܐܘܪܚܐ ܘܡܣܟܝܐ ܗܘܬ 𝕾 והות נפקת לפרשת אורחיא *Ar* ותצא אל הדרכים M η ωχ. . . . ημεραν] εξω οιας απηλθ. (-αν A) ημερας τε (ημ. τε > 𝕷) BA 𝕷 (*cf.* F) ει ερχεται ο υι. αυτης (αυ. > 44) 44, 106, 107 > 𝕾 בכל יום לראות אם יבא בנה M ביממא ובליליא אתר דברה ייתי ביה *Ar* κ. ουκ επειθ. ουδ.] αρτον ουκ ησθιεν

X. 2. κατῄσχυνται (Rᵛ, an unlucky substitute for κατεσχέθη of Rˢ, which is supported by *Ar* and F) must be translated 'are they disappointed?' (cf. בוש). Rᶜ omitted the clause because of this difficult expression, and most moderns who uphold Rᵛ are here compelled to emend on the basis of Rˢ. On -εσχεθη *v.* Th. *Gram.*, p. 238.

4–6. On the relation of these verses to Jub. ch. xxvii. *v.* R. Harris, *A.J.Th.* pp. 349 ff.

5. οὐ μέλει μοί (Rᵛ) is corrupt. It might be emended ὢ (cf. *Ar*) or ὡς or σὺ (Fri.) μέλει μοι or σὺ μέλει σοι (Tisch.).

6. περισπασμός (Rˢ) = 'distracting business, distraction' (e.g. Polyb. iii. 87, 9; iv. 32, 5), represents ענין (occupation, task) six times in Eccles. The words ὁ ἄνθρ. . . . μὴ λυποῦ (Rˢ) give the key to the difficult 'perfectus vir (et) verax . . . noli fiere' in Jub. ch. xxvii.

7. -λιμπ. -λιπ. (Rᵛ), Th. *Gram.*, p. 227. In *Ar* ארבסר (cf. viii. 20, ix. 3) may be original, but prob. it is a transformation by a late scribe of the numerical י"ד.

she said unto him, Hold thy peace at me and deceive me not; my child hath perished. And hastening forth early she spent every day watching the road, by which her son had gone, and would hearken to no one; and when the sun went down she would enter in, and mourn and weep the whole night, and have no sleep.

ii. Tobias sets out for home, *vv.* 7b–13.

And when the fourteen days of the wedding feast were expired which Raguel had sworn to
celebrate for his daughter, Tobias entered in to him and said, Send me away, for I know that my
father and my mother believe not that they will see me again; and now I pray thee, father, that
8 thou send me away that I may go to my father; already I have told thee how I left him. And Raguel
said unto Tobias, Abide, lad, abide with me, while I send messengers to Tobit thy father, and they
9 shall tell him concerning thee. And he said unto him, Nay, I pray thee that thou send me away to
10 my father. And Raguel arose, and handed over to Tobias Sarah his wife, and half of all his goods,
men-servants and maid-servants, oxen and sheep, asses and camels, clothing and money and chattels;
11 and he sent them away in peace, and he embraced him and said to him, Farewell, child, depart in
peace; may the Lord of heaven prosper you, and Sarah thy wife, and may I see children of you
12 before I die. And he said unto Sarah his daughter, Go unto thy father-in-law, because henceforth

(-ιε Bb) BA α β γ F > 44, 106, 107 𝔖 *Ar* κ. οτε εδυ . . . υπνον] τ. δε νυκτας (+ολ A) ου διελιμπανεν (Bb (vid) A -ιπ. B*) θρηνουσα T. τ. υι. αυτ. BA (*cf.* F) εως ου εδυ ο ηλ. κ. εισηλθ. εις τ. οικ. αυτ. (ܒܡܫܒܠܗ 𝔖) κ. ουκ εγευσατο ουδενος κ. ουκ ηδυνατο υπνωσαι (κ. ο. η. υ. > 44) 44, 106, 107 𝔖 ולא טעימת מדם אילהן דמעתא בליליא ולא נח לבה (ו׳ נ׳ ל׳ > M) *Ar* M κ. οτε 2°] εως ου BA F κ. εγενετο ως 106, 107 M κ. ως 44 τ. γαμ.] > 𝔖 ας ωμ. P.] > 44 *Ar* M F ας] καθως 106, 107 ποιησ. τ. θυγ. αυτ.] ποι. αυτον εκει BA > 44, 106, 107 𝔖 𝔏 *Ar* M F εισηλθ. . . . T. κ.] > BA 44, 106, 107 𝔖 *Ar* M F εισηλθ.] > 𝔏 ειπ. 2°] +δε (> *Ar*) T. τω (τ. > Bab) P. (ܠܗ 𝔖) BA 𝔖 *Ar* M (*cf.* F) +T. 44, 106, 107 +illi 𝔏 Εξαπ. . . . γαρ εγω] εξαπ. με BA *Ar* M F πορευσομαι προς τ. πατ. μου 44, 106 (+F) 107 > 𝔖 *pr.* ארוני F ου πιστ. . . . με ετι] ουκετι ελπιζουσιν οψεσθαι με BA *Ar* αγωνιωσιν (-ιουσιν 106) ει ετι (ετι > 44) οψονται τ. προσωπ. μου 44, 106, 107 ܕܟܡܐ ܟܠܗ ܥܡܝ ܘܡܨܛܒܝܢ ܘܠܐ ܡܣܒܪܝܢ ܠܡܚܙܝ ܠܝ 𝔖 מחשבים את הימים ואינם חושבים וג׳ M כי עד עתה נואשו ממני F ετι] > 𝔏 κ. νυν . . . αφηκ. αυτ.] > BA 44, 106, 107 𝔖 M F κ. νυν] nunc itaque 𝔏 πατ.] > *Ar* κ. πορευθ. . . . αυτ.] דלא יכילנא לאיתעכבא תוף *Ar* 8. κ. ειπ.] ειπ. δε BA P. τ. T.] αυτω ο πενθ. (+αυτου A) BA P. 44, 106, 107 𝔖 M ליה ר׳ *Ar* Μειν. 1° . . . μετ' εμου] μ. παρ' εμοι BA 𝔏 > 44, 106, 107 𝔖 Remane hic penes me 𝔏 M שב בני F κ. εγω αποστελλω] καγω εξαπ–λω (-λλω Ba) B* vid A α β γ εγω εξ–λω (-λλ 106) 44, 106, 107 αγγ.] > BA *Ar* M F T.] > BA 𝔖 𝔏 *Ar* M F τ. π. σ.] > *Ar* M +ולאמן F υποδειξ.] δηλωσ. BA υποδ–ωσιν 44, 106, 107 αυτῳ] לאבוך *Ar* M περι σου] τα κατα σε BA ܕܗܘܝܐ ܗܘܐ ܥܠܝܟ 𝔖 +συ δε μειν. ετι ολιγ. ημερας μετ' εμου (μ. ε. > 44) 44, 106, 107 𝔖 כל דעבדת *Ar* M הדבר F 9. ειπ. αυτ.] T. λεγει BA ειπ. T. 44, 106, 107 M F +T. 𝔖 ille dixit 𝔏 אתיב ליה ט׳ *Ar* Μηδαμως] > (ουχι Bab) B *Ar* ουχι αλλα A 23, 55, 64, 71 ܠܐ ܡܣܒܪ ܠܟ 𝔖 in totum 𝔏 +ω πατερ 44, 106, 107 𝔏 לא אל תאחר אותי M אדני אלא αξιω σε] > BA M F peto 𝔏 הב לי רשו *Ar* οπως] > BA 44, 106, 107 𝔖 *Ar* M F εξαποστειλης] -λον BA 44, 106, 107 למיתב *Ar* אלך F εντευθ.] > BA 44, 106, 107 𝔖 *Ar* F ואלכה M προς] ινα μη λυπησω 44, 106, 107 ܘܠܐ ܠܡܥܠ 𝔖 +ואל-אמי F 10. κ. 1°] > BA et continuo 𝔏 αναστας] +δε BA -εστη 44, 106, 107 > M P.] +κ. ελαβε Σ. (Σ. > 𝔖) τ. θυγ. αυτ. κ. 44, 106, 107 𝔖 *post* παρ. M παρεδ.] εδ. BA +αυτην 44, 106, 107 +ר׳ T.] αυτω BA F Σ. τ. γυν. αυτ. κ.] > 44, 106, 107 S. filiam suam 𝔏 κ. το ημισυ (א A* vid) τα (α *sup. ras.*) ημ. BA? κ. εδωκ. αυτῳ 44, 106, 107 παντων] > BA 𝔏 *Ar* M F παντα 106 αυτῳ] > BA +το ημ. 106, 107 +παντων τα ημιση αυτου 44 παιδ. κ. παιδ.] σωματα BA *Ar* β. κ. πρ.] κ. κτηνη BA πρ. 44 oves et boves 𝔏 (*post* καμ. *Ar*) *Ar* M > F ον. κ. καμ.] > BA F κ. κ. ον. 106, 107 καμ. 44 *post* σκ. 𝔏 *Ar* ιματ.] > BA 44, 106, 107 𝔖 F *plen.* M κ. αργ.] αργ. BA et pecuniam κ. σκ.] > BA *plen.* M (*cf.* F) 11. εξαπ.] *pr.* ευλογησας αυτους BA +בשלוה ובהשקט *Ar* > F αυτους . . . ησπασατο αυτον] > BA αυτ. κ. ησπασαντο αυτον 44, 106, 107 𝔖 illum salv. san. et vale illi fecit 𝔏. וברכינון *Ar* M F κ. ειπ. αυτῳ] λεγων BA κ. ε. P. 44, 106, 107 𝔖 et dixit 𝔏 M F ואמר להון *Ar* υγ. . . . υπαγε] > BA *Ar* M F βαδιζετε τεκνα υγιαινοντες 44, 106, 107 𝔖 vade fili salvus sanus 𝔏 ο κυρ.] ο θ. (*post* τεκνα BA) BA 44, 107 *Ar* M F *pr.* κ. 44, 106, 107 ουρ.] +ܘܢܘܬܪܘܢ 𝔖 > *Ar* אבותינו M ישראל F ευοδωσαι] -σει B 44, 106, 107 -λογησει A ישוי שלמא *Ar* יברך M υμας] +τεκνα BA -ιν 106, 107 דרכיכם F κ. Σ. τ. γ. σ.] > *Ar* M F κ. Σ. . . . παιδια] > BA κ. ιδ. τεκνα υμ. 44, 106, 107 𝔖 κ. ιδ.] ויחזי לי *Ar* M F παιδ.] בנים זכרים (ו)עוסקים בתורת יי M προ . . . με] > M με] *ante* αποθ. BA 12. κ. 1° . . . απελ. αυτ.] > 44 κ. 1°] +εφιλησε Σ. τ. θυγ. αυτ. κ. T. κ. 106, 107 𝔖

10. τὰ ἥμισυ (Rv), Th. *Gram.*, p. 180. σώματα (Rv) = *slaves* in classical Greek, e.g. Dem. (480. 10), Plut., but always with αἰχμάλωτα, οἰκετικά or some similar epithet, in the Ptolemaic papyri (cf. espec. Demophon's letter to Ptolemaeus *c.* 245 B.C. in *The Hibeh Papyri*, No. 54), in the LXX (e.g. Gen. xxxiv. 29, Bel and Drag. 32; 2 Mac. viii. 11), in Polybius and later writers, and in the N.T. See Deissm., *B.S.*, p. 160, *L.A.E.*, p. 151.

they are thy parents as they who begat thee; farewell, daughter. May I hear a good report of thee so long as I live. And he embraced them and let them go. And Edna saith unto Tobias, Child and brother beloved, may the Lord restore thee, and may I see children of thee while I live and of Sarah my daughter before I die. Before the Lord I commit my daughter unto thee in trust; vex her not all the days of thy life. Child, farewell; henceforth I am thy mother and Sarah thy sister. May we all be prospered in the same all the days in our life. And she kissed them both
3 (11, 1) and sent them away in peace. And Tobias departed from Raguel in peace and rejoicing and blessing the Lord of heaven and earth, the King of all, because he had prospered his journey. And *Raguel* said unto him, Mayst thou be prospered to honour them all the days of their life.

iii. Tobias' reunion with his parents and the return of Tobit's sight, xi. 1–17.

11 1, 2 And when they drew nigh to Caeserin which is over against Nineveh, Raphael said, Thou
3 knowest how we did leave thy father: let us run forward before thy wife, and prepare the house

+apprehendit illum et (+salutans *αβ*) osculatus est (+et *γ*) Sarram (+filiam suam *αβ*) et *αβγ* וגפיף להון ונשיק להון *Ar* M Σ.] > BA 106, 107 *αβγ* τ. θυγ. αυτ.] αυτη θυγατερ 106, 107 *αβ* illi *γ* > F Υπ. προς] τιμα BA 106, 107 𝔖 *αβγ Ar* M F +מאד M τον πενθ. σ.] τους π. σου (ου *sup. ras.* (*seq. ras.* 1 *lit.*) A1) BA +κ. την π. σ. 106, 107 𝔖 *αβγ Ar* M F οτι απο . . . γονεις σ.] αυτ. νυν γον. σ. εισιν BA *αβγ* οτι αυτ. σ. γον. απο τ. ν. εισι 106, 107 𝔖 > M απ. τ. ν.] תרויהון *Ar* ως οι γενν. σε] > BA *Ar* M F καθως ημεθα ημ. 106, 107 𝔖 *pr.* (*post* ως) pater tuus et mater tuus 𝔏 βαδ. . . . θυγ.] > BA F β. υγιαινουσα 106, 107 *Ar* M ακ. σ. αγ. ακοην ε. ζω] ακ. σ. ακ. καλ. BA > 106, 107 𝔖 +et gaudium 𝔏 ונשמע ··· בחיינו M והק"בה ישמעינו וגו' F ε. ζω] (+ M) וחדוא רבתא *Ar* M *cf.* F κ. απασπ. απελ. αυτ.] κ. εφιλησεν αυτην BA F et osculatus est eam et dimisit (+illam *γ*) *αβγ cf. Ar pr.* וישק להם M > 44, 106, 107 𝔖 κ.3°] > 106 Ε. λεγ. Τ.] Ε. ειπ. προς Τ. AB ειπ. Ε. πρ. Τ. 44, 106, 107 𝔖 ויאמר אל ט' M Τεκν. . . . αποθ.] αδελ. αγαπητε (ברי ואחי את *Ar* בני M) αποκαταστησει (-αι A) σε (salvum te perducat (ducet te *γ*) *αβγ Ar* M) ο κυρ. τ. ουρ. κ. δωη μοι ιδειν σου (σ. > *αβγ Ar*) παιδια (+ קשיטין *Ar* +טובים לפני יי M) εκ Σ. τ. θυγ. μου (+antequam moriar *αβγ* M) BA *αβγ Ar* M *simil.* F > 44, 106, 107 𝔖 ενωπ. τ. κυρ.] קדמי *Ar ante* εκ Σ. M ενωπ.] *pr.* ινα ευφρανθω BA *αβγ* του] > 44 κυρ.] +coeli *αβγ* παρατιθ.] *pr.* κ. ιδου BA 𝔖 F παραδιδ. 44, 106, 107 𝔖 F והא *Ar* M trado (-am *γ*) *αβγ* τ. θυγ.] *pr.* Sarram 𝔏 *Ar* M εν] επι 44, 106, 107 > 𝔖 παραθηκη] παρακαταθ. (κατα *sup. ras.* A1) BA παρ-ην (+ουτως 106) 44, 106, 107 > 𝔖 tanquam bonum depositum 𝔏 (+ F) בידך *Ar* M F μη λυπησ.] μη σκυλ. 44, 106, 107 𝔖 𝔏 *pr.* et 𝔏 πασ. τ. ημερ.1° . . . απεστ. υγιαιν.] > BA *aliter* F ημερ.] ימיך M τ. ζ. σου 1°] > 44, 106, 107 M חייה *Ar* παιδ. εις ειρ.] > 44, 106, 107 𝔖 vade f. salvus et sanus *αβγ* ולכו לשלום M παιδ.] > *Ar* απο τ. νυν . . . ζωη ημ.] ויברכם M απο τ. νυν] κ. ιδου 106, 107 𝔖 κ. 44 > *Ar* σ. μητ. κ. Σ. αδ.] μητ. σ. κ. Σ. η αδ. σ. 44, 106, 107 𝔖 αδελφη] uxor 𝔏 *Ar* ευοδ. . . . ζωη ημ.] > 44, 106, 107 𝔖 diligat (dirig. *γ*) te deus et illam ut sitis in loco sanctitatis omn. dieb. vit. vest. (diebus vestris *γ*) *αβγ* αμφοτ.] > *Ar* M אלהנא יצלח ארחיכון כל ימי חייכון *Ar* κ. απεστ. υγ.] κ. εξηλθοσαν 44, 106, 107 𝔖 υγ.] > *Ar* M 13. κ. απηλθ. . . . βασ. τ. παντ.] μετα ταυτα επορευετο κ. Τ. ευλογων τον θ. BA κ. επορ. Τ. χαιρ. κ. (κ. > 44) ευλ. τον θ. τ. ουρ. κ. τ. γης 44, 106, 107 𝔖 *aliter* M ואחרי כן הלכו משם וט' בירך את יי F απο Ρ.] > *Ar* υγ. κ.] > *αβγ Ar* κυρ.] deum *αβγ Ar* τ. βασ. . . . οτι] ו דשלח מלאכיה *Ar* οτι ευοδωκ. τ. οδ. αυτ.] οτι ευοδωσεν (-οδ. B*A -ωδ. Bab) τ. ο. α. BA > 44, 106, 107 𝔖 *aliter* M κ. ειπ. . . . ζ. αυτ.] κ. κατευλογει Ρ. κ. Ε. τ. γυναικα αυτ. (+et dixit iniunctum est mihi a Domino (אלהא יסעדנני *Ar*) honorari (-are *γ*) vos omnibus die. vit. vestr. (meae *γ*) *αβγ Ar*) BA *αβγ Ar* κ. προσηυξατο λεγων γενοιτο μοι τιμαν τον πενθ. μου ωσπερ τους εμαυτ. γον. π. τ. ημερ. τ. ζ. αυτ. 106, 107 𝔖 > 44 M F

XI. 1. *plen.* M ως ηγγισαν] επορευετο (+ט' *Ar* הלכו F) μεχρις ου εγγισαι αυτον (-τους Bb? c? F) εις BA *Ar* F επορευθησαν τ. οδον αυτων κ. ηλθον 44, 106, 107 𝔖 וילך ויבא M Κασερειν] > BA Καισαρειαν 44, 106, 107 ܟܣܪܝܢ (*v. l.* ܟܣܪܝܢ) 𝔖 Charam *αβ* Caracha *γ* Charan 𝔙 אַקְרִים *Ar* M > F η εστιν] > BA F κατεναντι] > BA F απεν. 44, 106, 107 in medio itinere contra 𝔙 Ν.] *pr.* της 44, 107 +undecimo die 𝔙 לנינוה F 2. ειπεν] *pr.* κ. BA 44, 106, 107 +προς Τ. BA 44, 106, 107 𝔖 *Ar* Ρ.] +המלאך F Συ] ου BA F γινωσκ.] +αδελφε BA *Ar* +Thobias frater 𝔏 M πως] > 𝔖 αφηκαμεν] -κες B -κας (ς *absciss.*) A 44, 107 *Ar* M F -κα 106 > 𝔖 reliqueris 𝔏 τ. πατερα] ܠܐܒܘܟ (? *l.* ܫܒܩܢ *vel* ܫܒܩܬ) ܫܒܩܢ 𝔖 σου] +ואת אמך M 3. προδρ.] +ουν 106, 107 ܩܘܡ ܢܪܗܛ ܩܕܡ 𝔖 τ. γυναικος σ.] *pr.* εμπροσθεν BA > 44, 106, 107 𝔖 *Ar* M F +et eamus 𝔏 ετοιμ.] ܢܛܝܒ 𝔖 > M εν ῳ ερχονται] > BA F η δε γυν. σ. παρεσται (-εστι 106) κατα σχολην (ܒܡܬܝܢܘܬܐ ܬܐܬܐ 𝔖) οπισω ημ. 44, 106, 107 𝔖 dum prosequitur nos (+puella *αβ*)

XI. 1. Rv followed by certain Vss. omits purposely to avoid the difficulty as to the precise name of the locality. Rs on the contrary, though possibly not absolutely original (Reusch conjectures Χαλάχ, cf. *γ* and Gen. x. 11), was the most ancient tradition and is presupposed by the majority of the variants.

4 while they are coming. And they went both together; and he said unto him, Take in thy hands the
5 gall. And the dog went with them, behind him and her son. And Anna sat watching the road by
6 which her son would come. And she espied him coming, and said unto his father, Behold, thy son
7 cometh, and the man that went with him. And Raphael said unto Tobias before he drew nigh to his
8 father, I know that his eyes will be opened; stuff the gall of the fish into his eyes and the medicament
will draw up and scale off the white films from his eyes, and thy father will see again and behold
9 the light. And she ran, and fell upon the neck of her son, and said unto him, I have seen thee, my
10 child; hereafter I can die. And she wept. And Tobit rose and stumbled with his feet and went forth
11 toward the door of the porch. And Tobias went towards him with the gall of the fish in his hand;

αβγ +עם גובריא דילן (pr. עם־העבדים M) Ar M 4. κ.1° . . . αυτῳ] > BA F κοινως] κ. ο κυων προετρεχεν εμπροσθεν αυτων 44, 106, 107 𝕾 κ. ειπ. αυτῳ] > BA Ρ. προς Τ. 44, 106, 107 𝕾 M +angelus 𝕷 Λαβε] +δε BA > Ar μετα χειρας] παρα χειρα BA > 44, 106, 107 tecum 𝕷 M > Ar χολην] +τ. ιχθυος (+מיד לקח ט׳ את המר׳ של דג בידו F) κ. επορευθησαν ([+וילחה] M) BA F M +τ. ιχθ. εν τ. χειρι σου 44, 106, 107 𝕾 de felle illo, et habe 𝕷 > Ar κ. συνηλ.] > 44, 106, 107 𝕾 Ar M et abiit 𝕷 αυτοις] > BA 44, 106, 107 𝕾 ο κυριος] ο κυων BA αβγ F > 44, 106, 107 𝕾 Ar M εκ τ. οπισω αυτου κ. τ. υιου αυτης] οπισθεν αυτων BA F εμπροσθεν αυτ. 58, 71, 74, 76, 236, 249 > 44, 106, 107 𝕾 Ar M cum illis 𝕷 5. > 44, 106, 107 𝕾 Αννα] ואשכחו אמיה Ar והנה אמו M εκαθητο] +invia et 𝕷 +בפרשת אורחיא Ar +על הדרך M περιβλεπ.] > F την οδον] pr. εις BA > Ar F τ. οδον] adventum 𝕷 > Ar F אם יבא M τ. υιου] παιδα BA Ar M filii 𝕷 6. > 44, 106, 107 𝕾 ερχομενον] מרחוק ותכירהו M מיד הכירם F κ. ειπ . . . μετ' αυτου] > Ar κ. ειπ.] ותרץ F κ2°.] > BA τ. πατρι αυτου] אישה M F pr. לט׳ M ιδου] +אדני F σου] μου B M > F 7. > Ar Ρ. ειπ.] 44, 106, 107 Τωβειᾳ] > B Τωβια post εγω A προς Τ. 44, 106, 107 לנער F προ τ. εγγ. . . . τ. πατ.] > BA M λαβε τ. χολην τ. ιχθ. εν τῃ χειρι σ. κ. εσται εν τ. εγγ. τ. πατρι σ. προσελευσεται σοι (πρ. σ. > 44 ܩܕܡ ܕܢܬܩܪܒ ܠܐܒܘܟ 𝕾) 44, 106, 107 𝕾 antequam adpropinquemus patri tuo 𝕷 אחי שמע בקולי ובשתכנם בבית F Επιστ.] +εγω B +εγω Τ. A > 44, 106, 107 𝕾 οτι] bis scr. A +ανοιξει B ανοιγει A κ. 106, 107 > 44 enim quia 𝕷 ܓܝܪ 𝕾 οι οφθ.] τους οφθ. BA F ܥܝܢܘܗܝ 𝕾 עור M αυτου] ο πατηρ σου. BA M F > 𝕾 ανεῳχθησονται] > BA M -ωγμενοι 44, 106, 107 𝕾 ויחבקך F 8. cf. סב מררתא דנונא ושוי בעינוי (post v. 10) Ar ובמרירה הזאת יפתחו עיניו וירפא M ενπλασον] συ εγχρισον B F συ ουν ενχ. A 23, 55, 58, 64, 71 εμπασον] 44, 106, 107 ܣܘܡ 𝕾 +ergo 𝕷 τ. ιχθ.] > BA 44, 106, 107 F ܗܢܐ 𝕾 αποστυψει τ. φαρμακον] δηχθεις διατριψει BA ܘܢܓܪܘܫ ܠܗ 𝕾 insidet medicamentum 𝕷 > F απολεπισει] αποβαλειται B βαλει A 23, 58, 71 pr. ܣܡܐ ܕܢܓܪܘܫ ܠܗ 𝕾 decoriabis 𝕷 ומיד יתרפא ויביט F απο τ. οφθ. αυτ.] > BA F αναβλεψει . . . κ.] > BA 𝕾 F τ. φως] σε BA +ܠܢܘܗܪܐ 𝕾 > F 9. sim. M 9[a]. sim. Ar κ.1°] והנה F ανεδρ.] προσδραμουσα BA Αννα ειστηκει επιβλεπουσα επι τ. οδον κ. ειδε τ. κυνα προτρεχοντα (περιτρ. 44 ܘܪܗܛܬ ܘܐܬܬ 𝕾) κ. εδραμε (κ. ε. > 44) κ. ειπεν (+ ܠܒܥܠܗ 𝕾) ιδου Τ. (> 𝕾) ο υι. σου (μου 44) ερχεται. κ. (+ ܟܣܬ ܦܪܨܘܦܗ 𝕾) ανεστρεψεν Α. εις απαντησιν του υι. αυτης (τ. υ. α. 44 αυτου) κ. περιελαβεν αυτον (κ. π. α. > 44) 44, 106, 107 κ.2°] Αννα BA mater sua αβ F επεπεσεν] επεσ. A 44 επι] εις 44 τ. υιου αυτης] αυτου 44, 106, 107 𝕾 F +ותבך F αυτω] ιδου 44, 106, 107 > 𝕾 F Ειδον κτλ.] בריך אלהא דאתיבך בשלם . . . . מה אוחרת למיתי והוי ליה כל עובדיא וחדיאת סגיא ואמרת לה זיל את לאביך ואנא קאימנא עד יתיתי אנתתך Ar אמותה הפעם אחרי ראיתי את פניך (אותך F) M F Ειδον] ιδον A vides 𝕷 παιδιον] τεκν. 44, 106, 107 fili 𝕷 απο τ. νυν] ܠܐ ܚܕܐ ܠܝ 𝕾 amodo 𝕷 αποθ.] +ܡܛܠ ܕܚܙܝܬܟ ܫܠܡܐ 𝕾 κ.4°] > 44, 106, 107 𝕾 εκλαυσεν] -σαν BA +ἀμφότεροι BA > 44, 106, 107 𝕾 Ar F +Thobias etiam lacrymatus est αβ et Th. lacr. est γ +על צואריו עוד M 10. cf. ואזל ט׳ ורפאל עמיה וכד שמע טובי . . . ואמר תב לותי . . . דאנא לא יכילנא למיזל לותך Ar ανεστη Τωβεις . . . αυλης] τ. εξηρχετο προς τ. θυραν κ. προσεκοπτεν BA cf. M (+כי לא ראהו) M ηλθε προς τ. (+ ܠܬܪܥܗ 𝕾) κ. συτος ειστηκει επι (προ 44) τ. θυρας κ. οτε ηκουσε τ. φωνης τ. υιου αυτ. ηλθεν (ܪܗܛ ܗܘܐ 𝕾) απαντησαι αυτῳ κ. αυτος προσεκοπτε (ܘܐܙܠ ܠܘܩܒܠ ܒܪܗ ܘܐܬܬܩܠ ܒܪܓܠܘܗܝ 𝕾) 44, 106, 107 𝕾 וטוביה עמד כנגד בנו לחבקו F κ. εβαδ. Τ. προς αυτ.] ο δε υιος (ט׳ M) προσεδραμεν αυτω κ. επελαβ. (κ. επ. > M) τ. πατρος αυτ. BA M κ. προσεδραμ. Τ. τ. πατρι αυτ. κ. ηρε Τ. φιλησαι αυτ. (τ. υιον αυτ. 106) κ. αμφοτερ. οι οφθ. αυτ. ηνεωγμενοι 44, 106, 107 ܘܪܗܛ ܛܘܒܝܐ ܒܪܗ ܘܐܚܕ ܠܐܒܘܗܝ ܘܢܫܩܗ ܘܗܘܘ ܥܝܢܘܗܝ ܕܬܪܝܗܘܢ ܦܬܝܚܢ ܘܥܝܢܘܗܝ ܕܛܘܒܝܛ ܦܬܝܚܢ ܗܘܝ 𝕾 וירץ ט׳ ויפל על רגלי אביו ויקם F 11. cf. ואסי אלהא ית עינוהי כיד מן אוולא Ar η χολη . . . αυτου κ.2°] > BA 44, 106, 107 ενεφυσησεν] προσεπασεν (α sup. ras. A[a]) τ. χολην BA F επασε 44, 106, 107 ܘܢܦܚ ܡܪܪܬܐ 𝕾 insufflavit 𝕷 וישם M εις] επι B 44, 107 > 106 αυτου2°] pr. τ. πατρος BA 𝕾 𝕷 +τ. χολ. τ. ιχθ. 44, 106, 107 κ.3° . . . αυτου3°] > BA M F εκκαμμυσε (ܘܟܡܫ 𝕾) τους οφθ. αυτου 44, 106, 107 𝕾 κ. ειπεν] λεγων BA +illi 𝕷 > M Θαρσει, πατερ] τι τουτο εποιησας τεκνον κ. ειπε Τωβιας (+ ܠܐܒܘܗܝ ܐܒܝ ܐܣܝܘܬܐ 𝕾) φαρμακον ιασεως εστιν πατερ (> 𝕾 +ܐܣܝܘܬܐ ܗܝ ܒܪܝ

5. dog, see Introd., p. 195.
8. ἀναβλέψει (א R[c]), Th. *Gram.*, pp. 232, 262.
9. Cf. Gen. xlvi. 29 f. for thought and language. 𝕾 with true Oriental instinct adds the detail of Anna's veiling herself.

(11, 12) and he blew into his eyes, and took hold of him and said, Courage, father! And *Tobias* threw the
12, 13 (13) medicament upon him, and gave it him; and he peeled off <the white films> with both his hands
14 from the corners of his eyes. And he fell upon his neck, and wept, and said unto him, I see thee,
child, the light of mine eyes. And he said, Blessed is God, and blessed is his great name, and blessed
15 are all his holy angels. May his great name [ ] be blessed [ ] to all ages; for he did chastise
me, and behold, I see my son Tobias. And Tobias went in rejoicing and blessing God in his whole
body, and Tobias shewed his father that his journey had prospered and that he had brought the
money, and how he had taken Sarah the daughter of Raguel to wife; and, Behold, she is at hand and
16 is nigh the gate of Nineveh. And *Tobit* went out to the gate of Nineveh to meet his daughter-in-
law, rejoicing and blessing God. And when the men of Nineveh saw him go and pass on with all
17 his strength and not led by the hand by anyone, they marvelled. And Tobit gave thanks before

ܠܡ 𝔖) 44, 106, 107 𝔖 > M κ. επεβ. . . . επεδωκ.] ως δε συνεδηχθησαν διετριψε (-ψεν A) τους οφθ. αυτ. BA > 44, 106, 107 ܘܐܣܬܟܡܗ ܠܐܦܘܗܝ 𝔖 et iniecit (introivit *γ*) medicamentum in oculis eius et morsum illi praebebat (et momordit eum *γ*) *αβγ* > F 12, 13. > *Ar* απελεπισεν . . . οφθ. αυτου] ελεπισθη απο τ. κανθ. τ. οφθ. αυτου τ. λευκωμ. BA απελ. τ. φαρμ. τ. λευκ. 44, 106, 107 ܘܟܕ ܐܣܝ ܗܘ ܠܗ ܡܢܗ ܗܘ ܥܡܠܐ ܗܘ ܡܢܚܡ ܣܘܪܦܐ 𝔖 + albugines (-em *γ*) *αβγ* ומיד נתפזרו התבלולים ופתח את עיניו M ויתברר עיניו ויפול חלובן מעיניו ונתרפא F וראה את בנו κ.2°] + ιδων τ. υιον αυτ. BA *αβγ* + ειδε (+ T. 𝔖) τ. φως 44, 106, 107 επεσεν (επεπ. B) . . . τραχ. αυτ.] ηυλογησε τον θ. κ. αναβλεψε εις τ. υιον αυτου (ܟܥܩܒܠܐ 𝔖) κ. εφιλησεν αυτ. (ܘܢܫܩܗ 𝔖) 44, 106, 107 𝔖 14. *aliter Ar* εκλαυσ.] > 44, 106, 107 *Ar* M + et benedixit Deum *αβ* αυτῳ] > BA 44, 106, 107 *αβγ Ar* M F Ειδον σε τεκν.] > BA *Ar* M F τ. φως . . . μου] > BA 44, 106, 107 𝔏 *Ar* M F κ. ειπ.] > BA 44, 106, 107 𝔏 *Ar* MF ο] *pr.* ει BA > 44, 106, 107 𝔏 θ.] κυριος 44, 106, 107 κ.2°] οτι ιδου βλεπω τον υιον μου 44, 106, 107 τ. μεγα] > BA 44, 106, 107 M כבוד מלכותו F αυτου 1°] σου BA F Κυριου 44, 106, 107 + εις τ. αιωνας BA M + του θαυμαστα ποιουντος 44, 106, 107 κ.3° . . . αυτ.2°] > 44, 106, 107 וברוכים כל משרתיך F αυτου 2°] σου BA γενοιτο τ. ονομα] > BA 44, 106, 107 *Ar* (*aliter* M) F τ. μεγα αυτου] > BA 44, 106, 107 F illius sanctum *αβγ Spec.* εφ ημ. κ. ευλογ. παντ. οι αγγ.] > BA 44, 106, 107 *αβ Ar* F benedictum *γ* et bened. *Spec. aliter* M εις παντ. τ. αιωνας] > BA 44, 106, 107 *Ar* F 15ᵃ. *plen. et aliter Ar* M οτι . . . μου] > 44, 106, 107 αυτος] > BA *γ Spec.* 28 εμαστιγωσεν] -σας BA + in redargutione mea *Spec.* 28 με] *pr.* κ. ελεησας BA + ipse misertus est mei *αβγ Spec.* 28 + ורופא *Ar* M (*cf.* F) κ. ιδου . . . μου] > *Ar* M et reddidit lumen oculis meis ut viderem filium meum *Spec.* κ.1°] > BA 𝔏 15ᵇ. *brev. Ar* > M Τωβειας 1°] ο υιος αυτ. BA Τωβιτ κ. Αννα η γυνη αυτ. εις τ. οικον 44, 106, 107 *αβ* (*γ* = א) > F χαιρων] κ. αυτοι εχαιρον 44, 106, 107 gaudentes *αβ* (*γ* = א) > F ευλογ. . . . κ.4°] > BA F ευλογων] -ουν 44, 106, 107 benedicentes 𝔏 εν . . . τ. σωματι] περι παντων τ. γεγενημενων αυτοις 44, 106, 107 toto ore suo pro omnibus quae sibi evenerant 𝔏 επεδειξεν] απηγγειλεν BA υπεδειξε 44, 106, 107 והגיד לי בני F Τωβειας 2°] > BA οτι 1° . . . Νινευη] τα μεγαλεια τα γενομενα αυτῳ [שעשה הקדש ברוך הוא F] εν τῃ Μηδειᾳ BA F > *Ar* ευοδωθη] + a Domino Deo 𝔏 οτι 2°] > 44, 106, 107 ενηνοχεν] ανηνεγκε 44, 106, 107 ως] οτι 44, 106, 107 γυναικα] *pr.* εαυτω 44, 106, 107 οτι 3°] > 44, 106, 107 παραγινεται κ.] > 44, 106, 107 συνεγγυς] εγγυς 44, 106, 107 Νινευη] εισερχομενη 44, 106, 107 16. κ.] *pr.* κ. εχαρη Τωβιτ κ. Αννα 44, 106, 107 *αβ* (> *γ*) *pr.* ופניו ביתא *Ar* εξηλθεν] -οσαν 44, 106, 107 *αβ* > *γ* + Τωβειας B F Τωβειτ B[ab] Τωβιτ A[vid] απαντησιν τ. νυμφης] συναντ. τῃ -φῃ BA > *γ* + ורפאל עמהון *Ar* αυτου] -των 44, 106, 107 *αβ* > *γ* χαιρων . . . Νινευη] > 44, 106, 107 *αβγ* πυλην] τῃ -λῃ B > *Ar* M Νιν.] > *αβγ Ar* M ιδοντες] εθαυμαζον οι εθεωρουντες BA (*cf.* M F) ειδον 44, 106, 107 *αβγ* > *Ar* οι εν Νινευη] > BA 44, 106, 107 qui erant in porta Ninive *αβγ* κ.2° . . . εθαυμασαν] οτι εβλεψεν BA (*cf.* M F) οι γειτονες αυτων κ. παν. οι συναντωντες κ. εθαυμαζον οτι διεβαινε T. ταχυ πασ. τ. ισχυι αυτ. κ. ουδεις οδηγει αυτον 44, 106, 107 venientem et ambulantem cum omni virtute sua nemine dante ei manum et mirabantur *αβγ* > *Ar* 17. 17ᵃ. *brev. Ar* > M T.] > 44, 106, 107 εξωμ.] εξομ. A ευλογει T. 44, 106, 107 מספר F εναντιον αυτων] ενωπιον αυτου (-των A) BA *pr.* μεγαλῃ τῃ φωνῃ 44, 106, 107 > F αυτων] -του B τον Θεον 44, 106, 107 הלם F εναντ. αυτ.] coram omnibus 𝔏 *pr.* et benedicebat magna voce Deum et ambulabat cum gaudio 𝔏 αυτον] -τους B ο Θεος] > 44, 106, 107 הקדוש ברוך הוא (*et saepe*) F οτι . . . κ.3°] > BA F ηγγισεν] *pr.* ως BA 𝔏 *pr.* οτι 44, 106, 107 כד חזאה *Ar* F > M Σαρρᾳ] adducens Sarram 𝔏 τῃ γυν. T. τ. υιου αυτου] τῃ νυμφῃ αυτ. BA 44, 106, 107 F uxorem suam 𝔏 κ. ευλογ.] κατευλογ. BA ευλογ. 44, 106, 107 αυτην] + Thobis 𝔏 κ. ειπ. αυτῃ] λεγων BA 𝔏 ואמר *Ar* F Εισελθ.1° . . . θυγ.3°] יתן אלהא לך מן אנתתא הדא בנין קשיטין ועיני ועיני אמך חמן *Ar brev. et aliter* M Εισελθ.] ελθ. BA δευρο ελ. 44, 106, 107. intra 𝔏 > F θυγατερ] + προς με 44, 106, 107 *pr.* Sarra 𝔏 > F κ.6° . . . κ.7°] > 44, 106, 107 κ.6°] > BA 𝔏 M F σου] > BA *αβγ* M F θυγατερ 2°] > BA 𝔏 M F ευλογημενος 1°] > BA M והנה ביתך F ο πατ. σου] + κ. μητηρ σου א[c a] BA 44, 106, 107 𝔏 > M κ. ευλ. T. . . . θυγατερ 4°] > BA M F τ. ο υιος μου] ο υ. μ. T. 44, 106, 107 > M F κ. εν τ. ημερ. . . . Νιν.] > *Ar*

12, 13. τὰ λευκώματα is to be restored after χερσὶν αὐτοῦ (from *αβγ*). 𝔙 alone states that Tobit held his father *quasi dimidiam fere horam* and that the peelings were *quasi membrana ovi*.

14. The second reference to the angels (which occasioned the insertion of ἐφ᾽ ἡμᾶς κ.) in א is a mere repetition from the preceding clause, being unknown to *αβγ* as well as to R[v] R[c] *Ar* M F.

them, because God had shewed mercy on him, and because he had opened his eyes. And Tobit
came near to Sarah the wife of Tobias his son, and he blessed her, and said unto her, Welcome,
18 daughter; and blessed is thy God which hath brought thee unto us, daughter, and blessed is thy
father and blessed is Tobias my son and blessed art thou, daughter; welcome, daughter, to thy
home, with blessing and joy, welcome, daughter. On this day there was joy to all the Jews which
were at Nineveh. And **Aḥiḳar** and **Nadab** his cousin [ ] came rejoicing unto Tobit.

E. The Self-revelation and Ascension of Raphael, xii. 1–22.

i. **The Offer of Wages**, *vv.* 1–5.

12 1 And when the wedding feast was ended Tobit called his son Tobias, and said unto him, Child,
see that thou give the wages to the man which went with thee, so that thou give him more for his
2 wages. And he said unto him, Father, How much shall I give him as his wages? It is no harm
3 to me to give him the half of the possessions which he has brought with me. He hath led me in
safety, and he cured my wife, and brought the money with me, and cured thee; how much shall I
4 give him further as wages? And Tobit said unto him, It is due unto him, child, to take the half of
5 all which thou hadst when thou camest. And he called him and said, Take the half of all that thou
hadst when thou camest for thy wages, and go in peace.

κ. 9°] > 44, 106, 107 εν τ. ημερᾳ ταυτ.] κ. BA 44, 106, 107 F (*cf.* M) χαρα] + εν τ. ημερᾳ εκεινῃ 44, 106, 107 + גדולה F Ιουδαιοις] εν Νινευη αδελφοις αυτου BA > F τοις . . . Νινευη] > BA τ. κατοικουσιν 44, 106, 107 F 18. > *Ar* Αχεικαρ ℵ*] Αχειαχαρος ℵ^{c a} Αχιαχαρος BA Αχιαχαρ 44 ܚܝܩܪ 𝕾 Achicarus αβ Achiacar γ Achior 𝔙 > M F Ναβαδ] Νασβας BA Ναβας 44, 106, 107 ܢܕܒ 𝕾 Nabal αβ in navis γ Nabath 𝔙 > M F οι εξαδελφοι ℵ*] ο -φος ℵ^{c b} BA ܒܪ ܚܬܗ 𝕾 avunculus αβ consobrini 𝔙 > γ M F αυτου] ܕܛܘܒܝܐ 𝕷 Tobiae 𝔙 > M F χαιροντες προς Τ.] (+ αβγ) κ. ηχθη ο γαμος Τωβεια μετ' ευφροσυνης επτα ημερας BA αβγ (*cf.* F) π. τ. χ. 44, 106, 107 + et data sunt ויתנו M illi munera multa (+ ויקרות M) αβγ M χαιροντες] > (*postea restituit*) ℵ^{c b} gaudens γ

XII. *aliter Ar* 1. οτε (ℵ^{1 (vid)} > οτε ℵ*) επετ. ο γαμ.] > BA M F εκαλ. . . . αυτῳ] ειπ. Τ. Τ. τ. υιω αυτ. 44, 106, 107 𝕾 M παιδ. ορα] ο. τεκν. BA τεκν. 44, 106, 107 > 𝕷 ορα] > M δουναι τον] > BA αποδωμεν 44, 106, 107 𝕾 𝕷 נתן M והשלים F πορευθ. μετ. σ.] συνελθοντι σοι BA qui tecum fuit 𝕷 προσθειναι] *pr.* κ. BA 𝕾 κ. (> 𝕷 M) -θωμεν 44, 106, 107 𝕷 M > F αυτῳ] > 44, 106, 107 F εις τ. μισθ.] δει BA + αυτου 44, 106, 107 𝕾 > F 2. αυτῳ] > B 𝕷 Τωβιας 44, 106, 107 𝕾 *pr.* 'ענה ט F ποσ. . . . μισθ.] > BA M F αυτ. δωσῳ] δῳ αυτ. 44, 106, 107 τον] > 44, 106, 107 𝕾 𝕷 μισθ.] > 𝕾 𝕷 ου βλαπτ.] ܠܐ ܓܝܪ ܣܓܝ ܠܝ ܠܐ 𝕾 non enim satis est 𝕷 > M ראוי לנו F διδους] δους BA γαρ (> 44) εαν δω 44, 106, 107 τ. υπαρχ.] > BA 44, 106, 107 𝕾 הכסף M F ενηνοχεν] -χα BA 𝕾 αβγ M F ηνεγκε 106, 107 μετ' εμ.] > BA משם M 3. εμε] οτι με με BA 𝕾 𝕷 *pr.* διοτι 44, 106, 107 *pr.* כי הרבה עשה לנו F αγιοχεν] -ηοχε B^b + σοι BA ετηρησεν 44, 106, 107 𝕾 duxit et reduxit 𝕷 הציל מן־הדנ F υγιαινοντα] -ιη BA εν τ. οδῳ 44, 106, 107 𝕾 + והביאני בשלום M αργυρ.] + μου BA μετ' εμου] > BA 44, 106, 107 𝕾 F מיד גביאל M κ. σ. εθερ.] > 𝕾 σε] + ομοιως BA את עיניך M ποσον . . . μισθον] > BA F ου βλαπτομαι οσον αν (εαν 106 > 44) δω αυτῳ 44, 106, 107 ܠܐ ܓܝܪ ܣܓܝ ܠܝ ܕܐܬܠ ܠܗ 𝕾 ומה ראוי לתת לו M ετι] > 𝕷 F על כל זאת M 4. > 𝕾 M κ.1°] *pr.* 'ענה ט F αυτῳ] > BA 44, 106, 107 𝕷 Τ.] ο πρεσβυτης BA Δικαιουται] Δικαιον δουναι 44, 106, 107 מן הדין ומן הצדק ראוי לו F παιδιον . . . ηλθεν] > BA F παιδιον] > 44, 106, 107 F λαβειν] > 44, 106, 107 F παντων] horum 𝕷 חצי הכסף F εχων ηλθες] ηλθεν (-θες 44) εχ. μετα σου 44, 106, 107 tecum attulit 𝕷 5. εκαλ.] + טוביה M *pr.* מיד F αυτον] τ. αγγ. BA *pr.* Τ. 𝕷 'אל־ר M למלאך רפאל F ειπ.] + αυτῳ BA 𝕾 𝕷 (M) F + [בא ו] עזריה אחי M 'עז' בני F παντων] horum 𝕷 הכסף M F εχων ηλθες] ενηνοχατε B ενηνοχας A εχω 44 ܕܐܝܬܝܬ ܥܡܟ 𝕾 שהבאת[י] משם M > F εις τ. μισθον σ.] > BA 𝕾 haec erit merces tua 𝕷 [כי הוא שכרך] M בשכר טורחך F

---

18. R^s (except γ) and R^c reproduce fairly faithfully the original form of the name Aḥiḳar, which R^v has by no means entirely lost. 𝔙 has Achior, an instance of 𝔙's affinities with some Syriac version (ܐܚܝܩܪ = ܐܚܝܘܪ). Nasbas in R^v (with which R^c is a compromise) may be meant for the younger brother of Nadan, but *Nadab* is the original, the second and third conss. having suffered metathesis in ℵ, characteristic transcriptional changes in αβ 𝕾 (ܢܕܒ into ܢܒܕ), vocalic confusion in 𝔙, and more serious textual corruption in γ. Cf. the variations in the Aḥiḳar story and Ed. Meyer, *Der Papyrusfund von Elephantine*, 1912, p. 106, footnote 2. αβ (cf. 𝔙) contain the original statement of R^s, from which ℵ only departed by mistaking the sing. for the plur. Granted this slight change, R^s is quite in conformity with the Aḥiḳar story.

XII. 3. ἁγίοχεν, Th. *Gram.*, p. 204.

ii. **Raphael's Wisdom and Self-revelation,** *vv.* 6–15.

His maxims of life, vv. 6–10.

6 Then he called them both privily, and said unto them, Bless God, and give him thanks in the
sight of all that live, for the good things which he hath done unto you, to bless and praise his name.
7 The words of God show forth to all men with honour and be not slack to give him thanks. It is
good to keep close the secret of a king, but to confess and reveal the works of God. And confess ye
8 them with honour. Do the good, and evil shall not find you. Better is prayer with truth, and alms
with righteousness than riches with unrighteousness; it is better to give alms than to lay up gold:
9 almsgiving doth deliver from death, and it purges away all sin. They that do alms shall be fed
10 with life; they that commit sin and unrighteousness are enemies to their own life.

His revelation of his own being and office, vv. 11–15.

11 I will show you all the truth and will keep close nothing from you. Already I have shown you
and have said, It is good to keep close the secret of a king, but the works of God to reveal gloriously.

κ.] > BA υπαγε] > BA βαδιζε 44, 106, 107 υγιαιν.] > BA 6. τοτε] κ. B > M F εκαλ.] καλεσας BA *pr.* Raph. 𝔏 ויאמר ר׳ M אמר F τ. δυο] *pr.* P. ομου 44, 106, 107 [Syriac] 𝔖 אל ט׳ ואל ט׳ M ר׳ להם F κρυπτ.] > 44, 106, 107 M *plen.* F κ. ειπ. . . . εξομ. αυτ.] *aliter* M κ.1°] > BA αυτοις] [Syriac] 𝔖 τον θ.] *post* ευλογ. BA αυτῳ] -τον 44, 106, 107 εξομ.] + μεγαλωσυνην διδοτε αυτῳ κ. εξομ. αυτῳ B μεγαλυνατε 44, 106, 107 + et ipsius maiestati date honorem et confitemini illi *a β γ* τ. ζωντ.] ανθρωπ. 44, 106, 107 𝔖 בקהל עם F α . . . εξομ. αυτ.] > γ α] περι ων BA quia *a β* > F υμ.] ημ. 106 > F αγαθα] -θον BA -θον γαρ 106, 107 > 44 [Syriac] 𝔖 נפלאותיו F του . . . αυτου] > 44 ευλογ.] + τον θ. BA 106, 107 *a β* 𝔖 *pr.* טוב F υμν.] υψουν (-οιν B) BA 106, 107 𝔖 τ. λογ.] + τ. εργων BA *pr.* κ. 44 et sermones de operibus *a β* του θ.] αυτου 44 *a β* υποδεικ.] -κνυοντες (-γν. A) BA *post* εντιμ. απαγγειλ. 44, 106, 107 [Syriac] 𝔖 πασιν ανθρ.] > BA 44, 106, 107 > *a β* [Syriac] 𝔖 εντιμ.] > 𝔖 κ. μη . . . αυτῳ] > 44, 106, 107 𝔖 et confitemini illi *a β* 7–12. > γ 7. *aliter* M *simil.* F μυστηριον] -ια 44, 106, 107 *pr.* quoniam *a β* βασιλεως] [Syriac] 𝔖 κρυπτ. . . . εντιμ.] > 𝔖 κρυπτ. καλ.] καλ. -ψαι B καλ. -πτειν A 44, 106, 107 εργα] + κυριου 44, 106, 107 εξ—θαι κ. ανακ. κ. εξ—θε εντιμ.] ανακ. ενδοξως BA αναγγελλειν εντιμως 44, 106, 107 revelare et confitere honorificum est *a β et mult. patr.* το αγ. . . . υμας] > A 44, 106, 107 *a β* το αγ. ποιειτε] αγ. -ησατε B [Syriac] 𝔖 ευρ. υμ.] [Syriac] 𝔖 8. *similiter* M [Syriac] 𝔖 αληθειας] νηστει. (-τιας A) BA 44, 106, 107 *a β Spec.* 24 *Cypr. Aug. Ps.-Aug.* F ελεημοσυνη] -ης BA > F μετα 2°] κ. BA *Cypr. Aug. Ps.-Aug.* (*a β Spec.* 24 = א) > F δικαιοσ.] + αγαθον το ολιγον μετα δικαιοσυνης BA μαλλον 1° . . . αδικιας] super utrumque autem melius est modicum cum iustitia quam plurimum cum iniquitate *a β* et in his omnibus etiam modicum cum iust. melius est quam plur. cum iniq. *Spec.* 24 > F μαλλον (*bis*)] > BA 44, 106, 107 η] υπερ 44, 106, 107 πλουτος] πολυ BA αμφοτερα 44, 106, 107 μετα αδικιας] > 44, 106, 107 καλον] κρεισσον 44, 106, 107 ποιησαι] *pr.* το A ποιειν 44, 106, 107 θησαυρισαι] -ζειν 44, 106, 107 9. ελεημ.1°] + γαρ A 44, 106, 107 *a β* αυτη] > 44, 106, 107 𝔖 αποκαθαιρει] -αριει BA καθαριζει 44, 106, 107 *a β* > 𝔖 M πασ. αμαρτιαν] απο π. αμαρτιας 44, 106, 107 > 𝔖 M peccata *a β* עון F ελεημ.2°] + κ. δικαιοσυνας BA + et miserationem et iustitiam *a β* > M χορτασθ.] πλησθ. BA *a β* εμπλ. 44, 106, 107 [Syriac] 𝔖 ישביעהו הק״בה F > M 10. > 𝔖 M *simil.* F οι] + δε BA ποιουντες αμ. κ. αδικ.] αμαρτανοντες BA ψυχης] ζωης BA 44, 106, 107 11. πασ. . . . υποδειξω κ.] > BA M F κ. νυν αναγγελω υμιν πασ. τ. αληθ. 44, 106, 107 πασ.] > 𝔖 κρυψ.] αποκρ. 106, 107 παν] > 44, 106, 107 𝔖 ρημα] > 𝔖 ηδη . . . υπεδειξα κ.] > BA 44, 106, 107 𝔖 M F ειπον. . . . ενδοξως] > 44, 106, 107 𝔖 M *simil.* F ειπον] ειρηκα δη (δε A) BA καλον κρυψαι] κρ. καλ. BA κ. τα] τα δε BA autem *a β Aug.* > *Cypr.* ανακαλυπτειν] + et confiteri *a β Cypr.* > *Aug.* 12. *simil.* M F κ. νυν] > 44, 106, 107 𝔖 et tunc *a β* οτε] ουτω 44 κ. Σ.] συ (+ Τ. 𝔖) κ. η νυμφη σου Σ. BA 44, 106, 107 𝔖 M F tu *a β Cypr. Aug. Spec.* εγω . . . υμων] εισηκουσθη (*pr.* κ. 44) η φωνη ([Syriac] 𝔖) αμφοτερων 44, 106, 107 𝔖 הכנסתי את דמעתכם F τ. δοξ. Κυρ.] τ. αγιου BA του θ. 44, 106, 107 𝔖 in clar. Dei et legi *a β* כסא הכבוד M לפני הק״בה F κ. οτε εθαπτ.] κ. εισηκουσθη ([Syriac] 𝔖) σου τ. εργα κ. ελεημοσυναι (*pr.* αι 44) σου (σ > 44) ας εποιησας επι 44, 106, 107 𝔖 ωσαυτως] + συμπαρημην (συνπ. A μην *sup. ras.* A[a?]) σοι BA M (*cf.* F) > 44, 106, 107 𝔖 similiter *a β Aug.* simpliciter *Cypr.*

6. Cod. Vat.'s ὑψοῖν is the only infin. in -οιν in LXX; among the papyri the earliest example of it belongs to the year 18 A.D., Moult., *Prol.* 53, n. 2.

τῶν ἔργων after λόγους probably once stood in R^s (as 𝔏 suggests), but was either a gloss or a doublet translation, which is rightly omitted in א and R^c but retained in R^v, exactly as in *v.* 9 R^v has retained the doublet δικαιοσύνην and inserted the copula before it. Müller's supposition that τ. ἔργων here points back to דברו (אמרו) מעשי אלהים misread as דברי (אמרי) מ׳ א׳ is untenable since the verse is already more than sufficiently well supplied with verbs.

12 And now, when thou didst pray and Sarah, I did bring the memorial of your prayer before the
13 glory of the Lord: and when thou didst bury the dead, likewise. And when thou didst not delay
14 to rise up, and leave thy dinner, but didst go and cover the dead, then I was sent unto thee to try
(14), 15 thee; and at the same time God did send me also to heal Sarah thy daughter-in-law. I am Raphael,
one of the seven angels, which stand and enter before the glory of the Lord.

iii. **Raphael's Commission and Ascension,** *vv.* 16–22.

16, 17 And they were both troubled, and fell upon their faces; and they were afraid. And he said
18 unto them, Be not afraid, peace be unto you; bless God to all eternity. I when I was with you,
was not with you of any favour of mine, but by the will of God; him bless ye day by day, him
praise.

19 **R**[S] And ye behold me that I have eaten nothing,
20 but a vision hath appeared to you. And now
bless the Lord on the earth and give God thanks:
Behold I ascend to him that sent me: write down
all these things which have been happened to you.
21 And he ascended. And they rose up and could

All these days did I appear unto you; and I **R**
did neither eat nor drink, but it was a vision ye
yourselves saw. And now give God thanks
because I ascend to him that sent me: and write
in a book all the things which have been done.
And they rose up and saw him no more. And

13. *plen.* M κ. οτε] et quia *αβγ Cypr. Aug.* ουκ ωκν.] > 44, 106, 107 M F ܡܬܚܡܠܬ 𝔖 αναστηναι] -στας > 44, 106, 107 𝔖 > M F κ.2° . . . κ.4°] 44, 106, 107 𝔖 καταλιπειν] -λειπιν A σου] *post* αριστ. BA κ.] οπως BA ωχου κ.] απελθων BA περιεστειλες] -στειλης BA -εστειλας 44, 106, 107 ܩܒܪܬ 𝔖 sepelisti 𝔏 M F +ובלילה F τοτε . . . πειρ. σε] ουκ ελαθες με (ς με *sup. ras.* A[a]) αγαθοποιων (αγαθον ποιων A) αλλα συν σοι ημην BA κ. ηλθεν επι σε πειρασμος 44, 106, 107 (*αβγ Cypr. Aug.*=א) +et S. nurum tuam (*ex v.* 14) *αβ plen.* M 14. > *αβ simil.* M κ.] > 𝔖 iterum *Cypr. Aug.* αμα] νυν BA F ο θ. 44, 106, 107 𝔖 ובעת צרתך M απεσταλκεν] -ειλεν BA 44, 106, 107 με] +ܘܐܢܣܝܟ 𝔖 ο θ.] > 44, 106, 107 𝔖 κ.2°] *pr.* σε BA 44, 106, 107 𝔖 γ *Cypr. Aug.* Σ.] *post* σου BA > 44, 106, 107 𝔖 15. εγω] *pr.* ܐܢܐ 𝔖 Ρ.]+המלאך M εις] +εκ BA επτα] > 44, 106, 107 M αγγελ.] *pr.* αγιων BA *αβγ Cypr. Ps-Aug.* (> *in altero loc. Ps-Aug.*) > 44, 106, 107 +iustis *Cypr. Aug. in alt. loc.* השרים M οι] > 44, 106, 107 𝔖 παρεστηκασιν] προσαναφερουσιν τ. προσευχας τ. αγιων BA τ. παρεστωτων 44, 106, 107 𝔖 κ. εισπορ.] > 44, 106, 107 𝔖 M τ. δοξ.] > 44, 106, 107 𝔖 F *pr.* כסא M Κυρ.] τ. αγιου BA του θ. 44, 106, 107 𝔖 Dei 𝔏 > M הק"בה F 16. εταραχθ.] ܘܫܬܓܫܘ ܘܕܚܠܘ 𝔖 οι δυο] αμφοτεροι 44, 106, 107 ויהי כשמעם את כל הדברים M (*cf.*) F επεσαν] -ον B 44 +αμφοτεροι 44 αυτων] > BA +επι τ. γην 44, 106, 107 𝔖 κ.3°] οτι BA 106, 107 > 44 𝔖 εφοβηθ.] > 44 𝔖 M 17. ειπ.] +R. 𝔏 M ειρηνη] *pr.* οτι A *ante* μ. φοβ. M υμιν] +εσται BA 44, 106, 107 τον] +δε BA τον θ.] *post* ευλογ. 44, 106, 107 εις] 44, 106, 107 𝔖 παντα] > BA 44, 106, 107 𝔖 τ. αιωνα] > 44, 106, 107 𝔖 *aliter* M (*cf.* F) 18. > M *aliter* F εγω . . . υμων 1°] > BA 44, 106, 107 𝔖 ουχι] οτι ου BA 44, 106, 107 𝔖 εμη] εμαυτου BA χαριτι] ܒܛܝܒܘܬܝ 𝔖 ημην μεθ' υμ.] > BA 44, 106, 107 𝔖 𝔏 θελησει] ܒܨܒܝܢܗ 𝔖 θεου] +υμων B +υ. ηλθον A +εγω ηλθον 44, 106, 107 +ܗܘܘ ܡܫܒܚܝܢ 𝔖 αυτον . . . υμνειτε] > 44, 106, 107 𝔖 αυτ. ευλ.] οθεν ευλ. αυτ. BA 𝔏 κατα . . . ημερ.] εις τ. αιωνα BA *pr.* et *αβγ* αυτῳ υμν.] > BA 19. et videbatis me *αβ* videbatis enim me quia manducabam sed visu vestro videbatis *γ* videbatis me manducare sed visu vestro videbatis *Aug.* 13122 vidistis me &c. *Aug.* *simil.* M F κ. θεωρειτε με] πασ. τ. ημερας ωπτανομην υμιν BA > 44, 106, 107 𝔖 οτι] κ. BA 44, 106, 107 𝔖 ουθεν] ουδε επιον BA 44, 106, 107 𝔖 ορασις . . . εθεωρειτο] ܐܢܬܘܢ ܚܙܝܬܘܢ ܐܢܬܘܢ ܗܘܝܬܘܢ ܠܝ ܕܐܟܠ ܠܐ ܐܟܠܬ ܘܫܬܝܬ ܠܐ 𝔖 ορασις] -σιν BA -σεις 44, 106, 107 υμιν] -εις BA > 44, 106, 107 εθεωρειτο] -ρειτε BA 44, 106, 107 20. וכהשלים את הדברים מיד נעלם מעיניהם F ευλογ. . . . Κυρ. κ.] > BA M αναστητε εκ τ. γης 44, 106, 107 𝔖 et nunc benedicite in terra *γ* et nunc surgite a terra *αβ* εξομολ. . . . αποστ. με] > 44, 106, 107 𝔖 M ιδου εγω] διοτι BA γραψ.] *pr.* κ. BA 44, 106, 107 𝔖 *pr.* ergo 𝔏 παντα] *pr.* ταυτα 44, 106, 107 ܐܝܟ ܗܠܝܢ 𝔖 ταυτ. τ. συμβαντα υμ.] τ. συντελεσθεντα BA > 44, 106, 107 𝔖 κ. ανεβη] εις βιβλιον BA 44, 106, 107 𝔖 (+*mult. verb.*) M +κ. τον θ. ευλογειτε εγω γαρ αναβαινω προς τ. αποστειλαντα με θ. (θ. > 𝔖) 44, 106, 107 𝔖 (*cf.* M) +וישלחוהו M 21. > (*cf. v.* 20) F κ. ανεστησαν] ויעל מלאך

16–22. The linguistic affinities with the records of the Transfiguration, Resurrection, and Ascension of Christ are remarkable. With the whole of *v.* 16 cf. Matt. xvii. 6, Luke xxiv. 5. With μὴ φοβεῖσθε in 17 cf. Matt. xxviii. 5, 10. εἰρήνη ὑμῖν cf. Luke xxiv. 36 (>D+ἐγώ εἰμι, μὴ φοβεῖσθε G old Lat.), John xx. 19, xxi. 26. (With *v.* 18 cf. John i. 13.) With ἐθεωρεῖτε (19) cf. Luke xxiv. 37, 39; οὐκ ἔφαγον contrast Luke xxiv. 43; with ὠπτανόμην (in LXX 3 (1) Kings viii. 8 and in papyri, e.g. ὀπτάεται in *Paris* No. 49. 33. *c.* 160 B.C., and ὀπτανομένων *Tebtunis* No. 245. 117 B.C.) cf. Acts i. 3 and the 'Great magical papyrus' of *c.* 300 A.D. (No. 574 of the *Supplément grec* in the Bibliothèque Nationale at Paris, reproduced in part by Deissm. in *L.A.E.*, pp. 250–60), in the Jewish text of which occur the words ὁρκίζω σε τὸν ὀπτανθέντα τῷ 'Οσραηλ. In *v.* 20 with ἀναβαίνω πρός cf. John xx. 17; πρὸς τὸν ἀποστ. με cf. John xvi. 5, xx. 21. With γράψατε and εἰς βιβλίον (R[V]) cf. John xx. 30, xxi. 25, Rev. i. 11; ἀνέβη (R[S]) cf. Ephes. iv. 9. With *v.* 21 cf. Acts xxi. 9, 10. With ηὐλόγουν in *v.* 22 (R[S]) cf. Luke xxiv. 53; ὤφθη αὐτοῖς ἄγγελος cf. 1 Tim. iii. 16 ὤφθη ἀγγέλοις.

22 no longer see him. And they blessed and praised God and they gave him thanks for these his great works, how the angel of God had appeared unto them.

they confessed the great and wonderful works of God, and how the angel of the Lord had appeared unto them.

iv. Tobit's Prayer of Joy, xiii. 1–18.

The Exile's prayer of exhortation and consolation, vv. 1–6.

13 1 And he said
Blessed is God that liveth for ever, and his kingdom,

2 For he chastiseth, and showeth mercy.
He leadeth down to Hades below the earth,
And he bringeth up from the great destruction;
And there is nothing that shall escape his hand.

3 Give thanks unto him before the Gentiles, ye children of Israel,
For he hath scattered you among them,
4 And there he hath shown you his greatness;
And extol ye him before all the living.

Because he is our Lord, and he our God, and he our Father,
Yea, he is God to all the ages:
5 He will chastise you for your iniquities,
And will show mercy unto you all.

6 When ye turn unto him out of all the nations
Whithersoever ye shall be scattered,

M לא יסף להראות ܚܙܝܢ ܗܘܘ 𝔖 ουκ ειδοσαν 106, 107 ουκετι ηδυν. ιδειν] ουκ ειδον BA 44 השמימה יי M αυτον] + ουκετι 106, 107 + ܘܠܐ ܐܬܚܙܝ ܠܗܘܢ 𝔖 22. ηυλογ. . . . αυτου] *ante* וישלחוה M *brev.* F ηυλογ. . . . θεον κ.] > BA ηυλογουν τ. θ. κ. 44, 107 𝔖 -ουντο τ. κυριον 106 αυτῳ] > BA 44, 106, 107 𝔖 επι] > BA αυτου] > BA τ. μεγαλα] > 44, 106, 107 𝔖 ταυτα] κ. θαυμαστα αυτου (του θ. A) BA > 44, 106, 107 𝔖 omnibus 𝔏 ως . . . θεου] α εποιησεν αυτοις 44, 106, 107 𝔖 > M ως] *pr.* κ. A αγγελος] *pr.* ο A θεου] Κυρ. BA

XIII. > *Ar* 1. κ.1°] *pr.* κ. T. εγραψεν προσευχην (την πρ. (ܠܬܫܒܘܚܬܐ 𝔖) ταυτ. 44, 106, 107 𝔖) εις αγαλλιασιν BA 44, 106, 107 𝔖 M וט׳ תקן תפלה והתחיל להתפלל F Tunc locutus est T. et scripsit orationem in laetitiam (-ia *a*) *aβγ* ειπ.] + ܗܕܐ 𝔖 M Ευλογ. ο θ.] Benedictus es (𝔖 *passim in vv.* 1–18) deus 𝔏 𝔖 ο ζων] quia magnus es et vivis 𝔏 הגדול המפליא לעשות (ם *solum*) פלאיו לעמו ועבדיו M εις τ. αιωνα] εις τ. -νας BA 44, 106, 107 > 𝔖 M κ.2°] οτι εις παντ. τ. αιωνας 44, 106, 107 𝔏 + ܠܐ ܥܒܪܐ 𝔖 η βασ. αυτ.] + est 𝔏 שם כבוד מלכותו F 2. *pr.* הוא טרף וירפאני F ελεᾳ] -εει B[ab] ורופא M F וממית ומחיה M εως ᾳδου] εις αδην BA κατωτ. τ. γης] > BA 44 𝔖 M F κατω 106, 107 𝔏 [κ. αυτ. αναγ. *usque ad cap. fin. aliter* M] αυτ.2°] > BA 44 𝔖 𝔏 εκ τ. απωλ.] > BA 44 𝔖 F τ. μεγ.] > BA 𝔖 F εν τ. μεγαλωσυνη αυτου 44, 106, 107 𝔏 ουδ.] > BA 44, 106, 107 𝔖 𝔏 F ο] ος BA 44, 106, 107 𝔖 𝔏 F εκφευξ.] effugiat 𝔏 τ. χ. αυτ.] ܡܢ ܐܝܕܘܗܝ 𝔖 > F 3. εξομολογεισθε] εξωμολογεισθαι A οι] > 44 Ισρ.] θεου 44, 106, 107 ενωπ. τ. εθνων] *pr.* שירו ··· בקשו פניו תמיד F υμας] ημ. BA 44, 106, 107 𝔖 4. *simil.* F κ.1°] > BA 44, 106, 107 𝔖 εκει] > 44, 106, 107 𝔖 υπεδειξεν . . . ζωντος] ܘܬܡܢ ܐܚܘܝ ܠܟܘܢ ܪܒܘܬܗ ܩܕܡ ܟܠ ܕܚܝ 𝔖 υπεδειξεν υμιν] υποδειξατε BA 44, 106, 107 *aβ* μεγαλωσ.] misericordiam 𝔏 κ.2°] > BA 44 καθοτι] διοτι 44, 106, 107 quoniam 𝔏 ημ.1° κυρ. εστιν κ.3° αυτ.2° θ.1° ημ.2°] κυρ. ημ. κ. θ. αυτ. (ο θ̅ς̅ ο A) BA κυρ. κ. θ. ημ. 106, 107 κυρ. θ. 44 est Dominus Deus noster 𝔏 κ.4° αυτ.3°] > BA κ. 106, 107 ο 44 κ.5° αυτ.4° θ.2°] > BA 𝔖 et deus 𝔏 5. μαστ.] *pr.* κ. BA flagellavit 𝔏 F μαστιγ. . . . υμων κ.] ܘܢܪܕܐ ܠܟܘܢ ܥܠ ܥܘܠܟܘܢ ܘܢܪܚܡ 𝔖 υμας] ημ. BA 44, 106, 107 επι] εν BA 44, 106, 107 ob 𝔏 υμων] ημ. BA 44, 106, 107 παντ. υμ.] παλιν BA 44, 106, 107 𝔖 > F ελεησ.] + באחרית הימים ולהושיעכם F κ. συναξει ημας BA 44, 106, 107 𝔖 *aβ* οπου αν] ου εαν BA ου 44, 106, 107 ubicumque 𝔏 διασκορπισθητε] σκορπ. B εσκορπισθητε A διεσκορπισθημεν 44, 106, 107 𝔖 dispersi fueritis 𝔏 6. *aliter* F οταν] εαν BA 44, 106, 107 κ.1° . . . υμων 2°] > 𝔏

---

22. ἐξομολ. (Cod. Vat.) cf. Th. *Gram.*, p. 199.

XIII. 3. ὅτι may be an error for οὗ or, as it is common to all recensions, a mistranslation of אשר (Müller, *op. cit.*, p. 33, n. 1).

6[b]–10[a]. ℵ's lacuna is due to that very common cause of such omissions, homoeoteleuton, and is not a proof of more than average frailty on the part of its scribe. After he had transcribed τ. βασ. τ. αιων, of 6[a], his eye returning to the MS. he was copying, lighted on τ. βασ. τ. αιων. in *v.* 10[a] and he proceeded to transcribe 10[b].

With your whole heart and with your whole soul, to do truth before him,
Then he will turn unto you, and will no longer hide his face from you.

And now see what he hath wrought with you,
And give him thanks with your whole mouth,
And bless the Lord of righteousness,
And exalt the everlasting King.

< I, in the land of my captivity, give him thanks,
And show his strength and majesty unto nations of sinners.
Turn, ye sinners, and do righteousness before him.
Who can tell if he will accept you and have mercy on you?

The New Jerusalem, vv. 7–18[a].

7 I exalt my God, and my soul [ ] shall rejoice in the King of heaven;
8 Of his greatness let all men tell,
And let them give him thanks in Jerusalem.

9 O Jerusalem, thou holy city! he will chastise thee for the works of thy hands,
And will again have mercy on the sons of the righteous.
10 Give thanks to the Lord with goodness, and bless the everlasting King, >

That thy tabernacle **may** be builded in thee again with joy,
And that he may make glad in thee all that are captives,
And love in thee all that are miserable and all the generations of eternity.

τη 1°] > B εν ολη. . . ψυχη] > 𝔖 υμων 2°] > B ενωπιον] εμπροσθεν 44, 106, 107 αληθ.] + ܒܟܠܗ ܘܨܠܐ 𝔖 τοτε . . . αφ. υμων] > 𝔖 επιστρεψει] ε *sup. ras.* A? ουκετι] > BA 44, 106, 107 κ. νυν . . . δικαιοσυνης κ.] > 44 νυν] > BA 106, 107 εποιησεν] ποιησει BA 106, 107 μεθ'] με *sup. ras.* B[ab] στοματι] σωματι B ܒܦܘܡܟܘܢ 𝔖 corde 𝔏 ευλογησατε] -γειτε A 106, 107 υμων 5°] + ut faciatis coram illo veritatem 𝔏 κυριον] ܠܐܠܗܐ 𝔖 שמו F τ. δικαιοσυν.] > F in iustitia 𝔏 τ. αιωνων] אשר מלכותו עומדת לעולם ועד F εγω—10[a] > א [*usque ad* 10[a] B:—] εγω . . . αμαρτωλων] > 𝔖 ואספר נפלאותיו וכחו וגבורתו לעיני כל חי F μου] > 44, 106, 107 εξομολογουμαι] -γησομαι 44, 106, 107 ισχυν] + ipsius 𝔏 εθνη αμαρτωλων B.] -νει -λῳ 248, 249 coram [in *Cypr.*] natione peccatrice αβ *Cypr.* αμαρτωλοι] > 44, 106, 107 *pr.* המורדים F κ. ποιησατε . . . αυτου] > F τις γιν. . . . υμιν;] > 44 τις γιν. (γιγν. A)] > 𝔖F η B*] ει A > B[b] ο 𝔖 אולי F θελησει] > F υμας] ημας 106, 107 > αβ (vos *Spec.* 5) κ. ποιησει] ut faciat 𝔏 υμιν] εις υμας A ημιν 106, 107 + כי אל רחום ··· ורב חסד ואמת F 7. τον] *pr.* εγω 44, 106, 107 F *pr.* ܡܫܒܚ ܐܢܐ 𝔖 τ. θεον μ.] > αβ υψω] אקרא F ego (*vide sub* τ. ουρ.) αβ τ. βασιλει] τ. βασιλεα A 44, 106, 107 ܠܡܠܟܐ 𝔖 τ. ουρ. (*v.* υψω)] > 𝔖 caeli laetationem (-orum -titiam *Fac. Herm. Def.*) dicimus αβ κ. 2°] + anima mea (*iterum*) αβ κ. 2° αγαλλιασεται] αγαλλιασομαι 44, 106 > 𝔖 הוד והדר לפניו F + omnibus diebus vitae meae αβ τ. μεγ. αυτ.] > 𝔖 עוז ותפארת במקדשו F maiestatem eius *post* laudate (*v.* 8) αβ 8. λεγετ. παντες] Benedicite domino omnes electi, et omnes laudate αβ λεγετ.] > 𝔖F παντες] *post* Ιεροσ. 44 > 𝔖 + העמים F κ. εξομ.] ܘܢܘܕܘܢ ܠܗ ܒܐܘܪܫܠܡ 𝔖 + נפלאותיו F et confitemini 𝔏 εν Ιεροσολ.] *seq. ras.* 2 *vel* 3 *litt. in* A + παντες 44 agite dies laetitiae *ante* κ. 3° 𝔏 9. Ιεροσ.] > 𝔖F [αγιου *usque ad cap. fin.* > 𝔖] αγιου] αγια A 𝔏 αγιασματος 44, 106, 107 μαστιγωσει] flagellavit 𝔏 μαστιγ. . . . δικ.] הוא שלם לך עונות בניך ועוד יושיעם ויש תקוה לאחריתך נאם יהוה ושבו בנים לגבולם F επι τ. εργ.] in operibus 𝔏 εργα] עונת F υιων] οικετων 44, 106, 107 manuum αβ κ. παλιν . . . δικαιων] > αβ 10. > 44 *plen. et aliter* F κυρ. αγαθως] αγαθω A in bono 𝔏 [κ. 1° *usque ad libri caput* א:—] κ.] ινα BA 106, 107 𝔏 η σκηνη αυτ. οικοδ.] *cf.* לשכן שמו בתוכך F η] > A σκηνη] σπουδη 106 σου] αυτου BA 106, 107 οικοδομηθησεται] -θη BA 106, 107 σοι 1°] *pr.* εν A 44, 106, 107 𝔏 ευφραναι] -ρανη A -ροσυνης 106, 107 παντας] > BA 106, 107 (*bis*) αιχμαλωτ.] *pr.* εκει A κ. 3°] > 106,

7, 8. A line seems to be lacking and λεγέτ. is awkward without an object. Metre, parallelism, and grammar are alike improved if καί in *v.* 7 is omitted, ψυχή taken as subject of ἀγαλλ., and τ. μεγ. as object of λεγετ. on the analogy of אמר and דבר with direct accus., Ps. cxlv. 6, 11, Sir. xxxiii. 10, John viii. 27.

9. *works of thy hands*, i.e. idols (with reference to Is. xxxi. 7), restored by Reusch from αβ in place of the colourless *sons* (derived from 9[b]) of R[v] and R[c].

10. The connexion of 10[b] with the earlier portion of the poem being lost after the omission of 6[b]–10[a], the scribe of א substituted καί for ἵνα, which must therefore be restored. The Semitic construction of the infin. (εὐφράναι) carrying on the finite verb was first altered in R[c].

11 A bright light shall shine unto all the ends of the earth;
Many nations <shall> come from afar,
And **the inhabitants** of the utmost ends of the earth unto thy holy name;

With their gifts also in their hands unto the King of heaven,
Generations of generations shall utter rejoicing in thee,
And thy name that is elect unto the generations of eternity.

12 Cursed shall be all they that shall speak a hard word;
Cursed shall be all they that demolish thee,
And throw down thy walls;

And all they that overthrow thy towers,
And set on fire thy habitations;
But blessed shall be all they that fear thee for ever.

13 Then go and be exceeding glad for the sons of the righteous:
For they all shall be gathered together,
And bless the everlasting Lord.

14 Blessed *shall* they *be* that love thee;
And blessed *shall* they *be*
That shall rejoice for thy peace:

And blessed *shall be* all the men
That shall sorrow for thee
For all thy chastisements:

Because they shall rejoice in thee
And shall see all thy joy for ever.

107 εν 2° σοι 3°] κ. 106, 107 > 𝔏 κ. 4°] εις BA 106, 107 *αβ* τ. αιωνος] υμων 106, 107 11. φως . . . γης] > BA 44, 106, 107 F φως λαμπ. λαμψει] luce splendida fulgebunt *αβ* luce clara fulgebis *Brev. Moz. Vig. Epiph.* ישאלו בשלומך ויבקשו F κ. κατοικ.] ηξει BA 44, 106, 107 venient tibi habitare (-tatores *Brev. Prosp.*) *αβ Brev. Ps.-Prosp.* παντ. . . . γης] > BA 44, 106, 107 παντ. τ. εσχ.] a novissimis partibus *αβ* τ. αγι. σου] κυρ. του θ. BA 44, 106, 107 *Brev. Ps.-Prosp.* dei mei *αβ* (*cf.* יהוה עליון מלכי תרשיש ואיום F) κ. 3°] > BA 44, 106, 107 τα δ. αυτων 1°] δ. BA 44, 106, 107 ταις χ. αυτων 2°] χ. BA 44, 106, 107 𝔏 εχ.] + κ. B 44, 106, 107 τῳ βασ.] *pr.* δωρα *iterum* BA 44, 106, 107 του ουρ.] caeli (-orum *Prosp.*) et terrae 𝔏 γενεαι γεν.] -εα γεν. A > F > (*sed v.* εις τας γ.) 𝔏 δωσουσιν] *pr.* αινεσουσιν σοι κ. A *post* in laet. offerentes *αβ* *post* terrae offerent *Prosp.* -runt *Brev.* (*cf.* מלכי שבא וסבא אשכר יקריבו F) εν σοι αγαλλιαμα] σοι αγ. B 44, 106, 107 -λιασιν A in laetitia *post* terrae *αβ* cum laet. *post* off. *Prosp.* κ. 3 ον. . . . αιωνος] > BA 44, 106, 107 F ον. της εκλ.] nomen magnum (*pr.* domini *Brev.*) erit *αβ* εις τας γεν. τ. αιωνος] in saecula saeculorum *αβ Prosp.* in omnibus -lis *Brev.* 12. επικατ.] *cf.* יבושו ויסוגו אחור F παντες] + qui spernunt (+ in *Brev.*) te et omnes q. blasphemant te: maledicti erunt omn. q. odiunt (-erunt *Brev.*) te et *αβ Brev.* ερουσιν . . . οικησεις σου] μισουντες σε BA 44, 106, 107 επικατ. 2° εσοντ. παντ.] *ante* q. odiunt *αβ Brev.* κατασπωντ.] *pr.* omn. q. *Brev.* εμπυριζ.] *pr.* omn. q. 𝔏 κ. 4° . . . σε] > F κ. 4°] > BA 44, 106, 107 ευλογητ.] -γημεν. BA 44, 106, 107 εις τ. αιωνα] *post* σε BA *αβ Brev.* οι φοβ. σε] οι αγαπωντες BA 44, 106, 107 qui aedificant te *αβ Brev.* 13. τοτε] > BA 44, 106, 107 πορευθητι] χαρητι B* A 44, 106, 107 *αβ Brev.* χαρηθι B[ab] + ירושלם F προς τους υι.] επι τοις υι. BA 44, 106, 107 in filiis *αβ Brev.* τ. υι. τ. δικ.] על קבוץ בניך השבים בקרבך F παντες] > BA 44, 106, 107 F επισυναχθ.] συναχθ. BA 44, 106, 107 וישם יודו F κυριον] שם יהוה F τ. αιωνος] δικαιων BA 44, 106, 107 > F 14. μακ. . . . σε] > 44 F μακ. 2°] *pr.* ω BA ως 106, 107 κ. μακ. οι] > BA F ευλογημενοι εσονται παντες 44, 106, 107 et qui 𝔏 χαρ. επι τ. ειρ. σου] οι αγαπωντες σε εις τ. αιωνα 44, 106, 107 > F χαρ.] gaudent 𝔏 κ. 2°] > BA 44, 106, 107 𝔏 F παντ. οι ανθρ. 1°] οσοι B 44, 106, 107 οι A επι σοι λυπηθησ.] ελυπηθησαν BA 44, 106, 107 contristabuntur 𝔏 πασαις] > B (*exc.* B[a?b]) 44, 106, 107 εν] επι BA 106, 107 κ. οψονται] θεασαμενοι BA 44, 106, 107 יתמהו F χαρ.] δοξ. BA 44, 106, 107 F σου 3°] + κ. ευφρανθησεται

---

11. The fine metaphor of R^s in 11^a finds support in *αβ Brev. Moz. Vig. Epiph.* The prosaic R^v omitted it along with the universalistic κ. κάτοικοι . . . γῆς which has been handed down by the scribe of א in a corrupt form. Reusch emends κάτοικοι ἀπὸ πάντ. and inserts ἥξει after μακρόθεν from 𝔏.

13. χάρητι B*A, cf. Sir. iv. 25 ἐντράπητι B*AC for -ηθι B^b. The emendation χαρ. for πορευ. (R^s) was so obvious that it was adopted not only in R^v and R^c but in 𝔏.

15 My soul doth bless the Lord the great King;
16 For Jerusalem shall be builded **again** as his house unto all the ages.

Happy shall I be if the remnant of my seed come to see thy glory
And give thanks unto the King of heaven.

And the gates of Jerusalem shall be builded with sapphire and emerald,
And all thy walls with precious stone.

The towers of Jerusalem shall be builded with gold,
And their battlements with pure gold.

17 The streets of Jerusalem shall be paved
With carbuncle and stones of Ophir.

18 And the gates of Jerusalem shall utter hymns of gladness
And all her houses shall say, Halleluiah.

Final benediction, v. 18^b.

Blessed is the God of Israel.
And the blessed shall bless the name
That is holy for ever and ever.

CONCLUSION OF THE HISTORY, xiv. 1–15.

i. **Tobit's Age**, xiv. 1, 2.

14 1 And the words of Tobit's thanksgiving were ended, and he died in peace being an hundred and
2 twelve years old, and was buried magnificently in Nineveh. And he was threescore and two years old
when he became maimed in his eyes; and after he recovered his sight he lived in prosperity and gave
alms, and he still continued to bless God, and to give thanks for the greatness of God.

B κ. ευφρανθησονται A 44, 106, 107 F 15. ευλογει] -γειτω A 44, 106, 107 benedic 𝕷 F κυριον] θ. BA 44, 106, 107 16. Ιερουσ.1°] > BA 44, 106, 107 liberavit Hierus. et 𝕷 οικοδομηθησεται] ι *sup. ras.* (*seq. ras.* 1 *lit.*) A[a] aedificabit *a β* -ur *Brev.* כי הוא יבנה F τη πολει . . . αι θυρ.] > BA 44, 106, 107 F τη πολει] iterum 𝕷 τῳ βασ.] nomini regis 𝕷 κ.2°] > 𝕷 σαπφειρ.] σαππειρ. B σαπφιρ A οικοδομηθ.1°] > BA 44, 106, 107 F λιθ. τιμι.] λιθ. εντιμῳ B 44, 106, 107 λιθ. επιτιμῳ A וברכת F παντα] > BA 44, 106, 107 +אבני אקדח F οι πυργ.] *pr.* κ. BA 44, 106, 107 Ιερουσ. χρυσ. οικοδομηθ.] > BA 44, 106, 107 F προμαχωνες] -μαχοι 44, 106, 107 αυτων] > BA 44, 106, 107 eius 𝕷 F χρυσιῳ 2°] *pr.* εν A 44, 106, 107 17. *pr.* κ. BA 44, 106, 107 𝕷 αι] > 44, 106, 107 πλατειαι] -ιαι A *pr.* כל F ανθρ.] *pr.* βηρυλλῳ κ. BA 44, 106, 107 נופך ואבני יקרה F ανθρ. . . . Σουφειρ] carbunculo lapide sternentur 𝕷 ψηφολογηθ.] *post* Σουφ. BA -λογησ. *post* Σουφ. 44, 106, 107 Σουφ.] *pr.* εκ BA 44, 106, 107 מאופור F 18. αι θυρ. . . . αγαλλ.] > BA 44, 106, 107 F Ιερουσ.] illius 𝕷 F κ.2° *et* ερουσιν 2°] λεγοντες (γον *sup. ras.* A[a]) *post* αινεσ. BA 44, 106, 107 οικι.] ρυμ. BA 44, 106, 107 𝕷 F Αλληλ.] + κ. αινεσιν BA + κ. αινεσουσιν (σουσιν *sup. ras.* A[a]) A[a] 44, 106, 107 > 𝕷 τ. Ισρ.] ος υψωσεν (-σε σε 44, 106, 107) παντας (*pr.* εις A 44, 106, 107) τ. αιωνας BA Dominus qui exaltat te et benedictus in omnia saec. (-nibus -lis *Brev.*) saeculorum *a β Brev.* יהוה אשר הרים קרן מלכותך לעולם ועד F κ. ευλογ. . . . κ. ετι] > BA 44, 106, 107 F quoniam in te benedicet (-cent? -etur *Brev.*) nomen (omne *Brev.*) sanctum (suum *a β*) in aeternum *a β Brev.*

XIV. > *Ar* M 1. συνετελ. . . . εξομολογησεως] επαυσατε εξομολογουμενος BA ܡܢ ܡܫܠܡܘܗܝ ܕܬܘܕܝܬܐ 𝕾 עוד כאן תפלה F συνετ.] *pr.* ut κ. απεθ. . . . εν N.] > BA F *pr.* ܘܗܘܐ ܗܘܐ ܕܡܫܠܡ 𝕾 δωδεκα] ܠܐܠܦܝܢ 𝕾 ενδοξ.] + ܘܫܟܪܐ 𝕾 2. ξβ' ετων ην] ην ετ. πεντηκοντα οκτω B 𝕾 𝕷 F ην ετ. ογδοηκοντα οκτω A εγεν. . . . οφθ.] απωλεσεν τ. οψεις BA F τ. αναβλ. . . . αγαθ.] ετη οκτω ανεβλεψεν BA F ܘܚܡܫܝܢ ܫܢܝܢ ܗܘܐ ܘܡܢ ܒܬܪ ܕܚܙܐ ܢܘܗܪܐ ܚܝܐ ܗܘܐ ܒܟܠܗܘܢ ܛܒܬܐ ܘܥܒܕ ܗܘܐ ܙܕܩܬܐ ܘܐܘܣܦ ܠܡܕܚܠ ܠܐܠܗܐ ܘܠܡܘܕܝܘ 𝕾 et quinquaginta quattuor annis postquam lucem recepit vixit in omnibus 𝕷 ελ. εποιησ.] εποιει ελ. BA F ετι] > BA 𝕾 προσεθ.] *bis scr.* κ. προς A* (*ras.* 1° A1) proposuit 𝕷 > 𝕾 ευλογ.] φοβεισθαι BA F colare 𝕷 > 𝕾 τον θ.] *pr.* κυριον BA שמו של הקדש ברוך הוא F εξομολογεισθαι] -ωμολογειτο (-εισθαι A) αυτω BA 44, 106 𝕾 F την μεγ. τ. θ.] μεγαλως (*cum* δε *v.* 3) BA μεγαλως 44, 106 ܩܕܡ ܐܠܗܐ 𝕾

16. As 𝕷 testifies πάλιν stood in R[s]. א has τῇ πόλει, τῇ being an incorrect repetition of the last three letters of the previous word, and πόλει a later scribal blunder for πάλιν under the influence of the τῇ. For the complete disappearance of the aspirate in σαππ. (Vat). see Th. *Gram.*, p. 121. For thought and language cf. Is. liv. 11, 12, Rev. xxi. 10–21.

XIV. 1. 𝕾 supports R[s], the difference resulting from the Syriac copyist's omission of *ten*, as in viii. 20 he omitted *four*.

2. ἀνάπειρ. not -πηρ., cf. 2 Macc. viii. 24 A.V.; Luke xiv. 13, 21; Th. *Gram.*, p. 83.

ii. **Tobit's last words and hopes for the Messianic Age,** *vv.* 3–11[a].

The future of Jerusalem, Israel, and the heathen, vv. 3–7.

3 And when he was dying he called Tobias his son, and charged him, saying, Child take thy
4 children ; and go into Media, for I believe the word of God upon Nineveh, which Nahum spake, that
all those things will be, and will befall Assyria and Nineveh. And all the things which the prophets
of Israel spake, whom God sent, shall befall ; and nothing shall be minished of all the words ; and all
things shall come to pass in their seasons. And in Media shall be deliverance more than among the
Assyrians and in Babylon ; wherefore I know and believe that all the things which God hath spoken
will be accomplished and will be, and there will not fall to the ground a word of the prophecies. And
as for our brethren which dwell in the land of Israel, **against all of them will God devise evils,** and they
will be carried captive from the goodly land, and all the land of Israel will be desolate, and Samaria and
5 Jerusalem will be desolate, and the house of God will be in grief and be burned up for a time ; and
God will again have mercy on them, and God will bring them back into the land of Israel, and they
will again build the house, but not like the first, until the time when the time of the seasons be
fulfilled ; and afterward they will return, all of them, from their captivity, and build up Jerusalem
with honour, and the house of God shall be builded in her, even as the prophets of Israel spake con-

+בכל עת F magnitudinem eius 𝕷 3. κ. οτε] δε (*pr.* μεγαλως *e v.* 2) BA ως δε 44, 106 απεθν.] εγηρασεν κ. BA +Thobis 𝕷 T.] > BA αυτου] +κ. τ. υιους (εξ υιους *nisi potius* εξυιους A) αυτου BA et septem filios eius 𝕷 ששה בני ט' F ενετ. αυτ. λεγων] ειπεν αυτ. BA 𝕾 precep. illis dicens 𝕷 Παιδιον . . . παιδια] τεκν. λαβε τ. υιους BA *pr.* ܒܪܝ ܘܐܡܪ ܠܗ ܘܦܩܕܗ 𝕾 > F απαγ.] dilige 𝕷 σου] +ιδου γεγηρακα κ. προς τ. αποτρεχειν εκ (απο A) τ. ζην ειμι BA (*cf.* F) 4. *plen. et aliter* F κ. αποτρ.] απελθε BA recurre 𝕷 Μηδειαν] -ιαν B* A *pr.* την BA +τεκνον BA regionem Medorum 𝕷 πιστ. εγω τ. ρ. τ. θ.] πεπεισμαι BA ܡܬܛܦܝܣ ܐܢܐ ܕܡܠܬܗ ܕܐܠܗܐ 𝕾 επι N.] περι N. *post.* προφ. BA > 𝕾 *post* ελαλ. 𝕷 α] οσα BA quod 𝕷 Ναουμ] Ιωνας ο προφητ. BA > 𝕷 ܥܠ ܢܝܢܘܐ 𝕾 οτι παντα . . . απαντ.2°] > 𝕾 παντα εσται . . . καιροις αυτων] καταστραφησεται B κατασκαφ. A κ. οσα . . . απαντ.] > 𝕾 κ. οσα] quae 𝕷 κ. ου μηθ. . . . ρηματ.] ܘܡܕܡ ܡܢ ܡܠܘܗܝ ܠܐ ܢܦܠ 𝕾 μηθεν ℵ* μη ουθεν ℵ[c a] κ. παντα . . . καιρ. αυτ] > 𝕾 κ. εν1°] εν δε BA Μηδεια] -ια A +παλιν 44, 106 σωτηρια] ειρηνη BA ܫܝܢܐ 𝕾 ηπερ . . . λογων] εως καιρου BA εν Ασσ.] *pr.* ܡܢ ܐܬܘܪ ܘܒܒܝܠ 𝕾 διο . . . λογων] > 𝕾 ο θ.] dominus 𝕷 διαπεσ.] excedet 𝕷 λογων] +dei 𝕷 κ. οι] κ. οτι οι BA οι κατοικ.] > BA εν τ. γη] > 𝕾 Ισρ. παντ. λογισθ. κ.] > BA Ισρ.] ܠܐܪܥܐ ܕܐܝܣܪܝܠ 𝕾 παντων] omnes 𝕷 ܟܠܗܘܢ 𝕾 λογισθ.] dispergentur 𝕷 αιχμαλωτ.] σκορπ. BA 𝕾 *pr.* ex illis 𝕷 εκ τ. γης τ. αγ.] απο τ. αγ. γ. BA ܘܢܬܒܕܪܘܢ ܡܢ ܐܪܥܐ ܛܒܬܐ 𝕾 ad terram optimam 𝕷 κ. εστι πασ. . . . ερημος2°] ܘܬܗܘܐ ܟܠܗ ܐܪܥܐ ܚܪܒܐ 𝕾 εσται πασ. . . . Σαμ. κ.] > BA 𝕷 Σαμ. . . . ερημ.2°] > 𝕷 εν λυπη] εν αυτ. BA ܘܒܝܬ ܡܩܕܫܐ 𝕾 quae in illa est 𝕷 κ. καυθησ.] κατακαησ. BA 𝕷 > 𝕾 μεχρι χρον.] *pr.* κ. ερημος εσται BA 𝕷 > 𝕾 5. *plen.* F ελεησ.] יזכר F αυτ.1°] > 𝕾 κ. επιστρ. . . . θ.2°] > 𝕷 ο θ.2°] > BA 𝕾 αυτ.2°] ܢܗܦܟ 𝕾 κ. επιστ. αυτ.] > 𝕷 εις τ. γην] > 𝕾 in terra 𝕷 τ. Ισρ.1°] > BA παλιν2°] > BA 𝕾 κ. ουχ . . . πρωτ.] ουχ οιος ο προτερος BA > 𝕾 εως . . . καιρων] εως (ως A) πληρωθωσιν καιροι τ. αιωνος BA > 𝕾 quoad usque repleatur tempus maledictionum 𝕷 κ. μετα ταυτα . . . οικοδ.3°] ܘܡܢ ܒܬܪ ܗܠܝܢ ܢܗܦܟܘܢ ܡܢ ܫܒܝܗܘܢ ܘܗܘܘ ܒܢܝܢ ܠܐܘܪܫܠܡ 𝕾 μετα ταυτα] > 𝕾 *cf.* לפי מלאות עולם אחד ועוד F της αιχμαλ. αυτ. παντες] των αιχμαλ. BA παντες] *post* κ. 𝕷 τ. θ. εν αυτ.] > 𝕾 του θ.] > 𝕾 οικοδομηθ.] +ενδοξως (ενδοξω B[b] *pr.* εις πασ. τ. γε|νεας τ. αιωνος οικοδομη (*seq. ras.*) B[ab mg] 𝕾) B 𝕾 +εις | πασ. τ. γεν. τ. αιων. | οικοδομη ενδοξω A (*cf.* F) +et in omnia saecula saeculorum aedificabitur 𝕷 ελαλ.] ܐܡܪܘ 𝕾 οι προφ.] *pr.* omnes 𝕷 τ. Ισρ.2°] > BA

---

3. The κ. ὅτε of R[s] was changed in R[v] into ὡς δέ, his favourite construction, e. g. vi. 10 (where R[s] also has καὶ ὅτε) ; viii. 4 (R[s] simply καί) ; xi. 12 (where the whole verse is edited by R[v]). R[c] has preserved this ὡς δέ of R[s], but it has fallen out of BA by haplography. μεγάλως therefore in R[v] originally belonged to *v.* 2 and appears to have been a conjectural abridgement (earlier than R[c]) of μεγαλωσύνην (R[s]) necessitated by a scribe's insertion of αὐτῷ before it and the consequent omission of τ. θ. after it.

4. Before the discovery of ℵ Grotius had correctly conjectured that Jonah had been inserted in place of Nahum under the influence of Jonah iii. 4. κατακαήσ. (R[v]) Th. *Gram.*, p. 237. Dr. Charles conjectures that λογισθ. (R[s]) is a translation of יתחשבון, which was a dittography of ישתבון, and regards πάντων as a solecism for πάντες. Marshall suggests that σκορπ. (R[v]) = יתפרשון, λογισθ. (R[s]) = יתפרעון, but this does not account for the difficult πάντων. Further σκορπ. in R[v] (followed by 𝕾) is a variation of αἰχμαλ. (to suit the circumstances of the Diaspora of that time), not of πάντων λογισθ. which was omitted on account of its difficulty and which is paraphrased in 𝕷 just as *ex illis* is inserted in the next clause with a definite motive. πάντων λογισθ. is an intentional corruption of ἐπὶ πάντας λογίζεται ὁ θεὸς κακά. οἱ ἀδελ. . . . Ἰσρ. was thus a *casus pendens*, and ἐπὶ πάντας (cf. the resumptive πάντες in 5[b]) was only corrupted into πάντων after λογίζεται ὁ θεός had been changed on dogmatic grounds into λογισθήσονται and κακά omitted. Cf. Mic. ii. 3 ἰδοὺ ἐγὼ λογίζομαι ἐπὶ τὴν φυλὴν ταύτην κακά, Ps. xxxiv. (xxxv.) 4, xl. (xli.) 7.

5. πρῶτον (R[s]) and πρότερος (R[v]) v. Th. *Gram.*, p. 183. For ܠܥܠܡ Ilgen would read ܠܥܠܡ.

6 cerning her. And all the nations which are in the whole earth, all shall turn and fear God truly, and
7 all shall leave their idols, who err after their false error. And they shall bless the everlasting God in
righteousness. All the children of Israel that are delivered in those days, remembering God in truth,
shall be gathered together and come to Jerusalem and shall dwell for ever in the land of Abraham
with security, and it shall be given over to them; and they that love God in truth shall rejoice, and
they that do sin and unrighteousness shall cease from all the earth.

Special injunctions to his descendants, vv. 9–11[a].

9 And now, children, I charge you, serve God in truth and do what is pleasing in his sight; and
upon your children it shall be enjoined to do [ ] alms, and that they be mindful of God and bless
8 his name at every season in truth and with all their strength. And now, child, depart thou from
10 Nineveh, and abide not here. In what day soever thou buriest thy mother with me, in the self-
same day abide not in the borders thereof; for I see that there is much unrighteousness therein,
and much guile is wrought therein, and they are not ashamed. See, child, what things Nadab did
unto **Aḥiḳar** that brought him up! Was he not brought down alive into the earth? and God
recompensed the shame upon his face, and **Aḥiḳar** came forth into the light, and Nadab went
into the eternal darkness, because he had sought to slay Aḥiḳar. Because I did alms, he came
forth from the snare of death which Nadab had set for him, and Nadab fell into the snare of death,

pr. ܟܠܗ ܥܡܡܐ ܕܒܟܠܗ̇ ܐܪܥܐ ܘܢܗܦܟܘܢ ܘܢܕܚܠܘܢ S 6. *simil.* F τα εν . . . παντες] > BA S terrae aβ ההם F επιστ.] +ܠܘܬ ܐܠܗܐ ܘܢܫܒܩܘܢ ܠܦܬܟܪܝܗܘܢ S κ. φοβηθ.] φοβεισθαι BA aβ לעבד F τον θ.] *pr.* κυριον BA ܠܗ S יהוה F αληθ.] *post* επιστρεψ. BA ܒܩܘܫܬܐ S > F κ. αφησ. . . . πλαν. αυτ.] κατορυξουσιν (*pr.* κ. A) τ. ειδωλα αυτ. BA > S τ. πλανωντ. . . . αυτ.] quae seducunt illos falso errore aβ 7. > S *plen.* F ευλογ.] +παντα τ. εθνη BA *pr.* omnes aβ τον θ. . . . εν δικ.] κυριον (*pr.* τον A) BA dominum in aeternum et in iustitia aβ παντες . . . ημερ. εκειν.] κ. ο λαος αυτου BA *pr.* et aβ οι σωζομ.] qui liberabuntur aβ μνημ. . . . αληθ.] εξομολογησεται τω θ. BA μνημ.] memores erunt aβ επισυναχθ. . . . παραδοθ. αυτ.] κ. υψωσει κυριος τ. λαον αυτου BA επισυναχθ.] *pr.* et aβ τ. αιωνα] *pr.* in aβ εν τ. γη . . . παραδοθ. αυτ.] in die illa cum diligentia et omnis iustitia in illis erit aβ οι αγ.] *pr.* παντες BA τον θ.] *pr.* Κυριον BA επ' αληθ.] εν αληθ. κ. δικαιοσυνη BA κ. οι ποιουντ. . . . τ. γης] ποιουντες ελεος τοις αδελ. ημων BA πασ. τ. γης] terris omnibus aβ 9, 8. *simil.* F 9. κ. νυν] S παιδ. . . . αληθ.1°] > S παιδια] τεκν. BA εγω υμιν . . . δικαι. κ. ελεημ.] συ δε τηρησον τ. νομον κ. τ. προσταγματα κ. γενου (γιν. A) φιλελημων κ. δικαιος *post* προφ. Ιωνας BA τῳ θ.] domino 𝔏 ενυποταγ.] ܘܦܩܕܘ S aβ *Spec. Cypr.* κ. ινα . . . ισχ. αυτων] ινα σοι καλως ην (η B[b]A) BA τον θ.] ܠܡܪܝܐ S > 𝔏 εν αληθ. κ.] ܒܟܠܗ ܠܒܐ S +in toto corde suo et 𝔏 8. κ. νυν συ παιδ.] > BA nunc vero fili 𝔏 εξελθε εκ N. κ. μη μειν. ωδε] απελθε απο N. οτι πα|ντως (παντως A) εσται α ελαλ. ο προφ. Ιωνας *ante* συ δε τηρ. BA ܘܡܢ ܗܪܟܐ ܦܘܩ ܠܟ ܡܢ ܢܝܢܘܐ S 10. > F εν η αν ημ. θαψης] κ. θαψον με καλως κ. BA ܒܝܘܡܐ ܕܬܩܒܪܝܗ̇ ܠܐܡܟ ܥܡܝ ܠܐ ܬܬܥܟܒ *ante* εξελθε *v.* 8 S *pr.* sed 𝔏 αυτ. τη ημ. . . . οριοις αυτ.] μηκετι αυλισθητε εις (εν A) N. BA > S ορω γαρ . . . αισχυν.] > BA ܡܛܠ ܕܚܙܐ ܐܢܐ ܕܣܓܝܐܐ ܒܗ̇ S εν αυτ.2°] > 𝔏 ιδε . . . Ναδαβ εποι.] τεκνον ιδε τι εποι. Αδαμ (Αμαν A) BA ܡܛܠ ܕܗܐ ܥܒܕ ܢܕܢ ܠܐܚܐܒ S ecce filius Nabad quid fecit aβ Αχεικαρῳ] Αχιαχαρω BA ܠܐܚܝܩܪ S Achicaro aβ τ. εκθρεψ. αυτ.] τ. θρεψ. αυτ. BA ܠܡܪܒܝܢܗ ܕܪܒܝܗ S ουχι ζων . . . γην;] ως εκ τ. φωτος ηγαγεν αυτον εις τ. σκοτος BA ܡܛܠ ܕܠܐ ܗܘܐ ܠܘܬ ܐܠܗܐ S quem vivum deduxit in terram deorsum aβ απεδωκ. . . . προσωπ. αυτ.] κ. οσα απεδωκεν αυτω BA > S τ. ατιμι.] malitiam illius aβ εξηλθ. . . . Αχικαρος] Αχιαχαρον (-ος A) μεν εσωσεν (-θη A) BA > (*vide infra*) S κ. Ναδαβ . . . αιωνος] εκεινω δε τ. ανταποδομα απεδοθη κ. αυτος κατεβη εις τ. (τ. > A) σκοτος BA ܘܠܐܚܐܒ ܫܠܡ ܦܘܪܥܢܗ S οτι εζητ. αποκτ. Αχεικαρον] > BA S εζητ.] +Nabad aβ εν τ. ποιησ. . . . απωλ. αυτ.] > aβ εν τ. ποιησαι με ελεημ.] Μανασσης εποιησεν ελεημ. BA > S εξηλθ. . . . Ναδαβ] κ. εσωθη εκ παγ. τ. θαν. ης επηξεν αυτω BA ܘܐܚܝܩܪ ܢܦܩ ܡܢ ܦܚܐ ܕܡܘܬܐ ܕܛܡܪ ܠܗ ܐܚܐܒ S πακ.] παγ. ℵ[ca] (*bis*) κ. Ναδαβ

6. τοὺς πλ. κτλ. in loose apposition to εἴδωλα, the gender of the original Hebrew or Aramaic probably being left unchanged, cf. Ezek. xlviii. 11.

9, 8. R[v] by no means placed *v.* 8 entire before *v.* 9, as Swete's verse-numbering (which is retained for convenience' sake) suggests.

10. 'Αδάμ in Vat. has arisen from Ναδάμ (= Nadab) by the attachment of its initial ν to the end of ἐποίησε while Cod. Al.'s 'Αμάν is an attempt to identify Aḥiḳar's nephew with the villain of the book of Esther. Μανασσῆς in R[v] is the result of textual confusion in that recension, possibly for Νασβᾶς (xi. 18 R.V.), possibly through a misreading of an anticipatory and partial excised με ἐλεημ. before ἐποι. In S the order is disturbed and the text possibly corrupt. ܠܡܪܒܝܢܗ after ܕܪܒܝܗ may be a gloss from ii. 10 (Ilgen) or a corruption of ܠܡܪܒܝܢܗ (Frit.). ܐܚܐܒ is not = Ahab (Fuller) but a corruption of ܢܕܢ and ܠܐܚܝܩܪ is a variation of ܐܚܝܩܪ.

11 and it destroyed him. And now, children, consider what alms-giving doeth, and what unrighteousness doeth, that it slayeth. And behold my soul fainteth.

iii. **Tobias' piety towards his parents and his long life,** *vv.* 11[b]–14.

11[b], 12 And they laid him upon his bed and he died; and he was buried magnificently. And when
his mother died, Tobias buried her with his father, and he and his wife departed to Media and
13 dwelt in Ecbatana with Raguel his father-in-law. And he sustained their old age in honour and
buried them in Ecbatana of Media, and he inherited the house of Raguel and of Tobit his father.
14 And he died, being an hundred and seventeen years old, full of renown.

iv. **The Dawn of the Messianic Age,** *v.* 15.

15 And before he died he saw and heard of the destruction of Nineveh, and saw her captivity led into Media which **Nebuchadnezzar** the king of Media took captive. And he blessed God for all he did unto the children of Nineveh and Assyria; and before his death he rejoiced over Nineveh, and blessed the Lord God for ever and ever. Amen.

επεσ. . . . απωλ. αυτον] Αδαμ (Αμαν A) δε ενεπεσεν εις τ. παγιδα κ. απωλετο BA ܘܗܘܐ ܠܗ ܠܗ ܠܦܚܐ 𝔖 11–15. > F 11. > 𝔖 α β κ. νυν . . . αποκτ.] ܘܗܫܐ ܚܙܝ ܙܕܩܘܬܐ ܡܟܠܡܘܗܝ ܠܗܘܢ 𝔖 ποι. ελ.] ελ. ποι. BA τι 2° . . . αποκτ.] δικαιοσυνη (*pr.* τ. ι. A) ρυεται BA κ. ιδου . . . τ. κλινην] κ. ταυτα αυτου λεγοντος εξελιπεν (-λειπ. A) αυτου η ψυχη επι τ. κλινης BA ܢܦܫܗ ܠܗ ܥܠ ܥܪܣܗ 𝔖 κ. απεθ.] ην δε ετων εκατον πεντηκοντα οκτω BA ܘܩܒܪܘܗܝ ܦܐܝܐܝܬ 𝔖 εταφη] εθαψεν αυτον BA 12. οτε απεθ. . . . απηλθ. αυτος] abiit T. postquam sepelivit parentes suos α β η μητ. αυτ.] Αννα BA 𝔖 T.] *post* απηλθ. δε BA τ. πατρ. αυτ.] *pr.* ܠܛܘܒܝܐ 𝔖 κ. απηλθ.] απ. δε BA αυτος . . . γυν. αυτου] μετα της γυν. αυτ. κ. τ. υιων αυτ. (αυτ. > A) BA ܐܬܬܗ ܘܒܢܘܗܝ 𝔖 ܘܪܕܐ *ante* κ. απηλθ. 𝔖 γυν. αυτ.] + et filii α β M. . . . Εκβ.] Εκβατανα BA εν Εκβ.] ܒܐܚܡܬܐ 𝔖 μετα P. του πενθ. αυτ.] προς P. τον π. αυτ. BA 13. εγηροβοσκ. αυτ.] εγηρασεν BA αυτους] τους πενθ. αυτου BA 𝔖 ετιμ.] ܒܐܝܩܪܐ ܪܒܐ 𝔖 εν Εκβ. τ. M.] ενδοξως BA ܒܐܚܡܬܐ 𝔖 οικ. P.] ουσι. αυτων BA ܟܠ ܩܢܝܢܗܘܢ 𝔖 T.] > 𝔖 14. απεθ.] + ܛܘܒܝܐ 𝔖 δεκα] > B 𝔖 εικοσι A nonaginta novem 𝔙 ενδοξως] εν Εκβατανοις τ. M. BA > 𝔖 15. ειδ κ.] > BA α β κ. ηκου.] > 𝔖 προ του] πριν η BA απωλιαν] -ειαν B[b] *(vid)* A κ. ειδ. . . . εις M] > BA κ. ειδ.] ܘܐܦ 𝔖 ην . . . Μηδ.] > 𝔖 ηχμαλωτισεν] -τευσεν A Αχιαχαρος ο βασ. τ. M.] Ναβουχοδονοσορ κ. Ασυηρος (Ασσ. ℵ[c a] Ασουηρ. A) ℵ[c a] BA κ. ευλογ. . . . Αθ.] > BA επιτ. . . . Αθ.] > 𝔖 Αθουρειας ℵ* Ασυερος ℵ[c a] α β εχαρη] *pr.* κ. A α β ܚܕܝ ܗܘܐ ܒ 𝔖 πριν] προ BA κ. ευλ. . . . αιωνων] > BA 𝔖 αμην] > α β

---

11. In R[v] 'if the text be right, there should be a strong stop after δικαιοσύνη', Dr. Harris, *Story of Aḥiḳar*, p. l, n. 1.

13. For ἐγηροβ. cf. Eur. *Med.* 1033, *Alc.* 663, and in the passive Ar. *Ach.* 678. R[v] is impossible since Tobit could himself scarcely have grown so old before he buried his parents! He has been influenced by a desire to emphasize the fulfilment of the prayer in viii. 7. Cf. Nestle, *Sept.*, iii, p. 24.

15. 'Ασύηρος seems originally to have stood in R[s], for which the scribe of ℵ wrote 'Αχιάχαρος, influenced by the frequent recurrence of the latter. Dr. Harris (*op. cit.* p. xxxii) however supposes that Ναβουχ. has been omitted and that in Cod. Vat. 'Ασύηρος is a corruption of 'Αθύρ or 'Αθυρείας and ἣν ᾐχμαλ. a gloss or displacement (*A.J.T.*, p. 354). Nestle, *Septuag.* iii, p. 24, argues that just as a corrector attached 'Ασύερος to 'Αθουρείας in ℵ, if Tisch. is right and it should not refer to 'Αχιάχαρος, so in R[v] καὶ 'Ασ[σ]ύηρος, for which two MSS. have 'Ασ[σ]ύριος whilst another omits the two words, may be a confusion with καὶ 'Αθυρείας, i.e. καὶ 'Ασσυρίας, which found a place in the text after Ναβουχ. instead of after Νινευή. The assumption of confusion with Cyaxares or Xerxes (Löhr) is improbable.

THE BOOK OF JUDITH

INTRODUCTION

§ 1. SHORT ACCOUNT OF THE BOOK.

THE *Book of Judith* falls naturally into two parts: (1) The Introduction (caps. 1–7). War was proclaimed by Nebuchadnezzar against Media, and a summons was sent to Persia, Syria, and Egypt to join in the expedition. The remoter parts of the Empire, however, treated the order with contempt (i. 11), whereupon Nebuchadnezzar determined, after conquering Media (i. 13, 15), to take vengeance on Syria and Egypt. This task was entrusted to Holofernes, the commander-in-chief (ii. 4), with 120,000 infantry and 12,000 cavalry (mounted archers, ii. 15). He marched three days' journey from Nineveh and encamped 'at the left hand of upper Cilicia', thence devastated 'the hill country', crossed the (upper) Euphrates as far as the coast, then turned south, 'compassing' the Midianites, to the plain of Damascus (ii. 27). After receiving the submission of Tyre and Sidon, Azotus and Ascalon, he went south to Esdraelon (iii. 9). The Jews, who were lately returned from the exile (iv. 3), resolved to resist, and Joakim the High Priest at Jerusalem sent instructions to Bethulia, which was near Esdraelon, to stop the passes leading to the capital (iv. 7). All Israel then fasted and prayed (iv. 9). Holofernes, hearing of the intended opposition, called a council of officers, when Achior the Ammonite gave a long account of Israelitish history (v. 5), pointing out that they could only be conquered if they had offended against their God (v. 20) and advising Holofernes to leave them alone. The advice was rejected, and Achior was handed over to the people of Bethulia (vi. 10), who received him in a friendly manner (vi. 20). Holofernes then moved his camp towards Bethulia, his army being now 170,000 infantry and 12,000 cavalry, besides accessories (vii. 2). It was decided to get possession of the water-supply at the foot of the mountain (vii. 7, 12) on which Bethulia stood, and thus to force the city to surrender, instead of risking a pitched battle. After thirty-four days, the stores of water within the city being exhausted (vii. 21), the people compelled Ozias and the leading men to agree to surrender in five days if no help came in the meantime (vii. 30).

(2) The story of Judith (caps. 8–16). This decision came to the ears of Judith (viii. 1, 9), the widow of Manasses, who lived in austere retirement (viii. 5, 6). She sent for the chief men (viii. 10), expostulated with them on their want of trust in God, and promised that she would herself effect their deliverance within the five days (viii. 33). They agreed to her project, without hearing the details, and departed (viii. 36). Judith then prepared for her plan by prayer (ix. 2). She put on her adornments, which had been laid aside since her husband's death (x. 3), took with her a single maid-servant with a bag of 'clean' food (x. 5), and went towards the Assyrian camp (x. 11). In an audience with Holofernes she informed him that what Achior had said was true (xi. 10), but that now the people had sinned by using first-fruits and tithes (xi. 13), and therefore God would deliver them up to their enemies (xi. 15). She would herself advise him when this was to take place (xi. 17). Holofernes, attracted by her appearance, invited her to his table (xii. 1), but she refused. She was allowed to go out of the camp every day to pray and bathe (xii. 6, 7). On the fourth day she consented to go to Holofernes' feast (xii. 10, 14), but partook only of her own provisions (xii. 19). The critical moment arrived when the guests departed (xiii. 1) leaving Judith alone with Holofernes. His excitement had caused him to drink immoderately, and he now lay on his couch helpless (xiii. 2). Judith, calling on God for strength (xiii. 4), took his sword and with two blows cut off his head (xiii. 8), which she put in the bag (xiii. 10) carried by the servant who was waiting outside. The two went out of the camp as if to pray, as usual, and escaped to Bethulia (xiii. 10). They were received with enthusiasm by the citizens (xiii. 17), and Achior became a convert to Judaism (xiv. 10). A sortie was made (xiv. 11), and the Assyrians, thus surprised, tried to rouse their general (xiv. 13), but found him dead (xiv. 15). They fled in a panic (xv. 2), pursued northward past Damascus (xv. 5), while their deserted camp was sacked (xv. 6, 7). The High Priest Joakim came in person from Jerusalem to bless Judith (xv. 8).

Chapter 16 contains a hymn of praise by Judith. The book ends by relating that Judith dedicated to God her share of the plunder (xvi. 19), that she remained a widow till her death at the age of 105 years (xvi. 23), and that the land was at peace all her lifetime and for long after.

The book is thus almost equally divided between the introduction and the story proper. The former is no doubt somewhat out of proportion, and the author dwells at rather unnecessary length on the military details. In spite, however, of these defects of composition, the literary excellence of the work is universally recognized even through the uncomely disguise of the Greek translation. It was originally written in Hebrew (now lost) for Jewish readers, with the object of encouraging and edifying the people in a time of trial or persecution. In order to carry conviction the more, it aims at the appearance of being historical, in its use of well-known names and of precise details, but this historical character is only apparent. The author is concerned with theology rather than with history, of which perhaps he had a not very exact knowledge, although he adopted this form as the most suitable for his purpose. He seems to have had in mind the time of Artaxerxes Ochus, with whose campaign in Syria many of the incidents agree, but it would be unsafe to assume that he is consciously depicting an episode in that campaign. The name and date of the author are alike unknown. He must have written at a time of oppression, such as the Jewish race often suffered, and various indications point to the second century B. C. as the most probable date. It is, however, possible that the author adopted an existing story or popular tradition, purposely confusing his historical allusions in order to disguise it.

§ 2. Title of the Book.

The title of the book in Greek is simply Ἰουδείθ (or Ἰουδήθ, or Ἰουδίθ). In Hebrew it would have been מגלת יהודית, like מגלת אסתר and מגלת אנטיוכוס, or מעשה יהודית, derived from the name of the principal character. The name, of course, simply means 'Jewess', and hence Grotius, explaining the story allegorically, makes it represent the Jewish people. But apart from the fact that this method of interpretation is forced and unconvincing, there is no need to suppose that the name suggested this meaning. It is used personally in Gen. xxvi. 34 as belonging to the Hittite wife of Esau, where at any rate it cannot mean 'Jewess'.

§ 3. MSS.

The Hebrew original (see § 5) being lost, the earliest form in which we have the book is that of the Greek translation, the only primary version existing. Of this there are three recensions: (1) the usual and no doubt the most original form, represented by the MSS. ℵ, A and B (Swete's text); (2) that contained in codd. 19, 108; (3) that of cod. 58, with which the Old Latin version (VL) and the Syriac (Syr) agree in a remarkable manner. All three recensions, however, represent the same version and go back to the same original. Their differences are due to corrections made not on a fresh comparison with the Hebrew, but subjectively by editors of the version, and though considerable, they concern the form rather than the matter. Such 'corrections' are most evident in the second and third classes of MSS., and vary even within the same class.

In the notes here added to the English (R.V.) variants are only mentioned where they materially affect the sense.

§ 4. The Ancient Versions.

The Greek version, at least as contained in ℵ A B, is as a rule easily intelligible and probably a correct rendering of the original, but it is very hebraistic. From it were made the Syriac and the Old Latin, both of them fairly close and agreeing in general with cod. 58, as will be seen from the notes. VL is rough, often merely latinized hebraistic Greek, and sometimes misunderstands the Greek which it translates. The MSS., of which Sabatier used five for his text, have been much corrected, perhaps from different Greek MSS., so that they vary considerably in minor details, though all derived from one text.

The Syriac version was first printed in Walton's *Polyglot*. It was derived from two late MSS., now in the Bodleian Library, of which one, dated 1614, belonged to Pococke (MS. Poc. 391), and the other was copied for Ussher in 1627 (MS. Bodl. or. 141). With these a Cambridge MS. was collated and the variants are given (by Thorndyke) in vol. vi of the *Polyglot*. The version has been edited by Lagarde, in his *Libri V. T. apocryphi Syriace* (Lipsiae, 1861), from a tenth-century MS. in the British Museum (from the Nitrian collection) with a full apparatus criticus. The Museum possesses two other MSS., of the twelfth and seventeenth century respectively.

A third version, the Vulgate, is of less value for textual purposes. Jerome's own account of it, in his preface, is not altogether clear. He says that he found great variations in the MSS. ('multorum codicum varietatem vitiosissimam amputavi') and implies that he endeavoured to produce a consistent text by embodying in his work only what he found in the 'Chaldee'. The questions which naturally present themselves are, What were these divergent MSS. and what was the 'Chaldee' text? The MSS. cannot have been Greek, because the Vulgate differs from that version in important particulars:

e. g. xiv. 5–7 comes at the end of xiii; i. 12^{b}–16 and iv. 3 are omitted; iv. 13–15 is altered; additions are made after xiv. 12 and elsewhere; names and numbers often differ. In fact, if compared with the Greek, the Vulgate presents the appearance of a paraphrastic recension. On the other hand, apart from these material differences, it often follows VL closely even in diction (cf. cap. 16), and the resemblance throughout is sufficient to show that Jerome used MSS. of the VL, which he merely adapted and corrected, as he considered, by the help of his 'Chaldee' text. It is evident from his own remarks ('huic unam lucubratiunculam dedi, magis sensum e sensu, quam ex verbo verbum transferens') that he spent very little time or trouble on it, and for this reason its style is less like Jerome's than the rest of the Vulgate.

As to the 'Chaldee' text, we have no other evidence. It will be remembered that he speaks in the same way of a Chaldee text of Tobit, and that an Aramaic recension of that book was actually found and published by Neubauer (Oxford, 1878). No such text of Judith is now known, but as Jerome's statement is explicit with regard to both books, we have to inquire what the text was. Probably the answer is to be found in a sentence in the preface to Judith, 'Chaldaeo tamen sermone conscriptus inter historias computatur.' If *historias* represents מעשיות, he means that the story of Judith was regarded as a מעשה, such as we find embodied in midrashim, or even composed separately for use on special occasions. Later forms of the story, in Hebrew (see § 8), were composed and so used, and in Neubauer's midrashic MS. the story of Tobit is called as a matter of course מעשה טוביה. We may therefore conclude that Jerome, finding no Hebrew text of the book, used an Aramaic מעשה (*historia*) containing a free treatment, not a translation, of the story, derived probably from the Greek. He evidently attached more importance to it than to VL, since he included in his own work only what he found in the Chaldee, but in language he was naturally influenced by VL where the two coincide. Thus the Vulgate of Judith is a hurried version of an Aramaic midrash containing a free presentation of the story, rather than a translation of any given text. It omits about one-fifth of the book.

§ 5. Date of the Original, and of the Versions.

(*a*) The existing versions thus all go back, through the existing Greek, to the same original, their differences being due to alterations within the versions. It is now generally agreed (against earlier scholars such as Fabricius, Jahn, and Eichhorn) that this original was Semitic, and Hebrew rather than Aramaic. Indeed there can be no possibility of doubt if we consider the style of the Greek and the nature of some of the mistakes in it. The language is not merely that popular Greek which we now know from papyri of the early centuries A. D. to have been identical with the κοινὴ διάλεκτος of the New Testament, even when independent of any Semitic idiom. The translation is so literal that it can be put back into Hebrew with ease, and in some cases becomes fully intelligible only when so re-translated. Moreover, the unusual lack of particles shows that the writer was under the influence of a foreign idiom, while the constant recurrence of phrases uncommon in late Greek but frequent in Hebrew shows incontestably the language of the original. Such are e. g. ἀπὸ προσώπου = מפני, εἰς πρόσωπον = לפני, the frequent use of σφόδρα = מאד, ἐν = בְּ, and many more: see the notes on iv. 2, v. 12, 19, vii. 10, 28, xii. 4, xiii. 4, 8, 13, 16, xiv. 2, 6, 11. The same conclusion is indicated by the confusion in the geographical names, due to uncertainty in the mind of the translator as well as to mistakes of copyists, so far as it is not intentional on the part of the author (see § 6). So also in other names, e. g. Achior no doubt = אחיהוד, chosen as meaning 'friend of the Jews', with the common confusion of ד and ר.

Against this comparative certainty we have the express statement of Origen (*ad Afric.* 13), οὐδὲ τῇ Ἰουδὴθ (χρῶνται) οὐδὲ γὰρ ἔχουσιν αὐτὰ καὶ ἐν ἀποκρύφοις ἑβραιστί, ὡς ἀπ' αὐτῶν μαθόντες ἐγνώκαμεν, as well as the fact that Jerome did not use a Hebrew text, which he certainly would have done if he had found one. It is possible that in the statement which Origen received from his Jewish informants, stress should be laid on χρῶνται rather than ἔχουσιν, and that it had fallen out of use and was not even included among the apocryphal books at the beginning of the third century. This must have been only temporary, since in 398 Jerome says 'Apud Hebraeos liber Judith inter apocrypha legitur'. Jerome's preface is all rather obscure, and it may be that he really means here to indicate a Hebrew text which he knew to exist but did not possess. In the very next sentence he speaks of the Chaldee which 'inter historias computatur', a degree lower than apocrypha, and seems to draw a distinction between them. No trace of the Hebrew original now survives.

The story is represented as taking place just after the return from the exile (iv. 3). The author does not, however, represent himself (as e. g. Daniel) as contemporary with the events recorded. In fact, he must have written much later. The return is far enough away to have become a sort of golden age, a time of simple happiness granted by God in consequence of the piety of the people. In this, as in its details, the description is wholly at variance with history (see § 6), either because the author did not know the facts, or because he was intentionally disguising them. He cannot have written as late as the first century A. D., for the book is quoted by Clement of Rome (1 *Cor.* 55). Moreover, there is no allusion to the final destruction of the temple, nor even to the Roman occupation of Palestine. Jewish tradition connects the story with the time of the Maccabees, making Judith the daughter of Johanan or Mattathia (Zunz, *Gottesd. Vorträge*, 2nd ed., p. 131), and this date agrees on the whole best with the author's point of view (see § 9). We must, however, be careful to distinguish between the date of composition and the real or supposed date of the events related (see § 6). The author evidently puts back into his post-exilic story the state of things under which he himself lived. There was no king, but the whole people is united under the High Priest (Joakim) governing with the γερουσία or Sanhedrim. The object of the book, too, is clearly to encourage the nation to resist the enemies of their religion and country even under the most desperate circumstances, and presupposes a time of great political or religious emergency. These several points, as well as the definitely Pharisaic theology, most naturally indicate an author living towards the middle of the second century B.C. Such is the view of Schürer, Hilgenfeld, and Nöldeke. (Cf. also Chajes in *Festschrift . . . Harkavy*, p. 105 Heb., who finds a number of parallels with the books of the Maccabees.) Ball proposes a date about 79–70 B.C., and argues with great ingenuity that Judith is modelled on Salome, successively wife of Aristobulus and Jannai, but this seems less probable than the earlier date.

The fact that the book is not mentioned by Josephus or Philo or in the New Testament proves nothing. Josephus does not refer to Job, besides other books, and Philo does not notice any of the Apocrypha.

(*b*) The versions can only be approximately dated. The earliest reference to the book, and no doubt to the Greek version of it, is by Clement of Rome (1 *Cor.* 55. 4 and 5) about 90 A. D. He alludes to the story as if it were well known to his Greek readers, very much in the same way as he goes on to speak of Esther. Allowing some time for the original book to become established before it was translated, and some time for the translation to become known, we should probably date the Greek not later than the beginning of the first century A. D.

The VL was made from the Greek, and as in Jerome's time (see § 4) it was already very corrupt, it must have been a long time in existence. The Syriac, which agrees closely with it, was possibly made about the same time from the same Greek text, for the use of oriental Christians. Fritzsche surmises vaguely that both were made between the first and third centuries A. D., and we have no means of dating them more precisely.

§ 6. Integrity of the Text; its Historical Framework.

It has been suggested that the story is founded on a popular tradition, true or imaginary. Reuss thought that the Song in cap. 16 was an early composition, like the song of Deborah, and that the story was built upon it. It is certainly remarkable that in xvi. 10 Persians and Medes, not Assyrians, are mentioned. There can be no doubt that Judith belongs to the family of Jael, Esther, and Joan of Arc. Such a theme appeals strongly to popular imagination, and even if based on fact, easily tends to be overlaid with fiction. Whatever may be the truth, the work, as we have it, is a consistent whole, and, with the possible exception of the song, shows no signs of being by more than one hand.

What then is the period which the author is proposing to describe, and how far is it in agreement with history? The question has been very variously answered. Attempts have been made to identify the Nebuchadnezzar of the story with Assurbanipal, Xerxes I, Artaxerxes Ochus, Antiochus Epiphanes: Arphaxad with Deioces or Phraortes. Without discussing these theories in detail, it may be said at once that none of them is consistent without a good deal of forcing. The historical Nebuchadnezzar did not reign at Nineveh (i. 1): he died in 562, and the return from the exile was not till about 536. He did not make war on Media (i. 7) nor capture Ecbatana. Nor do the annals of Assurbanipal, though they are very full, record anything of the kind, while Media had ceased to be a power before the time of the other kings whom it has been proposed to identify with Nebuchadnezzar. At the time of the Return, the Babylonian empire had passed to the Persians. They were not likely to send a punitive expedition against the Jews, who were not then in a position to offer any resistance. Moreover, Arphaxad is not the name of any Median king mentioned by Herodotus, and the fortifications of Ecbatana were not built by him but by Deioces (Hdt. i. 98): (H)olofernes (= Orofernes) and Bagoas, if they are historical names, are Persian, and belong to the time of Artaxerxes Ochus (see below). Again, there was no king in Israel, but the people was ruled by the High Priest Joakim (iv. 6, 8, 14, xv. 8) and a Sanhedrim (iv. 8, xv. 8). It has been suggested that this points to the reign of Manasseh when he was a prisoner in Babylon, or to the minority of Josiah. Either explanation is improbable. If a High Priest was acting for the king, so unusual a situation would have to be explained, whereas it is taken for granted, and also it is inconsistent with the references to the exile (iv. 3, v. 18). The suggestion that Joakim (Eliachim in the Vulgate) is the same as the Eliakim of 2 Kings xviii. 18, and that he may have survived as High Priest under Manasseh, is not supported by the list of High Priests. In fact the author clearly intends to put his story at the time of the Return, but makes no attempt to fill in the picture consistently. If it is to be made consistent, this can only be done by explaining the names as pseudonyms disguising really historical persons. This is the view taken by Ball, and it must be admitted that he finds some remarkable coincidences, on the assumption that Nebuchadnezzar is Antiochus Epiphanes, the Assyrians are Syrians, Nineveh is Antioch, and Arphaxad is Arsaces of Persia (= Media), against whom Antiochus made an expedition. But if the book is historical *fiction*, as it seems to be, we need not expect to explain all its statements. The writer selected such incidents as suited his purpose, without troubling about historical accuracy. The framework of the story was most probably suggested (so Schürer and others) by the campaign of Artaxerxes Ochus against Phoenicia and Egypt (about 350 B.C.). One of his generals was Holofernes, brother of the king of Cappadocia (Diod. Sic. xxxi. 19), who was sent against Egypt, though it is expressly stated that he died in his own country, and a certain Bagoas was his most trusted servant (Diod. Sic. xvi. 47). Sidon surrendered to the Persians (cf. Judith ii. 28 seq.), and the army then marched south towards Egypt, passing, no doubt, through Esdraelon (iii. 9). If any incident occurred in the campaign similar to that related here, we have no other record of it. The details are not meant to be historical. Nebuchadnezzar is introduced as the typical arch-enemy of Judaea: the time of the Return is chosen as being far away and little known, and the author is guilty of a further anachronism by describing his characters under the conditions of his own day. In the song (xvi. 10), if that is by the author of the rest, the mention of Persians seems to show that he was really thinking of the campaign of Artaxerxes Ochus. He also affects archaic names and allusions: hence with Nebuchadnezzar's army he includes princes of Moab and captains of Ammon (v. 2), the traditional enemies of Israel, who were in place, e.g. in 2 Kings xxiv. 2, but can surely not have been important in 150 or even 350 B.C. Similarly Midian (ii. 26) and Esau (vii. 8) are archaistic for Arabs and Idumaeans.

Such being the method of the book, we need not expect to identify all the geographical any more than the personal names. Bethulia, the scene of the story, is very like Shechem, and, if the author was thinking of Shechem, that may account for his using the name Βετυλούα = בית אלוה, since the Samaritans call Mt. Gerizim בית אל. It also fits the story, as a place of first-rate strategic importance, far better than Safed or Bait Ilfa, which have also been proposed. With regard to the other place-names, there is evidently a good deal of corruption either in the original or in the versions, or both. Many of them are too much distorted to be recognizable, but they may conceal actual sites, known or unknown. They can hardly be purely imaginary. Torrey (*JAOS*, 1899, pp. 160 sqq. and *Florilegium . . . de Vogüé*, p. 599) shows that, taking Bethulia to be Shechem, the other places agree, so far as they can be identified. See further on iv. 6.

§ 7. The Author of the Book.

As to the anonymous author there is no tradition. From his writing in Hebrew and from his detailed references to the geography of the Holy Land, it may be inferred that he was a Palestinian Jew. From his theological views (§ 9) it seems that he belonged to the Pharisaic party. He was a man of some literary skill. The story is well told, and apart from a certain tendency to exaggerate the magnitude of the military operations, the style is restrained and straightforward, without unnecessary elaboration. He was also well acquainted with the literature of his people, for, while his descriptions have vigour and originality, the book is full of reminiscences of the Old Testament, e.g. with the story of Achior in caps. 5, 6, cf. that of Micaiah in 1 Kings 22; with viii. 3 cf. 2 Kings iv. 18 seq.; viii. 16 is a quotation from Num. xxiii. 19; ix. 7, xvi. 3 from Exod. xv. 3; xiii. 18 from Gen. xiv. 19, 20. The fact that the quotations agree with the LXX rather than with the Hebrew text may be merely due to the translator. The author apparently knew some of the latest of the O. T. books (Esther and Daniel), and in v. 6–8 draws upon some midrashic source for the story of Abraham.

§ 8. Later Use of the Book.

(*a*) Although the Book of Judith was not received by the Jews, the story was well known to them, at least in the middle ages. It is mentioned in the liturgy for Ḥanukka (the feast of the Dedication of the temple, instituted by Judas Maccabaeus on Chisleu 25), and appears in various Hebrew forms among the minor midrashim (see Zunz, *Gottesd. Vorträge*, ed. 2, p. 131). A short recension of it is edited by Jellinek in his *Bet ha-Midrasch*, i, p. 130, a longer text, *ibid.* p. 132, and another, *ibid.* ii, p. 12. Three more forms of the story are found in MSS. of the Bodleian Library. See also

Gaster in *PSBA*, xvi, p. 156. A text translated from the Vulgate, and agreeing with that of two Bodleian MSS. (Heb. d. 11 f. 259 and MS. Opp. 712 f. 164), was published at Venice about 1651, under the title of מעשה יהודית. None of these is in any sense a translation of the Greek, still less the original form of the book. They are free sketches of a well-known story, set down from memory, like other מעשיות, in more or less detail according to the taste of the writer. They are usually short, and of no great antiquity. In the MSS. they are generally headed 'for Ḥanukka'. Hebrew translations of the Greek were published by Meir b. Ascher at Berlin in 1766, by Benseb at Vienna in 1819, and by Fränkel at Leipzig in 1830 (with other apocrypha). A Judaeo-German translation by S. Landau appeared at Frankfurt a. M. in 1715. A Persian version exists in a Bodleian MS. (Hyde 19). It is anonymous, but is made from the Vulgate, and the MS. was probably written about 1600.

(*b*) In the Church it was well known from the Greek (and Latin) translations, and was often quoted, not as canonical but as edifying, e.g. by Clement of Rome, Clement of Alexandria, Origen, Tertullian, Ambrose, Augustine (see Fritzsche, *Einleitung*, § 9), thus gradually acquiring a quasi-canonical recognition. On the use of the book in mediaeval times, see Pentin, *Judith*, London, 1908.

After the Council of Trent, the Protestants, though rejecting it from the canon, maintained the early view that it was good for edifying, and used it largely in preaching. It was never admitted to the English Church lectionary.

§ 9. Theology of the Book.

The theology of the book is strongly Pharisaic. The story is clearly intended for edification, to encourage the people in some time of trial, and to point out the true way to deliverance by showing that Israel's troubles are due to sin (v. 17, 18, xi. 10), that salvation comes through trust in God and obedience to Him, and that God uses the weak things to confound the strong (ix. 10 and frequently). But obedience to God, which is righteousness, consists in the strict observance of the Law. Judith is strong because of her consciousness of keeping the Law (xvi. 16). She observes not only the pentateuchal feasts of the Sabbath and New Moon, but also the eves of them (viii. 6), as required by the later teaching. She not only abstained from forbidden food, but she fasted continually, and underwent further mortification (viii. 5, 6) although she was rich. She is thus a perfect type of Pharisaic righteousness. She even dilates on these doctrines to Holofernes (cap. 11), laying stress on the sureness of punishment which would follow on such sins as the eating of forbidden things and the using of tithes and first-fruits by the citizens of Bethulia in their extremity. For even in the most desperate case God will find a means of deliverance for His faithful people and will punish the oppressor. This punishment is inflicted not only in the present life. There will be a day of judgement (apparently after death) when the wicked will be condemned to torment by fire and worms for ever (xvi. 17).

The objection which has been made to Judith's deceit (xi. 5) and approval of violence scarcely deserves notice. It could only be made in complete ignorance of the spirit of the time, and shows an utter inability to appreciate the position of a people struggling against overwhelming odds for their religion and their very existence.

THE BOOK OF JUDITH

1 1 In the twelfth year of the reign of Nebuchadnezzar, who reigned over the Assyrians in Nineveh,
2 the great city; in the days of Arphaxad, who reigned over the Medes in Ecbatana, and built at
Ecbatana and round about it walls of hewn stones three cubits broad and six cubits long, and made
3 the height of the wall seventy cubits, and the breadth thereof fifty cubits; and set the towers thereof
at the gates thereof, a hundred cubits *high*, and the breadth thereof in the foundation threescore
4 cubits; and made the gates thereof, even gates that were raised to the height of seventy cubits, and
the breadth of them forty cubits, for the going forth of his mighty hosts, and the setting in array of
5 his footmen: even in those days king Nebuchadnezzar made war with king Arphaxad in the great
6 plain: this plain is in the borders of Ragau. And there came to meet him all that dwelt in the hill
country, and all that dwelt by Euphrates, and Tigris, and Hydaspes, and in the plain of Arioch the
king of the Elymæans; and many nations of the sons of Chelod assembled themselves to the battle.
7 And Nebuchadnezzar king of the Assyrians sent unto all that dwelt in Persia, and to all that dwelt
westward, to those that dwelt in Cilicia and Damascus and Libanus and Antilibanus, and to all that
8 dwelt over against the sea coast, and to those among the nations that were of Carmel and Gilead,
9 and to the higher Galilee and the great plain of Esdraelon, and to all that were in Samaria and the
cities thereof, and beyond Jordan unto Jerusalem, and Betane, and Chellus, and Kadesh, and the
10 river of Egypt, and Tahpanhes, and Rameses, and all the land of Goshen, until thou comest above
Tanis and Memphis, and to all that dwelt in Egypt, until thou comest to the borders of Ethiopia.
11 And all they that dwelt in all the land made light of the commandment of Nebuchadnezzar king of
the Assyrians, and went not with him to the war; for they were not afraid of him, but he was before
them as one man; and they turned away his messengers from their presence without effect, and with
disgrace.
12 And Nebuchadnezzar was exceeding wroth with all this land, and he sware by his throne and
kingdom, that he would surely be avenged upon all the coasts of Cilicia and Damascus and Syria,
that he would slay with his sword all the inhabitants of the land of Moab, and the children of
Ammon, and all Judæa, and all that were in Egypt, until thou comest to the borders of the two
13 seas. And he set the battle in array with his host against king Arphaxad in the seventeenth year;
and he prevailed in his battle, and turned to flight all the host of Arphaxad, and all his horse, and
14 all his chariots; and he became master of his cities, and he came even unto Ecbatana, and took the
15 towers, and spoiled the streets thereof, and turned the beauty thereof into shame. And he took
Arphaxad in the mountains of Ragau, and smote him through with his darts, and destroyed him

I. 1. On the history see Introduction, § 6. **Nebuchadnezzar** reigned from 604 to 562 B.C. at Babylon. **Nineveh** and the Assyrian empire were destroyed about 607. **Arphaxad** is not known as a king of Media. It was Deioces (according to Herodotus i. 98) who fortified **Ecbatana,** about 700 B.C., and Cyrus who destroyed it in 550.

5. The apodosis begins here, with *καὶ* 'then'. **Ragau** = Ragae, the plain which begins about 100 miles north-east of Ecbatana.

6. **Hydaspes.** There is no river of this name in the region. Perhaps the Choaspes is meant. Syr. has Ulai.

and in the plain of Arioch the king, *καὶ πεδίῳ 'Αριὼχ ὁ βασιλεύς* (א* -εως). The nominative cannot be translated as in R.V. The sentence may originally have run 'they that inhabited the hills . . . and in the plain, and Arioch . . . and . . . Chelod assembled . . .' The plain is the plain of Elam. The name Arioch is borrowed from Gen. xiv. 1, in accordance with the author's love of archaism.

of the sons of Chelod . . . to the battle, *εἰς παράταξιν υἱῶν* X. properly 'many nations assembled to the army ('battle', 'camp', as below, xvi. 12) of the sons of Ch.' The name (otherwise unknown) may be a corruption of 'Chaldaeans'.

8. **those among the nations** (גוים), probably the non-Jewish inhabitants are meant. The Jews are mentioned later.

9. **beyond Jordan,** i. e. from the Babylonian point of view, though this should have come earlier in the verse.

Ball thinks that **Betane** is Beth-anoth (Jos. xv. 59), that **Chellus** is Allus in Idumaea, and that **Kadesh** is Kedesh in Judah (Joshua xv. 23) or Kadesh-Barnea. The **river of Egypt** is the Wadi-al-Arish, the boundary of Palestine and Egypt.

11. **as one man,** *ὡς ἀνὴρ εἶς,* א A and Fritzsche. The ordinary reading is *ὡς ἀνὴρ ἴσος.* If this is the original (and *εἶς* a correction of א A) it may represent כאיש שוה, a misreading of שוא 'a man of naught'.

12. **the two seas,** the Red Sea and the Mediterranean, or possibly two parts of the Mediterranean.

14. **beauty . . . into shame,** a play on words in the Hebrew יפי בדפי.

15. **destroyed him,** i. e. him and his kingdom.

16 utterly, unto this day. And he returned with them to Nineveh, he and all his company of sundry
nations, an exceeding great multitude of men of war, and there he took his ease and banqueted, he
and his host, a hundred and twenty days.
2 1 And in the eighteenth year, the two and twentieth day of the first month, there was talk in the
house of Nebuchadnezzar king of the Assyrians, that he should be avenged on all the land, even as
2 he spake. And he called together all his servants, and all his great men, and communicated with
3 them his secret counsel, and concluded the afflicting of all the land out of his own mouth. And
4 they decreed to destroy all flesh which followed not the word of his mouth. And it came to pass,
when he had ended his counsel, Nebuchadnezzar king of the Assyrians called Holofernes the chief
captain of his host, which was next after himself, and said unto him,
5 Thus saith the great king, the lord of all the earth, Behold, thou shalt go forth from my presence,
and take with thee men that trust in their strength, unto a hundred and twenty thousand footmen;
6 and the number of horses with their riders twelve thousand: and thou shalt go forth against all the
7 west country, because they disobeyed the commandment of my mouth. And thou shalt declare
unto them, that they prepare earth and water; because I will go forth in my wrath against them,
and will cover the whole face of the earth with the feet of my host, and I will give them for a spoil
8 unto them: and their slain shall fill their valleys and brooks, and the river shall be filled with their
9, 10 dead, till it overflow: and I will lead them captives to the utmost parts of all the earth. But thou
shalt go forth, and take beforehand for me all their coasts; and if they shall yield themselves unto
11 thee, then shalt thou reserve them for me till the day of their reproof. But as for them that are
disobedient, thine eye shall not spare; but thou shalt give them up to be slain and to be spoiled in
12 all thy land. For as I live, and by the power of my kingdom, I have spoken, and I will do this with
13 my hand. And thou, moreover, shalt not transgress aught of the commandments of thy lord, but
thou shalt surely accomplish them, as I have commanded thee, and thou shalt not defer to do them.
14 And Holofernes went forth from the presence of his lord, and called all the governors and the
15 captains and officers of the host of Asshur; and he numbered chosen men for the battle, as his lord
had commanded him, unto a hundred and twenty thousand, and twelve thousand archers on horse-
16, 17 back; and he ranged them, as a great multitude is ordered for the war. And he took camels and
asses and mules for their baggage, an exceeding great multitude; and sheep and oxen and goats
18 without number for their provision; and great store of victual for every man, and exceeding much
19 gold and silver out of the king's house. And he went forth, he and all his host, on their journey, to
go before king Nebuchadnezzar, and to cover all the face of the earth westward with their chariots
20 and horsemen and chosen footmen. And a great company of sundry nations went forth with them
like locusts, and like the sand of the earth: for they could not be numbered by reason of their
multitude.
21 And they departed out of Nineveh three days' journey toward the plain of Bectileth, and
encamped from Bectileth near the mountain which is at the left hand of the upper Cilicia. And he

16. B has 'and he returned with them (i.e. the spoils, &c.), he and his host, for 120 days'.

company is *σύμμικτος*, used here as a noun, 'a mixed multitude'; cf. *ἐπίμικτος* ii. 20 and Exod. xii. 38. Herodotus (vii. 55) uses *σύμμικτος* (adj.) of the army of Xerxes.

II. 1. **the twenty-second day of the first month** evidently ended the 120 days' rest, so that the return to 'Nineveh' took place just before the end of the ninth month of the seventeenth year of Neb. The precise date is meant to give the appearance of real history.

2. **communicated**, *ἔθετο*, lit. placed. The Greek of this verse is strange.

concluded, *συνετέλεσεν*. Fritzsche suggests that this translates ויכלה a misreading of ויגלה 'revealed (his purpose to destroy)'. If so, 'ended' in verse 4 is also for 'revealed'. Cf. the decree in Esth. iii. 13.

3. **all flesh**, a common Hebraism, כל בשר.

4. **(H)olofernes** (always with the smooth breathing in Greek) is usually taken to be for Orophernes, a Persian name borne by the kings of Cappadocia. It is quite out of place in the time of Neb.

6. **the west country** is Egypt and Syria, which were the objects of the campaign of Artaxerxes Ochus; cf. Introd. § 6.

7. **earth and water** as a sign of submission. The formula is Persian, not Assyrian or Babylonian (Ball, referring to Hdt. vi. 48, 49).

I will go, i.e. my power will go.

8. **river . . . overflow.** Rather 'even a strong, rushing river shall be choked up and filled . . .' *ποταμὸς ἐπικλύζων* translates נחל שוטף in Isa. lxvi. 12.

10. Rather 'and they shall yield . . . and thou shalt reserve . . .'. Resistance is not regarded as conceivable.

reproof. *ἐλεγμοῦ* is תוכחה, implying conviction with consequent punishment.

11. **thy land.** 58 VL Syr 19 108 omit 'thy'.

20. **company**, *ἐπίμικτος*, cf. *σύμμικτος* in i. 16. Note the exaggeration.

21. **Bectileth**, *Βαικτειλαίθ*. None of the proposed identifications is at all convincing. Apparently it was near N. Cilicia, about 300 miles from Nineveh—an impossible journey to perform in three days.

took all his host, his footmen and horsemen and chariots, and went away from thence into the hill
23 country, and destroyed Put and Lud, and spoiled all the children of Rasses, and the children of
24 Ishmael, which were over against the wilderness to the south of the land of the Chellians. And he
went over Euphrates, and went through Mesopotamia, and brake down all the high cities that were
25 upon the river Arbonai, until thou comest to the sea. And he took possession of the borders of
Cilicia, and slew all that resisted him, and came unto the borders of Japheth, which were toward the
26 south, over against Arabia. And he compassed about all the children of Midian, and set on fire
27 their tents, and spoiled their sheepcotes. And he went down into the plain of Damascus in the days
of wheat harvest, and set on fire all their fields, and utterly destroyed their flocks and herds, and
spoiled their cities, and laid their plains waste, and smote all their young men with the edge of the
sword.

28 And the fear and the dread of him fell upon them that dwelt on the sea coast, upon them that
were in Sidon and Tyre, and them that dwelt in Sur and Ocina, and all that dwelt in Jemnaan; and
they that dwelt in Azotus and Ascalon feared him exceedingly.

3 1, 2 And they sent unto him messengers with words of peace, saying, Behold, we the servants of
3 Nebuchadnezzar the great king lie before thee: use us as it is pleasing in thy sight. Behold, our
dwellings, and all our country, and all our fields of wheat, and our flocks and herds, and all the
4 sheepcotes of our tents, lie before thy face: use them as it may please thee. Behold, even our cities
and they that dwell in them are thy servants: come and deal with them as it is good in thine eyes.
5 And the men came to Holofernes, and declared unto him according to these words.
6 And he came down toward the sea coast, he and his host, and set garrisons in the high cities, and
7 took out of them chosen men for allies. And they received him, they and all the country round
8 about them, with garlands and dances and timbrels. And he cast down all their borders, and cut
down their groves: and it had been given unto him to destroy all the gods of the land, that all the
nations should worship Nebuchadnezzar only, and that all their tongues and their tribes should call
9 upon him as god. And he came towards Esdraelon nigh unto Dotæa, which is over against the
10 great ridge of Judæa. And he encamped between Geba and Scythopolis, and he was there a whole
month, that he might gather together all the baggage of his host.

encamped = נסעו (for which LXX three times has *στρατοπεδεύειν*, as here), 'they went a day's journey to their next camp at B.'

the left hand in Hebr. is the north, cf. Gen. xiv. 15.

23. **Put** (Pontus?) and **Lud** (Lydia?) are often found together in O.T. Probably Put (Phut) does not always represent the same country, but in any case neither name can be identified with any region bordering on Cilicia.

Rasses is also unknown. Vulg. has Tharsis (= Tarsus in Cilicia), VL Thiras et Rasis, Syr Tiras and Ra'amses.

Chellians, ℵ A, are unknown. B 58 Syr 19 108 read Chaldeans, which cannot be right.

24. As it stands, this verse can only mean that he left Cilicia, re-crossed the Euphrates, and then returned to Cilicia —a most unlikely proceeding. Or the verse is out of place, since he must have crossed the Euphrates to get to Cilicia. Evidently the writer had very vague ideas as to the relative positions of Mesopotamia, Cilicia, and the (Mediterranean) sea.

Arbonai is unknown. ℵ Χεβρών, B Ἀβρωνά, Syr Jabbok, VL Beccon, Vulg. Mambre.

25. He now turned south, towards Damascus, and, roughly speaking, in the direction of Arabia, but the meaning of the 'borders of Japheth' is obscure.

26. **Midian**, again an archaism for Arabs in general.

27. **wheat harvest** would be about the beginning of June. As the expedition started in the first month, the author has allowed far too little time (Ball), since there is no suggestion that this was the harvest of the next (nineteenth) year.

28. **Sur** looks like a dittography of Τύρῳ (צור); 19 108 have Σοὺδ (צור) a misreading of the Hebrew; ℵ has Τούρ; B has Ἀσσούρ, which is clearly out of place. Fritzsche proposes to read Dor, a port near Carmel.

Ocina, unknown. ℵ has Ἀμμάν (= Hamath?). Ball suggests Accho-Ptolemaïs, a haven north of Dor; Judges i. 31.

Jemnaan = Jamnia, Jabne, a well-known city on the south coast of Syria. The author evidently means to give a list of important towns going from north to south. His geography is more intelligible when he is dealing with Palestine, which he knew.

III. 1. **they**, i. e. the inhabitants of the non-Jewish towns just mentioned.

8. **borders**, *τὰ ὅρια*, is strange. Fritzsche and Ball think it is a mistranslation of הבמות, 'the high places.' Holofernes is represented as doing what a Jewish conqueror or reformer would have done, cf. 2 Kings xxiii. 14 (of Josiah).

as god, hardly an allusion to the title of Θεός assumed by Antiochus, &c. It is more probably imitated from the story in Dan. iii.

9. **Dotæa**, a Greek form of Dothan (= Dothayim). The plain of Jezreel was a suitable place for assembling a large army.

The **ridge**, *πρίων*, lit. 'saw' = sierra, must be the high ground on which Jerusalem stands. **over against**, *ἀπέναντι*, is a vague expression, which may only mean that you can see the ridge from Dothan. Fritzsche (following Reland) suggests that מישור, 'plain,' has been misread as משור, 'saw.'

10. **Geba**, about six miles due south of Dothan (Ball).

Scythopolis (= Bethshan) is the only purely Greek name occurring in the book. Elsewhere the translator uses Hebrew or Graecized Hebrew forms.

4 1 And the children of Israel that dwelt in Judæa heard all that Holofernes the chief captain of
Nebuchadnezzar king of the Assyrians had done to the nations, and after what manner he had
2 spoiled all their temples, and destroyed them utterly. And they were exceedingly afraid before
3 him, and were troubled for Jerusalem, and for the temple of the Lord their God: because they were
newly come up from the captivity, and all the people of Judæa were lately gathered together; and
the vessels, and the altar, and the house, were sanctified after the profanation.
4 And they sent into every coast of Samaria, and to Konæ, and to Bethhoron, and Belmaim, and
5 Jericho, and to Choba, and Æsora, and to the valley of Salem; and they possessed themselves
beforehand of all the tops of the high mountains, and fortified the villages that were in them, and
6 laid up victual for the provision of war: for their fields were newly reaped. And Joakim the high
priest, which was in those days at Jerusalem, wrote to them that dwelt in Bethulia, and Betomesthaim,
7 which is over against Esdraelon toward the plain that is nigh unto Dothaim, charging them to seize
upon the ascents of the hill country; because by them was the entrance into Judæa, and it was easy
to stop them from approaching, inasmuch as the approach was narrow, *with space* for two men at
8 the most. And the children of Israel did as Joakim the high priest had commanded them, and the
senate of all the people of Israel, which dwelt at Jerusalem.
9 And every man of Israel cried to God with great earnestness, and with great earnestness did they
10 humble their souls. They, and their wives, and their babes, and their cattle, and every sojourner
11 and hireling and servant bought with their money, put sackcloth upon their loins. And every man
and woman of Israel, and the little children, and the inhabitants of Jerusalem, fell before the temple,
and cast ashes upon their heads, and spread out their sackcloth before the Lord; and they put
12 sackcloth about the altar: and they cried to the God of Israel earnestly with one consent, that he
would not give their babes for a prey, and their wives for a spoil, and the cities of their inheritance
13 to destruction, and the sanctuary to profanation and reproach, for the nations to rejoice at. And
the Lord heard their voice, and looked upon their affliction: and the people continued fasting many
14 days in all Judæa and Jerusalem before the sanctuary of the Lord Almighty. And Joakim the high
priest, and all the priests that stood before the Lord, and they that ministered unto the Lord, had
their loins girt about with sackcloth, and offered the continual burnt offering, and the vows and the

IV. 2. **exceedingly**, *σφόδρα σφόδρα* = מאד מאד, a favourite expression with the author.

3. The sanctification after profanation might refer to what is narrated in 1 Macc. iv. 36, but for the definite statement that the people had just returned from the captivity. In v. 18, too, the temple had been actually destroyed. If the description here is suggested by the action of Judas Maccabaeus, the author purposely puts it back to the earlier period (soon after 516 B.C.).

4. **Samaria** in 516 was bitterly hostile to Judaea, and would not have been consulted. The political situation represented is imaginary.

Konæ. A reads *κωμας*, 'villages', and so VL.

Belmaim (א Abelmain) is unknown. Syr Abelmeholah.

Choba and **Æsora** are also unknown, and **the valley of Salem.**

5. **newly reaped**, cf. ii. 27. It was still the month of June.

6. The name of the high priest **Joakim** is no doubt derived from Neh. xii. 26. VL in this chapter and Vulg. throughout read Eliachim, El- being substituted for Jeho-.

Bethulia, *Βαιτουλούα*. A *Βετυλούα*. א here *Βαιτουλία*. The question of the historical value of the book turns largely on this name. As the town is the scene of the main action of the story, many details of its situation are incidentally mentioned. It can hardly be doubted that the author had in his mind some well-known and important site, although he may not have described it accurately in all points. No place of the name is known, however, and we can only suppose that a fictitious name has been adopted for some actual town. *Βαιτ(ο)υλούα* is now generally explained as בית אלוה = בית אל = Bethel = House of God, a name which might suitably be applied to any town which is to be represented as true to its faith in God, cf. e.g. viii. 20. It cannot, of course, be the historical Bethel, which was never of sufficient importance. The whole fate of the nation depended upon Bethulia, cf. viii. 21, 24. What place then is hidden under this assumed name? It would be natural to think of Jerusalem (בתולת בת ציון), but this is out of the question, since in this verse Joakim wrote from Jerusalem to Bethulia. On the whole, Torrey's view (see Introd. § 6) is most probable, that the author is describing Shechem, even if every detail is not exact. Supposing the story to be a romance, such exactitude is unnecessary. The importance of the position of Shechem is just what is wanted, while the antipathy to everything Samaritan affords a sufficient reason for not using the name, cf. on v. 16. For a description of the site see vi. 11, x. 10.

Betomesthaim is unknown. Apparently near Bethulia and Dothan. Torrey suggests that it is a pseudonym for Samaria, and that it is a corruption of בית מצפה, House of outlook, as שומרון from שמר, to watch.

8. **senate**, *γερουσία* = סנהדרין. Its constitution (seventy members and the president, נשיא) no doubt was modelled on the seventy elders of Exod. xxiv. 1, &c., but as an official body it probably is not older than the time of the Maccabees. It certainly did not exist in 516 B.C.

dwelt, *ἐκάθηντο*, rather 'sat' as a court or deliberative assembly.

13. **Jerusalem**, &c. א reads 'and those in Jerusalem fell down before . . .'

14. **continual burnt offering**, the תמיד, Num. xxviii. 3.

vows and **free gifts**, נדרים ונדבות, as in Num. xxix. 39 and often.

15 free gifts of the people; and they had ashes on their mitres: and they cried unto the Lord with all
their power, that he would look upon all the house of Israel for good.
5 1 And it was told Holofernes, the chief captain of the host of Asshur, that the children of Israel had
prepared for war, and had shut up the passages of the hill country, and had fortified all the tops of
2 the high hills, and had laid impediments in the plains: and he was exceeding wroth, and he called
all the princes of Moab, and the captains of Ammon, and all the governors of the sea coast, and he
3 said unto them, Tell me now, ye sons of Canaan, who is this people, that dwelleth in the hill country,
and what are the cities that they inhabit, and what is the multitude of their host, and wherein is
4 their power and their strength, and what king is set over them, to be the leader of their army; and
why have they turned their backs, that they should not come and meet me, more than all that dwell
in the west.
5 And Achior, the leader of all the children of Ammon, said unto him,
Let my lord now hear a word from the mouth of thy servant, and I will tell thee the truth
concerning this people, which dwelleth in this hill country, nigh unto the place where thou dwellest:
6 and there shall no lie come out of the mouth of thy servant. This people are descended of the
7 Chaldeans: and they sojourned heretofore in Mesopotamia, because they were not minded to follow
8 the gods of their fathers, which were in the land of the Chaldeans. And they departed from the
way of their parents, and worshipped the God of heaven, the God whom they knew: and they cast
them out from the face of their gods, and they fled into Mesopotamia, and sojourned there many
9 days. And their God commanded them to depart from the place where they sojourned, and to go
into the land of Canaan: and they dwelt there, and were increased with gold and silver, and with
10 exceeding much cattle. And they went down into Egypt, for a famine covered all the land of
Canaan; and there they sojourned, until they were grown up; and they became there a great
11 multitude, so that one could not number their nation. And the king of Egypt rose up against them,
and dealt subtilly with them, and brought them low, making them to labour in brick, and made
12 them slaves. And they cried unto their God, and he smote all the land of Egypt with incurable
13 plagues: and the Egyptians cast them out of their sight. And God dried up the Red sea before
14 them, and brought them into the way of Sinai, and Kadesh-Barnea, and they cast out all that dwelt
15 in the wilderness. And they dwelt in the land of the Amorites, and they destroyed by their strength
16 all them of Heshbon, and passing over Jordan they possessed all the hill country. And they cast
out before them the Canaanite, the Perizzite, the Jebusite, and the Shechemite, and all the
17 Girgashites, and they dwelt in that country many days. And whilst they sinned not before their

15. **mitres,** Exod. xxviii. 40 (A.V. bonnets).

V. 2. Moabites and Ammonites were employed against Judaea by the historical Nebuchadnezzar, see 2 Kings xxiv. 2.

and all the governors of the sea coast, omitted by א. The word for 'governors' is *σατράπας*, a Persian, not Babylonian, term.

3. A rhetorical question expressing scorn, cf. vi. 2.

Canaan is merely used archaistically for Syria, not (as Ball says) in its correct sense of Phoenicia and the coast. The name is rarely found in the later O.T. literature, and then only in reference to the early history of Israel (e.g. Neh. ix. 24). Holofernes, whether he was a Babylonian or a Persian, would not have used it.

5. **Achior** probably = Ahihud, by confusion of ר and ד as in LXX of Num. xxxiv. 27.

this people . . . thou dwellest. *τοῦ λαοῦ . . . πλησίον σοῦ οἰκοῦντος* probably go together, 'the people dwelling near thee.' The sentence is very awkward, and one of the two clauses would be better omitted. R.V. seems to me impossible.

6–8. This is rather the later midrashic development of the story of Abraham (refusing to worship the gods of Terah, incurring the wrath of Nimrod, and banished) than that contained in Gen. xi. 31–xii. 5, which is followed, e.g. in Neh. ix. 7–8, Acts vii. 2 f.

6. **descended of the Chaldeans,** i.e. Abraham came from Ur of the Chaldees.

7. **in Mesopotamia,** i.e. at Haran.

which were, *ἐγένοντο*, would naturally refer to 'fathers'. 58 VL Syr add *ἔνδοξοι*, 'which were worshipped,' making it refer to the gods.

8. **God of heaven,** cf. Dan. ii. 28, iv. 37, &c., and Sachau, *Aramäische Papyrus aus . . . Elephantine*, i. 2, &c. The expression was common in Persian times.

knew, *ἐπέγνωσαν*, perhaps 'whom they had come to know' or recognized as the only true God in consequence of a revelation, cf. Acts vii. 2.

9. See Gen. xii. 1.

10. **grown up,** *μέχρις οὗ διετράφησαν*. A.V. 'while they were nourished', which is correct. R.V. seems to mean 'until they increased in number', but that is said in the next clause. Possibly the Hebrew was עד שחיו 'as long as they lived (or were fed)'. Cf. Gen. l. 20.

11. B reads 'they dealt subtilly with them in (or with) labour (clay א, cf. Exod. i. 14) and brick, and they humbled them and made . . .'

12. The speech of Achior is part of the scheme of the book, to encourage the people in time of trouble by showing how God has given deliverance formerly when His people were worthy of it. Achior is represented as tending to a belief in the God of Israel, so that his sudden conversion later on is the less surprising.

out of their sight, *ἀπὸ προσώπου αὐτῶν* is merely the Hebrew מלפניהם, 'from them.'

16. Shechem is not named in the list in Joshua xii. It is introduced here out of hostility to the Samaritans.

18 God, they prospered, because God that hateth iniquity was with them. But when they departed
from the way which he appointed them, they were destroyed in many battles very sore, and were
led captives into a land that was not theirs, and the temple of their God was cast to the ground, and
19 their cities were taken by their adversaries. And now they are returned to their God, and are come
up from the dispersion where they were dispersed, and have possessed Jerusalem, where their
20 sanctuary is, and are seated in the hill country: for it was desolate. And now, my lord and master,
if there is any error in this people, and they sin against their God, we will consider what this thing
21 is wherein they stumble, and we will go up and overcome them. But if there is no lawlessness in
their nation, let my lord now pass by, lest their Lord defend them, and their God be for them, and
we shall be a reproach before all the earth.
22 And it came to pass, when Achior had finished speaking these words, all the people that
compassed the tent and stood round about it murmured; and the great men of Holofernes, and all
23 that dwelt by the sea side, and in Moab, spake that he should kill him. For, *said they*, we will not
be afraid of the children of Israel: for, lo, it is a people that hath no power nor might to make the
24 battle strong. Wherefore now we will go up, and they shall be a prey to be devoured of all thine
army, lord Holofernes.

6 1 And when the tumult of the men that were about the council was ceased, Holofernes the chief
captain of the host of Asshur said unto Achior and to all the children of Moab before all the people
of the aliens,
2 And who art thou, Achior, and the hirelings of Ephraim, that thou hast prophesied among us
as to-day, and hast said, that we should not make war with the race of Israel, because their God
3 will defend them? And who is God but Nebuchadnezzar? He shall send forth his might, and
shall destroy them from the face of the earth, and their God shall not deliver them: but we his
4 servants shall smite them as one man; and they shall not sustain the might of our horses. For with
them we shall burn them up, and their mountains shall be drunken with their blood, and their plains
shall be filled with their dead bodies, and their footsteps shall not stand before us, but they shall
surely perish, saith king Nebuchadnezzar, lord of all the earth: for he said, The words that I have
5 spoken shall not be in vain. But thou, Achior, hireling of Ammon, which hast spoken these words
in the day of thine iniquity, shalt see my face no more from this day, until I shall be avenged of the
6 race of those that came out of Egypt. And then shall the sword of mine army, and the multitude
of them that serve me, pass through thy sides, and thou shalt fall among their slain, when I shall
7 return. And my servants shall bring thee back into the hill country, and shall set thee in one of

18. **led captives**, by (the historical) Nebuchadnezzar in 588. Achior is telling this to a representative of Nebuchadnezzar seventy years later!

temple . . . cast to the ground. It was not merely desecrated as e.g. by Antiochus.

19. **are come up** (עלו), i.e. about 516.

the dispersion. *διασπορά* is the common word in Hellenistic times for the Jews scattered in various lands, not exiles in one place, as here.

20. Rather, 'if there is any fault due to ignorance (שגגה) . . . and we see that this offence (*σκάνδαλον*) is in them, then (*καί*) we will go up . . .'

21. **lawlessness**, *ἀνομία*, a breach of the Law, = *ἀγνόημα* in verse 20.

lest . . . for them, rather 'lest their Lord and their God defend (be a shield over) them'; *ὑπερασπίσῃ . . . ὑπὲρ αὐτῶν* = יגן עליהם.

and we shall be. *ἐσόμεθα* is not dependent (incorrectly) on *μή ποτε*, but means 'for then (*καί*) we shall be . . .'

VI. 1. **about the council**, i.e. were round about forming the council.

and to all the children of Moab is omitted by B, and transferred to the next verse by homoioteleuton, where it is evidently out of place. For 'Moab' 19 108, read 'Ammon', more appropriately, as Achior was an Ammonite.

aliens, *ἀλλόφυλοι* in LXX means Philistines, but here only 'non-Jews'.

2. **hirelings**, meaning that they were mercenaries in the 'Assyrian' army (Ephraim being then incorrectly used for 'Syrian'), or perhaps that they were bought over by Ephraim, i.e. Israel.

For **Ephraim** 19 108 read Ammon, and similarly 58 VL Syr.

as to-day. *καθὼς σήμερον* is no doubt כַּיּוֹם 'to-day', 'now'.

3. Cf. 2 Kings xviii. 32–5.

4. **burn them up**, *κατακαύσομεν* (בער), an unsuitable word. The variants *κατακλύσομεν* and *καταπατήσομεν* (בעט) are evident corrections.

for he said . . ., better 'for he hath spoken (it). The words of his sayings (א 19 108 "of his mouth") shall not be in vain'; cf. verse 9.

6. **the multitude of them that serve.** *Λαὸς τῶν θεραπόντων* passing through his sides is a strange expression. Fritzsche emends *χαλκός*, comparing VL and Syr. But it may mean 'cut him in two and march between the parts'; or, more probably, it is a mistranslation of חרב חילי וחיל עבדי (for *τοῦ λαοῦ*), 'the sword of my army and of my servants.' So above, i. 6 *βασιλεῖς*.

I shall return, B 'they'.

7. **bring thee back**, *ἀποκαταστήσουσί σε* used loosely for 'take thee away' (so Fritzsche), cf. Hos. xi. 12, LXX (not bring back).

8, 9 the cities of the ascents: and thou shalt not perish, till thou be destroyed with them. And if thou
hopest in thy heart that they shall not be taken, let not thy countenance fall. I have spoken it, and
none of my words shall fall to the ground.
10 And Holofernes commanded his servants, that waited in his tent, to take Achior, and bring him
11 back to Bethulia, and deliver him into the hands of the children of Israel. And his servants took
him, and brought him out of the camp into the plain, and they removed from the midst of the plain
12 country into the hill country, and came unto the fountains that were under Bethulia. And when the
men of the city saw them on the top of the hill, they took up their weapons, and went out of the city
against them to the top of the hill: and every man that used a sling kept them from coming up, and
13 cast stones against them. And they gat them privily under the hill, and bound Achior, and cast him
14 down, and left him at the foot of the hill, and went away unto their lord. But the children of Israel
descended from their city, and came upon him, and loosed him, and led him away into Bethulia, and
15 presented him to the rulers of their city; which were in those days Ozias the son of Micah, of the
16 tribe of Simeon, and Chabris the son of Gothoniel, and Charmis the son of Melchiel. And they
called together all the elders of the city; and all their young men ran together, and their women,
to the assembly; and they set Achior in the midst of all their people. And Ozias asked him of that
17 which had happened: and he answered and declared unto them the words of the council of Holofernes,
and all the words that he had spoken in the midst of the princes of the children of Asshur, and all
18 the great words that Holofernes had spoken against the house of Israel. And the people fell down
19 and worshipped God, and cried, saying, O Lord God of heaven, behold their arrogance, and pity the
20 low estate of our race, and look upon the face of those that are sanctified unto thee this day. And
21 they comforted Achior, and praised him exceedingly. And Ozias took him out of the assembly into
his house, and made a feast to the elders; and they called on the God of Israel for help all that
night.

7 1 But the next day Holofernes gave command to all his army, and to all his people which were
come to be his allies, that they should remove their camp toward Bethulia, and take aforehand the
2 ascents of the hill country, and make war against the children of Israel. And every mighty man of
them removed that day, and the host of their men of war was a hundred and seventy thousand
footmen, and twelve thousand horsemen, beside the baggage, and the men that were afoot among
3 them, an exceeding great multitude. And they encamped in the valley near unto Bethulia, by the
fountain, and they spread themselves in breadth over Dothaim even to Belmaim, and in length from
Bethulia unto Cyamon, which is over against Esdraelon.

4 But the children of Israel, when they saw the multitude of them, were troubled exceedingly, and
said every one to his neighbour, Now shall these men lick up the face of all the earth; and neither
5 the high mountains, nor the valleys, nor the hills, shall be able to bear their weight. And every man
took up his weapons of war, and when they had kindled fires upon their towers, they remained and
watched all that night.

6 But on the second day Holofernes led out all his horse in the sight of the children of Israel which
7 were in Bethulia, and viewed the ascents to their city, and searched out the fountains of the waters,

ascents, i. e. the hill-country of the enemy.
8. **with them**, i. e. the cities.
9. Meaning 'if you really believe what you have just said, you need not look dismayed as you do'.
10. **bring him back**, see verse 7.
Bethulia, Βετυλουά B, Βαιτουλουά א. Note that it was on a hill, and there were springs just below it (*v.* 11 and vii. 12).
12. **on the top of the hill**, though read by the chief MSS., is due to homoioteleuton from the line below. It is omitted by 58 VL Syr.
13. **cast . . . and left**, better 'left him lying'.
15. The forms of the names vary very much in the MSS.
Micah, Χειμά A: **of the tribe of Simeon**, as Judith was, ix. 2.
Charmis, Χαλμείς A.
Melchiel, Σελλήμ א*.
19. **those that are sanctified** . . . i. e. 'thy holy nation', מְקֻדָּשֶׁיךָ, which Syr seems to have taken as מִקְדָּשְׁךָ, 'thy sanctuary.'
20. VL adds, 'saying, As it shall please God (to do) concerning us, (so) shall it be also with thee.'
21. **feast**, πότον = משתה.

VII. 2. **the host** . . . properly 'their host of warriors'.
170,000. א* has 8,000, corrected to 120,000.
baggage and, B has 'baggage of'.
3. **The fountain** was below the city, cf. vi. 11.
Belmaim, א Abelmaim, cf. iv. 4.
Cyamon, Syr Kadmûn, VL Chelmona, is unknown.
5. **when . . . towers**, omitted by א* and added by the corrector.

and seized upon them, and set garrisons of men of war over them, and himself departed to his
people.
8 And there came unto him all the rulers of the children of Esau, and all the leaders of the people
9 of Moab, and the captains of the sea coast, and said, Let our lord now hear a word, that there be not
10 an overthrow in thy host. For this people of the children of Israel do not trust in their spears, but
in the height of the mountains wherein they dwell, for it is not easy to come up to the tops of their
11 mountains. And now, my lord, fight not against them as men fight who join battle, and there shall
12 not so much as one man of thy people perish. Remain in thy camp, and keep safe every man of thy
host, and let thy servants get possession of the fountain of water, which issueth forth of the foot of
13 the mountain: because all the inhabitants of Bethulia have their water thence; and thirst shall kill
them, and they shall give up their city: and we and our people will go up to the tops of the
mountains that are near, and will encamp upon them, to watch that not one man go out of the city.
14 And they shall be consumed with famine, they and their wives and their children, and before the
15 sword come against them they shall be laid low in the streets where they dwell. And thou shalt
render them an evil reward; because they rebelled, and met not thy face in peace.
16 And their words were pleasing in the sight of Holofernes and in the sight of all his servants; and
17 he appointed to do as they had spoken. And the army of the children of Ammon removed, and with
them five thousand of the children of Asshur, and they encamped in the valley, and seized upon the
18 waters and the fountains of the waters of the children of Israel. And the children of Esau went up
with the children of Ammon, and encamped in the hill country over against Dothaim: and they
sent some of them toward the south, and toward the east, over against Ekrebel, which is near unto
Chusi, that is upon the brook Mochmur; and the rest of the army of the Assyrians encamped in the
plain, and covered all the face of the land; and their tents and baggage were pitched upon it in
a great crowd, and they were an exceeding great multitude.
19 And the children of Israel cried unto the Lord their God, for their spirit fainted; for all their
enemies had compassed them round about, and there was no way to escape out from among them.
20 And all the army of Asshur remained about them, their footmen and their chariots and their horse-
21 men, four and thirty days; and all their vessels of water failed all the inhabitants of Bethulia. And
the cisterns were emptied, and they had not water to drink their fill for one day: for they gave them
22 drink by measure. And their young children were out of heart, and the women and the young men
fainted for thirst, and they fell down in the streets of the city, and in the passages of the gates, and
23 there was no longer any strength in them. And all the people were gathered together against Ozias,
and against the rulers of the city, the young men and the women and the children, and they cried
with a loud voice, and said before all the elders,
24 God be judge between you and us: because ye have done us great wrong, in that ye have not
25 spoken words of peace with the children of Asshur. And now we have no helper: but God hath
sold us into their hands, that we should be laid low before them with thirst and great destruction.
26 And now call them unto you, and deliver up the whole city for a prey to the people of Holofernes,
27 and to all his host. For it is better for us to be made a spoil unto them: for we shall be servants,
and our souls shall live, and we shall not see the death of our babes before our eyes, and our wives
28 and our children fainting in death. We take to witness against you the heaven and the earth, and
our God and the Lord of our fathers, which punisheth us according to our sins and the sins of our
fathers, that he do not according as we have said this day.

7. **to his people**, i. e. went back to the main body of his army.
8. **Esau**, archaistic.
10. **wherein they dwell**, *ἐν οἷς αὐτοὶ ἐνοικοῦσιν ἐν αὐτοῖς*, a Hebraism.
11. **as . . . battle.** *παράταξις* is battle-array; 'as a war is conducted in the field.'
13. **to watch . . .**, properly 'as an outpost, so that no one shall . . .'
17. **Ammon**, 19 108 VL Syr Moab. The same variant in vi. 1.
waters (i. e. reservoirs) and springs.
18. **Ekrebel** in A: the rest have Egrebel: probably Akraba, about ten miles south-east of Nablus or Shechem Ball and Torrey.
Chusi in A: the rest and VL, Chus: mod. Quzeh, five or six miles south of Nablus (Torrey).
Mochmur, omitted by A: mod. Makhueh, south of Nablus (Torrey).
in a great crowd, perhaps 'among a great throng of camp-followers' (Ball).
20. **four and thirty days.** 19 108 have fourteen days and a month; VL Syr four days and two months; Vulg. twenty days. The long siege by this large army is meant to emphasize the importance of Bethulia.
vessels, *ἀγγεῖα*, in which water was stored in private houses.
28. **witness**, cf. Deut. iv. 26.
Lord of our fathers is only used to vary the phrase, which is a translation of אלהינו ואלהי אבותינו.
that he do not . . . ought to mean 'we urge you (to take steps) that he do not . . .' If the text is correct, the subject of *ποιήσῃ* must be either God or Holofernes. The former is better, since they recommend surrendering to

29 And there was great weeping of all with one consent in the midst of the assembly; and they cried
30 unto the Lord God with a loud voice. And Ozias said to them, Brethren, be of good courage, let
us yet endure five days, in the which space the Lord our God shall turn his mercy toward us; for
31 he will not forsake us utterly. But if these days pass, and there come no help unto us, I will do
32 according to your words. And he dispersed the people, every man to his own camp; and they went
away unto the walls and towers of their city; and he sent the women and children into their houses:
and they were brought very low in the city.

8 1 And in those days Judith heard thereof, the daughter of Merari, the son of Ox, the son of Joseph,
the son of Oziel, the son of Elkiah, the son of Ananias, the son of Gideon, the son of Raphaim, the
son of Ahitub, the son of Elihu, the son of Eliab, the son of Nathanael, the son of Salamiel, the son
2 of Salasadai, the son of Israel. And her husband was Manasses, of her tribe and of her family, and
3 he died in the days of barley harvest. For he stood over them that bound sheaves in the field, and
the heat came upon his head, and he fell on his bed, and died in his city Bethulia: and they buried
4 him with his fathers in the field which is between Dothaim and Balamon. And Judith was a widow
5 in her house three years and four months. And she made her a tent upon the roof of her house,
6 and put on sackcloth upon her loins; and the garments of her widowhood were upon her. And she
fasted all the days of her widowhood, save the eves of the sabbaths, and the sabbaths, and the eves
7 of the new moons, and the new moons, and the feasts and joyful days of the house of Israel. And
she was of a goodly countenance, and exceeding beautiful to behold: and her husband Manasses
had left her gold, and silver, and menservants, and maidservants, and cattle, and lands; and she
8 remained upon them. And there was none that gave her an evil word; for she feared God
exceedingly.

9 And she heard the evil words of the people against the governor, because they fainted for lack of
water; and Judith heard all the words that Ozias spake unto them, how he sware to them that he
10 would deliver the city unto the Assyrians after five days. And she sent her maid, that was over all
11 things that she had, to call Ozias and Chabris and Charmis, the elders of her city. And they came
unto her, and she said unto them,

Hear me now, O ye rulers of the inhabitants of Bethulia: for your word that ye have spoken before the people this day is not right, and ye have set the oath which ye have pronounced between God and you, and have promised to deliver the city to our enemies, unless within these days the

Holofernes and in verse 31 Ozias promises to do so. 'That he do not . . .' then means 'that he let us not die of thirst'. But א omits *μή*, and VL reads *ut faciatis* (Vulg. 'ut tradatis civitatem,' &c.), which suggests a reading *ἵνα ποιήσητε*, 'that *ye* do as we say,' i.e. surrender, cf. verse 31.

32. **every man.** The Greek requires *ἕκαστον*, as in 58 VL Syr.

camp. *παρεμβολήν* is rather 'station' or 'post' of duty in guarding the walls, as shown by the next clause; cf. vii. 7 (garrisons).

he sent, 'they sent,' *ἀπέστειλαν*, is the common reading.

VIII. 1. **heard.** 58 VL Syr have 'was living in the city'.

If the genealogy is fictitious, it is strangely elaborate. The names are corrupt, and we have no means of checking them.

Ox, which is not a Hebrew name, may be for Uz (19 Oz) or Uzzi (VL Ozi).

son of Ananias . . . Ahitub, omitted by B.

Raphaim (cf. Gen. xiv. 5) cannot be right. Ball suggests Raphaiah or Raphael.

For **Ahitub** (א 19 108 VL Syr) A has Akitho.

After **Elihu** א B add *υἱοῦ Χελκ(ε)ίου.*

Eliab, א ENAB, VL Enar.

Salamiel, א Samamiel.

Salasadai, א Sarisadai (שׂרישׁדי ?), B Sarasadai.

3. Cf. 2 Kings iv. 18 f.

4. i.e. she had been a widow three years and four months up to the date of the siege.

6. **save the eves of the sabbaths,** VL 'praeter cenam puram'.

The observance of eves as well as the festivals was in accordance with the later Talmudic rule.

joyful days, *χαρμοσυνῶν*. We should expect a word answering to מועדים, the general term for festivals, since *ἑορταί* are חגים, the three great feasts. 58 adds *καὶ μνημοσυνῶν*, VL 'et memoriae', and so Syr.

7. 58 VL Syr have '. . . countenance and wise in heart and good in understanding (cf. xi. 23), and she was (exceedingly) rich, for her husband . . .'

After **Manasses** VL adds his genealogy, copied from verse 1.

remained, ישבה עליהם, she made her home on the property. Cf. Sayce and Cowley, *Aramaic Papyri* C 5, 6 ארקא זך . . . תב בגו עם אנתתך.

8. **gave her an evil word,** i.e. slandered her.

9. **how he sware.** 58 Syr 'how he hearkened (i.e. gave way) and sware'. So VL.

10. **maid,** *ἅβραν*, said to be a foreign word: possibly from the root חבר, and so 'companion': but she was a slave (xvi. 23). Ozias is omitted by א A B.

12 Lord turn to help you. And now who are ye that have tempted God this day, and stand instead of
13 God among the children of men? And now try the Lord Almighty, and ye shall never know
14 anything. For ye shall not find the depth of the heart of man, and ye shall not perceive the things
that he thinketh: and how shall ye search out God, which hath made all these things, and know his
mind, and comprehend his purpose? Nay, my brethren, provoke not the Lord our God to anger.
15 For if he be not minded to help us within these five days, he hath power to defend us in such time
16 as he will, or to destroy us before the face of our enemies. But do not ye pledge the counsels of
the Lord our God: for God is not as man, that he should be threatened; neither as the son of man,
17 that he should be turned by intreaty. Wherefore let us wait for the salvation that cometh from
18 him, and call upon him to help us, and he will hear our voice, if it please him. For there arose none
in our age, neither is there any of us to-day, tribe, or kindred, or family, or city, which worship gods
19 made with hands, as it was in the former days; for the which cause our fathers were given to the
20 sword, and for a spoil, and fell with a great fall before our enemies. But we know none other god
21 beside him, wherefore we hope that he will not despise us, nor any of our race. For if we be taken
so, all Judæa shall sit upon the ground, and our sanctuary shall be spoiled; and of our blood shall
22 he require the profanation thereof. And the slaughter of our brethren, and the captivity of the land,
and the desolation of our inheritance, shall he turn upon our heads among the Gentiles, wheresoever
we shall be in bondage; and we shall be an offence and a reproach before them that take us for
23 a possession. For our bondage shall not be ordered to favour: but the Lord our God shall turn it
24 to dishonour. And now, brethren, let us shew an example to our brethren, because their soul
25 hangeth upon us, and the sanctuary and the house and the altar rest upon us. Besides all this let
26 us give thanks to the Lord our God, which trieth us, even as he did our fathers also. Remember
all the things which he did to Abraham, and all the things in which he tried Isaac, and all the things
which happened to Jacob in Mesopotamia of Syria, when he kept the sheep of Laban his mother's
27 brother. For he hath not tried us in the fire, as he did them, to search out their hearts, neither hath
he taken vengeance on us; but the Lord doth scourge them that come near unto him, to admonish
them.

28 And Ozias said to her, All that thou hast spoken hast thou spoken with a good heart, and there
29 is none that shall gainsay thy words. For this is not the first day wherein thy wisdom is manifested;
but from the beginning of thy days all the people have known thine understanding, because the
30 disposition of thy heart is good. But the people were exceeding thirsty, and compelled us to do as
31 we spake to them, and to bring an oath upon ourselves, which we will not break. And now pray
thou for us, because thou art a godly woman, and the Lord shall send us rain to fill our cisterns, and
32 we shall faint no more. And Judith said unto them, Hear me, and I will do a thing, which shall go
33 down to all generations among the children of our race. Ye shall stand at the gate this night, and
I will go forth with my maid: and, within the days after which ye said that ye would deliver the

12. **instead of God.** ὑπὲρ τοῦ θεοῦ. Ball renders 'above God', but the meaning is probably as in R.V. VL has *pro Deo*, 'as God', and similarly Syr.

13. 58 VL Syr have καὶ νοῦν κυρίου . . . καὶ οὐθεὶς γνώσεται. Probably ἐξετάζετε is indicative 'ye are trying' (or tempting). Cf. Job xi. 7, and 1 Cor. ii. 11, 16, which is not a quotation.

14. 58 VL Syr have 'the depth . . . shall not be found', and διαλογισμούς for λόγους.

15. **For . . . days,** omitted by 58.
Syr has 'and to destroy our enemies before us'.

16. Cf. Num. xxiii. 19 (LXX), where διαρτηθῆναι (to be undecided) is used, as here by 19 23 44 55 al. R.V. 'turned by intreaty' is διαιτηθῆναι, the common reading.

17. **voice.** 19 23 44 55 al. δεήσεως, 'petition', as in ix. 12.

18. **age.** ἐν ταῖς γενεαῖς ἡμῶν = בדורותינו, i. e. within living memory, which might be true of the time after the exile.

18–20. This is the chief lesson of the book.

20. **we know . . .** ἡμεῖς . . . οὐκ ἐπεγνῶμεν, 'we (emphatic) have never recognized any . . .' 58 VL insert (οὐδ') ἀποστήσει τὸ σωτήριον ἔλεος αὐτοῦ, 'nec auferet salvationem *et* misericordiam suam a nobis et a . . .'

21. **all Judæa shall sit . . .** καθήσεται. 19 23 44 64 al. κλιθήσεται, others κληθήσεται. 58 VL Syr ληφθήσεται. Fritzsche conjectures καυθήσεται and Thilo παυθήσεται. But probably 'sit' is right, and some word for 'solitary' has dropped out. Cf. ישבה בדד, Lam. i. 1.
of our blood is the reading of the MSS., but the expression is unusual, and seems to be due to a mistranslation. Fritzsche reads στόματος (without MS. authority) which is no better. The meaning is 'he will punish us for its profanation'.

22. **turn upon our heads,** i. e. punish us for it, cf. Judges ix. 57 (Ball).

23. **to favour,** as in the case of Jehoiachin, 2 Kings xxv. 27 ff. (Ball).

24. **rest upon us.** Note the importance of Bethulia. It was the key of the whole situation.

27. **scourge,** cf. Heb. xii. 6. This verse is quoted by Clement of Alexandria, *Strom.* ii. 447.

31. 58 VL Syr have 'for us and God shall speedily hear us, because'.
godly, εὐσεβής; 58 Syr θεοσεβής (as in xi. 17), VL *sancta.*

32. 58 VL Syr 'a thing of wisdom'.

33. 58 VL Syr add 'as I trust' at the end.

34 city to our enemies, the Lord shall visit Israel by my hand. But ye shall not inquire of mine act:
35 for I will not declare it unto you, till the things be finished that I do. And Ozias and the rulers
said unto her, Go in peace, and the Lord God be before thee, to take vengeance on our enemies.
36 And they returned from the tent, and went to their stations.
9 1 But Judith fell upon her face, and put ashes upon her head, and uncovered the sackcloth wherewith she was clothed; and the incense of that evening was now being offered at Jerusalem in the
house of God, and Judith cried unto the Lord with a loud voice, and said,
2 O Lord God of my father Simeon, into whose hand thou gavest a sword to take vengeance of the
strangers, who loosened the girdle of a virgin to defile her, and uncovered the thigh to her shame,
3 and profaned the womb to her reproach; for thou saidst, It shall not be so; and they did so:
wherefore thou gavest their rulers to be slain, and their bed, which was ashamed for her that was
deceived, to be dyed in blood, and smotest the servants with their lords, and the lords upon their
4 thrones; and gavest their wives for a prey, and their daughters to be captives, and all their spoils
to be divided among thy dear children; which were moved with zeal for thee, and abhorred the
pollution of their blood, and called upon thee for aid: O God, O my God, hear me also that am a
5 widow. For thou wroughtest the things that were before those things, and those things, and such
as ensued after; and thou didst devise the things which are now, and the things which are to come:
6 and the things which thou didst devise came to pass; yea, the things which thou didst determine
stood before thee, and said, Lo, we are here: for all thy ways are prepared, and thy judgement is
7 with foreknowledge. For, behold, the Assyrians are multiplied in their power; they are exalted
with horse and rider; they have gloried in the strength of their footmen; they have trusted in
shield and spear and bow and sling; and they know not that thou art the Lord that breaketh the
8 battles: the Lord is thy name. Dash thou down their strength in thy power, and bring down their
force in thy wrath: for they have purposed to profane thy sanctuary, and to defile the tabernacle
9 where thy glorious name resteth, and to cast down with the sword the horn of thine altar. Look
upon their pride, and send thy wrath upon their heads: give into my hand, which am a widow, the
10 might that I have conceived. Smite by the deceit of my lips the servant with the prince, and the
11 prince with his servant: break down their stateliness by the hand of a woman. For thy power
standeth not in multitude, nor thy might in strong men: but thou art a God of the afflicted, thou

36. 58 VL 'returned and went down from the tent', which was on the roof of her house (viii. 5).

IX. 1. **uncovered**, i. e. rent the mantle which she wore over it, so 58 VL Syr, or took off her mantle.

2. Referring to Gen. xxxiv. 25.

girdle, *μίτραν*, is Grotius's emendation for *μήτραν* (as all MSS.). But 'to loose the girdle' is not a Hebrew expression in this sense, and *μίτρα* is used elsewhere in this book for head-dress, not girdle. *λύειν μήτραν*, if it is for פתח רחם, is quite unsuitable here. The verse is evidently corrupt, as the second *μήτραν* shows (which 248 has changed to *παρθενίαν*). We should expect in Hebrew גִּלָּה ערות בתולה. Can ערות have been misread עטרת and translated *μίτρα*? The result would be sufficiently unintelligible to lead to corrections in the Greek.

It shall not be so, as LXX in Gen. xxxiv. 7.

3. **bed . . . blood.** The text is difficult, and must be corrupt. B has *ἣ ᾐδέσατο τὴν ἀπάτην αὐτῶν ἀπατηθεῖσαν*, apparently meaning 'which was ashamed of their deceit (wherewith they had deceived)'. A and ℵ* omit *ἀπάτην*, and so R.V. Fritzsche omits *ἀπατηθεῖσαν*. 58 has *ἐδέξατο τὴν ἀγαπηθεῖσαν* (and similarly VL Syr) which must be a conjectural emendation. For *ᾐδέσατο* Fritzsche conjectures *ἠδύνατο*, Ball *ᾐδήσατο*, 248 has *ἠρδεύσατο*, others *ἠδεύσατο*, &c. None of these is an improvement on the ordinary reading, and some are impossible. The parallelism requires the whole relative clause to be omitted. Read 'thou gavest their rulers to slaughter and their bed to blood'.

with. *ἐπί* = על, and so the second *ἐπί* perhaps = 'with their thrones', cf. verse 10.

5. **those things, and.** *ἐκεῖνα καί* is very clumsy. ℵ omits *καί*. A omits *τά*. Syr has 'the middle things'. We should expect the Hebrew to be עשִׂיתָ קדמוניות ואחרניות, for which there may have been a variant ע׳ הק׳ ואלה האח׳ giving rise to the existing Greek. The present things are mentioned in the next sentence.

devise (1) is *διενοήθης*, 'intend'.

devise (2) is *ἐνενοήθης*, חשבתָ, 'thou hadst in mind'. Cf. Sir. xxxix. 30 and Midrash *Ber. R.* § 3, where creation is said to originate במחשבה.

6. **judgement.** A has 'judgements'. 58 VL Syr *αἱ κτίσεις*.

7. **breaketh . . . name,** from Exod. xv. 3 LXX.

8. **in thy power**, rather 'by', *ἐν* = בְּ as frequently.

58 VL Syr have 'dash down their strength, oh Eternal (*αἰώνιε*), break their multitude by thy power, smite (*πάταξον* for *κάταξον*) their force . . .' ℵ has *σύνραξον*, which may be the original reading for *σὺ ῥάξον*.

tabernacle . . . Cf. Deut. xii. 11 and frequently.

9. **the might . . .** i. e. strength to do what I have conceived.

10. **deceit.** Vulg. read *ἀγάπης* for *ἀπάτης*, as in ix. 3. 'Lips of deceit' is a Hebraism שִׂפְתֵי שקר, cf. Ps. cxx. 2. With this clause cf. ix. 3.

stateliness, *ἀνάστεμα*, a form also found in xii. 8 in some MSS. A has *ἀνάστημα*.

by the hand of a woman. She was thinking of Jael, cf. Judges ix. 54.

11. **might.** 58 VL Syr have *δόσις* 'gift', ℵ *δεξιά*.

art a helper of the oppressed, an upholder of the weak, a protector of the forlorn, a saviour of them
12 that are without hope. Yea, yea, God of my father, and God of the inheritance of Israel, Lord of
the heavens and of the earth, Creator of the waters, King of every creature, hear thou my prayer:
13 and make my speech and deceit to be their wound and stripe, who have purposed hard things against
thy covenant, and thy hallowed house, and the top of Sion, and the house of the possession of thy
14 children. And make every nation and tribe of thine to know that thou art God, the God of all
power and might, and that there is none other that protecteth the race of Israel but thou.
10 1 And it came to pass, when she had ceased to cry unto the God of Israel, and had made an end of
2 all these words, that she rose up where she had fallen down, and called her maid, and went down
3 into the house, in the which she was wont to abide on the sabbath days and on her feast days, and
pulled off the sackcloth which she had put on, and put off the garments of her widowhood, and
washed her body all over with water, and anointed herself with rich ointment, and braided the hair
of her head, and put a tire upon it, and put on her garments of gladness, wherewith she was wont
4 to be clad in the days of the life of Manasses her husband. And she took sandals for her feet, and
put her chains about her, and her bracelets, and her rings, and her earrings, and all her ornaments,
5 and decked herself bravely, to beguile the eyes of all men that should see her. And she gave her
maid a leathern bottle of wine, and a cruse of oil, and filled a bag with parched corn and lumps of
figs and fine bread; and she packed all her vessels together, and laid them upon her.
6 And they went forth to the gate of the city of Bethulia, and found standing thereby Ozias, and
7 the elders of the city, Chabris and Charmis. But when they saw her, that her countenance was
altered, and her apparel was changed, they wondered at her beauty very exceedingly, and said unto
8 her, The God of our fathers give thee favour, and accomplish thy purposes to the glory of the
9 children of Israel, and to the exaltation of Jerusalem. And she worshipped God, and said unto
them, Command that they open unto me the gate of the city, and I will go forth to accomplish the
10 things whereof ye spake with me. And they commanded the young men to open unto her, as she
had spoken: and they did so.
And Judith went out, she, and her handmaid with her; and the men of the city looked after her,
until she was gone down the mountain, until she had passed the valley, and they could see her no
11, 12 more. And they went straight onward in the valley: and the watch of the Assyrians met her; and
they took her, and asked her, Of what people art thou? and whence comest thou? and whither goest
thou? And she said, I am a daughter of the Hebrews, and I flee away from their presence; because
13 they are about to be given you to be consumed: and I am coming into the presence of Holofernes
the chief captain of your host, to declare words of truth; and I will shew before him a way, whereby
he shall go, and win all the hill country, and there shall not be lacking of his men one person, nor

oppressed, *ἐλαττόνων*, is right (not as R.V. margin) = those who are inferior to others, i.e. overcome by them. 58 VL Syr have 'saviour of the forlorn', omitting *σκεπαστὴς ἀπηλπισμένων*.

12. **of every creature**, *πάσης κτίσεώς σου* = כל בריאתך 'all (thy) creation', a common expression in late Hebrew.

13. **against thy covenant.** Ball cft. Dan. xi. 28, and suggests that this is an indication of Maccabean times, but the indication is too slight to be pressed.

top, i.e. mount, unusual with Sion.

14. **every nation . . . of thine**, ℵ B *ἐπὶ πᾶν τὸ ἔθνος σου*, A *ἐπὶ παντὸς ἔθνους σου*. 58 'every nation of every tribe to know thee'. VL also omits *σου*. The meaning is (as Syr) 'make thy whole nation (Israel) and every (foreign) tribe to know', not as R.V.

X. Ball rightly points out that x. 1–xi. 5 is modelled on the Greek Esther v. 1–15.

2. **maid**, *ἅβραν*, as in viii. 10 and in the parallel passage in Esther.

house. She lived usually in a tent on the roof, but went down into the house for festivals.

3. **braided**, *διέταξε*, properly 'arranged'. Syr 'anointed'. VL (cod. Corb.) and Vulg. *discriminavit*, 'she parted it.' ℵ *διέξανε*. 19 108 *διεξήνατο* = VL *pectinavit*, 'she combed it out.'

tire is *μίτρα*, cf. above on ix. 2.

4. **sandals** would not have been worn during her mourning.

chains, *χλίδωνας*, following sandals, are probably 'anklets', as VL.

decked herself. Vulg. adds that her beauty was miraculously increased because of her virtuous object.

to beguile, *εἰς ἀπάτησιν*. A B *ἀπάντησιν*, to meet.

5. **lumps of figs**, *παλάθης*. ℵ om. Syr has plural.

After **bread** 19 108 add 'cheese', and so 58 VL Syr.

It is in accordance with Judith's pious observance of the Law that she should make these careful preparations to ensure having clean (*kosher*) food while away from home. The vessels were for such cooking as might be necessary. Gentile vessels would be or might be unclean.

8. **give thee favour**, *δῴη σε εἰς χάριν*. A Hebrew expression = make thee to be favoured. 58 VL Syr have *δῴη σοι χάριν*.

10. Bethulia was on a mountain and was approached by a valley. The outposts (*προφυλακή*) of the enemy were at the other end of the valley.

12. **Hebrews.** Correctly used to distinguish them from foreigners, to whom she was speaking.

13. **lacking**, *διαφωνήσει*, a late Greek use of the word. In 1 Sam. xxx. 19 it renders נעדר. The end of the verse would be strange, even in Hebrew. It means 'no one shall be taken prisoner or killed'.

14 one life. Now when the men heard her words, and considered her countenance, the beauty thereof
15 was exceeding marvellous in their eyes, and they said unto her, Thou hast saved thy life, in that
thou hast hasted to come down to the presence of our lord: and now come to his tent, and some of
16 us shall conduct thee, until they shall deliver thee into his hands. But when thou standest before
him, be not afraid in thine heart, but declare unto him according to thy words; and he shall entreat
17 thee well. And they chose out of them a hundred men, and appointed them to accompany her and
her maid; and they brought them to the tent of Holofernes.
18 And there was a concourse throughout all the camp, for her coming was noised among the tents;
and they came and compassed her about, as she stood without the tent of Holofernes, until they told
19 him of her. And they marvelled at her beauty, and marvelled at the children of Israel because of
her, and each one said to his neighbour, Who shall despise this people, that have among them such
women? for it is not good that one man of them be left, seeing that, if they are let go, they shall be
20 able to deceive the whole earth. And they that lay near Holofernes, and all his servants, went forth
21 and brought her into the tent. And Holofernes was resting upon his bed under the canopy, which
22 was woven with purple and gold and emeralds and precious stones. And they told him of her; and
23 he came forth into the space before his tent, with silver lamps going before him. But when Judith
was come before him and his servants, they all marvelled at the beauty of her countenance; and
she fell down upon her face, and did reverence unto him: and his servants raised her up.

11 1 And Holofernes said unto her, Woman, be of good comfort, fear not in thy heart: for I never
2 hurt any that hath chosen to serve Nebuchadnezzar, the king of all the earth. And now, if thy
people that dwelleth in the hill country had not set light by me, I would not have lifted up my spear
3 against them: but they have done these things to themselves. And now tell me wherefore thou
didst flee from them, and camest unto us: for thou art come to save thyself; be of good comfort,
4 thou shalt live this night, and hereafter: for there is none that shall wrong thee, but all shall entreat
5 thee well, as is done unto the servants of king Nebuchadnezzar my lord. And Judith said unto him,
Receive the words of thy servant, and let thy handmaid speak in thy presence, and I will declare
6 no lie unto my lord this night. And if thou shalt follow the words of thy handmaid, God shall bring
7 the thing to pass perfectly with thee; and my lord shall not fail of his purposes. As Nebuchadnezzar
king of all the earth liveth, and as his power liveth, who hath sent thee for the preservation of every
living thing, not only do men serve him by thee, but also the beasts of the field and the cattle and
the birds of the heaven shall live through thy strength, in the time of Nebuchadnezzar and of all his
8 house. For we have heard of thy wisdom and the subtil devices of thy soul, and it hath been
reported in all the earth, that thou only art brave in all the kingdom, and mighty in knowledge, and
9 wonderful in feats of war. And now as concerning the matter, which Achior did speak in thy
council, we have heard his words: for the men of Bethulia saved him, and he declared unto them
10 all that he had spoken before thee. Wherefore, O lord and master, neglect not his word; but lay
it up in thy heart, for it is true: for our race shall not be punished, neither shall the sword prevail

14. The two halves of the verse are connected by *καί*. Perhaps the Hebrew original should be translated 'and noted her countenance, that (*or* for) it was very wonderful in beauty to look at (לעיניהם), then they said . . .'

16. **when,** properly 'if', i.e. if you are fortunate enough to be admitted.

17. **appointed them to accompany,** *παρέζευξαν*, lit. 'they yoked (them) alongside'.

18. Better 'until they had told him', i.e. she stood outside while some one went in and told him. The whole account is very vivid.

19. **because of her,** *ἀπ' αὐτῆς*, properly '(judging) from her'. 58 VL Syr 'they wondered at her beauty and received her words because they were very good, and marvelled . . .'

deceive, *κατασοφίσασθαι*, i.e. beguile with the beauty of their women.

20. **that lay near.** 58 *παρεδρεύοντες*, 'that were in attendance,' and so VL Syr.

21. **under** (prop. 'in') **the canopy,** which probably means the mosquito net.

22. 58 VL Syr 'very many silver lamps going before him, and they brought her in to him'.

23. **was come.** 58 VL Syr 'stood' more probably represents the Hebrew.

XI. 4. The construction is awkward. Lit. 'there is none who shall harm thee but shall entreat . . .' i.e. we (*or* all) will entreat. 19 44 al. VL Syr *ποιήσω*.

6. Ball suggests that the phrase 'God shall bring the thing to pass' is intentionally ambiguous, but the concluding words are against this. On the morality of Judith's device see Introduction.

7. Not very clear. At the end B has *ζήσονται Ναβ. καὶ πάντα τὸν οἶκον αὐτοῦ*, which will not translate. The other MSS. have *ἐπὶ* N. *καὶ πάντα* . . . , of which the meaning is not evident. R.V. follows Fritzsche's emendation *παντός*, &c., which may be the sense but has no MS. authority. VL has 'per virtutem tuam sciet N. et omnis domus eius'. Syr 'shall know (acknowledge) N. through thy strength'. Cf. Jer. xxvii. 6.

8. **brave,** *ἀγαθός*, rather 'a good general'. He was *ἀρχιστράτηγος*, ii. 4.

feats, *στρατεύμασι*, perhaps 'campaigns'.

9. **as . . . matter,** *λόγος* is a *nominativus pendens*. 58 VL Syr 'and now, my lord, the word which A. spake' (*ὃν ἐλάλησε λόγον* A.). At the end 19 108 add 'and all thy words'. 58 omits 'before thee', and 'lord and master' in verse 10.

11 against them, except they sin against their God. And now, that my lord be not defeated and
frustrate of his purpose, and that death may fall upon them, their sin hath overtaken them, where-
12 with they shall provoke their God to anger, whensoever they shall do wickedness. Since their
victuals failed them, and all their water was scant, they took counsel to lay hands upon their cattle,
and determined to consume all those things, which God charged them by his laws that they should
13 not eat: and they are resolved to spend the firstfruits of the corn, and the tenths of the wine and
the oil, which they had sanctified, and reserved for the priests that stand before the face of our God
in Jerusalem; the which things it is not fitting for any of the people so much as to touch with their
14 hands. And they have sent some to Jerusalem, because they also that dwell there have done this
15 thing, to bring them a licence from the senate. And it shall be, when one shall bring them word,
16 and they shall do it, they shall be given thee to be destroyed the same day. Wherefore I thy
servant, knowing all this, fled away from their presence; and God sent me to work things with thee,
17 whereat all the earth shall be astonished, even as many as shall hear it. For thy servant is religious,
and serveth the God of heaven day and night: and now, my lord, I will abide with thee, and thy
servant will go forth by night into the valley, and I will pray unto God, and he shall tell me when
18 they have committed their sins: and I will come and shew it also unto thee; and thou shalt go forth
19 with all thy host, and there shall be none of them that shall resist thee. And I will lead thee
through the midst of Judæa, until thou comest over against Jerusalem; and I will set thy seat in
the midst thereof; and thou shalt drive them as sheep that have no shepherd, and a dog shall not
so much as open his mouth before thee: for these things were told me according to my foreknowledge, and were declared unto me, and I was sent to tell thee.
20 And her words were pleasing in the sight of Holofernes and of all his servants; and they
21 marvelled at her wisdom, and said, There is not such a woman from one end of the earth to the
22 other, for beauty of face, and wisdom of words. And Holofernes said unto her, God did well to
send thee before the people, that might should be in our hands, and destruction among them that
23 lightly regarded my lord. And now thou art beautiful in thy countenance, and witty in thy words:
for if thou shalt do as thou hast spoken, thy God shall be my God, and thou shalt dwell in the house
of king Nebuchadnezzar, and shalt be renowned through the whole earth.
12 1 And he commanded to bring her in where his silver vessels were set, and bade that they should
2 prepare for her of his own meats, and that she should drink of his own wine. And Judith said, I
will not eat thereof, lest there be an occasion of stumbling: but provision shall be made for me of
3 the things that are come with me. And Holofernes said unto her, But if the things that be with
thee should fail, whence shall we be able to give thee the like? for there is none of thy race with us.
4 And Judith said unto him, As thy soul liveth, my lord, thy servant shall not spend those things that
5 be with me, until the Lord work by my hand the things that he hath determined. And the servants

11. Translate . . . 'purpose, death shall fall upon them, and (= for) their sin, wherewith they will provoke their God, has (already) got a hold on them, whensoever they may (actually) commit folly' (58 VL Syr 'commit it'). There are many small variants, but this (Swete's text) seems to give a suitable sense. They were already in the power of their sin by intending to commit it (see verse 12), although she does not know when the actual commission will occur.

13. **which . . . it is not fitting for any of the people** (but only for the priests) . . . **to touch** (much less to eat). The author feels so strongly on the point that he makes his heroine select this as her proof of wickedness even when speaking to an unbeliever.

14. **have done,** *ἐποίησαν*, i.e. did it on some former occasion.

to bring is Fritzsche's *μετακομίσοντας*. The ordinary reading *μετοικίσαντας* gives no sense.

Note their dependence on the Sanhedrin.

17. **religious,** *θεοσεβής*, rather 'god-fearing' (cf. Gen. xlii. 18), as the reason for her receiving a divine communication.

18. Properly 'there is none of them that shall . . .'

19. **a dog . . .** Cf. Exod. xi. 7. Here literally 'growl with his tongue'. **according to my foreknowledge,** *κατὰ πρόγνωσίν* (*μου* om. 19 108), probably means 'by way of revelation' (Ball).

20. 58 VL Syr 'at her beauty and wisdom'.

21. **for beauty of face.** *ἐν* (*καλῷ προσώπῳ*) is again the Heb. ־בְּ.

22. **that might should be . . .,** *τοῦ γενηθῆναι* . . ., rather 'send thee to be made a strength to us and a destruction to them' (להיות בידינו לחיל וכ׳).

23. **beautiful,** *ἀστεία*, 'pretty.'

witty, i.e. wise, *ἀγαθή*, 'acceptable.' The text may be right considering what follows, but it is tempting to suggest that after 'beautiful of countenance' (יפת מראה) the Hebrew had וטובת תאר 'and goodly in form' (cf. Esther ii. 7) which was misread וטוב תאמר 'and thou speakest well'. 19 108 have 'if thy God do as thou sayest', which would then be original and have been altered to agree with *ἀγαθὴ ἐν τοῖς λόγοις σου*. It is her *beauty* which should entitle her (as Esther) to dwell in the house of the king, not her intellectual qualities or her services to Assyria.

XII. 1. **prepare,** *καταστρῶσαι*, should no doubt mean 'spread a couch', &c., but here it must be 'set on the table'. Then *πίνειν* is simply epexegetical (לשתות) 'set before her of his own viands and of his wine to drink'.

2. As before, stress is laid on the duty of using only clean food.

4. B omits 'the Lord' wrongly.

of Holofernes brought her into the tent, and she slept till midnight, and she rose up toward the
6 morning watch, and sent to Holofernes, saying, Let my lord now command that they suffer thy
7 servant to go forth unto prayer. And Holofernes commanded his guards that they should not stay
her: and she abode in the camp three days, and went out every night into the valley of Bethulia,
8 and washed herself at the fountain of water in the camp. And when she came up, she besought
9 the Lord God of Israel to direct her way to the raising up of the children of his people. And she
came in clean, and remained in the tent, until she took her meat toward evening.
10 And it came to pass on the fourth day, Holofernes made a feast to his own servants only, and
11 called none of the officers to the banquet. And he said to Bagoas the eunuch, who had charge over
all that he had, Go now, and persuade this Hebrew woman which is with thee, that she come unto
12 us, and eat and drink with us. For, lo, it is a shame for our person, if we shall let such a woman
13 go, not having had her company; for if we draw her not unto us, she shall laugh us to scorn. And
Bagoas went from the presence of Holofernes, and came in to her, and said, Let not this fair damsel
fear to come to my lord, and to be honoured in his presence, and to drink wine and be merry with
us, and to be made this day as one of the daughters of the children of Asshur, which wait in the
14 house of Nebuchadnezzar. And Judith said unto him, And who am I, that I should gainsay my
lord? for whatsoever shall be pleasing in his eyes I will do speedily, and this shall be my joy unto
15 the day of my death. And she arose, and decked herself with her apparel and all her woman's
attire; and her servant went and laid fleeces on the ground for her over against Holofernes, which
16 she had received of Bagoas for her daily use, that she might sit and eat upon them. And Judith
came in and sat down, and Holofernes' heart was ravished with her, and his soul was moved, and
he desired exceedingly her company: and he was watching for a time to deceive her, from the day
17, 18 that he had seen her. And Holofernes said unto her, Drink now, and be merry with us. And
Judith said, I will drink now, my lord, because my life is magnified in me this day more than all the
19 days since I was born. And she took and ate and drank before him what her servant had prepared.
20 And Holofernes took great delight in her, and drank exceeding much wine, more than he had drunk
at any time in one day since he was born.

13 1 But when the evening was come, his servants made haste to depart, and Bagoas shut the tent
without, and dismissed them that waited from the presence of his lord; and they went away to their
2 beds: for they were all weary, because the feast had been long. But Judith was left alone in the
3 tent, and Holofernes lying along upon his bed: for he was overflown with wine. And Judith had
said to her servant that she should stand without her bedchamber, and wait for her coming forth, as
she did daily: for she said she would go forth to her prayer; and she spake to Bagoas according to
4 the same words. And all went away from her presence, and none was left in the bedchamber, neither
small nor great. And Judith, standing by his bed, said in her heart, O Lord God of all power, look

7. Properly 'she used to go out (of her tent, cf. verse 9) by night . . . and bathe in the camp at the spring'. This is awkward, but Movers' suggestion (quoted by Ball) that the Hebrew was מהנדה, which was misread במחנה, is impossible. 58 VL Syr omit 'in the camp'. It may be due to dittography from the line above. If it stands, it must mean that she was not allowed outside the limits of the camp, but went out of her tent and did her (merely ceremonial) washing (טבילה) at the spring, which was within the camp (cf. vii. 3).

8. **came up**, i.e. from the water, עלה, as e.g. in Mishna Yoma vii. 3.

direct, *κατευθῦναι*, to make it straight by removing the difficulties, cf. הישר דרך, Ps. v. 9.

10. **feast**, *πότον* = משתה.

called . . . banquet, *εἰς τὴν χρῆσιν* (*al.* *κλῆσιν*) *οὐδένα τῶν πρὸς ταῖς χρείαις* is difficult. *χρῆσιν* may be 'the enjoyment of it'. *κλῆσιν* (which is well supported), 'invited to the invitation,' is no better. *τῶν πρὸς ταῖς χρείαις* are the officers on duty. He only invited his personal friends.

11. **Bagoas**, a Persian name, בִּגְוַי, Ezra ii. 2, spelt בגוהי in the Elephantine papyri of 407 B.C. It is derived from O. Pers. Baga = god, as if Theodorus, &c. He was in charge of Judith.

15. **sit**, *κατακλινομένην*, prop. 'recline' (and so *ἀνέπεσεν* in ver. 16), according to the later practice. The earlier custom was to sit, cf. 1 Sam. xx. 24 with Amos vi. 4 (Ball).

16. **was watching**, *ἐτήρει*, a proper use of the imperfect: 'he had been waiting for an opportunity to seduce her.'

19. Again it is carefully noted that she ate only clean food.

20. **delight**, *ηὐφράνθη ἀπ' αὐτῆς*, 'was merry because of her.'

XIII. 1. **dismissed**, *ἀπέκλεισεν*, prop. 'shut out' those who had been in attendance on his lord, העומדים לפני אדונו, lit. *ἐν προσώπῳ τοῦ κυρίου αὐτοῦ*, which has been corrupted in the Greek to *ἐκ προσώπου*.

2. **lying along**, *προπεπτωκώς*, fallen forward.

overflown, lit. the wine was poured all over him.

3. **had said**, i.e. before starting out. **Spake**, i.e. had spoken.

4. **And** (= 'so') **all went**: resuming what was said in verse 1.

from her presence. The common reading is *ἐκ προσώπου*, as if = *ἐκποδών*, 'out of the way.' A adds *αὐτῆς*, others *αὐτοῦ*, &c. The Hebrew would naturally be מלפניו referring back to verse 1.

bed. 58 VL Syr *κεφαλήν*.

5 in this hour upon the works of my hands for the exaltation of Jerusalem. For now is the time to
help thine inheritance, and to do the thing that I have purposed to the destruction of the enemies
6 which are risen up against us. And she came to the rail of the bed, which was at Holofernes' head,
7 and took down his scimitar from thence; and she drew near unto the bed, and took hold of the hair
8 of his head, and said, Strengthen me, O Lord God of Israel, this day. And she smote twice upon
9 his neck with all her might, and took away his head from him, and tumbled his body down from the
bed, and took down the canopy from the pillars; and after a little while she went forth, and gave
10 Holofernes' head to her maid; and she put it in her bag of victuals: and they twain went forth
together unto prayer, according to their custom: and they passed through the camp, and compassed
that valley, and went up to the mountain of Bethulia, and came to the gates thereof.
11 And Judith said afar off to the watchmen at the gates, Open, open now the gate: God is with us,
even our God, to shew his power yet in Israel, and his might against the enemy, as he hath done
12 even this day. And it came to pass, when the men of her city heard her voice, they made haste to
13 go down to the gate of their city, and they called together the elders of the city. And they ran all
together, both small and great, for it was strange unto them that she was come: and they opened
14 the gate, and received them, making a fire to give light, and compassed them round about. And
she said to them with a loud voice, Praise God, praise him: praise God, who hath not taken away
15 his mercy from the house of Israel, but hath destroyed our enemies by my hand this night. And
she took forth the head out of the bag, and shewed it, and said unto them, Behold, the head of
Holofernes, the chief captain of the host of Asshur, and behold, the canopy, wherein he did lie in his
16 drunkenness; and the Lord smote him by the hand of a woman. And as the Lord liveth, who
preserved me in my way that I went, my countenance deceived him to his destruction, and he did
17 not commit sin with me, to defile and shame me. And all the people were exceedingly amazed,
and bowed themselves, and worshipped God, and said with one accord, Blessed art thou, O our God,
18 which hast this day brought to nought the enemies of thy people. And Ozias said unto her, Blessed
art thou, daughter, in the sight of the Most High God, above all the women upon the earth; and
blessed is the Lord God, who created the heavens and the earth, who directed thee to the smiting
19 of the head of the prince of our enemies. For thy hope shall not depart from the heart of men that
20 remember the strength of God for ever. And God turn these things to thee for a perpetual praise,
to visit thee with good things, because thou didst not spare thy life by reason of the affliction of our
race, but didst avenge our fall, walking a straight way before our God. And all the people said, So
be it, so be it.

14 1 And Judith said unto them, Hear me now, my brethren, and take this head, and hang it upon the
2 battlement of your wall. And it shall be, so soon as the morning shall appear, and the sun shall
come forth upon the earth, ye shall take up every one his weapons of war, and go forth every valiant
man of you out of the city, and ye shall set a captain over them, as though ye would go down to the

5. **now is the time**, sc. which thou didst appoint.
destruction, *θραῦμα* (B), *τραῦμα* (58), *θραῦσμα* (A), *θραῦσιν* (19, 44). The last would best express the Hebrew לְשַׁבֵּר קמינו.

6. **rail**, *κανών*, a bar at the head of the bed.
scimitar, *ἀκινάκης*, a Persian sword.

9. **took down** (*or* off) **the canopy**, cf. x. 21. She took it away as a trophy, verse 15.

10. **unto prayer**, omitted by B. 'As if to prayer,' 58 VL Syr. It would be past midnight, 'toward the morning watch' (xii. 5). This time they went out of the camp. **Compassed**, *ἐκύκλωσαν*, perhaps means 'took a circuitous route' along the side of the valley, so as not to be seen. **Went up . . .**, rather 'went up the mountain to B.' (which was on the top). For *τὸ ὄρος* ℵ* has *πρός*.

11. **now**, *δή* (one of the few particles used in the book) = נא.

12. **her city.** ℵ 44 106 58 VL Syr omit *αὐτῆς*, rightly.

13. **strange**, *παράδοξον*, i. e. unexpected.

14. **destroyed**, *ἔθραυσε*, 'broke,' the same stem as in verse 5.

16. **deceived**, *ἠπάτησεν*, 'beguiled.'

17. **Blessed . . .** ברוך אתה אדני אלהינו, the usual formula in later Hebrew.

18. A reminiscence of Gen. xiv. 19, 20, LXX.
directed thee to the smiting of the head . . . is a strange expression. 58 alters it to 'directed thee to the head'. The Hebrew must have been להכות ראש אויבינו, 'directed or inspired thee to smite the head (i. e. chief) of our enemies.' The incident of the head has caused ראש to be translated twice.

19. **thy hope.** 58 VL Syr have 'the praise of thee'. Hope, &c., may mean 'thy trust in God shall always be remembered when men recall (*or* talk of) the mighty works of God'.

20. **avenge**, *ἐπεξῆλθες*, 'you went to meet (and avert) our fall.'

XIV. 1. The account of Achior (*vv.* 5–10) precedes this in the Vulgate, certainly a better arrangement.

2. **a captain over them**, apparently over those who go out, but the change of person is strange.

3 plain toward the watch of the children of Asshur; and ye shall not go down. And these shall take
up their panoplies, and shall go into their camp, and rouse up the captains of the host of Asshur, and
they shall run together to the tent of Holofernes, and they shall not find him: and fear shall fall upon
4 them, and they shall flee before your face. And ye, and all that inhabit every coast of Israel, shall
5 pursue them, and overthrow them as they go. But before ye do these things, call me Achior the
Ammonite, that he may see and know him that despised the house of Israel, and that sent him to us,
as it were to death.
6 And they called Achior out of the house of Ozias; but when he came, and saw the head of
Holofernes in a man's hand in the assembly of the people, he fell upon his face, and his spirit failed.
7 But when they had recovered him, he fell at Judith's feet, and did reverence unto her, and said,
Blessed art thou in every tent of Judah, and in every nation, which hearing thy name shall be
8 troubled. And now tell me all the things that thou hast done in these days. And Judith declared
unto him in the midst of the people all the things that she had done, from the day that she went forth
9 until the time that she spake unto them. But when she left off speaking, the people shouted with
10 a loud voice, and made a joyful noise in their city. But when Achior saw all the things that the
God of Israel had done, he believed in God exceedingly, and circumcised the flesh of his foreskin,
and was joined unto the house of Israel, unto this day.
11 But as soon as the morning arose, they hanged the head of Holofernes upon the wall, and every
12 man took up his weapons, and they went forth by bands unto the ascents of the mountain. But
when the children of Asshur saw them, they sent hither and thither to their leaders; but they went
13 to their captains and tribunes, and to every one of their rulers. And they came to Holofernes' tent,
and said to him that was over all that he had, Waken now our lord: for the slaves have been bold
14 to come down against us to battle, that they may be utterly destroyed. And Bagoas went in, and
15 knocked at the outer door of the tent; for he supposed that he was sleeping with Judith. But when
none hearkened to him, he opened it, and went into the bedchamber, and found him cast upon the
16 threshold dead, and his head had been taken from him. And he cried with a loud voice, with
17 weeping and groaning and a mighty cry, and rent his garments. And he entered into the tent where
18 Judith lodged: and he found her not, and he leaped out to the people, and cried aloud, The slaves
have dealt treacherously: one woman of the Hebrews hath brought shame upon the house of king
19 Nebuchadnezzar; for, behold, Holofernes *lieth* upon the ground, and his head is not on him. But
when the rulers of the host of Asshur heard the words, they rent their coats, and their soul was
troubled exceedingly, and there was a cry and an exceeding great noise in the midst of the camp.
15 1 And when they that were in the tents heard, they were amazed at the thing that was come to
2 pass. And trembling and fear fell upon them, and no man durst abide any more in the sight of his
neighbour, but rushing out with one accord, they fled into every way of the plain and of the hill
3 country. And they that had encamped in the hill country round about Bethulia fled away. And
4 then the children of Israel, every one that was a warrior among them, rushed out upon them. And

3. **these**, i.e. the Assyrian outposts.
panoplies, *πανοπλίας*. 'Arms' would be less pedantic. Outposts when not expecting an attack would lay down some of their equipment. They would take this up again and so become *πανόπλοι* before going into camp.
4. **as they go.** Rather 'leave them lying in the paths by which they flee'.
5. Looks as if it had been put in to introduce an episode which had somehow got misplaced; see on verse 1.
7. **recovered**, *ἀνέλαβον αὐτόν* (א B) = 'had lifted him up'. *ἀνέλαβεν αὐτόν* (A, &c.) = 'he had recovered himself'.
tent. A reminiscence of Judges vi. 24?
troubled, i.e. alarmed at such things being possible.
9. **made a joyful noise**, *ἔδωκαν* (58, &c., *-κεν* א A B) *φωνὴν εὐφροσύνης* (A 58 VL, *-νου* א B) = ויתנו קול שמחה (Ball).
10. **God of Israel.** 58 VL Syr 'God had done for Israel'.
exceedingly, *σφόδρα*. The author's favourite word is not very suitable here. It must mean 'with all his heart'.
unto this day is really meaningless. The Vulgate applies it to his descendants.
Achior became a proselyte at once. The author overlooks the law of Deut. xxiii. 3.
12. **leaders**, i.e. subordinate officers, and they (the subordinates) went to their superiors, who eventually came to Holofernes' tent.
tribunes, *χιλιάρχους*, 'captains of thousands'. **Rulers**, *πάντα ἄρχοντα*, should be 'commanders'.
13. **to him.** 58 VL Syr 'to Bagoas'.
the slaves, העבדים, for which Movers suggests ('plausibly,' Ball) העברים, 'the Hebrews' (cf. VL), but this is unnecessary, cf. verse 18. Ball seems to prefer העכברים, 'the mice,' as Vulg.
14. **door** is necessary after 'knock', but *αὐλαίαν* is prop. 'curtain' (cf. verse 15). 19 108 *ἐκρότησε τῇ χειρὶ ἐν τῇ αὐλαίᾳ*, and similarly Vulg. 'stetit ante cortinam et plausum fecit manibus suis'.
15. **opened**, *διαστείλας*, 'drew aside the curtain.'
threshold, *ἐπὶ τῆς χελωνίδος*, more probably the step at the side of the bed (Ball).
18. **dealt treacherously**, *ἠθέτησαν*, alluding primarily to Judith's promises. The verb ought to have an object.

XV. 3. These were the Edomites and Ammonites, cf. vii. 18 (Ball).

Ozias sent to Betomasthaim, and Bebai, and Chobai, and Chola, and to every coast of Israel, such as
should tell concerning the things that had been accomplished, and that all should rush forth upon
5 their enemies to destroy them. But when the children of Israel heard, they all fell upon them with
one accord, and smote them unto Chobai: yea, and in like manner also they of Jerusalem and of all
the hill country came (for men had told them what things were come to pass in the camp of their
enemies), and they that were in Gilead and in Galilee fell upon their flank with a great slaughter,
6 until they were past Damascus and the borders thereof. But the residue, that dwelt at Bethulia, fell
7 upon the camp of Asshur, and spoiled them, and were enriched exceedingly. But the children of
Israel returned from the slaughter, and gat possession of that which remained; and the villages and
the cities, that were in the hill country and in the plain country, took many spoils: for there was an
exceeding great store.

8 And Joakim the high priest, and the senate of the children of Israel that dwelt in Jerusalem, came
to behold the good things which the Lord had shewed to Israel, and to see Judith, and to salute her.
9 But when they came unto her, they all blessed her with one accord, and said unto her, Thou art the
exaltation of Jerusalem, thou art the great glory of Israel, thou art the great rejoicing of our race:
10 thou hast done all these things by thy hand: thou hast done with Israel the things that are good,
and God is pleased therewith: blessed be thou with the Almighty Lord for evermore. And all the
11 people said, So be it. And the people spoiled the camp for the space of thirty days: and they gave
unto Judith Holofernes' tent, and all his silver cups, and his beds, and his vessels, and all his
furniture: and she took them, and placed them on her mule, and made ready her wagons, and
heaped them thereon.

12 And all the women of Israel ran together to see her; and they blessed her, and made a dance
among them for her; and she took branches in her hand, and gave to the women that were with
13 her. And they made themselves garlands of olive, she and they that were with her, and she went
before all the people in the dance, leading all the women: and all the men of Israel followed in their
16 1 armour with garlands, and with songs in their mouths. And Judith began to sing this thanksgiving
2 in all Israel, and all the people sang with loud voices this song of praise. And Judith said,

Begin unto my God with timbrels,
Sing unto my Lord with cymbals:
Tune unto him psalm and praise:
Exalt him, and call upon his name.
3 For the Lord is the God that breaketh the battles:
For in his armies in the midst of the people
He delivered me out of the hand of them that persecuted me.
4 Asshur came out of the mountains from the north,
He came with ten thousands of his host,
The multitude whereof stopped the torrents,
And their horsemen covered the hills.

4. **Betomesthaim**, see iv. 6. **Bebai** only in A. For **Chobai** ℵ* has Choba, cf. iv. 4. For **Chola** A has Kola, ℵ* Abelmaim, ℵ c.a Keïla. The sites are unknown.
5. **past Damascus.** This was the way they had come, cf. ii. 27.
6. **dwelt**, *κατοικοῦντες* = יושבים, 'remained (behind).'
7. **cities**, *αἱ πόλεις*, ℵ A; *ἐπαύλεις*, 'farmsteads,' B.
9. **they came.** 58 VL Syr 19 108 'when she went out to meet them', a correction in the interest of the high priest's dignity.
rejoicing, *καύχημα*, 'the boast.'
12. **for her**, i. e. 'in her honour'.
branches, *θύρσους*, a strange word to choose. It properly means the wands of the Bacchants. In the LXX only here and in 2 Macc. x. 7.
13. Lit. 'they crowned themselves with olive', a Greek, not a Jewish, custom, indicating a late date for the book (Ball).

XVI. 1. **sang with loud voices**, *ὑπερεφώνει*, so ℵ A B. The common reading is *ὑπεφώνει*, '(J. began and) they were singing in answer.'
2. **Begin**, *ἐξάρχετε* = ענו in Ps. cxlvii. 7.
and praise, *καὶ αἶνον*. A has *καινόν*, 'new' (cf. xvi. 13), as in Ps. xxxiii. 3, &c.
3. **breaketh the battles**, cf. Exod. xv. 3 LXX, as above, ix. 7.
The rest of the verse is corrupt. **in his armies**, *εἰς τὰς παρεμβολὰς αὐτοῦ* is properly 'into his camps'. For *ἐξείλατο*, ℵ has *ἐξελεύσεσθαι*, &c.; for *ἐκ χειρός* ℵ* has *ἕως χειρός*. Perhaps the Hebrew was אֵל בחנותו בתוך העם, 'God, when he encamped among . . .,' which was misread as אֶל־מחנותיו, *εἰς παρεμβολὰς αὐτοῦ.*
4. **from the north.** They came by way of Damascus.
stopped, i. e. blocked up.

5 He said that he would burn up my borders,
And kill my young men with the sword,
And throw my sucking children to the ground,
And give mine infants for a prey,
And make my virgins a spoil.
6 The Almighty Lord brought them to nought by the hand of a woman.
7 For their mighty one did not fall by young men,
Neither did sons of the Titans smite him,
Nor did high giants set upon him:
But Judith the daughter of Merari made him weak with the beauty of her countenance.
8 For she put off the apparel of her widowhood
For the exaltation of those that were distressed in Israel,
She anointed her face with ointment,
And bound her hair in a tire,
And took a linen garment to deceive him.
9 Her sandal ravished his eye,
And her beauty took his soul prisoner:
The scimitar passed through his neck.
10 The Persians quaked at her daring,
And the Medes were daunted at her boldness.
11 Then my lowly ones shouted aloud,
And my weak ones were terrified and crouched for fear:
They lifted up their voice, and they were turned to flight.
12 The sons of damsels pierced them through,
And wounded them as runagates' children;
They perished by the battle of my Lord.
13 I will sing unto my God a new song:
O Lord, thou art great and glorious,
Marvellous in strength, invincible.
14 Let all thy creation serve thee:
For thou spakest, and they were made,
Thou didst send forth thy spirit, and it builded them,
And there is none that shall resist thy voice.

6. **brought them to nought,** *ἠθέτησεν* as in xiv. 18, but here with a personal object. 58 19 108 add *κατῄσχυνεν αὐτούς*:—

'The Lord Almighty set them at nought,
By the hand of a woman he brought them to shame.'

7. **their mighty one,** גבורם = their champion, as 1 Sam. xvii. 51 (Ball). The next two lines look like alternative renderings of the same Hebrew. **Sons of the Titans** may be בני רפאים. Cf. 2 Sam. v. 18, LXX.

high giants, perhaps בני ענק.

9. For sandals as an adornment, cf. Cant. vii. 1. Chajes suggests that נעלה (her sandal) is a mistake for נעמה (her beauty).

10. **quaked,** *ἔφριξαν*, shuddered at it.

daunted, *ἐρράχθησαν* א B, *ἐταράχθησαν* א[c.a] A. Neither word could be construed with an accusative. VL and Vulg. omit the verb, thus making 'boldness' depend on *ἔφριξαν*. The mention of Persians here suggests that the author was really thinking of the time of Artaxerxes Ochus, and forgot for the moment that his invading army was Assyrian. Medes are naturally parallel to Persians, although, according to i. 13–16, Media had been devastated in the previous year.

11. **my lowly ones** must be Israelites. So also 'my weak ones' (VL 'aegrotantes in siti'), but *ἐφοβήθησαν*, 'were terrified,' is unsuitable as a parallel to *ἠλάλαξαν*, 'shouted in triumph.' Several cursives and VL Syr have *ἐβόησαν*, 'cried aloud.'

crouched. Apparently the subject changes to the enemy and the next three verbs form a climax, 'they crouched, they cried out, they fled,' as often in Hebrew poetry. 19 108 read *ἡττήθησαν* for *ἐπτοή(θη)σαν*, and add *οἱ ἐχθροί μου* at the end.

12. **sons of damsels,** i. e. of young wives, whose sons would be mere children. But *κοράσιον* in LXX often means 'maidservant', so that it may be contemptuous, 'the very slave-boys.'

runagates' children, properly 'sons of runaway slaves'. 19 108 VL Syr have *παῖδας αὐτομολοῦντας*, 'runaway slaves.'

by the battle, i. e. by means of the army . . . *παράταξις* (cf. i. 6) prop. 'an army in fighting order'.

13. Cf. Exod. xv. 11.

invincible, *ἀνυπέρβλητος*, prop. unsurpassed. Perhaps a loose rendering of עשה פלא.

14. **send forth,** *ἀπέστειλας*. א *ἐπέστρεψας*.

it builded is harsh. א has 'they were builded'. Probably the Hebrew was ונבראו (were created), not ונבנו (were built). Cf. Ps. xxxiii. 6–9, civ. 30 (Ball).

15 For the mountains shall be moved from their foundations with the waters,
And the rocks shall melt as wax at thy presence:
But thou art yet merciful to them that fear thee.
16 For all sacrifice is little for a sweet savour,
And all the fat is very little for a whole burnt offering to thee:
But he that feareth the Lord is great continually.
17 Woe to the nations that rise up against my race:
The Lord Almighty will take vengeance of them in the day of judgement,
To put fire and worms in their flesh;
And they shall weep and feel their pain for ever.
18 Now when they came to Jerusalem, they worshipped God; and when the people were purified,
19 they offered their whole burnt offerings, and their freewill offerings, and their gifts. And Judith
dedicated all the stuff of Holofernes, which the people had given her, and gave the canopy, which
20 she had taken for herself out of his bedchamber, for a gift unto the Lord. And the people continued
feasting in Jerusalem before the sanctuary for the space of three months, and Judith remained with
21 them. But after these days every one departed to his own inheritance, and Judith went away to
22 Bethulia, and remained in her own possession, and was honourable in her time in all the land. And
many desired her, and no man knew her all the days of her life, from the day that Manasses her
23 husband died and was gathered to his people. And she increased in greatness exceedingly; and
she waxed old in her husband's house, unto a hundred and five years, and let her maid go free:
24 and she died in Bethulia; and they buried her in the cave of her husband Manasses. And the
house of Israel mourned for her seven days: and she distributed her goods before she died to all
them that were nearest of kin to Manasses her husband, and to them that were nearest of her own
25 kindred. And there was none that made the children of Israel any more afraid in the days of Judith,
nor a long time after her death.

15. **For the mountains . . . waters.** *ὄρη γὰρ ἐκ θεμελίων σὺν ὕδασιν σαλευθήσεται* is obscure. Perhaps it means 'the mountains (or cliffs) shall be swayed down to their foundations, together with (i.e. just as much as) the waters which roll up against them'.

melt as wax, cf. Ps. xcvii. 5.

16. i.e. Any sacrifice is unworthy of God's acceptance as a sweet savour, but, while sacrifices are obligatory, it is the spirit which underlies them, namely the fear of the Lord, which is really important. Cf. Ps. li. 16–19.

17. Cf. the end of Deborah's song, Judges v. 31.

It is evident that the writer looks forward to a judgement after death, יום הדין, a later and more definite doctrine than the יום יהוה of Mal. iv. 5. The belief is indicated in Ecclus. vii. 17 (Ball), and developed in the Book of Enoch, thus corroborating the date assigned to the composition of Judith.

fire and worms are no doubt suggested by Isa. lxvi. 24, but applied to hell as in the N.T.

weep and feel, lit. weep at (or 'with') feeling, i.e. without losing consciousness of their pain.

18. Note again the insistence on purification (after contact with the dead) and sacrifice.

19. **stuff**, *σκεύη* = כלי, his silver plate.

gift, *ἀνάθημα* (or *ἀνάθεμα*) = חרם (Ball) as a thing devoted.

20. **three months.** Another instance of the author's love of exaggeration. Three days would be more likely.

21. **inheritance.** 58 VL Syr 'tents'.

to Bethulia. א 'to her house at B'.

23. **increased in greatness**, *ἦν προβαίνουσα μεγάλη*, is not clear. Prob. VL (and Vulg.) is right, 'she increased in reputation.'

24. She bequeathed her property according to the Law in Num. xxvii. 11.

25. Cf. again Judges v. 31. If Judith was twenty-five or thirty years old at the time of her exploit the land must have had peace for at least eighty years. Such a period can only have occurred 'under the Persian kings, and according to Jewish ideas under the Hasmoneans' (Ball).

The Vulgate adds that a festival was instituted to commemorate the deed of Judith, probably in imitation of Esther ix. 27, 28. No such festival is known, it is not mentioned in any other version, and cannot have been recorded in the original book. The statement may be founded on the fact that the story was read at the feast of Ḥanukka, see Introd. § 8 *a*.

THE BOOK OF SIRACH

INTRODUCTION[1]

§ 1. Short Account of the Book.

Ben-Sira's Book of Wisdom belongs, together with the Book of Job, a number of the Psalms, Proverbs, Ecclesiastes, and the Wisdom of Solomon (so-called), to the *Ḥokmah* or Wisdom Literature of the Hebrews. This literature represents the development of the crude philosophy of more ancient times, a philosophy which sought by means of proverbs and fables to express the results of reflections concerning the general questions of life. Such proverbs and fables were not necessarily of a religious character; see, e. g., Judg. ix. 8–15 (Jotham's parable), 2 Sam. v. 8, xx. 18; but they tended to become so more and more (cp. Jer. xxxi. 29, Ezek. xviii. 2); this is well exemplified by such parables as those contained in 2 Sam. xii. 1–4 (Nathan's parable of the ewe lamb), and Isa. v. 1–4 (the parable of the vineyard); and ultimately all wise sayings, upon whatsoever subjects they were uttered, came to have a religious content inasmuch as it was taught that all wisdom emanated from God. Ben-Sira, therefore, as a constructor of wise sayings, belonged to the class of Sages or *Ḥakamim* ('wise men') who already in the days of Jeremiah occupied a recognized position alongside of the priests and the prophets: 'For the law shall not perish from the priest, nor counsel from the wise (*ḥakam*), nor the word from the prophet' (Jer. xviii. 18). So that in presenting his book to his people he is making a justifiable claim when he says:

I, indeed, came last of all,
As one that gleaneth after the grape-gatherers:
I advanced by the blessing of God,
And filled my winepress as a grape-gatherer.

(xxxiii. 16–18 [= 𝔊 xxxvi. 16ᵃ and xxx. 25–27]).

The claim is modestly urged; but Ben-Sira, while whole-heartedly admitting his indebtedness to earlier sages, clearly reckons himself as one of the 'grape-gatherers', i.e. as one of the *Ḥakamim*, like the authors of Proverbs and Ecclesiastes, though the last in the succession.

A notable feature in our book is that it offers many examples of expanded proverbs; a little essay, as it were, is constructed on the basis of a proverb. A good example of this is xxxviii. 24–xxxix. 11; here the proverb, or text of the essay, is:

The wisdom of the scribe increaseth wisdom,
And he that hath little business can become wise.

Then Ben-Sira proceeds to expatiate upon these words by giving a number of illustrations showing that those who are occupied with ordinary trades and professions cannot possibly find the requisite leisure which must be possessed by those who would acquire wisdom (xxxviii. 25–35); and the essay concludes with an eloquent description of the ideal seeker after wisdom, thus presenting the positive side of his thesis.

Although Ben-Sira exhibits no great signs of originality there is plenty of individuality in his book; this is shown chiefly (in addition to what has just been said about the expansion of the proverb into the essay) by the use he makes of the Old Testament Scriptures. He does not merely quote from the Old Testament, but he utilizes the words and teaching of the inspired writers as the authority for what he has to say, and then proceeds to set forth his own ideas upon a given subject. An instructive example of this may be adduced. Ben-Sira's teaching on death and the hereafter is identical with that of the Old Testament, but in xli. 1–4 he offers some thoughts upon the subject of death which are evidently quite his own. He shows that two views concerning death exist among

[1] The two editors who are responsible for Sirach as a whole, apart from the Prologue and ch. xlix (the notes on which were written in consultation), shared the rest of the book between them as follows:

Mr. Box is primarily responsible for §§ 3, 6, 7, and 10 of the Introduction, and for the commentary on chs. ix. 1–xiii. 23, xxx–xl, xlii–xlv: Dr. Oesterley is primarily responsible for §§ 1, 2, 4, 5, 8, and 9 of the Introduction, and for the commentary on chs. i–viii, xiii. 24–xxix, xli, xlvi–xlviii, l, li.

men; to those who are living at ease and prosperity the thought of death is bitter, but it is welcome to such as are in sickness and adversity, who are broken and have lost hope. Then he goes on to utter a word of comfort to those to whom the thought of death is painful, by saying that it is the destiny of all men, and that it is the decree of the Most High; he concludes by reminding them also that:

In Sheol there are no reproaches concerning life.

For the rest, the book contains a large collection of moral maxims and sage counsels regarding almost every conceivable emergency in life; if the majority of these appear to be merely moral, it has to be remembered, as already pointed out, that to Ben-Sira the apparently most secular forms of wisdom partake of something religious fundamentally, because all wisdom is in its multifarious and varied expressions so many offshoots of the one primeval Wisdom which emanates from God. These maxims and counsels are applicable to people in every condition of life; a large proportion of them deals with the ordinary, every-day relationships between man and man, whether in regard to the rich or the poor, the oppressed, the mourners, &c., &c.; rules of courtesy, behaviour at table, politeness, respect for one's betters, and many other similar topics, abound. Ben-Sira's intimate knowledge of human nature meets one at every turn, and is certainly one of the most instructive features of the book. It was clearly Ben-Sira's object, in writing his book, to present to the Jewish public of his day an authoritative work of reference to which recourse could be had for guidance and instruction in every circumstance of life. In doing so, however, Ben-Sira makes it his great aim to set forth the superiority of Judaism over Hellenism. For some time previously the Hellenistic spirit had been affecting the Jews both in Palestine and in the Dispersion, and though there was immense good in the wider mental horizon fostered by this spirit, yet there can be no doubt that Hellenism had assumed a debased form in Palestine,[1] and a true Jew, such as Ben-Sira was, rightly felt bound to oppose its extension in the best way he could, namely, by offering something better in its place. Nevertheless, Ben-Sira was himself not unaffected by the Hellenic genius, probably unconsciously; and his admiration for Judaism of the orthodox, traditional type is unable to conceal altogether the newer tendencies of thought brought into existence through that Greek culture by which he, too, had become possessed. 'The results of the past and the beginnings of a future development were still in juxtaposition—not amalgamated, but as yet not separated, nor were their further sequences in view. Alike the close of the old and the beginnings of the new are side by side in *Ecclesiasticus*. The former reaches back to the early times of Israel's glory; the latter points forward to that direction which was to find its home and centre, not in Palestine, but in Alexandria.'[2] The traces of the influence of Greek modes of thought to be found in our book are not seen in definite form, but, as one would expect where the influence was at work unconsciously, they are to be discerned rather in the general outlook and conception; what is perhaps the most striking example of this is the way in which virtue and knowledge are identified; this is a distinct Hellenic trait, and is treated in the book as axiomatic. In the past, human and divine wisdom had been regarded as opposed, whereas, owing to Greek influence, both in our book and in the Wisdom Literature generally, it is taught that wisdom is the one thing of all others which is indispensable to him who would lead a godly life. The evil of wickedness is represented as lying in the fact that wickedness is foolishness, and therefore essentially opposed to wisdom. On the other hand, the Jews were faithful to the Law, the ordinances of which were binding because it was the revealed will of God; and, therefore, in order to reconcile this old teaching with the new teaching that wisdom was the chief requirement of the man of religion, wisdom became identified with the Law: 'The fear of the Lord is the beginning of wisdom'; by the 'fear of the Lord' is meant, of course, obedience to His commands, i.e. the observance of the Law. These words express what is, in truth, the foundation-stone of the Wisdom Literature, and this identification between wisdom and the Law formed the reconciling link between Judaism and Hellenism in this domain. Nowhere is this identification more clearly brought out than in the Book of Wisdom and in Sirach. This fully explains why Ben-Sira, following herein, without doubt, many sages before him, divides mankind into two categories, the wise and the foolish, which correspond respectively to the righteous and the wicked.

But while there is no sort of doubt that traces of Hellenic influence are to be discerned in the book, there is a danger which must be guarded against of seeing them where they do not exist.

[1] 'We have reason to believe that it was just in Syria that Hellenism took a baser form. The ascetic element which saved its liberty from rankness tended here more than anywhere else to be forgotten. The games, the shows, the abandonment of a life which ran riot in a gratification of the senses, grosser or more refined, these made up too much of the Hellenism which changed the face of Syria in the last centuries before Christ' (Bevan, *Jerusalem under the High-priests*, p. 41).

[2] Edersheim in the *Speaker's Commentary*.

Ben-Sira has here and there thoughts which at first sight look like traces of Hellenic influence, but are not so in reality; they are independent parallels, but have not otherwise anything to do with Greek culture. For example, the following might well appear at first sight to be an echo of Epicurean philosophy:

Give not thy soul to sorrow,
And let not thyself become unsteadied with care.
Heart-joy is life for a man,
And human gladness prolongeth days.
Entice thyself and soothe thine heart,
And banish vexation from thee:
For sorrow hath slain many,
And there is no profit in vexation.
Envy and anger shorten days,
And anxiety maketh old untimely.
The sleep of a cheerful heart is like dainties,
And his food is agreeable unto him (xxx. 21–25).

But quite similar thoughts are found in a fragment of the Gilgamesh epic found on a tablet written in the script of the Ḥammurabi dynasty (2000 B.C.), and published by Meissner in the *Mittheilungen der Vorderasiatischen Gesellschaft*, 1902, Heft i. On p. 8, col. iii, line 3, we read:

. . . *Thou, O Gilgamesh, fill indeed thy belly;*
Day and night be thou joyful,
Daily ordain gladness,
Day and night rage and make merry;
Let thy garments be bright,
Thy head purify, wash with water,
Desire thy children which thy hand possesses . . .[1]

There are other passages which might likewise seem to manifest the influence of Greek philosophy; in some of these it may well be that this is actually the case;[2] but it is well to be on one's guard, lest what appears to be a Hellenistic note is in reality nothing more than a parallel. While the Judaic elements in the book preponderate to an overwhelming degree, tinges of Hellenic influence are to be discovered here and there.

§ 2. The Title of the Book.

As the fragments of the Hebrew text of our book which are extant only begin with the concluding words of chap. iii. 6,[3] we do not know how the title ran, but the third line of the subscription reads: 'The Wisdom of Simeon, the son of Jeshua, the son of Eleazar, the son of Sira'; and the last line of the subscription in most of the Syriac manuscripts has: 'The writing or the Wisdom of Bar Sira is ended.' Jerome, however, says in his *Praef. in Libr. Sal.*, 'Fertur et πανάρετος Iesu filii Sirach liber, et alius ψευδεπίγραφος qui Sapientia Salomonis inscribitur; quorum priorem Hebraicum reperi, nec Ecclesiasticum, ut apud Latinos sed *Parabolas* praenotatum'; this title = מְשָׁלִי,[4] i.e. the Hebrew title for the Book of Proverbs, but that this was a title, in the ordinary sense, of our book is very improbable; it is more likely to have been a general title, descriptive of the contents, which was applied to the three books Ecclesiasticus, Ecclesiastes, and Canticles, for Jerome (in the context of the passage quoted above) says that these two latter were joined to Ecclesiasticus. In the Syriac Version the title is 'Wisdom of Bar Sira', while in most manuscripts of the Septuagint it runs: Σοφία Ἰησοῦ υἱοῦ Σειράχ, or abbreviated in Cod. B, Σοφία Σειράχ.[5] The probability is that the original title of the book was חכמת ישוע בן־סירא ('The Wisdom of Jesus Ben-Sira').[6] The title 'Ecclesiasticus' of the English Versions comes from the Vulgate, though it is one which has been in use in the Western Church ever since the time of Cyprian (d. A.D. 258). It meant the 'Church Book' *par*

[1] Quoted by Barton, *Ecclesiastes* (Intern. Crit. Com.), p. 39.
[2] e.g. when Ben-Sira controverts the fatalistic philosophy of the Stoics.
[3] According to Smend, a clause = ii. 18 *d* is placed after vi. 17.
[4] In later Jewish literature quotations from Sirach are sometimes prefaced with the words, 'the Parabolist said' (המשל אמר); see Cowley-Neubauer, p. xxiv. n. v. liv, and xx. n. x.
[5] In Cod. 248 Ἐκκλησιαστικός is placed before the ordinary title.
[6] In some Latin manuscripts the title is 'Liber Iesu filii Sirach'.

excellence among the 'Libri Ecclesiastici'. Among the early Greek Fathers the book is referred to as Πανάρετος Σοφία; see, e.g., Eusebius (*Chronicon*, ed. Scheone, ii. 122); and Jerome (*Comm. in Dan.* ix) speaks of it as ἡ Πανάρετος; Clement of Alexandria calls it Παιδαγωγός (*Paed.* ii. 10. 99, &c.), and sometimes quotes from it with the words ἡ σοφία λέγει.[1] In the Talmud it is called 'The Book of Ben-Sira' (*Hagigah* 13 *a*, *Niddah* 16 *b*, *Berakhoth* 11 *b*); [2] and Saʿadya speaks of it as ספר מוסר, 'The Book of Instruction,' while other Rabbis call it מוסר בן־סירא, 'The Instruction of Ben-Sira.' Schechter (*JQR*, xii. 460 f., 1900) quotes the words of a Rabbi Joseph that the 'Proverbs of Ben-Sira' (משלי בן־סירא) must be read because they contain useful matter.

§ 3. The Original Hebrew Text.

Apart from a few scattered citations in the Talmudic and post-Talmudic Jewish literature the Book of Ben-Sira was, until recent years, known only in the two principal ancient translations of it, viz. the Greek and Syriac versions, and the secondary versions based thereon. The disappearance of the Hebrew MSS. of the book may be explained as due, ultimately, to its exclusion from the Canon, for which early rabbinical evidence exists.[3] In spite of such exclusion, however, the book long retained its popularity in Jewish circles,[4] and in Jerome's time apparently MSS. of the Hebrew text were still accessible in Palestine. In his preface to the Books of Solomon, Jerome expressly mentions one of these which he had in his possession: 'Quorum priorem—sc. Iesu filii Sirach librum—Hebraicum reperi.' In the succeeding centuries, down to the eleventh, the book was still freely quoted in a Hebrew (and also an Aramaic) form. One of the most interesting references to the existence of copies of the Hebrew text is made by Saʿadya, Gaon of Bagdad (A.D. 920), who states that vowel-points and accents—usually reserved only for canonical writings—were to be found in copies of Ben-Sira.[5] Saʿadya also cites some seven (or eight) genuine sayings of Ben-Sira in classical Hebrew. Of the existence of the book in Spain, Provence, or among the Rabbis of France, the Rhineland, and Germany, there is no direct trace. The Hebrew text was apparently unknown (or at least inaccessible) to Rashi, the Tosafists, and even to Maimonides,[6] and seems to have completely vanished from knowledge in the eleventh century. The recovery of large portions of it has been one of the most striking discoveries of recent years.

(a) *The recovery of portions of the lost Hebrew original.*

It was in 1896 that the first portion of the lost Hebrew text came to light—a single leaf containing the text of ch. xxxix. 15–xl. 7, among some manuscript fragments brought from the East by Mrs. Lewis and Mrs. Gibson, together with the famous palimpsest of the Syriac Gospels. This leaf was examined by Dr. Schechter, then Reader in Talmudic in the University of Cambridge, who recognized its contents and published it, with an English translation, introduction and notes, in *The Expositor* for July, 1896. Almost simultaneously Professor Sayce presented to the Bodleian a box of Hebrew and Arabic fragments, among which Messrs. Cowley and Neubauer 'recognized another portion of the same text of Sirach, consisting of nine leaves, and forming the continuation of Mrs. Lewis's leaf from chapter xl. 9 to xlix. 11'.[7] Both fragments proved to be furnished with marginal notes 'giving the variants of another copy of Sirach, or more probably of two other copies.... In the Bodleian fragment there are also at least two Persian glosses (ff. 1 and 5ᵇ), which point to its having been written in Bagdad or Persia, possibly transcribed from Saʿadya's copy'.[8]

These fragments had come from the Genizah at Cairo. In consequence Schechter at once proceeded thither, and, having obtained the necessary authority, made an examination of the manuscript material there deposited, with the result that a considerable amount of the collection was brought to Cambridge. In this collection other fragments of Sirach were discovered by Schechter, all from the same MS. (denoted B by Schechter), covering parts of chapters xxx–xxxviii, as well as the final portion, covering chapters l–li. Two additional fragments of the same MS., containing xxxi. 12–31 and xxxvi. 24–xxxvii. 26, were secured for the British Museum, and edited by the Rev. G. Margoliouth (*JQR*, xii. 1–33). Meanwhile Schechter had discovered in the Genizah collection at Cambridge fragments of a second MS. of the Hebrew text (= MS. A), containing

[1] Cp. Hart, *Ecclesiasticus in Greek*, p. 333.

[2] *JE*, xi. 388 *a*.

[3] Cp. *Tosefta*, *Yadayim* ii. 13 (ed. Zuckermandel 683), which runs: 'The gilyōnîm and the books of the heretics (*mînîm*) do not defile the hands [i.e. are not canonical]; the books of Ben-Sira and all books written after the prophetic period do not defile the hands': cp. also T. J. *Sanh.* 28 *a*.

[4] For its influence on early Jewish and Christian literature cp. § 7 below.

[5] *Sefer ha-galuy*, p. 162 (cp. Cowley-Neub. *O. H.* p. x f.).

[6] Cowley-Neub. *op. cit.*, ibid.

[7] Ibid., p. xii.

[8] Ibid., p. xiii, where see a full description of the MS. and its peculiarities.

ch. iii. 6–xvi. 6, with a hiatus from vii. 29 to xi. 34, which was afterwards made good by some leaves that came into the possession of Mr. Elkan Adler. When the remaining contents of the Genizah were sold Israel Lévi discovered a fragment of a fresh MS. (= MS. D) in a single leaf covering ch. xxxvi. 24–xxxviii. 1 (thus providing a second text against that of MS. B for this portion of the book). Finally, Schechter, Gaster, and Lévi found in material derived from the same Genizah fragments of an anthology of the Book of Ben-Sira (= MS. C) embracing the following: iv. 23 *b*, 30, 31; v. 4–8, 9–13; vi. 18–19, 28, 35; vii. 1, 4, 6, 17, 20–21, 23–25; xviii. 30–31; xix. 1–2; xx. 4–6, 12 (?); xxv. 7 *c*, 8 *c*, 8 *a*, 12, 16–23; xxvi. 1–2; xxxvi. 16; xxxvii. 19, 22, 24, 26. The MSS. may be classified as follows:—

(*a*) MANUSCRIPT A, containing ch. iii. 6–xvi. 26; this consists of six leaves, and may be of the eleventh century. There are 28–29 lines to the page; in some places vowels are added, and, in one or two cases, accents. The size of the page is 11 x 11 cm.

(*b*) MANUSCRIPT B, containing xxx. 11–xxxiii. 3, xxxv. 11–xxxviii. 27, xxxix. 15–li. 30; this consists of 19 leaves, and may be of the twelfth century. 'The MS. is written on oriental paper, and is arranged in lines, 18 to the page, and the lines are divided into hemistichs.'[1] There are many marginal notes, containing, apparently, variant readings from two other codices, one of which is closely related to MS. D. 'As a rule, the body of the text corresponds to the Greek version, and the glosses in the margin to the Syriac; but occasionally the reverse is the case.'[2] The size of the page is 19·1 x 17 cm.

(*c*) MANUSCRIPT C (= Lévi's D), containing an anthology from chapters iv–vii, xviii–xx, xxv, xxvi, xxxvii (as specified above). This MS. consists of four leaves, and, according to Gaster, is older than the other MSS. It contains 12 lines to the page, the size of which is 14·6 x 10 cm. 'The text is often preferable to that of A, and offers variants agreeing with the Greek version, while the readings of A correspond to the Syriac.'[3]

(*d*) MANUSCRIPT D (= Lévi's C), containing xxxvi. 29–xxxviii. 1. This MS. consists of a single leaf; there are 20 lines to the page, which measures 16 x 12 cm. Words, and in some cases entire verses, are provided with vowels and accents.

It will thus be seen that the MSS. so far recovered yield a Hebrew text for something like two-thirds of the entire book. In some cases two MSS., and for four verses three, are available for the restoration of the text.

The following list shows the extent of the Hebrew MS. authority for different parts of the text:

(*a*) The portions of the text for which one manuscript authority only is available are: From MS. A, iii. 6–iv. 23 *a*, iv. 24–29, v. 1–3, 8, 14–15, vi. 1–17, 18 (C), 20–25, 27, 29–33, 36–37, vii. 3, 5, 7–16, 18–19, 22, 26, 29–36, viii. 1–xvi. 26: from MS. C, xviii. 30–31 [32–33], xix. 1–2, xx. 4–6 [5–7], 12 [13], xxv. 7 *c*, 8 *c*, 8 *a*, 12 [13], 16–23 [17–24]; xxvi. 1–2: from MS. B, xxx. 11–xxxiii. 3, xxxv. 11–xxxvi. 15, xxxvi. 17–28, xxxviii. 2–27; xxxix. 15–li. 30.

(*b*) The portions of the text for which two MSS. are available are: iv. 23 *b*, 30–31; v. 4–7, 9–13; vi. 19, 28, 35; vii. 1, 2, 4, 6, 17, 20–21, 23–25; xxxvi. 16; xxxvi. 29–xxxviii. 1.

(*c*) The portions of the text for which three MSS. are available are: xxxviii. 19, 22, 24, 26.

(*d*) The portions of the text for which no Hebr. MS. is yet available are: i. 1–iii. 5; xvi. 27–xviii. 3; xix. 3–xx. 4, 8–12; xx. 14–xxv. 6, xxv. 9–12, 14–16, 25–26; xxvi. 3–xxx. 10; xxxiii. 4–xxxv. 8 (10); xxxviii. 28–xxxix. 14.

(b) *The value and authenticity of the recovered fragments.*

The questions touched upon in this section have given rise to much controversy which it will be impossible to review here in detail. All that will be attempted will be to indicate the main lines and directions of the best critical opinion.

The problems raised by the Hebrew fragments are of an exceedingly complex character. The first point to determine, in a general way, is the relation of the MSS. to each other. The manuscript material that has been recovered, fortunately, is sufficiently extensive—overlapping as it does for certain parts of the text of the book—to make it possible to establish certain relations.

(i) *The relation of the Hebrew MSS. to each other.*

The most important point of relation between the MSS. is the frequent agreement of the marginal variants of B with D against the text of B in the section where comparison is possible, i.e. where the two MSS. overlap (xxxvi. 29–xxxviii. 1). A good example of this is to be seen in xxxvii. 16:

[1] Cowley-Neub., *op. cit.*, p. xiii. [2] I. Lévi in *JE*, xi. 393 *a*. [3] Lévi, *op. cit.*, xi. 392 *b*.

Here B [marg.] and D have

ראש כל מעשה מאמר
לפני כל פועל (פעל D) היא מחשבת

The beginning of every action is speech,
And before every work is the thought.

For this B [text] has

ראש כל מעשה דבר
וראש כל פעל היא מחשבת

Another good example is afforded by xxxvii. 25, where B [marg.] and D read ישרון against עם ישראל of B [text]. According to Peters[1], about 75 per cent. of the variants conform to this rule; in the other cases where D has a variant not attested in B [marg.] some are explicable as scribal errors in D, or as corruptions produced under the influence of the text of B. In several cases B [marg.] and D agree in purely orthographic variants, and even in reproducing identical scribal errors. The important conclusion deducible from these phenomena is that the marginal variants of B are not the emendations of the scribe, but represent readings derived from another MS. which has close affinities with D. Probably the marginal variants of the rest of B are derived from an identical or related source. Regarding the relation of C to B and D the material for comparison is too slight to enable any certain conclusions to be drawn. In one striking case, however, C = B [text] in reading גואל against B [marg.] and D which read נואל. Hence Peters concludes that C is to be ranked with the B type of text (against D + B [marg.]). The other important area of contact is iv. 23–vii. 25, where C and A partly overlap and comparison is possible. Here the divergence is occasionally considerable, as in iv. 30, 31 (see next subsection). But this must not be unduly exaggerated. The similarity of whole verses is so marked as to make it clear that we are confronted with different recensions of the same archetypal text, and not with independent types of text.[2]

(ii) *The general character of the Hebrew fragments and their relation to the Versions.*

The relation of the Hebrew fragments to the Versions presents many difficult textual problems which cannot be said yet to have been fully solved.[3] In the case of MSS. A and B, which may conveniently be considered first, the Hebrew sometimes agrees with the Greek version against the Syriac, sometimes differs from both, and occasionally explains one or the other, or both. The cases in which the Hebrew seems to follow the Syriac and to be dependent on it are, perhaps, the most crucial. In this connexion the doublets, which are particularly numerous in B, are most important. These have been indicated in the critical notes of the commentary. The following example will illustrate many others. In xxxi. 13 𝔥[B] has:

(1) זכור (*marg.* דע) כי רעה עין רעה
(2) רע עין שונא אל
(3) ורע ממנו לא ברא:
(4) כי זה מפני כל דבר תזוע (*marg.* תזיע) עין
(5) ומפנים דמעה תדמע (*marg.*? תזיע)
(6) רע מעין לא חלק אל
(7) על כן (*marg.* על כל) מפני (מלפני) כל נס לחה:

(1) *Remember that an evil eye is an evil thing;*
(2) *The man of evil eye God hateth,*
(3) *And He hath created nothing more evil than him.*
(4) *For this—by reason of everything the eye quivereth,*
(5) *And from the face it maketh tears.*
(6) *God hath created nothing more evil than the eye,*
(7) *Therefore by reason of everything its freshness is abated.*

[1] *Der jüngst wiederaufgefundene hebräische Text des Buches Ecclesiasticus* (1902), p. 23*.

[2] Schechter (*JQR*, xii. 458) pertinently remarks: 'Had we here to deal with different translations, it is impossible that they should agree as closely as they [MSS. C and A] do. Those who are inclined to doubt this obvious fact should take the trouble to compare these same fourteen verses [covering iv. 23–v. 13 + xxxvi. 24] in the three Hebrew versions we possess of Ben-Sira, viz. by Ben Zeeb, Fränkel, and Joshua Duklo, and he will see at once the difference between independent translations and families of MSS. differing but descendant from the same common origin. In the first case he will, before a closer reading, hardly be aware that they represent the same work, whilst in the latter it will take him some time before he detects their differences.'

[3] The most elaborate and detailed reconstruction of the text, taking the fullest account of all relevant data, is that of Smend (as cited in § 10).

Here (1) (6) (7) substantially = 𝔊: and (2) (3) and (4) = 𝔖 (see crit. note on xxxi. 23 in the following commentary): (5) is a doublet of (4) and (7). It is noticeable that ℌ does not, as it stands, yield an exactly corresponding text either to 𝔊 or 𝔖, while it provides one doublet (5) and (7) which corresponds to neither. The simplest explanation is that ℌ embodies variants from different recensions of the original text that lie behind 𝔊 and 𝔖.[1] Not improbably ℌ itself has been glossed and emended by scribes. The variant in (7) above ('its freshness is abated') may, perhaps, be explained in this way (from Deut. xxxiv. 7). As another example of a gloss in ℌ to which nothing corresponds in 𝔊 or 𝔖 xxxi. 2 may be cited. Here ℌ adds the following two lines:

רע נאמן תניד חרפה
ומסתיר סוד אוהב כנפשׁ

Reproach putteth to flight the faithful friend,
But he that hideth a secret loveth (a friend) as his own soul.

As this couplet does not harmonize with the context it is probably a gloss (? from the margin of a MS.). In general $\mathfrak{H}^{B}$ has many scribal errors and corruptions in its text, which is also marked by the occasional presence of strong Syriasms[2] and late Rabbinical expressions.[3]

In the case of $\mathfrak{H}^{A}$ the number of marginal variants is comparatively small. There are a certain number of doublets which exhibit features on the whole similar to those of $\mathfrak{H}^{B}$ illustrated above. But $\mathfrak{H}^{A}$ diverges more from the text of 𝔊 than is the case with $\mathfrak{H}^{B}$—it very rarely sides with 𝔊 against 𝔖. It has certain orthographical peculiarities of its own, and is marked by a number of errors due to the carelessness of the copyist.[4] In the case of $\mathfrak{H}^{D}$, which covers xxxvi. 29–xxxviii. 1, and provides (with $\mathfrak{H}^{B}$) a duplicate text for this section of the book, we have, on the whole, a text superior to that of $\mathfrak{H}^{B}$, though there are numerous cases of corruption. In two instances it yields a text which agrees with 𝔏 against the common text of 𝔊, viz. in xxxvii. 26[5], where it reads כבוד (= δόξαν 248 and 𝔏) against πίστιν of the ordinary text of 𝔊; and in xxxvii. 28 *b* where, against $\mathfrak{H}^{B}$ which = 𝔊, it reads:

ולא לכל נפשׁ כל זן תבחר

which = 𝔏 (*et non omni animae omne genus placet*). In this MS. late Hebrew expressions are of frequent occurrence. In the three fragments of selections which make up $\mathfrak{H}^{C}$ a type of text is preserved which is, on the whole, remarkably free from the corruptions and blemishes which disfigure the other MSS. It agrees sometimes with 𝔊, sometimes with 𝔖, and occasionally with neither (e.g. v. 11). In those parts of the book where it coincides with $\mathfrak{H}^{A}$ it often agrees with the text of 𝔊 against 𝔖.

The relation of the Hebrew fragments to the citations of Sirach that occur in the Talmudic and Rabbinic literature[6] is not easy to determine owing to the uncertain state of the Talmudic and Rabbinic texts, and also to the loose way in which such citations are often made. It would appear that in some cases the two Talmuds had different texts of Ben-Sira before them. Thus iii. 21 is cited in one form in T. J. *Ḥag.* 77 *c* (agreeing with $\mathfrak{H}^{A}$ in first and last word), and in another (doublet) form in T. B. *Ḥag.* 13 *a* (also in *Midr. rabba* Gen. viii). In the latter the first couplet agrees with 𝔖 and 𝔊 (and partly with $\mathfrak{H}^{A}$); the second diverges considerably from all the other forms of the text (though agreeing in one word with $\mathfrak{H}^{A}$, and in another with T. J. *Ḥag.*). The most natural inference to draw from these phenomena is that two divergent types of text of Sirach were current in the fifth century A.D. The citations from Sirach in Sa'adya (*Sefer ha-galuy*) are of a different character. They agree much more closely with the text of ℌ, give the impression of being more exact citations, and are apparently derived from substantially the same text as that represented in the Hebrew fragments.

It is important to note, in this connexion, that collections of detached sayings derived from Sirach were apparently in existence in the Talmudic period. The only long continuous quotation from Ben-Sira given in the Talmud (T. B. *Sanhedrin* 100 *b*) is apparently made from such a *florilegium*. It consists of the following passages in the following order: xxvi. 1–4; ix. 8, 9; xi. 29–34, and vi. 10. Another such collection is represented in the fragments denoted $\mathfrak{H}^{C}$. Such collections

[1] See further the discussion in the next subsection.

[2] e.g. ממחיו xlii. 5, which apparently = inf. Pael (Syr. *mĕmaḥāyu*); הִסְתַּוֵּיד xlii. 12, 'converse' = Syr. *'estawwed* = ὁμιλεῖν: בֵּית xlii. 12 = perhaps 'among' (Syr. *bêth*).

[3] e.g. כיוצא בו xxxviii. 17, 'such as befits him' (in $\mathfrak{H}^{B}$; also in $\mathfrak{H}^{A}$ x. 28); בבית מדרשי li. 23.

[4] Of differences of diction the following is the most notable: $\mathfrak{H}^{A}$ writes ניכיון where $\mathfrak{H}^{B}$ has ניסוי. See further Taylor-Schechter, *WBS*, pp. 7–12.

[5] This verse is wanting in $\mathfrak{H}^{B}$.

[6] For a collection of the citations conveniently grouped together see Cowley-Neub., pp. xix–xxx; also Schechter in *JQR*, iii. 682–706 (with full critical notes).

seem to have superseded the original Hebrew text of the entire book after it fell under the ban and was reckoned among 'the books of the heretics'. The 'good things' profitable for reading were excerpted; the rest consigned to neglect.[1] It is worth noting that some of the sayings of Ben-Sira are cited in an Aramaic form, which implies that an Aramaic translation of parts of the book was at some time or other made. This factor must be allowed for as a possible source of corruption in the diction of the fragments.

(iii) *The authenticity of the Hebrew fragments.*

The authenticity of the Hebrew fragments was early called in question by Professor D. S. Margoliouth,[2] who, noting the decadent nature of the diction, coloured as it is by the frequent presence of Syriasms and Arabisms, as well as of neo-Hebraisms, and struck by the presence of Persian glosses in 𝔋[B], propounded the theory that 𝔋 is itself a retranslation of a Persian version, which was based partly on the Greek and partly on the Syriac versions of the book. The hypothesis is that a Syriac version, which had been revised by the Greek, was used as the basis of a Persian rendering, and that this Persian translation was rendered by an unintelligent Persian Jew, who knew neither Syriac nor Greek, into Hebrew. 'The theory is incompatible with the known facts; the agreements (often literal) and the disagreements of the Hebrew with the primary versions make it practically inconceivable that it could have arisen in the way described.'[3] The obscurities in the Hebrew text alleged to be due to a misunderstanding of Persian expressions are all susceptible of a different—and more probable—explanation.[4] Consequently the hypothesis of a Persian basis for the text of 𝔋 may be ruled out. But in a modified form the hypothesis of retranslation may be made much more defensible, viz. on the basis of the Syriac—and Greek—versions. It is not, indeed, alleged that the whole of the recovered Hebrew text can be explained in this way, but the dependence of parts of the text on 𝔊 or 𝔖 is seriously maintained by some scholars. It will, therefore, be necessary to subject some of the crucial cases adduced to examination. Nestle[5] brings forward a number of cases from 𝔋[C] in which he concludes that the Hebrew text of these passages 'cannot be explained in any other way than by the supposition that' it rests 'on a corrupt and glossed text, sometimes of 𝔊, sometimes of 𝔖'. He, however, does not allege of 𝔋[C] as a whole that it is a *simple retranslation* of 𝔊, 'for even in 𝔋[C] there are passages which are at variance with 𝔊.' The passages in question are iv. 30, 31, v. 9 *b*, 13 *b*, vii. 25, xxv. 17. The first and last of these may be taken as crucial examples.

In iv. 30 𝔊 has:

μὴ ἴσθι ὡς λέων ἐν τῷ οἴκῳ (*v. l.* τῇ οἰκίᾳ) σου
καὶ φαντασιοκοπῶν ἐν τοῖς οἰκέταις σου.

𝔏 noli esse sicut leo in domo tua;
evertens domesticos tuos et opprimens subiectos tibi.

𝔖 Be not a *dog* (כלב) in thy house,
And rebuking and fearful in thy works.

𝔋[A] אל תהי ככלב בביתך
ומוזר ומתירא במלאכתך

𝔋[B] אל תהי כאריה בביתך
ומתפחז בעבודתך׃

Here 𝔋[A] 'like a dog' (ככלב) = 𝔖; and 𝔋[C] 'like a lion' (כאריה) = 𝔊. 'Can there be any doubt,' says Nestle, 'that A (𝔋[A]) agrees with 𝔖 and C (𝔋[C]) with 𝔊?' The mistake in 𝔖 (כלב) may be due to a misreading of כלבי (= כלביא) 'like a lion'. He, however, admits that the couplets as they stand cannot be explained entirely as retranslations. In particular, 'how would a late Jewish translator hit upon מתפחז to render so obscure a word as φαντασιοκοπῶν?' But if the two couplets are not retranslations the obvious inference is that they represent two recensions of the original Hebrew text, one of which lies behind 𝔖 and the other behind 𝔊. In 𝔋[A] ככלב is a corruption of כלב = כְּלָבִי (כלביא), which may be explained as a variant on the true reading (preserved in 𝔋[C]) כאריה: ומוזר may be a gloss: במלאכתך has come in by mistake from the previous verse; the correct reading is preserved

[1] Cf. Schechter in *JQR*, xii. 461.
[2] *The Origin of the 'Original' Hebrew of Ecclesiasticus* (1899).
[3] Toy in *EB*, ii, col. 1168.
[4] For a detailed criticism of these alleged cases see Taylor-Schechter, *WBS*.
[5] Art. 'Sirach' in Hastings's *DB*, iv. 547 f.

in 𝔥^c בעבודתך (cf. 𝔊 and 𝔖); ומתירא is probably original, and ומתפחז in 𝔥^c a corruption of ומתפחד a variant on ומתירא. Thus the original Hebrew of the couplet may be restored:

אל תהי כאריה בביתך
ומתירא בעבודתך:

Be not like a lion in thy family,
And timid among thy slaves.

[Smend, however, keeps ומוזר in line 2: then render

And shy and timid among thy slaves.]

In the text so read מתירא affords an excellent word-play (suggested by Amos iii. 8) on אריה in line 1 —quite in the style of Ben-Sira.[1]

Again, in xxv. 17:

The wickedness of a woman . . . darkeneth her countenance like sackcloth (A.V. marg. 'or like a bear'): R.V. *as a bear doth.*

𝔊^B &c. ὡς σάκκον: 𝔊^ℵAV 55, 106, 155, 157, 248, 253, Syro-Hex. ὡς ἄρκος: 𝔏 (combining both readings) *tanquam ursus et quasi saccum.*

𝔖 . . . *maketh pale the face of her husband, and*
Maketh it black like the colour of a sack.

𝔥^c רע אשה ישחיר מראה איש
ויקדיר פניו לדוב:

From these *data* Nestle concludes that 'all rules of textual criticism . . . must be naught, or C (𝔥^c) is here *the retranslation of a corrupt Greek text.*' The assumption is that ἄρκος is an inner (Greek) corruption of σάκκον, and that 𝔥^c here has followed a Greek text which had the corruption. But it should be noted that 𝔥^c *for the rest of the verse diverges strongly from* 𝔊, *and agrees with* 𝔖 *against* 𝔊 (1) in adding איש, and (2) in making the following word (פניו) refer to the husband (*his face*). We are, therefore, driven to suppose that 𝔥 has here followed 𝔊 *in one word only*, viz. in reading 'bear' for 'sack'; in the rest of the verse it is independent of 𝔊, and approximates to (though it does not coincide with) 𝔖. The phenomena point in the same direction as in the other case examined, viz. to the existence of divergent recensions of the text of 𝔥, one of which has been followed by 𝔊 and another by 𝔖, 𝔥^c partly agreeing with both. At least two alternatives are possible to Nestle's hypothesis, either of which is to be preferred to his solution; either (1) σάκκον is an inner (Greek) corruption of ἄρκος which has affected 𝔖, or (2) the readings שק and דוב existed in different recensions of 𝔥. In either case דוב is probably the true reading of the original Hebrew, which may be restored from 𝔥^c thus:

רע אשה ישחיר מראה
ויקדיר פניה כדוב:

The wickedness of a woman maketh black her look,
And darkeneth her countenance like a bear's.

The meaning of the couplet appears to be that wickedness makes a woman sinister of aspect and fierce; the alternative reading 'like sackcloth' would introduce the idea of sadness and mourning, which does not harmonize so well with the context. As the previous couplet[2] suggests the comparison of the wicked woman to a lion or dragon, the further comparison of her aspect to a bear's is in keeping. What is referred to, apparently, is the hardening effect of a course of wickedness, which makes a woman brazen. The context, therefore, does not really favour the idea that a woman's wickedness makes her sad of countenance ('darkeneth her countenance like sackcloth'). Schechter[3] aptly cites in illustration a passage from the *Midrash* (*Gen. rabba*, § 87. 4) where Potiphar's wife is compared to a bear ('I will incite against thee the bear'). The bear is proverbially associated with fierceness in the O. T.; cp. Prov. xvii. 12, 2 Sam. xvii. 8, Hos. xiii. 8.

The hypothesis of partial retranslation of 𝔖 in 𝔥 has been urged by Prof. I. Lévi with much force. It may be stated in his own words:[4] 'Certain details indicate that both A (𝔥^A) and B (𝔥^B) are derived from a copy characterized by interpolations due to a retranslation from Syriac into Hebrew. In a number of passages the same verse is given in two distinct renderings, one of which usually corre-

[1] So Taylor in *JQR*, xv. 611.
[2] *I would rather dwell with a lion and a dragon than keep house with a wicked woman.*
[3] *JQR*, xv. 464.
[4] *JE*, xi. 393 (art. 'Sirach').

sponds to the Syriac, even when this text represents merely a faulty or biased translation of the original. These verses, moreover, in their conformity to the Syriac, become at times so meaningless that they can be explained only as incorrect translations from that language. Such suspicious passages are characterized by a comparatively modern style and language, by a commonplace phraseology, and by a break in the parallelism which is affected by Ecclesiasticus. It may, therefore, be safely concluded that these doublets are merely additions made to render the Syriac version more intelligible. The same statement holds true of certain textual emendations made by the glossarist. In this, however, there is nothing strange, since it is a well-known fact that the Jews of certain sections were familiar with Syriac, as is shown by the quotations made by Naḥmanides from the Wisdom of Solomon, from Judith, and from Bel and the Dragon, and also by the introduction of the Peshiṭta of Proverbs into the Targum of the Hagiographa.' The alleged cases in the doublets of 𝕳 in which retranslation from 𝕾 is assumed by Lévi have been subjected to close examination by A. Fuchs,[1] who has shown good grounds for rejecting the hypothesis. The alternative view that these doublets represent variant readings derived from different recensions of 𝕳 is strongly upheld by Fuchs, and may be said to hold the field. With regard to the final acrostic hymn (li. 13–30), of which the version in $𝕳^B$ is, according to Lévi, a retranslation from 𝕾,[2] Levi's hypothesis is again rejected by Fuchs, and also by Dr. C. Taylor, who, after a careful discussion,[3] concludes as follows: 'Further study of 𝕳 has now brought out much positive evidence for its independence of 𝕾, and seemingly none to the contrary.' A word must be said in conclusion regarding the canticle which follows li. 12, and does not appear in any of the Versions. Is this a genuine part of the original Hebrew text of Ben-Sira? In favour of its authenticity may be urged the presence of the sentence:

Give thanks unto Him that chooseth the sons of Zadok to be priests,

which apparently contains an allusion to the pre-Maccabean high-priests who were descended from Zadok. The absence, too, of any reference to specifically Pharisaic ideas, such as the doctrine of the resurrection of the body, may also be cited in favour of its genuineness. Its omission in the Greek translation of Ben-Sira's grandson may be explained by the reference to the 'sons of Zadok'—which might have proved a source of offence at a time when the high-priesthood was no longer held by descendants of that line. On the other hand, the sentiment expressed in the line:

Give thanks unto Him that maketh the horn of the House of David to bud

is directly opposed to that expressed in ch. xxxvi, and in the entire 'Hymn of the Fathers' (ch. xliv–xlviii). Perhaps the solution reached by Fuchs[4] is least open to objection. Fuchs concludes that the Psalm, which is not a genuine part of the original Book of Ben-Sira, is old and originally existed in an independent form; it was inserted in the Hebrew text of Ben-Sira before the year 153 B.C. by a reader who thought the context, which already contained psalm-pieces, a suitable one. It may have emanated from the circles of the *Ḥasidîm* ('the Assideans'), who had already taken a stand against Hellenism before the Maccabean revolt.

Enough has been said to show that the text of 𝕳, though it is disfigured by scribal errors and corruptions, and—in some places—by the presence of glosses, is yet essentially independent of 𝕲 and 𝕾; the hypothesis of retranslation breaks down, at best a plausible case for the influence of such a factor can only be made out for an insignificant number of verses, where, however, an alternative—and, on the whole, more probable—explanation is possible.

On the other hand, it is all-important to remember that 𝕳 constantly explains the variations in the Versions. This is one of the surest indications of its essential genuineness. One or two examples will illustrate many others. In vi. 30 *a* 𝕳 reads: עלי זהב עולה and 𝕲 has κόσμος γὰρ χρύσεός ἐστιν ἐπ' αὐτῆς. Here the first word in 𝕳 can be corrected by 𝕲 to עדי ('ornament'), thus yielding the line:

An ornament of gold is her yoke.

At the same time the third word in 𝕳 explains 𝕲's ἐπ' αὐτῆς, which is obviously due to עולה being misread עָלֶיהָ.

The following is an example of a different kind. In xiii. 1 *b* 𝕳 has:

וחובר אל לץ ילמד דרכו

And he that associateth with a scorner will learn his way. 𝕲 has καὶ ὁ κοινωνῶν ὑπερηφάνῳ ὁμοιωθήσεται αὐτῷ. 𝕾 *He that associateth with a godless man is clothed with his way.*

Here 𝕾 reads ילבש דרכו for 𝕳's ילמד דרכו; 𝕲 has apparently corrected the expression (cf. 𝕷);

[1] *Textkritische Untersuchungen zum hebräischen Ekklesiastikus* (Freiburg i. B., 1907).

[2] 'The hymn, which follows the Syriac version closely throughout, is evidently a retranslation from the latter' (*JE.* xi. 393). For Lévi's detailed arguments see his *L'Ecclésiastique*, ii, pp. xxi–xxvii.

[3] *Journal of Philology*, xxx, pp. 95–132.

[4] *Op. cit.*, pp. 102–110.

ילמד and ילבש may have arisen by confusion; or ילמד may be a correction of an original ילבש. In any case 𝔥 independently throws light on the text; even its corruptions are illuminating. Another indication of originality in 𝔥 is the frequent word-plays. A good example of such is viii. 18: לפני זר על תעשׂ רז. Here זר and רז provide an excellent instance, and will serve to illustrate numerous others.

If any further confirmation be needed as to the value and genuineness of the Hebrew fragments as a whole it may be furnished from the words of Prof. Lévi, who, as has been pointed out above, feels constrained to adopt the hypothesis of retranslation in the case of a restricted number of verses (mostly doublets). Yet, despite these assumed 'corrections and interpolations', he declares that 'the originality of the text in these fragments of Ben-Sira cannot be denied. Besides the fact that many scholars deny the existence of any interpolations, there are portions in which it is easy to recognize the author's hand, for he has a characteristic technique, style, vocabulary, and syntax which are evident in all the Versions. It may safely be said that in the main the work of Ben-Sira has been preserved just as it left his hands, while the chief variant marginal readings recorded in the fragments and confirmed by the translations may be regarded as evidences of the existence of two separate editions written by Ben-Sira himself. It is self-evident, moreover, that Ecclesiasticus has undergone some alterations at the hands of scribes, and it would have been strange indeed if this book alone should have wholly escaped the common lot of such writings. No more conclusive proof could be found, were any necessary, of the fidelity of the Hebrew version than its frequent agreement, in citations from the Bible, with the text on which the Septuagint is based rather than with the Massorah, as in the case of 1 Sam. xii. 3 as compared with Sirach xlvi. 19, or Isa. xxxviii. 17 with Sirach l. 2.'[1]

(c) *The secondary Hebrew recension.*

The indications that point to the existence of a secondary Greek version of Sirach are discussed and set forth in the next section (§ 4). It is there shown that this secondary and amplified recension—undertaken clearly in order to make the teaching of the book more acceptable to later orthodox (Pharisaic) circles—is not fully represented in any group of Greek MSS.; it has affected most extensively the 248 group, and is largely in evidence in the Old Latin and also in the Syriac versions.[2] Originally, however, it seems probable that it existed in a complete and independent form, of which the readings mentioned above are traces. In other words, the secondary Greek recension has affected in varying degrees certain groups of the Greek MSS. of the book, and also the Versions. The question arises: was this secondary Greek version due to a purely Greek revision of the book, or does it depend upon a revised Hebrew text—in other words, upon a secondary Hebrew recension? The phenomena of the text point unmistakably to the latter alternative; *the secondary Greek text depends essentially upon, and is a translation of, a younger Hebrew recension of the book.*

Traces of this younger recension remain in the MSS. of 𝔥, though there are only traces; it has in fact affected these MSS. only partially, and its influence can also be seen in the Rabbinic citations. The following from among the examples cited by Smend[3] will illustrate what has just been said. In xvi. 3 *c* the ordinary Greek text (B, &c.), which represents the original Ben-Sira, has:

κρείσσων γὰρ εἷς ἢ χίλιοι.

For this 𝔥^{A} has an expanded text, viz.:

כי טוב אחד עשׂה רצון מאלף (so 𝔖 exactly).

Chrysostom, in citing the verse, has the doublet:

καὶ κρείσσων εἷς ποιῶν τὸ θέλημα κυρίου ἢ μύριοι παράνομοι.

ℵ$^{c.a}$ has the doublet:

κρείσσων γὰρ εἷς δίκαιος ποιῶν θέλημα κυρίου ἢ μύριοι παράνομοι.

𝔊 70 248 have for 3 *c*:

κρείσσων γὰρ εἷς δίκαιος ἢ χίλιοι (70 + ἁμαρτωλοί).

𝔏 *Melior est enim unus timens deum quam mille filii impii.*

What Ben-Sira wrote was:

כי טוב אחד מאלף

The addition עשׂה רצון belongs to the secondary Hebrew recension which underlies the revised Greek

[1] *JE*, xi. 394.

[2] The Syriac version, though made directly from the Hebrew, has apparently been influenced often by Greek MSS., which contained secondary readings; see § 5 below and cp. Smend, § 12 (p. cxxxix f.).

[3] *Op. cit.*, xcii f.

text. Another example shows the same verse as it appeared in the original Hebrew text and in the secondary recension. Ch. v. 11 is preserved in two forms in ℌ^{A} and ℌ^{C}. In ℌ^{A} it runs:

היה ממהר להאזין
ובארך רוח השב פתגם:

Be swift to give ear,
And with patience of spirit return answer.

In ℌ^{C} it runs:

היה נכון בשמועה טובה
ובארך ענה תענה נכונה:

𝔖 = ℌ^{A}.
𝔊 has:

γίνου ταχὺς ἐν ἀκροάσει σου (248 + *ἀγαθῇ*)]
καὶ ἐν μακροθυμίᾳ φθέγγου ἀπόκρισιν (248 &c. + *ὀρθήν*).

Here clearly the Greek MSS. 248 &c. have corrected the older text of 𝔊 according to the later Hebrew recension represented in ℌ^{C}; the ordinary text of 𝔊 and 𝔖 = ℌ^{A} (except that 𝔊 appears to have read בשמועה for להאזין, the latter being a variant of the former perhaps).

In some cases the doublets in ℌ, to which reference has been made in the former part of this section, are to be explained in this way, one couplet reproducing the older Hebrew text, another the younger.[1] It might be argued that these additions in the text of 𝔊 are merely glosses and independent amplifications made in the Greek MSS. which have affected the Hebrew fragments. But Smend, after a very close and exhaustive investigation, has made it probable (*a*) that the additions as a whole—though a certain small amount of inner Greek amplification, perhaps under Christian influence, must be allowed for—possess a number of striking and peculiar features which point to a common origin and their being part of a comprehensive and deliberate revision; in other words, they belong to a special recension: and (*b*) that this recension depends upon a Hebrew basis: many of the expressions and phrases used are fundamentally Hebrew, and are clearly translations of Hebrew originals.[2] The difficulties of the hypothesis which would account for the presence of such elements in the Hebrew MSS. as due to retranslation have already been discussed.

(d) *The reconstruction of the original Hebrew text.*

It has already been shown that the Hebrew fragments contain the genuine original text, though with many corruptions and with a certain amount of text-mixture due to the existence of different recensions. The first task of criticism, therefore, is to free the text, as it has been handed down in the MSS., from corruptions, glosses, and scribal errors. For this purpose the Hebrew text itself offers, in the first place, the most valuable aid. Ben-Sira's language constantly echoes that of the Old Testament, and it is remarkable how clearly and frequently these reminiscences display themselves in the text of ℌ.[3] Then, again, the form of the text in couplets of short lines of a certain approximately equal length and defined rhythm is of material assistance. It is often possible to reduce the lines to the normal length and rhythm by the removal of a superfluous word or words. The use of the ancient Versions—especially of 𝔊 and 𝔖—is often of great value for reconstructing the original Hebrew, though it must not be forgotten that these Versions are themselves beset with many drawbacks. Both have suffered much from textual deterioration; both are often free and not literal renderings; even the original form of 𝔊, as it was made by the author's grandson, does not, it would seem, depend upon the Hebrew text of Ben-Sira's autograph, but upon a later transcript. Yet, when all possible reservations have been made, the ancient Versions constantly afford aid of inestimable value for the work of reconstruction. Finally, the data derived from ℌ is often of the greatest possible value for criticizing those parts of the book for which no portions of the Hebrew text have been recovered. These points receive ample illustration in the text and textual notes which are printed in the following commentary. We are unable to subscribe to the verdict of Prof. Toy when he says:[4] 'In general the text of Ben-Sira remains nearly as it was before the discovery of the fragments.' On the contrary, a careful study of ℌ, and the use of it for the purpose of constructing

[1] Cp. xxxiv. 20 *a b*, xxxv. 22 in ℌ; xi. 15, 16, which appears in ℌ^{A}, apparently belongs also to the secondary recension, and so xvi. 15, 16.

[2] Such expressions as *ἐντολαὶ αἰώνιοι* (i. 5), *γνῶσις ἐντολῶν* (xix. 19), *μακρότης ἡμερῶν* are of this kind: *δένδρον ἀθανασίας* (xix. 19) = עץ חיים: in some cases the renderings amount to mistranslations, e.g. *φωτισμὸς ὑγιείας* (xvii. 26) = אור החיים: see further Smend, p. cxv f.

[3] See e.g. the elaborate list of parallel passages given in Taylor-Schechter, *WBS*, pp. 13–32.

[4] *EB*, iv, col. 4651.

a critical text of the book, has confirmed to us the verdict of the distinguished scholars who first made it available for the scientific world. How far-reaching and transforming its effect on the old currently received Greek Sirach really has been will be apparent to any careful reader who will take the trouble to compare the critical version of the text, as it appears in the following commentary, with that printed in the Authorized and Revised English versions.[1]

§ 4. The Greek Version and the Secondary Greek Text.

Among the versions of Sirach this is the most important as being the earliest. As the Prologue tells us, the Greek translation was made from the original Hebrew by the author's grandson; there was, therefore, not a long period of time between the original writing and its Greek translation. The Greek form of the book was that in which it was first officially received by the Church. Another fact which enhances the importance of this version is that in a number of instances the text represents a purer form of the original Hebrew than that contained in the manuscripts of the Hebrew text recently discovered. This fact makes the use of the Greek version extremely valuable, and indeed indispensable, for the reconstruction of the Hebrew text.

The text of this version, as the critical notes in the commentary will amply show, has come down to us in a bad condition; not infrequently it defies emendation. But in connexion with this two points must be taken into account when using the Greek text for the purpose of reconstructing the Hebrew. In the first place, there is in many cases of an apparently bad condition of the text the possibility that it was always so; that is to say, that it may be due to the initial inability of Ben-Sira's grandson to give a proper translation, so that what appears now as a bad text was so from the beginning. 'Ye are entreated, therefore,' says the translator in his Prologue, 'to make your perusal with favour and attention, and to be indulgent if in any parts of what we have laboured to interpret we may seem to fail in some of the phrases. For things originally spoken in Hebrew have not the same force in them when they are translated into another tongue.' And, secondly, Ben-Sira's grandson clearly does not consider it the duty of a translator to give anything in the shape of a literal translation of his original; he seeks, rightly, to present as far as possible a well-constructed Greek interpretation rather than a slavish reproduction of what he translates; and when, as in the present case, it is poetry which is in question, the translator's freedom is of course increased. These two points must, therefore, not be lost sight of. But when all allowance is made for this, the fact still remains that the Greek text is in a far from satisfactory state; it has suffered greatly from corruptions made in transmission, it has often been inflated by the addition of glosses, inserted sometimes for explanatory, at other times for doctrinal purposes, and further, marginal notes, not originally intended to be additions, have been later on incorporated into the text. Before proceeding, mention may here be made of the great displacement in the Greek text; we quote from Dr. Swete:[2] 'A remarkable divergence in the arrangement of the Septuagint and Old Latin versions of Ecclesiasticus xxx–xxxvi calls for notice. In these chapters the Greek order fails to yield a natural sequence, whereas the Latin arrangement, which is also that of the Syriac and Armenian versions, makes excellent sense. Two sections, xxx. 25–xxxiii. 13*a* (ὡς καλαμώμενος ... φυλὰς Ἰακώβ) and xxxiii. 13*b*–xxxvi. 16*a* (λαμπρὰ καρδία ... ἔσχατος ἠγρύπνησα), have exchanged places in the Latin, and the change is justified by the result. On examination it appears that these sections are nearly equal, containing in B 154 and 159 στίχοι respectively, whilst ℵ exhibits 160 in each.' There can be little doubt that in the *exemplar* from which, so far as is certainly known, all our Greek MSS. of this book 'are ultimately derived the pairs of leaves on which these sections were severally written had been transposed, whereas the Latin translator, working from a MS. in which the transposition had not taken place, has preserved the true order.'[3]

When the various MSS. of the Greek version are examined it is seen that they exhibit great divergences,[4] and these divergences are further increased when the other versions and the patristic quotations are taken into consideration. For English readers the most instructive way of being brought face to face with these variations found in the Greek MSS. is to compare the Revised and Authorized versions together, for in the margin of the Revised version the following note occurs again and again: 'Verse ... is omitted by the best authorities'; by these 'best authorities' are meant the great Greek uncials of the fourth century A.D. (B ℵ A). In the Authorized version, on the other hand, all the verses or parts of verses omitted by the Revised version find a place, the

[1] It should be noted that the displacement in chapter xxxi. 25 f., which has affected all extant Greek MSS., does not appear in 𝔓, which has the true order. See further on this point next section.

[2] *The Old Testament in Greek*, vol. ii. p. vi.

[3] The solution is due to O. F. Fritzsche, *Kurzgefasstes exegetisches Handbuch zu den Apokryphen*, v, pp. 169, 170.

[4] For examples recourse must be had to the *apparatus criticus* in the commentary.

reason for this being that the Greek text of which the Authorized version is a translation is that represented by a number of cursives belonging to the thirteenth and fourteenth centuries, a text which is also to a large extent represented in the Old Latin version, and in the quotations from Sirach in the writings of some of the Church Fathers. These great divergences, then, in the Greek MSS., all of which, as we have just seen, go back to one copy in which the great displacement was already present, occasion a difficult problem. Two points, however, emerge clearly; in the face of the striking and numerous divergences and additions it is evident that all the MSS. cannot ultimately all go back to one original form of text; and, again, since all the extant Greek MSS. are descended from one copy in which the displacement was already found, the divergences and additions must have been in existence at a very early period. The matter can be put in another way; Cod. B, for example, represents one type of Greek text, Codd. 248, 253 represent another type, that, namely, which contains the additions: both have the great displacement, and therefore both, presumably, must ultimately go back to one and the same copy, although in the actual dates of these two manuscripts there is a difference of, roughly speaking, a thousand years. But how can it be possible that these two manuscripts should go back to one original copy when one of them has so many variations and additions as compared with the other? Here let us note another factor which is of real assistance in helping to arrive at a solution of the problem—the Old Latin version, which is a translation of the Greek, has the additions, but has *not* got the displacement. Now the Old Latin version represents a condition of affairs which is older than either the great uncial codices or the cursives as we now have them; this, therefore, proves that the type of text represented by Codd. 248, 253 was extant in some MSS. before the existence of the archetypal MS. which contained the displacement.

It seems clear that there existed at a very early period, probably as early as the last century B.C., two types of the Greek text, a *primary* text, which lies at the back of *all* the Greek MSS., and which represents the original translation of Ben-Sira's grandson, and a *secondary* text. The former of these, the *primary* text, is represented by the great uncials B ℵ A and the group of cursives 68, 155, 157, 296, 307, 308, as well as in the Aldine and Sixtine editions. The *secondary* text is represented in varying degrees by the group of cursives 55, 70, 106, 248, 253, 254, and in the MS. used by the seventh-century corrector of Cod. Siniaticus, $\aleph^{c.a.}$; of these the foremost representative is 248; this type of text is also reflected in the Old Latin and the Syriac versions, as well as in the Syro-Hexaplar (in this latter many of the passages belonging to the secondary text are marked with the asterisk), and in the Complutensian text; it also has the support of Clement of Alexandria and Chrysostom in their quotations from our book. This secondary Greek text was, like the primary one, translated from the Hebrew.[1] In the Talmud, and in some other Jewish writings, there are Rabbinical Hebrew quotations from Sirach which vary from the text of the great uncials (the primary text), but which are represented in the secondary Greek text. Again, in some cases the secondary Hebrew text, remnants of which are preserved in the recently-found Hebrew MSS., is represented in the '248 group', but not in the uncials and their followers. And there is this further fact that many of the additions found in the '248 group' can, on account of their form, only be explained on the supposition of their having been translated direct from a Hebrew original. These points go to show that the additions which belong to the secondary Greek text are not interpolations, but are based in the main upon a secondary Hebrew original.

To come back again, then, to the question with which we started; how are the two (apparently contradictory) following facts to be explained? There are great divergences in our Greek MSS., and yet all go back to one archetype, because all have the same great displacement. The most probable hypothesis would seem to be that the archetype responsible for the displacement was a Greek MS. which contained the primary text represented by the uncials. From this MS. the uncials were directly derived, but at the same time other Greek MSS. were in existence which contained the secondary text and were without the displacement.[2] As copies were multiplied of the former group the distorted order was adhered to, while in some cases the variant text of the MSS. representing the secondary recension was adopted and embodied; hence two varieties of text, both of which contain the displacement, come into existence. The purest extant form of the text of the secondary recension is represented apparently by the Old Latin version; the text of Cod. 248 only partially embodies the variants and additions of the Greek MSS. behind the Old Latin.

But although there are some half-dozen Greek MSS., in addition to the Syriac and Old Latin versions and the Syro-Hexaplar, in which the secondary Greek text is represented, it is certain that no one of these actually contains that text as such; all that can be said is that these authorities

[1] On the primary and secondary *Hebrew* texts see the preceding section, § 3 (esp. (*c*)).
[2] It should be noted that 𝔥 agrees with 𝔏, &c., in having the true order; it has not the displacement.

have to a greater or less extent been influenced by it. Thus, apart from a great many minor additions, the '248 group' of MSS. (including א c.a and the Syro-Hexaplar), taken altogether, have about a hundred and fifty *stichoi* which are not found in the MSS. representing the primary Greek text;[1] of these additions thirty-two are found in the Syriac version, which has, besides these, thirty-seven more of its own; the Old Latin version has a much larger number of its own, together with thirty-three of those found in the '248 group'.[2] The other group of cursive MSS., mentioned above, which with the uncials represent the primary Greek text, were originally based on the secondary text, for they still contain traces of this latter, and must therefore be regarded as the descendants of manuscripts representing the secondary text which were corrected on the basis of the uncials.

Although the fragments of the secondary Greek text now extant are considerable, they are but fragments, and, as the sequel will show, it is reasonable to assume that at one time the divergences between the two types of text must have been considerably greater. The question, therefore, naturally arises why it was that a secondary type of text (in the first instance, as we have seen, existing in Hebrew) should ever have come into existence? The additions found in the '248 group' and other authorities are so considerable that they cannot be accounted for by the assumption that they are merely arbitrary expansions of the text or explanatory glosses; they must have some more specific purpose. We believe that Mr. Hart is right in saying that these additions are 'Fragments of the Wisdom of a Scribe of the Pharisees, and contain tentative Greek renderings of many of the technical terms and watchwords of the sect. As Jesus ben Sira dealt with the earlier Scriptures, so some unknown disciple dealt with his master's composition. He received the deposit and added to it;' the additions are 'traditional accretions, which—so far as external evidence testifies—descended from an immemorial antiquity', though 'they do not necessarily proceed from the hand of one individual'.[3] In fact, the secondary Greek text represents a Pharisaic recension of the original work of Ben-Sira. But before we deal more fully with the subject of this Pharisaic recension, it is important as well as instructive to indicate the standpoint represented by Ben-Sira himself in his work; this will help to explain and justify the existence of the later recension.

Dr. Taylor, in his edition of *Pirqe Aboth* (1897), p. 115, says in reference to the books of the Sadducees: 'We have no authentic remains of Sadducee literature, but it has been suggested with a certain plausibility that the book Ecclesiasticus approximates to the standpoint of the primitive Çaduqin as regards its theology, its sacerdotalism, and its want of sympathy with the *modern* Soferim.' The name of Ezra is significantly omitted from its catalogue of worthies. 'It remains singular', remarks Kuenen, 'that the man whom a later generation compared, nay, made almost equal, to Moses, is passed over in silence. . . . Is it not really most natural that a Jesus ben Sirach did not feel sympathy enough for the first of the Scribes to give him a place of honour in the series of Israel's great men?' The modern *Scribe* was to Ben-Sirach an unworthy descendant of the primitive *Wise*, in accordance with Eliʿezer ha-Gadol's lament over the degeneracy of a later age:

מיום שחרב בית המקדש שרו חכימיא למהוי כספריא כו׳:

'Ex quo Templum devastatum est,[4] coepere *Sapientes* similes esse *Scribis*; Scribae aedituis; Aeditui, vulgo hominum; Vulgus vero hominum in peius indies ruit, nec quis rogans, aut quaerens, superest. Cui ergo innitendum? Patri nostro coelesti?' Dr. Taylor points out, further, the important fact that in the Babylonian Talmud (*Sanhedrin* 100 *b*) the *Books of the Sadducees* and the *Book of Ben-Sira* are placed side by side on the 'Index expurgatorius':

תנא בספרי צדוקים רב יוסף אמר בספר בן סירא נמי אסיר למיקרי:

What Dr. Taylor says receives confirmation from the Hebrew text of the Canticle following l. 12, which was discovered subsequently to the publication of his book: 'Give thanks unto Him that chooseth the sons of Zadok to be priests; for His mercy endureth for ever.'[5] It is also in accordance with the Sadducean theology contained in the book. There is no mention of the existence of angels, and only the scantiest reference to demons (and even this is not certain), the central idea being that of a personified Wisdom.[6] Then, again, special prominence is given to the Law; here we may be permitted to quote again from Dr. Taylor's book, especially as in connexion with what he says a further Sadducean tenet, the denial of a resurrection, is included (in Sirach belief in a hereafter is restricted to the Sheol-conception): 'The Sadducees said, μὴ εἶναι ἀνάστασιν (Matt. xxii. 23), and our Lord answers by an indirect argument from the Pentateuch, instead of bringing

[1] Cod. 248 alone has a hundred and twenty-three.
[2] See Smend, *Die Weisheit des Jesus Sirach*, pp. xciv.
[3] *Op. cit.*, p. 274.
[4] Mishnah, *Sotah* ix. 5 (Surenhusius, vol. iii, p. 308).
[5] These words do not occur in either the Greek or the Syriac versions.
[6] See further § 9, iii.

proofs of a more obvious and direct kind from other parts of Holy Scripture. Hence it has been inferred that they accepted the Pentateuch only, and rejected the Nebiim and Kethubim. On the other side, it is asserted that this inference is wholly inaccurate; that they accepted the three divisions of the Old Testament, and rejected only the extra-scriptural 'Tradition' and scribe-law. The truth, perhaps, lies *in medio*. The Jews in general esteemed, and still esteem, the Pentateuch more highly than the Prophets and the Hagiographa:

ולכך אני אומ׳ שנקראו נביאים וכתובים דברי קבלה שהיו מקובלין [בהן] [1] ובאין מימות משה ומכל מקום אינן שוין לחמשה ספרים שכולן מצות וחוקים כו׳:

'And therefore I say that the *Prophets* and *Hagiographa* are called words of *Qabbalah*, because they were received by διαδοχή, and they came from the days of Moses; *and by no means are they equal to the Five Books*, which are all precepts and ordinances, &c.' If the Sadducees were of the number of those who insisted most strongly upon the superior authority of the Pentateuch, it might in certain cases be nearer to the truth to say that they rejected the Prophets and Hagiographa than to say that they accepted them. If a prophet were quoted in opposition to Moses they would have questioned the authority of the prophet.'[2] The antagonism between the Sadducees and the Pharisees on this point is clearly indicated by Josephus (*Ant.* xiii. 10. 6), where he says: 'The Pharisees have delivered to the people a great many observances by succession [cp. Dr. Taylor's quotation above] from their fathers, which are not written in the laws of Moses; and it is for this reason that the Sadducees reject them, and say, that we are to esteem as obligatory (only) those observances that are in the written word, but are not to observe those things that are derived from the traditions of our forefathers.' The prominence given to the Law in Sirach may, therefore, well indicate the Sadducean attitude. Again, the very meagre reference to the Messianic hope, which is also characteristic of our book, likewise points to its emanating from a Sadducean *milieu*, for the Sadducees did not share the Messianic hopes of the Pharisees; the latter, following the teaching of the Prophets, looked to God to guide the destinies of the nation, while the Sadducees disbelieved in such divine guidance; they 'take away fate, affirming that there is no such thing, and that the events of human affairs are not at its disposal, but they hold that all our actions are in our own power' (Josephus, *Ant.* xiii. 5. 9; cp. *Bell. Iud.* ii. 8. 14). Further, Ben-Sira shows himself to be a Sadducee by his comparatively favourable attitude towards the heathen world; it is true that one of the main objects of his book is to show the superiority of Jewish wisdom over that of the Greeks, but he does not show that contempt for non-Jews which was so characteristic of the Pharisees.

What has been said is sufficient to show that our book, in its original form, represented the Sadducean standpoint; and this fact offers a *prima facie* presumption that with the growth of Pharisaic influence a book which enjoyed so much popularity as Sirach should have been later on moulded, as far as possible, into a form more in accordance with the ideas of the dominant party, and that therefore the additions which constitute the main feature of the secondary Greek text should reflect specifically Pharisaic teaching. As an active movement Pharisaism emerges from the Maccabean conflict with surrounding heathenism and only becomes quiescent after the annihilation of the Jewish national life in the reign of Hadrian (from about 150 B.C.–A.D. 130). The work which the teachers of the Law had begun—viz. the application of the Torah to the practical affairs of everyday life—was continued and made effective by the Pharisees. Elbogen, in his *Religious Views of the Pharisees*, p. 2, says: 'The Pharisees are usually described as the party of narrow legalistic tendencies, and it is forgotten how strenuously they laboured, against the Hellenizing movement, for the maintenance of *Monotheism*; it is forgotten that they built up *religious individualism* and purely *spiritual worship*; that it was through them more especially that *belief in a future life* was deepened; and that they carried on a powerful mission propaganda. They are represented as merely the guardians of the Pentateuch, and the fact is overlooked that they no less esteemed the Prophets and the Hagiographa, and were not less careful to make it their duty, in the weekly expositions of the Scriptures, to preach to the people the truths and hopes of religion out of these books.' Fully in accordance with these religious views of the Pharisees are the three great watchwords in reference to practical religion to be found in Pharisaic literature, viz. תשובה ותפלה וצדקה, i.e. repentance, prayer, and almsgiving (lit. 'righteousness'); these three are mentioned together as the three things which 'avert the evil doom'.[3] In illustration of these Pharisaic religious views we

[1] [Read ואין for בהן ו. Then we get the right sense: 'though they came not' instead of 'and they came.'—Gen. Editor.]

[2] *Op. cit.*, p. 114.

[3] With what is said here regarding the Pharisees cp. Box's 'Survey of Recent Literature on the Pharisees and Sadducees', in the *Review of Theology and Philosophy*, vol. iv, No. 3, pp. 133 ff.

will take a few examples from the additions found in the secondary Greek text in order to show the high probability of their having been put in by a Pharisaic scribe or scribes for the purpose of bringing the book more into harmony with the views of what had become the dominant religious party in Palestine.

We have seen that in contra-distinction to Sadducean teaching the Pharisees believed strongly in the divine governance of the world and in a close relationship between God's children and their heavenly Father; in illustration of this we may turn first to xvi. 10, where the Hebrew text has:

Thus (did it happen) to the six hundred thousand footmen,
Who were destroyed in the arrogancy of their heart.

To this 55 70 248 add:

Chastising, showing mercy, smiting, beating,
The Lord guarded them in mercy and in discipline.

This addition is quite inappropriate where it stands, and has evidently got out of place, but it must evidently have been inserted for the purpose of emphasizing God's activity among His people. A similar emphasis is found in the addition to xvii. 17, where 70 248 insert:

Whom (i.e. *Israel*) *He brought up as His firstborn with severity,*
Yet loving them, imparting to them the light of love, and He forsook them not.

Further, in order to assert more strongly the divine guidance in the world, which, as we have seen from the words of Josephus above, the Sadducees denied, the Pharisaic scribe inserts in the middle of xvi. 19 (as preserved in 248), *The whole world was made, and existeth, by His will*; the fine passage in which Ben-Sira describes the transcendent might of Jahveh scarcely seems to require this insertion, but, as a matter of fact, it does afford a better answer to the words of the supposed sceptic which Ben-Sira uses; the point cannot be grasped unless the passage is quoted; in xvi. 17 it is said:

Say not: 'I am hidden from God,
And in the height who will remember me?
I shall not be noticed among so illustrious a people;
And what is my soul among the mass of the spirits of all the children of men?'

These are the words which a sceptic is supposed to utter, and Ben-Sira answers the objector thus, xvi. 18, 19:

Behold the heavens and the heavens of the heavens,
And the deep, and the earth;
When He treadeth upon them they stand firm,
And when He visiteth them they tremble;
Yea, the bottoms of the mountains, and the foundations of the world,
When He looketh upon them they tremble greatly.

Ben-Sira's reply is a fine one; it is probably true to say that he was a better Scribe than Sadducee in spite of the main tendency of his book (see the exegetical notes in the commentary for the Biblical references echoed in the lines above), but his answer was not sufficiently to the point for the practical Pharisee, whose added words offer in reality a more direct and pointed argument against the erroneous view expressed. Again, for practical purposes, as Hart well points out, 'it was necessary to guard against the tendency towards the Sadducean position, and to assert against them the fact that God governed the world'; and so the Pharisaic glossator adds after xviii. 29 (248):

Better is trust (lit. '*boldness*') *in a single Master* (i.e. *God*),
Than with a dead heart to cling to dead things (i.e. *idols*).[1]

With a similar object the following addition is made after xviii. 2 (70 248): Ben-Sira says, *The Lord alone shall be justified*; then comes the addition:

And there is none other beside Him,
Who guideth the world in the hollow of His hand,
And all things are obedient unto His will;
For He is king of all things, and they are in His power;
He separateth among them the holy things from the common.

[1] κρείσσων παρρησία ἐν δεσπότῃ μόνῳ
ἢ νεκρὰ καρδία νεκρῶν ἀντέχεσθαι (xviii. 29 Cod. 248).

And with the same purpose these striking words are added after xx. 31 (248):

Better is persistent endurance (ὑπομονή) *in seeking the Lord*
Than a driver (τροχηλάτης, 'charioteer') *of his own life without a master.*

Hart (*op. cit.*, p. 280) has some interesting remarks on these passages. 'The description of the typical Sadducee', he says, '*as clinging with dead heart to dead things* goes little beyond the account of Josephus. It is true he never identifies the sect formally with the Epicureans, but he describes them both in similar terms, and indicates his conviction that their denial of Providence leads to virtual atheism. A God who has no oversight of the universe is equivalent to a dead idol. Epicureans and Sadducees might acknowledge the distant existence of the gods of their respective nations,[1] but this formal acknowledgement could not save them from the lash of the orthodox. The Rabbis employ the word Epicurus to denote the fool who said in his heart, There is no God. And such were dead even in their lifetime, as the righteous live on even in death.[2] The picture of the charioteer, who drives his life, which is his chariot, at random, directed by no master, corresponds closely enough with one of the metaphors employed by Josephus: "The Epicureans", he says, "expel Providence from life, and do not admit that God oversees events, nor yet that the universe is guided by the blessed and incorruptible Essence for the permanence of the whole; they say that the world is borne along *lacking a charioteer* and uncared for."'[3]

The divine unity, together with the belief in God as the unique Saviour, is brought out by the addition in 70 248 (with slight variations) to xxiv. 23:

Faint not, but be strong in the Lord,
And cleave unto Him that He may strengthen you.
Cleave unto Him; the Lord, the Almighty, is the one and only God;
And beside Him there is no Saviour.

This passage offers one of the most striking instances of the Pharisaic doctrine of God, both as regards the Divine personality as well as the relationship between Him and His true worshippers. This double aspect of Pharisaic doctrine, which has not always been adequately recognized, has been insisted upon with some emphasis by a recent writer. 'It is well', he says, 'to lay stress upon the Pharisaic belief in the nearness of God and the directness of access to Him; also to make clear the fact that emphatic resistance was offered by the Pharisees to any idea of a plurality of Divine persons. . . . Of course it was never denied that God was the Almighty, the Lord of all worlds, supreme over everything. Indeed, that was affirmed over and over again, and is one of the axioms of Pharisaic belief. But, whatever other Jews may have done under the influence of Hellenism, the Pharisees never doubted for a moment that God Himself, the one supreme God, was actually near to every one of His people; "near in every kind of nearness," as it was said (*Jer. Berak.* 13 *a*).'[4]

The cleaving unto the Lord so strongly emphasized in the last-quoted addition leads us on to illustrate the Pharisaic characteristic of pietism; personal religion, that religious individualism which did so much to foster spiritual worship, is brought out in a number of the additions found in the secondary Greek text. Not that Ben-Sira was himself wanting in deep piety, but as compared with the Pharisaic ideal it is not surprising to find that the book was considered in some respects wanting, and that it seemed to the more ardent religious temperament of the Pharisees as not sufficiently expressive of the close relationship between God and His pious ones. For example, Ben-Sira says in i. 12:

The fear of the Lord delighteth the heart,
And giveth gladness, and joy, and length of days;

but the Pharisee deepens the sentiment by adding (70 253):

The fear of the Lord is a gift from the Lord,
For it setteth [men] upon paths of love.

In the same way, a few verses further on (16 f.), Ben-Sira's words:

To fear the Lord is the fullness of wisdom,
And she satiateth men with her fruits;

[1] Cp. xvii. 17.

[2] *Jer. Berakh.* ii. 3 (4 D): 'For the living know that they shall die; these are the righteous, who even in their death are called living. But the dead know not anything; these are the wicked, who though living are called dead, for it is said, For I have no pleasure in the death of המת.'

[3] *Antiq.* x. 11. 7. The word which Josephus uses for 'charioteer' is, however, not the same one which occurs in our book.

[4] Herford, *Pharisaism*, p. 259 f., and see also the pages that follow.

are supplemented by the similar thought (70 248):

And both are gifts of God unto [illegible].

Few better examples could be given illustrative of the trust which a pious Pharisee had in the mercy of God than the words added to xvii. 20. Ben-Sira says:

Their iniquities are not hid from Him,
And all their sins are [inscribed] before the Lord.

To this the Pharisaic glossator adds (70 248):

But the Lord, being merciful, knowing also (*that they are made in*) *His own image,*
Spared them, and forsook them not, nor cast them off.

The closeness of God to those who love Him—a characteristic Pharisaic doctrine, as we have seen—receives illustration from the following addition in 70 248 to xvii. 26*a*:

For He Himself will lead (*thee*) *out of darkness unto the light of salvation.*

The religious individualism of the Pharisee is brought out again in the addition of these words to xxiii. 5 in 248:

And Him that desireth to serve Thee
Do Thou ever hold up.

This is added in spite of the fact that the passage xxiii. 1–6 is one of the most striking ones expressive of personal religion in the whole book. One more example of this characteristic *trait* of the best Pharisaic spirit may be given; Ben-Sira says in xxv. 11:

The fear of the Lord surpasseth all things,
He that holdeth it, to whom shall he be likened?

The addition in 70, 248 breathes a deeper personal religion:

The beginning of the fear of the Lord is to love Him;
And the beginning of faith is to cleave unto Him.

Among the characteristic watchwords of the Pharisees few, if any, occupied a more prominent position than 'repentance' (תשובה); 'in their efforts to confirm the faith of their own people and to effect the conversion of those without, the Pharisees, like the Prophets and the Rabbis, were concerned to insist upon the paramount importanee of repentance. For the latter it was the condition of reception, and for the former it was the means of restoration. It was the function of the Pharisee to *convict* all men everywhere of their need of repentance.'[1] A good illustration of this occurs in the Pharisaic addition to xx. 2; Ben-Sira (according to the Syriac version, which has preserved the best text here,—the Hebrew is wanting) says:

He that reproveth a sinner getteth no thanks;
But let him that maketh confession be spared humiliation.

To this is added in 70 248 (the Old Latin version also has the words, but in a wrong place):

How good it is when he who is reproved manifesteth repentance,
For thus wilt thou escape wilful sin.[2]

The phrase *φανερῶσαι μετάνοιαν* certainly connotes more fullness of meaning than the one Ben-Sira uses in this connexion, *δεῖξον ἐπιστροφήν* (xviii. 21); the former, as Hart well puts it, 'includes all forms of outward manifestation of the inner change of mind.' Again, in xvii. 22, Ben-Sira says:

The righteousness of men is to Him as a signet,
And the mercy of man He preserveth as the apple of an eye;

but according to the Pharisaic glossator the real preciousness of man in God's sight lies in the fact that repentance, divinely accorded, is manifested; therefore he adds:

Granting repentance to His sons and daughters (70 248).

[1] Hart, *op. cit.*, p. 305. For instructive quotations from Rabbinical literature on the Pharisaic doctrine of repentance, see Herford, *op. cit.*, pp. 211–15.
[2] An almost identical addition occurs in 70 248 after xx. 8.

There are at least two of the additions in the secondary Greek text which contain a reference to the future life, a doctrine the development of which the Pharisees did much to foster. In xvi. 22, where Ben-Sira puts the following words into the mouth of a supposed sceptic:

My righteous dealing, who declareth it?
And what hope (is there), for the decree is distant?

The Pharisaic glossator adds what is evidently intended to be a reference to future judgement in saying:

And the trying of all things is not until the end (70 106 248).[1]

But more pointed is the longer addition found in 70 248 after xix. 17:

The fear of the Lord is the beginning of acceptance (by Him),
And wisdom will gain love from Him.
The knowledge of the Lord is life-giving instruction;
And they who do the things that are pleasing unto Him shall pluck the fruit of the tree of immortality.

There are also, as Hart points out (*op. cit.*, p. 312), one or two references among the additions to the Future Life under the term 'Holy Age', but as the references occur only in the Old Latin version 'they are perhaps to be relegated to a lower place in the succession of scribes who followed Ben-Sira . . . but their contexts contain nothing that is demonstrably Christian'. Thus in xviii. 27 the Old Latin has this addition:

Go to the lot of the Holy Age
With the living and them that offer thanksgiving to God.

And in xxiv. 32:

I will leave it to them that seek wisdom,
And I will not leave their progeny until the Holy Age.

'Speaking generally, there does not appear to be any definite demarcation of the future from the present in these fragments. The mercy which rewards the faithful here differs in degree perhaps, but not in kind, from that which awaits them hereafter.'

We have dealt only with some examples of the additions found in Greek MSS. which represent to a greater or lesser degree the secondary Greek text; the character of this text could be still further illustrated by taking the Old Latin version into consideration, for this version has retained a number of the additions belonging to the secondary Greek text which have disappeared from all extant Greek MSS.;[2] but enough has been said to show that this text, translated originally from the Hebrew, has with every justification been called the Pharisaic recension of Sirach. For illustrations from the Old Latin version reference may be made to Hart's book, pp. 289 ff., 313, in connexion with which should be read Herford's *Pharisaism*, pp. 267–281.

Turning now once more to the original translation of Ben-Sira's grandson, there are some special points to be noticed. His knowledge of the Septuagint is very considerable; as Smend has pointed out, he frequently utilized this for the purposes of a lexicon. But his use of the Septuagint varies with the different divisions of the Old Testament; thus, he appears to be most familiar with the Greek text of the Pentateuch, of which he makes a far greater use than of the two other divisions; for example, the words in xx. 29 *δῶρα ἀποτυφλοῖ ὀφθαλμοὺς σοφῶν* are a verbal quotation from the Septuagint of Deut. xvi. 19; the same is the case in xxiv. 23, which contains an exact quotation from Septuagint of Deut. xxxiii. 4; cp. also xxiv. 15 with the Septuagint of Exod. xxx. 23 f., 34; xlix. 1 with the Septuagint of Exod. xxxv. 28, &c. His use of the Greek version of the prophetical books is considerably less, though in a variety of instances he shows his knowledge of this (e.g. with xlviii. 10 cp. Mal. iii. 24, and xlix. 7 with Jer. i. 10). But he does not seem to have had any acquaintance with a Greek translation of the *Hagiographa*.

It is very probable that in his desire to attain a more than ordinary knowledge of Greek Ben-Sira's grandson was to some extent versed in the general literature of the Greeks; he uses over two hundred words which do not occur elsewhere in the Septuagint;[3] he is fond of using compound

[1] These words are also preserved in the Old Latin version.
[2] See further § 5, ii.
[3] Smend, *Die Weisheit des Jesus Sirach*, p. lxiv.

verbs instead of the simple forms, and he shows his liking for variety by rendering the same Hebrew word by different Greek ones. Not infrequently he expands his translation of the Hebrew by adding an explanatory word or two (see e.g. the Hebrew and Greek of viii. 12, xl. 19, xli. 9); he also often renders concrete words and expressions by abstract ones. The difference between the Greek of the Prologue and that of the book itself is so marked that Smend is justified in believing that Ben-Sira's grandson was helped in composing the former.[1]

§ 5. Other Ancient Versions.

i. *The Syriac Version.*

It is impossible to fix the date of the Syriac version of our book with any certainty; the earliest known MS. (Cod. Mus. Brit. 12142) belongs to the sixth century, but this MS. contains already a very large number of scribal errors, which points to a long previous history; it seems, however, to be the parent of all other extant Syriac MSS. of Sirach, for its corruptions occur in all of them. Wright, in speaking of the Syriac translations of the Old Testament Apocrypha, the dates of which are quite unknown, says that 'it seems tolerably certain that alterations were made from time to time with a view to harmonizing the Syriac text with that of the Septuagint',[2] a process which Burkitt thinks 'may have begun as early as the episcopate of Palut (about A.D. 200)', which would imply the existence of a Syriac version some time previous to this date.

Although some scholars long ago sought to show that the Syriac version of Sirach was a translation from the Hebrew, their contention was combated by Syriac scholars, who maintained that it was translated from the Greek.[3] The discovery of the Hebrew text has, however, definitely settled the matter; if there was reason to believe, as was certainly the case, that the Syriac text itself presented indications of its having been translated from Hebrew and not from Greek, there is absolutely no doubt about this now that we can compare the Syriac with the Hebrew. Nevertheless, the Syriac translation was not made from the *original* form of the Hebrew, though from a form which seems to have been in many respects nearer to the original form than that represented in the recently found Hebrew MSS. This fact makes the Syriac version valuable for correcting, where necessary, the Hebrew text in the form in which we now have it; and for those large portions of the book of which the Hebrew text has not been found the Syriac is, of course, indispensable. Another fact which makes the Syriac version valuable is that it contains a number of verses and parts of verses which are only found elsewhere either in the Hebrew alone, or in isolated Greek MSS., in some few cases also in the Old Latin version.[4] 'In some instances the Syriac has retained the correct text where both the Hebrew and the Greek agree in having gone astray. But in a considerable number of passages the Syriac is not a translation of the Hebrew, but of the Greek;[5] it is possible that the reason of this was that in such cases the Greek version represented what the original Syriac translator believed to be the reflection of a more original form of the Hebrew than that which he had before him; or else, and this is more probable, it may be that the Syriac, as we now have it, has been corrected on the basis of the Greek; this would have been a very natural proceeding (even if a comparatively speaking pure Hebrew text had been available) at a time when the Greek Bible was regarded in the Christian Church as more authoritative than the Hebrew. That the Syriac translator of Sirach was a Christian seems more than probable. The Greek MS. or MSS. which the Syriac translator made use of contained elements representing the secondary Greek text, and it was a text which had undergone deterioration in other respects.'[6] In any case, the Syriac version is one which has a distinct value; nevertheless it must be used with caution, for, in spite of what has been said about its usefulness and importance, it has some grave blemishes which must be taken into consideration when utilizing it. Smend says it is the worst piece of translation in the whole Syriac Bible, though in many cases it is uncertain in what proportion its mistakes are due to the translator himself, or to the Hebrew text which he had before him, or to some deteriorated Greek text which he utilized, or to textual corruptions which crept in during the process of transmission. But, however this may be, the fact remains that the work of translation has been done carelessly and without much trouble having been expended upon it; paraphrases abound; sometimes they are of a purely arbitrary character, at other times they

[1] For many examples illustrating what has been said about the Greek translation, see Smend, *op. cit.*, pp. lxii–lxvii.

[2] *Syriac Literature*, p. 4, quoted by Burkitt in *EB*, iv. 5026.

[3] Smend, *op. cit.*, p. cxxxvi.

[4] See e.g. ii. 18 *d*, xxv. 8 *b*, xlvii. 23 *e*, xlviii. 12 *c*, *d*, li. 11 *d*, 19 *d*, 26 *d*.

[5] See e.g. xxvi. 19–27, xliii. 1–10.

[6] Oesterley, *Ecclesiasticus*, in the Cambridge Bible, p. ci.

apparently represent what the translator believed to be the general meaning of the original, which he did not understand in all its details; in yet other cases these paraphrases were evidently due to the desire to give a Christian sense to a passage. But perhaps the most serious blemish in this version is the large number of omissions; Smend says that these amount to 370 *stichoi*, or one-ninth of the whole book. In many cases it is evident that the Syriac translator had what seemed to him good reasons for omitting certain passages; thus, as a Christian he felt justified in omitting such words as these:

Thanksgiving perisheth from the dead as from one that is not,
(But) he that liveth and is in health praiseth the Lord (xvii. 28).

It was probably owing to an anti-Jewish tendency that he omitted xxxvii. 25:

The life of a man (numbers) days but few,
But the life of Jeshurun days innumerable.

A similar reason would account for the omission of xxxviii. 11, xlv. 8–14, parts of l. 18–21, and the litany after li. 12, though this last is also omitted in the Greek version. Quite comprehensible are the omissions of xxxiii. 26 (𝔊 xxx. 35) and xxxvi. 21, 23 (𝔊 26, 28); but why such passages, e.g., as xli. 14—xlii. 2, and most of xliii. 11–33 should have been passed over it is impossible to say, excepting on the supposition that they are difficult ones to translate, and the Syriac translator did not feel inclined to undertake the task.

It will thus be seen that while the Syriac version has a distinct value of its own and can certainly not be neglected, it must nevertheless be used with great caution; indeed, the student will be wise never to utilize it without at the same time referring to the Greek. It should be added that in this version the right order of the chapters is preserved.

ii. *The Old Latin Version.*

This is the oldest [1] and most important of the daughter-versions of the Greek. Like the Syriac version, while in some respects it is valuable for correcting the Greek, in other respects it presents grave drawbacks. As we shall see later on (§ 8), Jerome left the Latin text of Sirach as he found it—a matter for congratulation, since as the version now stands it contains many really ancient elements which would probably have been lost altogether if Jerome had undertaken a translation of his own. That it contains, as we have already seen (p. 281), the chapters in the right order is also a fact of importance. But the text of the Old Latin version has come down to us in a deplorable condition, added to which it has the further disadvantage of having been made from a Greek text which was in a worse condition than that represented by any extant Greek MS. Moreover, the Old Latin text is full of scribal errors, and many arbitrary alterations have been introduced; quotations from this version in the writings of the Latin Fathers are of little use for emending its text. Emendation is made the more difficult in that the original translation was apparently subjected to constant correction on the basis of different Greek texts; one example out of a great many may be given: in xiii. 8 the Greek text runs:

πρόσεχε μὴ ἀποπλανηθῇς (V 106 248 253 Syro-Hex add *τῇ διανοίᾳ σου*),
καὶ μὴ ταπεινωθῇς ἐν εὐφροσύνῃ (248, &c. add *καρδίας*) *σου.*

For this the Latin has:

Attende ne seductus
In stultitiam humilieris.
Noli esse humilis in sapientia tua,
Ne humiliatus in stultitiam seducaris (= *vv.* 10, 11 in Latin).

In cases like this the question arises as to whether the additions have been inserted from other Latin texts, or whether they are doublets due to the incorporation of marginal notes into the text; in other words, do they represent different Greek texts from which Latin translations were made, or are they merely Latin variations of one and the same Greek text? It is by no means always possible to decide which, a fact which materially increases one's difficulties when utilizing the Latin version.

[1] Of its date nothing further can be said, but the earliest known citations are found in Cyprian.

The question as to whether the Old Latin version was made from a MS. representing the primary or secondary Greek text is one of extreme complexity; at first sight one would feel impelled to postulate the secondary Greek text as the basis of the Latin version, but the fact that many of the additions belonging to the secondary Greek text are preserved in the Syro-Hexaplar but not in the Old Latin goes to show that the latter cannot have been made *directly* from the secondary Greek text. And yet, as Smend has shown, the copy from which the Old Latin was made was more influenced by the secondary Greek text than any other known Greek MS., though that copy did not in itself represent the secondary Greek text; for, as Smend says, 'trotz aller sekundären Elemente, die die Vorlage enthielt, und trotz aller Bearbeitung, von der der ursprüngliche Text des Lateiners betroffen sein mag, — durch Massenbeobachtung lässt sich nachweisen, dass die Vorlage des Lateiners im Wesentlichen der griechische Vulgärtext war, den der Lateiner nicht nur in alten guten Lesarten, die freilich auch aus Gr. II' (i.e. the secondary Greek text) 'stammen könnten, sondern auch in höchst sekundärer Entartung vor sich hatte' (*op. cit.*, p. cxxiv). The proof of this is minutely worked out by him. The conclusion which Smend draws from this complicated state of affairs is that the foundation of the text from which the Old Latin Version was made was the primary Greek one, but that in that text was incorporated a later recension of the secondary Greek text, the offspring, perhaps, of a Hebrew original.[1] And it must be confessed that only on this hypothesis can all the phenomena of the Old Latin version be explained.

iii. *The Syro-Hexaplar.*

This is the Syriac version made by Paul of Tella from the Greek (*c.* A.D. 616). 'If we retain the designation Syro-Hexaplar,' says Nestle, 'we must bear in mind that Sirach had no place in Origen's Hexapla; but in one particular respect this Syriac version reminds us of the Hexapla; one of the critical marks of Origen, the asteriscus, appears also in Sirach, at least in its first part up to chap. xiii.'[2] Hart, on the other hand, remarks: 'Origen valued the Book of Jesus Ben-Sira, and its text required a settlement. It seems reasonable to accept the evidence—direct and indirect—as it stands, and to conclude that he attempted to purge the current Greek version of its accretions, and that his disciples removed them bodily, and sometimes parts of the true text with them' (*op. cit.*, p. 359). It is true we are nowhere told that Origen incorporated the books of the Apocrypha in his Hexapla, but the way in which he quotes from them, speaking of them as 'Holy Scripture' (see below, § 8), would naturally lead to the supposition that he did so incorporate them. There is also the fact that in the Syro-Hexaplar the Book of Baruch undergoes much the same treatment with regard to the Hexaplaric signs as the canonical books. As Smend says: 'The excellence of Syro-Hexaplaric Sirach text would not be unworthy of Origen.' In general the text of this version follows very closely a MS. with which Cod. 253 was intimately related, but the translator also utilized the Peshiṭta when for one reason or another he found it convenient to do so. The translation is in parts very free. There are a number of marginal notes which were presumably taken from the Greek MS. which the translator had before him; these not infrequently present the better reading.

iv. *The Sahidic Version.*

The MS. containing this version, which is based on a Greek text closely related to the Greek uncials, has suffered a good deal of mutilation; the Prologue is almost entirely wanting through this cause; in addition to this a good many *stichoi* are omitted. Other Coptic versions of more or less value are the Bohairic and Akmimic; only fragmentary remnants of these are extant. For the published texts of them see Smend, *op. cit.*, p. cxxx f.

v. *The Ethiopic Version.*

This version is rendered from the Greek, of which it is often a literal translation, but in his desire to make the meaning of the original before him clear the translator often interprets, i. e. he gives a paraphrastic rendering. Smend (*op. cit.*, p. cxxxii) gives as an example of this xxiv. 21, where for the Greek:

οἱ ἐσθίοντές με ἔτι πεινάσουσιν, καὶ οἱ πίνοντές με ἔτι διψήσουσιν,

[1] Cp. the words of Herkenne (*De Veteris Latinae Ecclesiastici capitibus i–xliii* [1899]): 'Nititur Vetus Latina textu vulgari Graeco ad textum Hebraicum alius recensionis Graece castigato'; quoted by Nestle in Hastings's *DB*, iv. 545.

[2] In Hastings's *DB*, iv. 544. There are altogether forty-five asterisks, about twenty of which are placed against words and sentences belonging to the secondary Greek text.

the Ethiopic has:

They that eat me, eat me and are not satisfied,
And they that drink me, drink me and are not satisfied.

The value of this version is not infrequently marred by the fact that its renderings only partially represent the Greek, the reason being presumably that the Ethiopic translator did not really understand what was before him and made a guess at the meaning. Smend quotes Dillmann (who has edited this version, *V.T. Aethiopici*, tom. v, Berol. 1894) to the effect that the Ethiopic has been subjected to revision in later times on the basis of the Greek text; he does not believe it possible to restore the Ethiopic text to its original form from the MSS. which are now extant. Upon the whole the Ethiopic follows the text of Cod. B; the MS. from which the version was made, however, represented in some cases a purer, in others a more corrupt, form of text than that of Cod. B. Here and there the Ethiopic is of value for correcting the Greek.

vi. *The Armenian Version.*

This version exists in two forms, one translated from the Old Latin, and the other from the Greek; the former is but of small value for text-critical purposes. The latter is of more use, but a good deal of the text is wanting, viz. xxxvi. 1–xxxviii. 14, xliii–li, besides a number of isolated passages. On the other hand, it has some additions which are singular to it; see Herkenne, *Armenischer Sirach*, p. 30 ff.

vii. *The Slavonic Version.*

One point of importance regarding this version is that it sometimes agrees with the Old Latin against all extant Greek authorities; moreover, in agreement with the Old Latin and against all known Greek MSS. (with the exception of Cod. 248) it has xxx. 25–xxxiii. 13 *a* in the right place. According to Margoliouth it 'follows a text similar to that of the Complutensian edition, but with only a portion of the additions'.[1] It has been revised from the Syro-Hexaplar.

viii. *The Arabic Version.*

This is a translation of the Peshiṭta (Syriac Vulgate). 'The translator', says Smend, 'was not concerned to offer a careful translation of his copy; he desired rather to present an elegantly-written Arabic book.' His translation is, therefore, throughout a free one, and he inserts additions of his own. The text, or that of the MS. from which it was made, has been influenced by the Greek. But the manifold *lacunae* of the Syriac version recur in the Arabic. The version is of but small value.

§ 6. Authorship and Date.

i. *The name and personality of the author.* In the MSS. of the Greek Bible the author of our book is called Ἰησοῦς Σειράχ, or more briefly Σειράχ[2]; among the later Jews בן סירא, and so in the MSS. of the Syriac Bible בר סירא (or in a less authentic form בר אסירא, i.e. *Son of the Captive*).

The full name of the author is given in the body of the book, in l. 27, which in 𝕳 appears as *Simeon the son of Jeshua (Jesus) the son of Eleazar the son of Sira* (in Hebrew שמעון בן ישוע בן אלעזר בן סירא).[3] For this 𝕲 has: Ἰησοῦς υἱὸς Σειρὰχ Ἐλεαζάρου ὁ Ἱεροσολυμείτης (but 248 Complut. Sixtine > Ἐλεαζάρου). In 𝕾 this passage is omitted altogether; the Syro-Hexaplar has: *Jesus the son of Sirach of Eliezer.* The usual designation of the author in the Syriac MSS. of the Bible is: *Jesus the son of Simeon.*[4]

Now as the author's grandson states explicitly in the Greek Prologue to his version of the book that his grandfather's name was *Jesus* (Ἰησοῦς), it is likely that the name *Simeon* is an intrusion in the text of 𝕳; this is made exceedingly probable when it is seen that the clause l. 27, as it appears in 𝕳, is overloaded; by the removal of שמעון בן symmetry is restored, and the line may be read with Smend:

לישוע בן אלעזר בן סירא:

Of Jesus ben Eleazar ben Sira.

[1] Quoted by Nestle in Hastings's *DB*, iv. 544.

[2] Σειράχ (Sirach) is the Greek form of Sira (סירא), the final χ being added in the Greek form of the word to indicate that it is indeclinable; so Ἀκελδαμάχ Acts i. 19, in some MSS., for Ἀκελδαμά: cp. Dalman, *Grammatik d. jüdisch-palästinischen Aramäisch*[2], pp. 137, 202.

[3] This form of the name reappears twice in the Hebrew subscription of the book, which follows li. 30.

[4] Nestle (*HDB*, iv. 541 *b*) remarks that the name Simeon 'is firmly attached to the author of this book in the Syriac Church'.

Thus the name of the author was *Jesus*, and his grandfather's name *Sira*; the use of a grandfather's (or earlier ancestor's) name as a patronymic (with *Ben* prefixed) was not uncommon, especially when a father's name was not sufficiently distinctive. The intruding *Simeon* may have been derived from l. 1 (the name of the High-Priest), and in this way may have come erroneously to be attached to the name of the author of the book.[1]

From the *data* supplied by the book itself it may be inferred that Ben-Sira was a professed student and teacher of 'wisdom'. As a 'scribe' (he is described in the Prologue as ἀναγινώσκων = סופר)—for by this time 'scribe' and 'wise' had become amalgamated—he imparted instruction to young members of the Jerusalem aristocracy, who assembled in his 'house of instruction' (בית מדרש li. 23); and there, doubtless, he lectured on matters of jurisprudence, as well as ethics, in the manner congenial to the Teachers of the Law (cp. xxiii. 11, 23). Ben-Sira, however, belonged to the earlier *Sōferîm* in whom the spirit pervading the Wisdom-Literature was still strong. Though possessed with a deep sense of Israel's unique position among the nations, the class of teachers to which Ben-Sira belonged was animated by a broad and tolerant spirit that could take a genial view of life as a whole. This spirit pervades the book. It is marked by sound piety mixed with a thorough knowledge of human nature, and a sympathetic and cultivated appreciation of the amenities of the social side of life. Both the follies and the heroism of the fanatic are carefully avoided by Ben-Sira. When he sings the praise of the ideal scribe (xxxix. 1–11) we doubtless have in the description a piece of self-revelation of the author:

Not so he that applieth himself to the fear of God,
And to set his mind upon the Law of the Most High;
Who searcheth out the wisdom of all the ancients,
And is occupied with the prophets of old;
Who heedeth the discourses of men of renown,
And entereth into the deep things of parables;
Searcheth out the hidden meaning of proverbs,
And is conversant with the dark sayings of parables.

Court life and foreign travel are part of his experience:

Who serveth among great men,
And appeareth before princes;
Who travelleth through the lands of the peoples,
Testeth good and evil among men.

It has been suggested that our author may have travelled as a young man, and at one time have been in the service of one of the Greek kings (successors of Alexander the Great), perhaps Ptolemy IV (220–204 B.C.). During these experiences, it would seem, he encountered much personal danger:

In my journeying I have seen much,
And many things have befallen me:
Often was I in danger even unto death,
But was preserved . . . (xxxiv. 11–12).

The opening verses of chap. li refer, in a tone of unusually deep feeling, to deliverance from a grievous danger which seriously threatened the author's life. This may have been, as has been suggested, some peril of a political kind, possibly connected with his life at court or with his responsible public life. He alludes in this passage more than once to 'cunning lips' and 'framers of lies', the result of whose machinations was that his

Soul drew nigh unto death . . . . . .
And I turned about on every side, yet there was none to help me.

The author's relation to contemporary Jewish life, as revealed in his book, could not be better summed up than in the words of Edersheim. 'The book of Ben-Sira', he says, 'represents an orthodox, but moderate and cold, Judaism—before there were either Pharisees or Sadducees; before these two directions assumed separate form under the combined influence of political circumstances and theological controversies. In short, it contains, as yet undistinguished and mostly in

[1] Schechter, however, thinks that the author's name may have been *Simeon* (or *Simon*): 'Probably he was so called after the High-Priest Simeon whose younger contemporary he was—a custom usual enough among the Jews at a very early period' (*WBS*, p. 65).

germ, all the elements developed in the later history of Jewish religious thinking. But beyond all this the book throws welcome light on the period in which it was written. If we would know what a cultured, liberal, and yet genuine Jew had thought and felt in view of the great questions of the day; if we would gain insight into the state of public opinion, morals, society, and even of manners at that period—we find the materials for it in the book Ecclesiasticus.'[1]

ii. *The date of composition of the Book.* The two crucial factors for determining the date of the book's composition are (*a*) the identity of the High-Priest Simon, who is the subject of the eulogium in ch. l; and (*b*) what is meant by 'the thirty-eighth year' in the Prologue of the Greek translation?

(*a*) *Simon I or Simon II?* With whom is the Simon son of Jochanan (so 𝔥: but 𝔊 Onias), mentioned in l. 1 f., to be identified? From the glowing description which is given by Ben-Sira of this High-Priest it has been surmised, with considerable plausibility, that our author wrote of one whom he had actually seen officiating in the sanctuary. The Simon referred to has been identified with 'Simon the Just' (שמעון הצדיק), who, again, is identified by some scholars with Simon I, son of Onias I, and grandson of Jaddua (he flourished 310–291 or 300–270 B.C.), according to others with Simon II (219–199 B.C.) son of Onias II. As far as Ben-Sira's description is concerned it would fit either of these identifications. The question of date must be determined on other grounds.

Josephus (*Ant.* xii. 2. 5) relates of Simon I that, on account of his piety, he was surnamed 'the Just'. Reference to Simon II is made in *Ant.* xii. 4. 10 f. Herzfeld identifies the 'Simon the Just' (שמעון הצדיק) of *Pirqe Aboth* iii. 1 with Simon II, and fixes the date of his high-priesthood as 226–198 B.C. (Zunz 221–201 B.C.); see Dr. C. Taylor's note on *Aboth* ii. 1. Derenbourg also (*Essai sur l'histoire et la géographie de la Palestine*, p. 46 f.) argues strongly in favour of the identification of Simon the Just, whose memory is preserved in Rabbinic tradition, with Simon II. It is this Simon, according to Derenbourg, who is the subject of Sirach l. Josephus' application of the epithet ('the Just') to Simon I is a mistake.

(*b*) *The date in the Prologue.* An explicit indication of date is given in the Greek Prologue written by the translator as a preface to his Greek translation of the book. In this the translator says he came to Egypt 'in the thirty-eighth year ἐπὶ τοῦ Εὐεργέτου Βασιλέως'. This, it is true, has been taken by some scholars to mean in the thirty-eighth year of the translator's age 'under king Euergetes'. If this were right it would be impossible to say what date is meant, as we have no other means for determining when the translator was born, or which king Euergetes is referred to. As there is no particular reason why the translator should have stated his age in this context, it is natural to interpret 'the thirty-eighth under king Euergetes' as referring to the thirty-eighth regnal year of the king so named. This limits the reference to the two Ptolemies, among the Egyptian kings, who were called Euergetes: of these Euergetes I reigned only twenty-five years (247–222 B.C.), and is thus excluded; Euergetes II, surnamed Physcon, reigned in all fifty-four years, partly as joint king (170–145) and partly as sole king (145–116). Reckoning from this king's accession his thirty-eighth regnal year would be 132 B.C. It may be concluded, therefore, that the translator reached Egypt in this year, and completed his translation of the book some few years later (between 132 and 116; see the note on line 15 of the Prologue in the following commentary).

The translator calls the author of the original book his πάππος, a term which may be interpreted in its usual sense of 'grandfather'.[2] The composition of the original book of Ben-Sira may, therefore, be assigned to the first quarter of the second century B.C. (200–175 B.C.). The author would thus have been a younger contemporary of the High-Priest Simon II, and could have witnessed a service on the Day of Atonement in the temple in which Simon took part. The tone of the references to Simon in ch. l suggests that when Ben-Sira wrote Simon had been dead for some time. This rather suggests a date about 180–175 B.C. for the actual composition of the book. As there is no allusion in the book to the events that led up to the Maccabean conflict the date cannot well be placed later than 175 B.C.

The internal evidence of the book itself favours the suggested date—especially the traces of Greek influence on the thought; notably the personification of Wisdom (cp. esp. ch. xxiv), and the acquaintance shown with Greek customs, such as the use of music at feasts (xxxv. 3–6).

Recently, however, a much earlier reckoning for the date in the Prologue has been proposed on new grounds and maintained by Mr. J. H. A. Hart.[3] Hart thinks it incredible that a Jew from the outside world should have visited and stayed for any length of time to work in Egypt in the reign of Euergetes II, who was notoriously hostile to Jews, and, in fact, to all foreigners. He

[1] In Wace's *Apocrypha* ii. 2 (Introduction to Ecclesiasticus).

[2] 'It sometimes means "ancestor"; but in such cases the connexion usually indicates the wider sense' (Seligmann, *EB*, ii, col. 1171, note 3).

[3] *Ecclesiasticus in Greek*, pp. 249 ff.

accordingly proposes to interpret the date in the Prologue as follows: the preposition ἐπί—though he allows that it is sometimes used in Greek translations of Hebrew date-specifications in a pleonastic sense = ὡς, and that this usage can be paralleled from the papyri and inscriptions (e.g. the Rosetta stone)—is not, as it is used in the Prologue, without definite significance, and merely a meaningless part of an established formula. While admitting that the words might conceivably mean the thirty-eighth year of Euergetes II, yet the number 'may equally well belong to some familiar and therefore unspecified era', and that this is the common Egyptian era which begins with the accession of each king and ends with his death. Ptolemy Philadelphus (284–247 B.C.) was succeeded by Euergetes I in the thirty-eighth year of the reign of the former, i.e. Euergetes I ascended the throne in the thirty-eighth year of the reign of Philadelphus (247 B.C.). The formula in the Prologue therefore means that the grandson of Ben-Sira came to Egypt in the thirty-eighth year of the era of Ptolemy Philadelphus, but after Euergetes I had come to the throne. Thus, according to Hart, the younger Ben-Sira came to Egypt in the year 247 B.C., and stayed there during the whole reign of Euergetes, till his death in 222 B.C.[1] These results would necessitate placing the composition of the original book of Ben-Sira at least a century before the commonly received date (i.e. 300–275 B.C.).

Hart's arguments are unconvincing. In particular he seems to exaggerate the hostility of Ptolemy Physcon to the Jews in Alexandria. The Jews were persecuted for a time by this king, not on account of their religion, but for political reasons. 'With the establishment of order, peace was doubtless restored to the Jews also.'[2] Willrich, indeed, has given good reasons[3] for believing that this Ptolemy was far from being hostile to the Jews in general. It has been shown that he possessed many Jewish officials, and that the Jews prospered and increased in Egypt under his rule exceedingly. The proposed explanation of the date is also anything but convincing. If the translator wished to say that he arrived in Egypt in the year which concluded the reign of Philadelphus and was marked by the accession of Euergetes (I) he might have written 'in the thirty-eighth year of Philadelphus ἐπὶ τοῦ Εὐεργέτου βασιλέως'. But it is difficult to imagine him writing at least twenty-five years after the era of Philadelphus had come to an end:[4] 'in the thirty-eighth year ἐπὶ τοῦ Εὐεργέτου βασιλέως'. On Hart's own showing a new era had intervened (that of Euergetes I); why then should not the first year of this era have been specified distinctly, if it was meant? Further, Hart's criticism of the very strong examples adduced by Deissmann[5] of the independent use of ἐπί in such date-specifications cannot be said to impair their cogency. The internal evidence of the book, as well as the character of the diction of the original Hebrew, also points to a later date than 300–275 B.C.

§ 7. The Influence of Sirach on Later Literature.

The influence of our book on the later literature of the Christian Church may be measured, in a general way, by the history of its relation to the Canon, which is summarized in the next section.[6] Restrictions of space will only allow of citations here to illustrate the influence of the book on (*a*) the New Testament, and (*b*) later Jewish literature.

(*a*) *The relation of Sirach to the New Testament.* When it is remembered that the New Testament writers, as a rule, use the Greek Bible in their citations of Scripture it is somewhat surprising to find so few direct quotations from the books which find no recognition in the Palestinian Canon. Not even all the books included in the latter are cited—no quotation occurring from Canticles, Qoheleth, Esther, or Ezra-Nehemiah. On the other hand, a rich use is made of the Pentateuch, Prophets, and Psalms, while the historical books are referred to more rarely. Still some quotations from deutero-canonical and extra-canonical books do occur, such as the citation from the Book of Enoch in the Epistle of Jude. In view of the important place occupied by Sirach in the Wisdom-Literature, and the popularity enjoyed by this literature, especially among the Jews of the Greek Dispersion, it would be surprising not to find any traces of its influence on those books of the New Testament which markedly reflect the Alexandrine spirit. If there are no actual citations of Sirach in the Epistle to the Hebrews, there are at least some possible indications of acquaintance with it (in its Greek form). Thus in Heb. xii. 12 a citation is made of Isa. xxxv. 3 (τὰς παρειμένας χεῖρας καὶ τὰ παραλελυμένα γόνατα) in a form which exactly agrees with that of Sirach xxv. 23, against the LXX (which has χεῖρες ἀνειμέναι). Such examples are not, it must be confessed, decisive. On the other hand, in the Epistle of St. James indications of direct acquaintance with our book are abundant and clear. The more important may be given here.

[1] συγχρονίσας, 'I stayed in Egypt as long as king Euergetes reigned.' But see our note on this word in the Prologue, line 15.

[2] Krauss in *JE*, x. 265 *a*.

[3] *Iudaica* (Göttingen, 1900), p. 11 f.

[4] This is involved in συνχρονίσας, according to Hart's explanation.

[5] *Bible Studies* (E.T.), pp. 339 ff.

[6] And also by the number of secondary versions based on the Greek text (see § 5 above).

Ep. of St. James.	*Sirach* (𝔊).
i. v: *But if any of you lacketh wisdom, let him ask of God, who giveth to all liberally and upbraideth not* (καὶ μὴ ὀνειδίζοντος).	xviii. 18: *A fool will upbraid* (ὀνειδιεῖ) *ungraciously,* &c. xx. 15: *He* [*the fool*] *will give little and upbraid* (ὀνειδιεῖ) *much.* xli. 22: *After thou hast given upbraid not* (μετὰ τὸ δοῦναι μὴ ὀνείδιζε).
i. 6, 8: *But let him ask in faith, nothing doubting; for he that doubteth is like the surge of the sea driven by the wind and tossed . . . a doubleminded man* (ἀνὴρ δίψυχος), *unstable in all his ways* (ἀκατάστατος ἐν πάσαις ταῖς ὁδοῖς αὐτοῦ).	i. 28: *Disobey not the Lord; and come not unto Him with a double heart* (ἐν καρδίᾳ δισσῇ). ii. 12 f.: *Woe unto fearful hearts, and to faint hands, and to the sinner that goeth two ways; woe unto the faint heart, for it believeth not,* &c.; cp. v. 9 (ὁ δίγλωσσος), vii. 10 (*Be not faint-hearted in thy prayer*).
i. 2–4: *Count it all joy, my brethren, when ye fall into manifold temptations,* &c. (cf. *v.* 12).	ii. 1 f.: *My son, if thou comest to serve the Lord, prepare thy soul for temptation,* &c. (cp. i. 23).
i. 13–15: *Let no man say when he is tempted, I am tempted of God: for God cannot be tempted with evil, and He Himself tempteth no man,* &c.	xv. 11–20: *Say not thou, It is through the Lord that I fell away. . . . Say not thou, It is He that caused me to err, For He hath no need of a sinful man,* &c.
i. 19: *Let every man be swift to hear* (ταχὺς εἰς τὸ ἀκοῦσαι), *slow to speak.*	v. 11: *Be swift to hear* (γίνου ταχὺς ἐν ἀκροάσει σου): cp. iv. 29.
i. 23: *For if any one is a hearer of the word, and not a doer, he is like unto a man beholding his natural face in a mirror* (ἐν ἐσόπτρῳ).	xii. 11: *And thou shalt be unto him as one that hath wiped a mirror* (ὡς ἐκμεμαχὼς ἔσοπτρον).
v. 5: *Ye have lived delicately on the earth, and taken your pleasure* (ἐσπαταλήσατε).	xxvii. 13: *The discourse of fools is an offence, and their laughter is in the wantonness of sin* (ἐν σπατάλῃ ἁμαρτίας).
v. 14: *Is any among you sick? let him call for the elders of the church; and let them pray over him, anointing him with oil in the name of the Lord.*	xxxviii. 9–15: *My son, in thy sickness be not negligent, but pray unto the Lord and He shall heal thee,* &c.

There are also many resemblances in thought and theme throughout the two books: cf. e.g. the treatment of humility (Jas. i. 9, Sirach iii. 18), pride (Jas. iv. 6, Sirach x. 7), of poor and rich (Jas. ii. 1–6, Sirach x. 19–24; cp. xiii. 9), of stumbling (Jas. iii. 2, Sirach xix. 16), and of true wisdom (Jas. iii. 13–17, Sirach xix. 18–22); and other parallels are to be noticed in the use of figure, such as that of the crown of life (Jas. i. 12, cp. Sirach xv. 6), and of rust (Jas. v. 2, 3, cp. Sirach xxix. 10, xii. 10).[1]

If these examples are not sufficient to establish a relation of direct dependence, they are sufficient to justify the inference—which is confirmed by the general character of the Epistle and its relation to other books of the Wisdom-Literature—that the author of St. James was well acquainted with, and was influenced by, Sirach.

It is difficult to believe that a book that enjoyed in the early centuries of the Christian era such popularity both among the Jews of Palestine and the Dispersion could have been entirely unknown to the writers of the other New Testament books. And, in fact, possible signs of acquaintance with it are not wanting. In this connexion the following parallels have been noted:[2]

Matt. vi. 14 ἐὰν γὰρ ἀφῆτε τοῖς ἀνθρώποις τὰ παραπτώματα αὐτῶν, ἀφήσει καὶ ὑμῖν ὁ πατὴρ ὑμῶν ὁ οὐράνιος.	*Sirach* xxviii. 2 ἄφες ἀδίκημα τῷ πλησίον σου, καὶ τότε δεηθέντος σου αἱ ἁμαρτίαι σου λυθήσονται.
Matt. vi. 19 f. μὴ θησαυρίζετε ὑμῖν θησαυροὺς ἐπὶ τῆς γῆς, ὅπου σὴς καὶ βρῶσις ἀφανίζει, καὶ ὅπου κλέπται διορύσσουσι καὶ κλέπτουσι· θησαυρίζετε δὲ ὑμῖν θησαυροὺς ἐν οὐρανῷ κτλ.	*Sirach* xxix. 12 σύνκλεισον ἐλεημοσύνην ἐν τοῖς ταμείοις σου, καὶ αὕτη ἐξελεῖταί σε ἐκ πάσης κακώσεως.
Matt. xvi. 27 καὶ τότε ἀποδώσει ἑκάστῳ κατὰ τὴν πρᾶξιν αὐτοῦ.	*Sirach* xxxii. 24 ἕως ἀνταποδῷ ἀνθρώπῳ κατὰ τὰς πράξεις αὐτοῦ κτλ.
Luke i. 17 ἐπιστρέψαι καρδίας πατέρων ἐπὶ τέκνα κτλ. (of Elijah).	*Sirach* xlviii. 10 ἐπιστρέψαι καρδίαν πατρὸς πρὸς υἱὸν κτλ. (of Elijah).

These parallels are, it must be confessed, not very convincing. On the other hand, the Parable of the Rich Fool (Luke xii. 15 f.) may have been suggested by more than one passage in Ben-Sira. The theme of the parable finds an exact parallel in Sirach xxxi. 3 ἐκοπίασε πλούσιος ἐν συναγωγῇ χρημάτων, καὶ ἐν τῇ ἀναπαύσει ἐμπίπλαται τῶν τρυφημάτων αὐτοῦ. St. Luke has parallels to some of the phrases used here (συνάξω, ἀναπαύου). There is also the remarkable parallel to the same passage, presenting similar features, in Sirach xi. 18–19:

[1] See, further, Mayor, *Ep. of St. James*³, pp. cxvi–cxviii; Zahn, *Einleitung*, i. 87.

[2] Cp. Nestle in *HDB*, iv. 550*b*.

There is that waxeth rich by his wariness and pinching,
And this is the portion of his reward:
When he saith, I have found rest,
And now will I eat of my goods;
Yet he knoweth not what time shall pass,
And he shall leave them to others, and die (R.V.).

It will be convenient in concluding this paragraph to note a passage from the *Didache*, which looks like a real quotation either from Ben-Sira or a common source.

Sirach iv. 31 runs:

Let not thy hand be stretched out to take,
And closed in the midst of giving (so 𝔋ᴬ).

This is apparently quoted in the *Didache* iv. 5:

Be not one that stretches out his hands to receive,
But draws them in when he should give.

It is difficult to believe that our book did not exercise a considerable influence on the formation of the *Didache* as a whole. There are many parallels both in thought and sentiment.

(*b*) *Sirach and later Jewish Literature.* In this connexion it will be convenient to note some of the more striking parallels between our book and (i) Aḥiqar, (ii) Tobit, (iii) other non-Rabbinical Jewish literature, and then (iv) to estimate and illustrate its influence on the Rabbinical literature.

It is difficult to determine priority of date in the case of Ben-Sira's relation to Aḥiqar and Tobit. The parallels may merely imply the presence of common matter from older sources. A strong case, however, can be made out for the priority of Aḥiqar. Thus the famous dictum, which is repeated over and over again in different forms in later literature, and appears in Tobit as

Alms delivereth from death,
And suffereth not to come into darkness (iv. 10, cp. xii. 9),

already implies the legend of Aḥiqar, and is only explicable by it.[1] In Sirach we meet with the same maxim, but in a form modified from that of Tobit:

Store up almsgiving in thy treasuries,
And it shall deliver thee from all evil;
Better than a mighty shield and a heavy spear
Shall (*this*) *fight for thee against an enemy.*[2]

i. *Parallels with Aḥiqar.* Of matter common to Sirach and Aḥiqar the following are striking examples:

Sirach iv. 26: *Stand not against the stream.*
Aḥiqar ii. 65: *Stand not against a river in its flood.*

Again,

Sirach xxii. 14, 15: *What is heavier than lead?*
And what is its name but 'Fool'?
Sand and salt and a weight of iron
(*Are*) *easier to bear than a senseless man.*

A close parallel occurs in Prov. xxvii. 3; but Aḥiqar (Syriac version) ii. 45 contains one even nearer:

My son, I have carried salt and removed lead: and I have not seen anything heavier than that a man should pay back a debt that he did not borrow.

My son, I have carried iron and removed stones, and they were not heavier on me than a man who settles in the house of his father-in-law.[3]

ii. *Parallels with Tobit.* The following may be cited to illustrate the parallels that occur in Tobit:

Sirach iv. 4: *Despise not the supplication of the poor,*
And turn not away from the afflicted soul.

Tobit iv. 7: *Turn not away thy face from any poor man,*
And the face of God shall not be turned away from thee.

[1] See the discussion in *The Story of Aḥikar*, ed. by Rendel Harris, p. xlviii. f. [2] xxix. 12, 13; cp. vii. 32, xii. 2.
[3] Cited by Rendel Harris, *op. cit.*, p. liv: see also Nau, *Histoire et sagesse d'Aḥikar*, pp. 60–63.

Sirach xxxviii. 16: *My son, let tears fall over the dead;*

. . . .

In accordance with what is due to him bury his body.

Compare with this the passages in Tobit which commend the pious duty of burying the dead; esp. xii. 13:

And when thou didst not delay to rise up . . . that thou mightest go and cover the dead, thy good deed was not hid from me, &c.

iii. *Parallels with other non-Rabbinical Jewish Literature.* Sirach has apparently influenced two other important books, viz. 2 Enoch (the Slavonic Enoch) and the Psalter of Solomon.

In 2 Enoch passages of Sirach are sometimes cited verbally; thus xlvii. 5 (*Who has numbered the dust of the earth, and the sand of the sea, and the drops of rain*, &c.) is cited from Sirach i. 2; in 2 Enoch li. 1–3 parallels occur with Sirach vii. 32, xiv. 13, xxix. 20, xxix. 10, and ii. 4.

The following further parallels are noted by Charles (*Secrets of Enoch*, p. 96): 2 Enoch xxx. 15 = Sirach xv. 14, 15; 2 Enoch xlii. 11 = Sirach vii. 3; 2 Enoch xliii. 2, 3 = Sirach x. 20, 22, 24; 2 Enoch lii. 5 = Sirach xxxix. 14; 2 Enoch lii. 8 = Sirach xxxi. 26; 2 Enoch lii. 12 = Sirach xxviii. 9; 2 Enoch lxi. 2 = Sirach xxxix. 25; 2 Enoch lxi. 4 = Sirach xxxi. 21–24, 28; 2 Enoch lxv. 2 = Sirach xvii. 3, 5; 2 Enoch lxv. 11 = Sirach xiv. 19.

In the case of the Psalms of Solomon there are many parallels, but dependence cannot be shown conclusively to exist. 'The language and thought of Sirach often illustrate' these Psalms; 'actual correspondences of expression are found, but the agreement is generally to be explained by some passage of Scripture from which both writers have borrowed' (Ryle and James).

The following passages are cited by Ryle and James in their ed. of the Psalms of Solomon (p. lxiii f.): Ps. S. ii. 19, cp. Sirach xxxii. 12; Ps. S. iii. 7, 12, cp. Sirach iii. 25, v. 5, xxi. 1; Ps. S. v. 15–17, cp. Sirach xviii. 12; Ps. S. v. 14, cp. Sirach xl. 14; Ps. S. ix. 16–18, cp. Sirach xxxvi. 17; Ps. S. xiii. 2, 3, cp. Sirach xxxix. 29, 30; Ps. S. xiv. 3, cp. Sirach xvii. 14; Ps. S. xvi. 2, cp. Sirach li. 6; Ps. S. xvi. 7, 8, cp. Sirach ix. 8; Ps. S. xvii. 6, cp. Sirach xlv. 18.

iv. *The influence of Ben-Sira on Rabbinical Literature.* That Ben-Sira's book has exercised a considerable influence on Rabbinic literature hardly needs any further demonstration. Allusion has been already made more than once, in the course of this Introduction, to the large number of quotations from the book that occur in the Talmuds, the Midrashim, and the works of some great Jewish scholars and poets like Saʿadya and Ibn Gebirol.[1] Even after the work had been banned by distinguished Rabbinical authority, and so became suspect to the orthodox, collections of extracts from it were still circulated and read (in the original Hebrew) among the Jews.[2] Apparently, also, it was at some time or other translated, either in whole or in part, into Aramaic for Jewish use. It was only in the Middle Ages that the original work entirely vanished from knowledge in Jewry. The extent of its influence in the earlier period can be measured by recalling one or two important facts. It apparently exercised a formative influence on such important Jewish works as the tractates *Pirqe Aboth* and *Derek 'ereṣ* (*rabba* and, perhaps, *zuta*). Not only is Ben-Sira actually cited in *Pirqe Aboth* iv. 7 (= Sirach vii. 17; see note), but a whole series of parallels can be traced throughout the tractate,[3] which shows that the book was, in the earlier period, closely studied and much esteemed in Rabbinical circles. For parallels in the tractate *Derek 'ereṣ rabba* reference must be made to the notes in the commentary. A good illustration is to be seen in the section concerning behaviour at banquets (xxxi. 12–24 and notes).[4] This tractate is mainly concerned with rules about behaviour in social intercourse. Ben-Sira's book also influenced the liturgy. At any rate, in the prayer contained in xxxvi. 1–17 there are some remarkable parallels to parts of the *Shĕmōnĕh ʿEsrēh* ('Eighteen Blessings'), which occupies so important a position in all the synagogue services.[5] Of course, it is possible that an earlier form of this liturgical prayer was already in existence in the time of Ben-Sira, and that he is quoting from or alluding to it. This is, on the whole, the most probable explanation. Ben-Sira's prayer has a liturgical ring about it which suggests that it is not his own individual composition. The following citations will illustrate the parallelism referred to:

[1] Ben-Sira's vogue among the Rabbis of the period before the Middle Ages is well brought out (in detailed references) by Zunz, *Die gottesdienstlichen Vorträge der Juden*, pp. 100–105.

[2] 𝔅c is an example of one such *florilegium*.

[3] Cp. e. g. the notes in the commentary on the following passages, where the parallels are cited: vii. 36, xi. 9, 28, xiii. 4, 9–13, xiv. 10, xxxi. 12, xxxviii. 24, &c.

[4] Cp. also xxxii. 1–10.

[5] The full form for week-days can be seen in Singer's *Authorized Daily Prayer Book*, pp. 44–54.

Sirach xxxvi. 4: *As Thou hast sanctified Thyself* (נקדשת) *before them*
So glorify Thyself in them before us.

Compare paragraph 3 of the *Shĕmōnēh 'Esrēh* ('the sanctification of the Name'):

Thou art holy and Thy name is holy . . .
Blessed art Thou the holy God.

The key-note here is 'holy' (sanctification).

Again, Sirach xxxvi. 11 *a* runs:

Gather all the tribes of Jacob,
That they may receive their inheritance as in the days of old.

The tenth paragraph of the *Shĕmōnēh 'Esrēh* is:

Sound the great horn for our freedom . . . and collect us from the four corners of the earth.

Possible parallels or allusions exist in this section to all except the sixth, eighth, and ninth paragraphs of the prayer, which it must be remembered in its present form contains nineteen sections. There is, however, at least one important part of the Jewish liturgy which is unquestionably dependent on Sirach. This is the rapturous description of the beautiful appearance of the High-Priest as he officiated in the temple on the Day of Atonement, which is still recited in the services of the day. It is largely based upon, and imitated from, the description of the High-Priest Simon the Just, given in Sirach l. It begins:

In truth, how glorious was the High-Priest as he came forth from the Holy of Holies in perfect peace.[1]

§ 8. Canonicity of the Book and its Use in the Early Church.

As is well known, Sirach owed its place and use in the Christian Church to the fact that it was included in the Alexandrine Canon; before coming to speak, therefore, of the early patristic evidence concerning our book, it will be well to draw attention to the ecclesiastical lists of the biblical books. 'Our earliest Christian list', says Prof. Swete (*Introduction to the Old Testament in Greek*, 1900, p. 221), 'was obtained from Palestine,[2] and probably represents the contents of the Palestinian Greek Bible. It is an attempt to answer the question, What is the true number and order of the books of the Old Testament? Both the titles and the grouping are obviously Greek, but the books are exclusively those of the Hebrew Canon.' Sirach, therefore, together with the rest of the books of the Apocrypha, is excluded. Origen, in his Commentary on Ps. i, gives the second list that we know of, which belongs to a time not later than A.D. 231; he reckons as belonging to the Canon the twenty-two books of the Hebrew Old Testament.[3] But, strange to say, Origen includes in his list the First Book of Esdras (he treats 1, 2 Esdras as one book) and the Epistle of Jeremiah, neither of which had ever been regarded as canonical by the Jews. Origen's list is adopted by Athanasius, Cyril, and Epiphanius,[4] as well as in the Laodicean Canon, in each case with the addition of Baruch. Furthermore, as Dr. Swete goes on to say (*op. cit.*, p. 222), 'Amphilochius mentions two books of Esdras, and it is at least possible that the Esdras of Gregory of Nazianzus is intended to include both books, and that the Epistle, or Baruch and the Epistle, are to be understood as forming part of Jeremiah in the lists both of Gregory and Amphilochius.' The point of importance which these facts reveal is that 'an expansion of the Hebrew Canon, which involved no addition to the number of the books, was predominant in the East during the fourth century'. Dr. Swete gives two other lists: one mentioned by Lagarde (*Septuagintastudien*, ii. 60 ff.), *Σύνοψις ἐν ἐπιτόμῳ*, in which the Wisdom of Jesus (the son) of Sirach is mentioned among the canonical Scriptures (so, too, Tobit and Judith); and the other is anonymous; in it Sirach is, together with Tobit and the Wisdom of Solomon, placed under Apocrypha, though Judith is reckoned among the canonical books.

[1] This composition is the work of the Jewish mediaeval poet Meshullam bar-Kalonymus. It forms part of the *Musaf*, or Additional' Prayer for the Day of 'Atonement, and can be seen in any of the Collections of Jewish Festival Prayers (in Routledge's edition, vol. ii of Day of Atonement Festival Prayers, p. 166 f.). See also *The Religion and Worship of the Synagogue* (Oesterley and Box), ed. 2, p. 428.

[2] Melito (*c.* A.D. 180) *ap.* Eusebius, *H. E.* iv. 26 *ἐπειδὴ μαθεῖν τὴν τῶν παλαιῶν βιβλίων ἐβουλήθης ἀκρίβειαν, πόσα τὸν ἀριθμὸν καὶ ὁποῖα τὴν τάξιν εἶεν . . . ἀνελθὼν εἰς τὴν ἀνατολὴν καὶ ἕως τοῦ τόπου γενόμενος ἔνθα ἐκηρύχθη καὶ ἐπράχθη . . . ἔπεμψά σοι.*

[3] Eusebius, *H. E.* vi. 25 *εἰσὶ δὲ αἱ εἴκοσι δύο βίβλοι καθ' Ἑβραίους αἵδε . . .*

[4] On the evidence of these Fathers see further below.

The following evidence of a more official kind may be added. It is conceivable that there is in the *Muratorian Fragment*[1] (which, as Westcott says, 'expresses with fair distinctness the first known judgement of the Catholic Church on the sum of the Christian Scriptures') a reference to the Wisdom of Sirach in the words: 'Et Sapientia ab amicis Salomonis in honorem ipsius scripta;'[2] it has to be remembered in this connexion that, as we shall see presently, the book of the Wisdom of Sirach, together with other books of the Apocrypha, seems from the beginning to have enjoyed greater esteem in the Western than in the Eastern Church. Next, the eighty-fifth of the Apostolical Canons gives a list[3] of the books of the Hebrew Canon, and adds the three first books of the Maccabees and the Wisdom of Sirach; these last four are not, however, included in the Canon, though the Wisdom of Sirach is specially recommended for the instruction of the young. Again, in the *Apostolical Constitutions*, vi. 14, 15 (= *Didascalia*), quotations from Sirach are given with the same formula as those from the books of the Hebrew Canon,[4] but in the list given in ii. 57 of the same work there is no mention of any of the books of the Apocrypha.[5] On the other hand, at the Council of Hippo (A.D. 393) Sirach was specially mentioned as being one of the canonical books, while at the Council of Carthage (A.D. 397) the 'five books of Solomon', i.e. Proverbs, Ecclesiastes, Canticles, Wisdom, and Sirach, are reckoned among the canonical Scriptures.[6] This was also confirmed by the Council of Carthage in A.D. 419.

Coming now to speak in some detail of what the Church Fathers[7] say as to the canonicity or otherwise of the book, we turn first to the Eastern Church.

In the *Didache* iv. 6 (*c.* 120) Sirach iv. 31 is quoted thus: Μὴ *γίνου πρὸς μὲν τὸ λαβεῖν ἐκτείνων τὰς χεῖρας, πρὸς δὲ τὸ δοῦναι συσπῶν*, which is sufficiently near the wording of Sirach iv. 31 to show that it is intended to be a quotation, viz. Μὴ *ἔστω ἡ χείρ σου ἐκτεταμένη εἰς τὸ λαβεῖν, καὶ ἐν τῷ ἀποδιδόναι συνεσταλμένη*. The same text is quoted in the Epistle of Barnabas, xix. 9 (*c.* 120). Eusebius, as we have already seen, quotes *Melito of Sardis* (d. *c.* 180), however, to the effect that the books of the Hebrew Bible are the only canonical ones; he excludes, therefore, Sirach.[8] The evidence of Clement of Alexandria (d. 220) is conflicting; in his *Paedagogus* he quotes very often from Sirach, and speaks of it as *ἡ γραφή* and *θεία γραφή* (e.g. II, chap. xxxiv. 4, xlviii. 4, lix. 4; III, chap. xviii, xxiii. 4, lxxxiii. 3), from which it would evidently appear that he regarded it as canonical Scripture; but, according to Eusebius, Clement reckoned Sirach among the 'Antilegomena', for in speaking of Clement's works he mentions the *Stromateis*, or 'Medleys', and says: 'He quotes in them passages from the disputed Scriptures, the so-called Wisdom of Solomon, for example, and (that) of Jesus the son of Sirach, and the Epistle to the Hebrews, and those of Barnabas, Clement, and Jude.'[9] Origen, too, gives conflicting evidence; we

[1] Published by Muratori in 1740 from a manuscript in the Ambrosian Library at Milan, though belonging originally to the great Irish monastery of Bobbio. 'It was found in a volume of Latin fragments and translations which dates apparently from the eighth century. But the fragment itself was evidently copied from a manuscript of much higher antiquity; for it was mutilated both at the beginning and end before it was transcribed. The writer claims to be a contemporary of Pius, who was bishop of Rome in the middle of the second century; so that its date may be fixed with tolerable certainty between A.D. 160 and 170' (Westcott, *The Bible in the Church* (2nd ed.), p. 112).

[2] See further on this G. Kuhn, *Das muratorische Fragment*, pp. 94, 112.

[3] Westcott says in reference to this: 'The list of the books of the Bible in the eighty-fifth of the *Apostolical Canons* was introduced into its present place at a much later date. Yet the list itself is remarkable, and probably Alexandrine in origin. . . . This canon, together with the canon of Carthage, was ratified at the Quinisextine Council [of Constantinople, A.D. 553], and had a powerful influence on many of the Eastern Churches' (*op. cit.*, p. 176).

[4] Cp. Herbst, *Hist.-krit. Einleitung in die heiligen Schriften*, ii. pp. 1 f.

[5] Μέσος δ' ὁ ἀναγνώστης ἐφ' ὑψηλοῦ τινος ἑστὼς ἀναγινωσκέτω τὰ Μωσέως καὶ Ἰησοῦ τοῦ Ναυῆ, τὰ τῶν Κριτῶν καὶ τῶν Βασιλειῶν, τὰ τῶν Παραλειπομένων καὶ τὰ τῆς Ἐπανόδου· πρὸς τούτοις τὰ τοῦ Ἰὼβ καὶ τοῦ Σολομῶνος καὶ τὰ τῶν ἑκκαίδεκα προφητῶν. Ἀνὰ δύο δὲ γινομένων ἀναγνωσμάτων ἕτερός τις τοὺς τοῦ Δαυὶδ ψαλλέτω ὕμνους καὶ ὁ λαὸς τὰ ἀκροστίχια ὑποψαλλέτω.

[6] The thirty-ninth canon reads as follows: 'Item placuit ut praeter Scripturas canonicas nihil in ecclesia legatur sub nomine divinarum Scripturarum; sunt autem Canonicae Scripturae hae': then follow the books of the Pentateuch, Joshua, Judges, Ruth, four books of Kings, two of Chronicles, Job, the Psalter, after which it continues: 'Salomonis libri quinque, libri duodecim prophetarum, Jesaias, Jeremias, Ezechiel, Daniel, Tobias, Judith, Esther, Esdrae libri duo, Machabaeorum libri duo': and then the books of the New Testament are enumerated. After this the following words occur: 'Let this be made known also to our brother and fellow-priest Boniface, or to other bishops of those parts, for the purpose of confirming that canon, because we have received from our fathers that those books must be read in the Church' (quoted by Westcott, *Canon*, pp. 439 f., 541 f.). As Westcott says further: 'Between the years A.D. 390 and 419 no less than six councils were held in Africa, and four of these at Carthage. For a time, under the inspiration of Aurelius and Augustine, the Church of Tertullian and Cyprian was filled with a new life before its fatal desolation.'

[7] Among the writings of the Apostolic Fathers there is only one citation from Sirach, viz. iv. 31, which is quoted in *Ep. Barn.* xix. 9.

[8] Eusebius, *H.E.* iv. 26. In *Strom.* II. chap. xiv. 5 (ed. Stählin), however, Sirach vi. 33 is referred to as Solomon's. And such a passage as the following suggests that Clement regarded Sirach as canonical Scripture: *Strom.* V. chap. ii. 1 "Μακάριος ὁ λέγων εἰς ὦτα ἀκουόντων·" (Sirach xxv. 9) *πίστις δὲ ὦτα ψυχῆς, καὶ ταύτην αἰνίσσεται τὴν πίστιν ὁ Κύριος λέγων* "*ὁ ἔχων ὦτα ἀκούειν ἀκουέτω*" (Matt. xi. 15).

[9] Eusebius, *H. E.* vi. 13.

have seen above that in the list of canonical Scriptures which he gives he only regards the twenty-two books of the Hebrew Canon as the genuine Scriptures of the Old Testament, but elsewhere he speaks of Sirach, the Book of Wisdom, and other books of the Apocrypha as 'authoritative Scripture', or as 'the Divine Word', or as 'Holy Scripture' (see e.g. Περὶ Ἀρχῶν, ii. 95, ed. Migne; *Contra Cels.* vi. 7, vii. 12); in these works he quotes Sirach vi. 4 and xxi. 18 as 'Holy Scripture'. As Westcott says, in speaking of Origen: 'In his other writings he uses apocryphal books as divine and authoritative, yet not without noticing the difference of opinion on the subject. But even in his case the familiar use of the Greek Bible practically overpowered his knowledge of the original Hebrew Canon, and in his famous "Letter to Africanus" he expressly defends the reception among Christians of the additions found in the Alexandrine Septuagint.'[1] Not that Origen was ignorant of the Hebrew Bible, for Eusebius (*H. E.* vi. 16) tells us that 'so accurate an examination was Origen undertaking with the Holy Scriptures that he even learned the Hebrew language, and acquired as his private possession original copies of the Scriptures in Hebrew characters, which were current among the Jews themselves'.[2] The evidence of Eusebius (d. 340) has been admirably summarized by Westcott as follows: 'Eusebius has left no express judgement on the contents of the Old Testament. In three places he quotes from Josephus, Melito, and Origen, lists of the books (slightly differing) according to the Hebrew Canon. These he calls in the first place "the canonical Scriptures of the Old Testament (lit. 'Scriptures in the Testament'), undisputed among the Hebrews"; and, again, "the acknowledged Scriptures of the Old Testament"; and, lastly, "the Holy Scriptures of the Old Testament." In his *Chronicle* he distinctly separates the Book of Maccabees from the "Divine Scriptures", and elsewhere mentions Sirach and Wisdom as "controverted" books. On the other hand, like the older Fathers, he quotes in the same manner as the contents of the Hebrew Canon passages from Baruch and Wisdom. On the whole, it may be concluded that he regarded the Apocrypha of the Old Testament in the same light as the books of the New Testament, which were "controverted and yet familiarly used by many". The books of the Hebrew Canon alone were, in his technical language, "acknowledged." One general characteristic of his judgement must not be neglected. It is based expressly on the collective testimony of antiquity expressed in the works of the chief ecclesiastical writers. There was no combined decision of any number of churches to which he could appeal. . . . According to Eusebius the only method by which the contents of the Bible could be determined was that of a simple historical inquiry into the belief and practice of earlier generations, and this did not appear to him to lead to a certain conclusion in every case.'[3] The evidence of Athanasius (d. 373) is likewise very important, both on account of his high ecclesiastical position as metropolitan of Egypt, as well as on account of his dominating personality. In the thirty-ninth of his *Festal Letters*[4] he writes as follows: 'As I am about to speak (of the divine Scriptures), I shall use for the support of my boldness the model of the Evangelist Luke, and say as he does, *Forasmuch as* some *have taken in hand to set forth in order* for themselves the so-called Apocrypha, and to mix these with the inspired Scripture *which* we *most surely believe, even as they delivered* it to our fathers *which from the beginning were eyewitnesses and ministers of the word; it seemed good to me also*, having been urged by true brethren, and having learned the truth *from the first*, to publish the books which are admitted in the Canon, and have been *delivered* to us, and are believed to be divine, that if any one has been deceived he may condemn those who led him astray, and he that has remained pure from error may rejoice in being again reminded (of the truth). All the books therefore of the Old Testament are in number twenty-two.' He then enumerates the books of the Hebrew Canon; these are followed by a list of the New Testament books, after which he continues: 'But for the sake of greater accuracy I add this also, writing of necessity, that there are also other books excluded from among these (ἕτερα βιβλία τούτων ἔξωθεν), not canonical, which have been framed by the Fathers to be read

[1] *The Bible in the Church*, p. 136; and cp. Eusebius's words (*H. E.* vi. 31): 'At this time Africanus also, the compiler of the *Cesti* [i. e. "Mystic Girdles"] as they are called, came into note. A letter of his, written to Origen, is extant, in which he intimates doubts about the Story of Susannah, in Daniel, as being ungenuine and fictitious, to which Origen wrote a very full answer.' It is true that Sirach is not mentioned by Origen in his letter to Africanus, but since he defends Susannah, much more would he have defended Sirach if the authority of this book had been specifically called in question; moreover, the objection urged by Africanus against the reception of Susannah, viz. that it did not exist in Hebrew, did not apply to Sirach, the Prologue of which was sufficient to prove its Hebrew origin even if Africanus did not know of any existing Hebrew copies.

[2] Cp. also the words of Jerome (*De viris illustr.* liv), who tells us that Origen had so much holy zeal for the Scriptures 'ut etiam hebraeam linguam contra aetatis gentisque suae naturam edisceret' (quoted by Hart, *op. cit.*, p. 348 note).

[3] *The Bible in the Church*, pp. 153 ff.

[4] Migne, *Patr. Gr.* xxvi, col. 1347. These Paschal, or Festal Letters, were pastorals issued by the bishops of Alexandria; they were originally written for the purpose of announcing the date of Easter, but gradually assumed the character of an annual metropolitan pronouncement in which topics of prominent interest were dealt with.

by those who are just approaching [entry into the Church], and who desire to be instructed in the word of godliness: the Wisdom of Solomon, and the Wisdom of Sirach, and Esther, and Judith, and Tobias, and the so-called Teaching of the Apostles, and the Shepherd. And, nevertheless, beloved, neither among those books which are canonical, nor among those that are read [i.e. those just enumerated], is there anywhere mention made of the apocryphal (books).' It is worth noticing here that Athanasius uses the word 'apocryphal' in an entirely different sense from that in which the word is now used in reference to the books of our Apocrypha; indeed, he goes on to say in this passage that such apocryphal books are 'a device of heretics', words which in view of the passage before us he could not possibly have ever applied to the books of what we now understand by the Apocrypha. One example, at least, exists of Athanasius quoting from Sirach, and speaking of it as 'Holy Scripture' (*Contra Arianos*, xii), but it is evident that, upon the whole, Athanasius did not regard Ecclesiasticus as belonging to the canonical Scriptures, for among these he included only the books of the Hebrew Canon.[1] Amphilochius (*c.* 380) enumerates the books of the Old Testament, but includes only the books of the Hebrew Canon, and makes no mention of the books of the Apocrypha.[2] Cyril of Jerusalem (d. 386) in his *Catechetical Lectures* (iv. 35) quotes the books of the Hebrew Canon (among which he, too, includes Baruch and the Epistle of Jeremiah as belonging to the Book of Jeremiah) as the canonical Scriptures of the Old Testament, after which he says: Τὰ δὲ λοιπὰ πάντα ἔξω κείσθω ἐν δευτέρῳ. He, however, quotes Sirach in his *Catechetical Lectures*, vi. 3. Gregory of Nazianzus (d. 389) divides the books of the Hebrew Canon, which alone he acknowledges as canonical Scripture, into three groups—historical,[3] poetical, and prophetical; in the second, besides Job and 'David', he includes three of 'Solomon', Ecclesiastes, Canticles, and Proverbs; no mention at all is made of any books outside the Hebrew Canon, there is only a reference to 'strange books', against which the reader is warned.[4] In the Preface to the *Synopsis Sacr. Script.* (pseudo-Chrysostom)[5] there is a threefold division of Scripture: τὸ ἱστορικόν, τὸ συμβουλευτικόν, and τὸ προφητικόν, in the second of which are included Proverbs, the Wisdom of Sirach, Ecclesiastes, and Canticles. Chrysostom himself quotes passages from Baruch, Sirach, and Wisdom as 'divine Scripture'. We come next to the evidence of Epiphanius (d. 404); in three places[6] he enumerates the canonical books, holding these to be only those of the Hebrew Canon; but he is not altogether consistent, for in one place he includes the 'letters of Jeremiah and Baruch' in Jeremiah, while in another he remarks that 'the letters of Baruch' are not found in the Hebrew Bible. 'He is equally inconsistent or uncertain', says Westcott, 'with regard to Wisdom and Ecclesiasticus. These', he says, 'occupy a doubtful place. They are useful, and still they are not reckoned among the acknowledged books, nor were they ever placed in the Ark of the Covenant,'[7] i.e. regarded as Scripture by the Jews. Yet again, after enumerating summarily all the books of the Old and New Testaments, he adds, 'and the books of Wisdom, that of Solomon, and of the son of Sirach, and generally all divine writings.' It is evident that he wishes to combine the practice of the early Fathers with their direct teaching. He will sacrifice nothing which had even the appearance of authority, and this characteristic of the man gives weight to his repeated statement that the books of the Old Testament 'were twenty-seven, counted as twenty-two'. The Hebrew Canon was that which he, like all the other Greek Fathers, wished to mark as definitely authoritative, though he admitted to a second place the books which had been sanctioned in some measure by Christian usage.[8] In the list given by Leontius (*De Sectis*, ii) and in the *Stichometria* of Nicephorus no mention is made of Sirach, though in the latter Baruch is mentioned among the canonical books.[9] Finally, John of Damascus (d. 750) in his *De fide orthod.* iv. 17 speaks of Wisdom and Sirach, after enumerating the books of the Hebrew Canon, in the following way: Ἡ δὲ Πανάρετος, τουτέστιν ἡ Σοφία τοῦ Σολομῶντος καὶ ἡ Σοφία τοῦ Ἰησοῦ, ἣν ὁ πατὴρ μὲν τοῦ Σιρὰχ ἐξέθετο Ἑβραϊστὶ Ἑλληνιστὶ δὲ ἡρμήνευσεν ὁ τούτου μὲν ἔγγονος Ἰησοῦς τοῦ δὲ Σιρὰχ υἱός· ἐνάρετοι μὲν καὶ καλαὶ ἀλλ' οὐκ ἀριθμοῦνται οὐδὲ ἔκειντο ἐν τῇ κιβωτῷ.[10] In his *De Imag.* i he speaks of Baruch as 'divine Scripture'.

[1] At the same time it is worth noting that Athanasius clearly did not feel himself bound by the Hebrew Canon, for he includes Baruch and the Letter of Jeremiah among the canonical Scriptures, and excludes Esther from the Canon.

[2] Migne, *Patr. Gr.* xxxvii, p. 1593.

[3] Ruth is treated as a separate book, and Esther is omitted altogether; Nehemiah is not mentioned, but included under Esdras among the historical books.

[4] *Haer.* I. i. 5; *De mens. et pond.*, §§ 4, 23.

[5] Migne, *Patr. Gr.* iii. 473 f.

[6] Migne, *Patr. Gr.* lvi. 513 ff. Westcott regards this as 'certainly a Syrian catalogue of Chrysostom's time' (*The Bible in the Church*, p. 174).

[7] i.e. the 'ark' in the Synagogue; the rolls of the canonical Scriptures read in the Synagogue service were kept there; κιβωτός = תֵּיבָה ('chest').

[8] *The Bible in the Church*, pp. 172 f.

[9] Cp. Swete, *op. cit.*, p. 207.

[10] Cp. Westcott, *The Canon of the New Testament* (5th ed.), p. 546.

We turn next to the Western Church. The earliest evidence is that of Irenaeus (d. 202); although he nowhere quotes from Sirach,[1] he has in his *Adv. Haeres.* iv. 26, v. 35, quotations from Baruch, which he cites as 'Jeremiah the prophet', and from the *Additions to Daniel*, which he cites as 'Daniel the prophet', and also from Wisdom;[2] presumably, therefore, he would have regarded the books of the Apocrypha as canonical. Tertullian (d. 220), in quoting from our book (e.g. *Contra Gnostic.* viii, *De Exhort. Castit.* ii, *De Hab. Mul.* iii), uses the same formula as that with which he introduces the quotations from the books of the Hebrew Canon, viz. *sicut scriptum est.* Cyprian (d. 258), in his *Testimonia* (e.g. iii. 95, 96)[3] and in his letters (e.g. *Ep.* lix. 20),[3] has many quotations from Sirach, and, like Tertullian, introduces them with the formula *sicut scriptum est*, or with the even more definite words *Scriptura divina dicit.* Methodius[4] (*c.* 311), who was bishop of Lycia, and afterwards of Tyre, quotes without reserve from Sirach, Wisdom, and Baruch, treating them all as 'Scripture'. Hilary of Poitiers (d. 368) has a list of the books of the Old Testament in his *Prol. in libr. Psalm.*[5] in which only the Epistle of Jeremiah among the books of the Apocrypha is included, but at the end of this list he adds the words: 'Quibusdam autem visum est additis Tobia et Judith xxiv libros secundum numerum Graecorum literarum connumerare'; nevertheless, he cites Ecclesiasticus and Wisdom as 'prophets', an expression which seems to imply his belief in their canonicity. Philastrius of Brescia (d. 397) gives an account of the Scriptures in his *De Haeres.* lx, lxi, in which he says that only the canonical books, meaning thereby the books of the Hebrew Canon, should be read in church; in the same work (lxxxviii) he says that the 'book of the Wisdom of Sirach' is used by a heretical sect, but he quotes Wisdom as the work of a 'prophet'. Rufinus (*c.* 410), in his *Comm. in Symbol. Apostol.*, §§ 36–38, gives a list of the Old Testament Scriptures comprised in the Hebrew Canon as those which 'the Fathers included in the Canon' (§ 37); he then continues, in the next section: 'Nevertheless, it should be known that there are also other books which by men of old were called not "canonical" but "ecclesiastical", namely, Wisdom, which is called Solomon's, and the other Wisdom, that of the son of Sirach'; he also includes other books in this category.[6] The important evidence of Jerome (d. 420) requires a little more detailed consideration. He was the first to make any thoroughgoing and successful attempt to differentiate between the canonical books of the Hebrew Bible and the books of the Apocrypha in the Christian Church; his intercourse with Rabbis and his knowledge of the Bible in Hebrew were the means of equipping him in a special way for his biblical studies. Jerome was, moreover, the first to use the term 'Apocrypha', in its present technical sense, in reference to the uncanonical books. In the *Prologus Galeatus* (the 'Helmed Prologue', with which he prefaces his translation of the books of Samuel and Kings), after enumerating the books of the Hebrew Canon, he says that every other book (referring, of course, to the Alexandrine Canon) is to be reckoned among the Apocrypha ('quidquid extra hos est, inter Apocrypha esse ponendum'); and he goes on: 'Therefore Wisdom, commonly entitled (The Wisdom) of Solomon, and the book of Jesus the son of Sirach, and Judith, and Tobit, and the Shepherd are not in the Canon.' To the same effect are his words in the preface to his Commentary on the Salomonic books: 'Porro in eo libro qui a plerisque *Sapienta Salomonis* inscribitur, et in Ecclesiastico, quam esse Iesu filii Sirach nullus ignorat, calamo temperavi, tantummodo canonicas Scripturas vobis emendare desiderans et studium meum certis magis quam dubiis commendare'; and, again, in the same preface he says: 'Sicut ergo Judith et Tobi et Macchabaeorum libros quidem legit Ecclesia, sed inter canonicas Scripturas non recipit, sic et haec duo volumina (i. e. Sirach and Wisdom) legat ad aedificationem plebis, non ad auctoritatem ecclesiasticorum dogmatum confirmandam.' But in spite of what Jerome says here, he not infrequently quotes from the books of the Apocrypha with the same introductory formula which he uses when quoting from the books of the Hebrew Canon; thus in his Commentary on Isaiah (ii. 3) he prefaces quotations from Sirach and Wisdom with 'sicut scriptum est'.[7]

Our next authority is Augustine (d. 430), whose authority over the Western Church was almost as great as that of Jerome. The following, from his *De Doctr. Christiana*, ii. 8, will show that he regarded the books of the Apocrypha generally as more authoritative than Jerome did. After enumerating the Old Testament books in the order—Pentateuch, Joshua, Judges, Ruth, 1–4 Kings,

[1] This silence does not of itself necessarily mean that Irenaeus did not regard Sirach as Scripture; it is worth noting that some books of the Hebrew Canon are never quoted or even alluded to in the New Testament, viz. Esther, Canticles, Ecclesiastes.

[2] He also mentions this book in a work of his which is now lost; see Eusebius, *H.E.* v. 26.

[3] Hartel's edition.

[4] Not to be confounded with the Methodius who, in conjunction with his brother Cyril, translated the Greek Bible into Slavonic in the ninth century, and preached the faith to the Slavs.

[5] Migne, *Patr. Lat.* i. 241.

[6] Ed. Migne, pp. 373 ff.

[7] It is worth noting that the books of Tobit and Judith were translated by Jerome from the Aramaic and incorporated in the Vulgate, but Wisdom, Sirach, the two books of the Maccabees, and Baruch as found in the Vulgate are not the work of Jerome, but are all ante-Hieronymian (cp. Swete, *op. cit.*, p. 103).

1, 2 Chronicles, he goes on: 'Haec est historia quae sibimet annexa tempora continet atque ordinem rerum: sunt aliae tanquam ex diverso ordine quae neque huic ordini neque inter se connectuntur, sicut est Job et Tobias et Esther et Judith et Machabaeorum libri duo et Esdrae duo, qui magis subsequi videntur ordinatam illam historiam usque ad Regnorum vel Paralipomenon terminatam: deinde Prophetae in quibus David unus liber Psalmorum, et Salomonis tres, Proverbiorum, Cantica Canticorum, et Ecclesiastes. Nam illi duo libri unus qui Sapientia et alius qui Ecclesiasticus inscribitur de quadam similitudine Salomonis esse dicuntur, nam Iesus Sirach eos conscripsisse constantissime perhibetur qui tamen quoniam in auctoritatem recipi meruerunt inter propheticos numerandi sunt.' Though he thus speaks with some reserve respecting Wisdom and Sirach he regards them as canonical, for at the end of his enumeration of the books of the Old and New Testaments he says: 'In his omnibus libris timentes Deum et pietate mansueti quaerunt voluntatem Dei.' In the *Speculum*[1] Augustine deals in the same way with Sirach as with the canonical books. John Cassian (*c.* 450) cites Sirach ii. 1 as Scripture in his *De Inst. Caen.* iv. 38.[2] Innocent II, in a list of the Scriptural books in his *Ep. ad Exsuperium*,[3] reckons five books of Solomon (i.e. he includes Sirach and Wisdom); the *pseudo-Gelasian* list[4] includes Sirach and Wisdom, as well as Tobit, Judith, and 1, 2 Maccabees, among the canonical books. And, lastly, Cassiodorus (d. 570), in his enumeration of the books of the Bible (*De inst. Div. litt.* 14)[5] also includes Sirach and Wisdom among the books of Solomon, and therefore regards them as canonical; so also Tobit, Judith, 1, 2 Esdras, 1, 2 Maccabees.

It is unnecessary to give further evidence, for from this time onwards all the books of the Apocrypha are usually found in the Old Testament undistinguished from the other books. So that the evidence of the early Church, taken as a whole, is in the direction of looking favourably upon Sirach as being, at the very least, a book which was both edifying and instructive; nevertheless, it is regarded as less authoritative than the books of the Hebrew Canon.

§ 9. The Theology of the Book.

i. *The Doctrine of God.* Ben-Sira's conception and teaching of the Almighty is very full; not only his orthodox belief, but still more his religious mind which so often expresses itself in his book, impelled him in the most natural way to refer very frequently to the Divine Personality, His attributes, and His relationship to men. First and foremost comes, of course, his teaching concerning the *Unity of God*, e.g. xlii. 21:

From everlasting He is the same;

and again in xxxvi. 5 (𝔊 xxxiii. 5):

That they may know, as we also know,
That there is none other God but Thee.

In the long section xliii. 1–26 Ben-Sira describes the divine activity in Nature, and he concludes (*v.* 27) with the words:

The conclusion of the matter is: He is all.[6]

The Greek (τὸ πᾶν ἐστιν αὐτός) might be thought to point to a pantheistic tendency, but the context makes it clear that all that Ben-Sira wishes to show is that God is to be discovered in all His works; the very definite personality which he always imputes to God amply proves that he was entirely free from all pantheistic tendencies. This teaching of God as the All-God leads on naturally to that of God as the *Creator of all*; here Ben-Sira gets his main inspiration from the Psalms, see the fine passage xlii. 15–xliii. 33, and cp. also xxxix. 16 and xlii. 21. In this last passage it is said that all created things are the products of the divine wisdom; this is further emphasized by the description of the *all-knowledge* of God in xlii. 18–25, see especially *vv.* 18, 19:

For Jahveh possesseth all knowledge,[7]
And seeth what cometh unto eternity.[7]
He declareth what is past and what is future,
And revealeth the profoundest secrets.

The *eternity* of God also frequently finds expression, e.g. xviii. 1 ff.:

He that liveth for ever created all things together . . .

[1] Chap. xxiii (ed. Weihrich). In the *pseudo-Speculum* almost every chapter of Sirach is quoted from.
[2] Ed. Petschenig. [3] Swete, *op. cit.*, p. 211. [4] Ibid. [5] Ibid.
[6] Cp. also xxxvi. 1: 'Save us, O God of all.' [7] These two lines are wanting in the Hebrew.

and xxxvi. 17 (𝕲 22):

. . . That all the ends of the earth may know
That Thou art the eternal God.

Belonging to this cycle of conceptions is also the *Holiness* of God ; this is taught, e.g. in xxiii. 9:

Accustom not thy mouth to an oath,
Nor make a habit of the naming of the Holy One.

See further iv. 14, xliii. 10, xlvii. 8, xlviii. 20.

Another side to Ben-Sira's doctrine of God is that in which he deals with the relationship of God towards Israel on the one hand, and towards the Gentiles on the other. The more usual Jewish view that God is the God of Israel only is taught, e.g. in xvii. 17:

For every nation He appointed a ruler,[1]
But Israel is the Lord's portion ;[1]

and the fact that the Wisdom of God belongs to Israel in a pre-eminent degree shows them to be in a special sense His people ; see the whole passage xxiv. 8 ff., especially *v.* 12:

And I [i.e. Wisdom] *took root among an honoured people,*[1]
In the portion of the Lord (*and*) *of His inheritance.*[1]

Moreover, the whole section on the praise of Israel's heroes of old (xliv–xlix) reveals the belief that Israel is a particularly favoured nation in the sight of God. On the other hand, Ben-Sira is not wholly particularistic ; he realizes that God is the God of all the world, and therefore he sometimes strikes a universalistic note, e.g. in xviii. 13, 14:

The mercy of man is (*exercised upon*) *his own kin,*
But the mercy of God is (*extended*) *to all flesh,*
Reproving, and chastening, and teaching,
And bringing them back as a shepherd his flock.
He hath mercy on them that accept (*His*) *chastening,*
And that diligently seek after His judgements.[2]

The attributes of mercy and forgiveness here portrayed find very frequent utterance, and of course the same is true of the converse ; God's wrath strikes the wicked whether they be Jews or Gentiles. The doctrine of the divine *Fatherhood* also finds expression in our book. As Toy says, referring to the older view : 'The old Israelitish idea of the divine love was, so far as we can gather from the literature, a purely national one. Jahveh was the father (Hos. xi. 1) or the husband (Jer. ii. 1, iii. 4 ; Isa. lxii. 5) of Israel. In the later psalms more individual relation is expressed ; Jahveh is said to pity them that fear Him as a father pities his children (Ps. ciii. 13). Gradually the paternal relation as expressing most completely the combination of guidance and tenderness came to be employed as the representative of God's relation to man' ;[3] and he quotes several passages from the Apocrypha, among them xxiii. 1 of our book:

O Lord, Father, and God of my life,[1]

which certainly witnesses to a real belief in the Fatherhood of God in regard to the individual.

ii. *The Law.* 'About half the passages in which the Law is mentioned in this book are wanting in the Hebrew ; in those which are extant in Hebrew the usual word rendered *νόμος* in Greek is תורה, but in ix. 15 the Hebrew is certainly corrupt,[1] in xliv. 20 the word is מצוה ("commandment"), and in xlv. 17 it is משפט ("judgement"). With three exceptions (ii. 16, xv. 1, xlix. 4) *νόμος* is used without the article. In the Prologue it is used with the article three times, but in each case it is in reference to the threefold division of the Canon (*ὁ νόμος, καὶ αἱ προφητεῖαι, καὶ λοιπὰ τῶν βιβλίων*). On the other hand, the concluding words in the Prologue are : . . . *ἐν νόμῳ βιωτεύειν*. In xxxvi. (EV xxxiii.) 3 the article is almost necessary grammatically.'[4] Ben-Sira gives great prominence to the Law both in its ethical and ritual aspects, differing in this markedly from Proverbs, to which he is in other respects so much indebted ; and the stress which he lays on the importance of the Law, and legal observances generally, marks his book out as perhaps the most striking link we have between the older and the newer Judaism, that is to say, the Judaism of post-

[1] Wanting in Hebrew. [2] The whole passage is wanting in Hebrew. [3] *Judaism and Christianity*, p. 83.
[4] But we should probably read בתורת יי. [5] Oesterley, *Ecclesiasticus* (Cambridge Bible), p. liii.

exilic times and Rabbinical Judaism. But he uses the word 'Law' in a wide sense; and herein, too, we are able to recognize the way in which the teaching of this book leads over in so many respects to the later Rabbinism, for what Schechter says regarding the meaning of the term 'Law' in Rabbinic literature applies also to its meaning in Sirach: 'The term Law or *Nomos* is not a correct rendering of the Hebrew word "Torah". The legalistic element, which might rightly be called the Law, represents only one side of the Torah. To the Jew the word Torah means a teaching or instruction of any kind. It may be either a general principle or a specific injunction, whether it be found in the Pentateuch or in the other parts of the Scriptures, or even outside the Canon. The juxtaposition in which Torah and Mitzvôth, "teaching" and "commandments", are to be found in the Rabbinic literature implies already that the former means something more than merely the Law. . . . To use the modern phraseology, to the Rabbinic Jew Torah was both an institution and a faith.'[1] Torah is, therefore, to be understood in both an extended and in a restricted sense according to the general purport of the passage in which the term occurs.

We may note, then, first of all the general emphasis which Ben-Sira lays on the observance of the Law as being the prime duty of the people to whom Jahveh has given the Law; he says, for example, in ix. 15:

With the intelligent let thy communing be,
And all thy converse in the Law of the Most High.

He teaches that there can be no honour for those who do not observe the Law:

A despicable race is that which transgresseth the commandment (x. 19).

The duty of seeking the Law, of believing it, and of meditating upon its precepts is insisted on in xxxii. 15–24:

He that seeketh out the Law shall gain her,
But the hypocrite shall be snared thereby. . . .
In all thy works guard thyself,
For he that so doeth keepeth the commandment.
He that observeth the Law guardeth himself,
And he that trusteth in Jahveh shall not be brought to shame;

and see also xxxix. 1 ff. Ben-Sira urges men not to be ashamed of the Law (xlii. 2), and recalls how the nation's great heroes in the past observed it and were enlightened by it, and taught it to others (see xliv. 20, xlv. 5, 17, xlvi. 14). The observance of the commandments of the Law is the one thing to be thought of at the approach of death (xxviii. 6).

Since the Law was given by God it is, like Him, eternal, and this brings us to what is perhaps the most interesting part of Ben-Sira's doctrine concerning the Law, namely, his identification of it with Wisdom; for this implies the pre-existence of the Law, as well as its divine character (see further the section on Wisdom). This conception of the Law, which, as far as is known, is found here for the first time in Jewish literature, became later on, with one exception (viz. the doctrine of the unity of God), the most important dogma of Rabbinical Judaism.[2] But the way in which the identification of Wisdom with the Law is taken for granted in Sirach makes it clear that Ben-Sira was not expressing a new truth, but one which had already received general acceptance. He says, for example, in xv. 1:

For he that feareth the Lord doeth this

[i.e. seeks Wisdom, which is the subject of the preceding verses],

And he that taketh hold of the Law findeth her [i.e. Wisdom].

Again, the Law and Wisdom are used synonymously in xxxiv. (𝔊 xxxi.) 8:

Without deceit shall the Law be fulfilled,
And Wisdom is perfect in a mouth that is faithful.

So also in xxi. 11:

He that keepeth the Law controlleth his natural tendency,[3]
And the fear of the Lord is the consummation of Wisdom.

[1] *Some Aspects of Rabbinic Theology*, p. 117 f.
[2] See the authors' book *The Religion and Worship of the Synagogue* (2nd ed.), pp. 161–177.
[3] See the note on this in the commentary.

This identification is further implied by 'the fear of the Lord' being both the true observance of the Law as well as the 'beginning' of Wisdom; both thoughts occur a number of times in the book. But the most direct assertion of the identity of the two is found in xxiv. 23, where it is said:

All these things [i.e. things concerning Wisdom which are mentioned in the preceding verses] *are the book of the covenant of God Most High,*
The Law which Moses commanded (as) an heritage for the assemblies of Jacob.

The same is taught in xix. 20:

All wisdom is the fear of the Lord,
And all wisdom is the fulfilling of the Law.

Ben-Sira taught, as we have seen, that the Law was eternal, a doctrine which is further illustrated by the way in which he identifies the Law with Wisdom, which is also eternal (see next section); the special point of interest in this connexion is that the doctrine of the existence of the Law before the Creation—a thoroughly Rabbinical doctrine—is seen to have been taught long before Christian times. As an example of the Rabbinical teaching reference may be made to the Midrash *Bereshith Rabba* viii, where it is said that the Torah is two thousand years older than the Creation; and in the first chapter (in the comment on Gen. i. 1) of the same Midrash it is said: 'Six things preceded the creation of the world; among them were such as were themselves truly created, and such as were decided upon before the Creation; the Torah and the throne of glory were truly created.'

Another important point concerning the Law is Ben-Sira's teaching on the spirit in which legal ordinances should be observed. 'It might seem doubtful', says Toy, 'whether the introduction of the finished Law was an unmixed good from the ethical point of view. The code was largely ritualistic; it fixed men's minds on ceremonial details which it in some cases put into the same category and on the same level with moral duties. Would there not hence result a dimming of the moral sense and a confusion of moral distinctions? The ethical attitude of a man who could regard a failure in the routine of sacrifice as not less blameworthy than an act of theft cannot be called a lofty one. If such had been the general effect of the ritual law we should have to pronounce it an evil. But in point of fact the result was different. What may be called the natural debasing tendency of a ritual was counteracted by other influences, by the ethical elements of the Law itself, and by the general moral progress of the community. The great legal schools which grew up in the second century, if we may judge by the sayings of the teachers which have come down to us, did not fail to discriminate between the outward and the inward, the ceremonial and the moral; and the conception of sin corresponded to the idea of the ethical standard.'[1] Now the teaching of Ben-Sira on the spirit in which the sacrifices prescribed in the Law are to be observed is a striking illustration of what is here so truly said: in xxxiv. 18, 19 (𝔊 xxxi. 21–23) he urges:

The sacrifice of the unrighteous man is a mocking offering,
And unacceptable are the oblations of the godless.
The Most High hath no pleasure in the offerings of the ungodly,
Neither doth He forgive sins for a multitude of sacrifices.

And again, a few verses later on, he says:

He who washeth after (contact with) a dead body and toucheth it again,
What hath he gained by his bathing?
So a man fasting for his sins
And again doing the same—
Who will listen to his prayer?
And what hath he gained by his humiliation?

Such words offer an eloquent proof of Ben-Sira's spiritual conception concerning the observance of the Law.

iii. *The Teaching on Wisdom.*

The divine character of Wisdom is graphically brought out in xxiv. 3–5:

I came forth from the mouth of the Most High (cp. i. 1),
And as a mist I covered the earth;

[1] *Judaism and Christianity*, p. 186.

In the high places did I fix my abode,
And my throne was in the pillar of cloud.
Alone I compassed the circuit of heaven,
And in the depth of the abyss I walked.

That Wisdom took her part in the creation of the world comes out clearly in the two following passages:

Before them all [i.e. the heavens and the earth] *was Wisdom created* (i. 4);

from the words which follow a little later on Ben-Sira evidently conceived of Wisdom having been created in preparation for the work of Creation which was to come, for he continues in verse 9:

He Himself created her, and saw, and numbered her;
And poured her out upon all His works . . .[1]

The existence of Wisdom before the creation of the world is again, and more definitely, stated in xxiv. 9 *a*:

He created me from the beginning, before the world.

This vivid personification of Wisdom is based on Proverbs, where the same thought finds expression in viii. 22, 23:

The Lord possessed me in the beginning of His way,
Before His works of old.
I was set up from everlasting, from the beginning,
Or ever the earth was. (See the whole passage, Prov. viii. 22–31.)

The intimate relationship between Wisdom and the Almighty naturally involves the eternity of Wisdom, a truth set forth in the opening words of our book:

All Wisdom cometh from the Lord,
And is with Him for ever.

The same is implied in xxiv. 9 *b*:

The memorial of me shall never cease.[2]

The personification of Wisdom is illustrated in another way when it is said that she takes up her abode among men, and invites them to come and dwell with her:

With faithful men is she, and she hath been established from eternity,[3]
And with their seed shall she continue (i. 15).
Come unto me, ye that desire me,
And be ye filled with my produce;
For my memorial is sweeter than honey,
And the possession of me than the honey-comb (xxiv. 19, 20).

It is characteristic of Ben-Sira's attitude in desiring to show the superiority of the wisdom of Israel over that of the Greeks that he should represent Wisdom as having sought a resting-place among the nations of the world, but that Israel alone was worthy of her, and that among them, therefore, God bids her abide;[4] he says in xxiv. 7, 8 f., 12:

With all these [i.e. every people and nation] *I sought a resting-place,*
And (said): In whose inheritance shall I lodge?
Then the Creator of all things gave me commandment,
And He that created me fixed my dwelling-place (for me);
And He said: Let thy dwelling-place be in Jacob,
And in Israel take up thine inheritance. . . .
And I took root among an honoured people,
In the portion of the Lord (and) of His inheritance.

[1] Cp. Ps. civ. 24: *O Lord, how manifold are Thy works!*
In wisdom hast Thou made them all.
Prov. iii. 19: *The Lord by wisdom founded the earth;*
By understanding He established the heavens.

[2] So the Syriac; the Greek and Latin read, 'Unto eternity I shall not fail.'

[3] So the Syriac; the Greek text is probably corrupt.

[4] Cp. with this the somewhat similar case of the Law, which, according to the later teaching of the Rabbis, was originally intended by God to be a revelation of Himself and of His will to all nations, but that Israel was the only nation that accepted it (see Oesterley and Box, *op. cit.*, p. 164).

The thought of Wisdom dwelling among men is already taught in Proverbs (e.g. viii. 31, 34 ff.), but Ben-Sira elaborates it, and in such a passage as that just quoted treats it with great poetical beauty.

Further, it is characteristic, not only of the Wisdom of Ben-Sira, but also of the Wisdom-Literature generally, that the term Wisdom is never used in the sense of pure knowledge; in its essence it connoted originally the faculty of distinguishing between what is good and what is bad, or, perhaps more accurately (in so far as earlier times are concerned), between what is advantageous and what is harmful. But in any case, regarding the nature of Wisdom, it is true to say that in the Jewish conception it had primarily a *religious* content from the beginning; that is to say, that it was in its origin essentially a divine attribute, the possession of which made man in some measure like God. In comparatively early times it must have come to this, that to be able to differentiate between good and evil, i.e. the exercise of the moral consciousness, enabled man to stand in a closer relationship to God than the mere external observance, however assiduously carried out, of a ceremonial law; this, at any rate, would have been the essence of the teaching of the prophets. It is in following such teaching that Ben-Sira inculcates the truth that the way to lead a wise life is to live according to the divine commandments; in contemplating the wisdom of God, as set forth in the commandments of God, and acting accordingly, man makes his human wisdom approximate to the divine, and worldly, practical wisdom, in its many and various forms, is thus of the same kind, only less in degree, as divine wisdom. It is thus easy to see, one may remark in passing, that the identification between the Law and Wisdom, referred to in the previous section, was inevitable. 'Human wisdom comes from the communion between the mind of man and the mind of God. The unity of the divine and the human attributes (implicitly contained in the book) appears to involve the conception that the divine wisdom fills and controls all things, including man's mind, and thus manifests itself in human thought;'[1] this is true, but it needs to be emphasized that Ben-Sira's strong insistence on human free-will makes it a matter of man's choice whether his mind is filled with divine wisdom or something else.

Wisdom is, therefore, in the first place, of a religious nature. How essential an element this was in Ben-Sira's conception of Wisdom will have been seen by what was said above as to the origin of Wisdom, namely, that it was an emanation from the Deity. This truth is further emphasized by the *dictum*, common to all the books of the Wisdom-Literature in one form or another, that:

The fear of the Lord is the beginning of Wisdom (i. 14).

Though Ben-Sira takes this thought over from earlier sages, he nevertheless makes it thoroughly his own, and elaborates it in such sayings as:

The crown of Wisdom is the fear of the Lord (i. 18);
To fear the Lord is the root of Wisdom (i. 20).

But besides this specifically religious content, Wisdom has, according to Ben-Sira, another element in its nature. While the knowledge of God may be said to describe its most exalted characteristic, it has also a less exalted, but extremely useful, further characteristic in that it connotes knowledge of the world; not that this would imply a non-religious element in Wisdom, for the man with knowledge of the world has acquired this lower form of Wisdom, too, by his observance of the divine commandments; so that it need cause no surprise to find that it is this latter element in the nature of Wisdom to which Ben-Sira devotes most attention in his book. Nor is this an unnatural thing when it is remembered that the writer, having none but the vaguest ideas about a life hereafter, is mainly concerned with the affairs of this life. So he says of Wisdom that:

They that love her love life (iv. 12);

and again:

The wisdom of the poor man lifteth up his head,
And causeth him to sit among princes (xi. 1).

The large number of precepts which Ben-Sira offers as to general conduct of life are the utterances of a sage whose whole life has been spent in the acquisition of Wisdom; they form part, at least, of the result of his labours in her service; and the contribution which he has to offer his fellow-creatures is to teach them what in very large measure is worldly wisdom. These moral precepts differ widely, of course, from divine wisdom, but, as we have seen, both emanate from the same source, and both are ultimately to be traced back to the Giver of all good things.

[1] Toy, in *EB*, ii. 1175.

It is owing to this practical nature of Wisdom that Ben-Sira insists on its being not only possessed, but also exhibited among men, so he says:

Hidden wisdom and concealed treasure,
What profit is there in either?
Better is the man that hideth his folly
Than a man that hideth his wisdom (xx. 30, 31).

To those who are desirous of acquiring Wisdom, Ben-Sira gives a piece of advice which well illustrates what has already been said above as to the religious element in every form of Wisdom:

If thou desire Wisdom, keep the commandments,
And the Lord will give her freely unto thee (i. 26).

That Wisdom is the gift of God is again declared to be the case in i. 10:

Without measure doth He grant her to them that love Him.

Wisdom is thus the free gift of God; but this does not mean to say that man has not his part to play in order to enjoy this free gift; he has a discipline to go through which is irksome, and which will test the sincerity of the seeker:

But I will walk with him in disguise,
And at first I will try him with temptations.
Fear and dread will I bring upon him,
And I will torment him with chastisements (iv. 17).

Wisdom will also make great demands upon those that would be her servants; it is a hard course of instruction through which they must go:

. . . Bring thy feet into her fetters,
And thy neck into her chain;
Bow down thy shoulder, and bear her,
And chafe not under her bonds (vi. 24, 25).

But if Wisdom can only be acquired by earnest and sustained effort, if to possess her requires concentrated zeal and self-denial, the reward of those who persist is great in proportion. In a beautiful passage Ben-Sira describes this great reward:

For at length thou wilt find her rest,
And she shall be turned for thee into gladness.
And her fetters shall become a stay of strength for thee,
And her bonds for robes of glory.
An ornament of gold is her yoke,
And her fetters a cord of blue.
Thou shalt array thee with her (*as with*) *robes of glory,*
And crown thee with her (*as with*) *a crown of beauty* (vi. 28–31).

Clearly such a reward cannot be for the many; only the best types of men are able to obtain her; so Ben-Sira says:

For Wisdom is according to her name,
And to most men she is not manifest (vi. 22).

Indeed, Ben-Sira holds that humanity is divided into two categories, the wise and the foolish, or the good and the evil—to him the two terms are respectively synonymous; Wisdom's attitude to each is thus expressed:

As a prison-house is Wisdom to a fool,
And the knowledge of the wise as coals of fire.
As chains on (*their*) *feet is instruction to the foolish,*
And as manacles on their right hand.
As a golden ornament is instruction to the wise,
And as a bracelet upon their right arm (xxi. 18–21).

So lasting is the power of Wisdom among those who truly possess her, that the possession is regarded as hereditary:

If he trust me, he shall possess me,
And his posterity shall hold me fast (iv. 16, see also i. 15).

Yet even he who possesses Wisdom may lose his treasure by sinning, so it is said:

If he turn away (from me), I will forsake him,
And will deliver him over to the spoilers (iv. 19).

The only truly blessed are they who persistently follow after Wisdom (xiv. 20–27); yet for this leisure is required; the ordinary occupations and callings of men are all good and necessary, but none are to be compared to that in which a man devotes himself wholly to the seeking out of the Wisdom of the ancients, which is none other than the fear of God and the Law of the Most High (see the whole of xxxviii. 24–xxxix. 11).

iv. *The Doctrine of Sin.* The great problem of the existence of sin had, of course, exercised the minds of men for ages before the time of Ben-Sira. How was one to reconcile the facts of daily experience with the belief in an all-righteous, all-powerful God, who governed the world? 'The ancient mythical religion had certainly connected physical evil with Adam's sin; but when, after the Exile, the individual, as contrasted with the nation, became more prominently an object of consideration, difficulties doubtless began to appear to which the answer of the old theology was felt to be incomplete.'[1] A suggested explanation of the difficulty is expressed in Ps. xxxvii, where it is said that the destruction of the wicked comes suddenly, while he is in the midst of his prosperity (*vv.* 35, 36); and again, in the same psalm the Psalmist seeks to explain the difficulty by contrasting the 'latter end' of the righteous and the wicked respectively:

Mark the perfect man, and behold the upright:
For the latter end of that man is peace.
As for transgressors, they shall be destroyed together;
The latter end of the wicked shall be cut off (*vv.* 37, 38).

In neither case was there any real solution of the problem. Later thinkers were impelled to offer another explanation; so, for example, the writer who explained that everything had been made for its own purpose:

The Lord hath made everything for its own end:
Yea, even the wicked for the day of evil (Prov. xvi. 4).

Ben-Sira was on safer ground when, in re-echoing earlier teaching, he said:

He that seeketh God will receive discipline (xxxii.[xxxv.]14),

i.e. any misfortune which befalls the righteous is looked upon as a discipline, and is, therefore, in reality for his benefit. None of these attempted solutions could, however, have been regarded as satisfactory, for they did not account for the divine acquiescence in the prosperity of the wicked, however much they might satisfy men as to the necessity of adversity for the righteous. In one passage Ben-Sira does strike out a somewhat original line of thought in seeking a solution of the mystery, though within the limits of the present life; a wicked man may, he says in effect, enjoy prosperity all his life, but so terrible may God cause his last hours to be that all his former enjoyment of life becomes wholly obliterated, and thus the apparent contradiction between the facts of life and the divine justice is harmonized; his words are:

For it is easy in Jahveh's sight
At the end to requite a man according to his deeds.
An evil time causeth forgetfulness of delights,
And the last end of a man will tell of him.
Pronounce no man happy before his death;
For by his latter end a man shall be known (xi. 26–28).

This attempted solution, if it does nothing else, witnesses at any rate to the very earnest desire to try and explain a grave difficulty; and if, as a matter of fact, no advance is made in our book towards a satisfactory solution of what must have constituted a cruel mystery to the God-fearing of

[1] Tennant, in the *Journal of Theological Studies*, ii, p. 209.

those days, it cannot cause surprise; with their lack of knowledge concerning the general laws upon which society is based and by which it exists, with their absolute ignorance concerning the laws of nature, with their very hazy conceptions concerning a fuller spiritual life hereafter, it was wholly impossible for the ancient Hebrew thinkers to frame any really satisfactory working theory whereby to harmonize the seeming contradiction between belief in the existence of an almighty, just God and the facts of human experience. Nevertheless, Ben-Sira had very definite ideas upon the existence of sin and its universal prevalence among men; he had also clearly thought and taught much about the nature and essence of sin, and the special importance of his book in connexion with this subject is that it is the only non-apocalyptic writing which unquestionably reflects light upon the Palestinian thought of its time concerning the introduction of sin and death into the world. 'It is a unique link', says Dr. Tennant, 'between the Old Testament and the ancient Rabbinism. It is also important as a guide to the views of the time from the fact that its author, though perhaps conscious of the inadequacy of his inherited theology to solve all the problems and difficulties which presented themselves to an educated mind, allows himself but little liberty of thought.'[1]

With regard to the origin of sin, Ben-Sira's treatment is highly instructive, for it reveals the difficulty in which he found himself involved as soon as he began to grapple with the subject. He mentions altogether three theories regarding the origin of sin; one of these he combats as erroneous. The first is that the existence of sin is due to God; this is the theory which he combats, though he does not seem to realize the difficulty in which he involves himself in doing so. The passage in which this is dealt with is xv. 11–20, where Ben-Sira replies to those who trace back the origin of sin to God; he says:

Say not: 'From God is my transgression,'
For that which He hateth made He not.
Say not: '(It is) He that made me to stumble,'
For there is no need of evil men.
Evil and abomination doth the Lord hate,
And He doth not let it come nigh to them that fear Him (xv. 11–13).

He says further in the course of his argument (and here his teaching on human free-will comes strongly to the fore):

God created man from the beginning,
And placed him in the hand of his Yeṣer.
If thou (so) desirest, thou canst keep the commandment,
And (it is) wisdom to do His good pleasure.
Poured out before thee (are) fire and water,
Stretch forth thine hand unto that which thou desirest.
Life and death (are) before man,
That which he desireth shall be given to him. . . .
He commanded no man to sin,
Nor gave strength to men of lies (xv. 14–20).

With regard to the word *Yeṣer* it may be noted in passing that in its primary meaning it denotes 'form' or 'framing', hence what is formed or framed in the mind, and it therefore comes to mean 'imagination' or 'purpose'. It is used in a good sense in Isa. xxvi. 3, 1 Chron. xxix. 18; on the other hand, in Gen. vi. 5, viii. 21 it is used of the evil imagination. In later times there arose the doctrine of a 'good' *Yeṣer* as opposed to the 'evil' *Yeṣer*, two opposing tendencies which, it was taught, were constituent elements in man's spiritual nature. Prof. Schechter says: 'The more conspicuous figure of the two *Yeṣers* is that of the evil *Yeṣer*. Indeed, it is not impossible that the expression good *Yeṣer*, as the antithesis of the evil *Yeṣer*, is a creation of later date.'[2] It is, therefore, probable that Ben-Sira, when making use of the expression in the passage just quoted, had the evil *Yeṣer*, or 'tendency', in mind; at any rate, the context shows that even if the word was used in a neutral sense it was at least *potentially* the evil *Yeṣer* to which he referred; but as this tendency or inclination to evil was part of man's nature it was created by God, so that Ben-Sira shows himself to have been in danger of falling, by implication, into the very error which he combats in the previously quoted passage (xv. 11–13); indeed, further on in his book he comes perilously near to a direct assertion that God created evil; see xxxiii. (𝔊 xxxvi.) 13–15, xxxvii. 3.

[1] *Op. cit.*, p. 207. [2] *Some Aspects of Rabbinic Theology*, p. 243.

So that, at least by implication, Ben-Sira might well be convicted of imputing the origin of evil to God, though he refrains from doing so explicitly.[1]

A second theory which Ben-Sira brings forward is expressed in xxv. 24:

From a woman did sin originate [lit. is the beginning of sin],
And because of her we all must die.

Dr. Tennant, in writing on this verse, says: 'It has to be borne in mind that when, in the second clause of the verse, the writer passes to the thought of death, to the relation of Eve's sin to our universal mortality, a causal connexion is distinctly asserted. The use of *teḥillah* ['beginning'] in the former clause does not perhaps in itself preclude the thought of such connexion, in the case of sin, having presented itself to Ben-Sira's mind, but it certainly does not suggest any such connexion. . . . If Ben-Sira intended to imply that Eve's transgression was the cause or origin of human sinfulness he was venturing further than was his wont beyond the letter of the Scriptural narrative which he had in mind, and was already in possession of a much deeper view of the first transgression than is to be met with in Jewish literature until we come to St. Paul's Epistles, the Slavonic book of Enoch, and 4 (2) Esdras.'[2] In any case, this second theory of Ben-Sira's only traces the history of sin from the time that it existed in humanity without following it further back.[3]

Finally, a third theory, though not expressed in definite form, can with much probability be shown to have been in the mind of Ben-Sira. In xxi. 27, 28 it is said:

When the fool curseth his adversary [lit. Satan],
He curseth his own soul;
The whisperer defileth his own soul,
And is hated wheresoever he sojourneth.[4]

This is a difficult passage, but it seems clear that by the words 'The whisperer defileth his own soul' Ben-Sira meant to express the truth that the evil in man is of his own making; it is also evident that the words are intended to be an illustration of the truth enunciated in the preceding couplet. Whatever is meant by 'adversary'—whether 'Satan' in the sense of the devil, or an adversary in its ordinary meaning—the words which follow ('He curseth his own soul') show that what Ben-Sira intends to teach is that the 'adversary' is synonymous with the ungodly man's own self; or, as Hart explains it, 'not Satan, but the man himself is responsible for his sin.'[5] The verse, as Cheyne has pointed out, can be illustrated by Ps. xxxvi. 1 (R.V. marg.): 'Transgression saith to the wicked within his heart . . .'[6] To explain the words by saying that when a man curses somebody else who is his enemy he curses himself, i.e. that the curse recoils upon his own head, would not only be contrary to the ideas of the times, but would also be out of harmony with the words which follow. The Syriac translator evidently saw the difficulty of making 'the adversary' refer to somebody other than 'the fool', but not perceiving the point of the words he put in a negative, thus giving a different turn to the whole, and rendered: 'When the fool curseth him who sinned *not* against him, he curseth his own soul.' The gist of the passage may then be taken to be that man is his own 'Satan'; in other words, that the origin of sin is to be sought in man himself. This may be illustrated by another passage:

What is brighter than the sun? Yet this faileth;
And (*how much more*) *man who* (*hath*) *the inclination of flesh and blood!*[7] (xvii. 31).

Dr. Tennant paraphrases the Greek thus: 'Even the sun darkens itself—the brightest thing in the world; how much more, then, frail man!' He says, further, in connexion with this verse, that if

[1] Some later Rabbis had no hesitation in directly asserting what Ben-Sira here implies; in the Midrash *Bereshith Rabba* xxvii it is definitely stated that God created the evil *Yeṣer*; and in *Qiddushin* 30 *b* (T. B.) the following words are put into the mouth of the Almighty: 'I created the evil *Yeṣer*; I created for him [i.e. for man, in order to overcome the evil *Yeṣer*] the Law as a means of healing. If ye occupy yourselves with the Law, ye will not fall into the power of it.'

[2] *Op. cit.*, pp. 210, 211.

[3] It is interesting to note that in a later, but pre-Christian, book the writer believes in the existence of sin before the creation of the human race; in the 'Book of the Parables' (1 Enoch lxix. 6), in reference to the evil angels, it is said: 'And the third was named Gadreel; he it is who showed the children of men all the blows of death, and he led astray Eve . . .'

[4] The Hebrew of these verses is not extant.

[5] *Op. cit.*, p. 154.

[6] *The Expositor*, series xi, p. 346.

[7] The Hebrew is not extant; the first clause of the above represents both the Syriac and the Greek; the second is based upon the Greek and the Syriac; the Greek runs: 'And an evil man will think on flesh and blood.' See the critical and exegetical notes in the commentary on this verse.

Ben-Sira offers any excuse for man's depravity 'it is that of his natural and essential frailty, referred to in such passages as xvii. 30–32, but never traced to an external cause'.[1] Difficult as the verse is, it may be concluded that its meaning illustrated Ben-Sira's teaching in the previously considered passage that the origin of sin is to be sought in man.[2] That this belief was held in certain Jewish circles may be gathered from the following words which occur in 1 Enoch xcviii. 4: 'I have sworn unto you, ye sinners, as a mountain has not become a slave, And a hill does not become the handmaid of a woman, Even so sin hath not been sent upon the earth, But man of himself hath created it, And under a great curse shall they fall who commit it.'[3]

The three passages discussed suggest, therefore, a belief that sin originates within man, and is of his own making, irrespective of any external agency; but there are other passages which point distinctly to a belief that sin *is* external to man; see, for example, xxi. 2, xxvii. 10.

So that Ben-Sira's teaching on the origin of sin may be summed up in the following way: He implies, though he does not definitely assert it, that the creation of sin is due to God; yet in one passage of considerable importance he strongly combats this theory. He teaches, further, that so far as the human race is concerned the origin of sin is to be sought in the fall of Eve; but he does not attempt to trace its history further back; this, however, was from his point of view unnecessary if, in accordance with his third theory, sin originates in each individual; nevertheless, he involves himself in a contradiction here in saying that because of Eve's sin all men must die. In addition to this, however, there is the further inconsistency regarding his third theory, for while teaching that sin originates within man, he speaks of sin as something external to man. These contradictory thoughts bring into clear relief Ben-Sira's inability to formulate a consistent and logical doctrine as to the origin of sin; and in this he but shows himself to be a forerunner of the Rabbis, from whose writings it can be seen that later thinkers were involved in precisely the same inconsistencies as soon as they attempted to construct a working theory on the subject.

But the theoretical difficulties in which Ben-Sira was involved did not in any way detract from his deep realization of the existence and universal prevalence of sin; he witnesses to this in many passages, as may be seen by a reference to the following passages among many others: iv. 26, vii. 8, viii. 5, xxiii. 4–6.

v. *The Doctrine of the Future Life.* In the main Ben-Sira's belief concerning the Hereafter was that of the normal teaching of the Psalms; such passages, for example, as Ps. vi. 5 ('For in death there is no remembrance of Thee: In Sheol who shall give Thee thanks?'), and cxx. 17, 18, cvi. 2, cp. Isa. xxxviii. 18, 19, are clearly the pattern on which he bases his teaching in xvii. 27, 28:

For what pleasure hath God in all that perish in Hades,
In place of those who live and give Him praise?
Thanksgiving perisheth from the dead as from one that is not,
(But) he that liveth and is in health praiseth the Lord.

Although death, as a rule, marks the end of all things and is usually connected with corruption (x. 11, xvii. 32, xxviii. 6), yet Ben-Sira does not speak of it as necessarily a cause of terror; indeed, under certain circumstances, it is preferable to life; he says, e. g., in xli. 2:

Hail! Death, how welcome is thy decree
To the luckless man, and that lacketh strength,
That stumbleth and trippeth at everything,
That is broken, and hath lost hope.

See also xxxii. 11, xxx. 17, xl. 28. On the other hand, death is terrible to him who is in prosperity and in the enjoyment of health (xl. 1). Sometimes death is spoken of as a punishment (vii. 17, xl. 9, 10); but there is nowhere any mention of punishment after death. The only sense in which, according to Ben-Sira, a man can be said to 'live' after death was by means of his wisdom which he had acquired in his lifetime:

His understanding many do praise,
And never shall his name be blotted out:
His memory shall not cease,
And his name shall live from generation to generation (xxxix. 9).

[1] *Op. cit.*, p. 212.

[2] On the question as to whether the evil *Yeṣer* is external to man or not there is much division in Rabbinical writings; see Schechter's very instructive chapters xiv, xv, xvi in *Some Aspects of Rabbinic Theology.* Further useful information on the Jewish doctrine of sin will be found in chap. viii ('The Doctrine of Divine Retribution in Rabbinical Literature') of the same writer's *Studies in Judaism* (First Series).

[3] Charles, 1 *Enoch*[2], p. 242.

Or, again, in the following fine passage (xli. 11–13):

Vanity is man (concerning) his body,
But the name of the pious shall not be cut off.
Be in fear for thy name, for that abideth longer for thee
Than thousands of precious treasures.
Life's goods last for limited days,
But the reward of a name for days without number.

In some few instances there seem to be the beginnings of what might naturally have developed into a somewhat fuller conception of life hereafter, the adumbration of a belief in something more than a mere shadowy existence beyond the grave. The instances are those in which the dead are said to 'rest', an idea very different from that of death being corruption and the end of all things, which is the more usual one in our book. The conception of the dead 'resting' must involve some sort of a belief beyond that of the bare existence of the spirit in the future state; thus, in xxii. 11 Ben-Sira says:

Weep gently for the dead, for he hath found rest (cp. also xxix. 17, xxxviii. 23).

It is of particular interest to note, in view of the development of ideas concerning the future life which took place during the second century B.C., that in at least two instances the Greek shows an advance upon the corresponding Hebrew conception; in vii. 17 the Hebrew has:

Humble (thy) pride greatly,
For the expectation of man is worms.

For this the Greek has:

Humble thy soul greatly,
For the punishment of the ungodly man is fire and the worm.[1]

The other passage is xlviii. 11, but for the details of this recourse must be had to the notes in the commentary.

§ 10. Bibliography.

Chief Editions of the Text:—

(*a*) Of the Hebrew Fragments: Schechter, *Ecclesiasticus* xxxix. 15–xl. 8 in *The Expositor*, July, 1896; Cowley-Neubauer, *The original Hebrew of a portion of Ecclesiasticus* (xxxix. 15–xlix. 11) together with the early versions, and an English translation and introduction (Oxford, 1897) (cited as 'Cowley-Neub.'); Halévy edited the same text in *Rev. Sém.* v. 148, 193, 383; I. Lévi, *L'Ecclésiastique*, Part I (containing xxxix. 15–xlix. 11) (Paris, 1898); Part II (containing all the rest of the recovered Hebrew text) (Paris, 1901): a very full and valuable text, translation, and commentary; Schechter (edition of xlix. 12–l. 22) in *JQR*, x. 197; Schechter and Taylor, *The Wisdom of Ben-Sira* (containing text of parts of iii–xvi, xxx–xxxiii, xxxv–xxxviii, xlix–li, with commentary, notes, introduction, &c.) (Cambridge, 1899) (cited as *WBS*); Halévy edited xlix. 12–l. 22 in the *Rev. Sém.* vii. 214–220; G. Margoliouth published, with notes, text of xxxi. 12–31 and xxxvi. 22–xxxvii. 26 in *JQR*, xii. 1–33; Schechter published *A further fragment of Ben-Sira* (containing iv. 23–v. 13, xxv. 8–xxvi. 2) in *JQR*, xii. 456–465; Elkan Adler edited and published *Some missing fragments of Ben-Sira* (containing vii. 29–xii. 1) in *JQR*, xii. 466–480; Lévi published *Deux nouveaux manuscrits hébreux de l'Ecclésiastique* (containing a new text of xxxvi. 24–xxxviii. 1, and a series of selections, vi. 18, 19, xxviii. 35, vii. 1, 4, 6, 17, 20, 21, 23, 25) in the *Revue des Études Juives* (*RÉJ*), xi. 1–30; finally Gaster edited and published *A new Fragment of Ben-Sira* (containing xviii. 31–33, xix. 1–2, xx. 5–7, xxvii. 19, 22, 24, 26, and xx. 13) in *JQR*, xii. 688–702. *Facsimiles of the fragments hitherto recovered of the Hebrew text* (of Ecclesiasticus) were published by the Oxford and Cambridge Presses in 1901. Editions of the complete (Hebrew) text (so far as recovered) have been published by Knabenbauer (Paris, 1902), with a valuable commentary, Peters (Freiburg, 1902), Strack (Leipzig, 1903); Lévi, *The Hebrew text of the Book of Ecclesiasticus*, with brief notes and a selected glossary (Leyden, 1904, in *Semitic Study Series*); Peters, *Ecclesiasticus Hebraice* (pointed Hebrew text and Latin translation on opposite pages; Freiburg, 1905); and Smend, *Die Weisheit des Jesus Sirach*, containing critically reconstructed Hebrew text, German translation covering the entire book (based on critical text), an elaborate commentary and index (Greek, Syriac, Hebrew): 3 vols., Berlin, 1906–7.

(*b*) Of the Ancient Versions. Important editions of the Greek text by Fritzsche (*Libri Apocryphi Veteris Testamenti Graece*, Leipzic, 1871); Holmes and Parsons (Oxford, 1827); Swete, *The Old Testament in Greek*, vol. ii. (Cambridge, 1891); of Codex 248 (with a valuable textual commentary and prolegomena) by J. H. A. Hart (*Ecclesiasticus in Greek*, Cambridge, 1909). Of the Syriac text (Peshitta): Lagarde, *Libri Veteris Testamenti Apocryphi Syriace* (Leipzig, 1871); Ceriani, *Translatio Syra Pescito Vet. Test. ex codice Ambrosiano* (Milan, 1876–1883); of the Syro-Hexaplar, Ceriani, *Codex Syro-Hexaplaris Ambrosianus photolithographice editus* (Milan, 1874): of the Old Latin, the various editions of the Vulgate; text of Codex Amiatinus, by Lagarde, in his *Mitteilungen* I (1884); of the Ethiopic,

[1] See the references to 'fire' and 'worm' given in the exegetical notes on this verse.

Dillmann, *Biblia Vet. Test. Aethiopice*, v (1894): see further the introductions in the commentaries of Smend and Peters (cited above).

COMMENTARIES AND CRITICAL DISCUSSIONS:—

(*a*) COMMENTARIES: Fritzsche, *Die Weisheit Jesus Sirach's erklärt und übersetzt* (Leipzig, 1859); Edersheim in Wace's *Apocrypha*, vol. ii (London, 1888); Ryssel in Kautzsch's *Apokryphen*, vol. i (Tübingen, 1900); Oesterley in the Cambridge Bible for Schools and Colleges (1912); the commentaries of Knabenbauer, Peters, Lévi, and Smend referred to above.

(*b*) CRITICAL AND GENERAL DISCUSSIONS: Herkenne, *De Veteris Latini Ecclesiastici*, &c. (Leipzig, 1899); Peters, *Die sahidisch-koptische Uebersetzung des Buches Ecclesiasticus* (Freiburg, 1898): A. Fuchs, *Textkritische Untersuchungen zum hebräischen Ekklesiastikus* (Freiburg, 1907); Perles, *Notes critiques sur le texte de l'Ecclésiastique* in *RÉJ*, xxxv. 48–64; Schechter and Taylor in *WBS*; Taylor, *The Wisdom of Ben-Sira* in *JQR*, xv. 440–474 and 604–626 (valuable for criticism of text); Gfrörer, *Philo*, ii. 18–52 (Stuttgart, 1831); Cheyne, *Job and Solomon*, pp. 179–198 (London, 1887); Drummond, *Philo Judaeus*, i, pp. 144–155 (London, 1888); D. S. Margoliouth, *An Essay on the Place of Ecclesiasticus in Semitic Literature* (Oxford, 1890); and (by the same) *The Language and Metre of Ecclesiasticus* in *The Expositor* (1890), pp. 295–320, 381–391 [on the literature of the controversy about the genuineness of the Hebrew Fragments see Schürer, *GJV*³, iii. 223]. Passages from Sirach, translated [into German] and explained, are included in the volume (of the series *Die Schriften des Alten Testaments*) entitled *Weisheit*, by P. Volz (Göttingen, 1911). See also the articles *Sirach* in *HDB* (by Nestle), in *JE* (by I. Lévi), and the articles *Ecclesiasticus* and *Sirach* in *EB* (by Toy), with the literature cited. For a full bibliography see Schürer, *GJV*³, iii. pp. 219–228 (brought up to 1909); in the *ET* of Schürer, *HJP* (1891), vol. v, pp. 27–30 (necessarily far from complete).

SYMBOLS AND ABBREVIATIONS.

𝔥 = The Hebrew text.
  𝔥^A 𝔥^B 𝔥^C 𝔥^D = The respective MSS. of the Hebrew text.
  𝔥¹ 𝔥² = These symbols are used occasionally to distinguish doublets in the text.
𝔊 = The Greek Version.
  A = Codex Alexandrinus.
  ℵ = Codex Sinaiticus.
  ℵ* = The uncorrected text of Cod. Sinaiticus.
  ℵ^{c.a} = The first seventh-century corrector of ℵ.
  B = Cod. Vaticanus.
  B^{a.b} = The second and third *instaurator* of B.[1]
  B^b = The third *instaurator* of B.[1]
  C = Cod. Ephraemi Rescriptus.
  V = Cod. Venetus Gr. 1.
  55 = Cod. Vat. Reg. Gr. 1.[2]
  68 = Cod. Venetus Gr. v.
  70 = Cod. Monac. Gr. 551.
  106 = Cod. Ferrarensis 187.
  155 = Cod. Hagensis Meerman II (Bodleian).
  157 = Cod. Basiliensis B vi. 23.
  248 = Cod. Vat. 346.
  253 = Cod. Vat. 336.
  254 = Cod. Vat. 337.
  296 = Cod. Vat. Palatino-Heidelbergensis 337.
  307 = Cod. Monac. Gr. 129.
  308 = Unknown; quoted by Holmes and Parsons.
𝔏 = The Old Latin Version.
  Cod. Am. = Cod. Amiatinus.
  Cod. Sang. = Cod. Sangermanensis.
𝔊^B = Cod. B. of the Greek Version.
𝔖 = The Syriac Version.
  𝔖¹ and 𝔖² = doublets in 𝔖 are sometimes so indicated.
Eth = The Ethiopic Version.
Ar = The Arabic Version.
Arm = The Armenian Version.
Boh = The Bohairic Version.
Sah = The Sahidic Version.
Slav = The Slavonic Version.
Syro-Hex = The Syro-Hexaplar.

A. V. = Authorized Version.
B. H. = Biblical Hebrew.
EB = Encyclopaedia Biblica.
E.T. = English Translation.
EV = English Version.
GJV = Geschichte des jüdischen Volkes im Zeitalter Jesu Christi (Schürer).
HDB = Hastings's Dictionary of the Bible.
HJP = History of the Jewish People in time of Christ (Schürer) E.T.
IJA = International Journal of Apocrypha.
JE = Jewish Encyclopaedia.
JQR = Jewish Quarterly Review.
RÉJ = Revue des Études Juives.
NH = Neo-Hebrew.
PBH = Post-Biblical Hebrew.
PEFQ = Palestine Exploration Fund, Quarterly Statement.
R. V. = Revised Version.
T. B. = Talmud Babli.
T. J. = Talmud Jerushalmi.
WBS = The Wisdom of Ben-Sira (ed. by Schechter and Taylor).
ZATW = Zeitschrift für die alttestamentliche Wissenschaft.
ZDMG = Zeitschrift der deutschen morgenländischen Gesellschaft.

[1] Swete, *The Old Testament in Greek*, i, p. xix.

[2] Swete, *Introduction to the O.T. in Greek*, p. 158 (1900).

SIRACH

PROLOGUE [a]

SINCE many things and great have been delivered unto us through the Law and the Prophets and the others who followed after them—for which things' sake we must give Israel the praise of instruction and wisdom—and as not only must the readers themselves become adept, but also the lovers of learning must be able to profit them which are without both by speaking and writing; my grandfather Jesus, having given himself much to the reading of the Law and the Prophets and the other books of our fathers, and having acquired considerable familiarity therein, was induced also himself to take a part in writing somewhat pertaining to instruction and wisdom, in order that those who are lovers of learning and instructed in[b] these things [c]might make so much the more progress[c] by a manner of life (lived) [d]in accordance with the Law[d]. Ye are entreated, therefore, to make your perusal with favour and attention, and to be indulgent, if in any parts of what we have laboured to interpret we may seem to fail in some of the phrases. For things

[a] *For the spurious Prologue found in cod.* 248, *in the Complutensian text and in the 'Synopsis of Holy Scripture', falsely attributed to St. Athanasius, see Edersheim (in Wace), p.* 25; *an English translation of it is given in the A. V. before that of the genuine Prologue.* Προλογος B A : πρ. σιραχ C : om. ℵ [*The whole is omitted in* 𝔖 *Eth and in* 157 248, *which have the spurious Prologue*] [b] *Reading* ενηχοι : Syro-Hex ℵ[c.a] A V 254 &c. *for* ενοχοι B C [c–c] *Reading with* B πολλῷ μαλλον επιπροσθωσιν : ℵ ετι (= Syro-Hex) προσθησουσιν [d–d] *Reading*

1. **the Law . . . after them.** The threefold division of the Hebrew Canon is here explicitly mentioned for the first time; it is noticeable, however, that the third division is referred to in a somewhat vague way (as again below), namely, as 'those that followed after them', 'the other books of our fathers', and 'the rest of the books'. It is clear that a third division was already in existence by the side of the Law and the Prophets; but the indefinite way in which it is referred to suggests that this third collection had not yet been delimited, and that it may still have been incomplete. The tripartite division of the Canon is also clearly indicated in Luke xxiv. 44, 'all things . . . which are written in the Law of Moses, and the Prophets, and the Psalms concerning Me'; but this is the only passage in the N. T. which makes explicit mention of it. See further Ryle, *The Canon of the O. T.*, passim; Buhl, *Canon and Text of the O. T.*; and Box, *Short Introduction to the Lit. of the O. T.*, p. 4. The expression 'followed after them' may imply chronological succession.

3. **instruction and wisdom.** Perhaps the order of cod. 253 'wisdom and instruction' (= חכמה ומוסר) may be more original; the foundation and first principle of true life is the moral culture implied by the term 'wisdom' (= the fear of the Lord), of which instruction, or discipline, is the specific application. Israel is worthy of praise because it has made the Law, which was graciously bestowed upon it by God, a means of imparting wisdom, and a means of discipline, to itself.

readers . . . lovers of learning. Both terms refer to one and the same class; perhaps, as Smend suggests, primarily teachers of the Law (i. e. Scribes) are meant; for 'reader' = scribe (ἀναγνώστης = סופר) cf. 1 Esdras (3 Ezra) viii. 8, 9, 19, ix. 39, 42, 49 (these correspond to Ezra vii. 11, xii. 21, Neh. viii. 1, 4, 9).

4. **them which are without.** i. e. either those that are 'in the land of their sojourning' (see below), or the laity; the latter, perhaps, suits the context better, as the original writer, Ben-Sira, wrote for the Palestinians, not for the Diaspora (so Smend).

by speaking and writing. Oral instruction was, of course, one of the most important departments of the Scribes' activity; the reference to writing in this connexion is interesting; doubtless other works besides Sirach were produced by members of the scribal class which were not embodied in the Canon; a specimen of such has recently come to light in the Aramaic version of the 'Sayings of Aḥikar' from the papyri of Elephantiné,—a work which reminds one of the Wisdom Literature; the Book of Tobit may also be thought of in this connexion. The literary activity of the earlier scribes, as well as the later, is also implied in a number of references in the Rabbinical literature; see Strack, *Einleitung in den Talmud* (4th ed.), pp. 12 ff.

8. **instructed in these things.** For the reading see critical note.

9. **a manner of life (lived) in accordance with the Law.** This expresses the practical aim which governed all the activities of the teachers of the Law; a good comment on this point may be read in Josephus (*Contra Apion.* ii. § 8): 'But, as for our people, if any do but ask one of them concerning our laws, he will tell all more readily than his own name, and this because of our learning them at once, as soon as we could understand anything, and because they were, as it were, graven upon our souls'; cp. also Philo ap. Eusebius, *Praep. Evangel.* viii. 7 (Migne); the expression ἔννομος βίωσις may be illustrated by βίος νόμιμος, which occurs in 4 Macc. vii. 15.

11. **to fail in some of the phrases. For things originally spoken . . .** The younger Sirach is acutely con-

originally spoken in Hebrew have not the same force in them when they are translated into another tongue: and not only these, but the Law itself, and the Prophecies, and the rest of the books, have no small difference when they are spoken in their original form. Now[e], in the eight and thirtieth year under king Euergetes, having come into Egypt and continued there, I found opportunity[f] for no small instruction. I, therefore, deemed it most necessary myself to devote some zeal and 'love-labour' to (the task of) interpreting this book; devoting, indeed, much sleepless care and skill in the interval in order, having brought[g] the book to an end, to publish it for them also who in the land of their sojourning desire to be lovers of learning, being already prepared in respect of their moral culture to live [h]by the Law[h].

(*a*) I. 1–10. *The Origin of Wisdom* (= 4+4 distichs).

𝔊 **1** 1 All wisdom cometh from the Lord,
  And is with Him for ever.
2 The sand of the seas, and the drops of rain,
  And the days of eternity,—who can number (them)?

with B εννομου: *but* ℵ*V εκ νομου: 70 253 εν νομῳ [e] *So* ℵ*V: γαρ B A C [f] *Reading* αφορμην *with* 254 *and two other cursives*: αφομοιον B ℵ A C [g] *Reading* αγαγοντα *with* ℵ[c.a] A C (ℵ* αγαγοντας) *and some cursives*: αγοντα B [h-h] εν νομῳ ℵ B: εννομως A C*V 253 Syro-Hex

scious of the difficulties which beset the translation of one language into another; he is thinking not so much of the original sense and meaning as of the wording of the Hebrew text, which he feels that he renders inadequately. The reference to the Greek translation of the Bible which follows is interesting; the Siracide wrote at a time when the work of translating the Scriptures into Greek was still unfinished, and he feels at perfect liberty to criticise it freely. The expression 'in Hebrew' (Ἑβραϊστί) occurs here for the first time.

12. **when they are translated.** The Greek word here used (μετάγω) occurs nowhere else in this sense, according to Smend.

13. **not only these.** 'These' refers to the present work. For the character of the Greek translation of Ben-Sira see Introd. § 4 (end).

14. **in the eight and thirtieth year.** The rest of the Prologue states the translator's reasons for undertaking his work. The date refers to the year in which the younger Sirach actually came into Egypt, probably the thirty-eighth regnal year of Euergetes II, viz. 132 B.C.; for a different view see Introd. § 6, ii b.

and continued there. The Greek word used (συγχρονίσας) seems to imply that he continued there till the end of the reign of Euergetes ('synchronize'), i.e. 117–116 B.C.; the Prologue was, therefore, in all probability written between the years 132–116 B.C. For a full discussion of the question of date see Introd. § 6, ii b.

16. **I found opportunity for no small instruction.** The alternative reading ἀφόμοιον (see critical note), which has the weight of manuscript evidence in its favour, is difficult to interpret. The word means 'unlikeness', 'difference', and, if read, the sentence would run: 'I found no small difference of culture,' namely, between the Palestinian and Egyptian Jews, with a depreciatory reference to the latter; but the context negatives such a meaning. The Latin understands ἀφόμοιον as equivalent to ἀφομοίωμα, 'copy' or 'book', cp. A.V. 'a book of no small learning', R.V. 'a copy affording no small instruction'; but it is best to adopt, with Smend, the reading ἀφορμήν, in spite of inferior attestation. This affords an excellent sense which harmonizes admirably with the context; the younger Sirach found large opportunities in Egypt for instruction in the wisdom of the Scribes. As in later times, the synagogues of the Egyptian Diaspora were the centres where such instruction was given, cp. Philo, *Vita Mos.* ii. 168: 'For what are the Jewish prayer-houses in the cities other than places of instruction, and wisdom, caution, moderation, and righteousness, in piety and holiness, in short, in every virtue which recognizes and accepts both human and divine goodness?' In another passage Philo (*De Septen.* ii. 282) says: 'The listeners sit in perfect order and absolute stillness, eagerly drinking in most excellent doctrines. For here one of the most experienced puts forth the most perfect and most useful teaching by which human life can be adorned in the most beautiful way.'

17. **love-labour.** φιλοπονίαν, R.V. 'travail'.

18. **sleepless care.** ἀγρυπνία, cp. xxxi. 1 (𝔊 xxxiv. 1), xxxviii. 26 ff.

in the interval. i.e., as suggested above, in the interval between the years 132–116 B.C.

19. **for them also . . . sojourning.** i.e. for those abroad in the Dispersion. The word παροικία is used of a sojourn in a strange land, as in Acts xiii. 17, 1 Pet. i. 17; so also the verb and adjective, e.g. Luke xxiv. 18, Acts vii. 6, 1 Pet. ii. 11, &c., and frequently in the Septuagint and in Philo.

I. 1—IV. 10. The general theme of this section is Wisdom regarded as the fear of God in its various relations. The subsections are indicated by (*a*), (*b*), (*c*), &c.

(*a*) I. 1–10.

I. 1. **wisdom.** See Introd. § 9, iii.

cometh from the Lord. Cp. Jas. i. 5.

And is with Him for ever. 𝔏 'et cum illo fuit semper et est ante aevum'. Cp. Job xii. 13, Prov. viii. 22, 23, 30, Wisd. vii. 26, John i. 1. 2.

2. **The sand of the seas.** Cp. Gen. xxxii. 12, 1 Sam. xiii. 5, Ps. lxxviii. 27.

the drops of rain. Cp. Job xxxvi. 27 (Sept.).

the days of eternity. יְמֵי עוֹלָם in the O.T. = 'the days of old' (cp. e.g. Isa. lxiii. 9), but according to the later

𝔊 3 The height of the heaven, and the breadth of the earth,
And the deep[a],—who can trace (them) out?
4 Before them all was Wisdom created,
And prudent insight from everlasting.[b]
6 The root of Wisdom, to whom hath it been revealed?
[c]And her subtle thoughts, who hath known them?[cd]
8 [e]One there is[f], greatly to be feared[e],
The Lord[g] sitting upon His throne;
9 He himself created her, and saw, and numbered her,
And poured her out upon all His works;
10 Upon all flesh [h]in measure[h],
But without measure doth He grant her to them that love Him.[i]

[a] +'and wisdom' 𝔊, >𝔖 𝔏 [b] 248 Syro-Hex 𝔏 Sah + *v.* 5: 'The source of Wisdom is the word of God in the heights, and her ways are eternal commandments' [c–c] >Arm [d] *Several cursives* (*not* 248) Syro-Hex 𝔏 Sah *add the following doublet* (= *v.* 7): 'To whom hath the understanding of Wisdom been manifested, and who hath realized the wealth of her experience?' [e–e] 'One (there is) who hath dominion over all her treasures' 𝔖 Ar [f] + 'who is wise' 𝔊 [g] 𝔊 (*exc.* B) *places this in the following clause* [h–h] *Lit.* 'according to His gift' [i] *Two cursives* (*not* 248) Syro-Hex* + 'The love of the Lord is glorious wisdom; He imparts it to those

---

usage the expression means (cp. xxiv. 9) the time eternal to come. In Rabbinical literature עוֹלָם (עלמא) is generally used of this world or the next, cp. e.g. *Chullin* 44 *b* (T. B.): עולם הזה עולם הבא ('this world and the world to come'); though this is not always so; in *Berakhoth* ix. 5 (Mishnah), for example, the word is used in reference to the eternal past.

who can number. Cp. *v.* 9.

3. **The height of the heaven.** Cp. Ps. ciii. 11.

the breadth of the earth. Cp. Ps. xix. 4.

the deep. ἄβυσσος = תְּהוֹם, the subterranean waters; cp. the phrase, 'the waters under the earth' (Deut. v. 8). 'It must be remembered that to the Hebrews the earth was not a large globe, revolving through space round the sun, but a relatively small flat surface, in shape approximately round, supported partly, as it seemed, by the encircling sea out of which it rose, but resting more particularly upon a huge abyss of waters underneath . . .' (Driver, *Genesis*, p. 8). Cf. the Greek 'Ωκεανός.

who can trace (them) out. Cp. xviii. 8, Rom. xi. 33.

4. **Before them all . . .** Wisdom is identified with the Law both by Ben-Sira (see i. 26, xv. 1, xxi. 11, xxiv. 23, xxxiv. 8), and by the Rabbis; cp., in view of this, the Midrash *Bereshith Rabba*, § 8, where among the comments on Gen. i. 26 it is said: 'According to R. Simeon ben Laqish the Torah was in existence 2000 years before the creation of the world'; the same is said in the Midrash *Pesiqta* 109 *a*. Cp. Prov. viii. 22–30.

prudent insight. σύνεσις φρονήσεως; in Job xxviii. 20 σύνεσις (= בינה) is also used as a synonym for Wisdom. The addition of φρονήσεως here seems unnecessary (but cp. Prov. viii. 12); 𝔖 'And firm faithfulness from of old', reading perhaps אמונה ('faithfulness'), for which 𝔊 apparently read תבונה ('understanding'). After this *v.* a number of cursives, including 248, add *v.* 5, see crit. note; with it cp. Wisd. ix. 17, Bar. iii. 11, 12. The verse is a later insertion, added probably to explain how it was that Wisdom existed before all things; Hart (p. 285, note) thinks it is a Pharisaic doublet to *v.* 4.

6. **root.** The source, not the origin, of Wisdom, cp. *v.* 20 and Job xix. 28.

her subtle thoughts. The Greek word occurs again in xlii. 18, where the corresponding Hebrew is מערומים in reference to hidden thoughts of the heart; the exact form is not used in the O.T., but ערומים occurs in Prov. xiv. 18 of 'prudent men'. This clause is wanting in Arm. On the doublet to this verse (= *v.* 7) see critical note.

8. **One there is.** Cp. xliii. 29; the words 'To fear the Lord is the beginning of wisdom' (*v.* 14, Prov. ix. 10, xxviii. 28, Ps. cxi. 10) must be understood in the light of this *v.*; wisdom and awe-inspiring might are correlative ideas (cp. Smend *in loc.*).

The Lord. See critical note.

sitting upon . . . Cp. Ps. xlvii. 8 (9 in Hebr.), Is. vi. 1.

9. **saw.** Cp. Prov. viii. 22, 1 Cor. ii. 7.

numbered. Cp. *v.* 2, Job xxviii. 27. 𝔏 adds 'et mensus est'.

poured her out . . . ἐξέχεεν, cp. Acts ii. 17 ff. (Joel ii. 28 ff.), where the same word is used of the pouring-out of the Spirit upon all flesh. In *Berakhoth* 58 *b* (T. B.) occur the words: 'Blessed art Thou, O Lord our God, King of the Universe, who hast imparted of Thy wisdom to flesh and blood.' In Wisd. i. 4–7 the Holy Spirit is identified with Wisdom; this is also the case in Rabbinical literature, e.g. in the Midrash *Bereshith Rabba* (§ lxxxv, to Gen. xxxviii. 26) it is said that the Holy Spirit was present in the judgement-hall of Solomon when he displayed his wisdom; the reference given is to 1 Kings iii. 27.

10. **Upon all flesh . . .** That Gentile rulers were believed to have some share of Wisdom is seen from Prov. viii. 15, 16.

in measure. κατὰ τὴν δόσιν αὐτοῦ, cp. xxxii. 10 (= 𝔊 xxxv. 12), =כמתנתו; and with the whole *v.* cp. Prov. iii. 13–17, as illustrating the richness and pleasantness of the gift of Wisdom.

to them that love Him. i.e. the Jewish people; a particularistic note, characteristic of the book generally; in the later Rabbinical literature this is, of course, still more emphasized; see e.g. *Qiddushin* 49 *b* (T. B.), where it is said: 'Ten measures of Wisdom came down from heaven, and nine of them fell to the lot of the Holy Land' (quoted

(*b*) I. 11–20. *The Fear of the Lord is the true Wisdom* (= 3+2+2+2+1 distichs).

𝔊 11 The fear of the Lord is glory and exultation,
And [k]gladness, and a crown of rejoicing[k].
12 The fear of the Lord delighteth the heart,
[kk]And giveth gladness[kk], and joy, and [l]length of days[l].
13 Whoso feareth the Lord, it shall go well with him at the last,
And in the day of his death he shall [m]be blessed[m].
14 [n]To fear[n] the Lord[o] is the beginning of Wisdom,
And with the faithful [p]was she created[p] in the womb[q].
𝔖 15 [s]With faithful men is she, and she hath been established from eternity[s];
ℌ [t]And with their seed shall she continue[t].
𝔊 16 To fear the Lord is the fullness[u] of Wisdom,
And she satiateth men with [v]her fruits.
17 She filleth all her house with [w]pleasant things[w],
And her garners with her produce[x].

to whom He appears, in order that they may behold Him'; 𝔏 *adds this after v.* 11. k-k C 'giveth gladness, and joy, and length of days', *added from v.* 12b kk-kk > 253 𝔖 Syro-Hex l-l 'eternal life'; *two cursives* (*not* 248) Syro-Hex* + 'The fear of the Lord is a gift from the Lord, for it sets [men] upon paths of love' m-m 'find grace' B n-n 'The fear of' C 𝔖 𝔏 o God B p-p > 𝔖 q + 'of their mother' 𝔖 s-s *So* 𝔖; *the text of* 𝔊 *is probably corrupt*; ℌ, *conjecturally emended, according to Smend*, 'Among faithful men hath she been established (𝔊 "nested herself") from eternity' t-t *So probably* ℌ; *the rendering of* 𝔊, 'shall she be had in trust,' *is due to a misunderstanding of the force of* תאמן, *which was most likely the word used in the Hebrew.* 𝔏 *adds another verse which is a combination of vv.* 11, 12 u 'beginning' 𝔖 v + 'the multitude of' 𝔖 w-w 'wisdom' 𝔖, 'from generations (of old)' 𝔏 x 'treasures' 𝔏; + 'And both [i.e. *the fear of the Lord and*

---

in *JE*, xii. 538 *a*). For the addition to this *v.* see critical note. The first clause of this addition (ἀγάπησις κυρίου ἔνδοξος σοφία) is quoted in the anthology of Antonius and Maximus (see Hart, p. 364).

(*b*) I. 11–20.

11. **The fear of the Lord.** As frequently in the O. T., this connotes in the Wisdom of Ben-Sira true piety; the Law has for its object the instilling of fear in the hearts of the Israelites (cp. Deut. iv. 10, 'Assemble Me the people, and I will make them hear My words, that they may learn to fear Me all the days that they live upon the earth'), and therefore the observance of the Law, which is the manifestation of divine Wisdom, is the visible proof that the fear of the Lord is in the heart of a man (cp. Ps. cxi. 10).

is. i.e. brings with it.

exultation. καύχημα, cp. x. 22 (Grk.).

a crown of rejoicing. Cp. *v.* 18, vi. 31, xv. 6, Prov. iv. 9.

12. **delighteth the heart.** Cp. Prov. xxvii. 9 (Sept.).

length of days. Cp. Deut. vi. 2; it is characteristic of the book (the same holds good of Prov., see e.g. iii. 2, 16, iv. 10, x. 27, 30) that attention is concentrated on this life; the rendering of 𝔖, 'eternal life,' shows Christian influence. For the addition to this *v.* see critical note.

13. **at the last.** ἐπ' ἐσχάτων; the reference is to the end of life in this world, cp. 𝔖 'at the last of his days'; in iii. 26, where the same expression occurs, the Hebr. equivalent is אחרית; see also xxxviii. 20, Prov. v. 11, Wisd. iii. 17.

he shall be blessed. Cp. 1 Chron. xix. 28, 'And he died in a good old age, full of days, riches, and honour'; the reading of B, 'he shall find grace,' is due apparently to Christian influence.

14. **To fear the Lord.** Cp. Ps. cxi. 10, Prov. i. 7, ix. 10, xxviii. 28.

the beginning. ἀρχή (= ראש) means either the starting-point of a thing, as e.g. in xv. 14, or the most important part of something, as e.g. in xxix. 21, xxxix. 26, or the essence of a thing, i.e. its best part, as in xi. 3; in the passage before us the meaning is that the fear of the Lord is the starting-point as well as the essence of true Wisdom.

the faithful. הנאמנים (cp. נאמני ארץ Ps. ci. 6) = הצדיקים, 'the righteous' (cp. Job xvii. 9).

was she created in the womb. The later Jewish doctrine of the *Yeṣer tob* ('the bias towards good') was based on passages like this, cp. Gen. viii. 21. An interesting passage occurs in *Nedarim* 32 *b* (T. B.), where, in discussing the parable in Eccles. ix. 14, 15, it is said that the poor wise man who by his wisdom delivered the city means the *Yeṣer tob*, 'for he delivered the city through his wisdom, namely, repentance and good works' (see Weber, *Jüdische Theologie*, p. 217); Wisdom is thus identified with the *Yeṣer tob*, which is implanted in man when he is created (see the Midrash, *Bemidbar Rabba*, § 22).

15. See critical note. For this *v.* and its addition, as found in 𝔏, see Herkenne, pp. 46–49.

With faithful men ... Smend, on the basis of 𝔖, supposes with much probability that the original Hebrew ran: עם אנשי אמת היא מעולם תְּקֻנָּה ('Among men of truth hath she been established for ever,' i.e. from of old).

shall she continue. So critical note. Cp. iv. 16, xxiv. 7–49.

16. **satiateth.** μεθύσκει, lit. 'intoxicates', cp. xxxii. 13 (= 𝔊 xxxv. 13), Ps. xvi. 11. xxii. 7 (Sept.).

her fruits. Cp. Prov. viii. 19, xi. 30.

17. **She filleth all her house ...** Cp. Prov. ix. 1–6. For the addition to this *v.* see critical note.

𝔊 18 The crown[y] of Wisdom is the fear of the Lord,
𝔖 [z]And increaseth peace and [a]life and health[a z].
19 [b]She is a strong staff and a glorious stay[b],
𝔊 And [c]everlasting honour to[c] them that hold her fast.
20 To fear the Lord is [d]the root of Wisdom[d],
And her branches are length of days[e].

(*c*) I. 22–30. *Wisdom is shown forth by the exercise of patience, self-control, and humility* (= 3+3+3+2 distichs).

22 [a b]Unrighteous wrath[b] cannot be justified,
For the wrath[c] of his anger (will prove) his ruin.
23 He that is patient [d]controlleth himself[d] until the (proper) time,
And afterwards joy springeth up for him.
24 He suppresseth his words until the (proper) time,
And (then) shall the lips of many[e] tell forth his understanding.
25 In the treasures of Wisdom (there are) wise proverbs[f];
But godliness is an abomination to sinners[g].

Wisdom] are gifts of God unto peace' 70 248 [y] 'beginning' 𝔖 [z–z] *So* 𝔖; 𝔊 *lit.* 'Making peace and health of cure to flourish'; + 'He increaseth glorying to them that love him' 248 [a–a] ℵ[c.a] 'life eternal' (αιωνιος *for* ιασεως) [b–b] *So* 𝔖; B ℵ A C *read:* 'He both saw and numbered her (> 248 253 Syro-Hex Sah); he rained down skill and knowledge of understanding' [c–c] 𝔊 *lit.* 'exalted the honour of' [d–d] 'eternal life' 𝔖 [e] 70 248 253 Syro-Hex* *add with slight variations v.* 21: 'The fear of the Lord driveth away sins; and he who abideth therein will avert all wrath'; + 'In the treasures of Wisdom is understanding and reverence of knowledge; but Wisdom is a curse to sinners' 𝔖

[a] 𝔖 *has in place of vv.* 22–27 *twelve distichs which differ almost entirely from* 𝔊; *if they were translated from Hebrew, which is probable, they belong to a later recension of* 𝔋 *and not to the original form; they run as follows:*—

Blessed is the man who meditateth therein,
For Wisdom is better to him than all treasures.

Blessed is the man who draweth nigh thereto,
And who occupieth himself with her commandments.

She prepareth (for) him an eternal crown,
And eternal righteousness among the holy ones.

He rejoiceth over her, and she rejoiceth over him,
And she rejecteth him not to all eternity.

The angels of God rejoice over him,
And tell forth all the glory of the Lord.

This whole book is full of life,
Blessed is the man who hearkeneth thereunto and doeth according unto it!

Hear me, ye who fear God,
Hearken unto, and mark, my words!

He who will inherit life,
As an eternal heritage and a great joy—

Hearken unto all my words and do them,
And thou shalt be inscribed in the book of life.

Love the fear of the Lord,
And stablish thine heart therein, so shalt thou have naught to fear.

Draw nigh unto her, and be not weary,
So shalt thou find life for thy spirit;

And when thou drawest nigh,
Do it as a hero and as a mighty one.

The text of 𝔏 *in these vv. is largely corrupt* [b–b] 'A wrathful man' 70 248 253 Syro-Hex [c] *So* ℵ* 𝔏; *all other Gk. MSS. including* ℵ[c.a] *read* 'sway' [d–d] *So* V 248 253 ανεξεται (= 𝔏); 𝔊 ανθεξεται, 'endures'; *the sense is much the same in either case* [e] 'of faithful (men)' B C [f] *plur. in* ℵ 70 248 253 𝔖 Syro-Hex;

18. **The crown of wisdom.** Cp. xxv. 6, Prov. xii. 4, xvi. 31, xvii. 6. For the addition to this *v.* see critical note.
19. See critical note. The rendering of 𝔊 is a partial repetition of *v.* 9, and is evidently out of place here.
20. Just as the fear of the Lord is the root, i.e. the very essence of Wisdom, so does it also bring forth the most desirable fruit, viz. prolonged life. Again the thought of reward hereafter for a godly life is quite absent. For the addition to this *v.* (= *v.* 21) see critical note.

(*c*) I. 22–30.

22. The abruptness with which this and the following *vv.* are introduced suggests that possibly something has fallen out between this and the preceding section. This appears the more probable on account of the form of 𝔖 and the state of the text of 𝔏 (see critical note, and cp. further Herkenne *in loc.*). Further, the later addition of *v.* 21 points to the desire of a glossator to smooth over the roughness of the passage.

wrath. Reading ὀργή with ℵ* (= 𝔏 iracundia), cp. xlv. 19, instead of ῥοπή of all other MSS. of 𝔊.

23. **until the (proper) time.** i.e. until the time is past during which the exercise of self-control was called forth.

springeth up. ἀναδώσει, a word used in the Bible elsewhere only in Acts xxiii. 33, of a letter being delivered to a ruler.

24. **the lips of many . . .** Cp. xxxix. 9.

25. **godliness.** Θεοσέβεια, 'the fear of God' = Wisdom. The word does not occur elsewhere in this book. In Job xxviii. 28 יִרְאַת אֲדֹנָי is translated Θεοσέβεια in the Sept., cp. Prov. i. 29. For the identification between the fear of God and Wisdom cp. *Pirqe Aboth* iii. 26: 'No wisdom, no fear (of God); no fear (of God), no wisdom.'

𝔊 26 If thou desire Wisdom, keep the commandments[h],
And the Lord will give her freely unto thee.
27 For the fear of the Lord is wisdom and instruction,
And faith and meekness are [i]well-pleasing unto Him[ik].
28 My son[l], disobey not[m] the fear of the Lord[n],
And approach it not with a double heart.
29 Be not a hypocrite in [o]the sight of [o]men,
And take good heed to thy lips.
30 Exalt not thyself lest thou fall,
And bring disgrace upon thyself[p],
And the Lord reveal[q] thy hidden (thoughts),
And cast thee down in the midst of the assembly,
Because thou camest not[r] unto the fear of the Lord,
And thy heart was full of deceit[s].

(*d*) II. 1–6. *On Faithfulness to God and Resignation to His Will* (= 3+3 distichs).

2 1 [a]My son, when thou comest [b]to serve[b] the Lord,
Prepare[c] thy soul for temptation.
2 [ed]Set thy heart aright[d] and endure firmly,
And [f]be not fearful[f] in time of calamity[e].
3 Cleave unto Him[g], and [h]let Him[i] not go[h],
𝔖 [k]That thou mayst be wise in thy ways[k].

in 𝔏 *v.* 25 *follows v.* 20 [g] *Plur. in* 70 253 Syro-Hex 𝔏, *otherwise sing.* [h] 'justice' 𝔏 [i–i] *Lit.* 'His good pleasure' [k] + 'and He filleth His treasures (therewith)' 𝔏 [l] *So* 𝔖 [m] 'be not unbelieving (in)' א 𝔏 [n] + 'when thou art in need' 70 248 253 Syro-Hex [o–o] *So* 253 𝔖 Syro-Hex 𝔏; 𝔊 'in the mouths of' (*reading* בפי *instead of* בפני) [p] *Lit.* 'thy soul' [q] + 'all' 70 248 253 Syro-Hex [r] + 'in truth' 248 253 Syro-Hex; '[Because thou didst draw nigh] unto the Lord with evil intent' (maligne) 𝔏 [s] 'guile and deceit' 𝔏
[a] 248 *inserts the title*: 'Concerning endurance' [b–b] '*to the fear of*' 𝔖; ad servitutem dei 𝔏 [c] 'Thou wilt deliver' 𝔖 [d–d] 'Humble thy heart' 𝔏 [e–e] > 𝔖 [f–f] 𝔊 *lit.* 'haste not' [g] 'God' 𝔏 [h–h] *So* 𝔖; 'depart not (from Him)' 𝔊 [i] 'her' 𝔖; *in* 𝔖 *the reference is to Wisdom* [k–k] *So* 𝔖; 'That thou mayst be increased' (א* 'and it shall be increased') 'at thy latter end' 𝔊; 'That thy life may increase at the last' 𝔏

26. **If thou desire . . .** Cp. Jas. i. 5; also *Berakhoth* 58 *b* (T. B.): 'Blessed art Thou, O Lord our God, King of the Universe, who hast imparted of Thy Wisdom to flesh and blood.' The *v.* before us offers a good example of the combination of grace and free-will.

27. **. . . is wisdom and instruction.** Cp. Prov. xv. 33, which must have been in the mind of Ben-Sira here.

faith and meekness. Cp. xlv. 4, where the same words occur together, and the Hebr. is אֱמוּנָה וַעֲנָוָה. On the meaning of 'faith' see Lightfoot's admirable note in his *Galatians*, pp. 154 ff.

28. **a double heart.** Cp. Ps. xii. 3, לֵב וָלֵב, and Jas. i. 8, iv. 8, ἀνὴρ δίψυχος; see also 1 Enoch xci. 4 (ed. Charles): 'Draw not nigh to uprightness with a double heart, and associate not with those of a double heart.'

29. **Be not a hypocrite.** Cp. xxxii. (𝔊 xxxv.) 15, xxxiii. (𝔊 xxxvi.) 2.

30. **Exalt not thyself . . .** Cp. *Erubin* 13 *a* (T. B.): 'He who humbles himself, him will God exalt; he who exalts himself, him will God humble.'

in the midst of the assembly. Cp. iv. 7, vii. 7, xxiii. 24, xli. 18, xlii. 11; Prov. v. 14.

full of deceit. Cp. xix. 26.

(*d*) II. 1–6.

II. 1. 248 has as title to this section Περὶ πομονῆς.

My son. In the Wisdom-Literature this is the regular mode of address to pupils; cp. vii. 3; Prov. ii. 1, iii. 1, &c., &c. The plural is also used at times; cp. xxxix. 13; Prov. iv. 1.

Prepare thy soul . . . Cp. xliv. 20 *d*; Prov. iii. 11, 12; Heb. xii. 7, 13; and especially Jas. i. 2–4, 12–15.

2. **Set thy heart aright.** Cp. xxxvii. 15; Ps. lxxiii. (Sept. lxxvii.) 8 = Hebr. לֵב (some MSS. הבין) הכין.

endure firmly. καρτέρησον, cp. Job ii. 9 μέχρι τίνος καρτερήσεις, where the Hebr. has עֹדְךָ מַחֲזִיק בְּתֻמָּתֶךָ ('Dost thou still hold fast thine integrity?'); cp. Heb. xi. 27.

be not fearful. μὴ σπεύσῃς; cp. 1 Sam. xxviii. 21 καὶ εἶδεν ὅτι ἔσπευσεν σφόδρα, where the Hebr. has וַתֵּרֶא כִּי־נִבְהַל מְאֹד ('and she saw that he was greatly afraid'); cp. Prov. xxviii. 20. The meaning, therefore, is not: 'Haste not (i.e. to forsake the Lord) in the time of calamity' (Ryssel), but that he is not to be afraid however much outward circumstances may be against him as a result of serving the Lord.

calamity. ἐπαγωγή, lit. 'that which is brought upon' a man by God; the word is often used in the book (𝔊), iii. 28, v. 8, x. 13, xxiii. 11, &c. This is one form of temptation, or 'trying', for which a man must prepare his soul.

3. **Cleave unto Him.** Cp. Deut. x. 20 πρὸς αὐτὸν κολληθήσῃ, Hebr. בּוֹ תִדְבָּק.

let Him not go. Cp. Prov. iv. 13; Cant. iii. 4.

That thou mayst . . . It is probable that both 𝔊 and 𝔖 have retained parts of the original, which was very likely a quotation from Prov. xix. 20 *b*, 'That thou mayest be wise in thy latter end.'

𝔊 4 Accept[1] whatsoever is brought upon thee,
𝔖 [m]And be patient in disease and poverty[m].
𝔊 5 For gold is proved in the fire,
And men acceptable [to God] in [n]the furnace of[n] affliction[o].
6 Put thy trust in God[p], and He will help thee,
[q]And hope in Him, and He will make straight thy ways[q].

(*e*) II. 7–11. *The Blessedness of those who fear the Lord* (= 3+3 distichs).

7 [qq]Ye that fear the Lord, wait for His mercy;
And turn not aside, lest ye fall.
8 Ye that fear the Lord, put your trust in Him,
𝔖 [r]He will not withhold your reward[r].
𝔊 9 Ye that fear the Lord, hope for [s]His benefits[s],
And for eternal gladness and mercy[t].
10 Look at the generations of old and see,
Who ever trusted in the Lord, and was put to shame?
Or who did abide in His fear, and was forsaken?
Or who did call upon Him, and [u]He did not hear him[u]?
11 For compassionate and merciful is the Lord[w],
[x]And He forgiveth sins, and saveth in time of affliction[x].

(*f*) II. 12–14. *A threefold woe against the faithless* (= 3 distichs)

12 Woe unto fearful[y] hearts and unto [z]faint hands[z],
And unto the sinner that goeth two ways.

[1] + 'readily' 70 248 253 Syro-Hex [m–m] So 𝔖; 𝔊 *lit.* 'And in the changes of thy humiliation be enduring'; 𝔏 'Be enduring in pain and be patient in humiliation' [n–n] >C [o] *Lit.* 'humiliation'; + 'in sickness and in poverty put thy trust in Him' ℵc.a 253 Syro-Hex [p] *So* 𝔖 𝔏; 'Him' 𝔊, 'the Lord' 253 [q–q] *So* 253 𝔖 Syro-Hex; + 'Observe the fear of Him, and grow old therein' 𝔏 [qq] 248 *has the order of this and the two following vv. thus:* 8, 9, 7 [r–r] *So* 𝔖; 'And your reward shall not fail' 𝔊 [s–s] *So* 𝔖; 'good things' 𝔊; 'Him' 𝔏 [t] + 'for an eternal gift with joy is His recompense' ℵc.a 253 Syro-Hex; + 'Ye that fear the Lord, love Him, and your hearts shall be enlightened' 𝔏 [u–u] *So* 𝔖; 'He despised him' 𝔊 𝔏 [w] + 'longsuffering and of great pity' ℵc.a 70 248 253 Syro-Hex [x–x] 'And heareth in time of affliction, and heareth all them that do His will' 𝔖; 'And forgiveth in time of affliction the sins of all them that seek Him in truth' 𝔏 [y] 'double' Syro-Hex 𝔏 [z–z] 'abominable

---

4. **Accept...** The reference is to adversity of any kind which Providence sees well to send, cp. Job ii. 10, Jas. i. 2.
be patient... Cp. v. 11; Job vi. 11; Jas. v. 7, 8. 𝔊 (see critical note) lit. 'in the changes of thy humiliation'.
5. **gold is proved.** Cp. Is. xlviii. 10; Prov. xvii. 3, xxvii. 21; Wisd. iii. 6; Jas. i. 12; 1 Pet. i. 7.
men acceptable. i.e. because they have been tried and purified, cp. Prov. iii. 10.
6. The *v.* is an adaptation of Ps. xxxvii. 3, 5, cp. Prov. iii. 5, 6.
He will help thee. Cp. Ps. xl. 17, xlvi. 1.
hope in Him. Cp. Ps. lxxi. 5.
He will make straight... Cp. Prov. iii. 6.

(*e*) II. 7–11.
7. **wait for...** Cp. Judith viii. 17.
And turn not... Cp. iv. 19.
8. **He will not withhold...** Cp. Lev. xix. 13; Tob. iv. 14.
9. **eternal gladness.** Cp. Is. xxxv. 10, li. 11, lxi. 7.
10. ... **the generations of old.** Cp. Ps. xxii. 4, 5; it is, of course, to the Scriptures that Ben-Sira is referring his pupils.
... **and was put to shame.** Cp. Ps. xxxvii. 25. Apparently Ben-Sira recognized that the Book of Job did not record history.
and He did not hear him. The rendering of 𝔖 seems to correspond better with the first part of this clause, see crit. note.
11. **compassionate and merciful.** Cp. Exod. xxxiv. 6 (Sept.); Ps. ciii. 8, cxlv. 8.
forgiveth sins. Cp. Ps. ciii. 3, 4.
and saveth... The compassion and mercy of God saves them from the result of sin.

(*f*) II. 12–14.
12. **fearful hearts.** Cp. xxii. 18; Deut. xx. 8; 2 Chron. xiii. 7.
faint hands. Cp. xxv. 23; Job iv. 3; Is. xxxv. 3.
that goeth two ways. Cp. 1 Kings xviii. 21; Prov. xxiii. 6, 18; Jas. i. 8, iv. 8; see note on i. 25.

𝔊 13 [a]Woe unto the faint heart, for it believeth not[a],
Therefore shall it not be sheltered.
14 Woe unto you that have lost your endurance[b],
And what will ye do when the Lord visiteth you?

(*g*) II. 15–18. *The Characteristics of those who fear the Lord* (= 3 + 2 distichs).

15 [c]They that fear the Lord [d]will not [e]be disobedient to[e] His words[d],
And they that love Him will keep His ways[f][c].
16 They that fear the Lord will seek His good pleasure,
And they that love Him [g]will be filled with[g] (His)[h] Law.
17 They that fear the Lord will make ready their hearts,
[i]And will humble[k] their souls before Him[i]:
18 [l][‘Let us fall into the hands of the Lord[m],
And not into the hands of men;’][l]
For as is His majesty, so also is His mercy,
𝔖 [n]And as is His name, so also are His works[n].

(*h*) III. 1–16. *On Filial Duty and its Reward* (= 7 × 2 + 1 distichs).

3 1 [a]Hearken, ye children, to the judgement of your father[a],
𝔊 And do thereafter, [b]that ye may be saved[b].

lips and harmful hands’ 𝔏 [a-a] ‘Woe unto the heart that believeth not’ 𝔖; + ‘in God’ 𝔏 [b] + ‘who have left the right ways and have turned unto evil ways’ 𝔏 [c-c] > 253 [d-d] ‘will seek His good pleasure’ A; ‘will not be unfaithful to God’ 𝔏 [e-e] ‘hate’ 𝔖 [f] ‘commandments’ ℵ[c.a] [g-g] ‘will learn’ 𝔖 [h] *expressed in* 𝔖 𝔏 [i-i] ‘But he that forsaketh Him destroyeth his own soul’ 𝔖; + ‘They that fear the Lord will keep His commandments, and will be patient until His visitation’ 𝔏; + ‘saying’ 253; ‘sanctify’ 𝔏 [l-l] > 𝔖 [m] ‘God’ 248 𝔏 [n-n] *So* 𝔖 *only*, > 𝔊 𝔏; + ‘He that feareth God will increase possessions, and his seed shall be blessed after him’ 𝔖. *That the words in the text are original is probable, for they occur in* ℌ, *though they have got misplaced in the extant form of the Hebrew, coming there after* vi. 17

[a-a] *So* 253 𝔖 Syro-Hex 𝔏; ‘Hear me your father, O my children’ 𝔊; *the Aldine text reads* κριμα *for* εμου, *and* 70 *adds* κρισιν *after* τεκνα, *to this* 𝔏 *prefixes*: ‘The children of Wisdom are assemblies of the just; their race is obedience and love’ [b-b] 𝔖 ‘that ye may live the life which is eternal’

---

13. **the faint heart.** Cp. iii. 26.
for it believeth not . . . Cp. Is. vii. 9.

14. **endurance.** If the equivalent Hebr. was תקוה, as in xvii. 24, xli. 2 *d*, the word should be, rather, ‘hope’ or ‘expectation’; cp. also xvi. 13, 22.
visiteth. ἐπισκέπτηται, a play on σκεπασθήσεται in the preceding *v.*

(*g*) II. 15–18.

15. **will not be disobedient . . .** Cp. xvi. 21; Ps. cv. 28, cvii. 11. כִּי־הִמְרוּ אִמְרֵי־אֵל, cp. xxxix. 31 (Hebr.).
His ways. Cp. Ps. xviii. 21, xxv. 4.

16. **will be filled with (His) Law.** Cp. *Pirqe Aboth* iv. 14: ‘Have little business, and be busied in the Law (Torah), and be lowly in spirit unto every man; and if thou idlest from the Law, thou wilt have idlers many against thee; and if thou labourest in the Law, He [i.e. God] hath much reward to give unto thee.’ Taylor, in his edition of *Pirqe Aboth*, p. 69, quotes from *Sanhedrin* 103 *a* (T. B.): ‘Whosoever starves himself for the sake of words of Torah in this world, the Holy One, blessed be He, will satiate him in the world to come.’

17. **will humble.** Cp. iii. 18, vii. 17, xviii. 21.

18. The first two lines of this *v.* are probably not part of the original; their contents have no connexion either with what precedes or follows; its omission by 𝔖 is significant. Cp. 2 Sam. xxiv. 14, of which it is an inexact quotation.
For as is His majesty . . . These words must be read in connexion with 17 *b*.
And as is . . . See critical note.

(*h*) III. 1–16.

III. 1. The words prefixed by 𝔏 (see critical note) are, as can be seen by their Latin form, of Hebrew origin (Breitschneider, Herkenne, Smend), though they probably do not represent part of the original Hebrew book, but belong rather to the secondary recension of this, see Introd. § 3 (*c*); the words in 𝔏 run: ‘Filii sapientiae ecclesia iustorum, et natio illorum oboedientia et dilectio.’
Hearken, ye children . . . 𝔖 𝔏 have evidently retained the more correct reading here, see critical note.
judgement. = מִשְׁפָּט (not דִּין), the right, or that which is due, cp. Deut. xviii. 3, xxi. 17; Jer. xxxii. 7.
that ye may be saved. ἵνα σωθῆτε, not in the Christian sense (as paraphrased by 𝔖, see critical note), but in reference to prosperity in this world (cp. Deut. v. 16); σώζεσθαι is often used in the Sept. as the equivalent of the Hebr. חָיָה (הֶחֱיָה), e.g. Gen. xlvii. 25; Ps. xxix. 4; Prov. xv. 28; Ezek. xxxiii. 12 (see Sept. in each case).

𝔊 2 For the Lord hath given the father glory as touching the children,
And hath established the judgement of the mother as touching the sons[c].
3 [d]He that honoureth his father [e]maketh atonement for sins[e d],
4 And as one that layeth up treasure is he that honoureth his mother.
5 He that honoureth his father shall have joy of his children[f],
And what time he prayeth he shall be heard.
6 He that giveth glory to his father shall have length of days,
𝔖 [g]And he that [h]giveth rest to[h] his mother[i] shall receive reward from God[g].
70 248 253 7 [k]He that feareth the Lord honoureth his father[k],
[l]And serveth his parents as masters[l].
𝔥[A] 8 My son[ll], in word and in deed honour thy father[m],
That [n]every blessing[n] may overtake thee.
9 The blessing of a father establisheth [o](his) seed[o],
But the curse of a mother rooteth up the [oo]young plant[oo].
10 Glorify not thyself in the dishonour of thy father,
For that is no glory to thee[p].
11 A man's glory is the glory of his father,
[pp]And he that dishonoureth[q] his mother [r]multiplieth sin[r pp].
𝔊 12 My son[s], [t]help thy father in his old age[t],
𝔥[A] And [tt]grieve him[tt] not [u]all the days of his[uu] life[u];

[c] 'her children' 𝔖 [d–d] 'He that loveth God obtaineth (forgiveness) for sins, and will keep himself from them; in the day of prayer he will be heard' 𝔏 [e–e] 'his sins are forgiven' 𝔖 [f] B *repeats v.* 4 *here* [g–g] *So* 𝔖; 'He that obeyeth the Lord giveth rest to his mother' 𝔊 [h–h] *So* 𝔥; 'honoureth' 𝔖 [i] + 'from anguish' 70 253 Syro-Hex [k–k] *So* 70 248 253 Syro-Hex 𝔏; > 𝔥 𝔊 𝔖 [l–l] > 𝔖 [ll] > 𝔊 [m] + 'and mother' 70 248 [n–n] *Lit.* 'all blessings'; + 'from him' (*i.e. the father*) 𝔊, + 'from them' (*i.e. the parents*) 248 253 [o–o] 𝔥 *lit.* 'a root'; 'habitations' 𝔖; 'the houses of children' 𝔊 [oo–oo] 'foundations' 𝔊 [p] + προς ατιμιαν (*doublet to* εν ατιμια *in the first clause, cp.* 248) 𝔊 [pp–pp] 'And a mother in dishonour is a reproach to her children' 𝔊 [q] *Reading* מְקַלֵּה *instead of* מקלל (= 𝔊 𝔖) [r–r] *Lit.* '(it is) increasing sin' [s] > 𝔊 [t–t] *So* 𝔊, *which, as the context shows, is preferable here to* 𝔥 𝔖 ('Be strong in the honour of thy father') [tt–tt] *Reading* תעצבהו (= 𝔊) *for* תעזבהו (= 𝔖; 'forsake him') [u–u] 'as long as he liveth' 𝔊 [uu] 'thy' 𝔥 𝔖 V 70 248

---

2. **hath given the father glory . . .** i.e. He has commanded the children to honour their parents, cp. Exod. xx. 12; Deut. v. 16; Matt. xv. 4; Mark vii. 10; Eph. vi. 2. Cp. the explanatory paraphrase of Sah: 'For the Lord gave the father more honour than the sons' (Smend).

the judgement of the mother. The mother's 'right', or 'due', must be equally respected with that of the father, cp. Prov. i. 8, vi. 20.

3. **maketh atonement for sins.** We are met here with the beginnings of the development (especially in one direction) of the Jewish doctrines of atonement and mediation, which assumed great prominence in later times. The honouring of father and mother was the fulfilling of a *mitzvah*, or 'commandment', of the Law, which being a meritorious act, effected atonement. The observance of the Torah, or Law, became, as time went on, to an ever-increasing extent the main basis of practical religion among the Jews; cp. *Pirqe Aboth* ii. 8: 'He who has gotten to himself words of Torah has gotten to himself the life of the world to come'; vi. 1: 'It clothes him with meekness and fear, and fits him to become righteous, pious, upright, and faithful; and removes him from sin, and brings him towards the side of merit'; vi. 7: 'Great is Torah, which gives life to those who practise it in this world and in the world to come'; and see the whole of vi (Pereq R. Meir). One of the most striking expressions of this honouring of the father is to be seen in the custom of a son praying publicly in the synagogue on the anniversary ('Jahrzeit') of a father's death; see further Oesterley and Box, *The Religion and Worship of the Synagogue* (2nd ed.), pp. 369, 434.

4. **as one that layeth up treasure.** ὡς ὁ ἀποθησαυρίζων; this form only occurs in the Bible elsewhere in 1 Tim. vi. 19, where it is used of making provision for the life to come.

5. **shall have joy.** Cp. Prov. xxiii. 24, 25 (Sept.).

6. **he that giveth rest to his mother.** Cp. v. 1; מניח אמו is all that is left of this *v.* in 𝔥.

7. **And serveth . . .** δουλεύσει implies the service of a slave; some Rabbis interpreted the Law to mean that the son was in the position of a slave to his father; cp. Exod. xxi. 7; Neh. v. 5. It was even taught by some Rabbis that a father had the right to exercise the power of life and death over a son, on the basis of such passages as Gen. xxii; Judg. xi. 39; 2 Kings xxiii. 10.

his parents. ἐν τοῖς γεννήσασιν αὐτοῦ; as Smend points out, the ἐν may represent ל. Cp. Hebr. of x. 18, xxiv. 22, and 1 Sam. iv. 9 עבד ל.

8. **in word and in deed . . .** Cp. Matt. xxi. 28–31; Luke xxiv. 9.

9. **The blessing of a father.** Cp. Deut. xxxiii. 1; Prov. xi. 11; *Test. Twelve Patr., Issachar* v. 6: 'Our father Jacob blessed me with blessings of the earth and of first-fruits.'

the curse of a mother. Cp. Jer. vi. 5; Zeph. ii. 4.

the young plant. נֶטַע in this particular sense occurs elsewhere only in Job xiv. 9.

10. **in the dishonour of thy father.** i.e. when a son does not honour his father.

11. **And he that dishonoureth . . .** Cp. Prov. xv. 20, xxiii. 22, xxx. 17.

12. **all the days of his life.** See crit. note on next *v.*

ℌ[A] 13 And even if his understanding fail, be considerate with him,
And dishonour him not [v]all the days of his life[v].
14 Benevolence to a father shall not be blotted out,
And as a substitute for sins it shall be firmly planted[w].
15 In the day of affliction it shall be remembered 'to thy credit',
It shall obliterate thine iniquities as heat (disperseth) hoar-frost.
16 [x]As one that acteth presumptuously[x] is he that despiseth his father,
And as one that provoketh his Creator is he that curseth[y] his mother.

(*i*) III. 17–25. *On the Need of Humility in all things* (= 3 + 3 + 1 + 1 distichs).

17 My son, when thou art in prosperity walk humbly,
And thou wilt be loved more than him that giveth gifts.
18 Humble thyself [z]in all greatness[z],
And thou wilt find mercy in the sight of God[a].
20 For many are the mercies of God,
And to the humble He revealeth His secret.

v–v *So* ℌ 𝔖; '(when thou art) in all thy strength' 𝔊 w *So* ℌ *mg.* 𝔖; 'it shall be added to build thee up' 𝔊
x–x *Reading* כמזיד *for* כי מזיד y *Reading* מְקַלֵּל z–z *Reading* בכל גדולה (*Smend*) *for* מכל גדולות עולם
a ℵ[c.a] 248 𝔖 Syro-Hex *add, with slight variations:* 'Many are exalted and esteemed; but the mysteries (of God)

13. **all the days of his life.** The rendering of 𝔊, ἐν πάσῃ ἰσχύϊ σου, suggests in ℌ בכל חילך, which is perhaps more satisfactory than the repetition of 'all the days of his life', see *v.* 12.

14. **Benevolence to a father.** Lit. 'righteousness (צדקה) (shown) to a father'; as is clear from the rendering of 𝔊 (ἐλεημοσύνη) צדקה has here the technical sense of 'almsgiving', i.e. righteousness *par excellence*; it is interesting to note that the word is used in this specific sense as early as the time of Ben-Sira. In Matt. vi. 12 'righteousness' and 'alms' are used synonymously. Cp. further *Sukkah* 59 *b* (T. B.): 'Greater is he that giveth alms (עשׂה צדקה, lit. "that doeth righteousness") than (he who offers) all sacrifices' (quoted by Weber, *Jüdische Theologie*, p. 285).

shall not be blotted out. ℌ is stronger than 𝔊 ('shall not be forgotten'). This *v.* offers another instance of the teaching of the efficacy of works, for the fulfilling of this *mitzvah* is reckoned as merit. The good deed is written down in God's book and therefore cannot be blotted out.

as a substitute for sins. The son's righteous act in succouring his aged father is written down to his credit, and thus counterbalances his sins; cp. *Qiddushin* 40 *b* (T. B.), where it is said that a man is judged 'according to that which balances', i.e. according as to whether the weight of sins or of good deeds weighs heavier; cp. also *Baba bathra* 10 *a* (T. B.): 'Almsgiving is a powerful mediator between the Israelites and their Father in heaven; it brings the time of redemption nigh.'

shall be firmly planted. i. e. set fast, cf. Eccles. xii. 11. With 𝔊 (see critical note) cp. Jer. i. 10, 'to build and to plant.'

15. **In the day of...** 𝔊 'In the day of thy affliction it shall remember thee', which obscures the sense of the *v.*, viz. that when affliction comes, as the result of sin, it will be mitigated, because his good deeds will be remembered to his benefit; *mitzvoth* are meritorious.

to thy credit. Lit. 'to thee'.

It shall obliterate... 'It' refers to the benevolence shown to the father; 𝔊 inexactly, 'As fair weather (acts) upon ice, so shall thy sins melt away.'

16. **As one that acteth presumptuously.** 𝔊 'is as a blasphemer' suggests מגדף (= 𝔖) in ℌ; the verb גדף (pi'el) is used of blaspheming God, cp. Num. xv. 30, 2 Kings xix. 6 = Is. xxxvii. 6; so, too, in Rabbinical literature, e. g. in *Shabbath* 75 *a* גדופי = 'one who blasphemes God' (Levy, *Chaldäisches Wörterbuch*, s. v.).

he that despiseth. בוזה (= 𝔖); 𝔊 'he that forsaketh', reading עוזב, cp. *v.* 12 above (crit. note).

And as one that provoketh... 𝔊 (so also 𝔖) has interchanged the verbs: 'And he that provoketh his mother is cursed of the Lord'; cp. Lev. xx. 9; Deut. xxvii. 16.

(*i*) III. 17–25.

17. **when thou art in prosperity.** Lit. 'in thy wealth' (בעשרך), which 𝔊 read as מעשיך 'thy works', or 'business'.

walk humbly. ℌ has התהלך, which 𝔊 ('go on with') misinterpreted owing to the mistake referred to in the last note.

more than him that giveth gifts. 𝔊 'of an acceptable man' is explanatory but misses the point of the comparison (מן) in ℌ (= 𝔖); cp. 𝔏 'super hominum gloriam'. The meaning of the *v.* is that the rich man who is humble in spite of his wealth is loved more than the rich man who is proud, even though he dispenses charity.

18. **Humble thyself in ...** Cp. Matt. xx. 26, 27; Phil. ii. 3; 1 Pet. v. 5. 𝔊 paraphrases: 'The greater thou art, humble thyself the more.' 𝔖 'Make thyself small (= ℌ lit.) in (the face of) all that is great in this world'; this agrees with the unamended text of ℌ, which Smend rightly regards as a later form. The pi'el of מעט ('make thyself small', i. e. 'humble thyself') occurs elsewhere only in xxxii. (𝔊 xxxv.) 8 and Eccles. xii. 3.

mercy. 𝔊 'grace'; cp. Prov. iii. 34.

God. 𝔊 'the Lord'.

For *v.* 19 see critical note.

20. **For many are ...** 𝔊 'For great is the potency of the Lord'; it is certainly possible that 𝔊 represents here a more original text than ℌ, for it corresponds better with the second clause of the *v.* whether we follow 𝔊 or ℌ there.

He revealeth His secret. Cp. critical note on *v.* 18. 𝔊 'he is glorified'. With ℌ cp. Amos iii. 7; Ps. xxv. 14; Prov. iii. 32.

ℌ[A] 21 [b]Seek not (to understand) what is too wonderful[c] for thee,
And search not out that which is hid from thee.
22 Meditate upon that which thou must grasp,
And be not occupied with that which is hid[b].
23 Have naught to do with that which is beyond thee,
For more hath been shown to thee than thou canst understand.
24 For many are the conceits of the sons of men,
And evil imaginations lead astray.
25 [d]Where (there is) no apple of the eye, light is lacking,
And where (there is) no knowledge wisdom is wanting[d].

(*j*) III. 26–28. *Retribution on the Sinner* (= 3 distichs).

26 [e]A stubborn heart shall fare ill at its latter end,
But he that loveth good things shall be led by them[e f].
27 (As for) the stubborn heart, its griefs shall be increased,
And the profane[g] man heapeth iniquity upon iniquity.

are revealed to the lowly' (= *v.* 19), cp. *v.* 20 ℌ   [b–b] *Quoted in Ḥagigah* 77 *c* (II) (T. J.): 'that which is too difficult for thee why shouldst thou know? That which is deeper than Sheol why shouldst thou search out?' Cp. also *Ḥagigah* 13 a (T. B.)   [c] *Reading* נפלא *for* מלאות (*Smend*) 'too hard' 𝔊   [d–d] 𝔊 𝔏 *omit this v., but it is preserved, with slight variations, by* 70 248 253 𝔖 Syro-Hex*; *in* ℌ *it is placed after v.* 27   [e–e] 𝔊 *with the exception of* א[c.a] 248 253 *transposes the order of these clauses*; 𝔖 𝔏 = ℌ   [f] + 'a stubborn heart shall be grieved at the last' 𝔊[B]   [g] *Reading* מתהולל *for* מתחולל   [h–h] *Following Smend's emendation of the text based*

---

21. **that which is hid from thee.** 𝔊 'the things which are above thy strength'. This and the following *v.* are quoted freely in *Ḥagigah* 13 *a* (T. B.) thus: 'For so it is written in the book of Ben-Sira, Inquire not concerning that which is too high for thee, and seek not out that which is hidden from thee; but meditate upon that which thou canst grasp, and be not occupied with that which is hid.' So, too, in *Ḥagigah* 77 *c* (T. J.): 'Rabbi Lezer (said) in the name of Bar-Sira, Why wilt thou know what is too high for thee, and why wilt thou search out what is deeper than Sheol? Meditate upon that which thou canst grasp, and be not occupied with that which is hid.' In the Midrash *Bereshith Rabba*, § viii (on Gen. i. 26), it is said in reference to Job xx. 4, 5 that the Torah alone knows what happened before the creation of the world when man was placed upon the earth, so that it is not for us to inquire about these things; then it continues: 'Rabbi Eleazar said in the name of Ben-Sira, Inquire not concerning that which is too great for thee, and search not out that which is beyond thy strength, seek not to understand what is too high for thee, nor (desire) to know what is hidden from thee. Meditate upon that which thou canst grasp, and be not occupied with that which is hid.' For the thought cf. 2 Esdras iv.

22. **that which thou canst grasp.** 𝔊 'the things that have been commanded thee'; the reference is to the commandments of the Law, cp. *Pirqe Aboth* ii. 18: 'Be diligent to learn the Law.'

And be not occupied with. 𝔊 'for thou hast no need of', a bad rendering of ℌ which means lit. 'and have no business (עֵסֶק) with'; for the Hebr. word cp. xi. 10, xxxviii. 24.

that which is hid. Cp. Deut. xxix. 29. For the ℌ בנסתרות cp. xlii. 19, xlviii. 25.

23. **Have naught to do with.** 𝔊 'Be not over busy' (μὴ περιεργάζου, cp. 2 Thess. iii. 11), cp. xli. 22.

that which is beyond thee. 𝔊, quite mistaking the point of ℌ, 'in thy superfluous works.'

For more hath been . . . Cp. 1 Cor. ii. 9, quoted from Is. lxiv. 4, lxv. 16 *a*.

24. **For many are . . .** 𝔊 'For the conceit of many hath led them astray'; the reference is no doubt to the philosophic speculations of the Greeks. The Hebr. word for 'conceit' (עֶשְׁתּוֹנָה) here is a late one, and occurs elsewhere only in Ps. cxlvi. 4, where it means 'purposes'. The corresponding Aramaic word, which is frequently used in the Targums, always has a bad sense, e.g. Targ. Is. xli. 29; Jer. xviii. 12. Here the meaning seems to be 'speculation', in a bad sense; cp. 248 which adds 'vain', and possibly represents, as Hart suggests, an original רע ('evil'), read רק ('vain'); cp. 𝔏 of next clause.

And evil imaginations . . . 𝔊 'And evil surmising hath caused their judgement to slip'; 𝔏 'Et in vanitate detinuit sensus illorum'. The words in 𝔊 refer to the teaching of Greek philosophers which led away from the Law.

25. See critical note.

Where (there is) no . . . i.e. just as a blind man cannot see, so a fool cannot acquire knowledge.

(*j*) III. 26–28.

26. **A stubborn heart.** לֵב כָּבֵד, lit. 'a heavy heart'; the same expression occurs in Exod. vii. 14, of Pharaoh.

But he that loveth . . . 𝔊 'And he that loveth danger shall perish therein'. 𝔏 adds: 'Cor ingrediens duas vias non habebit successus, et pravus corde (*or* pravicordius) in illis scandalizabitur.'

27. **shall be increased.** 𝔊 'shall be laden', a free rendering of ℌ.

the profane man. 𝔊 'the sinner.' The meaning of the *v.* is that just as troubles accumulate for one who is obstinate and will not understand, so do the sins of the ungodly man accumulate.

𝕳[A] 28 (As for) [h]the wound of the scorner, there is no healing for it[i],
For an evil growth[k] is his plant[hl].

(*k*) III. 29–31. *Reward for the Righteous* (= 1 + 2 distichs).

29 A wise heart understandeth the proverbs of the wise,
And the ear that listeneth to wisdom rejoiceth[m].
30 A flaming fire doth water quench,
So doth almsgiving atone for sin.
31 He that doeth good, it shall meet him on his ways,
And when he tottereth he shall find a stay.

(*l*) IV. 1–10. *On right behaviour towards the Poor and the Oppressed* (= 2 + 2 + 2 + 2 + 3 distichs).

4 1 [a]My son, [b]defraud not[b] the poor of his sustenance[c],
And grieve not [d]the eyes of him that is bitter in (his) soul[d].
2 [e]Despise not[f] the needy soul,
And vex[g] not the heart[h] of the oppressed.
3 Hurt not the feelings[i] of the afflicted,
And withhold not a gift [k]from the poor[k].

on 𝕲; 𝕳 *as it stands reads:* 'Run not to heal the wound of the scorner, for there is no healing for him' [i] + 'his ways shall be rooted out' 𝕲 (C 70 248 253) Syro-Hex [k] *Lit.* 'plant' [l] + 'and he shall not be known' 𝕲 (248) 𝕷 Syro-Hex [m] + 'Sapiens cor et intelligibile abstinebit se a peccatis, et in operibus iustitiae successus habebit' 𝕷

[a] 𝕷 *inserts the title:* 'Concerning almsgiving and the poor' [b–b] *So* 𝕲 𝕷; 𝕳 𝕾 'mock not'; *possibly for* תלעג *should be read* תגרע (=𝕲), *cp.* Ezek. xvi. 27 [c] *Lit.* 'life'; 'alms' 𝕷 [d–d] *Reading* עיני מר נפש *instead of* נפש עני ומר נפש [e] *In* 𝕳 *the clauses of vv.* 2–4 *have got misplaced* [f] Cp. 𝕷 ne despexeris (𝕲 μη λυπησης) [g] *Reading* תכעם, *the text is mutilated* [h] *Lit.* 'bowels' (מעי) [i] *Lit.* 'inward parts' (קרב) [k–k] *Reading*

---

28. See critical note. 𝕲 '(For) the calamity of the proud there is no healing, for a plant of wickedness hath taken root in him.'

(*k*) III. 29–31.

29. **A wise heart.** Spoken of in reference to God in Job ix. 4 (חכם לבב); cp. Prov. x. 8, xvi. 21. 𝕲 'The heart of the prudent' (cp. Eccles. viii. 5) is due to a misunderstanding. The expression is used in a different sense in Job xxxvii. 24.

the proverbs of the wise. 𝕲 'a parable'. מָשָׁל is used in the sense of 'parable' in Ezek. xvii. 2, xxi. 5, xxiv. 3.

And the ear that... Cp. Prov. ii. 2, xv. 31, xx. 12. 𝕲 'And the ear of a listener is the desire of a wise man'; cp. Prov. xxiii. 15.

30. **A flaming fire...** With the general thought of the *v.* cp. Prov. xvi. 6; Dan. iv. 27; and see notes on *v.* 14 above.

So doth almsgiving atone... Cp. *Baba Bathra* 10 *a* (T. B.), where a saying is preserved of Rabbi Aqiba to the effect that benevolence (= almsgiving) saves from the torments of hell (quoted by Bacher, *Agada der Tannaiten*, i, p. 295).

31. **He that doeth good...** i.e. he that shows kindness in its manifold expression will be rewarded. 𝕲 'He that requiteth good turns is mindful of the things (that come) after'; this paraphrase in so far gives the sense of 𝕳 that it refers to 'the things that come after', i.e. the reward for doing good.

And when he tottereth. Lit. 'And in the time of his shaking'; 𝕲 'in the time of his falling' gives the sense of 𝕳.

(*l*) IV. 1–10.

IV. 1. **defraud not.** See critical note. With 𝕲 (μὴ ἀποστερήσῃς) cp. Mark x. 19; 1 Cor. vi. 8; Jas. v. 4.

his sustenance. Cp. xxix. 21; Prov. xxvii. 27; Luke xii. 16.

grieve not. 𝕲 μὴ παρελκύσῃς, lit. 'defer not', cp. *v.* 3, xxix. 8; the word does not occur in the Bible elsewhere excepting in Ps. cxix. 5 (Symmachus), though ἕλκω, ἑλκύω often occur in the Sept.; cp. John vi. 44, &c. for ἑλκύω, and Acts xxi. 30, Jas. ii. 6 for ἕλκω. For the Hebr. אל־תדאיב cp. Ps. lxxxviii. 10.

the eyes of... 𝕲 'the needy eyes'.

2. See critical note.

Despise not. 𝕲 μὴ λυπήσῃς, cp. Job xxxi. 39. The Hebr. root פוח means lit. 'to puff at', cf. Ps. x. 5, implying contempt. In later usage it comes to connote the state brought about by being despised; cp. *Shabbath* 127 *b* (T. B.) הלך לביתו בפחי נפש 'He went to his house with downcast soul.'

the needy soul. 𝕲 'a hungry soul', which is explanatory.

vex not. 𝕲 'provoke not' (μὴ παροργίσῃς); cp. Gen. xxvi. 35 (Sept.). 𝕷 'non exasperes pauperem'.

the heart of the oppressed. 𝕲 'a man in his distress'. With 𝕳 מעים (lit. 'bowels') cp. Lam. i. 20, ii. 11.

3. **Hurt not...** 𝕲 'To a heart that is provoked add not more trouble'. The root כאב is used of causing both physical (e.g. Ezek. xxviii. 24) and mental (e.g. Ezek. xiii. 22) pain.

the feelings. The two words used here and in *v.* 2 for the inner emotions (מעי only used in the construct. plur. with suffixes, and קרב) occur together in Is. xvi. 11.

𝔥[A] 4 [l]Despise not the supplication of the poor[l],
[ll]And turn not away from the afflicted soul[ll].
𝔊 5 [m]From him that asketh turn not thine eye away[m n],
𝔥[A] And give him none occasion[o] to curse thee;
6 When in anguish of soul the broken-hearted[p] crieth[q],
[r]He that created him[r] heareth his plaint.
7 [s]Make thyself beloved in the assembly[s t],
And to the ruler[u] [uu]of the city[uu] bow thy head.
8 Incline thine ear to the afflicted[v w],
And return his salutation[x] in meekness.
9 Deliver the oppressed from his oppressors,
[y]And let not thy spirit hate[y] [z]just judgement[z].
10 Be as a father to orphans,
And in place of a husband [a]to widows[a];
Then God will call thee 'son',
And [aa]will be gracious to thee[aa], [b]and deliver thee from the Pit[b].

ממסכין *for* ממסכינך [l-l] *Reading* אל תבזה שְׁאִילוֹת דל (*Smend*) [ll-ll] > Sah [m-m] > 𝔥 𝔖 [n] + 'because of wrath' 𝔏 253 Syro-Hex* [o] *Lit.* 'place' [p] *Lit.* 'bitter of spirit' [q] 'curseth' 𝔊 𝔖 [r-r] *Reading* יוצרו (= 𝔊 𝔖) *for* צורו ('his Rock') [s-s] 248 𝔏 *follow* 𝔥 𝔖 *here* [t] + 'of the poor' 𝔏 [u] 'elder' א[c.a] 𝔏 [uu-uu] > 𝔊 [v] + 'without causing (him) pain' 70 248 253 𝔏 Syro-Hex [w] + et redde debitum tuum 𝔏, *cp. next clause* [x] *Lit.* 'peace' [y-y] Hebr. . . . אל תקוץ; 𝔊, *which is more logical*, μη ολιγοψυχησης (= אל תקצר). [z-z] 'when thou judgest' 𝔊 (*cp.* 𝔏 in iudicando) [a-a] 'unto their mother' 𝔊 [aa-aa] 'will love thee' 𝔊 [b-b] 'more

---

4. **Despise not . . .** 𝔊 'Reject not a suppliant in his affliction', a free rendering.

And turn not away . . . 𝔊 'And turn not away thy face from a poor man,' cp. Ps. xxii. 25 (Hebr.), Prov. xxviii. 25; Tob. iv. 7; in *Pirqe Aboth* i. 2 'the bestowal of kindnesses' (גמילות חסדים) is called one of the three things on which the world is stayed.

5. **From him . . .** Cp. Prov. xxviii. 27[b]; a saying of Rabbi Aqiba, preserved in *Baba Bathra* 10 *a* (T. B.), runs: 'By charity wealth is to be made a means of salvation; God, the Father of both the rich and the poor, wants the one to help the other, and thus to make the world a household of love' (quoted in *JE*, iii. 668 *a*); and cp. *Test. Twelve Patr.*, *Issachar* iii. 8: 'For on all the poor and oppressed I bestowed the good things of the earth in the singleness of my heart' (ed. Charles).

And give him . . . Cp. Prov. xxviii. 27. That such a curse was believed to entail evil consequences is seen from the words of the next verse, 'He that created him . . .' 'Talmudic literature betrays a belief amounting to downright superstition, in the mere power of the word (*Berakhoth* 19 *a*, 56 *a*; cp. *ZDMG*, xlii. 588). Not only is a curse uttered by a scholar unfailing in its effect, even if undeserved (*Makkoth* 11 *a*), but one should not regard lightly even the curse uttered by an ignorant man (*Megillah* 15 *a*)' (*JE*, iv. 390 *a*).

6. **When in anguish . . .** 𝔊 'For if he curse thee in the bitterness of his soul', a free rendering.

He that created him. See critical note. In Deut. xxxii. 37 צור ('Rock') is used as a divine name, and rendered Θεός in the Sept.; cp. 2 Sam. xxiii. 3; Ps. xviii. (xvii.) 3, 32, 47; in many of the Psalms, especially the later ones, צור is used for 'God' as One who is a refuge of His people. The rendering of 𝔊 here, however (ὁ ποιήσας αὐτόν), makes it probable that it read יוצרו; 𝔖 has בריה ('his Creator').

7. **Make thyself beloved.** i. e. by giving alms to those in need; for the phrase cp. xx. 13.

the ruler of the city. The 'ruler' in 𝔥 in שִׁלְטוֹן = 'Sultan'. 𝔖 reads 'rulers . . .'; there was no single ruler in Jerusalem, but a *Gerousia*, or assembly of great ones, which became known later on as the Sanhedrin.

8. **Incline thine ear.** Cp. Ps. xvii. 6; Jer. xi. 8.

And return . . . Cp. Gen. xli. 16. 𝔊, 'And answer him with peaceable words,' is a misunderstanding of the Hebrew form of salutation: 'Peace' (שלום).

9. **Deliver the oppressed . . .** Cp. Ps. lxxxii. 3, 4.

And let not . . . See critical note. 𝔊 'And be not faint-hearted in giving judgement', cp. Jas. ii. 9, and see Amos v. 10, 15.

10. **Be as a father . . .** Cp. Job xxix. 16, xxxi. 18; Ps. lxviii. 5; Is. i. 17.

to widows. Cp. Deut. xxiv. 17–21; Jas. i. 27.

Then God will call . . . Cp. Job xxxi. 18.

And will be gracious . . . 𝔊 'And He shall love thee more than thy mother doth'; Smend explains the words 'more than thy mother doth' in 𝔊 as due to a desire to beautify the text on the basis of such passages as Is. xlix. 15, lxvi. 13. For 𝔥 cp. li. 2; Job xxxiii. 18, 24, 30; Ps. ciii. 4; Is. xxxviii. 17.

The care of the fatherless and widows was reckoned by the Rabbis among the גמילות חסדים, lit. 'practice of kindnesses', which is constantly urged upon men in Rabbinical writings, e. g. in the T. B. *Nedarim* 39 *b*, 40 *a*, *Kethuboth* 50 *a*, *Sanhedrin* 19 *b*; cp. also the following words in the Apocalypse of Peter, § 15: . . . οὗτοι δὲ ἦσαν οἱ πλουτοῦντες καὶ τῷ πλούτῳ αὐτῶν πεποιθότες καὶ μὴ ἐλεήσαντες ὀρφανοὺς καὶ χήρας, ἀλλ' ἀμελήσαντες τῆς ἐντολῆς τοῦ Θεοῦ, and cp. Apocalypse of Paul, § 35.

(a) IV. 11–19. *The Reward of those who seek Wisdom* (= 1 + 2 + 2 + 1 + 2 + 2 + 1 distichs).

ℌ 11 Wisdom instructeth her sons,
And enlighteneth[a] all who give heed to her.
12 They that love her love life,
And they that seek her [b]shall obtain grace from the Lord[b].
13 They that take hold of her shall find glory [bb]from the Lord[bb],
And they shall abide in the blessing of the Lord.
14 They that serve her serve the Holy One,
[c]And God loveth them that love her[c].
15 He that hearkeneth unto me shall judge[d] (in) truth[e],
And he that giveth ear unto me shall dwell in my innermost chamber[f].
𝔊 16 [g]If he trust[h] me[i], he shall possess[k] me[l],
And his posterity[m] [n]shall hold me[o] fast[n g].
ℌ[A] 17 But I will walk with him in disguise[p],
And at first [q]I[r] will try him with temptations[q].
𝔊 [s]Fear and dread will I[t] bring upon him[u s],
ℌ[A] And I will torment him with chastisements,

than thy mother doth' 𝔊; > 𝔖 [a] *So* 𝔖; ℌ = 𝔊 'taketh hold of' [b–b] *Cp.* 𝔏 complectebuntur placorem eius (complebuntur placore illius); 'shall be filled with joy' 𝔊 [bb–bb] > 𝔊 [c–c] *Reading* ואל אוהב מאהביה (= 𝔊) [d] ישפט; *Smend suggests* ישכן = 'shall abide', *which forms a better parallel to the next clause* [e] אמת; 𝔊 *apparently read* אֻמּוֹת = 'peoples', *as in Num.* xxv. 15 [f] *Reading* בְּחַדְרֵי בְּחֶדֶר; *cp.* 1 Kings xx. 30 [g–g] > ℌ [h] *Reading with* ℵ A C εμπιστευση [i] *So* 𝔖 *only*; 'her' 𝔊 𝔏 [k] *Lit.* 'he shall inherit', *reading with* ℵ A C κατακληρονομησει [l] *So* 𝔖 *only*; 'her' 𝔊 Syro-Hex [m] *Lit.* 'generations'; 𝔖 'on behalf of all the generations of the world' [n–n] *Lit.* 'shall be (*plur.*) in possession'; 𝔖 'he shall receive' [o] *So* 𝔖 *only*; 'her' 𝔊𝔏 [p] *Lit.* 'in making myself a stranger', *cp.* 𝔊 διεστραμμενως = 'tortuously'; 253 Syro-Hex 𝔏 'with (in) temptation' [q–q] > 𝔊; eligit eum 𝔏 [r] *So* 𝔖; ℌ *erroneously* 'he' [s–s] > ℌ [t] *So* 𝔖 *only*; 'her' 𝔊 𝔏 [u] + ad proba-

---

IV. 11—VI. 17. This division falls into seven subsections. It further develops the general theme of Wisdom, but the subject-matter is somewhat miscellaneous.

(a) IV. 11–19.

11. **instructeth.** 𝔊 'exalteth'; cp. Prov. iv. 8, and *Pirqe Aboth* vi. 1, where it is said of the Law: 'It magnifieth him and exalteth him over all things.' 𝔏 'vitam inspirat', Clement of Alex. ἐνεφυσίωσε; perhaps 𝔊 had originally ἐνεψύχωσε (Ryssel).

her sons. Cp. Luke vii. 35 and Matt. xi. 19 (R. V. marg.); i.e. those whom Wisdom has begotten spiritually, cp. Gal. iv. 19.

enlighteneth. 𝔊 ℌ 'taketh hold of'; ℌ may have originally read תאיר (= 𝔖) instead of תעיד (Smend); cp. Ps. xix. 9, cxix. 130.

who give heed to her. Cp. 2 Chron. xxvi. 6; Ezra viii. 15; Neh. xiii. 7; Dan. ix. 23; 𝔊 'who seek her'. 𝔏 adds: 'Et praeibit in via iustitiae'.

12. **They that love...** 𝔊 'He that loveth ...'; cp. Prov. viii. 17, from which this verse is taken, and see Prov. iii. 18, viii. 35; Wisd. vii. 11 ff., viii. 16; Jas. iii. 17.

they that seek her. Cp. Prov. xi. 27. ℌ מבקשיה, but 𝔊 οἱ ὀρθρίζοντες πρὸς αὐτήν suggests משחריה. Cp. xxxii. 14, Eccles. vi. 36.

shall obtain grace. See critical note. Cp. Prov. xviii. 22, where the Sept. renders רצון ('grace') ἱλαρότης (synonym for εὐφροσύνη).

13. **They that take hold of her...** Cp. Prov. iii. 18.

shall find glory. 𝔏 'shall inherit life', cp. *v.* 12.

they shall abide... 𝔊 'And where he (*or* she) entereth, the Lord will bless'. The Hebr. חנה has the meaning 'to enter in', as well as 'to abide', in Neo-Hebrew. For the thought of this clause cp. Gen. xxxix. 5 (Peters).

14. **serve the Holy One.** Lit. 'the servers of the Holy One' (משרתי קדש); the term משרתי יהוה is used of the Levitical priests, cp. Deut. x. 8, xvii. 12, xxi. 5; Job vi. 10; Jer. xxxiii. 21; see also Joshua i. 9, 13, ii. 17. For 'the Holy One' cp. xxiii. 9, xliii. 10, xlvii. 8, xlviii. 20; Bar. iv. 22, v. 5; in later Jewish literature this term is that most frequently used when speaking of God; it is, as a rule, followed by the words ברוך הוא ('Blessed be He'); cp. Mark xiv. 61, where ὁ εὐλογητός is used as a name of God.

And God loveth... See critical note.

15. **unto me.** 𝔊 'unto her', so also in the next clause, oblique instead of direct narration.

shall judge (in) truth. See critical notes. Cp. Is. xlii. 3 (Hebr.). Smend understands אמת ('truth') in the sense of 'safety', and refers to 2 Kings xx. 19, which offers a good parallel to the next clause.

shall dwell in my... Cp. Prov. viii. 3 ff., ix. 1. 𝔊 'shall dwell securely', cp. xiv. 24 ff., li. 19; Deut. xxxiii. 14; Prov. i. 33; Is. xxxii. 18.

16. The omission of this verse in ℌ is probably an oversight. See the critical notes.

And his posterity... Cp. i. 15.

17. See critical notes.

I will walk... Cp. vi. 24, 25, 28; Prov. viii. 34.

Fear and dread... This is an interpolation in 𝔊; the oblique narration of 𝔊 is altered above in order to agree with the rest of the verse.

Until his heart is filled[uu] with me,
𝔊 [v]And I try him with my ordinances[v].
ℌ[A] 18 (Then) will I lead him on again[vv],
And will reveal to him my secrets.
19 [w]If he turn away (from me), I will forsake[x] him[w],
And will deliver him over to the spoilers.

(*b*) IV. 20–28. *Practical Precepts on Right-doing* (= 3 + 2 + 2 + 2 distichs).

20 My son, observe [y]times and seasons[y], and beware of[z] evil,
And be not ashamed[a] concerning thy soul.
21 For there is a shame[b] that bringeth sin,
And there is a shame (that bringeth) honour and favour.
22 [c]Respect no man to thine own detriment[c],
And be not ashamed[d], to thine own stumbling[e].
23 Withhold not speech[f] in due season[g],
ℌ[A] ℌ[C] [h]And hide not[i] thy wisdom[h].
ℌ[A] 24 For Wisdom is known [k]through utterance[k],
And understanding by the word of the tongue.
25 Speak not against the truth[l],
[m]And be humble towards God[m].

tionem 𝔏 [uu] 𝔊 ενπιστευση, 'he trust', *is perhaps to be preferred* (= יאמן *for* ימלא) [v–v] > ℌ 𝔖 (*it is a gloss on* 17 d), *cp.* 𝔏 donec temtet illum in cogitationibus illius et credat animae illius [vv] 𝔊 + 'and she will gladden him'; 𝔖 𝔏 > *with* ℌ [w–w] ℌ *has a variant to this clause*: 'If he turn away from (following) after me, I will cast him off' (= 𝔖) [x] *Reading, following* 𝔊, ונטשתיהו *for* ונטותיהו (*Smend*) [y–y] *Reading, with Schechter,* עת וזמון (*cp.* Eccles. iii. 1) *for* עת המון [z] *Lit.* 'be afraid of' [a] + 'to speak the truth' 𝔏; *see v.* 25 [b] *Reading* בשת (= 𝔊) *for* בשאת *due to the following* משאת [c–c] *Lit.* 'Lift not up thy face (*technical term for showing consideration*) against thy soul' [d] *Reading* אל תבוש (= 𝔊) *for* אל תכשל = 'stumble not', *due to the following* למכשוליך [e] *Lit. plur.* [f] *Lit.* 'a word' [g] *Reading* בעתו = 'in its time', *for* בעולם = 'in eternity', i.e. 'constantly' [h–h] > 𝔊, *but preserved in* 70 248 253 Syro-Hex 𝔏, *which add* εν καλλονη; + in decore eius 𝔏 [i] ℌ[C] 'shut not up' [k–k] *Lit.* 'by word'; Syro-Hex 𝔏 'by the mouth' [l] *So* 𝔊 𝔖 𝔏; 'God' ℌ; אמת, 'truth', *should probably be read instead of* האל = 'God', *cp. the next clause* [m–m] 'And be ashamed of thine

And I try him . . . See crit. note; 𝔊 has oblique narration as in the rest of the verse. With the whole verse cp. Matt. vii. 14; Heb. xii. 11.

18. **(Then) will I lead . . .** 𝔏 'Et firmabit illum'; the Hebr. word (אשר) has the meaning of 'strengthen' in xxv. 23.

And will reveal . . . Cp. xxxix. 3, 7; Job xi. 6; Dan. ii. 21, 22. 𝔏 adds: 'Et thesaurizabit super illum scientiam et intellectum iustitiae.'

19. **. . . to the spoilers.** 𝔊 lit. 'into the hands of his falls', cp. Ps. lxiii. 11 (Sept.); 𝔏 'in manus inimici sui'.

(*b*) IV. 20–28.

20. **times and seasons.** 𝔊 'the opportunity', cp. xxvii. 12.

And be not ashamed . . . i. e. Do nothing, by becoming entangled in anything evil, which will cause you to be ashamed of yourself. 'Soul' here = 'thyself', according to the frequent use of נפש in the O.T.

21. This verse is added to Prov. xxvi. 11 in the Septuagint.

a shame that bringeth sin . . . Cp. xx. 22 f., xli. 16.

a shame (that bringeth) honour . . . Cp. xxix. 14, xli. 17 ff.; 2 Cor. vii. 10.

22. See critical notes.

Respect no man . . . An instance of the wrong kind of shame (cp. *v.* 9); a man must not be ashamed to offend others if a right course of action necessitates it; in such a case it is to his own detriment if he spares the feelings of others.

And be not ashamed . . . If the precept given in the last clause be neglected, the result will be 'thine own stumbling', i.e. it will lead to sin.

23. **Withhold not speech . . .** To do so would be another example of false shame.

in due season. 𝔊 ἐν καιρῷ σωτηρίας; cp. viii. 9 . . . ἐν καιρῷ χρείας δοῦναι ἀπόκρισιν. Perhaps in the verse before us (in 𝔊) χρείας should be read instead of σωτηρίας. Smend ingeniously suggests that a copyist misread XPIAC instead of CPIAC, the usual abbreviation for σωτηρίας. Cp. Eccles. iii. 7, '. . . a time to keep silence, a time to speak'; cp. Prov. xv. 23.

And hide not . . . See critical note. Cp. xx. 31, xli. 15.

24. **Wisdom is known . . .** For Wisdom from another point of view cp. *Pirqe Aboth* iii. 20: 'A fence to Wisdom is silence,' a saying of Rabbi Aqiba.

And understanding by . . . Cp. Prov. xvi. 1[b]. 𝔏 adds: 'Et firmamentum in operibus iustitiae.'

25. **the truth.** Cp. *Sanhedrin* i. 18 *a* (T. J.), where it is said that 'Emeth' ('Truth') is the name of God; and cp. John xiv. 6, 'I am the Way, the Truth, and the Life.'

And be humble . . . See critical note.

𝔥A 26 Be not ashamed to confess[n] (thy) sins,
And stand not against the stream.
27 Prostrate not thy soul in the sight of a fool,
[nn]And accept not the person of one that is mighty[nn o].
28 Strive for the right[p] until death,
And the Lord will fight for thee[q].

(*c*) IV. 29—V. 3. *Further precepts for everyday life* (= 3+3 distichs).

29 Be not boastful[r] with thy tongue[s],
(Nor) slack and negligent in thy work.
𝔥A 𝔥C 30 Be not like a lion[t] in thy home,
And [u]tyrannous and terrible[u] towards thy servants[v].
31 Let not thy hand be stretched out[w] to take[x],
[y]And closed[z] [a]at the time of giving back[a y].
𝔥A 5 1 Trust not in thy wealth[b],
And say not, 'I have power[c].'

own ignorance' 𝔊; 'And keep thyself from thine own foolishness' 𝔖 [n] *Lit.* 'to turn from' [nn–nn] *Reading, on the basis of* 𝔊, ואל תשא פני מושל [o] 𝔥 *inserts* viii. 14 *here, but in a different form from* 𝔊, *see note below* [p] 'truth' 𝔊 𝔖; 𝔏 = 𝔥 [q] 𝔥 *inserts here* v. 14 a, b [r] ℵ[c.a] V 55 70 157 248 254 θρασυς (= 𝔥 𝔖); ℵ* A 155 ταχυς (= 𝔏 Syro-Hex) 'hasty'; B C τραχυς 'rough' [s] 'hearing' ℵ*; 'words' ℵ[c.a] 𝔖 [t] *So* 𝔥C (= 𝔊 𝔏); 𝔥A 'dog' (= 𝔖) [u–u] *So* 𝔥A (= 𝔖, *cp.* 𝔏 evertens domesticos tuos et opprimens subiectos tibi); 𝔊 φαντασιοκοπων, 'suspicious'; 𝔥C 'reckless' (מתפחז, *for which Smend would read* מתפחד 'terrifying'; *the hithpael form is not found in Biblical Hebrew*). [v] *So* 𝔥C, *reading* עבדיך (= 𝔊 𝔏); 𝔥A 'in thy work' (= 𝔖) [w] *So* 𝔥C (= 𝔊); 𝔥A 'open' (= 𝔖) [x] *So* 𝔥A (= 𝔊 𝔖); 𝔥C *lit.* 'to lift up' [y–y] *So* 𝔥C [z] *So* 𝔥A קפוצה; 𝔥C קפודה, 'gathered up' (= 𝔏) [a–a] 𝔥A 'in the midst of giving' (= 𝔖); 𝔏 ad dandum [b] *Lit.* 'strength' [c] εις ζωην 70 248

26. **to confess (thy) sins.** The root שוב is that from which the later Jewish word for 'repentance' comes, viz. *Teshubah*. In the O.T. this word does not occur, no noun being used for 'repentance'; the idea is expressed by the verb שוב, 'to turn,' i.e. from a wrong course. Ben-Sira's teaching on repentance is the same as that of the O.T.; the first step is confession of sins (cp. Lev. v. 5, Num. v. 7) and self-abasement in the sight of God (cp. 1 Kings xxi. 29). The later Rabbinical doctrine teaches that the act of repentance (the technical term is עשה תשובה 'to do repentance') is *per se* meritorious; cp. the Midrash *Bereshith Rabba* xxii, and on the whole subject see Weber, *Jüdische Theologie*, pp. 261 ff., and Schechter, *Some Aspects of Rabbinic Theology*, pp. 313–343.

In Rabbinical writings the confession of sins (the technical term is 'Widdui') is often insisted upon; e.g. Rabbi Aqiba in *Chagigah* 15 *a* (T. B.), says: 'As vessels of gold or of glass, when broken, can be restored by undergoing the process of melting, so does the disciple of the Torah, after having sinned, find the way of recovering his state of purity by repentance.' In *Sanhedrin* 14 *a* (T. B.) it is said that he who assumes a high public office after the confession of his sins in the past is 'made a new creature, free from sin like a child' (*JE*, ii. 280 *a*).

And stand not . . . Fritzsche takes these words in the sense of 'Swim not against the current of a river', i.e. Do not attempt the impossible; but the meaning seems to be that one might as well try and stop the current of a river as seek to hide sins, i.e. from God.

27. **Prostrate not thy soul . . .** 𝔊 'Lay not thyself down (lit. "spread not thyself out") for a fool to tread upon'; i.e. do not place yourself at the disposal of a fool. The Hebr. word translated 'prostrate', like the Greek equivalent, is used of spreading out sackcloth (see Is. lviii. 5, Hebr. and Sept.); so, too, in the Targums, e.g. in the Jerusalem Targum to Deut. xxxiv. 6 of spreading a bed. According to Smend, the word is also used of a slave who throws himself down before his master in order that the latter may step upon his slave in getting into the saddle.

accept not . . . Cp. Jas. ii. 1. The ignoring of either of the prohibitions contained in these two clauses brings shame.

28. **Strive.** The Hebr. היעצה should perhaps be read היעצם (Smend), or התעצם (Schechter); the latter means lit. 'Show proof of' = 'strive for'.

will fight. A different word in 𝔥 from the foregoing.

(*c*) IV. 29—V. 3.

29. **boastful.** See critical note. Cp. Jas. i. 19.

(Nor) slack . . . Cp. Prov. xviii. 9.

30. **thy home.** Cp. xi. 34 for this use of בית.

And tyrannous . . . See critical note.

31. **Let not thy hand . . .** Cp. Acts xx. 35. This *v.* is apparently cited in *Didache* iv. 5; cf. Introd. § 7 (*a*).

V. 1. **Trust not in.** Lit. 'Lean not upon.' 𝔊 'Set not thy heart upon,' the Greek word means lit. 'to be intent upon' something; cp. Ps. lxii. 10. With 𝔥 cp. xv. 4; Luke xii. 15; 1 Tim. vi. 17.

wealth. חיל is used primarily of physical strength, but also frequently of wealth, Is. viii. 4, x. 14, xxx. 6, &c.

I have power. Lit. 'There is to the "god" (אֵל) of my hand'. For the phrase cp. Gen. xxx. 29; Deut. xxviii. 32; Prov. iii. 27; Neh. v. 5; Mic. ii. 1; אֵל must be taken here in the sense of 'might' or 'power'. 𝔊 αὐτάρκη μοί ἐστιν, 'I have sufficient,' does not quite give the meaning of 𝔥, which refers to the sense of power which the possession of wealth inspires, not to the boast of possessing much.

𝔥^{A} 2 [b]Trust not in thy wealth,
[c]To walk after the desire of thy soul[c b].
[Go not after (the desire) of thine heart and of thine eyes,
To walk in the desires of thy soul[d].]
3 Say not, 'Who shall have power over me?'[e]
For Jahveh is an avenger [f]of the persecuted[f].

(*d*) V. 4–8. *The Wickedness of tempting God* (= 2 + 1 + 2 + 1 distichs).

𝔥^{A} 𝔥^{C} 4 Say not, 'I have sinned, [g]but what [i]happened unto me?'[g]
For Jahveh is longsuffering[h].
5 Count not upon forgiveness,
That thou shouldst add sin to sin.
6 [k]And say not, [l]'His mercies are great[l],
[m]He will forgive the multitude of mine iniquities'[m k];
For mercy and wrath are with Him,
And His indignation abideth upon the ungodly.
7 Delay not to turn unto Him,
And put (it) not off from day to day;
For suddenly doth His wrath come forth[n],
And in the time[o] of vengeance thou shalt perish.
𝔥^{A} 8 Trust not in unrighteous gains,
For they shall profit (thee) nothing in the day of wrath.

(*e*) V. 9—VI. 1. *On the Need of Straightforwardness in Speech* (= 2 + 1 + 1 + 1 + 2 + 2 distichs).

𝔥^{A} 𝔥^{C} 9 Winnow not with every wind,
[p]And walk not in every path[p q].

(= Syro-Hex); + Nihil enim proderit in tempore vindictae et obductionis, 𝔏 *cp. v.* 7 [b–b] > 𝔊 [c–c] > 𝔖 [d] *Reading* נפשך *for* רעה ('evil') [e] *Several Grk. cursives* Syro-Hex 𝔏 + 'Because of my works' [f–f] *Several Grk. cursives read* σου την υβριν (= Syro-Hex 𝔏) [g–g] 𝔥^{A} 'What will He do unto me?—Nothing!' [h] + ου μη σε ανη 70 248 [i] + λυπηρον 70 248 (= 𝔏) [k–k] > 𝔖 [l–l] 'Jahveh is merciful' 𝔥^{A1} [m–m] 'And He will blot out all mine iniquities' 𝔥^{A1} [n] + 'And if thou rememberest not thou shalt be destroyed ℵ$^{c.a}$ 248 [o] 𝔥^{A} 'day' [p–p] *So* 𝔥^{C}, *the text of* 𝔥^{A} *is corrupt:* 'Turn the way of the stream', *cp.* iv. 26 [q] + 'Thus

2. **Trust not . . .** This and the next clause are doublets based on *vv.* 1 *a*, 2 *b*; they are rightly omitted in 𝔊.
To walk in the desires . . . Cp. Job xxxi. 7.
3. **Who shall have . . .** Cp. Ps. xii. 4.
of the persecuted. 𝔊 'of thee'. Cp. Eccles. iii. 15, where almost the identical Hebrew of clause (*b*) occurs.
(*d*) V. 4–8.
4. **I have sinned . . .** Cp. Eccles. viii. 1; Ps. liii. 12. This verse is quoted in *Chagigah* 16 *a* (T. B.).
For Jahveh is longsuffering. With this rejoinder contrast the teaching of later sages, who, in accordance with a more developed belief concerning the hereafter, taught that retribution awaited the ungodly in the next world; cp. e. g. 1 Enoch li. 2.
5. **Count not.** Lit. 'trust not', 𝔊 'be not without fear'. This verse and *v.* 6 are quoted by Nissim ben Jacob (first half of eleventh century) in his *Sepher Ma'asiyoth*; also by Sa'adya (d. 942) (Smend).
forgiveness. Cp. Ps. cxxx. 4. 𝔊 'atonement'.
That thou shouldst . . . i. e. Do not think that because sins are forgiven you can therefore continue to commit sins. See further the note on xvi. 14.
6. 𝔥^{A} 𝔖 place the first two clauses of this verse before *v.* 5, the former repeats them here.
He will forgive. 𝔊 ἐξιλάσεται, 'He will be pacified.'
For mercy . . . This clause occurs again in xvi. 11; cp. the teaching of the books of Hosea and Amos in which the divine characteristics of mercy and wrath are respectively taught, with special emphasis.
7. This verse is quoted in *Shabbath* 153 *a* (T. B.).
Delay not . . . For the thought cp. Ps. cxix. 60, but the Hebr. word is different.
And put (it) not off. i. e. the turning = repentance; see note on iv. 26.
from day to day. For the phrase cp. 1 Chron. xvi. 23; Ps. xcvi. 2; Esther iii. 7 (Hebr.).
suddenly doth . . . Cp. Lev. x. 2; Num. xvi. 35; Is. li. 5; Mark xiii. 36.
in the time of vengeance . . . Cp. xviii. 24; for 'the day of vengeance' cp. Is. xxxiv. 8, lxi. 2, lxiii. 4; Prov. vi. 34.
8. **Trust not.** 𝔊 μὴ ἔπεχε.
unrighteous gains. Cp. Prov. x. 2; Ezek. vii. 19; Matt. xiii. 22; Mark iv. 19; Luke xvi. 11.
For they shall profit . . . Cp. Prov. xi. 14.
in the day of wrath. 𝔊 '. . . of calamity'; cp. ii. 2 and 1 Enoch lxiii. 10, 'Our souls are satisfied with the mammon of unrighteousness, but this does not prevent us from descending into the flame of the pain of Sheol.'
(*e*) V. 9—VI. 1.
9. The addition of 𝔊, &c. (see critical note), is from vi. 1 *c*.

ℌ[A]ℌ[C] 10 Be steadfast concerning [r]that which thou knowest[r],
And let thy speech[s] be one.
11 Be swift[t] to hear[u v],
[w]But with patience make reply[w].
12 If it lie in thy power answer thy neighbour;
And if not, —[x] thy hand upon thy mouth![y]
13 Glory and dishonour come through speaking[z],
And the tongue of a man [a]is his fall[a].
ℌ[A] 14 Be not called 'Double-tongued',
And slander not with thy tongue;
For shame hath been created for the thief,
[b]And sore reproach for[b] the double-tongued[c].
15 Deal not corruptly either in a small or a great matter;
6 1 And be not an enemy in place of a friend,
[d](For then) wouldst thou get an evil name, and reproach, and shame[d];
So it is with an evil man who is double-tongued.

(*f*) VI. 2–4. *A Warning against lustful passions* (= 3 distichs).

2 [e]Be not a slave to thy passions[e],
Lest they[f] consume [g]thy strength [h]like a bull[h];

(doth) the double-tongued sinner' 𝔊 Syro-Hex; + Sic enim peccator probatur in duplici lingua 𝔏 [r–r] 'thy word' ℌ[C] [s] 'words' ℌ[C] [t] 'firm' ℌ[C], *cp. v.* 10 [u] ℌ[C] *lit.* 'with a good hearing' (*see notes below*); +*good* 70 248 Syro-Hex. [v] + 'and let thy life be in truth' 70 248 𝔏 [w–w] ℌ[C] *has:* ובארך ענה תענה נבונה [x] ℌ[C] *inserts* 'place'; 𝔊 'let . . . be . . .' [y] + Ne capiaris in verbo indisciplinato et confundaris 𝔏, *cp. v.* 14 [z] 'one that babbleth' ℌ[C] [a–a] 'bringeth him into security,' *evidently a corruption* ℌ[C]; + 'evil' ℌ [b–b] *Reading, with Smend:* וחרפה רעה על [c] + susurratori autem odium et inimicitia et contumelia 𝔏 [d–d] *Reading, with Smend:* שם רע חרפה וקלין תוריש [e–e] *Lit.* 'Fall not into the hand of thy soul'; 'Deliver not thyself . . . .' 𝔖 [f] *Lit.* 'it' [g] *Reading* ותבער *for* תעבה (*Smend*) [h–h] *So* 𝔖 𝔊; > ℌ

---

10. **steadfast.** Cp. Ps. cxii. 8; Is. xxvi. 3.
let thy speech . . . i. e. be consistent in what you say.
11. **Be swift to hear.** Smend thinks that ℌ[C] (lit. 'Be steadfast with a good hearing') means 'Be attentive during a good lecture', or the like. ℌ[A], however, contains the right text; cp. Jas. i. 19.
with patience. Cp. Eccles. vii. 8, 1 Pet. iii. 15. Perhaps ארך רוח has here the sense of 'deliberation'.
make reply. With the Hebr. phrase חשב פתגם cp. Ezra v. 11; Dan. iii. 16.
12. **If it lie in thy power.** Lit. 'if there is with thee'; 𝔊 adds *σύνεσις* for clearness' sake; cp. Job xxxviii. 32.
thy hand . . . Cp. Job xxi. 5, xxix. 2; Prov. xxx. 32.
13. **Glory and dishonour.** Cp. Prov. xviii. 21.
come through. Lit. '(are) in the hand of'; cp. Prov. xviii. 21, '. . . in the hand (or, power) of the tongue.'
speaking. The Hebr. word (בטא, בטה) means properly 'to speak rashly', or 'unadvisedly', in the O. T.; cp. Lev. v. 4; Ps. cvi. 33; Prov. xii. 18. The root is a rare one, it occurs again in ix. 17; in Neo-Hebrew the noun means simply 'utterance' in a neutral sense (Smend), as in ix. 18.
And the tongue . . . Cp. Matt. xii. 37, Jas. iii. 2 ff., and *Abodah Zara* 11 *b* (T. B.): '. . . their tongue causeth them to stumble' (Peters, quoting Bacher).
14. In ℌ the first two clauses of the verse come also after iv. 29.
Double-tongued. Lit. 'master of two (tongues)'; 𝔊 'a whisperer'; cp. iv. 28, xxviii. 13; Prov. xvi. 28; 2 Cor. xii. 20; Schechter quotes *Baba mezia* 48 *a* (T. B.): '. . . who doth not speak one thing with his mouth and another with his heart.'
slander not. Cp. Ps. xv. 3; 𝔊 'lie not in wait', cp. Prov. xii. 13; 𝔏 '(ne) capiaris et confundaris', cp. *v.* 12.
hath been created. Cp. Prov. xii. 13, xviii. 7. 𝔊 'there is'.
the thief. The reference is to him who, through slander, has stolen the good name of another.
the double-tongued. See above.
15. **Deal not corruptly.** 𝔊 'Be not ignorant (concerning)'; a misunderstanding of ℌ.
VI. 1. **(For then) wouldst thou . . .** 𝔊 'For an evil name inheriteth shame and reproach', a free rendering.
get. Lit. 'inherit'.

(*f*) VI. 2–4.
2. **Be not . . .** 𝔊 'Exalt not thyself in the counsel of thy soul', which is difficult to account for excepting on the supposition that the point of ℌ was misunderstood. For the phrase נפל ביד ('to fall into the hand of') cp. Judges xv. 18; 2 Sam. xxiv. 14. In xxxvii. 7 𝔊 also renders יד as *βουλή* ('counsel'). The reference, as the context shows, is to impure passions.
Lest they consume . . . 𝔊 gives no sense: 'That thy soul be not torn in pieces like a bull'; ℌ as it stands is corrupt (see critical note). The original meaning was probably that lustful passions, if not resisted, consume a man's

ℌ[A] 3 Thy leaves will they[d] eat up, and thy fruits will they[d] destroy,
4 And they[d] will leave thee as a dried-up tree.
For[e] fierce passion destroyeth its possessor[f],
And[ff] [g]maketh him[g] the scorn[h] of his enemy.

(*g*) VI. 5–17. *Concerning true and false Friendship* (= 2 + 3 + 2 + 2 + 3 + 1 distichs).

5 [k]Gentle speech[k] multiplieth friends[l],
And [m]kindly words[m] [n]those that give greeting[n].
6 Let those [o]that are at peace with thee[o] be many,
But thy confidant[p] one in a thousand.
7 If thou makest a friend [q]test him[q],
And be not in haste to trust him.
8 For there is a friend (who is so) according to occasion,
And continueth not in the day of[r] affliction;
9 [s]And there is a friend that turneth to an enemy[t],
[u]And he revealeth strife to thy reproach[u].
10 And there is a friend who is a table-friend,
But he [v]is not to be found[v] in the day of affliction[w s].
11 [x]When thou art in prosperity he will be like thee[x],
𝔊 [y]And will lord it over thy servants[y].

[d] *Sing.* in ℌ [e] > 𝔊 *but* + γαρ 253 [f] *Reading* בעלה *for* בעליה [ff] + 'quickly' 70 [g–g] *Reading* תשימנו *for* תשיגם [h] *Lit.* 'joy' [k–k] 𝔊 *lit.* 'A sweet throat' [l] + 'et mitigat inimicos' (*cp.* Prov. xv. 1) 𝔏 [m–m] *Lit.* 'lips of grace'; 'the lips of the righteous' 𝔖; lingua eucharis 𝔏 [n–n] *Reading* שואלי שלום; 'peaceful greeting' 𝔖; in bono homine abundat 𝔏 [o–o] 'that greet thee' 𝔖 [p] *Lit.* 'the master of thy secret'; consiliarius sit tibi 𝔏 [q–q] *Lit.* 'acquire him by testing' [r] 𝔊 + 'thy' [s–s] > א* 𝔖 (*homoioteleuton*), *hab* א[c.a] [t] B א 'enmity'; A C &c. = ℌ [u–u] Et est amicus qui odium et rixam et convicia denudabit 𝔏 [v–v] 'will not continue' 𝔊, *cp.* v. 8 b, 12 b [w] 'thy affliction' 𝔊 [x–x] Amicus si permanserit fixus, erit tibi quasi coaequalis 𝔏 [y–y] 'And

strength; impure desire is aptly compared to a bull, because of the havoc it causes. The repetition of ψυχή is a mistake for ἰσχύς (= חיל). With the whole verse cp. Job xxxi. 9–12.

3. The metaphor is now changed, and the man who does not control his passions is compared to a sapless tree. 𝔊 makes the man himself the subject, in ℌ the lustful passion is the subject. Cp. Job xxxi. 12.

leaves . . . fruits. Figurative for youth and offspring; cp. Ps. cxvii. 3, cxxxii. 11; Is. xiii. 18.

a dried-up tree. Figurative for a man without posterity, a bitter thought to the Jew; cp. 1 Kings xvi. 3, xxi. 21; see also Ps. cxxviii. 3, 6 for a man's delight in his children. For the picture of a tree used figuratively for a man see Ps. i. 3, xxxvii. 35; Dan. iv. 10 ff.

4. **fierce passion.** i.e. uncontrolled desire (cp. Is. lvi. 11): 𝔊, 'a wicked soul,' apparently read רעה for עזה, and translated נפש literally.

its possessor. ℌ lit. 'its master'; 𝔊 τὸν κτησάμενον αὐτήν; cp. Is. xxvi. 13; Prov. xvi. 22 (Sept.).

the scorn. ἐπίχαρμα of 𝔊 well brings out the idea of malignant delight.

enemy. 𝔊 𝔖 𝔏 'enemies', probably correct.

(*g*) VI. 5–17.

5. **Gentle speech.** Cp. Cant. ii. 14; Prov. xvi. 21.

kindly words. 𝔊 'a fair-speaking tongue', cp. Prov. xi. 16 (Sept.), xv. 1. 𝔊 unnecessarily repeats the verb.

those that give greeting. ℌ lit. 'those that ask peace'; 𝔊 '. . . courtesies'.

6. This verse is quoted in the T. B. *Jebamoth* 63 *b*, *Sanhedrin* 100 *b*.

those that are . . . Cp. for the phrase Ps. xli. 10; Prov. xvi. 7; Rom. xii. 18.

thy confidant. i.e. thy most intimate friend; 𝔊 'thy counsellor', is too general, cp. Is. xl. 13; with ℌ cp. viii. 17.

7. **If thou makest.** The Hebr. word (קנה) means 'to acquire', and occurs often in Proverbs for acquiring wisdom.

test him. Lit. 'by testing' (בנסיון), cp. iv. 17.

be not in haste. Cp. xix. 4.

8. **according to occasion.** i.e. only in so far as it suits his own purpose. Cp. *Pirqe Aboth* v. 22: 'All friendship (אהבה) which depends on something, when the thing ceases, the friendship ceases; and such as does not depend on anything never ceases.'

9. **revealeth . . .** Cf. Prov. xxv. 9, 10, which offers an explanation of this clause.

10. **there is a friend . . .** i.e. his friendship only lasts as long as he receives hospitality. The Hebrew word *chabêr* means primarily, as here and in the O.T. generally, a companion, but later on it came to mean a companion in studying the Law, and thus came to be synonymous with 'scholar'. The word had, however, besides this the technical meaning of a member of a society or order (e.g. one who belonged to the sect of the Pharisees), whose aim was to observe in all strictness the laws of 'clean' and 'unclean'; in contrast to the *chabêr* was one who was not particular in the observance of these, viz. a *'am-ha'areṣ* (= 'one of the land'), i.e. one who knew not the Law, cp. John vii. 49.

11. **When thou art in . . .** Cp. xii. 8, 9; Prov. xi. 10, xix. 6. In *Shabbath* 32 *a* (T. B.) it is said: 'At the door of the rich all are friends; at the door of the poor there are none.'

he will be like thee. i.e. he will agree with you in everything.

ℌ[A] 12 [z][a]If evil overtake thee[z] he will turn against thee[a],
[b]And will hide himself from thee[c].
13 Separate thyself from thine enemies,
And be on thy guard against thy friends.
14 A faithful friend is a strong defence[d],
And [e]he that findeth him[e] findeth a treasure.
15 A faithful friend is beyond price,
And his worth cannot be weighed.
16 A faithful friend is a 'bundle of life',
He that feareth God [f]obtaineth him[f].
𝔊 17 [g]He that feareth the Lord directeth his friendship aright[g],
ℌ[A] For as he is, so is his friend[h].

(*a*) VI. 18–22. *Wisdom is a joy to those who seek her, but harsh to the foolish* (= 3+3 distichs).

𝔊 18 [i]My son, receive[k] instruction from thy youth up[i],
[l]And even unto hoar hairs[l] [m]shalt thou find wisdom[m].
ℌ[A]ℌ[C] 19 Draw nigh unto her as one that ploughеth and soweth[n],
And wait for the abundance of her fruits.

when thou art in adversity he will depart from thee' ℌ[A] 𝔖 [z–z] 'If thou fall' 𝔖 [a–a] Si humiliaverit se contra te 𝔏 [b] 𝔖 *inserts:* 'He will depart' [c] + unanimem habebis amicitiam bonam 𝔏, *rendered necessary by the misunderstanding of* 𝔊 *in the first clause* [d] *Reading* אהל (*lit.* 'tent') *for* אוהב (= 𝔊) [e–e] *Reading* ומוצאו (= 𝔊) *for* ימצא [f–f] *Reading* ישיגנו *for* ישיגם [g–g] > ℌ [h] 𝔖 + 'And as his name so are his works' ℌ (= ii. 18 *d* ℌ) [i–i] > ℌ 𝔏 *inserts the title:* 'De Doctrina Sapientiae' [k] *Reading* επιδεξαι (= 𝔖 𝔏) *for* επιλεξαι [l–l] > ℌ [m–m] *So also* ℌ[C]; '. . . grace' א Syro-Hex [n] *So* 𝔊; 'and reapeth' ℌ 𝔖

And will lord it . . . The reading of 𝔊 is, as the context shows (see *v.* 12), right. ℌ reads וברעתך יתנדה ממך, which should, on the basis of 𝔊, be emended to ובעבדיך יתנדב, as the antithesis does not come until the next verse. The meaning is that this false friend seeks in all things to identify his actions with those of him whom he calls his friend.

12. **If evil overtake thee . . .** Cp. Job xix. 19 (Hebr.); 𝔊 'If thou be brought low', cp. xxii. 26.

And will hide himself . . . See the contrast to this in xxii. 23 ff.

13. **And be on thy guard . . .** Cp. *vv.* 7, 10.

14. **defence.** 𝔊 σκέπη; cp. Exod. xxvi. 7 (Theod.), xxxv. 11 (Aq. Theod. Symm.); Job viii. 22 (Aq.), xxi. 28 (Theod.); where אהל is thus rendered.

a treasure. The word הון, lit. 'wealth', belongs especially to the Wisdom literature, cp. Prov. i. 13, vi. 31, viii. 18.

15. **A faithful friend . . .** Lit. 'For a faithful friend there is no price'; 𝔊 has for 'price' ἀντάλλαγμα, lit. 'exchange', cp. xxvi. 14, and for the Hebr. מחיר vii. 18.

And his worth . . . Lit. 'And there is no weight for his goodness', 𝔊 . . . τῆς καλλονῆς αὐτοῦ, cp. xxxiv. 23. Schechter (*Studies in Judaism*, second series, p. 93) quotes *Pirqe Aboth* i. 6 (T. J.): 'Let a man buy himself a friend who will eat and drink with him, who will study with him the written and the oral Law, and to whom he will entrust all his secrets . . .'

16. **a 'bundle of life'.** צרור חיים; the meaning is that a man's life is as safe in the hands of a faithful friend as his soul is in the bundle, or bag, of life. This latter expression occurs for the first time in 1 Sam. xxv. 29, where Abigail says to David: 'And though man be risen up to pursue thee, and to seek thy soul, yet the soul of my lord shall be bound in the bundle of life with the Lord thy God; and the souls of thine enemies, them shall He sling out, as from the hollow of a sling.' Mr. S. A. Cook, in the *JQR*, xiv, pp. 413 ff., refers to this in the words: 'Although Semitic examples of the belief of the external soul in its crude form appear to be exceedingly rare, the conception that a man's life can be wrapped up in some external object on the safety of which his immunity depends, is one that readily lends itself to development and refinement. Thus David's soul is bound up with (i. e. in the care and custody of) Jahweh (1 Sam. xxv. 29), and, according to 2 Sam. xxi. 17, the life of the nation is wrapped up in David, since the extinction of the "lamp of Israel" seems to entail that of the people.' The phrase is still used in the liturgies of the Ashkenazic and Sephardic Jews.

Schechter quotes the well-known Jewish saying from *Taanith* i. 23*a* (T. J.): 'Friendship or Death' (*op. cit.*, p. 93).

He that feareth . . . i. e. a faithful friend is to be regarded as a gift from the Almighty.

17. **He that feareth . . .** The accidental omission of this clause in ℌ is due to the fact that the opening words were the same as those of the preceding clause (ירא אל).

directeth . . . aright. εὐθυνεῖ, 'maketh straight,' cp. Isa. xl. 3; John i. 23; Jas. iii. 4.

For as he is . . . i. e. both are alike to him, his friend is as dear to him as he himself; cp. Matt. xix. 19: 'Thou shalt love thy neighbour as thyself.'

VI. 18—VIII. 7. The contents are again miscellaneous; Wisdom is still the main theme. The division falls into fourteen subsections.

(*a*) VI. 18–22.

18. **hoar hairs.** Cp. xxv. 4.

shalt thou find. The Hebr. תשיג means rather 'shalt thou attain', cp. xxv. 3.

19. **the abundance of her fruits.** 𝔊 'her good fruits'; with the clause cp. Jas. v. 7, 8.

ℌ[A] ℌ[C] For in cultivating her thou [needest to] toil[o] but for a little,
For to-morrow shalt thou eat her fruits.
ℌ[A] 20 How[p] harsh is she[q] to the fool[r],
And he that is lacking in understanding cannot abide in her.
ℌ[A] ℌ[C] 21 Upon him [s]she is like a burdensome stone[s],
And he is not slow to cast her off.
ℌ[A] 22 [t]For Wisdom[u] is according to her name[t],
And to most men she is not manifest.

(*b*) VI. 23–31. *They who seek Wisdom shall receive a crown of joy* (= 3 + 3 + 3 distichs).

𝔊 23 [w]Hearken, my son, and receive my judgement,
And refuse not my counsel;
24 And bring thy feet into her fetters,
And thy neck into her chain[w].
ℌ[A] 25 Bow down thy shoulder, and bear her,
And chafe not [x]under her bonds[x].
𝔊 26 [y]Draw nigh unto her with all thy heart[z],
And keep her ways with thy whole power[y].
ℌ[A] 27 Inquire and search, seek and find[a],
And take hold of her, and let her not go;

[o] *Reading* תעמל (= 𝔖 𝔊) *for* תעבוד [p] *Inserting* מה (= 𝔖 𝔊); 'exceeding harsh' 𝔊 [q] 'Wisdom' 𝔖 𝔏 [r] *plur.* 𝔊 𝔖 [s–s] 'like a mighty stone of trial' 𝔊, *reading* מסה *for* משא; quasi lapidis virtus probatio 𝔏 [t–t] 'Her name is like her teaching' 𝔖 [u] *Reading, with Smend,* החכמה *for* המוסר, *and* היא *for* הוא [w–w] > ℌ, *substituting instead* xxvii. 5, 6, *but in the marg.* [x–x] *Reading, with Smend,* בחבלותיה (= 𝔊) *for* בתחבולתיה 'at her counsels' [y–y] > ℌ [z] *So* 𝔖; 𝔊 'soul' [a] 'thou shalt find' 𝔖 [b] + 'and joy' 𝔖 [c–c] 'And thou shalt rejoice in her (*al.* thy) end' 𝔖 [d] 'her net' ℌ (𝔖 *plur.*) [e–e] in protectionem fortitudinis et bases virtutis 𝔏 [f–f] > 𝔖 [ff–ff] *Reading*

in cultivating her. Lit. 'in her cultivation'. Wisdom is compared to land which, though productive, requires labour to be expended upon it before its fruits can be enjoyed.

but for a little. Cp. xl. 6. The reference, as the context shows, is not to the smallness of the labour, but to the short time during which one need labour, so soon does Wisdom reward those who seek her.

to-morrow. Reading למחר; Peters may, however, be right in reading למהר 'quickly' (= 𝔊), but cp. Exod. viii. 19; Is. xvii. 11.

20. **harsh.** i. e. rough (𝔊 τραχεῖα; only B, wrongly, ταχεῖα). Wisdom is compared to a path, cp. iv. 17; Prov. ii. 9; and see the next clause, '. . . cannot abide in her.'

the fool. אויל is generally used of one who is morally bad, as well as deficient in understanding, cp. Prov. i. 7, vii. 22, xiv. 9, xx. 3.

in understanding. Lit. 'heart'; for the heart as the seat of the understanding cp. Prov. vi. 32, vii. 7, x. 13, &c.

cannot abide. Cp. xlix. 9 (Hebr.).

21. Wisdom is now compared to a great weight which to the fool is so burdensome that he flings it from him, thus forfeiting all the benefits which a little perseverance would have obtained.

a burdensome stone. Cp. Zech. xii. 3.

22. **For Wisdom . . .** Lit. 'For Wisdom—as her name so is she', i. e. her name expresses her essence.

manifest. Lit. 'plain', as in Prov. viii. 9.

(*b*) VI. 23–31.

23. **judgement.** γνώμην, i. e. estimate, or opinion, viz. of Wisdom; used only here in Sirach. With the whole verse cp. Prov. xix. 20.

24. **And bring . . .** Cp. *v.* 29.

25. **Bow down . . .** 𝔊 'Put thy shoulder under her'; Wisdom is compared to a yoke; with this metaphor cp. *Pirqe Aboth* iii. 8: 'Whoso receives upon him the yoke of Torah (Law), they remove from him the yoke of royalty and the yoke of worldly care (דרך ארץ); and whoso breaks from him the yoke of Torah, they lay upon him the yoke of royalty and the yoke of worldly care'; Matt. xi. 29, 30: 'Take My yoke upon you, and learn of Me . . . for My yoke is easy, and My burden is light.'

chafe not . . . Lit. 'loathe not'. Cp. *Erubin* 54 *a* (T. B.): 'If thou bring thy neck under the yoke of Torah she will watch over thee'; for the identification between Wisdom and the Law see Introd. § 9 (iii).

under her bonds. ℌ 'at her counsels', cp. Prov. i. 5; but the context justifies the reading based on 𝔊 (see critical note). Cp. the Midrash *Debarim Rabba* to x. 1: 'It is as if a lord said to his servants, "Here is a golden chain (if thou doest my will), but if not, here are iron fetters"'; the reference is to the obeying of God's will as revealed in the Law.

26. The omission of this *v.* in ℌ is probably accidental; there is no reason to doubt its genuineness; indeed the words of the next *v.*, 'Inquire and search,' seem to demand a reference to the walking in her paths, i. e. the ways that lead to Wisdom.

with all thy heart . . . with thy whole power. Cp. Deut. vi. 5.

27. **Inquire and search . . .** 𝔊 'Search (*lit.* trace out) and seek, and she shall be made known unto thee', a free rendering; cp. Deut. xiii. 15 (Sept.).

let her not go. Cp. Prov. iv. 13.

A 𝕳C 28 For at length thou wilt find her rest[b],
  [c]And she shall be turned for thee into gladness[c].
A 29 And her fetters[d] shall become[e] a stay of strength for thee[e],
  [f]And [ff]her bonds[ff] for [g]robes of glory[g].
30 An ornament of gold is her yoke,
  And her fetters a cord of blue[f].
31 Thou shalt array thee with her (as with) robes of glory,
  And crown thee with her (as with) a crown of beauty.

(*c*) VI. 32–37. *A reward awaits those who diligently seek Wisdom* (= 2 + 3 + 2 distichs).

32 My son, if thou desirest it thou shalt be made wise,
  And if thou set thy heart (thereon), thou shalt learn prudence.
33 If thou desire to hear, [h]thou shalt receive[h],
  [i]And if[i] thou incline[k] thine ear, thou shalt be wise.
34 [l]Stand thou in the assembly[m] of the elders,
  And whoso is wise, cleave unto him[l].
A 𝕳C 35 Desire to hear every discourse[mm],
  And let not a wise proverb[n] escape thee.
A 36 [o]Look for him who[p] is wise[o], and seek him out earnestly,
  And let thy foot wear out [q]his threshold[q].
37 Meditate in the fear of the Most High[r],
  [s]And think upon His commandments[s] continually;
Then will He instruct [t]thine heart[t],
  And He [u]will make thee wise[u] (in that) which thou desirest.

חבלותיה (*see v.* 25). g–g ‘robes of gold’ 𝕳; ‘a robe of life’ 𝔏 h–h *So* 𝔊; *the verb has fallen out in* 𝕳; ‘thou shalt learn’ 𝔖; + ‘understanding’ 70 248 253 Syro-Hex; + doctrinam 𝔏 i *So* 𝔊 𝔖; *the words have fallen out in* 𝕳 k 𝕳 *imperative, but probably the mistake arose through the falling out of the preceding letters* l–l > 𝕳 m *So* 𝔖; ‘multitude’ 𝔊 mm 𝔊 *inserts* ‘godly’; + dei 𝔏 n 𝔊 *plur.*; ‘the sayings of the wise’ 𝔖 o–o ‘See who is wise’ 𝔖 p *Reading* מי *for* מה q–q ‘the steps of his doors’ 𝔊 r ‘God’ 𝔖 s–s *Reading* ובמצותיו הגה (= 𝔖 𝔊); *the text is corrupt* t–t ‘thy ways’ 𝔖 u–u ‘will teach thee’ 𝔖

---

28. **her rest.** i. e. the rest which Wisdom finally gives to those who seek her.
she shall be turned . . . To follow after Wisdom seems hard and grievous at first, cp. *vv.* 24, 25, but to those who persevere Wisdom reveals herself as she really is.
gladness. תענוג, lit. ‘luxury’, cp. Prov. xix. 10.
29. **a stay of strength.** מכון עז, cp. Ps. lxxxix. 15 מכון כסאך (Smend).
bonds. Cp. *v.* 25[b]; 𝔊B *οἱ κλάδοι* (‘branches)’ is a corruption; AC read *οἱ κλοιοί* (‘bonds’), which probably represents the original reading.
robes of glory. Cp. l. 11, where 𝕳 has ‘robes of glory’; 𝔊 is to be preferred here (see critical note).
30. **her yoke.** עוּלָּהּ, which 𝔊 read עָלֶיהָ (‘upon her’); cp. *v.* 25.
a cord of blue. פתיל תכלת, the same as in Num. xv. 38, lit. ‘twisted threads of blue’. 𝔊 has the same rendering as the Sept. of Num. xv. 38.
31. **a crown of beauty.** Cp. Prov. iv. 9, xvi. 31; 𝔊 ‘a crown of rejoicing’, cp. i. 11, xv. 6.
(*c*) VI. 32–37.
32. **if thou set thy heart (thereon).** 𝔊 ‘if thou yield thy soul’.
thou shalt learn prudence. Lit. ‘thou shalt be shrewd’.
33. **If thou desire.** אם תובא, written defectively as in Prov. i. 10; but possibly it is a scribal error for אם תאהב (= 𝔊).
34. **Stand thou . . .** Cp. viii. 9.
in the assembly . . . Cp. xxxii. (𝔊 xxxv.) 3.
cleave unto. Cp. xiii. 16 *b*.
35. **discourse.** Cp. viii. 8, xi. 8. שיחה in the O. T. means a ‘complaint’, also ‘musing’ or a ‘meditation’; in Ps. cxix. 97 it has the sense of the ‘study’ of the Law. In Neo-Hebrew it means an edifying discourse.
escape. Lit. ‘go forth’, cp. Gen. xliv. 4; Jer. x. 20 (Hebr.).
36. **Look for him who is wise.** 𝔊 ‘If thou seest a man of understanding’, a free rendering.
seek him out earnestly. Cp. Job vii. 21. 𝔊 ‘Get thee betimes unto him’, cp. iv. 12.
let thy foot . . . Cp. Prov. viii. 34 and *Pirqe Aboth* i. 44.
wear. For the Hebr. word שחק cp. Job xiv. 19.
37. **the fear of the Most High.** 𝔊 ‘the ordinances of the Lord’. As Smend points out, Ben-Sira has יראת יי or יראת אלהים, but never elsewhere יראת עליון, this being the only place where it occurs; on the other hand, in xxxviii. 34 תורת עליון occurs, and perhaps that is what should be read here; the verb ‘meditate’ suggests this.
will He instruct. 𝔊 ‘establish’, reading יכין for יבין.
And He will make thee wise . . . 𝔊 renders freely: ‘And thy desire of wisdom shall be given unto thee.’

(*d*) VII. 1–3. *An Exhortation to keep from Sin* (= 2 distichs).

𝔥[A] 𝔥[C] **7** 1 Do no evil[a], and evil will not overtake thee;
2 Avoid iniquity, and it will turn from thee.
𝔥[A] 3 [b][c]Sow not in the furrows of unrighteousness[c],
Lest thou reap it sevenfold.

(*e*) VII. 4–7. *An Exhortation to follow after Humility* (= 2 + 3 distichs).

𝔥[A] 𝔥[C] 4 Seek not dominion[d] from God[e],
Nor[f] a seat of honour from[g] the king.
𝔥[A] 5 Justify not thyself in the sight of God[h],
[i]Nor display thy wisdom[i] before the king.
𝔥[A] 𝔥[C] 6 Seek not to be a judge[k],
[l]Lest thou be not able[l] [m]to put down presumption[m],
𝔥[A] (And) lest thou be in fear in the presence of a mighty[n] man,
And thou put a stumbling-block[o] in (the way of) thy uprightness.
7 [p]Sin not[p] against the assembly in the gate[q],
[r]That it cast thee not down[r] [s]among the multitude[s].

(*f*) VII. 8–10. *A warning against a false doctrine of Atonement* (= 3 distichs).

8 [t]Do not wickedly continue in sin[u][t],
For in respect of [v]one (sin)[v] thou art not without guilt.

[a] + ‘to thyself’ 𝔥[A] [b] 𝔊 *inserts* ‘My son’ (τεκνον) [c–c] *Reading* (*after* 𝔊 𝔖) אל תזרע חרושי עולה, *the text of* 𝔥 *is corrupt* [d] ‘pre-eminence’ 𝔊 [e] ‘from the Lord’ 𝔊; ‘from man’ 𝔏 [f] *So* 𝔊; 𝔥 *reads* וכן [g] ‘like’ 𝔥[C] [h] *Reading* אל (= 𝔖) *for* מלך ‘the Lord’; + quoniam agnitor cordis ipse est 𝔏 [i–i] noli velle videri sapiens 𝔏 [k] *Reading* שופט (= 𝔊) *for* מושל; > 𝔥[C] [l–l] *So* 𝔊; ‘If thou art not able’ 𝔥 𝔖 𝔏 [m–m] ‘to take away iniquities’ 𝔊 (= 𝔖 𝔏) [n] ‘rich’ 𝔖 [o] *Lit.* ‘a bribe’; ‘a blemish’ 𝔖 [p–p] *Lit.* ‘Make not thyself evil’ [q] *Reading* שער *for* שערי אל (‘the gates of God’) [r–r] ‘And cast not thyself down’ 𝔊 [s–s] ‘in its judgements’ 𝔖 [t–t] 𝔖 *lit.* ‘repeat not to sin sins’ [u] *Reading* חטאה (*Peters*) *for* חט [v–v] ‘the former (sins)’ 𝔖 [w] ‘my gifts’ 70 253 Syro-Hex 𝔏 [x–x] ‘Be not grieved’ 𝔖 [y] + ‘and tarry not to fulfil the commandment’ 𝔖 [z] > 𝔖 𝔊 𝔏 [a] 𝔏 *has the title* ‘De mendacio vitando ad amicum’ [b] ‘noli amare’ (*for*

(*d*) VII. 1–3.

VII. 1. Smend gives references to the Midrashic literature in which this verse is quoted several times, viz. *Wajjiqra Rabba* xxii. 190*c*, *Bemidbar Rabba* xviii. 272*d*, *Qoholeth Rabba* v. 97*b*.

2. **Avoid.** Lit. ‘be far from’.

3. **Sow not . . .** For the metaphor cp. Job iv. 8; Prov. xxii. 8; Gal. vi. 8.

sevenfold. Cp. xxxv. 11 (𝔊 xxxii. 13).

(*e*) VII. 4–7.

4. **Seek not . . .** The reason for the prohibition is not because these things are in themselves wrong, but because power becomes, for most men, a temptation to wrongdoing.

dominion. For the Greek ἡγεμονία cp. x. 1 *a*.

5. **Justify not thyself . . .** Cp. Job ix. 20; Ps. xliii. 2; Eccles. vii. 16; Matt. xix. 20; Luke xviii. 11.

Nor display thy wisdom. Lit. ‘be not wise’; 𝔊 μὴ σοφίζου, ‘play not the wise man’, cp. 𝔏 (see critical note). The form תתבונן does not occur elsewhere in this sense; Smend suggests תתחכם.

6. **Lest thou be not able.** See critical note; lit. ‘lest thou have not might’.

to put down. Lit. ‘to make to cease’; 𝔊 ‘to take away’.

lest thou be in fear . . . 𝔊 ‘Lest haply thou fear the person of a mighty man,’ lit. ‘lest thou act cautiously’ (μή ποτε εὐλαβηθῇς), used in a bad sense here, viz. not doing his duty for fear of offending the ‘mighty man’; cp. Lev. xix. 15; Mic. vii. 3.

uprightness. Cp. xlix. 3.

7. **Sin not against . . .** This would be done either by acting unjustly in deference to the ‘mighty man’, or else by taking a bribe; cp. 2 Sam. xix. 8; Amos v. 15.

in the gate. שער is rendered πόλις in the Sept. of Gen. xix. 1; Deut. xii. 12; Is. xlv. 1 and elsewhere; see also xxxi. (𝔊 xxxiv.) 24.

That it cast thee not down . . . i.e. that the multitude cast thee not down. The words are probably to be taken in a figurative sense, cp. Prov. v. 14.

(*f*) VII. 8–10.

8. **Do not wickedly . . .** Lit. ‘Conspire not to repeat sin’; 𝔊 ‘Bind not up sin twice’ (μὴ καταδεσμεύσῃς δὶς ἁμαρτίαν), cp. συνδεῖν in 1 Sam. xviii. 1, and συνδεσμός in 2 Kings xi. 14 (Hart).

For in respect of . . . i.e. each individual sin deserves, and receives, punishment.

9 Say not, 'He will look upon the multitude of my gifts,
And when I offer (them) to the Most High God He will accept (them)[w].'
10 [x]Be not impatient[x] in thy prayer,
And in righteousness be not behindhand[y].

(*g*) VII. 11–17. *Various precepts for conduct of life* (= 3 + 2 + 2 distichs).

11 Despise no man (who is) in bitterness of spirit,
Remember that[z] there is one who exalteth and humbleth.
12 [a]Devise not[b] evil[c] against a brother,
[d]Nor do the like[d] against a friend [e]or a neighbour withal[e].
13 Take no delight in lies of any[f] sort,
For the outcome thereof will not be pleasant.
14 Prate not[g] in the assembly of elders[h],
And repeat[i] not (thy) words in (thy) prayer.
15 [k]Hate not[l] laborious work,
[m]Nor husbandry, for it was ordained of God[m k].
16 [n]Number not thyself [o]among sinful men[o n],
Remember that wrath[p] will not tarry.

'arare') 𝔏 [c] *So* 𝔖; ℌ *lit.* 'violence'; 'a lie' 𝔊 [d–d] *So* 𝔊; ℌ *lit.* 'and thus' [e–e] > 𝔊 [f] *Reading* כל *for* על [g] 𝔖 'Hide not thy soul', *reading perhaps* תסתר for תסוד (*Smend*) [h] *So* 𝔊; ℌ *lit.* 'princes' (= 𝔖) [i] 'alter' 𝔖 [k–k] > 𝔖 [l] *Reading* תקוץ *for* תאיץ (*Smend*) [m–m] *The text is in part corrupt* [n–n] 'Love not thyself more than the men of thy people' 𝔖 [o–o] *Reading* במתי עון *for* במתי עם [p] *Reading* עברון (= 𝔊 𝔖) *for* עכרון

---

9. This verse has fallen out in ℌ; in its place *v.* 15 stands here. 𝔏 places *v.* 10 before *v.* 9.

Say not, 'He will look upon'... Cp. xxxiv. 19[b]; Prov. xxi. 27; on the false conception of atonement and satisfaction here combated cp. Is. i. 11–15.

10. **Be not impatient...** As Smend points out, תתקצר is an abbreviated form of קצרה רוח; for this phrase see Job xxi. 4; Prov. xiv. 29. 𝔊 μὴ ὀλιγοψυχήσῃς, cp. iv. 9, Jas. i. 6, and the Midrash *Debarim Rabba* iii. 24: 'Pray and pray, again and again; a time will come when thou wilt be answered'; see also Matt. xxi. 21, 22; Mark xi. 24.

And in righteousness... i. e. almsgiving, cp. xxix. 8; 𝔊 'Neglect not to give alms', cp. iii. 30. For almsgiving as the highest form of righteousness, as it is according to Rabbinical teaching, cp. Matt. vi. 1 ff.

(*g*) VII. 11–17.

11. **Despise no man.** 𝔊 'Laugh not a man to scorn', free rendering.

in bitterness of spirit. The more usual expression in the O.T. is 'in bitterness of soul' (= 𝔊), cp. Job iii. 20, vii. 11; Prov. xxxi. 6. The reference is to one suffering destitution who would be an object of scorn because his evil plight would be regarded as a visible sign of divine wrath for sin committed, cp. Is. liii. 34.

there is one who... Cp. for this thought 1 Sam. ii. 7; Luke i. 52, 53.

12. **Devise not.** Lit. 'plough not', so 𝔊; cp. Prov. iii. 29. חרש means both 'to plough' and 'to devise', cp. Prov. iii. 39, and for the metaphorical sense, as here, cp. Hos. x. 13 (Hebr.).

a friend or a neighbour. רע ('friend') is more intimate than חבר ('companion'); on the latter see also note on vi. 10.

13. **Take no delight...** Lit. 'Delight not to lie any lie'.

the outcome. תקוה means usually 'hope' or 'expectation', but it occurs in the sense of 'result' or 'outcome' several times in this book, cp. *v.* 17, xx. 2–6; Job xi. 20. 𝔊 misunderstands the clause in rendering: 'For the custom (lit. 'continuance') thereof is not for good.'

14. **Prate not.** 𝔊 μὴ ἀδολέσχει (lit. 'babble not'), seems to bring out the meaning, cp. xxxii. (𝔊 xxxv.) 9; Eccles. v. 2. The Hebr. word means simply 'to converse', cp. xlii. 12.

repeat not... Cp. Eccles. v. 1, and Matt. vi. 7, 'And in praying use not vain repetitions.'

15. **Hate not...** Lit. 'Hate not a warfare of work', cp. Job vii. 1 (R. V. marg.); the verse shows that already in the time of Ben-Sira manual labour, the honourableness of which is often emphasized in Rabbinical writings, was held in high esteem; cp. Matt. xiii. 55, Mark vi. 3, and *Pirqe Aboth* ii. 2: 'Excellent is Torah study together with worldly business... all Torah without work (i.e. manual labour) must fail at length, and occasion iniquity'; this is a saying of Rabbi Gamaliel, a grandson of the great Gamaliel; he lived at the end of the first century A. D. Cp. also *Qiddushin* 99*a* (T. B.): 'Whosoever doth not teach his son work, teacheth him to rob.'

husbandry. עבדה in this sense occurs in Exod. i. 14; 1 Chron. xxvii. 26; the verb is used in Deut. xxi. 4; Ezek. xxxvi. 9, 34; Eccles. v. 8.

ordained. Lit. 'apportioned', cp. xv. 9 *b* (Hebr.).

16, 17. The order of these verses varies in the Greek MSS.

16. **Number not thyself.** אל תחשובך, the pronominal suffix used reflexively is not found in the canonical books of the O. T. (Smend), cp. *v.* 7, where another example occurs in אל תרשיעך ('make not thyself evil'; in *Pirqe Aboth* ii. 17 this is expressed אל תהי רשע בפני עצמך). An analogous usage is found in Arabic, according to Smend.

among sinful men. 𝔊 'among the multitude of sinners', cp. xvi. 6, xxi. 9.

wrath. The Hebr. word עברון does not occur elsewhere; possibly it is a corruption of עברה, cp. Prov. xxii. 8 *b*. In ℌ there is a word-play in this clause: זכור עברון לא יתעבר.

ℌ[A] ℌ[C] 17 Humble (thy) pride[q] greatly,
For the expectation[r] of man is decay[s].
[[t]Hasten not to say, 'Violence';
Commit (thyself) unto God, and delight (in) His way[t].]

(*h*) VII. 18–21. *A man's duties to a friend, a wife, and a servant* (= 2 + 2 distichs).

ℌ[A] 18 Change not a friend for money,
Nor a natural[u] brother for gold of Ophir.
19 Reject not[v] a wise[w] wife;
And a well-favoured (wife) is above pearls.
ℌ[A] ℌ[C] 20 [x]Maltreat not [y]a servant that serveth truly[y],
Nor a hireling[z] who giveth his life (for thee).
21 A wise slave love[a] as thyself,
And withhold not from him (his) freedom.

(*i*) VII. 22–25. *A man's duties to his cattle and to his children* (= 2 + 2 distichs).

ℌ[A] 22 Hast thou cattle[b], look (to them)[c] thyself[d],
And if they are[e] profitable, keep them[f].
ℌ[A] ℌ[C] 23 [g]Hast thou sons, correct them,
[h]And give them wives[i] in their youth[h].

[q] 'soul' 𝔊 𝔖; 'spirit' 𝔏 [r] 'punishment' 𝔊 [s] *Lit.* 'worms'; 'for worms' ℌ[C] [t-t] > 𝔊 𝔖 𝔏; *the text is corrupt* [u] *Reading* תלים *for* תלוי [v] 'Forgo not' (μη αστοχει) 𝔊; 'Exchange not' 𝔖 (*cp. v.* 26); 'Depart not from' 𝔏 [w] > 𝔖; + 'and good' 𝔊; 𝔏 *adds* quam sortitus es in timore dei (*cp.* xxvi. 3) [x] 𝔏 *has the title* 'De bono servo' [y-y] 'a trusty servant' ℌ[C] [z] *Reading* שכיר *for* שוכר ('the hirer') [a] ℌ[A] *has* חבב (*cp.* Deut. xxxiii. 3, *a new Neo-Hebr. word*); אהב ℌ[C] [b] *Lit.* 'a beast' [c] *Or* 'to it' [d] *Lit.* 'with thine eyes' [e] *Or* 'it is' [f] *Or* 'it' [g] 𝔏 *has the title* 'De filiis' [h-h] 'And bow down

17. **Humble...** Cp. ii. 18.

decay. 𝔊 'fire and the worm', cp. Job xxv. 6, Mark ix. 48. A development of thought regarding the Hereafter had taken place in the intervening period between the time when Ben-Sira wrote his book and the grandson translated it, hence the addition in 𝔊; cp. with the latter 1 Enoch xlvi. 3 (The Book of Parables, *c.* 94–64 B.C.): '... Darkness will be their dwelling, and worms their bed...'; and 1 Enoch xcviii. 3 (*c.* 134–95 B.C.): '... and in shame and in slaughter and in great destitution will their spirits be cast into the furnace of fire.'

In *Pirqe Aboth* iv. 7 this verse is quoted thus: 'Rabbi Levitas of Jabneh said, Be exceedingly lowly of spirit, for the hope of man is the worm.'

Hasten not... These two additional clauses are certainly not original.

Commit (thyself) unto... Cp. Ps. xxii. 9, xxxvii. 5 (Hebr.); Prov. xvi. 3.

(*h*) VII. 18–21.

18. **for money.** 𝔊 ἀδιαφόρου ('a thing indifferent'), a mistake for διαφόρου ('profit').

a natural brother. The reading אח תלים is that suggested by Nöldeke (*ZATW*, xx. 85). The word occurs in the Targ. of Pseudo-Jonathan and in the 'Fragment' Targ. to Gen. xlix. 5 in the sense of 'twin', and seems preferable to the text as it stands אח תלוי; but Schechter thinks that the latter is correct, and compares it with the Rabbinical term אשם תלוי, 'which means the trespass-offering of one who is in *doubt* whether he has committed an act that has to be atoned for by a sin-offering; אח תלוי would then mean a doubtful, questionable friend, an indifferent friend.' The meaning of the verse would then be that a friend is so valuable a possession that even the semblance of one should not be exchanged for gold.

gold of Ophir. Cp. 1 Kings ix. 28; Job xxii. 24, xxviii. 16.

19. **a well-favoured (wife).** For the expression טובת חן ('well-favoured'), cp. Nahum iii. 4 (Smend); 𝔊 'her grace'.

pearls. The exact signification of פנינים is uncertain, whether 'pearls', 'corals', or 'rubies', cp. Job xxviii. 18; Prov. xxxi. 10, and R. V. marg.

20. **who giveth...** i.e. who devotes his whole life to thy service, cp. ix. 24*b*, li. 20; Deut. xxiv. 14.

21. **And withhold not...** In reference to the law according to which servants were to be granted their freedom after six years of service, cp. Exod. xxi. 2; Deut. xv. 12–15; Lev. xxv. 39–43; Jer. xxxiv. 8–18.

(*i*) VII. 22–25.

22. **cattle.** Lit. 'a beast'; Smend suggests that a riding-horse is meant, cp. Neh. ii. 12, 14, which seems probable. Cp. Prov. xxvii. 23 ff., of flocks and herds generally.

profitable. Lit. 'reliable'.

keep. Lit. 'let it stand firm', i.e. do not part with them.

23. **correct them.** Cp. xxx. 1–3, 13; Prov. xxii. 26, xxiii. 13.

And give them wives... Schechter (*Studies*, 2nd series, p. 96) refers to *Qiddushin* 30 *b*, where it says that the chief duties of a father towards his son consist in 'instructing him in the Torah, bringing him into wedlock, and

𝔥^{C} 24 Hast thou daughters[k], keep[l] their bodies,
And show them not a pleasant countenance.
25 Marry thy daughter, and sorrow will depart [from thy house],
But bestow her upon a man of understanding[m].

(*j*) VII. 26–28. *A man's duty to his wife and to his parents* (= 1 + 2 distichs).

26 Hast thou a wife[n], [o]abhor her not[o],
But trust not thyself to one that hateth (thee).
27 [p]Honour thy father with thy whole heart,
And forget not thy mother who bare thee [q]in pangs[q].
28 [qq]Remember that [r]of them thou wast born[r],
And how canst thou recompense them for what they have done for thee[p]?

(*k*) VII. 29–31. *A man's duties to God and to His ministers* (= 2 + 2 distichs).

29 [s]Fear God[t] with all thy heart[u],
And reverence His priests.
30 With all thy strength[v] love[w] Him that made thee,
And forsake not His ministers.
31 [x]Glorify God[x] and honour the priest,
And give (them) their portion as it is commanded (thee);
[xx]The food[y] of the trespass-offering, and the heave-offering of the hand[xx],
The sacrifices of righteousness, and the offerings [z]of holy things[z].

their neck from their youth' 𝔊 (= 𝔏)   i > 𝔥^{C} *by mistake*   k 'sons' 𝔥^{C} l 'give heed to' 𝔊   m + *και μισουμενω* (ℵ$^{c.a}$ *μισουση σε*) *μη εμπιστευσης σεαυτον* 𝔊^{ℵ}, *cp. v.* 26 b   n + 'after thy mind' 𝔊   o–o 'cast her not out' 𝔊; 'forsake her not' 𝔖   p–p > 𝔥   q–q > 𝔖   qq 𝔏 *has the title* 'De parentibus'   r–r 'if they had not been thou hadst not been' 𝔖 (= 𝔏)   s 𝔏 *has the title* 'De timore dei et honore sacerdotum'   t 'the Lord' 𝔊   u 'soul' 𝔊   v 'heart' 𝔖   w 'honour' 𝔖   x–x 'Fear the Lord' 𝔊   xx–xx 𝔏 *renders this clause in various ways*   y 𝔊^{B} *απ αρχης* (B^{ab} ℵA *απαρχην*)   z–z > 𝔊^{B}

---

teaching him a handicraft'. The point of the admonition is that fathers should, by marrying their sons while young, save them from temptation. With the rendering of 𝔊 (see critical note) cp. the interpolated passage xxx. 12 *a*.

24. **And show them not ...** Lit. 'And cause not thy face to shine unto them'; see xxvi. 10–12, xlii. 10, 11.

25. **Marry thy daughter ...** Lit. 'Let thy daughter go out, and sorrow will go out'. Marriages were arranged by the fathers; daughters had no say in the choice of their husbands.

But bestow her upon ... The Hebr. word זבד in this sense occurs elsewhere in the Bible only in Gen. xxx. 20. In the Midrash *Pesiqta* 49 *a*, it is said that a man should give up all he has (i.e. for the purpose of offering an adequate marriage-settlement) in order to marry his daughter to a learned man; and it goes on to say that if the daughter of a learned man marries one of the *'am-ha'areṣ* ('the people of the land', who were unlearned), the marriage would be a failure.

(*j*) VII. 26–28.

26. **abhor her not.** The reference is to Lev. xxi. 7, 14.

But trust not ... See critical note on the preceding verse.

27. The omission of this verse and the next in 𝔥 is probably due to the fact that *vv.* 27 and 29 both began with the same words בכל לבך ('with all thy heart').

Honour. Lit. 'give glory to'; cp. Exod. xx. 12, Deut. v. 16, where the Sept. uses τιμάω, instead of δοξάζω, as here.

28. **how canst thou recompense.** Cp. the saying of Rabbi Judah ha-Nasi (middle of second century A.D.): 'Be careful of the honour due to your mother; let the lamp be lit in its place, the table be set in its place, the couch be spread in its place' (T. B. *Kethuboth* 103 *a*, quoted in *JE*, ix. 99 *a*).

for what they have done for thee. 𝔊 καθὼς αὐτοὶ σοί.

(*k*) VII. 29–31.

29. **reverence.** Lit. 'regard as holy'; 𝔊 θαύμαζε, cp. xxxviii. 3.

30. **And forsake not...** Cp. Lev. ii. 3, vi. 16, vii. 7, 9, 34; Num. v. 9, xviii. 8–19; Deut. xii. 19, xviii. 1–5.

31. **their portion.** Cp. Lev. vi. 14–18.

The food of the ... Cp. Num. xv. 20 f., Lev. v. 6; 𝔊 'the first-fruits and the trespass-offering'.

the heave-offering of the hand. Cp. Exod. xxix. 27; Lev. vii. 32; Deut. xviii. 3; 𝔊 lit. 'the gift of the shoulders'.

sacrifices of righteousness. Cp. Deut. xxxiii. 19; the מנחה ('meal-offering') is most likely meant, it is called 'a thing most holy' in Lev. ii. 3, 10.

the offerings of holy things. Cp. Num. xviii. 5–11; 𝔊 'the first-fruits of holy things'.

(*l*) VII. 32–36. *A man's duties to the poor, to his departed friends, to mourners, and to the sick* (= 1 + 3 + 1 distichs)

𝔥[A]

32 [a]Also to the poor stretch out thy hand[a],
That the blessing may be perfected.
33 A gift is acceptable[b] in the sight of every man living,
[c]And also from the dead withhold not kindness[d].
34 Withdraw not thyself from them that weep[e],
And mourn with them that mourn.
35 Forget not [f]to visit the sick[f],
For thou wilt be loved for that.
36 In all thy doings[g] remember thy last end,
Then wilt thou never do corruptly.

(*m*) VIII. 1–3. *A caution against quarrelling with the powerful, the rich, and the boastful* (= 3 + 1 distichs).

8 1 [a]Contend not with a mighty man,
Lest thou fall into his hands[b].
2 Strive not against [c]the man that is rich[c],
Lest he weigh thy price[d], [e]and thou be destroyed[e].
For gold[f] hath made many reckless,
And wealth hath led astray the hearts of princes.
3 Quarrel not with a loud-mouthed man,
And put not wood on fire.

a–a *The text is somewhat mutilated* b *Reading* חן (*lit.* 'a grace') *for* תן; 'Grace is a gift . . .' 𝔖 c 𝔏 *has the title* 'De defunctis' d *Lit.* 'mercy' e + in conrogatione (*in reference to the funeral feast*) 𝔏 f–f *Reading* לבקר כואב *for* לב מאוהב ('thy heart from a friend') g 'words' 𝔊

a 𝔏 *has the title* 'De non litigando' b + *the doublet:* 'That thou needest not to turn against his heart, contend not with a man that is mightier than thou' 𝔥 c–c 'the possessor of gold' 𝔖 d *Reading* משקלך (*Smend*) *for* מחירך e–e > 𝔖 𝔊 𝔏 f + 'and silver' 𝔏 g–g 'an untutored man' 𝔊 h–h *Reading*

(*l*) VII. 32–36.

32. **Also to the poor . . .** The reference is to sharing with the poor, &c., the tithe of every third year, cp. Deut. xiv. 28, 29.

33. **And also from the dead . . .** The reference is to offerings for (or to?) the dead; cp. Deut. xxvi. 14; Hos. ix. 4; Jer. xvi. 7; Tob. iv. 17. 𝔊 seeks to tone down the point of 𝔥 by rendering: 'And for a dead man keep not back grace'; cp. xxx. 18 (Greek).

34. **mourn . . .** Cp. xxii. 11.

35. **to visit the sick.** This has always been regarded as a paramount duty among the Jews; the technical name for the visitation of the sick used in Rabbinical literature is *Biqqur Cholim.* Schechter (*op. cit.*, p. 99 f.) says: 'It is clear from certain injunctions in the Talmud in connexion with this duty, that it included, in case of need, also nursing, and sweeping the room (*Peah* iii. 9, Talm. J.). His friends also prayed for the patient, and it was part of their duty to remind him to make a will and to confess his sins, "for all those who were about to die had to confess their sins." They had also the belief that a confession, which concluded with a prayer for the forgiveness of sins, might bring about his recovery'; cp. Jas. v. 13–16. In the modern Jewish Liturgy there is a special Office for the visitation of the sick; see the *Jewish Authorized Daily Prayer Book* (ed. Singer), pp. 314–317.

36. **remember thy last end, Then . . .** Cp. *Pirqe Aboth* iii. 1: 'Consider three things, and thou wilt not come into the hands of transgression: know whence thou art come, and whither thou art going, and before whom thou wilt have to plead thy cause, and make thy reckoning.'

do corruptly. For the verb שחת cp. xxx. ii; Dan. ii. 9.

(*m*) VIII. 1–3.

VIII. 1. **Lest.** On the Hebr. למה here, see Smend *in loc.*

2. **Strive not.** Lit. 'devise not', cp. Prov. xiv. 22.

Lest he weigh thy price. i.e. lest he offer a larger bribe than thou art able to pay. 𝔊 'Lest haply he overweigh thee'.

reckless. Lit. 'boastful', i.e. the possession of much wealth has made men reckless in giving bribes. 𝔊 renders, 'And gold hath destroyed many.'

And wealth . . . 𝔊 'And turned aside the hearts of kings'.

3. **a loud-mouthed man.** Lit. 'a man of tongue', cp. ix. 18, xxv. 20; Jas. iii. 8.

And put not . . . Cp. xxviii. 8–12; Prov. xv. 1, xxvi. 20, 21; Jas. iii. 5, 6; in the Psalms of Solomon xii. 2 the tongue of a malicious man is compared to 'fire in a threshing-floor that burns up the straw'. 𝔊 has 'and heap not' (μὴ ἐπιστοιβάσῃς); for the word cp. Lev. i. 12 (Sept.).

(*n*) VIII. 4–7. *A warning against associating with a foolish man; the need of having respect for the penitent, the aged, and the departed* (= 1 + 3 distichs).

𝔥[A] 4 Associate not with a [g]foolish man[g],
Lest he despise [h](thy) sound (words)[h].
5 Reproach not a man who repenteth,
Remember that we are all guilty[i].
6 Dishonour not[k] a man that is old,
For [l]we shall be numbered among the aged[l].
7 Rejoice not over one that is dead,
Remember that we shall all be gathered[m] (to our fathers).

(*a*) VIII. 8–9. *An exhortation to learn from the wise and the aged* (= 2 + 2 distichs).

8 Neglect not the discourse of the wise,
And busy thyself with proverbs;
For therefrom[n] wilt thou learn instruction[o],
That thou mayst stand[p] in the presence of princes[q].
9 Reject not the tradition[r] of the aged,
Which they heard[s] from their fathers;
For therefrom wilt thou receive[t] instruction[u],
That thou mayst (be able to) return answer in time of need.

נכחים *for* נדיבים (' princes ')   [i] ' sinners ' 𝔖; ' worthy of punishment ' 𝔊   [k] ' Laugh not at ' 𝔖   [l-l] *Reading* נמנו מזקנים; *Smend emends the text* ממנו מזקינים ('from among ourselves some will grow old'); 'remember that . . .' 𝔖   [m] ' die ' 𝔊 𝔖   [n] ' From them ' 𝔊   [o] ' wisdom ' א   [p] + ' at ease ' 𝔊[v]; + ' readily ' 248 Syro-Hex; + sine querella 𝔏   [q] ' great men ' 𝔊   [r] *Reading* בשמועת; ' the discourse ' 𝔊   [s] ' learned ' 𝔊   [t] ' learn ' 𝔊   [u] ' understanding ' 𝔊

(*n*) VIII. 4–7.

4. **(thy) sound (words).** The emendation of the text (see critical note) is that suggested by Matthes and Dyserink (*ZATW*, iii. 163); cp. xi. 21; Prov. iv. 25, xxiv. 26. The rendering of 𝔊 πρόγονοι is probably based on the corrupt Hebr. text.

5. **a man who repenteth.** Lit. 'a man who turns from transgression'. Cp. *Baba mezia* iv. 10 (T. J.): 'When a man repenteth say not to him, "Remember thy former sins."'

6. **Dishonour not . . .** Cp. *Pirqe Aboth* iv. 28: 'He who learneth from the aged, to whom is he like? To one who eateth ripened grapes, and drinketh old wine.'

7. **Rejoice not . . .** Lit. 'boast not', i.e. because thou art still living, while another is dead.

we shall all be gathered . . . Cp. Gen. xxv. 8; Judges ii. 10; 2 Kings xxii. 20; Job xxvii. 19.

VIII. 8—X. 29. This division contains thirteen subsections; the contents are miscellaneous, consisting mainly of rules about conduct towards many classes of persons.

(*a*) VIII. 8–9.

8. **the discourse.** For שיחה cp. vi. 35.

busy thyself. This form of the Hebr. word does not occur elsewhere, and its meaning here is uncertain; Hart suggests דרש, following 𝔖, which in Hebr. means 'to seek out', and has become the technical term for studying the Scriptures, &c.; cp. Beth ha-Midrash, 'the house of study,' in li. 23.

That thou mayst stand . . . Cp. xxxviii. 3, xlvii. 1; 𝔊 'minister', cp. Prov. xxii. 29.

9. **Reject not.** אל תמאס, cp. vii. 19; 𝔊 μὴ ἀστόχει ('miss not'), as in vii. 19.

the aged. Cp. *v.* 6, vi. 34, xxv. 4, xxxii. (𝔊 xxxv.) 13.

Which they heard from . . . The reference is to the Oral Tradition, technically known as תורה שבעל פה (lit. 'The Law which is according to the mouth') in Rabbinical literature, cp. Ps. xliv. i. The following passage, from the preface to the *Yad ha-chazaqah* ('the Strong Hand') of Maimonides, shows the traditional belief of the Jews regarding this subject: 'All the commandments which were given to Moses on Sinai were given with their interpretation; for it is said, And I will give thee the tables of stone, and the Torah ("Law"), and the Mitzvah ("Commandment"), Exod. xxiv. 12; *Torah*: that is, the Written Law; *Mitzvah*: that is, its interpretation. He commanded us to observe the *Torah* in accordance with (על פה, lit. "according to the mouth of") the *Mitzvah*. And this *Mitzvah* is called the Oral Law. Moses, our teacher, wrote down the whole Law with his own hand before he died . . .; the *Mitzvah*, that is, the interpretation of the Law, he did not write down; but he commanded it (צוה בה) to the elders and to Joshua and to the rest of Israel; for it is written, "All the words which I have commanded you, these shall ye observe and do" (Deut. xii. 28). And therefore this is called "Oral Tradition" (תורה שבעל פה).' Cp. *Pirqe Aboth* i. 1: 'Moses received the Torah from Sinai, and he delivered it to Joshua, and Joshua to the elders (Joshua xxiv. 31; Judges ii. 7), and the elders to the prophets, and the prophets delivered it to the men of the Great Synagogue.'

(*b*) VIII. 10–11. *The danger of consorting with sinners* (= 2 distichs).

ℌ[A] 10 [v]Kindle not[w] the coals[x] of the wicked[v],
  Lest thou be burned with the flame of his fire.
11 [y]Be not enraged because of the scorner,
  That he should use[z] thy mouth[a] as an ambush.

(*c*) VIII. 12–13. *Warnings against lending and standing surety* (= 2 distichs).

12 Lend not to a man that is mightier than thou,
  And if thou lend, (thou art) as one that loseth.
13 Be not surety [b]for one who is more excellent[c] than thou[b],
  And if thou become surety (thou art)[d] as one that payeth.

(*d*) VIII. 14–19. *Warnings against having dealings with various types of evil men* (= 1+2+2+3 distichs).

14 Go not to law with a judge,
  For he will judge according to his good pleasure.
15 Go not [e]in the way[e] with a cruel[f] man,
  Lest thou be overwhelmed with misfortune:
For he will go[g] straight before his face,
  And through his foolishness thou wilt perish.
16 [h]Do not obstinately gainsay[h] a wrathful[i] man,
  And ride not[k] with him through the desert[l].
For blood is as nothing in his eyes,
  And where there is no helper, he will destroy thee.

v–v 'Be not a companion of him who is wholly bad' 𝔖   w *Reading* אל תצת (=𝔊) *for* אל תצלה ('rush not')
x *Reading* נחלת *for* גחלת   y 𝔏 *has the title* 'De vitandis malis'   z *Lit.* 'set'   a *Reading* לפיך (=𝔊) *for* לפניך
b–b 'above thy power' 𝔊   c 'stronger' 𝔖   d 'take thought' 𝔊; 'thou art become' 𝔖   e–e *So* 𝔊 𝔖; > ℌ
f 'rash' 𝔊; 'hard' 𝔖 (*lit.* 'heavy')   g ποιησει 𝔊, *a mistake for* πορευεται   h–h μη ποιησης μαχην 𝔊, *reading* אל תעש מַצָּה *for* אל תעיז מֵצַח   i 'an unrighteous' 𝔖   k 'strive not' 𝔖   l *Reading* במדבר (=𝔊 𝔖) *for* בדרך

(*b*) VIII. 10–11.

10. **Kindle not.** See critical note; cp. Is. ix. 17 (18 in E.V.).

the flame . . . Cp. xlv. 19. With the clause cp. the Mishna, *Aboth* ii. 10: 'Warm thyself at the fire of the wise; but beware of their coal (והוה זהיר בגחלתן), that thou burn not thyself (שלא תכוה).'

11. **Be not enraged.** זוח in Aramaic and Syriac means 'to set in movement', 'to become excited' (Smend) and this seems to be the meaning here (cp. 𝔊 μὴ ἐξαναστῇς). In Hebr. the cognate word זחח means 'to move away'; it only occurs twice in the O.T. (Exod. xxviii. 28, xxix. 21), each time in the Niphʿal voice; but in later Hebrew it is common, occurring frequently in the Targums.

scorner. Cp. Ps. i. 1; 𝔊 'an injurious man', or 'one who is insolent', cp. 1 Tim. i. 13.

That he should . . . 𝔊 'Lest he lie in wait as an ambush for thy mouth'. The meaning of the verse is that a man should not lose his temper before a scorner (i.e. one who scoffs at religion), because by doing so he gives his case away; the scorner gains the advantage through the intemperate speech of the other.

(*c*) VIII. 12–13.

12. **Lend not . . .** Cp. Prov. xxii. 7.

13. **Be not surety . . .** Cp. xxix. 14–20; Prov. vi. 1, 2, xi. 15, xvii. 18, xxii. 26, 27.

more excellent. i.e. of higher social standing, cp. Esther vi. 6; see also Gen. xlix. 3 (Hebr.).

(*d*) VIII. 14–19.

14. This verse occurs in a somewhat different form after iv. 27: 'Sit not with an unjust judge in order that thou judge not with him according to his good pleasure' (= 𝔖 here).

For he will judge . . . 𝔊 'For according to his honour will they give judgement for him'.

15. **a cruel man.** Cp. Job xli. 2 (Hebr.).

Lest thou be overwhelmed . . . Lit. 'Lest thou bear thyself down with thy evil'. 𝔊 ἵνα μὴ καταβαρύνηται κατὰ σοῦ ('Lest he be aggrieved against thee'), which Smend, on the basis of ℌ, emends thus: ἵνα μὴ βαρύνῃ τὰ κακά σου ('Lest thy evils bear thee down').

For he will go . . . i.e. he will follow his bent blindly, irrespective of consequences.

thou wilt perish. Lit. 'thou wilt be swept away'.

16. **Do not obstinately gainsay.** Lit. 'Harden not thy forehead', cp. Prov. vii. 13, xvi. 29, xxii. 24; Is. xlviii. 4; Ezek. iii. 7.

a wrathful man. Lit. 'a master of wrath' (בעל אף).

nothing. Lit. 'a lightly-esteemed thing' (קל), cp. Deut. xxv. 3; Prov. xi. 9; Is. iii. 5, xvi. 14.

17 Take no counsel with a fool,
For he will not be able [m]to keep thy secret[m],
18 [n]Do no secret thing before a stranger[n],
For thou knowest not what he will ultimately[o] do (therewith).
19 Reveal not [p]thy heart[p] to every man,
And [q]drive not away[q] from thee prosperity.

(*e*) IX. 1–9. *Of conduct towards women* (= 2 + 2 + 2 + 3 + 2 distichs).

9 1 [a]Be not jealous of the wife [b]of thy bosom[b],
[c]Lest she learn[c] [d]malice[d] against thee.
2 [e]Give not[e] thyself unto a woman,
[f]So as to let her trample down thy manhood[f].
3 [g]Meet not[g] [h]a strange woman[h],
Lest thou fall into her nets[i].
4 [j]With a female singer[j] [k]have no converse[k],
Lest thou be taken in her snares.
5 On a maiden fix not thy gaze,
[l]Lest thou be entrapped in penalties with her[l].

m–m ‘to conceal the matter’ 𝔊 n–n > 𝔖 o > 𝔊 p–p ‘what is in thy heart’ 𝔖 q–q *Reading* אל תדיח, *for which Smend suggests* אל ידיח (‘that he drive not away’)

a 𝔏 *inserts the title* ‘De mulieribus’ b–b *So* 𝔥 𝔊: > 𝔖 c–c *So* 𝔥 פן תלמד: 𝔊 μηδε διδαξῃς: 𝔏 ne ostendat (= μη δειξῃ) d–d *So* 𝔥 רעה; 𝔊 παιδειαν πονηραν (*so* 𝔖) = ? דעה רעה (? *conflation; but Peters reads so*) e–e *So* 𝔊 𝔖: 𝔥 אל תקנא (*dittography*); *read* אל תתן f–f *So* 𝔥 להדריכה על במותיך (‘To cause her to tread upon thy high places’; *cp.* Hab. iii. 19); επιβηναι αυτην επι την ισχυν σου 𝔊; ‘To give her power over all that thou hast’ 𝔖 g–g אל תקרב אל 𝔥 h–h אשה זזרה 𝔥; [μη υπαντα] γυναικι εταιριζομενῃ 𝔊 i 𝔥 + עם־זונה אל תסתייד פן תלכד בלקותיה: (*read* חלקותיה *for the last word or* בתקלותיה) *i.e.* ‘Consort not with a courtesan lest thou be caught in her flatteries *or* in her snares’ (תַּקָּלָה *in NH* = ‘snare’, ‘stumbling-block’: *B.H.* מִכְשׁוֹל). *The line is a doublet and variant on* 4 *a* j–j 𝔥 עם מנגינת (*point* מְנַגֶּנֶת) k–k *Read* אל תסתייד (*from variant in preceding line*) = 𝔖 *and* (?) 𝔊 (μη ενδελεχιζε): *so Smend*: 𝔥 text אל תדמוך = ‘do not sleep’ l–l *So* 𝔥 (*variant*) *i.e. reading* פן תלכד בתקלותיה (*see note* i–i *above*): ‘Lest haply thou be caught by her attempts’ 𝔊 = 𝔥 (*variant*): 𝔥 text פן יְשָׂרְפוּךְ בפיפיותם = ‘Lest they (*m.*) burn thee with their mouths’ (*sic!*) *is hardly possible.* 𝔖 ‘Lest she destroy thee with her utterances’ (*Smend keeps the reading* בלקותיה *of* 𝔥 *variant* = ? ‘with her punishments’: *cp.* לְקוּתָא = ‘punishment’, ‘disorder’, ‘defect’) l–l 𝔥 = 𝔊 (*lit.* ‘in her fines’: עוֹנֶשׁ = ‘fine’, ‘indemnity’): ‘Lest thou be mulcted in her dowry doubly’ 𝔖, *interpreting after* Deut. xxii. 29

---

17. **Take no counsel.** Cp. ix. 14 (Hebr.).
18. **secret thing . . . stranger.** זר . . . רז, evidently intended for a word-play; רז (‘secret thing’) does not occur elsewhere in the Bible, but it is used in the Targums.
what he will . . . do. Lit. ‘what he will bring forth’, i.e. what mischief he will do with the secret that has been confided to him. For the more general use of ילד cp. Prov. xxvii. 1.
19. **every man.** Lit. ‘all flesh’.
drive not away. i.e. If a man publishes his private concerns to all the world he will suffer for it.
(*e*) IX. 1–9.
IX. 1. **Be not jealous . . .** The Rabbis, as Edersheim points out, often warn against groundless jealousy. Ben-Sira here gives a good reason for avoiding it—it may promote the realization of the thing feared. For the subject cp. Num. v. 14. For the expression ‘wife of thy bosom’ cp. Deut. xiii. 6.
2. **Give not thyself unto a woman.** On the other hand, a man ought not to go to the other extreme, and be over-trustful.
So as to let her trample down thy manhood. Lit. ‘to cause her to tread upon thy high places’; cp. for the expression Hab. iii. 19. 𝔊 ‘that she should set her foot upon thy strength’. The term ‘high places’ in such connexions appears to have lost its original significance, and to have acquired the meaning ‘strength’ or the like: so 𝔖 renders the word in xlvi. 9; and the LXX (ισχυς) and Onqelos render similarly in Deut. xxxii. 13. The man who is ruled over by his wife is held up to pity and scorn as no man in several passages in the Talmud (see Edersheim on the verse).
3. **Meet not a strange woman.** 𝔥 has ‘draw not nigh’. ‘Strange woman’, as in Proverbs (cp. ii. 16, vii. 5) = courtesan. For the doublet in 𝔥 at the end of this verse see critical note.
5. **fix not thy gaze.** Cp. Matt. v. 28.
Lest thou be entrapped in penalties with her. Or ‘lest thou be caught in her punishments’. The verb might also be rendered ‘lest thou come to fall’ (in the penalties inflicted on her account). Perhaps ‘penalties on her account’ would be a better rendering. Such cases involved a fine of 50 shekels, and an indissoluble marriage according to Deut. xxii. 28–29.

ℌ[A] 6 Give not thyself unto the harlot,
[m]Lest thou lose[m] [n]thine inheritance[n].
𝔊 (𝔖) 7 [op]Look not round about thee[p] [q]in the streets of a city[q],
[r]And wander not about in the broad places thereof[r].
ℌ[A] 8 [st]Hide thine eye[t] from a lovely woman,
[u]And gaze not[u] upon beauty which is not thine;
[v]By the comeliness[v] of a woman many [w]have been ruined[w],
[x]And this way[x] [y]passion[y] flameth [z]like fire[z].
9 [sa]With a married woman[a] [b]sit not at table[b],
[c]And [mingle not] wine in her company[c];
Lest thou incline [d]thine heart[d] towards her,
[e]And in thy blood[e] [f][descendest][f] to the Pit.

m–m *So* 𝔊 ινα μη απολεσης: *so* 𝔖 = פן תאבד (*cp.* Prov. xxix. 3); ℌ פן תסוב ('Lest thine inheritance remove : *cp. Num.* xxxvi. 7). *Peters keeps* תסוב *and explains it as an Aramaism fr.* נסב = 'to take away'—'Lest she take away', &c. n–n *So* ℌ = 𝔊; 𝔖 'the inheritance of money' o ℌ *here is very corrupt* p–p *So* 𝔊 μη περιβλεπου = (?) אל תתנבט (*so Peters, Smend*): ℌ להתנבל = 𝔖 (ותצטער) q–q *So* 𝔊 = 𝔖 במבואי עיר (*so Smend: Peters* במבואות): ℌ במראה עיניך (*corrupt*) r–r 𝔊 και εν ταις ερημαις (א* ρυμαις: Eth 'streets') αυτης μη πλανω = ואל תשוטט בחרבותיה (*read* ברחובותיה *for last word, with Smend*). 𝔖 'And thou shalt be inscribed in the book of sins' (? *reading* ולשוטר בחובותיה): ℌ ולשומם אחר ביתה (*corrupt*) [ℌ *may be rendered:* 'to be treated with contumely in the sight of thine eyes and to be amazed behind her house'] s *vv.* 8–9 (*partly*) *are cited in Sanhedrin* (T. B.) 100 *b*, *Yebamoth* 63 *b as follows:*

העלם עיניך מאשת חן (= 8 a)
פן תלכד במצודתה: (= 4 b or 3 b)
אל תט אצלה (אצל בעלה .v.l) (= 9 a)
למסוך עמה יין ושכר: (= 9 b)
כי בתואר אשה יפה רבים הושחתו (= 8 c)
ועצומים כל הרוגיה:

i. e. Hide thine eyes from a lovely woman,
Lest thou be caught in her snares;
Turn not aside to her,
To mingle wine and strong drink with her:
For through the comeliness of a beautiful woman many have been ruined,
And 'all her slain are a mighty host' (Prov. vii. 26)

[𝔖 *has a double recension of ver.* 9, *one before and one after ver.* 8] t–t ℌ העלים עין = 𝔊 (οφθαλμον): Talmud (עיניך) + σου (א c.a C 106 157 254 Sah: *cp.* 𝔏 faciem tuam = 𝔖) u–u ℌ ואל תביט = 𝔊 και μη καταμανθανε = 𝔖 v–v *Reading* בתואר (*for* בעד *of* ℌ) = 𝔊 εν καλλει: *so* 𝔏 (70 248 Syro-Hex εν γαρ κ. = 𝔖 *and Talm.*) w–w *So* ℌ השחתו: 𝔊 επλανηθησαν: 𝔖 'have perished' x–x *So* ℌ וכן = 𝔊 και εκ τουτου: > 𝔖 y–y ℌ text 'her lovers' אהביה: *read* אהבה = 'love' = 𝔊: 'her love' 𝔖 z–z *So* 𝔊 = 𝔖 (*reading* כאש): ℌ באש 'in the fire' a–a ℌ עם בעלה (*i.e.* בְּעָלָה): 𝔖[1] 'With the mistress of a house' (= בַּעְלָה) 𝔖[2] = 𝔊 μετα υπανδρου γυναικος b–b *lit.* 'stretch not out thine elbow' (*reading* אל תט אצלך = 𝔖[1] 'prop not thine elbow'): *so the doublet in* 248 και μη κατακλιθης επ αγκαλων μετ αυτης (*so Clem. Alex. with* επ αγκωνα *for* επ αγκαλων): 𝔖[2] (*paraphrasing*) 'multiply not talking': 𝔊 μη καθου το συνολον: ℌ *text* 'do not taste' אל תטעם c–c *Reading* ואל תמסך עמה יין = 𝔖[1] (*which has* 'old wine'): *cp. the Talm. citation:* 𝔊 'And revel not (και μη συμβολοκοπησης) with her at the wine': 𝔖[2] 'Nor shalt thou protract conversations with her' (*with the variant* תמשך *for* תמסך): ℌ *text* ואל תסב עמו שכור (= ? ואל תסבא עמה ש"ש, *i.e.* 'And imbibe not strong drink in her company': *this may underlie* 𝔊) d–d *So* ℌ (לב) 𝔖: *also Clem. Alex.* η καρδια *and* 𝔏: 𝔊 η ψυχη σου e–e ℌ ובדמים 𝔊 και τῳ πνευματι (*but Clem. Alex.* αιματι: *so* 𝔖[1]

---

6. **Lest thou lose thine inheritance.** Cp. Prov. xxix. 3 ('he that keepeth company with harlots wasteth his substance'): cp. also Prov. v. 10, vi. 26.

7. **Look not round about thee in the streets . . .** A warning against giving opportunities to the courtesan: cp. Prov. vii. 8 f.

vv. 8–9 cited in the Talmud. See critical note.

8. **. . . many have been ruined.** Cp. Prov. vi. 26.

this way passion (*lit.* love) **flameth like fire.** Cp. Job xxxi. 12 (sinful passion compared to fire).

9. **With a married woman sit not at table.** Lit. 'stretch not out thine elbow' (corrected Hebr. text: see critical note). ℌ has 'do not eat' (contrast 9 *b*, which refers to drinking in her company—eating and drinking form, perhaps, a designed contrast). The verse is a general warning against undue familiarity. The married woman is the subject of the verse; but the reference is not intended to exclude her husband. Married women were often present with their husbands at banquets given to guests—such occasions are dangerous, says Ben-Sira. Cp. *Pirqe Aboth* i. 3 (a saying of Jose b. Jochanan): 'Prolong not converse with a woman' (and Taylor's note): cp. also John iv. 27, and, in our book, vii. 28.

And [mingle not] wine in her company. Or 'and imbibe not strong drink in her company' (see critical note).

Lest thou incline thine heart towards her. Or 'lest thine heart incline towards her'. Cp. Prov. vii. 25.

(*f*) IX. 10–16. *Precepts regarding friends and others* (= 2 + 2 + 3 + 3 distichs).

10 Forsake not [ff]an[ff] old friend,
For the new [g][is not his equivalent][g].
New wine is a new friend;
[h]But when old—then thou mayst drink it[h]!

11 Envy not [i]the ungodly man[i],
For thou knowest not what [j]his destiny shall be[j].
12 [k]Take no pleasure[k] [l]in the arrogant man that prospereth[l],
Remember that [m]he shall not escape unpunished[m] [n]till death[n].

13 Keep far from the man that hath power to kill,
[o]And so thou needest have no terror[o] [p]of death's terrors[p].
[q]But when[q] thou comest nigh (him) [r]commit no fault[r],
Lest he take away [s]thy life[s].
Know that thou marchest amid snares,
And walkest [t]upon nets[t].

14 As far as thou canst [u]associate with[u] thy neighbour,
And converse with the wise.
15 [v][w]With[w] [x]the intelligent[x] let [y]thy communing[y] be,
And all thy converse [z]in the Law of the Most High[z].

(+'guilty'): 𝔖[2] 'condemned to death': *so* 𝔏) σου [f–f] *Reading* תֵּחַת: *so* (?) 𝔊 ολισθησης *and* 𝔖: ℌ *text* תטה (*repeated by mistake from previous clause*) [ff–ff] *So* ℌ 𝔊: 'thy' 𝔖 [g–g] 𝔊 ουκ εστιν εφισος αυτω = לא ידמה לו (*so read with Peters, &c.*): 𝔖 'doth not attain unto him': ℌ יד.... (*partly illegible*) [h–h] ℌ וישן אחר תשתינו: *lit.* 'But when old—afterwards thou mayst drink it': (תשתינו = תִּשְׁתֶּנּוּ 'mater lectionis'): 𝔊 εαν παλαιωθη μετ ευφροσυνης (? *reading* חדוה *for* אחר: *so Levi*) πιεσαι αυτον (𝔖 *evades the difficulty of* ℌ) [i–i] ℌ באיש רשע 𝔊 δοξαν αμαρτωλου (𝔖 = ℌ) [j–j] *So* ℌ (*lit.* 'what his day [shall be]'): 𝔊 τι εσται (*so* ℵ* A = 𝔖: 70 248 τις εστιν: 106 τι εστιν: 55 254 τι τεξεται) η καταστροφη αυτου: 𝔖 'what his end shall be' [k–k] *So* 𝔊 (μη ευδοκησης) = אל תרצה (*so read with Peters*): ℌ *illegible for this word* (*Levi reads* תקנא = 𝔖; *Smend* תבחר) [l–l] בזדון מצליח (*i.e.* זֵדוֹן *adj. cp.* Ps. cxxiv. 5): 𝔊 εν ευδοκιας (B Sah ευδοκια *for* ευοδια) ασεβων = ℌ [m–m] ℌ לא ינקה = 𝔊 ου μη δικαιωθωσιν [n–n] 𝔊 εως ᾳδου = עד מות (*correct* ℌ עת *to* עד *with* 𝔊 *and* 𝔖) = 𝔖 [o–o] *So* ℌ: 'And thou shalt have no suspicion' (και ου μη [= ואל] υποπτευσης) 𝔊 [p–p] *So* ℌ (*cp.* Job xv. 21): φοβον θανατου 𝔊 [q–q] *So* ℌ ואם = 𝔖: εαν 𝔊 [r–r] ℌ לא תאשם: 𝔊 μη (? = אל) πλημμελησης: + נשמתך 𝔖 'make not thy breath guilty' (נ״ *from line* 13 d *which* 𝔖 *omits*) [s–s] נשמתך ℌ: την ζωην σου 𝔊 [t–t] ℌ על רשת: 𝔊 'upon the battlements of a city' (επι επαλξεων πολεως) = ? על אשית עיר (*Hart, comparing* Jer. xxvii. (l.) 15 *Hebr. and* LXX): 𝔊 *may, however, depend upon a variant* מצודות (*understood as* = 'strong places' *instead of* 'nets'): *Peters proposes* ראשת ('pinnacles': *cp.* Zech. iv. 7) [u–u] ℌ ענה *in Syr. sense* (*cp.* Eccles. i. 13, iii. 10 = 'be occupied', 'busied with'): *Hart renders* (Hebr. sense) 'answer kindly': 𝔊 στοχασαι (= 'have regard for', 'seek after': *cp.* 2 Macc. xiv. 8) [v] *ver.* 15 *follows* 16 *in* 𝔏 [w–w] *So* ℌ = 𝔖: + και 𝔊 [x–x] ℌ נבון = 𝔊 συνετων: 'him that feareth God' 𝔖 [y–y] ℌ חשבונך = 𝔊 ο διαλογισμος σου (ℌ ח״ = 'reckoning' *in B.H.*: *here* 'interchange of thought', 'communing': *cp.* xxvii. 5–6) [z–z] *So* 𝔊 (*and* 𝔖 *corrected text*): ℌ בינותם (*read* בתורת יי)

And in thy blood [descendest] to the Pit. For the expression 'in thy blood' (lit. 'with blood') cp. 1 Kings ii. 9 ('bring his grey hairs down to the grave with blood'). The reference is to the vengeance of the husband, who slays the adulterer. Cp. Prov. vii. 26, 27 (esp. 27 *a*, 'her house is the way to Sheol'). 'The Pit' = Sheol, as often elsewhere.

(*f*) IX. 10–16. The subject-matter is rather varied, ranging from friends (*v.* 10) to warnings as to the attitude to be adopted towards prosperous godlessness (*vv.* 11–12), and the tyrant (*v.* 13), and precepts regarding the value of good companionship (*vv.* 14–16).

10. **Forsake not an old friend.** The Alphabet of Ben-Sira has a similar admonition: 'An old friend repudiate not.'

11. **Envy not.** In the sense of desiring to be like him: cp. xlv. 18; Prov. iii. 31, xxiv. 1.

his destiny. Lit. 'his day', i.e. the day of his death (𝔊 'his overthrow').

12. **Take no pleasure in the arrogant . . . till death.** According to Ben-Sira's view the overthrow of the godless man who prospers for a time is certain: cp. xvi. 6–12 (also 13), xxi. 10, xl. 15 ff.

13. **Keep far from the man that hath power to kill.** Avoid contact with tyrants: cp. Prov. xvi. 14, xx. 2.

have no terror of death's terrors. For the terror of death cp. Job iii. 25, xv. 21, &c. (phrase).

. . . thou marchest amid snares, and walkest upon nets. Cp. Job xviii. 8, 9 ('. . . he walketh upon the toils', &c.). For 𝔊 see critical note.

vv. 14–16: an admonition to associate only with wise and pious men.

14. **associate with thy neighbour.** The meaning is not quite certain (see critical note). Smend renders: 'advise (*berate*) thy neighbour': teach and instruct others, but be careful, above all, to learn thyself of the wise.

converse with the wise. On the other hand, the wise have as little as possible to do with the ungodly; cp. viii. 17, xi. 9, xii. 13 ff., xiii. 17, &c.

ℌ[A] 16 Let men of rectitude be [a]the companions of thy board[a];
And in the fear of God be thy boast.

(*g*) IX. 17—X. 5. *The value of God-fearing wisdom as exemplified in rulers* (= 2 + 3 + 2 distichs).

17 [b]By the cunning-handed[b] [c]**a shapely work is devised**[c],
[d]Even so[d] one who ruleth over his people (must be) [e]wise in discernment[e].
18 A man (full) of tongue is dangerous [f]in the city[f],
[g]And he that is hasty in speech[g] is detested.
10 1 [h][i]A wise governor[i] [j]instructeth[j] his people;
And the rule of one that is discerning [k]is well-ordered[k].
2 As is the governor [l]of a people[l], so are his officers;
And as is the head of a city, [m]so[m] are its inhabitants.
3 [n]A reckless king[n] ruineth [o]his people[o],
But a city becometh populous through [p]the prudence of its princes[p].
4 [q]The rule over the world is in the hands of God,
And at the right time He setteth over it [r]one that is worthy[r].
5 [q]In the hand of God is [rr]the rule of every man[rr],
And He investeth [s]the commander[s] with his dignity.

(*h*) X. 6–18. *Pride in rulers ruins whole nations* (= 2 + 4 + 2 + 1 + 4 + 1 distichs).

6 [t]Requite not [evil to] thy neighbour[t] for any wrong,
[u]And walk not in the way of pride[u].

a–a ℌ בעלי לחמך = 𝔊 οι συνδειπνοι σου (*so* 𝔖 'eaters at thy table') b–b ℌ בחכמי ידים : 𝔊 εν χειρι σεχνιτων : 𝔖 'By the wisdom of the judge' (= בחכמת דין) c–c εργον επαινεσθησεται (=? ישבח עשׂה) : 'the city is established' 𝔖 (=? יושב העיר) : ℌ יחשך יושר = ? 'uprightness is preserved' *so Peters. Perhaps* יֵחָשֵׁב יֵצֶר *should be read* (יצר *might easily be corrupted to* עיר *as in* 𝔖 : *and* יחשב *is an easy correction of* ישבח *in* 𝔊 : יֵצֶר = 'something shaped or formed'). *Smend keeps* ℌ *which he renders:* 'a work of art' (יושר, *cp.* מְיֻשָּׁר 1 Kings vi. 35) 'is mastered' d–d *Lit.* 'and' (ℌ = 𝔊) e–e *Cp.* 𝔖 'wise and prudent' (= ? חכם בינה : *so read here with Peters*) σοφος εν λογῳ αυτου 𝔊. ℌ *text* חכם ביטה (*wrongly attaching* ביטה *to v.* 18) = 'wise of (?) speech' (ביטה *from* בטה = בטא ; *cp. Neo-Hebr.* ביטוי = 'vain speech'). 𝔊 ? = ℌ f–f *Reading* בעיר *for* בעד = 𝔖 : *cp.* 𝔊 g–g ℌ ומשא על פיהו (*part.* מַשָּׂא, *cp.* Syr. דנסב על פומה = 'to speak hastily, unadvisedly') = 𝔊 και ο προπετης εν λογῳ αυτου h 𝔏 *pr. tit.* 'de iudicibus' i–i ℌ שׁופט עם (*read* חכם *for* עם = 𝔊 𝔖) j–j ℌ יוסד (*read* יוסר = 𝔊 𝔖) k–k ℌ סדירה (*read* סדורה) = 𝔊 τεταγμενη : 𝔖 'settleth his city' l–l 𝔊 του λαου αυτου (*but* ℵ[c.a] 248 &c. Syro-Hex 𝔏 > αυτου = ℌ 𝔖) m–m *So* ℌ (כן) = 𝔖 : 𝔊 παντες (= כל) (*vv.* 2 *and* 3 *tr. in* ℌ) n–n ℌ מלך פרוע = 𝔊 βασιλευς απαιδευτος : 'An unrighteous king' 𝔖 o–o *So* 𝔊 = עמו : ℌ עיר p–p ℌ שׂריה = 𝔖 : 𝔊 δυναστων (= שׂרים) q *Vv.* 4 *and* 5 *tr. in* ℌ r–r *So* 𝔊 𝔖 (= ישר *or* כשר) ℌ איש rr–rr ℌ ממשלת כל גבר : 𝔖 'power of all' (*omitting* גבר) : 'prosperitas (*read* "potestas") hominis' 𝔏 = ℌ : Peters מצלחת : ευοδια (? *for* εξουσια) ανδρος 𝔊 s–s ℌ מחוקק = 𝔊 γραμματεως (*traditional rendering of* מחוקק : *the Targums render same word by* 'scribe' [ספרא] *in* Gen. xlix. 10) t–t ℌ אל תשלים רע לריע : 𝔊 'Be not wroth with thy neighbour' (μη μηνιασης [al. μηνισης] = ? אל תטור) τῳ πλησιον : 𝔖 'Offend not thy friend' [> 𝔖 𝔊 רע = 'evil' *of* ℌ : *probably added to produce word-play with* לריע] u–u *So* ℌ = 𝔖 : 𝔊

---

16. **Let men of rectitude be the companions of thy board.** Cf. vi. 19.

(*g*) IX. 17—X. 5.

17. **By the cunning-handed ... wise in discernment.** In spite of the uncertainty of the text (see critical notes) the general sense is clear; just as the skill of the trained adept produces a perfect piece of work, so insight (or ? wise speech) enables the wise man (or ruler) to govern his people successfully.

X. 1. **A wise governor ... well-ordered.** Cp. Prov. xx. 8. The word rendered 'governor' = lit. 'judge', 'magistrate'; here it is applied to rulers (cp. vii. 6, ℌ and 𝔊): cp. also verses 2 and 24 of this chapter, and xli. 18. 'Instructeth' has the idea of moral discipline.

2. **As is the governor ... his officers.** Cp. Prov. xxix. 12. The Hebrew word rendered 'officers' = lit. 'interpreters', i.e. those who represent the ruler and interpret his will to the people.

3. **A reckless king.** Lit. 'a king broken loose' (viz. from all restraints): cp. Exod. xxxii. 23 ('the people . . . broken loose').

4. **The rule ... of God ... setteth over it one that is worthy.** Cp. Dan. ii. 21. 'One that is worthy,' i.e. a worthy ruler: such good heathen kings as Cyrus are in the writer's mind, probably.

5. **In the hand of God is the rule of every man.** Or (pointing גִּבֹּר) of every man of power: i.e. the power of rulers comes from God. Cp. Wisd. vi. 1 ff. 𝔊 has 'success' (so Peters reads): the success which enables a man to secure power and rule well comes from God.

(*h*) X. 6–18.

6. **Requite not ...** Or ℌ may be rendered: 'in the case of every wrong requite not,' &c. Lévi renders:

ℌ[A] 7 [v]Pride is hateful to the Lord and to men,
[w]And before both oppression is an offence[w].
8 Sovereignty is transferred from nation to nation
[x]On account of the violence of pride[x].
9 How should he that is dust and ashes vaunt himself[y],
[z]He whose entrails rot (even) during his life[z]?
10 [a]A suspicion (?) of disease defieth (?) the physician[a]—
[b]To-day a king[b], and to-morrow [c]he shall fall[c]!
11 When a man dieth he inheriteth
[d]Worm and maggot, lice and creeping things[d].
12 The beginning of pride is [e]when a man becometh shameless[e],
And [f]his heart[f] departeth from his Maker.

(*freely*) και μη πρασσε μηδεν εν εργοις υβρεως [𝔖 *adds the doublet, perhaps translated from a Hebr. variant of the verse,* 'from all sins and lying depart, and walk not in a lofty spirit' (*reading* רוחא *for* אורחא)] [v] *Pr.* 'for' 𝔖 [w–w] ומשניהם מעל עשק ℌ = 𝔊[B] και εξ αμφοτερων πλημμελησει αδικα (*but for last two words* ℵ[c.a] 70 248 πλημμελεια αδικιας): et exsecrabilis omnis iniquitas gentium 𝔏 = ? ושנואה כל מעל עמים: 𝔖 = ℌ with + ו (מעל ועשק) [x–x] *So* ℌ בגלל חמס גאוה: δια αδικιας και υβρεις και χρηματα 𝔊 = 𝔖 'Because of sins and pride and Mammon': + diversos dolos 𝔏 = και διαφορα (*cp.* vii. 18, xlii. 5 = מחיר) [y] + 'there is not a more wicked thing than a covetous man: for such an one setteth his own soul to sale' 70 248 𝔏 (*so* A.V. = φιλαργυρου μεν γαρ ουδεν ανομωτερον ουτος γαρ και την εαυτου ψυχην εκπρακτον ποιει: 𝔏 nihil est iniquius quam amare pecuniam hic enim animam suam venalem habet—*a catechetical addition; see Hart*) [z–z] *Reading* (*with one correction of* ℌ) אשר בחייו ירום גויו: 𝔊 'Because in life I (*or* they) have cast away his bowels', οτι εν ζωη ερριψα (*so* B: *but* 248 &c. ερριψαν) τα ενδοσθια αυτου: proiecit 𝔏: Syro-Hex εξουδενωσε (*? a correction*): ℌ *text has* יורם *which yields no satisfactory sense: emend to* ירום *from* רמם = 'to rot'. 𝔖 (*correct text: see Lévi, Peters*) 'whose sides and bowels worms creep through during his life' [a–a] *Text very difficult.* ℌ שמץ מחלה יצהיב רופא = 𝔊 'A long disease the physician mocketh' (μακρον αρρωστημα σκωπτει (C σκοπτει, Sah σκοπει, 248 &c. κοπτει, 254 &c. εκκοπτει) ιατρος (ℵ[c.a] ιατρον). 𝔏 *has a doublet*: omnis potentatus brevis vita (= *tit. pr.?*). Languor prolixior (= μακραν) gravat medicum. Brevem (= μικρον) languorem praecidit medicus [*here* 'gravat medicum' = ℌ יצהיב רופא: *and* 'praecidit' = κοπτει *or* εκκοπτει, *suggesting a variant* יחצב 'cuts short']. שמץ *in* xviii. 32 = 'much' ('much luxury' שמץ תענוג): *but in* Job iv. 12, xxvi. 14 *it* = 'a little' ('the whisper of'): *so in Neo-Hebr.* (*suspicion of a thing*, 'particle'): *the meaning of* יצהיב *is also uncertain* (? gleam, provoke, grieve, defy): ℌ *might mean*: 'a long disease provokes (grieves, defies) the physician': *or* 'there is a suspicion of disease—the physician is alarmed'—*or as rendered above in text* [b–b] *So* ℌ = 𝔊 (+ και): 𝔖 'walking' (מהלך *for* מלך: 'walking to-day and dead to-morrow') [c–c] ℌ יפול: τελευτησει 𝔊 = 𝔖 [d–d] *So* ℌ רמה ותולעה כנים ורמש: 𝔊 ερπετα και θηρια και σκωληκας (σκωληκας = רמה ותולעה: ερπετα = רמש: 𝔊 *may not be in original order*): 𝔖 'and his worm before him creepeth' (= ותורעתם בנגדו ירמש) [*In Neo-Hebr.* כנה *pl.* כנים = 'vermin' *or* 'lice'] [e–e] ℌ אדם מועז = 𝔊 ανθρωπου αφισταμενου απο Κυριου (*free rendering*: מועז = *Hof. part of* עזז) [f–f] *Reading* לבו *with* 𝔊 *and* 𝔖: ℌ מלבו [𝔖 *renders the whole verse*: 'The

---

'Quelle que soit la faute ne punis pas ton prochain.' The sentiment (cp. Lev. xix. 27) seems hardly in place here, the sudden introduction of 'neighbour' having no apparent justification from the context. For this line the doublet in 𝔖 (see critical note) gives: 'from all sins and lying keep far away' (= ?מכל פשע וכחש רחק), which yields a satisfactory sense and harmonizes with the context. It may well represent a variant (and superior) Hebrew reading. The connexion would then be: from all sins and lying keep away, but especially avoid the sin of pride.

7. **And before both.** Lit. 'and from both of them', i.e. in the opinion of both God and men: (לפני = מן). 'Oppression' is not only an offence against men (in their social life), but also an offence against God.

8. **Sovereignty is transferred from nation to nation.** i.e. nations decline and fall (for reasons adduced in 8*b*).

On account of the violence of pride. The versions (see critical note) add a further reason—greed of money. Of this, however, there is no trace in ℌ, and it may be due to later revision. God will not allow pride in nations to go unpunished; much less in the case of individual men (cp. xvi. 11). There is probably an allusion to the transfer of the sovereignty of Syria from the Ptolemies to the Seleucidae, which was consummated by the victories of Antiochus III (a comparatively recent event when Ben-Sira presumably wrote). Ben-Sira, however, makes the principle one of universal application, and, perhaps, hints that the sovereignty of the Seleucidae is not likely to be more permanent than that of other oppressive world-powers.

9–11 have probably some contemporary historical incident in view: Smend suggests that it was the death of one of the Ptolemies; perhaps Ptolemy IV (died 204 B.C.). According to Dio Cassius, this monarch died of a painful disease (νόσῳ χαλεπῇ μεταλλάττει τὸν βίον).

9. . . . **he that is dust and ashes.** Cp. Gen. xviii. 27 (cp. also xvii. 32 and xl. 3 of our book).

10. **a suspicion of disease . . .** The logical gaps in the verse seem to be due to rapid description (adopted for graphic effect)—a sudden and (seemingly) trifling ailment defies the physician: the next day all is over.

11. **When a man dieth . . . worm . . .** Cp. Is. xiv. 11. Cp. also vii. 17 of our book.

12. **The beginning.** According to Smend the word so rendered denotes (like ראשית) the essence or chief part of a thing.

𝕳[A] 13 [g]For sin is the rallying-place of insolence[g],
[h]And its source overfloweth with depravity[h].
For this cause [i]hath God stricken such an one marvellously[i],
And smitten him to the uttermost.
14 [j]The throne of the proud[j] God overthroweth,
[k]And setteth[k] the humble in their place[l].
16 [m]**The roots of the proud**[m] God [n]**sweepeth away**[n],
[o]And extirpateth them to the foundations of the earth[o].
17 [p]He teareth them out of the earth[p] [q]and rooteth them up[q],
And extinguisheth their memory [r]from among men[r].
18 Insolence [s]was not the heritage of man[s],
[t]Nor savage wrath[t] (apportioned) to the earth-born.

(*i*) X. 19–25. *Honour to whom honour is due* (= 2 + 2 + 2 + 1 distichs).

19 An honourable race is what? The race of men!
𝕲 [u]An honourable race is that which feareth God.

beginning of the sins of men is their pride, and their deeds (=מעשהו) make foolish their heart'] [g–g] *So* 𝕳: αρχη υπερηφανιας 𝕲 *for* מקוה זדון: 𝕾 'the source of sin is pride' = αρχη αμαρτιας υπερηφανια *the reading of* 248 Syro-Hex *and Chrysostom* [h–h] *So* 𝕳 ומקורה יביע זמה: και ο κρατων αυτης εξομβρησει βδελυγμα 𝕲: 'and fornication is the source of both' 𝕾 (זמה *often in Biblical Hebrew of sins of unchastity*): 𝕲 *apparently read* וקונה *for* ומקוה (*so Lévi*) [i–i] *Reading* הפליא אלהים נגעו *with Smend* (*so Peters substantially*): παρεδοξασεν (=הפליא) Κυριος τας επαγωγας (=מכות) 𝕲: 'God separated (= ? הפלה) their conflicts' 𝕾: 𝕳 *has* מלא לבו אלהים נגע ('God filled his heart with a stroke': מלא לבו *corrupt*) [j–j] *So* 𝕳 = 𝕾: θρονους αρχοντων 𝕲 [k–k] 𝕳 וישב *i.e.* וַיֹּשֶׁב [l] 𝕲 *adds two lines* (= *v.* 15): ριζας εθνων εξετιλεν ο Κυριος και εφυτευσεν ταπεινους αντ αυτων =

(15 a) עקרי (שרשי) גאים עקר אלהים
(15 b) ויטע ענוים תחתם:

(15 a) 'The roots of the proud God plucketh up,
(15 b) And planteth the humble in their place': *so* 𝕾.

Here 15 a *is a doublet of* 16 a; *and* 15 b *a doublet of* 14 b (*with slight variants*). *Smend and Lévi* (*but not Peters*) *regard the verse, however, as original, and as omitted in* 𝕳 *accidentally* (*by homoioteleuton*) [m–m] 𝕳 עקבת גוים 'The traces of the nations' (*read* עקרי גאים *with Peters*): 𝕾 = עקבת גאים 'The traces of the proud' (*so Smend*): 𝕲 χωρας εθνων = 𝕳 (*cp.* xvi. 3 עקבת = τοπος) [n–n] 𝕳 טמטם = 'stoppeth up': *Fraenkel proposed* טֵאטֵא (Is. xiv. 23) *or* טאטְאָם *or* טאטָם (*indicated also in MS. of* 𝕳): 𝕲 κατεστρεψεν: 𝕾 עקר (𝕾 *suggests* עקרי גאים עקר אלהים, *cf.* 15 a *above*) [o–o] 𝕳 ושרשם עד ארץ קעקע = 'And their root (? root-offshoots) He cutteth down to the earth': *but* 𝕲 και απωλεσεν αυτας εως θεμελιων γης = וישרשם עד קרקע ארץ (*cp.* Amos ix. 3), *which is preferable* (*the first word of 2nd distich should be a verb on analogy of previous verses: hence* וישרשם *is preferable*). 𝕾 'And destroyed from the earth their memory' (*cp.* 17 b) [p–p] *Reading* (מארץ) נסחם (*cp.* xlviii. 15: *so Lévi, Smend*): 𝕳 (מארץ) וסחם = 'and He scoureth them from', &c. (*cp.* Ezek. xxvi. 4): εξηρανεν εξ αυτων (A א[c. a] *and some cursives* εξηρεν αυτους) 𝕲 [q–q] ויתשם 𝕳; και απωλεσεν αυτους 𝕲; 'He destroyeth them and uprooteth them and sweepeth them away' 𝕾 [r–r] *So* 𝕾 (= מאדם *or* מאנוש) 𝕳 מארץ = 𝕲 (*but repetition of this word cannot be right*) [s–s] 𝕲 ουκ εκτισται ανθρωποις = לא נחלק לאנוש (*so read*) = 𝕾: 𝕳 לא נאוה ('doth not befit') [t–t] ועזות אף 𝕳: ουδε οργη θυμου 𝕲 [u–u] *Lines* b *and* c *omitted in* 𝕳 *by homoioteleuton.* 𝕲 σπερμα εντιμον ποιον;

---

13. **For sin is the rallying-place** (מקוה) **of insolence, And its source** (מְקוֹרָה) **overfloweth with depravity.** 'Insolence', i. e. aggressive wrongdoing—sinning with a high hand, contemptuous both of God and men—finds its source or reservoir in sin, which also pours forth every form of depravity. The words rendered 'rallying-place' and 'source' occur together (as synonyms) in xliii. 20 = 'pond': but text doubtful; see critical note there.

such an one [lit. 'him'] . . . **him.** i.e. the proud and arrogant sinner.

14. **The throne of the proud** . . . Cp. 1 Sam. ii. 7 f.; Luke i. 52.

15. For this verse see critical note.

16. **The roots of the proud God sweepeth away** (*v. l.* 'rooteth out'). Cp. Ps. xliv. 2 (3): 'With Thy hand thou didst root up nations and plant them in' (corrected text). In 16 *b* ('extirpateth them,' &c.) there may be an allusion to Sodom. Cp. Ezek. xvi. 49.

17. **extinguisheth their memory.** The worst punishment of all: cp. xxxviii. 23; Deut. xxxii. 26.

18. **was not the heritage.** Or 'was not ordained'.

the earth-born. Lit. 'born of a woman', i.e. mortal: cp. Job xiv. 1.

(*i*) X. 19–25.

19. **An honourable race is what?** . . . Mankind may attain to honour or dishonour, in accordance with their relation to God.

𝔊 A despicable race is what? The race of men[u]!
ℌ[A] [v]A despicable race is that which transgresseth the commandment[v].
20 Among brethren their head is honoured,
And he that feareth God [a]**among his own people**[a].
22 [bc]Sojourner and stranger, alien and poor man[c]—
Their glory is the fear of God.
23 A poor man that hath understanding is not to be despised,
Nor is [d]any man of violence[d] to be honoured.
24 [e]Prince[e], ruler and governor are honoured,
[f]But none is greater than he that feareth God[f].
25 [g]Nobles will serve a servant that hath understanding[g],
[h]And a wise man will not complain[h].

(*j*) X. 26–29. *The wrong and the right kind of self-esteem* (= 2 + 2 distichs).

26 [i]Play not the wise man[i] when thou doest thy business,
[j]And glorify not thyself[j] in the time of thy need.
27 Better is he that worketh [k]and hath wealth in abundance[k],
Than he that glorifieth himself [l]and lacketh sustenance[l].

(*but* Syro-Hex Eth > ποιον;) οι φοβουμενοι (254 ο φοβουμενος) τον κυριον: = זרע נכבד ירא אלהים (*so* 𝔖 + 'the honourable race is that which observeth the commandment'): *for* c 𝔊 *has* σπερμα ατιμον ποιον; σπερμα ανθρωπου = זרע נקלה מה? זרע לאנוש (*so* 𝔖) v–v *So* ℌ = 𝔖: 𝔊 σπερμα ατιμον ποιον; (*but* Syro-Hex Eth > ποιον;) οι παραβαινοντες εντολας a–a 𝔊 εν οφθαλμοις αυτου = בעיניו (*so Peters*): 𝔖 = ממנו (*so Lévi*), *i.e.* ('is more honourable) than he': *Smend emends* בעמו b *Some cursives Complut.* + (= *v.* 21) προσληψεως (248 προ ληξεως) αρχη φοβος κυριου εκβολης δε αρχη (εκβολη δε αρχης 248) και (> 248) σκληρισμος και υπερηφανια—*a summary in gnomic form of verses* 7–25 (*Hart*) c–c *So* ℌ: 𝔊 πλουσιος και ενδοξος και πτωχος = עשיר ונכבד ורש (for גר וזר נכרי ורש): 𝔖 'Sojourner who is poor and troubled' d–d ℌ *defective* כל איש [חמ]ם (*Smend*): *Adler* כל איש [יור]ם 'every one that is exalted' (*so Lévi, with some reserve*): 𝔊 ανδρα αμαρτωλον: 𝔖 'the godless rich' (*reading* עשיר *for* איש) *cp.* 𝔏 (virum peccatorem divitem) e–e ℌ *defect.* 𝔊 μεγισταν και = נדיב (*so read with Smend and Strack*): *Adler, Peters* שר ו 𝔖 = 𝔊 f–f *So* ℌ = 𝔊 (+ αυτων): 𝔖 'And there is none who is greater than he that honoureth (= מכבד) the God-fearer' (+ מכבד ? *a variant from line above*) g–g *So* 𝔊 οικετῃ σοφῳ ελευθεροι λειτουργησουσιν = עבד משכיל חורים יעבדו (*so Smend, Peters*) = 𝔖: ℌ עבד משכיל הורם ועב[ד] h–h και ανηρ επιστημων ου γογγυσει = ואיש חכם לא יתאונן (*so read with Peters*); 𝔖 'And a wise man when he is corrected will not complain' = 𝔊 + πεπαιδευμενος (*so* 70 248 Syro-Hex: *cp.* 𝔏). [ℌ *has for both distichs*:

עבד משכיל הורם
ועב[ד חכם] לא יתאונן:

i.e. 'A slave that hath understanding is exalted;
And a slave that is wise will not murmur']

i–i *So* ℌ אל תתחכם — 𝔊 μη σοφιζου: 𝔏 noli te extollere = μη δοξαζου (b): 𝔖 'Be not slack' (תתחבנן ? *for* תתחכם) [𝔏 *transposes verbs in* a *and* b] j–j *So* ℌ 𝔊 𝔖: 𝔏 et noli cunctari (*verb transposed from* (a)) k–k ℌ ויותר הון = 𝔖: 𝔊 εργαζομενος και περισσευων εν πασιν (*so* א* V 70 248 Syro-Hex 𝔏 = Sah) = ℌ 𝔖 (*with* כל *for* הון): B εν πασιν η περιπατων *is not original* l–l *Reading* וחסר מזון (*so Lévi, Smend, &c.*): 𝔊 και απορων αρτων

20. **Among brethren their head is honoured, And he that feareth God . . .** A comparison is implied. Just as among a people (brethren) the leader is honoured, so the God-fearer is honourable among men. 'Brother' often = fellow-member of the same community or nation (cp. vii. 12). The alternative rendering (see critical note) is 'but he who feareth God is more honourable than he'.

[For *v.* 21 see critical note.]

22. **Sojourner and stranger, alien and poor man . . .** The reference is, perhaps, to poor Jews living in heathen lands (so Smend). 𝔊 ('The rich man, the honourable and the poor') makes the statement more general. All classes alike, whatever their condition, find their highest glory in the fear of God.

23. **A poor man that hath understanding.** i.e. a poor man who is pious, since piety (fear of God) is the only true source of wisdom according to Ben-Sira. Poverty and piety are often synonymous in the Psalms.

any man of violence. Even though he be rich. 𝔖 ('the godless rich') expresses this distinctly.

25. **Nobles will serve a servant that hath understanding.** Cp. Prov. xvii. 2 f. Character overcomes all the artificial barriers of social conventions.

(*j*) X. 26–29.

26. **Play not the wise man.** i.e. do not make a show of superior wisdom—do thy work quietly and honourably; do not pose as being superior to thy work (for then the work will suffer). Such superior wisdom is an excuse for idleness.

And glorify not thyself . . . Viz. as to what thou mightst have done. The fact remains that all that thou couldst have done has not availed to keep off want.

27. **Better is he that worketh . . .** The man who goes quietly about his work, and 'does' it, is infinitely superior to one who merely talks and boasts; cp. Prov. xii. 9.

And lacketh sustenance. i. e. through his own idleness.

𝔥A 28 My son, glorify thy soul in humility,
[m]And give it discretion[m] [n]such as befitteth it[n].
29 [o][p]Who will justify him that condemneth himself[p]?
And who will honour him that dishonoureth [q]himself[q]?

(*a*) X. 30—XI. 1. *Wisdom rather than mere wealth brings honour* (= 3 distichs).

30 There is a poor man that is honoured on account of his wisdom,
[r]And there is[r] he that is honoured on account of his wealth.
31 [s]He that is honoured (in his poverty)—how much more in his wealth[s]!
And he that is despicable in his wealth—how much more [t](in his poverty)[t]!
11 1 The wisdom of the poor man lifteth up [u]his head[u],
And causeth him to sit among princes.

(*b*) XI. 2–13. *Warnings against hasty judgements* (= 2 + 2 + 2 + 3 + 2 + 1 + 3 distichs).

2 Praise no man [v]for his beauty[v],
And abhor no man [w]for his appearance[w].
3 [x]Of no account[x] among flying things is the bee,
But her fruit is [y]supreme among products[y].

(= ? וחסר לחם *Prov.* xii. 9): *but* 𝔖 = מזון   m–m 𝔊 και δος αυτη τιμην = ותן לה טעם (𝔖 = טעם: 𝔊 τιμην *chosen for its sound-resemblance? see Smend*): 𝔥 . . . . ויתן לך ט (*Ryssel* וְיִתֵּן לך טוב)   n–n 𝔥 כיוצא בה (*a late idiom: cp.* xxxviii. 17)   o 𝔖 *pr.* 'My son'   p–p 𝔥 *has* מרשיע נפשו מי יצדיקנו: 𝔊 τον αμαρτανοντα εις την ψυχην αυτου τις δικαιωσει;   q–q 𝔥 נפשו: 𝔊 την ζωην αυτου (*? mistake for* την ψυχην αυτου)   r–r 𝔥 ויש: 𝔊 και πλουσιος (*? for* και εστιν ος): 𝔏 *suggests* ויש אשר (*also read* ויש עשיר: *so Hart*)   s–s 𝔊 ο δε δοξαζομενος (*but* ℵ* Syro-Hex > δε: *so* 𝔏 *in Cod. Am.*) (AC 248 &c. ο δεδοξασμενος) εν πτωχειᾳ και εν πλουτῳ ποσαχως; 𝔥 נכבד בעשרו איככה (= 'one honoured—in his wealth how much more!' *but* + בדלותו *after* נכבד: *so Smend, Peters*   t–t + בדלותו (*so Smend, Peters*): 𝔊 εν πτωχειᾳ [𝔥 *adds an explanatory doublet:*

המתכבד בדלותו בעשרו מתכבד יותר
והנקלה בעשרו בדלותו נקלה יותר]

u–u *So* 𝔥 𝔖: 𝔊 κεφαλην (+ αυτου ℵ A C &c. Syro-Hex 𝔏 = 𝔥)   v–v *So* 𝔥 𝔊: 𝔖 'that is beautiful in his appearance'   w–w *So* 𝔊 = במרהו (𝔥 מכוער ב״ = 'hateful in appearance' [*cp.* xiii. 22]: *but omit* מכוער *with* 𝔊 *Lévi, Peters, &c.*)   x–x 𝔥 אליל = 𝔖: 𝔊 μικρα (𝔖 + γαρ pr.)   y–y 𝔥 ראש תנובות: 𝔊 'the chief of sweetmeats'

---

28. **glorify thy soul** (i.e. thyself) **in humility.** In humility, not in pride and self-assertion, shall true honour be found.

give it discretion . . . i.e. cultivate sound sober sense in thyself, such as is worthy of thee. The implication seems to be that a proper self-respect is desirable.

29. **Who will justify . . .** Want of proper self-esteem, undue self-depreciation, are here condemned.

X. 30—XIV. 19. A series of warnings in connexion with various contingencies of life. This division contains eleven subsections.

(*a*) X. 30—XI. 1.

30. **that is honoured.** Even while he is still poor. The lives of many of the Rabbis would illustrate the truth of this remark.

31. **He that is honoured (in his poverty) . . .** i.e. wealth enhances the honour of the wise, and poverty the degradation of the foolish.

XI. 1. **The wisdom of the poor man . . . princes.** In both Talmuds and in the Midrashim clause *b* of this verse is quoted in combination with Prov. iv. 8 as from Ben-Sira: 'In the book of Ben-Sira it is written: '"Exalt her and she shall lift thee up (Prov. iv. 8) and set thee among princes."' (So *T. J. Berakhoth* vii. 2; cp. *T. B. Berakhoth* 48 *a*, &c.)

(*b*) XI. 2–13.

2. **Praise no man . . .** A warning against being misled by external appearance; cp. 1 Sam. xvi. 7.

3. **Of no account . . .** The bee is an excellent example to point the moral.

ℌ[A] 4 [z]Mock not the dress of the wretched[z],
[a]And scoff not[a] [b]at those whose day is bitter[b]:
For wondrous are [c]the works of Jahveh[c],
And His operation is hid [d]from man[d].
5 Many [e]downtrodden[e] have sat [f]upon a throne[f],
[g]And those who were never thought of[g] have worn [h]a crown[h].
6 Many exalted have suffered [i]great[i] abasement,
And also honourable [j]been delivered up[j].

7 Before thou hast examined [k]blame not[k];
Investigate first, and afterwards [l]rebuke[l].
8 [m]Answer not a word before thou hear,
And in the midst of [n]a discourse[n] speak not.
9 [o]In a matter where thou art not affected[o], [p]enter not into strife[p],
[q]And with the quarrels of the arrogant meddle not[q].

10 My son, [r]why multiply thy business (unduly)[r]?
[s]But if thou so doest thou shalt not go unpunished[s].

(αρχη γλυκυσματων): 𝔖 + כל *before* תנובות z–z *So* ℌ (מעטה אבד *might* = 'at him that is clothed with destruction') 𝔊 'Glory not in the putting on of raiment' (εν περιβολη ιματιων μη καυχησῃ = בעטה בגד אל תתהלל): 𝔖 = ℌ a–a *So* ℌ ואל תקלס: 𝔊 'And exalt not thyself' (*taking* קלס *in NH sense* = ואל תסתולל) b–b *So* ℌ במרירי יום: 𝔊 εν ημερᾳ δοξης [𝔖 'And do not despise the man whose throat is bitter'] c–c *So* ℌ 𝔊: 𝔖 'the secrets of God' d–d *So* ℌ = 𝔖: 𝔊 εν ανθρωποις (= באדם) e–e *So* ℌ נדכאים (*lit.* 'crushed ones') = 𝔖: 𝔊 τυραννοι = נדיבים f–f *So* ℌ = 𝔖 (*seat of kingship*): 𝔊 επι εδαφους (*? corruption or correction of* επι διφρου = 𝔏 in throno). g–g *So* 𝔖 = ובל עלו על לב עטו" (𝔊 *has singular* 'And one who was never thought of', &c.): ℌ *corrupt*: תבל על לב עטו צניף: *correct to* ובל עלו *as above*: *so Lévi*: *Peters* ובל עלה: *Smend* עלים. h–h *So* ℌ = 𝔊: 𝔖 'clothing of honour' i–i ℌ מאד = 𝔊: 𝔖 'together' (ℌ + והשפלו יחד *a variant*: יחד = 𝔖) j–j ℌ נתנו ביד: 𝔊 παρεδοθησαν εις χειρας εταιρων: 𝔖 'were brought low from their honour' k–k ℌ אל תסלף = 'distort not' (*sc. ? the judgement*): 𝔊 μεμψῃ: 𝔖 'associate not thyself' (לא תשתותף) l–l *So* 𝔊 = ℌ (תזיף *Hif. of* נזף = 'rebuke' *in NH*: *Hif. only here*: *if* תזעף *could be read the sense would be* 'be angry'; *cp.* Prov. xix. 3): 𝔖 *make* 'marriage' m ℌ *pr.* 'My son' n–n ℌ שיחה (*cp.* vi. 35): 𝔊 λογων = שִׂיחֹת: *so* 𝔖 o–o ℌ באין עצבה = 'When thou hast no concern (care)': 𝔊 περι πραγματος ου ουκ εστιν σοι χρεια (*but* ℵAC 248 &c. > χρεια): Syro-Hex περι πραγματος ου εστιν σοι αλυπως (*cp.* 𝔏 de ea re quae te non molestat) = ? 𝔊 II (= ℌ): 𝔖 (*corrected text*) = באין עצמה p–p *Reading* אל תתחר (*for* ℌ אל תאחר) = 𝔊 (*cp.* viii. 2): *so* 𝔖 q–q *So* ℌ וברב זדים אל תקומם: 𝔊 και εν κρισει αμαρτωλων μη συνεδρευε = ℌ (εν κρισει = בְּרִב *rightly*): 𝔖 'And in the midst of sinners multiply not thine exactions' r–r ℌ למה תרבה עשקך (עשק = עסק): 𝔊 μη περι πολλα εστωσαν αι πραξεις σου: 𝔖 = ℌ (*interpreting* עשקך *as from* עֹשֶׁק) s–s *Reading* ואם תרבה לא תנקה — 'But if thou multipliest it thou shalt not go unpunished' = 𝔊: ℌ ואין להרבות לא

4. **Mock not the dress of the wretched.** Or 'at him that is clothed with destruction' (less probable). For 'dress of the wretched' cp. Is. lxi. 3 (read 'garment of mourning'); and for 'those whose day is bitter' cp. Amos viii. 10 ('a bitter day'). As Edersheim remarks, great importance was attached by the Rabbis to dress. A saying attributed to Ben-Sira (in *Derek ereṣ zuta*, towards end) runs: 'The adornment (splendour) of God is man; the adornment of man is his dress.' It does not, of course, follow from this that a man would be estimated entirely by his dress, though Ben-Sira here enters a warning against conduct which may indicate the presence of such a tendency in certain quarters.

For wondrous are the works of Jahveh... God can (and often does) upset man's estimates by reversing in wonderful ways the conditions that determine a man's place in society. 'God may send sudden reversal in punishment of our pride, or else the prosperity of which we boasted may be only apparent and temporary: *vv.* 5 and 6 carry out this idea' (Edersheim).

5. **downtrodden.** Lit. 'crushed' = humble, lowly: cp. Is. lvii. 15. 𝔊 reverses the sense of 5*a* ('Many rulers have sat down upon the ground'). For the sentiment cp. Ps. cxiii. 7.

vv. 7–9. A warning against hasty action in regard to things heard.

7. **blame not.** The Hebrew word (see crit. note) perhaps = 'pervert not' (sc. the judgement): i.e. be not prejudiced. 𝔊 renders 'blame not' (so Lévi).

8. **Answer not... speak not.** For the sentiment of the verse cp. Prov. xviii. 13; it is also expressed in *Pirqe Aboth* v. 10: 'Seven things are in a clod, and seven in a wise man. (The wise man)... doth not interrupt the words of his companion, and is not hasty to reply...' Cf. also *Baba Bathra* 98*b* (cited by Edersheim): 'interrupt not in the middle of a discourse' (in a quotation from 'the book of Ben-Sira').

9. **And with the quarrels of the arrogant meddle not.** By the 'arrogant' are meant high-handed (presumptuous) sinners: the wise man will not trouble himself about the quarrels of such among themselves; he will confine himself to matters that concern the pious.

vv. 10–13. Warnings against hastiness in action.

10. **My son, why** (i.e. do not) **multiply...** In 10*b* an alternative rendering to 'thou shalt not go unpunished'

ℌ[A] [t]If thou runnest thou shalt not attain[t],
[u]And if thou seekest thou shalt not find[u].
11 There is one that toileth and laboureth [v]and runneth[v],
[w]And is so much the more[w] behind.
12 [x]There is (another) that is weak and wandering in misery[x],
[y]Lacking in strength and abounding in frailty[y];
[z]And the eye of Jahveh watcheth him for good[z],
[a]And He shaketh him up out of the stinking dust[a].
13 He lifteth up his head [b]and exalteth him[b],
So that many may marvel at him[c].

(*c*) XI. 14–28. *All things are in the hands of God* (= 1 [+3]+1+3+3+1+2+2+2 distichs).

14 Good and evil, life and death,
[d]Poverty and wealth come from Jahveh[d].
15 [e][Wisdom and insight [ee]and discernment 'of the Law'[ee]
Come from Jahveh:
[f]Love[f] and upright ways
Come from Jahveh.
16 Folly and darkness have been formed for sinners;
[g]And as for evil-doers—evil abideth with them[g e].]

ינקה = 'But he that hasteneth to multiply shall not go unpunished' = 𝔖 (*Lévi renders* נקה 'succeed' = זכא *in Aram.*) [t–t] *Reading* אם תרוץ לא תגיע = 𝔊 : ℌ *has* בני אם לא תרוץ לא תגיע = 𝔖 [u–u] *So* ℌ 𝔖 : 𝔊 'And thou shalt not escape by fleeing' (και ου μη εκφυγης διαδρας = ? ואם תאוץ לא תמלט (*Peters*). [*Thus according to* 𝔊 *the two lines would run:*

אם תרוץ לא תגיע
ואם תאוץ לא תמלט:]

[v–v] *So* ℌ : 𝔊 και σπευδων [w–w] ℌ וכדי כן = 𝔊 και τοσῳ μαλλον [x–x] ℌ יש רֹשֵׁשׁ ואבד מהלך (ℌ *MS. places* מהלך *at beginning of next stichos*) : רֹשֵׁשׁ = רשיש iv. 29 : 𝔊 (*freely*) εστιν νωθρος και προσδεομενος αντιληψεως (νωθρος = רשיש iv. 29 : προσ. αντι. = ? *a doublet of* υστερον ισχυι = חסר כח *of next line*) : 𝔖 'There is that toileth and laboureth (= *v.* 11 *a*) and is lacking in body' (= ? 𝔊 *above*) [y–y] ℌ *defective* : . . . . חסר כל ויותר א (*read* חסר כח ויותר אֹנֶשׁ : *Peters* דלות *for last word* = 𝔊 : 𝔖 = ℌ *in reading* חסר כל *and for rest of line* = 𝔊 [z–z] *So* 𝔊 (א* 248 &c. *have sing.* ο οφθαλμος . . . = 𝔏 𝔖 ℌ : *v. l.* οφθαλμοι) : 𝔖 'The word of the Lord shall be good upon him' [a–a] *So* ℌ : 𝔊 *weakens* 'stinking dust' *to* εκ ταπεινωσεως αυτου : 𝔖 *to* 'from dust and ashes' [b–b] *So* ℌ : 248 &c. Syro-Hex απο συντριβης : *other Codd.* > : 𝔖 = ℌ [c] 248 Syro-Hex + θεωρησαντες [d–d] *So* ℌ = 𝔊 : 𝔖 'Rich and poor are equal before God' [e–e] *vv.* 15–16 *are omitted in* א A B, *but are attested in* 248 &c. 𝔏 Syr Ar *as well as* ℌ : *they are regarded as original by Peters, but are rejected by Smend* (*who also thinks they do not form part of* 𝔏 *in its original form*). *Schlatter regards them* (*together with v.* 17) *as a glossator's addition to the text of* 𝔊 (*so Ryssel*). [ee–ee] *So* 𝔊 και γνωσις νομου = והבין תורה (*so Peters*) : ℌ והבין דבר : 𝔖 = 𝔊 [f–f] *So* 𝔊 = 𝔖 (חובא) = ? חִבָּה (*so read*) : ℌ חטא [g–g] 𝔊 'And evil shall wax old with them that glory therein' (τοις δε

---

is 'thou shalt not succeed' (see crit. note). Lévi compares the French proverb: 'Qui trop embrasse mal étreint.' Cp. also *Pirqe Aboth* iv. 14: 'Have little business (עסק as here) and be busied in Torah.' The idea expressed in our verse is that over-eagerness in business matters defeats its own ends.

If thou runnest (for text cp. crit. note): developing the thought of 10 *a*, *b*.

11. **There is one that toileth . . .** Cp. Qoh. ix. 11; Prov. xi. 24, xxi. 5 (toileth . . . runneth to amass riches).

12. **And He shaketh him up out of . . .** Cp. 1 Sam. ii. 8; Ps. cxiii. 7–8.

13. **So that many may marvel at him.** Cp. Is. lii. 14.

(*c*) XI. 14–28.

14. **Good and evil.** i.e. good fortune and misfortune: cp. xxxiv. 24–5 (and notes); also Is. xlvii. 7. God creates welfare and calamity.)

Come from Jahveh. 𝔖 comments: 'are equal before God.'

On *vv.* 15–16, which are considered secondary by Smend, see crit. note. They may be an addition due to later revision of the book (part of the secondary Hebrew recension: cf. Introd. § 3 *c*).

15. **Wisdom, insight . . . Law.** Note that 'wisdom' and 'insight' are equated with knowledge of the Law. This is characteristically scribal: the point of view is that of the doctors of the Law (cp. 1 Chron. xxv. 8 ['teacher' and 'scholar'] and xxvii. 32 ['a counsellor, a man of understanding, and a scribe']). The source of the passage is Dan. ii. 20–21 (Lévi).

Love and upright ways. The fruit of a real knowledge of and devotion to the Law.

16. **Folly and darkness . . .** The sinner, by his presumption in persisting in his evil ways, brings upon himself

ℌ[A] 17 [h]The gift of Jahveh abideth for the righteous[h],
And His good pleasure is ever successful.
18 There is that waxeth rich [i]from self-denial[i],
[j]And this is his allotted reward[j]:
19 [k]What time he saith: 'I have found rest,
And now [l]I will enjoy my goods'[l]—
He knoweth not [m]what lot shall befall[m];
He shall leave (them) to others and die.

20 [n]My son[n], [o]be steadfast[o] in thy task [p]and think thereon[p],
And [q]grow old[q] in thy work.
21 [r]Marvel not at the doers of iniquity[r]—
[s]Trust[s] in Jahveh and wait for [t]His light[t];
For it is [u]easy[u] in Jahveh's sight
Suddenly—in a moment—[v]to make a poor man rich[v].

γαυριωσιν επι κακιᾳ συγγηρᾳ κακα): ℌ *has* ומרעים רעה עמם (*Smend thinks a verb has fallen out of* ℌ = *συγγηρᾳ*: ? תשגה *foll.* מרעים: *Peters restores* ומתרבים ברעה רעה עמם = 𝔊 *and* 𝔖). h–h = 𝔊: ℌ *only partly legible* . . . . צדיק . . מ[תן] (*restore with Smend* מתן יי לצדיק יעמד): 𝔖 = 𝔊 (*with the reading εὐλαβεσιν* ℵ[ca] *for ευσεβεσιν*) i–i ℌ מהתענות 'from humbling himself' = 𝔊 (*free rendering*) 'by his wariness and pinching' (*απο προσοχης και σφιγγιας αυτου*): 𝔖 'from his poverty' j–j *So* 𝔊 *και αυτη η μερις του μισθου αυτου* = וזה חלק שׂכרו (*so read with Lévi*): ℌ יחיב שׂכרו . . . . = 'maketh his reward liable' ('mortgageth it'): *but the expression is a strange one*: 𝔖 'There is whose wealth does not follow him' k ℌ 𝔖 *pr.* 'And' l–l 𝔊 *φαγομαι εκ των αγαθων μου* = ℌ אכל (מטובתי) m–m ℌ *here defective*: *Smend* מה י[ום י]חלף = 'what sort of day' (*or* 'what day' = 'how much day') 'shall pass?' = 𝔊 *τις καιρος παρελευσεται*: *Strack* מה [יהיה] חלף: *Lévi* מה יהיה חלק: *Peters* מה יהיה חקו = 'what his (time)-limit shall be': *cf.* 𝔖 'what his end shall be' n–n *So* ℌ 𝔖: 𝔊 > o–o 𝔖 *στηθι* = עמח (*so read with Lévi, Peters*): ℌ *illegible* p–p 𝔊 *και ομιλει εν αυτῃ* = ובו תהגה (*so Adler, Lévi*): *Smend* ובו התרע = und lass sie dir gefallen: *Peters* ובו התהלך: 𝔖 'and thereon prop thyself' q–q 𝔊 *παλαιωθητι* = ℌ התי[שן] = 𝔖 r–r *Reading* אל תתמה בפעלי און = 𝔊 𝔖 (𝔊 *vocalized* פְּעָלֵי): *Lévi* בפעלי עול: *Smend* בדרכי רע: ℌ *defective* s–s *So* 𝔊 *πιστευε (τῳ κυριῳ)* = האמין [לייי]: 𝔖 'wait for' (סכר) = ? שחר = 'look diligently (for)' t–t *So* ℌ 𝔖: 𝔊 *τῳ πονῳ σου* (= ? לאונך *for* לאורו) u–u ℌ נכח = 'a straightforward thing', i.e. 'something plain and easily compassed': 𝔊 *κουφον* = 𝔖 v–v *So* 𝔊 𝔖 = להעשיר דל (ℌ *MS. defective*)

---

an inevitable doom—he is plunged into folly and darkness which have been created for him by God (predestinated for him).

evil abideth with them. Or 'waxeth old with them' (𝔊): i.e. it becomes inveterate.

17. **The gift of Jahveh abideth . . .** i.e. the good fortune that God bestows upon the righteous lasts—it is not transient like that of the wicked.

His good pleasure. Jahveh's goodwill always makes itself felt, and is seen in tangible evidences of it. [Schlatter regards *v.* 17 as part of the gloss, which includes *vv.* 15–17 according to him.] According to Smend the divine gift to the pious consists in the triumphant vindication which they enjoy at the latter part of their lives.

vv. 18–22. The subject of these verses is the old one of the prosperity of the wicked and the reward of the righteous (cp. e.g. Ps. lxxiii). Here *vv.* 18–19 are concerned with the rich fool, to which *vv.* 20–21 form an antithesis, having for their subject the poor righteous man: *v.* 22 sums up in favour of the righteous. Riches carefully amassed elude their possessor when he proposes to enjoy them; while piety leads to a good end of life.

18. **from self-denial.** Lit. 'from afflicting himself': 𝔊 interprets well 'by his wariness and pinching'.

his allotted reward. The same person is, of course, referred to as in clause *a* (for reading see critical note).

19. **What time he saith . . .** Cp. the parable of the rich fool (Luke xii. 16): also Ps. xlix. 10 (11) for the last line. The sentiment is common also in the Rabbinic literature: cp. e.g. *Qoheleth rabba* (on i. 4): 'In this world one man builds a house and another inhabits it; one plants a garden and another eats the fruit thereof' (cited by Edersheim).

20. **My son.** The form of address marked by the expression 'my son' introduces a new division, or a new paragraph.

be steadfast in thy task. i.e. in thy allotted task (בחוקך: cp. for this use of חק, Exod. v. 14), which in the case of the righteous is the fulfilling and carrying out of God's commands. (𝔊 renders: 'Be steadfast in thy covenant with God.')

in thy work: of leading a God-fearing life.

21. **Marvel not.** i.e. at the success of his works so as to envy: cp. Prov. iii. 31 ('Envy thou not the man of violence').

Trust in Jahveh and wait for His light. Cp. Is. lix. 9 ('we wait for the light'); Jer. xiii. 16; Job iii. 9, &c. 'Light' is a common metaphor for divine deliverance (so here).

to make a poor man rich. As Edersheim remarks: 'the moral of this verse can scarcely be considered elevated.'

ℌ[A] 22 [w]The blessing of God is [x]the portion[x] of the righteous,
[y]And at the right time[y] [z]his hope shall flourish[z].

23 Say not: [a]'What is (yet) my desire[a]?
[b]And what henceforth is left unto me[b]?'
24 Say not: [c]'I have enough[c],
[d]And what mischief can befall me[d]?'
25 [e]A day's happiness maketh misfortune to be forgotten[e],
[f]And a day's misfortune maketh happiness to be forgotten[f].
𝔊 26 [g]For it is easy in Jahveh's sight
At the end to requite a man according to his deeds[g].
ℌ[A] 27 [h]An evil time causeth forgetfulness of delights[h],
[i]And the last end of a man will tell of him[i].
28 [j]Pronounce no man happy before his death;
[k]For by his latter end[k] a man shall be known[j].

[w] *vv.* 22–26 *omitted in* 𝔖 [x–x] ℌ גרל : 𝔊 εν μισθῳ (= בְּגֹרָל *i.e.* ב *essentiae ; so Smend reads*) [y–y] ℌ ובעת : 𝔊 και εν ωρᾳ ταχινη (Sah > ταχινη) : 𝔖 = ℌ [z–z] ℌ תקותו תפרח : 𝔊 αναθαλλει ευλογιαν αυτου (? ευλογιαν *corrupt for* ευοδια = 𝔏 processus illius fructificet) [a–a] 𝔊 τις εστιν μου χρεια : ℌ 'כי עשיתי חפצ ..... *Read with Peters* מה חפצי = 𝔊 : ℌ *seems to embody an explanatory addition* (*it makes the line too long : Smend's restoration is hardly Hebrew*) [b–b] ℌ ומה עתה יעזב לי (*correct* עתה *to* מעתה *with* 𝔊) : 𝔊 και τινα απο του νυν εσται μου τα αγαθα = ומה מעתה ייטב לי? (*Lévi*) [c–c] 𝔊 αυταρκη μοι εστιν = דיי ישנו (*so read with Peters*) [d–d] ℌ *defect.* יהי עלי .... *Peters restores missing words* ומה אסון : *Smend* איה אנש : 𝔊 και τι απο του νυν κακωθησομαι ; (απο του νυν ? *from* 23 b) [e–e] *So* ℌ : 𝔊 εν ημερᾳ αγαθων αμνησια κακων [f–f] *So* ℌ : 𝔊 και εν ημερᾳ κακων ου μνησθησεται αγαθων [ℌ + ואחרית אדם תהיה עליו = 27 b *in* 𝔖 (*see note below*) : *v.* 27 *in the form preserved in* 𝔖 *seems to have been introduced as a doublet in* ℌ *and to have displaced v.* 26 ; *when this occurred its first stichos was omitted owing to its similarity with* 25 b. *See further Peters ad loc.*] [g–g] *So* 𝔊 (*omitted in* ℌ) : *Peters restores :*

כי נכח בעיני יהוה
באחרית להשיב לאדם כדבריו :

Peters plausibly explains the omission of vv. 22–26 *in* 𝔖 *as due to the similarity of* 21 b, c *and* 26 (*homoioteleuton*). [h–h] *So* ℌ : 𝔊 κακωσις ωρας (ℌ עת רעה) επιλησμονην ποιει τρυφης : 𝔖 'The evil of a day causeth forgetfulness of good' (*assimilated to* 25 b) [i–i] *So* ℌ וסוף אדם יגיד עליו : 𝔊 (*freely*) και εν συντελειᾳ ανθρωπου αποκαλυψις εργων αυτου : 𝔖 *exactly* = ואחרית אדם תהיה עליו (*doublet in* ℌ *added at end of v.* 25) : *here* תהיה *is a corruption of* תחיה, *and this and* ואחרית *are variants on* וסוף *and* יגיד [j–j] *So* 𝔊 = ℌ[2] : ℌ[1] = 𝔖. *The doublet* (ℌ[1]) *and the original text* (ℌ[2]) *appear in* ℌ *side by side, thus :*

בטרם תחקר אדם אל תאשרהו
כי באחריתו יאושר אדם } ℌ[1] = 𝔖

לפני מות אל תאשר גבר
כי באחריתו ינכר איש } ℌ[2] = 𝔊

Saadya (*as cited in Cowley*, iv, *p.* xxi) *quotes* ℌ[2] *with slight variants* (*omitting* גבר *at end of line* 1, *and reading* יתנכר *for* ינכר *in line* 2) [k–k] ℌ כי באחריתו *which* 𝔊, *misunderstanding, renders* και εν τεκνοις αυτου : *for* אחרית

22. **The blessing of God . . . flourish.** Cp. Prov. x. 22.
vv. 23–28 : God's retribution smooths away all inequalities at the last.
23. . . . **What is (yet) my desire?** i.e. what is there left for me to desire? (= 23 *b*).
25. **A day's happiness . . . a day's misfortune . . .** Developing the idea of 24 *b*. 'Past sufferings will be forgotten by the righteous when prosperity cometh, and the opposite will be the case with the wicked' (Edersheim). For 'a day's happiness' cp. xiv. 14 ('a good day'). For the general sentiment cp. xviii. 24 f.
26. **it is easy . . .** It is easy for God, because the retribution that comes at the last is final and complete.
27. **the last end of a man will tell of him.** The last circumstances of a man's life will reveal whether he has lived his life on the whole well or badly. This appears to be one of the main convictions of Ben-Sira.
28. **Pronounce no man happy before his death.** Cp. *Pirqe Aboth* ii. 5 (ed. Taylor) : 'Trust not in thyself until the day of thy death' (a saying of Hillel).

by his latter end a man shall be known. 𝔊 has 'in his children (by his posterity) a man shall be known'. The idea introduced by 𝔊's interpretation is not present in the original form of the verse. It is, however, one of the developments natural to speculation on the subject. It implies that the misdeeds of a man will involve his children in punishment, and that, if he dies unpunished, retribution will yet assert itself in their punishment. It was a common notion among the Jews that the sins of parents resulted in physical or moral defects in children (cp. John ix. 2). It is noticeable that the idea of a future life is entirely absent from the passage.

(*d*) XI. 29–34. *Beware of intercourse with strangers and bad characters* (= 3 + 1 + 2 distichs).

𝕳[A] 29 [l]Not every one is to be brought into [m]the house[m]—
[n]And how many are the wounds of a slanderer[n]!
30 [o]As a decoy partridge in a cage[o], so is the heart of the insolent (sinner),
And as a spy that seeth [p]the nakedness[p l].

=‘posterity,’ *cp.* Ps. cviii. (cix.) 13; xxxvii. (xxxviii.) 37; Jer. xxxviii. (xxxi.) 17. [l–l] *vv.* 29–30. *These verses have a number of additional lines appended to them in* 𝕳, *where they appear in the following form:*

29a = לא כל איש להביא אל בית
29b = ומה רבו פצעי רוכל
29c = [ככלוב מלא עוף } citation from
29d = כן בתיהם מלאים מרמה] } Jer. v. 27.
30a = כעוף אחוז בכלוב לב גאה
30b = כזאב אֹרֵב לטרף :
30c = מה ירבו פשעי בוצע
30d = ככלב הוא באכל (l. בא לכל) בית
30e = וחומס [כן] כל בוצע
30f = בא ומשים ריב (לכל.......) :
30g = אורב הרוכל כדוב לבית לצים
30h = וכמרגל יראה ערוה :

Here 29 c, d *is a citation from* Jer. v. 27 (𝕾 𝕲 >): 29 a, b, 30 a, *and* 30 h = 𝕲 *vv.* 29–30 *and represent the genuine text of* 𝕳. *These lines are also attested in* 𝕾. *Besides* 𝕾 *also represents* 30 c–f. (30 a, b *in* 𝕾 = 30 a, b *in* 𝕲: 𝕾 *thus preserves the two genuine clauses consecutively*). *In English* 30 a–h *may be thus rendered:*

‘As an imprisoned bird in a cage (so) is a proud man’s heart’ (= 30 a).
‘As a wolf that lieth in wait to tear’ (= 30 b).
‘How many are the iniquities of the pillager!’ (= 30 c).
‘Like a dog that entereth every house (= 30 d)
and stealeth (so) is every pillager’ (= 30 e).
‘He cometh and maketh strife in all ......’ (= 30 f).
‘The slanderer lieth in wait like a bear at the house of the scoffers (= 30 g)
and like a spy that seeth the nakedness’ (= 30 h).

A citation of the passage also occurs in T. B. Yeb. 63 b, *Sanh.* 100 b.

מנע רבים מתוך ביתך } = 29 a.
ולא הכל תביא (בתוך) ביתך }
רבים היו פצעי רכל (v. l. רוכל) = 29 b.
המרגלים לדבר ערוה (v. l. עבירה) = 30 h (i.e. 30 b in 𝕲).
כניצוץ מבעיר גחלת : = 32 a.

The origin of the additional clauses in 𝕳 *may be explained as follows:* [29 c, d *is a citation from* Jer. v. 27;] 30 b *is a gloss developing* 30 a; 30 c *is a doublet of* 29 b, *and* 30 d (*down to* וחומס *of* 30 e) *of* 30 a; 30 e (כן כל בוצע) *and* 30 f *a doublet of* 31 b; *and* 30 g *an expansion of* 30 h (= 30 b *in* 𝕲) [m–m] *So* 𝕳: 𝕲 𝕾 + ‘thy’ [n–n] *So* 𝕳: ומה רבו פצ[עי] רוכל (*in B.H.* רוֹכֵל = ‘trafficker’: רָכִיל = ‘slanderer’): 𝕲 πολλα γαρ τα ενεδρα του δολιου (248 διαβολου) = 𝕾: *hence Peters reads* ומה רב ארב נוכל [o–o] 𝕳 כעוף אחוז בכלוב: 𝕲 περδιξ θηρευτης (*but* 70 θηρευθεις = 𝕷) εν καρταλλῳ = קורא אחוז בכלוב (*so* 𝕾): *Peters so reads.* [p–p] 𝕳 ערוה = ‘nakedness’ (*cp.* Gen. xlii. 9, 12):

(*d*) XI. 29–34.

29. **Not every one is to be brought into the house.** The citation in the Talmud (see critical note) runs: ‘Keep away many from the midst of thy house, and bring not every man into thy house.’ To be ‘brought into the house’ = to be placed on terms of intimate friendship; to be made a ‘house-friend’.

30. **As a decoy partridge in a cage.** Lit. ‘as a partridge imprisoned in a cage’ (see critical note for text). The simile is drawn from the custom of employing a bird in a cage, provided with food, as a decoy, the cage being so arranged that other birds can enter, but, having once entered, cannot get out again: cf. Jer. v. 27: ‘As a decoy (cage) is full of birds, so are their houses full of deceit.’ This verse from Jeremiah has been inserted in the text of 𝕳 (at end of *v.* 29) to illustrate our passage here, which, indeed, is based upon it. The point of the comparison is the apparent harmlessness of the lure which is so dangerous.

the insolent (sinner). Lit. ‘the proud man’: ‘proud’ often = wicked, just as ‘meek’ often = pious in O. T. The heart of a sinner is as dangerous to know as a decoy bird is to other birds that come to it.

as a spy that seeth the nakedness. The phrase is to be explained by the full phrase ‘spies to see the

$𝔥^{A}$ 31 [q]The backbiter turneth[q] good into evil,
And in thy loveliest qualities he putteth [r]a stain[r].
32 [s]From a spark cometh much coal[s],
[t]And a villain lieth in wait for blood[t].
33 Shrink from an evil man, for he begetteth evil—
Why [u]shouldst thou incur[u] a lasting blemish?
34 [v]Let a stranger dwell with thee and he will estrange thy way of life,
And alienate thee from thine own house[v].

(*e*) XII. 1–7. *Against indiscriminate benevolence* (= 3 + 3 + 1 distichs).

12 1 [w]If thou do an act of kindness, know to whom thou doest it[w],
[x]That thou mayst have hope of thy kindness[x].
2 Do acts of kindness to the righteous and find recompense;
If not from him, [y]from Jahveh[y].
3 [z]No (return of) kindness (cometh) to him that giveth satisfaction to the ungodly[z],
[a]Nor hath he done any act of benevolence[a].

𝔊 *interpreting*) πτωσιν = 𝔖: *Talmud citation confirms* 𝔥 q–q 𝔥 יהפך נרגן = 𝔏 convertit insidiator: 𝔊 μεταστρεφων ενεδρευει (𝔖 > נרגן) r–r *So* 𝔊 μωμον = ? דוֹפִי (*Lévi*) *or* מום: 𝔥 קשר: 𝔖 'stumbling-block' (= ? מוקש) s–s *So* 𝔥 מנצוץ ירבה גחלת (*emend to* תרבה): 𝔊 απο σπινθηρος πυρος (248 μικρας) πληθυνθησεται ανθρακια: 𝔖 'From a little tow ('tow' = ? נערת) a fire is kindled' t–t *So* 𝔥 = 𝔊: 𝔖 (*freely*) 'So the man that is a sinner sheddeth blood like water' u–u *So* 𝔥: תשא [למה] 𝔊 = ישׂא לך *or* יתן לך v–v 𝔥 *has two forms of this v.: the first, which follows v.* 33, *runs:*

לא תדבק לרשע ויסלף דרכך
ויהפכך מבריתיך:

i. e. 'Cling not to a godless man lest he overturn thy way and turn thee from thy covenants' (*so* 𝔖): *a second form follows* xii. 1, *and runs:*

משוכן זריו זהיר דרכיך וינכרך במחמדיך

i. e. 'from a corrupt (?) neighbour (be) thy way warned, for he will estrange thee to them that are dear to thee'. *Prob. the Hebrew original of* 𝔊 *underlies this:* 𝔊 *has* ενοικισον αλλοτριον, και διαστρεψει σε εν ταραχαις και απαλλοτριωσει σε των ιδιων σου. *Correct* $𝔥^{2}$ (*with Smend*):

השכן זר ויזיר דרכיך
וינכרך מביתך:

This text prob. underlies 𝔊 (*see Smend*). מביתך *has been corrupted into* מבריתיך *in* 𝔥 1: במחמדיך *in* $𝔥^{2}$ *has prob. come in from v.* 31 w–w 𝔊 εαν ευ ποιῃς γνωθι τινι ποιεις = אם תיטיב דע למי תטיב (*so read with Peters, Smend, &c.*): 𝔥 אם טוב תריע למי תטיב = 'If thou doest evil to the good, to whom wilt thou do good?' 𝔖 'If thou doest good to the evil (= אם תטיב רע) thou doest nothing' (𝔖 *supports* 𝔊, *and the evidence shows that in* 𝔥 אם טוב תריע *is corrupt for* אם תטיב דע) x–x *So* 𝔥: 𝔊 και εσται χαρις τοις αγαθοις σου *which* = (?) ויהי טובה לטובתך, 'And thou shalt have kindness for thy kindness' (*so* 𝔖 *inserting* 'not'): *Smend so reads* (טובה *for* תקוה *in* 𝔥) y–y *So* 𝔥: 𝔊 παρα υψιστου: 𝔖 'from his Lord' z–z *Reading* אין טובה לְמֵנִיחַ רשע (𝔥 *has* למנוח *which Schechter takes as an infin. of a verb.* מנח = 'to bestow' [*cp.* מנחה]; *then render* 'No good cometh of bestowing upon him that is wicked)': 𝔖 'There is no good to him that honoureth (= ? למכבד, *cp.* Prov. iii. 9) the wicked':

---

nakedness of the land' (cp. Gen. xlii. 9, 12). A base and unscrupulous person, if admitted to intimacy, will use his opportunities of intimate knowledge merely for malicious purposes.

31. **The backbiter.** This word (Heb. נרגן) otherwise occurs only in Proverbs (xvi. 28, xviii. 8, xxvi. 20, 22).

32. **From a spark cometh much coal.** The general sense is: Do not play with fire.
lieth in wait for blood. Cp. Prov. i. 11.

33. **Shrink.** 𝔊 'take heed of'.
an evil man . . . begetteth evil. Cp. Is. lix. 4.
incur . . . blemish. Cp. xviii. 15, xx. 24, xxx. 31, xliv. 19, xlvii. 20.

(*e*) XII. 1–7.

XII. 1. **If thou do an act of kindness . . .** Lit. 'if thou do good'. This forms a sort of text for what follows.

1. **hope.** sc. of a return for thy benevolence.

2. **Do acts of kindness to the righteous . . .** This forms the complement of *v.* 1.

3. **No (return of) kindness (cometh) to him . . . benevolence.** i.e. acts of benevolence to the unworthy and

†5 (*b*) [b]Weapons of bread give him not[b],
†5 (*c*) [c]Lest he attack thee with them[c].
†5 (*d*) [d]Twofold evil[d] shalt thou obtain[e]
†5 (*e*) [f]For all the good thou shalt have brought him[f].
†6 For God also hateth them that are evil,
[g]And to the ungodly He repayeth vengeance[g].
†7 (4) Give to the good [h]and withhold[h] from the evil;
†5 (*a*) [i]Refresh[i] [j]the humble[j], and [k]give not[k] [l]to the arrogant[l].

(*f*) XII. 8—XIII. 1. *Against trust in false friends* (= 2+3+3+3+2+2+1 distichs).

8 A friend [m]is not known[m] in prosperity
And an enemy is not hidden in adversity.
9 [n]In a man's prosperity even an enemy is friendly[n],
But in his adversity even a friend [o]holdeth aloof[o].
10 Never trust [p]an enemy[p],
[q]For even as brass his wickedness rusteth[q].

𝔊 ουκ εστιν αγαθα τῳ ενδελεχιζοντι εις κακα (= לַמֵּנִיחַ רָשָׁע : 𝔖 *may* = לַמֵּנִיחַ רָשָׁע : *so Bacher*, *JQR*, xii. 278) a–a *So* ℌ וגם צדקה לא עשה = 𝔊 (*taking* ℌ *as a rel. clause*, 'And also to him who hath done no benevolence'): 𝔖 'And he that doeth alms loseth it not' †† (*vv.* 4–7): *these verses are out of order in* 𝔊 ℌ *and* 𝔖 (*they are numbered according to* 𝔊*'s reckoning*): *v.* 4 = *v.* 7 (*a doublet*) *and should be eliminated:* 5 a *should follow* 7: *thus the true order is most nearly preserved in* 𝔊, *and is* 5 b–e, 6, 7 (= 4), 5 a: *in* ℌ *and* 𝔖 (*but* 5 e *is omitted in* 𝔖) *the order of the clauses is:* 5 d, c, 5 b, c, 6, 7, 5 a (*both* ℌ and 𝔖 *rightly omit* 4). 𝔏 *also places* 5 a *after* 7 (*showing that this was original order of* 𝔊). b–b *So* ℌ כלי לחם אל תתן לו : 𝔊 'Keep back his bread and give it not to him' (εμποδισον τους αρτους αυτου [א* > αυτου: 248 Sah σου] και μη δῳς αυτῳ (𝔊 *took* כלי *as* = כלא, 'withhold'): 𝔖 'The instruments of thy warfare (= ? כלי מלחמתך) thou shalt not give him' [כלי לחם *is rendered by Schechter* 'weapons of war'; *cp.* Judges v. 8] c–c *So* ℌ למה בם יקביל אליך (למה = פן : *cp.* viii. 1, xi. 10, xi. 33, xii. 12, xxx. 12: 𝔊 ινα μη): 𝔊 ινα μη εν αυτοις σε δυναστευσῃ (*inexactly*): 𝔖 'Lest with them he war with thee' d–d 𝔊 διπλασια γαρ κακα = ℌ פי שנים רעה, 'a double portion of evil': *so* 𝔖 (𝔊 + γαρ) e ℌ 𝔖 + 'in the time of (thy) need' (בעת צורך): *omit with* 𝔊 f–f *So* ℌ = 𝔊 (οις αν ποιησῃς αυτῳ = תגיע אליו): 𝔖 >. g–g *So* ℌ 𝔊: 𝔖 'And upon the ungodly He bringeth His retribution' h–h ℌ ומנע : 𝔊 και μη αντιλαβῃ (*freely*) i–i ℌ הקיר, *i.e.* הָקֵיר, *Hif. of* קרר, 'to be cool': 𝔊 ευ ποιησον = 𝔖 j–j ℌ מך = 𝔊 ταπεινῳ k–k *So* ℌ 𝔊: 𝔖 'withhold' (כלי): l–l ℌ לזד = 𝔊 ασεβει m–m *So* ℌ לא יודע : = 𝔖: 𝔊 γνωσθησεται (א^{c.a} Syro-Hex: επιγνωσθησεται 253 𝔏) = ℌ: *the ordinary reading of* 𝔊 *is* εκδικηθησεται = ? יתנקם (*or* יִפָּקֵד) n–n *So* ℌ: 𝔊 'In a man's prosperity his enemies are grieved' (εν λυπῃ) = 𝔖 (+ γαρ) o–o ℌ בודד : 𝔊 διαχωρισθησεται = 𝔖 (𝔏 agnitus est = διαγνωρισθησεται) p–p *So* ℌ 𝔖: 𝔊 + σου q–q *So* ℌ כי כנחשת רועו יחליא : 𝔖 ('For even as brass is he that polluteth his comrade') = ℌ *with* ריעו for רועו = 𝔊 'For like as the brass rusteth so is his wickedness' (ιουται ουτως η πονηρια αυτου: *but* 𝔖

---

godless are not requited, and are not to be regarded as real benevolence. Cp. Midrash *Qoh. rabba* v. (*Tanch.* חקת § 1), where a proverb is attributed to Ben-Sira: 'Do not good to the evil and evil shall not befall thee' (*Qoh. rabba* adds: 'and if thou doest good to the evil thou hast done evil'). These citations illustrate the idea which is worked out in our passage, viz. that doing good to the evil will produce positively evil results to the doer (cp. *vv.* 5 *d*, *e* below). 𝔊 has entirely misunderstood the verse.

5. **Twofold evil.** The Hebrew expression here (פי שנים) = lit. 'a double portion (of evil'): it recurs xviii. 32 (ℌ), xlviii. 12 (ℌ); cp. in Biblical Hebrew 2 Kings ii. 9; Zech. xii. 8.

6. **For God also hateth them that are evil.** Justifying the advice given in the previous verse. With the whole contrast Rom. xii. 19–21.

7 (4). **Give to the good and withhold from the evil.** Cp. *T. B. Baba Bathra* 9 *b*: 'when given to undeserving persons it [alms] is not a meritorious act receiving reward.'

(*f*) XII. 8—XIII. 1.

8. **A friend is not known in prosperity . . .** This opening verse provides the text for what follows. A true friend is difficult to determine. Two Hebrew words are used for 'friend' in what follows, viz. אוֹהֵב, lit. 'one who loves', i.e. the true friend, and רֵיעַ = a friendly acquaintance.

9. **In a man's prosperity . . .** Cp. Prov. xix. 4: 'Wealth addeth many friendly acquaintances, but in the case of a poor man his friend separateth himself'; also *v.* 7.

10. **For even as brass his wickedness rusteth.** Just as the metal is ever liable to rust, so the wickedness of the enemy is ever active and assuming new forms. For the figure cp. xxix. 10 and Jas. v. 3.

ℌ[A] 11 Yea[r], when he is obsequious[r] [s]and walketh humbly[s],
[t]Take care[t] [u]to have a fear of him[u]:
Be to him [v]as one that brighteneth a mirror[v] [w]
[x]And so (thou shalt) know how to be rid of rust[x].
12 Let him not stand beside thee
Lest he thrust thee aside and stand in thy place:
Set him not at thy right hand
Lest he seek thy seat—
[y]And too late thou shalt comprehend[y] my words,
[z]And sigh o'er my plea[z]!

13 Who[a] pitieth[a] [b]the charmer that is stung[b],
Or any one that cometh nigh [c]a ravening beast[c]?
14 [d]So is he that associateth with an impious man[d],
[e]And polluteth himself with his iniquities[e][f].
15 [gh]So long as thou standest he doth not reveal himself[h],
But if [i]thou fall[i] [j]he no longer restraineth himself[j][g].

> *ουτως and* = ℌ: *ουτως due to a reviser*). r–r ℌ אם ישמע לך (= יִשָּׁמַע, 'is obedient, compliant'): 𝔊 (*freely*) *εαν ταπεινωθη* s–s ℌ ויהלך בנחת: 𝔊 *και πορευηται συνκεκυφως* ('and go crouching' R.V.) = 𝔖 (*which adds* לפניך: *so Peters*) t–t ℌ תן לבך = 𝔊 *επιστησον την ψυχην σου* u–u *So* ℌ: 𝔖 = 𝔊 *και φυλαξαι απ αυτου* v–v 𝔊 'as one that hath wiped a mirror' (*ως εκμεμαχως εσοπτρον*), *cp.* Syro-Hex 'as a wiped off mirror: *pointing to a reading* ראי: ℌ כמגלה רז, 'as one that revealeth a secret = 𝔖 (גַּלֵּה *here may* = 'brighten': *Smend compares Arab.* גלי = 'to polish bright', *of a sword, silver, &c.*) w ℌ + ולא ימצא להשחיתך, 'and he shall not find opportunity to harm thee' (*or* ? 'to rust thee'—*Aram. sense*): *so* 𝔖 *but* 𝔊 > (*prob. a gloss*) x–x ℌ 'And know thou the end of jealousy' (ודע אחרית קנאה) = 𝔖: *but* 𝔊 (*και γνωση οτι ουκ* [*but* Syro-Hex *prob. rightly* > *ουκ*] *εις τελος κατιωσεν*) *suggests* חלאה *for* קנאה: *so read with Smend* y–y ℌ ולאחור תשיג: 𝔊 *και επ εσχατῳ επιγνωση* = 𝔖: 106 *ευρησεις* (*cp.* xxxi. [xxxiv.] 12) z–z ℌ ולאנחתי תתאנח, *lit.* 'And sigh at my sighing': 𝔊 *και επι των ρηματων μου κατανυγηση* ('and be pricked with my sayings', R.V.)', 𝔖 'And wonder at my sayings' (? *reading* תתמה): 'at my sayings' (𝔊 𝔖) *suggested by* 'my words' *of preceding line.* a–a *Reading* יחון *with* 𝔊 𝔖: ℌ יוחן b–b *So* ℌ = 𝔊 *επαοιδον οφιοδηκτον* (𝔊 = 𝔖) c–c ℌ חית שן (*so* xxxix. 30) *lit.* 'beast of tooth': 𝔊 *θηριοις* d–d ℌ כן חובר אל אשת (l. איש) זדון: 𝔊 *ουτως τον προσπορευομενον ἀνδρι αμαρτωλῳ* (𝔏 *qui comitatur*) e–e ℌ ומתגלל בעונתיו: 𝔊 *και συνφυρομενον εν ταις αμαρτιαις αυτου*: 𝔖 > f ℌ + לא יעבר עד תבער בו אש, 'he will not cease until a fire be kindled in him' = xxiii. 16 f (= 𝔊 23 b) *ου μη παυσησαι εως αν εκκαυση πυρ* (*so* 𝔖 *here*): *the insertion of this clause in* ℌ *and* 𝔖 *is due to false reading* אשת זדון *in* 14 a: *in* 𝔖 *it has taken the place of* 14 b g–g ℌ *has* 4 *stichoi*:

(a) כאשר יבוא עמך לא יתגלה לך (c) עד עת עמד לא יופיע
(b) ואם תפול לא יפול להצילך: (d) ואם נמוט (l. תמוט) לא יתכלכל:

(a) 'When he cometh with thee, he doth not betray (*lit.* reveal) himself,
(b) And if thou fall he doth not fall to help thee;
(c) So long as thou standest he doth not show himself (as he is),
(d) But if thou stumble he doth not restrain himself.'

𝔖 = (*nearly*) (a) *and* (b); 𝔊 = (*nearly*) (c) *and* (d): *prob.* (a) *and* (b) *are doublets* (*with an explanatory tendency*) *of* (c) *and* (d)—יתגלה לך (a) *doublet of* יופיע (c) *and* תפול *of* נמוט (תמוט) *in* (d), *while* יפול (? *l.* יוכל) להצילך (b) *is a doublet of* יתכלכל (d). *Smend thinks* 𝔖 *at the end of* (b) *attests the reading* לא יתכלכל (𝔖 *reads* לא מצא אנת הילה) *and concludes that the translator of* 𝔖 *had the* 4 *stichoi before him which he reduced to* 2, *partly conforming to* 𝔊. 𝔊 (= (c) (d) of ℌ) *represents the original text.* h–h ℌ עד עת עמד לא יופיע: 𝔊 *ωραν μετα σου διαμενει* (= ? עד

---

11. **Yea, when he is obsequious** (*or* compliant) . . . Cp. Prov. xxvi. 24 f. ('he that hateth dissembleth with his lips', &c.). When a friend is especially compliant and humble be on your guard!

Be to him as one that brighteneth (*lit.* polisheth) **a mirror . . . rid of rust.** The danger of rust can be avoided in the case of the metal mirror by regular polishing; so one can avoid the dangers arising from an enemy's malice by constant watchfulness (being on one's guard against, and not confiding in such). For the text see critical note. For the figure of the mirror cp. Jas. i. 23.

13–18 (and xiii. 1) depict the consequences that follow neglect of the warning given in the previous part of the section.

14. **So is he that associateth with an impious man.** i. e. a man who runs risks by associating on terms of friendship with sinners (impious) is equally undeserving of pity when dire consequences ensue, as the cases referred to in the previous verse.

polluteth himself . . . The sinner is unclean and defiles all who come near him (Smend).

15. **So long as thou standest . . . restraineth himself.** i.e. so long as one sustains one's position the false friend

ℌ[A] 16 [k]With his lips [l]an adversary speaketh sweetly[l m],
But in his heart he deviseth [n]deep pitfalls[n].
[o]Yea[o], though an enemy [p]weep with his eyes[p],
[q]When[q] he findeth opportunity he will not be satiated with blood.
17 If misfortune have befallen thee [r]he is at hand[r];
[s]As though ready to help he seizeth the heel[s].
18 He shaketh [t]the head[t] [u]and waveth the hand[u],
[v]And with much whispering[v] [w]changeth[w] his countenance.
13 1 Whoso toucheth pitch, [x]it cleaveth to his hand[x],
And he that associateth with a scorner [y]will learn his way[y].

(*g*) XIII. 2–13. *Against dangerous and unequal association* (*a*) *with the rich*, (*b*) *with rulers* (= 2 + 1 + 2 + 2 + 2 + 1 + 2 + 3 + 1 distichs).

(*a*) *vv.* 2–8.

2 [z]What is too heavy for thee [a]do not lift[a],
[b]And with one that is richer than thyself[b] [c]associate not[c].

עת עמך עמד): *here* עמך *might be a mutilated* עמדך *which would be a variant on* עמד: *then the orignal form would have been, perhaps,* [לא יופיע] עת עמדך = 'what time thou standest,' &c. *Smend reads* עד עת תעמד לא יופיע: לא יופיע *is omitted by* 𝔊, *but its originality is guaranteed by the doublet* לא יתגלה. i–i *Reading* תמוט = 𝔊 (ℌ נמוט) j–j ℌ לא יתכלכל: 𝔊 ου μη καρτερηση k 𝔊 *pr.* και (*but* 254 &c. Syro-Hex 𝔏 > *with* ℌ 𝔖). l–l *Reading* ימתיק צר = 𝔊 (*so Peters*): 𝔖 'an enemy giveth a sign' (רמז): ℌ יתמהמה (*? due to assimilation with* xxvii. 23 b. m B[a·b] + και πολλα ψιθυρισει και ερει σοι καλα λεγων n–n ℌ מהמרות עמוקות (*cp.* Ps. cxl. 11): 𝔊 (*freely*) 'to overthrow thee into a pit' (αναστρεψαι σε εις βοθρον): 𝔖 'deep devices' o–o ℌ וגם = 𝔖: 𝔊 > p–p ℌ בעיניו ידמיע (*Hif. not attested in any other passage*) = 𝔖 ('cause tears to issue from their eyes'): 𝔊 δακρυσει q–q 𝔊 *pr.* και (254 &c. > και) r–r ℌ נמצא שם: 𝔖 'thou wilt find him there'; 𝔊 ευρησεις αυτον εκει προτερον σου (*or* προτερον σου εκει) (*Smend suggests that* προτερον σου *may have arisen from an uncorrected mistake in writing* πτερναν σου *of next line*) s–s ℌ כאיש סומך יַחְפֹּשׂ עקב = 'As a man that would help he seeketh reward' (*or* 'seeketh to supplant'): *read with Smend* יתפֹּשׂ *for* יחפש: 𝔊 υποσχασει πτερναν σου t–t 𝔊 + αυτου u–u ℌ והניף ידו: 𝔊 (*inexactly*) και επικροτησει ταις χερσιν (Syro-Hex 𝔏 τη χειρι) αυτου v–v ℌ *has* ולרוב הלחש (*read with Smend* ולרוב מְלַחֵשׁ) = 𝔖 'and whispering much': 𝔊 και πολλα διαψιθυρισει w–w ℌ ישנא = ישנה (*cp.* xiii. 25) x–x ℌ תדבק ידו (*read* בידו, *cp.* 𝔖): 𝔊 μολυνθησεται ('shall be defiled' R.V.), *? a correction for* κολληθησεται (248, 𝔏 Syro-Hex + εν αυτη) y–y *So* ℌ ילמד דרכו: 𝔖 'is clothed with his way' = ילבש דרכו, *cp.* 𝔏 induet superbiam (*Smend reads* ילבש ד"): 𝔊 ομοιωθησεσαι αυτῳ (= ? ידמה לו; *so Peters reads*) z 𝔏 *pr. tit.* (*before v.* 1) de societate divitum superborum a–a 𝔊 μη αρῃς = ℌ מה תשא (מה *sometimes* = אל, *just as* למה = פן *in later Hebrew: cp.* Cant. viii. 4; Qoh. v. 5, vii. 16: *another case of* מה = אל *occurs in ch.* xxxii. (xxxv.) 4) b–b *So* ℌ 𝔖: 𝔊 και ισχυροτερῳ σου και πλουσιωτερῳ (*double rendering*) c–c ℌ מה תתחבר

---

does not reveal his true character; but he comes out in his true colours when misfortune befalls. 𝔊 gives a different turn to the sentence, but expresses a similar general meaning (cp. R. V.).

16. **With his lips . . . speaketh sweetly . . . deep pitfalls.** i.e. when misfortune comes he professes to be sympathetic, but secretly plots further ruin for the victim: cp. Prov. xxvi. 24 f. ('he that hateth dissembleth with his lips'). The Hebrew word rendered 'pitfalls' (מהמרות) occurs only again in Ps. cxl. 11. The meaning 'pitfall' or 'pit' (Jerome, on the Psalm, renders *foveas*) is guaranteed by our passage.

Yea, though an enemy weep with his eyes . . . blood. Illustrate from Jer. xli. 6. The expression 'he will not be satiated with blood' is usually understood literally to mean that such an enemy will not be satisfied until the blood of the victim of misfortune has been actually shed. But Edersheim prefers to interpret the expression metaphorically (in conjunction with the following verse), as meaning that the false friend will not be satisfied with the mere coming of misfortune (= the shedding of blood), but will himself actively take part in making the ruin even more complete.

17. **he seizeth the heel.** i.e. to trip thee up. He actively assists in making the overthrow complete. For text see critical note.

18. **He shaketh the head . . . changeth his countenance.** His enmity now becomes open and undisguised.

He shaketh the head. A gesture of contempt; cp. xiii. 7; Job xvi. 4: 'with much whispering', i.e. secretly preparing all manner of evil devices.

changeth his countenance. i.e. becomes openly hostile; cp. xiii. 25; Qoh. i. 8.

(*g*) XIII. 2–13.

2. **What is too heavy for thee . . . richer than thyself associate not.** i.e. such a proceeding is too difficult to carry out successfully.

ℌ[A] What association can [d]jar and kettle[d] have in common
[dd]When[dd], if the one smite, the other is smashed[e]?
3 The rich man [f]if he perpetrateth a wrong[f] [g]plumeth himself[g],
While if a wrong is perpetrated upon a poor man [h]he must implore favour[h].
4 [i]If thou art useful to him[i] he maketh a slave of thee,
[j]But if thou be brought low[j] [k]he is sparing of thee[k].
5 [kk]If thou possessest anything[kk] [l]he will live with thee[l],
And will impoverish thee without a pang.
6 [m]Hath he need of thee[m]? [n]then he will deceive thee[n],
[o]And will smile upon thee[o] and raise thy hopes.
𝔊(𝔖) [p]He will speak thee fair[p],
7 [q]And shame thee with his hospitality[q].
ℌ[A] [r]So long as it profiteth he will cajole thee,
Twice (or) thrice he will . . . thee[r];

d–d ℌ פר ור אל סיר = 𝔊 χυτρα προς λεβητα (𝔖 'the vessel of clay to the cauldron of brass') dd–dd *So* ℌ אשר = 𝔏 quando: 𝔊 > (𝔖 'which [knocks it and breaks it'] = ℌ) e ℌ (𝔖) + או מה יתחבר עשיר אל דל 'or why should the rich associate with the poor': 𝔊 > (*rightly as a gloss*) f–f *Reading* יעוה *to correspond with* נעוה *in next clause* (*or* עוה): *so* 𝔊 (ηδικησεν) *and* 𝔖 g–g ℌ יתנוה = *Neo-Hebr.* נתנוה, 'to make oneself handsome, be vain (plume oneself)': 𝔊 προσενεβριμησατο (= ? יתכוה): 𝔖 'is unconcerned' (מהמא) h–h ℌ יתחנן: 𝔊 και προσδεηθησεται: 𝔖 (*misunderstanding* ℌ) 'he prays' i–i ℌ אם תכשר לו = 𝔖: 𝔊 εαν χρησιμευσης (> לו) j–j *So* ℌ (ואם תכרע): 𝔊 και εαν υστερησης (= ? ואם תגרע: *cp.* Num. ix. 7): 𝔖 'if thou art poor' (𝔊 and 𝔖 *may be free renderings of* ℌ) k–k ℌ יחמל עלך (= 'he pitieth thee'): 𝔊 καταλειψει σε = 𝔖 (*? interpreting* ℌ) kk–kk ℌ אם שלך: 𝔊 εαν εχης = אם יש לך (= 𝔖): *so read* (*with Peters, Smend*) l–l *So* 𝔊 συμβιωσεται σοι = יחיה עמך (*so read with Peters*): ℌ = 𝔖 ייטיב דבריו עמך = 6 c (*accidentally misplaced: so Peters*) m–m ℌ לו עמך (*l.* צורך) צריך: 𝔊 χρειαν εσχηκε σου: 𝔖 'while he does his will with thee' n–n ℌ והשיע לך = ? 'he will flatter thee' (*reading* וְהֵשַׁע *from* שעע: *cp. Aram. sense of verb*) *or* 'toy with thee': 𝔊 και αποπλανησει σε = והשיא לך: *so read with Peters*: 𝔖 'he will seem to do thy will' o–o ℌ לך (*l.* ושחק) ושוחק, *cp.* Job xxix. 24 (שחק אל) p–p *Reading* ייטיב דבריו עמך (= 5 a ℌ): 𝔊 λαλησει σοι καλα: 𝔊 + και ερει τις η χρεια σου, *which Peters regards as an explanatory doublet* (*but Smend keeps*). 𝔖 'and will call thee a fortunate man' (*? paraphrase of* 'will speak thee fair'): ℌ > q–q *So* 𝔊 and 𝔖 = ויבישך במאכליו (*so read with Peters, Smend*): ℌ > r–r ℌ

עד אשר יועיל יהתל בך
פעמים שלש יעריצך:

(𝔖 *prob.* = ℌ *substantially.*) 𝔊 εως ου αποκενωσῃ σε δις η τρις, και επ εσχατῳ καταμωκησεται σοι. *Peters thinks the Hebrew text underlying* 𝔊 *to have been*:

עד אשר ירששך פעמים שלש
ובאחרית יהתל בך:

But this can hardly be right (באחרית *foll. by* ובכן *next line*). ℌ *is essentially right: but the meaning of* יעריצך *is uncertain. Smend suggests that it may = a corresponding verb in Arab., which means* 'to deceive' s–s ℌ ובכן

What association . . . smashed? i.e. the weaker is bound to go to the wall: when a collision takes place the earthen pot (פָּרוּר, cp. Num. xi. 8) is bound to be smashed by the brass cauldron (סיר, cp. Ezek. xxiv. 3, 6). 'The one' =, of course, the cauldron or kettle, 'the other' the earthen pot. The latter was also used for boiling purposes; cp. Num. xi. 8.

3. **The rich man . . . perpetrateth a wrong. . .** 'The folly of the whole thing, viewed from the standpoint of the rich, could scarcely be more graphically set forth than in this and the following verses' (Edersheim).

4. **he maketh a slave of thee.** The same expression (עבד ב) occurs in Jer. xxiii. 13, xxvi. 14, xxx. 8: lit. = he uses thee as an instrument for work. For the Hebrew word here for 'to be useful' (כשר) cp. Eccles. v. 10 ('skill, success'). The original meaning is to be fit, suitable.

he is sparing of thee. The Hebrew word here used = usually 'to pity' ('he pitieth thee'). But here the meaning seems to be to neglect, leave alone: cp. Horace, *Odes*, i. 34. 1 'parcus deorum cultor et infrequens' (𝔊 gives the meaning correctly—'he will forsake thee'). Cp. *Pirqe Aboth* ii. 3.

5. **without a pang.** lit. 'and it will not pain him'.

7. **wag his head at thee.** In mockery and scorn; cp. xii. 18.

𝔥^A [s]And then[s] he will see thee [t]and pass thee by[t],
And wag his head at thee.
8 Take care [u]that thou be not overbearing[u],
[v]And that thou be not crushed by senseless folly[v].

(*b*) *vv.* 9–13.

9 Doth a noble [w]draw near[w]? [x]keep at a distance[x]—
[y]And so much the more[y] [z]will he cause thee to approach[z].
10 [a]Do not thyself draw near[a], lest thou be put at a distance;
And keep not (too) far away, lest [b][thou be forgotten][b].
11 [c]Venture not[c] [d]to be free[d] with him,
And mistrust his much conversation.
[e]For [f]by his conversation at large[f] [g]he is testing thee[g],
[h]And when he smileth at thee he is probing thee[h] [e].
12 [i]A ruthless one maketh **peace**,
While plotting against the life of many[i].

(*cp.* Prov. viii. 10, Esther iv. 16): 𝔊 μετα ταυτα t–t 𝔥 והתעבר בך (*cp.* Prov. xiv. 16) 𝔊 καταλειψει σε (א καλυψει σε = 𝔖 'be hid from thee') u–u 𝔥 אל תרהב מאד ('be not arrogant, overbearing, violent, overmuch'): 𝔊 μη αποπλανηθης (248 &c. Syro-Hex + τη διανοιᾳ σου, *i.e.* 'be not deceived in thy mind, act foolishly'—*an interpretation of* 𝔥): 𝔖 'be not given into his hands' = ?אל תתיהב בידיו. v–v 𝔥 ואל תדמה בַחֲסִירֵי מדע 'and be not like to them that lack intelligence' (*Schechter*): 𝔊 και μη ταπεινωθης εν ευφροσυνῃ σου (248 &c. + καρδιας *after* ευφροσυνῃ: *but* Sah 𝔏 εν τῃ αφροσυνῃ = *the original reading of* 𝔊): *the Hebr. text underlying* 𝔊 *is prob.*:

ואל תדכה בחסר מדע

i.e. 'and be not crushed by senseless folly' (*so read with Peters: Peters also reads in line* 1: אל תרהב בלבך: *cp.* 𝔊 τῃ διανοιᾳ σου) w–w *So* 𝔥 קרב, *i.e.* קָרֵב (*particip.*): 𝔊 προσκαλεσαμενου σε = קֹרֵא: 𝔖 = 𝔥 x–x 𝔥 היה רחוק: 𝔊 υποχωρων γινου, *so* 𝔖 + 'from him' y–y 𝔥 וכדי כן (*cp.* xi. 11) = 𝔊 και τοσῳ μαλλον: 𝔖 'and at every time' (ובכל זבן) z–z *So* 𝔥 יגישך = 𝔖: 𝔊 προσκαλεσεται σε [*Peters adopts* 𝔊 *in both clauses*: 'doth a noble invite thee . . . . . . will he invite thee'] a–a *So* 𝔥 אל תתקרב = 𝔖: 𝔊 (*freely*) 'do not press (upon him),' εμπιπτε b–b *So* 𝔊: 𝔥 תשנא, 'be hated (detested)' = 𝔖: *emend to* תִנָּשֵׁא = תִּנָּשֶׁה: *cp.* xlii. 9, 10 𝔥, *and* Isa. xliv. 21 תִנָּשֵׁנִי (*but text doubtful*) c–c 𝔥 אל תבטח = 𝔊 μη επεχε (επεχειν = בטח, v. 8, xiii. 11, xv. 4) d–d 𝔥 לחפש, *i.e.* לְחָפֹשׁ, 'to be free' (*Qal does not otherwise occur*): 𝔊 ισηγορεισθαι, 'to speak as an equal (with him)': 𝔖 'to speak' (*from context the word means* 'to speak freely'). *Bevan* (*so Strack*), *however, suggests the pointing* לְחַפֵּשׂ. e–e *These two lines are cited by Sa'adya* (*cp. Cowley-Neub.*, *p.* xxii) *as follows*:

כי ברב שיח מנסה אותך
ושחק לך ויחקרך:

'For with much talk will he try thee,
And will laugh at thee and probe thee.'

f–f 𝔥 מהרבות שיחו: 𝔊 εκ πολλης λαλιας (*read* שיח *for* שיחו, *so Sa'ad.*) g–g *Reading* ינסיך (*for* 𝔥 ו נסיון (*the* ו *of* שיחו)) = 𝔊 πειρασει σε (*cp. Sa'ad.* מנסה אותך): *so Smend*: 𝔖 = 𝔥 ('for in the multitude of his speech there are trials') h–h *So* 𝔥 = 𝔊 και ως προσγελων εξετασε σε (248 &c. Syro-Hex τα κρυπτα σου *instead of* σε: *cp.* 𝔏) i–i 𝔥:

אכזרי יתן מושל
ולא יחמל על נפש רבים קושר קשר:

𝔊 ανελεημων ο μη συντηρων λογους και ου μη φεισηται περι κακωσεως και δεσμων ('unmerciful is he that keepeth not words; and he will not spare injury and bonds'): 𝔖 'and he that is without pity exacts recompense (= שִׁלּוּם *for* מושל) and pitieth not the souls of many'. *Thus* 𝔊 *omits* לא יחמל *and* 𝔖 קושר קשר. *Smend attaches* ולא יחמל *to first line*

vv. 9–13 contain a warning against incautious intercourse with highly-placed members of the governing class (princes, governors, and their entourage). In *Pirqe Aboth* ii. 3, a passage occurs which expresses similar sentiments (attributed to Rabban Gamaliel, son of Judah ha-Nasi): 'Be cautious with (those in) authority, for they let not a man approach them but for their own purposes; and they appear like friends when it is to their advantage, and stand not by a man in the hour of his need.'

10. **Do not thyself draw near . . . be forgotten.** Avoid both extremes—pressing forward or holding back unduly.

12. **A ruthless** (or cruel) **one maketh peace, While plotting against the life of many.** A deliberate contrast

ℌ[A] 13 Take heed [j]and be wary[j],
[k]And go not about with men of violence[k] [l].

(*h*) XIII. 15–20. *Like consorteth with like: what common bond can there be between rich and poor?* (= 2 + 3 + 1 distichs).

15 [m]All flesh[m] loveth [n]its kind[n],
[o]And every man his like[o].
16 [p]All flesh consorteth according to its kind[p],
And with his kind man [q]associateth[q].
17 [r]What association[r] can wolf have with lamb?
[s]Even so is the ungodly that consorteth with the righteous[s].
18 [t]What peace[t] can the hyena have with the dog?
[u]Or what[u] peace rich with poor?
19 [v]Food[v] for the lion are the wild asses of the desert:
Even so the pasture of the rich are the poor.

and renders: 'the tyrant employeth (übt) cruelty and doth not pity, against the life of many he plotteth' (*but this is highly doubtful*): *Peters reads* אכזרי יתן מושָׁל ולא יחמל קושר קשר, *i.e.* 'the cruel one taunteth, and is without pity in his plotting'. *A better result is obtained if* שלום *is read* (*with* 𝔖) *in line* 1, *and* ולא יחמל (*? an explanatory gloss on* אכזרי) *is omitted; then read:* אכזרי יתן שלום על נפש רבים קושר קשר, *i.e. as rendered in text above* (*for* נתן שׁלֹשׁ *cp.* Lev. xxvi. 6, 1 Chron. xxii. 9) j–j ℌ והיה זהיר: 𝔊 και προσεχε σφοδρως (248 + ακουειν = 𝔏 auditui tuo): 𝔖 = ℌ k–k *So* ℌ: 𝔊 οτι μετα της πτωσεως σου περιπατεις = כי עם מכשולך תהלך, 'for thou goest with thine own fall' (𝔖 'for with the ravishers thou walkest'). *So Peters reads* l 248 253 𝔏 Amb + *verses* 13 c *and* 14 ('when thou hearest these things awake in thy sleep. 14 Love the Lord all thy life, and call upon Him for thy salvation'): *for text see Hart and Schlatter, p.* 108 f. *The verses are a late gloss* m–m ℌ כל הבשר : 𝔊 παν ζῳον n–n ℌ מינו = 𝔊 το ομοιον αυτῳ (*cp. v.* 16, xxvii. 9) o–o *So* ℌ וכל אדם את הדומה לו: 𝔊 και πας ανθρωπος τον πλησιον αυτου. *An echo of this line appears in a Talmud citation* (*T. B. Baba qama* 95 b). *Thirdly, in the Hagiographa; as it is written:* 'Every bird dwelleth according to its kind, and (so doth) man according to his like' (ובן אדם לדומה לך). *Note Talmud has* בן אדם *for* ℌ אדם p–p *Reading* כל בשׂר למינו יאצל = 𝔊 πασα σαρξ κατα γενος (Syro-Hex 254 + αυτης: *so* 𝔏 ad similem sibi) συναγεται (307 συναπτεται = 𝔏 coniungitur): ℌ מין כל בשׂר אצלו (𝔖 = ℌ *with* מִן *for* מין) q–q ℌ יחובר: 𝔏 sociabitur: 𝔊 προσκολληθησεται r–r ℌ מה יחובר : 𝔊 τι κοινωνησει s–s ℌ *has two forms of this line, viz.*:

(1) כך רשע לצדיק
(2) וכן עשיר אל איש נאצל:

𝔊 ουτως αμαρτωλος προς ευσεβη = ℌ (1): 𝔖 'and so the rich to the poor man' = ℌ (2): *read with Smend* כן רשע לצדיק נאצל: (כן = כך *in* ℌ (1) *is Neo-Hebr.*) t–t *Reading* מה יש שלום = 𝔊: ℌ (*corrupt*) מאיש ש״ (*cp.* איש = יש, 2 Sam. xiv. 19, Mic. vi. 10, Prov. xviii. 24) u–u 𝔊 και τις = ? או מה (*so Peters reads*): ℌ מאין 'whence?' v–v *So* ℌ = 𝔖: 𝔊 κυνηγια (*a free rendering: but Peters reads* ציד = κυνηγια, Gen. xxv. 27)

---

is drawn between the real character and the methods of the unscrupulous ruler. While pretending to make (or give) peace (i.e. to be full of active goodwill) he is secretly plotting murder. For the text see critical note. For a similar contrast cp. Ps. cxx. 7 ('I am for peace; but when I speak they are for war'). 𝔊 runs: 'Merciless is he that keepeth not words (i.e. betrays confidences in free and incautious conversation), nor will he spare (sc. to inflict) injury or bonds'.

13. **Take heed . . . men of violence.** For the second clause 𝔊 (cp. 𝔖) has 'For thou goest about with thy fall' (so Peters prefers to read): the expression is a figurative one (to have ruin as a companion in thy walk); cp. Job xxxi. 5; Prov. xiii. 20 (cp. also ix. 13 of our book).

14. See critical notes.

(*h*) XIII. 15–20.

vv. 15–16. A reference is made to this passage in the Talmud (see critical notes for the citation). Our passage is cited as from the *Hagiographa* in conjunction with passages from the Law and the Prophets (see Edersheim, *in loc.*).

15. **All flesh.** 𝔊 'Every living creature'. 'Flesh' has here a general sense, including the forms of animal life generally. Cp. Lev. xvii. 14 ('the life of all flesh . . . the blood thereof', &c.).

kind . . . like. Cp. xxvii. 9. The law of 'like consorteth with like' is 'a universal law in the physical and moral world, as well as of society'. 'Similis simili gaudet; aequalis aequalem delectat' (Edersheim).

17. **What association . . . wolf . . . lamb?** Cp. Is. xi. 6; Matt. x. 16.

18. **rich with poor.** Throughout these terms connote ungodly and pious respectively. Cp. Ep. James ii. 6 ('But ye have dishonoured the poor man. Do not the rich oppress you?' &c.).

19. **the wild asses of the desert** (or steppe). Cp. Job xxiv. 5, where the poor (as here) are compared to the wild asses in the desert. For the lion as a figurative expression for the rich cp. Ps. xxxiv. 10, xxxv. 17, lviii. 7; Zech. xi. 3.

ℌ[A] 20 [w]An abomination [x]to pride[x] is humility;
Even so an abomination to the rich are the poor.

(*i*) XIII. 21–23. *The world's treatment of rich and poor—a contrast* (= 1 + 2 + 2 distichs).

21 A rich man [y]when he is shaken[y] [z]is supported by a friend[z],
[a]But the poor man[a] [b]when he is shaken[b] is thrust away [c]by a friend[c].
22 A rich man [d]speaketh[d], and his helpers are many;
[e]And though his words be unseemly, they are pronounced lovely[e].
A poor man [f]speaketh[f], [g]and they jeer at him[g];
[h]Yea, though he speak with wisdom[h], [i]there is no place for him[i].
23 When the rich man [j]speaketh[j], all [k]keep silence[k],
And they extol [l]his intelligence[l] to the clouds.
When the poor man speaketh: 'Who is this?' say they;
And if [m]he stumble[m] [n]they will assist his overthrow[n].

(*j*) XIII. 24—XIV. 2. *A Collection of Miscellaneous Proverbs* (= 1 + 2 + 2 distichs).

24 Wealth is good if it be without sin,
And evil is poverty [a]which is due to presumption[a].
25 The heart[b] of a man changeth his countenance,
Whether for good or for evil[c].

[w] *v.* 20 *omitted by* 𝔖 x–x *So* ℌ גאוה: 𝔊 υπερηφανῳ y–y *So* 𝔊 σαλευομενος = נמוט (*so read*): ℌ מוט: 𝔖 'falls' z–z 𝔊 στηριζεται (= ? נסמך *or* יסמך: *so read*) υπο φιλων; ℌ בסמך מרע: 𝔖 'is cast into evil' (לרע) a–a ℌ ודל: 𝔊 ταπεινος δε (א* 248 πτωχος δε: '𝔊 *prefers the synonym* [ταπεινος] *which more easily admits of a spiritual interpretation*' (*Hart*)) b–b ℌ נמוט: 𝔊 πεσων = 𝔖 (*contrast renderings* 21 a) c–c 𝔊 υπο φιλων = מרע (*cp. v.* 21 a), *so read:* 𝔖 'from evil into evil' = ℌ מרע אל רע d–d ℌ מדבר = 𝔖: 𝔊 = נמוט (*in clauses* a *and* c *the two terms must correspond—either* 'speaketh' *or* 'falleth' *must be read in both*: 𝔊 *expresses in both* 'falleth'; 𝔖 *in both* 'speaketh'; ℌ *in* a 'speaketh', *in* c 'falleth') e–e *So* ℌ ודבריו מכוערין מהופין (מכוערין, *part. Hof. of* כער *common in Neo-Hebr.* = 'to be dark, ugly, repulsive, unseemly' (*cp.* xl. 2): מהופין, *part. Hof. of* יפה = *lit.* 'they are made beautiful': *note the pl. endings in* ־ין). *Schechter suggests reading* מחופין = 'they (his words) are veneered over', *as base with precious metal.* 'and his hateful words are glozed over' (*Hart*). 𝔊 ελαλησεν απορρητα και εδικαιωσαν αυτον = ? ודבר מכוערין ומופין (*so Peters reads*) f–f *So* 𝔖: ℌ נמוט = 𝔊 g–g *Reading* (*with Peters*): ונע גע ישאו (*lit.* 'and they raise [cries] of' גע, גע): 𝔖 'they say to him' גוע: 𝔊 (*freely*) και επετιμησαν αυτῳ: ℌ גע גע וישא גע h–h ℌ ודבר משכיל: 𝔊 εφθεγξατο συνεσιν i–i ℌ ואין לו מקום: 𝔊 και ουκ εδοθη αυτῳ τοπος j–j *So* ℌ (*part.*): 𝔊 ελαλησεν k–k *So* ℌ נסכתו (*cp.* Deut. xxvii. 9) = 𝔊: 𝔖 'hearkened' l–l ℌ את שכלו: 𝔊 (*freely*) σον λογον αυτου: 𝔖 'his favourers' m–m ℌ נתקל = 𝔊 n–n ℌ גם הם יהדפוהו = 𝔊

a–a *Lit.* 'according to the mouth of presumption' (על פי זדון); א A 55 157 248 253 307 εν στοματι ασεβους (= ℌ 𝔖 Syro-Hex 𝔏); B C 70 254 εν στομασιν ευσεβους b 𝔖 'sins' c 248 253 Syro-Hex + 'And a happy (*lit.* flourishing) heart maketh a face cheerful with delight'; *gloss on the following clause.*

20. **an abomination to the rich are the poor.** Cp. Prov. xxix. 27 *b* ('he that is upright . . . is an abomination to the wicked').

(*i*) XIII. 21–23.

21. **when he is shaken.** i.e. come into a dangerous and unfortunate situation; cp. Ps. xiii. 4 (5): 'mine adversaries rejoice because I am moved' ('shaken'), xvi. 8, x. 6 'I shall not be moved' (Hebr. בַּל־אֶמּוֹט = LXX οὐ μὴ σαλευθῶ, as here). Edersheim thinks the meaning need not be restricted to the decay of external fortunes, but may include a wider connotation.

22. **A poor man speaketh . . . no place for him.** Cp. Qoh. ix. 16: 'The poor man's wisdom is despised, and his words are not heard.' For the expression 'there is no place for him' cp. iv. 5; *Pirqe Aboth* iv. 6 (ed. Taylor), 'there is not a thing that has not its place' (a saying of Ben Azzai, second century A.D.); cp. also Rom. xii. 19. Here the expression may mean: they refuse to hear him.

23. **all keep silence.** From respect; cp. Job xxix. 9.
extol . . . to the clouds. Cp. for the expression Job xx. 6.

(*j*) XIII. 24—XIV. 2.

24. **Wealth . . .** After having pointed out the consideration shown to the rich for the sake of their wealth, Ben-Sira goes on to say that riches *per se* are not bad, but, on the contrary, good when they do not bring sin in their train.
And evil is poverty . . . See critical note. Poverty is an evil when it is the result of wickedness; this is a poverty to be ashamed of.

25. **The heart of a man . . .** i.e. the inward state of a man, not his outward circumstances, determines his happiness or otherwise, and this is reflected in the expression of his face; cp. Prov. xv. 11; Eccles. viii. 1; Luke ix. 47.
Whether for good . . . In the Midrash *Bereshith Rabba* to Gen. xxxi. 2 this verse is quoted verbatim, excepting that the אם . . . ואם of ℌ is, in accordance with the later Hebrew usage, expressed by בין . . . ובין.

ℌ[A] 26 The outcome[d] of a happy heart is a cheerful countenance,
But solitude and meditation *occasion* toilsome thoughts.

14 1 Blessed is the man whose mouth doth not grieve him,
[e]And (who) doth not mourn for the sorrow of his heart[e].
2 Blessed is the man whose soul doth not reproach[f] him,
And whose hope[g] hath not ceased.

(*k*) XIV. 3–19. *On the proper use of wealth* (= 2 + 3 + 3[+ 1] + 2 + 2 + 2 + 3 + 1 distichs).

3 To him that is small of heart wealth is unfitting[h],
And wherefore[i] should the evil-eyed have gold[k]?
4 He that withholdeth from himself gathereth for another,
And a stranger shall satiate himself with his goods.
5 He that harmeth his own soul, to whom will he do good?
For[l] [m]he hath no delight[m] in his own goods.

[d] *Lit.* 'result' [e–e] *Reading* ולא אנה על דוי לבו; *the text of* ℌ *as it stands cannot be right, it reads*: ולא אבה עליו דין לבו:, 'And his heart doth not desire judgement against him': 𝔊 'And (who) is not pricked at the heart (και ου κατενυγη) with sorrow for sin'; *excepting for* αμαρτιας (= עון) 𝔊 = ℌ *as amended above; αμ. may be an explanatory addition.* 𝔖 *reads:* ולא חבא דין מיעיו, 'And judgement is not hid from his eyes'; מיעיו *suggests a corruption of* עון (= 𝔊), *but* 'heart' *is required to correspond with* 'mouth' *in the first clause. Smend suggests the reading* ולא אנה על דון עונו, 'And (who) doth not sigh for sorrow of his sin.' *Another possible form might be* וְלֹא הֵעֵל דְּוַי בְּלִבּוֹ, 'And (who) doth not cause sorrow to enter into his heart' (*cp. Sanh.* 100 b, לא תעיל דויא בליבך 'Let not sorrow enter into thine heart,' *quoted by Levy*, i. 164); עלל *is only used in the Po'el in the O. T.*, *see* Job xvi. 15 [f] *Reading* חסדתו (*for* חסרתו), *cp.* Prov. xxv. 10: *cp.* 𝔏 qui non habuit animi sui tristitiam [g] V 248 253 Syro-Hex + 'in the Lord' [h] *Lit.* 'not comely', *as* 𝔊 [i] ℌ 𝔖 *repeat* 'not comely'; 𝔊 *is more probably correct here*, ινα τι (= למה) [k] 𝔏 = ℌ: 𝔊 'money': 𝔖 'mammon' [l] *Lit.* 'and' [m–m] *Reading* יחדה (= 𝔖 נקדא *and* 𝔊) *for* יקרה 'he shall not meet with' (*i. e.* 'will not retain possession of')

---

26. **a happy heart.** To be understood in accordance with *v.* 25. 𝔊 'a heart that is in prosperity'; cp. xii. 8.

But solitude . . . שיג ושיח (lit. 'withdrawing and musing') occur in the reverse order in 1 Kings xviii. 27, where Elijah says of Baal: '. . . for he is a god; either he is musing, or he is gone aside.' The clause seems a little inappropriate (possibly it expresses the thought of Eccles. xii. 12: 'Much study is a weariness to the flesh'), and Smend suggests as an emendation: 'Weary eyes (reading מחשיכים עינים for מחשבת עמל) are a sign of worry'; cp. xii. 9ff., xxv. 23*b*. At any rate the words as they stand must be taken in a general sense, and not in reference to Ben-Sira's own studies. 𝔊 has: 'And the finding out of parables is a weariness of thinking,' which is not far from ℌ; the meaning of the words which is intended is to offer a contrast to what is said in the previous clause.

XIV. 1. **whose mouth . . .** Cp. xxv. 8*b*; 1 Kings i. 6; Ps. xvii. 3, xxxix. 2, cxli. 3; Jas. iii. 2. 𝔊 'that hath not slipped with his mouth' is explanatory.

And (who) doth not . . . See critical notes.

2. **whose soul doth not . . .** Cp. 1 John ii. 19–22.

(*k*) XIV. 3–19.

3. **small of heart.** i.e. one who is grudging; cp. 𝔏 'viro cupido et tenaci'. 𝔊 μικρολόγος, one who cavils about trifles.

unfitting. Cp. xv. 9; 𝔏 'sine ratione'.

And wherefore . . . See critical notes.

the evil-eyed. i.e. envious, as 𝔊; cp. xviii. 8, xxviii. 11 *e*; Prov. xxiii. 6, xxviii. 22: it is equivalent to קנאה ('jealousy') in its bad sense. In *Pirqe Aboth* v. 29 the 'evil eye' is contrasted with the 'good eye' (cp. xiv. 10 below); in the same tractate (ii. 15) an 'evil eye' is reckoned among those things which 'put a man out of the world'. The expression here is used with reference to the envy which the miser feels at seeing riches in the possession of others.

gold. 𝔊 χρήματα is a free rendering; cp. Job xxvii. 13, where the Sept. has the same word for the Hebr. כסף ('silver').

4. **He that withholdeth . . .** The reference is to the miser who denies himself many things in order to increase his hoard; he is in reality only laying it up for others.

a stranger . . . Cp. Eccles. vi. 2; 𝔊 'others'.

satiate himself. The Hebr. root בעע means lit. to be full to bursting; the verb does not occur in the O. T., but in Exod. ix. 9 a derivative is used for 'blisters' or 'boils'.

5. **He that harmeth . . .** The reference is only to the miser; the 'harm' refers to the miser's denying himself every enjoyment.

𝕳A 6 None is worse than him that is evil to his own soul,
And the recompense of his evil is [n]in himself[n].
𝕲 7 [o]And even if he doeth good, [p]he doeth it in forgetfulness[p],
And at the last [q]he showeth forth[q] his wickedness[o].
8 [r]Evil is he that envieth[s] with his eye,
Turning away his face and despising men[t][r].
𝕳A 9 In the eye of the covetous[u] (too) small is his portion,
But he that taketh his neighbour's portion [v]destroyeth his own portion[v].
10 [w]The eye of the envious[w] hasteth[x] after bread,
And naught is on his table.
[y][A good eye causeth bread to increase,
And 'A dry fountain sendeth forth water' upon (his) table.][y]
bin 54*a* 11 [z]My son, [a]if thou possessest aught, do well to thyself[a],
[b]And prosper to the best of thy power[b].
𝕳A 12 [c]Remember that death tarrieth not,
Nor hath the decree of Sheol been told thee[c].
13 Before thou diest do good to him that loveth (thee),
And [d]as thou hast prospered[d], give to him.

n–n *Lit.* 'with him' o–o 𝕳 > p–p 248 'he doeth it not willingly': 𝕷 ignoranter et non volens facit q–q 𝕾 'he will look upon' r–r 𝕳 > s 70 248 + 'to look' t *Lit.* 'souls': 𝕷 'his soul' u *So* 𝕲: 𝕳 'of him that stumbleth' *is a corruption*: 𝕾 'of a fool' *is an attempt to improve upon* 𝕳 (כושל 𝕳, שכלא 𝕾) v–v 𝕾 'loseth his own soul', *so* V 248 Syro-Hex: 𝕲 'drieth up his soul': 𝕷 donec consumat arefaciens animam suam: *Smend is perhaps right in emending* 𝕳 *in accordance with these, reading* מיבש נפשו *instead of* מאבד חלקו w–w *Lit.* 'The eye of (him that hath) an evil eye' (עין רע עין): 𝕲 οφθαλμος πονηρος = עין רעה, *which perhaps represents the original* x 𝕲 '(is) envious' (= 𝕳 *inexactly*) y–y 𝕲 >: but 𝕾 = 𝕳 z 𝕷 *inserts the title* 'Concerning well-doing, for death tarrieth not' a–a *The Babylonian Talmud has preserved the right reading here:* 𝕳 𝕾 'Serve thy soul, and if thou hast [i.e. possessest aught], do well to thyself' b–b *Lit.* 'And according to the God [*i.e.* power] of thy hand, make thyself fat': *the rendering of* 𝕲, και προσφορας Κυριῳ αξιως προσαγε, *betrays ignorance of the Hebrew idiom here* c–c *In the Babylonian Talmud, Erubin* 54 a, *this verse is quoted thus:* 'For in Sheol there is no delight, and death hath no tarrying; and if thou say, I will give rest to my sons, the decree of (*lit.* in) Sheol who will declare (it) unto thee?' d–d *Lit.* 'according to the finding of thy hand',

---

6. **None is worse . . .** Cp. Prov. xi. 17.
that is evil to . . . 𝕲 'that is grudging to himself'; cp. Deut. xxviii. 54, 56 Sept. (Smend).
is in himself. 𝕲 'is this', i.e. being evil to his own soul, which does not fully bring out the force of 𝕳.
7. The omission of this and the next verse in 𝕳 is perhaps only accidental; 𝕾 has *v.* 7, though probably it is freely rendered ('And if by chance he doeth good, it is by mistake, and at the last he will see his wickedness'). The omission in 𝕳 can be accounted for by the similar beginning of *vv.* 6 (רע) and 8 (רעה); the beginning of *v.* 5 (רע) and the end of *v.* 6 (רעתו) may also have tended to confuse things.
in forgetfulness. i.e. not of set purpose.
And at the last . . . In spite of the apparent good done in forgetfulness, his true nature is sure to be revealed ultimately and seen of all the world.
8. **that envieth with his eye.** Cp. *v.* 6, where 𝕲 uses the same word (ὁ βασκαίνων).
despising men. ὑπερορῶν ψυχάς. Smend would read ὑπερορῶν ψυχὴν ἑαυτοῦ, as the verse is evidently intended to describe the harm done to the envious man himself; cp. the second clause in *vv.* 6, 7, 9, 10.
9. **In the eye of . . .** 𝕲 'A covetous man's eye is not satisfied with his portion'.
destroyeth his own portion. See critical note. With 𝕲 cp. Num. xi. 6, '. . . but now our soul is dried up,' i.e. there is no more enjoyment of good things; and Ps. xxii. 15 (16 in Hebr.).
10. **The eye of the envious.** See critical note.
hasteth. The Hebr. root עיט (cp. xxxi. [xxxiv.] 16) means to pounce greedily upon something, cp. 1 Sam. xiv. 32 (*Qeri*), xv. 19, xxv. 14 (probably corrupt); these are the only occurrences of the verb in the O.T.; the coll. noun עַיִט 'birds of prey' occurs more often, Jer. xii. 9, &c. The picture is that of a bird of prey darting upon its spoil.
And naught is on . . . 𝕲 καὶ ἐλλιπὴς ἐπὶ τῆς τραπέζης αὐτοῦ. Although the miser is ever grasping, he has naught to show for it.
A good eye. For the expression cp. xxxv. 8 (= xxxi. 10); Prov. xxii. 9; *Pirqe Aboth* v. 29.
A dry fountain . . . This seems to be a quotation. The bracketed clauses are secondary according to Smend.
11. See critical notes.
do well to thyself. Cp. Ps. xlix. 18.
12. **the decree.** חק, i.e. that which has been determined, cp. xli. 2.
13. **as thou hast prospered . . .** Cp. Lev. v. 11.

ℌ[A] 14 [e]Refrain not from the joy of the present[e],
𝔊 [f]And let not the portion of a good desire pass thee by[f].
ℌ[A] 15 Wilt thou not leave thy wealth to another,
And thy labour to them that cast the lot?
16 Give and take; yea, indulge thy soul,
Erubin 54*a* [g]For in Sheol there is no delight[g].
17 All flesh withereth[h] like a garment,
ℌ[A] And the eternal decree is: 'Thou shalt surely die!'
18 As the leaf that groweth on a luxuriant tree,
One fadeth, and another sprouteth;
[i]So (are) the generations of flesh and blood,
One dieth, and another flourisheth[j][i];
19 All his works will surely decay,
And the labour of his hands followeth after him.

(*a*) XIV. 20–27. *The Blessedness of him who seeks Wisdom* (= 4+4 distichs).

20 Blessed (is) the man that meditateth[k] on[l] Wisdom[ll],
And that giveth heed[m] to understanding,
21 That directeth[n] his heart upon her ways,
And giveth heed unto her paths[o];

reading כהשיגת *for* השיגת [e–e] *Lit.* 'Withdraw not (thyself) from the good things of a day' [f–f] ℌ, *which is corrupt, reads:* 'And upon the portion of a brother trespass not': אח ('brother') *is a corruption of* אוה ('desire'); טוב ('good') *should, according to* 𝔊, *be added; for* עבר *in the sense as used in* 𝔊 *cp.* Jer. xiii. 24, Isa. xxix. 5. 𝔖 > : ℌ𝔖 + 'And an evil desire, desire not', *a gloss, which, however, shows that* 𝔊 *has preserved the correct rendering* [g–g] ℌ 'For in Sheol there is no seeking of delight (= 𝔊); but all (that is) fitting to do, do in the sight of God'; *the addition is due to the desire to tone down the flippant sentiment of the verse.* 𝔖 > *the second clause, but has the addition* [h] *Lit.* 'wears out' [i–i] *In the Talmud, Erubin* 54 a, *these clauses are quoted thus*: 'the sons of men are like the herbs of the field, some flourish (*lit.* 'sparkle'), others fade' [j] *Lit.* 'ripeneth'. *At the end of the v.* 253 Syro-Hex + '(It is) by the decree of the Lord' [k] א[c.a] 70 248 253 μελετησει (= ℌ), *so* 𝔖 Syro-Hex: 𝔊 (τελευτησει) *is corrupt* [l] *Lit.* 'in' [ll] 𝔏 + Et in sensu suo cogitabit circumspectionem dei [m] *Lit.* 'that hath respect' [n] *Lit.* 'setteth' [o] *Reading* נתיבותיה (= 𝔖)

---

14. See critical notes.

15. **Wilt thou not leave . . .** Cp. Ps. xlix. 6–11, 17. Therefore why not enjoy it while you have it?

to them that cast the lot. 'In Palestine brothers divided their patrimony by lot as late as, and probably much later than, the second century' (*Baba Bathra* 106 *b* (T. B.); see *JE*, viii. 188 *a*).

16. **indulge thy soul.** Cp. Prov. xxix. 21.

17. **withereth like . . .** Cp. Job xiii. 21; Ps. cii. 26 (Sept.); Is. l. 9, li. 6.

Thou shalt surely die. 𝔊 'Thou shalt die the death'; cp. Gen. ii. 17 (Sept.), iii. 19. The Hebr. root גוע occurs mainly in the poetical books of the O. T.

18. **As the leaf . . .** The two first clauses of this verse are quoted in Erubin 54 *a* (see crit. notes above); cp. Is. xxxiv. 4, xl. 6, 8; 1 Pet. i. 24.

a luxuriant tree. 𝔊 'a thick tree', cp. Deut. xii. 2, &c.

One fadeth . . . 𝔊 'Some it sheddeth, and some it maketh to grow'.

So (are) the . . . This and the next clause were inadvertently omitted in the text of ℌ; they are added in the margin.

flesh and blood. בשר ודם (= σὰρξ καὶ αἷμα, also in the order αἷμα καὶ σάρξ; cp. xvii. 31; Matt. xvi. 17; 1 Cor. xv. 50; Gal. i. 16) does not occur in the O.T., but is frequent in Rabbinical writings; 'the writers use this form of speech infinite times, and by it oppose *men* to *God*' (Lightfoot, *Horae Hebr. et Talm.* [Gandell's ed.], ii. 234).

flourisheth. Lit. 'ripens', used of the 'ripening grape' in Is. xviii. 6; cp. 1 Kings xi. 20. 𝔊 'is born'. In ℌ there is added כן אחרית ('so is [their] latter end'); see Cowley in *JQR*, xii. 110.

19. **All his works . . .** 𝔊 'Every work rotteth and fadeth away'. 𝔖, in order to tone down this rather pessimistic note, substitutes: 'All his works shall be proved before Him' (i.e. God).

will surely decay. Cp. Is. xl. 20, where this word (רקב) is used of a tree rotting, and Prov. x. 7, where it is used in reference to 'the name of the wicked'.

And the labour . . . Just as man perishes and is forgotten, so it is with his works (cp. Job xxi. 13; John xii. 19); contrast with this thought Rev. xiv. 13. 𝔊 'And the worker thereof shall depart with it'.

XIV. 20—XVI. 23. The general theme of this division is Divine retribution. It contains six subsections.

(*a*) XIV. 20–27.

20. **that meditateth.** See critical note. Cp. vi. 37, l. 28; Ps. cxix. 15, 23, 148.

that giveth heed . . . Cp. Ps. cxix. 117; 𝔊 'And that shall discourse by his understanding'; some cursives add 'holy things'.

22 Going forth after her like a spy,
He looketh stealthily upon[p] her enterings-in[q].
23 [Blessed is he] that peereth into her window,
And hearkeneth at her doors;
24 Who encampeth round about her house,
And fixeth his pegs into her wall;
25 [r]Who pitcheth[s] his tent [t]close beside her[t r],
And dwelleth in a goodly dwelling;
26 And buildeth[u] his nest[v] in her foliage,
And lodgeth among her branches;
27 Seeking refuge from the heat in her shade,
He dwelleth within her habitations.

(*b*) XV. 1–10. *How Wisdom is to be attained* (= 2 + 2 + 2 + 2 + 2 distichs).

15 1 For[a] he that feareth the Lord doeth this,
And he that taketh hold of the Law findeth her.
2 And she will meet him as a mother,
And as a youthful wife will she receive him;
3 And she will feed him with the bread of understanding,
And will give him the waters of knowledge[b] to drink.

[p] *Reading* על *for* כל, *which the sense demands* [q] *Cp.* B εισοδοις: 𝕲 *otherwise* οδοις [r–r] 𝕾 > [s] *Lit.* 'stretcheth out' [t–t] *Lit.* 'upon her hand' [u] *Lit.* 'setteth' [v] 𝕲 'children', *misreading* קנו ('his nest') as בניו 'his children'

[a] 𝕲 𝕾 > [b] *Reading* תבונה *instead of* תבואה

21. **That directeth . . .** Cp. xxi. 17 *b*, xvi. 20; Is. xlvii. 7. 𝕲 'He that considereth her ways in his heart'.

And giveth heed unto . . . 𝕲 'And he shall take knowledge of her hidden things'; cp. iv. 18, vi. 22, xxxix. 3, 7. *Pirqe Aboth* vi. 1: '. . . and they reveal to him the secrets of the Torah.'

22. **Going forth . . . He looketh stealthily.** 𝕲 renders both verbs in the imperative.

like a spy. Cf. 2 Sam. x. 3. 𝕲 'as one that tracketh' (ὡς ἰχνευτής), using the metaphor of a hunter.

He looketh stealthily. Cp. Prov. viii. 34. 𝕲 'lieth in wait', continuing the metaphor of a hunter.

23. **into her window.** Cp. xxi. 23; Song of Songs ii. 9.

at her doors. Cp. li. 19; Prov. viii. 34.

24. **encampeth.** Cp. iv. 13, 15. 𝕲 'lodgeth'.

his pegs. The same Hebr. word as in Judges v. 26.

25. **And dwelleth . . .** Cp. Prov. i. 33.

26. **his nest.** See critical note.

in her foliage. Cp. Ps. civ. 12. 𝕲 'under her shelter'.

lodgeth among. 𝕲 'shall rest under'.

27. **Seeking refuge . . .** 𝕲 'By her he shall be covered from heat (cp. Eccles. vii. 12), and shall lodge in her glory' (cp. Is. iv. 5 f.).

(*b*) XV. 1–10.

XV. 1. **For.** Wrongly omitted by 𝕲, since this and the following verses are connected with what has preceded; the way in which men should seek Wisdom is now followed by a description of the reception accorded to those who find her.

doeth this. Referring to what has preceded.

he that taketh hold of . . . תופש תורה; cp. Jer. ii. 8, where four offices are enumerated, among which this is one, viz. priests, lawyers, rulers, prophets; the second of these ('handlers of the Law') came to be technically known as the Scribes (= 'Sopherim', cp. xxxviii. 24–xxxix. 11); in the N. T. γραμματεῖς, and, more rarely, νομικοί (Matt. xxii. 35; Luke vii. 30, x. 25, xi. 45 ff., xiv. 3) or νομοδιδάσκαλοι (Luke v. 17; Acts v. 34; 1 Tim. i. 7); they were those who occupied themselves with the study and teaching of the sacred Scriptures, and, above all, with the Law.

the Law. The most important point about Ben-Sira's teaching regarding the Law is that he identifies it with Wisdom; but the way in which this identification is taken for granted shows that Ben-Sira is not expressing a new truth, but one which in his time had already become generally accepted; cp. the following passages: i. 26, xix. 20, xxi. 11, xxiv. 23, xxxiv. (𝕲 xxxi.) 8.

findeth her. i.e. Wisdom; ידרכנה is more strictly 'shall attain her' or 'overtake', as in Judges xx. 43.

2. **. . . as a mother.** The same comparison is used in reference to Jahveh in Is. xlix. 14, 15.

a youthful wife. See the same expression in Prov. v. 18, 'a young wife'; 𝕲 γυνὴ παρθενείας, cp. Prov. vii. 4, 5; Jer. iii. 4; Joel i. 8 (see Sept. in each case); cp. also Wisd. vii. 8.

will she receive him. With 𝕳 cp. 1 Chron. xii. 18.

3. **bread of understanding.** Cp. Prov. ix. 5.

waters of knowledge. 𝕲 ὕδωρ σοφίας. In the later Jewish literature the 'water' and 'bread' of the Torah are often referred to; e.g. in *Shabbath* 120 *a* (T. B.) the words of Is. iii. 1, 'the whole stay of bread,' are explained as referring to the Torah; in the Midrash *Bereshith Rabba*, § lxx (to Gen. xxviii. 20), it is said that the proselyte may find in Israel 'the bread of the Torah'. In the Midrash *Shir Rabba* i. 4 it is said: 'As water refreshes the body, so does the Torah refresh the soul.'

𝔋[A] 4 And he that stayeth upon her will not fall,
Nor shall he that trusteth in her be ashamed;
5 And she will exalt him above his neighbour,
And will open his mouth in the midst of the assembly.
6 Joy and gladness shall he find,
And she will make him inherit an everlasting name.
7 [c]Ungodly men[c] shall not obtain her,
And the arrogant shall not look upon her.
8 Far from the mockers is she,
And liars do not think of her.
9 Praise[d] is not seemly in the mouth of the wicked,
For it hath not been apportioned [e]to him[e] by God.
10 In the mouth of the wise praise is uttered,
And [f]he who is mighty[f] with her shall teach her.

(*c*) XV. 11–20. *On Free-will* (= 2 + 1 + 2 + 2 + 2 + 1 distichs).

11 Say not: 'From God is my transgression,'
For that which He hateth made He not.
12 Say not: '(It is) He that made me to stumble,'
For there is no need of [g]evil men[g].
13 Evil and abomination doth the Lord hate,
And [gg]He doth not let it come nigh to them[gg] that fear Him.

c–c *Lit.* 'men of falsehood' d 𝔖 'wisdom' e–e 𝔊 > *exc.* 70 106 248 f–f *Lit.* 'he who ruleth'
g–g *Lit.* 'men of violence', cp. 𝔏 'homines impii' gg–gg *Lit.* 'he doth not cause it to encounter them'

---

4. **he that stayeth upon her.** On the other hand, in Ps. xviii. 18 Jahveh is man's stay.

5. **she will exalt him.** Cp. *Pirqe Aboth* vi. 1, where it is said: 'And it [the Torah] magnifies him and exalts him over all things'; cp. also Sirach iv. 11.

will open his mouth. In order that he may teach.

in the midst of the assembly. Cp. xxi. 17; Prov. xxiv. 7. The reference is probably to those gathered together for instruction in the temple, for, as Friedländer has shown (*Synagoge und Kirche in ihren Anfängen*), the synagogue did not exist in Palestine until the latter half of the second century B.C.

6. 𝔊 'Joy and a crown of gladness and an everlasting name shall he inherit'; for 'crown' cp. i. 9, vi. 31.

an everlasting name. Cp. Is. lvi. 3, where, however, this is given by God.

7. **Ungodly men.** 𝔊 'Foolish men'. 𝔋 מתי שוא, cp. Job xi. 11; Ps. xxvi. 4; 𝔏 homines stulti.

the arrogant. 𝔊 'liars'. 𝔋 אנשי זדון, cp. Jer. xliii. 2.

8. **the mockers.** 𝔊 'pride'; cp. Eth 'the proud'. The 'mockers' are the cynical free-thinkers to whom wisdom, as contained in the Law, is foolishness; cp. xiv. 6.

do not think of her. Cp. xxiv. 20.

9. This and the next verse belong to what has preceded, but form, at the same time, an introduction to what follows.

seemly. נאתה, cp. Ps. xxxiii. 1, cxlvii. 1 (Smend).

apportioned. 𝔊 'sent'. Cp. 𝔏 Quoniam a deo profecta est sapientia.

10. **In the mouth of . . .** 𝔊 'For praise shall be spoken in wisdom'. Cp. ii. 29; Prov. xi. 9.

And he who is mighty . . . 𝔊 *καὶ ὁ κύριος εὐοδώσει αὐτόν*, but, as the rendering of 𝔏 shows ('Et dominator dabit eam illi'), this is a corruption of *καὶ ὁ κυριεύων δώσει αὐτῷ*, which is much nearer to 𝔋; *αὐτῷ* must originally have been *αὐτήν*. Cp. Matt. vii. 29.

(*c*) XV. 11–20. Cp. with this passage James i. 13 f.

11. **From God is my transgression.** 𝔊 'Through the Lord I fell away'.

that which He hateth made He not. 𝔊 'For thou shalt not do the things that He hateth', a misunderstanding of the point in 𝔋. The reference is probably to the *Yeṣer ha-raʿ* (the 'Evil Tendency') which, according to the text, was evidently believed by some to have been created by God, a belief which is reflected in later Rabbinical writings, e.g. *Qiddushin* 30*b* (T.B.): 'I (God) created an evil tendency (*Yeṣer ha-raʿ*); I created for him (i.e. for man, in order to counteract this) the Law as a means of healing'; and in *Bereshith Rabba*, § xxvii (to Gen. vi. 6), Rabbi Ibo explains the text to mean: 'It repenteth Me for having created in him (i.e. in man) the evil tendency; if I had not created it in him, he would not have rebelled against Me.' In earlier days, too, it was believed that God was the cause of sin; see 2 Sam. xxiv. 1; Jer. vi. 21; Ezek. iii. 20.

12. **Say not.** פן תאמר, i.e. 'By no means say . . .'; cp. Is. xxxvi. 18 (Smend).

stumble. 𝔊 'err'.

evil men. 𝔊 'a sinful man'. With the whole verse cp. Job xxii. 2 ff.

13. **Evil and abomination.** 𝔊 'every abomination'.

He doth not let it come nigh. 𝔊 *οὐκ ἔστιν ἀγαπητόν* should be emended to . . . *ἀπαντητόν* (Knabenbauer).

14. **God.** 𝔊 'He himself'.

created man . . . Since man was created by God he cannot have been bad from the beginning; the teaching here implied seems to be that man became bad because he followed his evil inclination; contrast, however, xxxiii. (𝔊 xxxvi.)

𝔥A 14 God created man from the beginning,
[h]And placed[i] him in the hand of his *Yeṣer.*
15 If thou (so) desirest, thou canst keep the commandment,
[j]And (it is) wisdom[k] to do His good pleasure[j].
16 Poured out before thee (are) fire and water,
Stretch forth thine hand unto that which thou desirest.
17 Life and death[l] (are) before man,
That which he desireth shall be given to him.
18 Sufficient is the wisdom of the Lord,
(He is) mighty in power, and seeth all things.
19 And the eyes of God behold his works,
And He knoweth every deed of man.
20 He commanded no man to sin,
Nor gave strength to men of lies[m].

(*d*) XVI. 1–5. *The Curse of sinful Children* (= 2 + 2 + 1 + 1 distichs).

16 1 [a]Desire not the sight[b] of unprofitable sons,
And delight not in corrupt children;
2 Yea, and if they [c]are fruitful[c], exult not because of them
If they have no fear of the Lord.
3 Trust not thou in their life,
[d]Nor rely on their [e]end[e d];

[h] 𝔥 *inserts the following gloss*: 'And delivered him into the hand of him that spoileth him'; *added for doctrinal purposes* [i] *Lit.* 'gave' [j-j] 𝔖 >: 𝔥 𝔖 + 'and if thou trust in him, of a truth (*lit.* even) thou shalt live' [k] *Lit.* 'understanding' [l] 𝔏 + 'good and evil' [m] 𝔥 + *the gloss*: 'And He hath no mercy on him that committeth falsehood (*lit.* doeth vanity), nor on him that revealeth secrets.' 𝔖 + 'And He said not to the sons of flesh that they should sin, and He hath no mercy on them that commit falsehood.'

[a] 𝔏 *has the title* 'Concerning ungodly children' [b] *Lit.* 'beauty': 𝔊 𝔖 'multitude' [c-c] 𝔊 𝔖 'multiply' [d-d] 𝔖 'And trust not that there will be a good end for them' [e-e] 𝔊[BC] 'place'; ℵ A V 55 155 248 253 254 Syro-Hex Sah 'multitude'; 𝔥 + *the gloss*: 'For there will not be for them a good end'; ℵ[c.a] + στεναξις γαρ πενθει αωρω και εξεφνης αυτων συντελειαν γνωσεται

14, 15. *Yeṣer* is here used in a neutral sense (almost equivalent to Free-will) in which lay the power of doing right or wrong; the origin of evil is, therefore, in this passage, traced to man; cp. xxv. 24; Wisd. xii. 11; 4 Esdras iv. 29–31. A later scribe, realizing the difficulty which could be urged, that as the Creator of all things God must have created the *Yeṣer* with its tendency to evil as well as to good, added the gloss that God delivered man from his spoiler (i. e. Satan; see critical note); cp. iv. 19. This later scribe, in his turn, however, did not realize that the difficulty still remained.

Yeṣer. Cp. xxvii. 6, xxxvii. 3: 𝔊 διαβούλιον.

15. **If thou (so) desirest.** In this and the two next verses the normal Jewish doctrine of Free-will is well illustrated; it is characteristic of this that divine grace occupies a relatively subordinate position.

the commandment. מצוה, i.e. any precept of the Law; the keeping (עשׂא) of such is reckoned as of merit. Cp. x. 19, xxxii. (𝔊 xxxv.) 23, xxxvi. 12, xlv. 5; Prov. xix. 6; Eccles. viii. 5.

And (it is) wisdom . . . 𝔊 'And faithfulness (it is) to do (His) good pleasure, cp. Prov. xii. 22; for תבונה ('understanding') it is perhaps better to read אמונה ('faithfulness'), following 𝔊 (and see the addition of 𝔥, with which cp. Hab. ii. 4; see critical note); cp. 𝔏 'Et in perpetuum fidem placitam facere'.

16. **Poured out before thee.** 𝔊 'He hath set before thee'.

fire and water. Corresponding to 'life and death' in *v.* 17; opposing elements; cp. Light and darkness = Good and evil. For the synonym 'Fire' for 'Good', applied to God, cp. Deut. iv. 24.

17. **Life and death.** With the addition of 𝔏 (see critical note) cp. Deut. xxx. 15, 19; see also Jer. xxi. 8.

18. **Sufficient is . . .** i.e. God knows what each man chooses, cp. xlii. 17. 𝔊 'Great is . . .'

(He is) mighty in power. i. e. It lies within His power to punish those who choose the evil, and to reward those who choose the good.

and seeth all things. Cp. Ps. xxxiii. 13–15.

19. **And the eyes of God . . .** 𝔊 'And His eyes are upon them that fear Him', cp. Ps. xxxiii. 18, xxxiv. 16.

And He knoweth every deed . . . Cp. *Pirqe Aboth* iv. 31: 'He is the framer, and He the creator, and He the discoverer . . .'; cp. Ps. xxxiii. 15.

20. **to sin.** 𝔊 'to be ungodly' (ἀσεβεῖν).

nor gave strength . . . 𝔊 'And He gave no man licence to sin'. For the addition in 𝔥 see critical note.

(*d*) XVI. 1–5.

XVI. 1. **Desire not . . .** Cp. xlii. 12.

sight. 𝔊 'multitude', anticipating *v.* 2.

unprofitable sons. Lit. 'vain youths'. Cp. Philemon 11.

2. **If they have . . .** 𝔊 'Except the fear of the Lord be with them'.

3. **Trust not thou . . .** For the reason that it may suddenly come to an end cp. Job xxiv. 24.

on their end. For the Hebr. word עֵקֶב in the unusual sense of 'end' cp. Ps. cxix. 33, 112. Possibly the word is to be understood in the sense of 'gain', as in Ps. xix. 11 (12 in Hebr.); Prov. xxii. 4.

𝔜[A] For better is one[f] than a thousand[g],
And to die childless than [h](to have)[h] a presumptuous posterity.
4 From one that[hh] feareth the Lord a city is peopled,
But through a race of treacherous men it is desolated[i].
5 Many things like these mine eye hath seen,
And mightier things than these mine ear hath heard.

(*e*) XVI. 6–14. *God's righteous wrath against the Wicked* (= 1 + 2 + 2 + 1 + 2 + 2[+ 2] distichs).

6 In the assembly of the wicked a fire is kindled,
And in an apostate nation doth wrath burn.
7 He forgave not the princes[k] of old,
[l]Who revolted [ml] in their might.
8 He spared not [n]the place where Lot sojourned[n],
Who were arrogant in their pride;
9 Nor did He spare the nation accursed[o],
Dispossessed because of their sin[p].
10 Thus (did it happen) to the six hundred thousand footmen,
Who were destroyed in the arrogancy of their heart[q].
11 Yea, and if there be one who is stiff-necked,
A marvel it would be were he not punished.
For mercy and wrath are with Him,
He forgiveth and pardoneth, but [r]upon the wicked He causeth His wrath to rest[r].
12 As great as His mercy (is), so is His chastisement[s]:
(Each) man doth He judge according to his works.

[f] 248 + 'righteous'; ℵ[c.a] + 'doing the will of the Lord' (= 𝔜 𝔖): 𝔏 + timens deum [g] ℵ[c.a] + 'transgressors': 70 + 'sinners': 𝔏 + filii impii [h-h] 𝔜 + 'one that hath many unprofitable children and than' [hh] 𝔜 + 'is childless (but)' [i] 248 + 'quickly' [k] 𝔊 𝔏 'giants' [l-l] 𝔖 'who filled the world' [m] 𝔜 + 'of yore' [n-n] 𝔖 'the inhabitants of the city of Lot' [o] ℵ[c.a] + 'the nation of Canaan' [p] ℵ[c.a] + 'All these things did He do to the hard-hearted nations, nor was He appeased by the multitude of His holy ones' [q] 55 70 248 + 'Chastising, showing mercy, smiting, healing, the Lord guarded them in mercy and in discipline' [r-r] 𝔖 'punisheth sins' [s] 𝔊 + 'great'

---

4. **that feareth the Lord.** 𝔊 'that hath understanding'; 𝔖 'that feareth God'. To have understanding and to fear the Lord are synonymous terms in the Wisdom-Literature, cp. i. 14; Prov. i. 7, ix. 10; Ps. cxi. 10.

But through . . . Cp. Gen. xix. 24, 25. 𝔊 'But a race of wicked men shall be made desolate', misunderstanding the point of 𝔜.

5. **mightier things than . . .** These are enumerated in the verses that follow.

(*e*) XVI. 6–14.

6. **a fire is kindled.** Cp. Num. xvi. 35 for the thought, but probably the reference is not specifically to this as in the enumeration of events in the succeeding verses the chronological order is followed.

an apostate nation. The same phrase in Is. x. 6.

7. **He forgave not.** 𝔊 'He was not pacified towards'.

the princes of old. 𝔖 'the ancient kings'; 𝔊 follows the Sept. of Gen. vi. 4, 'the giants' of old time; cp. Num. xxi. 21–31; Wisd. xiv. 6; Judith xvi. 7; Bar. iii. 26 ff.; 3 Macc. ii. 4; Enoch vii. 2, ix. 9; Jubilees v. i.

Who revolted . . . 𝔏 Qui destructi sunt confidentes suae virtuti.

8. **He spared not . . .** Cp. Gen. xix. 14.

the place . . . sojourned. מגורי לוט as in Job xviii. 19, בִּמְגוּרָיו; not as 𝔊 𝔖.

Who were arrogant . . . Cp. Ezek. xvi. 49; 3 Macc. ii. 5 (Smend). 𝔊 'Whom He abhorred for their pride'.

9. **spare.** 𝔊 𝔖 𝔏 'pity'.

the nation accursed. i.e. Canaan, as ℵ[c.a] explains correctly in an addition. 𝔊 'the people of perdition'.

10. **to the six hundred thousand . . .** Cp. xlvi. 8, and see Num. ix. 21; it is improbable, as the context shows, that the reference is to Exod. xii. 37, as Ryssel thinks.

destroyed. Lit. 'taken away'; 𝔊 'gathered together'.

in the arrogancy of . . . For the Hebrew cp. Deut. i. 43; 𝔖 'because of their murmuring' (cp. Num. xiv. 12). 𝔊 'in the hardness . . .', cp. *v.* 11.

11. **stiff-necked.** Cp. Exod. xxxii. 9, xxxiii. 3, 5, and for 𝔊 Neh. vii. 51.

A marvel. תְּמָהּ; the noun (Aramaic) occurs, outside our book, only in Dan. iii. 32, 33, vi. 28.

For mercy and wrath . . . The same clause as *v.* 6*c* (𝔜 𝔊).

He forgiveth . . . 𝔊 for the whole clause, 'He is mighty to forgive (δυνάστης ἐξιλασμῶν, cp. Ps. lxxxvi. 5, cxxx. 4), and poureth out wrath.'

but upon the wicked . . . The same clause as *v.* 6*d* (𝔜 𝔊).

ℌ[A] 13 The sinner shall not escape with his spoil,
And He will not suffer the desire[t] of the righteous to fail for ever.
14 Every one that doeth righteousness shall receive his reward,
And every man shall find[u] (his reward) before Him, according to his works.
15 [[v]The Lord hardened the heart of Pharaoh who knew Him not,
Whose works were manifest under the heavens;
16 His mercies are seen by all His creation,
And His light and His darkness[w] hath He apportioned unto the children of men.][v]

(*f*) XVI. 17–23. *Man's insignificance in the sight of God* (= 2 + 3 + 3 + 1 distichs).

17 Say not: 'I am hidden from God,
And in the height who will remember me?
I shall not be noticed[x] among so illustrious a people,
And what is my soul among the mass of the spirits [y]of all the children of men[y]?'
18 Behold the heavens and the heavens of the heavens,
And the deep, and the earth[z];
19 [a]When He treadeth upon them they stand firm,
And when He visiteth them they tremble[a].
[b]Yea, the bottoms of the mountains, and the foundations of the world,
When He[c] looketh upon them they tremble greatly.

[t] 𝔊 𝔖 'patience' [u] *Reading* (*after* 𝔊 𝔖) ימצא *for* יצא [v–v] 𝔊 > (*exc.* 106 248): 𝔖 Ar = ℌ: *the two cursives vary only slightly from* ℌ [w] *Reading* (*after the cursives* 106 248 *and* 𝔖) חשכו *instead of* שבחו ('His blessing') [x] B C 'remembered' [y–y] 𝔊 > [z] 70 248 106 𝔏 + 'and all that in them is' [a–a] B 'when He visiteth them they are shaken' [b] 248 *inserts*: 'The whole world was made, and existeth, by His will' [c] 70 248 'the Lord'

12. **according to his works.** Cp. xv. 19, and *Pirqe Aboth* iii. 24: 'The world is judged by grace; and everything is according to work.'

13. **the desire.** Cp. Prov. x. 24, xi. 23; Ps. cxii. 10; Smend, on the basis of xliv. 10 (Hebr.), emends to 'hope (תקות for תאות).

for ever. Omitted in 𝔊.

14. **Every one that . . . to his works.** 𝔊 'He will make room for every work of mercy; each man shall find according to his works'. Concerning the efficacy of works, see iii. 14, 31, xi. 27, xvii. 22, xxix. 9, xxxi. 9, 10, &c.; the Hebr. phrase עשה צדקה is the technical one for fulfilling the commandments of the Law (*Mitzvoth*); Ben-Sira frequently lays stress on the need of this, though occasionally he finds it necessary to utter a note of warning, e.g. in v. 5, 6, where he combats the belief that any number of sins can be committed provided that a sufficient number of good works are done to atone for them (cp. xxxiv. 26 [xxxi. 31]). The danger of works assuming a mechanical character became a more urgent one as time went on, see e.g. Matt. vii. 15, 27; it is seen clearly also in the later Rabbinical literature (for many examples see Weber, *Jüdische Theologie*, pp. 279 ff.), though passages in which the efficacy of works is balanced by teaching on the need of grace are not wanting.

before Him. i.e. in His (God's) sight.

15, 16. These verses are probably not original, but they must have got into the text at an early period, as they are found in the Syriac and Arabic versions, as well as in two Greek cursives. They belong to the secondary recension of ℌ.

15. **The Lord hardened . . .** Cp. Exod. ix. 12 ff.

under the heavens. Cp. Exod. v. 2, xvii. 14; Deut. xxv. 19, xxix. 19; Job xli. 3.

16. **the children of men.** 𝔊 τῷ ἀδαμάντι, a corruption for τῷ ἀδάμ (לאדם).

(*f*) XVI. 17–23.

17. **I am hidden from God.** Cp. Ps. cxxxix. 7–12.

noticed. Lit. 'known', i.e. recognized.

among the mass . . . 𝔊 'in a boundless creation'; Saʿadya, who quotes this verse (Smend), omits 'of all the children of men', which overloads the clause, and is evidently not original.

18, 19. The whole-hearted acknowledgement of the divine glory and power contained in these verses cannot be intended to be spoken by the sceptic, in whose mouth they would sound strange; it is clear, on the other hand, that *vv.* 20–22 belong to the same speaker as *v.* 17. It would seem that *vv.* 18, 19 have got out of place; they would come more appropriately after *v.* 23, where, after having rebuked the sceptic's way of thinking, Ben-Sira utters his own confession of faith.

18. **the heavens of the heavens.** Cp. Deut. x. 14; 1 Kings viii. 27; 3 Macc. ii. 15.

the deep, and the earth. These, with the heavens, went to make up the universe, according to the ancient Hebrew conception. The 'deep' = *Tehom* (cp. Gen. vi. 11), i.e. the subterranean abyss of waters.

19. **treadeth.** Lit. 'cometh down', cp. Ps. xviii. 8, civ. 32.

And when He visiteth . . . פקד often has the sense of 'punish'; cp. Is. x. 12; Jer. ix. 24 (Hebr.); with the whole verse cp. *Test. 12 Patriarchs*, Levi iii. 9: 'When, therefore, the Lord looketh upon all creation, the heavens and the earth and the abysses are shaken.'

the bottoms of the mountains. Cp. Jonah ii. 6 (Hebr. 7); 𝔊 'the mountains'.

When He looketh . . . Cp. Ps. civ. 32; Nahum i. 5.

ℌ[A] 20 'In truth, unto me He will not have respect;
And as for my ways, who will mark them?[cc]
21 If I sin, no eye beholdeth it,
Or if I deal untruly in all secrecy, who will know it?
22 [d]My righteous dealing, who declareth it?
And what hope (is there)? for the decree is distant*[de].'
23 They that lack understanding think these things,
And the man of folly thinketh this.

(*a*) XVI. 24–30. *Wisdom as seen in Creation* (= 2 + 2 + 2 + 2 distichs).

24 Hearken ye unto me, and receive my wisdom,
And set your heart upon my words.
25 I will pour out my spirit[f] by weight,
And [g]by measure[g] will I declare my knowledge.
26 When God created His works from the beginning,
𝔊 [h]After making them[h] He assigned them (their) portions[i].
27 He set in order His[k] works for ever,
[l]And their authority unto their generations[l].
They hunger not, neither [m]are they weak[m],
And they cease not from their works[n].

[cc] א [c.a] + 'And according as a man asketh, his eye shall see (his reward'): *cp. v.* 14 b [d–d] 𝔖 > * *Reading* ירחק *for* אצוק (*Smend*) [e] 70 106 248 𝔏 + 'And the trying of all things is not until the end' [f] 𝔖 'words' [g–g] 𝔖 'in wisdom' [h–h] ℌ 'Concerning their life': *this is all that is left of* ℌ *in the clause; it is wanting from here to* xviii. 23 [i] 𝔖 'laws' [k] א 253 'their' (= 𝔖 𝔏) [l–l] 70 106 248: 'In His hand are their beginnings from generation to generation' [m–m] *So* א: 𝔊 'do they labour': 70 106 248 + 'in His works': 𝔖 'do they labour,' + 'nor are they weary' [n] 𝔖 'strength'

20. **In truth.** In this and the two next verses the sceptic's train of thought is continued from *v.* 17; he says, in effect, that neither evil actions nor righteous dealing matter since God is indifferent to both. 𝔊 misunderstands the point of the words, and renders: 'And no heart shall think upon these things, and who shall conceive his ways?'

21. **If I sin ...** It is difficult to make much out of 𝔊: 'And a tempest which no man seeth [א[c.a] adds: 'shall come upon him', to make sense], and the more part of his works are among hidden things'; with the second clause cp. xliii. 32. Smend ingeniously emends the first clause thus: κἂν κακοποιῇ ἄνθρωπος οὐκ ὄψεται ὁ ὀφθαλμὸς αὐτοῦ, but the unanimity of the Greek MSS. in reading καταιγίς points to an original misreading of ℌ. With the whole verse cp. xxiii. 18–20.

22. **who declareth it?** Since God Himself, according to the sceptic, does not see it (cp. *vv.* 20, 21), who is there to tell Him if a man deals righteously? The sceptic is represented as not believing in the ministry of angels (cp. Job xxxiii. 23, 24).

And what hope (is there)? 𝔊 'Or who shall endure them?' ὑπομενεῖ is probably a corruption of ὑπομονή (=תקוה in Job xiv. 19; Ps. ix. 19, lxi. 5).

for the decree is distant. i.e. the decreed reward for well-doing, or punishment for evil-doing, is, in any case, so far off that one need not be concerned with either.

23. **And the man of folly ...** 𝔊 paraphrastically: 'And an unwise and erring man thinketh follies.' Cp. Ps. xiv. 1 (Sept. xiii. 1), liii. 1 (Sept. lii. 1).

XVI. 24—XVIII. 29. Divine retribution further exemplified. This division contains seven subsections.

(*a*) XVI. 24–30.

24, 25. These verses form an introduction to this section, which deals with the wonders of Creation, in which the divine Wisdom is revealed.

24. **receive my wisdom.** Cp. viii. 9. שֵׂכֶל means 'insight', or 'good sense'; cp. Prov. iii. 4, xiii. 15, &c. 𝔊 'learn knowledge'.

set your heart. With 𝔊 πρόσεχε τῇ καρδίᾳ σου cp. Deut. xxxii. 46 (Sept.).

25. **I will pour out.** The Hebr. root נבע is a late one, and occurs only elsewhere in the poetical books, Psalms, Proverbs, and Ecclesiastes; cp. x. 13, l. 27.

by weight. Cp. xxi. 5, xxviii. 25.

by measure. 𝔊 ἐν ἀκριβείᾳ.

will I declare my knowledge. Cp. Job x. 17, xxxii. 6.

26. **When God created.** 𝔊 ἐν κρίσει (a scribal error for κτίσει) Κυρίου. Cp. 1 Enoch ii. 1–3.

... He assigned them ... Cp. Gen. i. 20, 25; Ps. cxxxvi. 6–9.

27. **He set in order ...** Cp. Ps. civ. 24, 31.

their authority. τὰς ἀρχὰς αὐτῶν. Cp. Gen. i. 16, 18; Ps. ciii. 22; i.e. the sphere of their activity. Ryssel refers to Philo (*De Monarch.* I. § i, II. § 5 ff.), where the sun and the stars are designated ἄρχοντες.

unto their generations. Cp. Ps. cxxxv. (cxxxvi.) 8 f. (Sept.).

They hunger not ... Cp. xliii. 10.

28 [o]Not one thrusteth aside his neighbour[o],
They never disobey His word.
29 And after this the Lord looked upon the earth,
And [p]filled it with His good things[p].
30 With every living thing He filled[q] the earth;
[r]And into it is their return[r].

(*b*) XVII. 1–14. *God's gifts to man* (= 2 + 2 + 4 + 2 + 2 distichs).

17 1 God[a] created man[b] out of dust[c],
And turned him back thereunto.
2 He granted them [d]a [fixed] number of days[d],
And gave them authority over all[e] things [f]on the earth[f].
3 [g]He clothed them with strength [gg]like unto Himself[gg][g],
And made them according to His own[h] image.
4 He put the fear of them[i] upon all flesh,
And [k]caused them to have power[k] over beasts and birds[l].
𝕾* 7*a* [m]With insight and understanding He filled their heart[m],
7*b* And taught[mm] them good and evil.
6*a* [n]He created for them[n] tongue, and eyes, and ears,
6*b* And He gave[o] them a heart to understand,

o–o 𝕾 'they hate not one another' p–p 𝕾 'blessed it with all its fruits' q *So* 𝕾; 𝕲 'covered' r–r 𝕾 'And gathered within it all His works'
a *So* 𝕾 𝕷: 𝕲 'The Lord' b 𝕾 Adam c *So* 𝕾: 𝕷 + 'and made him after His image' d–d *So* 𝕾 𝕷: 𝕲 'days by number': 𝕲 𝕷 + 'and a set time' e *So* 70 𝕾 f–f *Lit.* 'thereon' g–g 𝕷 *omits this clause here, but places it before v.* 2: 𝕾 'By His wisdom He clothed them with strength and covered them with fear' gg–gg *Reading* καθ' εαυτον *for* καθ' εαυτους h *So* ℵ A i So 𝕾: 𝕲 𝕷 'him' k–k *Cp.* B[b]: 𝕾 >: 70 248 + 'in His likeness' (*i.e.* like Him) l 70 248 +: 'They (*i.e.* men) received the use of five powers (*i.e.* the five senses) of the Lord; but as a sixth He also accorded them the gift of understanding (νους), and as a seventh the Word (λογος), the interpreter of His (*i.e.* God's) powers' (= *v.* 5) * *The order of the clauses here follows* 𝕾: 𝕲 *lacks logical sequence; the order in* 𝕷 *differs from both* m–m *So* 𝕾: 𝕲 𝕷 'He filled them with skilfulness of insight': 𝕷 + 'He created for them the understanding of the spirit, and filled their heart with reason' mm *So* 𝕾: 𝕲 'showed them' n–n *So* 𝕾: 𝕲 διαβουλιον, *the result of reading* וְיֵצֶר *instead of* וַיִּצֶר; *the omission of* לָהֶם ('for them') *followed from this* o 𝕾 *Lit.* 'granted as their portion'

---

28. **Not one thrusteth aside...** i.e. the heavenly bodies have been 'set in order', they follow their course without interfering with one another; cp. Ps. civ. 19.
They never disobey... Cp. Ps. cxlviii. 5, 6.
29. **And after this...** Cp. Gen. i. 20–31.
And filled it... Cp. Ps. civ. 24, 28.
30. **With every living thing.** 𝕲 ψυχὴν (ℵ ψυχή) παντὸς ζῴου; cp. Gen. i. 21 כל־נפש החיה, πᾶσαν ψυχὴν ζῴων...; cp. also Gen. i. 24.
And into it... Cp. Gen. iii. 19; Ps. civ. 29; Eccles. xii. 7.
(*b*) XVII. 1–14.
XVII. 1. After speaking of the Creation generally, Ben-Sira now deals more specifically with man and God's gifts to him.
God created... Cp. Gen. ii. 7.
And turned him back... Cp. Gen. iii. 19; Ps. cxlvi. 4.
2. **He granted them...** Cp. Ps. xc. 10.
And gave them authority. Cp. Gen. i. 28; Ps. viii. 6–8.
3. **like unto Himself... according to His own image.** Cp. Gen. i. 26, 27.
4. **the fear of them...** Cp. Gen. i. 28, ix. 2; Wisd. ix. 2.
caused them... Cp. Gen. i. 26, 28; Ps. viii. 6–8.
5. See critical note [l]. In reference to this insertion Grotius (quoted by Smend) says: 'Videtur ad marginem annotatum fuisse ab aliquo Stoicorum librorum lectore. Nam Stoici ad quinque sensus notissimos tres annumerabant alios, quorum hic omissum est τὸ σπερματικόν.' The verse is, on the face of it, not original.
6 ff. See critical notes.
7 *a*. **With insight...** Cp. Ps. viii. 5.
7 *b*. **... good and evil.** See, however, Gen. ii. 17, iii. 22.
6 *a*. **He created.** See critical note.
6 *b*. **heart.** As usually in the O. T., the seat of understanding.

𝔊 𝔖 8*b* [p]To show them the majesty of His works,
8*c* [q]And that they might glory in His wondrous acts[q];
*9 That they might evermore declare[r] His glorious works[r],
10 And praise[s] His holy name.
𝔊 11 He set before[t] them the covenant[tt];
The law of life [u]He gave them for a heritage[u].
12 He made an everlasting covenant with them,
And showed[uu] them His judgements.
13 Their eyes beheld [x]His[x] glorious majesty,
[y]And their ear heard His[z] glorious voice[y];
14 And He said unto them, [a]Beware of all unrighteousness[a];
And He gave them commandment, to each man concerning his neighbour.

(*c*) XVII. 15–24. *God's recompense to those who serve Him* (= 2[+1]+2+2 distichs).

15 Their ways [b]are ever[b] before Him,
They are not hid from His eyes[c].
17 [[d]For every nation He appointed a ruler,
But Israel is the Lord's portion[e]].

[p] 𝔖 > 8a: 𝔊 𝔏: 'He set His eye (254 Syro-Hex mg 'fear') upon their hearts' [q–q] *So, with some variation,* ℵ c.a 70 248 (*as v.* 9) 𝔖 𝔏 * *vv.* 9–10 *are misplaced in* 𝔊 [r–r] 𝔖 'the fear of Him in the world' [s] 70 248 'the elect shall praise' [t] προεθηκεν (= 𝔖) *instead of* προσεθηκεν ('He added') [tt] *So* 𝔖: 𝔊 'knowledge' [u–u] 𝔖 'He taught them': 248 + 'to perceive that they are mortal' [uu] 𝔖 'made known unto' [x–x] *So* 𝔖 𝔏: 𝔊 > [y–y] 𝔏 > [z] *So* ℵ C V 70 253 254 Syro-Hex Ar: BA &c. 'their' [a–a] 𝔖 'take heed and be not faithless' [b–b] 𝔖 'are manifest' [c] 70 248 + 'From their youth up every man (70 their way) was towards evil, neither were they able to make their hearts (to be) of flesh instead of stone' (= *v.* 16), *cp.* Ezek. xi. 19 [d] 70 248 *insert here*: 'At the separation of the peoples of the whole earth,' *cp.* Gen. vi. 5, vii. 21, Deut. xxxii. 8 [e] 70 248 + 'Whom (*i.e.* Israel, the Lord's portion) He brought up as His firstborn (*cp.* Exod. iv. 22) with severity, yet loving them, imparting to them the light of love, and He forsook them

8 *b*. **the majesty.** Cp. xviii. 4.
8 *c*. See critical note.
9, 10. The order as given above is that of 𝔖.
11. **He set before them.** Cp. Deut. iv. 44.
the covenant. 𝔊 read בינה for ברית.
The law of life. i.e. the law which gives life, the Law of Moses; cp. xlv. 5 (תורת חיים), Baruch iv. 1, and the Midrash *Sifre* 84*a*: 'As water giveth life to the world, so do the words of Torah give life to the world'; and *Pirqe Aboth* ii. 8: 'He who hath gotten to himself words of Torah hath gotten to himself the life of the world to come.' Ben-Sira is, of course, only referring to this life.
12. **made.** Lit. 'set up' (ἔστησεν); cp. xliv. 18*a*; Ezek. xvi. 60.
an everlasting covenant. Cp. Baruch iv. 1.
13. **Their eyes beheld ...** See Exod. xix. 16–20, xxiv. 16, 17.
His glorious voice. Cp. xlv. 5; Is. xxx. 30; Rev. i. 10, iv. 1.
14. **Beware of ...** A summary of all the prohibitory commandments of the Law, referring especially to that against worshipping other gods.
He gave them commandment ... This and the preceding clause sum up the 'great commandments' of the Law, love to God and one's neighbour; cp. Matt. xxii. 36–40.
(*c*) XVII. 15–24.
15. **Their ways are ...** Cp. Ps. xc. 8*a*; Is. xlix. 16.
They are not hid ... Cp. Ps. xc. 8*b*. See critical note.
17. See critical note for addition in 248. This verse (17) can hardly be original here. If genuine it has been misplaced (it breaks the close logical connexion between *vv.* 15 and 19, which form 2 distichs).
For every nation ... portion. This verse is of importance as illustrating the Jewish doctrine of God both in His relationship to Israel and to the Gentiles. By their acceptance of the Law the Israelites became God's 'peculiar people' (עם סגלה; cp. Deut. xiv. 2, xxvi. 18; Ps. cxxxv. 4), and were therefore His particular care (cp. the Sept. of Deut. xxii. 8, 9, 'But the Lord's portion was His people Jacob, the lot of His inheritance was Israel'). On the other hand, since He was the God of all the world, His interest in other nations could not be denied (cp. the Midrash *Sifre* 40: 'God doth not provide for Israel alone, but for all men'); thus the belief arose that, while God reserved the Israelites for His special care, He deputed angels to look after, and champion, the cause of other races. It is said, e.g. in the Targum of Pseudo-Jonathan to Gen. xi. 7, 8, that every nation has its own guardian angel who pleads the cause of the nation under his protection before God. It is interesting to observe that in later times even the divine guardianship over Israel was deputed to the archangel Michael; in *Ḥagigah* 12*b* (T. B.) he has the title of 'Advocate of the Jews'; and in the *Yalkut Shimeoni*, *Bereshith* 132, Michael is described as the prince over all the angels, because he is the guardian angel of the Israelite nation; he acts as Israel's representative and patron in the presence of God, and he intercedes there on behalf of his people.
For *v.* 18 see critical note.

𝔊 19 All their works [f]are [clear][f] as the sun before Him,
[g]And His eyes are continually upon their ways[g].
20 Their iniquities are not hid from Him,
And all [h]their sins[h] are [inscribed][i] before the Lord[k].
22 The righteousness[l] of men[m] [n]is to Him as a signet[n],
And the mercy[o] of man He preserveth[p] as the apple of an eye[q].
23 Afterwards [r]He will rise up[r] and recompense them,
And will visit[s] their deeds[t] upon their own head[u].
24 Nevertheless to them that repent doth He grant a return[v],
And [w]comforteth them that lose hope[w][x].

(*d*) XVII. 25–32. *An exhortation to turn to God and forsake sin* (= 2+2+2+2 distichs).

25 [y]Turn unto the Lord, [z]and forsake sins;
Supplicate before (His) face, and (so) lessen offence.
26 Turn unto the Most High, and turn away from iniquity[zz],
And vehemently hate the abominable thing[z].
𝔖 27 [a]For what pleasure hath God in all that perish[a] in Hades[b],
𝔊 In place of those who live and give Him praise?

not' (= *v.* 18) f–f *So* 𝔏 (*lit.* 'manifest'): 𝔖 'stand': 𝔊 > g–g 𝔖 'And all their thoughts are manifest before Him' h–h 𝔖 'the sins of men' i *So* 𝔖 *only* k 70 248 + 'But the Lord, being merciful, knowing also (that they are made in) His own image, spared them, and forsook them not nor cast them off' (= *v.* 21). l *Lit.* 'alms' m 𝔖 'of all men' n–n 𝔖 'is sealed and deposited with Him' o *Lit.* 'grace' p 𝔖 'is preserved' q 70 248 + 'granting (*lit.* allotting) repentance to his sons and daughters' r–r 𝔖 'shall He reveal Himself' s *Lit.* 'render' t *Lit.* 'retribution': 𝔖 'debts' u 𝔏 + 'and He will consign (*lit.* turn) them to the lower parts of the earth' v 𝔏 'a way of righteousness': 𝔖 'repentance' w–w 𝔖 'will destroy all who cause hurt to the righteous' x *Lit.* 'endurance': 𝔏 + 'and hath apportioned to them the lot of Truth' y 𝔏 *has the title* 'Concerning conversion': 248 'Therefore turn' z–z 𝔖 'and ye shall turn from destruction; turn from sin and cause not anger (unto the Lord)' zz 70 248 + 'For He Himself will lead (thee) out of darkness unto the light of salvation' (*lit.* 'health') a–a 𝔊 'who will praise the Most High in Hades': 𝔏 *has instead of v.* 27: 'and recognize the justice and judgements of God, and stand in the lot of the favour and prayer of the Most High; walk in the places of the holy world with the living and with those who give thanks unto God. Abide not in the folly of the wicked; confess (God) before death' b 𝔖 'the world': 70 248 + 'in heart'

---

19. **All their works...** Cp. xvi. 22; Eccles. viii. 9.
And His eyes... Cp. xxiii. 19; Ps. xciv. 11.
20. **Their iniquities...** Cp. Ps. xxxiii. 5, lxix. 5.
And all their sins... Cp. Jer. li. 5.
22. **righteousness.** ἐλεημοσύνη (=צדקה); almsgiving was reckoned as the greatest of the מעשים טובים ('good works'), and therefore righteousness *par excellence*. 𝔖 has זכותא, i.e. a state of justification in the sight of God brought about by the accomplishment of good works.
a signet. i.e. something which is especially precious; cp. xlix. 11; Job xiv. 17.
mercy. For χάρις (=חסד) used in reference to a human virtue see xl. 17, and cp. xiv. 1, where 𝔥 reads אנשי חסד, lit. 'men of mercy', for the Greek ἄνδρας ἐνδόξους.
He preserveth. i.e. He keeps in memory; cp. Acts x. 10: 'Thy prayers and thine alms are gone up for a memorial before God.'
the apple of an eye. Cp. Deut. xxxii. 10; Ps. xvii. 8; Prov. vii. 2; Zech. ii. 12.
23. **Afterwards...** The reference here is to those mentioned in *v.* 20; the words of *v.* 22 are parenthetic.
He will rise up. i.e. to judgement.
and will visit. For פקד על in this sense cp. Amos iii. 2, 14; Hos. i. 4, ii. 15, &c.
upon their own head. Cp. Joel iii. (Hebr. iv.) 4, 7.
24. **to them that repent...** Cp. *Shabbath* 32 *a* (T. B.): 'Repentance and works of charity are man's intercessors before the House of God'; and *Yoma* 86 *a*: 'Great is the power of repentance; for it reaches up to the throne of God; it brings healing...'
a return. i.e. to divine favour.
that lose hope. Cp. Hebr. of Ezek. xxxvii. 11.

(*d*) XVII. 25–32.
25. **Turn unto...** Cp. Ps. xc. 3; Mal. iii. 7.
Supplicate before (His) face. i.e. before the place in the temple where God's presence was believed to be, in the Holy of Holies.
offence. πρόσκομμα, cp. Rom. ix. 32, 33; 1 Cor. viii. 9.
26. **... the abominable thing.** Cp. xv. 13.
27. The thought is that God's delight is in those who live and can therefore praise Him, not in those who go down to Hades and are cut off from communion with Him; the teaching here coincides with the normal teaching of the O.T. (some passages in the Psalms show, however, a great development), that God's interest in man is restricted to this world; cp. the next verse.
... who live and give Him praise. Cp. Ps. cxvi. 2, cxx. 17, 18; Is. xxxviii. 18, 19.

𝔊 28 Thanksgiving perisheth from the dead as from one that is not,
(But) he that liveth and is in health praiseth the Lord[c].
29 How great is the mercy of the Lord[d],
And [e]His[f] forgiveness unto[e] them that turn unto Him[g].
𝔖 30 [h]For it is not like this in man,
Nor is (God's) thought like the thoughts of the children of men[h].
𝔊 31 What is brighter than the sun? Yet this faileth;
And (how much more) [i]man, who[i] (hath) the inclination[k] of flesh and blood!
32 He looketh upon [l]the hosts of heaven[l],
[m]And on men[m] who are dust and ashes.

(*e*) XVIII. 1–14. *The works of the Almighty are past finding out; the insignificance of man, and the magnanimity of God* (= 1 + 2 + 2 + 1 + 2 + 2 + 2 + 1 distichs).

18 1 He that liveth for ever created[a] all things together[b].
2 The Lord alone [c]shall be justified[c].
4 [de]Who is sufficient[e] to declare His works,
And who can trace out[f] His mighty deeds?

[c] 𝔏 + 'and thou shalt glory in His mercy' [d] 248 + 'our God' [e–e] 𝔖 'He forgiveth' [f] *Expressed in* 𝔏 *only* [g] 248 + 'holily' [h–h] 𝔊 𝔏 'For all things cannot be in men, for a son of man is not immortal': 𝔏 + 'and they take pride in the vanity of iniquity' [i–i] *Reading* αvηρ ος *instead of* πονηρος [k] *So* 𝔖: 𝔊 'thinketh', *reading* יצר *as a verb, cp.* xvii. 6, *where the verb is understood as a noun*: ℵ[c.a] και τι πονηροτερον ενθυμειται (= 𝔏): 70 253 και ανηρ ος ενθυμηθησεται (= Syro-Hex) [l–l] *So* 𝔖 [m–m] *So* 𝔖

[a] 𝔖 'tried', *or* 'proved' [b] 254 'by word (and) in order' [c–c] 70 248 'is just'; *adding*: 'and there is none other beside Him': 𝔏 + 'and He abideth as king, invincible for ever' [d] 70 248 *insert here*: 'who guideth the world in the hollow of His hand, and all things are obedient unto His will; for He is King of all things, and they are in His power; He separateth among them the holy things from the common' (= *v.* 3) [e–e] *So* 𝔖 𝔏: 𝔊 'to none' (248 'to whom') 'hath He given power' [f] 𝔖 'number'

---

28. The omission of this verse in 𝔖 is probably owing to the sentiments expressed, which would naturally be distasteful to a Christian translator.

Thanksgiving perisheth... Cp. Ps. vi. 5, xxviii. 1, xxx. 9, lxxxviii. 4, 5, cxv. 17.

29. **How great is...** Cp. Ps. lxxxvi. 5, 15.

forgiveness. ἐξιλασμός, lit. 'appeasement'; see further, note on xviii. 20.

30. The rendering of 𝔖 of this verse is to be preferred to that of 𝔊, according to which the meaning is that because man is imperfect and mortal, therefore he is entitled to appeal to God's mercy; 𝔖 accords better with the context.

it is not like this in man. Cp. xviii. 13.

Nor is (God's) thought... Cp. Isa. lv. 8, 9.

the children of men. 𝔊 υἱὸς ἀνθρώπου, i.e. a human being; cp. Judith viii. 12, the only other place in the Apocrypha where the expression occurs. (Cf. however 4 Ezra viii. 44, emended text.)

31. **What is brighter...** i.e. If the sun with all its brightness ceases at times to give light, is it to be wondered at that man, the victim of the manifold temptations which flesh is heir to, should sometimes fail? Logic of a somewhat similar incongruous character is found in Job xxv. 5, 6: 'Behold, even the moon hath no brightness, and the stars are not pure in His sight: how much less man, that is a worm! and the son of man, which is a worm!' But similes of the kind, especially in Oriental writers, must not, of course, be unduly pressed.

the man who (hath)... See critical notes.

𝔖 paraphrases the verse thus: 'When the sun, having run its course through the bright day, has sunk, it becomes dark; so also man, who, being flesh and blood, does not control his inclination' (יֵצֶר).

32. **the hosts of heaven.** Cp. xxiv. 2, xlii. 17; Deut. ix. 19, xvii. 3; Isa. xxiv. 21; 𝔊 'the power of the height of heaven', δύναμιν ὕψους οὐρανοῦ; in the Sept. δύναμις is the rendering of חַיִל even when it means 'a host'. Here the reference is to the sun, moon, and stars, regarded as eternal; God looks upon these as well as upon man who passes away.

on men. 𝔊, misunderstanding the point of the verse, viz. that God looks upon things eternal and also upon things transient, made an independent clause of the second half of the verse, and added 'all' to 'men'.

dust and ashes. Cp. x. 9; Gen. xviii. 27; Job xv. 14, 15.

(*e*) XVIII. 1–14.

XVIII. 1. **created.** ἔκτισεν, for which Ryssel would read κρίνει ('judgeth'), cp. 𝔖, and the reading of the cursives (see critical note) in *v.* 2; cp. the scribal error ἐν κρίσει for ἐν κτίσει in xvi. 26.

together. κοινῇ (= יחד as in l. 17), referring to Creation in its entirety.

2. **shall be justified.** δικαιωθήσεται, lit. 'shall be declared just'. For the additions to this verse see critical notes, and cp. Isa. xl. 12, 21; Ezek. xxii. 26.

4. **Who is sufficient...** Cp. i. 6. The similarity of language with that of the Psalms (Sept.) in this and the following verses is noteworthy.

to declare His works. ἐξαγγεῖλαι τὰ ἔργα αὐτοῦ; cp. Ps. cvi. 22 ἐξαγγειλάτωσαν τὰ ἔργα αὐτοῦ.

who can trace out. ἐξιχνιάσει; cp. Wisd. vi. 23.

His mighty deeds. Cp. Ps. lxx. 7 (Sept.).

𝔊 5 [g]Who can declare the might of His majesty,
And [gg]who can recount[gg] His[h] mercies[i]?
6 No man can take (from them) nor add (to them),
Nor can any one trace out the marvellous acts of the Lord[g].
7 When a man hath finished, then doth he but begin,
And when he ceaseth, he is in perplexity.
8 What is man, [m]and what profit is there of him[m]?
What is the good of him, and what is the evil?
9 The number of man's days
Is great (if it reach) an hundred years[n].
10 [o]As a drop of water[o] from the sea, or as[p] a grain[q] of sand,
[qq]So are [r](man's) few[r] years in the eternal days[s][qq].
11 Therefore is the Lord longsuffering towards them,
And poureth out His mercy upon them.
12 [t]He seeth[u] and knoweth[t] that their end[v] is evil,
Therefore doth He multiply His forgiveness[w].
13 The mercy of man is (exercised upon) his own kin[x],
But the mercy of God[y] is (extended) to all flesh[z],
Reproving, and chastening, and teaching[a],
And bringing them back as a shepherd his flock.
14 [b]He hath mercy on them that accept (His) chastening[b],
And that [c]diligently seek after[c] His judgements.

(*f*) XVIII. 15–18. *The right spirit in giving* (= 2 + 2 distichs).

15 [cc]My son, [d]bring no[e] blemish on thy good deeds[d],
[f]Nor in (giving) any gift[g] (cause) grief through words[f];

g–g 𝔖 > gg–gg 𝔊 *lit.* 'who shall add to make a description of' h C 'the Lord's' i C 'works': 307 μεγαλεια = נדלות, 'mighty works' m–m *So* 𝔖 'what is his loss and what is his gain?' n 70 248 + 'and eternal (*lit.* incalculable) is the sleep of such (which is common) to all' o–o 𝔖 'as when one fills a bottle' p *So* 70 248 𝔖 𝔏: 𝔊 > q *So* V 253 𝔖: 𝔊 𝔏 'pebble' qq–qq 𝔖 'So a thousand years of this world are not (even) as one day in the world of the righteous' r–r 248 'a thousand' s 𝔊 'in the day of eternity' (248 253 Syro-Hex 'days of') t–t 𝔖 'for He knew': ℵ c.a *places an asterisk before this v.* u 𝔏 + 'the pride of their heart, that it is evil' v *So* 𝔖: 𝔊 καταστροφη w 𝔖 + 'among them, and showed them the way of righteousness' (viam aequitatis) x *So* 𝔖: 𝔊 𝔏 'neighbour' y *So* 𝔖 𝔏: 𝔊 'the Lord' z 𝔖 'his works' a 𝔖 + 'them' b–b 𝔖 'Blessed are they that wait for His mercy': 𝔏 'He hath mercy on them that receive the teaching of mercy' c–c 𝔖 'accept' cc *ℵ has the title εγκρατεια ψυχης d–d 𝔖 'hinder not him that doeth a good deed to his neighbour' e 𝔊 *lit.* 'give not' f–f 𝔊 *lit.* 'nor in every gift grief of words'; *cp.* 𝔏 et in omni dato non des tristitiam verbi mali: 𝔖 'and on him that gives look not askance' g 248 'request'

---

5. **Who can declare.** τίς ἐξαριθμήσεται; cf. Ps. lxxxix. 12 (Sept.) = מנה.
who can recount. Cp. Isa. xlix. 16 (Sept.).
His mercies. Cp. Ps. xvi. 7 (Sept.).
6. **No man . . .** Lit. 'It is not (possible) to . . .'; so, too, in the next clause. Cp. xlii. 21 *c*.
the marvellous acts . . . Cp. Ps. lxxvi. 12, lxxvii. 12, lxxxvii. 11 (all in the Sept.).
7. **he is in perplexity.** i. e. because he realizes the impossibility of his task.
8. **What is man.** Cp. Ps. viii. 4 (Sept.),
what profit is there of him? i. e. that he should think it possible to trace out the wonderful works of God.
What is the good . . . i. e. neither are worth consideration in view of his insignificance in the sight of God.
9. **The number . . .** Cp. Ps. xc. 10. The addition to this verse (see critical note) probably represents something which the original contained; cp. with it Eccles. ix. 5, 6.
10. **As a drop of water . . .** Cp. Isa. xl. 15.
So are . . . i. e. man's few years of life are like a day compared with eternity.
11. **Therefore.** Because his time is short and fleeting.
12. **end.** Lit. 'overthrow'.
doth He multiply. Cp. Ps. xxxv. 8 (Sept.).
13. **his own kin.** See critical note. Cp. Peshitta of Lev. xviii. 6 (= שאר בשרו, lit. 'flesh of his flesh', i. e. 'near of kin'), quoted by Ryssel; cp. also Lev. xxv. 49.
as a shepherd. Cp. Isa. xl. 11.
14. **He hath mercy . . .** Cp. xxxii. (𝔊 xxxv.) 14.
chastening. i. e. 'instruction' which is given by means of chastening; cp. vi. 32, 33.
(*f*) XVIII. 15–18.
15. **Nor in (giving) . . .** i. e. do not humiliate the receiver of charity.

𝔊 16 [h]Just as[h] the rain[i] maketh the burning heat to cease;
[k]So a word changeth[l] (the character of) a gift[k].
17 [m]For there is a good word which is better than a gift[m],
And both belong to a saintly[n] man.
18 A fool upbraideth ungraciously[o],
And the gift of an envious[p] man consumeth[q] the eyes.

(*g*) XVIII. 19–29. *The need of foresight and preparation in view of many things which happen to men; this is true Wisdom* (= 3+2+3+1+2 distichs).

𝔖 19 [r]Before thou fight, seek thee a helper[r];
[s]Before thou art ill, seek thee a physician[s].
𝔊 20 [t]Before judgement [u]examine thyself[u][t],
And in the [v]hour of visitation[v] thou shalt find forgiveness[w].
21 Before thou fall[x], [y]humble thyself[y],
And [z]in the time of[z] (committing) sins, [a]show forth repentance[a].
22 Delay not[b] [c]to pay thy vow in due time[c],
[d]And wait not till death to be justified[d].

h–h *So* 𝔖: 𝔊 'doth not' i *So* 𝔖: 𝔊 *lit.* 'dew' k–k *So* 𝔖 l *Lit.* 'turneth': 𝔊𝔏 'is greater than' m–m *So* 𝔖: 𝔊𝔏 'Lo, is not a word above a good gift?' n *So* 𝔖: 𝔊𝔏 'gracious' o 𝔖 'before he doeth a gracious act' p 𝔊 *properly* 'evil-eyed': 𝔖 'evil' q *Lit.* 'melteth'; 𝔏 'maketh to waste away' r–r *So* 𝔖; 𝔊 'before speaking learn': 𝔏 'before judgement prepare justice for thyself,' *cp.* 20 *a* s–s *So* 𝔖: 𝔊 *lit.* 'before sickness heal': 𝔏 'and before thou speak learn, and before sickness apply to a physician' t–t 𝔖 'and before sorrow come upon thee, pray' u–u 248 'prepare thyself by well-doing' v–v 𝔏 'sight of God' w 𝔖 + 'and it shall help thee' x *So* 𝔖: 𝔊𝔏 'art sick' y–y 𝔖 'pray and beseech': 70 248 + 'with self-control' z–z 𝔖 'before' a–a 𝔖 'give alms' b 𝔊 *lit.* 'be not hindered' c–c 𝔖 'to cause thy sins to pass away': 𝔏 'to pray unceasingly' 𝔖 *inserts here two clauses:* 'be not careless until thou art in trouble, put not off the time of turning from thy sins' d–d 𝔖 'remember that death delayeth not': 𝔏 +'for

---

16. **Just as the rain . . .** Cp. xliii. 23.
17. **For there is a good word . . .** Cowley and Neubauer quote *Baba Bathra* 9 *b* (T. B.): 'He who giveth a farthing is blessed sixfold, but he who addeth words elevenfold'; the 'word' refers to the encouragement and words of cheer addressed to the recipient.

And both belong . . . Words as well as acts mark the truly charitable man.

18. **A fool . . .** He is a 'fool' because the efficacy of the gift in the sight of God is done away with by the churlish remark which accompanies it.

consumeth . . . The reference is to the humiliation suffered by him who receives when the gift is accompanied by cruel words; for the expression in Gr. cp. Lev. xxvi. 16.

(*g*) XVIII. 19–29.

19. 𝔖 is to be preferred in this verse; cp. 𝔏 (see critical note).

seek thee a physician. Cp. xxxviii. 12–15.

20. **Before judgement.** i. e. the judgement of God; the reference is to the 'hour of visitation' in the next clause; see note on vii. 35.

thou shalt find forgiveness. ἐξιλασμόν ('propitiation'). According to Jewish teaching suffering and sickness, as well as death itself, are in themselves means of atonement, and therefore of reconciliation with God, though the need of repentance as well is often insisted upon in Rabbinical writings. In the Midrash *Sifre* 73 *b* (belonging to the second century A. D.) it is said that a man should rejoice more in chastisement than in prosperity, because if he enjoyed good fortune all his life his sins would not be forgiven him. In the same Midrash (33 *a*) a saying is quoted to the effect that 'All who die are reconciled through death'. Very pointed are the words in the Midrash *Bereshith Rabba* 5 *a*: 'Suffering is more apt than sacrifice to win God's favour and to atone for man.' Teaching of this kind is only adumbrated by Ben-Sira, but it was greatly developed and elaborated by later teachers.

21. **humble thyself.** Cp. xxxiv. 26 (𝔊 xxxi. 31).

show forth repentance. Repentance is also, according to Jewish teaching, a mediating agency; cp. *Yoma* 86 *b* (T. B.), where it is said that repentance 'brings redemption, and is the cause of God's regarding sins as though they had been unconsciously committed, and even of His regarding them as good works and (therefore) meritorious. It prolongs the days and years of men.' Cp. also *Shabbath* 32 *a* (T. B.): 'Repentance and works of charity are man's intercessors before the House of God'; and *Sanhedrin* 43 *b* (T. B.): 'He who sincerely repents is doing as much as he who builds temple and altar, and brings all sacrifices.'

22. **Delay not to pay . . .** See critical note; perhaps the rendering of 𝔖 is to be preferred, for it seems to accord better with the words of the second clause; vowing is dealt with in the next verse. Smend adds the distich from 𝔖 to the text between verses 21 and 22. (See crit. note c–c.)

wait not till death to . . . As in the later Rabbinical literature (cf. on *v.* 20), Death is regarded as a means of atonement.

ℌ[A] 23 [e]Before thou vowest, prepare thy vows[ee],
And be not as one [f]that tempteth God[f e].
𝔊 24 Think of the wrath in the [g]latter day[g],
And (when), in the time of vengeance, He turneth away His face.
25 Remember [h]the time of famine[h] in the time[i] of fullness,
And poverty and want in the days of wealth.
26 From morning until evening the time changeth,
And all things[k] haste on[l] before the Lord.
27 [m]A wise man is discreet[n] in all things[o m],
And in days of sinning [p]keepeth himself from offence[p].
𝔖 28 [q]Every wise man teacheth[r] wisdom[s],
[t]And they who know her must give thanks[t q].
𝔊 29 They that are wise in words[u] also show that they are wise,
[v]In that they pour forth apt proverbs[v].

(*a*) XVIII. 30—XIX. 3. *An Exhortation to Self-control in all things* (= 2 + 3 + 2 distichs).

30 [w]My son[x], follow not the lusts of thy soul[y],
And refrain thyself [z]from its desire[z].
𝔖 31 [a]If thou fulfil the desire of thy soul,
Thou wilt be like him that fulfilleth his enemy's wish[a].
ℌ[C] 32 [b]Delight not thyself in overmuch luxury,
[c]For double is the poverty thereof[c].
33 Be not a squanderer and a drunkard,
Else there will be nothing in thy purse[d].

the reward of God abideth to eternity' [e–e] *So* ℌ, *of which this verse is extant* [ee] 𝔊 σεαυτον, *a correction of* την ψυχην σου (𝔏 animam tuam), *which is a mistake for* την ευχην σου (= 𝔖 *plur.*) [f–f] *So according to Smend's emendation* (= 𝔖 𝔏); *the text is corrupt* [g–g] *Lit.* ' days of the end' (א 'day') [h–h] 𝔏 'poverty' [i] A 254 𝔖 'days' [k] 70 248 𝔏 'these things' [l] *Lit.* 'are speedy' [m–m] 248 > [n] 𝔖 'is concerned' [o] 𝔖 'these things' [p–p] 𝔖 'feareth no evil': 70 248 + 'and the fool observeth not (248 > 'not') the opportunity' [q–q] *So* 𝔖: 𝔊 'every man of understanding knoweth, &c.' [r] 𝔊 𝔏 'knoweth' [s] 70 248 + 'and instruction' [t–t] 𝔊 𝔏 'and to him that findeth her he will give thanks' [u] 𝔖 'in teaching' [v–v] 𝔖 𝔏 *are paraphrastic*: 70 248 + 'unto life:' 248 *adds further* 'Better is trust (*lit.* boldness) in a single master (*i. e.* God), than with a dead heart to cling to a dead one (*i. e.* an idol)' [w] א A B C (> C[a]) 70 248 254 307 *have the title* 'Self-control of the soul' [x] *So* 𝔖 [y] *So* 𝔖 [z–z] *So* 𝔖: 𝔊 'from thine appetites': 𝔏 'from thy will' [a–a] *So* 𝔖: 𝔊 'If thou grant to thy soul the delight of (her) desire thou wilt make thee a rejoicing to thine enemies' (248 + 'who bear thee malice') [b] ℌ *is extant from here to* xix. 3 [c–c] 𝔊[B] 'neither be tied to the expense thereof': B μη προσδεθης *should be read with* א* A C μη προσδεηθης ('that thou be not in need besides'): 𝔖 'that thou become not twice as poor' [d] 70 248 𝔏 *add, with slight*

---

23. This verse is quoted in *Tanchuma* וישלח 13 *a* (Smend).
prepare. i.e. think over, so as not to vow rashly.
And be not as one that . . . In making a rash vow a man tempts God; for rash vows are not likely to be kept, and divine punishment will ensue on their being broken. Cp. Deut. vi. 16.
24. **in the latter day.** i.e. the day of death; cp. i. 13, xi. 26–8.
He turneth away His face. Lit. 'In the turning away', i.e. when God turns away His face, or 'hideth His face'; cp. Deut. xxxi. 17, 18, xxxii. 20; Ps. x. 10, xxx. 7, meaning that He repudiates the sinner.
25. **Remember . . .** Because evil days may come quite unexpectedly; cp. next verse; the reference is quite general.
26. **From morning . . .** i.e. within the space of a single day all may be changed; cp. Job iv. 19–21.
before the Lord. i.e. it is the will of God.
27. **is discreet.** εὐλαβηθήσεται, cf. Prov. xxviii. 14 (Sept.).
in days of sinning. i.e. when a man has succumbed to temptation and committed sin.
28. See critical notes.
29. **They that are wise . . .** i.e. their utterances proclaim their wisdom.
In that they . . . Perhaps in reference to the writer himself, who has just been pouring forth apt proverbs.

XVIII. 30—XX. 26. Warnings against various faults. This division contains nine subsections.

(*a*) XVIII. 30—XIX. 3.
30. The title in 𝔊 runs: Ἐγκράτεια ψυχῆς. In one or other of the Gr. MSS. titles are found before xix. 29, xx. 27, xxiv. 1, xxx. 1, 16, xliv. 1, li. 1; probably none of these belonged to the original.
the lusts of thy soul. Cp. 2 Tim. ii. 22; Jas. i. 14.
31. See critical note.
32. **For double is . . .** i.e. poverty in purse and poverty in health.
33. **Be not . . .** 𝔊 paraphrases: 'Be not made a beggar by banqueting upon borrowing'; this, when taken, as it must be, with the following clause, makes it tautologous.

ℌ^c **19** 1 He that doeth this will not become rich,
And [dd]he that despiseth small things[dd] [e]will become wholly poor[e].
2 Wine and women make the heart lustful,
𝔊 [f]And he that cleaveth to harlots [g]will perish[g][f].
3 [h]Moulder[i] and worms [k]will take possession of him[k][h],
ℌ^C [l]And a brazen soul will destroy its owner[l].

(*b*) XIX. 4–12. *A warning against too much talking* (= 2 + 3 + 3 distichs).

𝔊 4 [m]He that is hasty in reposing confidence [n]is unwise[n],
[o]And he that erreth sinneth against his own soul[o].
5 He that hath pleasure in wickedness[p] [q]shall be brought to destruction[q],
6 [r]And he that hateth[s] gossip is without malice[t].
7 Never repeat a word[u],—
[v]Then no one will reproach thee[v]—
8 [vv]Speak not of it to[vv] friend or foe—
Unless it be a sin to thee [w]reveal it not[w]—
𝔖 9 [x]Lest he who hear thee hate thee,
And regard thee as an evil-doer[x].
𝔊 10 Hast thou heard something[y]? let it die with thee[z];
[a]Be of good courage, it will not burst thee[a].
11 A fool travaileth in pain [b]because of[b] a word,
As a woman in labour [b]because of[b] a child.

variations, 'For thou wilt become a snare unto thine own life and much talked about' dd–dd 𝔖 'he that loveth the flesh' e–e *Lit.* 'will become altogether naked': 𝔖 'will inherit poverty': *the rendering of* 𝔊 (κατα μικρον πεσειται) *is due to a doublet* f–f ℌ > g–g *So* 𝔖: 𝔊 'will become reckless' (B A 'more reckless'): 𝔏 'will become bad (nequam)' h–h ℌ 𝔖 > i *So* B ℵ^{c.a} A C (σηπη): B^b *followed by R.V.* σητες (ℵ* σηπες) k–k 𝔊 *lit.* 'will inherit him' l–l *So* ℌ 𝔖: 70 248 'and he shall be destroyed as (*lit.* in) a terrible (*lit.* greater) example' m ℌ *is wanting from here to* xx. 4 n–n *So* 𝔖, *lit.* 'wanting in understanding': 𝔊 *lit.* 'empty of heart' o–o 𝔖 'He who accuseth his own soul, who will hold him guiltless?' p *So* ℵ* V 253 𝔏 Syro-Hex: B A C ℵ^{c.a} 70 'in his heart': 248 𝔖 'in evil living' q–q *So* 𝔖: 𝔊 'he shall be condemned': 70 248 + 'he that averteth his eye from pleasures crowneth his life' r 70 248 *insert* 'and he that controlleth his tongue liveth without strife' s 𝔖 'repeateth' t 𝔖 'understanding' (= A 'heart'): 𝔏 'life'. *In* 𝔏 *the text of this verse has got out of order* u 𝔏 'an evil and cruel (*lit.* hard) word': ℵ^{c.a} 253 + 'in ('thy' 253) prayer' v–v *So* 𝔖: 𝔊 'and thou wilt derive no disadvantage' vv–vv 𝔖 'deceive not' w–w 𝔖 '(then) pray for them, but accuse no one' x–x *So* 𝔖, *which on the whole is preferable to* 𝔊 'For if he hear thee he will guard himself from thee, and will hate thee (*i. e.* show himself thine enemy) at the (fitting) time' y *Lit.* 'a word': 𝔏 + 'against thy neighbour' z 𝔖 'in thy heart' a–a 𝔖 'it is not an arrow (*cp. v.* 12 a) that it should pierce through thee and come bursting forth' b–b *Lit.* 'in face of'

XIX. 1. **He that doeth this.** 𝔊 'A workman that is a drunkard'; cp. Prov. xxi. 17, xxiii. 21.

he that despiseth . . . It is not easy to see the connexion between the two clauses of this verse; this want of connexion probably accounts for the reading of 𝔖 (see critical note), which is apparently an attempt to make sense. Possibly these words are to be explained in the light of Eccles. x. 1: 'Dead flies cause the ointment of the perfumer to send forth a stinking savour,' i. e. looking upon any sins as venial must have evil results.

2. **Wine and women . . .** Cp. Hos. iv. 11; Prov. xxxi. 3–7.

make the heart . . . 𝔊 'make men of understanding to fall away' is a toning down of the directness of ℌ.

3. **Moulder and worms . . .** Cp. Prov. v. 5, vii. 26, 27, ix. 18.

a brazen soul. נפש עזה. Cp. vi. 4, xix. 3, and a similar phrase עַזֵּי־נֶפֶשׁ in Isa. lvi. 11. 𝔊 'And a reckless soul shall be taken away' is a free paraphrase; for τολμηρός cp. viii. 15.

(*b*) XIX. 4–12.

4. **He that is . . . confidence.** ὁ ταχὺ ἐνπιστεύων; cp. vi. 7 μὴ ταχὺ ἐμπιστεύσῃς, where the Hebr. has אל תמהר לבטח.

unwise. κοῦφος is not found elsewhere in the O.T. in this sense.

against his own soul. Cp. Prov. xx. 2 (Sept.).

5. **He that hath pleasure in wickedness.** The reading of ℵ* πονηρά is evidently the more correct one (see critical note). The addition in 70 248 may well contain an echo of the original.

6. See critical note.

7. **Never repeat.** Cp. xlii. 1.

Then no one . . . Cp. Prov. xxv. 10.

8. **Speak not of it.** Cp. 1 Pet. ix. 15. Possibly 𝔖 represents a more original text, 'Deceive not friend or foe.'

Unless it be a sin to thee. i. e. unless by keeping silence thou become a partaker in another's guilt.

9. **Lest he who . . .** Cp. Prov. xxv. 10. With 𝔊 (see critical note) cp. xxii. 26.

10. **it will not burst thee.** Cp. Job xxxii. 18, 19 (Hebr. and Sept.).

11. **because of a word.** ἀπὸ προσώπου λόγου = מלפני דבר.

𝔊 12 Like[c] an arrow that sticketh in the fleshy thigh,
So is a word in the [d]inward parts[d] of a fool.

(*c*) XIX. 13–17. *On taking a friend to task on any matter* (= 3 + 2 distichs).

13 Reprove a friend[e], [f]that he do no evil[f],
And if he have done anything, [g]that he do it not again[g].
14 Reprove a friend[h] [i]lest he speak[i] [evil],
And if he have said (it), that he do it not again.
15 Reprove a friend[k], for often there is slander[l],
And [m]believe not[m] every word.
16 [n]Many a man[n] there is that slippeth[o], [p]though unintentionally[p],
And who hath not sinned[q] with his tongue!
17 [r]Reprove thy[s] friend[r] [t]before thou threaten him[t],
[u]And give place to the law[v] of the Most High[u w].

(*d*) XIX. 20–30. *The Difference between Wisdom and Craftiness* (= 2 + 3 + 3 + 2 distichs).

20 [x]All wisdom is [y]the fear of[y] the Lord,
[z]And all wisdom is the fulfilling of the Law[z].
22 [a]But the knowledge of wickedness is not wisdom[a],
[b]And the counsel of sinners is not understanding[b].
23 There is a prudence[bb], [c]and the same is abomination[c],
And there is a fool [d]who is without[d] sins[e].
24 Better is one that hath small understanding, and feareth,
Than one that hath much prudence and transgresseth the Law.

[c] *So* 𝔖 [d–d] *So* 𝔖: 𝔊 'belly'; 𝔏 'heart' [e] 𝔖 'thy friend' [f–f] *So* 𝔖: 𝔊 'it may be he did it not' [g–g] 𝔏 'and shall not have perceived it, and he say, I did it not' [h] א C 253 𝔖 Syro-Hex 'thy neighbour' [i–i] *So* 𝔖: 𝔊 'it may be he said (it) not' [k] 𝔖 'thy friend' [l] 248 𝔖 'mere (*lit.* vain) slander' [m–m] 248 𝔖 'let not thine heart believe' [n–n] *Lit.* 'one' [o] 𝔖 'sinneth': 70 248 + 'in word': 𝔏 + 'with his tongue' [p–p] *Lit.* 'not from the soul' [q] 70 248 𝔖 'slipped' [r–r] 𝔖 'rebuke the evil man' (*reading* רַע *instead of* רֵעַ = 𝔊 'neighbour') [s] א 70 248 𝔏 > [t–t] 𝔖 'for he hath oppressed many' [u] 𝔖 'and believe not every word of his' [v] 𝔏 'fear' [w] 70 248 + 'being without wrath.' *These also insert here:* 'The fear of the Lord is the beginning of acceptance (by Him), and wisdom will gain love from Him. The knowledge of the commandments of the Lord is life-giving instruction (*lit.* instruction of life); and they who do the things that are pleasing unto Him shall pluck the fruit of the tree of immortality' (= *vv.* 18, 19) [x] 𝔖 *inserts* 'The words of prophecy and': 𝔏 *inserts* 'Because' [y–y] C 248 'from' [z–z] 𝔊 *lit.* 'and in all wisdom is the doing of the Law': 𝔖𝔏 'and the fear of God, that is wisdom'; 70 248 + 'and the knowledge of His omnipotence', *to which is added* 'A servant that saith unto his lord, I will not do according to thy will, though he do so afterwards, angereth him that feedeth him' (= *v.* 21) [a–a] 𝔖 'There is no wise man who is evil' [b–b] *So* א* A C 𝔖 𝔏: B א[c.a] 'and it is not (found) where the counsel of sinners (is deemed) prudence' [bb] *Reading* πανουργια (70 253) *instead of* πονηρια (*see exegetical notes*) [c–c] 𝔖 'that createth sins' [d–d] *Lit.* 'who is wanting in' [e] *So* 𝔖: 𝔊𝔏 'wisdom'

---

12. **inward parts of.** בתוך מעי (Edersheim).

(*c*) XIX. 13–17.

13. **Reprove . . .** Here in the sense of 'exhort'; if the reading of 𝔊 be accepted then it has the force of 'examine'. In these verses the various meanings of ἐλέγχειν are well illustrated.

14. **Reprove.** i. e. expostulate with, or the like.

15. **Reprove.** i. e. find out the truth concerning him.

16. **that slippeth.** Cp. xx. 18, xxi. 7, xxv. 8, xxviii. 26.

17. **Reprove.** i. e. call to account.

give place to the law. i. e. Lev. xix. 17.

18, 19. See critical note.

(*d*) XIX. 20–30.

20. **the fulfilling of the Law.** Cp. Jas. i. 25.

22. **the knowledge of wickedness . . .** Cp. Wisd. i. 4, 5.

23. **There is a prudence.** Although πανουργία ('subtlety', or 'prudence') is rarely used in a good sense, it is best to adopt this here. 'Subtlety,' as a form of wisdom, may be good; but in the sense of craft or sharp dealing it is bad. It is in this latter sense that it is spoken of as 'an abomination'.

And there is a fool . . . The meaning of the verse may be expressed thus: On the one hand, there is a good type of wisdom which can be made bad; on the other, there is a bad type of man which may be good—i. e. prudence, good in itself, may take the form of craft, and thus become bad; while, to be a fool, bad in itself, may take the form of guilelessness, and thus become good.

24. What has just been said is illustrated by this verse.

that hath small understanding. ἡττώμενος ἐν συνέσει, cp. iii. 13, xiii. 8, xxv. 2.

𝔊 25 There is [f]a subtle (form of) craftiness which is unrighteous[f],
[g]And there is the man who[g] dealeth tortuously to gain[h] a judgement[i].
26 There is one that walketh[k] [l]bent and mournfully[m][l],
But inwardly he is full of deceit[n].
27 There is[nn] one with downcast look, [o]pretending to be deaf[o],
But [p]when unobserved[p], [q]he will get the better of thee[q];
28 And there is one who[qq], if for want of power he be hindered from sinning,
Will do harm when he findeth opportunity.
29 A man is known by his appearance,
And the wise man recognizeth[r] him by his look[s],
30 A man's attire [t]proclaimeth his occupation[t],
And his gait[v] showeth what he is.

(*e*) XX. 1–8. *There is a time for silence and a time for speech* (= 3 + 2 + 2 distichs).

20 1 There is a reproof that is uncalled for[a],
Then he that is silent is wise.
𝔖 2 [b]He that reproveth a sinner getteth no thanks[b],
But let him that maketh confession [c]be spared humiliation[c].
𝔥[B] 4 [d]As is an eunuch that sojourneth with a virgin[dd],
So is he that would do right with violence[e].
𝔥[C] 5 [f]One[f] keepeth silence, and is accounted[g] wise,
[f]And another[f] is despised for his much talking.

f–f 𝔖 'a crafty man who rejoiceth in deceiving' g–g 𝔊 *lit.* 'and there is one that . . .': 𝔖 'and there is one that acteth perversely' h 𝔊 *lit.* 'to bring to light' i 248 + 'and there is a wise man who justifieth the judgement' k *Reading with two cursives*, πορευομενος (= Syro-Hex), *instead of* πονηρευομενος l–l 𝔖 'humbly and broken in spirit' m 𝔊 *lit.* 'with black' n 248 'burning deceit' nn *So* 𝔖 𝔏: 𝔊 > o–o 𝔖 'planning evil' p–p *Lit.* 'where he is not known' q–q *Lit.* 'he will be beforehand with thee': 70 248 + 'to harm (thee)' qq *So* 𝔖: 𝔊 𝔏 'And' r *So* 𝔖: 𝔊 'shall be known' s *Omitting with* 𝔖 απο απαντησεως t–t *So* 𝔖 ('occupation,' *lit.* 'deeds'): 𝔊 *lit.* 'and laughter of the teeth' v 𝔖 'appearance': 𝔊 *lit.* 'the footsteps of a man': ℵ[c.a] 'the step of the foot'

a *Lit.* 'not comely' b–b *So* 𝔖: 𝔊 𝔏 'how good it is to reprove rather than to be wroth': 70 248 + 'in secret' c–c *Lit.* 'be kept back from hurt'. *The interpolation* (= *v.* 3), *which* 70 248 *place after v.* 8, 𝔏 *after v.* 4, *but which logically belongs here, runs*: 'How good it is when he who is reproved manifesteth repentance, for thus wilt thou escape wilful sin' d 𝔥 *is extant from here to v.* 7 *incl.* dd 𝔥 + 'And the Lord will seek it at his hand' e 𝔥 *wrongly transposes the clauses of this verse: the whole verse has got misplaced;* 𝔥 B b mg, *several cursives*, Syro-Hex *place the second clause after* XXX. 20 f–f *Lit.* 'there is (one) that': *so frequently*

---

25. **dealeth tortuously.**] What the Greek is intended to express here is uncertain; διαστρέφων χάριν is lit. 'that distorts grace' (R.V. 'that perverteth favour'); but it is best to take χάριν (= the Hebr. למען, 'for the sake of') with τοῦ ἐκφᾶναι, and to regard διαστρέφων as the rendering of מתפתל ('that dealeth tortuously'); cp. the Septuagint of Ps. xviii. 28, 2 Sam. xxii. 27; διατέψεις = תתפתל (cp. also Deut. xxxii. 5); the clause then forms a good parallel to the other half of the verse.

26. See critical note, and cp. xii. 11.

that walketh bent and mournfully. Cf. Ps. xlii. 10; Mal. iii. 14.

full of deceit. πλήρης δόλου: cp. Acts xiii. 10 πλήρης παντὸς δόλου.

27. **one with downcast look.** συνκύφων πρόσωπον: cp. Job ix. 27 συνκύψας τῷ προσώπῳ.

28. 𝔖 is probably right, as against 𝔊, in not joining this verse on to the preceding.

30. **And his gait . . .** In the Babylonian Talmud directions are given as to how the inner worth of a man may be gauged by his outward appearance and behaviour, *Berakhoth* 43 *b*, *Erubin* 65 *b* (Ryssel).

(*e*) XX. 1–8. With this subsection cp. xix. 4–17.

2. **He that reproveth . . .** In this clause the rendering of 𝔖 is to be preferred as fitting in better with the context than 𝔊.

thanks. Cp. xii. 3, where the Hebr. טובה has the sense of 'thanks'.

But let him . . . Cp. viii. 5.

For *v.* 3 see critical note.

4. The point of the comparison is that in neither case is the design accomplished.

right. Lit. 'judgement'. 𝔊 for the second clause, 'So is he that executeth judgements with violence,' taking משפט in a legal sense. For the phrase עשה משפט, i. e. 'to do justice,' 'maintain the cause' of some one, see 1 Kings viii. 45, 49; Ps. ix. 5.

5. **One keepeth silence . . .** Cp. Prov. xvii. 28, *Pirqe Aboth* i. 18: 'Simon [the son of Gamaliel I] said, "All my days I have grown up amongst the wise, and have not found aught good for a man but silence; not learning, but doing, is the groundwork; and whoso multiplies words occasions sin."'

ℌ[c] 6 One keepeth silence, having naught to say;
And another keepeth silence, for he seeth (it is) a time (for silence).
7 The wise man is silent until the (proper) time,
But [h]the arrogant and the scorner[h] [i]take no note[i] of the time.
𝔊 8 *He that is abundant in word is abhorred[k],
And he that taketh to himself authority[l] is hated[m].

(*f*) XX. 9–17. *Things are not always what they seem* (= 2 + 3 + 3 + 2 distichs).

9 [n o]Sometimes it is advantageous[o] for a man[p] to be in adversity[n],
[q]And sometimes prosperity resulteth in harm[q].
10 [r]Sometimes a gift there is that profiteth thee nothing,
And sometimes a gift bringeth double recompense.
11 Sometimes cometh loss[s] through honour,
[t]And sometimes honour cometh through loss[t r].
12 [u uu]Some buy[uu] much for little[u],
And some pay sevenfold.
ℌ[c] 13 [v]The wise man with few words [vv]maketh himself beloved[vv],
But the pleasantries of fools are wasted[w].
𝔊 14 The gift of a fool profiteth thee nothing[x],
[y]For he looketh for recompense[z] sevenfold[a y];
15 He giveth little, and upbraideth much,
And openeth his mouth [b]like a crier[b];
To-day he lendeth, to-morrow he will demand it back:
Hateful is such an one [c]to God and men[c].

[g] 𝔊 𝔏 'found' [h–h] ℌ 'the fool': *the text is corrupt, for* וכסיל *read* וחד ולץ (*Smend*): 𝔊 'the braggart and the fool': 𝔖 'the arrogant and the unrighteous': 𝔏 'the haughty and the shameless' [i–i] *So* ℌ 𝔖 𝔏: 𝔊 'oversteppeth' * ℌ *is wanting from here to v.* 12 *incl.* [k] 𝔏 'injureth his soul' [l] 𝔏 + 'unjustly' [m] 𝔖 'his life will be hated': 70 248 + 'How good it is when he who is reproved manifesteth repentance, for thus wilt thou escape voluntary sin': *see v.* 2 *above* (*note*) [n–n] 𝔖 'there is that which is to a man's hurt' [o–o] 𝔊 *lit.* 'there is prosperity' [p] 70 248 𝔏 + 'that is a sinner' [q–q] 𝔊 *lit.* 'And there is a gain that turneth to loss' [r–r] *In place of these two verses* 𝔖 *has*: 'For as thou throwest a stone at a bird, thus causing it to fly, so dost thou destroy the friendship of thy true friend, and findest it no more' (= xxii. 20 + xxvii. 25, *Hart*) [s] 𝔊 *lit.* 'humiliation' [t–t] 𝔊 *lit.* 'And there is (the man) that hath lifted up his head from a low estate' [u–u] 𝔖 'One lendeth much like (*i.e.* as though it were) little' [uu–uu] 𝔊 *lit.* 'There is (the man) that buyeth' [v] *This verse is extant in* ℌ, *but is placed after* xxxvii. 26: 𝔖 *omits it* [vv–vv] *So* 𝔊, *inadvertently omitted in* ℌ [w] *Reading* ישפכו: ℌ 'poureth forth wisdom', *an obviously corrupt text*: 𝔊 *lit.* 'are poured out': ℌ *is wanting from here to* xxi. 21 *incl.* [x] 70 248 + '(who) receivest (it); so is it with the niggard who only giveth under compulsion' [y–y] 𝔊 *lit.* 'For his eyes are many instead of one': 248 *adds* 'with a view to receive' [z] *So* 𝔖 [a] *So* 𝔖 𝔏 [b–b] 𝔖 'and speaketh evil and lieth' [c–c] *So* 248 𝔖: 𝔊 𝔏 >

6. **having naught to say.** 𝔊 'for he hath no answer'; the discussions of the wise often took the form of question and answer; cp. Prov. xv. 23 *a*, xvi. 1 *b*.
7. **The wise man . . .** Cp. xx. 20 *b*; Eccles. iii. 7.
take no note. 𝔊 'oversteppeth', but in xviii. 27 ℌ is followed by 70 248 (see critical note there).
8. **he that taketh . . .** i. e. He who arrogates to himself the sole right to speak. For the addition to this verse in some Gr. MSS. and 𝔏 see critical note.
(*f*) XX. 9–17.
9. **prosperity.** Lit. 'gain', εὕρεμα, cp. xxix. 6 *b*.
10. **a gift.** i. e. which is given to another.
11. **honour.** Lit. 'glory'. With the verse cp. 1 Sam. ii. 4.
12. The original text probably presented a contrast, as indicated in the text; according to 𝔊 the meaning would be that a man thinks he has made a good bargain, but finds that he is ultimately a good deal worse off: 'There is that buyeth much for little, and payeth for it sevenfold,' i. e. apparent good fortune is in reality a loss.
13. This verse forms the antithesis to *v.* 8.
pleasantries. χάριτες, lit. 'kindnesses', cp. xxix. 15.
wasted. i. e. thrown away; for the Hebr. cp. Lam. iv. 1.
14. **profiteth thee nothing.** Because what is expected in return is much more than what has been received. The 'fool' is here, according to Ben-Sira, a rogue as well as a simpleton.
15. **He giveth little . . .** In *Berakhoth* iv. 2 (T. J.) reference is made to those 'who give little, and reprove much' (quoted by Smend).
upbraideth much. Cp. xviii. 18; the upbraiding refers to the reproaches made because he does not receive back as much as he expected.
And openeth . . . i. e. he complains to all the world.
Hateful . . . to God and men. Cp. x. 7.

𝕲 16 The fool saith: 'I have no friend,
And my good deeds receive no thanks;
They that eat my bread are evil-tongued[d].'
17 How oft—and how many there are—they laugh him to scorn[e].

(*g*) XX. 18–20. *Concerning unseasonable speech* (= 3 distichs).

18 [fg]A slip on the pavement is better than a (slip) of the tongue[g];
So doth the fall of the wicked come swiftly[f].
𝕾 19 [h]As the fat tail of a sheep, eaten without salt,
So is a word spoken out of season[h].
𝕲 20 A parable from the mouth of a fool is worthless[i],
For he uttereth it out of season.

(*h*) XX. 21–23. *Some are unintentionally without sin, while others sin intentionally* (= 3 distichs).

21 One, through want, is hindered from sinning,
[k]And when he resteth he will not be troubled[k];
22 Another destroyeth his life through sense of shame,
And perisheth[l] through [m]his want of frankness[m].
23 And another, for shame's sake, maketh promises to a friend,
[n]Thus making for himself[n] an enemy [o]without reason[o].

(*i*) XX. 24–26. *The Liar shall be destroyed* (= 3 distichs).

24 A lie is a foul blot in a man,
It is continually [found] in the mouth of the ignorant.
25 [p]Preferable is a thief to one who continually lieth[p],
[q]But both shall inherit destruction[q].

[d] 𝕲 *lit.* 'evil with their tongue': 𝕾 'like a rock of stone' [e] 70 248 + 'For he hath not honestly received [that which he possesseth]; likewise that which he hath not is unimportant (αδιαφορον) to him': *so* 𝕷, *excepting that instead of* 'received' *it reads* 'distributed' [f–f] 𝕾 'As waters poured out on a rocky stone, so is the tongue of the wicked among the righteous' [g–g] 𝕷 'The slip of a false tongue is as one falling upon the pavement' [h–h] *So* 𝕾: 𝕲 𝕷 'A man without grace is (as) a table out of season (𝕷 tabula vana)': 𝕲 𝕷 + 'It will be continually in the mouth of the ignorant' (= *v.* 24 b) [i] 𝕲 *lit.* 'will be rejected' [k–k] 𝕾 'and who that is righteous taketh his ease in (his) wealth?' [l] *So* 𝕾: 𝕲 𝕷 'destroyeth it' [m–m] *So* 𝕾: 𝕲 'by a foolish countenance' [n–n] 𝕲 *lit.* 'and hath obtained' [o–o] δωρεαν [p–p] 𝕾 'he loveth stealing as well as lying' [q–q] 𝕾 'and his

---

16. **I have no friend.** His good deeds have been unable to make friends for him, because his constant seeking for recompense has deprived them of all virtue.

receive no thanks. i. e. not sufficient thanks according to his estimate.

They that eat my bread. i. e. that live on his charity.

evil-tongued. φαῦλοι γλώσσῃ: i. e. they do not thank and praise him sufficiently.

17. **How oft . . .** The essence of folly is not to see how others scorn it.

(*g*) XX. 18–20.

18. **A slip . . .** Smend quotes Zeno: κρεῖττον εἶναι τῷ ποδὶ ὀλισθαίνειν ἢ τῇ γλώσσᾳ.

So doth . . . The point of the comparison is that each is sudden.

19. **fat tail.** Cp. Exod. xxix. 22. '𝕲 cuts the obscure allusion, compresses, and adds 24 *b* to make the couplet' (Hart).

20. **A parable . . .** Cp. Prov. xxvi. 7.

(*h*) XX. 21–23.

21. **want.** i. e. poverty.

hindered from sinning. Cp. xix. 28.

And when he resteth . . . i. e. he will not be conscience-stricken when, after the day's activities are over, he thinks over what he has done. Οὐ κατανυγήσεται, lit. 'he will not be pricked (at heart)'.

22. **Another destroyeth . . .** Cp. iv. 20–21.

want of frankness. Lit. 'the covering of his face'.

23. **an enemy without reason.** Because, being weak, he promises what he cannot fulfil, and thus makes enemies unnecessarily.

(*i*) XX. 24–26.

24. **A lie is . . .** Cp. xxv. 2.

of the ignorant. ἀπαιδεύτων, i. e. those uninstructed in wisdom.

25. **a thief.** Cp. v. 14, where a thief and 'one that hath a double tongue' are mentioned together.

. . shall inherit destruction. Cp. Ps. v. 6; Prov. xv. 5, 9.

26 The end[r] of a liar is dishonour[s],
And his shame is ever[t] with him.

(*a*) XX. 27–31. *The Reward of the wise and prudent; but wisdom must be apparent* (3 + 2 distichs).

27 [uv]The wise man advanceth himself by means of his words[v],
And a prudent man ruleth[w] the great.
28 [x]He that tilleth his[y] land raiseth high his heap[z],
And he that pleaseth the great atoneth for wrong[x].
29 Presents and gifts blind the eyes [a]of the wise[a],
And as a muzzle on the mouth turn away reproofs.
30 [b]Hidden wisdom and concealed treasure,
What profit is there in either[c]?
31 Better is the man that hideth his folly
Than a man that hideth his wisdom[bd].

(*b*) XXI. 1–10. *The Nature of Sin* (= 1 + 2 + 2 + 1 + 2 + 3 distichs).

21 1 [a]My son, hast thou sinned, (then) add not thereto;
And pray concerning thy former (sins)[ab].
2 [c]Flee from sin [d]as from the face of a serpent[d];
For if thou come nigh it, it will bite thee[e];
Like[f] the teeth of a lion [g]are the teeth thereof,[g]
It slayeth[h] the souls of men.
3 Like a two-edged sword is [i]all iniquity[i],
From the stroke thereof is no healing.

ways will bring him to destruction' [r] *So* 𝔖: 𝔊 'disposition' [s] 𝔖 'for a curse' [t] 𝔖 'destroyed' [u] 𝔊 𝔏 *insert the title*: Parabolic sayings: *lit.* 'words (𝔏 'word') of parables' [v–v] 𝔖 'he that is full of wise parables showeth himself humble (*lit.* small)' [w] *So* 𝔖: 𝔊 𝔏 'pleaseth' [x–x] 𝔖 > [y] *So* 248 𝔏 *only*: *others* > 'his' [z] 𝔏 + 'and he that doeth justice exalteth himself' [a–a] 𝔏 'iudicum': 𝔖 > [b–b] *These verses recur in* xli. 14, 15, *which see* [c] *Lit.* 'in both' [d] 248 + 'Better is persistent endurance (*lit.* patience) in seeking the Lord than a driver (*lit.* charioteer) of his own life without a master'

[a–a] 𝔖 > [b] 𝔏 + 'that they may be forgiven thee' [c] 𝔖 *inserts* 'my son' [d–d] 𝔖 > [e] δηξεται: *but* 70 248 &c. δηξεται = 𝔏 [f] *So* 𝔖 *only* [g–g] 𝔖 'is falsehood' [h] *Lit.* 'slaying' [i–i] 𝔖 'an harlot'

26. **The end . . .** The rendering of 𝔖 'is manifestly right, since אחרח even in the sense of "fate" does not suit here' (Smend).

XX. 27—XXIII. 27. Further Warnings and Contrasts. This division has eleven subsections.

(*a*) XX. 27–31.

27. **by means of his words.** ἐν (= ב of the instrument or means) λόγοις.

. . . ruleth the great. Smend thinks that the reference is to Jewish sages at the court of a Gentile king, and that perhaps Ben-Sira had here some particular historical personage in mind, who through his influence was able to be of help to his co-religionists; see *v.* 28 *b*.

28. **He that tilleth.** Cp. Prov. xii. 11. Just as proper attention to the land brings its reward, so does due attention paid to the great result in real advantage.

his heap. i. e. of corn.

atoneth for wrong. It is very possible that the reference here is to the wrongdoing of some Jew, which was overlooked through the kind offices of some influential Jewish person, perhaps Ben-Sira himself.

29. **Presents . . .** Cp. Prov. xxi. 14. For ξένια cp. Sept. of 2 Sam. viii. 2, 6; Hosea x. 16 (= מנחה).

the eyes of the wise. Cp. Deut. xvi. 19 (Sept.).

a muzzle. Lit. 'a gag'.

30, 31. See critical note.

(*b*) XXI. 1–10.

1. **And pray.** i. e. for forgiveness.

2. **Flee from . . .** Cp. Prov. xiii. 21.

it will bite thee. Cp. Prov. xxiii. 32, where strong drink is compared to a serpent that bites.

the teeth of a lion. Cp. xxvii. 10; Joel i. 6.

It slayeth . . . Cp. 1 Pet. v. 8.

3. **a two-edged sword.** Cp. Ps. cxlix. 6; Prov. v. 4; and the Sept. of Judges iii. 16.

no healing. Cp. iii. 28 *a*.

𝔊 4 [k]Tyranny and violence[k] make[kk] habitations[l] desolate,
And[ll] the house[m] [n]of the arrogant[n] is rooted out[o].
5 The supplication of the poor man cometh[p] unto His ears,
[q]And his vindication[r] cometh quickly[q].
6 He that hateth reproof [s][walketh] in the path of a sinner[s],
But he that feareth God[t] will turn [to Him] whole-heartedly[u].
𝔖 7 [v]The wise discerneth him that is before him,
And spieth out the sinner at once[v].
𝔊 8 He that buildeth his house with other men's money
Is as one gathering stones for his [w]sepulchral mound[w].
9 (Like) tow wrapped together is the assembly of the ungodly,
And their end is the flame of fire[x].
10 The way of sinners is [y]made smooth without[z] stones[y],
And at the end thereof is [zz]the pit of Hades[zz].

(*c*) XXI. 11–17. *The contrast between the godly man who is wise and the godless man who is a fool* (= 2 + 2 + 2 + 2 distichs).

11 He that keepeth the Law controlleth [a]his natural tendency[a],
[b]And the fear of the Lord is the consummation of Wisdom[bc].

[k–k] 𝔖 'from morning till evening' [kk] 𝔖 'she maketh' [l] *So* 𝔖: 𝔊 'riches' [ll] *So* 𝔖: 𝔊 𝔏 'so' [m] 𝔖 'many palaces': 𝔏 'the wealth' [n–n] 𝔖 > [o] *Reading, instead of* ερημωθησεται, *with* 𝔏, εκριζωθησεται: 𝔖 'she rooteth out' [p] *So* 𝔏 *only*: 𝔊 'is from the mouth' [q–q] 𝔖 'and it ascendeth unto the presence of the eternal Judge' [r] *Lit.* 'judgement' [s–s] 𝔖 'is an unrighteous man': 𝔏 '(it is) the mark of a sinner' [t] *So* A 𝔖 𝔏: א B C 'the Lord' [u] *Lit.* 'in heart': 𝔖 'from his heart' [v–v] 𝔊 'He that is mighty in tongue is known afar off, and the man of understanding knoweth when he slippeth' [w–w] *Read with* 248 εις χωμα (= 𝔖) *for* εις χειμωνα (𝔊): 248 + 'for his tomb' [x] 248 + 'unto destruction' [y–y] 𝔖 'is a stumbling-block to them' [z] εκ λιθων = מאבן [zz–zz] 𝔖 'a deep pit': 𝔏 inferi et tenebrae et poenae
[a–a] *So* 𝔖 (=יצר, *misunderstood by* 𝔊): א* > (*hab* א c.a) [b–b] 𝔖 'and he that feareth the Lord lacketh naught'

4. **Tyranny.** καταπληγμός is ἅπ. λεγ.; it might have also the meaning of 'intimidation'.
habitations. This rendering (of 𝔖) is preferable to that of 𝔊 because one expects a parallel to 'house' in the next clause; see further critical note.
is rooted out. Cp. Prov. xv. 25.
5. **His ears.** i.e. the ears of God; cp. Ps. xvi. 8, cx. 5, cxxxix. 10.
And his vindication . . . See the rendering of 𝔖 for this clause in the critical notes; perhaps it is to be preferred to 𝔊.
6. **in the path.** ἐν ἴχνει, lit. 'in the track' (cp. 𝔏 'vestigium est'); cp. Prov. xvi. 17.
7. The context makes it probable that the rendering of 𝔖 is nearer the original than that of 𝔊.
8. **He that buildeth his house.** A figurative expression for making a fortune; cp. Ps. xlix. 16.
sepulchral mound. See critical note.
9. **tow.** στιππύον = נערת; cp. Isa. i. 31 and Judges xvi. 9, the only occurrences of the word in the O.T.
the assembly of the ungodly. For the phrase συναγωγὴ ἀνόμων cp. vii. 16, xvi. 6.
the flame of fire. i.e. Gehenna; for the expression φλὸξ πυρός cp. viii. 10.
10. **without stones.** Cp. Isa. lxii. 10.
the end thereof . . . Cp. Prov. xiv. 12 *b*, xvi. 25 *b*. 'In Ecclesiasticus the problem of retribution takes a peculiar form. On the one hand it is uncompromisingly tory, and refuses to admit the possibility of the new views as to the future life. All retribution, without exception, is confined to this life (cp. xli. 3, 4). On the other hand, this writer supplements Ezekiel's theory of exact individual retribution with the older view which Ezekiel attacked, and seeks to cover its obvious defects with the doctrine of the solidarity of the family. A man's wickedness must receive its recompense either in his own person in this life, or, failing this, in the persons of his surviving children, since Sheol knows no retribution. Thus, on the one hand, he teaches the doctrine of individual retribution (see ii. 10, 11, ix. 12, xi. 26, 27 *b*, xii. 3). But this theory of individual retribution was inadequate, for obviously all men did not meet with their deserts. Hence a man's sins are visited through the evil remembrance of his name and in the misfortunes of his children after him. Thus our author declares that a man's character shall be manifest in the fortunes of his children (see xi. 28, xxiii. 24–6, xl. 15, xli. 6). On the other hand, the children of the righteous are blest (xliv. 11–13). Since there is thus no retribution beyond the grave, there is no organic relation between this life and the life in Sheol (in xxi. 10 thoughts of the penal character of Sheol do seem to be present, though not in harmony with the doctrinal system of the author). Sheol is out of the sphere of moral government; for there no account is taken of man's past life on earth (xli. 4); there is there no recognition of God (xvii. 28); in that region there is no delight of life (xiv. 16); its inhabitants are bereft of light (xxii. 11); they are plunged in an eternal sleep (xliv. 19)' (Charles, *Eschatology* . . ., pp. 162 ff.).
(*c*) XXI. 11–17.
11. **controlleth his natural tendency.** 𝔊 'becometh master of the intent thereof', as though the reference were to the Law (see critical note); cp. *Qiddushin* 30 *b* (T. B.): 'I created the evil tendency (יצר הרע) [and] I created the Torah for healing. If ye occupy yourselves with [the study of] the Torah, ye will not fall into the power of it (i. e. of the evil tendency)'; and cp. also *Pirqe Aboth* iv. 2: 'Who is mighty? He that subdueth his nature (יצרו).'

12 [d]He that is not wise[e] will not be instructed,
And[ee] there is a wisdom[f] which maketh bitterness to abound[d].
13 The knowledge of a wise man aboundeth like a [g]spring of water[g],
And his counsel [h]is like[h] [i]the water[i] of life.
14 The heart [k]of a fool is like a broken vessel,
[l]He holdeth no knowledge[l].
15 If a man of understanding hear a wise word,
He commendeth it, and addeth thereto;
[m]If a foolish man hear it, he mocketh at it[m],
And casteth it behind his back.
16 The discourse of a fool[n] is like a burden[o] on a journey,
But grace[p] is found [q]on the lips of the wise[q].
17 The utterance[r] of the prudent is sought for in the assembly,
And his words are pondered in the heart.

(*d*) XXI. 18–28. *Further contrast between the godly man and the fool* (= 2 + 1 + 1 + 3 + 2 + 2 distichs).

18 As a prison-house[s] is Wisdom to a fool,
And the knowledge of the wise[t] as [u]coals of fire[u].
19 As[v] chains[w] on (their) feet is instruction to the foolish,
And as manacles on their right hand.
21 As a golden ornament is instruction to the wise,
And as a bracelet upon their right arm.
20 The fool lifteth up his voice with laughter,
But the wise[x] man smileth[y] in silence[z].
22 *a* The foot of a fool hasteth into a house,
23 *b* But it is [a]good manners[a] [b]to stand outside[b].
23 *a* The fool through the door looketh into a house,
22 *b* But the cautious man [c]demeans himself humbly[c].

[c] 248 'the acceptation of Wisdom': 𝔏 + 'and understanding' [d–d] 𝔖 > [e] 𝔏 + 'in (that which is) good': 𝔊 *lit.* 'crafty' [ee] ℵ A C 'But' [f] *Lit.* 'craftiness' [g–g] *So* 𝔖: 𝔊 𝔏 'flood', *reading* מבול *instead of* מבוע [h–h] 𝔏 'abideth' [i–i] *So* 𝔖: 𝔊 'a fountain': 248 'a pure fountain (as)' [k] *So* 𝔖 𝔏: 𝔊 'the inward parts' [l–l] 𝔖 'he learneth no knowledge all the days of his life': 70 248 + 'in his life' [m–m] 𝔊 'The wanton man heareth it, and it displeaseth him' [n] 𝔖 'the ungodly' [o] 𝔖 𝔏 Syro-Hex 'a heavy burden' [p] A >: ℵ c.a 'parable' [q–q] 𝔖 'in all the speech of the righteous' [r] *Lit.* 'mouth' [s] *So* 𝔖: 𝔊 𝔏 'a house that is destroyed' [t] *So* ℵ* *only*: 𝔊 𝔖 𝔏 'unwise' [u–u] *So* 𝔖: 𝔊 *lit.* 'unexamined words' [v] *So* 𝔖: 𝔊 > [w] 𝔖 'a net' [x] *So* 𝔖 𝔏: 𝔊 'clever' (πανουργος) [y] *So* 𝔖: 𝔊 𝔏 + 'scarcely' [z] 𝔖 'in peace' [a–a] 𝔥 כבוד לאיש (= 𝔖) 'the glory of a man' (*Smend conjectures* מוסר *for* כבוד) [b–b] *So* 𝔊 𝔖: 𝔥 *corrupt* בבית עמו 'in the house of his people' (*Smend conjectures* בבר לעמוד) [c–c] 𝔥 יכנע רבים ('shall humble many'), *for which*

12. **a wisdom.** πανουργία, cp. xix. 23.
. . . which maketh . . . Craftiness is a kind of wisdom which is often a cause of sorrow and bitterness to others.
13. **aboundeth like a spring of water.** 𝔊 read מבול, the technical Hebrew word for the Flood, instead of מבוע ('a spring'). Cp. *Pirqe Aboth* vi. 1, where it is said that the man who is busied with the Law is like 'a spring that ceaseth not, and as a river that continueth to flow on'. In ii. 10 of the same tractate, Rabbi Eleazar ben Arak is called a 'welling spring' because of his devotion to the study of the Law.
. . . like the water of life. Cp. the Midrash *Sifre* 84 *a*: 'As water giveth life to the world, so do the waters of the Torah give life to the world.'
14. **like a broken vessel.** Cp. Jer. ii. 13.
15. **casteth it behind . . .** Cp. Ezek. xxiii. 35.
16. **grace.** For the word used in this connexion cp. vi. 5, xx. 19, xxxvii. 21; Ps. xlv. 3; Prov. xxii. 11; Eccles. x. 12.
17. **. . . are pondered in the heart.** Cp. xiv. 21.
(*d*) XXI. 18–28.
18. **coals of fire.** i.e. to a fool. 𝔖 is preferable here, because the context demands something that is disagreeable to the fool to correspond with 'prison-house' in the first clause.
19. Contrast vi. 24 ff.
21. That this verse should come before *v.* 20 is manifest, cf. *vv.* 22, 23.
20. **the wise man.** πανοῦργος.
22, 23. In 𝔥 these verses have got misplaced; both verses are preserved in a quotation in פרקא דרבינו הקדוש 14 *a* ('The Lecture of our holy Rabbi,' i.e. Judah ha-Nasi), an ethical treatise; *v.* 32 is also quoted in the Babylonian Talmud, *Nidda* 16 *b*, *Pesachim* 112 *a* (Cowley and Neubauer, p. xxiv).
23. **good manners.** For the Hebr. phrase cp. Prov. xx. 3.

𝕲 24 'Tis unseemly[e] for one to listen at the door,
And the wise man would be grieved [f]at the shameful act[f].
25 The lips of babblers[g] [only] repeat[h] [i]what others say[i],
[j]But the words of the wise are weighed in the balance[j].
26 The heart of fools is in their mouth,
But the mouth of the wise is [k]in their heart[k].
27 When the fool[l] curseth his adversary[m],
He curseth his own soul.
28 The whisperer defileth his own soul,
And is hated [n]wheresoever he sojourneth[n].

(*e*) XXII. 1–2. *The Despicableness of Sloth* (= 2 distichs).

22 1 The slothful man is like[a] a filthy stone[b],
𝕾 [c]Every one fleeth from the stench thereof[c].
𝕲 2 [d]A slothful man is like[a] the filth of a dunghill[d],
He who [e]taketh it up[e] shaketh out his hand.

(*f*) XXII. 3–6. *The shame and grief of evil children* (= 3 + 1 distichs).

3 [There is] shame to a father in [ee]the begetting of[ee] an uninstructed (son),
And a daughter is born to his loss.
4 [f]A prudent daughter [ff]is a treasure[ff] [g]to her husband[g],
But[gg] she that bringeth shame is a grief to him that begat her[f].
5 She that is bold[h] bringeth shame on father and husband[i],
And she is despised of both.
6 As[k] music in (time of) mourning, (so) is unseasonable talk[l],
But[m] stripes and correction are at all times wisdom[n].

read פנים . . . (= 𝕲)   [e] *Lit.* 'want of instruction'   [f-f] *Lit.* 'with the disgrace (of it)'   [g] *So* 248 : 𝕲 'strangers' : 𝕾 'ungodly' : 𝕷 'unwise'   [h] *Lit.* 'declare' : *so* א V 248 𝕾 𝕷 Syro-Hex : B A C 'are grieved'   [i-i] *Lit.* 'the things that are not theirs' : *so* 248 *only* : 𝕲 'at these things' : 𝕾 'in his own body', *i. e.* 'his inner thoughts' : 𝕷 'foolish things'   [j-j] 𝕾 'The wise man speaketh by measure' (*lit.* 'by weight')   [k-k] *So* 248 𝕾 𝕷 : 𝕲 'their heart'   [l] *So* 𝕾 : 𝕲 𝕷 'ungodly'   [m] 𝕲 *lit.* 'Satan' (*see note below*) : 𝕷 'the Devil' : 𝕾 'him who sinned not against him'   [n-n] *So* C V 248 253 254 (= Syro-Hex) ; 𝕲 εν παροικησει.   𝕾 *reads for this verse* : 'The soul of the wise is grieved at the fool, for he knoweth not what to say to him'

[a] *Lit.* 'is (to be) compared to'   [b] א c.a 𝕾 'a stone cast out' (𝕾 *lit.* 'thrown out into the street')   [c-c] 𝕲 'and every one hisseth at the shame thereof' : 𝕲 + 'every one keeps clear of him'   [d-d] 𝕾 'when a man goeth out into the street and disgraceth himself'   [e-e] 𝕾 'seeth it' : 𝕷 'toucheth it'   [ee-ee] 𝕾 >   [f-f] 𝕾 >   [ff-ff] 𝕲 'shall inherit' : 𝕷 'is an inheritance' : 𝕲 *misread* יְרַשָּׁה ('she shall inherit') *instead of* יְרֻשַּׁת ('treasure,' *lit.* 'inheritance')   [g-g] 𝕲 ανδρα αυτης   [gg] *Lit.* 'and'   [h] 𝕾 'foolish'   [i] 𝕾 'her mother' : 𝕷 *inserts* 'she will not be menaced by the ungodly' (*i.e.* 'they will be in sympathy with her')   [k] *So* 𝕾 *only*   [l] *Lit.* 'discourse'   [m] B 'and'   [n] *So* א* 𝕾 𝕷 : 𝕲 'of wisdom' : 70 248 + 'Children who live comfortably in good circumstances

---

24. **the wise man.** φρόνιμος means here 'discreet'.

25. **are weighed in the balance.** Cp. xvi. 25, xxviii. 25.

26. Fools talk without thinking, the wise think before they speak.

27. **his adversary.** 𝕲 evidently read השטן, the original meaning of which was simply 'adversary' (cp. Num. xxii. 22, 32 ; 1 Kings v. 18, xi. 22) ; the meaning is either, that in cursing Satan the curse recoils on the man's own head, or else that a man's real spiritual adversary is his own evil nature ; cp. the next verse.

28. Cp. v. 14, xxviii. 13.

(*e*) XXII. 1–2.

1. **a filthy stone.** Cp. the Midrash *Wayyiqra Rabba*, § xvii, chap. xiv. 34, where the passage Job xxxi. 34 is commented upon. Cp. Job ii. 8.

2. **A slothful man . . .** Ben-Sira's disgust for slothful people is coarsely expressed.

(*f*) XXII. 3–6.

3. **in the begetting of.** Cf. Prov. xvii. 21.

a daughter . . . According to Jewish ideas it was a misfortune to beget daughters ; cp. *Menachoth* 43 *b* (T. B.), where it is taught that a man ought to bless God every day for not having made him a woman or a slave. In the daily service for Morning Prayer in the Jewish Liturgy occurs the following Benediction : 'Blessed art Thou, O Lord our God, King of the Universe, who hast not made me a woman.'

4. **a treasure to . . .** See critical note. Cp. xxvi. 1–4.

she that bringeth shame. i.e. to her husband ; this is also a grief (εἰς λύπην) to her father, because her shame is a reflection on him, implying, as it does, that he did not bring her up properly.

5. **She that is bold.** ἡ θρασεῖα ; cp. Sept. of Prov. ix. 13, γυνὴ ἄφρων καὶ θρασεῖα.

6. **talk.** διήγησις (Syr. שועיתא) means the discourse of the sages ; this is 'unseasonable' at times when 'stripes and

(*g*) XXII. 7–18. *The Futility of the Fool* (= 2 + 3 + 3 + 2 + 2 + 1 + 2 distichs).

𝔊 7 He who teacheth a fool is (as) one that glueth together a potsherd[o],
(Or) as[p] one that awakeneth a sleeper out of a deep sleep.
8 [q]He that discourseth to a fool[qq] is as one discoursing to him that slumbereth[q],
And at the end he saith, 'What is it?'
11 Mourn for the dead, [r]for his[s] light hath failed[r];
And mourn[t] for a fool, for understanding hath failed (him).
[u]Weep gently[v] for the dead[u], for he hath found rest;
[w]But[x] the life of a fool is [y]worse than[y] death[w].
12 The mourning for the dead (lasts) seven days,
But [z]the mourning for a fool[z] all the days of his life.
13 Talk not much with a foolish man,
And consort not with a pig[a]:
Beware of him, lest thou have trouble,
And thou becomest defiled [b]when he shaketh himself[b];
Turn from him, and thou wilt find rest,
And (so) shalt thou not be wearied with his folly[c].
14 [d]What is heavier than lead[d]?
And what is its name but 'Fool'?
15 Sand and salt and a weight of iron
(Are) easier[e] to bear than [f]a senseless man[f].
16 As[g] timber girt and fixed into the wall[h]
[k]Is not loosened by an earthquake[k],

conceal the humble origin of their own parents; (but) children who grow up in arrogance and wantonness besmirch the noble descent of their kin (= *vv.* 9, 10) [o] V Syro-Hex *plur.*: 𝔏 + ('and as one) who telleth a tale (*lit.* word) to him that heareth not' [p] *So* 𝔖 𝔏 [q–q] 𝔖 'he that teacheth a fool is like one that eateth bread when he is not hungry' [qq] 𝔏 + 'wisdom' [r–r] 𝔖 *lit.* 'for he is kept from the light' [s] *Expressed in* 𝔏 [t] 𝔖 > [u–u] 𝔖 'it is not (fitting) to weep for the dead': Sah 'it is good to weep for the dead' [v] *Lit.* 'more sweetly': 𝔏 modicum [w–w] 𝔖 'For an evil life is worse than death' [x] *So* B *only* [y–y] 248 > [z–z] *So* 𝔖: 𝔊 𝔏 'for a fool and an ungodly man' [a] *So* 𝔖, *which adds* 'in the way': 70 248 + 'for being without sense he will altogether despise thee' [b–b] *So* 𝔖: 𝔊 'in his onslaught', *lit.* shaking': 𝔏 'in his sin' [c] 𝔖 'much talk' [d–d] 𝔖 'for he is much heavier than lead' [e] *So* 248 𝔏: 𝔊 'easy': 𝔖 'pleasanter' [f–f] 𝔖 'to dwell with a fool' [g] *So* 70 𝔖 [h] *Lit.* building': 𝔖 + 'of the corners of a house' [k–k] 𝔖 >

---

correction' are really what is required. Ben-Sira is laying stress on the need of firmness towards children; the lack of this in their earlier years results in the shame and grief which, later on, are brought upon a father (*vv.* 4, 5); cp. the gloss on *v.* 6 (see critical note).

stripes and correction. Cp. Prov. xxii. 15, xxix. 15.

(*g*) XXII. 7–18.

7. **He who teacheth . . .** Cp. Prov. i. 7, xxvii. 22. A potsherd glued together is useless for all practical purposes, one that is awaked out of a deep sleep is unfit for doing anything; nothing can be done with either—nor yet with a fool.

8. **He that discourseth . . .** A fool cannot understand sensible talk, although he hears, any more than one who is asleep and cannot hear. For *vv.* 9, 10, see critical note.

11. **Mourn . . .** Cp. vii. 34, xxxviii. 16.

his light hath failed. Cp. Prov. xx. 20 *b*, 27. On Jewish tombstones the following ancient formula is often inscribed: 'May his light continue to shine.'

12. **. . . (lasts) seven days.** This is still observed by modern orthodox Jews; the period is technically called 'Shibaʿ' (pronounced 'Shivaʿ'), 'seven'; cp. Gen. l. 10; Judith xvi. 24; and see below xxxviii. 17.

13. **Talk not much.** *μὴ πληθύνῃς λόγον* = אל תרבה שיחה, a phrase which occurs in *Pirqe Aboth* i. 5.

consort not. Lit. 'go not to'.

with a pig. This rendering of 𝔖 is evidently correct, as is shown by the context (see clause *d*); 𝔊 is a toning down. The swine is referred to as the emblem of filthiness in the T. B. *Berakhoth* 43 *b* (*JE*, xi. 609 *b*). The fool, like the man of sloth, is regarded as unclean; for the uncleanness of swine cp. Lev. xi. 7.

And thou becomest defiled . . . The outpouring of a fool's nonsense is compared to the filth carried about by a pig which it shakes from itself after having wallowed in the mire.

wearied. The verb *ἀκηδιάζω* occurs very rarely in the Sept.: Ps. lx. 3, ci. 1, cxlii. 4; Dan. vii. 15.

folly. *ἀπόνοια* means also 'madness', which is perhaps preferable here, as a strong word is required.

14. **What is heavier . . .** Cp. xxi. 16.

what is its name. i.e. the name of that which is heavier than lead.

15. **Sand.** Cp. Prov. xxvii. 3. See further Introd. § 7 (*b*).

16. The contrast offered by the wise man.

𝔊 So a heart established on well-advised counsel
[l]Will not be afraid[l] in time[m] [of danger].
17 [mm]A heart fixed on thoughtful understanding
Is as an ornament graven[n] upon[o] a polished wall[mm].
18 [p]Small stones[p] lying upon a high place
Will not remain against the wind,
[q]So will the fearsome heart (bent) on foolish imagination
Be unable to withstand any terror[q].

(*h*) XXII. 19–26. *How Friendship is dissolved; the duty of a friend* (=2+3+2[+1]+2 distichs).

19 A wound [r]in the eye maketh tears to flow,
And a (heart)-wound[r] [s]severeth friendship[s].
20 [t]He that throweth a stone at birds scareth them away,
And he that reproacheth[u] a friend dissolveth friendship.
21 Even if thou draw the sword against a friend,
Despair not, for there is [v]a way out[v];
22 And[w] if thou open thy[x] mouth against a friend,
Fear not, for there is a (way of) reconciliation;
[y]But reproach and arrogance, and betrayal of a secret, and a deceitful blow,—
In (face of) these every friend will depart[y].
23 Support[z] thy neighbour in his poverty,
That in his prosperity[a] thou mayst rejoice[b];
Remain true[c] to him in the time of his[d] affliction,
That thou mayst be heir with him in his inheritance[e].
24 [[ee]Before the fire is the smoke of the furnace[f],
So revilings before bloodshed].[ee]
𝔖 25 [g]Be not ashamed of a friend who becometh poor[g],
𝔊 [h]And [i]hide not thyself[i] from his face[h];
26 [k]For [kk]if evil happen unto him[l] through thee[ll k],
Whosoever heareth it will beware of thee[m].

[l–l] 𝔖 'no fear will shake him' [m] 70 248 𝔖 𝔏 'at any time': 248 𝔏 + 'with fear' [mm–mm] 𝔏 > [n] *Reading* γλυμματος (*Smend*) *for* ψαμμωτος [o] *So* 248 𝔖 [p–p] *Reading with* A C 70 248 *mg.* 254 χαλικες (=𝔏): B ℵ χαρακες, 'pales' [q–q] 𝔖 'So is the heart of a fool broken in his innermost being, and he cannot stand up against grief' [r] *Reading* νοσος (=𝔖) *for* νυσσων (=𝔏) [s–s] *So* 𝔖 (*lit.* 'changeth friendship'): 𝔊 'showeth feeling' [t] 𝔏 *inserts the title*: 'Concerning friendship' [u] 𝔖 'robbeth': *and adds* 'change not towards thy friend, but if thou change think not that thou wilt retain his love' [v–v] *Lit.* 'a returning' (=תשובה), *i.e.* 'a way of repentance' [w] *So* V 253 Syro-Hex. 𝔏: 𝔊 > [x] *So* 𝔖 [y–y] 𝔖 'He who reveals a secret is worthy of contempt (*lit.* is a son of contempt), and a deceitful blow puts friendship far away' [z] *So* 𝔖: 𝔊 𝔏 'acquire trust in' [a] *Lit.* 'good things' [b] *So* ℵA 25 248 253 254 Syro-Hex 𝔏 (ευφρανθης): B C V 70 ομου πλησθης: 𝔖 'thou mayst share' [c] *Lit.* 'steadfast' [d] *So* 𝔏 *only* [e] 248 + 'For not always is the (outward) appearance to be despised, nor is the rich man void of understanding to be respected' [ee–ee] *This verse seems to have got out of place, as it breaks the sequence of thought* [f] 𝔊 𝔏 + 'and smoke' (καπνος), *which* 𝔖 *rightly omits* [g–g] 𝔊 𝔏 'I will not be ashamed to shelter a friend' [h–h] 𝔏 > [i–i] 𝔊 𝔏 'I will not hide myself' [k–k] 𝔖 'If thy companion reveal to thee a secret, repeat it not'

---

17. **an ornament graven.** See critical note.

18. **Small stones . . .** The reference, as Ryssel points out, is to the small stones which were placed on the top of the walls surrounding gardens and vineyards; these were put there in order that, when jackals or foxes leaped on to the wall to enter the vineyard, the noise occasioned by the rattling of the displaced stones might warn the watcher. As these small stones were always lying in an exposed position they were easily blown down by a high wind.

(*h*) XXII. 19–26.

19. **A wound.** See critical note.
maketh tears to flow. Cp. Prov. xxx. 32, 33.

20. **reproacheth.** Cp. v. 22, xviii. 18, xx. 15.

21. . . . **for there is a way out.** Cp. xxvii. 21. The meaning of the verse is that every straightforward quarrel, however serious, is capable of adjustment, but when such things as those mentioned in the third clause of *v.* 22 sever friendship, then the breach is irremediable.

22. **if thou open . . .** The reference is to outspoken, straightforward differences between friends.
reproach. i. e. abuse.
betrayal of a secret. Lit. 'revealing . . .'; cp. Prov. xi. 13, xx. 19, xxv. 9.

23. **thou mayst rejoice.** See critical note.

24. **So revilings . . .** Cp. xxvii. 15.

25. **And hide not . . .** Cp. vi. 12.

26. The rendering of 𝔊 in this verse is clearly not in order, but its general sense agrees better with the context than

(*i*) XXII. 27—XXIII. 6. *The Need of Self-control* (= 2+4+1+2 distichs).

27 [no]O that one would set a watch over my mouth[o],
And a seal of shrewdness upon my lips,
That I fall not[p] by means of[q] them[r],
And that my tongue destroy me not[s]!
23 2 [a]O that one would set scourges over my mind[b],
And [c]a rod of correction[c] over my heart,
That they spare not [d]their errors[d],
[e]And overlook not their sins[e]!
3 That mine ignorances be not[f] multiplied,
And that my sins [g]abound not[fgh],
And [i]cause me to fall[i] in the sight of[k] mine[l] adversaries,
So that mine enemy rejoice over me[m].
(=4*a*) O Lord, Father, and God[n] of my[o] life,
Abandon me not [p]to their counsel[pq].
4 *b* Give me not[r] [s]a proud look[s],
5 [t]And turn away concupiscence[u] from me[v].
6 May [w]the lust of the flesh[w] [x]and chambering[x] [y]not overtake me[y],
[z]And give me[a] not over to a shameless soul[z].

(*lit.* 'give it not out') [kk] 𝔊 'and' [l] 𝔊 𝔏 'me' [ll] 𝔊 'him' [m] 𝔊 'him': 𝔖 + and will account thee a mischief-maker' (*lit.* 'one that doeth harm') [n] 254 *inserts here*: 'O that one would set scourges over my thought' (= xxiii. 2 *a*) [o–o] 𝔊 τις δωσει (= מי יתן) μοι (> ℵ A 𝔖 𝔏) επι στομα μου φυλακην [p] 248 + 'suddenly' [q] 𝔊 'from' [r] *So* V (= 𝔖 𝔏): 𝔊 'it': Sah 'through my mouth' [s] *The negative is preserved in* 248 253 (= 𝔖 Syro-Hex) [a] *For the reasons of the above order in the clauses of vv.* 1–5 *see note below* [b] *Lit.* 'thought' [c–c] *So* 𝔖: 𝔊 'a discipline of wisdom' [d–d] *So* 𝔏 (ignorationibus eorum): 𝔊 επι τοις αγνοημασι μου = 𝔖 [e–e] ℵ c.a *has the clause under the asterisk:* 248 'Overlook not the insults (υβρεις) of sinners, according to (*lit.* 'in') (Thy) promise': 𝔖 >, *but has instead:* 'that they in their assembly inherit not, nor take delight (נרחמון) in destroying (למחבלו)'; Sah > *the clause altogether*: 𝔏 et non appareant delicta eorum [f] 𝔏 > *the negative* [g–g] 𝔖 *lit.* 'be not strong' (נעשנון) [h] 70 248 + 'to (my) destruction' [i–i] 𝔖 'reveal me' (נגלונני), *a scribal error which should, according to Smend, be corrected to* נפלונני (= יפילוני), 'cause me to fall': 𝔊 𝔏 'I fall' [k] *Lit.* 'before' [l] *So* 𝔏: 𝔊 𝔖 > [m] 70 248 + 'from whom the hope of Thy mercy is far-distant' [n] 𝔖 'Master' [o] 70 248 'all my' [p–p] 𝔏 > [q] 𝔊 + 'and suffer me not to fall by them' (𝔖 'on their account'): 70 + 'as a (standing) example' (εν παραδειγματισμῳ): 𝔏 + in illa exprobatione [r] 𝔊 μη δῳς μοι [s–s] *Lit.* 'a lifting up of eyes': 𝔏 '... of mine eyes': 𝔖 'an exalted eye'; 248 + 'and an overbearing (*lit.* gigantic) soul' [t] 248 *inserts here:* 'Keep ever from Thy servant vain hopes' [u] 𝔖 'a lustful (בזוזא) heart': 𝔏 'every desire' [v] 248 + 'and him that desireth to serve Thee do Thou ever hold up': 𝔖 + 'and suffer naught that is good to escape me' [w–w] *So* 𝔖: 𝔊 𝔏 'the appetite (desire) of the (𝔏 'my') belly' [x–x] 𝔖 > [y–y] 𝔖 'not make me lustful' [z–z] 𝔖 'And let not a shameless soul have dominion over me' [a] 248 'Thy servant'

---

is the case with 𝔖; if the pronouns in 𝔊 are corrected on the basis of 𝔖 good sense can be made out of the verse. The first word of the verse should be 'For' instead of 'And'; this is demanded by the context.

(*i*) XXII. 27—XXIII. 6.

27. **O that...** Cp. Ps. cxli. 3.

that my tongue... Cp. Prov. xviii. 21, xxi. 23.

XXIII. 1–5. A reference to the text of 𝔊 will show that it is out of order as it stands: *v.* 1 breaks the sequence between xxii. 27 and xxiii. 2; the first clause of *v.* 1 = *v.* 4 *a*; *v.* 1 *b* is omitted by 𝔖, and inserted in *v.* 4; something has evidently fallen out in *vv.* 4–5. That there is something radically wrong with the text of these verses as they stand is evident from the variations in the Gr. MS. and the Versions (see critical notes). Smend (following 𝔖 partly) keeps 1 *a* and 1 *c* and 4 *a* of 𝔊, adding 1 *b* to 4 *a*.

2. **O that one would set.** Lit. 'who will set...', cp. xxii. 27.

a rod of correction. Cp. Prov. xxii. 15 *b*.

their errors... their sins: i.e. those of his heart and mind.

3. **So that mine enemy...** Cp. Ps. xiii. 4.

1. **... their counsel.** i.e. the counsel of his own heart and mind.

4 *b*. **a proud look.** Perhaps this should be interpreted in the sense in which the expression is used in Gen. xxxix. 7, in view of what follows (Ryssel).

6. **the lust of the flesh.** See critical note.

(*j*) XXIII. 7–15. *The need of keeping the tongue under control* (= 2 + 3 + 3 + 2 + 3 + 2 distichs).

𝔊 7 [b]Hear, O children, (concerning) the discipline of the mouth[c]:
He that keepeth (discipline)[d] [e]shall not be taken ⌊captive⌋[e]
8 But[f] the sinner is ensnared[g] through[h] his lips,
𝔖 [i]And the fool stumbleth through his mouth[i].
9 Accustom not[k] thy mouth to an oath,
[l]Nor make a habit of the naming of the Holy One[m l].
𝔊 10 [n]For as a servant who is constantly being questioned[n]
[o]Lacketh not[o] the marks of a blow,
So also he that [p]sweareth and is continually naming [q]the name of the Lord[q p]
Is not free[r] from sins.
11 A man of many oaths [s]is filled with iniquity[s],
And the scourge[t] departeth not from his house;
If he offend[u] his sin will be upon him[v],
[w]And if he disregard[x] it he sinneth doubly[w];
[y]And if he sweareth [z]without need[z], he shall not be justified[y],
[a]For his house shall be filled with calamities[b a].
12 [c]There is a manner of speech [d]that is to be compared[d] with death[c]:
Let it not be found in the heritage of Jacob.
𝔖 [e]He that keepeth[f] his soul from this shall live[e],
[g]And not wallow in sins[g].
𝔊 14 [h]Remember[i] thy father and thy mother
[k]When[l] thou sittest in council in the midst of the mighty[k],
Lest, perchance, [m]thou stumble[m] before them,
[In that] [n]thou showest thyself [to be] a fool[n] in thy manner [of speech],
[o]And dost wish thou hadst not been born[o],
And cursest the day of thy birth.
13 Accustom not thy mouth to impure manner [of speech],
For [p]that is a sinful thing[p].

[b] B 70 248 254 *insert the title*: 'Discipline of the mouth' [c] 248 + 'that is truthful' [d] *Not expressed* [e–e] 𝔖 'shall not suffer shame' [f] *So* 𝔖: 𝔊 > (ℵ[c.a] 'either') [g] *Lit.* 'overtaken', *reading* καταλη φθησεται *with* 157 (= 𝔖 𝔏) *for* καταλειφθ. 𝔊: 157 248 + 'in his folly' [h] *Lit.* 'in' (= ב 'by means of', *cp.* Ps. vi. 8) [i–i] 𝔊 'the reviler and the arrogant shall stumble through them': 𝔏 superbus et maledicus scandalizabitur in illis [k–k] 𝔖 'and thou wilt not (have to) sit before the judges' [l] 𝔖 'instruct not': 𝔏 + 'for there is great calamity therein' [m] ℵ[c.a] A 'the Most High': 𝔏 'God' [n–n] 𝔖 'for (as) every man that sweareth continually' [o–o] 𝔖 'is not free from' [p–p] 𝔖 'lieth and sweareth' [q–q] *So only* A ℵ[c.a] 55 157 254 [r] *So* 𝔖: 𝔊 𝔏 'is not cleansed' [s–s] 𝔖 'acquireth sins' [t] 𝔖 'strife' [u] 𝔖 'swear by mistake' (*i.e.* 'falsely'): 𝔏 frustraverit [v] 55 254 + 'he will hide it under his tongue' [w–w] 𝔖 'and if in truth he will not swear (at all)' [x] *Lit.* 'overlook': 𝔏 dissimulaverit [y–y] 𝔖 'For whosoever sweareth continually, it is detestable, and he shall not be justified' [z–z] *Lit.* 'in vain' [a–a] 𝔖 > [b] 248 𝔏 'retribution' [c–c] 𝔖 'And if there is another thing that is like it' [d–d] *Reading with* 70 253 (= Syro-Hex) αντιπαραβεβλημενη: 𝔊 αντιπεριβεβλ.: 𝔏 contraria [e–e] 𝔊 𝔏 'For from the godly (𝔏 'the merciful') all these things shall be put away' [f] *Lit.* 'shutteth up' [g–g] 𝔊 𝔏 'And they will not wallow (*lit.* roll) in sins' [h] *Vv.* 13 *and* 15 *belong together.* [i] 𝔖 + 'that thou hast' [k–k] 𝔖 'and from terror thou hast been preserved' [l] *So* 𝔖: 𝔊 𝔏 'for' [m–m] *So* 𝔖: 𝔊 'that thou be not forgetful': 𝔏 'lest He (*i.e.* God) forget thee' [n–n] 𝔖 'thou be despised' [o–o] 𝔖 'and sayest, O that I had not been created' [p–p] *Lit.* 'therein is the word of sin'

(*j*) XXIII. 7–15. With the whole of this subsection cp. Jas. iii. 1–12.

7. **shall not be taken [captive].** i.e. by his mouth; he will not fall under the dominion of his tongue.

9. . . . **to an oath.** Cp. Matt. v. 34 ff., xxiii. 20 ff.; Jas. v. 12.

10. **a servant.** *οἰκέτης*, 'a household servant'; the context suggests that *δοῦλος* (=עֶבֶד), 'a slave', would have been a more appropriate word here.

being questioned. *ἐξετάζω* means 'to examine closely', but the word is frequently used in the special sense of examining by torture (cp. Acts xxii. 24); *ἐξεταζόμενος* is, therefore, used quite appropriately here; so that Smend's suggestion that *ἐξουσιαζόμενος* (lit. 'one having authority over', i.e. here in the sense of 'one rebelling') should be read instead does not commend itself.

the marks of a blow. Cp. xxviii. 17; *μώλωψ* means the result of a blow, i.e. a bruise, as well as the blow itself.

the name of the Lord. Cp. Lev. xxiv. 16 (Sept.).

11. **A man of many oaths.** Cp. xxvii. 14. The last two clauses seem to be merely a variation of the first two.

12. **There is a manner of speech . . .** Cp. Lev. xix. 12, xxii. 2, 3, 32, and especially xxiv. 16.

the heritage of Jacob. In the O.T. this expression is used in reference to the Promised Land, cp. Isa. lviii. 14; here it refers rather to the Jews in contradistinction to the Gentiles.

14. As the text shows, this verse must come before *v.* 13, which has got out of place.

Remember thy father . . . i.e. so as not to bring disgrace on their name.

. . . **thou hadst not been born . . .** Cp. Job iii. 3; Jer. xx. 14.

𝔊 15 A man that doth accustom himself to [q]disgraceful talk[q]
[r]Will not learn[r] wisdom [s]all his days[s].

(*k*) XXIII. 16–27. *The Wickedness of Impurity* (= 4+3+4+1+3+3+2 distichs).

16 Two types (of men) [t]multiply sins[t],
And the third increaseth[u] wrath[v];
[w]A hot desire[x], burning like fire,
Which is not quenched till [y]it be consumed[y w];
A fornicator with the body of his flesh,
ℌ[A] (For) he ceaseth not till the fire consumeth him;
𝔊 17 [And] the man to whom all bread[z] is sweet,
(For) he will not leave off till he die.
18 A man[a] that [b]goeth astray[b] [c]from his own bed[c],
And saith in his heart: ‘Who seeth me?
𝔖 [d]The walls of my house hide me,
And the shadow of my roof covereth me,
And no one seeth me—
What hindereth me from sinning?’[d]
[e]He remembereth not the Most High[e];
𝔊 19 [f]The eyes of men are his (only) fear[f],
—And he perceiveth not that the eyes of the Lord
Are ten thousand times brighter than the sun,
Beholding all the ways of men,
[g]And looking into secret places[g];
20 For[h] all things are known unto Him before they are created,
[i]So also [doth He see them] after they are perfected[i],—
21 [k]Such a man shall be punished[l] in the streets of the city,
And shall be taken where he suspecteth it not[k m].

q–q *Lit.* ‘words of reproach’: 𝔖 ‘worthless words’ r–r *So* 𝔖: 𝔊 *lit.* ‘will not be instructed’ s–s 𝔊 ‘in all . . .’: 𝔖 ‘all the days of his life’: 𝔖 + ‘and the man that is impure in the shame of his flesh accepteth no instruction’ t–t 𝔖 ‘doth my soul hate’ u *Lit.* ‘will bring’: 𝔖 ‘causeth to arise’ v 𝔏 + ‘and perdition’ w–w 𝔖 > x *Lit.* ‘soul’ y–y ℵ[c.a] ‘it consume something’ (= 𝔏) z 𝔖 ‘flesh’ a A + ‘(that is) a fornicator’ b–b 𝔖 ‘committeth adultery’ c–c 𝔖 ‘on the covering of his bed’ d–d *So* 𝔖 (*pr.* ‘behold’): 𝔊 *inverts and abbreviates* 18 c d, *and misunderstands* 18 f e–e 𝔖 >: 𝔊 (*misnnderstanding*) ου μη μνησθησεται ο υψιστος f–f 𝔖 > g–g 𝔖 ‘and perceiveth the nature (*lit.* the form) of their works (done) in darkness’ h *Expressed in* 𝔖 𝔏 i–i 𝔖 ‘and judgeth them at the end of the world’ k–k 𝔖 *transposes the clauses* l 𝔖 ‘detected’ m 𝔏 + ‘and shall be a disgrace in the sight of (*lit.* to) all, because he knew not the fear of God’

---

15. **disgraceful talk.** Cp. Joshua v. 9 (Sept.).

(*k*) XXIII. 16–27.

16. **Two types . . . And the third.** With this form of expression cp. xxvi. 1, 5, 28, l. 25; Prov. xxx. 7, 15, 18, 21, 24, 29; cp. also the whole of chap. v of *Pirqe Aboth*.

increaseth wrath. Lit. ‘bringeth’, i. e. the wrath of God; for the Gr. word (ἐπάγω) cp. ii. 4, xlvii. 20.

he ceaseth not. 𝔊 ‘He will in no wise cease till he have made a fire to blaze’.

17. . . . **to whom all bread is sweet.** Cp. Prov. ix. 13–18, especially *v.* 17.

18. Cp. Job xxiv. 15.

19. **Beholding . . .** Cf. xvii. 19, 20; Prov. xv. 3, 11; Ps. xxxiii. 14 ff.

20. **For all things are known . . .** Cp. *Pirqe Aboth* iii. 24: ‘Everything is foreseen; and free-will is given’; and see Taylor’s comments on this in his edition.

So also . . . Cp. Gen. ii. 1, 2 (Sept.).

21. **shall be punished . . .** Cp. Lev. xx. 10; Deut. xxii. 22; the full rigour of the Law was evidently mitigated in later times, since there is no mention of punishment by death here. ‘Under the Talmudic law the severity of the Mosaic code was in many instances modified, and the laws relating to adultery came under the influence of a milder theory of the relation of crime and punishment. . . . Upon this mild view followed the entire abolition of the death penalty, in the year A. D. 40, before the destruction of the Second Temple (*Sanhedrin* 41 *a*), when the Jewish courts, probably under pressure of the Roman authorities, relinquished their right to inflict capital punishment. Thereafter the adulterer was scourged; and the husband of the adulteress was not allowed to condone her crime (*Sotah* vi. 1), but was compelled to divorce her, and she lost all her property rights under her marriage contract . . .’ (*JE*, i. 217 *a*).

shall be taken . . . i.e. to the public place of scourging. The transposition of these two clauses in 𝔖 is correct.

𝔊 22 So also a wife that leaveth[n] her husband,
And bringeth in an heir by a stranger.
23 For, firstly, she is disobedient[o] to the Law of the Most High;
And secondly, [p]she trespasseth[p] against her own husband[q];
And thirdly, she committeth adultery through (her) fornication,
And bringeth children in by a stranger.
24 She shall be led into the assembly,
And upon her children [r]there will be visitation[r].
25 Her children shall not spread out their roots,
And her branches shall bear no fruit.
26 She will leave her memory for a curse,
And her reproach will not be blotted out.
27 [s]And they that are left behind shall know
That there is nothing better than the fear of the Lord[t],
And nothing sweeter than to observe
The commandments of the Lord[u][s].

(*a*) XXIV. 1–34. [a]*The Praise of Wisdom*[a] (= 2 + 2 + 2 + 3 + 3 + 1 + 3 + 2 + 2 + 2 + 2 + 1 + 3 + 2 + 3 + 3 distichs).

24 1 Wisdom praiseth herself[b],
And is honoured among [c]her people
2 She openeth her mouth in the assembly [d]of the Most High[d],
And is honoured in the presence of His hosts[e].
3 'I came forth from the mouth of the Most High,
And as a mist I covered the earth.

[n] 𝔖 'sinneth against' [o] 𝔖 'she lieth against' [p–p] 𝔖 > [q] 𝔖 + 'of her youth' [r–r] 𝔖 'her sins will be remembered' [s–s] 𝔖, *which on account of its better rhythmical measure is perhaps to be preferred, reads*:

'And all the dwellers on earth will know,
And all the rest in the world will perceive,
That nothing is better than the fear of God,
Or sweeter than to keep His commandments.'

[t] 55 157 254 𝔖𝔏 'God' [u] 55 248 253 254 'God': 70 248 𝔏 + 'to follow after God (𝔏 'the Lord') is great glory, and length of days it is for thee to be accepted of Him' (= *v.* 28)
[a–a] V 106 157 253 𝔖 Syro-Hex > [b] 𝔏 + et in deo honorabitur [c–c] 𝔖 'the people of God' [d–d] 𝔖 'of God' [e] So 𝔖: 𝔊 'might'

23. **the Law of the Most High.** See Exod. xx. 14; Deut. v. 18.
bringeth children in by . . . For the result of this entailed upon such offspring see Deut. xxiii. 2.
24. **She shall be led . . .** i. e. for punishment.
upon her children . . . Their illegitimacy descended upon their children (*Qiddushin* 78 *b*).
25. **. . . shall not spread out . . .** They were not regarded as belonging to the congregation of Israel (cp. *Qiddushin* 78 *b*); for the belief that the children of adulterers do not come to maturity see Wisd. iii. 16–19, iv. 3–5.
26. **. . . will not be blotted out.** Cp. Ps. cix. 14.
27. **. . . shall know . . .** Cp. xlvi. 10. For the addition to this verse see critical note.

XXIV. 1—XXVII. 3. (In praise of Wisdom, with practical applications.) The division falls into twelve subsections.
XXIV. 1–34. A fine hymn in praise of Wisdom follows. The author, in declaring that Wisdom is honoured in heaven, as well as on earth, thereby shows that she is entitled to speak in her own name. The hymn falls into six strophes, each containing six distichs.
1. **Wisdom praiseth herself.** Lit. '. . . praiseth her soul'; she is entitled to do so on account of her inherent excellence; every utterance of hers is *ipso facto* the praise of herself because it witnesses to her transcendent perfection.
among her people. The rendering of 𝔖, 'the people of God,' suggests that Israel is meant (cp. *v.* 8); Smend thinks that the heavenly companions of Wisdom are meant, and the rendering of 𝔏 (in deo honorabitur) points to the scene being in heaven; but as the heavenly hosts are referred to in the next verse, it is probable that the Israelites are meant here, the intention of the writer being to indicate that Wisdom is honoured both on earth and in heaven.
2. **in the assembly of the Most High.** Cp. Ps. lxxxii. 1 בַּעֲדַת־אֵל (𝔖 reads 'of God'); here it is clear that the heavenly hosts are referred to.
. . . His hosts . . . *δυνάμεως αὐτοῦ*; cp. Isa. xxxiv. 4, where צבא השמים is rendered *αἱ δυνάμεις τῶν οὐρανῶν* in the Sept.; cp. Ps. xxxiii (Sept. xxxii) 6; Dan. viii. 10.
3. **I came forth . . .** Wisdom now speaks in her own name; for the personification of Wisdom cp. Prov. viii. 4 ff., and with the whole of this section cp. Prov. viii. 22–ix. 12, with which it has many points of similarity.
as a mist I covered the earth. Cp. Gen. i. 2, 'The Spirit of God brooded upon the face of the waters,' and Gen. ii. 6, 'There went up a mist from the earth, and watered the whole face of the ground.' In connexion with these

𝕲 4 In the high places did I fix my abode,
And my throne was [ee]in the pillar of cloud[ee].
5 [f]Alone I compassed the circuit of heaven[f],
And [g]in the depth of the abyss[g] I walked.
6 Over the waves of the sea, and over all the earth[h],
And over every people and nation I held sway[i].
7 With all these I sought a resting-place,
And (said): In whose inheritance shall I lodge?
8 Then the Creator of all things gave me commandment,
And He that created me fixed my dwelling-place (for me);
And He said: Let thy dwelling-place be in Jacob,
And in Israel[k] [l]take up thine inheritance[l].
9 He created me from the beginning, before the world;
𝕾 [m]The memorial of me shall never cease[m].
𝕲 10 In the holy tabernacle I ministered before Him,
Moreover[mm] in Zion was I established.

ee–ee 𝕾 'upon the pillars of the clouds' f–f 𝕾 'Together with Him did I dwell in heaven' g–g 𝕾 *lit.* 'in the roots of Tehom' h 𝕷 + steti i *So* ℵ$^{c.a}$ ηγησαμην (= 𝕾 𝕷): 𝕲 εκτησαμην ('I got possession') k 248 'Jerusalem' l–l 𝕾 'establish thyself' m–m 𝕲 𝕷 'And unto eternity I shall not fail' mm *So* 𝕾: 𝕲 και ουτως

---

the following should be considered: *v.* 5 *b*, 'in the depth of the abyss I walked,' and Prov. viii. 27, 'When He prepared the heavens I was there, when He set a circle upon the face of the deep...' Wisdom is here evidently thought of as the Spirit of God; in later Jewish literature Wisdom is identified with the 'Ruaḥ ha-qodesh' ('the Holy Spirit'). Here we have, therefore, the germ of the later teaching; but a great advance was made as early as the last quarter of the second century B.C., for in the Book of Wisdom the identification of Wisdom with the Holy Spirit is implicitly taught; see Wisd. i. 4–7, and especially xi. 17: 'And Thy counsel who hath known, except Thou give wisdom, and send Thy Holy Spirit from above?' In the Midrash *Bereshith Rabbah* lxxxv it is said that Solomon's wisdom was the Holy Spirit guiding him.

4. **In the high places.** Here again may be discerned the germ of the teaching of later Judaism, according to which there were a variety of 'Mehizoth', or dwelling-places on high; according to *Hagigah* 12 *b* there were seven heavens above (cp. 2 Cor. xii. 2), in the uppermost of which, called 'Araboth', God Himself dwells; in front of it a 'Pargôd' ('curtain') of clouds is placed; this is the 'Holy of Holies' of heaven (see further Weber, *Jüd. Theologie*², pp. 162 ff.).

the pillar of cloud. See Exod. xiv. 19, &c. (the 'Shekinah' of later Jewish teaching). According to Philo (*Quis Rer. Div. Heres.* § 42=§ 231 ff. in Cohn and Wendland's ed.) the 'pillar of cloud' was Wisdom; cp. *v.* 10, 'In the holy tabernacle I ministered before Him,' and Exod. xxx. 9, 10, '...the pillar of cloud descended and stood at the door of the Tent.' In *Sotah* 33 *a* it is said that the Holy Spirit and the 'Shekinah' dwelt in the Holy of Holies. In Wisd. x. 17 it is said of Wisdom that she 'became unto them a covering in the day-time, and a flame of stars through the night' (cp. Ps. lxxviii. 14); cp. the words of Philo in reference to the pillar of cloud (*De Vita Mos.* lib. i, § 29): τάχα μέντοι καὶ τῶν ὑπάρχων τις ἦν τοῦ μεγάλου βασιλέως, ἀφανὴς ἄγγελος, ἐγκατειλημμένος τῇ νεφέλῃ προηγήτωρ, ὃν οὐ θέμις σώματος ὀφθαλμοῖς ὁρᾶσθαι.

5. **the circuit of heaven.** γῦρον οὐρανοῦ; the same expression occurs in the Sept. of Job xxii. 14 (= חוג שמים); cp. xliii. 12; Prov. viii. 27.

in the depth of the abyss. Cp. i. 3, and Job xxxvi. 30 שָׁרְשֵׁי הים (= 𝕾 בעקׄרׄא דתהׄומׄא, see critical note), Amos ix. 3 בקרקע הים ('in the bottom of the sea'). Cp. the Babylonian belief of Ea, 'the lord of wisdom,' whose wisdom came forth from Apsu, 'the deep,' which is called also 'the house of Wisdom'.

6. **I held sway.** See critical note.

7. **With all these...** i.e. with every people and nation. 'On the thought here expressed the Rabbis based, later on, the legend (referring to Deut. xxxiii. 2 and Job iii. 3) that the Law was offered to all nations, but was refused by them, before it was accepted by the Israelites at Mount Sinai (*Abodah Zarah* 2 *b* towards the end)' (Ryssel *in loc.*). So the Midrash *Pesiqta* 186 *a* says that originally the Law was offered to all, but that Israel alone of the nations accepted it.

resting-place. ἀνάπαυσιν; so too in the Sept. of Is. xi. 10, '...and His resting-place (= מְנֻחָתוֹ) shall be glorious.'

...shall I lodge? αὐλίζομαι is the Sept. for שָׁכַן in Job xi. 14, xv. 28, xxxviii. 19 (cp. 3 Esdras ix. 2); as Smend points out, the expressions מנוחה and שָׁכַן are used in this sense of God also.

8. **the Creator of all things.** Cp. li. (12⁴) 'He that formed all things', as in Jer. x. 16, li. 19; cp. 1 Enoch lxxxiv. 3,

fixed my dwelling-place (for me). κατέπαυσεν τὴν σκηνήν μου, lit. 'made my tent to rest'; Wisdom, after having vainly sought a resting-place among a people who would welcome her, has finally to leave the decision with God.

Let thy dwelling-place be in Jacob... κατασκήνωσον, cp. John i. 14. Contrast with what is said in this verse 1 Enoch xlii. 1, 2: 'Wisdom found no place where she might dwell; then a dwelling-place was assigned her in the heavens. Wisdom came to make her dwelling among the children of men, and found no dwelling-place; then Wisdom returned to her place, and took her seat among the angels'; cp. lxxxiv. 3, xciv. 5. Wisdom is here identified with the Law, the perfect expression of divine Wisdom.

9. **He created me...** With this thought cp. John xvii. 5.

The memorial of me... This rendering of 𝕾 is preferable to that of 𝕲, since it is the Law (see the verses which follow) with which Wisdom is identified; this is thought of here; cp. Exod. xiii. 9, 16; Deut. vi. 8, 9, xi. 18.

10. **In the holy tabernacle...** The worship of the Tabernacle was the carrying out of the Law, so that, as personified, Wisdom could be said to minister before God.

in Zion... i.e. when the Temple took the place of the Tabernacle.

𝔊 11 In the Holy[n] City likewise[o] [p]He caused me to rest[p],
And in Jerusalem was my authority.
12 And I took root[q] among an honoured[r] people,
In the portion of the Lord (and) of His inheritance[s].
13 I was exalted like a cedar in Libanus,
And like an olive-tree[t] on the mountains of Zion[u].
14 I was exalted like a palm-tree on the sea-shore[v],
And as rose-plants in Jericho;
And as a fair[w] olive-tree in the plain[x];
Yea, I was exalted as a plane-tree [y]by the waters[y].
15 As cinnamon and aspalathus [z]have I given a scent of[z] perfumes,
And as choice myrrh I spread abroad a pleasant odour;
As[a] galbanum, and onyx, and stacte;
[b](I was) as the smoke of incense in the Tabernacle[b].
16 I as a terebinth[bb] [c]stretched forth my branches[c],
And my branches were branches of glory[d] and grace.

[n] *So* 248 𝔏 Eth: 𝔊 𝔖 'beloved' [o] 𝔖 '(. . . beloved) like me' [p–p] 𝔖 𝔏 Eth 'I rested' [q] 𝔖 'I was magnified' [r] ℵ^{c.a} 'approved' [s] 𝔖 + 'Israel': 𝔏 + 'and among the multitude of the saints was my abode' [t] *So* 𝔖 (*cp.* ℌ *in* l. 10). [u] *So* 𝔏 (*cp.* Deut. iv. 48, Sept.), *see exegetical note* [v] ℵ^{c.a} 253 𝔖 Syro-Hex 'in Engadi': 248 εν γαδδι: 𝔏 'in Cades' [w] 𝔖 > [x] 70 248 'the beautiful plain' [y–y] *So* 70 157 248 𝔖 𝔏: 𝔊 > [z–z] V 248 253 𝔖 Syro-Hex > [a] 𝔖 𝔏 *insert* 'incense and' [b–b] 𝔖 'I gave forth my perfumes as (that of) good oil' [bb] 𝔖 'oleander' [c–c] 𝔖 'fixed my roots' [d] 𝔏 'perfume'

11. **the Holy City . . .** ἡγιασμένῃ (cp. xxxvi. 18) instead of ἠγαπημένῃ is perhaps to be preferred, as the phrase 'the Holy City' (עיר הקדש) is supported by O. T. usage (Isa. xlviii. 2, lii. 1; Neh. xi. 1, 18; Dan. ix. 24), whereas 'the Beloved City' is not found (but cp. Ps. cxxxvii. 2).

He caused me to rest. Cp. Ps. cxxxii. 8, 14.

in Jerusalem was . . . It is possible that the thought of Wisdom having had her abode above (see *v.* 4) and coming to dwell in Jerusalem contributed to the later idea of Jerusalem having its counterpart above; cp. *Test. Twelve Patr.*, Dan. v. 12, 13; *Sib. Orac.* iii. 657 ff., iv; 4 Ezra vii. 26, viii. 52, 53, x. 44–59; 2 Bar. iv. 2–6, xxxii. 4; and in the N. T. Gal. iv. 26; Heb. xii. 22; Rev. iii. 12, xxi. 10; the same idea occurs often in Rabbinical literature; the earthly Jerusalem (ירושלים של מטה) is paralleled by the Jerusalem that is above (ירושלים של מעלה); cp. e.g. *Pesaḥim* 50 *a* and the Midrash *Pesiqta* 143 *a*.

12. **. . . of His inheritance.** Cp. xvii. 17, and Sept. of Deut. xxxii. 9; Zech. ii. 16.

13. **like a cedar . . .** Cf. Ps. xcii. 12.

an olive-tree. κυπάρισσος is the rendering of עץ שמן ('Oleaster') in l. 10 (= 𝔖 אילנא דמשחא).

Zion. 'Apparently Ἀερμών is a correction in the Greek ("innergriechische Korrektur"), which put the more usual name for the rarer one' (Smend); cp. Hebr. of Deut. iv. 48. 𝔖 'Senir,' cp. Deut. iii. 9.

14. **on the sea-shore.** See critical note. It is possible that the right reading is 'in Engadi', for, as Ryssel points out, palm-trees do not grow to any great height on the seashore, whereas Engadi was famed for them (see Buhl, *Geographie des alten Palästina*, pp. 58, 165).

rose-plants in Jericho. Cp. xxxix. 13, l. 8; i.e. 'the Rhododaphne' (= 'Oleander'), which grows on the banks of the Jordan (cp. the rendering of 𝔖 'field of roses'): see Buhl, *op. cit.*, p. 59.

a fair olive-tree. Still to be seen growing in great luxuriance in the plains round the site of Jericho.

a plane-tree. Hebr. ערמון as in Gen. xxx. 37; Ezek. xxxi. 8, the only occurrences in the O. T.; see further J. Löw, *Aramäische Pflanzennamen*, p. 107.

15. **cinnamon.** Cf. Exod. xxx. 23, 34; Prov. vii. 17; Cant. iv. 14 (קִנָּמוֹן).

aspalathus = *Genista acanthoclada* (cp. Löw, *op. cit.*, p. 340); according to Pliny (*Hist. Nat.* xii. 24) the root was used for making ointment.

choice myrrh. מָר־דְּרוֹר Exod. xxx. 23.

galbanum. חֶלְבְּנָה Exod. xxx. 34, a gum used as an ingredient for making incense (cf. Löw, *op. cit.*, p. 115).

onyx. שְׁחֵלֶת Exod. xxx. 34; 'unguis odoratus.' Onycha is 'generally believed to be the operculum of some species of marine mollusc. The operculum is a horny or calcareous plate attached to the foot of certain Gasteropodous molluscs, the function of which is to close the aperture of the shell when the animal has withdrawn into the interior' (*EB*, iii. 3511). The operculum when burned gives forth a strong but pleasant odour, and was likewise used as an ingredient for making incense.

stacte. נָטָף Exod. xxx. 34, an odoriferous gum; the Hebr. name was given, apparently, because this gum was gathered by *drops*. See further Nowack, *Hebr. Archäol.* ii. 64, 248.

as the smoke of incense . . . i.e. something holy, pleasant, and acceptable; its special sanctity is seen by the punishment meted out to those who offer it without being entitled to do so, cp. Num. xvi. 6 ff., 17 ff.; 2 Chron. xxvi. 16, and who use it for profane purposes, cp. Lev. x. 1 ff.; for its pleasantness, &c., cp. Ps. xlv. 8; Prov. vii. 17, xxvii. 9; Cant. iii. 6.

16. **terebinth . . .** It is still seen to be characteristic for its far-spreading branches (cp. Nowack, *op. cit.* i. 63).

𝔊 17 I as a vine put forth grace[e],
And my flowers are the fruit of glory and wealth[f].
19 Come unto me, ye[g] that desire me,
And be ye filled with my produce[h];
20 For my memorial[i] is sweeter than honey,
And the possession of me than the honey-comb.
21 They that eat shall still hunger [k]for me[k],
And they that drink me shall still thirst [k]for me[k];
22 He that obeyeth me will [l]not be ashamed[l],
And [m]they that serve me will not commit sin[m].'
23 All these things are the book of the covenant of God Most High,
The Law which Moses commanded (as) an heritage for the assemblies of Jacob[n],
25 Which filleth (men) with wisdom, like Pison,
And like Tigris in the days of [o]new (fruits)[o];
26 Which overfloweth like Euphrates, with understanding,
And as Jordan in the days of harvest[p];
𝔖 27 [q] [qq]Which poureth forth[qq], as the Nile, instruction[q],
𝔊 And[r] as Gihon in the days of vintage.
28 The first man knew her not perfectly,
So also the last will not trace her out;
29 [s]For her understanding is more full than the sea,
And her counsel is greater than the deep[s].
30 And as for me, I (was) as a [t]stream from the[t] river,
And I came forth as a conduit into a garden;
31 I said: 'I will water my garden,
I will abundantly water my garden beds';

[e] 248 'perfume': 𝔏 in suavitate odoris [f] 70 248 𝔏 (*with slight variations*) + 'I am the mother of beauteous love, and of fear, and of knowledge, and of holy hope; I, the ever-existing one, am given to all my children, to those who are called by Him' (= *v.* 18). [g] א 𝔖 'all ye' [h] 𝔖 'good fruits' [i] 𝔖 'instruction': 𝔏 'spirit' [k–k] *So* 𝔖: 𝔊 𝔏 > [l–l] 𝔖 'not fail' [m–m] 𝔖 'none of his works will be destroyed' [n] 70 248 (*with slight variations*) + 'Faint not, (but) be strong in the Lord, and cleave unto Him in order that He may strengthen you. Cleave unto Him; the Lord, the Almighty, is the one and only God, and beside Him there is no Saviour' (= *v.* 24) [o–o] 𝔖 'its fruits' [p] 𝔖 'Nisan' [q–q] 𝔊 (ως φως) *misread* יאור (= 'the Nile') *as* אור ('light'), *and wrote* εκφαινων ('maketh to shine forth') *in order to make sense* [qq–qq] = 𝔏 qui mittit [r] *So* 248 254 Syro-Hex 𝔏 𝔖 [s–s] *The rendering of* 𝔊 *is due to a misunderstanding of the Hebrew way of expressing the comparative* [t–t] 𝔖 >

17. **the fruit . . .** Cp. Prov. iii. 16, viii. 18, 19. See critical note.
19. **Come unto me.** Cp. Prov. ix. 4.
20. **sweeter than honey . . . honey-comb.** Cp. Ps. xix. 10 in reference to the Law; cp. Prov. xvi. 24.
21. With the thought of the verse contrast John vi. 58, iv. 14.
22. **will not commit sin.** Cp. *Pirqe Aboth*, ii. 2: 'Excellent is Torah-study together with worldly business, for the practice of them puts iniquity out of remembrance.' With the whole verse cp. *Test. Twelve Patr.*, Levi xiii. 7, 8. With this verse Wisdom concludes her speech.
23. **All these things . . .** The identification of the Law with Wisdom in this and the following verses comes out very clearly.
The Law which . . . assemblies. From Deut. xxxiii. 4, where the Hebr. reads קְהִלַּת (but Sept. συναγωγαῖς); Ben-Sira (so also the Sept. in Deut. xxxiii. 4) was thinking of the synagogues of the Dispersion.
25. **Pison.** Cp. Gen. ii. 11 ff.
new (fruits). Cp. l. 8; Num. xxviii. 26 (Sept.).
26. **in the days of harvest.** Cp. Joshua iii. 15.
27. See critical note.
And as Gihon. The addition of 'and' is well attested (see critical note); its omission (so 𝔊) would imply the identification of Gihon with the Nile, as in the Sept. of Jer. ii. 18 (Smend).
in the days of vintage. i. e. September to October, when the river is in full flood.
28. **The first man . . .** i. e. the first man who sought to fathom her (Fritzsche).
29. See critical note.
the deep. ἄβυσσος; cp. *v.* 5; Gen. vii. 11; Ps. xxxvi. 6.
30. **And as for me.** i. e. the writer, who speaks now of himself; he continues the metaphor of the river (as in *vv.* 25–27), and compares himself to a small irrigation canal leading out from the great river of Wisdom.
31. **I will water my garden.** i. e. he intended to use his waters of Wisdom for himself alone at first; but later on his stream 'became a river . . .', i. e. others were to benefit by it. Cp. Is. lviii. 11, 'thou shalt be like a watered garden'; John vii. 38.

𝔊 And lo, my stream became a river,
And my river [u]became a[u] sea.
32 Yet again will I bring instruction to light as the morning,
And will make these things shine forth afar off.
33 Yet again will I pour forth doctrine as prophecy,
And leave it for eternal generations.
34 [v]Look ye (and see), that I have not laboured for myself only,
But for all those that diligently seek her[w v].

(*b*) XXV. 1–2. *Three things which are beautiful, and three which are hateful* (= 2 + 2 distichs).

𝔖 **25** 1 [a]Three things hath my soul desired[a],
And [b]they are[b] lovely in the sight of God and men:
𝔊 The concord of brethren, and the friendship of neighbours,
And a [bb]husband and wife[bb] suited to each other.
2 Three types (of men) doth my soul hate,
And I am greatly offended at their life:
𝔥[A] The poor man that is haughty, and the rich man that is deceitful[c],
And an old man that is an adulterer [cc]lacking understanding[cc].

(*c*) XXV. 3–6. *A beautiful thing is wisdom and counsel among the aged* (= 1 + 2 + 1 distichs).

3 (If) in thy youth thou hast not gathered[d],
How wilt thou find in thine old age?
𝔊 4 [dd]How beautiful [e]to grey hairs[e] is judgement,
And for elders to know counsel!
5 How beautiful is the wisdom of princes[f],
And thought and counsel in those (who are) honoured!
6 The crown[g] of the aged is their much experience,
And their glorying is the fear of the Lord.

(*d*) XXV. 7–11. *Ten types of men who are blessed* (= 1 + 5 + 1 distichs).

7 [h]Nine (types of men) have I conceived of[h]; (these) I accounted blessed;
And a tenth will I speak of with my tongue:
A man that hath joy of his children[hh],
Who liveth to see his enemy's fall.

u–u 𝔖 'reached to the' v–v 𝔖 > w 𝔏 'truth'
a–a 𝔊 'In three things I was beautiful': ωραισθην *is perhaps a textual corruption of* ηρασθην (*Hart*): 𝔏 = 𝔖 b–b 𝔊 ανεστην ('I stood') *is probably a corruption of* α εστιν (= 253 𝔏) bb–bb *So* 𝔖 𝔏: 𝔊 'a wife and a husband' c 𝔊 'a liar' cc–cc 𝔥 > d 𝔖 + 'wisdom' dd 𝔥 *is wanting from here to v.* 8 e–e 𝔖 'among old men' f *So* 𝔖: 𝔊 'old men' (*cp.* 𝔏 veteranis) g 𝔖 'honour' h–h *Lit.* 'nine conceptions' (εννεα υπονοηματα), *to which* ℵ[c.a] + *the correction* ανυπονοητα (= 𝔖 𝔏) hh 𝔖 'posterity'

32. With this and the following verses cp. 4 Macc. i. 15–19.
afar off. i. e. to those of the Dispersion.
33. ... **doctrine as prophecy.** As Smend points out, these words show that there was no rigid idea as yet concerning a fixed canon of Scripture.
34. This verse occurs in almost identical form again as xxxiii. 17 (= 𝔊 xxx. 26).
(*b*) XXV. 1–2
1. **concord of brethren.** Cp. Ps. cxxxiii. 1.
a husband and wife. Cp. xl. 23 *b*.
suited to each other. ἑαυτοῖς συμπεριφερόμενοι; cp. Sept. of Prov. v. 19 συνπεριφερόμενος πολλοστὸς ἔσῃ.
2. **Three types.** τρία εἴδη; cp. xxiii. 16 δύο εἴδη (lit. 'species').
at their life. i. e. that they are alive. The two last clauses of the verse are quoted in *Pesaḥim* 113 *b* (T. B.).
lacking understanding. The Talmud quotation has instead of this: 'And a president who behaves himself proudly towards the congregation' (Cowley and Neubauer, p. xxiv); the same words occur also in *Ḥagigah* 5 *b* (פרנס המתגאה על הצבור).
(*c*) XXV. 3–6.
3. **(If) in thy youth ...** Quoted in *Aboth de R. Nathan*, c. 24, thus: 'If in thy youth thou hast had no delight in them, how wilt thou attain to them in thine old age?' (Cowley and Neubauer, p. xxiv); cp. vi. 18.
6. **The crown.** Cp. i. 18.
(*d*) XXV. 7–11.
7. **Who liveth ...** Cp. Ps. xviii. 37, 38, liv. 7, cxii. 8.

𝕳[C] 8 [i]Blessed is the husband of an understanding wife,
[ii]That doth not plough with ox and ass[ii].
[j]Blessed is he that hath not slipped with his tongue[j],
And he that hath not served one [jj]inferior (to himself)[jj i].
𝕲 9 *[k]Blessed is the man[k] that hath found a true friend[kk],
And that discourseth unto [l]ears that hear[l].
10 How great is he that findeth wisdom,
But he is not above him that feareth the Lord.
11 The fear of the Lord surpasseth all things:
[ll]He that holdeth it, to whom shall he be likened[ll]?

(*e*) XXV. 13–15. *Some of the worst forms of evil* (= 2 + 1 distichs).

𝕳[C] 13 Any wound, only not a heart-wound!
Any wickedness, only not the wickedness of a woman!
𝕲 14 †Any calamity, only not the calamity (brought about) by those who hate!
Any vengeance, only not the vengeance of enemies!
15 There is no poison [m]above the poison[m] of a serpent,
And there is no wrath above the wrath of a woman[mm].

(*f*) XXV. 16–26. *The evil of a wicked woman* (= 1 + 2 + 1 + 1 + 2 + 2 + 1 + 2 distichs).

16 I would rather dwell with a lion and a dragon,
Than [n]keep house with[n] a wicked woman.
𝕳[C] 17 The wickedness of a woman [nn]maketh black[nn] her look[o],
And darkeneth her countenance like that of a bear[oo].
18 In the midst of his friends her husband sitteth,
And involuntarily[p] he sigheth bitterly[q].

i–i 𝕳 *is much mutilated in this verse, and the order of the clauses is wrong, viz. c d a b* ii–ii 𝕲 > j–j *Most of this clause is mutilated in* 𝕳 jj–jj 𝕲 'that is unworthy of him' * 𝕳 *is wanting from here to v.* 13 k–k *So* א 𝕾: 𝕲 𝕷 > kk *So* 𝕷: 𝕾 'a friend': 𝕲 'prudence' l–l 𝕾 𝕷 'the ear of one that heareth' ll–ll 𝕾 'Hold it fast, my son, and let it not go; there is nothing to be likened unto it': 70 248 𝕷 (*with slight variations*) + 'The beginning of the fear of the Lord is to love Him, and the beginning of faith is to cleave unto Him' (= *v.* 12) † 𝕳 *is wanting from here to v.* 17 m–m 𝕲 'head', *misunderstanding of* ראש, *which means* 'poison' *as well as* 'head' mm *So* 𝕾: 𝕷 𝕲 'enemy' n–n *So* B א*: A א[c.a] 'dwell with' (= 𝕾) nn–nn 𝕾 'maketh pale' (*cp.* Jer. xxx. 6) o 𝕳 (*later hand*) + '(of her) husband' (= 𝕾) oo *So* א A *all the cursives*: B 'like sackcloth': א A *cursives* = 𝕳: 𝕾 'like the colour of a sack': 𝕷 *combines both renderings*: 'like a bear and like sackcloth' p *Reading* טעם מר *for* טעמו: 𝕲 ακουσας *is a corruption of* ακουσιως (248 𝕾) q 𝕾 >: 𝕷 modicum: 248 + 'through her'

8. **Blessed is the husband . . .** 𝕲 'Blessed is the man that dwelleth with . . .'; for ὁ συνοικῶν 𝕳 𝕾 have בעל ('husband'); 𝕳 is mutilated.

That doth not plough . . . This clause is undoubtedly genuine and occurs both in 𝕳 and 𝕾 (out of place in the former); it has dropped out of 𝕲 by mistake; without it there are only nine, instead of ten (see *v.* 7 *b*) types of men enumerated. Cp. Deut. xxii. 10; 2 Cor. vi. 14; the words are of course metaphorical.

that hath not slipped . . . Cp. xiv. 1; Jas. iii. 2.

9. **a true friend.** The second clause shows that 𝕲 ('prudence') is wrong here.

10. **that feareth . . .** Cp. i. 16.

11. **He that holdeth . . .** Cp. vi. 27. For the gloss added after this verse (= *v.* 12) see critical note.

(*e*) XXV. 13–15.

13. This verse is quoted in *Shabb.* 11 *a* (T. B.); see Cowley and Neubauer, p. xxiv; cp. Schechter, *JQR*, iii. 697 f.

14. **Any calamity . . .** Those that hate obviously desire misfortune to befall the object of their hatred, and what vengeance is there but the vengeance of an enemy? Smend rightly points out that שנא(ים) (= μισούντων) and צר(ים) (= ἐχθρῶν) were mistakes for שְׂנְאָה (vii. 26) and צָרָה (xxxvii. 11). The passage refers to the evils of polygamy, which, according to xxvi. 6, xxxvii. 11, was still in vogue in Ben-Sira's day.

15. **poison.** For ראש (see critical note) cp. Deut. xxxii. 33; Job xx. 16: in the former passage the Sept. renders the word by θυμός ('wrath'); see next clause. 𝕾 makes the same mistake.

(*f*) XXV. 16–26.

16. **I would rather . . .** Cp. Prov. xxi. 19, xxv. 24; εὐδοκήσω.

17. **maketh black.** 𝕲 'altereth'; the verb occurs elsewhere only in Job xxx. 30 in the O. T.; for the noun see Lam. iv. 8; Eccles. xi. 10, and for the adjective Lev. xiii. 31, 37; Cant. i. 5, v. 11; Zech. vi. 2, 6.

like that of a bear. In the Midrash *Bereshith Rabba* to xxxix. 7 God is made to speak of Potiphar's wife as a 'she-bear'. For the variant readings here see the discussion in the Introd. § 3 (*b*).

18. **In the midst . . .** 𝕲 ἀνὰ μέσον τοῦ πλησίον αὐτοῦ ἀναπεσεῖται ὁ ἀνὴρ αὐτῆς.

involuntarily. See critical note. With the expression בלא טעם (Neo-Hebr.) cp. בלא טעמא in *Gittin* 14 *a* (Schechter).

𝔥[c] 19 (There is but) little malice like the malice of a woman,
May the lot of the wicked fall upon her!
20 [r]As[rr] a sandy ascent to the feet of the aged,
So is a woman of tongue to a quiet man[r].
21 Fall not[s] because of the beauty of woman,
[ss]And [t]be not ensnared[t] for the sake of what she possesseth[ss];
22 For [tt]hard slavery[tt] and a disgrace it is,
(If) a wife support her husband.
𝔊 23 [u]A humbled heart and a sad countenance,
[uu]And a heart-wound, is an evil wife[u].
𝔥[c] Hands that hang down, and palsied knees,
(Thus shall it be with) a wife that maketh not happy her husband.
24 From a woman did sin originate,
And because of her [v]we all must die[v].
𝔊 25 [vv]Give not water an outlet,
Nor to a wicked woman power[x].
26 If she go not [xx]as thou wouldst have her[xx],
Cut her off from thy flesh[vv y].

r–r *So according to Smend's emendation* (*based on* 𝔊) *of the text, which is mutilated* rr 𝔊 (*exc.* 70 248) > : 𝔖 𝔏 = 𝔥 s 𝔖 'Be not enticed' ss–ss *So also* 𝔖 : *for* 𝔊 *see note below* t–t *Reading with Smend* אל תלכד : 𝔏 'look not upon' tt–tt *Reading* עבדה קשה (= 𝔖) *for* . . . בעדה *which* 𝔊 *read as* עברה ('wrath'): קשה *is wanting in the MS. of* 𝔥, *where a small hiatus occurs* u–u 𝔥 > uu 𝔖 *inserts* 'darkness' v–v *Lit.* 'we die altogether' (יחד) vv–vv *Wanting in* 𝔥 x ℵ A *and cursives* παρρησιαν : B εξουσιαν : 248 παρρησιαν εξοδον (*cp.* 𝔏 veniam prodeundi) : 𝔖 + 'For as the bursting forth of water goes on and increases, so does an evil woman continue to sin (more and more)' xx–xx *Lit.* 'according to thy hand' : 𝔏 + 'she will shame thee in the presence of thine enemies' y 248 + 'Give, and send her away' : 𝔖 + 'Give to her, and send her from thine house' : 𝔏 + Ne semper te abutatur

---

19. **(There is but) little . . .** 𝔊 renders freely: 'All malice is but little to the malice of a woman'; 𝔖 renders according to the sense of xlii. 14.

May the lot . . . i. e. may it be the lot of the wicked, not of the righteous, to have such.

20. **a sandy ascent . . .** i. e. one that is wearisome, and where it is difficult to get a foothold.

a woman of tongue. i. e. one that is abusive. The point of the comparison is that just as it is impossible for an aged man to ascend a slope where he can get no firm foothold, so it is impossible for a quiet man to get on with a woman who has an abusive tongue.

21. **Fall not.** For the expression נפל על of falling into a snare cp. Isa. xxiv. 18; Amos iii. 5; cp. also Prov. xxii. 14. 𝔊 incorrectly, 'throw not thyself upon.'

And be not ensnared . . . 𝔊[B] 'And desire not a woman': something has clearly dropped out; ἐν κάλλει is added by ℵ A and a number of cursives 𝔏 Syro-Hex; 70 248 add εἰς τρυφήν.

22. **For hard slavery . . .** See critical note; 𝔊 'There is anger, and impudence, and great reproach'.

23. The omission of the two first clauses of this verse (found in 𝔊 𝔖) by 𝔥 suggests that they are not original; the sense of them is contained in the two last clauses.

A humbled heart . . . 𝔖 'And the heart that is with her she covereth over', meaning probably that she suppresses all womanly feelings.

Hands that hang down. רִפְיוֹן יָדַיִם, lit. 'hanging down of hands', signifying helpless terror; the same expression occurs in Jer. xlvii. 3.

palsied knees. Lit. 'a tottering of knees'; the word כִּשָּׁלוֹן only occurs elsewhere in the O. T. in Prov. xvi. 18, where it means 'a calamity'. Cp. Ps. cix. 24: ברכי כשלו מצום ('my knees totter from fasting').

(Thus shall it be with). These words are unexpressed, but implied; fearfulness and calamity are to be the lot of the woman who does not make her husband happy.

24. **From a woman . . .** Cp. Gen. iii. 6; 2 Cor. xi. 3; 1 Tim. ii. 14, and see *The Life of Adam and Eve*, §§ 15–19.

did sin originate. 𝔊 '(was) the beginning of sin'.

And because of her . . . Cp. the Targum (Pseudo-Jonathan) to Gen. iii. 6, where it is said at the moment of Eve's succumbing to temptation Sammael, the Angel of Death (identified with Satan), appeared to her. In *The Life of Adam and Eve*, § 3, occurs the following: 'And Eve said to Adam, "My lord, if thou wilt, kill me; perchance the Lord God will then lead thee back into Paradise; for it was only through my fault that the anger of the Lord God was kindled against thee."' The later Jewish theology, however, generally points to Adam as the real cause for the entering of sin and death into the world (cp. 1 Cor. xv. 22), and that not so much on account of the 'Fall', as that he refused to show repentance for what he had done; see, e.g., the Midrash *Bemidbar Rabba*, chap. xiii: 'When Adam transgressed the command of the Holy One, and ate of the tree, the Holy One demanded of him penitence, thereby revealing to him the means of freedom [i.e. from the result of his sin], but Adam would not show penitence.'

25. **Nor to a wicked woman . . .** See critical note.

power. ἐξουσίαν, i. e. liberty to do what she likes; cp. 1 Cor. xiv. 34, 35.

26. **Cut her off from . . .** i. e. Give her a bill of divorcement (the later *Gêṭ*), cp. Deut. xxiv. 1 ff.; Matt. v. 31; hitherto they had been 'one flesh', cp. Gen. ii. 24; Eph. v. 31.

(*g*) XXVI. 1–4. *The happiness of the man who has a good wife* (= 2 + 2 distichs).

𝔥c **26** 1 A good wife,—blessed is her husband,
The number of his days is doubled.
2 A worthy wife cherisheth her husband,
𝔊 [a]And he fulfilleth the years of his life[b] in peace[bb a].
Yeb. 63*b* 3 A good wife [c](is) a good gift[c]:
Sanh. 100*b* She shall be given to him that feareth God, [cc]for his portion[cc].
𝔊 4 [d]Whether rich or poor, his heart is cheerful,
And his face is merry at all times.

(*h*) XXVI. 5–12. *The fearfulness of having a wicked wife* (= 3 + 3 + 2 + 2 distichs).

5 Of three things is my heart afraid,
And concerning a fourth I am in great fear[e]:
Slander in the city, and a concourse of the rabble,
[f]And a false accusation,—worse than death are they all.
6 Grief of heart and sorrow is a wife jealous of (another) wife[f],
The scourge of the tongue [g]all together[g] [are they].
7 Like[h] [i]a hard yoke[i] is[k] a wicked woman:
He that taketh hold of her is as one that graspeth a scorpion.
8 Great wrath (doth) a drunken woman (cause)[kk];
She doth not cover her own shame.
9 The whoredom of a woman is in the lifting up of her eyes,
And she will be known by her eyelids.
10 Upon a [l]headstrong daughter[l] keep strict watch,
[m]Lest, finding liberty, she use it for herself[m].

a–a 𝔥 > b *So* 248 𝔖 𝔏: 𝔊 > bb 𝔖 'joy' c–c 𝔖 > cc–cc *So* 𝔊: *Yeb. Sanh.* 'into his bosom' d 𝔥 *is wanting from here to* xxvii. 5 e προσωπῳ εφοβηθην, *so* A ℵ[c.a] 55 106 155 248 253 (= 𝔖 𝔏): B πρ. εδεηθην ('I made supplication'): ℵ* εδοθην f–f 𝔖 > g–g *So* 𝔖: 𝔊 'communicating to all' h *So* 𝔏: 𝔊 𝔖 > i–i *So* 𝔖; 𝔊 'a yoke of oxen shaken to and fro' k 𝔏 'so also is' kk 248 𝔖 + 'who strays about' l–l 𝔖 > 'daughter'; 'a wanton wife' m–m 𝔏 Ne inventa occasione utatur se

---

(*g*) XXVI. 1–4.

1. This verse is quoted twice in the Babylonian Talmud, *Yebamoth* 63*b*, *Sanhedrin* 100*b*; the only difference being that both these tractates read 'beautiful' for 'good'. With this and the next verse cp. Prov. xii. 4 *a*, xxxi. 10–12.

2. **worthy.** חיל; for this sense cp. Gen. xlvii. 6; Exod. xviii. 21, 25; Ruth iii. 11, and the references above to Prov.
cherisheth. Lit. 'maketh fat', cp. *v.* 13; 𝔊 'maketh glad'.
fulfilleth . . . Cp. Is. lxv. 20: לֹא־יִהְיֶה . . . וְזָקֵן אֲשֶׁר לֹא־יְמַלֵּא אֶת־יָמָיו.

3. **a good gift.** 𝔊 'a good portion'; cp. Prov. xviii. 22.
for his portion. Smend suggests that the rendering found in the Bab. Talmud בחיק ('into the bosom of') is a mistake for בחלק ('for [his] portion'), and refers to Num. xxvi. 53 for the use of ב.

4. **Whether rich or poor . . .** Lit. 'Of a rich man and of a poor man the heart is cheerful' (ἀγαθή), i.e. if he has a good wife.

(*h*) XXVI. 5–12.

5. **I am in great fear.** See critical note.
Slander in the city . . . Cp. Acts xix. 23 ff., xxiv. 12.

6. **a wife jealous . . .** The result of polygamy.
all together [are they]. i.e. All the four things enumerated, slander, the concourse of the rabble, a false accusation, and a wife's jealousy, are results of the scourge of an evil tongue.

7. **a hard yoke.** This rendering of 𝔖 simplifies matters; but the rendering of 𝔊, βοοζύγιον σαλευόμενον, suggests a misunderstanding of the original, which possibly had כמטת על ('like the bars of a yoke'), cp. Lev. xxvi. 13; Nahum i. 13; מוֹטָה ('a pole', or 'bar') was understood as though part of the verb מוט ('to shake'). In this case the point of the comparison would be that just as the bars of the yoke were constantly rubbing and chafing the neck of the ox, so a wicked woman was, by her behaviour, a constant source of irritation to her husband.
He that taketh hold . . . The thought seems to be that if a man attempts to assert his authority over a woman of this kind he will suffer grievously for doing so; deadly retaliation will be the result, i.e. some bitter slander or false accusation (see *v.* 5 *a*, and cp. Ezek. ii. 6). The simile of the scorpion is the more apt inasmuch as its sting was believed to be deadly (cp. Deut. viii. 15).

8. **She doth not . . .** i.e. Drunkenness leads her to adultery.

9. **. . . by her eyelids.** Cp. Prov. vi. 25; see also 2 Kings ix. 30; Jer. iv. 30; Ezek. xxiii. 40; for the Oriental customs and methods of painting the eyelids and eyebrows, &c., see *ZDMG*, 1851, pp. 236 ff.

10. **Upon a headstrong . . .** This clause occurs also in xlii. 11 *a*.
Lest, finding . . . Cp. xxiii. 16, 17.

𝔊 11 Look well after a shameless eye,
[n]And marvel not if it trespass against thee[n].
12 As a thirsty traveller that openeth his mouth,
And drinketh of any water that is near,
So she sitteth down at every post,
And openeth her quiver to every arrow.

(*i*) XXVI. 13–18. *The joy of the man who has a good wife* (= 3+3 distichs).

13 [o]The grace of a wife delighteth her husband,
And her understanding fatteneth his bones[o].
14 A silent woman (is) a gift from the Lord,
And [p]a well-instructed soul[p] [q]is above worth[q].
15 Grace upon grace is a shamefast[r] woman,
And there is no price worthy of [s]a continent soul[s].
16 As[t] the sun arising in the highest places of the Lord,
So[t] is the beauty of a good wife in the ordering of his[tt] [her husband's] house.
17 As the lamp shining on the holy candlestick,
So is the beauty [u]of a face[u] [v]on a stately figure[v].
18 As the golden pillars upon the silver base,
So are beautiful feet [w]upon firm heels[w].

(*j*) XXVI. 19–27. *A later appendix to the preceding* (= 3+4+1+1+1 distichs).

70 248 19 My son, [x]keep thyself healthy in the flower of thine age[x],
And give not thy strength unto strangers.
20 Having found a portion of good soil out of all the land,
Sow it with thine own seed, trusting in thine own good birth.
21 Thus will thine offspring flourish,
And, having confidence in their noble descent, will become great.
22 A hired woman is as spittle[xx],
But a married woman is reckoned as a tower of death [y]to them that use her[y].
23 A godless woman shall be given to the man who regardeth not the Law as his portion;
But a devout (woman) is given to him that feareth[yy] the Lord.
24 A shameless woman despiseth shamefastness;
But a shamefast daughter will show modesty even before her husband.

n–n 𝔖 'And tarry not lest she deceive thee' o–o 𝔖 > p–p 𝔖 *lit.* 'a lacking of throat', *i.e.* 'self-control in speech' q–q *Lit.* 'there is no exchange for' r 248 + 'and faithful' s–s 𝔖 *lit.* 'a lacking of mouth' t *So* 𝔖 𝔏: 𝔊 > tt *So* B*: B[a] ℵ A αυτης u–u 𝔖 'of a good woman' v–v 𝔖 'in keeping her house' w–w *Reading* επι πτερναις ευσταθεσι (*cp.* ℵ 248): B A επι στερνοις ευσταθους: 𝔏 super plantas stabiles mulieris: 𝔖 'in the ordering of her house' x–x 𝔖 'take heed to thyself in the time of thy youth' xx 𝔖 'naught' y–y 𝔖 'to them that cleave unto her' yy 70 'loveth'

---

11. **Look well . . .** The reference is still to 'a headstrong daughter'; in the second clause 𝔖 (see critical note) is perhaps to be preferred; there must be no hesitation in dealing with such a daughter.

(*i*) XXVI. 13–18.

13. **. . . fatteneth his bones.** i.e. is the means of giving him physical health and strength; cp. Prov. xv. 30.
14. **A silent woman.** Cp. xxxvi. 23 (28 in 𝔊).
15. **price.** Cp. vi. 15.
16. **the highest places . . .** Cp. xliii. 9.
17. **the holy candlestick.** Cp. 1 Macc. i. 21, iv. 49, 50.
18. **As the golden pillars . . .** i.e. the pillars of the Temple which were covered with gold; cp. 1 Macc. i. 22, 23.
upon firm heels. See critical note.

(*j*) XXVI. 19–27. These verses occur only in 70, 248 among the Greek MSS.; they are, however, preserved in the Syriac and Arabic versions, and some of the clauses are quoted by Clement of Alexandria and in the 'Commonplace Books' of the monks Antonius and Maximus (see Hart, pp. 321–370). In the main they are derived from the secondary recension of the Hebrew (see Introduction, § 3 (*c*)); this is proved by the fact that in 𝔖 there are various errors of translation which can only be explained on the basis of a Hebrew original (see Ryssel *in loc.*).

19. This verse is quoted in Antonius and Maximus (Hart, p. 367).
give not thy strength . . . Cp. Prov. v. 9, 10, xxxi. 3.
20. **a portion of good soil.** i.e. a good wife.
21. For the general sense of the verse cp. Prov. v. 15–19.
22. This verse is quoted by Clement of Alexandria (Hart, p. 330).
as spittle. ἴση σιάλῳ; cp. Sept. of Isa. xl. 15 ὡς σίελος = כרק (Smend).
. . . as a tower of death. See 2 Macc. xiii. 5 ff. (Nestle, quoted by Ryssel).
24. This verse is quoted by Antonius and Maximus (Hart, p. 367).

248 25 [z]A headstrong woman[z] will be regarded as a dog;
But she that hath shame feareth the Lord.
26 The woman that honoureth her own husband appeareth[a] wise unto all,
But she that dishonoureth (her husband) [aa]is known to[aa] all as one that is godless in (her) pride.
Happy is the husband of a good wife,
For the number of his years is doubled[b].
27 A loud-voiced and tongueful woman is reckoned as [bb]a trumpet[bb] that putteth enemies to flight;
[c]And the soul of every suchlike man will pass his life in the turmoils of war[c].

(*k*) XXVI. 28. *Three things that cause sorrow* (= 3 distichs).

𝔊 28 For two things my heart is grieved,
And for a third cometh wrath upon me:
A [cc]man of war[cc] suffering on account of poverty,
Men of understanding who suffer contempt,
(And) one that turneth from righteousness to sin;—
May the Lord prepare [d]him for the sword[d].

(*l*) XXVI. 29—XXVII. 3. *The temptations of trade* (= 3+1 distichs).

29 [e]Hardly[f] shall the merchant keep himself from wrongdoing[g],
And a huckster will not be acquitted of sin.
27 1 Many have sinned for the sake of gain[gg];
And he that seeketh to multiply (gain)[h] turneth away his eye.
2 [i]A nail sticketh fast between [k]the joinings of[k] stones[l],
[m]And [n]sin will thrust itself in[n] between buyer and seller.
3 [o]My son[o], if [p]thou hold not[p] diligently to the fear of the Lord,
[q]Thy[r] house will soon be overthrown[q].

(*a*) XXVII. 4–7. *The appraising of a man's value* (= 3+1 distichs).

4 [s]When a sieve is shaken, the refuse remaineth;
So (it is with) the filth of man in his reasoning[s].

z–z 𝔖 'A woman that hath no shame' a 𝔖 'is reckoned' aa–aa 70 'is accounted by' b 𝔖 + 'The strife of a woman is even in her gentleness, and as a burning fever so shall she appear' bb–bb 248 > c–c 70 > cc–cc 𝔖 'man of wealth' d–d *So* 248 253 (= 𝔏): 𝔊 'the sword for him': 𝔖 *is a paraphrase* e 𝔏 *inserts the clause*: Duae species difficiles et periculosae mihi apparuerunt f 𝔖 'with great difficulty' g 𝔖 + 'But in many things he stumbleth' gg *Reading, with* ℵ*, διαφορου (B A ℵ^c.a αδιαφορου). *Cp.* vii. 18 h 𝔖 'sins' i 𝔏 *inserts* 'As' k–k 𝔖 > l 𝔖 'one stone and another' m 𝔏 *inserts* 'So' n–n *Reading* συνθλιβησεται *for* συντριβησεται (𝔏 angustiabitur): 𝔖 'sins are fixed' o–o *So* 𝔖 p–p *So* 𝔏: 𝔖 'if thou transgress but a little' q–q 𝔖 'For long time wilt thou be in want' r *So* 𝔏 s–s 254 𝔖 >

25. **as a dog.** Used typically of some one without shame (cp. Deut. xxiii. 18).
26. **Happy is the husband . . .** These two clauses are almost identical with *v.* 1.
27. This verse is quoted by Antonius and Maximus (Hart, p. 368).
(*k*) XXVI. 28.
28. **A man of war.** Perhaps Smend is right in preferring here the rendering of 𝔖, 'a man of wealth'; in the two other types of men referred to in this verse contrasts are presented—a wise man suffering contempt, a righteous man committing sin—so that logically one would expect a similar contrast in this case as well—a rich man suffering poverty; the Hebrew may have had איש חיל ('a man of wealth,' lit. 'strength'), which was misunderstood by 𝔊; cp. Ruth ii. 1.
one that turneth from . . . Cp. Ezek. xviii. 24; Matt. xii. 45; 2 Pet. ii. 2.
XXVI. 29–XXVII. 3.
29. **Hardly shall the merchant . . .** Cf. *Pirqe Aboth* ii. 6: '. . . Nor is every one that hath much traffic wise.' In *Erubin* 55 *b*, where Deut. xxx. 13 is commented upon, it is said that the Torah 'is not found either among hucksters or among merchants', the reason being that their constant travelling from place to place prevents study. Schechter (*Studies in Judaism*, Second Series, p. 72) refers to *Qiddushin* 82 *a*, where it is said that the hawker and the shopkeeper are engaged in trades of bad odour, and the latter are said to practise 'the handicraft of robbery'.
XXVII. 1. **turneth away his eye.** i.e. will acquiesce in what is wrong; cp. Prov. xxviii. 27.
2. **nail.** Lit. 'tent-peg', cp. xiv, 24.
3. **My son . . .** 𝔊 'Unless (a man) hold on diligently . . . his house will soon . . .'; cf. Prov. xiv. 11.
XXVII. 4—XXIX. 28. This division continues the general theme of the preceding. It gives further illustrations of applied wisdom. Such topics as malice, anger, revenge, strife, calumny, and their baneful effects are dealt with; and lastly mercy in its several aspects. The whole falls into twelve subsections.
(*a*) XXVII. 4-7.
4. **a sieve.** i.e. the 'Kirbal-el-Kamachi', still used in Palestine. The corn which has been threshed for the first time is placed in it and sifted; the refuse, i.e. the dung of the oxen which has been trodden into the straw, remains behind,

𝔥[A] 5 [t]The furnace proveth[u] the potter's vessels,
[v]And the trying[v] of a man (is done) by examining him.
6 Upon the cultivation of the tree dependeth the fruit;
So (dependeth) man's[vv] thought upon his nature[t].
𝔊 7 [w]Praise no man [x]before taking stock (of him)[x],
For this (is) the (way to make) trial of men[w].

(*b*) XXVII. 8–10. *Reward and retribution* (= 3 distichs).

8 If thou follow after righteousness[y], thou wilt attain[z],
Baba Qamma And put it on as a robe of glory.
92*b* 9 Every bird[a] dwelleth[b] with its kind,
𝔊 And truth returneth[c] to them who practise her.
10 The lion lieth in wait for prey;
So do sins[d] for those who [e]work iniquity[e].

(*c*) XXVII. 11–15. *Concerning varieties of speech* (= 2 + 3 distichs).

11 The discourse of the wise[f] man continueth[g] [h]in wisdom[h],
But the fool changeth as the moon.
12 In the midst of fools [i]watch closely the time[i],
But [k]among the wise abide continually[k].
13 The discourse of fools[l] is an annoyance[m],
And their laughter is [n]sinful wantonness[n].
14 [o]The oath of the godless[o] maketh the hair stand upright;
Their strife maketh one stop his ears.
15 The strife of the proud is shedding of blood,
And their reviling is grievous[p] hearing.

t–t *vv.* 5, 6 *come after* vi. 22 in 𝔥[A]: *the text is in part corrupt* u *Reading* לבחר *for* לבער (*Smend*) v–v *Reading* ומסת *for* וכמהו (*Smend*) vv *Reading* אדם w–w *Wanting in* 𝔖: 𝔥 *is wanting from here to* xxxii x–x *Reading* προ διαλογισμου (*cp. v.* 5 *b*) *for* προ λογισμου y 𝔖 'truth' z 248 + αυτο (= 𝔖 𝔏) a 𝔖 'the birds of the heaven' b 𝔊 καταλυσει (*al.* καταλυει): 𝔏 conveniunt c 𝔖 'walketh' d 𝔖 'unrighteousness' e–e 𝔖 'commit sins' f *So* A (= 𝔖): 𝔊 'godly': 𝔏 sanctus in sapientia g *So* 𝔏: 𝔊 > h–h *So* 248 𝔖: 𝔏 'as the sun' i–i 𝔖 'bide thy time': 𝔏 serva verbum tempori k–k 𝔖 'among the wise speak continually' l 𝔏 'sinners' m 𝔖 𝔏 'hateful' n–n 𝔖 'impertinence' o–o *So* 𝔖 (*reading* מומתא *for* מוהבתא 'gift') p א[c.a] V 'evil'

while the grain passes through the sieve (cp. *Zeitsch. du deutschen Palästina Vereins*, xci. 2). The point of the comparison is that, in the case of the type of man under consideration, the bad qualities remain in him, just as the refuse remains behind in the sieve; while the good that is in him passes away.

5. With this verse cp. *Test. Twelve Patr.*, Naph. ii. 4: 'As the potter knoweth the use of each vessel, what it is meet for, so also doth the Lord know the body, how far it will persist in goodness, and when it beginneth in evil.'

by examining him. 𝔊 'in his reasoning'.

6. For this verse 𝔊 reads: 'The fruit of the tree declareth the husbandry thereof; so is the utterance of the thought of the heart of a man'; i.e. just as the yield of a tree depends upon the way in which it has been tended, so the utterances of a man depend upon the state of his heart, i.e. the way in which he has tended himself, in a spiritual sense.

7. **before taking stock (of him).** Lit. 'before his discourse', i.e. before discoursing with him.

(*b*) XXVII. 8–10.

8. **If thou follow after righteousness.** Cp. Zeph. ii. 3.

a robe of glory. ποδήρη (= מעיל) δόξης; cp. Isa. li. 10; Job xxix. 14 (מעיל צדקה); cp. the high-priestly robe mentioned in xlv. 8; Wisd. xviii. 24. In the *Test. Twelve Patr.*, Levi viii. 2, it is said: 'Arise, put on the robe of the priesthood, and the crown of righteousness, and the breastplate of understanding, and the garment of truth. . . .'

9. **Every bird . . .** Cp. xiii. 15; 𝔊 'Birds will resort unto their like'.

10. **The lion . . .** Cp. xxi. 2.

(*c*) XXVII. 11–15.

11. **. . . continueth in wisdom.** Cp. v. 10.

12. **watch closely the time.** συντήρησον καιρόν; cp. iv. 20, where the same phrase occurs. The meaning of the verse is that one must grudge the time wasted with fools, whereas among the wise one may well spend all one's time.

13. **annoyance.** προσόχθισμα is the Sept. rendering of שִׁקּוּץ ('abomination') in 2 Kings xxiii. 13, 24; Ezek. v. 11, vii. 20.

. . . sinful wantonness. Cp. Prov. x. 23, xiv. 9.

14. **The oath of . . .** Cp. xxiii. 11.

maketh the hair . . . Cp. Job iv. 15.

maketh one stop . . . Lit. '(is) a stopping' (ἐνφραγμός), א* στεναγμός ('groaning'). The strife of the godless man of oaths occasions language such as makes a man shut his ears.

15. **is shedding of blood.** i.e. their strife is as bad as shedding of blood in its results.

(*d*) XXVII. 16–21. *The evil consequences of betraying secrets* (= 2+3+1 distichs).

𝔊 16 He who revealeth secrets[q] loseth[r] credit,
And he findeth no friend to his mind[rr].
17 Prove[s] a friend, and [t]keep faith with him[t],
But if thou reveal his secrets, follow not after him;
18 For as a man that hath destroyed his inheritance[v],
So hast thou destroyed the friendship of thy[w] neighbour.
19 And as a bird which thou hast loosed out of thy hand,
So hast thou let thy[x] neighbour go, and thou wilt not catch him again.
20 Pursue him not, [xx]for he is gone far away[xx],
And hath escaped[y] like a gazelle out of a snare[yy].
21 For a wound may be bound up, and for slander[z] there is reconciliation,
But he that revealeth secrets [zz]hath no hope[zz].

(*e*) XXVII. 22–24. *The hatefulness of insincerity* (= 3+1 distichs).

22 [a]He that winketh with his eye planneth evil things,
70, 248 And he that knoweth him keepeth far from him.
𝔊 23 Before thy face he speaketh sweetly,
And will admire thy words;
But afterward he will alter his speech,
And with thy words will make a stumbling-block.
24 Many things I hate, but nothing like him,
And the Lord will hate him (too), [b]and curse him[b].

(*f*) XXVII. 25–29. *Nemesis* (= 3+2 distichs).

25 He that casteth a stone [bb]on high[bb] [c]casteth it on his own head[c],
𝔏 [d]And a deceitful blow apportions wounds to the deceiver[d].

q 𝔏 'of a friend' r *So* 𝔏: 𝔊 𝔖 'destroyeth' rr *Lit.* 'soul' (= 𝔖) s *So* 𝔖 (𝔊 𝔏 'love') t–t 𝔖 'put thy trust in him' v *So* 𝔖: 𝔊 'enemy': 𝔏 'friend' w *So* 248 𝔖: 𝔊 >: 𝔏 Syro-Hex 'his' x *So* 𝔏 Syro-Hex: 𝔊 𝔖 > xx–xx 𝔖 > y 𝔏 + quoniam vulnerata est anima eius yy 𝔖 + 'and like a sparrow out of the snare,' *cp.* Prov. vi. 5 z 𝔖 'a quarrel' zz–zz 248 'hath destroyed faith' a 𝔖 *in place of vv.* 22, 23 *has*: 'He who hath a proud eye it shall be his ruin' b–b *So* 𝔖: 𝔊 > bb–bb 𝔖 > c–c 𝔖 'it will return upon him': 𝔏 'it will fall upon his head' d–d 𝔊 'And a deceitful blow will open wounds': 𝔖 'He will be delivered over to destruction'

(*d*) XXVII. 16–21.
16. **He who revealeth secrets...** Cp. xxii. 22; Prov. xx. 19, xxv. 9.
17. **keep faith with him.** Cp. xxix. 3.
follow not after him. It is useless to do so because his friendship is lost.
18. **inheritance.** Smend's suggestion (following Böttcher) that *κλῆρον* should be read instead of *ἐχθρόν*, which is also the reading of 𝔖, is worth adopting, though 𝔊 makes good sense as it stands.
19. Friendship which has been forfeited by the betrayal of secrets is lost irretrievably.
21. **hath no hope.** i. e. of reconciliation, cp. xxii. 22.

(*e*) XXVII. 22–24.
22. **He that winketh with his eye.** *διανεύων ὀφθαλμῷ*; cp. Sept. of Prov. vi. 13 *ἐννεύει ὀφθαλμῷ*, x. 10 *ὁ ἐννεύων ὀφθαλμοῖς* (קרץ עין). A sign of insincerity.
planneth. *τεκταίνει*; cp. xi. 33, xii. 23; Prov. iii. 29, vi. 14 (חרש רע).
And he that knoweth him... This rendering agrees better with the context, and is preferable to 𝔊: 'And no man will remove him from it,' i.e. it is impossible to dissuade him from planning evil things.
keepeth far from him. Lit. 'will depart from him'.
23. **he speaketh sweetly.** Lit. 'he will sweeten his (B 'thy') mouth'; cp. xii. 16*a*; Prov. xvi. 21.
he will alter his speech. Lit. 'he will twist his mouth', *διαστρέψει τὸ στόμα αὐτοῦ*; cp. Prov. xii. 1 עקש שפתים.
And with thy words... Perhaps ובדבריך יתן קשר, cp. xi. 31; i. e. he will conspire against thee by wresting thy words and putting a wrong meaning upon them, and thus cause thee to give offence to others.
24. **but nothing like him.** See critical note. 𝔊 lit. 'and I likened (them) not unto him', i.e. he hated many things, but his hatred for them was not to be compared with his hatred for the insincere man who wrested his words.
will hate him. Cp. Prov. vi. 16, viii. 13. The addition 'and curse him' (from 𝔖) seems to be demanded, as otherwise the clause would be rather too short.

(*f*) XXVII. 25–29.
25. **casteth it on his...** i.e. he will wound himself.
a deceitful blow... So 𝔏. The meaning of 𝔊 is obscure, but 𝔏 gives good sense.

𝔊 26 He that diggeth a pit [e]shall fall into it[e];
And he that setteth a snare shall be taken therein.
27 He that doeth evil things, they shall roll[f] upon him,
And he will not know whence [g]they came[g] to him.
28 [h]Mockery and reproach (are the lot) of the proud,
And vengeance, like a lion, lieth in wait for them[ih].
29 [k]They that rejoice at the fall of the godly shall be taken in a snare,
And anguish shall consume them ere they die[k].

(*g*) XXVII. 30—XXVIII. 7. *Concerning forgiveness; vengeance belongs to God alone* (= 3+3+2 distichs).

30 Wrath[1] and anger, these also are abominations,
[m]And a sinful man clingeth to them[m].
28 1 [no]He that taketh vengeance[o] shall find vengeance from the Lord,
[oo]And his sins [p](God) will surely keep[p] (in memory)[oo].
2 [pp]Forgive thy neighbour the injury (done to thee)[pp],
[q]And then, when thou prayest, thy sins will be forgiven[q].
3 Man cherisheth anger against another;
And[r] doth he seek healing from God[s]?
4 [t]On a man like himself he hath no mercy;
And doth he make supplication for his own sins[t]?
5 He, being flesh[u], [v]nourisheth wrath[v];
Who will [w]make atonement[w] for his sins?
6 Remember thy [x]last end[x], and cease from enmity[y];
(Remember) [z]corruption and death[z], and [a]abide in the commandments[a].
7 Remember the commandments, and be not wroth with thy neighbour;
And (remember) the covenant of the Most High, and [b]overlook ignorance[bc].

e–e 𝔖 'shall fill it with his own body' f 𝔖 'shall fall' g–g 𝔖 'evil hath come' h–h 𝔖 > i *So* V 248: 𝔊 'him' k–k 𝔖 'Snares and nets are for those who make (*lit.* know) them; these shall cling to them till the day of their death': 𝔏 > l 𝔖 'envy' m–m 𝔖 'And a deceitful man destroyeth his own way' n 𝔏 *inserts the title*: De remissione peccatorum o–o 𝔖 'And' oo–oo 𝔖 'And all his sins are reserved for him' p–p *Reading* with 248 διατηρων διατηρησει (= 𝔏): 𝔊 διαστηριων διαστηρισει pp–pp 𝔖 'Put away what is in thy heart, and thereupon pray' q–q 𝔖 'And all thy sins will be forgiven thee' r 𝔖 'And why' s *So* 𝔖 𝔏: 𝔊 'the Lord' t–t 𝔖 > u 𝔖 'a man' v–v 𝔖 'will not forgive' w–w 𝔖 'forgive' x–x 𝔖 'death' y 70 248 + 'and be not wrathful with thy neighbour' z–z 𝔖 'Hades and corruption' a–a 𝔖 'keep thyself from sinning' b–b 𝔖 'give him what he needeth' c 𝔏 + 'of thy neighbour'

---

26. **He that diggeth . . .** Cp. Prov. xxvi. 27 *a*; Eccles. x. 8; Ps. vii. 15.
he that setteth . . . Cp. Ps. ix. 15, 16.
27. **they shall roll upon him.** See Prov. xxvi. 27, and cp. Sirach xxxvii. 3.
29. . . . **ere they die.** Cp. Job xxi. 19, 20.

(*g*) XXVII. 30—XXVIII. 7.
30. **these also . . .** i.e. in addition to the abominations above referred to.

XXVIII. 1. **He that taketh vengeance.** Cp. Deut. xxxii. 35; Rom. xii. 19.
will surely keep. 𝔊 διαστηριῶν διαστηρίσει, lit. 'will surely make firm'. For the reading διατηρῶν διατηρήσει of 248 'he will surely mark,' cp. Sept. of Ps. cxxix. (cxxx.) 3 (παρατηρήσῃ); Job xiv. 16, 17.

2. **Forgive thy neighbour.** With this and the next two verses cp. the following passage from the *Test. Twelve Patr.*, Gad vi. 3–7: 'Love ye one another from the heart; and if a man sin against thee, speak peaceably to him, and in thy soul hold not guile; and if he repent and confess, forgive him. But if he deny it, do not get into a passion with him, lest catching the poison from thee, he take to swearing, and so thou sin doubly. . . . But if he be shameless, and persist in his wrongdoing, even so forgive him from the heart, and leave to God the avenging.' In *Rosh Ha-shanah* 17 *a* occur the words: 'God forgives him who forgives his neighbour' (cp. Matt. vi. 14, 15, xviii. 35). In view of these passages, it is not necessary to regard the verse under consideration as a Christian interpolation (Edersheim).

3. With this verse cp. the Midrash *Sifre* 93 *b*: 'He only who is merciful with mankind may expect mercy from Heaven' (quoted by Schechter, *Studies in Judaism*, Second Series, p. 94).
healing. i.e. forgiveness, cp. next verse; for this sense of ἴασις cp. Sept. of Is. xix. 22, &c.

4. Cp. *Megillah* 28 *a*: 'So long as we are merciful, God is merciful to us; but if we are not merciful to others, God is not merciful to us.'

5. **being flesh.** Cp. xvii. 31; the 'flesh' is regarded in itself as evil; cp. Rom. vii. 25; 1 Cor. xv. 50; Gal. v. 19.
6. **Remember . . .** Cp. vii. 36, xxxviii. 20.
7. **be not wroth with . . .** Cp. x. 6, and *Shabbath* 20 *a*, where it is said that the most important law is: 'Thou shalt love thy neighbour as thyself'; cp. Matt. xix. 19.

overlook ignorance. πάριδε ἄγνοιαν = שא לשחיתות xxx. 11 (Smend). Ignore sins committed against you unconsciously.

(*h*) XXVIII. 8–12. *Warnings against quarrelling* (= 2 + 2 + 2 distichs).

𝔊

8 Keep far from strife, and [d]sins will keep far from thee[d]:
[e]For a passionate man kindleth strife[e];
9 And a sinful man [f]stirreth up strife among friends[f],
And casteth enmity[g] in the midst of the peaceful.
10 According to its fuel, so will the fire burn;
[h]And according to the vehemence of the strife, so doth it increase[h i];
And according to the [ii]might[ii] of a man, so is his wrath;
And according to (his) wealth, so doth he increase[k] his anger.
[kk]Strife begun in haste kindleth fire[kk],
11 And a hasty quarrel [l]leadeth to bloodshed[l].
If thou blow a spark it burneth, [m]and if thou spit upon it it is quenched[m];
12 And both [n]come out of thy mouth[n].

(*i*) XXVIII. 13–26. *The mischief that is wrought by a wicked tongue* (= 1 + 2 + 2 + 2 + 2 + 2 + 3 + 2 + 1 distichs).

13 [o]Curse the whisperer and double-tongued[o],
[p]For it hath destroyed many that were at peace[p].
14 The third tongue [q]hath taken many captive[q],
And hath dispersed them [r]among many nations[r];
Even strong cities hath it destroyed[s],
And laid waste[t] the dwellings of the great.
15 The third tongue hath cast out [u]brave women[u],
And deprived them of their labours[v].
16 [w]He that hearkeneth thereto shall not find rest,
Neither shall be dwell in quietness[w].
17 The stroke of a whip maketh a mark,
But the stroke of the tongue breaketh bones.

d–d *So* 𝔖: 𝔊 𝔏 'thou shalt diminish sins' e–e 𝔖 > f–f *Cp.* 𝔖: 𝔊 *lit.* 'troubleth friends' g *So* 𝔖 𝔏: 𝔊 'calumny' h–h 𝔏 > *In* B *this clause has got out of place, coming at the end of the verse* i *So* 70 248 αυξηθησεται (= 𝔖) *for* εκκαυθησεται ii 𝔖 *lit.* 'honour of the hands' k *Lit.* 'exalt' kk–kk 𝔖 'Gum and pitch kindle a fire' l–l *Lit.* 'sheddeth blood' m–m 248 > n–n 𝔖 'are from thee' o–o 𝔖 'May the third tongue be cursed' p–p 𝔖 'For it hath cast away many slain' q–q *So* 𝔖: 𝔊 𝔏 'hath shaken many' r–r *Lit.* 'from nation to nation' s *Lit.* 'pulled down' t *Lit.* 'overturned' u–u 𝔖 'many' v 𝔖 'wealth' w–w 𝔖 >

(*h*) XXVIII. 8–12.

8. **Keep far.** Cp. ix. 13. It is quite possible that, as Smend suggests, the clauses of *vv.* 8, 9 have got displaced, and that their order should be 8 *a*, 9 *a*, 8 *b*, 9 *b*. With *v.* 8 cp. viii. 1, Prov. xxvi. 21, xxix. 22.

10. **According to its fuel . . .** Lit. 'As is the fuel of a fire, so will it burn'; cp. Prov. xxvi. 20; Jas. iii. 5. The more inflammable the matter which is put on the fire the more fiercely it burns, and in the same way, the more contentious the cause of the strife, the more bitter will it be.

vehemence. στερέωσις = עצמה, cp. xi. 9 (Smend); cp. also Isa. xl. 29, xlvii. 9. The varying degrees of the vehemence of a quarrel are conditioned by the causes which give rise to it.

might. Not material strength here, but social rank.

according to (his) wealth . . . The richer a man and the more exalted his position the more will he resent any one crossing him.

11. **Strife begun in haste.** These words, in view of the next clause, evidently do not represent the original; 𝔖 (see critical note) very likely echoes the Hebrew, if it does not give the exact translation. Both in 𝔊 and 𝔖, as they stand, the parallelism between the two clauses is incomplete.

12. **If thou blow . . .** Quoted in the Midrash *Wayyiqra Rabba*, ch. xxxiii, thus: 'There was a glowing coal (גחלת) before him; he blew upon it, and it blazed up; he spat upon it, and it was extinguished.' Though Ben-Sira is not mentioned as the author of these words in the Midrash, they are evidently a quotation from his book. It may be gathered that in the Hebrew 'glowing coal' was read instead of 'spark'.

And both . . . The words are illustrated by Prov. xv. 1: 'A soft answer turneth away wrath, but a grievous word stirreth up anger.' The words which will kindle strife, as well as those which will avoid it, come from the same mouth; whether it is to be war or peace depends upon yourself.

(*i*) XXVIII. 13–26.

13. **the whisperer and . . .** Cp. v. 9, 14; and with the whole section cp. Jas. iii. 1–12.

14. **The third tongue.** A literal translation of the Hebrew, which is represented in Rabbinical literature by לישון תליתאי, a technical expression for the tongue of the slanderer; cp. e.g. *Arakin* 15 *b*: 'The third tongue kills three,' viz. the slanderer, the slandered, and he who believes the slander; on the last of these see *v.* 16.

15. **hath cast out brave women.** ἐξέβαλεν . . .; cp. vii. 26, where ἐκβάλλειν is used of divorcing a wife. For the expression 'brave women', i.e. noble women, cp. xxvi. 2.

16. **He that hearkeneth thereto.** This refers to the third person whom the third tongue 'kills'; see the quotation in note on *v.* 14. The husband is primarily thought of.

17. **. . . breaketh bones.** Cp. Prov. xxv. 15.

𝔊 18 [ww]Many have fallen by the edge of the sword,
But not (so many) as they that have fallen through the tongue[ww].
19 Happy the man that is sheltered[x] therefrom,
And that [xx]hath not passed through[xx] the wrath thereof;
That hath not drawn the yoke thereof,
And that hath not been bound with its bands.
20 For its yoke is a yoke of iron,
And its bands are bands of brass.
21 The death thereof is an evil death,
𝔖 [y]And the rest of Hades is better than hers[y].
𝔊 22 (But) it hath no power over the godly,
They will not be burned in her flame;
23 [z]They that[a] forsake the Lord shall fall into it[z],
And she will burn among them, and not be quenched;
As a lion shall she be sent upon them,
And as a leopard shall she destroy them[b].
𝔖 24(*a*) [c]For as thou enclosest thy vineyard with thorns[c],
70 248 25(*b*) So make [d]doors and bolts[d] for thy mouth.
𝔖 24(*b*) [e]Thou makest a bolt[f] for[e] thy silver and gold,
𝔊 25(*a*) Make a balance and weight for thy words.
26 Take heed that thou slip not thereby[g],
Lest thou fall before [h]him that ensnareth[h].

(*j*) XXIX. 1–13. *On lending and borrowing* (= 3+3+3+1+3+3 distichs).

29 1 [a]He that lendeth to (his) neighbour [b]showeth kindness[b],
And [c]he that taketh him by the hand[c] keepeth the commandments.
2 Lend to thy neighbour in time of his need,
And pay thou thy neighbour again at the appointed time.
3 Confirm thy word, and keep faith with him;
And (so) shalt thou always have what thou needest.

ww–ww 𝔖 'Many are they that are killed with the sword, but they are not (as many) as they that are killed by the tongue.' x 𝔖 'preserved' xx–xx 𝔖 'hath not mingled with' y–y 𝔊 'And more profitable is Hades than her' z–z 𝔖 'All who forsake the fear of God the fire shall burn' a 𝔖 'All who' b 𝔖 'tear them in pieces' c–c 𝔊 'See that thou hedge thy possession about with thorns' d–d 𝔊 'a door and a bar' e–e 𝔊 'bind up' f *Lit.* 'seal' g 𝔖 > : 𝔏 'in thy tongue' h–h 𝔖 'thine enemy'

a 307 *inserts the title*: 'Concerning loans' (= 𝔏) b–b 𝔖 'obtaineth good interest' c–c *So* 𝔖 : 𝔊 'he that

19. . . . **that is sheltered therefrom.** Cp. the Sept. of Ps. xxxi. 20: 'Thou shalt shelter them in a pavilion from the contradiction of tongues.'

hath not drawn the yoke. Cp. Deut. xxi. 3.

bands. Of the yoke, i. e. the tongue here.

20. **a yoke of iron.** Cp. Jer. xxviii. 14.

21. **The death thereof . . .** i. e. the death caused by the third tongue (see note on *v.* 14).

22. **They will not be burned.** Cp. Jas. iii. 5–8.

23. **into it.** i. e. the flame of the wicked tongue.

destroy. λυμαίνομαι; lit. 'to mutilate'.

24–25. The clauses of these verses have got out of order, as their contents show: the proper order should be as given in the text. 70 248 𝔏 read 25 *b* twice over, once after 25 *a* and again after 24 *a*; 𝔖 places 25 *b* after 24 *a*.

25 *b*. **make doors.** Cp. xxii. 27; Ps. cxli. 3.

24 *b*. **Thou makest a bolt.** For the rendering of 𝔊 (see critical note) cp. Deut. xiv. 25; 2 Kings v. 23.

25 *a*. **Make a balance.** Cp. xvi. 25, xxi. 25.

26. **that thou slip not.** For ὀλισθάνω cp. iii. 24, xiv. 1, xxi. 7, xxv. 8.

(*j*) XXIX. 1–13.

1. **showeth kindness.** Cp. xlvi. 7 (עשׂה חסד); also Exod. xxii. 25; Lev. xxv. 36; 2 Sam. ix. 3.

that taketh him by the hand. ὁ ἐπισχύων τῇ χειρὶ αὐτοῦ; cp. Lev. xxv. 35 (מחזיק בידו).

keepeth the commandments. Cp. xxxvii. 12 שׁומר מצוה, and the Rabbinical phrase עָשָׂה מִצְוֹת.

2. **Lend . . .** Cp. Prov. xix. 16, 17. In accordance with both Biblical and Rabbinical teaching there is no mention here of interest; in Lev. xxv. 36 it is said: 'Take thou no usury of him, or increase'; cp. *Baba Bathra* 90 *a*: 'A usurer is comparable to a murderer, for the crimes of both are equally irremediable' (quoted by Abrahams, *Jewish Life in the Middle Ages*, p. 237).

pay thou thy neighbour . . . Cp. iv. 31; Ps. xxxvii. 21. See also *Pirqe Aboth* ii. 13: 'Go and see which is the evil way a man should shun. . . . Rabbi Simeon said, "He that borroweth, and payeth not again."'

3. **keep faith.** Cp. xxvii. 17.

𝔊 4 Many have reckoned a loan as a windfall[d],
And have brought trouble[e] on them that helped them.
5 Until he receive it, he kisseth thy hand,
And speaketh humbly about his neighbour's money;
But when payment is due, he prolongeth the time,
𝔖 [f]And after much time he repayeth[f].
𝔊 6 If he is able [to repay], he [i.e. the lender] will hardly[ff] receive the half,
And counteth it as a windfall;
If not [able to repay], he hath deprived him [i.e. the lender] of his money,
And he hath made him an enemy unnecessarily[g].
He repayeth him with cursings and railings,
And instead of honour [gg]he repayeth him[gg] with insult[h].
7 Many, therefore[i], have turned away [from lending] because of wickedness,
(For) they feared [k]to be defrauded for naught[k].
8 [kk]But with the man of low estate be longsuffering,
[l]And let him not[m] wait for alms[l].
9 [mm]Help the poor man for the commandment's sake,
𝔖 [n]And grieve not for the loss[n].
𝔊 10 Lose money for the sake of a brother or a friend,
And [o]let it not rust[o] under a stone [p]or a wall[p].
𝔖 11 [q]Lay up for thyself a treasure of righteousness and love[q],
And it shall profit thee more than [r]all that thou hast[r].
𝔊 12 [rrs]Store up almsgiving [t]in thy treasuries[ts],
And it shall deliver thee from all evil;
13 Better than a mighty shield and a heavy spear
Shall (this) fight for thee against [u]an enemy[u].

strengtheneth him with his hand' [d] *Lit.* 'find' [e] *So* B: 𝔊 'grief' (= 𝔏 Syro-Hex) [f–f] 𝔊 'He returneth words of heaviness, and complaineth of the (shortness) of the time' [ff] 𝔖 > [g] So A ℵ c.a (= 𝔖 𝔏): ℵ*B 'not without cause' [gg–gg] 𝔖 > [h] *Lit.* 'dishonour' [i] B >: ℵ? V 253 307 𝔖 𝔏 Syro-Hex *have a negative* (ου *for* ουν) [k–k] 𝔖 'an empty quarrel' [kk] 307 *inserts the title* περι ελεημοσυνης [l–l] 𝔖 > [m] B *omits the negative* [mm] 𝔏 *inserts the title*: De dato in proximo [n–n] 𝔊 'And according to his need send him not away empty' (V 248 > 'empty') [o–o] 𝔖 'put it not': 248 𝔏 'hide it not': V 'let it not be saved' (σωθητω *for* ιωθητω) [p–p] *So* 𝔖: 𝔊 'for perishing' [q–q] 𝔊 'Lay up thy treasure according to the commandments of the Most High' [r–r] 𝔊 'gold' [rr] 𝔏 *inserts the title*: De misericordia [s–s] 𝔖 'Bind up alms and put them in thy store-chamber' [t–t] 𝔏 'in the heart of the poor' [u–u] 𝔖 'many'

4. . . . **as a windfall.** i. e. they did not repay the loan.

5. **he kisseth thy hand.** i. e. in insincere servility.

speaketh humbly. Lit. 'humbleth his voice', i. e. he speaks as one awestruck and humbled by his neighbour's wealth, thus implying that it would be but a trifling matter for one of such wealth to make a loan.

prolongeth the time. i. e. delays repayment.

And after much time . . . See critical note. The rendering of 𝔖 is to be preferred to that of 𝔊 because 'he returneth words of heaviness' forestalls what is said in 6 *ef*; it is probable that the words καὶ τὸν καιρὸν αἰτιάσεται are merely a bad translation of לְעֵת רַבָּה (Smend), 'after much time.' The two last clauses of *v.* 5 (as in the text above) are elaborated in *v.* 6: with the words, 'But when payment is due, he prolongeth the time,' must be read *v.* 6 *a–d*, and with the words, 'And after much time he repayeth,' must be read 6 *ef.* The rendering of 𝔖 in the clause under consideration must be understood ironically; the borrower repays indeed, but with 'cursings and railings'; that literal repayment is not meant is clear from 6 *a–c*.

7. . . . **because of wickedness.** i. e. many have refused to lend money because experience has taught them that they may not be able to get their money back owing to the unscrupulousness of the borrower.

to be defrauded for naught. The rendering of 𝔖 (see critical note) is perhaps to be preferred.

8. **But . . .** Nevertheless; the man is justified who will not part with his money for the reason just mentioned, nevertheless there are other reasons which should induce him to part with it.

9. **for the commandment's sake.** See Deut. xv. 7, 8, cp. xxxii. 7. In *Baba Bathra* 9 *a* it is said that 'almsgiving is equal in value to all other commandments' (quoted in *JE*, i. 435 *b*).

And grieve not . . . The rendering of 𝔖 accords better with the context, and is preferable to 𝔊.

10. **Lose money . . .** Cp. xxxvii. 6.

let it not rust. Cp. Matt. vi. 19; Jas. v. 3.

under a stone . . . For treasures hidden away cp. Isa. xlv. 3.

11. **Lay up for thyself . . .** The rendering of 𝔖 strikes one as more original than 𝔊, which reads as though it were explanatory.

12. **Store up . . .** The renderings of 𝔊 𝔖 have the same meaning.

it shall deliver thee . . . Cp. vii. 32, xii. 2; Tobit ii. 14, iv. 9–11.

13. **Shall (this) fight for thee . . .** Cp. iii. 30.

(*k*) XXIX. 14–20. *Concerning suretyship* (= 3 + 2 + 2 distichs).

𝔊 14 A good man becometh surety for his neighbour,
But he that hath lost the sense of shame [v]runneth away from his surety[v].
15 [w]Forget not the good offices of thy surety,
For he hath given his life for thee[w].
16 [x]A sinner disregardeth[y] the goodness of his surety,
17 [z]And the ungrateful[a] man faileth him that delivered him[z].
18 Suretyship hath undone many [b]that were prospering[b],
[bb]And tossed them about as a wave of the sea[bb];
Men of wealth hath it driven from their homes,
And they had to wander among strange nations.
19 The sinner falleth in (his) suretyship[c],
And [d]he that followeth after sins[d] falleth into judgements.
20 Help[e] thy neighbour according to thy power,
And take heed to thyself, that thou fall not.

(*l*) XXIX. 21–28. *The advantages of contentment and independence* (= 1 + 3 + 3 + 1 distichs).

21 [f]The chief thing for life[g] is water and bread,
And a garment, and a house to cover nakedness[h].
22 Better the life of the poor under a shelter of logs,
Than sumptuous fare [i]in the house of strangers[i].
23 With little or with much, be contented;
ℵ[c.A] 248 𝔏 [k]So wilt thou not (have to) hear the reproach of thy wandering[l k m].
𝔊 24 An evil life (it is) to go from house to house,
And where thou art[n] a stranger thou[n] (must) not open (thy)[n] mouth.
𝔖 25 [o]A stranger thou art [in that case], and drinkest contempt[o];
𝔊 And besides this thou wilt (have to) hear bitter things:
26 'Come hither, sojourner, furnish (my) table,
And if thou hast aught, feed me (therewith)';
27 (Or): 'Get thee gone, sojourner[p], from the face [q]of honour[q],
My brother is come as my guest, [r](I have) need of my house[r]!'

v–v *So* 𝔖 : 𝔊 'will fail him' w–w 𝔖 > x 𝔏 *inserts here* 'The sinner and the dishonourable man (immundus) fleeth from his surety': 248 *adds this* (*omitting* 'and the dishonourable man') *at the end of the verse* y *Lit.* 'will overthrow' z–z 𝔖 'He who forsaketh his Creator forsaketh him that delivereth him' a 248 'unprofitable in mind' b–b 𝔖 > bb–bb 𝔖 'And they went unto a strange people' c 70 248 𝔖 𝔏 + 'transgressing the commandments of the Lord' d–d *So* 𝔖 : 𝔊 'he that undertaketh contracts for work' e 𝔖 'Go surety for' f 𝔏 *inserts the title*: De frugalitate honesta et hospitalitate g A[a] *most cursives* 𝔖 𝔏 Syro-Hex + 'of man' h *Lit.* 'shame' i–i *Lit.* 'among strangers': 𝔖 'in exile': 𝔏 in peregre sine domicilio k–k 𝔊 >: 𝔖 'And what he doeth in his house none seeth' l *So* 𝔏 peregrinationis: *read* παροικιας *for* οικιας m 253 Syro-Hex + 'For there is one who humbleth and exalteth' n B 𝔖 𝔏 *3rd pers.* o–o 𝔊 'thou shalt entertain, and give to drink, without thanks' p 𝔖 𝔏 > q–q 𝔏 amicorum meorum r–r 𝔖 >

(*k*) XXIX. 14–20.

14. **becometh surety.** Cp. viii. 13. Contrast with this Prov. vi. 1 ff., xvii. 18, &c.

15. **the good offices.** Or 'kindnesses' (χάριτας).

For he hath given. Cp. Prov. xx. 16, xxii. 27.

16. **A sinner disregardeth . . .** Lit. 'A sinner overturneth the good things of (his) surety', i. e. disregards his obligations in spite of the kindness shown (cp. *v.* 15); it is also possible to take the words to mean that the sinner, by disregarding his obligations, involves his surety in ruin; but this is rather the meaning of *v.* 17.

18. Men, ruined by unscrupulous persons, have had to leave their homes and seek a living in foreign lands.

19. The preceding verse has described how good men have been ruined because they have become surety out of kindness; this verse refers to evil men who have been ruined because they became surety for evil purposes, e. g. for the sake of usurious practices.

20. Help others as far as you can, but be careful not to ruin yourself; cp. viii. 13.

(*l*) XXIX. 21–28.

21. **The chief thing for life.** Cp. xxxix. 26.

23. **. . . the reproach of . . .** i. e. the reproaches which the wanderer has to listen to when dependent on others. Although both 𝔊 and 𝔖 omit this clause, it is most probably genuine; cp. next two verses.

25. **A stranger . . .** The rendering of 𝔖 is, on the face of it, more genuine than that of 𝔊.

drinkest contempt. Cp. Prov. xxvi. 6.

27. **from the face of honour.** A literal translation of מִפְּנֵי יְקָר (Deut. xxviii. 20); cp. 𝔖 מן קדם איקרא (Ryssel),

𝔊 28 These things are grievous to a man of understanding:
[rr]Upbraiding concerning sojourning[s], and the reproach of a money-lender[rr t].

(*a*) XXX. 1–13. *The training of children*[a] (= 3+3+1+3+3+1 distichs).

30 1 He that loveth his son [b]will continue[b] (to lay) [c]strokes upon him[c],
That he may rejoice over him at the last.
2 He that disciplineth his son [d]shall have satisfaction[d] of him,
And among [e]his acquaintance[e] glory in him.
3 He that teacheth his son maketh his enemy jealous,
And in the presence of friends exulteth in him.
4 When his father dieth [f]he dieth not altogether[f],
For he hath left one behind him like himself.
5 In his life he saw[g] and rejoiced[h],
And in death he hath not been grieved.
6 [i]Against enemies he hath left behind [j]an avenger[j],
And to friends one that requiteth favour[i].
7 [k]He that pampereth his son[k] [l]shall bind up his wounds[l],
And his heart [m]trembleth[m] at every cry.

8 An unbroken horse [n]becometh stubborn[n],
And a son [o]left at large[o] [p]becometh headstrong[p].

rr–rr 𝔖 'Upbraiding and usury, and the loan of a money-lender' s *Reading* παροικιας *for* οικιας (*Smend*) t 𝔖 + 'Give very freely to the poor, and feed him from that which thou hast at hand; if he be naked clothe him; thus wilt thou be lending unto God, and He will repay thee sevenfold'

a B &c. *pr. tit.* περι τεκνων (307 λογος ετερος του αυτου περι τεκνων): *but* Syro-Hex. 253 &c. *omit*: 𝔏 de disciplina filiorum b–b 𝔊 ενδελεχησει: 𝔖 'will renew' c–c 𝔊 μαστιγας αυτῳ: 𝔖 'his strokes' d–d 𝔊 ονησεται (א^{c.a} αινεθησεται = 𝔏: ησθησεται 106, ευφρανθησεται 248 = 𝔖): ℌ? (בו) יִשִׂישׂ e–e 𝔊 γνωριμων: 𝔖 'his neighbours' f–f 𝔊 (ετελευτησεν αυτου ο πατηρ) και ως ουκ απεθανεν: 𝔖 'and is almost (= is not quite) dead' (וחבר דלא מות: חברדלא = 'wellnigh', 'almost', *as in* 4 Ezra vii. 48: *Lat.* 'pene', *Greek* ως ουκ) g 𝔖 + 'him' h 248 + επ αυτῳ = 𝔏 i–i 𝔖 *transposes clauses* (a) *and* (b) (*perhaps rightly*) j–j 𝔊 εκδικον: 𝔏 defensorem domus k–k 𝔊 (א* B A Sah Eth 𝔏) περι ψυχων υιων: *read with* 248 περιψυχων υιον (א^{c.a} A &c. *also read* υιον) = 𝔖 (דמפנק ברה: *cp.* מְפַנֵּק Prov. xxix. 21 = 'one pampering') l–l 𝔊 καταδεσμευσει τραυματα αυτου: 𝔖 'his wounds shall be increased' (𝔊 = ? ירפה: 𝔖 = ירבה [*Hart*]) m–m 𝔊 ταραχθησεται: 𝔖 'shall be empty' n–n 𝔊 αποβαινει σκληρος (= ? יקשה) o–o 𝔊 ανειμενος (= ? משלח) p–p εκβαινει προαλης (𝔖 *for whole verse*: 'like a young

---

meaning that the sojourner has now no more to expect any honour being shown to him, because a guest has arrived; the wanderer must only expect attention when there is no one else there to claim it.

brother. Used in the wide sense.

28. The addition to this verse in 𝔖 (see critical note) Smend regards as a translation from an original Hebrew text, though of a secondary character (see Introd. § 3 (*c*)).

XXX. 1—XXXII. 13 (= 𝔊. XXXV. 13). With ch. xxx a new division of the book begins, the change being marked not only by the difference of theme, but also by a difference in the method of treatment. A number of subjects now come in for brief and practical treatment. The division contains eight subsections, the subjects of which range over the upbringing of children, health, and conduct at meals and banquets.

(*a*) XXX. 1–13.

1. **He that loveth his son . . . strokes.** Cp. Prov. xiii. 24 ('He that spareth his rod hateth his son', &c.), xxiv. 13, 14, xxix. 15.

at the last. i.e. in the latter part of his (the parent's) life.

2. **He that disciplineth his son . . . satisfaction of him.** Cp. Prov. xxix. 17 ('Correct thy son . . . and he shall give delight unto thy soul'). The Greek word here rendered 'have satisfaction of' (ὀνίνασθαι) occurs only again in the Greek Bible in Philemon 20, where it is used with the same meaning as here. It was regularly employed in Greek of joy in children.

4. **When his father dieth he dieth not altogether . . . like himself.** i.e. the father lives on in his son. 'This and the following verse cast light on one of the great consolations and hopes which the writer entertained in regard to death: (viz.) continuance in one's children' (Edersheim). The son being regarded in this light, it was all-important that he should be pious.

6. **Against enemies . . .** Cp. Ps. cxxvii. 5 (a man who has a number of stalwart sons to support him will not be exposed to the danger of an unjust conviction at the place of trial (the gate)).

7. **shall bind up his wounds.** i.e. the wounds of his son, incurred in reckless play or adventure, when allowed to go on unchecked. 𝔖 (so Edersheim) understood the 'wounds' to be those of the indulgent father.

at every cry. Either of the son, or that caused by him (so Edersheim).

8. **a son left at large.** Cp. Prov. xxix. 15 ('a child left to himself').

𝔊 9 [q]Cocker[q] thy son [r]and he will terrify thee[r];
[s]Play with him[s] [t]and he will grieve thee[t].
10 [u]Laugh not with him[u], [v]lest he vex thee[v],
[vv]And make thee gnash thy teeth[vv] at the last.
ℌ[B] 11 [w]Let him not have freedom[w] in his youth,
[x]And overlook not[x] [y]his mischievous acts[y].
12 [z][a]Bow down ⌜his neck⌝ in his youth[a],
And smite his loins sore while he is little[z]—
Lest[b] he become stubborn[b] [c]and rebel against thee[c],
[d]And thou experience anguish of soul on his account[d].
13 Discipline thy son [e]and make his yoke heavy[e],
Lest [f]in his folly[f] [g]⌜he stumble⌝[g].

(*b*) XXX. 14–20. *The blessing of good health* (= 3 + 1 + 3 distichs).

14 Better is one that is poor, [h]and is healthy in his body[h],
Than a rich man who is plagued in his flesh.

horse that has not been broken, so is a rebellious son that listens not to his father' [q–q] 𝔊 τιθηνησον (=? אמן = 'nurture tenderly': *cp.* Lam. iv. 5): 𝔖 'chasten' [*read* 'thy son' *with* 𝔖: 𝔊 *has* τεκνον *only*] [r–r] *So* 𝔊: 𝔖 'lest thou be mocked' [s–s] *So* 𝔊: 𝔖 'and if thou laugh with him' (ℌ? שחק [t–t] 𝔊 και λυπησει σε = ? ויעצבך [u–u] *So* 𝔊: 𝔖 'do not go with him according to his pleasure' = ? אל תרצה עמו (*Smend*), *i.e.* 'be not complacent with him' (*cp.* Job xxxiv. 9, Ps. l. 18): *this may be right* [v–v] *So* 𝔖 = ? פן יכעיסך: 𝔊 ινα μη συνοδυνηθῃς (248 &c. Syro-Hex 𝔏 οδυνηθῃς) [vv–vv] 𝔊 *has* και . . . γομφιασεις τους οδοντας σου ('and thou shalt gnash,' &c.): *but* 70 *has* γομφιασει = 'he shall cause (thee) to gnash' (= 𝔖): *so read* [w–w] ℌ (*MS.* B *begins here*) אל תמשילהו, *lit.* 'let him not have rule' *or* 'independence' = 𝔊 μη δῳς αυτῳ εξουσιαν: 𝔖 = ℌ [x–x] ℌ ואל תשא ('and forgive not'): 𝔊 (248) και μη παριδῃς [y–y] ℌ לשחיתותיו: 𝔊 (248) τας αγνοιας αυτου (𝔏 cogitatus = εννοιας) [z–z] ℌ *has the first two stichoi of v.* 12 *in a double form, as follows:*

(a) כפתן על חי תפגע
(b) רציץ מתניו שעודנו נער:
(c) כיף ראשו בנערותו ⎫ = 𝔊, 𝔖
(d) ובקע מתניו כשהוא קטן: ⎭

Here (a) *and* (b) *form a doublet of* (c) *and* (d); (a) *is obviously corrupt, and yields no tolerable sense: Schechter emends to* כְּתֵפוֹ עַד חי תבקע: *then render* (a) *and* (b): 'beat his shoulder while it is yet tender, crush his loins while he is yet a youth' (*Lévi emends* כתפו בעלומו ת״, *i. e.* 'beat his shoulder in his youth'). *For* ראשו *in* (c) *read* צוארו *with* 𝔊 *and* 𝔖 (*cp.* li. 26) [a–a] *Reading* (*after* 𝔊 248) כַּיֵּף צוארו בנערותו [*owing to homoioteleuton all MSS. of* 𝔊 *except* 428 *and three other cursives omit* 11 *b and* 12 *a*: *in* 248 *the two lines run*: (11 *b*) και μη παριδῃς τας αγνοιας αυτου (12 *b*) καμψον τον τραχηλον αυτου εν νεοτητι] [b–b] *Reading* יקשה = 𝔊 (σκληρυνθεις), *so* 𝔖: ℌ ישקה (*scribal error*) ℌ *mg.* יקשיה [c–c] *So* ℌ ומרה בך = 𝔊 απειθησῃ σοι [d–d] ℌ ונולד ממנו מפח נפש ('and there will be born from him an expiry of soul'): 𝔊 και εσται σοι (+ εξ αυτου 106) οδυνη ψυχης: *so* 248 70 106 *and* 𝔏, *but uncials omit* (? *reading* מרת נפש *for* מפח נ״: *so Hart*) [e–e] *So* ℌ והכבד עולו: 𝔊 και εργασαι εν αυτῳ (= ? רהעביד עליו): 𝔖 'be hard towards him' [f–f] *So* ℌ: 𝔊 εν τῃ ασχημοσυνῃ σου (*but* 248 𝔏 &c. αυτου) [g–g] 𝔊 προσκοψῃ = יִתָּקֵל (*so read with Peters*): ℌ יתלע בך (ℌ *mg.* יתעל = 'lift himself up against thee') [h–h] ℌ וחי בעצמו (חי *often* = 'healthy' *in PBH*): 𝔊 υγιης (= חי) και ισχυων τῃ εξει (= *explanatory paraphrase for* בעצמו): 𝔖 'that is healthy and firm in his body' = 𝔊 [i–i] *Reading* חַיִּים וָשֹׁר = 𝔊 υγεια και ευεξια (שֹׁר = 'soundness,' 'strength': *Aram.* שְׁרַר, 'to be sound,' firm'); *so Peters:* ℌ חיי שׁר (*i. e.* שׁר = שׁאר, *so* ℌ *mg.*) 'bodily health' (𝔖 = ℌ) [j–j] *So* ℌ

---

9. **Cocker.** Nurture tenderly ('tend as a nurse', Edersheim; Heb. אמן); cp. Lam. iv. 5 ('they that were nurtured in scarlet').

10. **Laugh not with him.** Or 'be not complacent with him' (see critical note). Fritzsche quotes from Solon: 'liberis ne arrideas, ut in posterum non fleas' (cited by Edersheim).

12. **Bow down his neck.** Cp. li. 26 ('and bring your necks under her yoke'). ℌ has 'Bow down his head', i.e. humble him.; cp. iv. 7; Isa. lviii. 5.

smite his loins sore. Cp. Ezek. xxix. 7.

anguish of soul. Cp. Job xi. 20 ('giving up of the ghost').

13. **Discipline thy son.** Cp. vii. 23.

make his yoke heavy. Cp. 1 Kings xii. 10 (phrase).

(*b*) XXX. 14–20.

ℌ[B]

15 [i]Health and soundness[i] [j]have I desired[j] more than fine gold,
[k]And a cheerful spirit[k] [l]more than pearls[l].
16 There is no wealth [m]above the wealth[m] [n]of a sound body[n],
And no [nn]good[nn] above [o]a good disposition[o].
17 [p]Better death [q]than a wretched life[q],
And eternal rest [r]than continual pain[r][p].
18 Good things [s]poured out[s] before a mouth that is closed
[t]Are as an offering[t] [u]that is placed before an idol[u].
19 [v]How can (such) [w]profit[w] [x]the images[x] of the heathen
Which are unable either to eat or smell[y]?

אויתי = 𝔖: 𝔊 βελτιων k–k *So* ℌ ורוח טובה = 𝔖: 𝔊 και σωμα ευρωστον (? σωμα, *a corruption of* πνευμα: *so Lévi*) l–l ℌ מפנינים = 𝔖 ('pearls'): 𝔊 (*freely*) η ολβος αμετρητος m–m *So* ℌ: 𝔊 (βελτιων) *and* 𝔖 ('like') *omit* (*Peters omits second* עֹשֶׁר): *but* 𝔏 (census super censum) *and the parallelism with next line support* ℌ n–n ℌ שר עצם (*i. e.* 'soundness of body') = 𝔊 nn–nn ℌ טובה: 𝔊 ευφροσυνη = 𝔖 o–o ℌ טוב לבב = 'goodness of heart': 𝔊 χαραν καρδιας p–p ℌ *has this verse in a double form*:

(a) טוב למות מחיי שוא
(b) ונוחת עולם מכאב נאמן (Mg. מחיים רעים) } = 𝔊

(c) טוב למות מחיים רעים
(d) ולירד שאול מכאב עומד: } = 𝔖

𝔊 κρεισσων θανατος υπερ ζωην πικραν (ℵ[c.a] 70 + και αναπαυσις αιωνιος: *so* 𝔏 et requies eterna) η αρρωστημα εμμονον = ℌ (a) (b): 𝔖 = ℌ (c) (d) q–q *Reading* מחיים רעים = ℌ (c) *and* 𝔊: *so Peters, Smend* r–r *Smend reads* מכ״ עומד = ℌ (d) *and* 𝔖: *Peters* מכ״ נאמן = ℌ (b) s–s *So* ℌ = 𝔊: 𝔖 'shut up' = 𝔏 (bona abscondita) t–t ℌ תנופה 𝔊 θεματα (B Syro-Hex θεμα) βρωματων: *cp.* 𝔖 'as foods' u–u ℌ מצגת לפני גלול: 𝔊 παρακειμενα επι ταφῳ (𝔖 = 𝔊), *reading* גּוֹלֵל (גּוֹלָלָא) = 'the stone which closes a grave' v–v ℌ *has a lacuna in its text corresponding to vv.* 19 a–d *and* 20 a, *which is supplied by the margin*: ℌ *text has* 20 b *immediately after* 18 b:

19 (a) = מה י[עיל] לגלולי הגוים
19 (b) = אשר לא יאכלון ולא י[ריחון]:
19 (c) = כן מי ש[יש] לו עושר } ℌ *mg.*
19 (d) = ואין נהנה מהונו:
20 (a) = [רואה] בעיניו [ומתאנח]

20 (b) = כאשר סרים יחבק נערה ומתאנח: *in* ℌ *text.*

ℌ *adds the following to v.* 20:

20 c = [כן] עושה באונם משפט
20 d = כן נאמן לן עם בתולה } *in* ℌ *text.*
20 e = [ויי מבקש מידו]

[*These lines* 20 c–e *are unoriginal.*]

𝔊 τι συμφερει καρπωσις ειδωλῳ; = 19 (a)
ουτε γαρ εδεται, ουτε μη οσφρανθῃ = (19 b)
ουτως ο εκδιωκομενος υπο κυριῳ.
βλεπων δε οφθαλμοις και στεναζων = 20 (a)
ωσπερ ευνουχος περιλαμβανων παρθενον και στεναζων = 20 (b)

(+ ουτως ο ποιων εν βιᾳ κριματα) = 20 c (*so* 254 70 V &c., *but not uncials* = xx. 4 𝔊)
𝔖 = 19 (a) (b) (c) (d), 20 (a) (d) (e). Thus 19 (c) (d) *are attested in* ℌ *and* 𝔖, *but not in* 𝔊: *they are certainly*

15. **pearls.** So 𝔖: or 'corals' (ℌ פנינים).
16. **There is no wealth . . . disposition.** This verse is cited in Solomon ibn Gebirol's 'Choice of pearls' (see Cowley-Neubauer, p. xxx) as follows: 'There is no greater riches than health, no greater pleasure than a cheerful heart' (אין עושר כבריאות ולא נעימות כלב טוב).
17. **Better death than a wretched life.** Cf. Tobit iii. 13, 15 ('why should I live?'); the sentiment often comes to expression in classical literature (cp. e.g. Eur. *Hec.* 377).
And eternal rest. Omitted by 𝔊 (principal MSS.—see critical note), perhaps for dogmatic reasons (Edersheim). The omission may be due to later revision; note that 𝔏 ('requies eterna') attests the words, which probably belong to the original form of 𝔊.
18. **Good things . . . before a mouth that is closed . . .** i. e. riches which cannot be enjoyed (owing to ill health) are as futileas food offered to an idol that can neither taste nor smell.
an offering . . . placed before an idol. The heathen custom of offering food to idols is referred to (cp. e. g. the story embodied in Bel and the Dragon). 𝔊 ('as messes of meat laid upon a grave') makes the reference to the well-known heathen custom of providing food at the graves for the dead: cp. Tobit iv. 17 (and the notes there).
19. **unable either to eat or smell.** The phrase is borrowed from Deut. iv. 28 (cp. Ps. cxv. 4 f.).

𝔥[B] [z]So is he who possesseth wealth,
[a]And hath no enjoyment[a] [b]of it[bz]:
20 [c]He seeth it[c] with his eyes [c]and sigheth[c],
As [d]a eunuch[d] that embraceth a maiden[ev].

(*c*) XXX. 21–25. *An exhortation to dismiss sorrow and care* (= 2 + 2 + 2 distichs).

21 Give not thy soul [ee]to sorrow[ee],
[f]And let not thyself become unsteadied with care[f].
22 Heart-joy is life for a man,
And human gladness [ff]prolongeth days[ff].
23 [g]Entice thyself[g] [h]and soothe[h] thine heart,
And [i]banish[i] [j]vexation[j] from thee:
For sorrow [k]hath slain[k] many,
And there is no [l]profit[l] [m]in vexation[m].

original. 𝔊 *in its third line of v.* 19 *apparently preserves an unoriginal equivalent of* 19 (c) (d); *Peters regards the three original lines in* 𝔥 *as added to amplify the text from other parts of the book: v.* 20 (c) = xx. 4 b; *v.* 20 (d) = xx. 4 a, *and v.* 20 (e) = v. 3 b (כי יי״ מבקש נרדפים) [*in v.* 20 d נאמן, *lit.* 'trusted one' (*i.e. one entrusted with the care of the Harem*) = 'eunuch': *so* 𝔖 *renders* 20 d מהימנא; *but it is unnecessary to regard* נאמן *as a translation of* 𝔖; *see Peters* ad loc. *against Lévi*] w–w *Reading* יעיל = יועיל = 𝔊 𝔖 (*so Peters*); *others* ייטב; *Smend* יערכו ('what do men sacrifice, &c.') x–x *Smend* לגלולי: *Peters* לצלמי (*cp.* Ps. xxxix. 7, lxxiii. 20) = 𝔖: 𝔊 καρπωσις y 𝔖 + 'and drink not' z–z *So* 𝔥 𝔖: 𝔊 ουτως ο εκδιωκομενος (*read with* Syro-Hex εκδικουμενος) υπο κυριου = ? כן מיי מְבֻקָּשׁ = 19 c (כן) + 20 e a–a 𝔥 ונהנה (*Nif. of* הנה *a PBH word*) b–b 𝔥 *not quite certain: either* ממנו (= 𝔖) *or* מהונו, 'of his substance' (*the latter probably* = 𝔥'*s reading: so Schechter, Strack, Smend*) c–c *Reading* רוֹאֶה . . . ומתאנח = 𝔊 𝔖 d–d 𝔥 סרים, *a mistake for* סרים e 𝔥 + ומתאנח = 𝔊: *probably an addition from the previous clause* (*so Peters*) ee–ee 𝔥 לדין (*l.* לְדָוֹן: *the same graphical mistake in* xxx. 23, xxxviii. 18) f–f 𝔊 και μη θλιψης σεαυτον εν βουλη σου = ואל תִּכָּשֵׁל בעצתך (*so read with Peters*): 𝔥 *text* ואל ת״ בעונך (*? corrupt for* בעיניך, *but cp.* Ps. xxxi. 11): 𝔥 *mg.* בעצתך = 𝔊 𝔖: 𝔥 *mg.*[2] ואל תכשילך עצתך ff–ff 𝔊 μακροημερευσις: = האריך ימיו (*so read*): 𝔥 *text* ה״ אפו (*a scribal error*): 𝔖 'his life' *for* 'his days' (= חייו: *so Schechter reads*) g–g *So* 𝔥 פת נפשך = 𝔖: 𝔊 αγαπα (*but* ℵ[a.c] C V 253 254 &c. Syro-Hex απατα = 𝔥) h–h 𝔥 ופייג = 𝔖: 𝔊 και παρακαλει [פייג, *an Aramaism* = ? 'refresh' ('mitigate', 'soothe'), 'cause relaxation'] i–i 𝔥 הרחק = 𝔊 μακραν αποστησον j–j 𝔥 קצפון (= 'anger' *in PBH: cp.* קֶצֶף) k–k 𝔊 απεκτεινεν (*but* ℵ A C απωλεσεν: 248 *combines the two verbs*) l–l 𝔥 תעלה, *i. e.* תּוֹעָלָה (*or* תְּעָלָה) (*cp. PBH* תּוֹעֶלֶת = 'profit', 'use') = 𝔊 ωφελια m–m *So* 𝔥: 𝔊 εν αυτη [𝔖 *for the whole line*, 'And anxiety destroyed them'] n–n 𝔥 בלא עת תוקין = 𝔊 προ καιρου γηρας αγει (γηρας αγει = *the causative of* γηρασκειν [*Hart*]): 𝔖 'bring grey hairs' o–o 𝔥 שנות, *i. e.* שְׁנוֹת (*pl. constr.*); *cp.* Prov. vi. 10: 𝔊 *apparently omits.* 𝔖 *? transposes* (*see next note*) p–p 𝔥 לב

(*c*) XXX. 21–25 (= 𝔊 XXX. 21–24 + XXXIII. 13 *b c*).

21. **Give not thy soul to sorrow.** Cf. xxxviii. 20 *a* 𝔊. The sentiment expressed in this verse and also in *v.* 23 is also re-echoed in the Talmud. Thus in T. B. *Yebamoth* 63 *b* the following is cited as from the Book of Ben-Sira: 'Be not troubled for the trouble of to-morrow, for thou knowest not what the day may bring forth (= Prov. xxvii. 1). Perhaps on the morrow he will be no more, and be found grieving over a world that is not his' (so *Sanh.* 100 *b*). Edersheim also cites: 'Suffice sorrow for its hour' (T. B. *Berakh.* 9 *b*), and 'the sorrow of the hour (i.e. immediate sorrow) is sorrow' (T. J. *Abodah zarah* 39 *b*).

And let not thyself become unsteadied with care. 𝔥 text, 'and stumble not because of thine iniquity'; cp. Ps. xxxi. 10 ('my life is consumed in sorrow ... my strength stumbleth because of mine iniquity'). The rendering given above ('and let not thyself become unsteadied') = 'stumble not'.

22. **prolongeth days.** Lit. 'his days' (or 'his life'); see critical note. 𝔥 has 'prolongeth his anger' (maketh him slow to anger); cp. Prov. xix. 11 ('the discretion of a man maketh him slow to anger'). The mistake of the copyist may be due to his reminiscence of this passage (so Schechter).

23. **soothe thine heart.** The Hebr. word here rendered 'soothe' (פייג) 'is sometimes used in Rab. literature in the sense of calming and rejoicing' (Schechter).

banish vexation . . . For sorrow hath slain many. The Talmud cites a form of this passage as from Ben-Sira in T. B. *Sanh.* 100 *b* (in Aramaic): 'let not sorrow enter thy heart, for sorrow hath killed strong men' (לא תיעול דויא בליבך דגברין גיברין קטל דויא).

[At this point the dislocation of chapters, which has produced a different order in all extant Greek MSS., begins (Cod. 248 is not an exception). Chapters xxx. 25—xxxiii. 16 have been placed after xxxiii. 16—xxxvi. 11, thus

ℌ[B] 24 Envy and anger shorten days,
And anxiety [n]maketh old untimely[n].
(= 𝔊 xxxiii. 13 *b*, *c*) 25 [o]The sleep[o] [p]of a cheerful heart is like dainties[p],
[q]And his food is agreeable unto him[q].

(*d*) XXXI. (XXXIV.) 1-4. *The anxieties of poverty and riches* (= 2 + 2 distichs).

31 ℌ[B] 1 [r]Watchful care over wealth[r] [s]wasteth the flesh[s],
[t]And anxiety about it[t] [u]dissipateth slumber[u].
2 [v]Anxiety about sustenance[v] [w]breaketh off (?)[w] slumber,
[x]Even as severe sickness dissipateth sleep[x].
3 The rich man [y]laboureth[y] [z]to gather[z] riches,
And when he resteth, it is to [a]partake of delights[a].
4 [b]The poor man [c]toileth[c] [d]for the needs of his house[d],
And if he rest [e]he becometh needy[e] [b].

טוב תחת מטעמים: 𝔊 λαμπρα καρδια και αγαθη επι εδεσμασιν (= ? ℌ: ? λαμπρα . . . και αγαθη, *a double rendering of* טוב): 𝔖 'a good heart many (=? שׁנות *transposed—so Hart*) are its meats' (*but Smend suggests that both* 𝔊 *and* 𝔖 *may have read* לב טוב רב מטעמים). *Lévi thinks* שׁנות *in* ℌ *is a title* (= 'of sleep'), *and so is omitted by* 𝔊 *and* 𝔖 q–q ℌ ומאכלו יעלה עליו: 'and his food (𝔖 'all that he eats') goes up upon him' (𝔖 'upon his body'), *i. e.* 'agrees with him' 𝔊 *misunderstands* ℌ *and renders freely*: των βρωματων αυτης επιμελησεται. r–r *So* 𝔊 = שקד עשׁר: 𝔖 = ℌ עשׁיר (*l.* שׁקד) שׁקר (*so* ℌ *mg.* שׁקד) s–s ℌ ימחה שארו (*l.* שׁאר) 𝔊 εκτηκει = ? ימסה (*so* 𝔖) t–t *So* 𝔊 = ℌ *mg.* ודאגתו u–u ℌ *text* תפריע נומה = 𝔊 αφιστᾳ υπνον v–v ℌ דאגת מחיה; 𝔊 μεριμνα αγρυπνιας (αγρυπνιας *from previous line*): 𝔖 = ℌ w–w ℌ תפריג: 𝔊 απαιτησει (*but read with* 𝔏 [avertit] αποστησει = ? ℌ): 𝔖 = ℌ (פרג *in Aram.* = to break, divide, exchange) x–x *Reading* תפריע שנה (ℌ *mg.*) ומחלה חזקה (ℌ *mg.* תפריג *for* תפריע); ℌ *has* נומה *at end; but read* שֵׁנָה = 𝔊: 𝔊 και αρρωστημα βαρυ εκνηψει (= ? תפריג *so* ℌ *mg.*) υπνον: *but* 𝔖 *supports* תפריע. [ℌ *adds two lines, which are not original, to this verse: they are omitted by* 𝔊 *and* 𝔖 *and do not harmonize with the context.*

רע נאמן תניד חרפה
ומסתיר סור אוהב כנפשׁ:

'Reproach putteth to flight the faithful friend,
But he that hideth a secret loveth (a friend) as his own soul.'

Cp. xxii. 22, xxvii. 17, xli. 22] y–y *Reading* עמל with ℌ *mg.* = 𝔊 𝔖: ℌ *text* עמלי ('the labours of a rich man are to,' &c.) z–z *Reading* לקבץ *with* 𝔊 𝔖: ℌ לקבל (*from next line*) a–a ℌ לקבל תענוג: 𝔊 εμπιμπλασαι των τρυφηματων αυτου (𝔖 'to partake of banquets') b–b ℌ *gives a double recension of this verse:*

(a) יגע עני לחסר ביתו (c) עמל עני לחסר כחו
(b) ואם ינוח יהיה צריך: (d) ואם ינוח לא נחה לו:

According to Smend (c) *and* (a) *give the original text* of ℌ c–c ℌ (a) יגע: ℌ (c) עמל (*so Smend*) d–d ℌ (a) לחסר ביתו: ℌ (c) לחסר כחו = ? 𝔊 εν ελατσωσει βιου (לחסר כחו = ? 'for lack of means for himself' = 𝔖) e–e *So* ℌ (b): ℌ (d) 'he hath no rest'

---

producing the order in 𝔊 xxx. 24; xxxiii. 16—xxxvi. 11; xxx. 25—xxxiii. 15; xxxvi. 12 *et seq.* 'It is evident that this must have proceeded from a misplacement of the sheets in the archetype of our Greek MSS.' (Edersheim). Note that 𝔏 and 𝔖 have the right order; so ℌ.]

25. **The sleep of a cheerful heart is like dainties.** Cp. Prov. xv. 15 'he that is of a cheerful heart hath a continual feast'.

And his food is agreeable unto him. The Hebr. phrase here used (see critical note) = lit. 'and his food goes up upon him' (𝔖 'upon his body'). It may be illustrated from the *Aboth de Rabbi Nathan* (ed. Schechter), ch. xxvi: 'food which does not go up upon (i. e. which does not agree with) one's body' (אוכלים שׁאינם עלים על גופו).

(*d*) XXXI. 1-4 (= 𝔊 XXXIV. 1-4).

1. **anxiety about it dissipateth slumber.** Cp. (for the phraseology) xlii. 9.

2. **breaketh off (?) slumber.** The Hebr. word rendered 'breaketh off' occurs also in Rabbinic literature in the sense of 'to destroy', 'cause to disappear'. For the additional clauses in ℌ which are attached to *v.* 2 see critical note. They deal with the law of loving one's neighbour (cf. Lev. xix. 18, 34).

3. **The rich man . . . delights.** This verse may underlie Luke xii. 18-19 (so Peters). For the phrase 'to partake of delights' cp. xli. 4 *d* (ℌ).

4. **The poor man toileth . . .** Cf. with the sentiment here expressed the Rabbinic citation attributed to Ben-Sira

(*e*) XXXI. (XXXIV.) 5–11. *The perils of mammon-worship* (= 3 + 2 + 2 + 1 distichs).

ℌ[B] 5 He that [f]loveth[f] gold [g]shall not go unpunished[g],
And he that [f]pursueth[f] [h]hire[h] [i]erreth thereby[i].
6 Many there are that have [j]bound themselves to gold[j]
[k]And have put their trust in corals[k].
7 [l]It is a stumbling-block[l] [m]for the foolish[m],
[n]And whoso is simple is snared thereby[n].
8 Happy is [o]the rich man[o] that is found blameless,
And that hath not [p]gone astray following[p] mammon!
9 Who is he? that we may felicitate him—
For he hath done wondrously among his people.
10 Who [q]hath been tested[q] by it [r]and remained unharmed[r],
[s]So that it hath redounded to his glory?[s]

f–f *Reading* אוהב *in* (a) *and* רודף *in* (b) *with* 𝔊 𝔖: ℌ *inverts the order* g–g ℌ לא ינקה = 𝔊 ου δικαιωθησεται h–h ℌ מחיר: 𝔊 διαφθοραν (*corrupt for* διαφορον = ℌ): 𝔖 'mammon' i–i ℌ בו ישגה = 𝔊 αυτος πλησθησεται (+ αυτης 296 308 = 𝔏): *? l.* απ αυτης πλανθησεται = ℌ *and* 𝔖 (יִשָּׁגֶה: *but* 𝔊 *may* = יִשְׂגֶּה: *so Peters*) j–j ℌ חבולי זהב = 'bound of (given in pledge to) gold': 𝔊 εδοθησαν εις πτωμα χαριν χρυσιου: *but* 248 εδεθησαν χαριν χρυσιου = ℌ: 𝔖 'rich' (ℌ *might mean* 'have been destroyed of gold') k–k ℌ על פנינים (*l.* והבוטחים) והבוטח: 𝔖 'and have trusted (= והבוטחים) in their riches': 𝔊 και εγενηθη η απωλεια αυτων κατα προσωπον αυτων = וחבלם על פניהם ? (*or* והיה הוות ?: *Peters reads* והאבדון—'and destruction was before their face'): ℌ + (*so* 𝔖) 2 *lines*:

ולא מצאו להנצל מרעה
וגם להושע ביום עברה:

'And they found not how to deliver themselves from evil,
And also to save themselves in the time of wrath.'

(𝔖 'in the time of their end'.) *But* 𝔊 *rightly omits* (*the lines are a gloss*; *cp.* Prov. xi. 4) l–l *So* 𝔊 ξυλον προσκομματος = עץ תקלה (ℌ כי *for* עץ (*displacement*): 𝔖 *also inserts* כי) m–m ℌ לאויל 𝔊 τοις ενθυσιαζουσιν αυτῳ ('unto them that sacrifice unto it' R.V.): *but* א* *and three cursives give the right reading* ενθουσιαζουσιν (*? confusing* אוה *with* אויל: *so Hart*). *See also* 𝔏 n–n *So* ℌ 𝔊: 𝔖 'every one that erreth therein stumbleth' o–o 𝔊 πλουσιος = 𝔖 = עָשִׁיר: *so read for* ℌ איש (*Smend keeps* איש) p–p ℌ נלוז אחר: 𝔊 (*inexactly*) επορευθη οπισω q–q 𝔊 εδοκιμασθη = נבדק (*Peters* מי נבדק בו): ℌ *text* מי הוא זה שנדבק בו: ℌ *mg.* הנדבק (הוא זה *from previous line*): 'who is he that we should cleave unto him?' (= ℌ *text*) *or* 'who is he that cleaveth unto it?' (בדק *in PBH* = to examine, explore) r–r *Reading* וישלם = 𝔊 και ετελειωθη: ℌ והיה לו שלום s–s ℌ והיה לו

---

which is given in the notes on xl. 22. The alternative reading 'for the lack of his means' (for כח in this sense cp. Prov. v. 10; Job vi. 22) may possibly be right against 'for the lack of his house'. Cp. xi. 11.

(*e*) XXXI. 5–11 (𝔊 XXXIV. 5–11).

5. **He that loveth gold shall not go unpunished.** Cp. Prov. xxviii. 20 ('he that maketh haste to be rich shall not be unpunished'); also *Qoh.* v. 10 (Hebr. 9) ('he that loveth silver shall not be satisfied with silver', &c.). For the same theme (the dangers of love of money) cp. also 1 Tim. vi. 9.

that pursueth hire. Or rather 'gain, profit'; cp. xlii. 9, vii. 18.

erreth thereby. Or 'is led astray thereby' (i. e. 'falleth into sin on account of it').

6. **And have put their trust in corals.** Or pearls: for 𝔊 see critical note. For the two lines (a gloss) that are appended to this verse in ℌ and 𝔖 (see critical note) cp. Prov. xi. 4 ('Riches profit not in the day of wrath, but righteousness delivereth from death').

7. **It is a stumbling-block . . .** Cp. xiii. 23*c*.

simple. Cp. Job v. 2 (same word).

is snared. Cp. Eccles. ix. 12.

8. **the rich man that is found blameless.** Cp. for the phraseology xliv. 16, 17 (ℌ).

following mammon. The occurrence of the word 'mammon' (מָמוֹן) here is noticeable (= in Biblical Hebrew כסף or מטמון). Outside Ben-Sira its earliest attestation is in the N. T. (Matt. vi. 24; Luke xvi. 9, 11, 13). The spelling 'mamon' (so in Greek) seems to be probably correct; but both spelling and etymology are uncertain (see art. 'Mammon', col. 2912–5 in *EB*, vol. iii).

9. **Who is he? . . .** Apparently a pious rich man was as rare in Ben-Sira's time as an honest publican later in the provinces of the Roman Empire.

10. **Who hath been tested by it** (sc. by wealth) **and remained unharmed**? Cp. Matt. xix. 23; Luke xi. 24. ℌ (text) 'Who hath clung to it . . .'

Who could [t]fall away[t], and did not fall away;
[u]And (could) inflict[u] harm, [v]and did not[v]?
11 [w]Therefore[w] shall his good fortune [x]be steadfast[x],
And the congregation shall declare [y]his praise[y].

(*f*) XXXI. (XXXIV.) 12–24. [a]*Instruction concerning bread and wine together*[a] (= 3+2+2+1+3+1+2+2 distichs).

12 [b]If thou sittest [c]at a great man's table[c],
[d]Be not greedy upon it[d];
[e]Say not: [f]There is abundance upon it[f]—
13 [g]Remember that an evil eye is an evil thing[g],

לתפארת (ℌ *mg.* לתפארה: *so Peters reads*): 𝔊 και εστω εις καυχησιν (*but* ℵ[ca] 70 Syro-Hex εσται αυτῳ = ℌ) [ℌ *adds four lines which are not attested by* 𝔖 *or* 𝔊:

כי ברבות שלום חייו ‖ אהיה לך לתפארת
מי ברכו וישלם חייו ‖ הוא (m. אהיה) לך לתפארת

'For when the peace of his life multiplieth, I will be to thee a glory—who hath blessed it and made his life perfect? he (*m.* I) will be a glory unto thee.' *These lines form doublets to* 10 ab]   [t–t] ℌ לסור = 𝔊 παραβηναι   [u–u] ℌ ולהרע רעה (*so Cowley: Schechter* רע) = 𝔊 και εποιησεν κακα: 𝔖 'to evil entreat his comrade' (= רעו)   [v–v] *So* 𝔊 𝔖 = ולא הרע: ℌ ולא אבה   [w–w] ℌ על כן: > 𝔊 𝔖 (248, 70 𝔏 + δια τουτο)   [x–x] *Reading* יחזק *with* 𝔊 𝔖: ℌ חזק   [y–y] 𝔊 τας ελεημοσυνας αυτου = צדקתו: ℌ ותהלתו   [a–a] ℌ מוסר לחם ויין יחדו (*cp. similar headings in* xli. 16 *and* xliv. 1: *all doubtless secondary*): 𝔊 𝔖 > (*but* 254 *has title* περι βρωματων: *cp.* 𝔏 de continentia)   [b] ℌ *pr.* בני 'my son': *so* 𝔖 (*but* > 𝔊)   [c–c] *Or* 'at a great table' (*so* 𝔊) = ℌ על שלחן גדול (*may be rendered either way*)   [d–d] ℌ אל תפתח עליו גרנך (M גרון) *lit.* 'open not thy throat (*mg.* the throat) upon it' = 𝔊 𝔖   [e] 𝔊 *pr.* και (*so* 𝔖)   [f–f] ℌ ספוק עליו (*lit.* 'there is sufficient upon it') = 𝔊 πολλα γε τα επ αυτης: 𝔖 'I have not enough'   [g–g] *So* ℌ = 𝔊: > 𝔖: ℌ *here adds four lines, which are not attested by* 𝔊, *but are partly represented in* 𝔖:

(1) רע עין שונא אל
(2) ורע ממנו לא ברא:
(3) כי זה מפני כל דבר תזוע עין (M תזיע)
(4) ומפנים דמעה תדמע (M ? תזיע):

'The man of evil eye God hateth,
And He hath created nothing more evil than him.
For this—by reason of everything the eye quivereth,
And from the face it maketh tears.'

𝔖 *has*:—

(= 1) 'The evil of the eye God hateth,
(= 2) And He hath created nothing more evil than it.
(= 3) Therefore the eye quivereth by reason of everything.'

Here it is clear that (2) *is a doublet of* 13 b, *while* (1) *is prob. a gloss on the same stichus* (13 b); (3) *and* (4) *are*

Who could fall away . . . i.e. Who ever had the power and opportunity of falling away and inflicting mischief, and failed to do so? Such cases (see next verse) are so rare as to be marvellous. For 'inflict harm' (לְהָרַע) cp. Ps. xv. 4.

11. **his good fortune** (ℌ טובו). For this meaning cp. Prov. xi. 10; or it may mean 'his goods' (riches); cp. Deut. vi. 11.

And the congregation shall declare his praise. Cp. xliv. 15 (same expression). 𝔊 'his alms' (= צדקתו: so Peters reads) is probably an interpretation, but suggests the right meaning. A rich man who was pious would show his piety by generous almsgiving: cp. the Rabbinic dictum 'the salt of mammon is almsgiving'.

(*f*) XXXI. 12–24 (= 𝔊 XXXIV. 12–24). With the subject of this subsection cp. Prov. xxiii. 1–3.

12. **at a great man's table.** So ℌ preferably to 𝔊 ('at a great table', i.e. one well provided): cp. *Pirqe Aboth* vi. 5: 'lust not for the table of kings.' For the Rabbinic rules regarding table-manners cp. *Derek ereṣ rabba* vi–viii; also *Derek ereṣ zuta* and *Kallāh*.

Be not greedy upon it. Cp. *Derek ereṣ zuta* i: 'Be careful with your teeth (i.e. at your meals) that you do not eat too much.' The Hebrew phrase lit. = 'Open not thy throat upon it' (this possibly may mean, 'Make no remark': so Edersheim, cp. next note).

Say not: There is abundance upon it. The Syr. *it is not enough for me* 'is', says Edersheim, 'characteristic. The praising of the food in Oriental countries is done by the host; the mere act of admiration by any one else would be regarded as dangerous.'

13. **Remember that an evil eye . . .** 'When a person expresses what is considered improper or curious admiration

𝕳[B] [h]God hath created[h] nothing more evil than the eye;
[i]Therefore over everything must it weep[i].
15 [j] [k]Be considerate[k] to [l]thy companion as thyself[l],
And be mindful of all [m]thou detestest[m].
14 Stretch not out the hand [n]wherever he may look[n],
[o]And collide not with him[o] [p]in the dish[p] [j].
16 [q]Eat like a man [r]what is put before thee[r],
[s]And be not ravenous[s], lest thou become disliked[q].
17 [t]Leave off first[t] [u]for manners' sake[u],
[v]And devour not voraciously[v] [w]lest thou become offensive[w].

variants of 13 c [𝕳 *embodies a number of variants, &c. from different codices*]. *In* (3) כי זה *has displaced* על כן, *and* דבר *has been* (*erroneously*) *inserted; while* תזוע *has arisen, prob., from* תמעד *a corruption of* תדמע (*Perles*) h–h 𝕳 לא חלק אל (= *variant* (2) לא ברא): 𝕲 τι εκτισται; i–i *Reading* על כן מפני כל דמוע תדמע = 𝕲 δια τουτο απο παντος προσωπου δακρυει (*so Smend*: דמוע תדמע *from variant* (4)): 𝕳 *here for last two words yields a further variant, viz.* נס לחה, 'its freshness is abated' (*from* Deut. xxxiv. 7) j–j *vv.* 14, 15 *to be transposed* (*with Smend*): *in the usual order* 'may look' *has no proper antecedent* k–k *Reading* רעה (*cp.* xxxviii. 1 note) *with Smend*: 𝕳 דעה (*only again in this form* Prov. xxiv. 14) = 'know': 𝕲 νοει: 𝕾 = 𝕳 ('know that thy neighbour is like thyself') l–l *So* 𝕳 𝕾: 𝕲 (freely) τα του πλησιον εκ σεαυτου m–m 𝕳 ששנאת: 𝕲 [επι παντι] πραγματι = ? מעשה (𝕳 *mg.* אשר שנאת *is to be preferred*) n–n 𝕳 אל מקום יביט אל (אל *repeated accidentally: omit*) = 𝕲 ου εαν επιβλεψη (א* 155 Syro-Hex επιβλεψης = 𝕾) o–o 𝕳 *mg.* ואל תיחד עמו (תיחד = תֵּחַד) *lit.* 'and join not thyself with him': 𝕲 και μη συνθλιβου αυτῳ (70 αυτ αυτου: Origen μετ (αυτου)): 𝕾 'do not force thy hand' p–p 𝕳 בטנא = 'in the basket': 𝕲 'in the dish' (τρυβλιῳ) (*so* 𝕾) *give* טנא *an extended meaning* (*so Peters*) q–q *In* 𝕳 *v.* 16 *exists in a double form, as follows*:

(2) (1) הסב כאיש אשר נבחר ‖ ואל תעט פן תגעל:
(3) דע שרעך כמוך

---

of anything, he is generally reproved by the individual whom he has thus alarmed' . . . and especially when one is invited to partake of a meal 'he must reply if he do not accept the invitation "Heneeān" (i.e. "may it be productive of enjoyment"), or use some similar expression; else it will be feared that an evil eye has been cast upon the food' (Lane, *Modern Egyptians*, i. 183 (315), as cited by Edersheim). The thought of our passage, however, seems rather to be that the guest at the great man's table should not be envious and greedy in the presence of the abundance he sees upon it; such envy and greed is equivalent to 'the evil eye': cp. xiv. 10 *a*, 'The eye of him that has an evil eye darts greedily (𝕳 תעיט, cp. 1 Sam. xiv. 32) upon bread.' In the same passage Ben-Sira also says that the 'evil-eyed' man is not only greedy, but grudging (xiv. 10 *b*). For the Biblical senses of 'the evil eye' see *EB*, s.v. 'Eye' (ii, col. 1453), and for the later senses *JE*, s. v. 'Evil' Eye, v. 280 f. [For the variant additional clauses in 𝕳 see critical note.]

God hath created nothing more evil than the eye; Therefore over everything must it weep. The eye is a main cause of sin; cp. Num. xv. 38 f. (esp. 39: 'that ye go not about after . . . your own eyes'); Job xxxi. 1 ('I made a covenant with mine eyes', &c.); it is therefore punished by God in that when misfortune comes it must weep (so Smend).

15, 14. For the transposition of these verses see critical note.

15. **Be considerate.** i.e. treat in a friendly way; cp. xxxviii. 1 note (same Hebrew verb). 𝕲 here has 'know' (νοεῖ): see critical note [𝕲 for whole line has: 'Know the affairs of thy neighbour by thine own' (R.V. 'Consider thy neighbour's [liking] by thine own'). See next note.]

to thy companion as thyself. 'Thy companion' here =, of course, thy companion at table, thy fellow-guest. To see in this dictum an anticipation of the positive form of the Golden Rule of the Gospel[1], as Friedländer claims (*The Jewish Sources of the Sermon on the Mount*, p. 232 f.), is not justified by the context.

And be mindful of all thou detestest. Here, again, the reference is to the behaviour of the guest at table. In Tobit iv. 15, which is cited by Fritzsche and Ryssel in this connexion, the reference is more general and less restricted ('And what thou thyself hatest do to no man').

14. **wherever he may look.** i. e. wherever thy fellow-guest may look. Possibly, however, the reference is to the host.

16. **like a man.** i.e. as a grown-up man and not as a child, i.e. as becomes a man. Smend compares Qoh. x. 17.

16, 17. **be not ravenous . . . devour not voraciously.** Cf. xxxvii. 29: 'Indulge not excess in any enjoyment, nor immoderation in any dainties.' Prescriptions against gluttony are common in the Rabbinic literature.

---

[1] Matt. vii. 12: 'All things therefore whatsoever ye would that men should do unto you, even so do ye also unto them: for this is the law and the prophets.'

B 18 And, moreover, when thou art seated [x]in a large company[x]
Stretch not the hand out [y]before a neighbour[y].
19 Surely a little is sufficient for [z]a man of understanding[z],
And he need not [a]choke[a] upon his bed.
20 (*c*) [b]Pain and sleeplessness, and distress[b],
20 (*d*) [c]And inward disorder[c] [d]are with a foolish man[d].
20 (*a*) [e]Healthy sleep[e] [f]hath a purged belly[f],
20 (*b*) And when he riseth in the morning [g]his wits are with him[g].

(4) ואכול כאיש דבר ששם לפניך
[*This line added in smaller writing in MS.* ולא תהיה גרגרן פן תמאם] (5)

𝔊 φαγε ως ανθρωπος τα παρακειμενα σοι
και μη διαμασω μη μισηθης. } *v.* 16

[𝔖 *has for vv.* 15–16 *three stichoi* = (3) (4) (5) [*in same order*].

(1) 'Take thy seat like a man that is chosen,
(2) And dart not greedily (i. e. *be not voracious*) lest thou become abhorred.
(3) Know that thy neighbour is like thyself.
(4) And eat like a man what is placed before thee,
(5) And be not gluttonous, lest thou be rejected.'

The form of ℌ *as it exists in the MS. is a mixture of two recensions. Apparently* (3) (4) *and* (5) *represent the recension of the text which lay before* 𝔖. *It is clear that* (3) *is a doublet of v.* 15 a : *it divides the pairs of doublets* (1) (2) *and* (4) (5); (1) *is a variant form of* (4) *and* (5) *of* (2). *Peters adopts* (4) *and* (5) *as representing the original form of* ℌ, *and corresponding to* 𝔊; *but Smend adopts* (4) *and* (2) *thus :*

16 a = אכול כאיש דבר ששים לפניך
16 b = ואל תעט פן תגעל:

It should be noted that ℌ *mg. gives as a variant to* (1) אכל כאיש נכח, *from which Fuchs concludes that the original form of* 16 a *in* ℌ *was*: אכול כאיש אשר נכחך, i. e. 'eat as a man what is in front of thee': *this, he thinks, will explain* כאיש אשר נבחר *in* (1) *and* דבר ששים לפנך *in* (4): *but the latter is attested by* 𝔊   r–r *So* 𝔊 = ℌ (4): *the variant in* ℌ (1) נכח (*l.* נכחך) = 'what is in front of thee' (*cp.* Exod. xiv. 2, Ezek. xlvi. 9): ℌ (1) כאיש נבחר *perhaps arose from* כאיש נכח, *misread* נָכֹחַ = 'upright': *hence* הסב *in* ℌ (1)   s–s ℌ ואל תַּעַט = *lit.* 'and dart not (greedily) upon'; *variant* ℌ (4) ולא תהיה גרגרן (גרגרן = 'greedy': *a Neo-Hebr. word with Aramaic affinities*)   t–t ℌ (*partly damaged*) חדל ראשון = 𝔊: 𝔖 'be watchful'   u–u ℌ (*damaged*) בעבור מוסר = 𝔊 χαριν παιδειας   v–v ℌ . . . ואל תל i. e. תלע (*from* לוע *or* לעע 'to swallow greedily'; *cp.* Obad. 16): 𝔊 και μη απληστευου   w–w ℌ (*damaged*) פן תמאם: 𝔊 μη ποτε προσκοψης = ? פן תִּתָּקֵל (*Peters*)   x–x *Lit.* 'in the midst of many'   y–y *So* ℌ לפני רע: 𝔊 προτερος αυτων = לפניהם (*so* 𝔖): *Schechter, Ryssel propose* לפני ראש   z–z ℌ אנוש נבון = 𝔊 ανθρωπῳ πεπαιδευμενῳ (ℌ *mg.* נכון = 'honest, steadfast): 𝔖 'righteous' = ℌ *mg.*   a–a ℌ ישיק 'burneth': 𝔊 ασθμαινει = ? ישתנק (*from next line: so read*)   b–b 𝔊 πονος αγρυπνιας και χολερας: ℌ מכאוב ונדד ישינה וצער ותשניק: *but* 𝔊 = *the first four words of* ℌ: *prob.* ותשניק *is an error for* יתשנק = ישתנק *a variant of* ישיק *in previous line: it overloads the stichus here*   c–c ℌ הפוכות (M ופנים) ופני: 𝔊 και στροφος: 𝔏 'et tortura' (*but Cod. Tol.* 'et tortura ventris', *which suggests that* γαστρος *has fallen out of* 𝔊): και στροφος γαστρος = ? ומעים הפוכות (*so Smend: so read: Smend also reads* וְנדדי שנה *for* ונדד ישינה *in* 20 (c), *prob. rightly; cp. Targ.* Job vii. 4 נדדת שינתא)   d–d ℌ עם איש כסיל: 𝔊 μετα ανδρος απληστου = 𝔖; *but* ℌ *is implied by* אנוש נבון *in* 19 a   e–e ℌ שנות חיים (חיים = 'health' *as in* Prov. xiv. 30) = 𝔊 υπνος υγειας   f–f ℌ על קרב צולל (צלל *in PBH* = 'to clarify' (wine, &c.); *here* 'purge': ? *read* צלול *pt. pass.*) = 𝔊 επι εντερῳ μετριῳ (μετριῳ *a toning down*)   g–g ℌ ונפשו אתו = 𝔊 [*the right order of clauses in v.* 20 *is given in* ℌ, *as above, viz.* 20 (c) (d) (a) (b) *against* 𝔊]. *To v.* 20 ℌ *appends some additional clauses, six in number, which are partly destroyed* (*gaps in MS.*):

---

18. **Stretch not the hand out before a neighbour.** Cp. *Derek ereṣ rabba* vii: 'When two are sitting at table, the elder begins to eat first, and the younger after him; and if the younger begins first he is a glutton.' Cp. also Lane (*op. cit.* i. 183): 'The master of the house first begins to eat; the guests or others immediately follow his example' (this last passage is cited by Edersheim.)

19–22. Moderation in eating conduces to health.

19. **Surely a little . . .** Cp. Prov. xiii. 25: 'The righteous eateth to the satisfying of his soul.'
choke upon his bed. Or 'groan', viz. from the effects of indigestion.

20. **Pain and sleeplessness . . .** Cf. xxxvii. 29–31.

𝕳[B] 21 [h]And even if thou hast been constrained with dainties,
[i]Arise and vomit[i], and thou shalt have ease.
22 [j]Listen, my son, and despise me not,
[k]And in the end[k] thou shalt comprehend my words[j].
In all thy doings be [l]modest[l],
And no [m]mishap[m] shall touch thee[h].
23 [n]Him that is generous over meat[n] [o]the lip[o] blesseth;
[p]The testimony of his generosity[p] is lasting:
24 Him who is niggardly over meat [q]the city murmureth at[q];
[r]The testimony of his niggardliness[r] is lasting.

(*g*) XXXI. (XXXIV.) 25–31. *The use and abuse of wine* (= 2 + 2 + 2 + 1 + 2 distichs).

25 In wine [s]also[s] show not thyself valiant,
For [t]new wine[t] [u]hath been the ruin[u] of many.

(2) (1) ש . . . . ש נבון ‖ ילין עד בקר ונפשו עמו
(4) (3) . . . . ‖ . . . . ותמצא נחת
(6) (5) . . . . ‖ . . . .

𝕾 = (1) (2) *and by its aid* (1) *can be restored to* שנות חיים עם איש נבון: *thus* (1) *and* (2) *are doublets of* 20 (a) *and* (b): *the variant in* (a) *may be due to an attempt to refine away the somewhat coarse expression in* 20 a על קרב צולל. *In* (4) ותמצא נחת *is, apparently, a variant of* וינוח לך 21 b (*end*). [*Note that* 𝕷 in 20 b dormiet usque in mane = 𝕾 *and* 𝕳 (2) *against* 𝕲 (ανεστη πρωι)] h–h *The right order of vv.* 21, 22 *is preserved in* 𝕲 *and* 𝕾. *In* 𝕳 22 c d *is placed before* 21, *and a doublet* = 19 a *intruded* (הלא די אנוש נבון מזער), *thus producing the order* 22 c d *doublet*, 21, 22 a b i–i 𝕳 קוה קוה *i. e.* 'keep on hoping' (patiently): 𝕲 αναστα μεσοπορων: *but* 248, &c. + εμεσον = 𝕷 surge a medio et vome (*a conflation*): *read* קום קוה (*or* קִיא): 𝕾 'withdraw thyself from the midst of the company' j–j 𝕳 *has these lines in a double form thus:*

(a) שמע בני ואל תבוז לי
(b) באחרית תשיג אמרי
(c) שמע בני וקח מוסרי
(d) ואל תליג (M. תלעג) עלי ובאחרית תמצא דברי

Here, again, we have double readings: (c) *and* (d) *represent the recension of* 𝕳 *which lay before* 𝕾 (*reading* מוסרי = יולפני): (a) *and* (b) = 𝕲 k–k *Reading* ובאחרית = 𝕲 (*so* 𝕳 (d) *but* 𝕳 (b) > ו) l–l 𝕳 צנוע: 𝕲 'adroit' (εντρεχης = 𝕳: *cp.* Micah vi. 8, *where* הצניע = 'walk humbly' *is rendered by* LXX ετοιμον ειναι: 𝕲 *misunderstood*): *for* צנוע *cp.* xlii. 8 [*in* T. J. *Yoma* 43 c צנוע *is opposed to* גרגרן 'gluttonous': *Levi*] m–m 𝕳 אסון ('mischief'): 𝕲 αρρωστημα: 𝕾 'evil' n–n 𝕳 טוב על לחם = 𝕲 λαμπρον επ αρτοις: 𝕾 'the good eye over', &c. (*cp.* Prov. xxii. 9) o–o 𝕳 שׂפה: 𝕲 χειλη: 𝕾 > p–p 𝕳 עדות טובו = 𝕲 (+ και) 𝕾 'and a good witness' (*incorrectly*) q–q *So* 𝕲 διαγογγυσει πολις = ? ירגן עיר (*so Peters: but* עיר *fem.*): 𝕳 ירגז בשער 'shall be troubled in the gate' [*perhaps* יְרֻגַּן בשער *should be read* = 'he that is niggardly . . . shall be murmured at in the gate'] r–r *So* 𝕳 *mg.* 𝕲 (+ και): 𝕳 text *has* דעת *for* עדות—*a scribal error corrected by* 𝕳 *mg.* [𝕾 > *v.* 24] s–s 𝕳 וגם = 𝕾: > 𝕲 (𝕾 = גם) t–t 𝕳 תירוש: 𝕾 'the old (wine)' u–u 𝕳 הכשיל: 𝕲 απωλεσεν = 𝕾 v–v *Reading* ככור *with Smend* (*cp.* 𝕲 70 ως [*Clem. Alex.* ως αρα] καμινος *and* 𝕾): 𝕳 *text* כור = 𝕲 (*ordinary reading*)

---

21. **Arise and vomit.** This appears to represent the best attested text (see critical note). The custom of using an emetic after immoderate eating was prevalent among the Romans; cp. Cicero, *ad Att.* xiii. 52. 1, of Caesar: 'ἐμετικὴν agebat; itaque et edit et bibit ἀδεῶς' (cited by Edersheim). Here, however, the reference may be simply to natural action. In *Sifra* (אחרי מות end) on Lev. xviii. 25 ('and the land itself vomiteth out its inhabitants') the explanation is given: 'as a man vomiteth his food' (כאדם שמקיא את מזונו).

22. **be modest** (as opposed to gluttonous) (see critical note).

23. **Him that is generous . . . blesseth.** Cp. Prov. xxii. 9: 'He that hath a bountiful eye shall be blessed.'

24. **Him who is niggardly over meat . . .** Cp. xiv. 10.

(*g*) XXXI. 25–31 (= 𝕲 XXXIV. 25–31).

25. **In wine also show not thyself valiant.** An echo of Isa. v. 22.

new wine hath been the ruin of many. Illustrate from Judith xiii. 2. For the expression cp. xxx. 23 above. Note the change of words for 'wine' in the two clauses.

ℌ[B] 26 [v]Like a furnace[v] which proveth [w]the work of the smith[w],
[x]So is wine in the quarrelling of the scornful[x].
27 [y]Life-giving water[y] [z]is wine to a man[z]
If he drink it [a]in moderation[a].
[bc]What life[c] hath a man that lacketh new wine,
[d]Seeing it was created[d] [e]for rejoicing from the beginning[eb].
28 Joy of heart [f]and gladness and delight[f]
Is wine drunk [g]in season and (for) satisfaction[g].
29 [h]Headache, derision, and dishonour[h]
Is wine drunk [i]in strife and vexation[i].
30 [j]Much wine is for the fool a snare[j]—
It diminisheth strength and supplieth wounds.

31 At a banquet of wine [k]‹rebuke not›[k] a friend,
[l]And ‹grieve him not in his joy›[l]:

w–w ℌ מעשה לוטש = 𝔖: 𝔊 στομωμα εν βαφη (εν βαφη = 'by dipping' R.V., ? *an incorrect gloss*) x–x *So* ℌ: 𝔊 ουτως οινος καρδιας εν μαχη υπερηφανων (248 o. o. εν καρδια υπερηφανων εν μεθη): καρδιας *an addition*: 𝔖 'so is wine the provoker of the ungodly' [ℌ *has a doublet with inferior readings of v.* 26: נבון בוחן מעשׂה מעשׂה כן שכר לריב לצים, i. e. 'the discerning man proves work by work (every work); so is strong drink in the contention of the scornful'] y–y *Reading* למי חיים (*transposing* חיים *and* היין *with Smend*): 𝔊 εφισον ζωης = כמו חיים: 𝔖 = כמי היים z–z *Reading* היין לאנוש: ℌ *text for whole line has* למי היין חיים לאנוש = 'To whom is wine life? to the sick' (*cp.* Prov. xxxi. 6) a–a *Lit.* 'in its (due) proportion *or* measure': *so* ℌ = 𝔊 𝔖 b–b *A doublet of v.* 27 *c d occurs in* ℌ *text at the end of v.* 28, *which appears to yield a better text; read* (*following this*):

חיי מה לחסר תירוש ‖ והוא לגיל נחלק מראש:

(*so Smend*) (*inferior text of* 27 *c d* = ℌ[1]; *doublet* (*end of v.* 28) = ℌ[2]) c–c ℌ[1] מה חיים ℌ[2] חיי מה d–d ℌ[2] שהוא . . . . . נוצר : ℌ[1] והוא . . . נחלק e–e *So* ℌ[1 and 2]: 𝔊 εις ευφροσυνην ανθρωποις (*the last word an error for* απ' αρχης, *see Clem. Alex. paed.* ii. 23) [𝔖 *for whole line* 'for joy was created from the beginning] f–f ℌ וששׂון ועדוי (*l.* וְעִדּוּן = 'delight' *in late Hebr.*): 𝔊 και ευφροσυνη ψυχης (*cp.* עדי Ps. ciii. 5 = ? ψυχη: *so Peters reads here*): 𝔖 'and good times' g–g ℌ וראי (*so marg.*) בעת (ראי = רי 'saturation, moisture' Job xxxvii. 11; רויה Ps. xxxiii. 5): 𝔊 [εν καιρω] αυταρκης h–h ℌ כאב ראש לענה וקלון (*for* לענה 'wormwood' *l.* לעג *with Smend*): 𝔊 πικρια ψυχης (πικρια = לענה *often in LXX*): 𝔖 'pain, poverty, and headache' = *a double rend. of* כאב ראש i–i ℌ בתחרה וכעס = 𝔊 εν ερεθισμω και αντιπτωματι (𝔖 > וכעס) j–j ℌ מרבה (*l.* הרבה) חמר לכסיל מוקש = ? 𝔖: 𝔊 πληθυνει μεθη θυμον αφρονος εις προσκομμα ('Θυμον *perhaps marginal correction of* αντιπτωμα (29)' *Hart*) k–k 𝔊 μη ελεγξης = אל תוכח: ℌ *defective* l–l 𝔊 και μη εξουθενησης αυτον εν ευφροσυνη αυτου =

---

26. **Like a furnace . . . So is wine . . .** 'Furnace' and 'wine' are parallel; just as the furnace tests and proves the real character of the metal (gold and silver), so wine brings out the real character of the 'scornful'—their inherent pride and viciousness being revealed in the quarrelsomeness that is engendered by free indulgence in drinking wine. According to *Aboth de Rabbi Nathan* (p. 68, ed. Schechter) wine is one of three things by which a man's character is tested (business dealings, much wine, and much talk). 𝔊 has obscured the sense by the addition of an incorrect gloss ('by dipping'—'the furnace proveth the temper of steel by dipping,' R.V.)—a reference to the process of dipping red-hot iron in water to give it temper. See Edersheim *ad loc.*

[The word rendered 'smith' in 26*a* = lit. 'forger' or 'hammerer' (Heb. לוטשׁ); cp. Gen. iv. 22.]

27. **life-giving water.** Lit. 'water of life'; cp. for the expression Rev. xxi. 6, &c. (not in the O. T.).

If he drink it in moderation. Moderation in this connexion is often insisted upon in Rabbinic literature; cp. e.g. *Derek ereṣ rabba* vii: 'Wine drunk in large quantity is bad for the body; in moderation it is good.' Edersheim remarks on the verse as a whole: 'These sentiments were perhaps natural at a period when there were practically no drinks known save wine and water; cp. Virgil, *Georg.* i. *ad init.*' ['In moderation', lit. 'in its measure', or (due) proportion.]

Seeing it was created for rejoicing. Cp. Ps. civ. 15.

28. **Joy of heart . . . gladness . . . Is wine drunk in season . . .** Cp. T. B. *Yoma* 76 *b*: 'If he acts rightly (i. e. drinks in moderation, Rashi) it (wine) gladdens him; if he does not act rightly (i. e. drinks to excess) it ruins him' (Heb. זכה משׂמחו לא זכה משממו; see Cowley-Neubauer, p. xxv).

30. **Much wine . . . diminisheth strength . . .** According to *Aboth de R. Nathan* (ed. Schechter, p. 108 *b*, chap. 37) wine is one of seven things which if used in moderation are wholesome, and if in excess are harmful (wine, work, sleep, wealth, travel, warm water, and the letting of blood).

31. **At a banquet of wine . . .** This verse forms the transition to the following section which deals with behaviour at banquets generally. Logically, perhaps, it should be reckoned with what follows (xxxii. 1–13).

rebuke not a friend. Cp. xx. 1.

ℌ[B] [m]‘Speak to him’[m] no reproachful word,
[n]‘And quarrel not with him’[n] [o]in the presence of (other) people[o].

(*h*) XXXII. (XXXV.) 1–13. *On behaviour at a banquet* (= 3+2+2+2+2+2+1 distichs).

32 1 [p]‘If thou hast been appointed (banquet-)master, do not exalt thyself’[p];
Be [q]to them[q] as one of themselves;
Take thought for them, [r]and afterwards[r] be seated.
2 Supply [s]their needs[s], and [t]afterwards[t] recline;
That thou mayst rejoice [u]on their account[u],
And [v]receive consideration[v] [w]for politeness[w].

3 [x]Speak, O elder, [y]for it is thy privilege[y]:
[z]But be discreet in understanding[z], and [a]hinder not[a] song[x].

ואל (תוגהו בשׂמחתו): *so Smend* m–m *So* 𝔊 𝔖 n–n *So* 𝔖 = ואל תצה עמו: 𝔊 και μη αυτον θλιψῃς = ? ואל תעצבהו o–o ℌ *mg.* לעיני בני אדם = 𝔖: 𝔊 εν απαιτησει: *but* 248 εν απαντησει αυτου *suggests corruption of* εις απαντησιν ανθρωπων = ℌ *mg.* p–p linea ultima folii deest (*Strack*): 𝔊 ηγουμενον σε κατεστησαν; μη επαιρου = (*Peters* שׂר) ראשׁ (*Smend*) שמוך אל תתנשׂא = 𝔖 (𝔖 + ‘and at the head of the rich do not sit down’: *this may be a corrupt variant of, or a gloss on, the first line. It may have stood in the Hebr. MS.*) q–q *So* ℌ 𝔖: 𝔊 εν αυτοις (*but* א 248 > εν) r–r *So* ℌ *text* 𝔖: 𝔊 και ουτω = ℌ *mg.* ובכין (*cp.* xiii. 7) s–s *So* ℌ 𝔖: *but* 𝔊 την χρειαν σου (Sah > σου) t–t ℌ ואחר: 𝔊 𝔖 > u–u 𝔊 δι αυτους = בעבורם: ℌ בכבודם ‘in their honour’: 𝔖 ‘in their latter end’ (*correct to* בחדותהון ‘in their joy’: *so Smend*) v–v ℌ תשׂא שׂכל (*cp.* Prov. iii. 4: ומצא חן ושׂכל טוב ‘and find favour and good repute’): *Smend thinks* שׂכל *has come in from v.* 3; *possibly* חן *or* חסד *should be read for* שׂכל *here.* 𝔊 στεφανον = ? כליל: 𝔖 ‘honour’ = כבוד: *Schechter suggests* שׂכר w–w ℌ על מוסר = 𝔊 ευκοσμιας χαριν: 𝔖 ‘at table’ (? *misreading* מוסב *for* מוסר) x–x *v.* 3 *lacking in* 𝔖 y–y ℌ כי הוא לך = 𝔊 πρεπει γαρ σοι z–z ℌ והצנע שׂכל: ℌ *mg.* והצנע לכת = Micah vi. 8 (*in PBH* הצניע = ‘to hide, keep in the background’): 𝔊 εν ακριβει επιστημῃ = ? בהצנע שׂכל (248 εν ακριβειᾳ της επιστημης), *cp.* xvi. 25 a–a 𝔊 μη

---

31. **Speak to him no reproachful word.** Cp. xviii. 18, xx. 15, xxii. 22.

in the presence of (other) people. Lit. ‘of men’ (בני איש). The rendering of 𝔊 here (‘by asking back a debt’ = with a demand for repayment) depends upon a corruption in the Greek; see critical note.

(*h*) XXXII. 1–13 (= 𝔊 XXXV. 1–13).

1–3. The banquet-master should study not his own dignity, but the comfort and convenience of the guests.

1. **If thou hast been appointed (banquet-)master.** i.e. συμποσίαρχος or ἀρχιτρίκλινος: cp. John ii. 8. The reference is to the sumptuous banquets which were given by wealthy Jews, and conducted according to the rules of etiquette generally acknowledged by the polite society of the time (Greek or Roman). The ἀρχιτρίκλινος was apparently appointed either by lot or election in such circles. The rules governing his conduct ‘regarding the invitation and seating of the guests, the mixing of the wine and the serving of the dishes’, as also the methods of procedure to be adopted by the cook and the servant of the house (שַׁמָּשׁ), ‘were no less strictly observed by the Jews than by the Greeks and Romans’ (Kohler in *JE*, ii. 497). A vivid account of the more luxurious banquets of this kind, such as were given by wealthy heathen and even Jews, is set forth in Philo, *De vita contempl.*, §§ v, vii (cp. *JQR*, xii. 761–764; also Wisd. ii. 7 f.). The Rabbis often uttered warnings against the dangers of such banquets, and tried to guard against the worst evils by insisting on discussions of Scripture, sacred songs, and the presence of students of the Law at such gatherings. Ben-Sira's advice is less tinged with rigorousness, but insists on a standard of good manners, restraint, and consideration for the guests. He obviously has in mind banquets where such standards were not observed.

Be to them . . . 𝔖 adds a clause here which is probably not genuine; see critical note.

Take thought for them. ‘This, according to Plutarch (*Pollux*, vi. 11), would refer to the nature and quantity of the wine to be given to each’ (Edersheim).

be seated. Hebr. תסוב. This verb (in the Hif.) is used in Mishnaic Hebrew in the sense of ‘recline at table’ (lit.? ‘surround the table’), but does not occur in this sense in Biblical Hebrew. (In Mishnaic Hebrew מֵסֵב = ‘banqueting couch). Philo (*op. cit.* § 6) describes the couches used at a luxurious banquet thus: ‘Couches, both for three to recline upon, and which extend all round, are manufactured of tortoise-shell or ivory, and of the more valuable woods; and of them most parts are inlaid with precious stones. On them are laid cloths of purple with gold inwoven, as well as others dyed with divers bright colours, in order to attract the eye.’

2. **And receive consideration.** 𝔊 ‘and receive a crown’, which has been supposed by some (older) commentators to contain a reference to the custom, common at the drinking-parties of Greeks and Romans, and perhaps known to the Hebrews (cf. Wisd. ii. 8; Ps. xxviii. 1–5), of the guests crowning themselves with garlands. Fritzsche sees a reference to a supposed custom of crowning the successful *symposiarch*, which, however, lacks attestation. In any case our text probably did not read ‘crown’ originally (see critical note).

for politeness. Cf. xxxi. 17, ‘for manners' sake’ (same Hebr. word, מוסר).

3–6. The elder should not obtrude his ‘wisdom’ in an unseasonable manner; music and song also have their rights at a banquet.

3. **O elder.** The Hebr. word = lit. ‘grey-head’; cp. viii. 9, xlii. 8.

be discreet in understanding. Or keep thy wisdom in the background (see critical note for meaning of the Hebr. word). ‘Do not play the sage when others are laughing’ (Edersheim).

ℌ[B] 4 [b]In a place of music pour not forth talk[b],
[c]And at an unseasonable time[c] [d]display not thy wisdom[d].
5 [ef]As a signet-stone of carnelian[f] [g]on a necklace (?) of gold[g]
[h]Is a concert of song[h] at a banquet of wine[e].
6 [ij]Settings of fine gold and a seal of carbuncle[j]
Is the sound of music [k]with the pleasance of wine[k i].

7 [l]Speak, O young man, [m]if thou art compelled[m]—
[n]If thou art asked twice or thrice[n l].
8 [op]Sum up thy speech[p], [q]say much in little[q],
[r]And be like[r] one that knoweth and can keep silence[o].
9 Among [s]elders[s] [t]assert not thyself[t],
[u]And ply not [s]eminent persons[s] overmuch[u].
10 [v]In front of [w]hail[w] speedeth the lightning,
And in front of [x]the shamefast[x] speedeth favour[v].

εμποδισης = ℌ: *but* 248 *Chrysost.* xii. 248 (*Ben.*) > μη   b–b ℌ *has a doublet here,* (1) במקום היין אל תשפך שיח (2) ובלא מזמר מה תשפך שיח: *l.* במקום מזמר אל תשפך שיח = 𝔊 (οπου ακροαμα κτλ.): 𝔖 = ℌ[1]   c–c ℌ ובל (*lit.* ובלא) עת = 𝔊 και ακαιρως   d–d ℌ מה תתחכם   e–e *The true Hebrew text of this verse, which is preceded by a variant* (*two lines*), *runs*: כומז אודם על ניב זהב ‖ משפט שיר על משתה היין (*for* כומז Exod. xxxv. 22 *l. with variant* כחותם *cp.* 𝔊: *so Smend*)   1–f *Reading* כחותם אודם: 𝔊 σφραγις ανθρακος   g–g ℌ על ניב זהב (*meaning of* ניב *uncertain*): ℌ *variant* על כים זהב = 𝔖   h–h ℌ משפט שיר = 𝔊 συγκριμα μουσικων (ℌ *variant* שיר אל 'divine song' = 𝔖)   i–i *Here again the true Hebrew text is preceded by a variant* (*two lines*) *which corresponds to* 𝔖   j–j ℌ מלואות פז וחותם ברקת: 𝔊 (*freely*) εν κατασκευασματι χρυσῳ σφραγις σμαραγδου   k–k ℌ על נועם תירוש: 𝔊 εφ ηδει οινῳ [𝔖 *renders v.* 6 'As a collar of gold and gems and emeralds, so are pleasant words at a banquet of wine': *this corresponds to* ℌ *variant*: כרביד זהב ובו נפך וספיר ‖ כך נאים דברים יפים על משתה היין]   l–l *v.* 7 *wanting in* 𝔖   m–m ℌ אם צריך אתה = 𝔊 ει χρεια σου   n–n ℌ בחזק פעמים ושלש אם שאלך: 𝔊 μολις δις εαν επερωτηθῃς = ? בחזק פעמים אם יִשְׁאָלֶךָ (*so Peters* = 'at the most twice if thou art asked': *this may be right: Smend omits* בְּחֹזֶק (*cp.* בגבורות Ps. xc. 10) *and keeps* פַּעֲמַיִם ושלש = ? 'twice or thrice' *as above* (*but the expression is strange*)   o–o *v.* 8 *wanting in* 𝔖   p–p 𝔊 κεφαλαιωσον λογον = כַּלֵּל אֹמֶר (*Smend*): ℌ כל לאמר = ? 'finish saying'   q–q ℌ ומעט הרבה = ? 'and make little (*Piel*) of much': 𝔊 (*freely*) εν ολιγοις πολλα (*or ? reading* במעט *Schechter*)   r–r ℌ ודמה ל: 𝔊 γινου ως   s–s ℌ *in line* 1 *has* 'elders' *and in line* 2 'eminent persons' ('princes' שרים): 𝔖 *transposes*: *so* 𝔊 (μεγιστανων *and* γεροντες *true text*: *see note following*)   t–t 𝔊 μη εξισαζου ('behave not as their equal' R.V.): *but* א 𝔏 (praesumas) εξουσιαζου: ℌ אל תקומם = 𝔖   u–u *So* ℌ: 𝔊 και ετερου λεγοντος μη πολλα αδολεσχει, *but* 𝔏 ubi senes = οπου γεροντες (*cp.* 248 οπου λεγοντες): 𝔏 *preserves the true reading*   v–v *v.* 10 *wanting in* 𝔖: ℌ *has it in a double form with one variant, viz.* בוש ('shamefast') *and* דכא ('contrite')   w–w *So* ℌ = 𝔏 (grandinem): 𝔊 [προ] βροντης (*a correction*: 𝔏 *preserves original reading*)   x–x 𝔊 [προ] αισχυντηρου = ℌ בוש (*the variant is* דכא)

---

song. i.e. singing accompanied by music.

4. **In a place of music.** i.e. at an entertainment (𝔊 ἀκρόαμα). The entertainment here contemplated was, apparently, in the main musical (vocal and instrumental). It followed at the conclusion of the banquet. Heathen banquets included also at this point performances by jesters, story-tellers, and acrobats.

at an unseasonable time . . . Cp. for the general sentiment *Derek ereṣ rabba* vii (end): 'One shall not rejoice among those who are weeping, &c. This is the rule. One shall not have different manners from those of his friends, and of people in general among whom he is' (in reference to social gatherings).

5. **As a signet-stone of carnelian . . .** Cp. Prov. xxv. 11.

6. **Settings.** Cp. Exod. xxviii. 17 and 20.

7–13. The young should be modest and not self-assertive; respectful to their elders, and not unduly talkative. When the time comes they should return home quietly, and remember the duty of thankfulness to God.

7. **Speak, O young man, if thou art compelled . . .** For the general sentiment of the verse cp. *Derek ereṣ zuṭa* ii (beginning): 'Sit before the elders, and let thine ears be attentive to their words. Be not hasty in answering. . . . Do not speak in the presence of one who is greater than you in wisdom.'

If thou art asked twice or thrice. i.e. only speak after repeated invitations; or the clause may run: '(Speak) at the most twice if thou art asked' (see critical note). 𝔊 is rendered by R.V. 'Yet scarcely if thou be twice asked' (= same sense as rendering adopted in text.

9. **Among elders** (or 'eminent ones', see critical note) **assert not thyself.** Cp. Job xxxii. 6 (xxix. 7 f.).

ply not. viz. with questions. The verb (טרד) has the meaning of 'to weary', 'trouble' in later Hebrew.

10. **In front of hail . . .** Hail as well as thunder is inseparable from lightning our text says; but the lightning is swifter, and is seen first; even so the favour and winsomeness inspired by modesty anticipate the exhibition of the latter (Smend). The verse reads like a proverb. The Hebr. verb rendered 'hasten' here (נצח: κατασπεύδει, προελεύσεται)

ℌ[B] 11 [yz]At the time of departure[z] be not last,
Depart home [a]and linger not[a];
12 [b]And (there) whatsoever cometh up in thy mind, speak[b],
[c]In the fear of God and not in foolishness[cy].
13 [d]And for all these things[d] bless thy Maker,
Who satisfieth thee with His bounty.

XXXII. (XXXV.) 14–17. (*a*) *The god-fearing and the sinful man: a contrast* (= 2 + 2 distichs).

14 [ef]He that seeketh[f] God will receive discipline,
And he that resorteth to Him diligently shall obtain [g]favour[ge].

y–y ℌ *has:*
(1) בעת מפקד אל תתאחר ‖ (2) פטר לביתך ושלם רצון
(3) בעת שלחן אל תרבה דברים ‖ (4) ואם עלה על לבך דבר:
(5) [פטר] ל[בית]ך ושלם רצון ‖ (6) ביראת אל ולא בחסר כל:

(1) 'At the appointed time linger not (be not last);
(2) Depart to thy home and accomplish (thy) will.
(3) At table-time multiply not words;
(4) But if anything comes up in thine heart, speak.
(5) Depart to thy house and accomplish (thy) will,
(6) In the fear of God and not in foolishness' (לב for כל).

𝔊 *does not recognize* (3) *and* (4), *which* = 𝔖 *of v.* 11 *essentially:* (3) *is a variant of* (1), מפקד *and* שלחן *being corruptions of the variants* מפטר *and* שְׁלוּחַ (*so Smend*). *Smend adopts* (4) *as the true text of v.* 12 a; *while Peters follows* 𝔊 *and corrects it by* (5) z–z *Reading* בעת מפטר 𝔊 εν ωρᾳ εξεγειρου (*but* 𝔏 surgendi = αναστασεως *Clem. Alex. paed.* ii. 7. 56): *reading of* 𝔊 *is secondary.* ℌ *text* בעת מפקד = 'at the time appointed' a–a 𝔊 και μη ρᾳθυμει = ואל תתרא (Gen. xlii. 1): ℌ ושלם רצון ?*from* (5); *but Smend keeps here* b–b *So* ℌ (4) *above* (*and Smend*): 𝔊 εκει παιζε και ποιει τα ενθυμηματα σου. *This partly corresponds to* ℌ (5) *above; correcting by* 𝔊 *Peters reads* שם שחק ושלם רצון: c–c *So* ℌ (6) *above correcting* כל *at end to* לב: 𝔊 και μη αμαρτῃς λογῳ υπερηφανῳ, ?*reading* ולא בחטאת *and* בחסד d–d ℌ ועל כל אלה 𝔊 και επι τουτοις (*but* 𝔏 et super his omnibus) e–e *The genuine text of this verse runs in* ℌ *thus:* דורש אל יקח מוסר ‖ ומשחרהו ישיג מענה: *This is preceded by a variant which has* רצון *for* מוסר *in line* 1, *and gives as line* 2 ℌ *of v.* 15 b; *it is followed by another variant which runs:* דורש חפצי אל יקח לקח ‖ ויענהו בתפלתו: *i.e.* 'He that seeketh things pleasing to God will receive discipline, and He will answer him in his prayer' [*this* = 𝔖 *substantially:* 'he who seeketh the service of God receiveth instruction; and when he prayeth before Him He heareth him']: 𝔊 *has:* ο φοβουμενος κυριον εκδεξεται παιδιαν, και οι ορθριζοντες ευρησουσιν ευδοκιαν f–f 𝔊 ο φοβουμενος (?*from v.* 16): ℌ דורש g–g *Reading* רצון

---

means 'to make brilliant' in xliii. 5, 13 (where it is similarly rendered by 𝔊: see critical notes *ad loc.*): so here it might be rendered 'flasheth'—'In front of the hail flasheth the lightning, and in front of the shamefast flasheth favour'. [Prof. Schechter suggests ינחץ; cp. 1 Kings xx. 19 = 'be urgent'; but the word is a doubtful one. A common meaning of נצח is 'to be victorious'.]

12. **In the fear of God and not in foolishness.** ℌ text has 'in the fear of God and without lack of anything', which may be a reminiscence, as Schechter suggests, of Ps. xxxiv. 9: 'O fear Jahveh, His holy ones: for there is no lack (מחסר) to them that fear Him': but see critical note.

13. **And for all these things bless thy Maker.** This, according to Schechter (*Wisdom of Ben-Sira*, p. 32), implies the institution of grace over food (ברכת המזון), which was undoubtedly very old; it was, of course, based on Deut. viii. 10.

Who satisfieth thee. Lit. 'who saturateth thee' (המרוך); cp. 𝔊 (μεθύσκοντά σε).

XXXII. 14—XXXIII. 31 (= 𝔊 XXXV. 14—XXXVI. 16 *a* and XXX. 25–40). Here a new section of the book begins. The main themes that emerge in it are: (1) Wisdom above all else consists in foresight against danger. The imprudence of the ungodly man is the result of pride, and the blindness so engendered; the pious man, on the other hand, finds the right path by study of the Law and attention to its teaching (xxxii. 14—xxxiii. 6 = 𝔊 xxxv. 14—xxxvi. 6): (2) a justification of the apparent arbitrariness of providential choice (xxxiii. 7–15 = 𝔊 xxxvi. 7–15); (3) an appeal to the rulers and guides of the people to listen (xxxiii. 16–18 = 𝔊 xxxvi. 16 *a*, xxx. 25–27). All this, as Smend points out, is introductory to the teaching that follows on (*a*) the importance of maintaining independence (xxxiii. 19–23 = 𝔊 xxx. 28–32); and (*b*) on keeping slaves and subordinates in order (xxxiii. 24–31 = 𝔊 xxx. 33–40).

(*a*) XXXII. 14–17 (= XXXV. 14–17).

14. **And he that resorteth to Him diligently . . .** Cp. xviii. 14.

ℌ[B] 15 [h]He that seeketh out the Law [i]shall gain her[i],
[j]But the hypocrite[j] shall be snared thereby[h].
16 [kl]They that fear Jahveh discern His judgement[l],
[m]And elicit guidance from the darkness[mk].
17 [n]The man of violence[n] [o]wresteth reproofs[o],
[p]And forceth the Law to suit his necessity[p].

(*b*) XXXII. (XXXV.) 18–24. *Forethought before action* (= 2 + 2 + 2 distichs).

18 [qr]A wise man[r] [s]will not conceal understanding[s],
[t]And a scorner[t] [u]will not receive instruction[uq].
19 [v]Without counsel carry out nothing;
[w]And after the deed[w], [x]rue it not[x].

(*cp. first variant in* ℌ) = 𝔊 ευδοκιαν (𝔏 benedictionem = ευλογιαν): ℌ *text* מענה 'an answer' h–h *v.* 15 *wanting in* 𝔖 i–i *So* ℌ (יפיקנה): 𝔊 εμπλησθησεται αυτου j–j ℌ ומתלהלה (*cp.* Prov. xxvi. 18: 'as a madman') 𝔊 και ο υποκρινομενος k–k ℌ *has this verse in two forms: the variant runs:* יראי ייי יבינו משפטו ‖ וכחמות רבות יוציאו מלבם: (*m.* וחכמות) = 𝔖 l–l *Reading first line as variant above:* 𝔊 οι φοβουμενοι κυριον ευρησουσιν κριμα (ℌ^1 ירא ייי יבין משפט) m–m ℌ^1 ותחבולות מנשף יוציא (*l.* יוציאו): 𝔊 και δικαιωματα ως φως εξαψουσιν (? *a free rend. of* ℌ^1: *or possibly reading* כנשף יציתו): 𝔖 = ℌ *variant* (*see above*), *which may be a correction of the original* (*or paraphrase suggested* (?) *by a corrupt reading* מנפש *for* מנשף) n–n *Reading* איש חמס = 𝔊 ανθρωπος αμαρτωλος: ℌ איש חכם = 𝔖 o–o ℌ יטה תוכחות = 𝔊 εκκλινει ελεγμον ('reproof' *sing.*): 𝔖 'concealeth instruction' p–p ℌ ואחר צרכו ימשך תורה: 𝔊 και κατα το θελημα αυτου (= ? ואחר רצונו) ευρησει (248 εξευρισκει: *l.* ? ελκυσει [*Smend*]) συγκριμα: 𝔖 'and according to his will (= 𝔊) maketh his way' (*but l.* אוריתא *for* אורחו) q–q ℌ *has this verse in three forms; two in the text and one in the margin* (ℌ^1 ℌ^2 ℌ *mg.*) r–r ℌ (*all three forms*) איש חכם = 𝔖: 𝔊 ανηρ βουλης (= ? איש עצה: *so Smend reads*) s–s *Reading* לא יכסה שכל (*Smend*): 𝔊 ου μη παριδη διανοημα (διανοημα = שׂכל): ℌ^1 לא יכסה חכמה: ℌ^2 לא יקח שחד: ℌ *mg.* לא יקח שׂכל: 𝔖 'will not leave wisdom when it is hidden' (*combining* παριδη *with* ℌ^1) t–t *Reading* ולץ with ℌ^1: 𝔊 αλλοτριος και υπερηφανος (*misreading* זד *as* זר) = זד ולץ (ℌ^2 *and* ℌ *mg.*); *but the sing. verb that follows* (יקח *or* ישמר) *suggests that* זד *is an addition; the line ought also to begin with* ו: *so* 𝔖 (= ולץ) u–u *Reading* לא יקח תורה (*Smend*): ℌ *mg.* לא יקח מצוה: ℌ^2 לא ישמר תורה: ℌ^1 לא ישמר לשונו = 𝔖: 𝔊 ου καταπτηξει φοβον = ? לא יחת מורה (? *corruption of* לא יקח תורה) [*Peters reads line* 1: איש חכם לא יכחד שׂכל 'a wise man doth not dissemble wit': *in line* 2 *he follows* ℌ^1 'and a scorner guardeth not his tongue']. *At the end of v.* 18 𝔊 + και μετα το ποιησαι μετ αυτου ανευ βουλης (*but* 70 155 >; *and* ℵ$^{c.a}$ *marks the words with an asterisk*); *the words have arisen from a correction of* 19 b; *as they stand they yield no sense* (ανευ βουλης *repetition of* 19 a) v 𝔏 Eth *praem.* fili w–w *Lit.* 'and after thy deed': ℌ ואחר מעשׂיך: 𝔊 και εν τῳ ποιησαι σε (248. 155 > σε): *lit.* και μετα το ποιησαι (*from end of previous verse*) = 𝔏 et post factum x–x ℌ אל תתקצף: 𝔊 μη μεταμελου (μετ αυτου *end of v.* 18 *has*

15. **He that seeketh out the Law shall gain her.** Cp. iv. 12. The same Hebr. word (יפיקו) occurs in both passages, and 𝔊 renders in both passages 'shall be filled'. By 'seeking' (דורש) the Law is probably meant investigating it (searching out its meaning; cp. the technical use of the verb דרש in this sense in later Hebrew; also מדרש). Cp. Ps. cxix. 45.

the hypocrite. i.e. the man who is not in earnest about the Law or its fulfilment, and who therefore only pretends to be interested. Only those who love the Law will discover its secrets; cp. John vii. 17.

16. **They that fear Jahveh discern His judgement.** Cp. Prov. xxviii. 5.

And elicit guidance from the darkness. Knowledge of God's will, gained by the study of the revelation of it, will prove a beacon illuminating the darkness of life's journey. Possibly, as has been suggested, Ben-Sira has in mind the great lighthouse of Pharos off Alexandria, which he may have seen. For the idea cp. Prov. vi. 23; Ps. cxix. 105.

17. **The man of violence wresteth reproofs.** Cp. xxi. 6. He will accept no guidance.

And forceth the Law to suit his necessity. So ℌ. In 𝔊 σύγκριμα = prob. משפט, i.e. 'justice'. In its original form 𝔊 may have suggested (reading ἑλκύσει for εὑρήσει): 'and will drag justice to suit his will.'

(*b*) XXXII. 18–24 (= 𝔊 XXXV. 18–24).

18. **A wise man will not conceal understanding, And a scorner . . .** Here 'conceal' apparently = 'let be concealed', let lie dormant; and the verse, as a whole, seems to mean: the wise man will take care to discover what course is demanded by prudence, and then to follow it; while 'the scorner', i.e. the proud, wicked man, obsessed by his own conceit, is not willing to receive advice ('instruction'). Illustrate the general idea from Prov. xii. 15 ('The way of the foolish is right in his own eyes; but he that is wise hearkeneth unto counsel'). The verse states a general principle which is illustrated in what follows (forethought and prudence is necessary before an effective course of action can be followed). The alternative for line 2 offered by ℌ^1 (= 𝔖) is: 'And the scorner doth not guard his tongue,' i.e. is imprudent and reckless in speech; cp. Prov. xxi. 23 f. For 𝔊, the text of which is in much disorder, see critical note.

19. **Without counsel . . .** Cp. xxxvii. 16 (𝔊).

ℌ[B] 20 [y]In a way set with snares[y] walk not,
And stumble not [z]at an obstacle twice[z].
21 [ab]Be not careless[b] [c]in a way . . . . . .[c]
22 [d]And in thy paths be wary[da].
23 [ef]In all thy works guard thyself[f],
[g]For he that so doeth keepeth the commandment[ge].
24 [h]He that observeth the Law guardeth himself[h],
And he that trusteth in Jahveh [i]shall not be brought to shame[i].

(*c*) XXXIII. (XXXVI.) 1–3. *Loyalty to God's Law brings its own reward* (= 3 distichs).

33 1 Him that feareth Jahveh no evil befalleth,
But [j]in temptation[j] [k]‹he shall again be delivered›[k].
2 [lm]He that hateth the law is not wise[m],
[n]And is tossed about ‹like a ship in a storm›[nl].
3 [o]A man of discernment [p]discerneth the Word[p],
[q]And the Law ‹is faithful unto him as the Urim›[qo].

arisen from μεταμελου)   [y–y] ℌ בדרך מוקשת : 𝔊 εν οδῳ αντιπτωματος : 𝔖 'in a way of steepness'   [z–z] ℌ בנגף פעמים : 𝔊 εν λιθωδεσιν : *l.* εν λιθῳ δις (*Hart*) = 𝔖   [a–a] ℌ *has these two lines in a double form* (ℌ[1] *and* ℌ[2])   [b–b] ℌ[1] *and* [2] אל תבטח = 𝔊 𝔖   [c–c] ℌ[1] בדרך מחתף 'in the way of (?) the spoiler' : ℌ[2] בדרך רשעים = 𝔖 : 𝔊 εν οδῳ απροσκοπῳ = ? בדרך מנגף (*so Peters reads*). [*In Rabbinic Heb.* תָּפוּחַ *occurs in the sense* 'round and smooth' : מְתֻפָּח *might have some such meaning* : ℌ *apparently corrupt*]   [d–d] ℌ[2] ובארחתך הזהר (*so read*) = 𝔖 : 𝔊 και απο των τεκνων σου φυλαξαι = ובאחריתך השמר (ℌ[1])   [e–e] ℌ *has this verse in a double form* (ℌ[1] *and* ℌ[2])   [f–f] ℌ[2] בכל מעשיך שמור נפשך (ℌ[1] דרכיך *for* מעשיך) : ℌ[2] = 𝔖 : 𝔊 εν παντι εργῳ πιστευε τῃ ψυχῃ σου (? πιστευε *for* προσεχε : *cp.* 24 a)   [g–g] *Reading* כי עושה זה שומר מצוה (= ℌ[2]) : ℌ[1] *has* כי כל עושה אלה וגו" = 𝔖 : 𝔊 και γαρ τουτο εστιν τηρησις εντολων (= ? כי זה שמור מצוה : *so Peters reads*)   [h–h] ℌ נוצר תורה שומר נפשו : 𝔊 ο πιστευων (*cp. v.* 23) νομῳ (248 κυριῳ = 𝔏) προσεχει εντολαις : 𝔖 'he that keepeth his way keepeth the commandment of God' (*cp.* Prov. xvi. 17)   [i–i] ℌ לא יבוש : 𝔊 ελαττωθησεται (= יחסר : *this may be right*) : 𝔖 'shall not perish for ever'   [j–j] ℌ בניסוי (נִסּוּי *a late Hebr. formation ; also again in* xliv. 20 : נִסָּיוֹן *is more common, e.g.* iv. 17, vi. 7, xiii. 11)   [k–k] *Reading* ישוב יִמָּלֵט (*or* וישב ונמלט = 𝔖, *Smend*) : 𝔊 και παλιν εξελειται (ℌ *defective*)   [l–l] *v.* 2 *wanting in* 𝔖   [m–m] ℌ לא יחכם שונא תורה (*rightly*) : 𝔊 ανηρ σοφος ου μισησει νομον   [n–n] *Reading* ומתמוטט במס[ער כאניה] (*Smend*) : 𝔊 ο δε υποκρινομενος εν αυτῳ (= ? ומתלהלה *cp.* xxxii. 15) ως εν καταιγιδι πλοιον [מסער = סערה 'storm' ; *a noun not otherwise attested*]   [o–o] *v.* 3 *wanting in* 𝔖   [p–p] ℌ יבין דבר : 𝔊 εμπιστευσει νομῳ (νομος = דבר Ps. cxix. 57, 105)   [q–q] ℌ . . . . ותורתו : 𝔊 και ο νομος αυτῳ πιστος ως ερωτημα δηλων (*only* B δικαιων [ερωτημα *an explan. addition*]) = ותורה לו כאורים נאמנה (*so Peters, but without* לו) : *Smend* ותורה לו טטפת קשירת יד 'and the Law is for him an amulet, a band on the hand'   [r–r] *v.* 4 *wanting in* 𝔖. *From here to* xxxv. 11 *there is a gap in the Hebrew MS. consisting of two leaves* (= *seventy-two lines*). *Here again* ℌ *apparently must have contained doublets.*   [s–s] 𝔊 ετοιμασον λογον = הכין דבר   [t–t] 𝔊 και ουτως = ובכן (*cp.* xxxii. 2)   [u–u] 𝔊 ακουσθησῃ = ? והשמעת (*or* והשמיע) : 𝔊 ? *read Nif.*   [v–v] 𝔊 συνδησον : 𝔏 et conservabit (= ? συντηρησον = ℌ ? צרר (*cp.* Isa. viii. 16))   [w–w] *Reading* και τοτε *with* 248 &c. Syro-Hex 𝔏 (א 70 &c. και ουτως) : *cp.* ואחר xi. 7, xxxv. 1   [x–x] 𝔖 'like a swift wheel' : 𝔊 τροχος αμαξης (𝔏 quasi mota carri) : = ? כגלגל עגלה (*cp.* Isa. xxviii. 28)   [y–y] 𝔊 σπλαγχνα μωρου   [z–z] *Reading* כאופן חוזר : 𝔊 ως αξων στρεφομενος (αξων = אופן Exod. xiv. 25) : 𝔖 'like

20. **And stumble not at an obstacle twice.** For the figure of the obstacle (stumbling-block) cp. Isa. viii. 14. The verse appears to mean : do not persist in a course beset with pitfalls ; after stumbling at one obstacle, learn the lesson ; be warned and do not run the risk of stumbling a second time.

21, 22. **Be not careless . . . be wary.** Repeating the general sentiment of the preceding verses. Possibly the corrupt word at the end of *v.* 21 meant 'smooth' ; 'Be not careless in a way that is smooth'—a warning 'not to trust too much to the apparent ease and simplicity of a course' (Edersheim).

23. **In all thy works guard thyself . . . keepeth the commandment.** 'In the Rab. literature (T. B. *Berakoth* 32 *b*) the exposing of oneself to danger is regarded as a transgression of the Scriptural words (Deut. iv. 9) : רק השמר לך ושמר נפשך ('Only take heed to thyself and keep [guard] thy soul [self]')' (Schechter).

24. **He that observeth the Law . . .** Cp. Prov. xvi. 17, xix. 16 ('He that keepeth the commandment keepeth his soul'), xxii. 5. Good fortune and happiness are the reward of loyalty to the Law and its diligent observance. Therefore the observance of the Law appeals to the highest self-interest. This verse forms a natural transition to the paragraph that follows.

(*c*) XXXIII. 1–3 (= 𝔊 XXXVI. 1–3).

1. **no evil befalleth.** Cp. Job v. 19.
in temptation. Or 'trial'.
he shall again be delivered. viz. from the evil or misfortune that may threaten ; cp. Prov. xii. 21.

2. **And is tossed about . . .** And so is likely to founder. For the figure cp. 4 Ezra xii. 42.

(*d*) XXXIII. (XXXVI.) 4–6. *Against thoughtlessness, especially in teaching* (=3 distichs).

𝔊 4 [rs]Prepare thy speech[s], [t]and so[t] [u]let it be heard[u];
[v]Bind up[v] instruction, [w]and then[w] reply[r].
𝔊 (𝔖) 5 [x]Like a cart-wheel[x] [y]is the mind of a fool[y],
And his thought [z]like a rolling wheel-rim[z].
6 [a]Like a saddled horse is the love of a fool[a];
Under [b]whatever rider[b] he neighs.

(*e*) XXXIII. (XXXVI.) 7–15. *Divine preferences in Nature and Man justified* (=3+2+2+2+2 distichs).

7 [c]Why is one day distinguished from another[c],
[d]When all daylight in the year is from the Sun[d]?
8 [e]By God's ‹great› wisdom[e] they were distinguished,
[f]And He differentiated[f] [g]seasons and feasts[g].
9 Some [h]He blessed and hallowed[h],
And others He made [i]ordinary days[i].

a pig [are all his thoughts]' *misreading* חוזר *as* חזיר a–a *So* 𝔖: 𝔊 ιππος εις οχειαν (א[a] A.V. &c. οχειον: 307 ισοχιων: 253 Syro-Hex ισοχειος) ως φιλος μωκος (*but* א[c.a] *rightly* μωρος: *cp.* 𝔖): *for* μωκος V 70 *have* μοιχος (55 254 φιλομοιχος) b–b *So* 𝔊: 𝔖 (*inexactly*) 'whoever loves him' c–c *So* 𝔖 (+'of the year' *after* 'day') = למה יש יום מיום פרוש (*Smend*): 𝔊 δια τι ημερα ημερας υπερεχει d–d *So* 𝔊: 𝔖 'seeing that all lights serve' (*misreading* משמש = 'from the Sun' *as* מְשַׁמֵּשׁ = 'serve') 'the days of the year' e–e *So* 𝔖 (*corrected*): 𝔊 εν γνωσει f–f 𝔊 και ηλλοιωσεν (= שִׁנָּה) g–g = עתים ומועדים h–h *So* 𝔖 (*cp.* Gen. ii. 3): 𝔊 ανυψωσεν και ηγιασεν (253 V Syro-Hex ηυλογησε και ανυψωσε) i–i 𝔊 εις αριθμον ημερων

(*d*) XXXIII. 4–6 (= 𝔊 XXXVI. 4–6). From the theme of the desirableness of pious study of the Law the writer here passes to the work of the Teacher of the Law. The good teacher will take care that oral instruction is preceded by careful preparation. As in the preceding subsection the point is emphasized by a contrast.

4. **Prepare thy speech . . .** Apparently the writer is thinking of the teacher who is answering questions.

Bind up instruction. Cp. Is. viii. 16. 'The metaphor is from provisions for a journey that are packed up' (Edersheim). The subject to be taught should have been well thought out beforehand—made compact, and preserved for future use.

and then. i. e. and only then.

5. **Like a cart-wheel . . .** A contrast. The mind of a 'fool', i. e. an uninstructed person (the exact opposite of the type described in *v.* 4), is 'like a cart-wheel', i. e. has no fixed convictions, but changes constantly like a wheel that is ever revolving.

6. **Like a saddled horse is the love of a fool . . .** Not only the mind, but also the affections of a 'fool' are equally uncertain. Just as the saddled horse, in the joy of free movement and exercise, cares not who rides him, but neighs to signalize his exhilaration; so the careless 'fool' is indifferent as to the object on which (or on whom) he lavishes his transient affections. On the other hand, the pious are particularly careful to cultivate only the society of the pious, and to shun that of evil-doers. 𝔊 (cf. R.V. and critical note) has misunderstood the verse.

(*e*) XXXIII. 7–15 (= 𝔊 XXXVI. 7–15). God in His unfathomable wisdom has willed that creation should be organized in a series of opposites and contrasts. In themselves all men, so far as their creation is concerned, are on a level, just as all the days of the year derive their light equally from a common source, the Sun; but just as God has distinguished some days (the festivals and holy-days) from others, so has He distinguished some men from others—notably (the writer implies) Israel from the heathen nations. The passage, as Smend suggests, was probably directed primarily against the Hellenists, who were striving to break down distinctions between Israel and the outside world, at the time when he wrote. For the passage as a whole cp. 4 Ezra v. 23 f., and the following from the Midrash (*Tanch.* on Numbers נשׂא): 'Out of certain classes of things God has chosen one. Of days the seventh was chosen and sanctified. Of years, too, the seventh was chosen as the sabbatical year; and out of seven sabbatical years one was selected as the jubilee. Of countries God made choice of Palestine. Of the heavens Araboth (i. e. the highest of the seven heavens) was chosen for God's throne. Of nations Israel was the choice; and of the tribes of Israel that of Levi.' See further the *Midr. rab.* on Cant. ii. 1. The following passage from *Midr. Tanch.* (already referred to above) is cited by Cowley-Neubauer, p. xxvi (Exodus, תרומה ג, p. 109 *b*; cp. also T.B. *Sanhedrin* 65 *b*): 'Turnus Rufus asked this question of R. Aqiba, and said to him: Why is one day different from another? He said to him: And why is one man different from another? He said to him: Because the Lord wills; and the Sabbath also is because the Lord wills.'

7. **Why is one day distinguished from another.** viz. in length, according to Ryssel (see 7 *b*); but it is more natural to suppose that the distinctions of holy and profane are referred to, which are worked out in what follows. Note that the days are regarded as real entities (cf. Job iii).

8. **By God's great wisdom.** The answer to all questions is: God has so willed, and His will is unfathomable: 'they were separated by a divine decree' (Edersheim). Cp. the Midrash extract cited above.

9. **He blessed and hallowed.** Cf. Gen. ii. 3 (of the Sabbath).

others He made ordinary days. 'Lit. "He put into the number of days"; i. e. days distinguished by nothing further than their "number" (in the month or year). In this use of the word signifying "number", the Hebrew, Greek, and Latin languages agree' (Edersheim).

𝕲 (𝕾) 10 [j]Likewise also[j] all men [k]are made from the clay[k],
And Adam was created [l]of earth[l].
11 [m]In His great wisdom[m] God distinguished them,
And differentiated [n]their ways[n].
12 Some He blessed and exalted,
And others He hallowed [o]and brought nigh to Himself[o];
[p]Some He cursed [q]and abased[q],
[r]And overthrew them[r] [s]from their place[s].
13 [t]As the clay is in the power of the potter[t],
[u]To fashion it[u] according to his good pleasure;
[v]So is man[v] in the power [w]of his creator[w],
[x]To make him according to His ordinance[x].
14 Over against evil (stands)[y] the good, and against death[y] life;
[z]Likewise over against the godly[y] the sinner[z].
15 [a]Even thus look upon all the works of God[a],
[b]Each different[b], one the opposite of the other.

(*f*) XXXIII. 16–18 (XXXVI. 16 *a*, XXX. 25–27). *Ben Sira's right to give instruction asserted* (= 2+2 distichs).

16 [c]I, indeed[c], [d]came last of all[d],
(xxx. 25) [e]As one that gleaneth[e] after the grape-gatherers:

j–j *So* 𝕾 = וגם: 𝕲 και k–k *So* 𝕾: 𝕲 απο εδαφους l–l 𝕲 εκ γης: 𝕾 'of dust' m–m 𝕲 εν πληθει επιστημης: 𝕾 *renders as in v.* 8 *above* n–n 𝕲 τας οδους αυτων: 𝕾 '[and He made them] inhabitants of the earth' (*? confusing* ארחותם *and* ארצותם; *cp.* 1 Kings xviii. 6, LXX [*Smend*]) o–o 𝕲 και προς αυτον ηγγισεν (= ואליו הגיע): 𝕾 'and they attained unto Him' (= הגיעו ואליו) p 296 (= 𝕷 𝕾) *praem.* και q–q 𝕲 και εταπεινωσεν: 𝕾 'and overthrew' r–r 𝕲 και ανεστρεψεν (157 ανετρεψεν) αυτους: 𝕾 'and rooted them out' s–s 𝕲 απο στασεως αυτων (= ? ממצבם *or* ממעדם: *so Smend*): 𝕷 a separatione ipsorum (= A απο αποστασεως αυτων): 𝕾 'from their habitations' (= ? ממושבם) t–t 𝕲 ως πηλος κεραμεως εν χειρι αυτου (𝕾 *supports* 'in the hand of the potter') u–u *Reading with* 70 πλασαι αυτο (αυτον): *cp.* 𝕷 plasmare illud et disponere (+omnes viae eius); *a doublet: the ordinary reading of* 𝕲 πασαι αι οδοι αυτου *is a corruption of the true reading* [𝕾 *combines* 13 a *and* b *thus*: 'as the clay, which is fashioned in the hand of the potter'] v–v *Reading* ουτως ανθρωπος 248 = 𝕷 𝕾; *other MSS. of* 𝕲 ουτως ανθρωποι w–w του ποιησαντος αυτον 248 (*other MSS.* αυτους) x–x 𝕲 αποδουναι αυτοις κατα την κρισιν αυτου (*last three words* = כמשפטו): 𝕾 'to set him over all his works' (*misreading* כמשפטו *as* במעשיו: *the whole line in* 𝕳 *prob. ran*: לשים אתו כמשפטו) y, y, y 𝕾 + 'is created' *in each case* (*an unnecessary addition*) z–z 𝕲 ουτως απεναντι ευσεβους αμαρτωλος (248 70 Syro-Hex 253 V ουτως απεναντι [του] αμαρτωλου [ο] ευσεβης): 𝕾 'and over against light was created darkness' a–a *So* 𝕲: 𝕾 'so hath God manifested all His works' (*? confusion of* חוה *and* חזה: *so Smend*) b–b 𝕲 δυο δυο (= ? שנים שנים) = 𝕾; *cp.* xlii. 24 c–c 𝕲 καγω: 𝕾 (*one reading*) 'and I also' (= וגם־אני) d–d 𝕲 εσχατος ηγρυπνησα: 𝕾 'came last' (אחרית אתית) = ? באחרית בָּתִי (𝕲 ? *misunderstood* בָּתִי (*from* בות); *it* = בָּאתִי *as* 𝕾 *renders: so Edersheim*) e–e 𝕲 ως καλαμωμενος = ? כמעולל f–f 𝕲 εφθασα = קדמתי ('I went ahead'): 𝕾 'I stood' (= קמתי): 𝕷 speravi (= ? קויתי) *or emend to* superavi (*Bretschneider*) g–g *So* 𝕾: 𝕲 ληνον

10. **Likewise also all men are made from the clay.** Cp. Job x. 9.
11. **In His great wisdom.** i.e. for reasons known only to Himself; they are beyond the human mind to fathom.
their ways. i.e. their destinies (Smend).
12. **Some He blessed . . . others He hallowed . . .** Israel and the priesthood (within Israel) are referred to (Smend). For the phraseology cp. Num. xvi. 5 f. It was the special privilege of the priests to 'come near' (cp. 'bring nigh' in 12 *b*) to God; cp. Ezek. xl. 46, xlii. 13, xlv. 4.
Some He cursed and abased . . . The heathen nations outside Israel, regarded in the lump, are apparently referred to, especially, however, those (in Canaan) that were overthrown by Israel: cp. Gen. ix. 25–27.
13. **As the clay is in the power** (lit. hand) **of the potter . . .** For the figure cp. Jer. xviii. 4, and its application by St. Paul in Rom. ix. 21.
To make him according to His ordinance. For the text see critical note. 𝕲 ('to render to him according to his judgement') misunderstands the original, and introduces an alien thought.
15. **Even thus look upon all the works of God.** Cp. *Qohel.* vii. 13 ('Consider the work of God: for who can make that straight which He hath made crooked?').
Each different. Or 'two and two' (𝕲 𝕾); cp. xlii. 24.
(*f*) XXXIII. 16–18 (= 𝕲 XXXVI. 16 *a*, XXX. 25–27). Although he comes last in the succession of teachers Ben-Sira asserts his right to be heard. He is conscious that what he has to say has been gleaned largely from predecessors; but his labour has been directed towards one end—to select and gather together what is most important for practical wisdom in the affairs of life. Therefore the leaders of the people ought to pay close attention to his message. For the general idea cp. xxiv. 30 ff.
16. **came last of all.** sc. of the wise. 𝕲 ἠγρύπνησα might mean 'I was studious', i.e. strove by study to acquire wisdom; Wisd. vi. 16.

[f]I advanced[f] by the blessing of God,
And filled [g]my winepress[g] as a grape-gatherer.
17 (xxx. 26) [h]Consider that not for myself alone have I laboured,
[i]But[i] for all that seek [j]wisdom[j][h]!
(𝕾) 18 (xxx. 27) Listen [k]unto me[k], ye leaders [l]of the people[l],
And ye rulers of the congregation, give ear!

(*g*) XXXIII. 19–23 (XXX. 28–32). *Against surrendering one's independence to others* (=2+2+2 distichs).

19 (xxx. 28) To son or wife, to brother or friend,
Give no power over thyself while thou livest;
[m]And give not thy goods [n]to another[n]
[o]So as to have to ask for them again[o][m].
20 (xxx. 29) Whilst thou art yet alive and breath remaineth in thee,
[p]Give not any creature power over thyself[p].
21 (xxx. 30) For it is better that thy children ask of thee
[q]Than that thou shouldst look to the hand of thy sons[q].
22 (xxx. 31) In all thy works [r]remain uppermost[r],
And[s] [t]let no stain come on thine honour[t].
23 (xxx. 32) When[u] the days of thy life are ended,
[u]In the day[u] of death, [v]distribute thine inheritance[v].

(*h*) XXXIII. 24–31 (XXX. 33–40). *On the treatment of subordinates* (=1+2+2+1+2+1 distichs).

24 (xxx. 33) [w]Fodder[x] and stick and burdens[y] for an ass,
[z]Bread and discipline[z] and work for a servant!

h–h *v.* 17 *wanting in* 𝕾 i–i 𝕲 αλλα (+και ℵ^{ca}) i–j C 155 296 σοφιαν: *other MSS.* παιδειαν k–k *So* 𝕲 𝕾 (*but* 248 > μου) l–l 𝕲 λαου: *but* 55 254 λαων = 𝕾: *cp.* 𝕷 et omnes populi m–m 𝕾 *transposes these clauses so as to make them follow the next verse* (20) n–n 𝕾 'to others' = 𝕷 (*Cod. Amiat.* aliis); *so* Syro-Hex o–o 𝕾 'to return and beg from them': 𝕲 ινα μη μεταμεληθεις δεῃ περι αυτων (μεταμεληθεις *prob. a false transl. of* לשוב; *so Smend*) p–p *So* 𝕾: 𝕲 μη αλλαξῃς σεαυτον (= 'sell not thyself') παση σαρκι: 𝕷 non immutabit se omnis caro q–q 𝕾 (*freely*) 'than that thou shouldst beg from them' r–r *So* 𝕾 Sah = C (γινου υπερανω) = היה למעלה (Deut. xxviii. 13): B υπεραγων s *So* 248 70 Syro-Hex ℵ^{c.a} 𝕾; *others* > t–t 𝕲 μη δῳς μωμον εν τῃ δοξῃ σου u + u–u 𝕲 εν ημερᾳ . . . εν καιρῳ: *transpose with* 𝕾 v–v 𝕲 διαδος κληρονομιαν (= הנחל נחלה *cp.* Is. xlix. 8): 𝕾 'cause thy sons to inherit thy money' w *Certain MSS.* (248 &c.) *pr. tit.* περι δουλων (𝕷 de disciplina servorum) x 𝕲 χορτασματα (A 254 Sah χορτασμα = 𝕾) = מספא y *So* 𝕲: 𝕷 onus = 𝕾 z–z 𝕾 *transposes*

Here (in the middle of *v.* 16) occurs the great transposition in the Greek MSS. and the versions derived from the Greek. See further note on xxx. 24–25.

I advanced. viz. in wisdom. The Hebrew word (קדמתי = ἔφθασα) means 'I went to meet', 'anticipated'. The author attributes this advance to the grace of God ('by the blessing of God').

as a grape-gatherer. Ben-Sira here explicitly affirms his indebtedness to previous teachers. For the figure cp. Isa. xxiv. 13.

17. **Consider . . . wisdom.** = xxiv. 34.

18. **Listen unto me, ye leaders of the people . . .** For the address to rulers cp. xlv. 26; others, of course, are included: cp. Matt. xiii. 9, &c. ('He that hath ears to hear, let him hear'), and the similar passages in Rev. ii. 7, 17, 29, iii. 6, &c.

(*g*) XXXIII. 19–23 (= 𝕲 XXX. 28–32).

19. **Give no power over thyself.** So as to become dependent on them.

20. **Give not any creature power over thyself.** Ryssel thinks that 𝕲 (see critical note) = אַל־תָּמֵר נַפְשְׁךָ בְּכָל־בָּשָׂר, 'exchange not thyself with any flesh', i.e. do not allow any other person during thy lifetime to usurp thy place: following Edersheim he suggests that 𝕾 misinterpreted תָּמֵר by the Aram. מרא 'lord'.

21. **look to the hand of thy sons.** Cp. xl. 29 ('A man that looketh to a stranger's table'); Ps. cxxiii. 2 ('Behold, as the eyes of servants (look) unto the hand of their master'). Cp. the saying preserved in *Aboth de R. Nathan* (90 *a*): 'If a man eat of the property of his father or of his mother or of his children, his mind is not established; much more when he eateth of the property of others' (cited by Edersheim).

22. **And let no stain come on thine honour.** As would probably be the case in a position of dependence; for the expression cp. xviii. 15, xliv. 19.

23. **In the day of death, distribute thine inheritance.** In the so-called *Second Alphabet of Ben-Sira* the saying occurs in the following form: 'Hide, my son, thy wealth in thy life and conceal it; and to thy heirs give it not till the day of thy death.' Note that the dying man is to distribute the patrimony; written testamentary dispositions were apparently not usual (Smend).

(*h*) XXXIII. 24–31 (= 𝕲 XXX. 33–40).

24. **Fodder and stick . . .** Cp. Prov. xxvi. 3 ('A whip for the horse, a bridle for the ass, and a rod for the back of

𝔊(𝔖) 25 (xxx. 34) [a]Put thy servant to work[a], [b]and he will seek rest[b];
[c]Leave his hands idle[c], and he will seek liberty!
26 (xxx. 35) [d]Yoke and thong bow down the neck,
And for an evil servant (there are) [e]stocks and chastisement.[ed]
27 (xxx. 36) [f]Put thy servant to work[f], [g]that he be not idle[g];
(xxx. 37) For [h]idleness[h] teacheth much mischief.
28 (xxx. 38) [i]Appoint him (a task) in thy house[i] such as befitteth him,
And if he obey not [j]make his fetters heavy[j].
29 [k]But be not overbearing[k] against any creature,
And do nothing [l]that is without right[l].

30 (xxx. 39) [m]Hast thou an only servant[m], let him be as [n]thyself[n]—
[o]For [p]thou hast need of him as thy very self[po].
31 [m]Hast thou an only servant[m], treat him as [q]thy brother[q]—
[or]Be not jealous against thy very life[ro]!

a–a 𝔊 *εργασαι εν παιδι* = עבד בעבד : 𝔖 > (*by homoioteleuton*) b–b *So* 248 *και ζητησει αναπαυσιν* = 𝔏 (𝔖 'and give him no rest'): B &c. *και ευρησεις κτλ.* c–c *So* 𝔊 : 𝔖 'if thou raise his head' (*? reading* הָרֵם *for* הָרֶף) d–d 𝔖 > e–e 𝔊 *στρεβλαι και βασανοι* = ? מהפכת ויִסּוּרִים : *στρεβλωτηριον* (Symm.) = מהפכת Jer. xx. 2: *βασανιζειν* = יסר iv. 17 (*Smend*) f–f *So* 𝔖 = עבד בעבדך : 𝔊 *εμβαλε αυτον εις εργασιαν* g–g *So* 𝔊 = ולא(פן) יֶעְצַל h–h 𝔊 *αργια* = עַצְלָה i–i 𝔖 'give him power in thine house' = ? הפקידהו בביתך (*Smend*): 𝔊 *εις εργα καταστησον* (+ *αυτον* 𝔏 Syro-Hex) j–j 𝔊 *βαρυνον τας πεδας αυτου* (> *αυτου* א* A C &c.): 307 *βαρυνον ταις πεδαις cp.* 𝔏 curva illum compedibus k–k 𝔊 *και μη περισσευσης* = ואל־תותיר (*Smend*), *or better, perhaps, a misreading by* 𝔊 (תותיר) *for* תתיהר (*in Neo-Hebr.* = 'be boastful', 'overbearing', *cp.* יהיר Prov. xxi. 24) l–l 𝔊 *ανευ κρισεως* = בלא מִשפט : 𝔖 'which is not in the Law' m–m 𝔖 'If one is thy servant': 𝔊 *ει* (*read εις*) *εστιν σοι οικετης* n–n 𝔊 *συ* (*but* 248 = 𝔏 *η ψυχη σου*) o–o *In* 𝔊 *these clauses are transposed; the order adopted above is supported by* 𝔖 p–p 𝔊 *ως η ψυχη σου επιδεησεις αυτῳ*: 𝔖 'like thee is thy loss' (ℌ *read* תחסרהו *or* חסרונו : *so Smend*) q–q *Reading αδελφον* (*for σεαυτον* B) *with* א A C &c. Syro-Hex 𝔏 𝔖 r–r 𝔊 *οτι εν αιματι εκτησω* (= תקנה) *αυτον*: 𝔖 'do not fight against the blood of thy soul' = ? אל תקנא בדם נפשך (*so read*)

---

fools'). For 'discipline' in the second line the Armenian has 'the lash', which may be a correct interpretation of 'discipline' here; it corresponds to 'stick' in line 1. Cp. Prov. xxix. 19.

25. **Put thy servant to work.** Lit. 'work with thy servant'; cp. xiii. 4 ('make a slave of').

Leave his hands idle = הרף לו, which 𝔖 misread הָרֵם לו (so Edersheim).

26. **Yoke and thong bow down the neck.** The terms are applicable to a beast of burden, which is, no doubt, in the writer's mind. The word rendered 'thong' (*ἱμάς*) or 'strap' refers probably to some sort of rough harness. In Isa. v. 18 and Job xxxix. 10 it = עבות 'cord'—in the latter passage the cord or band by which an animal is controlled ('Canst thou bind the wild-ox with his band in the furrow?'). For the phrase 'bow down the neck' cp. vii. 23 𝔊.

stocks and chastisement. For the 'stocks' (מהפכת) cp. Jer. xx. 3, xxix. 26; 2 Chron. xvi. 10. It was an instrument of punishment which compelled a *crooked* posture, or *distorting* (הפך) apparently, and, though not recognized in the Law, is referred to (with the 'collar' or manacle [צינק] and the 'fetters' [see *v.* 28 below]) as a method of disciplining disobedient servants and other refractory persons. All these restrained personal liberty. By 'chastisement' (יסורים) probably scourging is meant. The right of a master to inflict excessive punishment was, however, limited by the Law, even in the case of non-Israelitish slaves; and the sabbath rest was a humane institution by which they benefited (cf. Exod. xxi. 26 f., xxiii. 12; Deut. v. 12 f.). It must be borne in mind that the case contemplated in our text is that of the '*evil* servant'.

27. **For idleness teacheth much mischief.** Illustrate from 2 Thess. iii. 11.

28. **make his fetters heavy.** Cp. for the phrase Lam. iii. 7 ('He hath made my chain heavy').

29. **be not overbearing.** The Hebr. text underlying 𝔊 is usually supposed to mean 'be not excessive' (אל־תותר), sc. in punishment; for another view see critical note. In any case the rights even of foreign-born slaves were safeguarded in the Law. Thus if a master struck his slave so as to cause the loss of an eye or tooth, the slave was to be free; if death resulted on the same day the deed was avenged as a murder, but not if it ensued on a subsequent day (cf. Exod. xxi. 20, 21, 26, 27). A fugitive slave, according to Deut. xxiii. 15, 16, was not to be delivered up to his master by those among whom he had taken refuge.

without right. i.e. contrary to the Law.

30. **an only servant.** For the reading cp. critical note. This reading explains the apparent contradiction between the advice given in this and the following verse and the section that immediately precedes. For the transposition of clauses *b* and *d* see critical note.

31. **Be not jealous against thy very life.** The original text probably ran אל תקנא בדם נפשך, lit. 'be not jealous against the blood of thy soul (or thyself)'; 'blood' = life according to Gen. ix. 3 f. and other passages. 𝔖 renders: 'and fight not with the blood of thy soul,' i.e. with thine own blood—a rendering of the same text, probably. Smend, following Drusius and other scholars, supposes 'with the blood' here to represent בְּדָמֵי, and explains this expression from the Aramaic sense of דמין = 'worth' or 'price': then the line may be interpreted: 'for in him thou possessest one worth thy very self': cp. A.V. (*v.* 30) 'because thou hast bought him with a price.'

𝔊 (𝔖) (xxx. 40) If thou treat him ill, [s]and he proceed to run away[s],
On what way shalt thou find him?

(*a*) XXXIV. (XXXI.) 1–8. *The vanity of dreams and divinations* (=3+1+3+1 distichs).

34 𝔖 1 [a]He who seeketh vanity findeth delusion,[a]
𝔊 [b]And dreams elate fools[b].
2 As one catching at a shadow [c]and pursuing the wind[c],
So is [d]he that trusteth[d] [e]in dreams[e].
𝔖 3 [f]Alike are mirror and dream[f],
[g]The likeness of a face opposite a face[g].
4 [h]From the unclean what can be clean[h],
And from the false what can be true?
5 Divinations and soothsayings and dreams are vain;
Even [i]as thou hopest (so) seeth thy heart[i].

s–s 𝔊 και απαρας αποδρᾳ: 𝔖 'and he goes and gets lost' (נפוק נאבד) = ? והלך וברח

a–a *So* 𝔖 (*cp. v.* 2 a): 𝔊 κεναι αι ελπιδες και ψευδεις ασυνετῳ ανδρι: 𝔏 *has sing.* (vana spes et mendacium) b–b *So* 𝔊: 𝔖 'and a dream is a vain delight' (? = תענוג הבל *for* (הרגיעו נבל(ים)) c–c *So* 𝔊 (ανεμον B, ανεμους 248 347 *Compl.*): 𝔖 'and as one startling a bird' d–d *So* 𝔖: 𝔊 ο επεχων (𝔏 qui attendit ad) e–e *So* 𝔊: 𝔏 visa mendacia: 𝔖 'to the vision of the night' f–f 𝔖 'thus is the vision' (= מַרְאָה *mirror*) 'and dream of the night': 𝔊 τουτο κατα τουτο (*so* א *et al* Syro-Hex 𝔏 Syr Sah: *but* B κατα τουτου) ορασις ενυπνιων (τουτο κατα τουτο = זה כזה *i.e.* 'like one another [are]', &c.): 𝔏 = 𝔊 (hoc secundum hoc, &c.) g–g *So* 𝔊 (κατεναντι προσωπου ομοιωμα προσωπου): 𝔏 ante faciem hominis similitudo hominis: 𝔖 'opposite a person (פרזופא) the likeness of a face' h–h *So* 𝔏: 𝔊 = מטמא מי יִטַּהֵר (יִטַּהֵר = καθαρισθησεται: *but read* יִטְהַר = καθαρευσει *cp.* αληθευσει *next clause: so Ryssel*): 𝔖 *has* 'and from the head of his people' = מראש עמו *misread from* מרשע מה 'it (*the dream*) expels innocency': 𝔖 *points to a Hebr. text* (?) ומרשע מה יזכה, 'out of wickedness what can be pure?' (*a variant on text underlying* 𝔊) [*Edersh., Ryssel suggest* צדק *for* יזכה *in Syr. variant*] i–i 𝔊 ως ωδινουσης φανταζεται καρδια (= ? כמו תחיל יוֹרֶה לבך: *cp.* Isa. xxvi. 17, LXX: *read* כמו תוחיל יראה לבך:

If thou treat him ill . . . 𝔖 renders: 'because if thou afflict him he will go away and perish (or get lost); and by what way shalt thou find him?' The runaway slave could not be recovered (see on *v.* 29 above).

XXXIV. 1—XXXVI. 16 (= 𝔊 XXXI. 1—XXXIII. 13*a*; XXXVI. 16 *b*–22). This division falls into six subsections, viz.: (*a*) xxxiv. 1–8; (*b*) xxxiv. 9–17; (*c*) xxxiv. 18–26; (*d*) xxxv. 1–11; (*e*) xxxv. 12–20; (*f*) xxxvi. 1–17. Its themes embrace a disquisition on the vanity of dreams, the practical value of true wisdom, acceptable and unacceptable sacrifice, the efficacy of the prayers of the oppressed, and, in conclusion, a prayer is set forth to God for His people.

XXXIV = (XXXI). Three of these subsections are included in chap. xxxiv, viz.: (*a*) xxxiv. (xxxi.) 1–8; (*b*) xxxiv. 9–17 (= xxxi. 9–20); (*c*) xxxiv. 18–26 (= xxxi. 21–31). The theme of (*a*) is the futility of dreams, divinations, and soothsayings as sources of knowledge; with this the writer contrasts (*b*) the outcome of his own much-travelled experience, viz. that nothing can exceed in practical value, for the stress of life, the possession of true wisdom and the fear of the Lord; in (*c*) he turns to another subject, the ineffectiveness of sacrifices unaccompanied by a proper spirit and true repentance (this is continued in xxxv. 1–11 [= 𝔊 xxxii. 1–13] by a paragraph on acceptable sacrifice).

(*a*) XXXIV. (𝔊 XXXI.) 1–8. In his strong repudiation of belief in dreams Ben-Sira is much in advance of his time. Even the later Rabbis failed to reach so discriminating a standard, belief in the efficacy of dreams being practically universal among them. 'The Jews of antiquity held almost the same views regarding dreams as did other ancient peoples' (*JE*, iv. 837). False divination is denounced in Jer. xxviii. 8: cp. *Qohel.* v. 6 (Hebr. v. 7).

1. **He who seeketh vanity findeth delusion.** So 𝔖. 𝔊 has 'A man without understanding hath vain and false hopes'. The aphoristic style of 𝔖 here is probably more original. For thought cp. *v.* 2 *a*.

dreams elate fools. For the variant of 𝔖 here ('A dream is a vain delight') cp. the dictum of R. Simon b. Yochai (2nd cent. A.D.): 'As there is no grain without chaff, so there is no dream without vain things.' The Greek ἀναπτεροῦν = 'to furnish with wings': then, metaph. 'to excite, elate'. It may here represent הרגיע (in Cant. vi. 4 it = הרהיב).

2. **pursuing the wind.** Cp. Hos. xii. 2 (xii. 1 Hebr.). 𝔖 ('as one startling a bird') is probably interpolated from xxvii. 18: cp. Prov. ix. 12 LXX.

3. **Alike are mirror and dream.** Dream and mirror are alike in this, that the image in both is a mere reflection as contrasted with the reality. There may be the further idea that as a mirror merely reflects what is placed opposite it, so a dream merely portrays what is read into it. It may be made to mean anything. 𝔏 ('hoc secundum hoc visio somnorum') can only = 'all dreams are alike'.

4. **From the unclean what can be clean.** Cp. Job xiv. 4.

5. **Divinations . . .** The Latin qualifies the terms employed ('divinations, soothsayings, dreams'): 'divinatio erroris, auguria mendacia, somnia malefacientium,' 'reserving the rights of legitimate divination' (Hart): cp. *v.* 6.

as thou hopest . . . The emended text yields an excellent sense. 𝔊 is rendered by R.V.: 'And the heart fancieth, as a woman's in travail,' i.e. is the victim of manifold self-delusions. The physical phenomenon alluded to is often referred to by ancient writers.

𝔖 6 [j]If they be not sent from the Most High providentially[j],
Do thou pay them no heed.
7 [k]For many there are that have been led astray by dreams[k],
𝔊 [l]And through placing their hopes thereon have fallen[l].
8 [m]Without deceit shall the Law be fulfilled[m],
[n]And wisdom is perfect in a mouth that is faithful[n].

(*b*) XXXIV. 9–17 (XXXI. 9–20). *The practical value of true Wisdom* (= 2 + 2 + 3 + 3 distichs).

9 [o]An ⁽experienced man⁾ knoweth much,
And ⁽one that is well versed⁾[o] [p]declareth understanding[p].
10 He that is without experience knoweth little,
(11) But [q]the well-versed[q] hath much [r]skill[r].

cp. Smend): 𝔖 'he that trusteth in them his heart is there' (248 *has* φανταζεται σου η καρδια: *so* 𝔏) [j–j] 𝔊 εαν μη παρα Υψιστου αποσταλη εν επισκοπη (א A C): + σου (248): επισκοπη (> εν) 106 = 𝔏 nisi ab Altissimo fuerit emissa visitatio: *so* Arm: *cp.* 𝔖 'even though it be ordained of God to err in thoughts of the night' [k–k] 𝔖 *lit.* 'for many there are that have missed their way (טעו אורחא) in a dream': 𝔊 (C &c.) πολλους (+ γαρ A 248 *et al.* Syro-Hex 𝔏 𝔖) επλανησε τα ενυπνια [l–l] *So* 𝔊 𝔏: 𝔖 'and have stumbled in their paths' [m–m] *So* 𝔊 𝔏 (verbum legis): 𝔖 'where there is no sin God is well pleased' (*Heb.* ? בלא שקר *misunderstood by* 𝔖: *so Ryssel*) [n–n] 𝔊 και σοφια στοματι πιστῳ (πιστων 253 296 308: *cp.* 𝔏 in ore fidelis) τελειωσις = וחכמה לפה שנאמן כליל ? (*cp. Ryssel*): 𝔖 'the wisdom of the ungodly at night is believed' = חכמה לְפֹּשֵׁעַ נאמנה בליל[ה] (*so Ryssel*) [o–o] 𝔊 ανηρ πεπαιδευμενος (*v. l.* א A *vid.* 248 347 &c. Syro-Hex πεπλανημενος) εγνω πολλα, και ο πολυπειρος: 𝔏 vir in multis expertus (= ανηρ πολυπειρος) cogitabit multa, et qui multa didicit (= και ο πεπαιδευμενος) *transposing the two Gk. words* [*in* xxi. 22 (25) ανθρωπος πολυπειρος *is rendered by* 𝔏 homo peritus: *in* xxi. 23 (26) ανηρ πεπαιδευμενος *by* vir eruditus]: *so* 𝔖 *which renders*: 'a wise man' (גברא חכימא = ανηρ πολυπειρος, *cp.* xxxvi. 25, xxi. 22) 'examines much, and the diligent man' (𝔖 כשיר [*so read*] = *Heb.* רגיל) *This would point to an original Hebrew text:*

איש וָתִיק (*cp.* xxxvi. 25) . . . . . .
וְרָגִיל . . . . . .

רגיל (= 'used to', 'well versed in', *parallel in meaning to* ותיק) *prob. gave rise to the variant reading* πεπλανημενος = 'travelled' (= רגיל *regarded as passive part of* רָגַל) [p–p] *So* 𝔊, 𝔏 (enarrabit intellectum): 𝔖 'searcheth out everything' [q–q] 𝔊 ο δε πεπλανημενος, *so* C 248 &c.: πεπαιδευμενος 55 106 157 254 (*variant renderings of* רגיל *as in v.* 9): 𝔏 in multis factus est (= ? πληθυνομενος, *corruption of* πεπλανημενος): 𝔖 'he who is tried (experienced)' (דנסי) [r–r] 𝔊 πανουργιαν = ערמה: 𝔏 malitiam (nequitia) = רעה: 𝔖 'wisdom' [*vv.* 9 a, 10, 11 *in* 𝔏 = *doublets*] [s–s] *So* 𝔊 𝔏: 𝔖 'when I tried (gathered experience)' [t–t] 𝔖 = ורבים דברים באוני: *this is confirmed by* 𝔏 *which has* et plurimas verborum consuetudines (consuetudines = συνηθειας, *a corruption ? of*

6. **If they** (i. e. dreams) **be not sent from the Most High providentially** (ἐν ἐπισκοπῇ, 'as a visitation'). The writer here makes an exception of God-given dreams, of which many are referred to in the O. T. The 𝔏, 'unless a visitation be sent from the Most High' (which may represent the true text), apparently means: unless the dream be followed by some definite and practical consequences, pay no heed to it—a good working precept which accords well with Ben-Sira's general view of the matter.

7. **through placing their hopes thereon have fallen.** For the phrase cp. 𝔊 xiv. 2.

8. **Without deceit shall the Law be fulfilled.** i.e. without the aid of such false and delusive *media* as dreams and divinations the Law will be realized (i. e. its threats and promises, dependent upon obedience or disobedience to its precepts, shall be realized): so Ryssel. Or the sentence might mean: those who practise the Law can and should fulfil its precepts without resort to such means (which, indeed, are contrary to it). Edersheim makes 'without deceit' = 'by telling the truth'—a harsh and strained construction.

wisdom is perfect in a mouth that is faithful. i. e. wisdom is only then perfect when it is allied with truthfulness. ('A mouth that is faithful and true': so Ryssel.) 'Wisdom when combined with sincerity is perfect' (Edersheim). Clem. Alex. *Strom.* ii. 26. 24, *Paed.* 441 cites the clause in the form: σοφία στόματι πιστῶν (without τελείωσις, cp. 𝔏). [For the equation of Law and wisdom cp. chap. xxiv, and see Introd. § 9, ii and iii.]

(*b*) XXXIV. 9–17 (= 𝔊 XXXI. 9–20). The writer in this subsection proceeds to enlarge on the benefit of true wisdom and sound piety, as shown in his own wide experience of life.

9. **An experienced man . . . one that is well versed.** The context shows that the writer is referring to experience gained in the school of life, especially by travel (cp. *v.* 11). Edersheim thinks skill in practice in the arts or sciences is meant (cp. *v.* 10 *b*).

10. **the well-versed.** For the reading (= Hebr. רגיל) see critical notes. 𝔖 'one who is tried' (in the school of experience) gives the sense well: cp. also 𝔏. [Against the view that נסע and נסה have been confused in original Hebrew here see Ryssel.]

𝔊 11 (12) [s]In my journeying[s] I have seen much,
𝔖 [t]And many things have befallen me[t].
12 (13) Often was I in danger even unto death,
But was preserved [u]because of these things[u].
13 (14) [v]The spirit of those that fear the Lord remaineth alive[v],
(15) [w]For their hope is upon Him that saves them[w].
14 (16) [x]He that feareth the Lord is afraid of [y]nothing[y],
And doth not lose courage—for He is his hope.
15 (17) Of him that feareth the Lord—happy the soul!
(18) On whom doth he trust? And who is his stay[z]?
16 (19) The eyes of the Lord are upon [a]them that fear Him[a],
[b]A mighty shield, and strong stay[b],
[c]A cover from scorching Sirocco[c], [d]a shadow from noontide heat[d],
[e]A guard from stumbling[e], and a succour from falling,
17 (20) Heart-gladdener[f] and eye-brightener,
[g]Healing, life, and blessing[g]!

(*c*) XXXIV. 18–26 (XXXI. 21–31). *Unacceptable sacrifice* (= 2 + 3 + 2 + 3 distichs).

18 (21) [h]The sacrifice of the unrighteous man is a mocking offering[h],
(22) And unacceptable are [i]the oblations[i] of the godless.

συνηλθε: *or* = ηθη *for* ηλθε): 𝔊 και πλειονα (248 τα πλασματα—*a secondary reading*) των λογων μου συνεσις μου (106 > μου) = ? ורבה מדברי בינתי (בינתי *may be a corruption of* באוני: *so Ryssel*) u–u 𝔊 τουτων χαριν = 𝔖: 𝔏 horum causa et liberatus sum gratia dei; ‘*double rendering of* χαριν *suggested by the familiar phrase* “saved by grace”’ (*Hart*). *Edersh. suggests that* בעברם *stood in the original Hebr. with the meaning* ‘when they passed over (me)’ (בְּעָבְרָם) *and that this was misread by the translators* בַּעֲבָרָם = ‘on account of them’ v–v *So* 𝔊 = רוח יראֵר יהוה תחיה: 𝔖 ‘the will of those that fear Him the Lord does’ = ? רְעוּת יראי יהוה תחיה (*Edersh.*): 𝔏 quaeritur = ζητηθησεται *for* ζησεται (*the following clause in* 𝔏 *is an amplification*) w–w *So* 𝔊 𝔏 + et oculi Dei in diligentes se (= *v.* 16 (19) a): 𝔖 ‘for great is his hope and He saves’ x 𝔖 > *the verse* y–y ουδεν א &c. Syro-Hex. 𝔏 𝔖: πολλα A: ου μη B &c. z 𝔊 αντιστηριγμα = משען Ps. xviii. 19 a–a 𝔊 (307) τους φοβουμενους αυτον (*so* 𝔏): τους αγαπωντας αυτον B &c. 248: 𝔖 ‘all His servants’ [𝔏 *really has both readings: cp. v.* 13 (15)] b–b 𝔖 ‘protecting (מגן) and delivering, and He is a great confidence’ c–c 𝔊 σκεπη απο καυσωνος: 𝔏 tegimen ardoris (𝔖 ‘from the enemy’) d–d *So* 𝔏 (umbraculum meridiani): 𝔊 σκεπη μεσημβριας (𝔖 ‘from the foe’) e–e *So* 𝔊: 𝔏 deprecatio (precatio) offensionis: 𝔖 ‘Saviour from affliction’ f–f 𝔊 ανυψων ψυχην = (לנפש) מְשַׂגֵּב: *so* 𝔏 (exaltans animam): 𝔖 ‘joy of heart’ = משמח לב: *so read here* (מְשַׂמֵּחַ) g–g *So* 𝔊 *adding* διδους (*cp.* 𝔏 dans sanitatem, &c.): διδους *prob. an addition of* 𝔊 (*so Ryssel*) [𝔖 *for the whole verse has:* ‘joy of heart and light of eyes and healing of life and blessings—all these doubly upon the righteous shall come’ (*last clause an addition: cp.* xl. 10)] h–h 𝔊 θυσιαζων εξ αδικου, προσφορα μεμωκημενη = ? זבח מעול מנחת תעתעים (*point* זֶבַח מְעַוֵּל: 𝔊 *read* זֹבֵחַ מֵעָוֶל): *so Ryssel*: 𝔖 ‘the sacrifices of the unrighteous are unrighteous’ (עלותהון דעולא דעולא אנון) = *Hebr.*: (*or* עַוְלָה) עולת מְעַוֵּל עָוֶל: *for* μεμωκημενη (*from* μωκασθαι = *to*

11. **In my journeying I have seen much.** An interesting autobiographical touch. Ben-Sira's travels are again alluded to in li. 13. Unfortunately no details are given.

And many things have befallen me. So 𝔖 (see critical notes): 𝔊 has ‘and more than my words is my understanding’, i. e. my knowledge and insight is greater than might be supposed from my words.

12. **because of these things.** i. e. because of the good sense, prudence, and skill referred to in the previous verses (*vv.* 9 and 10); or read: ‘when they (viz. the experiences mentioned in the previous verses) passed over (me)’; see critical notes.

13. **The spirit of those that fear the Lord remaineth alive.** sc. in danger: ‘spirit’ here = principle of life, as in Isa. xxxviii. 16.

14. **is afraid of nothing.** i. e. nothing daunts him, because he is sustained by a sublime faith in God's providence. The *v. l.* of 𝔊 (A) = ‘shall reverence much’ (taking εὐλαβεῖν in a religious sense, of God-fearing).

15. **On whom doth he trust?** τίνι ἐπέχει; (=על־מי יבטח), ‘And who is his stay?’ For the rhetorical questions cp. Ps. xxiv (end): ‘Who is the King of glory?’ (to introduce the answer that follows).

16. **The eyes of the Lord are upon them that fear Him.** = Ps. xxxiii. 17 (= Hebr. xxxiii. 18); cf. xxxiv. 15 (16). The clause is identical with xv. 19.

A mighty shield . . . ‘A mighty shield (ὑπερασπισμὸς δυναστείας = ? מגן חיל) and strong stay’ (στήριγμα ἰσχύος = משען עז); for the terms cf. Ps. xviii. (xvii.) 3 and 19 Hebr. and LXX; cp. also Ps. lxi. (lx.) 3 f., xci. (xc.) 1 f.

A cover from scorching Sirocco, a shadow from noontide heat. Cp. Is. xxv. 4.

17. **Heart-gladdener and eye-brightener.** Cf. Ps. xix. (xviii.) 8: ‘The statutes of Jahveh . . . rejoice the heart; the commandment of Jahveh . . . giveth light to the eyes.’

(*c*) XXXIV. 18–26 (= 𝔊 XXXI. 21–31). This subsection introduces a subject which is continued in the next

𝔊(𝔖)19(23) The Most High hath no pleasure in the offerings of the ungodly,
[j]Neither doth He forgive sins for a multitude of sacrifices[j].
20(24) [k](As) one that killeth the son before the father's eyes
Is he that offereth a sacrifice from the goods of the poor[k].
21(25) [l]A scanty bread is the life of the poor[l]:
[m]He that depriveth him thereof[m] is [n]a man of blood[n].
22(26) [o]He slayeth his neighbour who taketh away his living[o],
(27) [p]And a blood-shedder is he that depriveth the hireling of his hire[p].
23(28) One building [q]and another[q] pulling down—
What have they gained but [r]empty[r] toil?
24(29) One [s]praying[s] and [t]another[t] cursing—
To whose voice shall [u]the Lord[u] listen?
25(30) He who washeth after (contact with) a dead body [v]and toucheth it again[v],
[w]What hath he gained by his bathing[w]?

mock at: cp. Jer. ii. (xxviii.) 18 *where* מעשׂה תעתעים = εργα μεμωκημενα LXX): A 70 106 157 *Cyril. Alex.* vi. 311 *and* 𝔏 (maculata) *read* μεμωμημενη 'contaminated' (*so Smend*): *combining this last reading with* 𝔖 *we obtain as the possible text in the original Hebrew,* עוֹלָה מֵעַוְלָה מנחת מום, *i.e.* 'A burnt offering from that which is unjustly gotten (*cp.* Isa. lxi. 8 גָּזֵל וְעַוְלָה) is a blemished offering'. *This yields an excellent sense, and may be right* (*cp. Smend*) i–i 𝔊 (ℵ^{c.a} *mg.*, 248) δωρηματα ανομων (*cp.* 𝔖 'their oblations'): 𝔏 subsannationes iniustorum: *but* ℵ^{c.a} A 296 308 μωμηματα: B μωκηματα ανομων ('the mockeries of the godless') j–j *So* 𝔊: 𝔖 'neither for the multitude of their oblations (*cp.* 𝔏 nec in multitudine sacrificiorum eorum) doth He forgive them' k–k 𝔏 *transposes clauses* (a) *and* (b). [𝔊 *at beginning has* θυων: 𝔖 𝔏 Syro-Hex + ως 'as one that killeth': 𝔖 *also adds* ουτως *at beginning of clause* (b)] l–l 𝔊 αρτος επιδεομενων ζωη πτωχων: 𝔖 'bread of mercy', &c. (= לחם חסד *for* לחם חסר: *point* חֶסֶר = 'want, poverty' (Prov. xxviii. 22, Job xxx. 3)) m–m 𝔊 (B &c.): ο αποστερων αυτην: *for* αυτην ℵ^{ca} 248 𝔏 (qui defraudat illum) *read* αυτου: 𝔖 'he that exacts it from them' n–n *So* 𝔊 𝔏: 𝔖 'sheds innocent blood' (*cp.* 22 b) o–o *So* 𝔊 = ? הורג חברו הנוטל מחיה: 𝔏 qui aufert in sudore panem (*cp.* Gen. iii. 19, iv. 2) quasi qui occidit proximum suum: 𝔖 'he who kills his neighbour possesses his goods' (*Edersh. suggests* יוריש *as the verb* = ο αφαιρουμενος: *this would account for* 𝔖: ירשׁ = 'to dispossess' *as well as* 'possess') p–p *So* 𝔊: 𝔏 qui effundit sanguinem et qui fraudem facit mercenario, fratres sunt: 𝔖 *has a much extended text here* q–q 𝔊 και εις: 𝔖 'another': 𝔏 et unus r–r *So* 𝔖: > 𝔊 *and* 𝔏 s–s *So* 𝔊 𝔏: 𝔖 'blessing' t–t 𝔊 και εις: *so* 𝔏: Syro-Hex και ετερος: *so* 𝔖 u–u 𝔊 ο δεσποτης: 𝔏 deus, *so* 𝔖 v–v *So* 𝔊 𝔏: 𝔖 'and returns (= again draws nigh) to him' (*i. e. the dead*) w–w *So* 𝔊 (𝔖 'from his washing): 𝔏 quid proficit levatio illius? x–x 𝔏 *transposes these two clauses* y–y 𝔊 εν τῳ ταπεινωθηναι αυτον = 𝔏: 𝔖 'that he fasted' (*correctly interpreting*) = 𝔥? בְּעַנּוֹתוֹ נפשׁו *or* בתעניתו. z [*Throughout this chapter* 𝔖 *seems to*

---

chapter, viz. the value of sacrifices. The theme illustrated first is that of unacceptable sacrifice, which is defined as consisting in what is derived from unjust gain and oppression of the poor.

18. **The oblations of the godless.** The better attested Greek reading = 'mockeries', a term applied to the sacrifices of the godless. For the sentiment cp. Prov. xv. 8, xxi. 27.

19. **Neither doth He forgive sins for a multitude of sacrifices.** Cp. vii. 9; Isa. i. 11 f.; Ps. l. 8–15.

20. **(As) one that killeth the son before the father's eyes.** The point of the comparison is that a duty may not be fulfilled at the expense of committing a great wrong. The poor are dear to the divine heart as a son to a father.

21. **A scanty bread is the life of the poor.** 'Life' here = that on which their life depends and is sustained (= 𝔥 מחיה); cp. iv. 1. The reading of 𝔖 ('bread of mercy' = charity) yields the sense: 'Bread of charity is the livelihood of the poor,' i. e. the poor depend upon the doles of the rich for their livelihood: but this is probably not right. Ball (*Var. Apoc. ad loc.*) suggests the rendering: 'The bread of the needy, the living of the poor [he that depriveth him thereof,' &c.].

22. **his living.** The Greek word used (συμβίωσις) has here the unusual sense of 'living' (*victus*): 'living together' (of social or marital intercourse) would be more literal. Probably the word was chosen to represent מחיה as distinct from חיים (βίος). For the clause cp. the proverb cited in *Midrash Tanḥuma* 12 *b*: 'Any one who steals the worth of a farthing from his neighbour is as though he took away his life' (כל הגוזל שוה פרוטה מחבירו כאלו נוטל נשמתו ממנו).

who taketh away his living. The reading of 𝔏, 'he who takes away sweat bread' (see critical note), is remarkable. There is a clear reference to Gen. iii. 19; cp. iv. 2 (Cain) in a context which refers to unacceptable sacrifice.

And a blood-shedder is he that depriveth the hireling of his hire. Cp. the proverb cited in T. B. *Baba meṣia* 112 *a*: 'Every one who suppresses the hire of an hireling is as though he took from him his life' (כל הכובש שכר שכיר כאלו נוטל נפשו ממנו): cp. also vii. 20 and Lev. xix. 13; Deut. xxiv. 14 f.; Jer. xxii. 13; Mal. iii. 5; Tobit iv. 14; James v. 4.

23–24. In the case of the sacrifice contemplated one builds (= the poor man by his labour produces) something which the other pulls down (i. e. consumes by seizing it for an unjust sacrifice): one prays (i. e. the sacrificer) and the other (= the poor man who has been robbed) curses.

25–26. These verses give further illustrations of contradiction (between outward act and inward intention). It is futile

𝔊(𝔖) 26(31) So a man fasting for his sins
And again doing the same—
[x] Who will listen to his prayer?
And what hath he gained [y]by his humiliation[y x].

(*d*) [z]XXXV. 1–11 (XXXII. 1–13). *Acceptable sacrifice* (= 3 + 3 + 2 + 2 distichs).

35 1 (1) [a]He that keepeth the law multiplieth offerings[a];
(2) [b]He sacrificeth a peace-offering that heedeth the commandments[b].
2 (3) [c]He that practiseth kindness offereth fine flour[c],
(4) And he that doeth mercy [d]sacrificeth a thank-offering[d].
3 (5) A thing well-pleasing to the Lord it is [e]to avoid wickedness[e],
[f]And [g]a propitiation[g] to avoid what is wrong[f].
4 (6) Appear not with empty hands [h]in the presence of the Lord[h],
5 (7) [i]For all this (shall be done) because it is commanded[i].
6 (8) The offering of the righteous [j]maketh the altar fat[j],
[k]And its sweet savour (cometh) before the Most High[k].
7 (9) [l]The meal-offering[l] of a righteous man is acceptable,
[m]And its memorial shall not be forgotten[m].

have modified and altered the text to a considerable extent for dogmatic reasons. These alterations are in a Christian direction; direct references to sacrifices have been largely eliminated, and even allusions to words of Jesus introduced]
a–a *So* 𝔊 (*reading* προσφορας *with* א A &c. Syro-Hex: *against* συμφορας B): 𝔏 oblationem (*Hart* orationem): 𝔖 'If thou hast done that which is written in the Law thou hast multiplied service' b–b *So* 𝔊: 𝔏 sacrificium salutare est adtendere mandatis (*cp.* θυσια *a corrected reading of* A): 𝔖 'and he that keepeth the commandment blessed is his spirit' c–c *So* 𝔊: 𝔏 retribuet gratiam qui offert similaginem: 𝔖 'he earns good interest that offers an oblation (*or* that celebrates the Eucharist)' d–d 𝔊 θυσιαζων αινεσεως (א* θυσια κτλ.) = זבח תודה: 𝔏 offert sacrificium: 𝔖 'keepeth the Law' (? *reading* תורה *for* תודה) e–e 𝔊 αποστηναι απο πονηριας (απο αμαρτιας 55 106 254): 𝔖 'from all that is evil' f–f *So* 𝔊: 𝔖 'keep back thy strength from all that is hateful' g–g 𝔊 εξιλασμος (= סליחה, *cp. v.* 5): 𝔏 deprecatio pro peccatis h–h *So* 𝔊 𝔏: 𝔖 'before Him' i–i *So* 𝔊 (𝔏 propter mandatum Dei fiunt): 𝔖 'for every one that doeth what is pleasing keepeth the commandment' j–j *So* 𝔊 𝔏: 𝔖 'is the prayer of their mouth' k–k *So* 𝔊 𝔏: 𝔖 'their deeds penetrate the heavens' (*cp. v.* 17) l–l 𝔊 θυσια: *so* 𝔏: 𝔖 'the gift' (*Smend* 'Speiseopfer') m–m *So* 𝔊: 𝔏 et memoriam eius non obliviscetur

to pass through the ritual act of purification, if the defilement is to be immediately contracted again: so it is equally futile to ask for the divine forgiveness of sin (by a course of fasting) unless there is a real repentance: cp. for the thought 2 Pet. ii. 20–22; Heb. x. 26. Similar illustrations and language are employed in the Talmudic tractate on Fasting (*Ta'anith* 16 *a*); cp. also *Aboth de R. Nathan* (as cited both by Edersheim).

26. **humiliation** = 'fasting': cp. later Hebr. תענית (lit. 'humiliation', i.e. fasting).

(*d*) XXXV. 1–11 (= 𝔊 XXXII. 1–13). The governing thought of the section is that loyalty to God's Law, which is the expression of God's will, demands the offering of many sacrifices. But these are only acceptable if they are offered willingly, from a grateful heart, and if they are combined with high ethical standards of conduct.

1. **multiplieth offerings.** The various kinds of sacrifice are specified in what follows. The elimination of these references in 𝔖—who as a Christian recognizes no sacrifices—spoils the symmetry and appositeness of the original lines.

a peace-offering. 𝔊 σωτηρίου = probably περὶ σωτηρίου (so LXX 1 Chron. xvi. 1, 2, &c.): so αἰνέσεως *v.* 2 (cp. LXX 2 Chron. xxix. 31): Hebr. זבח שלמים. For the ritual prescriptions cp. Lev. iii.

2. **offereth fine flour.** i.e. a meal-offering (מנחה) of which fine flour (σεμίδαλις = סֹלֶת) was the principal constituent: cf. Lev. ii. The 'practice of kindness' (גמילות חסדים) is a regular phrase in late Hebrew for benevolence generally, which included much more than almsgiving.

he that doeth mercy. Hebr. prob. עושׂה צדקה.

3. **to avoid wickedness.** ἀποστῆναι ἀπὸ πονηρίας = סור מרע: cp. Job xxviii. 28.

4. **Appear not with empty hands** (lit. 'empty') . . . Cp. vii. 29–31.

in the presence of the Lord. i.e. in the temple. For phrase cp. Exod. xxiii. 15, xxxiv. 20; Deut. xvi. 16 and LXX.

5. **because it is commanded.** One of the main motives for observance of the Law is that such constitutes obedience to the divine will. The prescriptions of the cultus must be obeyed because God has commanded them to be obeyed. It is this only that gives the sacrifices religious value. Though the best sacrifice is a moral life, yet the sacrifices of the Law must be performed because God has enjoined them. This was the position later of the conservative Hellenistic Jews such as Philo.

6. **maketh the altar fat.** A sign from which it may be concluded that the sacrifice is accepted (Smend). 𝔖 here simply paraphrases in a Christian sense (see critical notes).

7. **The meal-offering.** 𝔊 θυσία here = מנחה (𝔖 'the gift'): and 'its memorial' = the אזכרה, i.e. that part of the meal-offering which was burnt as a 'memorial' (Lev. ii. 2): so μνημόσυνον in xxxviii. 11, xlv. 16. So also 'sweet savour' in *v.* 6 = ריח ניחח in reference to the fat pieces (of the burnt offering) which were burnt upon the altar (Lev. i. 6, iii. 5).

𝔊 8 (10) With a good eye [n]glorify the Lord[n],
And [o]stint not the heave-offering of thy hands[o].
ℌ[B] 9 (11) [p]In all thy deeds[p] let thy countenance shine,
[q]And with gladness dedicate thy tithe[q].
10 (12) Give [r]to God[r] as He hath given [s]to thee[s],
[ss]With goodness of eye[ss], and [t]as thine hand hath attained[t].
11 (13) For He is [u]a God of requital[u],
And [v]sevenfold[v] will He recompense thee.

(*e*) XXXV. 12–20 (XXXV. 14–26). *God hears the cry of the oppressed* (= 2 + 2 + 2 + 2 + 5 + 1 distichs).

12 (14) [w]Bribe not[w], for He will not receive[x];
(15) And put not thy trust [y]upon a sacrifice of extortion[y],
For He is [z]a God of justice[z],
And with Him is no partiality.
13 (16) [a]He will not show partiality against the poor man[a],
And the supplications of [b]the distressed[b] He heareth.
14 (17) He doth not ignore [c]the cry[c] of the fatherless,
[d]Nor the widow, when she poureth out (her) plaint[d].
15 (18) [e]Do not the tears[f] run down the cheek,
(19) [g]And sigh against ⌜him who causeth them to fall⌝[g]?

Dominus): 𝔖 'and the memorial of the righteous shall not be forgotten for ever' n–n *So* 𝔊 𝔏: 𝔖 'give to the poor' o–o *So* 𝔊 (απαρχην χειρων [70 χειρος] = תרומת ידך: *cp.* vii. 31, Deut. xii. 11, LXX), 𝔏: 𝔖 'stumble not (תמעד *for* תמעט) in thy gifts' p–p 𝔊 εν παση δοσει (*interpreting*): *so* 𝔖 q–q *So* ℌ (מעשׂר, *mg.* מעשרך *and* מעשׂיך) 𝔊 (δεκατην): 𝔖 'lend to him who doth not pay thee' (*cp.* Luke vi. 34 *Pesh.*) r–r ℌ *text* לו: *variant* (*under line*) לאל: *so* 𝔖: 𝔊 Υψιστῳ s–s 𝔊 > ss–ss *So* ℌ (בְּטוב עין) 𝔊 εν αγαθῳ οφθαλμῳ: *so* 𝔖 t–t ℌ כְּהַשָּׂגַת יד (השיג יד) = 𝔊 καθ ευρεμα χειρος: 𝔖 'with a large hand' (*reading* ב״ *and interpreting by Aram.* שגא). *For phrase cp.* xiv. 13 ℌ: 𝔖 + (*a gloss*: *cp.* Prov. xix. 17) 'for he who giveth to the poor lendeth to God; for who is a recompenser but Him' = ℌ *mg.*: מלוה ייי נותן לאביון ומי בעל גמולות כי אם הוא: u–u ℌ אלוה תשלומות: אֱלֹהֵי *as in v.* 12 (15) *would be expected, and should probably be read*: 𝔊 κυριος ανταποδιδους (אל גמלות Jer. li. 56) v–v 𝔖 'ten thousand times ten thousand' [𝔖 *transposes verses* 10 *and* 11] w–w ℌ אל תשחד = 𝔊 μη δωροκοπει (*cp.* Deut. x. 17 *Aq.*): 𝔖 'do not tarry' (= ? אל תאחר): 𝔏 noli offere munera prava x 𝔏 + illa. y–y ℌ על זבח מעשק: 𝔊 θυσιᾳ αδικῳ z–z *So* ℌ (*rightly*) אלהי משפט: 𝔊 κυριος κριτης (= ? אלהים שֹׁפֵט): 𝔖 'a doer of justice' a–a 𝔖 'the prayer of the poor man cometh up before Him' (*cp. clause* b) [248 *and* 𝔏 + κυριος] b–b ℌ מצוק (*read* מוצק: *cp.* iv. 9): 𝔊 ηδικημενου: 𝔖 'the weary of spirit' c–c ℌ צעקת (*mg.* אנקת 'groan' = 𝔖): 𝔊 ικετειαν (*cp.* 𝔏 preces) d–d 𝔊 και χηραν εαν εκχεῃ λαλιαν = ℌ (*mg.* כי תחבט שיח: *for* תחבט *text has* תרבה): 𝔏 *for last word has* loquelam gemitus e *v.* 15 (= 𝔊 18, 19) > 𝔖 f 𝔊 (𝔏) + (*incorrectly*) χηρας g–g ℌ *to be read* וַאֲנָחָה על מורידיה *or* מורידה = 𝔊: ℌ *text* מרודיה = 'her wanderings'. *A verb is required; hence point* וַאֲנָחָה (*subject* דמעה *repeated*): 𝔊 *takes as subst.* = 'sighing' (*rendering* και η καταβοησις: 248

---

8. **With a good eye.** i. e. with a thankful and joyful spirit. Cp. xiv. 10.
glorify the Lord. i. e. by sacrifices.
9. Here the Hebr. MS. B resumes the text.
In all thy deeds. Cf. xxxi. 21 (𝔊 xxxiv. 27).
thy tithe. Here tithe is expressly mentioned (contrast vii. 31; xlv. 20 f.). For the sentiment of the passage cp. 2 Cor. ix. 7.
11. **God of requital.** Cp. xii. 2: for 'sevenfold' cp. vii. 3, xx. 12; Ps. lxxix. 12.

XXXV. 12–20 (= 𝔊 XXXV. 14–26). This section is mainly concerned with the prayers of the poor and helpless oppressed. To such, prayer occupies the place of sacrifice in the case of the rich. The prayers of the distressed, indeed, will be heard by God, while sacrifices which are the outcome of unjust dealing are rejected. At the same time God will punish the oppressor who is the cause of bitter outcry (*vv.* 12–17). This thought suggests an appeal to God on behalf of His oppressed people. The section ends with the expression of a confident hope that God will yet vindicate His chosen people against their heathen tyrants (*vv.* 18–20).

12. **Bribe not, for He will not receive.** i. e. think not to bribe God to overlook sins unrepented by multiplying sacrifices. God is not like an unjust judge—such sacrifices are unavailing, and are not regarded. Cp. Job vi. 22.
a sacrifice of extortion. i. e. derived from the gains of extortion and unjust dealing.
with Him is no partiality (lit. 'respect of persons'). Cp. Deut. x. 17; 2 Chron. xix. 7.
14. **He doth not ignore . . . the widow.** Cp. Exod. xxii. 21 f.; Deut. xxiv. 17; Ps. lxviii. 6; Prov. xxxiii. 10.
15. **Do not the tears run down the cheek.** The question suggests that the subject is no longer the widow

ℌ[B] 16 (20) [h]A bitterness accepted[h] is (such)[i] [sighing][i],
[j]And (such) a cry[j] [k][bendeth] the clouds[k].
17 (21) The appeal of the lowly [l]traverseth the skies[l],
[m]And resteth not till it reach (its goal).
It shall not remove till God doth visit[m],
(22 *a*) [n]And (till) the righteous Judge executeth judgement .
18 (22 *b*) Yea, the Lord [o]will not tarry[o],
[p]And the mighty One will not refrain Himself[p],
Till He smite [q]the loins of the merciless,
(23) And requite vengeance [r][to the arrogant][r];
Till He [s]dispossess[s] [t]the sceptre of pride[t],
And [u]the staff of wickedness[u] utterly cut down;
19 (24) Till He render to man [v]his due[v],
[w]And recompense people[w] according to their devising;
(25) Till He plead the cause of His people,
And rejoice them [x]with His salvation[x].

Syro-Hex Sah 𝔏 *wrongly* + αυτης) h–h *So* ℌ (תמרורי רצון): 𝔊 θεραπευων εν ευδοκιᾳ = ? משרת ברצון (*cp.* θεραπων = משרת Exod. xxxiii. 11, LXX): 𝔏 qui adorat deum in oblectatione (*? pointing to a different text: Hart suggests* משמש אל: *then the doublet at end of previous verse* Dominus exauditor non = משמע אל אל): 𝔖 'the bitterness of the soul of the poor' = ? תמרורי [נפש] ריש. *Schechter reads* רצוץ *for* רצון: *so Smend* i–i ℌ (*text*) הנחה *to be emended with Lévi to* אנחה (*the subst. answering to the verb* אֲנָחָה *in previous line*). *For interpretations of* ℌ *text see exegetical notes below* j–j ℌ וצעקה: 𝔊 και η δεησις αυτου k *So* 𝔖 'boweth down the clouds' (= ? שחתה): ℌ *text* חשתה = 𝔊 'to the clouds hasteneth' (+ εως): *so* 𝔏. *Emend* ℌ *to* שחתה (*transp. two letters*). *Smend proposes* חשקה = (?) 'is attached to, attains'. [*For first clause Smend adopts Schechter's emend.*: וצעקת עני: *then read* וצעקת עני ענן חשקה] l–l *So* ℌ *mg.* עבים חלפה = 𝔊: ℌ *text* ענן חל עם: (חל = *shortened* חלפ *and* עם *a corruption of* עב, *Peters*): 𝔖 'above the clouds ascendeth' m–m ℌ = 𝔊: 𝔖 'and before the Lord of majesty it goeth, not passing away until He draw nigh upon it' n–n *So* ℌ: 𝔊 = ℌ *mg.*: 𝔖 'and judgement of truth judgeth [*for* και κρινει δικαιως א* A 248 *have* κρινει δικαιους = 'He shall judge the righteous (and execute judgement)'] o–o ℌ = 𝔊: 𝔖 'He will despise' p–p = ℌ *mg.*: 𝔊 ουδε μη μακροθυμησει επ' αυτοις (248 + ο κραταιος: *so* 𝔏): 𝔖 'and shall not forsake nor cease' q–q ℌ = 𝔊 (οσφυν = מתני): 𝔏 dorsum ipsorum r–r *Correcting* ℌ *text* לגוים (*so* 𝔊 𝔖) *to* לגאים: *cp.* x. 14 s–s ℌ יוריש = 𝔊 εξαρῃ (*cp.* xvi. 9). *Smend proposes to read* יָרוֹשׁ *or* ירשיש (*root* רשש) = 'beat down': *cp.* Jer. v. 17, Mal. i. 4 t–t = ℌ: 𝔊 πληθος υβριστων (= ? שפעת זדים: *cp. Hart ad loc.*): 𝔖 'the strength of sinners' u–u *So* ℌ *text* (*mg.* 'of the wicked' = 𝔊): 𝔖 'the unrighteous rulers' v–v *So* ℌ = 𝔖: 𝔊 κατα τας πραξεις αυτου w–w ℌ וגמול אדם = 𝔊 (*cp.* 𝔏): 𝔖 'to the workers of iniquity': *emend* ℌ *to* וגמל (*Smend*) x–x ℌ בישועתו = 𝔊 εν τῳ

(𝔊 adds χήρας incorrectly), but possibly oppressed Israel (so *v.* 18 onwards). The tears of Israel are often mentioned in the Psalms (so Smend). Cf. Lam. i. 2 ('She weepeth sore in the night, and her tears are on her cheeks'). If the subject is understood to be the widow clause *b* may be rendered (so Hebr. text): 'and she sigheth because of her miseries' (עַל מְרוּדֶיהָ: cp. Lam. i. 7).

16. **A bitterness accepted is (such) sighing.** i.e. the bitterness produced by such oppression is not allowed to pass by unheeded and unredeemed by God. The text of ℌ is here uncertain. If the last word of the line is retained (הֲנָחָה) and רצון altered to רצוץ, render: 'the bitterness of the crushed is accepted' (an accepted sacrifice): Peters, who keeps ℌ unaltered (pointing הֲנִחָה), renders: 'amaritudo gratiae adducit requiem ei' (see further critical notes).

(such) a cry bendeth the clouds. Cp. Ps. xviii. 10 ('He bowed the heavens and came down'). Perhaps the idea is that the cry or supplication of the oppressed pierces the clouds (= God's dwelling-place) and brings about the divine intervention. For God's dwelling-place in the skies (clouds) cp. Ps. lxviii. 34, lxxxix. 6 (7).

17. **The appeal of the lowly traverseth the skies, And resteth not till it reach (its goal).** Cp. Lam. iii. 44 ('Thou hast covered Thyself with a cloud that our prayer should not pass through'). A similar phrase occurs in the Zohar (according to Cowley-Neubauer) Lev. צו: 'this word ascends and cleaves the firmament.'

(till) the righteous Judge executeth judgement. Cp. Gen. xviii. 25.

18. **Yea, the Lord will not tarry . . .** i.e. will not delay His judgement on the oppressors. In this and the following verses the writer has in mind the heathen oppressors of God's elect people. For the thought cp. Luke xviii. 7 f.: 2 Pet. iii. 9.

Till He smite the loins. Cp. Deut. xxxiii. 11.

the merciless . . . the arrogant. Heathen ruling classes. (For phrase 'requite vengeance' cp. Deut. xxxii. 43.)

Till He dispossess the sceptre of pride. The expression 'dispossess' in such a connexion is unusual, but may be right, yielding a good sense. Smend proposes to read 'beat down'. For 'sceptre of pride . . . staff of wickedness' cp. Ps. cxxv. 3; Isa. xiv. 5; Ezek. vii. 11; Ps. lxxv. 11 ('all the horns of the wicked will I cut (hew) off').

19. **to man** (לאנוש). i.e. the heathen: cp. Ps. lvi. 2 (1).

And rejoice them with His salvation. Cp. Is. xxv. 9; 4 Ezra vii. 28, viii. 39, xii. 34.

ℌ[B]20(26) [y][Beauteous is His favour in a time] of stress[y].
[z]As a rain-cloud[z] in the season of [zz]drought[zz].

(*f*) XXXVI. 1–17 (XXXIII. 1–13*a*, XXXVI. 16*b*–22). *A prayer to God for Israel* (= 2+2+3+2+2+2+2+2 distichs).

36 1 [ab]Save us[b], [c]O God of all[c],
2 [d]And cast[d] Thy fear upon all the nations[e].
3 [f]Shake Thy hand[f] against [g]the strange people[g],
And let them see [h]Thy power[h].
4 As Thou hast sanctified Thyself in us before them,
So [i]glorify Thyself[i] [j]in them[j] before us;
5 That they may know[k], as we also know,
That there is none other God but Thee[l].
6 Renew [m]the signs[m], and repeat [m]the wonders[m];
(7) Make Hand and [n]Right Arm[n] glorious.
7 (8) Waken indignation and pour out wrath,
(9) [o]Subdue[o] the foe and [p]expel[p] the enemy.
8 (10) Hasten [q]the 'end'[q] and [r]ordain the 'appointed time'[r],
[s]For who may say to Thee: What doest Thou?[s]

ελεει αυτου (*cp.* Is. xlv. 8) y–y *There is a lacuna in the Heb. MS.*: 𝔊 *has* ωραιον ελεος εν καιρῳ θλιψεως αυτου (א 248 Syro-Hex 𝔏 *and* 𝔖 > αυτου, *which should probably be transposed to follow* ελεος): ℌ *may be restored* [נאה ר]צ[ונו בזמ]ן מצוקה: *so Smend.* *After* ελεος 𝔏 (Sang. Am.) + dei [*hence Peters restores* חסד יהוה]: 𝔖 'and put to shame the enemy'. [א 248 *prefix* ως (ως ωραιον = מה נאוה)] z–z ℌ כעת (*l.* כענן) חזיזים: *so* 𝔊 𝔖 zz–zz *So* 𝔊 𝔏: 𝔖 'vengeance' a 307 *pr.* αρχη λογου = ℌ פ(פרק = 'section') b–b *So* ℌ הושיענו = 𝔊 ελεησον ημας: *cp.* xxxv. (xxxii.) 25 c–c *So* ℌ: 𝔊 δεσποτα (A *and* 𝔏 >) ο θεος παντων (δεσποτα *and* ο θεος *variants*): 𝔊 + και επιβλεψον (𝔏 et respice nos)—*a dittograph from* επιβαλε τον *in foll. line* d–d *Read* ושים (*Smend*): *others* והר[ים]: ℌ *MS. defect.*: 𝔖 'and let [Thy wrath] come' [*from* Ps. lxxviii. (lxxix.) 6] e 248 (*so* 𝔏) + τα μη εκζητουντα σε (*cp.* Ps. xiv. 2): 𝔖 'that have not known Thee' (Jer. x. 25): 𝔏 + ut cognoscant, quia non est deus nisi tu et enarrent magnalia tua (*cp. vv.* 3, 5, 8) f–f 𝔊 επαρον την χειρα σου: ℌ הניף (*mg.* + יד) g–g *So* ℌ: 𝔊 εθνη αλλοτρια h–h 𝔊 την δυναστειαν σου = ℌ גבורתיך (*sing.*) i–i ℌ הִכָּבֵד: 𝔊 μεγαλυνθειης (= התגדל): 𝔖 'sanctify Thyself' j–j *So* ℌ *mg.* 𝔊 𝔖: ℌ *text* בנו (*a mistake*) k 𝔊 + σε ('and let them know Thee'): > σε ℌ 𝔖 l 𝔊 + κυριε (ℌ 𝔖 >) m–m ℌ *has* אות . . . מופת: 𝔊 σημεια . . . θαυμασια (= ? תמה *so* ℌ *mg.*: *cp.* xliii. 25, xlviii. 14) n–n *So* 𝔊 𝔖: ℌ 'and make strong arm and right hand': 70 248 + οπως διηγωνται τα θαυμασια σου (*from v.* 10) o–o ℌ והכניע: 𝔊 εξαρον (*but* εκτριβειν *in* xlvi. 18, xlvii. 7: *so* LXX, Neh. ix. 24) p–p ℌ והדוף: 𝔊 εκτριψον (*but in* xlvii. 5 εξαιρειν) q–q ℌ קץ = 𝔊 καιρον (*so often in* LXX) r–r *So* ℌ: 𝔊 μνησθητι (= פקוד Is. xxvi. 16) ορκισμου (*but* א Syro-Hex 𝔏 [finis] *read* ορισμου = ℌ מועד *rightly*): 𝔖 'let the time come' s–s *So* ℌ 𝔖 (*cp.* Job ix. 12): 𝔊 και εκδιηγησασθωσαν (248 + σοι) τα μεγαλεια (248 θαυμασια) σου t *v.* 9 (11) > ℌ

---

20. **As a rain-cloud.** Reading כעב חזיזים: חזיז = 'cloud' or 'rain' rather than 'lightning' as usually rendered (Job xxviii. 26; Zech. x. 1). So Smend.

(*f*) XXXVI. 1–17 (= 𝔊 XXXIII. 1–13*a*, XXXVI. 16*b*–22) forms an independent subsection, which is linked on naturally with what precedes. In the previous subsection the confident hope had been expressed that God would punish the arrogant heathen oppressors of Israel, and grant His people relief. In the present subsection the writer pleads with God, in the form of a prayer, that He will save His own, and strike fear into the nations in order that all may know that He is God alone (*vv.* 1–5); God is urged to assert Himself by gathering in the scattered nation, and by compassionating Sion (*vv.* 6–17). There are some striking parallels between this prayer and parts of the synagogue liturgy, especially the *Eighteen Blessings* (*Shĕmōnēh 'Esrēh*), some of the key-words of which seem to be echoed here.

1. **O God of all.** Cp. xlv. 23, l. 22 (𝔊); Rom. ix. 5.

2. **cast Thy fear upon all the nations.** Cp. 1 Chron. xiv. 17.

3. **Shake Thy hand.** Cp. (phrase) Is. x. 32.

against the strange people. i.e. the Greeks.

4. **As Thou hast sanctified Thyself . . . So glorify Thyself.** i.e. As Thou hast punished us in the sight of the heathen, so now punish them in the sight of us: cp. Ezek. xxxviii. 23.

5. **there is none other God but Thee.** Cp. Is. xlv. 14; 1 Kings viii. 43, 60; 1 Chron. xvii. 20, &c.

6. **Renew the signs, and repeat the wonders.** As in the deliverance from Egypt: renew the wonders of the Exodus.

Make Hand and Right Arm glorious. Cp. Exod. xv. 6; Is. li. 9, liii. 10, lxii. 8, lxiii. 12.

7. **Waken indignation.** Cp. Ps. lxxviii. 38.

pour out wrath. Cp. Ps. lxxix. 6 ('pour out thy wrath upon the heathen that know thee not').

8. **Hasten the 'end' and ordain the 'appointed time'.** The 'end' (Heb. קץ) = the end of the period of oppression: the 'appointed time' is that of the deliverance (the same terms are used, almost in a technical sense, in Dan. xi. 27, 35.) The Heb. word here rendered *ordain* (פקוד) means almost 'give the command that it may come'. Even though the 'end' has been fixed, God can, if He chooses, shorten the period: cp. Mark xiii. 20 (cp. also Is. lx. 22 *b*). 𝔊 mistranslates 'remember the oath'.

For who may say to Thee . . . Cp. Job ix. 12; Eccles. viii. 4.

𝔊 9 (11) [t]Let [u]him that escapeth[u] [v]be devoured[v] in the [w]glowing fire[w],
And may Thy people's [x]wrongers[x] [y]find destruction[y]!
ℌ 10 (12) Make an end of [z]the head of the enemy's princes[z]
That saith: There is none beside me!

a (𝔊 xxxiii. 13a) Gather all the tribes of Jacob[a],
11b (16b) [b]That they may receive their inheritance[b] [c]as in the days of old[c].
12 (17) Compassionate [d]the people[d] that is called by Thy name,
Israel, [e]whom Thou didst surname Firstborn[e].
13 (18) Compassionate Thy holy city,
Jerusalem, [f]the place of Thy dwelling[f].
14 (19) Fill Sion [g]with Thy majesty[g],
And [h]Thy Temple[h] with Thy glory.
15 (20) Give testimony [i]to the first of Thy works[i],
And establish [j]the vision spoken in Thy name[j].
16 (21) Give reward to them that wait for Thee,
That Thy prophets may be proved trustworthy.

u–u 𝔊 *ο* (א* Sah + *μη*: א^c.a + *ασεβης ο*) *σωζομενος* = שְׂרִיד v–v 𝔊 *καταβρωθητω* = יאכל (*cp.* xlv. 10): 𝔖 'destroy the enemy' = אכל שור (*for* יאכל שׂריד) w–w 𝔊 *εν οργῃ πυρος* = בחמת אשׁ: 𝔖 'in anger and in fire' x–x *αδικουντες* (B 68); *κατοικουντες* (70 A* *vid.* 306), *κατεχοντες* (106 *corr.*): *the rest* *κακουντες* y–y 𝔊 *ευροισαν απωλειαν*: *cp.* עדי אובד Num. xxiv. 20 z–z ℌ ראשׁ פאתי מואב (*mg.* אויב): 𝔊 *κεφαλας αρχοντων εχθρων* (ℌ *mg.* = 𝔊): 𝔖 'crown of the enemy' [*εχθρων v. l. εθνων* (106 157) *and εθνων εχθρων* (155)] a 𝔏 + *same clause as in v.* 5 (= 5 b) b–b ℌ ויתנחלו: 𝔊 *και κατακληρονομησεις αυτους* = ? ותנחילם (248 106 *κατεκληρονομησα*) c–c ℌ כימי קדם: 𝔊 = ? כמן קדם: 𝔖 'as Thou saidst from the days of old' d–d *So* ℌ 𝔊: 𝔖 *and* 𝔏 'Thy people' [𝔊 + *κυριε*: *but* א 253 23 𝔏 Sah >: > ℌ *and* 𝔖 *also*] e–e *So* ℌ 𝔖 = *ον πρωτογονον ωνομασας*, 157 248: *but* C &c. *ον πρωτογονῳ* (𝔏 + 'tuo') (א^c.a *πρωτοτοκῳ*) *ωμοιωσας* f–f ℌ מכון שׁבתיך: 𝔊 *πολιν* (*so* 𝔏: *but* א A Sah *τοπον*) *καταπαυματος σου* g–g ℌ את הודך (*mg.* מהדריך): 𝔊 *αρεταλογιας σου* (*so* B*: *on αρεταλογια, used of* 'glorifying' *God, cp. Deissmann, Bible Studies, p.* 93 f.: *it* = רנה *in* Ps. xxix. (xxx.) 6 Symm.): 253 307 Syro-Hex *αρρητα* (307 *αρετα*) *λογια σου* (A.V. 'Fill Sion with Thine unspeakable oracles'): *also misread αραι τα λογια σου* (B^b: R.V. 'exalt Thine oracles') h–h ℌ את היכלך *so* 𝔖: 𝔊 *τον λαον σου* (*read ναον*) i–i ℌ למראשׁ מעשׂיך: 𝔊 *τοις εν αρχῃ* (𝔏 ab initio) *κτισμασι σου* = 𝔖 'to Thy works as from the first' j–j ℌ חזון דָּבָר בשׁמך = 𝔊 *προφητειας* (= חזון Dan. xi. 14) *τας επ ονοματι μου* (248 *προφητας*): *cp.* 𝔏 𝔖 'the prophecies of Thy prophets that

9. **Let him that escapeth . . . destruction.** Num. xxiv. 19, 20 seems to have been in the writer's mind here.

10. **Make an end of the head of the enemy's princes.** ℌ text has 'of the princes of Moab', a correction by the text of Num. xxiv. 17. Here again there is probably a reminiscence of Num. xxiv. 17: 'princes' here = פאתי (R.V. 'corners'), which Ben Sira understands in the sense expressed by the LXX *ad loc.* (ἀρχηγούς). The 'head of the enemy's princes' means some one pre-eminent hostile person, probably either Antiochus the Great, or Seleucus IV, or Antiochus IV. [Perhaps Antiochus the Great (223–187 B.C.) is meant, who wrested Syria (including Judaea) from Egyptian rule (198), and made many other conquests. In 190 B.C. he was defeated by the Romans at Magnesia, and compelled to give up the greater part of his conquests (but not Coele-Syria). In *v.* 9*a* ('Let him that escapeth be devoured in the glowing fire') there may be an allusion to Antiochus's plight after this disastrous defeat.]

11 (11*b* = xxxvi. 16*b* 𝔊). **Gather all the tribes of Jacob, That they may receive their inheritance.** i.e. that they may once again receive possession of the whole of the Holy Land. The Restoration under Cyrus had been incomplete, the Jews only recovering a small part of their ancient inheritance. The greater part of the nation was still 'scattered' in foreign lands, and this state of things was never essentially altered. Technically, therefore, the 'Exile' still continued, and continues.

12. **Compassionate the people that is called by Thy name . . . Firstborn.** Cp. Exod. iv. 22. For 'that is called by Thy name' (κεκλημένον ἐπ' ὀνόματί σου) Syr. has 'over whom Thy name is called' = 𝔏 'super quam (*sc.* plebem) invocatum est nomen tuum'. Cp. Deut. xxviii. 10. See further xliv. 23*b* note.

13. **Jerusalem, the place of Thy dwelling.** Cp. 1 Kings viii. 39, 43, 49 (also 13); Exod. xv. 17. [𝔊 'place of thy rest' on account of the assonance between שבת (ישב) and שַׁבָּת.]

14. **Fill Sion with Thy majesty.** 𝔊 (R.V. 'Fill Zion; exalt Thine oracles'; cp. also A.V.) has been misread (see critical notes).

Thy Temple with Thy glory. Cp. Hag. ii. 7

15. **Give testimony to the first of Thy works.** i.e. openly acknowledge the position of Israel as firstborn. According to the Rabbis Israel was one of the six things created (or created in the divine thought) before the creation of the world. This was deduced from Ps. lxxiv. 2, 'O remember the congregation which Thou didst create of old,' עדותך קנית קדם (cited by Schechter *ad loc.*).

And establish the vision spoken in Thy name. Cp. (for phrase) 1 Kings viii. 20; the prophecies of the prophets are, of course, referred to; 'Vision' (חזון) often occurs as a title at the beginning of the prophetical books.

16. **be proved trustworthy.** 'Verified'; cp. Gen. xlii. 20 (same verb).

𝕳[B] 17 (22) Thou wilt hear[k] the prayer [l]of Thy servants[l],
[m]According to Thy good favour[m] towards [n]Thy people[n]:
That [o]all the ends of the earth[o] may know
[p]That Thou art the eternal God[p].

(*a*) XXXVI. 18–20 (23–25). *Moral discernment the fruit of experience* (= 3 distichs).

18 (23) [q]Every meat doth [r]the belly[r] eat,
Yet is [s]one meat more pleasant than another[s].
𝕳[C] 19 (24) The palate tasteth [t]the dainties that are bestowed[t],
And the discerning heart [tt]the dainties of falsehood[tt].
20 (25) [u]A deceitful heart[u] produceth sorrow,
But an experienced man [v]wardeth it off[v].

(*b*) XXXVI. 21–26 (26–31). *Concerning women* (= 3 + 2 + 2 distichs).

𝕳[B] 21 (26) [w]A woman will receive any man,
[x]Yet is one woman more pleasant than another[x].

spake in Thy name' [k] 𝔊 + κυριε (𝔏 = 𝕳 >) [l–l] 𝕳 עבדיך = οικετων σου (א A 155 253 𝔏 *and* 𝔖): C ικετων σου ('Thy suppliants') [m–m] *So* 𝕳: 𝔊 κατα την ευλογιαν Ααρων (*but* 307 κατα την ευδοκιαν: *the same mistake* xlii. 15): *after the misreading* ευλογιαν *had arisen the incorrect gloss* Ααρων *was added*: 𝔖 = 𝕳 [n–n] א* του υιου σου [o–o] *So* 𝕳: 𝔊 παντες οι επι της γης (𝔏 omnes qui habitant terram) [p–p] 𝕳 כי אתה אל [עולם] (*Hebr. MS. defect. at end of line*) = 𝔊 (248) οτι συ κυριος των αιωνων (*this the original reading*): C οτι Κυριος ει ο θεος των αιωνων (*also other variants*) [q] 𝕳 *pr.* פ (= פרק) *marking a new section* [r–r] = *one of the marginal readings of* 𝕳 *as restored by Smend, viz.* [כ]רש = 𝔊: 𝕳 *text* גרגרת ('throat'): 𝔖 'soul' [s–s] *Reading* 𝕳 (*which is defective*) אך יש אוכל [מא]ו[כ]ל [נ]עים (*Peters, Smend*) = 𝔊 [t–t] 𝕳 *mg.* מטעמי זבד (*text* דבר): 𝔊 βρωματα θηρας ('dainties of the chase' = ? מטעמי ציד, *cp.* Gen. xxvii. 4 f.) [tt–tt] *So* 𝕳: 𝔊 λογους ψευδεις (*adopting* דבר *from line* a 𝕳: *so Hart*): *so* 𝔖. [*The Hebr. readings of the verse are uncertain, there being several variants in mg. and in MSS.* B *and* C. *The more important may be exhibited thus*: חיך בוחן (C יטעם) מטעמי דבר (C זבד) ולב מבין (נבון ,בוחן .*v. l*) מטעמי כזב] [u–u] 𝕳 לב עקוב: 𝔊 καρδια στρεβλη = לב עקש [v–v] 𝕳 *text* ישיבנה בו: 𝕳 *mg.* ישיבנו: 𝔊 ανταποδωσει αυτῳ: 𝔖 'understands these things' [w] *This verse is misplaced in* 𝕳, *being inserted between vv.* 18–19 (23–24): 𝔖 > [x–x] 𝔊 *renders freely* (*in order to avoid repetition of* γυνη) εστι δε

---

17. **Thou wilt hear the prayer of Thy servants.** Or 'Thy servant' = Israel; cp. Dan. ix. 17; 1 Kings viii. 30.
According to Thy good favour towards Thy people. Cp. Ps. cvi. 4 (𝔊 'according to the blessing of Aaron' [cp. Num. vi. 22 f.] is due to a corruption in the Greek text; see critical note).
That all the ends of the earth may know (𝕳 mg. 'see'). Cp. Is. lii. 10.
the eternal God (אל עולם). Cp. Gen. xxi. 33; Isa. xl. 28. Cp. also 1 Kings viii. 60. Smend notes the significant omission in this prayer of all reference to the Messiah.

A new division of the book begins with xxxvi. 18 (𝔊 xxxvi. 23) which extends to xxxix. 11. Its contents, which are somewhat miscellaneous in character, may, perhaps, be grouped under the general title of 'Precepts for social life'. It falls naturally into the following sections: xxxvi. 18 (𝔊 xxxvi. 23)—xxxvii. 15; xxxvii. 16–31; xxxviii. 1–23; and xxxviii. 24—xxxix. 11, with an Appendix, xxxix. 12–35.

XXXVI. 18 (𝔊 XXXVI. 23)—XXXVII. 15 again falls into four subsections, the first of which treats of the moral discernment of a man of experience (xxxvi. 18–20 = 𝔊 23–25), the second of women (xxxvi. 21–26 = 𝔊 26–31), the third of friendship (xxxvii. 1–6), and the fourth of counsellors true and false (xxxvii. 7–15).

(*a*) XXXVI. 18–20 (= 𝔊 23–25). A parallel is drawn here between the senses and the moral faculties; in each case the educated sense or faculty discriminates.

19. **the dainties that are bestowed.** Perhaps the dainties set on the table before a distinguished guest are meant, or the 'portions' referred to in Neh. viii. 10, 12 (cf. Esther ix. 19, 22). For the Hebr. words = 'that are bestowed' (מטעמי זבד) cp. Gen. xxx. 20 [Hebr. text מטעמי דבר yields no sense. 𝔊 'dainties of the chase' may be due to reminiscence of Gen. xxvii. 4—possibly a Hebr. reading derived from the passage].
the dainties of falsehood. The deceptive and alluring appearance that disguises what is false. For the sentiment of the verse cp. Job xii. 11, xxxiv. 3.

20. **A deceitful heart.** Cp. Jer. xvii. 9 (same phrase). 'Produceth sorrow,' i.e. sorrow to itself; perhaps misdirected (tortuous) intelligence is referred to.
an experienced man wardeth it off. The Hebr. lit. rendered = causeth it (sorrow or trouble) to return by means of it (*sc.* the heart or intelligence), i.e. wards off its attack by foresight and intelligence. The word for 'experienced' here is ותיק, which occurs otherwise only in Neo-Hebrew.

(*b*) XXXVI. 21–26 (= 𝔊 26–31) forms a second subsection. Its general theme is women: happy is the man with a tactful wife.

21. **A woman will receive . . .** 𝕳 misplaces the verse, inserting it between verses 18 and 19. 𝔖 omits it.

ℌ[B] 22 (27) The beauty of a woman brighteneth the countenance[y],
And excels every [z]delight of the eye[z].
23 (28) [zz]When she possesseth also [a]a soothing tongue[a],
Her husband is not (like other) sons of men.
ℌ[BD] 24 (29) [b]He that getteth[b] a wife [bb](getteth) the choicest possession[bb],
[c]A help meet for him[c], and [d]a pillar of support[d].
25 (30) Without a hedge the vineyard is laid waste,
And without a wife (a man is) [dd]a wanderer and homeless[dd].
26 (31) Who trusteth [e]an armed band[e]
[f]That rusheth[f] from city to city?
So is the man that hath no [g]nest[g],
Who resteth where evening befalls him.

(*c*) XXXVII. 1–6. *Of friendship, good and bad* (= 3+3 distichs).

37 ℌ[D(B)] 1 Every friend saith: [h]I am a friend[h];
[i]But there is a friend who is (only) friend in name[i].
2 Is there not [j][a sorrow][j] [k]that cometh nigh unto death[k]—
[l]A deeply loved friend[l] [m]who changeth to an enemy[m]?
3 [n]O base nature! why then wast thou created[n],
[o]To fill[o] [p]the world's face[p] [q]with deceit[q]!

θυγατηρ θυγατρος κρεισσων [y] 307 + *ανδρος*: 𝔏 + viri sui: 𝔖 'her face' [z–z] = ℌ מחמד עין *so* 𝔖: 𝔊 *επιθυμιαν ανθρωπου* [zz] *v.* 23 > 𝔖 [a–a] ℌ מרפא לשון (Prov. xv. 4): 𝔊 *επι γλωσσης αυτης ελεος και πραυτης* (248 + *ιασις*): 𝔏 lingua curationis et mitigationis misericordia [b–b] ℌ[B] *mg. has part.* קונה = 𝔊: *so* ℌ[D] (*Lévi*): ℌ[B] (*text*) קנה 'get' (*imperative*) = 𝔖 [bb–bb] ℌ[B] ראשית קנין: 𝔊 *εναρχεται κτισεως*: 𝔖 'at the head of thy possession' [c–c] ℌ[B] *MS. reads* עזר ומבצר: 𝔊 *βοηθον κατ αυτον* = עזר כנגדו (Gen. ii. 18) = 𝔖 (*this probably original reading*): ℌ[B] *mg. and* ℌ[D] עיר מבצר (Jer. i. 18) 'a fortified town' [d–d] *So* ℌ: 𝔊 *στυλον αναπαυσεως*: 𝔖 'pillar over against thee' (𝔖 *may have read a faulty text*: עזר כמוך ועמוד כנגדך) [dd–dd] ℌ נע ונד (Gen. iv. 12, 14): 𝔊 *στεναζει πλανωμενος* (LXX Gen. iv. 12 *στενων και τρεμων*) = 𝔏 ingemiscit egens [e–e] ℌ בגדוד צבא (*cp.* 1 Chron. vii. 4) 'in a band of war' = 𝔊 *ευζωνῳ ληστῃ* (*ευζωνος* = גדוד *in Aquila*; *ληστης* = גדוד *in* LXX): 𝔖 'the youth like a gazelle' (גדוד *in Syr. sense: and* צבי *for* צבא: *cp. also* Cant. ii. 9) [f–f] ℌ המדלג: 𝔊 (B) *σφαλλομενῳ but εφαλλομενῳ* (248 106 155): *the rest αφαλλομενῳ* = ℌ 𝔖 [g–g] *So* ℌ 𝔊: 𝔖 'wife' [h–h] 𝔊 *εφιλιασα αυτῳ καγω* (*but all authorities omit αυτῳ except* B: *it is a dittograph of καγω* (*Smend*)) [i–i] ℌ[D] *text* אך יש אהב שם אהב 'but there is a friend the name of a friend' (*i. e.* 'only a friend in name'). *But the Hebr. is not smooth*: 𝔊 (*ονοματι μονον φιλος*) *suggests* בשם אהב 'a friend (only) in name': 𝔖 'whose name is friend' (= ? שמו אהב) [j–j] ℌ[BD] *text* דין: *but emend to* דָוֹן = tristitia [k–k] *So* ℌ: 𝔊 [*λυπη*] *ενι εως θανατου* (*so* א* B*: 𝔏 inest): *v. l. μενει* (B[b] א[c.a] Syro-Hex mg.): 𝔖 = ℌ [l–l] ℌ[D] ריע כנפש: ℌ[B] רע כנפשך: 'friend like the (thy) soul': 𝔊 *εταιρος και φιλος* [m–m] 𝔊 (A 155 254 296 308) *τρεπομενος εις εχθρον* = ℌ (*others εις εχθραν* = 𝔏): 𝔖 (*omitting* לצר *at end of v.* 2 *and confusing* יצר *of* 3 a *with* צר) *renders* 2 b '[a deeply loved friend] shall he be to thee'. (*v.* 3) 'Enemy and evil', &c. [n–n] ℌ[D] חוי רע יאמר מדוע נוצרתי (*so* ℌ[B] *substantially*) *i. e.* 'Woe to the evil man that saith: Why was I created?' (*cp.* Is. xxix. 16): 𝔊 *ω πονηρον ενθυμημα ποθεν ενεκυλισθης*, *i. e.* 'O wicked imagination! whence wast thou fashioned' (rolled, *sc. on the potter's wheel*): *by this correct* ℌ *and read*: הוי יצר רע מדוע כן נוצרת [o–o] ℌ למלא: 𝔊 *καλυψαι* [p–p] ℌ פני תבל: 𝔊 *την ξηραν* [q–q] ℌ תרמית:

22. **The beauty of a woman brighteneth the countenance** (for יהליל Hif. cp. Job xxxi. 26). Cp. xxvi. 16 f.
23. **a soothing tongue.** lit. 'healing of tongue' (Prov. xv. 4; cp. also Prov. xiv. 30 and Eccles. x. 4); 𝔊 'if there is on her tongue mercy and meekness' (248 adds 'and healing').
Her husband . . . lit. 'her husband is not of the sons of men,' i.e. is unusually fortunate.
24. **He that getteth a wife . . .** The other form of the text (see critical note) runs:
'Get a wife, (as) the choicest possession—
A fortified city, and a pillar of support.'
For the form of the distich see Prov. iv. 7. ['Get' has the idea of acquiring by purchase, as in fact was customary with a wife.]
25. **Without a hedge.** Cp. Ps. v. 5; Prov. xxiv. 30, 31.
a wanderer and homeless. Cp. Gen. iv. 12, 14 (Cain); same phrase.
26. **that hath no nest.** No wife, no house. For 'house' (בית) = wife. Cp. *Mishnah Yoma* i. 1.
(*c*) XXXVII. 1–6. This forms a third subsection. Its theme is true and false friendship (cp. what is said on the same subject in ch. vi).
1. **Every friend saith: I am a friend . . .** Cp. Prov. xx. 6 ('Many a man will meet one who is kind to him, but a faithful man who can find?')
there is a friend who is (only) friend in name. This agrees with 𝔊; but 𝔖 interprets otherwise: 'whose name is friend,' i.e. who deserves the name.
3. **O base nature!** יצר רע = 'the evil *Yeṣer*: cp. Gen. vi. 5. In order to avoid imputing the creation of 'the evil nature' to God 𝔊 rationalizes, translating 'wast thou created' by ἐνεκυλίσθης (see critical note).
To fill the world's face. Same phrase, Is. xiv. 21.

𝔥[D (B)] 4 [r]Base is the friend who hath regard to (one's) table[r],
But in the time of stress standeth aloof.
5 [s]A good friend contendeth with (one's) enemy[s],
[t]And[t] against [u]adversaries[u] holdeth the shield.
6 [v]Forget not[v] a comrade [w]in conflict[w],
[x]And forsake him not when thou takest spoil[x].

(*d*) XXXVII. 7–15. *Of counsellors true and false* (= 4 + 6 + 2 + 2 + 1 distichs).

7 Every counsellor [a]pointeth (with) the hand[a],
But there is he that counselleth [b]a way to suit himself[b];
8 Beware of the counsellor,
And inform thyself beforehand what is his interest:
[c]For he himself will also[c] take thought:
[cc]'Why should it fall out as he wishes?'[cc]
9 And will say to thee: [d]How good[d] is thy course!
And (then) stand off to watch [dd]thy misfortune[dd].
𝔥[D] 10 Consult not [e]with ⌈those opposed to thee⌉[e],
And hide thy counsel from him that is envious—

𝔊 εν δολιοτητι: 𝔏 malitia et dolositati illius. r–r *So* 𝔥 (= 𝔖 'evil is the friend who approacheth the table'): 𝔊 *misunderstanding* מרע *mistranslates the whole line* εταιρος φιλου εν ευφροσυνη ηδεται s–s *So* 𝔥[D]: 𝔊 *again mistranslates* (*but perhaps from a corrupt Hebr. text*) εταιρος φιλῳ συνπονει χαριν γαστρος (*? reading* אוהב נחמל עם רע בקרב: *i.e.* נחמל (= πονεῖν 1 Sam. xxiii. 21, LXX) *for* נלחם *and* רע *for* זר *with* בקרב *from next verse*) t–t 𝔊 > (*but* 70 248 *have* και: *so* 𝔏 *and* 𝔥) u–u 𝔥 ערים (*Neo-Hebr. for* צרים): 𝔊 πολεμου (*but* 248 πολεμιου) v–v 𝔥 אל תשכח = 𝔊: 𝔖 'praise not' = אל־תשבח w–w 𝔥 בקרב: 𝔊 εν τῃ ψυχῃ σου x–x *So* 𝔥 = 𝔊 (*but, perhaps,* εν χρημασιν σου = בשלך *for* בשללך): 𝔖 'make him not ruler' (*perhaps an interpretation of* אל־תעזבהו) 'in thy house' (? בביתך *for* בשללך). *Cp.* Gen. xxxix. 6 a–a 𝔥[B] יניף יד 'shaketh the hand': 𝔊 εξαιρει βουλην (*cp.* επαιρειν = הניף xxxiii. 3, xlvii. 4: *and* βουλη = יד vi. 2): 𝔥[B] *mg. and* 𝔥[D] אומר חזה 'saith behold': 𝔖 'behold' [*for* ἐξαιρει 23 296 *have* εξερει = 𝔏 prodit] b–b 𝔥[D] דרך עליו = *lit.* 'a way according to him' c–c 𝔥[D] כי גם הוא נפשו cc–cc 𝔥 למה זה אליו יפול: 𝔊 μηποτε βαλῃ επι σοι κληρον (𝔏 ne forte mittat sudem in terram): 𝔊 *perhaps read* עליך יפיל (*cp.* Job vi. 27: 1 Sam. xiv. 42): 𝔖 'lest he cast upon thee evil hurt' d–d 𝔥 מטוב = מה־טוב dd–dd 𝔥 רישך *lit.* 'thy poverty' (*cp.* iv. 29): 𝔊 το συμβησομενον σοι: 𝔖 'thy shame' e–e 𝔥[D] חמיך = 𝔏 socero tuo (𝔥[B] *illegible*): *but* חמיך *can hardly be right* (חָמִיךְ = 'thy father-in-law', *i.e. husband's father, always in ref. to a woman: Smend explained by Arab.* حمك = dux viae malus, 'an untrustworthy guide': *but this word is uncertain*): 𝔊 του υποβλεπομενου σε: *emend to* קָמֶיךָ (*with Lévi: this seems to be the best suggestion yet made, and may, perhaps, be accepted provisionally*): *cp.* 𝔖 'thine enemy'. [*Edersh., Margol. suggest* חֹמֵיךָ *as* = 𝔊 *from*

---

4. **standeth aloof.** Cf. 2 Sam. xviii. 13 (phrase).
[4 *a* is misunderstood by 𝔊; R.V. renders 'There is a companion, which rejoiceth in the gladness of a friend'. See critical note.]

5. **A good friend . . .** 𝔊 again misunderstands the text (see critical note; R.V. renders 𝔊 'There is a companion, which for the belly's sake laboureth with his friend'.

against adversaries holdeth the shield. Cp. Ps. xxxv. 2.

(*d*) XXXVII. 7–15. This forms a fourth subsection. It treats of counsellors base and faithful.

7. **Every counsellor pointeth (with) the hand.** The Hebr. expression means 'to shake the hand', and may be understood as = 'to beckon with the hand' as a preliminary to speech (cp. the phrase *κατασείειν τῇ χειρί*; e.g. Acts xii. 17, &c.). But this phrase is only used in reference to a public meeting, while here it is private counsel that is spoken of. It is better, therefore, with Smend, to understand the expression in the sense of Is. xiii. 2, of pointing the way = 'he points out a way or course of action'. The alternative reading of the Hebrew ('Every counsellor saith: Behold!' cp. the alternative Greek reading and 𝔖) certainly is well supported. It is preferred by Lévi. Smend, however, regards this as an interpretation. [𝔊 'extolleth counsel' misrepresents.]

he that counselleth a way to suit himself. Cp. *Derek 'Ereṣ zuta* 8: 'Beware of him that counselleth according to his own way' (= T. B. *Sanh.* 76 b): והוי זהיר מהיועץ לפי דרכו (cited by Edersheim).

8. **what is his interest** (lit. 'need') (cf. 𝔥 𝔊).

For he himself will also take thought: 'Why should it fall out as he wishes?' The thought is set forth. The metaphor of the lot underlies the expression (cp. also 𝔖) = why should matters fall out as he wishes (עליו = אליו)? Lévi arrives at a similar meaning for the text. He explains by the phrase נפל אל ('to fall to') = 'to go on the side of', 'espouse the cause of' (cp. 1 Chron. xii. 20); so here = why should it go to his benefit or interest? i.e. why should the matter result in benefiting him? 𝔊 has misread and misunderstood the clause (cp. R.V.).

10. **those opposed to thee.** See critical note. For words expressing hostility and envy in parallelism cp. Is. xi. 13.

ℌ[B (D)] 11 With[f] a woman [g]about[g] her rival,
[h]And from ⌈an enemy⌉[h] [i]about war with him[i];
With a merchant about [j]business[j],
And from a buyer about selling;
[k]With an evil-disposed man[k] [l]about benevolence[l],
And a merciless man [m]about human happiness[m];
[n](With) the worthless workman[n] about his work,
[nn]And the yearly hireling[nn] [o]about the sowing of seed[o];
𝔊 (With) the idle slave about much work—
Put no trust in these [p]for any counsel[p]!
ℌ[B (D)] 12 [q]But rather with a man that feareth always[q],
[r]Whom thou knowest to be a keeper of the Law[r];
[s]Whose heart is at one with thine own[s],
[t]Who[t], if thou stumblest, [u]will be grieved for thee[u].

Aram. חמא = 'to see'. *Here used in a hostile sense*] f 𝔏 *here inserts a doublet of clauses* (e) *and* (f) g-g ℌ על = περι (א C &c. *also* 𝔏): B > περι: *for* על צרתה 𝔖 *substitutes* 'lest thou commit adultery with her' (*to avoid sanctioning concubinage implied by text*) h-h ℌ[D] ומדד: 𝔊 και μετα δειλου (= מרך: *cp.* Deut. xx. 8): *but context requires* 'enemy' (*so* 𝔖): *read therefore with Smend* מזר (*cp. v.* 5) i-i ℌ[B] אל מלחמתו: 𝔊 (*so* 𝔖) περι πολεμου = ℌ[D] (*but parallelism with* צרתה *requires suffix*) j-j ℌ תתגר: 𝔊 περι μεταβολιας (א μεταβολης) 'concerning exchange' k-k ℌ עם איש רע: 𝔊 μετα βασκανου (= אם רע עין, *cp.* xiv. 13). *Perhaps* עין *has fallen out in* ℌ: 𝔏 cum viro livido *supports* ℌ *in reading* איש l-l ℌ[B] אל תגמל חסד (*cp.* תַּגְמוּל Ps. cxvi. 12): ℌ[D] על גמילות חסד (ג"ח *common in Neo-Hebrew*: ? *substituted in MS. for the earlier expression*): 𝔊 περι ευχαριστιας m-m ℌ על טוב בשׂר = 'about the happiness (welfare) of flesh' n-n ℌ[B] פועל שׁוא: 𝔊 μετα οκνηρου: 𝔏 cum operario agrario = μετα εργατου αγρου (*for* αργου *from next clause*): 𝔖 'with a cheating servant', *cp.* ℌ[D] פועל שׂכיר (? *misread* שקר) nn-nn ℌ[D] שׂכיר שנה (*so* ℌ[B] *mg.*: ℌ[B] שומך שוא): 𝔊 μετα μισθιου αφεστιου (B): *but for last word* Syro-Hex 253 23 εφεστιου: א* C 155 308 επεστιου: *the rest rightly with* 𝔏 επετειου (= 'yearly': *cp.* Deut. xv. 18 LXX) o-o ℌ[D] על מוצא זרע: 𝔊 (*freely*) περι συντελειας: 𝔏 consummatione anni p-p 𝔊 περι πασης συμβουλιας q-q ℌ אך אם (*read* עם) איש מפחד תמיד: 𝔊 αλλ η μετα ανδρος ευσεβους ενδελεχιζε, *cp.* 𝔖 'with men righteous be dwelling' r-r ℌ = 𝔊 (*but* εντολας): 𝔖 'for they fear to sin before God' s-s ℌ[B] אשר עם לבבו כלבבך = *lit.* 'with whose heart (it is) as thine own heart': 𝔊 = אשר בלבבו, *which may be right* t-t ℌ[B] אם: ℌ[D] ואם = 𝔊 𝔖 u-u 𝔊 συναλγησει σοι = יֶעֱבַר בך ('will be troubled on

---

11. **With . . . from.** The clauses that follow in 11 are in subordination to 'consult not (with)' and 'hide thy counsel (from)' in 10.

With a woman about her rival. i.e. with a wife about another woman whom one is intending to take as a second wife; the Hebr. word used here (צרה = ἀντίζηλος) has this technical meaning; cp. xxvi. 6 (also xxv. 11). In these passages Ben-Sira apparently has in mind some of the evil results of polygamy, which were in evidence when he wrote. The same word (= 'rival wife') is used in 1 Sam. i. 6; cp. also Lev. xviii. 18.

And from an enemy . . . 𝔊 'and with a coward about war'.

With a merchant about business. 𝔊 has 'concerning exchange', i.e. about what to buy (the goods that the merchant has to sell). The cases enumerated are of persons directly interested in the results of the transactions. From such the reader is warned not to seek advice.

And from a buyer about selling. i.e. about the price he should pay one. Such cautions as these are especially necessary in the East.

With an evil-disposed man . . . The list of unsuitable counsellors that follows consists of such as are incapacitated from giving advice on the particular matter by inherent defects of character. 'An evil-disposed man,' i.e. an ill-natured, grudging man (Lat. 'cum viro livido'). For 'benevolence' 𝔊 has περὶ εὐχαριστίας—εὐχαριστία apparently = display of kindliness.

about human happiness. i.e. about the good fortune and happiness of any one. 𝔊 'about kindness'.

And the yearly hireling about the sowing of seed. 𝔊 offers an interesting variety of reading here (see critical note). The reading of the cursives (55 106 248 254 296), viz. ἐπετείου (= 𝔏 'annuli'), is correct as against the uncials (B C א*), and is attested by ℌ. It is not 'the domestic (ἐφεστίου) servant', but the 'yearly hireling' that the verse is concerned with. Such an one remained in his employment not a day longer than he was obliged (cp. Isa. xvi. 14); hence it would be of all things most unprofitable to discuss with one of this class something which would be carried out after the termination of his year's contract—viz. the sowing of seed in the autumn.

(With) the idle slave about much work. i.e. the opinion of a lazy servant must not be asked on the question whether there is much work to be done (Edersheim).

12. **with a man that feareth always . . . keeper of the Law.** i.e. a man who is God-fearing and pious: such a counsellor will be guided by right principle. For the phrase 'that feareth always' cp. Prov. xxviii. 14; also xviii. 27 of our book.

Whose heart . . . i.e. a faithful counsellor must be one who can act in a disinterested way, and is not committed to any course by special interests of his own.

ℌ[B (D)] 13 Do thou also [v]take knowledge[v] of the counsel of (thine own) heart,
[w]For thou hast no one more true to thee[w].
14 The heart of a man [x]telleth (him) his opportunities[x]
Better than seven watchmen [y]on a tower[y].
15 But in all this intreat God,
That He may direct thy steps in truth.

(*a*) XXXVII. 16–26. *True and false wisdom* (= 3 + 2[+1] + 2 + 3 distichs).

16 [a]The beginning of every action is speech,
And before every work is the thought[a].
17 [b]The roots of the heart's deliberations
(18) Bring forth four branches[b]:
18 Good and evil, life and death;
[c]But the tongue ruleth over them altogether[c].
ℌ[B D (C)] 19 [d]There is a wise man who is wise for many[d]
But for himself [e]is a fool[e].

account of thee'), *which is the mg. reading of* ℌ[B] (*corrupted to* יעבד *in* ℌ[D]: ℌ[B] *text* יגיע אליך = ? (*pointing* יְגִיעַ) condolebit tibi [*Peters*]: 'shall be weary for thee') v–v ℌ הבין: 𝔊 στησον = הכין: 𝔖 *renders whole verse*: 'for his faith shall quicken him, and also he is faithful like thee' w–w ℌ[B] מי (ℌ[D] כי) יאמין (*l.* אין) לך אמן ממנו: 𝔊 ου γαρ εστιν σοι πιστοτερος αυτης x–x ℌ שעיותיו (מגיד) יגיד (*pl. of* שעה 'hour, time = opportunity': *form unusual*): 𝔊 απαγγελειν ενιοτε ειωθεν ('is sometimes wont to bring him tidings' R.V.) (157 + το αληθες: 106[b] αληθινα = 𝔏): 𝔖 'shall rejoice in (*for* shall show) his ways' y–y ℌ[B] על מצפה: 𝔊 επι μετεωρου καθημενοι επι σκοπης (καθημενοι *an addition*: ε. μ. *and* ε. σ. *a double rendering of* על מצפה): ℌ[D] *has* על שן 'upon a peak' [*possibly* επι μετεωρου = על שן *and* 𝔊 *gives a conflation*]. 𝔖 *renders* 'more than the riches of the world that profit not' ('*thinking of* Matt. iv. 8' [*Hart*]) a–a *So* ℌ[D] 𝔊: 𝔖 'before all men and before everything God hath created all'. [*For* לפני *in* (b) ℌ[B] *has* ראש.] 𝔏 ante omnia opera (*al.* omnem operam) verbum verax praecedat te et ante omnem actum consilium stabile b–b ℌ[B] עקרת (D עקר) תחבילות (D תחבולות) לבב ארבעה שכמים יפרחו (D יפריח) (*mg.* + D שרביטים): 𝔊 ιχνος αλλοιωσεως (= ? תחליפות) καρδιας τεσσαρα μερη ανατελλει [*Hebr. explains* 𝔊 *which yields no suitable sense*]: μερη = שכמים ℌ[B] (*cp.* שכם Gen. xlviii. 22) c–c *So* ℌ = 𝔊: 𝔖 'he that rules over his tongue shall be preserved from evil' d–d ℌ יש חכם לרבים נחכם: 𝔊 εστιν ανηρ (Syro-Hex 253 > ανηρ) πανουργος και πολλων παιδευτης (και > א A C &c. 𝔏, 𝔖 = ℌ) [𝔊 = ℌ: *possibly, however, reading* יחכם *for* נחכם, *and treating this as Hif.: Lévi considers* נחכם *a mistake for* יחכם: *Nif. not otherwise attested*) e–e ℌ[D] נואל (*so* ℌ[B] *mg.*) = 𝔊 𝔖: ℌ[B] *and* ℌ[C] גואל (*Peters renders*: et animam suam liberat): 𝔖 *renders whole verse:*

---

13. **take knowledge . . .** Self-reliance is, after all, best; for the maxim regarding the counsel of the heart cp. the *Alphabet of Ben-Sira* (I): 'Take sixty counsellors, but the counsel of thine own heart do not abandon.'

14. **The heart of a man telleth (him) his opportunities . . .** The Hebr. word rendered 'opportunities' = lit. 'hours', (שׁעה): the right opportune time for doing a thing (in this sense in Neo-Hebrew). The 'seven watchmen on a tower' of the second half of the verse may be an allusion to astrologers (Heb. is צופים lit. 'watchers'). For the number 'seven' in such a connexion cp. Prov. xxvi. 16, 25; Jer. xv. 9. The moral of the verse is that man should trust the instincts of his own heart most (so also 𝔊).

15. **But in all this intreat God.** 𝔊 has 'above all these'; counsel, to be fruitful, must be taken in conjunction with prayer. Prayer is of primary importance. The counsellors may be ranked in an ascending order of importance as one's friends, oneself, God (Edersheim). With the verse cp. Prov. xvi. 9.

XXXVII. 16–31. This section falls into two well-defined subsections, the first of which is concerned with wisdom true and false (*vv.* 16–26), and the second with wisdom or discretion applied to eating (*vv.* 27–31).

(*a*) XXXVII. 16–26 opens with some general remarks on reflection and thought. Thought precedes and determines action. Wisdom and folly bring in their train good and evil, life and death; but the fate of men is above all controlled by the tongue of the teacher (*vv.* 16–18). In the verses that follow (19–26) three classes of wise who are not really such (*vv.* 19, 20, 22) are contrasted with those who really deserve the name of 'wise' (*vv.* 23, 24, 26). 'Wise' throughout is a term for the well-instructed scribe or teacher.

17. **The roots of the heart's deliberations bring forth four branches.** The Hebrew (note the *v. l.*) may be rendered:

'The root of counsels is the heart;
It brings forth four branches.'

This accords well with *v.* 16. The workings of mind and the moral will issue in action which results in a harvest of good or evil, life or death. For the figure (root and branches) cp. i. 20. [𝔊 gives no coherent sense.]

18. **Good and evil, life and death.** Cp. xxxiii. (xxxvi.) 14; Deut. xxx. 19.

But the tongue ruleth over them altogether. Cp. Prov. xviii. 21 ('Life and death are in the power of the tongue').

19. **. . . who is wise for many But for himself is a fool.** The verse may be explained to mean either (*a*) there

ℌ[BD] 20 [fg]And there is a wise man who is loathed for his speech[g],
And is cut off [h]from all enjoyment[h];
𝔊 21 [For winning grace has not been bestowed upon him from the Lord,
And he depriveth himself of all honour].
ℌ[BD(C)] 22 [i]And there is [j]a wise man who is wise[j] for himself,
The fruit of whose understanding (is) [k]upon his body[k].
ℌ[BD] 23 [i]And there is a wise man [l]who is wise for his people[l],
The fruit of whose understanding is [m]lasting[m].
25 [n]The life of a man (numbers) [o]days but few[o],
[p]But the life of Jeshurun days innumerable[p].
ℌ[BD(C)] 24 [nq]Who is wise for himself[q] shall have his fill [r]of enjoyment[r],
And [s]all who see him[s] count him happy.
26 [t]Who is wise (for his) people[t] gaineth [u]honour[u],
And his name [v]abideth in life eternal[v].

(*b*) XXXVII. 27–31. *Wisdom or discretion applied to eating* (= 2 + 2 + 1 distichs).

ℌ[BD] 27 My son, prove thy soul [w]in thy life[w],
And see (that) what harmeth it [x]thou give it not.

'every one that is wise in his own conceit is a fool'. [𝔊 αχρηστος: 𝔏 insuavis = ℌ] [f] *Pr. tit.* 𝔏 de sofistica et versuta locutione [g–g] ℌ ויש חכם בדברו נמאס: 𝔊 εστιν σοφιζομενος εν λογοις (Syro-Hex + και) μισητος [h–h] ℌ מכל מאכל תענוג ('from all agreeable food'): 𝔊 πασης τροφης (א* 106 157 248 253 Syro-Hex σοφιας): Sah τρυφης = תענוג *rightly* (τροφη *for* τρυφη xli. 1). *Read* מכל תענוג: מאכל *in* ℌ *is an addition* (*a conflate reading*): 𝔖 'and he depriveth himself of all honour' (? = 21 b): *both* 𝔖 *and* ℌ *omit two lines: possibly* 𝔖 *omits* 20 b, 21 a *and this line* = 21 b (*so Smend*): ℌ > 21 a *and* b: *not improbably there is a doublet in* 𝔊 (*vv.* 20, 21), *and* 𝔖 *may represent a variant of* 20 b (ℌ 'is cut off from all enjoyment' = 𝔖 (*variant*) 'is deprived of all honour)' [i] 𝔖 *transposes vv.* 22, 23 (*wrongly: cp.* 24, 26) [j–j] *So* ℌ = 𝔏: 𝔊 σοφος [k–k] *So* ℌ: 𝔖 'from the sight of his face': 𝔊 επι στοματος (*read* σωματος) πιστοι (296 > πιστοι = *an interpolation from* 23 b) [l–l] *The verse is wanting in* ℌ[B]: ℌ[D] לעמו יחכם = 𝔊 τον εαυτου λαον παιδευσει: 𝔖 'who is wise at all times' = לעולם יחכם: *cp.* 19 a [𝔊 ανηρ *at beginning of line* = ℌ ויש *misread* איש] [m–m] *So* 𝔊 (= נאמן): ℌ[D] בגויתם = 'in their own bodies': *but* על (*not* ב) *would be expected here: cp.* 22 b. *Context supports* 𝔊. 𝔖 'for themselves' [n] ℌ *transposes vv.* 24, 25 (*rightly*): 𝔖 > *v.* 25 [o–o] ℌ[B] מספר ימים: ℌ[D] ימים מספר: 𝔊 εν αριθμῳ ημερων. *Read with Smend* ימי מספר (*cp.* (b) *and* xli. 13) [p–p] *So* ℌ[D]: ℌ[B] *has* עם ישראל *for* ישרון (= 𝔊 του Ισραηλ): *but* ישרון *original* [q–q] ℌ חכם לנפשו: 𝔊 ανηρ σοφος: ℌ = 𝔖 [r–r] ℌ תענוג (= 𝔖): 𝔊 ευλογιας [s–s] ℌ[D] כל רואיהו: 𝔊 παντες οι ορωντες (+ αυτον 10 b, *so* 𝔏 *and* 𝔖 = ℌ) [t–t] ℌ חכם עם: 𝔊 ο σοφος εν τῳ λαῳ αυτου [u–u] ℌ[CD] כבוד: 𝔊 πιστιν (*but* 248 δοξαν, *so* 𝔏 *and* 𝔖 = ℌ): πιστιν *may have been corrupted from* τιμην (*Smend*) [v–v] ℌ[D] עומד בחיי עלם: 𝔊 ζησεται (248 εσται) εις τον αιωνα (= לחיי עולם: *perhaps so read here with Smend*) [w–w] *So* ℌ[B] 𝔊 𝔖: ℌ[B] *mg.* ℌ[D] בחמר ('in wine') *probably a scribal mistake for* בחייך [x] ℌ[D] + ו ('and give it not'): *so* 𝔊: *but* ℌ[B] 𝔏 𝔖 > 'and'

---

are some who are wise where others' interests are concerned, but in their own affairs act as fools; or (*b*) there are some who pass as wise in the opinion of many, but who in their own estimation are as fools. Perhaps in view of the use of ל in 22 *a* the former interpretation (*a*) is to be preferred. Then 22 *a* is a contrast.

21. **winning grace.** 𝔊 χάρις = here also lovableness. Cp. xx. 19; xxi. 16.

depriveth himself of all honour. Cp. Num. xxiv. 11.

22. **The fruit of whose understanding (is) upon his body.** i.e. he experiences the results of his prudence in material comforts ('upon his body' = almost 'upon himself'). For the reading of 𝔊 see critical note, and cp. Prov. xii. 14, xiii. 2, xviii. 21.

23. **is lasting.** The result of such public-spirited wisdom is seen not merely in material comforts and success, but in lasting honour (fame among posterity).

25. **The life of a man . . . life of Jeshurun.** The verse gives interesting expression to one ancient view of immortality. A man's memory might live on in honour in the life of his people. The nation could be regarded as immortal. There is no hint of a survival of the personality of the individual. Cp. 2 Macc. xiv. 15. 'Jeshurun' is a poetic name for Israel under its ideal aspect (= 'upright one'); cp. Deut. xxxii. 15, xxxiii. 5, 26; Isa. xliv. 2.

24. **all who see him . . .** Cp. Job xxix. 11; Cant. vi. 9.

26. **And his name abideth in life eternal.** i.e. will live on honoured in the memory of future generations: cp. xxxix. 9, xli. 13 ('a good name endureth for ever'), xliv. 13, 14.

(*b*) XXXVII. 27–31. The theme of this subsection is prudence and self-restraint, especially as shown in eating. Discretion in this regard will ward off disease and prolong life. It forms a good transition to the following section, which deals with the physician and the healing art.

27. **My son, prove thy soul in thy life . . .** 'Experientia docet.' The wise man will learn from experience what to avoid as specially dangerous to himself.

$\mathfrak{H}^{B (D)}$ 28 For not [y]everything[y] is good for every one—
[z]Every soul maketh not its choice of every kind[z].
29 [a]Indulge not excess[a] [b]In any[b] enjoyment,
[c]Nor immoderation[c] in [d]any[d] dainties.
30 [e]For in much eating[e] [f]nesteth sickness[f],
[g]And he that indulgeth excess[g] cometh nigh to [h]loathing[h].
31 [i]By intemperance[i] many have perished,
But he that is on his guard prolongeth life.

(*a*) XXXVIII. 1–15. *The physician has been ordained by God and should be resorted to in sickness* (= 3+3+2+3+3+1 distichs).

38 $\mathfrak{H}^{B}$
1 [j]Cultivate[j] the physician [k]in accordance with the need of him[k],
For him also hath God ordained.

y–y *So* $\mathfrak{H}^{B}$ = 𝔊: $\mathfrak{H}^{D}$ תענוג ('luxury, enjoyment': 'for enjoyment is not good for every one'), *cp.* 𝔖 ('food is not,' &c. = ? אכל *for* לכל) z–z *So* $\mathfrak{H}^{B}$ = 𝔊: *cp.* 𝔖: $\mathfrak{H}^{D}$ ולא לכל נפש כל זן תבחר = 𝔏 et non omni animae omne genus placet a–a $\mathfrak{H}^{B}$ [ל] אל תזרע (*mg.* אל תזרו *and* [אל] תזר): $\mathfrak{H}^{D}$ [אל] אל תזד (*cp.* $\mathfrak{H}^{B}$ *mg.* 2): 𝔊 μη απληστευου. *Perhaps* $\mathfrak{H}^{B}$ *should be read* (*with a different division of the letters*) אל תזר על (*so Lévi, Strack*): *then point* אל תִּזָּר (*Nif. of* זרה) = 'scatter not thyself upon (dissipate not thyself)' = 'indulge not excess' (= 𝔊 'be not insatiable in'): *the reading of* $\mathfrak{H}^{D}$ אל תזד = 'be not excessive' (?). *Smend reads* אל־תזיע: *Hif.* (= *strengthened Qal*) *of* זוע 'to be restless': *he renders* 'sei nicht ausgelassen (bei)', *and regards the other readings as variants arising* (אל תזר[ו] *and* תזד אל) *from* תזר על *and this from* תזרע ל: *cp.* והמזיע *v.* 30 b $\mathfrak{H}^{B}$ *mg.* b–b $\mathfrak{H}^{B}$ לכל = 𝔊: $\mathfrak{H}^{B}$ *mg. and* $\mathfrak{H}^{D}$ > כל c–c $\mathfrak{H}^{B}$ ואל תשפך = 𝔊: $\mathfrak{H}^{B}$ *mg.* = $\mathfrak{H}^{D}$ ואל תתחנג = ? *a scribal error for* תתענג *which itself is a correction of* תשפך (*so Smend*): *Lévi reads* תתחנג *and explains from Syr. as meaning* 'desire' d–d *So* $\mathfrak{H}^{B}$: *but* $\mathfrak{H}^{B}$ *mg.* $\mathfrak{H}^{D}$ > 'any' (כל) e–e *So* $\mathfrak{H}^{D}$ = $\mathfrak{H}^{B}$ *mg. and* 𝔊 (εν πολλοις γαρ βρωμασιν): $\mathfrak{H}^{B}$ כי ברוב תענוג f–f *So* 𝔥: 𝔊 εσται πονος (B): *but other MSS.* (א A 248 &c.) νοσος (𝔏 infirmitas: *so* 𝔖) g–g $\mathfrak{H}^{D}$ המזיע (*cp. note* a–a *above*) = $\mathfrak{H}^{B}$ *mg.*: $\mathfrak{H}^{B}$ והמרבה: 𝔊 και η απληστια h–h 𝔥 זרא = 𝔊 (εως χολερας): *so* Num. xi. 20 (*Hebr. and* LXX) i–i 𝔥 בלא מוסר ('through lack of discipline': *cp.* Prov. v. 23 באין מוסר = *Symm.* δι' απαιδευσιαν): 𝔊 δι' απληστιαν: 𝔏 propter crapulam: 𝔖 'through much food' j–j $\mathfrak{H}^{B}$ רעי *i.e.* רְעֵי: *mg.* רעה רועה = $\mathfrak{H}^{D}$: 𝔊 τιμα = 𝔏 𝔖 *and the citation in Rabbinic sources* (כבד אוקיר): *see exeg. note for these, and also for the use of* רעה *in these connexions* (רעה *used in an Aram. sense* = *Heb.* רצה 'to take pleasure in, treat in a friendly way') k–k $\mathfrak{H}^{B}$ *mg.* לפי צרכך ($\mathfrak{H}^{D}$ לפי *here this MS. ends*): 𝔊 προς τας χρειας (+ αυτου א A V 155 253 254 307 Syro-Hex)

---

28. **For not everything is good for every one . . .** Cp. 1 Cor. vi. 12.

29. **Indulge not excess.** Cp. xxxi. (xxxiv.) 7, 'be not insatiable' (𝔊 μὴ ἀπληστεύου, as here).

Nor immoderation . . . lit. 'be not poured out' (𝔊 μὴ ἐκχυθῇς = 𝔥 אל תשפך), i.e. do not allow yourself to be given up excessively to. Cp. Ep. Jude 11 'rushed headlong (ἐξεχύθησαν) for wages in the error of Balaam'.

30. **sickness . . . loathing.** There is a clear allusion to Num. xi. 20. Possibly both here and in the Numbers passage the word translated 'loathing' (Vulg. 'nausea') may, as Smend suggests, denote something stronger, some severe illness like dysentery (Smend renders 'Brechruhr'). Oriental dysentery is especially dangerous. For the whole verse cp. xxxi. (xxxiv.) 20.

31. **prolongeth life.** Lit. 'will add life': cp. for the expression xlviii. 23; Ps. lxi. 6 (7); Prov. iii. 2, ix. 11.

XXXVIII. 1–23. This section falls into two well-defined subsections, the first of which treats of the physician and his healing art, which should be resorted to in sickness (*vv.* 1–15); and the second with mourning for the dead (*vv.* 16–23).

(*a*) XXXVIII. 1–15. God has ordained the physician, and given man the power and means to use the healing art, in order that these should be resorted to when needful (*vv.* 1–8). In time of sickness, together with prayer, repentance, and sacrifice, the skill of the physician should be called in to aid. The section seems to be addressed to people who, on religious grounds, were unwilling to consult the physician in times of sickness; cp. 2 Chron. xvi. 12 ('Asa . . . was diseased in his feet . . . yet in his disease he resorted not unto the Lord, but to the physicians'—the contrast is significant).

1. **Cultivate the physician in accordance with the need of him.** The line is cited more than once in Rabbinic works in the form—('The proverb says:) Honour thy physician before thou hast need of him' (*Midrash rabba* to Exod. xxi; cp. *Midr. Tanh.* Gen. מקץ § 10; also in an Aram. form in T. J. *Taanith* iii. 6). This form agrees with $\mathfrak{H}^{B}$ here in reading 'before (thou hast need of him)'; but the alternative reading (לפי = 𝔊) 'in accordance with the need of him' is to be preferred here, being supported by the logical connexion. The physician is to be cultivated and honoured 'because' God has ordained him for a special and necessary office in human affairs. This point the author is enforcing to people who were inclined to deny the necessity of the physician under any circumstances. The reading 'before' here may have arisen under the influence of xviii. 19 ('Have a care of thy health or ever thou be sick'); so Taylor. The word rendered 'cultivate' (רעה) occurs also in xxxi. (xxxiv.) 15, with the meaning to treat in a friendly and considerate manner; cp. רעי in Aram. = 'to delight in, welcome' (*B. H.* רצה).

ordained. The Hebr. word here rendered 'ordained' (חלק) sometimes has the meaning 'created' (so xxxi.

2 It is from God that [l]the physician getteth wisdom[l],
And from the king he receiveth [m]gifts[m].
3 The skill of the physician lifteth up his head,
[n]And he may stand before nobles[n].
4 God [o]hath created[o] medicines out of the earth,
And let not a discerning man reject them.
5 Was not [p]the water[p] made sweet [q]by the wood[q],
[r]That He might make known to all men His power[r]?
6 And He gave men discernment,
That they might glory [s]in His mighty works[s].
7 [t]By means of them the physician assuageth pain[t],
8 And likewise [u]the apothecary prepareth a confection[u]:

τιμαις (70 106 296 > τιμαις) αυτου: *Clem. Alex. has only* προς χρειαν αυτου: ℵ[c.a] προς τας χρειας = 𝔏 = לפי צרכו (*so read*): ℌ[B] לפני צרכו = 𝔖: *so Rabbinic citations* (? לפני *for* לפי *under influence of* xviii. 19) [l–l] ℌ יחכם רופא = 𝔖: 𝔊 (*freely*) εστιν ιασις [m–m] *So* ℌ: 𝔊 δομα (*but* V 248 253 Syro-Hex δοξαν) [n–n] *So* ℌ (*with mg.* מלכים *for* נדיבים): 𝔊 και εναντι μεγιστανων θαυμασθησεται: 𝔖 'and before kings they set him' [o–o] *So* 𝔊 𝔏 𝔖 = ℌ *mg.* (ברא [+שמים *i.e.* סמים]): ℌ (*text*) [תרופות] מוציא: *for* הוציא *used of creation cp.* Gen. i. 12. [*The marginal* שמים (סַמִּים) = 'spices' = 𝔖 *and occurs in the Rabb. citation* (*see exeg. note*), *but is not to be preferred to the text* תרופות = 'medicines'] [p–p] *So* ℌ 𝔊: 𝔏 aqua amara = 𝔖 (*amplifying ref. to* Exod. xv. 25) [q–q] ℌ *mg.* מעץ = 𝔊: ℌ *text* בעץ = 𝔖 [r–r] ℌ בעבור להודיע כל אנש כחו (*for* בעבור ל + *inf.*, *cp.* 1 Chron. xix. 3): 𝔊 εις το γνωσθηναι την ισχυν αυτου = 𝔖 (*but* 248 70 + υπο [248 απο] ανθρωπου [*so* 𝔏] = ℌ) [s–s] *So* 𝔊 𝔖: ℌ 'in His (*mg.* their) mighty work' (*but pl. is required by* בהם 7 a) [t–t] 𝔊 εν αυτοις εθεραπευσεν και ηρεν τον πονον αυτου (ℵ[c.a] 157 307 &c. Syro-Hex Sah Eth αυτων) = 'with them doth he heal and taketh away his (their) pain': 𝔏 in his curans mitigabit dolorem (*Aug. spec.* mitigavit dolorem ipsorum) = θεραπευων ανεπαυσεν = ℌ 𝔖 [𝔊 *may have added* ו *of* וכן *to* מכאוב] [u–u] 𝔏 unguentarius faciet pigmenta suavitatis + et unctiones conficiet

---

[xxxiv.] 13 ℌ, 27 mg.); the Greek so renders here (ἔκτισεν); cp. vii. 15, xxxix. 25, xl. 1, xliv. 2. But in all these passages the meaning 'allot' or 'ordain' is to be preferred. [The meaning 'create' in xxxi. (xxxiv.) 13 may be explained from the idea of smoothness, shape, according to Smend.]

2. **It is from God that the physician getteth wisdom . . .** The skill of the physician is derived from God, and is not dependent on the favour of earthly potentates for the high estimation with which it should be regarded. This seems to be the thought of the couplet. 'King' in clause *b* probably means an earthly king, and is not to be regarded as a title of God here (the King, i.e. the heavenly King). The verse, however, may not be intended to assert more than the fact that the physician derives his skill from God, and at the same time receives recognition and is honoured by the highest of earthly potentates. Physicians were regular officials of Oriental courts, and highly esteemed there. 𝔊 generalizes the statement ('from the Most High cometh healing').

3. **lifteth up his head . . . stand before nobles.** A physician specially skilful may rise to the highest honour. For the expression 'stand before nobles' (*v. l.* 'kings') cp. Prov. xxii. 29.

4. **created medicines out of the earth.** Herbs used for medicinal purposes are specially in the writer's mind. In the *Midrash rabba* on Gen. viii (cp. also *Yalqut*, Job, § 501) some sayings are grouped together which correspond to *vv.* 4 *a*, 7, and 8 *a* here:

(4 *a*) God causes spices to spring up out of the earth:
(7) With them the physician heals the stroke,
(8 *a*) And of them the perfumer compounds the perfume.[1]

5. **Was not the water made sweet by the wood . . .** The allusion is to Exod. xv. 23 f. Ben-Sira rightly interprets the miracle to have been effected by the nature of the wood: so Targ. Onq. *ad loc.* ('and the Lord instructed him (in the properties of) a tree, and he cast it into the waters, and the waters became sweet': cp. also Philo *de vita Moysi*, i. 33, and Josephus, *Ant.* iii. 1. 2).

That He might make known to all men His power. So ℌ rightly. God is the subject of the sentence (𝔊 makes the reference to the power (virtue) of the wood). God reveals His power through natural agents and properties.

6. **That they** (i.e. men) **might glory in His** (God's) **mighty works.** For the expression 'glory in' (התפאר ב) cp. xvii. 9, xxxix. 8, l. 20.

7. **By means of them the physician assuageth pain.** 'By means of them,' i.e. by the forces which God has placed in natural objects. The subject of the sentence in the text of ℌ is the physician: 𝔊 (wrongly) makes the subject of the sentence God. [𝔊 may have read בהם רופא ומרפא מכאובו (cp. Rabb. cit. above).]

8. **And likewise the apothecary prepareth a confection.** Or the clause (ℌ) may be rendered: 'And likewise the perfumer prepareth a perfume' (μίγμα). In B H רֹקֵחַ is a professional name = 'mixer, perfumer' (cp. Exod. xxx. 25, 35; Eccles. x. 1, &c.); in 1 Chron. ix. 30 cp. 'compounders of the ointment': מִרְקַחַת (the word used here) in Neo-Hebrew = 'ointment' (ointment-mixture) (so 1 Chron. ix. 30). Thus the line might be rendered: 'And likewise the apothecary (compounder) prepareth an ointment (ointment-mixture).' For רוקח (Gr. μυρεψός) cp. xlix. 1. The offices of apothecary (compounder) and physician were, of course, not distinct.

[1] אלוה העלה סמים מן־הארץ. בהם הרופא מרפא את המכה ומהם הרוקח מרקח את המרקחת

𝕳[B] That His work may not cease,
[v]Nor health[v] [w]from the face of His earth[w].
9 My son, [x]in sickness[x] [y]be not negligent[y];
Pray unto God, for He can heal[z].
10 [a][Turn] from iniquity, and [purify thy hands][a];
And from all [b]transgressions[b] cleanse thy heart.
11 [cd][Give a meal-offering with] a memorial[d],
[e]And offer a fat sacrifice[e] [f]to the utmost of thy means[f].
12 [g]And to the physician also give a place[g];
Nor should he be far away[h], for of him there is need.
13 For there is a time when successful help is in his power;
14 For he also maketh supplication to God,
[i]To make his diagnosis successful[i],
And the treatment, [j]that it may promote recovery[j].
15 He that sinneth before his Maker
[k]Shall be delivered into the hands[k] of the physician.

sanitatis (*a doublet*) v–v 𝕳 ותושיה : 𝕲 και ειρηνη [παρ' αυτου] (𝕷 *reading* γαρ *for* παρ : pax enim Dei) [? ειρηνη = שלוה *for* תושיה (*Hart*): *but Smend thinks it translates* 𝕳 = 'Heil'] w–w 𝕲 παρ αυτου εστιν επι προσωπου της γης = ממנו על פני ארצו [תושיה] = 'and that health from him may be upon the face of the earth' (*Smend thinks this may be the original text*): 𝕳 ותושיה מבני אדם, *mg.* מפני ארצו = 𝕾 ('from the face of the earth'): *in classical Hebrew* מעל פני *would be required* x–x *So* 𝕳 : 𝕲 + σου (*so* 𝕾 𝕷) y–y 𝕳 אל תתעבר = 𝕲 (*see further exeg. note*): 𝕾 > (𝕷 ne despicias te ipsum) z 𝕲 + σε (*so* 𝕷) a–a 𝕳 (*at beginning of line*) *is here defective*: (נום) מעול ומהכר פנים = 'flee from iniquity and from respect of persons' (*Schechter*): (נום *is supplied also by Lévi, Strack, Peters*): 𝕳 *mg. has* נסה = 'prove'. 𝕲 αποστησον πλημμελειαν (248 70—μειας) και ευθυνον χειρας = ? הסיר מעל והבר פפים (ευθυς = בר Ps. lxxviii. 1): *so Smend would emend the whole line*: סור מעול והבר פפים : *this is confirmed by parallelism of next clause.* 𝕾 *has* 'remove iniquity and falsehood' b–b 𝕲 αμαρτιας (*sing.*) c *v.* 11 > 𝕾 d–d *Hebr. MS. defective, only the final word of the line,* אזכרה, *being legible*: 𝕲 δος ευωδιαν και μνημοσυνον σεμιδαλεως : 𝕳 *mg.* אזכרתה : *Smend remarks that a fem. noun must have preceded this, and he restores the whole line*: תן מנחה וגם אזכרה : *Lévi* הגש ניחוח ואזכרה (*cp.* xlv. 16) = 'offer incense and a memorial' e–e 𝕳 ודשן ערוך = 'and make fat what is set in order or prepared' (*i. e.* 'the offering prepared'): *cp.* מערכות l. 14 *where* 𝕲 *renders by* προσφορα : 𝕲 *here* και λιπανον προσφοραν f–f 𝕳 בכנפי הוניך (*Schechter proposes* ככנפי הוניך 'according to the savings of thy substance'): 𝕲 ως μη υπαρχων = ? כפי אינך : *or as Lévi suggests* כבלי הון : *perhaps* כפי הונך (*Lévi*) *should be read.* 𝕷 > g–g *So* 𝕲 = 𝕳 (*MS. defective*): 𝕲 + και γαρ αυτον εκτισεν κυριος (*addition from v.* 1) h 𝕲 + σου : *cp.* 𝕳 *mg.* מאח (*corrupted for* מאתך ?) i–i אשר יצלח לו פשרה (פשרה = פֵּשֶׁר 'solution', Eccles. viii. 1): 𝕲 αναπαυσιν (*? from* αναλυσιν : λυσις = פשר Eccles. viii. 1. [𝕾 *here* 'health'.]) *For* יצלח (*read as Hif.*) 𝕳 *mg. has* ימנה (*i. e.* יְמַנֶּה) = 𝕾 : 𝕷 diriget j–j 𝕲 χαριν εμβιωσεως = 𝕳 : 𝕾 'in his hand and life' k–k *So* 𝕳 *mg.* יסתוגר על ידי = 𝕾 *and* 𝕲 (εμπεσοι εις χειρας): 𝕳 *text* יתגבר לפני 'is presumptuous before' l 𝕷 *pr. tit.* de exequiis m–m 𝕳 הזיב (*lit.* 'cause to flow') = 𝕲 καταγαγε : 𝕾 'multiply' (= הרב *Hart*) n–n 𝕳 התמרר : 𝕲 ως δεινα πασχων = כמתמרר o–o 𝕳 ואל תתעלם ('hide not thyself') p–p 𝕳 בגויעתם (*but sing. suff. is required: so read with versions*): 𝕲 (*for whole line*) και μη υπεριδης την ταφην

That His work may not cease, Nor health from the face of His earth. 'His (i. e. God's) work.' The idea is that God's mighty working manifests itself ceaselessly on the earth in the work of the physician. 'The reason . . . is a divine design to encourage science, which otherwise would vanish, being useless. "Miraculous" healing would never have suggested a study of botany or mineralogy' (Edersheim). 𝕲 obscures the meaning.

9. **in sickness be not negligent.** The Hebr. word rendered here 'be negligent' (so 𝕲) means 'to let oneself go', i. e. be careless: so Prov. xiv. 16; Sir. v. 7, vii. 10, 16; cp. xiii. 7, xvi. 8. It is not necessary to alter the text in these passages to התעכר, 'trouble oneself'.

Pray unto God, for He can heal. Cp. Exod. xv. 26.

10. **Turn from iniquity, and purify thy hands . . .** The expression 'clean of hands' ('he that hath clean hands') symbolizes innocence or freedom from guilt; cp. Job xvii. 9, &c. The idea that physical ills are a punishment for sin is here emphasized, as often elsewhere in the O. T.

11. **Give a meal-offering with a memorial.** The sacrifice as described in Lev. ii. 1–3 is meant; the 'memorial' is that part of the *minhah* which is burnt upon the altar. All incense was so burnt (cp. xlv. 16). Lévi restores here: 'Offer incense and a memorial.'

offer a fat sacrifice . . . Cp. vii. 31; Prov. iii. 9, &c.

12. **And to the physician also give a place.** Note the order of Ben-Sira's thought: In sickness first make thy peace with God; resort to prayer and sacrifice; then call in the physician ('for verily the Lord hath created him' is an addition in 𝕲 from *v.* 1).

14. **To make his diagnosis successful, And the treatment . . .** For the text see critical note. The word rendered 'treatment' lit. = 'healing'.

15. **He that sinneth . . . Shall be delivered into the hands of the physician.** This probably means that if a man sins against his Maker he will be punished by sickness and ill health, and will then have to depend upon the physician for relief—God will not help him (presumably till he has made his peace with God). 𝕲 (ἐμπέσοι : but 23 55 254 ἐμπεσεῖται) renders: 'let him fall!' but the alternative rendering is to be preferred.

(*b*) XXXVIII. 16–23. *On mourning for the dead* (= 2 + 2 + 2 + 2 + 2 distichs).

ℌ[B] 16 [l]My son, [m]let tears fall[m] over the dead;
[n]Show thy grief[n] and wail out thy lamentation.
In accordance with what is due to him bury his body,
[o]And hide not thyself[o] [p]when he expires[p].
17 [q]Let thy weeping be bitter and thy wailing passionate[q];
And make mourning such as befits him:
A day or two on account of [r]gossip[r]—
And be consoled [s]on account of (thy) ⌈sorrow⌉[s].
18 [t]For out of sorrow[t] proceedeth [u]bane[u];
[v]Even so[v] [w]sadness of heart[w] [x]⌈prostrateth⌉ vigour[x].
[y] 19 [z]⌈Worse than death is abiding sorrow⌉,
𝔊 (𝔖) And an unfortunate life is cursed by the heart[z].
ℌ[B] 20 [a]And let him no more occupy thy thoughts[a]:
[b]Dismiss the remembrance of him, and remember the end[b].

αυτου ('and neglect not his burial')   q–q ℌ מספד (*mg.* החם) והתם (*mg.* בכי) המר בני : 𝔊 πικρανον κλαυθμον και θερμανον κοπετον = המר בכי והחם מספד (*so Smend restores and reads*): החם מספד = *lit.* 'make hot lamentation'. *Lévi keeping* ℌ *text* התם מספד *renders* 'accomplis exactement les cérémonies funèbres'. 𝔖 (*reading* חמר 'wine' *for* המר) *renders*: 'wine and food for them that lament'   r–r 𝔊 διαβολης = ? דבה (*so read*): ℌ דמעה (𝔖 'of men' = ? העם *from* דמעה: *Lévi*)   s–s ℌ *text* בעבור עון: 𝔊 λυπης ενεκα = ? בעבור דָּוֹן: *so read*: 𝔖 'on account of life'   t–t *So* 𝔊 𝔖: ℌ מדין (*read* כי מִדָּוֹן)   u–u ℌ אסון: 𝔊 θανατος   v–v ℌ כן   w–w ℌ רֹעַ לֵבָב (*cp.* Neh. ii. 3) = 𝔊   x–x καμψει ισχυν = יענה עצמה (*so read*): ℌ *text* יבנה עצבה   y *v.* 19 > ℌ   z–z 𝔖 (*fusing* 18 b *and* 19 a) *has* '[for so an evil heart] more than death crushes through anxiety the poor man and brings distress, for the life of the poor is for a curse of the heart': 𝔊 (*clause* a) εν απαγωγη (א A &c. επαγωγη) παραβαινει (א[c.a] A &c. Syro-Hex 𝔏 παραμενει) και λυπη. *Smend proposes for this line* רע ממות דון עומד. 𝔖 *misread* רע *as* רש: 𝔊 *ignored* רע *and read* (ב)מכות *for* ממות (*cp.* iii. 28 επαγωγη = מכת): *so Smend. The second clause is in* 𝔊 και βιος πτωχου κατα (55 248 254 καταρα) καρδιας   a–a ℌ אל תשיב אליו לב עוד = 'turn not thy heart back to him again': ℌ *mg.* אל תשית עליו לב עוד *i.e. as rendered above*: 𝔊 *seems to have understood* עליו *as* = 'upon it (*i.e.* sorrow)' = 'set not thy heart upon sorrow' (μη δως εις λυπην την καρδιαν σου *which* = אל תתן לדון נפשך, xxx. 21): 𝔖 'upon oaths'   b–b *So* ℌ: 𝔊 (*mitigating the harshness*) αποστησον αυτην μνησθεις τα εσχατα

(*b*) XXXVIII. 16–23. Proper mourning and burial should be bestowed on the dead; but sorrow, unduly prolonged, can only harm the living, and cannot benefit the dead.

16. **let tears fall . . .** Cp. Jer. ix. 17–18.

In accordance with what is due to him bury . . . 'Perhaps in grave-clothes suited to his station' (Edersheim). For the Greek word here used (περίστειλον) cp. Tobit xii. 12 and Ezek. xxix. 5, LXX.

And hide not thyself when he expires. So ℌ (for the expression 'hide thyself', used absolutely as here, cp. Deut. xxii. 3). 𝔊 'And neglect not his burial': this, perhaps, gives the sense fairly correctly. A passage in the Babylonian Talmud, cited by Schechter (*Moed Qatan* 27 *b*), will illustrate the meaning: 'Formerly the funeral (lit. the bringing out) of the dead was more grievous to his relatives than his death—so much so that his relatives used to leave him and flee; until Rabban Gamaliel came and himself set the example of going forth (in the funeral procession) in linen garments,' &c. The abuse referred to is the burden of expense entailed by extravagant funeral fashions, which caused relatives to abandon the dead and take to flight rather than face the requirements. It would seem probable that some such abuse is aimed at in the text. Smend explains the verse as referring to the laws of ritual uncleanness in connexion with a corpse (cp. Num. xix. 14 f.). Rather than incur this impurity people would leave the dying man. But this is most improbable.

17. **Let thy weeping be bitter and thy wailing passionate.** Lit. 'make bitter weeping' (same expression Zech. xii. 10): the Syr. variant here, 'wine and food for them that lament' (see critical note), is interesting. It is an allusion to the customary funeral feast, mentioned in Jer. xvi. 7 (also ?Tobit iv. 17), but the reading is due to misunderstanding of the original text, though some allusion to the custom would have been expected.

A day or two on account of gossip. i.e. to avoid slander or public criticism. 𝔖 has 'on account of people' (generally).

be consoled on account of (thy) sorrow. i.e. after the prescribed days of mourning are ended. These, according to the strict letter of the law, were seven, but in ordinary life may have been reduced to one or two days. 𝔖 has 'on account of life', i.e. that thy own life and health may not suffer. The duty of burying the dead with proper respect is constantly enforced in Rabbinical literature; cp. also the Book of Tobit.

18. **bane.** 𝔊 renders θάνατος. The Hebrew word (אסון) may be understood of sudden death brought about by accident or misfortune; cp. Gen. xlii. 4, 38, xliv. 29; Exod. xxi. 22, 23 (Targ. Onq. renders מותא, 'death,' in all these passages). So again in our book xxxi. (xxxiv.) 21 ℌ (so Smend). Sorrow unduly prolonged will bring sudden misfortune (death).

19. **Worse than death is abiding sorrow . . .** Cp. xxx. 17. The verse is wanting in ℌ: for text see critical note. 𝔊 in clause *a* (B ἐν ἀπαγωγῇ παραβαίνει καὶ λύπη) is explained by Ryssel to mean: with the departure of the corpse from the house, sorrow also passes away (cp. *v.* 23 *a*). (ℌ for 19 *b*? וְחַיֵּי עָנִי קְלָלַת לֵב.)

20. **let him no more occupy thy thoughts.** 𝔊 'give not thy heart unto sorrow': cp. xxx. 21.

remember the end. The sense of the whole verse is: Give not up thy life and energies to vain regrets; remember thine own end, that thou thyself hast to die, and live thy life, while thou hast it, in the right way.

𝔥[B] 21 [cd]Remember him not, for he hath no hope[d];
Thou canst not profit him, while thou harmest thyself.
22 [c]Remember his doom, for it is the doom of thyself—
[e]His[e] yesterday, and thine to-day!
23 [f]When the dead is at rest, let his memory rest[f];
And be consoled when his soul departeth.

(*a*) XXXVIII. 24–30. *The superiority of the scribe over the labourer and artisan* (= 1 + 3 + 3 + 4 + 4 distichs).

24 The wisdom of the scribe [g]increaseth wisdom[g],
And [h]he that hath little business[h] can become wise.
25 How can he become wise that holdeth [i]the goad[i],
And glorieth [j]in brandishing the lance[j]?

[c] 𝔥 *transposes* (*wrongly*) *vv.* 21, 22 (*to* 22, 21)   [d–d] *So* 𝔥 : 𝔊 *again diverges, modifying the original sense:* μη επιλαθη ου γαρ εστιν επανοδος (R.V. 'forget it not, for there is no returning again'): 𝔖 *renders the whole verse:* 'Remember grief and dispel sins, and put not thy trust in riches, for there is no hope in them; for like a bird of the heavens that flieth and alighteth, so is wealth before the sons of men; thee it rejoiceth and another it harmeth'   [e–e] *So* 𝔥 𝔖 : 𝔊 εμοι (*so in clause* a 𝔊 *has* το κριμα μου *except* B 253 308 *which have* αυτου]): *so* A V Syro-Hex. 𝔏   [f–f] 𝔥 *mg.* [זכרו] כשבות מת ישבות = 𝔊 (*but* καταπαυσον *may* = השבת : *cp.* x. 17)   [g–g] *So* 𝔥 = 𝔖 (+'for him'): 𝔊 εν ευκαιρια σχολης (EV 'cometh by opportunity of leisure')   [h–h] *So* 𝔥 : 𝔊 ο ελλασουμενος πραξει αυτου : 𝔖 'he who is not busy with vain things' (ודלא מפרק סריקתא *cp.* 1 Tim. v. 13 *Pesh.*)   [i–i] 𝔥 מלמד = 'ox-goad' (*cp.* Judges iii. 31): 𝔊 αροτρου : 𝔖 'plough-share' (*cp.* LXX *Theod.* Judges iii. 31, αρατροπους : *Vulg.* vomer)   [j–j] 𝔥 *has* בחנית מהעיר = '(who glorieth) by reason of brandishing with the lance' (*cp.* 2 Sam. xxiii. 18): 𝔊 εν δορατι κεντρου = ? בחנית מַרְדֵּעַ : *so Smend reads here* (מרדע = *B.H.* דָּרְבָן)   [k–k] 𝔥 באלוף ינהג (אלוף Ps. cxliv. 14 = אלף) = 𝔊 βοας ελαυνων   [l–l] 𝔥 וישובב בשור (*mg.* וישובב בשיר : *over line*

---

21. **Remember him not, for he hath no hope.** So 𝔥. 𝔊 'forget it (i.e. thy latter end) not, for there is no returning' (? reading תקומה for תקוה, Lévi): for this sentiment cp. Job viii. 8; Wisd. ii. 1.

22. **Remember his doom . . .** Cp. xli. 2, 3.

23. **When the dead is at rest, let his memory rest . . .** Cp. for the sentiment 2 Sam. xii. 23.

XXXVIII. 24—XXXIX. 11, with an Appendix, XXXIX. 12-35. This forms an independent section which has for its general theme the scribes. It falls into three well-defined subsections (besides an Appendix), the first of which brings out the superiority of the scribe over the labourer and artisan (xxxviii. 24–30); then, the place of the craftsman in the civic economy is dwelt upon, but at the same time his inability to fulfil the higher offices of counsellor and judge is set forth (xxxviii. 31–34); the last subsection gives a glowing picture of the work and activity of the true scribe, and of his honourable status (xxxix. 1–11). The Appendix (xxxix. 12–25) contains a hymn of praise for creation.

The whole section is extremely valuable for the light it throws upon the position and character of the older Sopherim, and also, incidentally, on the trades that flourished in Jerusalem in Ben-Sira's days. These earlier scribes, in contrast with the later Teachers of the Law, appear for the most part to have belonged to the upper and wealthy classes (cp., however, xi. 1; Eccles. ix. 16), and to have been separated from the working classes (peasants, labourers, and artisans) by a wide social gulf. They were apparently a leisured class, raised above the necessity of earning a livelihood, who took the lead in public affairs and counsel, and acted as judges in pronouncing judicial decrees (cp. xxxviii. 33). They obviously belonged to the nobility, and perhaps to the noble families of the priesthood (hence their position as judges). They appear to have familiarized themselves with foreign affairs and countries, and to have sometimes occupied positions under foreign monarchs, in which capacity they would naturally act also as the representatives of their own people and state. Smend points out that originally the tradition of the scribes grew out of the priestly *Torah*, and, consequently, the earlier scribes were drawn from the priestly class. This was still the case in the time of Ben-Sira.

(*a*) XXXVIII. 24–30. This subsection is particularly interesting as containing a more or less representative enumeration of the handicrafts that flourished in Jerusalem, by the side of agriculture, when the author wrote. They appear in the following order of precedence: engravers of gems (signets and precious stones), smiths, and potters. Some of the more ordinary trades, such as weaving and carpentry, are passed over, as too obvious to mention, perhaps.

24. **The wisdom of the scribe increaseth wisdom.** Schechter cites *Baba bathra* 21 *a*: 'The emulation of scribes increaseth wisdom' (קנאת סופרים תרבה חכמה). 𝔊 apparently understood 'wisdom' at end of the line to mean 'learned leisure'.

he that hath little business . . . Cp. *Pirqe Aboth* iv. 14: 'R. Meir said: 'Have little business, and be busied in Torah.' But the rule in Mishnaic times was that study of the Law should be combined with a trade; cp. *Pirqe Aboth* ii. 2 ('Rabban Gamaliel said: Excellent is Torah study together with worldly business, for the practice of them both puts iniquity out of remembrance; and all Torah without work must fail at length and occasion iniquity').

25. **And glorieth in brandishing the lance.** The ox-goad is apparently meant here, as in the preceding line (so 𝔊 and Smend's restored text; see critical note). [For phrase 'brandish the lance' cp. 2 Sam. xxiii. 18; 1 Chron. xi. 11 and 20.]

[k]Who leadeth cattle[k] [l]and turneth about oxen[l],
[m]And whose discourse[m] is with bullocks?
26 [mm]He is careful [n]to harrow ⌈the seed-strip⌉[n],
And his anxiety is [o]to complete the provender[o].
27 [p]Likewise the maker of carving and cunning device[p],
Who by night as by day [q]hath no rest[q];
[r]Who engraveth signet-engravings[r],
[s]And whose art it is to make variety of design[s];
He is careful [t]to make the likeness true[t],
And his anxiety is to complete his work.
𝔊(𝔖)[tt] 28 So also [u]the smith[u] that sitteth [v]by the furnace[v],
[w]And regardeth the weighty vessels[w]:
The flame of the fire [x]cracketh[x] his flesh,
And with the heat of the furnace [y]he gloweth[y];
[z]To the sound of the hammer he inclineth his ear[z],
And to the pattern of the vessel [a]directeth[a] his eyes.

לשדר): 𝔊 *και αναστρεφομενος εν εργοις αυτων* m–m 𝔥 ושעיותיו = שׂוּעִיתוֹ = 𝔊 mm 𝔥 (*wrongly*) *transposes clauses* a *and* b *here. In transl. above the clauses follow the right order* n–n 𝔥 (*defective*) לב ישית .... לשד[ר] (*most scholars complete by adding* בתלמים [*cp.* 𝔊]: *but Smend reads* נבלת זרע, *cp.* 𝔖): 𝔊 *εκδουναι αυλακας*: 𝔖 'in his seed-row' (בגלתא דזרעה = *Smend's reading above: cp.* לגנה in *Neo-Hebr.* = 'row': לגנתא *in Targ.*) o–o 𝔥 לכלות מרבק (*Schechter* לבלות מרבק, 'to victual the stall'): 𝔊 *εις χορτασματα δαμαλεων* (= ? בקר (*vel* לכלכל] לאכל)) p–p 𝔥 (*defective: MS. mutilated*) אף עשה חר[ש וח]שב (*point with Peters* חָרָשׁ וְחֹשֵׁב: *others* חָרָשׁ וְחֹשֵׁב): 𝔊 *ουτως πας τεκτων και αρχιτεκτων* q–q 𝔥 *mutilated here: Smend* (*following* 𝔖 *partly*) *restores* [ו]יזיע = 'is (are) restless': 𝔊 *διαγει* = 𝔥 *mg.* ינהג (occupatus est) = *but* נהג *in v.* 25 = 'lead' (𝔖 *for v.* 27 a *and* b *has*: 'So also all the craftsmen are disturbed together, and night and day on them (*i.e. their works*) they think': *here* 'are disturbed' (= ? יזיעו) *has been transposed to the first clause: so Smend*) r–r 𝔊 *οι γλυφοντες γλυμματα σφραγιδων* = (?) מפתח פתחי חותם (*Smend*) s–s 𝔊 *και η υπομονη* (*so* B: *but* א A Syro-Hex 𝔏 *επιμονη*) *αυτου αλλοιωσαι ποικιλιαν*: *η επιμονη αυτου* = (?) אומנותו *and ποικιλιαν* = מחשבה: *αλλοιωσαι* = שׁנה ('change') t–t 𝔊 *εις ομοιωσαι ζωγραφιαν* (*ζωγραφειν* = חקה, חקק Ezek. xxiii. 14, Is. xlix. 16, LXX) [*for* 27 c–f 𝔖 *has*: 'on the work of carvings and signets and of pearls; also their thoughts are needed for the works of their craft'] tt xxxviii. 28–xxxix. 14 *is not extant in* 𝔥 u–u 𝔊 *χαλκευς* = חרשׁ (*worker in metal is meant*) v–v 𝔊 *εγγυς ακμονος* ('by the anvil'): *but* 𝔖 '[to sit] by the furnace' (*rightly*) = ? אצל כור (𝔊 = ? אצל סד: *or is ακμανος a corruption of καμινου*?) w–w 𝔖 'And to consider closely the implements of the balance' (*reading rightly* כלי משקל): 𝔊 *και καταμανθανων αργῳ* (*so* B *wrongly*; V *εργῳ*: 248 Syro-Hex *εν εργῳ*) *σιδηρῳ* (V *σιδηρου*: א 55 106 254 308 *εργα σιδηρου*): *orig. Hebr.* ? והתבונן בכלי משקל (*so Smend*) x–x *τηξει* (א A &c.) = ? יבקע (*cp.* Micah i. 4 LXX, *where τηκομαι* = התבקע): = 𝔖 ('cracketh'): B (V 253 308) *πηξει* ('stiffeneth') y–y 𝔊 *διαμαχησεται*: 𝔖 (*rightly*) 'he burneth' (𝔊 *a misrendering of* התחרה) z–z 𝔊 *φωνη σφυρης* (+ *ακμονος* 248) *καινιει το ους αυτου* ('The noise of the hammer reneweth his ear'): *but* 𝔖 ('Over against the model he will bend his hand') *suggests κλινει for καινιει*: *so read* (*and accentuate φωνῇ*) a–a *Cp.* 𝔖 'And over against the image of his work his eyes shall

---

Who leadeth cattle and turneth about oxen. 𝔥 mg. gives an excellent sense ('Who leadeth cattle and turneth them about with song'): the construction of the Hebrew is easier, and it may be right (so Smend).

26. **He is careful to harrow the seed-strip.** lit. 'he setteth his heart' (ישית לבו 𝔊 καρδίαν αὐτοῦ δώσει). In Palestine the field is arranged in separate seed-strips, which are ploughed and sown separately. See further on this point Krauss, *Talmudische Archäologie*, ii. 179 f.

his anxiety is to complete the provender. 𝔊 'his sleepless care is for provender of heifers'; cp. Gen. xv. 9, xxiv. 35. See further critical note.

27. **Likewise the maker of carving and cunning device.** 'Likewise,' i.e. is likewise prevented by the demands of his craft from enjoying the leisure necessary for a member of the learned class (a scribe). It is best to regard the verse as dealing with one class of workers only, viz. the engravers of precious stones (seals and gems; so 𝔖). For this form of art see Benzinger, *Archäol.*, 258 f., and cp. art. 'Engraving' in *JE*. Smend understands two classes to be referred to, the gem-engravers and the weavers of embroidered stuffs; he renders 27 *d* 'and he also whose art it is to weave embroidery' ('und auch der, dessen [Kunst] es ist, bunt zu weben'). But this is less probable.

28. **So also the smith that sitteth by the furnace.** The worker in metals is meant, here denoted by the Heb. term חרש probably. The work of the smith, as here described, is more particularly associated with the furnace, in which the ore was melted, and the anvil, on which the metal was beaten out (cp. Is. xliv. 12). With the present passage cp. also Ezek. xxii. 18–22; and see further *s.v.* 'metals' in *EB* and *JE*; cp. also Krauss, *op. cit.* ii. 299 f. [𝔊 reads 'by the anvil'; but the rendering adopted is supported by the context; see further critical note.]

And to the pattern of the vessel directeth his eyes. This clause apparently refers to the hammering out of the metal according to a model.

𝕲 (𝕾) He is careful to complete his work,
And his anxiety is [b]to measure it off exactly[b].
𝕾 (𝕲) 29 Likewise the potter who sitteth [c]at his wheel[c],
[d]And driveth the vessel with the soles of his feet[d];
[e]Who is all the time in anxiety over his work[e],
[f]And all his handiwork is [g]by number[g f];
30 [h]His arms are cracked by the clay[h],
[i]And ⌜before old age⌝ he is bent and bowed[i];
He is careful to complete [j]the glazing[j],
And his anxiety is [k]for the heating of[k] the furnace.

(*b*) XXXVIII. 31–34. *Though unfitted for the highest offices the craftsman fills an essential place* (=2+2+2 distichs).

31 All these [l]are deft[l] with their hands,
And each is wise [m]in his handiwork[m].
32 Without them a city cannot be inhabited,
[n]And wherever they dwell they hunger not[n].
33 [o]But they shall not be inquired of for public counsel[o],
And in the assembly [p]they enjoy no precedence[p].

be directed' (𝕲 > 'directeth') b–b 𝕲 κοσμησαι επι συντελειας (*cp.* xlvii. 10): κοσμειν = תקן xlii. 21; *cp.* xvi. 27 c–c *So* 𝕾 (על גיגלא): 𝕲 εν εργῳ αυτου d–d *So* 𝕾: 𝕲 και συστρεφων εν ποσιν αυτου τροχον (א^c.a πηλον) e–e *So* 𝕲 (𝕾 > *the line*) f–f *So* 𝕲: 𝕾 (*in disorder and corrupt*) 'And his eyes are upon the vessels of all his work' g–g 𝕲 εναριθμοις (B &c.), εν αριθμῳ (55 153), εν αριθμοις (307) h–h 𝕾 'His arms break up (split) the clay' (*transposing subject and object*): 𝕲 εν βραχιονι αυτου τυπωσει πηλον i–i 𝕾 'And until he die he is bowed down and bent': 𝕲 και προ ποδων καμψει ισχυν αυτου [*Smend conjectures* לפני שׁיבה *for* לפני מות *in* 𝕾] j–j 𝕲 (א A V &c. 𝕷) χρισμα = משחה (𝕾 'his work': ? *confusing with* מעשׂה) k–k 𝕲 καθαρισαι: 𝕾 'to build' (*context demands* 'to heat' = לבער: καθαρισαι *wrong transl. of* בער *in* LXX: *cp.* Hos. vii. 4, Jer. xxxvi. 22) l–l 𝕲 ενεπιστευσαν (εις χειρας αυτων): EV 'put their trust in their hands' (*probably mistranslating* אֻמָּן *or* אוּמָּן: *so Smend*): 𝕾 'for the sake of their advantage' (?) m–m 𝕲 εν τῳ εργῳ αυτου: 𝕾 'in the work of their craft' n–n *So* 𝕾: 𝕲 και ου (? *read* οὗ) παροικησουσιν ουδε περιπατησουσιν (? *last two words corrupted from* ου μη πεινασωσιν: *Edersh. suggests confusion between* יערבו *and* ירעבו) o–o 𝕲 (א^c.a) αλλ εις βουλην λαου ζητηθησεται: 70 248 εν βουλῃ λαου ου ζητηθησεται = 𝕾 p–p 𝕲 ουχ υπεραλουνται = ? לא ירומו (*so* 𝕾) q–q *This is the order of the clauses in* א A V = 𝕾: B *has them in the inverted order* r–r 𝕾 'covenants and judgements' (*suggests* 𝕳 חק ומשפט, *cp.* xlv. 17: *so read with Smend*): 𝕲 διαθηκην κριματος s–s 𝕲 εκφανωσιν = יביעו (*cp.* xvi. 25): 𝕾 'consider' (? *reading* יבינו *for* יביעו) t–t *So* 𝕾 (יולפנא דחכמתא) = ? מוסר שכל: 𝕲 (א A V &c. 𝕷) παιδειαν (B 253 308 δικαιοσυνην):

---

to measure it off exactly. R.V. (= 𝕲) 'to adorn them (the vessels made) perfectly'; the Greek κοσμῆσαι might be understood of the polishing of the metal, but probably = a Hebrew word meaning 'to measure off' (see critical note). The reference will then be to getting the dimensions of the finished vessel exact.

29. **Likewise the potter.** For the work of the potter as here described cp. the art. 'Pottery' in *EB* and *JE*; also Krauss, *op. cit.*, ii. 271 f.

who sitteth at his wheel. Cp. Jer. xviii. 3–4.

all his handiwork is by number. The meaning seems to be that the potter goes on mechanically multiplying his products, which are all of one uniform quality (the reading of some Gr. MSS. 'without number', i.e. endless, is a correction).

30. **His arms are cracked by the clay.** i.e. his hands are cracked and disfigured by his work. For the text see critical note (the correction is necessitated by the context, which describes what the potter suffers from his work. 𝕲 'he fashioneth the clay with his arm' does not yield a suitable sense: the clay is prepared by stamping [cp. Isa. xli. 25], and manipulated on the wheel with the hands).

the glazing. Probably smearing with paint, which was then polished; see *EB*, *s.v.* 'Pottery', § 10.

for the heating of the furnace. R.V. (= 𝕲) 'to make clean the furnace'; but the furnace of the potter required no cleansing, as the soot was destroyed by the great heat. What was necessary was to raise the furnace to the greatest possible heat, and maintain it there; cp. xxvii. 5.

(*b*) XXXVIII. 31–34. This subsection follows closely on the preceding in logical order, by bringing out the value of the craftsman for the community; but, at the same time, his inability to fill the higher public offices is emphasized.

32. **Without them a city cannot be inhabited.** Cp. xvi. 4.

they hunger not. i.e. have no difficulty in finding work and bread (𝕲 yields no coherent sense).

33. **But they shall not be inquired of . . .** The clauses that follow refer to the public work of the scribes, who must have included priests to some extent (cp. xlv. 17).

(𝕲) [q]On the seat of the judge they do not sit,
[r]And law and justice[r] they understand not[q].
[s]They do not expound[s] [t]the instruction of wisdom[t],
[tt]Nor understand the proverbs of the wise[tt];
34 [u]But they understand the work [they have wrought][u],
And [v]their thought[v] is on the practice of their craft.

(*c*) XXXIX. 1–11. *The ideal scribe described* (= 2 + 2 + 2 + 2 + 4 + 2 + 2 distichs).

39
1 Not so he that applieth himself [w]to the fear of God[w],
[x]And to set his mind[x] upon the Law of the Most High;
Who searcheth out the wisdom of all the ancients,
And [y]is occupied[y] [z]with the prophets of old[z];
2 Who [a]heedeth[a] [b]the discourses[b] of men of renown,
And [c]entereth[c] [d]into the deep things of parables[d];
3 Searcheth out [e]the hidden meaning[e] of proverbs,
And [f]is conversant[f] [g]with the dark sayings of parables[g];
4 [h]Who serveth among great men,
And appeareth before princes[h];
Who travelleth [i]through the lands of the peoples[i],
[j]Testeth[j] good and evil among men;
5 Who is careful [k]to seek[k] [l]unto his Maker[l],
And [m]before[m] the Most High [n]entreateth mercy[n];

𝕾 *here* = παιδειαν διδασκαλιας (*cp.* xxxix. 8) tt–tt *So* 𝕾: 𝕲 και εν παραβολαις ουχ ευρηθησονται u–u 𝕾 'for (= כי) they are skilled in the works of the world': 𝕲 αλλα (= כי) κτισμα αιωνος τηρησουσιν (*so* B: στηρισουσι, στηριουσι ℵ[c.a] 248): στηρισουσι = יכינו, *corrupt for* יבינו (= ? 𝕾): κτισμα = מעשׂה (*so* xxxvi. 24): *both* 𝕲 *and* 𝕾 *appear to have read* עולם, *which may have arisen, as Smend suggests, from* פעלם (*so read*) v–v *So* 𝕾 (רניהון): 𝕲 η δεησις αυτων (𝕳 ? הגותם: *so Smend*) w–w *So* 𝕾 (*rightly*): 𝕲 > x–x *So* 𝕾 (= ? להתבונן): 𝕲 και διανοουμενου y–y 𝕲 ασχοληθησεται: *cp.* ασχολια xl. 1 = עסק: 𝕾 'turns (to the', &c.) z–z 𝕷 in prophetis (*cp.* 𝕷 *of* xli. 3, xliv. 22): *cp.* 𝕾 ('to the prophets of old'): 𝕲 εν προφητειαις a–a 𝕲 συντηρησει = ישמר *or* ינצר ('treasureth'): *cp.* Prov. iii. 1: 𝕾 'learneth' b–b 𝕲 (B 248 308) διηγησεις (*but the rest and* 𝕷 Sah διηγησιν) c–c 𝕲 συνεισελευσεται: *cp.* בא Ps. lxxiii. 17: 𝕾 'thinketh' d–d 𝕲 εν στροφαις παραβολων: 𝕾 'on what is deep (= ? מעמקים) *corrupted in* 𝕲*'s MS. to* מעקמים √עקם *Aram.* 'perverse, crooked': *Edersh.*) e–e 𝕲 αποκρυφα = נסתרות (𝕾 *misplaces in next clause*) f–f 𝕲 αναστραφησεται: *cp.* viii. 8, l. 28 g–g 𝕲 εν αινιγμασι παραβολων h–h 𝕾 (*with clauses transposed*) 'and in the midst of the powerful he goeth, and in the midst of kings and of great ones he serveth': 𝕲 = *translation above* i–i 𝕲 εν γη αλλοτριων εθνων: 𝕾 'through the cities of the world' (? דעלמא *for* דעממא) — 𝕳 ? בארץ העמים — 'through the land of the peoples' j–j 𝕲 (αγαθα) γαρ . . . επειρασε (*but* ℵ* > γαρ: *so* 𝕾): 𝕷 tentabit (*rightly*: επειρασε *wrong tense*): *so* 𝕾 k–k 𝕲 ορθρισαι = לשחר (𝕷 ad virgilandum diluculo): 𝕾 'to pray' l–l 𝕾 >: 𝕲 προς κυριον τον ποιησαντα αυτον (κυριον *prob. gloss*: *omit*) m–m *So* 𝕲 (εναντι):

34. **their thought is on the practice of their craft.** Their mental horizon is bounded by the requirements of their craft.

(*c*) XXXIX. 1–11. This, the last of the three subsections (apart from the Appendix), gives a glowing picture of the work and position of the ideal scribe.

1. **Not so he that applieth himself . . . the Law of the Most High.** Cp. the description of Ezra, the ideal scribe, in Ezra vii. 10.

Who searcheth out the wisdom of all the ancients . . . the prophets of old. One, the principal, source of the scribe's knowledge is thus defined as the Law, the Wisdom books, and the Prophets. The other source of the scribe's wisdom, as described in *vv.* 2 and 3, is an oral tradition; but the descriptive terms employed do not suggest that it was legalistic or halakic in character, but rather of the type embodied in the Wisdom literature (proverbs, sententious sayings, maxims for the conduct of life, perhaps (?) allegories).

2, 3. **entereth into the deep things of parables . . . hidden meaning of proverbs . . . dark sayings of parables.** Cp. the description of Wisdom in Wisd. viii. 8 ('she understandeth subtilties of speeches and interpretations of dark sayings'). For 'deep things of parables' 𝕲 has 'subtilties (στροφαί) of parables': cp. Prov. i. 3 (also Wisd. viii. 8); what is meant is the process of investigation described in *v.* 3, by which the 'hidden meaning' is deduced—all that is implicit in the sayings.

4. **Who serveth among great men . . .** Cp. xxxi. (𝕲 xxxiv.) 9–12 and notes there. The wisdom of the scribe is culture—they are identical—and therefore the scribe has access to royal courts and enters into the service of kings. The high estimation of travel and foreign experience is particularly interesting. The education of the ideal scribe is broad and humanistic.

𝔖 (𝔊) Who openeth his mouth in prayer,
And [o]maketh supplication[o] for his sins.
6 [p]If[p] [q]it seem good to God Most High[q],
[r]He shall be filled[r] with the spirit of understanding.
[s]He himself poureth forth wise sayings in double measure[s],
And giveth thanks [t]unto the Lord in prayer[t].
7 He himself [u]directeth[u] [v]counsel and knowledge[v],
[w]And setteth his mind[w] on [x]their[x] secrets.
8 He himself declareth [y]wise instruction[y],
And glorieth in the law [z]of the Lord[z].
9 His understanding many do praise,
[a]And[a] never shall [b]his name[b] be blotted out:
His memory [c]shall not cease[c],
And his name shall live from generation to generation.
ℌ 10 [d][e]His wisdom[e] doth [f]the congregation[f] tell forth,
And [g]his praise[g] the assembly publisheth.
𝔖(𝔊) 11 [h]If he live long[h], [i]he shall be accounted happy[i] more than a thousand;
And when he cometh to an end, [j]his name sufficeth[j].

(*d*) Appendix. XXXIX. 12–35. *Hymn in praise of creation* (= 3+3 and 2+2+3+3+2+2+1+2+2+2 and 3+1 distichs).

12 [k]Yet again will I fix my thoughts and ⌈make my doctrine to shine forth⌉[k],
[l]As the full moon on the twelfth day[l].

𝔖 'from before' n–n *So* 𝔖: 𝔊 δεηθησεται o–o *So* 𝔊 (δεηθησεται): 𝔖 'seeketh good' (*perhaps* 'good' *belongs to next verse*) p–p 𝔊 εαν (+γαρ 106 155 157 296 307 308 𝔏) q–q 𝔊 (εαν) κυριος ο μεγας θεληση (κυριος ο μεγας = אל עליון: *cp.* xlvi. 5): 𝔖>(*but* 'good' *at end of previous verse may be a remnant of this clause: then the line may have run in* ℌ אם טוב בעיני אל עליון: *so Smend*) r–r *So* 𝔊: 𝔖 'he shall be made wise' s–s 𝔖 'he giveth out parables doubly' = ℌ הוא יביע משלים פי שנים: 𝔊 ανομβρησει ρηματα σοφιας αυτος t–t *So* 𝔊: 𝔖 'unto Him in his thoughts' (*reading* לו *for* ליי) u–u 𝔊 κατευθυνει (= יכין): 𝔖 'understandeth' (= יבין) v–v *So* 𝔊 (βουλην αυτου [א 254 𝔏>αυτου *rightly*] και επιστημην): 𝔖 'parables of the wise' w–w και . . . διανοηθησεται = התבונן (vi. 37: xlii. 18) x–x 𝔊 αυτου (*mistake for* αυτων *or* αυτης) y–y 𝔖 'instruction of wisdom' (= מוסר שׂכל): 𝔊 παιδειαν διδασκαλιας αυτου z–z 𝔊 διαθηκης κυριου (*probably* διαθηκη *and* νομῳ *original variants*): 𝔖 'of life' a–a א A C &c. Syro-Hex 𝔏 *have* και (εως): *so* 𝔖: B>και b–b *So* 𝔖 (*rightly*): 𝔊> c–c 𝔊 ουκ αποστησεται (= ?לא יחדל: *cp.* Job vii. 16 LXX) d *This verse follows* xliv. 14 *in* ℌ e–e *So* 𝔊: ℌ חכמתם f–f ℌ עדה 𝔊 εθνη g–g *So* 𝔊: ℌ תהלתם h–h 𝔊 εαν εμμεινῃ (= ?אם יעמד = 'if he abide' [*sc. in life*]) i–i 𝔊 'he shall leave a name' (*but does not harmonize with the context*') = ?ישאר, *a mistake for* יאשר [*so Smend*] = 𝔖 (ονομα *from next line in* 𝔊) j–j 𝔊 εμποιει αυτῳ (*? origin.* εμποιει τῃ ονοματι αυτου: *cp.* xlii. 17 = יספוק שמו) k–k 𝔊 ετι (א Sah + δε) διανοηθεις εκδιηγησομαι: 𝔖 'attend (understand) and I will say my doctrine': *but the next clause suggests that a verb meaning to* 'give light' *originally stood at end of first line—perhaps, as Smend suggests,* אאיר *which* 𝔖 *read* אומר (*so* xxiv. 32 𝔊 φωτιω = אמר *in* 𝔖): ?ℌ עוד אתבונן ואאיר מוסר l–l *So* 𝔖 ('as the moon on the day of the Twelfths'): 𝔊 και (248, 70 οτι: 𝔏 enim) ως διχομηνια επληρωθην (ℌ

5. **Who is careful to seek unto his Maker . . .** The note of true piety is strongly emphasized, as always. The cultivated humanists of Israel always kept a firm hold on the practical side of religion.

6. **If it seem good to God Most High.** Even when the conditions previously mentioned have been fulfilled, special grace is still required to inspire the scribe with the spirit of true wisdom.

He himself poureth forth wise sayings in double measure. i.e. he is not merely dependent upon the tradition which he has inherited, but puts forth what is his own: contrast the ideal of the later teachers of the Law—e.g. 'Eliezer b. Hyrqanos is a plastered cistern which loseth not a drop' (i.e. is a mere receptacle of tradition: *Pirqe Aboth*, ed. Taylor, ii. 10). The attitude of the earlier Sopherim to tradition was essentially freer and more independent. For 'in double measure' (a double portion) cp. xii. 5, xviii. 32 in ℌ.

8. **wise instruction.** Cp. l. 27, xxxviii. 33 *e*.

glorieth in. Cp., for expression, xxxviii. 6, l. 20.

9. **his name shall live . . .** Cf. xxxvii. 26, xliv. 14.

10. **His wisdom doth the congregation tell forth . . .** = xliv. 15 (10*b* = xxxi. [xxxiv.] 11*b*). 𝔊 misrenders 'congregation' (עדה) here by 'nations'; so by 'peoples' xliv. 15, cp. 'people', xlvi. 7.

11. **If he live long . . .** i.e. if long life is granted to him his reputation is assured; he reaps fame and honour; and when he dies 'his name sufficeth', i.e. in memory—his memory lives on and is cherished. For the text of verse see critical notes. The versions misunderstood it.

(𝔊) 13 Hearken unto me, [m]ye pious[m], and [n]your flesh shall grow[n],
[o]Like the cedar[o] that is planted [p]by streams of water[p].
14 [q]Your scent shall be sweet as Lebanon[q],
[r]And ye shall put forth blossoms as the lily[r].
[s]Lift up your voice[s] and [t]sing together[t],
[u]And[u] [v]bless[v] the Lord for all His works.
15 [w]O magnify His name,
And acknowledge Him with praise[w],
𝔥[B] [x]With songs of the harp[x] [y]and of stringed instruments[y];
And [z]thus shall ye say[z], [a]with a shout[a]:

16 The works of God [b]are all good[b],
[c]And supply every need in its season[c].
7 (21 c) [cc]None may say: This is worse than that;
(21 d) For everything availeth in its season[cc].
[d](By His word) He ordereth (the luminaries in the heavenly height)[d],
[e]And by the utterance of His mouth in His treasury[e].

? כירח מלא בשנים עשׂר, *cp.* l. 6) m–m 𝔊 υιοι οσιοι (*but* 248 Syro-Hex > υιοι; V 253 *have* οι *instead*): 𝔖 זדיקא n–n *So* 𝔖: 𝔊 και βλαστησατε o–o 𝔖 'like the lilies' (*from v.* 14) 'and like cedars': 𝔊 ως ροδον = 𝔏 (? 'rose' *substituted for* 'cedar') p–p 𝔊 επι ρευματος υγρου (*so* א A C V &c.: *but* B αγρου): = *Clem. Alex.* επι ρευματων υδατων: 𝔏 super rivos aquarum: 𝔖 'on the water' (*cp.* יבלי מים *l.* 8) q–q 𝔖 'and like pleasant odours (= לבונה) shall your scent be sweet, like the scent of Lebanon with its cedars' (*a double rendering*): = ? וכלבנון יריח ריחכם: 𝔊 και ως λιβανος ευωδιασατε οσμην r–r *So* 𝔊: 𝔖 'and like the root of the king's lilies' s–s *So* 𝔖: 𝔊 διαδοτε οσμην (*wrong rend.*) t–t αινεσατε ασμα—*but read* αμα = 𝔖 u–u *Clem. Alex.* 𝔏 *here* και (*so* 𝔖): 𝔊> v–v *So* 𝔊 (ευλογησατε = ברכו): 𝔖 = והודו ('and give thanks') w–w 𝔊 δοτε τῳ ονοματι αυτου μεγαλωσυνην (*cp.* הבו גדל Deut. xxxii. 3) και εξομολογησασθε εν αινεσει αυτου (*Clem. Alex. and* 𝔏 *have* αυτῳ *for* εν αινεσει αυτου: Eth *places* αυτῳ *after* εξομολ.: *read* αυτῳ εν αινεσι (*so Smend*)): 𝔖 'recount His mighty deeds with praises' x–x 𝔥 בשירות נבל: 𝔊 εν ῳδαις χειλεων (*corrupt for* χελυων) y–y 𝔥 וכלי מיני (*i. e.* מִנִּי *for* מִנִּים *as in* Ps. xlv. 9 = 'strings'): *so Smend, Strack*: *Lévi reads* וכל מיני שיר 'all kinds of music': 𝔊 και εν κινυραις z–z *So* 𝔊 𝔖: 𝔥 תאמר a–a 𝔥 בתרועה: 𝔊 εν εξομολογησει b–b *So* 𝔥: 𝔊 παντα οτι καλα σφοδρα (𝔖 + 'together') c–c *So* 𝔥 *mg.* (𝔥 *text* 'And He supplieth every need in its season'): 𝔖 'And they all for their functions were created': 𝔊 και παν προσταγμα εν καιρῳ αυτου εσται cc–cc *These two lines misplaced in* 𝔥—*transposed to follow* 21 a *and* b *on account of similarity with that verse: with v.* 16 *they form a sort of refrain, which is repeated in vv.* 33–34. 𝔖 *has also a misplacement: vv.* 16, 21, 17 d–d 𝔥 *is here defective* (*one word*, יעריך, *is legible*): 𝔊 εν λογῳ αυτου εστη ως θιμωνια υδωρ = ? בדברו יעמוד כנד מים (*cp.* Ps. xxxiii. 7): 𝔖 'at His word the sun rises and at His word it sets': *according to Smend* 𝔖 *read* בדברו יערוך נר *and paraphrased as above*: 𝔊 *read* נד *for* נר *and thinking of* Exod. xv. 8, Ps. xxxiii. 7 *rendered as above*: *Smend restores* בדברו יערוך נר [במ]ר[ו]ם (*in* xl. 11 מרום *is misrendered in* 𝔊 *by* υδατων): *Ryssel* בד' יעמיד על עמדים (—'He stations [them] at [their] stations': *cp.* 2 Chron. xxx. 16; Neh. xiii. 11): *Lévi* ומה תעריך אליו ('and what wilt thou compare unto Him?') e–e 𝔥 ומוצא פיו

(*d*) APPENDIX: XXXIX. 12–35.

With xxxix. 11 a distinct division of the book ends. The hymn that follows in xxxix. 12–35 may, perhaps, be regarded as an appendix to the preceding section, which extols the wisdom of the ideal scribe. It may be intended to serve as a specimen of such 'wisdom'—an example of the Sopheric teaching. Its theme is the creation and the divine government of the world, which are revealed everywhere as all-wise. *vv.* 12–15 form an introduction, 16–31 the song proper, and 32–35 an epilogue.

12. **Yet again . . . my doctrine shine forth . . .** The author means, 'I will set forth the best doctrine I can express.' For the figure cp. xxiv. 16.

the full moon on the twelfth day. The reckoning may depend upon an inaccurate observation of the time of the new moon (Smend).

13. **your flesh shall grow . . .** i. e. ye shall flourish and prosper (a promise). For the figures in this verse cp. xxiv. 17 f.; Hos. xiv. 6 f.; Ps. i. 3, xcii. 13, 14.

like the cedar . . . by streams of water. For cedars by water cp. Numb. xxiv. 6; Ezek. xxxi. 3 f.

15. **and of stringed instruments** (וכלי מיני [מִנִּים]). Cp. Ps. xlv. 9, cl. 4.

16. **The works of God are all good.** 𝔊 has 'exceedingly (σφόδρα) good'. Cp. Gen. i. 31, 33.

And supply every need in its season. So 𝔥 mg. 𝔥 text: 'He (God) supplieth.' 𝔊 'and every command (? וכל צִוּוּי for כל צורך) shall be'.

17 *a*, *b* (= 𝔥 21 *c*, *d*). **None may say: This is worse than that; for everything availeth in its season.** These two lines have been misplaced in 𝔥 (at beginning, cp. *v.* 21); 𝔊 has them in the right place (in a modified form); correct 𝔊 17 *a* (τί τοῦτο; εἰς τί τοῦτο; to τοῦτο τούτου πονηρότερον, as in *v.* 34 *a*). The four lines (beginning 'The works of God are all good') thus form a refrain, being repeated in *vv.* 33–34 at end of the poem. They express the burden of the whole composition.

(By His word) . . . treasury. For the text of this difficult verse see critical notes. The meaning of the rendering

ℌ[B] 18 [f]In His place (?) His good pleasure attaineth its end[f],
And there is no [g]restraint[g] to His deliverance.
19 [h]The works[h] of all flesh are before Him,
And there is nothing hid from before His eyes.
20 [i]From everlasting to everlasting He beholdeth[i],
[j]And there is nothing small or petty with Him;
Is there limit (?) to His deliverance?[j]
There is nothing too wonderful or hard for Him.

[k] 21 (*a*) None may say: [l]Wherefore is this[l]?
21 (*b*) For everything [m]is selected for its use[m].
22 [n]His blessing[n] overfloweth as the Nile,
And [o]saturateth[o] the world [p]like the River[p].
23 [q]Even so His wrath dispossesseth nations[q],
And He turneth a watered land into salt.
24 [r]His paths[r] [s]are plain for the blameless[s];
Even so [t]they offer obstacles[t] [u]to the presumptuous[u].

אוצרו ('And the utterance of His mouth is His treasure'): 𝔊 και εν ρηματι στοματος αυτου αποδοχεια υδατων (*so Smend corrects to* ובמוצא) f–f *So* ℌ (?): 𝔊 εν προσταγματι αυτου πασα η ευδοκια g–g 𝔊 ος ελαττωσει (*cp.* 𝔖): *but Clem. Alex.* ελαττωσις (= ? מחסור *for* מעצור) h–h *So* 𝔊, 𝔖: ℌ מַעֲשֵׂה i–i *So* ℌ *and* 𝔊: 𝔖 > j–j *In* ℌ *these clauses are inverted: probably they should stand as above so that clauses* b *and* d (*as in vv.* 18 *and* 19) *may begin with* אין (ואין): 𝔊 > *clauses* b *and* c (*? passing accidentally from first* ואין *to second*): *clause* b (c) ('there is nothing small', &c.) *is attested by* 𝔖 *as well as* ℌ (*against* 𝔊) k 𝔖 *places the two clauses corresponding to this verse after v.* 17. l–l ℌ זה למה זה: 𝔊 τι τουτο; εις τι τουτο; = 𝔖 m–m ℌ לצרכו נבחר: 𝔊 εις χρειας αυτων εκτισται (= נברא *for* נבחר: *so* 𝔖) n–n *So* 𝔊 𝔖: ℌ ברכות (*read* ברכתו) o–o ℌ רותה: 𝔊 επεκαλυψεν (*mistake for* επεκλυσεν = 𝔏 inundavit) p–p ℌ כנהר: 𝔊 ως κατακλυσμος (= כַּמַּבּוּל: *so Peters reads*) q–q *So* ℌ *and* 𝔏: 𝔊 ουτως οργην (א[c.a] Sah Eth *rightly* οργη) αυτου εθνη κληρονομησει (𝔖 *for* יוריש *has* 'judgeth') r–r *So* 𝔊: ℌ [תמים יישרו] ארחות = 'the paths of the blameless are straight' = 𝔖 (+ 'before his face') s–s *Read* לתמים יישרו: ℌ *mg.* = 𝔊 (ארחותיו [לי]שרים יישרו: 'His paths are straightforward to the straight'—*note word-play*) t–t ℌ יסתוללו: 𝔊 προσκομματα u–u *So* 𝔊 𝔖: ℌ לזרים (*read* לזדים) v–v *So* ℌ (חלק): 𝔊 εκτισται ('are

---

here given is that God, the great and all-wise Creator, disposes the heavenly bodies in their due order, and controls their movements. 'In His treasury' = in God's (celestial) treasury; cp. Deut. xxviii. 12 ('J. shall open to thee His good treasury, the heaven'); cp. Jer. l. 25. The lit. translation of 17 *b*, as the Hebr. text stands, is 'and the utterance of His (God's) mouth is His treasure': another suggestion is to read נוצרו for אוצרו; then render 'and (by) the utterance of His mouth they were formed'. Peters reads:

בדברו מים יערוך נד
ובמוצא פיו אוצרות:

'By His word the waters formed a heap (wall),
And by the utterance of His mouth treasuries.'

There is then an allusion to Ps. xxxiii. 7 and Exod. xv. 8; cp. 𝔊 (R. V.).

18. **In His place (?) His good pleasure attaineth its end.** 'In His place' = where He (God) is; cp. for the phrase 2 Sam. iii. 12. 𝔊 has 'in (*or* at) His command'. Peters, following this, reads: בְּצִוָּתוֹ רצונו יצליח = 'when He commandeth, His will attaineth its end' (an excellent sense, which may be right). For the last phrase cp. xi. 17 *b*, xliii. 26 *a*.

19. **The works of all flesh are before Him . . .** Cf. xvii. 15.

20. **From everlasting to everlasting He beholdeth.** Nothing escapes Him—past, present, and future are open before Him. For the thought cp. xlii. 18 f.

Is there limit (lit. number) **to His deliverance?** Cp. for phrase Job xxv. 3. Wellhausen and others would read לִתְשׁוּעָתוֹ (a formation from שׁעה like תבנית): then render 'Is there limit to His vision?'

21–27. God's works are a blessing to the pious, but a source of evil to the wicked.

21. **For everything is selected** (or **created**) **for its use.** Cf. *Qoh.* iii. 7 ('He hath made everything beautiful in its season').

22. **as the Nile.** The yearly overflow of the Nile is meant, which fertilizes the country adjacent.

like the River. i. e. the Euphrates; also much used for purposes of irrigation.

23. **His wrath dispossesseth nations.** The Canaanites are referred to; cp. xvi. 9.

turneth a watered land into salt. There is an allusion to Ps. cvii. 34; Sodom and Gomorrah are referred to.

24. **His paths are plain for the blameless.** Cp. Ps. xviii. 25 (26) f.

offer obstacles. The Hebr. word here (יסתוללו) may be taken to mean 'lift themselves up as a breastwork' (סללה) or obstacle; for the sentiment of the whole verse cp. Hos. xiv. 9 *b* ('for the ways of J. are right, and the just shall walk in them; but transgressors shall fall therein').

ℌ[B] 25 Good things for the good[v] hath He allotted[v] from the beginning;
Even so to the evil [w]good and evil[w].
26 [x](The chief of all the necessaries)[x] of life for man
Are water and fire, and iron and salt,
[xx]The fat of wheat[xx], milk and honey,
The blood of the grape, oil and clothing.
27 All these prove good to the good—
Even so for the evil they are turned [y]to evil[y].
28 [z]There are (winds) which are formed (for punishment)[z],
[a](And in their fury)[a] [b]remove moun(tains)[b].
𝔊 (𝔖) [c]In the season of destruction they pour out their force,
And appease the spirit of their creator[c].
ℌ[B] 29 Fire and hail, [d][famine][d] and pestilence—
These also are formed for judgement.
30 [e]Beasts of prey[e], scorpions and vipers,
And the avenging sword to exterminate the wicked—
[f]All these are created for their uses,
And are in the treasure-house (ready) to be requisitioned in due time[f]:
31 When He giveth them the command they rejoice,
And [g]in their prescribed tasks[g] disobey not His behest.

32 Therefore from the beginning [h]I was assured[h],
And when I had considered it I set it down in writing:

created')=𝔖 (= חֲלַק): *so* ℌ=𝔏 𝔖   w-w 𝔊 κακα   x-x ℌ *defective*: 𝔊 αρχη πασης χρειας (=ראש כל צורך: *so read with Peters*: *Smend* [ראש כל[היי)   xx-xx 𝔊 και σεμιδαλις πυρος (= ?חלב חטה: *cp.* 𝔖 'fat and wheat')   y-y ℌ לרעה = 𝔊 (𝔖 ?): ℌ *mg.* לזרא (= 'to loathing': *cp.* xxxvii. 30)   z-z ℌ *defective*: 𝔊 εστιν πνευματα α εις εκδικησιν εκτισται (*restore* ℌ יש רוחות למשפט נוצרו: *so Lévi, Peters, Smend* לנקם)   a-a ℌ *defective: the missing words* (= 𝔊 και εν θυμῳ αυτων) = ובאפיהם; *cp.* xlv. 24, xlviii. 10 (*Peters*): *but Lévi, Smend* ובאפם   b-b = ℌ הרים יעתיקו: 𝔊 εστερεωσαν μαστιγας αυτων (= ?עריהם ירקעו: *cp.* Jer. xv. 8, Hos. xi. 9, LXX, *and Hebr.*: *but Smend* צורים, *cp.* Job xiv. 18, xviii. 4)   c-c = 𝔊 = ℌ ובעת כלה חילם ישפכו ורוח בוראם ישביתו (*Peters*)   d-d *So* 𝔊: ℌ רע (*read* רעב): *cp.* xl. 9 (*where read* רעב *for* רעה)   e-e ℌ חית שֵׁן (*cp.* xii. 13) = 𝔊 θηριων οδοντες (ℌ *lit.* 'beasts of tooth')   f-f *Clauses* c *and* d *are preserved in* ℌ:

כל אלה לצורכם נבראו
והמה באוצר ולעת יפקדו:

but 𝔊 *in* 31 b (και επι της γης εις χρειας ετοιμασθησονται) *attests the genuineness of the clauses*: επι της γης = בארץ *for* באוצרו: *and* εις χρειας = לצורכם: 𝔊 *has shortened and misplaced the lines.* 𝔖 *attests them partly in v.* 34, *also shortening and misplacing*   g-g ℌ בחקם: 𝔊 (*inexactly*) εν τοις καιροις αυτων   h-h ℌ התיצבתי *Cowley-Neub.* (*or* התנצבתי): יַצִּיב *in Neo-Hebrew* = 'sure': *so* התיצבתי = 'I was assured (*or* assured myself') = 𝔊 εστηριχθην

25. **Good things for the good . . .** The verse is cited in the *Sefer Yeṣirāh* in the following form:
'Good is kept for the good,
And evil for the evil'
(טובה שמורה לטובים ורע שמורה לרעים): see Cowley-Neub., p. xxvi. 𝔊 and 𝔖 take ℌ חלק in the Arabic sense of 'create' as in xl. 1 (cp. xxxviii. 1 also); but this is unnecessary.

26. **(The chief . . . necessaries) . . . water . . .** Cp. xxix. 21. The place of iron in this list is certainly remarkable, as Edersheim remarks.

The fat of wheat. A poetical expression for the choicest wheat; cp. Deut. xxxii. 14; Ps. lxxxi. 17, cxlvii. 14.

The blood of the grape. Cp. l. 15 (in 𝔊); the expression (= wine) is derived from Gen. xlix. 11; it recurs in Deut. xxxii. 14; 1 Macc. vi. 34.

28. **There are (winds) . . .** The action of destructive winds (רוחות πνεύματα), not spirits, is meant, as the context shows. For the phrase 'remove mountains' cp. Job ix. 5 (of God). In Rabbinic Hebr. the phrase ('uproot' or 'remove mountains') = to accomplish what is seemingly impossible (cp. Edersheim, *Life and Times of Jesus the Messiah*, ii. 109, 376, notes). Here probably earthquakes and similar catastrophes are in the writer's mind.

29. **Fire and hail, famine . . . judgement.** Cp. Ps. cxlviii. 8. The judgements in view are such as are described in Gen. xix, Exod. ix, and 2 Sam. xxiv.

30. **Beasts of prey** (lit. of tooth) . . . The forces of judgement here are earthly, in *v.* 29 cosmic (Smend). For 'beasts of prey' cp. xii. 13 ('wild beasts' R. V.).

the avenging sword. Cp. Lev. xxvi. 25.

And are in the treasure-house (ready) to be requisitioned in due time. In xliii. 14 God's 'treasury' is also the armoury of judgement, as here; cp. Job xxxviii. 22 f.; contrast Deut. xxviii. 12 ('the good treasury' of heaven; see *v.* 17 above).

31. **in their prescribed tasks** (בחקם). Cp. Exod. vi. 14; Prov. xxxi. 15.

ℌ[B] 33 [i]The works[i] of God are all good,
[j]They supply[j] every need in its season.
34 None may say: This is worse than that;
For everything [k]availeth[k] in its season.
35 And now ring out [l]whole-heartedly[l]
And praise the name of the Holy One!

(*a*) XL. 1–17. *The woes of humanity and the destruction of evil*
(=3+3+4+2+2+1+2+2+1 distichs).

40 1 Much occupation [a]hath God apportioned[a],
And heavy is the yoke upon the sons of men—
From the day that he cometh forth from his mother's womb,
Until the day [b]when he returneth[b] [c]to the mother of all living:
𝔊 (𝔖) 2 [d]Preoccupation and anxiety of heart,
And watchfulness for the future, till the day of his death![d]
ℌ[B] 3 From him that sitteth in exaltation on a throne,
Unto [e]him that is clothed[e] with dust and ashes;
4 From [f]him that weareth[f] diadem and plate,
Even unto [f]him that weareth[f] [g]a garment of hair[g]:

i–i *Read* מעשי (*for* מעשה) *as in v.* 16 (*so* 𝔊, 𝔖) j–j 𝔊 χορηγησει = יספיק (*cp. v.* 16: *read pl.*) k–k ℌ *mg.* יגבר (*cp.* 21 d): ℌ *text* יגביר = 'displayeth strength': 𝔊 ευδοκιμηθησεται = ? נבחר (*cp.* 21 b) l–l ℌ בכל לב: 𝔊 εν παση καρδια και στοματι = ℌ *mg.* (+ופה)

a–a *So* ℌ: 𝔊 εκτισται παντι ανθρωπω (εκτισται = חָלַק *as in* xxxix. 25: *see note there*): 𝔖 'hath God created' b–b ℌ שובו = 𝔊 (248 157) [εως] επιστροφης [ημερας] (ℵ[c.a] επιστραφη: B επι ταφη *corrupted from* επιταφης: *cp.* 𝔏 usque in diem sepulturae) c–c ℌ אל אם כל חי (*mg.* ארץ): 𝔊 εις μητερα παντων: 𝔖 'to the earth of the living' (*Lévi adopts* ℌ *mg.* 'earth of all living') d–d > ℌ: 𝔊 τους διαλογισμους αυτων και φοβον καρδιας επινοια προσδοκιας ημερα τελευτης: 𝔖 'their praises (*reading a derivative of* שבח *for* חשב) and the perception of their heart and the last of their words till the day of their death': *perhaps* ℌ *underlying* 𝔊 *may have been*:

מחשבות ודאגת לבב
והקשבה לאחרית עד יום מותם (מותו)

the substantives in apposition to עסק *in v.* 1 (*cp. v.* 5). *Peters* (*following* 𝔖 *mainly*) *restores*:

מחשבותם ומשכית לבם
ואחרית דבריהם עד יום מותם:

[εως ημερας *may have stood originally in* 𝔊: 70 155 *have* ημερας] e–e *So* ℌ *mg.* (*read* לָבוּשׁ): ℌ *text* לשוב: 𝔊 (*freely*) τεταπεινωμενου (= לשח *according to Smend*): 𝔖 = ליושב (*cp.* עוטה *repeated in next verse*) f–f ℌ עוטה . . . עוטה: *but* 𝔊 φορουντος . . . περιβαλλομενου (*two different words*): *hence Peters reads* עוטה . . . עוטף (עטף = περιβ. Job xxiii. 9: Ps. lxxii. 6) g–g ℌ (*last word defective*) *read* (*vel* עור) שמלת שֵׂעָר ('a garment

33, 34. **The works of God are all good . . . season** = *vv.* 16–17 (refrain repeated).
35. **And now ring out . . .** Cp. Ps. cxlv. 21.

XL. 1—XLI. 13. With chapter xl a new section begins, which extends to xli. 13. Its contents may be grouped under the following subsections: (*a*) xl. 1–17; (*b*) xl. 18–27; (*c*) xl. 28–30; (*d*) xli. 1–4; (*e*) xli. 5–13.

(*a*) XL. 1–17. Following closely on the hymn of thanksgiving for God's goodness we have here, by way of contrast, a lamentation over the woes of humanity. Suffering is inherent in man's lot. His life must be passed in restless anxiety and misgiving, and constantly be visited by misfortune. But the godless experience the worst ills, viz. those which are inflicted by God in punishment for sins. What is false and unjust comes to destruction, but what is true abides. The two objects of the wicked man's desire, property (*vv.* 13–14) and children (*vv.* 15–16), are referred to, to illustrate the writer's main contention; in the final verse (17) he sets forth the blessedness which results from the fear of God.

1. **Until the day when he returneth to the mother of all living.** For the idea cp. Gen. iii. 19; cp. also in this book (Sirach) xvi. 30, xvii. 1 (ℌ mg. adopted by Lévi = 'land of (all) living', cp. Ezek. xxvi. 20, xxxii. 32). The conception of the earth being man's mother is worked out in 4 Ezra ix. 9–15; cp. also Job i. 21; Ps. cxxxix. 15.

2. **Preoccupation . . . death.** The substantives are in apposition to 'much occupation' in *v.* 1, the governing verb being '(God) hath apportioned'; cp. *vv.* 5 *a* and *b*. The text adopted by Peters may be rendered: 'Their thoughts and the imagination of their heart, and their last actions (*or* their fate) until the day of their death.' See further critical note.

3–4. **From him that sitteth in exaltation on a throne . . .** Nobody, high or low, enjoys rest from distracting care and peace.

5 (*a*) [h](Naught but) anger and jealousy[h], anxiety and fear,
Terror of death, [i]strife[i], and contention!
5 (*b*) And what time he resteth upon his bed,
The sleep of night [k]doubleth ⌈his distraction⌉[k].
6 For a little, vainly—[l]for a moment—he reposeth[l],
[m]And then is disturbed by dreams[m]:
[n]Deceived[n] by the vision of his soul,
He is like a fugitive fleeing [o]from before the pursuer[o]—
7 [p]⌈Now roused he waketh from his sleep⌉[p],
[q]And his vision (?) . . . .[q]
8 [r](There are) with all flesh, both man and beast,
Yea and upon the ungodly sevenfold[r]:
9 Pestilence and bloodshed, [s]blight and drought[s],
[t]Devastation and destruction, famine and plague[t].

of hair or skin'): 𝔊 ωμολινον ('a hempen frock' R.V.) h–h 𝔊 θυμος και ζηλος (𝔥 אך קנאה *read* אף וקנאה) i–i 𝔥 *mg.* תחרה k–k 𝔥 *mg.* תשנה דעתו = 𝔊 αλλοιοι την γνωσιν αυτου (? *read* רַעְתוֹ *or* רעיונו: *cp.* Qoh. ii. 22): 𝔖 'disturbeth them' l–l 𝔥 כרגע ישקוט: 𝔊 εν αναπαυσει (= ברגע *e.g.* Job xxi. 13): 𝔊 > ישקוט m–m 𝔥 (*defective*) ש . . . . ומבין בחל: 𝔊 και απ εκεινου εν υπνοις ως εν ημερᾳ σκοπιας (? *for* κοπιᾳ) (= Arm). *Read* (?) ובבין בחלומות ירגש (ובבין = וּבְבֵן: *cp.* xiii. 7, Qoh. viii. 10, Esther iv. 16: 𝔊 και απ εκεινου = ומבין, *corrupt for* ובבין) [*v.* 6 a b > 𝔖] n–n 𝔥 מעט עט (? *read* מוּטְעָה *Hof. part. as in Neo-Heb.* = 'misled': *Smend* מטעטע *i.e. Hithpalpel of* טעע = טעה: *cp.* 2 Chron. xxxvi. 16, *same form from* תעע: *but the existence of such a root is doubtful*): *Peters eliminates* מעט *as intrusion from previous line and reads here* נע (= 'trembling on account of', &c.): 𝔊 τεθορυβημενος 𝔖 (דמתמלך) = ? מתיעט = מתיעין ['for vision of his soul' 𝔖 *has* 'vision of the night'] o–o *So* 𝔥 𝔖: 𝔊 απο προσωπου πολεμου p–p 𝔥 (?) קין . . . . . מ עורך [ועד] = ? (יקיין) עוד עורך מלחמה מקיץ: *according to Lévi* = 'while still preparing to fight he awaketh': 𝔊 εν καιρῳ σωτηριας αυτου εξηγερθη: 𝔖 'according to the wish of his heart he awaketh' = ? ברצון בלבבו יקיץ. *Perhaps* 𝔥 *may be restored:* עַתָּ נעור משנתו יקיץ = 'now roused he waketh from his sleep': נעור *would account for* רצון *in* 𝔖 (ע *and* צ *often confused*) *and for* עורך *in* 𝔥 *MS.*: 𝔊 *apparently read the text* [ב]עת תשועתו יקיץ (תשועתו ? *a corruption of* נעור משנתו) q–q 𝔥 *defective* (מניה . . . . ומרא *can be made out with difficulty*): 𝔊 και αποθαυμαζων εις ουδενα φοβον, *whence Peters restores* וישתמם לאין יראה 'And marvels at there being nothing to fear': 𝔖 'And seeth that there is nothing therein' (= ? ויראה כי אין ממנה: *cp.* 𝔥 *MS.*) r–r 𝔥 *MS. defective here*: 𝔊 = עם כל בשר מאדם ועד בהמה אף על רשעים שבעתים: 𝔖 'All the sons of flesh their care is with them, and wealth driveth away their sleep' = ? עם כל בשר מגורם עמהם ועשר מעיר שנתם (*Lévi*). 𝔊 *is to be preferred* s–s 𝔥 חרחר וחרב (*point* חַרְחֻר וְחֹרֶב: *so in* Deut. xxviii. 22): 𝔊 (*with different points*) ερις και ρομφαια t–t 𝔊 (א A C V &c.: B > *the whole line*) επαγωγαι λειμος και συντριμμα και μαστιξ (א* μαστιγες) = ? מכות רעב שבר ושד = 𝔥 *inverted, viz.* שד ושבר רעה

3. **him that sitteth . . . on a throne.** Cp. Exod. xii. 29.

him that is clothed with dust and ashes. For the metaphor ('clothed with') cp. Job vii. 5 ('flesh clothed with . . . clods of dust').

4. **him that weareth diadem and plate.** The diadem or turban (צניף) of the High Priest is meant, with the metal plate (ציץ) attached to it. Cp. Exod. xxviii. 36–39; see also Josephus, *Ant.* iii. 7. 6, and *Jewish War*, v. 5, 7; cp. further Zech. iii. 5 and Exod. xxxix. 30 f.

him that weareth a garment of hair. Cp. Gen. xxv. 25; Zech. xiii. 4; Matt. iii. 4. 𝔖 renders 'garment of poverty'; the mantle of hair was such, and was worn sometimes as a protest against luxury and extravagance, or as a badge of simplicity.

5. **Terror of death.** Cp. Ps. lv. 4 (5).

what time he resteth upon his bed . . . Cf. *Qoh.* ii. 22 f. ('Even in the night his heart taketh no rest'). The words of 5 *a* = xlvi. 19 *a* 𝔥.

6. **And then is disturbed by dreams.** For this text see critical note. 𝔊 is here obviously corrupt; if, with the Armenian, ἐνυπνίοις and κοπιᾷ be read (for ἐν ὕπνοις σκοπιᾶς) (καὶ ἀπ' ἐκείνου ἐνυπνίοις ὡς ἐν ἡμέρᾳ κοπιᾷ) it may be rendered 'and after that he toils with dreams as in the day', i.e. he works hard during the greater part of the night by dreaming. Peters reads a Hebr. text (ומבין בֶּהָלוֹת יינע) which may be rendered, 'and then he wearies himself from the midst of terrors' (for בהלות cp. Jer. xv. 8).

7. **Now roused he waketh from his sleep.** For the conjectural restoration of the text here adopted see critical note. The line thus restored affords an excellent sense: distracted by fearful dreams the sleeper at length awakes—the disturbance of his rest is complete.

And his vision (?) . . . It seems impossible to restore 𝔥 here (but see critical note). But the sense of the verse is doubtless well preserved in 𝔊 and 𝔖: 𝔊 has 'And he marvelleth that the fear is naught'. For the general idea (the shock of awaking from the dream) cp. Isa. xxix. 8.

8–9. **(There are) with all flesh, both man and beast . . . Pestilence . . .** The two verses form one long sentence. Note that the whole animal world is here included (cp. Gen. vii. 23; Exod. ix. 25).

9. **Pestilence and bloodshed . . . destruction.** In 𝔥 the three pairs of words form a series of alliterations; cp. Is. li. 19 (where, perhaps, חֹרֶב 'drought' should be read for חֶרֶב 'sword').

𝕳[B] 10 [u]For the wicked[u] [v]evil[v] is created,
And on his account [w]⌈destruction is imposed⌉[w].
11 All things that are from the earth return to the earth,
[x]And what is from on high (returneth) on high[x].
𝕲 (𝕾) 12 [y]All that is false and unjust is destroyed,
But what is true abideth for ever[y].
𝕳[B] 13 [z]Wealth unjustly gotten[z] [a]⌈cometh to an end⌉ like a torrent[a],
[b]And like a water-course that is mighty in a thunder-storm[b]:
14 [c]With its onrush ⌈rocks are rolled away⌉[c]—
[d]Even so doth ⌈plunder⌉ suddenly come to an end[d].
15 [e]A branch (sprung) from violence[e] [f]⌈hath no tender twig⌉[f],
[g]For an impious root[g] [h]is on the point of a crag[h]:

ומכות (*l.* רעב) (𝕾 > *the verse*) u–u 𝕳 על רשע = 𝕲 επι τους ανομους (= 'to be a burden upon the wicked') v–v 𝕳 רעה: 𝕲 ταυτα παντα (= ? כֻּלָּהּ = *a variant* כָּלָה) w–w 𝕳 תמוש כלה (*to make sense the commentators propose to insert* לא = 'ruin departeth not, but'): *read* תְּוּשָּׂם *with Peters* = 𝕲 εγενετο (שׂוּם = γινεσθαι 1 Sam. xxx. 25, Job xxxviii. 33, &c.): 𝕾 > *v.* 10 x–x *So* 𝕳 ואשר ממרום אל מרום: 𝕲 και απο υδατων εις θαλασσαν ανακαμπτει (= ואשר ממים אל ים): 𝕾 = 𝕳 y–y > 𝕳: 𝕲 *has* παν δωρον και αδικια εξαλειφθησεται και πιστις εις τον αιωνα στησεται (= *in Hebrew*:

כל שֹׁחַד ועולה יִשָּׁחֵת
ואמונה לעולם תעמד:) (*so Peters*).

𝕾: 'Every one that sins and cheats shall cease,
But the diligent of the world, even they shall stand'

(כל חטא ומעול ישבת ? =
ונאמני עולם יעמדו:)

𝕾 *may have read* שקר *for* שחד *in line* 1: *so emend* (*with Smend*) z–z 𝕳 *mg.* חיל מחיל 'wealth born of wealth (*or* strength)': 𝕲 χρηματα αδικων (= ? חיל מעולים): 𝕾 'wealth of deceit' (? חיל מעל): *read* חיל מֵעָוֶל (*or* מֵעַוְלָה) a–a 𝕳 כנחל איתן = 'is like a perennial torrent'—*an unsuitable sense* [*Smend ad loc. argues that the meaning* 'perennial' *is not made out. He thinks the original idea is that of strength, then* (*of a stream*) *strongly flowing—a rushing current. So he retains the word here*]: *both* 𝕲 *and* 𝕾 *have a verb in place of* איתן: *viz.* 𝕲 ξηρανθησεται (= יִנָּתֵן *according to Peters*: *cp.* Isa. li. 12 LXX): 𝕾 'shall be swept away': *read, perhaps, with Ryssel* יִתֹּם (*Lévi, as well as Smend, keeps* נחל איתן = 'a swiftly flowing torrent') b–b *So* 𝕳 *mg.* = 𝕾 ('like rivers that are full of light clouds' [*reading* קַלּוֹת *for* קולות]): 𝕲 και ως βροντη μεγαλη εν υετῳ εξηχησει = 'And shall roar themselves out like great thunder in rain' (*a free rendering*) c–c 𝕳 *mg.* עם שׂאתו כפים יגילו (*emend to* יִגָּלוּ *and point* כֵּפִים): 𝕲 εν τῳ ανοιξαι αυτον χειρας ευφρανθησεται (*read* ευφρανθησονται) = 𝕳: 𝕾 *only has one line for this verse, which is usually supposed to represent clause* a: *but more probably clause* b (*see next note*) d–d 𝕳 כי פתאם לנצח יתם: 𝕲 ουτως οι παραβαινοντες (= ? פֹּתָאִם *for* פִּתְאֹם) εις συντελειαν εκλειψουσιν: 𝕾 'when they are taken away they come to an end' (= ? כי יִגָּלוּ יִתַּמּוּ). *Combining* 𝕳, 𝕲, *and* 𝕾 *read* כן פתאם גָּזֵל יתם (*or* גזלה תתם) e–e 𝕳 *text* נוצר מחמס *mg.* נצר חמס: 𝕳 *mg.* = 𝕲 εκγονα ασεβων: 𝕾 'and offspring to the wicked man' (= 𝕳 *mg.*?): *read* נֵצֶר מחמס f–f 𝕳 לא ינקה (= ? 'shall not be unpunished'): 𝕲 ου πληθυνει κλαδους

---

10. **For the wicked evil** (or calamity) **is created . . .** Cp. xxxix. 29.
11. **All . . . from the earth return to the earth.** Cp. Gen. iii. 19; Eccles. xii. 7; Job xxxiv. 15.
what is from on high (returneth) on high. The return of the spirit to its Maker is meant; cp. *Qoh.* xii. 7. The prosperity of the ungodly shares the fate of all created things; it comes to destruction (cp. Ps. xlix).
13. **Wealth unjustly gotten . . . torrent . . .** Cp. Job vi. 15–18 for the image. Just as the torrent suddenly swollen in a thunder-storm as suddenly goes down, so wealth unjustly gotten disappears. In clause *b* 'in a thunder-storm' = lit. 'in flashing of thunder'. For 𝕲 see critical note.
14. **With its onrush rocks are rolled away.** For the word rendered 'rocks' here (כֵּפִים) cp. Jer. iv. 29; Job xxx. 6. 𝕲 misread this as 'hands' (כַּפַּיִם), and may be rendered 'in the opening of his hands one shall rejoice' (i. e. when he is made to disgorge his ill-gotten wealth there is general rejoicing). 𝕳 might be rendered (understanding the word in this sense), 'when he (the wicked man) lifteth up his hands (*sc.* as a beggar) men rejoice'; or 'when He (God) lifteth up His hands (*sc.* against the wicked man to punish him and reduce him to poverty) men rejoice.'
Even so doth plunder suddenly come to an end. For text see critical note. 𝕳 as it stands = 'for suddenly doth he (? the wicked man) come to an end for ever' (cp. 𝕲). The words cannot be understood of the brook; they must refer to the riches, and this is well expressed by the emended text.
15. **A branch (sprung) from violence.** i.e. the wicked man himself (not his offspring); cp. the parallel expression in clause *b* 'an impious root'.
hath no tender twig. i.e. has no permanent posterity. For the idea cp. xxiii. 25; Job viii. 11 f.
an impious root is on the point of a crag. For 𝕾 see critical note, and cp. with its rendering Matt. xiii. 5.

ℌ[B] 16 [i]Like reed-stalks (?)[i] [j]on the bank of a torrent[j],
[k]Which are consumed before any (other) ⌈plant⌉[k].
17 [l]But kindness shall never be moved[l],
And righteousness is established for aye.

(*b*) XL. 18–27. *The fear of the Lord is the greatest of all good things* (= 10 + 2 distichs).

18 [m]A life of wine and strong drink[m] is sweet,
But better than both is [n]he that findeth a treasure[n].
19 Child [o]and city[o] establish a name,
[p]But better than both is he that findeth wisdom.
Young cattle and planting make ⌈abundance⌉ to flourish[p],
But better than both [q]is a woman beloved[q].
20 Wine [r]⌈and song⌉[r] rejoice the heart,
But better than both is [s]the affection of lovers[s].

(κλαδος = יונקת Hos. xiv. 7, LXX): *read* לֹא יָנֵק בו: *with Peters, &c.* [g–g] 𝔊 και ριζαι ακαθαρτοι (*? read* ακαθαρτου): ℌ כי שורש חנף = 𝔖 [h–h] ℌ = 𝔊: 𝔖 (*freely*) [‘ for the root of sinners] is like an ear of corn which sprouts upon a rocky crag’ [i–i] ℌ בקרדמות (*? pl. of* קרדם = καρδαμον, ‘ nasturtium *or* cress ’: *Cowley-Neubauer suggest* כְּקְרֹמִיּוֹת ‘ like reed-stalks ’: *pl. of* קְרֹמִית): 𝔊 αχει = ℌ אָחוּ (*cp.* Job viii. 11): *so Peters reads here: Hart suggests that* ℌ *may be a corruption of* כְּעֵרֶק (ערק = אחו *in Targ. of* Job viii. 11) [j–j] ℌ על גפת נחל (גִּפָּה = ‘ side ’, *only here: cp. Syr.* גף ‘ wing ’, *and Aram.* גיף ‘ bank ’): 𝔊 επι (παντος υδατος και) χειλους ποταμου (παντος υδατος και > *with* 𝔏): 𝔊 = ? על שְׂפַת נחל [k–k] ℌ *mg.* לפני כל מטר נדעכה (ℌ *text* נדעכו): 𝔊 προ παντος χορτου εκτιλησεται: *Peters conjectures:* לפני כל מטע נדעך (𝔊 παντος υδατος *in previous line* = ? כל מטר: *Hart*) [l–l] *So* ℌ: 𝔊 χαρις ως παραδεισος εν ευλογιαις = וחסד כעדן ברכה ‘ but kindness is like a blessed Eden ’ (*? from* xl. 27): 𝔖 ‘ But the works of the pious in season (= בעדן) are blessed ’ (*cp.* Isa. li. 3) [m–m] *So* ℌ חיי יין ושכר: *for* יין ושכר ℌ *mg. has* יותר שכל ‘ wealth of understanding ’: 𝔊 *has* ζωη αυταρκους εργατου (= חיי שָׂכִיר: αυταρκους *probably an addition in* 𝔊): ℌ *mg. may, as Peters suggests, be an independent attempt to emend* ℌ *in order to eliminate the offensive expression* ‘ a life of wine and strong drink ’ (*by substituting* ‘ a life of wealth of understanding ’). ℌ *text is certainly strange, but is supported* (*partly*) *by* 𝔊: 𝔖 > *line. Hart ingeniously proposes to read* חן ושכל ‘ grace and understanding ’ (חן *for* חיי יין): *cp.* Prov. iii. 4 [n–n] ℌ מוצא אוצר: 𝔊 *rightly takes* מוצא *as participle* = ‘ one finding ’ (*so most moderns*): *a subst.* מוֹצָא = ‘ finding ’ (*so Peters*) *is highly doubtful* [o–o] ℌ ועיר: 𝔊 και οικοδομη πολεως [p–p] 𝔊 > 19 b *and* c, *but the clauses are attested by* 𝔖 *as well as* ℌ: *omission in* 𝔊 *probably caused by homoioteleuton* (*so Peters, &c.*). *Smend, however, regards them as not a genuine part of the text, the double mention of* ‘ a name ’ (*in* 19 a *and* 19 c) *being alleged as suspicious. The repetition is certainly awkward: probably* ‘ a name ’ *in* 19 c *should be emended to* ‘ abundance (fatness) ’ (Heb. דשן) *as suggested by Fuchs:* שם *may easily have arisen out of this* (*? through* שמן), *perhaps under the influence of the previous* שם [q–q] ℌ אשה נחשקת: 𝔊 γυνη αμωμος λογιζεται (*possibly, as Smend suggests,* λογιζεται = נחשבת: αμωμος *an addition*) [r–r] 𝔊 και μουσικα = ושיר (*cp. for the equivalence* Gen. xxxi. 27, Ezek. xvi. 13 *in* LXX, &c.): 𝔖 ‘ old wine ’ = יין ישן: ℌ יין ושכר *under influence of v.* 18 [s–s] ℌ אהבת דודים:

---

16. **Like reed-stalks . . .** 𝔊 may have preserved the true reading here, ‘ sedge ’ (ἄχει = אָחוּ; see critical note), and also the true construction of the sentence. Then the whole may be rendered, ‘ Sedge on a torrent’s bank is consumed before any (other) plant: but kindness, &c.’ (so Peters). Cp. Job viii. 12.

17. **But kindness . . . righteousness.** Kindness and righteousness as between man and man are meant. ℌ in clause *a* (cp. Prov. x. 30) differs from 𝔊 and 𝔖 (see critical note). If the latter be followed the first line will run: ‘ But kindness is like a blessed Eden ’ (cp. *v.* 27).

(*b*) XL. 18–27. In this subsection the various good things of life are enumerated—in a series of ten contrasted sets of boons. The climax is that the highest good is the fear of God.

18. **better . . . he that findeth a treasure.** Both Lévi and Peters prefer to render—‘ the finding of a treasure ’. This certainly suits the construction of the verse, ‘ finding ’ rather than ‘ the finder ’ according with the predicate ‘ is sweet ’. But there is a grave philological objection to the rendering. ‘ Treasure ’ here may, perhaps, be explained by 19 *b* as = ‘ wisdom ’ (so Peters).

19. **Child and city.** 𝔊’s rendering ‘ children and the building of a city ’ gives the sense intended correctly. There may be an allusion to the building of such cities as were named after their founders (e.g. Alexandria). On the perpetuation of one’s name cp. xvi. 1 f., xli. 11 f.

Young cattle and planting. Operations which promote natural increase are referred to, breeding of stock and sowing of crops being mentioned as typical examples.

20. **Wine and song rejoice the heart.** Cp. xxxi. (xxxiv.) 27 f.

the affection of lovers. Or ‘ the love of friends ’. 𝔊’s ‘ love of wisdom ’ is probably a deliberate alteration due to revision; cp. Wisdom ii. 7 f.

ℌ[B]

21 Pipe and harp make sweet the song,
But better than both is [t]a tongue sincere[t].
22 [u]Grace and beauty[u] [v]charm the eye[v],
But better than both are [w]the crops of the field[w].
23 [x]A friend and companion will each conduct himself opportunely[x],
But better than both is [y]a discreet wife[y].
24 [z]A brother and helper will come to the rescue in a time of adversity[z],
But more than both doth righteousness deliver.
25 Gold and silver [a]make the foot stand sure[a],
But better than both [b]is good counsel[b].
26 Wealth and strength [c]lift up[c] the heart,
But better than both is the fear of God[d].
In the fear of Jahveh there is no want,
And with it there is no need to seek [e]support[e].
27 The fear of God is a very Eden of blessing,
And [f]its canopy[f] (stretcheth) [g]over[g] all that is glorious.

𝔊 αγαπησις σοφιας (? *a tendency alteration*) t–t ℌ לשון ברה : 𝔊 γλωσσα ηδεια (𝔖 = ℌ) u–u ℌ *defective*: 𝔊 χαριν και καλλος = יפי ותאר (*Peters*), יפי ונועם (*Smend*), יפי וחן (*Lévi*) (καλλος = תאר xlii. 12, xliii. 9, 18) v–v ℌ יחמידו עין : 𝔊 επιθυμησει ο οφθαλμος σου (σου > A &c. Syro-Hex 𝔏) w–w ℌ צמחי שׂדה ('the growing things of the field'): 𝔊 χλοην (*v. l.* χλοη) σπορου 'the green blade of corn' (א* σποριμου) x–x ℌ *defective* עת ינהגו . . . . : 𝔊 φιλος και εταιρος εις καιρον απαντωντες (*last word* = ? נֹגְעִים): 𝔖 *for last word* 'will receive greetings from one another' (נתברכון): *read* אוהב וחבר לעת ינהגו *and render as above* (*others render*: 'friend and companion give support at the right time') y–y *So* ℌ = 𝔖: 𝔊 γυνη μετα ανδρος z–z ℌ *defective*: אח . . . . ת צרה : 𝔊 αδελφοι και βοηθεια εις καιρον θλιψεως = 𝔖: *Peters, following Lévi mainly, restores*: אח ועוזר יצילו לעת צרה : *Versions do not support the insertion of verb: Smend restores* אח ושותף גם בעת צרה = 'a brother and a partner', &c. (שׁתף *occurs in Neo-Hebr.* = 'form a partnership or attachment'; *it occurs again in* ℌ *mg.* xli. 18, xlii. 3) a–a 𝔊 επιστησουσιν ποδα = רגל (יעמידו)—*only last word legible in* ℌ b–b 𝔊 βουλη (*only* B* 55 *have* γυνη) ευδοκιμειται: 𝔖 'good counsel' (𝔏 consilium beneplacitum): *read* עצה טובה c–c *The word is illegible in* ℌ (*MS. mutilated*): *Cowley-Neub. read* יגביהו = 𝔊 (ανυψωσουσιν): *Smend* יגוללו ('make to exult'): *Lévi* יגדלו d *In the MS. of* ℌ[B] *there is a marginal note by the side of vv.* 22–26 a b, *written in vertical lines, as follows*:

כל ימי עני רעים	בן סירא אום אף בלילה
בשפל גגים גגו	במרום הרים כרמו :
ממטר גגים לגגו	מעפר כרמו לכרמים :

'All the days of the poor are evil.	Ben-Sira says, At night also.
His roof is the lowest of roofs,	and his vineyard is in the height of the mountains;
The rain of other roofs falls on his roof,	and the earth of his vineyard falls on other vineyards.'

This citation agrees, with one slight variation (viz. אף לילות *for* אף בלילה*), with the passage as cited in T. B. Sanhedrin* 100 b. *It is probably excerpted from some compilation of selected sayings which circulated under the name of Ben-Sira, and contained, together with genuine quotations, a number of others which do not belong to the genuine text of Ben-Sira's book. The citation here given appears to belong to the latter class. A Persian gloss is added in the MS. (written in Hebr. characters) as follows*: 'It is probable that this was not in the original copy, but it is used as a proverb' (*see Cowley-Neub., p.* 7) e–e *Reading* מִשְׁעָן (ℌ *MS. defective*): *so Bacher, Smend, Peters.* 𝔊 βοηθειαν = 𝔖 [𝔖 *here adds a gloss on next verse*: 'the fear of God over everything is exalted; seize it, my son, and let it not go, for there is nothing like it'] f–f ℌ חפתה = 𝔊 (εκαλυψαν αυτον): 𝔖 'is praised' g–g 𝔊 και υπερ = ועל (*so* 𝔖): ℌ וכן (Isa. iv. 5 כי על) h–h ℌ חיי מתן 'a life of gift': 𝔊 ζωην

21. **Pipe and harp make sweet the song.** i.e. of course through their accompaniment.

22. **Grace and beauty . . . crops of the field.** For the sentiment cp. Matt. vi. 28–29.

23. **will each conduct himself opportunely.** Or 'will give support' (and guidance) 'at the right time'. The same verb (נהג), common in NH, is used in iii. 26.

a discreet (or prudent) **wife.** The expression is borrowed from Prov. xix. 14; cp. also Sir. xxv. 1.

24. **A brother and helper . . .** Possibly the original form of the sentence was exclamatory: 'A brother and helper in time of adversity.' Cp. Prov. xvii. 17.

But more than both doth righteousness deliver. Cp. Prov. x. 2, xi. 4, 6. 'Alms' (for 'righteousness') is a possible rendering.

25. **Gold and silver make the foot stand sure.** i.e. give a sure footing, a firm position. Neubauer cites the following from T. B. *Pesachim* 119 *a*: in reference to Deut. xi. 6 ('and every living substance that followed them' [lit. 'was at their feet']) R. Eleazar says: 'This means the wealth of a man, which makes him stand firm upon his feet.'

(*c*) XL. 28–30. *A beggar's life no life at all* (= 3 + 1 distichs).

ℌ[B] 28 My son, live not [h]a beggar's life[h];
Better is one dead [i]than importunate[i].
29 A man that looketh to a stranger's table—
His life is not to be reckoned as a life:
[j]A pollution of his soul[j] are [k]the dainties presented[k],
[l]And to an understanding man inward torture[l].
30 [m]In the mouth of an insatiable (man)[m] begging is sweet,
But inwardly it burneth as fire.

(*d*) XLI. 1–4. *Two views on death* (= 2 + 2 + 2 + 1 distichs).

41 1 [ab]Ah![c] Death, how bitter is [d]the remembrance of thee[db]
To him[e] [f]that liveth at peace[f] in [g]his habitation[g];
[h]To him that is at ease[h], and prospereth in all,
And that still hath strength to enjoy luxury[i].
2 Hail! Death, how[k] welcome is thy decree[l]
[m]To the luckless man[m], and that lacketh strength,
[n]That stumbleth and trippeth[n] [o]at everything[o],
[p]That is broken[p], [q]and hath lost hope[q].

επαιτησεως i-i ℌ ממסתולל: 𝔊 η επαιτειν (𝔖 *renders whole verse:* 'him that asks refuse not; and be not good to kill but to keep alive'—*misunderstanding* ℌ) j-j ℌ מגעל נפש (*so read for* ℌ *text* מעגל) = 𝔊 𝔖 (*possibly* נפשו *also to be read*) k-k ℌ *mg.* מטעמי זבד (𝔊 *read* זר *for* זבד) l-l ℌ (*with mg.*) לאיש יודע יסור מעים: 𝔊 *misunderstands* m-m 𝔊 εν στοματι αναιδους (*so* 𝔖) = בפי עז נפש (*for* ℌ לאיש עוז נפש): *so read.* a *Some MSS. of* 𝔏 *insert the title* De memoria et iudicio mortis b-b 𝔖 'Ah! Death, how evil art thou' c *So the margin; the text has* 'Life' d-d *So* 𝔊; *the text of* ℌ *is corrupt* e 𝔖 + 'rich': 𝔏 + et iusto f-f 𝔖 'sitting' g-g *Lit.* 'his foundation'; 𝔊 𝔖 'his possessions' h-h 𝔊 απερισπαστῳ (ευπρεπεστατῳ V 253): 𝔖 'strong' i 𝔊 τροφην; *read* τρυφην (= ℌ 𝔖) k *Reading* מה *for* כי (= א$^{c.a}$ 253 𝔖 Syro-Hex): > 𝔊 l *Reading* חֻקֶּךָ *for* חקוך (ℌ *marg.* חוק, חזק, *and* חוקו) m-m *Reading* לאיש אוֹנִים (*cp.* ℌ *marg. in v.* 10) ('to a man of sorrows'): 𝔊 επιδεομενῳ: 𝔖 'broken' n-n *Reading with* ℌ *marg.* כושל ונוקש: 𝔊 εσχατογηρῳ και περισπωμενῳ: 𝔖 'that is old and stumbleth' (*cp.* 𝔏 defecto aetate) o-o 𝔊 περι παντων p-p *Reading* שָׁבוּר (*Ryssel*) *for* סרב (= 𝔊): ℌ *mg. reads* אפס המראה ('lacking sight'): 𝔖 'lacking wealth' q-q 𝔖 'and is

---

26. **But better than both is the fear of God.** The fear of God is the one all-sufficing and all-important possession; cp. xxxiv. 10.
27. **its canopy** (**stretcheth**) **over all that is glorious.** Cp. Isa. iv. 5 (the source of the expression here).
(*c*) XL. 28–30. On begging: cp. xxix. 21 f.
28. **live not a beggar's life . . .** Perhaps this saying of Ben-Sira has influenced the dictum (cited from Ibn Gabirol by Cowley-Neubauer, p. xxx): 'Better the grave than a fall to poverty'. 'A beggar's life' is lit. in ℌ a 'life of gift' (or 'gifts'), i.e. a life dependent upon gifts.

In 28 *b* the word rendered 'importunate' (מסתולל) = lit. 'to make oneself a mound' (denom. from סֹלְלָה 'a mound' thrown up by besiegers); fig. to advance against, beset, cp. xxxix. 24; here 'to beset' (with requests) = 'to importune' (see Driver in the Glossary in Cowley-Neubauer, p. xxiii).

29. **A man that looketh . . . as a life.** Cp. the citation freely given in *T. B. Beṣāh* 32 *b*: 'There are three men whose life is no life. They are these—The man who watches the table of his neighbour, and he over whom his wife rules, and he whose body is ruled by pains.'

A pollution of his soul are the dainties presented. For 'dainties presented' cp. xxxvi. 19 (24) note. Such gifts pollute in so far as they are begged for, not because they have been presented.

30. **But inwardly it burneth as fire.** Cp. Jer. xx. 9.

(*d*) XLI. 1–4. Death fearful to some, welcome to others, inevitable for all.

1. **the remembrance of thee.** Lit. 'thy memory' (זכרך).

in his habitation. מְכוֹנָתוֹ, cp. Hebr. of xliv. 6, i.e. the conditions under which he is living.

that is at ease. Cp. Job xvi. 12, xxi. 23.

to enjoy. Lit. 'to receive' (cp. 𝔊 ἐπιδέξασθαι), cp. Hebr. of xxxiv. (A.V., R.V. xxxi.) 3.

2. **Hail.** האח, an expression of satisfaction, as in Isa. xliv. 16.

how welcome. Lit. 'how good'.

thy decree. Cp. xiv. 12, and see Isa. xxviii. 15, 18.

stumbleth. The word כושל has in Neo-Hebrew the meaning to be weak or ill (Smend).

broken. Cp. Ps. lxix. 21 (20 in R.V.), cxlvii. 3, where the same Hebr. word is used of being broken in heart. The text of ℌ reads סרב 'intractable', or the like (cp. 𝔊 ἀπειθοῦντι); but this word is out of place in its context.

𝔥[B] 3 [r]Fear not Death, (it is) thy destiny[r],
Remember that the former and the latter (share it) with thee.
4 This is the portion[s] of all flesh from God,
[t]And how canst thou withstand[u] the decree[v] of[t] the Most High!
[w](Be it) for a thousand years, for a hundred, or for ten (that thou livest)[w],
In Sheol there are no[x] reproaches concerning life.

(*e*) XLI. 5–13. *The end of the ungodly contrasted with the honour accorded to the name of the righteous* (= 3+3+1+3 distichs).

5 An abominable offspring is the generation[y] of sinners,
And [z]a godless sprout[z] is [a]in the dwellings of the wicked[a].
6 [b]From the son of the unrighteous man [c]shall the dominion be wrenched away[c b],
𝔖 [d]And want[e] shall ever abide with his seed[d].
𝔥[B] 7 A godless father do the children[f] curse,
𝔊 [g]For because of him do they suffer reproach[g].
8 [h]Woe unto you, ungodly men,
[i]Who have forsaken the Law of the Most High God[i h]!
𝔥[B] 9 [k]If ye increase (it will be) for mischief[k],
[l]And if ye bear children (it will be) for sighing;
If ye stumble (it will be) for everlasting joy[l],
And if ye die (it will be)[m] for a curse[n].

unable to work': 𝔊 '. . . patience': 𝔏 . . . sapientiam [r–r] μη ευλαβου κριμα θανατου [s] 𝔊 το κριμα: 𝔖 'the end' [t–t] 𝔖 > [u] *Lit.* 'reject', *or* 'despise' [v] 𝔊 ευδοκια [w–w] 𝔊 ειτε δεκα ειτε εκατον ειτε χιλια ετη [x] *Reading* אין (𝔥 *marg.*) *for* איש [y] *Reading* דור *for* דבר (*Smend*) [z–z] *Reading* ונכד אויל [a–a] *So* 𝔊 (= 𝔖 𝔏): 𝔥 *is mutilated, but may perhaps be read* מגורי רשע [b–b] 𝔊 τεκνων αμαρτωλων απολειται κληρονομια [c–c] *Reading* ממשלה תקרע (*Smend*) [d–d] 𝔥 *is almost entirely mutilated* [e] 𝔊 ονειδος [f] 𝔖 'his righteous sons' [g–g] 𝔥 *is almost entirely mutilated*: 𝔖 + 'in the world' [h–h] *In* 𝔥 *only three letters are preserved* [i–i] 𝔖 > [k–k] 𝔊 και εαν γεννηθητε εις καταραν γεννηθησεσθε; *pr.* εαν γαρ πληθυνητε εις απωλειαν 248 (*cp.* 𝔥) [l–l] 𝔊 > [m] 𝔊 μερισθησεσθε [n] *For the whole verse* 𝔖 *has*: 'A fruitful woman is the joy of her people, and if there die an

---

3. **thy destiny.** Lit. 'thy decree,' as in *v.* 2, i.e. to which thou art destined, cp. xxxviii. 22 *a*.
the former and the latter. The reference is probably to the generations that have gone before and those that will follow after.
(share it) with thee. The Hebr. might mean: '(are) with thee', i.e. they will all be together hereafter in Sheol (cp. the expression 'to be gathered unto the fathers', 2 Kings xxii. 20).
4. **This is the portion.** Cp. Job xx. 29, xxvii. 13.
how canst thou withstand . . . Cp. Lev. xxvi. 15 for this phrase in Hebr. אִם־בְּחֻקֹּתַי תִּמְאָסוּ.
withstand. See critical note.
the decree. 𝔥 reads 'the Law', see critical note, but this can hardly be right, because 'Torah' is never used in this connexion.
In Sheol there are . . . Since in Sheol it will be found that the same fate has overtaken all men, it will be immaterial whether one man lived longer on earth than another; men will not quarrel about that. Cp. Eccles. vi. 6.
(*e*) XLI. 5–13. Death means far different things to the godless and the pious. In the case of the latter their name lives on.
5. **offspring.** The Hebr. word נִין occurs in Gen. xxi. 23; Isa. xiv. 22; Job xviii. 19; in each case it is the parallel to נֶכֶד 'sprout' in the next clause.
the generation of sinners. The reference is most probably to the Hellenistic party in Israel (see *v.* 8), and especially to the high-priestly family, as *v.* 6 seems to show.
and a godless sprout . . . The Hebr. text is mutilated, and it is impossible to reconstruct it with certainty, but the general sense is probably as given above.
6. **From the son of . . .** Ryssel renders this clause 'Because of an unrighteous son a kingdom falls to pieces' (reading תֵּרַע), a rendering which the text may quite well bear, but if, as the present writers hold, the reference is to the high-priestly family, Ryssel's rendering seems too general. In the marg. of 𝔥 is read מבין ערל, 'from amongst the uncircumcized', a term which could well be applied to the Hellenistic ruling party (cp. 1 Macc. i. 48, ii. 46, &c.), so that at all events a later scholiast understood the passage as in reference to the Hellenizers.
the unrighteous man. עול, the regular term for a tyrannical ruler, cp. Job xviii. 18, xxvii. 7, xxix. 17, xxxi. 3.
. . . wrenched away. Cp. 1 Sam. xv. 28 (קרע יהוה את־ממלכת); 1 Kings xi. 11; 2 Kings xvii. 21.
8. **Who have forsaken . . .** This is a clear reference to the Hellenizers, cp. 1 Macc. ii. 23, iii. 6, 8, &c.
9. **If ye increase . . .** i.e. If they have children, these will likewise be godless.
if ye die . . . The reference is not to anything that would happen after death, but rather to the execration in which they will be held at the time of their death.

10 [o]All that is of naught returneth to naught[o],
[p]So the godless man,—from nothingness to nothingness[p].
11 [q]Vanity is man (concerning) his body[q],
[r]But the name of the pious shall not be cut off[r].
12 Be in fear for thy name, for that abideth longer for thee
Than thousands of [s]precious treasures[s].
13 [t]Life's goods last for limited days[t],
[u]But the reward of a name for days without number[u].

(*a*) XLI. 14—XLII. 8. *Moral duties enumerated under the category of shame.*

(i) XLI. 14–15. *Introduction to the section on the subject of shame* (= 2 distichs).

14 [[v]Hidden wisdom and concealed treasure,
What is the use of either?
15 Better the man who hideth his folly,
Than the man who hideth his wisdom.]

(ii) XLI. 16—XLII. 8. [x]*Instruction concerning shame*[x] (= 2 + 10 + 1 + 1 + 9 distichs).

16 [y]Hear, O children, instruction concerning shame[z y],
And be abashed [a]according to my judgement[a].
(16) For not every kind of shame is meet to retain,
[b]And not every kind of abashment is to be approved[b].
17 [c]Be ashamed of a father and a mother of whoredom,
Of a prince and a ruler[cc] of lies,

unrighteous father his righteous sons will not grieve over him' o–o *In place of this clause* 𝔊 *has a variant of* xl. 11 a: 𝔖> p–p 𝔊 ουτως ασεβεις απο καταρας εις απωλιαν: 𝔖 'the end of the ungodly man is for destruction', *so for the whole verse* q–q 𝔖>: 𝔊 πενθος ανθρωπων εν σωμασιν αυτων r–r ℵ^c.a *alone among the MSS. of* 𝔊 *has preserved the right reading:* ονομα δε αγαθον ουκ εξαλειφθησεται (= Arm): 𝔊 ονομα δε αμαρτωλων ουκ αγαθον εξαλειφθησεται s–s *So* 𝕳 *mg., the text reads* 'treasures of wisdom'; 𝔊 'great treasures of gold' t–t 𝔊 αγαθης ζωης αριθμος ημερων u–u 𝔊 και αγαθον ονομα εις αιωνα διαμενει: 𝔖> *from here to* xlii. 8, *except* 19 b, 20 a v *The order of the clauses of vv.* 14–16 *differs in* 𝔊 (= 14 b, c, 15) x–x 𝔖 𝔊> y–y *This clause* = 14 a *in* 𝔊 z 𝔊 'peace' a–a 𝔊 επι τῳ ρηματι μου b–b 𝔊 και ου παντα πασιν εν πιστει ευδοκιμειται c 𝔏 *inserts the title* De omnibus vitiis declinandum cc *So* 𝕳 *mg.* (= 𝔊)

---

10. **the godless man.** חָנֵף is often used in reference to one who is an apostate.

nothingness. Cp. xli. 10. In each case the Hebr. word is תהו ('tohu'), which in Gen. i. 2 is used of the 'waste' of chaos; it is also used in reference to moral worthlessness (cp. Isa. xxiv. 10, lix. 4). Both the words for 'naught' and 'nothingness' occur together in Is. xl. 17; cp. Is. lix. 4.

11. **But the name . . .** This thought of the memory of the righteous departed being held in honour was the beginning of a development regarding the conceptions about the future life; this memory involved, sooner or later, the question as to differentiation between the righteous and the sinners beyond the grave, and when once this point was reached further development of thought was inevitable. (Cp. Prov. x. 7; 1 Enoch ciii. 4, civ. 13; *Test. Twelve Patr.*, Naphtali viii. 5.)

12. **Be in fear for thy name.** Cp. Eccles. vii. 1, and *Pirqe Aboth* ii. 8: 'He who hath gotten a good name hath gotten it for himself'; iv. 19, 'Rabbi Simeon said, There are three crowns, the crown of Torah, and the crown of Priesthood, and the crown of Royalty, but the crown of a good name mounts above them.'

for that abideth. For the Hebr. word לוה cp. Eccles. viii. 15.

Than thousands of . . . Cp. Prov. xxii. 1.

13. **the reward.** Lit. 'goods' (טובת); the same word as in 'Life's goods'; in the Hebr. there is a play on the double meaning of טובת: 'The good things of life' = prosperity, 'the good things of a name' = its honourable remembrance.

XLI. 14—XLII. 14. With xli. 14 a new section begins, which extends to xlii. 14. It contains an enumeration of moral duties under the category of shame. It falls into two distinct subsections, (*a*) xli. 14–xlii. 8; (*b*) xlii. 9–14.

(*a*) XLI. 14—XLII. 8. After an introductory piece (xli. 14 *b*, 15) there follows the main part of the subsection, with the heading 'Instruction concerning shame'. It enumerates things to be ashamed of, and then the things not to be ashamed of.

14, 15. These verses, which occur also as xx. 30, 31, are evidently out of place here; possibly they were added from a marginal note (Smend), as seeming to offer an appropriate introduction to the section beginning at *v.* 16.

16. The title to this section is found in 𝕳 only.

according to my judgement. i.e. in accordance with my teaching concerning this subject; 𝔏 paraphrastically, 'quae procedunt de ore meo.'

17. **of whoredom.** i.e. guilty of whoredom.

ℌ[B] 18 [d]Of a master and a mistress[d] of deceit,
Of an assembly and a people of transgression,
Of a comrade and friend of treachery,
19 And of a place, where thou sojournest, of pride[e].
[ee][Be ashamed] to break an oath or a covenant[ee],
To stretch out thine elbow at meat,
[f]To withhold[g] a gift that is asked for[f],
21*a* (𝔊) [h]To turn away the face[h] of thy friend,
21*b* (𝔊) [i]To cause the dividing of portions to cease[i],
20*a* (𝔊) To be silent towards [j]him that greeteth (thee)[j],
20*b* (𝔊) To look upon a woman that is a whore,
𝔊 21*c* [k]To gaze on a woman that hath a husband,
22*a* To be busy with his maid[k] [l],
ℌ[B] 22*b* (𝔊) [m]And to violate her bed[m],
22*c* (𝔊) To [speak to] a friend with reproachful words;—
22*d* (𝔊) And after giving a gift contemn not,—
42 1 [n]To repeat [o]the word thou hast heard[o],
And to lay bare any secret counsel:
So shalt thou be truly [p]shamefast[p],
And find favour in the sight of all living.

[q]But of these things be not ashamed,
And accept not persons [r]unto sin[r]:
2 Of the Law of the Most High, and the statute;
And of justice, to do right by the wicked;

d–d απο κριτου και αρχοντος e *Reading* זד (ℌ *mg.*) *for* זר *in the text*: 𝔊 περι κλοπης ee–ee 𝔊 και απο αληθειας θεου και διαθηκης; ℌ *is much mutilated* f–f 𝔊 απο σκορακισμου λημψεως και δοσεως g *Reading* מִמְּנֹעַ h–h *Reading* (*on the basis of* 𝔊 απο αποστροφης προσωπου) מֵהָשִׁיב פְּנֵי (*Ryssel*) i–i *The text of* ℌ *is partly mutilated* j–j *So* ℌ *mg.* k–k ℌ *is wanting with the exception of two letters at the end of v.* 22 a l *Reading* נערה (*Cowley-Neubauer*) m–m ℌ *is much mutilated* n xlii. 1 a–d = xli. 23–24 *in* EV: xlii. 1–8 *omitted by* 𝔖 o–o *So* ℌ: 𝔊 και λογου ακοης p–p 𝔏 sine confusione: 𝔊 αισχυντηρος q *Here* xlii *begins in* EV r–r *Reading* לחטא = 𝔊 του αμαρτανειν (*with Cowley-Neub., Smend*): ℌ *text* וחטא (= ? 'And accept not persons and so bear sin': *cp. Peters*)

---

18. **a master and a mistress . . .** Smend thinks that the reference here is to Gentile kings and queens into whose service Jews of noble family entered.

. . . of treachery. Cp. Lev. vi. 2.

19. **of a place.** i.e. the people of a place; like עִיר ('city'), which is often used of the inhabitants of a city, see e.g. 1 Sam. iv. 13, v. 12; Isa. xxii. 2.

an oath or a covenant. Cp. Gen. xxvi. 28.

To stretch out thine elbow . . . Cp. xxxi. (𝔊 xxxiv.) 14. Peters thinks that the reference is either to the action of the arm when taking an oath, connecting this with the previous clause; or else to the withholding of a gift in the following clause. It is, however, best to take the words as referring to behaviour; the whole passage exhibits a curious variety of topics referred to.

21 *a*. **To turn away the face.** i.e. to make him turn away in anger because the gift asked has been withheld; 𝔏 adds, apparently by way of explanation, 'ne avertas faciem a proximo tuo'; but the reference is to the turning away of the face of the friend, cp. xviii. 24.

21 *b*. **To cause the dividing of portions . . .** The reference is possibly to the dividing of an inheritance (see xlii. 3), but more probably to the bestowal upon the poor of portions of the offerings for sacrifice, cp. 2 Sam. vi. 19 (Smend). Peters understands the words in a general sense as a prohibition against niggardliness.

20 *a*. **that greeteth.** Lit. 'that asketh peace'; the usual Oriental mode of salutation.

20 *b*. **that is a whore.** Lit. 'a stranger', cp. Prov. ii. 16, v. 3, 20, vii. 5, xxii. 14.

22 *c*, *d*. Cp. xviii. 15.

XLII. 1. **To repeat the word . . .** Cp. xix. 7; a warning against circulating mere unsupported rumours.

lay bare any secret counsel. Cp. xxii. 22 *c*, xxvii. 16 f.

shamefast. The Hebr. word used (בושׁ) occurs only here and in xxxii. (xxxv.) 10 in this sense (as an adj. = 'shamefast').

find favour in the sight of all living. Cp. xlii. 8.

But . . . be not ashamed, And accept not persons unto sin. This general exhortation applies to what follows: of certain things (following) the injunction is to be not ashamed, while some of the things enumerated also involve the application of a judicial and impartial mind. To the latter the injunction 'accept not persons (i.e. exhibit not partiality) unto sin' (i.e. so as to bring sin upon thyself) specially applies.

2. **Law of the Most High . . . statute . . . justice.** The 'Law of the Most High' = the Law generally, regarded as a body of principles invested with divine sanctions; 'the statute' = the particular enactments which result from

B 3 Of reckoning with a comrade [s]and (fellow) travellers[s],
And of the division of an inheritance [t]and a property[t];
4 [u]Of the small dust[u] of the scales and balance,
[v]And [w]of testing[w] measure and weight[v];
4(*b*) Of buying whether little or much,
5 [ww]And of profit from traffick with the merchant[ww];
[x]Of frequent correction of children,
And of smiting the side of an evil-disposed servant[x].
B 6 For an evil wife [y]a seal[y],
And where [z]many[z] hands are, [a]a key[a]!
7 [b]Upon what is deposited make a mark[b],
And let giving and receiving all be in writing.—
8 Of the correction of the simple and foolish (be not ashamed),
[c]Or of the tottering grey-head occupied with whoredom[c]:
So shalt thou be truly well-advised,
And a man (truly) modest before all living.

s–s *So* ℌ *mg.* וארח (*read* וְאֹרֵחַ) = 𝔊 και οδοιπορων (ℌ *text* 'and a master' ואדרן) t–t ℌ ויש (Prov. viii. 21): 𝔊 εταιρων (? *read* ετερων) = איש [ℌ *mg.* וישר ? *to be read* וִירֻשָּׁה: *so Ryssel*] u–u *So* ℌ (*omitting* ו *in* ועל) = על שחק (Isa. xl. 15): 𝔊 περι ακριβειας: *Smend supposes an infin. to be implicit in* שחק ('to rub off,' *then* ? 'to balance') v–v > 𝔊 w–w ℌ תמחות (*or read* המחות): *in Neo-Hebr.* מחה (המחה) = 'to prove, test' (*cp.* מוּמְחֶה = 'skilled, expert, tried') ww–ww ℌ (*difficult to decipher*) ועל ממהיר [מ]מכר תגר: 𝔊 περι αδιαφορου (*but* א A C 155 157 307 διαφορου = 'difference, profit' = מחיר) πρασεως (B + και) εμπορων (C εμπορου): *read* ועל מחיר ממכר תַּגָּר: x–x > ℌ (*but* ℌ *mg.* 5 a מוסר *points to the lines having been in text originally*): 𝔊 και (*probably to be omitted*) περι παιδειας τεκνων πολλης και οικετῃ πονηρῷ πλευραν αιμαξαι: *from which restore with Peters* (*cp. Lévi*):

על מוסר בנים רב
ועל הכות צלע לעבד רע
(*Lévi*: ולעבד רע הכות צלע)

y–y ℌ חותם חכם (> חכם *as marginal note*): 𝔊 καλον σφραγις (καλον *an addition*) z–z *So* 𝔊 = רבות *which read for* ℌ רפות a–a ℌ תפתח: 𝔊 κλεισον (? *originally* κλεις): *read* מפתח (*Ryssel*), *as parallelism demands* b–b 𝔊 'Whatsoever thou handest over (let it be) by number and weight' (ο εαν παραδιδῷς, εν αριθμῷ και σταθμῷ): ℌ יד תספור (*mg.* מפקד) על מקום תפקד: 𝔊 *may have read* על מפקד יד מספר ומשקל = 'upon a deposit number and weight' (מִפְקַד יָד = 'what is entrusted to a hand', *i.e.* 'a deposit': *cp.* תְשׂוּמֶת יד Lev. v. 21): *it will be nearer* ℌ, *however, to read with Peters* על מפקד יד תספור c–c ℌ *mg.* ושב כושל ועונה בזנות (ℌ *text* שב וישיש). *For* ועונה בזנות 𝔊 *has* κρινομενου περι πορνειας (*so* 253 307 Syro-Hex.) (*but* B προς νεους)

---

the application of these principles in practice; while 'justice' is a general term denoting the administration of such laws. The injunction is obviously addressed to the Scribes, who are responsible for the administration of law and justice. Smend explains the general meaning of the verse to be an admonition to the Scribes not to be ashamed of the Law of their fathers (i.e. their ancestral religion) in the face of Greek fashions and influences.

to do right by the wicked. i.e. probably not to hesitate to acquit the ungodly man when he is proved innocent of a particular charge.

3. **Of reckoning with a comrade and (fellow) traveller.** The meaning apparently is—do not allow feelings of false shame and pride to deter from settling accounts, involving mutual indebtedness, where friends and fellow travellers are involved. Lévi aptly quotes the French proverb, 'Les bons comptes font les bons amis.' Smend interprets differently. He takes 'reckoning with' to mean 'demanding from': 'Do not be deterred by feelings of false shame from asking a companion (on a journey) and a fellow traveller, who is staying for the night at the same inn, who he is.'

of the division of an inheritance . . . i.e. of determining exactly the details involved in the division of an inheritance or property (for the Hebr. of the last word cp. Prov. viii. 21).

4. **Of the small dust of the scales . . .** Cp. Is. xl. 15. 𝔊 gives the sense well, 'of exactness of scales.' Care must be taken that the exactness of the balance is not disturbed even by a fleck of dust. The scales, measures, and weights used by the trader must be tested ('measure and weight,' lit. 'ephah and stone').

Of buying whether little or much. Contrast xxvi. 29, xxvii. 2, where the dangers involved in buying and selling are dwelt upon.

5. **of smiting the side of . . . servant.** Cp. xxxiii. 24 f. (= 𝔊 xxx. 33 f.).

6–7. The construction changes in these verses, but it is not necessary for that reason to transpose them.

8. **Of the correction of the simple . . .** i.e. Be not ashamed to correct the foolish and ignorant, and also to correct the tottering grey-beard occupied with whoredom; for 8 *b* cp. xxv. 2.

a man (truly) modest. The Hebr. word here rendered 'modest' (צנוע) = 'lowly' in Bibl. Heb. (cp. Prov. xi. 2), but 'pious' in *PBH*. Smend renders it 'gesittet'. [It is supposed by some scholars that the word 'Essene' is equivalent to צָנוּעַ.]

(*b*) XLII. 9–14. *The care of daughters* (= 4 + 2 + 2 + 2 distichs).

ℌ[B] 9 [d]A daughter is to a father [e]a treasure of sleeplessness[e],
[f]And the care of her banisheth slumber[f]:
In her youth, lest [g]she pass the flower of her age[g],
And [h]when she is married[h], [i]lest she be hated[i];
10[d] [ii]In her virginity[ii], lest she be seduced,
[j][k]And in the house of her husband[k], [kk]lest she prove unfaithful[kk];
In her father's house, lest [l]she become pregnant[l][j],
[m]And in her husband's house[m], lest she be barren.
11 [n]Over thy daughter keep a strict watch[n],
[o]Lest she make thee a name of evil odour[o]—

[d] *The following version of vv.* 9 *and* 10 *is cited in T. B. Sanh.* 100[b]:

בת לאביה מטמונת שוא מפחדה לא יישן:
בקטנותה שמא תתפתה.
בנערותה שמא תזנה.
בגרה שמא לא תנשא.
נשאת שמא לא יהיו לה בנים.
הזקינה שמא תעשה כשפים.

(= 9 a) A daughter is a vain treasure to her father:
(= 9 b) for fear about her he does not sleep;
(= 10 a) in her youth, lest she be seduced;
(= 9 c) in her maidenhood, lest she play the harlot;
when she is marriageable, lest she be not married;
(= 10 d) when she is married, lest she have no sons;
when she is old, lest she practise sorcery.'

[e–e] ℌ *text* מטמונת שקר = 'a deceptive treasure' (*cp.* 'vain treasure' *in Talm. citation*): 𝔊 αποκρυφος αγρυπνια: *read* שָׁקֵד *for* שקר (*so Peters, Smend*): 𝔖 'great honour' [f–f] *So* 𝔊 𝔖: ℌ (*defective*): ודאגתה תפ[ריע] [נומה] (*cp.* xxxi. [xxxiv.] 1 𝔊 *and* ℌ) [g–g] *So* 𝔊 (παρακμαση) = ? תבגר (*cp.* בגרה 'when she is marriageable' *in Talm. cit.*): ℌ תגור ('she commit adultery') *corresponding to* תזנה *in Talm. cit.*: 𝔖 '[that she] be not blamed' [h–h] *So* 𝔊 (𝔖 'and by her husband') = בְּעוּלָה (*so read*): ℌ בבתוליה [i–i] *So* 𝔊 𝔖 (ℌ *text defective*): *read* פן תִּשָּׂנֵא: ℌ *mg.* תנשה 'she be forgotten' [ii–ii] *So* ℌ 𝔖: 𝔊 εν παρθενειᾳ (+ αυτης Syro-Hex 𝔏) [j–j] *Transposed in* 𝔊 (*right order in* ℌ *as given above in the translation*) [k–k] ℌ *text* (*defective*) ובבית [בע]ל[ה] (ℌ *mg.* בבית אישה) = 𝔊 μετα ανδρος ουσα [kk–kk] 𝔊 μη ποτε παραβῃ: ℌ *text lacking read with* ℌ *mg.* פן תשטה (*Peters; and Smend with* לא *for* פן) [l–l] 𝔊 εγκυος γενηται: ℌ *lacking* (*read* תהרה) [m–m] *So* ℌ: 𝔊 'And when she is married' (συνῳκηκυια = ובעולה) [n–n] ℌ *mg.* בני על בתך החזק משמר: 𝔊 επι θυγατρι αδιατρεπτῳ στερεωσον φυλακην: 𝔖 *with* ℌ *mg.* + 'my son' (ℌ *text defective: is restored by Lévi* [בני על בתו]ל[תך] הק[ם] מ[שמר]) [o–o] ℌ *text defective—the last two words are* (*l.* סרח) שם סרה: *read* [פן תעשה לך] שם סרח: ℌ *mg.* פ׳ תע׳ ש׳ לא׳ = ? פן תעשך שמצה לאויבים = 𝔊 μη ποτε ποιηση σε επιχαρμα (= שמצה Exod. xxxii. 25) εχθροις: *perhaps, however,* 𝔊 *read in Exodus* שמחה (= επιχαρμα *in Exodus*). *Lévi reads* ℌ *mg.* פן תעשך משל לאחרים: 𝔖 ('a bad name') = ℌ *text* [p–p] ℌ *text* וקללת עם (*so Lévi, Peters, Strack*): *but Smend reads it* וקהלת עם = 𝔊 (και εκκλητον λαου: *cp.* 𝔖 ורטוניא בעמא) [q–q] ℌ *text* (והושבתך) *corrected in left margin to* והובישתך = 𝔊: הוֹבִישׁ = הביש ℌ *right margin* והבשת (= ? וְהַבֹּשֶׁת) [r–r] ℌ בעדת שער: 𝔊 εν πληθει πολλων (? *read* πυλων) [s–s] *These two lines* (11 e f) *are*

(*b*) XLII. 9–14. The subject of this subsection is the care of daughters. The same subject is touched upon in vii. 24–25, xxvi. 10–12.

9. **A daughter . . . treasure of sleeplessness . . .** Edersheim cites some of the Talmudic *dicta* on the subject of daughters and women generally, among others the following: 'Happy he that has male children; woe to him that has female children' (*Qidd.* 82 *b*; *Baba bathra* 16 *b*, &c.); 'Women are of light mind' (*Shabb.* 33 *b*; *Qidd.* 80 *b*); and the well-known one in *Pirqe Aboth*, 'prolong not converse with a woman' (i. 5). The Blessing in the Jewish Morning Prayer may also be cited: 'Blessed art Thou, O Lord . . . who hast not made me a gentile . . . a slave . . . a woman.' But the harshness of tone manifest in Ben-Sira towards women generally was much mitigated in later (Rabbinical) Judaism under the influence of the Pharisees.

. . . lest she pass the flower of her age. i.e. without being married. Smend prefers to keep the reading of ℌ (פן תגור: Poel of גרר), which he renders 'lest she entice (men)': but 'lest she commit adultery' is a more probable rendering.

10. **be seduced.** For the Hebr. word here used cp. Exod. xxii. 15; Ezek. xiv. 9.

she prove unfaithful. Cp. Num. v. 12, 19 f., 29 (same Hebr. word שׂטה = 'go aside').

11. **Over thy daughter keep a strict watch.** Cp. xxvi. 10.

a name of evil odour. Cp. the Biblical expression 'to make odious' (lit. 'cause to stink', הבאיש e.g. Prov. xiii. 5).

B

A byword in the city [p]and accursed of the people[p]—
[q]And shame thee[q] [r]in the assembly of the gate[r].
[s]In the place where she lodgeth [t]let there be no lattice[t],
[u]Or spot overlooking the entrance round about[u][s].
12 [v]Let her not show her beauty to any male[v],
[w]And among[w] wives let her not converse.
13 For from the garment issueth the moth,
And from a woman a woman's wickedness.
14 [x][y]Better is the wickedness of a man than the goodness of a woman[y];
[z]And a disgraceful daughter poureth forth disgrace[z][x].

In praise of God as Nature's Lord.

(*a*) XLII. 15–25. *Exordium* (= 1 + 2 + 2 + 2 + 2 + 2 + 2 + 2 distichs).

15 [a]I would fain remember[a] God's works,
And what I have seen I would recount.
[b]By the word of God His works were formed[b],
[c]And what was wrought by His good pleasure according to His decree[c].

lacking in 𝔊 (*accidentally omitted: ? the translator's eye passing from* ובית *in* 11 f *to* ובית *or* רבין *in* 12 b *omitted two lines*) t–t *So* ℌ: 𝔖 *incorrectly* 'let her not go forth' u–u *So* ℌ ובית מביט מבוא סביב: 𝔖 (*?reading* ובית מבית מבוא סביב) 'And let her not be round about in houses' v–v *So* ℌ: 𝔊 *misunderstood the line* (παντι ανθρωπῳ μη εμβλεπε εν καλλει): *as also* 𝔖 ('Reveal not to every man what is in thine heart') w–w 𝔊 και εν μεσῳ = ובין: *so* 𝔖 *rightly*: ℌ ובית x–x > 𝔖 y–y *So* ℌ *mg.* = 𝔊 (η αγαθοποιος γυνη ? *an interpretation of* מְטוּב אשה: *but Lévi makes it* = ממטיב׳ אשה) z–z *Reading with* ℌ *mg.* (*correcting* ובית *to* ובת) ובת מחרפת תביע חרפה: *cp.* 𝔊 και γυνη καταισχυνουσα εις ονειδισμον (*? a free rendering of* תביע חרפה). *Smend reads* מחפרת = 'shame causing' *for* מחרפת a–a *So* ℌ = 𝔊 μνησθησομαι δε (δε *for* δη) b–b *So* 𝔖: 𝔊 εν λογοις Κυριου τα εργα αυτου = ℌ *mg.*: ℌ *text* באומר אלהים רצ[ו]נו: *read* מעשיו נוצרו *for last word* (? = 𝔖): *so Peters* c–c ℵ[c.a] και γεγονεν εν ευλογιᾳ αυτου κριμα (B &c. >): Sah και γεγονεν ευλογια των κριματων αυτου (ευλογιᾳ *for* ευδοκιᾳ): ℌ ופועל רצונו לקחו (*read* לְחֻקּוֹ *for* לקחו, *cp.* 𝔊): ℌ *mg. has* לקח *which Peters retains: then render*: 'and teaching (doctrine) is a work of His grace': *Cowley-Neub. render* ℌ *text* 'and him that doeth His pleasure He hath accepted'

Or spot. The Hebr. term (ובית) has here a general sense as in *NH*, 'place', 'spot'. Smend suggests ובית תבות for ובית מביט = and 'where she spends the night (let there be) no entrance,' &c.

12. **Let her not show her beauty . . .** Perhaps ℌ (אל תתן תֹּאַר) may be rendered 'Let her not give a look to any male', i.e. show herself, be visible to (cp. Smend). תואר has the meaning 'look', 'countenance' in *PBH*, cp. also xvi. 1.

And among wives . . . i.e. let her not mix on familiar terms with married women.

13. **For from the garment issueth the moth.** The reference is to daughters. If such mix with married women on familiar terms, and listen to the conversation of the latter, sexual impulses and desires will be stirred which will lead to sin. The sentence is couched in proverbial form. The moth issuing from the garment is a figure of something emanating spontaneously from within. 𝔖 interprets rather than translates, 'For as a moth falls upon a garment, so doth jealousy upon a woman from the wickedness of her fellow.'

14. **Better is the wickedness of a man than the goodness of a woman.** As Edersheim remarks: 'The misogyny of the author here reaches its climax.'

poureth forth disgrace. Cp. x. 13 ('poureth forth abomination').

XLII. 15—XLIII. 33. This piece forms a distinct division. Its theme is the praise of God—of God as the mighty and all-wise Lord of nature. The introduction (xlii. 15–25) sets forth God's omnipotence and omniscience. The main (central) part has for its subject the firmament and the sun (xliii. 1–5), the moon (xliii. 6–8), the stars and the rainbow (xliii. 9–12), the storm, the snow and the hoar-frost, the ice, and lastly the sea (xliii. 13–26). A concluding section (xliii. 27–33) has for its main thought that the highest praise man can offer to God is inadequate. As Smend points out, the question of the origin of the heaven, of the dry land and the sea, does not come into the writer's treatment of the theme (cp., however, xliii. 23) any more than the creation of vegetation, of the land animals, and of man. God shows Himself to be the Lord of nature in the wonderful adjustment and economy that are maintained in natural forces and life.

With xlii. 15 f. cp. xviii. 1–7.

(*a*) XLII. 15–25. EXORDIUM.

15. **I would fain remember . . .** Cp. Ps. lxxvii. 12.

And what I have seen . . . = Job xv. 17.

And what was wrought by His good pleasure according to His decree. For text see critical note. According to Peters' rendering ('and doctrine is a work of His grace') creation and the wisdom-teaching are placed side by side: cp. xliii. 33; Ps. xix (the light of creation and the light of revelation set together).

ℌ 17 The rising sun [d]is revealed[d] over all things,
And the glory of Jahveh [e]is over all His works[e].
16 [f]God's holy ones have not the power[f]
To recount [g]His wondrous works of might[g];
(Though) God hath given strength [h]to His hosts[h]
[i]To endure in the presence of His glory[i].
18 He searcheth out the deep and (man's) heart,
[j]And all their secrets[j] [k]He surveyeth[k]:
𝔊 [l]For Jahveh possesseth all knowledge,
And seeth what cometh unto eternity[l].
ℌ[B] 19 He declareth [m]what is past and what is future[m],
And revealeth [n]the profoundest secrets[n].
20 [o]No knowledge is lacking to Him[o],
[p]And no matter escapeth Him[p].
21 [q]The might of His wisdom[q] [r]is established[r],
From everlasting [s]He is the same[s]:
[t]Nothing hath been added and nothing taken away (therefrom)[t],
And He needeth none to give counsel.
𝔊 (𝔖) 22 [u]All His works are truly lovely,
And are ⌊like blossoms⌋ to behold[u].

d–d *So* ℌ: 𝔊 (*inexactly*) επεβλεψεν e–e *So* ℌ: 𝔊 (*inexactly*) πληρες το εργον αυτου f–f *So* ℌ: 𝔊 ουκ ενεποιησεν τοις αγιοις Κυριος g–g 𝔖 *has* גברותא דפרישתה = גבורותיו נפלאות (*so read with Smend*): 𝔊 παντα τα θαυμασια αυτου: ℌ *text* ייי נפלאות (*but* יהוה *here otiose with* אל *in clause* a: *probably only a variant on* אל) h–h *So* ℌ צבאיו: 𝔊 (*taking* אלהים צבאיו *together*) Κυριος ο παντοκρατωρ i–i *So* ℌ: 𝔊 στηριχθηναι εν δοξη αυτου το παν (*but* 𝔏 > το παν, *which is not original*) j–j ℌ ובכל מערומיהם: 𝔊 και εν πανουργευμασιν αυτων k–k ℌ יתבונן l–l > ℌ: 𝔊 εγνω γαρ ο Κυριος πασαν ειδησιν και ενεβλεψεν εις σημειον αιωνος *is restored in Hebrew by Peters thus:*

כי ידע יהוה כל דעת
ויביט אל אותות לעולם:

𝔖 *attests the two lines also, rendering* (*freely*): 'for before God nothing is hidden, and there lie revealed before Him all things that come into the world' m–m ℌ (*reading* ונהיות *mg. for text* נהיות) חליפות ונהיות = 𝔊 τα παρεληλυθοτα και επεσομενα (*so* 𝔖 *which, however, omits* מחוה = 'He declareth' *at the beginning of line*) n–n ℌ חקר נסתרות (חקר = 'what is to be explored', 'the whole range': *cp.* Job xxxviii. 16): 𝔊 ιχνη αποκρυφων: 𝔖 *paraphrases:* '[and there are revealed before Him] all things that are hidden' o–o *So* ℌ: 𝔊 'no thought' (διανοημα = ℌ שׂכל *as in* xxxv. 18) 'escapeth Him' (𝔖 'no wisdom') p–p *So* ℌ: 𝔊 'there is not a word hid from Him': *to* 'word (thing)' 𝔖 + 'of man' q–q ℌ *text defective:* ℌ *mg.* גבורת: 𝔊 τα μεγαλεια της σοφιας αυτου: *read* גבורת חכמתו r–r ℌ תכן (*point* תִּכֹּן: *cp.* 𝔖 'standeth fast'): *Smend prefers to point* תֻּכַּן = 'measured off', 'regulated' (*but parallelism favours* תִּכֹּן: *so Peters*): 𝔊 εκοσμησεν = תקן s–s ℌ אחד הוא: 𝔊 (B) και εως, ος (A 55 248 &c. Sah Lat Arm), ως (א 253 &c.) *are all corruptions of an original* [και] εις = אחד (𝔊 + και εις τον αιωνα) t–t *So* 𝔊: ℌ (*defective*) ל[א נוסף ו] לא נאצל (𝔖 > 21 b c d) u–u 𝔊 ως παντα τα

16. **The rising sun . . .** i.e. just as the sun shines over everything, so the glory of Jahveh is manifest in all His works.

17. **God's holy ones . . .** 'God's holy ones' here = the angels (cp. Job xv. 15). The meaning of the verse is: even the angels are unable to recount God's wondrous works—they need special strength to be given to them in order to stand in the divine presence. Sinful man can do neither. Cp. xliii. 27–33.

18. **He searcheth out the deep and (man's) heart . . .** i.e. the two inscrutable things. Omniscience = Almighty power (Smend). The word rendered 'deep' (ℌ תהום) recalls the stories of the subduing of the monsters of chaos (Rahab, Leviathan, the demons) by Jahveh as set forth in the old accounts of Creation (cp. e.g. Is. li. 9–10). For our verse cp. Dan. ii. 22 ('He revealeth the deep and secret things'), Judith viii. 14 (a good parallel), and Job xxxviii. 16.

For Jahveh possesseth all knowledge . . . what cometh unto eternity. For the thought cp. Is. xli. 21 ff., xliii. 9 f.

19. **He declareth what is past and what is future . . .** That God knows and reveals to men both the past and the future proves Him to be the controller of history and events—again a thought characteristic of Deutero-Isaiah: cp. also xxxix. 29 in our book.

20. **No knowledge is lacking to Him . . .** For the idea cp. Ps. cxxxix. 3 f.

21. **Nothing hath been added and nothing taken away (therefrom).** i.e. from 'the might of His wisdom' (*v.* 20). Cp. xviii. 6; *Qoh.* iii. 14.

And He needeth none to give counsel. Cp. Is. xl. 10, 14.

22. **All His works are truly lovely . . . like blossoms.** The beauty of creation is compared to the loveliness of flowers. For the text see critical note. The verse is regarded as a gloss by Schlatter (it is absent from ℌ).

ℌ[B](𝔊) 23 [v]Everything liveth and abideth for ever[v],
[w]And to every need all things respond[w].
24 [x]They are all different, one from the other[x],
But He hath not made any one of them [y]superfluous[y].
25 [z]The one exchangeth what is good (in it) with the other[z],
And who can be satiated with beholding [a]the beauty[a]?

(*b*) XLIII. 1–26. *Recital of the manifestations in Nature of God's might*
(= 1+4+1+4+2+2+4+4+4+3+1 distichs).

43 ℌ[B] 1 [b]The beauty of the (heavenly) height is the pure firmament[b],
[c]And the firm heaven[c] [d]poureth out light[d].

εργα αυτου επιθυμητα και ως σπινθηρος εστιν θεωρησαι [*here the first* ως *is probably due to assimilation to the second in second clause: so Smend:* σπινθηρος *has probably arisen from an original* σπινθηρ ος = 𝔏 tanquam scintilla quam (quae): *cp. Peters*]: 𝔖 *freely* 'And all His works He establisheth in truth for ever, and in holiness they are all of them praised'. 'in truth' *in clause* a (= באמת) *may be right. Perhaps* ℌ *of first clause may be restored thus:* כל מעשיו באמת נחמדים. *In clause* b και ως σπινθηρ ος = וכניצוץ אשר *according to Peters* (= 'and are as a spark which can be seen'). *But* וכניצוץ *is probably corrupt. Read* וכמו ציץ למראה (*Lévi suggests* וכציץ: וכמו *may easily have been corrupted into* וכני)   v–v 𝔊 παντα ταυτα ζη και μενει εις τον αιωνα: ℌ (*defective*) ל . . . . . הוא ח = ? הוא חי ועומד לעד: *so Smend, Lévi: Peters* (*following* 𝔊) *reads* הכל *for* הוא: ℌ *mg. has* וקים, *thus reading the line* [ועד] הוא חי וקים (*Peters thinks* הוא *of* ℌ *a correction for dogmatic reasons*). *Between this verse* (xlii. 23 a) *and its next half* (23 b) *the Hebr. MS. inserts v.* 25 *and* xliii. 1, *thus producing the dislocation* xiii. 23 a, 25, xliii. 1, xlii. 23 b, 24, xliii. 2. *At the top of the next folio the Hebr. MS. has against v.* 24 (כלם שונים זה מזה ולא עשה מהם שי . . .) *the following:*

זה על זה חלף טוב
ומי ישבע להביט תואר } xlii. 25

תואר מרום רקע על טהר
ועצם שמים מביט נהרה } xliii. 1

thus restoring the right order xlii. 24, 25, xliii. 1   w–w ℌ (*text damaged*) *can be read:* [ו]לכל צורך הכל ישמע (ℌ *mg.* נשמע): 𝔊 εν πασαις χρειαις και παντα υπακουει (*but* 𝔏 *places* και *at beginning* = ℌ: *so* Sah): 𝔖 *implies same text, but paraphrases*   x–x *So* ℌ (*text*): 𝔊 (*misunderstanding*) 'All things are double one against another' (παντα δισσα εν κατεναντι του ενος): *so* 𝔖 (*reading* שנים *for* ℌ שונים)   y–y 𝔊 εκλιπον (B), ελλιπον (A): 𝔏 aliquid deesse: ℌ שי . . *read* שוא *by Lévi, Peters* (= 'He hath not made one of them in vain'). *Smend restores* שי[שאיר]
z–z ℌ (*mg.* טוב) זה על זה חלף טובו: 𝔊 *inexactly* 'One thing establisheth (εστερεωσεν) the good things of another': 𝔖 'but one with the other (forms) pairs'   a–a ℌ *mg.* תואר: 𝔊 δοξαν αυτου (= 'God's glory'): 𝔖 (*interpreting rightly*) 'their glory', *i. e.* 'the glory (beauty) of all things (the whole world)'   b–b 𝔖>: ℌ *mg.* תואר מרום רקע על טהר: 𝔊 γαυριαμα υψους στερεωμα καθαριοτητος: *read* (*with Smend*) תואר מרום רקיע טהר   c–c ℌ *mg.* ועצם שמים (*cp.* Exod. xxiv. 10 כעצם השמים): 𝔊 ειδος ουρανου (*cp.* LXX Exod. xxiv. 10 και ωσπερ ειδος στερεωματος του ουρανου)   d–d ℌ *mg.* מביט נהרה (*to be emended to* מביע *with Bacher: cp.* xliii. 2). ℌ *text has* הדר *which Peters prefers to keep, reading* מביע הדר = 'bursteth with majesty': 𝔊 εν οραματι δοξης (𝔖>1 b *as well as* 1 a)

23. **Everything liveth and abideth for ever.** ℌ has 'He (i.e. God) liveth and abideth for ever' (ℌ mg. חי וקים is common in NH, but is always applied to God; often in the Synagogue Liturgy). The text as translated ('everything liveth', &c.) follows 𝔊 and 𝔖. It may have been altered for dogmatic reasons in ℌ; so Peters (cp. Smend).

And to every need . . . Cp. xxxix. 33.

24. **They are all different, one from the other.** The rendering of 𝔊, 'All things are double one against another' (see critical note), limits the reference in *vv.* 22–25 to living organisms that exist in pairs. But ℌ is to be preferred: in the text of ℌ the reference is to nature as a whole. Everything is distinct, but yet all things harmonize.

25. **The one exchangeth what is good (in it) with the other.** 'All things work together for good.' There is a constant interchange and mutual dependence.

the beauty. i.e. of the whole of nature.

(*b*) XLIII. 1–26. THE MAIN POEM.

1–5. *God's power manifested in the firmament and the sun.*

1. **The beauty of the (heavenly) height is the pure firmament . . .** There is a clear allusion (cf. ℌ) to Exod. xxiv. 10 ('as it were the very heaven for clearness'). The subject of the verse is the firmament, as clause *b* clearly shows: clause *a* in ℌ (see critical note) = 'the beauty of the (heavenly) height is spread upon purity'. This, as it stands, might be interpreted of the sun; but the context forbids it.

ℌ[B]

2 [e]The sun when he goeth forth maketh heat to shine[e]—
[f]How awe-inspiring is the work of Jahveh[f]!
3 [g]At noontide[g] he bringeth the world to boiling heat,
And before [h]his scorching (ray)[h] who can maintain himself?
4 [i](Like) a glowing furnace which keepeth the casting hot,
(So) the sun's dart setteth the mountains ablaze[i]:
[j]A tongue of flame consumeth the inhabited (world)[j],
[k]And with its fire the eye is scorched[k].
5 [l]For[l] great is Jahveh that made him,
[m]And His word maketh His mighty (servant) brilliant[m].
6 [n]Moreover, the moon He made for its due season[n],
[o]To rule over periods[o] and for an everlasting sign:

e–e *So* ℌ *mg. which reads* שמש מופיע בצאתו חמה (ℌ *text has* מביע בצרתו: ? מביע *confirms Bacher's emendation in previous clause*): 𝔊 'The sun when he appeareth bringeth tidings as he goeth forth' (ηλιος εν οπτασιᾳ διαγγελλων εν εξοδῳ) = ℌ *with reading* מביע בצאתו (חמה *interpreted by Aram.* חמא = 'to see') f–f ℌ מה נורא מעשׂי ייי (*read* מעשׂה): 𝔊 σκευος θαυμαστον εργον υψιστου *read* מָן *for* מה, *giving it its Aram. meaning* = σκευος g–g *Lit.* 'when he is at noon-tide' (בהצהירו: *denom. from* צהרים) = 𝔊 εν μεσημβριᾳ αυτου (*so* 𝔖) h–h *Lit.* 'his scorching heat' (חרבו) i–i ℌ *is very difficult here* (*mg.* מוצק) כור נפוח מהם מצוק = *line* 1; *line* 2: שמש (*mg.* שלוח) שולח הרים (*mg.* יסיק) ידליק: 𝔊 καμινον φυσων (*so* ℵ[c.a] A Sah: *for the erroneous* φυλασσων *of* B ℵ C &c. 𝔏) εν εργοις καυματος τριπλασιως ηλιος εκκαιων ορη: 𝔖 'As the furnace which blows in the work of the smith (so) three times more doth the sun burn up the mountains': 𝔊 *suggests the reading* מחם, *and* 𝔖 *a reading* נופח (*or* נפח): *in line* 2 *both* 𝔊 *and* 𝔖 *wrongly read* שלש *for* שולח *or* שליח. *A possible restoration is, perhaps:* (*vel* נוֹפֵח) כור נַפָּח מֵחֵם מוצק שליח וגו' = '(Like) a smith's smelting-pot which keepeth the casting hot, (so) the sun's dart', &c., *or* (*with the reading* נפוח *of* ℌ *text*) 'Like a glowing furnace which keepeth the casting hot' (*so Smend substantially*): *perhaps* יסיק *of* ℌ *mg.* (= 'kindleth') *is right* (*cp. v.* 21). *In line* 2 שלוח = *lit.* 'what is sent', *i.e. missile, dart, is to be preferred. For other possible renderings cp. exeget. note* j–j ℌ *mg.* לשון מאור (= מֵאוּר): ℌ *text* לשאון (תנמר נושבת = *the two remaining words in* ℌ): 𝔊 (*strangely*) ατμιδας πυρωδεις εκφυσων (ℵ A C: *but* B &c. εμφυσων) = ? נשׂיאים מאור נושבת (𝔊 *ignores* תגמר): 𝔖 = 𝔊 k–k ℌ ומנורה תכוה עין (נוּר = 'fire' *as in Aram.*: *cp.* Dan. iii. 6, &c.): 𝔊 'And sending forth bright beams he dimmeth the eyes' (και εκλαμπων ακτινας αμαυροι οφθαλμους) = ? ומנירה תכהה עין: 𝔖 = 𝔊 l–l ℌ כי: 𝔊 𝔖 > m–m ℌ ודבריו ינצח אביריו (ℌ *mg.* ינצה): 𝔊 και εν λογοις αυτου κατεσπευσεν πορειαν ('and at His word he hasteneth his course'): 𝔊 ? *due to reminiscence of* Ps. xix. 6 ('the sun rejoiceth as a mighty man to run his course'): *so Lévi* (*so that* 𝔊 *may have read* ובדבריו ירוץ ארח): *Bacher proposes to read* אבריו = 'his pinions': *cp.* Mal. iii. 20 Hebr. (*for the sun's wings*): *so Peters, who reads the whole line:* ובדבריו ינצה אבריו = 'and at His (Jahveh's) command he (*i.e.* the sun) stretcheth (*lit.* ? stirreth up) his pinions': *Smend reads the line:* ודברו ינצח אבירו = 'And His word assureth victory to His mighty servant' (*i.e.* to the sun): *this may be right.* 𝔖 = 𝔊 (*rendering* 'by the words of the Holy One he hastens his march') n–n ℌ *text* וגם ירח ירח עתות שבות (ℌ *mg.* עת עת *and* עד עת): 𝔊 και η σεληνη εν πασιν εις καιρον αυτης (248 και σεληνην εποιησεν εις στασιν [εν πασιν *of* B, &c., *corrupt for* εποιησεν): *hence Peters restores:* וגם ירח עשׂה לעתו (*so read*): *Smend reads:* וגם ירח זֹרֵחַ עת עת = ? 'Moreover, the moon shines from season

2. **The sun . . . maketh heat to shine.** 𝔊 here (= R.V.) has misunderstood the text; see critical note.

3. **And before his scorching . . . who can . . .** Cp. Ps. xix. 7 ('there is nothing hid from the heat thereof'). The sentence may be modelled on Nahum i. 6 ('Who can stand before His indignation?')

4. **(Like) a glowing furnace which keepeth the casting hot, (So) the sun's dart setteth the mountains ablaze.** The 'glowing furnace' (lit. 'furnace blown upon', i.e. to maintain the flame and heat; for the expression cp. Jer. i. 13) keeps the metal-casting in a fluid state by its great heat; in the same way the sun's dart (lit. 'what is sent', 'projection') sets the mountains ablaze with its great heat. This rendering and explanation of the difficult text agrees with that of Ryssel and Smend; Peters less probably: 'A furnace glows with imprisoned heat; the sun, let loose, sets the mountains ablaze.' This does not yield a good comparison; and the same remark applies to other renderings (collected by Lévi).

5. **And His word maketh His mighty (servant) brilliant.** His 'mighty servant' is, of course, the sun, the most wonderful and impressive object in creation, according to ancient conceptions. The creator of such an overwhelming source of power must Himself be all-powerful. For the alternative renderings see critical notes. In the preceding description a vivid sense of the searching heat of the Oriental sun is apparent.

6–8. *The Moon.* As Edersheim has pointed out, the moon occupied an all-important place in the ancient world, and more especially among the Jews, in the reckoning of time. The year was—and is—calculated among them by the moon. Their festal calendar is also arranged on a lunar basis. Consequently the determination of the new moon—by observation—was a highly important matter for the Jewish communities. Symbolically the moon in the Haggada represents Israel (the moon is in the sky both by night and by day): while the sun, visible by day only, stands for the Gentiles, and so on.

6. **Moreover, the moon He made for its due season.** ℌ text has: 'Moreover, moon by moon the seasons return', which can hardly be right.

To rule over periods. Cp. Gen. i. 16, 18. The Hebr. word rendered 'period' (קץ) = strictly 'end', and is used of time in Neo-Hebr.: = the determining point which marks the end of a period of time (long or short). In Apocalyptic it bears a technical sense.

7 [p]By her (are determined) the feasts and times prescribed[p],
[q]A light-giver waning with her course[q]:
8 [r]Month by month she reneweth herself[r]—
How wonderful is she in her changing!
[s]The army-signal of the cloud-vessels on high[s],
[t]She paveth the firmament with her shining[t].

9 [u]The beauty of heaven, and the glory, are the stars[u],
[v]And a gleaming ornament[v] [w]in the heights[w] of God.
10 [x]At the word of the Holy One[x] [y]they take their prescribed place[y],
[z]And they sleep not[z] at their watches.
11 Behold the rainbow and bless its Maker,
[a]For[a] [b]it is majestic exceedingly in majesty[b]:
12 [c]It encompasseth the (heavenly) vault with its glory[c],
And the hand of God hath spread it out [d]in pride[d].
13 [e]His might[e] [f]marketh out the lightning[f],
[g]And maketh brilliant[g] [h]the flashes of His judgement[h].

[𝔖 omits *vv.* 11–13.]

to season' [o–o] ℌ ממשלת קץ = 𝔊 αναδειξιν χρονων (*free rendering*) [p–p] *So* ℌ *text* (*read with mg.* בו) בם מועד וזמני חוק: ℌ *mg.* בו מועד וממנו חוק = 'by her is the appointed feast and from her is the prescribed ordinance': 𝔊 απο σεληνης σημειον εορτης: 𝔖 = 𝔊. *Smend reads* ממנו *and Peters* מירח *at beginning of line* [q–q] *So* 𝔊 φωστηρ μειουμενος επι συντελειας (𝔖 = 𝔊) = מוֹפֵעַ עיף בתקופתו (*so Peters reads*): ℌ וחפץ ע(שיו) בתקופתו = ? 'and the good pleasure of her Maker by her circuit' (*Smend proposes an impossible restoration* נר חפץ עופה) [r–r] *So* ℌ *text:* ℌ *mg.* חדש כשמו והוא מתחדש ('the new moon is like its name in that it reneweth itself') = 𝔊 μην κατα το ονομα αυτης αυξανομενη (*? from an original* ανανεομενη: *so Lévi*): *this reading is a good variant on that of text* [s–s] ℌ כלי צבא נבלי מרום (*cp.* Job xxxviii. 37): 𝔊 σκευος παραβολων εν υψει = ℌ *with* נבלי *omitted:* 𝔖 = 𝔊 [t–t] ℌ מרצף רקיע מזהריתו: 𝔊 εν στερεωματι ουρανου εκλαμπων = ? ℌ *with suppression of the obscure* מרצף (𝔖 = 𝔊 *with particip. at beginning*) [u–u] *So* ℌ תואר שמים והדר כוכב (כוכב *collective: or ? read* כוכבים) = 𝔖 (*which has* 'stars'): 𝔊 καλλος ουρανου δοξα αστρων [v–v] 𝔊 κοσμος φωτιζων = ℌ *mg.* ועדי משריק (*i.e.* משׂריק √שׂרק = 'to be bright red,' 'shine'): ℌ *text* ואורו מזהיר ('and her light shining') [w–w] *So* ℌ *text,* 𝔊: ℌ *mg.* כמרומי (כ *for* ב): [𝔖 > 9 b] [x–x] 𝔊 εν λογοις αγιου (B αγιοις) = 𝔖: ℌ בדבר אל: *read* בדבר קדוש (*so Peters*) [y–y] *So* 𝔊 στησονται κατα κριμα = יעמדו חק (*so read with Smend*): ℌ יעמד חק [z–z] 𝔊 και ου μη εκλυθωσιν: = ℌ *text* ולא ישח (*i.e.* יָשֹׁחוּ = 'collapse,' 'sink down': *cp.* Lam. iii. 20, *Qeri*): ℌ *mg.* ישון (*read* ישנו = 'sleep [not]': *so* 𝔖 *which misunderstood* ישנו, *taking it from* שנה 'to change') [a–a] ℌ כי: 𝔊 > [b–b] ℌ מאד נאדרה (בה)וד: *so Lévi, Peters:* 𝔊 σφοδρα ωραιον εν τῳ αυγασματι αυτου (ℌ *mg.* נהדרה *for* נאדרה) [c–c] ℌ הקיפה בכבודה (*l.* חוג) הוד = 𝔊 [d–d] *Reading* בגאון: 𝔊 > (*incorrectly*) [e–e] *So* ℌ (גבורתו): 𝔊 προσταγματι αυτου (= ? גערתו: *so Smend reads*) [f–f] *So* ℌ תתוה ברק: 𝔊 κατεσπευσεν (*so* B[ab] A C &c. 𝔏: κατεπαυσε *in* B* א* 248 &c. *is a mistake*) χιονα (*? χιονα corrupted from* χειμωνα): 𝔊 *misunderstood* תתוה *as a syn. of* תנצח (= ταχυνει *in* 𝔊) *in next line* [g–g] ℌ ותנצח: 𝔊 και ταχυνει (*cp. v.* 5 κατεσπευσεν) [h–h] 𝔊 αστραπας κριματος αυτου (= ? זִיקוֹת משפטו *or, possibly,* במשפט): ℌ *text* . . . . . . ותנצח זיקות (ℌ *mg. for the whole verse:*

גערתו תתוה בקר} *i.e.* 'His rebuke maketh signs in the morning,
ותזנח יקום במ״} And rejecteth what exists in judgement':

but ברק *and* ותנצח *are better readings:* יקום *also seems to be a corruption from* זִיקִים (Prov. xxvi. 18) *or* זִיקוֹת

7. **times prescribed.** 'dates légales' (Lévi).
8. **Month by month.** Cp. Isa. lxiii. 23 (same phrase). Note the variant to this line (cp. R.V.): see critical note. The word-play in ℌ is marked.

The army-signal (or beacon) **of the cloud-vessels on high.** The reference is to the fire-signal or beacon which in front of the camp or army serves to control and direct its movements. Edersheim refers to the haggadic story that the moon, because she had humbled herself to rule only by night, was, by God's appointment, to be attended by the stars as a retinue, both when she rose and when she went down. For 'cloud-vessels' (lit. 'water-skins' [of heaven] = 'clouds') cp. Job xxxviii. 37. Peters conjectures 'giants' (נְפִלֵי for נבלי = 'cloud-vessels') and renders the whole line: 'Weapons against the host of the giants on high' (the giants here = the stars as opposed to the moon).

9–10. *The Stars.*
9. **in the heights of God.** Cp. Job xxv. 2.
10. **At the word . . . prescribed place.** Cp. Ps. cxix. 91.

they sleep not . . . Cp. Baruch iii. 34 ('And the stars shined in their watches, and were glad; when He called them, they said, Here we are,' &c.).

11–12. *The Rainbow.* Cp. Ezek. i. 2.
13–17 *b. The Storm.* The storm-piece in Ps. xxix should be compared. As Smend remarks, the genuine Jewish

ℌ[B] 14 [i]On that account[i] [j]He hath created a treasure-house[j],
[k]And He maketh the clouds fly like birds[k].
𝔊 15 [l]By His mighty power He maketh strong the clouds,
And the hailstones are broken[l].
ℌ[B] 17 *a* [m]His thunder's voice maketh His earth to be in anguish[m],
16 *a* [n]And by His strength[n] [o]He shaketh mountains[o].
16 *b* [p]The terror of Him stirreth up the south wind[p],
17 *b* [q]The whirlwind of the north[q], [r]hurricane, and tempest[r];
[s]Like flocks of birds[s] He sheddeth abroad [t]His snow[t],
[u]And like settling locusts[u] [v]is the fall thereof[v].

(Is. l. 11): [זִק = 'fiery arrow, brand, *or* spark']. במשפט *may be right*) i–i ℌ *mg.* למענו = 𝔊 (ℌ *text* למען) j–j ℌ ברא אוצר: 𝔊 (*freely*) ηνεωχθησαν θησαυροι k–k ℌ ויעף ע̄ . . . . . : 𝔊 και εξεπτησαν νεφελαι ως πετεινα = ויעף ענן כרשף (*Lévi*): πετεινα = רשף *in v.* 17 c. [*Peters reads* עב] l–l *So* 𝔊: *Peters restores* ℌ: בגבורתו החזיק עב וישברו אבני ברד. [*In certain Greek MSS. the order of the clauses of vv.* 16–17 *is confused* (*as in Swete*); *the first line of v.* 17 (17 a) *is wrongly placed: it should precede* 16 a *and* b: *thus the right order is* 17 a, 16 a b, 17 b c d. *The translation in text above gives the correct order, though retaining the Greek numbering of the verses*] m–m ℌ *text has this line* (*it omits the two following lines* = 16 a b) *in the following form:* קול רעמו יחול ארצו: ℌ *mg. supplies the missing clauses, together with* 17 a:

קול רעמו יחיל ארצו (17 a)
ובכוחו יזעים הרים (16 a) } *this order is also found in certain MSS. of* 𝔊: *viz.* 106, 157, 248, 253.
אימתו תחרף תימן (16 b)
עלעול סופה וסערה: (17 b)

For יחיל 𝔊 (*original reading*) *has* ωδινησεν (*so* Sah &c. *altered to* ωνειδισεν *in* B א C 70 106 157 &c.) n–n ℌ *mg.* ובכוחו: 𝔊 και εν οπτασια αυτου (= ? *a different reading:* ? ובחזותו) o–o ℌ *mg.* יזעים הרים = 'He maketh mountains indignant': 𝔊 σαλευθησεται ορη (= זעים הרים): *read, perhaps,* יזיע הרים p–p *So* ℌ *mg.* (*above*): 𝔊 'at His will the south wind will blow' (εν θεληματι αυτου πνευσεται νοτος, ? *reading* אמרתו *or* אותו: *probably* 𝔊 *did not understand* ℌ) q–q *So* ℌ *text* זלעפו[ת צ]פון (*lit.* 'heats of the north') = 𝔊 καταιγις βορεου: ℌ *mg.* עלעול (= 'storm, whirlwind': *Aram. and Neo-Hebr.: cp. also* Job xxxvi. 33, *where* על־עולה *should probably be read* עַלְעוֹלֹה 'His storm'): *read* ℌ *mg.* r–r ℌ סופה וסערה: 𝔊 και συστροφη πνευματος (= וסופת סערה) s–s ℌ *mg.* כרשף: 𝔊 ως πετεινα καθιπταμενα t–t *So* ℌ: 𝔊 χιονα u–u ℌ וכארבה ישכון: 𝔊 και ως ακρις καταλυουσα v–v *So* ℌ *mg.* = 𝔊 w–w ℌ תואר לבנה (*this may be read* לְבְנָהּ = 'its whiteness') = 𝔊 καλλος λευκοτητος αυτης

---

view of nature is reflected throughout. Every storm may be regarded as in a sense a foretaste and anticipation of the world-judgement.

14. **On that account.** i.e. on account of His judgement.

He hath created a treasure-house. 𝔊 suggests the reading 'the treasure-house is opened' (reading נבקע or יבקע for ברא). This certainly accords well with the context. God's treasure-house (or houses), containing the winds, storm, &c., is opened, and the storm let loose: cp. Job xxxviii. 22 ('treasuries of snow . . . hail'); Deut. xxviii. 12 ('J. shall open unto thee His good treasury, the heaven to give thee rain,' &c.); Jer. li. 16 ('When He uttereth His voice . . . He maketh lightnings . . . and bringeth forth the wind out of His treasuries'); cp. also xxxix. 30 of our book. There is a reference to the treasuries of snow, hail, &c., and the chamber of the whirlwind and the storm in *T. B. Chagigah* 12 *b*.

like birds. Cp. 17 *c* ('like flocks of birds'). The Hebr. word here used (רשף) probably = 'birds' (so 𝔊) both in this chapter (*bis*), and also in Deut. xxxii. 24 (רשף = ὄρνεις LXX, *aves* Vulg.) and Job v. 7 (בני רשף = in LXX νεοσσοὶ γυπῶν); possibly also in Ps. lxxviii. 48, לרשפים = 'to the vultures' (so it is explained in *Exod. rabbah*, § 12, in reference to the Psalm passage): '*rĕshāfîm* means birds of prey' (רשפים אלו העופות). The more common meaning of the word is 'flame', 'spark'. The conception of the clouds pictured as flying birds of prey may be due to mythological associations; cp. Ps. xviii. 10 ('And He rode upon a cherub, and did fly eagle-like upon the wings of the wind').

15. **By His mighty power He maketh strong the clouds, And the hailstones are broken.** 'On the one hand, the light and elastic particles of cloud are combined into heavy masses; and, on the other, solid blocks of ice are splintered into hailstones' (Edersheim).

17. **His thunder's voice . . . anguish.** A reminiscence of Ps. xxix. 8 ('The voice of J. bringeth anguish upon the wilderness').

16 *b*. **The terror of Him stirreth up the south wind.** Cp. Ps. lxxviii. 26.

17 *b*. **The whirlwind of the north.** So ℌ mg. (עלעול צפון). ℌ text has 'the hot north winds' (זלעפות צפון, lit. 'the heats of the north'); cp. Ps. xi. 6, 'a glowing wind,' i.e. the sirocco. But this does not suit the north, which was a cold wind.

17 *c*–22. *Snow, hoar-frost, ice.*

17 *c*. **Like flocks of birds.** For this rendering cp. note on 14 *b* above. Cowley-Neubauer render 'like darting flashes'.

sheddeth abroad (ℌ יניף). Cp. Ps. lxviii. 9 (10), of rain (same Hebr. word).

17 *d*. **the fall thereof.** Cp. Num. xi. 9.

18 [w]The beauty of the whiteness[w] [x]⌈dazzleth⌉ the eyes[x],
And the heart [y]⌈marvelleth⌉[y] at the raining thereof.
19 The hoar-frost also [z]He poureth out[z] like salt,
[a]⌈And maketh the crystals sparkle⌉ like sapphire[a].
20 [b]The icy blast of the north wind He causeth to blow[b],
[c]And hardeneth the pond like a bottle[c].
Over every basin of water [d]He spreadeth a crust[d],
And the pond putteth on as it were a breastplate.
21 [e]It burneth up the produce of the mountains as a drought[e],
[f]And the sprouting pasture[f] as a flame.
22 [g]A healing for all such is the distillation of the clouds[g],
[h]Even the dew, alighting to bring refreshment after heat[h].
23 [i]By His counsel[i] [j]He hath stilled the deep[j],
[k]And hath planted[k] [l]the islands[l] in the ocean.

x–x ℌ *text* יגהה עינים (*? read* יגהר = 'dazzleth' [Syr. ܢܘܗܪ: *Afel* 'to blind', *of the sun*]: *or read* יכהה = 'dim'): 𝔊 εκθαυμασει οφθαλμος (*? reading* יתמה *and wrongly making* עין *subject of verb*): ℌ *mg.* יהגה (= ? 'remove, take away': *cp.* Prov. xxv. 4, 5) y–y *Read with* 𝔊 (εκστησεται) יִתְמַהּ: ℌ יהמה ('is disquieted'?) z–z *So* ℌ *mg.* ישפך = 𝔊 επι γης χεει (επι γης *an explanatory addition*): ℌ *text* ישכון (*copyist's mistake under influence of* 17 d) a–a ℌ ויציץ כספיר ציצים ('And maketh it to bloom with flowers like sapphire,' *Cowley-Neub.*): *emend with Peters* וְיָצִיץ כספיר צנינים (= *translation given above in text*): 𝔊 'and when it is congealed it is as points of thorns' (και παγεισα γινεται σκολοπων ακρα: *the last three words* = ? כסופי צנינים). *In emended text* יציץ *is Hif. of* נצץ = 'sparkle': *cp.* Ezek. i. 7 (צנינים = 'thorns' *lit.*) b–b ℌ צינת רוח צפון ישיב (צינת = צִנַּת *from* צִנָּה 'cold': *the word-play confirms* צנינים *in previous verse*): ℌ = 𝔊 'the cold north wind shall blow' (*reading* יָשׁוּב *for* ישיב) c–c *Reading with* ℌ *mg.* וכרקב יקפיא מקוה (ℌ *text has* מקורו *i.e.* מְקוֹרוֹ: קור = '*cold*': Gen. viii. 22): 𝔊 και παγησεται κρυσταλλος εφ (*so* Syro-Hex 307 &c. Sah &c.: *but* B αφ) υδατος = וקרח יקפיא מקוה [קרח 'ice' = κρυσταλλος Ezek. i. 22 *in* LXX]. רָקָב = Aram. רוקבא 'bottle' *probably in* Job xiii. 28. *Wellhausen and Bacher conjecture* וכרקיע ('and like a metal-plate'): *Smend suggests* וכקרם (= *Aram.* קְרָמָא 'skin', 'covering', 'surface') d–d ℌ יקרים (*Qal occurs* Ezek. xxxvii. 6, 8): 𝔊 καταλυσει (= ? יקום) e–e ℌ יבול הרים כחרב ישיק: 𝔊 καταφαγεται ορη και ερημον εκκαυσει (= יבלע הרים וחרב ישיק) f–f ℌ *text* ונוה צמחים (*cp.* נאות דשא Ps. xxiii. 2): ℌ *mg. has* צור 'form' (Ps. xlix. 15) *or* 'rock': 𝔊 και αποσβεσει χλοην = וְכִוָּה וגו״ g–g *So* ℌ מרפא כל מערף ענן: 𝔊 ιασις παντων κατα σπουδην ομιχλη (*? reading* מרדף *for* מערף) h–h ℌ טל פורע לדשן שרב(רטב *m.*): 𝔊 δροσος απαντωσα απο καυσωνος ιλαρωσει ('a dew coming after heat shall bring cheerfulness' R.V.) = *? reading* פוגע *for* פורע (*so Peters emends*) *and* (?) מִשָּׁרָב *for* שרב: *read* טל פוגע לדשן משרב = 'Even the dew, alighting to bring refreshment (*or* enrichment) after heat'. ℌ *text* פורע *is difficult*: = ? 'hastening' (*Aram. sense* פְּרַע: 'hastening to revive') i–i 𝔊 λογισμῳ αυτου = במחשבתו (*so read*): ℌ מחשבתו, ℌ *mg.* משובתו (? 'from His quietness') j–j ℌ [יע]שיק רבה (*Lévi* שיק [ינ]) = ? 'overpowereth the deep' (*but Hif. of* עשק *does not otherwise occur*): *Lévi* 'he maketh an arsenal of' (ינשיק *denom. from* נשק): 𝔊 εκοπασεν αβυσσον (= השקיע רבה: *so read with Peters*). רבה *is determined by* תהום *in next clause* (= תהום רבה): *Smend alters unnecessarily to* רהב k–k 𝔊 και εφυτευσεν = ויטע (*so read*): ℌ ויט: (*Bacher proposes* ויטל 'and uplifteth islands' *after* Isa. xl. 15) l–l *So* ℌ איים (*but* ℌ *mg.* אוצר) = 𝔊 νησους (*so* 23 55 106 155 157 248 253 254 308),

---

18. **The beauty of the whiteness.** Or 'of its whiteness' (i. e. the snow's whiteness); see critical note.

19. **The hoar-frost . . . like salt.** Cp. Ps. cxlvii. 6 ('like ashes'). Cp. Ps. cxlvii. 16–17 for *vv.* 17–19 generally.

And maketh the crystals sparkle like sapphire. The sapphire, as Peters remarks, besides blue, flashes with other colours, such as red, green, &c. The sense is: God makes the crystals of the frost sparkle with all sorts of colours. For the comparison to sapphires cp. Lam. iv. 7; Cant. v. 14. For 𝔊 see critical note. [For ℌ text = 'And maketh it to bloom with flowers like sapphires,' cp. Num. xvii. 8 (= 23 in Hebr. text).]

20. **The icy blast.** Lit. 'the cold' (cp. צִנָּה Prov. xxv. 13).

like a bottle. For this rendering see critical note. [In Joshua iii. 16 נֵד = 'heap' (of waters) is rendered רוקבא in the Targum (Strack): cp. ? נֹאד = 'bottle'.] For the conjectured alternatives see critical note.

as it were a breastplate. Cp. Isa. lix. 17.

21. **It burneth up the produce of the mountains as a drought.** 'It' = the north wind. The cold of the north wind is as destructive in its ravages as the heat of the east wind (sirocco). For 'produce of the mountains' cp. Job xl. 20.

22. **A healing . . . distillation of the clouds.** For the expression ('distillation') cp. Deut. xxxiii. 28.

Even the dew, alighting to bring refreshment after heat. 'Dew' (טל) and 'heat' (שָׁרָב = 'dry heat' in *NH*) are contrasted: in *NH* 'the time of dry heat' (שעת השרב), i. e. noon-day, is opposed to 'the time of dew' (שעת הטל).

23–26. *The Sea.* The passage shows reminiscences of Ps. civ. 25 ff.

23. **By His counsel He hath stilled the deep.** One of the mightiest evidences of Jahveh's power is that He tamed monsters of the deep; cp. Job ix. 13, xxvi. 12 (some scholars would read 'Rahab' in our passage for 'deep').

And hath planted the islands in the ocean. Apparently Ben-Sira shared the belief that the islands in the sea arose as the result of Jahveh's conflict with the dragon of the sea (Tiamat, Rahab). When the sea was overcome and sank, the islands appeared.

ℌ[B] 24 They that go down to the sea tell of [m]its extent[m],
[n]And[n] when our ears hear it we are astonished.
25 Therein are marvels, the most wondrous of His works,
[o]All kinds of living things[o], [p]and the monsters of Rahab[p].
26 By reason of Him [q]⌈business⌉ prospereth[q],
And at His word [r]what He wills is done[r].

(*c*) XLIII. 27–33. *Conclusion* (= 3 + 2 + 2 + 1 distichs).

27 [s]More like this we will not add[s],
And [t]the conclusion of the matter[t] is: He is all.
28 [u]We will sing praises, because we cannot fathom[u];
[v]For greater is He[v] than all His works.
29 Terrible is Jahveh [w]exceedingly[w],
[x]And wonderful are His mighty acts[x].
30 [y]Ye that magnify Jahveh, [z]lift up your voice[z],
As much as ye can[a], [b]for there is still more[b]!
[c]Ye that exalt Him[c], [d]renew your strength[d],
And weary not, [e]for ye cannot fathom (Him)[e]!

which has been corrupted into Ιησους *in* B א A C Eth &c. m–m *So* ℌ קצהו ('its bounds': *lit.* 'its end'): 𝔊 τον κινδυνον αυτης (*? interpreting: Lévi suggests that* 𝔊 *read* צרתו) n–n 𝔊 + και (*so read*): ℌ > o–o ℌ מין כל חי = 𝔊 ποικιλια παντος ζῳου p–p ℌ וגבורות רבה: 𝔊 κτισις κητων (א A C κτησις κτηνων): κητος = רהב Job xxvi. 12 *in* LXX: גבורות *to be taken in a concrete sense* (*cp.* Isa. iii. 25: גבורתך = οι ισχυοντες υμων: *Peters*) q–q ℌ יצלח מלאך = ευοδοι ο αγγελος αυτου (*Cod.* 248): B &c. ευωδια τελος αυτου (τελος *arose from* ΑΓΓΕLΟS *misread* ΑΤΕLΟS): *? read* מלאכה 'work, business' (= עשׂי מלאכה Ps. cvii. 24) r–r ℌ יפעל רצון (*point* יִפָּעֵל): 𝔊 συνκειται παντα s–s ℌ עוד כאלה לא נוסף: 𝔊 'we may say many things yet shall we not attain' (πολλα ερουμεν και ου μη αφικωμεθα), *i. e. ? reading* ולא נסוף *and interpreting this to mean* 'to attain the end' (סוף: *cp.* Dan. iv. 30): *then* ℌ *would* = 'even more things like these (we might say) and not attain the end' (*so Smend*): *an excellent sense, and suiting the next clause admirably: but* נסוף *is doubtful* t–t ℌ קץ הדבר: 𝔊 συντελεια λογων u–u ℌ עוד כי לא נחקור (*mg.* נגלה) נ[גד]לה: 𝔊 δοξαζοντες που ισχυσωμεν; = נגדלה כי לא נחקור (כי לא *rendered by rhetorical question*): *so read with Peters:* עוד *probably intruded into* ℌ *text here from previous line* (ℌ *mg.* נגלה = ? נָגִלָה 'we will exult') v–v ℌ והוא גדול: 𝔊 αυτος γαρ ο μεγας w–w ℌ [מ]אד מאד: 𝔊 (*freely*) και σφοδρα μεγας x–x ℌ *text* ונפלאות דבריו (ℌ *mg.* גבורתו *read* גבורותיו, *pl. demanded by* נפלאות): 𝔊 και θαυμαστη η δυναστεια αυτου = *emended text* (δυναστεια = גבורות xv. 18) y *here in* ℌ *four distichs are compressed into two lines: cp.* xlv. 26, xlvi. 17 b *foll. in same Hebr. MS.* (B) z–z ℌ הרימו קול: 𝔊 (*abbreviating*) υψωσατε a–a ℌ בכל תוכלו = 𝔊 καθ οσον αν δυνησθε b–b ℌ כי יש עוד: 𝔊 *freely* 'for even yet will He exceed' (υπερεξει γαρ και ετι) c–c ℌ מרומים: 𝔊 και (𝔏 > και) υψουντες αυτον: *read with* ℌ *mg.* מרוממיו (*so Peters, Smend*) d–d ℌ החליפו כח: 𝔊 πληθυνατε εν ισχυι e–e ℌ *mg.* כי לא תחק[רו]: 𝔊 *translates* תחקרו *by the same word as* נוסף (= ? נסוף) *in v.* 27 *above, viz.* [ου γαρ μη] αφικησθε f–f ℌ (*defect.*) מאלה . . . . . . רוב נ:

---

24. **They that go down to the sea.** Cp. Ps. cvii. 23 (same phrase).

25. **Therein are marvels . . .** This and the following verses reflect the phraseology of Ps. cvii. 23 f. 'Therein' (שׁם) may be due to Ps. civ. 25 (which passage has also influenced Ben-Sira here).

26. **business.** A reminiscence, perhaps, of the phrase 'they that do business in great waters' (Ps. cvii. 23), and so to be interpreted here (Lévi). Cp. Wisd. xiv. 2 f. (the vessel sailing for trade). The alternative rendering (cp. ℌ text), 'by reason of Him angels prosper' (i.e. in their various missions, which are controlled by God), introduces a more general thought, which not inappropriately concludes the section (cp. also clause *b*). It should be noted also that the angels, as God's ministers, are referred to in the Psalm (civ) which is in the author's mind here ('who maketh His angels of the winds, His ministers of the flaming fire', *v.* 4).

(*c*) XLIII. 27–33. CONCLUSION (CP. THE EXORDIUM, xlii. 15–25).

27. **More like this we will not add.** The sense is rather lame. Note the alternative reading: 'Even more such things we might say and not attain the end,' i.e. fail to exhaust the catalogue of God's mighty works—an excellent sense.

And the conclusion of the matter is: He is all. For the phraseology cp. Eccles. xii. 12, 13. The originality of this clause is guaranteed by ℌ, though it sounds very Hellenistic, and, in fact, was regarded by Dr. Edersheim as 'evidently a spurious addition by the younger Siracide'. The whole context shows that the words must not be interpreted in a pantheistic sense, though, taken alone, they might be so interpreted. What Ben-Sira means is that God is manifest in all His works (cp. 𝔏 'ipse est in omnibus'): cp. Col. i. 17 f.; Heb. i. 3.

28. **We will sing praises** (lit. magnify) . . . **all His works.** Cp. Ps. cxlv. 3.

29. **Terrible is Jahveh . . .** Cp. Ps. xcvi. 4 f.

30. **renew your strength.** Cp. Is. xl. 31, xli. 1.

31 Who hath seen Him, that he may tell thereof?
And who shall magnify Him as he is?
32 [f]The number of things mysterious is greater (even) than these[f],
[g]And I have seen (but) few[g] of His works.
33 [h]Everything[h] hath Jahveh made,
[i]And to the pious hath He given wisdom[i].

[j]*Praise of the fathers of old*[j].

(*a*) XLIV. 1–15. *General introduction* (= 2 + 7 + 3 + 3 + 3 distichs).

44 1 [k]Let me now hymn the praises[k] [l]of men of piety[l],
[m]Of our fathers[m] in their generations.
2 [n]No little glory[n] did the Most High [o]allot[o] them,
[p]And they were great[p] [q]from the days of old[q]:

𝔊 πολλα αποκρυφα εστιν μειζονα τουτων: *read* רוב נ[סתרות גדול] מאלה (*so Peters*) g–g 𝔥 מעט ראיתי: 𝔊 + γαρ (ολιγα γαρ κτλ.) h–h 𝔥 את הכל: 𝔊 παντα γαρ i–i *So* 𝔊: 𝔥 (*defective*) ול[חסידים נתן חכמה] j–j *The title appears as a superscription in* 𝔥: שבח אבות עולם, *and in* 𝔊 *as* πατερων υμνος (*but Codd.* 23 [V] 106 252 *and Complut.* >): *it is probably not original* k–k 𝔥 אהללה נא: 𝔊 αινεσωμεν δη l–l 𝔥 אנשי חסד = 𝔖: 𝔊 ανδρας ενδοξους (= ? אנשי כבוד — כבוד ? *influenced by* 2 a: *but* = אנשי הוד *according to Peters, who so reads*) m–m *So* 𝔥: 𝔊 + και n–n 𝔥 רב כבוד o–o 𝔥 חלק (*mg.* + להם) = 𝔊 εκτισεν (*see notes on* xxxix. 25). [*For* חלק עליון *of* 𝔥 *text* 𝔖 *has simply* 'He hath appointed to them' = ? חלק עליהם: *so Peters reads* + יהוה] p–p 𝔥 וגדלו *i.e.* וְגָדְלוֹ; *but* 𝔊 την μεγαλωσυνην αυτου = גָּדְלוֹ: *so Peters reads* וְגָדְלוֹ = ['No little glory did the Most High allot them] and His greatness' (𝔖 'and all their greatness') q–q 𝔥 מימות עולם: 𝔊 (*freely*) απ αιωνος: 𝔖 'to

---

31. **Who hath seen Him** . . . Only extant in 𝔊 (𝔥 omits). The verse is regarded as a gloss by Ryssel (cp. xlii. 15).

32. **The number of things mysterious** (hidden) . . . Cp. xvi. 21.

33. **Everything** . . . God has created all things; true wisdom consists in the fear of God (piety)—the two chief affirmations of the Jewish faith.

Chapters XLIV—XLIX form a well-knit and distinct division of the book, having for their theme the praise of the fathers of old. The heroes enumerated range from Enoch to Nehemiah (in a series of well-defined sections). The connexion with the preceding division is a natural one; God, whose glory is manifest in the mighty forces and phenomena of the natural world (xliii), is also worthy of praise both for and in the lives of the great heroes and pious men that shine through history. An appendix (l. 1–24) sets forth the praise of the high-priest Simon, who can hardly be reckoned, as Smend points out, with the fathers of old.

The whole forms a historical retrospect of Israel's history from the earliest age; cp. similar surveys in the O.T. in Psalms lxxviii, cv, cvi, cxxxv, cxxxvi, and Ezek. xx; in the apocryphal literature, Wisdom x ff., 1 Macc. ii. 51–60; and in the N.T., Heb. xi, &c. The subject throughout is Israel, regarded as the chosen and truly representative race. All that is best and highest in humanity is reflected in the Israelitish race, and comes to glorious expression in the long line of patriarchs, pious kings, heroes, prophets, and teachers, which stretches from the beginnings of history.

Ben-Sira lays special emphasis on the duty and privilege of the community to remember the pious of the past (cp. xliv. 9, 13, 15, xlv. 1, xlvi. 11, xlix. 1, 9, 13). He also lays stress upon the splendour of the cultus as the visible expression of Israel's unique relation to God. Thus Moses is subordinated to Aaron in importance, and David's greatest glory is that he was the founder of the Temple music and psalmody (xlvii. 8–10). This is all the more remarkable, as Ben-Sira was inclined, if anything, to depreciate the efficacy of sacrifices *per se*. Throughout Ben-Sira closely follows the narrative given in the canonical Scriptures, and reminiscences of scriptural phraseology are of frequent occurrence. It is clear that he values highly the written word (cp. xlviii. 10 = Mal. iii. 23, 24), which he obviously regards as among the most precious possessions of the chosen community of God. It is interesting to note, in this connexion, that the author shows clear indications of acquaintance not only with the Law (Pentateuch) and the Prophets (including Joshua, Judges, Samuel, and Kings), but also with Chronicles (xlvii. 8 ff.), Nehemiah (xlix. 13), the Psalms (xliv. 5, xlvii. 8 ff.), Proverbs (xliv. 5, xlvii. 17), Job (xlix. 9), and perhaps Ecclesiastes (*Qoheleth*) (xlvii. 23). No allusion is made to Daniel, which was not yet extant when the author wrote; and it is uncertain whether Ruth, Lamentations, and Canticles were yet regarded as sacred Scripture, as he makes no clear allusion to any of them.

The whole forms a carefully articulated composition, falling into strophes, and consisting of 211 distichs.

(*a*) XLIV. 1–15 forms an introductory section to the enumeration that follows, setting forth, in general terms and under twelve categories, the different classes of eminence into which Israel's heroes fall. The reference is to Israel only, and does not include the heathen (see on *vv.* 3–6). [The title is extant in 𝔥 and 𝔊, but is absent from certain Greek MSS. (see critical note). It is probably secondary, though the possibility remains that it may be an original feature due to the author (so Smend); Peters thinks it original in the form 'Praise of the Fathers' (omitting 'of old' = עולם; cp. 𝔊).]

1. **men of piety**. So 𝔥 (probably rightly). It is piety in its broadest sense of duty rendered to God that Ben-Sira sees manifested in various types of character and achievement. For the alternative reading ('famous men') see critical note.

in their generations. i.e. in chronological order.

ℌ[B] 3 [r](Men) who wielded dominion[r] over the earth [s]in their royalty[s],
And men of renown in [t]their[t] might;
[u]Counsellors[u] in their discernment,
[v]And all-seeing in their prophetic (power)[v];
4 [w]Princes of nations[w] [x]in their statesmanship[x],
[y]And (trusted) leaders in their penetration[y];
[z]Clever of speech[z] [a]in their (scribal) instruction[a],
[b]And speakers of wise sayings in their tradition[b];

eternal generations' r–r ℌ *mg.* רודי ארץ: 𝔊 κυριευοντες [𝔖 > *v.* 3 a b c] s–s ℌ במלכותם: 𝔊 εν ταις βασιλειαις αυτων t–t 𝔊 > *their* u–u ℌ *mg.* יועצים (ℌ *text+article*): 𝔊 βουλευοντες (55 106 155 157 248 254 Compl.: *v. l.* βουλευται 296 308 Eth: *the* βουλευσονται *of* B *is a mistake for* βουλευοντες): 𝔏 [prudentia sua] praediti v–v ℌ וחוזי כל בנבואתם (*cp.* וחוזה כל xv. 18): 𝔊 απηγγελκοτες εν προφητειαις (*but* א* 155 253 308 &c. *and* 𝔏 + εν προφηταις), *misreading* חוזי *as* חווי *and omitting* כל: *cp.* 𝔖 'And they declared by their prophecies signs' w–w ℌ שׂרי גוים: 𝔊 ηγουμενοι λαου: 𝔖 'and kings' (*omitting* גוים *to avoid reference to heathen: so Peters*) x–x ℌ במזמתם ('in their prudence,' *Cowley-Neub.*) = 𝔖: 𝔊 εν διαβουλιοις y–y ℌ ורוזנים במחקרותם: 𝔖 >: 𝔊 και εν (*so* 248 &c. Sah Eth: *but* B &c. > εν) συνεσει γραμματειας (א γραμματειαις: Sah Eth γραμματεις) λαου = ? ורוזני עם בחכמתם z–z ℌ חכמי שיח = 𝔊 σοφοι λογοι (? *originally* λογῳ: *note variants* λογοις 296, εν λογοις A &c.): 𝔖 'the wise taught' a–a ℌ בספרתם (*cp. Neo-Hebr.* ספרותה = 'office of scribe'): ℌ *mg. has* במס״ *i. e.* ? במספר *or* בְּמֹסָרָם (Job xxxiii. 16) *or* בְּמוּסָרָם = 𝔊 εν παιδειᾳ αυτων: 𝔖 'in their wisdom' b–b ℌ ומושלים במשמרותם: 𝔊 >: 𝔖 (*combining* 4 d *and* 5 a) 'And the rulers have explored their praises on lutes and harps'. *For other possible renderings of* ℌ *cp. exeget. notes. Bacher emends second word to* בממשלותם (= 'in their parables') c–c ℌ חוקרי מזמור על חוק (*note the word-play:* חוקר . . . . . חוק) ('who sought out music according to rule,' *Cowley-Neub.*): 𝔊 εκζητουντες μελη μουσικων (*ignoring* על חוק: *cp.* xxxii. [xxxv.] 6 *where* קול מזמור *is rendered* μελος μουσικων) d–d נושאי משל בכתב (+ ו *with best MSS. of* 𝔊: και διηγουμενοι ἐπη εν γραφῃ) e–e ℌ אנשי חיל = 𝔊 ανδρες πλουσιοι f–f ℌ וסומכי כח: *read* וסמוכי = 𝔊 και (*so* 155: *others* >) κεχορηγημενοι ισχυι g–g ℌ ושוקטים על מכונתם = 𝔊 (*point* מְכוֹנָתָם = 𝔊 εν παροικιαις αυτων)

3–6 (7). Twelve categories of men are here enumerated (for the number twelve in such a connexion cp. xxiv. 13–17 and l. 6–10); of men who 'were honoured in their generation and in their days had glory' (*v.* 7; it should be noticed that *vv.* 1–7 form a single logical period). It is then stated (*vv.* 8 and 9) that some of these have left a name which deserves to be honoured and remembered, while others have left no memorial. In other words, some were pious, and are remembered as such by posterity (the enumeration of these is introduced in *v.* 10), while others were not, and are deservedly forgotten (*v.* 9). Lévi and Ryssel think that the reference in *vv.* 3–6 is to heathen heroes—the great men of the pagan world—conquerors, warriors, counsellors, poets, writers, &c.; and that Ben-Sira draws a deliberate contrast between these and the heroes of Israel. The former are only partly remembered by their own people, while the memory of the pious in Israel never fades. But the terms of *v.* 3 *d* (ref. to the prophets) and *v.* 4 *c*, *d* (ref. to the scribes) can hardly be made to apply to the heathen; and it is doubtful whether Ben-Sira would have reckoned any heathen heroes among the truly pious. The terms used can all be applied more naturally to the heroes and great men of Israel. The absence of any specific mention of priests in these verses may be explained by supposing that Ben-Sira intends to include them among the princes and teachers.

3. **(Men) who wielded dominion . . . of renown . . .** Rulers like David and Solomon and warriors like Joshua are meant.

Counsellors . . . all-seeing in their prophetic (power). i. e. such men as Elisha and Isaiah, who were at once counsellors of the nation and prophets.

4. **Princes of nations in their statesmanship** (lit. in their devising), **And (trusted) leaders** (or potentates). 'Princes of nations' such as Joseph (a viceroy); leaders of Israel ('trusted leaders') like Zerubbabel and Nehemiah. 𝔊 misunderstands 4 *b* (rendering, according to the probable original Greek text, 'scribes of the people in understanding' (see critical note); 'scribes of the people' = שׁוטרי עם; cp. for the expression 1 Macc. v. 42). The Hebrew word rendered 'in their penetration' (בְּמֶחְקְרוֹתָם lit. 'in their searchings out') does not occur again, apparently, in this sense (in Ps. xcv. 4 מֶחְקָר = 'a place to be searched out', i.e. remotest part); but a form of the same word is used in Prov. xxv. 2 of the activities that characterize the life surrounding a royal court, 'It is the glory of God to conceal a thing: but the glory of kings is to search out a matter' (חֲקֹר דבר). Cowley-Neubauer render here 'in their care'.

Clever of speech in their (scribal) instruction. The Hebr. word here rendered '(scribal) instruction' does not occur in this sense in Biblical Hebrew (in Ps. lxxi. 15 סְפֹרוֹת = 'numbers'; but LXX γραμματεία: סְפֹרָה = ספר 'book', if it be a genuine form); but it can be justified from Neo-Hebrew (cp. סַפְרוּתָא (סַפְרוּתָה) = 'the office of scribe'; סְפִירוּת = 'the art of the scribe'). The reference in our text is doubtless to the work of the scribes as instructors, in which Ben-Sira was so deeply interested.

And speakers of wise sayings in their tradition. Lit. 'proverbialists (מוֹשְׁלִים) in their keeping' (viz. of the tradition); for the translation 'speakers of wise sayings' or 'proverbs' cp. Num. xxi. 27; and for 'keeping' used in this sense (viz. guarding a tradition) cp. Prov. iv. 21, vii. 1, xxii. 18. Lévi objects to this rendering on the ground that it anticipates *v.* 5 *b*, where 'the makers of proverbs' are the subject (thus involving an awkward repetition), but the objection is not a fatal one; in our present verse the author is thinking of the wise as a class of men who expressed their wisdom in proverbial form orally (in their teaching); in *v.* 5 *b* he refers specifically to the authors of

ℌ[B] 5 [c]Devisers of psalms according to rule[c],
[d]And authors of proverbs in books[d];
6 [e]Men of resource[e] [f]and supported with strength[f],
[g]And living at ease in their dwelling-places[g]:
7 All these [h]were honoured[h] [i]in their generation[i],
[j]And in their days[j] [k]had glory[k].
8 Some of them there are who have left a name,
[l]That men might tell of their praise[l]:
9 And some of them there are who have no memorial,
[m]So that there was an end of them when they came to their end[m];
[n]They were as though they had not been,
And their children after them[n].
10 [o]Nevertheless[o] these were men of piety,
[p]And their good fortune shall not come to an end[p];
11 With their seed [q]their prosperity[q] remaineth sure,
[r]And their inheritance to their children's children[r].
𝔊 12 [s]In their covenant their seed abideth,
And their children's children for their sakes[s];

h–h *So* ℌ *mg.* = 𝔊 𝔖: ℌ *text*> i–i ℌ בדורם: 𝔊 εν γενεαις (70 + αυτων): 𝔖 'in their generations' j–j *So* ℌ *mg.* (ובימיהם) = 𝔊 *and* 𝔖: ℌ *text* ומימיהם k–k ℌ תפארתם = 𝔖: 𝔊 καυχημα l–l 𝔊 του εκδιηγησασθαι επαινους = 𝔖 (+ 'their'): ℌ בנחלתם (*mg.* להשתעות) להשתענות ('That men might tell of it in their inheritance,' *Cowley-Neub.*): *read* להשתעות בתהלתם (*with Smend: so Peters, omitting* ב) [הִשְׁתָּעָה = *Aram.* אֶשְׁתָּעִי 'to narrate', 'tell'] m–m ℌ וישבתו כאשר שבתו: 𝔊 (*freely*) και απωλοντο ως ουχ υπαρξοντες (𝔖 = ℌ) n–n *So* ℌ *and* 𝔊: 𝔖> (*? for dogmatic reasons*) o–o ℌ ואולם = 𝔊 αλλ' η p–p ℌ ותקותם ל[א תשב]ת: 𝔊 ('whose righteous deeds have not been forgotten') ων αι δικαιοσυναι (248 Sah + αυτων) ουκ επελησθησαν (*reading* וצדקתם *for* ותקותם): 𝔖 'and their goodness shall not come to an end': *reading* וצדקתם (*so emend* ℌ) q–q ℌ טובם = טוּבָם, *i.e.* 'their prosperity' *or* 'their goods', 'property' (*parallel to* 'their possession' *next line*): 𝔊 αγαθη (𝔖 = ℌ) r–r ℌ (ונחלתם ל[בני בניהם) = 𝔖 ('and their root to their children's children): 𝔊 κληρονομια εκγονα αυτων *is obviously in disorder* (*? read* κληρονομια αυτων τοις εκγονοις αυτων): 𝔏 (*Codex Sang.*) hereditas nepotum illorum s–s ℌ>; *but the verse is attested by* 𝔊 *and* 𝔖. 𝔊 *has* εν ταις διαθηκαις (70 + αυτων = 𝔖) εστη σπερμα αυτων και τα τεκνα αυτων δι αυτους, *i.e.* בבריתם יעמד זרעם ובעבורם בניהם: 𝔖 *in second line reads* [הטובה] ובעבודתם *for* ובעבורם *and* (?) בני בניהם *for* בניהם (*Peters follows* 𝔖 *in line* 2, *and renders* 'and their children in their works')

---

certain books (Solomon and others) who have reduced this proverbial wisdom to writing. The alternative rendering adopted by Lévi and others makes the line refer to governors or officials. Thus Cowley-Neub. render 4 *c* and *d*:

'Wise of meditation in their writing,
And governing in their watchfulness.'

Lévi: 'Wise orators for their instruction,
And officials for their offices'

(the reference, according to Lévi, being to heathen orators and officers).

5. **Devisers of psalms according to rule.** Lévi, 'perfecters of poetry according to rule.' The reference is to the composition of psalms set to traditional melodies. In this connexion David and the guilds of temple-singers would be thought of primarily.

6. **Men of resource . . . living at ease in their dwelling-places.** The patriarchs, and perhaps Job, were in the writer's mind (so Smend).

8. **Some . . . have left a name.** Such are again referred to in *vv.* 10 f.

9. **And some . . . who have no memorial . . .** The reference is to godless kings, doubtless of the northern kingdom. As the Chronicler, so Ben-Sira passes these over in silence.

They were as though they had not been. For the expression cp. Job x. 19; Obad. 16.

10. **Nevertheless these were men of piety.** Cp. *v.* 1. This introduces the enumeration that follows of great and pious men in Israel.

And their good fortune shall not come to an end. Not only were they happy and fortunate in their lives, but their happy estate (reading וצדקתם with 𝔊 and 𝔖; צדקה = 'good fortune', 'prosperity' sometimes) lives on in their descendants' happy and prosperous lives (this is further developed in *vv.* 11 f.). The reading of 𝔊 affords a good sense—'their righteousness shall not be forgotten' (but anticipates *v.* 13 *b*). ℌ has 'their hope shall not come to an end'.

11. **With their seed their prosperity remaineth sure.** Cp. Job xxi. 8, 16; also xlv. 26 of our book.

12. **In their covenant** (or covenants) . . . Though this verse is absent from ℌ the variants in 𝔊 and 𝔖 (see critical note), which can only be explained by a Hebrew original, show that it must have formed part of the original Hebrew text. 'Covenant' in Ben-Sira's phraseology means always a gracious promise by God. The covenants in the author's mind are not only those with Abraham and Noah, but also those with Phineas, Aaron, and David (cp. xxiv. 25, xlv. 15). So Smend.

ℌ[B] 13 [t]Their memory[t] abideth for ever,
[u]And their righteousness shall not be forgotten[u];
14 [v]Their bodies were buried in peace[v],
[w]But their name liveth unto all generations[w].
15 [x]The assembly recounteth their wisdom,
And the congregation declareth their praise[x].

(*b*) XLIV. 16–18. *Enoch and Noah.*

16 [yz]ENOCH walked with Jahveh [*and was taken*][z],
[a]A miracle of knowledge to all generations[a].

t–t *So* ℌ 𝔖: 𝔊 το σπερμα αυτων (זרעם *for* זכרם) u–u ℌ *defective* ...... וצדקתם ל: 𝔊 και η δοξα αυτων ουκ εξαλειφθησεται: *read* (?) וצדקתם ל[א תשכ]ח: *so Lévi* (*Smend thinks there are faint traces of a* ה [*which may be* ח] *at end of line*): *Smend reads* תמחה: *Peters, following* 𝔊, וכבודם לא ינשה v–v ℌ *defective* [בש]ל[ום נאספו] .....: 𝔊 το σωμα αυτων εν ειρηνη εταφη: *read with Peters*: גְּוִיֹּתָם בשלום נאספו (*so* 𝔖) w–w ℌ *defective* ל[דור] ודור .....: 𝔊 και το ονομα αυτων ζη εις γενεας: *read* ושמם חי לדור ודור = 𝔖 x–x ℌ *text*> : *but* ℌ *mg. has* חכמתם תשנה עדה ותהלתם יספר קָהל: = 𝔊 (λαοι = עדה): 𝔖>*line* 1: *in line* 2 = 𝔊 *and* ℌ (*the whole verse* = xxxix. 10) y *v.* 16 *wanting in* 𝔖 z–z ℌ חנוך [נמצ]א תמים והתהלך עם יי ונלקח (*here* [נמצ]א תמים ו *must be deleted: came in from next verse*): *genuine Hebr. text*: 'Enoch walked with Jahveh [and was taken'] = 𝔊 Ενωχ ευηρεστησεν Κυριῳ (*so* LXX Gen. v. 24) και μετετεθη (*the last word* 'and was taken' *is probably an addition to the original text: see exeget. note*). a–a *So* ℌ אות דעת לדור ודור: 𝔊 'An example of repentance to all generations' (υποδειγμα μετανοιας ταις γενεαις) b–b ℌ *text* לעת כלה (ℌ *mg.* 'ב *i.e.* בעת): 𝔊 εν καιρῳ οργης c–c ℌ תחליף: 𝔊 ανταλλαγμα (𝔖 'he was taken in exchange for the world') d–d *So*

---

13. **Their memory abideth for ever.** Cp. xxxix. *c*, *d*.
14. **But their name liveth unto all generations.** = xxxix. 9 *d*.
15. = xxxix. 10 (see notes there).

(*b*) XLIV. 16–18. ENOCH AND NOAH.

16. **Enoch walked with Jahveh** [**and was taken**]. The phraseology is a reminiscence of Gen. v. 24 (for the text cp. critical note). The last word rendered 'and was taken' is probably an addition to the original form of the text; it overloads the line and spoils the rhythm (so Schlatter and Smend; the latter scholar points out that xlix. 10, which uses the same phrase of Enoch, implies that his being 'taken' has not previously been mentioned. See further notes on xlix. 10).

A miracle of knowledge to all generations. So ℌ. 𝔊 has 'an example of repentance to the generations'. The translation of 𝔊 reflects in an interesting way the influence of controversy. At an early period Enoch lived in popular legend as a heroic figure whose destiny was glorified by God. These features received elaborate and exaggerated development in the circles of the apocalyptists: thus Enoch's wisdom, a feature that belongs to the oldest form of the tradition (cp. Ezek. xxviii. 3 f., where read 'Enoch' for 'Daniel'; so also in Ezek. xiv. 14, 20[1]), receives elaborate development in the apocalyptic Enochic literature (cp. especially 2 Enoch), and Enoch becomes the exemplar of piety and wisdom, the friend and confidant of God, and the accredited revealer of divine secrets to men.[2] Against this, as it seemed, exaggerated estimate there was raised a protest in Rabbinical circles which is reflected in some of the early Rabbinical literature. Thus in the *Midrash rabba* on Gen. v. 24 the idea that Enoch was translated without dying is expressly refuted[3] (contrast the Christian view in Heb. xi. 5). Another view, reflected in Wisd. iv. 10–14, was that Enoch had been inconsistent in his piety, and was removed (? by death) before his time, in order that he might not fall into further sin ('he was caught away lest wickedness should change his understanding'). Cp. also Philo, *de Abrahamo*, § 3, where 'he was not' is explained to mean that his former blameworthy life was wiped out and effaced, being no longer 'found'. In 𝔊's version of our text, therefore, the influence of a later exegesis which had made its way to Alexandria is traceable. In ℌ, on the other hand, which represents the text of the original author, one primitive feature of the Enoch-tradition has been retained, viz. his wonderful knowledge. Ben-Sira, like some of the later Rabbis, would not have been predisposed to exaggerate unduly the claims of Enoch in the apocalyptic direction. Nor, in fact, has he done so. See further on xlix. 14, and cp. Fränkel, *Ueber den Einfluss der palästinischen Exegese*, p. 44 f.

[It should be added that in the Targ. of Pseudo-Jonathan (on Gen. v. 24) the old popular view of Enoch reappears. He is represented as a pious worshipper of the true God, who was translated to heaven, and received the names and offices of *metatron* and 'great scribe' (*Safra rabba*). This doubtless was made possible after controversy (with Christians) had ceased.]

---

[1] Cp. on this point *EB*, s. v. 'Enoch'.

[2] As Cheyne points out (*EB*, s. v. 'Enoch'), the Enoch-tradition shows traces of solar origin: 'A child of the "all-seeing" sun must be wise as well as pious.' This primitive idea will account for the later developments according to which Enoch was the inventor of writing, arithmetic, and astronomy (cp. *Jubilees*, ch. iv).

[3] In the same passage it is said that he had been reckoned among sinners, and was still inconsistent in his piety, and that God said if he continued pious He would take him out of the world. Cp. Wisd. iv. 10–14. Targ. Onq. says: 'God made him to die.'

ℌ[B] 17 NOAH the righteous was found blameless;
[b]In the season of destruction[b] he became [c]the continuator[c];
[d]For his sake there was a remnant[d],
[e]And by reason of the covenant with him the Flood ceased[e].
18 [f]By an eternal sign[f] [g](God) concluded it[g] with him,
Not to destroy (again) all flesh[h].

(*c*) XLIV. 19–23. *Abraham, Isaac, and Jacob* (3 + 3 + 1 + 3 distichs).

19 ABRAHAM, 'the father[i] of a multitude of nations',
[j]Tarnished not his glory[j];
20 Who kept the commandment of the Most High,
And entered into a covenant with Him:
[k]In his flesh[k] He engraved him an ordinance,
And in trial he was found faithful.
21 Therefore with an oath [l]He promised him[l]
[m]'To bless[m] [n]the nations[n] in his seed',
𝔊 (𝔖) [o]To multiply him '[p]as the dust of the earth[p]'[o],
And to exalt his seed 'as the stars';
ℌ[B] [q]To cause them to inherit 'from sea to sea,
And from the River to the ends of the earth'.

ℌ = 𝔖: 𝔊 δια τουτο (*for* δια τουτον = ℌ בעבורו) εγενηθη καταλιμμα τη γη (? τη γη *originally after* ανταλλαγμα: *cp.* 𝔖 *above*) e–e ℌ ובבריתו חדל מבול: 𝔊 δια τουτο (*reading* בעבורו *for* בבריתו) εγενετο κατακλυσμος (𝔖 *paraphrases*) f–f *So* ℌ באות עולם: 𝔊 διαθηκαι αιωνος (= ברית עולם) (𝔖 *may imply also* ברית: *rendering* 'oath') g–g ℌ *text* נכרת = 𝔊 επεθησαν: ℌ *mg.* כרת [𝔖 *renders the line*: 'an oath God sware to him in truth'] h 𝔊 + κατακλυσμῳ i 𝔊 + μεγας (μεγας πατηρ) j–j *So* ℌ (*lit.* 'Put not in his honour any blemish') לא נתן בכבודו מום: 𝔖 'and there was not put any blemish in his honour' = ℌ: 𝔊 και ουχ ευρεθη ομοιος (*read* μωμος) εν τη δοξῃ [ℌ *mg.* דופי *for* מום *cp.* Ps. l. 20] k–k 𝔊 + και (και εν σαρκι αυτου), *but* 𝔏 *and a number of Greek codices* (106 155 157 248 253), *also* Syro-Hex, > και (*so also* ℌ *and* 𝔖) l–l ℌ הקים לו = 𝔊 εστησεν αυτῳ = ? 'assured him': *in Aram.* קְיָם = 'to swear': *so* 𝔖 *here* 'God sware to him' m–m *So* ℌ: 𝔊 ενευλογηθηναι, *so* 𝔖 (*but* 248 ενευλογειν = ℌ) n–n *So* ℌ *and* 𝔊: 𝔖 'all the peoples of the earth' o–o *So* 𝔊 *and* 𝔖: *but* א* > *the line with* ℌ p–p *So* 𝔊 (*cp.* Gen. xiii. 6): 𝔖 'as the sand of the sea' (*cp.* Gen. xxii. 17) q 𝔊 + και (*preceding*): *but* ℌ 𝔖 > και

---

17. **Noah the righteous.** Cp. Gen. vi. 9, vii. 1 (Heb. xi. 7).

In the season of destruction he became the continuator. 𝔊 renders 'he became a substitute' (ἐγένετο ἀντάλλαγμα). The exact meaning of the Hebrew word rendered 'continuator' has been the subject of much discussion. Its form (תחליף) is similar to such Hifil noun-formations as תלמיד ('disciple'), and it seems best to explain its meaning from the Hifil of the verb (החליף) as it is used in Job xiv. 7 = 'to put forth fresh branches', 'sprout again'. So here the noun would mean 'continuator', 'renewer' (one who starts the race afresh). Cowley-Neubauer render 'successor', and in the Glossary this is explained as follows: 'i.e. humanity at large perished, but Noah was spared to carry on the succession and keep the race alive': cp. xlviii. 8 (in xlvi. 12 תחליף is probably a verbal form). With this meaning cp. the use of the verb in Hebrew החליף = 'to cause to come in place of', 'to make to succeed,' Is. ix. 9; in Aram. תחלופא = 'substitute', 'representative'. S. Krauss in *JQR*, xi. 156 f., discusses the word and proposes to render our passage: 'At the time of destruction there was a change (a reward, a compensation)'. See further Cowley-Neubauer in *JQR*, ix. 563.

ceased. i.e. probably ceased to come any more, was not to be repeated (so 𝔖 understands the meaning rightly).

18. **By an eternal sign . . .** Cp. xliii. 6; Gen. ix. 12 f., xiii. 17.

Not to destroy (again) all flesh. Cp. Gen. ix. 15.

(*c*) XLIV. 19–23. ABRAHAM, ISAAC, AND JACOB.

19. **Abraham, 'the father of a multitude of nations'.** Cp. Gen. xvii. 4 f. (xii. 2 f., xv. 5). 𝔊 ('Abraham was a great father of a multitude', &c.) combines with this the other explanation of the name Abram = 'exalted father' (so Hart).

Tarnished not his glory (or honour). The same phrase (cp. critical note) occurs in xlvii. 20.

20. **And entered into a covenant with Him.** Cp. Gen. xvii. 10; and for the phrase Ezek. xvi. 8 (בא בברית).

In his flesh . . . Cp. Gen. xvii. 9–11, 24.

And in trial . . . Cp. Gen. xxii.

21. **Therefore with an oath . . . seed.** Cp. Gen. xxii. 16–18 (also xii. 3, xviii. 18): see also Gal. iii. 8.

To multiply him 'as the dust of the earth' . . . his seed 'as the stars'. Cp. Gen. xxii. 17.

. . . to inherit 'from sea to sea . . . earth'. Cp. Gen. xviii. 18; Exod. xxiii. 31; Deut. xi. 24; Joshua i. 4; Ps. lxxii. 8; and Zech. ix. 10. 'The River' (i.e. the River *par excellence*) is, of course, the Euphrates.

𝕳[B]

22 And to ISAAC also [r]He promised it[r] [s]likewise[s],
For his father Abraham's sake;
[t]And the blessing of all predecessors
23 Rested upon the head of ISRAEL[t];
[u]And He titled him with the dignity of firstborn[u],
And gave him [v]his inheritance[v];
[w]And He set him in tribes,
So as to be divided into twelve[w].

(*d*) XLIV. 23—XLV. 5. *Moses* (=2+2+2+3 distichs).

[x]And He caused to issue[x] [y]from him[y] [z]a man[z]
[a]Who found favour[a] in the sight [b]of all living[b].
45
1 [c]Beloved of God and men[c]
Was MOSES [d]of happy memory[d].

r–r 𝕳 הקים = 𝕲 εστησεν   s–s 𝕳 *mg.* כן = 𝕲 ουτως: 𝕳 *text* בן *is a copyist's mistake* ('He raised up a son') t–t *So* 𝕾 = :וברכת כל ראשונים נחה על ראש ישראל: 𝕲 (ευλογιαν παντων ανθρωπων και διαθηκην και κατεπαυσεν επι κεφαλην Ιακωβ) *supports the reading suggested partly: ανθρωπων may have displaced an earlier* αρχαιων. 𝕳 *text has*

ברית כל ראשון נתנו
וברכה נחה על ראש ישראל: } *i.e.*

'The covenant of every ancestor (predecessor) He gave him,
And the blessing rested on the head of Israel'.

It is noticeable that 𝕲 *like* 𝕳 *has the two words* 'covenant' *and* 'blessing', *only in the reverse order. This suggests a double reading in the Hebr. text used by* 𝕲, *viz.* ברכת *and* וברית, *the latter a variant on the former* (*perhaps originally* וברכת). *Line* 2 *of* 𝕳 *is overloaded.* ראשון *was probably written in abbreviated form for* ראשונים: נתנו, *which is not attested in either* 𝕲 *or* 𝕾, *is probably a variant on* נחה   u–u *So* 𝕳 *mg.* ויכנהו בבכורה: 𝕳 *text* ויכוננהו בברכה 'and He confirmed (established) him in the blessing': 𝕲 επεγνω αυτον εν ευλογιαις αυτου: *reading* ויכירהו (*cp.* xv. 18) *for* ויכוננהו (*so Smend—then render*: 'and He (God) recognized him (*i.e.* singled him out) in blessing' (𝕾 = 𝕳 *mg. freely rendered*)   v–v *So* 𝕳: 𝕲 ἐν κληρονομιᾳ (κληρονομιαν 248 = 𝕷 𝕾) w–w *So* 𝕳 *may be rendered* (*see exeget. notes*): 𝕲 *misunderstanding* 𝕳 *renders*: 'and divided his portions; among twelve tribes did He part them': 𝕾 'He made him father to the tribes, and they went forth and He divided unto the twelve tribes'   x–x *So* 𝕲 = ויוצא: *so* 𝕳 (*which is defective in this word partly*) *is to be read* (*note the assonance with* מוצא *which follows at the beginning of next line*)   y–y *So* 𝕳 𝕲: *but* Sah Eth ἐξ αυτων (*sc.* 'the tribes'—*wrongly*)   z–z *So* 𝕳: 𝕲 ανδρα ελεους (=איש חסד: *so Peters*): 𝕾 'righteous men' (*but original reading probably* 'righteous man'): 𝕷 Eth *read* ανδρας ελεους (*so* 70)   a–a 𝕳 מוצא חן (*note* מוצא *a play on* משה)   b–b 𝕳 כל חי: 𝕲 πασης σαρκος   c–c *So* 𝕳 א[הוב א]להים ואנשים: 𝕲 ηγαπημενον . . . [Μωυσην] *wrong construction* (*making the clause dependent on preceding*): 𝕾 'beloved was he of God and also in the sight of men' d–d 𝕳 זכרו לטובה: 𝕲 ου το μνημοσυνον εν ευλογιαις: *Peters reads* זכרו לברכהה (*cp.* lxvi. 11); *so apparently* 𝕾 *here* (זכור לטוב *not uncommon in Neo-Hebrew*)   e–e 𝕳 *text defective*: 𝕳 *marg.* ויביי ייי: 𝕲 ωμοιωσεν αυτον δοξῃ

---

22. **And to Isaac . . . likewise . . .** Cp. Gen. xxvi. 3–5, where the covenant and the promises made to Abraham are repeated.

22–23. **And the blessing of all predecessors Rested upon the head of Israel.** i.e. the blessings promised to Abraham and Isaac, and possibly also those promised to Adam and Noah. For text cp. critical note.

23. **And He titled him with the dignity of firstborn.** The foundation-passage is Exod. iv. 22 (cp. also Hos. xi. 1): cp. further xxxvi. 12 (17) of our book. See further critical note (for variant forms of the text).

And He set him in tribes, So as to be divided (לחלק = לְחָלֵק for לְהֵחָלֵק: so Peters) **into twelve** (reading לשנים עשׂר for text, which omits ל: with Smend, Peters). Smend, however, renders substantially the same Hebrew text: 'and He assigned it (i.e. the inheritance) to the tribes to be a portion (לְחֵלֶק) for the twelve' (𝕳 ויציבה[ו] לשבטים לחלק [ל]שנים עשׂר). For the division by Jacob cp. Gen. xlix. But more probably God is here the subject of the sentence, in which case the laws issued by divine authority for the division of the land into twelve parts are in the writer's mind.

(*d*) XLIV. 23—XLV. 1–5 (MOSES).

He caused to issue. Cp. Isa. lxv. 9 (same verb הוציא).

from him. viz. from Jacob: Jacob's sons receive no further attention (but note the reference to Joseph, ch. xlix. 15).

found favour in the sight of all living. Cp. Exod. xi. 3. The author has also in mind, doubtless, the daughter of Pharaoh and the priest of Midian.

XLV. 1. **of happy memory.** The Hebrew expression used here (זכרו לטובה) is varied from the one commonly employed, 'his memory (be) for a blessing' (יחי זכרו לברכה), which, in an abbreviated form (ז״ל), is often used, as a pious interjection, after the mention of dead Israelites: e.g. 'our Rabbis of blessed memory' (רבותינו ז״ל), &c. The full phrase (in its usual form) occurs in xlvi. 11.

2 [e]And ‹He made him glorious as› God[e],
  And mighty [f]in awe-inspiring deeds[f].
3 [g]By his words[g] [h]he brought[i] ‹signs›[i] swiftly to pass[h],
  [j]And He emboldened him[j] in the presence [k]of the king[k].
 And He gave him a charge [l]‹unto his people›[l],
  And showed him [m]‹His glory›[m].
4 For his faithfulness and meekness[n]
  He chose him out of all [o]‹flesh›[o].
5 [p]And[p] [q]He caused him to hear His voice[q],
  And let him draw nigh [r]into the dark cloud[r].
 [s]And He placed[s] [t]in his hand[t] [u]the commandment[u],
  Even the Law of life [v]and discernment[v];
 That he might teach [w]His statutes[w] [x]unto Jacob[x],
  [y]And His testimonies and judgements[y] [z]unto Israel[z].

(*e*) XLV. 6–22. *Aaron* (3+4+4+4+4+4+4+4+3+2 distichs).

6 And He exalted a holy one [a]‹like unto him›[a],
  Even AARON of the tribe of Levi.
7 [b]And He made him an eternal ordinance[b],
  And bestowed [c]upon him His majesty[c]:

αγιων = ? ויכנהו באלהים (*so Smend: cp.* xxxvi. 17 *where* ωμοιωσας = כיניתה): 𝔖 *has* 'and He made him great in blessings': *Peters restores*: ויכבדהו כאלהים (*both* 𝔊 *and* 𝔖 *paraphrase* ℌ *in order to mitigate its boldness*) f–f *So* ℌ *marg.* במוראים = 𝔖; *cp.* 𝔊 εν φοβοις εχθρων: ℌ *text* במרומים g–g *So* 𝔊 = בדבריו: ℌ *marg.* בדברו (ℌ *text defective*) h–h ℌ מהר: 𝔊 κατεπαυσεν (*a mistake for* κατεσπευσεν) i–i *So* 𝔊 = אותות: ℌ *defective* [𝔖 > 3 *a*] j–j ℌ ויחזקהו: 𝔊 εδοξασεν (248 *pr.* και): 𝔖 'and set him' k–k *So* ℌ: 𝔊 βασιλεων (*but* 53 254 βασιλεως) = 𝔖 (*Peters reads* מלכים) l–l *So* 𝔊: ℌ *defective*: 𝔖 = העם (*so Peters reads*) m–m *Reading* את כבודו = 𝔊 𝔖: ℌ *defective* [𝔖 + *v.* 5 *a misplacing*] n 𝔊 + ηγιασεν (א 248 &c. 𝔏 Sah + αυτον) *wrongly* o–o *So* 𝔊 = בשׂר: 𝔖 'sons of men' p–p *So* ℌ (> 𝔊) q–q 𝔖 > *whole line* r–r *So* ℌ 𝔊: 𝔖 'His dark cloud' s–s ℌ *text* וישׂם, ℌ *marg.* ויתן t–t *So* ℌ: 𝔊 αυτῳ κατα προσωπον = 𝔖 (= ? לפניו) u–u *So* ℌ מצוה: 𝔊 εντολας: 𝔖 > v–v *So* ℌ ותבונה = 𝔊: 𝔖 'and blessings' (*misreading* ℌ) w–w *So* ℌ חקיו: 𝔊 διαθηκην: 𝔖 'His laws' x–x *So* ℌ *marg.* (ℌ *text* ביעקב): 𝔖 'those of the house of Israel' y–y *So* ℌ ועדותיו ומשפטיו: 𝔖 'and His laws and His covenants' z–z *So* ℌ 𝔊: 𝔖 'unto Jacob' a–a *So* 𝔊 𝔖 (= + כמהו): ℌ > b–b *So* ℌ = 𝔊 εστησεν αυτον (*inferior reading* αυτῳ) διαθηκην αιωνος: 𝔖 *reads* עם *for* עולם (*? an intentional alteration*) c–c ℌ *text* עליו הוד: ℌ *marg.* לו הודו: *read with Peters* עליו הודו: 𝔊 ιερατειαν λαου (*explanatory paraphrase*)

---

2. **And He made him glorious as God.** The author has in mind Exod. iv. 16 ('he shall be to thee a mouth, and thou shalt be to him as God'); cp. also Exod. vii. 1. ℌ *mg.* (which is adopted by Smend) has: 'And He titled him by the name of "God"': the boldness of the expression has led to its mitigation in the versions (see critical notes).

awe-inspiring deeds. i.e. the wonders performed in Egypt (see Exod. vii–xi); cp. Deut. iv. 34, xxvi. 8, xxxiv. 12 ('great terrors' = 'awe-inspiring deeds').

3. **he brought signs swiftly to pass.** There is a corruption here in 𝔊 which has obscured the meaning (see critical notes). As Smend points out, *vv.* 2–3 *a, b* set forth Moses' power in the face of the heathen.

in the presence of the king. Cp. Exod. vii. 1.

And He gave him a charge unto his people. Cp. Exod. vi. 13. In *vv.* 3 *c, d* and 4 the pre-eminence of Moses among his own people is set forth.

showed him His glory. Cp. Exod. xxxiii. 18, xxxiv. 6.

4. **his faithfulness and meekness.** Cp. Num. xii. 3, 7, also i. 27 of our book.

out of all flesh. 'All flesh' here means, apparently, all Israel (not all mankind): cp. l. 17 (ℌ): so Smend.

5. **His voice.** Cp. Deut. iv. 36.

let him draw nigh into the dark cloud. Cp. Exod. xx. 21, xxiv. 18.

placed in his hand the commandment ... Cp. Exod. xix. 7; Exod. xxxii. 15; Deut. vi. 1. The Decalogue is referred to.

the Law of life. Cp. xvii. 11. For 'life' in this connexion cp. Ezek. xx. 11.

teach His statutes unto Jacob ... unto Israel. Cp. Ps. cxlvii. 19.

(*e*) XLV. 6–22 (AARON). The great length of this section, which is devoted to Aaron, and the abundance of its detail, suggest that the subject of the Aaronite priesthood, as embodied in the High Priest, was one which specially interested Ben-Sira. See further the discussion in the General Introduction, § 9 ii.

6. **a holy one.** Cp. Ps. cvi. 16; Num. xvi. 3, 5, 7.

7. **And He made him an eternal ordinance.** In the Pentateuch the phrase 'an eternal ordinance' (חק עולם) is always applied to the rights, laws, and privileges of the Aaronite priesthood; here it is applied to Aaron himself; in the possession of the glorious priesthood he is himself an 'eternal ordinance'; for a similar turn of expression cp. Is. xlii. 6, xlix. 8 ('I make thee a people's covenant'): so Smend.

bestowed upon him His majesty. Cp. Num. xxvii. 20; 1 Chron. xxix. 25. 𝔊 has 'the priesthood of the people'; but such an expression is doubtful, as the 'priesthood' is always spoken of in the Bible as God's, not the people's.

𝕳[B] [d]And He blessed him[d] [e]with His glory[e],
And girded him [f]with beauteous magnificence[f][g]:
8 And He clothed him [h]with the perfection of adornment[h],
[i]And adorned him[i] [j]with splendid vestments[j][k]—
[l]The breeches[l], [m]the tunic and robe[m][n]—
9 And encompassed him [o]with pomegranates,
And with resounding bells[o] round about,
[p]That he might make music[p] with his steps,
So as to cause the sound of him to be audible [q]in the inmost shrine[q],
For a memorial for the children of his people:
10 [r](With) the holy garments of gold and violet
And purple[r], the work of the designer;
(With) the breastplate of judgement, [s](with) the ephod and waistcloth[s],
11 [t]And (with) scarlet[t], the work of the weaver;
(With) precious stones [u]seal-engraven[u]
[v]In settings[v], [w]<the work of the stone-engraver>[w][x];

d–d *Reading* ויאשרהו = 𝕲 εμακαρισεν αυτον (*so* 𝕾): 𝕳 *has* וישרתהו = 'and He ministered unto him' e–e *So* 𝕳 *text* בכבודו: 𝕳 *mg.* בברכה: 𝕲 εν ευκοσμιᾳ f–f *Reading with* 𝕳 *mg.* בתועפות תואר (*so Smend*): 𝕳 *text* בתועפות ראם (*? under influence of* Num. xxiii. 22, xxiv. 8): LXX περιστολην δοξης: 𝕾 'in the height of His glory' g 𝕳 + וילבישהו פעמונים (*a doublet made up of* 8 *a* + 9 *a to make up stichoi of verse after* 7 *a and* 7 *b had been fused into one line*) h–h 𝕳 כליל תפארת = 𝕲 συντελειαν καυχηματος: 𝕾 'with garments of purple' i–i 𝕳 ויפארהו: 𝕲 και εστερεωσεν αυτον (*read* εστεφανωσεν = 𝕷 coronavit): 𝕾 'and honoured him' j–j *Reading* בכלי עוז (*for* 𝕳 בכבוד ועוז) = 𝕲 *and* 𝕾 k *Verses* 8 *c*–14 *b are lacking in* 𝕾 l–l 𝕳 מכנסים: 𝕲 περισκελη m–m *Reading* כתונת ומעיל (𝕳 כתנות): 𝕲 και ποδηρη και επωμιδα (επωμις *often in* LXX *for* אפוד: *Smend and Peters regard* επωμιδα *as an error for* (?) διπλοιδα *which often* = מעיל *in* LXX) n *At v.* 9 *a in the margin the note occurs in Persian*: 'This MS. reaches thus far': *see Cowley-Neub., p.* 25 o–o *Reading* (*Nöldeke, Peters*) רמונים ופעמוני המון: *cp.* 𝕲 ροισκοις χρυσοις κωδωσιν πλειστοις: 𝕳 פעמונים ורמונים המון p–p 𝕳 לתת נעימה: 𝕲 (*freely*) ηχησαι φωνην [נעימה *only again in Neo-Hebrew* = 'chant', 'music'] q–q 𝕳 בדביר: 𝕲 εν ναῳ r–r *So* 𝕳 (+ ו *before* תכלת: *cp.* 𝕲): 𝕲 στολῃ αγιᾳ, χρυσῳ και υακινθῳ και πορφυρᾳ s–s *So* 𝕳 אפוד ואזור: 𝕲 δηλοις αληθειας = אורים ותמים (*so Peters reads, but* 𝕳 *to be preferred; see exeget. notes*) t–t 𝕳 ושני תולעת = 𝕲 κεκλωσμενῃ κοκκῳ (*in Bible always in reverse order,* תולעת שני) u–u = 𝕳 פתוחי חותם = 𝕲 γλυμματος σφραγιδος: *this is given in next line in* 𝕳 *which adds here the incorrect gloss* על החשן v–v 𝕳 במל[ואים] = 𝕲 εν δεσει χρυσιου (*cp.* Exod. xxxix. 13 *in* LXX) w–w 𝕲 εργῳ (*so read for* εργων) λιθουργου = מעשׂה חרשׁ אבן (Exod. xxviii. 11): *so read with Smend* x 𝕳 + כל אבן יקרה (*a gloss*: 𝕲 >) y–y *Reading* (מצנפת) מְעַל = 𝕲: 𝕳 מעיל ומצנפת z–z 𝕳 קדשׁ . . . . וציין >ו. *The missing words in* 𝕲 = פתוחי חותם: *but this does not suit the traces that*

And girded him with beauteous magnificence. For text see critical note. 𝕳 text has 'and girded him about (as) with the towering horns of a wild-ox', under the influence of Num. xxiii. 22, xxiv. 8. The word rendered 'towering horns' in the Numbers passages (תועפות) means here apparently 'magnificence'—a meaning for which there is some support in the LXX rendering of the word in Numbers (viz. δόξα).

The breeches. Cp. Exod. xxviii. 31.

the tunic. i.e. the ordinary outer garment: cp. Exod. xxviii. 39.

robe. i.e. the violet robe (מעיל תְּכֵלֶת) which was always worn with the ephod; cp. Exod. xxviii. 31.

9. **with pomegranates, And with resounding bells.** For text see critical note. Cp. Exod. xxviii. 33 f.

to cause the sound of him . . . audible . . . i.e. 'they were to call God's attention to Aaron as the representative of his people' (McNeile on Exod. xxviii. 33); cp. Exod. xxviii. 35 ('And the sound thereof shall be heard when he goeth in unto the holy place before the Lord, and when he cometh out, that he die not'). It has also been thought that their purpose was to apprise the people when Aaron had reached the Holy Place. They were probably a survival (some form of charm), the original meaning of which was forgotten. According to Josephus, *B. I.*, v. 5. 7, 'the bells signified thunder and the pomegranates lightning.'

10. **(With) the holy garments.** Cp. Exod. xxviii. 2–6. Here the ephod, girdle, and 'breastplate' are specially meant (see following verses).

the breastplate of judgement. Cp. Exod. xxviii. 4, 15. 'Breastplate' is a somewhat misleading translation of the Hebrew word (חֹשֶׁן), though it has become consecrated by usage. It probably denoted a bag or pouch of some kind, in which were contained the Urim and Thummim (= 'of judgement').

the ephod. Cp. Exod. xxviii. 6–12.

waistcloth. Otherwise spoken of as the 'girdle' (אבנט); cp. Exod. xxviii. 4, 39, 40.

10–11. **the designer . . . the weaver.** The division is only rhythmical—the same craftsmen are meant in each case.

scarlet . . . precious stones. Here, again, the division is rhythmical: 'scarlet' entered into the making of the 'breastplate of judgement', as well as of the ephod; and similarly precious stones (of both).

seal-engraven. Cp. Exod. xxviii. 21. The engraven stones (twelve) of the breastplate of judgement, inscribed with the names of the twelve tribes of Israel, are meant.

In settings. Cp. Exod. xxviii. 17.

For a memorial in graven writing,
  According to the number of the tribes of Israel.
12 (With) the crown of pure gold [y]‹(resting) upon› the mitre[y],
  [z]The diadem engraven, ‘Holy to Jahveh’[z]—
[a]Majesty most glorious, praise most puissant[a],
  [b]The desire of the eyes, and the perfection of beauty[b]!
13 [c]Before him there was nothing like them[c],
  [d]And no stranger shall He clothe therewith for ever[d]:
[e]So ‹He trusted him and› his sons[e],
  [f]And ‹his sons' sons›[f] [g]throughout their generations[g].
14 His (Aaron's) meal-offering is wholly consumed
  [h]Twice every day as a continual sacrifice[h].
15 [i]Moses consecrated him[i],
  And anointed him with the holy oil;
And it became for him [j]an eternal covenant[j],
  [k]And for his seed[k], [l]as long as the heavens endure[l];
[m]To minister (to God) and for Him to execute the priest's office[m],
  And to bless His people [n]in His name[n].
16 He chose him out of all living,
  To bring near [o]the burnt-offering and fat pieces[o],

remain in MS.: read with Lévi [וצ׳ץ] חרות ליי קדש   a–a ℌ הוד כבוד ותהלת עז   b–b *Reading with* 𝔊 (*επιθυμηματα οφθαλμων κοσμουμενα ωραια*: *last word belongs to v.* 12 *not to* 13 *a—so* Syro-Hex.) מחמ[ד עין ומכלל י]ופי   c–c *Reading* (לא היה כן) ל(פניו) = 𝔊   d–d *Reading* ועד עולם לא יַלְבִּשֵׁם זר (*cp.* 𝔊)   e–e ℌ *defective* הא . . . . . לבניו כזה: *Cowley-Neubauer suggest* האמין לו ולבניו כזה (*so read*): 𝔊 *πλην των υιων αυτου μονον* (*so Peters, reading* אך בניו לבדם)   f–f *Reading* ולבני בניו (*cp.* 𝔊 *και τα εκγονα αυτου*): ℌ וכן בניו   g–g ℌ (*restored*) ותם[לדור]: 𝔊 *δια παντος*   h–h ℌ וכל יום תמיד פעמים (> ו *before* כל *with* 𝔊)   i–i ℌ וימלא משה את־ידו = 𝔖 (‘And Moses placed upon him his hand’): 𝔊 *επληρωσεν . . . . . τας χειρας* (+ *αυτου* 70 248 𝔏)   j–j ℌ ברית עולם: 𝔊 *εις διαθηκην αιωνιον* = ״לברית: *so* 𝔖   k–k ℌ ולזרעו = 𝔖: 𝔊 *και εν τῳ σπερματι αυτου*   l–l ℌ כימי שמים = 𝔖: 𝔊 *εν ημεραις ουρανου*   m–m ℌ לשרת ולכהן לו: 𝔊 *λειτουργειν αυτῳ αμα και ιερατευειν*: 𝔖 > ולכהן לו, ‘*omitting the eternal priesthood here ascribed to Aaron and his seed*’ (*Hart*)   n–n *So* ℌ 𝔖: 𝔊 *εν τῳ ονοματι* (+ *αυτου* א^c.a &c. Syro-Hex. 𝔏: B א* A V 155 > *αυτου*)   o–o *So* ℌ: 𝔖 ‘burnt-offerings’: 𝔊 *καρπωσιν Κυριῳ* (= ? עלה לאלהים)

For a memorial . . . According to the number of the tribes of Israel. Cp. Exod. xxviii. 21, 29 (‘And Aaron shall bear the names of the children of Israel in the breastplate of judgement upon his heart, when he goeth in unto the Holy Place, for a memorial before the Lord continually’).

12. **the crown of pure gold . . . The diadem.** The terms are in apposition and synonymous; the ‘plate’ or ‘diadem’ which was fastened on to the ‘mitre’ or turban is meant: cp. Exod. xxviii. 36 f. For text of second clause see critical note. Cp. also Josephus, *B. J.*, v. 5. 7, and *Ant.*, iii. 7. 6.

Majesty most glorious . . . This emotional touch reveals the feeling of the writer that all the majesty and glory of Israel were embodied in the High Priest.

13. **Before him.** i. e. before Aaron was thus invested.

there was nothing like them. i. e. like the holy vestments.

no stranger. i. e. no unconsecrated person of another tribe in Israel. The emphasis laid on this point is noticeable. Evidently Ben-Sira would not have tolerated any breach in the legitimate succession to the High-priesthood, such as, as a matter of fact, occurred shortly after the period when he wrote.

shall He clothe therewith. ‘He,’ i. e. God.

So He trusted him and his sons. The text is uncertain (see critical note). That adopted might, perhaps, be rendered (following a Neo-Hebrew usage): ‘Such He entrusted to him and his sons,’ i. e. such a position of honour and responsibility.

And his sons' sons . . . The High-priesthood was to be maintained perpetually by legitimate succession.

14. **His (Aaron's) meal-offering . . . as a continual sacrifice.** The daily meal-offering of the High Priest was offered half in the morning and half in the evening; and it was specially distinguished by being wholly burnt upon the altar; cp. Lev. vi. 19–23 (= vi. 12–16 in Hebrew).

15. **Moses consecrated him, And anointed him . . .** Cp. Lev. viii.

And it became for him an eternal covenant . . . The anointing with the holy oil of Aaron was a solemn guarantee that the priesthood should remain perpetually in Aaron's line.

as long as the heavens endure. The same phrase recurs in l. 24 (‘as the days of heaven’); cp. also Ps. lxxxix. 30; Deut. xi. 21.

To minister . . . execute the priest's office . . . bless . . . Cp. Deut. x. 8; Exod. xxviii. 41, 43, &c.; Num. vi. 23, 27.

16. **He chose him out of all living.** Cp. *v.* 4 above; also Num. xvi. 5, 7, xvii. 20.

the burnt-offering and fat pieces. The burnt-offering was, of course, wholly consumed upon the altar; in the case of animal-sacrifices which were not wholly burnt the fat pieces were reserved for burning on the altar.

ℌ[B] [p]And to burn a sweet savour and a memorial[p],
And make atonement [q]for the children of Israel[q].
17 [r]And He gave him His commandments[r],
[s]And invested him with authority over statute and judgement[s],
[t]That he might teach His people statutes,
And judgements unto the children of Israel[t].
18 [u]But strangers were incensed against him[u],
And became jealous of him in the wilderness;
The men of Dathan and Abiram,
And the congregation of Korah [v]in their violent anger[v].
19 And Jahveh saw it [w]and was angered[w],
[xy]And consumed them[y] in His fierce wrath[x]:
[z]And He brought a sign to pass[z] upon them
[xa]And devoured them[a] [b]with His fiery flame[bx].
20 [c]And ⟨He increased⟩[c] Aaron's glory,
And gave him [d]his inheritance[d]:
[g] (20 *c*) [e]⟨The holy contributions⟩[e] [f]He gave him[f] for sustenance,
(21 *a*) [h]And[h] the fire-offerings of Jahveh they might eat:
(21 *d*) [i]⟨The presence-bread⟩[i] is his portion,
(21 *b*) [j]And the gift-sacrifice[j] for him and for his seed.

p–p *So* ℌ: 𝔊 θυμιαμα και ευωδιαν εις μνημοσυνον: 𝔖 'and sacrifices and incense' q–q *So* ℌ: 𝔊 περι του λαου σου (א* 248 > σου: 70 V 𝔏 *have* αυτου): 𝔖 'for all Israel' r–r *So* ℌ 𝔖: 𝔊 εδωκεν αυτον (*so* B Syro-Hex V 253: *the other MSS., also* 𝔏, *read* αυτῳ) εν εντολαις αυτου s–s *So* ℌ: 𝔊 εξουσιαν εν διαθηκαις κριματων (*reading* בחקי משפט): 𝔖 = ℌ (*though pointed as plural nouns*) t–t *Verses* 17 *c d* > *in* 𝔖: 𝔊 *has* διδαξαι τον Ιακωβ τα μαρτυρια (א[c.a] + αυτου) και εν νομῳ αυτου φωτισαι (*inferior reading* φωνησαι) Ισραηλ: *this may be more original than* ℌ, *and suggests*: ללמד ליעקב עדותיו ותורתו להורות את־ישׂראל: (*so Smend*) u–u *So* ℌ ויחרו בו בני זרים = 𝔖: 𝔊 επισυνεστησαν αυτῳ αλλοτριοι (*using the* LXX *word from* Num. xvi. 19, xxvi. 9, xxvii. 3) v–v ℌ בעזוז אפם: 𝔊 εν θυμῳ και οργῃ: 𝔖 'in strength' w–w *So* ℌ 𝔖: 𝔊 και ουκ ευδοκησεν x–x (x–x) *These clauses are transposed in* 𝔖 y–y *So* ℌ 𝔖: 𝔊 και συνετελεσθησαν (= ויכלו *for* ויכלם) z–z *Reading* ויברא (*for* ויבא) = 𝔊 𝔖 (*cp.* Num. xvi. 30) [𝔊 *has* τερατα: 𝔖 'a blow' *for* אות 'sign'] a–a *So* ℌ (ויאכלם) = 𝔖 *and* 𝔏 (consumsit eos): 𝔊 καταναλωσαι αυτους b–b ℌ בשביב אפו = εν φλογι πυρος αυτου (*so* 55 254 𝔏): *others* εν πυρι φλογος αυτου: 𝔖 'with flame' c–c *Reading* ויוסף (*Lévi, Peters*) = 𝔊 και προσεθηκεν: 𝔖 'and He put (upon Aaron)' [*Smend* וישנה 'and He doubled'] d–d *So* ℌ 𝔖: 𝔊 κληρονομιαν e–e *Reading* [תרומות קד]שׁ: 𝔊 απαρχας πρωτογενηματων = ? תרומות רשית (*a conflation*): 𝔖 = ראשית קדש; *apparently there were two readings, viz.* תרומות קדש *and* ראשית קדש: *the former is supported by* Num. xix. 18 f–f *So* ℌ: 𝔊 εμερισεν αυτῳ (B *against all other MSS. and* 𝔏 αυτοις) g ℌ *has the clauses rightly in this order*: 𝔊 (*wrongly*) 20 *c d* 21 *a b*: 𝔖 *compresses the four clauses into two, rendering*:

'The holy first-fruits and the presence-bread
To him and to his seed.'

h–h *So* 𝔊: ℌ > i–i *Reading* לחם פנים *with Peters* (*Nöldeke* לחם מערכת): *cp.* 𝔖 (*the translator of* 𝔖 *apparently passed accidentally from* לחם *at end of* 20 *c to the* לחם *at beginning of* 20 *d*: 𝔊 εν πρωτοις ητοιμασεν πλησμονην (*pr.* εις 70 106 &c. 248 &c. Sah εν πλησμονῃ) = ? לפנים ערך שבע (? *the first two words a corruption of* לחם מערכת): *for* εν πρωτοις = לפנים: *cp.* iv. 17 j–j ℌ ומתנה: 𝔊 ας εδωκεν [αυτῳ] k–k *Reading*

to burn a sweet savour and a memorial. The former ('to burn a sweet savour') is the technical term applied specially (but also in other connexions) to the burning of the sacrificial pieces and the fat upon the altar (cp. Lev. i. 8, 9); the latter ('a memorial') is applied specially to that portion of the meal-offering which was burnt upon the altar (cp. Lev. ii. 2, 9).

17. **And He gave him His commandments...** Cp. Deut. xxxiii. 10, xvii. 10 f., xxi. 5. Ben-Sira evidently applied Deut. xxxiii. 8 f. to Aaron. The divine authority of the priesthood in religious (ceremonial) enactments is emphatically asserted.

18. **But strangers were incensed against him.** In Num. xvi. 40 (Hebr. xvii. 5) 'stranger' is explained as = one 'who is not of the seed of Aaron'. Men not of the priestly tribe are here meant.

became jealous of him. Cp. Ps. cvi. 16.

The men of Dathan and Abiram. Cp. Num. xvi.

19. **with His fiery flame.** Cp. Job xviii. 5.

20. **And ⟨He increased⟩ Aaron's glory.** Not only did the abortive rebellion of Dathan and Abiram result in the Aaronite priesthood maintaining its position triumphantly (cp. Num. xvii), but the privileges of the position were strengthened (cp. Num. xviii. 1–7).

The holy contributions. Or 'offerings'. i. e. those parts of the sacrifice which were contributed to the priest (the 'heave-offerings' so called); cp. Num. xviii. 8 f.

ℌ[B] 22 Only [k]⟨in the land of the people⟩[k] might he have no heritage,
[l]And in their midst divide no inheritance[l];
[m]Whose portion and inheritance is Jahveh[m]
[n]In the midst of the children of Israel[n].

(*f*) XLV. 23–26. *Phinehas* (3+4+3 distichs).

23 Moreover PHINEHAS the son of Eleazar
[o]⟨Was glorious⟩ in might ⟨as a third⟩[o],
In that he was jealous [p]for the God of all[p],
And stood [q]in the breach for his people[q];
[r]While his heart prompted him[r],
[s]And he made atonement[s] [t]for the children of Israel[t].
24 Therefore for him, too, [u]He established an ordinance[u],
[v]A covenant of peace to maintain the sanctuary[v]:
That to him and to his seed should appertain
The High-Priesthood for ever.
25 [w]Also His covenant was[w] with David,
[x]The son of Jesse[x], of the tribe of Judah;
[y]⟨The inheritance of the king is his son's alone⟩[y],
While the inheritance of Aaron (belongs) [z]to him[z] and to his seed.

בארץ העם = 𝔊: 𝔖 'in their land' [l–l] *So* ℌ: 𝔊 και μερις ουκ εστιν αυτῳ εν λαῳ (*cp.* Num. xviii. 20): 𝔖 'And they did not divide a portion with them' [m–m] *Reading* אשר ייי חלקו ונחלתו: *cp.* 𝔊 αυτος γαρ μερις σου (248 70 Syro-Hex. 𝔏 αυτου) και (B א* 248 > και) κληρονομια: ℌ = 𝔖 [n–n] *So* ℌ (*cp.* 𝔖): 𝔊 > [o–o] ℌ (*defective*) בגבורה.......: 𝔊 τριτος εις δοξαν: 𝔖 'in his power received three honours' (= ? בגבורה נחל שלוש): *read* (*with Smend*) בגבורה נהדר שלישי: [p–p] *So* ℌ לאלוה כל: 𝔊 εν φοβῳ κυριου: 𝔖 'in the matter of the Midianitish woman and the son of Israel' (*from* Num. xxv. 6 ff.) [q–q] ℌ בפרץ עמו: 𝔊 εν τροπῃ λαου (155 εντροπῃ: 𝔏 reverentia): 𝔖 = בפרץ העם [r–r] *So* ℌ: 𝔊 εν αγαθοτητι προθυμιας ψυχης αυτου: 𝔖 > [s–s] *So* ℌ = 𝔊: 𝔖 'and he prayed' [t–t] *So* ℌ: 𝔊 περι του Ισραηλ = 𝔖 [u–u] ℌ הקים חק: 𝔊 εσταθη (*ignoring* חק *which is regularly rendered* διαθηκη, *in order to avoid repetition of the word* [διαθηκη]; *see following clause*): 𝔖 'with oaths God sware to him' [v–v] *So* ℌ: 𝔊 διαθηκη ειρηνης (*in previous stichus*). προστατειν (*so* 106 157 254 Sah: *other MS.* προστατην) αγιων και λαου (*so* 70 253 V א^{c.a} &c. Sah 𝔏: *others* λαῳ) αυτου—*the last clause is an addition of* 𝔊: 𝔖 'that he should build for Him an altar' (? *explanatory paraphrase*) [w–w] *So* ℌ: 𝔊 και διαθηκην (*read* και διαθηκη ην—70 106 Sah και διαθηκη) [x–x] *So* ℌ: 𝔊 υιῳ (70 א^{c.a} 𝔏 + Ιεσσαι) [y–y] *Reading* נחלת מלך לבנו לבדו: ℌ *MS. has* נחלת איש לפני כבודו—*which is obviously corrupt*: אש *is regarded as a miswritten* איש *by some scholars: then* (*reading* לבנו *for* לפני) *the sentence means*: 'The heritage of a man (passes) to his son alone': 𝔖 *has*: 'The heritage of kings he alone inherited' [z–z] *So* 𝔖: ℌ *and* 𝔊 >

---

21. **the fire-offerings of Jahveh they might eat.** Cp. Num. xviii. 9, 18, &c.

⟨The presence-bread⟩ is his portion. For the text see critical note. According to the Mishnah (*Sukk.* v. 7 f.), all the loaves were eaten by the priests, one half by the outgoing division for the week, the other half by the incoming division.

the gift-sacrifice. The word rendered 'gift' (מתנה) is twice applied (in the form מַתָּן) to sacrifices in the Pentateuch; cp. Num. xviii. 11 (Gen. xxxiv. 12). The usual word is *qorbān* (קרבן). It is a comprehensive term.

22. **⟨in the land of the people⟩ might he have no heritage...** Cp. Num. xviii. 20; Deut. xviii. 1; Joshua xiii. 14.

(*f*) XLV. 23–26 (PHINEHAS).

23. **Phinehas the son of Eleazar.** Cp. Num. xxv. 7 ff.

⟨as a third⟩. It is significant that Phinehas is set beside Moses and Aaron as 'third'; this may possibly point to disputed succession to the High-Priesthood (cp. 1 Macc. ii. 54: 'Phinehas our father ... obtained the covenant of an everlasting priesthood'; cp. also 4 Macc. xviii. 12).

In that he was jealous... Cp. Num. xxv. 11, 13.

24. **A covenant of peace... High-Priesthood for ever.** Cp. Num. xxv. 12 f.

to maintain the sanctuary. 𝔊 (see critical note) has a significant addition here; it renders ['to be leader of the sanctuary] *and of his people*'; i.e. not only leader in ecclesiastical but also in political affairs. When the grandson of Ben-Sira wrote, the political power of the High Priest had been strongly asserted. The High Priest had become ethnarch. One consequence was that the office became the sport of constant political intrigues.

25. **⟨The inheritance of the king is his son's alone⟩, While...** For the text see critical note. It is difficult to be sure what the exact point of the couplet is. Apparently the second line forms the antithesis to line one. If so, the meaning may have been: the power and privileges of the king, as sovereign, are transmissible only to his son, viz. by direct succession; whereas the power of the priesthood belongs to, in a sense, and is inherent in every member of the priestly tribe, all Aaron's descendants, in fact, together with Aaron himself. Others (cp. 𝔊 and 𝔖) see no antithesis, but, on the contrary, a parallel statement to the effect that in each case the dignity is only transmissible in direct and

ℌ[B] [a]And now bless ye Jahveh[b],
Who has crowned you with honour[a];
26 [c]May He grant[c] you wisdom of heart,
[d]⟨To judge His people in righteousness⟩[d];
That [e]your prosperity[e] [f]may never cease[f],
[g]Nor your power[g] [h]for perpetual generations[h].

(*g*) XLVI. 1–10. *Joshua, the son of Nun, and Caleb, the son of Jephunneh* (=3+3+4+3+2+3 distichs).

46 1 [a]A mighty man of valour[a] was Joshua [b]the son of Nun[b],
[cd]A minister of Moses in the prophetical office[d],
[e]Who was formed to be[e] according to[f] his name[g]
[h]A great salvation for his chosen[hc],
[i]To take vengeance upon [j]the enemy[ji]
[k]And to give an inheritance[k] to Israel[l].
2 [m]How glorious was he when he stretched forth [n]his hand[nm],
[o]And brandished the javelin against the city[o]!
3 [p]Who was he that could stand before him?[p]
[q]For he fought the wars of Jahveh[q].

a–a *So* ℌ : 𝔊 > [𝔖 > *last line*] b ℌ + הטוב : 𝔖 > c–c ℌ ויתן : 𝔊 δῳη = יתן (*so* ℌ, ch. l. 23 *a*) : 𝔖 'that giveth' d–d *So* 𝔊 = 𝔖 (*with* 'in His name' *for last words*) : ℌ > : *supply text* : לשפט עמו בצדק e–e ℌ טובכם = 𝔖 : 𝔊 τα αγαθα αυτων f–f ℌ לא ישכח *an error for* לא ישבת : *cp.* 𝔊 ινα μη αφανισθη : 𝔖 = ℌ g–g 𝔊 και την δοξαν αυτων : 𝔖 'their power' : ℌ *defective : read* ?וגבורתכם : *Peters* ותפארתם : *Smend* אמורתכם h–h *So* ℌ : *cp.* 𝔖 'for all generations for ever' : 𝔊 εις γενεας αυτων

a–a 𝔊 κραταιος εν πολεμοις (πολεμῳ ℵ A C 155 248 = 𝔏) b–b 𝔊 Ναυη, ℵ* ο Ναυη (ℵ[c.a] 248 ο του Ναυη), A V 70 155 Syro-Hex Sah Eth υιος Ναυη (= 𝔖 𝔏) c–c 𝔖 'By prophecy he was reserved to become like Moses the great one, to bring salvation by his hand to them that love him' d–d 𝔊 και διαδοχος Μωσῃ εν προφητειαις : 𝔏 successor Moysi in prophetis e–e 𝔊 ος εγενετο : 𝔏 qui fuit magnus f 𝔊 κατα (= 𝔏) g *Reading, with Smend,* כשמו (= 𝔊 𝔏) *for* בימיו h–h 𝔊 μεγας επι σωτηριᾳ εκλεκτων αυτου : 𝔏 Maximus in salutem electorum Dei i–i εκδικησαι επεγειρομενους (*reading* בקמי *for* נקמי) εχθρους (= 𝔏) j–j 𝔖 'the hateful men' k–k 𝔊 οπως κληρονομησῃ (κατακλ. ℵ A 55 157 248 254 Syro-Hex) : 𝔏 ut consequeretur haereditatem l 𝔖 'the children of Israel', *and adds* 'the land of promise' m–m 𝔊 ως εδοξασθη εν τῳ επαραι χειρας αυτου n–n 𝔖 'the spear that was in his hand' o–o 𝔊 και τῳ εκκλιναι ρομφαιαν επι πολεις p–p 𝔊 τις προτερον αυτου ουτως εστη (𝔖 = ℌ) q–q 𝔊 τους γαρ πολεμιους Κυριος (V ℵ[c.a] 70 248 253

---

legitimate succession, from father to son. In this case the external position and power of the High Priest is primarily thought of, not his spiritual authority. There is probably some allusion intended to contemporary events—the intrigues against the legitimate holder of the position of High Priest (Simeon, who would be regarded as a descendant of Phinehas) by the Tobiadae. For the covenant with David cp. 2 Sam. xxiii. 5; Jer. xxxiii. 21; Ps. lxxxix. 4; 2 Chron. xiii. 5, xxi. 7; Isa. lv. 3. See further in ch. xlvii of our book, especially *vv.* 11 and 22.

And now bless ye Jahveh. Cp. l. 22 *a*.

Who has crowned you with honour. Cp. Ps. viii. 6.

26. **May He grant you wisdom of heart.** Cp. l. 23. The reference is to the legitimate representative of Phinehas the High Priest.

(*g*) XLVI. 1–10 (Joshua and Caleb).

1. **A mighty man of valour.** Cp. Judges vi. 22, and 2 Chron. xxvi. 12 (Sept. and Hebr.).

A minister of Moses. משרת משה; cp. Exod. xxxiii. 11; with 𝔊 cp. 2 Chron. xxviii. 7 (משנה המלך . . .). 𝔊 is explanatory; the prophetic minister becomes in due course his successor, as in the case of Elisha, see 1 Kings xix. 21. For the prophetic succession see further the note on xlvii. 1.

the prophetical office. נבואה may rightly be rendered here 'prophetical office', though in the O.T. it is not used in this sense; it means 'prophecy' in 2 Chron. xv. 8 (genuine prophecy), Neh. vi. 12 (false prophecy), and 'prophetical writing' in 2 Chron. ix. 29. With 𝔊 cp. xliv. 3 *d*.

Who was formed to be according to his name. The emended reading is preferable, especially as it is supported by 𝔊; Joshua (= 'Jahveh is salvation'), as the leader of the Israelites into the Promised Land, would be appropriately called the saviour of his nation. For a somewhat similar word-play in the Hebrew see xlvii. 18.

for his chosen. Cp. xlvii. 22; Num. xi. 28 (Sept.).

To take vengeance upon the enemy. The reference is to Joshua x. 13.

to give an inheritance . . . Cp. Deut. i. 38, iii. 28.

2. **How glorious.** מה נהדר; cp. l. 5.

when he stretched forth his hand. See Joshua viii. 18, 26.

against the city, i.e. Ai.

3. **Who was he . . .** Cp. Joshua i. 5. The rendering of 𝔊 seems to have been based on Joshua x. 14.

the wars of Jahveh. Cp. Joshua x. 14 *b*; 1 Sam. xviii. 17, xxv. 28; and 'the book of the wars of Jahveh', Num. xxi. 14.

ℌ[B] 4 Was it not through him that the sun stood still[r],
(And) one day [s]became as two?[s]
5 [t]For he called upon the Most High God[ut],
[v]When he was in sore straits (and) his enemies around him[v];
And [w]the Most High God[w] answered him[x]
[y]With hailstones and bolts[zy];
[ℌ[B]] 6 [a]He cast them down upon the hostile people[a],
And [b]in the going down[b] he destroyed [c]them that rose up[c],
ℌ[B] In order that all[d] the nations [e](devoted to) destruction[e] might know
[f]That Jahveh was watching their fighting[f]:
[g]And also because[g] he fully followed after God[h],
7 And [i]did an act of piety[i] in the days of Moses,
He and Caleb, the son of Jephunneh,
[k]In that they stoo firm when the congregation broke loose[k].
[l]To turn away wrath from the assembly[l],
[m]And to cause the evil report to cease[m]—
8 [n]Wherefore also they two[n] were set apart[o]
From among the six hundred thousand footmen[p],
To bring them into their[q] inheritance,
(Into) a land flowing with milk and honey[r].

Syro-Hex πολεμους Κυριου, A πολεμιους Κυ) επηγαγεν [r] 𝔊 ανεποδισεν (A ενεποδισθη = 𝔏) [s–s] *Reading* כשנים היה (= 𝔊 𝔏, *cp.* xxv. 19) *following Smend; Peters reads* לשנים היה: 𝔖 'And one day became two days' [t–t] 𝔖 'For he prayed unto (*lit.* before) the Lord' [u] 𝔊 δυναστην [v–v] *Reading* כאכפה לו איביו מסביב (*Smend*): 𝔖 'And He heard him and put strength into his hand', *cp.* xlvii. 5 [w–w] 𝔊 μεγας Κυριος: 𝔖 > [x] 𝔊[B] αυτων [y–y] 𝔖 'And He cast down sulphur from heaven' [z] 𝔊 δυναμεως κραταιας [a–a] *Reading* השליך על עם אויב (*cp.* 𝔊 κατερραξεν επ εθνος πολεμον [*read* πολεμιον = 𝔖 𝔏 Eth] *and see* Joshua x. 11). *In* ℌ *the text of this and the following clause is almost wholly obliterated* [b–b] 𝔖 > [c–c] *Reading* קמים (= 𝔊 ανθεστηκοτας); *Smend reads* כנען ('Canaan'), *which* 𝔊, *he thinks, intentionally paraphrased*: 𝔖 'them all' [d] 𝔊 > [e–e] חרם, *which Smend thinks that* 𝔊 *misread as* חרבו ('his sword') *and paraphrases by rendering* πανοπλιαν, *or that perhaps* πανοπλιαν *is an error for* απωλειας [f–f] 𝔊 οτι εναντιον Κυριου ο πολεμος αυτου: 𝔖 'that God Himself was fighting against them' [g–g] 𝔊 και γαρ: 𝔖 'and he also': 𝔏 > [h] 𝔊 Δυναστου [i–i] 𝔊 εποιησεν ελεος [k–k] 𝔊 αντιστηναι εναντι εχθρου (V 248 253 Syro-Hex εκκλησιας) [l–l] 𝔊 κωλυσαι λαον απο αμαρτιας: 𝔖 'To turn back the assembly' ('*a compromise between* 𝔊 *and* ℌ' [*Smend*]) [m–m] 𝔊 και κοπασαι γογγυσμον πονηριας: 𝔖 + 'from the land of promise' [n–n] 𝔊 και αυτοι δυο οντες: 𝔖 'and they alone' [o] ℌ נאצלו, *which* 𝔊 (διεσωθησαν) *read as* נצלו = 𝔖 [p] 𝔖 > (*cp.* Num. i. 46) [q] 𝔊 > [r] *In* ℌ 8 c d *form a single clause*

4. **that the sun stood still.** ℌ follows Joshua x. 13 (Hebr. and Sept.); with 𝔊 cp. xlviii. 23; Isa. xxxviii. 8.
5. **For he called upon . . .** Cp. xlvi. 16, xlvii. 5, xlviii. 20.
the Most High God. The expression *'El 'Elyōn* occurs here, as far as we know from the Hebrew text now extant, for the first time in the book; it is used again in this verse and in xlvii. 5, 8, xlviii. 20; in l. 15 *d*, where ℌ is wanting, 𝔊 has . . . ὑψίστῳ παμβασιλεῖ, which probably represents *'El 'Elyōn.* The name *'Elyōn* alone occurs nine times. Both these names for God are, as far as can be seen, used only in chapters xli to the end; elsewhere in the book either *Elohim* or *Jahveh* is used; the latter is abbreviated as a rule in the MSS. thus: ייי or יי.
When he was in sore straits. Cp. Prov. xvi. 20; Smend says that the noun אֲכָפָה in the Talmud means 'oppression' or the like.
his enemies around him. Cp. *v.* 16.
With hailstones . . . Cp. Joshua x. 11.
bolts. אלגביש, cp. xliii. 15; Ezek. xiii. 11, 13, 'lumps of ice.'
6. **He cast them down . . .** 'The Lord cast down great stones from heaven upon them,' Joshua x. 11.
in the going down. Or 'descent', i.e. the pass of Beth-horon (the 'hollow way').
(devoted to) destruction. Cp. xvi. 9; Joshua vi. 17.
That Jahveh was watching their fighting. Cp. Joshua x. 14.
he fully followed after. מלא אחרי, cp. for the expression Num. xiv. 24; Joshua xiv. 8, 9, 14.
7. **did an act of piety.** עשה חסד, cp. xlix. 3; the reference is to Num. xiv. 6–10.
In that they stood firm . . . Cp. Num. xiv. 1 ff.
broke loose. Or 'cast off restraint'; for פרע cp. Exod. xxxii. 25; Prov. viii. 23, xxix. 18.
to cause the evil report to cease. Cp. Num. xlv. 3.
8. **were set apart.** For the root אצל see Ezek. xlii. 6, and cp. Gen. xxvii. 36; Num. xi. 17, 25.
the six hundred thousand. Cp. xvi. 10; Num. xi. 21, xiv. 38, xxvi. 65; Deut. i. 36, 38.
To bring them into . . . The subject, i.e. God, is understood.
their inheritance. Cp. Joshua xi. 23, where Joshua, as God's instrument, is spoken of as giving the whole land for an inheritance unto Israel.
a land flowing with milk and honey. The stereotyped description of the promised land: see Exod. iii. 8, 17, and often in the Pentateuch: cp. Jer. xi. 5, xxxii. 22; Ezek. xx. 6–15.

ℌ[B] 9 And He[s] gave strength unto Caleb,
And unto old age it remained with him,
[t]To cause him to tread[t] [u]upon the high places[u] of the land;
And also his seed obtained[v] a heritage,
10 In order that [w]all [x]the seed of Jacob[w] might know
[y]That it is good [z]to follow fully[z] after Jahveh.[y]

(*h*) XLVI. 11, 12. *The Judges* (=3 distichs).

11 Also the Judges, each with his name,
[a]All whose hearts were not beguiled[a],
Nor turned back [b]from (following) after God[b].
May their memory be [c]for a blessing[c].
𝔊 12 [d]May their bones flourish again out of their place[d],
ℌ[B] [e]And may their name sprout afresh for their children[e].

(*i*) XLVI. 13–20. *Samuel* (= 2+3+4+4 distichs ⌊+1 later add.]).

13 [f]Honoured by his people and loved by his Maker[f]
[g]Was [h]'he that was asked for'[h] from his mother's womb;
Sanctified [i]of Jahveh[i] in the prophetical office,—
Samuel, who acted as judge and priest.
By the word of God [k]he established the kingdom[k],
And anointed princes[l] over[m] the people[g].

[s] 𝔊 ο κυριος [t–t] *Reading* להדריכו *for* להדריכם (*cp.* 𝔊 επιβηναι αυτον) [u–u] 𝔊 επι το (B* *art.*) υψος [v] ℌ ירש: 𝔊 κατεσχεν: 𝔖 *has the future* [w–w] 𝔊 παντες οι υιοι Ισραηλ [x] 𝔖 > [y–y] 𝔖 'Who had fulfilled the law of Jahveh and His judgements' [z–z] 𝔊 το πορευεσθαι (*cp. v.* 6 *e where the same Hebr. word is differently rendered*) [a–a] 𝔊 οσων ουκ εξεπορνευσεν η καρδια [b–b] 𝔊 απο Κυριου: 𝔖 'from the law of God' [c–c] 𝔊 εν ευλογιαις (*cp. Sept. of* Zech. viii. 13) [d–d] *Wanting in* ℌ (*see, however,* xlix. 10 *b*): 𝔖 'May their bones shine like lilies' (*cp.* xxxix. 14) [e–e] 𝔊 και το ονομα αυτων αντικαταλλασσομενον εφ υιοις δεδοξασμενων αυτων: 𝔖 'And may they leave their good name behind for their children, and their glory for the whole nation': 𝔏 et nomen eorum permaneat in aeternum permanens ad filios illorum sanctorum virorum gloria. In ℌ 11 *c d and* 12 *b form one clause* [f–f] *Reading, with Smend,* נכבד עמו ואהוב עושהו (*the text has* אוהב עמו ורצוי עושהו): 𝔊 ηγαπημενος υπο κυριου αυτου ℵ A C + Σαμουηλ: 𝔖 'and loved by his Creator' [g–g] 𝔊 προφητης Κυριου κατεστησεν βασιλειαν (B βασιλεα) και εχρισεν αρχοντας επι τον λαον αυτου [h–h] ℌ המשואל, *for which Smend reads* המושאל ('he that was lent') *after* 1 Sam. i. 28 [i–i] 𝔖 > [k–k] 𝔖 'the kingdom was established' [l] 𝔖 'governors and kings'

9. **And He gave strength ...** Cp. Joshua xiv. 6, 11.

the high places of the land. i.e. the fortified places, cp. Deut. xxxiii. 29; and for the rendering of 𝔊 cp. Joshua xiv. 12.

And also his seed ... Cp. Num. xiv. 24; Joshua xv. 16 ff.; Judges i. 11 ff.

10. **to follow fully.** See note on *v.* 6.

(*h*) XLVI. 11, 12 (THE JUDGES).

11. **each with his name.** Ben-Sira desires to make some reference to the names of the Judges collectively without mentioning each by name.

All whose hearts were not beguiled. Cp. Is. xix. 13; the reference is to such passages as Judges xvi. 16–18 (Samson), viii. 27 (Gideon), &c.

May their memory be for a blessing. Cp. xlv. 1 note.

12. **May their bones ...** See xlix. 10.

And may their name ... Cp. Tob. iv. 12, 'we are the sons of the prophets'; a spiritual relationship is, of course, meant, and in that the good example of Israel's saints and heroes is emulated by succeeding generations it can be said that their names sprout afresh. See further xliv. 9, 13, 15, xlv. 1, xlix. 1, 9, 13.

sprout afresh. For the Hebr. תחליף cp. xliv. 17.

(*i*) XLVI. 13–20 (SAMUEL).

13. **'he that was asked for'.** Note the word-play in ℌ המשואל ('he that was asked for') and שמואל in 13 *d* ('Samuel'). Smend's emendation (see critical note) is most probably right.

Sanctified of Jahveh. נזיר ייי, cp. נזיר אלהים in Judges xiii. 5, xvi. 17; Ben-Sira interprets 1 Sam. i. 11 as though it referred to the Nazirite vow.

the prophetical office. See note on *v.* 1.

By the word of God. Cp. 1 Sam. ix. 27.

princes. נגידים; cp. 1 Sam. ix. 16, x. 1, xiii. 14, &c.

𝕳[B] 14 [n]By means of the commandment[n] [o]he commanded the congregation[o],
[p]And he mustered the tents of Jacob[p].
15 [qr]Because of his truthfulness they sought the prophet[r],
[s]And the seer[t] was also found reliable in his words[sq].
16 [uv]And, moreover, he called upon God[v]
[w]When his enemies surrounded him on every side[uw],
In that he offered up a sucking lamb,
[x][And cried unto the Lord][x].
17 [y]And Jahveh thundered from heaven[y],
[z]With a mighty crash His voice was heard[z],
18 [a]And He subdued the garrisons of the enemy[a],
[b]And destroyed[b] all the princes[c] of the Philistines.
19 [d]And at the time when he rested upon his bed[d],
He called [e]Jahveh and His anointed to witness[e]:
[f]'From whom have I taken a bribe, [g]even a pair of shoes?'[gf]
And no man accused him.
[h][And also to the time of his end he was found upright
In the eyes of Jahveh and in the eyes of all living[h].]
20 [i]Moreover after he died he was enquired of[i],
He declared unto the king his way[k];

m 𝕾 'for' n–n *Reading* במצוה (*the word is quite mutilated in* 𝕳): 𝕲 εν νομῳ Κυριου o–o 𝕲 εκρινεν συναγωγην: 𝕾 'he commanded the congregation' p–p 𝕲 και επεσκεψατο Κυριος τον Ιακωβ (*cp.* 1 Sam. vii. 16, 17, 2 Chron. xvii. 7 ff.): 𝕾 'And the Lord commanded Jacob': 𝕳 *reads* ויפקד אלהי יעקב ('and he visited the gods of Jacob'); *this is an obvious error which Peters emends by reading* ויפקד אלהים יעקב ('and God visited Jacob'), *but this sudden change in the subject of the sentence makes such an emendation improbable; it is better to read* ויפקד אהלי יעקב (*Lévi, Smend*); *see further exegetical note. The corruption must have found its way into the Hebr. text very early, since it was read by* 𝕲 q–q 𝕾> r–r *The text of* 𝕳 *is considerably mutilated; Smend reconstructs it thus*: באמונת פיו דרוש חזה; *Peters would read*: באמונתו נדרש חזה ('Because of his reliability the seer was enquired of'); *but, according to Smend, there is not room for* באמונתו, *while the upper halves of the letters of* פיו *are quite visible*; דרוש *is to be seen on the MS.; the form* נדרש, *which occurs in v.* 20, *has a different meaning*: 𝕲 εν πιστει αυτου ηκριβασθη προφητης s–s 𝕲 και εγνωσθη εν πιστει (ℵ A C 106 ρημασιν = 𝕷: ρηματι V 55 248 253 254 Syro-Hex) αυτου πιστος ορασεως t *Reading* רואה (*for* דועה) u–u 𝕾 'And moreover he conquered the enemies on all sides' v–v 𝕲 και επεκαλεσατο τον κυριον δυναστην w–w 𝕲 εν τῳ θλιψαι (70 248 Sah Eth + αυτον: ℵ* + αυτου) εχθρους αυτου (ℵ* > αυτου) κυκλοθεν x–x *A fourth clause is required, but it is wanting in* 𝕳 *as well as in all the Versions; the above is supplied from* 1 Sam. vii. 9 y–y *This clause is almost wholly mutilated; Smend reconstructs it thus*: וירעם מן השמים ייי *from* 𝕲 και εβροντησεν απ ουρανου Κυριος z–z 𝕲 και εν ηχῳ μεγαλῳ ακουστην εποιησεν την φωνην αυτου a–a 𝕲 και εξετριψεν ηγουμενους Τυριων (*reading* ציר [= 𝕾] *for* צר) b–b 𝕲> c 𝕲 αρχοντας (*in the Sept.* σατραπης *is used for* סרן). *In* 𝕳 17 *b and* 18 *form one clause* d–d 𝕲 και προ καιρου κοιμησεως αιωνος e–e 𝕲 εναντι Κυριου και χριστου (= 𝕾): + αυτου ℵ^c.a 70 248 f–f 𝕲 χρηματα και εως υποδηματων απο πασης σαρκος ουκ ειληφα g–g 𝕾> h–h 𝕲 𝕾>; *a later glossator added these two clauses* (*cp.* 1 Sam. xiii. 8–15, xvi. 1 ff., xix. 18 ff.) i–i 𝕲 και μετα το υπνωσαι αυτον επροφητευσεν (B προεφητευσεν) k 𝕲 την τελευτην αυτου

14. **By means of the commandment.** 𝕳 במצוה, cp. xliv. 20; the reference is to 1 Sam. vii. 2 ff.
the tents of Jacob. Cp. Num. xxiv. 5, 'How goodly are thy tents, O Jacob.'
15. **truthfulness.** i.e. reliability; cp. 1 Sam. ix. 6.
prophet . . . seer. See 1 Sam. ix. 9.
in his words. Cp. 1 Sam. iii. 19.
16. **he called upon God . . .** Cp. 1 Sam. vii. 5, 8, 9.
he offered up a sucking lamb. Cp. 1 Sam. vii. 9.
17. **And Jahveh thundered . . .** Cp. 1 Sam. vii. 10; 2 Sam. xxii. 14.
crash. פקע is Neo-Hebraic; it does not occur in the O. T.
18. **He subdued.** Cp. 1 Sam. vii. 13.
the garrisons. נְצִיב means in the first instance a 'pillar' (Gen. xix. 19), and then a small garrison or fore-post of which a pillar marks the site; cp. 1 Sam. xiv. 1, 4, 6, 11, 12, 15.
the princes. סרן is the special term used especially in Judges and 1 Samuel of the Philistine 'lords' or 'tyrants', five in number, who ruled over the five chief Philistine cities; cp. Judges iii. 3; 1 Sam. vi. 17.
19. **And at the time . . . his bed.** The identical words occur in xl. 5 *c*. Cp. 1 Sam. xii. 2 ff.
Jahveh and His anointed. See 1 Sam. xii. 5.
even a pair of shoes. i.e. something of a trifling nature; cp. Amos ii. 6, viii. 6. Both 𝕳 and 𝕲 follow the Sept. of 1 Sam. xii. 3, and depart from the Massoretic text.
20. **he was enquired of.** Cp. 1 Sam. xxviii. 7 ff.
his way. i. e. his destiny.

ℌ[B] And he lifted his voice from the earth,
[1]To blot out iniquity by prophecy[1].

(*j*) XLVII. 1–11. *David* (= 2 + 3 + 3 + 2 + 3 + 2 + 2 distichs).

47 1 [a]And moreover after him[a] stood up Nathan,
To serve[b] [c]in the presence of[c] David.
2 [d]For as[d] the fat is separated[e] [f]from the offering[f],
So was David (separated)[ff] from[g] Israel.
3 He played[h] with lions as with kids[i],
And with bears as [j]with calves of Bashan[j].

[1–1] *In* ℌ *only one word* (בנבואה) *is preserved in this clause*: 𝔊 εν προφητειᾳ εξαλειψαι ανομιαν λαου: 𝔖 'to destroy sins by prophecy' [a–a] 𝔊 και μετα τουτον (C 55 248 254 τουτο): 𝔏 post haec (= Sah) [b] 𝔊 προφητευειν (70 248 ο προφητης = 𝔖 𝔏): 𝔖 'to cause to hear' [c–c] 𝔊 εν ημεραις (𝔖 = ℌ) [d–d] 𝔊 ωσπερ: 𝔏 et quasi [e] מורם *lit.* 'lifted up': 𝔊 αφωρισμενον: 𝔏 separatus (𝔊 𝔏 = ℌ) [f–f] 𝔊 απο σωτηριου (= שלם, *cp.* Lev. vi. 12): 𝔏 a carne [ff] *Expressed in* 𝔖 [g] 𝔊 𝔏 + των υιων [h] 𝔊 επαιζεν (B[ab] ℵ επαιξεν, C επαισεν, 70 248 254 επεξενωσεν): 𝔖 'he slew': 𝔏 lusit [i] *Reading* גדיים (= 𝔊 𝔖) *for* גדי; *the plur. is required to correspond with the plur. in the next clause* [j–j] בני בשן *which Halévy, Peters, Smend, and others emend to* בני צאן; *cp.* 𝔊 εν αρνασι προβατων (*cp.* LXX *of* Ps. cxiv. 14,

---

To blot out . . . The reference is to the fact that by announcing the approaching death of Saul, Samuel prophesied the blotting out of the sins of the people, of whom Saul was the representative; Saul's death atoned for the sins of the people as well as for his own sins.

(*j*) XLVII. 1–11 (David).

1. **stood up.** עָמַד, as in *v.* 12, in the sense of 'appear upon the scene'; this is also frequently the force of the word as used in the later books of the O. T., especially in Daniel; see e.g. viii. 22, '. . . four kingdoms shall stand up [i.e. appear] out of the nation' (cp. Dan. xi. 2–4, xii. 1), almost equivalent to 'arise up' (קום); see also Ezra ii. 63; Neh. vii. 65; Ps. cvi. 30.

Nathan. It is noticeable that Ben-Sira lays stress on the succession of the prophets, cp. xlvi. 1, xlviii. 1, 12, 22, xlix. 8; his is the conviction of earlier writers and prophets, that the line of prophetical teachers in Israel has been uninterrupted since the time of Moses (cp. Amos ii. 10, iii. 7, 8; Hos. xii. 13; Jer. vii. 25, xv. 1, &c. &c.). As A. B. Davidson well says (*Old Testament Prophecy*, p. 16 f.): 'The real history of Israel is a history in which men of prophetic rank and name stand at the great turning-points of the people's life, and direct the movements. The inner progress of the people was throughout guided by prophets who fertilized the religious life of the nation with new thoughts, or nourished the seeds of truth and higher aspirations already planted in the heart of the people into fuller growth and fruitfulness. . . .' This offers a good comment on Ben-Sira's point of view in these chapters.

To serve in the presence of David. . . . לְהִתְיַצֵּב לִפְנֵי, lit. 'to present oneself before' some one with the implication of readiness for service (cp. e.g. Job i. 6, ii. 1; Zech. vi. 5). In 1 Kings i. 26 Nathan speaks of himself as the 'servant' of David; but this is exceptional: the true prophets are normally not the servants of any one but Jahveh; their unfettered freedom of speech and independent attitude towards those in authority were among their leading characteristics. It is probably owing to this that the Greek renders 'prophesy' instead of 'serve'. The reading of ℌ is, however, to be retained, as it more literally accords with the O. T. narrative. On the verse generally see 2 Sam. vii. 2 ff.

2. **as the fat is separated.** The reference is to the intestinal fat of the sacrificial victims (oxen, sheep, and goats), cp. Exod. xxix. 13, 22; Lev. iii. 3 ff., vii. 22 ff.; see also 1 Sam. ii. 15 ff. It is this part of the victim, 'the fat of the omentum with the kidneys and the lobe of the liver, which the Hebrews were forbidden to eat, and, in the case of sacrifice, burned on the altar. . . . The point of view from which we are to regard the reluctance to eat of them is that, being more vital, they are more holy than other parts, and therefore at once more potent and more dangerous' (Robertson Smith, *The Religion of the Semites*², p. 380 f.) The prohibition is only in regard to the fat about these more holy parts, and does not extend to the ordinary fat of an animal referred to in Neh. viii. 10, 'Go your way, eat the fat (מַשְׁמַנִּים, i.e. the tasty fatty morsels), and drink the sweet . . .'

separated. Lit. 'lifted up', the technical term used in Lev. iv. 8, 10, 19, &c. for separating the fat from the flesh. Schechter (*The Wisdom of Ben-Sira*, p. 31) pointedly refers to Ps. lxxxix. 20 (19 in EV): הרימותי בחור מעם, which may well have been in the mind of Ben-Sira.

from the offering. Lit. 'from the holy thing', cp. Lev. iii. 3 ff., xxi. 22; Num. v. 9, xviii. 17, 2 Chron. xxix. 33; Ezek. xxxvi. 38.

So was David . . . Cp. 1 Sam. xvi. 4–13.

from Israel. With the rendering of 𝔊 (see critical note) cp. l. 20.

3. **He played . . .** שׂחק ל in the O. T. means to 'laugh', usually in derision (cp. Ps. xxxvii. 13, lix. 9), whereas שׂחק ב means to 'play'; e.g. with beasts, in Job xli. 5 (xl. 29 in Hebr.). With the verse before us cp. 1 Sam. xvii. 34–36; Is. xi. 6 ff.

calves of Bashan. Properly 'bull-calves of Bashan', which is inappropriate as the parallelism requires a harmless and weak animal of some kind to correspond with 'kids'; it is scarcely to be doubted that 𝔊 𝔖 reflect the right text here.

ℌ[B] 4 In his youth[k] he slew the giant[k],
[l]And took away[ll] the reproach from the[m] people[l],
[n]When he swung his hand with[o] the sling[n],
And broke[p] the pride[q] of Goliath.
5 For [r]he called unto God[s] Most High[r],
And He gave strength to[ss] his right[t] hand,
So that he struck down[u] [v]the hero versed in war[v],
[w]And[ww] exalted[w] the horn of his people[x].
6 [y z]Therefore the daughters sang of him,
And honoured him with: '[Slayer] of ten thousand'[z].
When he had put on the diadem[zz] he fought,
7 And subdued the enemies on all sides,
[a]And plundered[a] the Philistine cities[b y],
And broke their horn unto this day[c].

16): 𝔖 'with lambs': 𝔏 cum agnis [k–k] 𝔊 ουχι απεκτεινεν γιγαντα (= 𝔏): 70 248 > ουχι: 𝔖 = ℌ [l–l] *Reading* ויסר חרפה מעל עם (*following* 1 Sam. xvii. 26 והסיר חרפה מעל ישראל); *the text, somewhat mutilated, reads apparently* חרפת עולם . . . (*cp.* Jer. xxiii. 40 ונתתי עליכם חרפת עולם *and the same in* Ps. lxxviii. 66) [ll] 𝔊 εξηρεν [m] 𝔖 'his' [n–n] 𝔊 εν τῳ επαραι χειρα (A V χειρας) εν λιθῳ σφενδονης [o] *Lit.* 'upon' [p] 𝔊 καταβαλειν (א C 155 κατεβαλεν = 𝔏) [q] 𝔊 γαυριαμα: 𝔖 'the whole (pride)' [r–r] 𝔖 'he prayed in the sight of God' (*perhaps in reference to* 1 Sam. xvii. 45, 47), *cp.* 𝔏 invocavit Dominum (*al.* Deum) omnipotentem [s] 𝔊 Κυριον [ss] *Lit.* 'into' [t] 𝔖 > [u] 𝔊 εξαραι [v–v] ℌ איש יודע מלחמות: 𝔊 ανθρωπον δυνατον (B* > δυνατον) εν πολεμῳ (Sah πολεμοις): 𝔖 'the mighty man' [w–w] 𝔊 ανυψωσαι (B ανυψωσει) [ww] 𝔊 𝔖 > (*expressed in* 254 𝔏) [x] 𝔖 + 'Israel' [y–y] 𝔊 *has mistaken the connexion between these verses and renders freely:*

ουτως εν μυριασιν εδοξασεν αυτον
και ῃνεσεν αυτον εν ευλογιαις Κυριου
εν τῳ φερεσθαι αυτῳ διαδημα δοξης.
εξετριψεν γαρ εχθρους κυκλοθεν
και εξουδενωσεν Φυλιστιειμ τους υπεναντιους . . .

In the last clause 𝔊 = ℌ [z–z] 𝔖 'Therefore the women praised him in myriads' [zz] 𝔖 'crown' [a–a] *Reading* ויבז (*so Peters*): ℌ *text has* ויתן *which Lévy adopts, as well as Cowley-Neubauer* ('and set nakedness among the Philistines'); *but the clause is corrupt; Halévy suggests* ויאבד. *See further exegetical note:* 𝔏 extirpavit: 𝔖 'he took vengeance on' [b] ערים (𝔊 *read* צרים, *which Smend and Halévy adopt, Cowley-Neubauer emend to* ערום 'naked') [c] 𝔏 in aeternum

---

4. **In his youth he slew the giant.** Cp. 1 Sam. xvii. 40 ff.

And took away . . . Cp. in addition to the references in the critical note, Isa. xxv. 8.

When he swung . . . Cp. 1 Sam. xvii. 49, 50.

And broke . . . Lit. 'broke in pieces'; referring to the cutting off of Goliath's head and the taking of his armour.

5. **he struck down.** In the O.T. הדף means to 'thrust out' or 'push away' (cp. 2 Kings iv. 27); in Is. xxii. 19, to 'depose' (in reference to Shebna).

the hero versed in war. With the Hebrew (see critical note) cp. the words in 1 Sam. xvii. 33 איש מלחמה מנעריו.

And exalted the horn of his people. The figure is taken originally from that of the wild-ox holding up his head in conscious strength, well illustrated, e.g., in the oracle of Balaam (Num. xxiii. 22), 'He hath as it were the horns of the wild-ox'; cp. for the expression 1 Sam. ii. 1; Ps. lxxxix. 17, cxlviii. 14; 1 Macc. ii. 48.

6. **Therefore the daughters . . .** Cp. 1 Sam. xviii. 6, 7; Ps. lxviii. 12 (Hebr.).

And honoured him. For כנה ב cp. xlv. 2; the word means properly to 'give a title', cp. Job xxxii. 21; Is. xliv. 5, xlv. 4; this seems to be the way in which it is used here.

When he had put on the diadem. צָנִיף is used in the O.T. of the high-priestly 'turban', see Zech. iii. 5; it is not used of a king's crown (the nearest to this being the metaphorical phrase צניף מלוכה, 'a royal diadem,' in Is. lxii. 3), for which the words עֲטָרָה (e.g. 2 Sam. xii. 30; 1 Chron. xx. 2; Esther viii. 15) and נֵזֶר (e.g. 2 Sam. i. 10; 2 Kings xi. 12; 2 Chron. xxiii. 11; Ps. cxxxii. 18) are used. It is possible that the term which Ben-Sira employs points to the idea of the high-priestly as well as the royal character of David, and this is not without significance from the point of view of the Messianic thought of his times. On the other hand צָנִיף is used quite generally in xi. 5, xl. 4.

he fought. i.e. he fought as the leader of the armies of Israel; he had, of course, fought before this on his own account many times (e.g. 1 Sam. xxiii. 1–5, xxvii. 7–12, xxx. 17–20); but Ben-Sira lays stress on the fact of David having fought because he was essentially a fighting king (cp. 1 Chron. xxii. 8).

7. **And subdued the enemies on all sides.** Viz. the Philistines (2 Sam. v. 17–25, viii. 1, xxi. 15–22); the Moabites (2 Sam. viii. 2); the Syrians (2 Sam. viii. 5–13, x. 1 ff., xii. 26–31); the Edomites (2 Sam. viii. 14); the Ammonites (2 Sam. x. 1 ff., xi. 1).

And plundered the Philistine cities. See critical note. The Philistines were the most inveterate foes of the Israelites during the early days of the monarchy; hence the special mention of them here.

unto this day. O.T. phraseology. The rendering of 𝔏 (see critical note) would be really more to the point.

ℌ[B] 8 [de]In all that he did[e] [f]he gave thanks[f]
[g]Unto God Most High[g] [h]with words of glory[hd].
[i]With his whole heart he loved[j] his Maker[i],
[k]And sang praise every day continually[k].
9 [l]Music of stringed instruments he ordained[m] before the altar,
And set [n]the singing[o] of psalms to harps[nl].
𝔊 10 [p]He gave comeliness to the feasts,
And set in order the seasons throughout the year
ℌ[B] [ppq]For that he gave praise[q] to His Holy Name;
[r]Before morning[r] the sanctuary[s] resounded[t] (therewith)[pp].
11 Jahveh also[u] put away his sin[v],
And lifted up his horn for ever.

[d–d] *In the margin of* ℌ 'David' *is inserted*: 𝔖 'Therefore he gave forth his voice in words of thanksgiving and honour' [e–e] *Lit.* 'in every work of his' (= 𝔊) [f–f] *Reading* נתן תודות *for* הודות . . . : 𝔊 εδωκεν εξομολογησιν (= 𝔏) [g–g] 𝔊 αγιῳ Υψιστῳ (= 𝔏) [h–h] *The text is mutilated; reading* באמרי כבוד (*Smend*) *following* 𝔊 ρηματι (155 ρημασιν) δοξης [i–i] 𝔏 laudavit dominum et dilexit deum, qui fecit illum et dedit illi contra inimicos potentiam [j] *Read* אהב *for* אוהב: 𝔊 υμνησε και ηγαπησε: 70 + κυριον [k–k] *The Hebrew text is much mutilated; Smend emends as follows*: ובכל יום יהלל תמיד (*of which the text above is the rendering*); *Peters emends* ובכל יום הלל בשיריו *which is based on the addition of* 70 248 *to v.* 9, *an addition which, as Schlatter has shown, belongs here, viz.* και καθ ημεραν αινεσουσιν εν ῳδαις αυτων: 𝔊 > *the whole clause, unless we are to discern a remnant of it in* υμνησε και: 𝔖 *joins the clause on to v.* 9, *see next note* [l–l] 𝔖 'and every day he sang praise (= 8 *d*) in a continual offering'; *perhaps in reference to* 1 Chron. xvi. 6, 37 . . . תמיד לפני ארון, *and* תמיד לדבר יום ביומו (*Smend*): 𝔊 *has*:

και εστησεν ψαλτῳδους κατεναντι του θυσιαστηριου
και εξ ηχους αυτων γλυκαινειν μελη

(*For the addition here of* 70 248 *see preceding note*) [m] *So the marg. of* ℌ [n–n] ℌ *marg.* קול מזמור הנעים [o] *Lit.* 'voice' [p–p] *The text of* ℌ *is wholly mutilated; Peters, on the basis of* 𝔊, *reconstructs it as follows*:

נתן לחגים הדר (εδωκεν εν εορταις ευπρεπειαν)
ויתקן מועדי תקופת שנה (και εκοσμησεν καιρους μεχρι συντελειας (= שנה בשנה))

𝔖 'he offered (*lit.* gave) great songs of praise year by year' [pp–pp] 𝔖 > [q–q] 𝔊 εν τῳ αινειν αυτους (Eth αυτον): 𝔏 laudarent [r–r] 𝔊[B] και απο πρωι (πρωιας א A C &c.): + φωνη א[c.a] [s] 248 + αυτου: 𝔏 dei sanctitatem [t] 𝔊 ηχειν (70 ηχει): 𝔏 amplificarent [u] 𝔊 𝔏 > [v] 𝔊 τας αμαρτιας (= 𝔖) [w–w] 𝔊 διαθηκην βασιλεων (55

8. **he gave thanks.** Cp. Joshua vii. 19 נתן תודה.
With his whole heart. Cp. Deut. vi. 5.
every day continually. For the phrase cp. xlv. 14 (Hebr.).

9. **Music of stringed instruments.** נגינות שיר; cp. the titles to Ps. iv, vi, liv, lv, lxi, lxvii, lxxvi, and cp. Is. xxxviii. 20; Hab. iii. 19. Cp. כלי שיר in 1 Chron. xvi. 42, and שירות נבל in xxxix. 15 above. From the time of David onwards stringed instruments seem to have occupied the most important place among musical instruments in the Temple worship; the *kinnor* ('lyre') and *nebel* ('harp') are the only two stringed instruments mentioned in the O. T. outside the Book of Daniel.

And set the singing of psalms to harps. Cp. 2 Chron. xvi. 4, 5. The meaning seems to be that David composed, or at all events introduced, harp accompaniments to the psalms when sung; תיקן means lit. to 'arrange' or 'put in order'; cp. Eccles. xii. 9, '. . . he set in order (תִּקֵּן) many proverbs.'

10. **He gave comeliness to the feasts.** The Zadokites of this period had become lax in the conduct of public worship; it was probably for this reason that Ben-Sira laid stress on David's work in this direction, and made special mention of the feasts (Smend).

And set in order the seasons. Cp. 1 Chron. xxiii. 31; i.e. the festive seasons. It is probable that Ben-Sira is reading back into earlier times the developed musical service in the Temple, of which details are given in the Mishnah; in *Yoma* iii. 11, *Tamid* vii. 3, e.g., we are told that there was a special Temple official whose duty it was to superintend the psalmody; there were under him a large number of musicians, including singers and instrumentalists; these had to accompany the daily burnt-offerings, as well as the solemn festival services, with the singing of psalms and playing on stringed instruments.

Before morning . . . Cp. Ps. lvii. 8 (9 in Hebr.), 'I will awake the dawn'; cxix. 62, 'At midnight I will rise to give thanks to Thee.' In reference to Ps. lxxii. 5 ('They shall fear Thee while the sun endureth') R. Jochanan taught that it was meritorious to worship at dawn. 'The *Wetiqin* (ותיקין = "the ancient pious") watched for the first rays of the sun to begin the *'Amidah* (*Berakhoth* 9 *b*, 29 *b*). There are now several societies of *Wetiqin* in Jerusalem who worship at that hour. They have prepared tables of the sunrise for the year round from special observations taken from Mount Olivet.' *JE*, x. 168 *a*.

11. **put away.** העביר, lit. to 'cause to pass away'; see 2 Sam. xii. 13, וגם יהוה העביר פשעו, which is quoted here almost verbatim, and cp. 2 Sam. xxiv. 10 (= 1 Chron. xxi. 8).
his horn. Cp. Ps. lxxxix. 23, cxxxii. 17.

𝔥[B] Also He gave to him [w]the decree of the kingdom[w],
[x]And established his throne[x] over Israel[y].

(*k*) XLVII. 12–22. *Solomon* (= 3+4+1+3+2+3 distichs).

12 [z]And [a]for his sake[a] there stood up after him[z]
[b]A wise son who dwelt in safety[b].
13 Solomon reigned in days of peace[c],
[d]And[dd] God gave him[e] rest round about[d],
[f]Who prepared[f] a house for [ff]His name[g],
[h]And set up[hh] a sanctuary for ever[h].
14 How wise wast thou in thy youth[i],
[j]And didst overflow like the Nile with instruction[k j]!
15 [lm]Thou didst cover the earth with thy soul[l],
[n]And didst gather parables like the sea[n m].
𝔊 16 [op]Thy name reached unto the isles afar off[p],
𝔖 [q]And they listened[r] for the report of thee[q o].

254 βασιλεως, 70 248 βασιλειας = Syro-Hex 𝔏): 𝔖 'the throne of kingship' [x–x] 𝔊 και θρονον δοξης (*cp.* 1 Sam. ii. 8, Is. xxii. 23, Jer. xiv. 21, xvii. 12): 𝔖 > [y] *So* 𝔊 𝔖 𝔏 (𝔥 'Jerusalem'): 𝔖 + 'for ever a mighty king' [z–z] 𝔊 μετα τουτον ανεστη υιος επιστημων (= 𝔏) [a–a] 𝔖 > [b–b] 𝔊 και δι αυτον κατελυσεν (א 70 κατεπαυσεν, *cp. v.* 13) εν πλατυσμῳ (= ? במרחב, *cp.* Ps. cxviii. 5): 𝔏 et propter illum deiecit omnem potentiam inimicorum, *cp. v.* 8 (*critical note*): 𝔖 'and Solomon dwelt in peace', *joining this verse to* 13 *a* [c] 70 248 + και εδοξασθη [d–d] 𝔏 cui subiecit deus omnes hostes: 248 + αυτον [dd] 𝔊 > [e] א* ως (𝔊 ῳ) [f–f] 𝔊 ινα στησῃ [ff] 𝔊 επ: 𝔏 in [g] 𝔖 + 'for ever' [h–h] 𝔖 > [hh] 𝔊 ετοιμασῃ [i] 𝔖 + 'Solomon' [j–j] 𝔊 και ενεπλησθης (εσοφισθη C*, -σθης C[a]) ως ποταμος συνεσεως [k] 𝔖 'wisdom' [l–l] 𝔊 *alters the construction*, γην επεκαλυψεν η ψυχη σου (70 248 + πασαν) [m–m] 𝔖, *joining this verse on to v.* 16, 'through thine understanding and through the height of the honour of kings' [n–n] *Reading* ותקלט כמו ים שיחה (*Smend*) *for* ותקלט במרום שירה ('And didst gather songs in the height'); *the Hebr. text is mutilated; Peters, following* 𝔊, *would read* ותמלא במשלי חידה ('And didst fill it with dark speeches'): 𝔊 και ενεπλησας εν (248 >) παραβολαις αινιγματων [o–o] 𝔥 > [p–p] 𝔖 = 𝔊 [q–q] 𝔊 και ηγαπηθης (*probably mistaking* יאב *for* אהב) εν τη ειρηνη σου (*mistaking* לשמעך *for* לשלומך) [r] *Lit.* 'yearned for'

---

the decree of the kingdom. i.e. the decree of perpetual sovereignty to David and his house; cp. *v.* 22; 2 Sam. vii. 12 ff.; Ps. ii. 7, lxxxix. 28, 29.

And established his throne. It is possible that 𝔊 read וכסא כבוד (see critical note).

over Israel. This is preferable to 'over Jerusalem' of the Hebrew text, which is possibly due to the influence of Messianic thought; cp. Is. xxiv. 23.

(*k*) XLVII. 12–22 (SOLOMON).

12. **And for his sake.** i.e. for his father David's sake; cp. xliv. 12, 22. As Solomon was not truly faithful to Jahveh (cp. 1 Kings iii. 3, xi. 1–8) his prosperous and peaceful reign is ascribed to the merits of his father David (cp. 1 Kings xi. 12, 13, 32–6). This doctrine of the merits of the fathers (זכות אבות) was much developed in later Jewish teaching, though one can see from a passage like that before us that the essence of the later teaching was already in existence long before. The thought of the solidarity of Israel often finds expression in Rabbinical writings; Israel is one self-contained organism, all the component parts of which are dependent upon each other in spiritual things, so that whatever may be lacking in righteousness to one can be supplied by others who are more righteous. Naturally those who were regarded above all others as righteous were the patriarchs of old, whose good deeds were so great and so many in number that some of them could be imputed to men of later generations, whose lives were not so rich in well-doing; cp. e. g. the words in the Midrash *Shir ha-shirim* ('Song of Songs') on i. 5 ('I am black but comely'): 'The congregation of Israel says, "I am black through my own deeds, but comely through the work of my fathers".' It is said of Solomon that before he sinned he had accumulated much merit; but after he sinned all the blessings which he received were due to the merits of his fathers (Midrash *Qoheleth rabba* to i. 1); it is precisely the same thought which lies at the base of the verse before us.

A wise son. Cp. 1 Kings ii. 3, iv. 21 (v. 1 in Hebr.).

who dwelt in safety. Cp. 1 Kings v. 4 (v. 18 in Hebr.).

13. **peace.** שלוה, lit. 'prosperity' (cp. Job xii. 5; Ps. cxxii. 6; Jer. xii. 1), but peace and prosperity are closely allied; the peace which Solomon enjoyed owing to his father's victories enabled him to live in prosperity.

And God gave him rest. Cp. 1 Kings v. 4 (v. 18 in Hebr.).

And set up a sanctuary for ever. Cp. Ps. lxxviii. 69, 70.

14. **How wise wast thou . . .** For this direct address cp. xlviii. 4–11; with the words cp. 1 Kings iii. 12, iv. 29 ff., x. 1.

like the Nile. Cp. xxiv. 27, xxxix. 22.

15. A continuation of the simile in the preceding verse.

with thy soul. i.e. with his influence; Smend compares the phrase שפך נפש ('to pour out the soul') in 1 Sam. i. 15; Ps. xlii. 5. Cp. also the words of the queen of Sheba in 1 Kings x. 6; 2 Chron. ix. 5.

16. **the isles afar off.** Cp. Is. xli. 5, and especially lxvi. 19 איים רחוקים; אי is not necessarily an island in the usual sense, indeed very rarely so in the O. T. (cp., however, Is. xl. 15); it refers originally to any land which a mariner can make for in order to gain shelter and rest; later on in the more general sense of 'border' or 'region'.

the report of thee. Cp. 1 Kings x. 1.

ℌ[B] 17 [s]By thy songs, parables, dark speeches[s],
[t]And satires[u] thou didst cause astonishment to the peoples[t].
18 [v]Thou wast called by the glorious name
Which is called over Israel[v].

Thou didst heap up gold like tin[w],
And [x]abundance of[x] silver like lead[y].
19 [z]But thou gavest[z] thy loins[a] unto women,
[b]And didst give them to rule over thy body[b].
20 Yea[c], thou broughtest a blemish upon thine honour,
And didst defile [d]thy bed[d],
So as to bring wrath upon thy progeny[e],
[f]And sighing concerning thy bed[f];
21 [g]So the people became[gg] two sceptres[h][g],
And out of Ephraim [i](arose) a sinful[j] kingdom[i].
22 Nevertheless[k] God[l] did not forsake His[m] mercy,
[n]Nor did He suffer any of His words to fall to the ground[n].
[o]He will not cut off [p]the posterity of His chosen[p][o],
Nor will He destroy [q]the offspring[r] of them that love Him[q];

s–s 𝔊 εν ῳδαις και παροιμιαις και παραβολαις : 𝔖 ‘he interpreted proverbs of wisdom in a book’ t–t 𝔊 και εν (248 𝔏 >) ερμηνιᾳ (א C -ιαις) απεθαυμασαν σε (248 >) χωραι u *In the text of* ℌ *this is joined to the first clause* v–v 𝔊 εν ονοματι Κυριου του θεου (70 248 Κυριου πασης της γης) του επικεκλημενου Θεου Ισραηλ, *joining it on to the rest of the verse*: 𝔖 ‘Thou wast called by the name of God, whose is the glory’ w *Reading* כבדיל (= 𝔊 𝔖) *for* כברזל (‘like iron’) x–x 𝔖 > y 𝔖 ‘like dust’ (*cp.* Job xxvii. 16, Zech. ix. 3) z–z 𝔊 παρανεκλινας a 248 τα σπλαγχνα σου : 𝔖 ‘thy strength’ (*cp.* Prov. xxxi. 3) b–b 𝔊 και ενεξουσιασθης εν τῳ σωματι σου : 𝔏 potestatem habuisti in corpore tuo c 𝔊 > (*hab* 253 Syro-Hex) d–d 𝔊 το σπερμα σου (*reading* זרעך *for* יצועיך, *but cp.* Ezra ix. 2, Mal. ii. 15) e 𝔖 ‘thy children's children’ f–f 𝔊 και κατενυγην επι τῃ αφροσυνῃ σου g–g 𝔊 γενεσθαι διχα τυραννιδα gg 𝔖 ‘divided itself into’ h 𝔖 ‘kingdoms’ i–i 𝔊 αρξαι βασιλειαν απειθη j 𝔖 ‘heathen’ k *Reading* אולם (*cp.* xliv. 10): 𝔊 > l 𝔊 ο δε Κυριος m ℌ > (*hab* 𝔊 𝔖) n–n 𝔊 και ου μη διαφθαρῃ (A א^c.a διαφθειρῃ) απο των εργων αυτου : 𝔏 et non corrumpet nec delebit opera sua o–o *Reading* לא יכרית לבחיריו נין (*Smend*); *Peter's reconstruction runs:* ולא יאביד בחירו נין ונכד; *the text of* ℌ *is much mutilated*: 𝔊 ουδε μη εξαλειψῃ εκλεκτου αυτου εκγονα p–p 𝔖 ‘the seed of those that love Him’ q–q 𝔊 σπερμα του αγαπησαντος αυτον : 𝔖 ‘the sons of His pious ones’ r *In the text of* ℌ *this is joined to the preceding clause* s–s *Reading with Smend* ויתן ליעקב

---

17. **By thy songs . . .** Evidently Prov. i. 6 was in the mind of Ben-Sira, where several of the same words occur (משל, מליצה, חידה).

thy songs. Cp. Cant. i. 1, ‘The Song of songs, which is Solomon's’; 1 Kings iv. 32, ‘and his songs were a thousand and five.’ שיר is used of both secular (e.g. Amos v. 23; Isa. xxiv. 9) and religious songs (e.g. Ps. xlii. 9, lxix. 31, &c.), and also specifically of the songs of the Levitical choirs in the Temple worship with musical accompaniment (e.g. 1 Chron. vi. 16, 17, xiii. 8; Neh. xii. 27, &c.).

parables. Cp. Prov. x. 1, xxv. 1 (משלי שלמה); משל is ‘a sentence constructed in parallelism, usually of Hebrew Wisdom, but occasionally of other types’ (*BDB*, s. v.).

dark speeches. חידה is a saying the meaning of which is not apparent on the surface; cp. Judges xiv. 12 ff.; 1 Kings x. 1; in Ezek. xvii. 2 it has the sense of ‘allegory’; something that needs interpretation.

satires. מליצה; cp. Hab. ii. 6 (‘a taunting riddle’, מליצה חידות); the root ליץ means to ‘scorn’.

18. **Thou wast called by the glorious name . . .** Cp. Deut. xxviii. 10; Amos ix. 12; and the Greek of James ii. 7. The reference here is to the original name given to Solomon, according to 2 Sam. xii. 25, viz. Jedidiah, ‘Beloved of Jahveh’; see Ryssel *in loc.* 𝔊 did not see the point, and probably altered the phrase deliberately, which it regarded as irreverent.

Thou didst heap up . . . Cp. 1 Kings x. 21, 27.

like lead. ‘Like stones’ in 1 Kings x. 27.

19. **But thou gavest . . .** Cp. 1 Kings xi. 1–3.

20. **thou broughtest a blemish . . .** Cp. xliv. 19.

And didst defile . . . Cp. Gen. xlix. 4.

And sighing concerning . . . i.e. Solomon's lax morality caused grief to men. It is strange that Ben-Sira makes no direct reference to Solomon's idolatry (cp. 1 Kings xi. 4–8), though it is implied by 21 *a*.

21. **So the people became two sceptres.** Cp. 1 Kings xii.

a sinful kingdom. Lit. ‘violent’; in Amos ix. 8 occurs הממלכה החטאה.

22. **did not forsake His mercy.** Cp. 2 Sam. vii. 15; Ps. lxxxix. 33 (34 in Hebr.).

Nor did He suffer any of His words . . . For the phrase cp. e.g. 1 Sam. iii. 19; 2 Kings x. 10, &c.

posterity. נין, cp. xli. 5; the word is a rare one, occurring only three times in the O.T. (Gen. xxi. 23; Job xviii. 19; Is. xiv. 22).

His chosen. בחיריו is used in reference to Israel in xlvi. 1.

ℌ[B] [s]And He will give to Jacob a remnant[s],
[t]And to the house of David [u]a root from him[u t].

(*l*) XLVII. 23–25. *The wickedness of the people under the kings who succeeded Solomon* (= 2 + 3 distichs).

23 And Solomon slept[v] [w]in Jerusalem[w],
And left after him [x]one that was overbearing[x].
[y]Great in folly[y] and lacking in understanding
[z](Was) he who[z] by his counsel made the people revolt.
[a]And (then) he arose—of him let there be no memorial[a]—
[b]Who sinned and made Israel to sin[b],
[c]And put [d]a stumbling-block (in the way)[d] of Ephraim[e c],
24 [f]To drive them from their land;
[g]And their sin became very great[g f],
[h]And they sold themselves to (do) all manner of evil[h].

(*m*) XLVIII. 1–11. *Elijah* (= 3 + 3 + 3 + 3 distichs).

48 1 Until[a] there arose[b] a prophet like fire,
Whose[c] word[d] was [e]like a burning furnace[e].

שארית (*the text of* ℌ *is much mutilated*) = 𝔊 [t–t] *Reading with Smend* ולבית דויד ממנו שורש (*the text of* ℌ *is again almost wholly obliterated*): 𝔊 και τῳ Δαυειδ εξ αυτου ριζαν [u–u] 𝔖 'a great kingdom' [v] 𝔊 ανεπαυσατο [w–w] *Reading with Peters* בירוש״ (*abbreviation for* בירושלים, *see exegetical note below*); *only the last letter* (ש) *of the word is preserved; Smend proposes* מיואש ('despairing', *cp.* Eccles. ii. 20): 𝔊 μετα των πατερων (+ αυτου א A Sah 𝔏 = עם אבותיו): 𝔖 > [x–x] *Reading* מנון (*see Hebr. of* Prov. xxix. 21 [*Smend*]): 𝔊 εκ του σπερματος αυτου (*cp.* LXX *of* Gen. xxi. 23 = מנין [*Smend*]): 𝔖 > [y–y] 𝔊 λαου αφροσυνην (Syro-Hex λαον αφροσυνης) [z–z] *Reading* אשר; *the present text has* רחבעם, *but this cannot have been the original reading as clauses c and d are enclosed within* רחב *and* עם; *this play on the name of Rehoboam makes it in the highest degree improbable that the name itself would also appear*: 𝔊 *reads* ος, *which reflects the original text, but places before it* 'Rehoboam'. *For another word-play see* xlviii. 17, 22 [a–a] *Reading with Smend* ויקם אל יהי לו זכר *for* עד אשר קם אל יהי לו זכר ירבעם בן נבט; *apart from the fact that this makes the clause too long, the mention of* 'Jeroboam the son of Nebat' *can hardly have originally stood together with* 'of him let there be no memorial'. *The words* עד אשר קם *presuppose a connexion with the preceding clauses which would give no sense; they are evidently taken from* xlviii. 1. *The present text has clearly suffered at the hands of a glossator*: 𝔊 και Ιεροβοαμ υιον (א υιος) Ναβατ: 𝔖 'let there be no memorial to him, (even) to Jeroboam the son of Nebat' [b–b] 𝔊 ος εξημαρτεν τον Ισραηλ [c–c] *Although these words are considerably mutilated in the text of* ℌ *sufficient remains to decipher them with reasonable certainty* [d–d] 𝔊 οδον αμαρτιας [e] 𝔖 'the house of Ephraim' [f–f] 𝔊 *wrongly transposes these two clauses* [g–g] 𝔊 και επληθυνθησαν αι αμαρτιαι αυτων σφοδρα: 𝔖 'And he made their sins many' [h–h] 𝔊 και πασαν πονηριαν εξεζητησαν + εως (A ως) εκδικησις ελθῃ επ αυτους: 70 248 + οργη και εκδικησις: 𝔏 + usque dum perveniret ad illos defensio et ab omnibus peccatis liberavit eos (dominus), *cp. v.* 11 *and* xlviii. 1–15 [a] 𝔊 'and' [b] 𝔊 + 'Elijah' [c] *Lit.* 'And his' [d] *Reading* דברו (= 𝔊 𝔖) *for* דבריו [e–e] 𝔊 ως λαμπας εκαιετο: 𝔖 *combines* 𝔊 ℌ 'burned like

---

a remnant. Cp. xliv. 17.

. . . a root. Cp. Is. xi. 1, 10; a reference to the Messianic hope, cp. 1 Kings xi. 39.

(*l*) XLVII. 23–25.

23. **slept.** שכב standing alone as here never has the sense of 'dying' in the O. T.; it is always followed by some words which explain it as referring to death, e.g. in 1 Kings xi. 43, 'he slept with his fathers'; in Isa. xiv. 8 the context shows that death is meant; otherwise it means simply to 'sleep' or 'lie down', &c.

in Jerusalem. Every suggested emendation must from the nature of the case be hypothetical; the one adopted in the text is that proposed by Peters; it commends itself on account of 1 Kings xi. 42, 43: 'And the time that Solomon reigned in Jerusalem . . . And Solomon slept with his fathers, and was buried in the city of David . . .' The abbreviation ירוש״ might, apart from other reasons, conceivably have been suggested by the false etymology ירוש שלם ('possession of peace'), which has been one of the etymologies put forward in the past (cp. *JE*, vii. 119 *a*). The rendering of 𝔊 (see critical note), which would commend itself on account of the phraseology, is ruled out because of the absence of a final ש involved, which is clear in the text; the omission of μετὰ τῶν πατέρων in 𝔖 is also against these words representing the original.

made . . . revolt. Lit. 'throw off restraint; cp. Prov. xxix. 18; with the whole clause cp. 1 Kings xii. 8, 13, 14.

and made Israel to sin. Cp. 1 Kings xiv. 16.

And put a stumbling-block . . . Cp. 1 Kings xii. 28.

24. **To drive them from their land.** Cp. 2 Kings xvii. 22, 23; Jer. xxvii. 10.

And they sold themselves . . . Cp. 1 Kings xxi. 20.

(*m*) XLVIII. 1–11 (Elijah).

1. **a prophet like fire.** Cp. Mal. iv. 1, 5 (iii. 19, 23 in Hebr.).

like a burning furnace. Cp. 2 Kings i. 10 ff.

ℌ[B] 2 [f]And he broke for them the staff of bread[f],
[g]And by his zeal[h] [i]made them few in number[i g].
3 By the word of God[k] [l]he shut up the heavens[l];
Fire[m] also[n] descended thrice[o].
4 [p]How terrible wast thou, Elijah[p]!
And he who is like thee shall be glorified[q].
5 Who didst raise up a dead man [r]from death[r],
And[s] from Sheol[t], [u]according to the good pleasure[u] of Jahveh[v];
6 Who broughtest down [w]kings to the Pit[x],
And[w] them that were honoured from their beds[y] [of sickness];
7 [z]Who heardest[a] rebukes[b] in Sinai,
[c]And judgements of vengeance in Horeb[c].
8 Who anointedst kings[d] [e]for retribution[e],
[f]And a prophet as successor in thy place[f].
9 Who wast taken upwards [g]in a whirlwind[g],
[h]And by fiery troops to the heavens[h].
10 [i]Who art ready for the time, as it is written[i],
[k]To still wrath before the fierce anger of God[l k],

a burning furnace' f–f 𝔊 (= 𝔖) ος (𝔖 και) επηγαγεν επ αυτους λιμον (+ ισχυρον 248) g–g 𝔏 et inritantes illum invidia sua pauci facti sunt + non poterant enim sustinere praecepta domini h + ισχυρῳ 70 i–i 𝔖 'he rent them asunder' k 𝔊 Κυριου l–l 𝔊 ανεσχεν ουρανον m 70 248: 𝔖 Syro-Hex Eth + 'from heaven': 𝔏 + terrae n 𝔊 ουτως (> ℵ[c.a] 70 248 253) o 𝔖 + 'upon the altar and upon the godless men' p–p 𝔊 ως εδοξασθης Ηλεια εν τοις θαυμασιοις σου: 𝔏 sic amplificatus est Elias in mirabilibus suis q *Lit.* 'shall glorify himself': 𝔊 καυχασθαι (ℵ A 106 155 296 καυχησεται = ℌ): 𝔏 potest gloriari r–r 𝔖 > s 𝔖 > t 70 248 253 Syro-Hex + ψυχην u–u *It is possible that* ℌ *read* ב *instead of* כ (= 𝔖): 𝔊 εν λογῳ, *cp. v.* 3 v 𝔖 𝔊 'the Most High': 𝔏 domini dei w–w 𝔖 > x 𝔊 εις απωλιαν: 𝔏 + et confregisti facile potentiam ipsorum y 𝔖 'thrones': 𝔊 κλινης z ℌ *transposes vv.* 7, 8 a *Reading* השומע (= 𝔊) *for* השמיע (= 𝔖 'who proclaimed') b 𝔖 'in his temptation' (*misunderstanding the whole verse*): 𝔊 ελεγμον: 70 248 253 Syro-Hex + Κυριου c–c 𝔖 > d *Reading* מלכי (= 𝔊 𝔖) *for* מלא e–e *So* 𝔊 εις ανταποδομα (ℌ תשלומות . . .) f–f 𝔊 και προφητας διαδοχους μετ αυτον: 𝔏 et prophetas facis successores post te g–g 𝔊 εν λαιλαπι πυρος h–h 𝔊 εν αρματι ιππων πυρινων: 𝔖 'by fiery horses to heaven': ℌ *is mutilated at the end of the verse,* 'to the heavens' *is added on the basis of* 𝔖 (*cp.* 2 Kings ii. 11 בסערה השמים) i–i ℌ *lit.* 'Who art written (as) ready for the time': 𝔊 ο καταγραφεις εν ελεγμοις (ελλεγμουις (*sic*) ℵ, ελεγμους 248, ελεγμος A) εις καιρους (V 55 254 Syro-Hex καιρον = ℌ); εν ελεγμοις *is probably a corruption of* ετοιμος: 𝔖 'And he who is ready to come' k–k *The end of this line in* ℌ *is mutilated, though the* ל *of* אל *is visible according to Smend and Peters*: 𝔊 κοπασαι οργην (+ κρισεως Κυριου 70 248) προ θυμου: 𝔖 'before the day of Jahveh comes' (= Mal. iii. 23 [iv. 5 *in* EV]) l 𝔏 domini m–m 𝔖 > n–n 𝔊 πατρος προς υιον: 𝔖 'the children unto the fathers' o–o 𝔖 *lit.* 'to proclaim'

---

2. **he broke for them . . .** Cp. Is. iii. 1; Ezek. iv. 16; Ps. civ. (cv.) 16.
And by his zeal . . . Cp. 1 Kings xix. 10, 14, 18.
3. **he shut up the heavens.** Cp. 1 Kings xvii. 1; James v. 17.
Fire also descended thrice. Cp. 1 Kings xviii. 38; 2 Kings i. 10, 12. For the addition of 𝔖 (see critical note) cp. 1 Kings xix. 38.
4. **How terrible wast thou . . .** For this direct address cp. xlvii. 14.
5. **Who didst raise up . . .** Cp. 1 Kings xvii. 17–24.
a dead man. For the Hebr. גוע cp. viii. 7.
6. **Who broughtest down kings . . .** Cp. 1 Kings xix. 17, xxi. 19 ff.
the Pit. See ix. 9, li. 2 (Hebr. and Gr.); cp. Ezek. xxviii. 7.
And them that were honoured . . . i.e. these he brought down to the Pit; the reference is to Ahaziah, 2 Kings i. 4, 16, 17.
7. **Who heardest rebukes . . .** Cp. 1 Kings xix. 9 ff., 15 ff. As in *v.* 6 the two clauses say the same thing in a different way. Ben-Sira regards Sinai and Horeb as identical, but it is questionable whether he was correct in this, though many modern scholars regard the two as identical. On the other hand, Cheyne (*EB*, iv. 4643) says that originally they were distinct: 'Horeb lay in the Sinaitic peninsula, Sinai in Midian, on the west coast of Arabia' (cp. Wellhausen, *Prolegomena*[3], p. 359; Moore, *Judges*, pp. 140, 179; Stade, *Entstehung des Volkes Israel*, p. 12). Von Gall regards the identification of the two as 'a post-exilic confusion' (*Altisraelitische Kultstätten*, p. 15). See further Driver on Exod. iii. 1.
8. **Who anointedst kings.** i.e. Hazael and Jehu; cp. 1 Kings xix. 15, 16.
retribution. Cp. xii. 2, where the Hebr. word is used in the sense of 'recompense'.
a prophet. Cp. 1 Kings xix. 19–21.
as successor. Cp. xliv. 17 (Hebr. and Gr.).
in thy place. Cp. 1 Kings xix. 16, 'and Elisha . . . shalt thou anoint to be prophet in thy room.'
9. **Who wast taken . . .** Cp. 2 Kings ii. 1, 11.
10. **Who art ready . . .** Cp. Mal. iii. 23, 24 (iv. 5, 6 in EV).

ℌ[B] To [m]turn the heart of[m] the [n]fathers unto the children[n],
And [o]to restore the[o] tribes of Israel[p].
11 [q]Blessed is he that seeth thee, and dieth[q],
[r]. . . . .[r]

(*n*) XLVIII. 12–16. *Elisha. The sinfulness of the people and their punishment* (= 2 + 3 + 4 distichs).

𝔖 𝔊 12 [s]Elijah was hidden in the [heavenly] chambers[s],
𝔊 [t]Then was Elisha filled with his spirit[t u].
ℌ[B] [v]In double measure did he multiply signs,
And marvellous was all that went forth out of his mouth[v].
All his days he moved [w]before no man[w],
[x]And no flesh[x] exercised authority over his spirit[y];

(*i. e. to preach the Gospel to ; due to Christian influence*) [p] 𝔊 Ιακωβ (= 𝔖), *cp.* Isa. xlix. 6 [q–q] 𝔊 μακαριοι οι ιδοντες σε και οι εν αγαπησει (*read* εν αναπαυσει) κεκοσμημενοι (248 253 254 κεοιμημενοι): 𝔖 'Blessed is he that hath seen thee and is dead' [r–r] *This line is almost wholly obliterated in* ℌ; *Smend, on the basis of* 𝔊 𝔖, *proposes to read*: ואשריך כי חיה תחיה ('And [more] blessed art thou thyself, for thou livest'), *making the words refer to Elijah; Peters, also following* 𝔊, *would read*: כי גם אנחנו חיה נחיה ('For we too shall live [again]'), *as though the words referred to Ben-Sira's readers* (*see further exegetical note*): 𝔊 και γαρ ημεις ζωη (א*A ζωης, 70 ζωην) ζησομεθα: 𝔖 'nay, he dies not but lives': 𝔏 post mortem autem non erit tale nomen nostrum (*in reference to Elijah*) [s–s] ℌ *is much mutilated, the text represents Smend's reconstruction*: אליהו שבאוצר נסתר, *based in part on* 𝔊 *and* 𝔖; Ηλειας ος (70 >) εν λαιλαπι εσκεπασθη (*in* LXX σκεπαζειν = סתר): 𝔖 'Elijah was gathered into the chambers in Heaven': *Peters reconstructs*: אליהו אשר בסערה נסתר [t–t] ℌ *is again almost entirely obliterated, only three letters remaining; the above is the rendering of* 𝔊: 𝔖 'And Elisha received a double (portion) of prophecy' [u] A 70 248 Syro-Hex + αγιου [v–v] 𝔊 >: 𝔖 'And many wonders and signs did his mouth utter' [w–w] 𝔊 υπο (55 248 απο) αρχοντος (70 248 αρχοντων) [x–x] 𝔊 και . . . ουδεις [y] 𝔊 αυτον (= 𝔖)

. . . **And to restore the tribes of Israel.** With 𝔊 καταστῆσαι φυλὰς Ἰακώβ cp. Mark ix. 12 ὁ δὲ ἔφη αὐτοῖς Ἠλείας μὲν ἐλθὼν πρῶτον ἀποκατιστάνει πάντα, with which Weber compares the מְתַקֵּן האומה by which Rabbi Saʿadya Gaon expresses Elijah's activity preparatory to the coming of the Day of Jahveh (*Jüdische Theologie*, p. 353).

This is one of the few passages in which Ben-Sira refers to the Messianic Hope (see also xliv. 21, xlv. 25, xlvii. 11, 22, xlviii. 24, 25, xlix. 12, l. 24, li. 12); but neither the nature of the book nor the historical circumstances of the time, by which Messianic conceptions were always conditioned, were such as to lead one to expect much stress to be laid on this subject. During the third century B.C. the Jews lived in quietude and prosperity, and the hopes concerning the Messianic Age seem to have dropped into the background; not that the Jews ever really abandoned (until quite modern times) their Messianic expectations; these only ceased, for the time being, to play an important part.

11. **Blessed is he . . .** i.e. those that saw Elijah in the flesh were blessed, though they died. The next line of this verse is almost entirely obliterated in ℌ (see critical notes). Peter's suggested reading can scarcely be right, as it presupposes conceptions concerning the future life which are too advanced for the time of Ben-Sira. By the time the Greek translation was made the beliefs regarding this subject had greatly developed. The rendering of 𝔖 is due to Christian influence. As regards Smend's proposed reading, the point is that Elijah was still alive, i.e. he had never died; the reference is not to life after death.

Elijah has been glorified in Jewish legend more than any other biblical personage. 'The Haggadah which makes this prophet the hero of its description has not been content, as in the case of others, to describe merely his earthly life and to elaborate it in its own way, but has created a new history of him, which, beginning with his death, or "translation", ends only with the close of the history of the human race. From the day of the prophet Malachi, who says of Elijah that God will send him before "the great and dreadful day", down to the later marvellous stories of the Ḥasidic rabbis, reverence and love, expectation and hope, were always connected in the Jewish consciousness with the person of Elijah. As in the case of most figures of Jewish legend, so in the case of Elijah, the biblical account became the basis of later legend. Elijah the precursor of the Messiah, Elijah zealous in the cause of God, Elijah the helper in distress—these are the three leading notes struck by the Haggadah, endeavouring to complete the biblical picture with the Elijah legends' (*JE*, v. 122 *a*).

(*n*) XLVIII. 12–16 (ELISHA, &c.).

12. **hidden in the [heavenly] chambers.** Smend is probably right in his reconstruction of the Hebrew text; the 'chambers in Heaven' of 𝔖 doubtless reflects the original Hebrew, though 'in Heaven' may well be an explanatory addition, and 'chambers' was most likely in the singular in the Hebrew as Ben-Sira speaks elsewhere of only a single 'chamber' in the realms above (see xxxix. 17, 30, xliii. 14); the division of the heavens into various departments of which the innermost is the *Mehiza*, or dwelling-place of the Almighty, is a later development (cp. 1 Enoch xxii. 9–12, 4 Ezra iv. 35, 41, v. 37, vi. 22; see also 2 Cor. xii. 14; *Nedarim* 32 *a* [T.B.], *Shabbath* vi. 8 *d* [T.J.], Midrash *Bereshith Rabbah*, I. lxviii).

was Elisha filled . . . Cp. 2 Kings ii. 9, 13.

In double measure . . . Cp. 2 Kings ii. 9, 20–22. Peters thinks that the omission of these two lines in 𝔊 (see critical note) may be due to the fact that they seem to give more honour to Elisha than to Elijah; the omission may, however, be merely due to an oversight.

All his days . . . Cp. 2 Kings iii. 13–15, vi. 15, 16, 30 ff.

moved. Cp. Esther v. 9, '. . . that he stood not up nor moved for him.'

𝔥[B] 13 Nothing was [z]too wonderful for him[z],
[zz]And [a]from his grave[a] his flesh[aa] prophesied[bzz].
14 In[c] his life he did wonderful acts,
And in his[d] death marvellous works.

15 For all this the people turned[e] not,
And ceased[f] not from their[g] sins[gg];
Until they were plucked[h] from their land,
And were scattered in all the earth.
[i]And there were left [k]unto Judah but a few[ki];
[l]But still a prince was left unto the house of David[l].
16 Some among them did [m]that which was right[m],
And some [n]among them[n] [o]committed fearful sin[o].

(*o*) XLVIII. 17–25. *Hezekiah and Isaiah* (= 2+2+2+2+2+3 distichs).

17 Hezekiah fortified[p] his[q] city,
[r]In that he brought[r] water[s] into the midst thereof,
[t]And hewed through the rocks with iron[t],
[u]And dammed up the pool with mountains[u].
18 In his days Sennacherib came up[v],
And sent Rabshakeh[w],
[x]And stretched forth[x] his hand[y] against Zion,
And blasphemed[z] God in[a] his arrogancy.

z–z 𝔊 *υπερηρεν αυτον*: 𝔖 'was hidden from him' zz–zz 𝔖> a–a מתחתיו, *lit.* 'from his place beneath': 𝔊 *εν κοιμησει* aa 𝔊 *το σωμα αυτου* b *Reading with Smend and Peters* נבא (= 𝔊) *for* נברא c 𝔊 *και* (70>) *εν* d 𝔊> (70 248 = 𝔥) *but* + *αυτου after* 'works' e 𝔊 *μετενοησεν* (*cp.* xvii. 4) f 𝔊 *απεστησαν* g B A C> gg 𝔖 'evil deeds' h 𝔊 *επρονομευθησαν*: 𝔖 'went into captivity i–i 𝔖 'And Judah alone remained a small dominion to the house of David' k–k 𝔊 *ο λαος ολιγοστος* l–l 𝔊 *και αρχων* (ℵ[c.a] *αρχοντες*) *εν* (> B C 55) *τῳ οικῳ Δαυειδ* m–m 𝔊 *τα αρεστον*: 𝔖 repentance' n–n 𝔊> o–o 𝔥 *lit.* 'did iniquity wondrously': 𝔖 'added sins unto sins': 𝔊 *επληθυναν αμαρτιας* p 𝔖 'built' q 𝔖> r–r 𝔊 *και εισηγαγεν* (= 𝔖) s B C *τον γωγ*, ℵ* V 253 *τον ηωγ* (ℵ[c.a] *τον αγωγον*), 70 Syro-Hex *τον νηωρ* (A 248 = 𝔥); *probably corruptions of υδραγωγον* ('a conduit') t–t 𝔖>: 𝔊 *ωρυξεν σιδηρῳ ακροτομον* u–u 𝔖>: 𝔊 *και ωκοδομησεν κρηνας* (*l.* *κρημνους*) *εις υδατα* v 𝔖 + 'against them' w 70 248 + *εκ Λαχεις* (*cp.* 2 Kings xviii. 17, xix. 8): 𝔊 + *και απηρεν* (*dittography*): 𝔏 + et sustulit manum suam contra illos (*a variant of the third clause*) x–x 𝔊 *και επηρεν* y B ℵ C *η χειρ* (A 70 248 *χειρα* [= 𝔏 Syro-Hex Sah Eth]) z 𝔊 *εμεγαλαυχησεν* a 𝔊>(*hab* V 70 &c.) b–b 𝔖> c *So* 𝔊, *and*

---

13. **Nothing was too wonderful** . . . i.e. too hard; cp. Gen. xviii. 14, 'Is any thing too hard (lit. too wonderful) for the Lord?'

And from his grave . . . Cp. 2 Kings xiii. 20, 21.

prophesied. i.e. exercised prophetic powers, though of course in a different way from that recorded of Samuel in xlvi. 20 *d*.

14. Practically a repetition of the preceding verse.

15. **For all this** . . . Cp. Is. ix. 12.

And ceased not from their sins. The repentance recorded in 1 Kings xviii. 39 was but of short duration.

Until they were plucked . . . Cp. Deut. xxviii. 63.

there were left unto Judah but a few. Cp. Is. xxiv. 6.

16. **did that which was right.** Cp. the oft-repeated formula in Kings, e.g. 1 Kings xv. 11, &c.

(*o*) XLVIII. 17–25 (HEZEKIAH AND ISAIAH).

17. **Hezekiah fortified.** Note the word-play in Hebrew יחזקיהו חזק. Cp. 2 Chron. xxxii. 5, 30.

In that he brought water . . . Cp. 2 Kings xx. 20; 2 Chron. xxxiii. 30.

And hewed through the rocks. The reference is evidently to the boring of the tunnel from the Gihon to the Pool of Siloam; see Driver, *Notes on the Hebrew Text of the Books of Samuel*, pp. xv, xvi, who says in reference to the inscription in the tunnel which leads to the Pool: 'The inscription will not be later than the time of Hezekiah, who is stated to have "made the pool, and the conduit, and brought water into the city", in terms which appear exactly to describe the function of the tunnel in which the inscription is.' On the inscription the word חצב, 'hew through', here used occurs twice in the sense of cutting through a rock; and צור, 'rock', which likewise occurs twice on the inscription, is the word used in the text.

And dammed up . . . Cp. Is. xxii. 11; Ezek. xxxix. 11.

18. **Sennacherib.** Cp. 2 Kings xviii. 13 ff.; 2 Chron. xxxii. 1 ff.; Is. xxxvi. 1 ft.

stretched forth his hand . . . Cp. Is. x. 32; and for the expression see Job xv. 25.

blasphemed God . . . Cp. 2 Kings xviii. 22; Is. xxxvii. 6, 23.

ℌ[B] 19 [b]Then[c] were they shaken [d]in the pride of their heart[d],
And they writhed as [e]a woman in travail[e b];
20 [f]And they called unto [g]God Most High[g f],
[h]And spread out their hands unto Him[h];
[i]And He heard [k]the voice of their prayer[k i],
And saved[l] them by the hand of Isaiah[m];
21 And He smote[n] the army of Assyria,
[o]And discomfited them by the plague[o].

22 [p]For Hezekiah did[p] [q]that which was good[q],
—And was strong[r] in the ways of David[s]—
𝔊 [t]Which Isaiah the prophet[u] commanded him[v],
Who was great and faithful in his vision.
23 [w]In his days the sun went backward[w],
And he added life unto the king.
ℌ[B] 24 By a spirit of might he saw the future[x],
And comforted [y]the mourners of Zion[y].
25 [z]Unto eternity he declared the things that shall be,
And hidden things before they came to pass[z].

(*p*) XLIX. 1–3. *Josiah* (2 + 2 distichs).

49 1 The name[a] of Josiah is as sweet-smelling incense,
That is well mixed, the work[b] of the apothecary.
[c]The mention of him[c] is sweet [d]in the palate[d] as honey,
And as music at a banquet of wine.

probably ℌ, *but the text is mutilated* d–d 𝔊 καρδιαι και χειρες αυτων e–e 𝔊 αι τικτουσαι f–f 𝔖 > g–g 𝔊 τον κυριον τον ελεημονα h–h 𝔖 'And Hezekiah spread out his hands before the Lord' i–i 𝔊 και ο αγιος εξ ουρανου ταχυ (V 248 >) επηκουσεν αυτων k–k 𝔖 'And God quickly heard their prayer': 𝔏 vocem ipsorum + non est commemoratus peccatorum illorum neque dedit illos inimicis suis l 𝔏 purgavit m 𝔏 + sancti prophetae n 𝔖 'broke up' o–o 𝔊 και εξετριψεν αυτους ο αγγελος αυτου: 𝔖 'And smote them with a great blow' p–p *So* 𝔊 𝔖; *the text of* ℌ *is mutilated* q–q 𝔊 το αρεστον Κυριῳ (א* >) r 𝔖 'walked' s 𝔊 (א* >) + του πατρος αυτου (*cp.* 2 Kings xviii. 3) t *In* ℌ *the remainder of this verse and v.* 23 *is wholly mutilated* u 𝔖 + 'the most praiseworthy of the prophets' v *So* 𝔖 𝔏 (𝔊 >) w–w 𝔖 'For by his hand the sun stood still' x 𝔊 τα εσχατα y–y 𝔊 τους πενθουντας εν Σειων z–z 𝔖 'And as long as he was in the world he saw signs and wonders before they came to pass' (*a misunderstanding, or conscious alteration of, the Hebrew text*): 𝔊 = ℌ a 𝔊 μνημοσυνον: 𝔏 memoria b א B 'by the work' (A = ℌ) c–c 𝔊 > d–d 𝔊 εν παντι στοματι

---

19. **they writhed . . .** Cp. 2 Kings xix. 3; Isa. xiii. 8.
20. **spread out their hands.** Cp. 2 Kings xix. 14, 15, where, however, only Hezekiah does so.
He heard the voice . . . Cp. 2 Kings xix. 20.
And saved them . . . Cp. 2 Kings xix. 20 ff.
21. **And He smote . . .** Cp. 2 Kings xix. 35.
And discomfited them . . . For 𝔊 (cp. critical note), which has perhaps the better reading, see 2 Kings xix. 35 (Hebr. and Sept.), and cp. 1 Macc. vii. 41, 2 Macc. viii. 19.
22. **Who was great . . .** Cp. Is. vii.
23. **the sun went backward.** Cp. 2 Kings xx. 9–11; Is. xxxviii. 7, 8.
he added life unto the king. Cp. 2 Kings xx. 5, 6; Is. xxxviii. 5.
24. **a spirit of might.** רוח גבורה, cp. Is. xi. 2 רוח עצה וגבורה.
the future. אחרית, lit. 'the end'; the reference is to the return from the Exile (Is. xl. 3–11), and to the glorious future in store for Jerusalem (Is. lxi. 1–7).
And comforted the mourners . . . Cp. Is. xl. 1, lxi. 2, 3.
25. With this and the preceding verse compare what is said in *The Martyrdom of Isaiah*, ch. iv.
(*p*) XLIX. 1–3 (JOSIAH).
1. **as sweet-smelling incense.** Lit. 'incense of spices', cp. Exod. xxxvii. 29.
That is well mixed. Lit. 'that is salted', cp. Exod. xxx. 35. For the use of salt in the cultus cp. Lev. ii. 13 ('With all thine oblations thou shalt offer salt'), see *EB*, iv. 4249.
in the palate. Cp. Prov. xxiv. 13.
as music . . . Cp. xxxii. 5, 6 (= 𝔊 xxxv. 5, 6).

𝔥[B] 2 [e]For he was grieved[f] at our backsliding[e],
And put an end to [g]the vain abominations[g];
3 And he [h]gave his heart wholly[h] unto God[i],
And in days of violence[k] [l]he practised piety[l].

(*q*) XLIX. 4–7. *Judah's evil kings; the persecution of Jeremiah* (2 + 2 + 2 distichs).

4 Except David[m], Hezekiah, [n]and Josiah,
They all dealt utterly corruptly[n],
And[o] forsook the Law [p]of the Most High[p]—
The kings of Judah, till [they came to] their end;
5 And their might[q] was given[r] unto others[s],
And their glory to a strange[t] nation;
6 And so [u]the Holy City[u] was burned,
And the ways thereof laid waste
Through[v] Jeremiah; 7. because they had persecuted[x] him,
And he a prophet formed[y] from the womb,

[e–e] αυτος κατευθυνθη εν επιστροφη λαου (א αυτου) 𝔊 [f] *Reading* נחלה *for* נחל (*Smend*) [g–g] 𝔊 βδελυγματα ανομιας [h–h] 𝔊 κατευθυνεν την καρδιαν αυτου: 𝔏 et gubernavit, &c. [i] 𝔊 𝔏 'the Lord' [k] 𝔊 ανομων (= 𝔏) [l–l] 𝔊 κατισχυσεν την ευσεβειαν (= 𝔏) [m] 𝔊 𝔖 + και (*so Peters*) [n–n] 𝔥 *text makes the second line begin with* 'and Josiah' (ויאשיהו כלם השחיתו), *but it is better to keep* 'and Josiah' *in the previous line and emend the second line by adding inf. abs.* (= 𝔊), *reading* כלם השחת השחיתו (*so Peters*) [o] 𝔊 'For' [p–p] 𝔖 > [q] *Lit.* 'horn' [r] *Lit.* 'he gave' [s] *Reading* אחרים (*instead of* לאחור) = 𝔊 𝔖 [t] 𝔥 + נבל (*variant from* l. 26 (?)) [u–u] 𝔊 εκλεκτην πολιν αγιασματος [v] *Lit.* 'By the hand of' (= 𝔊); 'In the days of' 𝔖, *a correction from* xlviii. 18, 23 [x] 𝔥 ענוהו: 𝔊 εκακωσαν [y] 𝔊 'sanctified (*cp.* Jer. i. 5) [z] 𝔊 'to harm'

2. **he was grieved . . .** 𝔥 (נחל) = 'he entered upon his inheritance' (?), yields no satisfactory sense; the reference is doubtless to the effect produced on Josiah by the newly-discovered Book of the Law, cp. 2 Kings xxii. 11 ff. For the Hebrew as emended cp. Amos vi. 6. The Greek ('He behaved himself uprightly in the conversion of the people') means that he showed his uprightness by converting the people to obedience to the Law; but possibly 𝔊 should be emended, ἀποστροφῇ for ἐπιστροφῇ (= 𝔥).

put an end to. Cp. 2 Kings xxiii. 5, 11.

abominations. Cp. 2 Kings xxiii. 13.

3. **gave his heart wholly.** Or 'perfectly'; the expression is formed on the model of such expressions as 'integrity of heart', cp. Gen. xx. 5. For the verb (Hiph'il form) cp. Job xxii. 3.

he practised piety. For the term as applied to Josiah see 2 Kings xxiii. 3, 25.

(*q*) XLIX. 4–7 (JUDAH'S EVIL KINGS).

4. **Except David . . .** Ben-Sira definitely excludes all other kings except the three mentioned; contrast, however, the representation of the Chronicler, according to whom Asa (2 Chron. xv. 8 ff.) and Jehoshaphat (2 Chron. xvii. 5 ff.) ought to be reckoned among the pious reforming monarchs. The Book of Kings also speaks favourably, though not with such marked emphasis, of these two rulers (see 1 Kings xv. 11 ff., xxii. 43).

the Law of the Most High. For Ben-Sira's attitude towards the Law see Introduction, § 9 ii.

till [they came to] their end. i.e. until their death, or, perhaps, until their line came to an end. The Hebrew is ambiguous; the context (see next verse) rather favours the latter.

5. **And their might was given.** 𝔊 ἔδωκαν γὰρ τὸ κέρας αὐτῶν; for the phrase cp. 1 Macc. ii. 48, also Ps. lxxv. 5.

others . . . strange nation. i.e. the Babylonians. By their sins the kings brought about the ruin of the nation, culminating in the Babylonian Exile.

a strange nation. גוי נכרי; cp. עם נכרי, Exod. xxi. 8; apparently the combination גוי נכרי does not occur in the O.T. elsewhere.

6. **the Holy City.** קרית קדש; the designation of Jerusalem as the Holy City (עיר הקדש) occurs first in Is. xlviii. 2, lii. 1, also in Neh. xi. 1, 18; cp. Dan. ix. 24; קרית is a poetical variation on the common עיר ('city'). For 𝔊 (a refinement) see crit. note.

was burned. Cp. 2 Kings xxv. 9.

the ways thereof. Cp. 'the ways of Zion', Lam. i. 4.

laid waste. Cp. 2 Kings xxv. 10; the same root is used in reference to the gates of the city in Lam. i. 4.

Through Jeremiah. Jeremiah prophesied the destruction of Jerusalem, cp. e.g. Jer. xxxvi. 29; the actual fulfilment of this prophecy is regarded by Ben-Sira as the inevitable result of the prophet's prediction; the prophecy produced its own fulfilment. From another point of view the prophet may be regarded as having been inspired to foresee the result which was inevitable from other causes. Ben-Sira here seems to regard the prophecy of woe as being invested with the same fatal power which, according to ancient ideas, belonged to the uttered curse.

7. **because they had persecuted him.** For the persecution of Jeremiah see Jer. xxxi–xxxviii. Because they persecuted God's chosen representative and servant (the prophet) they brought upon themselves destruction.

And he a prophet . . . Cp. Jer. i. 5.

𝔥B 'To pluck up, to break down[z], and to destroy,
And likewise to build, and to plant,' [a]and to strengthen[a].

(*r*) XLIX. 8–10. *Ezekiel, Job, and the Twelve Prophets* (2 + 2 distichs).

8 Ezekiel saw a vision,
And described the different beings of the chariot.
9 [b]He also made mention of Job [c]⟨among the prophets⟩[c][b]
[d][e]Who maintained[e] [f]all the ways of righteousness[f][d].
10 And, moreover, as for the Twelve Prophets,—
[g]May their bones ⟨flourish in their place⟩[g],
[h]Who recovered Jacob to health[h],
[i]And delivered him ⟨by confident hope⟩[i].

(= להרע, *cp.* Jer. xxxi. 28) a–a 𝔊 > b–b 𝔊 και γαρ εμνησθη των εχθρων εν ομβρῳ c–c *Restoring* "בנביא i.e. בנבאים: 𝔊 *misread* בנבע, *cp.* Aquila, Ps. lxxvii. 2 *for* ομβριω (= הביע); 𝔥 *MS. has space for this but is illegible*: 𝔖 > d–d 𝔖 'Whose ways were all righteousness' e–e 𝔊 και αγαθωσαι, *but* V κατορθωσαι, 248 &c. κατωρθωσε (= Syro-Hex.) f–f 𝔊 τους ευθυνοντας οδους g–g 𝔥 (*defective*) . . . תהי עצמתם; *supply* פרחת תחתם (*so Smend and Peters*) = 𝔊 τα οστα αναθαλοι εκ του τοπου αυτων (= 𝔖) h–h 𝔊 παρεκαλεσεν (-σαν A 55 155) δε τον Ιακωβ (70 𝔖 Ισραηλ) i–i 𝔥 (*defective*) . . . וישעוהו: 𝔊 και ελυτρωσατο (-σαντο A 254 𝔏) αυτους εν πιστει ελπιδος (*the*

'To pluck up . . .' Cp. Jer. i. 10.
and to strengthen. These words were added to the citation by Ben-Sira in order to fill up the line.

(*r*) XLIX. 8–10 (EZEKIEL, JOB, AND THE TWELVE PROPHETS).

8. **. . . vision.** Cp. Ezek. i; see also Ezek. x.

the different beings of the chariot. Lit. 'the sorts, or kinds, of the chariot'. The term 'chariot' here is a technical one to denote Ezekiel's picture of the heavenly beings who support Jahveh's throne-chariot. This is the earliest use of the term (מרכבה) in this technical sense of a sacred mystery. In early Rabbinical literature the term employed is מעשה מרכבה, and it was laid down that it 'should not be taught to any one except he be wise and able to deduce knowledge through wisdom of his own' (Mishnah, *Megillah* iv. 10, *Ḥagigah* ii. 1). The study of it was later developed into a whole system of theosophy. In its earliest form the conception of Jahveh riding on Cherubim upon the clouds seems to be a genuinely Hebrew one; cp. Ps. xviii. 11, lviii. 5; Deut. xxxiii. 26. In 1 Chron. xxviii. 15 the Ark with the Cherubim is called the 'Chariot'; the story of Elijah riding to heaven (2 Kings ii. 11) may have been suggested by the Assyrian sun-chariot drawn by horses (cp. 2 Kings xxiii. 11). Ezekiel, in his vision, apparently saw Jahveh riding on the throned chariot, supported by the Cherubim, when leaving the doomed Temple at Jerusalem. It is worth noting that the term 'chariot' does not actually occur in Ezekiel's vision, though it became the technical term describing it; nor must a chariot in the ordinary sense be thought of in this connexion. The divine 'chariot-throne' represents a transformation of the original conception, and has become something quite transcendental.

9. **He also made mention of . . .** Ezekiel (xiv. 14, 20) mentions Job in company with Noah and Daniel as one of the prophets, if this reading can be accepted as correct (see critical note). It is significant that Ben-Sira brings in the mention of Job in this way; he deliberately calls attention to the Job of older tradition as this is embodied in Ezekiel; in this tradition Job figures with Noah and Daniel, or possibly, in the original text of Ezekiel, Enoch (instead of Daniel). In the apocalyptic sense Noah and Enoch were certainly 'prophets', and a reflection of this view may perhaps be seen in the opinion held by some Rabbis that Job was one of the prophets of the Gentiles (*Seder Olam Rabba* xxi). A possible inference from the way and the position in which Ben-Sira mentions Job is that he was not acquainted with a canonical Book of Job, though he may have known some form of our Book of Job not yet canonical.

. . . all the ways of righteousness. Ezekiel in the two passages referred to above speaks of Job, in company with Noah and Daniel, expressly as a type of righteousness ('. . . by their righteousness').

10. **the Twelve Prophets.** It is interesting to note that the Twelve Prophets are treated as a single book; this implies, probably, that they had already assumed essentially the form in which they appear in the Canon; note, too, that they follow Ezekiel, as in the Hebrew Canon.

May their bones ⟨flourish . . .⟩ Cp. xlvi. 12, where this curious expression also occurs; there is, of course, no reference to a resurrection here. The word means literally 'to send out shoots'; here it has, no doubt, a metaphorical meaning such as, 'May their memory flourish,' or the like; but originally the idea of the bones 'sprouting' must be connected with some old-world superstition. Among the ancient Semites it was a regular custom to pour water on the graves, which suggests the idea of causing something to grow. Among the Arabs one of the usual prayers for the dead was that Heaven might send rain upon their graves (cp. Wellhausen, *Reste arabischen Heidenthums*, pp. 182 ff.). For the belief that the life of the deceased lies dormant in his bones, see Tylor, *Primitive Culture*, ii, pp. 150 ff.; Jevons, *Intr. to the Hist. of Rel.*, p. 56; Spencer and Gillen, *Northern Tribes of Central Australia*, pp. 530 ff.

Who recovered . . . ⟨hope⟩. This is an interesting summary of the outstanding teaching of the book of the Twelve Prophets, as Ben-Sira conceived it. Their book is to him essentially one of consolation and hope. This was also the view of the Rabbinic teachers who, in order to avoid a gloomy and threatening conclusion to the whole book (Malachi ends with the words, 'Lest I come and smite the earth with a curse'), directed (see the Massorah) that the last verse but one should be repeated in reading.[1] This is also the case with the books of Isaiah, Lamentations, and Ecclesiastes.

[1] So as to follow the actual last verse.

(*s*) XLIX. 11–13. *Zerubbabel, Joshua the son of Joṣedeq, and Nehemiah* (3 + 2 distichs).

𝔊 11 [k]How shall we magnify Zerubbabel—
He, indeed was as a signet on the right hand;—
12 [l]And also[l] Jesus, the son of Joṣedeq?
Who in their days[n] built the House[mk],
𝔥[B] And set up on high [o]the Holy Temple[o],
Which was prepared for everlasting glory.
13 [p]Nehemiah,—glorious is his memory[p]!
Who raised up [q]our ruins[q],
[r]And healed our breaches,
And set up gates and bars[r].

(*t*) XLIX. 14–16. *Conclusion* (*Enoch, Joseph, Shem, Seth, Enoch, and Adam*) (3 distichs).

14 [s]Few like[s] Enoch have been created on earth;
[t]He also was taken up[u] [v]⟨from off the face thereof⟩[vt].
15 [w]Like Joseph was ever a man born?[w]
His body[x] also [y]endured a visitation[y].
16 [z]Shem, Seth[z], [a]and Enoch were ⟨*highly* honoured⟩[a];
But above every living thing [b]was the beauteous glory of[b] Adam.

last words perhaps = בתקות אמת [*Smend*] *or* באמונת תקוה [*Peters*]) k–k 𝔥 *MS. damaged; restore with Smend* (*cp. Peters*) = 𝔊 *substantially*:

מה נגדלה את זרבבל
והוא כחותם על יד ימין:
וגם את ישוע בן יוצדק
אשר בימיהם בנו בית:

l–l *So* 𝔖: 𝔊 *and* Sah ουτως m A B* πυργον (?) (B[1] οικον) n 𝔖 'who in their poverty' o–o 𝔊 λαον (A ναον) αγιον Κυριῳ p–p 𝔊 και νεμουσιν (ℵ[c.a] A Νεεμιου) επι πολυ το μνημοσυνον, 70 248 και εν εκλεκτοις ην Νεεμιας (70 Ιερεμιας) ου επι πολυ το μνημοσυνον αυτου (70 αυτων) q–q 𝔊 ημιν (ℵ ημων) τειχη (ℵ* χειλη, ℵ[c.a] τειχη) πεπτωκοτα r–r 𝔊 *transposes these two clauses* s–s 𝔊 ουδε εις t–t 𝔖 > u A μετετεθη (𝔊 ανελημφθη) v–v *Reading with Bacher* (*JQR*, xii. 281) מעל פניה (*cp.* 𝔊 απο της γης) *for* פנים (= ? 'in person' [*Smend*] *or* 'within' [*Schechter*]) w–w 𝔊 ουδε ως (B 68 ο δε) Ιωσηφ εγενηθη (Textus Receptus εγεννηθη) ανηρ: 𝔖 'A mother' (*misunderstanding* אם) 'like Joseph was not born': 𝔊 + ηγουμενος αδελφων στηριγμα λαου (= l. 1 *a*, 𝔥 𝔖) x 𝔊 τα οστα y–y 70 248

(*s*) XLIX. 11–13 (Zerubbabel, Joshua, and Nehemiah).

11. **as a signet . . .** See Hag. ii. 23; cp. Jer. xxii. 24 for the full phrase.

12. **Jesus.** Or Joshua, cp. Ezra iii. 2, 3.

the House. As Smend points out, οἶκον may be a correction of πύργον, which can be used of any lofty building; cp. Josephus (*Bell. Iud.* vii. 10. 3), who speaks of the temple of Heliopolis as πύργῳ (παραπλήσιος).

set up on high . . . For the Hebrew phrase cp. Ezra ix. 9.

. . . for everlasting glory. An echo of the Messianic Hope, cp. Hag. ii. 7, 9.

13. **glorious is his memory.** The warmth of the terms with which Ben-Sira speaks of Nehemiah contrasts significantly with his silence regarding Ezra; apparently the latter did not occupy so high a place of estimation within the circle of the scribes to whom Ben-Sira belonged as was the case with the later scribes. These earlier *Sopherim* were profoundly affected by the spirit of the Wisdom-Literature, and had an altogether wider outlook. There is a marked contrast in this respect between Ben-Sira and the generality of the later Rabbis, with whom in so many other respects he has such striking marks of affinity. It would seem that Nehemiah's pious aspiration that he might be remembered for good (Neh. xiii. 14, xxii. 31) has met with a sympathetic response on the part of Ben-Sira.

Who raised up our ruins. See Neh. iii, *passim*.

gates and bars. Cp. Neh. vi. 1, vii. 1.

(*t*) XLIX. 14–16 (Conclusion).

14–16. In order to provide a fitting conclusion to the Praise of the Fathers, and at the same time to mark it off from the hymn in praise of Simeon which follows (ch. l.), Ben-Sira reverts to the most glorious of the Fathers of old. With the object of enhancing Israel's glory, Joseph is bracketed with Enoch, and Shem, Seth, and Enoch with Adam,—Israel's ancestors with those of the human race (Smend).

14. **Few like Enoch.** Enoch has already been referred to in xliv. 16. 𝔊 'not one . . .' involves a difficulty, seeing that Elijah was also taken up without dying (2 Kings ii. 11); 𝔥 removes the difficulty ('Few . . .').

He also was taken up. Cp. Gen. v. 24. The omission of this whole clause by 𝔖 (see crit. note) may be due to dogmatic reasons (𝔖 also omits xliv. 16, see notes *in loc.*).

15. **His body also . . .** i.e. a providential visitation in being transported from Egypt to the land of promise (cp. Gen. l. 25; Exod. xiii. 19; Joshua xxiv. 32). Enoch was translated into heaven in a wonderful way, but shared this distinction with Elijah; Joseph, however, enjoyed the unique distinction of having his body transported long after death from a foreign country to the Holy Land.

XLIX. 15 *b* and L. 1–24. *In praise of the High-Priest, Simeon, the son of Jochanan*
(1 + 3 + 1 + 3 + 2 + 2 + 3 + 3 + 3 + 2 + 2 + 2 + 3 + 1 + 2 + 3 distichs).

ℌ[B] 15 *b* [a]Great among his brethren and the glory[b] of his people
50 1 Was Simeon, the son of Jochanan[c] the priest[d a].
[e]In whose time[f] the House was renovated[g e],
And in whose days the Temple was fortified ;
2 [h i]In whose days the wall was built[i],
[k](Having) [l]turrets for protection[l] like[m] a king's palace[k] ;
3 [mm]In whose time a reservoir was dug,
A water-cistern[n] [o]like the sea[o] in its abundance[mm].
4 [p]He took thought for his people [to preserve them] [q]from robbers[q],
And fortified his city against the enemy[r p].

+ υπο Κυριου : 𝔖 'was buried in peace' z–z *tr.* 𝔖 𝔏 a–a 𝔊 εν ανθρωποις εδοξασθησαν : 𝔖 'and Enoch among men were created': ℌ נפקדו (*v.* 15) ואנוש, *for which read* נכבדו . . . : 𝔖 *combines* 𝔊 *and* ℌ *and misreads* נכבדו *as* נבר(א)ו b–b 𝔊 εν τη κτισει (= בבריאת *for* תפארת)

a–a . . . ηγουμενος αδελφων στηριγμα λαου Σιμων Ονιου (B* א* Ιονιου) υιος ιερευς ο μεγας b ℌ תפארת : 𝔖 כלילא (= עטרת 'crown') c 𝔖 Syro-Hex נתניא d 𝔖 + רבא (= 𝔊) e–e 𝔊 ος εν ζωη αυτου υπεραψεν οικον f 𝔖 *lit.* 'generation; in his days' g *Reading* נבדק (*Schechter*) *for* נפקד ('visited'): 𝔖 נבנה ('was built') h ℌ *places v.* 3 *before v.* 2 i–i 𝔊 και υπ αυτου εθεμελιωθη υψος διπλης k–k 𝔊 αναλημμα υψηλον περιβολου ιερου l–l *Reading* פנות מעוז *for* פ״ מעון m *Reading* כ *for* ב ('in') mm–mm 𝔊 εν ημεραις αυτου ηλαττωθη (*read* ελατομηθη *with Fritzsche*) αποδοχειον υδατων χαλκος ωσει θαλασσης το περιμετρον : 𝔖 'He dug a well' n *Reading* אשוח *for* אשיח o–o *Reading* כים (= 𝔊) *for* בם p–p 𝔖 'And he saved his people from the enemy' q–q 𝔊 απο πτωσεως : 𝔏 a perditione r . . . εντολιορκησαι ('to besiege')

---

16. **Shem . . .** For this juxtaposition of Shem, Seth, and Adam, cp. 1 Chron. i. 1. Shem, Seth (and Enoch) 'represent the ancestors of the pious part of the post-diluvian and antediluvian world respectively' (Edersheim).

But above every living thing. The thought implicit here seems to be that Adam, in virtue of having been directly created by God without human parentage, enjoys a glory which is not shared by any other member of the human race (cp. Luke iii. 38). This idealization of Adam is a notable feature, and occurs here for the first time in Jewish literature; it played later an important part in the development of Messianic doctrine (the Second Adam); but it is precarious to impute such an idea to Ben-Sira, whose thought here may merely have been that Adam in his ideal aspect was only adequately and worthily represented in his pious descendants, i.e. the Chosen People.

XLIX. 15 *b* + L. 1–24 (IN PRAISE OF THE HIGH-PRIEST SIMEON).

XLIX. 15 *b*. **Great among his brethren.** Cp. Lev. xxi. 10, 'He that is the high-priest among his brethren . . .'

the glory of his people. תפארה is used in Esther i. 4 in reference to the majesty of King Ahasuerus.

L. 1. **Simeon.** The second of the name, who lived at the beginning of the second century B.C.; it was this Simeon, not Simeon I, who was surnamed 'the Righteous', a title given, according to Smend, because he was the last of the house of Zadok to observe the Law. Josephus speaks of his father as Onias (*Antiq.* xii. 4. 10).

Jochanan. יוֹחָנָן is a shortened form of יְהוֹחָנָן; cp. יוֹיָכִין (Ezek. i. 2) for יְהוֹיָכִין, which is also contracted to יְכוֹנְיָה (Jer. xxvii. 20) and כָּנְיָהוּ (Jer. xxii. 24, 28). For the Greek Ἰονίας cp. the form יהוני, which occurs on an ossuary inscription found at Gezer (see *PEFQ*, 1904, p. 342).

In whose time. i.e. Simeon was no more living when this was written; the Greek makes this still clearer, see crit. note.

the House. Used in reference to the Temple in Ezek. xl. In the earlier literature it does not, as a rule, stand alone, but 'of God' or 'of Jahveh' is added; in 1 Kings vi (cp. also 2 Chron. i. 18, ii. 3, &c.), however, it stands alone.

renovated. Lit., according to the emended reading (see crit. note), 'to breach up'; the verb occurs in 2 Chron. xxxiv. 10 as parallel to חִזֵּק 'to repair', also in reference to the 'House'; this is its only occurrence in the O. T., though the noun בֶּדֶק ('a breach') is found fairly frequently.

the Temple was fortified. Cp. Josephus, *Antiq.* xii. 3. 3.

2. **turrets for protection.** i.e. battlements placed at intervals along a wall, cp. *v.* 4 *b*.

like . . . i.e. as in a king's palace.

3. **a reservoir.** מקוה, cp. Isa. xxii. 11.

A water-cistern. The Hebrew as it stands has אָשִׂיחַ ('I will talk'), which is clearly corrupt. Schechter, followed by Ryssel, reads שִׁיחָה, as in Jer. xviii. 22 (the *Qĕrî* has שׁוּחָה); but this does not account for the presence of the א. Bevan, followed by Smend, suggests אָשׁוּחַ, citing line 9 of the Mesha Inscription (ואבן את בעלמען ואעש בה האשוח, 'And I built Baal-Meon and made therein a reservoir'; cp. also line 23: ואנך עשתי כלאי האשו[ח למ]ין, 'And I made sluices (?) for the reservoir for water'); this seems to be preferable. The word does not occur in the O. T.; cp., however, שׁוּחָה 'a pit', Jer. ii. 6, xviii. 20, and שִׁיחָה, with the same meaning, in Ps. lvii. 7, cxix. 85.

in its abundance. הָמוֹן in reference to a mass of water occurs in Jer. x. 13, li. 16; cp. also 1 Kings xviii. 41.

4. **He took thought.** For the expression דאג מן in the sense of being concerned about something cp. Ps. xxxviii. 19.

from robbers. מִחֶתֶף lit. 'from (becoming) a prey'; cp. Prov. xxiii. 28, the only other occurrence of the word in the O. T.

fortified his city. Cp. xlviii. 17.

against the enemy. Smend, on the basis of what was probably the text before the Greek translator, reads 𝔥[B]

5 How glorious was he [s]when he looked forth from the Tent[t,s],
And[u] when he came out from the sanctuary!
6 Like a morning-star [v]from between the clouds[v],
And like the full moon [w]on the feast-days[w];
7 [x,y]Like the sun shining upon the Temple of the Most High[z],
And like the rainbow [a,b]becoming visible[b] in the cloud[a,y];
8 [c]Like a flower on the branches[c] in the days of [d]the first-fruits[d],
[e]And as a lily by the water-brooks[e],
As the sprout[f] of Lebanon on summer days,
9 And [g]as the fire of incense[g] in the censer[h];
Like a golden vessel[i] [k]beautifully wrought[l,k],
Adorned with [m]all manner[m] of precious stones;
10 Like a luxuriant[n] olive-tree [o]full of berries[o],
And like an oleaster[p] [q]abounding in branches[q].
11 [r]When he put on his glorious[s] robes[r],
And clothed himself in perfect[t] splendour,

s–s 𝔊 εν περιστροφη λαου t 𝔖 'Temple' u 𝔖 𝔊 > v–v 𝔊 εν μεσῳ νεφελης w–w 𝔊 εν ημεραις: 70 248 + αυτης (*leg.* εορτης): 𝔖 'in the days of Nisan' x 𝔥 𝔏 *insert* 'and' y–y *The clauses are transposed in* V 70 248 253 Syro-Hex z So 𝔊: 𝔥 'king': 𝔖 > a–a 𝔊 φωτιζον εν νεφελαις δοξης b–b 𝔖 > c–c *Reading* כנץ בענפים (*instead of* כנצפענפי): 𝔊 ως ανθος ροδων: 𝔖 'like spikenard' d–d *Reading* הבכורים (*Peters*) *for* מועד: 𝔊 νεων: 𝔖 'of the field': 𝔏 vernis e–e 𝔊 ως κρινα επ εξοδων υδατος f 𝔖 'trees' g–g 𝔊 ως πυρ και λιβανος: 𝔖 'as the smell of incense' h *Reading* המחתה (= 𝔖 𝔊) *for* המנחה i 𝔖 'necklace' k–k So 𝔖: *the Hebrew text is much mutilated*: 𝔊 ολοσφυρητον ('all of beaten [gold]') l *Lit.* 'enamelled' m–m *Reading* כל *for* על n 𝔊 >: 70 248 ευπρεπης (= 𝔖) o–o 𝔊 αναθαλλουσα καρπους: 𝔖 'great with branches' p 𝔊 κυπαρισσος q–q *Reading* מרבה ענף *instead of* מרוה ענף ('giving its branches to drink' = 𝔖): 𝔊 υψουμενη

'against a siege' (reading ממצור instead of מצר). 𝔖 renders according to the present Hebrew text. With regard to the text of 𝔊 Smend says: 'The infinitive is meaningless, for ἐμπολιορκῆσαι cannot well = τοῦ μὴ ἐμπολιορκηθῆναι.' It is true πολιόρκησις does not occur elsewhere, but ἐμπολιορκεῖν is also rare and is not found in the Bible. In any case 𝔊 did not read מצר, but מצור, i.e. במצור or ממצור.

5. **How glorious.** Cp. xlvi. 2.

when he came out. Ben-Sira is referring to the moment when the High-Priest, after having taken the ritual bath and being robed in the special garments, comes forth to offer the burnt-offering in atonement for himself and the people. It is the Day of Atonement that is referred to, the ritual of which is described in Lev. xvi; see especially *vv.* 23–25. Many further details of this ceremony are to be found in the Mishnic tractate *Yoma*; an English translation of this tractate with full notes by G. H. Box is published in *Church and Synagogue*, xi. 139 ff., xii. 49 ff.

from the sanctuary. מבית הפרכת, lit. 'from the house of the veil' (i.e. the Holy of Holies), so called because of the veil of blue, purple, and crimson which separated the Holy of Holies (*Debir*) from the Holy Place (*Hêkhāl*); but there was also a veil in front of this latter, separating it from the Court of the Priests; it must, however, be the former to which reference is made here, because the veil is spoken of as the *Paroketh*, whereas the veil before the Holy Place was known as the *Māsākh*.

6. **a morning-star.** Lit. 'a shining star'; cp. Ps. cxlviii. 3.

. . . feast-days. It was full moon at the two chief feasts, Passover and Tabernacles.

7. **Like the sun shining.** The Neo-Hebrew word (שרק Hiph.) occurs in xliii. 9 in the margin; it is not found in the O.T. Josephus thus describes the effect of the sun shining on the Temple: 'Now the outward face of the Temple in its front wanted nothing that was likely to surprise either the minds or the eyes of men; for it was wholly covered with plates of gold of great weight; and when the sun arose it reflected back a truly fiery splendour, and caused those who forced themselves to look upon it to turn away their eyes, just as they would have done at the rays of the sun itself' (*Bell. Iud.* v. 5. 6).

And like the rainbow . . . Ben-Sira evidently had the words of Ezek. i. 28 in mind: 'As the appearance of the bow that is in the cloud in the day of rain.'

8. **Like a flower on the branches.** Cp. the Midrash *Shir ha-Shirim* to ii. 3: 'Just as the apple-tree first brings forth the bloom and then its leaves.'

in the days of the first-fruits. Cp. Num. xxviii. 26 (Hebr. and Sept.).

as a lily. Cp. xxxix. 14.

by the water-brooks. Cp. Is. xxx. 25, xliv. 4.

the sprout of Lebanon. The same words (פֶּרַח לְבָנוֹן) occur in Nahum i. 4; the reference is to the cedars on Mount Lebanon.

9. **as . . . fire . . .** Cp. Lev. ii. 1, vi. 8; see also xlix. 1.

Adorned . . . Cp. xlv. 11.

10. **a luxuriant olive-tree.** Cp. Ps. lii. 10; Isa. xi. 16.

full of berries. Cp. Is. xvii. 6.

oleaster. In Neh. viii. 15 the oleaster (the wild olive-tree) and the olive-tree are also mentioned together. See further Nowack, *Hebräische Archäologie*, i, pp. 66, 238.

𝔥[B] When he went up [u]to the altar of majesty[u v],
[x]And made glorious the court of the sanctuary[x];
12 When he took the portions[y] from [z]the hand of his brethren[z],
While standing [a]by the blocks of wood[a],
Around him the garland[b] of his sons[c],
[d e]Like young cedar-trees[e] in Lebanon;
And [f]like willows by the brook[f] did they surround him[d],
13 [h]All the sons of Aaron in their glory,
And the Lord's[i] fire-offering[k] in their hands,
In the presence of the whole congregation[l] of Israel.

14 [m]Until he had finished the service of the altar[m]
[n]And arranging the rows of wood of the Most High[n],
𝔊 15 [o](And) stretched forth his hand to the cup,
[p]And poured out of the blood of the grape[p];
Yea, poured (it) out at the foot[q] of the altar,
A sweet-smelling savour [r]to the Most High, the All-King[r o].

εν (248>) νεφελαις (= מרומם ענן) r–r 𝔊 εν τῳ αναλαμβανειν αυτον στολην δοξης s 𝔖 + 'holy' t *Reading* כליל *for* בגדי (*Smend*) u–u 𝔖 'to receive the songs of praise' v 𝔊 'holy (altar)' x–x 𝔖 'In the beauty of the might of the sanctuary' y 𝔖 'the pieces of flesh' z–z 𝔊 εκ χειρων ιερων a–a 𝔊 παρ εσχαρᾳ βωμου b *Lit.* 'crown' c 𝔖 𝔊 'brethren' d–d 𝔖 > e–e 𝔊 ως βλαστημα κεδρου (*referring to the High-Priest*) f–f 𝔊 στελεχη φοινικων ('stems of palm-trees') h 𝔊 + και i 𝔖 > k 𝔊 προσφορα l 𝔖 'people' m–m 𝔊 και συντελειαν λειτουργων επι βωμων n–n 𝔊 κοσμησαι προσφοραν Υψιστου Παντοκρατορος: 𝔖 'and to serve the Most High with holy joy' o–o 𝔥 > *through homoioteleuton, both this and the preceding verse ending presumably with* עליון ('Most High'). p–p 𝔖 'And took old wine' q *Lit.* 'foundations'; 𝔖 'side' r–r 𝔖 >

---

11. **glorious robes.** For the description of the High-Priest's attire see Exod. xxviii. 36–42, xxix; cp. Sirach xlv. 6–13; *Yoma* vii. 5; also Josephus, *Ant.* iii. 7. 4–7, *Bell. Iud.* v. 5. 7.

When he went up . . . Cp. Lev. xvi. 18, 'And he shall go out unto the altar that is before the . . .'

the altar of majesty. הוד ('majesty') is not used in the O. T. in reference to the altar.

And made glorious the court of the sanctuary. עֲזָרָה (= περιβολή, precincts') is used of the ledge (R.V. 'settle') surrounding the altar of Ezekiel, see Ezek. xliii. 14, 17, 20, xlv. 19; but מקדש is never used of the altar, always meaning 'sanctuary'; we must, therefore, take עֲזָרָה in its later meaning, as in 2 Chron. iv. 9, where it is used in reference to the great, i.e. the outer, court; it is also used in this sense in the Mishnic tractate *Yoma*, where details concerning the ritual on the Day of Atonement are given; e.g. in i. 8 mention is made of the עֲזָרָה being 'full of Israelites', and in iv. 3 there is a reference to 'the pavement which is in the court' (הָרוֹבֵד שֶׁבָּעֲזָרָה).

12. **When he took the portions.** i. e. of the animals to be sacrificed; see the details in *Yoma* ii. 5–7. For נֵתַח used in the sense of portions of sacrificed animals cp. Exod. xxix. 17; Lev. i. 8, viii. 20, ix. 13.

blocks of wood. מערכות, lit. 'rows', i. e. the pieces of wood laid ready for use. The word comes from the root ערך 'to lay in order', which is used technically for laying the wood in order for the burning of the sacrifice; cp. Gen. xxii. 9; 1 Kings xviii. 23. According to Rabbi Eliezer ben Hyrqanus, who lived during the first century A.D. (*Megillath Ta'anith* v), the fifteenth day of Ab was the great day for wood-offering, 'when both priests and people brought kindling-wood in large quantities to the altar, for use in the burning of sacrifices during the whole year' (*EB*, i. 26 *a*). Josephus (*Bell. Iud.* ii. 17. 6) refers to this when he says: 'Now the next day was the festival of *Xylophoria*, upon which the custom was for every one to bring wood for the altar, that there might never be a want of fuel for that fire which was unquenchable and always burning.'

Like young cedar-trees. Cp. the somewhat similar expression in Ps. cxxviii. 3 כשתילי זיתים.

like willows by the brook. Cp. Lev. xxiii. 40; Job xl. 22; Is. xliv. 4; for the rendering of 𝔊 (see critical note) cp. Exod. xv. 27; Num. xxxiii. 6; Ps. xcii. 12, 13.

13. **In the presence of . . .** Cp. the same phrase in 1 Kings viii. 22.

14. **the service of the altar.** Lit. 'to serve the altar' לשרת מזבח; cp. the similar phrase in Joel i. 13 משרתי מזבח.

the rows of wood. See note on *v.* 12 *b*.

15. **poured out of the . . .** Cp. Josephus, *Ant.* iii. 9. 4: 'They bring the same quantity of oil which they do of wine, and they pour the wine about the altar.' See Num. xxviii. 1–8; cp. *Yoma* iii. 4. For the expression 'blood of the grape' cp. xxxix. 26; Gen. xlix. 11; Deut. xxxii. 14. The stress laid upon the drink-offering is noteworthy; in the Mishna (*Yoma*) it is merely mentioned, nothing more.

A sweet-smelling savour = רֵיחַ נִיחֹחַ, the technical term for an odour soothing to God; it is usually employed in reference to burnt-offerings (cp. Gen. viii. 21; Exod. xxix. 18; Lev. i. 9; Num. xv, &c., &c.); in, e.g., Exod. xxix. 41 the drink-offering is mentioned together with it; in Ezek. xvi. 19 it occurs in reference to offerings of flour, oil, and honey to idols; but in Ezek. xx. 28 it says: '. . . there they presented the provocation of their offering, there also they made their sweet savour, and they poured out there their drink-offerings.'

𝔋[B] 16 Then the sons of Aaron[s] sounded
With the trumpets [t]of beaten work[t];
Yea, they sounded and caused a mighty blast to be heard
[u]For a remembrance before the Most High[u].
17 [v](Then) all flesh[w] hasted together[v]
And fell upon their faces to the earth,
To worship [x]before [y]the Most High[x],
[z]Before the Holy One of Israel[z][y].
18 [a]And the sound of the song was heard[a],
And [b]over the multitude[b] [c]they made sweet melody[c];
19 [d][e]And all the people of the land cried[d]
In prayer before the Merciful,
[f]Until he had finished [g]the service of the altar[g][f],
[h]And His ordinances had brought him nigh unto Him[h].
20 Then he descended, and lifted up his hands
Upon the whole congregation of Israel[i],
[k]And the blessing of the Lord (was) upon his lips[k],
And he glorified himself with the name of the Lord[l].
21 [m]And again they fell down[m], (now) to receive[n]
[o]The pardon[p] of God from him[o][e].

[s] 𝔋 + 'the priests'; 𝔊 + 'shouted and' [t–t] 𝔖 'before all the people of Israel' [u–u] 𝔖 'in order to bless before all the people' [v–v] 𝔖 > [w] 𝔊 'the people' [x–x] 𝔊 'their Lord' [y–y] 𝔖 'God' [z–z] 𝔊 'the Almighty God Most High' [a–a] 𝔋 *lit.* 'And the song gave its voice': 𝔊 'And the singers praised (Him) with their voices': 𝔖 'They gave their voice to thanksgiving' [b–b] 𝔊 εν πλειστῳ οικῳ [c–c] *Reading* העריבו רנן (= 𝔊) *instead of* העריכו נרו ('they arranged his lamp') [d–d] 𝔊 'And the people besought the Lord Most High' [e–e] 𝔖 > [f–f] *See note on* 14 *a above* [g–g] 𝔊 κοσμος Κυριου [h–h] 𝔊 και την λειτουργιαν αυτου ετελειωσαν [i] 𝔊 υιων Ισραηλ [k–k] 𝔊 δουναι ευλογιαν κυριῳ (א V 70 253 Syro-Hex κυριου) εκ χειλεων αυτου [l] 𝔊 αυτου (157 κυριου) [m–m] 𝔊 και εδευτερωσεν εν προσκυνησει [n] *Reading* לשאת (= 𝔊) *for* שנית (*Smend*) [o–o] 𝔊 την ευλογιαν παρα Υψιστου [p] *Reading* זכיות (*Smend*); *the text is somewhat mutilated, but Smend says that the letters* 'כיו, namentlich יו, sind kaum zweifelhaft; von ת ist anscheinend der linke Fuss

16. **With the trumpets . . .** Cf. Num. x. 2 (R. V. marg.); for מקשה ('beaten work') cp. Is. iii. 24.
For a remembrance . . . Cp. Num. x. 10.
17. **To worship . . .** Cp. 2 Chron. xxix. 28.
18. **over the multitude . . .** i.e. the prostrate congregation.
19. **And His ordinances . . .** The Hebrew word משפט, which often has the sense of 'judgement', is also used as a technical term expressive of something that is due to somebody; thus in Deut. xviii. 3, 'this shall be the priest's *due* from the people . . .', cp. Deut. xxi. 17; in Num. xv. 24 reference is made to the offerings to the Lord 'in accordance with what is due', or, as the R. V. renders it, 'according to the ordinance' (כמשפט), cp. Job xxxvi. 6, Prov. xviii. 5.
20. **Then he descended.** According to Lev. ix. 22, Aaron does not descend from the altar until after he has pronounced the Blessing, and *Yoma* vi. 2 seems to agree with this.
And the blessing of the Lord . . . Cf. *Yoma* vi. 2, 'And the priests and the people who are standing in the court (בָּעֲזָרָה), when they hear the "Ineffable Name" (שֵׁם הַמְפֹרָשׁ) proceeding out of the mouth of the High-Priest, then they bow themselves down and worship, falling down upon their faces, and say: "Blessed be the Name of the glory of His Kingdom for ever and ever."' This was the only occasion on which the Holy Name was pronounced. As is well known, in the Hebrew text of the O. T. the name יהוה ('Jehovah' = *Jahveh*) is written with the vowels of *Adonai* ('Lord'), and pronounced so; if the title *Adonai* precedes יהוה (i.e. if the text has 'the Lord Jahveh') it is written with the vowels of *Elohim* ('God'). This was done in order to avoid pronouncing the Holy Name. In the Hebrew of Sirach, Jahveh is always written ''' or ''. This non-uttering of the Holy Name was not always due to reverential fear, but often also because of superstitious dread. 'The names of supernatural beings, such as gods and spirits, are commonly believed to be endowed with marvellous virtues, and the mere utterance of them may work wonders and disturb the course of nature' (Frazer, *The Golden Bough*², i, p. 441). This must certainly have applied at one time to the mass of the uncultured among the Israelites. There is a curious passage in *Pirqe Aboth* v. 14, where it is said that 'Noisome beasts come into the world for vain swearing, and for the profanation of the (divine) Name'.
he glorified himself. i.e. because he was privileged to utter the Holy Name.
21. **And again they fell down . . .** The verse presents us with the picture of the whole congregation falling down for the second time; the first time it was in order to receive the High-priestly blessing, now it is in order to receive divine justification, implying pardon for sin, through God's minister; cp. the somewhat similar thing mentioned in Lev. ix. 24, 'And there came forth fire from before the Lord, and consumed upon the altar the burnt-offering and the fat; and when all the people saw it, they shouted, and fell down on their faces'; the acceptance of the offering was an earnest of divine forgiveness which the whole congregation received prostrate. In Ben-Sira's day, apparently, the 'absolution' was pronounced by the High-Priest.

𝔥 22 Now [pp]bless [q]the God of all[q pp],
[r]Who doeth wondrously[s] on earth[r],
Who exalteth man[t] from the womb,
And dealeth with him according to His will[u].
23 May He grant you wisdom[v] of heart,
And may there be peace [w]among you[w].
24 May His mercy be established [x]with Simeon[x],
[xx y]And may He raise up for him the covenant of Phinehas;
May one never be cut off from him[y];
[z]And as to his seed[xx], (may it be) as the days of heaven[z xx].

L. 25, 26. *Three Detested Nations* (2 distichs).

25 For two nations doth my soul feel abhorrence,
(Yea), and (for) a third, which is not a people;
26 [a]The inhabitants of Seir[b] and[a] Philistia,
And that foolish nation that dwelleth in Sichem[c].

SUBSCRIPTION TO THE BOOK

L. 27–29. *The Concluding Words of Jeshua', the son of Eleazar, the son of Sira* (2 + 2 distichs).

27 [d]Wise instruction and apt proverbs[e d]
[ee f g]Of Jeshua', [gg]the son of Eleazar[gg], the son of Sira[g],

erhalten': 𝔊 την ευλογιαν: 𝔏 virtutem   [pp–pp] 𝔊 'bless ye all God'   [q–q] 𝔥 'the Lord God of Israel': 𝔖 'and the people of the land praised God'   [r–r] 𝔊 τω μεγαλοποιουντι παντη   [s] *Reading* המפליא *for* המפלא   [t] 𝔊 'our days'   [u] *Lit.* 'favour': 𝔊 'mercy'   [v] 𝔊 'joyfulness'   [w–w] 𝔊 'in our days in Israel (70> in Israel) for the days of eternity'   [x–x] 𝔊 μεθ ημων   [xx–xx] 𝔖 'and with his seed'   [y–y] 𝔊 >   [z–z] 𝔊 και εν ταις ημεραις αυτου λυτρωσασθω ημας (70>)   [a–a] 𝔊 οι καθημενοι εν ορει Σαμαρειας (A 155 + και): 𝔏 in monte Seir   [b] 𝔖 'Gebal': 70 248 Syro-Hex + και ανδρες οι κατοικουντες   [c] 𝔊 εν Σικιμοις   [d–d] 𝔊 παιδειαν συνεσεως και επιστημης: 𝔖 'all the proverbs of the wise and their riddles'   [e] *Reading* משלי *for* מושל   [ee–ee] 𝔖 'are written in this book', *omitting all the rest of vv. 27 b c d*   [f] 𝔥 *pr.* 'of Simeon the son of'   [g–g] 𝔊 'Jesus the son of Sirach, Eleazar the Jerusalemite': *in* 𝔊 *this and the next line are transposed*   [gg–gg] 70 248 𝔏>

The pardon. See crit. note. The reading of 𝔊, 'blessing,' can scarcely be right, as the preceding verse has just dealt with the High-priestly blessing.

22. **Now bless . . .** Martin Rinckart composed his hymn 'Nun danket alle Gott' ('Now thank we all our God') on the basis of this text.

doeth wondrously. Cp. Judges xiii. 19 (reading הַמַּפְלִא = Sept.).

23. **May He grant . . .** The clause also occurs as xlv. 26 *a*.

24. **with Simeon.** The alteration in 𝔊 is evidently intentional, and the same applies to the omission of the two next lines; the 'covenant of Phinehas' had come to an end by the time that Ben-Sira's grandson made his translation, so that the passage as found in 𝔥 would have appeared inappropriate. The mention of Simeon does not necessarily mean that he was still living when Ben-Sira wrote (see note on *v.* 1); 'Simeon' stands here for his house and lineage.

the covenant of Phinehas. Cp. xlv. 24, 25.

May one never be cut off . . . i. e. May his line always have a successor.

as the days of heaven. i. e. endless.

L. 25, 26 (THREE DETESTED NATIONS).

25, 26. These verses must probably have been added at the close of the book (if not by the author himself, which, however, is likely enough, then by a contemporary) with the special object of warning readers against those belonging to the three races mentioned. There was ample ground for the utterance of these words; the inhabitants of Seir, i. e. the Idumaeans (Edom), had been the bitter enemies of the Jews ever since the Return from Babylon; see e.g. Obad. 11–14; Ps. cxxxvii. 7; Lam. iv. 21; Ezek. xxv. 12–14, xxxv. 14, xxxvi. 3; Mal. i. 2–5; Judith vii. 8, 18: according to 1 Macc. v. 65 Hebron, and the villages thereof, were in possession of the Edomites ('the children of Esau') in the days of Judas Maccabaeus, cp. Josephus, *Ant.* xii. 8. 6, *Bell. Iud.* iv. 9. 7; they had probably occupied this territory, which was less unfertile than their own land, ever since the Captivity. The antipathy which Ben-Sira had for the Philistines is easily understood when it is remembered how strongly Hellenized their country had become; in the centuries following the Macedonian conquest the influence of Greek civilization was profound and wide-reaching (for details see *EB*, iii. 3725). But the most hated of all were the people of Sichem, i. e. the Samaritans, as is well known; they were, as Smend points out, especially dangerous to their neighbours at this time, because the Seleucidae had made common cause with them against the Jews.

that foolish nation. גוי נבל, cp. xlix. 5; Deut. xxxii. 21.

L. 27–29. SUBSCRIPTION TO THE BOOK.

27. **apt.** אופנים; cp. Prov. xxv. 11, דָּבָר דָּבֻר עַל־אָפְנָיו 'a word aptly spoken' (Symmachus renders it ἐν καιρῷ αὐτοῦ). Smend thinks that both here and in Prov. xxv. 11 the reference is to metrical form.

Jeshua' . . . 𝔥 inserts 'Simeon the son of', so also in the two subscriptions at the end of the book; but

ℌ[B] [hi]Which he declared in the explanation of his heart[h],
And which he taught with understanding[iee].
28 Blessed is the man[ii] who meditateth[k] on these things[l],
[m]And he that layeth them up in his heart shall become wise[m].
𝔊 29 [n]For if he do them, [o]he shall be strong for all things[n],
ℌ[B] [p]For the fear of the Lord is life[po].

APPENDIX TO THE BOOK (LI. 1–30)

(*a*) LI. 1–12. *A Prayer* (2+2+2+3+2+2+2+2+3 distichs).

51 1 [qab]I will thank Thee, [c]Jahveh, O King,[c]
[d]I will praise Thee, O God [e]of my salvation[eda],
I will declare Thy Name[f], [g](Thou) strength of my life[g];
2 [h]For Thou hast redeemed my soul from death[h],
[i]Thou didst keep back my flesh from the Pit[i],
[k]And from the power of Sheol Thou didst deliver my foot[k];
[l]Thou didst preserve me[m] from the scourge of a slanderous tongue,
And from the lips [n]of them that turn aside to lies[nl];
[o]Thou wast [p]on my side[po] in the face of those that rose up against me;
3 [q]Thou didst help me, according to the abundance of Thy mercy,
Out of the snare [r]of those that watch for my stumbling[r],
And from the hand of those that seek my life;
From manifold troubles didst Thou save me[q],

h–h *Reading* בפתור (*so Smend for* ניבע) אשר לבו ניבא i–i 𝔊 εχαραξα τῳ βιβλιῳ τουτῳ [*here follows* 27 *b*], ος ανωμβρησεν σοφιαν απο καρδιας αυτου ii 𝔊 ος k 𝔊 αναστραφησεται l 𝔏 + bonis m–m 𝔖 'and learneth them and becometh wise in them' n–n ℌ > o–o 𝔖 'the height of the fear of the Lord is excellent above all things; take hold thereof, my son, and let it not go' p–p *In* ℌ *these words form one line with* li. 1 *b a*; 𝔊 οτι φως (106 φοβος) Κυριου το ιχνος αυτου: 55 70 248 254 Syro-Hex + και τοις ευσεβεσιν εδωκε σοφιαν: 55 70 248 254 + ευλογητος κυριος εις τον αιωνα γενοιτο γενοιτο: 70 + δοξα σοι ο θεος ημων δοξα σοι q 70 Syro-Hex > *ch.* li.

a–a *Transposed in* ℌ b προσευχη Ιησου υιου Σειραχ *inserted as title by* 𝔊 c–c *So* 𝔊 𝔖: ℌ 'my God, my Father' d–d 𝔖 'Every day will I praise Thy Name, O Lord', *misplaced after v.* 11 e–e 𝔊 'my Saviour' f 𝔖 + 'in praises' g–g 𝔊 >: 𝔖 'my trust is (in) the Most High from everlasting' h–h 𝔊 οτι σκεπαστης και βοηθος εγενου μοι i–i 𝔊 και ελυτρωσω το σωμα μου εξ απωλιας k–k 𝔊 > l–l 𝔖 >: 𝔊 και εκ παγιδος διαβολης γλωσσης m ℌ + 'from the slander of the people' n–n 𝔊 εργαζομενων ψευδος o–o 𝔊 > p–p *Lit.* 'for me' q–q 𝔊 εγενου βοηθος, και ελυτρωσω με κατα το πληθος ελεου και ονοματος σου εκ βρυγμων ετοιμος εις βρωμα, (א και) εκ χειρος ζητουντων την ψυχην μου εκ πλειονων θλιψεων ων εσχον r–r *Reading* צופי צלעי (*Schechter*)

Ben-Sira's grandson, in the Prologue to his Greek translation of the book, calls the writer Jeshuaʿ, the son of Sirach. It is probable that the mention of Simeon here is due to the occurrence of this name in *vv.* 1, 24.

28. **Blessed is . . .** Cp. Ps. i. 1.

29. **For if he . . .** There can be no doubt that originally ℌ had this clause in some form.
. . . life. Cp. Prov. xiv. 27, xix. 23.

LI. 1–30 (Appendix to the Book).

(*a*) LI. 1–12 (A Prayer).

LI. 1. **Jahveh, O King.** Cp. Ps. cxlv. 1. The consensus of both 𝔊 and 𝔖 against ℌ favours the reading in the text; for *my God, my Father* of ℌ cp. Exod. xv. 2, and the *Abinu Malkenu* prayer in the Jewish Liturgy (Singer's ed., pp. 55–57), as well as the *Shemoneh 'Esreh* ('The Eighteen Benedictions') (see, further, Taylor's edition of *Pirqe Aboth*, Excursus v, p. 124; the Hebrew text of *Shemoneh 'Esreh* is given by Dalman in *Die Worte Jesu*, pp. 299–304).
O God of my salvation. Cp. Ps. xviii. 46, xxv. 5.
I will declare Thy Name. Cp. Ps. xxii. 22, cii. 21.
(Thou) strength . . . Cp. Ps. xxvii. 1.

2. **Thou hast redeemed.** Cp. Ps. xlix. 15, lv. 18, lvi. 13, lxix. 18.
Thou didst keep back . . . Cp. Job xxxiii. 18; Ps. lxxviii. 50.
Thou didst deliver my foot. Cp. Ps. xxv. 15.
that turn aside to lies. Cp. Ps. xl. 5.
. . . that rose up against me. Cp. Ps. iii. 1, lvi. 9.

3. **the abundance of Thy mercy.** Cp. Ps. v. 7, lxix. 13, cvi. 7, 45.
of those that watch for . . . For the Hebrew (see crit. note) cp. Jer. xx. 10.
that seek my life. Cp. Ps. xxxv. 4, xl. 14, lxiii. 9, lxx. 2.

ℌ[B] 4 And from the straits of the flame round about (me),
[st]From the midst of the fire that I kindled not[t],
5 [u]From the deep of the belly of Sheol[us],
[v]From the lips of wickedness, and from the framers of lies[v],
6 [x]And the arrows[x] of a deceitful tongue.
My soul drew nigh[y] unto death,
And my life[z] to the nethermost[a] Sheol[b].
7 [c]And I turned about on every side[c], [d]yet there was none to help me[ed],
[ee]And I looked for one to uphold[ee], but there was none.
8 Then did I remember [f]the loving-kindnesses of Jahveh[f],
And [g]His mercies[g] which have been from of old,
[h]Who delivereth them that trust in Him[h],
[i]And redeemeth them [k]from all evil[ki].
9 And I lifted up my voice[l] [m]from the earth[m],
[n]And cried out for help from the gates of Sheol[n].
10 [o]Yea, I cried[oo]: 'O Jahveh[p], my Father [q]art Thou[qo],
[r]For Thou art the hero of my salvation[r];
[rr]Forsake me not[rr] in the day[s] of trouble,
[t]In the day of wasteness and desolation[t].
11 I will praise Thy Name continually,
[u]And will sing Thy praise[u] in prayer[v].'

s–s 𝔖 > t–t *Reading* (*lit.* 'that was not kindled') מבתוך איש לא נפחה : 𝔊 και εκ μεσου πυρος ου ουκ εξεκαυσα u–u *Reading* מתהום רחם שאול (= 𝔊) v–v 𝔊 και απο γλωσσης ακαθαρτου και λογου ψευδους x–x 𝔊 βασιλει διαβολη: '*which presents a gloss* ("arrows of the tongue" = slander) *together with a corruption of an original* βολιδες (Jer. ix. 8) *or* βελη (*cp.* Job xxxix. 22, βασιλει B: βελει א^c.a A = ℌ)' (*Hart*) y B ηνεσεν (א A V = ℌ 𝔖): 𝔏 laudabit dominum z 𝔖 'spirit': 𝔊 + ην συνεγγος a א^c.a 248 κατωτατου (𝔊 κατω) b 𝔖 + 'and my spirit draweth near unto death' c–c 𝔊 περιεσχον με παντοθεν d–d 𝔖 'in order that I might be upheld' e 𝔊 𝔖 > 'me' ee–ee 𝔊 εμβλεπων (A εβλεπον, 248 επεβλεπον) εις αντιλημψιν ανθρωπων f–f 𝔊 του ελεους σου κυριε g–g 𝔊 της εργασιας σου h–h 𝔊 οτι εξελῃ τους υπομενοντας σε i–i 𝔊 και σωζεις αυτους εκ χειρος εθνων (א A εχθρων, V πονηρων) k–k 𝔖 'from him that is stronger than they' l 𝔊 ικετειαν m–m B επι γην, א A απο γης (*cp.* 248 απο οργης) n–n 𝔊 και υπερ θανατου (A απο αθανατου) ρυσεως εδεηθην: 𝔖 'and I made supplication' o–o 𝔊 επεκαλεσαμην κυριον πατερα κυριου μου oo *Reading* ואקרא (= 𝔊 𝔖) *for* וארומם ('Yea, I exalted') p 𝔖 > q–q 𝔖 'from on high' r–r 𝔊 >: 𝔖 'mighty Lord and Saviour' rr–rr 𝔊 μη με εγκαταλιπειν s 𝔊 εν ημεραις (248 253 εν ημερᾳ = 𝔏) t–t 𝔊 εν καιρῳ υπερηφανιων αβοηθησιας: 𝔖 > u–u *Reading* ואזמרך (*Smend*) = 𝔊 *for* ואזכרך ('And I will remember thee') v 𝔊 εν εξομολογησει: 𝔖 'in praises'

---

4. **the straits of the flame.** Cp. Is. xlvii. 14.
that I kindled not. Cp. Job xx. 26; a figurative way of expressing the presence of troubles not of one's own making.
5. **From the deep . . .** This rendering is uncertain, as רחם does not occur in this connexion in the O. T.; cp. Jonah ii. 3; note, however, בטן ('belly') is not used elsewhere in a similar connexion.
the framers of lies. Lit. 'them that plaster lies', cp. Job xiii. 4; Ps. cxix. 69.
6. **And the arrows . . .** See crit. note. Cp. Ps. lii. 2.
My soul drew nigh . . . Cp. Ps. lxxxviii. 3.
to the nethermost Sheol. Cp. Ps. lxxxvi. 13, lxxxviii. 6.
7. **I turned about . . .** Cp. Ps. cvii. 12; Is. lxiii. 5.
8. **. . . the loving-kindnesses . . .** Cp. Ps. xxv. 6.
. . . them that trust in Him. Cp. Ps. xvi. 1.
And redeemeth them . . . Cp. Gen. xlviii. 16; Ps. cxxi. 7.
from all evil. מכל רע, for which Smend would read מכף רע (=𝔊) 'from the hand of evil', cp. Hab. ii. 9; which Peters reads מיד צר ('from the power of the enemy'); 𝔊 possibly read this, cp. 1 Kings xxviii. 18.
9. **from the gates of Sheol.** Cp. Is. xxxviii. 10; Jonah ii. 3.
10. **. . . my Father art Thou.** See note on *v.* 1; cp. Ps. lxxxix. 26. The rendering of 𝔊 (see crit. note) is probably due to Christian influence. Cp. Ps. ii. 7, cx. 1.
the hero of my salvation. Cp. 'the rock of my salvation' in Ps. lxxxix. 26 (cp. Ps. lxii. 2), and 'the strength of my salvation' in Ps. cxl. 7 (cp. Isa. xxxiii. 6).
In the day of wasteness . . . See Zeph. i. 15, from which this is quoted.
11. **I will praise . . .** Cp. Ps. cxlv. 2.
And will sing Thy praise. This rendering of 𝔊 is preferable to that of ℌ 𝔖; the two verbs זמר and הלל occur together in Ps. cxxxv. 3.
in prayer. Cp. l. 19.

𝔥B [vv]Then did Jahveh hear my voice[vv],
And gave heed to my supplication;
12 [w]And He redeemed me from all evil[w]
[x]And delivered me[x] [y]in the day of trouble[y].
Therefore will I give and offer praise[z],
And bless [zz]the Name of Jahveh[zz]:—

(*b*) $12^{\text{i–xvi}}$ (*Extant only in Hebrew*): *A Thanksgiving* (=1+4+4+4+3 distichs).

i. Give thanks unto Jahveh, for He is good;
For His mercy endureth for ever.
ii. Give thanks to the God of praises;
For His mercy endureth for ever.
iii. Give thanks unto Him that keepeth Israel;
For His mercy endureth for ever.
iv. Give thanks unto Him that formeth all;
For His mercy endureth for ever.
v. Give thanks unto the Redeemer of Israel;
For His mercy endureth for ever.
vi. Give thanks unto Him that gathereth the outcasts of Israel;
For His mercy endureth for ever.
vii. Give thanks unto Him that buildeth His city and His Sanctuary;
For His mercy endureth for ever.
viii. Give thanks unto Him that maketh a horn to sprout for the house of David;
For His mercy endureth for ever.
ix. Give thanks unto Him that chooseth the sons of Zadok to be priests;
For His mercy endureth for ever.

vv–vv 𝔊 > w–w 𝔊 εσωσας γαρ με εξ απωλειας x–x 𝔊 και εξειλου με: V και εξελου μαι y–y 𝔊 εκ καιρου πονηρου A + και εξιλου (*sic*) μαι: 𝔖 'from all trouble' z 𝔊 + σοι zz–zz 248 'Thy Name, O Lord': 𝔖 'Thy holy Name'

gave heed to my supplication. Cp. Ps. cxl. 6, cxliii. 1.
12. **from all evil.** Cp. *v.* 8 *d*.
in the day of trouble. Cp. *v.* 10 *c*; Ps. xli. 1.
(*b*) $1^{\text{i–xvi}}$. (EXTANT ONLY IN HEBREW): A THANKSGIVING.

The Psalm which is here inserted is formed on the pattern of Ps. cxxxvi, that is, if this latter is prior in date; the possibility, however, of both having been composed on an earlier pattern (Peters) must be allowed for. It is probable that this Psalm is an amalgamation of two poems, a shorter one, *vv.* vi–ix, and a longer one, *vv.* i–v, x–xvi (=twelve verses). The first clause of each verse of the shorter poem is longer than the corresponding clauses of the longer poem. The place in which *vv.* vi–ix are inserted is the natural one, the word 'Israel' being the point of attachment. The omission of the whole by 𝔊 𝔖 favours the opinion that it did not form part of the original book; but Smend, who regards the whole as original, accounts for the omission by saying that 𝔊 took exception to its 'un-Greek character', as well as to the words in *v.* ix, while 𝔖 followed 𝔊 in omitting it because of the anti-Jewish tendency which is characteristic of 𝔖. This explanation seems inadequate, for the 'un-Greek character' would apply to the whole book, while the natural objection to *v.* ix (the downfall of the house of Zadok had taken place by the time the translation was made) would not account for the omission of the whole section. It seems more likely that *vv.* vi–ix are original, and that the rest was subsequently added, the amalgamation of the two taking place as suggested above. See, however, the discussion in the Introduction, § 3, iii.

i. **Give thanks . . .** This verse is identical with Ps. cxxxvi. 1; cp. the refrain at the end of each verse in this psalm as well as in Ps. cxxxvi.

ii. **the God of praises.** Cp. Ps. xxii. 3, lxxi. 6; and see also the *Shemoneh 'Esreh* (cp. note on *v.* 1 above) iii: 'The holy ones praise Thee every day.'

iii. **that keepeth Israel.** Cp. Ps. cxxi. 3–8.

iv. **that formeth all.** Cp. Jer. x. 16, li. 19.

v. **the Redeemer of Israel.** Cp. Is. xliv. 6, xlix. 7, and *Shemoneh 'Esreh* vii: 'Blessed art Thou, O Lord, the Redeemer of Israel.'

vi. **that gathereth the outcasts . . .** Cp. Ps. cxlvii. 2; Is. xi. 12, xxvii. 13, lvi. 8; and *Shemoneh 'Esreh* x: 'Blessed art Thou, O Lord, who gatherest the outcasts of Thy people Israel.'

vii. **that buildeth . . .** Cp. Ps. cxlvii. 2; Isa. xliv. 28; and *Shemoneh 'Esreh* xiv: 'Blessed art Thou, O Lord, the Builder of Jerusalem.'

viii. **that maketh a horn to sprout . . .** Cp. Ps. cxxxii. 17; Ezek. xxix. 21; and *Shemoneh 'Esreh* xv: 'Do Thou speedily cause the shoot of David to sprout forth, and do Thou lift up his horn through Thy victorious salvation; every day do we hope for Thy salvation. Blessed art Thou, O Lord, who causeth the horn of salvation to sprout forth.'

ix. **that chooseth the sons of Zadok . . .** Cp. l. 24 (𝔥); 2 Sam. viii. 17; 1 Kings i. 26; 1 Chron. vi. 8 (v. 34 in Hebrew), xxix. 22; Ezek. xl. 46, xliv. 15, xlviii. 11.

𝔥[B] x. Give thanks unto the Shield of Abraham;
For His mercy endureth for ever.
xi. Give thanks unto the Rock of Isaac;
For His mercy endureth for ever.
xii. Give thanks unto the Mighty One of Jacob;
For His mercy endureth for ever.
xiii. Give thanks unto Him that hath chosen Zion;
For His mercy endureth for ever.
xiv. Give thanks unto the King of the kings of kings;
For His mercy endureth for ever.
xv. And He hath lifted up the horn for His people;
The praise of all His pious ones,
xvi. For the children of Israel, a people nigh unto Him,
Hallelujah.

(*c*) LI. 13–30. *A Poem describing how Ben-Sira acquired Wisdom* (= 14+9 distichs).

𝔊 13 [a]When I was yet young, before I wandered abroad[a],
𝔥[B] [b]I desired her and sought her out[b].
14 [c]In my youth I made supplication in prayer[c];
𝔊 [d]And I will seek her out even to the end.
15 [e]She blossomed like a ripening grape[e],
My heart rejoiced in her[d].
𝔥[B] My foot trod [f]in her footstep[f],
From my youth [g]I learned Wisdom[g].

a–a 𝔥 *is mutilated; all that is left is* אני נער הייתי ('I was young') = 𝔖. *From here to v.* 15 *a incl.* 𝔖 *is wanting* b–b 𝔊 εζητησα σοφιαν προφανως εν προσευχη μου c–c *In* 𝔥 *this clause stands as v.* 16 *a, which it has displaced*: 𝔊 εναντι ναου ηξιουν περι αυτης d–d *Wanting in* 𝔥 e–e *Reading* ἐξήνθησεν ὡς περκάζουσα σταφυλή (*Bickell, cp. Sept. of* Amos ix. 13) *for* εξ ανθους ως περκαζουσης σταφυλης: *cp.* 𝔏 et effloruit tanquam praecox uva f–f *Reading* באשרה (*Smend*) *for* באמתה: 𝔊 εν ευθυτητι: 𝔥 𝔖 + 'O Lord' g–g 𝔊 ιχνευον αυτην

x. **the Shield of Abraham.** Cp. Gen. xv. 1; Ps. xviii. 2, and *Shemoneh 'Esreh* i: 'Blessed art Thou, the Shield of Abraham.'

xi. **the Rock of Isaac.** Cp. Deut. xxxii. 4; 2 Sam. xxiii. 3; Ps. xviii. 2, xlii. 9, lxxi. 3; Is. xxx. 29, li. 1; in *Shemoneh 'Esreh* xviii the expression 'Rock of our life' occurs.

xii. **the Mighty One of Jacob.** Cp. Gen. xlix. 24; Ps. cxxxii. 2, 5; Isa. i. 24, xlix. 26, lx. 16, and *Shemoneh 'Esreh* i: 'Blessed art Thou, O Lord our God, and God of our fathers, God of Abraham, God of Isaac, and God of Jacob, the great, the mighty, and the fearful God.'

xiii. **that hath chosen Zion.** Cp. Ps. lxxviii. 68, cxxxii. 13, cxxxv. 21, and *Shemoneh 'Esreh* xvii: 'Be pleased, O Lord our God, with Thy people Israel, and their prayer; and set up again the sacrificial service for the altar of Thine House . . . And may our eyes behold Thy merciful return to Zion. Blessed art Thou who restorest Thy *Shekinah* to Zion.' (On the withdrawal of the *Shekinah* from earth, and the reasons for this, see the Midrash *Bereshith Rabba*, c. 19; the passage is given in the authors' *The Religion and Worship of the Synagogue*[2], p. 219.)

xiv. **King of the kings of kings.** Cp. the title 'God of gods, and Lord of lords' in Deut. x. 17. In *Shemoneh 'Esreh* the title 'King' is applied to God five times, and in xi occur the words: 'Reign Thou over us, O Lord, alone in loving-kindness and mercy.' In *Pirqe Aboth* iv. 32 occurs the expression: 'The King of the kings of kings, the Holy One, blessed be He.'

xv, xvi. These two verses are identical with Ps. cxlviii. 14.

(*c*) LI. 13–30 (A Poem).

The Poem (*vv.* 13–30) which follows is an acrostic, each verse beginning with the letters of the Hebrew alphabet in their order; this had already been discerned by Bickell before the discovery of the Hebrew text (see the *Zeitschrift für katholische Theologie*, vi. 326–330; 1882).

13. **When I was yet young.** Cp. vi. 18; Wisd. viii. 2.

before I wandered abroad. For this use of πλανᾶσθαι cp. xxxiv. 11 (= 𝔊 xxxi. 12); Ben-Sira refers to his travels also in xxxix. 4.

14. **In my youth.** Smend is probably right in regarding ἔναντι ναοῦ of 𝔊 as a mistake for ἐν νεότητί μου (= 𝔥).

in prayer. ἐν προσευχῇ μου of 𝔊 belongs here, not in *v.* 13 *b*.

15. **My heart . . .** This clause was probably longer originally; it is unduly short as it stands.

in her footstep. See critical note; 𝔊, as Smend points out, may have read באשרה ('in her footstep') but misunderstood it; cp. Job xxiii. 11, 'My foot hath held fast to His steps'; for 𝔥 as it stands cp. Ps. xxv. 5, xxvi. 3.

I learned. Smend suggests the reading חקרתי ('I tracked'); cp. 𝔊, which certainly gives a better parallel to the preceding clause. For 𝔥 as it stands cp. Ps. lxxi. 17; Prov. xxx. 3.

𝔊 16 [h]I bowed down mine ear a little and received her[h],
ℌ^B And much knowledge did I find[i];
17 [k]And[l] her yoke was glorious to me[k],
[m]And to my Teacher do I offer thanks[m].
18 [n]I purposed to do good[n] ⟨with her⟩[o],
[oo]And [p]I was not put to shame[p], for I found her[oo].
19 My soul was attached[q] to her,
[r]And I turned not away my face from her[r];
𝔊 [s]I spread forth my hands to the heaven above[s],
ℌ^B [t]And for ever and ever I will not go astray from her[t].
[u]My hand opened her gates,
And I entered unto her, and looked upon her[u].
20 [v]I set my soul aright[v] [w]after her[w],
[x]And I found her in her[y] purity[x];
I gat me understanding [z]through her guidance[z].
𝔊 [a]Therefore [b]I shall not be forsaken[b][a].
ℌ^B 21 My inward part was troubled[c] [cc]like an oven[cc] [d]to look upon her[d],
Therefore have I gotten[e] a good possession.
22 Jahveh gave [f]me the reward of my lips[f],
And [g]with my tongue[g] do I praise Him.

23 Turn in[h] unto me, ye unlearned,
And lodge in my house of instruction.

h–h *This clause has been displaced by* 14 *a in* ℌ   i 𝔊 + εμαυτῳ: Sah + 'because of her' (*Smend*)   k–k 𝔊 προκοπη εγενετο μοι εν αυτῃ   l ℌ >, *but the* ו *is required as the sixth letter of the alphabet, this being the sixth clause*   m–m 𝔊 τῳ διδοντι μοι σοφιαν δωσω δοξαν   n–n 𝔊 διενοηθην γαρ του ποιησαι αυτην   o *A word has fallen out here*   oo–oo 𝔊 και εζηλωσα (*perhaps a mistake for* εζητησα = ℌ) το αγαθον και ου μη αισχυνθω   p–p *Reading* אבוש (= 𝔊) *for* לא אהפך ('I will not turn back')   q 𝔊 διαμεμαχισται (*reading* עשקה *for* חשקה): 𝔖 'clave'.   r–r 𝔊 και εν ποιησει λιμου διηκριβασαμην   s–s *Wanting in* ℌ, 20 *a stands in place of it*   t–t 𝔊 και τα αγνοηματα αυτης επενθησα   u–u 𝔊 >   v–v *Reading* כוננתי נפשי (= 𝔊) *for* נתתי נ״   w–w 𝔊 εις αυτην   x–x 𝔊^B *wrongly transposes this and the next clause*   y 𝔊 𝔖 > 'her'   z–z *Reading, with Smend,* מתחבלתה *for* מתחלתה ('from the beginning' = 𝔊 𝔖)   a–a *Only the first word and one letter of the second word are left in* ℌ   b–b 𝔖 'I shall not forsake her'   c 𝔖 'burned'   cc–cc 𝔊 >   d–d 𝔊 εκζητησαι αυτην   e ℌ 𝔖 + 'in her'   f–f 𝔊 γλωσσαν μοι μισθον μου   g–g 𝔊 εν αυτῃ   h *Reading* סורו (= 𝔖) *for* פנו: 𝔊 εγγισατε

16. **I bowed down mine ear.** Cp. iv. 8, vi. 53.
17. **her yoke . . .** Cp. vi. 24, 30, and *v.* 26 of this chapter.
to my Teacher. The Teacher is, of course, God.
18. The text is very corrupt here, and must be emended with the help of 𝔊.
19. In this verse 𝔊 apparently had a text before it which in part differed from that of ℌ as now extant.
My hand opened her gates. For the thought of Wisdom having her dwelling-house cp. xiv. 23–25, Prov. ix. 1 ff.
and looked upon her. Cp. xv. 7, 'Sinners shall not see her.'
20. **understanding.** Lit. 'heart'; cp. Prov. xv. 32, xix. 8, where the same verb as here is used (קנה).
21. **My inward part was troubled.** Cp. Jer. xxxi. 20.
Therefore have I gotten . . . Cp. Prov. iv. 7.
22. **the reward of my lips.** i. e. success as a teacher.
23. **Turn in . . .** Cp. Prov. ix. 4, 16.
house of instruction. The *Beth ha-Midrash*, or *Beth Midrash*, is the technical name for the 'house' where students gathered together for instruction in the Law. Great scholars had their own 'houses' where they gathered pupils together. The *Beth ha-Midrash* of Ben-Sira is the earliest of which we know; in *Yoma* 35 *b* (T. Babli) mention is made of the one in which Shemaiah and Abtalion taught, and which Hillel, when a youth, could attend only after having paid an admission-fee to the janitor; 'whether or not this charge of a fee, so contradictory to the maxim of the men of the Great Synagogue (*Aboth* i. 1, "Raise up many disciples"), was a political measure of the time, it seemingly stands in connexion with a principle pronounced by the Shammaites (*Ab. R. N.*, A. iii, B. iv, ed. Schechter, p. 14) that "only those who are wise, humble, and of goodly, well-to-do parentage should be taught the Law". On the other hand, the Hillelites insisted that "all, without exception, should partake of the privilege, inasmuch as many transgressors in Israel, when brought nigh to the Law, brought forth righteous, pious, and perfect men"' (*JE*, iii. 117 *b*). Ben-Sira says distinctly that the wisdom was to be acquired 'without money'; see *v.* 25 and cp. *Nedarim* 36 *a* (T. Babli): 'As I have taught you without payment, saith God, so must you do likewise.' Reference is made (*Tanna debe Eliyahu R.* ix [x], xvi, and elsewhere) to the *Beth ha-Midrash* in the Temple (cp. Matt. xxi. 23, xxvi. 55; Luke ii. 46, xx. 1, xxi. 37; John xviii. 20), which was called *Beth ha-Midrash ha-gadol*, 'the Great house of instruction.'

𝔥[B]
24 [i]How long will ye lack [k]these things[k i]?
And (how long) shall your soul be so[l] athirst?
25 I open my mouth and speak [m]of her[m],
Acquire Wisdom[n] for yourselves without money.
26 Bring[o] your necks under her yoke,
[p]And her burden let your soul bear[p];
[q]She is nigh unto them that seek her[q],
[r]And he that is intent (upon her) findeth her[r].
27 Behold with your eyes that [s]I laboured but (little)[s] therein[t],
[u]And abundance of peace[v] have I found[u].
28 [w]Hearken to my teaching, (though ye be but) a few[x w],
And much [y]silver and[y] gold shall ye acquire thereby.
29 May my[z] soul delight [a]in my *Yeshibah*[a];
And ye shall not be put to shame [b]in singing my praise[b].
30 Work your work [c]in righteousness[c],
And He will give you[d] your reward in its time.

[e][Blessed be Jahveh; and praised be His Name to generations.
Thus far the words of Simeon the son of Jeshua‘, who is called Ben-Sira.
The Wisdom of Simeon, the son of Jeshua‘, the son of Eleazar, the son of Sira.
May the Name of Jahveh be blessed from now and unto eternity.][e]

i–i 𝔊 και (τι ℵ A) οτι υστερεισθαι (υστερειτε ℵ A) λεγετε εν τουτοις k–k *Lit.* ‘from these things and those things’ l *Lit.* ‘very’ m–m 𝔊 > n 𝔊 > o 𝔊 υποθετε p–p 𝔊 και επιδεξασθω η ψυχη υμων παιδειαν (= 𝔖) q–q 𝔊 εγγυς εστιν ευρειν αυτην r–r 𝔊 > s–s *Reading, with Smend,* קטן עמלתי (= 𝔊 𝔖) *for* קטן הייתי ועמדתי (‘I was small and I persisted’) t 𝔊 > u–u *Reading, with Smend,* והרבה מצאתי מנוחה *for* . . . ומצאתיה (‘and I found her,—peace’) v 𝔊 + εμαυτῳ w–w 𝔥 *pr* רבים (‘many’): 𝔊 μετασχετε παιδειαν εν πολλῳ αριθμῳ αργυριου x *Reading* במספר (= 𝔖) *for* בנערותי (‘in my youth’) y–y 𝔊 > z 𝔊 𝔖 ‘your’ a–a 𝔊 εν τῃ ελεει αυτου: 𝔖 ‘in my repentance’ b–b 𝔊 εν αινεσει αυτου c–c *Smend would read* בלא עת, *Peters* לפני עת (= 𝔊 𝔖) d *So* 𝔊 𝔖: 𝔏 > e–e 𝔊 ‘Wisdom of Jesus, son of Sirach’: 55 70 248 254 ‘Blessed be the Lord for ever; Amen, Amen’: 𝔖 ‘Blessed be God for ever, and praised be His Name to generations. Thus far the words of Jeshua‘ the son of Simeon that is called the son of Asira [*so also Syro-Hex, but some Syriac MSS. read* Sirach]. The writing of the Wisdom of Bar Sira is ended’. *The subscription varies in the Syriac MSS.*

---

24. **shall your soul be so athirst.** Cp. Is. lv. 1; Amos viii. 11. Cp. *Pirqe Aboth* i. 4: ‘Let thy house be a meeting-house for the wise, and powder thyself in the dust of their feet; and drink their words with thirstiness.’

25. **without money.** Cp. Is. lv. 1, 2, and the Talmudic quotation in the note on *v.* 23.

26. **her yoke.** Cp. *v.* 17, vi. 25.

He that is intent. נותן נפשו, lit. ‘that giveth his soul’.

27. **(little).** For the use of קטן in a temporal sense cp. Is. liv. 7.

28. **(though ye be but) a few.** For this use of במספר cp. Gen. xxxiv. 30; Deut. iv. 27.

And much silver . . . Cp. *Pirqe Aboth* ii. 19: ‘If thou hast learned much Torah, they give thee much reward; and faithful is the maker of thy work, who will pay thee the reward of thy work; and know that the recompense of the reward of the righteous is for the time to come.’

29. *Yeshibah.* i.e. Circle of hearers, later an Academy of learning. ‘At first the *Beth ha-Midrash* was the place where the *Yeshibah* assembled. . . . Later, when the number of students increased, it became necessary to hold the sessions in a separate large hall adjoining the *Beth ha-Midrash*, and this hall was known by the name of *Yeshibah*’ (*JE*, xii. 595 *a*). For בישיבתי 𝔊 read בישועתי (‘in His salvation,’ referring it to God), while 𝔖 read בשיבתי (‘in my repentance’), neither understanding, presumably, what was meant by the *Yeshibah*.

in singing my praise. בשירתי.

30. **Work your work.** i.e. the work of seeking wisdom.

in righteousness. The reading of 𝔊 𝔖, ‘before the time,’ is probably the correct one, the reference being to the time of final reckoning; cp. John ix. 4.

THE WISDOM OF SOLOMON

INTRODUCTION

§ 1. Short Account of the Book.

The Book of Wisdom has long enjoyed the reputation of being the most attractive and interesting book in the Apocrypha. Nor is the reputation undeserved if attention is confined to the first ten or eleven chapters. In these chapters both thought and expression are of a high order. The thought, it is true, is not that of a systematic or consistent thinker, but of a writer imbued with a strongly religious spirit; one who felt the stress and perplexity of life and suffering, and yet resisted the temptation to abandon—like many of his co-religionists—his ancestral belief in a God of righteousness. These thoughts are expressed in the ancient Hebrew style of parallelism: in spite of rare words, the language is vigorous and the construction simple: the impression that he was well acquainted with the literature and philosophy of Greece grows upon one the more the book is studied, and he is not without boldness in revising some of the traditional beliefs of his religion.

The work falls naturally into three sections: (1) cc. i to vi. 8; (2) vi. 9 to xi. 1; (3) xi. 2 to xix. The first section has been well called 'the book of eschatology'; it portrays in vivid contrast the different destinies which await the righteous and the ungodly who oppress them. The impious and defiant speech of the ungodly, the picture of their despair and remorse after death, and the description of the divine vengeance upon them are the outstanding literary features in this part of the book. The religious teaching also of this section is interesting and important. The writer enunciates the doctrine of immortality immediately after death, denies that suffering presupposes sin, refuses to admit that early death is necessarily a calamity, or that childlessness is a mark of divine displeasure. It would be difficult to find five other chapters in the Old Testament Scriptures with so much departure from traditional views.

The second section consists of the panegyric on Wisdom which gives its name to the book. In beautiful and eloquent language the attractions of Wisdom as a heavenly Being are set forth. 'Wisdom is radiant and fadeth not away'; she seeks to know those that are worthy of her, and leads them to the enjoyment of immortality in the presence of God. According to the testimony of Solomon, who now speaks, her treasures are bestowed upon mankind in answer to prayer. The fine description of Wisdom is continued, and culminates in the statement that 'she is a breath of the power of God, and a clear effluence of the glory of the Almighty' (vii. 25). Solomon is not the only one who has been favoured by her. She guided the great ones of old, rescued them from all their troubles, and finally brought the holy nation itself out of captivity and 'prospered their works by the hand of a holy prophet' (xi. 1).

From this point onward a great change takes place. We have no longer a poem extolling goodness and celebrating Wisdom, but a Midrash in glorification of the Jews.

From xi. 2 to the end of the book we have an historical retrospect of Israel in Egypt and in the wilderness, broken by a dissertation on the origin and evils of idolatry in cc. xiii, xiv, xv. Chapters xi and xii with xvi to xix contrast the lot of Israel in the wilderness with that experienced by the Egyptians during the plagues. The writer sets himself to prove the two propositions that 'By what things a man sins, by these he is punished' (xi. 16), and 'By what things their foes were punished, by these they in their need were benefited' (xi. 5). First, the punishments of the Egyptians are said to have been framed in accordance with a variety of the *lex talionis*. This is shown most clearly in the plagues of frogs, lice, and flies. Because the Egyptians worshipped despicable animals, by despicable animals they were punished. But the writer's power of drawing parallels does not end here. He goes further and gives examples to prove his other contention that what was noxious to the Egyptians was beneficial to Israel. Historical facts are ingeniously selected and opposed to one another; if the main facts are intractable, the details are made to furnish the required lesson. If he cannot get a positive comparison, a negative one will do. The comparisons are mostly forced, except in the case of the last plague, where the slaying of the firstborn had a double effect. It punished the Egyptians and at the same time freed Israel. The first of these ideas, appropriateness of retribution, was doubtless based on Exod. iv. 22–23: 'Thus saith the Lord, Israel is my son, my firstborn: . . . (because) thou hast refused to let him go, behold, I will slay thy son, thy firstborn.' The second seems to be peculiar to this book.

In cc. xiii–xv the author discourses on idolatry and its attendant evils. He treats the worship of the heavenly bodies with some leniency, only marvelling that the worshippers did not go a step farther and find the Sovereign Lord of all through His works. He then turns to idolatry proper, and following Isa. xl pours scorn and sarcasm on those who worship a crooked piece of wood for which the workman can find no use save as an object of worship: a piece of wood not sound enough to be used for the building of a ship. The origin of idolatry is sketched after the manner of Euhemerus, and the methods of a second idol-maker—the worker in clay—held up to derision.

After this digression the writer turns once more to the Egyptians; and from here to the end the contrast between Egypt and Israel is resumed. The work concludes with a repetition of a favourite theme of the writer, that the world fights for the righteous: the elements by their transmutation into one another are used by God to punish the Egyptians and defend Israel.

The book is included in the so-called Wisdom Literature of the Hebrews, the chief object of which is to discuss the problem of life and its conditions. Some of the writers limited their teaching to directing men aright in their social relations. They saw that much of the failure and unhappiness of life arose from disregard of prudential considerations and rightly laid emphasis on this. Small troubles were the result of imprudence; serious troubles the result of deliberate wrongdoing; therefore, to avoid trouble small or great, be prudent and abstain from wrongdoing. We have examples of this teaching in Proverbs and Sirach. But the teaching of experience showed that this doctrine was very imperfect. The rich oppressed the poor, however prudent and pious the poor might be; and in times of religious persecution or national trial the theory broke down utterly. Some teachers faced these perplexing facts and tried to account otherwise for the mystery of suffering. Here they deserted the rôle of the sage inculcating prudential precepts, and became religious rather than moral teachers (though the difference would hardly be recognized by a Jew), endeavouring to penetrate the mysteries of God and explain them to suffering humanity. We have examples of this in Job, Ecclesiastes, and the well-known Psalms, xxxvii, xlix, and lxxiii. It is to this last division that the writer of Wisdom, cc. i–x, belongs: the later chapters, xi to xix, have nothing in common with either class of Wisdom literature.

The authorship of the book is unknown. It is perhaps the work of more than one writer, and dates probably from after 50 B.C. St. Paul undoubtedly knew and used the book, Romans and Ephesians showing clear traces of its influence; some other parts of the New Testament also show points of contact with it.

§ 2. TITLE.

The earliest mention of the book is perhaps found in p. 11 *a*, line 8 of the Muratorian Canon (A. D. 200). There the title is 'Sapientia', with the added words 'ab amicis Salomonis in honorem ipsius scripta'. Clement of Alexandria, head of the Catechetical School A. D. 190–203, speaks of it under the title Wisdom of Solomon. Tertullian (*circa* 200) quotes it as the Wisdom of Solomon. Origen (d. 250) speaks of it in the same way as Clement. Cyprian (d. 258) quotes it as Solomon or the Wisdom of Solomon. The Latin version has 'Liber Sapientiae'; the Peshitta, 'The great Wisdom of Solomon.'

In the fourth-century MSS. ℵ and B the title is Σαλομωντος and Σαλωμωνος respectively. The Alexandrine fifth-century MS. has Σολομωντος. Jerome (d. 420), who recognizes that the book is pseudepigraphic, says it was entitled 'Sapientia Salomonis'. Only the Latin omits the name of Solomon, and this may be due to Jerome's influence: although he did not alter the translation—'calamo temperavi' he says—he may have altered the title.

§ 3. THE MSS.

The most important uncials, ℵ A and B, contain the book in its entirety. C (Codex Ephraim) contains viii. 5–xii. 10, xiv. 19–xvii. 18, xviii. 24–xix. 22. V (23), eighth-ninth century, contains the whole. The cursives mentioned in Holmes and Parsons are numbered 23 (but this is a mistake: 23 is an uncial and is now called V), 55, 68, 106, 155 (omits vi. 22–xvi. 19), 157, 248, 253, 254, 261, 296. According to Klostermann (*Analecta*, Leipzig, 1895) 55 does not contain Wisdom. Klostermann has examined 248 and 253, while Nestle (*Urtext und Übersetzungen*) has investigated the readings of 68, 106, 157, 253, and 296. Of the cursives 248 seems to be the most important. It is frequently quoted by Prof. Margoliouth in *JRAS*, 1890, and Sanday and Headlam (*Romans*, p. 51 note) say, 'Cod. 248 embodies very ancient elements.' Grimm and Feldmann quote certain Parisian MSS. collated by Thilo of Halle, who contemplated an edition of the book (*c.* 1825).

The text of B is given in Swete, *O.T. in Greek*, with the variants of ℵ A and C. Many interesting variants in the cursives are given in Grimm, Holtzmann, and especially Feldmann. Feldmann's investigation (*Textmaterialien z. B. der W.*, Freiburg im B., 1902) is by far the most thorough yet published.

§ 4. THE VERSIONS.

The Latin version is the Old Latin; Jerome did not touch it: he says 'calamo temperavi'. It is generally faithful to the Greek, but includes several lines not in any Greek MS., one of which (ii. 8) is undoubtedly, another (i. 15) possibly, genuine; a third (v. 14) a very intelligent gloss: others, e.g. ii. 17, vi. 1, 23, viii. 11, ix. 19, xi. 5, are glosses pure and simple. The text has been exhaustively examined by Thielmann in the *Archiv für lat. Lex. und Gram.*, 1893, pp. 235–277.[1] Like previous investigators, Thielmann comes to the conclusion that the home of the version is North Africa. This he proves by full lists of words and constructions in Wisdom, only found elsewhere in North African Latin. A short list of such words is given in § 4 of Westcott's article on Wisdom in Smith's *DB*; a longer list may be found in Deane, *Index II.* As Tertullian and Cyprian used it, the version is placed by Thielmann in the latter half of the second century.

The Syriac (Peshitta) version is full of mistakes and paraphrases, but is of great interest on account of its striking relationship to the Latin. Prof. Margoliouth points out that the Peshitta agrees with the Latin 'in a way which cannot be the result of chance'. This relationship is probably that of assistant to the Latin translator. The reverse could not be the case, since, if the Syriac translator had had the Latin to refer to, he would have made far fewer mistakes. Both the Latin and the Syriac are from earlier Greek MSS. than any we now possess.

Some interesting instances of agreement between the Syriac and Latin, besides those mentioned by Prof. Margoliouth on p. 279, *JRAS*, 1890, are as follows: v. 14, x. 5, 12 (see note), xiv. 2, and especially xiv. 19, of which Prof. Margoliouth says 'the Latin rendering can only be accounted for as a rendering of either the Syriac or the (supposed Hebrew) original'.

There are numerous additions in the form of explanatory glosses, e.g. the proper names in c. x, Cain, Noah, Abraham, Lot, Jacob and Joseph, are inserted, and in xix. 17 (Syr. 16) ἐκεῖνοι rightly explained as the men of Sodom.

The text has been thoroughly examined by Joseph Holtzmann, *Die Pesch. z. B. der W.*, pp. 152, Freiburg im B., 1903. Of his conclusions, the two following deserve mention here: (1) the language of the copy before the translator was Greek, as is shown by mistranslations which could only have arisen from a misunderstanding of the Greek; (2) the Syriac version was used by the translator of the Latin version, therefore its date must be earlier.

The other versions (except the Arabic—which is said to be very late,—twelfth century or later) have been examined by Feldmann, who has collated the Coptic (Sahidic), Syro-Hexaplaric, and Armenian, and given the variants of each. He then (pp. 41–84) gives a most useful enumeration, with frequent discussions, of the various readings throughout the book.

§ 5. DATE.

The difficulty of arriving at a satisfactory date for the book is seen from the differences which exist between scholars as to the period of its composition. Grimm dates it 145–50 B.C., Thackeray 130–100 B.C., Gregg 125–100 B.C., Gfrörer 100 B.C., Bousset under the Empire, Farrar 40 A.D.

An indisputable *terminus a quo* is obtained from the fact that the writer made use of the LXX version of Isaiah, but that may be no later than 200 B.C. By common consent this date is far too early. It is, however, possible to get a later date for the *terminus a quo*. If the line in 1 Enoch v. 7 is the source of Wisd. iii. 9 the book must be later than the translation of Enoch into Greek, which was probably undertaken as a whole, seeing that the fragments which survive include chapter lxxxix. The latest part of Enoch consists of chapters xxxvii to lxxi, and the date of this according to Charles is 94–79 B.C. We may suppose Enoch to have been translated at some date between 70 and 50 B.C. and adopt this period as the *terminus a quo*.

Mr. Thackeray dates the book 130–100 B.C. on the ground that the two forms οὐδείς and οὐθείς occur in it, a characteristic which he would assign to that period (*Gr. of O. T. Gk.*, p. 62). On the ground, however, that only the δ forms of οὐδείς occur in LXX Proverbs, he assigns that book to about 100 B.C., making it later than Wisdom. But it is difficult to believe that the author of Wisd. i–xi was not acquainted with LXX Proverbs. If he was not, we must delete iii. 11 and vi. 12 *c* as interpolations based on Prov. i. 7 and viii. 12 *b*. It is no doubt possible that these lines may be interpolations, but it is more difficult to get rid of πάρεδρον γὰρ εὑρήσει τῶν πυλῶν αὐτοῦ (vi. 14), which seems to be a reminiscence of Prov. i. 21 ἐπὶ δὲ πύλαις δυναστῶν παρεδρεύει, and viii. 2 παρὰ γὰρ πύλαις δυναστῶν παρεδρεύει. Possibly, too, ἀγρυπνέω in Wisd. vi. 15 is a reminiscence of the

[1] There is an earlier work by Thielmann, *Die lat. Übers. d. Buches der Weisheit* (Leipzig, 1872).

same word in Prov. viii. 34. Moreover, the general description of Wisdom in c. vi. 9–16 seems based on that in Prov. i and viii.

Further, if the LXX version of Proverbs was not in existence when Wisdom was written—and this would be the case if Mr. Thackeray's dates are accepted—we must assume that the author was able to consult Proverbs in the Hebrew, and yet that he resorted to the Greek for such an important book as Isaiah. It seems impossible to deny that in c. ii. 12 he accepted the erroneous LXX translation of Isa. iii. 10 (as the writer of the second part accepted that of Isa. xliv. 20). This would be a strange circumstance if he were able to read the original.

The evidence, therefore, is strongly in favour of assuming the dependence of Wisdom on LXX Proverbs. We may, however, with Mr. Thackeray accept a date for Proverbs subsequent to Sirach, i. e. subsequent to 130 B. C., and take the order as Sirach, Proverbs, Wisdom. This would strengthen the conjecture made above that the date of Wisdom is not earlier than the middle of the first century B. C.

The *terminus ad quem* depends on the undoubted use made of the book by St. Paul: this would require a date not later than the first few years of our era: it would take some little time for the book to acquire a reputation and get into circulation. Grimm points out (page 34) that the writer's apparent ignorance of the Alexandrine doctrine of the Logos points to a date earlier than Philo. More than that, as Philo did not expound his doctrine of the Logos as though it originated with him, the date of Wisdom must be earlier than the acceptance of this doctrine by the Jewish scholars of Alexandria. This argument is no doubt valid, but it only means that the book must be earlier than the student life of Philo, which may be placed from 5 B. C. to A. D. 5. To place the book on this account a hundred years earlier than Philo, as Gregg does, seems quite uncalled for. But ignorance of the Alexandrine Logos doctrine can only affect the date of the first part of the book; the second part may with Bousset (*Religion des Judenthums*, p. 35) be dated after the beginning of the Empire (say 30 B. C.), on account of xiv. 17, where the likeness of an *absent* ruler is mentioned.

The present writer inclines to a date between 50 and 30 B. C. for the first part of the book, and 30 B. C. to A. D. 10 for the second part, which was written in continuation of part 1.

§ 6. Composite Nature.

The unity of the book was early disputed. In the eighteenth century the French scholar Houbigant pronounced the work to be composite, and was followed by Eichhorn, Bretschneider, and others. Houbigant divided the book at the end of ch. ix; Eichhorn, whose position is here adopted, at xi 1; Bretschneider, at vi. 8 and xii, taking ch. xi as the work of a redactor. Gfrörer (1835) and Grimm (1860) upheld the unity of the book, the former speaking with scorn of Eichhorn, the latter with respect; and the deservedly great influence of Grimm caused subsequent scholars to accept his decision. In 1900 Siegfried called it 'the well-arranged product of a single author'.

In 1903, however, Lincke in *Samaria und seine Propheten* divided the book into two parts. He attributed cc. i–xii. 8 to a writer living in Samaria in the time of the Seleucidae. It was a polemic against the hierocracy at Jerusalem. Ch. xii. 9 to the end is Alexandrian.

In the same year Stevenson, in *Wisdom and the Jewish Apoc. Writings*, a little volume in the Temple Bible Series, offered another division of the book. He agrees very nearly with Eichhorn in making the first part end at xi. 4; but in the remainder of the book he sees three different compositions—viz. (1) cc. xiii–xv, the section on idolatry; (2) xi. 21–xii. 22, the section on the love and mercy of God; (3) the strictly historical part, xi. 5–20, xii. 23–27, xvi–xix.

In 1904 Weber, in Hilgenfeld's *Zeitschrift*, attempted another analysis. He also divided the book into four parts: cc. i–v, the book of eschatology; cc. vi–x, the Book of Wisdom proper; c. xi to the end, the book of the method of retribution; in this last part the chapters on idolatry (xiii–xv) are an insertion. Feldmann, in *Bib. Zeitsch.* 1909, pp. 140–150, criticized and rejected Weber's attempt, scarcely noticing Lincke's work.

Kohler in the *Jewish Encycl.* maintains the composite authorship, apparently following Eichhorn. Toy in the *Ency. Bib.* and *Ency. Brit.* thinks that the question admits of no certain answer.

The arguments for the unity of the book (some of which are given by Grimm) may be set forth as follows: (1) Use of certain unusual words and expressions throughout the book—e. g. the word μεταλλεύω is used in the same *erroneous* meaning in both parts, iv. 12 and xvi. 25; ἀπότομος, a word which occurs nowhere else in the Greek Bible, is found in v. 20, 22, vi. 5, xi. 10, xii. 9, xviii. 15; ἀνυπόκριτος in v. 18, xviii. 16, nowhere else in the Greek Bible; κίβδηλος, ii. 16, xv. 9, only twice besides in the Greek Bible; συγγνωστός, vi. 6, xiii. 8, nowhere else in the Greek Bible. The phrase ἐν ὄψει is found in iii. 4, vii. 9, viii. 11, xiv. 17, xv. 19, but nowhere else in the Greek Bible (but see below); θηρίων θυμοί, vii. 20, xvi. 5, and λογισμοὶ ἀσύνετοι, i. 5 and xi. 15, both seem to be unique phrases; παντοδύναμος, vii. 23, xi. 17, xviii. 15, γεώδης, ix. 15, xv. 13, διέπω, ix. 3, xii. 15, διερευνάω, vi. 3, xiii. 7, occur nowhere else in the Greek Bible; κακότεχνος, i. 4, xv. 4, only once besides, 4 Macc. vi. 14. (2) The same extensive vocabulary, the similar use of compound and poetical words, assonances, and the like. (3) The rhythmical structure (see Thackeray, *JTS*, vol. vi, p. 232) throughout the book. (4) The use of philosophic theories in both parts—e.g. in part 1 the Stoic doctrine of the world-soul, in part 2 the Stoic doctrine of the metabolism of the four elements. (5) Omission of proper names in both parts.[1] (6) The occurrence in both parts of the striking conception of the 'world fighting for the righteous', which is found in v. 17, 20, xvi. 17, 24, xviii. 24 (perhaps), and xix. 6. The most formidable argument is the first. Many scholars would feel that the use of μεταλλεύω alone decides the question.

The arguments for the composite nature of the book are:—

(1) The difference in style, presentation, and tone.

(2) The omission of all reference to Wisdom in xi. 2 to the end, except in one doubtful passage.

(3) The abandonment of the transcendental view of the Deity.

(4) The absence of any reference to the doctrine of immortality, except a passing reference in xv. 3.

(5) Abandonment of parallelism.

(6) The numerous and striking linguistic differences.

The first five points may be explained away; it may be said that the writer is a philosopher in the first part, a preacher in the second; the sixth point, however, is more troublesome.

The most striking linguistic difference is found in the very different proportions in which certain particles are used[2] in the two parts—e.g. μέν is used three times only in the first part, v. 13, vii. 1, 30, and twenty-seven times (according to Swete's text) in the second, xi. 6, 10, xiii. 1, 3, 16, 17, xiv. 2, 8, 19, xv. 9, 17, xvi. 3, 9, 14, 18, 21, xvii. 5, 15, xviii. 1, 3, 4, 7, 16, 17, xix. 5, 10, 14. δέ is also unequally distributed, with fifty-two occurrences in part 1, eighty-two in part 2. ἵνα occurs seven times in the first part, viz. ii. 19, vi. 9, 21, ix. 2, 10, x. 8, 12, and twenty-one times in part 2—e.g. xi. 16, xii. 2, 7, 8, 13, 22, xiii. 9, 16, xiv. 4, 17, xvi. 3, 11, 18, 19, 22, 23, 26, xviii. 6, 19, xix. 4, 6. ἀλλά occurs four times in the first part, vi. 22, viii. 16, x. 8, 13, and seventeen times in part 2, viz. xi. 19, 20, xii. 8, xiii. 2, 6, xiv. 22, 31, xv. 7, 9, 12, xvi. 7, 12, 18, 26, xviii. 20, 22, xix. 15, and in connexion with this μόνον is of course more frequent in the second part than in the first. γάρ occurs 52 times in the first part, as against 102 in the second; καὶ γάρ twice in the first part, twelve times in the second.

In addition to these considerable differences the following smaller differences in the use of particles exist:—

ἄνευ, xiv. 4, xix. 13.
εἶτα, xiv. 16, 22, xvii. 16.
ἐπεί, xviii. 12, xix. 15.
ἔτι, x. 7, xiii. 6, xiv. 24, xix. 3, 10.

ὅτε, ix. 9, xi. 9, 13, xvi. 5, xix. 11, 17.
ποτε, v. 3, xiv. 15, xvi. 18, 19, xviii. 20.
τότε, v. 1, xi. 8, xiv. 15, xvi. 25, xviii. 17, 20.
πῶς, v. 5, vi. 22, xi. 8, 9, 25, xiii. 9, xvi. 4, xix. 10.
πάλιν, x. 4, xiii. 8, xiv. 1, xvi. 23, xix. 6.
ἀνάπαλιν, xix. 21.

This gives seven of these particles in part 1 to thirty-six in part 2.

The distribution of some other words is worthy of notice. The following occur only in the first part:—

ἀρετή, iv. 1, v. 13, viii. 7.
παιδεία, i. 5, ii. 12, iii. 11, vi. 17, vii. 14.
τρίβοι, in a metaphorical sense, ii. 15, v. 7, vi. 16, ix. 18, x. 10 (in xiv. 3 the singular is used in a literal sense).
ἐνθυμέομαι, iii. 14, vi. 15, vii. 15, ix. 13.
ἔσχατος, ii. 16, iii. 17, iv. 19.
συνίημι, iii. 9, vi. 1, ix. 11.
σύνεσις, iv. 11, ix. 5.

σημεῖον, v. 11, 13, viii. 8, x. 16.
κινέω, v. 11.
κίνησις, ii. 2, vii. 24.
κινητικός, vii. 24.
εὐκίνητος is in both parts, vii. 22 applied to Wisdom, xiii. 11 applied to a tree, nowhere else in the Greek Bible.
παροδεύω, i. 8, ii. 7, v. 14, vi. 22, x. 8.

πολύς is evenly distributed, but the compounds (seven) are all in part 1: πολυτελής ii. 7,

[1] The singularity of this largely disappears when we notice that Philo often omits the names of historical characters: see *Vita Mosis*, Bk. i, c. 42 (Caleb and Joshua), 43 (Edom), 59 (Reuben and Gad); Bk. ii, c. 10 (Lot); Bk. iii, cc. 21 and 38 (Korah, Dathan, and Abiram).

[2] It must be stated that the proportion of matter in the two parts is $11\frac{1}{2}$ to 13, or 23 to 26: the second part may be taken as one-eighth longer than the first: but in considering the particles it should be noticed that there are in B 556 stichoi in part 1, to 568 in part 2.

πολύγονος iv. 3, πολυετής iv. 16, πολυμερής vii. 22, πολυπειρία viii. 8, πολύφροντις ix. 15, πολυχρόνιος ii. 10, iv. 8.

The following words occur in the second part only :—

ἁμαρτάνω, xi. 16, xii. 2, 11, xiv. 31, xv. 2, 13.
ἀρνέομαι, xii. 27, xvi. 16, xvii. 10.
δεῖ, *necesse est*, xii. 19, xv. 12, xvi. 4, 28.
ἐπιταγή, xiv. 16, xviii. 16, xix. 6.
ἰσχύω, xi. 21, xiii. 1, 9, xv. 16, xvi. 20, xix. 20.
μεγαλύνω, xix. 22, μεγάλως, xi. 21, xiv. 22, μεγαλωσύνη xviii. 24.
τρύχειν, xi. 11, xiv. 15.

The following differences occur in the two parts :—

ἐπισκοπή, ii. 20, iii. 7, 9, 13, iv. 15, all in a favourable sense ; xiv. 11, xix. 15, in an unfavourable sense (pointed out first by Weber).

κἂν γάρ, iv. 4, ix. 6 ; καὶ γὰρ ἐάν, xv. 2.

ἴδιος occurs eleven or twelve times: two of these occurrences being in part 1, the remaining nine or ten in part 2. This difference could hardly be connected with difference in subject-matter.

The word ὄψις occurs three times in the first part, eight times in the second. In the first part it is used in a metaphorical sense in the phrase ἐν ὄψει; in the second, seven times literally, the eighth being doubtful. This should be considered with the similar cases of ἐπισκοπή and τρίβος.

The distribution of βίος and ζωή is worth noticing. βίος occurs ten times in the first part and five times in the second, ζωή once in the first part and six times in the second. ἐξετάζω and ἐτάζω and its derivatives five times in the first part, once in the second; κολάζω is a favourite word in part 2, eleven times as against once in part 1. This last, no doubt, is due to difference of subject-matter. The same reason holds good for σοφία, which occurs twenty-eight times in part 1 and twice in part 2.

The use of compound words is considerable in both parts, but there are differences to be observed. Of compounds of ἐπί there are nineteen in part 1 as against forty in part 2 ; compounds of πρό have nine instances in part 1 as against twenty-two in part 2 ; πρός seven in part 1 as against twenty in part 2; and ὑπό five in part 1 as against twenty-five in part 2. Compounds of κατά are twenty-one in part 1 to thirty-four in part 2, of μετά seven in part 1 to twelve in part 2. This gives sixty-eight of these compounds in part 1 to 153 in part 2. If the cumulative argument is worth anything, it should certainly be considered in deciding what weight should be assigned to these linguistic differences.

The difference in style, presentation, and tone between the two parts is undeniable. In style, as Eichhorn says, 'the first part is appropriate and concise, the second inappropriate, diffuse, exaggerated, and bombastic' (p. 145); though a few passages in part 2 may escape this censure.

With the exception of iv. 15–17, where the text is in disorder, there are no specially difficult or doubtful passages in the first part, while there are serious difficulties in xii. 5, 24, xv. 17 *c*, 18 *b*, 19 *a*, xvii. 6, 13, and xviii. 1, 2. It is also worth noting that the difference in style between the two parts led Siegfried, who accepts the unity of the book, to print his translation from xii. 19 to the end in prose. The presentation in the first part is varied: we have the author's own words, the speech of the apostates, Solomon's address and his prayer ; part 2 is one continuous apostrophe to the Deity. In tone the second part is pervaded by a narrow and bitter Jewish spirit, which is markedly absent from part 1.

In answer to this latter point, it may be said that part 1 deals with Jews only; that there was no opportunity of displaying narrow national feeling towards the Gentiles. It must then be asked what, on the supposition of its unity, was the object of the second part of the book? how does it fit in with the object of the first part? The first part is a polemic against the apostate Jews of Alexandria, and an appeal to them, by the example of the wise king, to return to the worship of Jehovah. But this object could hardly be helped forward by the contents of part 2. The teaching that by what things a man sins, by these he is punished, appears to be pointless with regard to the sins of the apostates. It is very far-fetched on the part of Bois to find this teaching in iii. 10. Again, these apostates who had adopted Greek or Epicurean views of life were in no danger of falling into idolatry ; they could scoff at the worshippers of a 'rotten piece of wood' as well as the author. The only way in which the appeal to history could be thought to influence them would be by pointing out that in plaguing the Egyptians and delivering Israel, Jehovah had shown Himself to be the true God, and that the Egyptians themselves had confessed Him to be so; but in view of the sceptical and scoffing attitude of the apostates towards the miraculous, as recorded by Philo (see end of note on i. 1), such an appeal could have no effect. It might uphold the courage of the faithful ; it could have no effect on unbelievers except to make them scoff the more.

The difference in the view of the action of the Deity adopted in the two parts (pointed out in the note on xi. 2) is seen most plainly in two parallel passages, where the very functions assigned to Wisdom in part 1 are assigned directly to God in part 2. In vii. 22 Wisdom is πάντων τεχνῖτις, in viii. 6 τῶν ὄντων . . . τεχνῖτις, while in xiii. 1 God Himself is called τεχνίτης. In viii. 1 it is said of Wisdom διοικεῖ τὰ πάντα, in xv. 1 God is addressed directly as διοικῶν τὰ πάντα. Moreover, when Heinisch (p. 47) affirms the God of the Book of Wisdom to be the living personal and almighty God of Israel, the passages he quotes in support of this position are drawn entirely from the second part of the book. He adduces xii. 18, xi. 17, 23, xvi. 13, 15, xi. 22, xiii. 1–7. This testimony is all the more valuable as it is given quite unwittingly. It shows plainly what part of the book a writer must resort to in order to find the action of the Deity portrayed in Jewish fashion.

In truth there are considerable difficulties in the way of accepting the unity of authorship which have not been met by its upholders. If we could assume that the writer of the second part had studied the first part carefully and wished to write a supplement to it, both resemblances and differences could be accounted for.

The proofs adduced by Thackeray (*JTS*, vi, pp. 232 ff.) and approved by Blass seem to show that the writer of the second part endeavoured to keep up the poetical form of the first: for this reason, although the second part is very prosaic, it has been thought well to keep the verse form of the Revised Version throughout.

§ 7. Authorship and Language.

The author of the book is generally assumed to be an Alexandrian Jew. But the opinion of scholars is not unanimous on the point. Bretschneider considered the first section, i–vi. 8, to have been written by a Palestinian Jew. Grimm in 1833 wrote a thesis entitled 'de Sap. libri indole Alexandrina perperam asserta', but he withdrew from this position in his great commentary of 1860, where the Alexandrian origin of the book is maintained. Grimm's later position was unanimously accepted till the appearance of Prof. Margoliouth's article in *JRAS*, 1890, entitled 'Was the Book of Wisdom written in Hebrew?'[1] He there maintains that 'the writer shows no acquaintance with Egypt beyond what he might have got from the Bible, and that he shows a familiarity with the interpretation of the Midrash which points to the Palestinian School'. This last clause can refer to the second part only, cc. xi–xix.

In 1903 Lincke, while accepting Greek as the original language, maintained that cc. i–xii were written in Palestine, and Bousset in *Die Religion des Judenthums* (1906), p. 212, writes, 'The early chapters of the Wisdom of Solomon are probably of Palestinian origin.' (He thus admits the composite authorship; see also p. 501, where he speaks of the second and third parts of the book.)

It seems difficult to accept the proposition that the book was written in Hebrew in face of the numerous instances where dependence on LXX seems undeniable, e. g.:—

ii. 12 ἐνεδρεύσωμεν δὲ τὸν δίκαιον, ὅτι δύσχρηστος ἡμῖν ἐστιν. Isa. iii. 10 δήσωμεν τὸν δίκαιον ὅτι δύσχρηστος ἡμῖν ἐστι. These passages have only to be put side by side to show the dependence of one upon the other (the fact that the passage from Isaiah is corrupt in the present Hebrew text, which should doubtless read אשרי צדיק כי טוב, does not enter into consideration here; though it shows how the LXX got δήσωμεν).

xi. 4 καὶ ἐδόθη αὐτοῖς ἐκ πέτρας ἀκροτόμου ὕδωρ. Deut. viii. 15 τοῦ ἐξαγαγόντος σοι ἐκ πέτρας ἀκροτόμου πηγὴν ὕδατος. Here the fact that ἀκρότομος, 'steep', is an incorrect translation of חלמיש, 'flint', makes for an undoubted connexion between the two passages.

xi. 22 ὅτι ὡς ῥοπὴ ἐκ πλαστίγγων ὅλος ὁ κόσμος ἐναντίον σου. Isa. xl. 15 πάντα τὰ ἔθνη . . . ὡς ῥοπὴ ζυγοῦ ἐλογίσθησαν. The thought is identical, and the writer could not have got it from the Hebrew, which has 'dust שחק of the balance'.

xv. 7 and Isa. xliv. 20 both refer to the idolater. The Hebrew has 'he feedeth on ashes, a heart deceived hath misled him'. The LXX divided the words in the Hebrew text wrongly and translated σποδὸς ἡ καρδία αὐτῶν. The writer of Wisdom followed this and wrote σποδὸς ἡ καρδία αὐτοῦ.

xvi. 22 πῦρ φλεγόμενον ἐν τῇ χαλάζῃ. Exod. ix. 24 τὸ πῦρ φλογίζον ἐν τῇ χαλάζῃ. The LXX translator was perhaps puzzled at the meaning to be assigned to the Hebrew word מתהלך, 'darting hither and thither'; at any rate he did not translate it literally, but put another word which would make sense: the writer of Wisdom borrowed directly from the LXX.

These examples seem to make it plain that Pseudo-Sol. did not use the Hebrew Bible and that he drew his quotations directly from the LXX.

The following resemblances also show the writer's acquaintance with LXX:

iii. 11 σοφίαν γὰρ καὶ παιδείαν ὁ ἐξουθενῶν ταλαίπωρος. Prov. i. 7 σοφίαν δὲ καὶ παιδείαν ἀσεβεῖς ἐξουθενήσουσιν.

[1] Prof. Margoliouth's thesis was contested by Freudenthal in an article entitled 'What is the Original Language of the Wisdom of Solomon?' *JQR*, iii. 722–53.

vi. 12 (if genuine) *καὶ εὑρίσκεται ὑπὸ τῶν ζητούντων αὐτήν.* Prov. viii. 17 *οἱ δὲ ἐμὲ ζητοῦντες εὑρήσουσιν.*
vi. 14 *πάρεδρον γὰρ εὑρήσει τῶν πυλῶν αὐτοῦ.* Prov. i. 21 *ἐπὶ δὲ πύλαις δυναστῶν παρεδρεύει.*
Compare also v. 17 with Isa. lix. 17, quoted below, p. 527. See also notes on vi. 7, xii. 26, and xiv. 8.

Again, throughout the book, compound words abound—a mark of Alexandrian Greek. Swete, *Introd. to O.T. in Greek*, p. 311, gives over fifty from the first six chapters.

Further, the knowledge of Greek philosophy displayed in the book speaks for its Alexandrine origin; though this is not absolutely decisive, as Proverbs and Ecclesiastes are supposed by some scholars to show traces of Greek philosophical influence. Moreover, the doctrine of immortality in all probability, and the doctrine of the transcendence of God certainly, are Alexandrian, not Palestinian. Finally, it seems likely that iii. 9 *c* is borrowed from the Greek translation of Enoch. As we cannot imagine a Palestinian writer borrowing from the Greek translation of a book originally written in Hebrew, the borrowing must have taken place outside Palestine, and the only possible alternative seems to be Alexandria.

But wherever the book originated the writer is unknown. In part I he plainly speaks in the name of Solomon, though the name itself is not mentioned, any more than it is in Ecclesiastes (where, accordng to McNeile, i. 1 is no part of the original text). The speaker is said to be of royal birth (vii. 5); he prays for wisdom (viii. 21), and says 'thou hast chosen me to be a king' (ix. 7). This is, of course, a literary device and would deceive no one. But it made the book anonymous, and anonymous it still remains.

The earliest record of any conjecture as to its authorship is given by Jerome, who says that some of the ancient writers affirm the author to be Philo. This may also have been the opinion of the writer of the document known as the Muratorian Canon. An interesting suggestion was made by Tregelles that in the Muratorian Canon, p. 11 *a*, lines 7 and 8, where the Latin has 'Sapientia ab amicis Salomonis in honorem ipsius scripta', there may have originally stood *ὑπὸ φίλωνος* instead of *ὑπὸ φίλων*. But though Jerome's testimony is interesting as showing that at an early period many saw the impossibility of ascribing the book to Solomon as Origen also did (*Contra Cels.* v. 29), the authorship of Philo does not recommend itself to modern scholars. The Philonian doctrine of the Logos, the pronounced dualism which said *σῶμα* = *σῆμα*, and almost certainly the doctrine of ideas, are all absent from Wisdom; while the personality of the devil is accepted as a fact in Wisdom, whereas in Philo it is allegorized into pleasure.

The suggestion that Apollos was the author (Noach, Plumptre) is generally rejected.

Like many other books in the Canon, both Hebrew and Greek, its authorship must remain unknown.

§ 8. Relationship to other Books in the Old and New Testaments.

The relationship of the Book of Wisdom to Ecclesiastes is generally admitted. The first section of Wisdom might be said to be a polemic against the words of Eccles. vii. 15, 'There is a righteous man that perisheth in his righteousness, and there is a wicked man that prolongeth his life in his evil doing.' That one book could be written in answer to another (both now sacred) is seen from Ecclesiastes itself, which was doubtless written in antagonism to the view propounded by Ezekiel and his followers that righteousness and unrighteousness were both rewarded in this life, a view which the author of Job also contests. Ruth, also, was probably written as a protest against the endeavours of Ezra and Nehemiah to enforce the Deuteronomic law (xxiii. 3) against mixed marriages. The first part of Wisdom, therefore, may have been written to oppose the despairing philosophy of Ecclesiastes and the opinions and practices of the apostates, who may have quoted it to support their views. The most striking passages, a full list of which is given in Grimm, p. 30, and McNeile, p. 38, are the following:—

Wisd. ii. 1, 'Short and sorrowful is our life.' Eccles. ii. 23, 'All his days are but sorrow, and his labour is grief.'

Wisd. ii. 2, 'By mere chance (*αὐτοσχεδίως*) were we born.' Eccles. iii. 19, 'The sons of men are a chance' (R.V. margin).

Wisd. ii. 4, 'Our name shall be forgotten and no one shall remember our works.' Eccles. i. 11, 'There is no remembrance of the former generations.' Eccles. ii. 16, 'For of a wise man, as of a fool, there is no remembrance for ever.' Eccles. ix. 5, 'The memory of them (i. e. the dead) is forgotten.'

Wisd. ii. 6–10 and Eccles. ix. 7–9 show a great similarity, the difference being only in tone. The tone of the apostates' words in Wisdom is defiant, that of Ecclesiastes is sad: 'Go eat thy bread in gladness, and drink thy wine with a cheerful heart. . . . At all times let thy garments be white, and let not oil on thy head be lacking. Enjoy life with the wife whom thou lovest all the days of thy transient life, which he hath given thee under the sun; for that is thy portion in life. . . . There is no work nor device nor knowledge nor wisdom in Sheol, whither thou goest.'

(The phrase 'this is our portion', Wisd. ii. 9*c*, is probably an echo of the words 'this is his or thy portion', which recur in Eccles. iii. 22, v. 18, ix. 9.)

Hitzig in his edition of Ecclesiastes (1847) refused to admit any connexion between the two books. According to Grimm, Hitzig did not give any reasons for his assertion. Mr. Gregg, in *CBS*, also rejects the idea of any connexion, and gives reasons, but they do not seem convincing. It is true that Epicureanism and Sadduceeism did not require Ecclesiastes to appeal to. The Sadducees in 1 Enoch cii. 6 say, 'As we die so die the righteous, and what benefit do they reap for their deeds? Behold, even as we, so do they die in grief and darkness, and what have they more than we? from henceforth we are equal.' These are the very same sentiments as those found in the speech of the apostates in Wisdom ii. Sadduceeism was a disease of the time, and the author of the first part of Wisdom combated it. That he would have opposed it had Ecclesiastes never been written is quite likely, but for all that the form of Wisdom ii. 6–10 probably owes something to Ecclesiastes ix. 7–9.

The influence of the Book of Wisdom upon the New Testament has been differently estimated. Eichhorn (p. 202) first pointed out resemblances in Romans and Ephesians, but Grimm declined to admit any direct connexion even in the case of Wisd. xv. 7 and Rom. ix. 21. Other scholars, however, maintain a direct connexion not only with St. Paul but with the Gospel of St. John, the Epistle of St. James, Hebrews, and the Apocalypse.

In his commentary Grimm gives, on p. 36, a large number of passages where connexion between Wisdom and the New Testament was affirmed by Nachtigal, Stier, and others; but all earlier investigations with regard to St. Paul's use of the book have been superseded by that of Grafe, *Das Verhältniss der Paulinischen Schriften zur Sapientia Salomonis*, Theol. Abhandl. in honour of Weizäcker, 1892, pp. 253–86.

Seeing that St. Paul nowhere quotes Wisdom by name, it is almost impossible to adduce a proof of connexion which will satisfy everybody; a parallel in expression or thought may be only a coincidence or go back to a common source. Take, for instance, passages that would occur to any one who knows both books, Rom. i. 20 and Wisd. xiii. 1, where the possibility of knowing God through His works is affirmed: here both writers might be independently using a well-known argument of the Stoics. The argument of course is cumulative: one or two resemblances would be of no value for proving connexion: but when in two short books like Wisdom and Romans a large number of parallelisms are found (Sanday and Headlam, p. 51, quote ten verses from the first chapter of Romans which have points of resemblance to Wisdom) it seems perverse to deny connexion. The most striking parallelism between Wisdom and Romans is found in the passages where St. Paul expounds his doctrine of predestination.

In Wisd. xii. 12 ff. and Rom. ix. 21–3 Grafe (p. 265) traces three thoughts:—

(1) The idea of the infinite power of God, which admittedly by itself proves nothing. Wisd. xii. 12; Rom. ix. 19–23.

(2) In the same context, however, both writers dwell upon the fact of God being longsuffering towards His enemies although He knows it will be unavailing. Wisd. xii. 8–10, 11*a*, 20*a*; Rom. ix. 22.

(3) In the same context also is found a contrast between the enemies and the sons of God in relation to their respective destinies. Wisd. xii. 20–2; Rom. ix. 22, 23.

The point to be noticed is that these three ideas occur in close connexion both in Wisdom and Romans.

In addition to the parallelism of thought there are also resemblances in language.

Wisd. xii. 12.	Rom. ix. 19, 20.
τίς γὰρ **ἐρεῖ** *τί* **ἐποίησας**; **ἢ τίς ἀντιστήσεται τῷ κρίματί σου**;	*μὴ* **ἐρεῖ** *τὸ πλάσμα τῷ πλάσαντι· τί με* **ἐποίησας** *οὕτως* . . . **τῷ γὰρ βουλήματι αὐτοῦ τίς ἀνθέστηκεν**;

Again, there is the parallel between Wisd. xv. 7 and Rom. ix. 21.

Here St. Paul uses in O.T. fashion the image of the potter and the clay as an illustration of God's dealings with man, but in addition to this he introduces the thought which is not found in the O.T. of the potter making out of the same clay some vessels for noble and others for ignoble purposes. The latter point is found only in Romans and Wisdom. But even here Grimm will not admit direct connexion. He thinks that both writers may have independently hit upon the same illustration. Here Grimm seems to be quite alone; all other expositors recognize the connexion.

Grafe was the first to point out in full the connexion between St. Paul's views on idolatry and those expressed in Wisdom, especially in regard to the lighter judgement passed on the more refined form of idolatry found in the worshippers of natural phenomena.

Taking *στοιχεῖα*[1] in Gal. iv. 3 as referring to the heavenly bodies, Grafe points out the lenient judgement passed by St. Paul here, and compares the lenient judgement on the same kind of worship in Wisd. xiii. 6. Against the grosser forms of idolatry St. Paul is scathingly severe, and the same attitude is found in Wisdom.

Again, after discussing the nature and folly of idol worship, both the writer of Wisdom and St. Paul dwell upon the immorality which they affirm to be the direct result of idolatry. Both give a long catalogue of vices, St. Paul 24, Wisdom 14, which naturally tally in several points.

Another similarity worth noticing is that between the striking and original thought in xi. 23 *b* that God's longsuffering is meant to lead sinners to repentance, and Rom. ii. 4 'not knowing that the goodness of God leadeth thee to repentance.'

An interesting comparison between Wisd. ix. 15 and 2 Cor. v. 1 ff. is pointed out by E. Pfleiderer (p. 317 note). He there shows the similarity both of thought and language. With reference to this, Otto Pfleiderer remarks (*Prim. Christianity*, vol. i. p. 454): 'It is true that 2 Cor. v. 1–5 has such close affinities with Wisd. ix. 15 that the conjecture is legitimate that this passage may have hovered before his (St. Paul's) mind and perhaps even suggested the choice of his words. But this close affinity by no means proves a direct borrowing of the Pauline doctrine from the Book of Wisdom.'

The connexion of Wisd. v. 17 ff. with Eph. vi. 11ff. is denied by Grimm on the ground that Isa. lix. 17 is the source of both. The passages are as follows:

Isa. lix. 17.	Wisd. v. 17 ff.	Eph. vi. 11.
καὶ ἐνεδύσατο δικαιοσύνην ὡς θώρακα, καὶ περιέθετο περικεφαλαίαν σωτηρίου ἐπὶ τῆς κεφαλῆς.	*λήψεται πανοπλίαν τὸν ζῆλον αὐτοῦ . . . ἐνδύσεται θώρακα δικαιοσύνην καὶ περιθήσεται κόρυθα κρίσιν ἀνυπόκριτον· λήψεται ἀσπίδα . . . ὀξυνεῖ δὲ ἀπότομον ὀργὴν εἰς ῥομφαίαν.*	*ἐνδύσασθε τὴν πανοπλίαν τοῦ θεοῦ . . . ἐνδυσάμενοι τὸν θώρακα δικαιοσύνης . . . ἀναλαβόντες τὸν θυρεὸν τῆς πίστεως . . . καὶ τὴν περικεφαλαίαν τοῦ σωτηρίου δέξασθε καὶ τὴν μάχαιραν.*

The decisive point for those who accept direct connexion is the fact that *πανοπλία* occurs in both Wisdom and St. Paul, but not in Isaiah: also 'shield' and 'sword' are in Wisdom and St. Paul, but not in Isaiah. On the other hand, *περικεφαλαίαν σωτηρίου* in Isaiah corresponds to *περικεφαλαίαν τοῦ σωτηρίου* in St. Paul.

The fact that St. Paul knew and used the Book of Wisdom makes it far easier to admit its influence on other parts of the New Testament. The parallels to St. John and St. James adduced by other scholars and rejected by Grimm have now more to be said for them. Mr. Gregg quotes a large number of parallels to St. John, the most interesting being 'This is life eternal, that they should know thee' (St. John xvii. 3) and Wisd. xv. 3. Prof. J. B. Mayor in his commentary on St. James, p. lxxv, gives twelve passages from Wisdom, echoes of which may be found in the epistle.

§ 9. Theology and Philosophy of the Book.

The theology of the Book of Wisdom is Alexandrine, a combination of Jewish religion with Greek philosophy.

The first part, cc. i–xi. 1, is more Greek than Jewish, and in nothing is this shown more clearly than in the idea of God presented by the two parts respectively. The idea of God in part 1 is that of Greek philosophy—a transcendent God who has no immediate contact with the world. It is true that in the later parts of the O. T. the writers had largely abandoned the conception of Jahveh as a God who had direct dealings with mankind. The theophanies which took place under the guise of the 'Angel of Jahveh' disappear, and in Daniel, for instance, the angel Gabriel gives to the seer the revelation which would have been given in earlier times by the 'Angel of Jahveh', i.e. by Jahveh Himself. God gradually became thought of as more and more remote, though even in Daniel the scene where the Ancient of Days sits in judgement on the nations shows that God could still be thought of as having immediate dealings with mankind. In Wisdom, however, in cc. i–x, we find that the author conceives God to be so remote, that He performs His will by means of an intermediary, whom He sends forth into the world (ix. 10). This intermediary is Wisdom, and possesses all the attributes of Deity. She is omnipotent (vii. 27), omniscient (viii. 8 and ix. 11), and puts these attributes into action: she administers all things well (viii. 1). At the Creation Wisdom stood by God and chose His works; the subsequent administration of the world was committed to her, since her relationship to God at the Creation ensured to her complete knowledge

[1] That R. V. here, following Lightfoot, must be given up, see the article 'Elements' in *Hastings' DB.*

of His commands (ix. 9). If God knows all things, it is because Wisdom takes her report to Him (i. 9–10). If for a moment it is said that God gave Solomon knowledge of things that are (vii. 17), it is immediately corrected by the statement, 'For she that is the artificer of all things taught me, even Wisdom' (vii. 21). In ix. 1 the direct action of God is not spoken of *simpliciter*; it is softened by the expressions 'word' and 'wisdom'—'who madest all things by thy word, and by thy wisdom formedst man.'

It must be admitted that the passages in which the writer speaks of the author of Creation are not at first sight consistent. We seem to have three views: (1) God as Creator, i. 14, vi. 7, ix. 1, ix. 9; (2) God as Creator while Wisdom is present and exercises the prerogative of choice, viii. 4, ix. 9; (3) Wisdom as creator, vii. 22, viii. 5 and 6, and by implication in vii. 23 (all-powerful), and vii. 27 (hath power to do all things). The only possible way of reconciling these utterances is to take (3) as representing the philosophic view of the writer, while in (1) God is spoken of as Creator on the principle that 'qui facit per alium facit per se'. No. 2 may represent the means by which the writer endeavoured to reconcile the biblical with his philosophic view of Creation. That the view expressed in vii. 22 and viii. 5 and 6 was deliberately adopted by the writer may be inferred by comparing vii. 22 with vii. 19, where he corrects an expression which might have been taken as attributing unmediated action to God. Yet it would appear that the writer felt unwilling to deny that man can have direct access to God. Solomon's prayer in c. ix presupposes that God hears man directly, and the belief in God as real, and not as a philosophical abstraction—to say nothing of the influence of the psalmists—caused the author, as it did Origen, to believe in direct access to God in prayer. This, it may be said, is inconsistent with a strictly philosophical belief in the abstract transcendence of God as ἐπέκεινα νοῦ καὶ οὐσίας, but it is an inconsistency our author shares in good company. On the other hand, the doctrine of the transcendence of God entirely disappears in part 2, where He is repeatedly spoken of as acting directly on the world (see note on xi. 2).

It is generally agreed that 'Wisdom' is not a 'person', i.e. a being capable of exercising understanding and will—a self-determining intelligence. What, then, is it? Is it an attribute of God personified? Personification is difficult to us: it is a device of the poet; but to the Oriental mind it came easily enough. The O. T. contains numerous instances of the personification of the nation: Rachel is pictured as weeping for her children: 'Ephraim hath grey hairs upon him, and he knoweth it not,' says Hosea; the nation is personified as the suffering servant in 2 Isaiah. The personification of an attribute or power would naturally come later. We perhaps see the first beginnings of it in 2 Isaiah (see the commentators on lxiii. 10) with respect to the Spirit of God. The belief in subordinate heavenly powers present at Creation (Gen. i. 26, Job xxxviii. 7) would help to give Wisdom its position in Prov. viii and Sir. xxiv; though probably without Greek influence Wisdom would never have been personified as it is there (Siegfried, *Hastings' DB*, iv, p. 925). In answering the question whether our author regarded Wisdom as personal or impersonal, we must remember that to the ancients, to whom even the stars were persons, the modern idea of personality was quite foreign, and that the same question with regard to the Logos of Philo cannot be satisfactorily answered (Caird, vol. ii, *Evol. of Theol.*, p. 200). But Philo did answer a somewhat similar question—was the Logos created or uncreated? 'The Logos, he declares, is neither uncreated like God nor created like us; but he is at equal distance between the extremes' (Caird, p. 202). 'The Logos is not unbegotten as God.' 'On the other hand it is not begotten as man' (Drummond, *Philo*, ii. 192). We shall perhaps not be far wrong if we attribute the same idea to our author with regard to the personality of Wisdom.

God created the world by means of Wisdom, and as Wisdom is φιλάνθρωπος, i. 6, vii. 23, the motive of Creation, though not explicitly stated, can be assumed to be God's love to man. This is expressed in both parts of the book, but with far greater emphasis on His love in part 2. 'It is he that made both small and great, and alike he taketh thought (προνοεῖ) for all' (vi. 7). 'But thou sparest all things, O Sovereign Lord, thou lover of souls' (xi. 26). But though there is more stress placed on love in the second part, in part 1 God assigns to man a higher destiny. In ii. 23 it is said, 'He made him an image of his own being,' while in xv. 11 He simply bestows on man the gift of life: accordingly, in part 1, a higher standard is demanded from man if he is to be worthy of His love: 'For nothing doth God love save him that dwelleth with Wisdom,' vii. 28; while in part 2 no such high demand is made; mere existence ensures God's love: 'For thou lovest all things that are, and abhorrest none of the things that thou didst make,' xi. 24. The Creator made man in His love, bestowed upon him the gift of likeness to Himself. From this being He looks for conduct worthy of his privileges, and therefore demands wisdom and righteousness (i. 6–8). In accordance with this demand Justice punishes those that sin (i. 8), while the righteous are rewarded with the 'wages of holiness' and the 'prize for blameless souls' (ii. 22). The reward is life, the punishment is death. But it is spiritual life, not so much upon earth—though the writer recognizes that as is seen from the blessings of Wisdom recounted in cc. vi and vii—as in the future; a blessed immortality with God entered upon immediately after death.

It is doubtful, however, whether the writer had realized that this belief involved the abandonment of the traditional Jewish eschatology. It certainly seems as though he could not give up the old Jewish idea of a visible triumph of the righteous over their enemies. The day of judgement also is mentioned more than once (iii. 18, iv. 20), and this is inconsistent with the belief that the soul immediately after death receives its full reward, happiness or misery, life or death. Again, ch. iii. 7 ff. clearly reflects ideas of a distinctly Jewish type. The righteous shall 'run to and fro like sparks amongst the stubble'. Here we seem to have an echo of the judgement by the sword inaugurating the Messianic Kingdom: then it is said, 'they shall judge nations and have dominion over peoples,' indicating a belief in a Messianic Kingdom which would naturally succeed the judgement. In v. 17, however, the conception is somewhat different. There it is Jehovah Himself who is to overthrow the ungodly by means of the forces of nature, while the spirits of the righteous are safe in His keeping. Probably iv. 18 *b* ff. is also equivalent to this.

With regard then to the future destiny of the righteous we must ask, what did the writer contemplate for them? The alternatives are (1) an everlasting Messianic Kingdom on earth, (2) a temporary Messianic Kingdom with heaven afterwards, or (3) immortality immediately after death—a purely Greek idea. If the first alternative is taken, he must have considered that the righteous were to descend from heaven at the day of judgement or decision and take up their position as rulers in an everlasting Messianic Kingdom. The mournful retrospect of the ungodly is said to take place when their sins are reckoned up, that is, on the day of decision. After this day of decision there will come for the righteous the time of their triumph, which is described in iii. 7. Against this arrangement of events Grimm affirms that in no known Jewish system of eschatology does this descent of spirits with (it is to be presumed) heavenly bodies take place: though Charles's translation of 1 Enoch cviii. 12 should be considered, 'And I will bring clad in shining light those who have loved my holy name, and I will seat each on the throne of his honour.' And it may be urged that a writer who could in these chapters propound four novel beliefs might have entertained a fifth.

The second alternative of a temporary Messianic Kingdom is found in 1 Enoch xci–civ, a book that has many points of contact with Wisd. i–x. There we find the wicked oppressing the righteous, encouragement given to the suffering righteous by the promise of reward in the next world: after their death their souls are guarded by angels: a temporary Messianic Kingdom comes into existence at the appointed time: at the close of this Messianic Kingdom the last judgement takes place, and all the righteous, including those whose souls had been kept in safety, enjoy everlasting life in heaven (see Charles's 1 *Enoch*², pp. 219–23). Wisd. iii. 7 deviates from this scheme, it is true, but v. 17 does not, nor perhaps iv. 18 *b* ff. Enoch makes it plain that the punishment of the unrighteous in the Messianic Kingdom is not effected by means of the righteous who have died; their souls are still in the keeping of angels; while in Wisd. iii. 7 it is the very same righteous who have suffered who are to 'run to and fro like sparks in the stubble', i. e. to consume their enemies. But in v. 17 Jehovah Himself overthrows the ungodly, the righteous being covered by His Hand. Thus iii. 7 fits in with the first alternative, v. 17 with the second.

The comparison of these different schemes of eschatology with Wisdom forces one to the belief that the writer simply added the idea of the immortality of the soul immediately after death to one or other of the current forms of Jewish eschatology, and did not, or rather could not, make them consistent. It is perhaps doubtful whether he felt the difficulty. Indeed, a much greater Alexandrian, Philo, found it impossible to have a consistent eschatology. He accepted the idea of a Messianic Kingdom though it was entirely 'foreign to his system' (Charles, *Eschatology*, p. 260): and with regard to a greater than either—St. Paul—we are told that it is impossible to get a systematic scheme of eschatology out of his writings (Stevens, *Theol. of New Test.*, p. 482).[1]

Lastly, it is no doubt just possible that the writer adopted a purely Greek view of immortality: that iii. 7 ff., iv. 18 *b* ff., and v. 17 ff. are survivals of a former method of thinking which he had discarded, traces of which, however, remain in his language: but the expressions used seem to be too forcible for this explanation to hold good.

But the belief in the future blessedness of the righteous cannot do away with the perplexing fact that at present they suffer, and suffer undeservedly. Death, and even premature death, seems to be their portion. How is this to be explained? This brings us to the discussion of the problem of undeserved suffering and the solution offered by the writer.

In the greater part of the Old Testament the problem of undeserved suffering does not appear.

[1] The reason in the last case is obviously that St. Paul's eschatological views advanced with his own spiritual experience and development.—General Editor.

Affliction is punishment, and the punishment is retributive. In Amos there is a hint given that punishment may be disciplinary and remedial. The Israelites have been punished, 'Yet ye have not returned unto me.' In one solitary place in Prov. iii. 12, 'Whom the Lord loveth he reproveth,' and in Job v. 17, 'Happy is the man whom God reproveth,' this idea recurs; in the Elihu speeches also (Job xxxv. 15 and xxxvi. 8) suffering is regarded as disciplinary and remedial; but the problem of undeserved suffering which gave rise to the book is apparently abandoned as insoluble. How great the perplexity continued to be is seen from the desperate argument in 2 Macc. vi. 12–17. There the writer says that the afflictions which came upon the Jews 'were not for the destruction but for the chastening of our race', and are 'a sign of great beneficence', while the reason of the heathen escaping such afflictions is that they may be punished 'when they have attained unto the full measure of their sins'.

In the first part of Wisdom a solution of the problem is offered in the theory that suffering is meant to test the righteous and prove them worthy of immortality and communion with God. 'As gold in the furnace, he proved them' (iii. 6). This corresponds to the conception in 1 Enoch cviii. 9: 'The righteous were much tried by the Lord and their spirits were found pure.' This world is not all: there is recompense and reward in the future. This belief may be said to be consoling, though it cannot be taken as a complete solution of the difficulty, which is perhaps to be found in the deeper thought suggested in Isa. liii. But even if the solution attempted is not quite satisfactory, the problem of the undeserved suffering of the righteous is fairly faced and an endeavour made to answer it. They will eventually be rewarded with life, while the wicked are punished with death.

The meaning of the word 'death', as used in part 1, is not at first sight apparent. Does it mean physical death only, or physical death in the first place and spiritual death afterwards? Or does the author always use it to denote spiritual death? He says 'God made not death; . . . for he created all things that they might have being: and all the created things of the world are serviceable to life, and there is no poison of destruction in them' (i. 13 ff.). From this it follows that our author, in accordance with ideas found in other writers (1 Enoch lxix. 11), probably held that death did not belong to the original purpose of Creation and that man would have been immortal if Adam had not sinned. This conclusion seems to follow also from ii. 23, 'God created man for incorruption, and made him an image of his own being,' i.e. immortal. 'By the envy of the devil death entered into the world, and those who belong to him experience it.' But what of those who do not belong to him? Do not they experience death? No, says our author; they only seem to die (iii. 2). The fact of physical death is passed over and attention directed solely to spiritual death. Other writers—St. Paul, for instance,—did not pass over physical death in this way; they accounted for it by saying that physical death came upon all men, good and bad, on account of Adam's transgression. We may suppose that our author would have accepted this theory: it is quite consistent with his views, and was a common belief of the time.

Physical death, however, is practically disregarded by our author: he fixes his attention upon spiritual death, and this can take place even on earth. The wicked are made to say, 'as soon as we were born we ceased to be' (v. 13). According to this statement spiritual death does not mean annihilation; the wicked are spiritually dead even on earth; and in the next world this miserable condition continues, with the additional fact that they are now conscious of their condition. That they are likened to a city razed to the ground, the very name of which is forgotten, does not mean that they are to be annihilated. They are still to be 'in anguish' (iv. 19 *c*). We can compare this with 1 Enoch cviii. 3, where we read 'their names shall be blotted out of the book of life . . . and their seed shall be destroyed for ever, and their spirits shall be slain, and they shall cry and make lamentation in a place that is a chaotic wilderness'. This seems to give exactly the view of the author of Wisdom. The opinion of Bois, therefore, reviving that of Bretschneider, that the writer believed the wicked suffered for a time and were then annihilated, must be rejected. An existence which was nothing but pain and misery could rightly be called 'death.'

The doctrine of retribution in part 1 is Life for the righteous, Death for the unrighteous, with the additional threat that the latter may be punished in this world and in their children. Suffering in the case of the righteous tests their goodness, while in the case of the unrighteous it is purely retributive.

In part 2 a different attitude is adopted. Undeserved suffering appears not to be thought of. Punishment is deserved, but it is remedial—God loves all men, otherwise He would not have created them; hence punishment inflicted by a God of love must be for the benefit of His creatures. In applying this theory to the Israelites the author, by means of ignoring much of the traditional narrative, is apparently consistent; but not so when he deals with the fate of the heathen, in xi. 16 and xii. 22. In truth, he adopts a very difficult rôle. He wishes to reconcile the O.T. statements of the action of God in exterminating the Canaanites with the higher view of the Deity due to

Ethical Monotheism. Ethical Monotheism cannot regard punishment as arbitrary or merely retributive; it must be reformative. Accordingly the writer ignores the biblical account and affirms that punishment in the case both of the Egyptians and the Canaanites was inflicted to give them the opportunity of repentance. But the fact remains that they did not repent. This is accounted for in the case of the Canaanites by saying that they were incorrigible. 'They were a seed accursed from the beginning;' while the Egyptians are punished because, when they knew the true God, they refused to obey Him; though subsequently they are placed in the same position as the Canaanites by the statement that Destiny (ἀνάγκη) was dragging them to their doom (xix. 4).

In addition to the eschatology in part 1, the anthropology differs from that of the Old Testament, in that it assumes the existence of the soul before birth. The question as to whether the writer accepted this belief at first sight admits of no dispute. In viii. 19, 20 he says, 'Now I was a child good by nature and a good soul fell to my lot; nay, rather, being good, I came into a body undefiled.' These words seem decisive. But granted that the writer believed in the pre-existence of the soul the question may be asked, What kind of pre-existence? Do the words of viii. 19 mean in his mouth, as they would in the mouth of Philo, not mere existence but self-conscious existence? It may help to answer this question, if we remind ourselves of the writer's attitude towards some other Greek ideas which he adopts, and ask whether they meant to him what they meant to the philosophers. We have seen that he adopted the Greek idea of immortality, but that it cannot be said that he did so fully and completely, since it is probable that he believed in a final day of judgement (iii. 18) to be followed or preceded by a Messianic Kingdom on earth. Again, he knew something of the philosophic theory of the inherent evil of matter, and says with reference to the body, that it 'weighs down the soul'; but there is no indication that he adopted the opinion that the body was no better than a tomb; i. 14 shows that he is very far from accepting the philosophical belief in the evil of matter as Philo subsequently did. It may therefore be fairly argued that as the writer perhaps did not accept the Greek philosophical belief in immortality, and certainly did not accept the belief in the evil of matter, without modification, it is quite possible that he also modified the philosophical belief in the pre-existence of the soul. In the case of the two former beliefs, however, it must be remembered that it would have been contrary to Jewish feeling to admit them completely. The complete and formal abandonment of the Messianic hope and the absolute worthlessness of the body were opinions too much opposed to Jewish tradition to be accepted by a writer who, though he had no great feeling for strict consistency, yet desired not to deviate too far from his ancestral beliefs. But there is no reason for thinking that the Greek doctrine of pre-existence was antagonistic to Jewish religious feeling. According to Harnack (*Hist. of Dogma*, vol. i, pp. 319 ff.), the early idea of some sacred object on earth being a copy of the original in heaven underwent development in the time of the Maccabees and the following decades. The conception became 'applied to persons'. Moreover, the Rabbis themselves adopted and worked it out, locating the unborn souls in the seventh heaven.[1] According to Porter[2] (p. 267), this Rabbinic idea of pre-existence is 'impersonal or half personal', and it is belief in this kind of pre-existence which he would ascribe to the author of our book. But it is doubtful if we have any more right to ascribe to the writer subsequent rabbinic than subsequent philosophic ideas; indeed, as the writer is an Alexandrian, it would seem less unjustifiable to ascribe to him the subsequent Philonic method of thinking on this point. Probably the writer of part 1 adopted the idea of the pre-existence of the soul without asking himself whether he was thinking of a mere vague general notion of existence, or a definite idea of self-conscious existence; it is worth noting, however, that he is far more definite than the writer of part 2 in xv. 8 and 11.

In regard to the writer's philosophical beliefs, it is generally agreed that he was well acquainted with the theories of the Greek philosophers, but whether his knowledge was first- or second-hand is a matter of dispute. Grimm considers that the writer's knowledge did not go beyond that possessed by every educated Alexandrian of the time: that he had no first-hand acquaintance with Platonism he infers from the absence of all reference to the doctrine of ideas, though it appears quite legitimate to ask whether a writer who admittedly had considerably more than a bowing acquaintance with Greek philosophy could have been ignorant of such a celebrated theory. Whether the writer's knowledge was first- or second-hand, it was certainly extensive. The views of the Stoics, of Plato, and of Heraclitus (to take them in order of importance) can all be traced in the book. In vii. 17 ff. he claims for his hero acquaintance with the whole range of philosophy and science; and he can hardly have failed to possess some of the knowledge which he attributes to Solomon.

[1] Weber, *Jüdische Theologie*, 1897, p. 205.

[2] 'The pre-existence of the Soul in the Book of Wisdom,' see below, p. 534. Porter takes viii. 19 to be by the same writer as xv. 11. Much of his argument would require restating if these are from different authors.

The influence of the Stoic philosophy appears in the idea of the world soul in i. 7, vii. 27, viii. 1. It is seen in the epithets 'alone in kind' (μονογενής) and 'manifold' (πολυμερής) applied to Wisdom in vii. 22, where the one world soul and its different manifestations are referred to, and especially in the use of technical Stoical terms. The reader can satisfy himself of this by referring to Ritter and Preller,[1] extract 513 (taken from Diog. Laertius' life of Zeno), where in the first few lines we find νοερός, τὸ διῆκον διὰ πάντων, διὰ τοῦ ζῆν κεχώρηκεν, all referring to the Deity. Like expressions are applied in c. vii to Wisdom. The four Cardinal Virtues (viii. 7) are Stoic, and also the metabolism of the elements, by the help of which the writer of part 2 endeavours to rationalize the miracles of the Exodus. The Sorites, a favourite figure of the Stoics, is used in vi. 17–20.

The influence of Platonism in the book is just as undeniable: the transcendence of God, the pre-existence of souls, the depreciation of the body (in part 2 also the pre-existence of matter (xi. 17)), all show platonic influence. Moreover, it seems difficult to deny a first-hand knowledge of Plato when we compare ix. 15 φθαρτὸν γὰρ σῶμα βαρύνει ψυχήν, καὶ βρίθει τὸ γεῶδες σκῆνος νοῦν πολυφρόντιδα, with the passage from the *Phaedo* 81 C Ἐμβριθὲς δέ γε τοῦτο (i. e. σωματοειδές) οἴεσθαι χρὴ εἶναι καὶ βαρὺ καὶ γεῶδες καὶ ὁρατόν. ὃ δὴ καὶ ἔχουσα ἡ τοιαύτη ψυχὴ βαρύνεται. The three points of connexion, βρίθει, γεῶδες, and βαρύνει, in one and the same sentence would be striking if they were all ordinary words; but when it is remembered that βρίθω occurs nowhere else in the Greek Bible, and that γεώδης occurs only here and in xv. 13, the argument for direct connexion seems very strong. Porter, who denies direct dependence, admits the probability of some indirect connexion. It should also be noticed that the Platonic classification of the Virtues is implicitly rejected in vii. 12.

With regard to Heraclitus, we have to remember that, as Zeller (*Stoics*, p. 371) says, 'there is hardly a single point in the Heraclitean theory of nature which the Stoics did not appropriate.' This increases the difficulty of deciding. His influence, direct or indirect, is to be found in ii. 3, 'reason is a spark kindled by the beating of our heart'; but, as mentioned in the note on the passage, the Stoics took up the idea. It is true that the Stoics considered that souls lived after death until the great conflagration, and our author puts into the mouth of the ungodly the exact view of Heraclitus—the belief in extinction immediately after death.[2] This, however, was also the view of the Epicureans, so we cannot be sure of the direct influence of Heraclitus here.

In vi. 24 the author announces his intention of making known the secrets of Wisdom, and apparently declaims against those who enviously keep knowledge to themselves: here all the commentators see a reference to the pagan mysteries, but E. Pfleiderer[3] wishes to see a reference to an individual philosopher—Heraclitus; the reference, however, seems quite general; the quotation from Philo by Grimm (see note) shows that the heathen mysteries were not identified with any individual. Our author's statement that 'a multitude of wise men is salvation to the world' is said by Pfleiderer to stand in direct opposition to the saying of Heraclitus, 'To me, one is ten thousand if he be the best' (Zeller, *Pre-Socratic Phil.* ii, p. 10), but neither observation is very original. The first is surely a commonplace, and as for the second, Milton's 'fit audience, though few', does not depend on Heraclitus.

The metabolism of the elements at the end of part 2 is traced by E. Pfleiderer to Heraclitus, and to him directly, rather than indirectly through the Stoics, on account of the allusion in c. xix to three elements only—fire, water, earth—since Heraclitus recognized only three. But it is difficult to see how the author could have brought in the idea of air changing into anything else: water changes into earth in the passage through the Red Sea, and earth becomes water again to overwhelm the Egyptians; fire lost its power and was unable to melt the heavenly food; what need or opportunity was there for adducing the change of air into another element? In this connexion it is worth noticing that Philo in *Vita Mosis*, iii, § 2, in speaking of the High Priest's robe (see note on xviii. 24) only mentions three elements and calls them 'the three elements', air, water, and earth, so that if we had no other passage to go by, we should be unable to prove that he accepted, as he certainly did, the doctrine of the four elements. It must, no doubt, be admitted that the Book of Wisdom has points of connexion with the system of Heraclitus, who was highly esteemed in Alexandria, but whether directly or indirectly it is impossible to say.

Heinisch,[4] who denies to the writer of Wisdom anything beyond a superficial knowledge of Greek philosophy, admits, or rather affirms, that he had read Xenophon's *Memorabilia*. He quotes *Mem.* 2. 1 (the choice of Hercules) side by side with Wisd. viii. 2–18, and points out that in nearly every one of these verses there is an echo of the passage in the *Memorabilia*. It is not merely that the writer knew the story of the choice of Hercules, but that he had read it in Xenophon, to which Heinisch commits himself. This is highly probable, but it is difficult to reconcile it with

[1] Eighth ed., 1898. [2] See Zeller, *Pre-Soc. Phil.* ii, p. 105. [3] *Die Phil. des Heraclitus*, see below, p. 533.
[4] *Die griech. Phil. im B. der Weisheit*, see below, p. 534.

Heinisch's denial of any direct acquaintance on the part of the author with other Greek writers. One who had studied the *Memorabilia* carefully enough to reproduce from memory a large number of the sentiments put into the mouth of Virtue in 2. 1 would not be a superficial student of the book; and if he had studied the *Memorabilia* carefully it is probable that he had paid the same attention to much more celebrated works such as the *Phaedo*. It may be added that Heinisch was the first to notice the close resemblance between these passages of Wisdom and Xenophon. It shakes one's confidence in a scholar to find that a resemblance discovered by himself is maintained to be the result of direct connexion, while those pointed out by other scholars are minimized or denied.

With reference to the general question of the indebtedness of our author to other thinkers, it may be noticed that Menzel[1] gives 135 places where connexion has been traced by one scholar or another. Most writers are children of their time, and their work cannot but show traces of the intellectual atmosphere which they breathed. We can admire the language and thought of the Book of Wisdom (i. e. cc. i–x), and yet admit that the parallels pointed out by the critics are valid.

In its method of interpretation of O.T. Scripture the book contains both haggadah and allegory. The haggadic treatment of the plague of darkness is equal to anything in the Rabbis, the allegory is of a milder type. We do not meet with that thoroughgoing kind of allegory where the literal truth of the narrative is denied as in Philo. The nearest approach to this is in the treatment of the serpent in Eden and the cloud which accompanied the Israelites on their wanderings. According to our author the serpent was not really a serpent but the devil, the cloud was not really a cloud but the form which Wisdom assumed. In some other instances historical events are regarded as parables. Lot's wife was turned into a pillar of salt as a warning against unbelief. The victory of Jacob in his struggle with the angel shows that piety is more powerful than even a supernatural opponent. That the manna was to be gathered before sunrise shows that prayer must be offered betimes: that it melted after sunrise shows that the hopes of the ungrateful come to naught. The successful intercession of Aaron, with his symbolical garments which represented the world, probably illustrates the truth that the world fighteth for the righteous. The ark of Noah shows that God blesses natural productions when they are put to a beneficial use, e. g. wood for the building of ships; and perhaps that He will protect men venturing on the high seas for the beneficent purposes of commerce. The narrative of the brazen serpent in the wilderness and its healing power is taken as historical; but the serpent has no magical power: it acts as a reminder to the Israelites who had forgotten God. This can hardly be called allegorical treatment unless allegory is taken to mean any interpretation of the narrative which goes beyond the literal one.

The allegorical traits in the book are not nearly so strong as the haggadic, but though the latter is generally associated with the methods of the Rabbis, both flourished vigorously amongst the Hellenistic Jews (Schürer, ii. 1, p. 341).

§ 10. Chief Critical Inquiries.

Eichhorn, *Einleitung in die apokryph. Schriften des A. T.*, pp. 86–207. Leipzig, 1795.

Grörer, *Philo*, vol. II (1831), pp. 200–72. An interesting review of the whole book.

Edmund Pfleiderer, *Die Phil. des Heraclitus*, 1886, pp. 289–348. Pfleiderer affirms that the writer of Wisdom had an intimate knowledge of Greek philosophy and in especial a direct acquaintance with Heraclitus. Heinisch (see below), pp. 18–30, subjects Pfleiderer's contention to a searching criticism. He denies that the writer of Wisdom had even a superficial knowledge of the system of Heraclitus.

Drummond, *Philo Judaeus*, 1888, vol. i, pp. 177–229. As a preliminary to his exposition of Philo's philosophy Dr. Drummond gives a most valuable discussion of the theology of the Book of Wisdom. The following statement deserves attention: 'There is little connected reasoning of any kind in the work. . . . It is as though the process of investigation had been conducted elsewhere, and led to results esteemed satisfactory by an important section of the Jewish community' (p. 186).

P. Menzel, *Der griech. Einfluss auf Prediger und Weisheit Salomos*, 1889, pp. 39–70. Menzel gives a useful table of passages (135)—which Professor Margoliouth says 'might be considerably reduced without disadvantage'—where connexion between Wisdom and Greek philosophy has been pointed out by Grimm and Pfleiderer. He has coined a somewhat question-begging epithet in the word 'parallelomania' which shows his attitude towards those who would trace the ideas of the author to their source. He admits, however, some of Pfleiderer's positions. Menzel is severely criticized by Heinisch, pp. 9 ff. Cheyne (*Origin of Psalter*, p. 423) calls the work 'a painstaking dissertation'.

H. Bois, *Essai sur les origines de la philosophie Judéo-Alexandrine*, 1890, pp. 211–311. Notes on the text 373–411. Bois undertakes a thorough examination of the theological principles in the Book of Wisdom, in a fresh and stimulating manner. In his notes on the text he suggests the rearrangement of certain passages, one of which is most probably right (see note on iv. 15). He also suggests several emendations, some of which are accepted by Siegfried. His exposition of the transmutation of the elements alluded to in ch. xix *ad fin.* deserves special attention.

Margoliouth. In the *JRAS* for 1890, pp. 263–97, Professor Margoliouth maintained that Bretschneider was on the right track in suggesting that the Book of Wisdom was originally written in Hebrew; and adduced many passages where he affirms that traces of mistranslation can be proved. This theory has not, however, found acceptance. Freudenthal in the *JQR*, 1901, contested it.

[1] *Der griech. Einfluss*, &c., see below, § 10.

Grafe. In 1892, in *Theol. Abhandl.* in honour of Weizäcker, pp. 253–86, Grafe published a convincing paper on the question of St. Paul's use of the Book of Wisdom.

Thielmann. In 1893 Thielmann published an exhaustive inquiry into the Latinity of the Latin version of the book in *Archiv für lat. Lex. und Gram.*, pp. 235–77.

Feldmann, *Textkritische Mat. zum B. der Weisheit gesammelt aus der sahidischen syrohexaplarischen und armenischen Übersetzung*, Freiburg im B., 1902, pp. 84. A most valuable contribution to the criticism of the text.

Joseph Holtzmann, *Die Peschitta zum B. der Weisheit*, Freiburg im B., 1903, pp. 152. A thorough investigation of the Syriac version.

Weber, in *Zeitschrift für wiss. Theol.*, 1904, upholds the composite authorship, tracing four different hands in the work. Feldmann in *Bibl. Zeitschrift*, Freiburg im B., 1909, contests this view.

Heinisch, *Die griech. Phil. im B. der Weisheit*, Münster i. W., 1908, pp. 158. An exhaustive inquiry into the relationship between the book and Greek philosophy; a work of great learning and ability. Unfortunately the writer, a Roman Catholic, seems to have made up his mind to prove that the author of the Book of Wisdom 'taught nothing which contradicted the faith inherited from his fathers. That which was new, which he expounded in his speculations on Wisdom and in his Eschatology, made no breach with the ideas of the O. T. . . . and if it has found acceptance in the N.T., that is only a proof that the sacred writer in his literary activity was under the guidance of divine inspiration' (p. 156). The author's knowledge of Greek philosophy was, according to Heinisch, 'very superficial.'

Porter, 'The pre-existence of the Soul in the Book of Wisdom and in the Rabbinical writings.' (In *Old Testament and Semitic Studies in memory of William Rainey Harper*, 1908, pp. 208–69.) A vigorous onslaught upon the prevalent view that the writer of Wisdom accepted the Greek doctrine of the pre-existence of souls. In this he is upheld by Heinisch (p. 86); though as Heinisch will not admit that Wisdom contains anything contrary to the doctrine of the Church, i.e. the Roman Catholic Church, his judgement is biased. An admirable summary of Porter's position is given by Prof. W. B. Stevenson in the *International Journal of Apocrypha*, April, 1912. Prof. Stevenson affirms that 'the argument is convincing'.

EDITIONS.

(The earlier editions of the book may be found in Grimm, p. 45, or Deane, p. 42.)

Grimm, 1860. In *Kurzgefasstes exeg. Handbuch zu den Apokryphen*, pp. 300. It is difficult to speak too highly of this masterly work. Grimm first published a commentary in 1837. For the next twenty-three years he was collecting additional materials, and the result was the work of 1860, which is and will probably long remain an indispensable quarry for all students of the book.

Deane, W. J., 1881, prints the Greek, Latin, and English A.V. in parallel columns. It contains very useful linguistic notes both on the Greek and the Latin.

Farrar, *Speaker's Comm.*, 1888. Abounds in apt illustrations from classical and English literature.

Zöckler, *Apocryphen und Pseud. des Alt. Test.*, 1891, pp. 355–95. Short introduction, translation, and notes.

Siegfried in Kautzsch's *Apocrypha*, 1900, gives a new and excellent translation, generally following Grimm. The notes, however, are very short.

Gregg, *Camb. Bible for Schools*, 1909. This is, perhaps, the best edition in English.

THE WISDOM OF SOLOMON

True religion leads to a blessed immortality: irreligion and apostasy to destruction.

Seek the knowledge of God by purity of life: such knowledge (i.e. wisdom) cannot be attained by the slaves of sin.

1 1 LOVE righteousness, ye that be judges of the earth,
Think ye of the Lord with a good mind,
And in singleness of heart seek ye him;
2 Because he is found of them that tempt him not,
And is manifested to them that do not distrust him.
3 For crooked thoughts separate from God;
And the *supreme* Power, when it is brought to the proof, putteth to confusion the foolish:
4 Because wisdom will not enter into a soul that deviseth evil,
Nor dwell in a body held in pledge by sin.
5 For the holy spirit of discipline will flee deceit,
And will start away from thoughts that are without understanding,
And will be scared away when unrighteousness approacheth.

The sinner cannot escape punishment: his very words are known.

6 For wisdom is a spirit that loveth man,
And she will not hold a blasphemer guiltless for his lips;

I. 1. **judges of the earth.** It is in his assumed character of Solomon that the writer speaks of 'judges of the *earth*'; in all probability, however, the judges really aimed at are the rulers of the Jewish community in Alexandria. As in the time of Philo the Jews in Egypt amounted to a million souls, we may presume that at least half a million lived in the capital. Strabo (died A.D. 21), quoted by Josephus, *Ant.* xiv. 7, says: 'There is also an ethnarch at their head who rules the people and dispenses justice, and sees that obligations are fulfilled and statutes observed, like the archon of an independent state.'

Doubtless many of the ruling classes in Alexandria, like those in Palestine, were of a Sadducean type and inclined to Hellenize. Indeed, some Jews, like Tiberius Julius Alexander who held high office under Nero, went over to the Gentiles completely. Bousset, *Rel. des Jud.* (p. 81, note 1), thinks that complete apostasy of this kind only rarely took place. The persecution of the pious by the freethinkers spoken of in ii. 10 may be paralleled by the oppression of the Pharisees under Alex. Jannaeus about 94 B.C. See Charles, 1 *Enoch*, p. 297. 'The rulers appear as the aiders and abettors of the enemies of the righteous. These enemies are the Sadducees, sinners, apostates, and paganizers.' Ch. ii. 12 shows that apostates are the object of the polemic: 'He upbraideth us with sins against the law.' Philo alludes to apostate Jews, *De Conf. Ling.*, ch. ii: 'Those who are discontented at the constitution under which their fathers have lived, being always eager to blame and accuse the laws, say—Do you boast of your precepts as if they contained truth itself? Behold, the books which you call sacred scriptures contain fables at which you are accustomed to laugh when you hear others relating them.' See also *Vita Mos.* i. 6.

Intermarriage with the Gentiles would facilitate apostasy, and as an act is not censured unless it has taken place, we may infer the existence of such marriages from Jubilees xxx. 7, 'If there is any man in Israel who wishes to give his daughter or his sister to any man who is of the seed of the Gentiles, he shall surely die, and they shall stone him with stones, for he hath wrought shame in Israel; and they shall burn the woman with fire, because she has dishonoured the name of the house of her father, and she shall be rooted out of Israel.'

with a good mind, Greek 'in goodness'. What a pious Jew would consider to be right thoughts about God may be gathered from Exod. xxxiv. 6-7, especially the last clause, 'Jahveh is a God full of compassion and gracious . . . forgiving iniquity and transgression and sin, and that will by no means clear the guilty.' The opposite is seen in Ps. l. 21, 'Thou thoughtest that I was even such a one as thyself.'

singleness of heart. A Hebraism: straightness of mind as opposed to crookedness; see *v.* 3, 'crooked thoughts.' The heart is the seat of the intellect in Hebrew; the reins (see *v.* 6) the seat of the emotions.

5. **discipline**: A.V. and R.V., but the idea of instruction must be included.

scared away: ἐλεγχθήσεται is a difficulty of long standing. Schultess (1820) declared the word to be corrupt. R.V. 'put to confusion', margin 'convicted'; Grimm, from a use of the word in Byzantine Greek, 'is scared away'. Siegfried, 'is filled with a spirit of reproof,' a very satisfactory meaning if allowable. The idea of being 'put to shame' like purity in the presence of iniquity is possible. This use of the word is found only in Homer, according to Liddell and Scott; and the book is admittedly full of poetical words.

6. **For wisdom,** &c. This line, which appears to have no connexion with what precedes or follows, has given great trouble to the commentators. Grimm takes the sense to be 'Wisdom is a spirit that loves mankind, and for that very reason will not leave wickedness unpunished'. The earlier commentators took φιλάνθρωπος in the sense of 'mild',

Because God is witness of his reins,
And is a true overseer of his heart,
And a hearer of his tongue:
7 Because the spirit of the Lord filleth the world,
And that which holdeth all things together hath knowledge of *every* voice.
8 Therefore no man that uttereth unrighteous things shall be unseen;
Neither shall Justice, when it punisheth, pass him by.
9 For the counsels of the ungodly shall be searched out;
And the report of his words shall come unto the Lord
For the punishment of his lawless deeds:
10 Because *there* is an ear of jealousy *that* listeneth to all things,
And the noise of murmurings is not hid.
11 Beware then of unprofitable murmuring,
And refrain your tongue from blasphemy;
Because no secret utterance shall go forth with impunity,
And a mouth that lieth destroyeth the soul.

God does not willingly afflict men: they bring punishment and death upon themselves.

12 Court not death in the error of your life;
Neither draw upon yourselves destruction by the works of your hands:
13 Because God made not death;
Neither delighteth he when the living perish:
14 For he created all things that they might have being:
And the products of the world *are* healthsome,
And there is no poison of destruction in them:
Nor hath Hades royal dominion upon earth;
15 For righteousness is immortal,
⟨But the gain of unrighteousness is death⟩.
16 But the ungodly by their hands and words called him unto them:
Deeming him a friend they were consumed with love of him,
And they made a covenant with him,
Because they are worthy to be of his portion.

'gentle', and connected it with preceding verse. The meaning then would be: 'Wisdom is put to confusion or scared away when wickedness enters in, because it is a mild and kindly spirit and cannot stay in the same abode as injustice.' Bois, p. 379, seeing that these explanations are unsatisfactory would transpose the line to the end of *v.* 13, and in this alteration Siegfried concurs. But the close connexion between the last line of *v.* 13 and the beginning of *v.* 14 militates against this. In face of these difficulties it does not seem rash to suggest that the line may be an interpolation on the basis of vii. 22–3, where Wisdom is said to be a πνεῦμα and φιλάνθρωπος.

Further, the fact that this line is out of harmony with its surroundings gives force to Weber's suggestion that *vv.* 4, 5, together with this line, have been interpolated; the connexion obtained after their omission is quite satisfactory. *v.* 3. 'The Power, when brought to the proof, chastiseth fools and (6) will not hold the blasphemer guiltless for his lips. For God, &c.'

7. **filleth**, as A.V.; R.V. 'hath filled'; but see Grimm's note, Burton, *N. T. Moods and Tenses*, § 76, and cf. St. John xi. 11.

holdeth all things together. We have here the Stoic idea of the world soul. The Stoics said of the world, εἰς ἅπαν αὐτοῦ μέρος διήκοντος τοῦ νοῦ, καθάπερ ἐφ' ἡμῶν τῆς ψυχῆς. See Dio. Laert. in Ritter and Preller, § 493; Zeller, *Stoics*, &c., p. 142.

8. For examples of **unrighteous things** see the quotation from *De Conf. Ling.* in the note on *v.* 1.

11. **blasphemy.** καταλαλιά in parallelism with murmuring, γογγυσμός, plainly means speaking against God: γογγυσμός is the word used in LXX Exod. xvi. 7, 8, 9, for the murmuring of the Israelites.

13–16. Man lost his uprightness and immortality through his own act according to this passage; in ii. 24, through the envy of the devil.

15. **For righteousness.** Either this line is in its wrong place and should be transferred perhaps to a position between *vv.* 22 and 23 of ch. ii, where it would be in a satisfactory context, or we must with Grimm accept the succeeding line found in some Latin MSS., 'iniustitia autem mortis acquisitio est.' Grimm renders this by ἀδικία δὲ θανάτου περιποίησις ἐστιν (the word περιποίησις is not found in the LXX with this meaning). As the line stands it has no connexion with what precedes or follows, and if the extra line is not accepted deletion or transference to the end of ii. 22 would seem to be justified. It should be noticed that the line summarizes the teaching of this part of the book, and may originally have been a marginal note. The Latin line *iniustitia autem* would then be a gloss like ii. 17, vi. 1, &c., and αὐτόν in the next line, referring to Hades, would not be separated from its antecedent.

16. Seems to be based verbally on Isa. xxviii. 15, though the context is quite different. There the covenant is that Death should spare the other contracting parties, while here they give themselves into the arms of Death. For τήκω used to denote a state of mind, see vi. 23, '*pining* envy.' E. Pfleiderer, followed by Bois, takes this verse as referring to the pagan mysteries, especially to the identification of Hades the God of death with Dionysus the God of life.

Some men even prefer the ways of death: they affirm that their souls are even as their bodies, that after this life nothing remains.

2 1 For they said within themselves, reasoning not aright,
Short and sorrowful is our life;
And there is no remedy when a man cometh to his end,
And none was ever known that returned from Hades.
2 Because by mere chance were we born,
And hereafter we shall be as though we had never been:
Because the breath in our nostrils is smoke,
And reason is a spark kindled by the beating of our heart,
3 Which being extinguished, the body shall be turned into ashes,
And the spirit dispersed as thin air;
4 And our name shall be forgotten in time,
And no man shall remember our works;
And our life shall pass away as the traces of a cloud,
And shall be scattered as is a mist,
When it is chased by the beams of the sun,
And overcome by the heat thereof.
5 For our allotted time is the passing of a shadow,
And there is no putting back of our end;
Because it is fast sealed, and none reverseth it.

They therefore will enjoy this life to the full, and crush those whose lives reprove their own.

6 Come therefore and let us enjoy the good things that *now* are;
And let us use creation with all earnestness as youth's *possession*.
7 Let us fill ourselves with costly wine and perfumes;
And let no flower of spring pass us by:
8 Let us crown ourselves with rosebuds, before they wither:
9 Let there be no ⟨meadow⟩ without traces of our proud revelry:
Everywhere let us leave tokens of *our* mirth:
Because this is our portion, and our lot is this.

Heraclitus had said ὡυτὸς δὲ ῾Αΐδης καὶ Διόνυσος (Ritter and Preller, § 49, Zeller, *Pre-Socratic Phil.*, ii, p. 100). If this is accepted and we assume that the writer is referring to the apostate Jews, we must infer that they had gone so far as to take part in the pagan mysteries. His 'portion' is the realm assigned to him.

II. The opinions here put into the mouth of the godless may easily have been known to the writer from his personal experience of Jews who adopted the tenets of Epicurus; most scholars also see a reference to Ecclesiastes, see Introduction, p. 525. It should, however, be noticed that the same sentiments are put into the mouth of the ungodly in 1 Enoch cii. 6–8.

1. It is impossible to say whether ὁ ἀναλύσας is transitive or intransitive. Grimm on 2 Macc. viii–xxv gives eight places where ἀναλύω = 'to return'; but it is used in the passive in iv. 12, so that if we take this as deciding the author's usage, it should be transitive here. Against this it may be urged, that in view of the liberties which the author allows himself to take with the Greek language, it is quite possible that he used the active and passive forms of an intransitive verb without any appreciable difference of meaning.

2. **reason is a spark.** A reference to the view of Heraclitus and others that fire (see note on xiii. 2) is the primitive substance. 'The soul of man is a part of this divine fire' (Zeller, *Outlines*, p. 70). 'It was conceived . . . as a transient individualization of the one primitive substance or force, and this individualization terminated at death' (Charles, *Eschat.*, p. 143). The Stoics adopted this view. 'The soul is . . . a part of the divine fire which descended into the bodies of men when they first arose out of the aether' (Zeller, *Outlines*, p. 244). Cic. *Tusc.* i. 19 'Zenoni Stoico animus ignis videtur'.

4. **overcome.** This is perhaps a justifiable paraphrase. The Greek means 'weighed down', which is incorrect from the point of view of Natural Science. But the writer merely wanted a parallel expression to 'chased away', and being unscientific chose an incorrect term.

5. **allotted time**, reading καιρός with ℵ A and Latin, as against βίος, B*. So most editors.

putting back. The explanation adopted by Grimm, Siegfried, and others, that no man can die twice, is not satisfactory. Gregg's reference to the shadow on a sundial is more acceptable, though there is a sudden change of metaphor in the next line in the word 'sealed'; the end is fast sealed = the end is predetermined.

The sense probably is 'while we are young', and Grimm gets this by reading ὡς ἐν νεότητι on the authority of 157, 248, 253, and the Complutensian polyglot. B reads ὡς νεότητι, ℵ and A ὡς νεότητος.

7. **spring**, reading ἔαρος for ἀέρος. So A, Latin, and most editions.

9 *a*. The Greek here has one line, μηδεὶς ἡμῶν ἄμοιρος ἔστω τῆς ἡμετέρας ἀγερωχίας; the Latin has two: 'nemo nostrum exors sit luxuriae nostrae', and 'nullum pratum sit quod non pertranseat luxuria nostra'. This is a doublet of the Greek line with λειμών in line 2 for ἡμῶν. As an old glossary to the book shows that it originally contained the word λειμών, this must be restored in place of ἡμῶν, and μηδεὶς λειμών κτλ. accepted as the true reading. See Feldmann.

proud revelry: ἀγερωχία, may be an allusion to the heathen mysteries (Bois, p. 295).

our portion; our only portion and lot. For connexion with Ecclesiastes see Introd., p. 525.

10 Let us oppress the righteous poor;
Let us not spare the widow,
Nor reverence the hairs of the old man grey for length of years.
11 But let our strength be *to us* a law of righteousness;
For that which is weak is found to be of no service.
12 But let us lie in wait for the righteous man,
Because he is of disservice to us,
And is contrary to our works,
And upbraideth us with sins against the law,
And layeth to our charge sins against our discipline.
13 He professeth to have knowledge of God,
And nameth himself servant of the Lord.
14 He became to us a reproof of our thoughts.
15 He is grievous unto us even to behold,
Because his life is unlike other men's,
And his paths are of strange fashion.
16 We were accounted of him as base metal,
And he abstaineth from our ways as from uncleannesses.
The latter end of the righteous he calleth happy;
And he vaunteth that God is his father.
17 Let us see if his words be true,
And let us try what shall befall in the ending of his *life*.
18 For if the righteous man is God's son, he will uphold him,
And he will deliver him out of the hand of his adversaries.
19 With outrage and torture let us put him to the test,
That we may learn his gentleness,
And may prove his patience under wrong.
20 Let us condemn him to a shameful death;
For according to his words he will be visited.

But they are wrong: a future life is in store for the righteous, who shall then triumph over the ungodly.

21 Thus reasoned they, being far astray,
For their wickedness blinded them,
22 And they knew not the mysteries of God,
Neither hoped they for wages of holiness,
Nor did they judge *that there is* a prize for blameless souls.
23 Because God created man for incorruption,
And made him an image of his own proper being;
24 But by the envy of the devil death entered into the world,
And they that belong to his realm experience it.
3 1 But the souls of the righteous are in the hand of God,
And no torment shall touch them.

12. The translation of *παιδεία* in the last line is difficult. Weber gives 'and reproaches us on account of the sins of our method of life' (*Bildung*). Mr. Gregg would omit. The line certainly looks like an addition.

let us lie in wait. Cf. LXX rendering of Isa. iii. 10, see Introd., p. 524.

20. **according to his words**, i.e. 'if what he says is true.'

visited. *ἐπισκοπή* is always used in a good sense in this part of the book, see Introd., p. 523. The word *ἐπισκοπή* is said to be used only once outside biblical and ecclesiastical Greek. It is a translation of the Hebrew word פְּקֻדָּה, which means a visitation to deliver, LXX Gen. l. 24, 25, Exod. iii. 16, or a visitation to punish, LXX Isa. xxiv. 22, xxix. 6. See Hort's full note on 1 Pet. ii. 12, and Charles's *Apoc. Bar.* xx. 2, note.

22. At the end of this verse i. 15 would be appropriate. There is a prize for blameless souls, viz. immortality.

mysteries of God, i.e. that suffering is not necessarily punishment, but is often a test of goodness which will be rewarded after death by immortality.

23. The difference between the author and Philo is seen very plainly here. In Philo, man is the image of the Logos (Drummond, *Philo Judaeus*, ii. 186–7).

his own proper being, *ἰδιότητος*, ℵ A and B. *ἀϊδιότητος*, 248, 253, and most of the patristic writers. But Gen. i. 26 seems to decide for the former, though Sanday and Headlam (*Romans*, p. 51) are doubtful, while Prof. Margoliouth prefers *ἀϊδιότητος*. He also suggests *κατ' εἰκόνα*, which is now upheld by Feldmann.

24. Bois (p. 297) suggests that the reference here is to Cain, the first murderer, and Mr. Gregg adduces additional arguments for this. All other expositors take it to refer to the temptation of Eve. In 1 Enoch lxix. 6 it is said that a Satan led Eve astray. This seems to favour the latter view.

2 In the eyes of fools they seemed to die ;
And their departure was accounted *to be their* hurt,
3 And their going from us *to be their* ruin :
But they are in peace.
4 For though in the sight of men they be punished,
Their hope is full of immortality ;
5 And having borne a little chastening, they shall receive great good ;
Because God tested them, and found them worthy of himself.
6 As gold in the furnace he proved them,
And as a whole burnt offering he accepted them.
7 And in the time of their visitation they shall shine forth,
And like sparks among stubble they shall run to and fro.
8 They shall judge nations, and have dominion over peoples ;
And the Lord shall reign over them for evermore.
9 They that trust on him shall understand truth,
And the faithful shall abide with him in love ;
Because grace and mercy are to his chosen,
And he will graciously visit his holy ones.

But the unrighteous shall be punished, both they and their ungodly offspring, while the righteous though childless shall be rewarded.

10 But the ungodly shall be requited even as they reasoned,
They which lightly regarded the righteous *man*, and revolted from the Lord
11 (For he that setteth at naught wisdom and discipline is miserable ;)
And void is their hope and their toils unprofitable,
And useless are their works :
12 Their wives are foolish, and wicked are their children ;
13 Accursed is their begetting.
Because happy is the barren that is undefiled,
She who hath not conceived in transgression ;
She shall have fruit when *God* visiteth souls.

III. 2. **seemed.** The righteous cannot die. For this spiritual idea of life and death see v. 13 and x. 3. Philo says (*Quod det. pot.* § 15), 'The wise man who appears to have departed from this mortal life lives in a life immortal.'

5. **tested.** The object of affliction is testing, proving ; not punishment. Cf. 1 Enoch cviii. 9 : The righteous 'were much tried by the Lord and their spirits were found pure'.

7. **visitation.** Cf. Ps. cvi. 4, 'visit me with thy salvation.' Salvation in the O. T. always means deliverance—deliverance from one's foes and triumph over them. So here ; the writer cannot refrain from picturing the visible triumph of the godly over the wicked, though it is quite inconsistent with the idea of reward or retribution coming immediately after death. For the figure cf. Obad. 18 upon the destruction of Edom : 'The house of Jacob shall be a fire, and the house of Joseph a flame, and the house of Esau for stubble.'

8. In the Messianic Kingdom. Cp. St. Paul, 1 Cor. vi. 2, 'Know ye not that we shall judge angels.'

9. **understand truth**, i. e. God's methods in governing the world.

9 *b.* With ὅτι χάρις καὶ ἔλεος τοῖς ἐκλεκτοῖς αὐτοῦ compare 1 Enoch v. 7 καὶ τοῖς ἐκλεκτοῖς ἔσται φῶς καὶ χάρις καὶ εἰρήνη. 1 Enoch i–xxxvi was written before the persecution under Antiochus Epiphanes ; but the translation of Enoch into Greek was probably undertaken as a whole. If this is later than the latest part of 1 Enoch (cc. xxxvii–lxxi) it must be subsequent to 94 B.C., and so has a bearing on the date of Wisdom itself, see Introd., p. 520.

9 *d.* So ℵ A and Syriac, καὶ ἐπισκοπὴ ἐν τοῖς ὁσίοις (ἐκλεκτοῖς ℵ) αὐτοῦ, which B Latin and R. V. omit. For justification of this see note on iv. 15. In addition, the line is suitable here as a rejoinder to ii. 20 *b*.

10. **reasoned.** This means that the annihilation after death proclaimed by the godless shall indeed be their lot, only the writer's idea of annihilation is different from that of the apostates.

11. **he that setteth**, &c. This line is almost a verbal reproduction of Prov. i. 7, 'The ungodly set at naught wisdom and discipline.'

13. **happy.** The reference here may simply be general ; but it is difficult to read Philo's account of the Therapeutae without feeling that the writer of these lines had them in mind. Of the virgins who were enrolled amongst the Therapeutae, Philo (*De Vit. Con.* § 8) says they 'yearn not for mortal but for immortal offspring', οὐ θνητῶν ἐκγόνων ἀλλ' ἀθανάτων ὀρεχθεῖσαι. This, and the statement in the text 'She shall have fruit when God visiteth souls', seem to belong to the same circle of ideas. It is not necessary to infer that the writer belonged to the sect ; Philo, in spite of his admiration for them, was not one of them. Whether he is referring to the Therapeutae or not the writer shows considerable independence in discarding the strong Jewish belief that a numerous offspring was the greatest blessing of mankind.

transgression. This refers to unlawful marriages with the heathen. See Jubilees xxx. 7, quoted on i. 1.

fruit. This may be a vague phrase for reward. Philo works out the idea contained in the words 'immortal offspring' as that 'which the soul that is attached to God is alone able to produce by itself and from itself', meaning perhaps what the Christian sums up in the word 'bliss'. This is subjective and may be contrasted with the more objective statement as to the reward of the childless man, which is to be a blissful position in the heavenly sanctuary.

14 And *happy is* the eunuch which hath wrought no lawless deed with his hands,
Nor imagined wicked things against the Lord;
For there shall be given him for his faithfulness a peculiar favour,
And a lot in the sanctuary of the Lord of great delight.
15 For good labours have fruit of great renown;
And wisdom's root cannot fail.
16 But children of adulterers shall not come to maturity,
And the seed of an unlawful union shall perish.
17 For if they live long, they shall be held in no account,
And at the last their old age shall be without honour.
18 And if they die early, they shall have no hope,
Nor in the day of decision *shall they have* consolation.
19 For the end of an unrighteous generation is always grievous.
4 1 Better *than this* is childlessness with virtue;
For in the memory of virtue is immortality:
Because it is recognized both by God and man.
2 When it is present, *men* imitate it;
And they long after it when it is departed:
And throughout all time it marcheth crowned in triumph,
Victorious in the strife for prizes undefiled.
3 But the multiplying brood of the ungodly shall be of no profit,
And with bastard slips they shall not strike deep root,
Nor shall they establish a sure hold.
4 For even if these put forth boughs and flourish for a season,
Yet, standing unsure, they shall be shaken by the wind,
And by the violence of winds they shall be rooted out.
5 *Their* branches shall be broken off ere they come to maturity,
And their fruit *shall be* useless,
Not ripe to eat, and meet for nothing.
6 For children unlawfully begotten are witnesses of wickedness
Against parents when *God* searcheth them out.

The premature death of the righteous is followed by immortality, but the very memory of the ungodly shall perish.

7 But the righteous, though he die before his time, shall be at rest.
8 (For honourable old age is not that which standeth in length of time,

14. **sanctuary.** Where is this sanctuary to be? In the Jerusalem which the seer saw 'descending out of heaven from God' (Rev. xxi. 10) or in heaven itself?

of great delight. θυμηρέστερος in an elative or intensive sense. Thackeray, *Gr.*, p. 181; Blass, *Gr. of N. T. Gk.*, p. 141.

15. **cannot fail.** These two lines are merely a variation of i. 15, 'For righteousness is immortal'; and iv. 1, 'For in the memory of virtue is immortality'; see also viii. 13. It may be that the writer could not get rid of the old Jewish idea of subjective immortality, Ps. cxii. 6, Prov. x. 7, or that he wished to oppose the repeated statement in Ecclesiastes i. 11, ii. 16, ix. 5, that there is no remembrance of the dead, righteous or unrighteous. See Introd., p. 525.

16. **adulterers.** Those who had contracted unlawful marriages, as is plain from the next line and from iv. 6.

17. In denying that affliction necessarily indicates God's displeasure and is therefore punishment, the writer advances beyond the view of Ezekiel and his followers. Here, in affirming that the children shall be punished for the parents' sins, he falls behind it. See also iv. 4.

18. Reading οὐκ ἕξουσιν with ℵ A Latin; οὐκ ἔχουσιν B.

hope. The idea seems to be that even if the children of the godless die young, before they have had much time to sin, they will have no hope of future happiness.

19. An involuntary and instinctive utterance of the old view that wickedness is always punished in this life.

IV. 3-6. This is taken by Grimm as referring not to a material but to a spiritual state. The children of the ungodly have an ineradicable taint. Here again the writer falls below Ezekiel and displays the spirit of the imprecatory psalms.

6. **witnesses of wickedness.** Their sufferings are a proof of the sin of their parents. Cf. St. John ix. 2.

8. **old age is not that,** &c. The writer has already departed from the traditional view that life without offspring cannot be regarded as happy; he now departs from the belief that length of days is necessary to the happiness of a godly man. Here again one cannot fail to be struck with the correspondence of the author's views with those of the Therapeutae. Philo (*De Vita Cont.*, ch. 8) writes: 'For they do not regard those as elders who are advanced in years and aged, but as mere youths if they have only lately devoted themselves to the vocation; but they call those elders who from their earliest years have spent time and strength in the contemplative part of philosophy.' Grimm gives a whole series of

Nor is its measure given by number of years:
9 But understanding is grey hairs unto men,
And an unspotted life is ripe old age.)
10 Being found well-pleasing unto God he was beloved *of him*,
And while living among sinners he was translated:
11 He was caught away, lest wickedness should change his understanding,
Or guile deceive his soul.
12 (For the fascination of wickedness bedimmeth the things which are good,
And the frenzy of desire perverteth an innocent mind.)
13 Being made perfect in a little while, he fulfilled long years;
14 For his soul was pleasing unto the Lord:
Therefore He hastened him out of the midst of wickedness.
16 But a righteous man that is dead shall condemn the ungodly that are living,
And youth that is quickly perfected the many years of an unrighteous man's age.
15 But as for the peoples, seeing and understanding not,
Neither laying this to heart:—
17 For they will see the wise man's end,
And not understand what the Lord purposed concerning him,
And for what he safely kept him:—
18 They will see, and despise;
But them the Lord shall laugh to scorn.
And after this they shall become a dishonoured carcase,
And a reproach among the dead for ever:
19 Because he shall dash them speechless to the ground,
And shall shake them from the foundations,

quotations from Greek and Latin authors emphasizing this thought. Perhaps the quotation from Bailey's *Festus* given by Farrar is as good as any:

'We live in deeds not years; in thoughts not breaths,
In feelings not in figures on a dial;
We should count time by heart-throbs.'

10. *εὐάρεστος*, &c. This looks like tautology. But reference to the LXX shows that the writer is thinking of Gen. v. 22, 24 (of Enoch); vi. 9; xvii. 1; and other places where *εὐαρεστέω*, a translation of הִתְהַלֵּךְ 'to walk', plainly refers to the spiritual condition of the person mentioned. In xvii. 1 *εὐαρέστει ἐναντίον μοῦ* addressed to Abraham shows this very clearly. Gen. v. 22, 24, shows that Enoch is referred to here. No one could say that Enoch's comparatively early removal was a punishment; it was plainly a blessing, and this supports the author's contention in *v.* 8 as to the early death of other righteous men.

12. **bedimmeth.** The editors point out that the word *ἀμαυρόω* was used by Greek philosophers to express the darkening of the moral sense.

things which are good, *τὰ καλά*. Moral and spiritual qualities.

perverteth. Greek *μεταλλεύει*, so again in xvi. 25. The word properly means 'to mine'. Here the author gives it the meaning of 'change', deriving it no doubt from *ἄλλος*. Commentators compare this mistake with that in St. Mark xii. 4.

13. **he fulfilled long years.** Of a Rabbi who died young it was said, 'In the twenty-eight years of his life he has learned more than others learn in a hundred years' (Oesterley and Box, *Rel. of Syn.*, p. 97).

14–16. The passage reads as follows in the R. V. according to B:—

14. For his soul was pleasing unto the Lord:
Therefore hasted he out of the midst of wickedness.
15. But as for the peoples, seeing and understanding not,
Neither laying this to heart,
That grace and mercy are with his chosen,
And that he visiteth his holy ones:—
16. But a righteous man that is dead shall condemn the ungodly that are living
And youth that is quickly perfected, the many years of an unrighteous man's old age.

Some rearrangement is plainly necessary. For (1) the passage is now impossible as it stands in B. (2) The MSS. show that there has been some transference to or from iii. 9. (3) Transference of 15 *c*, *d* to iii. 9 relieves this passage. (4) After 15 *c*, *d* have been returned to their proper place, the necessity of placing *v.* 16 before 15 is obvious. Bois (p. 387) would make a much more thoroughgoing rearrangement, but it has been thought better to be content with the minimum of alteration.

15. **the peoples.** *vv.* 17 ff. show that the ungodly are meant. ℵ B Latin give *λαοί*, A *ἄλλοι*. Mr. Gregg, on the basis of the latter, would emend to *ἄνομοι*. It looks, however, like a reminiscence of LXX Isa. vi. 9: 'Go, tell this people (*λαός*) . . . seeing ye shall see and not understand.'

18. This is best explained as the judgement by the sword at the beginning of the Messianic age, like *vv.* 17 ff.

19. **foundations.** The figure in the mind of the writer was probably that of a city razed to the ground. Cf. Ps. ix. 6: 'The enemy are come to an end, they are desolations for ever; and the cities which thou didst uproot, their memory is perished' (Driver, *Parallel Psalter*).

And they shall lie utterly waste, and be in anguish,
And their memory shall perish.

The remorse of the ungodly at the judgement. Their retrospect.

20 They shall come, when their sins are reckoned up, with coward fear;
And their lawless deeds shall convict them to their face.
5 1 Then shall the righteous man stand in great boldness
Before the face of them that afflicted him,
And them that make his labours of no account.
2 When they see *it*, they shall be troubled with terrible fear,
And shall be amazed at the marvel of his salvation.
3 They shall say within themselves repenting,
And for distress of spirit shall they groan,
This was he whom aforetime we had in derision,
And *made* a byword of reproach:
4 We fools accounted his life madness,
And his end without honour:
5 How was he numbered among sons of God!
And *how* is his lot among saints!
6 Verily we went astray from the way of truth,
And the light of righteousness shined not for us,
And the sun rose not for us.
7 We took our fill of the paths of lawlessness and destruction,
And we journeyed through trackless deserts,
But the way of the Lord we knew not.
8 What did our arrogancy profit us?
And what good have riches and vaunting brought us?
9 Those things all passed away as a shadow,
And as a message that runneth by:
10 As a ship passing through the billowy water,
Whereof, when it is gone by, there is no trace to be found,
Neither pathway of its keel in the billows:
11 Or as when a bird flieth through the air,
No token of *her* passage is found,
But the light wind, lashed with the stroke of her pinions,
And rent asunder with the violent rush of the moving wings, is passed through,
And afterwards no sign of *her* coming is found therein:
12 Or as when an arrow is shot at a mark,
The air disparted closeth up again immediately,
So that men know not where it passed through:
13 So we also, as soon as we were born, ceased to be;
And of virtue we had no sign to show,
But were utterly consumed in our wickedness.

V. 2. **When they see it.** Cf. 1 Enoch cviii. 15: 'And the sinners will cry aloud and see them (i. e. the righteous) as they shine, and they indeed will go where days and seasons are prescribed for them.'

4. **madness.** See ii. 15. The refusal to purchase material advantage at the price of apostasy.

6. **Verily,** ἄρα = 'as it now seems'. 'Hence it amounts sometimes to an expression of regret' (Donaldson, *Gk. Gr.*, p. 567).

7. **trackless deserts.** They now see that the 'primrose path of dalliance' is better described as 'a dry and weary land where no water is' (Ps. lxiii. 1).

knew: in a practical sense = 'pay heed to'. So frequently in the O. T. See especially Amos iii. 2, 'You only have I known (= regarded with favour) of all the nations of the earth'. See also Ps. i. 6.

9 ff. The images here used to denote the transitory nature of life are vivid and poetical: whether they are quite appropriate in the mouth of those in whom the agony of remorse is supposed to be working, is another question. The passage forms, however, an effective contrast to their defiant boasting in ch. ii.

12. **closeth,** ἀνελύθη. The active is used in ii. 1 and has been translated there as intransitive (see note). 'Various explanations are given of ἀνελύθη, but it seems most simple to take it in the sense of "returns" as ii. 1' (Deane). ἀνέλυσεν is read by 23 (V) and 253.

13. **ceased to be.** Another proof that the writer's view of life and death is spiritual.

At the end of *v.* 13 the Latin adds 'Talia dixerunt in inferno hi, qui peccaverunt'. This, if not genuine, is appropriate, as showing that the following verse is a reflection of the author and no part of the words of the ungodly.

14 Because the hope of the ungodly is like chaff carried off by the wind,
And like a thin spider's web driven away by a tempest;
And like smoke which is scattered by the wind,
And passeth away as the remembrance of a guest that tarrieth but a day.

The bliss of the righteous and the miserable fate of the ungodly.

15 But the righteous live for ever,
And in the Lord is their reward,
And the care for them with the Most High.
16 Therefore shall they receive a glorious kingdom,
And a diadem of beauty from the Lord's hand;
Because with his right hand shall he cover them,
And with his arm shall he shield them.
17 He shall take his jealousy as complete armour,
And shall make the *whole* creation his weapons for vengeance on *his* enemies:
18 He shall put on righteousness as a breastplate,
And shall take judgement unfeigned as a helmet;
19 He shall take holiness as an invincible shield,
20 And shall sharpen stern wrath for a sword:
And the world shall go forth with him to fight against *his* insensate *foes.*
21 Shafts of lightning shall fly with true aim,
And from the clouds, as from a well drawn bow, shall they leap to the mark.
22 And *as* from an engine of war shall be hurled hailstones full of wrath;
The water of the sea shall rage against them,
And rivers shall sternly overwhelm them;
23 A mighty blast shall encounter them,
And as a tempest shall it winnow them away:
So shall lawlessness make all the land desolate,
And their evil-doing shall overturn the thrones of princes.

Admonition to the rulers.

6 1 Hear therefore, ye kings, and understand;
Learn, ye judges of the ends of the earth:

14. **hope.** The object of their hope or that on which they found their hope, e.g. riches, &c.

spider's web. So Cursives 23, 106, reading ἀράχνη, and also R.V. margin. ℵ A B read πάχνη, 'hoar-frost', which is quite unsuitable. Some MSS. give ἄχνη, which was no doubt the reading of the Syriac (ܚܒܘܪܐ), and of the Latin *spuma*. Both πάχνη and ἄχνη can be explained from ἀράχνη better than ἀράχνη from the others. The strange mistranslation in LXX Ps. xc. 9 may be compared, τὰ ἔτη ἡμῶν ὡς ἀράχνη, 'our years are like a spider's web'.

16. **a glorious kingdom,** βασίλειον, occurs in i. 14 and here. In i. 14 it undoubtedly means kingdom, and there is no reason to adopt a different meaning here. In Dan. vii. 18 and 22 the kingdom is given to the saints.

17–23. These verses are not quite consistent with the similar passage in iii. 7 ff. There the righteous execute judgement on the ungodly: here, Jehovah Himself rouses the forces of Nature to fight against them. See Introd., p. 529.

17 *b*. See in note on xix. 18 the quotation there given from Philo.

18–20. Compare Eph. vi. 11–17, and see Introd., p. 527. The πανοπλία found both here and in St. Paul, which is taken by some scholars as conclusive evidence of direct connexion between the two writers, consisted of helmet, breastplate, greaves, and shield, as defensive, sword and lance as offensive armour.

18. **judgement unfeigned,** without respect of persons.

20. **stern,** or relentless, Greek ἀπότομος, also vi. 5, xi. 10, xii. 9, xviii. 15 and the adverb v. 22.

21. Possibly the rainbow is referred to: if so the translation should be, 'And from the well-drawn bow of the clouds' as in the Latin 'a bene curvato arcu nubium'. The association of Jahveh with a thunderstorm is frequent in Hebrew poetry, see Ps. lxxix. 17–20, xcvii. 3–5; Hab. iii.

15–23 *b*. This passage is 'eschatological'. 23 *c* suddenly brings the reader back to the present age.

23 *b*. Feldmann would omit ὡς on the authority of the Coptic. It is certainly better away. A 'mighty blast' is a tempest.

So shall lawlessness. The writer returns to the idea of i. 1. Those who follow these ungodly and lawless ways are in high positions in the community, and without any exaggeration may be addressed as judges and princes.

VI. The writer now apparently takes a wider outlook than in i. 1. Having dealt with the misdeeds of the governing body of the Jews in Alexandria, he turns in the manner of the prophets, e.g. Isa. viii. 9, Ps. ii. 10, to the rulers of the outside world. They too have a law which they have not kept, for the transgression of which they will be punished. It is not necessary to suppose that the writer ever thought of his words reaching the 'rulers of the ends of the earth', any more than Isaiah or the writer of Psalm ii imagined that their words would come to the ears of the foreign nations or rulers whom they apostrophized. The Jewish magnates at Alexandria are still the real object of the address.

1. The Latin begins the chapter with the words 'Melior est sapientia quam vires, et vir prudens quam fortis', a good introduction to the section.

2 Give ear, ye that have dominion over much people,
And make your boast in multitudes of nations.
3 Because your dominion was given you from the Lord,
And your sovereignty from the Most High;
Who shall search out your works,
And shall make inquisition of your counsels:
4 Because being officers of his kingdom ye did not judge aright,
Neither kept ye the law, nor walked after the counsel of God.
5 Awfully and swiftly shall he come upon you;
For a stern judgement befalleth them that be in high places:
6 For the man of low estate may be pardoned in mercy,
But mighty men shall be searched out mightily.
7 For the Sovereign Lord of all will not regard any *man's* person,
Neither will he stand in awe of greatness;
Because it is he that made *both* small and great,
And alike he taketh thought for all;
8 But strict is the scrutiny that cometh upon the powerful.
9 Unto you therefore, O princes, are my words,
That ye may learn wisdom and not fall away.
10 For they that have kept holily the things that are holy shall *themselves* be accounted holy;
And they that have been taught them shall find what to answer;
11 Set your desire therefore upon my words;
Long for *them*, and ye shall be instructed.

Wisdom desires to be found.

12 Wisdom is radiant and fadeth not away;
And easily is she beheld of them that love her,
And found of them that seek her.
13 She forestalleth them that desire *to know her*, making herself first known.
14 He that riseth up early to *seek* her shall have no toil,
For he shall find her sitting at his gates.
15 For to think upon her is perfection of understanding,
And he that keepeth vigil for her sake shall quickly be free from care.
16 For she goeth about, seeking them that are worthy of her,
And in their paths she appeareth unto them graciously,
And in every purpose she meeteth them.

The Sorites.

17 For her true beginning is desire of instruction;
And the care for instruction is love of *her*;

6. **searched out,** Greek ἐτάζω. The same word in ii. 19 probably means 'torture', so perhaps the A. V. and Latin are right in their interpretation, 'tormented', 'tormenta patientur'.

7. **regard any man's person,** R. V. 'refrain himself for'. The Greek ὑποστελεῖται πρόσωπον here is probably an echo of Deut. i. 17 LXX, where ὑποστείλῃ πρόσωπον is used to translate the Hebrew הִכִּיר פנים, to show partiality to any one. The injunction to Moses to make no difference between small and great appears in the same context.

12. This description of Wisdom is based on Prov. viii.

And found. This line looks so much like a variant of Prov. viii. 17 that some scholars have suspected it of being an insertion. But the writer probably had the chapter in Proverbs before his mind, so in spite of its omission in B* it may be genuine. It is found in ℵ B[a] and A.

15. **to think upon her.** Through the contemplation of Wisdom, a man gains a high moral standard: cf. 'His (i.e. Plato's) theory of education is dominated by the thought that the mind itself inevitably "imitates" the character of the things it habitually contemplates. Just because the aspiration after wisdom is the fundamental expression of the mind's true nature, it cannot be followed persistently without resulting in a transfiguration of our whole character' (A. E. Taylor, *Plato*, p. 35).

17–20. An instance of the logical figure called Sorites, or Chain-inference, of which the Stoics were very fond (Zeller, *Stoics*, p. 216 note). *v.* 20 contains the main conclusion consisting of the first and last step: Desire for wisdom promoteth to a kingdom. But the first premiss is not expressed in *v.* 17 and must be supplied, and another member is omitted in *v.* 19.

[The desire for wisdom is the beginning of wisdom;]
17. The true beginning of wisdom is the desire for instruction;
The care for instruction is love of wisdom;

18 And love *of her* is observance of her laws;
And to give heed to *her* laws is the assurance of incorruption;
19 And incorruption bringeth near unto God;
20 So then desire of wisdom promoteth to a kingdom.

Solomon promises to declare the nature of wisdom.

21 If therefore ye delight in thrones and sceptres, ye princes of peoples,
Honour wisdom, that ye may reign for ever.
22 But what wisdom is, and how she came *to me*, I will declare,
And I will not hide *her* mysteries from you;
But I will trace *her* out from her first beginning
And bring the knowledge of her into clear light,
And I will not pass by the truth;
23 Neither indeed will I take pining envy for my companion,
Because envy shall have no fellowship with wisdom.
24 But a multitude of wise men is salvation to the world,
And an understanding king is tranquillity to *his* people.
25 Wherefore be ye instructed by my words, and *thereby* shall ye profit.

Solomon at first like other men: wisdom given to him in answer to prayer.

7 1 I myself also am mortal, like to all,
And am sprung from one born of the earth, *the man* first formed,
2 And in the womb of a mother was I moulded into flesh in the time of ten months,
Being compacted in blood of the seed of man and pleasure that came with sleep.
3 And I also, when I was born, drew in the common air,
And fell upon the kindred earth,
Uttering, like all, for my first voice, the self-same wail:
4 In swaddling clothes was I nursed, and with *watchful* cares.
5 For no king had any other first beginning;
6 But all men have one entrance into life, and a like departure.
7 For this cause I prayed, and understanding was given me:
I called upon *God*, and there came to me a spirit of wisdom.

The value of wisdom.

8 I preferred her before sceptres and thrones,
And riches I esteemed nothing in comparison of her.
9 Neither did I liken to her any priceless gem,
Because all the gold *of the earth* in her sight is but a little sand,
And silver shall be accounted as clay before her.

18. Love of wisdom is the keeping of her laws;
The keeping of her laws is immortality;
19. Immortality bringeth near to God;
[To be near to God is to be a king;]
So the desire for wisdom promoteth to a kingdom.

There is remarkably little deviation from the exact logical form: what there is is justified by the poetical character of the composition.

22. **to me.** Ewald and Bois understand μοί after ἐγένετο.

from her first beginning. This (the A. V. and Latin) is the better translation; not 'from the beginning of creation', R. V.; as is seen from vii. 5, 'no king had any other first beginning,' where the Greek is practically the same.

mysteries. The Alexandrian Jews regarded their syncretism of Greek philosophy and Hebrew religion as a mystery, which, however, they were anxious to propagate in contrast to the heathen who kept their mysteries secret. Cf. Philo, *de Sacrificantibus*, 12 'Why, ye initiates, if these things are good and profitable, do ye shut yourselves up in darkness and benefit three or four only, instead of bringing the advantages into the market-place for all men, so that every one might enjoy a better and happier life? For envy does not dwell with virtue.' See vii. 13.

23. Cf. the last clause of the preceding quotation which strikingly resembles 23 *b*. The pride of the philosophers is no doubt referred to and perhaps the greed of the Sophists. For the Sophists see Philo, *de Congressu*, 23.

24. **a multitude of wise men.** This is a sounder view than that of Ecclesiastes i. 18, 'In much wisdom is much grief: and he that increaseth knowledge increaseth sorrow.'

VII. 1. **first formed.** The word πρωτόπλαστος first occurs here.

2. **was I moulded.** The man is here identified with the body in contrast to the soul which pre-existed, see viii. 19.

3. **kindred,** ὁμοιοπαθής. This is the usual significance of the word. But the commentators point out that the affinity is not between Solomon and the earth but between Solomon and the rest of mankind. Grimm gives 'equally trodden by all'. It is, perhaps, another instance of the author's free use of the language.

10 Above health and comeliness I loved her,
And I chose to have her rather than light,
Because her bright shining is never laid to sleep.
11 But with her there came to me all good things together,
And in her hands innumerable riches:
12 And I rejoiced over *them* all because wisdom leadeth them;
Though I knew not that she was the mother of them.
13 As I learned without guile, I impart without grudging;
I do not hide her riches.
14 For she is unto men a treasure that faileth not,
And they that use it obtain friendship with God,
Commended *to him* by the gifts which come through discipline.

Solomon's own great knowledge came from this gift of wisdom.

15 But to me may God give to speak with judgement,
And to conceive thoughts worthy of what hath been given *me*;
Because himself is one that guideth even wisdom and correcteth the wise.
16 For in his hand are both we and our words;
All understanding, and *all* acquaintance with divers crafts.
17 For he hath given me an unerring knowledge of the things that are,
To know the constitution of the world, and the operation of the elements;
18 The beginning and end and middle of times,
The alternations of the solstices and the changes of seasons,
19 The circuits of years and the positions of stars;
20 The natures of living creatures and the ragings of wild beasts,
The powers of spirits and the thoughts of men,
The diversities of plants and the virtues of roots:
21 All things that are either secret or manifest I learned,
22 For she that is the artificer of all things taught me, *even* wisdom.

The attributes of wisdom: her source: her activity.

For there is in her a spirit quick of understanding, holy,
Alone in kind, manifold,
Subtil, freely moving,

11. Cf. Matt. vi. 33, 'and all these things shall be added unto you.'

12. **mother**, *γενέτιν* (hapax); ℵ and B give *γένεσιν*, but *γένεσις* has already been used in vi. 22 and again in *v.* 5 in the abstract, and therefore is hardly likely to be used here with a concrete meaning. Wisdom is the 'mother' or root of all 'good things', not merely the chief. Plato's classification of the Virtues is rejected. See on viii. 7.

13. **without grudging**. See notes on vi. 22 and 23.

14. **friendship with God**. See on *v.* 27.

given. These gifts would be called 'graces' by the Christian. The R. V. takes the gifts as offered to God to win His favour.

15. **judgement**, or as R.V. margin, 'according to his (i. e. God's) mind', *κατὰ γνώμην*.

what hath been given. There are three readings here given by Feldmann. (1) *δεδομένων*: B, and three cursives, including 248; (2) *λεγομένων*: ℵ A, six cursives, Syriac and other versions; (3) *διδομένων*: comp. Latin (*quae mihi dantur*), Coptic, and Ethiopic. *λεγομένων* is generally rejected. *διδομένων* is preferred by Grimm and Feldmann. This reading, as Farrar points out, emphasizes the fact that the gift of Wisdom is continuous.

17–20. In these verses the writer shows his knowledge of the technical terms of Greek science. He highly esteems all branches of learning, including astronomy; which Philo, in spite of the remarkable contributions made by Alexandrian astronomers to the advancement of the science, strangely depreciated (Drummond, *Philo*, i. 264).

17. **things that are**, *τῶν ὄντων γνῶσιν* = 'philosophy'.

constitution of the world = 'cosmology'.

18. **beginning**, &c., **of times** = 'chronology'.

alternations, &c. = 'astronomy'.

19. **circuits**, i. e. cycles, e. g. the metonic and solar cycles.

20. **natures**, &c. = zoology.

powers of spirits. Latin gives *vim ventorum*, but Josephus, *Ant.* viii. 2, says that Solomon is said to have had power over spirits, so that demonology and not meteorology may be meant.

thoughts of men. The desires and passions which agitate the soul; part of the modern science of psychology.

22. The writer here takes care to emphasize his belief that the action of God is only indirect; thus differing from the presentation in the second part.

artificer, *τεχνῖτις*. It is suggested by Toy, following Grimm, that this is founded on Prov. viii. 30, where Wisdom is said to be אמון and where the LXX gives *ἁρμόζουσα*. It is doubtful, however, whether this can be accepted. It would involve the correction of LXX by the writer.

Clear in utterance, unpolluted,
Distinct, that cannot be harmed,
Loving what is good, keen, unhindered,
23 Beneficent, loving toward man,
Steadfast, sure, free from care,
All-powerful, all-surveying,
And penetrating through all spirits
That are quick of understanding, pure, subtil:
24 For wisdom is more mobile than any motion;
Yea, she pervadeth and penetrateth all things by reason of her pureness.
25 For she is a breath of the power of God,
And a clear effluence of the glory of the Almighty;
Therefore can nothing defiled find entrance into her.
26 For she is an effulgence from everlasting light
And an unspotted mirror of the working of God,
And an image of his goodness.
27 And she, though but one, hath power to do all things;
And remaining in herself, reneweth all things:
And from generation to generation passing into holy souls
She maketh them friends of God and prophets.
28 For nothing doth God love save him that dwelleth with wisdom.
29 For she is fairer than the sun,
And above all the constellations of the stars:
Being compared with light, she is found *to be* before it;

22, 23. Wisdom has twenty-one qualities, the number no doubt being purposely chosen as a multiple of the two sacred numbers, seven and three. Philo calls Wisdom *πολυώνυμος*.

Grimm quotes a fragment ascribed to Cleanthes the Stoic: *τἀγαθὸν ἐρωτᾷς μ' οἷον ἐστ'; ἄκουε δή· τεταγμένον, δίκαιον, ὅσιον, εὐσεβές, κρατοῦν ἑαυτοῦ, χρήσιμον, καλόν, δέον, αὐστηρόν, αὐθεκάστατον, αἰεὶ συμφέρον, ἄφοβον, ἄλυπον, λυσιτελές, ἀνώδυνον, ὠφέλιμον, εὐάρεστον, ὁμολογούμενον, εὐκλεές, ἄτυφον, ἐπιμελές, πρᾶον, σφοδρόν, χρονιζόμενον, ἄμεμπτον, αἰεὶ διαμένον.*

22. **in her,** *ἐν αὐτῇ* ℵ B Latin. *αὐτή* = 'She is a spirit' A. If *ἐν αὐτῇ* is right this is the nearest approach the author makes towards giving a distinct personality to Wisdom. But in ix. 17 he plainly makes Wisdom equivalent to the Holy Spirit.

quick of understanding. *νοερός*, a technical term of the Stoics applied to the world soul, see on i. 7. Other Stoical terms in this passage are *φιλάνθρωπος* (23), *χωρεῖν* (23), *διήκειν* (24), *διοικεῖν* (viii. 1). Three of these are found in one passage of Dio. Laert. quoted by Ritter and Preller, § 513. *ἀπόρροια* ('effluence') is also a philosophical term.

Alone in kind = 'the only one of its kind', *μονογενές*; **manifold**, *πολυμερές*, are opposed to one another and correspond to the Stoic idea of the world soul and its different manifestations. Compare St. Paul on the Holy Spirit, 1 Cor. xii. 4.

keen, unhindered. These words go together. Most commentators compare the *λόγος τομεύς* of Philo which divides, arranges, and unites the unarranged matter of chaos. Heinisch (p. 134) refuses to accept this.

23. **free from care,** *ἀμέριμνον*. This may be equivalent to the Aristotelian word *αὐτάρκης* applied to virtue in *Ethics Nic*. i. 7. 6.

subtil. R. V. 'most subtil', Latin *subtilis*, Greek *λεπτοτάτων*. *λεπτός* probably = 'ethereal'. In *v.* 22 Wisdom is said to be a *πνεῦμα λεπτόν*. Here it is said to penetrate spirits like itself intellectual, pure, and *λεπτοτάτων*. This can hardly mean that the spirits through which Wisdom penetrates must be *λεπτά* in a superlative degree, while Wisdom possesses the quality only in a positive degree. If it is not a mere rhetorical use of the superlative it must mean spirits which have the quality in as high a degree as is possible for men to possess it: an elative use of the superlative.

26. **effulgence,** *ἀπαύγασμα*. Cf. Heb. i. 3. The word can mean either (1) effulgence, radiance, or (2) reflection. The word 'effluence', *ἀπόρροια*, *v.* 26, upholds the first, the words 'unspotted mirror' uphold the second. Since the word 'mirror' seems to be in parallelism with *ἀπαύγασμα* the meaning 'reflection' is the more probable. Heinisch (p. 133) decides for 'effulgence' on the ground of Sir. i. 9, where it is said of Wisdom that God 'poured her out upon all his works'. So does Westcott on Heb. i. 3. Grimm and Gregg favour the rendering 'reflection'.

27. **all things.** Omnipotence is here ascribed to Wisdom.

remaining in herself, &c. Bois (p. 391) argues that this line contains a philosophical idea to be traced to Heraclitus or the Stoics. The primaeval fire, or the Logos, remains the same in its essence in spite of all its various manifestations in nature (see note on *πολυμερές*, *v.* 22). Grimm and Heinisch are content with a reference to Ps. cii. 27–28.

friends of God. See *v.* 15. Deissmann, *Bib. St.*, p. 167, thinks the word means favourites. 'Friend was the title of honour given at the court of the Ptolemies to the highest royal officials.' '*φίλος θεοῦ* denotes high honour in the sight of God, nothing more nor less.' But the thought was not peculiar to Egypt. If Heinisch is right in seeing direct connexion between ch. viii and the fable of the choice of Hercules (see note on viii. 2) the words may be an echo of *δι' ἐμὲ φίλοι μὲν θεοῖς ὄντες* in that passage. Compare also Plato, *Leg*. iv. 716 D *ὁ μὲν σώφρων θεῷ φίλος*. Philodemus (about 50 B.C.) quotes a *Stoic* saying 'that the wise are the friends of God and God of the wise' (Zeller, *Stoics*, p. 254 note).

and prophets. The Stoics also believed in prophecy and said that only a wise man could be a prophet. Cic. *De Div*. ii. 63 'Stoici negant quemquam nisi sapientem divinum esse posse.'

30 For to the light *of day* succeedeth night,
But against wisdom evil doth not prevail;
8 1 But she reacheth from one end *of the world* to the other with full strength,
And ordereth all things well.

Solomon desired wisdom for a bride to assist him both in public and private matters: but only God could give her.

2 Her I loved and sought out from my youth,
And I sought to take her for my bride.
And I became enamoured of her beauty.
3 She proclaimeth *her* noble birth in that it is given her to live with God,
And the Sovereign Lord of all loved her.
4 For she is initiated into the knowledge of God,
And she chooseth out *for him* his works.
5 But if riches are a desired possession in life,
What is richer than wisdom, which worketh all things?
6 And if understanding worketh,
Who more than wisdom is an artificer of the things that are?
7 And if a man loveth righteousness,
The fruits of wisdom's labour are virtues,
For she teacheth self-control and understanding, righteousness, and courage;
And there is nothing in life for men more profitable than these.
8 And if a man longeth even for much experience,
She knoweth the things of old, and divineth the things to come:
She understandeth subtilties of speeches and interpretations of dark sayings:
She foreseeth signs and wonders, and the issues of seasons and times.
9 I determined therefore to take her unto me to live with me,
Knowing that she is one who would give me good *thoughts* for counsel,
And encourage me in cares and grief.
10 Because of her I shall have glory among multitudes,
And honour in the sight of elders, though I be young.
11 I shall be found of a quick discernment when I give judgement,
And in the presence of princes I shall be admired.
12 When I am silent, they shall wait for me;
And when I open my lips, they shall give heed unto me;

VIII. 1. **ordereth,** διοικεῖ. A favourite term of the Stoics. They said τὸν δὲ κόσμον διοικεῖσθαι κατὰ νοῦν καὶ πρόνοιαν (Dio. Laert. 133, in Ritter and Preller, § 493).

2–18. In every one of these verses except 14 Heinisch finds an echo of the speech of Virtue in the apologue of the choice of Hercules in Xenophon, *Mem.* ii. 1. The fable was no doubt well known, but Heinisch insists that Pseudo-Sol. had a first-hand acquaintance with Xenophon's work. The passage runs as follows:—

Virtue says: 'I associate with gods and I associate with men who are good (cf. *v.* 3, it is given her to live with God), and no noble work divine or human is done without me (cf. *v.* 4, she is initiated into the knowledge of God, and she chooseth out for him his works). I am a beloved co-worker with artificers (cf. *v.* 6, Who more than wisdom is an artificer?) . . . a steadfast ally in the work of war (cf. *v.* 15, . . . I shall show myself a good ruler, and in war courageous), and the best companion in friendship (*v.* 18, in her friendship is good delight). . . . And the young rejoice in the praises of their elders, and those who are older are delighted with honour from the young (cf. *v.* 10). And when their destined end shall come they will not lie unhonoured in forgetfulness, but be celebrated in song and flourish in memory for all time' (cf. *vv.* 13 and 17).

In this case, as in that of the connexion between Rom. ix and Wisd. xii, it should be noticed that the resemblances are all found in one continuous passage in both authors.

3. **proclaimeth,** R.V. 'glorifieth'. δοξάζω = to cause the dignity and worth of some person or thing to become manifest and acknowledged, cf. 2 Thess. iii. 1. See Thayer's edition of Grimm's *N. T. Lexicon.* Does a man desire noble birth in a bride? Wisdom is noble enough to be the bride of God. Philo (*de Cherub.* 13. 14) calls God the husband of Wisdom.

6. ἐργάζεται has a pregnant meaning 'to work effectually or successfully'. If φρόνησις—earthly wisdom—works with success, much more does σοφία, the divine wisdom.

7. **self-control,** &c. The four cardinal virtues; a well-known philosophical classification originating with Plato and taken up by the Stoics. Zeller (iii. 2, p. 230, note) affirms direct Stoic influence here, since Chrysippus made Wisdom the root of the four virtues, whereas Plato made Wisdom one of them. See also note on vii. 12.

8. **dark sayings,** parables or allegories. The writer probably had Prov. i. 6 in mind, where the αἰνίγματα of the wise are spoken of.

signs and wonders. Probably a reference to the prediction of eclipses, &c., by astronomers.

12. See Job xxix. 9.

And if I continue speaking, they shall lay their hand upon their mouth.
13 Because of her I shall have immortality,
And leave behind an eternal memory to them that come after me.
14 I shall govern peoples,
And nations shall be subjected to me.
15 Dread princes shall fear me when they hear *of me*:
Among *my* people I shall show myself a good *ruler*, and in war courageous.
16 When I come into my house, I shall find rest with her;
For converse with her hath no bitterness,
And to live with her hath no pain, but gladness and joy.
17 When I considered these things in myself,
And took thought in my heart how that in kinship unto wisdom is immortality,
18 And in her friendship is good delight,
And in the labours of her hands is wealth that faileth not,
And in assiduous communing with her is understanding,
And great renown in having fellowship with her words,
I went about seeking how to take her unto myself.
19 Now I was a child good by nature and a good soul fell to my lot;
20 Nay rather, being good, I came into a body undefiled.
21 But perceiving that I could not possess *wisdom* except God gave *her* to me
(Yea and to know by whom the grace is given, this *too* came of understanding),
I pleaded with the Lord and besought him,
And with my whole heart I said,

He prays to God for this gift, pleading his own human weakness and the greatness of his task.

9 1 O God of the fathers, and Lord who keepest thy mercy,
Who madest all things by thy word;
2 And by thy wisdom formedst man,
That he should have dominion over the creatures that were made by thee,
3 And rule the world in holiness and righteousness,
And execute judgement in uprightness of soul;
4 Give me wisdom, her that sitteth by thee on thy throne;
And reject me not from among thy servants;
5 Because I am thy bondman and the son of thy handmaid,
A man weak and short-lived,
And of small power to understand judgement and laws.
6 For even if a man be perfect among the sons of men,
Yet if the wisdom that cometh from thee be not with him, he shall be held in no account.
7 Thou didst choose me before *my brethren* to be king of thy people,
And to do judgement for thy sons and daughters.
8 Thou gavest command to build a sanctuary in thy holy mountain,
And an altar in the city of thy habitation,
A copy of the holy tabernacle which thou preparedst aforehand from the beginning.

17. Wisdom is immortal. Those akin to her share her immortality. But in xv. 3 knowledge of the might of God is immortality. It may, however, be said that this knowledge could only arise from kinship with or the possession of Wisdom.

19. See Introd., p. 531, for the doctrine of pre-existence in the book. For the difference between the Jewish and Greek conception of pre-existence, see Harnack, *History of Dogma*, vol. i, pp. 318 ff.

20. This verse is a correction of *v.* 19. If *v.* 19 stood alone it would mean that the writer identified the Ego with the body or perhaps with the compound organism body and soul. But, strictly speaking, the soul is the Ego, hence the correction. In *v.* 19, as in vii. 2, the writer uses ordinary everyday language such as we find in the second part, 'the soul which was lent him', xv. 8, or in the N. T., 'this night thy soul shall be required of thee' (Luke xii. 20), where the soul seems to be regarded as distinct from the personality. It is generally accepted that the writer deliberately corrects himself in view of his doctrine of the pre-existence of the soul; but see Porter. Cf. note on xv. 8.

21. **possess wisdom,** i. e. ἐγκρατής in the sense of the Latin *compos*, understanding σοφίας. Grimm takes it in the sense of 'continent', but all other moderns take it as in the text.

IX. 1. **by thy word . . . by thy wisdom.** We may, perhaps, see here the truth of the statement that the writer of Wisdom was a forerunner of Philo. Word and Wisdom are here synonymous. Our author chose Wisdom, Philo chose the Word as the intermediary between God and the world.

3. God's purpose in Creation beneficent, see i. 13.

8. **A copy.** In Ps. cxxxv. 16, Exod. xxv. 9 we have the idea of heavenly archetypes of certain things on earth. This seems to have been a common Semitic idea. The temple of the goddess Nina was built by Gudea, King of

9 And with thee is wisdom, which knoweth thy works,
And was present when thou wast making the world,
And which understandeth what is pleasing in thine eyes,
And what is right according to thy commandments.
10 Send her forth out of the holy heavens,
And from the throne of thy glory bid her come,
That being present with me she may toil *with me*,
And *that* I may learn what is well-pleasing before thee.
11 For she knoweth all things and hath understanding *thereof*,
And in my doings she shall guide me in *ways of* soberness,
And she shall guard me in her glory.
12 And *so* shall my works be acceptable,
And I shall judge thy people righteously,
And I shall be worthy of my father's throne.
13 For what man shall know the counsel of God?
Or who shall conceive what the Lord willeth?
14 For the thoughts of mortals are timorous,
And our devices are prone to fail.
15 For a corruptible body weigheth down the soul,
And the earthy frame lieth heavy on the mind that is full of cares.
16 And hardly do we divine the things that are on earth,
And the things that are close at hand we find with labour;
But the things that are in the heavens who *ever yet* traced out?
17 And who *ever* gained knowledge of thy counsel, except thou gavest wisdom,
And sentest thy holy spirit from on high?
18 And it was thus that the ways of them which are on earth were corrected,
And men were taught the things that are pleasing unto thee;
And through wisdom were they saved.

The work of wisdom in history from Adam to Moses.

10 1 She guarded to the end the first formed father of the world, that was created alone,
And delivered him out of his transgression,

Lagash (3000 B.C.), after he had been shown a model of it in a dream (Maspero, *Dawn of Civilization*, p. 610). It is, therefore, not necessary to resort to the Platonic doctrine of ideas as Gfrörer does. Grimm prefers to take ἁγία σκηνή, as heaven itself. The temple would then represent the higher just as the high-priest's garments represented the lower world. Cf. xviii. 24.

9. Here Wisdom is only present as a spectator at the Creation in accordance with Prov. viii. 30. His devotion to Scripture in this place overcomes the writer's philosophical theories.

11. **glory.** The meaning of this is difficult. The Latin cuts the knot by translating *potentia*. Certain scholars follow this and refer to Rom. vi. 4. If, however, 'guard' can be taken as carrying on the idea in 'guide' in the preceding line, then 'glory' may, as Grimm suggests, refer to the brightness which Wisdom sheds over the path of her followers. As the author places great stress on the superiority of Wisdom to Light (see vi. 12, vii. 10, 26, 29) this interpretation seems most probable.

15. The writer was no doubt somewhat influenced by the Greek idea of the inherent evil of matter, though he probably did not accept it. It is quite possible to admit that the body is the occasion of evil without accepting the dualistic theory that it is the cause of evil. For the connexion of this verse with Plato's *Phaedo* see Introduction, p. 532.

cares. The cares are mentioned in the next verse. Grimm prefers the rendering which is given in R.V. margin, 'that museth on many things.' The thought is a common one in literature, sacred and profane. See St. Paul, 2 Cor. v. 4, 'For we that are in this tabernacle do groan, being burdened'; Seneca, *Ep.* 65 'Corpus hoc animi pondus ac poena est.' Philo made the body equivalent to a tomb, but according to Ritter and Preller, § 46, note b, he did not, as is sometimes said, get this from Heraclitus: 'Sed quod aiunt σῶμα esse quasi σῆμα, non est ab Her. inventum.'

16. **hardly.** If the mind were not weighed down by the body, knowledge would be easily acquired.

close at hand, τὰ ἐν χερσίν. ℵ 23 read ποσίν, also the Armenian according to Feldmann.

17. Here 'thy holy spirit' is plainly equivalent to Wisdom: this may have some bearing on the reading of vii. 22.

18. **through wisdom were they saved.** Houbigant divided the book here, and it must be admitted that it is a very good ending. It is in striking contrast to the ending of ch. xix.

X. 1. **alone.** According to Gen. ii. 7, Adam was created before anything was ready for him, therefore he required protection. The ingenious emendation of Bois, οὐ μόνον, the οὐ having dropped out after κόσμου, is accepted by Siegfried and Heinisch (p. 147). He would translate 'Wisdom not only guarded and delivered, but gave him', &c. For τέ used in this way he quotes Esther v. 3 (Bois, p. 399).

his, ἰδίου. This is doubtless, as already pointed out by Grimm, an instance of the 'use of the exhausted ἴδιος, which is confirmed by the Apocryphal books, especially by those in Greek from the first' (Deissmann, *Bible Studies*, pp. 123–4). In ch. xviii, *vv.* 13 and 21, there seem to be undoubted examples of this use. Opinions may differ as to the other cases, ii. 23, xi. 13, xii. 23, xvi. 23, xvii. 11, xix. 6, 13, 20, though Deissmann says the best course is 'to take

2 And gave him strength to get dominion over all things.
3 But when an unrighteous man fell away from her in his anger,
He perished himself in the rage wherewith he slew his brother.
4 And when for his cause the earth was drowning with a flood,
Wisdom again saved it,
Guiding the righteous man's course by a poor piece of wood.

5 Moreover, when nations consenting together in wickedness had been confounded,
Wisdom knew the righteous man, and preserved him blameless unto God,
And kept him strong when his heart yearned toward his child.

6 While the ungodly were perishing, wisdom delivered a righteous man,
When he fled from the fire that descended out of heaven on Pentapolis.
7 To whose wickedness a smoking waste still witnesseth,
And plants bearing fair fruit that cometh not to ripeness;
(*Yea and* a disbelieving soul hath a memorial *there*, a pillar of salt *still* standing.)
8 For having passed wisdom by,
Not only were they disabled from recognizing the things which are good,
But they also left behind them for *human* life a monument of their folly;
So that wherein they had offended could not but be known:
9 But wisdom delivered out of troubles those that waited on her.

10 When a righteous man was a fugitive from a brother's wrath, wisdom guided him in straight paths;
She showed him God's kingdom, and gave him knowledge of holy things;
She prospered him in his toils, and multiplied the fruits of his labour;
11 When in their covetousness *men* dealt hardly with him,
She stood by him and made him rich;
12 She guarded him from enemies,
And from those that lay in wait she kept him safe,
And in his sore conflict she guided him to victory,
That he might know that godliness is more powerful than all.

13 When a righteous man was sold, wisdom forsook him not,
But from sin she delivered him;
She went down with him into a dungeon,
14 And in bonds she left him not,
Till she brought him the sceptre of a kingdom,
And authority over those that dealt tyrannously with him;
She showed them also to be false that had accused him,
And gave him eternal glory.

ἴδιος in the old sense only when the context absolutely requires it'. See also Bois, p. 409. In xix. 13 ἴδιος is fortified by αὐτῶν and is certainly emphatic.

3. This is generally taken to mean that Cain underwent spiritual death when he slew his brother. Compare v. 13, 'As soon as we were born we ceased to be.' The writer's idea of life and death is a spiritual one. We find the same idea in Philo: 'Cain rose up and killed himself. . . . For the soul which destroys out of itself the virtue-loving and God-loving principle has died to the life of virtue' (*Quod det. pot.* § 14). There are two traditions as to the death of Cain, one that he was slain accidentally by Lamech who was blind, the other that he was overwhelmed in the fall of a house. See note on xi. 16.

4. **for his cause.** Like the author of the 'prophetic' narrative in Genesis, Pseudo-Sol. considers the evil on the earth before the flood to be due to the descendants of Cain.

5. **knew**, reading ἔγνω ℵ A C Latin and Syriac. B gives εὗρεν.

the righteous man. Abraham.

6. Lot.

7. Cf. 'Apples of Sodom'. See Josephus in his account of the Dead Sea, *Bell. Iud.* iv. 8. 4.

still standing. Josephus says 'I have seen it, for it remains even now' (*Ant.* i. 11. 4). 'Robinson (ii. 108) remarks that during the rainy season such pillars are constantly in the process of formation and destruction' (Driver, in *Hastings' DB*, vol. iii, p. 152).

8. **disabled**, i. e. they incur 'judicial blindness'.

10. Jacob.

holy things, or holy ones, i. e. the angels ascending and descending.

12. **guided him to victory.** Latin 'dedit ut vinceret'. R. V. 'watched as judge', but see βραβεύω in Liddell and Scott, ii. 2. The Syriac agrees in this interpretation.

13. Joseph.

15 She delivered a holy people and a blameless seed from a nation of oppressors.
16 She entered into the soul of a servant of the Lord,
And withstood terrible kings in wonders and signs.
17 She rendered unto holy men a reward of their toils;
She guided them along a marvellous way,
And became unto them a covering in the daytime,
And a light of stars through the night.
18 She brought them over the Red sea,
And led them through much water;
19 But their enemies she drowned,
And out of the bottom of the deep she cast them up.
20 Therefore the righteous spoiled the ungodly;
And they sang praise to thy holy name, O Lord,
And extolled with one accord thy hand that fought for them:
21 Because wisdom opened the mouth of the dumb,
And made the tongues of babes to speak clearly.

11 1 She prospered their works by the hand of a holy prophet.

Contrast between the fortunes of Israel and Egypt; the instrument of punishment to the Egyptians became the instrument of benefit to Israel.

2 They journeyed through a desert without inhabitant,
And in trackless regions they pitched their tents.
3 They withstood enemies, and repelled foes.
4 They thirsted, and they called upon thee,
And there was given them water out of the flinty rock,
And healing of their thirst out of the hard stone.
5 For by what things their foes were punished,
By these they in their need were benefited.
6 When *the enemy* were troubled with clotted blood instead of a river's ever-flowing fountain,
To punish the decree for the slaying of babes,
7 Thou gavest them abundant water beyond all hope,
8 Having shown *them* by the thirst which they had suffered how thou didst punish the adversaries.
9 For when they were tried, albeit but in mercy chastened,
They learned how the ungodly were tormented, being judged with wrath:
10 For these, as a father, admonishing them, thou didst prove;
But those, as a stern king, condemning them, thou didst search out.
11 Yea and whether they were far off *from the righteous* or near *them*, they were alike distressed;
12 For a double grief took hold on them,
And a groaning at the remembrance of things past.

15. **a holy people and a blameless seed.** This idealization of Israel is in strong contrast with Exod. xxxii. 9, Deut. ix. 6, and other similar passages. But the moral and spiritual superiority of the Jews to the heathen in the first century B.C. (see Bousset, *Rel. des Jud.*, p. 83) would naturally be carried back to their ancestors in a heightened degree.

17. This is the strongest instance of allegory in the book. It is quite of a piece with 'Philo's habit of allegorizing an angel into a Logos' (Drummond, ii, p. 268).

20. **spoiled.** According to a tradition mentioned by Josephus (*Ant.* ii. 16. 6) the arms of the Egyptians were washed up on the shore and so provided the Israelites with weapons.

21. **dumb.** In Exod. iv. 10 Moses says 'I am slow of speech'.

XI. 2. Here the second part of the book begins. In *v.* 7 the writer speaks of the direct action of God, and continues to do so in *vv.* 10, 15, 17. In *v.* 20, it is true, he speaks of 'Justice', and the 'breath of thy power': but reverts to the idea of the direct action of the Deity. Wisdom has disappeared and with it the Greek view of God as transcendant.

4. **called upon thee.** The writer prefers to follow Ps. cvii. 5 rather than Exod. xvii. 1–7.

ἀκρότομος = 'abrupt', 'precipitous': the LXX translation of חלמיש ('flint') in Deut. viii. 15. This shows direct dependence on the LXX.

5. The principles enunciated here and in *v.* 16 (appropriateness of retribution) are dwelt upon at considerable length in the rest of the book. The first point (elaborated in cc. xvi–xix), viz. that what injured the Egyptians benefited Israel, seems to be peculiar to the author. It appears later in Philo (*Vita Contem.* cii), 'For by the commandment of God the sea became to one party the cause of safety and to the other that of utter destruction'.

6. The R.V. margin says 'The text of this verse is perhaps corrupt'. B and C upheld by the Latin read ταραχθέντες: ℵ A ταραχθέντος. If the nominative is read, a subject must be supplied—'the enemy', as in R.V.; if the genitive, the translation must be 'Instead of a perennial fountain of a river turbid with clotted blood thou gavest them', &c. R. V. (i. e. Hort) takes the first; Grimm, Feldmann, and others adopt the second.

12. **things past**, reading παρελθόντων ℵ A. παρελθουσῶν is given by B and C agreeing with μνημῶν. Feldmann has a long discussion of the passage: he would emend to μνήμονας agreeing with αὐτούς.

13 For when they heard that by the very means wherewith they had been punished the others had been benefited,
They felt *the presence* of the Lord;
14 For him who long before was driven forth in hatred they left off mocking:
And marvelled at the events that had come to pass,
Having thirsted in another manner than the righteous.

Appropriateness of retribution shown to be the purpose of God.

15 But in requital of the senseless imaginings of their unrighteousness,
Wherein they were led astray to worship irrational reptiles and wretched vermin,
Thou didst send upon them a multitude of irrational creatures for vengeance;
16 That they might learn, that by what things a man sinneth, by these he is punished.
17 For thine all-powerful hand,
That created the world out of formless matter,
Lacked not means to send upon them a multitude of bears, or fierce lions,
18 Or new-created wild beasts, full of rage, *of* unknown *kind*,
Either breathing out a blast of fiery breath,
Or blowing forth *from their nostrils* noisome smoke,
Or flashing dreadful sparkles from their eyes;
19 Which had power not only to consume them by their violence,
But to destroy them even by the terror of their sight.
20 Yea and without these might they have fallen by a single breath,
Being pursued by Justice, and scattered abroad by the breath of thy power.
But by measure and number and weight thou didst order all things.

God, though almighty, is full of mercy and compassion.

21 For to be greatly strong is thine at all times;
And the might of thine arm who shall withstand?
22 Because the whole world before thee is as a grain in a balance,
And as a drop of dew that at morning cometh down upon the earth.

14. **in hatred**, reading ἐν ἔχθεσι with ℵ A C: B gives ἐν ἐκθέσει.

16. For the idea see Ps. vii. 15, 16 ('He hath made a pit,' &c.) and numerous other passages in the O. T. Jub. iv. 31 puts it very plainly: 'For with a stone he (Cain) had killed Abel and by a stone was he killed in righteous judgement.' As usual the writer does not trouble himself about literal accuracy. The Egyptians were punished, not by the identical animals which they worshipped, though in one district or another almost all animals were sacred, but by others, i.e. frogs and lice, quite as irrational and disgusting. Philo (*Vita Mos.* i. 17) says, 'For as the Egyptians used to honour the water in an especial degree . . . he thought it fitting to summon that first to the affliction and correction of those who honoured it.'

17. **That created.** Reading with all the versions, Lat., Syr., Arm., Kopt., ἣ for καί. B ℵ* A C all read καὶ κτίσασα. ℵ[a] exhibits a conflate reading ἣ καὶ κτίσασα. For the confusion between η and κ see Cobet, *Variae Lectiones*, p. 5, 'η et κ in veteri scriptura nil differunt.'

formless matter. As the words stand they convey a purely Greek philosophical idea. Matter was in existence from all eternity and God moulded it to His purpose. The question then arises—Did our author also conceive of matter as increate or did he assume that God first created formless matter and then brought it into order and arrangement? Grimm points out that the author's object was to adduce as great a proof as possible of the power of God. Creation *ex nihilo* would be even a greater marvel than the organization of matter; as the author does not mention this greater marvel it is urged that he did not accept it. Siegfried (*Philo*, p. 230) thinks that as Philo assumes the doctrine of the eternity of matter to be true and to require no proof, the Alexandrian Jews had accepted it before him. But even Philo, philosopher as he is, seems to waver in his acceptance of the belief (Siegfried, p. 232): 'God, when he begat all things, not only brought them into manifestation, but made things which did not exist before, being himself not only a Demiurge but also a Creator,' *De Somn.* i. 13. Caird (*Evolution of Theol.*, vol. ii, p. 191), speaking of Philo's views, says, 'In accommodation to Jewish notions God must be supposed to create the matter in which his ideas are realized.'

bears, or fierce lions. In *Vita Mosis*, i. 19, Philo says, 'Some one may ask why God punished the land with such insignificant and despised animals and not rather by bears, lions, and panthers . . . who devour human flesh.' The answer he gives bears a striking similarity to that in Wisd. xii. 20–25, 'God was desirous rather to admonish the Egyptians than to destroy them.'

18. **noisome smoke.** R. V. taking βρόμος, 'roaring', as a misspelling of βρῶμος, 'stench'.

19. The basilisk was supposed to kill by a glance.

20. **measure and number and weight.** Hence God deals out appropriate, not arbitrary retribution. This passage is referred to in Charles's *Testaments Naph.* ii. 3, where we read, 'By weight, measure, and rule was all the creation made.'

22. **a grain**: cf. Isa. xl. 15. Another indication of direct dependence on LXX.

23 But thou hast mercy on all men, because thou hast power to do all things,
And thou overlookest the sins of men to the end they may repent.
24 For thou lovest all things that are,
And abhorrest none of the things which thou didst make;
For never wouldst thou have formed anything if thou didst hate it.
25 And how would anything have endured, except thou hadst willed it?
Or that which was not called by thee, *how would* it have been preserved?
26 But thou sparest all things, because they are thine,
O Sovereign Lord, thou lover of souls;
12 1 For thine incorruptible spirit is in all things.
2 Wherefore thou dost chastise by little and little them that fall from the right way,
And, putting them in remembrance by the *very* things wherein they sin, dost thou admonish them,
That escaping from their wickedness they may believe on thee, O Lord.

As shown by his patience with the Canaanites.

3 For verily the old inhabitants of thy holy land,
4 Whom thou didst hate because they practised detestable works of enchantments and unholy rites,
5 Merciless slaughterers of children,
And sacrificial banqueters on men's flesh and blood,
6 Confederates in an impious fellowship
And murderers of their own helpless babes,
It was thy counsel to destroy by the hands of our fathers;
7 That the land which in thy sight is most precious of all *lands*
Might receive a worthy colony of God's servants.
8 Nevertheless even these thou didst spare as *being* men,
And thou sentest hornets as forerunners of thy host,
To cause them to perish by little and little;
9 Not that thou wast unable to subdue the ungodly under the hand of the righteous in battle,
Or by terrible beasts or by *one* stern word to destroy them at once;
10 But judging them by little and little thou gavest them a place of repentance,
Though thou knewest their nature was evil, and their wickedness inborn,
And that their manner of thought would in no wise ever be changed,
11 For they were a seed accursed from the beginning:
Neither was it through fear of any that thou didst pass over their sins.

23. **repent.** The thought that the goodness and mercy of God are calls to repentance does not seem to occur earlier than this. It was taken up by St. Paul, Rom. ii. 4, and is found in 2 Pet. iii. 9.

24 to xii. 2. This beautiful passage has nothing to compare with it in cc. i–x. Ch. i. 13, 14 do not speak of the love of God in the fervent way that the writer does here: while vi. 6–7 refer rather to God's compassion.

24. In Philo, as in his master Plato, the goodness of God is the motive of Creation. But we have not quite got this idea here. It only needs another step, it is true, but the author did not take it. He does not go beyond the O.T. The Jews did not ask what motive God had in creating man. The nearest approach to alleging a motive is found in Isa. xliii. 7, where the creation of Israel for the 'glory' of Jehovah is spoken of.

25. **called** = 'created'. A Hebraism, cf. Isa. xli. 4. 'Calleth' in Rom. iv. 17 is not quite the same, but probably = 'issues commands to'.

26. **lover of souls.** φιλόψυχος, in classical Greek, means 'cowardly'.

XII. The writer has set forth a very high ideal of God in xi. 24, and endeavours to illustrate it not only by His action towards the chosen people, but even by the treatment extended to His enemies, the Egyptians and Canaanites. He can only achieve his purpose by disregarding certain parts of the Biblical tradition. The Egyptians, according to the writer, were treated mercifully, in being afflicted at first with lighter plagues as a means of correction and admonition. It was only when they refused to be admonished and to obey the God whom they recognized to be the true God, that the punishment of death was inflicted. The difference between this view and that found in Exodus is considerable. There Jahveh hardens Pharaoh's heart to prevent the plagues from having a reformative effect. Again, the Canaanites, who, in spite of xi. 24, are described in xii. 4 as being hated by God, and as 'a seed accursed from the beginning', are said to have been leniently treated in order that they might escape from their wickedness by repentance. The reason given in Exodus (xxiii. 29, 30) why the Canaanites were destroyed little by little is that the land might not become the prey of wild beasts. The Deuteronomic editor of the Book of Judges gives two reasons why the Canaanites were not driven out at once: (1) To prove the Israelites; (2) To give them experience in war (Judges ii. 22–iii. 6).

5. **slaughterers,** φονέας. R.V. gives 'slaughters', emending to φονάς. This is probably on account of θοῖναν, 'banquet', in the next clause; but φονέας is supported by μύστας and αὐθέντας γονεῖς later on, so that it seems better to take 'banquet' as used by metonomy for 'banqueters' as in the Latin, which gives *devoratores*.

6. **Confederates.** The true reading of this line in the Greek seems beyond the possibility of recovery. The above rendering is that of the R.V. reading ἐκμυσοῦς from ἐκμυσής, a word coined by Grimm in his first edition (1837). Grimm, in the edition of 1860, read ἐκ μυσοῦς μύστας θιάσου, which equals 'impious initiates or confederates of a (secret idolatrous) fellowship'. The meaning is the same, but he avoids coining a word.

11. **accursed from the beginning.** Cf. Gen. ix. 25.

God's possession of almighty power shows that his leniency is due to his mercy.

12 For who shall say, What hast thou done?
Or who shall withstand thy judgement?
And who shall accuse thee for the destruction of nations which thou didst make?
Or who shall come and stand before thee as an avenger for the unrighteous?
13 For neither is there any God beside thee that careth for all,
That thou mightst show *unto him* that thou didst not judge unrighteously:
14 Neither shall king or prince meet thee *to plead* for those whom thou hast punished.
15 But being righteous thou rulest all things righteously,
Deeming it alien from thy power
To condemn him that doth not deserve to be punished.
16 For thy strength is the beginning of righteousness,
And thy sovereignty over all maketh thee to spare all.
17 For when men believe not that thou art perfect in power, thou showest thy strength,
And in dealing with them that know *it* thou puttest their boldness to confusion.
18 But thou, being sovereign over *thy* strength, judgest in gentleness,
And with great forbearance dost thou govern us;
For the power is thine whensoever thou willest.

His mercy an example to men.

19 But thou didst teach thy people by such works as these,
That the righteous must be a lover of men;
And thou didst make thy sons to be of good hope,
Because thou givest repentance when men have sinned.
20 For if the enemies of thy servants, even them that were due to death,
Thou didst punish with so great heedfulness and indulgence,
Giving them times and place to escape from their wickedness;
21 With how great carefulness didst thou judge thy sons,
To whose fathers thou gavest oaths and covenants of good promises!
22 While therefore thou dost chasten us, thou scourgest our enemies ten thousand times more,
To the intent that we may ponder thy goodness when we judge,
And when we are judged may look for mercy.

Those who did not respond to lenient treatment received a heavier punishment.

23 Wherefore also the unrighteous that lived in folly of life
Thou didst torment through their own abominations.
24 For verily they went astray very far in the ways of error,
Taking as gods those animals which even among their enemies were held in dishonour,
Deceived like foolish babes.
25 Therefore, as unto unreasoning children, thou didst send thy judgement to mock them.
26 But they that would not be admonished by a correction which was but as child's play
Shall experience a judgement worthy of God.
27 For because through their own sufferings they were moved to indignation
Against those creatures which they thought to be gods,

16. **beginning of righteousness.** So R. V.; Grimm, Deane, Farrar, and Siegfried, 'foundation.' Everywhere else in the book *ἀρχή* means 'beginning', though in xiv. 27 it is parallel with *αἰτία*; it may mean that God's power enables Him always to do justice. The word 'source' might be a good equivalent.

17. The Revisers say 'The Greek text here is perhaps corrupt'. B gives *εἰδόσι*, 'those that know'; A *οὐκ εἰδόσι*, 'those that know not'. Latin has *qui sciunt*, with which the Syriac agrees. Bois (p. 400) offers the emendation *ἐνδοιάζουσι*, which is accepted by Siegfried. To rebuke the audacity of those that doubt certainly seems at first sight a more likely statement than to rebuke the audacity of those that know; but if we compare the last two lines of the chapter we see that the Egyptians, who 'saw and recognized' the true God and may thus certainly be said to know Him, are thought of here, so that *εἰδόσι* is right. The Egyptians knew God's power but defied it.

20. **indulgence**, reading *διέσεως* ℵ. B reads *δεήσεως*, which gives no sense. A and Latin omit.

24. So R. V. Bois, however (p. 401), compares *ἐν ζώοις τῶν ἐχθρῶν ἄτιμα* with xv. 18 *τὰ ζῷα τὰ ἔχθιστα σέβονται*, and takes *ἐχθρός* with the same meaning in both places. If this is right we must probably translate 'taking as gods the most ignoble of hateful animals'. For the positive used as a superlative see Blass, *Gr. of N. T.*, p. 143.

26. The writer was misled by the LXX of Exod. x. 2 *ὅσα ἐμπέπαιχα*. There is no idea of child's play in the Hebrew word.

27. In opposition to R. V. and other renderings it is here suggested that *ἐφ' οἷς* is not prospective, anticipating *ἐπὶ τούτοις*, but simply means 'because' (on *ἐφ' ᾧ* and *ἐφ' οἷς* see Sanday's *Romans*, v. 12, and Lightfoot, Phil. iii. 12). The editorial comma after *ἠγανάκτουν* must be deleted.

Being punished by their means,
They saw, and recognized the true God whom before they refused to know;
Wherefore also the uttermost penalty came upon them.

Men being foolish by nature cannot know the true God, but worship, perhaps excusably, the works he has made.

13 1 For by nature all men were foolish, and had no perception of God,
And from the good things to be seen had not power to know him that is,
Neither by giving heed to the works did they recognize the artificer;
2 But either fire, or wind, or swift air,
Or circling stars, or raging water, or luminaries of heaven,
They thought to be gods that rule the world.
3 And if through delight in their beauty they took them to be gods,
Let them know how much better than these is their Sovereign Lord;
For the first author of beauty created them:
4 But if through astonishment at their power and influence,
Let them understand from them how much mightier is he that formed them;
5 For from the greatness and beauty of created things
Does man correspondently form the image of their first maker.
6 But yet for these men there is but small blame,
For they too peradventure do *but* go astray
While they are seeking God and desiring to find him.
7 For living among his works they make diligent search,
And believe their sight, because the things that they look upon are beautiful.
8 But again even they are not to be excused.
9 For if they had power to know so much,
That they could explore the course of *things*,
How is it they did not sooner find the Sovereign Lord of these *works*?

the true God. The indignation of the Egyptians at their gods, on finding them to be weaker than Jahveh, drove them to acknowledge Him to be the true God. The savage is often angry with his fetish. The statement in the text is founded either on Exod. viii. 8, ix. 28, x. 17, where Pharaoh requests Moses to 'entreat Jahveh' for him, thus recognizing that Jahveh was the true God, or on Exod. viii. 18, where the magicians, being unable to repeat the third plague, say, 'This is the finger of God.'

Wherefore. The writer takes it for granted that the reader will supply from the preceding words the thought that the Egyptians, though they recognized the true God, still refused to accept His admonition: 'Wherefore,' &c.

XIII. 1. **by nature . . . foolish,** as opposed to the intelligence that comes from wisdom. A solitary and indirect reference to the Wisdom of part 1.

the good things. The argument from design was a favourite one with the Stoics. 'They argued from the analogy of human art, and contended that the orderly movements and immutable constancy of the universe were just as clear an evidence of controlling reason as could be found in a statue or picture, in the course of a ship or a sundial' (Drummond, *Philo*, i, p. 77). Cf. Rom. i. 20, and see Sanday and Headlam, *in loco*.

him that is, τὸν ὄντα, from LXX Exod. iii. 14 Ἐγώ εἰμι ὁ Ὤν.

2. By the words 'fire', &c., Grimm, on the basis of Philo, *De Dec. Or.* ch. xii, and *De Vita Cont.* 1, takes the author to refer to the personification of natural phenomena under the names of Hephaestus, fire; Aeolus, wind; Hera, air; and Poseidon, water. E. Pfleiderer, who wishes to make the author a thoroughgoing Greek philosopher, takes the references to be to Heraclitus, who made fire the original element (i.e. fire as a vivifying and quickening power); Anaximenes, who proposed air; Pythagoras, who, with many others, considered the 'circling stars' to be gods; and Thales, who considered water to be the origin of all things. It is, of course, impossible to deny that the writer may have had these philosophers in his mind, but the reference is most probably a general one. See the statement of Prodicus in Zeller, *Pre-Socratic Phil.*, ii, p. 482.

luminaries of heaven. These were common objects of heathen worship. Cf. Deut. iv. 19, where it is also distinctly stated that Jahveh assigned the heavenly bodies to the nations to be worshipped.

3. **their beauty.** The commentators point out that the admiration of beauty is a Greek trait, not Hebrew. The beauty of the universe was a favourite subject with the Stoics.

5. **greatness and beauty.** Although ℵ B and A, the Latin and Peshitta, all read 'the greatness of the beauty', the editors (except R. V.) all accept the reading given in the text, which follows ℵ[a], various cursives, including 248, Athanasius, and other patristic authorities; and according to Feldmann is found in the Armenian, Syro-Hexaplar, Aethiopic, and probably the Coptic versions.

9. The writer, perhaps, forgot that he considered the Gentiles to be μάταιοι φύσει, 'foolish by nature', see *v.* 1. His question may be one of surprise, or he may, as Grimm and others suggest, insinuate that there was a moral failure. Philo makes it an intellectual failure, 'Therefore those persons are mere guessers who are anxious to contemplate the uncreated God through the medium of the things which he created; acting like those persons who seek to ascertain the nature of the unit through the number two when they ought to employ the investigation of the unit itself to ascertain the nature of the number two, for the unit is the first principle.'

But some men are without excuse because they worship objects which they themselves have made.

10 But miserable *were* they, and in dead things *were* their hopes,
Who called them gods which are works of men's hands,
Gold and silver, wrought with careful art, and likenesses of beasts,
Or a useless stone, the work of an ancient hand.
11 Yea, and if some woodcutter, having sawn down a tree he can handle,
Skilfully strippeth away all its bark,
And fashioning it handsomely maketh a vessel for the service of life;
12 And with that which is left he prepareth his food and is filled;
13 And taking that which is left again, for which no use can be found,
A crooked piece of wood and full of knots,
Carveth it with the diligence of his idleness,
And shapeth it by the skill of his indolence;
Then he giveth it the semblance of the image of a man,
14 Or maketh it like some paltry animal,
Smearing it with vermilion, and with paint colouring it red,
And smearing over every stain that is therein;
15 And having made for it a chamber worthy of it,
He setteth it in a wall, and maketh it fast with iron.
16 In order therefore that it may not fall, he taketh thought for it;
Knowing that it is unable to help itself;
(For verily it is an image, and hath need of help;)
17 And when he maketh his prayer for his goods and for his marriage and children,
He is not ashamed to speak to that which hath no life;
18 Yea for health he calleth upon that which is weak,
And for life he beseecheth that which is dead,
And for aid he supplicateth that which hath no experience,
And for a *good* journey that which cannot so much as use its feet,
19 And for gaining and getting and good success of his hands
He asketh power of that which with its hands is quite powerless.

Folly of the navigator who for safety prays to a useless piece of wood.

14 1 Again, one preparing to sail, and to journey through raging waves,
Calls on a piece of wood less sound than the vessel that bears him;
2 For that *vessel* the hunger for gain devised,
And an artificer by his wisdom built it;
3 And thy providence, O Father, guideth it along,
Because even in the sea thou gavest a way,
And in the waves a sure path,
4 Showing that thou canst save out of every *danger*,
That *so* even without art a man may put to sea;
5 And it is thy will that the works of thy wisdom should not be idle;
Therefore also do men intrust their lives to a little piece of wood,
And passing through the surge on a raft are brought safe *to land*.
6 For in the old time also, when proud giants were perishing,

10. **work of an ancient hand**, Acts xix. 35.
11 ff. Founded on Isa. xl, xli, xliv and xlvi.
13. **idleness.** The idol is made at odd times and no care spent upon it. A different method is mentioned in xiv. 19. ℵ B ἀργίας, A ἐργασίας.
indolence. ℵ* A B ἀνέσεως, συνέσεως ℵ[a] Latin.
18. ἀπειρότατον. An elative. A. V. margin 'that which hath no experience at all'. R. V. 'hath least experience'.

XIV. 1. **less sound.** Lit. 'more rotten'; see xiii. 13, where the wood of which the idol is made cannot be used for anything else.
2. **by his wisdom.** So the Vulgate and Syriac. ℵ B A give τεχνῖτις δὲ σοφία, and R. V. translates 'an artificer, even wisdom'. Nearly all the editors prefer the first, taking wisdom as the human quality. Blass (*Gram. of N. T. Gk.*, p. 6) points out that the mute ι in the dative was often omitted by scribes; also (see p. 8) η sometimes becomes ι. So read τεχνίτης δὲ σοφίᾳ. See also Thackeray, *Gr. of O. T. in Greek*, p. 85.
3. **Because.** This and the next three lines refer to Noah. The lines justify the statement that it is God's providence that guides a vessel rather than man's seamanship. Noah was not acquainted with navigation.
5. **a little piece.** ἐλαχίστῳ, elative sense = 'very little'. See Thackeray, *Gr. of O. T.*, p. 185.

The hope of the world, taking refuge on a raft,
Left to the race of men a seed of generations *to come*,
Thy hand guiding the helm,
7 For blessed was the wood through which cometh righteousness:

Idolaters shall be punished.

8 But the *idol* made with hands is accursed, itself and he that made it;
Because his was the working, and the corruptible thing was named a god:
9 For both the ungodly doer and his ungodliness are alike hateful to God;
10 For verily that which was made shall be punished together with him that made it.
11 Therefore among the idols of the nations shall there be a visitation,
Because, though formed of things which God created, they were made an abomination,
And stumblingblocks to the souls of men,
And a snare to the feet of the foolish.

The origin of idolatry.

12 For the devising of idols was the beginning of fornication,
And the invention of them the corruption of life:
13 For neither were they from the beginning, neither shall they be for ever;
14 For through the vain error of men they entered into the world,
And therefore has a speedy end been devised for them.
15 For a father worn with untimely grief,
Making an image of the child too quickly taken away,
Now honoured him as a god who then was a corpse,
And delivered to those that were under him mysteries and solemn rites.
16 Afterward the ungodly custom, in process of time grown strong, was kept as a law,
And by the commandments of princes graven images were worshipped.
17 And when men could not honour them in presence because they dwelt far off,
Imagining the likeness from afar,
They made a visible image of the king whom they honoured,
That by their zeal they might flatter the absent as if he were present.
18 But unto a yet higher pitch of worship
Did the ambition of the artificer urge forward even them that knew him not,
19 For he, wishing perchance to please the ruler,
Compelled his art to give the likeness greater beauty;
20 And so the multitude, allured by the grace of his work,
Now accounted as an object of worship him whom they had honoured before as a man.
21 And this became a hidden danger unto life,
Because men, under the power either of calamity or of tyranny,
Invested stones and stocks with the incommunicable Name.

Evil results of idolatry.

22 Afterward it was not enough for them to go astray in the knowledge of God;
But also, while they live in sore conflict through ignorance *of him*,

7. **righteousness**, i. e. 'the righteous purpose of God'. The ark preserved a righteous man, who was the ancestor of the righteous people. This is the highest example of the beneficial purposes for which wood has been used: other examples are seen in its enabling God's gifts to be conveyed from one part of the world to another; but wood which is put to a bad use is 'accursed'.

8. **idol made with hands.** χειροποίητος, the term used in LXX Isaiah to translate אליל, ii. 18, x. 11, *et al.*

11. **a visitation.** ἐπισκοπή used in an unfavourable sense as in xix. 15, the only other occurrence of the word in this part of the book.

14. **devised.** ἐπενοήθη is used as a paranomasia—which the R.V. keeps up—upon ἐπίνοια, 'devising', in *v.* 12. The A. V. prefers to give the meaning plainly, 'therefore shall they shortly come to an end.' Cf. 1 En. xcix. 9, where of the idolaters it is said, 'They shall have wrought all their work in a lie and shall have worshipped a stone: therefore in an instant shall they perish.'

15. The theory of Euhemerus was that idolatry arose from the worship of deceased heroes. The writer adopts this view with a slight modification.

17. On the basis of the words '*absent* ruler' Bousset (*Rel. des Judenthums*, p. 35) would date the book after Egypt had come under the Roman Empire. For the worship of the Emperors, cf. Dill, *Roman Society from Nero*, p. 617: 'But Egypt went rather too far for the western mind in its apotheosis of kings.'

22. Cf. Philo, *de Conf. Ling.* c. 12, 'For they do in peace everything that is done in war; they plunder, ravage, carry off booty; they assault, destroy, pollute; they murder treacherously; they murder openly if they are the more powerful.'

That multitude of evils they call peace.
23 For either slaughtering children in solemn rites, or celebrating secret mysteries,
Or holding frantic revels of strange ordinances,
24 No longer do they guard either life or purity of marriage,
But one slays another treacherously, or grieves him by adultery.
25 And all things confusedly are filled with blood and murder, theft and deceit,
26 Corruption, faithlessness, tumult, perjury,
Disquieting of the good,
Ingratitude for benefits *received*,
Defiling of souls, confusion of sex,
Disorder in marriage, adultery, and wantonness.
27 For the worship of those unnameable idols
Is the beginning and cause and end of every evil.
28 For *their worshippers* either make merry unto madness, or prophesy lies,
Or live unrighteously, or lightly forswear themselves.
29 For putting their trust in lifeless idols,
They wickedly swear *false* oaths and look not to be harmed.
30 But for both *sins* shall the just doom pursue them,
Because they had evil thoughts of God by giving heed to idols,
And swore unrighteously in deceit, despising holiness.
31 For not the power of them by whom men swear,
But Justice which hath regard to them that sin,
Punisheth always the transgression of the unrighteous.

Benefits of worshipping the true God.

15 1 But thou, our God, art gracious and true,
Longsuffering, and in mercy ordering all things.
2 For even if we sin, we are thine, knowing thy dominion;
But we shall not sin, knowing that we are accounted thine:
3 For to know thee is perfect righteousness,
Yea, to know thy dominion is the root of immortality.
4 For neither did any evil device of man lead us astray,
Nor yet the painters' fruitless labour,
A form stained with varied colours;
5 The sight whereof leadeth fools into lust:
Who desire the form of a dead image that hath no breath;
6 Lovers of evil things, and worthy to have such things to hope in,
Are both they that make them, and they that desire, and they that worship them.

Another example of the manufacture of idols.

7 For a potter, kneading soft earth,
Laboriously mouldeth each *vessel* for our service:
Nay, out of the same clay doth he fashion
Both the vessels that minister to clean uses, and those of a contrary sort,
All in like manner;
But what shall be the use of either sort,
The craftsman *himself* is the judge.

27. ἀνωνύμων, Latin *infandorum*. The meaning may be 'unspeakable', 'indescribable', referring to the immoralities of the mystery cults without any reference to Exod. xxiii. 13. The context favours this. Cf. Eph. v. 12.

XV. For a moment the writer turns aside to contrast the true worship with the false. The interruption has the effect, which was doubtless intended, of giving a slight rest to the reader before renewing the polemic against idolatrous worship.

2. **we shall not sin.** If the nation could be regarded as holy and blameless in the past in spite of the admissions in xii. 22, xvi. 11, xviii. 20, the future could be painted in the same colours.

5. **lust,** *ὄρεξιν.* ℵ A C and all the versions. *ὄνειδος* B and 68. *ποθοῦντες* in *v.* 6 justifies this. The reference, no doubt, is to Pygmalion, King of Cyprus, who fell in love with a statue of Venus.

7. For the connexion of this verse with Rom. ix. 21, see Introd., p. 526. E. Pfleiderer compares the saying of Heraclitus that 'the clay out of which things are made is for ever being moulded into new forms' (Zeller, *Pre-Soc. Phil.*, ii, p. 17), and affirms direct connexion.

8 And also, with evil labour, he mouldeth a vain god from the same clay,
He who, but a little before was made of the earth,
And will soon go his way *to the earth* out of which he was taken,
When the soul which was lent him shall again be demanded.
9 Howbeit his care is,
Not that his powers must fail,
Nor that his span of life is short;
But he rivals the workers in silver and gold,
And copieth moulders in brass,
And esteemeth it glory that he mouldeth counterfeit things.
10 His heart is ashes,
And his hope of less value than earth,
And his life of less honour than clay:
11 Because he was ignorant of him that moulded him,
And of him that inspired into him an active soul,
And breathed into him a vital spirit.
12 But he accounted our life to be but a game,
And our way of life a gainful fair;
For one must, saith he, get gain whence one can, though it be by evil means.
13 For this man beyond all others knoweth that he sinneth,
When out of the same earthy matter he maketh both brittle vessels and graven images.
14 But most foolish *were* they all, and of feebler soul than a babe,
The foes of thy people, who crushed them;
15 Because all the idols of the nations they reckoned as gods;
Which have neither the use of eyes for seeing,
Nor nostrils for drawing breath,
Nor ears to hear,
Nor fingers for handling,
And their feet are helpless for walking.
16 For a man it was that made them,
And one whose own spirit is borrowed moulded them;
For no one hath power, *being* a man, to mould a god like unto himself,
17 But, being mortal, he maketh a dead thing with lawless hands;
For he is better than the things he worshippeth;
Of the two, he indeed had life, but they never.

8. **the soul which was lent him.** This idea is repeated in *v.* 16, and must therefore be taken as a settled conviction of the writer. Whether in his mind it included the idea of pre-existence, it is perhaps difficult to say; it is, however, far less definite than the statement in viii. 20, 'I came into a body undefiled,' and it is immediately followed by words in *v.* 11 which are apparently inconsistent with pre-existence. From ψυχή here and πνεῦμα in *v.* 16 it appears that they were to our author only different names for the same thing. This shows without any elaborate argument that there is no trichotomy intended in *v.* 11.

9. **he rivals.** The clay idols were glazed and gilded.

10. For the connexion of this verse with LXX see Introd., p. 524. The word 'ashes' in Isa. xliv. 20, on which this passage is based, means that which is worthless. Cf. Job xiii. 12, 'Your memorable sayings are proverbs of ashes.' The words are a rhetorical statement that the whole being of the idolater is inferior to the clay he uses, though in *v.* 17 the opposite statement is made.

11. That the soul and spirit are here the same, cf. second part of note on *v.* 8. On the subject see the long and interesting note of Lightfoot on 1 Thess. v. 23 (*Notes on Epistles of S. Paul*).

12. **a gainful fair.** This comparison is traced by Grimm to Pythagoras, who said τὸν βίον ἐοικέναι πανηγύρει (Dio. Laert. viii. 1. 6). Cicero (*in Tusc. Disp.* v. 359) and other writers quote the saying. As the comparison was evidently well known, we cannot from its use here deduce any direct acquaintanceship by the author with the system of Pythagoras.

gain. The commentators quote the well-known passage of Horace, 'rem facias, rem. Si possis recte, si non, quocumque modo rem' (*Ep.* i. 1. 65).

15. It was a characteristic of heathen worshippers that they admitted the reality of the gods of other nations. This was natural enough to people who were not Monotheists. The Hebrews themselves before they were Monotheists acknowledged the existence of other gods besides Jahveh. Solomon recognized the gods of his foreign wives (1 Kings xi. 1–8). But the Egyptians went further than this. 'The Egyptian gods during the flourishing period of the country's history were not exclusive. They admitted into their number such of the gods of neighbouring peoples as had been found to be powerful and capable of resistance' (Wiedemann, p. 186 of *Hastings' DB*, extra vol.).

17. **Of the two.** R. V. 'Forasmuch as', reading ἀνθ' ὧν with ℵ. All other MSS. ὧν, except 157 and 253, which omit. For the disappearance of the dual see Thackeray, *Gr. of O.T.*, p. 22.

The Egyptians worshipped irrational and unclean animals and were therefore punished by means of them. Small animals, viz. quails, benefited the Israelites.

18 Yea, and the creatures that are most hateful do they worship,
For, being compared as to want of sense, these are worse than all others;
19 Neither, as seen beside *other* creatures, are they beautiful, so that one should desire them,
But are outcasts from the praise of God and his blessing.
16 1 For this cause were *these men* worthily punished through *creatures* like *those which they worship*,
And tormented through a multitude of vermin.
2 Instead of which punishment, thou, bestowing benefits on thy people,
Preparedst quails for food,
Food of rare taste, for the desire of *their* appetite;
3 In order that thine enemies, when they desired to eat,
Might for the hideousness of the *creatures* sent among them
Loathe even the necessary food;
But these *thy people*, having for a short space suffered want,
Might even partake of *food* of rare taste.
4 For it was needful that upon those tyrants inexorable want should come,
But that to these it should only be showed how their enemies were tormented.

It is true the Israelites had serpents sent against them, but that was for admonition.

5 For even when terrible raging of wild beasts came upon thy people,
And they were perishing by the bites of crooked serpents,
Thy wrath continued not to the uttermost;
6 But for admonition were they troubled for a short space,
Having a token of salvation,
To put them in remembrance of the commandment of thy law:
7 For he that turned toward it was not saved by that which he saw,
But by thee, the Saviour of all.
8 Yea, and in this didst thou convince our enemies,
That thou art he that delivereth out of every evil.
9 For them verily the bites of locusts and flies did slay,
And there was not found a healing for their life,
Because they were worthy to be punished by such *as these*;
10 But thy sons not the very teeth of venomous dragons overcame,
For thy mercy came to their help, and healed them.
11 For they were bitten, that they should remember thine oracles;
And were quickly saved, lest, falling into deep forgetfulness,
They should be irresponsive to thy beneficence:
12 For of a truth neither herb nor mollifying plaister restored them to health,
But thy word, O Lord, which healeth all things;
13 For thou hast power over life and death,
And thou leadest down to the gates of Hades, and leadest up again.
14 But though a man *can* slay by his wickedness,
Yet the spirit that is gone forth he bringeth not back,
Neither giveth release to the soul that *Hades* hath received.

19*b*. The writer probably considered that other animals besides the serpent were included in the curse of Gen. iii. 14: possibly all the creeping animals.

XVI. 3. **hideousness**, εἰδέχθειαν. This reading, a *hapax legomenon*, is generally accepted. It is given by C, some cursives, including 248, and the Syro-Hexaplar version. δειχθεῖσαν is given by ℵ B A, Complu., Latin, Syr., and some cursives. εἰδέχθειαν is accepted by most editors as referring to the frogs in the ovens and kneading-troughs, Exod. viii. 3.

3*c*. **food**. Literally, 'appetite.' As for the quails see note on xix. 12.

6. The allegory here is not so thoroughgoing as in xvi. 17. There Wisdom is identified with the cloud: here the serpent is a σύμβολον. Philo suggests that the serpent was chosen as a symbol of σωφροσύνη and καρτερία.

token. ℵ and A read σύμβουλον, 'counsellor'.

11. **irresponsive**, a paraphrase of ἀπερίσπαστος, 'unconcerned about'. R.V. 'unable to be roused by'. 23 (V) and 253 read ἀπερίστατοι, 'destitute of'.

12. **thy word**. Cf. Ps. cvii. 20, 'He sent his word, and healed them.' See on xviii. 15.

How the Egyptians were punished by fire and the Israelites benefited.

15 But thy hand it is not possible to escape:
16 For the ungodly, refusing to know thee, were scourged by the strength of thine arm,
Pursued with strange rains and hails and showers inexorable,
And utterly consumed with fire;
17 For, what was most marvellous *of all*,
In the water which quencheth all things the fire wrought yet more mightily;
For the world fighteth for the righteous.
18 For at one time the flame lost its fierceness,
That it might not burn up the creatures sent against the ungodly,
But that *these* might see and perceive that they were pursued by the judgement of God:
19 And at another time even in the midst of water it burns beyond the power of fire,
That it may destroy the fruits of an unrighteous land.
20 Instead whereof thou gavest thy people angels' food to eat,
And bread ready *for use* didst thou provide from heaven without *their* toil,
Bread having the virtue of every pleasant savour,
And agreeing to every taste;
21 For thy substance manifested thy sweetness toward *thy* children,
Ministering to the desire of the eater,
And transforming itself according to every man's choice.
22 But snow and ice endured fire, and melted not,
That *men* might know that fire was destroying the fruits of the enemies,
Burning in the hail and flashing in the rains;
23 And that this *element* again, in order that righteous men might be nourished,
Had even forgotten its power.
24 For the creation, ministering to thee its maker,
Straineth its force against the unrighteous, for punishment,
And slackeneth it in behalf of them that trust in thee, for beneficence.
25 Therefore at that time also, converting itself into all forms,
It ministered to thine all-nourishing bounty,
According to the desire of them that made supplication;
26 That thy sons, whom thou lovedst, O Lord, might learn

16 ff. Hail was rained down upon the Egyptians, but (*v.* 20) manna upon the Israelites.

strange rains. Rain is unusual in Egypt, see Deut. xi. 10. 'It is only the parts along the sea-coasts that are ever moistened with a few drops of rain' (Philo, *Vita Mos.* i. 20).

17. Philo (*Vit. Mos.* i. 20) notices this 'miracle within a miracle'. The lightning and the thunderbolts penetrated and descended through the hail, still they did not melt it nor were the flashes extinguished by it.

18. **that these**—and they alone: even the animals that formerly plagued them miraculously escaped. The writer has forgotten that the frogs are said to have been swept away by an east wind.

19. **fruits,** *γένημα*. A new *κοινή* formation distinguished from *γέννημα*, 'offspring', see Thackeray, *Gram.*, p. 118.

20. **provide.** Reading *παρέσχες* A C^{vid} Latin, and Syriac. *ἐπέμψας* B.

agreeing to every taste. This idea is found in the Talmud, *Yoma* 75, where it is said, 'Just as a child at the breast enjoys various flavours, so did the Israelites when they ate the manna find therein various flavours.' מה שד זה תינוק טועם בה כמה טעמים אף המן כל זמן שישראל אוכלין אותו מוצאין בו כמה טעמים. This fancy no doubt existed in the author's time, and he desired to explain it by the doctrine of the metabolism of the elements mentioned in the next note.

21. **substance,** Greek *ὑπόστασις*. This word has caused great difficulty. Early scholars proposed emendations; A. V. gives 'sustenance', and 248 altered *σου* into *αὐτοῦ*. It has been made equivalent to the Logos, and the R. V. translates it by 'thy nature'. It seems probable, however, that the writer was thinking of nothing more than the common substance which according to the Stoics underlay all four elements. As pointed out in the next note, he makes use of the doctrine of the metabolism of the elements to account for the manna being transformed to suit every taste. Here he goes back in thought to what the manna was before it assumed the attributes or accidents which differentiated it from other objects. The technical terms among the Stoics for substance and attribute were *τὸ ὑποκείμενον* or *οὐσία* and *τὸ ποιόν* (Zeller, *Stoics*, p. 97). The steps of the process were (1) *ὑπόστασις*, (2) manna, (3) transformation.

transforming itself. The author here gives a metaphysical basis to the events mentioned in *v.* 20 by the Stoic doctrine of the interchange of the four elements. Heraclitus first, and the Stoics after him, taught that the elements changed into one another by condensation and rarefaction, *πύκνωσις* and *μάνωσις*. See Dio. Laert. ix. 8, quoted in Ritter and Preller, § 36, for Heraclitus (Heraclitus recognized only three elements); and for the Stoics, Ritter and Preller, § 497, and Zeller, *Stoics*, &c., pp. 131 ff. See also the quotation from Philo given in the note on xix. 18.

22. **snow and ice,** i. e. the manna. See xix. 21.

23. **might be nourished.** See Num. xi. 8, where the manna is said to have been capable of being baked in the oven, though it melted before the sun.

24. **Straineth . . . slackeneth.** In addition to the interchange of the four elements with one another, the power of a single element—here in *vv.* 22 and 27 fire—could be increased or moderated.

That not the growth of *earth's* fruits do nourish a man,
But thy word which preserveth them that trust thee.
27 For that which could not be injured by fire,
Simply warmed by a faint sunbeam melted away;
28 To make known that *we* must rise before the sun to give thee thanks,
And must plead with thee at the dawning of the light:
29 For the hope of the unthankful shall melt as the winter's hoar-frost,
And shall flow away as water that hath no use.

The plague of darkness.

17 1 For great are thy judgements, and hard to interpret;
Therefore souls undisciplined went astray.
2 For when lawless men supposed they had overpowered a holy nation,
They *themselves,* prisoners of darkness, and bound in the fetters of a long night,
Close kept beneath their roofs,
Lay exiled from the eternal providence.
3 For while they thought that they were unseen in *their* secret sins,
They were scattered one from another by a dark curtain of forgetfulness,
Stricken with terrible awe, and sore troubled by spectral forms.
4 For neither did the recesses that held them guard them from fears,
But sounds rushing down rang around them,
And phantoms appeared, cheerless with unsmiling faces.
5 And no force of fire prevailed to give *them* light,
Neither could the brightest flames of the stars illumine that gloomy night:
6 But there appeared to them only the glimmering of a fire self-kindled, full of fear;
And in terror at that sight on which they could not gaze
They deemed the appearance
To be worse *than it really was*;
7 And the mockeries of magic art lay low,
And shameful was the rebuke of their boasted knowledge:
8 For they that promised to drive away terrors and troubles from sick souls
Were sick *themselves* with fear worthy of laughter:
9 For though no troublous thing affrighted them,
10 Yet, scared with the creepings of vermin and hissings of serpents, they perished for very trembling,
Refusing even to look on the air, which could on no side be escaped.
11 For wickedness in itself is a coward thing, and witnesseth its own condemnation,

27. **by fire,** i. e. the manna in the oven.

28. Several scholars have maintained that 'Wisdom' was written by a member of the Therapeutae, and have appealed to this passage as well as to iii. 13, 14, iv. 8, and viii. 28. Grimm, however, shows that the habit of prayer before sunrise was a Jewish practice.

XVII. 3. **secret sins.** The writer appears to attribute to the ancient Egyptians the mystery cults of his own time. He seems to picture some of them as engaged in their worship and suddenly scattered. It is true, he says in *v.* 16, every man remained in the place where he was; but, as he also says in xix. 17 that they tried to grope their way to their houses, it is plain that rigid consistency is not to be looked for in details due solely to the imagination of the writer, hence the literal translation 'scattered'—R. V. margin—is best. A and C read ἐσκοτίσθησαν. The description is a good example of the Jewish haggadic method of treating history.

4. **rushing down.** Reading δὲ καταράσσοντες with B^{ab} A C and Latin *descendens.* Feldmann prefers δ' ἐκταράσσοντες, the reading of B*. ℵ has ταράσσοντες, and so affords no help. If the more difficult reading is to be preferred that in the text—R. V. and Mr. Gregg—should be taken.

6. **And in terror,** &c. 'The form of expression is too obscure to be understood with certainty' (Farrar). If, however, we take ὄψις and τὰ βλεπόμενα to refer to the same thing, viz. the self-kindled fire, a good meaning can be obtained. The Egyptians did not or could not gaze directly upon the fire, but for all that could not avoid seeing it, and consequently were more terrified than they would have been had they deliberately looked at it. The endeavours of timid people to avoid seeing the flashes of lightning in a storm may be compared.

7. Reading κατέκειτο with ℵ B and Latin, as against the plural in A C and 248. The plural is no doubt the more difficult reading, and is perhaps supported by καταγέλαστον in 8 *b*. It is accepted by R. V.; but it is difficult to believe that a Jew would call the punishment sent by God μαγικῇ τέχνῃ. The R. V. gives 'and they lay *helpless,* made the sport of magic art'.

10. **the air.** The ancients considered the natural colour of the air to be dark—ὑάκινθος (Philo, *Vita Mos.* iii. 6 and 12). They shut their eyes so as not to look on the blackness of the air which surrounded them.

11. **in itself.** Reading ἰδίως ℵ A B and Latin, not ἰδίῳ ℵ^{a} and Comp. followed by Grimm and R. V. ἴδιος is used nine other times in this part of the book, and is never separated from the word it qualifies. This is upheld by Feldmann. The origin of the mistake was doubtless the itacism in ℵ and A, which both give μαρτυρι for μαρτυρει. See Thackeray, *Gram.*, p. 85.

And, being pressed hard by conscience, always forecasteth the worst:
12 For fear is naught but a surrender of the succours which reason offereth;
13 And when from within *the heart* the expectation thereof is o'erthrown
It reckons its ignorance worse than the cause that bringeth the torment.
14 But they, all through the night, which in truth was powerless
And which came upon them out of the recesses of powerless Hades,
All sleeping the same sleep,
15 Now were haunted by monstrous apparitions,
And now were paralysed by their soul's surrender;
For fear sudden and unlooked for came upon them.
16 So then each and every man sinking down in his place
Was shut up in ward in that prison which was barred not with iron:
17 For whether he were husbandman, or shepherd,
Or a labourer whose toils were in the wilderness,
He was overtaken, and endured that inevitable necessity,
For with one chain of darkness were they all bound.
18 Whether there were a whistling wind,
Or a melodious noise of birds among the spreading branches,
Or a measured fall of water running violently,
19 Or a harsh crashing of rocks hurled down,
Or the swift course of animals bounding along unseen,
Or the voice of wild beasts harshly roaring,
Or an echo rebounding from the hollows of the mountains,
All these things paralysed them with terror.
20 For the whole world *beside* was enlightened with clear light,
And was occupied with unhindered works;
21 While over them alone was spread a heavy night,
An image of the darkness that should afterward receive them;
But yet heavier than darkness were they unto themselves.

18 1 But for thy holy ones there was great light;
And *the Egyptians*, hearing their voice but seeing not their form,
Envied them because they had not suffered,
2 And because they do not harm them *now*, though wronged by them before, are thankful;
And for their *former* hostility besought their pardon.
3 Whereas thou didst provide *for thy people* a burning pillar of fire,
To be a guide for *their* unknown journey,
And withal a kindly sun for *their* proud exile.
4 For well did the Egyptians deserve the loss of light and imprisonment in darkness,
They who had kept in close ward thy sons,
Through whom the incorruptible light of the law was to be given to the race of men.

conscience. This is the first mention of conscience in the Scriptures. It is here regarded as the higher self, after the manner of Philo (see Drummond, *Philo*, ii, pp. 124 and 295).

forecasteth. Reading προείληφε with ℵ[a] and Latin *praesumit* instead of προσείληφε with ℵ A B C, which is accepted by Prof. Margoliouth and translated 'always increaseth its hardships'. In spite of the manuscript evidence all editors read προείληφε. According to Feldmann the Armenian and Coptic versions uphold it.

17. **in the wilderness,** κατ' ἐρημίαν, a Hebraism due to the LXX using ἔρημος to translate מִדְבָּר, the place where cattle are driven for pasture; not a wilderness in our sense of the word.

18. The birds are made to sing in the darkness, and in *v.* 20 the writer says the whole world besides was in light. It has therefore been suggested that he thought of a subjective darkness, which would, of course, simply be blindness. But *v.* 10 is against this, and in xix. 17 he distinguishes between the blindness of the men of Sodom and the 'yawning darkness' which encompassed the Egyptians.

21. **spread.** ἐπέτατο B A, ἐπέκειτο ℵ, ἐπετέτακτο 254. The right form is doubtless ἐπετέτατο, which is printed in the Roman text apparently without manuscript authority.

An image, &c. Mr. Thackeray, *JTS*, vol. vi, p. 232, thinks that this line may be a Christian interpolation. The repetition of σκότους looks suspicious.

XVIII. 1. **not suffered.** Grimm, Siegfried, Farrar, Gregg, all agree in reading οὐ with A and Latin, instead of οὖν ℵ and B. Grimm's explanation that οὐ was altered into οὖν by a scribe who took κἀκεῖνοι to refer to the Egyptians fully justifies the rejection of οὖν, though it is better supported by manuscript evidence. Deane, following Gutberlet, takes ὅτι and οὖν together = 'whatsoever they also had suffered (before), they (the Egyptians) counted them happy'. This is accepted by Feldmann and Stevenson.

4. **Through whom,** &c. Cf. *Test. of Twelve Pat.*, Levi xiv. 4: 'The light of the law which was given to lighten every man.'

The Egyptians counsel death against the Israelites, but are slain themselves.

5 After they had taken counsel to slay the babes of the holy ones,
†And when a single child had been cast forth and saved,
To punish them thou didst take away a multitude of their children,
And destroyedst all *their host* together in a mighty flood.
6 Of that night were our fathers made aware beforehand,
That, having sure knowledge, they might be cheered by the oaths which they had trusted:
7 *So* by thy people was expected the salvation of the righteous and destruction of the enemies;
8 For as thou didst take vengeance on the adversaries,
By the same act thou didst glorify us, and call us unto thyself.
9 For holy children of good men offered sacrifice in secret,
And with one consent took upon themselves the covenant of the divine law—
That the saints would partake alike in the same blessings and perils—
Singing the while the fathers' songs of praise.
10 But there sounded back in discord the cry of the enemies,
And a piteous voice of lamentation for children was borne abroad.
11 And servant along with master punished with a like just doom,
And commoner suffering the same as king,
12 Yea, all *the people* together, under one form of death,
Had *with them* corpses without number;
For the living were not sufficient even to bury them,
Since at a single stroke their noblest offspring was destroyed.
13 For though they had disbelieved all things by reason of their enchantments,
Upon the destruction of the firstborn they confessed the people to be God's son.
14 For while peaceful silence enwrapped all things,
And night in her swiftness was in mid course,
15 Thine all-powerful word leaped from heaven down from *the* royal throne,
A stern warrior, into the midst of the doomed land,
16 Bearing as a sharp sword thine unfeigned commandment,
And standing filled all things with death;
And while it touched the heaven it trode upon the earth.
17 Then forthwith apparitions in terrible dreams troubled them,
And fears came upon them unlooked for:
18 And one thrown here half dead, another there,
Declared the cause of his death:
19 For the dreams, perturbing them, did foreshow this,
That they might not perish without knowing why they were afflicted.

5. **To punish them.** Charles on Jub. xlviii. 14, p. lxxiv, shows that *εἰς ἔλεγχον* must be taken as in the text. He would emend by deleting 'and saved' in line 2 and 'of their children' in line 3. He shows that *πλῆθος* is probably a mistaken rendering of רבו, 'a myriad'. The meaning then would be that for every single Hebrew child cast into the Nile, ten thousand of the Egyptians were drowned. The passages here and in Jubilees are both based on a common tradition.

6. **our fathers**, i.e. the Patriarchs, as probably in *v.* 9.

9. **divine law,** reading *θειότητος* B A as against *ὁσιότητος* ℵ, Latin, Syriac, and other versions.

the saints, *τοὺς ἁγίους.* This is quite in accordance with the writer's idealization of the Israelites. R. V. with Grimm and others would take *τοὺς ἁγίους* with *αἴνους*, 'the sacred songs of praise', but, as Mr. Gregg points out, the rhythm of the Greek is against this.

the fathers', &c. The reading adopted in the text is that of R. V. margin, following ℵ[a] A, Complut., the Latin, and in all probability the Syriac. The writer attributes the custom of his own time—the singing of psalms at the Passover—to the Israelites at the Exodus. R. V. translates 'the fathers already leading', &c., reading *προαναμελπόντων* with B.

12. **noblest**, R. V. 'nobler'. For this rendering of the comparative, see Thackeray, *Gram. of O. T. in Gk.*, p. 181.

14. **her swiftness.** *ἴδιος* is here plainly used in its 'exhausted' meaning, see note on x. 1.

15. **Thine all-powerful word.** Eichhorn, p. 158, and Gfrörer, p. 236, affirm this passage to show a pre-philonian use of the Philonic Logos. But in view of xvi. 12, which is plainly based on Ps. cvii. 20, and the Jewish complexion of this part of the book, it seems better with Grimm to take it as founded on O. T. usage (cf. Hos. vi. 5 LXX, 'I slew them by the word of my mouth'; Jer. xxiii. 29, 'Is not my word like a fire? saith the Lord; and like a hammer that breaketh the rock in pieces?'; Ps. cxlvii. 29, 'His word runneth very swiftly'), though undoubtedly it differs from these passages in a far stronger personification. In 1 Chron. xxi. 16, which the writer may have had in his mind, the destroying angel is said to stand between heaven and earth.

16. **unfeigned,** *ἀνυπόκριτος.* The command was meant to be executed. It was no empty threat, feigned to terrify.

17. **terrible dreams.** The textual evidence for *ὀνείρων δεινῶν* is ℵ A, several cursives, Comp., and all the versions. B alone reads *δεινῶς* which R. V. renders.

19. The revelation by dreams to those about to be punished may be compared with the dream of Nebuchadnezzar,

The Israelites also experienced the punishment of death, but the plague was stayed by the intercession of Aaron.

20 But it befell the righteous also to experience death,
And a multitude were stricken in the wilderness:
Howbeit the wrath endured not for long.
21 For a blameless man hasted to be their champion:
Bringing the weapon of his ministry,
Even prayer and the propitiation of incense,
He withstood the indignation, and put an end to the calamity,
Showing that he was thy servant.
22 And he overcame the anger,
Not by strength of body, not by power of weapons;
But by word did he subdue the minister of punishment,
By bringing to remembrance oaths and covenants made with the fathers.
23 For when the dead were already fallen in heaps one upon another,
Standing between he stopped the *advancing* wrath,
And cut off its access to the living.
24 For upon *his* long *high-priestly* robe was the whole world *pictured*,
And the glories of the fathers *were* upon the graving of the four rows of precious stones,
And thy majesty *was* upon the diadem of his head.
25 To these the destroyer gave way, and these he feared;
For the mere proof of the wrath was enough.

But there was nothing to stay death in the case of the Egyptians.

19 1 But upon the ungodly there came pitiless wrath to the uttermost;
For what they would do He knew before,
2 How that, having pressed them to be gone,
And having speeded them eagerly on their way,
They would repent themselves and pursue them.
3 For while they were yet in the midst of their mourning,
And making lamentation at the graves of the dead,
They adopted another counsel of folly,
And pursued as fugitives those whom with intreaties they had cast out.
4 For the doom they deserved was dragging them unto this end,
And made them forget what things had befallen them,
That they might fill up the punishment yet lacking to their torments,
5 And that thy people might journey by a marvellous road,
But they *themselves* might find a strange death.

Dan. ii. E. Pfleiderer would see the influence of the Stoics here, and they certainly laid stress on the prophecies of the dying (Zeller, *Stoics*, p. 355, note 6).

21. Aaron, see Num. xvi. 47.

22. **anger.** Reading *χόλον* for *ὄχλον*, which gives no sense. So all editors (except Gutberlet and Deane), following Bauermeister.

24. **the whole world.** This is explained by passages in Philo, *Vita Mos.* iii. 12 and 13, where we learn that the high priest's robe and its adornments represented the *κόσμος*. The robe itself was blue, or rather dark purple (*ὑάκινθος*), and represented the air. The flowers on it symbolized the earth, and the pomegranates water, and (in *c.* xiii) the scarlet dye of the robe is the emblem of fire. The writer is thus able to get in another illustration of the idea found in v. 17, 20, xvi. 17, 24, and xix. 6, that 'the world fighteth for the righteous'.

25. **he feared.** *ἐφοβήθη* is supported by $\aleph^a$ A, some cursives, including 248, the Comp. and Latin. It is accepted by Grimm, Siegfried, Feldmann, and Deane. *ἐφοβήθησαν* is supported by $\aleph^*$ B C, some cursives, and Syr., and is adopted by R. V. and Mr. Gregg. Against the plural it may be urged that (1) the subject 'the people' has to be supplied, and (2) there seems to be no reason why the people should have feared the holy garments of the high priest.

XIX. 2. **pressed,** *ἐπιστρέψαντες*. R. V. 'changed their minds to let thy people go'. For the rendering here adopted see Jebb's note on Soph. *Trach.* 1182, where he says of *ἐπιστρέφω*, 'the primary notion is that of turning some constraining force upon a person.'

3. **adopted.** R. V. 'drew upon themselves'. For similar uses of the word in the sense here given see Liddell and Scott under *ἐπισπάω*, mid.

cast out, *ἐξέβαλον*. Probably a reminiscence of *ἐκβάλλω*, Exod. xi. 1 and xii. 33.

Creation fought for the chosen people,

6 For the whole creation in its several kind was fashioned again anew,
Performing their several commands,
That thy servants might be guarded free from hurt.
7 *Then* was beheld the cloud that shadowed the camp,
And dry land rising up out of what before was water,
Out of the Red sea an unhindered highway,
And a grassy plain out of the violent surge;
8 Through which they passed with all their hosts,
These that were covered with thy hand,
Having beheld strange marvels.
9 For like horses they roamed at large,
And they skipped about like lambs,
Praising thee, O Lord, who delivered them.
10 For they still remembered what came to pass in the time of their sojourn,
How instead of bearing cattle the land brought forth lice,
And instead of fish the river cast up a multitude of frogs.
11 But afterwards they saw also a new race of birds,
When, led on by desire, they asked for luxurious dainties;
12 For, to solace them, there came up for them quails from the sea.

And against the Egyptians.

13 And upon the sinners came the punishments
Not without tokens given beforehand by the force of thunders;
For justly did they suffer through their own *exceeding* wickednesses,
For grievous indeed was the hatred which they practised toward guests.
14 For whereas certain men received not strangers who came among *them*,
These made slaves of guests who were their benefactors.
15 And not only so, *but God* shall visit the former after another sort,
Since they received as enemies them that were aliens;
16 Whereas these *first* welcomed with feastings,
And *then* afflicted with dreadful toils,
Them that had already shared *with them* in the same rights.
17 And they too were stricken with loss of sight
(Even as those *others* at the righteous man's doors),
When, being compassed about with yawning darkness,
They sought every one the passage through his own door.

6. **fashioned again.** The writer again refers to the philosophical doctrine of the transmutation of the elements into one another; see xvi. 21 and xix. 18. Bois (p. 270) calls this 'a second edition of the Creation'.

12. The writer omits all mention of the murmuring of the Israelites. So does Philo, *Vita Mos.* i. 37, 'the Hebrews ... enjoyed the most exquisite meat, varying their food with this necessary and delicious addition.' Philo takes it that the supply of quails was as regular as that of the manna.

13. **beforehand.** Josephus, *Ant.* ii. 16, records the tradition that the overthrow of the Egyptians in the Red Sea was accompanied by a violent storm. Our author has perhaps slightly altered the tradition, though the reading is not absolutely certain, *γεγονότων* B, *προγεγονότων* ℵ A C Latin and Syriac. The tradition is probably founded on the poetry of Ps. lxxvii. 17–20.

own, *ἴδιος*, strengthened by *αὐτῶν*, is most probably emphatic. Grimm would make it very emphatic: their own extraordinary and peculiar wickedness.

14. **certain men,** i.e. men of Sodom.

15. The punishment, *ἐπισκοπή*, of the men of Sodom is to be lighter than that of the Egyptians. When is this *ἐπισκοπή* to take place? Grimm thinks in the Messianic age, or rather perhaps at the world judgement preceding it. This is the only certain reference in this part of the book to future retribution. In the earliest section of I Enoch there are different gradations of punishment for the wicked in Sheol (Charles, *Eschatology*, p. 188). The text is that of R.V., which is conjectural. Swete gives *καὶ οὐ μόνον, ἀλλ' ἧ τις ἐπισκοπὴ ἔσται αὐτῶν*, which means 'and not only so, but assuredly a certain kind of visitation, i.e. deliverance, shall be theirs'. But the author would not be likely to entertain any idea of a deliverance of the Sodomites, and to weaken the word *ἐπισκοπή* to mean 'consideration', 'allowance', is without justification. We can, dividing the words of B differently from Swete, read *ἄλλη τις ἐπισκοπή* = 'another kind of punishment', but as after *οὐ μόνον*, *ἀλλά* is necessary, and the Latin gives 'sed et alius quidam respectus', R.V. is probably right in seeing an instance of haplography in B and adopting the emendation of Grabe, *ἀλλ' ἄλλη τις ἐπισκοπή*.

The marvels explained by the theory of the transmutation of the elements.

18 For the elements changed their order one with another,
Just as the notes of a psaltery vary the character of the rhythm,
Continuing always *the same, each* in its *several* sound;
As may clearly be divined from the sight of what came to pass.
19 For creatures of dry land were turned into creatures of waters,
And creatures that swim trode *now* upon the earth:
20 Fire kept the mastery of its own power in *the midst of* water,
And water forgat its quenching nature:
21 Contrariwise, flames wasted not the flesh of perishable creatures that walked among them;
Neither melted they the ice-like grains of ambrosial food, that were *of nature* apt to melt.
22 For in all things, O Lord, thou didst magnify thy people,
And thou didst glorify them and not lightly esteem them;
Standing by their side in every time and place.

18. i.e. God deals with the elements as a musician handles his instrument. He arranges and rearranges them to produce the required results (Bois, pp. 410 ff.). Cf. Philo, *Vit. Mos.* i. 17, 'For all the elements of the universe, earth, water, air, and fire, of which the world was made, were all brought into a state of hostility against them, so that the country of those impious men was destroyed to exhibit the height of the authority which God wielded, who had fashioned those same elements at the creation of the universe so as to secure its safety, and who could change them all whenever he pleased to effect the destruction of impious men.'

Continuing. *μένοντα* is neuter, agreeing grammatically with *στοιχεῖα*, but the sense shows that it should agree with *φθόγγοι*.

20 and 21. See xvi. 18 and 23.

22. Contrast this verse with ix. 18, 'Through wisdom were they saved'; with x. 9, 'But wisdom delivered out of troubles those that waited on her'; and xi. 1, 'She (wisdom) prospered their works by the hand of a holy prophet.' The point of view has certainly changed, if not the writer.

THE BOOK OF BARUCH

OR I BARUCH

INTRODUCTION

§ 1. SHORT ACCOUNT OF THE BOOK.

THE *Book of Baruch*, of which the Greek version is found in all our editions of the LXX, forms one of a series of writings to which the name of Jeremiah's secretary is attached. Brief characterizations of these will be found in Charles's *Apocalypse of Baruch*, Introd., § 2 (p. xvi f.).

As will be shown in the sequel the tragic events of 597 (586) B.C., which heralded the exile, constitute a thin historic drapery which invests the yet greater tragedy of the Jewish race in A.D. 70. It is now generally accepted by recent critics that Nebuchadnezzar (Nabuchodonosor) and Belshazzar (Baltasar) represent the persons of Vespasian and Titus. Other corresponding traits between the Babylonian conquest here portrayed and the Roman conquest will reveal themselves to further scrutiny. Among alternative solutions which have been propounded from the days of Grüneberg (1797) to those of Ewald, Kneucker, and Schürer, none will be found to satisfy the conditions of the problem so well as that which we have just indicated (substantially that of Kneucker and Schürer).

§ 2. CONTENTS.

The contents may be briefly summarized as follows:

I. Ch. i. 1–14. Baruch wrote the words of this book in the fifth year and read them over to Jechonias and his fellow exiles in Babylon. These wept, made a money collection, and sent it to the High Priest in Jerusalem with a message that it was intended for the purchase of offerings on the altar, and also with a request for prayer on behalf of Nebuchadnezzar and his son, whom they desire loyally to obey, as well as on their own behalf, who have sinned against God. This book of confession of sin shall be read on the feast-day in God's house.

II. i. 15–iii. 8. The confession immediately follows. God is just. Their punishment is the result of sin and disobedience (i. 15–ii. 12). To this there follows a prayer for Divine mercy (ii. 13–iii. 8). God's previous utterances through Jeremiah are recalled, especially His command to serve the king of Babylon. Disobedience to this command has brought calamities on Israel and the destruction of the Jerusalem temple (ii. 21–26). Divine assurances follow that captivity will bring with it repentance and a final restoration to and rule over Palestine (ii. 27–35). This section closes with a cry to God not to remember Israel's past iniquities (iii. 1–8).

III. In the rest of the book we pass from the prose of the previous portion to poetry.

(*a*) iii. 9–iv. 4). Here, in the style of Hebrew Wisdom literature, we have the praise of God's laws of life. Neglect of them is the cause of Israel's calamities and exile. Learn, therefore, where wisdom is to be found (iv. 9–14). Not among the great and powerful rulers has it been found, nor even have those who are reputed wise discovered it (iii. 15–28). No one has found it in heaven or earth, but God, the all-wise Creator, alone is in possession of it, and has bestowed it on Jacob—the Law of God which is eternal and leads to life (iii. 29–iv. 1). This section concludes with a brief exhortation to Jacob to lay hold of Wisdom and walk in its light, and not to surrender the honour of this unique possession to any other.

(*b*) From this song of exhortation to Israel we pass to another of very different character: strains of lamentation and comfort in the style of the Deutero-Isaiah (iv. 5–v. 9): 'Be comforted' is the recurring refrain (iv. 5, 21, 27, 30) addressed (i) by Jerusalem to her children (iv. 5–29). 'Ye have been sold among the heathen, yet not to be destroyed. You have been surrendered to the enemy because you have angered God by past transgressions' (iv. 5–9). There follows a lamentation over the banishment of her children, and their harsh treatment at the hands of foreigners (iv. 10–17). 'But God, who has brought calamity, will also bring deliverance. I indeed trust in God for your salvation. Bear God's wrath in patience. You shall soon behold your enemy's destruction and set your foot on his neck. Joy shall come in place of sorrow' (iv. 18–29). (ii) God's word of comfort to Jerusalem (iv. 30–v. 9). Calamities are denounced against those cities that rejoiced at her fall. Fire shall come upon them. They shall be the habitation of demons. Jerusalem is exhorted to lift up her eyes and behold her children flocking to her from East and West, to divest herself of her garment of sorrow and array herself with a robe of salvation and a tiara of glory. Her enemies shall bring her children back to her. Mountain and hill shall be made low and valleys filled that Israel may return. Woods and fragrant trees shall yield their shade to Israel, whom God shall bring back in joy.

§ 3. Composite Character.

The *composite character* of the treatise is evident from the preceding survey. The *prose section* comprised in I and II stands *in marked contrast with both the poetical sections in* III (*a*) and (*b*). (I) in *contents*. The prose section is a confession of sin and a recognition that Israel's calamities and exile are the penalty for Israel's sins of disobedience. These will bring about repentance. It concludes with a cry for Divine mercy. On the other hand III (*a*), which is poetic in form, is based on a different conception. Here Israel's calamities are due to his neglect of Divine law regarded as Wisdom. This Wisdom, which belongs to God alone, He has bestowed on Israel as his precious privilege. Israel is exhorted to lay hold of it as the only means of safety. The contrast with III (*b*) is still more marked. We note the different attitude adopted towards Israel's conquerors. In i. 11, 12 Israel is exhorted to offer prayer on behalf of Nebuchadnezzar and his son, 'and the Lord will give us strength, and lighten our eyes, and we shall live under the shadow of Nabuchodonosor king of Babylon, and under the shadow of Baltasar his son, and we shall serve them many days, and find favour in their sight.' Here the tradition of Jeremiah and Ezekiel is followed (Jer. xxvii. 6–8, xxix. 4–7; Ezek. xxvi. 7–12, xxix. 17–20). So again, ii. 20–22, 24 ascribes the calamities which Israel suffered to his refusal to obey the prophetic injunction, 'Bow your shoulders to serve the king of Babylon, and remain in the land that I gave unto your fathers.' But when we turn to III (*b*) the attitude towards Israel's conquerors is that of *embittered subjugation leading to revolt* reflected in the literature of the late-exilian or early post-exilian period (Jer. l, li; Isa. xlvii). 'Thine enemy hath persecuted thee; but shortly thou shalt see his destruction, and shalt tread upon their necks' (iv. 25). The peoples who afflicted Israel and rejoiced in his fall, the cities where Israelites served in slavery, shall feel craven dread and grieve in their own desolation (iv. 31–33). (II) We note also great diversity *with respect to the O. T. sources from which they respectively borrow*. In ch. i. 11–iii. 8 we have frequent citations from Jeremiah, Daniel, and Deuteronomy. Specially noteworthy is the repeated employment of whole clauses of Dan. ix. 7–19 in Baruch i. 15–ii. 17. On the other hand, the Wisdom section, iii. 9–iv. 4, contains numerous borrowings from Proverbs, Job, Deutero-Isaiah, and Sir. xxiv. The last section (iv. 5–v. 9) is very largely based on Deutero-Isaiah. The concluding portion is evidently inspired by Ps. of Sol. xi.

§ 4. Critical Investigation of the above Documents.

We have arrived, therefore, at the following general result, viz. that in the Book of Baruch we have to deal with three distinct literary elements which possess all the signs of emanating from different hands. (A) A prose document to be found in ch. i. 1–iii. 8. (B) A poetical document of the character of Wisdom literature in ch. iii. 9–iv. 4. (C) A further document of exhortation and comfort is added in iv. 5–v. 9. These we shall now consider separately.

(A) Difficulties beset us when we examine the opening verses of the book.

(i) In verse 2 the fifth year is the date assigned to the writing, and this is reckoned from the date when Jerusalem was captured and burnt (2 Kings xxv. 9; 2 Chron. xxxvi. 19). This, we know, took place in the year 587–586 B.C. Accordingly Fritzsche, followed by Gifford (*Apocrypha*, ed. Wace), would identify the assigned date of the writing with 582 (583) B.C. This view, however, encounters difficulties. (*a*) The destruction of the temple in 587–586 B.C. hardly seems compatible with the offerings (burnt-offerings, sin-offerings, and incense) to be offered on the altar to which Baruch i. 10 makes reference. Accordingly Kneucker follows Eichhorn and other critics in dating the fifth year from the earlier capture of Jerusalem in 597 B.C. by Nebuchadnezzar, when Jehoiachin was made prisoner. Though the treasures of the temple and of the king's palace were carried off (2 Kings xxiv. 13), as well as the officers, household, artisans and soldiers (verses 12, 14–16), both city and temple were left intact. This, of course, rids us of one difficulty. Moreover, 597 is the date from which Ezekiel reckons (i. 2, viii. 1, &c.). On the other hand, it stands in complete variance with the explicit statement in Baruch i. 2 (last clause). Kneucker himself is aware of this contradiction (p. 16 NB). The difficulties which invest the alternative date 587–586 are far from insuperable. We learn in Jer. xli. 5 that offerings were made at the Jerusalem altar by men from Shechem and Shiloh after the temple had been destroyed. Therefore some form of cultus still persisted. (*b*) We have no evidence in Jeremiah or any other O. T. source that Baruch ever went to Babylonia. It is true that we have no personal details respecting Jeremiah's companion and scribe after he accompanied the prophet to Egypt (Jer. xliii. 5, 6); nevertheless such negative evidence contains no presumption against such a journey of Baruch to Babylonia and his residence there after 586 B.C. But in the presence of other features in Baruch i affecting its historic credibility it will be seen that this is a subject of minor significance.

(ii) Among these other features we note that Baltasar (who is called in Daniel Belshazzar or Belteshazzar) is spoken of as son of Nebuchadnezzar (Bar. i. 11, 12). This is in exact accordance with Dan. v. 2, 13, 18, 21, and is known to be due to historical confusion. The only Belshazzar known to the cuneiform documents is Bel-šar-uṣur ('Bel, protect the king'), son of Nabonidus (Nabûnaïd), the last king of Babylon, overthrown by Cyrus.

(iii) The text of verse 2 is uncertain. The omission of the number or name of the month is strange. As is well known, months were designated by numbers (beginning from Nisan as the first month of the ecclesiastical or Babylonian calendar) in all exilian and post-exilian Hebrew documents.

(iv) The following verses hang very badly together. (*a*) After verse 1 we naturally expect that the words of the book will soon follow; instead of this, thirteen verses of narrative succeed. (*b*) Verse 4 has all the appearance of a redactional prolongation of the final clause of the preceding verse. (*c*) Verse 8 (as Kneucker has clearly shown) stands out of its natural place. The subject of the sentence cannot be Joakim of the preceding verse, but is evidently Baruch who is last mentioned in verse 3. Moreover, verse 9 follows naturally after verse 7 rather than verse 8.

(B) The character of the document iii. 9–iv. 4, as based on the Wisdom literature of the O. T. (Proverbs and Job) and containing a citation from Eccles. xxiv. 8, has been already indicated in §§ 2, 3. It is a message of comfort and exhortation addressed mainly to the exiles who have long lived 'in the enemies' land' (iii. 10), in other words, to the Jewish Diaspora. Their calamities are due to their abandonment of the fountain of Wisdom, the way of life revealed in the Torah. This amid all his losses Israel possesses as his priceless and eternal privilege conferred by God. Hold fast to it, and walk in its light, happy and secure.

This entire section has a unity of its own, and it is quite evident that this is the book to which Bar. i. 1, 3 *a* refers. These verses, therefore, form the adequate and natural preface. That verse 2 originally belonged to this preface is extremely improbable. It probably formed part of the introduction to the document A (ch. i. 2, 3 *b*–iii. 8). The reference to the destruction of Jerusalem by fire, i. 2 and ii. 26, points to this conclusion. A redactor united A and B. It is this combined work which we shall first consider. C will be considered later.

§ 5. A Hebrew Original of Documents A and B.

A considerable number of the older critics held that the original of the Book of Baruch was in *Greek*. This was the opinion of Grotius, Eichhorn, Bertholdt, Hävernick, Keil, and Nöldeke (in his *Alttestamentliche Literatur*, p. 214). But this view has been abandoned by recent scholars. Even De Wette, who for a time held to the former view, saw reason to forsake it, and adopted the theory of a Hebrew original in the fourth edition of his *Introd. to the O. T.* (German), p. 443. Similarly Reusch, Ewald, Hitzig (*Die Psalmen*, vol. ii, p. 119), Fritzsche (*Exegetisches Handbuch zu den Apocryphen des A.T.*—Special Introd. to Baruch, pp. 171 foll.), and more decisively Kneucker, who in his elaborate work, *Das Buch Baruch* (1879), unhesitatingly (in contrast with Fritzsche) assumes for the whole book a Hebrew original which he devotes the utmost pains to reconstruct. Schürer, on the other hand, sustains the doubts of Fritzsche (*ibid.*, p. 172) as to the latter portion (iii. 9–v. 9), with this difference that he *decisively asserts* that Greek and not Hebrew was its original form (*Gesch. des jüd. Volkes im Zeitalter Christi*^{3}, iii, p. 340; *PRE*^{3}, i, p. 642). Similarly Reuss and Hilgenfeld (in *Zeitsch. für wiss. Theol.*). Bevan, in *Enc. Bibl.*, inclines towards this view. Marshall (art. 'Baruch' in *Hastings's DB*) propounds the ingenious theory that iii. 9–iv. 4 was originally composed in Aramaic. 'This view is based on a comparison of the Greek with the versions'—the Peshiṭta [as Marshall assumes it to be], the Syr. reproduction of Origen's Hexaplar, as well as the Vulg. Nine examples are given by Dr. Marshall, but the first of these, iii. 16, 'peoples' . . . 'world', is quite as easily explicable on a Hebrew basis עמם and עלם; the *second* (iii. 18), which has more attractiveness, might also be explained from two possible meanings of קנים in *Hebrew*. The meaning 'fashion' is probably late, and due to Aramaic influence. Cf. Gen. xiv. 19, 22; Ps. cxxxix. 13; Prov. viii. 22. In the *third* case (iii. 19) we have the two renderings of S and S$^{Hex.}$ respectively of ἠφανίσθησαν, 'they are vanished' (R.V.), which Kneucker rightly holds to have reproduced the original Hebr. אָבְדוּ 'perished'. This Hebr. word is rendered by S אתחבלו (the Ethpa.) 'were corrupted', hence 'perished'. Comp. the use of the Greek verb in Matt. vi. 19 f. (cf. Syr. where Pa. חבל is used) as well as in Attic Greek. On the other hand, S$^{Hex.}$ אסתרחו, the Ethpeel, does not mean 'sinned' nor does it arise out of אסתתרו 'disappeared'. We constantly find ܚܒܠ used for 'destroy' (as well as 'sin'), and as the equivalent of ἀφανίζω (in Exod. xii. 15; 2 Kings x. 28; Ezek. xix. 7; Jer. l. 21, &c.), and its passive or Ethpe. as the rendering of ἀφανίζεσθαι, Ezek. xxv. 3; Job. xxii. 20 (cf. 2 Macc. xii. 22). Comp. other examples in Payne Smith's *Thesaur. Syr.* In this case the S[Hex.] slavishly adheres to the Greek version. The *fourth* example (iii. 21) cited by Marshall, based on the diverse renderings, 'laid hold' and 'cared for', I am not able to follow. The S[Hex.] reading is not צדו but יצפו. The *fifth* (iii. 23), 'remembered' and 'trod', is due to a corruption of the Syriac translation (see notes) and therefore has no bearing on the question of the original. The *sixth* (iii. 31) accounts for the Vulgate *exquirat* by an Ethpeel form מתבעא instead of בעא. But the Ethpe. form of this verb has no other than a *passive* meaning which can hardly be fitted into the structure of the clause and verse. The *seventh* example (iii. 34), 'their watches', and the colourless Syr., 'their places', may be accounted for by the loose rendering of S or by the corruption of the Hebr. original suggested in the notes. The *eighth* (iii. 37), 'appeared' . . . 'was revealed', might just as easily be explained as variant translations of a Hebr. original נראתה (or נגלתה). In the general suspicion which regards the verse as a later Christian gloss, its evidential value counts for little. The *ninth* example (iv. 5), 'advantage' . . . 'dignity' (Vulg.), need not be dealt with, as it evidently possesses no cogency.

Nearly all living scholars, including Dr. Marshall, as well as Dr. Charles (in *Encycl. Brit.* (11th ed.)), are agreed that A (ch. i. 2, 3 *b*–iii. 8) was composed in Hebrew. For this there is strong evidence, and, in the opinion of the present writer, a fairly good case can be made for B (ch. i. 1, 3 *a*, iii. 9–iv. 4).

(*a*) The strongly-marked Hebraisms of the Greek version have been long recognized as affording unmistakable indications of a Hebrew original, viz. ch. i. 10 μάννα (cf. Jer. xvii. 26, xli. 5), or, as we should properly read with Codd. 22, 33, 36, 48, &c., μαναά, is evidently the Greek mode of writing מִנְחָה. In the same verse the formula περὶ ἁμαρτίας simply covers the Hebr. חַטָּאת 'sin-offering', as Lev. v. 10, 11, vii. 37, &c., clearly prove. Other significant traces of a Hebrew original may be cited, viz. ii. 23 ἀπὸ ἐνοικούντων, Hebr. מִיּוֹשֵׁב; εἰ μήν, 'surely', arising out of εἰ μή, Hebr. אִם לֹא idiomatically used for strong asseverations (ii. 29); βόμβησις (*ibid.*) for הָמוֹן; מתי misread as 'dead' in iii. 4. Still more significant are the frequently recurring relative constructions so characteristic of Hebrew. Thus in ii. 4, 13, iii. 8 οὗ . . . ἐκεῖ = אֲשֶׁר . . . שָׁם (cf. Mark i. 7, vii. 25). Similarly ii. 26 . . . τὸν οἶκον οὗ ἐπεκλήθη τὸ ὄνομά σου ἐπ' αὐτῷ אֶת־הַבַּיִת אֲשֶׁר נִקְרָא שִׁמְךָ עָלָיו—. Comp. ii. 17, 29. These relative constructions are obviously characteristic of prose rather than poetry in Hebrew, and therefore belong to the document A rather than B (ch. i. 1, 3 *a*, iii. 9–iv. 4). In the latter, however, we have variants in the Greek and Syr. renderings such as 'peoples' and 'world' (iii. 16), as well as iii. 18 'workers' in silver (LXX) and 'those who gain' silver (Syr.), included in Marshall's list which can best be explained on the basis of a Hebraic original. Similarly iii. 11 'thou art counted with them that go down into Hades', iii. 14 'length of days', iii. 18 'there is no searching (ἐξεύρεσις) of his works' are all Hebrew phrases. In some cases, as will be shown in the notes, the Syr. version points the way more clearly to a Hebr. original. See also Kneucker, p. 25, but the list requires sifting.

(*b*) So far at least as document A is concerned the hypothesis of a Hebr. original is rendered fairly certain by the marginal note which the Syro-Hexaplar version attaches to Bar. i. 17, ii. 3 'not recorded (*lit.* placed) in the Hebrew' ܠܐ ܣܝܡ ܠܘܬ ܥܒܪܝܐ. On the other hand, see Nestle in art. 'Septuagint' in *Hastings's DB.* iv. p. 450, footnote †.

§ 6. THE GREEK ORIGINAL OF C (Bar. iv. 5–v. 9).

It is, however, quite otherwise with document C. This document is a unity, not a series of lays, as Rothstein argues. Here evidences accumulate that the original was in Greek.

(*a*) The strongest support for this view is to be found in the close parallels between the *Greek* of Ps. of Sol. xi and Bar. iv. 36–v. 9.

Baruch.	*Ps. of Sol.* xi.
iv. 37 ἰδοὺ ἔρχονται οἱ υἱοί σου . . . συνηγμένοι ἀπ' ἀνατολῶν ἕως δυσμῶν.	3 ἴδε τὰ τέκνα σου ἀπὸ ἀνατολῶν καὶ δυσμῶν συνηγμένα.
v. 1 Ἰερουσαλήμ . . . ἔνδυσαι τὴν εὐπρέπειαν τῆς παρὰ τοῦ θεοῦ δόξης.	8 ἔνδυσαι, Ἰερουσαλήμ, τὰ ἱμάτια τῆς δόξης σου.
v. 5 ἀνάστηθι, Ἰερουσαλήμ, καὶ στῆθι ἐπὶ τοῦ ὑψηλοῦ. καὶ ἴδε σου συνηγμένα τὰ τέκνα ἀπὸ ἡλίου δυσμῶν ἕως ἀνατολῶν.	3 στῆθι, Ἰερουσαλήμ, ἐφ' ὑψηλοῦ. καὶ ἴδε τὰ τέκνα κτλ. as above.
v. 8 ἐσκίασαν δὲ καὶ οἱ δρυμοὶ καὶ πᾶν ξύλον εὐωδίας . . .	6–7 οἱ δρυμοὶ ἐσκίασαν αὐτοῖς ἐν τῇ παρόδῳ αὐτῶν. πᾶν ξύλον εὐωδίας ἀνέτειλεν αὐτοῖς ὁ θεός.

Comp. also Bar. v. 7 with Ps. of Sol. xi. 5. Here, as well as in the underlined phrases above, we have evident borrowings from the *Greek* of Deutero-Isaiah (see notes). But *in the case of Baruch the borrowing comes through Ps. of Sol.* This is made clear (*a*) by Bar. v. 8 compared with Ps. of Sol. xi. 6, 7; (*β*) by the repetitions. Note Bar. iv. 37 and v. 5 (the latter in closer approximation to Ps. of Sol. xi. 3). See also the careful investigation of this subject in Ryle and James's ed. of the Ps. of Sol., Introd. pp. lxxii foll. Other parallels between the document C and the Ps. of Sol., viz. iv. 26 ὁδοὶ τραχεῖαι, and Ps. of Sol. viii. 19; also Bar. iv. 20 and Ps. of Sol. ii. 21, 22 (Jerusalem clothed in sackcloth) are cited in Kneucker, p. 43 note, and also by Ryle and James (Introd., p. lxxvi), who extend the list so as to cover the whole of the Book of Baruch. Many of these, however, have very slight significance, while those which belong to the document C leave an irresistible impression of dependence by this document on the Ps. of Sol., and therefore become an important indication with respect to date.[1]

(*b*) Collateral evidence is supplied by the Syr. version. It will be seen hereafter that there are indications to warrant the belief that that version is based on the original Hebrew text as well as on the Greek version of the documents A and B; but when we come to the document C evidences abound that the only text on which the Syr. is based is the Greek. In iv. 20 and v. 1 the Greek word στολή is taken over into the Syriac. In iv. 34 Syr. even embodies a conflate reading. Thus in the LXX we have in B the original reading ἀγαλλίαμα, 'exultation', which was corrupted into ἄγαλμα, 'statue', 'idol', embodied in A. In Syr. we have the conflate reading 'I will take away from her the idols and the exultation'.

(*c*) Moreover, the phraseology is occasionally such as Hebrew could hardly employ. Thus in iv. 28 δεκαπλασιάσατε ἐπιστραφέντες ζητῆσαι αὐτόν, 'return and seek him ten times more', could scarcely be represented by עַשְּׂרוּ לָשׁוּב לְבַקְּשׁוֹ (so Kneucker). The Piel (or Aram. Pael) of עשׂר means only 'to tithe'. Only some such circumlocution as perhaps עֶשְׂרָתַיִם הַרְבּוּ לָשׁוּב וּלְבַקְּשׁוֹ would convey the idea expressed in the Greek. See also below on Greek style, § 9, I (Greek version).

(*d*) Lastly, the O.T. citations are based on LXX rather than the Hebrew text. This is especially clear in the Pentateuch.

Baruch.	*LXX.*
iv. 7 παροξύνατε γὰρ τὸν ποιήσαντα ὑμᾶς θύσαντες δαιμονίοις καὶ οὐ θεῷ.	Deut. xxxii. 16, 17 παρώξυνάν με . . . ἔθυσαν δαιμονίοις καὶ οὐ θεῷ.
iv. 15 ἐπήγαγεν γὰρ ἐπ' αὐτοὺς ἔθνος μακρόθεν, ἔθνος ἀναιδὲς . . . καὶ οὐκ ᾐσχύνθησαν πρεσβύτην οὐδὲ παιδίον ἠλέησαν.	Deut. xxviii. 49, 50 ἐπάξει κύριος ἐπὶ σὲ ἔθνος μακρόθεν . . . ἔθνος ἀναιδὲς . . . ὅστις οὐ θαυμάσει πρόσωπον πρεσβύτου καὶ νέον οὐκ ἐλεήσει.
iv. 20 ἐξεδυσάμην τὴν στολὴν . . . ἐνεδυσάμην δὲ σάκκον . . . cf. v. 1.	Isa. lii. 1 ἔνδυσαι τὴν ἰσχύν σου . . .

[On re-studying the question of the original language of this chapter I have come to the conclusion that it was Hebrew on the following grounds:

1°. There can be practically no doubt that the true text of *v.* 6 is: εἰσάγει δὲ αὐτοὺς ὁ θεὸς πρὸς σὲ αἰρομένους μετὰ δόξης ὡς θρόνον βασιλείας.

2°. A comparison of this verse with Isa. lxvi. 20, xlix. 22 makes it clear that the text is to be rendered as in the R.V. 'God bringeth them in unto thee borne on high with glory, as on a royal throne', but decidedly not 'as a royal throne'.

3°. Now since the Greek is vigorous and idiomatic, the author of the Greek does not think in Hebrew, he is more or less a master of the Greek of his period. Accordingly he could not have written ὡς θρόνου βασιλείας if he had meant ὡς ἐπὶ θρόνου βασιλείας. But since the context and the associations of the passage require us to translate ὡς θρόνου βασιλείας 'as on a royal throne', it follows that we have here a definite Hebraism = כבסא מלכות. See my note on § 5 of the Ps. of Sol. where this subject is discussed by Dr. Buchanan Gray. This Hebraism could only be explained in one of two ways: either the writer thought in Hebrew or the Greek is a mistranslation of the Hebrew. The rest of the Greek is wholly against the former hypothesis. Hence we must have recourse to the latter. The Greek of ch. v is a translation from the Hebrew.

4°. The peculiar form of the expression has not been noticed. In Isa. lxvi. 20 it is on actual wagons, horses, and litters that the returning Israelites are carried, since it is the Gentiles that convey them. But in our text, since it is God Himself that conveys them, the means by which He conveys them are not chariots, &c., nor anything that the writer can definitely describe. The Israelites are not borne 'on a royal throne' but on something resembling a royal throne. We have here the use of the Apocalyptic כְּ so frequently used in this sense in Ezekiel and Daniel, and 1 Enoch, and of its Greek equivalent ὡς in Revelation. The supernatural element (at all events imaginatively) is introduced here and in the verses that follow.

[1] See note on the Introduction to the Ps. of Sol., § 5. We cannot accept Rothstein's suggestion that Ps. of Sol. xi is based on Bar. iv. 36–v. 9.

5°. No real difficulty is caused by the fact of the very close resemblance of Ps. of Sol. xi and 1 Bar. iv. 36—v. 9. They can be explained as versions of two different recensions of the same Hebrew psalm. In the LXX and Theodotion we have Greek translations of two recensions of the Semitic text of Daniel, the older of which is lost. In the Testaments of the Twelve Patriarchs the two divergent Greek forms of the text presuppose two similarly divergent forms of the Hebrew original: while in the Zadokite Fragments, which are preserved only in Hebrew, we have two recensions of ch. ix. See *op. cit.* in vol. ii.

All, therefore, that we need to presuppose, is that the author of 1 Baruch adapted for his own purposes an existing Hebrew psalm, which is itself, or one form of it, preserved in Ps. of Sol. xi. *Possibly* also the translator of 1 Baruch had not only the Hebrew original of Baruch before him but also the Greek Version of Ps. of Sol. xi, just as Theodotion had the LXX, and the translator of the Hebrew original of β of the Testaments of the Twelve Patriarchs had *a* before him.—GEN. EDITOR.]

§ 7. DATE AND AUTHORSHIP.

We are now in a better position to consider the questions of *date* and *authorship*. The question of *date* has to be examined in relation to the three documents A, B, and C (*a*) separately and (*b*) in connexion with their redactional combination.

With reference to A (i. 2, 3*b*–iii. 8) the determining factor in deciding the date is the close connexion between Dan. ix. 7–19 and Bar. i. 15–ii. 17 as well as the historical confusion common to Daniel and this document (i. 11, 12), to which attention has already been called (§ 4). Now close literary parallels are often capable of alternative solutions. So here it might be argued that Baruch precedes Daniel. And this was the view taken by Ewald (*Gesch. des V. Isr.*[3] iv, pp. 265 foll.; *Propheten des Alten Bundes*[2], iii, pp. 252 foll.) ,who assigned the document to the close of the Persian Empire when the communities in and around Jerusalem were in a state of ferment (during the reign of Artaxerxes III (Ochus)) against Persian rule. This letter, under the name of Jeremiah's secretary Baruch, was intended to effect among Palestinian Jews what Jeremiah's own Epistle (Jer. xxix) effected among the Jews in exile, contentment with established foreign rule. Whatever view be taken as to the historical *prius*, whether it be Daniel or Baruch, it has been perfectly clear to nearly all except Roman Catholic critics that the document must have been composed long after the Babylonian exile. As in the case of Daniel, so also in that of this book, the historical confusion common to both can only have arisen long after the Babylonian Empire and its events had become a confused tradition. That the document A came after the Book of Daniel is indicated:

(1) By a comparison of Dan. ix. 7–19 with Bar. i. 15–ii. 17. The latter is longer and characterized by much repetition of phrase, e.g. 'have not hearkened unto the voice' . . . (= 'obeyed the voice', Dan. ix. 10, לא שמענו בקול) Bar. i. 18, 19, 21, ii. 10; 'plagues', i. 20, ii. 2. From repetitions the former is not entirely free.

(2) By the contents of A. Here the whole situation that is disclosed cannot be reconciled even with the late Maccabaean period. It is hardly conceivable that any Jew would have recommended at that time, with the retrospect of the great Maccabaean struggle behind him, and in the existing state of national feeling, a policy of loyal submission to their conquerors. Nor was that period one of utter gloom and national humiliation. Fritzsche's conjecture (p. 173) we may safely put on one side.

It is quite otherwise with the events of 63 B.C., when Pompey invaded Judaea and captured Jerusalem. Some of the indications in the document A might be held to accord with the humiliations and sufferings inflicted on the Jews when the Roman general espoused the cause of Hyrcanus against his brother Aristobulus, and laid siege to the temple quarter of Jerusalem, and even entered the Holy of Holies. The cup of humiliation was full when he carried off Aristobulus as his prisoner, and Jewish captives and spoil graced his triumph two years later. It might indeed be argued that the friendly attitude enjoined towards Israel's conquerors in A (i. 11, 12; ii. 21 f.) would accord with the date 48 B.C., when Julius Caesar's policy of clemency was extended towards the Jews. Cp. Joseph. *Ant.* xiv. 10 (*passim*); according to Suetonius (*Caes.* 84) large numbers of Jews bewailed his death. See Schürer, ed. 3, iii, p. 30. When we turn, on the other hand, to the document C evidences might be held to accumulate in favour of identifying the situation created by Pompey's invasion with that which underlies the Book of Baruch, e.g. the reference in iv. 15 to the 'shameless nation, and of a strange language' brought 'from far' points clearly to the Roman invasion, and might be compared with the phraseology of Ps. of Sol. xvii. 9. Other references, such as the 'captivity' of Jerusalem's 'sons and daughters' (iv. 14) and the denunciation of Rome, 'she that rejoiced' at Jerusalem's 'fall, and was glad of thy ruin' (iv. 33), 'her exultation and her boasting', become significant in the light of the captives which Pompey carried to Rome to adorn his triumph, which included not only Aristobulus, but also his son, Antigonus, and his two daughters.

But they become even more significant in the light of the later Roman triumph under the Flavian dynasty which wrought the greatest tragedy from which Israel has ever suffered. Ever since Kneucker's careful investigations (published in 1879) critical opinion has decisively inclined towards the view that the actual historical events which underlie the Book of Baruch belonged to the Jewish struggle against Rome of the years A.D. 66–70. The chief indications which point to this conclusion are:—

(i) The identification of Vespasian and his son Titus with 'Nabuchodonosor' and 'Baltasar his son' (i. 11, 12), whom Israel is commanded to serve loyally (ii. 21 f.). This expression of complaisance towards Rome finds its parallel in the attitude of the chief Pharisees in Judaea at a somewhat earlier period described in Josephus, *Wars*, ii. 17. 3, and in that of Josephus himself.

(ii) The fearful sufferings of the Jews to which reference is made (viz. 'great plagues', ii. 2; 'eating the flesh of children', ii. 3; 'bones of kings and ancestors cast forth', ii. 24) accord with the incidents in the siege of Jerusalem portrayed by Josephus (*Wars of the Jews*, vi. 3, 4, story of the daughter of Eleazar devouring her own son; cp. also iv. 5. 1, 2). The reference in ii. 25 to those who 'were cast out to the heat by day, and to the frost by night, and died in great miseries by famine' finds ample confirmation in the full record of Josephus, according to whom (*Wars*, vi. 9. 2–3) 'there perished for want of food 11,000' at one time. On the other hand, the references to the captivity and bondage (ii. 13, 14, 23, 29; iii. 8) are fully attested by Josephus. His numbers are doubtless exaggerated in many cases, yet he is probably not very wide of the truth when he reckons the numbers of those who were carried into captivity during the entire war to be 97,000 (*Wars*, vi. 9. 3).

(iii) The clear and definite reference to the destruction of the temple by fire in i. 2 and ii. 26 cannot be said to apply to the events of 63 B.C., when Pompey entered the temple, and its precincts were desecrated by slaughter (Josephus, *Wars*, i. 7. 4 f.). Bar. ii. 26 evidently points to the destruction of the temple by fire in A.D. 70 (Jos., *ibid.*, vi. 4).

When we turn to the document B the contents can hardly be said to reveal a distinct historical situation. It is a discourse on Wisdom embodied in the Torah. Israel has been for some considerable time dwelling in a foreign land (Bar. iii. 10) which can only refer to the very extensive *diaspora* in Egypt, Asia Minor, and other lands. It is difficult to found any definite conclusion as to date upon this. It is obviously intended to console Israel during the Roman dominion in Palestine. While Israel's temporal heritage had passed under Roman subjugation and paid tribute to the conqueror, the great spiritual possession, wisdom enshrined in the Torah, remained Israel's eternal glory of which none should deprive him (Bar. iv. 1–3). There can be little doubt that the significance of such a message to Israel would be enhanced during the years that followed the great overthrow in Vespasian's reign when Israel was bereft of temple and temple rites in the sacred city. The contents of B might seem to indicate Alexandria or Palestine as the place of its origin, but about this it is impossible to pronounce definitely on the basis of these contents only.

With the document A it is otherwise. Ch. i. 2, when connected with ii. 26, in its reference to the total destruction of Jerusalem and its temple by fire, decisively points to the conclusion that it belonged to the original introduction of the document. Here the date of the writing is fixed as the fifth year after the destruction of the temple, i.e. A.D. 74. The spirit of submission to the Roman authority, which it reflects, would be natural in the years which immediately followed the overwhelming and crushing blow to Israel's national aspirations which the capture of Jerusalem and the destruction of the temple involved. A spirit and policy like that of Josephus underlies the document. Israel's main consolation at this hour was the spiritual consolation of the Torah. That at least remained. The document B was equally appropriate to the years which followed the catastrophe of A.D. 70. On the whole it appears probable that both A and B proceeded from the circle of Joḥanan ben Zaccai, the first president of the School at Jabneh after the destruction of Jerusalem in A.D. 70. For (1) Joḥanan was a man of peace. He counselled peace in the struggle against Rome, and it is recorded of him that he prophesied imperial dignity for Vespasian in the days when he was a Roman general. (2) His pupils tore their garments and made lamentation as for the dead when they heard of the destruction of the temple of Jerusalem. (3) We read in Suc. 28 *a* that he was a devoted student of the Torah, 'He did not go four yards without reflecting on the Torah and without the phylacteries.' These are significant traits which are reflected in both the documents A and B. See *Jewish Encycl.*, art. 'Joḥanan ben Zaccai'. This view has been suggested to the present writer, independently of one another, by both Prof. Burkitt and Mr. I. Abrahams.

We have already seen that the attitude of the document C (iv. 5–v. 9) to the Roman power is altogether different. Instead of compliance we have notes of burning resentment and hostility (see above, § 3). As in the document A the events of the Flavian War against Judaea in A.D. 66–70 clearly stand in the background. The captivity of Jerusalem's children (iv. 14), like the references in A (ii. 13, 14, 23, 29; iii. 8), are in conformity with the well-known facts of history (Joseph. *Bell. Iud.* vi. 9. 3). 'Those that rejoiced' in Israel's fall and the 'exultation in her great multitude' (iv. 33, 34) receive a vivid illustration in the triumph of Vespasian and Titus. Such 'boasting' is to be 'turned into mourning' (iv. 34). We are unable to follow Kneucker in holding that the 'fire that shall come upon her from the Everlasting' is a reference to the volcanic eruption which destroyed Pompeii and Herculaneum in A.D. 79.

It is hardly possible to determine the date of such a document by any definite *terminus ad quem*. As *terminus a quo* we naturally have the tragedy of A.D. 70, whose events were still vivid in the memory of the writer. The minds of those to whom he appealed were beginning to recover from the shock of a quite recent disaster. Therefore, while the document A might appeal to those who were cowed by a quite recent calamity, the document C might be reasonably placed a few years later. Perhaps A.D. 78 might be a not improbable date. But it might well have originated later still.

§ 8. Redaction of the Documents.

We have already seen that there is strong evidence to prove that the document A was originally composed in Hebrew, and that arguments less cogent, yet valid, lead us to the same conclusion respecting the document B, which is poetical in form. The combination of both these documents into a single Hebrew roll probably followed not many years after their separate origination. In the prevailing gloom and depression awakened by such a catastrophe as that of 70 A.D.—the *année terrible* of the Jewish race—consolatory works and apocalyptic treatises would meet a widespread want. Documents A and B would appeal to minds that were disposed to bow to the inevitable—the cosmopolitan Jew, the liberal Pharisee whose sympathies were with Ananus rather than John of Gischala. 'The immediate result of the terrible calamity was a profound shock to the spirit. How could God permit such a disaster to overtake His chosen people?' Schürer (GJV^3, i, pp. 659 foll.) shows how these fundamental religious problems which meet us in the Psalms recurred with pressing intensity in the days that followed the destruction of Jerusalem. The solution of the problem of Israel's calamity was that it was a 'chastisement which God had inflicted on the people for their sin'. This conception meets us in both A and B (i. 17–19, 22, ii. 8–10, 24, iii. 8, 10–13), and also in C (iv. 7, 8). Cp. also Apoc. Bar. lxxvii. 3. 4.

It is difficult to decide how much in ch. i. 1–14 is the work of the editor who pieced together A and B. We have already seen that verses 3–9 hang badly together. We are confronted by an historical difficulty in i. 6–10, to which allusion has already been made. In § 4 we dealt with the apparent historic incompatibility of sacrificial offerings with the ruined temple. How can we reconcile these verses with the destruction of the temple in A.D. 70? Are we to regard i. 6–10 as unessential drapery? This seems hardly possible. We are driven, in fact, to raise the question discussed by Schürer (*ibid.*, pp. 653 foll.): Did sacrificial offerings actually cease immediately after the destruction of the temple? Putting aside Clem. Rom., ch. 41, and the Ep. to Diogn. 3, in which the allusion to sacrifices might be regarded as having reference to the past rather than the present, we come to the argument of Josephus, *contr. Ap.* ii. 6 *ad fin.* After stating that the law nowhere forbids Jews to pay honour to worthy men, provided it be inferior in kind to that which is paid to God, the writer proceeds to say 'we willingly testify our respect to our emperors and to the Roman people. We also offer perpetual sacrifices for them . . . although we offer no other such sacrifices at our common expense, not even for our own children, yet do we this as a special honour to the emperors.' Other confirmatory evidence is cited by Schürer; and though he is able to bring a considerable array of testimony on the other side, the statement of Josephus combined with Bar. i. 6–12 leaves behind a strong impression that such sacrifices were actually offered in Jerusalem after A.D. 70 by a party who were complaisant to the Roman power.[1] Probably these sacrifices ceased in the second century and subsequent Jewish writers ignored them as temporary and illegitimate.

The Greek translation of the Hebrew original of A and B was probably made at the close of the first century or soon after the beginning of the second. Whether it included from the first the document C (iv. 5–v. 9) or the latter came to be added subsequently it is impossible to determine. Kneucker, indeed, who regards the entire book as originally written in Hebrew, would make the *terminus a quo* of the Greek version about A.D. 118 or perhaps after the war of Bar Cocheba, A.D. 132–135. The *terminus ad quem* is A.D. 172, for Irenaeus (*Adv. Haereses*, v. 35) quotes the passage Bar. iv. 36–

[1] The view here adopted has the support of Mr. I. Abrahams. Schürer, GJV^3, i, p. 654, cites the passage in Taanith iv. 6 in which, when enumerating Israel's days of calamity, it is stated 'on the 17th Tammuz the Tāmîd came to an end'. The language of Josephus, which has been cited, practically admits this: 'although we offer no other such sacrifices at the public expense.' Abrahams therefore argues that the statement cited by Schürer from Taanith iv. 6, so far from contradicting the statement of Josephus, gives us a clue to its real meaning, since the *Tāmîd* was habitually bought at the public expense (paid for by the Sheḳālîm). Cf. *Pesikta Rabbati* (sect. Sheḳālîm). Josephus asserts that though the Tāmîd had ceased, contributions for a sacrifice for the emperor continued. It is therefore impossible to set aside such an express statement as that of Josephus, especially when taken in conjunction with the important collateral testimony of Bar. i. 6–10. We have sacrifices for the emperor in the days of Caligula (*Wars*, ii. 10. 4; cp. 17. 2–4.)

v. 9 as the words of Jeremiah. Somewhat later (A.D. 176–178) Athenagoras, in his *Apologia*, addressed to the emperor, M. Aurelius, cites (§ 69) Bar. iii. 35 as the words of an inspired prophet in close connexion with passages from Isaiah.

§ 9. The Versions.

I. Among the versions, the *Greek* was the first to appear, and secured thereby a wider currency for the entire work among the scattered Jewish population, and subsequently among the Christian communities of the Roman Empire.

Opinions are divided on the question whether a single hand or two hands have worked at the Greek translation. Both Fritzsche and Schürer have argued for a single hand, as earlier scholars (e. g. De Wette and Hitzig) have done. Fritzsche (p. 172) acknowledges that differences in style are to be found between ch. i. 1–iii. 8 and the remainder of the work, but the language in both portions is in the main the same, while other scholars account for the difference by difference of subject-matter. Kneucker, on the other hand, contends strongly that two hands have worked at the Greek translation, and submits the entire book to a careful scrutiny (pp. 76–82). It should be noticed, however, that in his comparisons a very large number of the divergences in style are found in ch. iv. 5–v. 9, which we have already shown good reason for regarding as originally composed in Greek. This of itself would involve a considerable difference in style from the earlier portion translated from an original Hebrew text. Thus Kneucker observes the frequent employment of the Greek particle *γάρ* in iv. 7, 9, 10, 11, 15, 18, 19, 22, 23, 24, 27, 28, 29, 33, 35, v. 3, 4, 6, 7, 9 (in nearly every case reproduced in Syr. by ܓܝܪ), also a more independent and free arrangement of words, iv. 9, 24, 25, v. 1, 2. In ch. iv. 10, 11 *τὴν αἰχμαλωσίαν τῶν υἱῶν μου καὶ τῶν θυγατέρων* without the repetition of *τὴν αἰχμ.* before *τῶν θυγ.* Also the genit. before the governing noun, iv. 25, 37, v. 5, 7, and the qualifying adj. or adjectival phrase preceding the noun: *τὴν παρὰ τοῦ θεοῦ ὑμῶν σωτηρίαν* (iv. 24), *τὴν παρὰ τοῦ θεοῦ ἐπελθοῦσαν ἡμῖν ὀργήν* (iv. 25); cf. iv. 29, 31, 33, 36, v. 3.

Another point to which the same writer calls attention is the close connexion between LXX on Jeremiah and our own text in those cases where borrowings from Jeremiah have taken place; e.g. Bar. i. 9, cf. Jer. xxiv. 1; Bar. ii. 3, cf. Jer. xix. 9; Bar. ii. 4, cf. Jer. xlii. 18; Bar. ii. 11, cf. Jer. xxxii. 21; Bar. ii. 13, cf. Jer. xlii. 2; Bar. ii. 21, 22, cf. Jer. xxxiv. 10, 9; Bar. ii. 23, cf. Jer. xxv. 10, 11, &c. These close resemblances are explained by some (Dillmann, Fritzsche, and Ewald) as due to the fact that the same Greek translator has produced the LXX of Jeremiah and the Greek rendering of Baruch. This theory, however, does not explain the differences as well as the coincidences of language. A more probable theory is that of Hävernick, Schürer, and (in later years) of Hitzig that the Greek translator of Baruch was acquainted with and made use of the LXX Jeremiah. This view will be found to be in some respects parallel to that which we shall have to adopt in reference to the Syriac version. The Greek translator of the document A was evidently familiar with Theodotion's version of Daniel (G^{θ}) or its groundwork, as we have indicated frequently in the notes.[1]

The MSS. of the LXX from which our text is obtained are, in the order of importance:

1. The *Codex Vaticanus* (B), written in uncials of the fourth century.
2. *Cod. Alexandrinus* (A), written in uncials of the fifth century, now in the British Museum.
3. *Cod. Marchalianus*, written in uncials not later, according to Ceriani, than the sixth century, designated Q.
4. *Codex Venetus* (numbered 23), 'written in sloping uncials of the eighth and ninth centuries' (Swete).

In addition to these we have twenty-two cursive MSS. The famous *Sinaitic codex* (א) and the *Codex Ephrêm Syri* (C) do not contain the Book of Baruch.

II. A *Syriac* version which ranks next in importance to the Greek must have been made before the time of Ephrêm Syrus (about the middle of the fourth century), who specially cites the Book of Baruch. This version is identified by Ewald, Ceriani, and Schürer with the Peshiṭta, while Kneucker disputes this view, holding that the Pesh. did not contain the books of the Apocrypha. We have a Syriac version in two forms:

(1) That which is contained in Walton's *Polyglott*, vol. iv, based on the Pocock Codex as well as the Cod. Usserianus. Upon this version we have chiefly relied in the accompanying commentary. This version has been amended by Paul de Lagarde in his work *Libri Veteris Testamenti Apocryphi Syriace*, &c. (1861).

(2) We have also the Syro-Hexaplar translation of Bishop Paul of Tela, executed at the instigation of the Monophysite patriarch Athanasius of Antioch in the year A. D. 617 at Alexandria.

[1] Theodotion is mentioned in the Syro-Hexaplar as textual authority for the Greek (cited in margin of Ceriani's edition with initial ܬ). Cp. *Encycl. Bibl.*, 'Text and Versions,' § 50.

It derives its name from the fact that it is based on Origen's Hexapla and closely follows the Greek text in the retention of Greek words and Hexaplaric signs. It thus becomes a valuable aid in the restoration of the Hexaplar text (De Wette, *Einleitung*, 8th ed., § 60). This Syro-Hexaplar version is contained in a codex belonging to the eighth century, written in Estrangelo, called *Ambrosianus*, reproduced in 1874 by photolithography (not by any means clearly in some places) by Ceriani. There is also an earlier reproduction (1861) by the same scholar (clearly printed and easily read).

We are here chiefly concerned with Walton's and Lagarde's text. A very cursory examination of this version when compared with LXX (A and B) clearly shows that it is no mere slavish reproduction of the latter, but contains numerous variants as well as expansions. We have already shown that there is clear evidence to indicate that the Syriac version (i.e. Walton's, and also Lagarde's amended version) in iv. 5–v. 9 is based on the Greek original for the simple reason that in document C there was no other. But it is otherwise with i. 1–iv. 4 (A and B). Here we are unable to follow in its entirety Kneucker's elaborate proof that the Syriac version is wholly based on the LXX. Reasons will be forthcoming in the commentary which point to the conclusion that the Syr. was based on the Hebrew original as well as on the LXX version. (1) This inference might be suggested by the Syr. rendering of ἐπὶ ποταμοῦ Σούδ, Bar. i. 4 *ad fin.* Here Σούδ is reproduced in Syr. by Ṣûr. This *may* point to a Heb. variant, since the confusion of ר and ד is exceedingly common, and Greek reproduces צ by σ (as in צִיּוֹן). Too much stress, however, cannot be laid upon proper names, which Syriac notoriously modifies and alters. (2) A more instructive example is i. 1, where ἐν Βαβυλῶνι corresponds to the Syr. ܠܒܒܠ 'to Babel' as though Baruch wrote the letter *to* Babylon. This variant is best explained by the Heb. original בבבל in which the first of the three letters ב was dropped and בבל was naturally interpreted as accus. 'to Babel'. (3) A more striking example is found in the enigmatic word ἐσχεδιάζομεν (B; in A ἐσχεδιάσαμεν) in i. 19. The word is a ἅπ. εἰρ. in the LXX. In Suidas and Hesych. the Greek word is explained by ἐγγίζειν, πλησιάζειν which yields no satisfactory sense and yet is reproduced in the Syro-Hexaplar by ܘܩܪܝܒܝܢ ܗܘܝܢ. Fortunately we have in Diod. Sic. i. 23 and Polyb. xii. 4. 4, xxiii. 9. 12, a guide to a signification which yields a better sense, 'act precipitately or rashly' (R.V. 'dealt unadvisedly'): 'We have acted precipitately in not hearkening to his voice.' We have, however, in Dan. ix the source from which many passages and phrases are borrowed, and here Dan. ix. 5, 11 enables us to restore the original וּמָרַדְנוּ לְבִלְתִּי שְׁמֹעַ בְּקוֹלוֹ. Here Kneucker is obliged to confess that the Syr. version (that of Walton) 'is relatively the most correct', ܘܡܪܕܢ ܘܠܐ ܫܡܥܢ ܒܩܠܗ which evidently closely follows the Heb. original. But how did ἐσχεδιάζομεν arise? It might perhaps be suggested that it arose by corruption of ἐστασιάζομεν. But it is a far more probable view that מרדנו became corrupted into מִהַרְנוּ. (4) For ἐκολλήθη εἰς ἡμᾶς τὰ κακά in the following verse (i. 20) we have in Syr. ܘܐܬܬ ܥܠܝܢ ܒܝܫܬܐ. With the former cp. Deut. xxviii. 60 (Heb. and LXX). The corresponding Heb. of the original may therefore have been וַתִּדְבַּק בָּנוּ הָרָעָה. But the Syr. rests on a variant וַתָּבֹא בָנוּ הָרָעָה which has greater inherent probability since we have in Dan. ix. 13 כל רעה הזאת באה, and we know that Dan. ix. 7–19 is the source from which phraseology is largely derived in Bar. i. 15–ii. 17. (5) In ii. 7 LXX ἃ ἐλάλησεν κύριος ἐφ' ἡμᾶς, πάντα τὰ κακὰ ταῦτα ἃ ἦλθεν ἐφ' ἡμᾶς. The original Heb. evidently was אֲשֶׁר יהוה דִּבֶּר עָלֵינוּ אֶת־כָּל־הָרָעָה הַזֹּאת הַבָּאָה עָלֵינוּ. Here Syr. renders the opening Heb. אֲשֶׁר by 'inasmuch as' ܡܛܠ ܕܡܪܝܐ ܥܠܝܢ ܡܠܠ . . . 'inasmuch as the Lord [our God] has declared concerning us all these evils which have come upon us'. This rendering of the relat. in Heb. is not only more accurate but brings with it better construction and sense. It is obviously not based on the Greek but on the Heb. original. (6) Another striking example may be found in ch. i. 9, on which consult the commentary. (7) Examples of dependence on a Hebrew original, sometimes on a variant corruption, may also be found in the document B (Bar. iii. 9–iv. 4), e.g. iii. 16 עלם for עמם, 18 מִסְפָּר for חֵקֶר. On these instances the notes should be consulted; also on iii. 21, 23, 34, 35. In not a few cases we have inferior renderings, and in a large number of passages indicated in the notes we have expansions[1] in the Syriac text itself, evidently in some cases added in later copies. But in some of the modifications introduced into the Syriac we may probably see primitive influences. And this concerns the document C (iv. 5–v. 9) as well as A and B.

[1] The most natural explanation of these variants and expansions is to be found in Prof. Sanday's article in *Studies in the Synoptic Problem*, pp. 17 foll., in which he describes the physical conditions under which a scribe or copyist worked with the roll, not spread out before him on a desk, but deposited in its *scrinium* or *capsa* for intermittent reference. A good example of a variant thus caused may be found in Bar. iv. 16 (on which see note). Still more would variations occur when we have to deal with translations and not copies. Here subtle motives would also co-operate, enhanced in the case of a rendering which was more or less paraphrastic.

We have therefore sufficient indications to show that the original author of the Syriac version as represented in Walton's *Polyglott* and Lagarde's edition made use of the Hebrew original of A and B, and not exclusively of the Greek translation as Kneucker insists (p. 163 f.). That it rested also on G Kneucker shows from many examples. Perhaps the most significant is to be found in iii. 32, in which κτηνῶν τετραπόδων corresponds to בְּהֵמוֹת in the Heb. original (cf. Exod. ix. 9, 10). This is the word which Delitzsch employs in his Heb. N. T. for τετράποδα in Acts x. 12. But Syr. has no corresponding word, and so there renders ܡܫ̈ܬܘܬܐ ܕܐܪܒܥ ܪ̈ܓܠܐ just as in Bar. iii. 32 ܚܝܘܬܐ ܕܐܪܒܥ ܪ̈ܓܠܝܗ. Cp. i. 14 note.

Accordingly the conclusion to which we are guided is analogous to that to which Cornill was led in his memorable critical edition of Ezekiel (1886) when dealing with the Peshiṭta: 'It is apparent at every stage that S has rendered its Heb. original freely, and does not contemplate a literal translation' (p. 148). This will be found abundantly illustrated in the notes on Baruch, where additions and variations of phrase will be found, 'additions of the most varied character' (p. 150). 'S is no pure recension but a mixed one. In the first place LXX has exercised over it an important influence' (p. 153). A similar result is even recorded in far different conditions and a very different field, where divergences of rendering are naturally restricted, viz. in Genesis, by Hänel in his careful investigation of the Peshiṭta ('Die aussermasoretischen Übereinstimmungen zw. der Septuaginta und der Peshiṭta in der Genesis'). This writer shows from a large number of instances that S is there based not only on LXX but also on a Heb. text which stands considerably nearer to the LXX than the Massoretic version (pp. 68 foll.).[1]

From slight yet significant indications we may derive some inference as to the date of the Syriac version in its origin.

(*a*) In Bar. v. 2 Jerusalem is exhorted to put on the diadem (μίτρα), but when we turn to the Syr. we find the diadem is exchanged for the military *helmet* (ܣܢܘܪܬܐ as in 1 Sam. xvii. 5, Eph. vi. 17). Again, in v. 5 'by tents' takes the place of 'on the height'.

(*b*) We note the expansion given in Syr. of iv. 31, 32: 'The cities shall be in dread that treated thee ill and rejoiced in thy downfall. The cities shall be in terror that enslaved thy sons. Thou shalt rejoice in their downfall. They shall be alarmed who treated thee ill. She shall be in dread who received thy sons.' An extra clause is added. The last clause refers to Rome specially, which we know possessed a large population of Jews (cf. Juven. *Sat.* iii. 12–16 and Schürer[3], vol. iii, p. 35). The cities to which reference is here made are probably those to which the large number, to which Josephus refers, was deported. See above under § 7 (ii).

From these indications, of which (*a*) is the more significant, we infer that the Syriac version arose at a time when there was a considerable reawakening of the martial spirit of revolt against Rome. This points to a date about 130 B.C. and after, when the struggle, headed by Bar Cocheba, was impending—the last uprising of Judaism against the power of Rome. At that time a large population of Jews (considerably augmented by those who had escaped from Judaea under the Flavian dynasty) had settled down in the Euphrates lands. Among these Jews Syriac versions, not only of the O.T. but also of such works as the Book of Baruch, would find ready acceptance. The reader who has studied Prof. Burkitt's *Early Eastern Christianity* (see esp. pp. 75 foll.) will not find this date unreasonably early. Lastly, we know that the Jews were persecuted under Trajan, and that before the outbreak of Bar Cocheba's rebellion Rabbi Aḳiba made a final journey throughout Parthia and Asia Minor and preached against Hadrian and his legions (see art. Aḳiba in Hastings's *Enc. R. E.*) The Syriac version in its earliest form may have arisen 132 A.D.

III. We have two ancient Latin versions, (*a*) the *Vetus Latina a*, sometimes called the *Itala*, which also included Wisdom, Ecclesiasticus, 1 and 2 Macc., Prayer of Manasseh, and fourth Esdras. That this version originated before the time of Jerome is evident from the fact that Cyprian (*Test. adversus Jud.* ii. 6) quotes Bar. iii. 35–7 and Tertullian (*Adv. Praxean* 16) makes a reference to verse 37. The version was, however, incorporated into the Vulgate. Fritzsche in Schenkel's *Bibel-lexicon* characterizes the style of the *Itala* as a patois full of provincialisms and violations of grammatical and syntactical rules. Not a few Greek terms are retained in Latin form. The careful investigation of this version by Kneucker (pp. 143–9) shows how closely the Greek version is followed, but not the exact text of any existing codex. (*b*) *Vetus Latina b* was first published at Rome in 1688 by Jos. Caro from an old MS. Since then it has been republished by Sabatier in the *Bibliotheca Casinensis*, vol. i (1873), on the basis of three additional MSS. Where *Vet. Lat. a* differs from the Greek text, *Vet. Lat. b* follows the latter. It is, however, also clear that *Vet. Lat. b* follows in a considerable number of details *Vet. Lat. a*, but has a better Latin style.

[1] Also Burkitt (*Enc. Bibl.*, 'Text and Versions,' Peshiṭta, § 60) remarks that the Syr. Ecclesiasticus is partly a rendering of the Hebrew.

IV. The *Arabic* version contained in Walton's *Polyglott* closely adheres to the Greek text. Kneucker has shown in his detailed examination (pp. 177 foll.) that in the vast majority of instances G^A is followed and not G^B.

V. The *Ethiopic* version similarly is based on G^A in abbreviated form. It is contained in Dillmann's *Biblia Vet. Test. Aethiopica*, vol. v (1894).

VI. The *Coptic* version was first published in 1870 by Father Bsciai (see Kneucker *in loc.*) in an edition on the basis of the Cairo codex of the Prophets. Brugsch published subsequently (1872–4) a Sahidic (Thebaic) version of the Book of Baruch (including the Epistle of Jeremiah) in Lepsius' *Zeitschrift für ägyptische Sprache und Alterthumskunde*, series x, pp. 134–6; xi, pp. 18–21; xii, pp. 46–9, from a careful, though not faultless, copy made by the learned Copt Kabis. We have also an edition by Schulte, 1892 (pp. 37–9). This version, like the Arabic and Eth., adheres on the whole to G^A, though there are *omissions* of individual words such as καί and of particles and pronouns, and even of phrases, and there are also *additions*.

VII. The *Armenian* version likewise follows, with few exceptions, G^A.

§ 10. Influence on Christian and Jewish Literature.

The influence of the book on ecclesiastical *Christian literature* has been far greater than upon the Jewish. We have already referred to the use made by Athenagoras of Bar. iii. 35 (see § 8, *ad fin.*), as well as by Irenaeus, who quotes (*Adv. Haeres.* v. 35) the passage in Bar. iv. 36–v. 9 as the words of Jeremiah. It seems at this time to have been assumed that because Baruch was the secretary of the prophet, and wrote out many of his discourses, the Book of Baruch must have also contained the utterances of Jeremiah. Thus Clemens Alexandr. (*Paedag.* I. x. 91–2) cites several passages from the Book of Baruch as the words of Jeremiah. Hippolytus, in his treatise *Contra Noëtum*, takes note of the fact that Noëtus and his followers make use of the passage Bar. iii. 35–7 as a support to their patripassian views of Christology. On the other hand, Origen, like Melito, follows the Jewish Canon, and so ignores what Roman Catholic theologians (including the latest commentator Schneedorfer) call the Deutero-Canonical books (Apocrypha), though Lamentations and Epistle of Jeremiah are included in the canonized writings. It is probable, however, that (as in the case of Clemens Al.) he included the Book of Baruch under Jeremiah, since he cites the oft-quoted Bar. iii. 38 in his *Commentary on St. John's Gospel*, and also Bar. iii. 9–13 in his *Jerem. Homil.* vii. 3. Similarly his pupil, Dionysius of Alexandria, quotes Bar. iii. 14, 15, while *Apost. Const.* cite Bar. iv. 4. So also references are to be found in Tertullian and Cyprian. Lactantius cites Bar. iii. 36 f. as the words of Jeremiah along with citations from Isaiah and the Psalms (*Inst.* iv. 38). Ephrêm Syr. regarded Bar., as well as the other Apocrypha, as Scripture.

Yet in fact many *Greek* Fathers of the fourth century separated the Apocryphal (or so-called Deutero-Canonical) writings from the Canonical. Baruch, however, formed an exception, since it was treated as an appendix to Jeremiah, and so formed part of what Athanasius calls κανονιζόμενα καὶ παραδοθέντα, πιστευθέντα τε θεῖα εἶναι βιβλία. Similarly, Cyril of Jerusalem and the Provincial Synod of Laodicea. Thus we find Chrysostom frequently quoting passages from Baruch as words 'of the prophet' or Jeremiah.

As we follow the *Latin* Fathers from Hilary of Poitiers and Ambrosius onwards we find a similar tradition. On the other hand Jerome, who studied and followed Hebrew tradition, forms a unique exception. He separates the Book of Baruch, together with the Epistle of Jeremiah, from the book of the prophet Jeremiah as non-Canonical: 'Librum autem Baruch notarii eius, qui apud Hebraeos nec legitur nec habetur, praetermisimus.' This is the more remarkable since in subsequent times Pope Felix III, Cassiodorus, and others cite Baruch as authoritative scripture. In the Latin Bible (as revised by Jerome) Baruch and the Epistle of Jeremiah are omitted. Thus they are not to be found in the Cod. Amiatinus, the oldest known MS. of the Vulgate. On the other hand, at the Council of Trent it was recognized as part of the O.T. among other Deutero-Canonical books. Our English Bible follows the Protestant tradition in placing it among the Apocrypha as non-Canonical. For further detail we would refer to Reusch's work, pp. 2–21, and to Schürer, *GJV*[3], iii, p. 342 f. Among Protestant German divines till Ewald there was a tendency to depreciate the value of the book.

With reference to the Book of Baruch as a part of *Jewish* literature, we have already shown that there are strong grounds for the belief that a Hebrew original of Bar. i. 1–iv. 4 existed for a time among the Jewish communities of the Diaspora during the last quarter of the first century, and that the rest of the book must have been published within that period in Greek. During the early part of the second century the whole must have circulated in Greek and somewhat later in Aramaic (among the Jewish settlements of Mesopotamia). But the history of the book both then and later among the Jewish communities is most obscure. Probably the note of complaisance towards the

Roman power in ch. i. 1–iii. 8 did not commend the book to Jews after the suppression of Bar Cocheba's insurrection in A.D. 135. The testimony of the *Apostolic Constitutions* (v. 20) that on the 10th of the month Gorpiaeus it was read along with the Lamentations of Jeremiah as a portion in Jewish worship is subject to some difficulty, as we are unable to identify the date assigned with that of the Jewish Calendar, though the statement is confirmed by a reference to synagogue-worship accompanied by a citation of Bar. iv. 9 in Ephrêm Syrus. See Schürer, *GJV*³, iii, p. 342. The express statement of Jerome (Preface to Jerem.) that in his day the Book of Baruch and the Epistle of Jeremiah were 'not read among the Hebrews' would lead us to the conclusion that in the fourth century A.D. both had ceased to have any recognized place in current Jewish religious literature.

§ 11. The Religious Ideas of the Book of Baruch.

Since the book is composite in authorship and tendency, it cannot be said to present in its three documents any uniformity of ideas, except in certain positive general features common to all three parts and also in the general absence of others to which allusion will be made.

(*a*) *Doctrine of God.* In all the three documents God is recognized as the absolute ruler of Israel's destiny, the fountain of righteousness and power, i. 15, 19, ii. 6, iii. 1, 32 foll. The document B (iii. 9–iv. 4) naturally emphasizes God's wisdom and universal knowledge (iii. 32–7). On the other hand, God's mercy, which listens to the cry of His people, is assumed throughout the penitential supplication of i. 15–iii. 8, and is expressly affirmed in ii. 35, iii. 2. These features are, however, most prominent in document C (iv. 5–v. 9), which is greatly influenced by the Deutero-Isaiah, in which God's love and mercy to His people is the dominant theme. This divine compassion is the ground of the repeated exhortation 'Be of good cheer'. 'He that called thee by name will comfort thee.' This document C is specially characterized by the designation of God as 'Everlasting' (*αἰώνιος*), iv. 22, 35, v. 2, and as 'Holy One', iv. 22. On the other hand, when we turn to the document A (i. 2, 3 *b*–iii. 8), Lord God (יהוה אלהים) is the usual combination, frequently with the 1st pers. plur. added, 'Lord *our* God.' In fact 'Lord' (= יהוה) belongs to this document and not to the other two. To this in two passages (iii. 1, 4) is added the epithet 'Almighty' (*παντοκράτωρ*, Heb. צבאות) or 'All-ruler' (iii. 1, 4). See Gifford's Introd. *ad fin.*

(*b*) *The doctrine of Sin* and of *Suffering* as the divinely inflicted chastisement for sin is strongly emphasized throughout the book, especially in i. 13, 18–ii. 10, 22 foll., iii. 10–13, iv. 6–8, 12, 13. Moreover, the sin of the fathers is visited in chastisement on the children, though the obverse doctrine of merit through the righteousness of ancestors which plays so large a part in Jewish Soteriology (cp. Matt. iii. 9, Weber, *Jüdische Theologie*, § 63) is repudiated in ii. 19.

(*c*) *Silence on other points of doctrine.* One is impressed by a certain meagreness in the religious conceptions presented to us in this brief book. In this respect it stands sharply contrasted with the wealth of ideas contained in 2 Baruch, i. e. the Syriac Apocalypse of Baruch. Of the Angelology of the latter (2 Bar. vi. 4 f., vii, viii, temple destroyed by angels, with which the Epistle to the nine and a half tribes should be compared, lxxx. 1, 2 in Charles's ed. of 2 Bar.) we have not a trace, nor have we mention of Sirens, Liliths, and dragons (2 Bar. x. 8); only a stray reference to demons in 1 Bar. iv. 35, a borrowed feature. Even the Messianic element prominent in 2 Bar. (xxix. 3–8, xxxix. 7) is conspicuous by its absence, as in fact are apocalyptic and eschatological ideas generally. Of the resurrection of the righteous, to which 2 Bar. alludes (xxx), not a word is said in 1 Bar., though we cannot go so far as to assert (with Toy in *Jewish Encycl.*) that it is denied in ii. 17, where the language respecting the dead in Sheôl is merely an echo of Ps. cxv. 17. Nor have we the pessimistic forecast of a coming age of decay such as we find in 2 Bar. xxxi. 5, xxxii. 5, 6 (cf. Epistle to the nine and a half tribes, lxxxiii. 9–23, lxxxv. 10). The 2 Baruch and the Epistle to the nine and a half tribes evidently belong to a school and atmosphere of thought entirely different from that of 1 Baruch.

(*d*) *Great message of document B.* Ch. iii. 9–iv. 4, with its praise of Wisdom embodied in the Torah, strikes the highest note that meets the ear throughout the whole book. There is something profoundly impressive and pathetic in the closing verses of this document which direct Israel's thoughts away from his national humiliation, the temple-ruins and the vanished material pomp of religious ritual, to the eternal glory of that wisdom enshrined in the Torah which was to be Israel's inalienable possession for ever: 'Turn thee, O Jacob, and take hold of it: walk toward her shining in the presence of the light thereof.' We can afford to miss the grandiose and bizarre effects of apocalyptic as we stand in the clear sunlight of this sublime utterance. In place of the ruined temple the broad universe is the 'house of God' (iii. 24, 25).

§ 12. SELECTED LITERATURE.

The articles on the Book of Baruch in the *Encycl. Bibl.*, *Hastings's DB*,[1] *Encycl. Brit.* (11th ed.), *Jewish Encycl.*, and in *PRE*³, i, p. 640 f. under 'Apocryphen des A.T.'—Perhaps the most complete and useful is by SCHÜRER, *GJV*³, iii, pp. 338–44.

Among commentaries specially to be mentioned are FRITZSCHE, *Exegetisches Handbuch zu den Apocryphen*, Leipz., 1851; REUSCH, *Erklärung des Buches Baruch* (1853), which is from the Roman Catholic standpoint, useful for its survey of the book's place in patristic literature, [also from same standpoint *Das Buch Jeremias, des Propheten Klagelieder u. das Buch Baruch* by SCHNEEDORFER (1903)]; EWALD in *Die Propheten des Alten Bundes*, iii (*Die jüngsten Propheten*). The most important, however, is that by KNEUCKER (1879), which contains not only an ample Introduction but also a very complete textual apparatus with a careful examination of the different versions, a full commentary, a translation, and a reproduction of the original Hebrew. In English should be specially mentioned the *Commentary on the Apocrypha*, edited by Dr. Wace, to which the Ven. E. H. Gifford, D.D., contributes the commentary on the Book of Baruch. Lastly, *Die Apocryphen des A.T.*, by KAUTZSCH, to which ROTHSTEIN contributes Baruch, will be found useful and suggestive.

Among other contributions we should mention HITZIG, *Zeitsch. für wissensch. Theol.*, 1860, pp. 262–73; HILGENFELD, *ibid.*, 1862, pp. 199–203; 1879, pp. 437–54; 1880, pp. 412–22, and KNEUCKER, *ibid.*, 1880, pp. 309–23; GRÄTZ, 'Abfassungszeit und Bedeutung des Buches Baruch,' *Monatsch. für Gesch. u. Wissensch. des Judenthums*, iii. 1887, pp. 5–20.

---

[1] Attention should have been drawn above under § 2 to the two parts of the confession of Israel, noted in his article by Dr. Marshall. The *first* and shorter portion (i. 15–ii. 5) appears to have been intended more especially for use by the inhabitants of Judah. Hence the distinction in ii. 4 'round about *us* . . . hath scattered *them*'. The *second* part (ii. 6–iii. 8) is the confession more especially of the exiles. Hence in ii. 13, iii. 8 'scattered *us*'. This distinction is useful since it accounts for the repetition of phrase in the two parts, e.g. i. 15 and ii. 6; ii. 4 and ii. 13 (iii. 8). Both portions obviously proceeded from the same hand, rested on like presuppositions (such as the solidarity of Israel and Judah), and are based very largely on Danielic phraseology.

THE BOOK OF BARUCH

1 1 And these are the words of the book, which Baruch the son of Nerias, the son of Maaseas, the
2 son of Sedekias, the son of Asadias, the son of Helkias, wrote in Babylon, in the fifth year, *and* in
the seventh day of the month, what time as the Chaldeans took Jerusalem, and burnt it with fire.
3 And Baruch did read the words of this book in the hearing of Jechonias the son of Joakim king of
4 Judah, and in the hearing of all the people that came to *hear* the book, and in the hearing of the
mighty men, and of the kings' sons, and in the hearing of the elders, and in the hearing of all the
people, from the least unto the greatest, even of all them that dwelt at Babylon by the river Sud.
5, 6 And they wept, and fasted, and prayed before the Lord; they made also a collection of money
7 according to every man's power: and they sent *it* to Jerusalem unto Joakim the *high* priest, the
son of Helkias, the son of Salom, and to the priests, and to all the people which were found with
8 him at Jerusalem, at the same time when he took the vessels of the house of the Lord, that had been
carried out of the temple, to return *them* into the land of Judah, the tenth day of *the month* Sivan,

TITLE. G S$^{Hex.}$ Baruch; S 'In addition the Second Ep. of Baruch the Scribe'; S (Lag.) 'The Second Epistle'; Arm. 'Ep. of Baruch'; Vet. Lat. *a b* 'Prophecy of Baruch'; Copt. 'Baruch the prophet'. [The 'Second Ep.' in S title refers by implication to the earlier preceding Ep. in S addressed by Baruch to the nine and a half tribes beyond the Euphrates.]

INTRODUCTION 1-14 [1, 3 *a* belong to document B; 2, 3 *b*–14, excluding redactional insertions, to document A].

1. On the personal details respecting Baruch see *Ency. Bibl.*, *sub voce*, and cf. Joseph. *Ant.* x. 9. 1, Kneucker Introd., pp. 2 foll. *Maaseas* here is obviously the Maḥsēiah of Jer. xxxii. 12; *Asadias* is the Hebr. Ḥasadiah. We find the name in 1 Chron. iii. 20. In S, through omission of the opening character and the frequent confusion of ר and ד, the name takes the form ܣܪܝܐ. This form of the name may, however, have arisen through Jer. li. 59. Baruch's genealogy is here traced further back than Maḥsēiah (Jer. xxxii. 12). S reads '*to* Babylon', as though the letter were dispatched from Palestine. How this may have textually arisen has been already explained, Introd., § 9 (ii. Syr. Version). In this way the so-called Second Ep. (in S) accords with the preceding epistle addressed to the nine and a half tribes beyond the Euphrates (cf. Title above), which is given in Walton's *Polygl.* and as an addendum in Charles's *Apoc. of Baruch*, pp. 124 foll.

2. The omission of the numeral before μηνός is certainly unusual, and points either to a defective original or to an omission by the translator. S leads us to the conclusion that the omission belonged to the original. We have no warrant, therefore, for the insertion of the name of the month Sivan (with Ewald).

In Ezek. i. 2, viii. 1, &c., the years are reckoned from the date of the first capture of Jerusalem by Nebuchadnezzar when Jehoiachin was made prisoner (597 B.C.). In this year, however, Jerusalem was not burnt, but in the subsequent and final capture when the temple was destroyed 587–586 B.C. (cf. Bar. ii. 26). It is from this date, therefore (with Fritzsche, as against Eichhorn and others), the fifth year should be reckoned. See Introd., § 4.

3, 4. The language reminds us of 2 Kings xxiii. 2; 2 Chron. xxxiv. 30. πρὸς τὴν βίβλον, i. e. to hear the book. βίβλος instead of βιβλίον in 3 *a*. Similarly βίβλος in iv. 1. We know nothing of the locality of Sud. Grotius conjectures that it refers to the city Soïta. Bochart would emend to *Sur*, i. e. the city Sora. S, in fact, renders 'river of Ṣûr', which may be founded on the original צור, but it is precarious to base a conclusion on the Syr. treatment of proper names. Cheyne's suggestion of Shihor (in *Ency. Bibl.*) is pure conjecture. L and Ar. follow G in reading *Sud*; so also characteristically S^{Hex}.

5. With the phraseology comp. 2 Chron. xxiv. 5, 11; Lev. v. 7, &c.

7. ἱερέα (as contrasted with following ἱερεῖς) is used in the pregnant sense of the head-priest of the Jerusalem sanctuary as in 1 Kings iv. 2; 2 Kings xi. 9, xii. 8; cf. Lev. xiii. 2; Num. iii. 6; Neh. xiii. 4; 1 Chron. xvi. 39, &c. (cf. 1 Macc. xv. 1). In assigning this position to Joakim the writer departs from earlier tradition. According to 1 Chron. v. 39 the succession of High Priests was Shallum, Hilkiah, Azariah, Seraiah. Esdras (A) viii. 1 interpolates Zichri between Hilkiah and Azariah. In only quite late times we find a tradition (in Joseph. *Ant.* xi. 5. 1) that on the death of Darius a certain Jehoiakim, son of Jeshua, was High Priest contemporary with Ezra. But this was more than 120 years after the time to which this passage refers. The chief priest in Jerusalem at the time of its final overthrow (587–586 B.C.) was Seraiah, 2 Kings xxv. 18 (= Jer. lii. 24).

8. As already shown (Introd., § 4) the reference of αὐτόν is vague. 'He' might be referred to Joakim (Jehoiakim) of the preceding verse (so Herzfeld, Hilgenfeld, &c.). But this is evidently not intended. Baruch, the subject of verse 3, is meant, since his presence in Babylon and not in Judaea fits the situation (so Fritzsche, Reusch, Ewald, Hävernick, Hitzig, and Kneucker).

The restoration of the vessels to Jerusalem is another departure from the older tradition. According to the latter, the vessels which had been carried off by Nebuchadnezzar (2 Kings xxiv. 13, i. e. 597 B.C., and xxv. 14 f., i. e. 586 B.C.) were restored by Cyrus (Ezra i. 7–11). The statement in this verse seems to ignore Jeremiah's polemic against Hananiah and the false prophets (Jer. xxvii. 16, xxviii. 3, xxix. 4). Zedekiah's preparation of silver vessels is another addition to the later story. The angelic vision in 2 Bar. vi. 4–10 respecting the concealment of the furniture of the Holy of Holies is another example of the freedom with which later writers dealt with history. The month Sivan (May-June) belongs in origin to the Babylonian Calendar (Schrader, *COT*, ii, p. 69 f.), borrowed by exilian and post-exilian Judaism and made the third month of their ecclesiastical year. It is mentioned in the late post-exilian Esther viii. 9. S reads here Nisan and om. 'silver' (perhaps as derogatory to national dignity).

9 *namely*, silver vessels, which Sedekias the son of Josias king of Judah had made, after that Nabuchodonosor king of Babylon had carried away Jechonias, and the princes, and the captives, and the
10 mighty men, and the people of the land, from Jerusalem, and brought them unto Babylon. And
they said, Behold, we have sent you money; buy you therefore with the money burnt offerings, and
sin offerings, and incense, and prepare an oblation, and offer upon the altar of the Lord our God;
11 and pray for the life of Nabuchodonosor king of Babylon, and for the life of Baltasar his son, that
12 their days may be as the days of heaven above the earth: and the Lord will give us strength, and
lighten our eyes, and we shall live under the shadow of Nabuchodonosor king of Babylon, and
under the shadow of Baltasar his son, and we shall serve them many days, and find favour in their
13 sight. Pray for us also unto the Lord our God, for we have sinned against the Lord our God; and
14 unto this day the wrath of the Lord and his indignation is not turned from us. And ye shall read
this book which we have sent unto you, to make confession in the house of the Lord, upon the day
of the feast and on the days of the solemn assembly.
15 And ye shall say, To the Lord our God *belongeth* righteousness, but unto us confusion of face, as
16 at this day, unto the men of Judah, and to the inhabitants of Jerusalem, and to our kings, and to
17 our princes, and to our priests, and to our prophets, and to our fathers: for that we have sinned
18 before the Lord, and disobeyed him, and have not hearkened unto the voice of the Lord our God,
19 to walk in the commandments of the Lord that he hath set before us: since the day that the Lord
brought our fathers out of the land of Egypt, unto this present day, we have been disobedient unto
20 the Lord our God, and we have dealt unadvisedly in not hearkening unto his voice. Wherefore the
plagues clave unto us, and the curse, which the Lord commanded Moses his servant *to pronounce* in

9. Obviously an echo of Jer. xxiv. 1. There δεσμώτας corresponds to the doubtful word מַסְגֵּר = 'prison' (Isa. xxiv. 22, xlii. 7; Ps. cxlii. 8), and there applied apparently to those who are imprisoned. The 'people of the land' corresponds to עַם הָאָרֶץ of Zech. vii. 5, but meaning here, as in 2 Kings xxiv. 14, Jer. i. 18, Dan. ix. 6, the common people as opposed to the aristocracy (in Zech. the laity as distinguished from the priesthood). S varies considerably after 'princes', viz. 'and the officers and the workmen and the armies from Jerusalem'. Here 'the workmen' (τεχνίτας = הֶחָרָשׁ) takes the place of 'the people of the land' in G and Syr.-Hex., and stands in closer accord with both Jer. xxiv. 1 and the history of the year 597 B.C. (comp. 2 Kings xxiv. 14). We are in fact led to conclude that S here rather than G is based on the original Hebrew text.

10. μάννα (more correctly μαναά in many codd.), 'oblation', is obviously an attempt to reproduce the Hebr. מִנְחָה Jer. xvii. 26, xli. 5. ποιήσατε, 'prepare', is a literal rendering of the Hebr. וַעֲשִׂיתֶם, as in Exod. xxix. 36, &c., Lev. ix. 7, xv. 15. Similarly καὶ ἀνοίσατε, 'and offer', most probably corresponds to והעליתם (Jer. xxxiii. 18 G^A; Exod. xxiv. 5, xxx. 9; Lev. xiv. 20, &c.).

11. The exhortation to pray for the life of Nebuchadnezzar reflects the tone of prophecy in Jeremiah and Ezekiel towards Babylonia. In later exilian prophecy the tone becomes embittered (Isa. xlvii, Jer. l, li, contrasted with Jer. xxvii. 6–8, xxix. 4–7; Ezek. xxvi. 7–12, xxix. 17–20). προσεύξασθε περὶ . . . seems an echo of Jer. xxix. 7 (xxxvi. 7 G^B). On the historical questions involved see Introd., § 8.

Baltasar appears in Dan. v. 1 as Belshazzar (H, in $G^{o \text{ and } \theta}$ Baltasar). Both here and in Daniel we have the same confusion of names. Belshazzar (in Babyl. *Bêl-šar-uṣur*, 'Bel, protect the king') was son of Nabonidus (*Nabû-naïd*, 'Nebo is gracious'), the last Babylonian king, not of Nebuchadnezzar (as in Dan. v. 2, 13, 18, 22, and in the present passage).

12. S introduces characteristic variations in the opening of the verse, 'and that the Lord grant unto us that we may serve him.'

13. ἀπέστρεψεν ('is . . . turned') is here intransit., whereas in verse 8 above ἀποστρέψαι is transit. On this tendency of transit. Greek verbs to become intransit., see Radermacher, *NTliche Gram.* (1911), pp. 18 foll.; comp. below, ii. 8. The Hebrew equivalent may be easily restored from Isa. ix. 11, 16, &c. (G ἀπεστράφη), lv. 10, viz. לא שב ממנו אף יהוה וזעמו. S adds 'our God' to 'Lord' in all three cases where the Deity is mentioned. This combination is the usual formula in 1 Baruch.

14. **make confession** (ἐξαγορεῦσαι), evidently the rendering of לְהִתְוַדּוֹת, as in Lev. v. 7, xvi. 21; Num. v. 7. καιρός here stands for מוֹעֵד in the sense of festival season or 'solemn assembly' (πανήγυρις), whereas ἑορτή, 'feast', is the translation of חָג. Comp. Hos. ix. 5, xii. 10. But while $S^{Hex.}$ reproduces here G, S has 'days of the *Lord*'. This is evidently due to the influences of a corrupted Greek text (κυρίου for καιροῦ). G^B S ἡμέρᾳ . . . ἡμέραις, but $G^{A \text{ and } Q}$ harmonize by reading plur. in both cases, L by reading sing. S, moreover, introduces additions, 'make confession *on behalf of us* in the Lord's house *before the Lord*.'

CONFESSION OF THE PALESTINIAN REMNANT, i. 15–ii. 5 (document A. See note on p. 582).

15–18 is closely modelled on Dan. ix. 7–10, yet abbreviated.

15. **as at this day** is the familiar Hebr. כַּיּוֹם הַזֶּה in 1 Kings viii. 24 and Dan. ix. 7. On this pregnant use of כְּ in Hebrew see Gesen.-Kautzsch, *Hebr. Gr.*,[26] § 118. 6; comp. below, ii. 26 note.

17. **before the Lord.** ἔναντι G^B belongs to the κοινή, Radermacher, *NTliche Gram.*, p. 117. $G^{A\,Q}$ ἐναντίον; 'for that we have sinned,' &c. = אֲשֶׁר חָטָאנוּ לַיהוָֹה (לִפְנֵי י״י), Dan. ix. 8, 11.

19. On ἐσχεδιάζομεν (G^A ἐσχεδιάσαμεν), a ἅπ. εἰρ. in LXX ('dealt unadvisedly'), see Introd., § 9, ii (Syr. Vers.). S and Dan. ix. 5, 11 clearly show that we have in G a rendering based on a corrupt text. Translate: 'We have *rebelled* in not hearkening . . .' ἐσχεδιάζομεν arose out of the corruption of מרדנו into מהרנו.

20. **clave** (ἐκολλήθη). A strong phrase which occurs again in iii. 4. This and other expressions in this verse are

the day that he brought our fathers out of the land of Egypt, to give us a land that floweth with
21 milk and honey, as at this day. Nevertheless we hearkened not unto the voice of the Lord our
22 God, according unto all the words of the prophets, whom he sent unto us: but we walked every
man in the imagination of his own wicked heart, to serve strange gods, and to do that which is evil
2 1 in the sight of the Lord our God. Therefore the Lord hath made good his word, which he pronounced against us, and against our judges that judged Israel, and against our kings, and against
2 our princes, and against the men of Israel and Judah, to bring upon us great plagues, such as never
happened under the whole heaven, as it came to pass in Jerusalem, according to the things that
3 are written in the law of Moses; that we should eat every man the flesh of his own son, and every
4 man the flesh of his own daughter. Moreover he hath given them to be in subjection to all the
kingdoms that are round about us, to be a reproach and a desolation among all the people round
5 about, where the Lord hath scattered them. Thus were they cast down, and not exalted, because
6 we sinned against the Lord our God, in not hearkening unto his voice. To the Lord our God
7 *belongeth* righteousness: but unto us and to our fathers confusion of face, as at this day. *For* all
8 these plagues are come upon us, which the Lord hath pronounced against us. Yet have we not
intreated the favour of the Lord, in turning every one from the thoughts of his wicked heart.
9 Therefore hath the Lord kept watch over the plagues, and the Lord hath brought *them* upon us;
10 for the Lord is righteous in all his works which he hath commanded us. Yet we have not hearkened
unto his voice, to walk in the commandments of the Lord that he hath set before us.
11 And now, O Lord, thou God of Israel, that hast brought thy people out of the land of Egypt
with a mighty hand, and with signs, and with wonders, and with great power, and with a high arm,
12 and hast gotten thyself a name, as at this day: O Lord our God, we have sinned, we have done
13 ungodly, we have dealt unrighteously in all thine ordinances. Let thy wrath turn from us: for we

obviously Deuteronomic, cf. Deut. xxviii. 60 (Hebr. and G). In the original there would stand ותדבק בנו הרעה והאלה (cf. also Dan. ix. 11). But S has a variant which is more probable. See Introd., § 9, ii (Syr. Version).

21–22 continue in the Deuteronomic strain (esp. of Deut. xxviii) reflected in Dan. ix. 5–17. S contains an interpretative expansion 'to do all the words of his servants the prophets'.

22. G[A] (followed by Vet. Lat. *a* and Ar.) wrongly places ἡμῶν instead of αὐτοῦ after καρδίας.

II. 1–2 follow Dan. ix. 12, 13 with many close resemblances in G to the corresponding version in Dan. of G[θ], but δικαστάς for κριτάς and δικάσαντας for οἳ ἔκρινον. Note ὑπὸ παντὸς τοῦ οὐρανοῦ common to both. καὶ ἔστησεν . . . δικάσαντας is almost a literal reproduction of Dan. ix. 12. S + 'and Judah' in both cases to 'Israel'. Corresponding to ἔστησεν, 'made good', we should have the familiar וַיָּקֶם. This Hif. is used in the sense of keeping a command or promise by fulfilling it. Cf. verse 24 and Gen. xxvi. 3; Lev. xxvi. 9; Deut. ix. 5: 1 Sam. i. 23, xv. 13; 1 Kings ii. 4, vi. 12, xii. 15; Jer. xi. 5, xxxiii. 14. S ܘܐܩܝܡ appears to reproduce the Hebr. original, but this is not a necessary conclusion; cf. S[Hex.] and Ar.

ἄνθρωπον Ἰσρ. Here Hebr. original would be אִישׁ יִשְׂ׳ where אִישׁ is used *collectively* as in Joshua ix. 6 and Judg. vii. 23 (where G more correctly has ἀνήρ).

G[A Q] preserve the full original text, since they add τοῦ ἀγαγεῖν (Q* ἀναγαγεῖν) ἐφ' ἡμᾶς κακὰ μέγαλα ἅ, 'to bring upon us great plagues such as', just as in Dan. ix. 12, i.e. in Hebr. original . . . להביא עלינו רעה גדולה אשר. So S[Hex.] (with asterisks) and Ar. S, however, has ܘܐܝܬܝ ܒܝܫܬܐ ܪܘܪܒܬܐ, perhaps based on וַיָּבֵא עלינו יהוה, and after 'heaven' adds 'upon all the earth' (evidently an expansion; cf. Dan. ix. 12).

3. ἄνθρωπον, Hebr. אִישׁ in sense of 'every one'. We have here language based on Jer. xix. 9, Deut. xxviii. 53 (cf. Lev. xxvi. 29); G[A] 'sons' (plur.); so Ar. S has *sing.* as G[B].

4. ὑποχειρίους, 'in subjection', ויתן אתם ביד [cf. Gen. xiv. 20 (H and G)], closely followed in S. The latter part of the verse is an echo of Jer. xlii. 18 (G closely corresponds), 'reproach and a desolation', לְחֶרְפָּה וּלְשַׁמָּה; οὗ . . . ἐκεῖ (cf. verse 13 and Mark i. 7, vii. 25), Heb. אֲשֶׁר . . . שָׁם.

5. Borrowed from Deut. xxviii. 13.

Confession of the Exiled Community in Babylon, ii. 6–iii. 8 (document A).

6. Repetition of i. 15 with slight variation.

7. S renders 'seeing that the Lord our God hath uttered against us all these evils', &c., ܡܛܠ ܕܡܠܠ ܒܝܫܬܐ ܪܘܪܒܬܐ [ܟܠܗܝܢ] . ., which is a better rendering of the original Hebr. אֲשֶׁר דִּבֶּר יהוה עָלֵינוּ אֶת־כָּל־הָרָעָה הַזֹּאת הַבָּאָה עָלֵינוּ. See Introd., § 9, ii (Syr. Vers.). Here, however, S[Hex.] follows G as usual. On ὡς ἡ ἡμέρα αὕτη cf. Bar. v. 6 note.

8. G is here nearly identical with G[θ] in the corresponding portion of Dan. ix. 13. νοημάτων, 'thoughts'; S ܪ̈ܢܝܢ, 'inclinations', 'desires', as in i. 22 (διανοίᾳ), corresponds to Hebr. מַחְשָׁבוֹת.

9. An almost exact replica of Dan. ix. 14, which in its turn echoes Jer. xliv. 27. Note that for 'works which he hath *done*' in the Dan. passage, we have here 'which he hath *commanded* us' (in S ܕܦܩܕ just as in G and S[Hex.], Hebr. צִוָּנוּ). Yahweh is watching over the calamities in order to bring them to pass as retribution for transgression.

10. Repeats with variations i. 18, which closely follows Dan. ix. 10, G partly following the Dan. passage in G[θ].

11. Reproduces Dan. ix. 15 in its earlier part with Deuteronomic phrases added. Here again G follows the Dan. version of G[θ].

12. Continues the Danielic phraseology at the close of ix. 15 (cf. 5). G, however, prefers δικαιώματα to the κρίματα of G[o and θ] in Dan. as rendering of מִשְׁפָּטִים. Cf. verse 1.

13. The language is borrowed from Jer. xlii. 2, כִּי נִשְׁאַרְנוּ מְעַט מֵהַרְבֵּה 'for we are left but a few *out of many*' (cf.

14 are but a few left among the heathen, where thou hast scattered us. Hear our prayer, O Lord, and
our petition, and deliver us for thine own sake, and give us favour in the sight of them which have
15 led us away captive: that all the earth may know that thou art the Lord our God, because Israel
16 and his posterity is called by thy name. O Lord, look down from thine holy house, and consider
17 us: incline thine ear, O Lord, and hear: open thine eyes, and behold: for the dead that are in the
grave, whose breath is taken from their bodies, will give unto the Lord neither glory nor righteousness:
18 but the soul that is greatly vexed, which goeth stooping and feeble, and the eyes that fail, and the
19 hungry soul, will give thee glory and righteousness, O Lord. For we do not present our supplication
20 before thee, O Lord our God, for the righteousness of our fathers, and of our kings. For thou hast
sent thy wrath and thine indignation upon us, as thou hast spoken by thy servants the prophets,
21 *saying*, Thus saith the Lord, Bow your shoulders to serve the king of Babylon, and remain in the
22 land that I gave unto your fathers. But if ye will not hear the voice of the Lord, to serve the king
23 of Babylon, I will cause to cease out of the cities of Judah, and from without Jerusalem, the voice
of mirth, and the voice of gladness, the voice of the bridegroom, and the voice of the bride: and the
24 whole land shall be desolate without inhabitant. But we would not hearken unto thy voice, to serve
the king of Babylon: therefore hast thou made good thy words that thou spakest by thy servants
the prophets, *namely*, that the bones of our kings, and the bones of our fathers, should be taken out
25 of their places. And, lo, they are cast out to the heat by day, and to the frost by night, and they
26 died in great miseries by famine, by sword, and by pestilence. And the house which is called by
thy name hast thou laid *waste*, as at this day, for the wickedness of the house of Israel and the house

Deut. iv. 27). *ἀπὸ πολλῶν* has been accidentally dropped out of G[A B] and is inserted in S. ܡܢ ܣܓܝܐܐ. We are justified in restoring מֵהַרְבֵּה to the Heb. 1 Baruch, since some G codd. (22, 36, 48, 51, and others) retain *ἀπὸ πολλ.* and its omission is indicated in the marg. of S[Hex.]. S supplies us here with a parallelism: 'because we have been left a few out of many and are scanty among these peoples among whom thou hast scattered us.'

14. *ἀποικίζω* corresponds to שבה (cf. Jer. xliii. 12, H and G). So here S ܫܒܐ.

15. S adds 'holy' to 'name'.

16–17. *ἐννόησον εἰς ἡμᾶς* = הָבֵן בָּנוּ (or בִּין Dan. ix. 23, G[θ] *ἐννοήθητι ἐν*). S repeats ܚܘܪ, *κάτιδε*, הַבֵּט (or הַשְׁקִיפָה, Deut. xxvi. 15).

incline . . . thine eyes repeat Dan. ix. 18. On *ὧν . . . αὐτῶν* Hebr. relat. cf. verses 4, 13 above.

We have here the ordinary O. T. teaching of life in Sheôl taught in Ps. vi. 6, lxxxviii. 11, cxv. 17. *πνεῦμα* corresponds in meaning to רוּחַ חַיִּים of Gen. vi. 17 (cf. נִשְׁמַת חַיִּים, ii. 7). *σπλάγχνα* usually corresponds to Hebr. רַחֲמִים (cf. S), but here it is more likely that the original had מֵעִים (as Kneucker suggests). *δικαίωμα* here = *δικαιοσύνη* (verse 18 *ad fin.*). Comp. Isa. xlv. 23 foll. The corresponding Hebr. צְדָקָה describes 'that aspect of Yahweh's activity which has for its object the salvation of His people' (Kautzsch in *DB*, v, p. 683).

18. *ἐπὶ τὸ μέγεθος* has caused difficulty to interpreters. S affords no help. Fritzsche rightly suspects that there lurks behind it a corrupted Hebr. original. The passage seems to reflect the spirit of Deut. xxviii. 65 f.

19. *καταβάλλομεν τὸν ἔλεον*, 'present our supplication', is fairly clear. S paraphrases: 'We seek from Thy presence compassion and cast our supplication in Thy presence.' It is nearly certain that we have here the rendering of the original Hebr. אֲנַחְנוּ מַפִּלִים תְּחִנָּתֵנוּ, Jer. xxxviii. 26, xlii. 9; Dan. ix. 20. In all these passages G renders תְּחִנָּה (which means 'pity' and thence is used in the pregnant sense '*prayer for* pity') by the corresponding *ἔλεος*, properly 'compassion', 'pity', like the Hebr. equivalent, and similarly used in a pregnant sense.

This verse exhibits a reaction against the prevalent Jewish doctrine of merit. It is not on account of the righteousness of ancestors and kings that we found our claim to divine compassion. See Weber, *Jüd. Theol.*, §§ 63 foll. *δικαιώματα*, 'acts of righteousness' (צְדָקוֹת); comp. Rom. v. 18.

20. Phraseology borrowed from Jer. xxxvi. 7, הָאַף וְהַחֵמָה 'wrath and indignation'. So also as in Dan. ix. 6, עֲבָדֶיךָ הַנְּבִאִים (G[o] *παιδων*, G[θ] *δουλων*). Here Dan. LXX for 'servants' is followed.

21. Based on Jer. xxvii. 11, 12 and xxix. 5 f., 'bow your shoulders,' in Hebr. הָבִיאוּ צַוַּארְכֶם (or perhaps הַטּוּ שִׁכְמְכֶם, Gen. xlix. 15), reflecting the attitude of Jeremiah and Ezekiel towards Babylonia; cf. i. 11–12 above.

23 reproduces Jeremiah's words repeated in Jer. vii. 34, xvi. 9, xxxiii. 11. *εἰς ἄβατον*, 'desolate', probably = *εἰς ἐρήμωσιν* in Jer. vii. 34, לְחָרְבָּה; comp. S ܠܚܘܪܒܐ. *ἀπὸ ἐνοικούντων* is an obvious Hebraism, viz. מִיּוֹשֵׁב (= מֵאֵין יוֹשֵׁב, Jer. xxxiii. 10).

24. *ἔστησας*, 'thou hast made good', cf. ii. 1, 12, note.

should be taken out, *τοῦ ἐξενεχθῆναι* = לְהוֹצִיא, Jer. viii. 1. S has also the act., viz. ܢܦܩܘܢ (Aph.).

25. Based on Jer. xxxvi. 30; latter part of the verse follows Jer. xiv. 12, xxxviii. 2.

sword, famine, pestilence, but in the order 'famine, sword, pestilence'. That *ἀποστολή* represents 'pestilence' (דֶּבֶר) is clear from Jer. xxxii. 36, where *ἀποστολή* is given in G. This use of the Greek word appears to arise from the use of *ἀποστέλλειν* as the equivalent of שִׁלַּח when employed as in Jer. xxiv. 10 (H and G) of Yahweh sending plagues as chastisement. S and Ar. 'exile' appears to have arisen from a misunderstanding of the true meaning of *ἀποστολή* as S[Hex.] marg. indicates.

26. *οὗ . . . ἐπὶ αὐτῷ*. Heb. relat. constr. as in ii. 4, 13. There are no sufficient grounds, as Kneucker alleges, for regarding the first part of this verse as not genuine. Of the genuineness of the entire verse we have clear evidence in its thoroughly Hebraic diction. Not only the relat. construction already noted, but also *ὡς ἡ ἡμέρα αὕτη* reflects the pregnant use of כְּ (Gesen.-Kautzsch, *Hebr. Gr.*[26], § 118. 6, cf. Hos. ii. 5, 17, ix. 9, xii. 10). Moreover, the verse stands in full harmony with i. 2. The mere fact of repetitions of phrase (Kneucker cites i. 15, ii. 15) constitutes no argument against genuineness in a document crowded with repetition.

27 of Judah. Yet, O Lord our God, thou hast dealt with us after all thy kindness, and according to all
28 that great mercy of thine, as thou spakest by thy servant Moses in the day when thou didst command
29 him to write thy law before the children of Israel, saying, If ye will not hear my voice, surely this
very great multitude shall be turned into a small *number* among the nations, where I will scatter
30 them. For I know that they will not hear me, because it is a stiffnecked people: but in the land
31 of their captivity they shall lay it to heart, and shall know that I am the Lord their God: and I
32 will give them a heart, and ears to hear: and they shall praise me in the land of their captivity, and
33 think upon my name, and shall return from their stiff neck, and from their wicked deeds: for they
34 shall remember the way of their fathers, which sinned before the Lord. And I will bring them
again into the land which I sware unto their fathers, to Abraham, to Isaac, and to Jacob, and they
35 shall be lords of it: and I will increase them, and they shall not be diminished. And I will make
an everlasting covenant with them to be their God, and they shall be my people: and I will no
more remove my people of Israel out of the land that I have given them.

3 1 O Lord Almighty, thou God of Israel, the soul in anguish, the troubled spirit, crieth unto thee.
2 Hear, O Lord, and have mercy; for thou art a merciful God: yea, have mercy upon us, because we
3, 4 have sinned before thee. For thou sittest *as king* for ever, and we perish evermore. O Lord
Almighty, thou God of Israel, hear now the prayer of the dead Israelites, and of the children of
them which were sinners before thee, that hearkened not unto the voice of thee their God: for the
5 which cause these plagues clave unto us. Remember not the iniquities of our fathers: but remember
6 thy power and thy name *now* at this time. For thou art the Lord our God, and thee, O Lord, will
7 we praise. For for this cause thou hast put thy fear in our hearts, to the intent that we should
call upon thy name: and we will praise thee in our captivity, for we have called to mind all the

27. S adds after 'kindness' the clause 'and according to all thy purpose' (ܨܒܝܢܟ). Comp. Ps. li. 3.

29. Comp. Deut. xxviii. 62. The reading *εἰ μὴν* ($G^{A.B}$) [in Q^a *ἢ μήν*], 'surely', arose out of *εἰ μή*, a literal rendering of the original Hebr. אם לא idiom used to express a strong asseveration which would be unintelligible in its literal Greek form. S, on the other hand, reproduces the Hebr. original. See Winer, *Grammar of N. T. Greek*, 8th ed., p. 553, footnote 7 (on Heb. vi. 14), and especially p. 627, footnote 3, where useful parallels are given. *βόμβησις*, 'multitude', corresponds to הָמוֹן in the original (so Fritzsche, who compares Jer. xxxi. 34 *ἐβόμβησε*, ויהמו), rendered 'people' in S, which expands into a parallelism, 'shall be turned into a small number and shall be diminished among the peoples.' Hebr. relat. constr. *οὗ . . . ἐκεῖ* as in verses 4, 13, 26, above.

30. **lay it to heart** is hardly satisfactory. The phrase is an echo of 1 Kings viii. 47, where R. V. rightly renders 'bethink themselves' (cf. Luke xv. 17 and Delitzsch's Hebr.), יָשִׁיבוּ אֶל־לִבָּם, almost literally reproduced in G S and L (*convertetur ad cor suum*). *ἀποικισμός* = שְׁבִי, Jer. xliii. 11.

31. Hebr. אֹזֶן 'ear' (sing. and du.) is used to express 'mind', 'intelligence' (cf. Assyr. *uznu*). Comp. 1 Sam. ix. 15, xx. 2, &c.; Isa. vi. 10; Matt. xiii. 9, 15.

32. A parallelism.

33. **stiff neck,** עֹרֶף קָשֶׁה, as in verse 30 (קְשֵׁה ערף, Exod. xxxii. 9, &c.; Deut. ix. 6, &c.), though we have *τράχηλος* in 30 and *νῶτος* here (S has same word) for 'neck'.

34. Deuteronomic (Deut. vi. 10, &c.); last clause echoes Jer. xix. 6 *b*.

35 recalls Jer. xxxi. 31, xxxii. 40, **remove,** probably אָמִישׁ as in Isa. xlvi. 7 (cf. Num. xiv. 44), though S suggests a stronger word. Kneucker prefers אֶתּשׁ, cf. Jer. xii. 14 foll., xlii. 10.

III. 1-8. Bitter cry of appeal to God from the exiles, and confession of past sin.

1. *Παντοκράτωρ*, 'Almighty', Hebr. צבאות, as in 2 Sam. v. 10, vii. 8, 26, &c., appended to יהוה. So S (as in 2 Sam. vii. 8, 26). *ἐν στενοῖς* (בְּצָרוֹת or בְּצָרָה, cf. Ps. xxv. 17, xxxi. 8). *ἀκηδιῶν* must be the partic. and would correspond to כֵּהָה (רוּחַ). Comp. Isa. lxi. 3 (H and G).

crieth, צְעָקָה (as in Ps. lxxvii. 2). S + 'afflicted body' (perhaps גְּוִיָּה מְעֻנָּה).

2. S characteristically adds 'God' to 'Lord'. G^B 'Hear, O Lord, and have mercy'. $G^{A\,Q\,\text{marg.}}$ + 'for thou art a merciful God, yea have mercy'. S + 'for thou art merciful and kind'. L and Ar. + 'because thou art a merciful God'. In the original we might therefore assume, with Kneucker, חָנֵּנוּ כִּי חַנּוּן וְחָסִיד אַתָּה.

3. *καθήμενος* corresponds to ישב, used of sitting on a throne, Exod. xi. 5 (H and G). We should probably follow Ps. xxix. 10 (rather than Isa. lvii. 15, with Kneucker), i. e. יֹשֵׁב לְעוֹלָם. S 'abidest for ever'.

4. For 'dead' of G S and other versions, read with R. V. marg. 'men', מתי of the original Hebrew being misread מֵתֵי instead of מְתֵי. A more literal rendering of G would be: 'and [so] the evils clave unto us.' S prefixes 'curses' to 'evils'. The original would then be וַתִּדְבַּקְנָה בָּנוּ הַמְּאֵרוֹת וְהָרָעוֹת (cf. Deut. xxviii. 20), or in sing. וַתִּדְבַּק בָּנוּ הָאָלָה וְהָרָעָה.

5. S 'iniquity and folly', apparently based on an alliterative combination, הָעַוְלָה וְהַנְּבָלָה אֲשֶׁר לַאֲבֹתֵינוּ, but here probably, as in many other cases, S expands the original text.

7. With the opening cf. Jer. xxxii. 40 *b*. The original has become corrupted. Hence we have several variants. S 'that we may invoke (call upon) thy holy name', where 'holy' is evidently added as in ii. 15. In other respects this accords with $G^{A\,Q}$, which substitute *τοῦ* for *καί* before *ἐπικαλ*. In the latter part of the verse G^B reads 'because we have put away from our mind all the iniquity', &c. Similarly Ar. and Vet. L. *a convertimur ab iniquitate.* But $G^{B^{ab}\,A\,Q\,et\,al.}$ 'because we have recalled to our mind' (*ἐπὶ καρδίαν*), &c. S 'because *thou* hast recalled to our mind

8 iniquity of our fathers, that sinned before thee. Behold, we are yet this day in our captivity, where
thou hast scattered us, for a reproach and a curse, and to be subject to penalty, according to all the
iniquities of our fathers, which departed from the Lord our God.

9 Hear, O Israel, the commandments of life:
Give ear to understand wisdom.

10 How happeneth it, O Israel, that thou art in thine enemies' land,
That thou art waxen old in a strange country,

11 That thou art defiled with the dead,
That thou art counted with them that *go down* into the grave?

12 Thou hast forsaken the fountain of wisdom.

13 *For* if thou hadst walked in the way of God,
Thou shouldst have dwelled in peace for ever.

14 Learn where is wisdom, where is strength,
Where is understanding; that thou mayst know also

Where is length of days, and life,
Where is the light of the eyes, and peace.

15 Who hath found out her place?
And who hath come into her treasuries?

16 Where are the princes of the heathen,
And such as ruled the beasts that are upon the earth;

17 They that had their pastime with the fowls of the air,
And they that hoarded up silver

And gold, wherein men trust
And of whose getting there is no end?

18 For they that wrought in silver, and were so careful,
And whose works are past finding out,

all the evils and iniquity . . .', where we have an expanded version, but may perhaps infer that in the Hebrew original stood הֲשֵׁבֹתָ לִלְבָבֵנוּ וְגוֹ.

8. οὗ . . . ἐκεῖ, Hebr. rel. constr. as in ii. 4, 13, 26, and also recurrence of the phraseology of ii. 4 and 29, comp. Jer. xlii. 18. S lengthens the series: curse, reproach, derision, and condemnation (= ὄφλησις R.V. to be subject to penalty), the last word in S being the same as that which renders κρίμα in 1 Cor. xi. 34 (cf. Delitzsch, *Heb. N.T.*, *ad loc.*). The Jer. parallel has also four terms: curse, horror, malediction, reproach (in which 'malediction' in G is rendered ἀρά). Accordingly S restores to our text the 'curse' of the *Jer.* passage, whereas the condemnation (subjection to penalty) might be regarded as a weakened form of the 'horror'. The original of S we might accordingly conjecture to be לְאָלָה וּלְחֶרְפָּה וְלִקְלָלָה וּלְאַשְׁמָה.

BARUCH'S PRAISE OF AND EXHORTATION TO WISDOM REVEALED IN THE LAW, iii. 9–iv. 4 (document B).

9. S 'understanding and wisdom'. Comp. Prov. iv. 1 *b*. The fuller expression in S maintains a more equable and rhythmic parallelism, הַקְשִׁיבוּ לָדַעַת בִּינָה וּלְחָכְמָה. The influence of the Wisdom literature (esp. of Prov.) throughout this document is obvious and natural.

10–12. R.V. rightly follows $G^{A\,Q}$ in omitting in verse 10 the second τί of G^{B}. It is quite possible that we ought here to follow S and read:

Wherefore, O Israel, art thou waxen old in thine enemies' land,
Hast polluted thyself (הִטַּמֵּאתָ) in a strange land (cf. Hos. ix. 4),
Art counted (נֶחְשַׁבְתָּ) with the dead who go down to the grave (יֹרְדֵי שְׁאוֹל, Ps. lv. 16; Prov. i. 12),
Hast forsaken the fountain (מְקוֹר) of Wisdom? (Prov. xviii. 4).

14. Echoes of Prov. iii. 16, viii. 14.

16–17. Wisdom is not to be found among the rich and mighty of this world. There seems to be a subtle reference to Nebuchadnezzar. Cf. Dan. ii. 37, iv. 20 f.; Jer. xxvii. 6.

16. It would be best to render here by 'peoples' (עַמִּים) rather than 'heathen', since ἔθνος also stands as the equivalent of עַם (Gen. xvii. 16; Lev. xxi. 1; Prov. xxx. 26). So Kneucker. Moreover S reads here עולם (עָלָם) 'age', which is evidently a corruption of עמם.

17 portrays the luxury and amusements of the rich. Comp. Judith xi. 7.

18. **they that wrought in silver** might correspond to חָרָשֵׁי כֶסֶף, as Kneucker suggests. Prov. xi. 27 (R.V. margin)

19 They are vanished and gone down to the grave,
And others are come up in their steads.

20 Younger men have seen the light,
And dwelt upon the earth:

But the way of knowledge have they not known,
21 Neither understood they the paths thereof:

Neither have their children laid hold of it:
They are far off from their way.

22 It hath not been heard of in Canaan,
Neither hath it been seen in Teman.

23 The sons also of Agar that seek understanding, [which are in the land,]
The merchants of Merran and Teman,
And the authors of fables, and the searchers out of understanding;

None of these have known the way of wisdom,
Or remembered her paths.

24 O Israel, how great is the house of God!
And how large is the place of his possession!

25 Great, and hath none end;
High, and unmeasurable.

26 There were the giants born that were famous of old,
Great of stature, *and* expert in war.

would lead us on a wrong scent. We should rather find the original through S, 'who gain silver', קֹנֵי כֶסֶף, which might also mean 'makers' or 'fashioners' in silver. This is really an Aramaic use of קנה, reflected in the later Hebrew diction of Gen. xiv. 19, 22; Prov. viii. 22; Ps. cxxxix. 13. Both this and the following verse begin with the interrog. 'Who?' in S, in continuation of the series of interrogations that follow after 'Learn where', &c., in verse 14. On the other hand, G begins verse 18 with ὅτι, 'for', as though it gave the reason for the preceding verses. As these are interrog., we can only obtain an intelligible sequence with verse 18 in G by assuming (with Fritzsche) that a negative answer ['They no longer exist'] is implied after verse 17. But this anticipates verse 19. It would be better, therefore, to read at the opening of this verse with S, 'who are they who gain (are makers in) silver . . .?'

whose works are past finding out. A relat. sentence, more literally 'There is no searching (ἐξεύρεσις) of their works'. S 'There is no numbering of their works'. The Hebrew original of G would be וְאֵין חֵקֶר לְמַעֲשֵׂיהֶם, and of S וְאֵין מִסְפָּר לְמ׳. The latter is perhaps an inferior reading. But both are quite consonant with the Wisdom literature on which this document (B) in 1 Baruch is modelled. Prov. xxv. 3; Job v. 9, ix. 10, xxxvi. 26 (cf. Isa. xl. 28).

19. The answer to the preceding queries. All these devotees of worldly pomp have vanished.

20. 'The young' would be a better translation of νεώτεροι = הַנְּעָרִים, as opposed to הַזְּקֵנִים (πρεσβύτεροι), Ps. xxxvii. 25, cxlviii. 12 (cf. Judges viii. 20). 'Have seen the light' = 'have been born', Job iii. 16, 20, xxxiii. 30. For 'knowledge' S has 'loving intelligence' (sûkolô dᵉreḥmᵉthô) or 'intelligence *and* love' (Lag.), an evident later expansion.

21. **their children,** i.e. the third generation, viz. sons of the young men of verse 20, who are themselves the sons of those who are referred to in verse 19.

are far off. S 'have removed themselves far and revolted from *its* way', i.e. of knowledge. Fritzsche rightly restores the sing. with S in place of the plur. (αὐτῶν) with G., so also Rothstein. Moreover, the fuller rendering in S points to a more rhythmic length of line in the original וּמִדַּרְכָּהּ רָחֲקוּ וַיִּמְרְדוּ.

22. Teman, situated in Edom, was celebrated for its wisdom, Jer. xlix. 7.

23 is at variance with the passive construction of the previous verse (contained in G). From this defect S is entirely free, which shows the impress of the Hebrew original. This verse is obviously a continuation of the preceding 'nor among the Hagarenes who seek after understanding', וּבִבְנֵי הָגָר מְבַקְשֵׁי תְבוּנָה. The error in G probably arose from the omission of the first ב in בבני (cf. i. 1). The force of the preceding negatives continues in this clause. Hence there is no need to write ולא בבני. The emendation of תְּבוּנָה into תְּבוּאָה 'gains', by Kneucker (who reads סֹחֲרֵי תְבוּאָה, 'die um Erwerb das Land durchziehen'), is utterly unwarranted, and tends to destroy the parallelism. Probably 'Merran' has arisen by corruption from 'Midian' through the constant confusion that arises between ד and ר (so Gifford, who cites 'Medan and Midian', Gen. xvi. 15, xxv. 2, sons of Keturah). Comp. Gen. xxxvii. 36. The Hagarenes are mentioned in Gen. xxv. 12 f. They are the nomads referred to in 1 Chron. v. 20 f., xxvii. 31. They inhabited the district east of Gilead. Comp. Ps. lxxxiii. 7.

It is impossible to resist the suspicion that this verse has received undue extension. S has 'followed up' for 'remembered', through corruption of its own text, i.e. ܐܬܪܕܘܗ instead of ܐܬܕܟܪܘ.

24. S prefixes 'Lord' to 'God', thus securing the usual combination. For 'large' it reads 'long and spacious'.

25. S has here an abbreviated text which spoils parallelism and rhythm, viz. 'And it has no end and is lofty and has no measure.' The 'house of God' here is evidently the *Universe* (not heaven exclusively as in ii. 16).

26. Gen. vi. 4 plays a considerable part in later Jewish writings, as 1 En. vii; Sir. xvi. 7; Wisd. xiv. 6.

27 These did not God choose,
Neither gave he the way of knowledge unto them :

28 So they perished, because they had no wisdom,
They perished through their own foolishness.

29 Who hath gone up into heaven, and taken her,
And brought her down from the clouds?

30 Who hath gone over the sea, and found her,
And will bring her for choice gold?

31 There is none that knoweth her way,
Nor any that comprehendeth her path.

32 But he that knoweth all things knoweth her,
He found her out with his understanding:

He that prepared the earth for evermore
Hath filled it with four-footed beasts:

33 He that sendeth forth the light, and it goeth ;
He called it, and it obeyed him with fear:

34 And the stars shined in their watches, and were glad :
When he called them, they said, Here we be ;
They shined with gladness unto him that made them.

35 This is our God,
And there shall none other be accounted of in comparison of him.

27–28. For ‘knowledge’ S has ‘wisdom’. 28 *a* (= 27 *b*) in S ‘wisdom and understanding’.

29–30. The interrog., as frequently in Hebrew, anticipates a negat. answer. Comp. as parallels Deut. xxx. 12, 13; Prov. xxx. 4; Sir. li. 28. Here again S expands beyond the original (which was probably מִי עָבַר אֶל־עֵבֶר הַיָּם) into ‘who hath passed over the sea's bounds and extremities’.

31. From the interrog. form we pass to the direct negat. For ‘comprehendeth’ (ἐνθυμούμενος), S ‘meditateth’, ‘pondereth’, perhaps Hebr. מֵבִין (Prov. xxiii. 1), or מִתְבּוֹנֵן (Isa. xliii. 18, lii. 15, Job xxxvii. 14).

32. Only God can discover wisdom with His omniscience—a clear echo from the Book of Job (xxviii. 12–24, which evidently underlies the thought of this passage). For ‘understanding’ S has ‘wisdom’, cf. verse 27 above. For ‘prepared’ read with S ‘established’ (מֵכִין). ‘For evermore’, perhaps, as S indicates, in Hebr. לְעוֹלַם עוֹלָמִים. ‘Four-footed beasts’ (τετράποδα) corresponds to Hebr. בְּהֵמוֹת. G has evidently influenced here S, which renders ‘beasts of four feet’; see Introd., § 9, ii (Syr. versions).

33. **fear** is an inadequate rendering of τρόμῳ. S has a different conclusion to the verse which might appear to indicate a lost line: ‘Who sendeth forth the light and it goes, and called it and it obeyed him, and the earth responded to him with trembling.’ Here the introduction of the earth comes in abruptly after the reference to the light of heaven in the previous couplet:

קָרָא לוֹ וַיִּשְׁמַע אֵלָיו
. . . . . .
וַתַּעֲנֵהוּ הָאָרֶץ בִּרְעָדָה

‘trembling’ (τρόμος) is more consonant with the earthquake, and is therefore more in place when connected with the earth than in reference to light. Cf. Ps. xviii. 8, xlvi. 7, civ. 32. Rothstein interprets ‘light’ as lightning (Job xxxvii. 3, xxxviii. 35), but this does not harmonize with verse 34, though readily compatible with such an intervening couplet as S indicates.

34. **their watches.** S ‘their places’. We have to choose between the original readings: בְּמִשְׁמְרוֹתָם and בִּמְקוֹמוֹתָם. The latter is colourless, and might have arisen by corruption from the former, which yields a picturesque and appropriate metaphor, the stars being represented as keeping sentinel duty at their night-watches. Cf. Sir. xliii. 10. Hom. *Iliad* viii. 555, 556. ‘Here we be’ (πάρεσμεν), S ‘behold us’ reproduces the Hebr. original הִנֵּנוּ.

35 exhibits evident echoes of Isa. xliii. 10, 11, xliv. 6, xlv. 18, which in S become more apparent than in G, since we have three clauses, the third being a parallel of the second. S omits ‘our’, and for ‘in comparison of (πρός) him’ in the third clause renders ‘above him’ (ܡܢܗ):

This is God, and there is none other beside Him,
And none other shall be reckoned above Him.

הוּא הָאֱלֹהִים וְאֵין אַחֵר מִבִּלְעָדָיו
לֹא יֵחָשֵׁב אַחֵר עָלָיו (לְפָנָיו or)

36 He hath found out all the way of knowledge,

37 And hath given it unto Jacob his servant,
And to Israel that is beloved of him.

4 1 [Afterward did she appear upon earth,
And was conversant with men.]

This is the book of the commandments of God,
And the law that endureth for ever:

2 All they that hold it fast *are appointed* to life;
But such as leave it shall die.

3 Turn thee, O Jacob, and take hold of it:
Walk towards her shining in the presence of the light thereof.

4 Give not thy glory to another,
Nor the things that are profitable unto thee to a strange nation.

O Israel, happy are we:
For the things that are pleasing to God are made known unto us.

5 Be of good cheer, my people,
The memorial of Israel.

6 Ye were sold to the nations,
But not for destruction:

Because ye moved God to wrath,
Ye were delivered unto your adversaries.

7 For ye provoked him that made you
By sacrificing unto demons, and not to God.

36. For 'knowledge' S has 'wisdom', probably in accordance with the original. Comp., however, verses 27 and 32 above. The passage reflects Jewish particularism, and is evidently based on Sir. xxiv. 8 foll. Cf. Prov. viii. 31.

37 has long been suspected as a Christian gloss (Grotius, Hitzig, Hilgenfeld, Kneucker, Rothstein). Greek and Latin Fathers cite it in the interests of the Logos doctrine. See Introd., § 10. In S the subject is masc., i. e. God: 'revealed himself and was seen.' So L and Ar. In G the subject is probably God as in verse 36, but it might be wisdom (knowledge); cf. Prov. viii. 31.

IV. 1 is evidently connected with iv. 36 (rather than 37). The wisdom which God has bestowed on Jacob is identified with the Torah, which is eternal. S 'book and memorial of the commandments . . . to all who hold it fast it shall be (for) life'. The addition 'and memorial' is evidently an extension of the original.

2. The expression is varied in S:

Turn and incline, O Jacob;
Lay hold and go in its path (cf. Prov. iii. 18, iv. 13)
Toward the brightness of its light (cf. Isa. lx. 3).

3. For 'glory', S 'praise and honour', and for 'profitable' (συμφέροντα G), S 'good and advantageous', which are evidently paraphrastic expansions. 'Glory' prob. in Hebr. original הוד (Dan. xi. 21).

4. S 'Happy are we, happy art thou . . . What is pleasing to God we know.' This last clause conforms to the Hebrew idiom, which would here be הַטּוֹב לֵאלֹהִים יָדַעְנוּ (cf. Deut. xxiii. 17).

Songs of lamentation and comfort addressed (*a*) by Jerusalem to her exiled children, and (*b*) of consolation addressed by God to Jerusalem, iv. 5–v. 9 (document C). (Verses 5 to 9 *a* should be regarded as introductory.)

(*a*) *Lamentation and comfort addressed by Jerusalem to her banished sons* (iv. 9 *b*–29). The situation is that of the Jews in exile (verses 8, 10), just as in chap. i, and the language is obviously moulded on that of the Deutero-Isaiah, but, unlike the Deutero-Isaiah, the language of lamentation is more prominent, and the situation is painted in darker colours. In verses 7 foll. confession is made of past transgression (as in i. 17–ii. 12) for which the present calamities are the penalty (iv. 6). In iv. 17–29 the exiles are exhorted to cry to God and deliverance from their enemies will come. Though the present be painful it shall speedily end, and better days shall come (21–24); destruction shall befall their foes (25 foll.), and for the exiles joy in place of the evils of the past.

5. S renders here, as in verses 27, 30, 'be comforted', which is evidently a Deutero-Isaianic trait (cf. Isa. xl. 1, liv. 11). Also for 'my people', S 'people of God'. 'Memorial' ('remembrance' = Hebr. זֵכֶר) is the equivalent of 'name', to which it frequently stands in parallelism (Exod. iii. 15; Job xviii. 17; Prov. x. 7). Cf. Deut. xxv. 19 and LXX (Kneucker). The word 'memorial', therefore, means those who preserve Israel's name (Grotius, Fritzsche).

6. S '*your* adversaries' (as R. V.), giving greater definiteness than G (τοῖς ὑπεναντίοις). For '*ye* moved God to wrath' (G^B S L Ar.) G^A has '*we*', by obvious textual error.

7 contains an evident reminiscence of Deut. xxxii. 16, 17. S appends to 'him that made you' the appositional

8 Ye forgat the everlasting God, that brought you up;
Ye grieved also Jerusalem, that nursed you.

9 For she saw the wrath that is come upon you from God,
And said,
Hearken, ye *women* that dwell about Sion:
For God hath brought upon me great mourning;

10 For I have seen the captivity of my sons and daughters,
Which the Everlasting hath brought upon them.

11 For with joy did I nourish them;
But sent them away with weeping and mourning.

12 Let no man rejoice over me,
A widow, and forsaken of many:
For the sins of my children am I left desolate;

Because they turned aside from the law of God,
13 And had no regard to his statutes,

Neither walked they in the ways of God's commandments,
Nor trod in the paths of discipline in his righteousness.

14 Let them that dwell about Sion come,
And remember ye the captivity of my sons and daughters,
Which the Everlasting hath brought upon them.

15 For he hath brought a nation upon them from far,
A shameless nation, and of a strange language,

Who neither reverenced old man,
Nor pitied child.

16 And they have carried away the dear beloved sons of the widow,
And left her that was alone desolate of her daughters.

17 But I, what can I help you?

phrase 'the everlasting God', an evident expansion, since it recurs in the following verse. This appellation 'everlasting' attached to God (*αἰώνιος*) is a Deutero-Isaianic trait (Isa. xl. 28 G אלהי עולם) which is a special characteristic of the document C (iv. 10, 14, 20, 22, 24, 35, v. 2). Gifford indeed remarks that *αἰώνιος* seems to take the place of *κύριος* (יהוה).

8. An equally evident reminiscence of Deut. xxxii. 18 *b*. S applies the term 'nurse' in both clauses, i. e. to both God and Jerusalem. 'God, that *nursed* you . . . Jerusalem, that *reared* you' would be a closer rendering of the Greek. G^A, again, in the first clause substitutes 'us' for 'you' (as in verse 6), i. e. *ἡμᾶς* for *ὑμᾶς*, against G^B S L Ar.

9. S characteristically prefixes 'Lord' to 'God' in both places, and introduces the parallelism 'the wrath which has come upon you and the anger from the presence of the Lord God'; to 'great' it adds 'eternal' as epithet of 'mourning'. In 9 *b* ('Hearken ye . . .') begins Jerusalem's lamentation over the exile of her sons (9 *b*–16).

10. S 'everlasting *Lord*' and 'upon *me*' (not 'them'). The latter is probably due to a harmonizing tendency.

11–12. S + 'and groaning (sighs)'. Also 'rejoice in my widowhood who am abandoned and desolated of much people'. The language and ideas are cast in the Deutero-Isaianic mould (Isa. xlix. 21, liv. 1, 4). S also appends an extra parallel clause with variation in phraseology:

'Because of the sins of my sons,
because they turned aside from the *path* of the *Lord* God.'

13. S 'statutes and judgements', the familiar combination in Deut. (Deut. iv. 1, &c.) The rest of the verse in S runs: 'Nor did they walk in the way of God's statutes, nor did they tread or betake themselves to the paths of true instruction (lit. instruction of truth) in righteousness.' Here 'instruction' (discipline) and 'betake themselves' are expansions. 'Truth', however, rests on a more secure textual foundation, being found in $G^{Q* al.}$ (+ *ἀληθείας*) L (om. *disciplinae*). And it has O.T. warrant. Cf. 1 Kings iii. 6.

14. We have here a change from 3rd to 2nd person. This, however, should probably be consistently carried out through the entire verse, as in S (so Kneucker). S om. 'come', and has in its place the pers. pron. 'ye' ('ye inhabitants of Zion, remember'), but this is probably due to inner-Syriac corruption of ܬܘܘ 'come ye' to ܐܢܬܘܢ 'ye'.

15. Evidently echoes Deut. xxviii. 49, 50.

16. S 'And they took captive and carried away the beloved (sons) of the widow *and her daughters*.' The 'daughters' are inserted in this clause perhaps owing to the influence of verse 14 above. S omits 'daughters', however, in the latter part of the verse: 'And her alone and solitary left they desolate.'

17 foll. After the lamentation there now begins a message of comfort. Jerusalem can afford no help, but God can. The question here, as frequently in O. T., implies a negation; and this S directly expresses.

18 For he that brought these plagues upon you
Will deliver you from the hand of your enemies.

19 Go your way, O my children, go your way:
For I am left desolate.

20 I have put off the garment of peace,
And put upon me the sackcloth of my petition:
I will cry unto the Everlasting as long as I live.

21 Be of good cheer, O my children, cry unto God,
And he shall deliver you from the power and hand of the enemies.

22 For I have trusted in the Everlasting, that he will save you;
And joy is come unto me from the Holy One,
Because of the mercy which shall soon come unto you
From the Everlasting your Saviour.

23 For I sent you out with mourning and weeping:
But God will give you to me again with joy and gladness for ever.

24 For like as now they that dwell about Sion have seen your captivity:
So shall they see shortly your salvation from our God,
Which shall come upon you with great glory, and brightness of the Everlasting.

25 My children, suffer patiently the wrath that is come upon you from God:
For thine enemy hath persecuted thee;

But shortly thou shalt see his destruction,
And shalt tread upon their necks.

26 My delicate ones have gone rough ways;
They were taken away as a flock carried off by the enemies.

27 Be of good cheer, O my children, and cry unto God:
For ye shall be remembered of him that hath brought *these things* upon you.

28 For as it was your mind to go astray from God:
So, return and seek him ten times more.

18. G^{Q} + ὑμῖν after ἐπαγαγών, G^{A} after τὰ κακά.

19. 'My' before children om. G L, and inserted in S Ar.

20. Jerusalem clothed in sackcloth of sorrow and supplication, the reverse of the picture in Isa. lii. 1, lxi. 3 (cf. 1 Bar. v. 1 below). S takes over στολήν of G. S 'I will cry unto thee that livest for ever in my days', G 'unto the Everlasting in my days' (= 'in my life-time', i.e. 'as long as I live').

21. **Be of good cheer.** S reproduces the form of Isa. li. 17, cf. lii. 1, 'awake'. G^{B} 'power and hand', also Ar. Vet. Lat. *a, b de manu principum inimicorum* appears to presume a reading ἐκ χειρὸς δυναστῶν ἐχθρῶν (Kneucker). G^{A} om. 'power', prob. due to paraphrastic expansion. S carries expansion further: 'from the hands of the mighty and from the hands of rulers and from the hands of adversaries.'

22. S for 'Holy One' has 'Lord God Everlasting', after which it renders 'because he hath at once taken compassion on them on account of the compassion of God your everlasting Saviour'. G^{A} om. 'because of the mercy' (compassion). There can be little doubt that extensions have crept into the text.

23. S 'God' + 'from whom I received you' (obvious expansion).

24. S prefixes 'Lord' to 'our God', and continues: 'and he shall bring you with great joy.' Also 'everlasting *Lord*'. It may be noted, however, that this appellation of deity, κύριος (יהוה), while frequent and indeed characteristic of the document A, is in reality foreign to C (see Introd., § 11, and note on iv. 7). It is evidently introduced by S, which has a tendency to combine 'Lord' with other designations of deity. Comp. S, verses 27 *bis*, 28, 36, v. 1, 2.

25. S 'My sons, be patient and endure the wrath' (+ 'Lord'). 'Thine enemy' G^{AQ} S L Ar. G^{B} om. 'thine'.

26. S expands: 'have gone into captivity and have travelled on hard rough ways', apparently an attempt to represent Isa. xl. 4 (including עקב and רכסים). S continues: 'They have been scattered on difficult ways, they have been scattered like a flock that is carried off by enemies.' 'Scattered as a flock' is a combination which meets us in Ezek. xxxiv. 4, 5, 12; Zech. xiii. 7 (cf. Mark xiv. 27), &c.

27. Cf. verse 5. S 'for there shall be for you *with the Lord* remembrance from him that brought *these* [evils] upon you'. G om. obj. to 'brought'.

28–29. The phraseology is singularly unpoetic and non-Hebraic. See Introd. § 6 (*c*).

(*b*) *Message of comfort addressed by a prophet in God's name* (iv. 34) *to Jerusalem* (iv. 30–v. 9). Obviously a pendant to the address to the exiles by Jerusalem (iv. 5–29) which precedes. The enemies of Jerusalem shall receive divine chastisement (iv. 31–35). In this we see the influence of Jer. li. Help shall come from the east (iv. 36, v. 5), i.e. her exiled sons in Babylonia and the Euphrates lands. The language and ideas of the Deutero-Isaiah resound in chap. v (esp. verses 5 and 7).

29 For he that brought these plagues upon you
Shall bring you everlasting joy again with your salvation.

30 Be of good cheer, O Jerusalem:
For he that called thee by name will comfort thee.

31 Miserable are they that afflicted thee,
And rejoiced at thy fall.

32 Miserable are the cities which thy children served:
Miserable is she that received thy sons.

33 For as she rejoiced at thy fall,
And was glad of thy ruin:
So shall she be grieved for her own desolation.

34 And I will take away her exultation in her great multitude,
And her boasting shall be turned into mourning.

35 For fire shall come upon her from the Everlasting, long to endure;
And she shall be inhabited of devils for a great time.

36 O Jerusalem, look about thee toward the east,
And behold the joy that cometh unto thee from God.

37 Lo, thy sons come, whom thou sentest away,
They come gathered together from the east to the west [at the word of the Holy One],
Rejoicing in the glory of God.

5 1 Put off, O Jerusalem, the garment of thy mourning and affliction,
And put on the comeliness of the glory that *cometh* from God for ever.

2 Cast about thee the robe of the righteousness which *cometh* from God;
Set a diadem on thine head of the glory of the Everlasting.

3 For God will show thy brightness unto every *region* under heaven.

4 For thy name shall be called of God for ever
The peace of righteousness, and the glory of godliness.

30. **Be of good cheer** recurs here, as previously, iv. 5, 21, 27. **called thee by name** is naturally expressed in S analogously to Dan. i. 7 (cf. Phil. ii. 9).

31–32. **Miserable** is not an adequate rendering of δείλαιοι. (Shall be) 'alarmed' or 'affrighted' (S) is nearer the true meaning. Versions render variously. S expands the clauses of the verse: 'The cities shall be in dread that treated thee ill and rejoiced in thy downfall. The cities shall be in terror that enslaved thy sons. Thou shalt rejoice in their downfall. They shall be in dread who treated thee ill. She shall be in dread who received thy sons.' S seems to luxuriate in repetition of the phrase.

33. S om. second clause of parallelism *in protasi*, but amplifies the *apodosis*: 'So shall she be grieved and vexed.' The city (sing.) which is vaguely referred to in verses 32–5 is evidently Babylon (= Rome).

34. A strange confusion has arisen in G^A^, which reads ἄγαλμα, 'statue', 'idol', for ἀγαλλίαμα, 'exultation' (G^B^). This is reflected in the conflate reading of S, 'I will take away from her the idols and the exultation of great assemblies, and the joy shall become mourning.'

35. The conception is evidently derived from Jer. li. 58. Kneucker thinks that we have here a reference to the eruption of Vesuvius in A.D. 79, which would of course furnish a *term. a quo* as regards date of document C (Introd., pp. 51 foll.), but the expression in the text is far too general in character.
The demons who are to inhabit the desolated city are a feature borrowed from Isa. xiii. 21, 22; Jer. li. 37.

36. The opening clause reflects Isa. xlix. 18, lx. 4.

V. 1. Again, as in iv. 20, S reproduces στολήν of G. **affliction**, S + 'and suffering', 'and array thyself in the splendour which is from the Lord God unto glory everlasting'. Both conceptions and language resemble Isa. lii. 1.

2. διπλοΐς, 'robe', should rather be rendered by 'tunic', viz. the Hebr. מְעִיל of Isa. lxi. 10, of which this passage is evidently an echo. G there renders by χιτῶνα, but διπλοΐς is the rendering in other passages where the same Hebrew word occurs, 1 Sam. ii. 19, xv. 27, xxiv. 12 (11 Hebr.); Ps. cviii. 28 (cix. 29 Hebr.).
This Baruch passage is the reverse of Ps. of Sol. ii. 21, 22, where the μίτρα or 'diadem' (Heb. פְּאֵר) is put off. We have already seen (Introd., § 6) how close is the parallel between 1 Bar. iv. 37–v. 8 and Ps. of Sol. xi. 3–7. Here it may be noted that in S the military 'helmet' (*Sānûrtâ*) takes the place of the 'diadem' as the woman's head-dress. See Introd., § 9, ii (Syr. Versions) *ad fin.*

3. S 'unto every man upon all the earth'.

4. θεοσέβεια, 'godliness', is the equivalent of the Hebr. 'fear of the Lord' (so S) as in Job xxviii. 28; comp. Gen. xx. 11. L. *pietas*.

5 Arise, O Jerusalem, and stand upon the height,
And look about thee toward the east,

And behold thy children gathered from the going down of the sun unto the rising thereof [at the word of the Holy One],
Rejoicing that God hath remembered them.

6 For they went from thee on foot,
Being led away of their enemies:

But God bringeth them in unto thee
Borne on high with glory, as *on* a royal throne.

7 For God hath appointed that every high mountain, and the everlasting hills, should be made low,

And the valleys filled up, to make plain the ground,
That Israel may go safely in the glory of God.

8 Moreover the woods and every sweet-smelling tree have overshadowed Israel [by the commandment of God].

9 For God shall lead Israel with joy in the light of his glory
With the mercy and righteousness that cometh from him.

5. Evidently reflects the Isaianic passages, Isa. li. 17 and lx. 4, and these either affect the version in S (e.g. 'awake' repeated, a Deutero-Isaianic trait) or S reflects the existence of a variant G in closer adhesion to the Isaianic model. Similarly 'gathered', S + 'and coming to thee'; cf. Isa. lx. 4. Note in S the military feature 'by the tents' in place of 'upon the height' (G), though possibly this might arise by corruption; see Kneucker, p. 133.

6. G^B ὡς θρόνου, 'as [on] a royal throne', lit. 'throne of the kingdom', has occasioned some difficulty. This seems to have been early felt, for in $G^{A\,Q}$ L and Ar. we have 'children of the kingdom', i.e. royal sons. The passage is obviously based on the Isaianic passages, Isa. xlix. 22, lx. 4, 9, and lxvi. 20, descriptive of the restoration of Jewish exiles. Are we to interpret ὡς θρόνου as meaning that the children are to be carried in state as a royal throne (a palanquin or sedan chair (Isa. lxvi. 20)), or, as seems more natural and as S ('carried aloft in glory on a royal throne') warrants us in supposing, should we interpret ὡς θρόνου as equivalent to 'as on a throne'? This has the appearance of, and probably is, a Hebraism = כְּכִסֵּא, the well-known pregnant use of כְּ, *GK*, § 118. 6. It would be perilous to base upon such a slender sporadic example any argument for a Hebraic original of the document C in face of the evidence already set forth (Introd., §§ 6, 9. i). Let us remember that this document came from a patriotic Hellenic Jew familiar with his O. T., both in Greek and Hebrew. Examples of the pregnant use of כְּ he would find reflected in his Greek Scriptures, 1 Kings viii. 24; Hos. ii. 5, 17, ix. 9. xii. 10. Before deciding upon a Hebr. original we must give due play to the considerations that should weigh with us as to the effect produced upon the Greek diction of Jews familiar with the Hebr. Scriptures as well as with 'the LXX, the constant reading of which by Hellenist Jews has unconsciously affected their Greek'. See Moulton, *Gr. of N. T. Greek*, vol. i, p. 13.[1] Cf. also above, i. 15, ii. 26.

7. Evidently based in idea and phraseology on Isa. xl. 4. S om. 'and the everlasting hills (mounds)' of G and after 'made low' + 'and rough places shall become smooth and level', in closer approximation to the Isaianic original; comp. iv. 26 above.

8. S 'all trees of the wood'

9. S 'For the God of Israel shall go before you', in closer adherence to Isa. lii. 12, lviii. 8; Exod. xiii. 21. For 'Him' (of G^B L) G^A S Ar. read 'God'.

[1] See the note by General Editor in Introd., § 6, and that in the Ps. of Sol. (vol. ii), § 5.

EPISTLE OF JEREMY

INTRODUCTION

PROBABLY most readers approach these relics of the past with a controlling opinion or prejudice in their minds, whether they are conscious of the fact or not. If, however, we wish to form a just appreciation of the significance of an ancient document, we must clear our minds of prepossessions and let it speak to us. We must be careful neither to overlook things which are there, nor to read into it things which are not there. It may have been mere chance which caused it to survive the wreck of much else that we could wish had been saved; but it is more likely that it was preserved because of some intrinsic merit, or because of something in it which specially appealed to the sympathies of its earliest readers.

§ 1. NATURE AND SCOPE OF THE WORK.

The so-called *Epistle of Jeremy* reads more like a sermon or hortatory address than a letter; a fact which may account for its characteristic repetitions. The author is very much in earnest, as becomes a preacher. The idolatry he denounces is no imaginary picture, but the reality of his own environment. And it is not the idolatry of Canaan, so strongly condemned by the prophets of Yahweh, nor that of Egypt, which Jeremiah might have denounced had he long survived his forced migration to that uncongenial region. It is the idolatry of Babylon. For 'Babylon', in the author's use, is evidently not a mask for some other land or city. Not only is he aware of a very peculiar custom there prevalent, which Herodotus has also noted (*v.* 43; cf. Hdt. i. 199); but many incidental allusions and individual touches agree with other known features of Babylonian religion. (See the notes on *vv.* 4, 11, 15, 30–32, 41, 43.) Had 'Babylon' meant Egypt, the degrading animal-worship, of which the author of Wisdom makes so much, would hardly have escaped the shafts of his eager though not very profound satire.

§ 2. PROBABLE DATE.

But what Babylon was it? Was it the Babylon of Nebuchadnezzar the Great, whose magnificent temples were enriched with the plunder of nations and maintained by the tribute of a subject world? Was it Babylon in its imperial splendour, as Jechonias and the men of the First Captivity saw it—Babylon as it was when the susceptible heart of the poet-priest Ezekiel was so powerfully impressed by the carven and painted symbols of its immemorial faith? Not Babylon in its glory, but Babylon in its decay, as Herodotus saw it more than a century afterwards; or rather as Alexander saw it, crumbling slowly away, yet still, in its ruined majesty, preserving enough of its ancient splendour to induce the conqueror of the world to choose it for his future capital and seat of empire. When our author makes Jeremiah predict a sojourn of the Jews in Babylon for 'seven generations', he does it deliberately. He can hardly have been ignorant of the famous prophecy of the seventy years, or of the less-heeded estimate of three generations involved in the statement that the exiles were to serve Nebuchadnezzar and his son and his son's son (Jer. xxv. 12; xxvii. 7). He seems, in fact, to be giving us a clue to his own period. Seven generations, allowing forty years to the generation according to Old Testament reckoning, would cover 280 years. If we count from the exile of Jechonias (597 B.C.), this brings us to the year 317 B.C., or counting (as the author may have done) from 586 B.C., the year of the final Captivity, we arrive at 306 B.C., some thirty years after the arrival of Alexander in Babylon. It must not be forgotten that the Jews who returned to Palestine in consequence of the Edict of Cyrus were only a small part of the Jewish population of Babylonia. Great numbers of them were perfectly satisfied with their adopted country, and no more desired to return to Judaea than our own colonists in Australia or New Zealand desire to return to the narrower conditions of English life. What is more, they not only went beyond the advice of Jeremiah (xxix. 4–7) in the matter of regarding the land of their exile as their permanent home. Many of them assumed Babylonian names, implying at least an identification of the God of Israel with Bel-Merodach or Nebo; and there must always have been a strong temptation to assimilate themselves entirely to their neighbours in the customs and manners of life. Doubtless there was considerable leakage from the synagogue to the indigenous worships. Some might sincerely believe that the destruction of the Jerusalem Temple and the overthrow of their national independence were proof enough of the superiority of the Babylonian gods. Others would surrender themselves to the influence of more sordid considerations (cf. Jer. xliv. 17 f.). The zeal of loyal spirits would naturally be roused by this state of things; and pieces like the one before us might have been circulated among the weak believers and waverers as dissuasives from the folly of exchanging the religion of the prophets for any lower form of faith and life.

§ 3. Original Language.

If the author belongs to anything like so early a date, he probably wrote in Hebrew, not Greek. But this probability is greatly strengthened by a careful study of the phenomena of the Greek text. It is incredible that a piece so formless, so confused, so utterly destitute of the graces of style, as this 'Epistle' now is, should have been thought worthy of preservation in the Alexandrian Canon of Scripture, had such been its original condition. Our translators and their Revisers have done their best; but what a poor halting semblance of sense, not to say manifest nonsense, the result too often is! Harmony with context and logical connexion of thought are often untraceable. We are presented with a voluble but ill-connected succession of propositions, bearing little visible relation to each other beyond a general animus against idolatry. But almost every verse exhibits peculiarities which suggest translation, and that from a Hebrew original, as will be seen by reference to the notes on the text. It is, of course, often easier to see that the Greek is more or less suspicious than to divine the true reading of the lost Hebrew archetype. A suggestion may seem plausible, even probable, without being right. But a possible sense is better than nonsense and may be accepted provisionally, in preference to the assumption that we have before us nothing better than the crude effusion of an illiterate fanatic. Amid all such uncertainties one thing appears to be certain. It is that in this *Epistle of Jeremy* there are places where the strange phraseology of the Greek can only be accounted for by assuming that the writer of it supplied the wrong vowels to some Hebrew word which he was translating, or mistook some Hebrew consonant for another resembling it, or could only guess at the meaning of a corrupted text. His MS. may have been badly written or have become illegible in places through time and use. Perhaps also, like some of his modern commentators, he was not himself a too expert Hebraist, though capable enough of a certain careless and misleading fluency in Greek, which enabled him to conceal lack of knowledge under a surface of smoothly-expressed inaccuracies. It may suffice to examine a few of the more striking instances here, referring to the notes on the text for a more complete presentation of the evidence.

(1) *V.* 12: 'from rust and **moths**'. The true meaning; but the Greek has ἀπὸ ἰοῦ καὶ βρωμάτων = 'from rust and foods'. In LXX βρώματα = אֹכֶל (Gen. xli. 35 f) or מַאֲכָל (Gen. vi. 21) *food.* The translator read the latter word here, instead of מֵאֹכֵל *from a devourer* (= moth or grub; cf. Mal. iii. 11; Isa. li. 8; Matt. vi. 19 σὴς καὶ βρῶσις = עָשׁ וְאֹכֵל *moth and devourer*). The translator supplied the wrong vowel-points in reading his unpointed Hebrew text.

(2) *V.* 20: 'They are as one of the beams of the temple; and men say their hearts are eaten out,' &c. Here there is no apparent connexion of thought, and the Greek does not help us. But the words τὰς δὲ καρδίας αὐτῶν φασίν suggest a corruption of the common Hebrew phrase 'to say in one's heart' = *to think*. The original sense may thus have been: **And he** (the idol) **is like a beam** (i.e. a mere log) **inside** *the temple* (cf. 1 Kings vi. 15); **yet they think that he eats!** (i.e. consumes the offerings made to him). For eating, as a proof of being a 'living god', see Bel 6. Our translator pointed יְלַחֵךְ instead of יְלַחֵךְ (Num. xxii. 4).

(3) *V.* 31: Gk. διφρεύουσιν, *drive chariots.* Not even a Jew of 100 B.C. would have accused the Babylonian priests of careering about in chariots inside their temples, and that with all the outward signs of mourning upon their bodies, rent clothes, shaven heads, &c. But read 'they weep' instead of 'they drive chariots', and the context is satisfied, and all becomes clear. It is merely a matter of writing יבכו, which was perhaps miswritten ייבכו in the translator's MS., for ירכבו *they ride.* Cf. *v.* 32, and the notes *in loc.* The reference is to services of mourning for the gods, especially Dumuzi = Tammuz (see *Cuneiform Texts*, vol. xv).

(4) *V.* 35. 'They can neither give riches *nor money*' (χαλκόν): a false antithesis, and incongruous with the context (*v.* 34; cf. 1 Sam. ii. 7). What is obviously required is οὔτε πενίαν, 'nor poverty'. Prov. xxx. 8. The translator may have mistaken a badly written ריש *poverty* for נחש, and then guessed that this was a remnant of 'נחש (= χαλκός). But if חלכה in Ps. x. 8, 10 really means ὁ πένης (LXX and Syr.), it may be that חלכות (= πενία) stood in the Heb. MS. of our *Epistle*, and the Greek translator, not being acquainted with the rare word, identified it with the like-sounding χαλκός; cf. the transliterations of Heb. words in LXX.

(5) *V.* 54. 'Neither can they judge . . . being unable: *for they are as crows between heaven and earth.*' The point of the comparison is obscure. Moreover, a verb seems wanting, as crows are not always in the air. 'Αδύνατοι ὄντες is perhaps a misrendering of כי דלו (cf. Job xxviii. 4 with v. 16, xxxi. 16), and ὥσπερ αἱ (AQ[mg] *recte*) κορῶναι may be due to misreading כערבים for כעבים. We thus get the sense: *for they hang suspended—like the clouds—between heaven and earth.* The reference would be to plated wooden images hung against the walls of the temples.

(6) *V.* 59. 'Therefore it is better to be *a king that showeth his manhood* . . . than such false gods.' Was such a feeble truism worth writing or worth preserving? Could it ever have proved edifying to any readers whatever? But let us look at the context. The other comparisons of the verse are a vessel, a door, a wooden pillar—all inanimate objects. Emend *Better is a stick* (Ezek. xxxix. 9) *in the hand of a mighty man . . . than the false gods*, and harmony and sense are restored to the whole verse. (Heb. טוֹב מַקֵּל בְּיַד גִּבּוֹר instead of טוֹב מֶלֶךְ מַרְאֶה גְבוּר'.)

(7) *V.* 68. 'The (wild) beasts are better than they: for they can get under a covert, and *help themselves.*' The object of getting under a covert is surely *to hide*; and it is almost self-evident that αὑτὰ ὠφελῆσαι represents Heb. להעלם *to hide themselves.* The translator vocalized the word wrongly, reading לְהֹעִלָם *to profit them* (cf. Isa. xxx. 5) instead of לְהֵעָלֵם *to hide.*

(8) *V.* 72. 'The **bright purple** that rotteth upon them.' The Greek has 'the purple *and the marble* that rotteth upon them'. As I pointed out long ago (*Var. Apocr.* in loc.), this is clearly a case of confusion between שש *byssus, fine linen*, and its homophone שש *alabaster* or *marble* (Cant. v. 15). 'Marble' does not 'rot', 'fine linen' does; and 'purple and fine linen' go together (Exod. xxvi. 1; Prov. xxxi. 22; Luke xvi. 19).

For a not inconsiderable amount of similar evidence the notes on the text may be consulted. Altogether it would seem difficult to avoid the conclusion that our *Epistle* is a free translation of a lost Hebrew original. In that case, the Greek version may very well be considerably later in date, and may even belong to the age of the Maccabees.

THE EPISTLE OF JEREMY

1 A copy of an epistle, which Jeremy sent unto them which were to be led captives into Babylon
by the king of the Babylonians, to certify them, as it was commanded him of God.
2 Because of the sins which ye have committed before God, ye shall be led away captives into
3 Babylon by Nabuchodonosor king of the Babylonians. So when ye be come unto Babylon, ye

1. **copy of an epistle, which Jeremy sent.** (*Ἀντίγραφον ἐπιστολῆς ἧς ἀπέστειλεν Ἰερεμίας* = פרשגן אגרתא די שְׁלַח י׳; cf. Ezra iv. 11; v. 6.) It is nowhere stated in the body of the letter that Jeremiah wrote it. The statement might be only the guess of an editor or translator who remembered Jer. xxix and 2 Macc. ii. 2. Some such introductory formula, however, seems almost necessary to the understanding of what follows; and, upon the whole, the superscription is probably an integral part of the original composition. Cf. the last clause 'as it was commanded him *of God*' with *v.* 3 '*I* will bring you out' and *v.* 7 '*mine* angel'.

Why does not the author say 'Jeremiah *the prophet*', after the precedent of Jer. xxix. 1 and 2 Macc. ii. 1? He assumes that every reader will know who 'Jeremiah' was, although others besides the prophet bore the name (e.g. 2 Kings xxiv. 18 = Jer. lii. 1). But doubtless in his day the others would not be thought of. The mention of the name would at once suggest the great prophet whose importance had come to overshadow that of all the other great figures of the past in the imagination of later generations.

them which were to be led: i.e. were about to be led, or were on the point of being led (*τοὺς ἀχθησομένους*). There is no mention of such a letter being sent by Jeremiah to the captives deported by Nebuzaradan in 586 ('the remnant of the people'; Jer. xxxix. 9). The prophet was, however, so kindly treated by the Chaldeans that, had he wished to do so, he would probably have been permitted to communicate with his unfortunate countrymen. But the record is silent; and, besides, the whole character of the letter is quite unlike the sort of appeal which the dreadful circumstances of the time would have elicited from the tender heart and powerfully stirred sympathies of the prophet. No satire on idolatry, however brilliant, no series of gibes and jests at the gods of the conquerors, however ingeniously conceived and bitterly expressed, could seem other than strangely ill-timed to the poor captives, cowering in abject fear before their conquerors, in the very hour of what seemed to be the irretrievable ruin of their country and the triumph of the gods of Babylon.

The letter of Jer. xxix is expressly stated to have been sent to the exiles (of 597) when already established in Babylon (see *vv.* 1, 4, 7); not when they were on the point of leaving their own country, as our superscription affirms in regard to the captives to whom this 'Epistle of Jeremy' is supposed to be sent.

the king of the Babylonians. The same expression recurs in *v.* 2, and is, so far as it goes, an indication that the heading is due to the composer of the letter. The phrase of the canonical books is 'the king *of Babylon*' (Kings, Jer., Ezek., &c.), which the Syriac has in both places here also. See also Baruch i. 9, 11 f. It would be somewhat strange if a Greek translator had rendered so easy and common a phrase as the Heb. מלך בבל in this unnatural way. (Was the original phrase מַלְכָּא דִּי בָבְלָיֵא? Cf. Ezra iv. 9 for 'the Babylonians'.)

to certify them. Rather, 'to report unto them.' This word *ἀναγγέλλω* in LXX mostly represents Heb. הגיד, 'announce, report, give a message'; e.g. Jer. xvi. 10 *et saep.*

2. Rather, 'It is on account of your sins which ye have sinned before God, that ye will be brought to Babylon as captives.' Cf. Jer. xxxix. 7; 2 Kings xxv. 7. The writer is not *predicting*, as the English of both A. V. and R. V. seems to imply. He is declaring the moral cause of the banishment which, as they well knew, awaited them. It is as though the people had asked the question supposed in Jer. xvi. 10.

Since it was, strictly speaking, Nebuzaradan who carried away the people after the fall of Jerusalem in 586, 2 Kings xxv. 11, while (according to 2 Kings xxiv. 10–16) Nebuchadnezzar himself carried away Jehoiachin and his fellow-captives, it would seem that our author really intends the earlier captivity of 597. The next verse, in fact, summarizes the message of the prophet to the exiles of the first captivity, Jer. xxix. 4–11.

3. Lit. 'ye shall be there many years and a long time unto seven generations; but after this I will bring you out thence with peace.' Cf. Jer. xxix. 10, 11. The datum 'unto seven generations' is quite inexplicable if the author was acquainted with the writings of Jeremiah and felt himself bound by their data in such a matter. It is difficult to imagine any Jew of literary pretensions ignorant of that prophet's limit of 'seventy years' for the Babylonian Captivity (Jer. xxv. 12; xxix. 10). It is, of course, possible that the author was thinking of another passage of Jeremiah, viz. xxvii. 7. There the prophet estimates the divinely appointed duration of Babylonian dominion at three generations. 'All the nations', he says, 'shall serve *him*' (i.e. 'Nebuchadnezzar the king of Babylon'), '*and his son, and his son's son*, until the time of his own land come.' This might be regarded as limiting the duration of the Captivity also to three generations; and we might suppose that a Hebrew ג (= 3) has been confused with ז (= 7) in the original text of our Epistle. But see the Introduction,

shall remain there many years, and for a long season, even for seven generations: and after
4 that I will bring you out peaceably from thence. But now shall ye see in Babylon gods of
5 silver, and of gold, and of wood, borne upon shoulders, which cause the nations to fear. Beware
therefore that ye in no wise become like unto the strangers, neither let fear take hold upon you
because of them, when ye see the multitude before them and behind them, worshipping them.
6, 7 But say ye in your hearts, O Lord, we must worship thee. For mine angel is with you, and
8 I myself do care for your souls. For their tongue is polished by the workman, and they

§ 2, for what appears to be a more probable solution of the difficulty. The Syriac cuts the knot, reading 'until *seventy years*; and after *seventy years* I will bring you forth from thence in peace'. 'With peace' (μετ' εἰρήνης = בשלום) occurs in LXX Gen. xxvi. 29; Exod. xviii. 23.

Since Jer. xxvii. 7 does not appear in the LXX (see Q^{mg}), it would seem that our epistoler was not dependent on that source for his knowledge of Jeremiah's writings, but was acquainted with the Heb. text.

4. **But now shall ye see.** Νυνὶ δὲ ὄψεσθε = ועתה תראו, *And now, ye will see*: cf. Gen. xxxii. 11; Exod. xxxii. 34.

gods of silver, and of gold, and of wood. Vulgate: 'gods of gold, and of silver, and of stone, and of wood.' But cf. Ps. cxv. 4, cxxxv. 15; Jer. x. 4 for 'silver and gold'. For the addition (found also in Syr.), see Deut. iv. 28, xxix. 17; Dan. v. 4. Obviously, stone would be too heavy a material for gods which were to be 'borne upon shoulders'; i.e. carried in procession by the priests on their festivals, as depicted in the Assyrian sculptures. The 'gods of silver and of gold', moreover, were not of solid metal; but of wood overlaid with the precious ores. See Isa. xl. 19 f., xli. 6 f., xliv. 12–17, xlvi. 6 f.; Jer. x. 3–5.

which cause the nations to fear. Lit. 'showing (or *displaying*) a fear to the nations' (δεικνύντας φόβον τοῖς ἔθνεσιν = מראים את־הגוים מורא, 'making the nations behold an object of fear'). A 'fear' or 'dread' denotes a deity in Aramaic (דַּחְלָא, Syr. ܕܚܠܐ) as well as in Hebrew (מוֹרָא); Isa. viii. 12 f.; Ps. lxxvi. 12; פַּחַד, Gen. xxxi. 42. The curious Greek phrase, which is usually explained by reference to Ps. lx. 5 ('Thou hast made thy people see hard things'), suggests the Hebrew original given above, with its characteristic paronomasia or play upon like-sounding words (*mar'îm môrā'*), which the translator failed to reproduce in Greek. So the LXX everywhere ignores this feature of Hebrew style.

5. Rather, 'Beware, then, lest ye also become wholly assimilated to the foreigners, and fear at them (i.e. the idols) seize you, when ye see a crowd before and behind them bowing down to them.' This again suggests a Hebrew original. ונשמרתם פן דמה תדמו גם אתם לבני נכר ויראה אתכם תאחז עליהם וגו׳. Note especially the ἀφομοιωθέντες ἀφομοιωθῆτε = דמה תדמו (the compound Greek verb seems peculiar to this Epistle in LXX: see Tromm), and ἐπ' αὐτοῖς = עליהם 'on account of them', as the source of the fear. For the phrase 'fear take (or seize) you', see Ps. xlviii. 7; Exod. xv. 15. 'Before and behind them': i.e. in the procession.

6. **But say ye in your hearts.** The Greek has 'your understanding' (τῇ διανοίᾳ), as in Gen. xvii. 17; xxvii. 41. Heb. בלבבכם 'in your heart' (sing.). The Greek of what follows (σοὶ δεῖ προσκυνεῖν, Δέσποτα) might represent Heb. לך להשתחוות אדני. The verse, however, may be an interpolation. It breaks the connexion between *vv.* 5, 7 (see note on *v.* 7), and is omitted by LXX^A.

7. **For mine angel is with you:** recalls Exod. xxiii. 23, xxxii. 34; Gen. xxiv. 7, xlviii. 16; Exod. xxiii. 20; Num. xx. 16.

The next clause should run: 'And *he* (*emphatic*) careth for your lives.' The original verse may have been something of this kind:

כי מלאכי אתכם
והוא דורש (ל)נפשכם:

Cf. Gen. xxvi. 24; Isa. xliii. 5; Ps. cxlii. 5; Jer. xxx. 14, 17. (For the plur. τὰς ψυχάς = נפש sing., cf. Ps. xix. 8, xxxiii. 19 LXX.)

God is represented as speaking directly, as in *v.* 3. No doubt, the author felt that the whole message was a 'word of God', like all prophetic utterances. But the present verse may perhaps be a direct quotation from some poetical or prophetical piece. It does not seem likely that an author writing in Greek would have chosen to use the phrase ἐκζητῶν τὰς ψυχὰς ὑμῶν in this special sense, unless he had had such a word as דרש (or בקש, Prov. xxix. 10) before him. 'To seek a man's soul or life' generally implies a murderous, not a benevolent motive. See Ps. xxxv. 4, xxxviii. 13, &c.; 2 Sam. iv. 8 (all בקש). For דרש = ἐκζητῶ, see also Gen. ix. 5. Perhaps the author intended this last use: 'And he requireth *or* will require (i.e. avenge) your lives.' (So Syr. 'The A. of the Lord—מלאך י׳ for מלאכי—is with you, and he will avenge your souls.') Further, why ἐκζητῶν, and not ἐκζητεῖ (or ἐκζητήσει), if the author was not translating a Heb. participle?

8–16. *Idols, though made of costly materials and richly adorned, are powerless to help or to hurt.*

8. **For their tongue is polished by the workman** (*more lit.* a craftsman. τέκτων = חרש, Isa. xl. 18, 20; a carver or graver in wood, metal, or stone). Heb. perhaps: כי לשונם שנונה ביד חרש (*sharpened* rather than *polished*); a paronomasia. Cf. Ps. lxiv. 4, cxl. 4. κατεξυσμένη here only in LXX (Tromm). If 'polished' were what the author intended, this might represent Heb. מרוקה or ממורטה. It is implied that the images' mouths were open,

9 themselves are overlaid with gold and with silver; yet are they but false, and cannot speak. And
taking gold, as it were for a virgin that loveth to go gay, they make crowns for the heads of their
10 gods: and sometimes also the priests convey from their gods gold and silver, and bestow it upon
11 themselves; and will even give thereof to the common harlots: and they deck them as men with
12 garments, *even* the gods of silver, and gods of gold, and of wood. Yet cannot these gods save
13 themselves from rust and **moths**, though they be covered with purple raiment. They wipe their
14 faces because of the dust of the temple, which is thick upon them. And he that cannot put to

as if to speak (*scil.* oracles). The connexion of thought with what precedes may be: 'Fear them not, for,' &c. The verse is reminiscent of Ps. cxv. 4, 5 a.

and they themselves: i. e. their bodies (Greek αὐτά τε: cf. *Iliad* i. 4). Heb. ועצמם or וגופם. The whole clause may have been: ועצמם נחפה בזהב ובכסף.

yet are they but false. ψευδῆ = שקר, Jer. x. 14, xiii. 25, *a deception* or *fraud*, of an idol. Render: 'but they are a fraud.' Heb. והם שקר; after which the verse concludes with ולא יוכלו לדבר.

9. Lit. 'And as for a virgin fond of adornment, taking gold they make crowns upon the heads of their gods.' φιλόκοσμος only here in LXX. Heb. וכאשר לבתולה חפצה עדי לקחו זהב ויעשו עטרות על־ראש אלהיהם. Cf. Jer. ii. 32, iv. 30; Zech. vi. 11.

10. Lit. 'But there are also times when the priests, filching from their gods gold and silver, spend it on themselves'. Heb. perhaps ויהי היום וגנבו הכהנים וגו'; ὑφαιρεῖσθαι = גנב, Job xxi. 18. καταναλίσκω εἴς τι, 'to spend upon a thing,' is a classical phrase. The verb renders Heb. אכל 'to eat, consume,' Jer. iii. 24 et al. Possibly εἰς ἑαυτοὺς (= להם) is due to the translator's having misread לחם 'bread' as להם. The Heb. will then have been: ואכלו לחם or ולחם יאכלו 'and eat bread' (= feast: Gen. xliii. 25; Ps. xiv. 4; Jer. xli. 1; Luke xiv. 15). Otherwise, cf. 2 Kings xii. 12 and suppose an original like ולנפשם יוציאו 'and would spend it on themselves': so the Syriac (מפקין).

11. Render: 'while they will give part of them (i. e. the gold and silver ornaments) even to the harlots on the roof'; i. e. apparently, the roof of the temple, where perhaps they slept for coolness, as on an ordinary house-roof (cf. Joshua ii. 6). These would be hierodules or temple-harlots such as we know to have been connected with some of the Babylonian temples, e. g. that of Ishtar at Erech (πόρναι = קדשות; cf. Gen. xxxviii. 21 f.; Deut. xxiii. 17). στέγος, *roof* (Syr. om.), was also used for a brothel in late Greek; and the variant τέγος (A Q) is Aquila's equivalent of קֻבָּה in Num. xxv. 8 'a vaulted tent', rendered by the Vulg. *lupanar*, and so used in Neo-Hebrew. Cf. Lat. *fornix*, 'vaulted cellar; brothel.' Was this the author's meaning here, and did he write ונתנו מהם גם לזונות על הקבה ('and they would give part of them even to the whores by the arched bower')? In view of the Babylonian custom, the former interpretation seems preferable. Indeed, it seems possible, and even probable, that the original reference was to the supposed brides of Bel, who slept in the shrine on the top-stage of his great pyramidal temple (see Hdt. i. 181).

and they deck them as men with garments, &c. = ויעדו אותם כאדם לבוש את אלהי כסף ואת אלהי זהב ועץ (cf. Ezek. xvi. 11; 2 Kings x. 22). This sentence resumes the thread of the narrative from *v.* 9, *vv.* 10, 11 *a* constituting a parenthesis.

12. Lit. 'But these are not saved from rust and fret, arrayed in purple apparel' = ואינם נושעים מחלאה ומאכל מְלֻבָּשִׁים בגדי ארגמן: cf. Num. x. 9; Ezek. xvi. 18, xxiv. 6; Esther viii. 15; Mal. iii. 11; Job xiii. 28; 1 Kings xxii. 10, for the vocabulary. The second clause probably belongs to this rather than to the following verse (Vulg., Arab.); since, if 'rust' refers to the tarnishing of metal, 'fret' (βρώματα) seems to indicate the ravages of moths or grubs in clothing. The genitive absolute is, therefore, incorrectly used by the translator. But, further, βρώματα in the LXX generally means *food* (Heb. אֹכֶל or מַאֲכָל). Tromm. gives twenty-one instances of βρώματα = אכל (e. g. Gen. xli. 35 f.) and ten of βρώματα = מאכל (Gen. vi. 21). It is evident that '*from rust* and food' cannot be right. We probably have here another instance of error in translation from the Hebrew original. If ומאכל stood in the unpointed text, the translator may be supposed to have pointed וּמַאֲכָל (= καὶ βρ.) instead of וּמֵאֹכֵל 'and from a devourer' (i. e. moth or grub; Mal. iii. 11; cf. Job xiii. 28; Amos iv. 9). LXX makes the same blunder in Isa. lv. 10, giving εἰς βρῶσιν for לאכל ('to the eater'). In Matt. vi. 19 also σὴς καὶ βρῶσις may represent עָשׁ וְאֹכֵל 'moth and devourer' (Isa. li. 8. Cf. also Assyr. *âkilu*, 'eater,' 'grub,' 'worm,' &c.).

13. **They wipe their faces.** ἐκμάσσονται is strange, if this be the meaning. We should have expected ἐκμάσσουσιν. The middle voice denotes 'to wipe away one's own tears', *Anth. Palat.* 5. 43. If the Heb. was ימחו פניהם 'they wipe their faces', the translator might have pointed the verb as a passive, יְמֻחוּ, understanding 'they are wiped as to their faces' = 'they have their faces wiped'; though the sense might rather be simply 'their faces are wiped'. (For the verb see Prov. xxx. 20; Isa. xxv. 8.)

the temple is τῆς οἰκίας = הבית 'the house'. Cf. 1 Kings vi. But בית in the sense of temple or God's house (Assyr. *bît ili*) is usually οἶκος in LXX, while οἰκία is an ordinary dwelling-house. Did the translator use the latter word purposely, to express contempt for the heathen temple?

14. Lit. 'And a sceptre holdeth he, as a man judge of a place, who will not destroy him who offendeth

death one that offendeth against him holdeth a sceptre, as though he were judge of a country.
15 He hath also a dagger in his right hand, and an axe: but cannot deliver himself from war and
16, 17 robbers. Whereby they are known not to be gods: therefore fear them not. For like as a vessel
that a man useth is nothing worth when it is broken; even so it is with their gods: when they
18 be set up in the temples their eyes be full of dust through the feet of them that come in. And
as the courts are made sure on every side upon him that offendeth the king, as being committed
to suffer death; *even so* the priests make fast their temples with doors, with locks, and bars, lest
19 they be carried off by robbers. They light them candles, yea, more than for themselves, whereof

against him' = ושבט תומך כאיש שופט מדינה אשר לא יהרג את חוטא לו: (cf. Amos i. 5; Exod. ii. 14; Gen. xx. 9). ἀνελεῖ may also stand for יַכֶּה *will smite* (Gen. iv. 14); a suitable word in connexion with שבט (Isa. xi. 4). The Babylonian gods are represented on the sculptures and seal-engravings as holding sceptres, swords, axes, and other emblems of authority. Some of the Hittite deities at Boghaz Keui carry sceptres; and an axe is the common Egyptian symbol for a god.

15. Lit. 'But he holdeth a dagger in (A Q) the (A) right hand and an axe' = Heb. ... ותמך חרב בימינו וגרזן. LXX has ἐγχειρίδιον for Heb. חרב 'sword' in Ezek. xxi. 3, 4, 5 and elsewhere. Syr. adds: 'in his left,' which may very well be right. Restore therefore: וגרזן בשמאלו. 15b. Lit. 'but himself from war and brigands he will not deliver'. The collocation '*war* and brigands' is improbable; and it seems natural to suppose a confusion of πόλεμος and πολέμιος, such as we observe in Esther ix. 16, where we find ἀπὸ τῶν πολέμων (but B πολεμίων) for מאיביהם. Restoring πολεμίων (cf. A πολέμων), here, we conjecture the following original text: ואת נפשו מאיבים ושודדים לא יציל, *and himself from enemies and spoilers he cannot deliver* (cf. Isa. xliv. 20; Obad. 5).

16. **they are known.** Gk. γνώριμοί εἰσιν, which, according to the ordinary use of the LXX, should mean 'they are kinsfolk' (Ruth ii. 1) or 'friends' (2 Sam. iii. 8). The translator probably had the Heb. מודעים in his MS., and possibly confused the participle with the substantive. The verse, which is rhetorically repeated in almost the same words at *vv.* 23, 29, 65, 69, may be reconstructed in Hebrew somewhat thus: על־אלה מודעים לא־אל(הים) על־כן אל־תיראו מהם. Cf. Isa. xxxi. 3, lvii. 6; Jer. x. 5, v. 7.

17–23. *The senseless idols are patient of all indignities.*

17. A reminiscence of Jer. xxii. 28, Hos. viii. 8, as regards the language of the first half of the verse. But σκεῦος ἀνθρώπου is suspicious, as it hardly means 'a vessel *that a man useth*'; and if it did, the description would be quite superfluous. It looks as if חרש *earthenware* (Jer. xxxii. 14: כלי חרש) had been misread אדם by confusion of letters (ש or ש is sometimes mistaken for מ or ם), or perhaps rather אנש. Cf. also the Syr., which gives 'a potter's vessel'. Lit. the Greek says: 'For just as a vessel of a man, if broken, becometh useless, such are their gods.' The Heb. may have been: כי ככלי חרש נפוץ אין חפץ בו כן היו אלהיהם 'For like an earthen vessel broken, useless, so are their gods.' A broken vessel is a proverb of worthlessness, Jer. xxii. 28. (The full stop is rightly placed here; what follows is a new thought.) The next statement may be rendered: 'When they have been established in their houses, their eyes are (become) full of dust from the feet,' &c. But it seems probable that, in the Hebrew, the clause מֻצבים בבתים 'set up in the houses' (= temples), or whatever the phrase was which the Greek represents by καθιδρυμένων (? מוסדים נסכים) αὐτῶν ἐν τοῖς οἴκοις, was connected with the preceding words. The sense will then have been: 'So are their gods, set up in their temples.' Then followed in the Hebrew, as a new sentence: עיניהם מלאו עפר מרגלי הבאים: 'their eyes are filled with dust', &c. LXXA gives κήποις for οἴκοις; an interesting variant, which recalls Isa. lxv. 3. Cf. also *v.* 21 and the note there.

18. **the courts are made sure on every side.** Gk. περιπεφραγμέναι εἰσὶν αἱ αὐλαί, 'the courts (of the palace) are fenced in all round'; cf. Job i. 10 (שׂוך = περιφράσσω; Hos. ii. 6 (8) = φράσσω, 'hedge in'). αὐλή generally = חצר 'court'; but 'the courts are fortified' does not give a good sense, and αὐλή sometimes represents Heb. שער 'gate' (Ps. cxxii. 2; Esther ii. 19). Perhaps the Heb. was נסגרו השערים 'the gates are shut'. αὐλαί can hardly be the courts of a prison, as in Jer. xxxii. 2, xxxiii. 1 (Gifford); for that would require the addition of τῆς φυλακῆς.

as being committed to suffer death. Lit. 'as having been led off for death' (execution). This is not very intelligible; and A prefixes the conjunction ἤ *or*, which improves the sense, and may be right. ἀπηγμένος in LXX renders Heb. אסיר 'prisoner' (Gen. xxxix. 22; cf. xl. 3 אָסוּר = ἀπῆκτο, xlii. 16 הֵאָסְרוּ = ἀπάχθητε; Isa. xiv. 17 τοὺς ἐν ἀπαγωγῇ = אסירים). Either this (אסור למות) might have been the phrase here, or we may suppose an original לַמָּוֶת מוּבָל 'one led to death' (Isa. liii. 7; Jer. xi. 19). The rest of the verse is easy. The whole may have run in the Hebrew pretty much as follows: וכאשר בעד איש חוטא למלך נסגרו השערים ובעד אסור למות (איש למות מובל) כן את בתיהם יחַזקו הכהנים בדלתות ובמנעלים ובבריחים פן ביד שודדים יושדו: 'And just as around an offender against a king the gates are shut, or around one bound for execution (*or* a man led to execution); so do the priests strengthen their (the idols') houses with doors, and locks, and bars, lest by the hand of spoilers they should be despoiled'. (Syr. 'And like a man who is condemned by the king, *their arms are stretched out*—like the condemned (pl.) to death. Their houses their priests strengthen,' &c. This points to a different Greek exemplar.)

19. **They light them candles.** Rather: 'Lamps they burn'; Gk. λύχνους καίουσιν, which probably represents Heb. נרות יערכו 'lamps they arrange'; see Lev. xxiv. 4.

20 they cannot see one. They are as one of the beams of the temple; and men say their hearts
21 are eaten out, when things creeping out of the earth devour both them and their raiment: they
22 feel it not when their faces are blacked through the smoke that cometh out of the temple: upon
23 their bodies and heads alight bats, swallows, and birds; and in like manner the cats also. Whereby
24 ye may know that they are no gods: therefore fear them not. Notwithstanding the gold wherewith
they are beset to make them beautiful, except one wipe off the rust, they will not shine: for not even
25 when they were molten did they feel it. Things wherein there is no breath are bought at any cost.

yea, more than for themselves. A's reading πλείονας αὐτοῖς = רבים להם 'many for them', is preferable. The rest of the verse might have been: אשר לא יוכלו לראות גם־אחת מהן 'of which they cannot see even one'.

20. **They are as one of the beams of the temple; and men say their hearts are eaten out,** &c. Evidently there is something wrong here. The connexion of thought, if any exist, between the first and second members of the verse is hopelessly obscure. The Greek does not help us. 'He is, indeed, as a beam of those out of the house; but their hearts they say are licked up': surely a false contrast. It is likely that the words τὰς δὲ καρδίας αὐτῶν φασίν conceal the common Hebrew phrase 'to say in one's heart' = to think, and that the sense of the original was: 'And he (i. e. the idol) is like a beam of the temple, yet they think that he eats.' See Bel 6 ff. for eating as a proof of being a 'living god'. ἐκλείχειν = לקק 'to lap' or 'lick up', 1 Kings xxii. 38, and the syn. לחך, ibid. xviii. 38; Num. xxii. 4 (of eating). The Hebrew may have been: והיה כקורת הבית ובלבם יאמרו ילַחך *And he is like a beam of the house* (or read: כקורה מבית = ὥσπερ δοκὸς τῶν ἐκ τῆς οἰκίας); 'And they say in their heart, "He licketh up!"' (The translator pointed יְלֻחַךְ, as he renders by a passive infin.) The verse continues, if we translate literally: 'Of the reptiles from the earth eating up both themselves and their dress they are not aware.' This may have sprung from Heb. רמש האדמה אוכל אותם ובגדיהם ולא ידעו:, 'The creeping things of the ground (Gen. i. 25) eat them and their robes (1 Kings xxii. 30), and they know not.' (Syr. 'They are like beams, &c.; *and their heart is foolish and goeth astray*; and they are destroyed by the reptiles of the earth, and are eaten—they and their garments.')

21. Lit. '(They are) blackened as to their face from the smoke out of the house'. The Hebrew may have been: חשכו פניהם מעשן הבית 'Their faces are black from the smoke of the house'. Cf. Lam. iv. 8. In that case, μεμελάνωται (Q*) τὰ πρόσωπα (Q[mg]) would represent the Hebrew more correctly than the reading of B. But A's τοῦ ἐκ τῆς γῆς καιομένου is more likely to be original than B's τοῦ ἐκ τῆς οἰκίας (dittogr. from *v.* 20). It points, moreover, to the Heb. (בעשן) העלה מן־האדמה '(through the smoke) which goeth up from the ground' (cf. *v.* 54 note). The Greek translator seems to have vocalized העלה as הַעֲלֵה = καίειν, *to light* a lamp (Ex. xxvii. 20; Lev. xxiv. 2).

22. **swallows, and birds** (Gk. *the birds*) is a curious collocation. We should expect the name of some other species to be added to that of the swallow. The Syriac, accordingly, has *ravens*, which may be right, as the dominant idea would seem to be that of unclean birds (Lev. xi. 14, 15, 19). But 'bats and swallows and [all] the birds' is also possible; especially if 'the cats' be correct in the next clause. The mention of the (domestic?) cat is unique in LXX. The word (οἱ αἴλουροι) might conceivably represent שונרים (= Aram. שׁוּנְרִין, Arab. سنانير) or חתולים (see Talmud Bab. *Hor.* 13 a). The Targum renders איים by this last word in Isa. xiii. 22, xxxiv. 14. Was the word here איות 'kites' or 'hawks', which the translator misread איים and rendered 'cats'? Then the Heb. of the verse may have been על־גופתם ועל־ראשם ינוחו העטלפים והסוסים והערבים וגם האיות:. (The Syriac has: 'And on their heads sit bats and swallows *and ravens* together, and also *weasels*.' For *ravens*, cf. *v.* 54.)

23. γνώσεσθε = תדעו = 'ye *may* know'. מאלה תדעו כי לא־אל המה על־כן אל־תיראו מהם:.

24. Lit. 'For the gold which they wear for beauty,—unless one have wiped off the rust, they will not *make to* shine; for not even when they were being cast, were they aware (of it)'. There is no obvious relation between the two statements of this verse, the connecting γαρ notwithstanding. But it is at least evident (*pace* R.V.) that στίλβω is used transitively in the former of them, as in Diosc. i. 111 and Aristaen. i. 25. The Heb. might be יאירו (Job xli. 24) or יגיהו (Ps. xviii. 29). In the second, 'they were molten' or rather *cast* (ἐχωνεύοντο = הוצקו) can hardly be right; for the verse has in view, as the first member shows, idols overlaid or plated with the precious metal, not images of solid gold. The sense required, and indicated, by the context is: 'for they do not know when (*or* that) they are dirty (*or* tarnished).' Possibly the translator mispointed חֹלָלוּ 'were brought forth, produced', the real word being חֻלָּלוּ *were defiled* (cf. Ezek. xxviii. 7 'defile thy brightness': Isa. xxx. 22). ὃ περίκεινται, 'which they have round them, which they wear'; cf. Acts xxviii. 20; also τὰ περικείμενα χρυσία, plates of gold *laid on* an ivory statue, Thuc. ii. 13. Heb. כי את הזהב אשר צֻפּו ליפעה (נחפו לתפארת) אם לא ימחה איש את החלאה לא יאירו (יגיהו Ps. xviii. 29) כי לא ידעו כי (מחללים המה) חללו:

25. **at any cost.** Gk. ἐκ πάσης τιμῆς = מכל מחיר; a misreading of בכל מ׳. The Heb. may have been: בכל מחיר לקוחים הם אשר אין רוח בם:: cf. Jer. x. 14; 2 Chr. i. 16. Better: 'At all cost they are acquired, in whom is no breath.'

26 Having no feet, they are borne upon shoulders, whereby they declare unto men that they be
27 nothing worth. They also that serve them are ashamed: for if they fall to the ground at
any time, they cannot rise up again of themselves: neither, if one set them aright, can they
move of themselves: neither, if they be set awry, can they make themselves straight: but the
28 offerings are set before them, as if they were dead men. And the things that are sacrificed
unto them, their priests sell and spend; and in like manner their wives also lay up part thereof
29 in salt; but unto the poor and to the impotent will they give nothing thereof. The menstruous
woman and the woman in childbed touch their sacrifices: knowing therefore by these things that
30 they are no gods, fear them not. For how can they be called gods? because women set meat
31 before the gods of silver, gold, and wood. And in their temples the priests sit on seats, having
32 their clothes rent, and their heads and beards shaven, and nothing upon their heads. They roar

26. Rather *being footless . . . exposing their own shame to mankind.* Cf. Isa. xlvi. 7, xlix. 22, for the first reproach; for the second, Jer. xiii. 26, Nah. iii. 5. Indecent figures of gods were perhaps commoner in Egypt than in Babylonia, where they usually appear draped. See the procession in my *Light from the East*, p. 173. But nude and phallic figures occur on the seals. Heb. באין רגלים על־כתף ינשׂאו | מראים את־האדם קלונם:.

27. Lit. *And even they who attend on them are ashamed* = ובשו גם־עבדיהם. The participle θεραπεύων = עֶבֶד in Isa. liv. 17 also (LXX θεράπων = עֶבֶד saepe). Perhaps the translator pointed עֹבְדֵיהֶם (Zech. ii. 13). The next sentence is lit. 'On account of the rising by help of them, lest (= if?) ever he have fallen upon the ground'. Instead of 'by help of them' (δι' αὐτῶν), i. e. of the attendants, LXX[A] gives 'by themselves' (δι' ἑαυτῶν), i. e. unassisted. δι' ἑαυτοῦ would have been better after πέσῃ, sing. Further, the negative must be supplied: 'On account of their not rising by themselves, if ever he have fallen,' &c. Heb. perhaps: על קומו בְּיָדָם אִם נָפַל אַרְצָה 'because of his rising by their hand if he have fallen to earth'. Cf. 1 Sam. v. 3, xxviii. 20. The Chinese say 'A fallen Buddha rise!' (Pi Fou-tu k'i), of a hopeless case (Giles, *Dict.* 3600). The verse continues: 'nor, if one have set him upright, will (= 'can'—a Hebraism) he move of himself, nor if he be bowed, will he stand erect; but as before corpses the gifts are set before them.' The Heb. might have been: ואם איש יזיבהו במקמו לא ימיש לבדו ואם יכרע לא יַעמד כי כמתים לחם שים להם: 'And if a man set him up in his place, he will not move alone; and if he bow, he will not stand up; but as (before) the dead bread is set before them'. Cf. Isa. xlvi. 1, 7; and for the offerings to the dead, Ps. cvi. 28, Ecclus. xxx. 18 f., Tobit iv. 17. τὰ δῶρα = לחם, Lev. xxi. 6, 8; and παρατιθέναι = שים, Gen. xliii. 32 al. The change from plur. to sing. exemplified in this verse is a common characteristic of Hebrew style (see Driver, *Samuel*, p. lxix).

28. Lit. 'But their sacrifices their priests sell and use up; but in like manner the women (A their wives) also, salting part of them, neither to a beggar nor to a pauper give any share'. In Hebrew: וזבחיהם ימכרו כהניהם וּבִעֲרוּ (Isa. iii. 14) וכן גם הנשים (A = נשיהם) מולחות (Lev. ii. 13) מהם עני ואביון לא תאכלנה: (cf. μετέδωκα: Job xxxi. 17). Instead of ובערו 'and greedily consume', perhaps וְכִלּוּ 'and use up' (cf. Deut. xxxii. 23; Gen. xxi. 15); and instead of מולחות 'salting', perhaps חונטות 'spicing' or 'pickling' (cf. Gen. l. 2, 3, 26). (The Syriac 'their priests *eat them* and their wives *gorge themselves with them*' may indicate a more original text: יאכלו *edunt* pr. יכלו *consumunt*; לוחמות *vorant* pr. מולחות *condiunt.*)

29. See Lev. xii. 4, 7, xx. 18. ἀποκαθημένη '(a woman) *sitting apart* during menstruation' = דוה; λεχώς (for which Q's λεχώ is more correct), 'a woman in childbed,' or 'one who has just given birth' = יולדת. Heb. therefore: בזבחיהם הדוה והיולדת נוגעות:, an argument which would appeal to none but orthodox Jews. (For the construction γνόντες οὖν κτλ., cf. Isa. xxvi. 11: γνόντες δὲ αἰσχυνθήσονται = יחזו ויבשו. Here perhaps: ודעו מאלה כי לא־אל ואל וגו׳; cf. Q's γνῶτε.) (γνόντες is rare in LXX. It occurs otherwise only a few times in the idiom γνόντες γνώσεσθε = יָדֹעַ תדעו, Jer. xxvi. 15 et sim.)

30. Another objection from a purely Jewish point of view. There were no priestesses or female attendants of Jahweh. πόθεν γὰρ is perhaps equivalent to כי איך, 'For how?' B κληθείησαν and A κληθήσονται might either of them represent a Heb. impf. See *v.* 27 for παρατιθέασιν θεοῖς, 'they set (food) before gods.' The Heb. verse might be: כי איך יִקָּרְאוּ אלהים | כי נשים שָׂמוֹת לאלהי כסף וזהב ועץ.

31. **sit on seats**. So Syr.; but it is very doubtful whether διφρεύω, 'drive a chariot' (Eurip. *Androm.* 108), can bear this meaning, although δίφρος may be a chair or throne (כסא; Deut. xvii. 18; 1 Sam. i. 9). Q cuts the knot by substituting καθίζουσιν, 'they sit.' The sense is perhaps not unsuitable, if the word could bear it; but the whole context shows that the author is thinking of the mourning for dead gods, which was a well-known feature of Babylonian religion. We may, therefore, suppose that the original text had יבכו *they weep*, which the Greek translator misread ירכבו *they ride* (see the Introduction, § 3). For the other phrases of the verse, cf. Lev. x. 5, 1 Sam. iv. 12, 2 Sam. xv. 32, Jer. xli. 5, Lev. xiii. 45; whence we may infer an original text: ובבתיהם הכהנים יבכו קְרוּעֵי כֻתָּנֹתָם ומְגֻלְּחֵי ראש וזקן וראשם פרוע:. 'Ακάλυπτοι (here only) should probably be ἀκατακάλυπτοι, as Q[mg] = פרוע 'unbound' (by unwinding the turban); a thing forbidden to priests, Lev. xxi. 10.

32. Lit. 'But they roar, shouting before their gods, as persons at a dead man's wake'. Τὸ περίδειπνον, 'a funeral-feast,' perhaps renders מַרְזֵחַ (Jer. xvi. 5; cf. Amos vi. 7) = targumic מרזיחא, מרזחא 'the funeral-

33 and cry before their gods, as men do at the feast when one is dead. The priests also take off
34 garments from them, and clothe their wives and children withal. Whether it be evil that one
doeth unto them, or good, they are not able to recompense it: they can neither set up a king,
35 nor put him down. In like manner, they can neither give riches nor money: though a man make
36 a vow unto them, and keep it not, they will never exact it. They can save no man from death,
37 neither deliver the weak from the mighty. They cannot restore a blind man to his sight, nor
38 deliver any that is in distress. They can show no mercy to the widow, nor do good to the
39 fatherless. They are like the stones that be *hewn* out of the mountain, *these gods* of wood, and
that are overlaid with gold and with silver: they that minister unto them shall be confounded.
40 How should a man then think or say that they are gods, when even the Chaldeans themselves
41 dishonour them? Who if they shall see one dumb that cannot speak, they bring him, and intreat

feast', eaten soon after the burial of the corpse. Cf. Jer. xvi. 7: 'And they shall not break bread unto the mourner, to comfort him for the dead' (so Giesebrecht). The Heb. of the verse may have been: וזעקו לפני אלהיהם כאנשים במרזח מת: (Ps. xxxviii. 9 ושאגו). These rites of mourning for the gods recall the 'women weeping for Tammuz' of Ezek. viii. 14 and the Babylonian festivals of mourning for the same deity (Dumuzi).

33. Lit. 'From their dress taking away (a part), the priests will clothe their wives and children'. In Heb. מבגדיהם יקחו הכהנים והלבישו את נשיהם וטפם:.

34–39. *Unlike Jahweh, they do nothing*. Carlyle's cry to Froude, 'He (God) never does anything!' may be remembered. The prophets of Israel thought otherwise. They thought He did everything.

34. Lit. 'Neither if they have suffered evil by any one, nor if good, will they be able to repay'. Cf. Deut. xxxii. 35, Jer. xvi. 18, Prov. xxv. 22, and many other places. Heb. perhaps: אם רע ואם טוב קבלו מאת איש לא יוכלו לשלם 'If evil or good they have received from a man, they cannot repay'. See Jer. xlii. 6; Job ii. 10.

put him down: lit. 'remove him'. The Heb. of the second sentence might have been: לא להקים מלך יוכלו ולא להסיר. With this and the next two verses cf. 1 Sam. ii. 6–8.

35. **money**; Gk. χαλκός = copper, a copper coin, and then collectively, money. The original phrase may have been עשר ונכסים 'wealth and riches', which is rendered πλοῦτον καὶ χρήματα, 'wealth and money,' 2 Chron. i. 12. Probably, however, χαλκός = נחשת, as usual, and this Heb. term is a disguise or corruption of some word meaning poverty, e.g. ריש (cf. Prov. xxx. 8). This gives a better parallel to what precedes (ὡσαύτως). Heb. כן עשר וראש לא יוכלו לתת. The next sentence is based on Deut. xxiii. 22, and must have run pretty much as follows: אם ידר איש להם נדר ולא ישלם לא ידרשו:.

36. Heb. ממות אדם לא יצילו | ודל מיד חזק לא יחלצון:. Ἥττων = דל, Job xx. 10. Perhaps rather וחלש מיד גבור; cf. Joel iv. 10.

37. Lit. 'A blind man into seeing (= *visus*) they will not bring round' (περιστήσωσιν, B. A's παραστήσωσι = *set beside* or *near* is less suitable). The Greek is rather peculiar and suggests translation. Perhaps εἰς ὅρασιν should have been εἰς ὁρῶντα; and ישיבו may have been misread יציבו (= στήσωσιν). Hence we get: אדם עור לְרֹאֶה לא ישיבו 'A blind man into one seeing they restore not' (cf. Lev. xiii. 16, Isa. xxix. 17). There follows: אדם בצר לו לא יצילו 'A man in straits (Isa. xxv. 4) they will not deliver'.

38. Cf. Isa. ix. 16, Ex. i. 20, for the language. The verse falls back easily into Hebrew: אלמנה לא ירחֵמו | וליתים לא ייטיבו:.

39. *these gods* **of wood.** The italicized words probably represent the Heb. correctly. Cf. Isa. xxi. 9, where LXX renders אלהיה by τὰ χειροποίητα αὐτῆς, and Isa. xxxi. 7, where אלילי כספו ואלילי זהבו is rendered τὰ χειροποίητα αὐτῶν τὰ ἀργυρᾶ καὶ τὰ χειροποίητα τὰ χρυσᾶ. The Heb. of the clause may have been: לאבני ההר דומים אלהי העץ ואלהי הזהב ואלהי הכסף 'To the stones of the mountain are like the gods of wood and the gods of gold and silver'. The second clause is simply ועבדיהם יבשו: 'and their servants shall be ashamed'. See note on *v.* 27 a. The priests are intended.

40. Lit. 'How then is it to be thought or proclaimed that they are gods?' Cf. the classical use of νομίζω, '*to believe in* or *acknowledge as* a god'; e.g. in the indictment of Socrates: οὓς ἡ πόλις νομίζει θεοὺς οὐ νομίζων, 'not believing in the gods in which the state believes.' Heb. perhaps: ומה נאמין ומה נקרא כו הם אלהים: 'And how should we believe and how proclaim that they are gods?'

41. **they bring him, and intreat him to call upon Bel.** Or, 'having brought Bel, they expect him to speak.' But the man would be taken before the god. And ἀξιῶ in LXX is 'to beg, pray, request' (Dan. i. 8, ii. 16, vi. 11; Esther iv. 8, viii. 3). Φωνῆσαι = 'to speak', as in Ps. cxv. 7 (לא יהגו בגרונם). The Heb. of the verse might have been ואף המה הכשדים מקלים אותם כי אם ראו אלם אשר לא יוכל לדבר והביאו ומבל יבקשו אשר יהגה לאמור כי הוא יודע: 'And also they, the Chaldeans, dishonour them' (Deut. xxvii. 16); 'for if they have seen a dumb man who cannot talk, they will bring him in (to the temple) and beg of Bel that he may speak, thinking that he (Bel) is aware.' (Syr. 'They bring him *before the gate*': perhaps אבלא *gate* was

42 him to call upon Bel, as though he were able to understand. Yet they cannot perceive this
43 themselves, and forsake them: for they have no understanding. The women also with cords
about them sit in the ways, burning bran for incense: but if any of them, drawn by some that
passeth by, lie with him, she reproacheth her fellow, that she was not thought as worthy as herself,
44 nor her cord broken. Whatsoever is done among them is false: how should a man then think
45 or say that they are gods? They are fashioned by carpenters and goldsmiths: they can be nothing

somehow confused with אל בל *unto Bel*. Cf. Jer. l. 26 where Syr. renders מאבסיה by *her gates*, reading or guessing אבליה.)

42. **Yet**; rather, *And*. The idolaters themselves cannot see all this (A: τοῦτο νοήσαντες), and abandon them (the idols); for they are devoid of sense (Jer. x. 8). Hebrew: ולא יוכלו להבין (זאת) ולעזוב אותם כי דעת אין להם:.

43. This verse describes a well-known custom of Babylonian religion, which, according to Herodotus (i. 199), was observed in honour of the goddess Mylitta (Μύλιττα). 'Mylitta,' he says, 'is the name the Assyrians give to Aphrodite.' Aphrodite is, of course, Ishtar, the goddess of love and procreation; and 'Mylitta' is simply a contracted or corrupted form of the epithet *mu'allidtu*, 'she who causes to bring forth' (i.e. Eileithyia or Lucina), or 'she who brings forth' (intensive) all living, the Great Mother, as the Deep (Tiâmat) is called mu-al-li-da-at gim-ri-shu-un, 'the Mother of them all,' in *Creation-Tab.* i. See also Ishtar's lament over mankind when drowned by the Deluge (Flood Legend, *NE*, xi. 119 ff.), where she seems to claim them as her offspring. Heb. והנשים חֲגֻרוֹת חבלים (Jo. i. 8) בדרכים תשבנה מקטרות גֶּרֶשׂ (עור חטים) וכאשר אחת מהן תִּמָּשֵׁךְ ביד איש עובר וְשָׁכְבָה עמו (cf. Gen. xix. 35) אֶת־רעותהּ תְּחָרֵף כי לא נחשבה גם כמוה ולא חבלהּ נִתָּקָה: 'And the women, girt with ropes, sit in the ways offering groats (or chaff); and whenever one of them is dragged off by a passer-by, she reproaches her companion, because she has not been valued even as herself, and her rope has not been broken'. 'Bran' (τὰ πίτυρα) perhaps means *crushed* or *pounded* grain, since the ancients did not separate the skin from grain, as is done in modern milling.

The account of Herodotus is as follows: 'But quite the most disgraceful of the customs which the Babylonians have is the following. Every native woman is bound to sit in the temple of Aphrodite and, once in her life, have carnal intercourse with a foreigner. Many, moreover, not condescending to mix with the others, as being proud of riches, drive in a closed carriage-and-pair and stop at the temple, with a great following of attendants. But the majority proceed in this way. In Aphrodite's precinct sit, with a fillet of cord round their heads, many women (for some are coming, others going); while rope-drawn passages keep every direction of ways through the women, by which the foreigners pass through and make their choice. And when a woman seats herself there, she does not go home before one of the foreigners has thrown money into her lap and dealt with her outside the temple. But when he throws it, he has to say this much: "I invoke over thee the goddess Mylitta!" (The Assyrians call Aphrodite "Mylitta".) The money may be ever so little in amount, for she may not refuse it, for it is not lawful for her (to do so); for this money becomes sacred: but she follows the first that throws, rejecting no man. But after the intercourse, she makes expiatory offerings to the goddess, and goes home. And after this, thou wilt not give her so much when thou receivest her in marriage.

'All, then, who are possessed of beauty and stature soon go home; but all of them who are plain wait a long time, unable to fulfil the law. Some even wait three or four years' time. A similar custom prevails in some places in Cyprus.'

Our verse seems to describe something similar but not identical. There is no mention here of the Sanctuary (ἱερόν) of Aphrodite. The women 'sit in the ways' or streets, instead of repairing thither: cf. Gen. xxxviii. 14 ff., Prov. vii. 8, 12. Herodotus does not mention the offering of 'bran'; and it is not clear whether the 'cords' (σχοινία) of our verse are to be identified with his 'fillet of cord' (στεφανὸν θώμιγγος) or his 'rope-drawn passages' (σχοινοτενέες διέξοδοι), or with neither. The expression ἐφελκυσθεῖσα, 'dragged after him,' seems to imply a cord round the woman's waist, a sort of Venus's girdle, which is then symbolically broken.

44. **Whatsoever is done among them is false.** This agrees with A's reading παρ' αὐτοῖς, and seems to refer to the Chaldeans or their priests. Q's ἐν αὐτοῖς = בהם, which would more naturally mean 'upon them', i.e. the idols (cf. Num. xxxiii. 4, Dan. ix. 12), in the sense of punishment. Heb. perhaps: כל הנעשות להם שקר 'All the things that are done unto (or *for*) them are a fraud'; or כל אשר יֵעָשֶׂה להם שקר 'Everything which is wont to be done for them is a fraud' (so Syr.). πάντα τὰ γενόμενα = כל אשר עשה, 1 Kings xxii. 54. Perhaps, therefore, כל אשר עשו להם שקר (שוא) הוא = 'All that they do in their honour is a fraud (folly)'. (Both ψευδῆ adj. and ψεύδη subst. appear for שקר in LXX.)

For the rest of the verse see *v.* 40. The ὡς (= ὥστε: so A Q) seems superfluous as well as difficult. Ὡς θεοὶ αὐτοὶ ὑπάρχοιεν would be more intelligible. Cf. Soph. *Oed. Tyr.* 780: καλεῖ με πλαστὸς ὡς εἴην πατρί.

45–52. *Idols are merely works of art* ('the work of men's hands', Ps. cxv. 4).

45. Heb. perhaps: מעשה ידי חורש וצורף המה 'handiwork of carpenter and smelter are they': cf. Jer. x. 9,

46 else than the workmen will have them to be. And they themselves that fashioned them can never
47 continue long; how then should the things that are fashioned by them? For they have left lies
48 and reproaches to them that come after. For when there cometh any war or plague upon them,
49 the priests consult with themselves, where there may be hidden with them. How then cannot
men understand that they be no gods, which can neither save themselves from war, nor from
50 plague? For seeing they be but of wood, and overlaid with gold and with silver, it shall be
51 known hereafter that they are false: and it shall be manifest to all nations and kings that they
52 are no gods, but the works of men's hands, and that there is no work of God in them. Who
53 then may not know that they are no gods? For neither can they set up a king in a land, nor
54 give rain unto men. Neither can they judge their own cause, nor redress a wrong, being unable:

Ps. cxv. 4. Since עשה *fecit* is often rendered by γίνομαι in LXX, e.g. Gen. xlii. 25, 2 Kings xxiii. 23, Jer. viii. 8, we may suppose the original of the second clause of the verse to have been something of this kind: לא יֵעָשׂוּ למעשה אחר אשר לא חפצו חרשים לעשות: 'They are not made into another thing which the craftsmen did not want to make'. This implies γένωνται (A Q) for γένηται (B). Literally rendered, B's text says: 'no other thing will result than what the craftsmen wish them to become.' In 2 Kings ii. 10, οὐ μὴ γένηται = לא יהיה; and so here the Heb. may have been לא יהיה כל שונה מאשר חפצו וגו׳ 'there will not come into being aught different from that which', &c. (cf. Esther i. 8, iii. 7 for שונה with מן = 'different from').

46. B wrongly omits εἶναι θεοί from the second clause, where A Q [Syr.] preserve those words. Heb. והם עושיהם לא יאריכו ימים ומה מעשי ידיהם יהיו אלהים (cf. Gen. xxvi. 8, Deut. iv. 26) 'And they, their makers, cannot prolong days; And how shall works of their hands become gods?' Gods *are* πολυχρόνιοι and, indeed, eternal.

47. Lit. 'for they left lies and a reproach to those who are born after' (i.e. to posterity). The connexion of thought would seem to be: for the idolaters bequeath, not gods, but a *damnosa haereditas* of disappointment or deception (ψεύδη = שקר, Jer. x. 14) and reproach (ὄνειδος = חרפה) to after generations. Posterity is not likely to regard as gods things which had failed to help in the hour of national danger and disaster, and whose impotence was a subject of mockery to the conquerors (cf. 2 Kings xviii. 33 ff.), and of shame and mortification to their worshippers (Isa. xlii. 17, Jer. xlviii. 13). Heb. כי עזבו שקר וחרפה לאחרונים:. For אחרון in this sense, see Job xviii. 20, Eccles. i. 11, iv. 16.

48. **when . . . or plague.** Rather, 'Whenever . . . and evils' (κακά = רעה, as in Mic. iii. 11: οὐ μὴ ἐπελθῇ ἐφ' ἡμᾶς κακά). Heb. of verse: כי בבוא עליהם מלחמה ורעה יועצו הכהנים יחדו (or איש אל רעהו) אי־זה (אנה) יתחבאו עמם: B: ἐπ' αὐτά = upon the idols; A: ἐπ' αὐτούς = upon the idolaters. The Heb. עליהם might mean either; but A is probably right. Βουλεύονται πρὸς ἑαυτούς. Cf. 2 Kings vi. 8 for the construction (נועץ אל).

49. Lit. 'How then is it not possible to perceive', &c. = Heb. ומה אין לדעת וגו׳; see for this construction Ezra ix. 15, Eccles. iii. 14. Instead of 'themselves' (ἑαυτούς) A gives 'them' (αὐτούς). 'Plague' should be 'evils' (κακά), as in *v.* 48. The Heb. of the rest of the verse may have been: כי לא אלהים הם אשר לא יושיעו את נפשם (אותם :A Q) ממלחמה ומרעה (ומצרה Isa. xlvi. 7).

50. Heb. possibly: כי (om. Q) כאשר הם עץ וּמְצֻפִּים (cf. *v.* 6, and Deut. xxviii. 42 ξυλινά = עץ; Exod. xxvi. 32, also Exod. xx. 23) זהב וכסף תִּוָּדַע אחרי כן כי שקר המה: 'For inasmuch as they are wood and overlaid with gold and silver, it will become known hereafter that they are a fraud'.

51. **and that there is no work of God in them** = καὶ οὐδὲν θεοῦ ἔργον ἐν αὐτοῖς ἐστίν; a somewhat strange statement, and suggestive of mistranslation. If the Hebrew were ואין אלהים עֹשֶׂה בהם ('And there is no god working in or through them'), we have here a parallel to the error of LXX in Job iv. 17 (ἀπὸ τῶν ἔργων αὐτοῦ = מעשהו) and Joel ii. 11 (עֹשֵׂה דברו = ἔργα λόγων αὐτοῦ). Cf. also Prov. xx. 12 (κυρίου ἔργα = יְהוָה עָשָׂה).

52. B has: τίνι οὖν γνωστέον ἐστὶν ὅτι οὐκ εἰσὶν θεοί; 'By what then must it be known that they are not gods?' an inept question, surely, after all that has been already said. A's reading is preferable: Τίνι οὖν γνωστὸν οὐκ ἔσται κτλ. = 'To whom then shall it not be known', &c. ולמי לא יִוָּדַע אפוא כי אינם אלהים: (cf. Exod. xxxiii. 16).

53. The verse falls back into Hebrew quite naturally. כי מלך (ה)ארץ לא יקימו (1 Kings xiv. 14) ולא אֶת־מְטַר הָאֲדָמָה יתנו: 'For a king of a (the) country they cannot set up, and the rain of the ground they cannot give'. Apparently the Greek translator misread האדם (= ἀνθρώποις) for האדמה: see Deut. xxviii. 12, 24, xi. 14; 1 Kings xvii. 14.

54. The position of ἑαυτῶν (A Q αὐτῶν) is remarkable. It looks as if the word were an attempt to render Heb. הֵמָּה or הֵם; an emphatic *they*. Heb. ודין לא ידינו המה: cf. Jer. v. 28. The next clause, οὐδὲ μὴ ῥύσωνται ἀδίκημα ('nor redress a wrong'), appears to be a reminiscence of Isa. i. 17, where LXX[B] has ῥύσασθε ἀδικούμενον = אשרו חמוץ. Here also A has ἀδικούμενον for B's ἀδίκημα. We may therefore suppose an original text ולא יאשרו חמוץ 'nor can they correct an oppressor', or 'right one that is wronged'. (Cf. also 2 Sam. xxii. 49: ἀδίκημα = חָמָס.) 'Being unable' (ἀδύνατοι ὄντες) probably belongs to the next clause; where A Q[mg] read αἱ instead of γάρ (no doubt correctly). This gives the sense: 'being powerless as the crows

55 for they are as crows between heaven and earth. For even when fire falleth upon the house of
gods of wood, or overlaid with gold or with silver, their priests will flee away, and escape, but
56 they themselves shall be burnt asunder like beams. Moreover they cannot withstand any king
57 or enemies: how should a man then allow or think that they be gods? Neither are those gods
of wood, and overlaid with silver or with gold, able to escape either from thieves or robbers.
58 Whose gold, and silver, and garments wherewith they are clothed, they that are strong will take
59 from them, and go away withal: neither shall they be able to help themselves. Therefore it
is better to be a king that showeth his manhood, or else a vessel in a house profitable for that
whereof the owner shall have need, than such false gods; or even a door in a house, to keep
the things safe that be therein, than such false gods; or a pillar of wood in a palace, than such
60 false gods. For sun, and moon, and stars, being bright and sent to do their offices, are obedient.

between the heaven and the earth.' The point of the comparison, however, is still obscure, for 'crows' (or ravens: see Jer. iii. 2 כַּעֲרָבִי במדבר = ὡσεὶ κορώνη ἐρημουμένη, LXX reading or misreading 'כְּעֹרֵב במ) do not give the impression of powerlessness, especially when flying in mid-air. Moreover, a verb seems wanting, as crows are not always in the air. Now in Job v. 16, xxxi. 16, ἀδύνατος represents Heb. דַּל, *weak, helpless.* It seems possible, therefore, that the Hebrew text here had כִּי דַלּוּ (*for they hang suspended*: cf. Job xxviii. 4), which the Greek translator ignorantly rendered ἀδύνατοι ὄντες. The reference would be to images hanging on a wall (cf. *v.* 21 note): Heb. כי דלו כערבים בין השמים ובין הארץ. We may further suggest that כעבים ('like the clouds') has been mistaken for כערבים ('like the ravens'). The Syriac has: 'And not like the ravens between heaven and earth *do they fly in the air*' (פרחין באאר).

55. Hebrew possibly: גם כי תפול אש (וגם בנפול אש) בבית אלהי עץ וזהב וכסף כהניהם ינוסו ונמלטו והם כקרות בַּתָּוֶךְ יִשָּׂרֵפוּן (cf. Gen. xv. 10: διεῖλεν αὐτὰ μέσα).

56. Heb. may have been: ועל מלך ועל איבים לא יקומו (Deut. xxviii. 7) ומה לקחת ולהאמין (cf. *v.* 40) כי אלהים המה: (For לקח '*to receive* a lesson', cf. Jer. ii. 30.)

57. Διαθῶσιν (B) is evidently wrong. The syllable σω has been accidentally omitted. Q presents the right reading διασωθῶσιν [so Syr.]: cf. *v.* 55. The Heb. was probably something like the following: לא מגנבים ולא משודדים יִמָּלְטוּ אלהי עץ וכסף וזהב: 'Neither from thieves nor from robbers' (Obad. 5) 'can gods of wood and silver and gold escape'.

58. Lit. 'From whom the strong will (= may) strip off the gold and silver; and the raiment that lies about them they will (may) go off with.' Heb. אשר הגבורים יפשיטום את כספם ואת זהבם ואת הבגדים אשר עליהם יקחו והלכו: (cf. Gen. xxxvii. 23, Ezek. xvi. 39, Isa. xlix. 25, for the language). In the third member of the verse, A's οἱ δέ, *but they*, seems better than B's οὔτε = ולא 'and not'. Heb. והם לנפשם לא יושיעו (Joshua x. 6), 'and they (the idols) will not save themselves.'

59. What writer, thinking in Greek, would have expressed himself in this fashion? Lit. the words run more like this: 'So that it is better to be a king exhibiting his own courage, or a vessel in a house useful for what the possessor shall use it for, than the false gods.' The fitness of the first comparison is far from being self-evident. It goes without saying, that a king giving proof of life and vigour in the face of attack is superior to a 'god' who can do nothing to defend his own person. But why a 'king' and not rather a 'man', i. e. any one whatever? Possibly because god and king are synonymous terms in Oriental use (cf. 1 Sam. xii. 12; Ps. v. 2, xx. 9, xxiv. 7, lxviii. 24; Isa. vi. 5, viii. 21, xli. 21); and a 'king' who fights for crown and kingdom (he was perhaps thinking of the struggles of some contemporary sovereign) is certainly 'better' than a *roi fainéant.* Heb. על כן טוב (להיות) מלך מראה את גבורתו וכלי בבית מועיל לאשר יעשה אתו קֹנֵהוּ (מאלהי שקר): It seems questionable whether the Hebrew had 'It is better to be a king', as the Greek has it (cf. Prov. xxi. 9), or 'Better is a king', &c. (cf. Prov. xix. 1, Eccles. iv. 13), of which A Q's κρείσσων (B κρεῖσσον) looks like a reminiscence. The nominatives in what follows (ἢ καὶ θύρα ἐν οἰκίᾳ . . . καὶ ξύλινος στύλος) may point in the latter direction. They at least show that the author of the Greek forgot the construction with which he started, and support the view that he was translating from a language destitute of Case-inflexions, viz. Hebrew. The LXX rendering of the Canonical Books often exhibits the same error. [I leave this note as originally written, in order to show how little can be made of the text as it stands; but see Introd. § 3 (6) for a conjectural emendation of the first clause of the verse.] The Heb. of the rest of the verse might be: וגם דלת בבית שומרת את אשר בו (מאלהי שקר) ועמוד עץ בהיכל מאלהי שקר: (τὰ βασίλεια = ההיכל, Nahum ii. 6). The triple ἢ οἱ ψευδεῖς θεοί is hardly original. The first two occurrences look like artless insertions intended to make the meaning clearer. (Cf. Wisd. v. 9–13.) I have therefore enclosed them in brackets. The Syriac omits all, perhaps correctly.

60. Unlike the things just mentioned, and those enumerated in *vv.* 60–63, the false gods are useful for no purpose whatever.

כי שמש וירח וכוכבים מאירים
ושלוחים על חֵפֶץ ושומעים:

61 Likewise also the lightning when it glittereth is fair to see; and after the same manner the wind
62 also bloweth in every country. And when God commandeth the clouds to go over the whole
63 world, they do as they are bidden. And the fire sent from above to consume mountains and woods
doeth as it is commanded: but these are to be likened unto them neither in show nor power.
64 Wherefore a man should neither think nor say that they are gods, seeing they are able neither
65 to judge causes, nor to do good unto men. Knowing therefore that they are no gods, fear them
66, 67 not. For they can neither curse nor bless kings: neither can they show signs in the heavens
68 among the nations, nor shine as the sun, nor give light as the moon. The beasts are better than

'For sun and moon and stars do shine;
They are sent on a business and obey.'

For χρείας = חֵפֶץ, see Eccles. iii. 1 Symm. and ib. 17 Aq. For the sense of חפץ, cf. Isa. liii. 10, lviii. 13. Εὐήκοος = שומע, Prov. xxv. 12. It is evident that the Greek closely follows, while partially misunderstanding, the Hebrew.

61. **Likewise also the lightning when it glittereth is fair to see.** The attribution of beauty to lightning is quite contrary to Biblical conceptions, which rather associate awe and terror with this phenomenon: Ex. xix. 16; Ps. xviii. 14, lxxvii. 18; Rev. iv. 5. Εὔοπτος might be 'well-seen' = conspicuous. But it is probable that we have here another instance of error in translation; the author of the Greek version having connected נורא *terrible* with נראה *seen*. The Heb. may have been: ואף ברק בהראותו נורא 'And also lightning when it appeareth is awful'; or וכן גם ברק בהאירו נורא, 'And so also lightning when it shineth is terrible'. In either case there is a paronomasia on the two like-sounding words, such as is characteristic of Hebrew style. (In Zeph. ii. 11 נורא is rendered by LXX ἐπιφανήσεται, and in 2 Sam. vii. 23 נוראות = ἐπιφάνειαν, while נורא is rendered by ἐπιφανής six or seven times. In these cases there is a similar confusion of the above Heb. roots.) The rest of the verse might be: וכן גם רוח בכל ארץ נושבת: 'And so also wind bloweth in every land'. For τὸ δ' αὐτὸ καὶ . . . see Phil. ii. 18 (Gifford).

62. Lit. 'And to clouds whenever it is commanded by God to go over all the inhabited (world), they accomplish what was commanded'. The Hebrew may have been simply: ועבים בצותם אלהים לעבר על תבל יכלו (יעשו) את המצוה (יעשו כן): Isa. xiii. 11, xiv. 17 תבל = ἡ οἰκουμένη ὅλη; but ib. xiv. 26 ἐπὶ τὴν οἰκουμένην ὅλην = על כל הארץ. The translator possibly connected the מ of בצותם with אלהים, supposing the verb to be passive. Cf., however, Isa. v. 6: ועל העבים אצוה = καὶ ταῖς νεφέλαις ἐντελοῦμαι. See Ezek. xxxix. 14 for ἐπιπορεύεσθαι = לעבור. The paronomasia with עבים was probably intentional.

63. **the fire**: i.e. lightning, which is 'the Fire of God'. Instead of 'to consume' (ἐξαναλῶσαι, 'to spend' or 'destroy utterly'), Q gives ἐξερημῶσαι, 'to desolate utterly'. The latter might be an attempt to render Heb. להחריב or להשם more exactly (= to *lay waste*), but the Heb. may have been simply לבער *to consume* (cf. Syr.). Q's addition καὶ βουνούς, *and hills* (so also Syr.), may be original: cf. Isa. lv. 12. Δρυμούς may represent a sing. יער, as in Isa. x. 18, though plur. יערים (Ezra ii. 25) or יערות is perhaps more probable. The Heb. of the verse might be: והאש שלוחה (Amos i. 7, 10, &c.) ממעל לבער הרים (וגבעות) ויערות תעשה כן . והם לא דמו אליהם במראה ובגדל: (cf. Ezek. xxxi. 18, Dan. i. 13, 15 מראה = ἰδέαι). (Syr. 'They are not like *one of these things*'; cf. A Q: ἑνὶ αὐτῶν or τούτων.)

64. Heb. על כן לא יֵאָמֵן ולא יֵאמר הם אלהים כי לא יוכלו לשפוט משפט ולהיטיב לאדם: The last word was probably intended to be vocalized לָאָדָם = τοῖς ἀνθρώποις. For היטיב ל, see Joshua xxiv. 20. (Syr. adds: *nor do evil* after *do good*.)

65. See *vv.* 23, 29, *supra*.

66. **curse . . . kings.** See Eccles. x. 20. Cf. also Num. xxii. 6. Heb. כי מלכים לא יקללו ולא יברכו: 'For kings they will (= can) not curse nor bless.'

67. **in the heavens among the nations.** It is probable that this is an instance of a 'conflate reading'. בעמים = בשמים (out of which it might easily have originated). The Heb. of the first clause may well have been: ואתות בשמים לא יתנו 'and signs in the heavens they cannot set'. Cf. Joel iii. 3 (Heb.), Neh. ix. 10. (Syr. corrects: 'and signs in heaven *to* the nations they *show* not.' Cf. Matt. xvi. 1.) The fluctuation of the Greek codd. between ὡς σελήνη (B) and ὡς ἡ σελήνη (A Q; recte) again suggests a Heb. original; for the unpointed כירח might, of course, be read either way (כְּיָרֵחַ or כַּיָּרֵחַ). The Heb. of the latter half of the verse may have been: ולא כַשמש יגיהו ולא יאירו כַירח:.

68. **The beasts are better than they** = החיה טובה מהם. For החיה, see Gen. vii. 21, viii. 1. (Perhaps חית השדה, Jer. xii. 9. Syr. *beasts of the wilderness*.) There seems to be something wrong about the reason. Literally the Greek says: 'which are able by escaping into a covert to profit themselves.' Αὑτά or ἑαυτὰ ὠφελῆσαι is a strange expression for ὠφεληθῆναι. Now, the verb ὠφελεῖν in LXX usually renders Heb. הועיל 'to profit', as in Isa. xxx. 5; and it is likely that the translator mistook להעלם 'to hide' for 'to profit them'. It is merely a question of vowel-points (לְהֹעִלָם instead of לְהֵעָלֵם Niph. Inf.). Obviously, the motive for 'fleeing into a covert' would be to *hide*, rather than to 'help' or 'profit' oneself.

69 they: for they can get under a covert, and help themselves. In no wise then is it manifest unto
70 us that they are gods: therefore fear them not. For as a scarecrow in a garden of cucumbers
that keepeth nothing, so are their gods of wood, and overlaid with gold and with silver. Likewise
71 also their gods of wood, and overlaid with gold and with silver, are like to a white thorn in
an orchard, that every bird sitteth upon; as also to a dead body, that is cast forth into the dark.
72 And ye shall know them to be no gods by the bright purple that rotteth upon them: and they

69. Heb. perhaps: אין דבר במה נודע לנו כי הם א׳ 'There is nothing whereby it is known to us that they are gods'. Cf. Gen. xv. 8.

70. **a scarecrow.** Strictly speaking, *προβασκάνιον* is an amulet or safeguard against witchcraft, such as, according to Plutarch, workmen hung up before their shops. Cf. *βάσκανος* = רע עין, Prov. xxiii. 6. Since *βασκαίνω* is to 'slander, disparage, envy, grudge', is it not just possible that the translator misunderstood Isaiah's מלונה (Isa. i. 8), connecting it with לון 'to murmur' (perhaps rather 'be evil, *hostile*'; cf. Assyr. *lawânu, lamânu, limnu,* be evil, evil, hostile) rather than with לון 'to lodge?' The Syriac actually renders ערזלא דמקטיא, as in Isa. i. 8. But the context rather suggests a post or pillar (perhaps a terminal figure, like Priapus), set up to scare birds and other pilferers, cf. Hor. *Sat.* I. viii. 1–7); and the original phrase may have been modelled on Jeremiah's כתמר (ב)מקשה 'like a post (scarecrow) in a garden of gourds' (Jer. x. 5), which is said of idols as being speechless blocks. Heb. of verse: כי כאשר תֹּמֶר במקשה אין נוטר דבר כן אלהיהם עץ וזהב וכסף: 'For as a post in a cucumber-plot protecteth nothing, so their gods (of) wood and gold and silver' (protect nothing). Their 'terrors are empty terrors, like those of the palm-trunk, rough-hewn into human shape, and set up among the melons to frighten the birds away' (see my exposition of Jer. x. in *Prophecies of Jer.*, pp. 227–9, *Expositor's Bible*).

71. **white thorn,** the Greek *ῥάμνος*, a kind of prickly shrub, also called *παλίουρος*; *Rhamnus paliurus*, of which Theophrastus mentions two kinds, a white and a black, as we have our 'whitethorn' and 'blackthorn' in the hedgerows. Ῥάμνος is the equivalent of אטד 'bramble', 'buckthorn', in Judges ix. 14, 15, Ps. lviii. 10, where it is mentioned as the inferior of all the trees (Judges l.c.), and as used for fuel (Ps. l.c.). Here, the idols are as contemptible as this common hedge-growth, upon which any bird might settle and foul it (cf. *v.* 22). Tristram enumerates sixteen species of Rhamneae in Palestine (*Enc. Bib.* s.v. 'Thorns'). It is not evident why the *Rhamnus* should be '*in* a garden' (*τῇ ἐν κήπῳ ῥάμνῳ*), as it was not a garden plant. Probably a hedge of thorns *round* the garden (not 'orchard') is intended. Or the idea may be that of a wild growth in a neglected garden.

a dead body... cast forth into the dark is a comparison by which the writer intends to signify the extreme of contempt. Cf. Amos viii. 3; Jer. xiv. 16, xxii. 19; Isa. xxxiv. 3; Baruch ii. 25; 1 Macc. xi. 4. For a corpse to be left unburied was the height of indignity. 'Into the dark' may be a vivid touch, suggesting in one word (בחשך) an entire picture. We see the helpless body, perhaps of an infant, thrown out furtively under cover of night into the darkness of the deserted street, to become a prey to pariah dogs. (For the construction *ἐρριμμένῳ ἐν σκότει*, instead of *εἰς σκότος*, cf. 2 Kings ix. 25, 26, xiii. 21.) But it seems more likely that בחשך is a corruption or alteration of בחוץ 'into the street' (Jer. xiv. 16). The original text of the verse may have been something like the following: וכן גם לאטד בגן אשר כל צפור יושב עליו וגם למת (לפגר) מֻשְׁלָךְ בחוץ דמו אלהיהם [עץ וזהב וכסף]: (The concluding words may be due to inadvertent repetition from the preceding verse.) Or perhaps ... וגם כמת ... וגם כאטד נמשלו אלהיהם.

72. Lit. 'And from the purple and the marble that rotteth upon them it shall (= *may*; Hebraism) be known that they are not gods'. The Greek word *μάρμαρος* means any *stone* or *rock* which *sparkles* (*μαρμαίρει*) in the light; and then specially *marble* (= Lat. *marmor*). The margin and R.V. are both wrong in supposing that the term is here used as an epithet of *πορφύρα*, with the sense of 'brightness' or 'bright', which the word never bears. As I pointed out long ago in the *Variorum Apocrypha*, the Greek translator has here confused the Hebrew שֵׁשׁ 'linen' (Exod. xxv. 4; = Greek *βύσσος*) with its homophone שֵׁשׁ 'marble' (Cant. v. 15; עמודי שש = *στύλοι μαρμάρινοι*). Byssus is coupled with purple in Exod. xxvi. 1, and elsewhere; see especially Prov. xxxi. 22 (*ἐκ δὲ βύσσου καὶ πορφύρας ἐν αὐτῇ ἐνδύματα*). The robes of the idols might 'rot' upon them, but 'marble' hardly. The Syriac at least shows a sense of the fitness of things, with its 'purple and *silk stuffs*'. Heb. ומן הארגמן והשש הרוקב עליהם יודע כי אינם אלהים. For רקב = *σήπομαι*, cf. Job xix. 20, where LXX has *ἐσάπησαν* = דבקה (obviously reading רקב׳). The variations *ἐπ' αὐτούς* (B), *ἐπ' αὐτῶν* (A), *ἐπ' αὐτοῖς* (Q), might all be attempts to represent Heb. עליהם 'upon them'. 'And they themselves' (*αὐτά τε*); in contrast with their apparel. Heb. perhaps simply והם 'and they'; or וגופם 'and their body'; or וגרמם (Aramaism). Cf. *v.* 8.

shall be consumed; rather *devoured* (*βρωθήσονται* = יאכלו or יאכל; cf. Isa. li. 8). The idea might be *devoured by fire*; but then בָּאֵשׁ seems necessary, as in Ezek. xxiii. 25, Neh. ii. 3 al. The word may have been passed over accidentally; but it seems more likely that the Greek translator misread יכלו 'shall perish' (Isa. i. 28) as יאכלו 'shall be eaten up'. This gives us as Heb. for the rest of the verse: והם אחר יכלו והיו חרפה בארץ:. [*v.* 20 may possibly give the clue to the sense: 'Things creeping out of the earth devour both them and their raiment.' But I prefer the preceding suggestion.] After plur. *βρωθήσονται*, with subject *αὐτά*,

73 themselves afterward shall be consumed, and shall be a reproach in the country. Better therefore
is the just man that hath none idols: for he shall be far from reproach.

the following clause καὶ ἔσται ὄνειδος ought to mean 'And it shall be a reproach' = והיתה חרפה; but Q's ἔσονται is preferable.

73. An apparently lame conclusion. Idols will evidently become a reproach to their worshippers; therefore one who has nothing to do with idols will be far from reproach; a *non sequitur*, unless idolatry be the sole ground of reproach. Further, there is no obvious reference for the comparative κρείσσων. Better than whom? A vague ἢ αὐτοί, *than they*, meaning 'the Chaldeans' (*v.* 40), may have fallen out; cf. οἱ θεοὶ αὐτῶν, 'their gods,' in *vv.* 70 sq. Or the omitted phrase may have been ἢ οἱ θεραπεύοντες αὐτά, 'than they that serve them,' *v.* 27. See the repeated ἢ οἱ ψευδεῖς θεοί, *v.* 58 (Eng. 59). The Hebrew of the verse may thus have been: על כן טוב איש צדיק ועצבים אין לו מהמה (מעבדיהם) כי הוא יהיה רחוק מחרפה: 'Therefore better is a righteous man who hath no idols than they (than their worshippers); for he (A: αὐτός) will be far from reproach'. The phrase ἄνθρωπος δίκαιος = 'a non-idolater', in the sense of the writer; cf. the use of ἄνομοι, ἀσεβεῖς, υἱοὶ παράνομοι, ἁμαρτωλοί, for the heathen and renegade Jews in 1 Macc. *passim*. And it would perhaps give a more coherent sense if the statement of the verse were: 'Better is a "righteous" man (= a non-idolater) than one that hath idols; for (unlike the latter) he will be far from reproach' (which the latter must share with his discredited gods) = Heb. טוב איש צדיק מאשר לו אלילים וגו׳. The translator may have confused לו with לוא (לא), *not*, and omitted to notice the particle of comparison. (Possibly his Heb. MS. was worn at the end.) The Syriac ends thus: 'Well is it, then, for the righteous man who is far from reproach, *and is looking for the Lord God!*' (that is, the Parousia). 'Finished is the Epistle of Jeremiah the Prophet. His Prayers be with us!'

THE PRAYER OF MANASSES

INTRODUCTION

§ 1. Description of the Book.

'The Prayer of Manasses, King of Judah, when he was holden captive in Babylon,' is the title of a short penitential Psalm. It is written in Greek, and contains thirty-seven στίχοι. In Fritzsche's *Libri Apocryphi Vet. Test. Graece* it is divided into fifteen verses; and this division has been very generally adopted.

The Psalm consists of (*a*) an invocation of the Deity (*vv.* 1–7), (*b*) a confession of sin (*vv.* 8–10), (*c*) an entreaty for forgiveness (*vv.* 11–15).

§ 2. Its Origin.

Its literary origin is obscure. There seems, however, to be little reason to doubt that the author was a Jew, i.e. not a Christian. While, in the case of so short a fragment, it is difficult to decide with absolute certainty, it seems most probable that the Prayer was originally written in Greek; and that the existing Greek text is not, as has sometimes been maintained, a translation from the Hebrew or Aramaic.[1] If this view be correct, 'The Prayer of Manasses' should be classed with such writings as 'The Song of the Three Children', and be regarded as, in all probability, the composition of a Hellenistic Jew, who in the interests of his people's faith wrote the penitential Prayer to suit the special circumstances under which the prayer, ascribed to Manasseh, King of Judah, in 2 Chron. xxxiii. 18, 19, was supposed to have been uttered.

It will be convenient to quote the whole passage in which this mention of the king's prayer occurs, 2 Chron. xxxiii. 11–13, 18, 19:

(11) 'Wherefore the Lord brought upon them the captains of the host of the king of Assyria, which took Manasseh in chains (Or, *with hooks*), and bound him with fetters, and carried him to Babylon. (12) And when he was in distress, he besought the Lord his God, and humbled himself greatly before the God of his fathers. (13) And he prayed unto him; and he was intreated of him, and heard his supplication, and brought him again to Jerusalem into his kingdom. Then Manasseh knew that the Lord he was God. . . . (18) Now the rest of the acts of Manasseh, and his prayer unto his God, and the words of the seers that spake to him in the name of the Lord, the God of Israel, behold, they are written among the acts of the kings of Israel. (19) His prayer also, and how *God* was intreated of him, and all his sin and his trespass, and the places wherein he built high places, and set up the Asherim and the graven images, before he humbled himself: behold, they are written in the history of Hozai (Or, *the seers*).'

According to this account, a Prayer of Manasseh[2] was reputed, in the Chronicler's time, (*a*) to have been preserved among 'the acts of the kings of Israel', and (*b*) to be contained in the records of Hozai (or, *the seers*). Whether the Chronicler himself was acquainted with any such Hebrew prayer, or whether he is simply repeating a popular tradition, we have no means of determining. No such writing was ever contained in the Hebrew Scriptures; nor, if it ever existed, has it survived in any Hebrew or Aramaic form.

It is easy to understand that the Chronicler's story of Manasseh's repentance and prayer and deliverance from captivity must have produced upon the minds of devout Jews a profound impression. The record of his idolatry and of his persecution of the servants of Jehovah had stamped his name with infamy in the annals of Judah. But side by side with his wickedness were commemorated the unusual length of the king's reign and the quiet peacefulness of his end. The Chronicler's story of the repentance and conversion of Manasseh provided the explanation of a seemingly unintelligible anomaly. Henceforth his name was associated by Jewish tradition not only with the grossest acts of idolatry ever perpetrated by a king of Judah, but also with the most famous instance of Divine forgiveness towards a repentant sinner. What more remarkable example could be found of the long-suffering compassion of the Almighty and of His readiness to hear and to answer the supplication of a contrite penitent?

Nothing would be more natural than for a devout Jew to endeavour to frame in fitting terms the kind of penitential prayer, which, according to the tradition, Manasseh had poured forth when he was in captivity in Babylon. The sentiments embodied in such a form of petition might conceivably be

[1] See note on § 7.—Gen. Ed.

[2] The oldest non-canonical reference to this prayer is to be found in 2 Baruch lxiv. 8.

appropriate to those of his countrymen who had fallen into idolatry, and who might yet be reclaimed from the error of their way.

According to this hypothesis, the Psalm was composed for a practical devotional purpose.

§ 3. Its Literary History.

'The Prayer of Manasses' makes its first appearance in extant literature, so far as is known at present, in the so-called *Didascalia*. This was an early Christian writing, composed probably in the second or third century, and incorporated into the *Apostolical Constitutions*, a work of the fourth or fifth century, of which the first six books consist of the *Didascalia*.

The author of the *Didascalia* was probably a member of the Christian Church in Syria, and wrote in Greek. In a long extract, apparently derived from some other writing, he records at length the narrative of Manasseh's idolatry and punishment, of his repentance and prayer, of his miraculous deliverance from captivity and restoration to Jerusalem. The object which the author of the *Didascalia* has in view is to illustrate God's mercy towards a repentant sinner. After briefly mentioning the classical instances of David's repentance at the rebuke of Nathan, of Jonah's repentance and the answer to his prayer uttered in the whale's belly, of Hezekiah's supplication and the pardon of his sin of pride, he continues, 'But hearken, ye bishops, to an excellent and apposite example; for thus is it written in the Fourth Book of the Kingdoms (i.e. 2 Kings) and in the Second Book of Chronicles.' Then follow extracts from the LXX of 2 Kings xxi. 1–18 and 2 Chron. xxxiii. 1 ff., which are welded together and expanded by four Additions, to which there is nothing corresponding in the Hebrew text. The order in which these extracts follow one another is as follows:

(1) 2 Kings xxi. 1–4.
(2) 2 Chron. xxxiii. 5–8.
(3) 2 Kings xxi. 9–16.
(4) 2 Chron. xxxiii. 11.
(5) Addition A.
(6) 2 Chron. xxxiii. 12–13ª (*προσηύξατο*).
(7) Addition B. *λέγων*, followed by 'The Prayer of Manasses'.
(8) Addition C.
(9) 2 Chron. xxxiii. 13ᵇ.
(10) Addition D.
(11) 2 Chron. xxxiii. 15, 16.

The Additions are as follows:

(A) An insertion between 2 Chron. xxxiii. 11 and 12: *καὶ ἦν δεδεμένος καὶ κατασεσιδηρωμένος ὅλος ἐν οἴκῳ φυλακῆς, καὶ ἐδίδοτο αὐτῷ ἐκ πιτύρων ἄρτος ἐν σταθμῷ βραχύς, καὶ ὕδωρ σὺν ὄξει ὀλίγον ἐν μέτρῳ, ὥστε ζῆν αὐτόν, καὶ ἦν συνεχόμενος καὶ ὀδυνώμενος σφόδρα.*[1]

(B) After 2 Chron. xxxiii. 13 *καὶ προσηύξατο πρὸς κύριον* (LXX *αὐτόν*) is added *λέγων· κύριε παντοκράτωρ . . . εἰς τοὺς αἰῶνας. Ἀμήν.*

(C) Instead of 2 Chron. xxxiii. 13 *καὶ ἐπήκουσεν αὐτοῦ· καὶ ἐπήκουσεν τῆς βοῆς αὐτοῦ*, is substituted *καὶ ἐπήκουσε τῆς φωνῆς αὐτοῦ κύριος, καὶ ᾠκτείρησεν αὐτόν· καὶ ἐγένετο περὶ αὐτὸν φλὸξ πυρός, καὶ ἐτάκησαν παντὰ τὰ περὶ αὐτὸν σίδηρα· καὶ ἰάσατο κύριος Μανασσῆν ἐκ τῆς θλίψεως αὐτοῦ.*

(D) Instead of 2 Chron. xxxiii. 14 is substituted *καὶ ἐλάτρευσε μόνῳ κυρίῳ τῷ θεῷ ἐν ὅλῃ καρδίᾳ αὐτοῦ καὶ ἐν ὅλῃ τῇ ψυχῇ αὐτοῦ πάσας τὰς ἡμέρας τῆς ζωῆς αὐτοῦ· καὶ ἐλογίσθη δίκαιος.*

§ 4. Its Preservation.

The preservation of this short disconnected Psalm may thus, with good reason, be ascribed to the accident of its occurrence in the *Didascalia* and the *Apostolical Constitutions*. There is no evidence to show that it was ever included in the Septuagint, the Judaeo-Greek Canon of Holy Scripture. But, very possibly, in consequence of the popularity of the *Apostolical Constitutions*, 'The Prayer of Manasses' became well known in the Eastern Church; and it was a natural step to take, to detach the Prayer from its context and to insert it among the Canticles (*ᾠδαί*, *Cantica*) used and sung for liturgical purposes, and to be found appended to the Psalter 'in certain uncial MSS. and a large proportion of the cursives' (Swete, *Introd. to the O. T. in Greek*, p. 253).

In the Codex Alexandrinus (A) there are fourteen Canticles appended to the Psalter in the following order: (1) Exod. xv. 1–19 (*ᾠδὴ Μωυσέως ἐν τῇ Ἐξόδῳ*): (2) Deut. xxxii. 1–43 (*ᾠδὴ Μωυσέως ἐν τῷ Δευτερονομίῳ*): (3) 1 Sam. ii. 1–10 (*προσευχὴ Ἄννας μητρὸς Σαμουήλ*): (4) Isa. xxvi. 9–20 (*προσευχὴ Ἐζεκίου*): (5) Jonah ii. 3–10 (*προσευχὴ Ἰωνᾶ*): (6) Hab. iii. 1–19 (*προσευχὴ Ἀμβακούμ*): (7) Isa. xxxviii. 10–23 (*προσευχὴ Ἐζεκίου*): (8) 'The Prayer of Manasses' (*προσευχὴ Μανασσή*):

[1] On the Jewish Midrashic legend respecting Manasseh's deliverance see Ball's 'Introduction to the Prayer of Manasseh' in Speaker's Comm. on Apoc. ii. 362 ff. Compare 2 Baruch lxiv. 8, part of the section (liii–lxxiv) assigned by Dr. Charles to 50–70 A.D. Cf. Anastas. *in Ps.* 6 *Canis. thes. Monum.* iii, p. 112 *φασὶν οἱ ἀρχαῖοι τῶν ἱστοριογράφων, ὅτι ἀπενεχθεὶς Μ. κατεκλείσθη εἰς ζῴδιον χαλκοῦν ἀπὸ βασιλέως Περσῶν καὶ ἔσω ὢν ἐν τοιούτῳ ζῳδίῳ προσηύξατο μετὰ δακρύων.* Ioh. Damasc. *Parall.* 2. 15, Opp. ii, p. 463 *ἱστορεῖται παρὰ Ἀφρικάνῳ, ὅτι ἐν τῷ λέγειν ᾠδὴν τὸν Μ. τὰ δεσμὰ διερράγη σιδηρᾶ ὄντα καὶ ἔφυγεν.* Suidas *s.v.* *Μανασσῆς: ὑπὸ Μεροδὰχ βασιλέως Ἀσσυρίων δέσμιος εἰς Νινευὴ τὴν πόλιν αἰχμάλωτος ἀπήχθη καὶ εἰς τὸ χαλκοῦν ἄγαλμα καθείρχθη . . . ἐδεήθη τοῦ κυρίου . . . καὶ τὸ μὲν ἄγαλμα θείᾳ δυνάμει διερράγη . . . δεδεμένῳ δὲ ὄντι ἐν φυλακῇ, ἐν πέδαις χαλκαῖς ἐν Βαβυλῶνι ἐδίδοσαν αὐτῷ ἐκ πιτύρων ἄρτον βραχὺν καὶ ὕδωρ ὀλίγον σὺν ὄξει μετρητῷ πρὸς τὸ ζῆν αὐτὸν καὶ μόνον, καὶ τότε προσηύξατο πρὸς κύριον· κύριε παντόκρατορ.*

(9) Dan. iii. 23 (προσευχὴ Ἀζαρίου): (10) ὕμνος τῶν πατέρων ἡμῶν: (11) Magnificat (προσευχὴ Μαρίας τῆς θεοτόκου): (12) *Nunc Dimittis* (προσευχὴ Συμεών): (13) *Benedictus* (προσευχὴ Ζαχαρίου): (14) The Morning Hymn (ὕμνος ἑωθινός). Similarly, in the Codex Turicensis (T), the liturgical Canticles are appended to the Psalter; and 'The Prayer of Manasses' appears ninth in the list. But the evidence of Codex Alexandrinus would alone suffice to show that in the Eastern Church the Prayer was in use for liturgical psalmody in the fifth century A.D.

§ 5. The Title.

To the Psalm is prefixed the title 'The Prayer of Manasses' (προσευχὴ Μανασσῆ) in Codex Alexandrinus (A); 'The Prayer of Manasses the son of Hezekiah' (προσευχὴ Μανασσῆ τοῦ υἱοῦ Ἑζεκίου) in Codex Turicensis (T); and in the editions of the Vulgate 'The Prayer of Manasses, King of Judah, when he was holden captive in Babylon' (*Oratio Manassae regis Iuda cum captus teneretur in Babylone*).

There is no sufficient reason to call in question the correctness of the title. (1) The title is derived from the narrative in the *Didascalia* in which the Prayer has been incorporated. (2) There is no evidence to show that the Prayer had existed before its inclusion in this Manasseh tradition. (3) Though it is noteworthy that the Prayer contains no mention of any proper name of personage or place, by which the legitimacy of the title might be confirmed, there are nevertheless to be found in it allusions which are most naturally interpreted on the assumption that the Prayer is put into the mouth of Manasseh, King of Judah. Thus, (*a*) the speaker describes himself as 'weighed down with chains', κατακαμπτόμενος πολλῷ σιδήρῳ (ver. 10): (*b*) he dwells with emphasis upon his many sins in past time, ἥμαρτον ὑπὲρ ἀριθμὸν ψάμμου θαλάσσης . . . ἀπὸ πλήθους τῶν ἀδικιῶν μου (ver. 9): (*c*) he makes particular mention of the forms of idolatrous sin whereby he had provoked the wrath of God, στήσας βδελύγματα καὶ πληθύνας προσοχθίσματα (ver. 10).

The objection must be admitted for what it is worth that there is no reference to the Temple of Jerusalem or to the religious worship of Israel. But this omission is intelligible, if we are correct in assuming that the composer is concerned with the tradition of Manasseh's repentance in its religious rather than in its historical bearings.

§ 6. Date of Composition.

It seems probable that the *Didascalia* (lib. ii. 21), in which the Prayer was preserved, was composed in the first half of the third century A.D. (F. X. Funk, *Die Apostol. Konstitutionen*, 1891, p. 50), and in Syria (*ibid.*, p. 54). If we may assume that the author of the *Didascalia* borrowed from some Jewish, or Hellenistic, source the whole passage relating to Manasseh, then the Prayer, and the writing in which it stood, must have been well known in the beginning of the third century A.D. Its composition must be assigned to an earlier date than this.

The inclusion of the Prayer among the liturgical Canticles in the Codex Alexandrinus implies a high degree of estimation; and if those Canticles were copied from a yet earlier MS., we might be justified in inferring that its adoption for liturgical use had its origin not later than in the fourth century, and that a considerable interval of time must have elapsed between its becoming known in the Eastern Church and its being transcribed for liturgical use in MSS. of Scripture. Perhaps, however, we cannot say more than that (1) 'The Prayer of Manasses' probably found its way into liturgical use after becoming known to the Church through the *Didascalia*: (2) that the citation, in the *Didascalia*, of the long extract in which the Prayer occurs, points to an earlier date for the period of its composition: (3) that the position of the Prayer, in a setting of passages cited from the Greek versions of Kings and Chronicles, suggests that the Prayer itself is of considerably later date than the translations which were used as a framework into which the penitential Psalm was inserted.

§ 7. Original Language.

'The Prayer of Manasses' is too brief to admit of any degree of certainty in the reply to the question whether we have to do with a Greek original, or with a Greek translation from a Hebrew or Aramaic original.[1] If it be a translation, it deserves to rank high. But the general impression

[1] [There is, I think, one real piece of evidence on behalf of a Semitic original. This is to be found in ver. 7:

σύ, κύριε, κατὰ τὸ πλῆθος τῆς χρηστότητός σου ἐπηγγείλω μετανοίας ἄφεσιν τοῖς ἡμαρτηκόσιν σοι
καὶ τῷ πλήθει τῶν οἰκτιρμῶν σου ὥρισας μετάνοιαν ἁμαρτωλοῖς εἰς σωτηρίαν.

Here μετανοίας ἄφεσιν is clearly anomalous and unintelligible. Furthermore, if we compare the two στίχοι, we discover that it is just this phrase that destroys the otherwise exact parallelism of the στίχοι. Originally the first line contained five elements parallel to the five elements still preserved in the second. Three of these still exist: κατὰ τ. πλῆθος τ. χρηστότητός σου || τ. πλήθει τ. οἰκτιρμῶν σου, ἐπηγείλω || ὥρισας, τ. ἡμαρτηκόσιν σοι || ἁμαρτωλοῖς. Over against

produced by the flexible style and ample vocabulary favours the view that Greek is the language in which it was composed: and it receives further support from the consideration that the manner in which it is inserted in the *Didascalia* extract among quotations from the Greek renderings of Kings and Chronicles, combined with Greek 'Haggadic' Additions, would suggest an originally Greek compilation.

The language may be described as a good specimen of the *κοινὴ διάλεκτος*, and contains phrases which show the usual Semitic colouring, e.g. *ἀπὸ προσώπου* (ver. 3), *ἐνώπιόν σου* (ver. 10), *εἰς τὸν αἰῶνα* (ver. 13). The occurrence of such adjectives as *ἀμέτρητος*, *ἀνεξιχνίαστος*, *ἀνυπόστατος*, *ἄστεκτος* (*vv.* 6, 7), of such substantives as *ἀγαθωσύνη* (ver. 14), *ἐπαγγελία* (ver. 6), *ψάμμος* (ver. 8), and of such verbs as *ἀνανεύειν* (ver. 10), *ἀτενίζειν* (ver. 9), *κατακάμπτειν* (ver. 9), would suggest a freedom from the usual restrictions of translation.

The employment of phrases based on, or derived from, the LXX seems to indicate an acquaintance with the Greek version rather than the work of an independent translator; e.g. *ὁ ποιήσας τὸν οὐρανὸν καὶ τὴν γῆν σὺν παντὶ τῷ κόσμῳ αὐτῶν* (ver. 1), cf. Gen. i. 1, ii. 1: *μετανοῶν ἐπὶ κακίαις ἀνθρώπων* (ver. 7), cf. Joel ii. 13: *μὴ συναπολέσῃς με ταῖς ἀνομίαις μου* (ver. 13), cf. Gen. xix. 15: *εἰς τὸν αἰῶνα μηνίσας* (ver. 13), cf. Ps. cii. (ciii.) 9: *ἐν τοῖς κατωτάτοις τῆς γῆς* (ver. 13), cf. Ps. cxxxviii. (cxxxix.) 15: *πᾶσα ἡ δύναμις τῶν οὐρανῶν* (ver. 15), cf. Ps. xxxii. (xxxiii.) 6.

Strange constructions such as *ὡρίσας μετάνοιαν . . . εἰς σωτηρίαν* (ver. 7); *ἥμαρτον ὑπὲρ ἀριθμὸν ψάμμου θαλάσσης* (ver. 9); *εἰς τὸ ἀνανεῦσαί με ὑπὲρ ἁμαρτιῶν* (ver. 10); *κλίνω γόνυ καρδίας μου* (ver. 11); *διὰ παντὸς ἐν ταῖς ἡμέραις τῆς ζωῆς μου* (ver. 15) seem to indicate the freedom of one who wrote in Greek.

It has been strongly urged by Sir Henry Howorth that the current LXX version of 2 Chronicles should be identified with the work of Theodotion; and that as we have 'a free rendering of parts of Chronicles, Ezra, and Nehemiah grouped round a fable (1 Esdras), and by the same hand a paraphrase of parts of Daniel, also with legendary additions' (Thackeray, *Grammar of O.T. in Greek*, p. 15), so we should be prepared to recognize in the Manasseh narrative, Prayer, and Additions, preserved in the *Didascalia* a reproduction of the original LXX version, for which the more literal version of Theodotion was afterwards substituted.

This view has been supported in *Old Test. and Semitic Studies in Memory of W. R. Harper: Apparatus for the Textual Criticism of Chronicles, Ezra, Nehemiah*, by C. C. Torrey (Chicago, 1908).

§ 8. THE THEOLOGY OF 'THE PRAYER OF MANASSES'.

The two main religious ideas which pervade the Prayer are (1) the infinite compassion of the Almighty, and (2) the efficacy of true repentance.

The opening Invocation portrays in striking terms the Omnipotence of the Deity, and this leads up to the consideration of the yet nobler attributes of His mercy and goodness (*vv.* 6–7). An effective prelude is thus furnished to the sinner's confession of his iniquities, the climax of which had been reached by his having set up idolatrous abominations. The glory of God and the abasement of the sinner having thus been set over against one another in sharpest contrast, the way is prepared for the ardent supplication for forgiveness which occupies the remainder of the Prayer.

The reader should take notice of the emphasis laid upon the Israelite patriarchs and their true spiritual lineage. The God of 'our fathers Abraham, Isaac, and Jacob' (ver. 1) is 'the God of the righteous seed' (ver. 1) and 'of the righteous' (ver. 8). The Patriarchs had not sinned against God (ver. 8). Those only were the righteous seed who had not yielded to idolatry. The range of view of the Psalmist is limited: it has regard to the sin of idolatry and to the pardon of the repentant

μετάνοιαν . . . εἰς σωτηρίαν in the second line we have the corrupt phrase *μετανοίας ἄφεσιν* in the first, which on the analogy of the former phrase should obviously be *ἄφεσιν . . . εἰς μετάνοιαν*. If we ask how this corruption arose I reply that it is possible to explain it as due to a transposition of לתשובה (= *εἰς μετάνοιαν*) from the end of the line to the place immediately after סליחה (= *ἄφεσιν*). In this new position the translation rendered סְלִיחָה לִתְשׁוּבָה by *μετανοίας ἄφεσιν*—a rendering that is quite possible though wrong in this context. On the order of the Greek cf. ver. 11 *τῆς παρά σου χρηστότητος*. Thus we should read:

'Thou, O Lord, according to thy great goodness hast promised forgiveness to them that have sinned against thee that they may repent;
And in the multitude of thy mercies hast appointed repentance unto sinners that they may be saved.'

If the above evidence is valid, then we can also recover the right rendering of ver. 4 *ὃν πάντα φρίσσει καὶ τρέμει ἀπὸ προσώπου δυνάμεώς σου*. Here the two verbs should be taken together. Then *ὃν . . . ἀπὸ προσώπου δυνάμεώς σου* is a pure Hebraism = אשר · · · מלפני חילך. Hence render—

'Before whose power all things shudder and tremble.'—GEN. ED.]

idolater. But a warning seems to be conveyed against the notion that Divine acceptance was ensured by Jewish lineage. The same note is struck, though it may not ring so clear, as in Luke iii. 8: 'Bring forth therefore fruits worthy of repentance, and begin not to say within yourselves, We have Abraham to our father.' Cf. John viii. 39; Rom. ix. 6, 7.

Other points, characteristic of Jewish religious thought and deserving of attention, are the following:

(*a*) supernatural efficacy ascribed to the sacred Name (ver. 3);

(*b*) the statement that 'repentance' is appointed by God for certain persons, and not for others (ver. 8);

(*c*) the representation of the under-world (*Sheol*, or Hades) as a region containing various grades of remoteness from the light of heaven (ver. 11);

(*d*) the description of the angels as the 'host of heaven' (ἡ δύναμις τῶν οὐρανῶν, ver. 15).

§ 9. Versions.

(*a*) 'The Prayer of Manasses' was never included in the LXX version of the Old Testament Scriptures. Its position among 'the Canticles' appended to the Psalter, in certain MSS., is due to liturgical reasons.

The Greek text was first printed by R. Stephanus in his edition of the Vulgate. 'The Prayer' follows 2 Chron.; and a short Preface contains this sentence: 'Graecam hanc Manassae regis Iuda orationem, nunquam antehac excusam, peperit tibi, candide lector, bibliotheca Victoriana.'

It does not appear in the majority of the printed editions of the LXX. In the Complutensian Polyglott (1514–17) it is printed in small type, in Latin, at the end of 2 Chron. It was not contained in the Sixtine edition (1586–7) of the LXX; nor does it appear in the editions of Holmes and Parsons, or of Tischendorf.

In Walton's Polyglott (although not mentioned in the index of contents) it is found in vol. iv (the Apocrypha) placed before 3 Esdras, and is printed both in Greek and in Latin. The note is prefixed: 'Orationem Manassae regis Iudae Graece non extare affirmatur in praefatione Bibl. Vulg. Lat. Edit. Antwerp. 1645. Quam tamen Graece iuxta exemplar Bibliothecae Victorianae in Bibliis latinis Roberti Stephani, Edit. 1540, fol. 159 excusam atque insuper in MS. A post Psalmos inter Cantica exaratam invenimus: ipsamque hic subiunximus.' The variants of Cod. A are recorded.

On the other hand, it is found in three reprints of the Sixtine edition, that of Frick (1697), that of Reineccius (1730), and that of Kirchner (1750). It was also included in Grabe's edition of the LXX, following Codex Alexandrinus. But there was no foundation for the note: 'Προσευχὴ Μανασσῆ, 2 Paral. cap. xxxiii iuxta quaedam exemplaria' (1817, iv. 165). This statement has led to a very general misapprehension. No ancient Greek MSS. of 2 Chron. xxxiii exist containing 'Oratio Manassis'.[1]

(*b*) *The Latin.* As it was not extant in the Hebrew or the Greek Bible, it was not included in the work of Jerome. In all probability he was not aware of its existence. Otherwise, he would scarcely have failed to make some allusion to it in the passage referring to the repentance of Manasseh: 'Legimus Manassem post multa scelera et post captivitatem in Babylone egisse poenitentiam et ad meliora conversum Domini misericordiam consecutum. Unde et fidei suae, per quam crediderat Deo, filium vocavit ἐπώνυμον, id est Ammon' (*In Sophoniam Liber I*, ed. Migne, P. L., vi, § 675, p. 1340).

At what date the Latin version, which is a good specimen of translation, was made is not known. It is probably much later than Jerome's version. The Prayer, however, is very commonly found in mediaeval MSS. of the Vulgate, immediately after 2 Chronicles, and often with the title 'Oratio Manassae'.

In his *Septuagintastudien*, iii, p. 20, Nestle states that he had been assured both by Ph. Thielmann in Landau and by S. Berger in Paris that, so far as they knew, there was no MS. of the Vulgate containing 'The Prayer of Manasses' of an earlier date than the middle or first third of the thirteenth century. A list of fifteen Latin MSS. in the British Museum containing 'The Prayer of Manasses' at the end of Chron. has been most kindly furnished me by Mr. J. P. Gilson of the MS. Department; all belong to the thirteenth century. It would be extremely interesting to know whether there exists any copy of the Vulgate containing 2 Chron. followed by 'The Prayer of Manasses' which is of an earlier date. It is also an at present unsolved problem to determine the influence which from the beginning of the thirteenth century led to the common inclusion of the Prayer in the Latin Scriptures.

An eleventh-century MS. of the Mozarabic Psalter gives a text which differs considerably from

[1] See the valuable discussion in Nestle's *Septuagintastudien*, iii, pp. 6–22. Stuttgart, 1899.

that in the thirteenth-century Latin Bibles, and with the title 'Oratio Manasse Regis De Libro Paralipomenon'. See below, Note B.

The three Latin MSS. (Colbert 273, Colbert 933, Remig. 4) which Sabatier collated with the Clementine Vulgate for his *Bibl. Sacr. Lat. Vers. Ant.* (iii. 1038 sq.) belong to the same period, and have no special claim to distinction (see Fritzsche, *Libri Apoc. Vet. Test. Praefat.*, p. 15).

It was printed in the Latin Bible of Stephanus (1540) together with the Greek text, and it appeared also in Joh. Brentius' edition of the Vulgate (Leipzig, 1544), in two columns, one in Greek, the other in Latin, side by side.

The edition of the Vulgate issued by Sixtus V (1590) did not contain the Prayer.[1] But in the revised edition of Clement VIII (1592) it was inserted, together with 3 and 4 Esdras, as an appendix after the New Testament. The *Praefatio ad Lectorem* written by Cardinal Bellarmine contains the following statement: 'Porro in hac editione nihil non canonicum, nihil adscititium, nihil extraneum, apponere visum est; atque ea causa fuit, cur libri iii et iv Esdrae inscripti, quos inter canonicos libros sacra Tridentina Synodus non annumeravit, ipsa etiam Manassae regis Oratio, quae neque hebraice neque graece quidem exstat, neque in manuscriptis antiquioribus invenitur, neque pars est ullius canonici libri, extra canonicae Scripturae seriem posita sint.' This statement, as Sir Henry Howorth has pointed out (*Soc. Bibl. Arch.*, vol. xxxi, pt. 3, p. 90), 'was probably unwittingly taken over from the Dominican Pagnini's revised version of the Vulgate which was published in 1527, before Stephen had published his Bible. In Pagnini's edition the Prayer is put at the end of 2 Chronicles, and is headed: "Oratio Manasse regis Iuda quae neque in Hebraeo neq. in Graeco habetur."'

In modern Greek Bibles 'The Prayer of Manasseh' has a place immediately after the Books of Chronicles (e.g. St. Petersburg, 1876).

§ 10. Syriac Version.

An account of the Syriac Version of the Prayer appeared in *Hermathena* xxxvi, 1910, from the competent pen of Professor George Wilkins, of Trinity College, Dublin. In his article he published a collation of a Paris MS. (*Anc. fonds* 2, *Biblioth. Nat.*, Syr. 7) which is probably a transcript of the Syriac MS. (*Vat.* viii) written by Sergius Risius, Maronite Archbp. of Damascus, circ. 1610.

The Syriac Version of the *Didascalia* is preserved, according to Professor Wilkins, in the following four MSS.:

(1) Cod. Syr. 62 (= Saint Germain 38), Paris, ninth century, = P.
(2) Harris Codex (Mrs. Gibson's *Horae Semiticae*), eleventh century, = H.
(3) University Library, Cambridge, thirteenth century, = C.
(4) Cod. Borgia, Museo Borgia, Rome.

§ 11. Other Versions.

Armenian MSS. of the O. T. Scriptures contain the Prayer among the Canticles appended to the Psalter.

It is also stated to occur in the old Slavonic Version (cf. article by Sir Henry Howorth, *Soc. Bibl. Arch.*, March, 1909, p. 90).

It is found appended to the Psalter in the Ethiopic Version of the Psalms (ed. Ludolf, Frankfort, 1701).

And the Ethiopic Version of the *Apostolical Constitutions* (ed. Thomas Pell Platt, London, 1834) contains the Prayer.

§ 12. Text.

The principal authorities for the text are (*a*) the two Greek uncial MSS. Alexandrinus and Turicensis; (*b*) the Latin and Syriac Versions; (*c*) the *Apostolical Constitutions* and *Didascalia*.

The text of cursive MSS., containing the Canticles appended to the Psalter, has yet to be critically investigated.

The MSS. of the *Apostolical Constitutions* are given by Pitra in his *Iuris Ecclesiastici Historia et Monumenta*, tom. 1, p. 163 (Romae, 1864). Pitra himself seems to have relied especially upon 'Vatic. 1' (= Vatic. 839, f. 1–175, saec. x, membr.), and 'Vatic. 2' (= Vatic. 1506, f. 1 ad. 77, a. 1024 membr.).

The important edition by P. de Lagarde, Lipsiae, 1862, contains an apparatus criticus.

The old edition of Cotelerius (1672) is well worth consulting.

[1] The Bull of Sixtus V (*Aeternus ille*), by which it was prefaced, had simply this allusion: 'Orationem Manassae, quae neque in Hebraeo, neque in Graeco textu est, neque in antiquioribus manuscriptis Latinis exemplaribus reperitur; sed in impressis tantum post librum secundum Paralipomenon affixa est, tanquam insutam, adiectam et in textu sacrorum librorum locum non habentem repudiavimus.'

The principal problems presented by the text of 'The Prayer of Manasses' are to be found in:

(1) ver. 7; the additional clauses found in the Latin and in the *Apostol. Const.* at the close of the verse;

(2) ver. 9; additional clause in the Syriac Version and in the Mozarabic Psalter;

(3) ver. 10; various readings arising from the obscurity of the verb ἀνανεῦσαι;

(4) ver. 10; the gloss added in Cod. T (μὴ ποιήσας τὸ θέλημά σου καὶ φυλάξας τὰ προστάγματά σου) and the Latin.

§ 13. English Versions.

'The Prayer of Manasses' was not included in Coverdale's Bible, 1535. But it appears in Cranmer's Bible (Grafton), 1539 (being given a place in the Apocrypha after 'Bel and the Dragon' and before 1 Maccabees), and in the subsequent editions (1541, 1549, 1562, 1566).

It receives the same position in the Bishops' Bible, 1st ed., 1568. It does not appear in the Genevan version. In the 'Authorized' (1611) and 'Revised' versions it stands between 'Bel and the Dragon' and 1 Maccabees.

In the Douai Bible of 1609 the Prayer precedes 2 Esdras and follows 2 Maccabees. It is headed by the note: 'The Prayer of Manasses, with the second and third Bookes of Esdras, extant in most Latin and Vulgare Bibles, are here placed after al the Canonical Bookes of the Old Testament, because they are not received into the Canon of Divine Scriptures by the Catholique Church.'

In Luther's Bible it stands at the end of the Apocrypha, after the Additions to Daniel.

Summary of the Prayer.

(1) *The Invocation*: (*a*) O God of Israel (ver. 1), Lord and Creator of the Universe (*vv.* 2, 3), infinite in power (ver. 4) and in anger against the sinner (ver. 5); (*b*) infinite also in mercy (ver. 6), Thou hast proclaimed forgiveness for repentance, and appointed me the sinner unto repentance (*vv.* 7, 8).

(2) *The Confession*: my sins are innumerable; I am unworthy to look upwards: I am justly punished, loaded with chains, in misery (*vv.* 9–11).

(3) *The Entreaty*: I beseech Thee (ver. 11); I acknowledge all (ver. 12); grant pardon; consume me not; nor let Thine anger burn for ever (ver. 13).

(4) *The Ascription*: Thou, the God of them that repent, wilt graciously save me (ver. 14); and I will praise Thee for ever.

(5) *Doxology*: Angels hymn Thy praises; Thine is the glory for ever (ver. 15).

A[1]. *Note on the Latin MSS. containing the Prayer of Manasses.*

In the British Museum, the following MSS., all of the thirteenth century, contain the Prayer of Manasses at the end of 2 Chron.:

(1) Add. 31,831 (f. 271 B): early thirteenth century.
(2) Eg. 2867.
[3 Lansd. 453: first half of thirteenth century. Does not contain Prayer, but has marginal note on f. 127 B: 'M[in]us Oracio Manassé regis qué sic incipit "Domine deus . . ."']
(4) Stowe 1.
(5) Harl. 1748 (f. 130).
(6) Royal 1 A. viii (f. 155).
(7) „ 1 A. xvii.
(8) „ 1 A. xix. (f. 106 B, insertion by a different hand).
(9) „ 1 C. i. (f. 106 B).
(10) Burn 3 (f. 390 B).
(11) „ 10 (f. 232 B).
(12) Ar. 303 (f. 166).
(13) Add. 28,626 (f. 210).
(14) „ 35,085 (f. 228 B): A.D. 1233–53.
(15) „ 37,487.

B. *Mozarabic Psalter: Eleventh (?)-Century MS. of Prayer of Manasses.*

In the 'Mozarabic Psalter (MS. British Museum, Add. 30,851) edited by J. P. Gilson, M.A., of the Department of Manuscripts in the British Museum', vol. xxx of the Henry Bradshaw Society (London, 1906), Canticum xxii contains *Oratio Manasse Regis De Libro Paralipomenon* 7–15; and the text differs sufficiently

[1] For this list I am indebted to the kindness of Mr. Gilson.

widely from that which is found in the Latin Bibles to justify its transcription here ('the character of the handwriting', says Mr. Gilson in the Prefatory Note (p. viii), 'points to the eleventh century as the date at which the MS. was written').

XXII [Canticum] Oratio Manasse Regis De Libro Paralipomenon.

Antiphona. *Peccabi domine peccaui et iniquitatem meam ego agnosco.*

Deus altissimus magnanimis . miserator et multe misericordie . patiens super mala hominum.

Tu ergo domine secundum multitudinem bonitatis tue promisisti indulgentiam et remissionem delinquentibus tibi . et habundantia misericordie tue statuisti penitentiam peccatoribus ad salutem.

Tu ergo domine deus iustorum . non posuisti penitentiam iustis tuis Abraham Ysaac et Iacob . qui non peccauerunt tibi . sed posuisti penitentiam mihi peccatori.

Quoniam super numerum arene maris habundauerunt iniquitates mee . et non est declinatio delictorum meorum.

Et nunc iuste contineor . (et)[1] digne comprimor percurbat(u)s (in)[2] multis vinculis ferreis . ad non erigendum caput.

Quoniam non sum dignus aspicere et videre altitudinem celi . pre iniustitiis meis.

Quoniam irritabi furorem tuum . et feci malum coram te.

Statuens abominationes . et multiplicans odiositates.

Et nunc flecto genua cordis mei . precans a te bonitatem.

Peccaui domine peccaui . et iniquitatem meam ego agnosco.

Ne perdas me cum iniquitatibus meis . neque in finem iratus contineas mala mea neque condemnaueris me cum (h)is[3] qui sunt in inferiora terre.

Tu es enim deus penitentium . ut in me hostendas bonitatem tuam.

Indignum me saluabis secundum multitudinem misericordie tue . et glorificabo nomen tuum in omni uita mea.

Quoniam te laudat omnis uirtus celorum . et tibi est gloria in secula seculorum.

[1] et] interlined. [2] percurbatus] *u* on erasure ; *in* interlined. [3] his] *h* interlined.

THE PRAYER OF MANASSES

1 O Lord Almighty, *which art in heaven*,
Thou God of our fathers,
Of Abraham and Isaac and Jacob,
And of their righteous seed;
2 Thou who hast made the heaven and the earth,
With all the array thereof:
3 Who hast bound the sea by the word of thy command;
4 Who hast shut up the Deep, and sealed it
With thy terrible and glorious Name;
5 Whom all things do dread; yea, they tremble before thy power:
For the majesty of thy glory cannot be borne,
And the anger of thy threatening against sinners is unendurable:

A = Codex Alexandrinus. T = Codex Turicensis. Const. Apost. = Constitutiones Apostolorum, lib. ii, cap. xxii (apud Cotelerium *Patres Apostolici*, tom. 1, p. 171; et apud Pitram *Iuris Eccles. Graecorum Historia et Monumenta*, tom. i. 162). Syr. = Syriac Version. Lat. = Latin Version, in Vulgate. Moz. = Mozarabic Psalter: Canticum xxii. See Note B, above.

TITLE. Cod. A Η προσευχη Μανασση: + του υιου Εζεκιου T: Latin *Oratio Manassae regis Iuda cum captus teneretur in Babylone* 1. επουρανιε om. T, Const. Apost., Syr., Lat. 2. ο κλεισας: και κλεισας T σφραγισαμενος: + αυτην T, Const. Apost., Lat. 4. φριττει: φρισσει T, Const. Apost. 5. τε και. Some edd. δε και: *vero et* Lat.

---

1. *κύριε παντοκράτωρ.* On the opening words of this invocation, compare 1 Chron. xvii. 24 κύριε παντοκράτωρ θεὸς Ἰσραὴλ κτλ. (= 2 Sam. vii. 27).

The reading ἐπουράνιε, omitted in Codex Turicensis, is possibly a gloss on παντοκράτωρ. In the Ὕμνος ἑωθινός (the fourteenth of the Ὠιδαί in Codex Alexandrinus) we find an elaborate ascription, κύριε βασιλεῦ ἐπουράνιε θεὲ πατὴρ ἐπουράνιε.

ὁ θεὸς τῶν πατέρων. Cf. 1 Chron. xxix. 18 κύριε ὁ θεὸς Ἀβ. κ. Ἰσ. κ. Ἰσ. τῶν πατέρων ἡμῶν.

τοῦ σπέρματος αὐτῶν τοῦ δικαίου. The writer implies the distinction between the true seed of the Patriarchs ('the righteous', cf. *v.* 8) and the nominal, which is found in Tobit xiii. 9, 13: 'O Jerusalem, the holy city, he will scourge thee for the works of thy sons, and will again have mercy *on the sons of the righteous.*' 'Rejoice and be exceeding glad for *the sons of the righteous.*' We are reminded of St. Paul: 'For they are not all Israel, which are of Israel; neither, because they are Abraham's seed, are they all children' (Rom. ix. 6).

2. *ὁ ποιήσας κτλ.* This verse is based upon the LXX of Gen. i. 1 ἐν ἀρχῇ ἐποίησεν ὁ θεὸς τὸν οὐρανὸν καὶ τὴν γῆν, and Gen. ii. 1 καὶ συνετελέσθησαν ὁ οὐρανὸς καὶ ἡ γῆ καὶ πᾶς ὁ κόσμος αὐτῶν. Cotelerius, commenting on these words, cites 'Theophanes Cerameus Homilia' 56 κόσμος καὶ ἡ τοῦ κάλλους ἁρμονία καὶ διακόσμησις κατὰ τὸ ὑμνούμενον ἐν ᾠδῇ Μανασσῇ. Ὁ ποιήσας τ. οὐρανὸν κ. τ. γῆν σὺν παντὶ τῷ κόσμῳ αὐτῶν (*Patres Apostolici*, vol. ii, p. 150).

σὺν παντὶ τῷ κόσμῳ αὐτῶν. Latin 'cum omni ornatu eorum'. The word κόσμος is here evidently introduced from the LXX of Gen. ii. 1, and may be regarded as an indication that the Prayer was written in Greek. The precise meaning of κόσμος is not certain. The fact, that in Gen. ii. 1 κόσμος = צָבָא 'host', causes Ryssel to consider that the reference is to 'the host of heaven', i.e. 'the stars', as e.g. in Deut. iv. 19, xvii. 3; Isa. xl. 26; Ps. xxxiii. 6. But in the first three passages the words 'of heaven' are added; in Isa. xl. 26 'the host' of the stars is clearly meant. Here the word κόσμος is followed by αὐτῶν, by which, strictly speaking, is denoted τὴν γῆν, as well as τὸν οὐρανόν. On the other hand, the literal renderings 'ornament' (R.V.) or 'order' (R.V. marg.) are too limited; and the second alternative, 'array,' seems best to combine the ideas of splendour and orderliness.

3. *ὁ πεδήσας κτλ.* There is a reference here to the passages in the O. T. describing the power of the Almighty in restraining the sea within its bounds, and in imprisoning the waters of the Abyss. See especially Job xxxviii. 8, 10, 11: 'Or who shut up the sea with doors, when it brake forth ... when I ... prescribed for it my decree, and set bars and doors, and said, Hitherto shalt thou come, but no further.' Ps. civ. 9: 'Thou hast set a bound that they may not pass over; that they turn not again to cover the earth.'

ὁ κλείσας τὴν ἄβυσσον. ἄβυσσος is the rendering of תְּהוֹם in Gen. i. 2, vii. 11, viii. 2. Here it evidently denotes the subterranean watery depths upon which the ancient Israelites believed the earth to be upheld. Cf. Apoc. ix. 1 κλεὶς τοῦ φρέατος τῆς ἀβύσσου, and xx. 3 καὶ ἔβαλεν αὐτὸν εἰς τὴν ἄβυσσον καὶ ἔκλεισεν καὶ ἐσφράγισεν ἐπάνω αὐτοῦ, where we may observe the association with κλείειν and σφραγίζειν.

σφραγισάμενος. Cf. Job ix. 7, 'which commandeth the sun ... and sealeth up the stars.' The seal denoted possession, security, and inviolability.

ἐνδόξῳ. Cf. Tob. viii. 5 τὸ ὄνομά σου τὸ ἅγιον καὶ ἔνδοξον. The rabbinic belief in the magical efficacy residing in the sacred Name is here referred to. Solomon was reputed to have wrought miracles by a seal engraved with the Tetragrammaton. Cf. Sirach xlvii. 18 and *Gittin* 68 *a*. The Name was often mentioned as the embodiment of power and attributes. Cf. Baruch iii. 5.

4. *ὃν πάντα φρίττει.* For φρίττειν with acc. cf. Judith xvi. 10 ἔφριξαν Πέρσαι τὴν τόλμαν αὐτῆς.

ἀπὸ προσώπου κτλ. Latin has 'a vultu virtutis tuae'. It admits of doubt whether this phrase simply amplifies the object of the verb expressed in ὃν = מִלִּפְנֵי 'in the presence of'; or whether it introduces a fresh thought, 'because of', 'by reason of' (= מִפְּנֵי). In the former case it would grammatically be closely conjoined with φρίττει and τρέμει; in the latter case it would introduce with τρέμει an explanatory clause. See, however, note on p. 615.

6 Infinite and unsearchable is thy merciful promise;
7 For thou art the Lord Most High, of great compassion,
long-suffering and abundant in mercy, and repentest thee
for the evils of men.
Thou, O Lord, according to thy great goodness hast promised repentance and forgiveness to them that have sinned against thee; and in the multitude of thy mercies hast appointed repentance unto sinners, that they may be saved.

7. οτι συ: συ γαρ T: *quoniam tu* Lat. om. υψιστος Const. Apost., Syr. om. και [1] Const. Apost. om. και [2] T, Moz. Insert *συ κυριε . . . σωτηριαν* Const. Apost., Syr., Lat., Moz.: om. A T 8. εμοι: pr. επ T, Const. Apost.; Lat. *propter me*

5. ἄστεκτος. The Latin renders by 'importabilis'. The adjective does not occur in the LXX. Hesych. ἄστεκτος, ἀφόρητος, ἀβάστακτος. Cf. Aesch. Fragment 220.

ἡ μεγαλοπρεπία τῆς δόξης σου. The phrase is evidently derived from Ps. cxliv. (cxlv.) 5 τὴν μεγαλοπρεπίαν τῆς δόξης τῆς ἁγιωσύνης σου, and 12 καὶ τὴν δόξαν τῆς μεγαλοπρεπίας τῆς βασιλείας σου.

ἀνυπόστατος. Latin 'insustentabilis'. An adjective of rare occurrence in the LXX: cf. Ps. cxxiii. (cxxiv.); 2 Macc. i. 13, viii. 5. Cf. Symmachus in Job iv. 11, ix. 19; Ps. lxxxv. (lxxxvi.) 14; Prov. xvi. 27.

6. ἀμέτρητον. Another uncommon adjective in the LXX. Cf. Isa. xxii. 18; Baruch iii. 25; 3 Macc. iv. 17.

τε καί. The reading of some editions, δὲ καί, and the Latin, seems to deserve support on internal grounds. (1) At this point the main subject which occupies the thought of the Prayer, i. e. the mercy of God, is first reached. The power (*v.* 4), the majesty and the wrath (*v.* 5), have been described; but here, in *v.* 6, another note of infinite graciousness is to be recorded. (2) The variation of thought between the two adjectives, ἀμέτρητος and ἀνεξιχνίαστος, is not sufficient to make the τε prefixed to the καί strongly preferable.

ἀνεξιχνίαστον. Latin 'investigabilis'. In LXX Job v. 9, ix. 10. Comp. Rom. xi. 33; Eph. iii. 8.

τὸ ἔλεος τῆς ἐπαγγελίας σου, 'the mercy of thy promise', or 'thy merciful promise', referring to the promise of forgiveness to them that repent implied in *vv.* 8, 11, 13, which forms the nucleus of the prayer.

ἐπαγγελίας. ἐπαγγελία, in the sense of 'promise' or 'declaration', is a common word in the N. T., e. g. Luke xxiv. 49; Acts i. 4, ii. 33–9; Rom. iv. 13–14, and often in Ep. to Heb. But it occurs rarely in LXX, e. g. 1 Esdras i. 7; Esther iv. 7; Ps. lv. (lvi.) 8; Amos ix. 6; 1 Macc. x. 15; 4 Macc. xii. 9.

7. ὅτι σύ (or, σὺ γάρ). The present verse develops the claim to the Divine mercy. It appeals to the language which would be familiarly known from passages in the O. T.

ὕψιστος. The omission of this adjective by Const. Apost. and Syr. has been explained on the ground that it is out of place at the head of a list of epithets of a moral character and bearing upon the mercy and forbearance of the Almighty: 'At in Editionibus, in Horologio, et in quinque MSS. Regiis, σὺ γὰρ εἶ κύριος ὕψιστος' (Cotelerius). The passage in Ps. xcvii. 9, 'For thou, Lord, art most high above all the earth,' has led to the insertion in Latin texts of 'super omnem terram'.

εὔσπλαγχνος. Not found in LXX; Eph. iv. 32 (Robinson, *ad loc.*); 1 Pet. iii. 8.

εὔσπλαγχνος κτλ. In this rehearsal of the merciful attributes of Jehovah we have the key to the whole Prayer of Repentance. The language reminds us of Exod. xxxiv. 6; Ps. cxxxvi. 15; Joel ii. 12, 13; Jonah iv. 2. Of these passages, the words of the prophet Joel are probably uppermost in the author's mind. For (1) it is a classical appeal for repentance, and hence would be appropriate to the subject of the Prayer; and (2) the expression μετανοῶν ἐπὶ κακίαις is derived from the LXX of Joel ii. 12, 13. The passage runs as follows: 'Yet even now, saith the Lord, turn ye unto me with all your heart, and with fasting, and with weeping, and with mourning; and rend your heart, and not your garments, and turn unto the Lord your God: for he is gracious, and full of compassion, slow to anger, and plenteous in mercy, and repenteth him of the evil' (LXX μετανοῶν ἐπὶ κακίαις).

ἐπὶ κακίαις ἀνθρώπων. Latin 'et poenitens super malitias hominum'. The word κακίαις seems to be borrowed from the LXX of Joel. The prophet's own phrase 'of the evil' (על הרעה) had reference to 'the evils' of calamity which befell the people as the punishment for their sins. But the LXX rendered by κακίαι, which ordinarily denotes 'wickedness' (Lat. 'malitia'), the source of sorrows; and not by τὰ κακά = 'evils', or *mala*, as the consequence of sin. The common meaning of κακίαι may be illustrated from Gen. vi. 5 (LXX) ἐπληθύνθησαν αἱ κακίαι τῶν ἀνθρώπων, in which context it 'repented' the Lord that He had made man, because the wickedness of men was increased. But κακίαι may have reference to the punishment arising from the sin: 1 Chron. xxi. 15 εἶδεν κύριος καὶ μετεμελήθη ἐπὶ τῇ κακίᾳ; Jonah iii. 10 μετενόησεν ὁ θεὸς ἐπὶ τῇ κακίᾳ (cf. iv. 2); Matt. vi. 34 ἀρκετὸν τῇ ἡμέρᾳ ἡ κακία αὐτῆς. Probably an intentional contrast is here drawn between the μετάνοια ascribed to the Almighty (cf. Gen. vi. 6; 1 Sam. xv. 11; 2 Sam. xxiv. 16), in His pity relenting towards suffering, which is sin's penalty; and the μετάνοια of the sinner for his own sin which calls down Divine judgement. The addition to the text contained in Const. Apost. and in the Latin, though omitted in Codd. A and T, is an important expansion of the main theme of repentance. It particularizes the promise (ἐπαγγελία, *v.* 6) as one that proclaimed 'forgiveness of repentance', i. e. forgiveness of sin, to the repentant sinner; it decrees for sinners the duty of repentance, with a view to their being saved. If only a gloss, it constitutes a very substantial addition to the Prayer. But it is, more probably, part of the original document. (1) It was very possibly accidentally omitted, because these two στίχοι both commence with the same words (ὅτι σύ) as the preceding στίχος. (2) Arguing from the contents of the passage, it is more reasonable to suppose that such remarkable phrases as ἐπηγγείλω μετανοίας ἄφεσιν and ὡρίσας μετάνοιαν . . . εἰς σωτηρίαν should have been included in the original Psalm, than that they should have been inserted as a gloss. (3) Against their being a gloss, it is to be observed that the next verse, σὺ οὖν . . . οὐκ ἔθου μετάνοιαν κτλ., seems to imply some such sentence, and would not follow so naturally upon μετανοῶν ἐπὶ κακίαις ἀνθρώπων.

μετανοίας ἄφεσιν. Latin 'poenitentiam et remissionem'. The Mozarabic Psalter, 'indulgentiam et remissionem,' avoids the difficulty by a paraphrase. The introduction of μετάνοια with ἐπηγγείλω seems at first sight incongruous. The 'promise' of ἄφεσις is conditional upon μετάνοια. The object of the Prayer is to unite the two ideas of the sinner's repentance and the Divine pardon as closely as possible. For general sense compare Luke v. 32. For a restoration of the text on the basis of a Semitic original see note on pp. 614, 615. μετάνοια in the LXX, Prov. xiv.

8 Thou, therefore, O Lord, that art the God of the righteous, hast not appointed repentance unto the righteous, unto Abraham, and Isaac and Jacob, which have not sinned against thee:
But thou hast appointed repentance unto me that am a sinner;
For *the sins* I have sinned *are* more in number than the sands of the sea.
9 For my transgressions were multiplied, O Lord:
My transgressions were multiplied,
And I am not worthy to behold and see the height of heaven by reason of the multitude of mine iniquities.
*And now, O Lord, I am justly punished and deservedly afflicted;
For lo! I am in captivity,*
10 Bowed down with many an iron chain,
So that I cannot lift up mine head by reason of my sins,

9. οτι om. T, Const. Apost. μου [1]: + κε επληθυναν T; Lat. *domine multiplicatae sunt* κυριε επληθυναν αι ανομιαι μου Const. Apost. ουκ ετι Const. Apost. *And now . . . captivity* insert Syr., *And now . . . afflicted* insert Moz., omit Codd., Const. Apost., Lat. 10. σιδηρου Const. Apost.; σιδηρω T; Lat. *ferreo* ανανευσαι: pr. μη, om. με T; Lat. *ut non possim* υπερ αμαρτιων την κεφαλην T, Syr., Lat. μοι ανεσις: ανεσις μοι T

15; Sirach xliv. 16; Wisd. xi. 23, xii. 10, 19. For ἄφεσις cf. Isa. lxi. 1 κηρύξαι αἰχμαλώτοις ἄφεσιν (דְּרוֹר). For forgiveness through repentance see Hos. ii. 1–4, vi. 1 ff., xiv; Isa. i. 16 ff.; Ezek. xviii. 21 ff.

τῷ πλήθει τῶν οἰκτιρμῶν σου. Cf. κατὰ τὸ πλῆθος τῶν οἰκτιρμῶν σου, Ps. l. (li.) 1, lxviii. (lxix.) 19.

ὡρίσας. Lat. 'decrevisti'. Cf. 3 Macc. vi. 36 κοινὸν ὁρισάμενοι περὶ τούτων θεσμόν.

εἰς σωτηρίαν (Lat. 'in salutem') after μετάνοια has a suggestion of N. T. phraseology. Cf. 2 Cor. vii. 10 ἡ γὰρ κατὰ θεὸν λύπη μετάνοιαν εἰς σωτηρίαν (Vulg. 'poenitentiam . . . in salutem') ἀμεταμέλητον ἐργάζεται. But both the idea and phraseology are pre-Christian: cf. T. Gad v. 7 ἡ γὰρ κατὰ θεὸν ἀληθὴς μετάνοια . . . ὁδηγεῖ . . . πρὸς σωτηρίαν. Had the author of the Prayer been a Christian, he could hardly have omitted a reference to 'salvation through Jesus Christ'. There is no higher conception here than that of deliverance from the penalty of Divine wrath.

8. ὁ θεὸς τῶν δικαίων. This is not a Biblical phrase. Compare with it *v.* 1 ὁ θεὸς . . . τοῦ σπέρματος αὐτῶν τοῦ δικαίου. 'The righteous' are the elect Israel, as distinguished from the οἱ ἁμαρτωλοί, οἱ ἀσεβεῖς, οἱ ἄνομοι. Compare the contrast in Luke xv. 7 between the ἁμαρτωλός and the δίκαιοι.

τοῖς οὐχ ἡμαρτηκόσι σοι. The Patriarchs were invested with sinlessness in the estimation of the reverent few. Such treatment of patriarchal virtue was based on such passages as Gen. xvii. 17–19, xxii. 18, and Exod. xxxii. 13.

ἐπ' ἐμοὶ τῷ ἁμαρτωλῷ. Lat. 'propter me peccatorem'. Cf. Luke xviii. 13 ὁ θεός, ἱλάσθητί μοι τῷ ἁμαρτωλῷ. The article gives distinctiveness to the self-condemnation.

9. ὅτι. The confession of his exceeding sinfulness occupies the following four verses, and, as the expression of repentance, forms the basis of entreaty for pardon.

ὑπὲρ ἀριθμὸν ψάμμου θαλάσσης. The construction is obvious, though grammatically harsh: 'to sin more than the number of the sand of the sea' is equivalent to saying that it was easier to count the sands of the sea than the number of his offences.

ψάμμος in the LXX is found only in Wisd. vii. 9 ὁ πᾶς χρυσὸς ἐν ὄψει αὐτῆς ψάμμος. The more common word is ἄμμος, as in Gen. xxxii. 12, xli. 49; Joshua xi. 4; Isa. x. 22; Hos. i. 10 (ii. 1).

ἐπλήθυναν κτλ. Cf. Isa. lix. 12: 'For our trangressions are multiplied before thee.'

πληθύνω. Used intransitively.

οὐκ ἄξιος. Cf. Luke xv. 19, 21, which may be the origin here of the variant reading οὐκέτι.

ἀτενίσαι, 'to look at with intent gaze'. Lat. 'intueri'. The word is of rare occurrence in the LXX, 1 Esdras vi. 28; 3 Macc. ii. 26. But in the N. T. it is not infrequent, e. g. Acts i. 10, iii. 4, 12, vi. 15, vii. 55, &c.

τὸ ὕψος τοῦ οὐρανοῦ. 'The height of heaven' is the Throne of the Most High. Cf. Isa. xxxviii. 14 ἐξέλειπον γάρ μοι οἱ ὀφθαλμοὶ τοῦ βλέπειν εἰς τὸ ὕψος τ. οὐρανοῦ πρὸς τὸν κύριον. For the thought see Ps. cxxiii. 1: 'Unto thee do I lift up mine eyes, O thou that sittest in the heavens.'

9, 10. Between *v.* 9 and *v.* 10 the Syriac version inserts the verse: 'And now, O Lord, I am justly punished and deservedly afflicted; for lo! I am in captivity.' The Mozarabic Psalter reads: 'Et nunc juste contineor, et digne comprimor.' In favour of some such insertion there are certainly the following considerations: (1) *v.* 10 opens with μὴ κατακαμπτόμενος, which stands in no suitable relation either to *v.* 9, οὐκ εἰμὶ ἄξιος, or to the following clause, διότι παρώργισα; (2) the clause beginning with μὴ κατακαμπτόμενος has no main verb, and is grammatically disconnected; (3) if there is any consistency in the arrangement of the στίχοι, it is noticeable that, whereas in *v.* 9 we find a group of three στίχοι, (1) διότι ἥμαρτον κτλ., (2) ὅτι ἐπλήθυναν κτλ., (3) καὶ οὐκ εἰμί κτλ., and in *v.* 10 *c d e* a group of three στίχοι, (1) διότι παρώργισα κτλ., (2) καὶ τὸ πονηρὸν κτλ., (3) στήσας βδελύγμ. κτλ., and in *v.* 11 a group of three στίχοι, (1) καὶ νῦν κλίνω κτλ., (2) ἡμάρτηκα κτλ., (3) καὶ τὰς ἀνομίας κτλ., this grouping breaks down in *v.* 10 *a b*, κατακαμπτόμενος κτλ. and εἰς τὸ ἀνανεῦσαι κτλ. The reading of the Syriac and Mozarabic would thus supply grammatical coherency and rhythmical balance. Hence it is quite conceivable that they may have preserved the true text. Its opening words, καὶ νῦν, being identical with the opening of *v.* 11, may have led to the accidental omission. If genuine, it conveys a further reference to the position of the speaker as a captive in prison. There is, of course, another alternative, which is only conjectural, and yet is not altogether impossible, that the line κατακαμπτόμενος . . . σιδηρῷ has been inserted to identify the utterer of the Prayer with Manasses; and that the following line, εἰς τὸ . . . ἄνεσις, is a further expansion of the gloss. On the other hand, if κατακαμπτόμενος κτλ. is original, the probability seems to be strong that some clause, like that of the Syriac version, has fallen out of the Greek text.

10. κατακαμπτόμενος. If not conjoined to some clause such as that which the Syriac version supplies, the present clause follows very awkwardly upon what has gone before; and grammatically the sentence is extraordinarily disjointed and prolonged. In consequence, the Latin and the English version begin here a new sentence.

Neither have I any respite:
Because I provoked thy wrath, and did that which was evil in thy sight.
I did not do thy will, neither kept I thy commandments:
I set up abominations, and multiplied detestable things.
11 And now I bow the knee of mine heart, beseeching thee of thy gracious goodness.
12 I have sinned, O Lord, I have sinned,
And I acknowledge mine iniquities.
13 But, I humbly beseech thee,
Forgive me, O Lord, forgive me,

εις το . . . ανεσις om. Const. Apost. **μη ποιησας το θελημα σου και φυλαξας τα προσταγματα σου** insert T and Lat. but not Moz. *στησας . . . προσοχθισματα* om. T 11. *καρδιας*: + *μου* T, Const. Apost. Lat. 12. *εγω γινωσκω* Codd. A T, Const. Apost., ed. Fritzsche: *αναγινωσκω* Vulgo; Lat., Moz. *agnosco* 13. *αιτουμαι . . . ανες μοι*: om. Moz.:

κατακαμπτ. Lat. 'incurvatus sum'. This verb is rare in the LXX, Ps. xxxvii. 6, lvi. (lvii.) 6; cf. Symmachus Ps. xli. (xlii.) 6, xliii. (xliv.) 26.

πολλῷ δεσμῷ σιδηρῷ. Latin 'multo vinculo ferreo'. Cf. 2 Chron. xxxiii. 11: 'The captains of the king of Assyria . . . took Manasseh in chains [Or, *with hooks*], and bound him with fetters, and carried him to Babylon.' There is no sufficient reason to explain, as Zöckler and Ball, this sentence metaphorically of sin and its chains, like Ps. cvii. 10, 'being bound in affliction and iron.' The whole context of this verse is occupied, not with the iniquities that produced the punishment, but with the penalty, of a quite real and overwhelming kind, which had befallen the speaker. Again, the metaphorical use of iron chains applied to sin is not a common one; and there is nothing in the character of the Prayer which would favour the theory of a metaphorical use of these simple words.

The precise meaning of *πολλῷ* is doubtful; it may either be rendered as if it were the same as *πολλοῖς δεσμοῖς*, or the singular number may denote 'a weighty chain'. For the use of *πολύς* with a singular substantive—most of the examples usually given are with an abstract noun—cf. *v.* 14 *κατὰ τὸ πολὺ ἔλεός σου.*

εἰς τὸ ἀνανεῦσαί με κτλ. This is the most difficult expression in the whole Prayer, and the difficulty has given rise to the variety in the readings.

ἀνανεύειν in the LXX is employed to translate מָאֵן and נוֹא (Hiph.) in the sense of 'to refuse': cf. Exod. xxii. 17; Num. xxx. 6; Neh. ix. 17. Here, however, it is used in a sense that represents the physical motion of the verb (*νεύειν*) and the preposition (*ἀνά*), and means 'to incline upward', as Ps. xl. 12, 'so that I am not able to look up.' We have, therefore, three alternative renderings: (1) Fritzsche, 'so that I shake (my head) over my sins' (cf. Polyb. xviii. 13. 3 *ἀνανενευκώς* = 'with the head up'; Dionys. Areop.; Basil, Ps. vii, p. 140; Chrys. *De Zelo et Piet.* (ap. Suicer.). (2) *εἰς τό* with inf., equivalent to *τοῦ* with inf. (= Hebr. מִן with inf.) = 'more bowed down . . . than to lift up *my head*, because of my sins', in the sense of 'bowed down . . . so that I cannot lift up my head, or look upwards'. This gives a good sense, but grammatically it is a harsh construction. (3) *εἰς τὸ μὴ ἀνανεῦσαι τὴν κεφαλήν*, as Cod. T, 'so that I cannot lift up my head.' This text is evidently emendational. The insertion of the *μή* gives the same sense as No. 2. So Latin, 'ut non possim attollere caput meum.' The omission of the whole line, *εἰς τὸ . . . ἄνεσις*, in Const. Apost. may have been due to the obscurity of the meaning; but see note on *vv.* 9, 10 above.

ἄνεσις. Latin 'respiratio', in the sense of 'release', or 'cessation', or 'relief'. Cf. LXX in 2 Chron. xxxiii. 15; 1 Esdras iv. 62; 2 Esdras iv. 22. In the N. T. it occurs of St. Paul in prison, Acts xxiv. 23. Cf. 2 Cor. vii. 5.

παρώργισα. The verb *παροργίζω*, 'to anger', is of frequent occurrence in LXX with a personal object; e.g. Judges ii. 12 *παρώργισαν τὸν κύριον.* But there is no instance in the LXX of the phrase here used, *παροργίζειν τὸν θυμόν τινος.*

The line *μὴ ποιήσας . . . τὰ προστάγματά σου* added by Codex Turicensis, and in the Latin version, 'non feci voluntatem tuam et mandata tua non custodivi,' seems certainly to be a gloss, expanding the words *τὸ πονηρὸν ἐνώπιόν σου ἐποίησα.* It adds nothing to the sense of the verse, it overloads the arrangement of the lines, it places *μὴ ποιήσας* immediately after *ἐποίησα*, and interposes a general negative between the assertion of wicked action (*τὸ πονηρὸν ἐνώπιόν σου ἐποίησα*) and the statement of its most conspicuous instance of enormity. The line should not, therefore, be included in the text.

στήσας βδελύγματα κτλ. Latin, 'statui abominationes et multiplicavi offensiones.' Mozarabic, 'Statuens abominationes et multiplicans odiositates.' *βδέλυγμα* is the usual rendering in the LXX for תּוֹעֵבָה 'abomination'. Cf. 2 Kings xxi. 2: 'And he (Manasseh) did that which was evil in the sight of the Lord, after the abominations of the heathen.' *προσοχθίσματα* is the word used for 'the abomination' (שִׁקֻּץ) of the Zidonians and of Moab in 2 Kings xxiii. 13 *τῇ Ἀστάρτῃ προσοχθίσματι Σιδωνίων καὶ τῷ Χαμὼς προσοχθίσματι Μωὰβ καὶ τῷ Μολχὸλ βδελύγματι υἱῶν Ἀμμών.* On the outrages committed by Manasseh upon the worship of Jehovah and upon the Temple at Jerusalem see 2 Chron. xxxiii. 1–9.

11. *καὶ νῦν κτλ.* The confession is complete; the entreaty for compassion now begins.

κλίνω γόνυ καρδίας. In the LXX *κάμπτω* is the regular verb to be used with *τὰ γόνατα.* With *κλίνω* we find another construction in 2 Esdras ix. 5 *κλίνω ἐπὶ τὰ γόνατά μου.* The heart of the suppliant is here represented as a person kneeling. For this personification of the heart cf. Rom. ii. 29, 'circumcision is that of the heart.' The teaching of the prophet Joel is perhaps still influencing the writer: 'Rend your heart, and not your garments' (Joel ii. 13).

δεόμενος τῆς παρὰ σοῦ χρηστότητος, i. e. begging for the kindness which continually proceeds from thee. It is more than *τῆς χρηστότητός σου*, while the Latin 'precans a te bonitatem' fails to reproduce the Greek idiom.

12. *ἡμάρτηκα.* The perf. tense gives the sense of the continued result of the sin, 'I have sinned, and am in a state of sin.' This is a different shade of thought from that of the aorist *ἥμαρτον* (*v.* 9). For this acknowledgement of sin compare the cases of Balaam, Num. xxii. 34; Saul, 1 Sam. xv. 24, xxvi. 21; David, 2 Sam. xii. 13.

ἐγώ. Emphatic: 'I—the guilty one—am alone cognizant of my guilt, and therefore alone can perceive and acknowledge my transgression.'

γινώσκω. Latin 'agnosco'. Cf. Ps. l. (li.) 5 'iniquitatem meam ego cognosco'. In this passage some editions have *ἀναγινώσκω.* Cf. Ps. xix. 12: 'Who can discern his errors?'

13. *αἰτοῦμαι.* The reading *ἀλλ'*, which is found in Cod. T and Const. Apost., expresses the fresh departure made at this point in the Prayer: 'Nevertheless, in spite of my sinfulness, I beseech,' &c. Latin, 'quare peto rogans te.'

And destroy me not with mine iniquities.
Neither, in thy continual anger against me,
  Lay up evil in store for me;
Nor pass thou sentence against me,
  When I am in the lowest parts of the earth.
For thou, O Lord, art the God of them that repent;
14 And in me thou wilt show forth *all* thy goodness:
For thou wilt save me, unworthy that I am,
  According to thy great mercy.
15 And I will praise thee for ever all the days of my life:
  For all the host of heaven doth sing thy praise,
    And thine is the glory for ever and ever. Amen.

αιτουμαι: pr. αλλ T, Const. Apost.; Lat. *quare* μη: pr. και T, Const. Apost.; Lat. *et ne* οτι συ ει κυριε ο θεος A T: οτι συ θεος θεος Const. Apost. 14. εν εμοι A T; επ εμοι Const. Apost. δειξης A T; δειξεις Const. Apost.; Lat. *ostendes*, ed. Fritzsche την αγαθωσυνην: pr. πασαν T; Lat. *omnem*, ed. Fritzsche 15. εν ταις ημεραις A T: εν πασαις ταις ημεραις Const. Apost.: Vulgo πασας τας ημερας

ἄνες μοι. The repetition of the prayer for forgiveness corresponds with the repetition of ἡμάρτηκα in the previous verse. For ἄνες cf. Ps. xxxviii. (xxxix.) 13 ἄνες μοι ἵνα ἀναψύξω = 'O spare me, that I may recover my strength'.

μὴ συναπολέσῃς με τ. ἀνομ. μ. The phrase is evidently based upon the LXX of Gen. xix. 15 ἵνα μὴ συναπόλῃ ταῖς ἀνομίαις τῆς πόλεως. Cf. Wisd. x. 3. Used of persons, the same verb is found with μετά and the gen., Ps. xxv. (xxvi.) 9 μὴ συναπολέσῃς μετὰ ἀσεβῶν τὴν ψυχήν μου; xxvii. (xxviii.) 3 μετὰ ἐργαζομένων ἀδικίαν μὴ συναπολέσῃς με.

εἰς τὸν αἰῶνα μηνίσας. Latin 'in aeternum iratus'. Another phrase borrowed from the LXX: Ps. cii. (ciii.) 9 οὐδὲ εἰς τὸν αἰῶνα μηνιεῖ; Jer. iii. 12 οὐ μηνίω ὑμῖν εἰς τὸν αἰῶνα.

τηρήσῃς τὰ κακά μοι. Latin 'reserves mala mihi'. The meaning is: 'do not, by long-continued anger, retain, or lay up in store against me, the evils which I have deserved.'

τὰ κακά: not the sins I have committed; but the evils I have brought upon myself as the punishment of sin.

καταδικάσῃς, 'pass sentence of condemnation upon.' The verb renders the Hiph. of רשע in Ps. xxxvi. (xxxvii.) 33. The punishment of physical suffering, disease, want, injury, exile, was deemed to be inflicted for offences against the law of God.

The Mozarabic Psalter renders 'neque in finem iratus contineas mala mea neque condemnaueris me cum his qui sunt in inferiora terre'.

ἐν τοῖς κατωτάτοις τῆς γῆς. This phrase renders תַּחְתִּיּוֹת־אָרֶץ in the LXX of Ps. cxxxviii. (cxxxix.) 15, where Codd. A B read ἐν τοῖς κατωτάτοις τῆς γῆς. In that passage, as in Isa. xliv. 23, the lowest region in the under-world of the departed is denoted by this term. It does not indicate the place of torment; but rather the most remote and inaccessible locality in the unknown region of departed spirits. Here, as in Ps. cxxxviii. (cxxxix.) 15, the meaning is: 'When I am most remote, and abide in the lowest parts of the earth, condemn me not.' 'Do not prolong, or delay, the punishment of my sins, so that they may be visited upon me, however inaccessible in the lower world.' The other rendering, 'nor condemn me to (i. e. for punishment in) the lowest parts of the earth', follows the Latin, 'neque damnes me in infima terrae loca.' 'The lowest regions' were not a locality of torment, like the mediaeval hell, but the most inaccessible place in the shadowy under-world.

14. *ὁ θεὸς τῶν μετανοούντων.* Another Divine title, which does not elsewhere occur in Holy Scripture.

δείξεις or *δείξῃς.* The former reading gives the simplest meaning, and is supported by the Latin 'ostendes' and Const. Apost. δείξῃς, which is read by Codd. A and T, is grammatically harsh. The subjunctive must be dependent on the μηδέ in *v.* 13; but the prohibition closes with *v.* 13, and if in *v.* 14 the positive side of the injunction is to be continued in the subjunctive, the construction is almost intolerable, especially with the clause ὅτι σὺ . . . μετανοούντων interposed.

τὴν ἀγαθωσύνην. Cf. LXX in Judges ix. 16; 2 Chron. xxiv. 16. The insertion of πᾶσαν (Cod. T) is a very natural amplification: Latin 'omnem bonitatem tuam'.

ἀνάξιον. A rare adjective in the LXX. See Esther viii. 13; Sirach xxv. 8; Jer. xv. 9.

σώσεις. The deliverance here contemplated is from the manifold punishment he had deserved.

κατὰ τὸ πολὺ ἔλεός σου. Cf. *v.* 7.

15. *διὰ παντὸς κτλ.* Latin 'semper omnibus diebus vitae meae'. Mozarabic Psalter, 'in omni vita mea.' The more usual phrase in the LXX would be πάσας ἡμέρας τῆς ζωῆς μου. Cf. Ps. xxii. (xxiii.) 6, xxvi. (xxvii.) 4, cxxvii. (cxxviii.) 5.

πᾶσα ἡ δύναμις τῶν οὐρανῶν. Lat. 'omnis virtus caelorum'. The meaning is 'all the heavenly host of angelic beings'; and the phrase is probably derived from Ps. xxxii. (xxxiii.) 6 πᾶσα ἡ δύναμις αὐτῶν. Cf. Dan. viii. 10. See 2 Chron. xviii. 18, 'all the host of heaven standing on his right hand and on his left'; and Luke ii. 13, 'a multitude of the heavenly host praising God.'

καὶ σοῦ ἐστιν ἡ δόξα εἰς τοὺς αἰῶνας. A short concluding doxology reminding us of the Lord's Prayer (Matt. vi. 13). For instances of Jewish doxologies cf. 1 Chron. xxix. 11; 1 Esdras iv. 59.

Ἀμήν. For the liturgical use of Amen see 1 Chron. xvi. 36 = Ps. cvi. 48, Judith xiii. 20 (γένοιτο), Tobit viii. 8; and compare, in N. T. illustration of this usage, 1 Cor. xiv. 16 and Rev. v. 14.

THE PRAYER OF AZARIAH AND THE SONG OF THE THREE CHILDREN

INTRODUCTION

§ 1. Short Account of the Book.

The subject of this introduction is not really a 'book'; and it is sometimes known as the 'First Addition' to the canonical Book of Daniel. It is an illustrative interpolation inserted in that book after iii. 23; and is found there, forming an integral part of the book,[1] in Theodotion, the LXX, Vulgate, and some other versions dependent on the LXX. It is absent from the Aramaic text.

It consists of four parts:

(*a*) *Verses* 1, 2. An introductory verse or verses connecting it with the narrative. This introduction occurs in two different forms in the LXX and in Theodotion.[2]

(*b*) *Verses* 3–22. A 'Prayer' ascribed to Azariah, one of the 'Three Children' who were thrown into the fiery furnace.

This 'Prayer' begins with praise to God (3) and an acknowledgement of His justice (4), especially in the judgement executed upon Israel (5–10). There follows a prayer for deliverance, for His Name's sake (11); because of His promise to the Patriarchs (12, 13); because of their great sufferings and true repentance (14–19). The Prayer concludes with an appeal for deliverance, for the punishment of the enemies of Israel, and for the world-wide manifestation of the glory of God (20–22).

(*c*) *Verses* 23–27. A narrative as to the further heating of the furnace, the burning up of the Chaldeans round about, and the descent of the Angel of the Lord into the furnace to protect the 'Three Children'.

(*d*) *Verses* 28–68. The Song of the Three Children with an introductory verse.

The Song is an ascription of praise to God, in which all His creatures, animate and inanimate, are called upon to glorify Him.

Verses 35–65 have the same refrain, 'Sing His praise and highly exalt Him for ever,' slightly varied in verse 52. These verses form the *Benedicite*.[3]

§ 2. Title of the Book.

Just as this 'Addition' is not really a book, so originally, being merely a section of the Greek *Daniel*, it had no separate title. Thus Swete[4] says, 'In the Greek MSS. no break or separate title divides these Greek additions from the rest of the text.'[5] But the Alex. MS. gives the Prayer and the Song under the titles 'Prayer of Azarias' and 'Hymn of our Father' as two of the fourteen hymns which it inserts as an appendix to the Psalter. Other MSS. head the Song 'Hymn of the Three Children'. The Vulgate inserts after Dan. iii. 23 the note *Quae sequuntur in hebraeis voluminibus non reperi*. Then follows our 'Addition' and then another note, *Hucusque in Hebraeo non habetur; et quae posuimus de Theodotionis editione translata sunt*.

Lagarde in his edition of the Syriac version of the Apocrypha gives the heading 'Prayer of Hananiah and his companions' from one MS., and from Walton (literally) 'Prayer of the House of Hananiah'; the meaning of the latter phrase being the same as the former.[6]

In the A.V. and R.V. the whole 'Addition' is placed under the title 'The Song of the Three Holy Children', adding the note, 'Which followeth in the third Chapter of Daniel after this place,—*fell down bound into the midst of the burning fiery furnace.*—Verse 23. That which followeth is not in the Hebrew, to wit, *And they walked*—unto these words, *Then Nebuchadnezzar*—verse 24.'

In the Prayer Book verses 35–65 form one of the canticles of the Morning Service, the opening words of the Latin version, *Benedicite, Omnia Opera*, being used as a title.

[1] But cf. below, § 2. [2] Cf. below and notes on verses 1 f. [3] Cf. below, § 7.
[4] *Introduction to the O.T. in Greek*, p. 260.
[5] Tischendorf in his edition of the Vatican LXX inserted titles in brackets, hence the statement sometimes made that these titles are given in the Vatican MS.
[6] pp. xxi, 126.

§ 3. THE MSS.

The LXX version of *Daniel* was almost universally displaced at an early date by that of Theodotion, made in the first half of the second century A.D. The English versions are made from Theodotion.

The MSS. may be classified thus:

(*a*) *MSS. of Theodotion's Version.*[1]

A. *Codex Alexandrinus* contains the whole 'Addition' as part of *Daniel* and also the Prayer and Song as two of the Canticles.

B. *Codex Vaticanus.*

V. *Codex Venetus.*

Q. *Codex Marchalianus*, a complete copy of the Prophets preserved in the Vatican Library, written in Egypt not later than the sixth century. The margins supply copious extracts from the various Greek versions.[2]

Γ. *Codex Cryptoferratensis*, in the Basilian Monastery of Grotta Ferrata, a volume consisting partly of palimpsest leaves of an uncial MS. of the Prophets of the eighth or ninth century. This is available for Dan. i. 1–11 *a*, iii. 1–5 *a*, 37 *b*–52 *a*, vii. 1–viii. 19 *a*, ix. 15 *b*, 26 *a*, xii. 4 *b*–13.[3]

R. *Psalterium Graeco-Latinum Veronense*, 'a bilingual Psalter of Western origin and attributed to the sixth century . . . the property of the Chapter of Verona,' includes the Song as one of eight canticles supplementary to the Psalter.[4]

T. *Psalterium Purpureum Turicense*, a Western uncial, ascribed by Tischendorf to the seventh century, containing the Psalter, followed by canticles, including the Prayer and the Song. Verses 14–19 are wanting. It is in the municipal library of Zurich.[5]

Swete, pp. 165 ff., further enumerates a large number of cursive MSS. of, or including, Daniel.

(*b*) *MS. of the LXX.*

This version is only extant in the cursive MS. 87, the *Codex Chisianus*, in the library of the Chigi family at Rome. It contains Jer., Baruch, Lam., Ep. of Jeremiah, the LXX Daniel, Hippolytus on Daniel, Theodotion's Daniel, Ezek., and Isaiah. It is usually assigned to the ninth century.[6]

§ 4. THE ANCIENT VERSIONS.[7]

(*a*) *The Old Latin of Daniel* is extant in various fragments and patristic quotations. These show that the version included our 'Addition'. F. C. Burkitt's investigations seem to point to the conclusion that before the time of Jerome there were current Latin versions of both the LXX *Daniel* and Theodotion's *Daniel*.[8]

(*b*) *The Vulgate of Daniel* is made from Theodotion, and includes the additions.

(*c*) *The Peshitta Syriac.* Swete [9] states that 'From the first the Peshitta seems to have included the non-canonical books of the Alexandrian Bible except 1 Esdras and Tobit'. A. A. Bevan, however, writes that 'The apocryphal pieces are found even in the oldest MSS. of the Peshiṭta, but seem not to have belonged to it in its original form'; this he infers from the statement of Polychronius, early fifth century, that the *Song of the Three Children* is not contained in the Hebrew and Syriac Bibles.[10] The version is made from Theodotion, but differs considerably from both Theod. and LXX, probably through corruption and free handling.

(*d*) *The Syro-hexaplaric Version* is a literal version of the LXX column of Origen's Hexapla, and supplements the testimony of Codex Chisianus as to the text of the LXX.

(*e*) A Syriac version of *Daniel* and other books of Jacob of Edessa, A.D. 704–5, exists in MSS. at London and Paris, but only specimens have been printed.[11]

(*f*) *Egyptian Versions.* (i) *The Bohairic Coptic*, based on Theodotion, but influenced by the LXX.[12] (ii) *The Sahidic.*

(*g*) *The Ethiopic Version*, based on Theodotion.

(*h*) *The Arabic Version*, based on Theodotion.

(*i*) *The Armenian Version*, from the text of Theodotion.[13]

[1] For details of MSS. merely named, see Swete, *Int. to the O. T. in Greek.*
[2] Swete, pp. 144 f. [3] Swete, p. 146. [4] Swete, *O.T. in Greek*, II. ix.
[5] Swete, *O. T. in Greek*, II. xi. [6] Swete, *O. T. in Greek*, III, xii.
[7] For further details as to these versions, see Swete, *Int. to the O. T. in Greek.*
[8] *The Old Latin and the Itala*, p. 28. [9] p. 112. [10] *The Book of Daniel*, x. 3.
[11] Swete, p. 116. [12] Bevan, p. 3. [13] F. C. Conybeare, *Hastings's DB*, i. 152.

§ 5. Original Language.

This problem might seem to belong to the realm of pure scholarship; but it is involved in the controversy between the Protestant Churches and Rome as to the canonicity of the Apocrypha. Protestant divines have been inclined to regard original composition in Hebrew as one mark of canonicity, though they have never formulated any rigid doctrine to that effect. Dr. Barry, for instance, wrote of 'the true Hebrew Canon of the Old Testament'.[1] He probably only meant the canon current amongst Palestinian Jews, but the use of the term 'Hebrew' lays emphasis on the fact that the books of the Palestinian canon are extant in Hebrew or Aramaic; while the Apocrypha, when he wrote, were not extant in Hebrew.

Thus, according to Rothstein,[2] most Protestant scholars since Eichhorn, including Fritzsche, Schürer, König, Cornill, and Strack, have decided for Greek as the original language; while Catholic scholars have held that the 'Addition' was written in Hebrew. But some Protestant scholars have also taken this view, e.g. Delitzsch, Zöckler, Bissell,[3] Ball, Vatke, and Reuss. Further, Rothstein himself is inclined to accept a Hebrew original.

Bissell's statement[4] that 'the majority of critics of all schools have always held to the opinion that this composition was originally written in the Hebrew or Aramaic language' is too sweeping; but perhaps on the whole the balance of authority inclines that way. The theory of a Hebrew original is also favoured by J. T. Marshall:[5] 'The evidence for a Hebrew original is not irresistible, but probable'; Kamphausen[6] states that it cannot be conclusively proved that the 'Additions' were written in Greek; J. E. H. Thomson[7] argues for a Hebrew or Aramaic original; Swete[8] writes, 'The addition to Dan. iii. 23 is clearly midrashic, and probably had a Semitic original.'

The present writer is clear that there was a Hebrew original probably for the bulk of our 'Addition', and certainly for the *Prayer of Azariah*. It must not, of course, be overlooked that various considerations, partly drawn from the study of the newly-discovered papyri, reduce the force of much evidence which would prima facie point to a Hebrew original. Idioms and words supposed to be Hebraisms or Aramaisms seem to belong to ordinary Hellenistic Greek, unless, indeed, the Jewish population of some districts gave a Semitic flavour to the local dialect. Moreover, it is always possible that if a Jewish author were more familiar with Aramaic and Hebrew than with Greek, or were soaked in the language of the LXX and had read nothing else in Greek, he might write original Greek as if he were translating from Hebrew. These considerations, accordingly, have been borne in mind, and due weight has been given to them; they lessen, but do not destroy, the force of the general arguments advanced, and there are specific items of evidence which are not affected by them. The conflicting views of various scholars show that there is not obviously an overwhelmingly strong case for either view.

Allowing for a very little editing or corruption of the text, there is not much that could not have been written in Hellenistic Greek, and nothing which could not have been translated from Hebrew. The present writer admits that, as he is mainly interested in the Old Testament, he may have some slight bias in favour of a Hebrew original, but he believes that he has made due allowance for his personal equation. In studying the 'Addition' for the purposes of this work, he has felt that for the most part the Greek goes into Hebrew of its own accord, and many passages are most easily understood as unidiomatic renderings of a Hebrew original. The vocabulary is almost entirely confined to that of the LXX.

Moreover, some little weight may be given to the argument that a pre-Christian Jew would compose prayers and hymns in Hebrew rather than in Greek, Hebrew being the language of devotion. Thus Reuss maintains[9] that a Jew in prayer could only think in Hebrew. But if our 'Addition' was originally composed to supplement a Greek *Daniel*, it would naturally be written in Greek. We do not think it was so composed, partly because of other evidence of a Hebrew original, but were such evidence entirely lacking, the use of Greek might thus be explained by the purpose for which the passages were written.[10]

It must, however, be admitted that, with a very few exceptions to be mentioned later, the different texts and versions do not present the kind of variations which would arise from the independent use of a Hebrew or Aramaic text. Theodotion and the LXX are so similar that they are clearly texts of the same Greek original. It is true that the Peshitta Syriac has some striking differences from both of them, so that Thomson maintains[11] that 'The Syriac could not have been

[1] *Teacher's Prayer Book*, p. 280 *g*. [2] p. 178.
[3] So Rothstein, but apparently Bissell does not expressly adopt this view. [4] p. 443.
[5] *Hastings's DB*, iv. 756 *a*. [6] *Encycl. Bibl.*, iv. 1014.
[7] *Daniel*, *Pulpit Comm.*, pp. 113–17. [8] p. 261.
[9] *Apud* Rothstein, p. 174; somewhat similarly Thomson, p. 114.
[10] Cf. further below, p. 629. [11] p. 114.

made from the Greek, nor the Greek from the Syriac; they must have had a common source', probably Hebrew. We think, however, that the history of the Peshitta version of our 'Addition' makes this unlikely.[1] A Syriac translator some centuries after Christ would hardly have known or used a copy of the Hebrew original. The variations of the Peshitta are probably due to a tendency to paraphrase.

When we turn to detail, it is desirable to examine separately (*a*) the Prayer, (*b*) the Song, (*c*) the narrative verses.

Let us take first the *Prayer of Azariah*.

Verse 4. 'All thy judgements truth', ἀλήθεια;[2] the use of the substantive is a familiar Hebrew idiom. Similarly 'judgements of truth'—so literally, in verse 5.

Verse 6. 'We have dealt lawlessly in departing from thee,' ἠνομήσαμεν ἀποστῆναι ἀπὸ σοῦ, i.e. 'We have lawlessly departed from thee', a familiar Hebrew use of the dependent infinitive.

Verse 9. The peculiar word ἀποστατῶν, R.V. 'forsaken of God', is most easily understood as a rendering of the Hebr. מרדים 'rebels', as in LXX, cf. notes.

Verse 14. 'Low in all the world,' where perhaps we might have expected 'lowest' or 'lower than all', is often explained as due to the confusion of two similar Hebrew letters, see note.

Verse 16. 'Humble spirit,' lit. 'spirit of lowliness', a familiar Hebrew idiom.

Verse 17. 'Wholly *go* after thee,' lit. 'complete' or 'be complete after thee', ἐκτελέσαι ὄπισθέν σου, a literal rendering of the Hebr. phrase מַלֵּא אַחֲרֶיךָ, cf. מִלֵּא אַחֲרֵי and similar phrases, found in Joshua xiv. 8 f., 14, &c., in the sense of 'follow with perfect obedience and fidelity'. This instance is conclusive as LXX does not render this phrase by ἐκτελέσαι, so that the Greek cannot be got from the LXX of the passages in the canonical O.T. Aquila in Deut. i. 36 renders מלא by πληρῶσαι; otherwise Aquila, Symm., and Theod. are not extant for the passages where this phrase occurs. The LXX of this verse has a double rendering for the phrase, in one of which τελειῶσαι, 'complete', is an alternative rendering of the original Hebr., and the other ἐξιλάσαι, 'make thou atonement', is a guess by way of correction; LXX has many such guesses. We have not seen this explanation of ἐκτελέσαι κτλ. elsewhere. Cf. note.

Verse 21. 'Let them be brought to shame *and deprived* of all their dominion.' R.V. 'Let them be ashamed of all their power and might',[3] καταισχυνθείησαν ἀπὸ πάσης τῆς δυναστείας, cf. Ps. cxviii. (LXX Hebr. cxix.) 116, μὴ καταισχύνῃς με ἀπὸ τῆς προσδοκίας μου, 'Make me not ashamed of my hope,' מִשִּׂבְרִי. Similarly Sirach xxi. 22 (which is known to be a translation from Hebrew) ἰασχυνθήσεται ἀπὸ προσώπου, R.V. 'will be ashamed of entering', lit. 'from (the) face', probably 'from', i.e. 'so as to keep away from the presence of the master of the house.' The phrase in our passage may be a mere Hellenism, but makes much better sense if taken as a case of the pregnant use of the Hebr. מִן. Cf. note.

Numerous minor Hebraisms might be cited. It is true that the majority of these apparent Hebraisms, taken individually or to the number of three or four, might be explained away as due to the influence of the LXX or otherwise. But some of them, notably ἐκτελέσαι in verse 17, cannot be thus disposed of; and this fact, together with the concurrence of so many in a few verses, shows that the original language was Hebrew. Aramaic, indeed, would be possible,[4] but much less probable.

The scheme of the *Song of the Three Children* is so simple, that for the most part it might equally well have been written originally in Greek or translated from Hebrew. The predilection for compounds with ὑπερ- is a matter of taste that may be due to a translator, just as much as to the original author.[5] But we find Hebraisms in the few places where there is an opportunity for them to occur. The genitive of the substantive is used for an adjective in verse 30, 'the name of Thy glory' for 'Thy glorious name', and in verse 31, 'the temple of Thy holy glory' for 'Thy holy and glorious temple'. In such a case the balance of probability seems in favour of a Hebrew original.

The *Narrative Verses* include a good deal of curious Greek, e.g. καίοντες τὴν κάμινον νάφθαν for 'heating the furnace with naphtha', which might represent a too literal rendering of a Hebrew or Aramaic original. Here, too, the vocabulary and idiom are largely that of the LXX. On the other hand, there are several touches that do not look like translations from a Semitic original, e.g. τοῖς περὶ τὸν Ἀζαρίαν, but this and others might quite conceivably be somewhat free renderings from Hebrew or Aramaic. On the whole, too, verses 23–27, which connect the Prayer and the Song, seem some-

[1] Cf. above, p. 626, § 4 (*c*).
[2] Theodotion; the LXX corrects to ἀληθιναί.
[3] 'Power and,' an addition found in some authorities.
[4] The Targum of Num. xiv. 24 translates מלא lit. by אשלים.
[5] Cf. notes on verses 29, 30.

what rhetorical, and are not so simple and straightforward as the Greek of the narratives which precede and follow the 'Addition'. Moreover, Theodotion and the LXX differ considerably. It is possible that we have to do with a Greek expansion of an Aramaic original.[1]

In any case the section or sections originally written in Hebrew or Aramaic were to a certain extent edited after they were translated into Greek.

§ 6. Composition of the Book, Date, etc.

The 'Addition' was not part of the original Book of Daniel. As we shall show later, the Prayer of Azariah could not have been composed with reference to the rest of the book. It seems, however, just possible that the 'Addition' as a whole was part of the book before it was translated into Greek, but that it was somewhat amplified in the course of translation or afterwards. For the most part the Greek of the 'Addition' is very similar to that of the canonical part of the book, and indeed to the LXX of the canonical books generally.[2] We will return to this subject after discussing the separate sections.

The 'Addition' as a whole probably belongs to the first century B.C. It is later than the canonical Daniel, i.e. later than 168 B.C.; the LXX is apparently by the same hand as that of the canonical Daniel, which was probably in existence at the beginning of the Christian Era or somewhat later.

The Prayer of Azariah was not originally composed in reference to the incident of the Three Children. If it had been, it would have been put into the mouth of Hananiah (Shadrach), who always stands first of the Three. Thus the Peshitta heads the 'Addition', 'Prayer of Hananiah and his companions.' There is nothing whatever in the Prayer to connect it with the incident to which it is attached. Moreover a Jew, writing a Prayer for the beginning of the Exile, would hardly have forgotten Jeremiah and Ezekiel, to say nothing of Daniel himself, and spoken of the people as having been without a prophet. On the other hand verse 15, which states that there was neither priest, prophet, nor leader, neither sacrifices nor place for public worship, points to the dark days at the beginning of the Maccabean struggle. Probably, therefore, it was composed by, or in the name of, some unknown Azariah, about 168–170 B.C.[3]

The Song of the Three Children is expressly connected with the incident by verse 66; but probably this was not part of the original Song. The jubilant tone of this poem is in marked contrast to the despondency of the Prayer. The 'holy and glorious Temple' and its services seem to be flourishing.[4] Apart from verse 66, it might belong to any prosperous period after the reforms of Ezra and Nehemiah, probably some time after the success of the Maccabean revolt. There is nothing to indicate that it was composed with reference to the incident of the Three Children.

The Narrative Verses were obviously put into their present form in order to connect the Prayer and the Song with the rest of the book; but they may be based on a section of the original Daniel, no longer included in the canonical book. In the latter the sequence between verses 23 and 24 seems imperfect. In 23 we read that the Three Children 'fell down bound into the midst of the burning fiery furnace'. We are not told how they fared, but verse 24 goes on at once 'Then Nebuchadnezzar the king was astonied', nothing so far having happened to astonish him. Apparently originally something like the apocryphal narrative verses 1, 2, 23–27 stood between the canonical verses 23 and 24, and may have provided the basis for the apocryphal narrative verses.

These facts seem to point to some such conclusions as the following: Two independent Hebrew poems, the Prayer and the Song, were inserted, either at the same time or at different times, in the Hebrew-Aramaic Daniel;[5] the narrative section originally connecting the canonical verses 23, 24 was modified in order to connect the poems with the rest of the book. There were then in circulation copies of two editions of Daniel, one with the 'Addition', the other without; the former, longer, edition was the more popular and the more widely circulated. But later on it was held that the shorter form was the more authoritative; and in copies of the longer form our verses 1–68[6] were marked as an addition. From a copy or copies so marked, fresh copies were made which omitted our 'Addition', without restoring the section which originally stood in the canonical chap. iii, between verses 23 and 24.

The various authors and editors were clearly Jews; nothing whatever is known of them, beyond what may be gathered from the 'Addition' itself.

[1] See further § 6, on the composition of our 'Addition'.
[2] See notes, *passim*.
[3] So Thomson, *Daniel*, p. 115.
[4] Verses 30 f., cf. notes.
[5] We are not concerned here with the history of the Book of Daniel apart from our 'Addition'.
[6] LXX Dan. iii. 24–90.

§ 7. Influence of the Book on Later Literature, Canonicity, etc.

As the 'Addition' was current in early times as part of the longer Daniel, it is difficult to know how far it was accepted as canonical. When Daniel is mentioned in a list of canonical works, there is usually nothing to show whether or no it includes our 'Addition'. Its absence from the Massoretic edition of the Old Testament probably shows that the 'Addition' was not included in Daniel as it was received into the Palestinian Canon.

On the other hand, it was generally accepted in the early and mediaeval Christian Church, being included in the LXX, Latin, Syriac,[1] Egyptian, Arabic, Ethiopian, and other versions. The 'Additions' to Daniel are freely used by the Greek and Latin Fathers;[2] a Father who accepted Susanna and Bel and the Dragon would *a fortiori* accept the Prayer and the Song.

At the Reformation our 'Addition' shared the fate of the rest of the Apocrypha. The Roman Church kept it as an integral part of Daniel and of the Old Testament; the Reformed Churches took it out of Daniel and made it a separate *Apocryphon.*

Philo apparently makes no use of Daniel, and Josephus in his version of the incident of the Three Children and the Fiery Furnace, *Ant.* x. 10. 5, entirely ignores this 'Addition'.

Most of the parallels between the New Testament and the 'Addition' are also parallels with the canonical Old Testament; and the two or three that remain may be mere coincidences. We may, however, note one. In verse 64 we have 'spirits and souls of the righteous',[3] with which we may compare Heb. xii. 23, 'the spirits of just men,'[4] and Apoc. vi. 9, 'I saw ... the souls[5] of them that had been slain for the word of God.' But here there need be no literary connexion; moreover, in Wisdom of Solomon iii. 1, we have 'The souls of the righteous are in the hand of God'. Thus there is no sufficient evidence that the writers of the New Testament made use of this 'Addition'.[6]

Verses 35–66 form the *Benedicite* which stands in the Morning Service of the Prayer Book as an alternative to the *Te Deum.* The S.P.C.K. *Prayer-Book with Commentary* states, 'The rubric of 1549 directing its use during Lent was done away with in 1552, and there is now no special direction when it should be used. But it is still deemed more suitable for that season than the exultant strain of the *Te Deum*, and to those days when the Lessons relate to the wonders of creation.'[7]

§ 8. Theology.

These few verses, about one long Biblical chapter, are mostly secondary and imitative, largely a cento of phrases from the Old Testament. They illustrate, however, some of the features of Jewish theology about the beginning of the Christian Era. Thus the unique deity of one God is set forth in verse 22 and at length in the appeal of the Song to all things animate and inanimate to praise God. Yet this one God is still specially the Champion of Israel against their enemies, verse 21. It is possible that the 'worshippers' of verses 10, 68 are proselytes, or, at any rate, include Gentiles.

In verses 5, 6, 14 the misfortunes of Israel are explained by their sins, whereas in Psalm xliv, commonly regarded as Maccabean, the Jews protest that they are innocent martyrs, persecuted for loyalty to their God. But the sins confessed here are probably those of the nation in the past. Azariah says for himself and those for whom he speaks, 'But in a contrite heart and a humble spirit let us be accepted ... now we follow thee with all our heart, we fear thee and seek thy face,' verses 16–18.

Further, in verses 16, 17 we have the idea that penitence is an acceptable sacrifice, cf. Psalm li.[8]

§ 9. Bibliography.

See the list of works dealing with the Apocrypha as a whole,[9] and in addition the following:—

(*a*) Chief Editions of the Text (and of the Ancient Versions).

(i) LXX of Daniel, S. de Magistris (?), Rome, 1772: 'Daniel secundum LXX. et tetraplus Origenis nunc primum editus e singulari Chisiano codice.' Reprinted ... at Milan, 1788 (Bugati); and at Leipzig, 1845 (Hahn). The LXX text is also given in the editions of Holmes and Parsons, Tischendorf, and Swete.[10] These authorities also give the text of Theodotion; Theodotion was also used for Daniel in the Complutensian, Aldine, Sistine, and Grabian editions of the LXX, and in the minor editions based upon them.[11]

[1] But perhaps not in the original Peshitta, cf. 4 *c*.
[2] *Smith's DB*, i. 258.
[3] Πνεύματα καὶ ψυχαὶ δικαίων.
[4] Πνεύμασι δικαίων.
[5] Τὰς ψυχάς.
[6] Cf. W. Dittmar, *Vetus Testamentum in Novo*, p. 351.
[7] p. 43.
[8] Cf. Maldwyn Hughes, *The Ethics of Jewish Apocryphal Literature*, p. 69.
[9] See Introd. to Vol. I.
[10] Swete, p. 193.
[11] Swete, pp. 171 ff.

(ii) Peshitta Syriac. *Libri Veteris Testamenti Apocryphi, Syriae*, Lagarde, London, 1861.
(iii) Syro-hexaplaric Version. The Daniel of this version was published by Bugati in 1788.
(iv) Egyptian, Coptic, or Bohairic Version, Tattam, Prophetae Majores, Oxford, 1852.

(*b*) CHIEF CRITICAL INQUIRIES.

BEVAN, A. A. *Daniel*, 1892, Section on 'LXX', pp. 43 ff.
BLUDAU. *Die alexandrin. Uebersetzung des B. Dan.*, &c., 1897.[1]
BRÜLL. 'Das Gebet der drei Männer im Feuerofen,' *Jahrbuch für jüd. Gesch. u. Litt.*, viii, 1887, pp. 22 ff.[2]
BURKITT, F. C. *The Old Latin and the Itala*, Camb., 1896, Section on 'LXX Text of Dan.', pp. 18 ff.
Dictionary of the Bible (Hastings), 1902. J. T. MARSHALL, 'Three Children, Song of the', iv. 754.
DRIVER, S. R. *Daniel* (*Camb. Bible*), pp. xviii ff., and Section on 'Versions and Comm.', pp. xcviii ff.
Encyclopaedia Biblica, 1899, A. KAMPHAUSEN, 'Daniel, Book of', i. 1013.
*PRE*³, 1896, E. SCHÜRER, 'Apokr. des A.T.,' i, pp. 638 ff.
THOMSON, J. E. H., in *Pulpit Commentary on Daniel*, 1897, Excursus on 'Song of the Three Holy Children', p. 112.

[1] *Encycl. Bibl.*, i. 1015.
[2] *PRE*³, i. 639.

THE PRAYER OF AZARIAH AND THE SONG OF THE THREE CHILDREN

The Prayer of Azariah, 1–22.

1, 2 AND they walked in the midst of the fire, singing the praise of God, and blessing the Lord. Then
Azarias stood *up* with *his companions* and prayed on this manner; and opening his mouth in the
3 midst of the fire said, Blessed art thou, O Lord, thou God of our fathers, and worthy to be praised:
4 and thy name is glorified for evermore: for thou art just in all the things that thou hast done, and
5 all thy works are true, and thy ways right, [and all thy judgements truth]. In all the things that
thou hast brought upon us, and upon the holy city of our fathers, *even* Jerusalem, thou hast executed
true judgements: for according to truth and justice hast thou brought all these things upon us
6 because of our sins. For we have sinned and committed iniquity in departing from thee, and we
7 have sinned grievously in all things, and have neither hearkened unto thy commandments nor kept

Our version follows the text of Theodotion; variations found in the LXX are given in the notes.

1. In the Greek MSS. this verse follows iii. 23 of our Daniel.

they, the 'Three Children'. In the account of this incident in the canonical Daniel they are referred to by their Aramaic names, 'Shadrach, Meshach, and Abednego'; but in this 'Addition' they are called Ananias, Misael, and Azarias, the Hellenized forms of their Hebrew names, Hananiah, Mishael, and Azariah.

God . . . the Lord. In the Pentateuch the divine names often alternate through the combination of clauses from documents using 'God' and 'Yahweh' respectively. This alternation seems to be sometimes imitated, as a point of style, by later writers; cf. Jonah iii. 10, iv. 2.

the Lord, *κύριος*, representing the Hebrew divine name, *Yahweh.*

2. **stood up with his companions,** *συνστάς*, R.V. 'stood'. The verb is used in 1 Kings xvii. 26 LXX to translate עמד 'stand'. In Dan. iii. 23 the three 'fell down bound'.

1, 2. Instead of these two verses, LXX has the following: 'Thus then prayed Hananias and Azarias and Misael, and sang praise to the Lord, when the king commanded them to be thrown into the furnace. And Azarias stood and prayed thus and opened his mouth and gave thanks to the Lord, [together with his companions in the midst of the fire, the furnace being brought to an exceeding great heat by the Chaldeans].' Rothstein regards the words in brackets as a later addition. On the words 'brought . . . to a heat', i. e. *ὑποκαιομένης*, cf. Jer. i. 13, where *ὑποκαιόμενον* renders נָפוּחַ, R.V. 'seething (cauldron)'.

There is no apparent reason why the following 'Prayer' should be put into the mouth of *Azariah.* Where the three names are given in the canonical Daniel, his name, whether as Azariah or Abednego, stands last, and in verse 66 of our 'Addition' it stands second. As the 'Prayer' itself does not connect in any way with the incident in Daniel, and the name is a common one, the Azariah of the 'Prayer' may originally have had nothing to do with the Azariah of Daniel.

3. Cf. 1 Chron. xxix. 10, 20 (Yahweh, the God of their fathers); 2 Chron. vi. 3, 4.

and worthy to be praised, *αἰνετός*. LXX has *αἰνετόν* connecting with the following, 'and thy name is worthy to be praised,' &c.

4. **thou art just,** &c. Neh. ix. 33 R.V., 'thou art just in all that is come upon us; for thou hast dealt truly'; 2 Esdras, *καὶ σὺ δίκαιος ἐπὶ πᾶσι τοῖς ἐρχομένοις ἐφ' ἡμᾶς, ὅτι ἀλήθειαν ἐποίησας.*

thy works, &c. Cf. Deut. xxxii. 4.

true, *ἀληθινά*. This Greek word is frequently used in the LXX for the genitive of the Hebr. *'ĕmeth*, 'truth', such genitives in the Hebrew often doing the work of an adjective. The idea in the Hebrew is rather 'faithful' than 'true'; faithful, as corresponding to the nature, promises, and commands of God.

right, *εὐθεῖαι*. Often in LXX for Hebr. *yāshār*, 'straightforward'; so Hos. xiv. 10 LXX.

[and all thy judgements truth]. Apparently a variant arising by dittography from the clause 'and judgements of truth', which immediately follows in the Greek; so Rothstein. The words for 'judgements' are different, *κρίσεις* and *κρίματα* respectively.

truth. LXX and Syr. marg. have 'true', *ἀληθιναί*; Syr. text agrees with Theodotion.

5. **the holy city,** &c. Cf. Isa. lxiv. 10 f., also lii. 1, Neh. xi. 1, and Deut. ix. 24.

brought . . . upon, *ἐπήγαγες* as in the earlier part of the verse; LXX has 'wrought', *ἐποίησας*.

6, 7. Cf. Isa. lix. 12; Ezra ix. 6, 7, 13; Neh. i. 7.

6. **sinned** (first occurrence). LXX adds 'in all things'.

in departing from thee. A more idiomatic rendering of the first part of this verse would be, 'We have sinfully and lawlessly departed from thee.'

sinned . . . sinned grievously, *ἡμάρτομεν . . . ἐξημάρτομεν*. The *ἐξ* of the latter may be used of erring *from* the mark, emphasizing the nature of sin as a divergence from a standard, an aberration. *'Εξαμαρτάνω* is occasionally used in LXX in the sense of 'sin', but more often in that of 'cause to sin'; it does not occur in N. T. In view of the similarity of the first and last clauses of this verse, Rothstein regards 'sinned and' as a later addition; but *ἡμάρτομεν* and *ἐξημάρτομεν* probably represent two different Hebrew words.

thy commandments. The LXX reads 'the commandments of thy Law'.

8 them, nor done as thou hast commanded us, that it might go well with us. So all that thou hast
9 brought upon us and everything that thou hast done to us, thou hast done in true judgement. And
thou didst deliver us into the hands of lawless enemies, and most hateful forsakers *of God,* and to
10 a king unjust and the most wicked in all the world. And now we cannot open our mouth; shame
11 and reproach have befallen thy servants, and them that worship thee. Deliver us not up utterly, for
12 thy name's sake, neither disannul thou thy covenant; and cause not thy mercy to depart from us,
for the sake of Abraham that is beloved of thee, and for the sake of Isaac thy servant, and Israel
13 thy holy one; to whom thou didst promise that thou wouldst multiply their seed as the stars of
14 heaven, and as the sand that is upon the seashore. For we, O Master, have been made less than all
15 the nations, and are brought low this day in all the world because of our sins. Neither is there at
this time prince, or prophet, or leader, or burnt offering, or sacrifice, or oblation, or incense, or place
16 to offer before thee and to find mercy. But in a contrite heart and a humble spirit let us be

8. The first two clauses are practically identical, and Rothstein and others may be right in regarding one of them as a gloss, probably the former.

9. **lawless,** i. e. Gentiles who had not the Jewish law. LXX inserts 'our' before this word.

most hateful forsakers of God, *ἐχθίστων ἀποστατῶν*. *ἐχθίστων* might mean 'most hostile' or 'most hateful'; either would suit the sense, but in the Apocrypha it occurs with the latter meaning, e.g. Wisd. xv. 18.

ἀποστατῶν and cognate words in the LXX would usually represent the Hebrew root מרד 'rebel'; so Num. xiv. 9, Joshua xxii. 19. In Acts xxi. 21 Paul is accused of teaching *ἀποστασίαν ἀπὸ Μωϋσέως*, i.e. 'apostasy' in the modern sense, and *ἀποστάτης* in ecclesiastical writers has the sense of 'apostate'. In 1 Macc. ii. 15 we read of agents of Antiochus compelling the people to apostatize, *καταναγκάζοντες τὴν ἀποστασίαν*. Here it may represent the Hebr. מרדים 'rebels', i.e. against God; but it would be understood by the later Greek reader in the sense of 'apostate'. Probably the phrase does not refer to the Gentiles but to apostate Jews. In the time of the revolt of the Maccabees we read of 'renegade and wicked Jews', *Ant.* xii. 7. 1, who took the side of the oppressor, cf. xii. 5. 4.

a king, &c. In the present setting of the Prayer the king will be Nebuchadnezzar. What we read of him elsewhere does not convey the impression that he was 'unjust and most wicked in all the world'. In Jer. xxv. 9 Yahweh speaks of him as 'my servant'. But the author of this clause was probably thinking of Antiochus Epiphanes.

the most wicked in all the world. The Greek is *πονηροτάτῳ παρὰ πᾶσαν τὴν γῆν*, an unusual construction, probably elliptical for 'more wicked than any of the kings of the whole earth'.

10. **them that worship thee,** *τοῖς σεβομένοις σε*; the participle also occurs in verse 68. In Acts *οἱ σεβομένοι* are the proselytes, e.g. xvii. 17 *τοῖς Ἰουδαίοις καὶ τοῖς σεβομένοις*. Possibly the word has the same sense here and verse 68. Rothstein thinks the clause an addition; a reference to proselytes might well be added as an afterthought.

11. **utterly,** *εἰς τέλος*. This phrase and *εἰς τὸ τέλος* frequently occur in the LXX and represent numerous Hebrew originals, most often לָנֶצַח 'for ever', or in the Psalm headings לַמְנַצֵּחַ, apparently understood in the same sense.

disannul, *διασκεδάσῃς*, lit. 'scatter abroad'. This verb, with *διαθήκην* for object, is the regular LXX rendering of הֵפֵר בְּרִית 'annul a covenant', e.g. Judges ii. 1.

12. **that is beloved of thee.** In 2 Chron. xx. 7 LXX Abraham is called *τῷ ἠγαπημένῳ σου*; the Hebrew has אֹהַבְךָ, R.V. 'thy friend'. In Isa. xli. 8 he is called אֹהֲבִי, R.V. 'my friend', LXX *ὃν ἠγάπησα*, 'whom I loved'. The root אהב is the regular word for 'love'. In James ii. 23 Abraham is called 'the friend (*φίλος*) of God', and this is his common title amongst Mohammedans.

thy servant . . . thy holy one. These epithets are not applied elsewhere to Isaac or Israel (the patriarch) respectively. In Deut. ix. 27 Abraham, Isaac, and Jacob are called 'thy servants', and the *nation* of Israel is constantly spoken of as, or exhorted to be, holy, e.g. Deut. vii. 6.

13. LXX has, 'As thou didst speak unto them, saying that *thou* wouldst greatly multiply (*πολυπληθῦναι*) their seed as the stars of heaven for multitude,' &c.

Cf. Gen. xxii. 17 *πληθύνων πληθυνῶ τὸ σπέρμα σου ὡς τοὺς ἀστέρας τοῦ οὐρανοῦ καὶ ὡς τὴν ἄμμον τὴν παρὰ τὸ χεῖλος τῆς θαλάσσης*, 'Multiplying I will multiply thy seed as the stars of heaven and as the sand by the seashore.'

14. **Master,** *δέσποτα*. Very occasionally used by LXX to render *'Adonai, 'Adon, 'Elohim, Yahweh*; fairly common in the Apocrypha as a divine title, and so used in Luke ii. 29; Acts iv. 24; 2 Pet. ii. 1; Jude 4; Apoc. vi. 10. The word expresses 'the absolute control of a master over a slave' (R. J. Knowling on Acts iv. 24).

in all the world. It has been suggested that we should read '(lower) than all the world', an original Hebrew מכל having been misread as בכל. In some forms of the Hebrew script מ and ב are very similar.

15. Cf. Hos. iii. 4; Ps. lxxiv. 8, 9, perhaps Maccabean.

prophet. In the time of Nebuchadnezzar there were Jeremiah, Ezekiel, and others.

burnt offering, *ὁλοκαύτωσις*, עֹלָה. The sacrifice in which the victim was wholly consumed on the altar.

sacrifice, *θυσία*. Used in LXX both for זֶבַח, the general term for the sacrifice of an animal (so probably here), and for מִנְחָה, sometimes limited to bloodless offerings.

oblation, *προσφορά*. Only once in LXX, Ps. xxxix. 7, where it is used for מִנְחָה; it is fairly common in the Apocrypha.

to offer. The Greek *καρπῶσαι* is a derivative of *καρπός*, 'fruit'; Liddell and Scott explain its use in the sense of 'offer' by suggesting that it meant to 'bring' or 'offer fruit'. In classical Greek it is most often used in the passive or middle to mean 'to derive profit', 'to enjoy'. The noun *κάρπωμα* is the regular LXX for אִשֶּׁה 'an offering made by fire', which had nothing specially to do with fruit, but was commonly used of animals. The verb occurs in the sense of 'offer' in Lev. ii. 12, 16; cf. Ps. li. 18 LXX. According to Deissmann, LXX uses *καρπόω* in the sense of 'burn'.[1]

heart, Gk. *ψυχῇ*, which is occasionally used by the LXX to render the Hebr. לֵב 'heart'.

---

[1] *Bible Studies*, pp. 135 ff.

17 accepted, like as in the burnt offerings of rams and bullocks, and like as in ten thousands of fat
lambs; so let our sacrifice be in thy sight this day, and *grant* that we may wholly *go* after thee, for
18 they shall not be ashamed that put their trust in thee. And now we follow thee with all our heart,
19 we fear thee and seek thy face. Put us not to shame, but deal with us according to thy forbearance,
20 and according to the multitude of thy mercy. Deliver us also according to thy marvellous works,
21 and give glory to thy name, O Lord: and let all them that do thy servants hurt be confounded, and
let them be brought to shame *and deprived* of all their dominion, and let their strength be broken;
22 and let them know that thou art the Lord, God, sole and glorious over the whole world.
23 And the king's servants, that put them in, ceased not to make the furnace hot with naphtha, pitch,
24 tow, and small wood; so that the flame streamed forth above the furnace forty and nine cubits.
25, 26 And it spread, and burned those Chaldeans whom it found about the furnace. But the angel of the
Lord came down into the furnace together with Azarias and his fellows, and he drove the flame of
27 the fire out of the furnace; and made the midst of the furnace as it had been a moist whistling
wind, so that the fire touched them not at all, neither hurt nor troubled them.
28 Then the three, as out of one mouth, praised, and glorified, and blessed God in the furnace
saying:

The Song of the Three Children, 29–68.

29 Blessed art thou, O Lord, thou God of our fathers,
And to be praised and highly exalted for ever.

17. **burnt-offerings.** LXX and B of Theodotion have the singular.

grant that we may wholly go after thee. The Greek ἐκτελέσαι ὄπισθέν σου is obscure as Greek. It is a literal rendering of the Hebr. מִלֵּא אַחֲרֵי, R.V. 'followed fully', Num. xiv. 24, xxxii. 11 f.; Deut. i. 36; Joshua xiv. 8 f., 14. LXX of these passages renders the phrase by ἀκολουθέω and cognate or synonymous words. The LXX reading ἐξιλάσαι, 'make thou atonement', is a correction to improve the sense.

At the end of the verse the LXX adds καὶ τελειῶσαι ὄπισθέν σου, a variant of our clause, which was originally placed in the margin as a correction of the LXX ἐξιλάσαι ὄπισθέν σου, and then inserted in the text in the wrong place.

19. **deal with us.** LXX adds ἔλεος, giving the sense 'show us mercy'.

forbearance, ἐπιείκεια. In 2 Cor. x. 1, St. Paul exhorts the Corinthians by the meekness (πραότητος) and forbearance (ἐπιεικείας) of Christ. Dean Bernard on this passage (*Exp. Gk. Test.*) points out that ἐπιείκεια, 'gentleness', 'sweet reasonableness', is one of the qualities of the Righteous Man in Wisd. ii. 19; and that in Greek ethics the ἐπιεικής is the 'equitable' man who does not press for the last farthing of his rights.

The noun does not occur in the LXX of the canonical books, but in Ps. lxxxv. 4 LXX (Heb. lxxxvi. 5) God is said to be 'good and forgiving' (Hebr. סַלָּח, LXX ἐπιεικής) 'and of great mercy'.

20, 21. Cf. Ps. xxxiv. 26, xxxxix. 15, LXX; xxxv. 25, xl. 14, Hebr.

21. **do . . . hurt,** ἐνδεικνύμενοι, 'show', as in LXX of Gen. l. 15, 17.

let them be brought to shame and deprived of all their dominion, καταισχυνθείησαν ἀπὸ πάσης τῆς δυναστείας. Some MSS. insert 'power and' before 'dominion', R.V. 'let them be ashamed of all their power and might'. This does not make sense, and would not be the natural way of expressing 'let them be ashamed of the use they have made of their dominion', as it is sometimes explained. The sense 'ashamed of their dominion or authority' because it had failed them in their hour of need would be more probable. Perhaps, however, the Greek renders a pregnant use of the Hebrew *min* as suggested by the translation; cf. the next clause. See also p. 628.

22. **the Lord, God,** &c., Κύριος Θεὸς μόνος; LXX has μόνος Κύριος ὁ Θεός, 'alone the Lord God.'

23. **to make the furnace hot with naphtha,** &c. The construction is peculiar, or rather impossible, καίοντες τὴν κάμινον νάφθαν. In the LXX text νάφθαν κτλ. is the direct object of ὑπέκαιον, and it is possible that Theodotion's text is an ungrammatical abbreviation. In the rendering of the Aramaic Dan. iii, ἡ καιομένη is used for יָקִידְתָּא 'fiery', the epithet describing the furnace. After 'make the furnace hot', the LXX continues, 'And when they had cast the three all at once into the furnace, and the furnace was thoroughly aglow with seven times its usual heat' (this rendering requires παρά rather than κατά), 'and when they had thrown them in, those who had thrown them in were above them, but the others kindled under them,' then follows 'naphtha', &c., as in Theodotion. The broken construction indicates a gloss or glosses. According to Aram. of Dan. iii. 22 (LXX, iii. 23), the men who threw the Three Children into the furnace have already been burnt to death, and therefore could not go on kindling fuel. The LXX gloss is an unsuccessful attempt to explain away the difficulty.

25. **spread,** διώδευσεν; LXX διεξώδευσε, 'escaped'.

26. **the angel.** LXX has no article, but probably is intended to be definite. The article is not written before 'angel' in the Hebrew phrase for 'the angel of the Lord'.

drove, ἐξετίναξεν, lit. 'shook out', but the verb is the regular LXX rendering of נער 'shake, shake out'.

27. **moist . . . wind,** lit. 'wind of dew'.

28. **Then.** LXX ἀναλαβόντες, 'taking up', i.e. 'speech'. An English writer might have said, 'broke forth into song,' &c.

blessed. LXX adds after this word, 'and exalted.'

29. **highly exalted,** ὑπερυψούμενος. The verb is used in LXX of canonical books in Ps. xxxvi. 35, xcvi. 9; Dan. iv. 34 (Theod.). Compounds with ὑπερ- in the intensive sense are not common in LXX of canonical books, e.g. 'highly-praised', ὑπεραινετός (verse 30), 'highly sung', ὑπερυμνητός, 'highly glorified', ὑπερένδοξος (verse 31), do not occur in LXX, except in this 'Addition'. At the same time a translator with a turn for hyperbole, having appreciated the effect of the ὑπερ- in ὑπερυψούμενος, might readily introduce ὑπερ- to strengthen other epithets. In several places the texts vary as to the insertion or omission of ὑπερ-.

30 And blessed is thy glorious and holy name,
And to be highly praised and highly exalted for ever.
31 Blessed art thou in the temple of thy holy glory,
And to be highly sung and highly glorified for ever.
32 Blessed art thou that beholdest the depths and sittest upon the cherubim,
And to be praised and highly exalted for ever.
33 Blessed art thou on the throne of thy kingdom,
And to be highly sung and highly exalted for ever.
34 Blessed art thou in the firmament of heaven,
And to be sung and glorified for ever.
35 O all ye works of the Lord, bless ye the Lord,
Sing *his praise* and highly exalt him for ever.
36 O ye heavens, bless ye the Lord,
Sing *his praise* and highly exalt him for ever.
37 O ye angels of the Lord, bless ye the Lord,
Sing *his praise* and highly exalt him for ever.
38 O all ye waters that be above the heaven, bless ye the Lord,
Sing *his praise* and highly exalt him for ever.
39 O all ye powers of the Lord, bless ye the Lord,
Sing *his praise* and highly exalt him for ever.
40 O ye sun and moon, bless ye the Lord,
Sing *his praise* and highly exalt him for ever.
41 O ye stars of heaven, bless ye the Lord,
Sing *his praise* and highly exalt him for ever.
42 O every shower and dew, bless ye the Lord,
Sing *his praise* and highly exalt him for ever.
43 O all ye winds, bless ye the Lord,
Sing *his praise* and highly exalt him for ever.
44 O ye fire and heat, bless ye the Lord,
Sing *his praise* and highly exalt him for ever.

31. **the temple of thy holy glory.** The reference may be to the Temple at Jerusalem; verses 62 f. seem to imply that the Temple services were observed at the time this poem was written. On the other hand, verses 14 f. state that there were neither Temple nor services. Thus it would seem that the Prayer and the Song belong to different periods. In this verse, however, the reference may be to the Heavenly Temple; the following verses refer to God as in heaven.
32, 33. LXX has these verses in the reverse order.
32. **sittest upon the cherubim.** A favourite title of Yahweh, e. g. 2 Sam. vi. 2. The original reference was to the Ark, but the Ark disappeared before the Exile and was not replaced, Jer. iii. 16. Unless this is the mere repetition of a conventional phrase, the cherubim here, as in Ezek. i, are supernatural beings.
highly exalted, ὑπερυψωμένος; LXX 'glorified', δεδοξασμένος.
33. **on the throne.** LXX 'on the throne of glory', i. e. 'glorious throne'.
34. **of heaven.** LXX and Syr. omit.
35–65. The Prayer Book *Benedicite*; cf. Introd., § 7.
35. Cf. Ps. ciii. 22.
Sing his praise and highly exalt him for ever. This refrain, slightly varied in verse 52, is repeated up to and including verse 66. Cf. Ps. cxxxvi, where the refrain, 'For his mercy endureth for ever,' is repeated in each of the twenty-six verses; cf. cxlviii, cl, and cxxxv. 1–3, 19–21.
36, 37. LXX reverses the order of these two verses.
36. Cf. Ps. cxlviii. 4.
37. Cf. Ps. cxlviii. 2.
38. Cf. Gen. i. 7; Ps. cxlviii. 4.
all ye waters. Some texts have 'ye waters and all things'.
39. **O all ye powers of the Lord, bless ye the Lord.** So LXX of Ps. ciii. 21, except that the psalm has 'his' for 'of the Lord'. The Hebr. is צבאיו, E.V. 'his hosts'; cf. 'Yahweh Ṣebaoth', 'Lord of hosts'; in which phrase 'hosts' referred at various times to (*a*) the actual Israelite armies, (*b*) the heavenly bodies, (*c*) the angels. As the present writer is using a conventional phrase, he may have had no definite idea of what he meant by it. The Vatican MS. of Theodotion has 'Let every power bless the Lord'.
40, 41. Cf. Ps. cxlviii. 3.
40. Syr. marks this verse as spurious, but it is well supported and is required by the context.
42. **every.** Rothstein proposes to omit with Pesh.; cf. 44 ff., where there is no 'every' before the various pairs.
43, 44. Ps. cxlviii. 8.
The Alexandrine MS. of Theodotion and LXX insert here the verses numbered 45, 46, in A.V., thus:—
'45. O ye winter and summer (LXX, frost and cold), bless ye, &c.
46. O ye dews and storms of snow, bless ye, &c.
'Winter and summer', in Alex. MS. 'cold and burning wind'.
45–51. The order of these verses varies in different authorities. Thus LXX has 45, 46, 49, 50, 47, 48, 51.
45 is a doublet of 48 or, according to LXX, of 50, of which 46 is also partly a doublet.

47 O ye nights and days, bless ye the Lord,
Sing *his praise* and highly exalt him for ever.
48 O ye light and darkness, bless ye the Lord,
Sing *his praise* and highly exalt him for ever.
O ye cold and heat, bless ye the Lord,
Sing *his praise* and highly exalt him for ever.
50 O ye frosts and snows, bless ye the Lord,
Sing *his praise* and highly exalt him for ever.
51 O ye lightnings and clouds, bless ye the Lord,
Sing *his praise* and highly exalt him for ever.
52 O let the earth bless the Lord,
Let it sing *his praise* and highly exalt him for ever.
53 O ye mountains and hills, bless ye the Lord,
Sing *his praise* and highly exalt him for ever.
54 O all ye things that grow on the earth, bless ye the Lord,
Sing *his praise* and highly exalt him for ever.
56 O ye seas and rivers, bless ye the Lord,
Sing *his praise* and highly exalt him for ever.
55 O ye fountains, bless ye the Lord,
Sing *his praise* and highly exalt him for ever.
57 O ye whales, and all that move in the waters, bless ye the Lord,
Sing *his praise* and highly exalt him for ever.
58 O all ye birds of the heaven, bless ye the Lord,
Sing *his praise* and highly exalt him for ever.
59 O [all] ye beasts and cattle, bless ye the Lord,
Sing *his praise* and highly exalt him for ever.
60 O ye sons of men, bless ye the Lord,
Sing *his praise* and highly exalt him for ever.
61 O Israel, bless ye the Lord,
Sing *his praise* and highly exalt him for ever.
62 O ye priests of the Lord, bless ye the Lord,
Sing *his* praise and highly exalt him for ever.
63 O ye servants of the Lord, bless ye the Lord,
Sing *his praise* and highly exalt him for ever.
64 O ye spirits and souls of the righteous, bless ye the Lord,
Sing *his praise* and highly exalt him for ever.
65 O ye saints and meek-hearted, bless ye the Lord,
Sing *his praise* and highly exalt him for ever.

48. **cold and heat,** *ψῦχος καὶ καῦμα.* Alex. MS. of Theod. 'frost (*πάγος*) and cold', apparently a variant of the LXX (verse 49, A.V.) 'O ye frosts (*πάγοι*) and cold, bless ye', &c.

50. **frosts,** *πάχναι.* Vatican MS. 'frost'. Both *πάγος* and *πάχνη* render כְּפוֹר 'hoar-frost', and *πάγος* also renders קֶרַח 'frost'.

53. Cf. Ps. cxlviii. 9.

56, 55. LXX has these verses in reverse order, i.e. 55, 56, as in A.V.

55. **fountains.** LXX 'showers and fountains'.

57. **whales,** *κήτη*, sea-monsters or huge fishes; *κῆτος* is used in the LXX for תַּנִּינִים 'sea-monsters', Gen. i. 21, for Jonah's 'fish', דָּג, and for the mythical sea-monsters, Leviathan, Job iii. 8, and Rahab, Job xxvi. 12.

all that move, &c. Cf. Lev. xi. 46.

58, 59. Cf. Ps. cxlviii. 10.

59. **[all].** Alex. MS. omits, cf. on 42.

beasts and cattle, *τὰ θηρία καὶ τὰ κτήνη*; LXX *τετράποδα καὶ θηρία τῆς γῆς*; cf. LXX of Gen. i. 24, 'quadrupeds and beasts of the earth.'

61, 62. Cf. Ps. cxxxv. 19.

62. **O ye priests of the Lord.** Vat. MS. of Theod. omits 'of the Lord'; the margins of LXX and Syr. have 'ye priests, servants of the Lord'.

63. **O ye servants of the Lord.** Vat. MS. of Theod., LXX, and Syr. omit 'of the Lord'. These are temple ministrants, perhaps Levites; cf. Ps. cxxxiv. 1, cxxxv. 1, 20.

64. **O ye spirits and souls of the righteous.** 'Spirit', *πνεῦμα*, represents רוּחַ, sometimes the divine element in man; 'soul', נֶפֶשׁ, often the vital principle. The verse is one of a series appealing to various classes of living men, so that it also refers to the living, 'righteous souls,' not souls of the departed.

65. **saints and meek-hearted.** 'Saint', *ὅσιος*, and 'meek-hearted', *ταπεινὸς τῇ καρδίᾳ*, represent the Hebr. *ḥāsîd* and *ʿānāv* or *ʿānî*, which in post-Exilic times were technical terms for members of the nationalist party which insisted

[66 O Ananias, Azarias, and Misael, bless ye the Lord,
Sing *his praise* and highly exalt him for ever.
For he hath rescued us from Hades, and saved us from the power of death,
And delivered us from the midst of the burning fiery furnace, even out of the midst of the fire hath he delivered us.
67 O give thanks unto the Lord,
For he is good; for his mercy *endureth* for ever.
68 O all ye that worship the Lord, bless the God of gods,
Sing *his* praise, and give thanks unto him;
For his mercy endureth for ever.]

on the strict observance of the Law. *Hāsîd* and *'ānāv* or *'ānî* occur in the same context of the true believer in Ps. xviii. 25, 27; lxxxvi. 1 f.; cxlix. 1, 2, 5, 9. In Matt. xi. 29, Christ speaks of Himself as *πραΰς καὶ ταπεινὸς τῇ καρδίᾳ*, 'meek and lowly of heart.'

Verses 66–68 are probably an addition; verse 66 was added to connect the hymn with the 'Three Children'. Verses 67, 68 were added from the psalm as a closing doxology, the clause 'O all ye that worship the Lord' being introduced later, possibly in order to bring in a reference to proselytes; cf. on verse 10. These verses probably displaced an original conclusion, less suitable to the present context of the hymn.

66. Cf. on verse 1.

Hades, *ᾅδου*, the Hebr. *Sheol*, the abode of the dead.

burning fiery furnace, lit. 'furnace burning of flame'; LXX and some texts of Theod. omit 'furnace', leaving 'from the midst of the burning flame'.

67 exactly = LXX of Ps. cxxxv. 1 (Hebr. cxxxvi. 1).

good, *χρηστός*, 'benevolent and benevolent.' In Ps. cxxxv. 1 and elsewhere in LXX it is used to render *ṭōb*, 'good'.

68. **ye that worship the Lord,** *οἱ σεβόμενοι τὸν κ.* Cf. on verse 10.

the God of Gods. Cf. Ps. cxxxvi. 2.

LXX adds at the end, 'and for ever and ever,' *καὶ εἰς τὸν αἰῶνα τῶν αἰώνων.*

SUSANNA

INTRODUCTION

§ 1. Contents of the Story of Susanna, and Summary of Results in Introduction.

Two elders are made judges in a Jewish community. One evening they see a Jewess walking in her husband's garden, and both become enamoured of her. Next morning they detect each other near the garden, acknowledge to each other their passion, agree to accost the woman, and are repulsed with scorn. To protect themselves they must accuse the woman; they betake themselves to the synagogue of the city and issue a summons to Susanna. She appears with her household, and is ordered to be unveiled. The elders appear as witnesses before the assembled people. They aver that while they were walking in her husband's garden, they detected the woman in company with a youth who escaped. Being arrested she refused to tell who her paramour was. The official standing of the elders leads the whole synagogue to believe the evidence and to condemn Susanna.

On her way to execution, a youth (Daniel) questions the verdict, reopens the trial, and examines the two elders separately. The one says the crime took place under a mastick tree; the other says under a holm tree. The contradiction condemns both. The synagogue applauds the young man because he had proved them to be false witnesses. 'And as the Law prescribes, they did unto them as they had wickedly devised against their sister.' The elders are gagged, cast into a ravine, and destroyed by fire from heaven.

The inspired sincerity of youth, by means of cross-examination, prevented a judicial murder, therefore let youth be honoured.

The later version of Theodotion locates the scene in Babylon when Daniel was 'a young lad'. The house of Joakim, husband of Susanna, is the resort of the people and place of trial. The scene in the garden is more detailed.

This story of Susanna is a parable intended to illustrate the value and necessity of cross-examination of witnesses. It also seeks to vindicate the execution of false witnesses, although their victim may be delivered before his sentence was carried out. The story is a product of the Pharisaic controversy with the Sadducees in the later years of Alexander Jannaeus, *c.* 95–80 B.C. The original language was the literary Hebrew of that period. A later recension of the Hebrew named the Deliverer Daniel, and associated the story with Daniel conceived as an historical person living in Babylon in the early years of the Captivity. This subsequent association with Daniel is the main cause of the differences between Theodotion's version and the LXX. The story circulated independently, and was sometimes associated with the name of Habakkuk. The LXX before the Christian era placed it in an appendix to Daniel; Theodotion and the Uncials, in the interests of chronology, make Susanna the opening chapter of Daniel. The Hebrew MSS. now extant have no claim to be considered the original of the Greek versions.

§ 2. Title.

In the earliest MSS. the story has no name, being part of Δανιηλ B A; Δανιηλ κατα του Θευδοτιωνος Q. In Codex Chisianus, LXX Dan. is entitled Δανιηλ κατα τους Ō. This title is repeated at the end of Dan. xii; Dan. xiii is headed Σουσαννα. Codex Chisianus gives Theodotion's version under the curious title το ειρ αγρυπνος Δανιηλ, Susanna being *c.* 13; c. 14, which follows, has the superscription ἐκ προφητείας ʽΑμβακοὺμ υἱοῦ ʼΙησοῦ ἐκ τῆς Φυλῆς Λευί. The Syriac Hexapla makes the latter title include Susanna. A codex from Athos: ὁράσεις (*l.* ὅρασις?) ἕνδεκα τοῦ προφήτου Δανιήλ deinde sequitur περὶ τοῦ ʽΑββακούμ. His omnibus praemittitur περὶ τῆς Συσάννης.[1] Another Greek title is Διακρισις Δανιηλ.[2]

Syriac Versions ܬܫܥܝܬܐ ܕܫܘܫܢ History of Shushan Pesh., Lag. 1; ܟܬܒܐ ܕܫܘܫܢ ܛܘܒܢܝܬܐ Lag. 2; 'the book of the youthful Daniel, the history of Shushan ܫܘܫܢ ܡܫܡܫܢܝܬܐ Harkleensian edition; 'Book of the Women' (i.e. Susanna, Judith, Ruth, Esther) in Bible of Jacobite Syrians.

[1] *De Habacuci prophetae vita atque aetate*, § 13, Franz Delitzsch, 1842.
[2] Walton, *Polyglot*, vi, p. 191.

The Vulgate places Daniel between Ezekiel and Hosea as 'propheteia Danielis', Susanna being c. 13.

The Arabic version has an invocation of the Trinity, and 'begins to translate the prophecy of the prophet Daniel whose prayer be for us! Amen.'

In general literature the designation varies, e.g. τὸ δρᾶμα τῆς Σωσαννίδος, Nicolas (of Damascus?); 'Pistill (epistle) of Swete Susan', Scots poems of the fourteenth century.

The position in which Susanna is inserted is variable. It precedes the canonical Daniel in B A Q Old Latin and Copto-Memphitic Versions; it is appended after Dan. xii in LXX, Syro-tetraplar Version of LXX, Vulgate and Versions based on it.

These titles reflect variety of opinion as to the origin, authorship, and character of the story. There is uncertainty as to whether the book is history, prophecy, apocalypse, apocryphal or canonical scripture.

§ 3. The MSS.

The Codex Chisianus 87, first published at Rome in 1772, is for Susanna, as for Daniel, the sole authority for the Greek of the Septuagint. It is a ninth-century cursive, and at the end of Dan. xii says it was copied from an exemplar with this subscription: ἔγραφη ἐκ τῶν τετραπλῶν ἐξ ὧν καὶ παρετέθη. Its text is thus only once removed from the recension of the LXX made by Origen *c.* A.D. 240. The Codex Chisianus receives important corroboration from the Syro-Hexaplar Codex, written in Alexandria A.D. 616–617 by Mar Paulus of Mesopotamia. The LXX text from Origen's Hexapla is rendered literally into Syriac. The agreement of Chisianus with the Syro-Hexaplar gives assurance for the LXX text of Susanna as approved by Origen. The Old Latin versions and quotations in the Fathers do not suffice to fix a generally received text at an earlier period.

Theodotion's version of Susanna was adopted into the Greek Bible in place of LXX. It has thus all the MS. evidence available for the Greek Daniel in the Church Bible, and is found in Codex Vaticanus B, Codex Alexandrinus A, and in Cod. Marchalianus Q, sixth century. The text here used is that of Swete, vol. iii.

Among MSS. two in Hebrew require notice, because the question of a Semitic original is much discussed, and because one of these MSS. has been supposed to contain the Semitic original of certain apocryphal books.[1]

In Bodley's Library at Oxford is a MS. (Heb. d. 11, Catalogue No. 2797) called *Sepher haz-Zikhronoth*, compiled by Asher hal-Levi about A.D. 1325, written in German rabbinical character. It contains legendary matter illustrating Biblical history from the Creation to the time of the Maccabees. The catalogue describes the contents of the part preceding Susanna as a Hebrew translation of the Aramaic passages in Daniel by Yeraḥmeel, . . , the Aramaic text of the Song of the Three Children, the history of Bel and the Dragon in Syriac in Hebrew characters without a Hebrew translation. In fol. 74 *b* begins the Midrash concerning Ahab and Zedekiah (Jer. xxix. 21). Fol. 75 *a* and 75 *b* contain the Story of Susanna in Hebrew, occupying fifty-three lines. A later hand has headed the page: מעשה שושנה בימי דניאל. The story itself begins a new paragraph headed זה מעשה שושנה. After Susanna the history of Nebuchadnezzar is resumed. The compiler considered the elders identical with the false prophets mentioned by Jeremiah, and located the story in Babylon. Has this Hebrew text any claim to be considered the original of the LXX and Theodotion? The Greek versions have some thirty verses nearly identical; in these passages this MS. omits much, adds not a little, and freely paraphrases the rest. Two translators, however arbitrary, could not make this text responsible for the agreements or divergences that exist in LXX and Theodotion. The language is in parts a fair imitation of Biblical Hebrew: in other parts it is not; e.g. v. 23 θ′ fol. 75, l. 18, מוטב לי ואפולה ביד ∴ הצדיק והטוב הגדול הגיבור והנורא מציל ומושיע גאל חזק ∴ צבאות שמו׳; fol. 76, l. 29, a supplement to θ′ v. 59 שאין בגן לא זה אילן ולא זה אילן והלכו וראו האמת; for הִנֵּה we find הרי three times; for 'thereupon' מיד with a Perf. three times; twice there appears גינת הביתו for 'the garden of his house'. The compiler of the MS. evidently knew Syriac, and may have carelessly followed some Syriac version in writing the story for the amusement of his heirs male. His object appears in his preface: 'Blessed be my descendants, and may they be established if they fulfil my wishes.'

The second Hebrew MS. is also in the Bodleian (Heb. MS. e. 12, Catal. No. 2777). The volume, with which the leaf containing Susanna is bound up, contains hymns, astronomical tables, &c., disorderly arranged. The copyist of fol. 3 signs himself Mordecai ben Samuel, and finished his work A.D. 1691. A note on f. 71 implies the date A.D. 1737.

[1] *Proceedings of the Society of Biblical Archaeology*, vol. xvi, 1894, 'The Unknown Aramaic Original of Theodotion's Additions to the Book of Daniel,' pp. 280–90, 312–17.

Susanna occupies both sides of one folio, 55, thirty-five lines on the first page, thirty-four on the other. The story conforms closely to the Greek of Theodotion, so closely that either the Vulgate or Theodotion must have been used by the translator into Hebrew. The additions and omissions in Heb. e. 12 are not many and not important. The garden, *v.* 3, 'has all kinds of trees'; the elders are called 'priests'; the maids fetch soap going out 'by the doors of the house'. The Hebrew is more idiomatic than in MS. d. 11. Yet here too we have a version. The writer has not understood *v.* 5, yet has tried to be faithful to the obscurity of the Greek. ונעשו אז באותו הזמן שני כהנים ברצון ה׳ שופטים כי סר העין [העון] מבבל מהשופטים הראשונים ויקומו שופטים אחרים וילכו אחרי ה׳. Again, in *v.* 15 he has failed to recognize the Greek form of כִּתְמוֹל שִׁלְשֹׁם and renders: ויהי כראותם אותה בכל יום קרה ביום השלישי ורצתה לילך עם שתי נערות לרחוץ עצמה .... In *v.* 18 he ignores the gender in the verbs; *περιπατούντων ἡμῶν* = כשהלכנו *v.* 36; the comparative he renders by יותר, *ἐνδοξότερον* = יותר נכבד *v.* 4; *αἱρετόν μοι* = יותר טוב. That he used Theodotion and not the Vulgate appears to follow from his treatment of *v.* 22: *καὶ ἀνεστέναξεν Σ. καὶ εἶπεν Στενά μοι πάντοθεν* = ותאנח שושנה ותאמר אנחה תהיה לי. Here he reproduces the repetition of the sound. He ignores the play on the names of the trees.

These two Hebrew MSS. are of some interest as showing the Jewish attitude to the story during the fourteenth and fifteenth centuries. They also illustrate the facility with which every phrase of the Greek can be reproduced in Hebrew.

§ 4. The Ancient Versions.

Two forms of the *Old Latin* version of Daniel can be traced. Burkitt[1] finds that the tract *De Pascha computus*, dated A.D. 243, is the earliest Latin follower of Theodotion's Greek for Daniel. But 'the earliest Latin version of Daniel as witnessed by Tertullian, S. Victorinus of Pettau, and partly by S. Cyprian was made from the LXX'. 'The text of Daniel used by Tertullian is a form of the LXX differing slightly from Origen's edition, but agreeing most closely with the quotations of Justin Martyr' (ib. p. 23). In Sabatier[2] the Versio Antiqua preserves about forty-four verses of Susanna out of the sixty-five in the Vulgate. In these Theodotion's version is much more obvious than the LXX. The verses at the beginning are given; and Sabatier adds, 'Haec Susannae historia, si Flaminio Nobilio fides, in omnibus vetustis libris est principium Danielis, . . . in multis inscribitur Daniel ut in nostra; in quibusdam Συσαννα: in aliquo Διακρισις Δανιηλ.'[2] In Cod. Wirceburgensis Palim. sixth century, Susanna *vv.* 2–10 survive.[3]

The Vulgate. St. Jerome's preference for Theodotion's Susanna led to the disappearance of the LXX Susanna. St. Jerome says the churches of his time read Daniel according to Theodotion, the LXX Daniel being long ago discarded. 'Hoc cur acciderit, nescio'; but after comparing both versions with the Semitic original in the rest of Daniel, he agrees that sound judgement has been shown in substituting Theodotion. The Vulgate therefore puts Theodotion's Greek into Latin. At the end of Dan. xii, this note precedes Susanna: 'Hucusque Danielem in Hebraeo volumine legimus. Quae sequuntur usque ad finem libri de Theodotionis editione translata sunt.' Jerome therefore had never seen a Hebrew or an Aramaic Susanna. The Vulgate has an extra verse at the end, *v.* 65 'Et rex Astyages appositus est ad patres suos et suscepit Cyrus Perses regnum eius.' This error in chronology belongs to *Bel and the Dragon*, which follows in c. 14.

Syriac. The LXX Susanna is faithfully reproduced in Syriac in the Codex Siro-estrangelo Bibliothecae Ambrosianae. Bugatus[4] gives this note after Dan. xii from the Syriac: 'Descriptus est ab exemplari in quo erat adnotatio haec: descriptus est a Tetraplis cum quibus etiam collatus est.' Swete and others refer to the MS. as 'Codex Syro-Hexaplaris Ambrosianus'. As Origen had no Hebrew for Susanna, he must have had two columns blank in his Hexapla; the names Tetrapla and Hexapla here evidently refer to the same text. This version was made at Alexandria by Mar Paulus of Mesopotamia, in the years A.D. 616–617. It is an exact translation, and serves to fix the LXX text as approved by Origen A.D. 240.

Walton's *Polyglot* gives two Syriac versions, W_1 the Peshitta, W_2 the Philoxenian or Harkleensian made by Thomas, Bishop of Heraklea about A.D. 616. Both are based on Theodotion, but make additions in sympathy with the story. Two other Syriac versions are edited by Lagarde,[5] from two codices in the British Museum. These MSS. belong, one to the ninth, the other to the tenth century.

[1] Burkitt, *The Old Latin and the Itala*, p. 7.

[2] *Bibliorum Sacrorum Latinae versiones antiquae*, 1751.

[3] Kennedy, *DB* (Hastings), art. 'Old Latin Versions'.

[4] 'Daniel secundum editionem LXX interpretum ex tetraplis desumptam, ex codice siro-estranghelo Bibliothecae Ambrosianae Syriace edidit Caietanus Bugatus Mediolani 1788.'

[5] *Apocryphi Syriace*, Lagarde, 1861.

They resemble Walton's first Syriac version 'Apud Waltonem versio duplex est, altera fere cum nostris consonans'. In the last twenty verses the variations between these two versions (L_1 L_2) are considerable.

Coptic Versions. The *Copto-Memphitic* was based on Theodotion's version. It may have been made by the beginning of the fourth century. 'Hoc unum statuemus, interpretem nempe copto-memphiticum magnam semper fidem Theodotioni habuisse, quam vero textus Theodotionei recensionem secutus fuerit, certo definiri non posse.'[1] In this version Susanna is found at the beginning of Daniel.

No fragments of Susanna appear to have survived in the *Sahidic* version.[2] The 'Song' appears in c. 3.

Arabic. John, Bishop of Seville A.D. 719, made an Arabic version of the Bible from the Latin Vulgate as it is supposed.[3] The version in the Polyglots is derived from an old MS. of Greek akin to A.[4] The version of Susanna in Walton conforms to the Vulgate. The two trees are called *sandayān* سَنْدَيَانِ and سُمَّاق *summāq*; but no attempt is made to reproduce these sounds in the verbs.

The new elements in the versions have been supposed, especially in the Harkleensian Syriac, to be independent gleanings from tradition (Brüll, Ball). The fidelity of the translators has been impaired by the warmth of their feelings; e.g. Susanna is only a few days betrothed to Joachim, and the rest of her life is passed in widowhood, day and night being devoted to the service of the Lord (Syr. Harkl.). Susanna is set free from her chains, ibid. Hebrew 'the elders, the accursed rascals', &c.

§ 5. The Original Text.

'Things originally spoken in Hebrew have not the same force in them when they are translated into another tongue.' So testified the younger Ben-Sira, *c.* 130 B.C., when he 'laboured to interpret' in Greek the Hebrew composition of his grandfather. The Semite and the Aryan had created their language in different worlds. Between them there was no aboriginal kinship such as embraced the Greek and the Roman. The verbal paradigm of Arabic cannot be forcibly adjusted to the moods and tenses of the Greek verb. A Greek could neither pronounce nor write the sound 'Shoshanna'. Ben-Sira's 'labour' was in some respects like trying to graft the laurel on the palm.

The two tense-forms of Semitic, aided in Hebrew by the potent Vav consecutive, offer perceptible resistance to expression in the Greek idiom. One effect is a monotonous repetition of *καί* introducing clauses which can be more subtly linked by Vav in Hebrew. In the LXX of Susanna *καί* introduces clauses, where Hebrew Vav consec. or conj. would conveniently replace it, over fifty times; an equal extent of narrative and dialogue in St. John's Gospel yields such a *καί* twenty times; St. Luke fifteen; Josephus twelve times. A Greek-speaking Jew, or a Greek influenced by the LXX, when composing in his own conversational Greek, thus by this test exhibits a freedom which is conspicuously absent from Susanna.[5] A similar test shows that *αὐτός* for Hebrew pronominal suffix occurs much oftener than in the Greek, which an Alexandrian Jew (Philo) writes spontaneously; cf. Susanna *v.* 30, *v.* 9 *τὸν νοῦν αὐτῶν* LXX, *τὸν ἑαυτῶν νοῦν* Theodotion *et passim*. Redundant auxiliary verbs, e.g. *ἀναστάντες εἶπαν vv.* 29, 34, reflect the superfluous וַיָּקוּמוּ of Hebrew. *καὶ ἐγένετο* for ויהי *vv.* 7, 15, 19, 28, 64, Theodotion; the so-called *σχῆμα Χαλδαικόν vv.* 24, 42, 46, 53, 60, Theodotion; *καθὼς ἐχθὲς καὶ τρίτης ἡμέρας* Theodotion *v.* 15, for כִּתְמוֹל שִׁלְשֹׁם; *σφόδρα* = מְאֹד *vv.* 4, 27, 31; 'Ἰδού for הִנֵּה; *εἷς τὸν ἕτερον* and *ἀλλήλους* for אחד אל אחד or איש אל אחיו; infinitive with prep. לַהֲמִיתָהּ, *ἵνα θανατώσουσιν αὐτήν* LXX; *τοῦ θανατῶσαι αὐτήν* Theodotion *v.* 28; *σχίσει σου τὴν ψυχήν* LXX *v.* 55; *πεπαλαιωμένε ἡμερῶν κακῶν* LXX *v.* 52. Article for vocative *οἱ υἱοὶ 'Ισραήλ* Theodotion *v.* 48, LXX omits *οἱ*.[6] The versions have *οἱ γονεῖς αὐτῆς v.* 3 which Hebrew would express by אביה ואמה (Hebrew MS. e. 12 אבותיה), but in *v.* 30 LXX lets the literal Hebrew appear *ἡ γυνὴ σὺν τῷ πατρὶ ἑαυτῆς καὶ τῇ μητρί*, Theodotion *οἱ γονεῖς αὐτῆς*.

The names of the trees and the paronomasia *σχῖνον . . . σχίσει v.* 54 f, *πρῖνον . . . καταπρίσῃ v.* 58 f. have caused the assumption of a Greek original since Africanus. 'The history of Susanna is even very certainly a Greek original, as Julius Africanus and Porphyry already showed from the play on the words.'[7] Theodotion often resorts to transliteration of Hebrew words: *νωκεδείμ* Amos i. 1, *σαβείρ* Dan. xi. 16. He is especially timid about trees: Isa. xli. 19 *βραθὺ καὶ θαδαὰρ καὶ θαασούρ*,

[1] Daniel, *Copto-Memphitice*, p. xiv, Bardelli, Pisis, 1849.
[2] *Fragmenta Copto-Sahidica*, Ciasca ii, Rome, 1889.
[3] Scrivener[3], xii. 414.
[4] *Encycl. Bibl.*, art. 'Texts and Versions', § 64.
[5] The English version has skilfully hidden the offensive 'and' by 'albeit, now, then, but, yet, also'.
[6] Most of these Hebraisms are corroborated and others are indicated by Scholz, *Susanna*, p. 148, and Bludau, *Die Alexandr. Übersetzung des B. Daniel*, p. 183.
[7] Schürer, II. ii. § 33 (Eng.).

the fir, the pine, and the box-tree. Had his Hebrew text regarded the tree-names as suggesting the verbs to be used, Theodotion would *more suo* have transliterated them. But LXX is here so apt as to be irresistible to Theodotion. The LXX translator will guess rather than transliterate Hebrew. In Dan. iv–vi, as a translator he exhibits that *effrenata licentia*[1] for which he was dismissed from the Greek Bible, and his version of Daniel and Susanna imprisoned in Cod. Chisianus for 1000 years. This free and lively translator made the pun which has puzzled translators from Mar Paulus to Luther. From internal evidence we conclude that both Greek texts are versions dependent on a Hebrew original.

This conclusion is confirmed by a comparison of the texts of LXX and Theodotion. Half the story coincides in both, sometimes verbally identical, sometimes agreeing in sense though differing in terms. The variation consists in the use of a synonym, or a different construction, or a different order of words, e. g. *κάλλιον δέ με* LXX 23, *αἱρετόν μοί ἐστιν*, Theod. = טוב לי ; cf. *vv.* 10, 14, 28, 35, 61. The nature of the resemblances in the two Greek texts shows that neither writes independently. Where they disagree, they write constrained Greek, e. g. LXX 29, 32, 55, 62 *b*, and in parts peculiar to Θ′ *vv.* 15, 24, 39 *b*, 43. Apart from Semitic idioms in either text, the identity, the nature of the resemblances, and the divergences suggest the dependence of translators. Independent writers could not deal with a common Synoptic tradition as these writers do. Theodotion is a critical reviser of the LXX, but he too defers to an authority superior to the Greek.

Had Susanna been written in Greek to scourge certain officials in Alexandria it could scarcely have been represented as Babylonian history, where Greek was unknown. Its association with the Canon would be unlikely, and, had there been no Hebrew original, it is difficult to see why Symmachus and Theodotion should have taken the trouble to revise a casual tract about an Alexandrian *fama*. Origen and Jerome could find no Hebrew archetype; but the second century A. D. produced versions enough to secure a place for Susanna in the Tetrapla of Origen *c.* A. D. 240. It appears doubtful whether Aquila included Susanna. Akiba was his tutor, and the Jewish Canon, which was definitely settled *c.* A. D. 90, excluded Susanna. The story would not be popular with elders, and it was the elders who fixed the Canon. Susanna was useless for the polemical purposes of Judaism; it reflected on the good name of the daughters of Israel and the probity of the judges. It was, therefore, an encumbrance to the Canon and excluded. Hippolytus, Bishop of Rome, already suggests this explanation before A. D. 230. The lemnisci in Syro-estrangelo Tetrapla are accompanied by the marginal note Σ. Θ′, implying that Aquila had no Susanna. But unless there had been a Hebrew archetype in the time of Symmachus and Theodotion (A. D. 150–200) there is no sufficient reason why Susanna should have been included in Origen's Tetrapla.

§ 6. Integrity or Composite Nature of the Text.

The story of Susanna is skilfully compacted. Its characters are few and vividly contrasted; the issues at stake are of universal interest, death or dishonour are the calamities imminent, suspense deepens as the story proceeds, there is an impressive reversal (*περιπέτεια*) of the intended effect into its direct opposite, at the end nothing requires to be added except the applause of heaven and earth. A feeble woman in the right (cf. Esther, Judith) has triumphed over tyranny in the wrong. The genius of the writer is more important than his material, whether that were chiefly legendary, traditional, or suggested by contemporary politics. Nobody remembers the raw material, nobody forgets the story.

Though the story is coherent and homogeneous, it appears to have suffered alteration in some features. The earlier form of the story seems to have had no connexion with Daniel or Babylon. In LXX Daniel is an intruder. He does not appear till *v.* 45 and is introduced awkwardly in apposition to *νεώτερος*. His name is mentioned only four times—*vv.* 48, 51 *a*, 52, 59; the original *νεώτερος* maintains his anonymous part in *vv.* 52 *a*, 55, 60; and in the epilogue *οἱ νεώτεροι* are the heroes, while Daniel is forgotten. The contrast is not between youth and age, but between such an one as the son of Simon ben Shetach and the pair of Sadducean informers and judges who secured his condemnation by false witness. The son, who chose death in order that his father might be able, even on Sadducean principles, to inflict the penalty of death on his false accusers, is the *νεώτερος* come to judge justly. This requires us to omit the preface which never belonged to LXX, and which is superfluous in view of LXX *v.* 7, to delete *ἐκ βαβυλῶνος* in the dubious and difficult *v.* 6, and either to read *νεώτερος* four times for *Δανιήλ*, or else merely to omit the proper name.

The transference of this original story to Babylon offends against verisimilitude. Recent captives

[[1] This is practically the universal opinion of these chapters, but I hope in a future work to show that it is wrong.—General Editor.]

were not likely to have synagogues, popular election of judges, the right to carry out a sentence of death. Joakim is too comfortable with a pleasure garden and 500 famuli. The disastrous trees and the stadion have no place in Babylon. 'Other cities' (*v.* 6) could be Judaean villages with fewer than 120 families; they are a curious addition to 'Babylon'. Such features are proper to Judaea in the time of John Hyrcanus and his successors.

The career of the individual Daniel also affects the question. The book became known *c.* 165 B.C.; by its merit and in the temper of the time it became instantly popular, and was translated into Greek before 1 Maccabees was written. Meanwhile Daniel himself was a nebulous personality, half-angelic, wholly admirable. Theodotion's version of Daniel in Cod. Chisianus bears the title *το ειρ αγρυπνος Δανιηλ*. Ειρ is explained as 'angelus, quo nomine Daniel a barbaris etiam dictus est', and stands for העיר 'the Watcher'. To Theodotion *c.* A.D. 150, Daniel is still associated with the 'Sleepless Angel keeping Watch'. Josephus apologizes to his Roman readers *c.* A. D. 90 for summarizing the Book of Daniel as history: 'I have described these matters as I have found and read them; but if any one is inclined to another opinion about them, let him enjoy his different sentiments without any blame from me.'[1] In the time of Alexander Jannaeus Daniel was still a semi-angelic figure, not yet regarded as an historical person who lived during the time his book describes. In the fervour of the struggle between Pharisee and Sadducee a polemical tract would have been derided which made such use of his name as Susanna does. There is evidence that Susanna circulated independently of Daniel. Jerome[2] (Pref. to Commentary on Daniel) cites the opinion of Eusebius and Apollinarius: 'Susannae Belisque ac Draconis fabulas non contineri in Hebraico, sed partem esse prophetiae Abacuc filii Iesu de tribu Levi.' In Cod. Chisianus Bel (Dan. xiv) still retains the superscription *ἐκ προφητείας Ἀμβακοὺμ υἱοῦ Ἰησοῦ ἐκ τῆς φυλῆς Λευί*. Suidas[3] derives Ἀμβακούμ from אַבָּא and קוּם, and comparing *ταλιθὰ κούμ* in the Gospel, gets the sense *πατὴρ ἐγέρσεως*. The additions to Daniel were thus by a section of early tradition connected with the name of Habakkuk.

The intrusion of Daniel and Babylon into the story explains the chief differences between the LXX as conceived above and Theodotion's version. The preface is new and locates the scene in Babylon. The epilogue ignores the *νεώτερος* of LXX and sings the praise of Daniel. Joakim resembles the Chief of the Captivity ראש גלות: at his house justice is administered, in it the trial is conducted. It is easier to identify Joakim with the captive king Jehoiachin; no children are mentioned; anxiety for the continuance of the Davidic lineage may supply a motive for the methods of Ahab and Zedekias. Details are added chiefly in the scene in the garden. Doors are shut, the maids are dismissed, no other observer is present, the guilty youth escapes though the elders try to prevent him. These variations make the evidence of the elders more telling against themselves. The LXX hurries over the garden scene; its interest is in the trial.

Theodotion as a translator is 'simplex et gravis'. His habitual deference to the Hebrew text would not allow him to invent the additions to LXX of Susanna. A second edition in Hebrew adapted to Babylon appears to be the source of his revision and extension of the LXX. When the story had achieved its purpose, when the dictum of Simon ben Shetach, 'Make full examination of the witnesses,'[4] became dominant, then it became possible to identify the youthful champion of the right with Daniel. Daniel's name 'El is my Judge' commended his claim to be the *νεώτερος* of the first edition.

§ 7. Authorship and Date.

Judaea was vigorous under John Hyrcanus and his sons, 139–79 B.C. Not content with subduing the Idumaeans, they also circumcised them: disapproving the Samaritan heresy they demolished the Temple on Gerizim. They did hard fighting, sustained serious reverses, yet kept adding to their territory. At home in Jerusalem Pharisee fought Sadducee with persistent energy. Points in dispute seem trivial: should Pentecost be kept on a Sabbath? should there be a procession at the Feast of Tabernacles? should certain vessels of the Temple be ritually cleansed? ('better wash the Sun too,' sneered the Sadducee); should informers be executed before or after their victim has suffered punishment? does the intent to slay in a false witness merit death?

During the first ten years of his reign, 105–95 B.C., Alexander Jannaeus was too busy with foreign war to take an active part in these disputes. At the Feast of Tabernacles, 95 B.C., while acting as high-priest, he poured the libation of water, not on the altar as the Pharisees required, but at his feet. The indignant worshippers pelted their king and high-priest with the festive fruits they carried in their hands. The king called in his Pisidian and Cilician mercenaries, who slew 6,000 people in the Temple. Six years of civil war followed. After his defeat at Shechem Jannaeus had

[1] *Ant.* x. 10. 7.
[2] Migne, xxv, § 620.
[3] *De Habacuci prophetae vita atque aetate*, Delitzsch, 1842.
[4] *Pirqe Aboth* i. 10.

800 Pharisees crucified in Jerusalem in one day. To save themselves 8,000 Pharisees fled into exile. Weary of strife, the king asked the rival party what terms might satisfy them. 'The first condition is thy death,' was the reply. Nearing his end, the king appointed his queen Salome (Alexandra) regent and left her this advice, 'Fear not the true Pharisees or their honest opponents; but fear the painted ones who look like the Pharisees, whose works are like the work of Zimri, and who seek the reward of Phinehas.' The Pharisees made the day of his death an annual festival.

The leader of the Pharisees in this period was Simon ben Shetach. While the Sadducees had control of the law courts, informers by false witness secured a verdict of death against the son of Simon. Before the sentence was carried out, the perjurers confessed; according to Sadducean views, 'life for life', 'eye for eye', the perjurers could not be executed. The son of Simon, however, refused to be tried again, preferring to die that his accusers might also suffer that penalty. 'Father,' said he, 'if thou desirest that help should come through thee, use me as a threshold.'[1] Another point contended for by Simon ben Shetach was that informers should be carefully cross-examined. 'Simon ben Shetach said, "Make full examination of the witnesses; but be guarded in thy words, perchance from them they may learn to lie."'[2] Both these contentions were realized when the Pharisees came into power at the death of Jannaeus 79 B.C. The Synhedrion was reorganized. 'Witnesses in the law courts were no longer to be questioned merely upon the place where, and the time when they had seen a crime committed, but they were expected to give the most detailed and minute evidence connected with it, so that the judge might be more certain of pronouncing a correct judgement, and also more able to entrap the witnesses should they make contradictory statements.'[3]

Satire of the Sadducees, the vindication of the need and value of cross-examining informers, the application of the *ius talionis* to convicted perjurers are the aim of Susanna. The story appears to belong to the period 95–80 B.C. and to have been written by a supporter of Simon ben Shetach. In the heat of controversy neither party could well call the young detective Daniel. That identification would suggest itself when the tract had achieved its purpose. The language would be Hebrew. Though Aramaic was the common language in Jerusalem at this time, writers, especially a Pharisee, would share the temporary revival of interest in Hebrew. The Semitic idioms in the Greek texts in many cases favour a Hebrew rather than an Aramaic source.

The LXX version may have been made before the Christian Era, but its Hebrew exemplar had already a slender attachment to Daniel. Theodotion, not later than A.D. 180, possibly as early as the latest N. T. writers, used a Hebrew text which contained a new preface and epilogue emphasizing Babylon and Daniel. This conception led to the identification of the two elders with Ahab and Zedekiah and the assimilation of legends about the captive king Jehoiachin.

§ 8. Influence of the Book on Later Literature.

In Jewish circles the story would prepare the general mind to appreciate the announcement of the Golden Rule. The domestic scandal would not win credit for Judaism from Gentile readers. Josephus does not care to make the story known to the Romans; Akiba about the same time secures its exclusion from the Jewish Canon. It is doubtful whether Aquila included Susanna in his literal Greek version of the Hebrew Bible. Origen can find among learned Jews only vague stories about the elders. Africanus says the story is a fiction of recent date, which had never been in Hebrew. Henceforward Judaism knows the story only as gossip about the methods of the false prophets Ahab and Zedekiah (Jer. xxix. 20–23). Brüll[4] asserts that Nachmani is the only Jewish author of the Middle Ages who mentions Susanna, and his quotation is part of Judith, which he refers to the Roll of Shoshan. The Hebrew MSS. of the fourteenth and fifteenth centuries show that individuals were sufficiently interested to make careful copies; and that Jewish tradition still identified the elders with the false prophets in Babylon.

Influence in Christian Literature. The plea for cross-examination of informers may have coloured the arguments of Justin in his *Apology*. The rescripts of Hadrian and Antoninus Pius adopt the principle advocated in Susanna. Antoninus says: 'If any one hereafter shall go on to inform against this sort of men, purely because they are Christians, let the persons accused be discharged, although they be found to be Christians, and let the informer himself undergo the punishment.'

In the Greek O.T. of Alexandria the story acquired authority by its attachment to the Book of Daniel, and thus secured the attention of the Church while it lost the regard of the synagogue. The Church hesitated to pronounce it prophecy, or vision, or history. Matt. xxiv. 15 cites Daniel as

[1] Jerus. Sanhed. vi. 3. [2] *Pirqe Aboth* i. 10.
[3] Graetz, *Hist. of the Jews* (Eng.), ii. 50.
[4] Brüll, *Das apokryphische Susanna-Buch*, 1877, p. 6. A good summary of Brüll's important essay is given by Ball, *Apocrypha*, Dr. Wace, ii. 325–30.

a prophet; the parallel passage in Mark xiii. 14 omits 'the prophet' in the earliest MSS. Theodotion and the Syriac and later versions regard Susanna as history; Jerome, with some hesitation, includes it under prophecy. The allegorical interpretation soon became dominant in the Church. Hippolytus, Bishop of Rome, A. D. 230, writes: 'Susanna is a type prefiguring the Church; Joachim her husband prefigures the Christ. The garden is the election of the saints, who like trees that bear fruit are planted in the Church. Babylon is the world; the two elders are typical of the two nations who plot against the Church, the one being of the circumcision, the other from the Gentiles.'[1] The same conception is ably represented in the latest expositor of the Latin Church, Dr. Anton Scholz.[2]

An incipient phase of this view can be traced in Irenaeus before A. D. 200. In his work *contra Haereses*, iv. 26,[3] Irenaeus quotes, as from Daniel, Susanna *vv.* 20, 56, 52, 53. He is explaining how prophecy has a new meaning after its fulfilment. Any process is mysterious till it is finished. The Jews who deny the Advent fail to understand the prophecies. The true interpretation belongs to sincere disciples of Christ. There are impostors among presbyters who do evil secretly, saying, 'No one sees us.' To them apply the words of Daniel the prophet, 'Seed of Chanaan, not of Judah,' &c. He enforces this view by reference to Matt. xxiv. 48 f. Irenaeus has no doubt that Daniel is a prophet, that Susanna belongs to his book and describes something that really happened, and that the Divine purpose in the history of the world is made manifest in the Christian revelation. In the light of this new Revelation, casual phrases in the old records acquire a new significance.

Tertullian, *de Corona Militis*, iv,[4] discussing women's dress (1 Cor. xi. 5) argues that the interference with Susanna's veil does not warrant the inference that the veil was customary or necessary for women. He quotes the word *στάδιον* as in LXX.

Origen defends the canonicity of Susanna and often refers to the book. Jerome gave it a place in the Vulgate. Before the Reformation the story had taken popular and dramatic form. Hildebert, Archbishop of Tours, 'Egregius Versificator,' had made it the subject of a Latin poem (*c.* 1100). From German an Ober-Engadine version had adapted the story for a play; as the alliterative poems had done for the Scots. Luther's Bible gave Susanna currency in the North as far as Iceland. The Council of Trent made its place in the Canon more secure. In the nineteenth century the Bible Societies, by refusing to circulate the Apocrypha, diminished the fame of Susanna in a section of Christendom. The Anglican Church reads from Susanna in November; the Latin Church makes use of it on the vigil of the Fourth Sunday in Lent, also in the 'Ordo commendationis animae', 'Libera Domine animam servi tui, sicut liberasti Susannam de falso crimine.'

The subject has been treated pictorially in the Catacombs and also by modern artists.

§ 9. THEOLOGY.

In Daniel, as in post-exilic literature generally, יהוה tends to become *nomen ineffabile* and is replaced by אלהים and אֲדֹנָי. Only in Dan. ix does יהוה occur, and there it is used seven times: LXX renders *Κύριος* six times, omits once; Theodotion has *Κύριος* seven times. In the same chapter (Dan. ix) אֲדֹנָי for the Divine Name appears eleven times: LXX renders by *Κύριος* five times, *δεσπότης* four times, omits twice: Theodotion by *Κύριος* consistently eleven times. Further, in this chapter, אלהים with or without suffixes appears eleven times: LXX renders by *Θεός* eight times, *Κύριε* twice, *δέσποτα* once; whereas Theodotion renders uniformly by *Θεός* eleven times. Theodotion avoids *δεσπότης*, which by his time would mean the Roman Emperor denuded of divine honours. Thus Theodotion is scrupulous and consistent in rendering the Divine Names; the LXX is irregular and careless of Jewish feeling on the subject. The same motive can be traced in Dan. ix. 26, where Theodotion avoids the LXX term *Χριστός* for מָשִׁיחַ. The Hebrew of Susanna as reflected in Theodotion would use אֲדֹנָי. *Οὐρανός* for שָׁמַיִם *vv.* 9, 35 is an evasion due to reverence.

In Susanna, *vv.* 44, 62, LXX refers to an angel, while Theodotion does not. This is likely due to inexact translation. In Dan. ii. 11 LXX renders אֱלָהִין by *ἄγγελος*: Dan. iii. 25 Aram. = iii. 92 LXX דָּמֵה לְבַר אֱלָהִין by *ὁμοίωμα ἀγγέλου θεοῦ*: Dan. iv. 10 עִיר וְקַדִּישׁ מִן שְׁמַיָּא נָחִת by *ἄγγελος ἀπεστάλη ἐν ἰσχύι ἐκ τοῦ οὐρανοῦ*: Dan. x. 21 מִיכָאֵל שַׂרְכֶם *Μιχαὴλ ὁ ἄγγελος*. The term *ἄγγελος* is thus too elastic in LXX to allow any inference as to its difference from Theodotion on the doctrine of angels. Theodotion also refers to *ἄγγελος vv.* 55, 59. A Sadducee would not have written מַלְאָךְ.

The story does not intend to teach anything new in theology. Its theism is incidental and generally accepted. The Law of Moses expresses the will of God: His Word condemns injustice.

[1] Greek Text in Pitra, *Analecta Sacra*, ii, p. 256.
[2] *Commentar über das Buch 'Esther' mit seinen 'Zusätzen' und über 'Susanna'*, Anton Scholz, Würzburg, 1892.
[3] Migne, vii. 1054.
[4] Migne, Latin, ii.

Belief in God makes Susanna prefer death to sinning against God; she trusts in God, Who is not of one generation only, Who perceives the causes of events, knows her innocence, answers her prayer, and inspires her deliverer. On the other hand, an error in theism is the most deadly of errors. Unbelief in God, although veiled by hypocrisy, perverts the elders, leaves them a prey to passion, allows them deliberately to plan murder, and blinds them to the penalties of their conduct. Injustice is the fruit of atheism. That Susanna should represent the Messianic kingdom, Joakim and Helkias the God of Israel, the elders the ungodly powers of the world, can hardly be the intention of the writer (Scholz). Allegory and apocalypse have come from students of the story, not from its author.

§ 10. Bibliography.

See also in Bibliography for the other Additions to Daniel.

(a) Text.

LXX. Cod. Chisianus, ed. Rome, 1772, Bugati, Cozza.
Syro-Hexaplar Ambrosianus, Ceriani, 1874.
Theodotion, as in Swete, *O.T. in Greek*, vol. iii.
Versions. Walton, *Polyglot*, vi. 191 f.; Lagarde, *Apocryphi Syriace*, 1861.
Old Latin. Sabatier, II, 1751.
Copto-Memphitic. Joseph Bardelli, Pisis, 1849.
Hebrew Versions in MS. Bodleian Hebr. MSS. d. 11 and e. 12.

(b) Critical Inquiries.

Commentary by Hippolytus, Bishop of Rome, *c.* A.D. 230.
Part of the Commentary of St. Hippolytus on Daniel, lately discovered by Dr. Basilios Georgiades. J. H. Kennedy, Dublin, 1888.
Analecta Sacra, ed. Pitra, ii. 253 ff., 1884.
Origen. Fragments of Commentary based on Theodotion in Jerome.
Discussion of views of Africanus and Porphyry.
Jerome. Preface to Commentary on Daniel.
Vulgate.
Handbuch zu den Apokryphen des A.T. Fritzsche, Leipzig, 1859.
Apokryphen des A.T. Strack und Zöckler, 1891.
Apocrypha of the O.T. Bissell, 1880.
Commentar über das Buch Esther mit seinen Zusätzen und über Susanna. Anton Scholz, Würzburg, 1892.
Die Alexandrinische Übersetzung des Buches Daniel. August Bludau, Freiburg i. B., 1897.
Das apokryphische Susanna-Buch by Dr. N. Brüll in *Jahrbücher für Jüdische Geschichte und Literatur*, III. Jahrgang, Frankfurt am Main, 1877.
Commentary on the Apocrypha, ed. by Henry Wace, D D., 1888; *Susanna*, by C. J. Ball.
Die Apokryphen des A.T., ed. by E. Kautzsch, 1890; *Susanna*, by W. Rothstein.

General.

In Susannam Danielicam. De Celada, 1656, appendix 'de S. figurata in quo Virginis Deiparae laudes in Susanna adumbratae praedicantur'. fol. 672 + pp. Fine-spun exhortation based on fantastic allegory.

Susanna. Ein oberengadinisches Drama des XVI. Jahrhunderts. Jakob Ulrich, 1888. This is a literal translation from German into Ladino, e.g. 'Unna bella histoargia da quella seinchia et prusa duonna Susanna.' The elders are called Achab and Sedechias; the maids are Spondea and Promptula; there is a Judex Dadan, a Notarius, &c.

ιστορια εκ του Δανιηλ περι της Σωσαννης. Venice, 1682. A paraphrase of the story in Greek elegiacs extending to about 400 lines. Modern Greek constructions are often used.

Scottish Alliterative Poems in riming stanzas, edited by F. J. Amours. Scottish Text Society, 1896–7. 'The Pistill of Susan, Four Versions from MSS. of Fifteenth Century.' The Vulgate and Wiclif are here much adorned. The garden has palms, poplars, pears, plowine, junipers, and roses:

'There were popinjays present (?), nightingales upon nest.
Blithe birdies of the best, on blossoms to sit.'

Susanna, or the Arraignment of the Two Unjust Elders. Robert Aylett, D.C.L., 1622. An edifying exposition in English verse for the benefit of 'our Judges in Westminster Hall'.

The Apocrypha Controversy. Edinburgh, 1826. Susanna 'is justly characterized as a fable'. The British and Foreign Bible Society was forbidden to expend subscribers' money in circulating the Apocrypha—'these unhallowed productions of the wisdom and folly of men that have been so presumptuously associated with the sacred oracles of God,' Resolution, p. 38.

THE HISTORY OF SUSANNA

Set apart from the beginning of Daniel, because it is not in the Hebrew, as neither the Narration of *Bel and the Dragon.*

Susanna according to the Septuagint.

1 There dwelt a man in Babylon, and his name
2 was Joakim: and he took a wife, whose name
was Susanna, the daughter of Helkias, a very
3 fair woman, and one that feared the Lord. Her
parents also were righteous, and taught their
4 daughter according to the law of Moses. Now
Joakim was a great rich man, and had a fair
garden joining unto his house: and to him
resorted the Jews; because he was more honour-
5 able than all others. And the same year there
were appointed two of the elders of the people to
be judges, concerning whom the Lord had spoken
when He said that iniquity went forth from
Babylon through elder-judges who were thought
worthy to govern the people.
6 And cases from other cities also came before
them for decision.
7 Now these men observing a
woman of beautiful form, the wife of one of their
own brother-Israelites, who was called Susanna,

The Revised Version of the Greek of Theodotion.

There dwelt a man in Babylon, and his 1
name was Joakim: and he took a wife, whose 2
name was Susanna, the daughter of Helkias, a
very fair woman, and one that feared the Lord.
Her parents also were righteous, and taught 3
their daughter according to the law of Moses.
Now Joakim was a great rich man, and had a 4
fair garden joining unto his house: and to him
resorted the Jews; because he was more honourable than all others. And the same year there 5
were appointed two of the ancients of the
people to be judges, such as the Lord spake
of, that wickedness came from Babylon from
ancient judges, who were accounted to govern
the people.
These kept much at Joakim's house: 6
and all that had any suits in law came unto them.
Now when the people departed away at noon, 7
Susanna went into her husband's garden to walk.
And the two elders beheld her going in every day, 8

PREFACE. 1–5 *a.* These verses are marked with *lemnisci* in LXX and the margin has Α Σ Θ, i.e. Aquila, Symmachus, Theodotion. The Syro-Tetrapla has obeli ÷ and margin Σ Θ. These marks apparently signify that Origen's Tetrapla inserted this preface in the LXX, borrowing it from other versions. The Syriac suggests that Aquila did not include Susanna. The Jewish Canon had rejected Susanna *c.* A.D. 90, and Aquila conformed closely to Jewish views. The preface comes from a later form of the story, which locates the scene in Babylon, and calls the young detective Daniel. The LXX had some other introduction, probably connecting the story with Palestine, in the time of Alexander Jannaeus.

1. **Babylon.** The preface (*vv.* 1–5 *a*) definitely places the scene in Babylon; cf. § 6, Introd.

Joakim. The proper names Joakim, 'the Lord will establish,' Helkias, 'the Lord is my portion,' Daniel, 'my judge is El,' may have been as significant as Melchizedech Howler and Habakkuk Mucklewrath were to readers of Scott.

2. **Susanna,** שׁוֹשַׁנָּה in Hebr., is reproduced Σουσαννα, also Σωσαννα Breser.. Hos. xiv. 6, 'Israel shall grow as the lily.' The 'lily' is used as simile of a bride, Cant. ii. 2; of flower-shaped capitals of pillars, 1 Kings vii. 19; in titles of Psalms xlv. 1, lx. 1, lxix. 1, lxxx. 1. Erman derives from Egyptian *šôšen*; and the lotus was an emblem from early times in Egypt. Lane (*Arabic Dict.*) derives from Persian. In O.T. Susanna is not found as a proper name of a person, but appears in Luke viii. 3. What is called the 'poppy-head' on the coins of John Hyrcanus might come under the name 'Shoshanna'. Like Esther and Judith, Susanna might thus be an emblem of right ultimately vanquishing might, cf. Scholz, Comm. *in loc.* The story has doubtless been the cause of the use of 'Susan' as a personal name.

'O model of a chaste and constant Dame,
The world all chaste ones hence Susanna name.'—Robert Aylett, 1622.

The Latin Catalogue of Saints has more than twenty who bear the name 'Susanna'.

5. **the same year.** This phrase applies to a context which is lost. The Syriac Harkleensian begins: 'When Daniel was twelve years old, there was . . .' Daniel was בר מצוה when his insight began.

ancients, R.V. for πρεσβύτεροι; **assembly** for ἡ συναγωγή, *vv.* 41, 60. The R.V. hesitates to use the terms 'elders' and 'synagogues' because their existence in Babylon *c.* 590 B.C. might be felt to be an anachronism. The technical use of the terms suits the conditions in Judaea *c.* 150–50 B.C.

such as the Lord spake of, that wickedness . . . This rendering is inexact, cf. LXX.

concerning whom. περὶ ὧν ἐλάλησεν ὁ δεσπότης ὅτι ἐξῆλθεν . . . A Hebrew split-relative with ὅτι for כִּי introducing *oratio recta.* Cf. LXX Jer. xxiii. 15 ὅτι ἀπὸ τῶν προφητῶν ἐξῆλθεν μολυσμὸς πάσῃ τῇ γῇ. The false prophets Ahab and Zedekiah whom Nebuchadrezzar roasted in the fire for sins like those of the elders, Jer. xxix. 21–23, may be present in the recollection of the writer, and may be responsible for the insertion of this verse. Jewish tradition names the elders Ahab and Zedekiah, and has much to say of their methods. Before the birth of a child they would promise the mother that the child would be a boy; to the neighbours they would say 'That woman expects a son but it will be a daughter'. In either case they got a reputation.

daughter of Helkias, wife of Joakim, as she walked
8 about in her husband's garden at eventide, were
9 inflamed with love for her; and they perverted
their mind and turned away their eyes so as
neither to look toward Heaven nor to be mindful
of right decisions.
10 And though both were smitten by desire of
her, yet each concealed from the other the evil
that possessed them in regard to her; neither
12 was the woman aware of this matter. And as
soon as it was daylight they came stealthily,
evading each other, hurrying *to see* which should
be first to show himself to her and to speak with
13 her. And behold! she was taking her walk
according to her wont and the one elder had
barely arrived, when lo! the other came up. Then
the one began to cross-examine his fellow, demanding,
'Why art thou gone forth so very early,
14 leaving me behind?' With that they made confession
each to the other of his painful state.

19 Then said the one to the other, Let us repair
to her; and having agreed together on a plan,
they made advance to her and sought to constrain
her.

22 But the daughter of Judah answered them, I
know that if I do this, it is death to me: and if
I do it not, I shall not escape from your hands.

23 Yet it is better for me not to do this and to fall
into your hands rather than to sin before the
Lord.

and walking; and they were inflamed with love
for her.
And they perverted their own mind, and 9
turned away their eyes, that they might not look
unto heaven, nor remember just judgements.

And albeit they both were wounded with her 10
love, yet durst not one show another his grief.
For they were ashamed to declare their lust, that 11
they desired to have to do with her. Yet they 12
watched jealously from day to day to see her.
And the one said to the other, Let us now go 13
home: for it is dinner time.

So when they 14
were gone out, they parted the one from the
other, and turning back again they came to the
same place; and after that they had asked one
another the cause, they acknowledged their
lust: and then appointed they a time both
together, when they might find her alone. And 15
it fell out, as they watched a fit day, she went
in as aforetime with two maids only, and she
was desirous to wash herself in the garden: for
it was hot. And there was nobody there save 16
the two elders, that had hid themselves, and
watched her. Then she said to her maids, 17
Bring me oil and washing balls, and shut the
garden doors, that I may wash me. And they 18
did as she bade them, and shut the garden doors,
and went out themselves at the side doors to
fetch the things that she had commanded them:
and they saw not the elders, because they were
hid. Now when the maids were gone forth, the 19
two elders rose up, and ran unto her, saying,
Behold, the garden doors are shut, that no man 20
can see us, and we are in love with thee; therefore
consent unto us, and lie with us. If thou 21
wilt not, we will bear witness against thee, that a
young man was with thee: and therefore thou
didst send away thy maids from thee. Then 22
Susanna sighed, and said, I am straitened on
every side: for if I do this thing, it is death unto
me: and if I do it not, I cannot escape your
hands. It is better for me to fall into your 23
hands, and not do it, than to sin in the sight of
the Lord. With that Susanna cried with a loud 24
voice: and the two elders cried out against her.
Then ran the one, and opened the garden doors. 25
So when the servants of the house heard the cry 26
in the garden, they rushed in at the side door, to
see what had befallen her. But when the elders 27

9. **Heaven.** *οὐρανόν* for God; cf. Dan. iv. 23, שְׁמַיָּא 'the heavens' for 'God'. So in Matt. *ἡ βασιλεία τῶν οὐρανῶν* = Mark, Luke, *ἡ βασιλεία τοῦ θεοῦ.*

17 *θ.* **washing balls,** *σμήγματα.* The same word is used, Esther ii. 3, 9. Hebr. תַּמְרוּקִים 'things for purification'.

22. Death is the penalty imposed on the unfaithful wife, Lev. xx. 10; Deut. xxii. 22; for unchastity, death by stoning, Deut. xxii. 21; cf. John viii. 4, 5.

28 So these transgressors of the law turned away,
vowing vengeance and planning together how
they might put her to death. And they came
into the synagogue of the city in which they
dwelt, where were assembled in council all the
Israelites of the place.
29 Then the two elders and judges arose and
said, Send for Susanna, daughter of Helkias,
the same who is the wife of Joakim. And
30 straightway they summoned her. And when
the woman appeared with her father and mother,
her bondmen and her bondwomen to the number
of five hundred also presented themselves, as well
31 as the four little children of Susanna. Now the
woman was very delicate.
32 Yet the lawless pair ordered that she should
be unveiled, that they might sate themselves
with the beauty of her attraction.
33 Whereat all her attendants and all who knew
34 her began to weep. Then arose the elders and
judges and laid their hands upon her head.
35 But her heart was stayed upon the Lord her
God, and looking upward she wept within her-
35a self, saying, O Lord the eternal God, who
knowest all things before they come into being,
Thou knowest that I have not done what these
lawless men maliciously allege against me. And
36 the Lord hearkened to her entreaty. Then the
two elders affirmed, We were walking about in
37 her husband's garden, and as we came round the
stadion, we saw this woman dallying with a
man; we stood still and observed them consort-
38 ing together, but they were not aware that we
were standing by. Then when each of us had
confirmed the other, we said, We must find out
39 who these persons are. So we came forward
and her we recognized; but the young man
40 escaped us being concealed by a mask. And
having arrested her, we put the question, Who
41 is the fellow? but she refused to tell us who he
was. These things we declare as witnesses.
And the whole synagogue believed them inasmuch
as they were elders and judges of the people.

had told their tale, the servants were greatly
ashamed: for there was never such a report made
of Susanna. And it came to pass on the morrow, 28
when the people assembled to her husband
Joakim, the two elders came full of their wicked
intent against Susanna to put her to death; and 29
said before the people, Send for Susanna, the
daughter of Helkias, Joakim's wife. So they 30
sent; and she came with her father and mother,
her children, and all her kindred. Now Susanna 31
was a very delicate woman, and beauteous to
behold.

And these wicked men commanded her 32
to be unveiled (for she was veiled) that they
might be filled with her beauty. Therefore her 33
friends and all that saw her wept. Then the two 34
elders stood up in the midst of the people, and
laid their hands upon her head. And she weep- 35
ing looked up toward heaven: for her heart
trusted in the Lord.

And the elders said, As 36
we walked in the garden alone, this *woman* came
in with two maids, and shut the garden doors, and
sent the maids away. Then a young man, who 37
there was hid, came unto her, and lay with her.
And we, being in a corner of the garden, saw 38
this wickedness, and ran unto them. And when 39
we saw them together, the man we could not
hold; for he was stronger than we, and opened
the doors, and leaped out. But having taken 40
this *woman*, we asked who the young man was,
but she would not tell us: these things do we
testify. Then the assembly believed them, as 41
those that were elders of the people and judges:
so they condemned her to death. Then Susanna 42
cried out with a loud voice, and said, O ever-

32. Regulations for dealing with a wife suspected of adultery are given in Num. v. 11–31. The way in which these rules were applied is discussed in detail in Mishna. Sota i. 5 contains the following: 'Sacerdos arreptis eius vestibus . . . quoad sinum mulieris denudaret: crines quoque eius explicabat. R. Iuda (tamen hic limitat) dicens, si sinum venustum ipsa haberet, non fuisse eum a Sacerdote revelatum: nec capillos solutos, si essent decori.' The elders are *παράνομοι* because they broke this limitation, for the very purpose the rule was intended to prevent. The spectators see in the unveiling an indignity and a foregone assumption of guilt.

that they might sate themselves, &c. The phrase *ἵνα ἐμπλησθῶσιν κάλλους ἐπιθυμίας αὐτῆς* LXX = θ′ *ὅπως ἐμ. τοῦ κάλλους αὐτῆς* appears to be due to a mistranslated construct:

θ′ לְשָׂבְעָם יְפִי תָאֳרָהּ

LXX — תַּאֲוַת יָפְיָהּ

34. **laid their hands upon her head.** Cf. Lev. xxiv. 14, 'Bring forth him that hath cursed without the camp: and let all that heard him lay their hands upon his head, and let all the congregation stone him.' The elder-judges are not assessors in this trial, but witnesses. This is the reason for the laying on of hands; cf. Bab. Kam. 90*b*: אין עד נעשה דיין 'a witness cannot be made a judge'. Death by stoning imposed the responsibility on the whole congregation; no one could say whose missile caused death. Here the whole synagogue, guided perhaps by three or twenty-three of its leaders (Synhed. I), is considered responsible for the verdict.

37. Greek influence in the second century B.C. had induced Jewish youth to practise athletics. Some cities had a race-course. מָבוֹא is used to indicate something like a *στάδιον* in Jerusalem.

1105 U u

44–45 And as she was being led away to be destroyed,
behold! *there came* an angel of the Lord; and
as it had been commanded him, the angel bestowed a spirit of discernment upon a young man,
48 *this* being Daniel. Then separating the crowd
Daniel stationed himself in the midst of them and
said, Are ye so foolish, O sons of Israel, that
without examination and knowledge of the truth
ye have condemned a daughter of Israel to
51[a] die? Now therefore take these men apart from
each other, that I may cross-examine them.
51[b] And when they were separated, Daniel said to
the synagogue: Now consider not that these men
are elders nor say, They can never be false; but
I will examine them with reference to that which
52 is suggested to me. And he summoned one of
the two, so they brought forward the elder before
the young man. Then said Daniel to him:
Hearken, hearken, thou ancient of evil days!
now have overtaken thee thy sins which thou
hast committed in time past.
53 Being trusted to hear and to decide capital
cases, thou hast both condemned the innocent
and hast acquitted the guilty, although the Lord
saith: 'The innocent and the righteous slay thou
not.'
54 Now therefore under what tree and at what
sort of place in the garden hast thou seen them
together? The impious man answered, Under
55 a mastick tree. Then said the youth, Right
well hast thou borne false witness against thine
own soul; for the angel of the Lord will cleave
thy soul this day.

lasting God, that knowest the secrets, that
knowest all things before they be: thou knowest 43
that they have borne false witness against me,
and, behold, I must die; whereas I never did
such things as these men have maliciously
invented against me.
And the Lord heard her 44
voice. Therefore when she was led away to be 45
put to death, God raised up the holy spirit of a
young youth, whose name was Daniel: and he 46
cried with a loud voice, I am clear from the blood
of this woman. Then all the people turned them 47
toward him, and said, What mean these words
that thou hast spoken? So he standing in the 48
midst of them said, Are ye such fools, ye sons of
Israel, that without examination or knowledge of
the truth ye have condemned a daughter of Israel?
Return again to the place of judgement: for these 49
have borne false witness against her. Wherefore 50
all the people turned again in haste, and the
elders said unto him, Come, sit down among us,
and show it us, seeing God hath given thee the
honour of an elder. Then said Daniel unto 51
them, Put them asunder one far from another,
and I will examine them. So when they were 52
put asunder one from another, he called one of
them, and said unto him, O thou that art waxen
old in wickedness, now are thy sins come *home*
to thee which thou hast committed aforetime, in 53
pronouncing unjust judgement, and condemning
the innocent, and letting the guilty go free;
albeit the Lord saith, The innocent and righteous
shalt thou not slay. Now then, if thou sawest 54
her, tell me, Under what tree sawest thou them
companying together? Who answered, Under
a mastick tree. And Daniel said, Right well 55
hast thou lied against thine own head; for even
now the angel of God hath received the sentence
of God and shall cut thee in two.

44–45. Mishna Synhed. vi. 1, 2 prescribes appeals for fresh evidence after the verdict is given, 'When the person to be stoned is led out, a herald must precede proclaiming these words: This person N. M., son of N. M., is on the way to be stoned, for the crime (specified), on the testimony of N. M. and N. M.; whosoever can show his innocence, let him approach and set forth his reasons.' If none appeared, when they came within ten cubits of the place of stoning, the condemned was invited to confess, in deference to Joshua vii. 19.

51[b]. **with reference to that which is suggested to me,** *κατὰ τὰ ὑποπίπτοντά μοι.* Divine inspiration is the source of his suspicion. The Philoxenian Syriac says 'according as God has given to me'. Daniel condemns the first elder before his evidence is proved inconsistent with that of the second elder. His insight into their past is not the result of the examination. 'Any indication of the will of the Invisible King was sufficient in the Theocracy to supersede the operation of ordinary rules and restrictions; the theory being that the Divine Sovereign chose His own ministers when and how and whence He pleased' (Ball, *in loc.*). The elders of *v.* 50, Theodotion, are thus not the two who have given witness, but their colleagues on the bench.

53. **The innocent and the righteous slay thou not.** Quoted exactly from Exod. xxiii. 7 LXX *ἀθῷον καὶ δίκαιον οὐκ ἀποκτενεῖς.*

54–59. **Under a mastick tree,** &c. *ὑπὸ σχῖνον . . . σχίσει* and *ὑπὸ πρῖνον . . . καταπρίσῃ*, *v.* 59. Origen says (Epistle to Africanus, 48 f.): 'This passage gave me no rest and I often wondered about it, so I betook me to several Hebrews, asking what *πρῖνος* was called in their language, what was the verb for *πρίζειν*, also how they rendered *σχῖνος* and *σχίζειν*.' His inquiry was intended to refute the contention of Africanus that the play on the words proved that Susanna had been composed in Greek, not in Hebrew. That Hebrew could use paronomasia even in a death sentence appears from Achan's condemnation by Joshua, vii. 25. That the LXX would copy a play upon words appears, e.g., in Judges x. 4: עירים . . . עירים 'colts . . . cities', Gk. *πώλους . . . πόλεις.* Some of the versions succeed in preserving the Greek play in Syriac. With some liberty in choosing the trees, the play can be furnished by Hebrew, e.g. אֱגוֹז, which occurs in Cant. vi. 11:

וַיֹּאמֶר תַּחַת אֱגוֹז׃ וַיַּעַן הַנַּעַר הֵיטֵב קָשַׁרְתָּ עַל נַפְשְׁךָ כִּי גָּזוֹז יָגוֹז מַלְאַךְ י׳ אֶת־נַפְשְׁךָ בְּעֶצֶם הַיּוֹם הַזֶּה׃

Other ways are given in Ball, *Apocr.* ii. 324.

56 Then removing the one he gave command to
bring the other before him, to whom he said:
Wherefore is the seed that is in thee become
perverted as *that* of Sidon and not as *that* of
Judah? beauty has beguiled thee, base passion!
57 Even so were ye wont to do with daughters of
Israel, who through their fear companied with
you; but a daughter of Judah scorned to endure
58 your pestilent licence. Now therefore tell me,
Under what tree and in which spot of the
enclosure didst thou detect them consorting
together? Who answered, Under a holm tree.
59 Then said Daniel, Thou sinner! even now the
angel of the Lord is standing with drawn sword,
till the people shall make an end of thee, that
he may cut thee to pieces.

60–62[a] Then the whole synagogue shouted aloud in praise of the young man because from their own mouth he had proved them both to be confessedly false witnesses. And they dealt with them according as the Law prescribes, *doing to them* just as they maliciously intended against their sister.

So when they had gagged them, they led them out and hurled them into a chasm; then the angel of the Lord cast fire in the midst of them. And thus was innocent blood kept safe on that day.

62[b] For this cause the young men are beloved of
62[c] Jacob by reason of their sincerity. And as for
us, let us watch over young men that they may
become men of worth, for *so* young men will be
God-fearing, and there shall be in them a spirit
of knowledge and discernment for ever and ever.

So he put 56
him aside, and commanded to bring the other,
and said unto him, O thou seed of Canaan, and
not of Judah, beauty hath deceived thee, and lust
hath perverted thine heart. Thus have ye dealt 57
with the daughters of Israel, and they for fear
companied with you: but the daughter of Judah
would not abide your wickedness.

Now there- 58
fore tell me, Under what tree didst thou take
them companying together? Who answered,
Under a holm tree. Then said Daniel unto him, 59
Right well hast thou also lied against thine own
head: for the angel of God waiteth with the
sword to cut thee in two, that he may destroy
you.

With that all the assembly cried out with 60
a loud voice, and blessed God, who saveth them
that hope in him. And they arose against the 61
two elders, for Daniel had convicted them of
false witness out of their own mouth: and accord- 62
ing to the law of Moses they did unto them in
such sort as they maliciously intended to do to
their neighbour: and they put them to death,
and the innocent blood was saved the same day.

Therefore Helkias and his wife praised God for 63
their daughter Susanna, with Joakim her husband,
and all the kindred, because there was no dis-
honesty found in her. And from that day forth 64
was Daniel had in great reputation in the sight of
the people.

60–62. **the Law prescribes.** Deut. xix. 16–21 prescribes the treatment of a false witness, *v.* 19, וַעֲשִׂיתֶם לוֹ כַּאֲשֶׁר זָמַם לַעֲשׂוֹת לְאָחִיו, LXX καὶ ποιήσετε αὐτῷ ὃν τρόπον ἐπονηρεύσατο τῷ πλησίον ποιῆσαι (cf. θ′). On the application of this rule the Pharisees and Sadducees differed acutely during the reign of Alexander Jannaeus, 105–79 B.C. If the person falsely accused has actually suffered death, only then shall this regulation be carried out, said the Sadducees. The Pharisees maintained that if the perjury has been detected before its victim has suffered, then the same penalty must be inflicted on the false witnesses. The elders must therefore perish, in accordance with the Pharisaic interpretation of Deut. xix. 19 (*Hamburger Real-Encycl. für Bibel und Talmud*, ii. 1050; Mishna *Makkoth* i. 6; Sifre on Deut. xix. 19; Gemara *Makkoth* 5 β).

Cf. Code of Hammurabi, § 3: 'If a man in a case pending judgement . . . has not justified the word that he has spoken, if that case be a capital suit, that man shall be put to death.'

60. ἐφίμωσαν, 'muzzle', 'put in the pillory'. Cf. Matt. xxii. 34, 'The Pharisees when they heard that He had *put* the Sadducees *to silence* . . .'. Possibly more than a mere verbal coincidence. Strangling or suffocation is mentioned in the Talmud as the mode of death for false witness (Brüll on *v.* 60–62). Here it denotes symbolically that silence is imposed, no further defence can be offered.

62[b]. **beloved of Jacob.** The patriarch Jacob trusted his younger sons Joseph and Benjamin, and of Joseph's sons preferred the younger, Gen. xlviii. 14 (Brüll). For ἁπλότης cf. 1 Macc. ii. 60.

62[c]. **let us watch over young men,** καὶ ἡμεῖς φυλασσώμεθα εἰς υἱοὺς δυνατοὺς νεωτέρους. Meaning must be sought from the Semitic original: וַאֲנַחְנוּ נִשְׁמְרָה נְעָרִים לִבְנֵי חָיִל For εἰς = לְ as translated above, *v.* LXX, 1 Sam. xviii. 17; 2 Sam. ii. 7, xiii. 28; Dan. xi. 33, &c. בְּנֵי חָיִל = υἱοὺς δυνατούς, 2 Sam. ii. 7; = υἱοὺς δυνάμεως, 1 Sam. xiv. 52; 2 Sam. xiii. 28, xvii. 10. The Semitic metaphor 'son of valour' forbids Fritzsche's emendation of εἰς into ὡς, 'let us guard as sons virtuous young men.'

If the epilogue enforcing the didactic side of the story is an addition (Brüll), it has been added in Hebrew, not in Greek. Cf. 'One of the objects that Simon ben Shetach had greatly at heart was the promotion of better instruction. In all large towns high schools for the use of young men from the age of sixteen sprang up at his instance' (*c.* 75 B.C.) (Graetz, *History of the Jews*, Engl. edition, vol. ii, p. 50).

BEL AND THE DRAGON

INTRODUCTION

Bel and the Dragon forms the third of the Apocryphal Additions to Daniel, and was written originally almost certainly in Hebrew, though none of the Hebrew original has survived. The other two Additions are the Song of the Three Children and Susanna. In the Greek and Latin texts the three Additions to Daniel constitute an integral part of the canonical Book of Daniel, and were recognized as such, and therefore as themselves canonical, by the Council of Trent. The Song of the Three Children is, however, the only one of the three which has a necessary connexion with the Hebrew canonical Book of Daniel, standing in the Greek and Latin texts between Dan. iii. 24 and 25. The other two Additions are appended, and appear to have an origin independent of the book to which they are attached and also of each other, though in all three, as also in the canonical book, the name and fame of Daniel forms the principal theme.

§ 1. Name and Position in the Canon.

In the Greek Codd. Bel and the Dragon stands at the end of the canonical Book of Daniel, bearing therefore no distinct title. In Codd. A and B of Θ[1] it is, however, preceded by the words 'Vision (ὅρασις) xii'; i. e. it forms the twelfth and last of the series of visions into which this enlarged Book of Daniel is divided. In the LXX it is called 'Part of the prophecy of Habakkuk the Son of Jesus of the tribe of Levi': see note on *v.* 1. In the Vulgate Bel and the Dragon forms ch. xiv of Daniel.

In Syr W (see § 3) the Story of Bel is preceded by the heading 'Bel the idol', that of the Dragon having at its beginning the words, 'Then follows the Dragon.'

Bel and the Dragon is the title in all the Protestant versions of the Apocrypha, these versions keeping the books now known as Apocryphal apart as being, it was thought, deutero- or non-canonical. In a Nestorian list of biblical works mentioned by Churton[2] it is called 'The Lesser Daniel'.

§ 2. Contents.

The two stories as told in common by LXX and Θ may be thus summarized.

1. *The Story of Bel, vv.* 1–22. There is in Babylon an image of Bel (Marduk, Merodach) which Daniel refuses to worship, though no form of worship is mentioned besides that of supplying the god with food. The king, identified in Θ with Cyrus, remonstrates with the delinquent Hebrew, pointing him to the immense quantity of food consumed daily by Bel as a proof that the god thus recognized is a living, true deity. Daniel denies that the food is eaten by the god, and asks permission to put the matter to a test. This request being granted, he is shown the lectisternia, the sacred tables, covered with food which it is alleged the god will consume during the night. It is agreed that the doors of Bel's temple shall be closed and sealed for the night after the departure of the priests. But in addition, Daniel takes the precaution of having, without the priests' knowledge, the floor of the temple strewn lightly with ashes. When the morning breaks, the doors are still closed and the seals intact, but the food has disappeared, evidence, the king thinks, that it has been consumed by Bel. Daniel, however, points to the tracks of bare feet on the ash-strewn floor as evidence that the priests have entered the temple by secret doors and removed the food. Angered by the trick which the priests had played on him, the king has them put to death and the image destroyed.

On the word 'Bel' see note on *v.* 3.

2. *The Dragon Story, vv.* 23–42. There is in Babylon a great live serpent (dragon) worshipped by a large number of the inhabitants, who feed it lavishly. In the present case the god is represented by a living creature which can be fed and which needs feeding. Daniel refuses to bow down before the serpent, and throws out a challenge to the king, that, if permission is given him, he will destroy the creature alleged to be a god. Receiving the requested permission, Daniel makes a mixture of

[1] i. e. Theodotion's version, see § 3.
[2] *The Uncanonical and Apocryphal Scriptures*, p. 398 f.

which pitch is the principal ingredient, and thrusting it down the serpent's throat this creature bursts asunder and dies. Infuriated at the death of their god, the populace demand the death of this god-murderer. The king yields, and has Daniel cast into the den of lions, the usual punishment of persons found guilty of capital charges. But though Daniel remained in the company of seven lions for seven days, he suffers no injury. On the sixth day Daniel, being naturally hungry, is miraculously supplied with food. The prophet Habakkuk has prepared the midday (?) meal for his reapers, and is on the way to the field where they are. An angel arrests him, telling him he is to carry the meal to Daniel in the lions' den in Babylon. On his alleging his ignorance of the location of the lions' den, and even of Babylon itself, the angel lays hold of the hair on the crown of his head and conveys the prophet to the den, where, seeing Daniel, he hands him the food, and seems as safe among the lions as Daniel himself. The angel then restores Habakkuk to his Palestine home. Seeing that Daniel was preserved (the Habakkuk incident is an evident interpolation), the king magnifies God, sets Daniel at liberty, and substitutes for him in the den Daniel's accusers, who are at once devoured by the lions.

The meaning of the word 'dragon'. The Greek word (δράκων) translated 'dragon' denotes originally a large serpent. Homer uses δράκων and ὄφις interchangeably without the least apparent difference. Even the *drakōn* of Greek mythology remains essentially a serpent. In the East the serpent came to be commonly used as a symbol of the principle of evil. In the LXX δράκων translates most frequently (twelve times) the Hebrew תַּנִּין (*tannin*), rendered in the A. V. generally (eight times) 'dragon', sometimes (thrice) 'serpent.' In two passages (Amos ix. 3, Job xxvi. 13) the usual Hebrew word for serpent (נָחָשׁ) is represented in the LXX by δράκων. There is no good reason for departing from the simple impression which the narrative gives that in the present tale the dragon is a live snake worshipped as a god. Perhaps such worship is to be regarded as a survival of totemism. There is abundant evidence of snake worship in various parts of the ancient world, and there is good reason for believing that it obtained in Babylon. (1) The god Nina was worshipped in the form of a serpent.[1] (2) On Babylonian seals men are figured worshipping gods apparently serpentine in form, their lower parts consisting of serpent coils with worshippers in front. (3) Both Berosus and Helladius speak of gods worshipped as serpents in Babylon.[2] (4) Jensen, quoted by Baudissin (*PRE*³, v, p. 6), says there was a serpent god called in Sumerian *Seraḫ*. For traces of serpent worship among the Hebrews, see Num. xxi. 8 f., 2 Kings xviii. 4. There is no certain proof that in ancient Babylon the live serpent as in distinction from the image of a serpent was worshipped, but there is no conclusive evidence to the contrary, and the analogy of other countries favours a decision in the affirmative.

Fritzsche[3] holds that the story was composed in Egypt, where serpent worship is known to have existed in early times, but that the author inaccurately transferred it to Babylon. But since Fritzsche's time fresh evidence of such worship in Babylon has presented itself.

Modern writers generally maintain that the dragon in this story represents a mythical monster with a serpent's head and neck, an eagle's legs, a lion's body, and a unicorn's horn.[4] In this or some similar form a very large number of Babylonian inscriptions picture this monster or other monsters (we can never be quite sure as to this) as in conflict with Marduk or some other Babylonian deity. The monster has been very commonly identified with the mythological dragon, but no decisive proof of the identity has been furnished. W. Hayes Ward has made a careful attempt to bring together the various forms in which the 'dragon-myth' has been portrayed on Babylonian-Assyrian inscriptions,[5] and he assumes throughout that in all it is the Marduk-Tiamat conflict of the Babylonian Creation legend that is set forth, but he gives no proof of this, for the name Tiamat is not once connected with the representation. Indeed it seems now generally understood that Tiamat was a snake deity, and that the dragon of the story now under consideration is no other than Tiamat: so Sayce, Ball, Gunkel, Marshall, Toy.

The present writer ventures with Jensen and Baudissin to dispute and even deny this, and for the following reasons:

1. There is no evidence in the Babylonian-Assyrian inscription that Tiamat was conceived as a serpent. The serpentine forms pointed out cannot be shown to be intended for Tiamat.

2. Berosus does not once translate the Babylonian Tiamat by dragon or by any word denoting serpent. He uniformly transliterates the word, though not as we should do now, but as *Thalatth*.

3. The idea embodied in Tiamat differs from that of the dragon or serpent. In Babylonian mythology Tiamat stands for the female principle, expressing itself in darkness and disorder, older

[1] See Sayce, *Hibbert Lectures*, p. 282 f.
[2] e.g. Rawlinson, *Five Great Monarchies*⁴, i. 122 f., ii. 14.
[3] *Exeg. Handbuch zu den Apoc.*, i, p. 121.
[4] See figures in Gressmann, *Altor. Texte und Bilder*, ii. 90 f.
[5] See *American Journal of Semitic Languages*, xiv. 94–105.

than the gods themselves, since the birth of the gods took place through their separation from the primaeval chaos (= Tiamat). Tiamat is usually identified with the primaeval ocean, wild and rebellious, needing to be subdued. We are probably to see a reference to it in the תהום rendered by English versions 'the deep': LXX ἄβυσσος: Vulg. *Abyssus*.

4. In the present story the dragon is a god alongside of Bel in the preceding story: there is not the remotest hint that he is regarded other than as a Babylonian deity worshipped in the form of a serpent or dragon.

The present writer would like to add that he does not now, as he once did (see Century Bible, *Psalms*, ii, pp. 50, 63, 112, 141, 177), agree with Gunkel and the bulk of recent Bible scholars in seeing reflections of the Marduk-Tiamat legend in innumerable passages of the O. T. Later writers have too blindly followed Gunkel (see his *Schöpfung und Chaos*).

§ 3. Textual Authorities: Manuscripts and Versions.

1. *Manuscripts.* The Greek text exists in two principal forms throughout the Book of Daniel including the Apocryphal Additions.

(1) 𝔊 (i. e. the LXX) has been preserved in but one MS., the Codex Chisianus (from the Chigi family which owned it), published in Rome in 1772, in Cozza's *Sacrorum Bibliorum Vetustissima Fragmenta Graece et Latine*, in Swete's 𝔊 (in parallel pages with Θ), and in Tischendorf's 𝔊. This unique MS. is quoted by Field and Swete as Cod. 87, which must be distinguished from that so designated by the Oxford editors, Holmes and Parsons.

(2) Of Theodotion's text (Θ) of Bel and the Dragon the following MSS. exist: B, A, Γ (*vv.* 2–4 only), Δ (from *v.* 21 to *v.* 41).

Besides the above majuscules (uncials) there also several valuable minuscules (cursives), as e. g. those numbered 34, 49.

For details and explanations, see Swete's edition of 𝔊 and his *Introduction to the O. T. in Greek*.

2. *Versions.* (1) *Greek.* It may not be strictly correct to speak of the two best known texts (𝔊 and Θ) as versions since no Hebrew or Aramaic original has come down to us. Yet according to the view of a Hebrew lost original advocated by the present writer (see below) these so-called versons are correctly thus described.

A careful comparison of 𝔊 and Θ of Bel and the Dragon has led the present writer to these conclusions. (*a*) That 𝔊 is a translation from a Hebrew original. This is made exceedingly probable by the presence of a large number of Hebraisms (see § 4, Original Language), though there is another possible explanation (see below, § 4, (*c*) 5). (*b*) That Θ contains a much larger number of Hebraisms than 𝔊: see on *vv.* 1 f., 5 f., 16, 18, 27, 28, 39, &c., suggesting what other considerations make likely that Theodotion corrected 𝔊 with the aid of a Hebrew original before him.

Yet, on the contrary, Θ corrects at times the Greek of 𝔊 (see on *vv.* 26, 40, 42), and it avoids the Hebraism Κύριος without the article (= Hebrew יהוה), preferring Θεός: see *v.* 5.

Theodotion's version of Daniel displaced that of 𝔊 at a very early time, for though in his Hexapla it is the true 𝔊 that he uses, yet in his own writings Origen almost invariably cites Θ. In his preface to Daniel Jerome points to the fact that in his own time the Christian Church had rejected 𝔊 in favour of Θ on account of the defective renderings in the former. Even Irenaeus (*ob.* 202) and Porphyry (*ob.* 305) preferred Θ to 𝔊. Field was the first to indicate clearly that what has for centuries been treated as 𝔊 of 1 Esdras, &c., including Daniel and its Additions, is really the version of Theodotion.

(2) *Syriac.* In this language there are two principal versions:

(*a*) The Peshiṭta, best preserved in the Cod. Ambrosianus B 21 (sixth century), reproduced in Walton's *Polyglot* and critically edited by Lagarde (Leipzic, 1861). In Bel and the Dragon this version follows Θ very closely, though at times (see on *vv.* 2, 18, 25) it agrees with 𝔊 against Θ. There are several cases where this version and Θ agree against 𝔊 (see on *v.* 21). In a few cases this version diverges from both the Greek texts (see on *v.* 27). In the notes Walton's *Polyglot* has been used, the version consulted being designated Syr W. But Lagarde's critical edition has always been compared.

(*b*) The Hexapla's Syriac version is that made by Paul of Tella in 617 from Col. VI (𝔊) of Origen's Hexapla. It exists in manuscript form (Cod. Ambrosianus, C. 313). This most valuable MS. has been edited, photographed, and published by Ceriani (Milan, 1874). In the notes it is quoted as Syr H. As might have been expected from its origin, it is in general agreement with 𝔊, rather than with Θ, and thus differs from the other Syriac version, which follows Θ closely.

(3) *Aramaic other than the Syriac.* For the Aramaic text of parts of Bel and the Dragon see § 4, Original Language.

There are no Targums on Ezra, Nehemiah, or Daniel, a lack easily explained if it could be assumed that all these books were written originally in Aramaic as portions of the existing books of Ezra and Daniel are.

(4) *Latin.* (*a*) Fragments of the Old Latin version occur in Sabatier's work, *Bibliorum Sacrorum Latinae Versiones Antiquae*, 1743, &c., vol. ii. Judging from the specimens therein preserved it may be confidently stated that in Daniel and its Additions this version follows Θ closely.

(*b*) Jerome's version—Vulgate simply reproduces it—is also based on Θ, though in some parts (see on *v.* 42) it is independent of any other version or text known to us.

(5) *Arabic.* The Arabic version of Saadias (A.D. 892–942) was made from the Hebrew and therefore lacks the Apocrypha. The Arabic version of Bel and the Dragon in Walton's *Polyglot* has no critical value, being due to a priest living in Egypt in the sixteenth century; see Walton, *Proleg.* xiv. 17 f., and Cornill on Ezekiel, p. 49.

§ 4. The Original Language.

Until comparatively recent years the prevailing view was that Bel and the Dragon was composed and first edited in the Greek language: so Eichhorn, Ewald, De Wette, Schrader, Fritzsche, Schürer, and König.

(*a*) In favour of this conclusion the following reasons have been given:

1. No traces of any Semitic original with reasonable claims have been discovered. Origen, Eusebius, and Jerome distinctly say that no Hebrew (or Aramaic) form of this tract was known in their day.

2. It is denied that the Hebraisms are more numerous than can be accounted for on the assumption of a Greek original. See below, (*b*) 3, 4.

3. In the Greek of Susanna there are certain word-plays inconsistent with a translation: e.g. *v.* 54 f. ὑπὸ σχῖνον . . . σχίσει, and 58 f. ὑπὸ πρῖνον . . . πρίσαι. No such word-plays have been discovered in Bel and the Dragon, and where in Susanna they do occur they can be easily due to a translator. Why cannot a translator adopt alliteration? Moreover, it is noteworthy that Bel and the Dragon is more Hebraic than Susanna, though less so than the Song of the Three Children.

(*b*) On the other hand, the opinion has been growing among recent scholars that the work was written originally in Semitic (Hebrew or Aramaic). Drs. Marshall and Gaster contend for an Aramaic original. But there is evidence conclusive to the present writer that the author of Bel and the Dragon wrote in Hebrew.

1. It has been pointed out (see § 3, 2 (1)) that Θ introduces Hebraisms which are absent from 𝔊, a change due undoubtedly to the fact that Theodotion had before him a Hebrew text as well as 𝔊, which latter he corrected by means of the former.

2. The extraordinary extent to which the syntactical construction called parataxy (co-ordination) exists points to a Hebrew, not an Aramaic original. The recurrence of the Greek καί with all the shades of meaning borne by the Hebrew *waw* and the Arabic *waw* and *fa* is characteristic of Hebrew very much more than of Aramaic. The latter is much richer than Hebrew in conjunctions and adverbs, so that in it hypotaxy (subordination) of sentences exists, very much in the manner of Greek; especially is this last true of Syriac which came under Greek influence.

3. There are many examples in the LXX and especially in Θ which imply the Hebrew '*waw* consecutive' construction and cannot be otherwise explained. Thus sentences often begin with καὶ ἦν (= וַיְהִי) and also with καὶ ἐγένετο, followed in this latter case by a finite verb; see *vv.* 14 and 18. This *waw* consecutive construction is peculiar to Hebrew at its best, even late Biblical Hebrew has almost lost it (cf. Ecclesiastes, &c.).

4. There are many other Hebraisms: thus *v.* 14 in Θ begins with words implying וַיְהִי וַיִּתֵּן. In *v.* 27 (Θ) καὶ ἔδωκεν is good Hebrew (וַיִּתֵּן) but bad Greek, cf. 𝔊 ἐνέβαλεν. The use of θύρας, 'doors', in the sense of the singular is Hebraic, see note on *v.* 18. οὐδὲ εἷς (*v.* 18 Θ) is the Hebrew אֵין אֶחָד. The constant recurrence of καὶ εἶπεν with the various shades of meaning possessed by וַיֹּאמֶר is a Hebraism: see *v.* 20, &c.: ἄγγελος κυρίου = מַלְאַךְ יְהוָה, the anarthrous ἄγγελος following the rule for nouns in the construct: see on *v.* 34; ἀναστάς (קוּם) followed by another verb: see on *vv.* 37 (𝔊) and 39 (Θ).

5. There are sometimes textual mistakes best explained on the assumption of a Hebrew original: see for examples the notes on *v.* 14 (𝔊).[1]

6. It is in favour of a Hebrew original that these two tales have been actually found in that language in a more or less complete form, as in the Midrash *Rabba de Rabba*.

[1] See Franz Delitzsch, *de Habacuce*, p. 82; Neubauer, *Tobit*, viii.

(*c*) Dr. M. Gaster discovered an Aramaic form of the Dragon story embedded in the *Chronicles of Jerahmeel*, a work of the tenth century, and he maintains that in this fragment we have a portion of the original text of Bel and the Dragon,[1] an opinion with which Dr. Marshall seems to be in sympathy. In that case the original text of the three 'Additions' was Aramaic, as these two scholars maintain. The present writer does not think that Dr. Gaster has proved his case.

1. There are constructions in all the 'Additions' which are not Greek and which can be explained from Hebrew but not from Aramaic. See above, (*b*) 2.

2. Two only of the three 'Additions' occur in the Aramaic version found by Dr. Gaster, and only a part (Dragon story) of the third; what has become of the rest?

3. This Aramaic form of the Dragon story differs from that in the Greek and Syriac in many particulars. In *v.* 24 the two Greek versions and Syr W have 'the king (said)', which the Aramaic text omits. In *v.* 35, after 'And Habakkuk said', the Aramaic document adds 'to the angel', which 𝔊, Θ, and Syr are without.

4. The compiler of the *Chronicles of Jerahmeel* distinctly says that he had taken the Song of the Three Children and the Dragon story from the writings (i. e. the translation) of Theodotion, he having himself, it is implied, turned the Greek into Aramaic. Dr. Gaster lays stress on the compiler's words[2] that what he gives in Aramaic is that which Theodotion himself found, but the reference can be only to 𝔊, which Theodotion made the basis of his own translation, and not to an Aramaic original, though it must be admitted that the compiler does not express himself unambiguously. But when such ambiguity does exist the decision must be according to facts otherwise authenticated.

5. There is of course another explanation of the apparent Semiticisms in Bel and the Dragon. It is probable, as Wellhausen holds,[3] that the language of 𝔊 represents a Hebrew-Greek jargon actually spoken, as is the Yiddish of the present day. In favour of this are, in addition to the innumerable Hebraisms, many of them due to translation, the large number of Hebrew words transliterated instead of being translated even in cases where the sense is not obscure: e. g. βεδέκ for בֶּדֶק, 'breach', 2 Kings xxii. 5; χεττιείμ (χεττιείν) for a restored כתנים = בָּתְּנוֹת, 2 Kings xxiii. 7; ἰαμείν for יָעִים, 'shovels', 2 Kings xxv. 14. These and other Hebrew words were perhaps taken over into the Greek spoken by these Jews, just as Polish-Russian-German Jews to-day talk in a German interlarded with Hebrew words.

§ 5. Authorship, Date, and Place of Origin.

Nothing whatever is known of the author of this work and nothing that is definite of the place or date of composition. We have no Hebrew or Aramaic original from the style of which it might have been possible to draw conclusions as to date.

It is quite certain that Bel and the Dragon imply the canonical Book of Daniel and belong therefore to a later date, for they show subsequent developments of Daniel legends. The canonical Daniel is dated by modern scholars at about 160 B.C. The general character of this tract suggests that, like the canonical Daniel, it arose at a period when the Jewish religion was bitterly persecuted. Such a period was the reign of Antiochus VII (Sidetes) (139–128 B.C.). This Syrian monarch reconquered Palestine and did his utmost to suppress Judaism. At that time Hebrew was, even in Palestine, more a literary than a spoken language, and this might explain the fact that the use of the *waw* consecutive—a feature of the classical language—is preserved. It is assumed that the place of origin was Palestine, and not, as Bissel and most hold, Babylon. The references to Babylon are the same in the canonical Daniel, but they are only a literary device; and this can be said also of the mention of clay and bronze (*v.* 7), which Bissel cites as proof of a Babylonian origin.

It is to be noted that Judaism in the narrow technical sense is entirely absent from these two stories—what is taught is the absurdity of idolatry and the duty of worshipping the only true God—Yahweh. The Judaism of Babylon was of a definite orthodox kind and could hardly have given rise to a tract so vaguely religious as the one under consideration. The universalism of Bel and the Dragon stamps it as a product of the Wisdom school of Judaism, though the positive characteristics of the literature of that school (Ecclesiastes, &c.) are lacking.

Assuming a date of about 136 B. C. for the Hebrew text the LXX must be later. It may be taken for granted that when 1 Macc. ii. 59 f. was written (i. e. about 100 B. C.) the three Additions

[1] See *PSBA*, 1894, 280 ff. (Introduction), 312 ff. (text); and 1895, 75 ff. (translation and notes).
[2] *PSBA*, 1895, p. 83.
[3] F. Bleek, *Einleitung in das Alte Test.*[5], 535. Deismann, however, says (*Bible Studies*[2], 68) that in a private communication to him Wellhausen abandons the above view.

formed no part of the Book of Daniel and did not perhaps even exist in Greek. Yet these Additions exist in all extant MSS. of the Greek and Syriac texts. The character of the Greek in 𝔊 and other considerations suggest that this version was made at Alexandria at a date not much later than 100 B. C. Yet the evidence for reaching such a conclusion is slight.

Theodotion is generally believed to have lived and to have completed his translation at Ephesus towards the close of the second century of our era. This accords with the fact that Irenaeus, who died A. D. 202, used Θ and preferred it to 𝔊.

§ 6. Integrity.

With the exception of small parts to be indicated in the notes, and *vv.* 33–39, these two tales seem to have been written by one author, who, however, used pre-existing materials. The incident of the miraculous transportation of the prophet Habakkuk from his home in Palestine to the lions' den in Babylon (*vv.* 33–39) is certainly a later piece having no necessary connexion with the rest of the story.

§ 7. Teaching.

These two stories teach the doctrines of the oneness and absoluteness of Yahweh, called Κύριος in 𝔊, a translation of the Hebrew word substituted by Jews from about 300 B. C. for Yahweh, which near that time took on a mystic and esoteric sense.

Little is told us of Yahweh's character. He is great, the only true God (*v.* 11), a living God in contrast with Bel (*v.* 5). Nothing is said of the nature of the demand He makes, ritual or ethical.

There is no allusion to any distinctively Jewish beliefs or practices. The law is not mentioned nor is the existence of a Divine revelation to man implied. This tract is silent as to sacrifice and temple, and even as regards priesthood, except that in 𝔊 Syr W (not Θ) Daniel the prophet is spoken of as a priest; all this strong evidence of the low place assigned by the writer to the external side of the Jewish religion. We do, however, read of an angel, but in a part of the Dragon story (*vv.* 33–39) which is certainly introduced by an editor *ab extra.*

For further Introductory notes, including references to special literature, see 'Bel and the Dragon' (by the present writer) in *The International Standard Bible Encyclopaedia* (Chicago), vol. i.

BEL AND THE DRAGON

The translation of Θ is that of the R. V., that of 𝔊 is by the present editor. See Introd., § 3, 1, 2.

I. The Story of Bel, *vv.* 1–22

𝔊 87

1 From the prophecy of Habakkuk the son of Jesus of the tribe of Levi.

2 There was a certain man a priest, by name Daniel, son of Abal, a companion of the King of Babylon.

3 And there was an idol Bel whom the Babylonians worshipped. And they expended on him daily twelve artabas of fine wheaten flour, and four sheep, and six measures of oil.

Θ

And king Astyages was gathered to his 1
fathers, and Cyrus the Persian received his kingdom.
And Daniel lived with the king, and was 2
honoured above all his friends. Now the Baby- 3
lonians had an idol, called Bel, and there were
spent upon him every day twelve great measures
of fine flour, and forty sheep, and six firkins of
wine.

1. Syr H begins the Story of Bel exactly as does 𝔊. But Θ and Syr W begin with a chronological notice which in the Vulg. closes Susanna.

Habakkuk. Greek Ἀμβακούμ, Syr. H ʿΑβακούκ. So also in *vv.* 33 ff. It is certain that Habakkuk the prophet is meant (see on *v.* 33), though the tradition that he was a Levite, based on Hab. iii. 19 *b*, is probably inaccurate. According to *The Lives of the Prophets* he was of the tribe of Simeon. See Stonehouse, *The Book of Habakkuk*, pp. 61 ff., for this and other traditions regarding Habakkuk. This title in 𝔊 and Syr H (not in Syr W) owes its existence to the interpolated incident in *vv.* 33–39.

Cyrus . . . received his kingdom. According to this verse, identical in Syr W, Cyrus succeeded his grandfather Astyages immediately upon the death of the latter. But Herodotus (i. 130) says distinctly that Cyrus took the kingdom from Astyages by force. Ancient authors disagree on this matter, as also as to whether in fact Cyrus was the immediate successor of his grandfather or not. Recent cuneiform inscriptions confirm the testimony of Herodotus That the incidents related in Bel and the Dragon could not have occurred during the reign of Cyrus goes without saying.

the Persian. On these words see Century Bible, *Ezra*, *Nehemiah*, *Esther*, pp. 19, 41.

2. **a priest, by name Daniel.** That Daniel was a priest is stated in 𝔊 and in Syr W, one of the rare instances in which the Peshitta agrees with 𝔊 against Θ. Dan. i. 3, 6 proves that Daniel could not have been a priest. That he is so described is due to priestly influence, and belongs to the period of priestly domination.

Abal. Ἄβαλ (so Fritzsche, Tisch., and Ball) for Ἀβιήλ (God my father) or Ἀβιχαιλ (= strong one, lit. father = possessor of strength, Num. iii. 35). But probably we should write with Swete and Rothstein ʿΑβάλ for Hebr. הֶבֶל, Gen. iv. 2. According to Epiphanius (*Adv. Haeres.* lv. 3) Σαβαάν (שבעין, שמעין) was father of the prophet Daniel.

a companion. The Greek word συμβιωτής denotes strictly one that lives (βιόω) with another. Cf. Vulg. *conviva.* Plutarch (*Julius Caesar*, 211) employs the word for the confidants of the emperors.

lived with the king. Render, as in 𝔊 above (the same Greek word being used), 'And Daniel was a companion of the king.' Syr W 'And Daniel's glory equalled that of the king, and he dwelt with the king and was more praised than any of the king's friends'.

King of Babylon. In 𝔊 and Syr W the particular king of Babylon meant is not named.

3. **Bel.** The Hebr. word בֵּל, a short form of בַּעַל, occurs in the O.T. in Isa. xlvi, Jer. l. 2, li. 44, in all which passages it stands for Marduk (Merodach), chief of the Babylonian deities. Originally it denoted any one of the Babylonian local gods, and in particular the principal one worshipped at Nippur. Cf. the generic use of בַּעַל (Baal).

worshipped. That the Babylonians worshipped Bel is in 𝔊 distinctly stated: in Θ and Syr W it is implied. The word translated 'worship' (σέβομαι) = 'to revere', especially as God.

artabas (in 𝔊 and Θ ἀρτάβαι): R.V. (Θ) renders 'great measures'. The artaba (ἀρτάβη) was a Persian measure = about half a hectolitre.

four. So 𝔊 and Syr H. But Θ Syr H^{mg} Fri τεσσαράκοντα (forty), which gives a better proportion. In Syr W 'forty rams'.

measures. The Greek μετρητής (R.V. 'firkin') = about nine gallons. Note the large quantity supposed to be consumed by Bel.

oil. So 𝔊: but read (with Θ Syr W Syr H^{mg}) οἴνου (wine). Cf. *vv.* 11, 14, 21 in 𝔊. Note the three kinds of sacrifices: meat offering (מִנְחָה), animal offering (זֶבַח), and drink offering (נֶסֶךְ), which accord with the regulations of the Priestly Code.

𝔊 87

4 The king also used to worship him, and the
king used to go daily to do homage to him ; but
Daniel used to pray to *the* Lord. So the king
said to Daniel, Why bowest thou not down to
5 Bel? Then Daniel said to the king, None do
I worship save *the* Lord, the God who created
the heaven and the earth, even Him who has
sovereignty over all flesh.
6 Then the king said to him, Is this then
not a god? Dost thou not see how much is
7 spent on him daily? Daniel therefore said to
him, Let no one by any means mislead thee by
false reasoning, for this is within of clay and
without of bronze: and I swear by *the* Lord the
god of gods that this never did eat anything.
8 So the king became angry and summoned the
overseers of the temple, and said to them, Show
me who eats the things prepared for Bel, other-
9 wise ye shall die. Or (if ye do show that Bel
devours them), Daniel, who alleges that these
things are not eaten by him, (shall die). But they
said, It is Bel himself who devours these things.
Then Daniel said to the king, Let it be thus. If
I shall not show that it is not Bel who devours
these things, let me suffer death together with
10 all my friends. Now Bel had seventy priests
besides (their) wives and children. So they conducted the king into the idol temple.

Θ

And the king did honour to it, and went daily 4
to worship it: but Daniel worshipped his own
God. And the king said unto him, Why dost
thou not worship Bel? And he said, Because I 5
may not do honour to idols made with hands, but
to the living God, who hath created the heaven
and the earth, and hath sovereignty over all flesh.

Then said the king unto him, Thinkest thou 6
not that Bel is a living God? or seest thou not
how much he eateth and drinketh every day?
Then Daniel laughed, and said, O king, be not 7
deceived: for this is but clay within, and brass
without, and did never eat or drink anything.

So the king was wroth, and called for his 8
priests, and said unto them, If ye tell me not who
this is that devoureth these expenses, ye shall die.
But if ye can show me that Bel devoureth them, 9
then Daniel shall die: for he hath spoken blasphemy against Bel. And Daniel said unto the
king, Let it be according to thy word. Now the 10
priests of Bel were threescore and ten, beside
their wives and children. And the king went
with Daniel into the temple of Bel.

4. **worship.** The Greek verb (σέβομαι) means to revere, usually as one does a god. The imperfect tenses in this verse denote habitual actions.

him. Rather than 'it', as the Greek has the masc., though εἴδωλον, for which the pronoun stands, is neuter.

the Lord. The anarthrous Κύριον translates the word (אדני) read for the tetragrammaton (יהוה) from about 300 B.C. Θ and Syr W have 'God'. Here, as in the foregoing Hebraism in 𝔊 ('used to go and bow down'), Θ corrects in the direction of classical Greek. Theodotion often does this, though in other cases he corrects 𝔊 according to the Hebrew. It is quite according to the usual policy of the early Persian kings to fall in, at least outwardly, with the worship of the peoples they conquered. See Century Bible, *Ezra*, *Nehemiah*, *Esther*, p. 40.

5. **idols made with hands.** This description of idols is not in 𝔊. Syr W gives 'I worship not images or sculptured things or idols because they are the work of men's hands'. In Θ and Syr W there is a contrast drawn between man-made idols and the God who is Himself the *Maker* of heaven and earth.

all flesh = every human being. See Gen. vi. 12.

6. The proof that Bel is a true, living god is the immense quantity of food he is able to eat daily!

7. **Let no one . . . reasoning.** It is difficult to account for the differences between 𝔊 and Θ in this verse. The words in 𝔊, 'Let no one . . . reasoning,' would be in Hebr. רַמֹּה אַל יְרַמְּךָ אִישׁ; the Greek παραλογίζομαι standing in 𝔊 generally for the Hebr. רִמָּה, 'to deceive'. Θ has simply μὴ πλανῶ, 'deceive not thyself'. Probably the two texts represent independent attempts to translate the above Hebrew, Θ as usual avoiding a peculiarly Hebrew construction—the absolute infinitive before a finite verb strengthening it.

I swear. Not in Θ. Probably in the original Hebrew no such verb was employed, but the conjunction אִם, which implies a negative oath. This Hebrew construction might easily give rise to the construction in 𝔊 and to that in Θ, though in 𝔊 ביהוה אֵל אֵלִים (see Dan. xi. 36) is also implied.

laughed. So *v.* 19 (𝔊 and Θ): 𝔊 here omits this verb.

brass (Θ). Render 'bronze'. Brass was unknown in the times when this tract was written.

eat. $Θ^{A}$ has, as 𝔊, simply 'eat'; $Θ^{AQ}$ add 'or drink'.

8. **the overseers of the Temple.** In Θ 'his priests'. Probably 𝔊 translates the Hebrew freely, Θ literally.

these expenses. Better 'this outlay', i.e. the things on which money has been expended. The Hebrew word thus rendered is perhaps the late הוֹצָאָה (see Ezra vi. 4, 8). 𝔊 seems to translate freely.

9. **(if ye . . . them).** The words bracketed in the translation are added because implied in the Greek 𝔊, or at least are necessary for the sense.

Let it be thus, &c. 𝔊 ascribes more words to Daniel than Θ.

for he hath spoken blasphemy against Bel. Θ and Syr W give the reason, 𝔊 does not.

10. With the seventy priests of Bel cf. the four hundred of Baal in 1 Kings xviii. 22.

children. $Θ^{A}$ παιδίων, 'little children'.

the idol temple. Greek εἰδώλιον, as in 1 Esdras ii. 9; 1 Macc. i. 47; 1 Cor. viii. 10. Θ has 'the house' (τὸν οἶκον), i.e. 'temple' (see 1 Kings vi. 1; 2 Kings xix. 33) 'of Bel'. It is probable that Θ follows the original Hebr. (הַבַּיִת).

𝔊 87

11 Then the food was laid out in the presence of
the king and of Daniel, and mixed wine was
12 brought on and set out for Bel. And Daniel
said, Thou thyself seest that these things are in
13 their places, O king. Do thou therefore seal the
bolts of the temple, when it is shut. And the
utterance pleased the king.

14 Then Daniel ordered those with him to put
out of the temple all (the rest) and to besprinkle
the temple with wood ashes, none of them outside
the same knowing (it). And then he shut the
temple and gave orders to have it sealed with the
king's signet ring and with the signet rings of
certain priests of high rank: and this was done.
15 And it came to pass on the morrow that they
came back to the place, but the priests had, in
the meantime, entered through secret doors and
devoured all that had been placed before Bel
16 and drunk up the wine. Then Daniel said, O
priests, look at your seals, whether they remain
(intact); and do thou, O king, mark well whether
anything has happened of which thou disapprovest.
17 And they found (the state of things) as it was

Θ

So Bel's priests said, Lo, we will get us out: 11
but thou, O king, set on the meat, and mingle
the wine and set it forth, and shut the door fast,
and seal it with thine own signet; and when thou 12
comest in the morning, if thou find not that Bel
hath eaten up all, we will suffer death: or else
Daniel, that speaketh falsely against us. And 13
they little regarded it: for under the table they
had made a privy entrance, whereby they entered
in continually, and consumed those things.
And it came to pass, when they were gone 14
forth, the king set the meat before Bel. Now
Daniel had commanded his servants to bring
ashes, and they strewed all the temple *with them*
in the presence of the king alone: then went they
out, and shut the door, and sealed it with the
king's signet, and so departed. Now in the night 15
came the priests with their wives and children, as
they were wont to do, and did eat and drink up
all. In the morning betime the king arose, and 16
Daniel with him.

And the king said, Daniel, are the seals whole? 17

11–17. These verses differ in 𝔊 and Θ considerably. How can we account for this if both the Greek versions were made from one Hebrew original?

11. **the food,** lit. 'things eaten'.

mixed wine. What is meant is probably that the wine was mixed with certain aromatic spices which gave it a more pungent flavour. See Isa. v. 22; Ps. xvi. 2. This is according to common Oriental custom; many, however, think that the allusion is to the Greek and Roman practice of diluting wine by water. See Isa. i. 22.

signet, i. e. *δακτυλίῳ*, 'finger-ring signet'. Θ^{A} *δακτύλῳ*, 'finger'.

13. **bolts.** The Greek word (*κλεῖδας*) means primarily 'keys'; then, as here, 'bolts', 'locks'.

they entered in, &c. Cf. 1 Kings xviii. 25, 'put no fire under.' Such deceptions were, according to Chrysostom, common in heathen temples (*Hom. in Petrum et Helicum*, Opp. (Ben. ed.), vol. ii, p. 880. Syr W adds to *v.* 13 in Θ, 'and carried away what remained.'

14. **besprinkle.** 𝔊 *καταστῆσαι*, a Hebraism (שִׂים); Θ^{B} and Syr H[mg] *κατέσησαν*, 'they shook through a sieve' (Θ^{A} *κατέσεισαν*, 'they shook'), implying וַיְנַפּוּ (= וַיְנִיפוּ)—this yields no sense. Read, with Θ 34 49 *κατέστρωσαν*, representing the Hebr. וַיְזָרוּ, which might easily have been misread as either of the above Hebrew words.

temple. The Greek word *ναός* is used in 𝔊 and N.T. for the temple building proper in distinction from the temple and its enclosures (*ἱερόν*).

wood ashes. The word *σποδός* in 𝔊 denotes specially wood ashes. *τέφρα* is the word used in Θ. See Tobit vi. 17, viii. 22.

sealed. 𝔊 *σφραγισάμενος*. Read *κλείσας*; the sealing followed the shutting. The Hebr. verb סָתַם ('shut') could easily be read חָתַם ('seal'). We have in this confusion, as well as in that in the verbs noticed above, strong evidence of a Hebrew (not an Aramaic) original. The temple door was sealed, according to Θ, with the signet ring of the king. Syr W adds, 'and with Daniel's signet ring'; 𝔊 adds, 'and with the signet ring of certain priests of high rank' (see Dan. vi. 17).

set the meat before Bel (Θ). Syr W + 'and filled the vessels with wine according to the custom'; probably this should be added.

15. Verse 15*b* in 𝔊 corresponds to *v.* 15 in Θ, 15*a* answering to 16 in Θ.

it came to pass . . . that. Note the Hebraism. In good Greek, as in English, the usual expression would be, 'On the morrow they came back.' Θ avoids the Hebraism.

secret doors. *ψευδοθυρίδων*, lit. 'false doors'. See *v.* 21.

16 foll. In Θ it is the king who takes the initiative—rises early, asks about the seals. In 𝔊 it is Daniel that speaks, the priests (not Daniel) testing the seals.

16. **remain.** The Greek word (*μένουσιν*) perhaps to be understood absolutely 'remain *as they were*', the Hebr. for which would probably be יַעַמְדוּ; but it is most likely that the original Hebr. word was יִשְׁלְמוּ (are intact, literally 'complete'), misread as above. Θ (*σῷοι* in *v.* 17) favours this.

17. This verse in 𝔊 has been variously rendered: 'they found that the seal had lasted' (lit. 'was'), and 'they found how the seal *really* was'. But we should have expected 'seals'—the plural—as in *v.* 16, and as in Θ, *v.* 17. Fritzsche is probably right, therefore, in regarding (ἡ) *σφραγίς* as an interpolation. In the second part of the verse

𝔊 87

(the day before); so they cast away the seals.
18 But on opening the door they saw that what had
been set out for Bel had been consumed and that
the tables were empty. The king accordingly
rejoiced, and said to Daniel, Great is Bel, and
19 with him is no deception. And Daniel laughed
heartily and said to the king, Come, see the
deception of the priests. Then Daniel said, O
king, whose footprints are these?
20 And the king said, (Those) of men, women,
21 and children. Then he went to the house in
which the priests resided, and found Bel's food
together with the wine. And Daniel showed
the king the secret doors through which the
priests entered for the purpose of consuming
22 what had been set before Bel. The king therefore led them out of Bel's temple and delivered
them up to Daniel; and what had been provided
by purchase for him he gave to Daniel, but Bel
he destroyed.

Θ

And he said, Yea, O king, they be whole. And 18
as soon as he had opened the door, the king
looked upon the table, and cried with a loud
voice, Great art thou, O Bel, and with thee is no
deceit at all. Then laughed Daniel, and held 19
the king that he should not go in, and said,
Behold now the pavement, and mark well whose
footsteps are these.

And the king said, I see the footsteps of men, 20
women, and children. And then the king was 21
angry, and took the priests with their wives and
children, who showed him the privy doors, where
they came in, and consumed such things as were
upon the table. Therefore the king slew them, 22
and delivered Bel into Daniel's power, who overthrew him and his temple.

The Dragon Story, *vv.* 23–41.

𝔊 87

23 Now there was a dragon in the same place,
24 and the Babylonians worshipped (it). And the

Θ

And in that same place there was a great 23
dragon, which they of Babylon worshipped.

we are to read 'seals' (plural). Translate then as above. Syr H has 'that the seal remained', reading, perhaps, ὡς ἔμενεν.

And the king. So Θ^{AQ} Syr W Fritzsche. But Θ^{B} (Swete) om. ὁ βασιλεύς.

18. Note the double Hebraism with which Θ begins *v.* 18, though 𝔊 has the regular classical construction. This suggests that Θ corrects 𝔊 from the Hebrew original. See Introd. § 3, 2 (1).

door. Greek has 'doors', plural, a literal rendering of the Hebr. דְּלָתַיִם, a two-leaved door. For such a door see *H. D. B.* iv. 700 *b*. Another confirmation of a Hebrew, not an Aramaic, original. Syr W has the singular (*tar'a*), as has Θ in *v.* 14.

tables. So 𝔊: Θ 'table'. After the latter word Θ needs, and seems to have had, words similar to if not identical with those in 𝔊. Probably we should restore according to Syr W, which usually follows Θ closely: (after 'door') 'the king looking upon the table and seeing that what had been set for Bel had been consumed, cried out,' &c.

with thee is no deceit at all. This last clause of *v.* 18 in Θ is a literal translation of a Hebraism absent from 𝔊: 'there is no deception, . . . not one', אֵין מִרְמָה . . . אֵין אַחַת. Cf. Prov. xiv. 3.

19. That Daniel laughed *heartily* (σφόδρα) is stated in 𝔊, not in Θ. It represents probably the Hebrew absolute infinitive. On the other hand, that Daniel held back the king from looking in appears in Θ, not in 𝔊.

see the deception of the priests. Referring probably to the king's acclamation (*v.* 18), 'there is no deception in him' (Bel). His priests deceive if *he* does not, and indeed cannot.

and said. Θ^{B} Syr W 𝔊; > Θ^{A}.

whose. Θ^{Q} om. τινος; render then, 'find out these footprints.' Θ^{Qmg}, Θ^{B}, 𝔊, Syr W +. The sense requires it.

20. The ὁρῶ ('I see') of Θ translates probably the Hebr. הִנֵּה. It is not represented in 𝔊.

21. Θ and Syr W omit the words in 𝔊 in the beginning of *v.* 21, but they are necessary for the sense and should probably be restored. Verse 21 in Θ would in that case read: 'Then the king, becoming angry, went to the house in which the priests resided, and found Bel's food together with the wine. He thereupon seized the priests and their wives and children, so that (καί) they showed,' &c.

found. Syr H ευρον ('they found').

secret doors. In 𝔊 the doors are lit. 'false doors' (ψευδοθύρια); see on *v.* 15. In Θ the doors are literally hidden' (κρυπτάς).

22. **Bel's temple.** τὸ Βήλιον = 'the temple of Bel' only here; but cf. Πυθεῖον. See the reference in Fritzsche.

delivered them (𝔊). 𝔊 says the king delivered up the priests to Daniel; Θ and Syr W say he delivered up Bel. Syr W Arab., translating the Greek ἔκδοτον of Θ as 'gift', render 'gave Bel as a gift to Daniel'. 𝔊 adds that what had been expended on Bel (the residue) was also delivered up to Daniel.

destroyed, lit. 'overthrew' (κατέστρεψεν).

23. **dragon,** or 'serpent'. See Introduction, § 2, 2. Θ Syr W have 'great dragon'.

in the same place. Θ^{B} om., reading simply, 'and there was a great dragon.' εν τω τοπω Θ^{AQ}: εν αυτω τω τοπω Θ^{Qmg}.

worshipped. See on *v.* 4.

it. Θ Syr H Syr W; > 𝔊.

𝔊 87

king said to Daniel, Thou wilt not, wilt thou, say
of this also that it is bronze? Lo, he liveth,
eateth, and drinketh: do homage to him.

26 But Daniel said, Give me the power and I will
destroy the dragon without sword or staff. So
the king conceded this to him, and said, It is
27 granted thee. Then Daniel took thirty minas of
pitch, fat, and hair, and boiled them together,
and made a cake (out of them) and threw (it)
into the dragon's mouth; and after it had eaten
(the cake) it burst asunder. And he showed it
to the king, saying, Is it not the case that ye
worship these (fragments)?
28 Then there assembled against **the king** all the
inhabitants of the country, and they said, The
king has become a Jew; Bel he has overthrown
and slain the dragon.

30 And when the king saw that the mob from
the country was gathered against him he called
his companions, and said, I give (up) Daniel to
be destroyed.
31 Now there was a den in which seven lions
were kept to which those who plotted against the
king used to be delivered up, two bodies of

Θ

And the king said unto Daniel, Wilt thou also 24
say that this is of brass? lo, he liveth, and eateth
and drinketh: thou canst not say that he is no
living God: therefore worship him. Then said 25
Daniel, I will worship the Lord my God: for he
is a living God.
But give me leave, O king, and I shall slay 26
this dragon without sword or staff. The king
said, I give thee leave. Then Daniel took pitch, 27
and fat, and hair, and did seethe them together,
and made lumps thereof: this he put in the
dragon's mouth, so the dragon did eat and burst
in sunder: and *Daniel* said, Lo, these are the gods
ye worship.

When they of Babylon heard that, they took 28
great indignation, and conspired against the king,
saying, The king is become a Jew, and he hath
pulled down Bel, and slain the dragon, and put
the priests to the sword. So they came to the 29
king, and said, Deliver us Daniel, or else we will
destroy thee and thine house. Now when the 30
king saw that they pressed him sore, being constrained, the king delivered Daniel unto them:
who cast him into the lions' den: where he was 31
six days. And in the den there were seven lions, 32
and they had given them every day two carcases,

24. **Daniel.** + *μη και τουτον ερεις οτι χαλκους εστιν· ιδου ζη και εσθιει και πινει* (this is translated in the R.V. (Θ) above; Θ^B (Swete) and Vulg. om.) $\Theta^{B\ a\ b\ mg\ AQ}$. + *μη εις . . . χαλκ. εστιν ιδου . . . και πεινει* Δ.

brass (Θ). See *v.* 7, and render 'bronze'.

do homage. The same verb (*προσκυνέω*) occurs in *v.* 4. It is the one used in 𝔊 to translate the Hebr. הִשְׁתַּחֲוָה. It represents סגד in the Aramaic parts of Daniel.

25. Verse 25 of Θ has no counterpart in 𝔊. See Deut. vi. 13; Matt. iv. 10; and cf. Dan. vi. 20, 26; 1 Thess. ii. 9.

26. **power** (𝔊); **leave** (Θ). The Greek word (*ἐξουσία*) denotes delegated authority.

sword. The word in 𝔊 denotes strictly iron; then an iron weapon. 𝔊 uses it in Job v. 20 for חֶרֶב (sword). Cf. a similar use of the Lat. *ferrum*. Θ has *μάχαιρα*.

27. **thirty minas.** The weight is not given in Θ. The mina (Greek *μνᾶ*, Hebr. מָנֶה) is a Babylonian weight adopted after the exile by the Hebrews. The heavy mina weighed 1·636 lb. avoir., the light mina half this. See 1 Macc. xiv. 24.

together. *ἐπὶ τὸ αὐτό* = the Hebr. יַחְדָּו. See Exod. xxvi. 9.

a cake (𝔊). *μάζα* usually = 'a barley-cake'; cf. *ἄρτος*, 'a wheaten cake'. Θ Syr H have the plural. Syr W has a transliterated form of the Greek *σφαίρας* (cf. 'sphere'), i.e. 'round things', 'balls', 'pills'. The R.V. renders 'lumps', following the Vulg. *massas*.

dragon's mouth. + 'and the dragon swallowed them' (to complete the sense) Syr W. Perhaps it is original and should be restored.

and after . . . asunder. + 'so that it died' Syr W.

these (fragments). In 𝔊 *ταῦτα* has a touch of irony, 'these bits!' The words in Θ should be rendered, 'see what things ye worship!' (lit. 'See the objects of your worship', *σεβάσματα*). See Acts xvii. 23. Θ^A, for *ιδετε* in $𝔊^B$, has *ιδου δη*.

28 foll. differ much in 𝔊 and Θ. Verse 29 of Θ is wholly lacking in 𝔊.

28. **against the king.** 𝔊 reads 'against Daniel' (*τὸν Δανιήλ*), but the sense requires *τὸν βασιλέα* as in Θ.

a Jew. *περι του βασιλεως λεγουσι ως γεγονεν Ιουδαιος* Syr H^{mg}. Grotius omits the article before *βασιλεύς*, and translates Θ, 'a Jew has become a king,' which is against the context.

has overthrown. The verb used in *v.* 22, often rendered 'destroy'. Θ^B has a different verb here (*κατέσπασεν* = 'pulled down'). But Θ^A reads as 𝔊 (*κατέστρεψεν*).

29. Lacking in 𝔊.

30. This verse is fuller than the corresponding verse of Θ, the latter giving what appears to be a kind of summary. Verses 31 foll. in 𝔊 correspond in matter to *vv.* 32 and 31 in Θ.

31, 32. **den.** The Greek word *λάκκος* (cf. the English 'lake') = a water-pond, a reservoir, then a pit or dungeon, as in Dan. vi. 8, &c., where it translates the Hebr. and Aram. גֹּב. Lions were kept in such places for the chase. See Bevan on Dan. vi. Fritzsche holds that the den in Dan. vi. 8, &c., is a mere cistern, whereas here it is a proper vivarium into which people looked from above. But in regard to Dan. vi. 8, &c., he is hardly right.

𝕲 87

persons condemned to death being provided for
32 them daily (as food). So the crowds cast Daniel
into that den that he might be devoured and
find no burial. And Daniel was in the lions'
33 den six days. Now it happened on the sixth
day that Habakkuk had wheaten loaves crumbled
in a bowl, cooked, and an earthen jar of mixed
wine, and that he was proceeding into the field
34 to the reapers. Then the angel of the Lord
spake to Habakkuk, saying, Thus says the Lord
God to thee: The dinner which thou holdest,
take it away to Daniel to the lions' den in
Babylon.

35 But Habakkuk said, O Lord God, I have not
seen Babylon and the den—I do not know where
36 (it) is. Then the angel of the Lord laid hold of
Habakkuk by the hair of his head and set him
37 over the den in Babylon. And Habakkuk said
to Daniel, Arise, and eat the dinner which the
38 Lord God has sent thee. Then said Daniel,
(Yea), for the Lord God who forsakes not those
who love Him has remembered me.

39 So Daniel ate; and the angel of the Lord set
Habakkuk down (in the place) whence he had

Θ

and two sheep: which then were not given to
them, to the intent that they might devour
Daniel.

Now there was in Jewry the prophet Habak- 33
kuk, who had made pottage, and had broken
bread into a bowl, and was going into the field,
for to bring it to the reapers. But the angel of 34
the Lord said unto Habakkuk, Go carry the
dinner that thou hast into Babylon unto Daniel,
in the lions' den.

And Habakkuk said, Lord, I never saw Baby- 35
lon; neither do I know where the den is. Then 36
the angel of the Lord took him by the crown,
and lifted him up by the hair of his head, and
with the blast of his breath set him in Babylon
over the den. And Habakkuk cried, saying, O 37
Daniel, Daniel, take the dinner which God hath
sent thee. And Daniel said, Thou hast remem- 38
bered me, O God: neither hast thou forsaken
them that love thee.

So Daniel arose, and did eat: and the angel of 39
God set Habakkuk in his own place again imme-

(two) bodies. *σώματα*: not necessarily the bodies of dead persons. It = bodies of living or dead persons; persons, human beings. Here it = criminals condemned to death. In Gen. xxxvi. 6 (𝕲), Tobit x. 10, Rev. xviii. 15, and Polyb. xii. 16. 5, *σῶμα* = a slave. 'Two carcases', R.V. of Θ, should be 'two human bodies' or 'two persons'. The addition in Θ and Syr W to *v.* 32 (𝕲 31), 'which then,' &c., was suggested by Dan. iii. 19.

32. **the crowds** (𝕲). > Θ^{AB} Syr W in *v.* 31.

that he might be devoured. The reason is given in 𝕲 only. The ancients dreaded non-burial as a dire calamity, no doubt for superstitious reasons. See Century Bible on Psalm lxxix. 3.

six days. Daniel was in the den six days (so 𝕲, *v.* 32, Θ, *v.* 31). According to *v.* 33 (𝕲) it was on the sixth day that Daniel was miraculously fed. Θ, *v.* 40, says he was delivered on the seventh day.

33–39. The miraculous incident in which the prophet Habakkuk plays so prominent a part has no vital connexion with the rest of the narrative, and is certainly a late interpolation. The legend belongs to an age when the heroes of the past, such as Daniel, Habakkuk, were becoming more and more idealized.

33. 𝕲 alone gives the time—the sixth day—and also the earthen jar and the mixed wine (see on *v.* 11); the place in Judaea (R.V. 'Jewry') is given by Θ and Syr W only. Θ and Syr W speak of Habakkuk 'the prophet'; not so 𝕲. The Greek form of the name, Ἀμβακούμ, is due to the change of the first of two 'b's' for euphony ('mb' for 'bb') and the dissimilation of the final 'k' to 'm'. See König, ii. 465 and 473.

34. **the angel**, &c. The definite article rightly prefixed, though it is absent from the Greek (𝕲 and Θ). It is really a Hebraism, cf. מַלְאַךְ יְהוָה, the article in a construct noun being unnecessary in Hebrew, as in Welsh. See Introduction, § 4, (*b*) 4.

The dinner. The Greek *ἄριστον* denotes more commonly the mid-day (dinner) than the morning meal (breakfast), but it is not necessarily either. See Susanna, *v.* 13, where the R. V. renders *ἀρίστου ὥρα* as 'dinner time'.

35. **den.** After *λάκκον* in Θ^{B}, Θ^{C} adds *τῶν λεόντων*: cf. *v.* 34 (𝕲 and Θ).

is. Θ^{A}; > Θ^{B}. So R.V. Syr W has 'and the den I do not know'.

36. The verb *ἐπιλαμβάνομαι* takes after it two genitives in both versions, an unusual but not unprecedented construction. According to 𝕲 the angel laid hold of the hair of the prophet's head; Θ says it was of the crown (*κορυφή*) of his head that the angel laid hold, though he was lifted up by his hair.

the angel of the Lord. Θ^{A} omits *Κυρίου*: the article before *ἄγγελος* supports this. See on *v.* 34.

with the blast of his breath. Only in Θ. Render 'with the swiftness of wind', omitting *αὐτοῦ* (dittograph). Syr W and Midrash *Bereshith Rabba*, 'by the might of the Holy Spirit'; Jer. Vulg. *in impetu spiritus sui* ('by the force of His spirit'), Douay version. See Dan. ix. 21; Ezek. viii. 3. In one instant Habakkuk is transferred from Palestine to Babylon, and in another he is brought back.

37. **Habakkuk.** Syr W. Ἀμβακούμ 𝕲 Θ^{B} (see on *vv.* 1, 33). Ἀμβακούκ Θ^{Δ}. Θ^{A} omits Ἀμβακούμ, reading 'and he cried out'.

Arise and. *ἀναστάς*, &c., a Hebraism, though found in Syr W. Cf. קום followed by another verb = 'set about'. See Introd. §§ 4, (*b*) 4, and cf. Century Bible, *Ezra, Nehemiah, Esther*, p. 145.

38. In 𝕲 Daniel speaks of God in the 3rd person; in Θ he addresses God.

who forsakes not. *ἐγκαταλείπων* 𝕲: *ἐγκατέλειπες* Θ: *ἐγκαταλιπών* Syr H. Syr W gives 3rd person as 𝕲.

39. Note the Hebraism in Θ, *ἀναστάς*; so Syr W. See on *v.* 37 (𝕲).

the angel of the Lord. Θ changes 'Lord' to 'God'. Syr W has simply 'an angel'.

in his own place (Θ). For *εἰς* (Θ^{B}), $\Theta^{A\Omega}$ reads *ἐπί*.

𝔊 87

taken him on the same day. But the Lord God
40 remembered Daniel. (Then) the king after these
things went forth bewailing Daniel; and as he
stooped to pry into the den he saw him sitting
41 (there). So the king cried out and said, Great
is the Lord God, and there is no other (god)
42 besides Him. And the king led Daniel out of
the den, and those who would have brought
about his destruction he cast into the den in the
presence of Daniel, and they were devoured.

Θ

diately. Upon the seventh day the king came to 40
bewail Daniel: and when he came to the den, he
looked in, and, behold, Daniel was sitting. Then 41
cried the king with a loud voice, saying, Great
art thou, O Lord, thou God of Daniel, and there
is none other beside thee. And he drew him out, 42
and cast those that were the cause of his destruction into the den: and they were devoured in
a moment before his face.

on the same day (τῇ αὐτῇ ἡμέρᾳ 𝔊); **immediately** (παραχρῆμα Θ): 'in that hour' = 'immediately' Syr W. The bracketed words in the rendering of 𝔊 above occur in Syr W, which usually follows 𝔊.

But the Lord God remembered Daniel. This last clause in 𝔊 is absent from Θ.

40. **after these things** in 𝔊 corresponds to 'on the seventh day' in Θ.

41. In 𝔊 the king speaks of God in the third person; in Θ he addresses God. See on *v.* 38. Syr W omits last clause of verse ('there is no other').

the king (Θ^{Q}). Θ^{B} om. ὁ βασιλεύς.

and there is none other beside thee. > και ουκ εστιν πλην σου αλλος Θ^{AQ}. In 𝔊 (followed by Syr H) these words are appended: Δανιηλ κατα τους ό: in Θ^{BQ} Δανιηλ: in Θ^{A} τελος Δαν. προφητου.

THE ADDITIONS TO ESTHER

INTRODUCTION

§ 1. Character of the Additions.

The Additions to Esther consist of six passages (containing 107 verses not in the Hebrew text), inserted in the LXX text by way of amplification of subjects referred to in the canonical chapters.

It cannot be said that these Additions, which are imaginative reconstructions of a forgotten past, are of great interest or importance. Perhaps as much as two centuries separate their date from that of the canonical portions of Esther, and they emanate from a different centre of Jewish life and thought, which possessed no independent sources of historical information.

Any interest, therefore, that these fragments possess lies not in their power to enlarge our knowledge of the story of Esther, but in the reflection they offer of the religious development of the circle in which they originated.

If we are to attach any weight to the postscript found in the LXX (Esther xi. 1)—and Ryssel's reason for rejecting its witness is not sufficient—the translation of canonical Esther dates from not later than 114 B.C.; but it seems unlikely that the Additions were incorporated with the translated portions until after this postscript was appended. The Additions may not all be the work of one author, but they are not translations, and Greek was their original language.[1] It is probable that the Additions, with their slightly Egyptian flavour (cf. the use of ἀδελφός in D 9, φίλοι in E 5, the application of the word 'Macedonian' to Haman in E 10, and ἐκτιθέναι in E 19), were composed in Egypt, where the veneration for the canonical book was naturally not so high as in Palestine, rather than in Palestine by Egyptian Jews temporarily residing there.[2]

But were the Additions made immediately upon the reception of the translation of Esther in Egypt, or only after some time had passed, and interest in the book had been awakened, and a desire aroused in the minds of patriotic Jews to hear the story of Esther in greater detail?

The latter hypothesis seems the more probable. Not only is time required for the creative activity of the imagination to get to work; but the postscript, which with its explicit reference to the *translation* of Esther must have been appended immediately on the introduction of the translation into Egypt, would surely have been worded differently, if the Additions had been already incorporated.

The date of the Additions, therefore, may be placed in the earlier part of the first century, and they may be regarded as contemporaneous with the Book of Wisdom. They can be referred to Maccabean times (as e.g. by Jacob and V. Ryssel) only by a complete rejection of the witness of the postscript.

Wisdom is the work of an Alexandrian Jew keenly distressed by Egyptian idolatry and by the growing laxity and indifference to the national religion on the part of a large number of the Jews resident in Egypt. The writer of Wisdom represents that more conservative section of the Egyptian Jews in whom the forces of reaction were at work, and who became the more ardently patriotic in proportion as they saw the traditions of their religion neglected.

The Additions to Esther may be accounted for in a similar way. The relations between the domiciled Jews of the Diaspora and the natives of the country were at times far from cordial, and in periods of trial and oppression, when the Jews were driven in upon themselves, it was natural for them to take refuge in the study of their sacred books, and of those especially, such as Esther, which told of the subjection of the heathen to the chosen people. It was only natural that elaborations of these favourite narratives should spring up, and in course of time take their place as authentic parts of the original works.

The Additions are free from all trace of Alexandrine doctrine, but there is no reason to suppose

[1] Cf. Ryssel, in *Kautzsch*, i. p. 196; André, *Les Apocryphes de l'A. T.* pp. 203, 204.

[2] Cf. Jacob, *ZATW*, x, 1890, pp. 274–90; and Jellinek, *Beth-ha-Midrash*, v, p. viii. The 'Additions' to Esther sprang out of the imagination of an Alexandrian Jew, and hence their original language was Greek.

that every Jew residing in Egypt surrendered to the influence of the philosophic atmosphere of Alexandria. The practical purpose with which the Additions were composed would cause their author to eschew the introduction of all foreign elements. His hearers would be of the simpler type, not versed in speculation, but familiar only with the religious ideas of the O. T.; his object would be rather to confirm them in the old than to provide a meeting-place for the old with the new. Accordingly, the Additions might be expected to be strictly orthodox and conservative in tone; and this is exactly what we find. The spirit of simple prayer breathes in them, and trust in God and remembrance of God's mercies to Israel are especially emphasized.

The object of the author is purely practical, and speculative questions are altogether beyond his range. It has been thought that the object of the Additions was 'to remove the uneasiness arising from the secular tone of the original story'.[1] This is a proposition very difficult to accept, suggesting as it does a deliberate effort to correct the canonical book, and thereby an implied censure on its character. The difference between the tone of the canonical book and the additions can be less invidiously accounted for, on the supposition that the latter came into existence to meet an historical need, and that floating legendary material was drawn upon for the purpose of consoling and strengthening a simple-minded people in adversity. If it is true that the Additions have introduced the religious note, it cannot be said that they have a materially higher tone. Hatred of the heathen and thirst for revenge appear in undiminished vehemence.

It has been assumed so far that we are justified in speaking of these six passages as additions, which first took shape in Greek. It is true that they are not all homogeneous, and that some of them are more Hebraic in character than others. But of two (Adds. B and E) it may be said[2] that any re-translation of these rhetorical and florid pieces into Hebrew would be impossible, while of the rest it is enough to say that the Hebraisms they contain are fully accounted for by the fact that the Jew who composed them could not divest himself altogether of the idioms of his people.[3] A somewhat paradoxical contention has been put forward by Langen, Kaulen, and Scholz, who are concerned to prove the authenticity of the Additions, the effect of which would be to show that the LXX form of Esther is the original, and the Hebrew only an abbreviated edition of the book. This hypothesis rests on the existence of various Midrashic compilations,[4] and especially of an Aramaic piece known as 'Mordecai's Dream', containing the Dream and the Prayer of Mordecai and the Prayer of Esther, of which the so-called Additions to Esther are *ex hypothesi* the Greek form.

But there is much more reason to regard these diffuse Aramaic fragments as being indirectly based on the LXX Additions than vice versa;[5] and, further, inasmuch as not more than one of these pieces can be proved to have existed as early as even the middle of the fourth century, they are quite valueless as proofs of a Hebrew original earlier than that known to St. Jerome.

Almost equally baseless is the argument that the older and fuller Hebrew text was deliberately expurgated of the name of God, in order that it might not suffer dishonour when the Esther-roll was read during the course of the rather secular festival of Purim. Such editing of the book is far more difficult to credit than the hypothesis of subsequent additions.

One of the surest arguments against the original integrity of the book in its LXX form lies in the many discrepancies between the canonical Esther and the so-called Additions.[6] Some of these may be noted here:—

(1) A 2. Mordecai is represented as holding a high position at court in the second year of Artaxerxes; but Esther ii. 16 speaks of the seventh year.

(2) A 13. Mordecai himself informs the king of the conspiracy of the eunuchs; but Esther ii. 21–23 says that Esther told the king in Mordecai's name.

(3) A 16. Mordecai is rewarded for his services, but Esther vi. 3, 4 shows that Mordecai had been forgotten.

(4) A 17. The reason for Haman's grudge against Mordecai is that Mordecai had caused the death of the eunuchs, but in Esther iii. 5 it is that Mordecai will not bow before Haman.

(5) C 26, 27. Esther protests her hatred of the position of queen to an uncircumcised alien. But the Hebrew makes no such suggestion.

(6) E 10. Haman is called a Macedonian, but in Esther iii. 1 his father's name is Persian.

[1] Streane, *Esther*, p. xxix.

[2] Cf. Fuller, p. 365, note 4.

[3] Cf. S. I. Fränkel, *Hagiographa posteriora . . . e textu Graeco in linguam Hebraicam convertit*, &c., 1830; André, op. cit. pp. 203, 204; Jellinek, *Beth-ha-Midrash*, v, p. viii.

[4] e.g. a treatise on Esther in the *Babylonian Talmud*, Megillah 10^b ff.; in the *Pirke Rabbi Eliezer*, ch. 49 f.; in Josippon, cent. x; *Midrash Esther Rabba*, cent. xi or xii. For an exhaustive list see Ryssel, p. 195; cf. André, p. 198; Fuller, Apocr. of O.T., p. 363.

[5] Bissell, p. 202.

[6] Cf. André, pp. 202, 203.

(7) E 22. The Persians as well as the Jews are required to keep the feast of Purim; but in Esther ix. 20–28 the Jews alone are charged to observe it.

The Additions are six in number, distinguished by Dr. Swete in his edition of the O. T. in Greek by the letters A to F in accordance with a suggestion made by the late Prof. Hort. As they stand in A.V. and R.V., they are practically unintelligible.[1] Jerome's relegation of the Additions to an appendix, in which their relation to the canonical chapters was altogether obscured, is responsible for this.

Not finding them in the Hebrew, he desired in his translation to mark the distinction between them and the authentic portions; and this arrangement was carried over into A.V. and R.V.[2]

Their contents are as follows:—

A. Mordecai's Dream, and the conspiracy of the two eunuchs (a double of Esther ii. 21–23). Precedes Esther i. 1.

B. The king's Edict commanding the destruction of the Jews. Follows Esther iii. 13, and expands iii. 8–13.

C. Prayer of Mordecai, and Prayer of Esther. Follows Esther iv. 17.

D. Esther's appearance before the king. Follows D, and is an amplification of Esther v. 1, 2.

E. The king's second Edict in favour of the Jews. Follows Esther viii. 12.

F. Interpretation of Mordecai's Dream. Follows Esther x. 3.

§ 2. MANUSCRIPTS.

The current and unrevised text of the third century is more or less closely represented by the uncials:

B. Vaticanus, cent. iv.

A. Alexandrinus, cent. v.

ℵ. Sinaiticus, cent. iv.

N. Basilio-Vaticanus, cent. viii–ix; and by many cursives, of which the most important are (as numbered by Holmes and Parsons, *Vet. Test. Graecum cum var. lect.*, Oxford, 1798–1827)—

55. Rome (Vat. Reg. Gr. I).

108. Rome (Vat. Gr. 330), containing two recensions, the first of which, known as 108 *a*, represents the unrevised text.

249. Rome (Vat. Pius I).

Other nearly allied cursives are—

52. Florence (Laur. Acq. 44).

64. Paris (Nat. Reg. Gr. 2).

243. Venice (St. Mark's, cod. 16), with which the Aldine edition is connected.

248. Rome (Vat. Gr. 346), of which the Polyglot of Alcala (Complutensian, 1514) is a reproduction.

The recension made by Origen in the third century is represented by the cursive numbered 93, which contains two recensions of Esther, that known as 93 *b* having the critical signs employed by Origen.

The readings of 93 *b* correspond very closely with the corrections inserted in Cod. Sinaiticus by the first of three seventh-century hands, known as $ℵ^{c.a}$, who acknowledges his indebtedness to the work of Origen.[3]

The Hesychian, or Egyptian, recension, of the fourth century, is represented by 44, 68, 71, 74, 76, 106, 107, 120, 236.

The Lucianic, or Antiochian, recension, of about A.D. 300, is represented by 19, 93 *a*, 108 *b*. P. de Lagarde,[4] who designates these MSS. respectively by the letters h_1 m_1 d_1, has reconstructed the Lucianic text, and placed it in parallel columns with that of the uncials. There is a very wide difference between the two types of text, but the Lucianic (known by Lagarde as *a*) contains all the six longer additions.

Certain resemblances between the details in Josephus' account and those in the Lucianic text led Langen[5] to argue that Josephus had in his hands the so-called Lucianic recension, and that therefore this text is not a recension of the third or fourth century, but an independent translation

[1] Cf. Swete, *Intr. to O. T. in Greek*, p. 257.
[2] Cf. Jer., *Prol. in Esth.* ch. x, ed. Vallarsi, ix, p. 1581.
[3] Swete, *Intr. to O. T. in Greek*, p. 131, and *O. T. in Greek*, ii, p. 780.
[4] *Lib. V. T. Can. Gr.* i, 1883.
[5] *Tüb. Theol. Quart.* 1860, pp. 244 ff.

from the Hebrew. But there are too many correspondences between the two types of text, especially in the Additions, for this theory to be possible.[1]

§ 3. The Ancient Versions.

No Syriac version of Esther is known ; the book is altogether absent from the Nestorian MSS.[2] Paton[3] writes that the Coptic versions, which would presumably give a Hesychian type of text, have never been published, while the Ethiopic version, fourteen MSS. of which are known to contain the Book of Esther, is equally inaccessible. An Armenian version of Esther also exists, but in too corrupt a form to be of any service.

The only ancient versions extant and available are the Old Latin and the Vulgate.

(1) The Old Latin belongs to the middle of the second century, and is a useful witness to the LXX text as it existed before the time of the three recensions. It is the work of one who, though not a good Greek scholar, made a faithful effort to translate the Greek original, and where he failed to understand the Greek, as in the case of the two edicts, reproduced it word for word in Latin. This makes it possible in many cases to reconstruct with comparative certainty the Greek text which lay in front of him.[4] The Old Latin version contained all the six Additions (except A 12–17), together with certain others peculiar to it, e.g. after B 7, in C 14, a very long addition in C 16, after C 30, in D 7. On the other hand it omits A 12–17, and (in Cod. Pechianus) C 17–23.

(2) The Vulgate was undertaken by St. Jerome at the request of Pope Damasus, and was produced between A.D. 390 and 405. He devoted himself particularly to the books which belonged to the Hebrew Canon, and paid less attention to those which were only known through the LXX.

In the case of Esther, he gathered all the non-Hebraic additions together, and placed them somewhat contemptuously at the end of his translation of the canonical book. In the *Prol. in Esth.* he writes : 'Quae habentur in Hebraeo, plena fide expressi. Haec autem quae sequuntur scripta repperi in editione vulgata quae Graecorum lingua et litteris continetur, et interim post finem libri hoc capitulum ferebatur, quod iuxta consuetudinem nostram obelo, id est veru, praenotavimus.'

Jerome's translation differs very largely from the Old Latin, the former being as free as the latter is slavishly literal. Very often he is content to give only the general sense of the Greek, and his work is more like an original Latin composition than a translation.[5]

§ 4. Date of the Additions.

The Additions belong to that mass of floating legendary material which in the course of years gathered around the name of Esther.

It is impossible to assign a single date to them, as they are written in different styles, and may be the work of different authors, some of the additions (e.g. A C D F) having probably grown up gradually and assumed their present shape after an existence of some years in an oral tradition.

The two edicts (B and E), on the other hand, are of a quite different character from the four already mentioned which have strong Hebraic affinities : B and E belong undoubtedly to Egypt, and their periodic style shows that they could have originated in no other way than as formal written compositions. They show considerable resemblance to 2 Macc., which clearly emanated from Egypt (cf. B 5 *πρὸς τὸ μὴ τὴν βασιλείαν εὐσταθίας τυγχάνειν* with 2 Macc. xiv. 6 *οὐκ ἐῶντες τὴν βασιλείαν εὐσταθείας τυχεῖν*) ; but although the place of origin is clear, the date (in so far as internal evidence is concerned) is in both cases equally indeterminate.

No conclusion, again, as to the lateness of A and F is to be drawn from the failure of Josephus to employ them. It is quite as likely that they did not suit his purpose as that they were absent from the MS. he employed or from all the MSS. of that period.

The present writer is not satisfied with the arguments of Jacob against the validity of the postscript in Esther xi. 1 : 'In the fourth year of the reign of Ptolemy and Cleopatra, Dositheus, who said he was a priest and a Levite, and Ptolemaeus his son, brought the Epistle of Phrurai here set forth, which they said was true, and that Lysimachus the son of Ptolemaeus, that was in Jerusalem, had interpreted it.' Jacob's objection is based on the assumed impossibility of a translation with so many clearly marked examples of Egyptian vocabulary[6] having been made in Palestine ; but he

[1] See Paton, *Esther*, pp. 37, 38 ; Fuller, p. 365 ; André, p. 207. A very full statement concerning the MSS. may be found in Paton, *Esther*, pp. 29–38.

[2] André, *Les Apocryphes*, p. 207.

[3] *Esther*, pp. 36, 37.

[4] Cf. Jacob, *Das Buch Esther*, Giessen, 1890, pp. 13–22.

[5] Cf. André, *Les Apocryphes*, p. 208.

[6] Cf. Jacob, *Das Buch Esther*, p. 51, *(ἐν)θρονίζεσθαι, ἐκτιθέναι, καταχωρίζειν, ἀρχισωματοφύλακες, διαγράφειν.*

ignores the assertion of Dositheus and Ptolemy who brought it to Egypt, that it was made by Lysimachus son of Ptolemy, whose very name proclaims him to have been connected with Egypt, even if a temporary resident at Jerusalem. The postscript may be regarded as reasonably trustworthy, and various inferences may be drawn from it.

(1) It was appended to the translation of the canonical Esther immediately on its introduction into Egypt.

(2) That date was 114 B.C.[1]

(3) The postscript refers so definitely to the *translation* of Esther, that it cannot be held to cover the Additions, which were not translations.

(4) Some time must have passed between 114 B.C., the date of the introduction of the translation into Egypt, and the incorporation therewith of unauthentic matter. Its sacredness would have protected it from formal alterations for at least a quarter of a century.

(5) The most probable date then for the incorporation of the Additions would be from about 80 B.C. onwards, the *terminus ad quem* being about A.D. 90, the date of their employment by Josephus.

If the postscript is rejected (as by Jacob followed by Ryssel), the dating of the Additions is rendered even more indefinite. Jacob can only name one certainty with regard to date derivable from the Greek form of canonical Esther, i.e. that it must have been made at some time long or short before the destruction of the Ptolemaic régime in 30 B.C.[2] He also argues that Esther must have been one of the earliest of the Old Testament books to have been translated into Greek after Kings, Chronicles, and Job, which Freudenthal has shown were translated about 150 B.C.;[3] but Jacob's argument is mere hypothesis, however reasonable. Apart from the postscript, we are left without any means of dating the Additions more closely than between about 125 B.C. and A.D. 90.

§ 5. Authorship.

The Additions are not a homogeneous whole, and are bound together by no community of style. This does not prevent them from being the work of one hand; for an even greater dissimilarity exists between the earlier and later chapters of the Book of Wisdom.

But there is no evidence of any kind to show whether the Additions were all composed at the same time, or were all intercalated at the same time. All that can be said is that the Additions originated among the Egyptian Hellenistic Jews, and that they are based on familiar legendary materials.

In view of the more Hebraic tone of A C D F and their simple narrative style, as contrasted with the Greek tone and self-conscious rhetoric of B and E, it is not unnatural to view the former as the written form of a tradition long known and finally reduced into its present shape by dint of frequent repetition, and to regard the latter as having originated with a single individual. It is hardly likely that the agent in the two cases was one and the same.

§ 6. Influence on Later Literature.

(*a*) *Jewish.* The direct influence of the Additions is to be seen in Josephus, *Ant.* xi. 6. He draws upon Adds. B C D E, following them closely and yet employing them with by no means a slavish dependence. He introduces a few details not found in the Additions, which were either his own invention or copied from embellishments in the MS. he used. He makes no reference to the Dream of Mordecai (Add. A) or its interpretation (Add. F); he alters the time of the conspiracy of the eunuchs, and relates that the services rendered by Mordecai were forgotten, whereas the Additions say that he was rewarded. Josephus gives the reason adduced in Esther iii. 5 for Haman's hatred of Mordecai, and not that given in the Additions. He introduces new features into the Prayers of Esther and Mordecai, and into the account of Esther's appearance before the king. Similarly, he deviates from the exact language of the Greek in the Royal Edicts.

But the dependence of Josephus on the Additions is in the main beyond doubt.

The so-called second Targum gives a very free reproduction of the Edict in Addition E. This Targum dates from about A. D. 800.[4]

The Prayers of Mordecai and Esther were used by Josephus ben-Gorion in his history composed about the beginning of the tenth century.[5]

From this work has been borrowed the abbreviated form of the same prayers in *Midrash Esther*

[1] Jacob, *Das Buch Esther*, p. 43.
[2] Jacob, *op. cit.* p. 52.
[3] *Op. cit.* p. 53.
[4] Targum Sheni on Esther, viii. 13, quoted by Fuller, p. 400.
[5] Ed. Breithaupt, Gotha, 1707, ii, pp. 72–84.

Rabba (cent. xi, xii), and also the Prayer of Esther in *Midrash Lekach Tob* (*c.* 1100). It is also the source of the Prayers of Esther and Mordecai which are found in an Aramaic fragment of cent. xi or xii.[1] This fragment, which was claimed by Langen[2] as a witness to a Hebrew original of the Additions, is now clearly recognized by Bissell[3] and Fuller (p. 364) as being derived, through Josephus ben-G., from the Greek Additions. Fuller quotes the Prayer of Mordecai in this version, p. 385, and that of Esther, p. 391.

(*b*) *Christian.* The Additions are occasionally mentioned in the Fathers, but they can hardly be said to have exercised any influence. Clement of Rome (ch. lv) makes a reference to the Prayer of Esther, ἠξίωσεν τὸν παντεπόπτην δεσπότην, cp. Add. D 2 ἐπικαλεσαμένη τὸν πάντων ἐπόπτην Θεόν; while Origen writes (*ad Africanum* 3): 'From the Book of Esther neither the Prayer of Mordecai nor that of Esther is accepted among the Hebrews; and similarly neither the Edict of Haman for the destruction of the Jews nor that of Mordecai.'

Nevertheless, he held these Additions 'to be fitted to edify the reader', and he regarded their absence from the Hebrew Canon as no reason for 'rejecting as spurious the copies in use in the Christian Churches', or for 'enjoining the Brotherhood to put away the sacred copies in use among them'. References to the Additions are found in Clem. Alex. *Strom.* iv. 19; Rufin. *Apol.* ii. 33; Aug. (cf. Sab. *Bibl. Sacr. lat. vers. ant.*) *Contr. Epist. ii Pelag.*, col. 428; *l. de grat. et lib. arb.*, col. 741.

§ 7. Theology of the Additions.

The theology of the Additions is strictly conservative and Palestinian in type. It stands in the same category with that of Ecclesiasticus, ch. xxxiii (xxxvi), xlii, xliii, the Prayer of Daniel (Dan. ix), and the Prayer of Judith (Judith ix).

The absence of all trace of Alexandrine doctrine can only be accounted for on the assumption that the Additions took their rise in a pious and simple-minded stratum of orthodox Egyptian Judaism, or else were based on legendary material belonging to Palestine which had nearly crystallized into the shape we know when it was carried in an oral form to Egypt. The truth probably lies somewhere between these alternatives.

The points which find illustration in the Additions are:—

God as Creator, C 3; as omniscient, C 5, 26, 27, D 2; as supreme, C 2, 4, 23, 30, E 16, 18; as the only true God, C 14; as the God of Abraham, C 8, 29, and of Israel, C 14; as having chosen Israel, C 9, 16, E 21; as the Redeemer from Egypt, C 9; His disposing Providence, D 8, E 16, F 1, 7; His readiness to hear prayer, F 6, 9; and to help the needy in trouble, C 14, 24, 30; His holiness, C 17; His righteousness, C 18; His jealousy of His honour, C 7, 8, 20, 22, 28, 29; His punishment of sin, C 17, 22, E 18; His mercy and pity, C 10.

There is no mention of the Law or of a future life; the temple and the altar are only mentioned metaphorically (D 20). There is one reference to angels (D 13).

§ 8. Bibliography.

(*a*) **The Text.**

(i) *Reproductions.*

Vaticanus (B), *V. T. e. cod. Vat.* 1209 . . . *phototyp. repraes.*, 1890.

Alexandrinus. Facsimile reproduced under the direction of Sir E. Maunde Thompson, London, 1881–1883. 3 vols.

(ii) *Editions.*

Holmes and Parsons (with variants of 12 uncials and 261 cursives), *V. T. Graecum cum variis lectionibus*, Oxford, 1798–1827. 5 vols.

O. F. Fritzsche, *Libri Apocr. V. T. Graece*, Leipzig, 1871.

Tischendorf, *V. T. Graece iuxta LXX interpretes* (ed. 7, Nestle), Leipzig, 1887.

H. B. Swete, *O.T. in Greek according to the Septuagint*, Cambridge, 1891.

J. Ussher, *De Graeca LXX interpretum versione syntagma, cum libri Estherae editione Origenica et vetere Graeca altera*, London, 1655 (from cod. 93).

O. F. Fritzsche, ΕΣΘΗΡ, *Duplicem libri textum ad opt. codd. ed.*, Zürich, 1848.

A. Scholz, *Commentar über das Buch Esther.* [Two Greek texts, in parallel columns with text of Josephus.]

P. de Lagarde, *Lib. V. T. Can. Pars Prior Graece*, Göttingen, 1883. [Two types of text.]

(*b*) **The Ancient Versions.**

(i) *The Old Latin.*

P. Sabatier, *Bibliorum Sacrorum Latinae Versiones antiquae seu Vetus Itala et caeterae . . . quae cum Vulgata*

[1] Ed. de Rossi, *Spec. var. lectt. sacri textus et Chald. Estheris additamenta*, Tüb. 1783, and Jellinek, *Beth-ha-Midrash*, v, 1873, pp. 1–8.

[2] *Deuterokanon. Stücke im Buche Esther*, Freiburg, 1862.

[3] *Apocr. O. T.* 1880, p. 202.

Latina et cum textu Graeco comparantur, 3 vols., Paris, 1751. [Based on Cod. Corbeiensis, and giving variants of Cod. Oratorius (to end of ch. 2) and Cod. Pechianus.]

Berger, *Notices et extraits des manuscrits de la Bibl. Nat. et autres bibl.* xxxiv, pt. 2, 1893 (pp. 141-52).

(ii) *The Vulgate.*

Hieronymi opp. ed. Vallarsi, vol. ix.

(*c*) Critical Inquiries.

S. I. Fränkel, *Hagiographa posteriora . . . e textu Graeco in linguam Hebraicam convertit*, &c., Leipzig, 1830.

Langen, 'Die beiden griechischen Texte des Buches Esther' (*Tübingen Theol. Quart.*, 1860, pp. 244–72).

Langen, *Die deuterokanon. Stücke im Buche Esther*, Freiburg, 1862.

F. Field, *Origenis Hexaplorum quae supersunt*, 1875, vol. i, p. 793 ff.

W. J. Deane, 'The LXX Adds. to the Hebrew text,' *Expositor*, Sept. 1884.

Kaulen, *Einleitung in das A. T.*, Freiburg, 1890.

Jacob, 'Das Buch Esther bei den LXX,' *ZATW*, x. 1890, pp. 241–98. [See also *Inauguraldissertation von B. Jacob*, Giessen, 1890.]

L. E. T. André, *Les Apocryphes de l'A. T.*, Florence, 1903.

L. B. Paton, 'A Text-Critical Apparatus to the Book of Esther,' in *O. T. and Sem. Studies in Mem. of W. M. Harper*, vol. ii, pp. 1–52, Chicago, 1908. [See also L. B. Paton, *A Critical and Exeget. Comm. on the Book of Esther*, pp. 29–47 (in Intern. Crit. Comm.), Edinburgh, 1908.]

H. B. Swete, *Introd. to O. T. in Greek*, pp. 257, 258, Cambridge, 1902.

(*d*) Chief Editions of the Additions.

Fritzsche, *Kurzgefasstes exegetisches Handbuch zu den Apokryphen des A. T.*, vol. i, pp. 67–108, Leipzig, 1851.

Bissell, *The Apocr. of the O. T.*, New York, 1880.

J. M. Fuller, in *Speaker's Commentary*, 'Apocrypha,' vol. i, pp. 361–402 (ed. Wace), London, 1888.

Ball, *The Eccles. or Deuterocanon. Books of the O. T.*, London, 1892.

Scholz, *Commentar über das Buch Esther mit seinen Zusätzen*, 1892.

V. Ryssel in Kautzsch's *Die Apokryphen und Pseudepigraphen des A. T.*, vol. i, pp. 193–212, Tübingen, 1900.

G. Jahn, *Das Buch Esther nach der LXX hergestellt*, Leiden, 1901.

A. W. Streane, *Book of Esther*, Cambridge, 1907.

THE ADDITIONS TO ESTHER

ADDITION A.

The Dream of Mordecai.

1 (xi) (2) In the second year of the reign of Artaxerxes the great king, on the first day of Nisa, Mardocheus the son of Jairus, the son of Semeias, the son of Kiseus, of the tribe of Benjamin, saw a dream.
(3) 3(4) *He was* a Jew, dwelling in the city of Susa, a great man, serving in the king's court; and he was of the captivity, which Nabuchodonosor the king of Babylon carried from Jerusalem with Jechonias, the king of Judaea.
4 (5) And this *was* his dream; and behold noise and tumult, thunderings and earthquake, confusion upon the earth.
5 (6) And, behold, two great dragons came forth, both of them ready to fight, and their cry was great.
6 (7) And at their cry every nation made itself ready for war, to make war upon a nation of righteous men.
7 (8) And behold a day of darkness and of gloom; tribulation and anguish; affliction and great confusion upon the earth.
8 (9) And the whole righteous nation was troubled, fearing the evils that threatened them, and they made ready to perish.

ADDITION A, *vv.* 1–11. *The Dream of Mordecai.* Addition A consists of 17 *vv.*, and in the LXX is placed at the beginning of the canonical Book. These *vv.* are numbered in Vulg. xi. 2–xii. 6. By an easily explained process of inversion, it follows Add. F in Vulg., which thus places the interpretation of the dream before the dream itself.

In Vulg. this Add. is separated from Esther xi. 1 by the following note: 'Hoc quoque principium erat in editione Vulgata, quod nec in Hebraeo, nec apud ullum fertur interpretum.' Josephus shows no acquaintance with any part of this Addition.

1. **In the second year.** There is a discrepancy between the dates as given in canon. Esther and in the Additions. In Esther i. 3 the king's feast occurs in the third year of his reign, and in Esther ii. 16, 19 Esther entered the palace and Mordecai sat at the gate in the seventh. But here the dream is seen in the second year. Ryssel (Kautzsch, p. 193) makes an elaborate attempt to reconcile the discordant dates, but it is better to acknowledge the difficulty than to try to explain it away.

Artaxerxes. For the identity of this king with Xerxes I (486–465 B.C.) see Paton, *Esther*, Intr., § 22. In canon. Esther LXX renders Ahasuerus by Artaxerxes, but Persian monuments make it plain that Ahasuerus represents *Khshayarsha*, the Persian form of the name Xerxes. Uncial texts of the Adds. give *Artaxerxes*, though some of the later Lucianic recensions correct to *Assuerus*.

the great king, the customary title of the Persian king. Cf. Isa. xxxvi. 4, 13. So Add. B 1, E 1, though > βασιλέως ℵ A.

first day of Nisa. Vulg. *Nisan*, the Heb. form of the Bab. *Nisannu*, which after the exile replaced the old Isr. name Abib. This month corresponds to March–April. Lucianic texts give the name according to Macedonian reckoning, 'Adar-Nisan, which is Dystrus Xanthicus.'

Mardocheus, the Gr. form of Mordecai. His genealogy is borrowed from canon. Esther ii. 5. Shimei and Kish are doubtless not his grandfather and great-grandfather, but remote ancestors belonging to the tribe of Benjamin. For Shimei cf. 2 Sam. xvi. 5 ff., and for Kish, father of Saul, cf. 1 Sam. ix. 1, xiv. 51. See Paton, *Est.* p. 167.

of the tribe of Benjamin. Mordecai was thus, as a member of the family of Saul, the hereditary enemy of Haman, who was of the house of Agag, whom Saul destroyed (1 Sam. xv).

2. **a Jew.** Mordecai, though a Benjamite, may be classed as a Jew, because during the exile men of all tribes came to be known as Judaeans. After the fall of Israel, Judah had given its name to the nation.

city of Susa. One of the three capitals of the Persian empire, on the river Choaspes, which separated the city of Susa from the fortress of Susa.

serving, see Esther ii. 19, vi. 10. Vulg. 'inter primos aulae regiae'.

3. **of the captivity**, cf. Esther ii. 6; 2 Kings xxiv. 15. He was not himself a captive, but was sprung from an exiled family.

Jechonias (Jehoiachin) was carried away in B.C. 596, and therefore it is a chronological impossibility for Mordecai to have been himself one of those deported from Judaea.

4. **his dream.** For the interpretation see Add. F.

noise and tumult. φωναὶ θορύβου A.

confusion. καὶ τάραχος ℵ[c.a] A.

5. **came forth.** προσῆλθον A.

their cry. ἐγένοντο αὐτῶν φωναὶ μεγάλαι A.

6. **made itself ready.** For a similar concourse cf. Joel iii. 2, Zech. xiv. 2.

righteous men. A conventional epithet for the people of God, cf. Wisd. x. 15, 'A holy people and a blameless seed,' and xvii. 2. The enemies of Israel were similarly ἀσεβεῖς, ἄνομοι.

7. **gloom.** Vulg. *discriminis.* For the idea cf. Joel ii. 2; Matt. xxiv. 29.

8. **that threatened them.** Gr. τὰ ἑαυτῶν κακά.

9 (10) And they cried unto God; and from their cry, as it were from a small spring, there came up a great river, *even* much water.
10 (11) A light and the sun rose, and the humble were exalted and consumed the glorious.
11 (12) And Mardocheus, having seen this dream and *observed* what God had determined to do, awoke and kept it in his heart, and sought by all means to understand it until the night.

Mordecai discovers the plot of the two eunuchs.

12(xii)(1) And Mardocheus took his rest, as was his custom, in the court with Gabatha and Tharra, the two eunuchs of the king who kept the court.
13 (2) And he heard their communings, and searched out their counsels, and learned that they were preparing to lay hands upon Artaxerxes the king; and he informed the king concerning them.
14 (3) And the king examined the two eunuchs, and they confessed *their intention* and were led forth and executed.
15 (4) And the king wrote these things for a memorial, and Mardocheus wrote concerning these things.
16 (5) And the king charged Mardocheus to serve in the court, and gave him gifts in respect of these things.
17 (6) And Haman, the son of Hamadathus, a †Bugaean†, was in honour in the king's sight, and sought to bring evil upon Mardocheus and his people because of the two eunuchs of the king.

9. **cried unto God.** The name of God is not present in canon. Esther. The Additions offer a strong contrast in this respect, 'God' and 'Lord' appearing forty-two times.

from their cry. Mingled, i.e., with their tears.

10. **light and the sun.** For these as pictures of happiness cf. Wisd. v. 6.

the humble. The Old Lat. has *humiles*, but Lucianic MSS. have οἱ ποταμοί by a copyist's error.

the glorious. The adj. is plural, but Haman is specially thought of. Cf. A 17: 'Haman . . . was in honour in the king's sight.'

11. **having seen.** ὁ ἑωρακώς ℵ A.

had determined. βουλεύεται A.

kept it. Cf. Luke ii. 19.

until the night. > Vulg. There is nothing in the Adds. to suggest that the conspiracy of the eunuchs did not follow immediately upon the dream of Mordecai. But canon. Esther places the former in the seventh year of the king's reign. The Luc. texts endeavour to harmonize the accounts by reading: 'And M. being raised from his sleep pondered what the dream might be, and his dream was hidden in his heart, and at every opportunity he was searching it out, until the day in which M. slept in the king's court.'

ADDITION A, *vv.* 12–17. *Mordecai discovers the plot of the two eunuchs.* This piece (cf. Esther ii. 21–23) which forms part of Add. A is omitted by Old Lat. Josephus depends on LXX for his account of the plot.

12. **as was his custom.** ἡσύχαζεν ℵ$^{c.a}$. Mordecai's circumstances were still humble. Cf. Esther ii. 19–21.

Gabatha. The names of the eunuchs are borrowed from Esther ii. 21, vi. 2, though the names are given by LXX only in ℵ$^{c.a\ mg}$. For *Gabatha* (Bigthan, Bigthana, Heb.) Vulg. has 'Bagatha', and Jos. Βαγάθωος.

Tharra (Teresh, Hebr.). Θάρα ℵ*, Θάρρας ℵ$^{c.a}$, Θεοδόσιτος Jos., 'Thara' Vulg.

13. **counsels**, lit. *anxieties*, concerning the success of the plot.

informed the king. In Esther ii. 22 he informed Esther.

concerning them. *Super eo* Vulg.

14. **led forth.** Complut. has the curious ἀπήγχθησαν (*were strangled*). 'iussit duci ad mortem' Vulg.

15. **for a memorial.** In the book of the chronicles of the kings of Media and Persia (Esther x. 2).

16. **charged Mardocheus to serve.** In canon. Esther no recompense is made to Mordecai. His deed is embalmed and forgotten in the royal chronicles. Cf. Esther ii. 23, vi. 2, 3. In the Adds. his reward is service in the king's court, an advancement from a merely tolerated presence there.

in respect of these things. περὶ τούτων, i.e. not on account of the eunuchs, but in return for services rendered (*pro delatione*, Vulg.).

17. **And Haman.** It is not easy to see how much is implied by *and*. The mention of Haman follows in the Adds. immediately on the discovery of the plot, and suggests that the grudge borne by Haman (who was already in high favour) against Mordecai was in some way due to the action which M. had taken and which had led to their death. Canon. Esther iii. 1, on the other hand, states that 'after these things' the king exalted Haman, as though H. received credit for the discovery of the plot. Haupt (*Purim*, p. 37) suggests that instead of telling the queen (Esther ii. 22) M. had revealed the plot to Haman, who had taken to himself the credit of saving the king. This would explain the advancement of Haman, and M.'s refusal to bow before him. But Haupt's suggestion is too subtle: the reason is probably to be found in H.'s jealousy of a successful underling, whose vigilance might one day be directed against himself.

a †Bugaean†. Undoubtedly a corrupt reading, though found also in Esther iii. 1 and ix. 10 LXX.

Whatever the epithet may mean, it is derived from the LXX rendering of Esther iii. 1 (Heb. האגגי, Vulg. 'qui erat de stirpe Agag'), which prompted its gratuitous introduction into ix. 10 LXX. It is obvious that the LXX version of Esther iii. 1 was earlier than the composition of any of the Additions, and therefore that Βουγαῖος did not originate with their author. It should be noted that in Esther ix. 24 the Heb. text is as in Esther iii. 1, but is there rendered by LXX ὁ Μακεδών (Vulg. 'stirpis Agag'): this rendering is borrowed by the author of Addition E (*v.* 10).

What then does Βουγαῖος mean? Is it a false transliteration for what should have been Ἀγαγαῖος (cp. Γωγαῖος 93 *a*), or has it a meaning of its own?

There is no reasonable ground for identifying the word with the Homeric *bully*, or *braggart* (*Il.* xiii. 824), nor can

ADDITION B.

The Letter of Artaxerxes.

1 (xiii) (1) Now the copy of the letter is as follows. The great king Artaxerxes writeth these things to the princes of one hundred and twenty-seven provinces from India to Ethiopia, and to the subordinate governors.

2 (2) Having become lord of many nations and attained dominion over the whole world, not *as though I am* elated with the presumption of power, but as one who ever rule my life with moderation and mildness, I desire to establish the lives of my subjects in a lasting tranquillity, and, making my kingdom peaceable and safe for passage to its *furthest* bounds, to restore that peace which is desired of all men.

3 (3) But having made inquiry of my advisers how this might be brought to pass, Haman, who excels in prudence among us, and is approved for his unswerving goodwill and firm faithfulness and is
4 (4) exalted to the second place in the kingdom, has shown us that among all the nations in the world there is scattered a certain evilly-disposed people, which sets itself in opposition to every nation by its laws, and which habitually neglects the ordinances of the kings, so that the consolidation of the kingdom honourably intended by us cannot be brought about.

5 (5) Having understood therefore that this nation stands alone in opposition to all men continually,

it be regarded as a Grecized form of Bagoas (Judith xii. 11). Its presence here is due to a mistake which first occurred in Esther iii. 1, either in the original transliteration from the Hebrew, or in subsequent MS. transcription. What was originally a piece of inadvertence was confirmed into an error by a copyist who did not see in the expression a reference to the predestined antipathy between Mordecai of the family of Saul, and Haman of the family of Agag (cf. 1 Sam. xv). Amalek was Israel's most ancient enemy. Γωγαῖος of 93 *a* and Μακεδών (Esther ix. 24 LXX) bring out the idea better than Βουγαῖος, even if incorrectly.

For **Haman, the son of Hamadathus**, see Paton, *Est.* p. 69.

because of the two eunuchs. Luc. texts have ὑπὲρ τοῦ λελαληκέναι αὐτὸν τῷ βασιλεῖ περὶ τῶν εὐνούχων διότι ἀνῃρέθησαν.

ADDITION B. *The Letter of Artaxerxes.* Addition B (xiii. 1–7) is preceded in Vulg. by Add. A, being separated from it by the following note: 'Hucusque prooemium. Quae sequuntur, in eo loco posita erant ubi scriptum est in uolumine *Et diripuerunt bona, uel substantias eorum*, quae in sola Vulgata editione reperimus, *Epistolae autem hoc . . .*'

The place of Add. B in LXX is between Esther iii. 13 and Esther iii. 14. Josephus (*Ant.* xi. 6. 6) has made copious use of this Add.

Its Greek provenance is betrayed by its turgid style, which is altogether foreign to other Persian decrees to be found in the Bible (Ezra i. 2–4, iv. 18–22, vi. 3–12, vii. 11–26). The same trait appears in Add. F, both these rescripts being of Graeco-Egyptian composition.

1. **The great king**, cf. A. 1. Cf. the inscription on the rock of Behistun, 'the great king, the king of kings.'

one hundred and twenty-seven provinces. This number is drawn from Esther i. 1, viii. 9, and may reasonably be regarded as symbolic and indicating ($12 \times 10 + 7$) the universal dominion of Xerxes.

If, on the other hand, it is treated as historical, we are reminded of Dan. vi. 1, which tells how Darius appointed satraps over 120 provinces, and the suggestion is that the kingdom of Xerxes was greater even than that of Darius. According to Herodotus (iii. 89) there were only twenty satrapies in the kingdom of Darius, or, according to his own inscriptions, twenty-nine; hence, *provinces* (Hebr. *medinah*) would refer to subdivisions of satrapies corresponding to racial groupings. Paton, *Est.* p. 124, mentions that in Ezra ii. 1 the 'province' means no more than Judaea, which was only a part of the great satrapy of Trans-Euphrates (Syria, Phoenicia, and Cyprus).

India. Not modern India, but its north-west portion which is watered by the Indus. For the conquest of India by Darius see Hdt. iii. 94–106.

Ethiopia. The modern Nubia. Hdt. iii. 97 relates the subjection of Ethiopia by Cambyses.

India to Ethiopia is borrowed from Esther i. 1, viii. 9 LXX (cf. Dan. iii. 1 LXX), the former representing Hebr. *Hôddû* and the latter rightly *Kush.*

2. **I desire**, lit. *I desired*, in the epistolary manner.

and, making . . . furthest bounds. > Vulg. There is a slight anacoluthon here, which is removed if for παρεξόμενος we read παρασχεῖν.

peaceable. For ἥμερον, lit. *tame*, i.e. through building cities and roads, A and many cursives read ἤρεμον.

3. **my advisers.** Cf. Esther i. 13–15.

among us, i.e. at our court.

unswerving. Reading with Complut. ἀπαραλλάκτῳ for -ως B ℵ A.

second place in the kingdom, i.e. next after the king. Cf. Dan. v. 7. But Haman is not named among the counsellors of the king in Esther i. 14. There is something to be said for Fritzsche's βασιλείων ℵ B instead of Swete's βασιλειῶν. The latter is what we should expect, but in Esther i. 10 LXX Haman is called one of the seven eunuchs that ministered to the king. However, 'the second place in the palace' is a comparatively inferior position.

4. **evilly-disposed people.** Cf. Jos. *Ant.* xi. 6. 5; Esther iii. 8.

in opposition. ἀντίθετον B, ἀντίτυπον ℵ A.

ordinances. προστάγματα B, διατάγματα B^{ab} (δια- over an erasure) ℵ A.

be brought about. κατατίθεσθαι. Fritzsche's καθίστασθαι is hardly necessary.

5. **in opposition.** ἐν ἀντιπαραγωγῇ, a military metaphor, lit. *lies in hostile formation against.* Cf. 1 Macc. xiii. 20.

observing perversely an alien manner of life in respect of its laws and being ill-affected towards our
6 (6) government, working all the damage it can that our kingdom may not attain to security, we have
decreed accordingly that they that are indicated to you in the letters of Haman, who is set over our
affairs and *is* our second father, be all with wives and children destroyed root and branch by the
sword of their enemies without pity or mercy, on the †fourteenth† *day* of the twelfth month Adar in
7 (7) the present year; that they who in days past and *even* now are malicious may in one day go down
violently into Hades, and may henceforth leave our state secure and unthreatened.

ADDITION C.

The Prayer of Mordecai.

1 (xiii) (8) And *Mardocheus* besought the Lord, calling to remembrance all the works of the Lord, and said,
2 (9) 'Lord, Lord, King that rulest over all, for in Thy power is the whole world, and there is none that
3 (10) gainsayeth Thee when Thou willest to save Israel: for Thou didst make heaven and earth, and
4 (11) every wondrous thing beneath the heaven; and Thou art Lord of all, and there is not *one* that shall
resist Thee, the Lord.
5 (12) 'Thou knowest all things; Thou knowest, Lord, that it was not in insolence or in pride or in
vainglory that I did this, *to wit*, that I did not bow before proud Haman.

observing perversely. παραλλάσσον, by a solecistic use. This seems to make ξενίζουσαν superfluous; accordingly Fritzsche suggests παραφυλάσσον, but Jos. supports the text. παράλλαξιν ℵ$^{c.a}$ A.

manner . . . laws, i. e. the Mosaic law. νόμων is very loosely joined to διαγωγήν.

that our kingdom. συντελοῦν κακὰ καὶ πρός. I omit καί which has crept in through dittography. ℵ* points in this direction.

6. **accordingly.** > οὖν ℵ$^{c.a}$.

set over our affairs. Vulg. renders 'qui omnibus prouinciis praepositus est, et secundus a rege'. Cf. Dan. v. 7.

our second father. Vulg. has 'quem patris loco colimus'. Cf. Add. E 11. The expression reflects the king's regard for Haman (cf. Esther vi. 11) rather than Haman's solicitude for the welfare of the king. Cf. 1 Macc. xi. 32, 'Demetrius the king to Lasthenes his father, greeting.'

be . . . destroyed. ἀπολέσαι B ℵ A, *deleantur* Vulg. In some ways ἀπολέσθαι would be smoother, as the subject of ἀπολέσαι is not named.

sword of their enemies. ἐθνῶν μάχαις A can hardly be intentional.

on the †fourteenth† day. This should no doubt be *thirteenth*; cf. Esther iii. 13, viii. 12, ix. 1, E 20. The error is due to a confusion between the day fixed for the massacre and the day fixed for the commemorative festival; cf. Esther ix. 16–19. No very careful attempt was originally made to remove discrepancies between the canonical book and the Additions.

Adar. Luc. texts have the Macedonian 'Dystri'.

7. **our state.** πράγματα B ℵ rightly, but A, recalling *v.* 4, has προστάγματα. After πρ. Old Lat. has (cf. E 24) 'qui autem celebrauerit gentes Iudaeorum inhabitabilis non solum inter homines sed nec inter aves; et igni sancto comburetur et substantia eius in regnum conferetur. Vale.'

ADDITION C. *The Prayer of Mordecai*, *vv.* 1–11. Add. C follows Esther iv. 17 in LXX, and immediately precedes Add. D. In Vulg. it is numbered xiii. 8–xiv. 19. It is separated from xiii. 7, which forms the conclusion of Add. B, by the following words: 'Hucusque exemplar epistolae. Quae sequuntur, post eum locum scripta reperi, ubi legitur: *Pergensque Mardochaeus fecit omnia quae ei mandaverat Esther.* Nec tamen habentur in Hebraico, et apud nullum penitus feruntur interpretum.'

Josephus makes free use of Add. C in *Ant.* xi. 6. 8.

1. ℵ$^{c.a}$ A read Μαρδοχαῖος ἐδεήθη.

2. **Lord, Lord.** κύριε θε͞ κύριε A.

for in Thy power. This clause introduced by ὅτι establishes the assertion of the Divine Sovereignty.

the whole world. For τὸ πᾶν, *the universe*, cf. Sir. xlii. 17, xliii. 27, and Plat. *Tim.* 28 C, *Crat.* 436 E. Heaven and earth are specified in next *v.* as the chief constituents of τὸ πᾶν. Cf. Isa. xlv. 18.

that gainsayeth Thee. For ἀντιδοξεῖν, a late Gr. word, cf. ἀντοφθαλμεῖν, Wisd. xii. 14, 'Neither king nor tyrant shall be able to gainsay Thee in Thy punishments.'

when Thou willest. ἐν τῷ θέλειν, *si decreueris* Vulg.

4. **And Thou.** > καί A.

shall resist. Cf. Wisd. xii. 12, 'Who shall say "What hast Thou done?" or who shall resist Thy judgement?'

5. **that it was . . . Haman.** > Old Lat.

not in insolence. Mordecai disclaims any personal prejudice against Haman as the reason for his refusal, and in *v.* 7 puts forward a reason savouring strongly of the morbid scrupulosity of later Judaism. Any reason which would have been valid in the case of Haman, the king's representative, would have been valid also when M. appeared before the king, and yet not only did M. have to bow to the king, when he became vizier, but he must have himself received the homage of the people (Esther viii. 15). Ezra and Nehemiah appear to have observed the court regulations without protest.

Various conjectures as to the ground for M.'s refusal are noted by Paton, *Est.* pp. 196, 197. The reason is not given in canon. Esther, and that given here is purely imaginary.

6 (13) 'For I had been content to kiss the soles of his feet for the salvation of Israel.
7 (14) 'But I did this that I might not set the glory of a man above the glory of God: and I will bow
before none save before Thee, my Lord, and I will not do it in pride.
8 (15) 'And now, Lord, God *and* King, the God of Abraham, spare Thy people; for the eyes *of our*
enemies are against us to consume us, and they seek to destroy the heritage that is Thine from
the beginning.
9 (16) 'Despise not Thy portion which Thou didst redeem unto Thyself out of the land of Egypt.
10 (17) Hearken to my prayer, and be gracious unto Thine heritage; and turn our mourning into
feasting, that we may live and sing Thy Name, O Lord; and destroy not the mouth of them that
praise Thee.'
11 (18) And all Israel cried out with their might, for their death was before their eyes.

The Prayer of Esther.

12(xiv)(1) And Esther, the queen, fled *in prayer* unto the Lord, being seized with an agony of death. And
13 (2) taking off her glorious raiment, she put on garments of anguish and mourning; and instead of the
choice ointments, she covered her head with ashes and dung, and she humbled her body *with* much
14 (3) *fasting*, and every place of the ornament of her joy she filled with her tangled hair. And she
besought the Lord God of Israel and said, 'My Lord, our King, Thou art *God* alone; help me who
15 (4) stand alone, and have no helper save Thee: for my danger is in my hand.
16 (5) 'I have heard ever since I was born in the tribe of my family that Thou, Lord, didst take Israel
out of all the nations, and our fathers from their progenitors, for an everlasting inheritance, and that
Thou didst for them all that Thou didst promise.

6. Mordecai acknowledges that his attitude towards Haman has brought this calamity on his people.

to kiss the soles. Cf. Xen. *Cyr.* vii. 5. 32, a token of homage apparently reserved for kings. Cf. Isa. xlix. 23, 'lick the dust of thy feet.'

7. **the glory of a man.** Ryssel quotes Dan. iii. 18; 2 Macc. vii. 2.

will not do it, i.e. will refuse to give homage to Haman.

8. **God and.** > ὁ θεός ℵ A Vulg.

eyes . . . are against us. ἐπιβλέπουσιν. Cf. Lat. *in-videre.*

heritage. For κληρονομία in the sense of God's special possession of Israel cf. Ps. xxviii. 9, xciv. 5.

9. **Thy portion.** For μερίς cf. Sir. xvii. 18. These words seem to be a reminiscence of Deut. ix. 26 LXX μὴ ἐξολεθρεύσῃς . . . τὴν μερίδα σου ἣν ἐλυτρώσω . . . ἐκ γῆς Αἰγύπτου.

10. **heritage.** For κλῆρος cf. Deut. ix. 29; 'sorti et funiculo tuo' Vulg.

mourning into feasting. Cf. Isa. lxi. 3, and for εὐωχία 3 Macc. vi. 30.

destroy not. μὴ ἀφανίσῃς, lit. 'blot not out'; Vulg. suggests the idea of the cessation of spoken praise and renders freely, 'ne claudas ora te canentium.' It is the living who praise God, cf. Isa. xxxviii. 19. For στόμα B, τὸ στ. A, ℵ* has τὸ αἷμα, which is impossible, but ℵ$^{c.a}$ corrects to στόμα.

11. **all Israel.** With this *v.* cf. Esther iv. 16.

with their might. ἐξ ἰσχύος αὐτῶν. Cf. Dan. iii. 4, iv. 11, ἐν ἰσχύι, and Isa. xlii. 13. Vulg. has 'pari mente et obsecratione'.

vv. 12–30. *The Prayer of Esther.*

12. **fled.** Cf. Ps. cxx. 1.

an agony. For ἐν ἀγῶνι some cursives have ἀγωνίᾳ. Cf. Luke xxii. 44. Esther's condition was one of great perplexity; she was beset on one side by the stringent rules of the court etiquette, and on the other by her patriotism and the outspoken insistency of Mordecai (Esther iv. 13, 14).

13. **taking off.** Cf. Jonah iii. 6.

glorious raiment, including the διάδημα (Esther i. 11, ii. 17). Cf. Ps. xlv. 14; Isa. iii. 18 ff.

garments of anguish. Cf. Judith viii. 5. Sackcloth is no doubt intended.

ointments. As symbols of joy. Cf. Ps. xlv. 8, cxxxiii. 2; Isa. lxi. 3.

covered her head. κεφαλὴν αὐτῆς ℵ A. Cf. Judith ix. 1.

humbled her body. σῶμα αὐτῆς ℵ A. Cf. 'to afflict the soul with fasting', Lev. xvi. 29; Ps. xxxv. 13.

every place. It would be most natural to interpret this of her apartments, but as the entire passage refers to the disfigurement of Esther's person, it must mean that her torn hair fell over the sackcloth she was clothed in.

14. **And . . . Israel.** Old Lat. substitutes 'and she fell upon the earth with her maidens from morning until evening'.

My Lord. κύριε ὁ θς̄ μου A. Cf. *v.* 2.

My Lord . . . alone. Old Lat. substitutes 'Deus Abraham et Deus Isaac et Deus Iacob, benedictus es'.

Thou art God alone, following Swete's punctuation, lit. 'Thou alone hast being'. Cf. Ps. lxxxvi. 10. R.V. has 'Thou only art our King'. But this does not bring out the idea of God's absolute sovereignty so well. Note the Gr. σὺ εἶ μόνος· βοήθησόν μοι τῇ μόνῃ.

15. ἐν τῇ χειρί μου A.

16. **I have heard.** Cf. Deut. xxxii. 7; Ps. xliv. 1.

didst take Israel. Cf. Deut. iv. 20, 34, xxvi. 5; Joshua xxiv. 3.

progenitors. So R.V. for προγόνων, better than A.V. *predecessors.*

inheritance. Deut. xxxii. 9.

didst promise. A inserts αὐτοῖς.

For *vv.* 16–23 (ὅτι σύ . . . θλίψεως ἡμῶν) Old Lat. has 'quoniam Noe in aqua diluvii conservasti. Ego audivi in libris paternis meis Domine quoniam tu Abrahae in trecentis et decem octo viris novem reges tradidisti. Ego audivi

17 (6) 'And now we have sinned before Thee, and Thou hast delivered us into the hands of our enemies,
18 (7) because we have given glory to their gods. Righteous art Thou, O Lord.
19 (8) 'And now they have not been satisfied with the bitterness of our captivity, but they have laid
20 (9) their hands ⟨in the hands of their idols⟩, to remove the ordinance of Thy mouth, and to destroy
Thine inheritance, and to stop the mouth of them that praise Thee, and to quench the glory of Thy
21 (10) house, and Thy altar, and to open the mouth of the nations to give praise to vain *idols*, and that
a king of flesh should be magnified for ever.'
22 (11) 'Surrender not, O Lord, Thy sceptre unto them that be not *gods*; and let not them *that are our*
enemies mock at our fall; but turn their counsel against themselves, and make an example of him
that began *to do this* against us.
23 (12) 'Remember ⟨us⟩, O Lord; make Thyself known *to us* in the time of our tribulation, and give me
courage, O King of the gods and Lord over all dominion.
24 (13) 'Put eloquent speech into my mouth before the lion; and turn his heart to hatred of him that
fighteth against us, that there may be an end of him and of them that are likeminded with him.
25 (14) 'But save us by Thy hand, and help me who *stand* alone, and have none save Thee, O Lord.

in libris paternis meis Domine quoniam tu Ionam de ventre ceti liberasti. Ego audivi in libris paternis meis Domine quoniam tu Ananiam Azariam Misahel de camino ignis liberasti. Ego audivi in libris paternis meis Domine quoniam tu Daniel de lacu leonum eruisti. Ego audivi in libris paternis meis Domine quoniam tu Ezechiae regi Iudaeorum morte damnato et oranti pro vita misertus es et donasti ei vitae annos quindecim. Ego audivi in libris paternis meis Domine quoniam tu Annae petenti in desiderio animae, filii generationem dedisti. Ego audivi in libris paternis meis Domine quoniam tu complacentes tibi liberas Domine usque in finem.'

17. **And now.** *ὅτι* A.

we have sinned. Cf. Dan. ix. 16. The Prayer of Esther recalls the tone of the Prayer of Daniel.

delivered us. Cf. Deut. iv. 27.

18. **given glory.** Ryssel thinks this refers to a declension into idolatry on the part of Israel while in exile. But it cannot be so: the exile is viewed as the punishment of pre-exilic idolatry. Cf. 2 Kings xvii. 10–16, 29–41, xxi. 7, 21.

Righteous. Cf. Dan. ix. 7.

19. **satisfied.** A late use of *ἱκανοῦσθαι*.

laid their hands. Vulg., failing to understand the meaning, renders 'robur manuum suarum idolorum potentiae deputantes'.

We must either render literally, 'they have applied their hands,' &c., or, following the hint supplied by ℵ* *τὰς χεῖρας τῶν εἰδώλων αὐτῶν*, read with ℵc.a mg. *ἔθηκαν τὰς χεῖρας αὐτῶν ἐπὶ τὰς χεῖρας τῶν εἰδώλων*, and render as in text. The mistake, as Lagarde saw, was caused by the double *χεῖρας*.

For the custom of striking hands as the outward expression of a contract or bargain cf. 2 Kings x. 15; Prov. xi. 21 LXX; Ezra x. 19; Lam. v. 6; 1 Macc. vi. 58; xi. 50, 66.

20. **ordinance.** *ὁρισμός*. Cf. Dan. vi. 7, 8, 12, 15. If the *ὁρισμοί* of the Medes and Persians were unchangeable, what an impiety to seek to overthrow those of the living God! The destruction of Israel would invalidate the determination of God to make Israel His inheritance.

mouth . . . praise. *στόματα ὑμνούντων* A. For *ἐμφράξαι* cf. Job v. 16; Ps. lxiii. 11, cvii. 42.

house, i.e. the Temple. Cf. Isa. vi. 1. That the reference must be to the Temple of Jerusalem, still the ideal centre of the people's religion even though destroyed and its worship suspended, is plain from the mention of the altar. With the destruction of the people the altar-fire would be finally quenched. Cf. Judith ix. 8.

21. **vain idols.** *μάταια*, a conventional word for false gods. Cf. Lev. xvii. 7 LXX.

should be magnified. The passive *θαυμασθῆναι* follows very loosely upon the active infinitives which depend on *ἔθηκαν τὰς χεῖρας*. The Persian king is referred to, who will win glory for all time, as a king of flesh who has defeated the King of heaven. Vulg. loosely renders 'et laudent idolorum fortitudinem'.

22. **Surrender not.** For God to permit the destruction of His people is tantamount to an abdication of His throne and the power symbolized (in the case of an earthly king) by the sceptre.

them that be not gods. *τοῖς μὴ οὖσι*, i.e. *those who have no being*, in contrast to Jehovah, in whom being resides. Cf. *v.* 14 *σὺ εἶ μόνος*, and Wisd. xiii. 10–19, xiv. 13 *οὔτε γὰρ ἦν* [*εἴδωλα*] *ἀπ' ἀρχῆς, οὔτε εἰς τὸν αἰῶνα ἔσται*, and 1 Cor. viii. 4.

mock. Either the subject of the verb is changed, and 'our enemies' is now the subj.; or the gods are thought of as mocking. Cf. Wisdom's mocking, Prov. i. 26, and Jehovah's, Ps. ii. 4. The former seems to suit the context better.

their counsel. *αὐτοῦ* ℵ*, i.e. Haman.

make an example. *παραδειγμάτισον*. Cf. Num. xxv. 4; Ezek. xxviii. 17; Heb. vi. 6.

him that began. Haman. 'qui in nos coepit saevire' Vulg.

23. **make Thyself known.** Cf. Ps. xliv. 23–26.

give me courage. In this verse Esther passes from prayer for national deliverance to prayer for personal safety (*vv.* 24–9). In support of her entreaty she urges (*vv.* 26–28) that for religious reasons, none of which is even hinted at in canon. Esther, she hates the position she is forced to occupy, and distinguishes her official duties from her personal predilections. Here again, as in *v.* 7, we find ourselves in the atmosphere of later Judaism.

King of the gods. Cf. Ps. xcv. 3.

24. **eloquent speech.** Cf. Luke xxi. 15.

before the lion. Strength is suggested, cf. Jer. xlix. 19; and terribleness, cf. Prov. xix. 12, xx. 2; Sir. xxviii. 23. The Aramaic 'Mordecai's Dream' has, 'For Thy maid feareth before him, as the kid before the lion' (Merx, *Chrest. Targ.* p. 164).

turn his heart. For *μετατίθημι* in this sense cf. Sir. vi. 9 *φίλος μετατιθέμενος εἰς ἔχθραν*.

an end. *συντέλεια* in this sense is used with *ἀπώλεια* 1 Macc. iii. 42.

25. **have none.** A assimilates to *v.* 14 by adding *βοηθόν*.

26 (15) ‘Knowledge hast Thou of all things, and Thou knowest that I hate the glory of the wicked, and I
27 (16) detest the bed of the uncircumcised and of any alien. Thou knowest my necessity, that I abhor the
sign of my proud estate, which is upon my head in the days when I show myself openly; I abhor it
as a menstruous rag, and I wear it not in the days of my leisure.
28 (17) ‘And Thy servant hath not eaten at the table of Haman, and I have not honoured the king's
feast, neither have I drunk the wine of the libations.
29 (18) ‘And Thy servant hath known no joy since the day I was brought here until now, save in Thee,
30 (19) Lord God of Abraham. O God, whose strength is over all, hear the voice of the hopeless, and save
us from the hand of them that deal wickedly, and save me out of my fear.’

ADDITION D.

The appearance of Esther before the king.

1 (xv) (4) And it came to pass on the third day, when she had ceased praying, she put off her garments of
2 (5) humiliation, and clothed herself in her glorious apparel. And being majestically adorned, she called
3 (6) upon the all-seeing God and Saviour, and took with her two maids: and upon the one she leaned as

26. **Knowledge hast Thou . . . and Thou knowest.** Cf. St. Peter's appeal to the universal knowledge of Christ, John xxi. 17.

I hate the glory. It is no personal vanity that keeps Esther where she is; the glory of her high place is shame to her. Cf. Esther ii. 8–17.

of any alien. The prohibition of marriages with those outside the covenant dated from very early times (cf. Deut. vii. 3, 4), and came to rest on religious sentiment blended with national prejudice. In Ezra x. 2, Neh. xiii. 23 ff., we learn something of the abhorrence in which the marriage of Jewish men with heathen women was held. A, through a simple oversight, omits from ‘the bed of’ (*v.* 26) down to ‘that I abhor’ (*v.* 27).

27. **my necessity.** She is under compulsion, and as wife of a heathen king she must wear the token of her dignity, the royal crown, her badge of shame.

sign of my proud estate. The crown royal, a kind of peaked turban, which had to be worn when the queen appeared in public. Cf. Esther i. 11, ii. 17. For ὀπτασία, *appearance*, cf. Mal. iii. 2.

rag. Cf. Isa. lxiv. 6.

28. **hath not eaten.** Cf. Dan. i. 8, 13, 15.

king's feast. Cf. Esther i. 5, ii. 18.

the libations. Cf. Deut. xxxii. 38 LXX. One reason for Esther's abstention from the royal feasts was their heathen character. Cf. Dan. v. 3, 4. Fuller suggests that there is a reference here to the Haoma-drink, which ‘was drunk by the faithful for the benefit of themselves and the gods’. Cf. Sayce, *Ancient Empires*, p. 269.

29. **since the day I was brought,** lit. ‘since the day of my change’, i.e. since the day of entry into the palace.

30. **the hopeless.** For ἀπηλπισμένων cf. Isa. xxix. 19; Judith ix. 11.

save us . . . save me. Cf. *v.* 23. Old Lat. adds ‘transfer luctum nostrum in laetitiam, dolores autem nostros in hilaritatem: surgentes autem supra partem tuam Deus palam facito, aperi Domine; cognoscere Domine’.

ADDITION D. *Esther's interview with the king, vv.* 1–16. Add. D consists of sixteen verses, and follows in LXX immediately upon Add. C. In Vulg. it is numbered xv. 4–19, and is separated from xiv. 19 by the following words, which are not unlike Esther iv. 13 ff.:

‘*Haec quoque addita reperi in editione Vulgata.*

(1) Et mandavit ei (haud dubium quin esset Mardochaeus) ut ingrederetur ad regem, et rogaret pro populo suo et pro patria sua.

(2) Memorare, inquit, dierum humilitatis tuae, quomodo nutrita sis in manu mea, quia Aman, secundus a rege, locutus est contra nos in mortem;

(3) Et tu invoca Dominum, et loquere regi pro nobis, et libera nos de morte.

Nec non et ista quae subdita sunt.’

Jos. (*Ant.* xi. 6. 9) draws largely upon Add. D, which endeavours to show in detail what is briefly stated in Esther v. 1 f. The danger of Esther's enterprise is emphasized by the king's wrath, which serves also to set off the power of God which could turn the king's heart.

1. **the third day.** Cf. Esther iv. 16, v. 1. A. W. Streane quotes the Midrash, ‘Never did the Israelites find themselves in trouble longer than three days,’ and refers to Gen. xxii. 4, xlii. 17; Jonah i. 17; and Hos. vi. 2.

when she had ended her prayer. > Vulg.

garments of humiliation. ἱμάτια θεραπείας, cf. D 13; so A.V. *garments of mourning*. Esther's θεραπεία (or *service*), cf. Esther iv. 16, consisted in mortification and prayer. Accordingly, Fritzsche is perhaps right in emending *vest. ornatus* Vulg. to *vest. oratus*. After these words Old Lat. has ‘et lavavit corpus suum aqua et unxit se unctione’.

glorious apparel. Cf. Esther v. 1 and Judith x. 3.

2. **majestically adorned.** γενηθεῖσα ἐπιφανής. Vulg. ‘cum regio fulgeret habitu’; Jos. ‘adorned herself as became a queen’.

she called. The religious element is as usual emphasized in non-canonical Esther.

two maids. So ℵ A, instead of τὰς δύο B, *her two maids*. She was waited upon by seven maids (cf. Esther ii. 9), and of them she took with her only two.

For ἅβρα (Vulg. *famula*, but elsewhere *delicata*, i.e. pretty, delicate) cf. Gen. xxiv. 61; Judith x. 5.

The ἅβραι were maids of honour for the queen's personal service.

3. **she leaned.** ἐπηρείδετο, cf. Prov. iii. 18.

4 (7) 5 (8) one that walked delicately, and the other followed *her*, holding up her train. And she herself was
radiant in the perfection of her beauty, and her countenance was happy and lovely: but her heart
6 (9) was stricken with fear. And when she had passed all the doors, she took her stand before the king:
now he was sitting upon his royal throne, clad in all his array of majesty, all *adorned* with gold and
precious stones. And he was very terrible.
7 (10) And lifting up his face that flamed with glory, he looked *upon her* in fierce wrath. And the
queen fell down and changed colour and swooned, and she bowed herself down upon the head of the
maid who went before her.
8 (11) And God changed the spirit of the king into mildness, and in alarm he sprang up from his throne,
and raised her in his arms until she came to herself again, and comforted her with reassuring words,
9 (12) and said unto her, 'What is it, Esther? I am thy brother. Be of good cheer, thou shalt not die.
(13) 11 (14) For our commandment is *only* for our subjects. Draw near.'
12 (15) Then he raised the golden sceptre and laid it on her neck, and embraced her and said, 'Speak
to me.'
13 (16) And she said unto him, 'I saw thee, my lord, as an angel of God, and my heart was dismayed for
14 (17) fear of thy glory. For wonderful art thou, lord, and thy countenance is full of grace.'

walked delicately. ὡς τρυφερευομένη, Vulg. 'quasi prae deliciis et nimia teneritudine corpus suum ferre non sustinens'. Esther adopted the languishing manner of deportment cultivated by the pampered ladies of the harem. The impression of delicateness is heightened by Esther's having a train-bearer. ὡς τρυφ., lit. 'like a pampered, effeminate woman'.

4. **train.** ἔνδυσις, a very rare use, and ἅπ. λεγ. in LXX.

5. **the perfection.** ἀκμῇ B ℵ A, ὡς ἀκμῇ ℵ*, ἐν ἀκ. ℵ c.a. Cf. *v.* 7, ἐν ἀκμῇ θυμοῦ, *in fierce wrath.*

happy and lovely, lit. 'happy like a lovely (face)'. Old Lat. adds 'oculi autem gratissimi'.

6. **passed all the doors.** Cf. Esther v. 1, '[she] stood in the inner court of the king's house, over against the king's house: and the king sat upon his royal throne in the royal house, over against the entrance of the house.' Esther had entered into the inner court, in itself an act of presumption. Cf. Esther iv. 11. The throne-room opened upon the inner court, and through this door Esther passed into the immediate presence of the king.

took her stand. κατέστη, but ἔστη ℵ c.a A.

majesty. ἐπιφάνεια; cf. *v.* 2 ἐπιφανής. The regular use of ἐπιφ. in LXX is in connexion with the *visitations* of heavenly beings; cf. 2 Macc. (six times). The sculptures of Persepolis present a striking picture of the splendour of a Persian king (cf. Rawlinson, *Ancient Mon.* iv. 153). The Greeks assessed at 12,000 talents the value of the precious stones worn by Xerxes.

7. **flamed with glory.** > δόξῃ A, which reads καὶ ἦρεν τὸ πρόσωπον αὐτοῦ πεπυρωμένον ἐν ἀκμῇ θυμοῦ, and 'he lifted his face, which flamed in fullness of wrath'. For ἀκμῇ θυμ. cf. *v.* 5.

fierce wrath. Esther had violated the rule (see Esther iv. 11) which forbade any one to approach the king unsummoned. After ἔβλεψεν Old Lat. has 'et cogitabat perdere eam rex, et erat ambiguus clamans, et dixit, quis ausus est introire in aulam non vocatus?'

fell down. Cf. Esther viii. 3. But this seems to be a fall due to fear, rather than in token of obeisance. Vulg. *corruit.*

changed colour. μετεβάλετο ℵ, but μεταβάλλειν has an intr. use.

swooned. ἐν ἐκλύσει. But LXX more commonly gives a milder meaning to ἔκλυσις, i.e. *weariness*, and Vulg. does so here, taking ἐν ἐκλ. with the following clause, 'lassum super ancillulam reclinavit caput.'

bowed herself down. ἐπέκυψεν ἐπὶ τῆς κεφαλῆς τῆς ἅβρας τῆς προπορευομένης αὐτῆς A, προπορ. ℵ, i.e. '*who was coming towards* (the king)'.

8. **changed the spirit.** Cf. an intr. use of μεταβ., Hab. i. 11 τότε μεταβαλεῖ τὸ πνεῦμα. Old Lat. has 'Deus autem iram convertit in miserationem et furorem ipsius in tranquillitatem'. For μετεβ. ℵ* has μετέλαβεν, and conversely for ἀνέλαβεν below A has ἀνέβαλεν.

in alarm. ἀγωνιάσας, Vulg. 'festinus ac metuens'.

from his throne. > αὐτοῦ A.

with reassuring words, lit. *with peaceable words.* For the expr. λόγοι εἰρηνικοί cf. Deut. ii. 26; Mic. vii. 3; and 1 Macc. (seven times); also Sir. iv. 8 ἀποκρίθητι αὐτῷ εἰρηνικὰ ἐν πραΰτητι.

9. **What is it, Esther?** Old Lat. adds 'soror mea Hester es et consors regni'.

thy brother. An expression of intimacy, intended to show that the king regarded Esther as really entitled to special consideration. Cf. Song of Solomon viii. 1. For the Egyptian use of ἀδελφός as 'husband' cf. Witkowski, *Epist. Priv. Graec.* xxvi, p. 37, where we find a wife so addressing her husband. For the converse use of ἀδελφή cf. Pap. Oxyr. iv, No. 744, and Tobit vii. 15, viii. 4, 7.

10. **our commandment.** Lit. *our comm. is common*, i.e. it governs the king's subjects generally, but not so favoured a one as Esther. Cf. Vulg. 'non enim pro te, sed pro omnibus haec lex constituta est'. The words, preceded by 'Thou shalt not die', are a reminiscence of Esther iv. 11. Paton, however (p. 220), quotes Herodotus to the effect that people might send in a message to the king, and request an audience.

11. **Draw near.** Vulg. 'Accede igitur et tange sceptrum'.

12. **embraced her.** τὴν Ἐσθήρ A. The pronoun is better as in B ℵ.

13. **as an angel of God**, i.e. radiant and terrible. The expression does not accord well with the scrupulosity shown by Esther in Add. C; it comes strangely from a Jew to a heathen. Perhaps this is why it does not appear either in Josephus, or the Midrash, or Ben-Gorion. Cf. 1 Sam. xxix. 9 (cod. Al.); 2 Sam. xiv. 17, 20; xix. 27.

for fear of. > φόβου A, but Vulg. has 'prae timore gloriae'.

14. **full of grace.** χαρίτων μεστόν. Cf. Ps. xlv. 2 ὡραῖος κάλλει παρὰ τοὺς υἱοὺς τῶν ἀνθρώπων, ἐξεχύθη ἡ χάρις ἐν χείλεσίν σου.

15 (18) But while she was speaking, she fell swooning.
16 (19) And the king was troubled, and all his servants sought to comfort her.

ADDITION E.

The Decree of Artaxerxes concerning the Jews.

1 (xvi) Of which letter that which follows is a copy.
The great king Artaxerxes to the rulers of countries in one hundred and twenty-seven satrapies
from India to Ethiopia, and to those who are well affected to our government, greeting.
2 Many, the more often they are honoured by the all too great goodwill of their benefactors, have
3 become the more proud; and not only do they seek to injure our subjects, but, being unable to
4 endure abundance, they take in hand to devise schemes against their own benefactors. And not
only do they take thankfulness away from men, but also, being lifted up with the ostentatiousness
of the foolish, they suppose that they shall escape the evil-hating justice of the all-surveying God.
5 Yea, and oftentimes many of those who have been placed in *the highest* positions of authority
have been moved by the specious words of *those their* friends who have been entrusted with the
administration of the government to become partakers of innocent blood, and have become involved

15. **swooning.** ἀπὸ ἐκλύσεως B + αὐτῆς ℵ A, lit. *because of her fainting*. She fell a second time. Cf. *v.* 7.
16. **servants.** θεραπεία, *curia* Old Lat. Cf. Gen. xlv. 16 Φαραὼ καὶ ἡ θεραπεία αὐτοῦ.

ADDITION E. *The decree of Artaxerxes concerning the Jews*, xvi. 1–24. Add. E consists of twenty-four verses, and is placed in LXX between Esther viii. 12 and viii. 13. In Vulg. it is numbered xvi. 1–24, and is separated from Add. D by the words 'Exemplar epistolae regis Artaxerxis, quam pro Iudaeis ad totas regni sui provincias misit; quod et ipsum in Hebraico volumine non habetur'. It presents an imaginary reconstruction of the edict mentioned in Esther viii. 13, which, while cancelling the earlier rescript (Add. B), instructs all the king's subjects in the most precise way to render all the aid in their power to the Jews on the thirteenth day of Adar. For the style of this Add. see note on Add. B. Josephus, *Ant.* xi. 6. 12 reproduces this letter very fully.

1. **Of which letter**, lit. *of which things*, i.e. *the letter, that which follows is a copy*. ὧν > X*.

to the rulers . . . Ethiopia. The recipients are described in almost identical terms with those in Add. B. Here σατραπείαις (σατράπαις ℵ*, σατραπίαις ℵ[c.a]) precedes χωρῶν. On *satrapies* see B 1. ἰδίων χωρῶν ℵ*.

to those who . . . government. τοῖς τὰ ἡμέτερα φρονοῦσι takes the place of τοπάρχαις ὑποτεταγμένοις in B 1. ℵ[c.a mg] A have wrongly καὶ σατράπαις τοῖς τὰ . . . Two classes of officials are thus referred to, (*a*) the governors in 127 satrapies, (*b*) the other officials, less prominent than satraps. Vulg. supports this view with 'ac principibus qui nostrae iussioni oboediunt', and this is better than to refer the clause (with Fritzsche) to subjects generally, who are mentioned unambiguously in *v.* 3. Jos. seems to favour 'subjects'.

2. **Many.** A veiled reference to Haman. Cf. Esther iii. 1.

their benefactors. Cf. Luke xxii. 25. Their benefactors are the kings who have elevated them to their high position. A. W. Streane recalls how Ptolemy III (247–242 B.C.) obtained the actual title of εὐεργέτης (benefactor) through his restoration of the images of Egyptian gods, carried off by Cambyses to Persia.

the more proud. μεῖζον ἐφρόνησαν. The general is interpreted by the particular in *vv.* 12–14.

3. **abundance**, i.e. the excess of the honour bestowed on them in particular. Ryssel recalls the old proverb τίκτει τοι κόρος ὕβριν. Satiety is shown in thanklessness, *v.* 4.

against their own benefactors. It has been suggested that Haman was not altogether free from participation in the plot of the two eunuchs, discovered by Mordecai (Add. A), and that Haman's hatred of Mordecai was due to his having been thwarted by him. Cf. A 17. Haman's part in the plot may be referred to here. See also Esther vii. 8.

4. **thankfulness.** καὶ κατὰ τὴν εὐχ. ℵ A wrongly, by dittography.

lifted up . . . foolish. 'Avidorum praesumptionibus inflammati' Old Lat. This is a nearer translation of τοῖς τῶν ἀπειραγάθων κόμποις ἐπαρθέντες than in Vulg. 'humanitatis in se iura violare'. ἀπειραγάθων has given much concern to copyists (ὑπεραγάθων 52, ἀπειρωπάθων 93 *a*) and to commentators, but it is a late ecclesiastical word, and (like ἀπειρόκαλος) is not to be translated literally, but with the general sense of *foolish*. 'Men ignorant of benefits' is very clumsy. *The foolish* are either the parasites who fawn upon the *nouveau riche*, or the too highly honoured man himself.

suppose. For ὑπολαμβ. ℵ[*cb] A have διαλαμβ.

evil-hating. An attribute properly belonging to God, but here by a rhetorical licence applied to His justice. With μισοπόνηρος cf. μισοπονηρία, 2 Macc. iii. 1, and μισοπονηρεῖν, 2 Macc. iv. 49, viii. 4.

5. **those placed . . . positions**, i.e. kings, such as Xerxes himself, who have been misled by their underlings.

specious words. παραμυθία in the Greek is the subject of the verb, but the sentence runs more smoothly if it is turned as in text.

friends . . . entrusted. Ryssel suggests with much probability that φίλων should be rendered as in text, and not as often 'entrusted with the management of the affairs of their friends', since a king would be slow to speak of kings as the 'friends' of their subordinates. Ryssel speaks of φίλοι as the universal title of honour borne in Egypt by the highest officers of the king (cf. 1 Macc. ii. 18 and Jacob in *ZATW* x. 283), and translates *Statthalter*. Fritzsche emends φίλων to φιλοφρόνως or φιλοτίμως, but this is unnecessary.

partakers. For μετόχους B 93 *b* have μεταιτίους, which seems better in sense, and explains the corruptions μετένους ℵ* and μεταγνοῦσα A.

innocent blood. For αἵματα ἀθῷα cf. Jer. xix. 4. Cf. Jer. ii. 34 αἵματα ψυχῶν ἀθῴων.

6 in irretrievable disasters, *these men* beguiling the innocent goodwill of their lords with the false
trickery of their evil disposition.
7 And the things impiously accomplished through the pestilent behaviour of men who *thus* exercise
their power unworthily may be seen not so much by an examination of the more ancient records
8 which have been handed down as by observation of the things near at hand; and care must be
taken for the future, in order that we may render the kingdom tranquil and peaceable for all men,
9 not by relying upon †informations†, but by ever passing judgement with clemency and attentiveness
upon the matters that are brought to our notice.
10 For Haman, the son of Hamadathus, a Macedonian (an alien in very truth from the Persian blood
11 and one who is fallen far from our favour), having been a guest among us, so far enjoyed the goodwill which we display towards every nation, that he was called our father, and continued to receive
the honour of all as the second person after the royal throne.
12 13 But he, not bearing his proud position, took counsel to deprive us of our kingdom, and *to deprive*
of life not only Mardocheus who is at once our saviour and perpetual benefactor, but also Esther the
blameless partner of our kingdom, together with their entire nation, by manifold chicanery and
14 deceits asking for them *to be delivered up* to destruction. For through these wiles he thought to
catch us isolated and to transfer the kingdom of the Persians to the Macedonians.
15 But we find that the Jews whom this trebly-dyed villain had delivered to destruction are no evil-

6. **with the false trickery.** *τῷ τῆς κακοηθείας τρόπῳ* ℵ$^{c.a.}$ ‘while they after the fashion of their maliciousness (i.e. as malice is wont to do) by lying craft overreached.’

7. The text of this verse is slightly corrupt, though the sense is plain. *ὡς* B A > ℵ*, *παραδεδώκαμεν* ℵ$^{c.a}$, *παρεδώκαμεν* B A, *ὅσα* B A, *ὅσον* ℵ, *ὑμᾶς* B ℵ A, *ὑμῖν* ℵ*, *ἐκζητοῦντας* B ℵ A, *ἐκζήτουν* ℵ*. Accepting Fritzsche's *ὧν παρέδωκαν* (‘which they, i.e. our predecessors, handed down’), I read as follows: *σκοπεῖν δὲ ἔξεστιν, οὐ τοσοῦτον ἐκ τῶν παλαιοτέρων ὧν παρέδωκαν ἱστοριῶν ὅσον τὰ παρὰ πόδας ὑμῖν ἐκζητοῦντας, τὰ ἀνοσίως συντετελεσμένα.*

exercise . . . unworthily. The text here is corrupt. *ἀνάξια δυναστευόντων* B, *ἀξιας δυναστευω | το* ℵ*, *ἄξια δυναστευοντω̄* ℵ$^{c.a}$, *αξιοδυναστευοντων* A. Fritzsche's *ἀναξίᾳ, . . . λοιμότητι* is not very satisfying, besides which *τῶν* is in the wrong place. I suggest either to read with Cod. 248 *τῶν ἀναξίως δυναστευόντων*, or to follow the hint given by A and accept the rather long compound *τῇ τῶν ἀναξιοδυναστευόντων λοιμότητι*. It is just possible that *ἀνάξια* as in B might be right, the use being adverbial as in *ἀνάξια πράττειν*; but a suggestion made by Ryssel, *ἀναξίᾳ* (dat. of subst. formed from *ἀνάσσειν*), cannot be entertained.

which . . . handed down. *ὡς παρεδώκαμεν* would mean ‘as we handed down’, but it would not fit with *τῶν παλ. ἱστ.*, which refer to chronicles of an earlier age. A. W. Streane refers to the inscription on the rock of Behistun, which, recording events in the reign of Xerxes' predecessor, Darius Hystaspes (522–485 B.C.), tells of the rebellions of Smerdis and Gomatas. Fuller's ‘as we have made clear’ might be a translation of *παραδεδείχαμεν*, but not of *παραδεδώκαμεν*.

the things near at hand. *τὰ παρὰ πόδας ὑμῖν.* Cf. the prov. *τὰ πρὸς ποσὶν σκόπει.*

8. **care must be taken.** Before *προσέχειν* supply *ἔξεστιν* from *v.* 7.

in order that we. Unless *εἰς τὸ . . . παρεξόμεθα* is a colloquialism, which is not to be expected in this passage, we must emend *εἰς τὸ* to *ὅπως*, or else, following Codd. 52, 64, 243, 248, read *ὥστε*, and emend *παρεξ.* to *παρέχειν* or *παρέξειν*.

9. **†informations†.** Fritzsche, following ℵ$^{c.a}$ A, inserts *οὐ*, and for *μεταβολαῖς* B ℵ A suggests *διαβολαῖς*, which is found in Luc. texts, and is perhaps supported by *varietatibus* in Old Lat., and *si diversa iubeamus* Vulg., both of which may point to an earlier corruption *διαφοραῖς*. *οὐ χρώμενοι ταῖς διαβολαῖς*, as translated in text, is supported by Jos. *Ant.* xi. 6. 12, ‘it is not fit to attend any longer to calumnies.’

With this change of text, there is no longer the question of the formal revocation of the earlier edict (Add. B), a step which would seem to be opposed to the Persian rule stated in Dan. vi. 8, 12. Cases are indeed cited where Persian kings have repealed their edicts, but the strongest argument for a change of text seems to lie in the evident antithesis between the first and second clauses of *v.* 9.

10. *ὡς γὰρ Ἁμάν* B ℵ A. I suggest *ὁ γάρ*.

a Macedonian. Vulg. ‘et animo et gente Macedo’. Cf. Esther ix. 24 LXX, which renders by Μακεδών the same Hebr. expression as in Esther iii. 1 is rendered Βουγαῖος. The word is no doubt intended to represent Haman as a traitor, but it is probably employed as a word held in odium by the Jews, who associated it with Antiochus Epiphanes, the hated reversionary in Syria of the Macedonian power.

an alien. Both ‘Agagite’ and ‘Macedonian’ describe Haman as a foreigner. Cf. also the plot ascribed to him in *v.* 14. His malignity is emphasized by *ἐπιξενωθείς*: he had enjoyed the privileges of hospitality.

11. **our father.** Cf. Add. B 6 and *v.* 3. For ‘father’ as a complimentary title cp. Witkowski, *Ep. Priv.*, p. 50.

as the second person. Cf. Esther iii. 1; see also 2 Chron. xxviii. 7, and 1 Esdras iii. 7 *δεύτερος καθιεῖται Δαρείου, καὶ συγγενὴς Δ. κληθήσεται.*

12. **deprive . . . kingdom.** For Haman's motive, however, cf. A 17 and Esther iii. 5. See also Esther iii. 11. It is difficult to see what Haman could hope to gain by the motive attributed to him here and in *v.* 14.

13. **benefactor.** As recorded in the royal chronicles, Esther vi. 1. Paton writes (p. 245): ‘It was a point of honour with the Persian kings to reward promptly and magnificently those who conferred benefits upon them (cf. Her. iii. 138, 140; v. 11; viii. 85; ix. 107). According to Her. viii. 85 the Persians had a special class of men known as *Orosangai*, or “benefactors of the king”.’

14. **these wiles.** > *τούτων* A.

transfer. *μετάξαι* B ℵ A, *μεταλλάξαι* 44 74 76 106 120 236.

15. **trebly-dyed.** *τρισαλιτήριος.* Cf. 2 Macc. viii. 34, xv. 3.

16 doers, but govern themselves with the most righteous laws, and are sons of the Most High, Most
Mighty, Living God, who ordereth the kingdom both for us and for our fathers with the most
excellent governance.
17 Ye will do well therefore not to give effect to the letters sent by Haman the son of Hamadathus,
18 because the man himself who wrought these things has been hanged with all his house at the gate
of Susa; for God that ruleth over all hath speedily rendered unto him the justice that he merits.
19 Now *therefore* display the copy of this letter openly in every place, and suffer the Jews to obey
20 their own laws, and reinforce them so that on the thirteenth day of the twelfth month Adar, on the
selfsame day, they may defend themselves against those who attacked them in the time of their
21 affliction: for this day hath the God who ruleth over all made to be unto them *a day of* gladness
instead of the day of destruction for the chosen race.
22 Do ye also therefore, among your commemorative festivals keep *it* a notable day with all good
23 cheer, that both now and hereafter it may be a day of salvation to us and to the Persians friendly to
us, but a memorial of destruction to those who conspire against us.
24 And every city or country without exception which shall not do according to these commands
shall fall under our wrath and be destroyed with fire and sword; it shall be rendered not only
unpassable for men, but also hateful for all time to beasts and birds.

ADDITION F.

The interpretation of the Dream of Mordecai.

1 (x) (4) And Mardocheus said, 'These things are from God.

16. **sons of the Most High.** Cf. Hos. i. 10 LXX κληθήσονται καὶ αὐτοὶ υἱοὶ θεοῦ ζῶντος. The Jews are members of the people which God has created as His 'son'.

who ordereth. 'Darius Hystaspes, the father of Xerxes, was wont to attribute—judging from the inscription over his tomb at Naksh-i-Rastám—all that he had done to the favour of Ormuzd' (*Speaker's Comm.* ad loc.). For the likeness between Persian and Jewish language on the subject cf. Ezra i. 3, vii. 21; Dan. iv. 34 ff., vi. 27; Jer. xxvii. 6.

18. **hanged.** ἐσταυρῶσθαι, i.e. *impaled.* Cf. Esther vii. 10.

with all his house. Haman's sons were not actually impaled till the fourteenth day of Adar, though they died on the thirteenth day. Cf. Esther ix. 12–14. It was indeed a Persian custom to execute the family with the guilty one (cf. Dan. vi. 24), especially in the case of a traitor, but here Haman evidently suffered alone. Cf. Esther vii. 10, viii. 7, ix. 10.

19. **display.** ἐκθέντες. For ἐκτιθέναι, a specially Greek-Egyptian word, cf. Esther iii. 14, iv. 8, viii. 13, ix. 14.

openly. With μετὰ παρρησίας cf. Esther viii. 13 ὀφθαλμοφανῶς.

obey their own laws. For νομίμοις B ℵ A have νόμοις. The same permission was given by Artaxerxes to Ezra (Ezra vii. 25 f.). Cf. Jos. *Ant.* xii. 3. 3.

20. **thirteenth day.** So Esther ix. 1, but Add. B 6 has *the fourteenth day.*

the selfsame day. The very day appointed for the destruction of the Jews. Cf. Esther iii. 13, viii. 11.

21. **ruleth over all.** ὁ ἐπὶ πάντα A.

chosen race. The Jewish fabricator of the decree betrays himself here by an expression that a Persian king would not have used. For ἐκλεκτός applied to Israel cf. Ps. cv. 6; Isa. xliii. 20.

22. **commemorative festivals.** Fritzsche, thinking ὑμῶν out of place in a decree addressed to Persians, and unsuitable in connexion with ἐπωνύμοις, which when so used could not bear its full meaning, suggests ἐν ταῖς ἐπωνύμοις κλήρων ἑορταῖς. We should thus have κλήρων as the translation of פּוּרִים, translating 'on the feasts known by the name of Lots'. The suggestion is good, but not essential.

a notable day. Cf. 2 Macc. xv. 36. Translate, supplying ταύτην, 'Keep it (i.e. the 13th day of Adar) a notable day.'

23. **it may be.** After σωτηρία many Codd. add ᾖ.

a day of salvation. σωτηρία stands in antithesis to ἀπωλείας, and should therefore have this accent; Fritzsche, neglecting this, reads σωτήρια (i.e. ἱερά), but wrongly. The day is to be a 'salutary' day for the Persians, as well as a memorial of their king's deliverance. But they are not called upon to observe the feast in the Jewish way.

salvation to us. ὑμῖν ℵ* ὑμῶν A. Fritzsche suggests ὑμῖν here for ἡμῖν, which is in harmony with ὑμεῖς at beginning of *v.* 22.

24. **fire and sword**, lit. 'spear and fire'.

unpassable . . . hateful. Cf. Jer. xxxii. 43, li. 62; Ezek. xxv. 13, xxxii. 13.

for all time. > εἰς . . . χρόνον A.

ADDITION F. *The interpretation of the Dream of Mordecai*, x. 1–10. Add. F consists of 10 *vv.*, and is numbered in Vulg. x. 4–13, and is the only one of the six Adds. which is given there in its right place. But while in relation to the canonical portions its position is correct, it stands in an inverted relation to the uncanonical, Jerome having gathered out of the text all the Adds. which preceded, and placed them after it in a kind of appendix. Jerome prefixed to this Add. the following words which separate it from Esther x. 3: 'Quae habentur in Hebraeo plena fide expressi. Haec autem quae sequuntur, scripta reperi in editione Vulgata quae Graecorum lingua et litteris continetur; et interim post finem libri hoc capitulum ferebatur; quod iuxta consuetudinem nostram obelo, id est veru,

2 (5) ‘For I remember concerning the dream which I saw respecting these things; and nothing thereof
is unfulfilled.
3 (6) ‘The little spring became a river, and there was a light and the sun and much water.
4 (7) ‘The river is Esther, whom the king married and made queen. And the two dragons are I and
5 (8) Haman. And the nations *are* those that were gathered together to destroy the name of the Jews.
6 (9) And my nation, this is Israel, which cried unto God and were saved. And the Lord saved His
people, and the Lord delivered us out of all these evils. And the Lord wrought great signs and
wonders, such as have not been done among the nations.
7 (10) ‘Therefore *the Lord* made two lots, one for the people of God and the other for all the *other*
8 (11) nations; and these two lots came at the hour and the moment and the day of judging before God
⟨for His people⟩ and for all the nations.
9 (12) ‘So God remembered His people, and justified His inheritance.
10 (13) ‘And these days shall be unto them in the month Adar, on the fourteenth and fifteenth day of the
same month, with an assembly and joy and gladness before God, from generation to generation for
ever among His people Israel.’
11 (xi)(1) In the fourth year of the reign of Ptolemy and Cleopatra, Dositheus, who said he was a priest and

praenotavimus.’ In LXX Esther this Add. is the concluding portion of the book. Josephus shows no acquaintance with either the Dream of Mordecai or its interpretation.

1. **These things**, i.e. the history recorded in the chapters of canonical Esther.

from God. Cf. Ps. cxviii. 23 (Matt. xxi. 42), of an event determined by God's providence.

2. **the dream.** See Add. A.

respecting these things. ‘Haec eadem significantis’, Vulg. The interpretation of the dream in detail occupies *vv.* 3–6.

3. **spring became.** The style of this verse is naturally rather abrupt. *πηγὴ ἐγένετο* ℵ* A seems better than *πηγὴ ἣ* B. Vulg. quite unnecessarily translated ‘the little spring became a river, and was turned into light and the sun, and overflowed into many waters’. There is nothing in the Greek of either the dream or its interpretation to suggest this. The elevation of Esther answers to ‘the spring [which] became a river’, while the safety and joy of the Jews upon their deliverance are pointed to by ‘the light and the sun’ (cf. Esther viii. 16). But cf. Luc. MSS., *ἥλιος καὶ φῶς οἳ ἐγένοντο τοῖς Ἰουδαίοις ἐπιφάνεια τοῦ θεοῦ.*

4. **the two dragons.** > *δύο* A. See Add. A 6.

5. **the nations.** See Add. A 6. The suggestion is that the whole world was arrayed against the people of God.

destroy the name, i.e. the very existence of the Jewish people.

6. **my nation.** We should have expected *τὸ δὲ ἔθνος τὸ δίκαιον* from Add. A 6.

cried unto God. See A 9.

signs and wonders. Cf. Ps. cxxxv. 9.

7. **Therefore.** This verse is omitted by A.

two lots. Cf. Esther iii. 7, which shows Haman seeking to obtain a lucky issue by lot; cf. 1 Sam. xiv. 41. Here God's making two lots means simply that God took into His own arbitrament the decision between His people and their enemies.

8. This verse is omitted by B*, but is inserted in the lower margin.

came . . . before God. Hardly, with Ryssel, that ‘the destinies represented by them *were fulfilled*’. They came before God, and God passed judgement on them.

moment. *καιρὸν* B, *κλῆρον* B^ab ℵ A.

⟨for His people⟩ and. Fritzsche's suggestion is good, and has been incorporated into the text. The question is of both lots, but the mention of ‘the people’ in *v.* 9 may be the cause of its omission in *v.* 8.

9. **justified.** *Servavit*, Old Lat.; *misertus est*, Vulg. But the meaning is the characteristic meaning of *δικαιοῦν*, cf. Deut. xxv. 1; Sir. xiii. 22 ‘pronounced their cause righteous’.

10. **fourteenth and fifteenth day.** *καὶ τῇ πεντ.* > ℵ* A* (*καὶ τῇ ε′ καὶ ι′* ℵ^c.a mg). The actual day of deliverance was the 13th day of Adar, but the fact of the observance of the festival on the 14th and 15th days caused Jewish writers to seek for an explanation.

The explanation as given in Esther ix. 16–19 is as follows: the Jews in the provinces avenged themselves on the 13th Adar, and rested on the 14th; but the Jews in Shushan required two days for their vengeance, and did not rest till the 15th Adar.

The 14th day was the principal day, and is referred to in 2 Macc. xv. 36 as *ἡ Μαρδοχαϊκὴ ἡμέρα.*

11. Esther and the Wisdom of the Son of Sirach are the only books of the Greek O. T. which offer any information as to their authorship and date.

The objection has been raised against the authenticity of this subscription that it represents the author of the version as a Palestinian Jew, whereas his speech has an Egyptian colour; but his name ‘Lysimachus son of Ptolemaeus’ suggests a distinctly Egyptian origin, and it is legitimate to assume that he was an Egyptian Jew who through residence at Jerusalem became acquainted with this Hebrew *Megillah*, and having acquired a knowledge of Hebrew, sought to benefit his Egyptian brethren by providing them with a Greek version.

It is indeed impossible to say whether the subscription was appended by the translator of the canonical Hebrew portions, or by the author or incorporator of the Additions; but there is nothing in the subscription to make us hesitate to accept its witness. The Wisdom of the Son of Sirach was translated 132 B.C., and it is probable that Hebrew Esther was translated about the same time.

It used to be thought that the date indicated by the subscription was 178 B.C., Ptolemy Philometor, who reigned at that period, being well disposed towards the Jews. But further investigation has shown that of the four Ptolemies who were married to a Cleopatra only one (Ptolemy VIII, Soter II, Lathyrus) was married to a Cleopatra in the

a Levite, and Ptolemaeus his son brought in *to Egypt* the Epistle of Phrurai *here* set forth, which they said was *true*, and that Lysimachus the son of Ptolemaeus, of the dwellers in Jerusalem, had interpreted it.

fourth year of his reign. The date therefore is plainly 114 B.C. (see Jacob, 'Das Buch Esther bei den LXX,' in *ZATW*, 1890, p. 241 ff.).

This entire verse is omitted by the Luc. MSS. (except 19) and Old Lat.

In the fourth year, i.e. 114 B.C.

Epistle of Phrurai. *Φρουραί* B, *Φρούραια* ℵ* A, cf. Jos. *Ant.* xi. 6. 13, *Φρουρίμ* ℵ[c.a]. The 'Epistle' does not refer merely to the instructions of Esther ix. 20–28, but to the whole Book of Esther, which is regarded as an Epistle from Mordecai to the Jewish people concerning the feast of Purim.

For the connexion of the feast of Purim (Phrurim) with the Persian *Farvardigân*, the Feast of the Dead, cf. Paton, *Est.* pp. 84–87.

of the dwellers. *τῶν ἐν* B ℵ, but Fritzsche and Lagarde read *τόν*.

After the last word in *v.* 11 B ℵ A have the subscription Ἐσθήρ.

Oxford: Horace Hart M.A. Printer to the University